D1529984

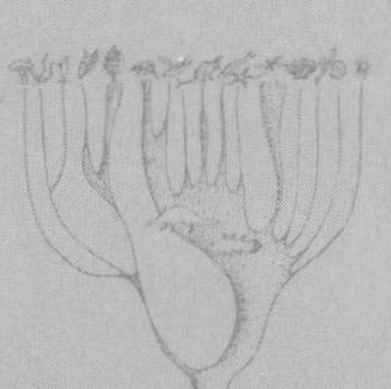

BIOSPHERE □ A STUDY OF LIFE

N. M. Jessop

United States International University

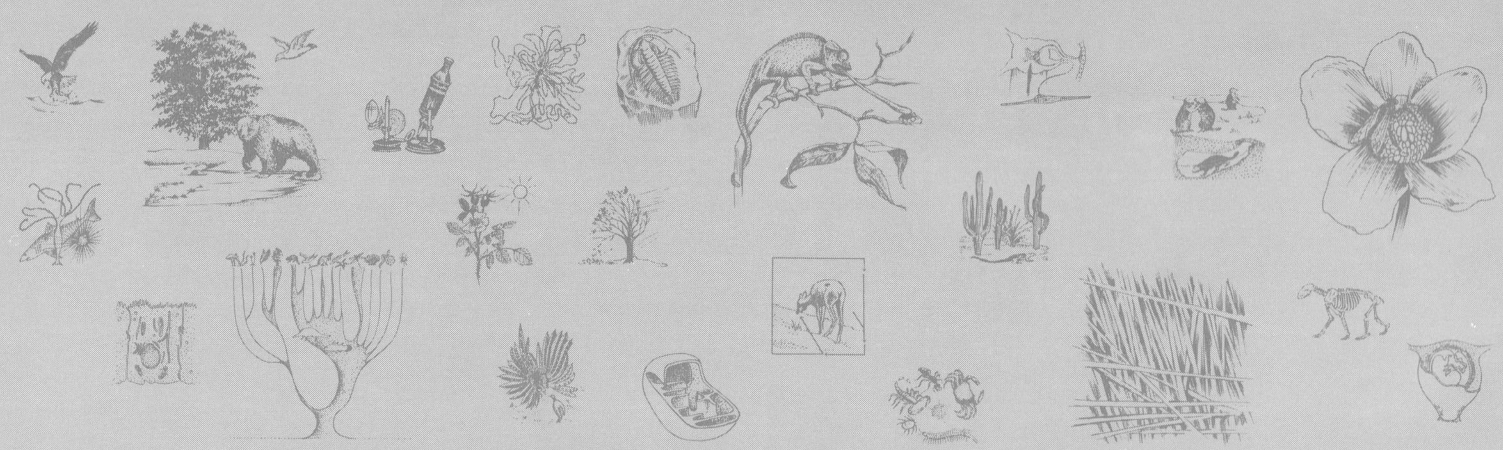

BIOSPHERE □ A STUDY OF LIFE

Prentice-Hall, Inc.

Englewood Cliffs, New Jersey

BIOLOGICAL SCIENCE SERIES *William D. McElroy and Carl P. Swanson, editors*

N. M. JESSOP *Biosphere: A Study of Life*

Printed in the United States of America.

13-077206-2

LIBRARY OF CONGRESS CATALOG CARD NUMBER *70-79114*

CURRENT PRINTING 10 9 8 7 6 5 4 3 2 1

☐ This book has been composed on film in Zenith, a version of a contemporary typeface designed by Hermann Zapf, with headings and captions in boldface Laurel, adapted from a typeface by W. A. Dwiggins.

The line illustrations were executed by Eva Cellini and Patricia Collins.

The quotations introducing the parts are taken from the following sources: (Part 1) I. I. Rabi, *Center Diary*, 18 (Santa Barbara, Calif.: Center for the Study of Democratic Institutions, 1967); (Parts 2 and 4) Charles Darwin, *On the Origin of Species By Means of Natural Selection, or the Preservation of Favoured Races in the Struggle for Life* (London: John Murray, 1859); (Part 3) L. Eiseley, *The Immense Journey* (New York: Random House, Inc., 1957); (Part 5) Lucretius, *On the Nature of Things*, Book I, in *Great Books of the Western World*, R. M. Hutchins, ed. (trans. by H. A. J. Munro) (Chicago: Encyclopaedia Britannica, Inc., 1952).

Prentice-Hall International, Inc., *London*
Prentice-Hall of Australia, Pty. Ltd., *Sydney*
Prentice-Hall of Canada, Ltd., *Toronto*
Prentice-Hall of India Private Ltd., *New Delhi*
Prentice-Hall of Japan, Inc., *Tokyo*

TO COUGAR AND DOG

Preface

THIS BOOK HAS GROWN OUT OF THE conviction that an introductory textbook of college biology can both do justice to the customary aims of the first-year biology course and undertake the more difficult task of providing a perspective on the biosphere that may promote concern for its future and man's role in it.

It is thus important for a general biology text to impart a sense of the spirit and procedures of scientific inquiry while clearly setting forth the functional and organizational principles of life from the molecular to the organismal level; and such objectives have always been kept in sight during the preparation of *Biosphere: A Study of Life.* However, the intensifying crises of population expansion and environmental destruction make it apparent that the pursuit of these aims must not preclude a thorough consideration of ecological relationships, which alone can form the basis of a renovated world view. These relationships—within species, among species, and between life and its abiotic milieu—have been particularly explored through five chapters in Part 2, where considerable attention has been given to such topics as competition-minimizing adaptations, animal communication, and the organization of animal societies. Instead of adhering to a strictly holistic approach to the study of life's interactions with its environment, this text presents ecological relationships throughout as selective factors operating to shape the evolution of life at all its levels of organization, molecular as well as organismal: surely the exquisitely adapted mechanisms of cell and organism nutrition and integration are more appreciated if they are viewed not as isolated phenomena but as products of dynamic evolutionary and developmental interactions operating within a unitary "organism-environment complex."

Remarkably, although biologists assume that life has had a past and is subject to continued change, biological courses of study at the beginning college level still tend to present the living world primarily as a *fait accompli,* imparting little sense of the dynamic processes of genetic change and adaptation that have shaped and will shape the biosphere. Today there is particular urgency in studying life as a stream emerging from a past not wholly unknown and moving into a future not utterly unforeseeable. From reasonable extrapolations we can predict the probable outcomes of continued adherence to philosophies that view man as the ultimate product of creation, destined to subdue the earth and multiply without limitation. Indeed, failure to consider present trends implies acquiescence in the ongoing destruction of much of the biosphere, which, if continued unabated, is likely to impoverish our descendants and lead to the disruption of the planetary ecosystem, with the extinction of many species and perhaps of mankind itself.

The nature and effectiveness of the solutions proposed will depend largely on how effectively our outlook can be expanded and transformed through the study of biology: Will these solutions be aimed strictly at improving the lot of mankind, or will they operate on a larger scale to ensure as well the survival of the host of endangered nonhuman species? Man-centered man is obsolete; we must move expeditiously, making the most of whatever brief grace period may remain.

However, it is less the intention of this book to dwell upon all the particulars of the crisis, which scarcely can be encompassed in a balanced textbook, than to provide sufficient emphasis on ecology within the scope of the biology curriculum. As indicated above, the organizational scheme places ecological relationships and evolutionary mechanisms early in the course of study. A general perspective is thus developed that makes more meaningful subsequent consideration of cellular and organismal structure and function. However, each part is sufficiently self-contained (and a comprehensive Glossary is also provided) so that the reader can progress from microscopic to macroscopic studies by proceeding to Chapter 9 directly after completing Chapter 1, returning at a later point to Chapters 2 through 8. Each chapter deals with a major topic integrated to include consideration of both plant and animal life. However, the instructor wishing to bypass sections of certain chapters that seem peripheral to his main thrust will readily find it feasible to do so. A biologically oriented introduction to chemistry is provided in Chapter 9 for those students who have not yet had adequate chemistry to comprehend the essential aspects of bioenergetics and cell metabolism. Although it has not been assumed that most students have prior acquaintance with biology, a sustained attempt has been made to furnish fresh examples and present materials in new contexts and at a fairly sophisticated level.

The author appreciates the efforts of the many undergraduate students whose comments on portions of the manuscript have assisted in the development of this book. Especial thanks are also extended to those colleagues who have devoted time and energy to the reading and constructive criticism of the entire manuscript or portions of it, in particular Professors Howard Bern, Peter Buri, John Hopperton, Raymond Jessop, William McElroy, and Carl Swanson. I should also like to thank a number of other reviewers (invited by the publisher to examine portions of the manuscript) whose names remain unknown to me but whose comments have been invaluable in improving various aspects of the presentation and in minimizing errors. Errors of fact or interpretation that remain are, of course, the author's responsibility; corrections or suggestions from readers will be gratefully received. I am indebted as well to the many persons and organizations providing illustrative materials or granting permission for use of figures or excerpts from previous publications. Finally, I should like to express warm appreciation to John R. Riina, David R. Esner, and Bert N. Zelman of Prentice-Hall, Inc., for their sustained encouragement and help that made possible the publication of this book.

N. M. JESSOP

Contents

Part 1

THE DIVERSITY OF LIFE

. . . a knowledge of a basic science is not a skill—it's a point of view, it's a citadel, it's a whole intellectual structure against which one can measure other intellectual structures. This is a home, from which man can have a view of the world. Only when you learn something that is still developing and has a seemingly endless frontier do you get a vision of the future.

I. I. RABI

Diversity and fecundity are conspicuous attributes of the living world. The biosphere (that film of life sandwiched between the upper atmosphere and the earth's rocky crust) is made up of vast numbers of individual organisms constituting no less than a million and a half known kinds of plants and animals. Among the fundamental problems facing the science of biology are (1) analysis of those factors of heredity and environment which interact to bring about the diversification of life and (2) recognition of common characteristics that underlie this diversity. In Part 1 we shall first consider the nature of the science of biology, which examines and classifies the living world. We shall trace the development of this science through a preliminary consideration of key concepts that have contributed to the science of biology. Next we shall summarize the basic characteristics of living things and shall briefly review the distinguishing characteristics of the major groups of organisms—plants, animals, and intermediate forms. We shall consider the entire mosaic of life—the fruit of three billion years of organic evolution. This study of organismal types once made up nearly the whole of biological science and is of course still essential in gaining a complete view of the biosphere. But today we place greater emphasis on questions of causation: through what interactions of internal and external factors has the biosphere evolved to its present level of diversity and complexity? These questions have been posed for centuries, but only in recent decades have satisfactory answers begun to be formulated.

Chapter 1  ANALYZING THE LIVING WORLD

NO FORMAL SCIENTIFIC TRAINING IS needed to help us distinguish mosquitos from mushrooms, magpies from men. Long before the first scientific expedition reached New Guinea, the natives of that island had accomplished the considerable feat of correctly distinguishing among and conferring names upon all but one of the well over 500 species of resident birds. The phenomenon of biotic diversity is apparent to the most casual observer and is a cardinal attribute of life. The biosphere comprises a bewildering variety of living things (*organisms*), some of which are fitted to survive in the most hostile environments found on this planet. Algae, fungi, and delicate pink mites are at home barely 600 km from the South Pole. In the sunless deeps far below the surface of the sea, bizarre forms stave off extinction through escape from the fierce competition of the surface waters, instead coping successfully with their difficult environment.

The hordes of species that make up the biosphere range in size from viruses measurable in nanometers (such as the tobacco mosaic virus, which is about 300 nm long and 16 nm in diameter) to comparatively large bacteria and protozoans ranging from 2 to 100 μm (2,000 to 100,000 nm) in length, and finally to those species which represent the upper limits of organic size, the 30-m baleen whales and 100-m redwood trees (Figure 1.1).* On a scale in which 1 Å (one angstrom unit, 10^{-10} m), the diameter of a hydrogen atom, arbitrarily represents one, the dimensions of representative objects in the living world and the physical universe

*See Appendix 1 on the metric system.

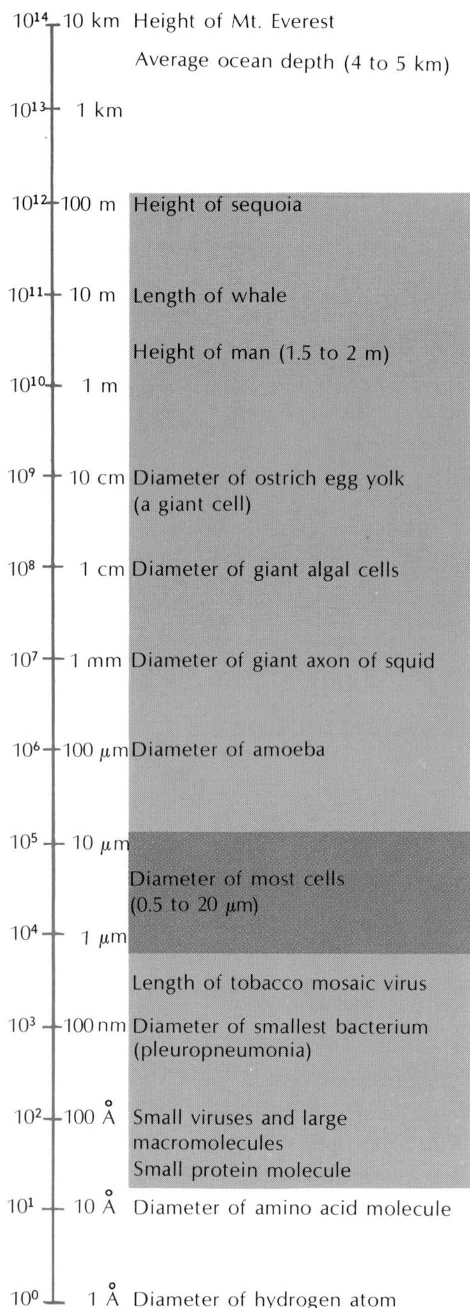

Figure 1.1 □ Representative size relationships expressed exponentially, with 1 Å (0.1 nm) as equivalent to 1 (10^0). The colored region represents the range of size in the biotic world, darker color delimiting the size range of most kinds of cells.

may be represented as exponents of 10. On such a scale we find that the range of organic size generally lies between 10^2 (100 Å) and 5×10^{11} (50 m). It is interesting to note that despite the susceptibility of giant organisms to extinction, the largest species of plants and animals that have ever lived are in existence today (although precariously so as a result of man's recent depredations).

Not only is life richly diverse in terms of *kinds* of organisms, but the number of *individual* organisms living at any given moment is unimaginably vast. For instance, most life in the ocean depends nutritionally upon the floating "meadows of the sea" (*phytoplankton*), unicellular algae that normally occur near the surface at a density of around 100,000 per liter. However, during occasional favorable periods when mineral nutrients are made available by the upwelling of deeper waters, the phytoplankton may proliferate explosively to densities of several million per liter! By comparison, Charles Darwin's classic census of earthworms in good English soil—25,000 to 50,000 per acre—appears insignificant. Even foods that are processed prior to human consumption, commonly considered to be free of microbial contaminants, contain a surprisingly large population of organisms that have ruggedly survived the purification procedures. Pasteurized milk, for example, often qualifies for grade A rating if its bacterial count is below 30,000 per cubic centimeter: a glass of freshly pasteurized milk could hold 7 million inhabitants!

If we are impressed by the fecundity of life and the vast assemblage of different types *now* in existence, we should also note that many other forms of life have already become extinct and that others now unforeseen may yet appear. Furthermore, beyond our solar system we can speculate that wherever in the universe life *can* arise it probably *does* arise, assuming forms compatible with the environment.

In Chapter 2 we shall examine the diverse patterns of organization that make up the living world. In so doing we shall in a sense retrace the early history of the science of life, for one of the achievements of biology prior to the nineteenth century was discovering and categorizing these gross organizational patterns. While studying the basic organizational patterns of plant and animal life, it was natural for early biologists to be preoccupied with formulating names for different types of organisms and with trying to categorize them on the basis of gross structural similarities. During this period students of animal life considered themselves *zoologists* whereas students of plant life were known as *botanists;* these divisions persist today, but the more general term *biologist* now encompasses all professions analyzing the living world.

Creating a vocabulary of names for organisms and additional terms to designate parts of their bodies was a task that began with the birth of human language and, because of the tremendous variety of living things, is not yet finished. Unfortunately for our deeper understanding of the living world, there is a tendency to equate a verbal symbol with the object itself—which sometimes produces the naïve conviction that knowledge of the man-made name of an organism or body part somehow confers intuitive understanding of its basic nature. Such holds true whether the vocabulary employed consists of "common names" or of scientific terms—in fact, the feeling is often accentuated when we have managed to tag on a scientific label; this is such an accomplishment that we tend to forget that we are still ignorant of the nature of the object in all other respects.

Naming and classifying organisms was nevertheless one of the significant accomplishments of the young science of biology, for it promoted the development of a systematic approach to the living world that facilitated later more sophisticated attempts at analysis. Attempting to impose some order upon that which at first seemed chaotic, early biologists tried to fit various kinds of living things into groups that might reflect their actual relationships. The attempts to categorize organisms into logical groupings based upon similarities of structure demanded acceptance (as a working hypothesis at least) of the idea that structural similarities serve as valid indicators of degrees of *relatedness;* this idea in turn implies a *common ancestry,* at least for certain groups of organisms. These two assumptions by early biologists were taken more on faith than as a result of scientific inquiry. Although it required no more than casual observation to perceive the *diversity* of life, it took centuries of hard scientific work, assisted by occasional flashes of genius, to establish the fundamental *unity* of organization underlying the living world. Faith in the then largely undisclosed orderliness of the natural world strengthened the assumption that if relatedness were sought among the welter of organic forms, it would indeed be found. Thus without benefit of modern techniques of genetic, physiological, and biochemical analysis, the science of *taxonomy* (*systematics*) was launched, supported mainly by studies in comparative anatomy. This science represented the first sustained effort toward an orderly study of the world of life as a whole.

1.1 □ THE SCIENCE OF BIOLOGY

We shall explore the development of systematics in Section 1.2; for the present let us examine the science of biology as a whole and the nature of scientific inquiry per se. Bestowing names upon living things has always been only the beginning of inquiry. None but the most incurious can share the world with a host of other living things without wondering how they live and what internal and external forces shape their lives. Scientists are distinguished by their intense curiosity—their determination to find out how things work, leaving little privacy to even the most retiring of creatures.

To a point all men are scientists, for we all observe our surroundings and even ourselves and then attempt to explain what we have observed. But those of us who are not easily satisfied by ready explanations (and are willing to devise tests to challenge their validity) are the kinds of individuals who tend to become scientists by vocation. Science is one of the most rewarding of human endeavors. It can be as exciting as geographical exploration, for scientific research is an adventure of the mind and each new vista gained provides a glimpse of regions still uncharted.

A science is made up of a compilation of data, together with certain basic principles derived from these data, which have been assembled over many years by individuals who have devoted their lives to the perennial inquiry. All that we shall discuss in the following chapters therefore represent fruits of the labors of countless biologists, living and dead, some renowned but most obscure. We shall often summarize particular experiments or observations that have opened the way for further understanding, but as a rule we shall not attempt to link these investigations to the names of individual biologists. The reason for this general anonymity is twofold: (1) to give fair recognition to the many investigators working in the nineteenth and twentieth centuries is not feasible, for even to weave into our story more than a few names of prominent biologists would result in a "Who's Who" compilation as formidable as any encyclopedia of taxonomic names; (2) the scientific revolution has so accelerated in the present century that the number and variety of biological investigations now in progress greatly exceeds the sum total of all of those undertaken since the dawn of civilization. It is apparent that even the most distinguished of contemporary biologists have reached prominence by virtue of the fact that they do not stand alone: they are members of a scientific culture rooted in the past and sustained today by the energies of thousands of dedicated workers the world over, all helping to build the edifice of a still-developing science, stone by stone.

A Characteristics of scientific inquiry

Throughout our course of study we should keep in mind that the descriptions, conclusions, and general principles presented here have been arrived at by application of one or both of the most effective tools of scientific inquiry: (1) *direct observation and measurement* of natural phenomena not manipulated by the observer; (2) *controlled experimentation,* in which the investigator strives to identify the factors operating causally in a given situation by varying each factor separately while attempting to hold the other factors constant.

In biology, as in astronomy, direct observation without experimental intervention remains a valuable tool and is steadily being improved by the extension of human senses through the appropriate instrumentation. Sounds inaudible to the human ear (such as a bat's cry) may now be recorded, electronically analyzed, and played back at frequencies which our ear *can* detect. The familiar *light microscope* first opened to investigation the microbial world, which the unaided eye could not resolve. The more recently developed polarizing, X-ray, and electron microscopes have revealed further details of microscopic structure, down to the level of molecular resolution. *High-speed cinephotography* may be used to capture movements too rapid to be observed by direct means (such as the movement of a bee's wing in flight); *time-lapse* photography can compress a time sequence so that movements too slow to be detected otherwise (such as the opening of a flower) may be accelerated to an observable rate. Many other instrumental techniques now exist for the visual, acoustic, physical, and chemical analysis of biotic materials.

The *controlled experiment* is one of the most fruitful of scientific methods. By "controlled" we mean that to be valid an experiment must be so designed that it includes both a control and an experimental group maintained under conditions that are held constant so that only the variable being tested (that is, the factor being subjected to experimental variation) differs between the two groups. For instance, to determine the effects on rats of vitamin C deprivation, we should first obtain a sufficient number of animals so that the effects of chance incidence of disease or injury may be minimized. The animals should be as alike as possible in age, sex, initial weight, and heredity; they should be subdivided into two groups, each receiving identical care except that the preparation fed to the experimental group lacks vitamin C. Under such conditions defects consistently arising in the experimental group but absent in the control group may legitimately be attributed to vitamin C deficiency. Without the control group it would be impossible to rule out the intervention of some other pathological factor. Finally, the incidence of observed differences between the control and experimental groups should be analyzed for *statistical significance* (indicating probability that the experiment can be repeated, that is, *replicated,* with the same results). Obviously an investigation involving only two or three organisms would be statistically insignificant, although possibly of great value in formulating a hypothesis to be tested in a more extensive set of experiments.

A *hypothesis* is a proposed answer to a question, an assumption which, no matter how logical and reasonable it appears to be, must be put to the test of observation or controlled experimentation. To be scientifically useful, a hypothesis must be amenable to testing; it may in fact suggest the form such testing must take. If the testing of a hypothesis is impossible because of technological limitations, it remains of interest only in terms of speculation. For instance, many biologists believe that life may exist on planets of other solar systems, and speculate that life may assume quite unfamiliar forms under nonearthlike conditions. These hypotheses cannot be proved or disproved without direct evidence, which will not be forthcoming until interstellar travel becomes a reality or until the unlikely event that radioastronomers receive a reply to the messages they have been transmitting into space. Nevertheless, such untestable hypotheses are still of value in that they may influence our thinking regarding the uniqueness of man as a form of intelligent life, and may promote the expectation that extraterrestrial life may eventually be encountered.

A flow diagram of scientific inquiry (Figure 1.2) is useful in showing the relationship between hypothesis, testing, and generalization. However, we should note

Figure 1.2 □ **Flow diagram of scientific inquiry. Not depicted here but operating at all stages of inquiry are the factors of *insight* and *serendipity*. The former determines the nature of the question perceived and the approach to its solution; lack of insight often results in pursuing a more pedestrian inquiry while questions of greater significance remain unrecognized. Serendipity is the factor of fortuitous discovery—stumbling upon one thing in pursuing another; insight is often required in the recognition of a serendipitous happening.**

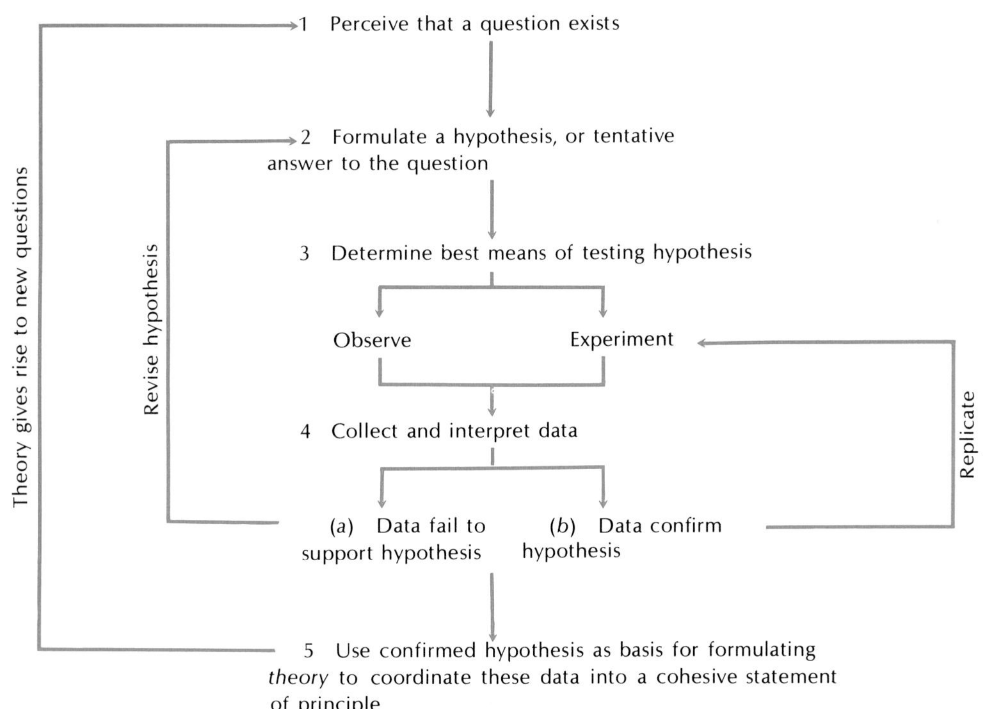

that there really is no such thing as *the* "scientific method." It is tempting to be wise after the fact when relating the story of a scientific discovery, and to speak as if the investigation had been planned with a clear knowledge of the outcome and then carried forth inexorably in a perfectly predictable sequence. This is sometimes true, especially in the later stages of a scientific investigation, but in the initial stages a great deal of random casting about may be required even to define what questions may be asked that are amenable to being answered. Further trial and error may ensue until a legitimate testing procedure has been worked out. In the course of testing something quite unforeseen may transpire, and insight is then required to determine whether this unpredicted outcome should be pursued or ignored. *Serendipity,* the chance discovery of one thing while in pursuit of another, is a phenomenon that occurs surprisingly often during scientific investigation; such happenings cannot of course be planned in advance, but must be seized upon by the alert investigator.

It is also characteristic of scientific inquiry that when the answer to one question is sought, discovery of a solution may not bring an end to inquiry but rather opens many additional questions that lead to further investigation. Insight is once more required to determine which of these new questions are amenable to testing and which deserve priority in terms of possible significance.

Regardless of the procedure used in obtaining them, if accurate results (*data*) are compiled eventually they may provide the basis for a generalization, a scientific *theory.* Years of collecting and analyzing data may be needed before a scientific theory may be formulated that fits all of the results into a meaningful whole. Once formulated, a theory can serve as impetus for further inquiry; it must be challenged from all possible angles before it becomes firmly incorporated into the structure of science as an accepted *principle.* If a theory is accepted uncritically, it may gain the status of scientific dogma without having been thoroughly tested; however, since each new scientific theory tends to strike at the root of some previously established doctrine, it is unlikely that any new theory will be adopted without argument. When one scientific theory is proposed to supplant another, there is often a vigorous clash of minds until all the necessary data are assembled to decide the issue, but the sounds of battle rarely penetrate outside the scientific world. On the other hand, if scientific theory challenges some cherished nonscientific doctrine (as did Charles Darwin's proposal of the theory of evolution by natural selection), the reverberations are heard around the world. In such disputes the value of scientific *objectivity* comes to the fore. Although scientists may fight to retain their pet ideas, ideas sometimes not easily relinquished, if the objective data fail to support the theory, the data cannot be ignored and the theory, however attractive, must be revised or abandoned. This is because scientists, although often guilty of prejudice and error, are fundamentally committed to *inductive reasoning:* facts must be sought and then a generalization formulated which is consonant with those facts; unscientific are a priori generalizations for which only supporting facts are sought and other data rejected.

In other words, the nature of their work demands that scientists practice the virtues of *honesty* and *willingness to recognize truth* no matter who discovers it or how the discovery may affect their most cherished beliefs. Science is thus ideally a truly democratic human endeavor; respect and recognition are ultimately accorded any effectively executed, creatively designed piece of research, without regard to the investigator's race, sex, economic status, or national origin. Of course scientists must also be skeptical of the results of any investigation until the data pass the test of replicability by other workers and thus become firmly established. To this end, scientists forego secretiveness with regard to their procedures, for these must be spelled out explicitly so that others may accurately replicate the conditions under which the original investigation took place. The general adherence of scientists to standards of honesty, skepticism, openness, and willingness to relinquish opinions in the face of contradictory data is *not* the outcome of adherence to a moral code or doctrine; it results of necessity from the fact that scientific inquiry cannot proceed effectively when scientists practice deceit, prejudice, gullibility, and secretiveness.

B Methods of data collection and evaluation

Whatever instrumentation may be available, the ultimate instrument of scientific inquiry is the human mind; although tools like the electron microscope are needed to resolve the question of how living matter is organized at subcellular levels, the essence of inquiry is to know how to ask questions, to work out means of testing these questions, and to interpret correctly the data obtained. The methods summarized in this section have significance far beyond direct application in the science laboratory, for they are relevant to everyday experience as well. It is all too common for human actions to be based on intuition or on generalizations and assumptions drawn from too few facts. It is an interesting and worthwhile mental discipline, when faced with a "nonscientific" dilemma, to see how far the methods of scientific fact finding and analysis can be applied to bring about an effective solution of that problem.

When undertaking an inquiry it is important to seek out the *measurable* aspects of the problem. A qualitative, narrative description has merit, but is severely limited in contributing to the development of sound generalizations. Much more can be learned by obtaining quantitative data. Let us take as an example the manner in which honeybee communication by "dancing" can be analyzed. This phenomenon was discovered around 1940 by the Austrian zoologist Karl von Frisch and is especially useful as an example of the manner in which scientific inquiry proceeds; to investigate this phenomenon one needs neither sophisticated equipment nor an extensive scientific background. Men have domesticated honeybees for thousands of years but with little knowledge of the behavior of these useful insects. An uncritical observation of the bustling life of the hive might lead us to conclude that it is impossible to dissect out of this constant bustle any recognizable behavioral elements suitable for analysis. Assumptions have been made of a mystical "hive intelligence," the bees behaving like individual brain cells, incapable of independent thought but in the aggregate composing some formidable "bee mind" capable of advanced thought processes. Now the concept of a composite mind has been abandoned, for evidence has been produced that bees are capable not of reasoning either alone or in the aggregate but of communicating with one another.

How can we discover some of the ways in which bees communicate? The first necessity is to *observe* bees directly within their hives; this demands that an observation hive be designed and constructed that allows the investigator to watch the bees while they remain undisturbed by his presence. This is one of the basic methods of the science of *ethology,* the biological study of animal behavior: to allow the animal insofar as possible to pursue its normal mode of life while its activities are objectively observed, qualitatively described, and quantitatively measured. First, out of the constant stream of activity specific behavior patterns of the bees must be *described* and *categorized:* self-grooming, grooming other bees, foraging, packing pollen into cells, caring for larvae, and so forth. Next, as an initial step in obtaining *quantitative* data, we can determine what proportion of the bee's life is spent in performing each of these activities; this requires that *individual* bees be marked for identification (such as by affixing a very small numbered tag to the body). In the process of tabulating bees' activities and the time spent in each, we should discover that bees returning from foraging (recognizable by their heavy load of pollen) spend some time moving about rapidly and performing a peculiar repeating pattern like a dance before going off to clean themselves of pollen. We should also notice nearby bees clustering about the "dancer" and attempting to follow her. Is it possible that this dancing communicates some definite information to the surrounding bees, or is it merely a way of alerting them to the floral odors borne by the returning forager, exciting them to forage in turn? We can observe whether or not the dance really does promote foraging by bees that have associated with the dancer; if some of these bees have been marked to permit individual recognition we can trace their subsequent activities. These bees are found soon to leave the hive and return later laden with pollen. This allows us to conclude that dancing does in fact seem to recruit new foragers, but is there any additional information content?

To test this possibility, we can resort to *experimentation:* we can set an artificial feeding station at a distance of perhaps 200 m from the hive and watch to see what happens when the stand is discovered by the first bee: soon after this bee has drunk its fill of sugar water and flown away, bees begin to visit the stand in ever increasing numbers—somehow they have gotten the message and are locating the stand other than by chance. How is information on the location of the feeding stand imparted? To discover this, one investigator may mark with lacquer each bee visiting that stand, while a colleague observes these marked bees' behavior on their return to the hive. The watcher at the hive will see that all bees returning from the same feeding place tend to perform the same dance. This dance, when performed on the vertical face of the honeycomb, is found to be oriented at a constant angle to gravity. The dancing bee performs a repetitious figure-8 pattern: it runs in a tight counterclockwise semicircle, makes a short straight run wagging its abdomen vigorously from side to side, turns clockwise through 180° and then makes another straight "waggle run" and so forth (see Figure 7.26*b*). By careful observation we see that the waggle run is performed at the same angle to gravity by all bees returning from the feeding stand. Since other bees that have been foraging elsewhere may orient the dance differently, we must be able to identify individual bees if we are to discover that the orientation of the waggle run is correlated with the location of a given food source.

This discovery should lead to the formulation of a testable question: if the waggle run is now performed in one consistent direction, what will happen if we change the location of the feeding stand? Maintaining the same absolute distance from stand to hive, we relocate the stand through 90° or 180° of arc. Soon we should find that the orientation of the bees' dances has altered by an equivalent number of degrees. This leads us to conclude that the angle to gravity of the waggle run provides information on the location of a food source.

Next, how can we determine in what manner this information is given? If we place the food stand due west of the hive and observe the bees visiting it in the morning, we find their waggle runs to be performed head downward on the honeycomb; were our observations made at the same time each day we might well conclude that "head down" meant "fly west" and might confirm this by moving the feeding stand to the east of the hive, whereupon the bees would commence to make their waggle runs upwards on the comb. We might conclude that making the runs upward meant "fly east" and then proceed to formulate a generalization—that the direction of the waggle run indicated a consistent compass direction. And we should be wrong! For, having reached this satisfying (but unfortunately incorrect) conclusion, should we chance to visit our bees in the afternoon, we would find to our dismay that when returning from a stand placed to the west of the hive the bees now perform the waggle run head up, and when returning from a stand to the east of the hive they perform this run head down! Thus our correlation was erroneous and we must now pose a further question: if the angle of the waggle run to gravity does *not* correlate with a consistent compass direction, is there some other environmental factor with which it *does* correlate?

Correlation, like quantitative measurement, is an important method of analysis: biotic activities do not take place in a vacuum but within a milieu in which certain other factors may correlate consistently with the performance of that activity. When a consistent correlation between two phenomena exists, they *may* be causally related. Performance of the bee dance correlates with return to the hive after foraging, hence foraging may in some way be causally related to dancing. Association with a dancing bee correlates with ability to locate a distant food source, hence this ability may be the result of having associated with the dancer.

These two correlations appear to have been validated, but our third correlation, between angle of waggle run and absolute compass direction, has proven false. What other natural phenomenon may correlate consistently with the angle of the waggle run and cause the direction of the run to change through 180° in the course of a day? A plausible answer soon presents itself: the sun moves across the sky from east to west each day, describing an arc of 180° from rising to setting; therefore the sun must be used as a direction finder by honeybees.

It is tempting to leap to the conclusion that this logical assumption is correct, but our previous mistake should warn us not to make another correlation on the basis of inadequate data. How can we test it? First we can leave the feeding stand in place and watch the bees from dawn to dark, taking compass readings hour by hour on the angles described by the sun, hive, and food source, and the angles of the waggle runs to gravity. (A plumb line hung across the observation window of the hive allows us to measure the angle of the dance to the gravitational axis.) After making these observations a number of times the correlation appears firmly established: the angle of the waggle run at any given time is equivalent to the angle described by the relative positions of sun, hive, and food source (see Figure 7.26c).

How do we know when we have collected enough data to be statistically significant in establishing this correlation? Results obtained by watching one bee for one day may not suffice. Several *statistical* tests can be applied both to determine how well the data fit the hypothesis and how adequate is the sample size. One of the most widely used is the *chi-square* (χ^2) test, which takes sample size into account when indicating the *probability* that any discrepancy between the *observed* results and those *expected* on the basis of the hypothesis can be ascribed to chance alone. The χ^2 test and a few other useful statistical measures are given for reference in Appendix 2.

When the number of dances observed is great enough for the data to be statistically significant, we can make a prediction: if one set of angles has been consistently obtained with the feeding stand in it's original position, moving the stand to another position should result in a predictable shift in the angle of the bee dances. This can be checked in turn, thereby strengthening the generalization. Extending our generalization by this type of prediction is an example of *deductive reasoning:* an assumption is made on the basis of a premise previously established. Deductive reasoning is very useful but its limitations should be noted; the predictive assumption just made can be tested, but sometimes assumptions are made by deduction that are not as easily verified. For instance, from our premise, "Bees communicate by means of a waggle dance when returning from foraging," we may proceed to the assumption, "Therefore, bees *always* communicate by means of a waggle dance when returning from foraging." One implication of this assumption is that bees in all parts of the world use the waggle dance; over a period of time other investigators may provide corroborative or contradictory data. A second implication is that the waggle run is the honeybee's sole means of communicating about a food source. But again our deduction has led us into error: we discover that other means of communication exist. In our experiments let us say that 200 m has been used as the standard distance of the feeding place from the hive. One day (perhaps by chance) we place the feeding stand less than 100 m from the hive and discover that bees returning from the stand now do not perform the wagging dance at all! Were all our previous conclusions wrong? Certainly not, but another variable has been introduced: the distance between hive and food source has been altered. Apparently the wagging dance is used to communicate direction of the food source only when the latter is so far from the hive that odors from the food are unlikely to attract the bees once they have been stimulated to forage.

Is any other consistent behavior now performed that might provide this stimulus? Indeed there is: another dance pattern exists that we may previously have noticed but not considered significant. Returning foragers now perform a "round dance," describing a partial circle, then turning abruptly about and circling the opposite direction for the same distance, back and forth, followed by other bees. After sufficient study we can conclude that the round dance is used to recruit foragers when a food source is within 100 m of the hive but gives no directional information, whereas a wagging dance is used both to recruit foragers and to give directional guidance to a food source at a greater distance than 100 m from the hive. We now have discovered a second "word" in the honeybee "vocabulary."

We might not discover the third word at all unless in the process of seeking measurable components of bee behavior we also happened to measure the *rate* at which the wagging dance is performed, that is, how many complete patterns are performed per unit time. If we measured this rate, we would find it to be fairly consistent when the feeding stand remains at a constant distance from the hive (provided that variations due to temperature are taken into account). Unless the distance is varied, we would not discover that the rate of dance can be varied significantly also. However, we might notice that while bees returning from the feeding stand dance at one rate, bees returning from other feeding areas dance at other rates. This prompts us to seek another correlation: what measurable variable correlates consistently with changes in the rate of dancing? Only after considerable trial and error do we discover that rate of dancing correlates *inversely* with the distance of the food source from the hive: the more distant the food source, the more slowly the dance is performed!

It is obviously infeasible to measure changes in the rate of dance as the food stand is moved away from the hive a meter at a time. Instead, by moving the stand in 100-m steps we can get a manageable quantity of data, and by graphing these data can fill out the story in two ways: (1) by *interpolation* we can determine the dance rates between the points actually measured; (2) by *extrapolation* from the data as graphed we can predict dance rates of bees reporting food sources still more distant than the farthest location used in our experiment. The *mean* (average) dance rate obtained at each sampling distance is first plotted as a point on two axes: rate of dance (vertical axis) and distance of food source from hive (horizontal axis). In Figure 1.3*a*, taken from the data of Von Frisch, each dot represents the mean of 100 bee dances. However, to use an average or mean value is misleading if there is much variation about the mean: if we found from 4 to 8 dance turns taking place in a given group per unit time, we would calculate the mean for that group as 6 turns, but this figure would not be significant since so wide a spread of variation would not permit a close correlation with distance. If on the other hand, we found the range for a group to be only from 5.5 to 6.5 turns, the mean of 6 turns would be very significant. The spread about a mean is calculated as the *standard deviation* (see Appendix 2).

If there is a low deviation from the mean, we can accept the mean values as useful points on our graph. The change of dance rate with increasing distance can now be shown by connecting consecutive points with a line. Since our data represent only samples and not a total census of *all* bee dances, the line obtained will be somewhat irregular; however, it is acceptable to draw a smooth curve passing close to but not through each dot (Figure 1.3*b*). Dance rates between points on the horizontal axis are therefore derived by *interpolation,* or filling in between the measured samples. Could we have interpolated with confidence by measuring dance rates only at 100 m and at 6,000 m and then connecting these points by a straight line, as shown in Figure 1.3*c*? We can see that it would have been incorrect to do so, for the true rate of change describes a curve and not a straight line. When interpolating data it is necessary to have a sufficient number of established reference points or error may result.

From the data actually collected we can also attempt to predict the results to be obtained should the range of our experiment be extended. For instance, simply by extending the line on our graph, we can try to predict the bee's rate of dance when the food source is 10 km from the hive. Such a procedure is called *extrapolation.* It is less safe to extrapolate than to interpolate: unless bees are found foraging this far from

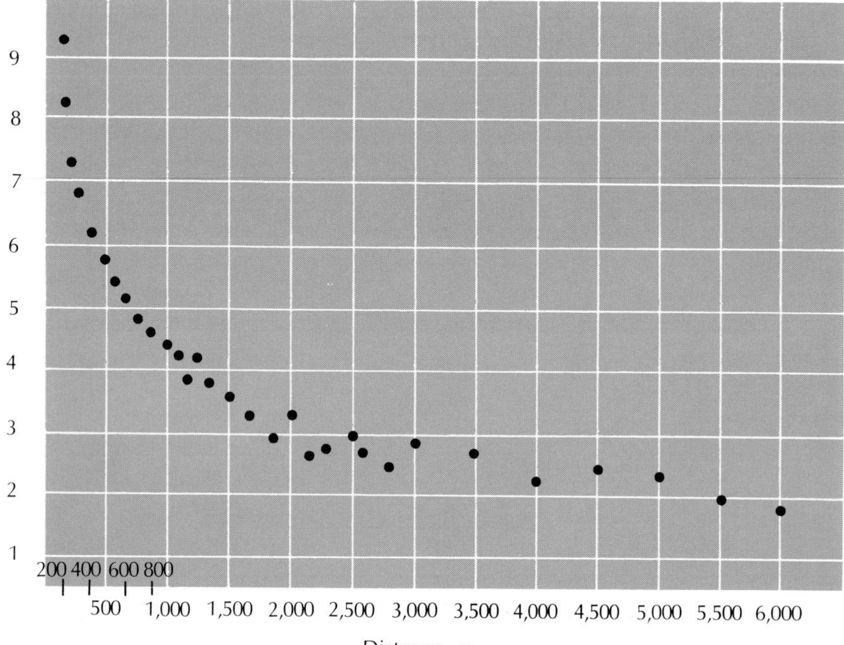

(*a*)

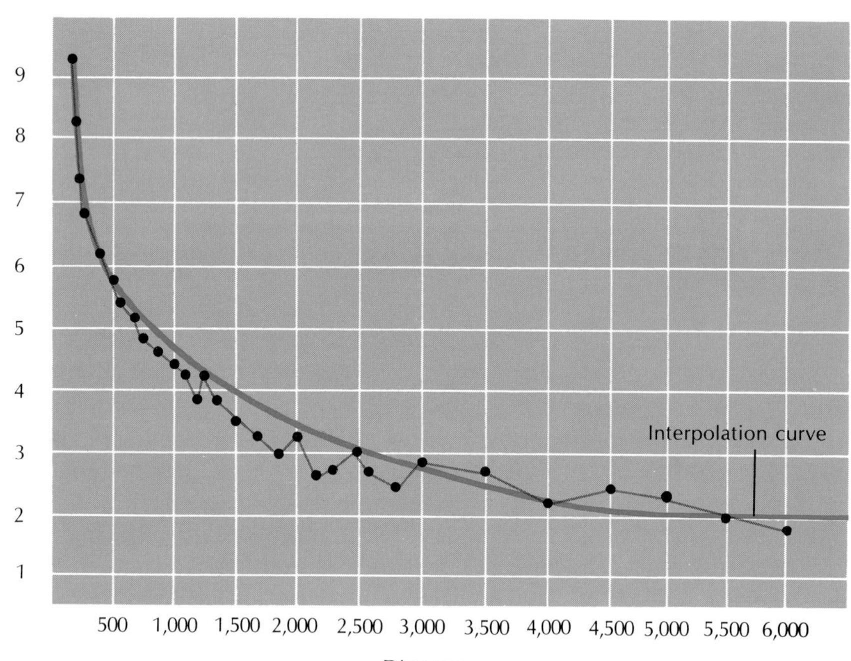

(*b*)

Figure 1.3 □ **(See text for explanation.)**

the hive, the validity of the extrapolation cannot be checked. As long as it is kept in mind that the method of extrapolation must be considered a speculative device, the technique can be of great value in predicting the probable outcome of observable trends. Had we measured dance rates up to a distance of 3,000 m and then extrapolated to 6,000 m, our extrapolation would have proven reasonably correct. But if we had extrapolated from measurements taken only to 1,000 m, the curve obtained would have deviated greatly from that obtained by testing. The more extensive an extrapolation, the less we find ourselves able to trust its validity.

In the preceding example we have seen how it is possible to attack a problem by: (1) careful *observation* and *description;* (2) *quantification,* or seeking measurable variables; (3) arranging *experimental* situations to test hypotheses; (4) seeking *correlations* between factors that may vary together (directly or inversely); (5) using *statistical measurements* to ascertain significance of results obtained; (6) extending data by *interpolation* and *extrapolation;* (7) making *deductive* predictions and testing them; and (8) arriving at verifiable *generalizations* by *inductive reasoning* from the data collected by the preceding steps.

We said earlier that a characteristic of scientific inquiry is that answering one question typically poses new questions that demand investigation. Have any further questions been suggested to you by the example given above?

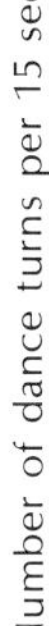

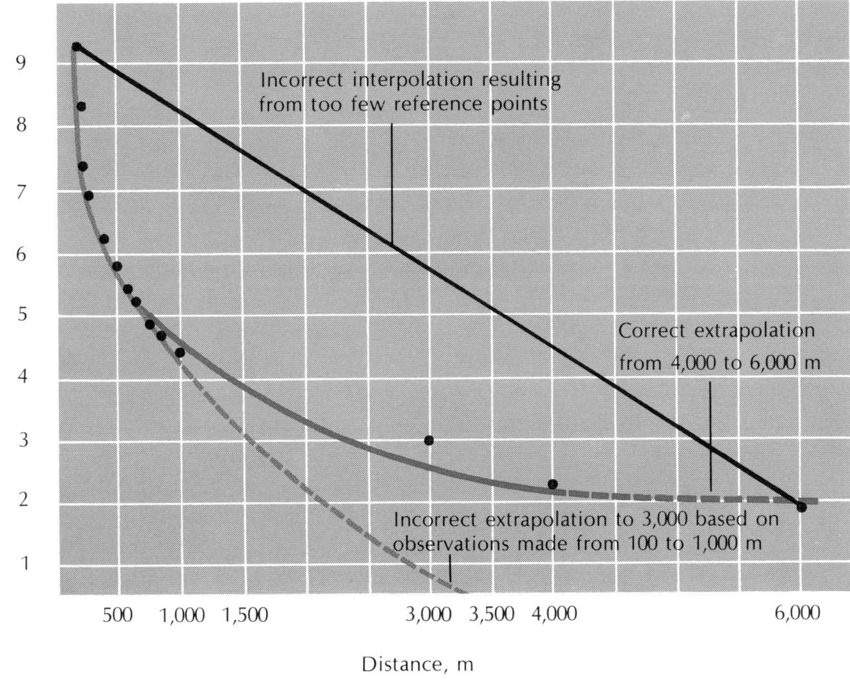

(c)

C Key concepts of biology

The foregoing discussion of the characteristics of scientific inquiry is relevant to our consideration of the development of the science of biology. Conferring scientific names upon organisms challenged no doctrine; however the concurrent development of a mode of thinking in which principles were derived by collecting and evaluating facts, rather than by selecting facts to fit principles, set the stage for the eventual biological revolution. As early as the fourth century B.C. the celebrated Greek philosopher and naturalist Aristotle compiled a vast quantity of zoological and anatomical data and attempted to synthesize valid principles, sometimes on the basis of these data but other times (unfortunately) by processes of a priori reasoning. A number of his observations have proved erroneous, but a substantial number have been validated. The writings of Aristotle therefore reflect the earliest known systematic application of direct observation and experimentation to analyzing the living world. It was no fault of Aristotle's that in later centuries his works were treated as dogma—so that while his *conclusions* were accepted as truth, few dared adopt his *procedures.*

Not until the sixteenth century A.D. is there a record of significant rebellion against the authoritarianism that had paralyzed biological inquiry for nearly two millenia: in 1543, Andreas Vesalius published his outstanding work on the anatomy of the human body. His accurate and artistic anatomical drawings are still noteworthy, but Vesalius's greatest contribution was that he dared employ direct observation—he studied the human body itself and did not rely on ancient writings. Specifically, Vesalius challenged the works of Galen (a physician to Roman gladiators in the second century A.D.), whose writings, filled with error, were accepted as ultimate authority for 1,400 years! Gradually thereafter the abandonment of authoritarianism gained momentum and students of life followed Vesalius's lead in returning to the practices of direct observation and experimentation.

We can trace the development of biological thought over the past 2,000 years by summarizing key concepts or theories that revolutionized the study of life. In so doing we must remember that although it is often possible to ascribe an important concept to a specific individual (usually because that person published writings clearly formulating the concept and presenting supportive evidence), new concepts tend to arise not in the mind of any one individual but out of the intellectual climate of the day and have their origins in earlier, less well known, and often more speculative works. Except for the twentieth century, we shall limit our summary to those concepts which have stood the test of time to become principles of modern biology. Much of the biological work of the present century has served to test theories formulated in the last century and has firmly established some of them as principles. Theories developed in this century generally require further testing and may yet be modified, refuted, or established as principles. In previewing these concepts we should bear in mind that those requiring further explanation and discussion will be considered at greater length in later chapters. Their introduction at this time serves to provide a frame of reference that will give greater meaning to the material following.

KEY CONCEPTS DEVELOPED PRIOR TO THE NINETEENTH CENTURY *The ladder of nature* (scala naturae) Aristotle (fourth century B.C.) proposed that living things form a hierarchy in terms of organizational complexity, from forms barely distinguishable from the inanimate, to the highest forms of animal life.

Theory of biological inheritance The concept that traits of the parents are perpetuated in their offspring is stated by Aristotle in his great work *De Generatione Animalium* as ". . . the offspring always changes rather toward the likeness of the nearer ancestor than the more remote, both in the paternal and in the maternal line." (This generalization, not quite correct, may have been partly responsible for the blending theory of inheritance, refuted by Gregor Mendel in the nineteenth century.)

Mechanism In the seventeenth century a school of thought developed that attempted to liken the functioning of living bodies to that of machines. Broadened to the status of a generalization, mechanistic theory holds that life processes can be explained in terms of physicochemical laws applying to inanimate matter and need not be explained on the basis of a "vital force" not subject to such analysis. Important in establishing this theory were the works of the French philosopher and mathematician René Descartes, who formulated a concept of reflex action that integrated the functions of sense organs, nerves, and muscles, and the English physician William Harvey, who proved that human blood circulates through a closed system of blood vessels much as water does through a system of pipes. Mechanism changed the tenor of biological investigation, for previously it had been generally conceded that life processes could not be explained on the basis of known principles applying to the inanimate and any analytical investigation of these processes was hampered by being undertaken in an atmosphere of anticipated frustration.

Theory of epigenesis In 1759, C. F. Wolff published evidence that refuted the theory of preformation, which held that sex cells contained tiny preformed individuals that needed but to increase in size during embryonic development; he proposed the concept that the characteristics of the new individual must instead develop from the undifferentiated material of the sperm and eggs. Although requiring subsequent modernization, this theory set the stage for a new approach to the study of development. It also held implications for evolutionary theory, for according to the preformation theory (if carried to its logical conclusion) the gonads of the first creature created to represent each species must have contained the preformed individuals of the next generation, which in turn bore within their gonads the fully formed but even tinier individuals of the next generation, and so on, to the last possible generation of that species. Preformation implied both that there would be a finite life for a species, determined at the moment of its initial creation, and that significant hereditary changes could not take place since the pattern of all future generations was set in the sex organs of the first individual created.

KEY CONCEPTS DEVELOPED DURING THE NINETEENTH CENTURY *Cell theory* The results of microscopic studies carried on ever since Anthony van Leeuwenhoek invented the microscope around 1675, were finally synthesized in 1838 and 1839 by the zoologist T. Schwann and the botanist M. J. Schleiden into the important generalization that organized units of living matter known as *cells* are the basic units of structure and function in the bodies of all plants and animals. Twenty years later, R. Virchow added the concept that all cells come from preexisting cells and do not under present conditions arise from inanimate matter.

Theory of organic evolution The concept that living things are not unchanging but that new forms of life arise in the course of time while other forms become extinct was known to have been tentatively proposed by several biologists in the course of the eighteenth century but met with little acceptance at that time. At the dawn of the nineteenth century (1801) the renowned French zoologist and paleontologist Jean Baptiste Lamarck, who specialized in studying living and extinct invertebrates (animals without backbones), set forth a clear formulation of the theory of organic evolution. Unfortunately, current ignorance of hereditary mechanisms led him to propose that evolutionary change depended upon the inheritance of acquired characteristics: that is, through exercise and use a trait could be developed that would then be transmitted in this improved form to the offspring, which could develop it still more through further use. He proposed that in this manner giraffes developed long necks. Lamarck's concept of inheritance of acquired characteristics proved impossible to verify experimentally, and thus strengthened the arguments of those opposed to the idea of evolution, including the celebrated paleontologist Georges Cuvier, a colleague of Lamarck.

In 1859 Charles Darwin published his monumental work, *The Origin of Species by Means of Natural Selection,* which presented a staggering quantity of observational data in support of the theory of organic evolution and also proposed a mechanism of evolutionary progress that has proven valid in all major respects. Darwin's evidence was mostly obtained from specimens collected during his youthful voyage as ship's naturalist on *H.M.S. Beagle.* During this voyage he was particularly intrigued by the unique fauna and especially the bird life found inhabiting the Galápagos Islands off the coast of Peru. He noted that the resident songbird species seemed related to one type of ground finch found on the mainland, but that on the islands these birds had apparently become diversified for different modes of life. That these volcanic islands, obviously much less ancient than the mainland, should have a group of indigenous songbird species and a variety of other types of creatures found nowhere else in the world, seemed to him inconsistent with the accepted idea that all species had come into being at the same moment of divine creation. Darwin postulated instead that a gradual process of adaptation had taken place through an interaction between the organism and its environment. This process he termed *natural selection.* The conditions under which an organism lives constitute a set of *selective factors* that favor the survival of organisms possessing certain hereditary traits while simultaneously mitigating against survival of individuals having less favorable traits. In this way the hereditary makeup of a population changes generation by generation. Unlike the proposed evolutionary mechanism of Lamarck, natural selection has proved to be consistent with modern genetic theory.

The debate over organic evolution characterized the entire nineteenth century. Near its close (1898) H. F. Osborn, curator of vertebrate paleontology of the American Museum of Natural History, added new weight of evidence by establishing the concept of *adaptive radiation* (adaptation by diversification from a common ancestral type), developed on the basis of his studies of fossil vertebrates.

Theory of particulate inheritance While the conflict raged over evolutionary theory, Gregor Mendel, an Austrian monk, was quietly laying the experimental basis for the formulation of the basic laws of heredity. His data, published in 1865, clearly refuted the accepted doctrine of blending inheritance (that is, that the traits of the parents were blended in the offspring by some "mixing of blood") and established the fact that traits are inherited as unit characters or particles that are neither changed nor lost in the process of transmission and recombination. The significance of Mendel's work remained unrecognized until the close of the century; it was rediscovered and verified in 1900 by three investigators working independently (K. E. Correns, E. Tschermak, and H. de Vries).

Morgan's canon The work of seventeenth century mechanists and their successors enabled biologists to investigate physiological processes in terms of physicochemical laws, but the behavior of man and other animals still seemed exempt from mechanistic analysis. Then in 1894 the psychologist C. L. Morgan proposed a working concept: an animal's behavior should be interpreted in terms of the simplest mental process capable of producing this behavior. Adoption of this concept, known as Morgan's canon, opened the door for the objective study of behavior, starting with attempts to dissect even the most complex forms of behavior into simple units such as reflexes.

KEY CONCEPTS DEVELOPED DURING THE PRESENT CENTURY The twentieth century has seen the development of a scientific culture—one in which so many people are engaged in scientific pursuits that a milieu has been created in which the pace of scientific research is accelerating. Significant discoveries in chemistry and physics have led to important advances in biology, and interdisciplinary attacks upon formidable problems have become common practice. Methodologies developed in the physical sciences are now being applied to the life sciences and those developed in the life sciences are being extended to the social sciences. It is too early to compile a definitive roster of ordering principles of biology that have originated in the twentieth century, but we can enumerate important theories now being subjected to rigorous testing that may become accepted principles in the future.

Important as these newer concepts are, one of the greatest contributions of the present century has been the firm establishment of the principle of organic evolution, which is undoubtedly the fundamental unifying principle of biology. The concept of organic evolution makes sense of both similarities and differences among organisms; it holds true for the organization of life at the molecular level as well as for the gross characteristics of organisms. In the last century evolutionary theory rested strictly upon observational data; in the present century its foundations have been reinforced by genetic and experimental data.

If evolutionary theory was the keynote of the nineteenth century, perhaps we can say that the concept of the *universality of biotic mechanisms* has been the keynote of the twentieth century. This century began with the rediscovery of Mendel's laws of heredity and their extension to a wide variety of plants and animals, giving evidence that universal mechanisms of heredity may operate in all forms of life. From this beginning, investigations of life processes at the cellular and molecular levels have continued to lend support to the concept that common molecular organizational patterns exist throughout the living world; for instance, a biochemical pathway found to exist in the cells of a protozoan or a plant may also be found to occur in virtually the same form in human tissues.

Important concepts developed in the present century include the following:

Mutation theory of evolution In 1901, Hugo deVries proposed the theory that evolutionary progress depends upon changes in genetic factors; mutation and natural selection are now considered to be the two major mechanisms by means of which organic evolution takes place.

Theory of the gene Work done between 1910 and 1920 by Thomas H. Morgan and his coworkers with the fruit fly *Drosophila* linked Mendel's unit characters to visible bodies within the cells, namely, chromosomes. A gene was proposed to be the portion of a chromosome responsible for transmission of a single trait or Mendelian character. This theory provided a physical explanation for the behavior of Mendel's unit characters.

Organizer concept in embryology In 1921, Hans Spemann proposed an extension of the epigenetic theory, with the idea that developmental patterns in the embryo are controlled by means of inductive interactions among embryonic tissues; certain regions of the embryo having a particularly powerful inductive influence on surrounding tissues, he termed *organizers*. Induction, the channeling of a tissue's developmental potential, is seen as a means whereby the maturation of different types of tissues is integrated so that an effectively organized multicellular body is produced.

Concept of the ecosystem In 1935, A. G. Tansley formulated the concept that organisms and environment are parts of a unit (the *ecosystem*) within which mass and energy are utilized cyclically; perpetuation of the ecosystem depends upon a complex web of ecological interrelationships among plants, animals, microbes, and their physicochemical environment. The looming problems of habitat destruction, environmental pollution, and the derangement of natural balances due to human activities make the ecosystem concept one of the most significant today in terms of the survival of man and other species.

One gene–one enzyme The Nobel prize was awarded in 1958 to G. W. Beadle and E. L. Tatum for their years of research during which they established the hypothesis (now considered a theory) that genes function by controlling the production of cellular proteins, most of which are enzymes (substances that affect the rates of specific cellular activities), and that the action of each enzyme is required for expression of a given hereditary trait. This concept helped to bridge the gap between observed genetic traits and genes, the physical carriers of heredity.

Theory of abiogenesis Replication of possible "primitive earth conditions," pioneered by H. Urey and S. L. Miller in 1953, demonstrated that organic compounds can arise from inorganic precursors. This supports the theory that under certain conditions living systems can originate from the inanimate.

Theory of perpetuation of life by nucleic acid replication A number of investigators have established the hereditary role of compounds (nucleic acids) that constitute the genes postulated by Morgan. In 1953, F. H. C. Crick and J. D. Watson investigated the chemical structure of DNA (deoxyribonucleic acid) and proposed a mechanism whereby this compound can reproduce itself. Nucleic acids are the carriers of heredity and, being capable of self-replication, form the basis for reproduction of all forms of life including viruses. Furthermore, deVries' mutations can now be explained in terms of alterations in nucleic acid molecules, which in turn produce changes in protein molecules. This latter finding was largely the outcome of the work of V. M. Ingram, who in 1956 determined the chemical compositions of normal and mutant forms of the blood pigment hemoglobin.

Theory of universality of basic metabolic mechanisms We do not yet know how many exceptions to this generalization may exist, but data obtained to date imply that the genetic code may be universal or at least very similar throughout the living world (the "genetic code" being the nucleic acid pattern that governs protein synthesis), and that important biochemical pathways may exist in essentially identical form in widely different groups of organisms. This theory can be considered an extension of the cell theory of Schleiden and Schwann, for if the cell is the basic unit of structure and function in all plants and animals it is not surprising that cellular mechanisms may also be alike.

Theory of innate behavior Konrad Lorenz and N. Tinbergen have largely been responsible for development of the concept that many important patterns of animal behavior can be termed *innate* in that they need not be learned but can be genetically transmitted (in the sense that any bodily trait is inheritable). This concept extends evolutionary and genetic theory to the study of behavior, for innate behavior is as much subject to genetic change, natural selection, and evolution, as any other genetically based character. In fact, selection toward a given behavioral change may precede selection toward relevant morphological changes.

Theory of intrinsic population-density control mechanisms This concept, proposed by V. C. Wynne-Edwards and others, suggests that the rate of increase of many species is controlled less by predation, starvation, and disease (the extrinsic population-control factors proposed by Darwin) than by evolved mechanisms operating *within* a species. These mechanisms maintain numerical stability by balancing mortality and the recruitment of new individuals to the breeding population, and keep animal numbers at a level well below that at which the habitat would be overexploited. These important control mechanisms, apparently both behavioral and physiological, are now under investigation and will be discussed later in this book.

The developing and testing of these ordering concepts has brought our understanding of life to a level at which the study of biology has become much more satisfying than was possible only a generation ago. Details of anatomy and taxonomy are now largely deferred to more advanced courses in the biological curriculum and their place taken in the beginning course of study by considerations of ecological relationships, genetic and evolutionary mechanisms, and the organization and functioning of life especially at the molecular and cellular levels. The study of the organism itself has become less a matter of examining body functions at the gross systemic level than of relating general physiological processes (such as digestion or circulation) to events taking place within the cell. In addition, the riddle of integration—the manner in which the development and subsequent functioning of a multicellular body is coordinated—must now receive greater attention, although much remains to be known concerning the mechanisms of integration. Above all, every aspect of life can now be viewed in the light of modern genetic and evolutionary principles: the mechanisms of genetic change at the molecular level and of evolutionary progress at the organismal and population levels are now reasonably well understood, allowing us to interpret biotic phenomena with increasing confidence and logic. Nevertheless, many fundamental questions have not yet been resolved; these remain to test the ingenuity of coming generations.

1.2 □ ORDER IN DIVERSITY

Faced with a horde of diverse living things and lacking understanding of how such diversity could have come about, early naturalists set forth to assemble living things into taxonomic groups (*taxa;* singular, *taxon*) indicative of relatedness. Early attempts to systematize the living world in this manner were crude and often inaccurate, for gross similarities may be superficial. For instance, Aristotle proposed the catch-all taxon Vermes (worms) for all slithering creatures of dubious antecedents. This category has long been superseded by a number of more valid categories known as *phyla* (singular, *phylum*). In the light of more careful description we can no longer say that "a worm is a worm," but must recognize separate phyla of flatworms, ribbon worms, roundworms, segmented worms, and arrow worms. Each phylum is characterized by a common organizational pattern or body plan, expressed with variations in the different specific types of creatures that make up the phylum.

A The development of modern systematics

During the past two centuries systematics has adhered, at the level of lower taxa in particular, to the framework established in the eighteenth century by Carl von Linné (Linnaeus). Linnaeus set forth criteria for defining *genera* (singular, *genus*) and *species,* and proposed an international system of naming organisms that has become universally recognized as the Linnaean system of *binomial nomenclature.* Under this system each kind of living thing is designated by two names (or sometimes three), customarily derived from Latin or Greek. The first name indicates the genus to which it belongs, the second, the particular species within the genus, and the third (when present) the *variety, race,* or *subspecies.* A genus may be conveniently defined as a taxon encompassing a group of closely related species. A species is considerably more difficult to define adequately and in fact our understanding of the species concept is still incomplete. For the present a species may be thought of as an interbreeding population of organisms possessing a unique group of traits by which it may more or less readily be recognized. A robin is one species of bird, a tanager is another, and the two do not interbreed when they occur together in the same habitat. In size, plumage, song, and diet, the two species differ. However, our simplified definition falls short when it must encompass physical diversity as seen in the great dane, bulldog, and dachshund, all belonging to the species *Canis familiaris* (domestic dog) but greatly differing in size and overall appearance because of selective breeding practices. While there are exceptions, the usual rule (which we shall understand better after reading Chapter 8) is that organisms of one species cannot breed successfully with those of another species: offspring produced by such *heterospecific* ("different species") matings are usually infertile.

Linnaean nomenclature possesses the advantages of (1) indicating relatedness, insofar as allied species may be grouped into genera, (2) being relatively stable and internationally recognized, and (3) often imparting minor descriptive information about the organism. Linnaeus, who was primarily a botanist, contributed significantly to plant systematics by recognizing that although the vegetative forms of plants may differ radically even within closely related groups, the morphology of their reproductive organs (pistils and stamens in seed plants) is conservative and may be employed as the most reliable basis for determining degree of relatedness. (This brilliant suggestion can be considered an instance of the operation of *insight,* mentioned in the caption to Figure 1.2.) He also lent impetus to the acceptance of an international scheme of nomenclature by originating scientific names for many plants and animals native to Europe or available in museum collections of the day, a contribution attested to by the many species to which his name is appended as the describing taxonomist.

Over the two centuries following Linnaeus's work various systematists contributed to the establishment of higher categories forming a hierarchy of taxonomic levels ascending with increasing inclusiveness from the *specific* to the *phyletic* level. According to this *Linnaean hierarchy,* related genera are grouped into *families,* related families into *orders,* related orders into *classes,* and related classes into *phyla.* Additional levels of grouping have been fitted into this construct as needed. Each taxon features a group of attributes that serve as distinguishing characteristics of the organisms assigned to that taxon. Each lesser taxon must possess the distinguishing features of those higher taxa encompassing it in addition to characteristics peculiar to itself.

The continuing task of classification is centered upon the study of evolutionary relationships. This is now facilitated by comparisons of embryonic development, comparative chromosome analysis, comparative ethology (studies of normal adaptive behavior), determination of degree of biochemical similarity, and other comparisons of structure and function. Additional paleontological data also continue to accumulate as new fossil species come to light.

The approximate age of fossils can now be determined by calculating the extent to which radioactive materials associated with the fossils have decayed. Uranium (^{238}U) undergoes a series of changes that ultimately result in the production of lead (^{206}Pb). Over a period of about 4.5×10^9 (4,500,000,000) years, half of those ^{238}U atoms originally present in a rock sample would have turned to ^{206}Pb. The *half-life* of a radioactive element is the time required for half of the atoms present to disintegrate;

the half-life of ^{238}U is considered to be 4.5×10^9 years. This figure means that 1 g of ^{238}U would, at a constant rate over a period of 4.5×10^9 years yield 0.5 g of ^{206}Pb. During the next 4.5×10^9 years the remaining ^{238}U would undergo disintegration of half of its atoms, yielding 0.25 g of ^{206}Pb. By the end of a third period of 4.5×10^9 years half of those ^{238}U atoms then remaining would have decayed, yielding 0.125 g of ^{206}Pb, and so forth. This regular and predictable rate of disintegration permits radioactive elements of long half-life to serve as "geological clocks." Rock samples are dated by measuring the relative quantities of radioactive materials and their stable decay products present in unweathered crystals of the sample. Radioactive elements of shorter half-life than ^{238}U may allow fossils to be dated with even greater precision. A particularly useful element is radioactive potassium (^{40}K) which decays to argon (^{40}Ar) with a half-life of 1.4×10^9 years. The well-known carbon 14 technique is actually of more value to physiologists and ecologists than to taxonomists, for it can reliably establish the age only of materials less than 50,000 years old (^{14}C having a half-life of only 5,600 years), but is very useful as a means of tracing carbon compounds in living tissue.

One of the most significant outcomes of the development of radioactive dating techniques is that the biosphere (and of course the earth itself) has been shown to be much older than was commonly supposed only a century ago. Traces of life in rock samples estimated to be well over 2×10^9 years old have made inescapable the conclusion that the biosphere has reached its present state through the gradual process of change that we call organic evolution. As we said above, this conclusion has not only opened the past to the science of biology (for the life of the past need no longer be thought virtually identical with that of the present), but it has enabled us to approach the study of existing life from a new and exciting perspective. Like detectives in pursuit of clues we attempt to reconstruct the past, unearthing the roots from which have sprung the forms and functions of the living world as we see it today. Furthermore, the evolutionary process, set in motion perhaps 3×10^9 years ago, certainly has not come to a halt today, and so we are faced with the additional challenge of trying to detect evolutionary trends now in operation and to extrapolate from present data the future outcomes of those trends. To deflect, accelerate, or counteract these trends may be vital to the continuance of human life, for already in our ignorance we may have been instrumental in giving impetus to forces leading toward extinction.

Today most students of evolution are not primarily taxonomists, but are geneticists, ecologists, ethologists, comparative anatomists, and molecular biologists. Nevertheless they contribute to the continuing task of systematics by discovering additional properties characteristic of specific forms of life, which may reveal their evolutionary origins. The resultant massing of data has made imperative the application of computer technology to taxonomic problems. Evolution-centered systematics (*phylogenetic* taxonomy) utilizes computer techniques primarily for data retrieval and rapid identification, but there has recently developed a school of taxonomy known as *numerical phenetics,* which by submitting for computer analysis almost every measurable trait of an organism seeks to discover the affinities of present-day groups without drawing deductions about their evolutionary descent. Pheneticists contend that since evolutionary branchpoints must remain obscure, it is less fruitful to trace relationships through comparisons with the fossil record than to analyze numerically the characteristics of living species. The proportion of traits held in common by any two groups is considered indicative of the degree of affinity between those groups. Phylogenetic taxonomists feel this philosophy to be in error, for in according a numerical designation to each trait all are given equal value and the historical significance of particular characteristics may therefore be overlooked.

The future of systematics may lie in a fruitful amalgamation of the phylogenetic and phenetic approaches. Meanwhile, pending the centralized computer storage of phenetic data on all known species, most biologists must continue to identify organisms unknown to them by making reference to published *keys* which backtrack *downward* through the Linnaean hierarchy, a procedure somewhat the reverse of that employed in originating the hierarchical construct itself.

B Keying out an unknown

If we had in hand a small furry being with two pairs of jointed limbs, a long and relatively hairless tail, and four prominent cutting teeth or incisors, we could classify it by making a serial comparison of its attributes with those distinguishing various taxa. Beginning with phyletic characteristics, we would find that only two animal phyla, Arthropoda and Chordata, contain members with jointed appendages (limbs). Of these two phyla, only Subphylum Vertebrata of Phylum Chordata is characterized by having only two pairs of such limbs and by having an *internal* articulated skeleton. Within Subphylum Vertebrata we could at once eliminate our unknown from the various classes of fishes by virtue of its land-adapted legs. Among the classes of tetrapods (four-footed vertebrates) we can recognize our specimen as a mammal because of its hair and mammary glands as well as other mammalian traits disclosed only by an internal examination. Among the orders of the Class Mammalia only Lagomorpha and Rodentia are characterized by possession of long, chisel-shaped gnawing teeth. Because the lagomorphs have six such incisors and the rodents only four, the conformity of our unknown with the latter trait indicates that it is a rodent. At this point recourse could be made to a taxonomic key to the Rodentia. A key consists of a series of usually paired comparisons of selected traits, involving successive refinements. By comparing the specimen with the selected traits it is usually possible to arrive at a correct conclusion regarding the genus and species.

In the present example our unknown is the black rat, named *Rattus rattus rattus* in what was possibly a moment of creative fatigue. In orderly fashion the systematics of the black rat may be presented in the following scheme:

Phylum: Chordata (possessing a hollow brain and a notochord)
Subphylum: Vertebrata (having a backbone of vertebrae and a cranium)
Class: Mammalia (having hair, mammary glands, and so forth)
Order: Rodentia (having two pairs of chisel-like incisors)
Family: Muridae (resembling a mouse)
Genus: *Rattus* (a rat)
Species: *Rattus rattus* (a black rat as opposed to, say, a Norway rat)
Subspecies: *Rattus rattus rattus* (a specific race of black rat)

Utilizing the Linnaean system, about half a million species of plants and over a million species of animals have been named and classified, together with a number of forms that do not permit themselves gracefully to be categorized as either plant or animal. The task is far from complete and each year newly described species or revisions of earlier classifications appear. Indeed, it is possible that insect species may actually evolve more rapidly than we have to date been able to classify them!

C Advantages and disadvantages of systematics

As is the case with many conceptual devices, schemes of classification confer both advantages and disadvantages on those who use them. The *advantages* are fairly obvious: (1) they provide convenient means for cataloging living things in a manner indicative of their relationships; (2) they facilitate data retrieval by adhering to accepted conventions of nomenclature and organization. The *disadvantages* reside mainly in the fact that taxonomic categories purport to be much more definite than are the organisms which they categorize. In the first place, there is no reliable means for "weighting" taxa. One may mistakenly assume that there is a well-defined "jump" from genus to family or from order to class which is identical in the case of all genera, families, orders, and classes. One may also wrongly conclude that a genus, for example, is a genuine *entity* having a definite form and aspect, rather than a *concept* within the elastic boundaries of which it is possible for a given genus to be either small and uniform or large and varied. Furthermore, taxonomic schemes, while of great utilitarian merit, do not recognize the fact that life forms display *intermediate* conditions of structure and function that often make the decision extremely difficult (and arbitrary) as to where to draw the line relegating a given organism to this group or that. This problem of intergradation was recognized over 2,000 years ago by Aristotle, who wrote:* "Nature proceeds little by little from things lifeless to animal life in such a way that it is impossible to determine the exact line of demarcation, nor on which side thereof an intermediate form should lie." This is a remarkably perceptive statement from one who knew nothing of those microorganisms which are true intermediates between living and inanimate and between plant and animal!

D The species problem

The problem of defining a species is illustrated by a salamander of the western

*Aristotle, Historia Animalium, Book VIII, in *The Works of Aristotle Translated into English*, Vol. IV, J. A. Smith and W. D. Ross, eds., trans. by D'Arcy W. Thompson (London and New York: Oxford University Press, 1910), p. 588b.

United States, *Ensatina eschscholtzi*. As stated before, one criterion of "species" is the extent to which the members of a population will interbreed under natural conditions and produce progeny that are themselves fully fertile. Hybridization between species is uncommon in nature and when it does occur typically yields sterile offspring (such as the mule, the hybrid offspring of horse and donkey). Virtual *absence of spontaneous interbreeding* between two similar types of organisms can thus be used to indicate separate species.

In the case of *E. eschscholtzi* the major and presumably original population of the species occurs throughout the humid Pacific Northwest. Proceeding southward into California, climatic conditions compatible with the well-being of salamanders are largely restricted to two separate mountain chains: the coastal range and the Sierra Nevada. *Ensatina* has apparently extended its range southward along each of these mountain ridges, the two populations being isolated from one another by the great Central Valley—at present a region of natural aridity and seasonal heat, at other times an inland sea. In southern California the most southerly races of *E. eschscholtzi* meet in a common habitat (that is, are *sympatric*). But here they do not seem to interbreed freely and display dissimilarities, particularly of coloration, that would lead us to conclude that these two races are actually separate species (Figure 1.4). However, other races exist which interbreed where their ranges overlap and which thus maintain a degree of reproductive compatibility along each mountain chain from north to south. Each race can interbreed with adjacent races to the north and south, but are progressively less able to interbreed with races occuring in more distant ranges. Presumably the farther apart any two races live, the longer they have been isolated from one another.

Figure 1.4 □ A problem in speciation: the salamander *Ensatina eschscholtzi*. Two subspecies are shown that do not interbreed in nature: (*a*) *E. e. eschscholtzi* (*courtesy of General Biological, Inc., Chicago*) and (*b*) *E. e. klauberi* (*Zoological Society of San Diego*). Note the salamanders' moist skin, which restricts them from inhabiting arid habitats and has confined the races of *Ensatina* to the more humid mountainous regions during their extension of range from Oregon to southern California.

Should the two southern races of *Ensatina* persistently fail to interbreed, and should the linking races eventually be eradicated (perhaps as a result of climatic changes or habitat destruction), future systematists no doubt would assign them to separate species.

The preceding example should serve to point up the problem that faces taxonomists: not only may contemporary species be at times difficult to define, but living things possess the unsettling attribute of being subject to change. Some of these changes occur in the hereditary material (mutations) and may be transmissible to future generations. No one generation has a genetic constitution exactly like that of the preceding generation. Therefore, when we attempt to describe a particular species, we are in fact only naming and describing a *limited segment of a population's lifeline:* that segment which exists here and now. The greater taxa such as phyla and classes persist through long periods of time, measured in hundreds of millions of years. Lesser taxa such as genera and species represent relatively ephemeral manifestations of the fundamental body plans of the phyla to which they belong. Rarely is the record of past life sufficiently complete to permit us to reconstruct in full the progressive alteration by which species *A* may imperceptibly become species *B*, or by which geographically isolated (*allopatric*) populations of species *X* may evolve independently into species *W* and *Y*, respectively (see Figure 8.15).

E Homology, analogy, and homomorphism

A perennial problem in the study of biotic diversity is that of distinguishing among *analogous, homologous,* and *homomorphic* traits. Characteristics alike in origin but differing in function may become so different that a basic relationship is obscured. Conversely, characteristics of different origin but of similar function may come to resemble one another so closely that they appear to indicate a close relationship where none actually exists.

ANALOGY AND CONVERGENCE Under similar environmental influences, organisms

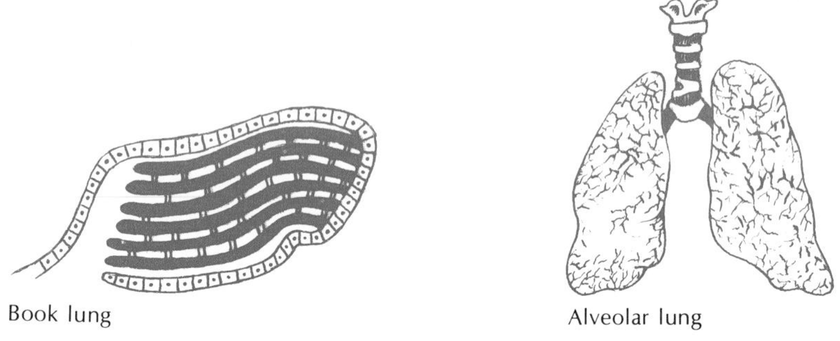

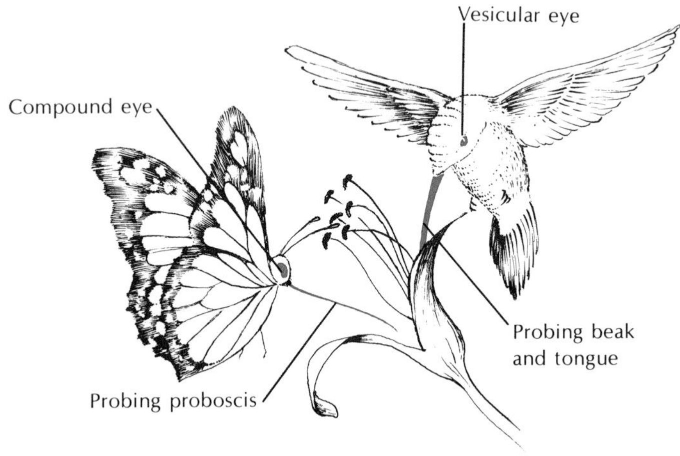

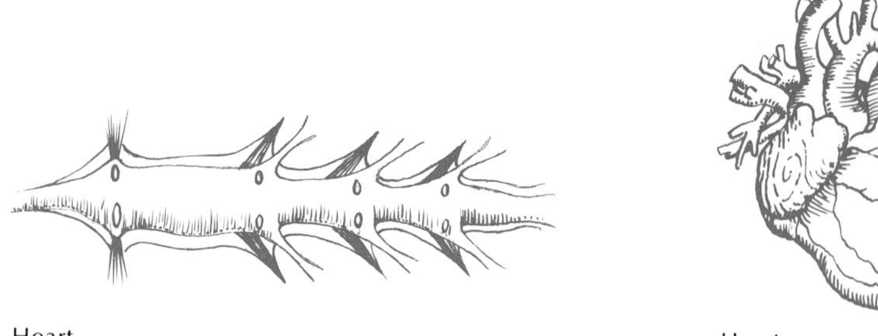

Figure 1.5 □ Analogous structures have comparable functions but often follow very different evolutionary histories although structurally they may resemble one another more or less closely. (*a*) Respiratory organs of spider and man, both used for breathing in terrestrial habitats. (*b*) Eye and mouth parts of insect and bird are built on different structural patterns; yet each eye type allows perception of color and form, and both butterfly and hummingbird have slender, elongated mouthparts with which to probe tubular flowers. (*c*) Hearts of insect and mammal each serve to circulate blood.

Squid

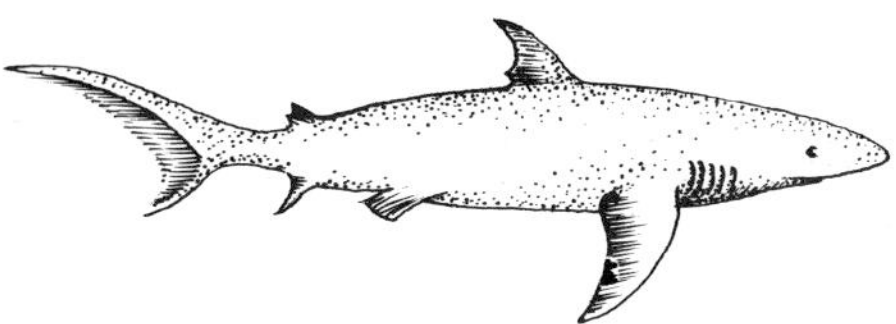

Shark

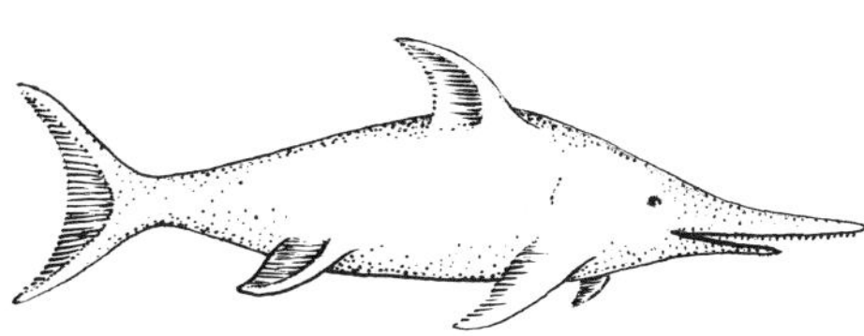

Ichthyosaur

Penguin

Seal

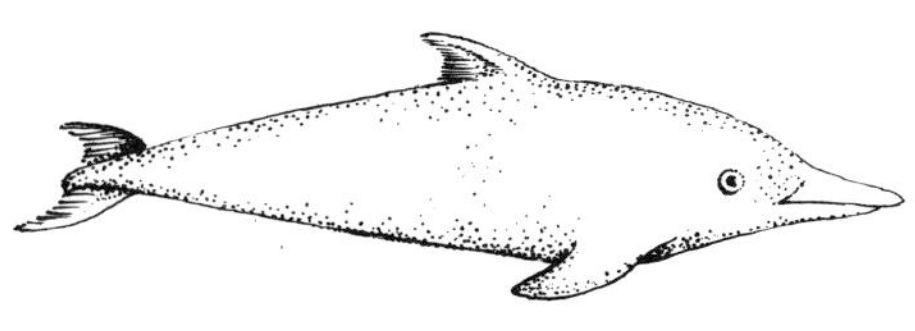

Porpoise

only distantly related may develop similarities of structure and function which adapt them to that environment. These similarities imply a degree of relatedness that is in fact nonexistent. Structures *performing the same function* without necessarily sharing a close common origin are considered to be *analogous* to one another (Figure 1.5). They may be as different in construction as the wing of an insect and that of a bird, both of which are employed in flight yet are so dissimilar as to pose no problem for the taxonomist or student of evolution. On the other hand, analogous structures of unlike origin sometimes tend to become almost identical to one another by a process of *convergence*. Convergence is seen in the case of the streamlined bodies of efficient swimmers of diverse ancestry, such as the squid, shark, seal, porpoise, penguin, and ichthyosaur (Figure 1.6). All of these except the squid are vertebrates and share certain structural homologies, but since the latter four have all descended from different terrestrial ancestors, their close resemblance is basically due to analogous convergence.

In Australia pouched mammals (*marsupials*) enjoyed a long history of evolutionary development free from competition with the more modern placental mammals (*eutherians*) that had successfully expanded throughout the other continents but were long barred from Australia because of its relatively isolated position. This geographical barrier allowed marsupials and eutherians to evolve along separate but frequently parallel or convergent lines of descent. As a result, many equivalent forms came into being, pursuing similar modes of life and exhibiting analogous adaptations with strong convergence. These analogs include the wolf and the marsupial "wolf," the mole and marsupial "mole," the flying squirrel and flying phalanger, and so forth (Figure 1.7). The marsupial wolf (now nearly extinct) is so wolflike in appearance and mode of life that we may be surprised to find that in ancestry and embryonic development this animal is more closely related to the kangaroo than it is to the true wolf (Figure 1.8). Conversely, the wolf is more closely related to the whale than it is to its marsupial analog!

Figure 1.6 □ Evolutionary convergence. These marine animals are all efficient swimmers and show similar adaptations of form resulting from the selective influence of their similar mode of existence. All shown are vertebrates except the squid (a mollusc). Except for the shark, the vertebrates shown have descended from different terrestrial ancestors and are air-breathers, the ichthyosaur being a reptile (extinct), the penguin, a bird, and the seal and porpoise, mammals belonging to two different orders. All have developed comparable adaptations for reducing friction, increasing buoyancy, providing forward thrust, and minimizing roll and pitch.

Physiological processes and behavioral patterns may also undergo analogous convergence. For example, egg-guarding behavior has evolved independently in such different animals as cobra, stickleback, octopus, and spider.

HOMOLOGY AND RADIATIVE ADAPTATION Homologous characteristics are those which have a *common evolutionary and developmental origin* but may have diverged in structure and function. They are taken as evidence of common descent. Homology stemming from the common ancestry of a group of species is known as *phylogenetic homology* (Figure 1.9). Another type, *serial homology,* is seen in animals

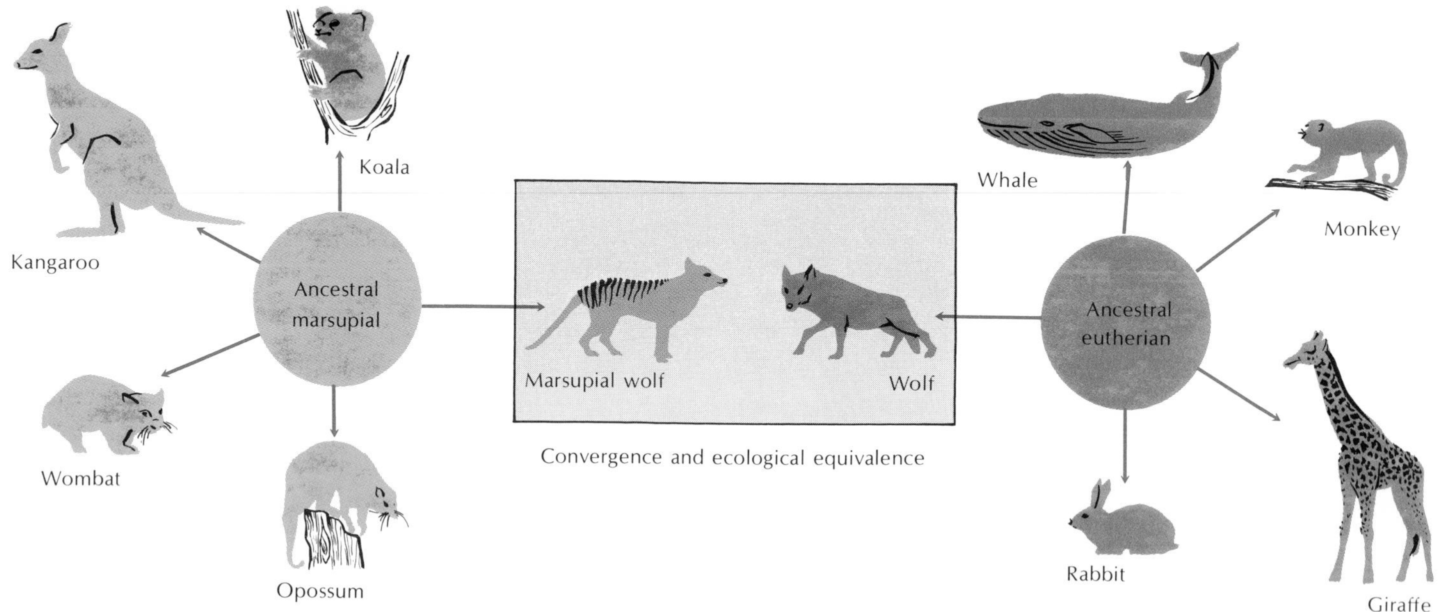

Figure 1.7 □ **Ecological equivalence. Organisms playing comparable roles in different biotic communities are termed *ecological equivalents.* The isolation of Australia from other continents in early mammalian history favored the development of equivalent forms of marsupial (pouched) and eutherian (placental) mammals. Some of these also show remarkable *convergence* in structure, physiology, and behavior, such as the wolf and the marsupial "wolf," or thylacine.**

Figure 1.8 □ **Marsupial analogs of familiar eutherian mammals. (*a*) Thylacine. This last captive specimen died in Australia in 1933. If not actually extinct, thylacines are now confined to secluded wilds of Tasmania, having vanished from the Australian continent. The striking physical similarity between this marsupial and the eutherian wolf exemplifies structural convergence in unrelated animals of similar modes of life. (*Courtesy of Australian News and Information Bureau.*) (*b*) Tasmanian devil (*Sarcophilus*). This carnivorous marsupial resembles the North American wolverine in its ferocity, strength, and surprisingly powerful jaws. It can kill prey considerably larger than itself (such as sheep) and here is seen working upon a bone. (*Courtesy of Australian News and Information Bureau.*)**

Figure 1.9 □ **Phylogenetic homology. Vertebrate forelimbs, derived from a generalized ancestral type, have undergone diversification toward different types of employment but continue to feature homologous skeletal elements (indicated by shades of black and color). Digits are numbered in parallel.**

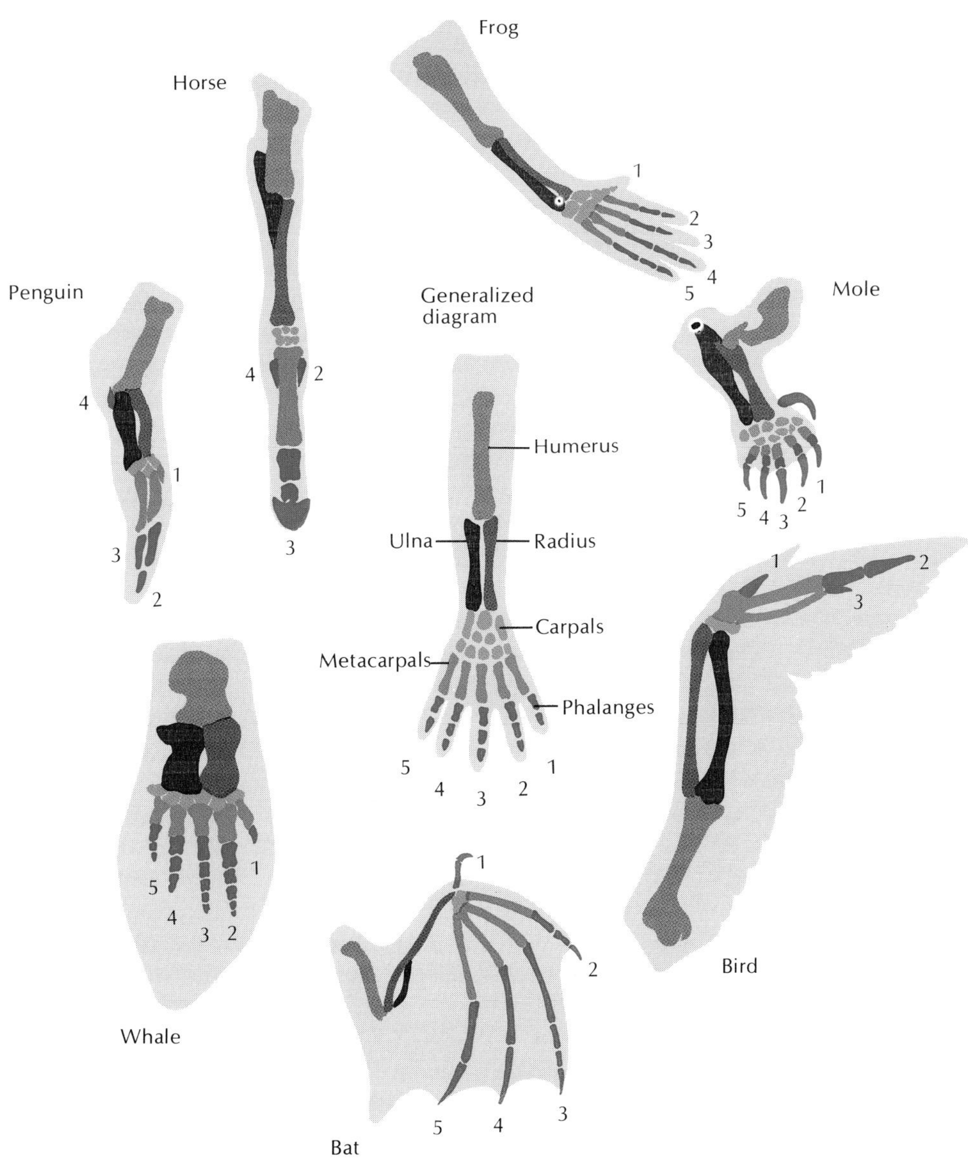

having a segmented plan of body construction. In these species the "unit of construction" is the individual segment (which is repeated along the length of the body). This serial repetition is readily detectable in animals composed of a series of similar body segments such as the clamworm (Figure 1.10*a*), in which the internal organs and flaplike appendages of each segment are largely identical. In such animals as insects and vertebrates, the basically homologous body parts have undergone diversification so that they are no longer alike in form or function (Figure 1.10*b*). Serially homologous structures are taken to be consecutive repetitions of a basic structural "package" produced by reiteration of part of the organism's hereditary code.

Structures of similar origin come to *diverge* in appearance as they become adapted for different uses; this process is termed *radiative adaptation*. Flipper of whale, foreleg of horse, wing of bird, and arm of man are all phylogenetically homologous and show parallel embryonic development. Similarly, the serially homologous appendages of the lobster are variations on a simple Y-shaped basic pattern that has become diversified for locomotion, food handling, copulation, defense, and sensory perception (Figure 1.11): even lobster antennae and crushing jaws are modified legs!

Radiative adaptation and convergence both come about through the interaction of organisms and their environments: mutational changes take place in the hereditary materials, causing variation in any population of living things. Selective factors in the environment then define the survival value of these traits, so that some individuals survive and contribute more offspring to the

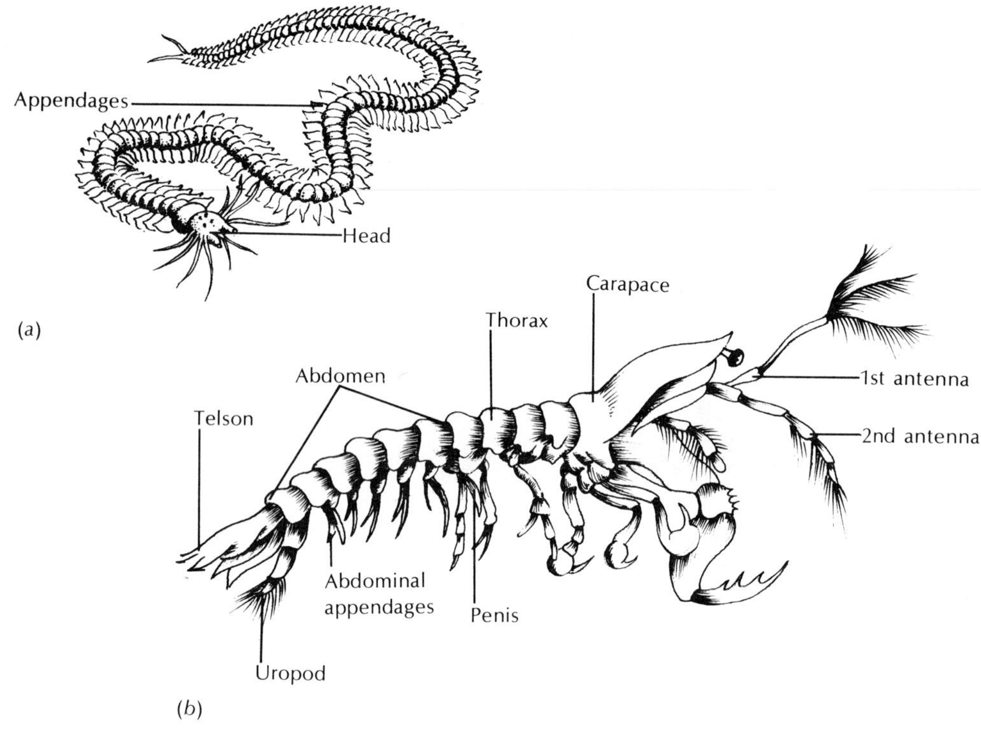

Figure 1.10 □ **Two successful patterns of body organization. (*a*) Homonomous metamerism: the body of the clamworm, *Nereis*, consists of a series of similar segments, each bearing a pair of appendages identical with all the rest. (*b*) Heteronomous metamerism: the mantis shrimp, *Squilla*, exhibits a moderate degree of modification and fusion of body segments, together with functional diversification of the serially homologous appendages.**

next generation than do others. In this manner unrelated species living in similar habitats and pursuing similar modes of life tend to become alike, whereas related species occupying different habitats and pursuing different modes of life tend to become more and more different from one another.

HOMOMORPHISM When comparing similar structures we must note instances in which such structures are neither homologous nor convergent—they may be alike simply because of genetic and developmental limitations that dictate the range of choice possible for constructing a viable organism. For instance, planar (watchspring-type) coils occur among shelled protozoans, nautiloids, and snails. Such shells are better considered *homomorphic* (of like form) than analogous (of like function), for the incidence of planar coiling in these three groups probably results from the fact that a shell can coil in relatively few ways.

Furthermore, functionality often demands that efficient organs be constructed along similar lines, in which case structures appearing independently in unrelated groups may be both analogous and homomorphic. The architecture of an eye, for example, can be of only a few types, all of

Figure 1.11 □ **Serial homology. The serially homologous appendages of the lobster display diversification adaptive to the assumption of a variety of functions. All appear to have been derived from an ancestral two-branched (biramous) pattern, best illustrated by the swimmeret, in which a medial *endopodite* (colored dots) and a lateral *exopodite* (dark-colored area) spring from the basal *basopodite* (uncolored). Both lateral and medial branches are not present in all appendages.**

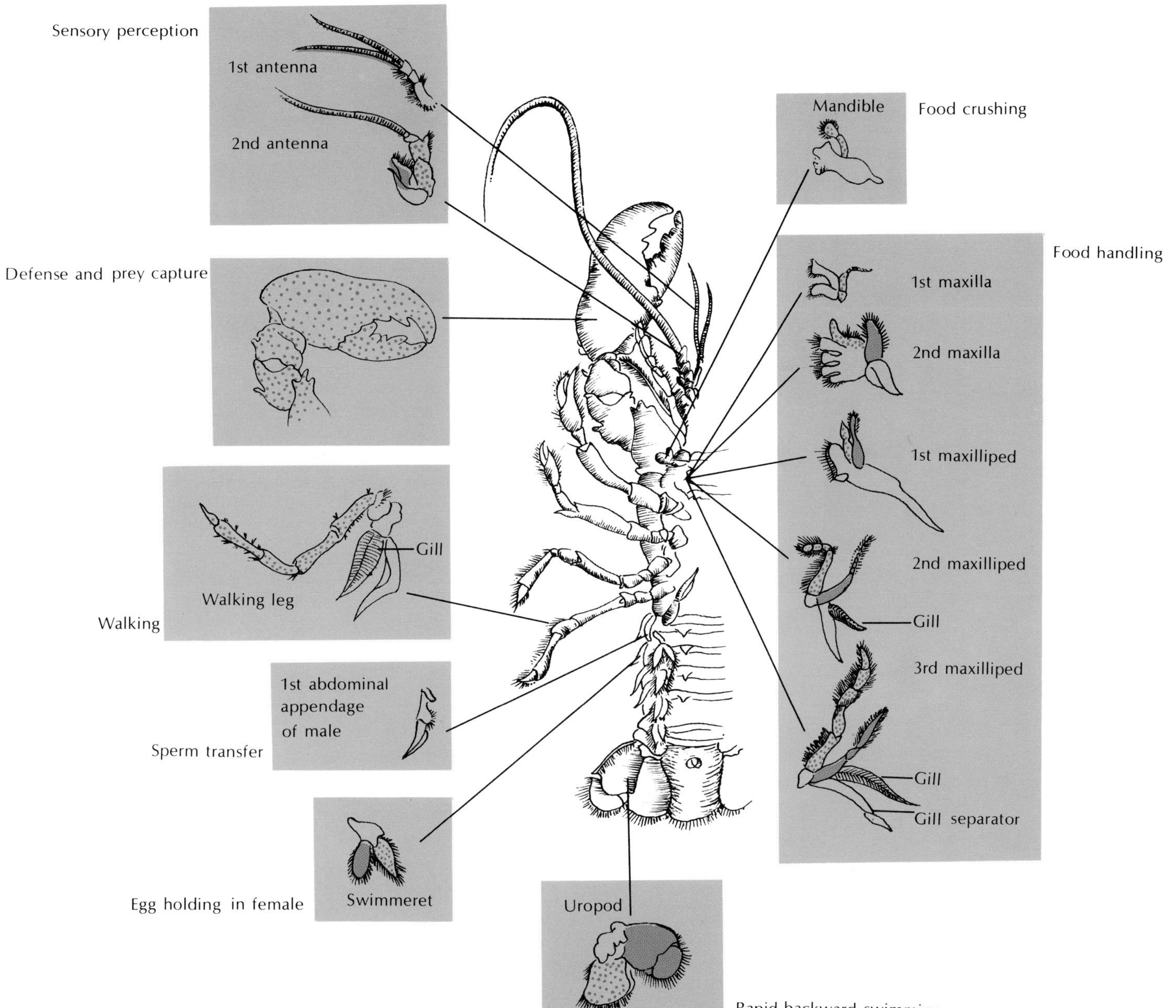
Sensory perception
1st antenna
2nd antenna
Defense and prey capture
Walking leg
Gill
Walking
1st abdominal
appendage
of male
Sperm transfer
Egg holding in female
Swimmeret
Uropod
Rapid backward swimming
Mandible
Food crushing
Food handling
1st maxilla
2nd maxilla
1st maxilliped
2nd maxilliped
Gill
3rd maxilliped
Gill
Gill separator

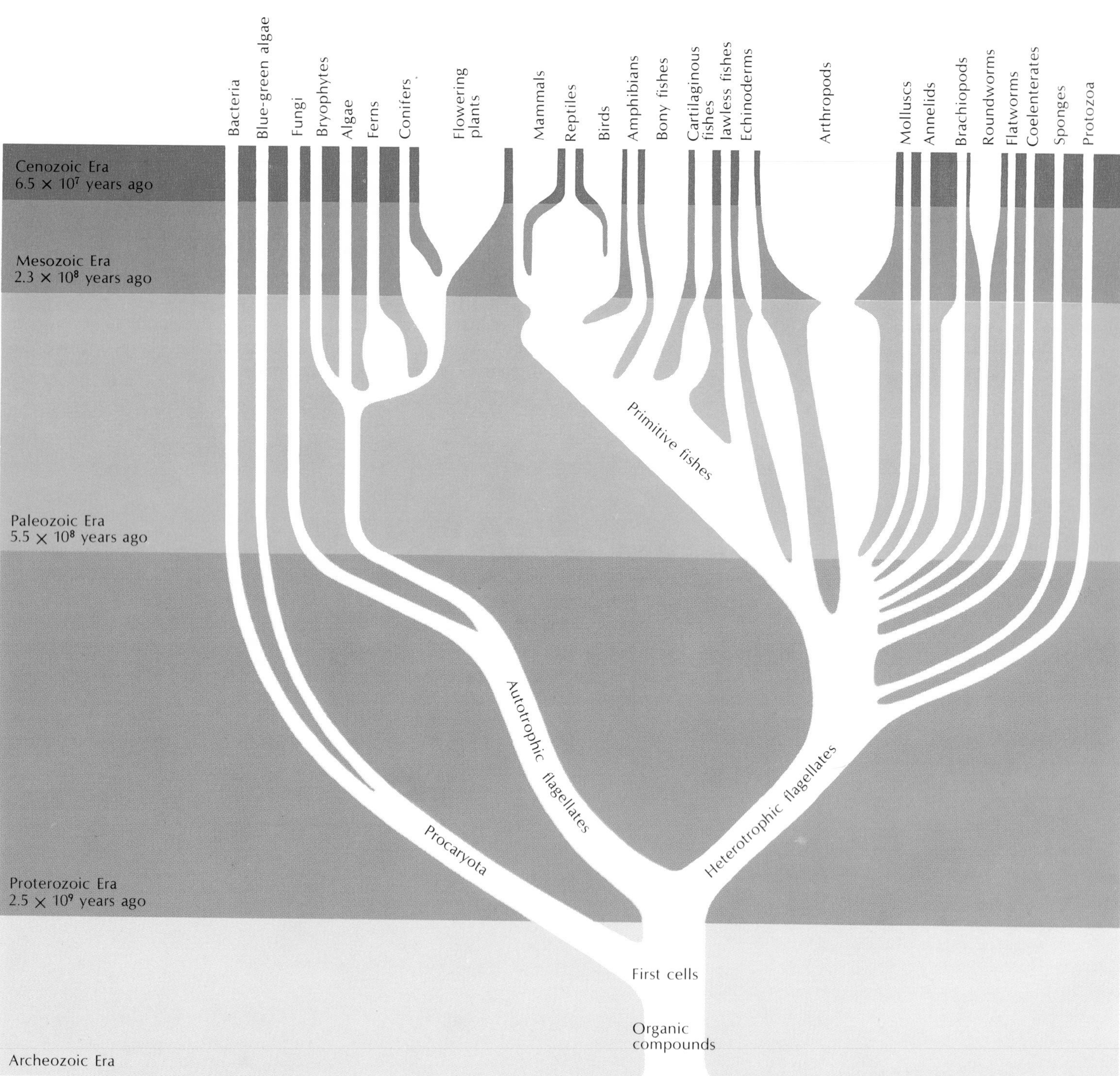

Bacteria
Blue-green algae
Fungi
Bryophytes
Algae
Ferns
Conifers
Flowering plants
Mammals
Reptiles
Birds
Amphibians
Bony fishes
Cartilaginous fishes
Jawless fishes
Echinoderms
Arthropods
Molluscs
Annelids
Brachiopods
Roundworms
Flatworms
Coelenterates
Sponges
Protozoa
Cenozoic Era
6.5 × 10^7 years ago
Mesozoic Era
2.3 × 10^8 years ago
Paleozoic Era
5.5 × 10^8 years ago
Proterozoic Era
2.5 × 10^9 years ago
Archeozoic Era
Primitive fishes
Autotrophic flagellates
Heterotrophic flagellates
Procaryota
First cells
Organic compounds

which appear in widely separated groups as well as within related groups (see Figure 15.20). Vesicular eyes (in which the eye is a fluid-filled sac) occur in coelenterates, flatworms, molluscs, and vertebrates. Such structural similarity is due less to convergence than to homomorphism (that is, the vesicular eye is one successful plan for the construction of a sense organ receptive to light). Whenever a hitherto eyeless group starts along the evolutionary pathway toward the construction of eyes, it is not very surprising that some new departure in eye architecture is less likely to occur than repetition of one of the few plans already in use, so that the newly evolving eyes become homomorphic with some type already in existence. During their subsequent refinement, of course, homomorphic structures may undergo convergence toward even greater similarity. Thus the basically homomorphic eyes of man and octopus have converged as well, both having a lens-adjusting mechanism, an iris, and other such parts.

If we successfully avoid the pitfalls inherent in a fragmentary fossil record, incomplete knowledge of hereditary mechanisms, and the possibility of confusing homology, convergence, and homomorphism, we may arrive at a taxonomic construct that will represent with reasonable validity the evolutionary relationships of contemporary and known fossil species. "Phyletic trees," depicting different forms of life as branches springing from a common trunk, attempt the ultimate synthesis by schematizing the probable common ancestry and divergent descent of all known forms of life (Figure 1.12). Being theoretical models, such schemes are seldom in perfect agreement but are subject to dispute and to continued revision and refinement as the acquisition of new knowledge permits.

1.3 □ CHARACTERISTICS OF LIFE

Traditionally biologists have recognized two major divisions of the world of life: the plant kingdom and the animal kingdom. Although this schism is useful in reminding us that pansies and chimpanzees have certain rather basic differences, it is also somewhat impeding because the separate concepts of "plant" and "animal" tend to obscure the fact that the two kinds of organisms are *much more alike than they are different*—they are both *alive,* and both share certain fundamental structural and biochemical attributes.

Figure 1.12 □ Phyletic tree. Theoretical model representing contemporary life forms as branches arising in the past from a common trunk. The width of individual branches roughly indicates the relative number of species in existence at any given point in time.

What is life? In considering this question we must stipulate whether we are comparing *biotic* systems (those living or having once been alive) with *abiotic* systems (those never having been alive), or are instead contrasting the living with the dead. That which is dead by definition was once alive, since death can be considered the irreversible cessation of vital activities. However, even dead tissues show many characteristics of biotic organization, for until they decay, they continue to have the high level of structural complexity that is one of the unique attributes of biotic systems. No abiotic matter approaches the organizational complexity which the biotic world achieves. But in death organisms do of course forfeit those functional attributes which comprise life. These functional attributes include the following.

THE CAPACITY TO ADAPT The capacity to change in a manner favorable to survival is perhaps the most important attribute of the living world. We can view all other biotic characteristics as evolved manifestations of this basic attribute. There are two aspects of adaptation: (1) *adaptability,* used here to mean the capacity of an organism to change in ways conducive to its own survival; (2) *mutability,* the capacity for change inherent in the hereditary material, which brings about the adaptation of populations over a period of generations but cannot bring about specific changes needed at any particular time to abet survival of the individual.

Adaptability Individual organisms often adjust to changing conditions through appropriate behavioral or physiological (occasionally also morphological) adjustments.

These adjustments are often flexible and readily reversible. Even microorganisms demonstrate adaptability in being able to adjust to a variety of culture media or in secreting a protective cyst when conditions become unfavorable for active existence.

Much of an organism's adaptability depends on physiological steady-state (*homeostatic*) mechanisms that, like gyroscopes, restore normal body conditions in the face of external or internal perturbations. For example, when the human body is in need of more oxygen, mechanisms are activated that increase the depth and rate of breathing, the rate and force of the heartbeat, and the quantity of red blood cells that are circulating. *Homoiothermal* (warm-blooded) animals can adapt to changing environmental temperatures more effectively than *poikilothermal* (cold-blooded) organisms, for homiothermal species can regulate their internal production and dissipation of heat so as to maintain a relatively stable body temperature despite wide environmental fluctuations. Poikilothermal species cannot maintain thermal stability by physiological mechanisms and their body temperature therefore tends to fluctuate with that of their surroundings.

Behavioral adaptability depends mainly on the capacity to *learn*—to modify responses on the basis of experience. Both learned and genetically determined behavior patterns contribute to adaptation, but the latter must depend on evolutionary change whereas the former are readily modifiable and can keep pace with rapidly changing demands. Of course, the potential for adaptability is itself inheritable and subject to evolutionary change.

Adaptability also includes an organism's capacity to change its *environment* in ways favorable to its survival. Such outward extension of steady-state mechanisms is shown by various animals that construct and furnish shelters for themselves and lay up stores of food against times of scarcity.

Mutability The second aspect of adaptation is mutability, the tendency of the hereditary material to change. Structural and functional patterns of life are primarily encoded in a series of nucleic acid molecules that constitute a "blueprint" for building a new organism. A few of these changes (*mutations*) are potentially adaptive, that is, they enable the organism to survive certain environmental changes that would otherwise prove lethal. Through mutation any population becomes genetically diverse (heterogeneous). As a result of this heterogeneity, when some environmental change causes the death of most members of a population, there are usually a few survivors that carry a mutation allowing them to adapt to the new conditions.

USE OF NUTRIENTS All living things possess means for obtaining materials from the external environment and converting them into substances characteristic of their own organization, or breaking them down and using the energy thus released. Such materials taken from the environment and used for growth and maintenance are called *nutrients*. The term *nutrition* encompasses all processes involved in obtaining and utilizing nutrients:

In animals *nutrient procurement* involves *ingestion* (eating), whereas in the case of plants nutrients are inorganic substances such as carbon dioxide (CO_2), water (H_2O), and minerals, which may be directly absorbed into the cells.

Digestion is the mechanical fragmentation of food and the chemical breakdown of large molecules to smaller ones that can readily be absorbed and distributed.

Respiration is the process whereby gaseous molecules (mainly O_2 and CO_2) are exchanged between the organism and its environment.

Excretion is the removal of waste products of metabolism.

Metabolism is the sum total of intracellular chemical activities by which organisms utilize nutrients for growth, repair, and energy. This includes *anabolism* (constructive metabolism) and *catabolism* (degradative metabolism). Energy released by catabolic processes (cell respiration) is used to maintain the organization of living systems in opposition to the universal tendency of all systems to proceed toward disorganization and randomness.

CONSTRUCTION OF MACROMOLECULES Using various kinds of nutrients, living things construct macromolecules, giant molecules with a mass equal to that of thousands or even millions of hydrogen atoms. Primary among these large molecules are proteins and nucleic acids, compounds that occur in all living things and which will be considered in depth in Chapter 9.

THE CAPACITY TO REPRODUCE As well as being capable of change, living systems are also capable of producing new entities of like kind, passing on their characteristics fundamentally unchanged. As we shall see later, this attribute actually depends on the self-replicating properties of nucleic acids. The simplest known naturally occurring biotic systems, viruses, are composed only of nucleic acids associated with a structural framework of protein. Viruses may not grow in the usual sense, but they can replicate, organizing protein and nucleic acid constituents into their own unique structure. In their limited complexity viruses approach the zone of intergradation between the abiotic and the biotic.

IRRITABILITY Irritability is the capacity of living things to perceive and respond to certain changes in the environment (*stimuli*). Irritability makes possible *adaptive* responses to stimuli, rather than merely *random* ones. In most multicellular animals irritability is enhanced by the specialization of certain tissues for reception and transmission. However, even single-celled organisms exhibit irritability without benefit of brain or sense organs. They move away from noxious substances and toward regions rich in nutrients, or along gradients of light intensity into zones of optimal illumination. Plants too show irritability in their directional growth movements oriented by light, gravity, and chemical factors.

THE CAPACITY FOR SPONTANEOUS MOVEMENT The forces causing living things to move or come to rest are not merely external, but are a complex combination of extrinsic and intrinsic factors involving the interaction of external and internal stimuli including physiological states (such as hunger). This type of dynamic mobility is an aspect of organismal *responsiveness* and is dependent upon irritability. Many organisms, both plant and animal, scamper freely from place to place (*locomotion*). Others may be attached to the substratum yet exhibit *motility* of body parts. According to our own time sense many plants appear motionless, yet when plants are viewed by time-lapse cinephotography we see that this seeming immobility is an illusion caused by our own perceptual limitations: stems move from side to side as they elongate, tendrils describe wide arcs until they contact a support around which they can twine, and roots bend around obstacles as they grow downward through the soil. Individual cells also move by amoeboid streaming or by means of motile fibrils (cilia and flagella). Even within the rigid walls that enclose the cells of multicellular plants the living material or protoplasm flows in a rotary and streaming motion (cyclosis).

1.4 □ HOW MAY PLANTS AND ANIMALS BE DISTINGUISHED?

As explained above, it is conceptually hampering to attempt to distinguish rigidly between plants and animals. The genetic and biochemical mechanisms possessed by both are so similar as to indicate common ancestry. Furthermore many intermediary forms exist that defy classification as either plants or animals and must be referred to as "plant-animals." These intermediates have been variously classified as protozoans (one-celled animals) or as unicellular algae.

The most fundamental difference between plants as a whole and animals in general is *not* that which seems most obvious: that animals move about more freely than do plants. This criterion for distinguishing plants from animals holds true only in part, and even insofar as it does hold true is merely a secondary outcome of basic differences in the *nutritional* processes of these two kinds of organisms. Actually, the primary distinction between the two great branches of the biotic world—plant and animal—is that in general *plants can make organic compounds out of inorganic ones,* trapping energy from the abiotic world (usually radiant energy) in the chemical bonds of the molecules they build. (By organic compounds we mean substances such as sugars, proteins, nucleic acids, and fats, in which the essential element of molecular structure is *carbon.*) This type of *autotrophic* ("self-nourishing") nutrition is characteristic of a few bacteria and of all plants that contain *chlorophyll,* a pigment that serves to trap radiant energy, thereby making *photosynthesis* possible. Animals lack chlorophyll and are incapable of converting radiant energy to chemical energy within their own bodies; therefore they cannot utilize inorganic molecules in constructing organic materials. Consequently animals (as well as chlorophyll-lacking plants such as fungi) exhibit *heterotrophic* ("other-nourishing") nutrition, in that they must obtain organic compounds from other living things (or from their dead tissues or excrement) and make use of the chemical energy stored in the intramolecular bonds of these compounds.

Probably the first animal was a unicellular plant-animal, a motile cell capable of photosynthesis, which irreversibly lost this capacity and thereafter had to seek organic food. For this protoanimal and all of its descendants, loss of the capacity for photosynthesis might fancifully be equated with banishment from a primeval Garden of Eden, following which the Animal Kingdom was destined to prowl hungrily forever in a widening search for sustenance. Nevertheless, this loss was no unmitigated curse, for it served as a new selective force in influencing the evolution of this part of the living world. Where there was need to seek organic food rather than utilizing as nutrients inorganic materials of nearly universal availability, there would be survival value in any inheritable change that would permit more acute perception of stimuli and more effective response. Changes in the nutrient-seeking animal that would tend to be conserved and perpetuated were those that increased the level of metabolic activity (for more energy would be needed to move about, eat, and digest food), enhanced the effectiveness of respiratory exchanges and excretion of toxic waste materials, accelerated the rate of distribution of materials throughout the body, facilitated locomotion, sharpened and expanded sensory acuity, and improved nervous integration. Thus animals have developed a variety of adaptations not needed by plants: nerves, brains, legs, wings, tentacles, eyes, ears, stomachs, hearts, kidneys, lungs, gills, and all of the other structures needed for procuring and processing complex food materials while at the same time minimizing the probability of becoming another animal's prey.

For higher animals there has been a bonus. Many adaptations initially associated with the need to seek food can also be utilized for the performance of other activities: seeking of mates, care of young, satisfaction of curiosity, and—in the case of advanced vertebrates—the development of new types of activity such as play and creativity.

The manifold differences between cows and carrots accordingly may be traced to the organism's ability or inability to construct chlorophyll (see Figure 9.4*b*), for it is by means of this compound that the living world taps the energy resource of sunlight to power life's activities.

Plants and animals differ in certain other biochemical capacities. Plants in general (but only a few animals) synthesize *cellulose,* a rigid structural material. Excess fuel is stored as *fat* and *glycogen* ("animal starch") by animals, but mainly as *oils* and *starch* by plants.

The overall body architecture of higher plants is comparatively diffuse in contrast with the animal body, for plants typically exhibit *indeterminate* growth, proliferating new parts throughout their entire life span. Most animals exhibit *determinate* growth, ceasing to grow after having attained a size and form characteristic of their species. This distinction suffers from a number of exceptions, but where it holds true is merely another outcome of the basic nutritional difference. Multicellular plants have little need for locomotion but do need a large surface area through which radiant energy can be absorbed and gases exchanged. Most metazoa (many-celled animals) on the other hand, must be mobile in their search for food, and mobility is favored by a compact size and form. Furthermore, plants are commonly preyed upon by herbivorous animals and would be killed off unless capable of regenerating the parts lost (Table 1.1). In fact, pruning a plant is one way that has been found that will spur it to accelerated growth.

One significant outcome of the potential of multicellular plants for indeterminate growth is that shed foliage and other plant tissues accumulate in the soil, improving its porosity and providing organic materials that nourish heterotrophic soil organisms such as bacteria, fungi, and earthworms.

Table 1.1 □ Summary of differences between plants and animals

PLANTS	ANIMALS
Nutrition typically autotrophic	Nutrition heterotrophic
Chlorophyll typically present	Chlorophyll lacking
Growth indeterminate	Growth generally determinate
Cellulose usually present in cell walls	Cellulose of rare occurrence
Carbohydrate stored as starch	Carbohydrate stored as glycogen
Higher forms nonlocomotory	Typically locomotory
Digestive, excretory, respiratory organs lacking	Digestive, excretory, respiratory organs often present

The simplest biotic units capable of self-replication in the presence of appropriate nutrient materials are viruses; however, these nutrients are only usable by the virus when it is within the living cells of a host organism. There is reason to suspect that the earliest forms of life were viruslike and therefore represented a form of *molecular* life not yet evolved to the cellular level of organization. The least complex forms of *cellular* life known today are bacteria and blue-green algae, which are usually placed in a separate division, *Kingdom Procaryota,* because of their simple cell organization (to be described in Chapter 10). The Procaryota are very tiny, only a few micrometers in length, and are basically unicellular although chains and clumps of cells may be formed. Although nutritionally the blue-green algae may be considered plants (and bacteria are sometimes also termed plants although most are heterotrophic) their cell structure indicates that they have been distinct from other forms of life for a very long time, probably over 2×10^9 years. Although living bacteria and blue-green algae may closely resemble ancestral forms of cellular life, it is unlikely that such ancestral forms could have persisted to the present without acquiring evolutionary innovations which disqualify them from representing truly ancestral types.

Also to be described in Chapter 10 is the more complicated cell structure of higher organisms, which is *eucaryotic* (having a real nucleus). Not only are the individual cells much larger than those of Procaryota, but these cells may be organized to form multicellular bodies. Eucaryotic organisms are usually grouped into three kingdoms. We shall use the taxonomic scheme in which *Kingdom Protista* includes all organisms of eucaryotic grade that are basically *unicellular.* Protists include one-celled animals (protozoans), several types of unicellular aquatic plants, and certain plant-animal types probably resembling the common ancestor of plants and animals. However, it is a general principle that *no contemporary species can be considered identical to a primeval ancestor of any other contemporary species.* These simple organisms are not really "primitive" but have continued to perpetuate themselves and to undergo further evolutionary changes in parallel with the evolution of more complex forms of life.

The two other kingdoms of eucaryotic organisms are *Metaphyta* (many-celled plants) and *Metazoa* (many-celled animals). Plants and animals diverged very early in the history of life and pursued ever-diverging pathways of evolutionary advancement, which has led metaphytes and metazoans progressively away from their common origin.

It is not surprising that among the Protista there are colonial forms that appear to reflect the transition from a unicellular to a multicellular condition of life. In plants this gradual transition is best seen in the green algae (Phylum Chlorophyta), which include unicellular, colonial, and multicellular species of varying degrees of complexity. Fungi also include unicellular forms (such as yeasts), simple multicellular forms (such as molds), and more complex multicellular forms (such as mushrooms and cup fungi). This gradation from unicellular to multicellular makes somewhat arbitrary the assignment of fungi and green algae to either the Metaphyta or the Protista. In animals the transition from unicellular to multicellular organisms is seen in certain colonial protozoans. Whether the adult form be unicellular or multicellular, however, all organisms begin life as a single cell. For most sexually reproducing species this cell is the fertilized egg (*zygote*). The form that the organism assumes as the zygote develops is primarily dictated by its heredity, adapted throughout the history of life by the interacting forces of genetic mutation and natural selection.

The adaptive radiation of metaphytes and metazoans into various major phyla began in the sea more than a billion years ago, with the emergence of a variety of body plans that proved successful in an aquatic milieu. Only in about the last 3.5×10^8 years has life diversified on land, and the success of those comparatively few groups of organisms which have made an effective transition to a terrestrial existence is one of the most remarkable events of organic evolution.

1.6 □ SUMMARY

In this chapter we have seen that living things range in size from around 100 Å to 50 m, are incredibly numerous, and constitute well over 1.5×10^6 recognizable species inhabiting almost every conceivable locus on the earth's surface. The science of biology, which investigates the principles by which the living world is organized, comprises many specialities, but in general individual biologists tend to conduct research at particular levels of biotic organization—the molecular and cellular, the organismal, and the supraorganismal (or population) level. Biology has advanced through steadily improving techniques of scientific inquiry involving observation, measurement, and experimentation, nowadays often requiring the use of sophisticated instrumentation; this advance has depended primarily upon the critical faculty, imagination, and insight of biologists, together with the occasional "lucky" breakthrough that must be credited to serendipity. By these means a number of ordering principles have been discovered, which constitute the framework of modern biological science. These key concepts include the following: (1) hierarchical organization of the living world; (2) transmission of hereditary traits from parents to progeny; (3) mechanism; (4) epigenesis; (5) cells as the universal units of structure and function; (6) evolution of life; (7) inheritance of unit characters; (8) mechanistic nature of animal behavior; (9) hereditary change by mutation; (10) genes as the units of heredity; (11) inductive interactions in embryonic development; (12) organization of the biotic world into ecosystem units; (13) production of enzymes by genes; (14) origin of life from the inanimate; (15) perpetuation of life by self-replicating nucleic acids; (16) universality of basic metabolic mechanisms; (17) inheritance of the neural basis for certain forms of behavior; (18) existence of intrinsic population-regulating mechanisms.

The development of modern systematics rests upon perception of natural relationships and is based upon evolutionary theory. Systematists, attempting to reconstruct the history of contemporary organisms, rely not only on the fossil record but on many techniques of genetic, chemical, and developmental analysis; even so, disagreements often cannot be resolved at present as to which taxonomic scheme most closely reflects actual lines of descent. Phylogenetic taxonomy seeks to distinguish among analogous forms that have undergone convergence, homologous forms that have undergone adaptive radiation, and homomorphic forms that resemble one another due to the limited number of organizational patterns available to the living world.

Many biologists recognize only the plant and animal kingdoms while acknowledging the existence of numerous intermediary forms; others prefer a scheme in which organisms of simple cell structure constitute Kingdom Procaryota, while all other species, having a more complex cell structure constitute the Kingdoms Protista (basically unicellular forms), Metaphyta (multicellular plants), and Metazoa (multicellular animals). (Others place multicellular algae and fungi with the protists, considering only mosses, ferns, and seed plants truly deserving of the designation Metaphyta.) Whatever the divisions used, intermediate forms exist, but these cannot be considered ancestral to contemporary types, for although many comparatively simple forms of life persist to the present time they cannot be considered truly primitive for they must have changed, albeit slightly, to meet the demands of the present. The basic unit of taxonomy, the species, is not unchanging, but represents a relatively ephemeral point on a population's lifeline, and reflects the genetic makeup of that population at only a given point in time

We have seen that living things, which are the concern of the science of biology, share certain characteristics that *en bloc* distinguish them from the abiotic: (1) an intensive degree of organization maintained in opposition to the tendency for disorderliness; (2) the capacity to change through adaptability and genetic mutability; (3) use of nutrients in constructive and degradative metabolism; (4) the construction of specific giant molecules such as proteins and nucleic acids; (5) the property of irritability; (6) the potential for spontaneous movement; (7) the capacity to conserve and perpetuate biotic organization by reproduction of kind. Although sharing these attributes, plants and animals differ in various particulars, most of which stem from a basic nutritional difference: most plants can synthesize organic compounds from simple inorganic precursors, whereas animals must ingest and process complex organic foodstuffs.

REVIEW AND DISCUSSION

1 In Figure 1.1 we saw that the radius of a typical cell (10 μm) can be expressed as 10^5 on an exponential scale using the angstrom unit as 10^0. Calculate the *volume* change between the smallest bacterium (pleuropneumonia) and this typical cell, and between the typical cell and the ostrich egg.

2 Explain the nature and value of scientific hypotheses. In view of the requirement for testability, define the limitations of science and specify—with explanations—the types of questions with which science may not deal effectively. Postulating the necessary cultural and technological changes, can you predict certain areas in which scientific methods may ultimately be effectively employed? What precautions need be observed in such potential extensions of scientific method?

3 Compare inductive and deductive reasoning and explain how each is useful in scientific inquiry.

4 Defending your selections, specify which of the key concepts of biology developed prior to the nineteenth century, during the nineteenth century, and during the twentieth century to date may have the farthest-reaching significance in terms of changing human existence.

5 Differentiate, with examples, between analogy and homology. Under what circumstances would you expect organisms of diverse ancestry to undergo analogous convergence? Under what circumstances would you expect to find that homologous structures are becoming different from one another? What is the significance of homomorphism?

6 Enumerate and define the major divisions of the Linnaean hierarchy. What is meant by the system of binomial nomenclature? Specify the advantages and disadvantages that are inherent in the adoption of any taxonomic scheme.

7 Summarize the characteristics that may be used, in the aggregate, to distinguish between the biotic and the abiotic. Which of these apply to viruses? Explain, with an example, why other vital characteristics can be viewed as evolved manifestations of the biotic world's potential for adaptation. Distinguish, with examples, between adaptability and mutability. How does the one depend upon the other?

8 Summarize the differences generally cited in distinguishing plants from animals, and explain how each difference between higher plants and higher animals is an outcome of their basic nutritional differentiation.

9 Why may no species living today (even the viruses or the plant-animals such as *Euglena*) be considered identical to a primitive ancestor of any other contemporaneous species?

REFERENCES

BRONOWSKI, J. *Science and Human Values.* New York: Harper & Row, Publishers, 1959. Contrary to the popular belief that science cannot render value judgments, a distinguished scientific philosopher contends that the structure of modern science rests upon acceptance of certain ethical principles.

DICE, L. R. "Quantitative and Experimental Methods in Systematic Zoology," *Syst. Zool.,* **1** (1952).

EVANS, H. E. "Comparative Ethology and the Systematics of Sand Wasps," *Syst. Zool.,* **2** (1953). A well-known ethologist points to the value of behavioral studies to recognition of taxonomic relationships.

HULL, D. L. "Consistency and Monophyly," *Syst. Zool.,* **13** (1964). A scientific philosopher notes that phylogenetic systematists are frustrated by limitations imposed on classification by the Linnaean hierarchy.

INGLIS, W. G. "The Observational Basis of Homology," *Syst. Zool.*, **15** (1966). The difficulties of establishing true homologies are considered; it is suggested that similar characters of unknown origin be termed *paralogous*.

MAYR, E. "Numerical Phenetics and Taxonomic Theory," *Syst. Zool.*, **14** (1965). An important student of evolution compares current schools of systematics and criticizes the school of computer taxonomy known as numerical phenetics. This paper should be read along with that by Sokal and Camin cited below.

NOVIKOFF, M. M. "Regularity of Form in Organisms," *Syst. Zool.*, **2** (1953). Discusses the incidence of similarity in form among living things, owing to fundamental limitations of living systems, which can form efficient organs in only a limited number of ways.

SABROSKY, C. W. "How Many Insects Are There?" *Syst. Zool.*, **2** (1953).

SIMPSON, G. G. *Principles of Animal Taxonomy.* New York: Columbia University Press, 1961. A useful reference on the practise and philosophy of phylogenetic taxonomy.

SOKAL, R. R., AND J. H. CAMIN "The Two Taxonomies: Areas of Agreement and Conflict." *Syst. Zool.*, **14** (1965). Presents a defense of numerical phenetics. Should be read with Mayr's article cited above.

TERMAN, L. M. "Are Scientists Different?" *Sci. Amer.*, **192** (1955).

Chapter 2 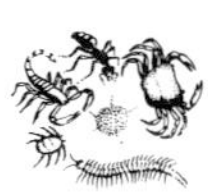 A SURVEY OF THE LIVING WORLD

THROUGH THE EFFORTS OF GENERATIONS of taxonomists and students of evolution, living things have been found to fall into groups of allied forms each of which shares some basic type of body plan or architecture. Each of the major taxonomic groups or phyla is distinguishable from the others by a constellation of traits typical of that group. In this chapter we shall examine the basic distinguishing characteristics of 25 important phyla, making especial note of phyla in which some important innovation in biotic organization or function may first have taken place. Without delving extensively into anatomical particulars we can profit by early familiarity with these phyla as a basis for understanding references to be made to various types of organisms during subsequent chapters. A synopsis of the living world at the end of this chapter should prove convenient for rapid reference.

We shall use one of the several acceptable schemes of classification (Figure 2.1):

VIRUSES These are forms of "molecular life" that in some respects may stand between the biotic and abiotic worlds.

KINGDOM PROCARYOTA Included here are organisms with simple cell structure lacking a true nucleus (that is, *procaryotic*): Phylum Schizophyta (bacteria) and Phylum Cyanophyta (blue-green algae).

KINGDOM PROTISTA This group comprises unicellular organisms with complex cell structure having a true nucleus (*eucaryotic*): Euglenophyta (euglenoids), Protozoa (acellular animals), Pyrrophyta (dinoflagellates and cryptomonads), and Chrysophyta (diatoms).

KINGDOM METAPHYTA These are

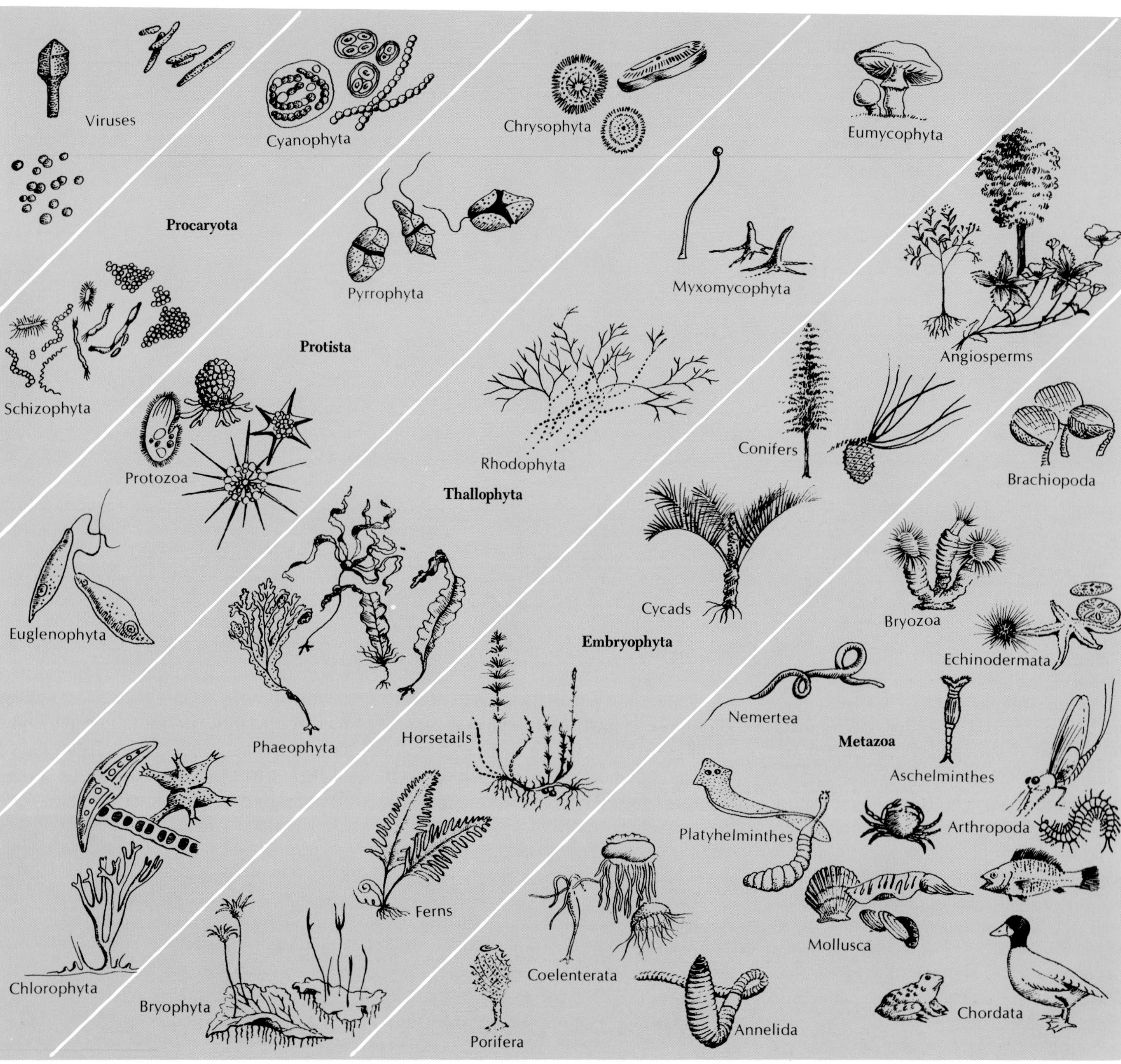

Viruses
Cyanophyta
Chrysophyta
Eumycophyta
Procaryota
Pyrrophyta
Myxomycophyta
Angiosperms
Protista
Schizophyta
Rhodophyta
Conifers
Brachiopoda
Protozoa
Thallophyta
Cycads
Bryozoa
Euglenophyta
Embryophyta
Echinodermata
Nemertea
Horsetails
Phaeophyta
Metazoa
Aschelminthes
Platyhelminthes
Arthropoda
Ferns
Mollusca
Coelenterata
Chlorophyta
Bryophyta
Porifera
Annelida
Chordata

Figure 2.1 □ Major groups of living things.

multicellular plants, which may be grouped into two subkingdoms:

Subkingdom Thallophyta This group contains simple metaphytes lacking protective structures for the embryo: Chlorophyta (green algae), Phaeophyta (brown algae), Rhodophyta (red algae), Myxomycophyta (slime molds), and Eumycophyta (fungi).

Subkingdom Embryophyta These are complex metaphytes that have protective structures to guard the embryo: Bryophyta (mosses and liverworts) and Tracheophyta (vascular plants: ferns and seed plants).

KINGDOM METAZOA Included here are multicellular animals, which may be grouped into two subkingdoms:

Subkingdom Parazoa These are metazoans below the tissue grade of organization: Porifera (sponges).

Subkingdom Eumetazoa This group comprises metazoans having true tissues, of which we shall consider only twelve major phyla: Coelenterata, or Cnidaria (polyps and medusae), Platyhelminthes (flatworms), Nemertea (ribbonworms), Aschelminthes (roundworms and rotifers), Ectoprocta (bryozoans), Brachiopoda (lamp shells), Annelida (segmented worms), Mollusca (including univalves, bivalves, and squid), Arthropoda (joint-footed animals such as insects, crustaceans, and spiders), Echinodermata (spiny-skinned animals such as starfish and sea urchins), and Chordata (including tunicates and vertebrates).

In several cases diversification within a phylum is such that individual consideration must be given to the major classes of the phylum, but the special features of these classes should not be allowed to obscure the basic characteristics common to the entire phylum. In Chapter 12 organisms selected from several of these phyla will serve to represent various levels of complexity of organismic construction; our present concern is less with organization per se than with gaining a panoramic view of the products of biotic evolution. Although the fundamental unity of life is apparent in the persistence of common mechanisms operating at the cellular level—mechanisms of such import that their significance has recently tended to eclipse both organism and ecosystem in the attentions of many biologists—the fact is inescapable that much of the success of the biosphere resides in its potential for diversification along contrasting lines of organization adapted toward a variety of modes of existence. Nearly all of these 25 phyla have been in existence for more than 0.5 billion years and in the aggregate they represent "the best" and most durable products of 3 billion years of organic evolution. As such, they deserve our respectful attention.

Substantial discontinuities occur in the record of biotic intergradation from one phylum to another. Such gaps exist because phyla represent groups of organisms that diverged from one another in a past so distant that no fossil records of ancestral forms common to two or more phyla have endured. (Fossils are evidences of ancient life, preserved in the rocks of the earth's crust.) Furthermore, only organisms with hard parts (shell, woody, or skeletal materials) usually leave meaningful traces. Fossils of soft-bodied creatures such as jellyfish are rare. Perhaps because of a low concentration of calcium in the ancient seas, limiting the production of limy shells and skeletons, the fossil record is fragmentary in sedimentary rocks more than about 550 million years old. By that time the major phyla of animal life together with most plant phyla already existed as distinct types. Vertebrates, insects, and land plants appeared later and thus left a less fragmentary record of their origins. Despite such major discontinuities it is often possible to formulate reasonable hypotheses concerning the relations between various phyla based on such evidence as developmental similarities or the existence of modern forms possessing characteristics typical of two or more different phyla.

2.1 □ VIRUSES

Little agreement exists on the taxonomic status of viruses. They may perhaps be conceded to be "living" on the basis of their capacity to reproduce (although only within the cells of a host), and because they consist of protein and nucleic acid molecules, the

Figure 2.2 □ Viral organization. Three architectural types revealed by electron microscopy: (*a*) *cubic* (adenovirus), (*b*) *helical* (tobacco mosaic virus—TMV), and (*c*) *complex* (bacteriophage). The outer shell of adenovirus consists of 252 protein subunits, and its core contains an equivalent number of nucleic acid units. The internal nucleic acid helix of TMV is covered by a sheath of about 2,130 protein subunits that form a cylinder about 300 nm in length by 16 nm in diameter. (*d*) Bacteriophage T4 attacking its host, the bacterium *Escherichia coli.* The host is seen in cross section, showing the thick cell wall to which the parasite's slender tail filaments are anchored. The protein sheath of the virus will remain outside while the nucleic acid strand (chromosome) contained within is injected into the host. (*Courtesy of Lee D. Simon and Thomas F. Anderson, The Institute for Cancer Research, Philadelphia.*)

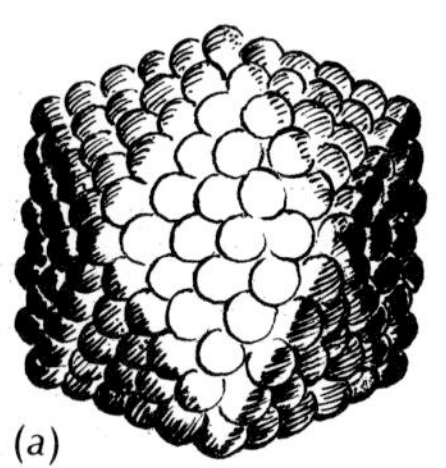

(*a*)

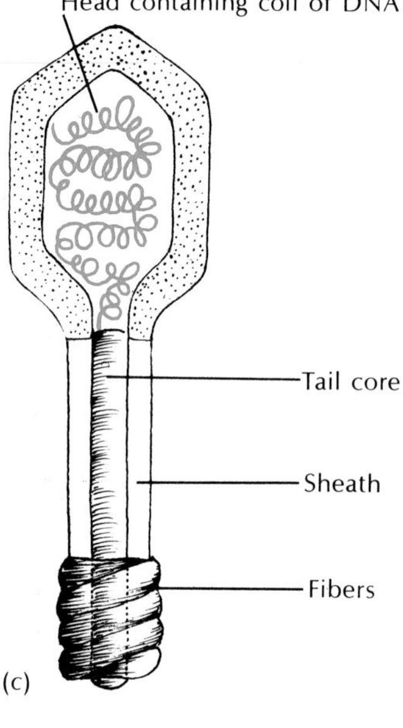

(c)

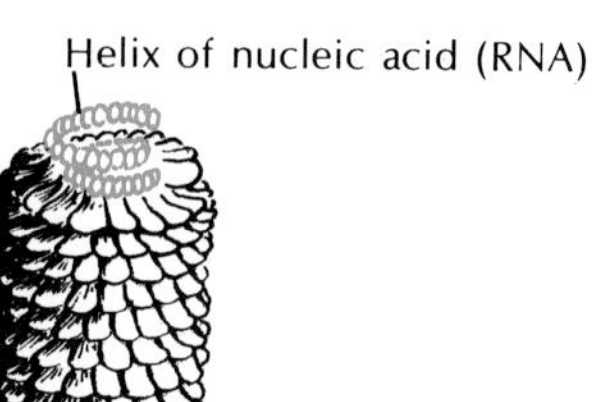

(*b*)

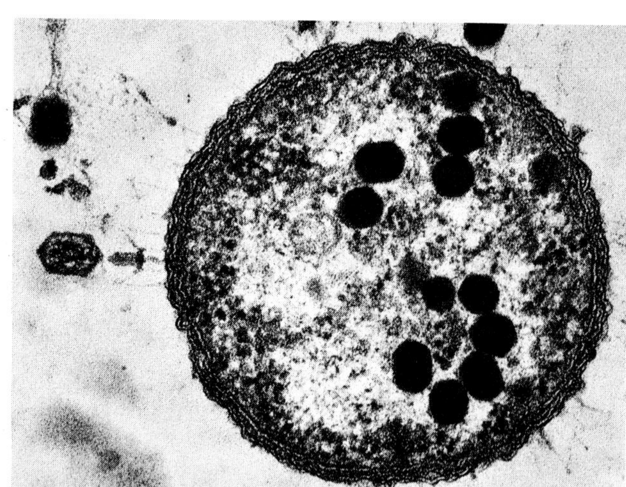

(*d*)

latter encoding hereditary information in the same way that it is encoded throughout the rest of the living world. Generally a virus consists of a supportive framework of protein and a single long thread of nucleic acid that makes up its chromosome. Viruses exhibit several distinct types of architecture (Figure 2.2). Simpler kinds may be cubic or helical, whereas such types as the well-studied bacteriophage T2 are much more complex.

The bacteriophage ("bacteria-eating") viruses attack susceptible bacteria by adhering to their outer membranes with tail filaments that are thought to fit into specific sites on the host's membrane somewhat as a key fits a lock. Such host-parasite specificity implies a history of adaptive evolution of the parasite parallel to that of the host. After entering its host, the virus takes over the cell's metabolic machinery and uses it to produce more viral protein and nucleic acid. Finally the new viruses kill the bacterium, escaping to infect new hosts.

Viruses may represent the descendants of extremely primitive microorganisms that did not attain the cellular level of complexity but resorted to parasitism as other sources of organic nutrients became depleted. Alternatively they may represent simplified descendants of a formerly more complicated intracellular parasite that has kept only the "bare essentials" for survival.

Rickettsias are infective agents (causing such diseases as typhus) that are simpler than bacteria but more complex than viruses, and may represent an intermediate step in evolution from viral to bacterial status (or, conversely, a step down from a more complex ancestral condition toward the viral level by elimination of nonessential structural components). Like viruses, rickettsias can carry out life processes only within the cells of a host.

Because of their simplicity, viruses have proved to be valuable subjects of genetic research. Much of our present knowledge concerning hereditary mechanisms is the outcome of studies performed upon viruses, bacteria, and molds.

2.2 □ PROCARYOTA: PHYLA WITH SIMPLE CELL STRUCTURE

A Phylum Schizophyta ("fission plant"): bacteria (approximately 2,500 species)

These minute organisms, usually only a few micrometers in length, may have been the first living things to achieve a *cellular level of organization*. The bacterial cell, the structure of which will be further considered in Chapter 10, is bounded by a membrane that regulates the passage of substances into and out of the cell. This membrane encloses numerous tiny bodies known as ribosomes that play an essential role in protein production and several ring-shaped chromosomes that may be loosely gathered toward the center of the cell but are not enclosed within a membrane to form a true nucleus. Typically a bacterium is covered by a celluloselike coating resembling the outer walls of plant cells.

Bacteria are more advanced than viruses in several ways: (1) they are forms of cellular

Figure 2.3 □ Bacteria. (*a*) Large bacilli containing fat bodies. (*Courtesy of Carolina Biological Supply Company.*) (*b*) *Proteus vulgaris*, a flagellated bacillus. (*Courtesy of Carolina Biological Supply Company.*) (*c*) *Streptococcus pyogenes*, a pathogenic species, showing typical clusters of spheroidal cocci. (*Ward's Natural Science Establishment, Inc.*) (*d*) *Spirillum rubrum*, showing typical corkscrew shape. (*Courtesy of General Biological, Inc., Chicago.*) (*e*) *Spirochaete recurrens* in blood. The spirochetes are protozoalike bacteria having the shape of a flexible, coiled spring (spirilla are rigid and flagellated). The causative agents of syphilis and relapsing fever are spirochetes. (*Courtesy of General Biological, Inc., Chicago.*)

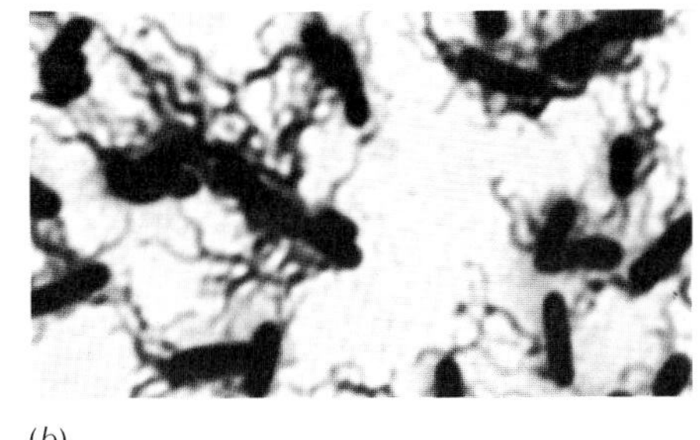
(*b*)

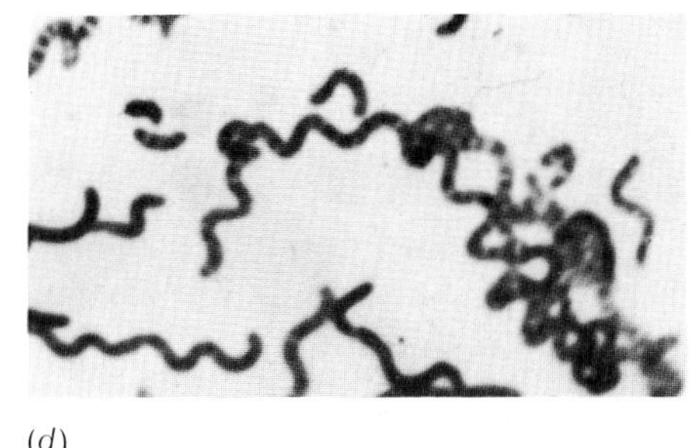
(*d*)

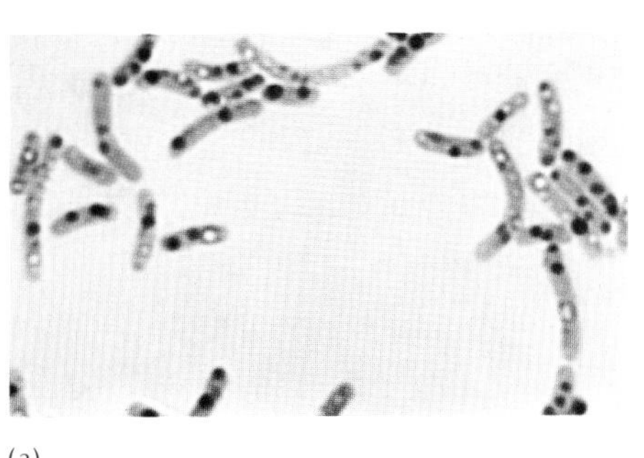
(*a*)

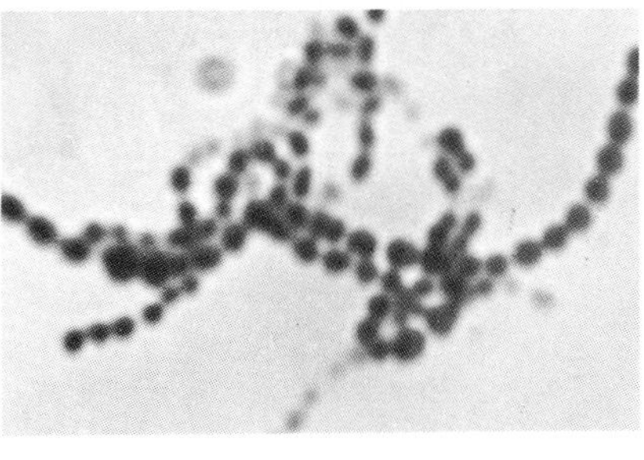
(*c*)

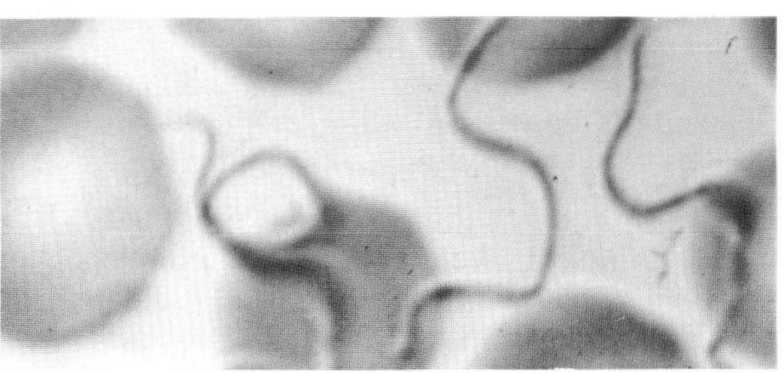
(*e*)

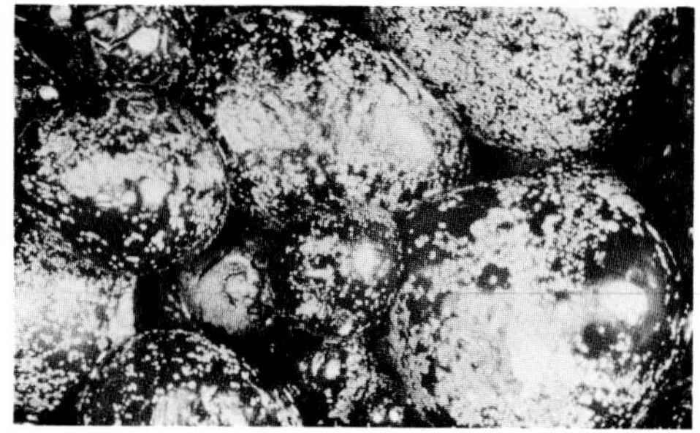

(a)

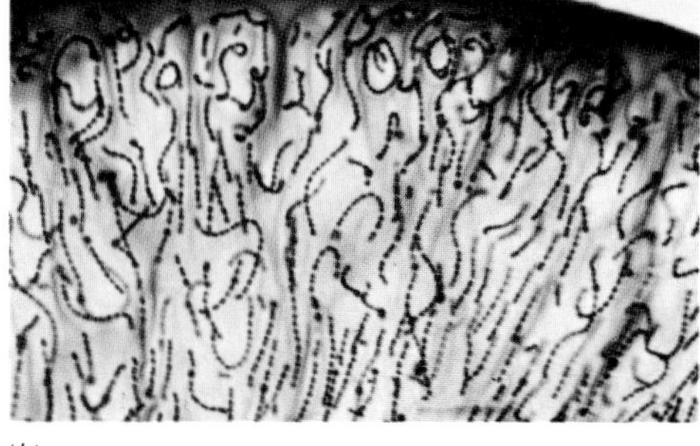

(b)

(c)

Figure 2.4 □ ***Nostoc*, a cyanophyte. (*a*) Nodules a few centimeters in diameter. (*Courtesy of General Biological, Inc., Chicago.*) (*b*) Portion of nodule showing chains of cells embedded in gelatinous matrix and a section of the outer surface. (*Courtesy of General Biological, Inc., Chicago.*) (*c*) Chains of cells at higher magnification; these are little larger than bacteria and have no distinct nucleus. (*Ward's Natural Science Establishment, Inc.*)**

life (although their cell structure is much less complicated than that of higher organisms); (2) they are not restricted to only a parasitic life within the cells of a host; (3) they can selectively control the passage of materials through their bounding membrane; (4) they can produce and store food reserves (mainly glycogen).

On the basis of body form three major types of bacteria are distinguishable (Figure 2.3): spherical *cocci* (singular, coccus), rod-shaped *bacilli* (singular, bacillus), and helical *spirilla* (singular, spirillum). Many bacteria possess motile filaments or flagella (singular, flagellum, that is, "little whip") used in locomotion. Bacteria may be solitary or may associate in pairs, clumps, or chains.

Most bacteria feed by absorbing organic nutrients from the living or dead tissues of other organisms, or from their excrement. Only a few bacterial species can synthesize organic compounds from inorganic materials, exploiting either radiant or chemical energy in the process. Bacteria that utilize light energy possess granules containing a unique form of chlorophyll, *bacteriochlorophyll.* Certain other bacteria gain the energy needed for building organic compounds by oxidizing inorganic materials such as nitrites (NO_2^-) to nitrates (NO_3^-).

Relatively few species of bacteria are pathogenic (disease-producing) parasites. By far the greater number are free-living (nonparasitic) species that are essential to the continuance of life in general because they are instrumental in bringing about decay, permitting the cyclic reuse of nitrogen, carbon, sulfur, and other materials.

Allied to true bacteria are the spirochetes (see Figure 2.3e), such as *Treponema pallidum,* the causative agent of syphilis. The body is spiral, flexible, and as much as 500 μm long. Locomotion may be effected by spinning about the longitudinal axis.

B Phylum Cyanophyta ("blue plant"): blue-green algae (approximately 2,500 species)

Some cyanophytes are as blue as their name implies for they possess, in addition to chlorophyll *a* (the most universal form of chlorophyll, other variants known as chlorophylls *b, c,* and *d* being of more sporadic distribution), a blue pigment (*c-phycocyanin*), which is restricted to this phylum but is often masked by red or yellow pigments.

Cyanophytes can be considered advanced over the majority of bacteria in being capable of photosynthesis. Excess food materials are stored as a unique type of starch. Cyanophytes occur mainly in fresh water, on damp soil and bark, and in a typical "black zone" just above the high-tide level of oceans the world around. Visitors to Yellowstone National Park may notice the cyanophyte ring around the thermal pools.

Like bacteria, cyanophytes are basically unicellular and their structure is that of the primitive procaryotic type (see Figure 10.5*a*). However, unlike most bacteria, the cyanophyte cells, each encased in a cell wall formed partly of cellulose, are embedded in a gelatinous matrix to form spheres, filaments, or flat plaques (Figure 2.4).

Cyanophyta is the only phylum in which reproduction is always *asexual* (that is, only one parent is needed), and sexual reproduction (the recombination of hereditary material by exchanges between individuals) is not known to occur.

Figure 2.5 ☐ *Euglena,* a chlorophyllous flagellate. Chlorophyll needed in photosynthesis is contained in the chloroplasts. The light-sensitive eyespot enables *Euglena* to locate regions of optimum illumination. Locomotion is by rotatory beating of the anterior flagellum or by wormlike elongation and shortening of the entire body (except in species where the pellicle is too rigid to allow this).

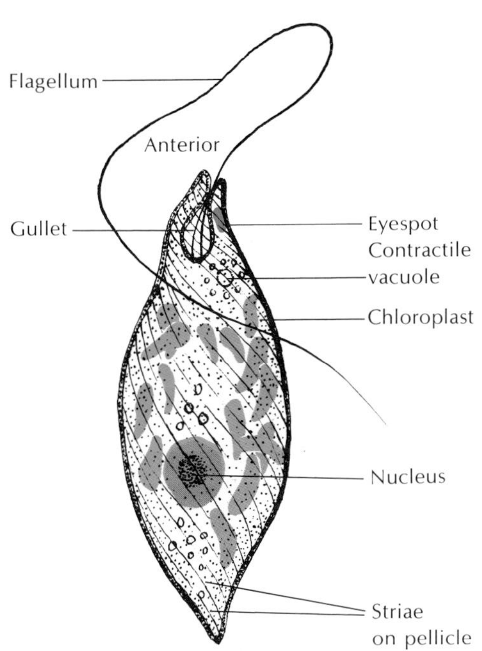

A Phylum Euglenophyta: euglenoids (approximately 350 species)

The euglenoids are motile unicellular organisms having one or two flagella that emerge from a deep gullet, which in some species is employed for the ingestion of organic material, although most euglenoids are also capable of photosynthesis (Figure 2.5). The autotrophic types possess both chlorophylls *a* and *b,* and also often have concentrations of photosensitive red-pigment granules ("eyespots") that help the organism find favorable illumination.

Modern euglenoids may well be linear descendants of those ancestral plant-animals which gave rise to all higher organisms, for in several ways they are intermediate between plants and animals: (1) they lack a cellulose wall, the body instead being encased by an outer covering or pellicle similar to that of protozoans, which may be rigid or flexible, in the latter event permitting a wormlike method of locomotion (euglenoid movement); (2) reserve food is stored as *paramylum,* a carbohydrate intermediate in form between glycogen (typically found in animals) and starch (typically found in plants); (3) when deprived of light, normally photosynthetic euglenoids may permanently lose their chlorophyll and become heterotrophic. Some euglenoids (such as *Astasia*) never possess chlorophyll and feed like animals. *Astasia* is morphologically identical with *Euglena* save for the absence of chlorophyll. Nutritionally, *Euglena* is a plant and *Astasia* an animal.

If ancestral euglenoids were indeed the original plant-animals, they were also the first organisms to evolve a *eucaryotic cell structure.* Eucaryotic ("true-nucleus") cells are both larger and more complex than the procaryotic cells characteristic of bacteria and cyanophytes. Their chromosomes are contained within a membrane to form a true nucleus, and a number of other subcellular structures are present which procaryotic cells lack (Figure 10.5*b*). All the higher phyla that may have descended from these primitive euglenoids have eucaryotic structure.

B Phylum Protozoa ("first animal"): protozoans (probably exceeding 100,000 species)

As usually defined, this phylum consists of organisms that are mainly unicellular (although a few are colonial) and mostly lack the capacity to produce organic molecules by photosynthesis. The term "acellular" is often applied to these animals because although their bodies are not subdivided into many cells they may nevertheless be elaborately organized at a subcellular level. In various protozoa specialized *organelles* (subcellular structures) perform functions similar to those carried out by multicellular

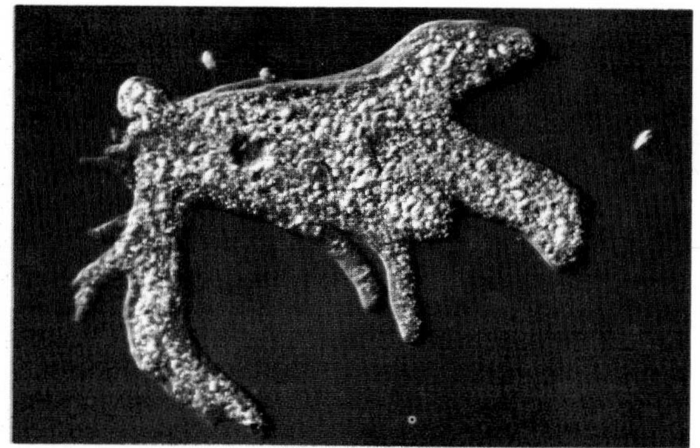

Figure 2.6 □ ***Amoeba.*** **This comparatively simple protozoan has no constant body form but moves by protruding temporary pseudopodia into which the cytoplasm flows. (*Courtesy of Carolina Biological Supply Company.*)**

Figure 2.7 □ **Protozoan types. *Plasmodium,* causal agent of malaria, is shown in several life stages within the red blood corpuscles of its mammalian host. *Trichomonas* lives symbiotically in the termite gut. Foraminiferans are among the most abundant marine protozoans; their chambered calcareous shells contribute to the building of limestone strata.**

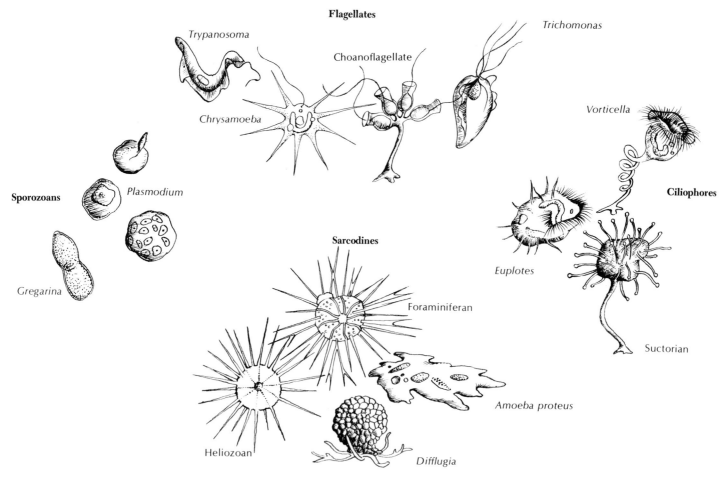

Flagellates
Trypanosoma
Choanoflagellate
Trichomonas
Chrysamoeba
Sporozoans
Plasmodium
Gregarina
Ciliophores
Vorticella
Euplotes
Suctorian
Sarcodines
Foraminiferan
Heliozoan
Amoeba proteus
Difflugia

organs in the bodies of larger animals. This phylum includes a number of apparently primitive forms such as *Amoeba* (Figure 2.6); but, by and large, modern protozoans are not at all primitive and have undergone a long evolutionary history through which they have become adapted to various modes of existence (Figure 2.7). Most protozoans are aquatic or marine, whereas others live in moist soil. A number are internal parasites, although the majority are free-living forms that feed upon bacteria, microscopic algae, and other protozoans.

The phylum is subdivided according to whether the major locomotory mechanism is pseudopodial, flagellar or ciliary. Pseudopodial locomotion involves changes in body form with the extension of cytoplasmic processes termed *pseudopodia* ("false feet"), while ciliary and flagellar locomotion depends on the beating or undulation of motile fibrils (cilia and flagella) which extend from the surface. (These types of locomotion will be considered further in Chapter 16.)

Flagellates are protozoans that typically propel themselves by whiplike, undulating, or rotatory movements of one to many flagella; however, some are also capable of movement by pseudopodia. Some flagellates are photosynthetic; these *phytoflagellates* may also be classified with various phyla of unicellular algae, such as the Euglenophyta. Other types, the *zooflagellates,* are incapable of photosynthesis and consume organic nutrients. Some zooflagellates are parasitic like the trypanosomes (Figure 2.8), which cause such diseases in man as African sleeping sickness and Chagas' disease. Others live within the intestinal tracts of higher organisms and aid their digestive processes; for instance, certain flagellates help termites digest wood.

Figure 2.8 □ ***Trypanosoma gambiense*, the parasitic flagellate causing African sleeping sickness, seen among red blood corpuscles having a diameter of only 8 μm. This parasite is disseminated by the blood-sucking tsetse fly. (*Courtesy of Carolina Biological Supply Company.*)**

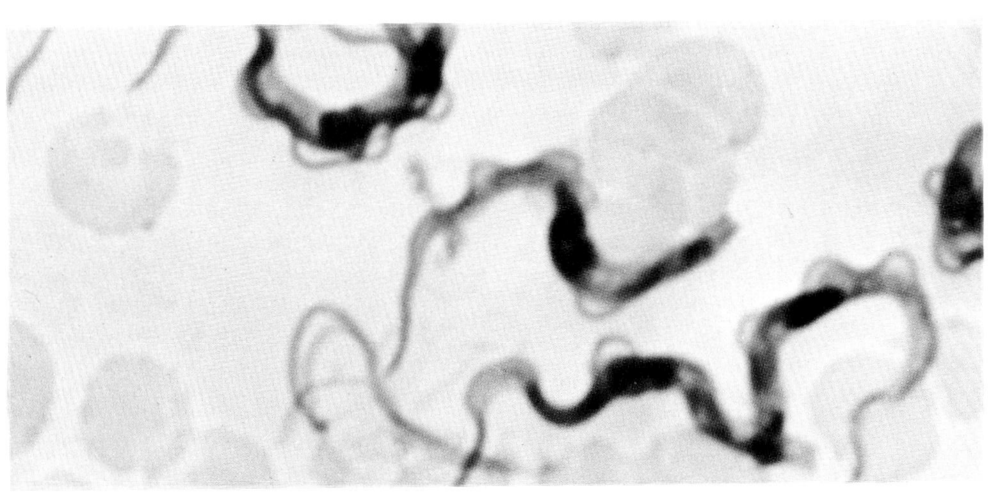

Flagellates display a number of interesting affinities to other groups of organisms. Occasionally an amoeboid zooflagellate will reabsorb its flagellum and thereafter be indistinguishable from a small amoeba. This suggests the possible flagellate ancestry of the sarcodines (see below). Alternatively, phytoflagellates can round up like a ball and lose their flagella, behaving thereafter like nonmotile unicellular algae. *Chrysamoeba* is a *phyto*flagellate that can also extrude pseudopodia and feed like an amoeba. Certain colonial flagellates bear conical "collars" about the flagellated end of the cell; these *choanoflagellates* closely resemble the choanocytes, or collar cells, of sponges, which may indicate that sponges descended from ancient choanoflagellate colonies.

Sarcodines possess pseudopodia that may be either flexible, retractable, lobose protrusions of the cytoplasm, or rigid, raylike, nonretractable extensions. The latter are typical of floating types such as radiolarians and heliozoans. Other sarcodines creep upon the substratum by extending temporary pseudopodia into which the internal cytoplasm flows. Some secrete protective external shells or supportive internal "skeletons." *Difflugia* constructs a caplike shell of microscopic sand grains cemented together; its pseudopodia are extruded through a single opening on the underside. *Foraminiferans* secrete multichambered calcareous shells with numerous pores (*foramina*) through which branching pseudopodia ex-

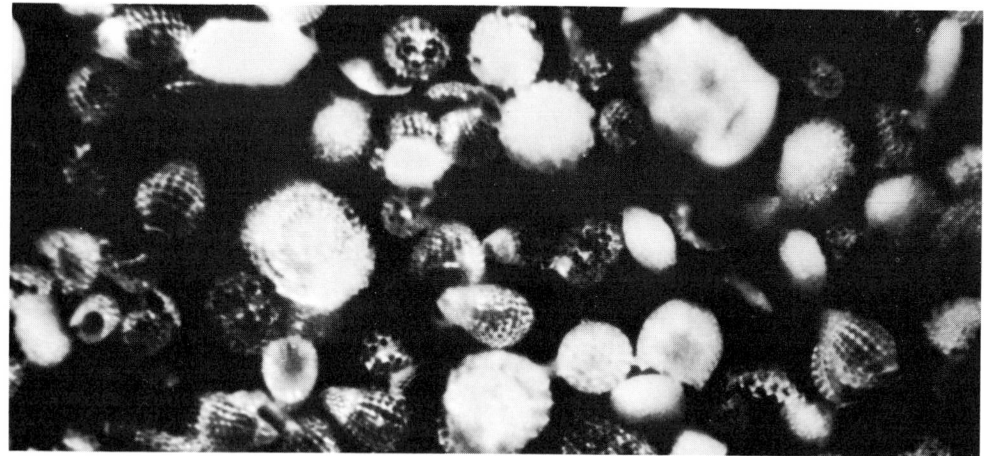

Figure 2.9 □ **Radiolarian shells. Mainly composed of silicon compounds, these protozoan shells resist the solvent action of carbon dioxide (which forms carbonic acid) and therefore can sink to the deep ocean floors; where they accumulate to great depths as radiolarian ooze. Modern concepts of organic symmetry were worked out by E. Haeckel through studies of the variety of radiolarian shells collected on the first oceanographic expedition (that of *H.M.S. Challenger* in 1872).**

Figure 2.10 □ ***Paramecium*, a ciliate, stained to show pellicular structure. (*Courtesy of General Biological, Inc., Chicago.*)**

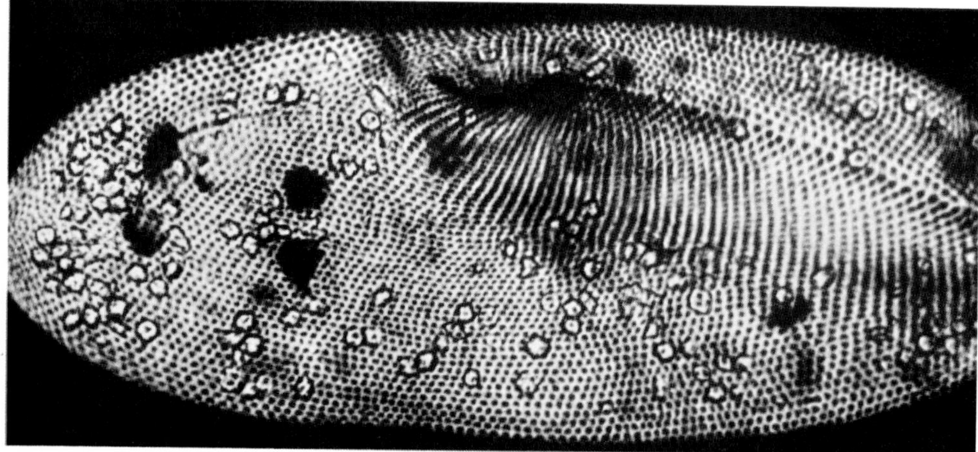

tend. Beautiful, symmetrical siliceous endoskeletons are produced by *radiolarians* (Figure 2.9). Millions of square miles of the sea bottom are deeply covered with deposits of the shells of foraminiferans and of radiolarians.

Sporozoans are internal parasites that inhabit either the cells or the body cavities of their hosts. They have complicated life histories in which both sexual and asexual reproduction occur and new individuals are produced by the multiple fission of a zygote (fertilized egg) or a vegetative cell (see Figure 6.28). Sporozoan diseases include coccidiosis and malaria. Sporozoans lack special locomotory structures but may move by changing body shape. The name of the class is derived from the fact that a nonmotile "spore" typically forms one stage in the life cycle.

Ciliates (Figure 2.10) possess few to many short protruding fibrils termed cilia that differ from flagella mainly in their shorter length and mode of action (consisting of a rigid effective stroke followed by a relaxed recovery stroke). When many cilia are present their action is coordinated by means of interconnecting fibrils. In certain ciliates the cilia are restricted to a whorl around the mouth and are used to create water currents that collect food, rather than as an aid to locomotion. Some ciliates are among the most complex of acellular animals (see Figure 12.4).

Suctorians are ciliated when immature but later lose the cilia and develop tentacles used in prey capture. Small animals that come in contact with the tentacles are paralyzed by a toxin and their contents ingested by way of fine canals within the tentacles. Suctorians are very common in fresh and salt

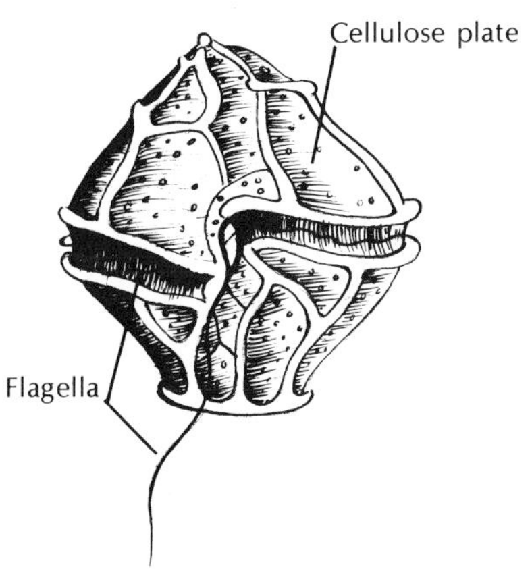

Figure 2.11 □ ***Gonyaulax*, a dinoflagellate. Some species produce a toxic alkaloid lethal to fish in sufficiently high concentrations. However, most dinoflagellates are nontoxic and represent an important food source for marine animals.**

water. They are sedentary and often attach to the bodies of other organisms for support.

C Phylum Pyrrophyta ("flame plant"): dinoflagellates and cryptomonads (approximately 1,000 species)

Pyrrophytes are red to yellow-brown unicellular aquatic organisms that typically bear two flagella and have cellulose cell walls. They possess the brownish pigment dinoxanthin as well as chlorophylls *a* and *c*. Although most are autotrophic, some feed like animals. The luminescent dinoflagellate, *Noctiluca* ("night light"), can both carry on photosynthesis and ingest prey. The cryptomonads *Chilomonas* and *Cryptomonas* are nearly identical, except that the latter is photosynthetic and the former is not. Cryptomonads are ovoid and their two flagella spring from the base of a deep gullet.

Dinoflagellates ("terrible flagellates") are by far the most abundant pyrrophytes and form an important component of the marine phytoplankton. Despite the existence of a few toxic forms that justify the name of the group, dinoflagellates constitute an important food source for tiny marine animals (the zooplankton). Dinoflagellates are characterized by a cell wall composed of overlapping cellulose plates and by the peculiar arrangement of their flagella, one of which vibrates within an equatorial groove that encircles the cell, while the other trails. The summer shellfish quarantine along the coast of California results from seasonal increases in the toxic form, *Gonyaulax,* which causes "red tides" (Figure 2.11). Mussels and other bivalves that feed upon these organisms accumulate the toxins in their tissues and so become temporarily poisonous.

Figure 2.12 □ **Diatoms. These unicellular planktonic organisms are the most abundant of marine plants and as such constitute the most important single food source for marine animals. Their siliceous valves are constructed with such precision that their fine markings can be used to test lenses. Like those of radiolarians, diatom shells resist dissolution and accumulate as diatomaceous ooze on the ocean floor. When compressed, this ooze becomes diatomaceous earth, mined for use as a fine abrasive and an absorptive element in filters.**

D Phylum Chrysophyta ("golden plant"): diatoms and the like (approximately 5,800 species)

Diatoms, by far the most numerous chrysophytes, are unicellular or colonial organisms of exceeding abundance in fresh and salt water, where they serve as food for small animals. Diatoms are photosynthetic and, by virtue of their vast numbers, their annual growth in terms of dry weight may equal that of all land plants put together. Tremendous quantities of diatom shells accumulate on the ocean floor, where they may be compressed by the weight of overlying sediments into *diatomaceous earth,* useful as a fine abrasive and an adsorptive agent in filters. Diatoms are characterized by a siliceous shell or capsule consisting of two overlapping halves (Figure 2.12). The beautiful, precise etching of the capsule is functional, for it increases the effective surface area and aids flotation (see Figure 12.2a). Buoyancy is also increased by the storage of food, primarily as lipid droplets rather than

Table 2.1 □ Comparison of unicellular phyla

PHYLUM	CELL STRUCTURE	FLAGELLA	OUTER COVERING	CHLOROPHYLL	OTHER MAJOR PIGMENTS	MAJOR STORAGE COMPOUND
Schizophyta	**Procaryotic**	**When present, few to many**	**Variable; polysaccharide or protein**	**Rare; when present, bacteriochlorophyll**	—	**Glycogen**
Cyanophyta	**Procaryotic**	—	**Cellulose plus slime sheath**	***a* only**	**c-Phycocyanin, c-phycoerythrin (both unique)**	**Cyanophycean starch (unique)**
Euglenophyta	**Eucaryotic**	**One or two**	**Rigid or flexible proteinaceous pellicle**	***a* and *b***	**Carotenes; xanthophylls**	**Paramylum**
Protozoa	**Eucaryotic**	**When present, one to many**	**Flexible proteinaceous pellicle**	—	—	**Glycogen, fats**
Pyrrophyta	**Eucaryotic**	**Two, one often in equatorial groove**	**Cellulose, often rigid plates**	***a* and *c***	**Fucoxanthin**	**Starch, oils**
Chrysophyta	**Eucaryotic**	**Lacking in most**	**Siliceous, two overlapping valves**	***a* and *c***	**Fucoxanthin**	**Oils**
Chlorophyta (unicellular types)	**Eucaryotic**	**When present, one or two**	**Cellulose and pectin layers**	***a* and *b***	**Carotenes, xanthophylls**	**Starch**

as starch. Much of our present petroleum resources may represent oil accumulated by diatoms over millions of years and deposited with their shells on the ocean floor.

Chrysophytes have chlorophylls *a* and *c* and the brown pigment fucoxanthin, as well as red and yellow pigments of more restricted distribution. Although only one group of chrysophytes is flagellated, the diatoms (which are unflagellated) can nevertheless creep in the manner of a tractor upon a thin film of cytoplasm extruded from between the valves of the shell.

The major characteristics of the unicellular phyla are summarized in Table 2.1.

2.4 □ THALLOPHYTA: SIMPLE METAPHYTES

Multicellular plants in general, whether of simple or complex tissue structure, are characterized by the typical alternation in their life cycle of two different organisms: an asexually produced *gametophyte* (gamete-producing plant) and a sexually produced *sporophyte* (spore-producing plant). The tissues of the gametophyte are *monoploid,* that is, contain only one set of chromosomes per cell. The tissues of the sporophyte, on the other hand, are *diploid,* containing two sets of chromosomes per cell, one set from each parent. A typical metaphyte life cycle proceeds as shown in the following diagram:

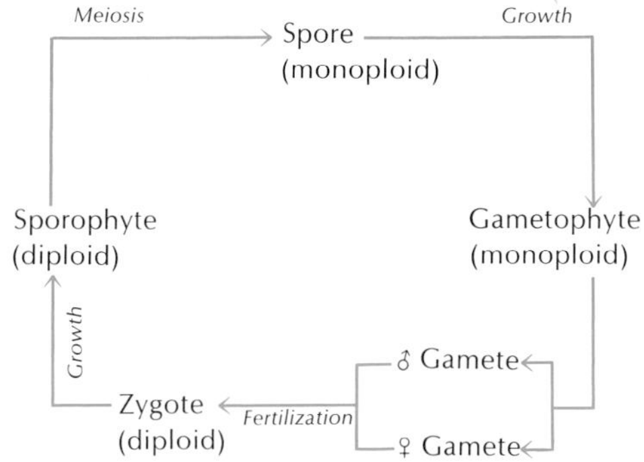

Plant evolution has tended toward the increasing ascendancy of the sporophyte generation with concomitant reduction of the gametophyte generation (see Figure 17.17). In green algae the gametophyte may be the only organism in the life cycle; or independent gametophyte and sporophyte generations indistinguishable in gross form may be present; or gametophyte and sporophyte may be dissimilar but roughly equal in size. In only one known kind of green algae is the sporophyte predominant and the gametophyte reduced and dependent nutritionally on the sporophyte. Brown algae typically alternate gametophyte and sporophyte generations of similar form, but in some the former is reduced and the latter more complex and conspicuous.

The life cycle of red algae is unusually complicated. In some types the gametophyte is essentially the only organism in the life cycle. In others the sporophyte genera-

Table 2.2 ☐ Comparison of multicellular plant phyla

PHYLUM	GAMETOPHYTE (G) AND SPOROPHYTE (S) GENERATIONS	VASCULAR TISSUE	BODY FORM	MAJOR HABITAT	CHLOROPHYLL	OTHER CHARACTERISTIC PIGMENTS	MAJOR STORAGE COMPOUND
Chlorophyta (multicellular types)	G only; or isomorphic G and S; or dissimilar but more or less equal G and S	None	Filament or thallus	Aquatic	*a* and *b*	Carotenes, xanthophylls	Starch
Phaeophyta	Isomorphic; or G reduced and S dominant	None	Thallus, with gas bladders	Marine	*a* and *c*	Fucoxanthin	Laminarin
Rhodophyta	G only; or G and S isomorphic; or equal but anisomorphic; or unequal with S smaller and free or dependent; or 1 G and 2 S generations	None	Thallus, often lacy	Marine	*a* and *d*	r-Phycoerythrin r-phycocyanin (both unique)	Floridean starch
Myxomycophyta	—	None	Plasmodium	Moist terrestrial	None	—	Glycogen, oils
Eumycophyta	—	None	Mycelium	Moist terrestrial	None	—	Glycogen, oils
Bryophyta	G dominant, S dependent	Lacking or rudimentary	Thallus or leafy shoot	Moist terrestrial	*a* and *b*	Carotenes, xanthophylls	Starch
Tracheophyta	S dominant, G much reduced and either independent or dependent	Present	True organs: roots, stems, leaves	Terrestrial	*a* and *b*	Carotenes, xanthophylls	Starch

tion is present but is small and dependent nutritionally on the gametophyte. In still other species the gametophyte and sporophyte are independent and either similar or dissimilar in form. Sometimes the life cycle consists of one gametophyte and two consecutive sporophyte generations, the first producing diploid (not monoploid) spores.

A few bryophytes lack the sporophyte generation, but in most a sporophyte is produced which does not live long and which is nutritionally dependent on the gametophyte. In the vascular plants, however, the gametophyte is much smaller than the sporophyte and in seed plants is microscopic and completely embedded within the tissues of the sporophyte (see Section 17.2B). The evolutionary ascendancy of the sporophyte is probably due to the advantages of having a double quantity of hereditary material (as we shall see in Chapter 8).

The metaphytes that are grouped together in Subkingdom Thallophyta are simple-bodied and their tissues are not distinctly differentiated into specialized types. In multicellular algae the body is filamentous or consists of a *thallus* (a ribbonlike, flattened, or branching body lacking true roots, stems, and leaves). The thallus usually branches dichotomously, that is, by forking repeatedly into two branches of equal size. In fungi the plant body consists of a network of filaments forming a *mycelium* that may be diffuse or densely packed to form bodies such as mushrooms. In bryophytes, the simplest members of Subkingdom Embryophyta, the plant body may be a simple leafy shoot or a flattened algalike thallus.

Multicellular plant types have been compared in Table 2.2.

A Phylum Chlorophyta ("green plant"): green algae (approximately 6,000 species)

Green algae are indubitably plants, for they not only generally possess chlorophylls *a* and *b* and carry on photosynthesis, but they also produce cellulose cell walls and store true starch. Aside from this, they are exceedingly diverse, ranging from flagellated or nonmotile unicellular species to colonial forms and truly multicellular types with a simple body consisting of a filament or a thallus (Figure 2.13). *Desmids* are nonmotile unicellular chlorophytes that are especially abundant in freshwater plankton, forming an important food source for tiny animals. In this regard, their importance parallels that of diatoms in the marine plankton community.

In addition to chlorophylls *a* and *b,* green algae often contain as accessory pigments yellow *xanthophylls* and orange-red *carotenes,* which are of wide occurrence among land plants. Because chlorophytes possess both forms of chlorophyll that occur in mosses and vascular plants, they are thought to represent the stock from which these higher phyla arose. The other eucaryotic algal phyla (Chrysophyta, Pyrrophyta, Phaeophyta, and Rhodophyta) are evidently early offshoots that developed along independent lines with evolution of unique variants of chlorophyll (*c* and *d*) and other pigments and storage products of restricted distribution. They are not thought to have contributed to the evolution of land plants.

A few chlorophytes lack chlorophyll and are heterotrophic. These forms seem to be farther along the path of plant evolution than the euglenoids and therefore do not resemble the ancestral "protoanimals." They depend nutritionally upon the absorption of dissolved organic substances from the milieu and thus resemble yeasts and other fungi. This suggests that fungi may have evolved from unicellular chlorophytes that had long ago lost their photosynthetic capacity.

The reproductive processes of chlorophytes are especially interesting because varying methods of combination apparently reflect stages in the evolution of sexual reproduction. Certain chlorophytes reproduce asexually, but most types are capable of both sexual and asexual reproduction. (1) The simplest type of sexual reproduction occurs when two unicellular organisms come together and fuse to form a *zygote* that later divides to produce several new individuals. (2) A number of filamentous green algae reproduce by conjugation (Figure 17.10), a process in which neighboring cells form an interconnecting bridge and fuse to become a zygote that eventually germinates to produce a new filament. (3) Some green algae produce morphologically indistinguishable flagellated sex cells termed *isogametes,* which fuse in pairs to form the zygote from which a cluster of new vegetative (nonreproductive) cells are ultimately released (see Figure 17.13). (4) In other species motile gametes of two different sizes are formed (see Figure 17.14). (5) Finally, there are species in which distinctive male and female sex cells are produced: large, nonmotile female gametes or *ova,* and small, motile male gametes or *sperm.* Production of ova and sperm is characteristic of sexual reproduction in all metazoans and higher plants.

Figure 2.13 □ **Green algae: (*a*) *Chlamydomonas*, a unicellular flagellate containing a single large cupshaped chloroplast. (*b*) Desmids: top left, two *Micrasterias* species; bottom, *Cosmarium;* right, *Closterium.* In freshwater plankton, desmids play a role comparable to that of diatoms in the sea, forming an essential food source for small herbivorous freshwater animals. (*c*) *Volvox*, a colonial form, with young colonies developing within the parent colony. (*Courtesy of Carolina Biological Supply Company.*) (*d*) *Codium*, a marine seaweed characteristic of the intertidal zone. Note regular *dichotomous* (Y-type) branching characteristic of seaweeds in general. (*Courtesy of General Biological, Inc., Chicago.*)**

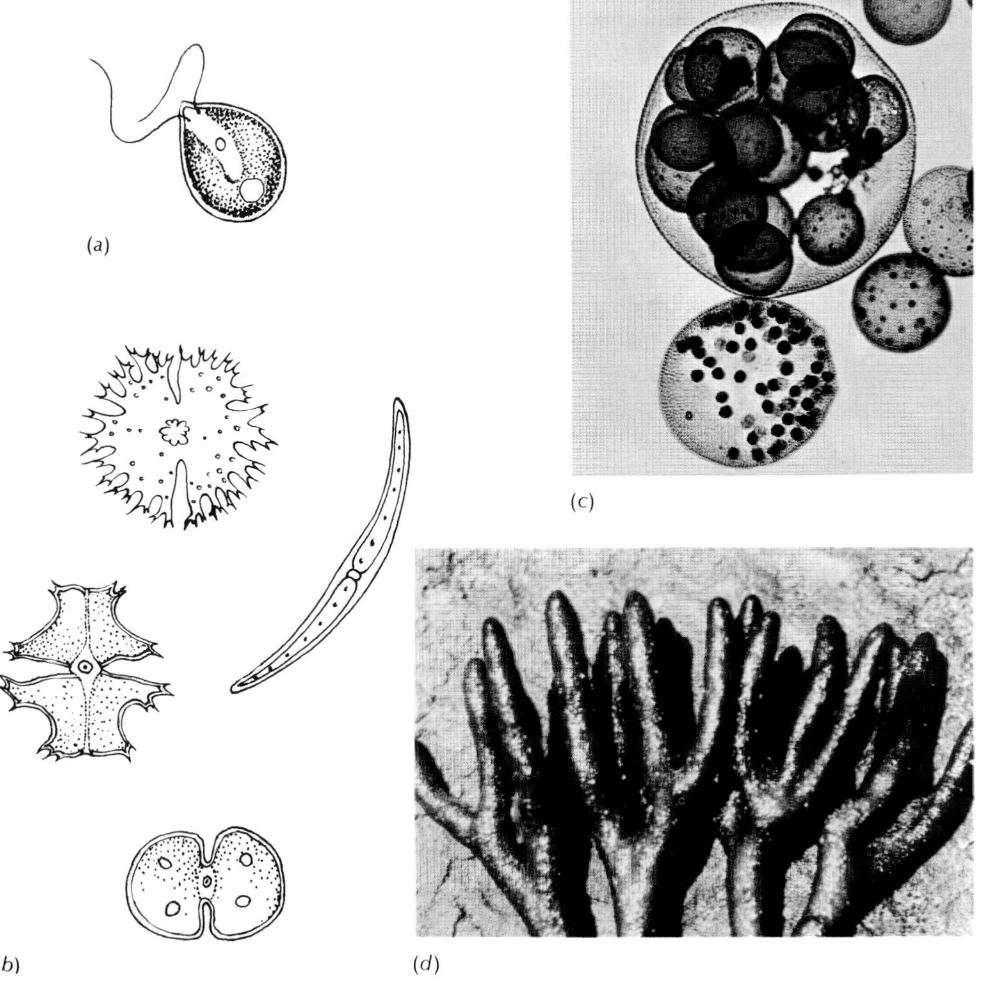

B Phylum Phaeophyta ("dusky plant"): brown algae (approximately 1,000 species)

Brown algae are multicellular and almost exclusively marine. They include the largest seaweeds, the kelps, which may attain a length of 100 m. A phaeophyte attaches to rocks or other solid surfaces by means of a strongly adhesive holdfast, from which there extends a stemlike stipe bearing flattened leaflike blades (Figure 2.14). Deeper-water species in particular possess air bladders, located at the base of each blade, which serve to raise the plant toward the light.

Phaeophytes produce flagellated reproductive cells. Sexual and asexual reproduction alternate in the life cycle, with gametophyte and sporophyte generations usually being similar in form. All phaeophytes are autotrophic and contain chlorophylls *a* and *c* together with such heavy concentrations of fucoxanthin that the plant may range in color from tan to a dusky blackish brown. Fucoxanthin assists chlorophyll by absorbing light of wavelengths that penetrate deeply into the water but are not absorbable by chlorophyll. The major storage product of brown algae is a unique carbohydrate, *laminarin.* Brown algae are important commercially as a source of *algin,* a carbohydrate derivative used to make ice cream and candies "creamy."

Kelps are ecologically important, for they form dense offshore "forests" along coastlines where rocky substrates permit their attachment. These kelp forests provide food, shelter, and support for many species of marine mammals.

Figure 2.14 □ *Laminaria*, a common genus of brown alga. Seen here are the branching adhesive holdfasts with which the plants cling to rocks in strong surf and the slender, stemlike stipes from which spring the ribbonlike blades. Such seaweeds furnish food and shelter for animals inhabiting the sea margins. (*Courtesy of General Biological, Inc., Chicago.*)

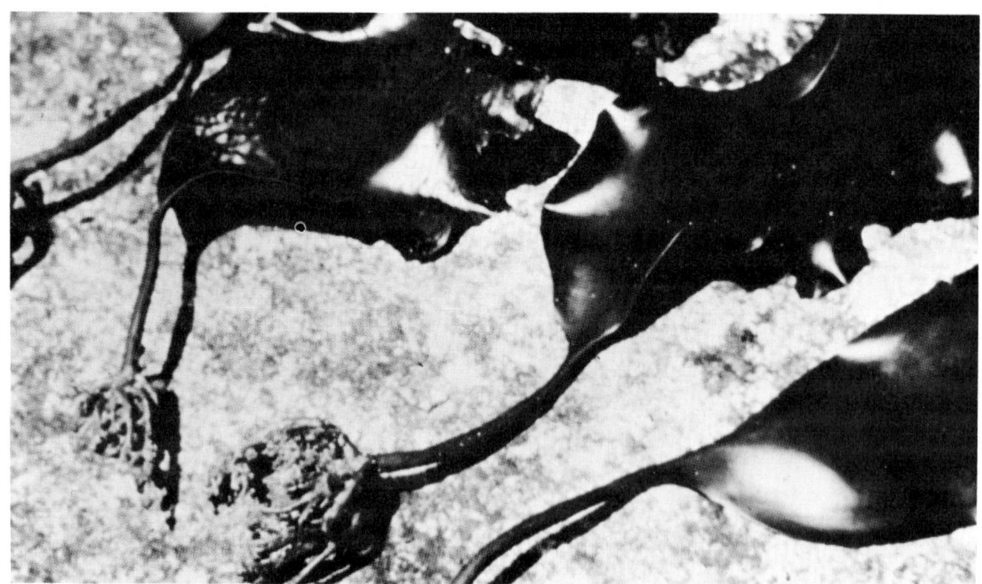

C Phylum Rhodophyta ("red plant"): red algae (approximately 2,500 species)

Red algae are multicellular and mostly marine, but unlike the phaeophytes they contain chlorophylls *a* and *d* in addition to dense concentrations of a unique pigment, *r-phycoerythrin*. The latter absorbs light of the short wavelengths that penetrate more deeply into water than do the longer wavelengths. This permits red algae to grow at considerable depths. Rhodophytes are generally small and feature a delicate, lacy thallus suited to quiet subtidal waters (Figure 2.15). Like the phaeophytes, red algae require a rocky substratum for the attachment of their branching rhizoids or single holdfast cell; however one group, the *coralline* red algae, accumulates calcium carbonate ($CaCO_3$), which imparts structural rigidity to the thallus and persists after death as limy deposits that provide a solid surface for the attachment of new generations of algae and for other organisms as well. Some "coral reefs" are composed in equal portions of materials contributed by coral polyps and coralline algae.

The reproductive cells of red algae are not flagellated. Asexual spores and the nonmotile sperm are transported by water currents. Sexual and asexual generations commonly alternate in the life cycle, a typical example of which is seen in Figure 17.17*a*.

Rhodophytes manufacture a unique glycogenlike type of starch and their cell walls consist of cellulose and pectin. The latter is the source of *agar,* which is extracted in quantity from the alga *Gelidium* and used as a bacterial culture medium.

Figure 2.15 □ **Red algae: (*a*) *Gelidium*, source of commercial agar, and (*b*) *Bossiella*, a coralline alga. Note the delicate, finely divided thallus of *Gelidium* and the stiff, calcium-impregnated thallus of *Bossiella*. Coralline red algae contribute as much as 50 percent to the construction of coral reefs, along with coral polyps. (*Scripps Institution of Oceanography.*)**

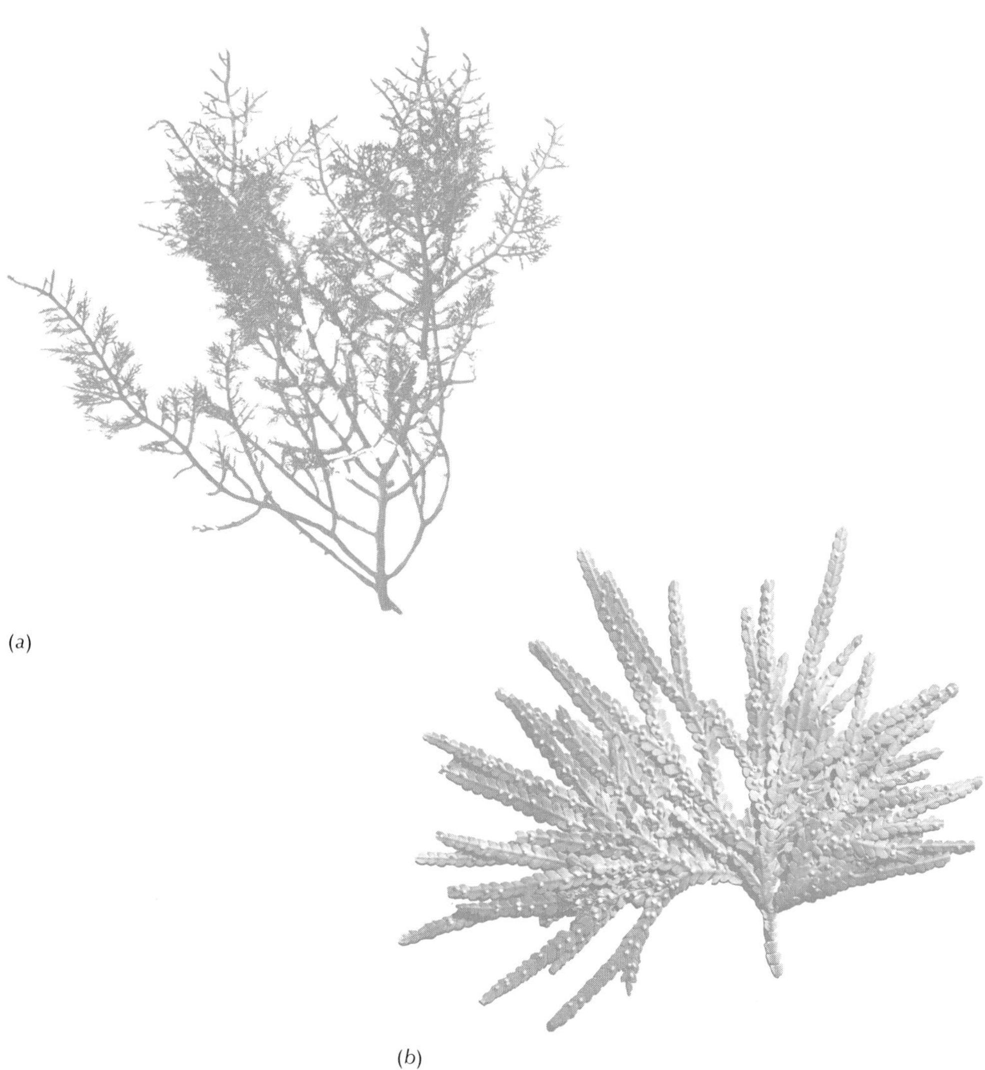

(*a*)

(*b*)

D Phylum Myxomycophyta ("slime-fungus plant"): slime molds (approximately 500 species)

Slime molds are heterotrophic organisms that live saprophytically (that is, by absorbing nutrients from decaying wood and other decomposing organic material). Their life history is unusual (Figure 2.16*a*) and of special interest to biologists who are engaged in the investigation of aggregation and differentiation of cells (see Figure 11.6). The initial stage in a representative life cycle begins with individual motile cells resembling zooflagellates. Lacking rigid cell walls, these cells are capable of amoeboid as well as flagellar locomotion. Eventually they fuse in pairs, forming zygotes that become amoebalike and creep about engulfing solid particles of food. After a feeding period these amoeboid individuals aggregate to form a multicellular organism. Cells in this mass often lose their separating membranes and fuse into a *plasmodium* ranging from less than 1 mm to more than 25 cm in diameter. The plasmodium (or multicellular aggregation, as the case may be) creeps by extending pseudopodia and feeds saprophytically or in some cases even by ingesting solid food (Figure 2.16*b*). At last it ceases to move and produces spherical spore-bearing bodies (*sporangia*) that are often brightly colored and are borne on stalks above the plasmodium. Within each sporangium four flagellated cells are produced that are released to initiate a new cycle.

The origin and affinities of the slime molds are unknown; they may represent a group diverging early in fungal evolution.

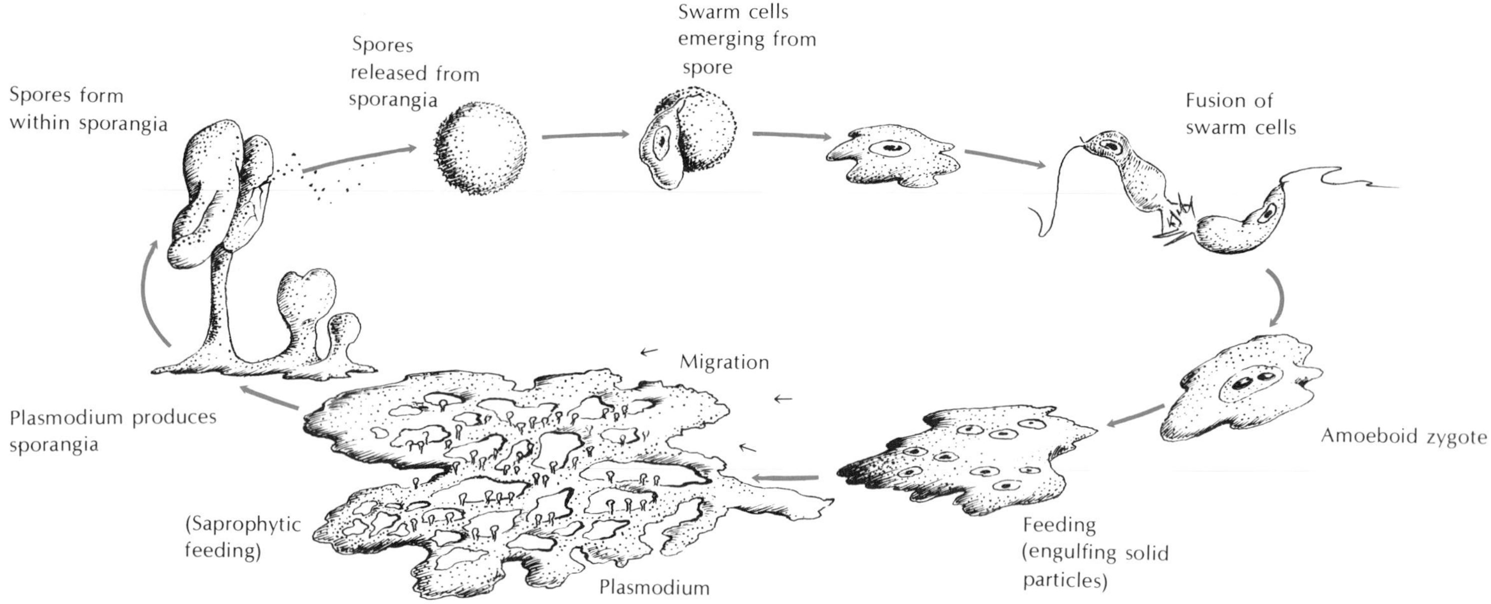

(*a*)

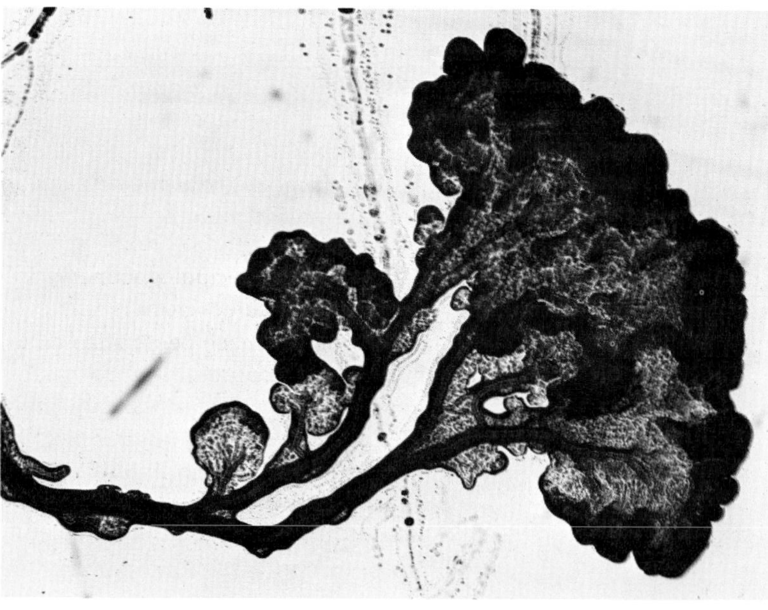

(*b*)

Figure 2.16 □ Slime molds. (*a*) Life cycle of *Physarum polycephalum.* Flagellated swarm cells fuse in pairs, producing an amoeboid zygote that feeds and grows into a plasmodium; small plasmodia may come together and fuse to form one larger. After a period of moving about while feeding upon decaying material, the plasmodium puts forth sporangia, within which are formed the spores that give rise to a new generation of swarm cells. (*b*) Photograph of feeding plasmodium of *Physarum.* (*Courtesy of Carolina Biological Supply Company.*)

(*a*)

(*b*)

Figure 2.17 □ *Eumycophyta,* true fungi: (*a*) *Morchella angusticeps,* the edible morel, a sac fungus (ascomycete) (*courtesy of Carolina Biological Supply Company*), and (*b*) *Lepiota rachodes,* a mushroom and club fungus (basidiomycete) (*Los Angeles County Museum of Natural History*). Only the fruiting bodies are shown and not the extensive underground mycelium producing them.

E Phylum Eumycophyta ("true-fungus plant"): fungi (over 100,000 species)

The true fungi are nonphotosynthesizing plants, mostly multicellular, which live either as saprophytes or as parasites. A few are even predatory and capture and kill small animals.

The main body of a fungus consists of a *mycelium,* a tangled mesh of filaments (*hyphae*). Each hypha consists of a series of cells, usually separated by cellulose crosswalls; in the more primitive fungi crosswalls are often lacking and adjacent cells are fused to form a syncytium. The mycelium grows by elongation of the hyphae and eventually produces tiny spherical sporangia or larger and more elaborate "fruiting bodies" made of highly organized masses of hyphae. Because of the tremendous nutritional capacity of the mycelium that produces them, such fruiting bodies emerge into the air and develop with prodigious haste (hence the common saying, "growing like a mushroom"). Puffballs, mushrooms, morels, and bracket fungi (Figure 2.17) are fruiting bodies produced by extensive mycelia which, because they are buried in the soil or rotting wood, may escape observation though they may be meters long.

Four classes of fungi are recognized: (1) *phycomycetes,* or algalike fungi, which are unicellular or filamentous with syncytial hyphae, lack elaborate fruiting bodies, and when aquatic produce motile flagellated spores resembling those of algae (including black bread mold, water molds, and downy mildews); (2) *ascomycetes,* or sac fungi, so called because their spores are produced in slender sacs termed *asci* that are often grouped into cup-shaped fruiting bodies (including red and blue molds such as *Neurospora* and *Penicillium,* morels, yeasts, and powdery mildews); (3) *basidiomycetes,* or club fungi, so called because the spores are borne externally on the ends of club-shaped cells termed *basidia* (including mushrooms, puffballs, bracket fungi, and the parasitic smuts and rusts, which are serious agricultural pests); (4) *deuteromycetes,* a heterogeneous group of fungi of obscure relationships that apparently lack a sexual stage in the life cycle (including many parasitic forms such as the causative agents of ringworm, athletes' foot, and sprue).

Many fungi kill competing bacteria by secreting inhibitory chemicals termed *antibiotics.* The first antibiotic to be isolated in quantity and purified for medical use was penicillin, a secretion of the blue mold, *Penicillium.* The discovery of penicillin by Alexander Fleming is a classic case of the operation of serendipity in scientific investigation, for the mold entered his bacterial cultures as a chance contaminant. Since then, purposive investigations have brought to light many other fungus products with antibiotic properties, including actinomycin, streptomycin, and aureomycin.

Most fungi are much better adapted to life on land than any phyla considered up to this point, but tend to be restricted to sites rich in organic nutrients. However, several types of ascomycetes (or more rarely basidiomycetes) associate with green or blue-green algae to form dual organisms termed *lichens.* The structural form of the lichen is contributed by the fungal mycelium. Algal cells occupy the spaces between

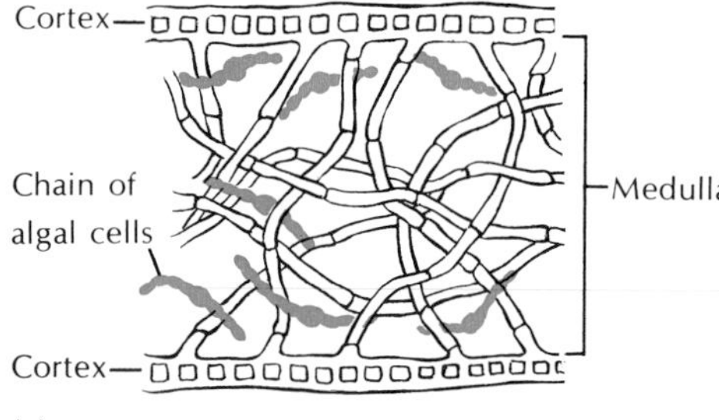

(a)

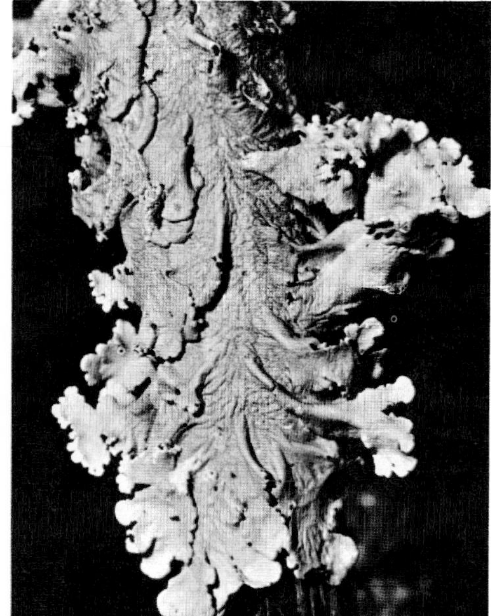
(b)

Figure 2.18 □ **Lichens.** ***(a)*** **Section of portion of lichen thallus (*****Leptogium*****), showing fungal thallus with interstices occupied by short chains of algal cells.** ***(b)*** **Foliose lichens on twig. (*****Courtesy of Carolina Biological Supply Company.*****) Lichens do not need to obtain water from the soil but can grow on bark and even bare rock, which they break down by secreting dilute acids.**

the fungus filaments and are protected from dehydration by the surrounding hyphae (Figure 2.18). The photosynthetic activity of the algae results in a surplus of organic food that serves to sustain the fungal member of the association. Reproduction is by means of fungal spores that are dispersed by wind but only germinate to become a new lichen thallus if appropriate algal spores are present. Over 16,000 types of lichen are known; many subsist on bare rock, which they disintegrate by releasing acidic secretions. "Reindeer moss," a tundra species, constitutes an important food source for herbivorous mammals that live in the Arctic regions.

2.5 □ EMBRYOPHYTA: COMPLEX METAPHYTES

The Subkingdom Embryophyta is in a sense an artificial grouping because the two phyla that it contains, Bryophyta and Tracheophyta, are thought to have arisen independently from ancestral green algae. Nevertheless they share the characteristics of having *multicellular sex organs* (sperm-producing *antheridia* and egg-producing *archegonia*) and of *sheltering their embryos* within the archegonia during early development. The archegonial tissues also provide nourishment for the sporophyte embryo.

A Phylum Bryophyta ("moss plant"): mosses and liverworts (approximately 23,000 species)

Bryophytes are small autotrophic plants that frequent moist terrestrial habitats (Figure 2.19). Fossil and developmental evidence indicates their descent from green algae. Bryophytes were among the earliest land plants and their adaptation to land is still imperfect for they lack well-developed water-absorbing organs and produce flagellated sperm that must swim through water to reach the egg. Their small size is dictated by the fact that they lack tissues specialized for effective conduction of water and mineral nutrients from soil to growing tips.

The gametophyte is the conspicuous organism in the life cycle: it grows from an algalike filamentous *protonema* ("first-thread") stage which arises from an asexual spore (see Figure 17.19). The protonema puts out fine absorptive rhizoids into the soil and then develops a main gametophyte body, consisting of a flattened, prostrate thallus that shows algalike branching (in some liverworts), or an upright, leafy shoot (in mosses and certain liverworts). Vegetative proliferation of the gametophyte may continue indefinitely by way of underground runners, but for sexual reproduction sperm and eggs are produced in antheridia and archegonia; in mosses these sex organs are often borne at the apex of separate shoots. The egg remains in the archegonium during fertilization; it develops into a sporophyte that remains attached to the gametophyte (on which it is nutritionally dependent) and disappears once it has produced and liberated its spores.

Figure 2.19 □ **Bryophytes. (*a*) *Polytrichum*, a moss; living clump, showing leafy gametophytes and slender sporophytes. (*Courtesy of Carolina Biological Supply Company.*) (*b*) *Marchantia*, a liverwort; photograph of glass model, showing prostrate thallus bearing asexual reproductive bodies (gemmae) and upright fruiting bodies on the underside of which sex cells are formed and the small sporophyte generation develops. (*Field Museum of Natural History.*)**

(*a*)

(*b*)

B Phylum Tracheophyta ("tracheid plant"): vascular plants (exceeding 250,000 species)

Tracheophytes represent a highly diversified phylum that has exploited land habitats more successfully than any other plant group. They are characterized by a dominant sporophyte that is differentiated into *roots, stems,* and *leaves,* made up of various types of specialized tissues. All parts of the body are interconnected by way of special conductive or *vascular* tissues that carry water and solutes throughout the plant (see Figure 14.12). (One type of vascular element is the tracheid, from which the phylum name is taken.) Many tracheophytes attain great size, requiring both a highly efficient conduction system and the development of supportive mechanical tissues that enable the plant to assume an upright habit of growth.

Tracheophyte reproductive cycles will be considered in further detail in Chapter 17 (see Figures 17.21 and 17.22). In the more primitive tracheophytes (such as ferns) sexual reproduction is still dependent upon water, for the sperm must swim from the male to the female sex organs of the gametophyte. In the higher tracheophytes, the seed plants, this swimming-sperm stage has been replaced by a new male gametophyte form—*pollen*—which can be dispersed by the wind or by insects. The emergence of this type of male gametophyte was a major evolutionary breakthrough in the conquest of the land, for it set seed plants free from dependence on water for completion of the sexual phase of their life cycle.

Phylum Tracheophyta is divided into

Figure 2.20 □ *Equisetum,* a primitive vascular plant; photograph of glass model, showing conelike strobilus within which the small gametophyte generation is produced. The sphenopsids, or horsetails, are also known as scouring rushes because their silicon-impregnated stems were once commonly used for scrubbing. (*Field Museum of Natural History.*)

(*a*)

(*b*)

Figure 2.21 □ Ferns. (*a*) Tree ferns occupying a gully in a eucalyptus forest, Australia. (*Courtesy of Australian News and Information Bureau.*) (*b*) Photomicrograph of fern gametophyte or *prothallium,* ×2.25. The prostrate thallus sends rootlike rhizoids into the ground and can nourish both itself and the young sporophyte produced from the gametes it bears. (*Ward's Natural Science Establishment, Inc.*)

four subphyla, the first three of which are relics of the geologic past and are represented today by only a few surviving species: (1) *psilopsids,* which have only rudimentary vascular tissue and display algalike body form; (2) *lycopsids,* including club mosses and ground pines, which were dominant during the Carboniferous Period (about 250 million years ago) when some were giant trees; (3) *sphenopsids,* the horsetails, which grew to heights of 30 m during the Carboniferous Period, have stems impregnated with silica, leaves borne in regular whorls, and spores produced in a terminal cone (Figure 2.20); (4) *pteropsids,* the ferns and seed plants, which have well developed leaves and vascular tissues and bear spores upon specialized leaves termed *sporophylls.*

The hypothesis that tracheophytes did not evolve from bryophyte ancestors but arose independently from the green algae is supported by the flagellated algalike sperm and algalike branching of the psilopsids. Psilopsids are thought to have given rise to the other groups of tracheophytes.

Among pteropsids, only ferns produce independent gametophytes, tiny prostrate organisms that produce the eggs and sperm and nourish the sporophyte embryos that develop into the familiar fern plant. Some ancient ferns attained great size, but today only a relatively few tropical forms remain treelike (Figure 2.21*a*). Fern sporophytes produce asexual spores in sporangia grouped on the undersides of the leaves. These require moist conditions to germinate into the simple thalluslike gametophyte (Figure 2.21*b*). The sporophyte can also persist indefinitely, spreading by underground runners without passing through the sexual stage of the life cycle.

Figure 2.22 □ **A gymnosperm, *Pinus aristata* (bristlecone pine), branch with 1-year-old cone. The term "gymnosperm" refers to the fact that conifers and their relatives (cycads and gingkoes) bear naked seeds, that is, seeds not enclosed in fruits. (*Los Angeles County Museum of Natural History.*)**

Figure 2.23 □ **Angiosperms. In contrast to gymnosperms, angiosperm seeds are enclosed by ovarian tissues, forming a fruit; specializations of fruits abet seed dispersal and have greatly contributed to the outstanding success of flowering plants. (*a*) Characteristics of dicots (subclass Dicotyledoneae). (*b*) Characteristics of monocots (subclass Monocotyledonae). (Additional distinguishing features are described in the text.)**

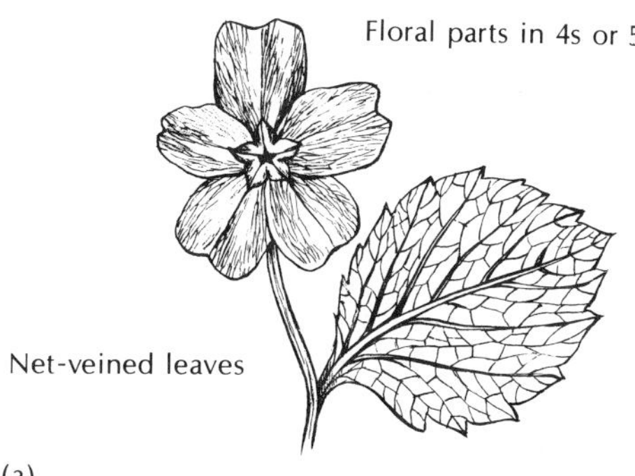

(*a*)

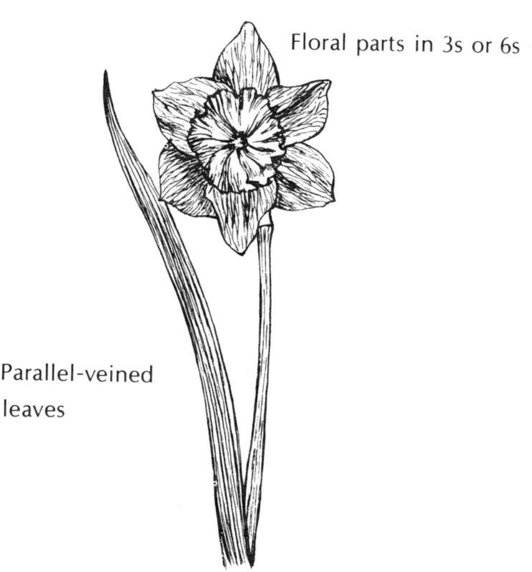

(*b*)

Seed plants include gymnosperms (conifers, cycads, and ginkgoes) and angiosperms (flowering plants). They are characterized by (1) having a nearly microscopic gametophyte that is entirely embedded within the tissues of the sporophyte, and (2) the production of a sporophyte embryo that is provided with stored food and passes through a period of arrested development as a *seed* prior to germination. This period of dormancy favors dissemination by wind, water, or animals, and many seeds are enclosed within tissues especially modified to effect dispersal.

Gymnosperm ("naked-seed") seeds are borne in a comparatively exposed condition, ripening on the scales of the female cones (Figure 2.22). These seeds, when shed, are protected only by their seed coat. In the angiosperms (literally, "vessel seed," implying that the seeds are enclosed within maternal tissues that serve as a *vessel* for their protection and dispersal), the seeds are completely embedded *within* the ovary of the flower, which matures into a protective covering about the seed.

Flowers are usually adapted for the attraction of insect pollinators. Flowering plants form two major groups, the Monocotyledoneae ("monocots"), including grasses, lilies, palms, orchids, sedges, reeds, and bananas, and the Dicotyledoneae ("dicots"), comprising almost all flowering plants other than those specified above. Monocots are the most recently evolved plants; a number are wind-pollinated and consequently bear inconspicuous flowers. Monocots and dicots may be distinguished on the basis of morphological differences in the flowers, stems, leaves, and seeds (see Figure 2.23 and Table 2.3).

Table 2.3 □ Morphological differences between dicots and monocots

CHARACTERISTIC	DICOTS	MONOCOTS
Floral parts	**Borne in fours and fives**	**Borne in threes and sixes**
Stem anatomy	**Vascular tissue forms a cylinder; annual growth rings present**	**Vascular tissue in scattered bundles; no growth rings**
Leaf venation	**Netted**	**Parallel**
Cotyledons (seed leaves)	**Two**	**One**

The most significant advances made by angiosperms over gymnosperms are (1) their general use of insects as pollinating agents, and (2) the specialization of tissues of the maternal sporophyte to surround and protect the female gametophyte and later to protect the seed and abet its dispersal. These tissues, when ripe, constitute a *fruit.*

2.6 □ METAZOA: MULTICELLULAR ANIMALS

A Phylum Porifera ("pore bearer"): sponges (approximately 15,000 species)

Sponges, the most primitive multicellular animals, possess no true tissues or organs. They are probably descended from choanoflagellate protozoa but have not themselves contributed to the evolution of other metazoan phyla; they are therefore considered a side branch of metazoan evolution, often separated into the Subkingdom *Parazoa.*

Only the larval stage is motile. The adult is sedentary and capable of only limited contractility. A number of specialized cell types are present that perform various duties, including setting up water currents, controlling the incurrent and excurrent apertures, secreting supportive fibers or spicules, digesting and storing food, and forming gametes (see Figure 12.6). The body plan basically resembles a vase, the walls of which are perforated by countless minute openings (Figure 2.24). The diameter of these pores sets the upper limits of size for particles that may be carried into the sponge with the water currents set up by the *choanocytes* or collar cells. These particles are captured as they pass through canals or chambers lined with choanocytes and are digested within the individual cells. The water exits by way of a single excurrent opening, the osculum. The large central cavity (spongocoel) is *not* a stomach but a chamber through which water circulates. The body wall consists of an outer layer of somewhat contractile, flattened cells (pinacocytes), an inner, irregularly discontinuous layer of choanocytes, and a middle layer of noncellular gelatinous material forming a matrix through which glide assorted amoeboid cells. Some of these cells are concerned with reproduction; others secrete a supportive skeleton of protein fibers or hard spicules of calcium or silicon salts.

The three classes of sponges are (1) the *calcareous* sponges, having a skeleton of limy spicules; (2) the delicate *siliceous* sponges, which are supported by a lattice of glassy fibers and six-pronged siliceous spicules (see Figure 4.25); and (3) the *horny* sponges, possessing a supportive framework of proteinaceous spongin fibers together with siliceous spicules bearing one to four rays. Three levels of complexity of the sponge body plan are diagrammed in Figure 2.24. Comparison of these body plans reveals a trend toward increase in internal surface area, allowing more effective capture of food particles from the water passing through.

Sponges are advanced over protozoans because they are multicellular and have various types of specialized cells that permit a division of labor. Although the activity of individual cells is largely autonomous and not as well coordinated as in tissues of higher multicellular animals, their aggregate performance is quite effective in, say, pumping water and drawing food particles into the body of the sponge. A large sponge may filter more than 1,500 liters of water per day; thereby it is able to render unnecessary locomotion and active food seeking.

B Phylum Coelenterata ("hollow intestine"); also called Cnidaria: polyps and medusae (approximately 10,000 species)

Sea anemones, sea fans, hydroids, corals, and jellyfish are coelenterates, members of the simplest phylum of *eumetazoan* (true metazoan) animals. Their embryonic development differs markedly from that of sponges, in essence resembling that of all other metazoan phyla. This supports the hypothesis that coelenterates evolved directly from some protozoan line (probably flagellates) rather than from sponges, and that an ancestral coelenterate may have been the progenitor of more advanced metazoan groups. A candidate for this common ancestor is the *planula* larva of modern coelenterates (an ovoid mass of cells clothed in cilia), which matures into a polyp; by alternative developmental routes it is possible that it had given rise to the flatworm body plan.

Coelenterates are more advanced than sponges in several ways. (1) Their specialized cell types are functionally coordinated into true tissues and can cooperate in bringing about effective movement and prey capture. (2) Sponges are not mobile as adults, but coelenterates move by coordinated muscular contractions. (3) Such coordination is made possible by the presence of a simple *nerve plexus.* (4) Tentacles armed with stinging cells are used to capture large prey. (5) The prey is digested extracellularly in a large central digestive (*gastrovascular*) cavity, thereby liberating coelenterates from dependence on microscopic food suitable for intracellular digestion.

The coelenterate body plan is that of a double-walled sac, with outer epidermal and inner gastrodermal cell layers enclosing the large gastrovascular cavity that serves for both the digestion and distribution of nutrients (see Figure 12.8). The mouth, being the single opening into the gastrovascular cavity, serves both for ingestion and egestion. Between the epidermis and gastrodermis may lie a layer of nonliving material (mesoglea) of variable thickness, which may contain few to many contractile and amoeboid cells. The mouth is located centrally, ringed with tentacles bearing batteries of stinging capsules (*nematocysts*). These discharge when stimulated and penetrate or adhere to the integument of appropriate prey (see Figure 12.9). Coordinated movements of the tentacles bring the prey to the mouth through which it is drawn into the gastrovascular cavity. Both epidermis and gastrodermis feature a mixture of several cell types, some of which are common to both layers. Most abundant are the contractile epitheliomuscular cells that are controlled by the underlying nerve plexus. The gastro-

Figure 2.24 □ **Sponges are simple multicellular animals without mouth and digestive cavity and must subsist upon food captured and digested by individual cells. Flagellated *collar cells* (*choanocytes*) line portions of the internal surface; they set up a constant flow of water entering through the pores in the body wall and expelled by way of the central osculum. From simplest to most complex, three body plans are (*a*) *asconoid* (choanocytes line the main internal cavity), (*b*) *syconoid* (the body wall is expanded as fingerlike outgrowths enclosing radial canals lined with collar cells), and (*c*) *rhagonoid,* or *leuconoid* (collar cells are restricted to numerous chambers communicating by canals to the exterior and reduced central cavity). Bath sponges are rhagonoid.**

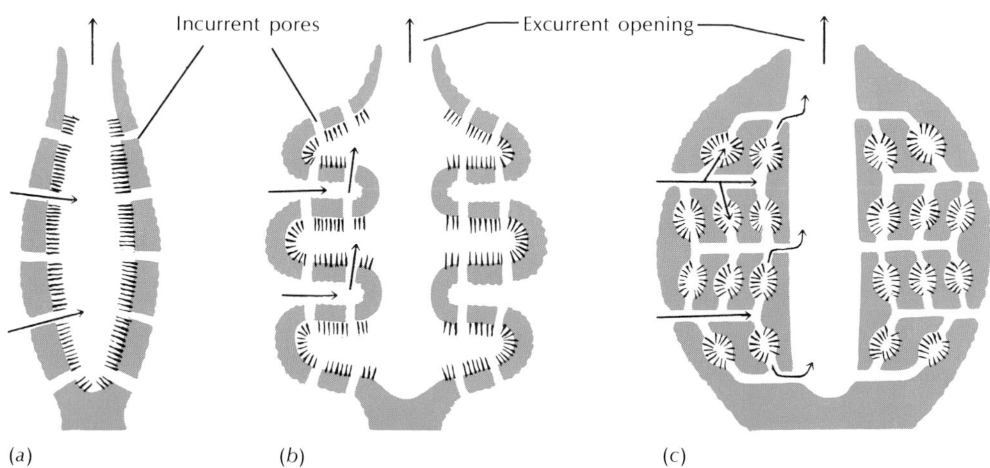

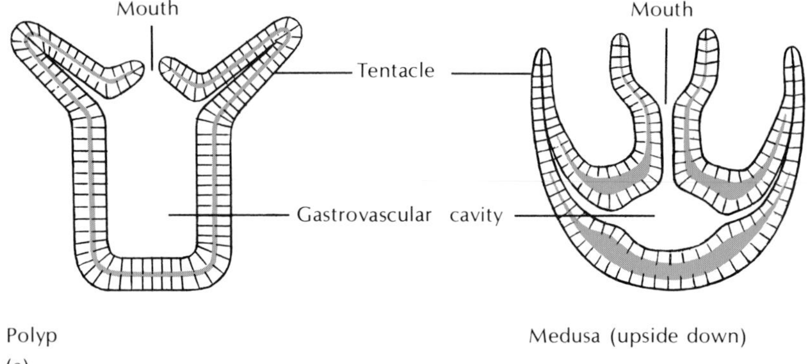

(b)

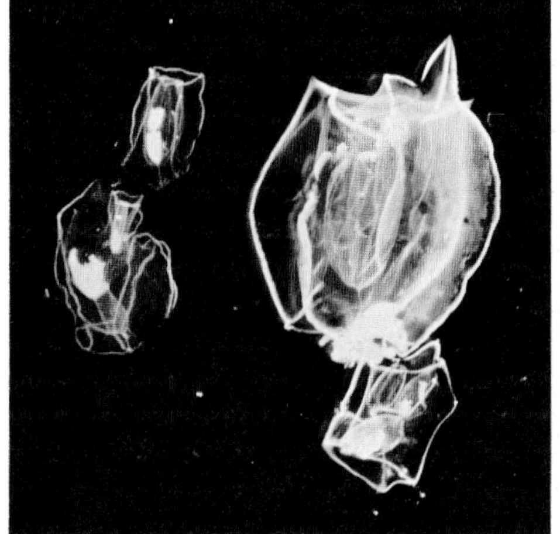
(c)

Figure 2.25 □ **(*a*) Coelenterate body plans. The sedentary polyp and free-swimming medusa are alternative expressions of the saccular body plan, in which a centrally located mouth, ringed with tentacles, opens into a large digestive cavity. The body wall consists of two distinct cell layers, the outer epidermis and inner gastrodermis, separated by a variable amount of gelatinous material (*mesoglea*) inhabited by amoeboid wandering cells and contractile fibers. (*b*) *Gonionemus*, a hydrozoan medusa. (*Courtesy of Carolina Biological Supply Company.*) (*c*) *Ablyopsis erscholtzii*, a siphonophore. These floating colonies each consist of only two zooids: (left) asexual colony, (right) sexual colony. (*Courtesy of Dr. A. Alvariño de Leira and Scripps Institution of Oceanography.*)**

dermis also contains glandular cells that secrete digestive fluids and also stir the contents of the digestive cavity with their flagella. Sensory cells and nematocysts are abundant in the epidermis. The coordinated activities of these cells will be further considered in Chapter 12.

Coelenterates typically alternate a *polyp* and a *medusa* form in their life history. These two manifestations of the phylum's body plan are basically similar (Figure 2.25), but the medusa swims about more freely and has a thicker mesoglea. The polyp generation produces medusae asexually; the medusae then produce gametes, which upon fertilization give rise to the ciliated planula larva that matures into the polyp (see Figure 7.6). A medusa generation is lacking in anemones and corals.

Ecologically perhaps the most significant single type of coelenterate is reef-building coral. By the building up of fringing and barrier reefs, coral polyps create quiet-water areas and provide substratum and protection for a variety of organisms.

C Phylum Platyhelminthes ("flatworms"): flukes, tapeworms, turbellarians (approximately 7,000 species)

The three major types of flatworms are *turbellarians, flukes,* and *tapeworms* (Figure 2.26). Although flukes and tapeworms are highly specialized for a parasitic existence, the free-living turbellarians such as polyclads and planarians demonstrate several important biotic innovations that apparently originated with this phylum. These soft-bodied, unsegmented, and conspicuously flattened worms are the most primitive ani-

Figure 2.26 □ Flatworms. (*a*) Turbellarians, nonparasitic carnivorous species. The drawing shows a common planarian (*Dugesia*), representative of typical flatworm structure. The photograph is of the marine polyclad *Prostheceraeus vittatus.* (*Courtesy of Dr. Douglas P. Wilson.*) (*b*) A fluke, *Opisthorchis sinensis*, inhabitant of the human liver. (*Photograph courtesy of Carolina Biological Supply Company.*) (*c*) Tapeworms. Diagram indicates body parts of a typical tapeworm (*Taenia*). Photograph shows the dog tapeworm *Echinococcus granulosus*, consisting of scolex and three proglottids, the largest of which contains a gravid uterus filled with eggs. (*Ward's Natural Science Establishment, Inc.*) This small cestode is dangerous because its eggs when swallowed give rise to large hydatid cysts in the muscles or organs of the new host.

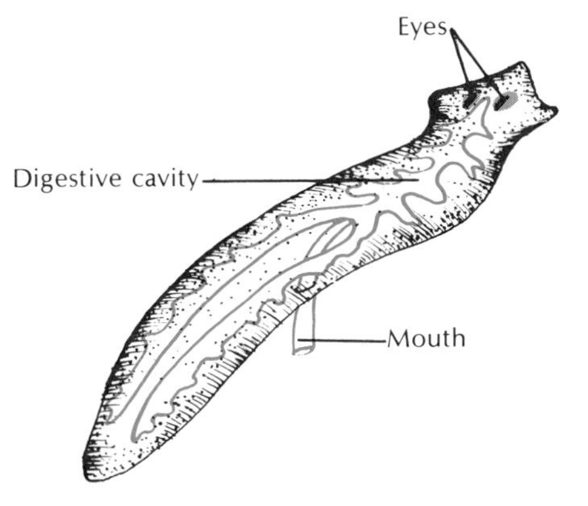

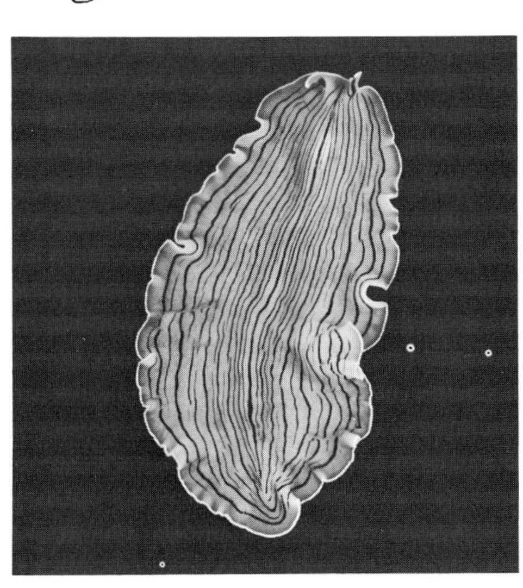

(*a*)

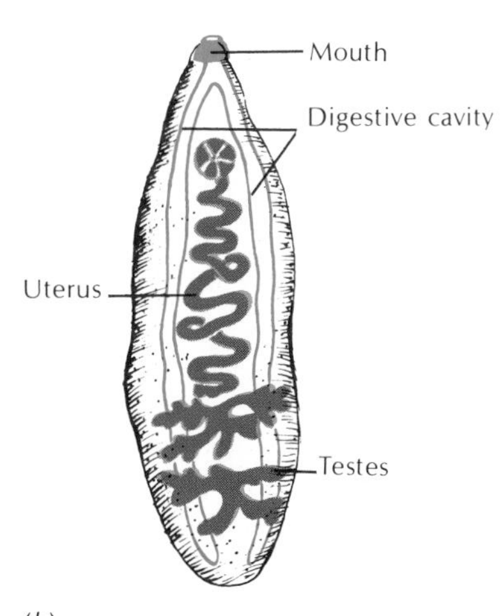

(*b*)

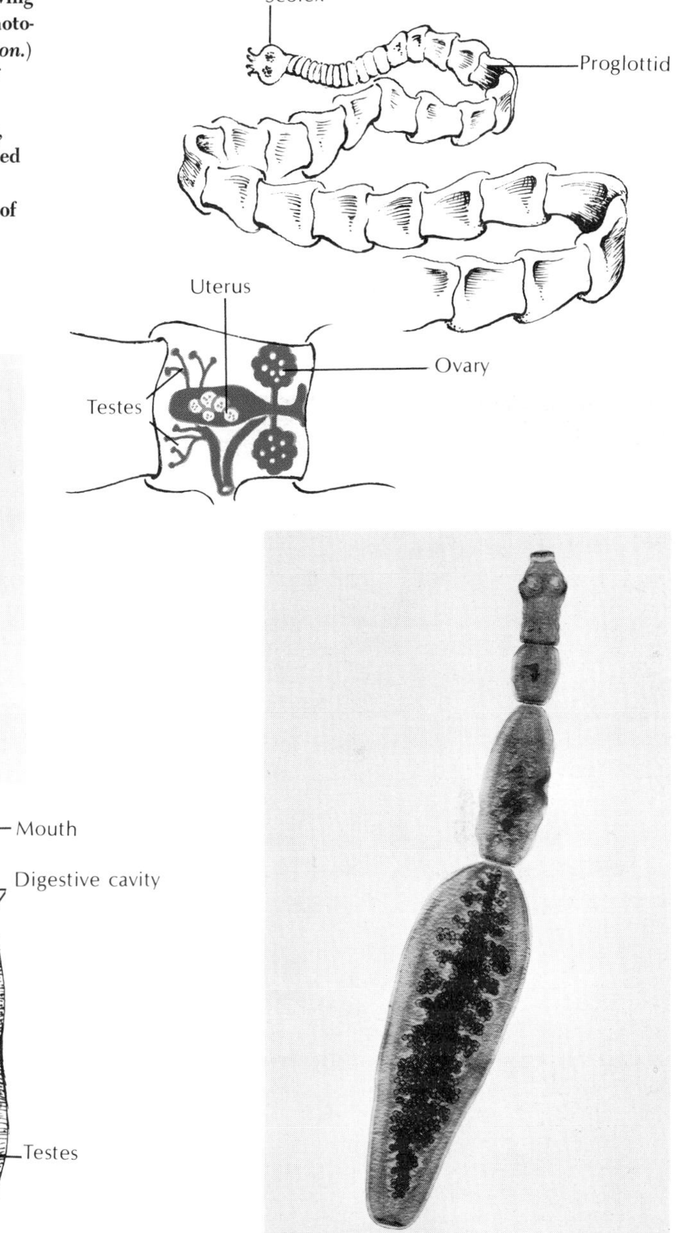

(*c*)

mals to display *bilateral symmetry*—the type of symmetry in which the body is divisible into two equal halves along only one plane, a longitudinal plane separating the right and left halves of the body. Bilateral symmetry is typical of the actively moving animal, while the *radial* (wheel-like) *symmetry* displayed by coelenterates reflects a sedentary or a floating existence in which the animal may meet the environment in any direction with equal facility. The bilaterally symmetrical animal is said to possess an *anterior* (front) end, a *posterior* (hind) end, *dorsal* (upper) and *ventral* (lower) surfaces, and right and left sides (see Figure 12.1). The anterior end is the first part of the animal to meet the environment; consequently, there has been a progressive tendency in such animals for the sense organs, nervous tissues, and mouth to move to that end of the body. This tendency, termed *cephalization,* is first manifested by flatworms and becomes more pronounced in higher animal phyla. Cephalization in turbellarians involves the massing of nerve cells in the head to form a simple "brain" and the clustering of eyes and other sense organs in the head.

Other advances shown by flatworms as compared to coelenterates include the first appearance of a true layer of cells (*mesoderm*) between the outer epidermis and the inner gastrodermis that lines the highly branched gastrovascular cavity. (The developmental significance of mesoderm will be considered in Chapter 11.) Special excretory structures and a complicated reproductive system, both derived from the mesoderm, first appear in flatworms. Flatworms may be either *monoecious* ("one house," that is, housing both ovaries and testes in the same individual), or dioecious ("two houses," that is, having the male and female organs in different individuals). In both the monoecious and dioecious types, transfer of sperm is often effected by copulation rather than by release of gametes into the water as is common with coelenterates and sponges. The eggs are provided with yolk furnished by yolk glands, and are encapsulated by material secreted from a shell gland.

Most flukes and tapeworms combine asexual and sexual generations in their life cycle, which begins with the fusion of sperm and egg to produce a zygote that develops into the first larval stage. This larva eventually reproduces asexually, by budding, giving rise either to secondary and tertiary larval generations (which in turn reproduce asexually) or to the sexually reproducing generation. Representative life histories will be considered later from the standpoint of their ecological significance.

In regions where chronic poverty, overcrowding, and lack of education combine to produce unsanitary living conditions, human infection with flukes, tapeworms, and other helminths may become widespread and acute, representing a public health problem of major proportions.

D Phylum Nemertea ("unerring"): ribbon worms (approximately 500 species)

Nemerteans are predominantly marine, soft-bodied, unsegmented worms with greatly extensible bodies ranging in length from a few centimeters to several meters (one species reputedly exceeds 20 m!). The phylum name is derived from the presumed accuracy with which the proboscis, often as long as the worm's entire body, is protruded from its sheath to pierce or wrap about the prey (Figure 2.27), which is then pulled into the mouth (Plate 1a).

Ribbon worms are of especial interest because they are the simplest animals to show two important evolutionary advances in body structure. First, the digestive cavity is no longer saccular, with its only orifice being the mouth, but instead is *tubular,* extending from the anterior mouth to a posterior eliminatory opening, the *anus.* A tubular digestive tract permits a one-way passage of material so that ingestion, digestion, and elimination can all go on simultaneously.

A second major advance shown by nemerteans is the possession of a system of contractile *blood vessels.* The function of internal distribution of nutrients is thereby removed from the digestive tract and relegated to a separate circulatory or vascular system. Association of the excretory tubules with the walls of the major blood vessels also occurs in nemerteans, facilitating removal of waste materials from the blood.

E Phylum Aschelminthes ("cavity worm"): roundworms, rotifers, and the like (approximately 13,000 named species*)

The scientific name of this large and somewhat heterogeneous phylum is derived from the fact that its body plan features a fluid-filled cavity, the *pseudocoel,* which separates the tubular digestive tract from the

*The actual number of species probably exceeds 500,000 owing to the large number of parasitic forms that appear to be restricted to single host species.

body wall (see Figure 12.23). The resultant "tube within a tube" body plan is highly successful and has apparently arisen analogously on several different occasions in metazoan evolution, with a body cavity being formed by one of several alternative developmental processes. In the aschelminths the fluid within the pseudocoel serves as a medium of transport and blood vessels are lacking. The sex organs lie coiled within the pseudocoel. The digestive tract is complete, from mouth to anus, and is a simple nonmuscular tube except in the vicinity of the mouth, which is usually armed with biting teeth and specialized for sucking or chewing. The body wall typically consists of an outer, noncellular cuticle secreted by the underlying epidermis (which is often a continuous sheet of living matter not divided into separate cells) and a layer of more or less longitudinally oriented *muscle fibers.*

By far the most numerous representatives of this phylum are the *nematodes* or roundworms (Figure 2.28). Nematodes range in size from microscopic to about 1 m in length. Their smoothly cylindrical bodies taper to pointed ends. Swimming nematodes are readily recognized by their distinctive whipping or lashing movements, caused by the inelastic but flexible cuticle, which can be bent but which prevents the body of the worm from shortening or elongating. Many nematodes are parasitic in the tissues of plants and animals; others are free-living in the soil, the ocean, and fresh water. Nematodes that cause a significant incidence of human infection in the United States include *Trichinella,* the causative agent of trichinosis, usually contracted by eating inadequately cooked pork; hookworm (*Necator americanus*), which penetrates the skin (usually between the toes) and eventually lodges within the intestine where the worms' blood-sucking activity causes severe anemia; and the less serious but highly infectious intestinal pinworm (*Enterobius vermicularis*), which may infect more than 40 percent of the children in certain communities. Old World hookworm (*Ancylostoma*) is responsible for much human debility throughout both hemispheres.

The more than 1,500 species of *rotifer* ("wheel bearer") predominantly inhabit fresh water (Figure 2.29). These small (0.5 to 1.5 mm) but complex animals are characterized by a double crown of cilia at the anterior end, the rotary beating of which justifies the name. The cuticle covering the posterior third of the body is segmented, allowing this part of the body to be telescoped, so that the rotifer can move by wormlike contraction and elongation as well as by the propeller action of its crown of cilia. Anchored by its posterior "toe," a rotifer also uses its cilia to set up water currents that sweep microorganisms into the mouth. Males are rare or unknown in some species and reproduction is often *parthenogenetic.* This means that the eggs can develop without being fertilized, usually producing females or (less frequently) males.

Figure 2.27 □ Ribbonworms: (*a*) a nemertean capturing its prey (an annelid) by means of its extensible proboscis and (*b*) longitudinal section showing proboscis in its sheath (*rhynchocoel*) lying above the digestive tract. Note complete tubular digestive tract extending from mouth to anus, allowing ingestion, digestion, and elimination to proceed simultaneously.

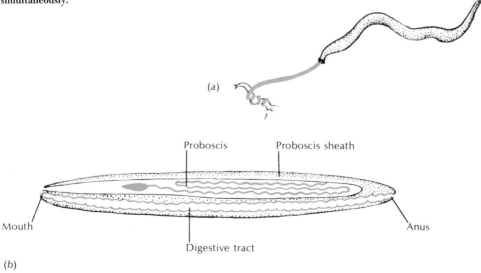

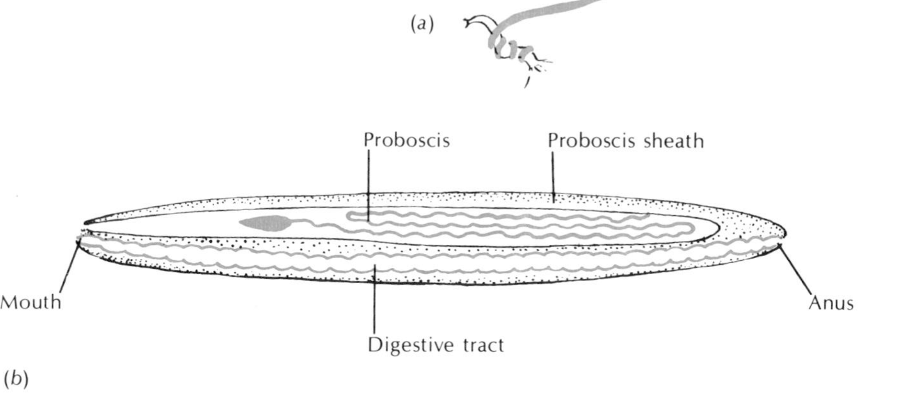

Figure 2.28 □ Nematodes. (*a*) Internal structure of the intestinal roundworm *Ascaris.* Note that the internal organs lie within a "false" body cavity, the pseudocoel. (*b*) *Trichinella spiralis,* causative agent of trichinosis, encysted in muscle tissue. (*Courtesy of Carolina Biological Supply Company.*) (*c*) *Strongyloides,* the threadworm, an intestinal parasite (female). The dark material seen through the transparent body wall is the alimentary tract and sex organs. (*Ward's Natural Science Establishment, Inc.*)

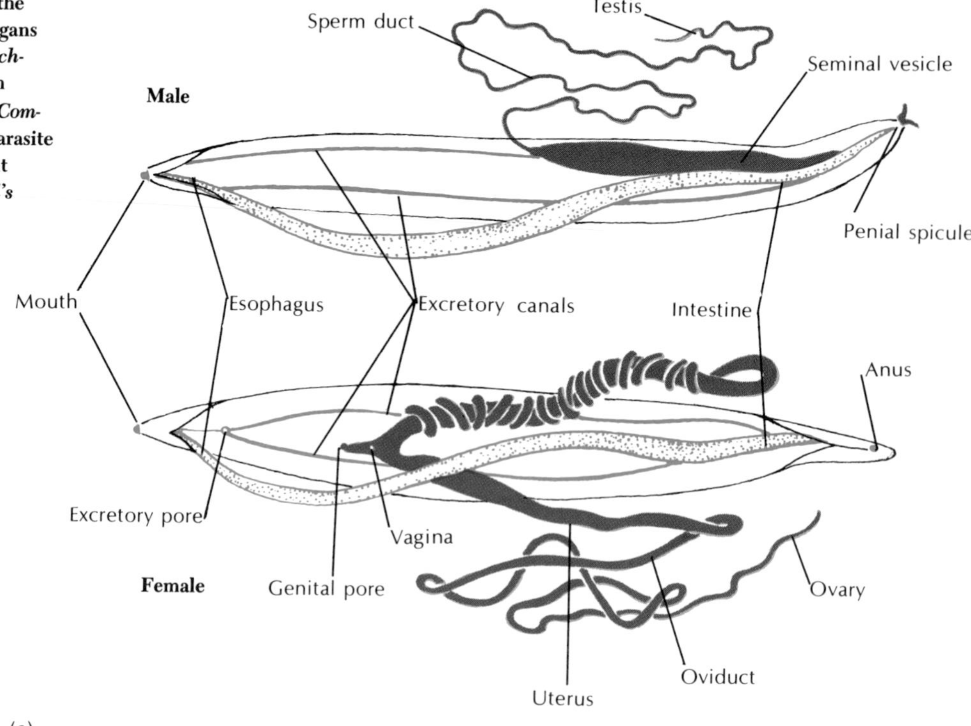

(*a*)

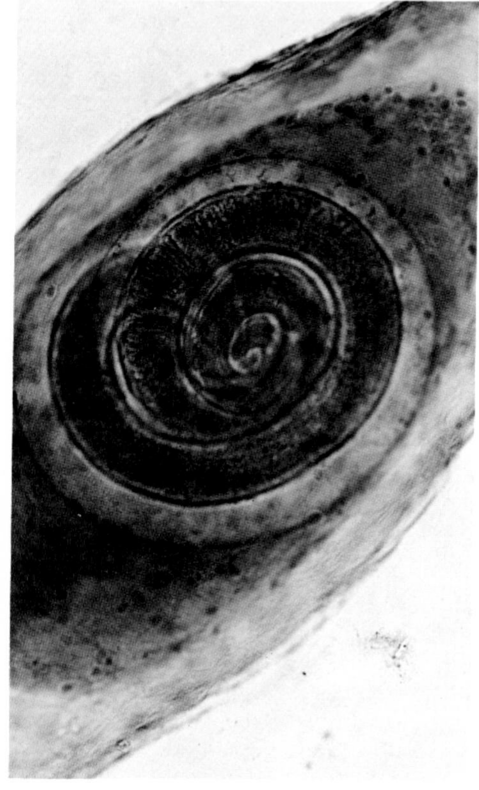

(*b*)

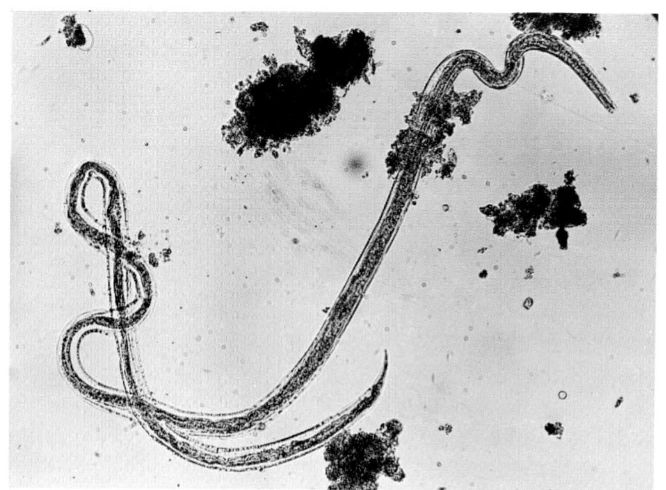

(*c*)

Figure 2.29 □ *Philodina*, a rotifer. This minute freshwater animal, no larger than many protozoans, has complicated digestive, excretory, nervous, and reproductive organs. Food is captured and rapid swimming effected by the double crown (corona) of cilia flanking the mouth, the rotatory beating of which is responsible for the name "rotifer" (wheel bearer). A semirigid pellicle restricts bending, but the rear portion of the body can be telescoped. The cement gland and toes are used in clinging to vegetation.

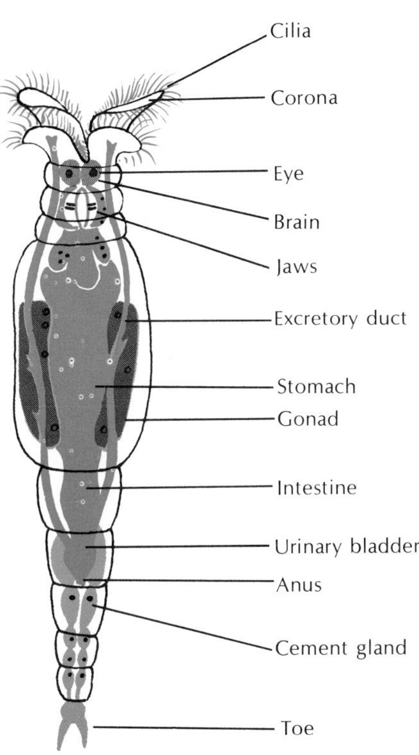

F Phylum Ectoprocta ("exterior anus"), or Bryozoa: bryozoans (over 2,000 species)

These nearly microscopic yet highly organized animals form encrusting or upright colonies on any solid surface in fresh or salt water (Figure 2.30). Most species are marine. Each individual occupies a rectangular or cup-shaped cavity within the chitinous or limy framework that supports the colony. A horseshoe-shaped or circular whorl of ciliated tentacles, forming a distinctive feeding organ termed the *lophophore,* surrounds the mouth. The digestive tract is U-shaped, with the anus opening outside of the lophophoral region. Bryozoans and all other phyla to be discussed hereafter have a true body cavity (*coelom*). This is an important adaptive innovation. Unlike the pseudocoel, the coelom arises in the embryo in such a way as to divide the developing musculature into an outer layer concerned with locomotion and an inner one around the gut, concerned with moving food.

G Phylum Brachiopoda ("arm foot"): lamp shells (approximately 300 contemporary and 30,000 extinct species)

Brachiopods are a marine coelomate phylum allied to the bryozoans and not as closely related to the molluscs as their superficial resemblance might indicate. The two movable shells (valves) that enclose the body are dorsal and ventral valves (Figure 2.31) rather than being right and left valves as is the case with bivalve molluscs. In most brachiopods there is a hole at the apex of the ventral valve through which passes a muscular stalk by which the brachiopod is attached to the substratum. When empty the shells thus bear some resemblance to an ancient oil lamp (hence the common designation, "lamp shells"). Much of the space within the valves is occupied by a large lophophore, and brachiopods, like bryozoans, feed upon small organisms that are swept toward the mouth by the beating of cilia on the tentacles of the lophophore. The digestive tract is basically tubular and U-shaped, but often secondarily lacks an anus and terminates as a blind pouch. Although blood vessels are lacking, a muscular heart circulates the fluid within the coelom.

Living brachiopods represent but a remnant of a phylum that was most abundant in the Paleozoic Era (500 to 200 million years ago). The valves of fossil lamp shells may exceed 15 cm, but those of living species seldom reach 5 cm.

The lophophorate phyla are of especial interest to students of evolution, for they appear to be forms that ancestrally were close to the point at which an important new line of evolutionary ascent (the *deuterostome* line leading to the echinoderms and chordates) branched off the more ancient *protostome* line (leading to the annelids, molluscs, and arthropods).

H Phylum Annelida ("ringed"): segmented worms (approximately 15,000 species)

The major classes of annelids are the *polychaetes, oligochaetes,* and *leeches* (Figure 2.32). Polychaetes such as the clamworm *Nereis* (see Figure 1.10) are marine

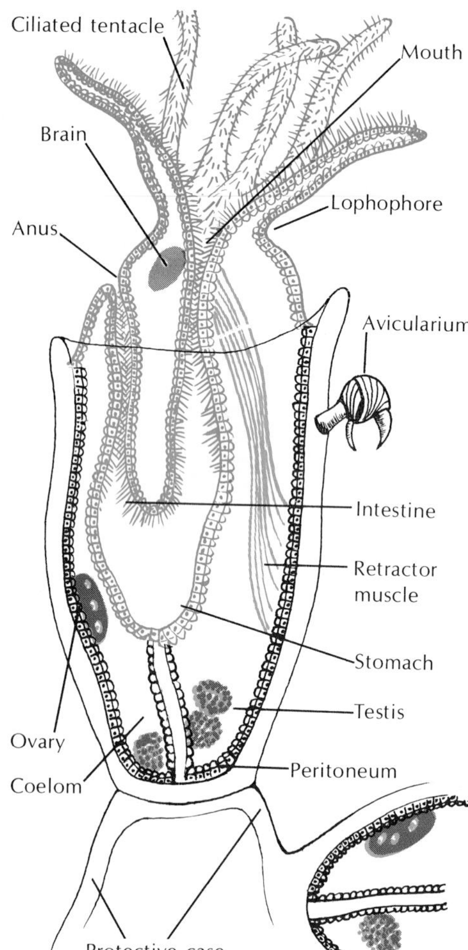

Figure 2.30 □ *Bugula*, a colonial bryozoan. One zooid is represented in longitudinal section, showing the U-shaped digestive tract extending from mouth to anus. The horseshoe-shaped lophophore bears ciliated tentacles to collect planktonic organisms. The mouth opens in the center of the lophophore; the anus opens outside—hence the phylum name Ectoprocta (exterior anus). On the side of the feeding zooid is a defensive zooid, or *avicularium*, that cannot feed but bears a snapping beak for crushing small organisms that might settle on the colony and, if not disturbed, overgrow it.

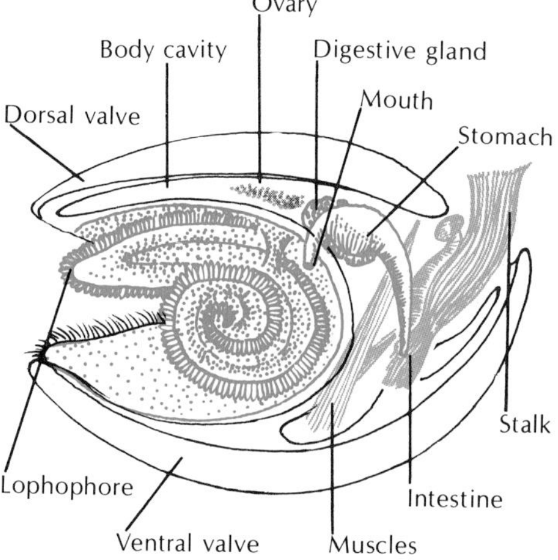

Figure 2.31 □ Although superficially resembling a clam, a brachiopod (shown here in section) is entirely different within. The two valves are dorsal and ventral (and not left and right as in the clam), and much of the space within the valves is occupied by the huge coiled lophophore used in food gathering. Through a hole in the ventral valve passes a tough stalk by which the animal is anchored to the substratum. Geologically ancient, brachiopods nearly underwent extinction at the end of the Paleozoic Era around 230 million years ago.

forms having a well-developed head, often featuring eyes, chitinous jaws, sensory palps and/or ciliated feeding tentacles. They bear numerous *setae* or chitinous bristles (hence the name polychaete, meaning "many bristles"). Segmentally arranged flaplike appendages may be present as an aid to swimming. Filamentous gills sometimes occur, serving as respiratory organs. The errant (freely wandering) polychaetes are predacious and may subdue large prey such as other worms. The sedentary, tube-dwelling polychaetes are mainly filter feeders, collecting minute plankton on their ciliated tentacles.

Oligochaetes live mainly in fresh water or moist soil, and are characterized by reduced setae (hence the name oligochaete, signifying few bristles) and a degenerate head lacking eyes, jaws, and tentacles. The pointed anterior end terminates in a fleshy lobe, the prostomium, used in burrowing and in grasping the vegetable matter on which these worms feed. Earthworms are considered beneficial to the soil because their burrowing activities increase its porosity and water permeability.

Leeches are moderately specialized for a parasitic existence. The dorsoventrally flattened, leaf-shaped body bears anterior and posterior suckers by which the leech adheres to its host while it pierces the skin either with a muscular proboscis or with a set of three chitinous teeth. The anterior portion of the digestive tract is extremely distensible, permitting the leech to feed sporadically, storing blood to be digested gradually over several months. A fully engorged leech may weigh ten times more than one which has not recently fed! Feeding may therefore take place as seldom as twice a year.

Figure 2.32 □ **Annelids. (*a*) Stereoscopic representation of earthworm internal organs, lateral aspect. Only two excretory tubules (*nephridia*) are shown here although a pair is borne in nearly every body segment. Note the segmented nerve cord running ventral to (below) the digestive tract. The latter is muscular and regionally specialized. Blood is propelled by rhythmic waves of contraction along the dorsal blood vessel, which constitutes the true heart. Segmental vessels are given off from the dorsal vessel, and the capillaries of these drain into the ventral blood vessel. Both male and female sex organs are present in the earthworm, but most annelids are not hermaphroditic. (*b*) Polychaete larva, showing four dark eyes in head, pronounced homonomous metamerism, and the numerous long chitinous bristles (*setae*) that increase buoyancy. Planktonic as a larva, the adult lives on and in the substratum. (*Courtesy of General Biological, Inc., Chicago.*) (*c*) Parchment worm, *Chaetopterus pergamentaceus.* This marine polychaete secretes and inhabits a leathery tube. The expanded, fanlike segments serve to circulate water through the tube, aerating the gills and drawing in food. (*Courtesy of General Biological, Inc., Chicago.*) (*d*) *Hirudo*, a leech, ectoparasitic on aquatic vertebrates. Note large posterior and smaller anterior suckers used in adhering to host while the skin is penetrated with three strong teeth and blood is withdrawn. (*Courtesy of Carolina Biological Supply Company.*)**

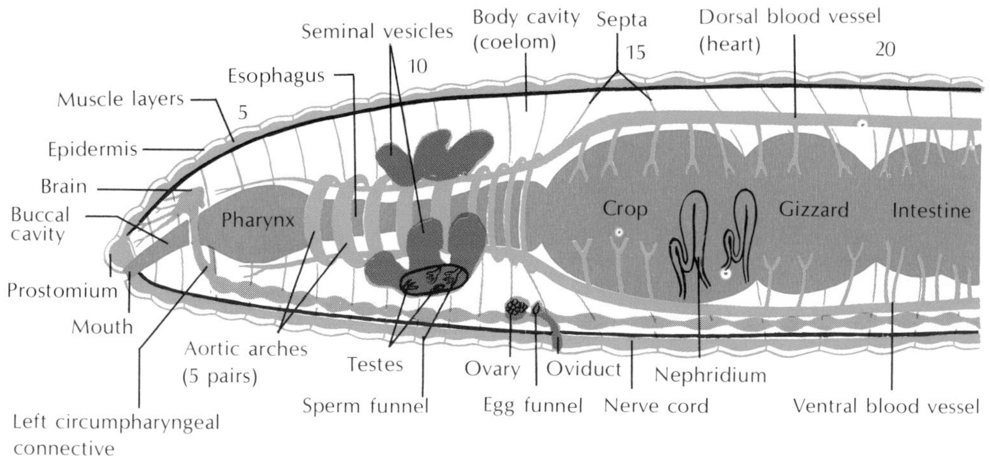

(*a*)

(*d*)

(*b*)

(*c*)

Figure 2.33 □ Trochophore. Top-shaped larvae resembling the generalized type shown here occur among marine bryozoans, brachipods, annelids, nemerteans, and molluscs, which suggests that these phyla may have arisen from a common ancestral form with trochophorelike features.

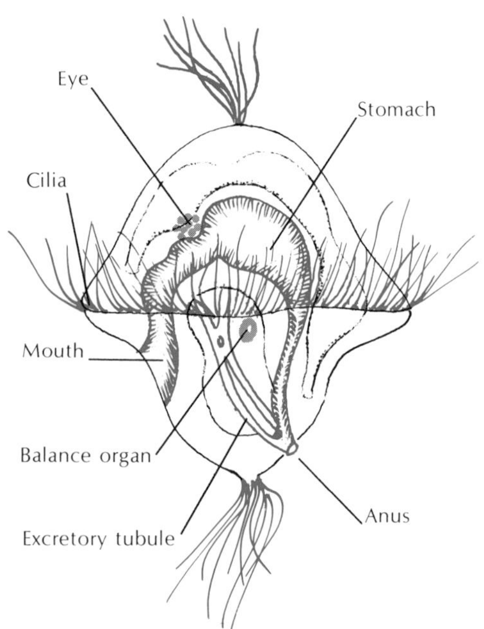

The most conspicuous feature of annelids, their *metamerism,* is also their most outstanding evolutionary innovation. The body is segmented and consists of a linear series of homologous (and often nearly identical) segments or metameres; a simple structural "package" is repeated down the length of the body. Most annelid organ systems—circulatory, excretory, nervous, and reproductive—are therefore metamerically organized. Appendages, when present, are also segmentally arranged, one pair per metamere. Metameric body plans have proved markedly successful, as evidenced by the fact that the two animal groups which have generally achieved the highest level of structural organization, the vertebrates and arthropods, both have exploited this type of body plan.

I Phylum Mollusca ("soft"): molluscs (approximately 100,000 species described to date*)

Molluscs apparently share a close common ancestor with annelids and certain other phyla including bryozoans and brachiopods, for at least some members of these phyla develop from a similar larval form, the *trochophore* (Figure 2.33). The trochophore is a ciliated, top-shaped organism about as large as a rotifer and of about the same level of complexity, containing a complete tubular digestive tract, a balance organ, and other structures that allow it to fend for itself while it forms part of the marine plankton before metamorphosing to a more advanced stage. The trochophore is thought perhaps to resemble closely the common ancestor from which this group of phyla arose. In fact, an ancestral trochophore may have been the first organism to have a complete tubular digestive tract and coelom.

*About a third of these species are known only as fossils.

One recently discovered group of molluscs (the Monoplacophora) shows a certain amount of segmentation, which suggests that metamerism may have begun to arise in one branch of this phylum, but its potential has not been exploited and molluscs have instead evolved an unsegmented but nevertheless complex body plan. The major features are as follows: (1) a muscular *foot* used in locomotion and food getting; (2) a *visceral hump* containing the internal organs and usually terminating anteriorly in a more or less well developed head bearing the mouth and occasionally eyes, sensory palps, or tentacles; (3) a cloaklike *mantle* that

Figure 2.34 □ Molluscan body plans: (*a*) chiton, (*b*) snail, (*c*) scaphopod (tusk shell), (*d*) clam, and (*e*) *Nautilus,* a cephalopod. Features common to all include one or more shells (*valves*) secreted by the underlying *mantle,* a muscular *foot* (divided into siphon and tentacles in cephalopods), and a *visceral hump* housing the internal organs. In this drawing of the clam, the shell muscles ("anterior protractor," and so on) are bisected, half attached to each valve. Diversification from a common ancestral body plan has enabled molluscs to play many roles in aquatic communities; only a few gastropods are terrestrial. Note the eight overlapping valves characteristic of chitons and the chambered gas-filled shell of *Nautilus.* Although the shell provides buoyancy, a healthy *Nautilus* is found not near the surface of the sea but upon the bottom. Shelled cephalopods (nautiloids and ammonites) were highly successful and very numerous in the past but have been mostly extinct since the close of the Mesozoic Era some 70 million years ago.

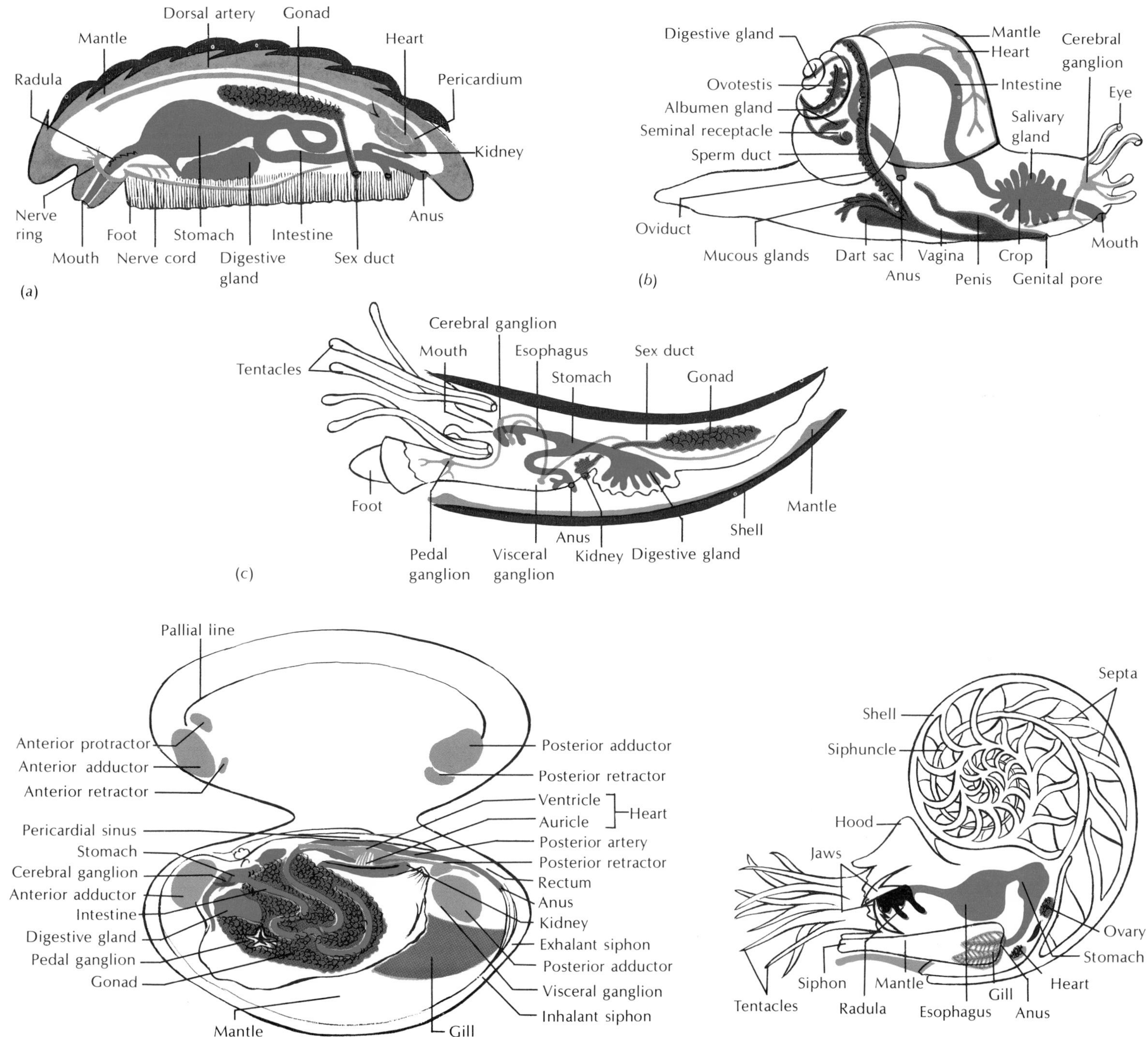

Dorsal artery
Gonad
Mantle
Heart
Radula
Pericardium
Kidney
Nerve ring
Foot
Stomach
Intestine
Anus
Mouth
Nerve cord
Digestive gland
Sex duct
(a)
Digestive gland
Mantle
Heart
Cerebral ganglion
Ovotestis
Intestine
Eye
Albumen gland
Salivary gland
Seminal receptacle
Sperm duct
Oviduct
Mouth
Mucous glands
Dart sac
Vagina
Crop
Anus
Penis
Genital pore
(b)
Cerebral ganglion
Mouth
Esophagus
Sex duct
Tentacles
Stomach
Gonad
Foot
Mantle
Shell
Anus
Pedal ganglion
Visceral ganglion
Kidney
Digestive gland
(c)
Pallial line
Anterior protractor
Posterior adductor
Anterior adductor
Posterior retractor
Anterior retractor
Ventricle
Auricle
Heart
Pericardial sinus
Posterior artery
Stomach
Posterior retractor
Cerebral ganglion
Rectum
Anterior adductor
Anus
Intestine
Kidney
Digestive gland
Exhalant siphon
Pedal ganglion
Posterior adductor
Gonad
Visceral ganglion
Inhalant siphon
Mantle
Gill
(d)
Septa
Shell
Siphuncle
Hood
Jaws
Ovary
Stomach
Siphon
Mantle
Heart
Gill
Tentacles
Radula
Esophagus
Anus
(e)

covers the visceral hump and secretes (4) one or more internal or external shells or *valves* usually made up of crystalline calcium carbonate and covered by a protective proteinaceous membrane (the periostracum).

Internally the coelom contains the tubular and usually coiled and functionally regionalized digestive tract associated with a large digestive gland, sex organs, kidneys, a heart, and blood vessels. The molluscan nervous system typically includes three "brains" or paired masses of nervous tissue: (1) the cerebral ganglia located in the head, which receive sensory information from various sense organs and control the motor aspects of feeding; (2) the pedal ganglia that control the foot; (3) the visceral ganglia regulating the internal organs.

This basic body plan has undergone diversification in the five major classes of the phylum (Figure 2.34). The chitons and their relatives are considered the most primitive living molluscs; they are entirely marine. Their nervous system lacks centralized masses or ganglia, the digestive tract is relatively straight and simple, and the foot is large and flat, comprising most of the lower surface of the body. Chitons are covered dorsally by a series of eight overlapping valves. The head is reduced but the mouth contains a chitinous feeding organ, the *radula,* bearing teeth used in scraping algae off rocks. A number of simple eyes may be embedded in the valves.

Gastropods (snails and slugs) may be marine, freshwater, or terrestrial (Plate 2). The shell is single and may be external, internal, or lacking. Typically the shell is coiled, reflecting a coiling of the elongate body (Figure 2.35). During development the internal organs of the gastropod undergo *torsion,* that is, they become twisted about so that the anus opens close to the mouth. This adaptation is thought to aid survival of the swimming veliger larva (a modified trochophore) of marine gastropods by allowing it to withdraw into its rudimentary shell and thereby sink out of danger. The gastropod head is well developed, bearing eyes and one or two pairs of sensory tentacles. A radula is present, which may be used in rasping vegetation or even to drill holes in the shells of other molluscs on which carnivorous gastropods feed (see Figure 3.2*b*).

Tusk shells (scaphopods) are marine and have a tubular shell that is open at both ends, allowing water to circulate through the mantle cavity. The foot is conical and used in digging. The head is reduced but the mouth bears a radula and is ringed by feeding tentacles with suckerlike tips. Tusk shells were widely used by primitive peoples for jewelry and in trade.

Bivalves occur in the ocean and fresh water, where most types burrow in the bottom although some attach to rocks and pilings, a few (such as scallops) may actively swim, and others burrow in rock or wood [such as piddocks (see Figure 3.2*a*) and the destructive shipworm, *Teredo*]. The bivalve

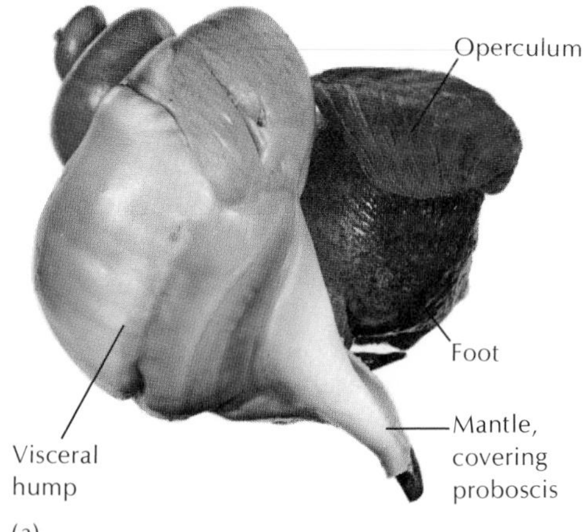

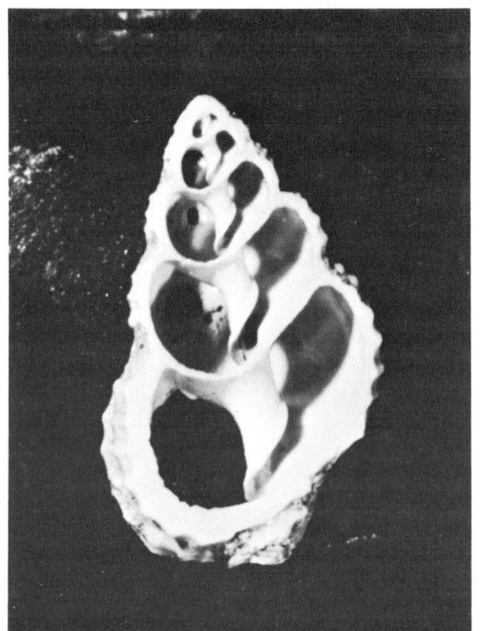

Figure 2.35 □ Gastropod structure: coiling of both shell and body makes for a more compact body form. (*a*) A whelk (*Busycon*), shown removed from its shell. (*Courtesy of Carolina Biological Supply Company.*) (*b*) Gastropod shell sectioned longitudinally. The animal's body fills the entire shell cavity and is accordingly elongate and somewhat wormlike. (*Los Angeles County Museum of Natural History.*)

foot is wedgeshaped (hence the class name, Pelecypoda, "hatchet foot") and used in digging. When engorged with blood the foot extends and becomes rigid, pushing through the substratum; its end then swells like a bulb, becoming anchored in place while the rest of the foot contracts, drawing the body of the mollusc downward. Bivalves lack a head, but have food-handling palps around the mouth. Their laterally flattened bodies are enclosed by two shells, left and right valves that are hinged dorsally. Under the mantle are platelike or filamentous gills used both in respiration and food collecting. Cilia clothing the gills set up a current that enters through a siphon (formed from part of the mantle), circulates through the mantle cavity and over the gills, and leaves by way of another siphon; food particles are trapped and carried to the mouth, where they are collected by the labial palps (see Figure 13.16).

Cephalopod ("head-foot") molluscs are the most advanced members of the phylum, alert and mobile, most possessing excellent eyes and a complex brain, and under experimental conditions demonstrating considerable learning capacity. They are restricted to the sea and include squid, octopus, cuttlefish, and nautilus. Except for the nautilus, which has an external shell coiled flat like a watchspring, the shell is internal or lacking. Locomotion is by jet propulsion, water being taken into the mantle cavity and then expelled forcibly through a muscular funnel. The mouth is surrounded by eight, ten, or many prehensile (grasping) arms, and is often armed with both a set of biting jaws and a rasping radula.

Molluscs are among the most successful and diversified of animal phyla, although with few exceptions they have been unable successfully to invade the land or, in most cases, fresh water. Generally they lack effective means of preventing water loss by evaporation when on land and have failed to overcome the excretory problems involved in living in fresh water. Although molluscs lack the structural support necessary for attaining large size on land, certain marine molluscs such as giant clams and squid reach a length and mass unequaled by any other invertebrate. Tentacles of giant squid exceeding 12 m in length have been taken from the stomachs of sperm whales that prey upon these great cephalopods. Such tentacle length implies a body length of about 8 m or more, a total estimated length of 20 m from apex to tentacle tip!

J Phylum Arthropoda ("jointed foot"): arthropods (approximately 1,000,000 described species*)

Arthropods are segmented animals of great diversity but of mostly small size that inhabit almost every conceivable habitat. Several classes of the phylum, the insects, centipedes, millipedes, and arachnids, are predominantly terrestrial. These arthropods have adapted more successfully to a land existence than have any other invertebrates. Their success in this environment is due to: (1) the development of an impervious cuticle that resists water loss; (2) internalized and highly efficient respiratory organs; (3) jointed appendages made rigid by a chitinous exoskeleton, permitting efficient locomotion on land. Furthermore, insects have developed wings and their capacity for flight has greatly assisted their dissemination to all parts of the world. The remarkable success of insects is also due to dietary diversification, aided by specialization of the mouthparts for chewing, biting, piercing, lapping, and sucking. Insects may be predacious or herbivorous, they may suck blood or plant sap, feed upon nectar and pollen, or even subsist largely upon dung. Such diversification allows many kinds of insects to share the same habitat without competing for food.

Arthropods resemble annelids in a number of features, and are probably descended from a common ancestor. [In fact, a form considered intermediate, the "walking worm," *Peripatus,* still exists (Figure 2.36).] However, arthropods manifest a number of important advances over the annelids including the following: (1) the development of a jointed, chitinous *exoskeleton,* often hardened by deposits of calcium salts, which affords protection and support, and provides sites for muscle attachment (see Figure 4.27); (2) differentiation of body segments (*heteronomous metamerism;* see Figure 1.10*b*); (3) development of one pair of *jointed appendages* per metamere; (4) diversification of these *serially homologous* appendages for a variety of uses other than locomotion (see Figure 1.11); (5) development of a greater variety of sense organs, including in some groups the efficient *compound eye;* (6) accumulation of a repertory of *instinctive behavior patterns* of considerable complexity that are concerned with obtaining food, construction of shelters or traps, care of eggs and young, courtship, and social communication.

Fusion of adjacent segments is a com-

*The total number of species has been estimated as high as 10^7.

Figure 2.36 □ *Peripatus*, the "walking worm," inhabitant of New Zealand and other moist terrestrial habitats, is thought to be a modern descendant of a common ancestral form linking the annelids and arthropods. Its characteristics include a mixture of annelidan and arthropodan traits. *Peripatus* stumps along on pairs of stubby unjointed appendages. (*Ward's Natural Science Establishment, Inc.*)

mon feature of more advanced arthropods but the appendages belonging to those segments are often retained, becoming closely grouped for functional cooperation. Thus, the complexity and diversity of insect mouthparts depends upon the fact that the insect head actually develops by the fusion of *six* segments, the appendages of three of which persist as the mouthparts.

Few arthropods attain large size, probably due to limitations imposed by their possession of an *exoskeleton* covering the outside of the body rather than an *endoskeleton* lying within it (see Figure 4.27). Because an exoskeleton encases the body it must be molted periodically to permit growth, and until the new skeleton hardens the animal is helpless. The greatest size attained by any living arthropod is seen in certain spider crabs, the spindly legs of which may span 4 m; the extinct water scorpions (eurypterids; see Figure 8.21a) were more massive, for their total body length reached 3 or 4 m. Even such comparative giants are small when compared with a number of vertebrates and certain molluscs.

Several important groups of arthropods are now extinct; trilobites, for instance, account for about 70 percent of all fossils found in rocks laid down around 500 million years ago. Living forms are grouped into two great subphyla, *chelicerates* and *mandibulates*, each having several classes. Chelicerates have no antennae or true jaws; instead the first pair of legs is modified to form clawed fangs (*chelicerae*), which in spiders are specialized to deliver venom into the wound they make. The second pair of legs are food-handling *pedipalps* (which in scorpions bear pinchers like those of a crab). The body is divided into only two major divisions (cephalothorax and abdomen), the former typically bearing four pairs of walking legs as well as the fangs and pedipalps (Figure 2.37 and Plate 3*a, b*). Mandibulates have true jaws (mandibles) used in biting and chewing. The anterior part of the body is an externally unsegmented head or cephalothorax bearing simple or compound eyes, one or two pairs of sensory antennae, and (besides the mandibles) one or two pairs of accessory food-handling legs (maxillae). At least two pairs of legs are borne on the thorax (midregion of the body), and the hind region (abdomen) may or may not bear appendages (Figure 2.38 and Plate 3*c, d*).

A significant adaptive radiation has taken place in each subphylum, both groups having members that have successfully invaded the land and fresh water. By extensive diversification arthropods have succeeded in adapting to many different modes of life, so that in terms of total numbers of individuals, of species, and of roles played in the ecosystem, arthropods are perhaps the most successful of all phyla.

Marine chelicerates include the horseshoe "crab" (*Limulus*) and the pycnogonids ("sea spiders"). The latter are ungainly animals appearing to be all legs, for the trunk is much reduced and bears from eight to twelve slender, multijointed walking legs plus a pair of egg-carrying legs. So small is the trunk that the internal organs must extend into the legs! Most pycnogonids span but a few millimeters, but some span half a meter.

The most successful chelicerates are the arachnids, which are mainly terrestrial, have four pairs of walking legs, and breathe by means of internalized respiratory organs

Figure 2.37 □ **Chelicerate arthropods. (*a*) Scorpion, shown in striking position. (*Courtesy of Carolina Biological Supply Company.*) The pinchers are used in grasping prey while the venomous tail lashes forward over the back. (*b*) Tick (*Amblyomma*), a blood-sucking ectoparasite. (*Courtesy of Carolina Biological Supply Company.*) (*c*) Solpugid shown in defensive posture with the five pairs of walking legs drawn under in readiness for springing and the pedipalps, which bear adhesive tips and can be used in climbing, raised in threat. Note the thick fangs (*chelicerae*), characteristic of this subphylum (Chelicerata), tapering to slender piercing tips and the eyes at the top of the head. (*Photograph by J. Honey, Los Angeles County Museum of Natural History.*)**

(*a*)

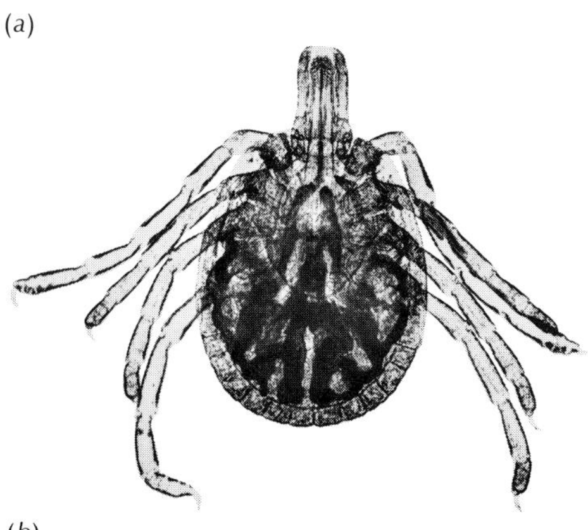

(*b*)

(*c*)

(typically book-lungs; see Figure 14.30). They include spiders, harvestmen, scorpions, and the parasitic mites and ticks.

Mandibulate arthropods include crustaceans, centipedes, millipedes, and insects. Crustaceans are predominantly aquatic but the other groups are mainly terrestrial. Crustaceans gain their name from the fact that their exoskeleton is usually hardened by calcium deposits to form a protective "crust" or armor; a fused, shieldlike carapace often covers the head and thorax. The appendages, including two pairs of antennae, are most characteristically biramous (two-branched; see Figure 1.11), and the abdomen terminates posteriorly in a spinous or spatulate telson. Many different kinds of crustaceans develop from a swimming larval stage known as a *nauplius* (Figure 2.39) and may pass through a number of different larval stages before reaching adulthood. Some of the most abundant plankton types of crustaceans are copepods (see Figure 4.24), which form an essential food supply for larger marine and freshwater animals. The largest, most advanced crustaceans, the malacostracans (that is, "soft shell," thus called because they are soft-bodied and helpless after molting), include wood lice, gribbles, beach hoppers, and decapods (forms with ten walking legs, such as crabs, lobsters, and shrimp).

Centipedes and millipedes were once grouped together because the elongated bodies of both are composed of a series of similar segments, but in fact the two groups are quite different. Both are terrestrial and breathe by means of branching internal air tubules (tracheae). The head bears one pair of antennae and similar pairs of appendages run the length of the body. Here the re-

Figure 2.38 □ **Mandibulate arthropods. (*a*) Internal anatomy of female lobster. (*b*) A crab, *Planes minutus*, which "hitchhikes" on driftwood and is never found ashore except when its "ship" grounds. Totally a creature of the open sea, *Planes* has spread to all oceans. (*c*) A millipede, *Spirobolus*, showing small legs borne two pairs to each conspicuous body segment. (*Courtesy of Carolina Biological Supply Company.*) Millipedes feed on vegetation and may defend themselves by rolling up and exuding a noxious odor. (*d*) Head of centipede, ventral aspect, showing poison claws. (*Los Angeles County Museum of Natural History.*) The small mandibles are seen between the tonglike poison claws, modified legs used in seizing and injecting venom. (*e*) Lace bug (family Tingidae), an insect. (*Los Angeles County Museum of Natural History.*) Note the tracery of supportive veins in the nearly transparent wings and exoskeletal extensions. Such breakup of the body outline makes it difficult for predators to recognize this insect for what it is.**

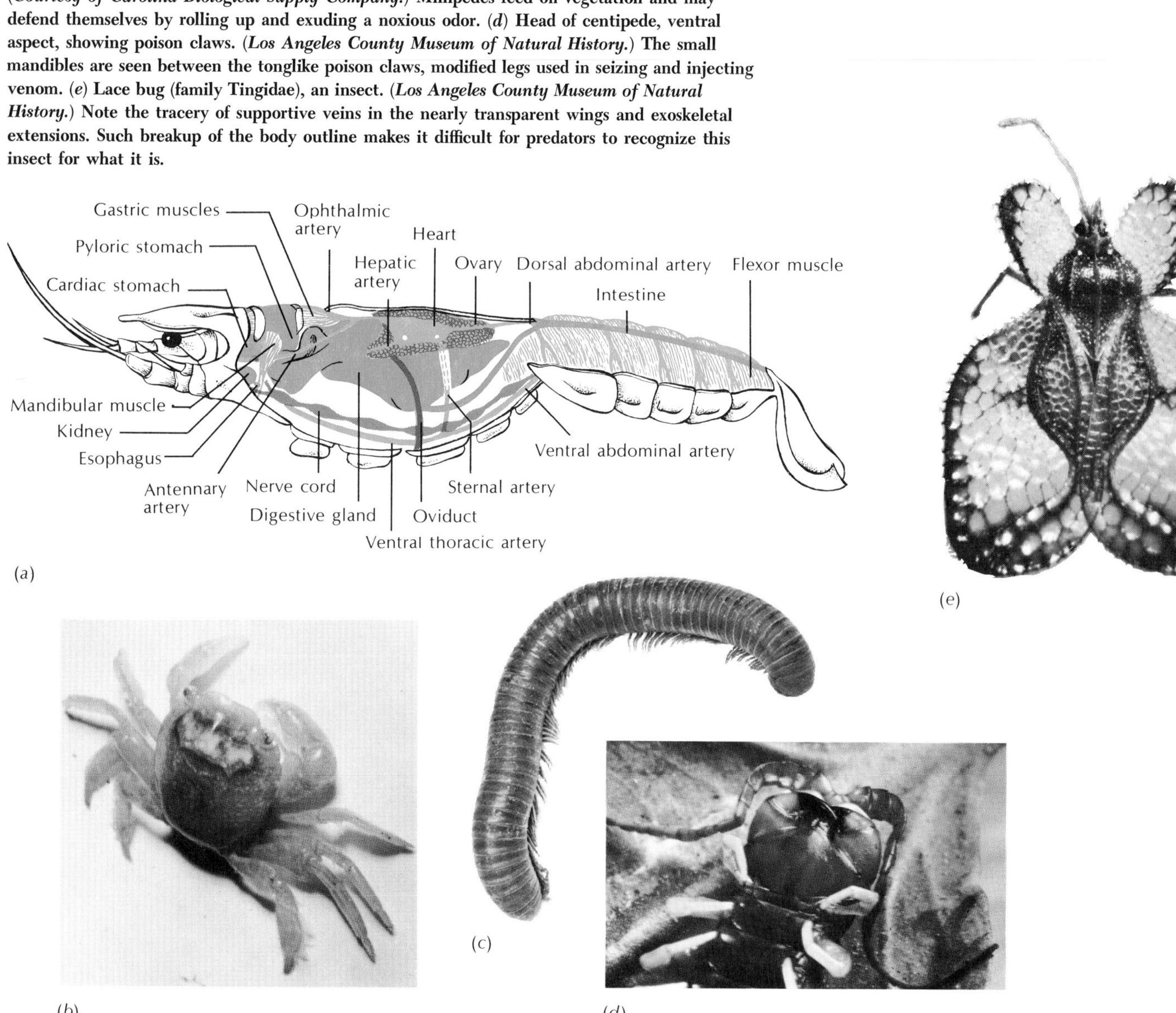

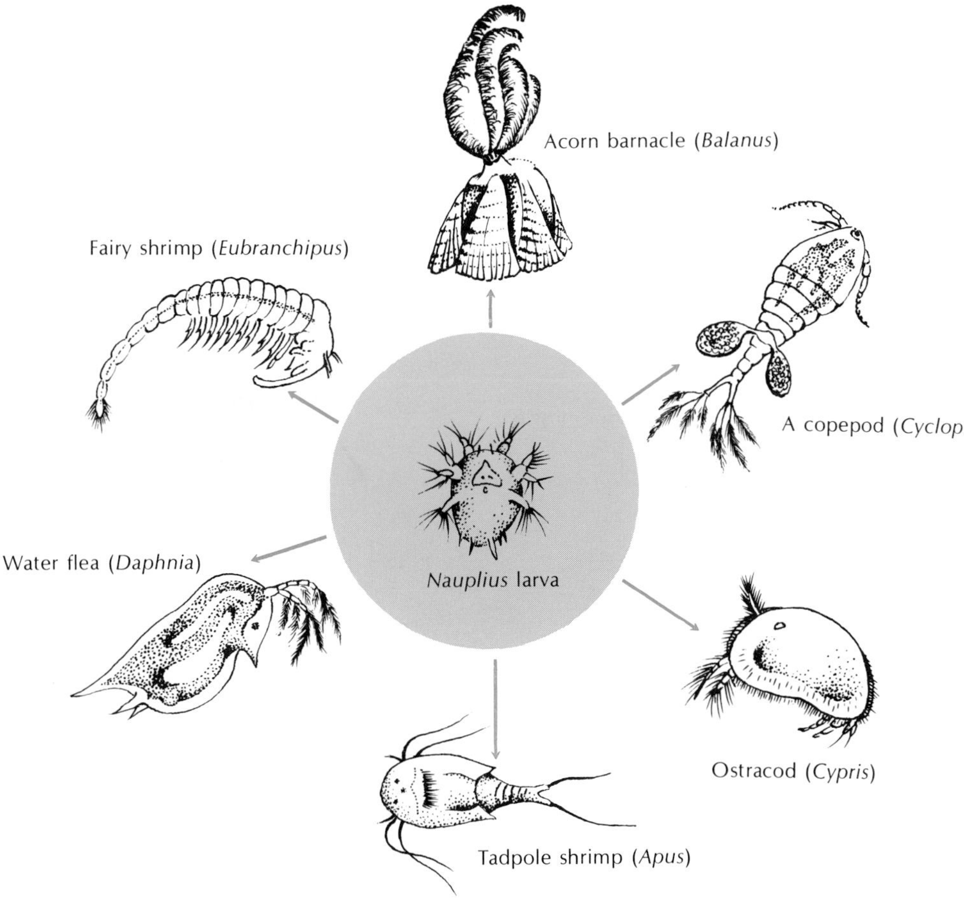

Figure 2.39 □ Small crustaceans developing from a nauplius larva stage. Fairy and tadpole shrimp are exclusively freshwater, and barnacles entirely marine; various members of the other groups may be either freshwater or marine. The nauplius may resemble the ancestral crustacean type, for a nauplius stage is passed through in the egg of advanced crustaceans such as lobsters and crabs.

semblance ends. Centipedes are carnivorous and their first pair of legs posterior to the mouthparts are modified into poison claws for piercing and injecting venom into the prey; millipedes are vegetarians and can defend themselves only by coiling up and giving off a noxious fluid. Centipedes' walking legs are comparatively strong and clawlike and number about 15 pairs. Millipedes' legs are much more numerous and may number about 80 pairs; they are short and weak, and there seem to be two pairs per segment (actually the body segments are fused in pairs). The centipede body is dorsoventrally flattened, while that of the millipede is nearly cylindrical in cross section. Although certain tropical centipedes attain a length of over 20 cm and can inflict a dangerous bite, the harmless, long-legged house centipede is sometimes kept as a "pet" to control household insect pests like cockroaches.

The most diversified and successful of arthropods are insects, the named species of which outnumber the named species of all other kinds of organisms. Most are terrestrial and breathe by tracheae. The insect body is divided into three sections: head, thorax, and abdomen. The head bears one pair of antennae (see Figure 15.13), mouthparts that are specialized for various types of diet, and both simple and compound eyes (see Figure 15.21). The thorax bears three pairs of walking legs and usually two pairs of wings. The abdomen typically consists of eleven segments, more or less fused and lacking walking legs. Although man tends to look upon insects as his most serious competitors because of their vast numbers and propensity for sharing his crops, in fact relatively few species represent agricultural pests or carriers of disease. Many are predatory on other insects and therefore serve as man's allies in controlling insect pests. In fact, insects become pests usually following the disturbance of natural balances caused by human activities. A number of insects serve as essential pollinating agents and their eradication would bring extinction to innumerable species of flowering plants.

Figure 2.40 □ **Starfish water-vascular system, a unique echinoderm adaptation. The water-vascular system is used in locomotion, in clinging by suction to rocks in surf, and in food getting (starfish use their tube feet to pull open the valves of shellfish on which they feed). Contraction of the ampullae extends the tube feet. When they contact a surface, the ampullae relax, and a strong suction is set up, which the animal can maintain indefinitely without further effort. Water can enter or leave the system by way of a small opening, the madreporite.**

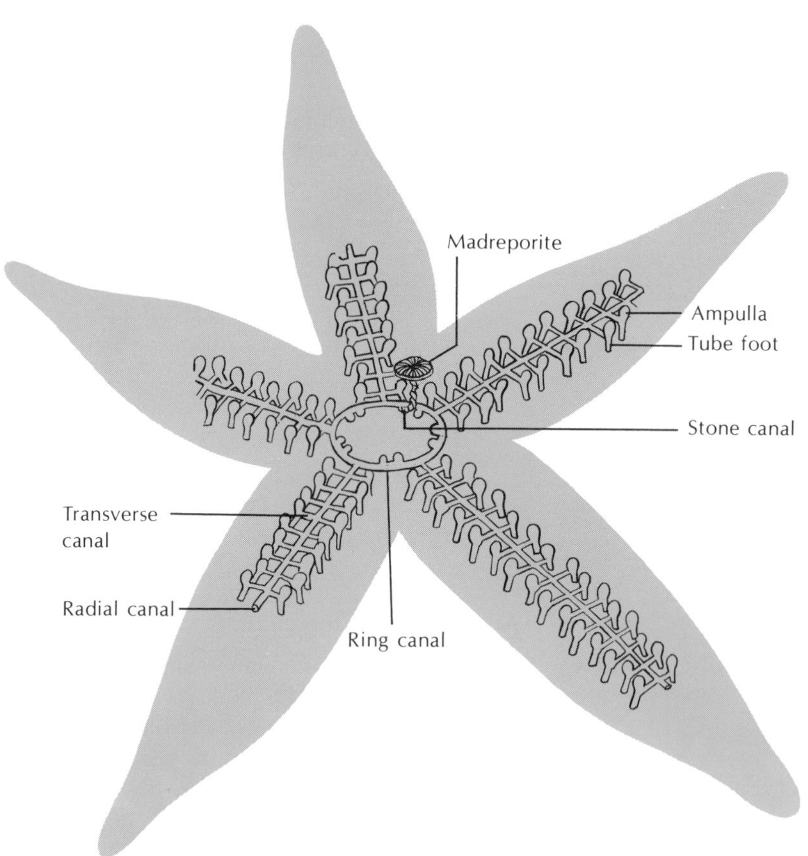

K Phylum Echinodermata ("spiny skinned"): echinoderms (approximately 6,000 living and 20,000 known fossil species)

This exclusively marine phylum is allied by developmental similarities to the chordates and certain minor phyla, including the tongue worms, arrow worms, and beard worms. Adult echinoderms are sedentary or sluggishly creeping forms, which in keeping with this mode of life have abandoned the bilateral symmetry characteristic of their freely swimming larvae and have adopted a secondary radial symmetry of a unique five-partite type best seen in starfishes and brittle stars (Plate 1). The phylum is marked also by the possession of numerous *spines* that arise from the calcareous endoskeleton of plates or ossicles lying just below the epidermis. In sea urchins the spines are movable and articulate by way of ball-and-socket joints with the underlying part of the skeleton, which is solidly fused to form a discoid or ovoid *test.*

A unique feature of echinoderms is their *water-vascular system,* a system of internal tubes communicating to the exterior by way of a sieve plate (which regulates the amount of water in the system) and

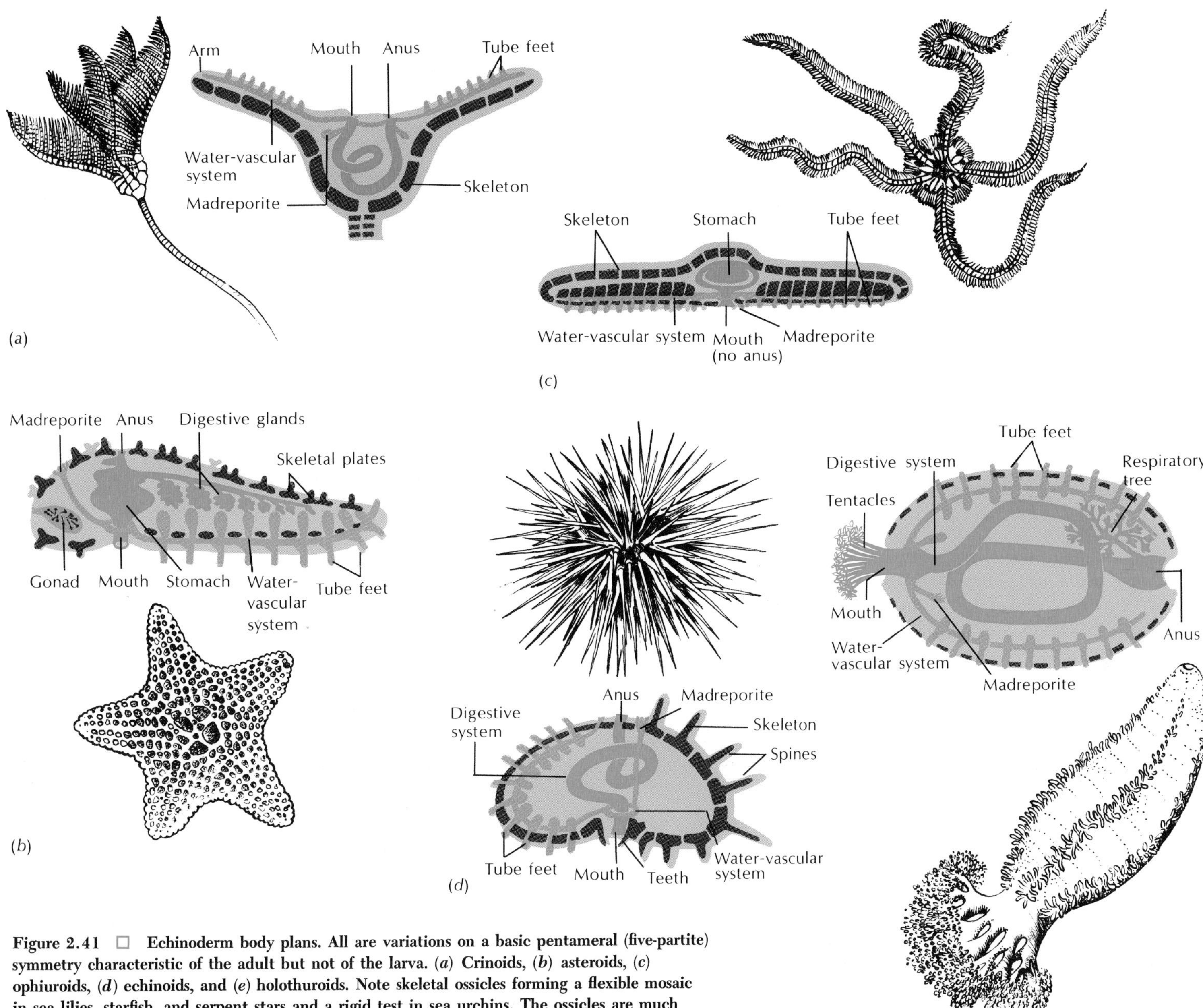

Figure 2.41 □ **Echinoderm body plans. All are variations on a basic pentameral (five-partite) symmetry characteristic of the adult but not of the larva. (*a*) Crinoids, (*b*) asteroids, (*c*) ophiuroids, (*d*) echinoids, and (*e*) holothuroids. Note skeletal ossicles forming a flexible mosaic in sea lilies, starfish, and serpent stars and a rigid test in sea urchins. The ossicles are much reduced in the sea cucumbers. All echinoderms are marine bottom dwellers except for the swimming feather stars (a type of crinoid).**

Figure 2.42 □ **Basket star, *Gorgoncephalus caryi.* This unusual starfish clings to seaweeds and collects food with its finely divided, tendrillike rays. (*Courtesy of Dr. Martin Johnson and Scripps Institution of Oceanography.*)**

terminating in a paired series of *tube feet* running the length of each ray or along each section of the pentamerous test (Figure 2.40). The tube feet are extended by the contraction of muscular bulbs (ampullae) at their inner ends that forces water into the feet, making them turgid. When the tube feet are brought in contact with a suitable surface, the ampullae relax, permitting water to flow out of the tube feet into the main vessels of the water-vascular system. This creates a powerful suction that permits the echinoderm to adhere strongly to the surface without further expenditure of energy. Little wonder that many echinoderms can withstand the force of crashing surf in the intertidal zone. The tube feet are also used in food getting, especially by starfishes that mainly prey upon bivalve molluscs. Creeping over an oyster or mussel, a starfish affixes its tube feet to both valves and then exerts a steady outward pull, which eventually tires the bivalve so that the shell opens. The starfish then everts its stomach through its mouth, digesting the bivalve in its shell.

Five extinct and five living classes of echinoderms are recognized. The major body plans of the existing classes are shown in Figure 2.41. Crinoids or sea lilies are usually attached to the bottom by means of a jointed stalk. The body is cup-shaped and the mouth is ringed by delicately branching arms that trap small organisms that are carried to the mouth along the ciliated ambulacral grooves (Plate 1c).

Starfish typically have five fairly stiff arms (rays), each having on its underside an ambulacral groove within which lie the tube feet. Ophiuroids [brittle, serpent, and basket stars (Figure 2.42)] typically have five slender, very flexible rays that are sharply demarcated from the central disc which houses the internal organs. In the brittle stars these rays are often cast off voluntarily in self-defense, but can be regrown. The ambulacral grooves are closed and the tube feet reduced so that instead of holding firmly to rocks as starfish can, ophiuroids creep or swim by sinuous movements of the rays. A variety of food items can be chewed with the five wedge-shaped spine-toothed jaws.

Echinoids, the sea urchins and sand dollars, have the most prominent spines, which are movable and can be used in walking as well as in self-defense. The slender tube feet must extend beyond the spines to enable the animal to attach itself to rocks against the surge of waves. The food, usually algae, is chewed with the five strong teeth.

Sea cucumbers are difficult to recognize as echinoderms. The body is wormlike or cucumber-shaped and is secondarily bilaterally symmetrical although retaining the five-partite arrangement of the tube feet (when these are present). The endoskeleton is reduced in this class to scattered ossicles embedded in the skin, and spines are lacking. Modified tube feet form branching tentacles that surround the mouth. When these tentacles are short they do not aid much in food getting; instead the sea cucumber swallows large quantities of sand and mud that pass through its gut and are expelled from the anus while organic residues are digested. If the tentacles are longer, they are extended to snare small organisms that become trapped in the sticky mucus covering the tentacles; the tentacles are then taken into the mouth one at a time and the food wiped off (much like a child sucking jam off its fingers).

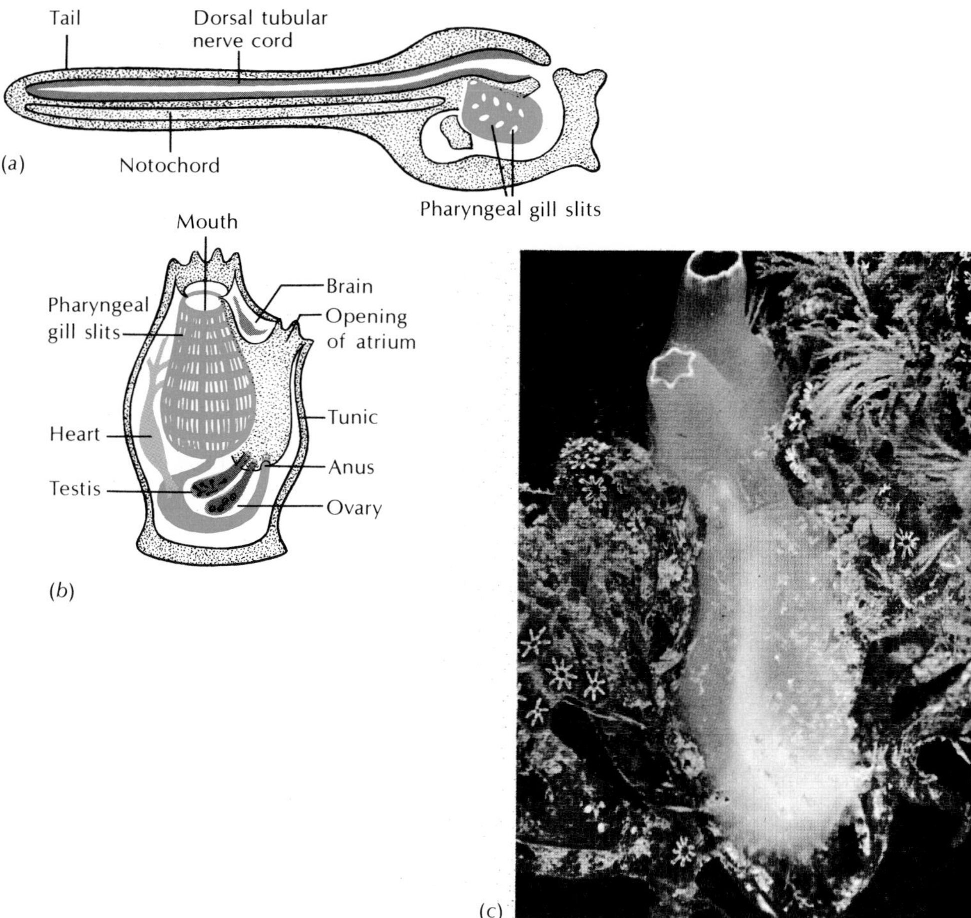

Figure 2.43 □ **(*a*) Tunicate "tadpole" larva, longitudinal section showing characteristics of chordates. In tunicates the gill slits are located in the walls of the large pharyngeal basket that traps planktonic organisms for food. The anterior end of the larva is not a head but a *tunic* surrounding a water-filled cavity, the *atrium*, into which water is expelled by way of the gill slits. (*b*) Internal structure of adult tunicate. Water is drawn in through an incurrent siphon surrounding the mouth, is strained through the pharyngeal basket, and passes out of the atrium via an excurrent siphon. (*c*) Tunicates in the intertidal habitat: the solitary, transparent glass tunicate, *Ciona*, and the colonial star tunicate, *Botryllus*. (*Courtesy of General Biological, Inc., Chicago.*)**

L Phylum Chordata ("corded"): vertebrates, tunicates, amphioxus (approximately 50,000 species)

Chordates are distinguished from other animals by the possession during some part of their life history of three unique characteristics: (1) a flexible supportive rod, the *notochord,* that extends along the longitudinal axis of the body; (2) a *hollow nerve tube* running dorsal to the notochord; (3) a paired series of *pharyngeal clefts* running along each side of the throat, which originally functioned in filter feeding but later came to bear gills. Except for adult tunicates, the phylum is notably metameric.

Perhaps the most significant single innovation of the chordates is the hollow character of their central nervous system, for the heavy nutritional demands of nerve cells can be met by exchanges between the blood and the cerebrospinal fluid that bathes both the outer and inner surfaces of the brain and spinal cord.

There are three major chordate subphyla: (1) *tunicates,* which are headless, unsegmented, and usually sedentary as adults, but have a free-swimming larva (Figures 2.43 and 5.18); (2) *cephalochordates* (known today by only one type, amphioxus), which lack a brain but have a notochord and neural tube that extend the length of the body and persist throughout life, and also a metameric arrangement of muscles, gonads, blood vessels, and the skeletal bars that support the pharyngeal clefts (Figure 2.44); and (3) *vertebrates,* which have a brain consisting basically of five hollow vesicles, and a jointed endoskeleton consisting

Figure 2.44 □ Comparison of (*a*) an amphioxus (*Branchiostoma*), a cephalochordate, and (*b*) a larval lamprey (*Ammocoetes*), a vertebrate. Note that they have many similarities, including the dorsal nerve tube, notochord, large pharynx used for filtering food, oral hood overhanging the mouth, and segmental muscles (*myotomes*). Unlike the amphioxus, the nerve tube of the ammocoetes is expanded anteriorly to form a hollow brain, and eyes and ears (otic vesicles) are present. Jaws are lacking in both. The endostyle of ammocoetes is considered to be a forerunner of the thyroid glands.

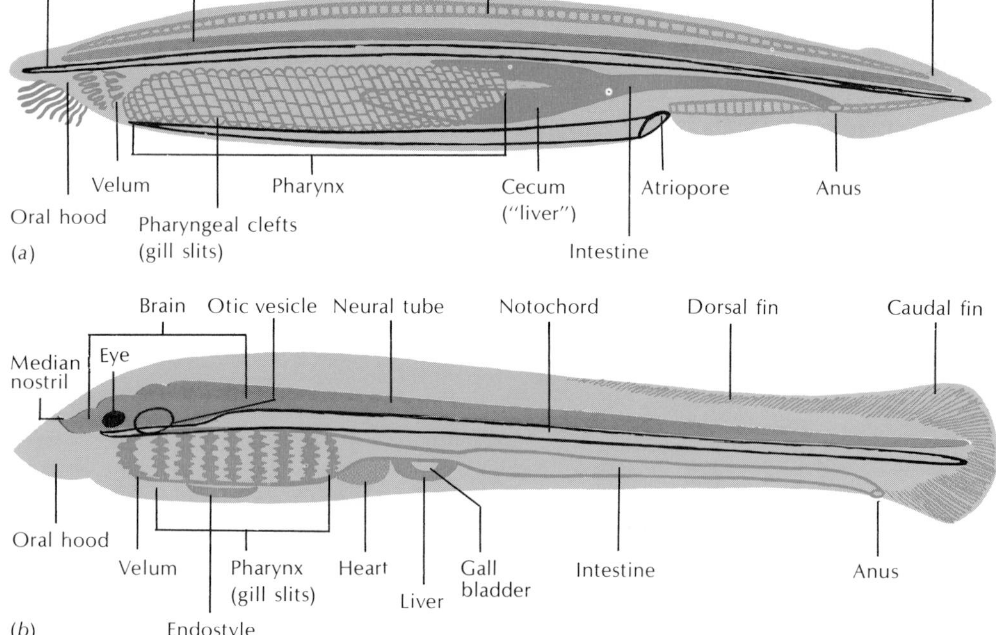

primitively of bone and including a cranium (which encloses the brain) and a backbone of segmental vertebrae that largely replaces the notochord during postembryonic life. The tendency for major sense organs to be concentrated in the head is more pronounced in vertebrates than in any other animal group: the head bears paired nostrils, eyes, ears, and organs of equilibrium, notably the semicircular canals.

Chordates are thought to have evolved from an ancestral form of a little-known group of sedentary marine arm feeders, the *pterobranchs*. Modern species of these tiny, soft-bodied animals bear paired ciliated arms above the mouth. Food particles are collected on the arms but are drawn into the mouth partly by means of a water current entering through the mouth and leaving by way of slitlike clefts in the sides of the pharynx. In the proposed ancestral pterobranch line leading to the chordates, improvement of the pharyngeal filtering mechanism rendered the arms superfluous and encouraged their eventual disappearance. The armless, sedentary, filter-feeding ancestral chordate was probably not unlike modern tunicates except that it lacked the specialized tunic and huge pharynx of the latter. How could a mobile, fishlike form arise from such an ancestor? Modern tunicates have a motile tadpole-shaped larva, with a muscular propulsive tail and a "head" consisting of little more than an enlarged pharynx serving for filter feeding. Larval forms are known occasionally to attain sexual maturity without metamorphosing to the adult form (this event is termed *neoteny*). A line of neotenous tunicate "tadpoles" could well have been the ancestors of both the cephalochordates and vertebrates, neither of which have a sedentary adult stage.

The enlarged pharynx of a modern cephalochordate, amphioxus, occupies up to two-thirds of its total body length. Water is drawn through the mouth by ciliary action and exits by way of the numerous pharyngeal clefts, while food particles are carried posteriorly to the esophagus on a ciliated band forming the floor of the pharynx. In these small animals use of the pharynx for respiration is unnecessary and gills have not developed from the pharyngeal lining. Pharyngeal gills are an innovation of vertebrate fishes; because of their increasing size and the development of an armored skin through which gases could not freely be exchanged, such respiratory organs became essential.

The most ancient known vertebrates, the *ostracoderms* ("shell skin"), did not depart greatly from the filter-feeding ancestral plan, for the small mouth opened into an enormous pharynx. However, the presence of a heavy armor composed of bony plates and the ventral position of the mouth indicate that ostracoderms were bottom feeders and sucked food particles out of the mud (Figure 2.45*a*). Evidence based in part on studies of vertebrate excretory physiology, as well as on the nature of sedimentary deposits in which ostracoderm remains have been found, indicates that these jawless creatures inhabited fresh water rather than the sea. In this habitat they largely escaped competition and had but one serious predator—water scorpions (eurypterids) many times their own size (see Figure 8.21*a*). The threat posed by these huge arthropods was reduced by the development of bony armor within the skin. After the eurypterids became extinct, the amount of bone deposited in vertebrate skin declined and the bone-secreting cells began instead to contribute to the development of an endoskeleton (see Figure 4.31).

The adaptive radiation of vertebrates into many specialized types took place during only the past 300 million years, a substantial period, yet recent enough so that fossil records exist even for the several orders of ostracoderms. These records permit us to reconstruct the history of the vertebrate radiation with more assurance than is possible for any major invertebrate group (Figure 2.46). In fact, the rise of vertebrates has been so conspicuous a feature of this period that its earlier portion, the Upper Paleozoic Era, is commonly referred to as the "age of fishes and amphibians," while the Mesozoic Era is known as the "age of reptiles," and the Cenozoic, as the "age of mammals and birds." The evolution of vertebrates and their successful invasion of the land constitutes a fascinating story, the

(*a*)

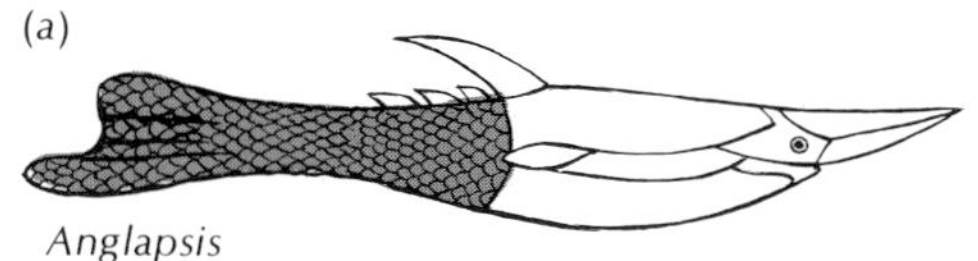

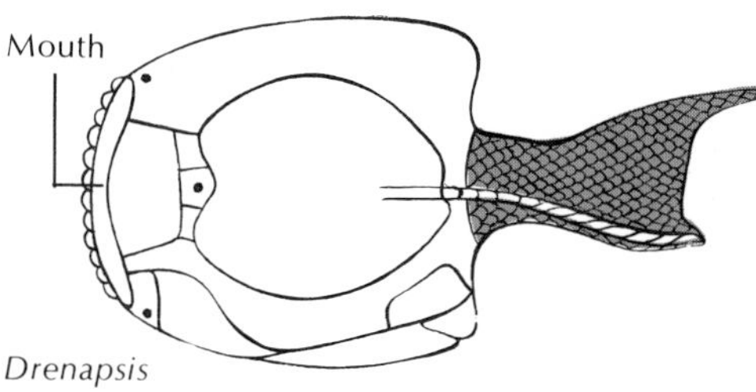

(*b*)

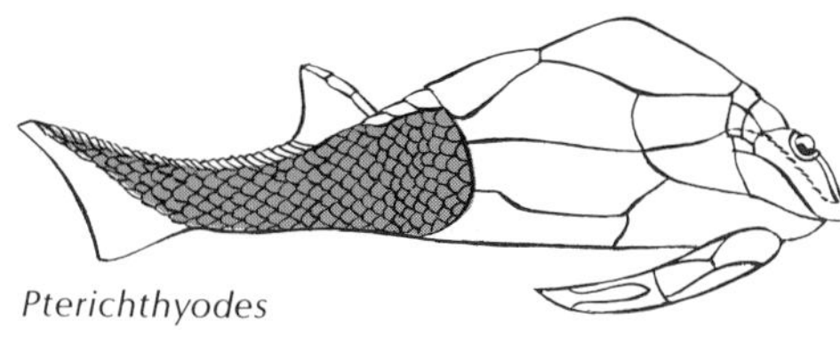

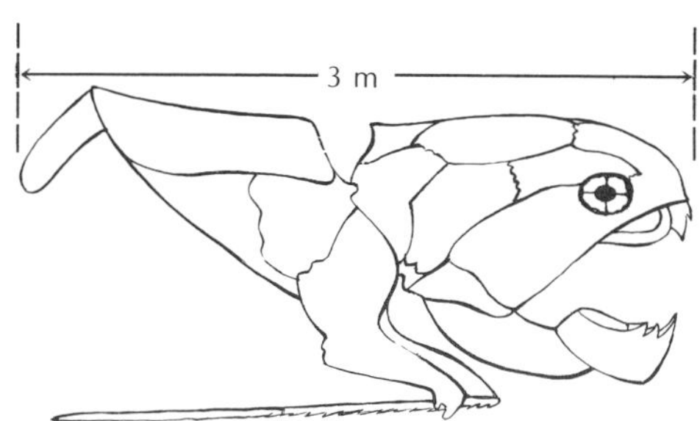

Figure 2.45 □ Extinct primitive fishes. (*a*) Ostracoderms: above, *Anglapsis*, side view; below, *Drenapsis*, dorsal aspect (note median third eye). The anterior part of the body of these ancient jawless mud grubbers was sheathed in bony armor plates, while bony scales covered the more flexible tail portion. Such protection reduced predation by the large water scorpions that also lived in fresh water and were the worst enemies of these early vertebrates. (*b*) Placoderms: *Climatius*, the spiny shark; *Pterichthyodes;* armored portion of *Dinichthyes*, a predacious fish that may have attained lengths of 10 m. Note that the upper jaw and skull of *Dinichthyes* could be elevated while the lower jaw was dropped. Jaws and paired appendages originated in the vertebrate line with the placoderms, descendants of the ostracoderms and themselves ancestral to all other vertebrates.

major outline of which is well established through paleontological data although details may remain obscure.

In time the lowly, mud-sucking ostracoderms became extinct, but not before leaving as descendants the first jawed fishes (the *placoderms,* that is, "plate skin"), and two jawless, degenerative groups, the lampreys and hagfish, which have persisted to the present time. The placoderms were not only the first vertebrates with jaws, but the first to develop paired appendages. Originally they were heavily armored but as time went on the dermal bony plates became thinner and divided into separate scales. Efficient locomotion apparently had become more essential than the protection afforded by armor. Some placoderms reinvaded the sea where a giant 10-m form, *Dinichthys,* eventually dominated the scene as the most formidable predator of the day (Figure 2.45*b*). Others remained in fresh water and gave rise to two important groups of more advanced bony fishes, the ray-finned fishes (*actinopterygians*) and the lobe-finned fishes (*crossopterygians*). The majority of fish which remained in the freshwater habitat at that time developed lungs that enabled them to survive in stagnant ponds poor in oxygen. Most of the ray-finned fishes eventually returned to the sea, where they successfully underwent diversification in competition with another group of fishes that had arisen separately from the placoderms, the sharks or cartilaginous fishes (*chondrichthyes*). Eventually the primitive lungs of those bony fishes which returned to the sea moved dorsally and united into a single structure, the swim bladder, which now serves a hydrostatic function, enabling these fish to adjust their buoyancy. The cros-

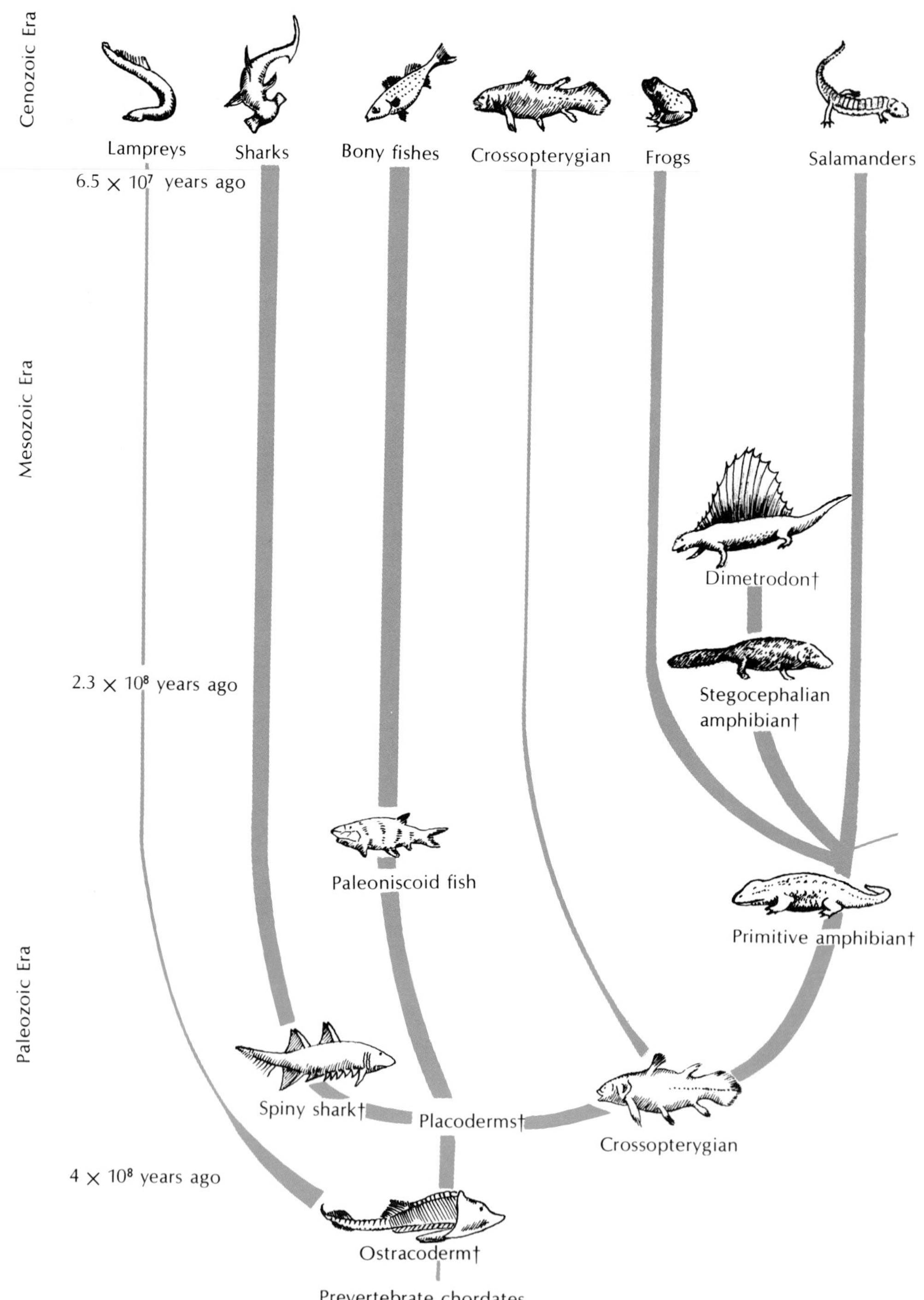

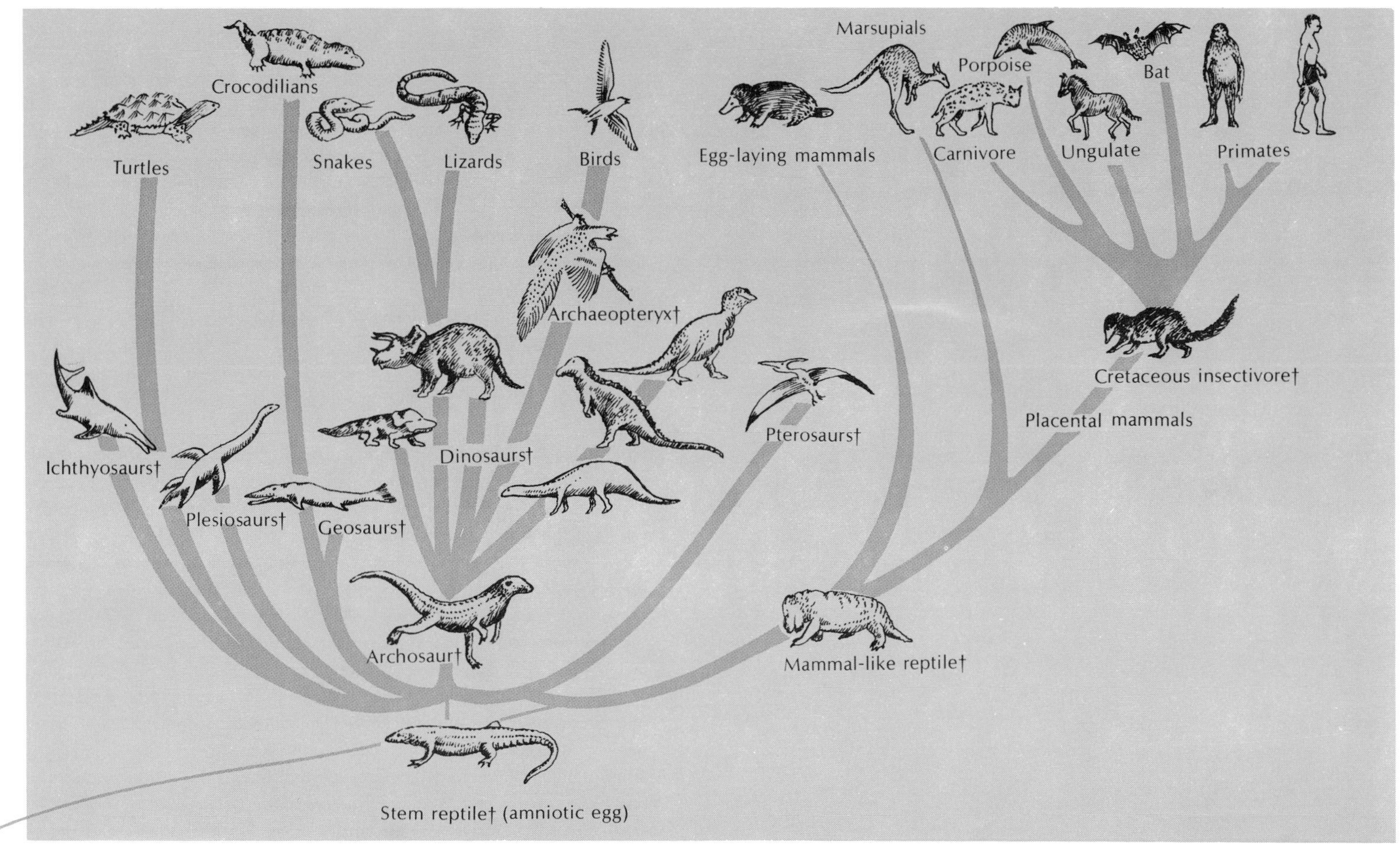

Figure 2.46 □ The vertebrate radiation. Extinct groups are designated by a special symbol (†). Amniotes are shown within the tinted area on this page. Note especially the diversification occurring within the reptilian and mammalian lines.

Table 2.4 □ Comparison of metazoan phyla

PHYLUM	LEVEL OF ORGANIZATION[a]	SYMMETRY[b]	BODY CAVITY[c]	DIGESTIVE TRACT[d]	OTHER IMPORTANT CHARACTERISTICS
Porifera	**C**	***r***	***A***	—	**Marine or freshwater; choanocytes; lacking nerve tissue; spicular endoskeleton; body wall with numerous pores; digestion intracellular**
Coelenterata	**T**	***r***	***A***	s	**Marine or freshwater; nerve net lacking brain; tentacles with nematocysts ringing mouth; polyp and medusa forms; many are colonial**
Platyhelminthes	**O (OS)**	***b***	***A***	s	**Marine, freshwater, endoparasitic, or terrestrial; dorsoventrally flattened; ladder-type nervous system; flame cells; complex reproductive systems; many are parasitic and metagenetic**
Nemertea	**OS**	***b***	***A***	t	**Marine; extensible proboscis dorsal to mouth; closed circulatory system with red blood cells; flame cells**
Aschelminthes	**OS**	***b***	***P***	t	**Marine, freshwater, endoparasitic, or terrestrial; body often cylindrical, tapering; cuticle inelastic; epidermis syncytial; blood vessels lacking; many are parasitic**
Bryozoa	**OS**	***b***	***C***	t	**Marine or freshwater; lophophorate, colonial, digestive tract U-shaped; two types of zooids, feeding and protective**
Brachiopoda	**OS**	***b***	***C***	t	**Marine; lophophorate; dorsal and ventral valves; often pedunculate; digestive tract U-shaped, may end blindly without anus**
Annelida	**OS**	***b***	***C***	t	**Marine, freshwater, or terrestrial; metameric (mainly homonomous); chitinous bristles (setae) typical; main nerve trunk ventral; closed circulatory system**
Mollusca	**OS**	***b***	***C***	t	**Marine, freshwater, or terrestrial; body soft, unsegmented, of visceral hump, mantle, foot; head often present; 0, 1, 2, or 8 calcareous valves; circulation open or closed; 3 major ganglia (pedal, cephalic, visceral)**
Arthropoda	**OS**	***b***	***H*(*C*)**	t	**Marine, freshwater, terrestrial, or endoparasitic; metameric (mostly heteronomous); chitinous exoskeleton; jointed appendages; open circulation; main nerve trunk ventral; many with compound eyes**
Echinodermata	**OS**	***b,r***	***C***	t	**Marine; adult symmetry pentamerous; endoskeleton of calcareous plates or ossicles; fixed or movable spines; water-vascular system with tube feet**
Chordata	**OS**	***b***	***C***	t	**Marine, freshwater, or terrestrial; mostly metameric (heteronomous); dorsal, hollow nerve tube; notochord; pharyngeal clefts (vertebrates with vesicular brain; cranium; jointed endoskeleton with vertebrae; 2 pairs jointed appendages typical; circulatory system closed, with red blood cells)**

[a] **C,** cellular; **T,** tissue; **O,** organ; **OS,** organ system.
[b] ***b,*** bilateral; ***r,*** radial.
[c] ***A,*** acoelomate; ***P,*** pseudocoelomate; ***C,*** coelomate; ***H,*** hemocoelomate.
[d] **s,** saccular; **t,** tubular.

sopterygians, however, remained in fresh water; eventually they had to contend with conditions somewhat similar to those of the modern tropics, where most present-day types of air-breathing, land-walking fishes such as mudskippers (see Figure 2.50*d*) and climbing perch now live. The sturdy skeletal support of the fin base (see Figure 4.33) allowed crossopterygians to stump across land from pond to pond. Hence, during a period of recurrent seasonal drought, some may have been able to survive the drying up of their habitat by escaping to other waterholes. Thus the first vertebrate adaptations relevant to future life on land did *not* come about as a conscious adoption of a terrestrial mode of life, but rather in response to an immediate predicament, allowing them to remain in fresh water even when that water had become scarce.

Meanwhile, land plants and insects had become abundant, providing a ready and heretofore virtually unexploited food source. Over a considerable period of time, probably quite gradually, certain crossopterygian populations altered imperceptibly into the first amphibians. All crossopterygians are now extinct save for a single marine genus, *Latimeria,* which lurks in the depths of the Indian Ocean, a blue, 1.5-m recluse that has only recently been viewed alive by man (see Figure 2.50*a*).

Most amphibians still are imperfectly adapted for life on land, for their skin is thin and provides only a partial shield against dehydration; most return to the water to lay their eggs, which hatch into an aquatic larval stage. Modern amphibians, including salamanders, legless caecilians, and the tailless frogs and toads, represent but a remnant of an extensive amphibian radiation that took place during the late Paleozoic Era.

The next major innovation following the appearance of the land-adapted leg was the *amniote* egg, which had membranes that protected the embryo from dehydration and could therefore be laid on land. In another chapter we shall consider the structure of this excellent egg in further detail (Figure 4.3). The land egg probably developed at a time when amphibians still spent much of their time in the water and served to protect the young from aquatic predators or from death in the drying mud of evaporated ponds. The development of the embryo within a yolky, protective amniote egg allowed the deletion of the aquatic larval stage; the animals which first laid those eggs, although otherwise amphibianlike, were in fact the first reptiles. The reptiles and their descendants, the birds and mammals, are therefore known as *amniotes,* while amphibians and fishes are termed *anamniotes.*

The metazoan phyla have been compared in Table 2.4.

In Chapter 8 we shall trace the radiative adaptation of reptiles throughout the Mesozoic Era. These vertebrates survived the increasing aridity of climate that accompanied the end of the Paleozoic Era, for the egg that had previously served to reduce larval mortality in a still moist habitat now proved adaptive in another sense. In addition, a start toward keratinization of the skin (that is, deposition of a water-impervious protein, keratin, within the epidermal cells) had been made by amphibians, but their potential in this respect remained limited. Now, under the selective pressure of increasing aridity, reptilian skin underwent further keratinization with the development of an effective "epidermal seal" consisting of densely packed horny cells. Forced to adopt a new way of life by the disappearance of their accustomed habitat, the reptiles crept forth to conquer a new world.

During the rise and diversification of the reptiles, two different reptilian lines each gave rise to a new type of vertebrate—birds arose from the bipedal *archosaurs* (ancestors also of the dinosaurs), and mammals from the quadrupedal *therapsids,* many features of which already foreshadowed mammalian structure. Although both appeared early in the Mesozoic Era (the age of reptiles), the primitive birds and mammals were ecologically overshadowed by the reptiles until climatic changes toward the end of the era led to extinction of most reptilian orders.

The cooler climate of the past 75 million years (the Cenozoic Era) favored the survival of forms that could generate their own body heat independent of the temperature of their surroundings. At some point in their evolution, birds and mammals each became *homoiothermal,* or capable of maintaining a stable body temperature by internal physiological regulation. This now contributed to their success and they diversified to occupy the habitats formerly dominated by reptiles. Homoiotherms are not only capable of year-round activity, but their metabolism and development are accelerated.

Birds have specialized toward flight, becoming both the least typical and most homogeneous class of vertebrates. They have developed a complex of structural peculiarities by which the ability to fly has been promoted and refined (see Figures 4.15 and 4.16). At the same time, diversification *within* the class has been mainly restricted to specializations of the bill and foot that are favorable to particular methods of food getting (Figure 2.53). Mammals, on the other hand, remained pedestrian or adopted arboreal or burrowing habits. Only one group, the bats, specialized for flight; they could not have competed successfully with birds save for their remarkable sonar method of prey detection, which enables them to seek flying insects in the dark.

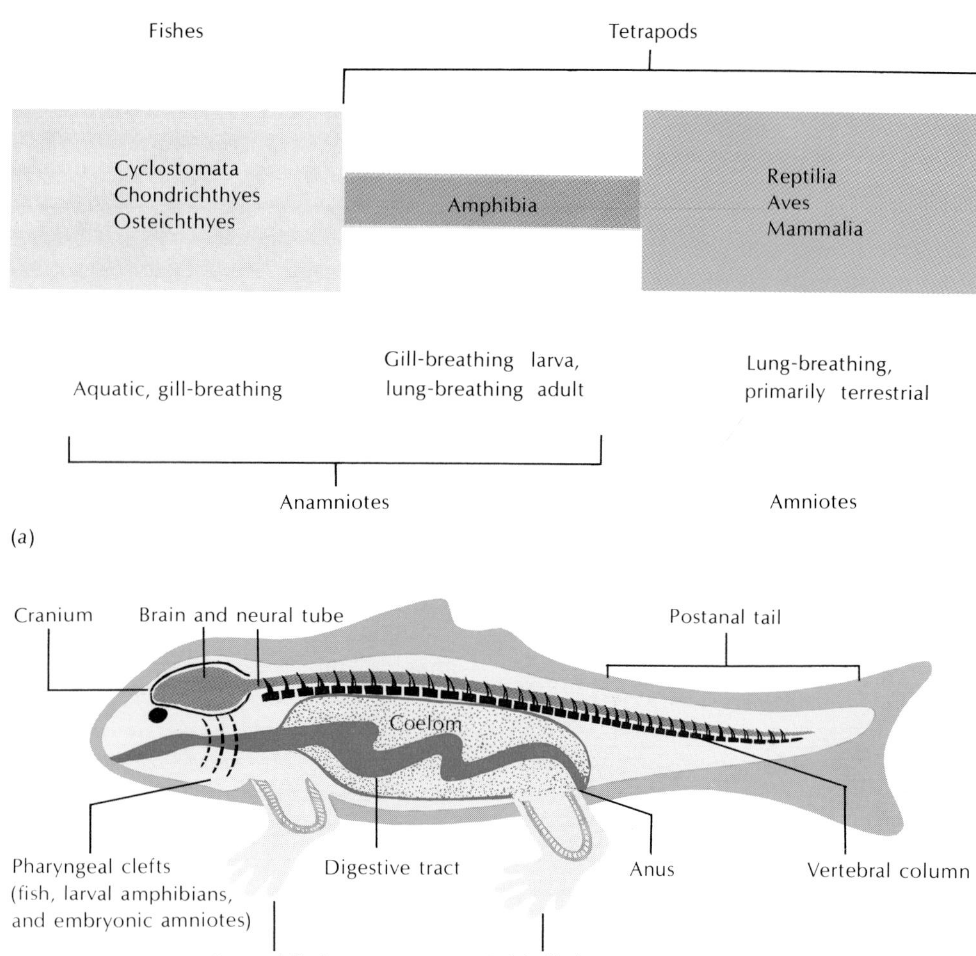

Figure 2.47 □ **(*a*) Living vertebrate classes. Amphibia, which are terrestrial tetrapods as adults, have not developed an amniote egg and must therefore as a rule lay their eggs in water and pass through an aquatic larval stage. They are therefore shown to occupy an intermediate position between aquatic and land-adapted vertebrate classes and were indeed the first vertebrates to invade the land. (*b*) Vertebrate characteristics in fish and tetrapod.**

Avian and mammalian adaptations for care of the young are far advanced over those of other vertebrates. Birds incubate their eggs and provide food for their young until the latter are mature enough to succeed on their own. The most primitive mammals also laid eggs. The only surviving egg-laying mammals (*monotremes*) are the Australian duckbilled platypus and echidna (Figure 2.55), both highly specialized and possessing effective antipredator adaptations, including the echidna's covering of stout quills and the male platypus' venomous hindleg spur. Egg-laying mammals incubate their young as birds do, but they have an additional adaptive advantage in being able to suckle their young on milk secreted by *mammary glands.*

Other than the monotremes, mammals are *viviparous:* rather than laying eggs, the female retains the embryos in her uterus during early development. Viviparity is of sporadic occurrence in the animal world, but only *eutherians* (placental mammals) have effective means of providing nourishment from the mother's bloodstream to the developing young. The *placenta* is a complex organ (see Figure 17.45) consisting of both embryonic and maternal tissues, which provides intimate contact between the bloodstreams of mother and young, facilitating exchanges of nutrients and metabolic wastes. Whenever they have shared the same habitat with more primitive nonplacental mammals such as the pouched marsupials, placental mammals almost invariably have replaced the nonplacental species.

Contemporary eutherians represent some 16 orders, diversified for different modes of life. The great adaptive radiation

Figure 2.48 □ Lamprey, *Entosphenus tridentatus:* (*a*) clinging to rock by means of jawless sucking mouth; (*b*) closeup of mouth, showing rows of rasping teeth used in perforating the body wall of the host (a fish). (*Courtesy of Carolina Biological Supply Company.*)

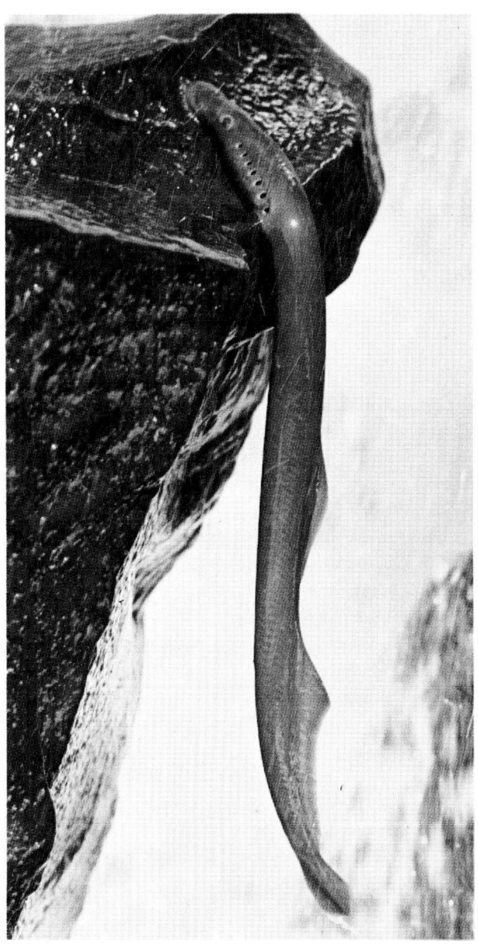

(*a*)

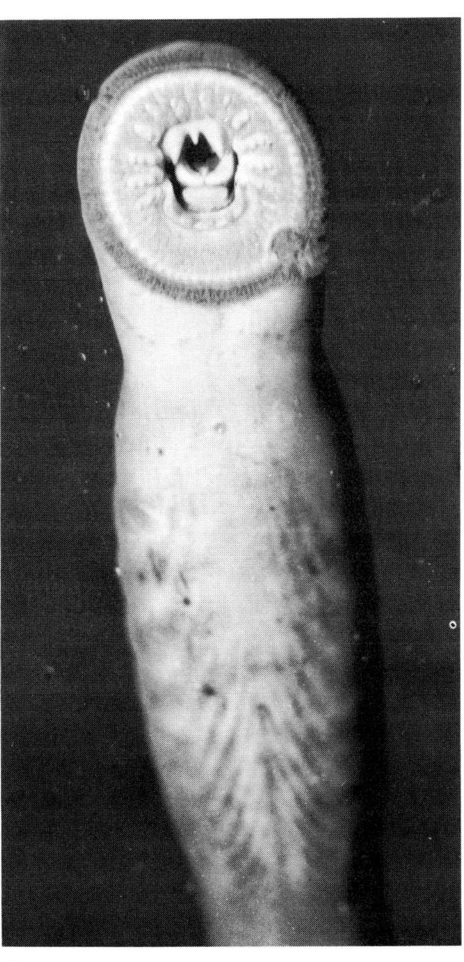

(*b*)

of the Cenozoic Era produced bats, cetaceans (whales and porpoises), rodents, lagomorphs (rabbits and hares), elephants, primates (monkeys, apes, and man), insectivores (shrews, hedgehogs, and moles), edentates (sloths, armadillos, and anteaters), carnivores (seals, dogs, cats, bears, weasels, and otters), odd-toed hoofed mammals (horses, tapirs, and rhinoceroses), even-toed hoofed mammals (cattle, swine, sheep, antelopes, giraffes, and others), and a number of other, less familiar groups. Most mammals are terrestrial, but cetaceans and sea cows have resumed a totally aquatic life although they have continued to be breathers of the air at the surface of their habitat.

The living classes of vertebrates are schematized in Figure 2.47. Three of these classes—Cyclostomata, Osteichthyes (bony fishes), and Chondrichthyes (cartilaginous fishes)—are aquatic and are gill breathers throughout their entire lives; three more, the *amniotes* (forms having an amniote egg)—reptiles, birds, and mammals—are air breathers throughout their lives and are primarily terrestrial; one class, Amphibia, still spans the gap between the aquatic and terrestrial classes, having an aquatic, gill-breathing larval stage and air-breathing adulthood. In Chapter 12 the body plan of the shark will be studied as representative of primitive vertebrate architecture, and in Parts 4 and 5 we shall consider much more comparative material on the organization and functioning of the vertebrate body. Additional characteristics of the individual classes are summarized in the synopsis provided for reference at the close of this chapter, and representatives of each of the living classes are shown in Figures 2.48 through 2.55.

Figure 2.49 □ Chondrichthyes. (*a*) *Isurus oxyrhynchus* (mako shark). Note the broad-based, relatively nonmaneuverable pectoral fins (the pelvic fins have been partly removed), the gill slits exposed on the sides of the pharynx, and the undershot mouth armed with rows of teeth. (*Photograph by G. Mattson, U.S. Bureau of Commercial Fisheries.*) (*b*) *Raja binoculata*, a bottom-dwelling species. (*Courtesy of General Biological, Inc., Chicago.*) Note the wide, flattened body as compared with the streamlined shark outline. The rays and skates swim by winglike undulations of the enlarged pectoral fins; the large pelvic fins of the male, here spread to each side of the tail, are modified for use in copulation. *Raja* feeds on shellfish collected from the bottom.

(*a*)

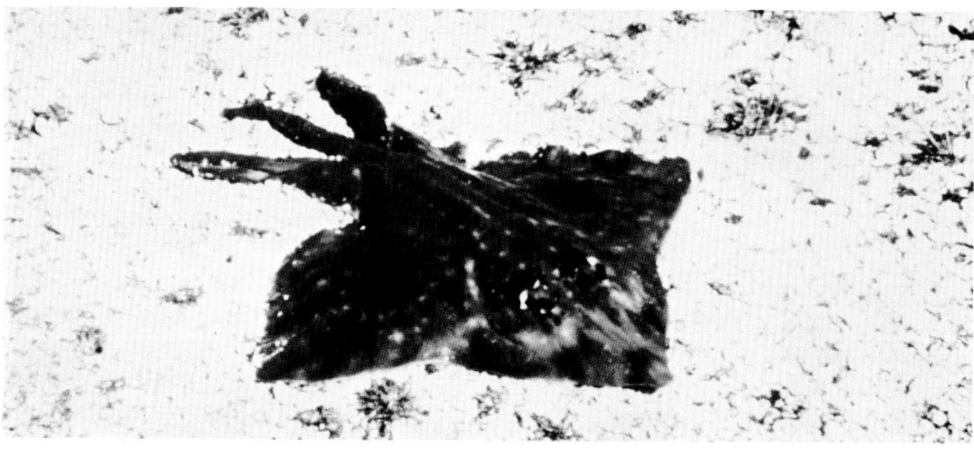

(*b*)

Figure 2.50 □ Osteichthyes (facing page). (*a*) Coelacanth (*Latimeria*), last survivor of crossopterygian line (lobe-finned fishes). (*Los Angeles County Museum of Natural History.*) (*b*) Sea dragon (*Hippocampus* species), a sea horse that resembles its background of seaweed. (*Los Angeles County Museum of Natural History.*) (*c*) Sturgeon, living relic of an ancient line. The skeleton is mostly cartilaginous. Note barbels, used in sensing food, and the heterocercal tail, the prominent dorsal lobe of which tilts the fish downward at the head end, assisting bottom feeding. Sturgeons may attain lengths of 2 to 3 m and live many years in captivity, their eggs being used as caviar. (*Scripps Institution of Oceanography.*) (*d*) Mudskipper (*Periophthalmos*), a modern fish adapted for climbing trees and walking on land. (*Los Angeles County Museum of Natural History.*) Note the armlike pectoral fins used in crawling and leaping over the mud as well as in climbing into mangrove trees overhanging the water. *Periophthalmos* is a ray-finned fish unrelated to the ancient lobefins.

(*a*)

(*b*)

(*c*)

(*d*)

Figure 2.51 □ Amphibians. (*a*) Salamander larvae (*Typhlotriton spelaeus*), showing external gills. The paler variety inhabits caves, whereas the darker form was collected from a spring. (*Courtesy of General Biological, Inc., Chicago.*) (*b*) Bullfrog tadpole (*Rana catesbiana*) undergoing metamorphosis. (*Courtesy of General Biological, Inc., Chicago.*) Note well-developed hind legs; the forelegs are not yet evident, nor has the tail begun to shrink. (*c*) Toad (*Bufo valliceps*), which, with a semihorny skin, is less confined to humid habitats than are either frogs or salamanders. (*Courtesy of Carolina Biological Supply Company.*)

(*a*)

(*b*)

(*c*)

(*a*)

(*b*)

(*c*)

Figure 2.52 □ Reptiles. (*a*) Newly hatched sea turtle, showing paddlelike limbs adapted for swimming. (*Scripps Institution of Oceanography.*) Although air breathers, sea turtles come ashore only to lay their eggs, feeding on sea grasses, executing overseas migrations to their breeding grounds, and mating underwater. When the eggs (buried by the mother) hatch, the young turtles find their way to the sea without instruction. (*b*) American alligator, with an egg like that from which it has recently emerged. (*Zoological Society of San Diego.*) The epidermal scales that protect reptiles from dehydration show to advantage here. (*c*) Cobras (*Naja*) hatching from their amniote eggs. (*Zoological Society of San Diego.*) Spreading the hood is a defensive display that may save the snake from having to bite in self-defense.

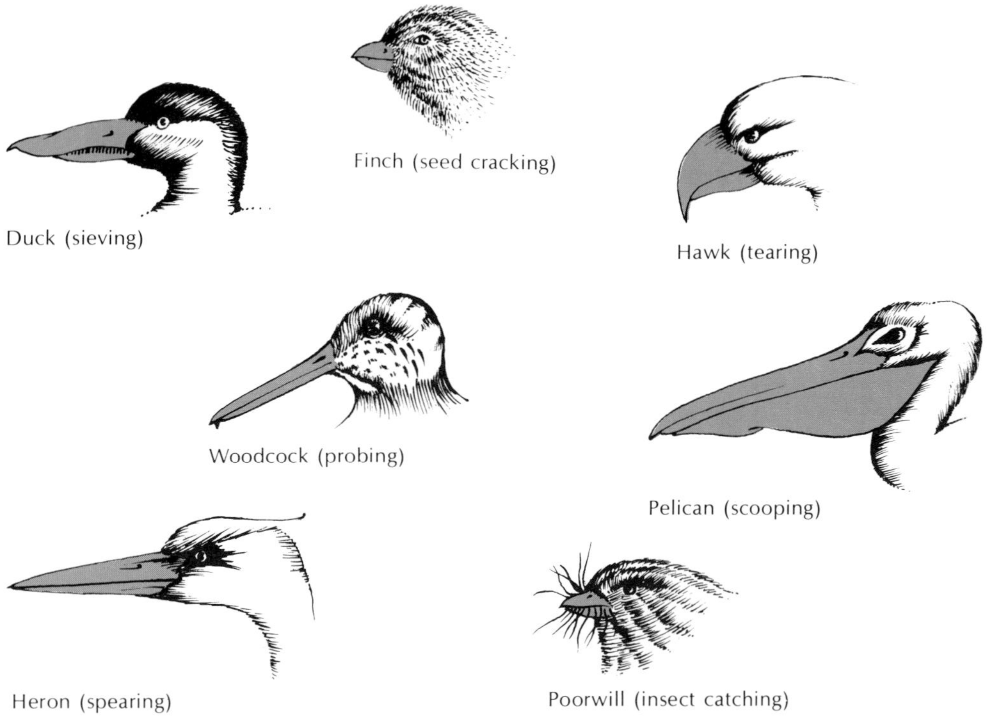

Figure 2.53 □ Birds' beaks demonstrate adaptive radiation toward different methods of food getting.

(a)

(b)

(c)

Figure 2.54 □ Birds. (*a*) Blue-footed booby (*Sula*) with young, on Isla San Pedro Martín, Gulf of California. (*Courtesy of California Academy of Sciences.*) These relatives of cormorants and pelicans have all four toes directed forward and webbed for effective swimming. Note the sharp, fish-catching bill. (*b*) Secretary bird (*Sagittarius serpentarius*), a ground-dwelling raptorial bird, killing a snake, a regular dietary item. (*Los Angeles County Museum of Natural History.*) Otherwise hawklike, the secretary bird favors running, and selection has operated toward survival of longer-legged forms. (*c*) Rockhopper penguins (*Eudyptus crestatus*), showing low-intensity threat by individual on right and withdrawal indicative of submission by bird on left. (*Zoological Society of San Diego.*)

Figure 2.55 □ Mammals. (*a*) Echidna (*Tachyglossus aculeatus*), one of two species of egg-laying mammals surviving to the present. (*Courtesy of Australian News and Information Bureau.*) The spiny anteater rolls up in self-defense and can dig rapidly with its clawed toes. (*b*) Platypus (*Ornithorhynchus anatinus*), the other surviving monotreme. (*Courtesy of Australian News and Information Bureau.*) The platypus is specialized for an amphibious life. Found only in streams of eastern Australia, it must eat nearly its own weight daily in worms, crayfish, and other freshwater animals. The eggs are laid in streamside burrows and incubated by the female, which then suckles the young. The male is armed with a stout venomous spur on each hindleg. The platypus's ducklike snout serves for grubbing food out of muddy stream bottoms. Hunted nearly to extinction for its otterlike fur, the platypus is now protected and on the increase. (*c*) Kangaroo "joey" at age of 130 days. (*Courtesy of Australian News and Information Bureau.*) This infant marsupial was taken from its mother's pouch for weighing and examination. Note that nearly 4 months after birth the joey is still hairless and its eyes sealed, resembling a fetal eutherian mammal. At birth the joey was only 1.5 cm long. (*d*) Female polar bear (*Thalarctos m. maritimus*) nursing twin cubs (order Carnivora). (*Zoological Society of San Diego.*) (*e*) Golden-bellied mangabey (*Cercocebus galeritus chrysogaster*); placating approach of one individual to another with food (order Primata). (*Zoological Society of San Diego.*)

(*c*)

(*d*)

(*a*)

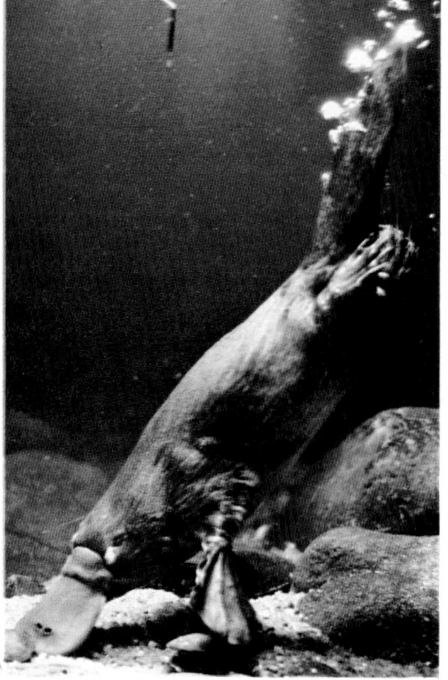

(*b*)

(*e*)

Figure 2.56 □ Circle graphs depicting relative numbers of identified plant (*a*) and animal (*b*) species. Note that speciation has taken place to the greatest extent in those groups which have most successfully adapted to life on land and have accordingly diversified toward occupancy of the great variety of terrestrial habitats available.

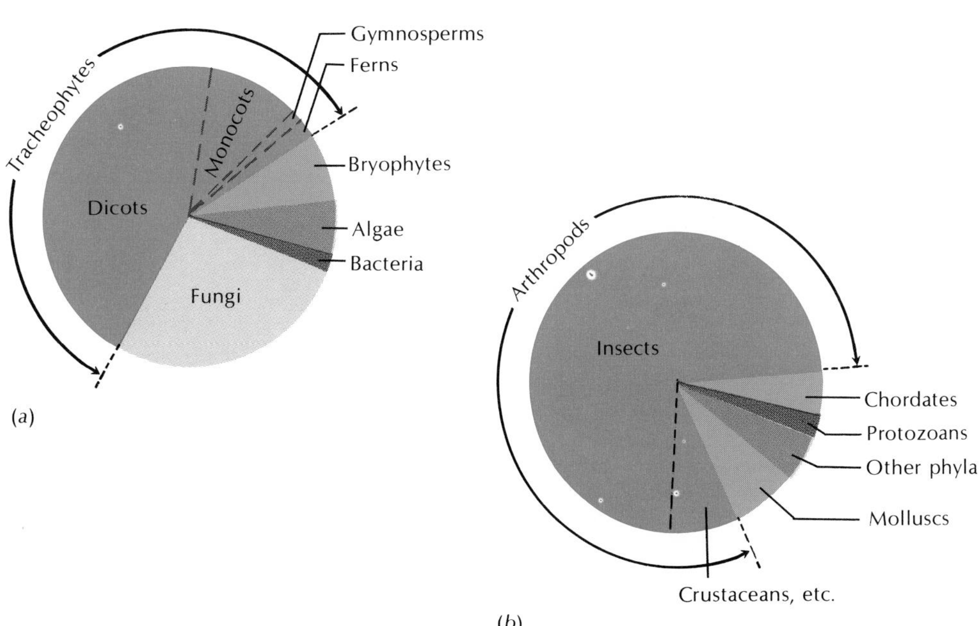

Despite the prominence of the vertebrates and the relatively large size that a number of them attain, if the total picture of biotic diversity and fecundity is viewed in terms of numbers of species and of individual organisms, this is still mainly a world of invertebrates and plants. Figure 2.56 depicts the relative numbers of named species of plants and animals in graphic form (not taking into account the probable large number of nematode species yet to be named). For purposes of review the major biotic innovations seen in various phyla are summarized in Figure 2.57; it should be kept in mind that although a given advance is cited in relation to the simplest type of creature that shows this innovation today, the actual advance was probably made by some ancestral form perhaps not closely resembling its modern descendants (or possibly resembling its descendants' larval stages more closely than it does their adult form).

For centuries botanists and zoologists have been engaged in describing and classifying the host of living things that make up the biosphere. The task is far from finished, and for comparatively few species do we even have a complete picture of how they live and reproduce. Many are difficult to maintain in captivity and nearly inaccessible for prolonged study in their natural environment. Today the "naturalist," or student of plants and animals under natural conditions, is far from obsolete. Instead, there is more need than ever for trained personnel to study the natural relationships of living things in order to understand and, where necessary, to manipulate the complex web of interdependencies that characterize communities of living things.

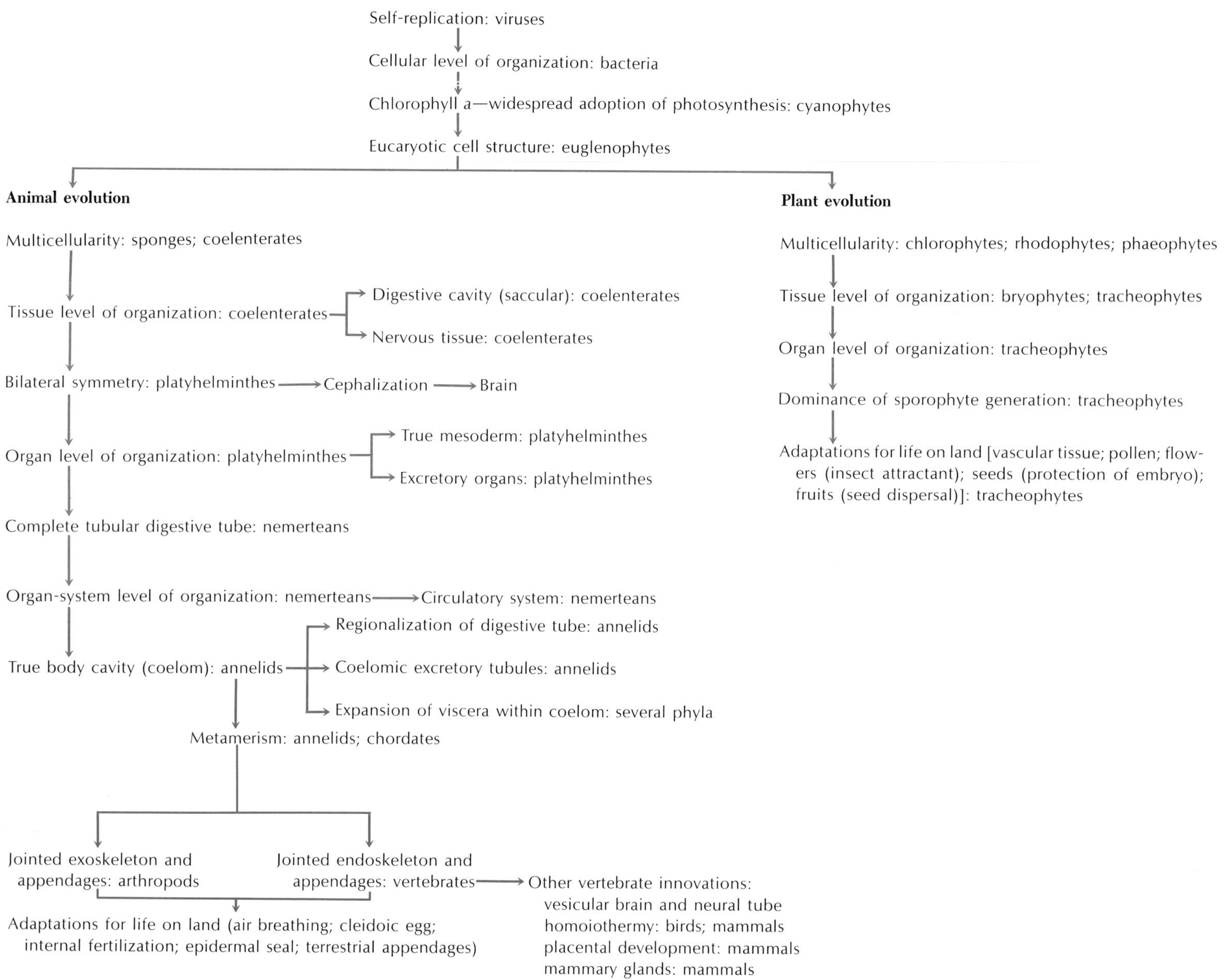

Figure 2.57 □ Important biotic innovations. Groups in which innovations may first have appeared are shown following colons.

Viruses

"Molecular life" capable of reproduction only within cells of host, consisting only of protein framework and nucleic acid chromosome

Kingdom Procaryota

Unicellular organisms with simple procaryotic cell structure lacking nuclear envelope and other organelles characteristic of eucaryotic cells; rarely exceed 2 μm diameter although variable in length

PHYLUM SCHIZOPHYTA Bacteria, spirochetes; mostly heterotrophic; synthesize cellulose and store fuel as glycogen (*Escherichia coli*)

PHYLUM CYANOPHYTA Blue-green algae; autotrophic, containing chlorophyll *a* and c-phycocyanin, excess fuel stored as cyanophycean starch; invested by cellulose cell wall and gelatinous matrix; sexual reproduction unknown (*Nostoc*)

Kingdom Protista

Unicellular organisms with eucaryotic cell structure; true nucleus and other advanced organelles present; cell diameter usually exceeds 20 μm

PHYLUM EUGLENOPHYTA Euglenoids; autotrophic and/or heterotrophic; have one or two flagella emerging from deep gullet; autotrophic types have chlorophylls *a* and *b*; cellulose lacking, fuel stored as the carbohydrate paramylum (*Euglena*)

PHYLUM PROTOZOA Acellular animals; mostly heterotrophic

SUBPHYLUM PLASMODROMA Have flagella, pseudopodia, or no locomotory structures

Class Flagellata Move by means of flagella (*Trypanosoma*)

Class Sarcodina Move and capture food by means of pseudopodia (*Amoeba*)

Class Sporozoa Parasitic; no locomotory organs, may move by changing body shape; one stage of life cycle is infective spore or sporozoite (*Plasmodium*)

SUBPHYLUM CILIOPHORA Bear cilia at some time of life

Class Ciliata Possess many to few cilia throughout life; have two kinds of nuclei, macronucleus and micronucleus (*Paramecium*)

Class Suctoria Young, ciliated; adults, sessile and bearing tentacles used in prey capture (*Podophyra*)

PHYLUM PYRROPHYTA Dinoflagellates and cryptomonads; have two flagella and cellulose cell walls; autotrophic forms have chlorophylls *a* and *c* and the brown dinoxanthin; fuel stored as oil, fat, or starch

Class Dinophyceae Dinoflagellates; naked or armored with cellulose plates; two flagella, one trailing, one in equatorial groove (*Gonyaulax*)

Class Cryptophyceae Cryptomonads; ovoid, flagella springing from deep gullet; both autotrophic and heterotrophic species (*Cryptomonas*)

PHYLUM CHRYSOPHYTA Diatoms; autotrophic, containing chlorophylls *a* and *c*, brown fucoxanthin and other pigments; siliceous test of overlapping halves; food stored mainly as oils (*Arachnoidiscus*)

Kingdom Metaphyta

Multicellular plants; characteristically alternate monoploid gametophyte and diploid sporophyte in life cycle (or equivalent monoploid and diploid forms in fungi); have cellulose cell walls and mainly store food as starch and oils

Subkingdom Thallophyta Tissues poorly differentiated, body filamentous or a flattened, dichotomously branching thallus lacking true roots, stems, and leaves; gamete-producing structures unicellular, do not house embryo

PHYLUM CHLOROPHYTA Green algae; unicellular, filamentous, or thallose; mostly autotrophic, with chlorophylls *a* and *b*, carotenes and xanthophylls (*Ulva*)

PHYLUM PHAEOPHYTA Brown algae; mainly marine; autotrophic with chlorophylls *a* and *c*, fucoxanthin and other pigments; food stored mainly as laminarin (a starchlike carbohydrate built up of units of mannitol); thallus usually consisting of holdfast, stipes, and blades with air bladders for flotation; algin extracted commercially from cell walls (*Macrocystis*)

PHYLUM RHODOPHYTA Red algae; mainly marine; thallus feathery, straplike, or branching and impregnated with calcium salts; autotrophic, containing chlorophylls *a* and *d* and other pigments including red phycoerythrins; fuel stored as floridean starch and sterols; reproductive cells not flagellated (*Gigartina*)

PHYLUM MYXOMYCOPHYTA Slime molds; heterotrophic, with amoeboid stages capable of ingesting solid food

Class Myxomycetes Major feeding stage is a multinucleate plasmodium; unicellular stages interchangeably flagellated or amoeboid (*Physarum*)

Class Acrasiomycetes Major feeding stage is unicellular myxamoeba; aggregative stage is multicellular pseudoplasmodium (*Dictyostelium*)

PHYLUM EUMYCOPHYTA Fungi; heterotrophic; body a mycelium of filamentous hyphae; cellulose cell walls prevent ingestion of solid food, allow only absorption of dissolved nutrients

Class Phycomycetes Algalike fungi; reproductive cells flagellated in aquatic types; hyphae syncytial without crosswalls (*Rhizopus*)

Class Ascomycetes Sac fungi; sexual spores (ascospores) produced in an ascus; mycelial cells binucleate (*Morchella*)

Class Basidiomycetes Club fungi; sexual spores produced on club-shaped cells (basidia); mycelial cells binucleate (*Amanita*)

Class Deuteromycetes Imperfect fungi; sexual stages unknown; most parasitic (*Candida*)

Subkingdom Embryophyta Tissue differentiation slight to complex; sex organs multicellular antheridia and archegonia; sporophyte embryo protected and nourished by archegonium of parent gametophyte; mainly terrestrial; autotrophic, containing chlorophylls *a* and *b* and other pigments found in green algae

PHYLUM BRYOPHYTA Mosses and liverworts; gametophyte predominant, consisting of thallus or erect "leafy" shoot; true roots, stems, and leaves lacking; vascular tissue lacking; tissue differentiation slight to moderate; sporophyte nutritionally dependent on gametophyte

Class Musci Mosses; aerial portion of gametophyte a "leafy shoot" with green leaflike scales, bearing sex organs at apex (*Sphagnum*)

Class Hepaticae Liverworts; gametophyte thallose or forming leafy shoot; archegonia and antheridia often borne on separate vertical stalks above thallus; asexual reproduction often by buds known as gemmae (*Marchantia*)

PHYLUM TRACHEOPHYTA Vascular plants; tissues well-differentiated with vascular tissues (phloem and xylem) present; sporophyte predominant, consisting of true roots, stems, and leaves; gametophyte reduced and either independent or dependent and embedded within tissues of sporophyte; well-developed cuticle protects against dehydration; autotrophic, possessing chlorophylls *a* and *b*, carotenes, and xanthophylls

SUBPHYLUM PSILOPSIDA Most primitive; sporophyte with rudimentary vascular tissues and upright shoots having algalike dichotomous branching; gametophyte small and independent, but heterotrophic and nutritionally aided by soil fungi, bisexual, producing both archegonia and antheridia on same thallus; widely distributed about 350 million years ago, now only 2 surviving genera (*Psilotum*)

SUBPHYLUM LYCOPSIDA Club mosses and ground pines; sporophyte shoot upright, usually dichotomously branching, bearing spiral whorls of minute leaves; spores borne on specialized leaves (sporophylls) forming club-shaped strobili (cones) at shoot apices; gametophytes either bisexual or of distinct male and female types, independent or dependent and enclosed within walls of sporangium; ecologically dominant during Carboniferous Period about 250 million years ago, some attaining heights of 30 m and diameters of 2 m (*Lycopodium*)

SUBPHYLUM SPHENOPSIDA Horsetails; sporophyte predominant with hollow, distinctly jointed stems giving rise to whorls of reduced leaves at each joint; tissues impregnated with silica; spores borne in sporangiophores clustered to form ovoid strobili (cones) at tips of shoots; gametophytes independent and bisexual; important during Carboniferous Period, attaining heights of 30 m, only one genus now living (*Equisetum*)

SUBPHYLUM PTEROPSIDA Ferns and seed plants; leaves larger and more complex than in lower tracheophytes; break in vascular tissue (leaf gap) separates leaf from stem, allowing leaf drop to occur; spores borne in sporangia on margins or lower surfaces of sporophylls

Class Filicae Ferns; sporophylls resemble other leaves; gametophyte thallose, autotrophic, and usually bisexual; swimming-sperm stage present as in all lower tracheophytes (*Polypodium*)

Class Gymnospermae Conifers, cycads, and ginkgoes; sporophylls scalelike, clustered to form cones; develop two kinds of spores (microspores that develop into male or microgametophytes, and megaspores that develop into female or megagametophytes); male gametophyte adapted for dispersal as pollen, there being no free-swimming-sperm stage; female gametophyte remains within ovule of sporophyll; sporophyte embryo has more than two cotyledons (seed leaves) and develops within ovule to form a seed; seeds are not enclosed within fruits but borne on surface of cone scales (*Pinus*)

Class Angiospermae Flowering plants; sporophylls form stamens and pistils of flowers; flowers usually adapted for attraction of insect pollinators; two types of spores produced: microspores within stamens, megaspores within ovary of pistil; male gametophyte is pollen grain; sporophyte embryo develops within ovary to form a seed; tissues of ovary become modified to form a fruit about the seeds

Subclass Dicotyledoneae Dicots; embryos have two seed leaves (cotyledons); flower parts typically in fours or fives; vascular bundles form cylinder in stem; leaves with net venation; diversified into over 50 orders, of which one of the largest is *Asterales* (composites such as daisies)

Subclass Monocotyledoneae Monocots; embryos have one cotyledon; flower parts typically in threes; vascular bundles scattered throughout stem; leaves usually narrow with parallel venation; flowers inconspicuous in wind-pollinated species; 14 orders including *Liliales* (lilies), *Orchidales* (orchids), and *Graminales* (grains and grasses)

Kingdom Metazoa

Multicellular animals; eucaryotic cellular structure; heterotrophic, generally lacking cellulose and storing fuel as glycogen and fat

Subkingdom Parazoa Metazoa below tissue grade of organization; specialized cell types present but nervous tissue lacking and little functional cooperation among cells; embryonic development not parallel to that of other metazoans

PHYLUM PORIFERA Sponges; body wall perforated by pores; water circulated by flagellated choanocytes; digestion intracellular, no mouth or stomach; supportive skeleton of spongin fibers and/or mineral spicules; flagellated larvae free-swimming, adults sedentary

Class Calcispongiae Calcareous sponges; entirely marine; spicules limy, porocytes present; asconoid, syconoid, and rhagonoid levels of organization (*Sycon*)

Class Hyalospongiae Siliceous or glass sponges; marine; spicules siliceous, six-rayed, often fused; rhagonoid (having complex of flagellated chambers); body form often cylindrical or funnel-shaped (*Euplectella*)

Class Demospongiae Horny sponges; marine and freshwater; skeleton of spongin fibers and siliceous spicules (not six-rayed); rhagonoid; some used commercially as bath sponges (*Spongilla*)

Subkingdom Eumetazoa Have true tissues of epithelial, contractile, nervous, and supportive or connective types; embryonic development passes through true gastrula stage with ectoderm and endoderm layers

PHYLUM COELENTERATA (CNIDARIA) Polyps and medusae; all aquatic; radially symmetrical, characteristically alternating polyp and medusa generations in life cycle; true organs lacking; digestion intracellular and extracellular in gastrovascular cavity having only one opening (the mouth); mouth ringed by tentacles bearing stinging capsules (nematocysts); body wall of outer epidermis, central mesoglea, and inner gastrodermis; nerve plexus lacking brain

Class Hydrozoa Hydroids, hydrozoan medusae, hydras; marine and freshwater; alternation of generations present or lacking, either polyp or medusa may be more conspicuous stage; gastrovascular cavity of polyp not subdivided by radial mesenteries (septa); polyps often colonial; bell-shaped medusa lacks oral tentacles and has a velum (shelf around margin of bell) (*Hydra, Physalia, Obelia, Polyorchis*)

Class Scyphozoa Jellyfish; medusa generation predominant, polyp generation reduced in size; medusa lacks velum and has large oral tentacles around mouth; all marine (*Cyanea, Aurelia*)

Class Anthozoa Sea anemones, soft corals, stony corals; medusa generation lacking, polyp bears gonads and reproduces both sexually and asexually; gastrovascular cavity internally subdivided by radial septa; mouth flanked by one or two ciliated grooves (siphonoglyphs); soft corals produce internal, horny, or calcareous skeleton; polyps tiny, bearing eight branching tentacles; stony corals produce calcareous skeleton external to the polyps (secreted by epidermis), have more than eight nonbranching tentacles (*Metridium, Gorgonia*)

PHYLUM CTENOPHORA Comb jellies; marine; biradially symmetrical, most with pair of retractile, bilaterally-placed tentacles bearing colloblasts (glue cells) for prey capture; locomotion by radially arranged ciliated comb plates (*Pleurobrachia*)

PHYLUM PLATYHELMINTHES Flatworms; marine, freshwater, parasitic (a few terrestrial in moist conditions); dorsoventrally flattened, bilaterally symmetrical; eyes and brain in head, mouth anterior or ventral; gastrovascular cavity often much branched; complex reproductive system; excretory tubules with flame cells; true mesoderm present

Class Turbellaria Nonparasitic flatworms including triclads (forms with a three-pronged digestive cavity such as planarians) and polyclads (marine types with a many-branched digestive tract); eyes and more or less well-developed head present (*Dugesia, Planocera*)

Class Trematoda Flukes; parasitic on or within bodies of vertebrate and invertebrate hosts; *monogenetic* flukes require only one host in the life cycle and are mainly ectoparasitic whereas *digenetic* flukes require two or more hosts (one of which is usually a snail) and are mainly endoparasitic; characteristically have several generations of asexual reproduction (sporocyst, redia, and cercaria) before maturing into sexual form (*Fasciola, Opisthorchis*)

Class Cestoda Tapeworms; cysticercus larva typically encysts within muscles of herbivorous host, maturing into adult strobila within intestinal tract of carnivorous host; strobila consists of scolex specialized for attachment and series of proglottids produced by transverse budding or strobilation; epidermis and digestive tract lacking, food being absorbed directly from gut of host; each proglottid contains male and female sex organs

PHYLUM NEMERTEA (RHYNCHOCOELA) Ribbonworms; mostly marine; predatory, capturing prey with long proboscis extended from sheath above mouth; soft, unsegmented, cylindrical body has complete digestive tract, simple blood vessels, and excretory tubules with flame cells (*Amphiporus*)

PHYLUM ASCHELMINTHES Roundworms, rotifers and minor groups; body usually cylindrical, unsegmented, and tapering, covered with a cuticle that prevents wormlike elongation or shortening; epidermis syncytial or cellular, cilia usually absent; muscle fibers usually arranged longitudinally; pseudocoel contains tubular digestive tract and sex organs; excretory tubules sometimes with flame cells; major classes are:

Class Nematoda Roundworms; body cylindrical, wormlike, covered with thick cuticle; epidermis syncytial; aquatic, terrestrial, or parasitic (*Necator*)

Class Rotifera Rotifers; 0.5 to 1.5 mm long, with shell-like cuticle segmented to allow telescoping of posterior part of body; forked toe with cement gland for attachment; aquatic (mostly in fresh water), feeding and swimming by means of double whorl of cilia on head; males much smaller than females; reproduction often parthenogenetic (*Asplanchna*)

PHYLUM ECTOPROCTA Bryozoans; aquatic, minute colonial forms with trochophore larva; each zooid has U-shaped digestive tract with anus opening outside the coiled feeding organ (lophophore) that surrounds the mouth; excretory organs and blood vessels lacking, true body cavity (coelom) present; colonies bear protective nonfeeding individuals (avicularia) that crush small organisms settling on colony (*Bugula*)

PHYLUM BRACHIOPODA Lamp shells; marine, particularly abundant in Paleozoic Era; body enclosed by movable dorsal and ventral valves, the latter often perforated for passage of a stalk for attachment; feeding by tentacled lophophore; coelomate, with tubular digestive tract (anus often secondarily lacking), heart and blood vessels, kidneys; sexes separate, reproduction only sexual, producing a form of trochophore larva (*Terebratulina, Lingula*)

PHYLUM ANNELIDA Segmented worms; marine, freshwater, and terrestrial; body elongate and metameric, consisting of more or less similar segments; bristlelike chitinous setae usually present; appendages when present are paired flaplike swimming organs; coelomate; complete, muscular, regionalized digestive tract; nervous system with paired ventral nerve trunks and segmental ganglia; closed system of blood vessels with dorsal tubular heart; excretion by paired segmentally arranged metanephridia (with open coelomic funnels); monoecious or dioecious, marine forms often producing trochophore larva

Class Polychaeta Marine annelids, usually with numerous setae, paired appendages (parapodia), well-developed head with eyes, jaws, palps, or ciliated feeding tentacles (*Nereis, Chaetopterus*)

Class Oligochaeta Freshwater and terrestrial worms, with reduced setae and no parapodia; head small, bearing anterior lobe (prostomium); monoecious, with no larval stages (*Lumbricus*)

Class Hirudinea Leeches; marine and fresh water, mostly ectoparasitic with anterior and posterior suckers; body leaf-shaped, of 34 segments, with distensible esophagus; parapodia and setae lacking; monoecious, with no larval stages (*Hirudo*)

PHYLUM MOLLUSCA Molluscs; highly diversified phylum occuring in marine, freshwater and terrestrial habitats; coelomate with regionalized digestive tract, accessory digestive glands, heart, kidneys; monoecious or dioecious, most marine forms having trochophore larvae; body consists of foot, visceral hump (head present or lacking), mantle, and may have one, two, or eight calcareous valves (or none); nervous system usually contains paired cerebral, pedal, and visceral ganglia

Class Amphineura Chitons and related forms; marine; head reduced, ganglia lacking; mouth usually with radula; foot ventral, used for creeping; chitons with eight overlapping valves; trochophore larva (*Stenoplax*)

Class Gastropoda Snails and slugs; marine, freshwater and terrestrial; marine types with trochophore larvae; torsion (twisting of internal organs) takes place during development; shell single, usually coiled, or lacking; mouth with radula; head well developed with eyes and tentacles; foot used in creeping (*Helix*)

Class Scaphopoda Tusk shells; marine, with trochophore larva; shell tubular and open at both ends; foot conical, used in digging; head and circulatory system reduced; mouth with radula, ringed by tentacles with suckerlike ends (*Dentalium*)

Class Pelecypoda Bivalves (clams, oysters, scallops); marine and freshwater; left and right valves hinged dorsally; feeding usually by ciliary circulation over gills; head reduced and radula lacking but mouth bears labial palps; foot bladelike, used in digging; marine types with trochophore larva (*Pecten, Ostrea*)

Class Cephalopoda Octopus, squid, cuttlefish, nautilus; marine; no larval stages; eight, ten, or many prehensile arms; mouth usually with chitinous jaws and radula; nervous system highly developed; shell external, internal, or lacking; gristlelike endoskeleton present; muscular funnel formed from foot used in "jet propulsion" (*Sepia, Octopus, Nautilus, Loligo*)

PHYLUM ARTHROPODA Arthropods; body metameric, segments often fused or specialized; jointed appendages arranged in segmental pairs, usually functionally diversified; jointed chitinous exoskeleton present, serving for protection, support, and muscular attachment; coelom reduced; circulatory system open, allowing blood to flow into tissue spaces (hemocoel); cilia lacking; sexes separate; development direct or through larval stages

SUBPHYLUM CHELICERATA No true jaws or antennae; first appendages form piercing fangs (chelicerae), second appendages are food-grasping pedipalps; two major body divisions, cephalothorax and abdomen, the former typically bearing four or more pairs of walking legs, abdominal locomotory appendages lacking

Class Xiphosurida Horseshoe crab; marine, covered dorsally with domed carapace; abdomen ends in spinous telson; eyes compound; development by way of a "trilobite" larva resembling this extinct type (*Limulus*)

Class Pycnogonida Sea spiders; marine; abdomen reduced, cephalothorax bears eight to twelve walking legs and a pair of egg-carrying legs; mouth at tip of sucking proboscis (*Nymphon*)

Class Arachnida Arachnids; mainly terrestrial, usually predatory or parasitic; cephalothorax typically unsegmented bearing four pairs of walking legs; eyes simple; breathing by tracheae, book lungs, or both; larval stages usually absent; important orders include *Scorpionida* (scorpions), *Araneida* (spiders), *Phalangida* (harvestmen) and *Acarina* (mites and ticks)

SUBPHYLUM MANDIBULATA Anterior part of body is an externally unsegmented head or cephalothorax bearing one or two pairs of antennae, simple and/or compound eyes, true mandibles, and typically two pairs of food-handling legs (maxillae); at least two pairs of thoracic appendages; abdomen may bear or lack appendages

Class Crustacea Predominantly aquatic, breathing by gills; exoskeleton hardened with limy impregnations; thorax and abdomen usually segmented, the former often covered dorsally by a shieldlike carapace; appendages include two pairs of antennae and are mainly biramous (two-branched); abdomen ends in spinous or spatulate telson; many with nauplius and other larval stages; important subclasses include:

Subclass Branchiopoda Brine shrimp, water fleas and other small planktonic forms, mostly freshwater

Subclass Ostracoda Planktonic; covered by bivalved carapace; swim mainly by moving antennae

Subclass Copepoda Copepods; planktonic; have single median eye; female bears large lateral brood pouches

Subclass Cirripedia Barnacles; marine, adults sedentary, lacking eyes and antennae; monoecious; carapace enclosing body can be opened for extrusion of feathery legs for feeding

Subclass Malacostraca Typically have eight thoracic and six abdominal segments, all bearing appendages; eyes often compound and stalked; important orders include *Isopoda* (sow bugs), *Amphipoda* (beach hoppers), *Stomatopoda* (mantis shrimp), *Euphausiacea* (krill), and *Decapoda* (forms with ten walking legs including crabs, lobsters, crayfish, prawns, shrimp)

Class Chilopoda Centipedes; terrestrial, breathe by tracheae; body elongate, dorsoventrally flattened, homonomously segmented except for head which bears one pair of antennae, one pair of mandibles and two pairs of maxillae; predatory, with first trunk legs modified as poison claws; other trunk legs ambulatory (15 pairs or more); eyes compound, simple, or absent (*Scolopendra*)

Class Diplopoda Millipedes; terrestrial herbivores, breathing by tracheae; head bears one pair each of antennae, mandibles, and maxillae; body elongate, cylindrical, homonomously segmented; first four trunk segments single, rest fused in pairs so that each visible segment appears to bear two pairs of small legs totaling about 80 pairs; eyes simple (*Iulus*)

Class Insecta Insects; mainly terrestrial, breathing by tracheae; three distinct body parts, head, thorax, and abdomen; head of six fused metameres bearing compound and simple eyes, labium, one pair each of mandibles, maxillae, and antennae; mouthparts variously specialized; thorax of three fused segments bearing three pairs of walking legs and typically two pairs of wings; abdomen usually of eleven segments, lacking walking legs

Subclass Apterygota Silver fish and springtails; primitively wingless; no metamorphosis

Subclass Pterygota Winged (a few secondarily wingless); metamorphosis

Superorder Exopterygota Metamorphosis gradual, without pupal stage; development of wings external on body of juvenile; important orders include *Orthoptera* (crickets, roaches, and grasshoppers), *Isoptera* (termites), *Odonata* (dragonflies), *Hemiptera* (true bugs), *Homoptera* (aphids, scale insects)

Superorder Endopterygota Metamorphosis abrupt, with pupal stage; wing development internal within larval body; important orders include *Lepidoptera* (butterflies, moths), *Diptera* (two-winged flies), *Siphonaptera* (fleas), *Coleoptera* (beetles), *Hymenoptera* (bees, ants, wasps)

PHYLUM ECHINODERMATA Echinoderms; marine; larva bilaterally symmetrical; adults with secondary pentamerous radial symmetry, often sessile or creeping; calcareous endoskeleton and dermal spines; water-vascular system with tube feet

SUBPHYLUM PELMATOZOA Usually attached by stalk to substratum, oral surface upward; ambulacral grooves and tube feet used in food getting; digestive tract U-shaped with both mouth and anus opening on oral surface; only one existing class

Class Crinoidea Crinoids; arms branched, feathery, endoskeleton limited to aboral side of cup-shaped body; stalked and sedentary (sea lilies) or free-swimming without stalk (feather stars) (*Antedon*)

SUBPHYLUM ELEUTHEROZOA Unattached; mouth downward or at one end, anus aboral or lacking; tube feet used in locomotion

Class Asteroidea Starfishes; star-shaped, typically with five stiff arms bearing ambulacral grooves within which lie the tube feet (*Pisaster*)

Class Ophiuroidea Serpent and brittle stars; star-shaped, typically with five slender, flexible rays that are sharply set off from the central disc and can often be cast off voluntarily; ambulacral grooves closed and tube feet reduced; intestine and anus lacking (*Ophioderma*)

Class Echinoidea Sea urchins; endoskeleton fused to form solid, spherical to discoidal test bearing movable spines; mouth with "Aristotle's lantern" bearing five strong movable teeth (*Arbacia*)

Class Holothuroidea Sea cucumbers; body wormlike or cucumber-shaped, secondarily bilaterally symmetrical; tube feet present or absent; ambulacral grooves closed; branching tentacles ring mouth; endoskeleton as scattered ossicles (*Cucumaria*)

PHYLUM CHORDATA Chordates; notochord, dorsal hollow neural tube, and pharyngeal clefts present some time during life

SUBPHYLUM TUNICATA Ascidians, salps and larvaceans; marine; ascidian adults sedentary, others planktonic; usually with free-swimming larvae; notochord and neural tube present only in larva; adult covered by a tunic enclosing the mouth and enormous pharyngeal basket used in food gathering (*Styela, Salpa*)

SUBPHYLUM CEPHALOCHORDATA Amphioxus; marine, burrowing in sand; notochord and neural tube run length of body, persist throughout life; no brain; head rudimentary; pharynx huge, about half of total body length; metameric arrangement of muscles and other organs (*Branchiostoma*)

SUBPHYLUM VERTEBRATA Vertebrates; marine, freshwater, and terrestrial; notochord largely replaced postembryonically by backbone of segmental vertebrae; neural tube expanded anteriorly as brain of five linearly arranged vesicles; brain partly or almost wholly encased in cranium; articulated endoskeleton primitively bony, some forms secondarily lacking bone and having cartilaginous endoskeleton; typically two pairs of jointed appendages; head with nostrils, eyes, ears, and semicircular canals; heart ventral, circulatory system closed, with red and white blood corpuscles; skin two-layered with outer epidermis and inner dermis, latter primitively bony

Superclass Agnatha Lack jaws and appendages; endoskeleton limited to vertebral column and cranium; single median nostril

Class Ostracodermi Ostracoderms; extinct; body armored with dermal bone; filter feeding by means of expanded pharynx; lungs probably present; probably originally freshwater (*Cephalaspis*)

Class Cyclostomata Lampreys and hagfish; dermal armor and bone lacking, endoskeleton cartilaginous; skin scaleless; lungs absent; mouth suctorial with horny teeth; metamorphose from filter-feeding larva to parasitic adult; hagfish hermaphroditic (*Entosphenus, Myxine*)

Superclass Gnathostomata Have jaws and two pairs of limbs (pectoral and pelvic)

Class Placodermi Placoderms; extinct, probably ancestors of bony and cartilaginous fishes; extensively armored with dermal bone (*Dinichthyes*)

Class Chondrichthyes Cartilaginous fishes; mostly marine; bone lacking; body dorsoventrally flattened, tail heterocercal (with larger dorsal lobe), mouth and nostrils ventral; scales toothlike (placoid); fins broad-based; carnivorous

Subclass Elasmobranchii Gill clefts not covered by operculum; pair of spiracles open dorsally behind jaw; includes orders *Selachii* (sharks) and *Batoidei* (skates and rays)

Subclass Holocephali Chimaeras; gill opening covered by operculum, no spiracle; scales lacking (*Chimaera*)

Class Osteichthyes Bony fishes; endoskeleton of bone and cartilage; dermal scales flat, discoidal or rectangular, not toothlike; mouth usually terminal; body usually laterally compressed; fins narrow-based and maneuverable, tail usually with both lobes equal (homocercal)

Subclass Actinopterygii Ray-finned fishes; pectoral and pelvic fins supported by dermal rays, without fleshy basal lobes; nasal sacs do not open into mouth cavity

Superorder Chondrostei Sturgeons, polypterus; scales of thick, rectangular ganoid type; other primitive features present (*Acipenser, Polypterus*)

Superorder Holostei Bowfin, garpike; scales ganoid or cycloid (*Amia, Lepidosteus*)

Superorder Teleostei Modern ray-finned fishes; body scaleless or with nonbony cycloid or ctenoid scales; swim bladder seldom with connection to gut, not used in respiration; two major orders are *Isospondyli* (soft-rayed fish such as salmon) and *Acanthopterygii* (spiny-rayed fish such as perch)

Subclass Choanichthyes Scales cycloid, nostrils open into mouth cavity; paired fins typically with fleshy lobe at base

Superorder Crossopterygii Lobe-finned fishes; mostly extinct, ancestral to amphibians (*Osteolepis, Latimeria*)

Superorder Dipnoi Lungfish; single or paired air bladder specialized for breathing; paired fins lobed or vestigial (*Protopterus*)

Class Amphibia Amphibians; endoskeleton bony; metamorphosis from aquatic fishlike larva with gills to four-footed (tetrapod), terrestrial adult having lungs; toes commonly webbed and clawless; skin soft and moist; most orders extinct, surviving ones being *Apoda* (limbless burrowing caecilians), *Caudata* (tailed salamanders), and *Anura* (tailless frogs and toads)

Class Reptilia Reptiles; endoskeleton bony, exoskeleton of epidermal horny (keratinized) scales or plates; dermal bony plates or ossicles also may be present; legs land-adapted with clawed toes; no aquatic larval stage; egg amniotic, laid on land, with hard or leathery shell; important extinct orders include *Therapsida* (mammal-like reptiles, the ancestors of mammals), *Archosauria* (ancestors of dinosaurs, crocodiles, and birds), *Saurischia* (lizard-hipped dinosaurs), *Ornithischia* (bird-hipped dinosaurs), *Pterosauria* (flying reptiles), *Ichthyosauria* (fish-shaped marine forms), and *Plesiosauria* (long-necked marine forms); living orders include *Testudinata* (turtles), *Rhynchocephalia* (tuatara), *Crocodilia* (crocodilians), and *Squamata* (lizards and snakes)

Class Aves Birds; endoskeleton bony, highly modified for flight with trunk vertebrae fused, forelimbs modified into wings, stance bipedal, breastbone usually keeled, mouth with toothless beak; exoskeleton of epidermal feathers and scales (on legs); homoiothermal; egg amniotic, large-yolked, hard-shelled, incubated by parent; about 27 living orders including *Anseriformes* (geese, ducks), *Falconiformes* (hawks, eagles), *Galliformes* (poultry, quails), *Charadriiformes* (gulls, sandpipers), *Columbiformes* (pigeons), *Psittaciformes* (parrots), *Strigiformes* (owls), and *Passeriformes,* by far the largest order (perching birds, including sparrows, robins, crows, jays, and many others)

Class Mammalia Mammals; endoskeleton bony, exoskeleton of epidermal hair and some scales; red blood corpuscles lacking nuclei; muscular diaphragm separates thorax and abdomen; homoiothermal; egg amniotic but lacking yolk except in monotremes; young fed on milk from mammary glands; teeth diversified for various diets

Subclass Prototheria Egg-laying mammals (*Order Monotremata*); duckbilled platypus and echidna

Subclass Theria Viviparous (live-bearing) mammals

Infraclass Metatheria Pouched mammals (*Order Marsupialia*) including koala, kangaroos, opossums

Infraclass Eutheria Placental mammals, that is, forms in which a placental attachment forms between embryo and mother's uterus allowing unborn young to receive nourishment from mother's bloodstream; important orders include *Insectivora* (shrews, hedgehogs, moles), *Chiroptera* (bats), *Carnivora* (seals, walruses, dogs, cats, bears, weasels), *Rodentia* (gnawing mammals including squirrels, rats, woodchucks, beavers), *Lagomorpha* (rabbits, hares, pikas), *Edentata* (forms with degenerate or no teeth, including anteaters, sloths, armadillos), *Cetacea* (fish-shaped marine mammals including whales and porpoises), *Proboscidea* (elephants), *Perissodactyla* (odd-toed hoofed mammals such as horses and rhinoceroses), *Artiodactyla* (even-toed hoofed mammals such as pigs, camels, and ruminants including cattle, deer, and sheep), *Sirenia* (sea cows and manatees), and *Primates* (lemurs, monkeys, apes, man)

REVIEW AND DISCUSSION

1 What properties of viruses make it appropriate to consider them as intermediate between the biotic and abiotic?

2 List each phylum described in this chapter in which one or more major evolutionary breakthroughs or innovations have taken place. Summarize these innovations, and provide an explanation of their impact upon the further history of plant evolution or animal evolution.

3 Explain why each of the following groups of organisms are of particular interest to students of evolution: (*a*) euglenophytes; (*b*) flagellate protozoans; (*c*) chlorophytes; (*d*) ostracoderms; (*e*) crossopterygians; (*f*) amphibians.

4 Summarize the various kinds of reproductive mechanisms found in Phylum Chlorophyta, and discuss alternation of generations as it occurs in algae, bryophytes, and tracheophytes.

5 Explain why euglenophytes are considered to be *plant-animals* while fungi, which are heterotrophic like animals, are classified as being true *plants*.

6 Why are the chlorophytes considered the most probable ancestors of land plants? What evidence is there that the tracheophytes arose directly from the chlorophytes and not from the bryophytes?

7 Each of the following groups has at least some terrestrial members; explain why each is imperfectly adapted to life on land: (*a*) bryophytes; (*b*) molluscs; (*c*) chlorophytes; (*d*) ferns; (*e*) amphibians.

8 Specify the ways in which each of the following is important for the well-being of the rest of the living world: (*a*) bacteria; (*b*) fungi; (*c*) diatoms; (*d*) dinoflagellates; (*e*) insects; (*f*) desmids.

9 What evidence is presented in this chapter that the phaeophytes, pyrrophytes, and chrysophytes belong to one line of algal descent, the rhodophytes to a second line, and the chlorophytes to a third?

10 For what modes of life is *radial* symmetry most appropriate? *Bilateral* symmetry? Explain, giving examples.

11 What specific advances are shown by (*a*) amphibians over fish; (*b*) reptiles over amphibians; (*c*) birds over reptiles; (*d*) mammals over reptiles; (*e*) eutherians over marsupials?

12 What peculiarity of the chordate nervous system may have made it more suited for enlargement and increase in complexity than those of nonchordates?

REFERENCES

BOLD, H. C. *The Plant Kingdom.* Englewood Cliffs, N.J.: Prentice-Hall, Inc., 1960. A useful reference on major plant groups.

BUCHSBAUM, R., AND L. J. MILNE *The Lower Animals.* Garden City, N.Y.: Doubleday & Co., Inc., 1960. A nontechnical discussion of invertebrates, distinguished by outstanding photographs.

DELEVORYAS, T. *Plant Diversification.* New York: Holt, Rinehart and Winston, Inc., 1966. A synopsis of plant evolution.

DITTMER, H. J. *Phylogeny and Form in the Plant Kingdom.* Princeton, N.J.: D. Van Nostrand Company, Inc., 1964. An advanced treatment of plant-structure evolution.

DOYLE, W. T. *Nonvascular Plants: Form and Function.* Belmont, Calif.: Wadsworth Publishing Company, 1964. A useful compendium of information on the lower plants.

ECHLIN, P. "The Blue-green Algae," *Sci. Amer.,* **214** (1966).

HANSEN, E. D. *Animal Diversity.* Englewood Cliffs, N.J.: Prentice-Hall, Inc., 1961. Provides a succinct and lucid résumé of major body plans in the animal kingdom.

HORNE, R. W. "The Structure of Viruses," *Sci. Amer.,* **208** (1963).

PESSON, P. *The World of Insects.* New York: McGraw-Hill Book Co., Inc., 1959. A fascinating exposition of insect life, with numerous colorful photographs.

ROMER, A. S. *Man and the Vertebrates.* Chicago: University of Chicago Press, 1941. A now classic exposition of vertebrate structure and evolution, comparing modern and fossil types.

——— "Major Steps in Vertebrate Evolution," *Science,* **158** (1967). A master comparative anatomist succinctly traces the rise of vertebrates through a series of adaptive innovations.

WEISS, F. J. "The Useful Algae," *Sci. Amer.,* **187** (1952).

YOUNG, J. Z. *The Life of Vertebrates* (2nd ed.). London and New York: Oxford University Press, 1962. A comprehensive yet highly readable volume, excellent for reference upon specific aspects of vertebrate life.

Part 2

CAUSES OF BIOTIC DIVERSITY

It is interesting to contemplate an entangled bank, clothed with many plants of many kinds, with birds singing on the bushes, with various insects flitting about, and with worms crawling through the damp earth, and to reflect that these elaborately constructed forms, so different from each other, and dependent on each other in so complex a manner, have all been produced by laws acting around us. These laws, taken in the largest sense, being Growth with Reproduction; Inheritance which is almost implied by reproduction; Variability from the indirect and direct action of the external conditions of life, and from use and disuse; a Ratio of Increase so high as to lead to a Struggle for Life, and as a consequence to Natural Selection, entailing Divergence of Character and the Extinction of less-improved forms. Thus, from the war of nature, from famine and death, the most exalted object which we are capable of conceiving, namely, the production of the higher animals, directly follows. There is grandeur in this view of life, with its several powers, having been originally breathed into a few forms or into one; and that, whilst this planet has gone cycling on according to the fixed law of gravity, from so simple a beginning endless forms most beautiful and most wonderful have been, and are being, evolved.

CHARLES DARWIN

Diversity, as we have seen in Part 1, is a cardinal attribute of the living world. In the following chapters the adaptive significance and causes of biotic diversity will be examined, and the principles summarized below will be illustrated by a number of examples drawn from various aspects of the living world.

Diversity contributes to the success of the biotic world by reducing competition and increasing the capacity of life to exploit various potential habitats.

The nature of living systems is such that diversification is easier to achieve and energetically less costly than a condition of complete adaptability, which would be an alternative to diversification as a means of exploiting all possible modes of life.

Biotic diversity is an outcome of the interplay between the mutable hereditary mechanisms of life and environmental factors, both biotic and abiotic, that define the survival value of chance alterations in heredity.

The organism is an inextricable component of an indissoluble "organism-environment complex," which is in a sense the functional unit of adaptation. Living things shape their environment and in turn are shaped, both in form and function, by their environment. A constant flow of matter and energy passes between organism and environment, and therefore no living thing is ever static in composition.

Biotic communities consist of diversified aggregations of species that not only share certain tolerances of prevailing environmental conditions but have evolved toward a state of stability in which competition is minimal and cooperation and mutual exploitation maximal.

Competition is a selective factor that operates primarily among individuals of the same species and results in certain individuals contributing more progeny than others. Nevertheless, competition within a species is often minimized in various ways, such as diversification within the species.

Living things are subject to change: evolution is the change, through successive generations, of the hereditary composition of a population. As such, it is a universal and unending process.

At all levels of biotic organization from the molecular to the supraorganismal, the living world constantly evolves toward a condition of adaptation (fitness to survive and perpetuate itself under particular conditions of life); however, the state of adaptation possessed by any organism or population always falls short of the optimum, both because of limited genetic potentialities and because the total adaptive state represents a compromise resulting from the need to adapt to a variety of selective factors that may have opposing effects on the survival of the organism.

Chapter 3

THE INTEGRATION OF ORGANISM AND ENVIRONMENT

BIOLOGY, LIKE GEOLOGY, IS A SCIENCE that deals with the fourth dimension: *time*. Biologists interpret the present in the light of the past, not merely describing life as it is today but seeking to understand the forces that have brought into being the myriad forms of life that constitute the biosphere. These forces exist both within the organism and in its environment. They are as operative now as in the past and will inexorably determine the future of life—including that of man.

There is scarcely an aspect of life that does not represent a manifestation of organic adaptation, that is, "fitness" to survive and propagate. The diversity of life, overviewed in Chapter 2, is itself an outcome of the process by which life adapts to its environment. Underlying this diversity is a common foundation of essential life processes that developed to a high level of efficiency long before life began to diversify into the more than a million and a half species recognized today.

Although the effectiveness of adaptation is tested in terms of individual survival and prolificacy, it is important to understand that this capability depends on effective adaptation at every level of biotic organization, from molecule to ecosystem. The interactions between chance inheritable changes and environmental factors operate at all levels of life and have been largely responsible for determining the nature of the biosphere. In turn, living things have radically altered the face of the earth and at the same time have caused profound changes in the composition of its atmosphere.

3.1 □ THE ADAPTIVE VALUE OF DIVERSITY

Is diversification merely an incidental by-product of the mutability of living matter or does the very fact of biotic diversity somehow enhance the potential for survival of the living world as a whole? Biotic diversity abets the success of the biosphere in two ways: (1) it promotes the capacity of living things to make use of a variety of habitats and allows them to withstand or exploit various factors in their physicochemical environment; (2) it allows many kinds of creatures to coexist without competing too severely for environmental commodities and allows various types of adaptive interactions among organisms to be built up.

If all living things were alike they would require similar habitats, would obtain nutrients in the same manner, and would be identical in their capacity for enduring or exploiting their environment. Were they alike, they would probably interact in only one major way—competitively—for as they proliferated they would vie increasingly for space, light, nutrients, and other needs.

Few types of organisms are capable of exploiting a wide range of habitats. The capacity to survive under a wide range of physical conditions depends either upon great physiological adaptability or upon genetic flexibility. The versatility that would permit a single kind of organism to exploit a number of greatly differing habitats with equal facility is difficult to achieve. For one thing, the total amount of hereditary material that an individual organism can contain is limited, and it is doubtful that the genetic mechanisms of any given creature could become sufficiently elaborate to allow it to modify itself rapidly and efficiently in both form and function so as to cope with many different environments. Furthermore, to develop and maintain enough physical equipment, for example, to permit an animal to run, swim, and fly with equal skill would so increase its energy requirements that it might be unable to meet them even by constant feeding. No type of organism has yet evolved total adaptability; man has vastly augmented his physical capabilities by the invention of artificial adjuncts, such as aqualungs.

Diversification through genetic flexibility is far easier to achieve than complete adaptability and for the biotic world as a whole has proven just as effective. Through diversification the living world has gained access to almost every type of physical environment found on the surface of this planet. At the same time, biotic diversity permits a host of creatures to share each habitat, forming communities in which competition is mitigated because the diverse needs seldom directly conflict.

There is still another value to the diversification of life: higher organisms have evolved many capabilities which less advanced creatures lack, but these advances have been made at the cost of giving up other vital capabilities possible for lower organisms. For instance, animals can move about and perform complex types of behavior but they are unable to make materials such as carbohydrates and vitamins, which they must have to survive; plant life, while incapable of many of the activities of animals, can perform these necessary tasks. Since animals rely on plants for food, their hereditary potential has been developed in other directions.

3.2 □ THE SIGNIFICANCE OF ADAPTATION

The term *adaptation* may be used correctly in several ways. First, it may designate the *process* of hereditary change and selection by which various kinds of organisms attain fitness for survival and reproduction. This process never ceases, for circumstances are never static. Habitats change both cyclically (as in annual and longer-phase climatic cycles) and progressively (as in the case of the ever-increasing salinity of the ocean), and living things must adapt accordingly or become extinct.

In its second context, adaptation may refer to the *condition* or state of fitness possessed by an organism at a certain time under a given set of conditions. As a state or condition of being, adaptation depends on how stable the environment may be: species that have achieved a high level of adaptation to a certain set of conditions by becoming highly specialized often fail to survive when the conditions change.

In its third usage, the term adaptation may designate some particular structural or functional *attribute* that enhances the survival of the organism possessing it. When used in this sense it is important to remember that not only are certain specializations (such as a giraffe's long neck or a duck's webbed feet) correctly termed adaptations, but that *all* functional organs, all of the body's finely adjusted metabolic machinery, constitute adaptations, for all contribute toward survival by enabling the organism to cope with the conditions under which it lives. Each species is characterized by an assemblage of adaptations that not only fit it for its mode of existence much as a key fits a lock but also allow individual parts of the organism to function in harmonious integration. Every important attribute of a species, as well as nearly all of the features that appear to be inconsequential until the appropriate investigation discloses their adaptive value, may be considered adaptations. For example, the colored spot near the tip of a mature sea gull's beak was once considered a mere item of adornment until it was demonstrated that this spot stimulates and directs the pecking response of the gull chick, and this pecking in turn causes the parent bird to regurgitate food for the chick. With regard to feeding in general, we may say that mouth, jaws, teeth, tongue, alimentary tract, and digestive glands are all adaptations that have proved successful for various animals as means of obtaining and processing food. The perfection of these adaptations has required a gradual process of chance genetic change, followed by perpetuation of favorable variants and elimination of unfavorable ones.

A An example of adaptation: a leaf

A leaf is a complicated organ of a vascular plant, made up of several kinds of specialized cells or tissues. It is the major organ within which the chemical reactions of photosynthesis are carried out and sugars are produced. As such, it has evolved a number of adaptive characteristics (Figure 3.1). (1) A leaf characteristically has a high ratio of surface to volume, which facilitates the absorption of light and exchange of gases with the air. (2) Leaf tissues are rich in chlorophyll, the pigment that absorbs light energy used in chemical reactions by which sugars are built. (3) The leaf's surface is shielded from dehydration by a waxy cuticle that is perforated by microscopic pores or stomates through which gaseous exchange takes place. (4) Each stomate is flanked by a pair of guard cells that open and close the stomate, allowing the leaf to conserve water when necessary by reducing its evaporation from the stomate. (5) The leaf's network of veins is composed of conductive or vascular tissue by means of which materials in solution may be efficiently transported from the roots to the leaves and from the leaves to other parts of the plant.

These properties of a leaf contribute to the plant's survival by (1) enabling it effectively to exploit certain abiotic environmental factors (namely, light, water, carbon dioxide, and various minerals) and (2) helping the plant to function as an integrated organism, utilizing materials manufactured in the leaf for the growth and energy requirements of all the other portions of the plant.

A leaf can also serve to illustrate the principle of *coadaptation*. By this we mean that living things must not only adapt to their external environment, but that *internal* adaptation is equally important. The various parts of the whole organism must be coadapted so that they improve one another's functional efficiency. For example, the overall shape of the typical leaf, with extensive surface area, contributes to the efficiency of chlorophyll molecules within the leaf cells by exposing them to light more effectively. This increased exposure to light would however be futile were there no means for facilitating gaseous exchange, since the absorption of CO_2 and the elimination of O_2 are also necessary for photosynthesis. The leaf's activities in combining inorganic molecules into organic ones rich in chemical energy would again be of little use if the plant were not equipped to transport water and minerals from the roots to the leaves and to carry the products of photosynthesis to other parts of the plant for use or storage. Thus we see that the various tissues of a leaf are not only adapted for exploiting the external environment, but are also coadapted to allow the plant to live as an effectively coordinated unit.

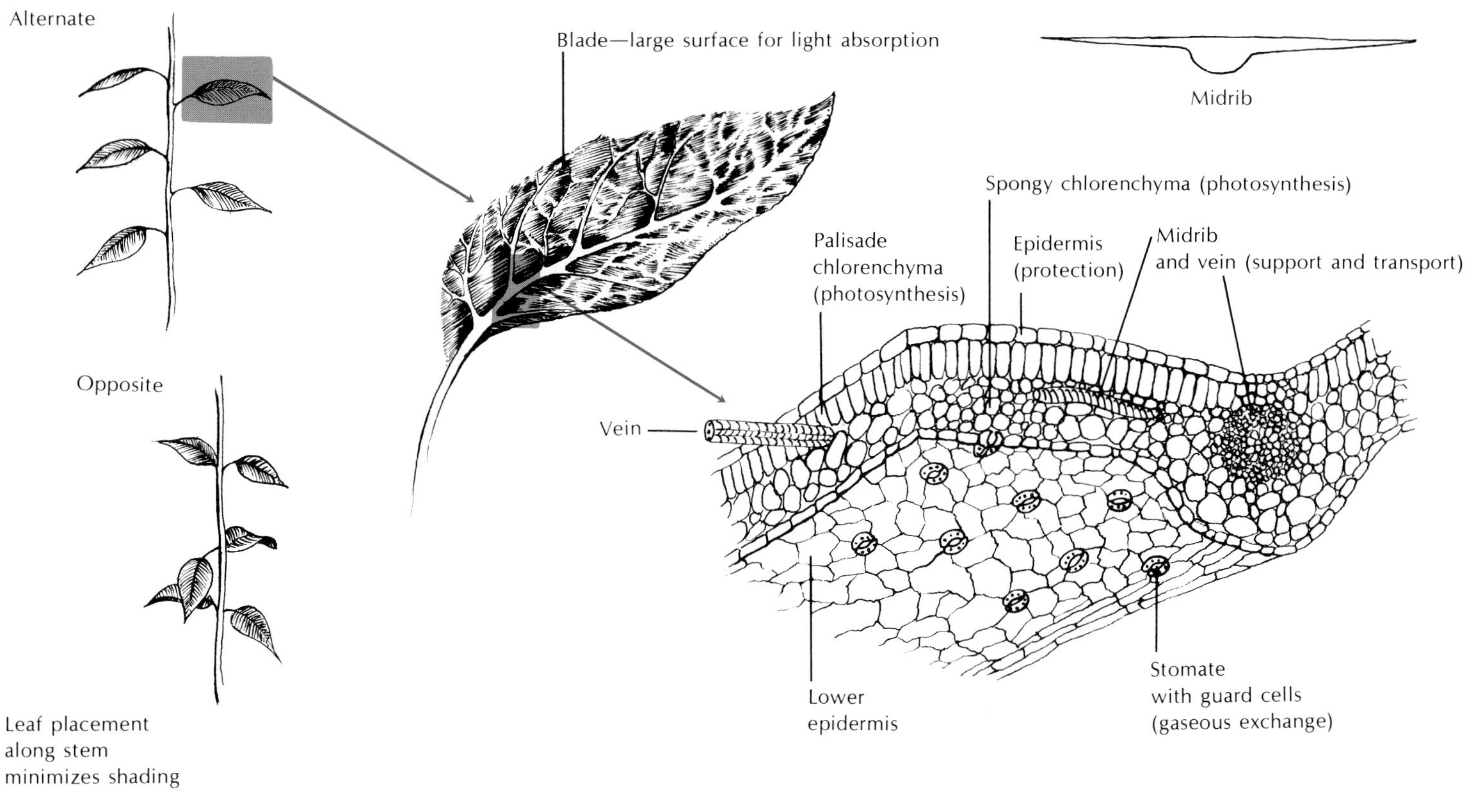

Figure 3.1 □ **Adaptation to environment: leaf structure seen at successive levels of magnification.**

B The origins of adaptation

Adaptation is not achieved by some mystical prior planning. It is attainable in only two ways: (1) through physiological and behavioral adjustments made by the individual organism during its own lifetime; (2) through the chance occurrence of effective changes in heredity. Although various external and internal factors define the survival value of hereditary changes, these factors cannot cause favorable genetic changes to occur. On the contrary, hereditary changes or mutations arise at random, and *selection* is the ensuing process by which these factors test the capacity of the mutant to survive and reproduce itself. Individuals with favorable characteristics tend to leave more progeny: favorable traits are thus conserved and eventually become the norm for the population, while unfavorable traits tend to be eradicated.

The process of selection may be either natural or artificial. *Natural selection* results in adaptation of organism to environment and in coadaptation of body parts to one another, for here the selective factors that test survival are natural ones, arising from the organism's natural conditions of existence. *Artificial selection* is practiced by man in selecting domestic plants and animals for his requirements. Here the selective factors are artificial, in that they represent arbitrary criteria that enhance the organism's usefulness to man. Such artificial selection may reduce the organism's fitness for the kind of existence normal to its species. For instance, through selective breeding of spontaneously occurring genetic variants man has developed breeds of cattle that are short-legged, broad-chested, short-horned, and docile to the point of stupidity. These features, while making cattle more manageable and more likely to put on weight rather than becoming lean, muscular, alert, and decidedly dangerous, are actually *maladaptive* for the cattle in the sense that they lower the chance for survival in the wild state. Similarly, through natural selection plants that produce large quantities of seed would be more likely to perpetuate the species; however man has selected a number of seedless variants that would die out in the wild and perpetuates them by grafting and root cuttings.

As a rule, artificial selection tends to reduce genetic diversity by making the population more homogeneous for the desired traits; natural selection, on the other hand, operates to preserve diversity and genetic heterogeneity: in the first place, outbred organisms are frequently more vigorous than inbred ones (a condition known as "hybrid vigor"); in the second place, only through preserving genetic heterogeneity can a population maintain a broad capacity for variability so that responses may be made that permit it to survive sudden crises. In the face of environmental change the inbred, homogeneous population is less likely to have survivors than the population that is genetically diverse.

To summarize, spontaneous changes in the hereditary material coupled with the influence of natural selective factors bring about a more or less enduring state of adaptation for living things. Any hereditary change that confers even a slight benefit in terms of helping the organism survive and reproduce tends to be conserved while any change that acts to the contrary is minimized or eliminated. In Chapters 8 and 9 we shall examine the nature of genetic changes and how they are transmitted. The importance of environmental factors in natural selection will now be considered.

3.3 □ THE "ORGANISM-ENVIRONMENT COMPLEX"

Men often frame ideas in terms of paired opposites: good-evil, true-false, plant-animal, mind-body, organism-environment. Such dichotomies are misleading when they overlook intergradations (as with "true-false" and "plant-animal") or contradict a fundamental unity (as in "mind-body" or "organism-environment"). It is impossible to comprehend the extent of the reciprocal involvement of organism and environment if we think of an organism as complete in itself and therefore separable from its environment. The body of each individual organism must be totally constructed of materials obtained from the environment. Furthermore, during the course of evolution the forms that life has taken have largely been dictated by living and nonliving factors in the environment. Conversely, the organism affects both its biotic and abiotic environments.

This interaction is all-pervasive and endless: mass and energy perpetually pass back and forth across the boundary between organism and environment. Tracer studies conducted with radioisotopes demonstrate convincingly the constant exchange of materials between a living body and its environment. For instance, plants grown in an atmosphere artificially enriched with radioactive carbon (^{14}C) in the form of carbon dioxide gas ($^{14}CO_2$) incorporate these tagged atoms into their own tissues; if these tissues are then eaten by an animal, the ^{14}C becomes detectable in the animal's flesh. In time it may reappear as tagged $^{14}CO_2$ breathed out from the animal's lungs or as tagged bicarbonate ion in its urine. In the form of bicarbonate, ^{14}C may next be taken up to become part of a snail's shell; as $^{14}CO_2$ it may once more enter the leaf of a plant. This perpetual cycling carries materials back and forth between the living and nonliving worlds and from organism to organism.

We see, therefore, that the individual living thing is an inextricable component of an organism-environment complex consisting of itself, other members of its species, creatures of other types, and physicochemical factors of the abiotic environment. It is senseless in its broadest context to consider

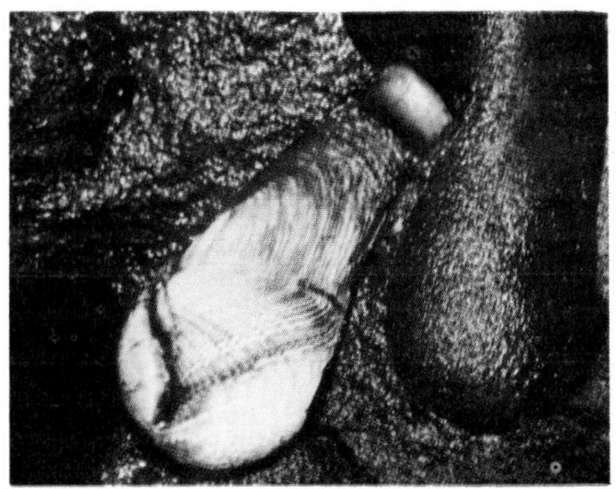

(a)

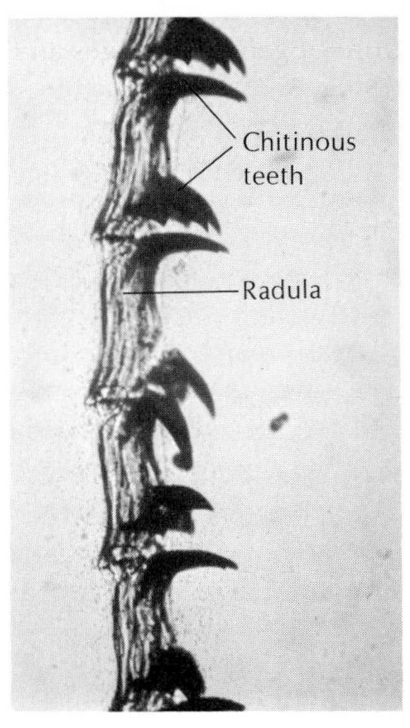

(b)

Figure 3.2 □ Animals as agents of erosion. (*a*) Piddock in its burrow in rock (*courtesy of General Biological, Inc., Chicago*). (*b*) Radular teeth of limpet (*courtesy of Dr. James H. McLean*). The radula, a chitinous band, here shown dissected out of the limpet's mouth, bears rows of teeth used in rasping algae off rocks. Limpets also wear away the rock itself and excavate cavities in which they lie protected to await high tide.

adaptation outside the frame of reference of the total complex.

The relationships of an organism with all factors in its environment are termed *ecological relationships.* For clarity we should stipulate that these relationships are *reciprocal* and that they operate at *all levels of biotic organization.* Ecological relationships do not only involve the organism in toto (such as a rabbit, man, or snake) but involve life at all levels down to its ultimate molecular organization. We shall illustrate this statement (1) by considering ways in which living things affect their environment, including the surface of the earth and its climate and atmosphere, and (2) with an example that will demonstrate how the biotic world at all of its organizational levels is adapted for utilizing a particular environmental factor (oxygen).

3.4 □ THE IMPACT OF ORGANISM ON ENVIRONMENT

Each living thing affects other living things in its environment as well as exerting effects upon its abiotic environment. A skein of mutual relationships, cooperative, competitive, and exploitative, ties all organisms into the vast fabric that is the biotic community. *Conspecific* relationships having to do with mating, rearing of young, and other aspects of social life exist among members of the same species; *heterospecific* relationships (such as the use of one creature by another for food) exist among organisms of different species. These relationships exert a powerful and continuing influence on the evolution of living things: for instance, the appearance of mammals in the habitats of flowering plants encouraged perpetuation of variants in fruit structure that aided seed dispersal by allowing the fruit (such as the cocklebur) to be caught in the fur of mammals. Hereditary changes that affect conspecific and heterospecific interactions are as subject to natural selection as are changes that affect the organism's adaptation to its abiotic environment.

Let us now consider through a few specific examples how living things alter their nonliving environment.

A Effects on the earth's surface

Many living things contribute to the erosion of rock (Figure 3.2). Lichens and bacteria secrete rock-etching acids, plant roots mechanically fragment it, and animals such as the piddock (a boring clam) honeycomb soft rocks, accelerating their decomposition. The soil formed by the decomposition of rock is protected against further erosion by the binding action of plant roots. Organic residue in the form of humus accumulates in the soil, which becomes a community of microorganisms, burrowing animals, and plant roots. Thus organisms help to form soil and then proceed to exploit it as a supportive, nutritive, and protective substratum.

The effectiveness of plants as soil binders is seen dramatically wherever watersheds are destroyed by fire or improper cultivation (Figure 3.3). Rainwater, no longer held by sod until it can penetrate deeply into the ground, runs off the surface, carrying away the denuded soil, clogging river channels with silt, and flooding lowlands. Man's attempts to cure these conditions, which have often resulted from his mishandling of the habitat, have frequently been shortsighted. Flood-control dams constructed downriver accelerate the upstream deposition of sediments, extending flood damage farther and farther up the watercourses. Restoring the watersheds by sodding and reforestation generally ameliorate the problem by correcting its causes.

Living things also change the face of the earth by contributing extensively to the production of sedimentary rock. Strata of limestone thousands of meters thick originate as vast deposits of the tiny shells of foraminiferan protozoans. As the shells accumulate on the floor of shallow temporary seas that from time to time cover parts of the continents (as is the case whenever a long period of warm climate causes the polar icecaps to melt and the sea level to rise correspondingly) they are compressed by their own weight and that of overlying sediments and gradually are altered into layers of limestone or chalk, which upon further compression and heating may be changed into marble. Continental elevation or a drop in sea level eventually may expose these sedimentary layers as dry land, whereupon they become subject to erosion and exploitation by terrestrial organisms. They may be quarried as building materials by man. Eroding, they yield calcium carbonate ($CaCO_3$) which is taken up by plant roots and utilized in their tissues; eaten by animals, plant tissues then contribute calcium for animal skeletal parts and other organs. In due time, calcium released by weathering of rock and by organic decay returns to the sea and is once again used by marine organisms and eventually built into limestone (Figure 3.4).

Figure 3.3 □ **Erosion following fire, where disappearance of plant cover leads to watershed destruction (Limestone Hills, Montana). Note soil loss and accumulation of rubble in small draw. (*Photograph by J. Harvey and D. Rittersbacher, U.S. Forest Service.*)**

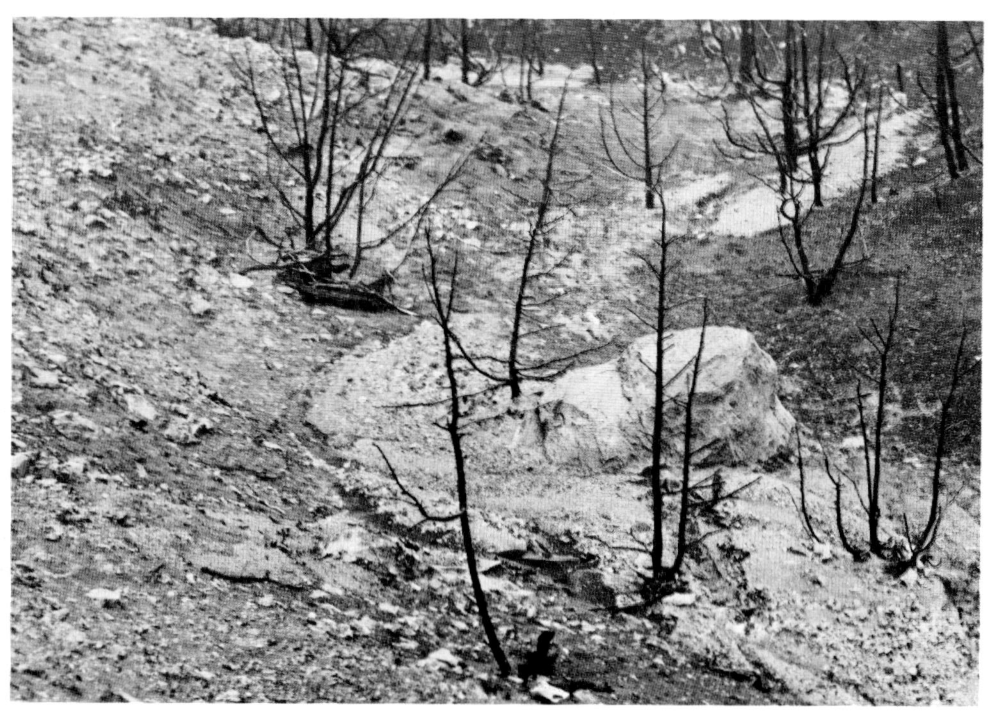

Between latitudes 30°N and 30°S the earth's geography is altered by extensive coral reefs built up through the combined efforts of coral polyps and coralline red algae. Coral reefs form the foundations of many islands and peninsulas (including the state of Florida). Coral land masses, together with their quiet-water lagoons rich in marine life, have supported the development of human societies, particularly throughout the southern Pacific area.

B Effects on climate and atmosphere

Both local and world climate may be changed by living things. An extensive forest creates its own climate, both because its foliage breaks the force with which rain strikes the soil and consequently preserves the soil's permeability to water and because it contributes large quantities of water to the atmosphere as vapor. A single sunflower plant has been found to transpire about 24 liters of water during its 4.5-month growing period, but a maize plant is capable of transpiring as much as ten times that amount (about 240 liters) during a life span of 3 months! It is easy to see that an entire forest transpires vast amounts of water and that local humidity and rainfall are substantially affected by it. In regions where man has cut away the forests, such dramatic changes in climate have sometimes ensued that even deserts have been created.

World climate and the composition of the atmosphere are greatly influenced by the activities of living things. The proportions of atmospheric oxygen, carbon dioxide, and water vapor are most susceptible to biotic influences. It is estimated that annually the world's flora fixes some 30 to 60 billion tons (possibly much more) of carbon derived from atmospheric CO_2 and releases around 60 to 120 billion tons of O_2 liberated by the breakdown of water molecules!

Many scientists believe that prior to the evolution of photosynthesis the earth's atmosphere was devoid of free oxygen and that photosynthesizing plants have been responsible for producing all of the O_2 that now makes up about 20 percent of the atmosphere. If so, plant life is responsible for all oxidizing reactions in which atmospheric oxygen is used in combustion and in oxidizing materials of the earth's crust (such as the rusting of iron to iron oxides). At present it is estimated that photosynthesis could completely replenish atmospheric O_2 within only about 30 years. Since micro-

Figure 3.4 □ The calcium cycle.

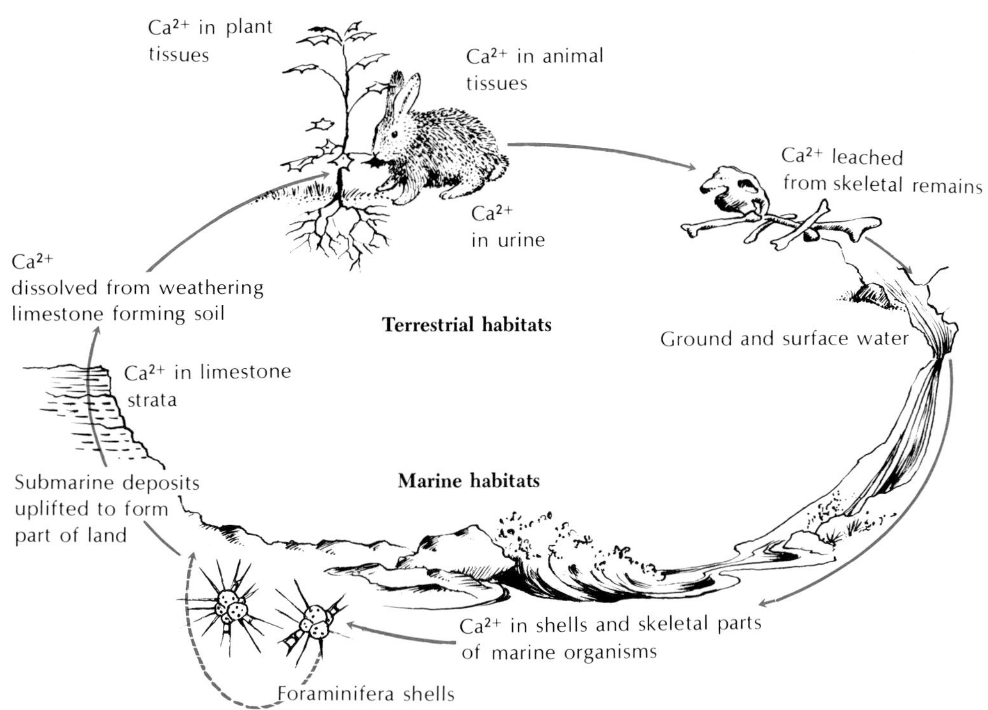

scopic marine plants contribute about 80 percent of the O_2 on which all forms of animal life depend for survival, it is a matter of concern that recent evidence indicates that the photosynthetic activity of these plants is being jeopardized by the accumulation of insecticide residues (especially DDT) in sea water.

At present CO_2 comprises only about 0.044 percent of the atmosphere; it is removed from the air by photosynthesizing plants and returned to the air by decay, combustion, and oxidative metabolism. Fluctuations in the concentration of atmospheric CO_2 can alter world climate significantly, for this gas is especially effective in trapping heat and producing a thermal-blanketing effect. Some scientists are concerned about the rate at which CO_2 is now being released to the atmosphere as a result of industrial combustion and other human activities involving the burning of fuel; they fear the earth's mean temperature gradually will rise due to the heat-trapping effect of this added CO_2.

Human technological activities are also changing the atmosphere by the liberation of contaminants that do not break down readily but accumulate in the air and other parts of the ecosystem. A number of toxic compounds are detectable in the air many miles from the industrialized areas where they are produced. In the presence of light some pollutants such as butene and propylene enter into photochemical reactions with other atmospheric components such as oxides of nitrogen to form even more noxious substances (including peroxides, ozone, and various acids). Vehicles with internal combustion engines are responsible for a large proportion of these contaminants. For example, at one time the average automobile driven in the state of California was estimated to contribute to the atmosphere nearly 3 kg of contaminants daily; though this amount is reduced by use of "smog-control" devices, the increased number of automobiles in use (an estimated 6 million in Los Angeles County) has so far offset the advantage gained.

Atmospheric contamination with finely dispersed radioactive materials has resulted from open-air nuclear testing. Microscopic particles of "fallout" remain in the atmosphere indefinitely and may be breathed in; most however eventually settle and can then be incorporated into the bodies of organisms where they may accumulate to concentrations many times greater than that at which they occurred in the atmosphere. Strontium 90 and cesium 137 are particularly dangerous fission products because of their relatively long half-life (about 30 years) and because strontium can be incorporated in living tissues in place of calcium (particularly in skeletal materials), while cesium can take the place of potassium in all tissues. Besides harming the individual organism, these radioisotopes can cause changes in the hereditary material for generations to come.

We can see that the effects of living things (notably man) upon the composition of the earth's atmosphere produce an unavoidable feedback upon the living world, sometimes to its detriment.

3.5 □ LEVELS OF BIOTIC ORGANIZATION

To understand the manner in which ecological relationships involve all levels of biotic organization, we must first briefly summarize the way in which the complexity of the living world has been built up through succeeding levels of organization. (This important concept will be considered in depth in Part 3.) Life has advanced in complexity by developing the potential of one level of organization and then passing to a higher level, into which all lower levels are integrated. This concept may seem novel to those whose mental image of the living world tends to be restricted to a consideration of organisms per se. The biologically uneducated often view life in terms of a Noah's ark procession of "animals [marching] two by two, the elephant and the kangaroo," from aardvark to zebu. With further insight we come to realize that the organismic level of biotic organization is merely life's most conspicuous manifestation and not necessarily its most fundamental or significant aspect. The organism, which appears to be an independent, singular entity, a discrete "parcel of life," is made up of many smaller functional units, and is at the same time a unit in a higher organizational construct.

Eleven levels of organization may be discerned in the world of life. At the lowest level is the *molecule*. Many kinds of molecules are unique to living systems and some may be unique to single individual organisms. Molecules are organized into *macromolecular complexes* consisting of integrated groups of giant molecules. Some of these form subcellular bodies known as *organelles,* specialized for carrying out specific functions within the *cells*. The cell is the unit of structure and function in all organisms. Metabolism takes place almost exclusively within cells, and cellular activities in turn are the product of the coordinated activities of interdependent organelles and macromolecular complexes. Many organisms consist of but a single cell, but in multicellular organisms cells are specialized into functional types, resulting in an efficient division of labor. A functionally coordinated mass of similar cells is termed a *tissue*. Tissues in turn are associated to form *organs,* which again are specialized for carrying out some particular bodily function. The stomach, for example, is an organ consisting of many kinds of tissues. It is lined internally and covered externally by sheets of cells known as epithelia; its walls contain glands, muscle fibers, blood vessels, and nerves. Its adaptive value rests on the fact that it permits the storage and digestion of food in quantities much greater than could be accomodated if digestion took place solely within individual cells. Sponges are multicellular animals without stomachs, dependent exclusively on microscopic particles captured and digested by individual cells; accordingly, they feed constantly. A sea anemone, on the other hand, may swallow a fish nearly as large as itself, this single meal lasting for many hours.

Coadapted groups of organs are functionally integrated at the level of the *organ system*. The functional efficiency of a stomach, for instance, is greatly augmented if it is part of a digestive system consisting of other organs such as tongue, salivary glands, teeth, pancreas, liver, and intestines. Organ systems in turn constitute the body of the *organism* and, like organs, must be functionally coordinated to bring about integrated bodily activities.

The individual organism is an ephemeral embodiment of the genome (genetic constitution) of its *deme*. A deme is a breeding unit; it is a population of a species that inhabits a particular location and consequently consists of potentially interbreeding individuals. A deme of field mice may occupy a meadow only a few meters in diameter and may exchange little hereditary material with neighboring demes. Within each deme, a complicated web of social bonds may be built up. These social bonds, which include interactions between mates and between parents and offspring, augment both the individual's and the group's potential for survival.

Both the individual organism and the deme are inextricable components of the biotic *community;* this in turn interacts with the abiotic environment to form a balanced system termed an *ecosystem,* in which mass and energy are cyclically exchanged.

A Integration of the levels of life

No single level of biotic organization may be adequately understood if its position relative to other levels of organization is not considered. Problems arise when biologists, because of specialized training or interests, become exclusively preoccupied with a single level of biotic organization. Such an impasse, arising out of an inadequate concept of the multilevel nature of biotic phenomena, long hindered the analysis of the nature of inheritance. Prior to the middle of the nineteenth century, observers concerned mainly with the entire organism ("holists") thought of heredity as a process in which the characteristics of the parents were *blended* in the offspring. (This misconception persists in common parlance in terms such as "mixed blood.") Then Gregor Mendel, an Austrian monk, demonstrated that heredity consisted of the transmission of individual units controlling specific traits. These units might not be expressed, but are not diluted, lost, or permanently blended in the offspring. Later investigators linked Mendel's "unit characters" to visible cellular structures, the chromosomes. At this point dissent arose, for it was plain to some biologists that chromosomes were the determinants of heredity, whereas others contended that only molecules could bring about the reactions required for the development of the organism. According to F. O. Schmitt:*

Both groups—the molecular reductionists on the one hand and the cellular, organismic, or naturalistic holists on the other hand—were right, and both were wrong. The molecular reductionists piled up on the Scylla of molecular componentry because their conceptual models lacked a systems-type organization in which the stored information might be meaningfully processed: the cellular and organismic holists, on the other hand, foundered in

*F. O. Schmitt, "The Physical Basis of Life," *Science,* **149** (1965), 932.

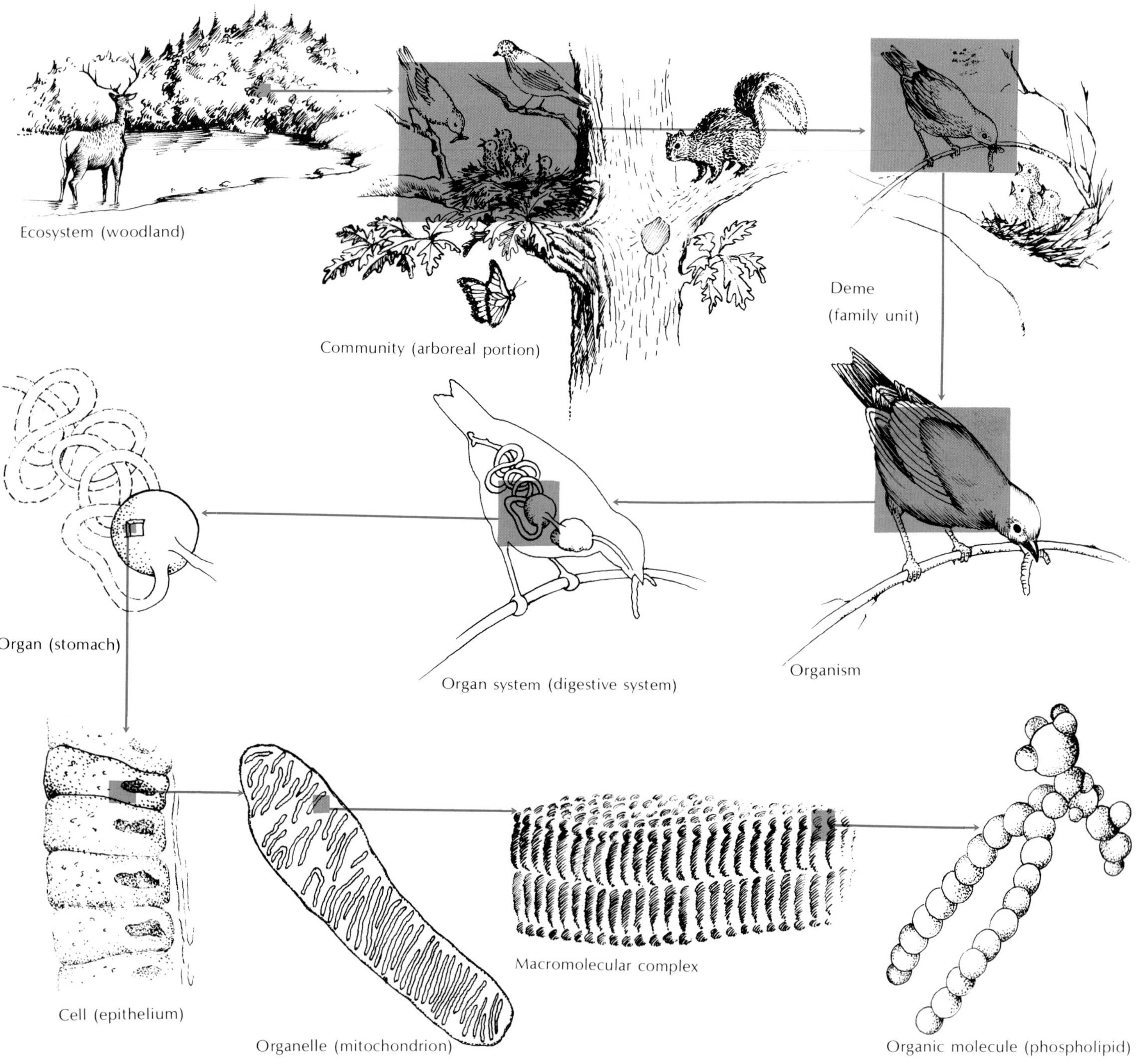
Ecosystem (woodland)
Community (arboreal portion)
Deme
(family unit)
Organism
Organ system (digestive system)
Organ (stomach)
Cell (epithelium)
Organelle (mitochondrion)
Macromolecular complex
Organic molecule (phospholipid)

the Charybdis of reliance on mystical emergent properties of systems devoid of demonstrable information-containing molecular components. In this hierarchical molecule-chromosome-organism impasse, created by artificial professional and parochial barriers of communication, the two groups were prevented from joining forces in a common assault on the problem at all levels . . .

Just as a multilevel approach finally made possible an effective attack upon the riddle of inheritance, so the analysis of organism-environment interactions will also be facilitated if they are thought of as involving all levels of biotic organization: the ecosystem, the community, the deme, the organism, the organ system, the organ, the tissue, the cell, the organelle, the macromolecular complex, and the molecule. Figure 3.5 shows how each level of biotic construction may be resolved into finer levels of organization down to the ultimate atomic components. It depicts part of a forest, including trees, soil, stream, and atmospheric backdrop: an ecosystem. Within the woods a bird family is shown, nesting in a tree and engaged in capturing insect prey. Tree, birds, and insects comprise a portion of the local community. The birds, parents and nestlings, represent a socially integrated portion of a deme. Each bird is a single organism. Using X-ray vision, we see one bird's digestive system. With the aid of a microscope we can examine the wall of one organ, the stomach, noting that it is comprised of various tissues, layers of specialized cells. In a more highly magnified view, we can see that each cell consists of an organized aggregation of organelles composed of macromolecular complexes. The structure of a single organelle (a mitochondrion) is shown. And passing below the level of resolution of the electron microscope, we attempt to visualize the proposed molecular structure of part of the mitochondrial membrane. Finally, there is depicted within this membrane a single phospholipid molecule, of which only the constituent atoms cannot be considered as products of biotic activity.

Figure 3.5 □ Levels of biotic organization, each level a magnified portion of the preceding one.

B Adaptations for the use of oxygen

If the earth's atmosphere contained no oxygen during the early history of life, the most primitive living things neither needed nor could use oxygen. Only after gaseous oxygen (O_2) was released by plants as a waste product of photosynthesis did it become available for biotic use. The first adaptations for making use of this gas must have occurred at the subcellular level when enzyme systems were involved that were capable of using oxygen atoms to rid cells of excess hydrogen atoms liberated during cell metabolism. Some simple organisms still exist that do not use oxygen, but their means of recovering energy from foodstuffs is much less efficient than in those forms which have evolved the molecular means for *aerobic* metabolism.

For unicellular organisms the only special adaptations required for using oxygen are found to be certain enzymes. For multicellular organisms further adaptations are necessary. Active aquatic animals such as fishes need both gills and blood vessels for adequate uptake of oxygen and its transport to the cells; terrestrial animals require lungs or other internal respiratory organs for effective gaseous exchange. In man these organs include the lungs and air passages, including nasal cavity, pharynx, windpipe, and bronchi. In addition, muscles such as the diaphragm and rib muscles are needed to ventilate the lungs. These muscles in turn will not contract unless stimulated by nerve fibers coming from the brain and spinal cord. When oxygen is taken into the bloodstream at the lungs, it is carried within the red blood corpuscles in combination with a protein known as hemoglobin; circulation of the blood is dependent upon the pulsing of the heart, which in turn is regulated by nerve fibers from the brain.

At how many levels of biotic organization have adaptations been developed for the use of oxygen? First, at the ecosystem level, oxygen liberated by green plants is used by many organisms, animal life being completely dependent on plants for survival; animals would be doomed to suffocation were all plant life destroyed (even if food could somehow still be synthesized). Also, free oxygen affects both soil and atmosphere, and combines with other elements to form substances such as nitrous and nitric oxides and iron oxides. Further adaptations permit organisms to use these mineral oxides. Oxygen use is based on adaptations at the molecular level: (1) the oxygen-using metabolic systems are molecular; (2) cellular and organismal structures concerned with uptake and transport of oxygen are built according to a hereditary code spelled out by nucleic acid molecules. At the organelle level we find that the particular substances concerned with oxidative energy release are organized within the bodies known as mitochondria. In higher animals, the uptake and transport of oxygen involve three organ systems: nervous, circulatory, and respiratory. Within the bloodstream, oxygen transport depends upon the capacity of red blood corpuscles to synthesize and store hemoglobin, a molecule that is adapted to accept oxygen at one concentration and to release it at another.

We thus see that no one level of biotic organization can be considered out of context—that is, without taking into account its evolution within the organism-environment complex.

REVIEW AND DISCUSSION

1 Explain, with examples, the adaptive value of biotic diversity.

2 Explain why the term *adaptation* should not be restricted to designating unique specializations such as a stork's beak or a duck's webbed feet. What is meant by coadaptedness, both as seen within the body of a single organism and as seen among the various species making up a given community?

3 Distinguish between artificial and natural selection in terms of the selective factors operating in each case and the effect of each on the fitness for survival of the individual and the population as a whole. How do you think artificial (that is, cultural) and natural selection may be operating today upon mankind?

4 Explain with examples how organisms affect their environment as well as being affected by it; what factors constitute the organism's environment?

5 What two major factors interact to shape the structural and functional characteristics of living things? Explain why the organism cannot be thought of as a discrete entity having an existence independent from that of the rest of the world.

6 What is meant by biotic *levels of organization?* What are the hazards of studying any one of these levels to the exclusion of the others? Can you think of *any* biotic activities which occur exclusively on a single level of organization? Explain your answer.

7 Why is it important for man's well-being for him to realize that ecological relationships operate at all levels of biotic organization? Develop an explanatory example *other* than the one presented in this chapter.

REFERENCES

EVANS, F. C. "Ecosystem as the Basic Unit in Ecology," *Science,* **123** (1956). Stipulates that the ecosystem concept is relevant to tracing the cyclic utilization of matter and energy at any level on which life is being examined.

GROBSTEIN, C. *The Strategy of Life.* San Francisco: W. H. Freeman and Company, 1965. A concisely written exposition of many aspects of life; Chapter 4 deals with biotic levels of organization.

HECHT, M. K. "The Role of Natural Selection and Evolutionary Rates in the Origin of Higher Levels of Organization," *Systematic Zool.,* **14** (1965). The "levels" referred to are taxonomic groups above the species level. Discusses various aspects of natural selection, and postulates that directional selection contributes to the evolution of higher taxa.

KELLOGG, C. E. "Soil," *Sci. Amer.,* **183** (1950).

NASH, L. K. *Plants and the Atmosphere.* Cambridge, Mass.: Harvard University Press, 1952.

REDFIELD, A. C. "The Biological Control of Chemical Factors in the Environment," *Amer. Scientist,* **46** (1958).

REID, L. *The Sociology of Nature.* Baltimore, Md.: Penguin Books, 1958. A highly literate presentation of basic material on ecological relationships and organic evolution.

SHEPARD, P. "The Place of Nature in Man's World," *Atlantic Nat.,* **13** (1958).

THOMAS, W. L., JR. (ED.) *Man's Role in Changing the Face of the Earth.* Chicago: University of Chicago Press, 1958. A useful reference detailing the impact of man's activities upon various biotic communities.

WALLACE, B., AND A. M. SRB *Adaptation (2nd ed.).* Englewood Cliffs, N.J.: Prentice-Hall, Inc., 1964. A brief, readable discussion of the genetic basis of adaptation, together with specific examples of the adaptive process.

Chapter 4 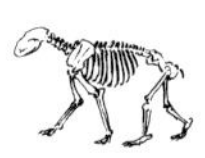 ADAPTATION TO ABIOTIC FACTORS

THE PHYSICOCHEMICAL CHARACTERISTICS of the earth and its atmosphere have set prerequisites that determine the nature of life on earth. During the evolution of life organisms have had to develop their capacity for enduring abiotic factors present in their habitats; alternatively, they have also succeeded in developing capabilities for actively exploiting these factors to satisfy their requirements for survival.

Some of the most important abiotic factors that organisms either endure or exploit include water, light, temperature, wind and waves, atmospheric gases, gravity, and pressure. In this chapter we shall discuss those biotic adaptations which have come about primarily through the selective influence of abiotic environmental factors upon organisms. Traditionally, such adaptations have been studied chiefly as part of the physical equipment of existing organisms, but we shall study them here in the context of evolution, as products of natural selection with respect to particular factors in the physicochemical environment. For instance, skeletal support systems are necessary only because organisms live in the earth's gravitational field: should life evolve in interstellar space such support systems would be redundant. Furthermore, in the transition from water to land the support systems of both plants and animals have become modified; creatures that have failed to adapt successfully in this respect have neither attained large size on land nor, if animals, achieved a rapid mode of locomotion.

Through the study of this chapter and Chapters 5, 6, and 7, we hope to establish a perspective that will serve as a guide during subsequent study of the organization and functioning of living systems: at all of its levels of organization the development of life has been determined less by emergent properties of living matter than by the manner in which biotic and abiotic factors in the environment define the survival value of each inheritable change in living matter.

4.1 □ WATER AND LIFE

A How is water important to life?

Terrestrial life has always depended upon water. Data to be considered in detail later (Chapter 10) indicate not only that life originated in the water, but that water molecules themselves probably were involved in chemical reactions to produce simple organic molecules from which more complex aggregations could be formed.

Water makes up over 80 percent of the bodies of most organisms, serving as a medium of transport and as a solvent. More substances can be dissolved in water than in any other solvent, and since nearly all chemical reactions take place while the reacting molecules are in solution, it may be seen that most metabolic activities and diffusion processes in living systems depend on materials so dissolved or suspended.

Water molecules directly enter into several essential biochemical reactions including *photosynthesis* (in which water is used as the source of hydrogen atoms needed in making sugars) and *hydrolysis* (in which large organic molecules such as starches are broken into smaller sugars).

Water molecules cling together very strongly; this *cohesive* tendency may have helped living systems to evolve by stabilizing primitive groups of molecules at water-air interfaces, allowing them to remain together and interact. Although the role played by the cohesive properties of water in the origin of life is speculative, its *present* importance is seen in such processes as water conduction in plants, for if water molecules did not cling together, they could not be elevated (against the force of gravity) from roots to treetops.

Water has a *high heat capacity:* it can absorb proportionately great amounts of heat while its own temperature rises only slightly. Water therefore serves to protect sensitive organic molecules from excessive changes in temperature. Water also absorbs and conducts heat released by metabolic processes, which otherwise would tend to build up at the site of release.

The *thermal conductivity* of water is high for a liquid. As heat is generated by cell metabolism it is conducted by movements of water molecules through the cell and out to the surrounding medium; thus the cell's internal temperature is barely higher than that of the fluid surrounding it.

As well as performing these essential functions within the bodies of living things, water also serves as the *habitat* of most kinds of organisms. Most phyla are predominantly or exclusively aquatic, living in the ocean or in fresh water. Those groups which have evolved to a terrestrial existence still carry in themselves, enclosed against evaporation, their own watery worlds.

B Adaptations for water use

Organisms have developed a wide variety of adaptations related to the utilization of water. These adaptations are of three types: (1) those enabling living things to utilize water chemically; (2) those related to the use of water as a habitat; and (3) those enabling organisms to obtain and conserve water in habitats where water is limited or tends to be lost from the organism.

ADAPTATIONS FOR THE BIOCHEMICAL USE OF WATER Adaptations that enable living things to utilize water chemically include water-splitting enzymes. Such enzymes make possible the utilization of water as a source of hydrogen atoms in photosynthesis. So great are the photosynthetic water requirements of plants that land plants have evolved structural adaptations related to their metabolic use of water. These include extensive *root systems,* through which water is absorbed, and *vascular tissue* providing for water transport from roots to leaves.

Water molecules are also involved in hydrolytic reactions whereby organic compounds are degraded into smaller constitu-

Figure 4.1 □ Water-conserving adaptations.

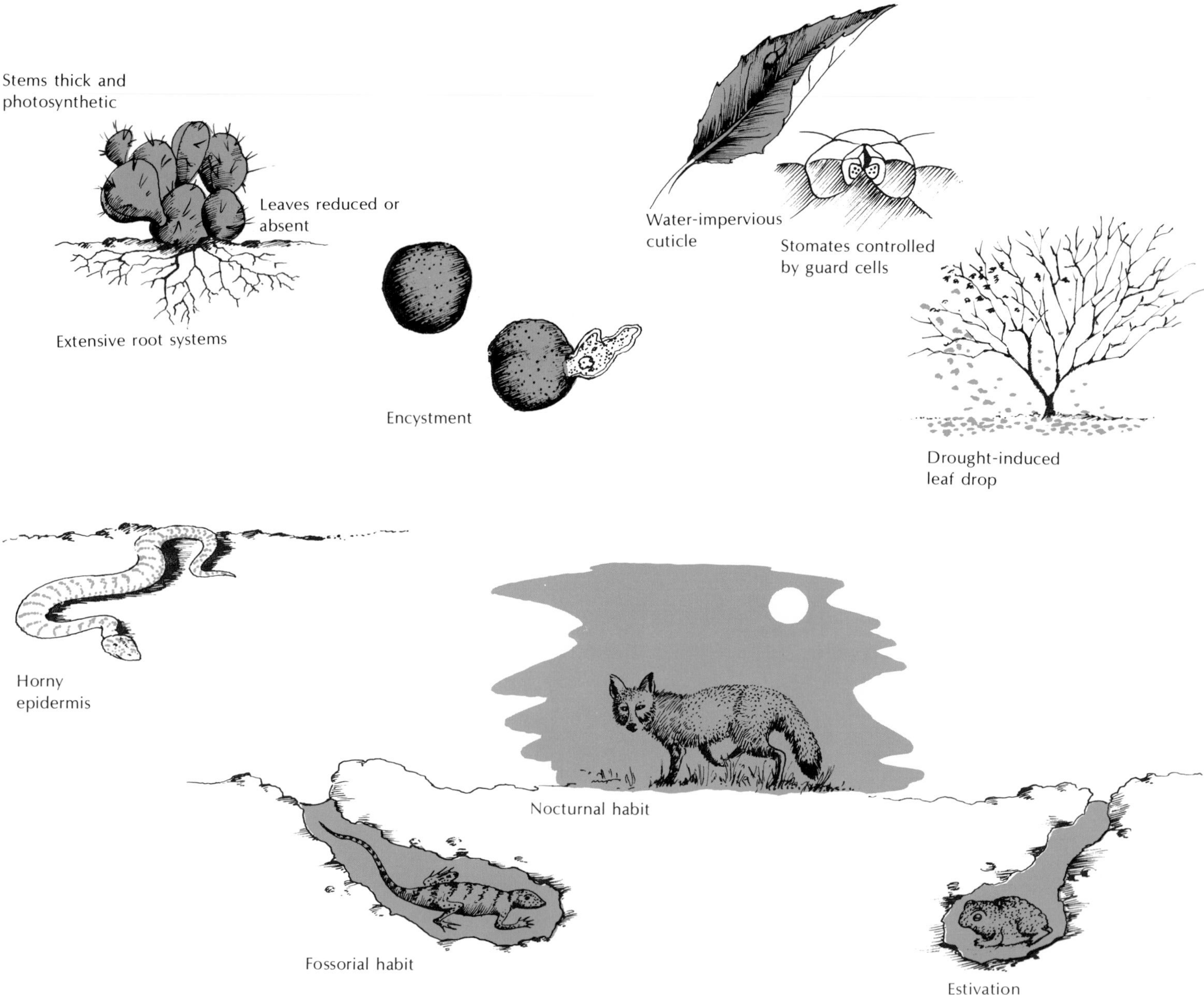

ents, such as during the digestive process. Hydrolysis in biotic systems requires the assistance of enzymes (hydrolases). Such enzymes qualify as biotic adaptations that evolved with the presence and potential exploitability of water as a selective factor.

ADAPTATIONS FOR SWIMMING AND FLOATING Aquatic organisms have developed many adaptive devices that assist flotation or facilitate swimming. As a medium, water is more viscous and consequently more supportive than air (and sea water owing to its greater salt concentration, is more supportive than fresh water). Since aquatic organisms gain support from the medium in which they live, they tend to lack the structural strength demanded of terrestrial animals and woody plants. On the other hand, the viscosity of water impedes rapid locomotion and thus favors selection toward a smoothly tapering, streamlined form in those species for which swiftness is a necessity. As we have seen, analogous convergence in body form is shown by many swimming animals—including squid, most bony and cartilaginous fishes, and vertebrates of terrestrial ancestry that have secondarily reinvaded aquatic habitats (see Figure 1.6). Buoyancy mechanisms are adaptations by which organisms overcome the pull of gravity; they will be considered in detail in Section 4.4.

C Water-conserving adaptations

Whenever organisms adopt a terrestrial habitat or a formerly freshwater species moves into a saltwater habitat, mechanisms for obtaining and conserving water are mandatory (Figure 4.1).

Occupancy of any terrestrial habitat requires that the problem of water loss (desiccation) be overcome. Few kinds of plants and animals have successfully made the transition to a truly terrestrial mode of life. Those that have include seed plants, several classes of arthropods (particularly the insects and arachnids), and three classes of vertebrates (the reptiles, birds, and mammals). Their successful invasion of an extensive habitat that is inimical and in fact lethal to most of the living world has enabled these few groups to proliferate and diversify tremendously; they now occupy the great variety of terrestrial environments that were previously uninhabited.

REDUCING THE NEED FOR WATER IN REPRODUCTIVE PROCESSES The sex cells and embryos of aquatic organisms require water for both fertilization and development. Most groups of lower plants, including algae, mosses, and ferns, produce sperm cells similar to those of animals, which swim through water to reach the female gametes. In a dry environment sperm cells perish; therefore sexual reproduction in terrestrial habitats is restricted to those organisms which have either developed some means of protecting the sperm during transfer or have evolved a counterpart of sperm that does not need water for transport.

The only terrestrial organisms that have developed a substitute for sperm are the conifers and flowering plants. The virtual loss of sperm cells from the life history of seed plants was made possible by the evolution of hard-walled pollen grains containing the male hereditary component. Pollen, incapable of active locomotion, is carried passively by wind or insects. Pine pollen (Figure 4.2) is winged, facilitating wind dispersal. Pollen grains spread by insects have elaborately sculptured coats that cause the grains to cling to each other and to the bristly bodies of their insect carriers.

The reproductive processes of animals that have succeeded well in terrestrial habitats have been freed from dependence on water in two ways: (1) by *insemination* (direct transfer of sperm to the female genital tract); (2) by development of eggs resistant to dehydration.

Animals accomplish the transfer of sperm directly from the male to the female genital tract by *copulation,* thereby eliminating the transfer of sperm through the external milieu. Reptiles, mammals, insects, and certain other terrestrial arthropods developed special copulatory organs that effect this exchange. In birds special organs do not occur; instead the female's cloaca (terminal chamber of the intestine, into which the oviduct also opens) is extruded and inserted into the male's cloaca. In spiders one of the male's pedipalps is modified into a copulatory organ: the tip of this specialized leg is swollen into a bulblike syringe that is used to withdraw semen from the male's genital pore and inject it into the female's.

When copulatory organs are lacking sperm may be transferred encased within a protective *spermatophore.* Male scorpions of certain species place a spermatophore on the ground and then perform a mating dance during which the female is gradually maneuvered over the spermatophore and pressed down upon it.

By the development of a *cleidoic* egg (one which resists dehydration) reptiles, birds, mammals, and terrestrial arthropods

Figure 4.2 □ Pine pollen, winged for wind dispersal. (*Ward's Natural Science Establishment, Inc.*)

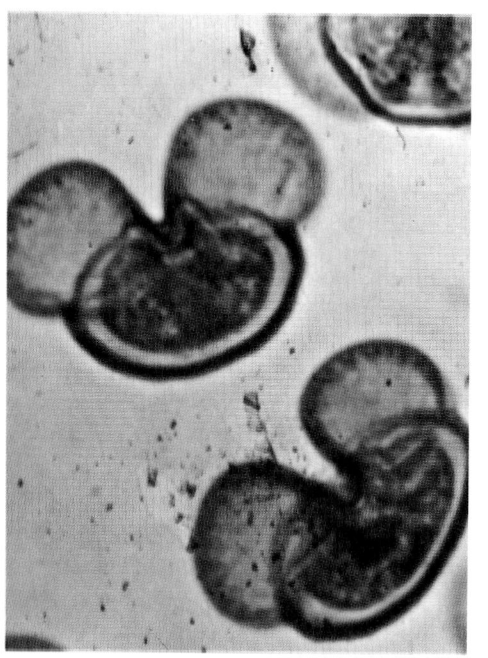

have eliminated the need to lay their eggs in water (Figure 4.3). The vertebrate cleidoic egg is termed an *amniote* egg because it is invested by several protective embryonic membranes including the amnion, which directly encloses the embryo and surrounds it with protective amniotic fluid. This provides an aquatic microhabitat for the embryo, which is not yet ready to withstand the dry outside world.

EPIDERMAL SEALS Water conservation is a continuing problem, not only for the embryo but for the adult terrestrial plant or animal as well (Figure 4.4). Both plants and animals have developed an effective epidermal seal to reduce the loss of water by evaporation from body surfaces. In plants the seal consists of a waxy cuticle secreted by underlying epidermal cells of the leaves and smaller stems. Larger stems are protected by layers of cork composed of a waxy material called *suberin*. The cork cells, secreting suberin, eventually cut themselves off from further nourishment (much like the man who paints himself into a corner) and die, leaving tiny empty spaces in the mass of protective cork.

Animals such as earthworms and soil nematodes burrow in the ground or hide beneath rocks or logs and thus are largely protected from desiccation by their moist surroundings. They also secrete a thin cuticle, which is moderately protective but cannot prevent dehydration when the animal is fully exposed to air and sun. Terrestrial arthropods possess a more effective seal in the form of a chitinous exoskeleton, which is not only supportive but is also relatively impervious to water.

The reptiles and their descendants, the birds and mammals, have developed an epidermal seal analogous to that of arthropods. They do not secrete a waxy cuticle or a chitinous exoskeleton; instead, epidermal cells become horny by producing and storing large quantites of *keratin*, an insoluble protein. These keratinized cells die and form a densely packed waterproof seal. They eventually slough off, but are replenished by the proliferation of underlying cells in the basal layer of the epidermis (Figure 4.5). The highly effective epidermal seal of amniotes is foreshadowed in the amphibian skin, which is moderately keratinized but cannot long protect the animal from desiccation in arid surroundings.

In the birds and mammals the horny epidermis in turn is overlain by feathers or hair, which serve to retain body heat. The development of these structures, composed of dead, keratinized cells, was made possible by the *prior evolution of keratinization* as a means of preventing water loss.

WATER RETENTION DURING EXCRETION Animals conserve water either by excreting solid waste products or by reclaiming water from the urine before it is voided. Insects and mammals have developed especially effective means of water reclamation (see Chapter 16). Some insects and vertebrates such as birds, lizards, and snakes have evolved metabolic mechanisms for converting some of these wastes into nontoxic solid products that may either be harmlessly stored or released from the organism with very little loss of water. The colorful scales of butterfly wings, for instance, are actually storage depots for metabolic wastes that (owing to the adaptive ingenuity of biotic systems) do double duty as pigments!

In the preceding paragraphs we have

Figure 4.3 □ **Cleidoic eggs. (*a*) Insect egg (*Lepidoptera*), showing chitinous shell protecting against dehydration. (*Los Angeles County Museum of Natural History.*) (*b*) Tortoise (*Testudo elephantopus*) hatching from an amniote egg. (*Zoological Society of San Diego photo by Ron Garrison.*) (*c*) Structure of amniote egg, showing protective membranes. The embryo rests in amniotic fluid, protected by the *amnion* from loss of water and mechanical injury. The *yolk sac* encloses a mass of stored food, and the *allantois* serves for respiratory exchange and as a repository for metabolic wastes. In eutherians the outer membrane or chorion participates with the allantois in forming the embryonic part of the placenta. Terrestrial animals lacking fully cleidoic eggs must protect them in other ways, such as by burying them in soil.**

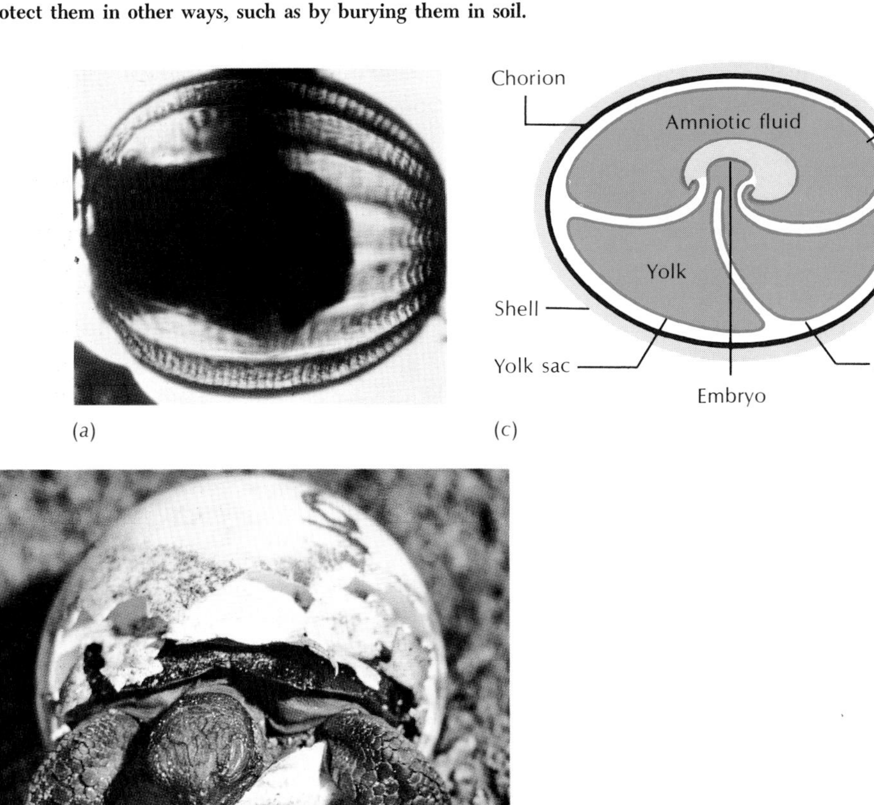

seen that successful terrestrial organisms are those which have developed effective means for protecting themselves, their gametes, and their embryos from an arid environment. However, no organism can complete this process of self-immurement and continue to live. Nutrients must be obtained, some in aqueous solution, and in the case of most organisms, water itself must be taken in to serve either as a nutrient (for photosynthesizing plants) or as a solvent and agent of hydrolysis. Gaseous exchange also requires water, for effective diffusion of gases occurs only when the membranes exposed to the air are kept moist. Moist membranes line the respiratory organs of terrestrial animals and despite various protective devices water will be lost in the air exhaled. Air spaces within the leaves of plants communicate to the exterior by way of stomates controlled by guard cells that close the stomates when evaporation is excessive and thereby preserve the humidity of the intercellular air spaces. Despite this, plants lose water, for the stomates must be opened to allow photosynthesis to proceed. However, the stomates may be restricted to the shaded underside of the leaf or sunk into pits in the epidermis. In addition to losing water by evaporation from the stomates (*transpiration*), plants also may exude water droplets from glands along the leaf margin or from the open ends of veins (*guttation;* Figure 4.6). Transpiration and guttation are water-wasting processes, yet they must take place to allow continuous upward movement of water and solutes from the roots to the leaves. Perennial desert plants cannot indulge freely in such profligate tactics; they maintain their water economy at the cost of a very slow rate of growth,

Figure 4.4 □ Xerophytic adaptations of a grass, *Ammophila arenaria:* cross sections of leaf, (*a*) low-power and (*b*) high-power magnification. The blade remains curled up, reducing the amount of surface area exposed to an arid atmosphere; the stomata occupy a protected position on the inner surface. (*Triarch Incorporated, Geo. H. Conant, Ripon, Wis.*)

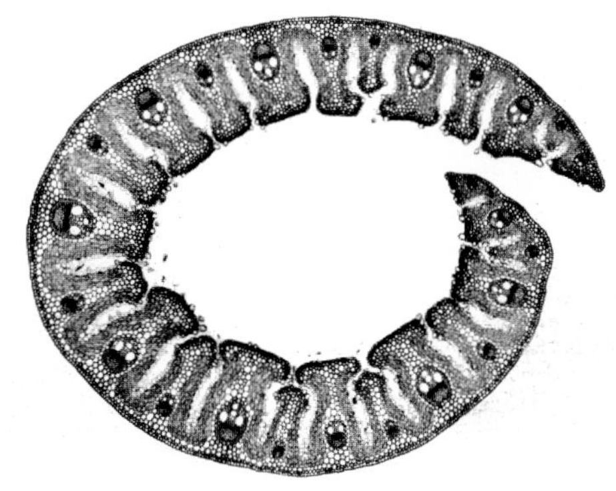

(*a*)

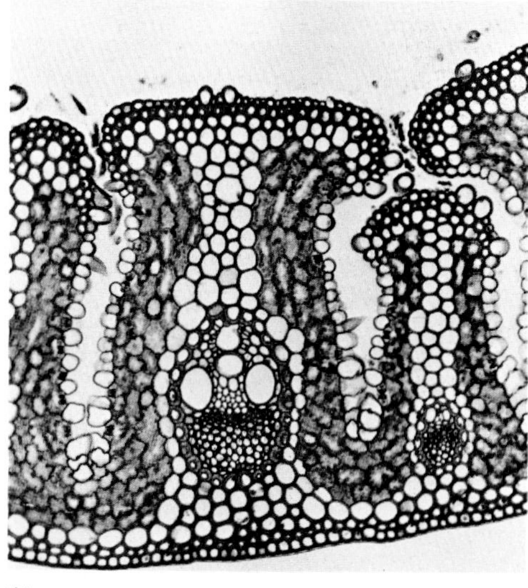

(*b*)

which however is often compensated for by a long lifespan.

No organisms can totally avoid water loss, and so if they are unable to replenish the loss, they soon die. Most terrestrial animals fulfill this need by drinking water or by eating moist food. However, a few desert species such as the kangaroo rat drink no water and subsist on dry seeds, their water needs being met by metabolic water, which is that produced when hydrogen combines with oxygen during oxidative metabolism or that released by dehydration synthesis.* Terrestrial plants obtain water through the finely divided terminal portions of their root systems, the total cross-sectional area of which may far exceed the aboveground parts of the plant.

XERIC ADAPTATIONS The more arid the habitat, the more effective must be the organism's adaptations for obtaining and conserving water. Tremendous root systems are often required to sustain perennial desert plants (*xerophytes*). Some xerophytes such as the creosote bush develop tap roots that can reach the watertable at depths exceeding 20 m. The roots of other species such as saguaro spread horizontally over a large area, the extent of which is reflected by the ordinarily wide spacing between individual plants. Within the radius of each root system, the established roots of the mature plant take up water to such an extent that the roots of young saguaros cannot take hold. Intraspecific competition for water is thereby reduced.

*For instance, when sugar molecules are combined to make starch or glycogen, one molecule of water is liberated for each sugar molecule added to the chain.

Extensive root systems, thickened or reduced leaves, stems modified for water storage, and thick, water-impervious cuticles make up a complex of xeric adaptations that permit plants to survive in arid habitats. In the main these represent extreme manifestations of water-conserving tendencies demonstrated by plants in less arid environments. For instance, the more arid the habitat, the smaller will be the total surface area of the leaves relative to their thickness. Plants in humid habitats often have large, thin leaves, and even within the same species a well-watered specimen will produce larger, thinner leaves than one subjected to drought. Subdesert chaparral (scrub forest) species tend to have small, hard leaves with thick cuticles. In desert plants the leaves may be few and fleshy, may appear temporarily and be quickly shed, or may be modified into spines, the photosynthetic function being assumed by the stems.

Many desert plants also conserve water by opening their stomates only at night. They take up carbon dioxide at night, when it cannot be used in photosynthesis, and convert it to organic acids. In the daytime the stomates are closed but carbon dioxide is made available by the breakdown of these acids, allowing photosynthesis to proceed.

As commonly occurs when organisms of diverse ancestry come under the selective influence of a similar habitat, *convergence* has taken place among desert plants belonging to several different families: these have independently been able to develop similar complexes of xeric adaptations and are therefore all "cactuslike" or "succulent-like."

BEHAVIORAL MECHANISMS FOR CONSERVING WATER Without resorting to

Marine invertebrates. (*a*) A ribbonworn, *Tubulanus polymorphus.* The soft, unsegmented body houses a long proboscis that can be shot forth to capture such prey as annelid worms. (*Courtesy of Carolina Biological Supply Company.*) (*b*) A denizen of rocky coasts in the lower intertidal zone, the starfish *Henricia leviuscula* displays the pentamerous symmetry of adult echinoderms. (*Courtesy of Carolina Biological Supply Company.*) (*c*) The feather star, *Antedon,* is a free-swimming relative of the stalked sea lilies and a living representative of a subphylum of echinoderms now mainly known as fossils. The feathery projections along the arms both increase buoyancy and assist in food capturing. (*Courtesy of General Biological, Inc., Chicago.*)

(*b*)

(*a*)

(*c*)

(*a*)

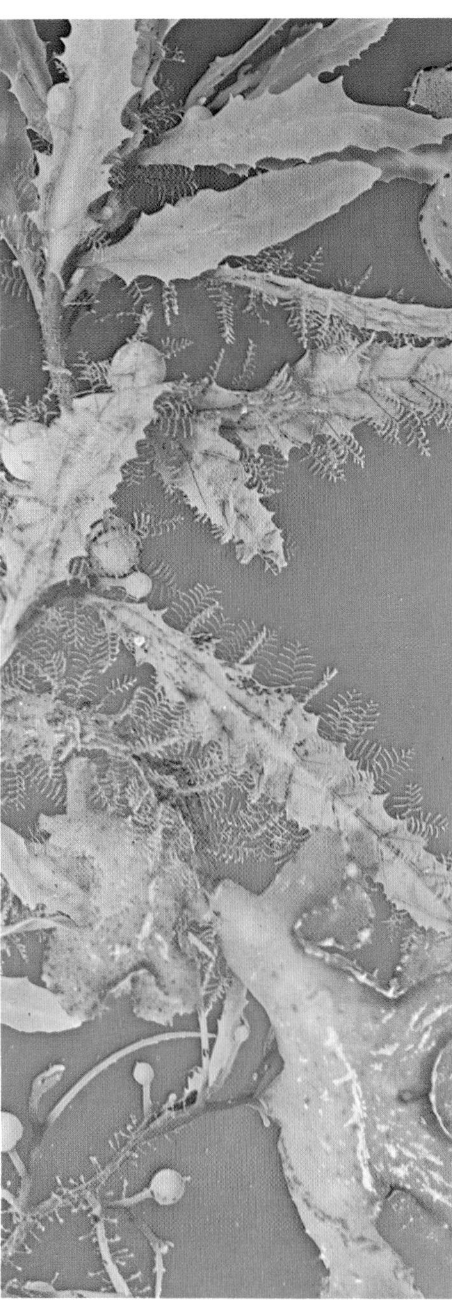

(*b*)

Protective coloration in sea slugs. (*a*) The brilliantly colored eolid nudibranch ***Flabellina iodinea*** advertises its unpalatability by contrasting vividly with its background of surf grass or algae. (***Ward's Natural Science Establishment, Inc.***) (*b*) Sargassum nudibranchs in their natural habitat of floating sargassum weed match the vegetation in both form and color, thereby escaping the attention of predators. (***Marineland of Florida.***)

encystment or estivation (summer dormancy), many animals exhibit behavioral mechanisms for conserving water. Numerous soil-dwelling invertebrates (as insects, centipedes, earthworms, and so forth) migrate vertically according to the amount of moisture in the soil, burrowing more deeply as the surface soil becomes dry. This directional response or *hydrotaxis* was exploited by the Italian entomologist, A. Berlese, who invented a collecting device now known as the Berlese funnel. The metal funnel is filled with an appropriate amount of soil (as much as a cubic meter) and is then heated from above by an incandescent bulb, thereby accelerating the evaporation of water from the exposed surface of the soil. The small lower end of the funnel terminates in a sieve, below which is placed a bottle of fixative. As the soil is dehydrated from above, the animals within the sample burrow more and more deeply until at last they force their way through the sieve and plummet obligingly into the waiting fixative. In this particular situation, they are betrayed by the behavioral pattern that normally would have been most effective in preserving their lives.

Another behavioral device for water conservation is displayed by the majority of desert animals: they are nocturnal. Restriction of the period of activity to the dark hours not only protects animals from excessive water loss but also reduces exposure to the extremes of heat that characterize some deserts in summer.

ESTIVATION Estivation is a physiological adaptation for enduring seasonal drought. Lungfish lie dormant in the mud of vanishing ponds, becoming immovably imprisoned as the mud dries. Their torpor reduces the need for water and thus they survive until restored to activity by the advent of seasonal rains. Similarly, desert spadefoot toads of the southwestern United States estivate in deep burrows, emerging in an emaciated and dehydrated state only when stimulated by adequate rainfall. During such brief episodes of arousal, the toads quickly hydrate, becoming plump as water swells their bodies. As if to make the most of their opportunity, they promptly mate and then feed before returning to their dungeons. These bouts of activity can be so infrequent that up to 20 years may be required for spadefoot toads to mature, for they do not grow or age appreciably during estivation.

Drought-induced dormancy may persist for incredibly long periods of time. It is always fascinating to watch the emergence of life in some temporary puddle or in a culture made by adding dry soil to a vessel of water. Within a few days the water abounds with protozoans, bacteria, unicellular algae, and even tiny metazoans such as nematodes and rotifers. Whence has this assemblage so mysteriously appeared? The answer lies in the capacity of many small organisms to respond to drought by encysting within an impervious wall of their own secretion, thus protecting their moist bodies from further desiccation. These cysts may lie inactive for months or even years until water is again available. Other inhabitants of temporary ponds cannot encyst and therefore perish as the water disappears. These species however spend most of their brief lives mating and producing eggs invested by

Figure 4.5 □ Rattlesnake shedding its "skin." Only the outer, horny epidermis is molted, usually separating in one piece from the underlying living skin. This highly effective epidermal seal even extends (as a transparent spectacle) over the eyeball. During the premolting period the spectacle becomes opaque and loose, partially blinding the snake and making it irritable. (*U.S. Fish and Wildlife Service.*)

drought-resistant membranes. Fairy shrimps, delicate crustaceans that abruptly appear in great numbers gracefully swimming upside down in temporary woodland ponds, hatch from eggs that may have lain in the soil for a year or more. Similarly seeds, which are actually arrested plant embryos, may remain inactive within the protective seed coat for years or even centuries until a favorable combination of moisture and temperature permits hydration of the seed, bursting of the seed coat, and the resumption of growth, an event known as *germination*. As an extreme example, lotus seeds buried in sediment for up to six centuries were found to germinate when finally exhumed and provided with water!

Figure 4.6 □ **Strawberry leaf, showing loss of water by guttation around margins.** (*Courtesy of J. Arthur Herrick.*)

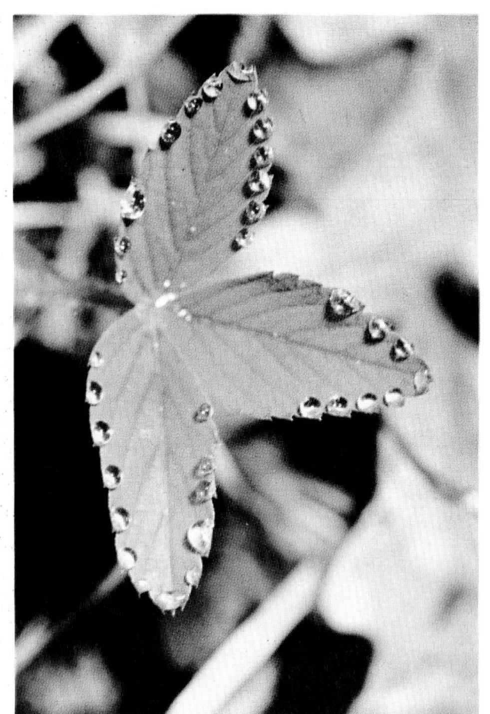

D Physiological drought and winter survival

The desert is the most demanding of habitats with respect to the need for water conservation, but in other habitats seasonal conditions may prevail that produce *physiological drought* even though water may in fact be present in some form. Physiological drought may result whenever low temperatures change water to ice. Freezing of water in the environment takes place at temperatures higher than those required for freezing water within the bodies of organisms. Body fluids contain more solutes than does fresh water and therefore have a freezing point nearer that of sea water. When water in and on the soil is bound as ice, it becomes unavailable for absorption by the roots of plants, which may therefore suffer from drought just as if no water at all were present. Fortunately, metabolic processes of most organisms are carried on at a rate which is directly temperature-dependent. Only mammals and birds are capable of intrinsic regulation of heat production. These "warm-blooded" animals (homoiotherms) maintain a stable body temperature in the face of environmental fluctuations and therefore are not inactivated by falling ambient temperatures. All other organisms—plants and poikilothermal animals—are incapable of such intrinsic regulation and their internal temperature tends to vary with that of the environment. For these organisms physiological drought caused by the freezing of water is endurable because the time of drought coincides with a period of cold-induced dormancy in which metabolism nearly ceases. However, the winter dormancy of terrestrial plants and poikilothermal animals cannot be explained entirely as an unavoidable outcome of chilling, for *marine* plants, invertebrates, and fishes do not become dormant even when the surrounding water is at or below 0°C. Sea water does not freeze at these temperatures and consequently is available for photosynthesis; as long as plant growth continues, animals have adequate food and need not overwinter in a dormant state. On land, on the other hand, there is little adaptive advantage in becoming capable of remaining active throughout the winter, for if plants cannot grow, food for animals must soon become scarce, leading to starvation.

The foliage of conifers, adapted for water conservation, consists of small scales or thick needles having a low surface-to-volume ratio, a waxy cuticle, and sunken stomates (Figure 4.7); this foliage is not shed during winter, but cannot grow back when eaten by mammals such as deer that remain

Figure 4.7 □ **Xeric adaptations of pine: thickened cuticle, multiple epidermis, sunken stomata, and low surface-to-volume ratio of the pine needle, all representing adaptations for moisture conservation. The whole leaf shown in cross section was photographed by polarized light; the central conductive tissue appears pale, and the chlorenchyma black. Small resin ducts are seen in section below the epidermis. (*Ward's Natural Science Establishment, Inc.*)**

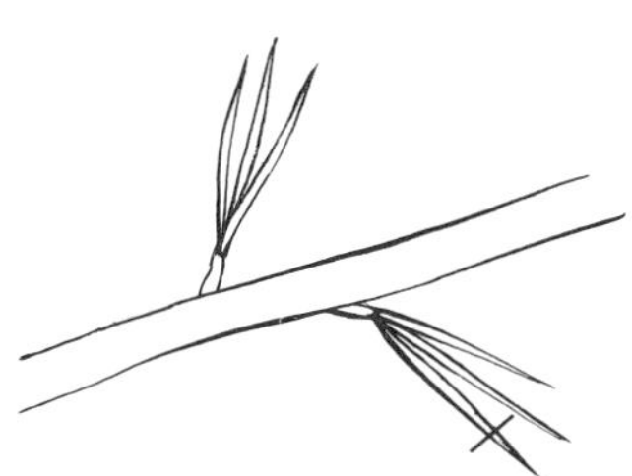

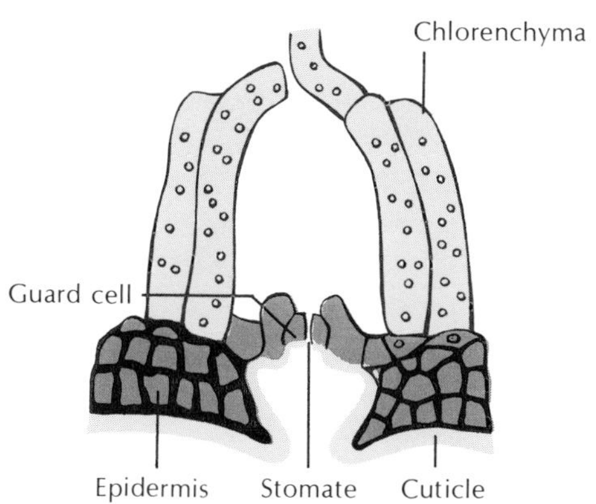

active throughout the winter. The foliage of angiosperm species native to regions characterized by freezing winters is shed through a *deciduous process* that allows the leaves to fall without the plant's losing sap by bleeding: solid plugs develop within the veins at the base of the leaf stalk, blocking the flow of sap, and a corky line of abscission is formed, along which the dead leaf later breaks off.

As long as ground water remains solidly frozen, the physiological drought of plants continues and they can produce no new foliage, flowers, or seeds. Animal survival may then depend on the capacity to overwinter in an inactive, nonfeeding state. The problem is automatically solved in terrestrial poikilotherms, for their metabolic processes are geared to activity only at temperatures above 0°C. A number of mammals sleep to escape the need to find food. The winter sleep of bears is called *somnolence,* a condition in which body temperature and metabolic rate remain near the waking level but the animal sleeps, subsisting only on stored fat. Other mammals such as woodchuck *hibernate:* body temperature and metabolic rate decline drastically and heartbeat and breathing nearly cease (see Section 16.2B). Hibernation was once considered a response to falling temperatures, but its independence of temperature has been demonstrated by experiments in which rodents of hibernatory species were found to remain active even when subjected to extreme cold, as long as they were well fed and watered.

Some mammals solve the problem of winter food scarcity by hoarding food during the autumn. The preoccupation of a well-fed animal with the collection and storage of food, the future need for which it can scarcely foresee, is a remarkable example of instinctive behavior. An alpine hare, the pika, actually cuts grass, spreads it to dry in the sun, stores the dried material in its burrow, and thus starts the winter with a supply of hay!

Other homoiotherms escape starvation by altitudinal or latitudinal migration. Elk and mountain birds move to warmer lowlands, returning to higher altitudes in the spring. Many temperate birds migrate south for the winter, but (as we shall see in Section 7.2B) such migratory behavior may have evolved as an outcome of factors other than the need to escape winter cold and food scarcity. In any case, latitudinal bird migrations are not triggered by falling or rising temperatures but they are brought about by annual changes in photoperiod.

4.2 □ RADIANT ENERGY

The stars, including our sun, are the major natural emitters of waves of the electromagnetic spectrum (Figure 4.8). The shorter waves of this spectrum (X rays and ultraviolet rays) may affect the living world by producing "spontaneous" mutations of genetic material. A narrow band of waves of intermediate length is detectable either as *light* or as *heat,* and it is vibrations of these wavelengths that are most widely detectable by animals and most effective in influencing metabolic and developmental processes.

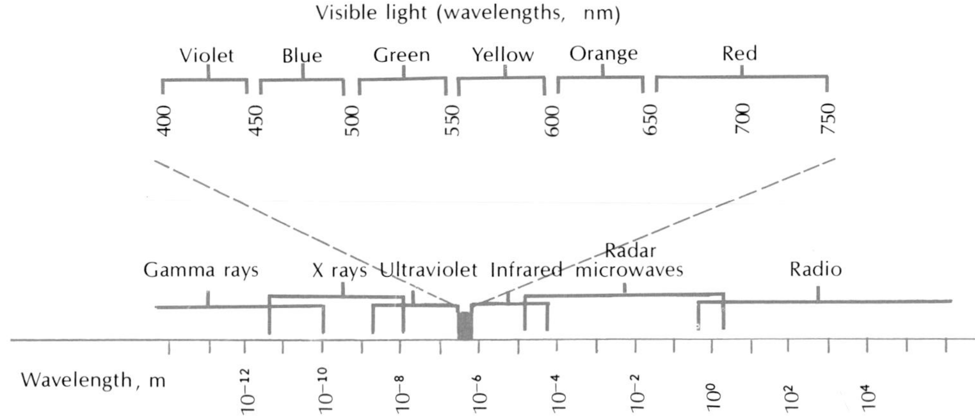

Figure 4.8 □ **The electromagnetic spectrum.**

A Light and heat

Men in all ages have worshipped the sun. Their reverence was not misdirected, for without the vast quantity of energy that continually falls upon our planet from the sun, life as we know it could not exist. Solar energy reaches the surface of the earth mainly as electromagnetic radiation of the wavelengths perceived as visible light, together with some shorter ultraviolet and longer infrared rays. When sunlight passes through a prism, it is found to consist of a mixture of radiations of different visible wavelengths ranging from 400 to 700 nm. Because waves of different lengths are refracted at different angles as they pass through a prism, they are sorted into a rainbowlike *spectrum.* We see the shortest rays of visible light as purple and the longest rays as red. The series of colors ranging from violet through blue, green, yellow, orange, and red is termed the *visible spectrum,* that is, the spectrum visible to the *human* eye. Since the lens of the human eye absorbs ultraviolet rays, we cannot usually perceive these shorter wavelengths. (Persons who have undergone surgical removal of the lens can, in fact, perceive ultraviolet rays as light.) Insects detect ultraviolet, but they are blind to the red light that is visible to the human eye.

Most radiant energy is absorbed by the surface of the earth and reradiated as waves longer than those of the visible spectrum, which we detect as heat. In equatorial regions, where the sun's rays strike the earth vertically after passing through a minimal thickness of atmosphere, each square centimeter of the earth's surface receives the equivalent of 2 cal of heat energy per minute, or 0.033 cal/cm^2-sec. (A *calorie* is the amount of heat required to raise the temperature of 1 g of water by 1°C.) This is by far the greatest source of heat available to the earth's surface. The flow of heat outward from the interior of the planet, although appreciable, amounts to only 1.2×10^{-6} (or 0.0000012) cal/cm^2-sec and is inadequate to maintain water in the liquid state or, for that matter, to keep most of the atmosphere in a gaseous state. Life processes as we know them can be carried on only in a fairly narrow range of temperature, lying between the extremes of the freezing point and the boiling point of water (0° to 100°C). Organisms that remain active at subzero temperatures do so because they maintain internal temperatures well above the freezing point of water. Conversely, temperatures above 80°C are lethal to all but a few species found in hot springs, for proteins such as enzymes are permanently inactivated at temperatures well below the boiling point of water. Variations in solar output may have been responsible for major climatic fluctuations throughout the earth's history, and only a slightly greater deviation in the direction of increased solar radiation or decreased output could end all terrestrial life.

B Temperature preference and tolerance

Within vital limits, an organism's metabolism tends to vary directly with its body temperature. Mammals maintain a body temperature of about 38°C and birds a temperature of about 40°C, whereas other organisms are mainly dependent upon heat absorbed from the environment. When placed in a thermal gradient, many poikilothermal animals show a behavioral preference for a specific range of temperature that presumably represents the physiological optimum for the species. For example, stable flies aggregate most densely at 28° to 29°C (Figure 4.9) and blowflies tend to remain in a thermal zone of about 30°C. In this manner, many animals that cannot regulate their body heat *physiologically* may do so *behaviorally,* warming themselves with a sunbath and then retreating from the heat source when on the verge of overheating.

Whether organisms of a given species die when deprived of heat or overwinter in an active or dormant state is dependent upon their capacity to make the required physiological adjustments. Excessive heat can kill both homoiotherms and poikilotherms if it overloads their cooling mechanisms (which include automatic responses such as perspiring, panting, and lethargic behavior); the exact point of *heat death* depends on the temperature range to which the species is adapted. *Cold death,* on the other hand, is escaped by many species through appropriate behavioral or physiological regulation. Homoiotherms are capable of activity even at temperatures well below 0°C, but (as we have seen earlier) many are forced to migrate or hibernate because of lack of food. Some poikilotherms, particularly marine polar species, remain metabolically active even at temperatures below zero. Their enzyme systems are adapted to operate at low ambient temperatures so that they do not become torpid, but they are usually killed if their tissues freeze solidly.

Comparison of cold resistance in aquatic insects, Japanese beetles, and woodborers indicate that some species of aquatic insects are able to remain active at temperatures close to 0°C although they have little resistance to temperatures at which their tissues freeze; Japanese beetles tolerate cold to about −10°C, overwintering in soil below the frost line; woodborers, on the other hand, increase their resistance to cold by spontaneously losing much of their body water. Thus dehydrated, they can survive temperatures as low as −40°C.

Figure 4.9 □ Thermal preferendum of the stable fly, *Stomomyx calcitrans.* The ordinate indicates percentage of individuals aggregating at any particular temperature. Note that the preferred temperature represents a zone mainly lying between 24 and 32°C, rather than a distinct point. Other species have different preferenda. (*After Nieschulz.*)

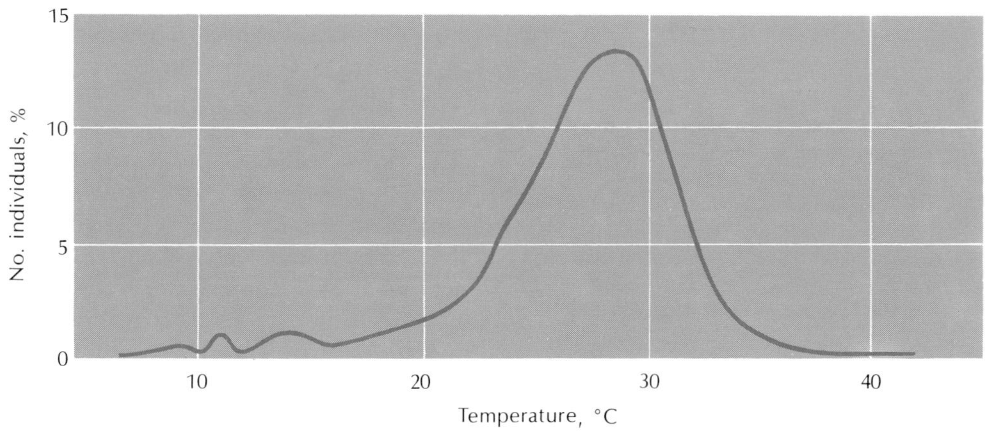

C Radiant energy and the atmosphere

Most of the solar radiation that strikes the earth's surface is reradiated as infrared, which would be dissipated into space were it not for the overlying blanket of atmospheric gases. Atmospheric carbon dioxide and water vapor absorb infrared energy, converting it into kinetic energy (the energy of motion). The heated gas molecules move about more rapidly, colliding with other molecules to which they impart some of their kinetic energy. In this manner the atmosphere is heated and thus serves as a heat trap, conserving a portion of the sun's energy and thereby maintaining over most of the earth's surface a range of temperature compatible with life. The insulating effect of the heated atmosphere retards the loss of heat by reradiation. Mountains are usually cold in any latitude at heights of 5 to 6 km above sea level, for at such altitudes the atmosphere is rarified and most of the thermal blanketing effect is lost. On the other hand, polar regions are colder than the lower latitudes because sunlight penetrates obliquely through the atmosphere to reach the earth's surface near the poles, and much of its energy is therefore reflected rather than absorbed.

As a result of the earth's curvature, solar radiation contacts the earth's surface at an increasing angle of incidence toward each pole, thus heating the earth's surface unequally. This in turn results in the unequal heating of the atmosphere, which receives greater amounts of energy by reradiation from the earth's surface in equatorial regions. Thus, near the equator, the rapidly moving heated air tends to diffuse and expand upward. As the warm equatorial air rises, it is displaced by gases flowing from cooler areas north and south of the equator. These convection currents, products of the unequal heating of the earth's surface by the sun, are modified by the rotation of the earth into great systems of prevailing winds. The importance to living things of these movements of the atmosphere is discussed in Section 4.3; here we should note that these movements are mainly caused by the conversion into kinetic energy of radiant energy that originated as sunlight.

D How do organisms exploit radiant energy?

It would be astonishing if in the course of nearly 3 billion years of organic evolution living things had failed to develop some means of using this gratuitous flood of solar energy otherwise than by passively benefiting from the heat provided. Such failure has indeed not occurred. Various light-utilizing adaptations have been developed, of which the most significant has been the evolution of the photosynthetic mechanism of plants.

THE USE OF LIGHT IN PHOTOSYNTHESIS Photosynthesis is the only efficient natural means by which energy from the abiotic world is trapped for utilization by the biotic world. (It will be discussed in detail in Chapter 13.) The trapping of solar energy is mainly accomplished by means of chlorophyll (see Figure 13.5). Radiant energy particularly of the blue-violet (440 nm) and short-red (655 nm) wavelengths is absorbed by chlorophylls *a* and *b* (Figure 4.10). Chlorophylls *c* and *d* occur in red and brown algae living at depths where light of longer wavelengths fails to penetrate. Of these four types, chlorophyll *a* is most directly concerned in photosynthesis, for only this form is capable of transferring energy to power the carbohydrate-building reactions. The variants *b*, *c*, and *d*, together with other accessory pigments, assist chlorophyll *a* by absorbing light of wavelengths other than those which chlorophyll *a* absorbs most effectively and then passing energy along to the latter. Although photosynthesis is a highly efficient process, only about 2 percent of the solar energy that reaches the earth's surface is trapped as chemical energy by photosynthesizing plants.

PHOTOSYNTHESIS AS A SELECTIVE FACTOR IN PLANT EVOLUTION Once the capacity for photosynthesis had evolved, this capacity itself became a powerful selective influence in the evolution of plants. Many aspects of plant structure and function

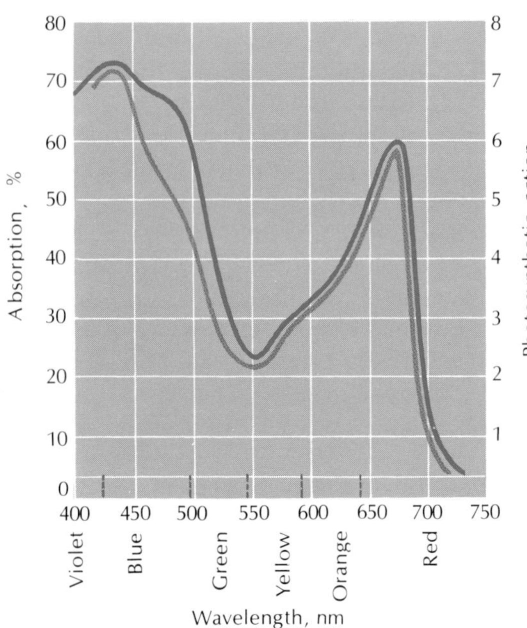

Figure 4.10 □ Light absorption spectrum (dark colored curve) and photosynthetic-action spectrum (tinted color line) of the water plant *Elodea*. The two curves correspond most closely in regions of the spectrum where most of the light is absorbed by chlorophyll. The deviation seen in the blue and green regions is due to absorption of light of these wavelengths by accessory pigments (carotenoids). (*From V. A. Greulach and J. E. Adams, after M. H. Hommersand and F. T. Haxo.*)

increase the plant's efficiency in obtaining and utilizing light energy. The foliage provides great surface area for light absorption. The arrangement and spacing of individual leaves along the stem is genetically regulated in ways that provide most effective exposure to light: leaves may alternate along the stem, be produced in opposite pairs, or emerge in a gradual spiral. Prostrate plants often produce flat rosettes of leaves. In each case, the arrangement maximizes exposure.

The responsiveness of plants is expressed in directional growth responses (*tropisms*). One of the most characteristic plant responses is positive *phototropism,* the tendency of a plant to respond to a directional source of illumination by growth toward it. A seedling grown inside an opaque container provided with a small hole for the admission of light directs its growing tip toward and through that hole. Motile unicellular autotrophs exhibit positive *phototaxis,* moving toward a directional source of illumination until they reach a zone of optimal (usually moderate) intensity. Many heterotrophic organisms, on the other hand, exhibit some degree of *negative* phototaxis and move away from a directional light source.

Figure 4.11 □ **Photoreception. Diagram of planarian head, showing primitive eyes consisting of a pigmented cup and cluster of nerve cells, the distal portions of which are sensitive and therefore form a retina. The light-absorptive pigment in the cells forming the cup prevents light from entering except through the open end of the cup. This allows the worm to determine the direction of illumination and results in a negatively phototactic response, the worm turning away from the light.**

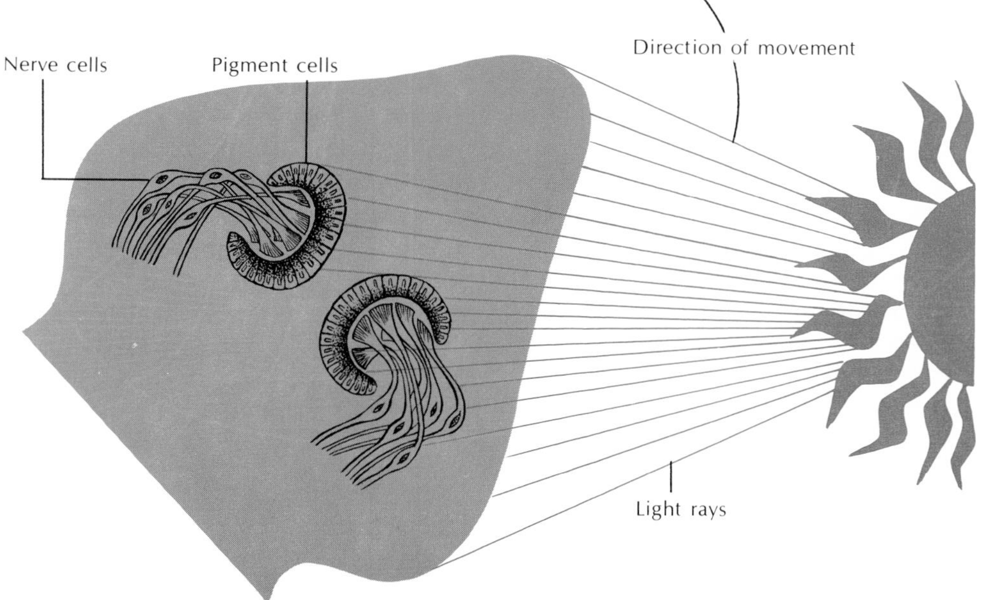

REGULATION OF REPRODUCTIVE PROCESSES BY LIGHT The length of daylight (*photoperiod*) fluctuates seasonally over much of the earth's surface. Many organisms can respond physiologically to photoperiodic changes. In particular, reproductive processes such as flowering and mating are photoperiodically governed in such a way that seeds or offspring are produced at the time of year most conducive to their survival. (We shall consider photoperiodic responses further in Chapter 5.)

THE USE OF LIGHT IN SENSORY PERCEPTION The capacity to perceive light is of general occurrence in the living world and is even demonstrated by phototropic or phototactic organisms that lack demonstrable photoreceptors. In such cases we assume that sensitivity to light is due to the fundamental irritability of living matter. Such organisms may *feel* light as we feel heat. Certain unicellular organisms such as euglenoids possess "eyespots" containing photosensitive pigment. Most metazoans have developed specialized photoreceptive cells that tend to be clustered into organized units, namely eyes. Fundamentally, an eye consists of a layer of photosensitive cells, the retina, which is partially enclosed by a pigment layer so that light can enter from one side only (Figure 4.11). This permits the location of the light source to be detected. The open side of the eye is often covered by a transparent lens, which serves

Figure 4.12 □ Vision in a scallop. (*a*) Eyes of *Pecten irradians* along edge of mantle. (*Courtesy of General Biological, Inc., Chicago.*) (*b*) Escape response of queen scallop (*Chlamys opercularis*) swimming to avoid attack by common starfish (*Asterias rubens*). The scallop's prominent eyes can be seen as black dots along the mantle edge. (*Courtesy of Dr. Douglas P. Wilson, Marine Biological Laboratory, Plymouth.*)

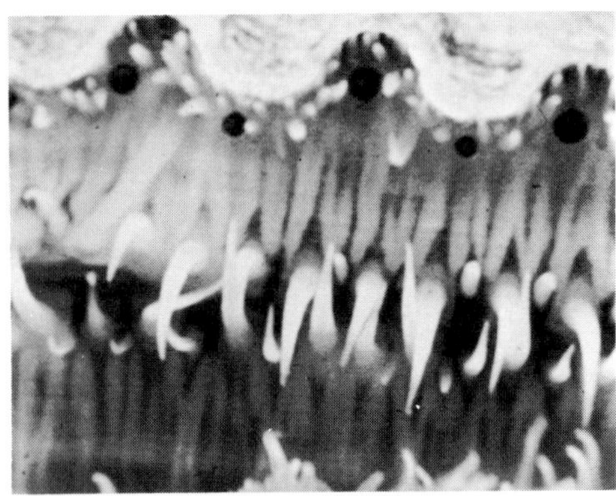

(*a*)

(*b*)

to focus light upon the retina. So great is the adaptive value of photoreceptors that analogous types have arisen in many different kinds of eumetazoans: the well-developed eyes fringing the scallop's mantle assist this bivalve in its escape from an approaching predator, such as a starfish (Figure 4.12).

Primitive photoreceptors probably yield limited information of only two kinds: (1) the direction and intensity of light may be determined; (2) objects may be perceived as shadows if they come between the organism and the light source. More advanced photoreceptors yield another, more significant type of information: objects may be perceived in detail by means of the wavelengths they reflect. The ability to see objects by reflected light furnishes the animal with a tremendous amount of information about its environment, provided that it possesses a brain capable of analyzing and integrating the data.

Photoreception takes place through the eye, but most visual analysis (perception) occurs in the brain. Equal note is *not* taken of all visual stimuli and response is made only to particular signals. Visual cues that elicit instinctive reactions are termed *sign stimuli.* A sign stimulus may be identified by the fact that it retains its effectiveness even when presented out of normal context. This indicates that such stimuli possess characteristics that may bear a "lock-and-key" type of relationship to some inherited configuration within the nervous system. An example of this is the response of a male stickleback in breeding condition to simplified models depicting only particular features of male and female sticklebacks (Figure 4.13). A realistic model lacking red underparts is ignored, while a crude oval with the lower part painted red is attacked. Similarly, an ovoid shape featuring the outline of a swollen belly is courted as though it were a living female. Thus the sign stimulus eliciting attack is the red underparts, and that releasing courtship behavior is a swollen belly. Such innate responses imply an evolutionary history in which central nervous mechanisms have become specifically adapted to being "triggered" by the perception of particular visual cues.

The "filtering" effect which perception exerts upon vision is also evinced by the fact that birds, with visual acuity often exceeding our own, also respond to sign stimuli presented out of context. An example of this is the European robin's aggressive response to a mere tuft of red feathers mounted in perching position (see Figure 7.18). The eye of the bird can certainly detect the difference between such a simplified model and the "real" object, yet so irresistable is the cue presented that the attack behavior has a high probability of taking place.

Despite considerable differences in the structure of photoreceptors in animals of different phyla, it is generally true that photoreception depends upon light sensitivity of *visual pigments,* compounds that occur in retinal cells such as the rods and cones of the vertebrate retina (see Figure 15.18). Some visual pigments absorb light over a wide range of wavelengths. If the organism possesses only one such pigment, it can discern only various shades of gray. Other visual pigments are known that absorb light only through a narrow band of wavelengths. Several such pigments must be present in the photoreceptor to provide the organism with color vision. The rods of the vertebrate retina contain *rhodopsin,* a pigment that absorbs light through a wide range of wavelengths, providing discrimination between light and dark but no ability to discriminate among various colors. The *cones* are color receptors and are thought to be of three types, each containing one of three different visual pigments (*iodopsins*) having different light-absorption properties: one iodopsin absorbs mainly light of longer wavelengths (red); the second, light of intermediate wavelengths (green); the third, light of short wavelengths (blue-violet). Color perception therefore depends on the *relative proportion* of red-sensitive, green-sensitive, and blue-sensitive cones that are excited (see Section 15.2D).

The incidence of color vision is sporadic. It is difficult to establish experimentally whether or not a given species can perceive colors. Cephalopods, insects, and vertebrates (but excepting most nocturnal mammals, which lack color vision) react to specific colors under controlled conditions, which implies that these three advanced groups of animals have evolved color vision independently of one another. This parallel evolution is not unlikely, since the amount of additional information obtained by color vision greatly augments the organism's potential for survival. On the other hand, it is possible that pigments required for color vision are of nearly universal occurrence throughout the animal world but that many lower animals do not have brains capable of making use of this much visual information.

Figure 4.13 □ **A series of experimental models used to identify the specific sign-stimulus configuration releasing aggressive behavior in the male three-spined stickleback. A realistic model (at right) lacking red underparts is ignored; simplified models painted red on the underside evoke attack. Such experiments demonstrate that animals do not respond to all that they see but that instinctive responses can be released by specific stimuli even when the latter are presented out of normal context. (*After N. Tinbergen.*)**

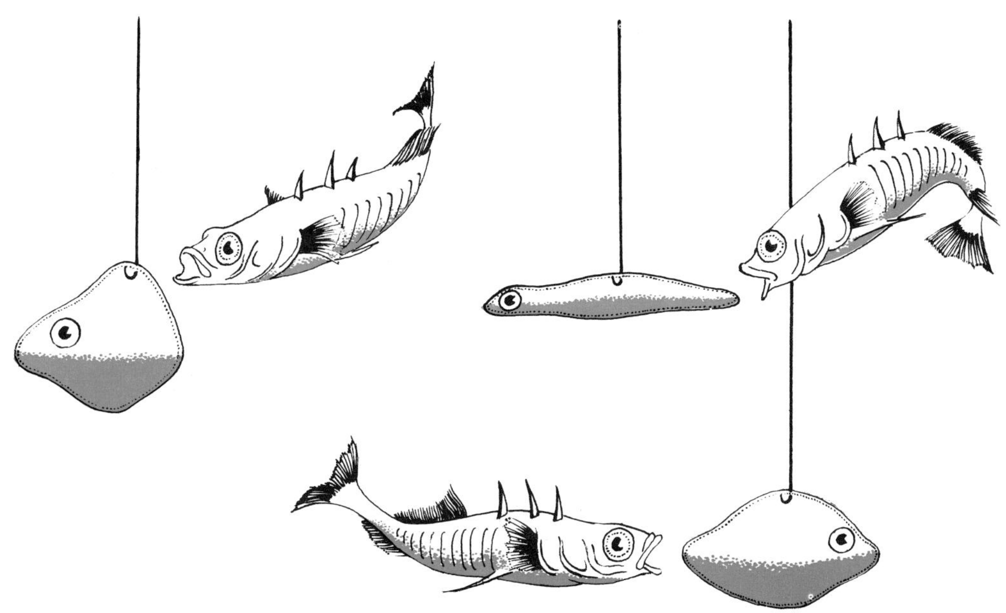

The living world profoundly affects the composition of the atmosphere, as we saw in Chapter 3. In turn the atmosphere has influenced the evolution of the biosphere in two essential ways: (1) Winds and the water currents they generate can be powerful destructive forces that living things must avoid or withstand; alternatively, they can be exploited for locomotion and dispersal. (2) Atmospheric gases such as nitrogen, oxygen, and carbon dioxide can serve as a ready source of materials for general metabolic use once means are evolved for processing these gases.

A Wind and waves

Movements of the atmosphere are complex, but result mainly from the interaction of two factors: (1) unequal heating of the atmosphere at different latitudes, producing convection currents; (2) the Coriolis effect, produced by the earth's rotation, causing wind systems to rotate clockwise in the northern hemisphere and counterclockwise in the southern hemisphere. Winds are important to organisms as agents of transport and dispersal, as destructive and erosive forces, and as factors that profoundly influence local climate and weather conditions.

TRANSPORT AND DISPERSAL Winds implement the dispersal of many species, a number of which have developed adaptations that enhance the effectiveness of wind dissemination. The spider that unreels a length of silk and casts itself adrift upon the sea of moving air is utilizing a device analogous to that of the airborne thistle seed; however, the spider's adaptation is mainly behavioral while the thistle's is entirely structural. Both have evolved as a result of survival benefits accruing to those species having efficient means of dispersing themselves. Structural adaptations that facilitate wind dispersal are those which increase the surface-to-volume ratio and decrease the object's density. They consist mainly of flattened vanes or finely divided projections analogous to those used for flotation by aquatic organisms. They have appeared independently in many different species and particularly in plants, which—being mainly nonlocomotory—must rely on other means of getting about. Adult plants are immobilized by root systems, but their spores or seeds and pollen can be disseminated by agencies such as wind. Plants such as conifers and grasses, which utilize the wind for pollen transport, have tended to evolve alate (winged) pollen grains (see Figure 4.2). Adaptations for wind dispersal of seeds are shown by milkweeds, maples, and other plants (see Figure 7.7). Many small organisms are carried great distances by winds because of their insignificant mass, even though they possess no special modifications facilitating wind dispersal. Such is the case with bacteria, encysted protozoans, small metazoans, and the reproductive spores of fungi, mosses, and ferns. The greater the force of the wind, the more massive are the organisms it can transport.*

The preceding examples pertain to *passive* wind dispersal. Several groups of animals actively *fly,* utilizing the atmosphere as a milieu and exploiting its currents in their locomotion. These will be considered below.

INJURY AND EROSION Air currents may be strong enough to damage organisms directly, by the transport of abrasive solids or by the production of waves in bodies of water. Many species must seek protection from the wind or must be capable of anchoring themselves securely against the force of wind or wind-generated waves. As an agent of erosion, wind may strip soil from areas lacking effective plant cover, leaving the region incapable of supporting life. Wind-blown sand dunes are highly destructive to life. A stationary dune can be anchored by plant roots and may thus eventually be stabilized. But a *moving* dune, advancing several centimeters a day, smothers all living things that cannot move out of its path. Dune deserts are truly among the most *deserted* of habitats.

Waves in bodies of water are the direct product of moving air. The molecules of

*Occasional "rains" of fish are due to the previous passage of a whirlwind over a body of water. Both water and fish may be drawn aloft, to be dropped elsewhere when the wind's force is spent.

atmospheric gases impart some of their kinetic energy to the water over which they pass. This kinetic energy is translated into a series of vertically oriented rotatory movements of the water. Over wide expanses of open water where air currents flow without obstruction, the perpetual energy transfer from atmosphere to water generates great waves that travel forward in the direction of the wind until they reach some barrier, usually a land mass. Here the energy of the wave becomes translated into shearing forces as the wave crashes in surf. The hydraulic force exerted by surf is enormous. According to H. B. Moore,* a wave front 3 m high and 30 m long can strike a vertical surface with a force of about 80,000 newtons†/m²; a wave 13 m high and 150 m long can exert 303,000 newtons/m². Furthermore, if such a wave breaks upon a *slope* rather than a *vertical* face, its energy is converted into forward thrust, which may produce a force up to six times greater than that which the wave would exert against a vertical surface. Such wind-generated wave action not only erodes coastlines, undermining cliffs, pulverizing rocks to sand, and then transporting and redepositing the products of erosion, but is also a factor of prime significance in the lives of all organisms inhabiting the sea margins.

The animals and plants of the *littoral zone*, the habitat between the extreme limits of the tides, must be able to withstand or escape from the tremendous impact of crashing surf. On sandy beaches the fauna typically burrows into the substratum, extending only a small portion of the body for feeding. Mole crabs extend only their plumose antennae used in collecting small organisms from the water. Clams protrude tips of siphons that may be two or three times the length of the rest of the animal. The biota (fauna and flora) of rocky coasts exposed to surf has evolved adaptations for firm attachment to the substratum and for deflection of the force of waves. These adaptations include the tough holdfasts of algae, the strong byssus threads secreted by mussels, and the conical shells of limpets and acorn barnacles (see Figure 5.23). Barnacles cement themselves immovably to the substratum and thrust out feathery legs for feeding. Limpets, on the other hand, creep freely over the rocks, but their "chinese-hat" shells deflect the wave force.

METEOROLOGICAL EFFECTS Atmospheric movements influence climate and produce a variety of meteorological phenomena, which we refer to in the aggregate as *weather*. As water evaporates from the surface of lakes and oceans it coalesces into clouds, which are then transported by wind. When a moving mass of air meets another air mass markedly different in temperature, the likely result will be precipitation, strong local convection currents, and electrical discharges along the *front* (interface of the two air masses). Movement of gas molecules from a "mountain" of air (an atmospheric *high*) follows a spiral path into an adjacent "valley" in the atmosphere (a *depression* or *low*). Such movement from a high-pressure area to a low-pressure area takes the form of a circular (*cyclonic*) wind system. These winds sometimes attain high velocity and can be quite destructive.

In addition to the effects on living things exerted by the kinetic force of the wind per se, the precipitation associated with fronts and cyclonic air movements may have both beneficial and detrimental effects on life. Although normally contributing to the watertable, in regions where massive destruction of plant cover has been brought about by overcultivation or fire the precipitated water may act as an erosive force, transporting and redepositing large quantities of soil with consequent destruction of life.

The static electricity generated by violent air turbulence within cloud masses is discharged as lightning. Lightning affects the biotic world both favorably and unfavorably. It may ignite fires that destroy vegetation and expose the burnt area to erosion. On the other hand, lightning is responsible for uniting gaseous nitrogen with oxygen, producing oxides, which, dissolved in water and precipitated in thundershowers, enter the soil as nitrite ion (NO_2^-); this ion is readily converted by bacterial action to the nitrates on which plants depend. As we shall see shortly, most living things are unable to utilize atmospheric nitrogen (N_2) directly; hence the abiotic fixation of nitrogen by lightning is significant for the living world.

B Adaptations for flight

We have seen that many organisms profit by wind dispersal, which may be enhanced by various adaptive specializations. In addition to passive dispersal, four major groups of animals (insects, bats, birds, and pterosaurs) evolved means for active flight. Birds and insects have been particu-

Marine Ecology (New York: John Wiley & Sons, Inc., 1958), p. 55.

†A newton is a metric unit of force equal to about 0.2248 lb.

Figure 4.14 □ **Insect flight. High frequencies of wingbeat can be generated by means of slight deformations of the elastic exoskeleton. In flies, for example, the wings are inserted at the junction of the dorsal and lateral skeletal plates; as tension is generated by contraction of the intrathoracic muscles, the wing base snaps over the edge of the lateral plate, moving the wing tip rapidly through as much as 180°. Forward movement occurs because the wings do not merely move up and down but, during each cycle, their tips describe figure 8s and therefore act like propellers to pull the insect forward.**

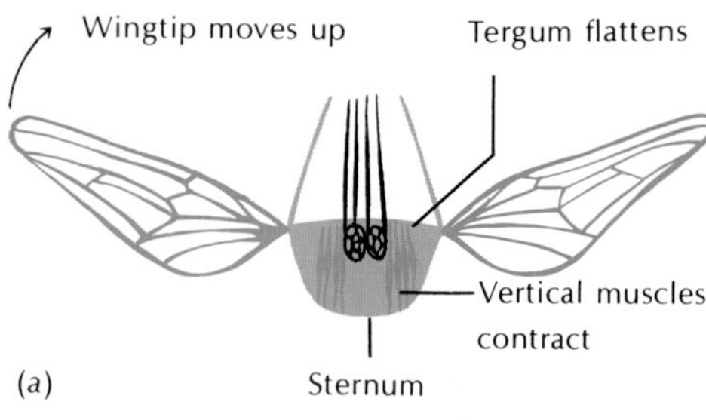

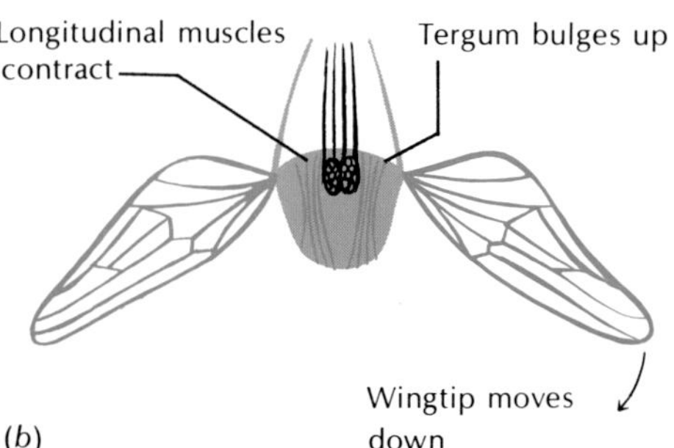

larly successful in developing an efficient wing structure coupled with the necessary neural and physiological mechanisms. These two groups have become expert fliers and this accomplishment has greatly increased their potential for dispersal and survival.

INSECTS The wings of insects are radically different from those of winged vertebrates, for they do not represent modified legs. They develop as outgrowths of the thoracic body wall and are filled with air spaces and strengthened by supportive "veins" (see Figure 12.33*a*). The flight muscles are not attached directly to the wings, but are attached instead to the inner walls of the thorax. One pair of flight muscles runs the length of the thoracic cavity. When these *longitudinal* muscles contract, the upper plate of the exoskeleton is bowed upward. This deformation in turn forces the wings through a downward arc. An opposing set of muscles (the *tergosternals*) runs obliquely from the top to the bottom of the thoracic cavity, being attached to both the dorsal and the ventral plates of the thoracic exoskeleton (the tergum and the sternum). When the tergosternal muscles contract, they depress the tergum and cause the wing tips to rise (Figure 4.14). This highly efficient mechanism permits the wing tips to be moved through an arc of 180° at frequencies exceeding 50 times per second! Insects are seldom large enough to fly against wind currents and while in flight may be carried downwind for great distances. Their presence on oceanic islands is best explained by wind displacement. The conspicuous biotic success of insects is largely attributable to their power of flight for this has permitted their dispersal over the entire globe.

FLYING VERTEBRATES At different times, three separate groups of vertebrates have undergone evolutionary changes that enabled them to use the atmosphere as a medium for active locomotion. In each case, the forelimb has been modified into a wing but each time the modification has taken a different form. In pterosaurs (the extinct flying reptiles) and bats, the wing surface was formed by the development of a membrane of skin stretching from the forelimb to the sides of the trunk. The bones of four fingers of the bat's hand are extremely attenuated for support of the flight membrane and are correspondingly fragile and susceptible to fracture (see Figure 1.9). The flight membrane of pterosaurs was supported along its outer edge by the prodigiously elongated fifth finger. Because of its flimsy skeletal support the pterosaur wing probably could be utilized only in gliding.

Wing development took quite a different evolutionary path in birds (Figure 4.15). The bird's hand and finger bones are not elongated but reduced and sturdily fused, and the wing surface is formed primarily by the light, strong flight feathers. This type of construction is less susceptible to serious injury than that of other types of vertebrate wings, for although the plumage may occasionally be damaged it is molted and regenerated. Each feather is supported by a horny shaft, off each side of which run parallel series of barbs. Adjacent barbs are hooked together by barbules bearing minute hooks (barbicels). Should the barbules become unhooked, preening with the beak sets them in order. Each feather develops from a feather follicle in the skin and is composed of densely packed keratinized

Figure 4.15 □ **Bird adaptations for flight. (*a*) Position of bird in flight, showing skeletal specializations. Note fusion of hand and wrist bones. Only digits 2, 3, and 4 of the typical five remain, the second supporting the alula, a tuft of feathers important in maneuvering. The third and fourth digits and metacarpals support the primary flight feathers, the secondary flight feathers are supported by the lower arm bones (ulna and radius), and the tertiaries are supported by the upper arm bone (humerus). Note short, fused backbone, long, rigid pelvis, and extended and flexible neck. Weight is lightened by the absence of teeth and by other adaptations mentioned in the text. (*b*) Structure of a flight feather. Smaller contour feathers smooth the body outline, reducing air friction, and down feathers conserve body heat.**

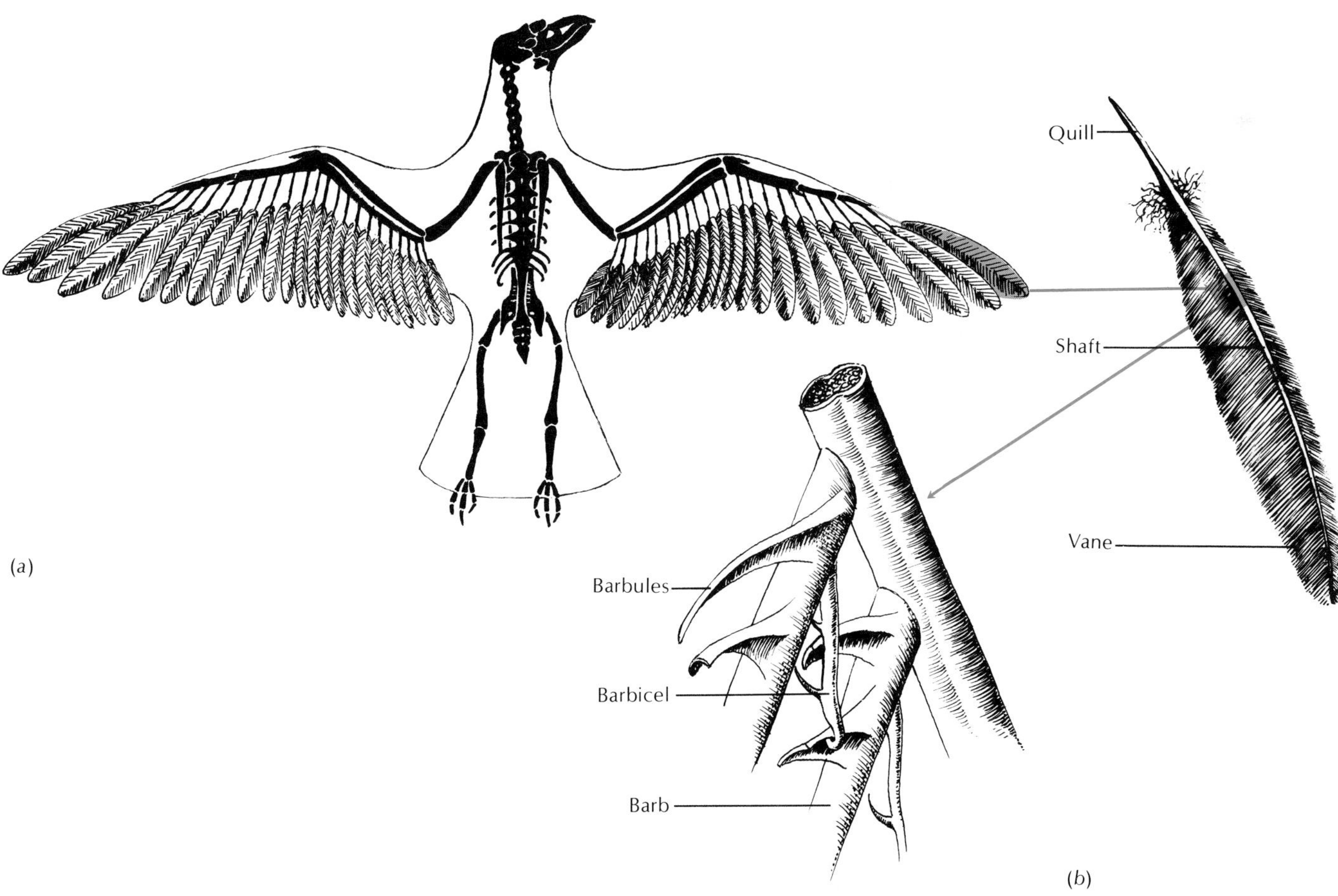

Figure 4.16 ☐ **Flight maneuvers. Note the positions assumed by wings and tail during (*a*) the landing maneuver of a pintail duck and (*b*) the hovering of a hummingbird. The hummingbird's wing moves as a whole, like a paddle, making possible both speed and extreme maneuverability.** [*Zoological Society of San Diego photos, (b) by Ron Garrison.*]

(*a*)

(*b*)

cells. The small down and filoplume feathers, which help to retain body warmth, are of simpler construction, but the contour feathers of which we have just spoken are an outstanding example of functional morphology, as precise and elaborate as any human architectural venture.

As an outcome of having adopted flight as a means of locomotion, birds have evolved a complex set of flight-related structural and functional specializations. Ancient birds had short grasping fingers on each hand, which were used in climbing; but as the power of flight began to act as a selective factor in further evolution, these fingers were lost and many additional modifications of the skeleton and internal organs took place. In modern birds, weight has been lessened by the elimination of teeth, gall and urinary bladders, and one of the formerly paired ovaries. Large air sacs occupy part of the body cavity and extend into the arm bones. The metabolic rate is elevated over that of any other vertebrate. The backbone is rigidly fused in the trunk region, while the neck, in compensation, is extraordinarily long and flexible. The breastbone protrudes as a bladelike keel to which the powerful chest muscles are attached. These and other specializations have made the bird the most successful of flying vertebrates. Both wings and tail can be deployed expertly for hovering and landing (Figure 4.16). For vertical takeoff and landing a duck can shorten its wingstroke and move the wingtips somewhat in the manner of helicopter rotors. The hummingbird's arm is shortened so that its wing can be moved like a paddle and rotated for hovering.

The undisputed masters of atmospheric currents are soaring birds; the wandering albatross, a great oceanic bird that spends most of its life out of sight of land, glides on wings that may exceed 3 m from tip to tip. Birds that spend much time aloft have become adept at conserving their energy resources by taking advantage of atmospheric currents and updrafts, used to gain altitude. Rarely flapping its wings, the soaring bird makes delicate adjustments in its glide path by small wing movements that change the angle of the primary feathers. Flapping flight requires expenditure of from 10 to 100 times the amount of energy required for soaring with the wings held motionless.

C The metabolic use of gases

All organisms make physiologic use of various gases, which they take in by way of the skin, stomates, or specialized respiratory organs. Terrestrial organisms obtain needed gases directly from the air, whereas aquatic creatures must depend upon gases passing into solution at the air-water interface or released by respiration or decay within the aquatic habitat itself. The dissolved gases are circulated by water currents and eventually reach even the extreme depths of the ocean. The amount of dissolved gases that water may hold in solution varies inversely with temperature. Water at 0°C, for example, may hold twice as much gaseous oxygen as an equal quantity of water at 30°C. Ocean currents moving poleward at the surface retain as they are chilled increasingly greater quantities of the atmospheric gases that enter solution as waves mix with the overlying air. As the surface water becomes colder its density increases until at last it sinks, carrying with it the dissolved gases. Atmospheric gases are also dissolved in rain and carried to the ground, where they become available to soil organisms. Gases released by the processes of metabolism and decay pass from the soil into the atmosphere or may be taken up by other organisms before they seep out of the ground. Gases pass cyclically between the biotic and abiotic components of the ecosystem, being combined with other molecules within organisms and then being released once again into the atmosphere.

NITROGEN AND THE NITROGEN CYCLE Nitrogen in the molecular form (N_2) comprises 79 percent of the atmosphere. It is required by the entire biotic world for the construction of proteins, nucleic acids, and other nitrogenous compounds, yet in the gaseous state it is virtually unavailable to the living world. Animals cannot utilize inorganic nitrogen but must ingest nitrogen-containing organic compounds manufactured by plants. Plants, in turn, generally can utilize nitrogen only when it is available to them as the *nitrate ion* (NO_3^-) and not as atmospheric molecular nitrogen. We noted earlier that appreciable amounts of atmospheric nitrogen are converted to oxides, including nitrate, by the action of lightning. In addition to this sporadic abiotic source of nitrate, a few species of microorganisms, particularly the *nitrogen-fixing bacteria,* can accomplish this conversion and subsequently utilize the nitrogen in manufacturing nitrogenous compounds. Eventually these are broken down and released to the soil as ammonia (NH_3), which other soil bacteria convert to nitrite (NO_2^-) and nitrate. Some species of nitrogen-fixing bacteria inhabit soil or water, whereas others flourish within swellings or nodules on the roots of legumes, such as peas, beans, and alfalfa (Figure 4.17). Legumes therefore are crops of great importance because they enrich rather than deplete the soil nitrogen.

While the trapping of atmospheric nitrogen is performed by microorganisms such as nitrogen-fixing bacteria and certain blue-green algae, other types of bacteria and fungi promote the putrefaction of dead organisms and voided wastes, during which various nitrogenous compounds are broken down to ammonia. With H_2O, NH_3 reacts to yield ammonium ion (NH_4^+), which can be oxidized to NO_2^- by *nitrite bacteria.* Nitrite bacteria not only use NH_4^+ as a nitrogen source but also utilize the energy released by its oxidation to NO_2^- in their constructive metabolism. Not all of the NO_2^- produced by these bacteria remains available for conversion to NO_3^-: *denitrifying bacteria* use NO_2^- and NO_3^- in their oxidative metabolism and release N_2 to the atmosphere as a waste product.

Most higher plants cannot utilize NO_2^- as a nitrogen source but must depend upon nitrate bacteria for its further oxidation to NO_3^-. Such nitrifying bacteria derive the energy needed for their own metabolism from the conversion of NO_2^- to NO_3^- and in so doing incidentally produce a byproduct of inestimable significance to the rest of the living world. The continuance of life on earth thus depends on a few species of microbes that convert nitrogen into forms usable by the rest of the biosphere. This fact should be seriously weighed in these days of careless contamination of soil and water, when pollutants which cannot be broken down by ordinary decay processes fre-

Figure 4.17 □ **Nitrogen fixation in legume-root nodules. (*a*) The photographs show a legume (soybean) root system with nodules (*The Nitragin Co., Inc.*) and a section through both root and nodule (*Triarch Incorporated, Geo. H. Conant, Ripon, Wis.*). (*b*) At higher magnifications, dense concentrations of nitrogen-fixing bacteroids are seen within the nodule cells. When cultured in the laboratory, these unusually shaped bacteria revert to the form of ordinary bacilli.**

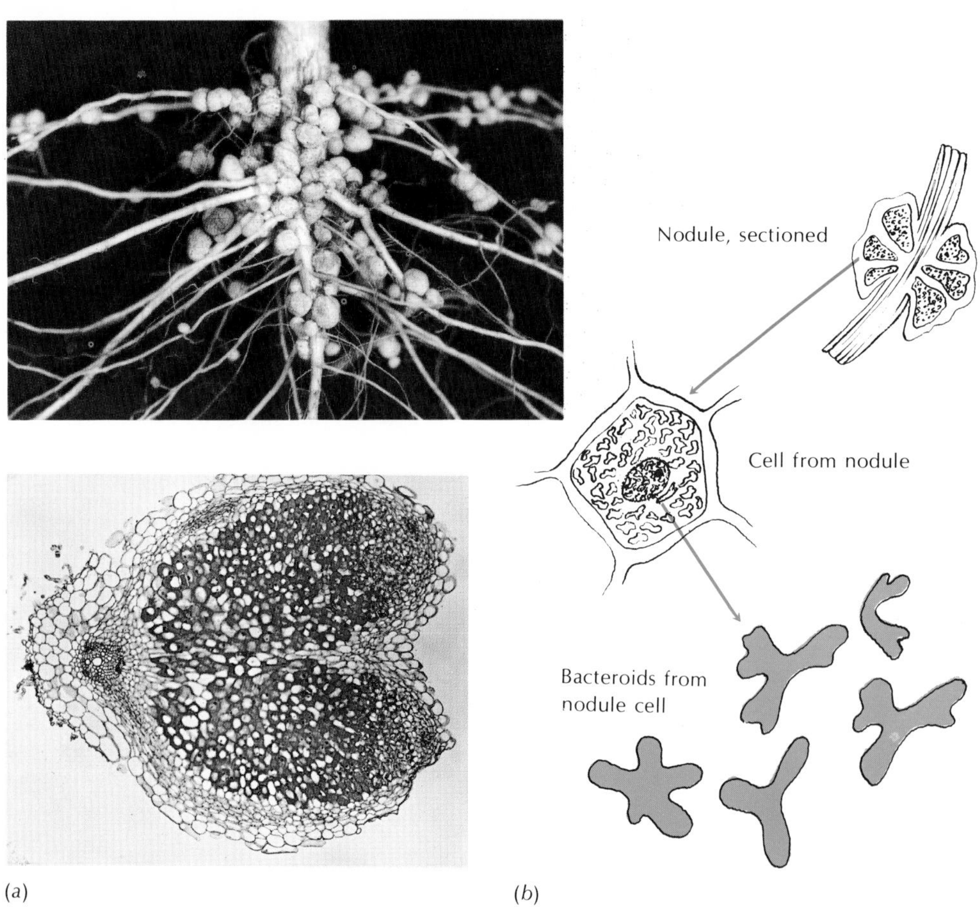

quently accumulate in concentrations toxic to the microorganisms on which the cycling of nitrogenous materials depend.

The circular pathway of nitrogen between the atmosphere and the biosphere, termed the *nitrogen cycle*, is schematically illustrated in Figure 4.18.

CARBON DIOXIDE AND THE CARBON CYCLE Although today CO_2 comprises only about 0.044 percent of the atmosphere, its significance for life is second to none, for it is the source of the carbon atoms employed by living things in constructing the great variety of organic compounds of which their bodies are composed.

The fixing of CO_2 molecules involves their chemical combination with hydrogen atoms derived from H_2O molecules. These reactions require energy, usually in the form of light; however a number of bacteria that do not possess chlorophyll (the pigment responsible for absorption and transfer of radiant energy) are nonetheless able to fix CO_2 by using energy obtained by simple oxidative conversions of inorganic compounds. Such nonphotosynthetic, CO_2-fixing organisms include nitrite and nitrate bacteria, sulfur bacteria, which obtain energy from the conversion of sulfide (S^{2-}) to sulfate (SO_4^{2-}),

$$H_2S \longrightarrow H_2SO_4$$

and iron bacteria, which derive energy from oxidizing ferrous (Fe^{2+}) to ferric (Fe^{3+}) compounds. An interesting side effect of the activity of iron bacteria is that in providing for their own energy needs these microbes convert soluble iron compounds into less soluble ones, thus causing the precipitation of iron as sedimentary iron ore. At present such deposits are being formed mainly in

Figure 4.18 □ Nitrogen cycle. Atmospheric nitrogen cannot be utilized directly by most organisms but is fixed as soil nitrates through the action of soil bacteria, soil algae, and bacteria in legume root nodules. (Lightning and sunlight also convert a certain amount of nitrogen to nitrate.) Nitrate ion is used by plants in building proteins and other nitrogenous compounds. These are converted into compounds typical of animal tissue when the plants are consumed by animals. Nitrogen is returned to the soil in animal excreta (as urea, ammonia, uric acid, and so on) and by the death of plants and animals. Decay bacteria process the dead matter, liberating ammonia. This may be converted to nitrogen gas by the action of denitrifying bacteria or may be oxidized first to nitrite ion by soil nitrite bacteria.

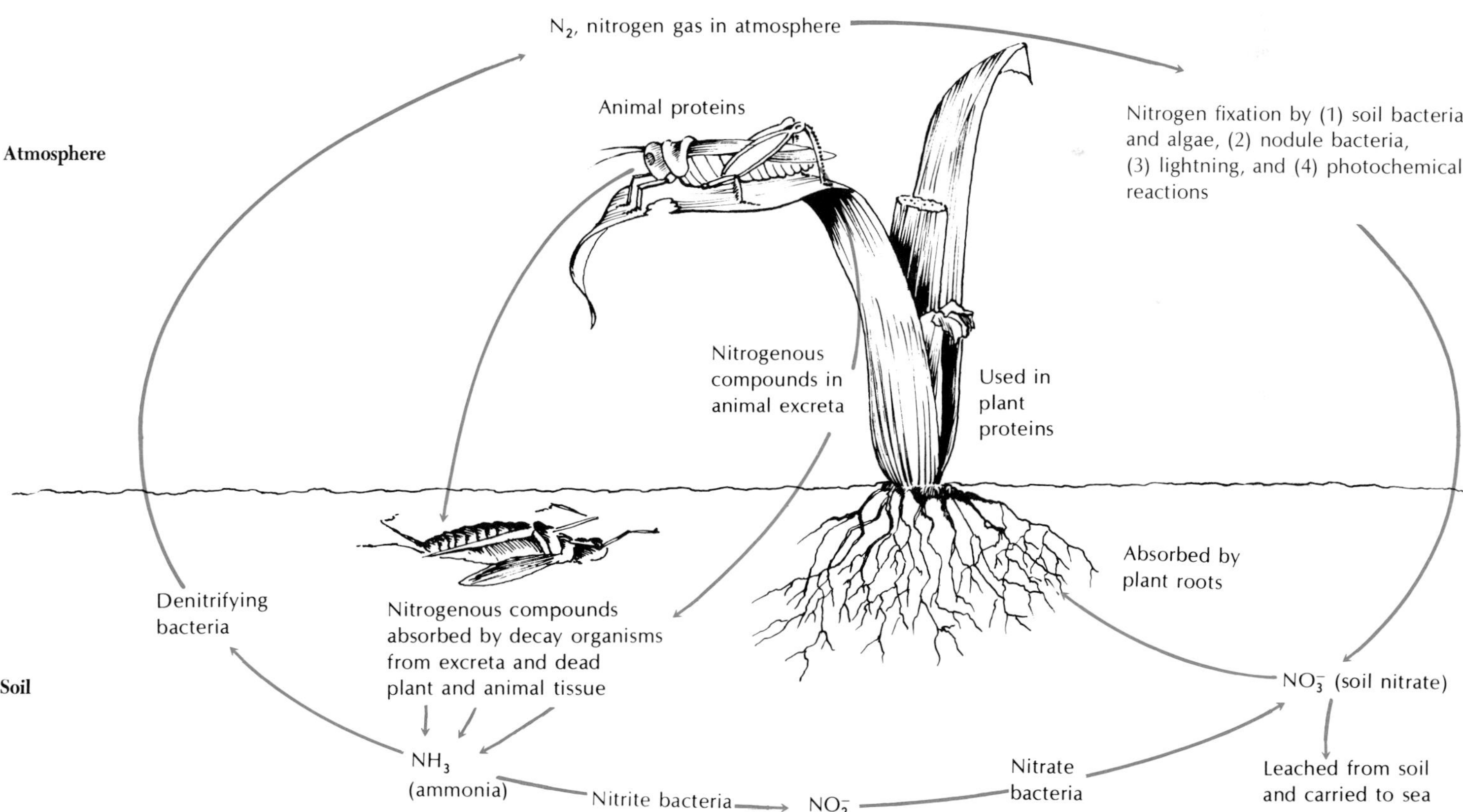

Figure 4.19 □ **Carbon cycle. To indicate the relative importance of various agencies in moving carbon dioxide between the atmosphere, hydrosphere, and biosphere, we may cite the following quantities: atmospheric carbon dioxide, 7.5×10^{11} tons; land-plant photosynthesis uses 0.2×10^{11}; aquatic-plant photosynthesis, 2×10^{11}; fossil-fuel reserves, 45×10^{11}; dissolved carbon dioxide and carbonates, 180×10^{11}; total respired, 1.08×10^{11}. Carbon locked in fossil fuels is liberated by combustion.**

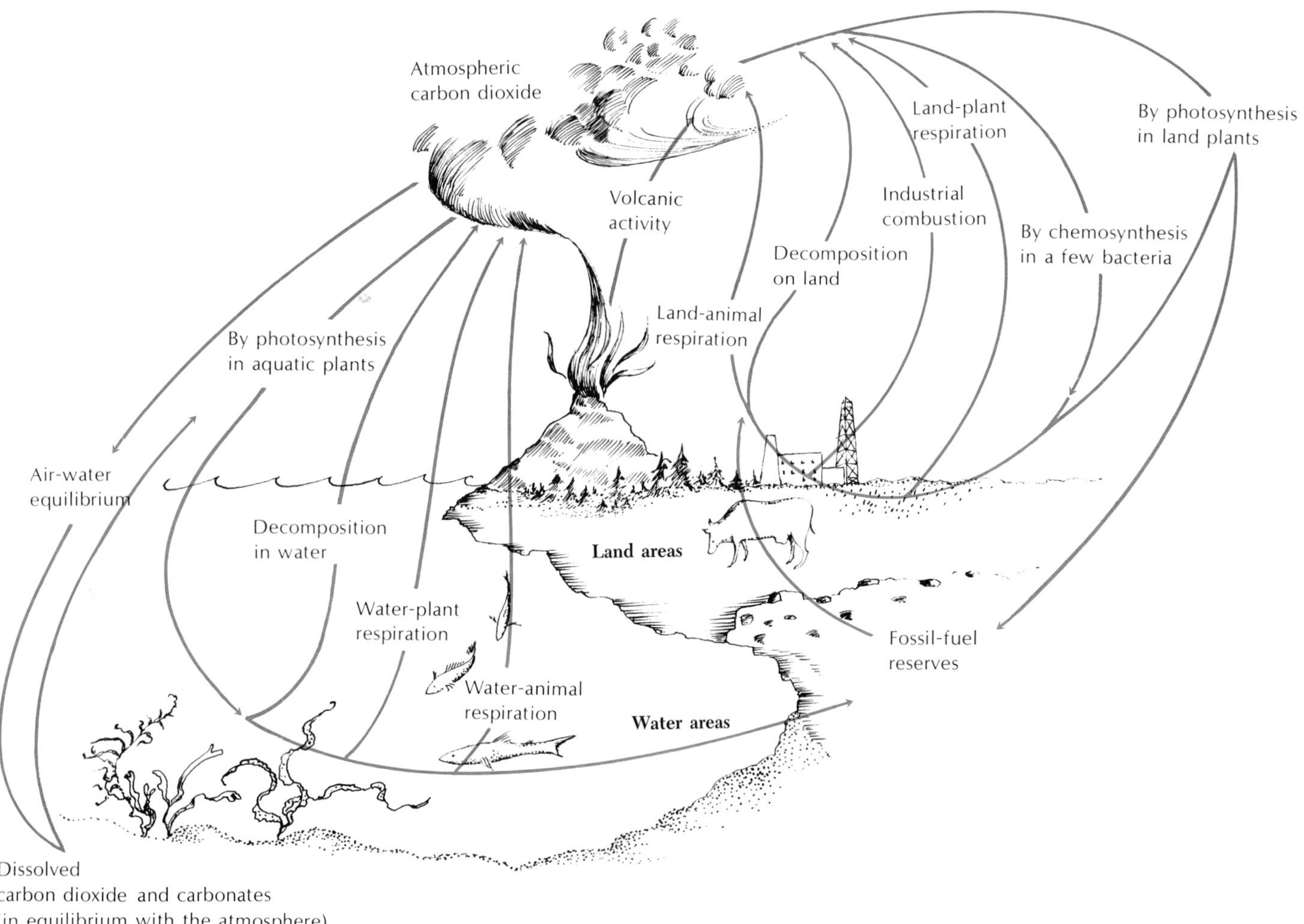

bogs. Extensive beds of sedimentary iron now being mined accumulated on the beds of ancient lakes as much as 1.5×10^9 years ago, primarily as a result of bacterial action. These iron-fixing bacteria therefore not only represent some of the earliest living things, but also have left us a legacy of importance in the present industrial age.

With the evolution of photosynthesis, the use of *radiant* energy instead of *chemical* energy for the fixing of CO_2 put the living world on a profit economy. Once the boundless supply of solar energy could be tapped, the potential of living things for development was restricted only by their genetic limitations and the supply of available carbon.

Carbon can pass from the abiotic world into the biotic world only as CO_2 or, more limitedly, as carbonate or bicarbonate ion (CO_3^{2-} or HCO_3^-). Deposits of carbon compounds such as coal, consisting of material derived from ancient plants, remain inaccessible for metabolic use until converted to CO_2 and H_2O by oxidation (as in combustion). Atmospheric CO_2 is mainly replenished by the slow combustion of decay, brought about chiefly through the agency of bacteria and fungi. Without the activity of these simple organisms, the continued photosynthetic activity of higher plants would rapidly deplete atmospheric CO_2 to a level at which plant growth would virtually cease and the earth would no longer be capable of sustaining most of the present biosphere.

Both plants and animals must constantly tap reserves of chemical energy, which they make available by the degradation of carbon compounds, thereby releasing CO_2 into the atmosphere. However, the net production of solid material by plants so greatly exceeds their need for oxidative breakdown of these materials that plant and animal metabolism alone cannot replenish atmospheric CO_2 at a rate equal to the rate of its fixation. Combustion and decay are required to restore the equilibrium.

The carbon cycle is presented in Figure 4.19, which depicts the manner in which carbon atoms are repeatedly utilized and released by the living world. It may be seen that the reaction of CO_2 with H_2O to produce CO_3^{2-} and HCO_3^- is important in that it provides materials used in the construction of shells, coral reefs, and the like.

HYDROGEN SULFIDE AND THE SULFUR CYCLE Anyone familiar with the rotten-egg odor of hydrogen sulfide (H_2S) will appreciate the fact that this gas is not present in perceptible concentrations in the atmosphere as a whole, although its release may be conspicuous in the vicinity of volcanoes and hot springs, as well as in bogs where it is given off by rotting materials. Much H_2S is converted from the gaseous state by bacterial action before it can diffuse out of the soil into the air. That which escapes to the atmosphere eventually is fixed by *sulfur bacteria* (for example, *Thiobacillus*). Sulfur, like nitrogen, is an element necessary for life that becomes available for general use only through the activities of a relatively few species of microorganisms. Sulfur passes cyclically between the biotic and abiotic worlds (Figure 4.20), being made accessible to the living world as a whole primarily through the activities of microbes that can accomplish the conversion of H_2S to SO_4^{2-}, the only form in which higher plants can use sulfur. Plant proteins containing sulfur are in turn eaten by animals and transformed into animal proteins; some sulfur may be excreted as urinary SO_4^{2-} released by the breakdown of proteins during metabolism. Upon the death of both plant and animal tissue, these proteins are decomposed by putrefying bacteria and the constituent sulfur is eventually released as H_2S. Sulfur bacteria then oxidize H_2S either directly to SO_4^{2-}, or first to elemental sulfur and then to SO_4^{2-}, which again is taken up by higher plants.

OXYGEN IN CELL METABOLISM As part of the carbon dioxide molecule, oxygen atoms are incorporated into most organic compounds. However, *gaseous* oxygen (O_2) can*not* be directly utilized by organisms in constructing organic molecules. Instead, it functions as a *hydrogen acceptor*. This means that it combines with hydrogen atoms released by the breakdown of organic compounds to produce water. Water, as we have said, is the source of hydrogen atoms used in the production of carbohydrate. The oxygen atoms derived from water molecules are released to the atmosphere as waste products of photosynthesis.

The photosynthetic pathways of carbon, hydrogen, and oxygen atoms may be traced experimentally. If a plant is placed in a sealed vessel containing H_2O and a measured quantity of CO_2, it may be seen that the amount of free CO_2 decreases in inverse proportion to the amount of O_2 set free. That is, apparently one molecule of O_2 is liberated for each molecule of CO_2 fixed. A logical but erroneous conclusion would be that each molecule of O_2 released has come from the breakdown of CO_2 to C and O_2. That this is not the case may be shown by conducting the previous experiment using *heavy* H_2O [that is, H_2O containing a

Figure 4.20 □ **Sulfur cycle.**

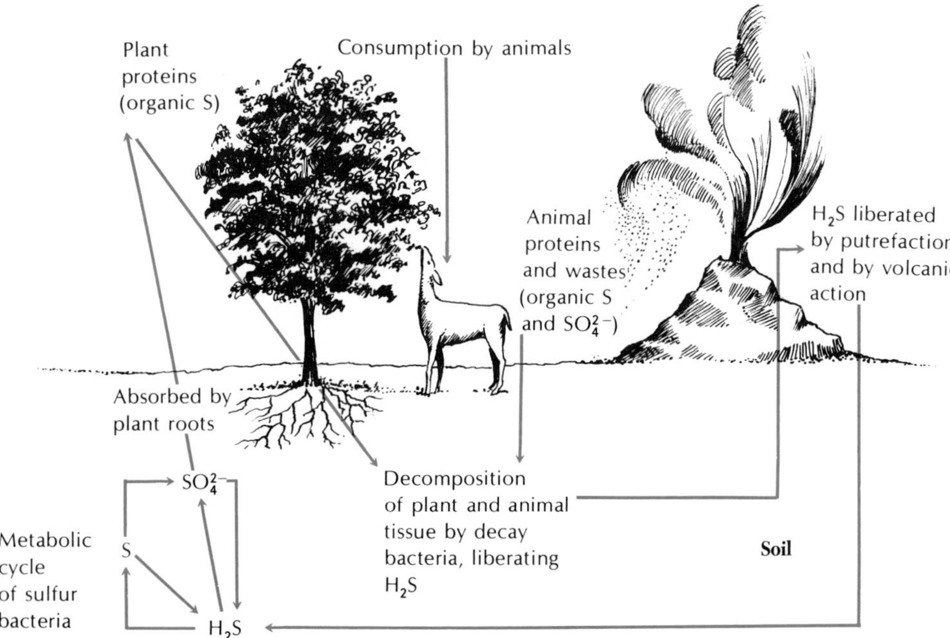

heavy form of oxygen (^{18}O), instead of the commoner form (^{16}O)]. By this means it can be proved that all of the O_2 released during photosynthesis consists of O atoms derived from the heavy -H_2O molecules (Figure 4.21) and that none comes from CO_2. Similar studies have shown that O_2 can be used metabolically only in the formation of *water* molecules, combining chemically with hydrogen released by the breakdown of organic compounds. Except for a few species that can utilize substances other than gaseous oxygen as hydrogen acceptors, oxygen deprivation causes death. The great majority of plants and animals must take in O_2 and are accordingly termed *aerobes*. Species that do not need O_2 to live (mostly certain bacteria) are termed *anaerobes*. For a few of these (*obligate* anaerobes), O_2 is actually poisonous.

It should be noted that with respect to O_2 and CO_2, the dependence of animals on plants is not fully reciprocated. Animal life is directly dependent on plant life for the replenishment of atmospheric O_2 (Figure 4.22). Plants, on the contrary, liberate ample O_2 to meet their own metabolic needs. Animal respiration is often cited as being responsible for the release of the CO_2 required by plants. This conclusion applies only to conditions in which both organisms are confined together in small sealed containers. On a world scale, plant respiration coupled with the decay and combustion of plant materials would be adequate to replenish atmospheric CO_2 without appreciable assistance from animals.

EXTERNAL RESPIRATION: EXCHANGE OF GASES Both carbon dioxide and oxygen can pass into and out of the body of an organism by simple *diffusion,* following their respective *concentration gradients:* any gas (or substance in solution) tends to diffuse or spread from an area where it is more concentrated into adjacent areas where it is less concentrated. The tendency of molecules to diffuse may be demonstrated simply by uncapping a bottle of ether or perfume. In time the container will be virtually emptied of the substance previously contained and molecules of that substance will be equally dispersed throughout the air of the room. Each kind of substance diffuses along its *own* concentration gradient; if containers of ether and of perfume are opened together both substances will diffuse until the air of the room contains both kinds of molecules, each evenly dispersed.

In nonphotosynthesizing cells, as O_2 diffuses into the cells it is converted to H_2O; therefore the intracellular concen-

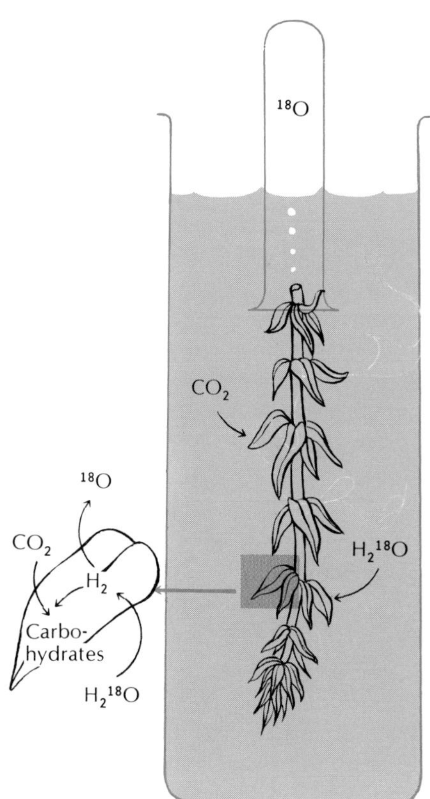

Figure 4.21 □ **Experiment demonstrating that all O_2 liberated during photosynthesis comes from H_2O and not from CO_2. A piece of *Elodea* immersed in heavy water ($H_2{}^{18}O$), made with the heavy isotope of oxygen (^{18}O), during photosynthesis liberates bubbles of O_2, which when analyzed are found to consist almost entirely of ^{18}O. The CO_2 present contains the ordinary isotope of oxygen (^{16}O).**

Figure 4.22 □ **Gaseous exchanges in plants and animals. Plants both release O_2 (as a byproduct of photosynthesis) and consume it during oxidative respiration (using it as a H acceptor, to make H_2O). Animals too use O_2 as a H acceptor in cell respiration. As a product of oxidative metabolism, CO_2 is released in both plants and animals. Plants either liberate excess CO_2 to the atmosphere or store it as CO_3^{2-} until it can be converted to carbohydrate during photosynthesis. For animals excess CO_2 is toxic, and they release it from the respiratory organs or (as HCO_3^- and CO_3^{2-}) in the urine.**

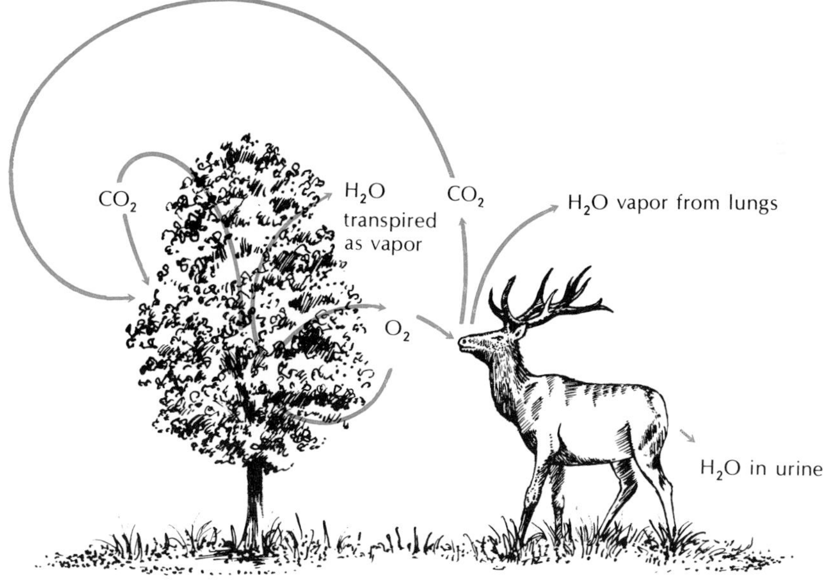

tration of free O_2 remains consistently less than in the surrounding medium and more O_2 tends to enter the cells. A reversal of the concentration gradient for O_2 occurs during photosynthesis, when O_2 is liberated within the cells and consequently tends to diffuse out of the plant.

Carbon dioxide also follows a concentration gradient in diffusing into or out of cells. In plants kept in the dark (hence not photosynthesizing) and in animals, the carbon dioxide produced by cell metabolism tends to follow its concentration gradient *out* of the cell and thence out of the organism. During photosynthesis, carbon dioxide is fixed about as rapidly as it is released by oxidative metabolism; therefore the concentration gradient remains such that carbon dioxide diffuses *into* the plant cells.

Plant metabolism ordinarily proceeds at a rate slow enough that its requirements for gaseous exchange with the environment may be met simply by diffusion of gases through the stomates or, in the case of aquatic plants, through any portion of the surface. The higher energy requirements of animals, an outcome of their more mobile existence, generally requires the evolution of adaptive devices for facilitating gaseous exchange. When an animal is aquatic and small (or has a low metabolic rate), there may be no need for special respiratory organs. Exchange of gases may take place over most of the body surface. However, as the mass of an organism increases its volume becomes too great in comparison with its surface area for this surface exchange to be adequate. The problem becomes still more acute when the body is partly encased in some type of shell, tube, armor, or horny skin, which will impede gaseous diffusion. Furthermore, the more active the animal, the more exacting are its requirements for gaseous exchange. Thus, the evolution of more effective means for facilitating gaseous exchange was prerequisite to increases in size and metabolic rate and adoption of a terrestrial mode of life. The respiratory organs of aquatic and terrestrial animals (see Figure 14.30) share some fundamental characteristics: (1) they provide a very large *surface area* in contact with the surrounding milieu; (2) the respiratory membrane through which gases diffuse is thin and moist. In animals in which a circulatory system is employed for the transport of dissolved gases, the respiratory membrane is *highly vascularized* (that is, provided with a rich network of very small, thin-walled vessels, the capillaries, into and out of which gas molecules will readily diffuse). Various muscles (such as the mammalian diaphragm) are employed in breathing, to refresh the supply of air or water in contact with the respiratory membrane.

Gases effectively diffuse across membranes only when in solution. In aquatic animals the respiratory membranes often occur externally as feathery gills that are bathed by the surrounding water, but in terrestrial animals these membranes are located internally, forming the moist lining of *lungs* (vertebrates), *booklungs* (arachnids), and *tracheal systems* (insects); see Figure 14.30. All animals that have successfully made the transition from water to land have had to evolve some means of keeping their respiratory membranes moist.

4.4 □ GRAVITY

Organisms not restricted to lying flat upon the substratum must be provided with some means for resisting the pull of gravity. Aquatic organisms would tend to sink to the bottom if they did not have a way of increasing their buoyancy. Land plants would lie in sheets upon the ground; terrestrial animals could only inch along on flattened bodies. The adaptations that plants and animals have developed for resisting the pull of gravity will be this section's theme.

A Buoyancy devices

Buoyancy is increased in two ways (Figure 4.23): (1) by modifications of body form *increasing the surface-to-volume ratio;* (2) by *reducing the density of the body* so that it is either in equilibrium with the surrounding water or even somewhat less dense than the latter. Density may be reduced by the storage of fats and oils (these being lighter than water) or by the possession of gas-filled bladders such as those of siphonophores (Coelenterata), kelps, and many vertebrate fish. Lipid storage is a par-

Figure 4.23 □ Buoyancy mechanisms in aquatic organisms. (*a*) Density-reducing mechanisms (organisms not drawn to same scale). (*b*) Surface-increasing adaptations: striae on diatom shell at bottom (*courtesy of Bausch & Lomb*) and numerous radiating pseudopods of protozoan (*Actinosphaerium*) at top (*courtesy of Carolina Biological Supply Company*).

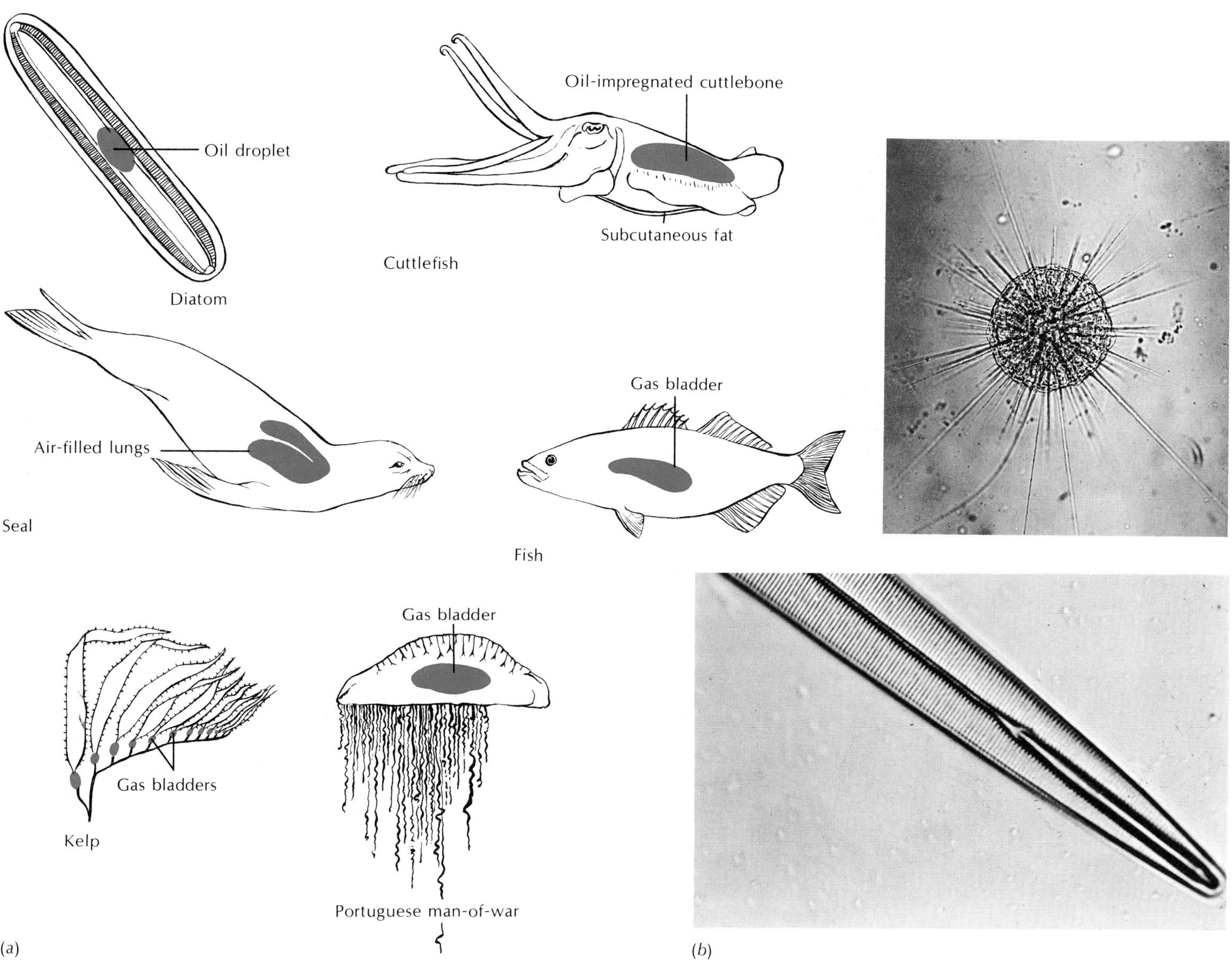

ticularly important means of flotation for phytoplankton, such as diatoms, which would die were they to sink below the level of light penetration. Where subject to physiological regulation, changes in density allow aquatic organisms to remain at a given level in the water without continued energy expenditure. Many fish have internal gas-filled sacs (swim bladders) supplied with glandular tissue that can rapidly secrete additional gases into the bladder as needed; thus the specific gravity of the fish's body remains in equilibrium with the density of the surrounding water. In the case of deep-water fish, the gases of the bladder are under such compression that the fish are killed by explosive decompression if brought quickly to the surface.

Where rapid forward movement is not necessary, the buoyancy of an aquatic organism may be increased by the development of projections of the body wall that augment the surface area and favorably alter the surface-to-volume ratio. The adaptive significance of a high ratio of surface to volume in terms of buoyancy is readily realized if one compares the behavior of a feather with that of a pellet of the same weight: the pellet promptly sinks, whereas the feather remains afloat for some time. Because warm water is less dense than cold water, flotation structures may assume bizarre proportions in tropical species. Figure 4.24 compares three species of copepods, small crustaceans that form an essential part of plankton communities. The species with the simplest body outline lives in cold and temperate regions, while those with an elaborately extended body outline inhabit warmer seas.

Figure 4.24 □ Three species of pelagic copepods. The long processes and bristles abet flotation and are most conspicuous in forms inhabiting such warmer waters as the Mediterranean Sea.

Attached aquatic plants are limited in distribution by the depth to which light can penetrate. The possession of gas-filled bladders, which lift the stipes and blades into the better-illuminated levels, has enabled the larger phaeophytes to extend their range into waters up to 100 m deep.

Bottom-dwelling aquatic species supplement buoyancy mechanisms with some means of mechanical support by which their bodies may be lifted free of the substratum. In unicellular organisms such as *Amoeba,* adequate support can be provided simply by *viscosity changes in the cellular protein,* which assumes a gelatinous consistency. In this condition the pseudopodia are so rigid that only their tips need contact the substratum.

Multicellular organisms characteristically depend for support upon specialized *mechanical tissues* that combine the qualities of rigidity and tensile strength. In terrestrial plants and animals, such mechanical tissues must be particularly sturdy.

B Support in terrestrial plants

Land plants, particularly tracheophytes, possess well-developed mechanical tissues formed by lignification of thick cellulose walls secreted around certain types of cells termed *fiber cells* and *sclerenchyma* (see Figure 11.36). During lignification the

(a)

Two groups of terrestrial arthropods. *Chelicerates:* (*a*) velvet mites, showing the apparently unsegmented trunk and four pairs of walking legs characteristic of these ectoparasitic arachnids and their close relatives, ticks; (*b*) a spider, *Diaea pictilis*, illustrating the effectiveness of disruptive coloration in that the abdomen is brightly colored and pebble-shaped, whereas other body parts match the background, to make it unlikely that predators would perceive the entire body form. (*Los Angeles County Museum of Natural History.*) *Mandibulates:* (*c*) a millipede, *Brachycybe rosea*, from the Mt. Lassen area of California; (*d*) the praying mantis, a predatory insect, grips its prey with the jackknifed terminal joint of its forelegs—such insectivorous insects are of great importance in reducing the numbers of herbivorous insects. (*Los Angeles County Museum of Natural History.*)

(b)

(d)

(c)

(*a*)

(*b*)

Color adaptations among vertebrates. ***Warning colors*** are frequently displayed by venomous species such as (*a*) the small but deadly South American tree frog ***Dendrobates pumilio*** (***courtesy of General Biological, Inc., Chicago***) and (*b*) the coral snake, ***Micrurus fulvius*** (***courtesy of Carolina Biological Supply Company***), a Western-hemisphere representative of the cobra family. ***Dendrobates*** is protected from predators by venom glands in the skin; the venoms of various species of tree frog have long been used by South American Indians for poisoning arrow tips. The reddish, black, and yellow banding of the coral snake also serves to break up its body outline, but its primary role in warning predators is confirmed by the occurrence of various harmless coral mimics occurring sympatrically with one or another species of coral snake. ***Breeding coloration,*** as shown by (*c*) a male shiner, ***Notropis cornutus*** (***courtesy of General Biological, Inc., Chicago***), often renders a male vertebrate conspicuous during the mating season. Such conspicuous pigmentation advertises the individual's physiological readiness to mate, allows rivals to recognize the male in his territory, and attracts females in breeding state but is often lost during the rest of the year, when the male becomes protectively colored.

(*c*)

cellulose cell walls, themselves fairly rigid, are further strengthened by impregnation with a stony material, lignin. After forming these thick surrounding walls, the secretory cells often die, so that the mature mechanical tissue consists only of the deposited noncellular material. In addition to the support provided by fibers and sclerenchyma, *woody* plants gain additional strength from deposits of lignin filling the cavities of old conductive elements.

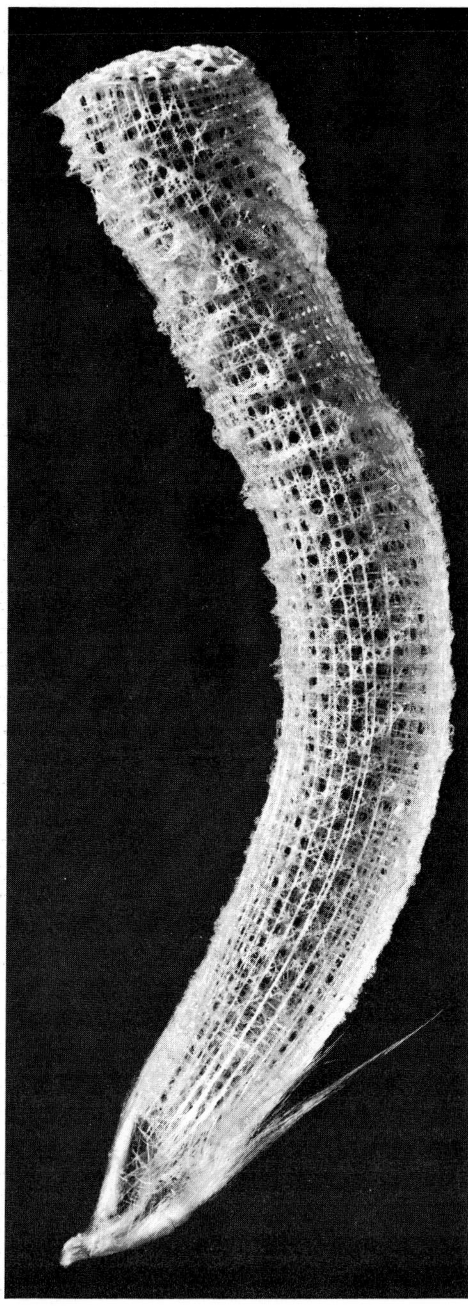

Figure 4.25 □ Skeleton of the siliceous sponge *Euplectella*. (*Los Angeles County Museum of Natural History.*)

C Invertebrate support systems

A variety of supportive tissues occur among metazoans. Some of these are located internally, forming *endoskeletons;* others form external *exoskeletons*. Sponges are supported by an internal framework of branching protein (spongin) fibers or of spicules, which are either calcareous or siliceous. The spicules may remain separate or may fuse to form a reticulate lattice (Figure 4.25). Spicules and spongin fibers are secreted by wandering amoeboid cells similar to those which secrete connective fibers in higher animals.

Many sedentary coelenterates possess exoskeletons (Figure 4.26). Hydroids such as *Obelia* are supported by a chitinous envelope (the *perisarc*), which is secreted by the underlying epidermis. The exoskeletons of stony corals consist of conjoined cup-shaped units, each of which supports a single polyp. The skeletal cups, bearing numerous radiating ridges, are almost entirely composed of calcium carbonate secreted by the epidermis of each polyp. In the "soft" corals (including sea fans and organpipe coral) the skeleton is deposited

Figure 4.26 ☐ **Support in sedentary coelenterates. (*a*) Stony corals, Great Barrier Reef, Australia. (*Courtesy of Australian News and Information Bureau.*) (*b*) A branching gorgonian, or soft, coral, with a horny rather than limey skeletal support, elastic instead of rigid. (*Los Angeles County Museum of Natural History.*) (*c*) Sea fan (*Gorgonia*), showing development of a wide planar surface from a small base. The broad surface of the fan tends to be oriented across the direction of water currents, facilitating food capture by the zooids. (*Courtesy of Carolina Biological Supply Company.*)**

(*a*)

(*b*)

(*c*)

as calcareous spicules or as strands of horny organic material secreted by amoeboid cells that wander through the matrix (*mesoglea*) in which the polyps are embedded. Supportive skeletons such as that of the sea fan *Gorgonia* provide a large surface area on which many polyps can live: if a single larva finds room to settle, it can grow into a colony of hundreds of polyps, supported above the original point of attachment by the fan-shaped skeleton.

Articulated skeletons providing for effective locomotion as well as support occur only in arthropods and vertebrates. The arthropod epidermis secretes a chitinous exoskeleton that molds the body form and permits the trunk to be supported upon the jointed legs. The exoskeleton is composed of protein and a carbohydrate, chitin (see Figure 9.8*d*), and may be further hardened by deposits of calcium phosphate. It remains thin and flexible at intervals along the trunk and limbs, permitting these to bend. The voluntary muscles are attached to the inner surface of the exoskeleton.

Figure 4.27 ☐ **The arthropod exoskeleton. (*a*) Cross section of an arthropod trunk bearing an appendage. Note segmented exoskeleton consisting of external cuticle secreted by underlying epidermis. Major trunk and limb muscles are shown; note tendonous insertion onto distal segment of leg. (*b*) Cross section of arthropod integument. Prior to molting, digestive enzymes begin to dissolve the endocuticle, and a new exocuticle is secreted internally to it. The new exoskeleton is still capable of being stretched at the time of molting and enlarges at this time to accommodate body growth. The integument is studded with sensory bristles, pegs, and pits, served by nerve fibers. Note that muscle fibers insert through the epidermis onto the exoskeleton proper.**

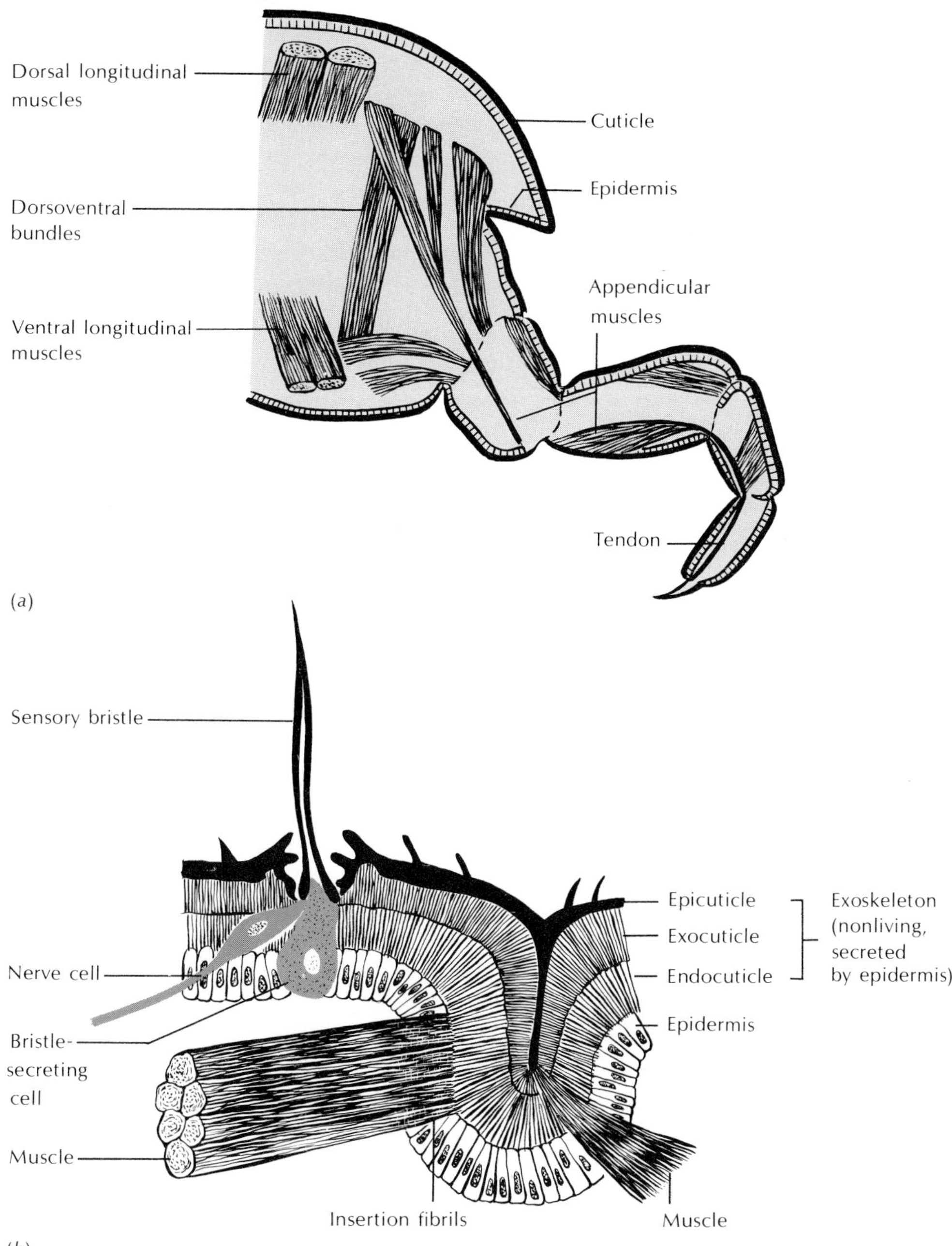

Their contractions bend or straighten the joint, making possible walking and swimming movements (Figure 4.27). Periodically the exoskeleton must be molted to accommodate growth. Molting (*ecdysis*) is hormonally regulated (see Figure 15.46) and is preceded by the secretion of a new but unhardened cuticle interior to the old one. The latter then separates from the underlying layer and splits, allowing the arthropod to withdraw its body (including every bristle) from the old encasement. Following ecdysis the body quickly swells by taking up water, stretching the still-flexible new exoskeleton. The larger arthropods such as crabs and lobsters are helpless for a while after molting until the new skeleton hardens, for their legs cannot bear the body's weight. Adult insects cannot molt and therefore do not grow.

D The vertebrate endoskeleton

The endoskeleton of vertebrates serves for support, for muscle attachment, and for the protection of certain vital organs such as the brain. It consists of bone, cartilage, and connective tissue (see Figure 11.37). Since the skeleton lies internal to the muscles, these attach to the outer surfaces of the skeleton rather than to its inner surface as with exoskeletons (Figure 4.28).

In the evolution of more advanced types of skeletons adaptation must proceed along three more or less contradictory lines: (1) toward increased supportive strength; (2) toward reduced weight (favoring mobility); (3) toward more effective muscular attachments for moving parts of the skeleton. Vertebrate skeletal structure is a compromise resolution of these three conflicting demands.

THE STRUCTURE AND ADAPTABILITY OF BONE *Bone* is perhaps the most complexly organized of all mechanical tissues and shows a remarkable capacity for adjusting to changing stress. Bone is built up of microscopic cylindrical units termed *Haversian systems* (or *osteons;* Figure 4.29). Each osteon consists of matrix secreted in a series of concentric layers about a central cavity (the *Haversian canal*), which encloses an artery, vein, and nerve. The bone cells become trapped within the matrix they secrete but receive nourishment by way of minute canals extending radially through the matrix from the central canal. The matrix consists of the fibrous protein *collagen* (see Figure 10.7*d*) and crystalline calcium phosphate (*hydroxyapatite*). Far from being static, this matrix constantly interchanges materials with the bloodstream. Under hormonal regulation, bone deposits calcium or yields it to the bloodstream as needed.

Bone responds to changes in mechanical load by redepositing and realigning its materials in such a way that maximum support continues to be provided with minimum weight. Throughout maturation, changes in the internal organization of bone accompany the necessary increases in length and diameter. The needs of a growing body are often best met by a comparatively flexible cartilaginous skeleton. As growth proceeds, the cartilage is digested by amoeboid cells (*chondroclasts*) that operate in localized centers of ossification that enlarge as bone deposition proceeds (Figure 4.30). The primary supportive skeleton thus undergoes *endochondral* ("within cartilage") ossification, whereas bones derived from the skin (dermal bones), which serve less for support than for protection, ossify directly (membraneous ossification).

The shaft of a bone consists of a cylinder of dense bone composed of tightly packed osteons. The greater the weight the shaft must bear, the more compressive force is exerted upon the osteons; this results in further deposition of bone and the production of a thicker shaft. The outer cylinder is sturdy enough that weight can be saved; the center of the shaft has a marrow cavity filled with fat tissue or maturing blood cells. The heads of the bone consist mainly of spongy bone in which osteons are deposited along internal lines of stress to form an elaborate lattice that again furnishes maximal support with minimal weight.

Although the overall organizational pattern of the skeleton is a product of evolution dictated by the support needs of animals of various sizes and modes of life, bony tissue itself is highly adaptable and can be dissolved and redeposited to adjust to changing stress. This adaptability has been investigated experimentally. It may be explicable on the basis of the finding that an electrical current is generated within bone when it is put under stress. Both the calcium phosphate and collagen molecules in bone are arranged in a regular crystalline configuration: when these crystals are bent, a flow of electricity passes between them. This flow of electricity seems to affect the behavior of materials being deposited to form new matrix. In the laboratory, when an electrical current is passed through a solution of collagen, the molecules turn with their long axes at right angles to the flow of the current and aggregate to form fibers. In an isolated strip of bone that is being

Figure 4.28 □ **Endoskeletal and exoskeletal muscle attachments. (*a*) One of the major flexors of the vertebrate forelimb, the brachialis, is shown originating on the humerus and inserting on the ulna. Its contraction bends the limb. The major extensor, or triceps brachii, originates on the shoulder blade and humerus and inserts on the ulna; its contraction straightens the limb. (*b*) Arthropod muscles are also arranged in antagonistic pairs, but since they attach to the inner surface of the skeleton, the positions of flexors and extensors are reversed from those of the corresponding vertebrate muscles.**

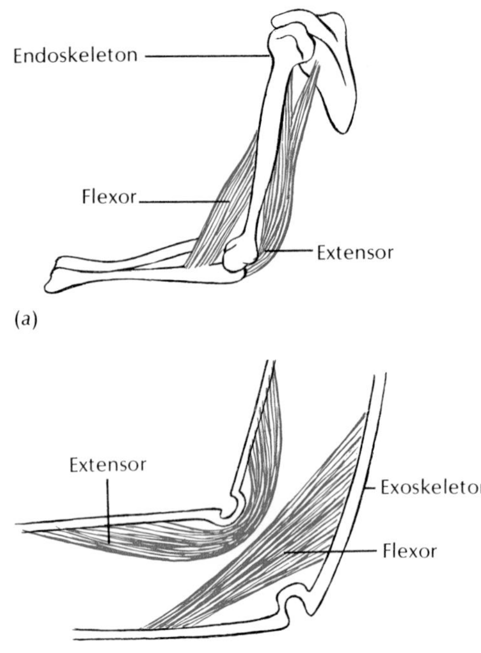

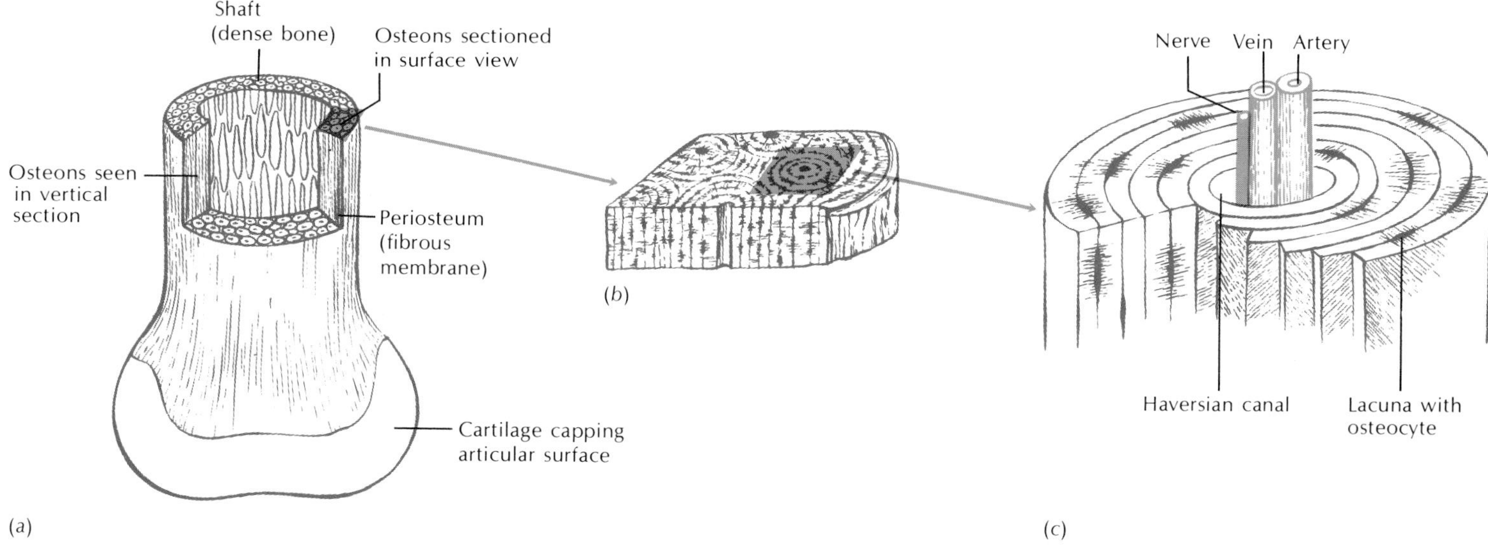

Figure 4.29 □ The structure of vertebrate bone. (*a*) Portion of a long bone, showing section of shaft. (*b*) Enlargement of portion of dense bone, showing its organization into parallel tubular Haversian systems. (*c*) Portion of a single Haversian system. Note deposition of bony matrix in concentric layers (lamellae) surrounding the central nerve and blood vessels. Note also that the crystalline structure of each lamella is oriented at right angles to that of adjacent lamellae.

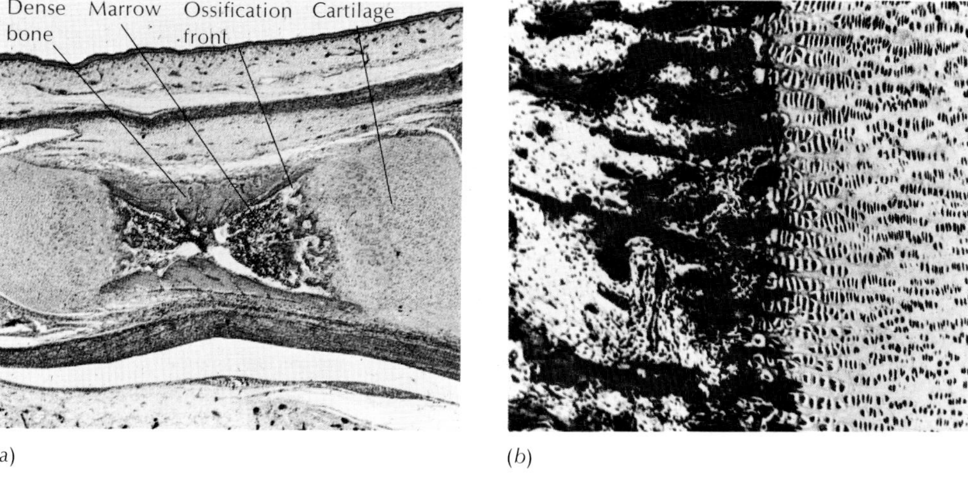

Figure 4.30 □ Endochondral bone formation. (*a*) Longitudinal section of entire fetal finger bone, showing process of ossification taking place in center of bone. Both ends of the bone still consist of hyaline cartilage, but in the shaft the cartilage is being digested away and replaced by marrow and bony tissue. (*b*) Ossification front in developing bone. At this higher magnification the interface between the retreating cartilage (at right) and advancing bone can be seen. Bony matrix is deposited irregularly in the area to left and is stained darkly. Marrow occupies the pale areas. (*Courtesy of General Biological, Inc., Chicago.*)

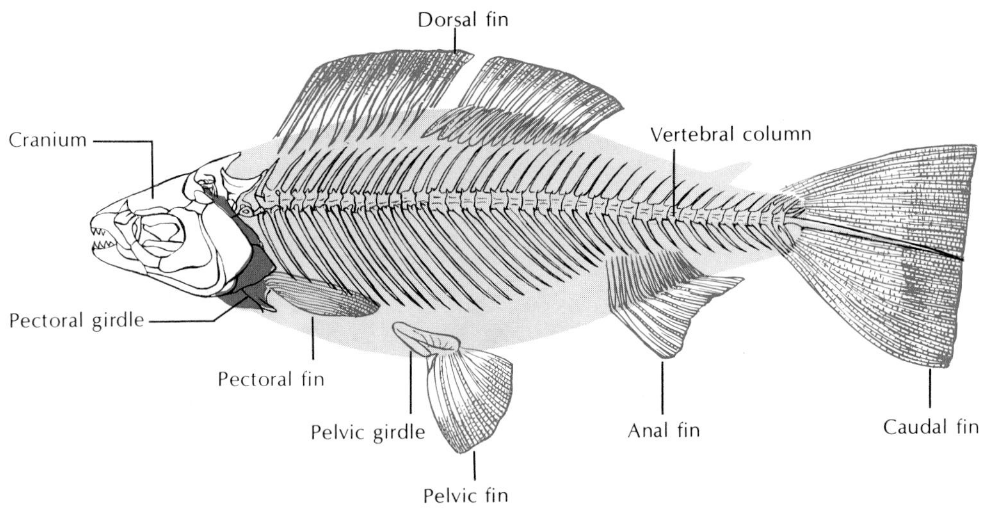

Figure 4.31 □ Fish skeleton: axial support. The axial skeleton consists of the cranium, jaws, gill arches, and vertebral column. The appendicular skeleton consists of the pectoral and pelvic girdles that support the pectoral and pelvic fins, respectively. The pectoral girdle of fish is braced against the skull, but the pelvic girdle lacks attachment to the axial skeleton.

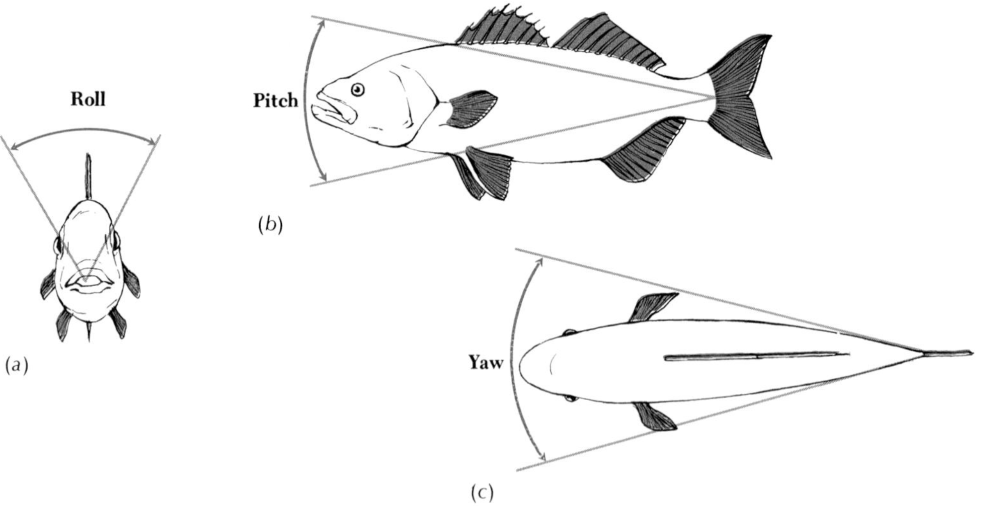

Figure 4.32 □ A fish's fins act as horizontal and vertical stabilizers that reduce deviation from the line of motion about three axes: (*a*) the longitudinal axis, (*b*) the transverse axis, and (*c*) the vertical axis. Fish models tested in wind tunnels exhibit various types of deviation when one fin or another is removed. The pectoral and pelvic fins can also be maneuvered for turning and braking. Major forward thrust is provided by the trunk and tail muscles that move the caudal fin from side to side.

bent, the direction of flow of the electrical current generated by this stress is determined by the direction of bending: the concave side of the strip (which is being compressed) becomes negatively charged, while the convex side (which is being stretched) becomes positively charged. New bone is then deposited along the concave side, in the negatively charged region. When electrodes are inserted into a living bone in the intact body, new matrix is deposited only around the negative electrode. These electrical properties of bone may explain why it is so adaptable and hence so useful for the support of large, mobile land animals.

THE FUNCTIONAL ORGANIZATION OF THE VERTEBRATE SKELETON During the evolution of vertebrates a number of adaptive changes have taken place in the organization of the endoskeleton. At first it was little more than a means of protecting the spinal cord and brain and affording attachment for muscles that bent the trunk from side to side during swimming. Ostracoderms were bottom dwellers with a rudimentary endoskeleton; when paired pectoral and pelvic fins arose in their placoderm descendants (foreshadowed by the appearance of lateral flaps in certain ostracoderms) they may have served mainly for support in these heavily armored forms that at first could not swim rapidly. As bony fishes separated into two diverging groups, skeletal evolution began to proceed along two contrasting lines. In most fishes, fins came to have little supportive role and the vertebrae developed long vertical processes that served to limit the tendency of the trunk to bend in a dorsoventral plane while allowing it to be bent freely from side to side for swimming (Figure 4.31). The fins became useful mainly in maneuvering and in reducing the tendency of the fish's streamlined body to roll, pitch, or yaw about its longitudinal axis (Figure 4.32). In the lobefinned fishes, on the other hand, the ability to move about on land became more critical for survival than the ability to swim rapidly; in this group the fin skeleton continued to strengthen, developing sturdy bones considered to be the forerunners and homologs of the limb bones of tetrapod vertebrates (Figure 4.33).

Basically, the two major parts of the vertebrate endoskeleton are (1) the *axial skeleton,* consisting of the vertebral column, skull, and (where present) the ribs and breastbone; (2) the *appendicular skeleton,*

Figure 4.33 □ Primitive support on land: walking in lobefinned fish and salamanders. (*a*) Comparison of skeletal elements in fin of lobefinned fish and pentadactylous limb of tetrapod. A lobefinned fish is shown resting upon its fins. Note apparent origin in these fish of the major bones that have undergone further evolutionary development into the limb bones of land vertebrates. (*b*) Salamander walking, showing straddling stance (*after F. G. Evans*). All four-footed vertebrates walk by advancing the left front and right rear legs at almost the same time and then advancing the right front and left rear. This progression is thought to be an outcome of inherited motor patterns stemming from the sinuous lateral trunk flexions used by fish in swimming. Such trunk movements are shown by salamanders in a hurry. In higher tetrapods new muscles develop to make the use of limbs more efficient, and the limbs are rotated under the trunk, allowing it to be kept free of the ground during walking and standing.

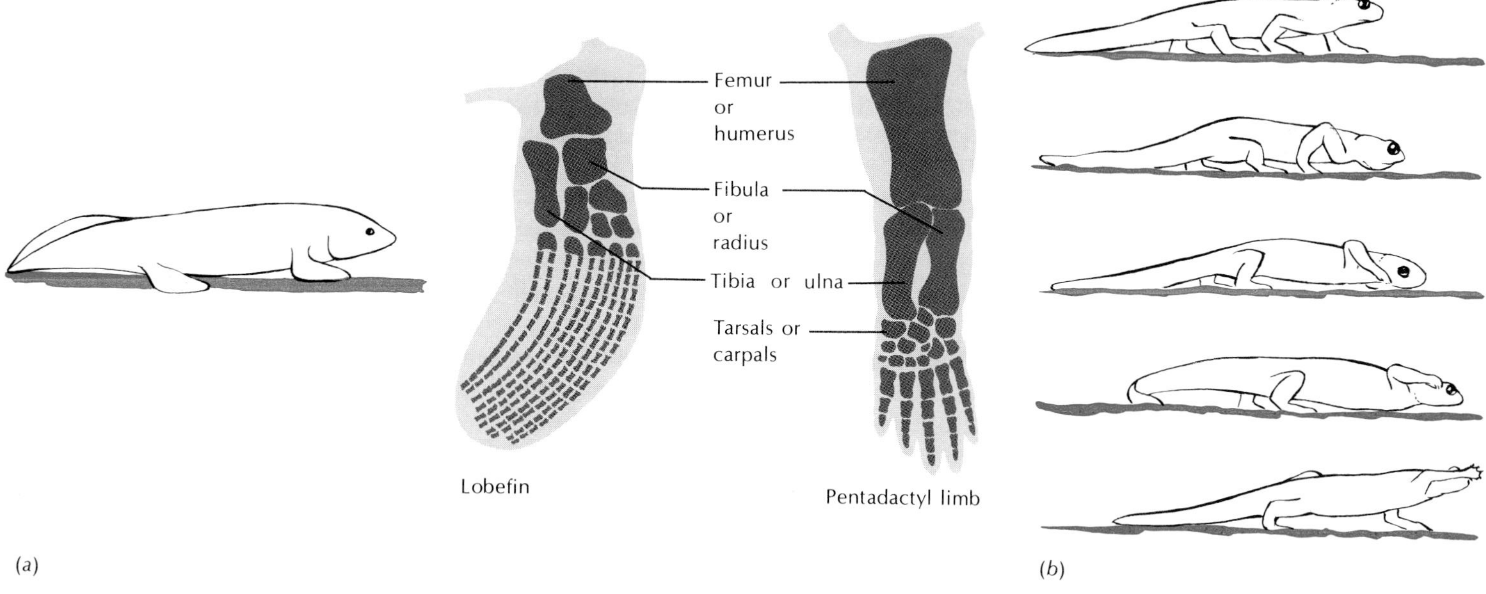

consisting of the limb bones and the pectoral and pelvic girdles that support the forelimbs and hindlimbs, respectively (Figure 4.34). It is the appendicular skeleton that has had to undergo a much greater modification in terrestrial vertebrates (see Figure 1.9).

ADAPTATIONS FOR SUPPORT ON LAND Adaptive changes in most parts of the skeleton have come about during the adjustment of vertebrates for life on land. Most conspicuously, the limbs have become land-adapted legs that serve for elevating the trunk from the ground and for walking and running. Supporting the trunk required certain changes in the limb girdles. The pectoral girdle remained unattached to the vertebral column but its major bone, the scapula, came to form the main support for a muscular "sling" that bears the weight of the anterior part of the trunk (Figure 4.35a). The narrow and deep shape of the mammalian trunk in cross section allows the legs to be brought toward the midline close to the body's center of gravity; in reptiles and amphibians this trend is less advanced and the legs tend to spraddle to the sides.

The pelvic girdle, rudimentary in fish, has enlarged in tetrapods and has become firmly anchored to the vertebral column; in the region of attachment vertebrae have become fused to form a broad plate (the sacrum) furnishing a longer surface for the union. In most tetrapods the two pelvic bones also articulate ventrally, so that a complete bony ring supports the hindquarters (Figure 4.36), but in birds the passage of large eggs has made necessary a wide separation of the ventral parts of the girdle.

Figure 4.34 □ **Skeleton of a dog. Note various terrestrial adaptations as mentioned in the text. Note also digitigrade condition of the feet, with the animal standing only upon the toes.**

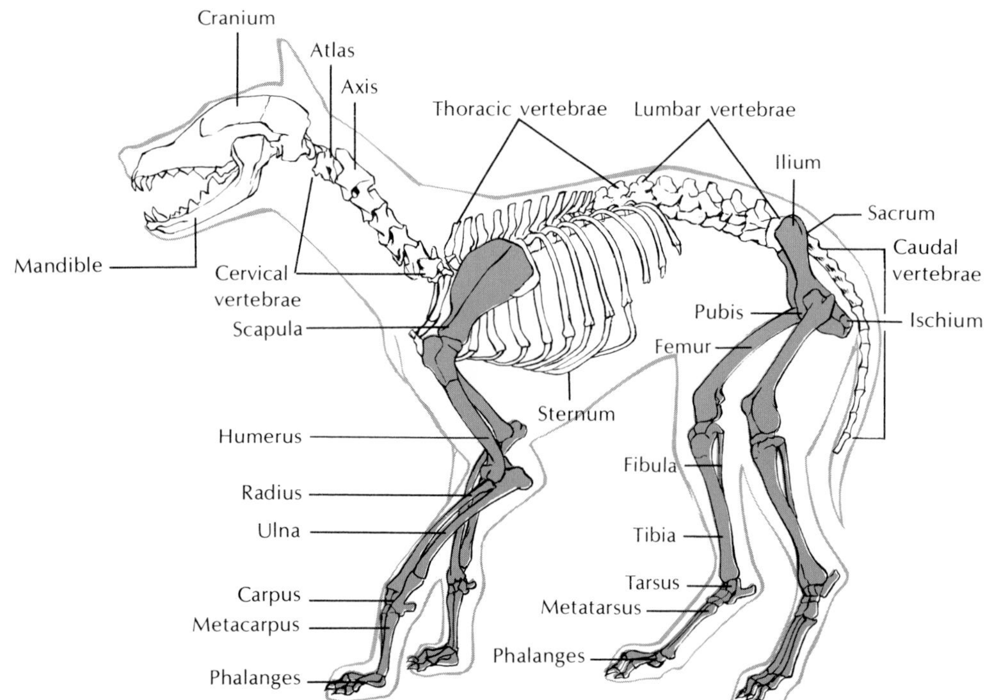

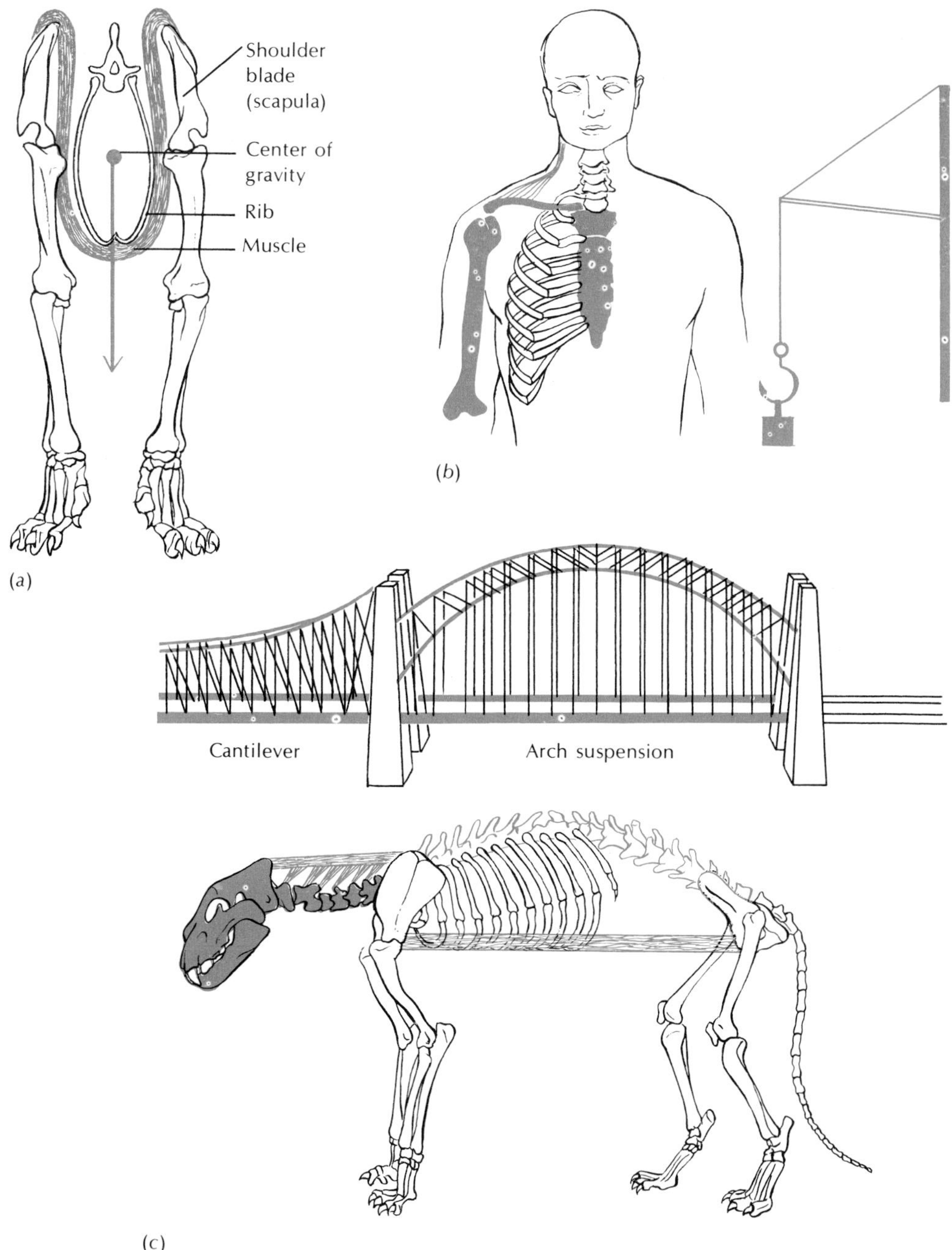

Figure 4.35 □ The role of skeletal muscles in support. (*a*) Trunk suspension in mammals. The full weight of the anterior portion of the trunk is borne by a suspension sling made up of muscles running from the top of the scapula to the ventral part of the chest. (*b*) The human shoulder girdle is designed like a swinging boom, with the weight of the arm supported by muscles extending from the cranium to the outer part of the pectoral girdle. (*c*) The architecture of the mammalian skeleton resembles that of an arch-suspension bridge. Longitudinal belly muscles, maintaining a mild state of sustained contraction (tonus) keep the arch of the backbone from collapsing to a swaybacked condition. The head is cantilevered from the trunk by way of dorsal longitudinal muscles that attach by tendinous slips to the cervical vertebrae and to the occipital region of the skull. (*Biological Sciences Curriculum Study.*)

The vertebral column of land vertebrates has also become modified for additional support. Excessive twisting of the backbone resulting from walking movements has been counteracted by the development of articular processes by which each vertebra is braced against both sides of the next in line. We have already mentioned the specialization of the sacral region of the column for bracing the pelvic girdle. The cervical (neck) vertebrae have become specialized in another direction—for enhanced flexibility of the neck and mobility of the head; the first two vertebrae are modified to allow the head to swivel on the neck. The trunk vertebrae (thoracic and lumbar) bear sturdy transverse processes providing sites for muscular attachment.

THE SUPPORTIVE ROLE OF SKELETAL MUSCLES Besides providing for mobility by moving the parts of the skeleton, the skeletal muscles also furnish support against gravity. At all times they preserve a mild state of contraction in which their *tone*

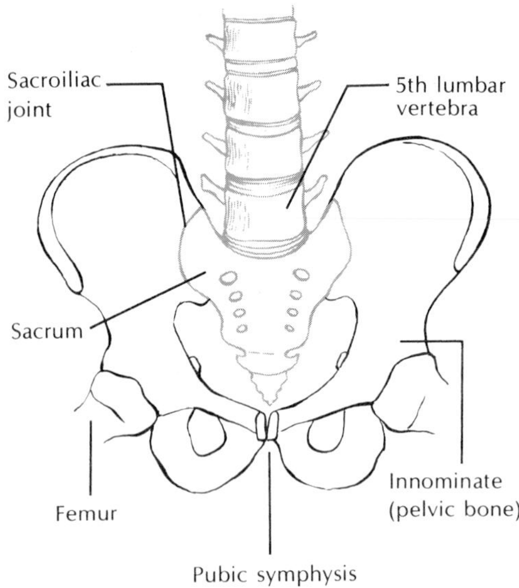

Figure 4.36 □ Pelvic support in man. The three original elements of the pelvic girdle (*ilium*, *ischium*, and *pubis*) fuse to form a single innominate, or pelvic, bone on each side. The two halves of the girdle meet ventrally at the *pubic symphysis*, a fibrocartilage articulation, and dorsally are firmly joined to the *sacrum*, a broad bony plate formed by the fusion of several vertebrae. This forms a sturdy ring of support important for bipedal locomotion.

(internal tension) is maintained without a change in the muscle's length. Reflex postural adjustments help the animal to retain its balance even when motionless. The constant work performed by muscles in resisting gravity is actually necessary for maintenance of their proper tone, blood supply, and health. A chronically bedridden patient suffers from loss of muscle tone and muscular atrophy, involving a reduced blood supply to the muscles and shrinkage of the fibers with reduction in the amount of contractile protein present. Such problems may also be encountered in conditions of prolonged weightlessness attending space travel and may need to be compensated for by various specially devised programs of exercise.

Besides their contribution to support through coordinated contractions and tonal adjustments, certain skeletal muscles help support the body against gravity merely by the way in which they are attached to the skeleton. For instance, the human arm hangs from a skeletal brace formed by the articulation of the collar bone (clavicle) with the scapula (Figure 4.35*b*). This bony brace is kept from sagging by the lateral neck muscles (particularly the trapezius), originating on the rear (occipital) bone of the skull and the cervical and thoracic vertebrae and attached to the clavicle and the scapula. The muscles support their articulation in a manner similar to that seen in a swinging boom.

The dorsal longitudinal neck muscles and ventral longitudinal trunk muscles help support the tetrapod head and trunk (Figure 4.35c). An adaptive property of muscle tissue is that it contracts upon being stretched. The weight of the head places the dorsal longitudinal neck muscles under tension; this causes a reflexive contraction that holds the head erect. Thus the head is actually cantilevered from the trunk. Similarly, any tendency of the backbone to bow downward under its load stretches the ventral longitudinal muscles and their compensatory contraction tends to keep the backbone straight or even to force it into an upward bow. If these abdominal muscles weaken, a "swaybacked" condition will be the result.

E Gravity sense

In addition to the development of various adaptations for obtaining support against gravity, living things are also *sensitive* to gravity and employ the information obtained through their gravitational sensors to orient themselves in space and to maintain positions relative to the substratum. *Geotropic* growth movements are exhibited by plants, the shoots being negatively geotropic and turning upward, while the roots are *positively* geotropic, bending downward. This response is due to differential rates of growth on the upper and lower sides of the stem and root (see Figure 15.56).

The gravity sensors (*statocysts*) of animals are much alike in construction regardless of the phylum in which they occur. They consist of fluid-filled saccules lined with sensitive "hair cells" and containing one or more stony pellets that are free to move about within the saccule (Figure 4.37). These pellets (*statoliths*), which may be granules of calcium carbonate or calcium phosphate secreted by the organism or grains of sand introduced from the environment, stimulate

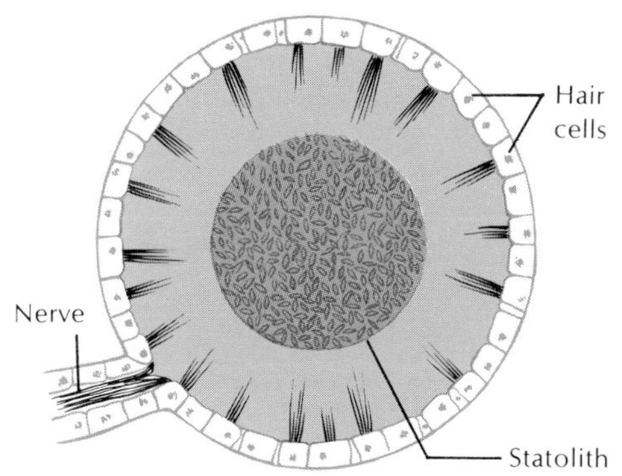

Figure 4.37 □ Statocyst of a mollusc, a gravity receptor. This spherical sense organ is lined with sensory hair cells and contains fluid within which are suspended one or more statoliths. Changes of the body's position in the earth's gravitational field cause the statolith to press against some of the hair cells, alerting the brain to such changes.

the hair cells by their movements, causing nerve impulses to be sent to the brain. In some animals gravitational cues can be demonstrated to be more effective than visual ones when the two are contradictory. In shrimps the statoliths are sand grains that are lost at each molt and must be replaced. If at this time iron dust is substituted for the sand in an aquarium, the iron is incorporated in the statocysts. The shrimp now respond to magnetism; and when a magnet is passed over the top of the aquarium, they begin to swim upside down.

The vertebrate analogs of invertebrate statocysts are the sacculus and utriculus, inflated bulbs associated with the semicircular canals. The former monitor head *position,* whereas the semicircular canals are adapted to the detection of head *movements* (see Figure 15.29).

4.5 □ PRESSURE

At sea level the overlying atmosphere exerts a pressure of 1.014×10^6 dynes* upon every square centimeter of the earth's surface. This amount (equivalent to 14.7 lb/in.^{2}), equals 1 atmosphere (atm). Above sea level atmospheric pressure decreases, while below sea level it increases at the rate of 1 atm per each 10-m increase in depth. Most organisms are capable of withstanding fluctuations of no more than 1 or 2 atm, although a number of *eurybathic* species (those tolerant to wide changes in pressure) normally execute vertical movements of up to 400 m, equivalent to a pressure change of 40 atm. These species possess a degree of physiological adaptability sufficient to permit extensive homeostatic regulation during their ascents and descents. Organisms collected from deep water by routine dredging procedures usually die while being brought to the surface. In the case of animals having gas bladders we have already noted that death results from the rapid expansion of the stored gases, but invertebrates such as sea urchins, sea cucumbers, and bivalves, which have no gas-filled spaces, die also. In this event death is probably due less to pressure reduction per se than to other intervening factors, such as temperature change and physiological disturbances, that overtax the animals' homeostatic mechanisms. Painful "bends" experienced by divers after a too-rapid ascent are caused when excess gases that have permeated their tissues during underwater breathing of compressed gases expand in the joint cavities. Death may also result, due to *air embolism* (the formation in the bloodstream of air bubbles that block the circulation).

*The dyne equals 10^{-5} newton.

If our own experience is any criterion, organisms do not actually *detect* pressure unless they execute vertical movements of considerable magnitude, for they customarily inhabit regions where pressure change is small and thus are well adapted to it. Sensory receptors detect *changes* in the environment rather than *constant* conditions; where the density of the organism is in equilibrium with its environment, no matter how great the surrounding pressure may be it will not crush the organism. This does not mean that the tremendous pressures characteristic of the ocean depths do not affect the organisms living there but rather that the effects are primarily *biochemical* rather than *mechanical.* This has been aptly summarized in the following words of J. A. Colin Nicol:†

It is generally believed that the most significant effect of pressure on biological systems lies in the volume changes which it brings about. At high pressures protein molecules are compressed, denatured and altered in structure and chemical activity. In the ocean

†*The Biology of Marine Animals* (2nd ed.) (London: Sir Isaac Pitman & Sons, Ltd., 1967), p. 24.

depths two factors, low temperatures and high pressures, both of which affect the rate of biological processes, are acting concomitantly, and the animals of the abyss must be genotypically modified to withstand the conditions obtaining there. . . .

REVIEW AND DISCUSSION

1 Evaluate the statement "Organisms must struggle to survive in a hostile environment."

2 Explain why, to most organisms, life on land is as forbidding as life in outer space would be for us. What are the major water-conserving adaptations by which particular groups of plants and animals have succeeded in exploiting the land as a habitat?

3 What are the properties of water that make it a particularly suitable compound for incorporation into biotic systems? Can you conceive of any conditions under which some other compound might take the place of water in the evolution of life?

4 Why are such seasonal adaptations as hibernation, leaf-drop, and migration better interpreted as responses to lack of available water than to low temperatures? Cite experimental evidence bearing on this conclusion.

5 In what ways do living things alter the composition of the atmosphere? Evaluate the effect of human activities on the concentration of carbon dioxide and contaminants. Suggest specific corrective measures that could be initiated. Determine recent pollution data for your area and ascertain which local ordinances attempt to control pollution. Do these ordinances seem to be working effectively?

6 Describe the manner in which nitrogen and sulfur atoms pass cyclically through the ecosystem. What could be the ultimate effect if accumulated soil contaminants were to make life impossible for sulfur bacteria and nitrogen-fixing organisms? Explain.

7 Specify exactly how CO_2 and O_2 are utilized by the living world. Do sugar and O_2 interact directly?

8 Explain how H_2O is used in photosynthesis. Cite an experiment by which the source of the O_2 released in photosynthesis may be determined.

9 Describe and compare various means used for support against gravity by *aquatic* plants and animals. How do the support requirements differ for aquatic and terrestrial organisms? Compare the supportive adaptations of a kelp plant and an oak tree.

10 Compare the structure of insect wings and those of flying vertebrates. How does *behavior* enhance the effectiveness of flight in soaring birds?

11 Compare the advantages and disadvantages of exoskeletons and endoskeletons.

12 What adaptive properties does bone exhibit? How does the generation of electricity in living bone affect the deposition of new matrix?

13 What changes in the vertebrate skeleton took place in those forms which invaded the land?

14 What peculiarities of bird anatomy and physiology may be considered to be adaptations for increasing the efficiency of flight? In what ways does this flight-related specialization constitute a kind of penalty for birds?

15 What are the major effects upon life that can be attributed to atmospheric pressure?

REFERENCES

BASSETT, C. A. L. "Electrical Effects in Bone," *Sci. Amer.*, **213** (1965). Bone is presented as an adaptive crystalline system which reacts to stress by generating piezoelectricity.

CARSON, R. *Silent Spring.* Greenwich, Conn: Fawcett Publications, Inc., 1962. The author brings together many data indicating long-term damage inflicted on biotic communities (with special reference to bird life) by the promiscuous use of insecticides.

COLE, L. C. "The Ecosphere," *Sci. Amer.*, **198** (1958). The living and abiotic worlds interact in a balanced system of matter and energy exchange, which man's activities threaten to disrupt.

DENTON, E. "The Buoyancy of Marine Animals," *Sci. Amer.,* **203** (1960). Explores ways in which animals overcome gravity in an aquatic environment.

HENDERSON, L. J. *The Fitness of the Environment.* Boston: Beacon Press, 1958 (reprinting). A classic work demonstrating that the physiochemical conditions prevailing on earth, far from being inimical to life, have properties conducive to the evolution and perpetuation of life.

HENDRICKS, S. B. "How Light Interacts with Living Matter," *Sci. Amer.,* **219** (1968). Photosynthesis, photoperiodic responses, and vision are discussed in terms of the photosensitivity of specific pigments.

IRVING, L. "Adaptations to Cold," *Sci. Amer.,* **214** (1966).

JACOBS, W. P. "What Makes Leaves Fall?" *Sci. Amer.,* **193** (1955).

JAMES, W. O. "Succulent Plants," *Endeavor,* **17** (1958). Examines xerophytic adaptations to conserve water and minimize the effects of excessive heat.

KAMEN, M. D. "Discoveries in Nitrogen Fixation," *Sci. Amer.,* **188** (1953).

MIDDLETON, J. T., AND OTHERS "Man and His Habitat: Problems of Pollution," *Bull. Atom. Sci.* (March, 1965). Sources of pollution of soil, water, and atmosphere are examined and prospects hypothesized.

MILNE, L. J., AND M. J. MILNE "Temperature and Life," *Sci. Amer.,* **180** (1949).

PLASS, G. N. "Carbon Dioxide and Climate," *Sci. Amer.,* **201** (1959). Discusses levels of atmospheric carbon dioxide in relation to world climate.

REINERT, J. "Phototropism and Phototaxis," *Ann. Rev. Plant Physiol.,* **10** (1959). Discusses differential growth responses and oriented locomotion directed by light.

SCHMIDT-NIELSEN, K. *Desert Animals.* London and New York: Oxford University Press, 1964. A valuable compendium of knowledge concerning the adaptations of desert animals to drought and heat; brings together data from numerous experiments and field observations.

STORER, J. H. "Bird Aerodynamics," *Sci. Amer.,* **186** (1952).

WALD, G. "Life and Light," *Sci. Amer.,* **201** (1959).

WENT, F. W. "The Ecology of Desert Plants," *Sci. Amer.,* **192** (1963).

WOODWELL, G. M. "The Ecological Effects of Radiation," *Sci. Amer.,* **208** (1963).

——— "Toxic Substances and Ecological Cycles," *Sci. Amer.,* **216** (1967). Presents data indicating the persistence of toxic contaminants such as pesticides and fallout, and their concentration in human and animal tissues resulting from the passage of these substances through food chains.

WURSTER, C. F., JR. AND D. B. WINGATE "DDT Residues and Declining Reproduction in the Bermuda Petrel," *Science,* **159** (1968).

Chapter 5  ADAPTATION TO HABITAT

THE HABITAT HAS SHAPED THE EVOLUtion of life to a profound extent. In Chapter 4 we saw that biotic systems have evolved along such lines as to exploit or withstand the general physicochemical conditions prevailing on the earth. In addition, most organisms have become specifically adapted toward the efficient utilization of their own limited environments. In this chapter we shall consider major types of habitats—terrestrial, freshwater, and marine—in terms of the dominant conditions characterizing each and shall note how these conditions have served as selective factors in determining the forms that life has taken in each environment.

A great variety of habitats exists on earth both because the earth's surface is not homogeneous and because the sun's rays do not strike all parts of the earth's surface with uniform intensity. In consequence there are available a number of potential habitats, each characterized by certain physicochemical conditions to which living things must adapt if they are to survive. These conditions include temperature range, length of day, intensity and quality of light, weather conditions, and the relative proportions of water, solutes, and solids in the substratum or milieu. These factors vary particularly with *latitude* and *altitude*.

The species found in any given habitat either must develop a *tolerance* for the prevailing abiotic conditions or must be able to escape them in some way. The state of adaptation of any given species typically represents a *compromise adjustment to the entire complex of factors* in the habitat. It is usually impossible for an organism to achieve a state of *optimal* adaptation to any *one* factor, for in so doing it may reduce its tolerance for some other. Thus a compromise state of *suboptimal* but adequate adaptation to all factors is maintained.

Any given species is characterized by a set of tolerances, some of which are broad while others are narrow. The *limiting factor* to distribution of a species is that which comes closest to the limits of its range of tolerance. A habitat may be ideal in all other respects, yet if in one particular it violates the range of tolerance of a species it will be uninhabitable by that species. The limiting factor for the vertical distribution of marine algae is the depth of light penetration. All other factors needed for life (H_2O, O_2, CO_2, minerals, and favorable temperature) may be abundantly present, but in the absence of light algae cannot synthesize organic compounds and hence cannot survive. Most of the sea is therefore uninhabitable by algae, which are limited mainly to the upper 100 m.

In Chapter 4 we considered a number of abiotic factors—radiant energy, atmospheric gases, water, gravity, pressure—that the biosphere as a whole must either tolerate or exploit. These factors have served as *general* agents of natural selection, determining the general direction of biotic evolution by favoring or discouraging the perpetuation of particular genetic variations throughout the three billion year history of life. The *specific* combination of factors characterizing any given habitat influences the evolution of its inhabitants even more precisely, for hereditary alterations will tend to persist that specifically enhance the fitness of an organism to survive within that habitat.

The more perfectly a species has adapted to one habitat, the more *unlikely* it is that this species will succeed equally well in another. The actual range of a species is set not so much by the outer limits of its ability to *survive,* but by the limits within which it can *procreate.* Many marine fish, for example, fail to breed in captivity even though they may survive in apparent good health for years (probably longer in some cases than they would have survived in the wild). We have said that life can exist within a temperature range of 0°C to nearly 90°C, and this is indeed true. Yet it is equally true that few *individual* species can tolerate both extremes of this range for any length of time. In fact many species, particularly marine fish, can reproduce only within a temperature range that deviates from a set optimum by no more than about 5°C.

Such adaptive limitations apply to all environmental factors. It is by means of diversification into various species adapted to different sets of conditions, rather than by achieving extensive physiological adaptability, that life has successfully expanded into the wide range of habitats available on earth. However, the relative impermanence of many habitats is responsible for the repeated extinction of groups of species that have become adapted to one specific habitat. The modification of habitat inexorably spells death to all but a few genetically favored individuals and the process of specific adjustment to the new environmental conditions must take place over and over again.

5.1 □ THE EFFECTS OF LATITUDE

From equator to pole the habitats of life are latitudinally graded through a continuum that may be subdivided into *tropical, subtropical, temperate, subtemperate,* and *polar* zones. These zones differ in two major respects: (1) *mean temperature;* (2) *annual fluctuations in photoperiod* (length of daylight). Temperature is influenced by the angle at which the sun's rays strike the earth's surface. Because of the earth's curvature, as one moves from the equator toward either pole, the angle of incidence of the sun's rays gradually increases, and the amount of solar energy penetrating the atmosphere and reaching the surface decreases. This phenomenon results in a declining mean temperature from the region of the equator to that of the poles.

Annual cyclic changes in photoperiod result from the earth's axial inclination. As the earth proceeds about the sun in its annual revolution, the northern and southern hemispheres are alternately presented more directly to the sun. This results both in seasonal fluctuations in mean temperature, and in seasonal changes in the length of daylight (Figure 5.1). The beginning of summer coincides with the greatest extension of photoperiod in each hemisphere. The annual lengthening and shortening of photoperiod is most marked toward the poles and is virtually nonexistent at the equator, where the length of day remains nearly constant throughout the year. High mean temperature and a stable photoperiod thus characterize the tropical zone, whereas low mean temperatures and maximal annual fluctuation in photoperiod are typical of the polar zones. Zones intermediate in latitude are also intermediate with respect to mean temperature and seasonal changes in climate and photoperiod.

The composite fauna and flora (also called the *biota*) of a region vary with latitude, mostly as a result of differences in tolerance to temperature. Many animal species are severely restricted because of their limited tolerance for low temperatures. Reptiles, for instance, are largely excluded from the subtemperate and polar zones. In the case of birds and mammals, ability to maintain a stable body temperature allows some species to occupy polar habitats. In these homoiotherms it is found that species occupying the higher latitudes typically are larger, lighter in color, and (in the case of mammals) have shorter extremities (ears, paws, tails) than similar species living nearer the equator. The tendency for body size to correlate directly with latitude actually represents an adaptation to lower temperatures, for with increased size the volume-to-surface ratio is altered favorably and less body heat is lost by radiation. This generalization (*Bergmann's rule*) is exemplified by the three species of penguin depicted in Figure 5.2. The large King penguin with a body length of 90 cm lives as far south as 55°S; the Magellan penguin ranges to 52°S and is 60 cm long; and the Humboldt penguin, which inhabits the west coast of South America at lower latitudes, is only 45 cm long. Another adaptation for minimizing heat loss is reduction in the size of the extremities. This tendency (*Allen's rule*) is shown by Arctic hares and foxes in comparison with their tropic- and temperate-zone relatives (Figure 5.3). The tendency of species living closer to the equator to be darker in color than those living further north or south (*Gloger's rule*) is less well understood but may relate to the fact that dark fur or plumage absorbs harmful ultraviolet radiation (which increases in intensity toward the equator) and prevents it from penetrating the skin.

The biota of the temperate, subtemperate, and Arctic life zones exhibit physiological rhythms, each coordinated with the annual climatic rhythm of their environment. According to the species, either changes in *temperature* or alterations in *photoperiod* (or both) initiate physiological changes that permit the organism to adjust to the coming

Figure 5.1 □ Photoperiod: variation with latitude. Such seasonal oscillations profoundly affect the activities of living things. Note that the oscillation becomes more pronounced with increasing distance from the equator.

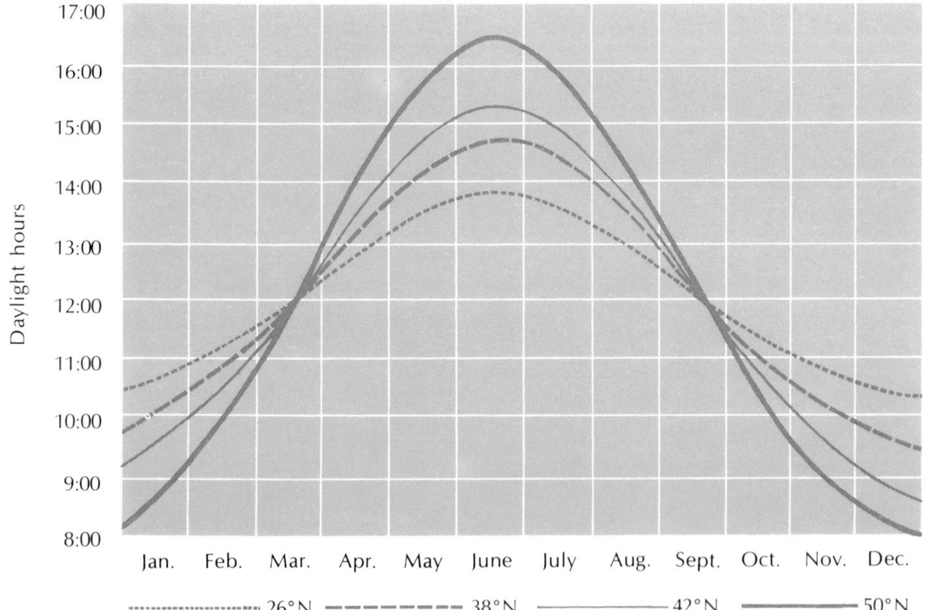

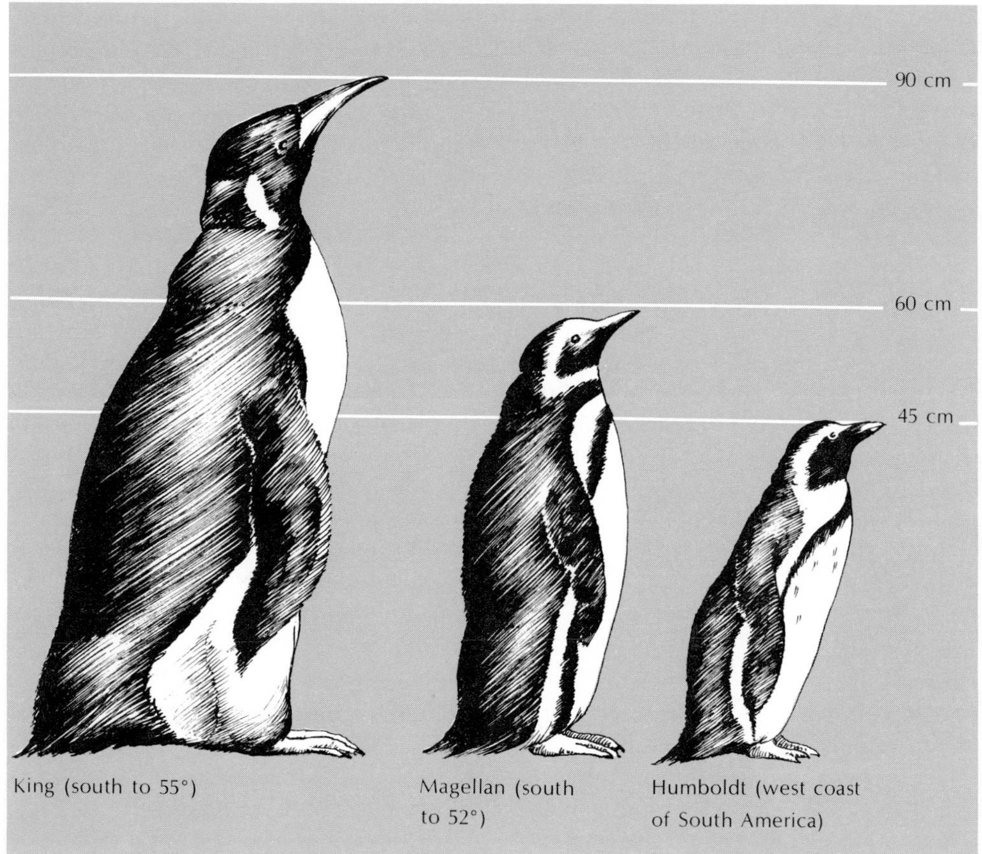

Figure 5.2 □ **Bergmann's rule states that, in closely related species of warm-blooded animals, larger members inhabit colder climates; this is exemplified in three species of penguin. The emperor penguin, even larger than the king (although little taller), breeds on the Antarctic continent during the winter. (Considerably smaller species of penguins breed there in summer.) (*Adapted from C. P. Hickman,* Integrated Principles of Zoology, *2nd ed. St. Louis, Mo.: The C. V. Mosby Co., 1961.*)**

Figure 5.3 □ **Allen's rule exemplified in two species of fox: (*a*) Arctic fox (*Alopex lagopus*), (*b*) fennec (*Fennecus zerda*) (*Zoological Society of San Diego*). The fennec inhabits the Sahara Desert near the equator; its enormous ears serve for heat dissipation as well as for funneling sound into the ear canal. The ears of the Arctic fox are even smaller than those of the red fox of temperate woodlands.**

(*a*)

(*b*)

seasonal change. The adequacy of this regulatory process depends on the fact that it is usually set in motion long *before* the seasonal change threatens survival. Migratory birds, for instance, apparently are subject to photoperiodic regulation, for as the length of the day decreases, they first begin to store fat, then to exhibit a typical premigratory restlessness, and finally to aggregate into flocks and begin the migration. During winter, the lengthening photoperiod stimulates the onset of the annual growth cycle of the birds' sex organs so that by spring they are ready to breed and their young are therefore hatched at the time of year most conducive to survival. These physiological responses of birds to light therefore must involve coordinated activity of the eyes, the nervous system, and the endocrine glands.

Diapause, an arrestment of development during either the embryonic or the pupal stage, is an adaptation that permits a number of insects to overwinter successfully. Photoperiod has been found to regulate the onset of diapause, and temperature to control its termination. In the silkworm moth, a species in which the control of diapause has been intensively studied, the regulatory mechanism is remarkably sophisticated, for the stimuli provided by photoperiod act not upon the embryo itself but upon its *mother.* Furthermore, these stimuli are effective only during the mother's *larval* life and *not* when she is actually engaged in egg laying! When a female silkworm larva is reared under conditions of *long* photoperiod (about 16 hr of light per day), she produces a *diapause hormone* that acts upon her developing egg cells so that a delayed effect is initiated. Embryos developing from egg cells exposed to diapause hormone will grow to only a certain stage and then will enter diapause. They must remain in this arrested state until winter is past, because diapause cannot be broken until the egg is chilled to nearly 0°C for at least a period of 40 days and then gradually rewarmed.

Female silkworm larvae reared under conditions of *short* photoperiod (about 12 hr of light per day) lay eggs that develop without undergoing diapause because their mothers were not stimulated to produce the diapause hormone. The adaptive significance of the control of diapause by photoperiod is that eggs laid late in summer cannot develop to adulthood before the onset of winter. On the other hand, eggs laid early in summer by females that were larvae in the spring (having themselves emerged from diapause) have ample time to develop to maturity and to reproduce before the following winter.

In certain aphids, both photoperiod and population density serve as stimuli which, acting upon the sense organs and nervous system, bring about hormonal changes that affect the mode of reproduction and the type of offspring produced. Under conditions of *long* photoperiod, *isolated* aphids always produce *wingless* progeny. These offspring are all female, for they develop parthenogenetically (from eggs not fertilized). These eggs are held within the mother's body while they develop. *Crowded* aphids, however, produce *winged* progeny under long-day conditions, facilitating dispersal at a season when food is abundant. Under *short* photoperiods both the winged and the wingless long-day forms lay eggs that develop into *wingless* individuals of *both sexes.* This shows that under conditions of long photoperiod development is influenced by population density; when the photoperiod is short, however, population density is not an effective stimulus and day length alone regulates the reproductive and developmental processes.

Many flowering plants depend upon changes in photoperiod for the regulation of flowering and seed production; this is especially true for annual plants, in which these processes take place within a single growing season. *Short-night* (long-day) species such as lettuce and petunias produce only vegetative organs until the nights shorten to a certain critical duration, whereupon they begin to flower (Figure 5.4). *Long-night* (short-day) species such as marigolds bloom only when the night becomes longer than a certain critical period. Experiments show that flowering of long-night plants is suppressed if the dark period is interrupted by even a brief flash of light; the plant's internal "clock" is reset under these conditions as though a full period of daylight had intervened (see Section 15.4D).

Flowering is influenced by photoperiod according to the annual growth pattern and rate of maturation of the species. Natural selection has favored those plants which bloom early enough so that their reproductive processes are completed before the onset of winter. A plant that blooms too late in the year to produce mature seeds will not pass on this late-blooming characteristic to subsequent generations.) On the other hand, an opposing selective factor is also at work: if all species of flowering plants in one locale were to bloom at the same time of year, they might seriously compete for the services of pollinator insects and the

(a)

(b)

Figure 5.4 □ Effects of photoperiod on flowering. (*a*) A short-day (long-night) species, Double Eagle marigold grown on 8-, 12-, 14-, and 16-hr photoperiods, blooms on 8- and 12-hr regimens but not under 14 or 16 hr of light. (*b*) A long-day species, Pink Cascade petunia grown on 8-, 12-, 14-, and 16-hr photoperiods, blooms on 14- and 16-hr light schedules but not on 8- or 12-hr schedules. These effects will be discussed further in a later chapter.

incidence of accidental cross pollination among species would be increased. Furthermore, the survival of those insects on which plants depend is increased if the insects can feed upon nectar throughout most of the year. Accordingly, within any given community, the various native plant species tend to develop different maturation rates and times of flowering. We should stress that they have not diversified purposively *in order to* survive—they survive because they have become diverse.

5.2 □ THE EFFECTS OF ALTITUDE

At any given *latitude,* habitats also vary *altitudinally.* Altitude zero has been established as equivalent to the present mean sea level, though over a period of several thousand years the sea level may rise or fall many meters according to the proportion of the earth's water that is bound as ice in glaciers and in the polar ice caps. The minus altitudes (below sea level) are largely occupied by *water* and represent the marine habitats. Since the oceans are to some extent inhabitable at any depth, they present not only a vast surface area but a tremendous three-dimensional habitat for numerous species. Most terrestrial and freshwater habitats lie above sea level. The mean temperature of these varies inversely with altitude, with the result that at a given altitude life forms occur similar to those characterizing a latitude of comparable temperature.

The thermal gradient from sea level to mountaintop results in a *vertical* stratification of life forms, particularly the flora, that closely parallels the *horizontal* stratification observed when one travels from equator to pole (Figure 5.5). This vertical stratification is of course most fully realized in mountainous regions located close to the equator, such as the equatorial Andes. Here, at low altitudes, typical tropical biota occurs, but with increasing altitude the biota becomes successively like that of the subtropics, the temperate zone, the subtemperate, and above the timberline the Arctic regions (called the *alpine zone*), beyond which lies perennial snow.

The particular expression of life in each of these vertical zones is affected by the availability of water as well as by the mean temperature, and this of course also holds true in equivalent *latitudinal* life zones. Desert or semidesert conditions can occur at any altitude or latitude. Given an adequate water supply, in the tropical or subtropical life zone a rain forest will develop at the lower altitudes, whereas under conditions of less rainfall, grassland, chaparral, or desert may result.

Figure 5.5 □ **Latitudinal and altitudinal life zones. Although the specific vegetation varies according to the amount of local rainfall, in travelling from equator to pole, one finds communities similar to those encountered in going from base to peak of a high mountain near the equator. Full vertical zonation is seen in the crossing of the Andes from Peru as one descends from perennial snows to the tropical rain forest to the east.**

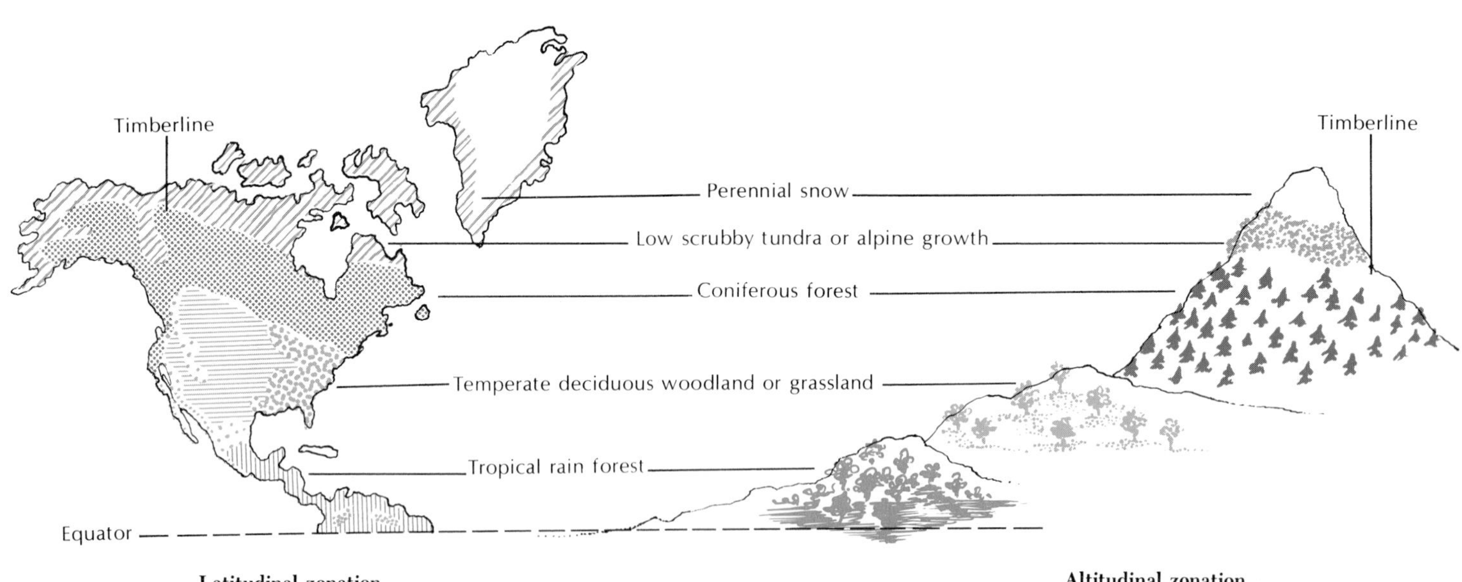

A *biome* is an area within which the most conspicuous species of vegetation comprise some particular uniform type. The uniformity of vegetation results from the need of the major plant species to adapt to the prevailing abiotic conditions. Six major terrestrial biomes are recognized: *desert, rain forest, grassland* or *savannah* (grassland dotted with trees), *deciduous woodland, taiga* (coniferous forest), and *tundra.* These biomes usually intergrade through transition zones in which the biotas of two adjacent biomes intermix. Each biome contains a number of biotic communities that may be relatively stable and self-supporting. In proceeding from equator to pole or from mountain base to peak, one typically finds that tropical and subtropical rain forest gives way to subtropical and temperate grasslands, savannahs, or deciduous forest. These in turn are succeeded by taiga or taigalike associations at the appropriate altitude or latitude. The taiga is replaced at the altitudinal or latitudinal timberline by treeless arctic or alpine tundra. The global distribution of biomes is depicted in Figure 5.6, which also shows the extent of the six major biogeographic *realms*—the Palearctic, Nearctic, Neotropical, Oriental, Ethiopian, and Australian. Each realm is separated from the others by a major land or water barrier of long standing, which has served to restrict the continental distribution of terrestrial species. For instance, the Himalayan mountains form a barrier that few organisms can cross, separating northern and southern Asia. Similarly, Wallace's line, which traces the path of a submarine trough, divides Australia from southern Asia; this division came into being in the Mesozoic Era and since then no land bridge has united the island continent with the mainland.

A **Desert**

A desert is by definition a "deserted" place, usually made so by extreme limitations of atmospheric and surface water. Lack of water vapor in the atmosphere reduces the thermal-blanketing effect so that daily and seasonal temperatures tend to fluctuate more drastically than do those in more humid regions. Groundwater may be accessible to plants with deeply penetrating tap roots, but surface water is so scanty that abundant vegetation cannot develop. When rainfall occurs, the sparse plant cover is ineffectual in preventing erosion; great alluvial fans of sand and rubble cover the foot of each promontory.

ADAPTATIONS OF DESERT BIOTA Species that survive under desert conditions are those which have successfully evolved toward the extreme expression of various water-conserving devices possessed to some degree by all terrestrial plants and animals (Figure 5.7a). As we saw in Section 4.1C, perennial desert plants tend to develop a heavy waxy cuticle, few and sunken stomates, reduced or absent leaves, thick stems, which are also green for conducting photosynthesis, and great root systems. Their leaves are often modified into formidable spines that curtail browsing by desert herbivores (excepting the enterprising pack rat). These spines also protect certain animals: for instance, cactus wrens construct nearly invulnerable nests among them, as shown in Figure 5.7*b*. Annual desert plants exhibit unique adaptive adjustments in maturation rate. They may remain dormant, as seeds, for months or even years until an adequate amount of rainfall permits germination. Development is then swift, flower- and seed-production are accelerated, and death shortly ensues.

Desert animals obtain water from the food they eat. They conserve water by excreting metabolic wastes in concentrated form, by staying in the shade, or by spending the day in burrows, where the temperature is lower and the humidity higher.

THERMOREGULATORY ADAPTATIONS IN DESERT ANIMALS Low-altitude deserts not only pose problems in water conservation for the animal inhabitants but present equally formidable problems in thermoregulation. Where ambient temperatures routinely exceed tolerable physiological limits, heat dissipation is most economically effected by water loss, such as by panting or perspiring. However, cooling by evaporation cannot be afforded by desert fauna, which must conserve water while

Figure 5.6 □ Major terrestrial biomes and Wallace's six biogeographical realms, with characteristic fauna.

- Tundra
- Northern conifer forest (taiga)
- Temperate deciduous and rain forest
- Temperate grassland
- Chaparral (temperate scrub forest)
- Desert
- Tropical rain forest
- Tropical deciduous forest
- Tropical scrub forest
- Tropical grassland and savannah
- Mountains (complex vertical zonation)

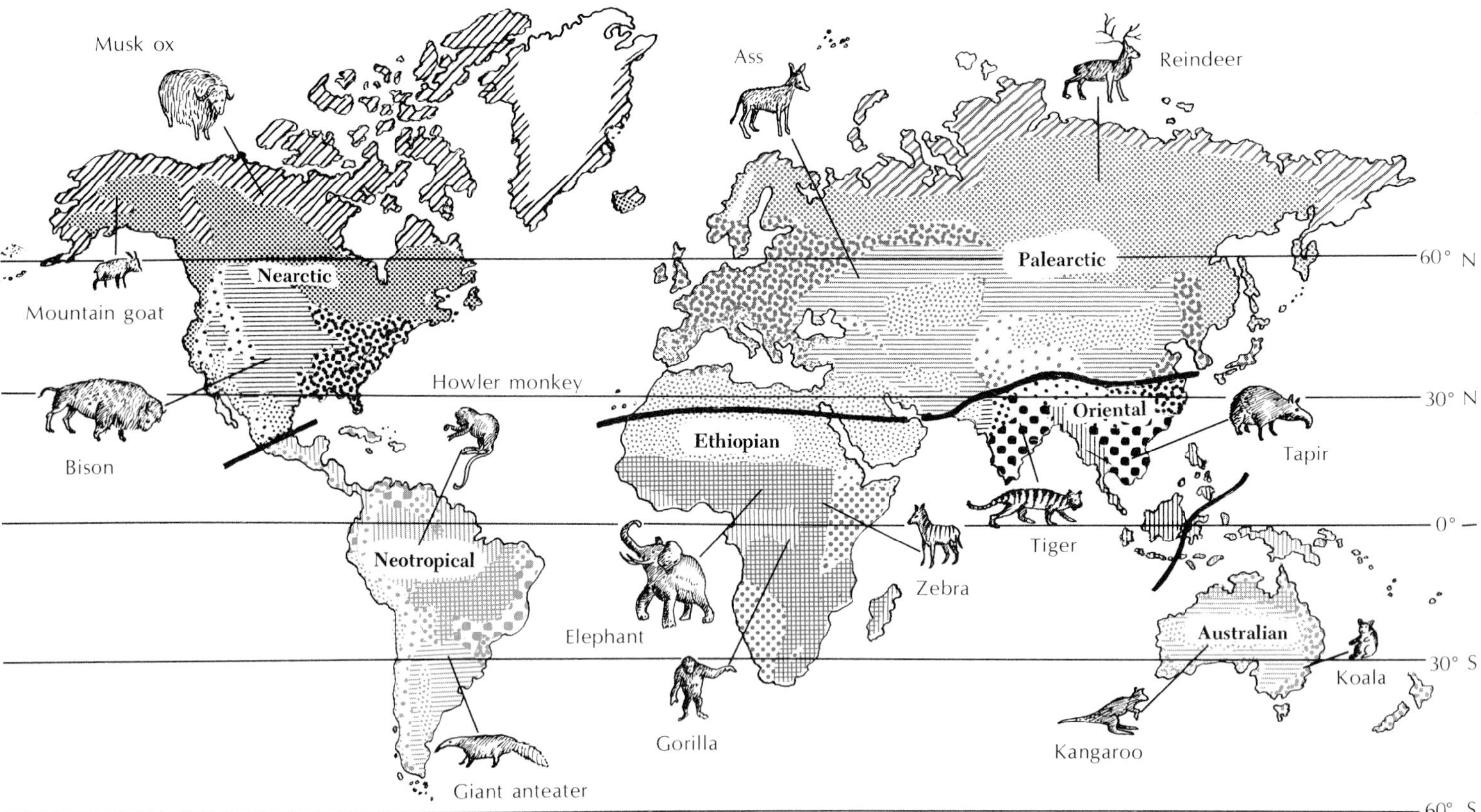

Figure 5.7 □ (*a*) **Characteristic flora of the Sonoran desert. (*b*) Nest of cactus wren, showing manner in which desert animals may exploit the adaptations of desert flora (*courtesy of General Biological, Inc., Chicago*). In such a position the wren's nest is virtually immune from attack.**

(*a*)

(*b*)

dissipating heat. This dual problem is surmounted either (1) by tolerance of *hyperthermia* (excess body heat) or (2) by behavorial adjustments. Large desert animals such as the dromedary demonstrate great tolerance both for dehydration and for hyperthermia. During the day their bodies can absorb large quantities of heat, which at night is lost by radiation to the now cooler atmosphere. The dromedary's rectal temperature can rise to 40.7°C on a summer day and then drop to about 34.7°C at night. The dromedary, though a mammal, thus by no means maintains a stable body temperature (Figure 5.8).

Small desert animals avoid overheating by the same behavioral adaptations that serve for water conservation. Most are nocturnal and burrowing and thereby escape the necessity for heat loss by either evaporation or radiation. A burrow extending only a few centimeters below the surface maintains a moderately stable *microclimate* with higher humidity and less thermal variation than at the surface; the temperature of a burrow only about 10 cm undergound may be as much as 6°C below the daytime surface temperature. Small diurnal animals pursue a relatively precarious existence, approaching their physiological limits of tolerance for both drought and heat. They commonly seek shelter from the direct rays of the sun and by resting intermittently allow the heat produced by muscular exertion to be dissipated. Jackrabbits of the American western desert are conspicuously successful at remaining active during the day and may lose heat by radiation from their large, highly vascularized ears.

Two California ground squirrels, the antelope ground squirrel (*Citellus leu-*

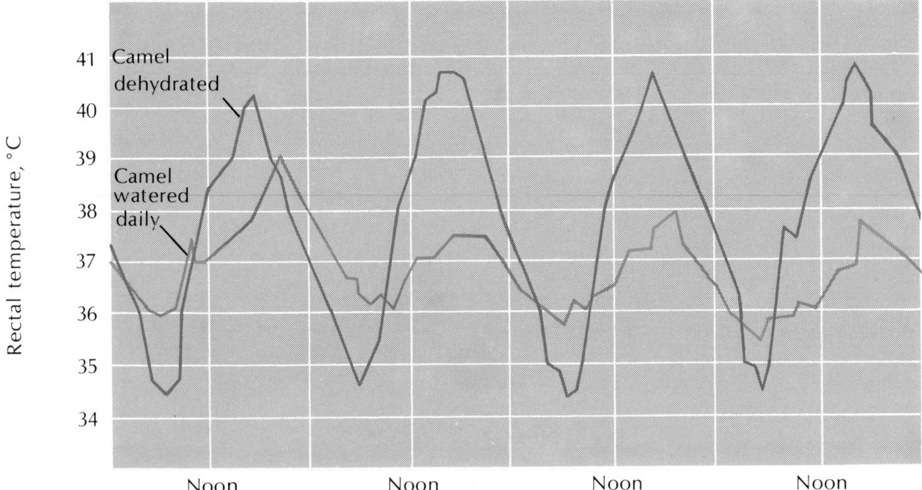

Figure 5.8 □ Relation of body temperature to water economy in the camel. The rectal temperature of a camel deprived of drinking water may fluctuate as much as 5 to 6°C each day, whereas that of a camel watered daily fluctuates only 2 to 3°C. Thus close thermoregulation demands some water loss (by evaporation); if water is scarce, the camel conserves water while bearing greater oscillations in body temperature. Other desert mammals also tolerate severe heat loads. (*From K. Schmidt-Nielsen,* Desert Animals. *London and New York: Oxford University Press* (*Clarendon*), *1964.*)

ceurus) and the Mojave ground squirrel (*Citellus mohavensis*), although anatomically similar survive in the desert by very different means. The former remains active throughout the summer. During brief bouts of vigorous food-hunting activity it builds up a great heat load; it then gives up this excess body heat by retiring to its burrow and stretching out on the cool floor. The Mojave ground squirrel, on the other hand, avoids the problem of adjustment to heat and drought by becoming dormant during the more demanding times of the year.

B Rain forest

Rain forests are typically confined to humid continental areas lying between latitudes 30°N and 30°S, although in scattered regions of high rainfall they may be found considerably farther north and south (Figure 5.9). The dominant plant species of tropical and subtropical rain forests are *evergreen hardwoods* such as mahogany and ebony. Water is abundant and temperatures are relatively uniform both throughout the day and through the year, partly because of the high atmospheric humidity. Under these conditions vegetation grows luxuriously, providing abundant food and a substratum for numerous animals (many of which are arboreal).

STRATIFICATION OF THE COMMUNITY In the rain forest, the limiting factor for plant life is *access to light and substratum.* The dominant trees form an almost solid canopy of foliage that absorbs most solar radiation and deprives the undergrowth of all but dim illumination. Differences in light requirement result in a vertical stratification of the flora. Species tolerant of dense shade throughout their entire lifespan (those which do not photosynthesize, such as fungi, and those which can endure the limitation of photosynthesis that light deprivation may involve) form the permanent *undercanopy.* Other species, which endure dense shade as seedlings but must have access to more intensive illumination in maturity, form the *canopy* or rise above the canopy as scattered lofty *emergents.* In this biome, plants of several families have converged toward a climbing mode of growth. Such species are less tolerant of shade than is the undergrowth but they do not have the structural strength to hold themselves erect at the level of the canopy; they gain elevation by using other plants as a support or a substratum. *Epiphytes* ("air plants"), such as orchids and bromeliads, need no contact with the soil (Figure 5.10). However, they do not parasitize the plants on which they live. Their nutritional requirements are met by atmospheric gases, by rainfall, and by whatever substances may be dissolved in the rainwater that accumulates in crevices

Figure 5.9 ☐ **(*a*) Tropical rain forest, Puerto Rico. Note that undergrowth must tolerate dense shade. (*Photograph by P. F. Heim, U.S. Forest Service.*) (*b*) Olympic rain forest, Washington, climax of Pacific silver fir, Sitka spruce, and western hemlock, undergrowth of fern and vine maple, and stand of young hemlocks coming up in open area in foreground. (*Photograph by L. J. Prater, U.S. Forest Service.*)**

(*a*)

(*b*)

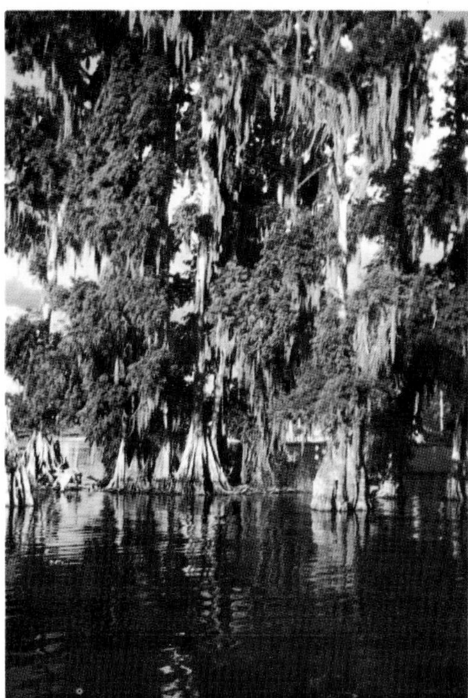

Figure 5.10 ☐ **Epiphytes on bald cypress, Florida. "Spanish moss," a member of the pineapple family, depends on its host only for support and not for nourishment.**

and depressions in the bark of the host.

ECOLOGY OF THE SOIL IN THE RAIN FOREST The lush vegetation of the rain forest deceptively implies fertility of the soil supporting this rank growth. Actually, rain-forest flora must be tolerant of soil that is very poor in both mineral and organic content. The soil is *lateritic,* that is, produced mainly by the weathering of rock: it is rich in iron and aluminum oxides, which are of little use to plants; because of many generations of plant growth, it is largely depleted of calcium, potassium, and phosphate, which are only slowly replenished by the decay of underlying rock. Heavy rainfall leaches the soil of such solutes as sulfates and nitrates formed during processes of organic decay.

The native forest plants have become adapted to these conditions. When man clears and cultivates the rain forest, however, his agricultural ventures frequently fail. Stripped of its normal cover the soil proves nearly sterile and soon bakes to the hardness of brick. Cultivation of lateritic soils destroys an essential association between soil fungi and the roots of native forest plants: this *mycorrhizal* association serves to trap soil nutrients before they can be leached away. Native plants are dependent on soil fungi for nutrition and use the soil itself for little more than support.

Further understanding of tropical ecology might enable man to utilize the unique resources of the rain-forest biome rather than to destroy it for short-term profit. The agricultural productivity of land cleared of rain forest is marginal and of very short duration, and the forest can reclaim this land only if clearing is not widespread. The present practice is to farm an area for only a few years and then to move on, allowing the land to revert to brush. As the human population increases, however, the rate and extent of deforestation is accelerating. If present trends continue, even the great Amazonian basin may become desert like the Sahara (a man-made desert).

RAIN-FOREST COMPETITION AND DIVERSIFICATION Animal life has undergone more extensive diversification in the tropical rain forest than it has in any other terrestrial biome. There is an abundance of food and water, the climate is stable and warm enough for rapid maturation of poikilothermal species (such as insects), and the vegetation provides shelter and abundant substratum. These favorable conditions make possible exponential population increases that greatly intensify biotic competition. Diversification is especially favored, for it results in the evolution of numerous species able to meet their needs in many ways. Competition, though not eliminated, is thereby considerably reduced. Within any given species, however, competition remains acute, and it is therefore under these tropical conditions that natural selection resulting from intraspecific competition proceeds most expeditiously.

Figure 5.11 □ **Hardwood deciduous forest (St. Francis National Forest, Arkansas). Young stand of hardwood reclaiming cut-over area; black, white, and red oaks, poplar, and beech are present. (*Photograph by D. O. Todd, U.S. Forest Service.*)**

C Deciduous woodland

Deciduous forests are still the most characteristic biome of the temperate zone (Figure 5.11) although they are retreating before the advancing front of grasslands. Grasses are among the most recently evolved angiosperms and, with their efficient means of wind pollination and asexual (vegetative) proliferation by runners or rhizomes, are formidable competitors of the dicot species of the deciduous forest. Climatically, woodland biota has become adapted so as to withstand seasonal temperature variations that in winter customarily fall below 0°C and in summer occasionally exceed 35°C. Water is usually abundantly available, with rainfall (averaging about 80 cm/year) distributed almost evenly throughout the year. But the cold winter temperatures serve as a limiting factor for both plants and animals, namely by binding water as ice, and thus impose a strict annual cycle on their periods of growth and activity (Figure 5.12). Declining temperatures bring death to "annual" plants (which may be perfectly capable of living several years when cultivated at lower latitudes), and perennial deciduous species shed their leaves and cease to photosynthesize.

Figure 5.12 □ **Acorn woodpeckers (*Melanerpes formicivorus*) storing food. Food-caching behavior characterizes a number of temperate-woodland species. Such stores may supplement the winter food supply. (*Los Angeles County Museum of Natural History.*)**

D Grassland

The grassland biome, either treeless or—as *savannah*—studded with well-spaced trees, extends over vast areas of the subtropical and temperate zones, forming the African veldt, the Argentinian pampas, the Russian steppes, and the North American prairies. Grassland was the most recent biome to appear, for grasses have evolved in only the past 3×10^7 years. Grasslands are most prevalent where winters range from mild to freezing and rainfall is intermittent and sparse to moderate (20 to 90 cm/year). The absence of tall vegetation permits winds to sweep across the land. Wind dispersal and wind pollination thus become significant factors. The tough, finely divided fibrous root systems and rhizomes of the grasses prevent severe wind erosion. As man has learned to his sorrow the grassland biome, when deprived of its protective sod and put to the plow, may soon succumb to the ravages of wind and become a "dust bowl" or a desert.

Grasses possess great regenerative powers and are not irreparably injured by moderate grazing or traffic. They also produce and release large quantities of seed that may fail to germinate for want of rooting space. The seeds and vegetative parts of grasses thus provide nourishment for herbivorous animals, and it is in this biome that most species of socially aggregative herbivorous grazing mammals (including antelope, bison, and horses) have tended to evolve. These are among the most fleet-footed of terrestrial animals, for the terrain permits headlong flight without danger of encountering obstructions. Two different orders of mammals (together known as *ungulates,* or hoofed mammals) have undergone convergence in becoming adapted to the grassland biome, with its opportunity for unrestricted running. In both of these orders the *foot* has become greatly elongated and the *leg* commensurately shortened, bunching the leg muscles near the trunk and increasing the power and length of arc through which the foot can be moved. In both of these orders the number of toes has been reduced, the nails of the remaining toes thickening into sturdy hooves. The *artiodactyls* ("even-toed"), including cattle, camels, antelopes, and bison, have two remaining functional toes, whereas *perissodactyls* such as the horse and rhinoceros possess either one functional toe, or three, justifying the common name of "odd-toed" hoofed mammals.

Grasslands tend toward monotony, both

in appearance and in biota, for the relatively few dominant species of plants are repeated to the distant horizon and the occasional great nomadic animal herds consist of hundreds to thousands of similar individuals. Nevertheless, in the grassroots and among their stalks lives a microcosm of lesser beings—mice, voles, reptiles, and a horde of invertebrates—the existence of which escapes the eye of the casual observer. The grassland biome also long served as the home of nomadic human tribes such as the American Plains Indians and the Asiatic Mongols, who lived as predators, following their migratory prey and being as much a part of the natural ecology of their habitat as were the herbivores on which they fed.

E Taiga

This biome, characterized by *coniferous forest* (Figure 5.13) occupies most of Siberia, northern Europe, and Canada. There is little taiga in the southern hemisphere for want of land masses at the appropriate latitudes. Taiga tends to succeed grassland or deciduous woodland at about 40 to 45° latitude but extends far into the lower latitudes at increasingly higher *altitudes*. For example, the Douglas fir (*Pseudotsuga taxifolia*), an important timber species, occurs at sea level in Canada and the northwestern United States but in California becomes limited to progressively higher altitudes, tending not to occur below 650 m in its southerly range.

Figure 5.13 □ **Coniferous forest (stand of Englemann spruce, Colorado). Similar coniferous forests (with different dominant species) occur farther north at lower altitudes. (*Photograph by R. W. Mosher, U.S. Forest Service.*)**

The dominant plants in taiga are a few species of conifers, having needlelike or scalelike foliage adapted for water conservation. Although the foliage persists perennially in conifers, the growing season is short: temperatures low enough to freeze water during at least half of the year inhibit photosynthesis and the transport of nutrients from the roots to the leaves. Few reptiles inhabit the taiga (the pine snake and the mountain king snake are exceptions), but insects are abundant, together with many species of birds, mammals, and freshwater fish. Prolonged winter torpor or hibernation is the lot of most animal species. The more mobile mammals and birds often migrate to lower altitudes or to lower latitudes.

The evergreen foliage of the taiga has adaptive value in that photosynthesis can resume as soon as rising temperatures have made liquid water available for absorption by the plant roots. Time and energy need not be lost in putting forth a completely new set of leaves. Instead, stored nutrients are mobilized for an abrupt surge of growth, in which a "candle" of new foliage several centimeters long suddenly burgeons at each growing tip. The rudiments of the new shoots were formed during the previous growing season but remained enclosed within protective bud scales throughout the winter. Taiga species are highly adapted toward making the most of a season of activity much shorter than that available to species of the temperate deciduous forest.

F Tundra

At the present time, tundra is predominantly restricted to the northern hemisphere and lies mainly within the Arctic Circle. During warmer periods of world climate, when the Antarctic ice cap is less extensive, tundra is probably the dominant biome of that continent also. In the extreme poleward extension of its range, the taiga becomes progressively more stunted, until at last the terrain becomes treeless, a phenomenon similar to that occurring at the timberline of a mountain. The tundra in this respect resembles the alpine zone. Treeless and low, it consists of shrubby conifers and angiosperms, lichens, and mosses (Figure 5.14). Herbaceous annuals spread a carpet of color when they bloom simultaneously during the short summer. Water is abundant, though made unavailable by freezing through most of the year. A short distance below the surface the ground is perennially frozen (*permafrost*). Repeated thawing and freezing of groundwater breaks up the soil into large blocks that are forced up and tilted by the expansion of water during freezing.

Figure 5.14 □ Tundra (Colville River delta, Alaska). Small ponds that melt early allow marsh marigold (*Coetha palustris*) to bloom while ice still covers the larger lakes in background. (*Photograph by U. C. Nelson, U.S. Bureau of Sport Fisheries & Wildlife.*)

Precipitation at these high latitudes actually tends to be scanty since the cold air can hold so little water vapor. Therefore the plants may not be deeply buried in snow at any time of year and can quickly thaw and resume their metabolic activity when summer comes. Fortunately, the highest temperatures of the year necessarily coincide with the greatest length of photoperiod, which in fact becomes continuous in summer though of relatively low intensity. This extremely long photoperiod in part compensates for the brevity of the period of favorable temperatures, for plants can photosynthesize and grow continuously and animals can feed uninterrupted by darkness. Many birds use the tundra as a breeding ground, profiting by the long photoperiod: the explosive proliferation of plants and insects makes it possible for birds to rear their young more rapidly and perhaps have more than one brood per season. These birds are almost exclusively migratory, abandoning the tundra well ahead of the first autumnal storms.

Big Arctic mammals include reindeer, caribou, and musk oxen. These ungulates are nomadic, following a circular annual trek that takes them daily to new grazing areas and, in winter, to more southerly portions of the tundra or into the taiga. Lichens such as "reindeer moss" form a substantial part of their diet. These mammals have been extensively preyed upon and domesticated by man. Other mammals of the tundra include lemmings, Arctic foxes, Arctic hares, and ermine. The polar bear is not actually a tundra animal, for it preys largely on seals and is amphibious by nature, spending much of its time on the pack ice.

One of the main features of freshwater habitats is their relative *impermanence.* The water is on the move, destined to descend to altitude zero and become one with the sea. Originating primarily as snow and rainfall, water is precipitated onto the land and begins to move downhill, either as surface runoff or as percolating ground water. In its downward course, water may temporarily be impounded in lakes and ponds, forming quiet-water habitats for many species of aquatic organisms. But viewed from the perspective of geologic time, these bodies of water are transient, for they become filled with silt and organic residue and eventually disappear.

The physical characteristics of the still-water and running-water habitats are so different and impose such divergent selective forces on their inhabitants that they will be considered separately below.

A Problems of water balance

Osmosis (the diffusion of water across differentially permeable membranes, such as the cell membrane) and *osmoregulation* (the maintenance of a correct water balance in the cell or organism) will be considered in detail in Chapter 14. Problems of osmoregulation are most acute in organisms that inhabit milieus not in osmotic balance with their tissues. Osmotic balance depends upon there being equivalent concentrations of dissolved materials (*solutes*) in living tissues and in the milieu. When this is the case, the tendency of water to enter the tissues is in equilibrium with its tendency to flow out of them. If an organism is immersed in a solution having a *higher* concentration of solutes than does its tissues (that is, in a *hyperosmotic* solution), water tends to pass into the milieu and the organism may suffer dehydration. On the other hand, freshwater species must adapt to a milieu that is *hyposmotic* to their tissues (that is, too *low* in solutes to be in osmotic balance with living material).

Living things can adjust to a seawater environment (which has a heavy solute concentration) by active excretion of salts or by gradually *increasing* their own internal solute concentrations until an osmotic balance is achieved. However, organisms can never *reduce* their solute concentrations to arrive at equilibrium with a freshwater milieu. In consequence, water molecules, following their own concentration gradient, tend to diffuse *into* the bodies of freshwater organisms; they eventually would burst if they had no active or passive means for restricting excessive water uptake. The impervious exoskeletons of aquatic arthropods help to restrict the penetration of water, as do the scales and mucus-covered epidermis of freshwater fish. The cellulose cell walls of aquatic plants are permeable to water; but as the enclosed cells swell, they press with increasing force against the cell walls, impeding the further entrance of water. Under these conditions, *hydrostatic* pressure* balances *osmotic pressure* (the tendency of water to cross the cell membrane in the direction of its lower concentration), and the influx and outflow of water molecules is finally equalized. Freshwater animals, on the other hand, must expend energy to rid their bodies of excess water. Freshwater protozoans have contractile vacuoles, vesicles that collect water and forcibly eject it from the cell. In more complex freshwater organisms, the kidneys produce a dilute copious urine, reabsorbing needed solutes from the urine before it is voided.

B Lakes and ponds

The physicochemical factors influencing the lives and evolution of the inhabitants of still-water (*lentic*) habitats vary greatly according to the size and surface-to-volume ratio of the body of water. Therefore, lakes and ponds will be considered separately.

PONDS Ponds are small and shallow bodies of water. Consequently much of their bottom is within the range of light penetration and can support a growth of rooted aquatic plants. These plants in turn increase the amount of substratum and food available for animals. The depth of light penetration varies with the quantity of material in sus-

*Hydrostatic pressure is the pressure exerted by a liquid on an immersed body.

pension, including concentration of microscopic floating plants and animals that form the freshwater plankton.

Ponds are comparatively uniform in their distribution of gases and in temperature, for they are shallow enough so that their waters may be mixed from top to bottom. However, they experience greater seasonal fluctuations in temperature than do larger bodies of water and are also subject to rapid short-term perturbations caused by changes in weather and alterations in the balance of organisms present. Even slight winds mix pond water and increase its turbidity. Precipitation or evaporation can cause the concentration of solutes to vary markedly. In fact, smaller ponds may dry up entirely in summer, necessitating estivation or transition to a terrestrial mode of life for those organisms which can survive the temporary disappearance of their normal habitat.

Sunny weather accelerates photosynthetic activity and at such times bubbles of oxygen stream from the leaves of submerged plants. Conversely, on cloudy days the oxygen content of a pond decreases considerably. As the proportion of animal life increases seasonally following the burgeoning of vegetation, carbon dioxide may accumulate to excess, especially during overcast weather. We may thus conclude that ponds are precarious habitats, subject not only to abiotic disturbances but also to imbalances in biotic community relationships, which demand the utmost in physiological adaptability on the part of their inhabitants.

LAKES The deeper a lake, the more definite is its thermal stratification (the tendency for water of different temperatures to form layers that remain separate). As summer progresses, the surface water is increasingly warmed by the sun. Warming reduces its density and causes it to remain at the surface. Below the depth of light penetration, lake water remains relatively unheated by the sun and is markedly colder and denser than the overlying water of the *photic* (lighted) zone. At the interface between these two layers is the *thermocline,* a narrow zone within which water temperature declines steeply with increasing depth. The thermocline may become so stable that it cannot be disturbed even by violent storms. It constitutes a barrier to the distribution of gases, minerals, and small organisms.

Below the thermocline the waters lie cold, stagnant, and often nearly devoid of oxygen, until the autumnal and vernal *overturns,* when the surface and deeper waters mix. In autumn the surface water begins to cool. When it reaches the same temperature as the deeper water, the thermocline disappears and there is a period of redistribution of solutes and suspended materials. Again, in spring, as surface waters are warmed but before the thermocline is reestablished, there is a period of expansion and upwelling, bringing dissolved minerals to the surface where they serve as "fertilizer" for the phytoplankton. Desmids, diatoms, and other unicellular autotrophs are important constituents of the freshwater plankton.

The oxygen content of the waters below the thermocline may serve as a strict limiting factor in the distribution of life. The rotting of organic debris accumulated on the lake floor may use up all available oxygen so that the deeper waters may lack oxygen for as much as 5 months of each year! Under such conditions only organisms capable of anaerobic metabolism can survive. These anaerobes include certain bacteria and a few animals (such as larvae of the midge, *Chironomus*).

The freely swimming fauna (*nekton*) of lakes and ponds tends to favor the photic zone where food and some measure of protection are afforded by the attached plants. This fauna consists of bony fishes such as trout, bass, pike, and sturgeon.

In summary, it may be said that the smaller a body of water, the more subject it is to seasonal and short-term fluctuations in temperature, turbidity, gaseous and mineral content, and composition of the living community. On the other hand, the larger and deeper the body of water, the more restricted will be the proportion that is lighted and the more limited will be the circulation of its surface and deeper water, with consequent disparity in the distribution of oxygen and other solutes. The qualities that determine what species can succeed in a *pond* habitat include physiological adaptability with respect to tolerance of acute and rapid fluctuations in many physical and chemical factors and, for residents of temporary ponds, the capacity to estivate or become temporarily terrestrial. Biotic distribution in *lakes* is determined by the extent of the organism's dependence on light and oxygen.

C Running water

A *lotic* habitat is an environment in which the waters are usually flowing. There is, of course, a transition between quiet-water and lotic conditions, especially in the larger, more sluggishly flowing rivers. A current requires that most lotic species have some means of preventing themselves from being swept away; otherwise, they would not come to rest until they had reached a quiet-water habitat (or the ocean), in which they would be unlikely to survive. The lotic *plankton* is therefore impermanent but is continuously replenished from streamside pools and from the ponds and lakes that drain into the stream or river. When the current is swift, fixed plants are few and much of the fauna is carnivorous. Unlike the condition in lakes and ponds in which the relative quietude of the waters forces animals to move about in search of food, the currents of the lotic habitat perpetually transport fresh supplies of food to animals, and thus they have little need for locomotion. Many insects spend their larval lives in the lotic habitat, where they employ food-getting adaptations related to the extraction of microorganisms from running water. Certain caddis-fly larvae spin small funnellike nets across the current and gather their prey from the net. Other larvae, such as mayflies and black flies, have bristly appendages modified into "plankton baskets," within which diatoms and other microorganisms are concentrated before ingestion. Upon these plankton feeders live the carnivorous lotic species (such as dragonfly and damselfly larvae) and fish (such as brook trout). Most permanently lotic species are *benthonic* (living on the bottom) and either are *sessile* (attached) or retire under stones or burrow into the substratum. Only vertebrates are generally large and strong enough to maintain a nektonic existence in the face of rapidly flowing water. Freshwater clams succeed in lotic habitats because their larvae are parasitic on the gills of fish and thereby escape downstream displacement.

In contrast with quiet waters, running water tends to be more turbid (thus limiting light penetration), more uniform in temperature and solute concentration throughout its depth, and more fully saturated with atmospheric gases. The fauna is typically adapted to a high oxygen concentration and may perish if the oxygen content falls much below saturation. The lotic habitat is more subject to seasonal variation than are the deeper still-water habitats. The motion of the water and the relatively large surface exposed to the air cause the temperature of the water to conform closely to that of the atmosphere. Extensive freezing may occur in rivers in the temperate and Arctic zones, resulting in a high winter mortality.

5.5 □ MARINE HABITATS

A folk rhyme begins, "If all the seas were one sea, what a great sea that would be . . ."; since all the major oceans actually are continuous with one another, the world ocean is indeed "a great sea"! Although each basin—the Pacific, Arctic, Atlantic, and Indian—is characterized by its own particular current systems and tidal rhythm, these being influenced by the shape, size, and depth of the basin, in the southern hemisphere all the seas meet and are one. No permanent barrier blocks the gradual dispersal of marine organisms so that eventually many become cosmopolitan in distribution. The earth's eastward rotation, coupled with the inertia of the atmosphere, produces west-moving winds near the equator. Corresponding westward-flowing currents are set up in the oceans. When they meet a land mass, these currents are deflected, so that a great current system rotating clockwise occurs in the ocean basins north of the equator, while an equivalent counterclockwise rotational system exists in the southern hemisphere (Figure 5.15). These great oceanic currents profoundly affect the biosphere: not only do they bring about the dispersal of marine life, but they affect the climate of bordering land masses and distribute equatorial solar heat.

Although a thermocline does exist in the sea at the lower limit of the photic zone (a depth of about 100 m), the anaerobic conditions that may prevail below the thermocline in deep lakes do not develop. This is because convection currents resulting from the unequal solar heating of the earth's surface cause the deep and surface waters of the ocean to circulate. Since cool water can hold more dissolved gases than warm water, water at about 0°C can contain twice as much dissolved oxygen as water at 30°C. As the currents passing poleward become cool, they sink, bearing their freight of dissolved gases into the depths.

Averaging a depth of over 4 km, the world ocean fills its basins and overlaps the edges of the continental masses. That portion of a continent which is overlain by ocean at any given time is known as the continental shelf. At its outer limit, the continental mass terminates in a more or less abrupt declivity (the continental slope), which marks the actual boundary of the ocean basin proper (Figure 5.16). During periods when the world climate is mild and little water is bound as ice, the surface of the sea may lie as much as 0.5 km above its present level and most continental lowlands are inundated. At such times the continental shelf is very extensive and shallow seas penetrate far into the interior of the land masses, occupying areas (such as the Mississippi Valley and the Great Plains) that today are relatively level land. More startling is the recovery of fossils of marine organisms from layers of rock being weathered at high altitudes. The buckling of the earth's crust has repeatedly elevated mountain chains from strata that were deposited as sediments on the floor of these shallow and temporary extensions of the sea.

Figure 5.15 □ **Major oceanic currents. Note that the major rotatory systems of the Pacific and Atlantic basins move clockwise in the northern hemisphere and counterclockwise in the southern hemisphere. The westbound equatorial current is set up by the eastward rotation of the earth, and is deflected to the left and right upon meeting a land mass.**

A Sea water as a medium for life

Sea water has a composition much more complex than that of fresh water. It not only contains large quantities of dissolved inorganic material, primarily ions such as sodium ion (Na^+), chloride ion (Cl^-), magnesium ion (Mg^{2+}), calcium ion (Ca^{2+}), carbonate ion (CO_3^{2-}), and sulfate ion (SO_4^{2-}), but also contains small but detectable quantities of many organic compounds such as vitamins, as well as nitrates, phosphates, and other products of biotic activity and decomposition. These organic materials are frequently adsorbed onto solid particles of such minute dimensions (1 to 2 μm) that they tend to remain indefinitely in suspension. Considerable nutrition may be obtained by zooplankton that collect and ingest these microscopic particles along with their digestible coating of organic material.

Since water is perpetually evaporated from the surface of the sea and returns as runoff from the land, bearing minerals in solution, the solute content of sea water is slowly but perpetually increasing. Up to the present the problem of adapting to ever-increasing salinity has posed no insuperable obstacle to those groups of organisms which originated in the sea and have never forsaken it for another habitat. Such marine organisms have undergone a gradual increase in their own internal solute concentrations, which has kept pace with the change in composition of sea water. They thus experience little difficulty in regulating their balance of water and ions. For organisms that have reinvaded the sea from fresh water or from the land, the problem is more severe. Vertebrates are thought to have evolved from prevertebrate ancestors that entered estuaries and became established in rivers, which at that time were sparsely populated and presented fewer problems of predation and competition than did the neighboring shallow seas. During this upstream transition the prevertebrates carried with them in their blood and body fluids a solute content similar to that of the ocean that had been their home. The composition of vertebrate body fluids probably has

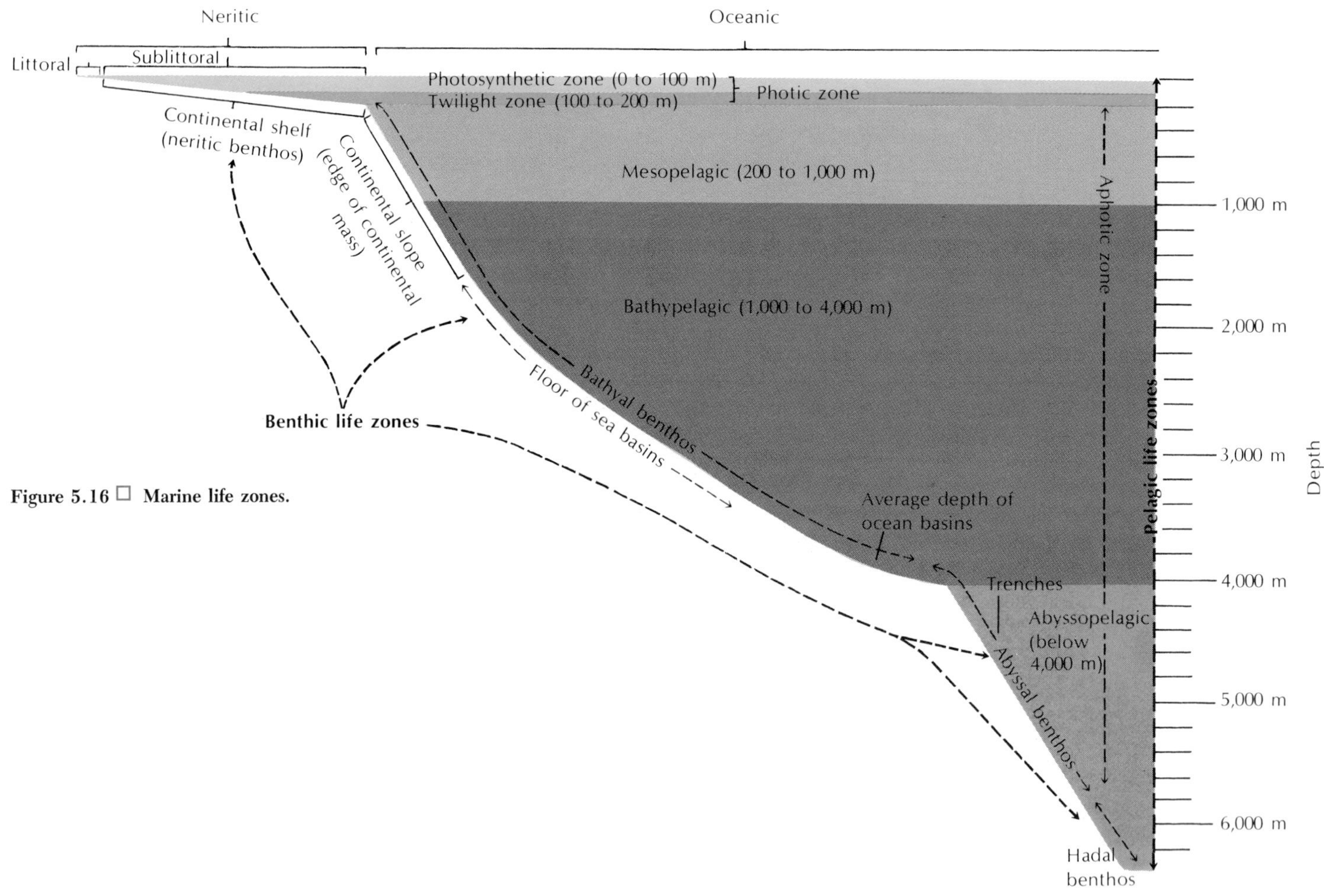

Figure 5.16 □ Marine life zones.

changed much less since that time than has the saltiness of the sea. Vertebrate fish, having evolved in fresh water, soon reinvaded the sea, where ever since they have had to cope with the problem of retaining water and ridding their bodies of excess salt. The marine environment contains proportionately less water and more salts (especially Na^+ and Cl^-) than do the bodies of most marine vertebrates and consequently is not in osmotic balance with their tissues. Sharks are an exception, for their mode of adaptation to sea water has been to tolerate ever greater concentrations of such nitrogenous waste materials as urea, which ordinarily would be removed by the kidneys. The high urea content of shark blood, which would probably be fatal to other animals, allows it to be in osmotic balance with the surrounding sea water. Other marine fish, as well as marine birds, mammals, and turtles, must actively excrete salt from their bodies. Seabirds and turtles have salt-excreting glands located in their heads. Sea turtles seem always to be weeping, for the briny exudate from these glands flows from the corners of their eyes. The salt glands of birds vent into their nostrils, from which the birds can expel the saline liquid. Marine mammals do not have such glands, but they accomplish the removal of salt and the conservation of water by means of their specially adapted kidneys (see Section 16.2A).

B The pelagic habitat

As with lakes, the open water of the sea constitutes one habitat and the bottom or floor represents another: these two major marine habitats are called, respectively, the *pelagic* and the *benthic;* each is further zonated on the basis of depth. The pelagic habitat includes all open water, while the benthos includes the floors of the continental shelf, slope, and sea basin proper. Pelagic organisms may be categorized as *plankton* or *nekton,* whereas those forms which are bottom-dwelling are termed *benthonic.*

THE MARINE PLANKTON Plankton consists of those organisms which, because of small size or weakly developed locomotory powers, cannot move against the ocean currents but are involuntarily carried with them. Marine *phytoplankton* is composed mainly of diatoms and dinoflagellates. Being photosynthesizers, these microscopic plants must remain in the lighted levels (photic zone) where they can absorb the needed radiant energy (Figure 5.17). Much of the marine *zooplankton* (Figure 5.18), on the other hand, remains near the lower edge of the photic zone, rising toward the surface each evening as the light wanes and descending again as the sun rises. Why these minute animals spend so much time swimming upward or downward remains a mystery. Since performing vertical movements that may exceed 200 m/day involves a high energy expenditure for animals often less than 0.5 mm long, the survival value of these movements must be considerable. It is thought that the downward migration allows the zooplankton to enter subsurface currents flowing in a different direction or at a different rate than the surface current. This may carry them to new locations where phytoplankton is less depleted or, by transporting them in opposition to the surface current, may prevent them from being carried out of their range of thermal tolerance.

Marine plankton differs from freshwater plankton in three main respects: (1) the marine zooplankton characteristically exhibits a daily rhythm of vertical migration that freshwater plankton lacks; (2) a wider variety of phyla are represented in the marine plankton; (3) marine zooplankton includes not only permanently planktonic species (*holoplankton*) that spend all of their lives in the plankton but also a great variety of *meroplankton* species that are planktonic as larvae, maturing into nektonic or benthonic adults. Included in the meroplankton are the larvae of echinoderms, molluscs, annelids, arthropods, and many other phyla. Holoplankton includes arrow worms, comb jellies, medusae, siphonophores, pteropods ("sea butterflies," or swimming snails), and small crustaceans, including the prodigiously abundant copepods and shrimplike krill. The zooplankton is an essential food source for larger marine animals, and it must counteract this depredation through the means of its tremendous fecundity.

THE NEKTON The *nekton* includes those pelagic animals which are sufficiently powerful swimmers to oppose the ocean currents [although they usually prudently swim with these currents and thus exploit them (Figure 5.19)]. Nekton includes squid, vertebrate fishes, marine mammals, and turtles.

Oceanic ("open-sea") nekton species are almost exclusively carnivorous, whereas species that inhabit the shallow coastal waters may be found to browse upon seaweed as well as hydroids, coral, and other benthonic forms.

Figure 5.17 □ Marine phytoplankton. (*Courtesy of Dr. Douglas P. Wilson and Marine Biological Laboratory, Plymouth.*) The species numbered are diatoms, (1) *Coscinodiscus concinnus,* (2) *Biddulphia sinensis,* (3) *Ceratulina pelagica,* (4) *Stephanopyxis turris,* (5) *Chaetoceros affinis,* (6) *Chaetoceros curvisetum,* (7) *Chaetoceros didymum,* and (8) *Chaetoceros* sp., and dinoflagellates, (9) *Ceratium tripos,* (10) *Ceratium longipes,* (11) *Ceratium* sp., and (12) *Ceratium fusus.*

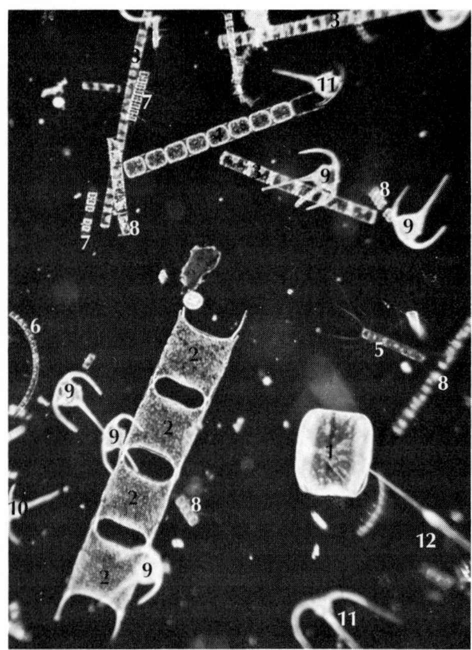

Figure 5.18 □ Marine zooplankton, a sample taken in the California Current off central California. (*Photograph by G. Mattson, U.S. Bureau of Commercial Fisheries.*) The items numbered are (1) euphausid, (1*a*) euphausid egg mass, (2) amphipod, (3) copepod, (4) ostracod, (5) zoea larva (*Emerita analoga*), (6) pteropod, (7) polychaete larva, (8) siphonophore, (9) chaetognath, (10) salp, (11) doliolid, (12) fish, (12*a*) fish egg, and (13) decapod larva.

Figure 5.19 □ Nekton: portion of school of sardines (*Sardinops caerulea*). (*Photograph by G. Mattson, U.S. Bureau of Commercial Fisheries.*)

C Benthic habitats

The texture of the benthos—rocky, sandy, muddy, or soft ooze—determines the adaptations of benthonic species. Most attached marine plants are seaweeds—red algae, kelps, and multicellular green algae. These require a solid substratum and are restricted to waters shallow enough for light to penetrate to the bottom. A few species of grasses, including surf grass and eel grass, flourish in the intertidal zone and in shallow bays. Having true root systems instead of adhesive holdfasts, these grasses are more successful than seaweeds in exploiting sand or mud as a substratum. The lightless benthos cannot be occupied by photosynthesizing plants, but bacteria are abundant, feeding upon organic detritus in the oozes covering much of the sea floor.

Figure 5.20 □ **Epifauna. The largest bivalve, sometimes weighing 200 kg, is the giant clam, *Tridacna*, being inspected by a diver in this underwater photograph taken over the Great Barrier Reef, Australia. The clam's thickened mantle edges are dark with symbiotic algae that are exposed to sun when the mantle is spread. Part of the clam's food supply consists of carbohydrates manufactured by these tiny symbionts. (*Courtesy of Australian News and Information Bureau.*)**

Benthonic animals may live upon or within the substratum. Sedentary animals such as corals, sea lilies, oysters and giant clams (Figure 5.20) live attached to the bottom; other species such as starfish, crabs, octopus, and snails, are unattached and mobile. Burrowing animals include most kinds of clams, scaphopods, and many worms.

The character of the benthic habitat alters abruptly at the edge of the continental shelf. Upon the shelf proper, the benthos usually receives some light and the type of life is influenced by whether the substratum is sand, mud, or rock. The continental slope plunges swiftly to the floor of the true sea basin, where far below the depth of light penetration a permanent abyssal biota of surprising diversity exists in darkness unrelieved save for the occasional eerie glow of bioluminescence. Most of the floor of the ocean basins is deeply covered with drifts of soft sediments: red clays of presumably volcanic origin and extensive deposits of oozes mostly made up of the loosely compacted calcareous or siliceous tests of protozoa (foraminiferans and radiolarians) and diatoms. The fauna living upon the surface of these soft sediments typically has developed delicately elongate appendages that might surprise us by their fragility until we recall that these creatures are as well-adapted to the tremendous pressures under which they live as we are to the overlying blanket of the atmosphere. Abyssal benthonic animals are mainly *detritus* feeders, subsisting upon bacteria and ooze enriched by decaying organisms that have sunk into the black depths from the upper waters. However, some predators are also present, including a slender polyp nearly 3 m tall.

According to whether they occupy a sea basin proper or overlie part of a continental shelf, the pelagic and benthic habitats are grouped into *oceanic* and *neritic regions*.

D The oceanic region

This region, the "open sea," is bounded peripherally by the continental slopes. It includes both pelagic and benthic habitats, zonated according to depth. The oceanic *benthos* lies entirely below the photic level, from about 150 m to the greatest depths of the sea. Its biota must live on or within the soft clays and oozes and must tolerate darkness, cold, and great pressure. Approximately the upper 200 m of the oceanic pelagic habitat represents the *epipelagic* zone, extending from the surface to the farthest depth of light penetration. The epipelagic zone consists of an upper, well-lighted region, in which photosynthesis may be carried on (0 to about 100 m), and a twilight zone, in which light is insufficient for photosynthesis to occur (approximately from 100 to 200 m). Within the twilight zone lies the thermocline, where the warmer surface waters are sharply divided from the cold waters of the lightless zones. The rest of the pelagic habitat is in perpetual dark-

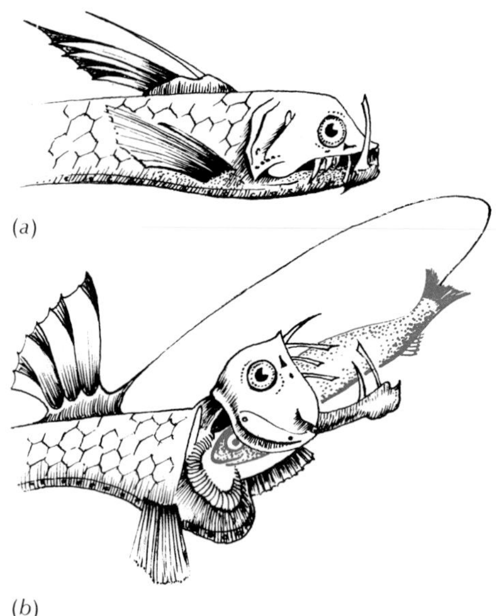

Figure 5.21 □ A deep-sea fish, *Chauliodus* (*a*), showing unusual adaptation for swallowing large prey (*b*); as described in text, a portion of the gill skeleton is added to the lower jaw, extending the gape. (*From Colin Nicol, after Tchernavin.*)

Figure 5.22 □ Deep-sea angler female with "parasitic" male attached to her forehead. The pair are shown approximately life size. This remarkable adaptation ensures that, despite low population density and perpetual darkness, individuals of the same species and of opposite sex are together at the time of mating. The luminescent projection above the female's mouth may attract prey.

ness. Its biota must feed on one another and upon the slow rain of detritus and dead organisms from the upper waters.

Deep-sea nekton are predators and scavengers adapted to living in virtually lightless conditions. Their eyes are either degenerate or huge and capable of detecting luminescent organisms. Some of these animals ascend sufficiently far to prey upon epipelagic animals at the lowest point of their daily vertical migration. Many deep-sea fish exhibit bizarre specializations for devouring prey larger than themselves. In *Chauliodus* some of the skeletal gill supports are enlarged and modified as accessories to the jaw (Figure 5.21). During feeding the head of *Chauliodus* is thrown back while the huge jaw mechanism shoots forward forming a trap that engulfs the prey. The stomachs of most deep-sea fish are enormously distensible, allowing meals to be taken infrequently.

Many deep-sea animals are *bioluminescent* (see Section 16.3J). In some cases light is given off merely as an incidental by-product of metabolism (as in the case of luminescent bacteria), but it is of practical use to deep-sea animals both in the capturing of food and the finding of mates. Some have luminescent extensions of the body that seem to function as lures for prey, since the rest of the body is nonluminescent and hence invisible. In other species the light-emitting organs (*photophores*) may be so arranged that a species-specific light pattern is produced. These patterns help animals of the same species to recognize one another. Such recognition signals can also be hazardous since they may attract predators instead of the sought-for mate.

Certain deep-sea anglers have solved the mating problem in a less dangerous but very unusual manner. In these species, the male need find the female only once, for at the first meeting he attaches himself to her body and assumes a parasitic existence. Since the young of a species always tend to be more numerous than the adults, the probability of young males meeting females is enhanced. Natural selection has favored ever-earlier attachment of the male: the tinier the male at the moment of attachment, the less will be his nutritional demands upon the economy of his host-wife. Natural selection would also favor his remaining as small as possible throughout life. Upon locating a female, the male attaches himself to any portion of her body, their integuments and bloodstreams fuse, and they become as inseparable as "Siamese twins" (Figure 5.22). Probably a hormonal exchange occurs between the two, for the female ovulates at the same time that the male produces and voids sperm.

E The neritic zone

That part of the sea which overlies the continental shelf constitutes the neritic zone: landwards, the neritic terminates in the coastal or *littoral* habitat; peripherally, it is continuous with the open sea although its outer limit is demarcated by the edge of the continental shelf. Because they overlie a continental mass, the waters of the neritic are shallow and its benthos lies largely or wholly within the range of the penetration of light. Here substratum is afforded for attached seaweeds, which in turn provide food, shelter, and substratum for a great variety of animals. The neritic is accordingly

Figure 5.23 □ **Littoral-zone biota. (*a*) *Fucus vesiculosus*, a rockweed. Note globular floats. The alga clings to rocks in surf by means of tough holdfasts. (*b*) Limpets, *Acmaea scabra*, clinging by suction to rocks exposed to full surf. The sloping "Chinese-hat" outline deflects wave force. (*c*) Mussel-barnacle association. Mussels cling by tough, elastic byssus threads. Barnacles cement themselves to the shells of mussels or to the substratum. Such dense aggregations, characteristic of the middle littoral zone of exposed rocky coasts, harbor many more vulnerable species.**

(*a*)

(*b*)

(*c*)

the most abundantly and diversely populated of any region of the sea. Silt carried into the sea from the land changes the character of the bottom and occasionally smothers its life especially off the mouth of rivers. Such buried organisms are candidates for fossilization and eventually turn up once again in shales to edify everyone from paleontologists to small boys. The shoreward portion of the neritic is especially interesting to the biologist because of the peculiar conditions that its biota must endure.

THE LITTORAL ZONE The landward border of the neritic, the littoral zone, is characterized by unique conditions of *surf* and twice-daily *tidal* fluctuations. The sea-land interface is a changing margin, oscillating rhythmically with the tides. It also alters as cliffs crumble and as sand builds shifting spits and beaches; subsidences create salt marshes and elevations raise bluffs. To some extent the littoral biota represents the uppermost extension of the range of offshore species. In general, however, those species which can withstand the powerful force of surf and exposure to air at low tide are uniquely littoral forms. This fact should be borne in mind by persons who prey immoderately upon seashore life, for this fauna cannot be replenished by the shoreward movement of animals from greater depths.

On sandy beaches animals can avoid both surf and exposure at low tide merely by burrowing (as done by clams) or seeking deeper water (as done by swimming crabs). For want of secure attachment, algae (which as we know lack roots and depend upon adhesive holdfasts) do not succeed well on sandy shores, although surf grasses may adapt well to these conditions.

The dominant species found on rocky

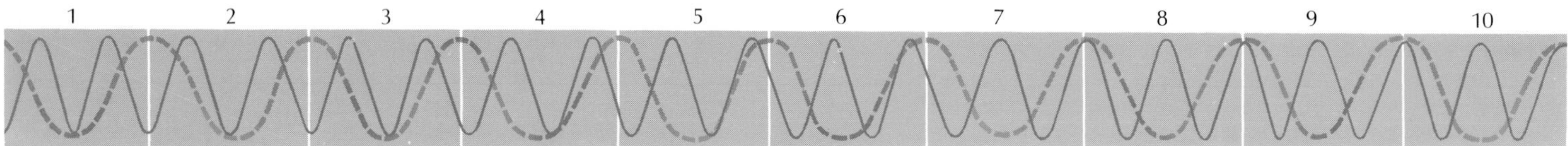

Figure 5.24 □ **Endogenous activity rhythms in the fiddler crab. The solid line represents a 12.4-hr tidal rhythm, with the animal's activity peak (crest of each wave) coinciding with low tide but falling gradually out of phase with the actual tide schedule when the crab is kept for prolonged periods under constant conditions in the laboratory. The broken line shows a diurnal rhythm of pigment changes, the crab darkening by day (wave troughs) and becoming pale (wave crests) at night (noon is midway between the lines demarcating each day). The period of this circadian rhythm is very close to 24.0 hr; it persists for weeks or months even when the crab is constantly in darkness or under illumination.**

coasts are those which have developed surf-defying methods of attachment to the substratum (Figure 5.23). Plants include kelps such as rockweed (*Fucus* and related species), the tough stipes and firm holdfasts of which withstand the most severe wave action. Animals of rocky coasts are often anchored more or less permanently by suction, by cement, or by secreted threads of great tensile strength. Other animals actively seek protection in crevices or among attached organisms during the periods when surf action is most severe.

Littoral organisms must possess wide tolerance for fluctuations in temperature, salinity, and acidity and alkalinity; they must also withstand exposure to air and direct sunlight. Tidepools are subject to heating by the sun, dilution by rainfall, and concentration by evaporation. At night the combined respiratory requirements of both plants and animals may largely deplete the tidepool's oxygen content. Even more serious is the accumulation of carbon dioxide, which reacts with water to form carbonic acid (H_2CO_3), thus making the pool acidic. During the day the carbon dioxide is used up by the algae, and the water of the tidepool becomes neutral or even alkaline. Such acid-alkaline fluctuations are not tolerated by most animals of the open sea but must be endured by tidepool species. Direct exposure to the rays of the sun is potentially as detrimental as desiccation, not only because of the heat produced but because rays of some wavelengths promote photochemical reactions. Penetration of harmful rays is reduced if the organism possesses an impervious integument, shell, or exoskeleton or actively seeks shelter. It is thus clear that many littoral species operate near their tolerance limits; the mortality rate is high whenever any one of the abiotic factors fluctuates beyond the critical limit or when the animal is under severe stress in one respect so that its tolerance for other factors may be reduced.

ACTIVITY RHYTHMS IN LITTORAL ANIMALS The intertidal fauna has undergone selection toward the establishment of physiological and behavioral rhythms that reflect daily and monthly tidal rhythms. Barnacles and mussels, for example, close their valves and cease to feed when receding water leaves them exposed to the air. Feeding commences as soon as they are again submerged by the rising tide. Conversely, at low tide crabs emerge from their burrows and scamper about the beach hunting for food (Figure 5.24). Such activity rhythms might at first appear merely to be responses to the direct stimulus of contact with air or water; but under constant laboratory conditions, where diurnal and tidal rhythms are abolished, these activity rhythms tend to persist—although they may gradually fall out of phase with the actual times of day and night and of high and low tides on the shores from which the animals were taken. The innate physiological rhythms demonstrated by littoral fauna have their own periods, which are usually slightly longer or shorter than the environmental rhythm that caused them to evolve. However, under normal circumstances, stimuli from the environment keep the innate rhythm entrained to the exogenous one. True *circadian* rhythms (so called because they approximate a 24-hr cycle) occur in littoral animals together with rhythms attuned to the tides and to the moon.

The spawning activities of many littoral species are related to the lunar cycle, with the result that egg-laying coincides with the highest tides of the month. During each lunar month (28.3 days) there are two cycles of *neap* tides and two of *spring* tides. Neap tides occur at the first and third quarters of the moon, when the tidal oscillation is damped by the opposing gravitational forces of moon and sun, which are exerted at right angles to one another at these times. Spring tides occur when the sun and moon are in line and exert their attraction in the same plane, either on the same side of the earth or on opposite sides (at the new and full moons, respectively). At these times, the tidal oscillation is exaggerated, and low water is lower and high water is higher than they are at any other times of the month.*

At the high spring tides, animals that are exposed to air during the greater portion of their lives are briefly submerged. If their larvae require aquatic development, the eggs must be shed at this time.

TRANSITION TO LAND The littoral is a transitional zone where many forms of life have experimented with terrestrial existence. Life did not *once* come ashore from the sea—it is still in the process of coming ashore. A case in point are three related species of small snails or periwinkles, *Littorina littoralis, L. rudis,* and *L. neritoides.* Of these species, *L. littoralis* cannot endure long exposure to air but lives among masses of rockweed that protect it at low tide. It breathes in a manner typical of aquatic gastropods by circulating water across a gill enclosed in the mantle cavity under the shell. The eggs of *L. littoralis* are laid in gelatinous masses on rockweed, and the young emerge as miniatures of the adult, there being no planktonic larval stage in this species. *Littorina rudis* and *L. neritoides* can obtain oxygen from either air or water. In these two species the gill is reduced and the mantle itself richly provided with capillaries, a condition similar to the "lung" of true land snails. The female of *L. rudis* retains the eggs within her body until they hatch into shelled juveniles resembling the adult. Thus from the standpoint of both respiration and reproduction, *L. rudis* is capable of a terrestrial existence and in fact does live exposed to air except at the highest tides; *L. neritoides,* on the other hand, inhabits the spray zone even higher up than *L. rudis* ranges but has failed to develop means of brooding its young. Consequently the reproductive cycle of *L. neritoides* is coordinated with the monthly tidal rhythm so that every fortnight it sheds eggs into the sea coincident with the high water of the spring tides. The larvae that hatch from these eggs are briefly planktonic and then migrate inshore and metamorphose into young snails that gradually move upward beyond the reach of mean high tide to the spray zone, where their adult lives are spent.

REVIEW AND DISCUSSION

1 Explain, with examples, what is meant by a "limiting factor" in the distribution of a species.

2 Is it likely that any given organism can achieve a state of optimal adaptation to all factors in its environment? Explain your answer.

*For more information on tides and their cause, see E. J. Cable, R. W. Getchell, W. H. Kadesh, W. J. Poppy, and L. L. Wilson, *The Physical Sciences,* 5th ed. (Englewood Cliffs, N.J.: Prentice-Hall, Inc., 1969), pp. 30–31.

3 Summarize the specifications for an animal having complete adaptability for any mode of life. Why do you think that the living world has gained access to various habitats by way of diversification rather than by total adaptability?

4 What are the major ways in which habitats vary with latitude and with altitude? How do latitudinal and altitudinal life zones resemble one another? In what important respects do they *not* resemble each other?

5 Summarize the characteristics of the major terrestrial biomes. Why is it likely that hoofed mammals evolved in the grassland biome although some now live in forests? Explain why attempts to cultivate grassland and rain forest often end disastrously.

6 How does the problem of water conservation complicate the problem of thermoregulation in desert animals? In what ways are these problems met? Are poikilotherms capable of any type of thermoregulation? Explain.

7 What contrasting requirements do quiet- and running-water habitats impose on the organisms inhabiting them? Contrast the living conditions of lakes and ponds, and the different demands placed on organisms in these two types of environments. Why are lakes the biotic habitats most subject to damage by sewage and industrial wastes?

8 What is the major limiting factor to the vertical distribution of life in the sea? Explain.

9 Distinguish between holoplankton and meroplankton, with examples. What may be the adaptive value of the daily vertical migration of marine zooplankton? Why may we assume that this behavior has *any* adaptive value? How do marine and freshwater plankton differ?

10 In what habitats would you expect to find forms of life that appear to be evolving from an aquatic to a terrestrial existence? From a marine to a freshwater existence? From a terrestrial to an aquatic mode of life? What particular problems of existence would have to be solved in order that each of these transitions be made successfully? What species do you think may be making such transitions at the present time?

11 What are circadian rhythms? How do you think innate "biological clock" mechanisms are established and perpetuated? Suggest an experimental method for distinguishing a true innate rhythm from an activity rhythm induced by some external periodicity. If an animal isolated in a laboratory under constant conditions continued to demonstrate an activity rhythm that stayed in phase with a rhythmic occurrence in the outer world, how could you experimentally rule out the possibility that the animal was still responding to some environmental cue that could not be eliminated?

12 How do annual fluctuations in mean temperature and length of photoperiod affect the lives of plants and animals of the temperate, subtemperate, and polar zones? Why are annual rhythms not prevalent among tropical species to the extent that they are in the other groups? Why do you think so many temperate-zone birds migrate to the Arctic to raise young?

13 In what ways do photophores serve deep-sea fish? What other unique adaptations are found in fish of the deep sea?

REFERENCES

AMOS, W. H. "The Life of a Sand Dune," *Sci. Amer.*, **201** (1959).

BATES, M. *The Forest and the Sea.* New York: The New American Library of World Literature, Inc., 1960. A discussion of basic ecological principles at a popular level.

BLISS, L. C. "A Comparison of Plant Development in Microenvironments of Arctic and Alpine Tundras," *Ecol. Monogr.*, **26** (1956).

BUCHSBAUM, R., AND M. BUCHSBAUM *Basic Ecology.* Pittsburgh, Pa.: The Boxwood Press, 1957. A short, basic presentation of ecological principles, nicely illustrated.

CARPENTER, J. R. "The Grassland Biome," *Ecol. Monogr.*, **10** (1940). Describes the composition of three major climax grassland associations of North America.

DEEVEY, E. S. "Life in the Depths of a Pond," *Sci. Amer.*, **185** (1951).

FARB, P. *The Forest.* New York: Time Incorporated, 1961. A popular exposition with fine illustrative material.

HANSON, H. C. "Ecology of the Grassland," *Bot. Rev.*, **16** (1950). New methods for analyzing the characteristics of grassland communities are described and evaluated.

HARDY, A. C. *The Open Sea: The World of Plankton.* Boston: Houghton Mifflin Co., 1956. A very readable description of the animals of the marine plankton, stressing morphological adaptations and discussing some unusual and interesting forms of life.

INGER, R. F. "Ecological Aspects of the Origins of the Tetrapods," *Evolution*, **11** (1957). Studies of present-day air-breathing fishes point toward probable conditions of climate and habitat under which lobefinned fishes evolved. Read with paper by Romer cited below.

INGLE, R. M. "The Life of an Estuary," *Sci. Amer.*, **190** (1954). Estuarine conditions pose special problems for animal life.

JAEGER, E. C. *The North American Deserts.* Stanford, Calif.: Stanford University Press, 1957. A classic in its field, presenting a comprehensive discussion of the deserts of this continent and their wildlife.

LEOPOLD, A. S. *The Desert.* New York: Time Incorporated, 1961. Description of the desert and its life at a popular level, with excellent photographs.

MOORE, H. B. *Marine Ecology.* New York: John Wiley & Sons, Inc., 1958. An advanced presentation with much useful reference material.

NEAL, E. *Woodland Ecology* (2nd ed.). Cambridge, Mass.: Harvard University Press, 1965.

NICHOLAS, G. "Life in Caves," *Sci. Amer.,* **192** (1955).

NORRIS, K. S. "The Ecology of the Desert Iguana *Dipsosaurus dorsalis,*" *Ecology,* **34** (1953). Field research upon the adaptations of a lizard to drought and thermal extremes; records a voluntarily tolerated body temperature of 46.4°C! The annual activity cycle is described and seasonal changes in diet noted.

OVINGTON, J. D. *Woodlands.* London: The English Universities Press, Ltd., 1965. A simplified account of woodland structure and nutritional processes in the woodland community, together with a discussion of woodland management for profit and recreation.

PEARSE, A. S. *The Emigrations of Animals from the Sea.* Dryden, N. Y.: The Sherwood Press, 1950. Discussion of the adaptive adjustments shown by many species which occupy transition zones between the marine and freshwater or marine and terrestrial habitats.

PEDERSON, O. *Polar Animals.* New York: Taplinger Publishing Co., Inc., 1966. Interesting naturalistic account of the lives of animals of northeast Greenland.

RICHARD, P. W. *The Tropical Rain Forest.* London and New York: Cambridge University Press, 1952. A comprehensive treatment of this fascinating biome.

ROMER, A. S. "Tetrapod Limbs and Early Tetrapod Life," *Evolution,* **12** (1958). A noted paleontologist replies to the argument of R. F. Inger (cited above) concerning the selective role of climatic factors during vertebrate evolution to life on land.

STEPHENSON, T. A., AND A. STEPHENSON "The Universal Features of Zonation between Tide-marks on Rocky Coasts," *Jour. Ecol.,* **37** (1949).

VEVERS, H. G. "Animals of the Bottom," *Sci. Amer.,* **187** (1952).

WALFORD, L. A. "The Deep-sea Layers of Life," *Sci. Amer.,* **185** (1951).

WEATHERSBEE, C. "Research to Save the Fragile Green Hell," *Science News,* **95** (1969). Reviews meetings of the International Association for Tropical Biology concerned with means of saving the Amazonian rain forest from destruction.

WECKER, S. C. "Habitat Selection," *Sci. Amer.,* **211** (1964).

YONGE, C. M. *The Sea Shore.* New York: Atheneum, 1963. A classic work, lately reprinted, which presents in brief and eminently readable form a discussion of the life and adaptations of littoral biota, with special reference to species of the British Isles.

Chapter 6  ADAPTATION TO OTHER SPECIES

THERE IS A WIDER TRUTH TO JOHN Donne's statement, "No man is an Iland, intire of it selfe; every man is a peece of the Continent, a part of the maine," although it strictly refers to man's involvement in mankind. In essence, this wider truth bears upon the broad concept of an integrated organism-environment complex, discussed earlier. In preceding chapters we have considered the following facts: (1) the bodies of organisms are wholly constructed of components derived from the environment and accordingly living things have had to develop a number of structural and functional adaptations enabling them to obtain and utilize such materials; (2) the earth in general and different kinds of habitats in particular provide sets of selective factors that have greatly influenced the evolution of living things.

In this chapter and the next we shall explore the often complex relationships existing among the various organisms that coexist in integrated units known as *biotic communities.* We have noted that biotic diversity comes about through chance hereditary changes, of which only those that aid survival will tend to be perpetuated. We have seen that many aspects of biotic diversity represent adaptations for enduring or exploiting the abiotic environment. Now we shall consider how the need to adapt to the presence of other living things has influenced the evolution of each species. *Every organism has a biotic as well as an abiotic environment.* No creature exists in isolation from other species and from other individuals of the same species. The relationships among organisms are as influential in shaping the genetic constitution of a population as are the abiotic selective factors previously considered. The operation of natural selection upon populations interacting in the same community has led to the establishment of coadapted groups of sympatric species knit together into a complicated fabric of communal life and coexisting with minimal competition while exploiting one another for survival.

6.1 □ CHARACTERISTICS OF BIOTIC COMMUNITIES

A biotic community consists of an assemblage of sympatric plant and animal species that share a common habitat. The species comprising a community are in part selected on the basis of their tolerance of the same abiotic conditions: climate, temperature, availability of water, type of substratum, and so forth. Thus in a desert we find species that have achieved effective resistance to drought and in polar regions, species that can endure extreme cold. In addition these species, which may coexist merely because they have similar tolerances for the abiotic conditions, *themselves create new physical conditions that make possible the existence of other species.* For example, the canopy of sun-tolerant forest trees creates a shaded, humid subcanopy environment in which shade-tolerant plants and moisture-requiring species live. The composition of a littoral marine community is, as we have seen, largely determined by the distribution of attached algae, which in turn depends upon the nature of the substratum. On a sandy coast seaweeds lack anchorage, while a rocky substratum affords opportunity for their attachment. Where algae succeed, they support a multitude of animal species that use the plants both for food and for attachment and shelter. Rocky reefs exposed to strong surf may be inhospitable to most algae but may be colonized by animals adapted for firm anchorage, such as barnacles and mussels. The dense mussel-barnacle association in turn affords protection for other species that have no structural means of withstanding surf but avoid its force by sheltering among attached species. We see from these examples that, as a community diversifies, it modifies and expands the range of physical conditions beyond the original limitations set by the abiotic environment. One species is able to exploit the adaptive devices of other species. Although the limiting factor in the distribution of a species is that factor for which its range of tolerance is most restricted, the limits of one species may be stretched if it can take advantage of the greater tolerance or greater adaptive capacity of some other species. As a further example, a moisture-dependent creature such as a liver fluke may inhabit a desert by virtue of the fact that its host, perhaps a pack rat, is adapted to withstand the aridity of the habitat. Furthermore, the pack rat, feeding upon moisture-containing vegetation, in turn takes advantage of the adaptations that desert plants have developed for obtaining and storing water. A desert fox, dining upon pack rat, profits indirectly from the adaptations of the plants upon which the rat had fed. Thus a community is built up as *an assemblage of species not only drawn together by the coincidence of similar tolerances but also aggregated by virtue of a web of interdependences, within which one species makes possible the existence in that habitat of still other species.*

During its development, a community is unstable and each species tends to pass through a phase of increase characterized by a sigmoid growth curve involving an initial phase of gradual acceleration, a period of exponential increase followed by a declining rate of productivity, eventually reaching an equilibrium state (*asymptote*) in which reproduction and mortality are in balance (Figure 6.1). Eventually a community attains a high degree of *stability* and *self-sufficiency.* In this mature stabilized condition, the numbers of individuals of each species in the community either remain quite steady or fluctuate together. Increase in a population of prey organisms is followed with a slight lag by a compensatory increase in their predators. Such controls exerted by species upon themselves and upon one another lead to a state of natural balance that is disturbed only when the community is subjected to a perturbation such as unusual climatic changes, fire, flood, cultivation, or invasion by some new and competitive species. Like an organism, a community tends to evolve toward the coadaptedness of its parts; like an organism, it tends to develop steady-state (homeo-

Figure 6.1 □ **Population growth curve. Increase in numbers describes a typical sigmoid curve, flattening out at an asymptote at which the population density of that species either is stabilized or oscillates (dashed curve) about a mean value. This equilibrium phase is perpetuated indefinitely by a combination of extrinsic (physical and heterospecific) and intrinsic (intraspecific) influences that tend to keep proliferation and mortality in balance. The phases leading up to equilibrium are seen when a population is introduced into a new habitat. In a climax community most species are at their asymptotes and serious deviations rarely occur.**

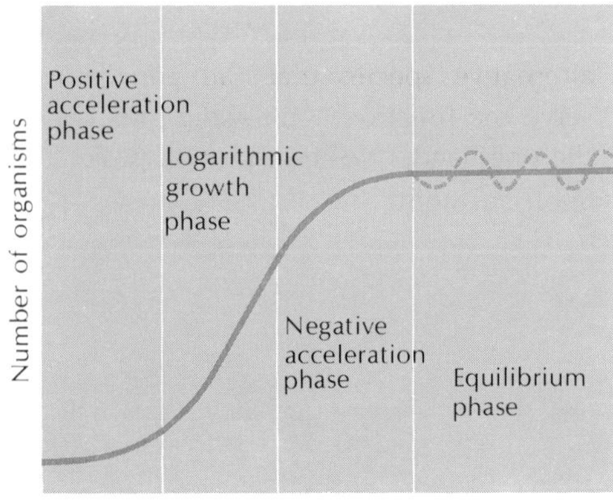

static) mechanisms by which it resists perturbation; and like an organism, a community may perish if it is subjected to a greater disturbance than its homeostatic mechanisms can overcome.

A community in equilibrium constitutes the living portion of an *ecosystem*. This has been defined earlier as a balanced system in which mass and energy pass cyclically through the living and nonliving components of the system. The ecosystem concept implies a balanced economy, in which *production* of organic material by photosynthesizing plants is balanced by *consumption* on the part of animals and decay organisms. Within an ecosystem, atmospheric CO_2 is fixed as organic carbon by plants; atmospheric N_2 is fixed as nitrates by bacteria; atmospheric and soil H_2S is fixed as sulfates by bacteria; chemical and mechanical action of plant roots fragments rock into soil, and ground water dissolves minerals. Plants then incorporate these components into various organic molecules. Herbivorous animals derive these compounds from the plants on which they feed. Carnivores in turn feed upon herbivores. Ultimately, various scavengers and decay organisms effect the dissolution of the dead members of the community, releasing their constituent molecules for reuse by other members of the community. This cyclic reuse of materials makes the ecosystem a self-perpetuating entity except for its dependence on solar energy and (in the case of terrestrial ecosystems) rainfall.

Community interactions involve a process of coadaptation, which operates at all levels of biotic organization. The multilevel nature of this involvement deserves emphasis because we often tend to view community interactions as if they operated exclusively at the gross organismal level, when in fact, the evolution and maintenance of the community results from inheritable changes occurring primarily at the *molecular* level of organization. The web of interdependence within which the members of a community operate is a product of evolution and is the outcome of interaction between genetic and selective factors. Most sympatric species interact directly or indirectly to an extent such that they operate as selective factors upon the further evolution of one another. Just as adaptations related to the use of radiant energy, for instance, have been achieved by the perpetuation of favorable genetic variations, so adaptations for obtaining food, for reproducing, and for minimizing the chances of becoming prey must be achieved by the evolutionary process. These latter adaptations play a role primarily in interactions among organisms.

That biotic communities may persist long enough for their members to evolve adaptations based upon particular heterospecific interactions is implicit in numerous cases of exceedingly specific mimicry and crypsis. *Mimicry* is a protective resemblance between two or more different kinds of organisms. *Crypsis,* or form- and color-matching, is the resemblance of an organism to the background against which it is seen. Evolution toward mimicry or crypsis is usually a unilateral process, involving selective factors operative only upon that species which will derive protection from the resemblance. In other instances, a *mutually* adaptive selective process is involved, whereby two species of organisms may coevolve and in so doing acquire characteristics that are adaptive mainly with respect to their reciprocal dependence. An example of this is the coevolution of flowering plants and insects, a process that commenced at least 2×10^8 years ago and is still in progress, operating at various levels of specificity in every terrestrial habitat. From the general statement that most flowering plants depend on insect pollinators and that such pollinators feed upon nectar and pollen and only incidentally disseminate pollen in the course of their quest for food, we can go on to numerous examples of evolved interdependence between *particular* species of insects and plants, such as the yucca and the yucca moth. The yucca moth lays its eggs nowhere but within yucca blossoms; in so doing it serves as the only natural agency by which pollen is transferred from one yucca flower to another. In such cases as this the relationship has become *obligate* to one or both members of the association, to such a degree that the elimination of one species would most likely result in the extinction of the other.

Sometimes a common selective factor may operate to bring about coadaptedness within an entire *complex* of species in a given community. By way of example, in the chaparral or scrub forest of southern California live several species of flowering shrubs with tubular blossoms, which primarily depend upon hummingbirds as pollinators. The blooming period of each species is short, and were all of these species to bloom simultaneously, the hummingbirds would be forced to migrate during the months when suitable nectar-yielding flowers were unavailable. However, the flowering times of these sympatric species barely overlap, with the result that food is available for hummingbirds throughout the year, and one kind (Anna's) remains in residence all year although hummingbirds are ordinarily migratory. We can only speculate about how this state of adaptive asynchrony in flowering time has come about. Were these species originally asynchronous in blooming but mostly *allopatric* (isolated from one another), and did the presence of a suitable pollinator species through part of their range encourage the development of a sympatric range of distribution? Or did these plants evolve sympatrically and undergo selection toward asynchronous flowering periods as a result of the adaptive advantage of keeping a pollinator in residence? In either event, adaptation of these plants to a *biotic* factor, their pollinator species, is evident. On its part, the hummingbird's elongate beak and tongue and its hovering flight are adaptations that permit it to feed by probing tubular flowers, incidentally bringing about pollen transfer (see Figure 4.16*b*). Each relationship in the community shows evidence of having developed through such processes of coadaptive evolution. As a result, a community becomes a highly integrated and self-perpetuating biotic unit.

The relationships operating among the members of a biotic community are of two kinds: *conspecific* relationships, among organisms of the *same* species (these are the topic of Chapter 7); *heterospecific* relationships, involving organisms of different species, which are the subject of this chapter. Heterospecific relationships may be either symbiotic or nonsymbiotic. *Symbiotic* ("living-with") relationships are those in which two species are intimately associated in an obligate relationship, that is, one which is necessary for the survival of at least *one* of the species concerned. *Nonsymbiotic* relationships are those in which the relationship is less intimate and less obligate, at least with respect to the interdependence of any *particular* two species.

For example, the relationship of a tapeworm with its host is intimate, and obligate for the tapeworm, which would die without a host. There may be several possible host species and the relationship is certainly neither obligate nor desirable from their standpoint. Nevertheless, the parasite-host relationship is considered to be symbiotic because it is obligate for one member of the association. A symbiotic relationship of *mutual* advantage, which is obligate for both species involved, is the previously mentioned example of the yucca and yucca moth. The former is completely dependent on the latter for pollination, while the latter is behaviorally incapable of laying its eggs anywhere but within the tissues of the yucca. The mutual interdependence of flowering plants and pollinator insects as a whole, however, is a *non*symbiotic association, for there is usually available to both members of the association a number of alternative species that can equally well serve the function of providing nectar, on the one hand, or of transporting pollen, on the other. Similarly, although it is essential that a predator find prey, several potential prey species are usually available, so that the predator-prey relationship is not considered to be symbiotic. There are, however, many heterospecific associations intermediate between the symbiotic and nonsymbiotic, which may in fact be in the process of evolving from one category to the other.

Nonsymbiotic relationships include: (1) neutralistic relationships; (2) use of another species as shelter or substratum; (3) inhibitory relationships; (4) predator-prey relationships; (5) competitive relationships; and (6) cooperative relationships.

A Neutralism

Neutralism implies that any two species under consideration do not directly interact. Thus a deer and a centipede may be neutralistic until the former treads upon the latter or the latter bites the former. Species neutral to one another do not directly compete for any of the commodities of the habitat, nor does one depend directly upon the other for food. Nevertheless, the relationship is seldom truly indifferent in the wider sense of the ecosystem. Adequate analysis of community structure may reveal indirect interdependence that superficial observation failed to perceive.

B Use as shelter or substratum

Use of one species by another as a shelter or a substratum is of widespread occurrence. Many animals find refuge in and on vegetation. Larger plants shelter smaller ones. Animals such as coral and sponges provide protection and support for more vulnerable species. Coral reefs provide both shelter and substratum for so many other organisms that such a reef may come to constitute the basis for an entire ecosystem.

Some organisms live permanently attached to their living substratum, which they use only for support. These include the epiphytes of the rain forest, such as the Spanish moss seen in Figure 5.10.

Any burrowing or tube-dwelling animal may become unwilling host to a variety of shelter-seeking guests, some of which may eventually have the obligate status of a symbiont. By way of example, the tube of the worm *Urechis caupo* ("fat innkeeper") is typically inhabited not only by *Urechis* itself, but by three guests: a small goby,

Figure 6.2 □ **The echiuroid worm *Urechis caupo* with its three commensals.** (*Adapted from Fisher and G. E. MacGinitie and N. MacGinitie.*) **See the text for explanation.**

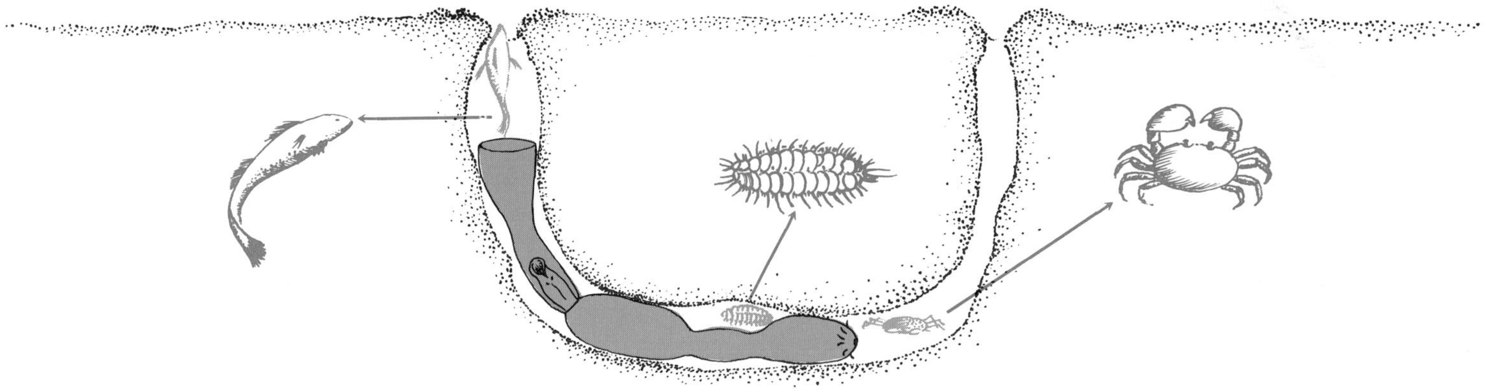

which forages outside the burrow, returning to it only for shelter; a pea crab, which never leaves the tube but snatches particles of food that fall into *Urechis'* slime net; and a very dependent scale worm, which remains almost constantly in contact with the apparently comforting body of the host, turning when it turns, and directly nibbling upon the slime net that *Urechis* first exudes and then devours together with entrapped food particles. Here in one example we find three levels of dependency, ranging from a casual burrow-sharing relationship to a fully obligate symbiotic association (Figure 6.2).

C Inhibition

Inhibition occurs whenever one species secretes a noxious exudate that blocks the survival of another potentially competitive species in its vicinity. Many fungi release such inhibitory chemicals, or *antibiotics,* which by impeding bacterial growth discourage potential competitors. Certain antibiotics exert their effects by suppressing the activity of particular hereditary factors in the organisms against which they act. Inhibitors are also released by phytoplankton that control the proliferation of competitive species.

D Predator-prey relationships

Predation involves the use of one species, the prey, as food by another species, the predator. Predation usually implies death of the individual prey organisms, but it also may include situations in which the predator merely consumes *portions* of the body of the prey, such as foliage of a plant, without causing the death of the entire organism. Because of their potential for indeterminate growth, most plants are capable of extensive *regeneration* of lost parts and therefore can withstand the recurrent depredations of herbivorous animals. Some animal species also demonstrate considerable regenerative capacity, such as hydroids which are often browsed upon by sea slugs.

An unprecedented type of predation, independent of the need for food, is exhibited by man, who often slays merely to possess. In addition to the traditional trophies of the hunt, large numbers of marine animals are marketed annually for the enrichment of personal collections or for home decor. A number of attractive butterflies, moths, and birds have been brought to the brink of extinction because their wings and feathers are sought as ornamentation. Despite concerted efforts to protect them, several species of large African mammals are approaching extinction because they are hunted not for food but for other uses: elephants are slain for the ivory of their tusks, and rhinoceroses for their horns, which are powdered and sold as an oriental love potion or aphrodisiac. In the United States excessive picking of wild flowers resulted in the near extinction of some species before they came to be protected by law. In the case of annual plants that produce a single bloom, picking the flowers prevents the plants from producing seeds for the next year and is tantamount to castration.

The acquisition of exotic pets is also on the upsurge in affluent nations such as the United States. Although affection and intelligent care may be lavished upon the captives, they often fail to reproduce, and thus have been as effectively removed from their breeding population as if they had furnished a meal for a hungry predator. As mankind increases in numbers this type of gratuitous predation looms as a factor of increasing significance in all biotic communities. There is scarcely a major community that does not now experience the effects of human intervention. Compounded with widespread habitat destruction, the human urge to *possess* is critically reducing numerous populations of living things that have made the world interesting and beautiful. Enhanced understanding of ecological relationships may enable mankind to develop wisdom in its treatment of other living things. Much of the harm that has been done may still be undone, although the margin of survival for many species is becoming dangerously narrow.

A number of well-intentioned persons kill predatory animals with the intent of protecting the species being preyed upon. These persons fail to recognize that although from the point of view of the *individual* prey organism predation may appear distinctly disadvantageous, the predator-prey relationship is actually of *reciprocal benefit to both species* involved in the association. Many forms of life exhibit a potential for fecundity that would soon outstrip the resources of the habitat if permitted uninhibited expression (Figure 6.3). Predation exerts an exogenous control on the population of prey species, and the population level of predators is reciprocally determined by the availability of prey. This is shown in Figure 6.4, where the population growth curves for phytoplankton and zooplankton are graphed. A proliferation of

Figure 6.3 □ **Overpopulation due to community disturbances. (*a*) Overbrowsing of trees by deer establishes a browse line, below which foliage is lacking. Such conditions occur where natural predators, such as cougar, have been killed off by hunters. Eventually the population level will be restabilized —but by starvation instead of predation. (*Photograph by C. Mcdonald, U.S. Forest Service.*) (*b*) Rabbit "plague" following introduction of a prolific species into a continent where its natural enemies are lacking. Introduced for sport at several different times, the European rabbit at first failed to establish itself; but once favorable circumstances were met, the population proliferated explosively and overran the countryside, destroying the grass cover that supported sheep and such indigenous herbivores as kangaroo. Control was sought by introducing a fungus parasite fatal to rabbits, but this led only to the selective survival of genetically resistant individuals, which soon repopulated the area. Eventually this population too must reach its asymptote, but at the probable cost of extinction of less prolific native species in competition with these alien invaders. (*Courtesy of Australian News and Information Bureau.*)**

Figure 6.4 □ **Seasonal cycle of phytoplankton (tinted-color line) and zooplankton (solid-color line) on George's Bank. Note that proliferation of the prey species results in closely following increase in zooplankton and that subsequent decline in phytoplankton is followed by equivalent decline in zooplankton. (*From H. B. Moore, after Riley.*)**

(*a*)

(*b*)

phytoplankton is followed by a proportional increase in the zooplankton feeding on it. Depletion of the phytoplankton soon concomitantly reduces the zooplankton.

Among vertebrates, alert, healthy adults are nearly immune from predation, which operates almost exclusively upon the very young and upon individuals debilitated by age, injury, or disease. Hunting can play a role in preserving natural balances where native predators have become scarce, but the human hunter tends to select not debilitated individuals but those in fine physical condition, often the dominant males of a herd; the hunter's effect as an agent of selection is therefore likely to be very different than that of predators, which perform a valuable culling function for the prey species and help reduce the incidence of disease.

The importance to man of insectivorous

insects (Figure 6.5) can scarcely be overestimated. Few plant-eating insects can multiply to "pest" status in the presence of their natural enemies, of which the most effective are birds, lizards and amphibians, spiders, and predatory insects. Biocontrol of economic pests can often be achieved by breeding predatory insects in the laboratory and releasing them en masse upon the insect population to be controlled.

SERIES OF NUTRITIONAL RELATIONSHIPS In any ecosystem the ultimate prey species are those which utilize abiotic substances to build organic compounds. Essentially these are photosynthesizing plants. Such autotrophic species are the *producers* in the ecosystem, forming the basis for any series of nutritional relationships.

Figure 6.5 □ **Predatory bug, *Nabis*, feeding on leafhopper. The bug's long stylet is piercing the leafhopper's exoskeleton, while the prey is secured by the predator's forelegs. Insectivorous insects such as *Nabis* are invaluable to man in the control of economically harmful insects. Leafhoppers suck plant juices but do not reach harmful densities when held in check by their natural predators. (*U.S. Department of Agriculture.*)**

All heterotrophic organisms, including animals and most bacteria and fungi, are nutritionally dependent on the autotrophs. Animals that feed upon living prey may be mainly carnivorous (flesh-eating), herbivorous (plant-eating), omnivorous (eating both plant and animal material), and so forth, according to their dietary selectivity. Scavengers such as vultures do not kill prey but feed upon animals already dead. Most nonparasitic bacteria and fungi subsist upon dissolved organic materials liberated during decay; they may first secrete enzymes that promote decomposition of dead material and then absorb the substances thus made available.

Herbivorous animals are the *primary consumers* in a community, for they feed directly upon the producers (the autotrophs). Omnivores and carnivores constitute various levels of *secondary consumers*. Large carnivores, such as lions, tigers, and killer whales, are relatively safe from predation (except by man) but are nonetheless subject to attack by parasites and ultimately become food for decay organisms, which liberate nutrients promoting plant growth.

The nutritional relationships of an ecosystem are therefore cyclic and may be depicted as a circular *food chain* (Figure 6.6) or, where more complex, as a branching (but still circular) *nutritional web*. Such schemes are useful in conceptualizing what eats what, but the quantitative aspect of nutritional relationships must be expressed as a *pyramid of biomass* (Figure 6.7a). At each step in a food chain, only about 10 to 15 percent of the materials forming the body of the prey organism will be utilized in building the tissues that form the body of the predator. The remainder will be broken down to obtain energy needed for carrying out various activities, including maintenance of body heat, building of chemical compounds, and the like. A portion will also be used up in the work of digestion and some of the material eaten will be lost because it is not digestible.

Mathematically, the *nutritional efficiency* of an animal species may be expressed as a fraction: the numerator is the amount of energy that the animal can derive from its plant or animal prey and utilize for growth; the denominator is the amount of energy that the prey population can derive from *its* source of nutrients for use in building tissues. In the case of most species for which nutritional efficiency has been calculated, this fraction approximates $\frac{1}{10}$. Thus, 90 percent of the chemical energy available for work is lost at each step of the food chain, and this is roughly reflected by an exponential decrement in *biomass* (the net weight of living matter produced). In Figure 6.7*b*, we see that about 10^4 kg of phytoplankton are required to make 10^3 kg of zooplankton; when the zooplankton in turn is eaten by small fish such as anchovies, 10^3 kg of zooplankton are required to produce only 10^2 kg of anchovy; 10^2 kg of anchovy yields only 10 kg of tuna; and when 10 kg of tuna in turn is consumed by ultimate predators such as killer whales or man, only 1 kg of biomass is produced! Thus, for *every kilogram* of human flesh built up by eating tuna, approximately *10,000 kg* of phytoplankton have been required. Actually, since human beings eat only the muscle tissue and discard the fishes' internal organs, the loss of biomass in this last conversion is even greater than the usual 90 percent. It takes no great acumen to realize that, if mankind persists in its rather illogical drive toward multiplication without limitation, it may become necessary to by-pass several levels of the biomass pyramid and to feed the multitudes exclusively on plant materials such as soybeans, grains, and algae.

THE ADAPTATIONS OF PREDATORS The fundamental difference between plants and animals is that most plants are autotrophic while all animals are heterotrophic. This single difference, which stems primarily from the capacity or incapacity to synthesize chlorophyll, has caused two very different complexes of selective factors to operate on evolving plants and animals. Plants adapt in ways that facilitate their access to inorganic nutrients and the solar energy that they require. Animals, on the other hand, require organic nutrients, and have elaborated a variety of adaptive mechanisms that enable them either to seek food or to capture food which comes to them. Sedentary animals like sponges and sea anemones succeed mainly in habitats where water currents continuously replenish the available prey. Most animals, however, move about in search of food. Natural selection in the case of animals has thus tended to favor any hereditary changes that have

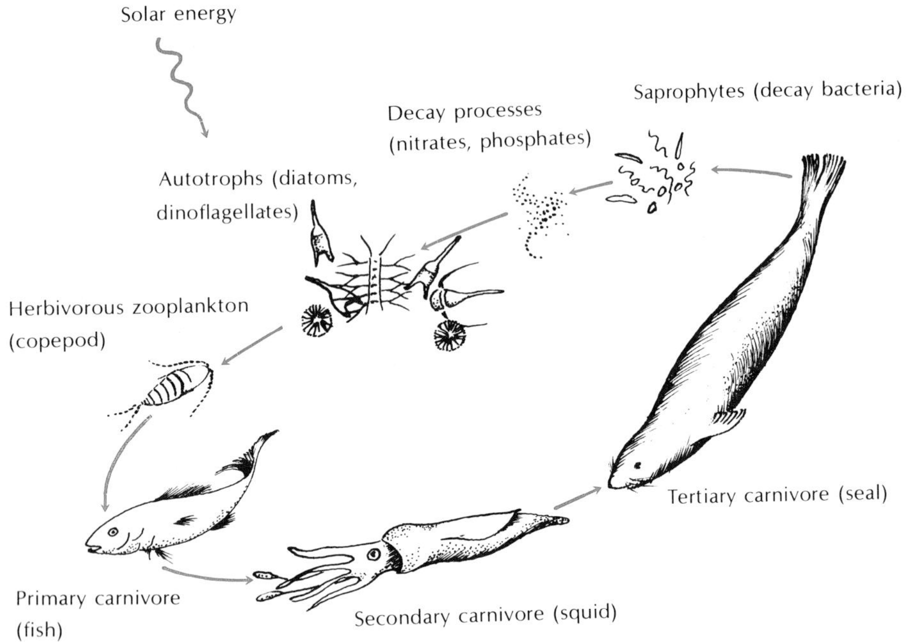

Figure 6.6 □ **A food chain (organisms not drawn to same scale). Arrows point from the organism serving as food toward the organism nourished. Decay bacteria complete the cycle by reducing the bodies of deceased carnivores to components that enrich the water and act as fertilizer for phytoplankton.**

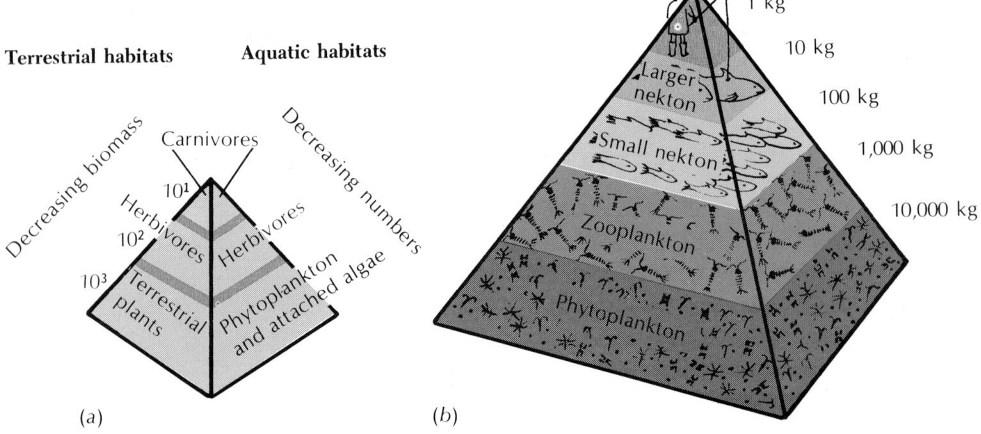

Figure 6.7 □ **(*a*) Generalized pattern of nutritional pyramids, showing quantitative relationships that cannot be depicted in a diagram of a food chain or web. Note that at each step there is an approximately exponential decrease in biomass. (*b*) Biomass pyramid in a marine community. At each ascending step there is reduction in both number of organisms and total biomass. For a net gain of 1 kg of human flesh, from consumption of such fish as tuna, approximately 10,000 kg of phytoplankton must have been produced!**

enhanced locomotory and sensory capacity. Although sensory acuity and locomotor efficiency are also useful to prey species in *escaping* from predators, these qualities evolved primarily with respect to the basic need of animal life to seek organic food.

Dependence upon organic sources of nutrients has also required the development of means for mechanically and chemically digesting such nutrients before they become accessible for metabolic use. *Mechanical digestion,* by which solid food is dissolved or reduced to a finely divided suspension, is aided by such structures as jaws, teeth, and gut muscles. *Chemical digestion,* in which large molecules are broken down into smaller ones that are more readily absorbed into cells, require the secretion of *enzymes* that catalyze the reactions. The various adaptations directly involved in the digestion of nutrients will be considered further in Chapter 13.

DEFENSIVE ADAPTATIONS OF PREY As a rule, although plants are extensively preyed upon by animals, they have evolved few antipredator mechanisms, perhaps because their capacity for indeterminate growth permits them to regenerate the lost parts at a rate that under natural conditions would more than keep pace with the demands of herbivorous animals. Occasional species have reduced the amount of predation to which they are subject by producing noxious substances (for example, locoweed and digitalis) or deterrents such as spines.

Animal species that are preyed upon either must be limitlessly fecund or must develop active or passive means of defense. The more effective these defenses, the less prolific the species need be to maintain its numbers.

Active defense A potential victim may react behaviorally to the appearance of the predator by fleeing, threatening, counterattacking (including biting or stinging), displaying (Figure 6.8), or activating some special defense mechanism (such as the release of noxious chemicals by skunks or "ink" by cephalopods). The prey's mode of life per se may also serve to reduce predation: it may move secretively, or may construct and inhabit an elaborate burrow system complete with emergency escape tunnels.

Some animals actively *autotomize,* or cast off, a limb that has been seized by a predator. Two expert autotomists are brittle stars and porcelain crabs. A brittle star can break off its rays until nothing remains but the immobile and inconspicuous central disc. The cast-off rays writhe about for some time and may divert the predator. The disc eventually regenerates the lost rays. The porcelain crab autotomizes its pincers, which continue to snap convulsively after being cast off while the crab flees from the scene of action. The lost claws are restored at subsequent molts.

Animals may camouflage themselves by

Figure 6.8 □ Defensive displays: threatening behavior may ward off attack by predators. (*a*) Frilled lizard erecting neck frill at the photographer; (*b*) burrowing owl spreading wings, fluffing plumage, and hissing. (*Zoological Society of San Diego.*)

(*a*)

(*b*)

Figure 6.9 □ Crypsis by self-decoration. Some animals hide themselves beneath a covering provided by other organisms: (*a*) the decorator crab (*Loxorhynchus crispatus*), here covered with barnacles, also plants its back with sponges and algae; (*b*) the decorator clam, *Xenophora pallidula*, incorporates shell fragments into its own shell. (*Los Angeles County Museum of Natural History.*)

(a)

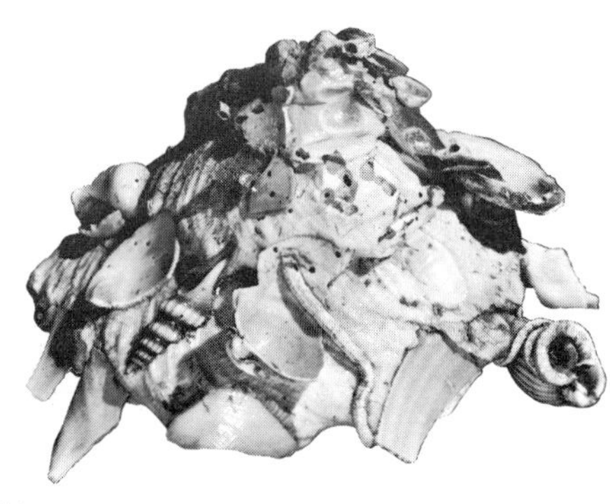

(*b*)

(*a*)

(*b*)

Figure 6.10 □ Eyespot display: (*a*) *Polyphemus* moth at rest with eyespots on underwings hidden from view; (*b*) response of moth when lightly touched. (*Courtesy of Thomas Eisner.*)

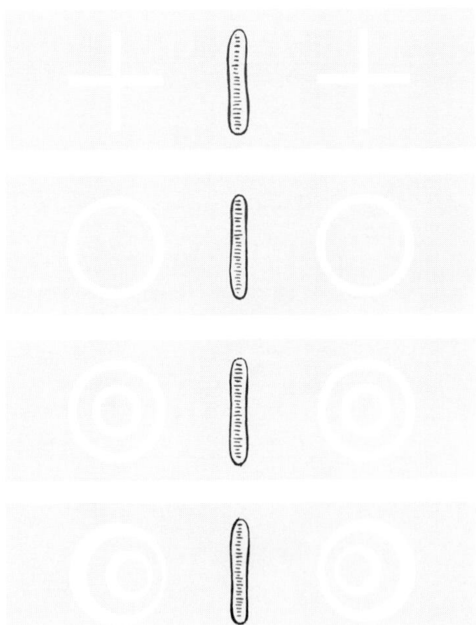

Figure 6.11 □ Four patterns used in D. Blest's experiments on the effectiveness of eyespots in discouraging predators. The birds were offered mealworms positioned midway between two patterns that could be illuminated from below. The more eyelike the pattern, the greater its "scare value" was found to be. (*From Niko Tinbergen,* Curious Naturalists. *New York: Basic Books, Inc., Publishers, 1959; © 1958 by N. Tinbergen.*)

self-decoration if their natural color and form are not protective. Decorator crabs literally "plant" their backs with algae and may even tolerate a heavy load of barnacles that effectively hides them from view (Figure 6.9*a*). The decorator clam, *Xenophora,* camouflages itself by incorporating fragments of other shells into its own growing shell (Figure 6.9*b*). The sponge crab, *Dromia,* covers itself with a piece of living sponge, neatly trimmed with its pinchers and hollowed out to form a cap that the crab holds over its back. The crab's specialized hind legs are bent upward over its back and though useless in walking serve to hold the sponge cap in place. If this cap is forcibly taken from the crab but left nearby, *Dromia* retrieves it and puts it on again. When deprived of its cap, *Dromia* hustles about until a suitable sponge is located and then sets to work cutting and shaping a replacement. If no sponge can be found, the crab covers itself with anything available, even a scrap of paper.

Passive defense Prey species tend to evolve protective devices that do not have to be specially activated but are merely part of their anatomy. Active defensive responses then become merely ancillary to the possession of the protective attribute. By way of example, the echidna (Figure 2.55*a*) is protected by a covering of stout spines. Its response to danger can be merely to roll up, guarding its vulnerable underparts.

Another passive defense that requires only a supplementary behavioral act to enhance its effectiveness is the so-called *horror mask.* The wings of certain insects feature large, vivid "eyespots" that normally are hidden from view when the wings are folded at rest. If the insect is disturbed, it abruptly spreads its wings to disclose the two conspicuous eyespots (Figure 6.10). Field observations verify the efficacy of this sudden display of eyespots in frightening birds, and experiments have supported the hypothesis that such eyespots do indeed have survival value. In one such experiment (conducted by D. Blest), captive birds were presented with mealworms placed midway between a symmetrical pair of symbols that could be illuminated from below (Figure 6.11). The relative effectiveness of these patterns in discouraging predation was tested by presenting each bird with two mealworms simultaneously. The pair of symbols which flanked each worm were lighted up as soon as the bird approached. If the lighted symbols were frightening, the bird would fly off and thereafter would avoid that mealworm. In each test the more eyelike of the two pairs of symbols proved to elicit the more pronounced fright response. In commenting upon the above experiment, the eminent ethologist N. Tinbergen* has written:

While Blest's study seems to leave little doubt as to the real function of eye spots, it raises one new problem. If it is of advantage to the insects to scare the birds away, then it is disadvantageous to these birds to be scared of eyespots. Why have not these birds been able to get rid of this harmful response? There seem to be two possible answers to this. One is that the organization of a bird's vision is so formed that a round pattern such as an eye-spot is more conspicuous than any other pattern, and that it is of benefit to birds to be scared of anything that appears suddenly. Another is that the escape responses of these birds are adapted in such a way that they are released by sign stimuli which characterize their own predators. If such birds recognize Owls, Cats, and Stoats, etc., partly by their eyes, it would be impossible for them to give up this in order to gain the small advantage of an occasional snack.

Coloration can serve protectively in several ways. Poisonous or inedible animals may bear conspicuous *warning colors* that enhance their recognition and avoidance (Plate 4*a,b*). Whereas the edible sargasso sea slug fades into its background, many other sea slugs advertise their unpalatability by brillant pigmentation (Plate 2). An animal's coloration may allow it to rest unseen against its background, so that color-matching is an important aspect of crypsis; alternatively, its color may so faithfully resemble that of some inedible or noxious species living in the same community that predators tend to avoid both. The effectiveness of camouflage and mimicry in promoting survival cannot be assumed a priori, but must be tested experimentally; several of these experiments will be described in the following sections.

Crypsis Crypsis is a form of passive defense in which the organism escapes recognition by blending in with its background or resembling some object less attractive to predators. It may involve *color-matching, form-matching, countershading,* or *disruptive coloration.* In countershaded animals, including a number of birds, mammals, and fish, the underparts are lighter than the upper parts. Experiments with models show that countershading neutralizes the effect of shadow, which a dark

**Curious Naturalists* (New York: Basic Books, Inc., Publishers, 1959), pp. 155–156.

underside would accentuate. Disruptive coloration breaks up the total body outline. The body may be blotched or bear light and dark bands, which out of context may appear highly conspicuous yet in the normal habitat effectively destroy the body form. The spider seen in Plate 3*b* has a brightly patterned abdomen and inconspicuous legs and foreparts; it not only escapes recognition by birds, but the colorful abdomen may entice flower-seeking insects.

Modifications of body form producing a resemblance to some other object presumably less attractive to predators are especially common among insects but occur widely in other groups as well (a few desert plants even resemble stones!). Form matching and disruptive or matching coloration are well shown by a number of animals frequenting floating masses of sargassum weed, including the sargasso sea slug seen in Plate 2*b* and the frogfish (Figure 6.12). Plate 5 depicts several kinds of insects that are protected by their resemblance to foliage, including a tree cricket with a *compressed* (that is, flattened from side to side) leaflike body, and a praying mantis with a *depressed* (that is, flattened from top to bottom) leaflike form. The mantis, itself insectivorous, is cryptically protected from its own predators, birds and lizards. The development of leaflike forms by both compression and depression shows that *analogous convergence* has occurred under the influence of similar selective factors. Insects of various orders have come independently to resemble twigs or leaves with incredible fidelity. Resemblance to a leaf may be so faithful as to include petiole, midrib, veins, and sometimes even irregular notches as though the "leaf" had been nibbled upon (Figure 6.13*b*). The dead-leaf butterfly, *Kallima* (Plate 5*d*), even changes color seasonally as the foliage changes, becoming brownish and pale in the dry season and dark when foliage is burgeoning during the rainy season.

Figure 6.12 □ **Form and color matching in the frogfish, *Histrio histrio*, shown here in native sargassum habitat (*From A. Portmann, "Tarnung im Tierreich,"* Verständl. Wiss., *61, Berlin: Springer Verlag, 1956.*)**

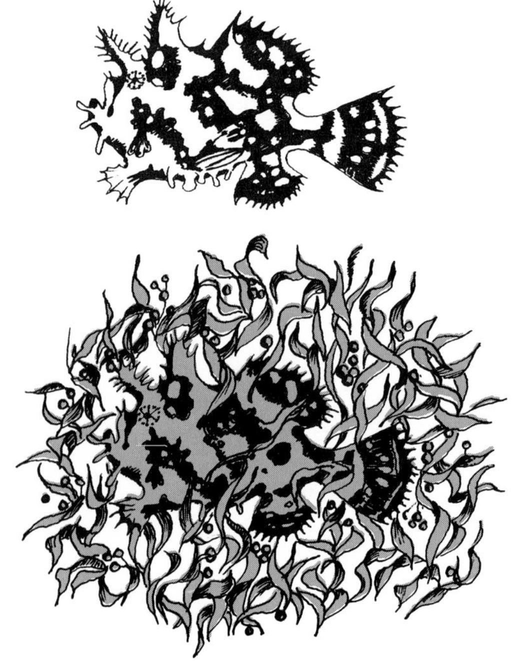

The effectiveness of crypsis is dependent upon the appropriateness of the accompanying behavior. Color matching is effective only if the animal remains on the appropriate background. The animal may even have to orient itself in a certain direction to fit the background pattern. In this case the orienting behavior probably preceded the development of crypsis and served as a selective factor in determining the orientation of the pattern of coloration. Note that the plume moth shown in Plate 6*b* must rest only upon the specific type of cactus, the spines of which it has come to resemble, and must actually position itself according to the pattern of distribution of the spines. Similarly, the leaf hoppers seen in Figure 6.13*a* are well protected only if they frequent thorny stems. The behavior of two cryptically striped moth species has been compared. In one of these species the striping runs the length of the wing, whereas in the other it runs across the wing. The first species typically orients itself vertically on the trunks of trees; the other rests at right angles to the vertical axis of the tree. In such positions, the respective patterns match the vertical furrows of the bark.

Immobility much enhances the survival value of crypsis. A twig-resembling caterpillar may hold itself rigidly motionless throughout the day, with its body extended at an appropriate angle from the limb of the plant on which it is at rest (Plate 6*a*). This condition of stiff immobility (*catalepsy*) is retained even under handling. Only at night does the animal become active.

The effectiveness of crypsis accompanied by catalepsy has been experimentally investigated. Certainly it is unwarranted to assume that because an animal appears to *our* eyes to bear a protective resemblance to some other object, that a less imaginative predator would be similarly deceived. Observations made by Tinbergen* on the re-

* *Curious Naturalists* (New York: Basic Books, Inc., Publishers, 1959), pp. 126–127.

sponse of a jay to the twiglike caterpillar *Ennomos* illustrates the effectiveness of this behavior:

Some of them (i.e. Ennomos *caterpillars) were offered to the Jays on leafy twigs, sitting in their natural position; others were laid out on the ground and, in addition, we gave some real twigs about the size of the larvae . . . Being admitted into the aviary had come to mean being fed and, consequently, every Jay, upon entering the aviary, began to search around. It could not know, however, what kind of food to expect; every Jay began the test completely "open-minded".*

To our delight our first Jay failed to find the larvae at first. It hopped past and over several of them, giving an exploratory peck here and there. This went on for about 20 minutes . . . when suddenly the Jay stepped on a larva. This was too much for even an Ennomos *and giving up the advantage of keeping motionless, it began to wriggle. At once the Jay picked it up, beat it on the ground once or twice, and swallowed it. This gave us already an indication of the importance of stillness in combination with camouflage. But what happened next was a complete surprise to us. The Jay, immediately after swallowing the larva, looked around and hopping briskly through the cage, picked up—a twig. It nibbled at it, threw it away, hopped on, took another twig, and so on, one after the other, in quick succession. Then, after several of these mistakes it calmed down and ignored twigs and caterpillars alike . . . Thus we had seen in one test: (1) that the Jay did not see the larva until it moved, (2) that it would eat it eagerly once found, (3) that it confused twigs with caterpillars, and (4) that, therefore, it had originally ignored twigs and caterpillars alike because they were all "just twigs" to it.*

Figure 6.13 □ Crypsis in insects. (*a*) *Umbonia*, a thorn-shaped leafhopper, shown in typical resting position on thorny stem. (*Ward's Natural Science Establishment, Inc.*) (*b*) *Phalacrana*, the tattered-leaf mantis, also seen in natural resting position. (*Los Angeles County Museum of Natural History.*)

(*a*)

(*b*)

Once a species has started on the evolutionary road toward crypsis, natural selection tends to promote the fidelity of the resemblance. Such passive defense is no unmitigated blessing, for the selective encouragement of immobility reduces the chance of the animal's escaping from a predator that has penetrated its disguise. Cryptic animals are "sitting ducks" for alert and intelligent predators systematically hunting them. Intervention of various disturbing factors, however, reduces the likelihood of a systematic search being carried out.

Mimicry Mimicry is a type of passive defense involving the close resemblance of two or more sympatric species, at least one of which is in some manner noxious or dangerous to would-be predators. Two major types, Batesian and Müllerian mimicry, are recognized.

Batesian mimicry is the resemblance of an edible species, the *mimic,* to a noxious species, the *model* (Plate 7*a,b*). Mimic and model must of course be sympatric and the model species should be more numerous than the mimic. It is probable that, the more noxious the model, the greater the protection afforded the mimic and the *less* faithfully it need resemble the model. Conversely, if a model is less virulently noxious, the mimic must resemble it very closely to achieve protection. This is because the protection afforded the mimic depends upon the capacity of a predator to *learn* from its experience. The more painful the lesson, the less likely is the predator to forget or to chance another bite. A simple but clever experiment demonstrating the efficacy of Batesian mimicry was conducted by L. and J. Brower. Utilizing naive (inexperienced) toads as predators, the Browers first presented them with harmless robberflies, which are mimics of bumblebees. These were routinely accepted by the toads. Next, bumblebees were offered and most of these, upon being seized, stung the toads. Thereafter, most of the toads manifested avoidance movements, hunching up when presented with either robberfly or bumblebee. They readily accepted dragonflies, however, which did not resemble the bumblebees, and so demonstrated their willingness to feed.

Müllerian mimicry involves mutual resemblance among two or more sympatric species, all of which are noxious to predators. The survival value to the mimics is that the resemblance reduces the number of lessons an individual predator must learn. Experience with any *one* of the noxious species produces a disinclination to trifle with any other species in the group. A Müllerian mimic complex often sports a brilliant and conspicuous *warning pattern,* which apparently facilitates recognition by potential predators (Plate 7*c*). A good many noxious insects that neither sting nor bite are distasteful by virtue of poisonous chemicals which they derive from their food plants and store rather than degrade. Such insects (including monarch butterflies) tolerate concentrations of plant poisons that would be fatal or at least physiologically embarrassing to other animals. It is likely, however, that these accumulated poisons may put stress upon the insect's bodily economy. If so, this would encourage some members of a Müllerian complex to become "free-loaders," that is, to degrade a large portion of the toxic molecules and ride along on the reputation of the other members of the group. In such a case, an evolutionary transformation from Müllerian to Batesian mimicry would be under way.

In any consideration of crypsis and mimicry, as well as of organic adaptation generally, it is essential to avoid any implication of purposive foreknowledge on the part of the organism. Viceroy butterflies did not come to resemble monarchs "in order to" escape predation on the strength of the resemblance. On the contrary, ancestral viceroys that resembled monarchs were less likely to be taken by predators familiar with monarchs and thus were more likely to survive and perpetuate the resemblance. Over a period of time, selection operated in the direction of improving the resemblance, for in each generation the more faithful mimics would be most likely to survive.

An adaptive conflict may arise during the process of selection toward mimicry (especially in the case of Müllerian mimicry, in which an entire group of species may be involved): if a visual resemblance fools predators, may it not also confuse insects in search of mates? Final recognition of an appropriate mate may depend on cues other than overall appearance, but an interesting fact has been noted: certain butterflies that look alike to vertebrate eyes look very different when seen by ultraviolet light (a part of the spectrum visible to insects but invisible to most vertebrates). This double optical effect gives the butterflies protection against vertebrate predators such as birds and lizards, while allowing the insects readily to recognize their own kind.

E Competition

Competition for materials or space only available in restricted quantities is more acute among members of a single species than among the various species of an *established* community. It is however an important factor during the maturation and evolution of a community. Competition acts as a selective force in encouraging biotic diversification (Figure 6.14). The numerous species of a diversified biota can coexist with a minimum amount of competition, for they have become adapted to fulfill particular roles in the ecosystem—that is, they

Figure 6.14 □ **Reduction of competition between related species: two species of cormorants avoid competition for nesting sites. (*a*) The double-crested cormorant nests in trees on a refuge in North Dakota. (*b*) Brandt's cormorant nests on sea cliffs. Selection of widely separated breeding sites could serve as a factor leading to the breaking up of a population into two species, for hereditary exchanges between the two breeding populations would cease to take place. Such diversification in nest-site preference helps to minimize competition. (*Photographs by C. J. Henry and V. B. Scheffer, U.S. Bureau of Sport Fisheries & Wildlife.*)**

(*a*)

(*b*)

occupy separate *niches.* An ecological niche is not a *place:* it represents the position or *role* in the ecosystem that a given species occupies and is the product of that species' own requirements and its interactions with the rest of the community. *Gause's rule,* stating that two species cannot occupy the same niche in a given community (or, briefly, that "complete competitors cannot coexist"), is seen in action mainly when an established community is perturbed by the introduction of a new species or characteristic. This may occur when a geographical barrier is surmounted (as in the case of the Mediterranean fruit fly and the Japanese beetle, which—held in check by the structure of their native communities—attained the status of pests only when they were transported to new habitats as an accident of human commerce). It may also operate when one species evolves an adaptive innovation that gives it an unprecedented advantage over some other species in the community (as when the more prolific and intelligent placental mammals began to compete with marsupials for niches that the latter had long held.)

In the struggle for possession of a particular niche, the adaptive advantage of one species need be only *slightly* greater than that of another: a slightly more effective means of defense, a more aggressive demeanor, a higher prolificacy, or a more effective means of caring for the young—any of these can serve as the tiny advantage enabling one competitor eventually to eliminate the other from the community.

An advantage may lie with one of two competitive species because of its higher tolerance of some abiotic factor in the habitat. A study of the flour beetles

Tribolium castaneum and *T. confusum* revealed that each species when cultured separately could survive indefinitely under a wide variety of conditions of temperature and humidity. However, when populations of the two species were grown in the same culture, one eventually exterminated the other. Warm and wet conditions proved favorable to *T. castaneum,* while under conditions of low temperature and low humidity the advantage lay with *T. confusum.* Considered theoretically, a set of intermediate conditions could be found at which humidity and temperature would no longer determine the outcome of this heterospecific competition, but under such neutral abiotic conditions no doubt some hitherto undetected advantage would show up in one species that would again prevent an equilibrium from being maintained between the two competing populations.

The starling, which was introduced into the United States from Europe, competes severely with native woodpeckers because, despite great differences in mode of life, both are hole-nesting birds. While woodpeckers construct nestholes, the starling must use a preexisting cavity. However, starlings have been observed attacking woodpeckers and driving them away from their own nests. In this instance, heterospecific *aggression* appears to be of importance in the success of starling over woodpecker. This example is also of interest because starlings and woodpeckers are by no means "complete competitors," but instead they come into conflict over only *one* critically limited commodity—nesting cavities. Obviously the supply of trees suitable for excavation is not unlimited, nor is the strength and endurance of the woodpeckers equal to providing a series of nestholes both for themselves and for piratical starlings. It is not difficult to foresee the probable outcome of this case of heterospecific competition. As we have said, whenever two species are in competition for the same niche, or for any critically restricted aspect of the habitat, *no equilibrium will be achieved,* for with even the slightest selective advantage, one of the competitors will finally exclude the other from the community.

This fact should be borne in mind when one attempts to assess the role of competition in biotic communities. A stabilized biotic community is one in which evolution has proceeded toward a state of *coadaptation,* in which diversification of needs and modes of life have finally reduced competition among species to an operable minimum.

ECOLOGICAL DOMINANCE A few species that contribute largely to the biomass of the community and strongly influence its character are said to hold a position of *ecological dominance* in that community. These organisms are large enough or numerous enough to exert profound effects on the structure of the community. Ecological dominants are usually large perennial plants that determine the basic nature of the community. The ecological dominants of the southern California coastal chaparral are mountain lilac (*Ceanothus*) and chamise (*Adenostoma*). This community is therefore referred to as the *Adenostoma-Ceanothus* association. North American forest communities include the *Thuja-Tsuga* (cedar-hemlock) association of coastal forests, *Acer-Fagus* (maple-beech) deciduous woodland, *Picea-Abies* (spruce-fir) subalpine forest, and others.

Among animal species, the most widespread and effective of ecological dominants is *Homo sapiens.* To date, human actions have been so largely predicated on short-term expediency that the emergence of man as an ecological dominant has been catastrophic for most of the biosphere. If mankind can to some extent outgrow its not unnatural preoccupation with what it conceives to be its own immediate interests, it may come to realize that *no biotic community is secure in which the proliferation of a single species diminishes or eradicates so many others.* In the interests of the future of life on earth, man should assist in the preservation of biotic diversity. The roll call of animal and plant species that have been brought to the point of extinction by human agency is already of formidable length. Heterospecific competition, predation, and parasitism no longer check the proliferation of the human population. Whether or not we can successfully control our population growth is of immediate concern. The vital question is whether such control will be exercised through educated free choice, through authoritarian dictation, or by warfare. Or will we permit limitations of food supply and living space to prescribe the ultimate maximum for the human population? Even if we are able to meet the immediate demands of increasing population by bringing more land under cultivation, applying agricultural practices to the sea, and seeking means of food synthesis, sooner or later birthrate and deathrate *must* be brought into equilibrium. If we can attain this equilibrium in time, uncultivated and unexploited parts of the world may yet be preserved, in which biotic communities can flourish relatively free of human domination.

If this is done, our descendants will not have to inherit a world from which all traces of the wild, the exciting, and the unknown have vanished.

THE REDUCTION OF COMPETITION Returning to a consideration of the structure of established, evolved communities, we find that diversification has reduced heterospecific competition through the development of: (1) different nutritional requirements; (2) varying needs for shelter and support; (3) periodicity; and (4) stratification. The first two are implicit in our earlier studies of biotic diversity. The latter two deserve further clarification.

By periodicity is meant the various daily and seasonal rhythms shown by species in a community.

On a 24-hr basis, the community leads a double life: as the sun goes down, one set of inhabitants goes to sleep and another set awakes. There may, in fact, be diurnal and nocturnal species that occupy virtually the same niche except that one is active while the other sleeps. Much activity and predation occur at the junctions of day and night, the dusk and the dawn, when the two populations, the *diurnal* and the *nocturnal,* are both partially astir.

Seasonal periodicity also serves to increase the number of species that a given habitat can accommodate. Many communities are significantly affected by the influx and departure of migratory species, particularly birds. They are also profoundly affected by the annual growth and reproductive cycles of plants. We have already considered the effects of photoperiod on flowering in short-night and long-night species. Flowering plants that bloom at different times of the year do not compete for the services of pollinator species such as honeybees. Nocturnal bloomers like *Cereus* also escape this competition for they attract and are pollinated by moths.

Stratification of a community expands the *vertical* component of the *space* occupied, even as periodicity expands the *temporal* factor. Some species occupy the abiotic substratum proper, as either surface or subsurface fauna and flora. The soil is richly populated with burrowing animals, bacteria, fungi, and the root systems of plants. Its surface supports pedestrian animals and numerous autotrophic plants. The vegetation in turn provides further substratum for arboreal animals and epiphytes. Particular species are often confined to certain strata of the community. Studies of howling monkeys (*Alouatta palliata*), have revealed that this species is exclusively arboreal, never voluntarily forsaking the canopy of the rain forest. Occasionally, a fallen youngster is retrieved by the troop, which howls loudly to discourage predators as a few adults descend and collect him, all the while gripping a branch with their prehensile tails.

A community may include a number of potentially competitive species that in fact do *not* compete, due to differential uses of *space*. The feeding zones of five sympatric species of North American warblers, which feed upon insects picked off vegetation, have been mapped spatially, and it has been found that although birds of all five species may be feeding simultaneously in a single spruce tree, they do not compete appreciably, since their major feeding zones overlap only partially (Figure 6.15). The tree is stratified, as though by invisible fences, into vertical zones each approximately 3 m high. A spruce tree about 20 m tall contains six such strata, and no single species frequents more than two of them. In addition, each stratum is further divided into three horizontal zones: an outer zone of young foliage; a middle zone of older foliage; and the inner, bare or lichenous branches. Each of these zones offers a somewhat different supply of insects. As with the vertical strata, so the outer, middle, and inner foliage zones are differentially preferred by the various warbler species.

ECOLOGICAL EQUIVALENCE The nature of communities and habitats is such that similar niches often recur in widely separated communities. Any terrestrial habitat of suitable climate has the potential for supporting a subsurface, surface, and arboreal biota. Any community will develop its complexes of producer and consumer species. Diversity will be favored by virtue of its value in reducing competition and permitting the biota full exploitation of the habitat. In due time, all available niches tend to become occupied. As this takes place, in different geographical regions species evolve that are ecologically equivalent to one another—that is, they occupy equivalent niches in their separate communities. Striking examples of ecological equivalence are seen by comparing the Australian marsupial fauna with the eutherians of other continents (Figure 1.7). Ecological equivalents tend to develop analogous specializations related to their niche. Equivalents such as wolf and marsupial "wolf" show marked convergence in appearance as well as in way of life. Other ecological equivalents may not converge structurally. For example, marsupial grazing animals include kangaroos and wallabies; their eutherian equivalents are antelope, bison, cattle, and the like. Given earthlike conditions on planets of other solar systems, it is entirely possible that life forms may have evolved that are ecologically equivalent to those we know and perhaps analogously convergent to some of them.

Figure 6.15 □ **Feeding zones of five species of North American warblers in a spruce tree. The tree is vertically stratified into zones about 3 m high. At each level are three additional zones: (1) an outer region of new foliage and buds, (2) a middle region of old needles, and (3) an inner zone of branches lacking foliage. Shading indicates the area in which each species spends at least 50 percent of its feeding time. (*Adapted from E. D. Hanson,* Animal Diversity, *2nd ed. Englewood Cliffs, N.J.: Prentice-Hall, Inc., 1964.*)**

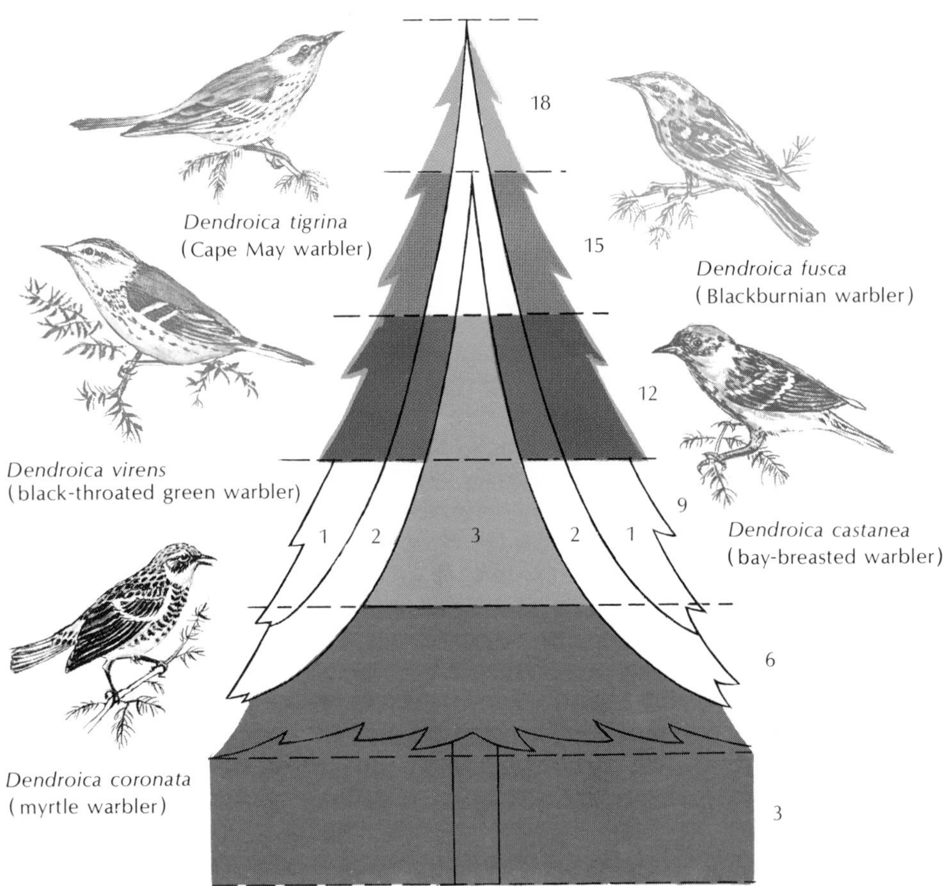

F Cooperation

Cooperative relationships among the species of a community are both direct and indirect. One of the most conspicuous instances of direct cooperation exists between flowering plants and pollinator insects. The insects profit by the edible secretions of the plant, and the plants are aided by transference of their pollen (Figure 6.16). Many aspects of floral structure represent adaptations that attract insect pollinators—vivid colors perceptible to insect eyes, pigment streaks serving as guidelines into the flower's interior, petals or sepals forming flat landing platforms, nectaries filled with palatable secretions and emitting an attractive odor—all part of plants' insect-luring repertory. Certain blossoms that appear white to our eyes have been found to emit strongly in the ultraviolet, appearing brilliantly "purple" to insect eyes.

Insects in turn exhibit numerous adaptations related to the exploitation of flowers: elongated mouthparts, sensory acuities attuned to floral emanations, and, in the case of honeybees, various modifications of the legs related to the transport of pollen, upon which the bees feed. The first and second legs of the honeybee bear bristly "pollen brushes" used in removing pollen that clings to the body. In addition, each foreleg bears a bristle-lined notch (the "cleaning brush"), while a curved spine borne on the next

Figure 6.16 □ **Cooperation between species. (*a*) Museum mount of sphinx moth in feeding attitude (*Los Angeles County Museum of Natural History*). The long proboscis, ordinarily not seen because deeply inserted into the blossom when not coiled up, probes the nectaries at the base of the trumpet-shaped corolla. Such tubular blossoms depend for pollination on animals with probing mouthparts, such as hummingbirds, moths, and butterflies. (*b*) Honeybee pollinating alfalfa blossom, shown with pollen basket loaded (*photograph by W. P. Nye, Agricultural Research Service*). (*c*) Detail of specializations of honeybee legs for transporting pollen.**

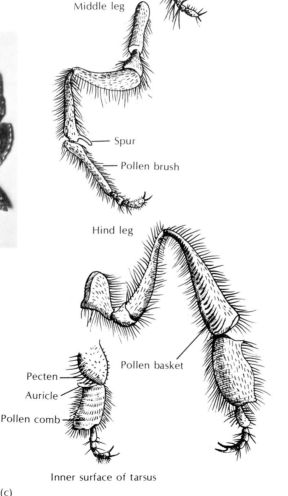

(*a*)

(*b*)

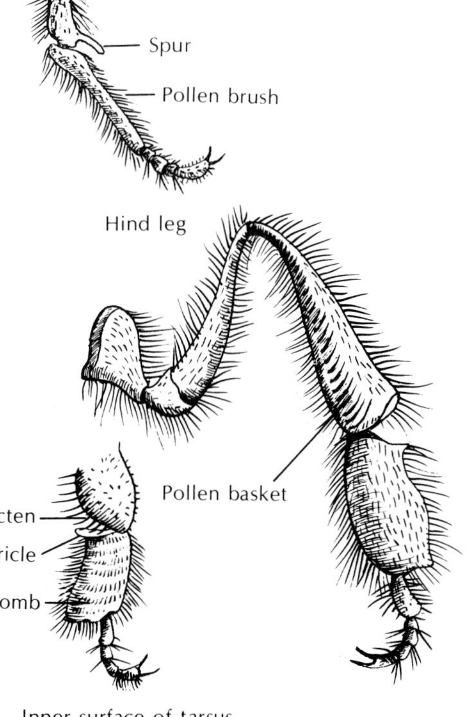

(*c*)

segment of the leg fits over the top of this notch. Together they constitute a device for cleaning pollen off the antennae as the latter are drawn through the notch. The hind legs are most highly adapted for pollen carrying, for they bear the "pollen basket," "pollen comb," and "pollen packer." After a bee has industriously plunged into the heart of a flower, she emerges drenched with pollen. A brisk grooming session ensues, during which each pollen comb is cleaned by a row of stiff bristles (the pecten) forming part of the pollen packer. A flat plate (the auricle) forming the other component of the pollen packer is then used as a tamp in transferring pollen from the pecten into the pollen basket of the opposite leg. The pollen basket is a concavity edged with long bristles, which the bee periodically keeps moistened with saliva. When the pollen baskets are filled, the bee returns to the hive bearing pollen gleaned from many flowers that she has visited. In the course of this series of visitations, she has of course inadvertently left some pollen grains adhering to the pistils (female organs) of the flowers.

A number of *behavioral* adaptations of honeybees enhance the effectiveness of the *morphological* specializations: (1) The pollen-cleaning and -transporting structures would be valueless if appropriate motor patterns for their use had not been evolved; in fact, grooming activities no doubt *preceded* the structural adaptations and served as selective factors in the development of the latter. (2) Bees tend to visit only one species of plant at a time; this augments the likelihood of pollen being transferred from one flower to another of the same species and enhances the survival value of the bee-angiosperm association. (3) As described in Sections 1.1B and 7.3C, honeybees have developed methods of communicating information to one another concerning the location of food sources. With this assemblage of sensory, motor, and structural adaptations, the honeybee (*Apis mellifera:* "sweet-carrying bee") has become the single most important insect species to the survival of flowering plants of the temperate zone.

Another type of cooperative relationship is exhibited by ants and aphids (plant lice). An aphid feeds upon plant sap, piercing the tissues with its long proboscis. As the aphid feeds, excess sap is expelled from its anus, sometimes in such quantities that droplets fall like fine rain. Ants seek out aphid-infested plants and feed upon this anal exudate, for they themselves are unable to withdraw sap. Up to this point, the relationship is of unilateral benefit, but certain kinds of ants assist the aphids by gathering their eggs and keeping them through the winter in the safety of the ants' underground nests. This is true in the case of the corn root aphid. After having kept the eggs in their nests, the ants carry them out in spring and place them on the roots of certain native plants. Then when the corn has begun to grow, the ants transfer the aphids onto the corn roots and visit them throughout the summer. In this cooperative relationship (in which the aphids play the more passive role), the overwintering and dissemination of aphids is abetted by the behavioral adaptations of the ants.

6.3 □ SYMBIOTIC RELATIONSHIPS

Symbiotic relationships have been defined as those which involve an intimate relationship between two particular species which is necessary for the survival of at least one of the members of the association. They include *mutualism, commensalism,* and *parasitism.*

A Mutualism

An obligate relationship that is of reciprocal benefit to *both* partners is termed *mutualism* or *mutualistic symbiosis.* Such a relationship exists between termites and their intestinal flagellate protozoans. Although termites eat wood, they are incapable of digesting cellulose because they lack the appropriate digestive enzymes. Only a few animals manufacture *cellulase* (cellulose-splitting enzyme). Among these are certain flagellates, which can digest fragments of wood if these are small enough to be engulfed (Figure 6.17). The termite-flagellate association has apparently been of long duration, for the protozoans have developed many long flagella that help them move through the viscid intestinal contents of their host. They engulf wood fragments, which the termites have reduced to microscopic size by chewing, and digest the cellulose to simple sugars. These sugars nourish not only the protozoans themselves but are actually taken into the tissues of the host as well. Each generation of termites infects itself with symbionts by eating fecal pellets voided by the adults.

A number of heterotrophs profit by the activities of autotrophic symbionts, particularly one-celled blue-green, green, or golden-brown algae. The algal symbionts profit by their protected status within the tissues of their host. Lichens, as we have seen, are "dual organisms": their structural framework usually consists of an ascomycete fungus; among the hyphae live numerous unicellular algae (see Figure 2.18). The organic products of algal photosynthesis nourish algae and fungus alike. Their impervious covering permits lichens to survive in very dry habitats where algae alone would perish. In similar fashion, the nutrition of green anemones (*Anthopleura*), green hydra (*Chlorohydra*), and giant clams (*Tridacna*) is enhanced by their symbiotic algae. The giant clams open their valves in the daytime and extrude the edges of their mantles, thus giving their symbionts periods of exposure to the sun essential for photosynthesis (see Figure 5.20).

Animals containing algal symbionts rarely depend solely upon them, but ingest food as well. However, an experimental study of a two-species system involving green hydra and brown hydra (*Pelmatohydra*), the latter lacking symbionts, has shown that under controlled conditions green hydra eventually displace brown hydra. The efficiency of brown hydra in using food for growth is the usual 10 percent, while that of green hydra is about *40 percent.* In other words, the nutritional efficiency of green hydra is four times that of most animal species. Thus, under conditions of normal illumination, about three-fourths of the green hydra's energy requirements are met by materials produced by its algal symbionts. The symbionts cannot, however, totally provide for the needs of their host, for when deprived of prey green hydra eventually starve. On the other hand, when provided with ample prey (such as the small crustacean, *Daphnia*), green hydra kept in the dark can maintain themselves indefinitely by predation alone. While green hydra eventually displace brown hydra under lighted conditions, in the dark green hydra will *not* displace brown hydra. Victory in the competition for survival will then depend on the *size* of available prey: *Pelmatohydra* feeds upon considerably larger prey than *Chlorohydra* can accept.

This example illustrates the selective advantage a mutualistic relationship may offer in the context of other community relationships: while algal symbionts are not required for the survival of the *individual* animal, the success of the green hydra *population* in heterospecific competition *is* dependent upon its symbiotic algae.

There is no clear-cut demarcation between cooperation and mutualism. Intermediary conditions are known, and it is likely that simple cooperation may occasionally evolve into obligate mutualism. Such may be the case with the unique relationship found among certain marine animals, known as *cleaning symbiosis.* The well-being of many marine fish seems to depend upon the removal of parasites from their skin and gills, and the trimming of decaying flesh from wounds. Certain kinds of shrimp and small fish have adopted the role of cleaners, and obtain much if not all of their food by cleaning the bodies of larger fish. These "cleaner" organisms advertise their calling by remaining in one location and sporting conspicuous colors. Fish come to recognize the stations of individual cleaners, and aggregate at the cleaning station until they are serviced. During the cleaning operation, the "patient" extends its fins, opens its mouth, and spreads its gill covers, allowing the cleaner access to all parts of the body including the interior of the mouth. The cleaner on its part works methodically over the mouth, gills, and integument of its patient, exhibiting no reluctance at entering the mouth of fish capable of swallowing it with ease. The cleaning sym-

Figure 6.17 □ Mutualism. The protozoan *Trichonympha* is one of several genera of flagellates that inhabit the gut of the termite, engulfing and digesting fragments of wood that have previously been masticated and ingested by the insect host. Without these symbionts the insect could not digest cellulose to sugar. Young termites become infected with the symbionts by feeding upon fecal pellets voided by the adults. At each molt a new infection must be established through fecal ingestion since the chitinous lining of the hindgut is molted too, thereby thoroughly emptying the intestines. The symbiont's unusually numerous flagella enable it to navigate through the viscous intestinal contents.

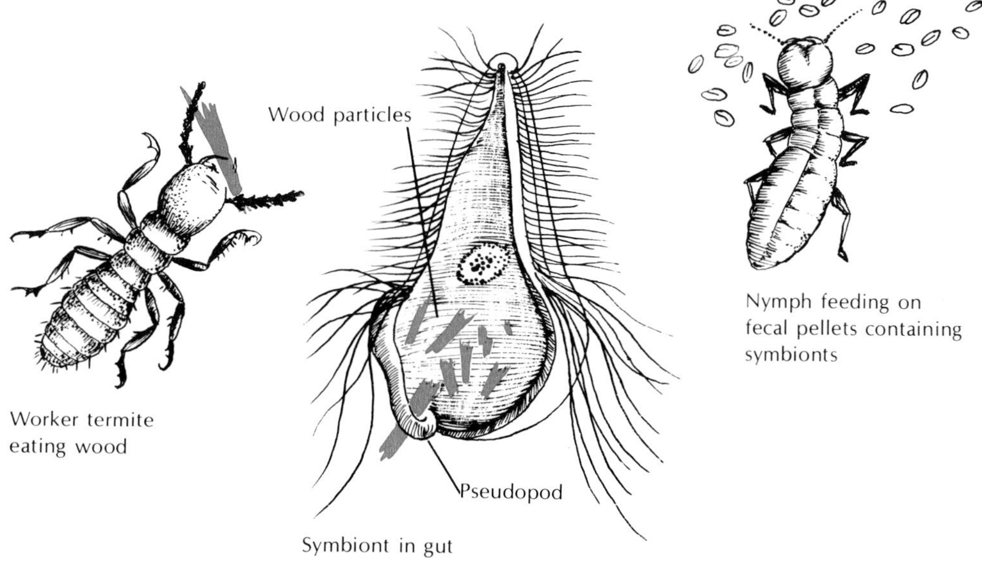

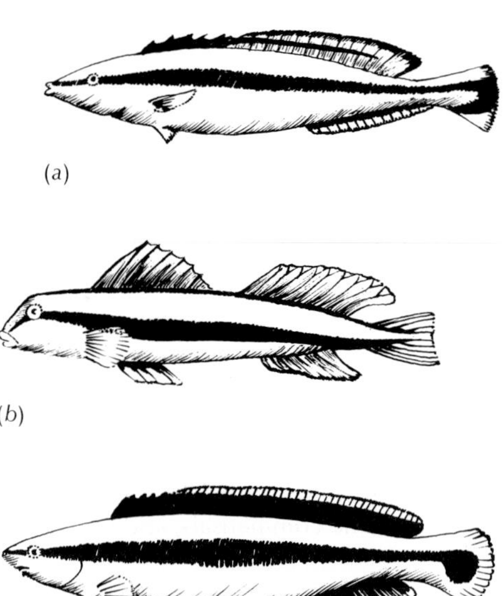

Figure 6.18 □ A false symbiosis. A number of shrimp and small marine fish make their living by cleaning ectoparasites and dead tissue off the bodies of larger fish that actually congregate to await the attentions of the cleaning symbiont. This has paved the way for another relationship, a false symbiosis, in which the true cleaners, *Labroides dimidiatus* (*a*) and *Elancatinus oceanops* (*b*), are mimicked by a predator, *Aspidontes taeniatus* (*c*), which bites chunks of flesh from larger fish as they approach expecting to be groomed. (*From B. Wallace and A. M. Srb,* Adaptation, *2nd ed. Englewood Cliffs, N. J.: Prentice-Hall, Inc. After Eibl-Eibesfeldt.*)

biosis relationship itself has paved the way for the development of yet another niche in the neritic community. One small fish (*Aspidontes*), which resembles sympatric cleaner species in size, shape, color, and pattern, positions itself in a conspicuous attitude of waiting (Figure 6.18). This combination of signals attracts fish which approach and open their mouths, only to have the mimic dart within and grab a bite of the fish's tongue before executing a speedy departure. This amazing opportunism, so typical of the process of organic adaptation, demonstrates the way in which *the development of relationships in a community can make possible the induction of further relationships.* Thus the fabric of interdependence elaborates itself, and the community grows in complexity.

B Commensalism

Commensalism is a symbiotic relationship in which one partner profits by the association while the other is not demonstrably harmed. Again, many intermediate conditions exist, gradated from commensalism to mutualism or to parasitism. The word *commensal* means "eating at the same table." This sharing of meals is in fact generally characteristic of commensal associations. The relationship is more or less obligate for the beneficiaries (witness our earlier example of the three "guests" of the fat innkeeper, *Urechis;* see Figure 6.2). For the host, the association may range from slightly detrimental to mildly beneficial, but is never obligate. Three types of commensalism are *ectocommensalism, endoecism,* and *inquilinism.*

An *ectocommensal* lives primarily attached to the exterior of the body of its host, which may be exploited primarily for transport or for obtaining food that the commensal then shares. Ectocommensals often possess adaptive structures that facilitate attachment, such as the modified dorsal fin of the remora (shark-sucker), which forms an effective adhesive organ when the remora butts its head against the body of its host. Not itself a sturdy pelagic swimmer, the remora is passively transported by its host and, when the shark feeds, appropriates a portion of the kill. The whale barnacles shown in Figure 6.19 are of particular interest in that whereas one species can cling directly to the skin of the whale, the other cannot gain purchase on the host's slick hide and must attach instead to the shell of the first commensal.

The hydroid *Clytia bakeri* occurs nowhere except attached to the valves of the coquina and the Pismo clam. Both of these clams inhabit sandy coasts, but do not burrow deeply, for their siphons are short. The hydroids, clustered at the upper end of the valves, protrude above the surface and have through ectocommensalism provided themselves with a solid substratum on a sandy shore which they otherwise could not inhabit.

Endoecism is the obligate sharing by one species of the shelter (such as a tube or burrow) of another. The crab *Scleroplax,* for instance, inhabits the tube of *Urechis* or the burrow of a ghost shrimp (*Callianassa*). The ghost shrimp is also host to a regularly occurring endoecist, the blind goby. The commensal preempts a portion of its host's food and thus benefits not only from the shelter provided, but also from the food-getting adaptations of its host. The annelid *Nereis fucata* is an endoecist that shares with a hermit crab the mollusc shell that the latter has appropriated for its own use. At rest, the commensal occupies the smaller whorls of the shell close to the apex, thus remaining out of contact with the crab's body. But when the crab begins to feed the worm swiftly approaches the opening of the shell, thrusts its head out and seizes a morsel of the host's meal.

Inquilinism is a commensal relationship in which the commensal resides *within* the body of its host. Although perhaps guilty of an occasional ungrateful sampling of the host's tissues, inquilinists are not true parasites, for their primary source of nutrition is food collected by the host. In the case of the mussel crab, *Fabia,* only the female is a soft-shelled inquilinist, inhabiting the mantle cavity of mussels and scraping from the host's gills the food being carried by ciliary action toward the host's own mouth. The male is an active, tough-shelled individualist, who slips between the open valves of the mussel only long enough to inseminate the female and then departs for the free life of the outer world.

A pair of inquiline shrimp inhabits the central cavity of the Venus' flower-basket (see Figure 4.25) with such regularity that the dried sponge skeletons together with their equally desiccated inhabitants have been traditionally given to newlyweds in the orient, as a symbol of marital fidelity. Since the shrimp grow so large that they are unable to leave the sponge in which they live, we may wonder whether this gift serves best to exemplify wedded bliss or to warn against marital entrapment!

Inquiline crabs and fishes inhabit the intestinal tract of sea cucumbers, where they feed upon the intestinal contents. This situation approaches that of the endoparasitic tapeworms, which as adults inhabit the intestine of a host, absorbing digested nutrients rather than feeding upon the host's tissues. The larval stage of the tapeworm, however, actually does penetrate the host's tissues and encysts there.

Inquilinism may represent one evolutionary route to parasitism. Within one group of crustaceans, the copepods, there occur species that represent all stages: free-living forms (see Figure 4.24), ectocommensals, inquiline commensals, and highly specialized endoparasites (Figure 6.20).

Figure 6.19 □ **A remarkable double-commensal relationship is seen with these two genera of whale barnacles: the acorn barnacle can attach directly to the whale's slick hide, to which the stalked barnacle cannot cling; the latter must gain purchase instead on the shell of the first commensal. Both kinds of barnacle thereby gain free transportation through waters rich in the plankton on which both host and barnacles feed.** (***Courtesy of Dr. W. Newman and Scripps Institution of Oceanography.***)

C Parasitism

Parasitism is a symbiotic relationship that is obligate for one member, the parasite, and harmful to the host. It is of such interest in terms of the impact of the relationship upon the adaptation of both parasite and host that we shall consider it in some detail. Parasites may be strictly limited to a single host (that is, be host-specific) or be able to exploit a number of potential host species. In some cases the parasitic relationship may have evolved from an earlier commensal association, but in other cases it may represent a modification of frank predation. A parasitic infection may occasionally cause the death of the host, but more usually a light infestation is not particularly disabling. Especially in the case of endoparasites, to which the host is both food and habitat, death or serious debility of the host is highly undesirable for the parasite and may even be fatal to it. It is therefore advantageous

Figure 6.20 □ Female parasitic copepod (*Pionodesmotes phormosomae*) in gall within test of sea urchin. Compare this figure with Figure 4.24 of nonparasitic copepods. Note reduction of antennae and legs, and other morphological simplifications of the parasite. (*From Colin Nicol, after Koehler.*)

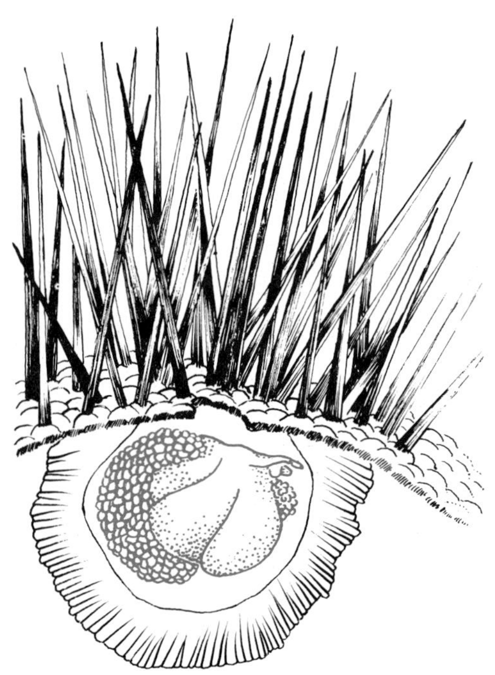

to the parasite that the host survive and remain in as good health as possible. Accordingly, *selection against pathogenicity* is operative in the evolution of parasites. Is the virulently pathogenic smallpox virus, which winnows a host population until none survives but the most resistant, more or less successful than the viruses of the "common cold," which seldom kill a host and consequently are of cosmopolitan distribution?

The *parasitoid* habits of spider wasps and caterpillar wasps are only a step removed from predation. The prey, a spider or caterpillar, is seized and stung, and thus paralyzed is borne to the burrow that the wasp has prepared (Figure 6.21). She then lays one or more eggs on each host, and seals the burrow. The wasp larvae are thus provided with fresh meat that sustains them until they are ready to pupate. The related ichneumon and braconid flies do not paralyze the host, but use their needlelike ovipositors to inject eggs under the host's integument. The host, often a caterpillar, survives for some time, but since it is literally being eaten alive, it eventually succumbs at about the time that the parasitic grubs pupate (Figure 6.22).

Most parasites do not, however, cause the death of the host, in sharp contrast to the situation that obtains between a predator and its animal prey. Charles Elton has drawn the analogy that the predator lives on *capital,* while the parasite lives on *income.* Predators destroy their prey (except for most herbivores, since plants generally regenerate the lost parts and are not seriously inconvenienced by normal grazing or browsing). When the prey population is sufficiently depleted the predators may starve. As the defensive adaptations of prey species evolve toward greater efficacy, predators are increasingly forced to spend more time and energy in the hunt. Parasites, on the other hand, seldom kill and may not even debilitate their hosts unless persistent reinfection occurs. Cumulative human parasitic infection has occurred mainly in densely populated parts of the world, where ignorance, poverty, congestion, lack of sanitation, and unwise agricultural practices (like the use of untreated sewage as fertilizer) have raised the incidence of human infestation by parasitic worms to such a level that debilitation is the rule and death not uncommon. Such situations of heavy parasitic infestation are usually attributable more to the customs of the afflicted populace than to any particular virulence on the part of the parasites.

In this regard, we should note that, as mankind has spread throughout the world, it has come in contact with many parasitic species that were *not* originally parasitic on human beings. These parasites may be much more pathogenic to man than to the species that they normally infested throughout their evolutionary history. For instance, many species of native African mammals harbor the protozoan *Trypanosoma gambiense,* exhibiting no ill effects from the infestation. When *Trypanosoma* is transferred to man by the bite of the blood-sucking tsetse fly, the human host may develop African sleeping sickness. Usually, the longer a parasitic species has been associated with its host species, the more likely it is that the two have evolved to a condition of mutual tolerance.

TYPES OF PARASITISM Various forms of parasitism include *nest parasitism, cleptoparasitism, ectoparasitism,* and *endoparasitism,* as well as the *parasitoid* behavior

Figure 6.21 □ **Tarantula wasp, *Pepsis cerberus*, with paralyzed prey, a tarantula that will be carried to the wasp's burrow and used as food for her larva. (*Los Angeles County Museum of Natural History.*)**

Figure 6.22 □ **Larval parasitism. (*a*) *Microbracon* preparing to lay egg under skin of caterpillar of Mediterranean flour moth. Note sharp ovipositor extending from tip of female wasp's hunched abdomen. (*U.S. Department of Agriculture.*) (*b*) Chalcid larvae seen within body of host, caterpillar of *Autographica brassicae*. (*Los Angeles County Museum of Natural History.*) (*c*) Pupae of *Apanteles* attached to integument of the host within which their larval life was spent. The host is a tobacco hornworm, caterpillar stage of sphinx moth. (*U.S. Department of Agriculture.*)**

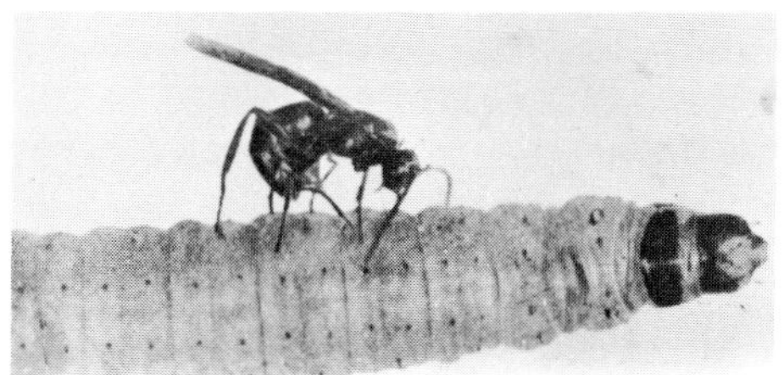

(*a*)

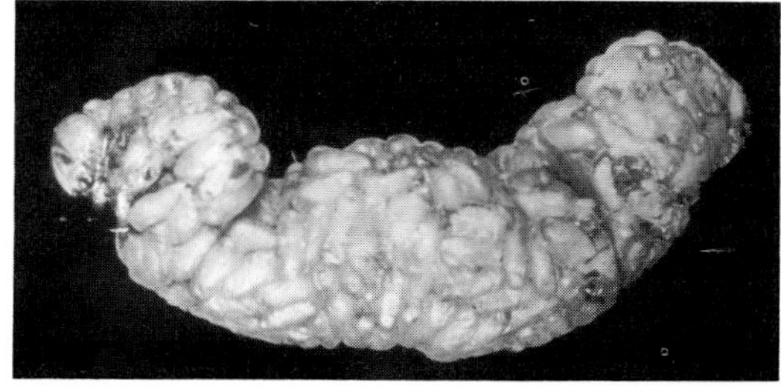

(*b*)

(*c*)

of wasps and ichneumons as described above (Figure 6.23).

A classic example of the nest parasite is the cuckoo, which lays its single egg in the nests of other birds, neither building a nest of its own nor attempting to incubate. These normal avian proclivities have been lost by the cuckoo as an outcome of the success of its parasitic mode of life.

Unless the foster parents reject the cuckoo's egg, it hatches ahead of their own clutch. One of the first acts of the infant cuckoo's life is to exert its puny strength to oust the remaining eggs or nestlings, pushing them out upon its back.

Parasitic nestlings must furnish stimuli so irresistible that they can overcome any tendency of the foster parents to recognize that these youngsters are not of their own kind. The efficacy of the cries and gaping of young cuckoos has been tested in field experiments in which fledgling cuckoos were tethered to posts where their entreaties could affect birds of other species passing by bearing food for their own nestlings. Numerous birds, returning with food to their own nests, were lured from their proper errands by the irresistible stimuli provided by the young cuckoos (see Figure 16.19*b*). It is noteworthy that although early learning plays an important role in the ability of most bird species to recognize their own kind, it can play no such role in parasitic birds: until adulthood one cuckoo may never see another.

If the host species should develop effective defenses against nest parasites (as in the case of some birds that now regularly recognize a cuckoo egg as something undesirable and solve the problem of its disposal by either abandoning that nest or constructing

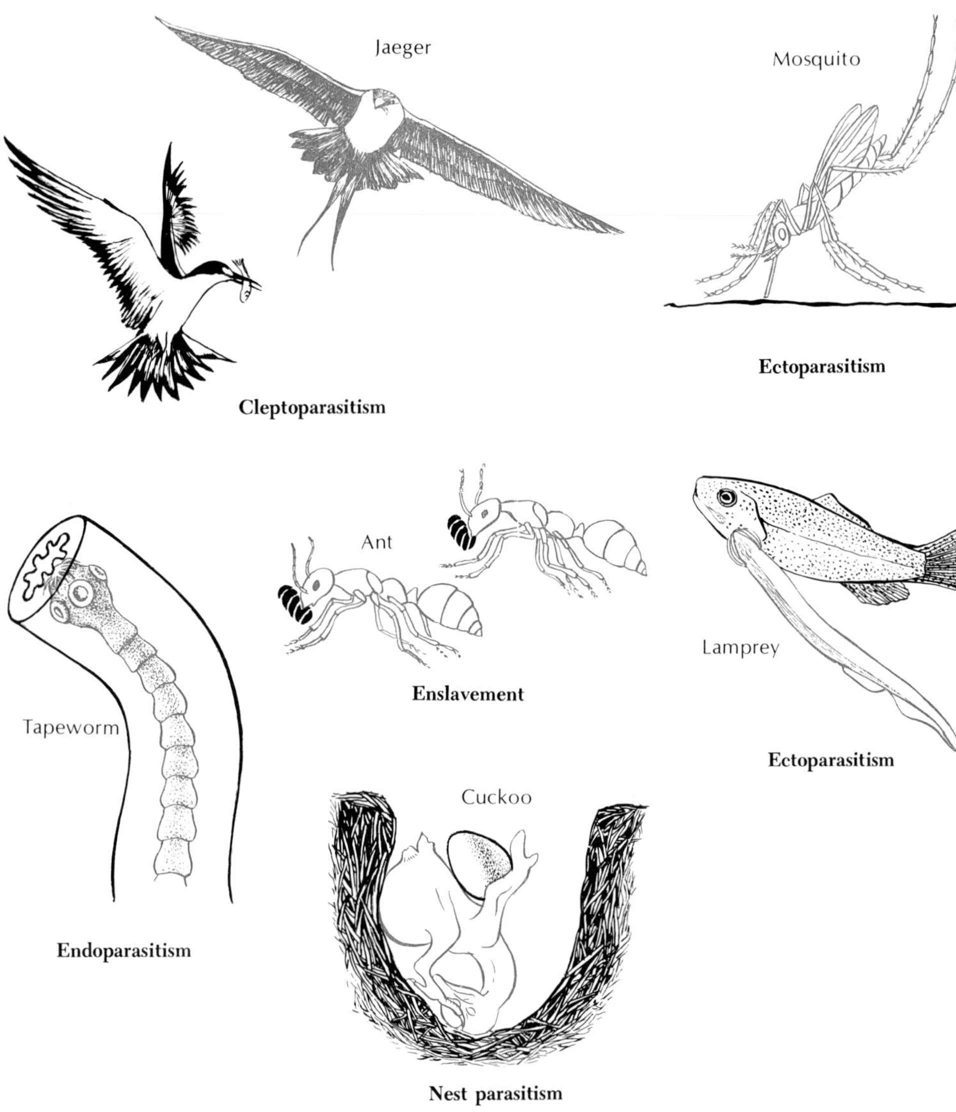

Figure 6.23 □ **Types of parasitism. (Enslavement is seen in ants that raid the nests of other species to carry away larvae that will mature to serve as workers in their captors' nest. The "slavemasters" are so dependent on this raiding practice that they can no longer produce the workers necessary for maintaining their own nests.)**

a new floor over the cuckoo's egg), the cuckoo and other parasitic birds may find themselves in an adaptive trap from which escape may be impossible. Any attribute, structural or functional, that has been lost by a species is unlikely to reappear if again needed. The deletion of nesting and incubating behavior patterns from the instinctive repertory of parasitic birds may therefore eventually contribute to their extinction.

Cleptoparasites steal something from animals of other species. The parasitic jaeger is a marauding gull that catches no fish itself but finds another fish-laden gull and pursues and harries it until the victim relinquishes its catch. *Enslavement* is a specialized type of cleptoparasitism. It is obligate for certain species of ants which produce no worker caste of their own but must raid the nests of ants of other species, kidnapping the larvae. These larvae mature to become the workers of the cleptoparasitic colony. Since these displaced workers are not employed on behalf of their own kind, they are indeed slaves. Under normal circumstances the major function of worker ants is care of the young of their own species. The energies of the abducted workers are instead expended to rear the young of their captors. Man is another organism which enslaves members of other species, rearing them under conditions in which they contribute mainly to the welfare of man and not of their own species. *No* species other than man, however, has been known to enslave *its own kind.*

Ectoparasites attach themselves permanently or temporarily to the exterior of the host's body, penetrating its integument to withdraw nutrients in the form of blood or tissue fluid. Such plants as mistletoe and dodder (Figure 6.24) are parasitic on other plants, their roots penetrating the host's bark. Ectoparasitic animals such as fleas, mosquitoes, bed bugs, and aphids, are not usually greatly different from their free-living relatives. They may bear one or more adhesive suckers, such as those of the leech (Figure 2.32*d*), and their mouthparts must be capable of piercing the host's integument. Ectoparasites often secrete an *anticoagulant,* which inhibits the clotting of the host's blood. The anticoagulant hirudin was formerly extracted from leeches and used to prevent clotting during physiological experimentation.

Figure 6.24 □ **Mistletoe, section through root of parasite, showing penetration into tissues of host. Mistletoe can carry on photosynthesis but depends on the host's sap for a supply of water and minerals. (*Courtesy of Carolina Biological Supply Company.*)**

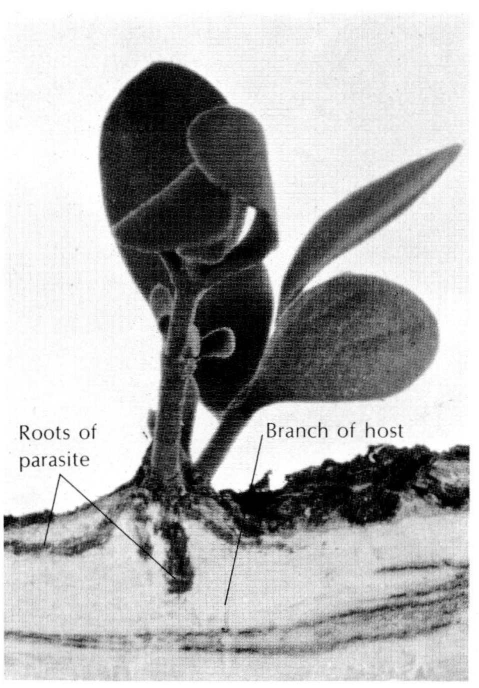

Many animal phyla have contributed ectoparasitic members to the community. At least one kind of hydroid is parasitic; growing on the skin of fish, it sends feeding stolons into the tissues of its host. Among the annelids are the leeches and a few parasitic polychaetes. A few marine gastropods are ecto- or endoparasites, primarily of starfish or sea cucumbers. The *glochidia larvae* of freshwater clams are transiently parasitic on the gills of fish; since these clams inhabit an environment in which planktonic larvae are subject to downstream displacement, attachment of the larval parasites to the gills of fish primarily serves to prevent them from being swept away and to permit dispersal further upstream. One type of freshwater clam has developed a mantle flap that some investigators believe is effective in attracting fish (Figure 6.25). When the clam's larvae are ready to leave the mother's mantle cavity, in which they have been harboring, the clam is seen to open its valves and wriggle the mantle flap. If a fish approaches, the larvae are expelled and they speedily attach to the fish's gills. If this mantle flap actually does attract fish, it serves to reduce the proportion of larvae that will be swept away before they can locate a host.

Few vertebrates are parasitic. Exceptions are adult lampreys and hagfish (the larvae are free-living). Lampreys have a jawless circular mouth armed with rasping teeth and leading posteriorly into a muscular pharynx used in sucking. Attached by its mouth to the body of a fish, the lamprey rasps the flesh and may cause death by perforating the host's body cavity (see Figures 2.48 and 13.14c). The hagfish is more nearly an unusual predator than a parasite, for it enters the host's body by way of the mouth, and proceeds to devour the fish from the inside out.

Phylum Arthropoda includes a particularly rich variety of both ecto- and endoparasites, including many insects, arachnids, and crustaceans that parasitize plants and animals of many phyla. Occasionally, as with mosquitoes, only the female is parasitic. Some arthropods are parasitic throughout their lives (such as fleas and ticks); others are parasitic as larvae but become free-living as adults (ichneumons and botflies); and still others metamorphose from free-living larvae into parasitic adults (mosquitoes and most parasitic crustaceans). A number of ectoparasitic arthropods are of medical interest as *vectors* (carriers) of endoparasites. The rickettsia which causes Rocky Mountain spotted fever, for example, is transmitted by the bite of the wood tick and the malarial parasite (the protozoan *Plasmodium*) is carried by the *Anopheles* mosquito.

An *endoparasite* spends at least one stage of its life cycle *within* the body of a host. Endoparasitism is of particular biological interest, for here we see realized to the

Figure 6.25 □ **Parasite luring host? The mantle edge of the freshwater clam *Lampsilis* is extended to form what some investigators claim to be a fish-shaped "lure" for attracting fish. The lure is most fully developed and is said to exhibit peculiar "swimming" movements only during the time the clam's glochidia larvae are ready to leave the mother's gill chamber for that of a fish. If this structure serves as a lure, it would promote survival when a suitable host fish is nearby, for fewer of the larvae would then be swept downstream. What experimental procedures might be used to determine whether or not this mantle flap actually attracts fish? Can you explain the development of such a structure in terms of differential prolificacy of clams in which the mantle flap is more or less fully developed? (*Photograph by John H. Welsh, Harvard University.*)**

utmost the effects of the parasitic existence upon the evolution of parasites themselves. The evolutionary effects of endoparasitism are displayed in the parasite much more than in the host, although the evolution of the host's defensive system has taken place as an outcome of the presence of parasites in the community. Endoparasites are some of the most precisely and specifically adapted of living things. Several major animal groups including tapeworms, sporozoans, and most nematodes and flukes are exclusively endoparasitic. A number of bacteria and fungi are also endoparasites.

EFFECTS OF PARASITISM ON THE PARASITE Several conspicuous evolutionary tendencies are shown by endoparasitic animals. These include: (1) structural and physiological *simplification* of the parasitic stage of the life cycle; (2) tremendous *fecundity;* (3) *metagenesis,* or development of several stages or generations in the life history, which utilize different hosts or pursue different modes of existence; and (4) intercalation of one or more *asexually reproducing generations* between the sexual generations.

Simplification of morphology and physiological processes may often be noted when one compares an endoparasite with its free-living relatives, a parasitic larva with its own free-living adult stage, or a parasitic adult with its own free-living larva. Comparison of a free-living flatworm such as *Dugesia* with a parasite such as the tapeworm shows that *Dugesia* has a well-developed gut or gastrovascular cavity employed both in digestion and internal distribution, a brain, and well-developed eyes (Figure 2.26a). The anterior end of a tapeworm (the scolex), on the contrary, possesses neither eyes nor brain, but does develop hooks and suckers that are adaptive in retaining a hold on the wall of the host's alimentary tract. A gastrovascular cavity is lacking, and nutrients are obtained by absorption of the products of the host's digestive activities. Muscles are degenerate and active locomotion is restricted to the larval stages. Each segment, or *proglottid,* produced by budding from the posterior end of the scolex, is almost exclusively devoted to the housing of reproductive organs (Figure 6.26).

Regression also occurs in crustacea that metamorphose from free-swimming nauplius larvae, similar to those of other nonparasitic crustaceans (Figure 2.39), into endoparasitic adults. A radical elimination of unneeded organs may accompany this metamorphosis. One of the most dramatic of such changes occurs in parasitic barnacles such as *Sacculina.* Any barnacle larva undergoes great modifications during metamorphosis to adulthood, but most retain the jointed appendages and well-developed nervous, sensory, digestive, and circulatory systems characteristic of arthropods. The larval sacculinid, on the other hand, seeks out a crab and attaches itself to the base of one of the host's integumentary bristles. It then penetrates the exoskeleton (which is thin at the base of the bristle) and proceeds to inject itself into the host by way of its own hollow antennae! The degenerative process has thus begun ahead of the attachment to the host.

Within the host, the sacculinid migrates through the bloodstream to the gut, attaches near the host's stomach, and begins to grow rootlike processes that extend throughout all parts of the crab's body (Figure 6.27). The host molts only once after having been

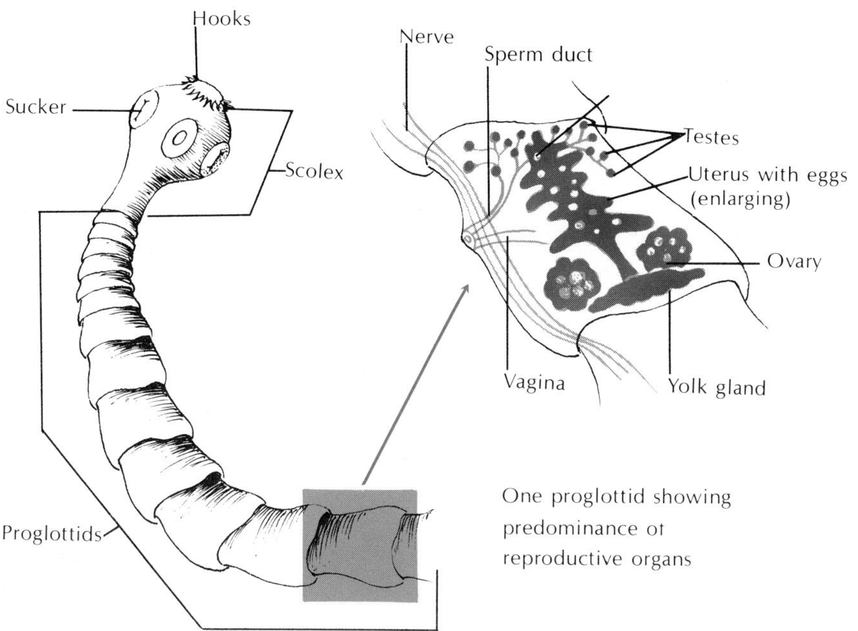

Figure 6.26 □ Life cycle of a tapeworm, *Taenia*.

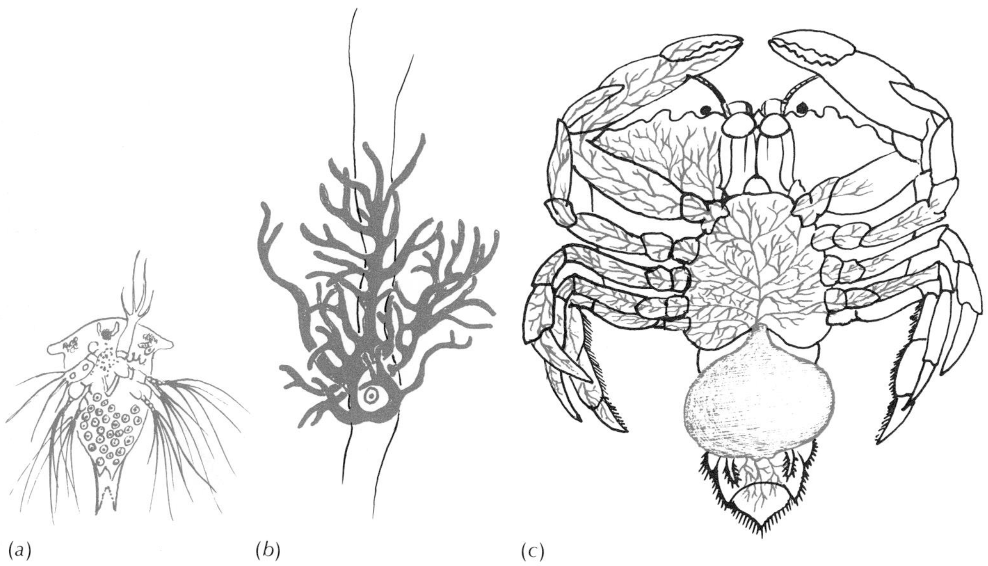

parasitized, and during this molt the portion of the parasite that underlies the junction of the host's thorax and abdomen erupts to the surface as a tumorous mass, which thereafter constitutes the main portion of the parasite's body. From this mass the gametes of the parasite are discharged. The sacculinid may live for 3 or 4 years and eventually perish while the host may live on. Strangely enough, this massive infestation does not inevitably kill the host but renders it sterile, sluggish, and unable to molt. The infection, while sterilizing a female host, merely accentuates her female sexual characters (such as the U-shaped abdomen). A male host, on the other hand, is not only sterilized but feminized by the destruction of the gland that secretes male sex hormone. In his final molt the crab develops the small claws and wide abdomen typical of the female. If he should survive the eventual death and disappearance of the parasite, he may thereafter produce both eggs and sperm, having been rendered hermaphroditic by the hormonal maladjustments caused by the parasite.

The loss of unneeded structures by endoparasites demonstrates an important evolutionary precept: *the unused tends to be lost.* The survival value of such deletion

Figure 6.27 □ Stages in life cycle of the parasitic barnacle *Sacculina carcini.* (*a*) Nauplius larva, resembling that of nonparasitic barnacles. (*After Smith.*) (*b*) Rootlike processes of parasite growing along intestine of host, a crab. (*After Smith.*) (*c*) Rhizoids of parasite extending throughout trunk and limbs of host (depicted as if host's body were transparent). The main body of the parasite emerges as a bulbous mass at host's thorax and abdomen junction. (*From Colin Nicol.*)

is apparent; less developmental energy need be used in the elaboration of structures that will be of no use to the organism. Development is thus abbreviated by deletion of the useless structure and energy is conserved.

Great fecundity is characteristic of endoparasites. Larval life is apt to be hazardous, for few are fortunate enough to find an appropriate host before their resources are depleted and they perish. A typical parasitic roundworm, *Ascaris,* lays millions of eggs at the rate of 200,000 per day, which are shed with the host's feces. These eggs embryonate in the soil for 2 or 3 weeks, after which the larva remains within the protective eggshell for several more weeks, during which time the eggs may be accidentally swallowed by an appropriate host (man, swine, or horses). Flukes also produce great quantities of eggs. Particularly noteworthy is the Japanese blood fluke, *Schistosoma japonicum,* the female of which releases about *five million eggs per day* over a lifespan of several years!

Precise mechanisms govern the *hatching* of the eggs: moisture and temperature must be favorable; also, in the case of liver flukes of the genus *Opisthorchis,* for example, the egg will not hatch until it is ingested by the specific snail that serves as its larval host.

Metagenesis, a condition in which the life history of the parasite involves several consecutive generations differing in appearance and mode of life, makes possible both the exploitation of alternative hosts, and the opportunity for the inclusion of both asexually and sexually reproducing stages in the life cycle. The malarial parasite, *Plasmodium,* exploits alternate hosts in a life cycle involving several specialized generations (Figure 6.28). A female *Anopheles* mosquito is the host during the sexually reproducing part of the life cycle and a vertebrate is host for the asexually reproducing forms. While feeding, the mosquito transmits infective sporozoites to a host such as man. Within this host, the sporozoites typically concentrate in such organs as the liver, where they feed and undergo asexual reproduction by multiple fission, each giving rise to several merozoites only 2 or 3 μm in diameter. Each merozoite enters a red blood cell and changes to an amoeboid feeding form (the trophozoite). The trophozoite grows and in turn undergoes multiple fission, yielding 6 to 36 merozoites. The infected red blood corpuscles then burst, releasing the merozoites into the blood stream. Each merozoite again invades a red blood cell, and the cycle of growth, multiple fission, and release is repeated with a periodicity that varies according to the species of *Plasmodium* involved. Because the reproduction and release of each generation of merozoites is synchronous, each such release elicits a toxic chill-fever reaction. In malignant tertian malaria, caused by *P. falciparum,* a new generation of merozoites is liberated every 24 to 48 hours, causing an acute chill-fever response that may prove fatal.

After a while some of the merozoites change into sexual forms or gametocytes. These can develop no further until they are transferred into the body of a mosquito that feeds upon the infected blood. Within the mosquito's gut, the gametocytes mature into male and female types, which fuse in pairs to form zygotes. Each zygote changes into a motile ookinete ("moving egg"), which burrows into the wall of the mosquito's stomach and enlarges to form an oocyst. This soon divides internally, producing a number of sporozoites, which migrate to the mosquito's salivary glands preliminary to being passed again to the vertebrate host. The life cycle of *Plasmodium* thus involves one sexual and an indefinite number of asexual generations, each having a characteristic morphology and mode of life, the sexual generation exploiting an insect host, the asexual generations, a vertebrate host.

Flukes commonly exploit two or even three alternate hosts, within only one of which the sexual generation can occur (Figure 6.29). The sexual generation, or so-called adult, of the Chinese liver fluke (*Opisthorchis sinensis*) inhabits the bile passages of various fish-eating mammals including man. The flukes are monoecious, each producing both eggs and sperm. Cross insemination occurs by copulation, and the fertilized eggs, protectively encased, pass down the bile ducts of the host to the intestine and are voided with the feces. These eggs develop into microscopic ciliated larvae (miracidia) but do not hatch unless ingested by an aquatic snail. Within the snail, each miracidium grows and changes shape, becoming a saclike sporocyst. After further growth, each sporocyst buds internally, producing an asexual generation of rediae. Each redia has an alimentary tract, a nervous system, and an excretory system. The young rediae burst out of the sporocyst and grow, feeding upon the snail's liver. Eventually they in turn reproduce asexually, forming internal buds that become tadpole-shaped cercariae. Cercariae are in fact the juveniles of the "adult" or sexual generation, but they must undergo several more adventures before reaching maturity. The cercariae abandon their snail host and search for

Figure 6.28 □ **Life cycle of malarial parasite, *Plasmodium*, in mosquito and mammal.**

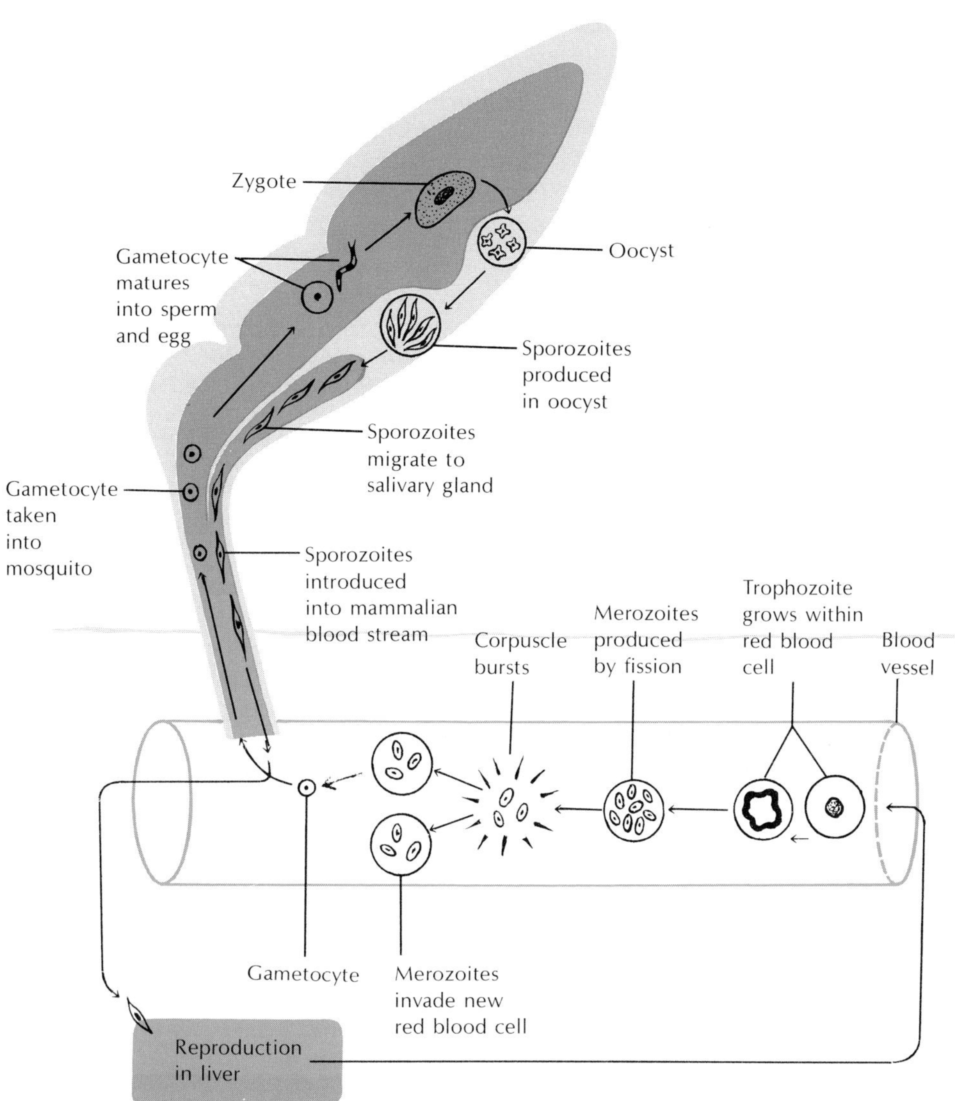

certain species of fish, to which they attach by suckers. They burrow through the integument of their new host, penetrate the muscles, and encyst as quiescent metacercariae. Eventually the fish may be eaten by a mammal, whereupon the mammal's digestive juices activate the metacercariae, which then migrate up the bile duct to their new host's liver. Here they grow to sexual maturity and may live as long as 30 years, continuously producing eggs. The exploitation of three such different hosts permits *Opisthorchis* greatly to enhance its distribution and to have a better chance to survive.

Asexual reproduction is a common adaptation of endoparasites: it greatly promotes survival because each of the primary sexually produced larvae that finds a suitable host can give rise to a large number of parasites asexually, by fission or budding. A single *Plasmodium* sporozoite can divide to yield from 6 to 36 merozoites, *each of which,* after feeding as a trophozoite, can yield another 6 to 36! Within as few as six such asexual generations, an initial infection by a *single* sporozoite could produce nearly a *billion* merozoites! The asexual budding of the sporocyst and redia in flukes also makes possible an astronomical rate of increase within the snail host. A single miracidium of the blood fluke *Schistosoma* may yield 200,000 cercariae, each of which is capable of growing into an "adult" fluke. Coupling this asexual prolificacy with the tremendous egg-laying capacity of the female, one can readily understand why this fluke is so successful.

In summary, we have seen that assumption of a parasitic mode of life, especially in the case of endoparasitism, where the

Figure 6.29 □ **Life cycle of human liver fluke, *Opisthorchis sinensis.* Stages: (1) adult sheds egg; (2) egg ingested by snail in which miracidium hatches and develops into sporocyst; (3) rediae are produced in sporocyst and in turn (4) produce cercariae, which (5) leave snail to find fish host and encyst in muscle; (6) ingestion of raw fish releases metacercariae, which find their way to bile duct, where they mature into adults.**

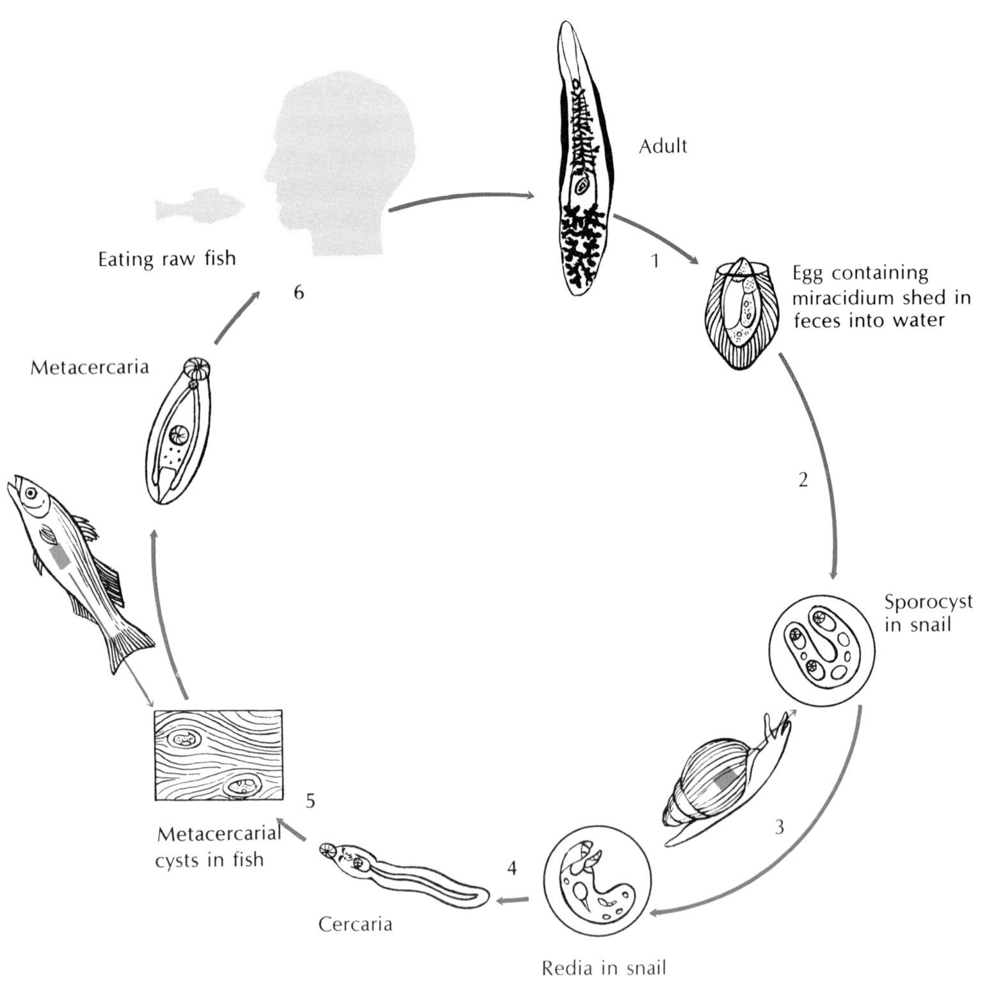

host serves the parasite as both larder and habitat, imposes on the parasite an entirely new set of selective factors. These factors encourage the perpetuation of genetic variants that increase the efficiency of the parasite, reduce its pathogenicity, and enhance its prolificacy. Organs, behavioral patterns, and so forth, which may be essential to the free-living relatives of the parasites, may be useless in the new existence, and thus selection favors any mutation that tends toward their elimination. Endoparasites are so highly specialized and so well adapted to their peculiar and often elaborate modes of existence that, in spite of the loss of their independence, they cannot usually be considered truly *degenerate.*

D Attraction of symbionts to host

Symbionts—parasitic, commensal, or mutualistic—locate their hosts by means of specific tactile, thermal, and chemical cues emanating from the host. Ticks that parasitize mammals respond to a limited series of cues. The first of these is the odor of butyric acid, a component of mammalian skin oils. The tick's response to this cue is simply to drop off the vegetation where it may have clung motionless for months. If it falls onto the mammal's fur, contact with the hair serves as a tactile cue, setting off a random running response. When, in the course of these random movements, the tick comes close to the host's skin, a third stimulus, warmth, extinguishes the running response and initiates the boring response. Thus only three stimuli—one chemical, one tactile, and one thermal—serve to trigger the three major motor components of the tick's food-seeking repertory. A fourth, climbing up vegetation after the host has been abandoned and a molt or egg-laying period has ensued, apparently is a geotaxis, a movement away from the pull of gravity. The long wait for a suitable host is not difficult for a tick to endure, for these arthropods can fast for very long periods. It has been reported that a tick kept at the Zoological Institute at Rostock survived without food for 18 years!

Chemical cues are probably the most important in initially guiding a symbiont to its host or partner. Studies conducted on a polychaete commensal on starfish showed that these worms could distinguish between plain sea water and sea water in which their potential host had lived, even if the host had been removed. Given a choice, the worm would swim through a tube connecting its aquarium with one inhabited by its preferred host species, in preference to alternative routes leading to tanks of species with which it did not associate. Maintenance of a symbiotic association probably involves not only *chemotaxis* (movement toward an attractive chemical) but also *thigmotaxis* (the tendency to remain in contact with the host due to meaningful tactile cues). If the association improves the chances for survival of at least one of the partners, any means by which these cues may be genetically fixed as innate "memories" will be selectively favored.

E Host defenses

The parasitic relationship has served as a selective force favoring evolution of defensive mechanisms on the part of the host. An organism's first line of defense against parasitic invasion is its intact integument. If this should be breached, or entrance made by way of the respiratory or digestive tracts, a number of other defensive responses are set in motion that may culminate not only in the repulsion of the invaders but in the acquisition of immunity against further attack. These responses have been most thoroughly studied in laboratory rats, mice, and rabbits, and our comments will therefore be restricted mainly to a consideration of these species. It is likely that invertebrates use similar although less effective ways of combatting parasites, but the *particular* cells and organs discussed below, which serve defensively in vertebrates, are not identifiable as such in invertebrates.

Once parasitic organisms have actually entered the tissues of the host, their presence attracts large numbers of amoeboid cells; these are components of a diffuse defensive system made up of various blood and tissue cells, all of which are motile and capable of concentrating at sites of infection. The relationships among these cells are uncertain, and it is likely that several types are actually morphological variants of the same cell in different functional states.

The two major types of defensive wandering cells in mammals are *granulocytes* and *agranulocytes* (Figure 6.30), the former having conspicuous granules in their cytoplasm and the latter lacking cytoplasmic granules except when engaged in active secretion. The generally recognized kinds of mammalian granulocytes are neutrophils, with granules that do not take up differential stains, eosinophils, with acid-staining granules, and basophils, with alkaline-staining granules. These cells most commonly occur in the bloodstream, which they enter from their main site of origin in the red bone marrow. Neutrophils constitute 70 percent of all *leucocytes* (white blood corpuscles) in man, but only 30 percent of the total in rodents. A fourth type of granulocyte, the mast cell, wanders through the tissues rather than frequenting the bloodstream. The roles of neutrophils and mast cells are fairly well understood, but those of eosinophils and basophils remain only vaguely defined. Invasion by parasitic worms specifically mobilizes the eosinophils; these cells also play a part in the inflammatory response, which helps to recruit other defensive cells to a site of infection.

Agranulocytes include lymphocytes and monocytes, cells with large, round to kidney-shaped nuclei, and clear, nearly agranular cytoplasm. Monocytes are thought by some to be merely overgrown lymphocytes, while others consider them to be a distinct cell type. Lymphocytes are produced in the *lymphoid organs:* the thymus, the spleen, and the lymph nodes that are scattered along the course of the lymph vessels, veinlike vessels which collect tissue fluid and drain it into the bloodstream. Entering the lymphatic drainage, lymphocytes ultimately reach the bloodstream, where they represent some 25 to 30 percent of all circulating leucocytes in man, while in rodents they constitute nearly 70 percent. In man the total number of circulating leucocytes averages 5,000 to 7,000/mm^3, as compared with a red corpuscle count averaging 5,000,000/mm^3, but during the course of infection the leucocyte count may double or treble.

A lymphocyte is thought to have two alternative courses of development open to it. It may become *phagocytic* (capable of devouring microbes and damaged tissue cells), and grow into a *macrophage* ("large eater"). Alternatively, lymphocytes may multiply rapidly, forming secretory cells known as *plasma cells* that are the producers of *antibodies;* these are specific proteins that attack parasites or neutralize their toxins.

Figure 6.30 □ Sites of production of defensive cells in the human body and major types of defensive cells. Only a few lymph nodes are shown of the many actually present, and only one locus of red bone marrow is indicated.

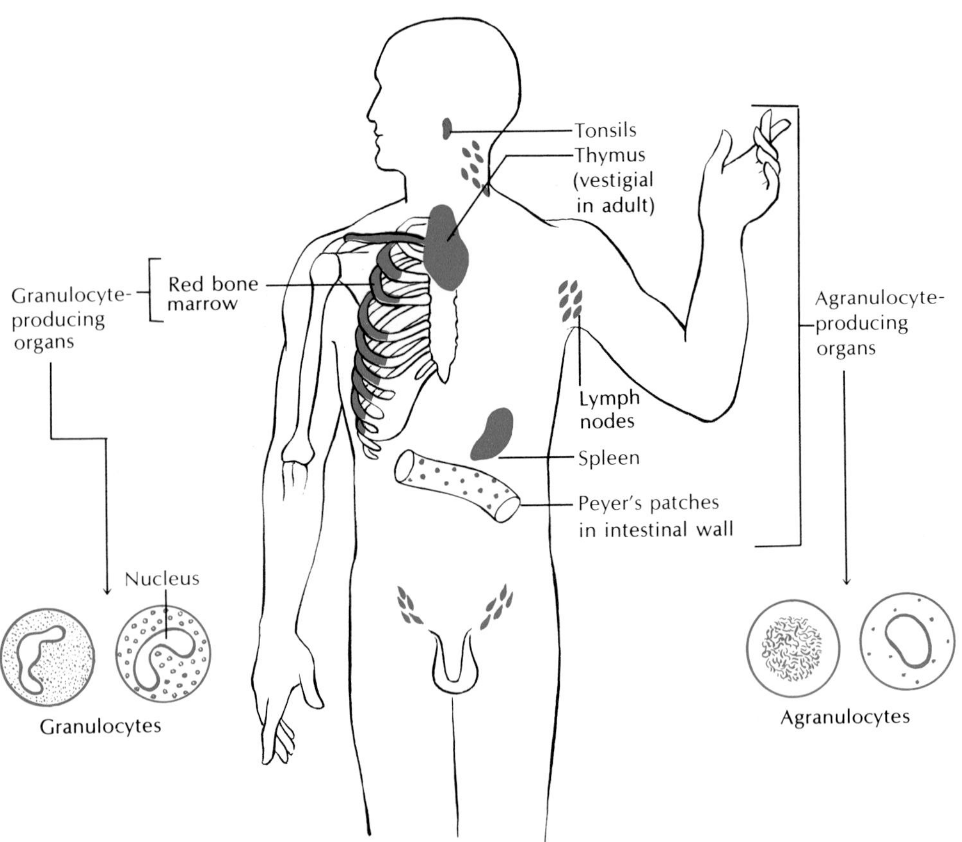

Thus, if the phagocytic defensive cells have been unable to accomplish the immediate destruction of the invaders by eating them, further defensive measures are taken: (1) plasma cells are proliferated and begin to secrete antibodies; (2) should the parasite resist the host's antibodies (as tuberculosis bacilli may, because of their protective capsule), connective tissue cells congregate and wall off the invaders in a nodule of scar tissue. Such nodules secreted around concentrations of tuberculosis bacilli become impregnated by calcium deposits and form hard tubercles. Within the tubercles the bacilli remain alive but unable to spread throughout the host's body. Walnut-sized nodules are constructed around larger parasites such as lung flukes, usually confining but not killing the parasite.

Antibodies are produced in response to the presence of some *foreign protein* in the body. During embryonic development there is a period of "self-recognition," in which the tissues come to "recognize" the body's own native proteins. After this, the defensive cells respond to all other proteins as alien substances. Proteins not native to a particular organism are termed *antigens* because they elicit an *immune response*—the production of specific antibodies. The immune response is normally elicited by the presence of a parasite; however, it also must be taken into account during certain medical procedures such as blood transfusion and organ transplantation. In transplantation of organs (such as the kidney or heart), unless donor and recipient are identical twins, rejection of engrafted tissue normally takes place, simply because the graft contains proteins foreign to the body of the host. The success of organ transplants thus depends on a hazardous suppression of the recipient's defensive mechanisms.

Chemically, all antibodies must be similar, for they probably stem from a single precursor, *gamma globulin,* a protein found in blood plasma. Functionally, they are categorized as *antitoxins* (which neutralize the toxins released by the parasite), *agglutinins* (which cause affected microbes to clump together), *lysins* (which cause the microbes literally to disintegrate), and *opsonins* (which make the parasites more susceptible to attack by phagocytes). The differences in action may be due less to differences in the antibodies themselves, than in the nature of the parasite's susceptibility to their action.

Study of the host's defensive responses has been made easier by the discovery that they may be elicited merely by an injection of purified antigen, instead of by the introduction of the living parasite. The antigen alone cannot multiply or "fight back," and thus it is relatively easy to determine what takes place in defense mobilization.

Following the introduction of antigen, granulocytes—neutrophils and mast cells in particular—are quickly attracted to the area. Here the neutrophils begin to ingest and destroy the antigen molecules. The mast cells, on the other hand, disintegrate, releasing substances that increase inflammation and attract other defensive cells. The neutrophils also soon begin to break up, but by this time the agranulocytes have arrived on the scene. Some of these begin to feed upon the antigen together with fragments of neutrophils and mast cells, quickly growing into large cells that begin to multiply. Meanwhile, certain lymphocytes also start to multiply, producing plasma cells that commence to secrete an antibody specific for that particular antigen. This takes place even when the organism has never before been exposed to that antigen! If the combination of phagocytosis and local antibody production completely destroys the antigen (that is, the parasite), the defensive cells soon depart, after devouring any remaining debris. Wandering connective tissue cells stay to effect repairs with scar tissue.

If the antigen reaches the lymphatic drainage (see Figure 14.21) rather than being disposed of locally, changes occur in the lymphoid organs—first in the lymph nodes concentrated along the course of the lymph vessels draining the area. Within these nodes certain lymphocytes begin to proliferate rapidly, each forming a cluster of identical cells. Most of the lymphocytes in each cluster change into actively secreting plasma cells. These produce large quantities of antibody that pass into the lymph and eventually reach the bloodstream, persisting there as *plasma antibody.* The blood antibody level may rise so high during infection that it affects the parasites wherever they may lodge in the body.

Up to this point, the host's defenses have operated primarily at the *cellular* level, but a persistent infection ultimately provokes generalized (*systemic*) reactions. The body temperature may rise, usually damaging the parasite more than the host (although sustained or acute fever may itself prove debilitating). In addition, an endocrine gland, the adrenal cortex, now puts out increased amounts of a hormone that fortifies the body in general against stress and reinforces the response of the scattered defensive cells.

IMMUNITY If the organism successfully overcomes an initial infection, it achieves a state of *active immunity* that prevents future reinfection. Active immunity is of variable duration. In man, immunity to the common cold virus, for instance, lasts but a few weeks, whereas immunity to measles virus lasts a lifetime.

The persistence of a high concentration of circulating antibody for some time after infection suggested the use of "serum antibody" to confer *passive immunity* on the recipient. (Serum is blood plasma from which the cells and clotting factors have been removed merely by allowing the blood to stand in a container until a clot forms.) Purified serum antibody can be obtained from horses that have been inoculated with bacteria causing human disease. It aids recovery if a patient's own immune response is feeble, but such passive immunity does not last and the individual can be reinfected.

Because the active immunity that results from the mobilization of the body's own immune response is relatively permanent, weakened antigen (toxoid), killed pathogens, or strains of reduced virulence bred specifically for this purpose are inoculated into the body in controlled dosages that stimulate the production of antibody while minimizing the systemic involvement. Such use of the parasites themselves, or their products, to stimulate active immunity was first made near the close of the eighteenth century by Edward Jenner. This English physician noted that milkmaids who contracted a mild disease, cowpox (*vaccinia*), from their bovine associates were immune to the deadly smallpox. Jenner successfully immunized people against smallpox by *vaccinating* them with fluid from cowpox vesicles, containing (as we now know) active vaccinia virus. Cowpox and smallpox are caused by viruses so closely related that immunity to one confers immunity to the other. This historic event founded the science of immunology and made it possible for large portions of mankind to be protected against its most deadly parasites.

At the same time, *immunological procedures have relaxed the operation of natural selection,* for without such intervention only the more resistant individuals previously survived attack. The genetic basis of human resistance to certain parasites is shown by the fact that Europeans, who have over the centuries undergone selection toward resistance to parasites to which they were routinely exposed (such as measles virus and tuberculosis bacilli), inadvertently communicated these parasites to non-European peoples with whom they came in contact in the course of exploration and commerce. These peoples, including Polynesians and Eskimos, proved much less resistant to such parasites (because they had not previously lived in contact with them) and suffered heavy loss of life; the measles virus, for instance, was responsible for the virtual eradication of native Hawaiians and the collapse of their culture. This severe selection toward resistance took place within a generation or two, rather than gradually over many generations.

THE MECHANISM OF ANTIBODY PRODUCTION The theoretical capacity of the body to produce a specific antibody against *any* of the millions of proteins foreign to that body has yet to be explained satisfactorily. We also understand little of what constitutes "immunological memory," the basis of the accelerated immune response elicited by reinfection with some antigen previously experienced.

By using antigen tagged with a radioactive tracer it has been found that particles of antigen remain within the macrophages for a year or more after the initial infection, being engulfed by other phagocytes when the old cells die. When the animal is experimentally reinoculated with the same antigen during this period, the defensive response takes a somewhat different course than it did on the first occasion. Once more, the infected area attracts phagocytes, of which a number still carry particles of antigen stored from the previous encounter. As these begin to feed upon the new antigen particles, they prove *hypersensitive* to them and soon disintegrate. Eosinophils, attracted in much greater concentrations than during the first infection, penetrate the sensitized macrophages and accelerate their disintegration. Some factor liberated by the eosinophils or the disintegrating macrophages (very likely the antigen particles or some combination product thereof) promotes the immune response: now, much more quickly than on the previous occasion, plasma cells are produced that begin to release antibody.

The apparently indefinite retention of antigen particles within the macrophages points to a possible explanation of lasting immunity. Two alternative proposals have been put forth concerning the mechanism by which specific antibodies are made: (1) the *instruction* and (2) the *selection theories.*

According to the instruction theory any plasma cell (or its precursor, the lymphocyte) is capable of converting gamma globulin into a specific antibody by using the particular antigen as a *template* on which a complementary antibody molecule can be shaped. Such "instructed" cells, and their descendants, would retain a "memory" of the shape of that antigen, and therefore be capable of rapidly synthesizing more antibody should the antigen once more be introduced.

The selection theory suggests that in early life the rapidly dividing lymphocytes mutate frequently, resulting in a diversification of the genetic code that controls the manufacture of gamma globulin. Each mutant cell type would be capable of making only one or a few specific antibodies; that is, it would be *competent* to react to only certain antigens—but the millions of possible mutant types produced could *collectively* recognize and respond to any possible foreign protein. During this period of genetic diversification, mutants would appear that would produce antibodies to the cell's own proteins, but these would quickly be destroyed leaving only those that were nonreactive to the body's own proteins. Actually, since the antibody reacts with only a small portion of the antigen molecule, it is estimated that, instead of *millions* of types of mutant lymphocytes, only about 160,000 types would be needed to recognize any protein as either "native" or "foreign." According to the selection theory, the presence of a given antigen would stimulate the proliferation of *only* those lymphocytes which were genetically competent to respond to it. This would explain why at the outset of an immune response only *certain cells* in the lymph nodes begin to multiply, while other lymphocytes "stand by" without participating in this proliferation.

It is interesting to note that these two theories account for the immune response on the basis of alternative means of achieving adaptation, namely, functional adaptability, and genetic mutability. The instruction theory proposes that any lymphocyte is originally competent to react with any antigen; it adapts functionally when confronted with an antigen and thereafter becomes incompetent to respond to any other antigen. The selection theory proposes genetic diversification of lymphocytes in early life, producing many strains that will then be selectively activated by the presence of the appropriate antigen.

Possibly both theories are true in part. Mutation may serve to create a number of genetic variants, each of which can be further committed by "instruction." "Uncommitted" lymphocytes would be those still competent to respond to a certain group of foreign proteins, while "committed" ones would have contacted *specific* antigens to which they were competent to respond and after this made but *one* kind of antibody.

DEFENSIVE ROLE OF THE THYMUS The thymus is a lymphoid organ of birds and mammals, in the latter lying under the breastbone near the heart. It is largest at birth, and in man starts to shrink when the individual is only 10 years old. In newborn mice, the thymus constitutes 0.5 to 1 percent of the entire body weight. It is strange that the functions of so conspicuous an organ should have been clarified only recently. One function of the thymus can be disclosed by removing this organ from newborn mice. These animals grow normally for some time, but eventually succumb to a wasting disease. Upon autopsy, they are found to have a severe lymphocyte deficiency. Such thymectomized animals are completely incapable of producing antibodies, for even though a few lymphocytes are present from birth in their other lymphoid organs, these cells apparently cannot respond to antigens. This failure of the immune response may be tested by transplanting patches of foreign skin to the thymectomized subjects: although grafts even from mice of another strain are rejected by normal mice, thymectomized mice will actually accept grafts of *rat* skin! Experiments such as these have led to the conclusion that the thymus is the source of most of the lymphocytes that later populate the spleen, lymph nodes, and other lymphoid tissues. During early life, the thymic lymphocytes multiply some ten times more rapidly than the rest of the tissues. It would be during this time of rapid proliferation that the proposed mutation and genetic diversification would take place, as discussed above.

Another recent investigation appears to have resolved the long-standing dispute as to whether or not the thymus secretes a hormone. Mice thymectomized within 12 hr of birth each received 3 or 4 weeks later an implant consisting of an entire thymus removed from a newborn mouse. The implant was enclosed in a small chamber or capsule sealed with a filter of 0.5 μm mesh, which prevented the escape of the enclosed cells. To determine whether any lymphoid cells could pass a filter of such gauge, the investigators first used as controls animals that received implants of such capsules containing not normal but highly malignant lymphoid tumor tissue. The malignancy of the tumor was such that the escape of only a few cells would shortly cause the animal to develop the cancer. Since none of this control group became cancerous, it was considered certain that no lymphocytes could pass the filter. Therefore, any effect which the implanted thymus exerted on its thymectomized host would necessarily be due to the passage through the filter of some material of subcellular dimensions. It was in fact found that the implant exerted profound effects on all of the host's lymphoid organs. The few lymphocytes that were already present in the spleen and lymph nodes not only began to proliferate under the influence of the implant, but also became competent to respond to antigens. Thus it appears that the mammalian thymus is doubly responsible for immunological competence, serving both as a site where most of the body's lymphocytes are originally produced, and as an endocrine gland secreting a hormone that renders lymphocytes competent to respond to antigens. The thymus of mammals and birds is therefore of primary importance in the superior defensive response of these animals against parasitic invasion.

The preceding discussion of the immune response exemplifies the principle that ecological relationships operate as selective factors at all levels of biotic organization, for although the parasite-host relationship involves the interaction of organisms, the battle for survival goes on also at the cellular and molecular levels. When, through natural selection, a balance is struck between the parasite's adaptive potential and the host's defensive mechanisms, both species can coexist with minimal harm to either.

REVIEW AND DISCUSSION

1 What evidence is there that the structure of biotic communities is often shaped as much by evolution toward coadaptation of the sympatric biota as by tolerance of the prevailing abiotic conditions?

2 Several times in the earth's geologic past mass extinctions have occurred in which anywhere from one-third to two-thirds of the known fauna became extinct. Can you think of any conditions in which the loss of one or a few species from a community might lead to a mass extinction of many other species in that particular community?

3 Distinguish between each of the following pairs of terms, using specific illustrations: (a) *ecosystem* and *community;* (b) *inquilinist* and *endoparasite;* (c) *cooperation* and *mutualism;* (d) *mimicry* and *crypsis;* (e) *Batesian mimicry* and *Müllerian mimicry;* (f) *producer* and *consumer;* (g) *autotroph* and *photosynthesizer.*

4 Design an experiment to ascertain whether a given situation involving mimicry among sympatric species involves Müllerian or Batesian mimicry.

5 Design an experiment (other than the one described in this chapter) to test whether a certain case of apparent crypsis is actually effective in protecting the cryptic species against predators.

6 Summarize and evaluate Blest's experiment on the adaptive significance of "eyespots." Can you think of other animals that rely for protection on some comparable defensive display?

7 What are at least three prerequisite conditions that must pertain for a Batesian mimic to gain protection from a resemblance?

8 Why are antipredator mechanisms rare among plants? Where might you expect to find the greater majority of plants that have developed means of discouraging the depredations of herbivorous animals? Explain why such devices are especially necessary for these particular plants in this habitat.

9 Why must one be cautious in concluding that a certain community relationship represents a neutralistic situation? Explain, with examples.

10 Explain the conceptual difference between a *food chain* and a *biomass pyramid.* What relationships are shown better by each type of diagram?

11 Explain the concept of *nutritional efficiency.* Why is there so great a decrement in biomass at each step in a food chain? How does the biotic world compensate for this energy depletion? Explain how the contribution of symbiotic algae to the ecological efficiency of green hydra is sufficient to tip the balance in a situation involving heterospecific competition.

12 Explain the concept of the *niche* and its implications for community relationships. Summarize *Gause's rule* and explain why it is rarely seen in operation in an evolved community. Give examples of situations in which you would expect to see this rule in operation. Need the competitors always be in competition for an entire niche? Explain.

13 Why is the predator-prey relationship of benefit to both the species that are concerned?

14 Postulate a situation in which species that are ecologically equivalent may come into competition with one another. Can you think of any specific instances in which this has taken place?

15 Distinguish, with examples, among the three main types of symbiotic relationships, and explain how symbiotic relationships as a whole differ from those which are nonsymbiotic.

16 Specify at least three different behavioral adaptations shown by cuckoos that are necessary for the success of their parasitic life. What adaptive behaviors common to birds have been sacrified by cuckoos? Do the host species exhibit any defenses against these parasites?

17 Contrast the effects of parasitism and of predation upon the animal populations that serve respectively as host or as prey.

18 What selective factors operate upon endoparasites, and with what results? How does natural selection operate upon pathogenicity?

19 What defenses have host species evolved against their parasites? Compare and contrast the "instruction" and the "selection" theories of antibody production. What kinds of experiments might you use to determine whether one, both, or neither of these theories are correct?

20 Distinguish between active and passive immunity. How do immunological procedures affect the operation of natural selection on human populations?

AHMADJIAN, V. "The Fungi of Lichens," *Sci. Amer.,* **208** (1963).

BILLINGS, W. D. *Plants and the Ecosystem.* Belmont, Calif.: Wadsworth Publishing Company, Inc., 1964. Plant distribution and major terrestrial biomes are examined in this excellent work.

BROCK, T. D. "The Ecosystem and the Steady State," *Bioscience,* **17** (1967). Homeostatic mechanisms operate at the ecosystem level.

BROWER, L. P. "Ecological Chemistry," *Sci. Amer.,* **220** (1969). Insects may become unpalatable by feeding upon plants poisonous to vertebrates but not to insects.

BURNET, M. "The Mechanism of Immunity," *Sci. Amer.,* **204** (1961).

——— "The Thymus Gland," *Sci. Amer.,* **207** (1962).

CLAUSEN, C. P. *Biological Control of Insect Pests in the Continental United States,* U.S. Dept. of Agriculture Tech. Bull. No. 1139. Washington, D.C.: U.S. Government Printing Office, 1956. Summarizes progress in controlling insect pests by nonchemical means.

CLEVELAND, L. R. "An Ideal Partnership," *Sci. Monthly,* **67** (1948).

CRUDEN, R. W. "Birds as Agents of Long-Distance Dispersal for Disjunct Plant Groups of the Temperate Western Hemisphere," *Evolution,* **20** (1966). Migrating birds may be responsible for carrying plant seeds from temperate North America to temperate South America.

DARLING, F. F. "Wildlife Husbandry in Africa," *Sci. Amer.,* **203** (1960).

DICE, L. R. "Effectiveness of Selection by Owls of Deer-mice (*Peromyscus maniculatus*) Which Contrast in Color with Their Background," *Contrib. Lab. Vert. Biol., Ann Arbor,* **34** (1947). An experiment on the protective value of crypsis.

——— *Natural Communities.* Ann Arbor: University of Michigan Press, 1952. A significant discussion of the self-regulatory aspects of animal communities.

DUNBAR, M. J. "The Evolution of Stability in Marine Environments: Natural Selection at the Level of the Ecosystem," *Amer. Nat.,* **94** (1960). A discussion of selective factors operating within marine communities.

EHRLICH, P. R., AND P. H. RAVEN "Butterflies and Plants," *Sci. Amer.,* **216** (1967).

ELTON, C. S. *The Ecology of Invasions by Animals and Plants.* New York: John Wiley & Sons, Inc., 1958. An advanced and well-documented consideration of the effects on established communities of invading species.

LACK, D. *The Natural Regulation of Animal Numbers.* London and New York: Oxford University Press, 1954. Presents the theory that the population levels of animal species are kept in balance with the carrying capacity of the habitat by conspecific as well as heterospecific interactions.

LAMB, I. M. "Lichens," *Sci. Amer.,* **201** (1959).

LEOPOLD, A. S. "Too Many Deer," *Sci. Amer.,* **193** (1955).

LEPPIK, E. E. "Evolutionary Relationship between Entomophilous Plants and Anthophilous Insects," *Evolution,* **11** (1957). Six distinguishable levels in floral evolution are correlated with corresponding stages in the sensory development of pollinating insects.

LEVEY, R. H. "The Thymus Hormone," *Sci. Amer.,* **211** (1964). An ingenious experiment establishes the existence of a thymic hormone.

LIMBAUGH, C. "Cleaning Symbiosis," *Sci. Amer.,* **205** (1961). A new heterospecific relationship is discovered in marine communities.

MEEUSE, B. J. D. "The Voodoo Lily," *Sci. Amer.,* **215** (1966).

MURPHY, R. C. "The Oceanic Life of the Antarctic," *Sci. Amer.,* **207** (1962). The biota and nutritional relationships of an Antarctic marine community are examined.

RIPPER, W. E. "Effect of Pesticides on Balance of Arthropod Populations," *Ann. Rev. Entomol.,* **1** (1956). Presents information concerning the effects of insecticides on natural balances.

ROGERS, W. P. *The Nature of Parasitism.* New York: Academic Press, Inc., 1962. An important reference work on an interesting and unusual type of heterospecific relationship.

ROTHSCHILD, M., AND T. CLAY *Fleas, Flukes and Cuckoos.* London: William Collins & Co., Ltd., 1952. An entertaining consideration of parasitism.

SEARS, P. B. *The Ecology of Man: Condon Lectures.* Eugene, Oregon: University of Oregon Press, 1957. A well-known ecologist examines man's role in the ecosystem.

SIMMONS, K. E. L. "Interspecific

Territorialism," *Ibis,* **93** (1951). Certain birds defend their territories not only against their conspecifics but also against potential competitors of other species, by means of persistent aggressive behavior.

SMITH, R. F., AND W. W. ALLEN "Insect Control and the Balance of Nature," *Sci. Amer.,* **190** (1954).

SPEIRS, R. S. "How Cells Attack Antigens," *Sci. Amer.,* **210** (1964). Describes reactions to antigens of defensive cells in culture.

STEINHAUS, E. A. "Living Insecticides," *Sci. Amer.,* **195** (1956).

SUMNER, F. B. "Studies of Protective Color Changes, III. Experiments with Fishes Both as Predators and Prey," *Proc. Natl. Acad. Sci. U.S.,* **21** (1935). Classical experiments on animal camouflage are detailed in this research paper.

Chapter 7  ADAPTATION WITHIN THE SPECIES

RELATIONSHIPS AMONG CONSPECIFICS (members of the same species), are particularly characterized by the opposing factors of *competition* and *cooperation*. Both act as selective factors in the evolution of a species. We have seen that biotic diversification lessens competition within ecosystems by enabling each species to occupy a unique niche or role in the community. However, members of the *same* species must occupy the same niche; accordingly, competition for the necessities of life is more acute among conspecifics than among organisms of different species. At the same time, opportunity for cooperation is greater within a species than it is between different species, provided that competition is not so intense as to preclude such cooperation.

Although intraspecific competition is unavoidable and even beneficial in terms of maintaining the species' level of adaptation, in practice most species have evolved means whereby competition is somewhat alleviated and its effects upon the individual and group are tempered. Once it was held that living things characteristically interacted with their own kind in a "dog-eat-dog" savagery bred of overcrowding and near starvation. This fallacious concept served to justify such human institutions as warfare, enslavement of conspecifics, and genocide. Intensive study of a wide range of conspecific relationships has disclosed little precedent for such forms of behavior, which may in fact represent pathological outcomes of man's emancipation from the evolved safeguards that normally minimize overpopulation, overexploitation of the habitat, and mortal conflict within the species.

The effects of competition within a species are modulated by two factors: (1) *The prolificacy of the population.* In every generation the progeny outnumber the parents: this increase is regulated and usually balanced by premature mortality, only a certain proportion of the young surviving to become part of the breeding population. (2) *The heterogeneity of the population.* No sexually reproducing population is absolutely homogeneous. Changes in the hereditary material occur spontaneously and may be distributed throughout the breeding population (deme). Some of these variations are advantageous in competitive situations; so the carriers are likely to survive and reproduce—thus "survival of the fittest," a phrase that requires further inspection.

In the first place, this concept is *circular:* the fittest survive; *ergo,* those which have survived *are* the fittest. Observing contemporary forms of life, we are faced with a *fait accompli,* at least as regards the evolution of life to the present time. We assume that these survivors are the fittest because they have survived, but in fact it is possible that chance may have eradicated at their outset certain life forms potentially fitter to survive than are some now alive.

In the second place, "fitness" cannot be defined solely on grounds of superiority in size or vigor. For instance, under some circumstances smallness may equate with enhanced fitness. This was apparently the case in the development of a dwarf race of horse discovered trapped in a box canyon in the southwestern United States, as well as the dwarf elephants that once inhabited the coastal islands of California. In these restricted environments, any factor decreasing food requirements would favor survival. Hence the tinier individuals of each generation were more likely to survive than were

Figure 7.1 □ Genetic variation and survival: industrial melanism. Environment determines the survival value of coloration in the peppered moth, *Biston betularia.* Both peppered and dark (melanistic) forms appear in each photograph, (*a*) resting on pale, lichen-encrusted bark characteristic of trees in rural England and (*b*) resting on soot-blackened bark characteristic of trees in industrialized regions. (*From the experiments of Dr. H. B. D. Kettlewell, University of Oxford.*) The peppered form predominates in the countryside but in industrialized areas is outnumbered by the melanistic variant. Ever since the Industrial Revolution, the proportion of melanistic moths and other insects has been on the upswing.

(*a*)

(*b*)

larger ones with greater food requirements. Many factors, some quite difficult to analyze, contribute to the capacity to survive intraspecific competition.

In the third place, "survival" implies being able not merely to live but also to *produce progeny*. Less "fit" individuals do not necessarily die—they may in fact live just as long as their fitter brethren but produce *fewer* progeny. For example, competition for nesting space may result in only a portion of the birds of a breeding group being able to nest and produce young. In the case of sea gulls, the beginning of the mating season is marked by frequent aggressive encounters that determine the acquisition of small territories within which nesting will take place. Birds that fail in the competition for nesting space usually do not merely move to another area and nest but loiter about the edges of the established breeding area and rear no young that year. Similarly, aggressive encounters among males of such species as elk, deer, and sea lions influence the size of the "harem" of females that each male will control during that mating season. A single male American elk may impregnate a harem of 30 to 40 females in one season, fending off all other potential swains. Another male may control a harem of no more than 5 or 6 females. Others may be incapable of gathering a harem at all and thus will fail to transmit their hereditary traits, though leading long and healthy (but frustrated) lives.

Fourth, fitness is determined largely by the *particular set of circumstances* under which the organism lives. Should the habitat alter, there will be a concomitant change in the requirements for survival. As an example, in peppered moths the pale and melanistic (dark) color phases have varying survival value according to the environment in which a particular population lives. Pale moths are protectively colored when at rest on light surfaces such as the lichenous bark of trees in rural areas. Melanistic moths are at a selective disadvantage under these circumstances. However, in urbanized regions where soot blackens walls and bark and pollutants kill the lichens, dark moths are less conspicuous than are the paler members of their species (Figure 7.1). Statistical analyses of moth populations in Great Britain have indicated a shift in the frequency of these alternative traits, with melanistic moths being the more common in industrialized regions while the light phase remains more abundant in the agricultural areas. *Fitness, therefore, requires a combination of characteristics that make possible effective propagation under the given environmental conditions.*

7.2 □ COMPETITION-REDUCING ADAPTATIONS

Competition among conspecifics, although unavoidable, may be minimized by means of adaptations that (1) increase diversity within the species, (2) extend the range of the species, (3) decrease the prolificacy of the species, and (4) facilitate the social organization of demes in such ways that conflict is restricted and a better-than-marginal life is possible for most members.

A Diversification within the species

Adaptations that increase diversification and thereby alleviate competition within a given species include polymorphism, metamorphosis, and metagenesis. Any or all of these may be encountered within a single species.

POLYMORPHISM When a population of a species includes at the same time and within the same generation, various types of individuals that differ from one another structurally, functionally, and behaviorally, the species is said to be polymorphic ("many-formed"). Polymorphism occurs primarily in social and colonial species, in which the various specialized individuals do not compete severely, but rather *cooperate* in carrying out particular functions important for the existence of the whole group. The development of *castes* in social insects such as termites, ants, and bees makes possible a degree of *division of labor* that could not be realized in any nonpolymorphic insect species. Besides the obvious morphological differences, the castes differ markedly in behavior. Since insect behavior is chiefly determined by heredity, members of each caste will perform in predictable ways. Specialization in behavior is economical for the species, for the insect brain can accommodate only a limited repertory of motor patterns. Ant and termite castes include reproductive males and females and neuter workers and soldiers (Figure 7.2). Polymorphism in social insects frequently serves also as a means for *regulating prolificacy,* for in these insects all reproduction is carried out by a relatively few fertile individuals. All of the workers and drones in a given beehive, for example, are offspring of that hive's single queen. Building, food-gathering, care of young, and defense are conducted exclusively by infertile individuals, the workers.

The maintenance of a worker caste by social insects depends upon the action of chemical regulators termed *pheromones,* produced by the reproductive castes. Pheromones are either detected as odors, are absorbed through the integument, or are ingested by the individuals that they affect. Pheromones alter the organism's physiological state or influence its behavior. In termites the sexual development of the majority of juveniles or *nymphs* of both sexes is pheromonally repressed and they become neuter workers.

Figure 7.2 □ Model of portion of termitary, including royal chamber within which the queen is attended by workers. A developing queen is seen at upper left; a winged male ("king"), at lower right. (*Buffalo Museum of Science.*)

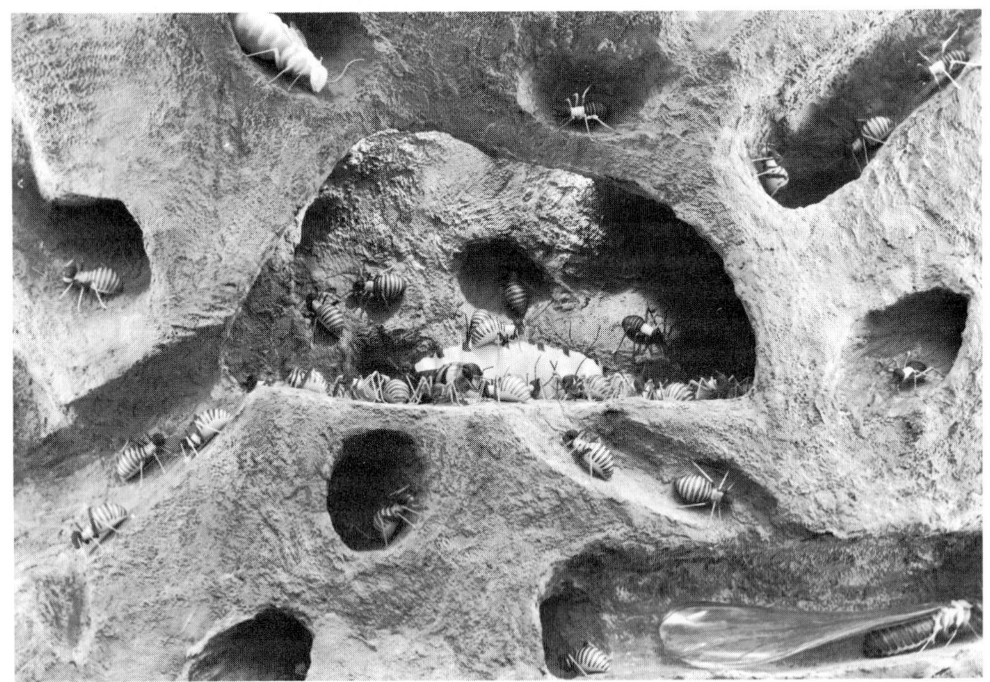

There are three caste-controlling pheromones in termites: (1) a *queen pheromone* secreted by sexually mature females, which inhibits female nymphs from developing into queens; (2) a *king pheromone* secreted by sexually mature males, which suppresses the sexual maturation of male nymphs; and (3) a *female-stimulating pheromone,* also secreted by the male, which *promotes* the maturation of nymphs into queens (but is effective only when the amount of queen pheromone is reduced). Death of members of either of the two "royal castes" results in a decrease in the concentration of the pheromone produced by that caste. In consequence, the development of nymphs of the same sex is no longer inhibited and a few mature sexually, making up the deficit of reproductive individuals. For example, if a queen were to die, the amount of queen pheromone taken in by the nymphs would correspondingly decrease, and a few would mature into queens. As these matured, they would begin to secrete queen pheromone, thereby inhibiting the sexual maturation of younger nymphs.

The sexual maturation of worker bees is also suppressed by means of pheromones that the queen bee produces and feeds to her workers. Many social insects engage in *mutual feeding,* during which the workers feed the reproductive females and then while grooming them eat their anal or oral exudates. The significance of this activity in disseminating ingestible pheromones responsible for caste development has only recently been discovered.

Polymorphism is also common among colonial animals such as hydroids. The term *colony* is loosely used in several connotations, but it is defined here as an aggregation of asexually produced individuals physically attached to one another. A single sexually produced larva initiates the colony, producing other individuals by asexual budding. The individuals that make up a colony are termed *zooids*. When colonialism is accompanied by polymorphism, division of labor is made possible. Otherwise, the only gain attendant upon a colonial mode of life may be that of increased size and structural strength (as in the case of reef corals). The colonial hydroid *Obelia* (Figure 7.3) produces on a common stalk two types of zooids: feeding polyps (hydranths) and reproductive polyps (gonangia). The hydranths capture prey by means of tentacles armed with nematocysts and digest it with their saccular gastrovascular cavities. The nutrients digested by one hydranth, however, are not only utilized by that one polyp but pass to neighboring zooids by way of intercommunicating branches of the gastrovascular cavities. Gonangia cannot capture prey or carry on digestion but are nutritionally dependent upon the hydranths. The gonangia bud off tiny medusae that represent the free-swimming sexual generation of the hydroid.

Figure 7.3 □ Colonial polymorphism. *Obelia* colony, with feeding polyps (hydranths) and reproductive polyps (gonangia), interconnected by a common gastrovascular cavity. The two types of individual arise by asexual budding from the common stalk; the entire colony develops from a single larva. (*Courtesy of Carolina Biological Supply Company.*)

An even more remarkable instance of colonial polymorphism in coelenterates is found in the Portuguese man-of-war, *Physalia* (Figure 7.4). Developed by budding from one original larva, the mobile colony includes individuals of several types. The original zooid differentiates into a gas-filled float (the pneumatophore), which provides buoyancy for the entire colony. The other zooids hang down from the float and are specialized for reproduction, feeding, or prey capture. The "tentacles" of *Physalia* are in fact dactylozooids ("finger animals"), slender polyps up to 8 m long armed with heavy batteries of nematocysts. The dactylozooids sting the prey (usually a fish) and, by contracting, laboriously raise it to the underside of the float. Here the gastrozooids carry out digestion. These zooids expand to become "all mouth," pressing themselves against the body of the prey and secreting digestive enzymes onto its surface. Clusters of sexual zooids (male and female gonophores) are produced from the base of the pneumatophore but remain attached to the colony rather than becoming independent medusae. These sexual individuals release eggs and sperm, which upon fertilization give rise to ciliated larvae, each having the potential to develop into a complete *Physalia* colony. Along with the other float-possessing hydrozoans (siphonophores), *Physalia* exploits colonial polymorphism as a means of creating its own floating support system, enabling it to live in the open sea. Through polymorphism it also has realized a significant degree of division of labor and thus can function in a much more sophisticated fashion than is possible for a solitary polyp.

METAMORPHOSIS A change in form (and often in manner of existence) during the lifetime of a single individual, called *metamorphosis*, often serves to reduce competition between adults and juveniles of the same species. Both the habitat and the food requirements of the larvae may differ from those of the adults (Figure 7.5). Some degree of metamorphosis always accompanies maturation, but the more abrupt the transition, the more dramatic it is and the more likely it is that adults and young are removed from competition with one another. A familiar example is the division of the amphibian life cycle into an aquatic, gill-breathing larval stage and a terrestrial, air-breathing adulthood. Frogs are carnivorous inhabitants of humid terrestrial environments. Their larvae, tadpoles, are legless aquatic vegetarians.

Dragonflies also are terrestrial air-breathers as adults but develop from gill-breathing aquatic juveniles (naiads). Both stages of the life history are carnivorous but

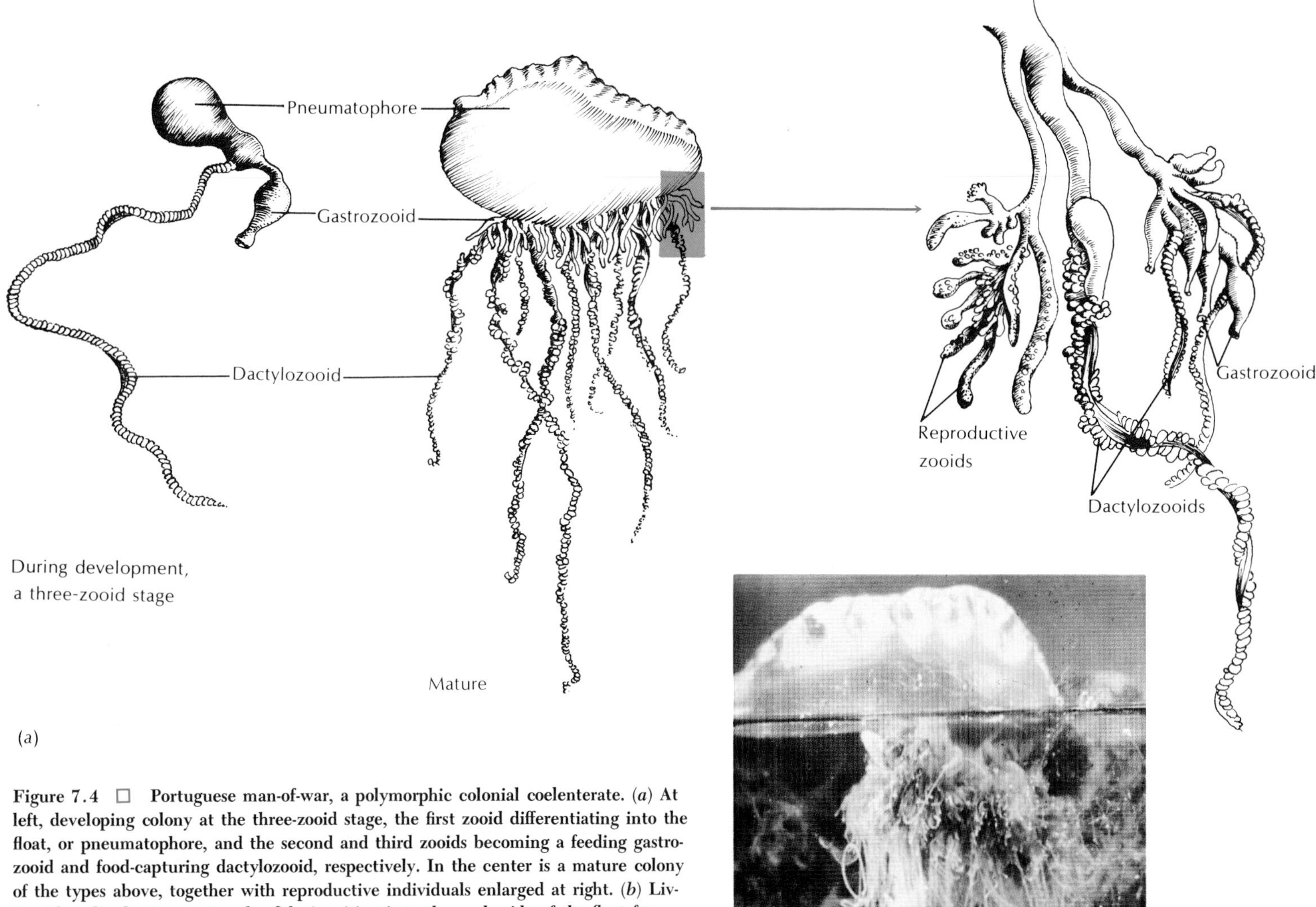

Figure 7.4 □ Portuguese man-of-war, a polymorphic colonial coelenterate. (*a*) At left, developing colony at the three-zooid stage, the first zooid differentiating into the float, or pneumatophore, and the second and third zooids becoming a feeding gastrozooid and food-capturing dactylozooid, respectively. In the center is a mature colony of the types above, together with reproductive individuals enlarged at right. (*b*) Living *Physalia*, having captured a fish, is raising it to the underside of the float for digestion. (*Courtesy of General Biological, Inc., Chicago.*) Through polymorphism this colony can perform as a single organism of a complexity much greater than that of any single zooid.

of course do not compete for prey, nor do they employ the same prey-capturing devices. The naiad has a formidable "underjaw," which shoots forward like a great scoop capable of trapping even small fish and tadpoles. The adult is a competent aerial performer, employing its legs as a basket with which to scoop up other insects in midflight. Just before the final molt to adulthood, the naiad becomes negatively geotactic; forsaking the bottom where it has lived for about two years, it clambers up any available reed and emerges into the air. The juvenile exoskeleton then splits and the adult emerges, expands its wings, and flies away. Although they may range far from water, adult female dragonflies must return to some quiet pond in order to lay their eggs.

Many insect larvae and adults do not compete because a "complete" metamorphic transition (that is, one in which a quiescent *pupal* stage separates the larval and adult stages) separates the two active phases of life. Caterpillars usually feed upon foliage, which they chew with biting jaws. During metamorphosis very different mouthparts develop. The coiled, tubular proboscis, which replaces the chewing mandibles of the larva, is used by the adult butterfly or moth in extracting nectar from flowers. The separation of adult and juvenile stages by diapause in the egg or pupal stage also

Figure 7.5 □ Metamorphosis as a competition-reducing adaptation: larval and adult mosquitoes do not compete with one another because the former are aquatic and feed upon plankton, whereas the adults live on land, the female as a parasitic bloodsucker and the male as a nectar feeder.

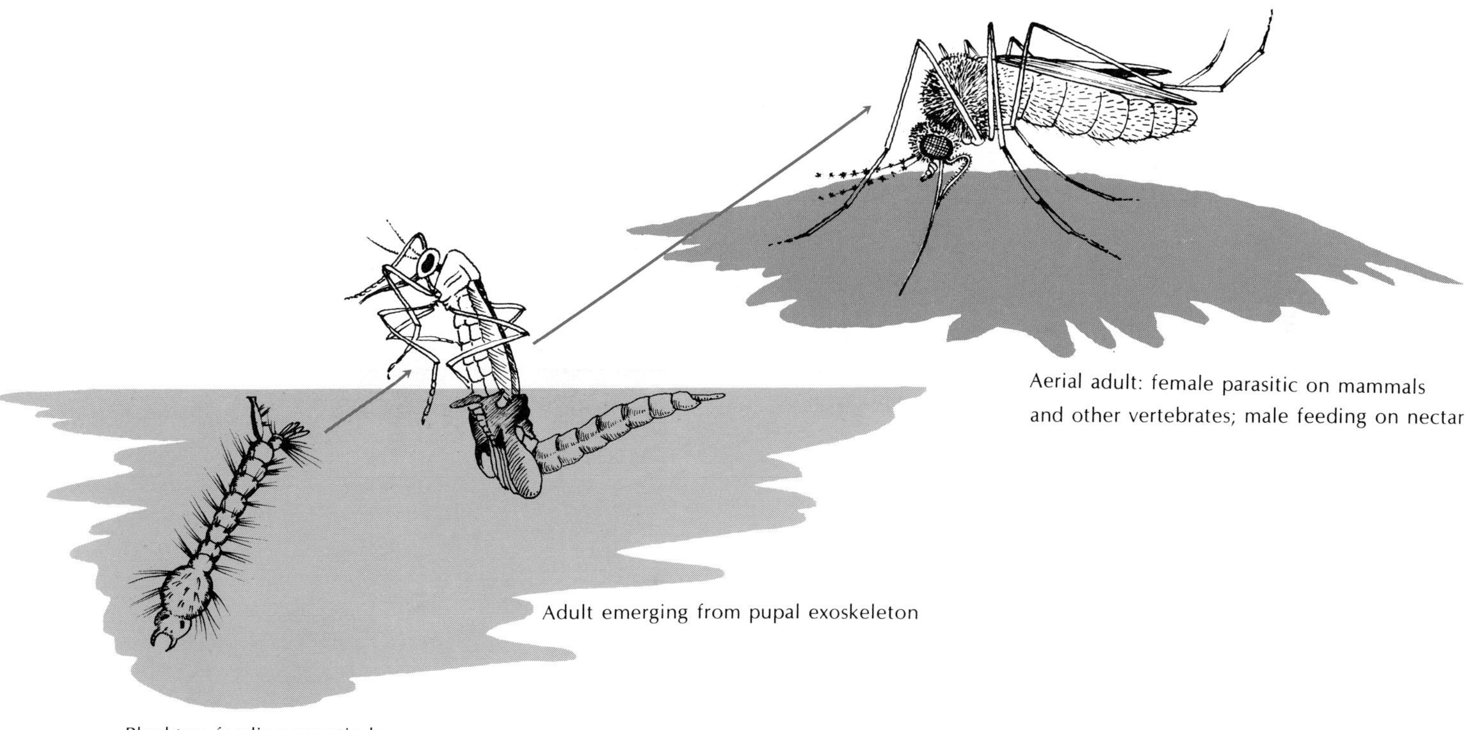

Figure 7.6 □ **Metagenesis or alternation of generations in the moon jelly, *Aurelia*. The free-swimming jellyfish is the sexual generation; the eggs, held on the long oral tentacles of the female, are fertilized with sperm from another individual and develop to the planula stage before being set free. The asexual polyp generation (scyphistoma) often overwinters on the bottom before undergoing strobilation to produce new sexual individuals.**

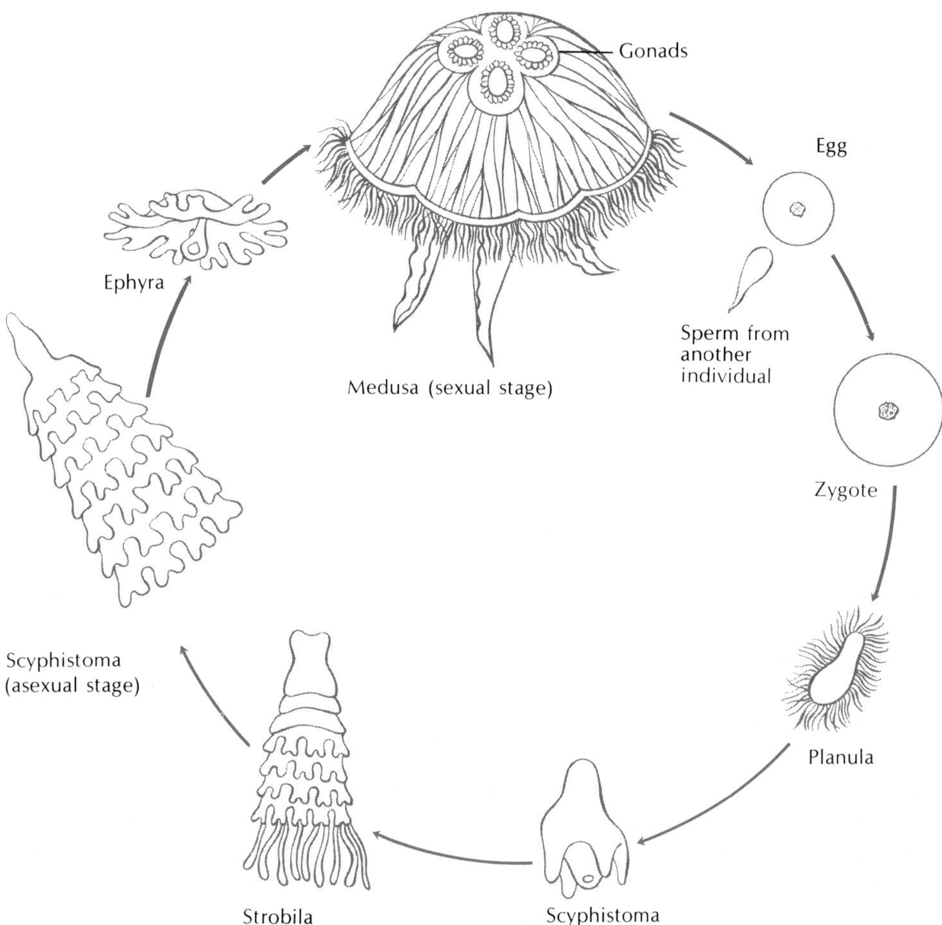

serves to reduce competition by prolonging the developmental period. Thus in many species the old adults have died (often killed by winter cold) before their young attain adult status.

The role of metamorphosis in facilitating dispersal will be discussed below and its physiology will be considered in Chapter 15.

METAGENESIS "Alternation of generations" (metagenesis) involves the intercalation of one or more *asexual* generations between each *sexual* generation within the life cycle of the species: each generation differs from the others in form and mode of existence and may also differ strikingly in habitat. Metagenesis is displayed by many plants, protists, coelenterates, and such flatworms as tapeworms and flukes (see Figures 6.28 and 6.29). As seen in Chapter 6, metagenesis alleviates intraspecific competition in parasitic animals such as flukes, for the sexual and asexual generations inhabit different hosts.

The life cycles of *Obelia* and *Aurelia* (Figure 7.6) demonstrate metagenesis as it occurs in coelenterates. In the case of *Obelia,* the most conspicuous and persistent generation is the sedentary colony composed of hydranths and gonangia; this colony proliferates asexually by budding. The gonangia in turn bud off tiny medusae resembling diminutive jellyfish. These are the sexual generation, producing eggs and sperm. The fertilized egg develops into a ciliated larva that settles upon a suitable substratum and develops asexually into another *Obelia* colony. In this case, competition is mitigated by the fact that an intervening motile generation enhances the distribution of the species. The prey of both

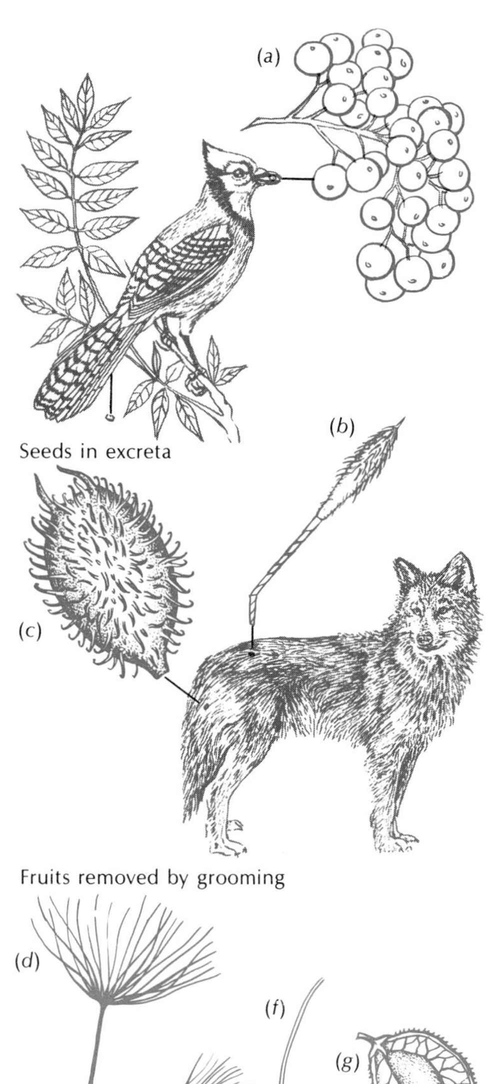

hydranths and medusae is the same—small planktonic organisms—but the hydranths must feed on the plankton that reaches the inshore area where these colonies can grow, while the medusa itself is planktonic and is briefly a part of the fauna of the open sea.

In *Aurelia* the conspicuous generation is the sexual organism—the motile medusa, known as the moon-jelly, which is planktonic and large enough to prey upon fish. The minute polyp generation, or scyphistoma, feeds upon small plankton and overwinters in the shelter of some overhanging ledge. New medusae are produced asexually by strobilation of the polyp, which occurs in spring after medusae of the previous year have died (see Figure 17.3*b*).

B Extension of range

The range of a deme or a species may be extended in several ways, including dispersal (commonly in an immature stage), occupancy of different habitats by adult and juvenile or by alternate generations, emigration, nomadism, and migration.

DISPERSAL There must be some stage in the life cycle of plants and sedentary animals when dispersal away from centers of population can be accomplished. Dispersal is effected most simply by spore-producing plants such as algae and fungi. Spores are single cells encased in a protective wall; they require no fertilization, but develop asexually into new plants. Spores are so light that they are readily transported by wind or water currents.

Figure 7.7 □ Adaptations of fruits for seed dispersal. Edible fruits, such as the berries of mountain ash (*a*), are often eaten by birds and the seeds eliminated at a distance from the parent plant. The spinous fruits of porcupine grass (*b*) and cocklebur (*c*) are caught in the fur of mammals and later removed during grooming. The fruits of dandelion (*d*), cottonwood (*e*), maple (*f*) and elm (*g*) are specialized for wind dispersal.

Many seed plants have developed special adaptations related to the dispersal of their seeds. A seed is an arrested embryo plant and contains much stored food; it is consequently much heavier than a spore. Its outer covering may be a *seed coat* derived from the embryo's own tissues, or a *fruit* derived from the "mother's" tissues. The seeds of gymnosperms such as conifers are not encased in a fruit. However, the seed coat is winged, facilitating wind dispersal. In the angiosperms, the ovarian wall ripens into a fruit that encloses one to many seeds. A fruit may be fleshy, perhaps edible, or hard, dry, and sometimes spinous. The specialization of the ovarian wall for aiding seed dispersal is one of the most important evolutionary innovations of flowering plants and has been largely responsible for their present dominance in most terrestrial habitats (Figure 7.7). Edible fruits enhance dispersal because seeds that are swallowed with the fruit often pass undamaged through the animal's alimentary tract and are voided at a distance from the parent plants. Birds in particular are exploited by angiosperms. We readily recognize the fact that a waxwing is exploiting a mountain ash as it feeds hungrily upon the tree's berries. What may escape us is the fact that the ash is reciprocally exploiting the bird as a vehicle for dispersing its seeds.

The evolution of barbed or spinous

Figure 7.8 □ **Planktonic larvae of benthonic adults. (*a*) Brachiolaria larva of starfish. (*Ward's Natural Science Establishment, Inc.*) (*b*) Third-stage larva of spiny lobster (*Panulirus interruptus*); (*c*) late tenth- or eleventh-stage larva of spiny lobster. (*Courtesy of Dr. Martin W. Johnson and Scripps Institution of Oceanography.*)**

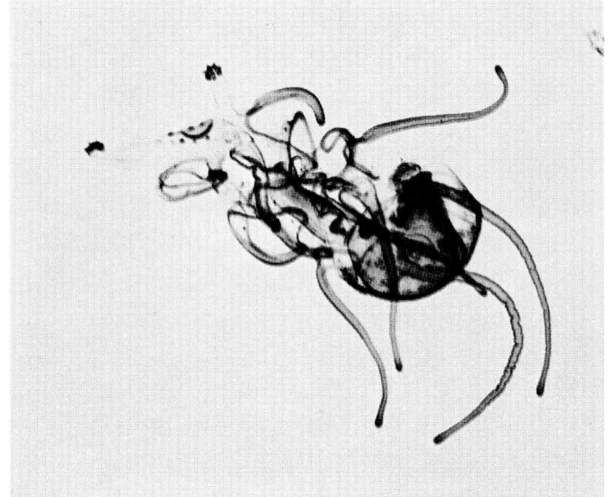

(*a*)

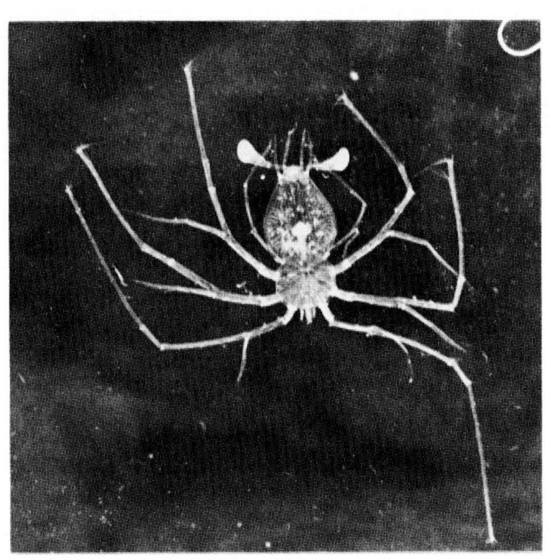

(*b*)

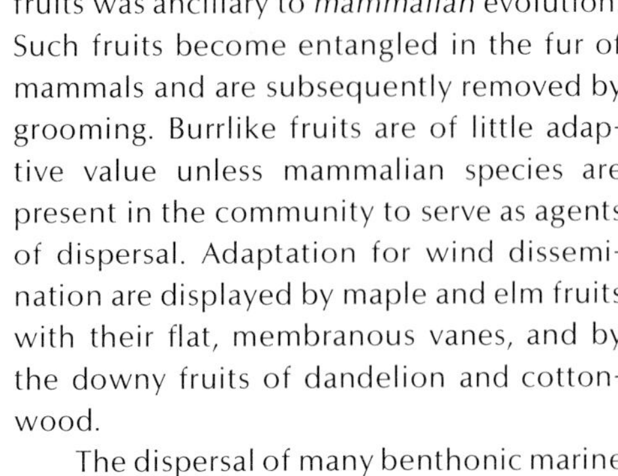

(*c*)

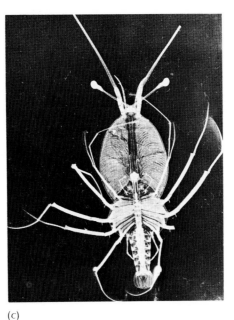

fruits was ancillary to *mammalian* evolution. Such fruits become entangled in the fur of mammals and are subsequently removed by grooming. Burrlike fruits are of little adaptive value unless mammalian species are present in the community to serve as agents of dispersal. Adaptation for wind dissemination are displayed by maple and elm fruits with their flat, membranous vanes, and by the downy fruits of dandelion and cottonwood.

The dispersal of many benthonic marine animals depends upon their possession of a larval form, or a generation, which is free-swimming (usually planktonic) (Figure 7.8). Many benthonic molluscs produce planktonic *trochophore* larvae (see Figure 2.33), top-shaped juveniles having a ring of cilia for locomotion. Echinoderms and crustaceans typically pass through several planktonic larval stages before reaching adulthood.

Planktonic larvae may be transported great distances. Mortality is high: they are not only vulnerable to predators but will also perish if unable to find a good site for their final metamorphosis. The tremendous abundance of these larvae is exhibited whenever a jetty or pier (providing a solid surface for attachment) is constructed on a long stretch of sandy coast. Within a few weeks the structure is colonized by rocky-coast species, even though there may not be a naturally occurring rocky shore within hundreds of miles; this indicates that great numbers of larvae have been widely displaced from their point of origin.

Although it is more common for the young of a species to be more involved with dispersal than the adults, we find a remarkable "turnabout" in certain insects such as the *Cecropia* and clothes moths. Here the adult stage merely serves for reproduction and dispersal. The mouthparts of the adult moths are atrophic and accordingly they cannot feed. They survive for only a few hours, during which mating and egg laying occur. The female disperses her eggs here and there on appropriate food plants—or, in the case of the clothes moth, on our favorite woolens—where they feed with little competition from one another and of course with no competition at all from the adults of their kind (Figure 7.9).

EMIGRATION Emigration implies movement away from a population center, with *no subsequent return* to that area. Emigration may result from accidental displacement, or may be an outcome of excessive population density or of a system of territoriality. The emigrant is placed in particular jeopardy, for it is unprotected by its group and deprived of its optimal habitat. It may readily perish, a victim of predators, starvation, or abiotic factors that violate its limits of tolerance. On the other hand, the emigrant may by chance become established in a habitat hitherto unexploited by its species and succeed well there.

Figure 7.9 □ **Life stages of *Cecropia* moth: caterpillar, pupa, imago. The adult does not feed but mates and disperses its eggs on an appropriate host plant before death. (*Courtesy of General Biological, Inc., Chicago.*)**

Emigration not only expands the range of a species but paves the way for its diversification into new species. Emigrant populations are geographically isolated from the rest of their kind and cannot interbreed with other populations. They are also subject to the influence of a habitat that may differ in important respects from that which was their ancestral home.

Settlement of islands Oceanic islands that have never been attached to the mainland (such as the Hawaiian and Galápagos Islands) are typically colonized on a random basis by fortuitous emigrants from other habitats, in a process termed *sweepstakes dispersal.* This means that an island well removed from the continent is usually reached by only a few displaced individuals, representing a handful of species. These scattered representatives of continental plant and animal groups often perish, but those which survive find available for exploitation a number of potential niches that their descendants may fill by diversification. In this case diversification has such high adaptive value (because there is a potential role in the evolving community for almost any conceivable genetic variant) that in a relatively short time a single original species may fragment into a number of different species occupying the various available niches. Any such *group* of species arising by divergence from a common ancestor represents an *adaptive radiation.* An adaptive radiation is likely to develop any time that a new habitat is invaded and a large number of potential niches are available. A classic example of an adaptive radiation in island fauna is seen in the many species of sicklebills found in the Hawaiian Islands, filling niches that other birds would occupy on the mainland (Figure 7.10).

Another illustration is the adaptive radiation of ground finches (*Geospiza*) in the Galápagos Islands. A typical finch has a stout, seed-cracking beak, but the beaks of the various species of *Geospiza* have become diversified for as many different types of diet as there are species of these birds. In the absence of competing insectivorous birds, some populations of *Geospiza* became adapted to a diet of insects, with concomitant selection toward the slender beak characteristic of insectivorous birds throughout the world. The woodpecker finch evolved a sturdy bill that it employs in the manner of a woodpecker to drill holes in bark. However, it failed to develop the flexible tongue with which the woodpecker seeks grubs under the bark. This deficiency has been remedied by an unusual behavioral adaptation: the woodpecker finch uses twigs or cactus spines, held in its beak, to probe the holes which it has drilled!

Two large types of lizards, both iguanas, also inhabit the Galápagos Islands, where they probably arose from a common ancestor—perhaps an egg-bearing female carried on driftwood from the coast of South America. Now different species, these lizards may have first diverged in feeding habits, thereby ceasing to compete for food: the land iguana feeds upon land vegetation; the marine iguana, which rests and breeds along the rocky coast, feeds by diving into shallow water and browsing upon seaweeds.

Figure 7.10 □ **Radiative adaptation of Hawaiian sicklebills. Diversification in bill structure reflects diversification in modes of food getting that has enabled these finchlike birds to occupy many niches in their habitat that would have been filled by other kinds of birds on the mainland.**

Both of these reptiles show the remarkable tameness and lack of fear so characteristic of island fauna, traits that often have threatened their survival when their habitats have been invaded by man and his domestic animals. Commenting on the land iguana's defenselessness against predators, Charles Darwin* wrote:

I watched one [burrowing] for a long time, till half its body was buried; I then walked up and pulled it by the tail; at this it was greatly astonished, and soon shuffled up to see what was the matter; and then stared me in the face, as much as to say, "What made you pull my tail? . . .

He noted that, although wary of sharks, the marine iguanas lacked fear of man:

They do not seem to have any notion of biting; but when much frightened they squirt a drop of fluid from each nostril. I threw one several times as far as I could, into a deep pool left by the retiring tide; but it invariably returned in a direct line to the spot where I stood. . . . Perhaps this singular piece of apparent stupidity may be accounted for by the circumstance, that this reptile has no enemy whatever on shore, whereas at sea it must often fall a prey to the numerous sharks. Hence, probably, urged by a fixed and hereditary instinct that the shore is its place of safety, whatever the emergency may be, it there takes refuge. . . .

The ultimate fate of emigrants that colonize islands is uncertain, for the pioneers carry with them but a fraction of the total gene pool (sum total of hereditary material) of their species, thereby sacrificing much variability. However, the circumstances are such as to encourage the perpetuation of many genetic variants and in due time adequate heterogeneity may be reestablished through mutation.

Mass emigration and population control Sporadic mass emigration is less a means for extending the range of the species than a means by which population density is regulated. One of the most renowned cases of mass emigration is that of the Norwegian lemming. The surplus lemming population does not merely drift away by gradual departure of individual animals; instead the population density mounts to a critical level, whereupon a mass movement is triggered. Boiling out of their burrows, the lemmings move downhill and often into the sea, where most drown. The residual population that has not participated in this fugue remains behind to repopulate the original range. The few surviving emigrants may be able to establish themselves in a new area if they do not first starve or fall victim to predators.

Territoriality Many vertebrates and certain arthropods as well manifest territoriality, defined as the tendency to prevent a particular area from being occupied by other animals of the same species. For some species, a typical territory must be measured in square meters or kilometers; for others it may constitute merely the "envelope" of space within which the animal moves. Territory may be either stable or impermanent, and in many species belongs not to the individual but to a family unit or to an entire deme. The deme may be a herd, pack, or troop, which carries its territorial boundaries with it through a nomadic route of travel.

**The Voyage of the Beagle* (New York: Bantam Books, Inc., 1958), pp. 335–336.

It is generally thought that one of the primary adaptive values of territoriality is that it brings about an efficient spacing out of the units of population—the individuals, family units, or demes—to a level of dispersal at which the habitat can sustain the population without being detrimentally exploited. Animals that operate under a territorial scheme often reserve for themselves (or for their families or deme) an area extensive enough to contain adequate food and shelter. A study of prairie-dog towns revealed that these aggregations are in fact highly integrated social units, each of which commands a territory adequate to its needs. Far from leading wretched lives eked out at the edge of starvation, these gregarious rodents are ordinarily well fed, free of stress, and (by virtue of communal watchfulness) nearly immune from predation. How then is their increase compensated? Death of diseased and aging animals helps to balance reproduction, but in addition young animals are forced to emigrate away from the group territory. Many of these, of course, fall victim to predators, but their sacrifice preserves the integrity of the social group as a whole.

The lusty singing of male birds may play a role in attracting potential mates, but it serves the major function of *territorial advertisement*. The males of migratory songbird species often arrive at the nesting area in advance of the females, and there they establish themselves in conspicuous positions, each male in the heart of his territory. Newcomers can intercalate themselves between territories previously established only by dint of vigorous battles. However, once they have been accepted, their individual songs become familiar to the other males, and then it is only a new interloper that provokes attack. That the animals themselves have a keen sense of the extent of their territories is shown by the fact that two individuals (such as gulls) may stand eye to eye in mutually threatening postures at a territorial boundary which, though invisible, may nonetheless be rigidly defined. A territorial bird, fish, or mammal that pursues another individual into its own territory seems to realize the extent of its trespass, for it displays progressively less aggressiveness and more timidity as the neighboring territory is encroached. At last an equilibrium is struck and the retreating victim turns upon its attacker, which in turn now flees to the "safety zone" of its own territory. Such seesawing across territorial boundaries diminishes as mutual recognition of the boundary becomes established.

In summary, the adaptive value of territoriality appears to be that it enforces emigration of surplus population and permits the remainder to utilize the habitat with less competition than would otherwise be possible.

NOMADISM Nomadism is a form of range extension in which the individual or group has no fixed home but wanders along a route of travel that is either random or cyclic. What appears to be *random* nomadism is shown by various species of army ants, which wander through New World rain forests without ever establishing a permanent nest. During egg-laying periods, the ants cluster in a globular mass which protects the queen. The workers then carry the eggs, larvae, and pupae as the procession continues on its way. The destructiveness of army ants to other fauna makes this nomadic way of life obligate, for they soon would destroy the fauna of an area if they did not move on, thereby allowing the community to recover from their depredations. The army ant column has become a veritable community in itself, because various "camp followers" have become associated with the procession. These species, mostly insects also, have converged toward mimicry of the ants themselves. Saturated with the ants' odor, these interlopers resemble the ants sufficiently for the latters' weak eyes to accept the resemblance (see Figure 15.21*b*). Protected from other predators by their voracious hosts, these uninvited guests share their hosts' food and even devour their larvae.

New World caribou and bison undertake annual nomadic movements of a roughly cyclic character, influenced by the availability of food and by seasonal climatic changes. Nomadic animals never overgraze their habitat; in fact caribou feed while constantly on the move, browsing lightly upon lichen as they go. Nomadism not only takes the herds to new food supplies and more favorable climates, but also provides escape from parasites that tend to build up when the animals are confined to a permanent pasturage. *Nomadic* animals feed all along their route of travel, and in fact rarely cease to move along. Strictly *migratory* species, on the other hand, spend substantial periods of time at *both ends* of the migratory route, and may feed only intermittently (if at all) during the migration proper.

MIGRATION Migratory behavior commonly extends a species' range by enabling it to utilize one habitat in summer and another in winter. It may involve nutritional and climatic considerations, but it is also intimately tied to the reproductive cycle and to the production and rearing of young. Two major types of migration may be recognized: altitudinal and latitudinal.

Altitudinal migration Altitudinal migratory movements are associated with climatic changes and are mainly executed by birds and mammals. The elk herds of the Yellowstone area move from their summer range at about 3,000 m altitude to winter in relatively protected valleys at around 2,000 m. As the climate becomes warmer in spring they again ascend, following their food supply as far up as timberline.

Latitudinal migration Pronounced latitudinal migrations are accomplished mainly by birds and marine mammals such as whales and seals. Gray whales spend the summer in Arctic waters, feeding upon the abundant planktonic crustaceans. In late autumn they migrate southward along the west coast of North America or the east coast of Asia, seeking protected bays and estuaries where they bear their young. When the infants are strong enough, they and their parents move north to feed. Because the southern waters are relatively poor in plankton, the breeding migration is a time of partial fasting for these great animals.

The pathways and possible mechanisms of migration have been most intensively studied in migratory birds. About 15 percent of all bird species are migratory, dividing their time between a breeding range (usually to the north) and a winter range to the south. Since most land masses occur in the northern hemisphere, it is not surprising that the greater part of most bird migratory routes lies north of the equator. The temperate, subtemperate, and polar zones are widely utilized for breeding. It is tempting to conclude that many bird migrations originated with the need of Arctic and temperate birds to abandon their homes because of winter cold (particularly during glacial periods). However, there is evidence that it is not the *northern* but the *southern* range which more probably represents the original home of the species; if so, the northward trek for breeding must involve other selective factors. This hypothesis rests upon the observation that widely dispersed populations of a single species may converge upon a sometimes highly delimited southern range. A extreme illustration of this is the chimney swift that nests throughout temperate North America. Because of their propensity for adopting chimneys as nesting sites (in lieu of hollow trees), chimney swifts were easily banded for ornithological study, and by the time some 400,000 bands had been affixed the fact that not a single banded swift had yet been recovered in winter was becoming a deepening mystery. Eventually, Peruvian Indians from the isolated Yanayaco Valley brought a few legbands to a missionary. These were in time identified as having been attached to swifts nesting in Ontario, Tennessee, Alabama, Georgia, Connecticut, and Illinois. No data so far obtained refute the conclusion that the whole North American population of chimney swifts funnels into this small Peruvian valley as though pulled by invisible strings. Concentration of the entire swift population in this confined area strongly suggests that this valley may have been the species' ancestral point of origin.

If by moving north in summer, migratory birds are in fact leaving their ancestral homes, what is the survival value of this northward movement? A clue is provided by the fact that the more northerly populations of *non*migratory birds produce more young per year, both in terms of clutch size and number of clutches brooded, than do the more southerly populations of the same species. If this is true for nonmigratory birds, it should apply as well to migrants. The explanation of this phenomenon probably is that the extended daylight of the higher latitudes permits the birds to forage longer and to collect more food for their offspring. The long photoperiod encourages plants to grow at a nearly explosive rate, with a concomitant burgeoning of the insect fauna upon which many birds feed. These favorable conditions do not persist the year around in northern latitudes, of course, and as the summer wanes the birds start to become restless, then aggregate, and finally fly southward heading "home"—according to this hypothesis.

Some bats and a few insects also execute latitudinal migrations. The monarch butterfly is the only known insect species in which individuals live long enough to pass north and south over the migratory route for several years. Most insect "migrations" are in fact unidirectional emigrations, and the fate of the emigrants remains in doubt.

The physiological and behavioral mechanisms involved in initiating and executing migratory movements are not fully understood. The navigational cues appear to be genetically rather than experientially acquired. Evidence for the hereditary acquisition of cue-utilizing mechanisms rests not only upon observation of the performance of migratory birds, but on experimental studies as well.

One of the most impressive pieces of observational data concerns the golden plover, a shore bird that annually flies an elliptical route exceeding 16,000 miles, from the Arctic region of North America to Argentina. Golden plovers rear their broods along the shores of the Arctic Ocean. As soon as the young are independent, the adults abandon them and begin their southward migration. This early withdrawal of the adults from the northern range lessens competition for food for the younger birds, which must become stronger before undertaking the southward journey. The adults pass southeast to Nova Scotia and then cross the open Atlantic to South America, flying nonstop until they reach the Argentinian pampas. The young plovers, departing later, pursue quite a different route, arriving in Argentina by an overland passage that crosses the high Andes. Here they rendezvous with their parents! Returning northward at the close of the southern hemisphere's summer, the plovers both young and old now retrace the course which the inexperienced plovers used in their first southward movement. In the years following their initial migration, the young plovers adopt the oversea route southward for the rest of their lives. This modification is perhaps learned from their elders, but the initial migration obviously was not. A Pacific race of the golden plover nests along the west coast of Alaska. This race does not migrate to South America, but crosses trackless ocean to a diminutive target, the Hawaiian Islands. Thence they continue to islands of the South Pacific. Over most of their route, no fixed landmarks are available to assist navigation.

Figure 7.11 □ **Migratory route of the Arctic tern.** (*After R. W. Hines and U.S. Fish and Wildlife Service.*)

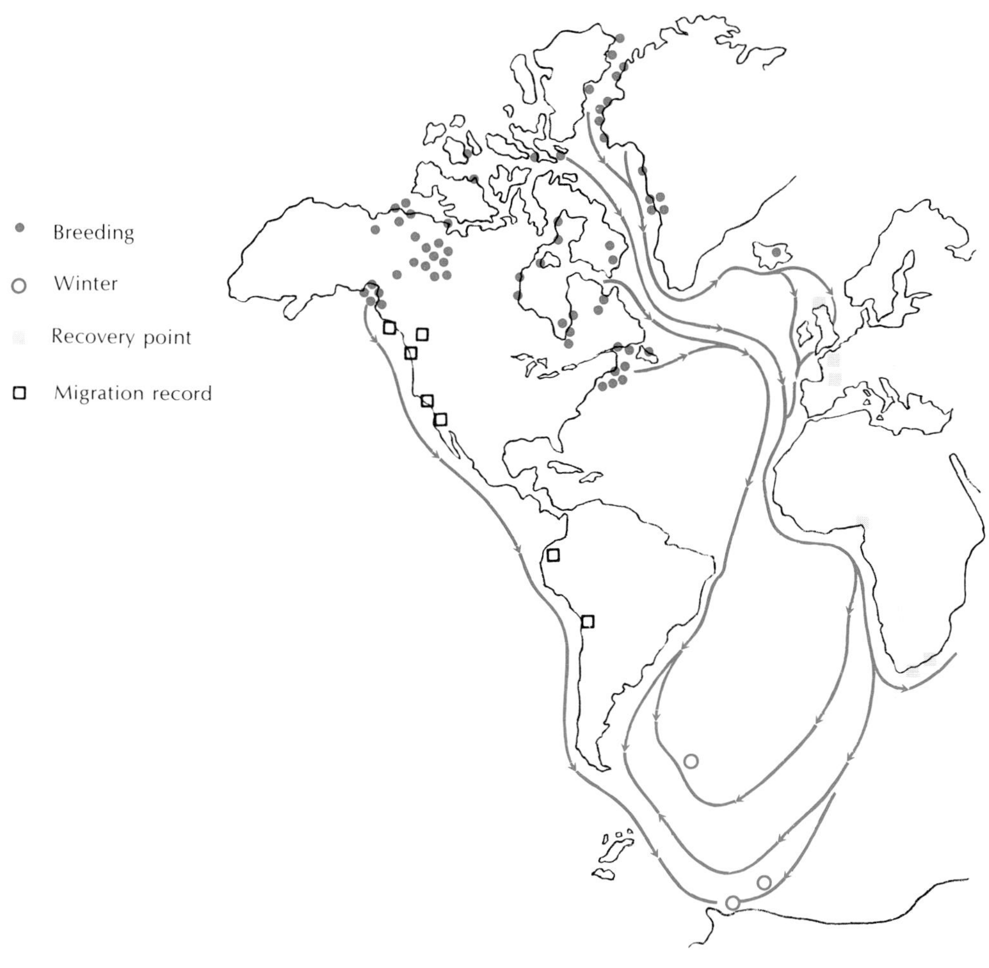

Another champion migrant is the Arctic tern, the annual migratory route of which exceeds 22,000 miles (Figure 7.11). Breeding in the north, this species also exploits the extended photoperiod of the *opposite* polar region, for its "winter" range is actually the Antarctic Ocean where it spends the Antarctic summer. The Arctic tern thus follows "summer" from pole to pole, and by so doing experiences more hours of daylight than any other animal known.

Experimental investigations concerned with determining the extent to which a migratory route is learned or genetically acquired have involved two major approaches: (1) hand-raising of birds in *isolation* from the parental populations; (2) *cross-fostering* of nestlings between species, or between two populations of a single species that follow different migratory routes. The second of these techniques was used in a study of the European stork. The West German stork population migrates south to Egypt by a route that passes southwest over France and Spain, crosses the Straits of Gibraltar, and follows the north coast of Africa eastward to the Nile Valley. The East German population rounds the eastern end of the Mediterranean in reaching the same objective. Clutches of eggs laid by East German storks were transferred to the nests of West German storks, and the nestlings subsequently banded. Later, some of the banded juveniles were recaptured in the course of their first migration to winter quarters. It was found that these East German storks, although hatched and reared by *West* German storks, had nevertheless flown eastward following the migratory route of the *East* German stork population. None had gone with their foster parents, although these did not differ in species or appearance from their true parents.

Young birds about to undertake their initial migration have been banded and released after being moved several hundred miles east or west of their normal starting point. These birds rarely found their way "home" but pursued a course parallel to the correct one and flew for approximately the right distance.

It is apparent that the major features of a migratory route must be encoded in some type of "memory bank" that develops under the control of the hereditary material, and yet it seems unlikely that an animal can "remember" what it has never seen. Perhaps what is inheritable is the tendency to adopt some particular bearing and to maintain this bearing over a certain distance or for a given period of time, after which some new bearing may be adopted. During the animal's lifetime learned cues, such as landmarks, may reinforce or modify the innate disposition. But how does the animal know what bearing to adopt? In the course of evolution, rather than by individual learning, the tendency may have been strengthened for members of migratory species to orient with respect to specific stimulus patterns such as constellations. Neither the mechanisms of inherited nor those of learned pattern recognition are yet understood.

Navigational mechanisms Migrating birds are thought to navigate by a *light-compass reaction:* the bird takes its bearings from the positions of the sun and stars, and navigates toward a fixed compass point despite the earth's rotation and the consequent movements of these celestial bodies across the sky. Much bird migration takes place at night, with constellations serving as navigational cues for the birds much as they also serve human voyagers. The use of celestial objects for navigation requires that the animal possess an internal time-keeping mechanism (*biological clock*) that allows it to compensate for the earth's rotation (causing the apparent movement of the sun and stars across the heavens). Biological clocks are of widespread occurrence and are often expressed in endogenous physiological and behavioral rhythms, which by sensory input are kept in phase with the rhythms of the environment.

Extensive research is still being conducted into the mechanisms whereby animals follow annual migratory routes or successfully come home after being displaced. So far, these mechanisms have defied definitive analysis. It is possible that some animals orient by detecting magnetic lines of force, but use of magnetic cues by migrating birds has never been irrefutably established.

Fish migration Another type of migration is performed by certain fish that migrate between marine and freshwater habitats, exploiting both environments during their life cycle. *Anadromous* fish, including salmon and sea lampreys, spend their adult lives at sea, but migrate upstream to spawn (Figure 7.12). The young may spend from one to several years in fresh water before migrating to the sea. The upstream migration of salmon has been particularly well studied, and it has been found that when the fish are ready to breed, they follow olfactory cues to the mouth of the river which they once descended, and ultimately find their way back to the very stream where they had been hatched and lived as juveniles. Salmon with their eyes covered are successful in homing, but those with nostrils blocked with vaseline, or with olfactory nerve tracts severed, often get lost.

Electrodes can be used to monitor the response of a salmon's olfactory nerve when a few drops of water are introduced into its nostrils. By this means, it has been found that water taken from the fish's home stream elicits a pronounced neural response, whereas water from other sources does not provoke such a response. In fact, water from the home stream exerts this effect even when several years have elapsed since the fish left that stream and migrated to the sea. These findings serve as evidence that the homing of breeding salmon depends upon early experience, in which olfactory cues are imprinted upon the fish's memory. (Imprinting will be further considered in Chapter 11.)

Freshwater eels are *catadromous* species, which spend their adult lives in fresh water, and migrate down to the sea for spawning. American and European species converge upon an area of the Atlantic termed the Sargasso Sea, the quiet "eye" of the rotatory current system of the North Atlantic, and are seen no more. Their larvae, or elvers, grow for some time in this habitat, and then set out for the continents from which their parents came. No European eel becomes confused and ends up in American waters, nor does the reverse occur to American species. Ascending rivers, they make their homes in fresh water until, with the onset of sexual maturity, the downstream migration is initiated. Unlike salmon, the upstream migration of eels cannot be due to learned scent recognition, for the eels moving upstream are of a new generation. The mature eels may return to the Sargasso Sea for breeding by following olfactory cues remembered from their youth, but another explanation must be sought for the ability of young eels to find their way to the continent of their parents' origin. This may involve the same type of inherited pattern recognition that may govern bird migratory routes, but it probably involves innate recognition of certain olfactory rather than visual cues.

Figure 7.12 □ **Fish migration: sockeye salmon leaping Brooks Falls, Bristol Bay, Alaska, on way to spawning grounds. (*Photograph by G. B. Kelezy, U.S. Bureau of Commercial Fisheries.*)**

Conclusion Migration serves to reduce competition among conspecifics by making two habitats alternatively available to a single species. Altitudinal migration permits a species to escape climatic extremes and to utilize different ranges for winter and summer foraging. Latitudinal migration such as that exhibited by many bird species enables these species to exploit the long photoperiods of higher latitudes for the rearing of large numbers of young. Latitudinal migratory routes may be followed by means of light-compass orientation coupled with a time sense that sets the distance over which a given bearing is held. The breeding migrations of anadromous and catadromous fish are partially oriented by olfactory cues and serve to eliminate competition between young and adults as well as enabling them to occupy two habitats during different stages of the life history.

C **Regulation of rate of increase**

The numerical stabilization of a population involves both extrinsic and intrinsic factors by which the production of new individuals is balanced against rate of mortality. Analysis of population growth rates shows that they describe a sine curve (see Figure 6.1), in which an initial phase of slow increase (when the population is just becoming established in a habitat) is succeeded by a period of exponential increase, leveling off at an asymptote when a certain density has been reached. This eventual stabilization is governed in part by limitations of food and living space, and by the action of predators. However, there appear to be still other factors, operating *within* a given species, which serve to maintain a stable population level *well below* that at which the productivity of the habitat is threatened. The nature and occurrence of endogenous controls on fertility have yet to be fully clarified. Certainly some species are capable of increasing to "plague" proportions if not held down by predation or lack of food. A veritable "rabbit plague" followed the introduction of these prolific animals into Australia (see Figure 6.3).

There are other species, however, in which increasing population density seems to trigger physiological changes that result in a reduction of the number of young produced and reared to maturity. Crowded mice, although provided with adequate food, exhibit symptoms of stress. The size of their adrenal glands has been used as an index of the intensity of stress. During prolonged stress the adrenal glands (which are indirectly controlled by the brain) first become overactive and enlarge. Eventually they may be damaged by this overactivity, and death may ensue. According to some investigators, the social stress produced by overcrowding may prove sufficient to cause death from adrenal exhaustion. At less critical levels, stress may interfere with maternal behavior, cause abortion of embryos, and even prevent pregnancy.

"Olfactory pregnancy block" (the Bruce effect) occurs in female mice that are caged close to a large number of male mice, even when they can neither see nor touch these males. When a male is allowed access to such a female, she rarely becomes pregnant; it is thought that this is due to an inhibitory effect on ovulation exerted by the concentrated odor produced by the large number of male mice. Presumably this effect might operate to prevent pregnancy in crowded groups of wild mice as well.

Territoriality has been cited previously as a factor in forcing emigration and causing a population to space itself in such a way that the habitat is not overexploited and the animals accordingly do not suffer want. Since it results in the departure of surplus population from the area, territoriality also exerts an effect on the rate of increase. Many animals unable to hold a territory die of starvation or by predation. A study of grouse in Scotland has shown that no males lacking

Figure 7.13 ☐ **Territoriality and social dominance in breeding success. (*a*) Adelie penguin pairs on breeding territories in Antarctica. Nests are spaced about 1 m apart and are built of rounded stones often pilfered by neighboring penguins. When densely aggregated, Adelie penguins can repulse attacks of skua gulls, which prey upon abandoned chicks and may rob nests on the fringes of the breeding area. (*Zoological Society of San Diego photo by Ron Garrison.*) (*b*) Flamingo breeding ground in San Diego zoo. Each pair constructs a mound of earth on which the egg is placed. Nesting territories may be only about 0.5 m^2 but are defended against encroachment by neighboring birds, as seen in background. Note the adult's unusual bill, adapted for sieving shellfish out of mud; the chick's bill has not yet developed the adult specialization. (*Zoological Society of San Diego photo by Ron Garrison.*) (*c*) Most seals are territorial, but male elephant-seal breeding success is affected by rank in a social hierarchy. High-ranking males hold desirable resting places near the water and control large harems. (*Scripps Institution of Oceanography photo by John B. MacFall.*)**

(*c*)

(*a*)

(*b*)

a territory are able to survive the winter. Furthermore, the possession or lack of a territory or appropriate breeding place may physiologically affect the organism's reproductive state. As previously stated, gulls that do not succeed in laying claim to a territory in the breeding grounds neither mate nor lay eggs. This regulation of reproduction also applies to parrots that lack a nesting cavity. Sexual activity can thus be regulated according to whether or not an animal controls a territory or an appropriate breeding place (Figure 7.13).

Endogenous control of reproduction in birds includes the regulation of egg laying by the number of eggs already in the nest. Egg laying ceases when a clutch is laid that is of appropriate size for the species. Many birds can be induced to lay eggs indefinitely if their nests are systematically robbed. This is done routinely with domestic chickens, which are also forced to continue egg laying throughout the year by being exposed to an artificially extended photoperiod. Inviable eggs can also limit clutch size. Seabirds such as gulls produce only a few eggs per clutch. A cracked egg is broken and eaten. However, unhatched but unbroken eggs remaining in the nests may inhibit further egg laying, not only during that season but during subsequent ones. A demonstration of this phenomenon occurred when a seabird colony was damaged by radioactive fallout. The deserted eggs remained intact upon the nests and in subsequent years the returning survivors laid no new eggs but reincubated the old ones. This situation might eventually have led to the extinction of the colony were it not for the intervention of concerned naturalists, who removed the stimulus inhibiting egg laying.

D The role of social organization in reducing competition

Almost all vertebrates together with higher invertebrates exhibit some degree of *social organization and interaction* within the species. Social organization and communication will be taken up in more detail in the following paragraphs: it is by these means that cooperation among conspecifics is maximized. In considering the alleviation of the effects of competition among conspecifics, we shall next focus upon aggressive behavior, its ritualization, and its employment in the establishment and maintenance of social hierarchies.

HIERARCHICAL ORGANIZATION OF DEMES It has already been said that aggressive encounters occur during competition for mates and territories, and that successful combatants are rewarded by possession of the territories containing their worldly needs as well as the opportunity to inseminate more females and produce more progeny. In many social groups, individuals of both sexes resort to aggression in the establishment of a more or less stable social hierarchy. Linear "pecking orders" exist in flocks of domestic hens. In such a hierarchy the dominant individual gives way to none, while the lowest subordinate can be attacked with impunity by any other member of the flock. An alert observer can often identify the dominant member of a group merely by its independent and carefree demeanor. A dominant male deer or antelope literally struts. A dominant hen approaches the feeding trough with poise and certainty, while the subordinates melt away without resistance. An individual at the bottom of the hierarchy, on the other hand, may be recognized by its fearful mien and by the manner in which it favors obscure corners and avoids the other members of the group. Although the hierarchy is established by combative means, it actually serves to *reduce* conflict, for each animal comes to accept its position in the hierarchy, and gives way to those which exceed it in rank. Among social primates one of the roles of the dominant male is to break up fights between females or subordinate males. More harmonious group relations are therefore maintained and possible fighting injuries reduced.

In any hierarchical social organization natural selection operates against the subordinate individual but in favor of the group as a whole. Under conditions of acute food scarcity, it is the lowest subordinates that starve while individuals of higher rank may still obtain enough food not only to survive but to remain in good health. From the standpoint of the species, this undemocratic state of affairs is no doubt better than having the entire deme resort to internal conflict and eventually succumb to starvation.

The hierarchical organization of a deme has important effects upon its heredity. Not all males have equal access to the females and hence will not contribute equally to the next generation. In chickens social rank determines the extent of a cock's opportunity to inseminate the hens. In Figure 7.14, we see the effect of social dominance on breeding success. Three roosters, a Rhode Island Red, a barred Plymouth Rock, and a White Leghorn were penned with white hens. The color of the chicks permits determination of the number fathered by each rooster. We can see that the dominant, barred cock produced the most chicks, while the subordinate White Leghorn fathered only a single chick! These data illustrate the extent to which social hierarchy may affect genetic selection.

Figure 7.14 □ **Effect of social dominance on breeding success. White Leghorn hens were penned with three roosters: a dominant Rhode Island Red, a barred Plymouth Rock, and a White Leghorn subordinate to the other two males. Since the chicks' color reflects their paternity, the number of successful matings by each cock can be determined.** (*Data from A. M. Guhl.*)

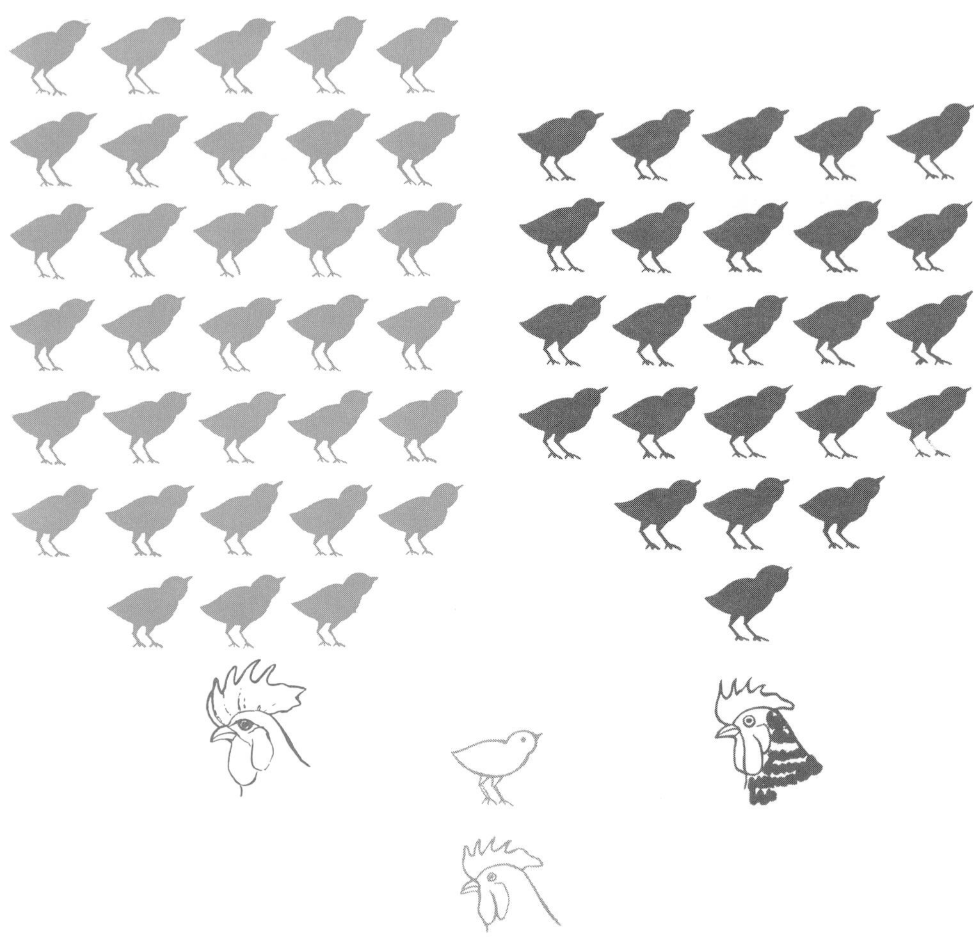

RITUALIZATION OF AGGRESSIVE BEHAVIOR The motor patterns involved in aggressive exchanges are often *ritualized* in such a manner that severe injury of the combatants is avoided (Figure 7.15). The antagonists assume sterotyped threat postures and may emit vocalizations indicating readiness to attack. If an engagement ensues, much ferocity may be displayed, of which most is bluff. Physical contact may be almost completely avoided. The bouts are terminated when the loser runs away or assumes a submissive posture that apparently inhibits the winner from further attack. Fighting in marine iguanas consists mainly of a pushing contest in which two males stand snout-against-snout, pushing, until one is forced backward. The loser then drops flat on his belly, this serving apparently as a gesture of submission to which the champion responds by withholding further attack. Fighting rhinoceros clash horn-to-horn instead of using the horn to rip open each other's belly, and stags in rut lock antlers and push. Aggressive encounters between *confined* antagonists may have abnormally severe consequences because the loser cannot implement its urge to leave the scene of action. Encounters between imprisoned game cocks often lead to the death of one combatant, particularly when the spectators' amusement requires that the cocks' natural spurs be augmented with sharp metal caps. Such prolonged and injurious battles seldom occur in the wild, where the loser can take to its heels if submission should prove inadequate. Some ethologists contend that aggression is usually an expression of *territorial* defense and does *not* usually directly involve competition for mates.

Figure 7.15 □ Ritualization of aggression. Animals capable of inflicting serious injury upon their conspecifics seldom do so owing to the tendency for agonistic encounters to be ritualized. (*a*) Threat display of male iguana, involving extension and reddening of dewlap accompanied by head bobbing. (*b*) Combat dance of rattlesnakes. The encounter ends when the loser is forced down and backward. (*c*) Rhinoceros head butting, a horn-to-horn clash preferred to gashing the soft underparts. [*Zoological Society of San Diego, photo* (*a*) *by Ron Garrison.*]

7.3 □ COOPERATION AMONG CONSPECIFICS

Groups of organisms can control their environment much more effectively than solitary individuals can. Even as *competition* is more severe among conspecifics, so the possibilities of organized *cooperation* are most capable of attainment within a given species. Even simple, socially unorganized aggregations may enhance the survival of both the individual and the group.

A Unstructured aggregations

The simplest type of aggregations are those which are incidental to a food supply or a common substratum and which lack any kind of social structure. Feeding aggregations in animals may be more competitive than beneficial. A similar aggregation of plants, however, benefits by the proximity of individuals in that, although there may be competition for light and root space, there is enhanced opportunity for cross pollination, and as a group the plants also more effectively build soil and bind it against erosion. A forest is capable of altering the physical conditions of its habitat to an extent that scattered single trees could never achieve. The tendency of honeybees to collect nectar from plants of only one species at a time also lends survival value to aggregation and synchronous blooming in any bee-pollinated plant species.

Aggregation is essential for reproduction in barnacles, for these sedentary crustaceans cross-fertilize by reciprocal copulation. Barnacles are monoecious, and each possesses a penis that can be extended to a length about twice the diameter of the animal's entire body! Any barnacle that has attached itself to the substratum at a distance greater than its penis' length from other barnacles is unable to reproduce for it cannot exchange sperm. The behavior of the motile larva of the barnacle suggests that selection of a suitable site for attachment depends not only on the physical characteristics of the substratum, but on chemical cues furnished by other barnacles. In searching for a permanent place of attachment the nearly microscopic larva will come to rest on any solid surface and begin to walk about, anchoring itself by adhesive pads on its antennae. Sometimes it rejects what appears to an observer to be a quite acceptable substratum, and breaking free is carried away to another location. On the other hand, if the substratum provides both tactile and chemical cues that encourage settling behavior, the larva attaches itself permanently and molts to the sessile adult form. Adult barnacles are thought to secrete a chemical attractant that induces larvae of their own species to settle nearby. This attractant is correctly considered a pheromone, because it influences the behavior of other members of the same species.

A number of observations point to the *protective* effects of aggregations, even when these are not socially structured. Birds may crowd together in favorite roosting trees, where presumably a warning given by one would serve to rouse the entire group. Even certain butterflies form nightly sleeping aggregations, possibly with similar benefit. Alarm pheromones released by agitated ants, minnows, and tadpoles serve to alert other individuals in the vicinity. Flocks of birds and schools of fish maneuver together with uncanny precision, this coordinated behavior depending upon *social facilitation*—the tendency of each individual to respond to cues from others in the group with such rapidity that the group responds as a whole. Traveling in such coordinated groups may afford protection from predators. For instance, a flock of starlings flying in loose formation closes ranks when approached by a falcon. The falcon, which would readily dive upon a straggler, refrains from plummeting into the bunched group, for this would be tantamount to striking a solid wall. The birds of course cannot consciously predict the result of their action, but the tendency to aggregate is reinforced by the fact that individuals with a penchant for straying from the group are less likely to live to have progeny.

The ecologist W. C. Allee observed that aggregated organisms show superior resistance to toxins when compared with isolated organisms. In one experiment he exposed grouped and isolated goldfish to a highly toxic chemical, colloidal silver, and found that the mean survival time for 70 isolated fishes was 182 min, whereas that for 7 accompanying groups of 10 each was 507 min, or nearly 3 times as long. This protective effect was attributed to properties of the fishes' mucus, which caused most of the silver to be precipitated harmlessly out of solution. Although the concentration of the poison was so great that death eventually resulted even in the grouped fish, in the wild such a protective mechanism would probably suffice to neutralize most naturally occurring toxins.

Similarly, it has been found that aggregations of the small crustacean *Daphnia* can endure overalkaline water that is lethal to solitary *Daphnia*. In this case, the grouped animals give off enough CO_2 to neutralize the medium in their immediate vicinity.

More mysterious are the winter aggregations of hibernating animals such as ladybird beetles, which form clusters containing thousands of individuals. These clusters lack sexual significance but may be protective. Ladybirds exude a noxious odor that repels predators. During hibernation little of this exudate is produced, but the massed beetles may retain a trace of the protective odor and will thus continue to discourage predation throughout the winter.

B Colonial aggregations

Colonies, in the strict sense, are groups of organisms that have arisen by asexual budding from a single original individual and retain some degree of physical continuity; they realize their greatest adaptive potential when they consist of polymorphic individuals that fulfill different functions. However, even colonial aggregations which are not polymorphic have survival value in that they permit a group of organisms to elaborate its own substratum. The sea fan (Figure 4.26), as we have seen, secretes a horny framework that enlarges as the zooids proliferate. This skeletal framework furnishes two large plane surfaces that support thousands of zooids even though its base may occupy only 3 or 4 cm² of the substratum.

We have already considered the division of labor possible in polymorphic colonies such as *Obelia* and *Physalia*. Bryozoans are also colonial, with two types of zooids present, tentaculate zooids which both feed and reproduce (see Figure 2.30), and defensive zooids (avicularia). The latter are shaped like tiny, beaked parrots' heads and employ their "beaks" in crushing small organisms that settle upon the colony. They thus protect the colony from being overgrown.

Figure 7.16 □ **Vigilance stance of prairie dog. "Altruistic behavior" is characteristic of many social animals. If danger threatens, this individual will whistle vigorously, alerting neighboring prairie dogs, before retreating into the safety of its own burrow. At all times one or more adults of the colony maintain a vigil while others forage. (*Zoological Society of San Diego.*)**

C Societies and their integration

Colonialism is of course an obligate situation for the individual zooid, which would die if separated from the colony. It is perhaps less obvious that for the *social* organism integration into its *society* is almost equally obligate. Although not physically fused with other individuals of the society, as is the case with colonial species, the social animal is bound to its society by functional and behavioral ties that are as powerful as a structural link. Animal societies exhibiting various degrees of stability and exerting some measure of homeostatic control over their members have evolved particularly among vertebrates, and in a few orders of insects. Group construction of nests and shelters, group defense, group action in subduing prey, group activities in courtship, breeding, and care of young—all are observable in various animal species (Figure 7.16). For an aggregation to become organized into a society there must be effective means of *communication* among members of the same species. Animals of one species may also communicate their intent to those of other species (for instance, few would mistake the intent of a crouched and snarling dog or a handstanding skunk), but the greatest value of communicative devices is their facilitation of social interaction among conspecifics.

THE EVOLUTION OF SOCIAL SIGNALS The evolution of communicative devices requires the coadapted and more or less simultaneous development of two complementary factors: (1) the *signal* itself; (2) the *receivers,* which are the sense organs and the integrative brain centers that permit the signal to be apprehended and its meaning determined. Each of these factors acts as a selective force in the evolution of the reciprocal component. It would be useless, for example, for an acoustic signal to be emitted by a species at a frequency that its auditory receptors could not detect. It is equally unlikely that a species entirely lacking color perception would develop any visually perceived signal (such as the epaulette of redwing blackbirds) the reception of which depends upon the capacity for color discrimination.

Signals that achieve social significance tend to evolve toward *specificity* and *stereotypy.* That is, they tend to become *unambiguous.* Through ritualization, a motor pattern primarily belonging to one category of behavior may come to have a secondary or *derived* meaning that other members of the species would never mistake for the original, unritualized act. For example, many species of ducks, though generally protectively colored, sport a conspicuous patch of plumage that is displayed during courtship. Stereotyped movements derived from ordinary preening activities are made use of in the act of "drawing attention to" these patches (Figure 7.17).

Figure 7.17 □ Visual signals in courtship. (*a*) Displacement preening of courting drakes. These stereotyped postures appear to be derived from ordinary preening movements but are exaggerated and performed during courtship rather than normal preening. The movement is thought to direct attention to the brilliant patch of color (*speculum*) on the wing, by which the recognition of individual species appears to be facilitated. (*After K. Lorenz.*) (*b*) "Bridling" display of Cape teal, exposing iridescent wing patch. (*Courtesy of Dr. P. A. Johnsgard.*)

Movements that serve as social signals in turn act as selective factors in the adaptive evolution of the *structures* associated with them, so that the combination of a stereotyped, conspicuous movement and an equally conspicuous structure provides a signal of unequivocal meaning.

The simplicity and clarity of social signals are adaptive because such lack of ambiguity minimizes the demands on the nervous system for their interpretation. Fixed action patterns typical of innate behavior are thought to be released or triggered by specific "sign stimuli" which may represent only a fraction of the total stimulus configuration. Sign stimuli can be presented out of normal context and much simplified from the "real" stimulus object, and still be capable of eliciting the appropriate response. Lack's study of the European robin, the original "robin redbreast" (not the same species as the American robin), revealed that the male was provoked to attack by the sign stimulus provided by red breast feathers of another male. Lack found that an isolated tuft of red feathers in no way resembling an actual bird was sufficient to elicit attack (Figure 7.18). A stuffed immature male robin, lacking the red breast, was ignored. We have already noted the response of male sticklebacks to simplified models with red underparts or swollen bellies—the one eliciting attack, the other initiating the ritual of courtship (see Figure 4.13).

The evolution of communicative behavior patterns is difficult to reconstruct because behavioral acts seldom leave fossil evidence. Comparative studies of behavior patterns of related species indicate that *communicative behavior patterns are ritualized components derived from other motor activities.* Courtship behavior in gulls, cormorants, grebes, and other birds consists of ritualized postures and vocalizations, performed synchronously by male and female alike (Figure 7.19). These activities have been interpreted as representing stereotyped components of the agonistic (aggressive-submissive), nest-building, and caregiving repertories.

A group of related species of balloon flies (or dance flies) show a spectrum of courtship activities which, if they reflect an evolutionary progression, show how communicative behavior may become ritualized. Balloon flies earn their name by their habit of carrying prey encased within a shiny balloon of hardened secretion. Such a balloon is carried by the male in flight as he searches for a mate. Should he find a female, he presents her with the balloon. While she is engaged in tearing it open and eating the prey contained therein, the male takes advantage of her preoccupation by initiating copulation. These diversionary tactics are important for survival because balloon flies are predatory and the female might otherwise devour her admirer before copulation could take place. In a second species of balloon fly, the gift is ritualized to the extent that the male merely encases scraps of his prey—a few legs or wings—within the balloon and presents this to the female. In a third species, the male still produces and carries a balloon, but puts nothing at all inside of it. The female of this species does not appear to take the balloon seriously. She does not open the balloon, but accepts the male that brought it as a suitable mate.

TYPES OF SIGNALS Social integration is effected through chemical, visual, acoustic, and tactile stimuli.

Pheromones Chemical signals may either be detected at a distance or only upon direct contact. They are sometimes detected as tastes or odors. Others exert their effects

Figure 7.18 □ Releasers of aggressive behavior in the European robin, as determined by David Lack. A mere tuft of red feathers serves to elicit threat displays and attack, whereas a mounted immature robin lacking the red breast characteristic of adult males is usually disregarded.

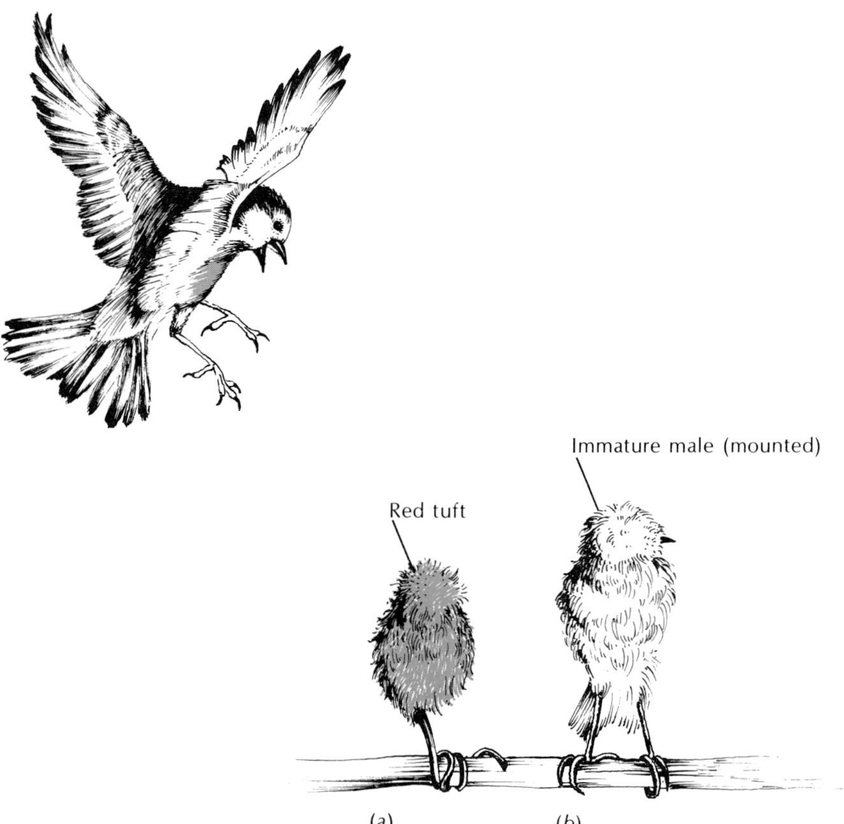

Figure 7.19 □ **Mutual displays in the herring gull: (*a*) mew calling, (*b*) choking, (*c*) facing away. Synchronous performance of these seems to overcome fear and aggressiveness and allow pair formation to take place. Each of these stereotyped activities resembles displays in aggressive encounters between birds of the same sex. The stimulation provided by participation in such mutual displays may be required to bring both birds into a full breeding state, ready to build a nest and lay eggs. [*After N. Tinbergen,* Behaviour, 15 (*1959*).]**

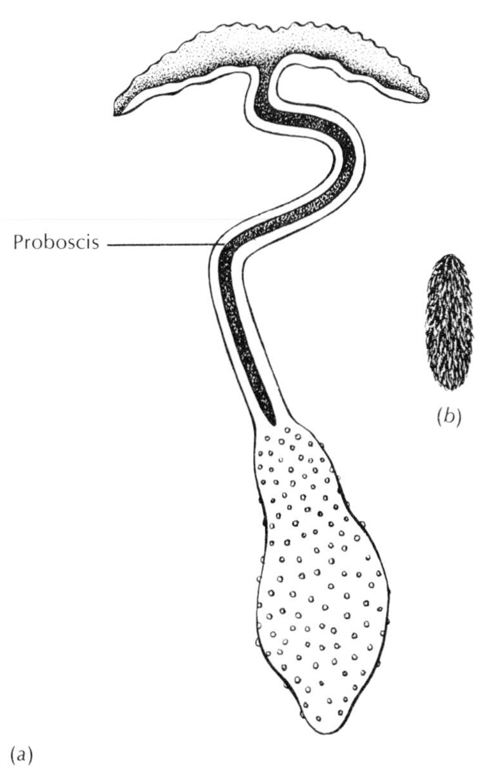

Figure 7.20 □ **Effect on larval development of pheromone secreted by female *Bonellia viridis*. The female (*a*), shown about life size, secretes a pheromone that induces nearby larvae to enter her egg organ and differentiate into small males (*b*)—one shown here magnified somewhat more than 10×—which obtain their nourishment from the female's body. Larvae developing without exposure to the pheromone become females instead of males.**

only when ingested. We have already defined a *pheromone* as a regulatory chemical secreted by some members of a species, that serves to modify the physiology, behavior, or morphology of other individuals of the same species. In their mode of action pheromones are either *primers* or *releasers*. The latter serve directly as cues that elicit specific behavioral responses. The former affect the physiological state of the organism in such a way that its response to various sensory cues is altered. For instance, certain pheromones stimulate the organism's reproductive physiology so that it will respond positively to the presence of a potential mate; this would be a primer effect. The evocation of defensive behavior by alarm pheromones is, on the other hand, a releaser effect.

The physiological activity of pheromones in suppressing the sexual development of the worker castes in termites and bees has already been mentioned. A remarkable instance of pheromonal regulation of development and maturation occurs in the echiuroid worm, *Bonellia* (Figure 7.20). *Bonellia* larvae are capable of differentiating into either males or females. A larva that settles in an area where there are no mature female *Bonellia* will itself become a female. But a larva that is attracted to a mature female will enter her egg-organ and there will differentiate into a tiny "parasitic" male with all organs degenerate save for the testis. This profound regulation of development is caused by a pheromone produced by glandular cells in the proboscis of female *Bonellia*.

Pheromones may also serve to synchronize reproductive activities, such as the production and release of gametes, and may promote the settlement of planktonic larvae such as those of barnacles.

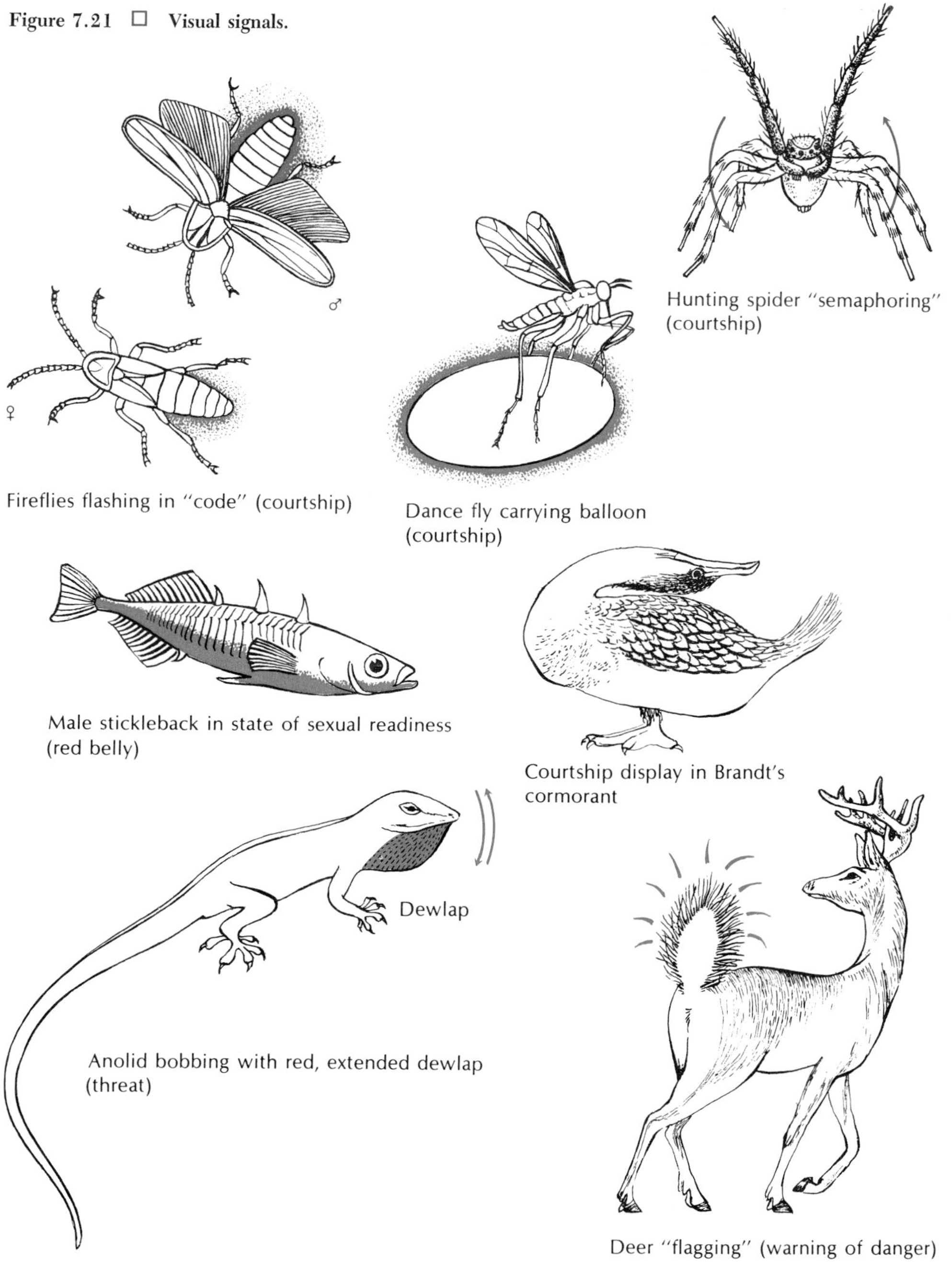

Many pheromones serve as *sex attractants*. Some stimulate sexual behavior, while others serve as means of identifying sexually mature organisms of the same species. A number of vertebrates have special glands which become active only during the mating season and release musky odors that provide olfactory cues for the attraction of mates. Current research on using such pheromones to lure insect pests may permit selective control of individual species by means that are more effective and less hazardous than the present massive use of chemical insecticides. Exposure to insecticides merely results in selection for pesticide resistance, since such resistant individuals will survive and reproduce. However, because a species must depend upon its sex attractants to bring potential mates together, it cannot develop a resistance to these substances and still reproduce at an effective rate. The necessity for the coadaptation of signals and receivers also makes it extremely difficult for a species to replace one attractant by another.

A number of pheromones are employed by ants in recruiting workers to particular tasks. If the nest is attacked, the ants release an alarm substance that elicits attack behavior. If a portion of the anthill caves in, workers are pheromonally recruited to excavate the area. Foraging workers mark their trails with a series of invisible chemical "dashes" secreted onto the ground. These odor trails persist long enough for other workers to track them, reinforcing the trails with their own signals.

Visual communication Visual signals consist of meaningful postures and movements, and also of conspicuous structural

Figure 7.21 □ **Visual signals.**

Fireflies flashing in "code" (courtship)

Dance fly carrying balloon (courtship)

Hunting spider "semaphoring" (courtship)

Male stickleback in state of sexual readiness (red belly)

Courtship display in Brandt's cormorant

Dewlap

Anolid bobbing with red, extended dewlap (threat)

Deer "flagging" (warning of danger)

attributes that convey information regarding the species, sex, and state of maturity of the individual (Plate 4c). They may be used to facilitate mating, to threaten rivals, or to help a group stay together during flight from a predator (Figure 7.21). The conspicuous plumage of male songbirds apparently attracts females of the same species, while simultaneously warning other males to remain in their own territories. The communicative value of brilliant colors must be highly significant to warrant even a temporary suspension of protective coloration. Danger to the male is often minimized, however, by the molting of nuptial plumage soon after courtship is over. Any signals that facilitate recognition of conspecifics have adaptive value because heterospecific matings rarely produce fertile offspring. The more readily potential mates can recognize one another, the less energy is wasted in approaches made to individuals of the wrong species.

Visual signals are employed by fireflies, in which the *flashing patterns* are species-specific and guarantee that a male and a female of the same species will come together. The male's flashing evokes an answering flash from the wingless female. These flashing patterns must be particularly distinctive in regions where several species of fireflies live (Figure 7.22). Although evolved as a device to facilitate mating, flashing is put to a second use in one species: the female of this species responds not only to males of her own kind but also answers the flashing of males of other species. The male, in either case, responds by alighting near the female, but her next response depends upon the kind of male that approaches her: if he belongs to her own kind, she allows him to copulate with her; but if he is of another species and has been mistakenly lured to her side, his fate is less pleasant, for she seizes and devours him. A similar fate may befall the male of any carnivorous species if a "communications breakdown" takes place. Little wonder that male hunting spiders approach their females cautiously, while maintaining striking postures that serve as recognition signals.

Figure 7.22 □ **Flash patterns of four species of fireflies occurring sympatrically. The male's signals are shown above the horizontal lines, the female's responses below. Tick marks represent time in seconds. Females ordinarily respond only to males of their own kind. These species also differ in color of light emitted, daily and seasonal peaks of mating activity, and preferred habitat. [*From B. Wallace and A. M. Srb,* Adaptation *(2nd ed.) (Englewood Cliffs, N.J.: Prentice-Hall, Inc., 1964).*]**

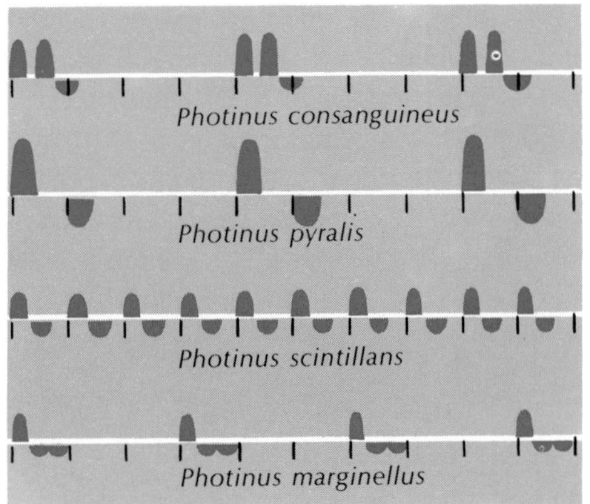

Acoustic communication Animal sounds are more versatile and susceptible to refinement and elaboration in complexity than either visual or chemical signals. Acoustic communication reaches its epitome in man, but many vertebrates possess vocabularies consisting of several characteristic sounds that evoke particular responses from other individuals of the same species. The domestic chicken has at least a nine-word repertory. The crowing of a cock advertises territory or social dominance. Readiness to attack is indicated not only by ruffled plumage and extended head, but by a throaty, growling vocalization. Contented chicks emit soft chirps, while chicks in need of attention give voice to prolonged and plaintive cheeps. These cries evoke solicitous behavior on the part of the mother hen and in fact are much more effective than visual signals, for a chick penned under a soundproof bell jar in full view of the hen is ignored by her so long as she cannot hear its cries. The hen in turn uses one sound to summon her chicks to be hovered and another to call them to food. Any bird may warn the flock of an approaching predator, using one of two informative vocalizations. One heralds the slow approach of a ground predator, for instance a fox, and causes the chickens to run and hide. The other, noting the sudden appearance of an aerial predator such as a hawk, causes them to crouch motionless. Finally, when a bird is actually seized by a predator, it emits rasping squawks which sound like cries for help, although they elicit no attempted assistance on the part of the other birds.

In some species, acoustic signals produced by members of one sex serve to attract individuals of opposite sex over a distance. Male mosquitoes cluster about a tuning fork that hums like a female in flight (Figure 7.23). Female crickets, tested in the field, will actually crawl into a loudspeaker that is projecting the recorded stridulations of the male. These calls, as well as those of male frogs and toads, are species-specific,

Figure 7.23 □ **Acoustic signals. Male mosquitoes (*Aedes aegypti*) are attracted to a tuning fork vibrating at 480 Hz, as they would be to a female *Aedes*. (*a*) Fork at rest. (*b*) Fork vibrating. (*Photographs by Edwin R. Willis.*)**

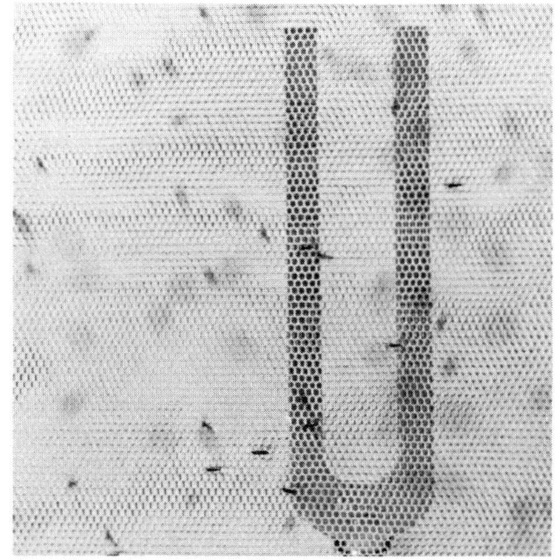

(*a*)

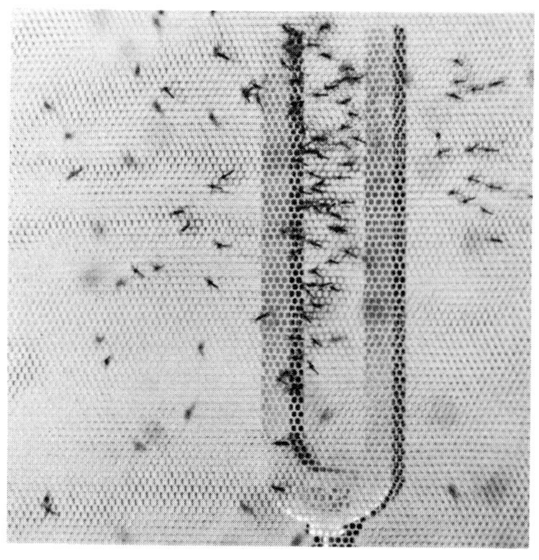

(*b*)

and thus attract only females of the same kind. When two closely related species are *sympatric,* their calls tend to become even *more differentiated* than in *allopatric* populations of those two species; natural selection promotes this divergence of signal in related sympatric species, for a call which is ambiguous may attract individuals of the wrong species and result in infertile matings. Since many female insects mate only once in their lives, should they mate with the wrong male their total egg production is forfeit.

The analysis of acoustic signals has been greatly facilitated by the use of recorders, oscilloscopes, and acoustic analyzers (such as the sound spectrograph) which identify the component frequencies, their sequence, and their duration.

Tactile communication Tactile stimuli may impart information or may trigger specific responses. Bodily contact may also be necessary for developing social integration. A number of animals, including many mammals, are *contact species:* their well-being depends on the opportunity to be in physical contact with other members of their species during at least part of their lives. Pigs, hippopotamuses, walruses, hedgehogs, parrots and many primates are examples of animals that seek bodily contact with their conspecifics throughout their lives (Figure 7.24). This tendency apparently bears no correlation with feeding; nor is it related to sexual activity, since the aggregation may be composed entirely of either sex or indifferently of both; it does not even seem to be elicited by a need to conserve body heat. Many contact species engage in *mutual grooming,* which not only serves to keep the animals free of ectoparasites but is an important factor in the reinforcement of social bonds.

All homoiothermal animals necessarily begin their lives in contact with the body of their parent. In many species of birds, both parents incubate the eggs and hover the young. Young mammals nestle against their mothers to suckle and rest; or, if deprived of a mother, the siblings huddle together. Infant primates normally spend the first weeks of their lives tightly clinging first to the mother's belly and later to her back. Studies by H. F. Harlow on the development of social relationships in rhesus monkeys showed that stimuli that attract young monkeys to their mothers are independent of the need for food. In one experiment, each monkey was raised in isolation with a pair of surrogate mothers. One "mother" consisted of a wire framework on which the bottle was mounted at each feeding. The other was a softly padded "cloth mother," which never provided food. The young monkey would, of course, mount the wire mother for feeding, but would at once return to cuddle against the cloth mother. Any fright sent the infant scurrying in panic to the cloth mother (Figure 7.25), but never to the food-providing wire mother. Such studies suggest the importance of bodily contact in the development of social bonds in human babies as well. In fact, some studies suggest that the incidence of severe mental disturbances such as schizophrenia may occur more frequently in individuals deprived of bodily contact during infancy; however, this remains unproven. Other data point to an inherited susceptibility to such derangements as schizophrenia and manic depressive psychosis. The effects of contact deprivation may be more akin to lasting

Figure 7.24 □ Contact species. (*a*) California sea lions. (*Scripps Institution of Oceanography.*) (*b*) Ring-tailed lemurs. Female at right, with young clinging to her own underside, displays interest in her neighbor's infant; she may gently remove this infant from its mother's back, using her paws as hands. All adults in the group, especially females, appear solicitous of juveniles and tend to pick up any that are untended. Adults too will huddle in groups containing individuals of both sexes. (*c*) Young orangutans at play. (*d*) Male Gelada baboon grooming female. Grooming is an important means of social integration in addition to its value in removing ectoparasites and salt granules (from sweat); females groom males and other females, males less often groom females, juveniles groom adults, and adults juveniles. (*Zoological Society of San Diego photos by Ron Garrison.*)

(*a*)

(*c*)

(*b*)

(*d*)

anxiety neurosis than to actual psychosis.

After infancy, many homoiotherms are *noncontact species,* each individual maintaining between itself and its conspecifics a species-typical *personal distance,* which may vary from a few centimeters to many meters. This personal distance is violated only for mating, for rearing the young, and sometimes briefly during aggressive encounters. In these species, tactile contact with conspecifics seems to be aversive and results in the spacing out of individuals in a group.

COMMUNICATION IN HONEYBEES One of the most elaborate repertories of communication found among invertebrates occurs in the honeybee. In Chapter 1 certain aspects of bee communication, the now-famous "dances," were described. Performed in the darkness of the hive these dances scarcely qualify as *visual* signals. A bee returning from foraging is made conspicuous by the odors of the plants she has been visiting; as she begins to dance the noise made by her vibrating wings attracts other workers, which attempt to follow her movements by placing their antennae against her body. In the words of K. Von Frisch* (translated from the original German):

> *. . . she starts whirling around in a narrow circle, constantly changing her direction, turning now right, now left, dancing clockwise and anti-clockwise in quick succession, describing between one and two circles in each direction. This dance is performed among the thickest bustle of the hive. What makes it so particularly striking and attrac-*

* *The Dancing Bees* (London: Methuen & Co., 1954), pp. 102–103.

Figure 7.25 □ **Responses of mother-deprived rhesus-monkey infants. (*a*) Although it must nurse upon wire mother, infant prefers to remain in contact with cloth mother, returning to it whenever frightened. (*b*) Four motherless rhesus juveniles find comfort in mutual huddling; raised together without adult care, these infants will prove to be normally socialized, whereas infants reared in solitude with cloth and wire mothers prove incapable of normal social relationships. (*Courtesy of Dr. H. F. Harlow and University of Wisconsin Primate Laboratory.*)**

(*a*)

(*b*)

tive is the way it infects the surrounding bees; those sitting next to the dancer start tripping after her, always trying to keep their outstretched feelers in close contact with the tip of her abdomen. They take part in each of her manoeuverings so that the dancer herself, in her madly wheeling movements, appears to carry behind her a perpetual comet's tail of bees. . . . What is the meaning of this round dance? One thing is obvious; it causes enormous excitement among the inmates of the hive sitting nearest to the dancers. Moreover, if we watch one of the bees in the dancer's train, we may actually see her preparing to depart, cleaning herself perfunctorily, then hurrying off in the direction of the entrance hole to leave the hive. . . . After returning with their loads, the new bees will dance in turn; the greater the number of dancers, the greater will be the number of newcomers crowding around the feeding place. . . .

From our discussion in Chapter 1 we may recall that this "round dance" (Figure 7.26*a*) is performed by honeybees returning from food sources within 100 m of the hive, while foragers coming from food sources at a greater distance perform a "wagging dance" in the pattern of a figure 8, with the wagging run oriented to gravity in such a way that directional information is imparted with respect to the location of the food source (Figure 7.26*b*,*c*).

The directional component of the wagging dance can be corrected to compensate for the passage of time: a forager that has been trapped and kept in the dark for several hours before being allowed to perform her dance in the presence of other workers will orient the wagging run correctly even though the sun has moved during her period of isolation. This indicates that bees, like migratory birds, have an internal timekeeping mechanism that compensates for the earth's rotation.

The wagging dance indicates not only direction but the approximate distance that must be flown to reach the food source. Von Frisch concluded that the rate at which the wagging dance is performed provides sufficient cue as to distance (see Figure 1.3), whereas certain other investigators hold the acoustic signals to be more important in this regard; however, the rate of dance and frequency of wing vibration no doubt are related and both may be of importance in "putting across" the message. A study of different races of honeybees, in which workers of two races were mixed in the same hive, showed that communication between races is imperfect: the directional component of the wagging dance is understood but the distance cue is not. After following the dances of a worker belonging to one race, workers of the second race tend to fly in the correct direction but not for the right distance.

Studies of various species of wild bees shed some light on the possible evolution of bee communication. Species considered to represent the most primitive types seem to have no special means of communicating information on food sources; some of these bees may be excited to forage by the flower odors clinging to returning foragers. Tropical bees, living in a region of the world in which the sun passes directly overhead each day, can make little use of the sun as a reference point; furthermore, so high is the forest canopy that much of their foraging is done vertically, and we have seen that honeybee dances have no *vertical* informational content. Such tropical bees instead rely on scent

Figure 7.26 □ Honeybee communication by dancing. (*a*) Round dance that alerts workers to a food source near the hive. (*b*) Wagging dance that gives directional information on the location of a food source more than 100 m distant from the hive. (*c*) Relation of orientation of waggle run to position of sun, hive, and food source.

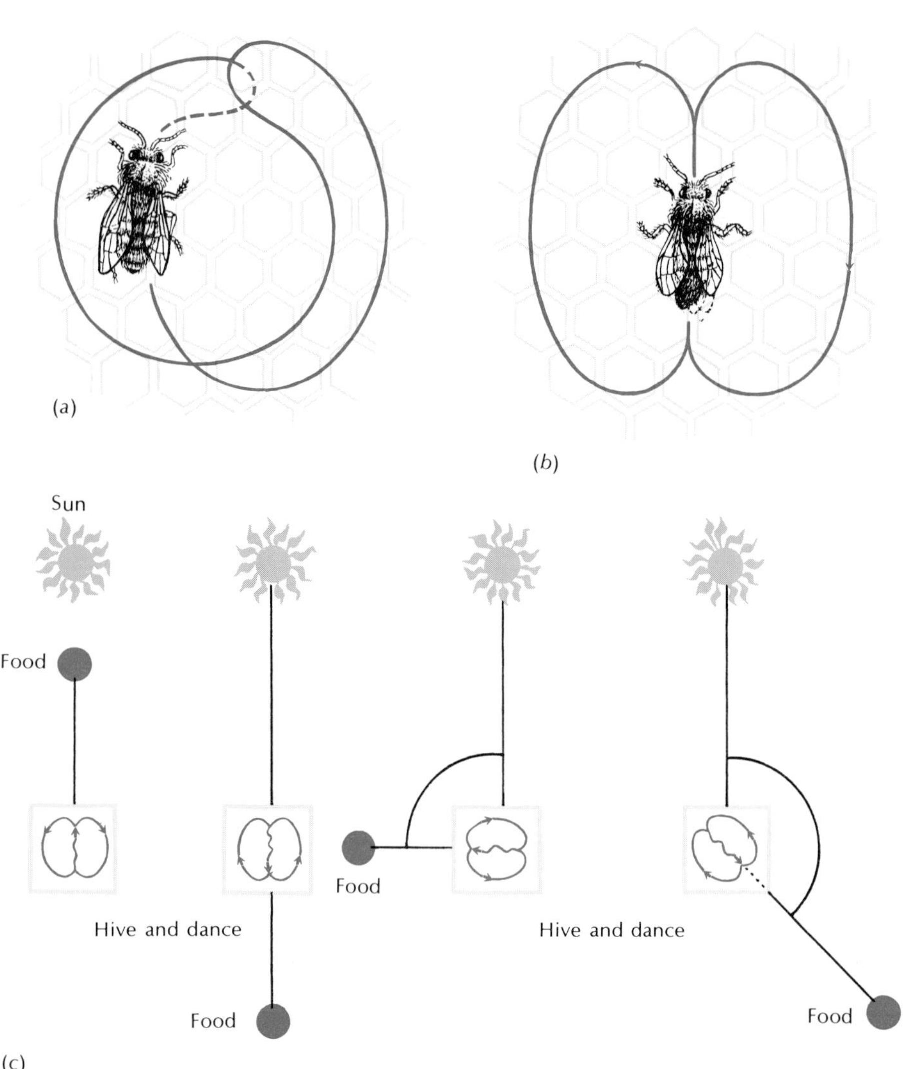

markers laid down at intervals, which may be followed by other bees and reinforced by them so that the signal does not fade away. In certain other species definite dance patterns are performed, but these are enacted out of doors on a flat platform trampled smooth on top of the hive; these bees keep an eye on the sun as they dance and use the sun directly as a reference point indicating direction to the food source. In these species the translation of visual cues into gravitational cues has not taken place. This final translation perhaps was demanded by the more rigorous climate of regions to which honeybees were native: a hive hidden for warmth within a hollow tree, for instance, would not allow the bees to dance in sight of the sun.

COMMUNICATION AND PREDATION An adaptive conflict exists between achieving effective communication between conspecifics and avoiding predators. The animal which dons bright colors and assumes conspicuous postures or which vocalizes noisily is advertising its presence not only to other members of its species but to potential predators as well. As mentioned previously, the bright coloration associated with mating in some birds and fishes is transitory. In the bowerbird family, some species have apparently abandoned nuptial plumage in favor of adorning a "bower" with brightly colored fruits and pebbles. The male constructs a more or less elaborate bower typical of his species, weaving thousands of twigs into the structure. This bower will *not* serve as the nest but functions in bringing male and female together. He furnishes the bower with an assortment of shells, spider silk, egg-sized fruit, pebbles, and fresh flowers replaced daily. His activities are reminiscent of nest-building behavior, though later the male will play no part in construction of the actual nest. The bower serves to attract the female. When she enters it, the male enters also, and courting and copulation take place within the bower. The female then departs to build a nest and rear her young with no assistance from the male, who remains near his bower awaiting visits of additional females. The bowerbirds are much less resplendent than the closely related birds-of-paradise. Within the bowerbird family, an inverse correlation commonly exists between the gaudiness of the male's plumage and the complexity of the bower: the more resplendent the bower, the drabber the male. Noting this phenomenon, E. T. Gilliard,* who has made a detailed study of the gardener bowerbird (*Amblyornis*), comments:

> *I believe that in these birds the forces of sexual selection have been transferred from morphological characteristics—the male plumage—to external objects and that this "transferral effect" may be the key factor in the evolution of the more complex bowerbirds. This would explain the extraordinary development and proliferation of the bowers and their ornaments; these objects have in effect become externalized bundles of secondary sexual characteristics that are psychologically but not physically connected with the males. The transfer also has an important morphological effect: once colorful plumage is rendered unimportant, natural selection operates in the direction of protective coloration and the male tends more and more to resemble the female. . . .*

These observations and many others point up the fact that selection with respect to social factors operating within a species may be as instrumental in influencing the evolution of structure, function, and behavior as are selective forces originating in the abiotic environment or with other species.

Through the interaction of biotic and abiotic factors the character of a species is shaped; as long as conditions remain relatively stable, the future evolution of the species may involve only minor adaptive adjustments and it may be thought of as "fully evolved." However, we shall see in the next chapter that change is inevitable and that if a population is long to persist, it cannot indefinitely remain static. Should it prove incapable of the necessary modification, some other form of life will rise to take its place. A niche vacated by extinction will eventually be reoccupied by a newly evolved species or, at least, by some species new to that community.

REVIEW AND DISCUSSION

1 Explain the adaptive value of each of the following: (*a*) social facilitation; (*b*) latitudinal migration (both ways); (*c*) systems of social hierarchy; (*d*) systems of territoriality; (*e*) substitution of bowers for bright plumage in bower birds; (*f*) mass emigration; (*g*) unstructured aggregations.

2 Explain the phrase "survival of the fittest." Why are its implications often misinterpreted? Give examples.

3 Discuss the roles of polymorphism, metamorphosis, and metagenesis in mitigating the intensity of competition among conspecifics. Provide illustrative examples. Explain how polymorphism affects the effectiveness of colonial organisms.

4 What types of organisms depend primarily upon their juvenile stages for dispersion? What kinds of adaptations for dispersal do you find in these cases?

5 What *endogenous* controls operate to control the growth of a population? Give examples of reproductive-rate regulation by intraspecific factors.

6 Explain the selective factors that operate on a given behavior or structure when it becomes of use in communication. What factors act concomitantly on the animal's receiving apparatus? Why are such signals likely to be more different in sympatric populations of related species than they are in the allopatric parts of the range?

7 Give examples of the pheromonal control of social behavior, development, and caste determination.

8 Distinguish between primer and releaser effects of pheromones. Why are sex attractants likely to be more successful in controlling insect pests than the application of insecticides?

9 Explain the nature of ritualization and how natural selection operates toward the ritualization of movements that have a signal function. What is the adaptive value of the ritualization of aggression?

*"The Evolution of Bowerbirds," *Sci. Amer.*, **209,** 43 (1963).

ARLING, G. L., AND H. F. HARLOW "Effects of social deprivation on maternal behavior of rhesus monkeys," *J. Comp. Physiol. Psych.,* **64** (1967). Early experience is shown to have ineradicable effects on behavior at maturity.

BONNER, J. T. "A Colony of Cells," *Sci. Amer.,* **182** (1949).

BRIAN, M. V. *Social Insect Populations.* New York: Academic Press, Inc., 1965. The structure and dynamics of insect societies is concisely examined and the importance of intraspecific, interspecific, and intergeneric competition is evaluated.

CALHOUN, J. B. "Population Density and Social Pathology," *Sci. Amer.,* **206** (1962). Experiments indicate that conspecific interactions become abnormal under conditions of overcrowding.

CARR, A. "The Navigation of the Green Turtle," *Sci. Amer.,* **212** (1965). Radio tracking devices permit study of the trans-Atlantic migrations of green turtles.

CARTHY, J. D. *Animal Navigation.* New York: Charles Scribners' Sons, 1963. Summarizes various studies into the mechanisms of navigation in animals.

DARLING, F. F. *A Herd of Red Deer.* New York: Doubleday & Co., Inc., 1964. A classic field study reveals an interesting pattern of social organization in British red deer herds.

EIBL-EIBESFELDT, I. "The Fighting Behavior of Animals," *Sci. Amer.,* **205** (1961). Natural selection favors the ritualization of aggressive behavior and the evolution of submissive signals which inhibit continued attack. Has man no such evolved controls?

EMLEN, J. E., AND R. L. PENNEY "The Navigation of Penguins," *Sci. Amer.,* **215** (1966). Field experiments show that displaced penguins can "home" over trackless Antarctic snow fields.

ESCH, H. "The Evolution of Bee Language," *Sci. Amer.,* **216** (1967).

FRINGS, H., AND M. FRINGS "Uses of Sounds by Insects," *Ann. Rev. Entomol.,* **3** (1958).

——— *Animal Communication.* Waltham, Mass.: Blaisdell Publishing Co., 1964. This work, authored by a competent research team investigating acoustic signals in the animal world, summarizes ways in which animals communicate.

GRIFFIN, D. *Bird Migration.* Garden City, N.Y.: Doubleday & Co., Inc., 1964. A brief, interesting account, mainly anecdotal, of the author's and others' investigation of bird homing and navigation.

GUHL, A. M. "The Social Order of Chickens," *Sci. Amer.,* **194** (1956). Social hierarchies affect the genetic composition of the flock.

HARCOURT, D. G., AND E. J. LEROUX "Population Regulation in Insects and Man," *Amer. Scientist,* **55** (1967). Density-dependent factors responsible for the regulation of insect populations are compared with those which may operate to bring human birth and death rates into balance.

HARLOW, H. F., AND M. K. HARLOW "Social Deprivation in Monkeys," *Sci. Amer.,* **207** (1962). Monkeys deprived of normal social contacts during infancy show persistent failure to develop normal conspecific relationships.

——— AND R. R. ZIMMERMANN "The Development of Affectional Responses in Infant Monkeys," *Proc. Amer. Phil. Soc.,* **102** (1958). Experiments with models elucidate factors involved in the maintenance of bonds between mothers and young.

HOWARD, H. E. *Territory in Bird Life.* New York: Atheneum, 1964. This reprinted classic represents an early exposition of the importance of systems of territoriality.

JACOBSON, M., AND M. BEROZA "Insect Attractants," *Sci. Amer.,* **211** (1964).

KNIPLING, E. F. "The Eradication of the Screw-worm Fly," *Sci. Amer.,* **203** (1960). The monogamous behavior of insects is used to good account in eliminating a serious parasite of livestock.

LANE, C. E. "The Portuguese Man-of-War," *Sci. Amer.,* **202** (1960). Describes the development and morphology of a polymorphic colonial coelenterate.

LINDAUER, M. *Communication Among Social Bees.* Cambridge, Mass.: Harvard University Press, 1961. Comparative studies of communication in the tropical bees shed light on the evolution of honeybee dances.

LORENZ, K. Z. *King Solomon's Ring.* New York: Thomas Y. Crowell Co., 1952. A pioneer ethologist relates his experiences in the study of animal behavior, especially with his flock of jackdaws.

——— *Evolution and Modification of Behavior.* Chicago: University of Chicago Press, 1965. An advanced but readable defense of studies which indicate that behavioral potentials can be genetically transmitted and are subject to evolution through natural selection.

SHAW, E. "The Schooling of Fishes," *Sci. Amer.,* **206** (1962).

SOUTHWICK, C. H. (ED.) *Primate Social Behavior.* Princeton, N.J.: D. Van Nostrand Co., 1963. A compilation of articles reporting the results of field and experimental studies of the organization of primate social groups.

THORPE, W. H. *Bird Song.* Cambridge, Mass.: Cambridge University Press, 1961.

TINBERGEN, N. "Social Releasers and the Experimental Method Required for Their Study," *Wilson Bull.,* **60** (1948). An eminent ethologist discusses experimental means of identifying the sign stimuli which release innate patterns of social behavior.

——— "A Note on the Origin and Evolution of Threat Display," *Ibis,* **94** (1952). Threat behavior is the outcome of the simultaneous activation of tendencies to attack and escape. An evolutionary increase in the strength of the fighting tendency would interfere with courtship, hence the "relentless fighter" is selected against.

VON FRISCH, K. *Bees: Their Vision, Chemical Senses and Language.* Ithaca, N.Y.: Cornell University Press, 1950. Reviews the author's experiments on the sensory acuities of honeybees, and describes the transmission of information via the bee "dances" first discovered by Von Frisch.

——— "Dialects in the Language of the Bees," *Sci. Amer.,* **207** (1962).

WASHBURN, S. L., AND I. DE VORE "The Social Life of Baboons," *Sci. Amer.,* **204** (1961). Field studies disclose the social organization of baboon troops.

WENNER, A. M. "Sound Production During the Waggle Dance of the Honey Bee," *Animal Behav.,* **10** (1962). The significance of acoustic communication in the honeybee is discussed.

WIGGLESWORTH, V. B. "Metamorphosis, Polymorphism, Differentiation," *Sci. Amer.,* **200** (1959). Larval stages are not merely steps on the road to adulthood but have evolved their own particular complexes of adaptive characteristics whereby they exploit different habitats and pursue modes of life different from those of the adult.

WILSON, E. O. "Pheromones," *Sci. Amer.,* **208** (1963). The significance of a recently discovered class of "external hormones" is discussed.

WYNNE-EDWARDS, V. C. "Population Control in Animals," *Sci. Amer.,* **211** (1964). Endogenous mechanisms for regulating population levels may exist in many animal species.

Chapter 8  THE DYNAMICS OF ADAPTATION

IT WAS LONG A MATTER OF ACCEPTED opinion that each specific kind of living thing represented an immutable entity, which had remained the same from the moment of its creation. Only a century ago most biologists still accepted the concept of the *fixity of species,* for they had little idea of the tremendous reaches of time through which life has come to reach the present. Working within a frame of reference of a few thousand years since the beginning of the earth and life upon it, they neither accepted the significance of the fossil record nor recognized the evidences of ongoing biotic change. Even as the acceptance of Copernicus's revolutionary heliocentric theory of the solar system in place of the classical Ptolemaic earth-centered concept involved a profound philosophical readjustment, so the realization that life on earth probably spans a period exceeding 2.5×10^9 years has enabled us to view biotic phenomena in quite a new perspective. Within the past century the concept of the *dynamic fluidity of life* has replaced that of the unchanging *fixity* of life forms. One of the major prerequisites for static inflexibility in living things would be that their environment be equally static and unchangeable. In a changing milieu, the cost of inflexibility is extinction. Living things are now known to be in a constant state of adjustment to changes in their biotic and abiotic environments. Through genetic modifications and physiological regulation, they strive not only to maintain their own steady state but also to exert homeostatic control over the environment. In the living world the criterion of success is simple and unequivocal: *sur-*

vival. Any population that fails to cope with changes in its environment becomes extinct. On the other hand, in successfully meeting the challenge of habitat alteration, a population can evolve into something new and descendants may come to differ markedly from their ancestors.

Neither the species nor the community is exempt from change. These changes are of two major types: (1) those which occur in the course of *ecological succession;* (2) those which occur as a result of *organic evolution.* The former involves changes in the composition of a community, whereas the latter involves changes in the hereditary makeup of populations. Both of these processes operate over prolonged periods of time, so that many of the phenomena we see today are understandable only when viewed as stages in an ongoing process. The dynamic character of the adaptive process is best comprehended when we can decipher its past history; it is then sometimes possible to predict its future.

8.1 □ ECOLOGICAL SUCCESSION: CHANGE IN COMMUNITY STRUCTURE

By *ecological succession* we mean the series of changes that a biotic community undergoes in its maturation toward the stable, or *climax,* condition (Figure 8.1). As we have noted earlier, the initial assemblage of a group of species in a given area requires that the pioneer forms have similar tolerances for the prevailing abiotic conditions. However, the actions and interactions of these pioneer populations set up new conditions that make possible the success of still other species. Thus a process of succession is set in motion, which carries the community through many transient phases until the climax condition is reached; this may remain stable for some time, but as the environment continues to change, one climax is succeeded by another. This replacement can occur by the incursions of better-adapted species or by the further evolution of the biota of the previous community.

A The process of succession

Studies of ecological succession have been conducted in areas where some catastrophe, such as a massive landslide or a lava flow, has utterly destroyed the existing community. It has been found that certain plant species that can grow on rock in the absence of soil, notably lichens, are among the first to resettle the denuded area. By secreting acids lichens accelerate the weathering of stone and soon pockets of soil appear in which small vascular plants of especially rugged constitution, such as club moss (a lycopsid) can take root. These species in turn add to the accumulation of soil and their dead tissues form humus. Soil bacteria and fungi take hold and begin to decompose this organic detritus. Seeds of higher plants are soon introduced by wind dispersal or in the droppings of birds, and these germinate wherever the pioneer species have prepared the way. As the vegetative cover thickens it provides food and shelter for animals from adjacent areas. In time the denuded land tends to return to the original climax condition that prevailed before catastrophe struck. Most areas disturbed by cultivation or fire can be seen to be undergoing ecological succession toward the reestablishment of the former climax community. However, in some cases the disturbance is so severe that the original climax can never be restored, and a different community may succeed it. For instance, overcultivation or overgrazing may promote desert conditions where forest or grassland once prevailed. A long-term climatic change, such as a gradual decline in annual rainfall, may be coped with successfully for some time by the capacity of a major climax community to create its own microclimate. However, in this situation the homeostatic mechanisms of the community become so stressed that the same climax may not be reestablished should a severe perturbation occur. Once the microclimate is destroyed, the original community is unable to take hold again; then a new set of ecological dominants will eventually hold sway.

During the course of ecological succession, one biota, constituting a *subclimax community,* may literally "put itself out of business" by altering the conditions requisite for its own survival. This is the case in the succession of pond to marsh to woodland. The aquatic plants themselves accelerate the disappearance of the pond that gave

Figure 8.1 □ Ecological succession. (*a*) Succession from old field to woodland. From left to right, three photographs taken of the same scene at intervals of several years; in the third stage, woodland is fully established and grass cover is missing. (*b*) Succession from pond to coniferous forest, showing characteristic changes in flora and fauna: (1) pond stage with phytoplankton, zooplankton, leeches, fish, pond snails, and rooted aquatic vegetation; (2) marsh stage with great blue herons, redwing blackbirds, and reeds and sedges encroaching upon the water, pond basin filling with silt; (3) bog stage with Venus' flytrap, pitcher plants, peat moss, and salamanders, soil saturated with water; (4) woodland succession to coniferous forest, showing seedlings of climax species under canopy of subclimax trees; (5) climax community: mainly coniferous.

(a)

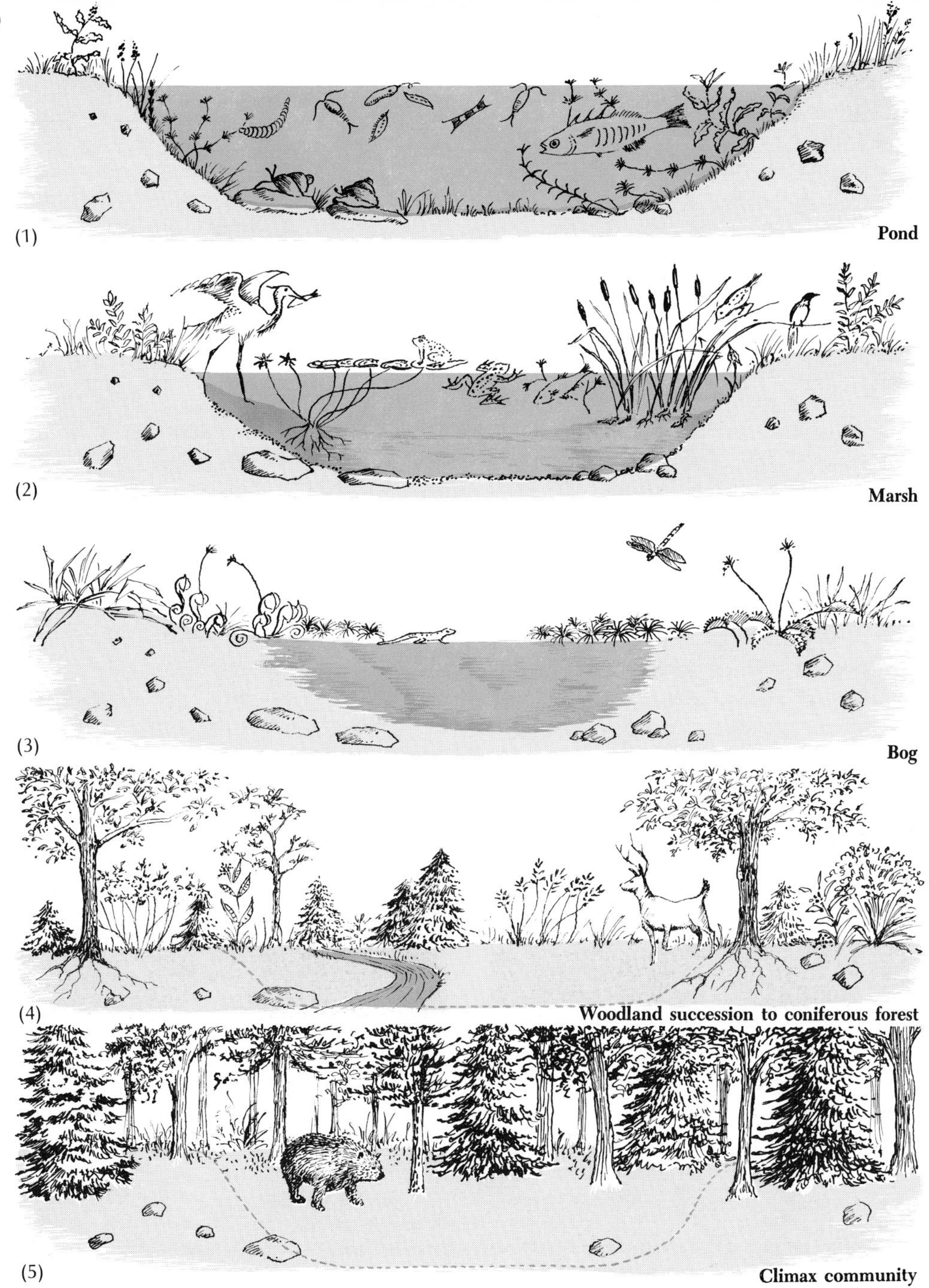

them life. Organic detritus from these plants accumulates, promoting the growth of other plants, which encroach ever further upon the open water. Not only does this organic debris glut the pond, but it causes settlement of sediments brought from upstream. Eventually a streamside marsh community succeeds the former pond community. Continued sedimentation and accumulation of detritus from the marsh community at last builds up the marshy substratum into solid soil that can support the invading biota of the neighboring woodland community. Thus each subclimax community in turn contains the seeds of its own destruction and facilitates the establishment of the next phase (*sere*) to take place in the process of succession.

B Disturbance of the climax community

An established biotic community is one that has undergone coadaptive evolutionary changes as a result of selective influences exerted by the various members of the community upon one another. Accordingly, the climax community is a precisely integrated biotic entity. Nevertheless it can be disrupted by such factors as habitat changes, invasions, or the development of some biotic innovation by an existing member of the community.

HABITAT CHANGES An established community usually exhibits great resilience in overcoming the effects of relatively transitory disturbances, such as those caused by fire or flood. A succession of subclimax stages leads eventually to the reestablishment of the original climax condition, as described above.

Long-term cyclical changes in abiotic factors may take place gradually over centuries or millennia. These include slow climatic modifications, changes in altitude resulting from warping or folding of the earth's crust or from the erosion of mountains, and fluctuations in sea level. The more *slowly* these changes occur, the more likely they are to be met by compensatory evolutionary adjustments in the original biota. New species exhibiting new ranges of tolerance may evolve from the preexisting species. A more rapid change, on the other hand, is more likely to cause extinction of the inhabitants and to result in the subsequent resettlement of the area by populations derived from other habitats of suitable character.

INVASIONS Invasion of an established community by a new species may have temporary or lasting effects depending upon the degree of difficulty with which the newcomers are assimilated into the fabric of the community. If a vacant niche exists or a new niche can be created, the new species merely enriches the community. This seems to be the case with the cattle egret, which recently crossed the Atlantic to the United States. These birds feed with cattle, upon insects that the cattle disturb while grazing. They occupy a niche that was vacant before their coming and are in competition with no previous inhabitant of the grassland biome.

If, however, the invader seriously competes with species already established in the community (as European starlings do with native American woodpeckers), then in time either the invader or the previous inhabitants give way before the other species.

ADAPTIVE INNOVATIONS Development of an adaptive innovation—an evolutionary breakthrough—by one portion of the community may profoundly stress the whole. The innovation may require compensatory adjustments that other members of the community are unable to make. One of the most dramatic examples of this is seen in the innovations developed by early mammals, which their reptilian predecessors lacked: (1) *homoiothermy,* the capacity for maintaining a stable body temperature; (2) *viviparity,* the capacity for providing embryos with nourishment from the maternal bloodstream during intrauterine development; (3) development of the *neopallium* (the modern cerebral cortex), providing extensive new brain areas in which neural integration and association take place. The neopallium is absent or rudimentary in other vertebrates and has reached its highest level of complexity to date in the primates, particularly man. Adaptive innovations developed by man have included (1) development of language of sufficient complexity to facilitate cultural transmission and (2) manufacture and use of tools and weapons, with concomitant selection toward improved prehensility and manipulative ability of the hand.

In modern times, the impact of man's adaptive innovations upon the entire biosphere has increased markedly. Development of his nervous system to that critical point at which the fruits of individual experience could be culturally transmitted from generation to generation has enabled *Homo sapiens,* a single species, to compete successfully with or to control nearly all other creatures in communities that man has invaded. Man's "cultural evolution" has widened the gap between *Homo sapiens* and the other intelligent mammalian species to an extent much greater than would have resulted from organic evolution alone. A child deprived of its cultural inheritance, if it survives at all, will develop not much of a language nor any but the most rudimentary uses of tools. The differences among various human populations are much more cultural than they are genetic. Inventions such as the wheel and key concepts such as numerals, the alphabet, and the notion of zero have arisen independently in particular cultures and then have been disseminated to others.

Unfortunately, during its cultural evolution certain portions of humanity developed philosophical aberrations that have had disastrous consequences on the rest of the living world and may yet bring catastrophe upon humanity itself. These include the assumptions that (1) the human species is both psychologically and ecologically divorced from the rest of the biosphere, and (2) any exploitation by man of his living and nonliving environments is justifiable on the grounds that the universe was expressly created for the use and amusement of mankind. Increasing evidence of serious ecological disturbances caused by human activities suggests that mankind's long-term survival may depend on its ability to become integrated harmoniously with the wider biotic community. Otherwise the planetary ecosystem may collapse, and should this happen, humanity will fall with it.

One aspect of the dynamism of biotic diversity is the change in community structure we have called ecological succession. A second aspect is *evolution,* by which we mean the change through successive generations of the hereditary characteristics of a population. Not all evolutionary change is adaptive, yet in general we can consider evolution to be *the process of adaptation as viewed in the perspective of time.* Evolution is the product of the interaction of two sets of factors: (1) alterations that take place in the hereditary material itself; (2) the complex of internal and external factors that define the adaptive value of each hereditary trait.

We noted in Chapter 1 that in all organisms this hereditary material is made up of enormous molecules known as nucleic acids (the chemical nature of these interesting macromolecules will be discussed in Chapter 9). Our sequence of study will continue approximately to parallel the history of biological science (although with benefit of hindsight that enables us to interpret earlier discoveries in the light of later knowledge). The role of natural selection in evolution was recognized prior to the discovery of the laws of heredity that would explain the internal mechanisms by which evolutionary change takes place. In turn, these laws of inheritance, describing the behavior of inheritable traits during their transmission from parents to progeny, were worked out decades before it was known that such traits were governed by threadlike bodies seen in dividing cells, which were named *chromosomes* ("colored bodies," due to their affinity for basic dyes) long before their real significance was understood (see photographs of chromosomes in Figures 8.11*b* and 8.13*a*). Even the "mapping" of chromosomes—the assigning of specific locations (*loci*) to particular unit characters—had been undertaken successfully (in the fruit fly, *Drosophila*) many years before the fundamental nature of these genetic units (*genes*) was finally worked out.

In Part 2 we concentrated upon the need of the biosphere to adapt successfully to factors in the external environment, for it was the study of these factors that contributed most heavily to Darwin's development of the theory of evolution by means of natural selection. Now we shall turn our attention to the more recently discovered internal mechanisms of heredity, first studying these at the level of the organism and population (as Mendel did) and at the chromosomal level (as did Thomas Hunt Morgan); next, in Chapter 9 we shall study these mechanisms at the molecular level, according to the model worked out by Francis Crick and James Watson. In Parts 3 and 4 we shall find that adaptation to *internal* factors has also played a profound role in the evolution of life—molecules must be effectively organized into biochemical reaction systems and cellular structures; cells within multicellular bodies must be both structurally and functionally coordinated to maintain the life of the individual organism. The hereditary mechanisms of living systems must therefore interact with *two* environments: the external environment that surrounds the organism and the internal environment that exists within its very own body.

A Heredity and evolution

Changes in the hereditary material occur *randomly,* without reference to potential adaptive value. For every change of positive adaptive value, there will be many that are *maladaptive* with respect to either coping with the environment or carrying out the body's own metabolic processes. How do populations of organisms tolerate the load of maladaptive hereditary mutations that they must carry as the inescapable price of genetic flexibility?

THE ADAPTIVE VALUE OF DIPLOIDY The accumulation of maladaptive traits may lead to the extinction of a population. However, almost all animals and higher plants have developed a means that permits them to carry a variety of altered and sometimes harmful genetic characters in the population while still minimizing their detrimental effects: this means is *diploidy,* a condition in which each hereditary trait is represented by a *pair* of basically identical factors known as *alleles.* This condition was discovered by Gregor Mendel, who found that sweet pea plants have a double set of hereditary factors, half contributed by each parent. We now know that in diploid species generally, this "double dose" results from the fact that one complete set of chromosomes is contributed to the individual by each of its parents. In each body cell, therefore, every chromosome is usually a member of a homologous pair, each of which carries a fundamentally identical set of unit factors or genes. Within homologous chromosomes, homologous genes or alleles occupy corresponding positions or loci. Although alleles are originally identical, when one is altered by mutation they are no longer exactly alike and are then capable of exerting different effects upon the *phenotype* (physical constitution) of the organism. For now we may consider a gene to be a portion of a chromosome that determines a specific inheritable trait. Small alterations in a gene, as we shall see, may have drastic effects upon the phenotype. Through a long process of adaptive change each gene has become capable of encoding the structure of some essential protein responsible for carrying out some vital function in the living body; mutations in these adapted genes are likely to interfere with performance of some essential physiological process and thereby cause death or at least produce some detectable metabolic or developmental defect. On the other hand, all evolutionary progress rests on the fact that now and then some change will take place in a gene that enables it to produce a substance more useful than ever.

The survival value of diploidy rests in the following advantages: (1) *it doubles the "margin for error" of the individual organism* (that is, if one gene is altered by mutation, its "normal" allele remains functional and may be able to carry out the job that both alleles ordinarily accomplish together); (2) *it increases the potential of a population for effectively coping with crises by means of genetic adjustments* (that is, a genetically heterogeneous population has more alternatives from which to draw). Originally useless or even detrimental traits may prove useful under new circumstances.

TYPES OF MUTANT ALLELES Genes considered to be the *normal* alleles of a population are those which have arrived at an optimal state of functionality through a period of gradual selection toward increased functional efficiency of the gene products (proteins). Any mutation may thus impair the functionality of a gene, rendering it amorphic, hypomorphic or neomorphic. The majority of such mutants are—at least initially—less adaptive than their normal alleles, for the genetic mechanism, like any fine precision instrument, is more likely to be damaged than improved by random tampering. *Amorphic* ("no form") alleles are those which no longer contribute *positively* to the development or functioning of an organism. They are apparently "silent" or nonfunctional. The effects that they exert on the phenotype are due to the *deficiency* of some necessary product of gene action rather than to the *presence* of some new substance manufactured by the allele.

Hypomorphic ("reduced form") alleles are not "silent" but "crippled," for they are still capable of producing basically the same kind of protein as that produced by the normal alleles, but in a form that is functionally impaired. For instance, if the trait in question is hair pigmentation, a hypomorphic allele may cause production of less pigment than usual, and the hair color is accordingly less intense than in *wild type* individuals (those showing the trait considered typical of the population).

It is possible to discriminate experimentally between amorphic and hypomorphic mutants by increasing the *gene dosage* (the number of alleles present). If a hypomorphic mutant gene is multiplied so that not two but several alleles for a given trait are present, with each increment the phenotype more closely approaches normalcy. If, for instance, the hypomorphic gene is only 50 percent as effective as its normal allele, when *two* identical hypomorphic alleles are present their combined efforts approximate the effectiveness of *one* of the normal alleles. On the other hand, experimentally increasing the gene dosage for an *amorphic* allele will *not* cause the phenotype to become more nearly normal because amorphs are completely inactive.

A *neomorphic* ("new form") allele is a mutant gene that produces a protein that is so significantly altered that it can be termed a "new" substance. A neomorph exerts a *new* effect on the phenotype. Increasing the gene dosage for a neomorphic allele causes the phenotype to *deviate* further from that produced by the normal allele. This is an effect opposite to that obtained by increasing the dosage of a hypomorph. The neomorphic mutant is most important to evolutionary advancement, for its altered product may prove capable of assuming a new function, and some desirable trait may result. For instance, a new digestive enzyme may be produced that is capable of digesting some substance hitherto found indigestible; a new source of food is then available to individuals carrying this trait.

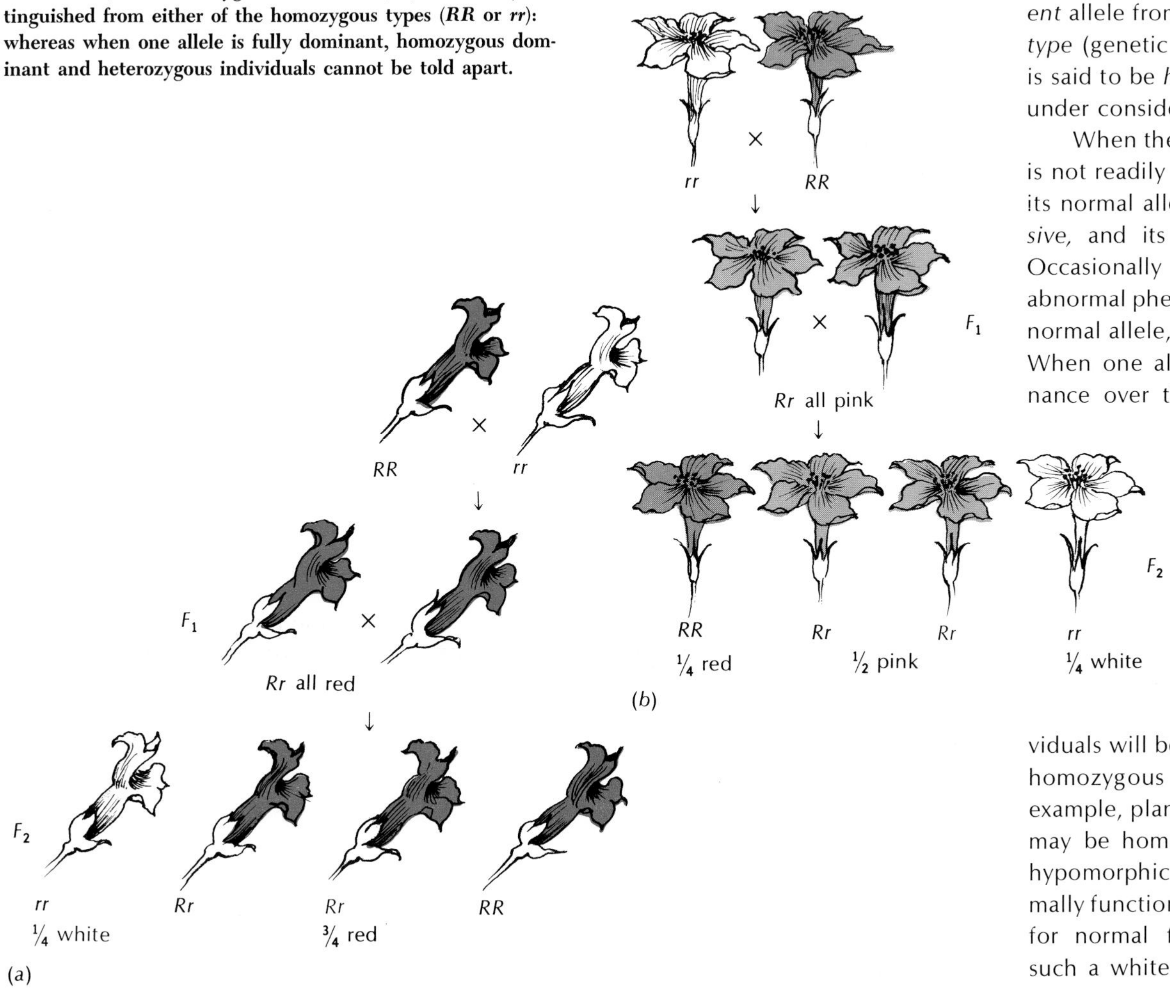

DOMINANCE, CODOMINANCE, AND RECESSIVENESS Amorphic and hypomorphic alleles often do not produce readily discernible effects on the phenotype unless one of them has been inherited from each parent. An individual that inherits two *identical* alleles is said to be *homozygous* for that trait. If an organism inherits a *different* allele from each of its parents, its *genotype* (genetic constitution for a given trait) is said to be *heterozygous* for the character under consideration.

When the effect produced by one gene is not readily detectable in the presence of its normal allele, the gene is termed *recessive,* and its functional allele, *dominant.* Occasionally a mutant gene producing an abnormal phenotype will be dominant to its normal allele, but this is not the usual case. When one allele exhibits *complete* dominance over the other, heterozygous individuals will be indistinguishable from those homozygous for the *dominant* alleles. For example, plants that produce white flowers may be homozygous for the amorphic or hypomorphic alleles of a gene which normally functions to produce a protein needed for normal floral pigmentation. Crossing such a white-flowered strain with a strain

Figure 8.2 □ Dominance and codominance. (*a*) In snapdragons red flower color is determined by a single dominant gene (*R*), which completely masks the presence of its allele for white coloration (*r*). The first hybrid generation (F_1) has fully red flowers. Their progeny (F_2) are red or white in the proportions $\frac{3}{4}$ red to $\frac{1}{4}$ white. (*b*) In four o'clocks the flowers are red only when two pigment-producing genes are present and the genotype is *RR*. Mating red and white individuals produces an F_1 generation that has only pink flowers. Crossing these *Rr* individuals yields red-, pink-, and white-flowering plants in the ratio $\frac{1}{4}:\frac{1}{2}:\frac{1}{4}$. When alleles are codominant, the heterozygous individuals (*Rr*) are readily distinguished from either of the homozygous types (*RR* or *rr*): whereas when one allele is fully dominant, homozygous dominant and heterozygous individuals cannot be told apart.

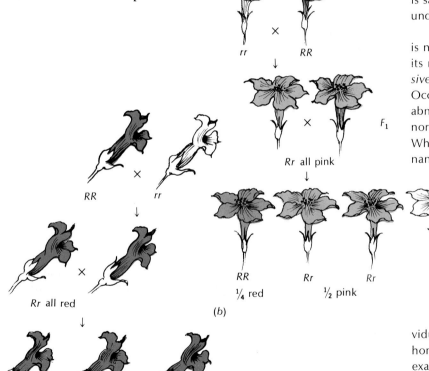

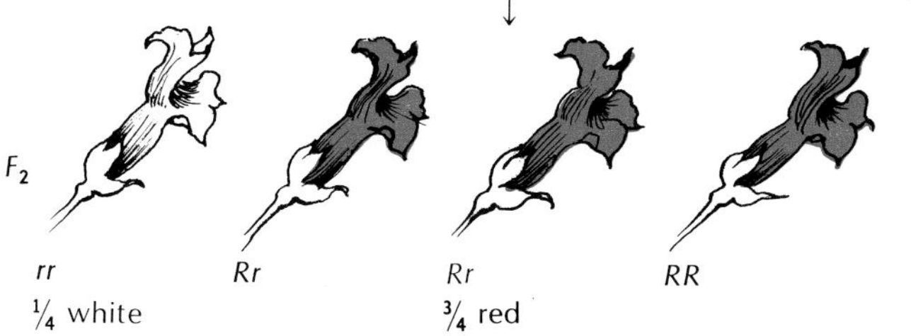

bearing red flowers results in a hybrid progeny that may be either red-flowered or pink-flowered, according to whether or not the "red allele" is completely dominant (Figure 8.2). In snapdragons, such heterozygotes are fully red, because a single functional allele is capable of producing complete floral pigmentation. In four o'clocks, on the other hand, *two* normal alleles are required for full pigment production and the presence of one amorphic or hypomorphic allele results in production of only about half the normal amount of pigment. In this case the hybrid progeny are *pink*-flowered. This condition of phenotypic intermediacy exemplifies one type of *codominance*. Codominance is a condition in which two contrasting alleles exert approximately equal effects upon the phenotype of the heterozygote. Codominance does *not* necessarily imply that each allele carries on a different activity. In the preceding examples, the "white" allele does *not* function by producing a "white pigment." It merely *fails* to produce a compound needed for manufacturing *red* (or other) pigments. Thus the codominance effect in four o'clocks really results from the fact that *one* "red" allele alone cannot produce enough red pigment to enable the fully red phenotype to develop. This type of codominance therefore is actually a dilution effect due to a 50 percent deficiency of the needed gene product.

Another kind of codominance, which is genuinely due to differing functions of two alleles rather than being produced by the nonfunctionality of one allele, results when a mutant gene is neomorphic. As we have said, neomorphic mutants produce a protein the *presence* of which alters the phenotype. An individual that inherits a given neomorphic allele from *both* parents produces only the new protein, whereas a heterozygous individual carrying both the normal and neomorphic alleles will produce equal quantities of the two different proteins, which, as we have said, exert different effects on the phenotype. In man, a neomorphic allele concerned with synthesis of the blood pigment hemoglobin causes an altered form of this pigment to be produced. A person heterozygous for this pair of alleles has in his red blood corpuscles equal quantities of two kinds of hemoglobin, known respectively as *hemoglobin A* (*Hb-A*, the normal type), and *hemoglobin S* (*Hb-S*, sickle-cell hemoglobin). Chemically, Hb-S molecules differ only slightly from Hb-A, but they behave abnormally under conditions of low oxygen concentration, changing from the globular configuration characteristic of Hb-A, to an elongate state that twists the red blood corpuscles into characteristic sickle shapes (Figure 8.3). These deformed cells are destroyed by the body's defensive cells, resulting in a condition known as *sickle-cell anemia*. In the heterozygous individual enough Hb-A is produced to alleviate the sickling tendency so that it will not become acute except when the blood is very low in oxygen, such as during extreme physical exertion. In homozygous individuals, however, who have received an Hb-S allele from each parent, the red blood cells sickle extensively with the production of a profound anemia, of which the result is usually death.

GENETIC POLYMORPHISM The existence in a population's gene pool of two or more kinds of alleles for a given trait is termed genetic polymorphism. It is not always easy to ascertain whether a specific polymorphism is balanced, transient, or indifferent. Sickle-cell trait constitutes a *balanced* (stable) genetic polymorphism in some human populations and a *transient* (changing) polymorphism in others. This is because the survival value of the alleles for Hb-A and Hb-S is in part *environmentally* determined. Each death of a child homozygous for sickle-cell trait removes two Hb-S alleles from the population. At this rate one could predict the eventual elimination of this trait. However, the Hb-S allele is maintained in the human species despite its detrimental effects on the carriers. Such persistence of a physiologically detrimental trait is due to an *ecological* relationship which promotes the survival of persons carrying the trait. In regions where malignant tertian malaria is endemic, persons heterozygous for the sickle-cell trait prove more resistant to malaria than those homozygous for normal hemoglobin. This is not surprising in the light of the fact that the malarial parasite feeds and reproduces within the red blood corpuscles. Changes in these cells tend to affect the parasite adversely. As an outcome of this parasite-host relationship, the lethal effects of two Hb-S alleles on the homozygote are counterbalanced by the enhanced malaria resistance of the heterozygote. Therefore, both the Hb-S and Hb-A alleles persist in equilibrium in the population. The mortality of the sickle-cell homozygotes is offset by the reproductive advantage of the heterozygotes over normal persons, who are more subject to malaria. Such persistence of a basically detrimental allele because of a selective advantage favoring heterozygous individuals is known as *balanced polymorphism*. If

Figure 8.3 □ Malaria and sickle-cell anemia. (*a*) Distribution of malignant tertian malaria (colored areas), together with occurrence of sickle-cell anemia in man (hatched lines). [*Data from Motulsky,* Human Biology (*Detroit, Mich.: Wayne State University Press*).] (*b*) Human blood showing abnormal sickle cells (deformed red blood corpuscles). (*Courtesy of Carolina Biological Supply Company.*) Despite the fact that the condition is fatal to individuals homozygous for the trait, sickle-cell anemia persists in populations inhabiting parts of the world where malignant tertian malaria is endemic since persons heterozygous for the trait are more resistant to malaria than normal individuals are.

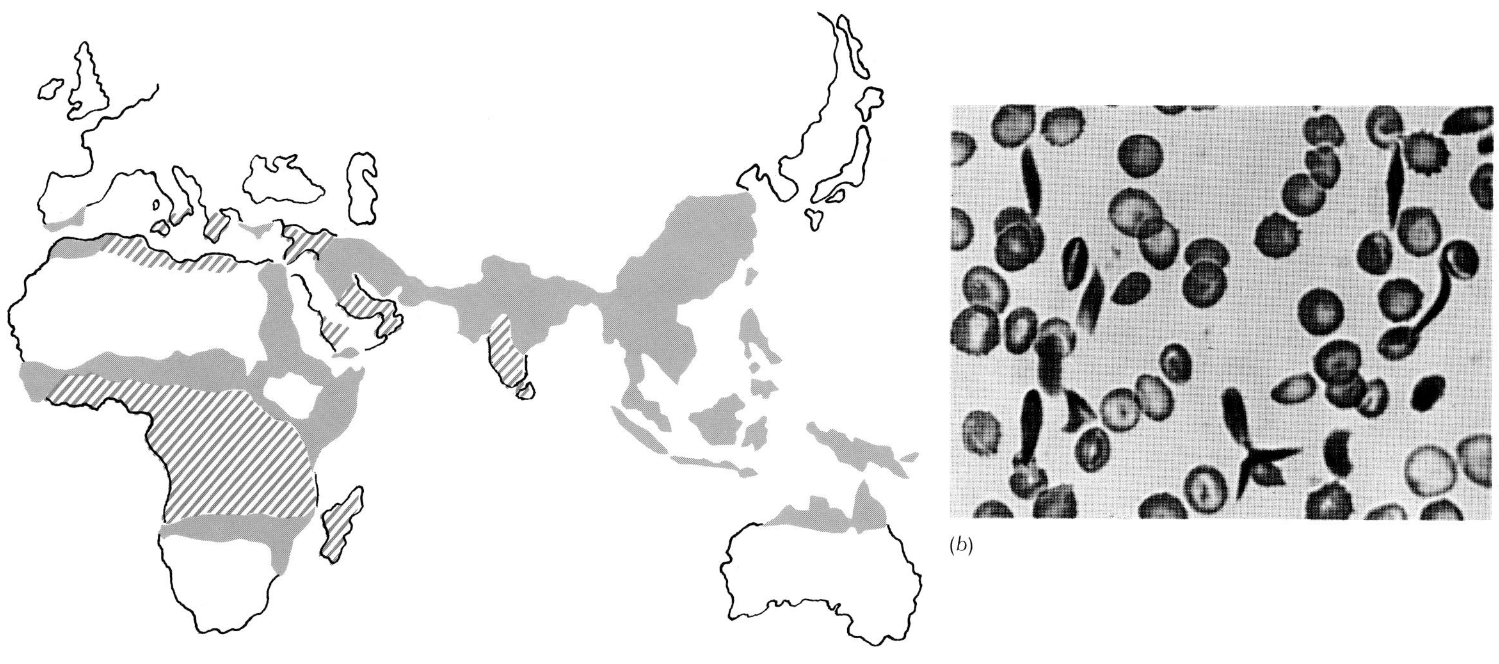

malaria were eradicated as a threat to human health the selective advantage of the heterozygote would be lost and the balanced polymorphism would become a *transient* one.

Thus, *transient polymorphism* is a situation in which a gene exists in more than one allelic state but the *relative frequency* of the alleles is in fact shifting with each generation due to selection against carriers of the less beneficial allele. If it were not for recurrent mutation, a transient polymorphism would finally end with the disappearance of the less adaptive trait. The frequency of the Hb-S allele is in fact declining in the American Negro because malaria is insignificant in North America; in time the population should be nearly homozygous for Hb-A.

Populations are also polymorphic with respect to sets of alleles in which neither trait possesses a selective advantage over the other. Human populations are polymorphic for various alternative traits, such as widow's peak versus straight hair line, and straight hair versus curly hair. In such cases there seems to be no difference in the survival value of either allele. Such *indifferent polymorphism* is merely a result of genetic mutability and will persist in a population indefinitely, so long as the survival value of the alternative traits remains equal.

TRANSMISSION OF HEREDITARY TRAITS Many genetic changes (or mutations) occur during the life of an organism. In fact, senescence may be due largely to the cumulative effects of mutations taking place in the various body tissues (*somatic* mutations). As many as 10^6 cells in the human body may mutate daily, but many of these cells die and are replaced. Somatic mutations affect only the individual, unless asexual reproduction takes place. In *sexually* reproducing organisms, for a mutation to be transmissible to the next generation it must take place in cells which are fated to become gametes. When reproduction is sexual, the slim bridge from one generation to the next is a single pair of sex cells, each of which contributes about half of the hereditary material to the new individual. Gametes of certain lower plants are morphologically alike (isogametes) but in most organisms two types of gametes are produced: motile sperm and larger, nonmotile ova. The paternal hereditary contribution enters the ovum at the moment of fertilization and a zygote is produced that undergoes repeated cell divisions, begins to accept nourishment, and so becomes a new and independent organism. Gametes must differ from the other cells of diploid organisms in one essential respect: *they themselves cannot be diploid.* No sex cell may contain a full double set of hereditary factors, for if this were the case the amount of genetic material would double in each generation. Species diploid during any part of their life cycle must have a means of reducing the gametic chromosome number in an *orderly* fashion so that each gamete receives *only one allele of each pair of genes;* this is known as meiosis.

Essentials of meiosis Meiosis is the process whereby a diploid cell is reduced to the *monoploid* (haploid) state in which only one set of chromosomes is present. Details of cellular events during meiotic division may be more clearly understood after a full consideration of cell structure in Chapter 10, but its essential features are not hard to grasp at this time, for we shall concentrate only upon the behavior of the chromosomes. Genes, as we have said, occur in linear assemblies visible to the microscope as elongated bodies within the cells, namely the chromosomes. In all phyla except bacteria and blue-green algae the chromosomes are confined within a membranous envelope to form a central body or *nucleus* within each cell. In diploid species, as we have noted above, each cell contains one set of chromosomes inherited from each parent, each maternal and each paternal chromosome contributing one allele of each gene pair. All genes that make up a single chromosome are said to be *linked;* if they are not linked, they are said to *assort independently* during meiosis, as we shall see.

The number of chromosomes per cell is fairly constant within any given species, but differs from one species to another. In man the diploid number is 46, that is, 23 pairs: nearly all the estimated million billion (10^{15}) cells that make up the adult human body contain 23 homologous pairs of chromosomes. (Exceptions are mature red blood corpuscles, which lose their chromosomes before entering the general circulation.) The germinal cells that mature into ova and sperm originally contain a full double set of chromosomes. During the process of maturation homologous chromosomes will be separated so that each mature gamete contains only one chromosome of each pair and only one allele of a kind. In animals meiosis is directly associated with the maturation of germ cells (see Figure 17.24), but in plants meiosis is typically separated from germ cell production by an entire generation. Earlier we reviewed a generalized plant life cycle and noted that in most metaphytes a spore-

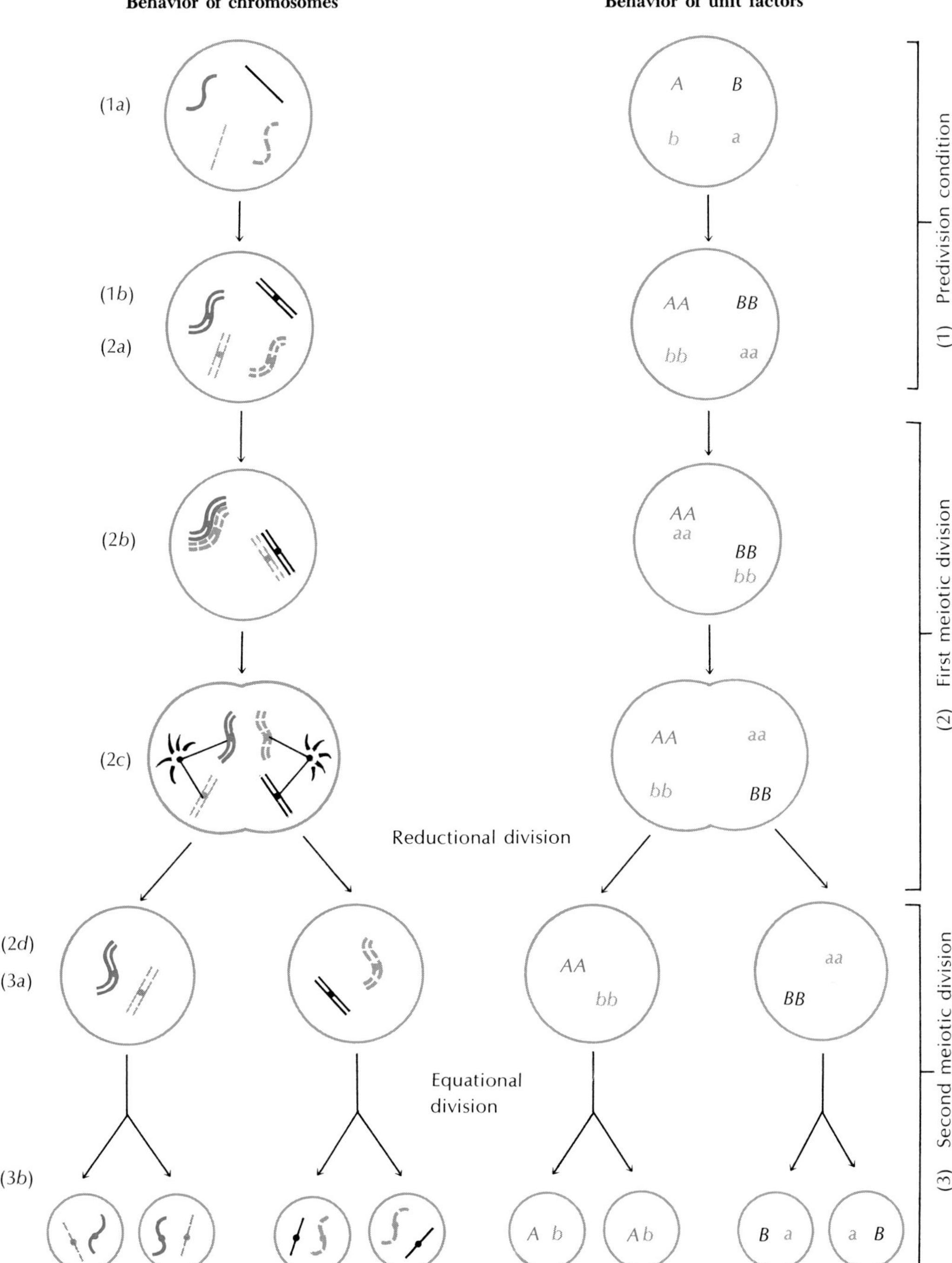

Figure 8.4 □ Essential features of meiosis. Behavior of chromosomes is shown to far left; behavior of two pairs of alleles, at near left. Each pair of alleles is designated by the same letter, capitals representing dominant alleles, lower-case letters recessive ones. Homologous chromosomes have the same shape, one member of each pair being designated by a solid line, the other member by a broken line. For simplicity only two pairs of chromosomes are represented, and only one gene is considered to be on each chromosome. (1*a*) Diploid condition in nucleus of cell prior to chromosome reproduction. (1*b*) Chromosomal reproduction actually takes place before the onset of cell division, but the daughter chromosomes (*chromatids*) adhere so intimately that their separateness is not apparent until later (2*a*) in the division process. At this stage the homologous chromosomes begin to move together in the first phase (*prophase*) of the first meiotic division. (2*b*) The coming together of homologous chromosomes (*synapsis*) is the essential feature of the first meiotic division, for it is prerequisite to separation of alleles and reduction of the chromosome number from the diploid to the monoploid condition. (2*c*) Homologous chromosomes and allelic unit factors are separated and move to opposite poles of the dividing cell. (2*d*) At this point the cells are essentially monoploid since homologous chromosomes and alleles have already been separated from one another. (3*a*) However, a second division is needed to separate the chromatids from one another. This second division immediately follows the first and is unique in that no metabolic ("resting") period or chromosome reproduction intervenes. (3*b*) Four cells of equal size often result from the two meiotic divisions of the original diploid cell. However, when meiosis takes place as part of the process of maturation of the egg (*oögenesis;* see Figure 17.24), cell division takes place unequally so that only one functional ovum is formed from each original diploid cell. The genotype shown is heterozygous for both pairs of alleles. What other possible combinations of the genes *A*,*a* and *B*,*b* could have resulted from these divisions?

producing generation, the sporophyte, alternates with a gamete-producing generation, the gametophyte. The sporophyte is a diploid organism and meiosis takes place within its spore capsules, producing monoploid spores. The gametophytes that develop from these spores are also monoploid and when they in time begin to produce gametes no further chromosome reduction is necessary. Thus a diploid, asexually reproducing generation and a monoploid, sexually reproducing generation alternate in the life cycles of many plants, with the sporophyte generation gaining ascendancy in higher plants probably as a result of the adaptive value of diploidy.

Whenever it takes place during the life cycle, meiotic cell division is preceded by *synapsis,* the coming together of homologous chromosomes (Figure 8.4). Each paternal chromosome is attracted to the corresponding maternal chromosome, and vice versa. This event is visible in the microscope because the nuclear envelope, which ordinarily hides the chromosomes from view, has disappeared. Homologous chromosomes move together and "zip themselves up" in such a way that every gene lies directly opposite its allele. Synapsis seems to result from attractive forces operating between specific alleles, for if the linear order of some of the genes has been accidentally reversed in one chromosome of the pair, the synapsing homologs must take up peculiar looped positions that permit the alleles to come together despite the rearrangement. Prior to the onset of meiosis each chromosome has reproduced itself and consists of two identical strands (*chromatids*), which at first are so closely intertwined as to appear one. Thus, the synapsed chromosome pairs form *tetrad* configurations—bundles of four chromosomal strands.

In the first meiotic division each chromosome is precisely separated from its homolog and each gene correspondingly parted from its allele. *Which* member of each chromosome pair ends up in which daughter cell is, however, a matter of *random distribution.* A second cycle of division follows *without* an intervening period of chromosomal reproduction, and this separates the chromatids. In Figure 8.4, we see that from the meiotic division of a diploid cell containing only *two* pairs of chromosomes *four* kinds of monoploid cells may be produced containing the alleles *A* and *B*, *a* and *b*, *A* and *b*, or *a* and *B*. If the diploid precursor contains *three* pairs of chromosomes, *eight* (2^3) possible types of monoploid cells may be produced. In man, since the normal diploid chromosome complement is 23 pairs, there are 2^{23} possible combinations of maternal and paternal chromosomes in human sperm and ova—more than eight million possible combinations. In addition, since it is a matter of chance as to which sperm fertilizes a given ovum, the chromosomal recombinations possible in producing a new human being are theoretically on the order of $2^{23} \times 2^{23}$! Of course many genes borne on these chromosomes exist in only one state throughout the entire species and therefore do not contribute to diversity, but the number of polymorphic genes and possible chromosomal recombinations is so large that an almost infinite number of individually distinctive persons may be conceived.

The Mendelian Laws and the particulate theory of inheritance Meiosis is the physical basis for the two Mendelian laws of heredity, derived from data obtained by Gregor Mendel during a series of experimental hybridizations with garden peas.

Mendel's *law of segregation* stipulates that alternative characters (alleles) are separated from each other when the germ cells are formed. The *law of independent assortment* states that *non*allelic factors assort at random during the formation of the germ cells. In the light of our present knowledge of hereditary mechanisms, this second law must be amended: nonallelic factors assort independently in meiosis, *as long as they are not in the same chromosome.* Part of the remarkable quality of Mendel's work rests on the fact that he worked out the principles governing the behavior of hereditary factors during their transmission without any knowledge of the meiotic events responsible for this behavior. Proof that Mendel's "factors" were physically parts of chromosomes was not forthcoming until the early part of the twentieth century, more than half a century after Mendel's data were published.

Even more significant than his two laws was Mendel's formulation of the *particulate theory of inheritance.* The tendency of progeny to be intermediate to their parents in quantitative characteristics such as height and skin coloration had lent credence to the commonly held idea that heredity involved a *blending* process, in which parental "bloodlines" were amalgamated and diluted. Quite to the contrary, Mendel discovered that the transmission of traits from parents to progeny involved the passing along of a number of discrete particles or units of inheritance, which *could be recombined and transmitted indefinitely without being altered or diluted* in the process. This was

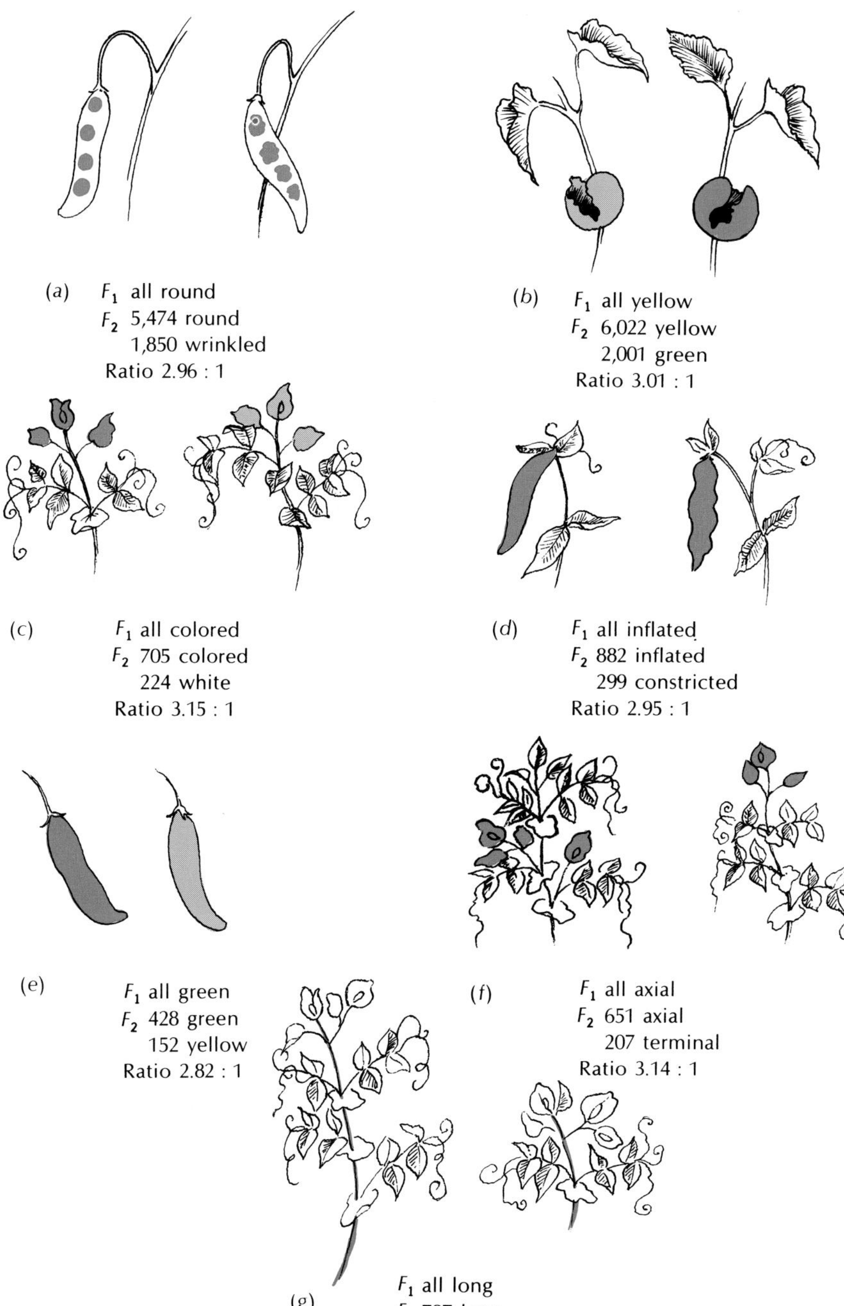

Figure 8.5 □ Experiments from which Mendel developed his postulates. Each pair of mutually exclusive traits constitutes an allelic pair. In each experiment the dominant trait is given first. (*a*) Round seed, wrinkled seed; (*b*) yellow seed, green seed; (*c*) colored flowers, white flowers; (*d*) inflated pod, constricted pod; (*e*) green pod, yellow pod; (*f*) axial flowers, terminal flowers; (*g*) long stem, short stem.

a discovery of inestimable significance for the understanding of hereditary transmission, variation, and evolution. Mendel's experiments were simple and well designed and are still worthy of study. He selected for breeding analysis seven pairs of traits in which the action of each allele was reflected by a clear-cut difference in phenotype and in which one allele was dominant and the other recessive (Figure 8.5).

Mendel noticed that in each pair the alternative traits were mutually exclusive: a single plant did not have both inflated and constricted pods nor could it be both tall and dwarf simultaneously. Therefore he referred to these traits as *differentiating characters.* Today we would describe them as being the contrasting phenotypic effects of alternative alleles. In Figure 8.5, the phenotypes produced by the dominant alleles are given first, the second phenotypes appearing only in plants homozygous for the recessive alleles. Mendel selected for analysis seven pairs of alleles, all of which were later found to be located on different chromosomes—none were linked. Since the sweet pea has only seven pairs of chromosomes, every chromosome was represented by these seven pairs of traits. (If Mendel had dealt with linked traits, his conclusions would have been less unambiguous.)

By crossing pure strains of garden peas that differed mainly with respect to the expression of *one* of these pairs of characters, Mendel first demonstrated that no progeny exhibited phenotypic intermediacy for the trait under consideration. For instance, hybrid progeny (F_1, or first filial generation) resulting from the cross pollination of a tall plant and a dwarf plant were all tall—none were intermediate in height. In turn, the second-generation progeny (F_2, or second filial generation) produced by interbreeding the hybrid F_1 (a *monohybrid* cross) turned out to be either tall or dwarf and not of medium height. In Mendel's words (in translation), "Transitional forms were not observed in any experiment." This simple statement should have been startling to a world which thought exclusively in terms of intermediate or "transitional" forms as being the expected products of inheritance. Unfortunately, conventional habits of thinking prevented the significance of Mendel's data from being realized until 1900, some 35 years after they had been published. By that time, other investigators had approached the same conclusions with different organisms and were surprised to find that Mendel had preceded them. Since then, Mendel's laws have served as valuable guidelines for the analysis of *inheritance,* the transmission of traits from parents to progeny.

The fact that segregation and recombination of alleles does not involve a blending process can be shown by crossing individuals heterozygous for a given pair of alleles. Such a cross yields progeny three-fourths of which show the dominant trait and one-fourth of which show the recessive trait, reappearing unchanged after having been hidden for a generation. This 3:1 phenotypic ratio (first described by Mendel) is only obtained when one allele is dominant over the other; the *genotypic* ratio is actually 1:2:1 ($\frac{1}{4}AA : \frac{1}{2}Aa : \frac{1}{4}aa$). In cases of codominance like that of four o'clocks, the phenotype of the heterozygotes differs from those of the two homozygous classes, and a 1:2:1 phenotypic ratio, which thus accurately reflects the genotypic ratio, will be obtained in the progeny of the monohybrid cross.

Independent assortment Following his demonstration that (1) each pair of mutually exclusive traits is controlled by a corresponding pair of alternative hereditary factors, (2) these factors or alleles are separated in the germ cells and transmitted unchanged to each new generation, and (3) one member of each pair is dominant and the other recessive, Mendel next interbred pure (homozygous) strains of garden peas that differed with respect to more than one pair of characters. The first generation of progeny (F_1), as might be expected, showed the phenotype for each of the dominant characters. But in the progeny of the hybrid F_1 plants, new phenotypic combinations appeared that represented recombinations of the grandparental traits. For example, he crossed a strain producing round, yellow seeds with one yielding wrinkled, green seeds and found that all first-generation progeny produced round, yellow seeds. Interbreeding these dihybrids (individuals heterozygous for two traits), Mendel* found that they

... yielded seeds of four sorts, which frequently presented themselves in one pod. In all, 556 seeds were yielded by 15 plants, and of these there were:

315 round and yellow,
101 wrinkled and yellow,
108 round and green,
32 wrinkled and green.

These data disclosed the now well-known 9:3:3:1 dihybrid phenotypic ratio, which upon inspection turns out to be merely the product of two independent 3:1 monohybrid phenotypic ratios. Using the symbol *R* to designate the factor producing round seeds, and *r* to designate its recessive allele, which produces wrinkled seeds, *Y* to designate the dominant factor producing yellow cotyledons, and *y* its recessive allele, which produces green cotyledons, we may represent the genotypes of the original strains as: *RRYY* (homozygous round, yellow) and *rryy* (homozygous wrinkled, green). Each of these strains can produce sex cells of only one type. The *RRYY* strain produces germ cells with the monoploid genotype *RY*; the *rryy* strain, only germ cells with the genotype *ry*. When these two types of gametes are joined in fertilization, only one genotype is possible for the progeny, *RrYy*, which will be phenotypically round and yellow.

These dihybrid individuals (*RrYy*) will, by meiosis, produce sex cells containing either *R* or *r*, but not both, and either *Y* or *y*, but not both. The four possible monoploid combinations are *RY*, *Ry*, *rY*, and *ry*. These four types of germ cells are produced in equal quantities. When two plants with the genotype *RrYy* are crossed, any one of the four types of pollen can unite with any one of the four possible female germ cells,

*"Experiments in Plant-Hybridization," in *Classic Papers in Genetics,* J. A. Peters, ed. (Englewood Cliffs, N.J.: Prentice-Hall, Inc., 1959), pp. 11, 12.

Figure 8.6 □ **Independent assortment of two pairs of genes. Note that in the F_2 two phenotypic classes emerge (round, green and wrinkled, yellow) that are unlike the phenotypes of the original homozygous strains. The four phenotypic classes occur in the ratio $\frac{9}{16}:\frac{3}{16}:\frac{3}{16}:\frac{1}{16}$.**

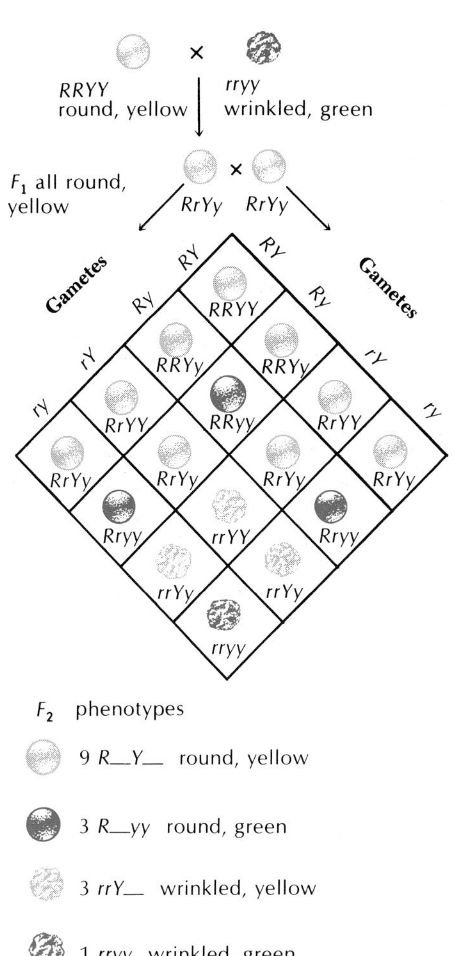

as shown in Figure 8.6, yielding the four phenotypic combinations in the proportions shown.

Any phenotypic ratio such as 9:3:3:1, which represents the *product of the separate phenotypic ratios* [that is, $(3:1)^2$] obtained with individual pairs of traits, indicates that *the characters under consideration are not linked* and therefore behave independently of one another in the meiotic divisions that produce the monoploid germ cells. As noted earlier, meiosis results in the separation of each chromosome from its homolog, but it is a matter of chance as to *which* homolog of each pair goes into a given germ cell. If we stipulate that the character designated *R* above is actually a part of chromosome *C*, then its allele *r* is part of the homologous chromosome *C′*. The chromosomes *C* and *C′* cannot normally coexist in the same germ cell: only one will be present. Similarly, if we stipulate that the character *Y* is part of chromosome *D′*, its allele *y* will occupy a corresponding position in chromosome *D*.

The two members of each homologous pair—*C* and *C′*, and *D* and *D′*—are thus separated during meiosis. If we now consider the possible kinds of germ cells producible with respect to only these two pairs of homologous chromosomes, we find that four possible combinations will be produced in equal proportions: *C* and *D*; *C* and *D′*; *C′* and *D*; and *C′* and *D′*. If we now compare these results with those obtained for the segregation of the genes *R*, *r*, *Y*, and *y*, we shall find that *there is a strict correspondence between the behavior of the chromosomes in meiosis, and the behavior of the Mendelian characters.* In the present example, the gametes containing chromosomes *C* and *D* would also have the genotype *R* and *y*; those with chromosomes *C* and *D′* would carry the factors *R* and *Y*; those containing chromosomes *C′* and *D* would contain the alleles *r* and *y*; and those with chromosomes *C′* and *D′* would thus have the genotype *rY*.

Linkage of genes on chromosomes We now know that each Mendelian factor represents a *gene* or functional unit of a chromosome. Each chromosome constitutes a *linkage block* comprising all of the genes in that chromosome. That these genes occur in a *regular linear sequence* in the chromosomes has been demonstrated by breeding experiments in which the locations of individual genes have been *mapped* along the length of the chromosome. Chromosome mapping is made possible by the occurrence of interchanges of genes between homologous chromosomes, an event known as *crossing over.* The frequency with which two linked genes are separated from one another by this process of reciprocal exchange is directly proportional to the linear distance between the two genes along the length of the chromosome.

Evidence that two particular genes may be linked comes first from the fact that a dihybrid cross may fail to yield the expected 9:3:3:1 Mendelian phenotypic ratio. The actual proportion of phenotypes obtained depends on the relative locations of the two genes on the chromosome, which in turn is reflected by the amount of crossing over that occurs between them.

As an example, in the wasp *Habrobracon* the genes *Vl* and *Ho* are linked. *Vl* is responsible for normal wing venation; its recessive allele *vl* is incapable of producing normal wing venation, and so the wings of the homozygotes *vl*-*vl* are veinless. The gene *Ho* is necessary for the production of normal (dark) body pigmentation; its recessive allele *ho* cannot produce dark pigment, and so the homozygotes *ho-ho* have pale, honey-colored bodies. The progeny of a wasp with the genotype (*Vl-Vl, Ho-Ho*) and one with the genotype (*vl-vl, ho-ho*) will exhibit a normal phenotype for both characters: normally veined wings, normally pigmented body. If these genes were not linked, matings between hybrid wasps of the genotype (*Vl-vl, Ho-ho*) *should* produce an F_2 with the following phenotypic ratio:

Normal wings, normal body (Vl- , Ho-)	9
Normal wings, pale body (Vl- , ho-ho)	3
Veinless wings, normal body (vl-vl, Ho-)	3
Veinless wings, pale body (vl-vl, ho-ho)	1

What actually happens, however, is that all four possible phenotypes do appear in the F_2 but *not* in the 9:3:3:1 ratio of independent assortment. Instead, those phenotypes representing the original grandparental types (in this case, *normal wings–normal body,* and *veinless wings–pale body*) predominate, while the *recombinant* types (*normal wings–pale body,* and *veinless wings–normal body*) are less frequent, being the products of crossing over. This may be shown as follows, with the linkage relationships indicated by horizontal lines representing the chromosomes:

Original parents $\frac{Vl\ \ Ho}{Vl\ \ Ho} \times \frac{vl\ \ ho}{vl\ \ ho}$

Normal wing, dark body — *Veinless wing, pale body*

F_1 $\frac{Vl\ \ Ho}{vl\ \ ho}$

All normal wing, dark body

These F_1 hybrids can produce four types of gametes, of which two types represent the original or noncrossover combinations

$\underline{Vl\ \ Ho}$ and $\underline{vl\ \ ho}$

and two represent the products of recombination resulting from exchange of genes between homologous chromosomes

$\underline{Vl\ \ ho}$ and $\underline{vl\ \ Ho}$

The amount of crossing over which regularly occurs may be most readily detected if the dihybrid individual (*Vl-vl, Ho-ho*) is crossed with one homozygous for both recessive alleles. This is known as a *testcross,* and is extensively used by plant and animal breeders:

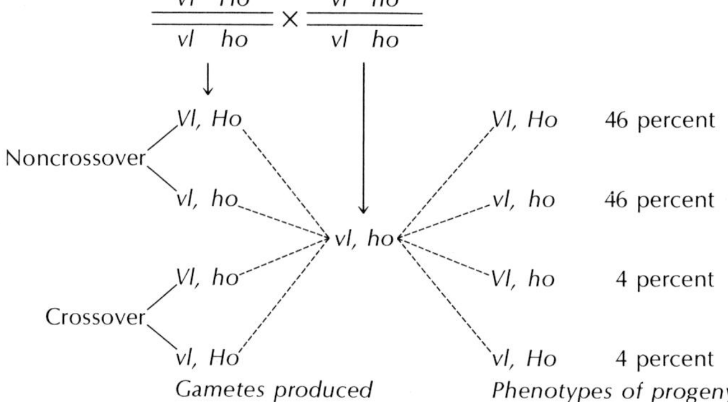

In a testcross involving two pairs of *unlinked* genes, the four phenotypic classes of progeny should ideally be present in *equal* proportions, a 1:1:1:1 ratio that reflects the proportions of the gametes. The actual results indicate that the genes *Vl* and *Ho* are linked with about 8 percent crossing over (the sum of the frequency of the two recombinant types). If we divide this chromosome into equal map units, each presumably the locus of one gene, we may place these two genes eight map units apart; however their *actual* positions relative to the length of the chromosome will be clarified only when a number of other genes have been mapped.

SEX LINKAGE AND SEX DETERMINATION In animals, certain characters are termed sex-linked traits because they are carried upon one particular pair of chromosomes, the so-called *sex chromosomes.* The sex chromosomes are influential in determining the sex of the individual, although they do not carry all genes relating to sexual characteristics. The sex chromosomes are distinct in that they are of *two kinds:* a functional chromosome of normal size, called X, and a much reduced chromosome bearing few functional genes, known as Y. An individual accordingly may be XX or XY. Alternatively, in certain species a Y chromosome is lacking and individuals merely carry one or two X chromosomes, being XX and XO, respectively. The XY or XO individual is said to be *hemizygous* for genes borne on the X chromosome; in any given species individuals of the hemizygous sex have only one allele for those genes which are sex-linked.

The sex of the individual is usually determined by the *balance* between the sex chromosomes and all of the other chromosomes (which are sometimes called *autosomes* to distinguish them from the sex-determining pair). In *Drosophila melanogaster,* the fruit fly that has served genetic research so well, the presence of two X chromosomes determines that the fly will be female. If only one X chromosome is present, the fly is male because the "masculine" genes scattered among the autosomes are not overbalanced by the "feminine" genes concentrated on the X chromosome. In *Drosophila* the Y is apparently nonfunctional, for abnormal individuals having only one X and lacking a Y (hence, XO) are male, whereas unusual individuals with two X chromosomes and a Y (XXY) are female.

In mammals, on the other hand, the Y chromosome does carry a "maleness" factor: whereas XY individuals are male and XX individuals female, unusual genotypes such as XXY are also male and XO individuals are female, both types being somewhat abnormal.

The *male* is the hemizygous sex in mammals and in such insects as *Drosophila,* whereas females may be either homozygous or heterozygous for genes borne on their X chromosomes. In birds and such insects as butterflies and moths, the *female* is the hemizygous (XO) sex. In either event, it is the gametes produced by the hemizygous parent that determine the sex of the offspring. In mammals the female, being XX, can produce only X-carrying gametes. The male, being XY, produces equal quantities of X-carrying sperm and Y-carrying sperm. The fertilization of an ovum (X) by an X-bearing sperm results in female progeny (XX); fertilization by a Y-bearing sperm produces a male (XY).

The hemizygosity of male mammals explains why certain hereditary abnormalities, such as colorblindness and hemophilia, are much more prevalent in men than in women. Any recessive sex-linked abnormality carried by a man will show up in his phenotype, while a woman must be homozygous for the trait. To be homozygous, she must inherit one of the recessive alleles from *each* of her parents (each of whom donated one X chromosome). The man, on the other hand, need inherit the trait from only *one* of his parents. Since a sex-linked gene is almost invariably borne on the X chromosome and not on the Y chromosome, he must inherit such traits from his *mother* and can transmit them only to his daughters (Figure 8.7).

The fact that individuals of one sex can get along with only one allele of a kind for the sex-linked genes and that individuals of the opposite sex have two alleles for each of these genes may pose a problem in coordinating the effects of sex chromosomes and autosomes upon bodily processes other than those concerned with sex. This problem of adjusting the dosage for sex-linked genes has been solved in female mammals by the partial inactivation of one or the other X chromosome in each cell. Because it is a matter of chance as to which X chromosome is inactivated in each cell, a female mammal heterozygous for some sex-linked trait proves to be a genetic *mosaic:* about half of her body cells show the effect of one allele and the rest show the effect of the other allele. This mosaicism is externally visible in cats of tortoise-shell coat coloration. Yellow and black pigmentation are determined by a pair of sex-linked alleles that are codominant: males can be either yellow or black but never tortoise-shell; females homozygous for one allele have yellow fur and those homozygous for the other allele have black fur. Heterozygous females, on the other hand, are covered with patches of yellow and black fur—the so-called tortoise-shell coat. This patchwork quilt effect results from the fact that, instead of both alleles being active in all hair follicle cells (producing a blended agouti coloration), the yellow alleles are active in some patches of skin and the black alleles in others. The size of the individual patches depends on the stage in development when one or the other X chromosome was inactivated: all cells descended from the embryonic cell in which the inactivation took place will contribute to the same patch of fur. Presumably the genes responsible for feminizing the individual remain active on both X chromosomes. Only the genes not concerned with sexual characteristics are inactivated, clumping into a dense, darkly staining *Barr body* that is visible within the nucleus of nondividing cells.

POLYGENIC INHERITANCE The hereditary traits with which Mendel dealt and which we have considered in the example involving *Habrobracon* have all been examples of *monogenic* traits—that is, of discrete phenotypic characters produced under the control of a single pair of alleles. In actuality, the performance of most genes is integrated in such a manner that although each gene has a specific role in metabolism and development, *a number of genes together* influence the expression of a particular trait. This is known as *polygenic inheritance.* The genes concerned often act *additively,* each contributing an increment of height or weight or pigmentation. The fact

Figure 8.7 □ Sex-linkage: inheritance of colorblindness in man. Note that a woman cannot be colorblind unless she receives an allele for the trait from each parent. A man transmits the gene only to his daughters, for the sons receive the Y chromosome that lacks this gene.

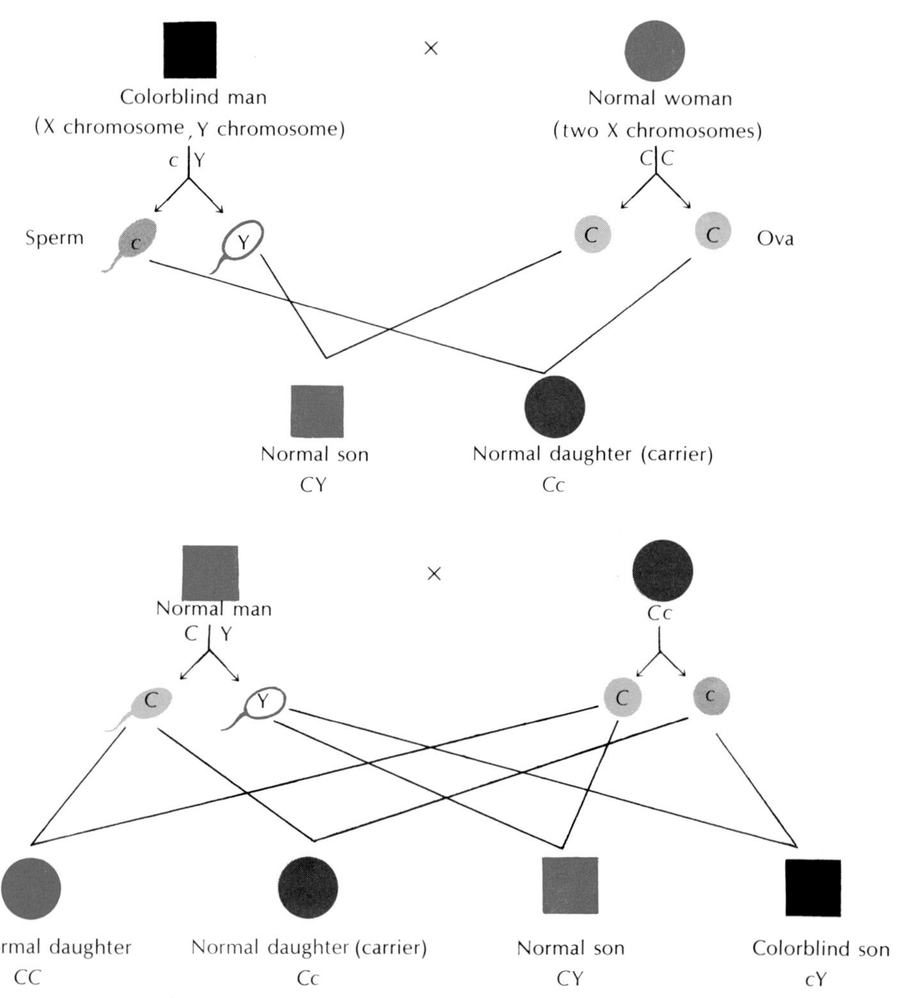

that many traits are polygenically inherited is the basis for the occurrence of transitional or intermediate phenotypes in the progeny of parents representing phenotypic extremes for the character. Polygenic inheritance is more difficult to analyze than monogenic inheritance, yet it has been demonstrated that each gene involved in producing a quantitative or additive effect actually behaves simply as a single Mendelian factor. The intermediate condition of the progeny, once thought indicative of a "blending" inheritance, can be explained satisfactorily on the basis of a *number* of genes acting quantitatively upon the character. In fact, no other hypothesis serves to explain why the F_2 resulting from a cross of two such "intermediate" individuals are not themselves exclusively intermediary forms, but represent a *normal distribution curve* for the trait, ranging from one phenotypic extreme to the other (Figure 8.8). For example, if a breed of short-eared rabbits with ears about 4 cm long is crossed with a long-eared breed with ears about 8 cm long, the progeny, or F_1, will have ears of intermediate length, about 6 cm long. Matings between F_1 individuals will produce not only an F_2 with an ear length of 6 cm but rabbits with ear length ranging from 4 cm to 8 cm, the majority being about 6 cm. If, out of 500 F_2 progeny, two rabbits had ears as short as the short-eared grandparent and two had ears as long as the long-eared grandparent, this would indicate that *four* pairs of genes were involved in producing the variation in ear length. The genotype of the original short-eared strain could therefore be written *aa, bb, cc, dd,* and that of the long-eared strain, *AA, BB, CC, DD*. Each dominant allele would be responsible for an increment of 0.5 cm

Figure 8.8 □ **Polygenic inheritance. Normal distribution curve for ear length, as seen in 500 progeny obtained from hypothetical crosses of hybrid rabbits heterozygous for four pairs of independently assorting genes with equal and additive effects on ear length.**

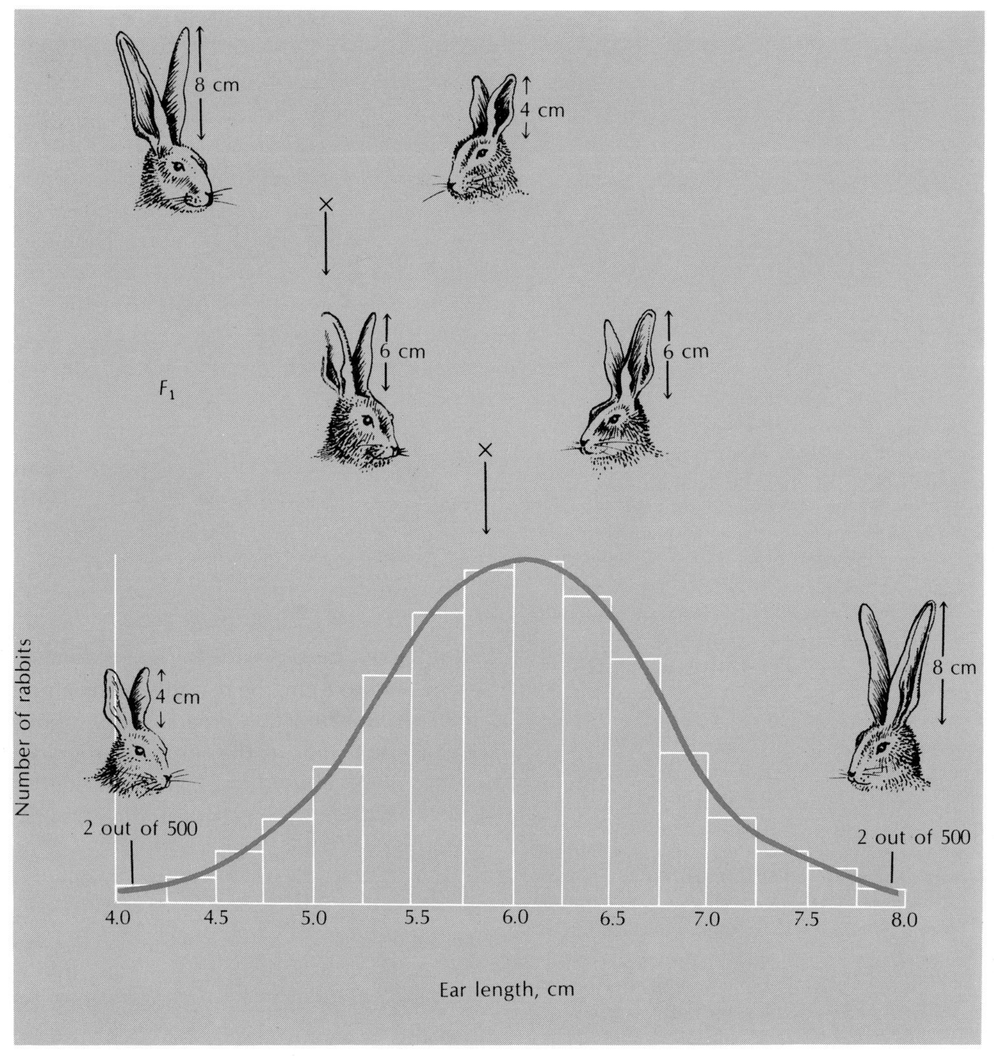

in ear length. The F_1, with a genotype of *Aa, Bb, Cc, Dd,* would have four effective alleles more than were present in the genotype of the short-eared parent. At a contribution of 0.5 cm per effective allele, the F_1 would have gained a total increment of 2 cm in ear length over the short-eared parent. Since each of the four gene pairs involved in determination of ear length is located on a different chromosome, they assort independently. Therefore the F_2 will consist of individuals possessing from 0 to 8 of the "length" genes, each of which could add 0.5 cm to the minimal length of 4 cm (seen in the short-eared strain).

The number of gene pairs *additively* concerned in the production of a polygenic trait may be calculated on the basis of the proportion of F_2 showing a phenotype as extreme as that of one of the other of the grandparents (as is shown in the following table):

PROPORTION OF F_2 AS EXTREME AS ONE OF THE GRANDPARENTAL TYPES	NUMBER OF GENE PAIRS CONCERNED
1 out of 4	**1**
1 out of 16	**2**
1 out of 64	**3**
1 out of 256	**4**
1 out of 1,024	**5**
1 out of 4,096	**6**
⋮	⋮

These calculations have been arrived at as the product of the ratios of single gene pairs *without dominance,* that is, 1:2:1 or 1*AA*: 2*Aa*:1*aa,* where *AA* represents one extreme and *aa* the opposite extreme. Where only two pairs of genes are involved additively,

$$(1:2:1)^2 = 1:4:6:4:1$$

the smallest categories representing the genotypes that yield the phenotypic extremes, namely, *AABB* and *aabb*. When three gene pairs are involved, the following distribution is obtained:

$$(1:2:1)^3 = 1:6:15:20:15:6:1$$

in which the smallest categories represent the extreme genotypes and phenotypes, *AABBCC* and *aabbcc*.

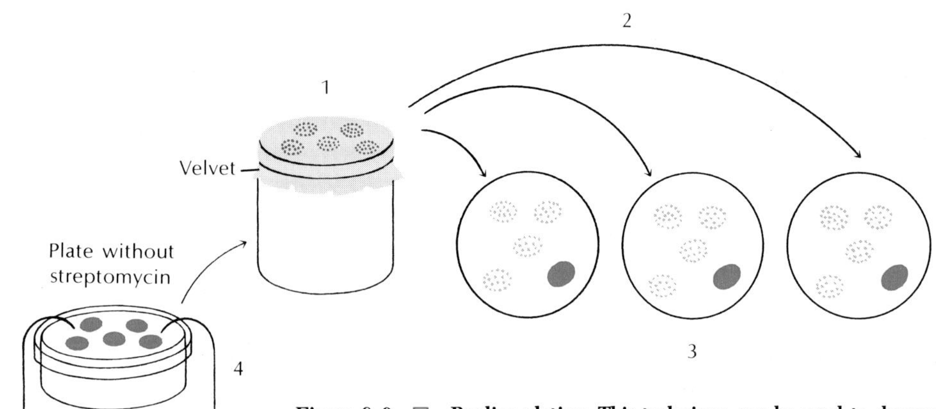

Figure 8.9 □ Replica plating. This technique can be used to demonstrate that mutations for antibiotic resistance in bacteria do not take place in response to need (that is, in the presence of the antibiotic) but are already present owing to chance genetic variation in populations not previously exposed to the antibiotic. The technique permits identification of resistant clones because the relative positions of all colonies are maintained during replica plating. (1) Bacteria from clones grown on the plate lacking streptomycin are transferred by pressing plate onto a velvet disc. (2) A series of fresh culture plates containing medium with streptomycin are inoculated by being pressed against the velvet disc. (3) Few (if any) bacteria survive in the presence of the antibiotic. Stippled clones represent those that failed to survive. Should any clone survive, it is found to occupy the same relative position on all the culture plates. (4) On the original, streptomycin-free plate, the resistant clone that gave rise to the surviving clones on the other plates can be identified by its position. Bacteria from this clone are now inoculated directly into culture tubes containing streptomycin, while, as a control, bacteria from a nonresistant clone are inoculated into another series of tubes with streptomycin. (5) Growth occurs in all tubes inoculated from the resistant clone, whereas no growth occurs in tubes inoculated from the sensitive clones. It can therefore be concluded that mutation for streptomycin resistance did not take place in response to need but that selection in favor of the resistant bacteria took place rapidly in the presence of the antibiotic.

B Genetic change

The genetic composition of a population may be altered in two major ways: (1) by *changes in the hereditary material itself*—alterations in the genetic code, in the total amount of hereditary material, and in its arrangement on the chromosomes; (2) by *shifts in gene frequency* (that is, in the relative proportions of alternative alleles) through successive generations. In this section we shall restrict ourselves to a consideration of changes in the hereditary material per se, deferring discussion of the chemical aspects of gene mutation until Chapter 9.

MUTATION *Gene mutations* generally affect single Mendelian factors, for they usually involve chemical alterations in individual genes. However, an amorphic mutation often reflects the complete loss of an allele through the *deletion* of a small portion of a chromosome. A deletion may actually be detectable upon microscopic examination if the chromosome is a giant one such as those in the salivary glands of the fruit fly *Drosophila* (see Figure 8.13). Whether or not it is visible to the microscope, a mutation due to a deletion can be identified by the fact that it can never regain its lost function by back-mutating to the normal state. A mutation that is not due to a deletion but to a chemical change in a gene may occasionally back-mutate.

Various studies indicate that mutations take place *at random* in time and space, having no relation to possible survival value. Most significant is evidence pointing to the randomness of mutation with respect to *adaptive need.* The *replica-plating* technique is admirably suited for testing whether or not mutations occur in response to specific needs. Bacteria are sparsely inoculated onto agar plates, where each individual bacterium will form a separate clone of descendants. From one original plate, subcultures may then be made by pressing onto a disc of velvet first the original culture and then a series of fresh sterile culture plates. The subcultures that develop will be true replicas of the original, for each clone will occupy the same relative position on every plate. A few bacteria from each clone adhere to the velvet disc and are subsequently transferred to a comparable location on each plate in the series (Figure 8.9). To test the incidence and time of occurrence of mutations that permit the bacteria to resist the action of an antibiotic such as streptomycin, colonies grown on a control plate lacking streptomycin are replica-plated to a series of dishes in which streptomycin has been added to the medium. If mutations were to occur in *response* to the presence of streptomycin in the medium, they would occur at random in the various plates. But in fact only a very few clones survive and, instead of occurring at random, they occupy the *same relative positions* on each of the plates. Each surviving clone represents, in

Figure 8.10 □ **Translocation: its effects upon meiosis and the genotype of subsequent generations. (*a*) Translocation taking place in a diploid cell: a piece of one chromosome breaks free and fuses to the end of another chromosome. At subsequent cell divisions, the translocated fragment is reproduced upon and segregated with the chromosome to which it has become attached. (*b*) Typical figure seen during synapsis at first meiotic division due to attraction between translocated and nontranslocated alleles. (*c*) Separation of the synapsed chromosomes may result in one daughter cell's receiving one normal chromosome and one that lacks the translocated genes, while the other daughter cell receives a normal chromosome plus one that also bears the translocated fragment. The first daughter cell will probably die, but the second now contains a number of duplicated genes. If this cell is a sex cell and participates in fertilization, the new individual will have an extra set of genes *F, G,* and *H.* Mutations occurring in these extra genes should not threaten survival but may provide "raw material" for evolutionary advancement.**

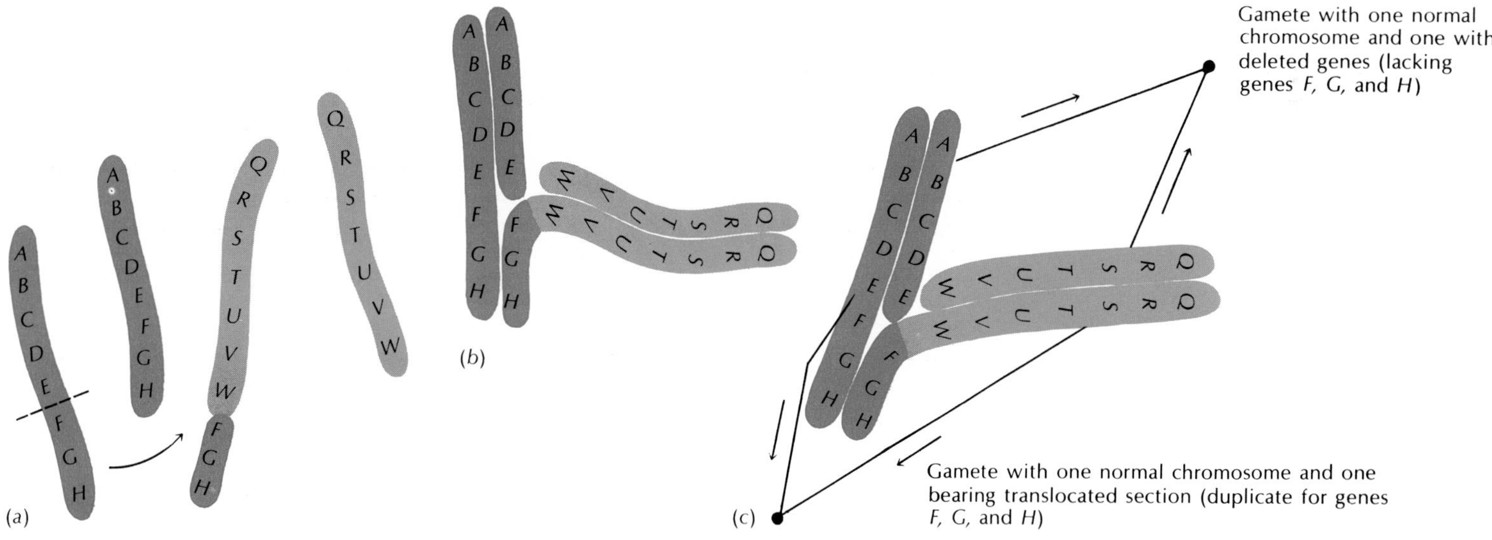

fact, descendants of a mutant bacterium that arose on the *original* plate at a time when *no* streptomycin was present. Now it is possible to refer back to the original plate, and to identify by position alone the mutant clone or clones in which mutations for streptomycin resistance *did* take place. As a further test, bacteria from the original resistant clone and from a nearby nonresistant clone may be inoculated into tubes of broth containing streptomycin. Inocula from the resistant clone proliferate at a normal rate, showing that all members of this clone are resistant to the antibiotic, while cells from the susceptible clone all die in the streptomycin-containing broth unless a fortuitous mutation appears. It is found that mutations for streptomycin resistance take place with *no greater frequency* in a medium containing streptomycin than when no streptomycin is present. In the light of such findings, we can conclude that bacteria do not routinely become resistant *because* they are exposed to antibiotics; instead, exposure to antibiotics merely gives a selective advantage to any preexisting mutations that enable their carriers to survive in the presence of the antibiotic. In the preceding example, the environmental stress (to wit, the antibiotic) did not *induce* the appropriate genetic change to occur, but it did serve to alter the relative proportions of the streptomycin-resistant and streptomycin-sensitive alleles in the population. This serves as experimental proof of the invalidity of the Lamarckian concept of evolution by the inheritance of characters acquired in response to specific needs.

CHANGES IN THE TOTAL AMOUNT OF GENETIC MATERIAL *Duplications, deletions,* and *changes in chromosome number* all serve to change the total amount of genetic material in the gene pool of a species. Small *losses* of genetic material by deletion do not necessarily prove fatal; however, the *enrichment* of the genome by the addition of genetic material is very significant in that it provides raw material for building a more complex organism. Although the genetic code is thought to be essentially identical throughout the living world, the *genome* (total genetic constitution) of a simple organism like *Amoeba* obviously needs carry much less information than the genome of man. In fact, estimates of the total amount of genetic material in the cells of several representative organisms indicate that a typical bacteriophage virus (see Figure 2.2) has a genome consisting of only about 10^5 nucleotide pairs (these being the basic chemical units of which genes are built). This is enough genetic material to control the production of about 50 different proteins. By contrast, some 3,000 different proteins theoretically may be encoded by the genetic material present in the genome of a typical bacterium, some 6×10^6 nucleotide pairs. The genome of *Drosophila* includes 8×10^7 nucleotide pairs per chromosome set, whereas each chromosome set in the mouse is made up of an estimated 5×10^9 nucleotide pairs. This represents a thousandfold increase over the bacterial genome. How has this increase in genetic material occurred in the evolution of life?

Genetic "accidents" that increase the amount of chromosomal material present include *duplication* of parts of chromosomes, *aneuploidy,* and *polyploidy.* Mere

Figure 8.11 □ Origin of a linear series of duplicate genes, due to a breakage-fusion cycle. (*a*) Sequence of events involved in creating a series of identical genes: (1) A portion of one arm of a chromosome has become inverted. (2) During synapsis, a loop must be formed to allow homologous alleles to come together despite the inversion (for purposes of simplicity, only one chromatid of each chromosome is shown; crossing over may involve any two, three, or four chromatids in the tetrad; distances between consecutive genes must be distorted in order to render this two-dimensionally). (3) Crossing over within the inversion loop results in the production of two abnormal chromatids: one having two centromeres and the other having none. (4) In the ensuing cell division, the acentric chromosome fails to move to either pole of the dividing cell and may be lost (or attached as a translocated fragment to some other chromosome); meanwhile, the two centromeres of the dicentric chromatid move apart, tearing the chromosome in two. (5) The fate of one of the broken halves is now traced through later cell divisions. (Only the asterisked portion is carried on to the next diagram.) Prior to such division, the broken chromosome reproduces, and the daughter chromatids fuse together by their broken ends. (6) Once more a bridge is formed, and the chromatids that have fused endwise are pulled apart; if the breakpoint is to one side of the point of fusion, one chromatid now has two identical genes. (7) Once more the broken chromosome reproduces, and the chromatids fuse by their broken ends. (8) Again the chromosome is pulled in two. At each such cycle of fusion and breakage, one chromatid may receive additional duplicate genes until an entire linear series results. (9) Eventually the cycle of breakage and fusion ends when the chromatids fail to fuse endwise and the broken ends "heal." In this illustration, the chromosome followed through several divisions now has three *F* genes. Mutation of the extra *F* genes should not be deleterious and may in fact result in an "assembly line" of genes producing similar, functionally related products. (*b*) Normal chromosomes of *Trillium erectum* in anaphase of first meiotic division (*Courtesy of Dr. A. H. Sparrow*). (*c*) *Trillium* cell in anaphase of first meiotic division after irradiation (50 r), showing acentric chromosome fragments and dicentric chromosomes forming bridges (*Courtesy of Dr. A. H. Sparrow*).

duplication of genes that are already present does not change an organism very greatly, but over a period of thousands or millions of years, diversification of the duplicated material through mutation could result in the acquisition of new functions and in consequent evolutionary advances.

Enrichment by duplication of parts of chromosomes Perhaps the simplest way in which part of a chromosome can be duplicated is as the result of an error during chromosomal replication: one portion may become looped over so that it is "read" twice as the new strand is produced. As a result of such a *replication error,* the genes in a chromosome might read:

ABCDEFGEFGHIJK . . .

Duplication can also result when a piece of one chromosome is broken off and becomes attached to another chromosome that is not its homolog. Such *translocation* places these genes in a new linkage block, where they will *assort independently of their own alleles* during any subsequent meiotic division. As a result, some gametes will lack the translocated segment and probably be inviable, while other gametes will contain a "double dose" of these genes (Figure 8.10). In the latter case, after fertilization the

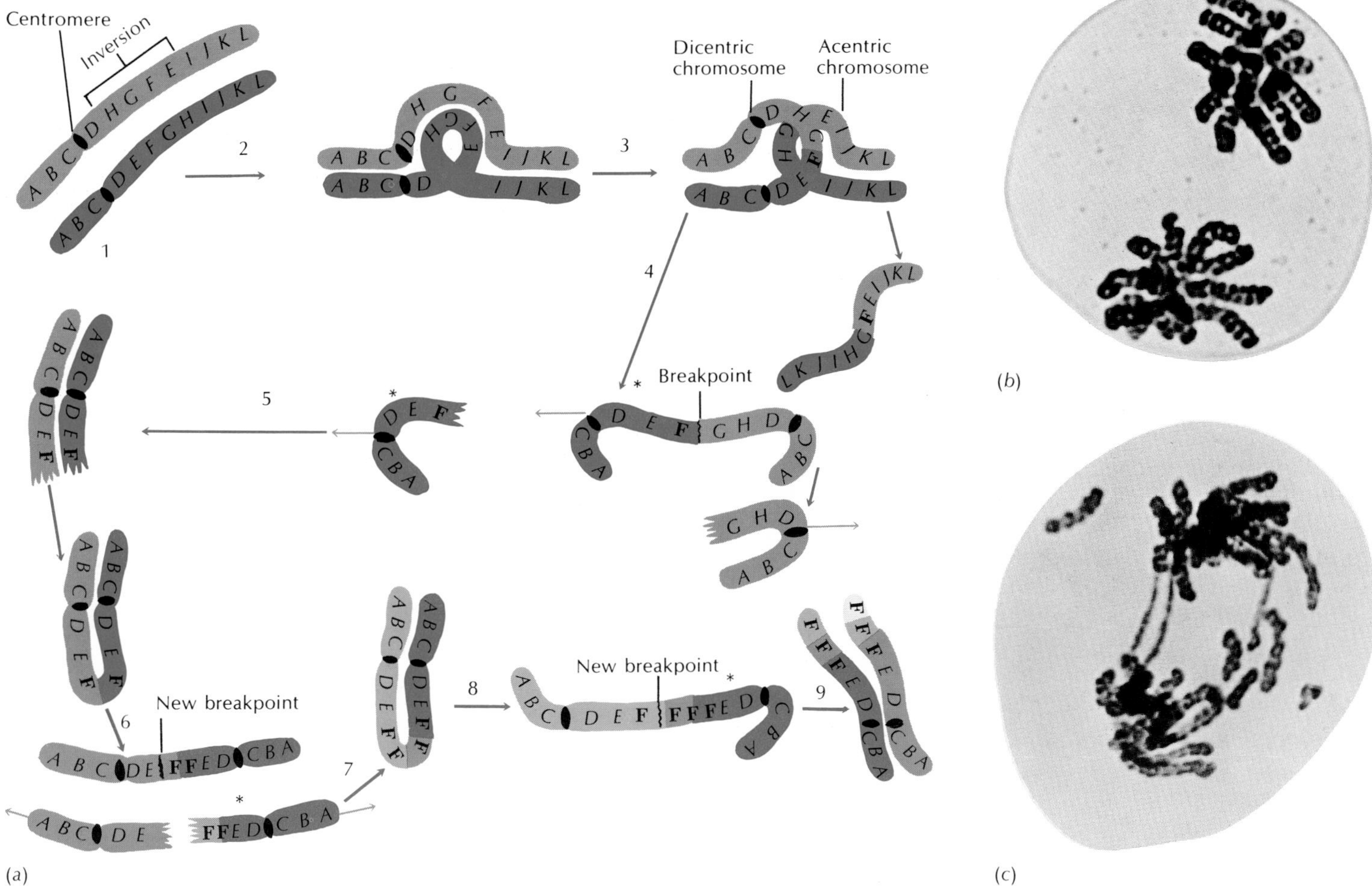

zygote will have *three* alleles for each gene involved in the translocation. As the chromosomes reproduce during subsequent cell divisions the translocated fragment reproduces in its new position as if it had always been a part of that chromosome. With an additional set of alleles present, two possible phenotypic results may follow: (1) there may be a simple *additive* effect (for instance, in rabbits another pair of alleles for ear length may be added); (2) since the basic needs of the organism are met by alleles already present, then no harm should result if any of the extra genes mutate. Should the mutant genes lose the function for which they had originally become adapted, their duplicates carry on the task and survival is not jeopardized.

Duplication of genes may also take place as the result of an interesting phenomenon known as the *breakage-fusion cycle* (Figure 8.11). Such a cycle arises when the chromatids of a dividing chromosome fuse endwise and are pulled apart during cell division so that one daughter cell receives the genes that occupied the terminal positions on both chromatids (*ABCDEFF*) while the other suffers a comparable deletion. At subsequent cell divisions the once-broken chromatids tend to fuse again by their broken ends and once more may be torn apart so that more of the terminally placed genes pass to one daughter cell than to the other. The cycle usually eventually terminates when the broken ends of the chromatids heal instead of fusing, but by that time it is possible for a chromosome to bear a linear series of duplicate genes (*ABCDEFFFFFFF*). The adjacent position of the redundant alleles may have importance in the evolution of genetic "assembly lines" such as are known to occur in some bacteria; in these cases a series of adjacent genes is concerned with a specific metabolic sequence, in which each gene apparently produces an enzyme needed to promote the next reaction in line. Because of mutations in individual duplicated genes of the series, each enzyme may be just different enough from the one controlling the preceding reaction to be able to use the products of that reaction as substrates of the next. Such a series of eight linked genes occurs in the bacterium *Salmonella typhimurium,* all of which are concerned in the same reaction pathway. Eventually, analysis of molecular structure should make it possible to ascertain whether the enzymes produced by this series of eight linked genes are the results of variation in the same basic molecule, and thus could have arisen by mutation of a series of originally identical genes.

Transduction is a fourth way in which duplication of part of a chromosome can take place. In this case, new genetic material in the form of chromosome fragments is carried by a *virus* from its old host cell to a new one. Transduction is only known to occur in bacteria subject to infection with bacteriophage viruses. Such viruses commonly invade a bacterium, reproduce, and escape by rupturing the host cell. During this process a virus occasionally carries away a piece of the host's chromosome. This fragment is *transduced* into another host when it is entered by the virus [Figure 8.12 (1)]. Occasionally a virus fails to reproduce within the host and is lost from one daughter cell when the host bacterium divides. However, the transduced piece of bacterial chromosome persists, often attaching itself to the host's chromosome and reproducing in phase with it. The bacterium is thus rendered *diploid* for that part of its genome and, if the diploid condition persists, duplicate genes are now available for eventual diversification. Although it is not known how widespread is the incidence of transduction of hereditary material by viruses, since viruses afflict most kinds of organisms it is unlikely that transduction is limited to bacteria. In fact, in some cases the *virus itself* becomes part of the host's genome and may replicate in phase with the host's genetic material indefinitely, altering the host phenotypically. Such incorporation of viral material into the host's genome occurs in bacteria, where it is known as *lysogenic conversion* [Figure 8.12 (2)]. There is little doubt but that in the long history of life, viral chromosomes may have become parts of the genome of many organisms originally serving as hosts.

Chromosome fragments from disintegrating cells may also be picked up by other cells. Ordinarily these are digested, but occasionally genetic *transformation* takes place, in which the material incorporated becomes a permanent part of the genome of the cell that took it in. In bacteria such material makes its presence known by exerting permanent phenotypic effects upon the progeny of the "transformed" bacteria (see Figure 9.15). Recently, transformation has been experimentally induced in animals, and is viewed as a potentially useful tool for modifying the genome in specific ways, with the hope of remedying genetic defects in man. Spontaneous transformation by the incorporation of material taken from disintegrating cells may be a much more common phenomenon than we now realize.

Chromosomal abnormalities that result in fragmentation and the establishment of breakage-fusion cycles occur spontaneously, but their incidence is greatly increased by exposure to mutagenic agents such as X rays. Figure 8.11c shows radiation-damaged plant chromosomes in division, with chromosome fragments and breakage-fusion bridges.

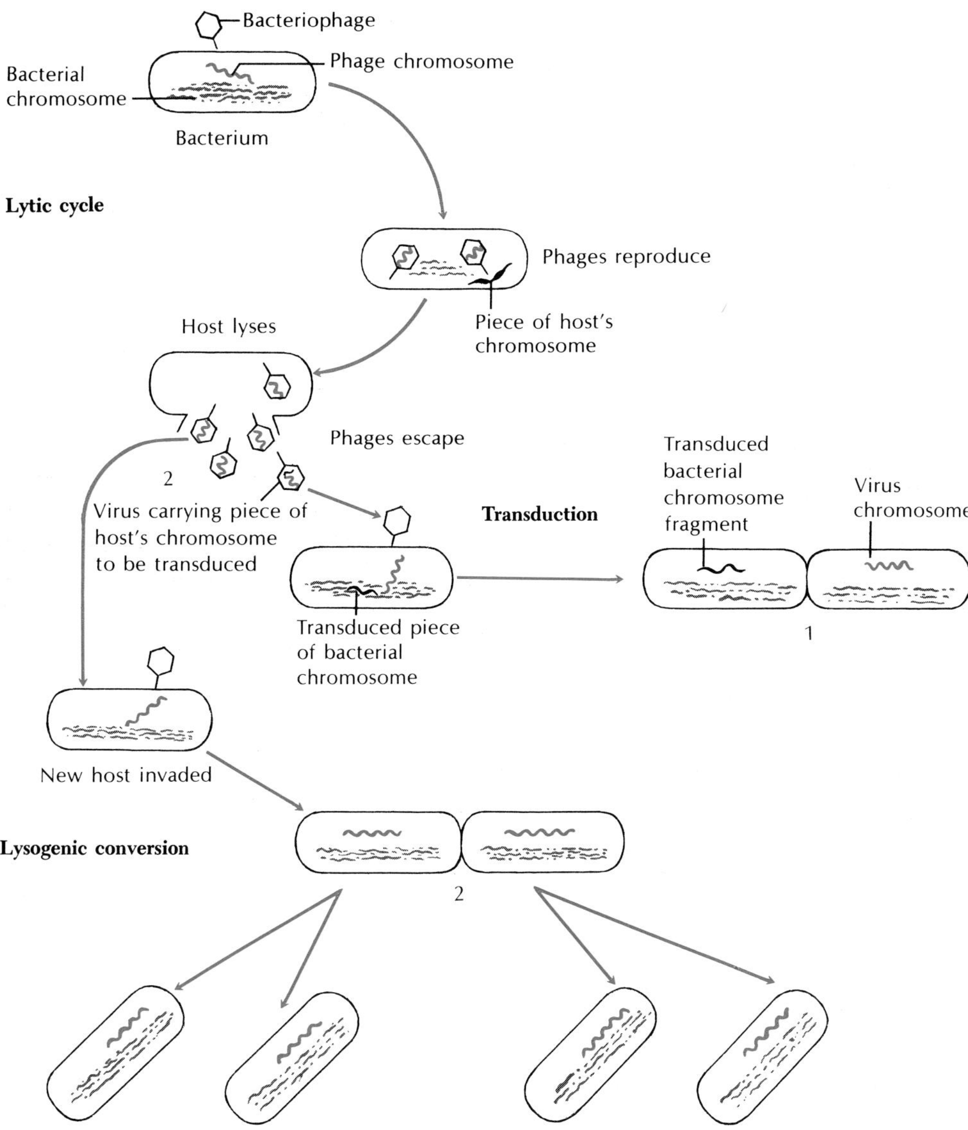

Changes in chromosome number: aneuploidy and polyploidy The genome may also be enriched by the accidental *duplication of one or more entire chromosomes.* Changes in chromosome number can take place in several ways. One such genetic accident is *nondisjunction* (the failure of homologous chromosomes to separate after having synapsed in meiosis). As a result, after meiosis one cell will have an extra chromosome, while the other, lacking a complete chromosome, will be inviable. The condition in which one or more extra chromosomes is present (but not a multiple of the complete set) is termed *aneuploidy.* Aneuploids may be phenotypically distinct from regular diploid members of the population because of the effects of increased doses of the genes located on the extra chromosomes, even when those genes have not altered through mutation. In man certain abnormalities are associated with the occurrence of extra chromosomes. Persons having an extra chromosome of the pair designated

Figure 8.12 □ Transduction and lysogenic conversion: virus effects upon bacterial heredity. A bacteriophage virus typically reproduces within its host and then escapes by destroying the host (lytic cycle). A virus may incorporate a piece of the chromosome of its former host and carry it into the new host [transduction (1)]. If the new host divides before the virus begins to reproduce, one daughter cell may receive the transduced chromosome but not the virus and may incorporate this new material into its own chromosome. In lysogenic conversion (2) a virus fails to kill its host and reproduces only in phase with the host's reproductive cycle; only the virus chromosome remains and may alter the host's heredity, for instance, making it resistant to future attacks by viruses of the same strain.

number 21 develop Down's syndrome—mongoloid idiocy. Recent chromosome studies on men imprisoned for crimes of violence including murder have revealed the startling fact that due to nondisjunction a significantly high proportion of these men have an extra Y chromosome! The genotype XYY may predispose the individual toward antisocial behavior, perhaps due to overaccentuation of masculine traits promoting aggressive tendencies. These studies, already considered statistically significant, indicate that a criminal XYY individual may be as genetically abnormal as one with Down's syndrome—and no more to blame for his condition. Early identification of XYY males may forestall the expression of these antisocial tendencies.

Polyploidy, or the duplication of entire *sets* of chromosomes, occurs frequently in plants, but its occurrence in animals is sporadic and may be restricted to specific tissues such as liver and pancreas, in otherwise diploid organisms. *Autopolyploidy,* or the duplication of the complete set of chromosomes normal to the species, adds no *different* genes, but does make available material for future mutational diversification. Autopolyploidy may take place spontaneously when cell division fails to be completed after the chromosomes have reproduced themselves. If this occurs before the first division of the fertilized egg, the entire organism will be polyploid, in this case *tetraploid* ($4n$). *Triploid* ($3n$) individuals may be produced by the fusion of a normal monoploid gamete with one in which reduction of chromosomes has failed to occur. Triploid plants are partially sterile since in meiosis the extra set of chromosomes cannot synapse normally and will be randomly scattered between the sex cells. Nevertheless, a number of potentially viable aneuploids are produced by the mating of two triploid organisms. Multiples of the *diploid* set ($2n$) pose no problems in synapsis, and there is consequently no reduction in fertility in tetraploid, hexaploid ($6n$), or octoploid ($8n$) plants. Many plant species apparently have arisen by spontaneous autopolyploidy. According to some authorities, a third or more of all angiosperm species are polyploids of some type.

As well as occurring spontaneously, autopolyploidy can be experimentally induced by treating plants with the chemical *colchicine.* In colchicine-treated cells the chromosomes reproduce normally, but cell division is inhibited and the treated cells are left with a doubled chromosome complement. Polyploid plant varieties are generally larger and produce bigger fruits and flowers than the diploid species from which they are derived. Artificial induction of polyploidy is therefore an important technique in horticulture. In general, the phenotypes of known autopolyploids merely represent exaggerations of the diploid phenotype; but over a long period of time many mutations may accumulate to change a phenotype so that its polyploid origin is obscured.

Allopolyploidy, the combination of diploid chromosome sets from two different species, occurs in plants but is not definitely known to occur in animals. It makes possible the origin of a new species in a *single generation.* Allopolyploidy must be preceded by a cross between individuals of different species. Ordinarily such heterospecific crosses are inviable, because the genes brought together in the hybrid are likely to be more or less incompatible. Artificial insemination of goat by lion, for instance, would bring together sets of genes so poorly adapted to one another that no offspring could result. On the other hand, more closely related species, such as the horse and jackass, may occasionally mate, particularly in domesticity where barriers of behavior and range do not pertain. In this case, a hybrid offspring known as a mule is produced, which is vigorous and sturdy, but almost invariably sterile because the maternal and paternal sets of chromosomes are too unlike to synapse successfully in meiosis. This prevents the mule from forming normal gametes. In plants, however, hybridization between species is occasionally followed by a doubling of both sets of chromosomes, producing an organism that is an allopolyploid having a genome consisting of two complete diploid sets, one derived from each of the parental species. Such an organism is fully fertile, for synapsis can proceed normally during meiosis, and gametes will be produced containing one chromosome of each homologous pair. If self-pollination occurs, an entire population of allopolyploid plants, breeding true and representing a new species, may appear.

The first new species experimentally produced by man was an allopolyploid obtained by the Russian geneticist G. D. Karpechenko, who crossed cabbage (*Brassica*) and radish (*Raphanus*) plants and ultimately obtained a fertile, true-breeding allopolyploid which he named *Raphanobrassica.* Rather than being agriculturally useful, *Raphanobrassica* had a head like a radish and a root like a cabbage. On the other hand, domestic wheat seems to be a naturally occurring allopolyploid that is more useful than the wild species from which it originated. A number of other cases are known in which new species of plants have evolved in the wild by allopolyploidy. The new species may have adaptive advantages over the parental species. For example, certain populations of the composite *Crepis* inhabiting the Mount Hamilton region in California appear to be allopolyploids that originated from the hybridization of two species, one of which requires a cold, dry climate, while the other needs mild, fairly moist conditions. The allopolyploid population combines the climatic preferences of the progenitor species in such a way that it can tolerate both situations, for its habitat is characterized by a hot, dry summer and a mild, rather damp winter.

New World cultivated cotton is thought to have arisen as an allopolyploid hybrid of two species, one a native American cotton with 13 pairs of small chromosomes, and the other, Old World cotton, which has 13 pairs of large chromosomes. This hypothesis was based on the discovery that cultivated American cotton has 26 pairs of chromosomes, of which 13 are small and 13 large. To test the hypothesis, Old World cotton and the American wild cotton were crossed and the chromosome complement of the hybrid doubled by colchicine treatment. The prog-

Figure 8.13 □ **Normal and abnormal synapsis. (*a*) Normally synapsed giant chromosomes of *Drosophila melanogaster.* The homologs are so intimately united that they cannot be distinguished as separate entities. (*Ward's Natural Science Establishment, Inc.*) (*b*) Synapsis in an interspecific hybrid, *D. pseudoobscura* mated with *D. miranda.* Long segments of the chromosomes are sufficiently alike to pair closely, but other portions, as shown here, are so unlike that synapsis can occur only at intervals. This does not necessarily mean that large numbers of genes of these closely related species have mutated to the point of becoming so unlike that they will not synapse but, more probably, that repeated rearrangements in gene sequence have taken place so that synapsis is blocked. Hybrid sterility may result from such interference with synapsis, which prevents proper segregation of homologous chromosomes. Numbered regions represent homologous portions of the chromosomes. [*After Th. Dobzhansky and C. C. Tan,* Zeitschrift für induktive Abstammungs- und Vererbungslehre, 72 (*1936*), *courtesy of Springer-Verlag.*]**

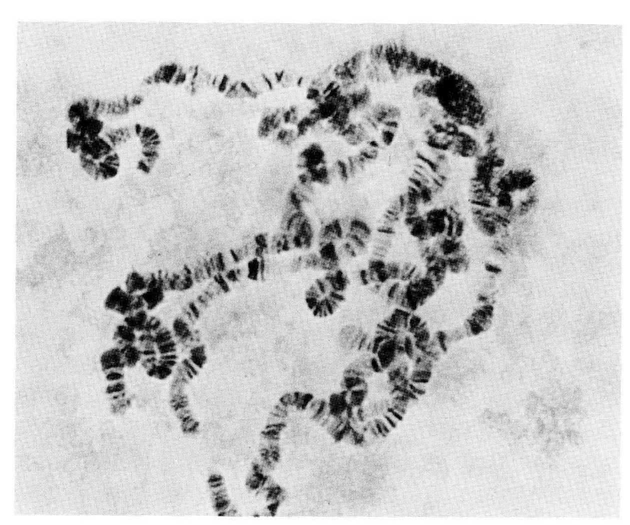

(*a*)

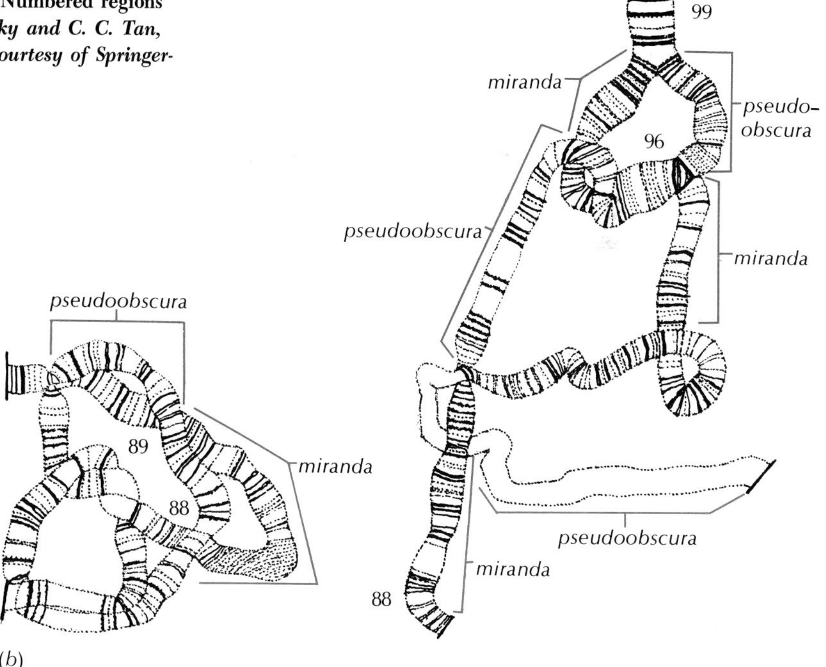

(*b*)

eny thus obtained were fertile and closely resembled present-day cultivated cotton, lending support to the hypothesis.

CHROMOSOMAL REARRANGEMENTS Rearrangements in the linear organization of the chromosomal material are constantly occurring. Portions of chromosomes undergo inversion. Materials are exchanged between homologous and nonhomologous chromosomes (crossing over and translocation). Chromosome breakage and fusion take place. The linear sequence of genes on chromosomes becomes gradually jumbled. Such rearrangements may become common to the genome of a particular deme, but are likely to be different from rearrangements occurring independently in other demes; eventually such populations may become unable to interbreed because of a loss of fertility resulting from interference with synapsis in meiosis (Figure 8.13). Chromosomal rearrangements thus contribute to the *genetic* isolation of populations that have also been *geographically* isolated from one another during the period in which the genetic changes have been taking place. Chromosomal rearrangements may in fact be more instrumental in separating isolated populations into different species than are the accumulated mutations built up by each population separately. *Enrichment* by duplication and polyploidy; *diversification* by mutation and rearrangements: these are the genetic alterations that provide the raw materials for organic evolution.

C The fate of genetic innovations

Changes in the hereditary material take place at the level of the *molecule* (DNA) and the subcellular *organelle* (the chromosome), but they are of significance to the survival of a species only if they can be transmitted at the *cellular* level, in a gamete that will contribute 50 percent of the heredity of a new organism. Whether or not these changes will persist and be passed on to yet another generation also depends on the effects which they exert at the level of the *organism*. Many genetic changes so severely disrupt metabolism and development that they are lethal, particularly to the homozygote. Finally, their fate depends upon the effects which they exert at the level of the breeding population or *deme*, according to whether or not they improve the carrier's state of adaptation and confer a reproductive advantage in comparison with the mean prolificacy of the population. Any genetic innovation must stand the test of how it affects both the organism's adaptation to its environment and the coadaptation of the body's internal functions.

THE EVOLUTIONARY SIGNIFICANCE OF DEMES Genetic change is fundamentally a subcellular phenomenon, but the long-term effects of genetic modification are often *ecologically* determined. In this regard, the fact that species tend to be broken up into smaller breeding units, the demes, among which gene flow is somewhat restricted, assumes particular significance. Most mutations are recessive and do not affect the phenotype unless they are inherited from both parents; if a genetic change were to take place in a single member of a large, freely interbreeding population, the mutation would tend to disappear into the gene pool of the species, perhaps never to reach the homozygous state in which its phenotypic effect could be manifested. Thus the *deme* is especially significant as a "testing ground" for evolutionary innovations, for its restricted size increases the incidence of consanguineous matings and thereby accelerates the appearance of recessive traits. If the mutation is incompatible with the harmonious functioning of the rest of the individual's genome, the homozygote probably will fail to survive long enough to reproduce. If, on the other hand, the individual genome can incorporate the new factor harmlessly, it still must stand the test of exposure to extrinsic factors: how does the new trait affect the relationships of the individual organism with its conspecifics, with organisms of other species, and with the abiotic habitat in which it must live? The fate of a genetic modification is thus ultimately determined at the level of the *organism-environment complex,* and its testing ground is the deme.

It should be reemphasized that *evolution is a population phenomenon*—it is not the individual that evolves, but the population, through gradual changes in its hereditary composition. Any population living today is not merely a duplicate of a population that lived a century ago. In fact, the genetic makeup of a given population does not even persist without modification from one generation to the next. This is because *all individuals in the population do not contribute equally to the production of progeny* (Figure 8.14). Many will die without having transmitted their genetic traits at all, while others will be highly prolific. It is estimated that even at the current nearly exponential rate of increase in the human population, considerably fewer than *half* of the individuals *initially* present in each generation produce progeny. This may seem surprising until we recall that the total census for a single generation must include *all of the zygotes* produced when ova are fertilized by sperm. Many of these new individuals perish during embryonic development. To these must be added all who fail to live to sexual maturity or who, having attained maturity, do not have progeny because of sterility, failure to secure a mate, or other factors. Since in most species the best-adapted individuals are most prolific, their contribution, generation after generation, improves the adaptation of the population, producing favorable evolutionary change.

THE HARDY-WEINBERG EQUILIBRIUM PRINCIPLE Analysis of the mechanics of inheritance has been facilitated by the controlled breeding of homozygous stocks of plants and animals that have been inbred for many generations. When Mendel crossed garden peas of genotype *RRYY* with those of genotype *rryy,* he introduced into the hybrid population exactly as many recessive alleles as there were dominant alleles. Yet in nature it is most *unusual* for the two or more alternative allelic states of a given gene to be present in equal proportions in the gene pool of a population. Ordinarily the phenotype recognized as the norm or *wild type* for a particular species is that which reflects the action of alleles that have been conserved in the population because they conferred a selective advantage on the individuals which carried them. Nevertheless, populations are always somewhat heterogeneous in their genetic constitution, so that a good many different recessive alleles are represented in the gene pool. The question then arises as to whether or not a given allele will be eliminated from a population merely because it is recessive. The mathematicians W. Weinberg and G. H. Hardy independently and simultaneously concluded that, unless disturbing factors intervene (which we shall discuss shortly), *the pro-*

Figure 8.14 □ **Schematic diagram to show change in genetic composition of a population through five generations. Individuals dying without progeny are designated by grayed circles. Note that, although the population level remains stable, by the fifth generation only four of the original lines are still represented, and of these nearly two-thirds are descendants of the line originally marked by an asterisk. If mortality appears excessive, recall that the original census of a generation must include all *zygotes* and that considerable mortality takes place during embryonic development.**

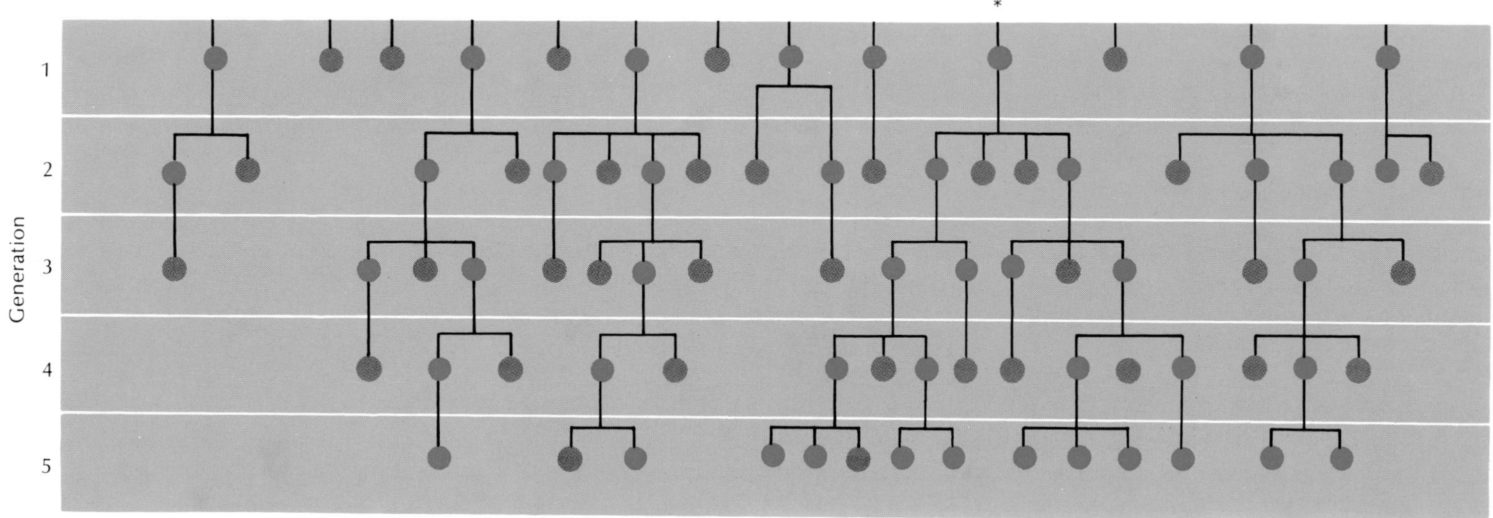

portion of alleles in a population tends to remain stable, regardless of their respective dominance or recessiveness. This tendency toward stability is expressed by

$$p^2 + 2pq + q^2 = 1$$

where p^2 equals the percentage of individuals in the population that are homozygous for one allele (conventionally the dominant, or AA), q^2 equals the percentage of individuals homozygous for the other allele (conventionally the recessive, or aa), and $2pq$ equals the percentage of individuals heterozygous for the allelic pair under consideration. This equation can be modified to apply as well to cases in which there are three or more alternative alleles for a given gene, but it is more simply understood if we limit our consideration to only two alternative alleles.

To demonstrate the Hardy-Weinberg equilibrium principle, let us consider an imaginary situation in which a spaceship bearing a crew of ten sets forth to colonize a distant planet. Of these ten colonists, nine are dark-eyed homozygotes and the tenth is a blue-eyed Dane. The initial gene pool therefore represents only two alleles for blue eyes (b), these being concentrated in the genotype of one person, and 18 alleles for brown eyes (B). In the first generation of offspring, and probably for several subsequent generations, blue eyes will disappear from the colony since any children of the blue-eyed Dane would be brown-eyed heterozygotes (Bb). If the colony flourishes, in around a century it may have grown to 1,000 persons, and if all of the original crew and their descendants have contributed equally to the population increase we shall find that the alleles b and B are *still present in their original proportions,* even though only about *one person in 100,* rather than the original one in ten, are actually blue-eyed. The frequency of the alleles B and b may be calculated if the percentage (q^2) of blue-eyed individuals (bb) is known, and this of course is a matter for simple observation. If there are ten blue-eyed persons in a population of 1,000, $q^2 = 1$ percent or 0.01. The total number of b alleles, however, must include not only those detectable phenotypically in the homozygotes (q^2), but also those hidden in the heterozygous portion of the population ($2pq$). Thus the total percentage of b alleles equals

$$q^2 + \tfrac{1}{2}(2pq) = q^2 + pq = q(q + p)$$

Since $p = (1 - q)$, the expression $q(q + p)$ actually equals $q[q + (1 - q)]$, which equals $q \times 1$, or q. Thus the total frequency of b alleles equals

$$q = \sqrt{q^2} = \sqrt{0.01} = 0.1$$

Our population of 1,000 colonists therefore represents a gene pool of 2,000 B and b alleles, of which, as we have shown, 10 percent (or 200) are b and 90 percent (or 1,800) are B. The proportions have not changed from those of the original crew with two b and 18 B alleles!

Taste polymorphism The preceding example was hypothetical, but the results of an actual analysis of random samples of the population of the United States demonstrate that *allelic frequency* has nothing directly to do with dominance or recessiveness, for in this analysis it is the *recessive* allele that is shown to be the more numerous. The human species is polymorphic for a gene that determines the ability to taste the chemical phenylthiocarbamide (PTC). The fundamental action of this gene is not known, but the detection of PTC is probably only ancillary to the main gene function. Since this organic compound, which "tasters" call bitter, is neither a normal ingredient of the diet nor a naturally occurring poison, there does not seem to be any particular advantage in being able to taste it. On the other hand, the *inability* to taste PTC is sometimes associated with a type of goiter, suggesting that this gene may be involved somehow in proper thyroid function. The ability to taste PTC is due to a dominant allele, T. Tasters therefore may have the genotypes TT or Tt, while nontasters are tt. In the United States, about 70 percent of the population tested are tasters and 30 percent are nontasters. At first glance, these findings might appear to indicate that the dominant allele is also the more frequently occurring allele, but the application of the Hardy-Weinberg formula to the data shows that the reverse is true:

$$q^2(tt) = 0.3$$

and

$$q = \sqrt{0.3} = 0.547$$

In other words, about 55 percent of the alleles are t, and only about 45 percent are T!

Other taste polymorphisms are known in man. Another bitter chemical, brucine, was briefly adopted for use in denaturing tax-exempt ethyl alcohol, until it was found that delighted brucine nontasters were taking advantage of the situation.

Blood type polymorphism In man a number of different genes affect the composition of blood proteins and thus are responsible for the so-called blood groups. These include the rhesus (Rh), M and N, and

Landsteiner (A, B, O) factors. What may well be a stable genetic polymorphism exists for three alternative alleles that control the production of a red-cell factor which determines if the major blood type is A, B, AB, or O. These alleles are designated I^A, I^B, and *i*. (The symbol *I* is an abbreviation of *isoagglutinogen,* a technical name describing the antigenic nature of the red-cell factor.) The alleles I^A and I^B are codominant, and each causes a distinctive variety of protein to be produced in the red blood corpuscles. That produced by the allele I^A is called "red-cell antigen A," although of course it does not behave antigenically unless introduced into plasma of an incompatible type. The variant produced by allele I^B is accordingly termed "red-cell antigen B." If type A erythrocytes (containing antigen A) are introduced by transfusion into the bloodstream of a person whose erythrocytes contain only antigen B, a factor in the recipient's blood plasma reacts against antigen A as a foreign protein, causing the clumping or agglutination of the A-type corpuscles. The reciprocal effect occurs when type B blood, with red corpuscles containing antigen B, is transfused into the bloodstream of a person whose red cells contain only antigen A. The plasma antibodies that react against these red-cell factors act as *agglutinins,* affecting the outer surface of the erythrocytes so that they clump together (agglutinate). These clumps can fatally block the capillaries.

Persons with blood type A may be genotypically I^AI^A or I^Ai. Those with type B blood are genotypically I^BI^B or I^Bi. Persons with blood type AB are always I^AI^B, while type O blood results only from the genotype *ii*. The recessive allele *i* produces neither red-cell antigen A nor B. Individuals with type AB blood, on the other hand, have *both* antigens A and B in their erythrocytes. Accordingly, their plasma contains neither the anti-A nor the anti-B factor. Consequently, persons with blood type AB are *universal recipients* because their blood plasma will not react adversely against any type of erythrocytes that may be introduced by transfusion. The transfused plasma in which the donated cells are suspended may contain anti-A or anti-B agglutinins, but it is quickly diluted and does not adversely affect the recipient's red blood corpuscles.

Type O blood is known as the *universal donor* type, because its erythrocytes, lacking both antigens A and B, will not be agglutinated by any type of plasma into which they may be introduced. On the other hand, the plasma of type O individuals contains both anti-A and anti-B agglutinins. Therefore persons of blood type O can *receive* transfusions only of type O.

There seems to be no particular selective advantage or disadvantage to having blood of any one of these types (with the exception that duodenal ulcers have been found to occur predominantly in type O individuals). Nevertheless, the frequency of the various alleles is by no means equal, as seen in Table 8.1, showing blood-type frequencies in population samples from various parts of the world. Even cursory inspection reveals that the commonest allele in all samples is *i*, and the rarest, I^B. The absence of the allele I^B from Australian aborigines and of both alleles I^B and I^A from the Bororo Indian tribe is explicable on the basis of chance loss of a rare allele from a small population, a phenomenon known as *genetic drift.* Probably the alleles I^A and I^B arose by mutation from the allele *i*, which may have been the original form of the gene, and since these variants were not harmful (and possibly were beneficial if they

Table 8.1 □ Blood-type frequencies[a]

	BLOOD TYPES AND GENOTYPES, %			
POPULATION	O (*ii*)	A (I^AI^A, I^Ai)	B (I^BI^B, I^Bi)	AB (I^AI^B)
Scottish	**52.2**	**34.2**	**11.8**	**2.7**
French	**41.6**	**47.0**	**8.0**	**3.3**
Russians (Moscow)	**33.3**	**37.4**	**22.8**	**6.5**
Chinese (Peking)	**28.6**	**26.6**	**32.0**	**12.8**
Japanese (Tokyo)	**30.1**	**38.4**	**21.9**	**9.7**
Kikuyu (Kenya)	**60.4**	**18.7**	**19.8**	**1.1**
Egyptian	**32.6**	**35.5**	**24.4**	**7.5**
Australian Aborigines	**60.7**	**39.3**	**0.0**	**0.0**
Navajo	**72.6**	**26.9**	**0.2**	**0.2**
Bororo (Brazil)	**100.0**	**0.0**	**0.0**	**0.0**

[a]Data taken from T. Dobzhansky, *Heredity and the Nature of Man* (New York: The New American Library, Inc., 1966), p. 99.

contribute to resistance against duodenal ulcer), they have remained in the genome and may be on the increase.

FACTORS THAT DISTURB ALLELIC EQUILIBRIUMS Evolution takes place only when various factors disturb the genetic equilibrium defined by the Hardy-Weinberg principle. In point of fact, the equilibrium is only a mathematical model, seldom actualized in life. The three main factors that act in conjunction or in opposition to modify gene frequencies in a population are *mutation pressure, selection pressure,* and *genetic drift.*

Mutation pressure A gene tends to fluctuate back and forth among its various mutually exclusive allelic states. This tendency is not necessarily uniform: the probability of allele A mutating to become allele A' may be greater than that for allele A' to become A by mutation. This difference in directional rate of mutation may be expressed as $A \rightleftarrows A'$, in which the larger size of the upper arrow indicates that allele A tends to mutate to A' more frequently than A' to A. We would say that, in this case, mutation pressure favors A'. Even if A' were detrimental to its carrier, it still would not be eliminated from the population because it would continue to arise *de novo* by mutation of allele A.

Genetic drift The action of drift may be illustrated by reference to our earlier example of the extraterrestrial colony founded by ten space mariners. Such a small original population is highly subject to changes in gene frequencies by *chance alone.* For example, if our blue-eyed Dane were to fall on his head the first time he stepped out of the spaceship, the colony would irrevocably lose the opportunity to produce blue-eyed descendants, unless a new b allele were to arise by mutation. Genetic drift, the *loss of alleles by chance alone,* is particularly significant in the evolution of small populations. In fact, any tiny deme colonizing a new habitat is in great danger of extinction, for it can contain only a fraction of the total gene pool of the species, and thus lacks flexibility in coping with environmental changes by means of genetic adjustments. If the new colony survives this initial hazard, in time new mutations will restore the population heterogeneity, bettering the probability of survival.

Natural selection Natural selection is the process whereby the most effectively adapted individuals in a population (in terms both of extrinsic adaptation to the environment and of intrinsic coadaptation of body functions) contribute the most progeny to the next generation, while less well-adapted individuals fail to contribute equally. If the adaptive value of two particular alleles is not equal, then in each generation *selection pressure* will bring about a shift in the relative frequency of these alleles. Selection pressure may be measured in terms of the effect of an allele on the prolificacy of the heterozygote or homozygote, as compared with the reproductive rate of the population as a whole. Selection pressure may operate for or against a given allele, but *not* on the basis of chance. Instead, the fate of the allele is determined by its effect on the organism's reproductive capacity. If the gene enhances the *fitness* of the organism, that is, *increases its prolificacy,* it will tend to increase in the population at the expense of its less beneficial allele. The rate of increase is dependent upon the size of the population and the intensity of selection. If the trait is produced by a recessive allele, its rate of increase will correlate *inversely* with the size of the population. This is because selection cannot operate upon a recessive allele unless it is brought into the homozygous condition in which it can exert its phenotypic effect. Selection pressure operates simultaneously both positively and negatively—obviously, if one gene confers a selective *advantage* on its carrier, its allele by comparison confers a selective *disadvantage;* if selection is operating in favor of one allele (*positive selection pressure*) it is simultaneously operating against the alternative allele (*negative selection pressure*).

The factors that operate in producing positive and negative selection pressure are both intrinsic and extrinsic, originating within the individual organism, or in its environment. If a mutant allele is unable to fulfill its required metabolic function, the health and fitness of the individual may be seriously impaired. This is the case with the recessive allele in man that causes phenylketonuric idiocy. The mutation blocks a sequence of chemical reactions by which the amino acid phenylalanine is metabolized. This substance then accumulates to toxic levels, impairing structural and mental development. The recessive homozygote consequently fails to reproduce, and two of the recessive alleles are thereby removed from the gene pool of the population. Thus the allele that causes phenylketonuric idiocy is decreasing in frequency because of negative selection pressure.

Even if an allele does not produce an effect that is intrinsically harmful to the normal functioning of the individual body, it is still subject to the influence of selective factors originating in the environment. Often the contributory factors are quite complex, and may involve the impact of both abiotic and biotic influences on the individual. In our imaginary extraterrestrial colony, several factors may influence the frequency of the alleles for brown or blue eyes. Should the new habitat be characterized by intense illumination, blue-eyed homozygotes might suffer visual impairment, because blue irises are less efficient than dark irises in screening radiation from the interior of the eye. Since visual acuity usually has importance for survival, selection would then operate against the blue-eyed allele. On the other hand, selection might favor blue eyes: their rarity might well enhance the attractive potential of our Dane and his blue-eyed descendants, and they might be particularly desired as mates. The value of rarity is easily understood in human populations because of the human tendency to delight in novelty. What is less readily explained is a comparable *minority effect* in other animals such as fruit flies. Female fruit flies (*Drosophila pseudoobscura*) exhibit a penchant for selecting mates with novelty value. In fruit flies it is the female that exercises selection in the choice of a mate, for the male will often court promiscuously, even females of the wrong species. He cannot copulate, however, unless the female accepts his advances. In one recently performed study flies of the Californian and Texan races of *D. pseudoobscura* were mixed in various proportions, and the number of successful copulations recorded. When both the Texan and Californian flies were present in equal numbers, neither showed any reproductive advantage, but when the two strains were present in unequal proportions, in every case males of the less numerous type were involved in proportionately more successful copulations than the commoner type! Such preference for the rarer type is difficult to explain, but its adaptive value lies in promoting the genetic heterogeneity of the population.

As long as the circumstances to which a population is adapted remain stable, there is a tendency (known as *normalizing selection*) for phenotypic deviants to be at a disadvantage when compared with individuals more closely representing the phenotypic norm for the population. It is often noted that predators concentrate their attention on animals that look or act even slightly differently from the rest of their group, and despite the incidence of minority effects as described above, individuals that deviate too widely from the norm usually fail to secure mates. Normalizing selection therefore limits the variability of populations by operating against individuals that "stand out in a crowd," even when the traits that make them distinctive are not otherwise disadvantageous to survival. If we think of a population's range of variability as describing a normal distribution curve, in each generation the normalizing tendency operates to chop off both extremes of the curve. Should the environment change, however, selection pressures will change in intensity or reverse in direction, and a new norm must be sought.

The *intensity* of selection pressure may be quantitatively expressed on the basis of the estimated impact of the trait on the organism's ability to survive and reproduce. Negative selection pressure is expressible in terms of the estimated *reproduction deficit* caused by possession of the trait. This may usually be taken as the difference between the net productivity of the recessive homozygotes and the net productivity of the phenotypic dominants. This difference is called the *coefficient of selection,* or k. When the recessive homozygote is totally unable to reproduce, the coefficient is unity: $k = 1$. In this case there is complete selection against the recessive allele. Each *genetic death* of a recessive homozygote removes two of the recessive alleles from the population. Genetic death is not necessarily synonymous with the actual death of the organism—it merely means failure to reproduce: the genome of that organism is removed from the gene pool of the population. Conversely, a gene may operate as an outright *lethal,* bringing about the death of its carrier (usually but not invariably the homozygote), but unless death occurs before reproductive age is attained the lethal gene may not actually cause *genetic* death. This is the case with the dominant allele in man that causes Huntington's chorea, a degenerative disease of the nervous system, terminating in death. The individual carrying this allele is apparently normal until about 40 years of age, when the first symptoms appear. Unfortunately, the victim has had ample previous opportunity to produce children, 50 percent of whom have probably received the allele and eventually also will die of the disease.

The change in allelic frequency that takes place over a given number of generations may be calculated as a function of the estimated value of k, the coefficient of selection against the more detrimental (or less adaptive) allele. The shift occurring in a single generation is given by the formula

$$q_1 = \frac{q_0 - kq_0^2}{1 - kq_0^2}$$

in which q_0 represents the frequency of the recessive allele in the initial generation under consideration and q_1 is the frequency of that allele in the next generation. If the recessive homozygotes do not reproduce at all, then $k = 1$ and

$$q_1 = \frac{q_0 - (1 \times q_0^2)}{1 - (1 \times q_0^2)}$$

The initial frequency of the alleles is first determined by counting the number of recessive homozygotes in the population (q^2) and solving the Hardy-Weinberg equation for the values of p and q. When an allele acts as a lethal during embryonic development, the value of q^2 may be arrived at only by inference.

Under *partial* selection, the value of k is less than 1. If, for instance, individuals with the genotype *cc* tend to produce only one fourth the number of progeny produced by individuals with the genotypes *CC* or *Cc*, then $k = 0.75$. If the initial value of q^2 is 0.25, or 25 individuals of the genotype *cc* per thousand, then the frequency of the allele *c* in the first generation is 0.5, or 50 percent. After one generation of selection,

$$q_1 = \frac{0.5 - (0.75 \times 0.25)}{1 - (0.75 \times 0.25)} = 0.385$$

As we can see, the frequency of the allele *c* has been reduced from 50 to 38.5 percent in a single generation and the proportion of recessive homozygotes, from 25 per thousand to about 15 per thousand. This would seem to indicate that an allele responsible for such a reproduction deficit could be swiftly eliminated from the population; but in fact the more rare the allele becomes, the less effective will be selection against it, because of the infrequency with which it comes into the homozygous state.

We can calculate the number of generations of *complete* selection required to effect a specified reduction in the frequency of an allele by employing the equation

$$n = \frac{1}{q_n} - \frac{1}{q_0}$$

in which n represents the number of generations required for the specified reduction in allelic frequency. One person in 10,000 is an albino (*aa*). Although under civilized conditions natural selection against albinism is negligible, *artificial* selection could be employed in an attempt to eliminate the allele *a* from the human species. If every albino child were sterilized, how many generations would it take to reduce the proportion of albinos from the present 1 in 10,000 to 1 in 50,000 (that is, to reduce the value of q^2 from 0.0001 to 0.00002)? We find that

$$n = \frac{1}{\sqrt{0.00002}} - \frac{1}{\sqrt{0.0001}}$$
$$= \frac{1}{0.00465} - \frac{1}{0.01} = 115$$

It would take 115 generations, or about 2,500 years! It is thus apparent that eugenics programs aimed at the elimination of *rare* alleles causing genetic diseases are of limited value. On the other hand, voluntary abstinence from further child bearing in the case of families that have already produced a child suffering from a genetic abnormality might prevent the recurrence of personal tragedy, for in producing one defective recessive homozygote the parents have demonstrated that each is a carrier of the detrimental allele and that there is consequently a 25 percent probability of future offspring also exhibiting the trait.

D Characteristics of organic evolution

EVOLUTION AS A CONTINUOUS PROCESS We have said that evolution is the change that takes place through successive generations in the genetic composition of a population. Since only a fraction of each generation contributes gametes to produce the next generation, it can be seen that no generation is genetically identical with the preceding one. It follows that *evolution is a continuous process* that will not end as long as life itself persists.

THE UNIVERSALITY OF EVOLUTION Since alterations are continuously taking place in the genes and chromosomes, spontaneously or under the influence of mutagenic agencies such as radiation, *no kind of living thing is exempt from evolutionary change*. Populations will evolve whether their primary mode of reproduction is asexual or sexual, although sexual reproduction facilitates the dissemination of beneficial mutations and accelerates evolution. The rate at which genetic change takes place is not the same in all groups of organisms and consequently some types evolve more rapidly than others. No form of life, however conservative, can exist utterly unchanged even in a relatively stable environment.

PRODUCTION OF NEW FORMS OF LIFE Evolution is not synonymous with *speciation* (the origin of new species), yet new forms of life eventually do arise, either by phyletic evolution or by schistic evolution (Figure 8.15). *Schistic evolution* requires

Figure 8.15 □ **Types of evolutionary change. (*a*) *Schistic evolution:* geographical isolation of subpopulations leads toward speciation because of the restriction of gene flow among the subpopulations and the operation of different selective factors in each habitat. Eventually, a cluster of related species will result, which will not interbreed if their numbers should increase until their ranges once more overlap (making intermating geographically possible). (*b*) *Phyletic evolution:* genetic change in a population through successive generations. Geographical isolation of subpopulations is not necessary for this type of evolutionary change, for each generation is separated in *time* from those preceding or following it.**

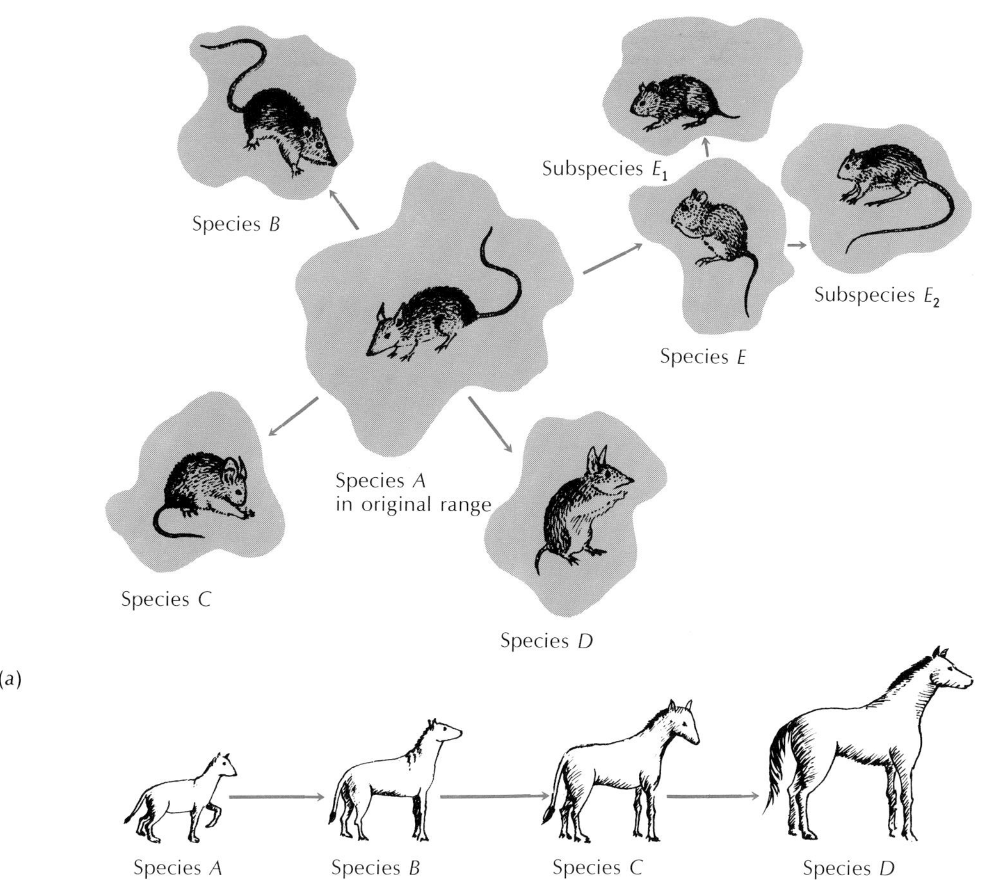

that subpopulations of a species be geographically isolated from one another. Such allopatric populations are subjected to different selective factors in their separate environments. In addition, they cannot share by gene flow the mutations and chromosomal rearrangements that spontaneously occur in each population. *Phyletic evolution* occurs over a period of time within a *sympatric* population. In this case, gene flow occurs freely and geographical (or other) barriers do not fragment the gene pool. As the environment gradually alters and genetic changes accumulate in the population, one species imperceptibly grades into a new one. No real extinction of a population takes place, and it is difficult to establish the precise point at which species *A* becomes species *B*.

ADAPTIVENESS Evolution is usually adaptive, because gene frequencies are subject to alteration through intrinsic and extrinsic selection pressures. The fundamental characteristic of life is adaptability, but since no environment remains static in either its abiotic or biotic constituents, perfect adaptation can never be achieved. The population that *overspecializes* in the course of adaptation eventually finds that extinction is the price of genetic inflexibility in a dynamic milieu.

UNDIRECTED NATURE OF EVOLUTION Evolution is not purposive, nor does it guarantee survival. Many a population follows a trend that is originally adaptive, only to find itself trapped in an evolutionary *cul-de-sac.* Adaptive specializations may fit a species to a particular niche with extreme precision—a fit so exact that the species is incapable of surviving if its niche disappears. The mutualistic association between yucca and yucca moth may be cited as an example. The requirements of both species have become so narrow that extinction of either species would probably result in the extinction of the other. Birds have become highly specialized for flight. Having once committed themselves to flying as a means of locomotion, food seeking, and escape from predators, their entire evolution has tended toward the refinement of the mechanisms of flight. Modifications of the nervous, muscular, skeletal, respiratory, and even urogenital systems have occurred. Much has been gained, for birds have become the best flying machines produced by organic evolution, and yet much has also been sacrificed. Prehensile use of the forelimbs has been ruled out; teeth have been jettisoned in favor of a lightweight toothless beak; fixed behavior patterns have become more important in the bird's life than learned behaviors, possibly permitting simplification of neural organization. The urinary and gall bladders have also been eliminated, and a solid urine is produced; one of the two ovaries fails to develop, reducing the weight of the reproductive tract; sensory perception depends mainly upon sight and hearing, taste and olfaction being absent or undeveloped in many. Defense adaptations have been minimized, for birds can respond to danger by merely flying away from it. In all these respects birds have become highly specialized organisms, committed to the accumulation of adaptations relating to flight and equally committed to forgoing other valuable capabilities when these tend to impair the efficiency of flight.

EVOLUTIONARY OPPORTUNISM In evolution use is made of *whatever is available in the genome at the time of need.* Since genetic change does not occur in response to need but only randomly, the *timing* of environmental stress is a key factor. A given population that responds in a certain way to a critical change in the environment at one time might respond in a very different manner if the crisis were to take place at another. By analogy, an unarmed man meeting a grizzly would probably run away or climb a tree, but the same man, armed, would probably attempt to kill or frighten the bear. The difference in response would depend on what resources were available at the time of crisis. It follows that many adaptive adjustments are far from ideal; they are merely the best that may be achieved with the genetic resources available at the time. At some point in their early history vertebrates apparently developed and fixated upon two pairs of limbs, which proved to be adequate for their survival. Arthropods had no such limitations but developed many pairs of appendages modifiable for diverse uses. If vertebrates had developed *three* pairs of limbs instead of *two,* flying vertebrates would not have had to sacrifice manipulative capacity in favor of flight, and quadrupeds could have been like the mythological centaurs: running on four legs but still possessing two limbs for handling things. Arthropod development, on the other hand, fixated upon an exoskeleton in lieu of an articulated endoskeleton. Thereafter, they have been burdened with the limitations of an exoskeleton: its weight, the necessity for its being molted to permit growth, and the barrier to sensation that it imposes between the organism and its environment. Calcification of the exoskeleton affords protection but increases the weight of the skeleton; small size and aquatic habit compensate for the skeletal encumbrance. Insects, however, in developing the capability for flight, came to need lightness more than armor. In these arthropods the exoskeleton is rarely calcified but is sometimes strengthened by horny protein. Above all, for flying arthropods, small size is dictated. The size limitations dictated by their type of skeletal support have necessarily imposed limitations on the size and complexity of the arthropod brain and nervous system. Although complicated fixed motor patterns have evolved, modifications of behavior by learning are severely restricted.

COMPENSATORY EVOLUTION A certain amount of evolutionary change is *compensatory,* in the sense of having to "make up for" past mistakes. Some such "mistakes" are the result of adaptive opportunism—of taking the only possible way out at the time. Behavioral patterns that partly compensate for the absence of hands are often seen among birds. A bird may stand on one foot, holding an object with its other foot, or may employ its beak dexterously in weaving together strands of nest material. The bird's absence of teeth may be compensated in grain-eating species by the swallowing of stones which, during the contractions of the gizzard, serve to pulverize coarse food.

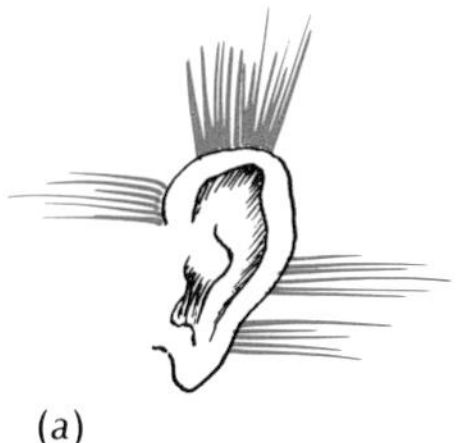

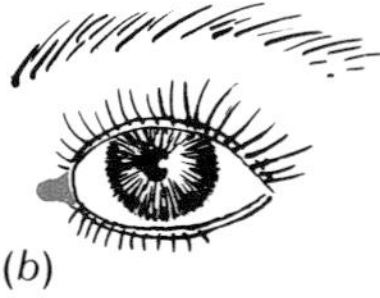

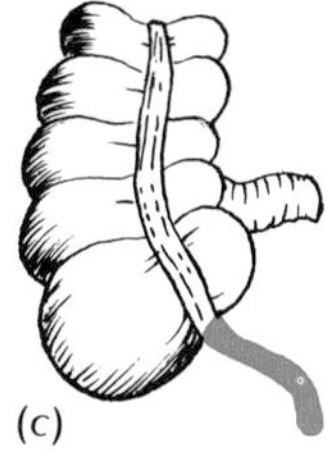

Figure 8.16 □ Vestigial characters in man. (*a*) Extrinsic muscles move the pinna in most mammals but are largely functionless in man. (*b*) The nictitating membrane (seen at inner corner of eye) is a vestige of the movable third eyelid of birds and many reptiles and amphibians. (*c*) The vermiform appendix is a vestigial portion of the cecum, a long pouch at the proximal end of the large intestine that serves in many herbivorous mammals as a storage place for food residues that can only be utilized if digested by cecum bacteria.

Figure 8.17 □ Flightless cormorant. Resident of the Galápagos Islands, this species knew no enemies on land and now fails to develop the large wing feathers that, though necessary for flight, may restrict its speed and maneuverability under water, where it feeds upon fish. The posture shown here is a favorite of sunning cormorants and may help in drying the plumage after diving. (*Zoological Society of San Diego.*)

Compensatory adaptations may also occur in response to certain evolutionary advances. For instance, during vertebrate evolution the sequence of development from zygote to adult has become longer and more complicated. This *developmental hypertrophy* has been compensated in various ways which will be considered in Chapter 11.

USE AND DISUSE AS FACTORS IN EVOLUTION Structures or processes no longer needed for survival *tend to be lost or to become adapted for a new use.* The elimination of useless characters is an outcome of the selective advantage inherent in avoiding the wasteful expenditure of energy in maintenance of something valueless. During the course of the disappearance, useless characters become *vestigial,* persisting as mere remnants of what they were earlier in ontogeny (individual development) or in evolution (Figures 8.16 and 8.17). A *rudimentary* character is one which appears to be underdeveloped as compared with its condition *later* in ontogeny or evolution. By comparing them with earlier conditions in evolution or development, vestigial characters may be distinguished from those which are rudimentary or on the ascendancy. The limbs, for instance, first appear in the embryo as rudimentary limbbuds, which subsequently grow larger. During vertebrate evolution the ear is at first almost exclusively an organ of equilibrium, the acoustic function evolving gradually. The acoustic portion of the fish ear, the *lagena,* therefore represents a rudimentary form of the mammalian *cochlea* (see Figures 15.29 and 15.30).

Many characteristics of organisms are best understood when considered in the light of evolutionary change. The vestigial hindlimbs and pelvic girdles of whales and pythons reflect a four-legged ancestral condition. Air-breathing vertebrates have vestigial pharyngeal pouches that reflect their aquatic ancestry.

Animal species that live underground or in caves tend to become eyeless (Figure 8.18). Eyeless mutations are selectively favored since embryos that need not waste energy in constructing these useless organs tend to develop more rapidly than their eyed contemporaries and therefore compete more successfully with them in the darkness of the habitat. Furthermore, animals living constantly underground may be hampered by having to keep the eyes free of dirt.

Figure 8.18 □ **Adaptations of a burrowing lizard. This two-legged species shows many adaptations common to burrowing animals: reduction in number of appendages; modification of the remaining legs into broad, molelike digging tools; reduced pigmentation; and elongate, worm-shaped body with well-developed trunk muscles. Many burrowing animals are blind or, as this lizard, have vestigial eyes. (*Zoological Society of San Diego.*)**

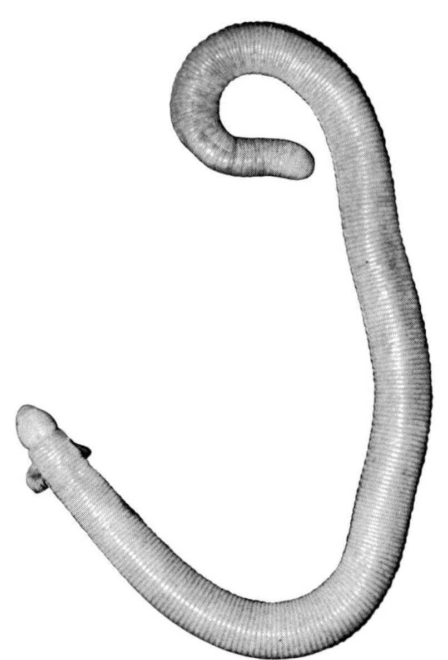

Assumption of new functions by preexisting organs A character that has lost its previous adaptive value may be "salvaged" by its taking on a new function. Here, the *opportunism* of the adaptive process becomes evident. If the character has become useless, any mutations that affect its development will probably not be very deleterious. If it is even slightly modified in such a way that a new adaptive use is made possible, its further evolution will be subject to regulation by selective factors quite different from those which operated upon it previously. Occasionally it is possible to trace the probable history of such a salvaged characteristic, especially if it happens to be a skeletal structure which leaves a fossil record. Such a record exists in the case of the *branchial skeleton,* which supports the gills of vertebrate fish (Figure 8.19). The most primitive vertebrates, the small fishlike ostracoderms (see Figure 2.45) were jawless, but the walls of the pharynx contained skeletal supports which kept the gill slits from collapsing. From the ostracoderms arose the first jawed vertebrates, the placoderms, in which the first gill arch became the upper and lower jaw, while the others retained their original function of gill support.

The next significant change in the evolution of the branchial skeleton occurred when certain lobefinned fishes (see Figure 2.50*a*) evolved into the first amphibians. The branchial skeleton persists in modern amphibians as gill supports that are functional during the aquatic larval stage but remain as a cumbersome and mostly useless tongue-supporting skeleton in the adult possessing lungs. One of the more posterior elements of the branchial skeleton became the *glottis,* a pair of semicircular cartilages flanking the opening of the windpipe into the pharynx and serving to close it during the swallowing of food.

There is no functional gilled stage in the life history of reptiles, birds, and mammals, hence no need at any time for gill-supporting skeletal elements. Some of these have been deleted perforce, whereas others have contributed to the voicebox (larynx; see Figure 16.37), to the hyoid (tongue-supporting bone), and to the articulation of the lower jaw with the skull.

The transition in land vertebrates from the detection only of sound waves conducted through solids (such as the ground) to the detection of sound waves conducted through air was made possible by other changes in the branchial skeleton: certain bones formerly concerned with the articulation of the lower jaw with the skull instead became concerned with sound conduction. In fishes a bone derived from the second gill arch (the hyomandibula), functions both in the suspension of the lower jaw and in the conduction of sound vibrations. In nonmammalian tetrapods the hyomandibula serves only for sound conduction, becoming the single middle ear ossicle (columella). The columella receives vibrations from the eardrum by conduction through two bones derived from the former first gill arch and also involved in the suspension of the lower jaw (the quadrate and articulare). Finally, in mammals, as the articulation of the jaw

Figure 8.19 □ **Evolution of vertebrate branchial skeleton. (*a*) Jawless vertebrate: branchial skeleton of nine gill arches supports walls of pharynx, providing attachment for muscles to open and close gill slits. (*b*) Placoderm: arch I forms upper jaw (1, palatoquadrate) and lower jaw (2, mandible). (*c*) Later fish: dorsal part of arch II (3, hyomandibula) for suspending jaw from cranium. (*d*) Adult primitive amphibian: arch I is further subdivided to form quadrate (4) and articulare (5), both used in jaw suspension, freeing hyomandibula of suspensory function (it now becomes a middle-ear bone—columella—for sound conduction); arch VII gives rise to laryngeal cartilages (6) and cartilage rings supporting trachea (7); other arches support the larval gills but persist in adult only as a tongue-supporting apparatus. (*e*) Primitive reptile: arches IV and V disappear, except in premammalian forms, in which they give rise to thyroid cartilage of larynx; arch VI becomes epiglottis, which protects larynx during swallowing. (*f*) Most mammals: jaw suspension shifts anteriorly, releasing quadrate and articulare from suspensory duties; these become incus and malleus of middle ear, while columella becomes stapes. [*After H. M. Smith,* Evolution of Chordate Structure (*New York: Holt, Rinehart & Winston, Inc., 1960*).]**

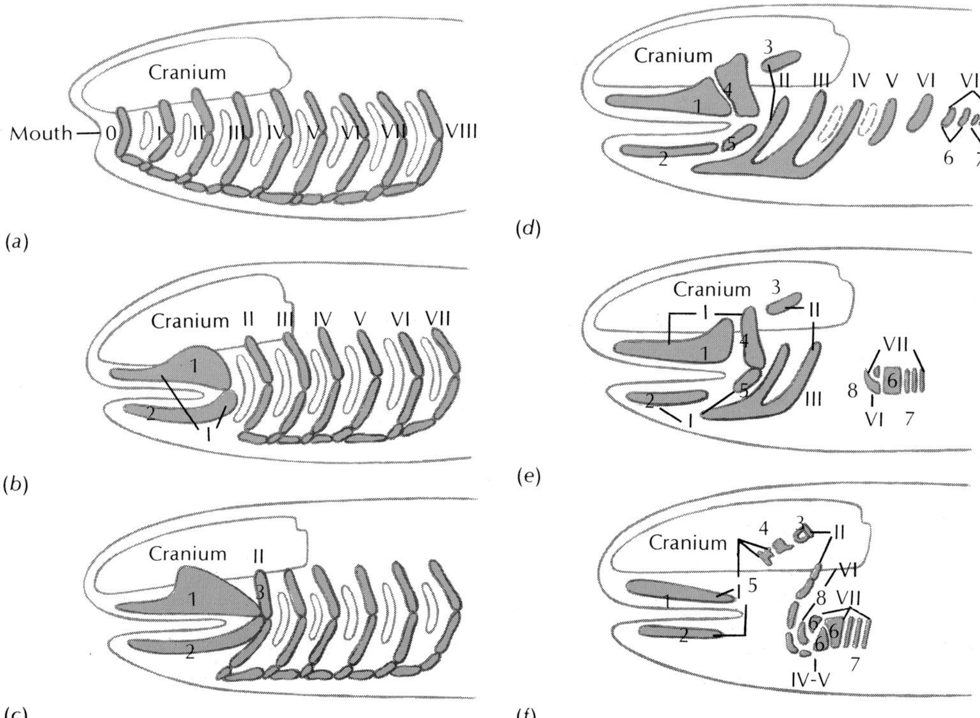

shifts forward, shortening the jaw and permitting a more efficient chewing action, the quadrate and articulare lose their function in jaw suspension, and become wholly concerned with sound transmission as the anvil and hammer of the middle ear. The columella persists in mammals as the stirrup (see Figure 15.30), and is the innermost of the three ossicles. These three small ear bones are set in motion by the vibration of the eardrum. Their movement increases the pressure of vibrations reaching the middle ear, making mammalian hearing more acute than that of other tetrapods.

The vertebrate *pineal organ* serves as an example of an organ that is thought to have evolved a new physiological function as its original one was lost. The physiological change from a *visual* organ to a *gland* has been accompanied by concomitant structural changes. The most ancient vertebrates generally show evidence of an opening in the top of the skull for the apparent accommodation of a third, median eye. The "living fossil," tuatara, a lizardlike reptile with a very ancient skeletal structure now found only on certain islands near New Zealand, actually *has* a small third eye, considered to be a pineal eye, on the top of its head. The pineal organ of other modern cold-blooded vertebrates is completely covered over by the roofing bones of the skull but lies close to the surface of the brain and presumably is exposed to light penetrating the thin cranium. Electrophysiological studies have demonstrated that the frog pineal is indeed a photoreceptor: nerve impulses are generated in the pineal organ when it is exposed to light of certain wavelengths. As a result of the enlargement of the forebrain, the pineal organ of mammals lies deep below the surface, between the two cerebral hemispheres that have overgrown it. This position, together with the opacity of the skull to light, makes it highly unlikely that the mammalian pineal can detect light directly. However, recent evidence indicates that this tiny organ (in man weighing only about 0.1 g), although vestigial as a photoreceptor, has developed a new functional significance in mammals as an endocrine gland. Although no longer capable of receiving light stimuli directly, the pineal nevertheless appears to be controlled by nerves so that it is responsive to changes in *photoperiod.* Mediated by way of nerve impulses, light induces the pineal to secrete the hormone *melatonin,* which by way of the bloodstream affects other organs, particularly the gonads. Melatonin suppresses gonadal activity. Further experimentation has indicated that the actual effect of light, acting through nerve fibers to the pineal, is to modify the rate at which the synthesis of an enzyme necessary for the production of melatonin takes place. We seem in this case to be observing a mechanism whereby enzyme synthesis at the molecular level is indirectly regulated by an environmental factor, to wit, light. This new function of the pineal in mammals may serve to correlate various physiological cycles, especially those concerned with reproduction, with seasonal changes that are marked by changes in photoperiod. Accordingly, the time of reproductive activity may be coordinated with annual seasonal changes so that the young are born at the time of the year most conducive to their survival. The new role of the pineal organ would thus seem to be that of a *biological timekeeper,* responding to annual rather than daily environmental cycles.

IRREVERSIBILITY OF EVOLUTION Evolution appears generally to be irreversible. A structure or capacity that has been lost does not seem to reappear in the history of that group. This is not surprising in view of the extreme unlikelihood of any adaptive characteristic arising in the first place. The history of life is filled with aborted beginnings and unactualized potentialities. A myriad of types fail while only a few succeed. Survival is the product of the population's successful adaptations. Should circumstances favor the loss of some of these adaptations, the chances are great that, when further environmental changes again make them necessary, they will most likely not reappear.

INCONSTANCY OF RATE It should be stressed that *evolution does not proceed at a constant rate.* Its rate depends upon: (1) the relative constancy or inconstancy of the environment; (2) the rate of mutation; (3) the size of the breeding population; (4) the intensity of competition; (5) the intensity of selection pressure; and (6) the variety of selection pressure. The most slowly evolving organisms are those which inhabit relatively stable environments such as the open sea. A variety of selection pressures acting simultaneously on a population may also act to slow down evolutionary change, since the organism may need to adapt to a number of somewhat opposing factors. Improvement in one respect may be counterbalanced by a reduction in adaptation with respect to another factor, in such a manner that change in any direction is blocked. The more intense the competition and selection pressure and the higher the rate of mutation, the more rapidly will evolutionary change proceed. Finally, as we have said before, the smaller the breeding population, the more rapidly can innovations be tested and either eliminated or fixed in the gene pool of the population.

8.3 □ EVENTS IN THE HISTORY OF LIFE

The earliest phases of organic evolution cannot be traced through the fossil record. They took place over a prolonged period, during which organic molecules must first have been formed spontaneously under the prevailing abiotic conditions; at a later stage these molecules combined into larger and larger molecules that finally associated into macromolecular complexes from which the first primitive cells arose; and, still later, the products of cell division remained together, forming undifferentiated clusters and then simple multicellular organisms with certain cells specialized to perform specific func-

Figure 8.20 □ Geologic history exposed in the walls of the Grand Canyon of the Colorado River.

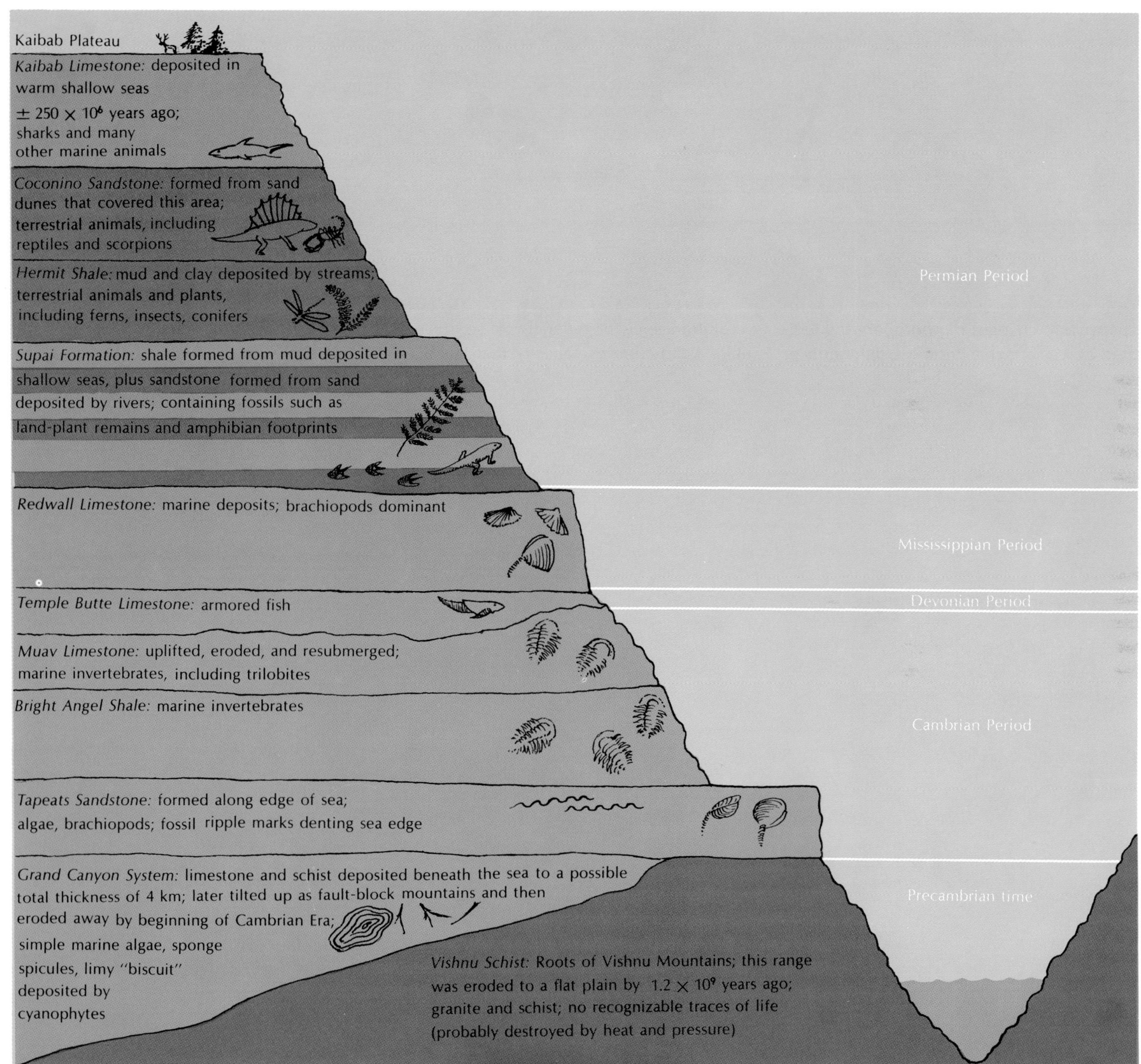

Kaibab Plateau
Kaibab Limestone: deposited in warm shallow seas ± 250 × 10^6 years ago; sharks and many other marine animals
Coconino Sandstone: formed from sand dunes that covered this area; terrestrial animals, including reptiles and scorpions
Hermit Shale: mud and clay deposited by streams; terrestrial animals and plants, including ferns, insects, conifers
Supai Formation: shale formed from mud deposited in shallow seas, plus sandstone formed from sand deposited by rivers; containing fossils such as land-plant remains and amphibian footprints
Permian Period
Redwall Limestone: marine deposits; brachiopods dominant
Mississippian Period
Temple Butte Limestone: armored fish
Devonian Period
Muav Limestone: uplifted, eroded, and resubmerged; marine invertebrates, including trilobites
Bright Angel Shale: marine invertebrates
Cambrian Period
Tapeats Sandstone: formed along edge of sea; algae, brachiopods; fossil ripple marks denting sea edge
Grand Canyon System: limestone and schist deposited beneath the sea to a possible total thickness of 4 km; later tilted up as fault-block mountains and then eroded away by beginning of Cambrian Era; simple marine algae, sponge spicules, limy "biscuit" deposited by cyanophytes
Precambrian time
Vishnu Schist: Roots of Vishnu Mountains; this range was eroded to a flat plain by 1.2 × 10^9 years ago; granite and schist; no recognizable traces of life (probably destroyed by heat and pressure)

Figure 8.21 □ **Fossils of ancient life. (*a*) Eurypterid, water scorpion (Silurian Period); (*b*) trilobite (Devonian Period). (*Ward's Natural Science Establishment, Inc.*) (*c*) Ammonite (Mesozoic Era); (*d*) toothed carp (Tertiary Period); (*e*) millipede (Quaternary Period). (*Los Angeles County Museum of Natural History.*)**

tions. Finally came major types of plant and animal body plans and diversification.

The duration of the earlier phases of the history of life can be estimated by means of radioactive dating, which indicates that the earth's crust contains rocks that solidified from the molten state more than 4.5×10^9 years ago. The biochemical phase of organic evolution may have commenced more than 3×10^9 years ago, for a variety of fairly complex organic molecules can be extracted from sedimentary rocks of that age. Well-preserved microorganisms have been found in strata about 2×10^9 years old, showing that cellular life had appeared by that time. However, an abundant fossil record exists for only about the past 6×10^8 years, by which time life had already attained a level of complexity at which most of the major phyla of multicellular organisms had already appeared and had begun to undergo a moderate degree of diversification. Hypotheses of the molecular and cellular phases of evolution are considered in Chapter 10. Now we shall take up only events of the fossil record (Figure 8.20).

Fossils are records of ancient life (Figure 8.21). They may be actual body parts, such as shell or bone, but in more ancient fossils all organic residues have usually been leached away, leaving an imprint, a cast, or a replacement fossil. The prerequisites for fossilization are that an organism have hard parts (although occasionally even the imprints of soft-bodied organisms remain recorded in stone) and that it suffer immediate burial. Most fossil beds have been formed wherever organisms can be buried in sediments—in bogs, river beds, at the mouths of estuaries, and on the floor of shallow seas. Fossilization may first involve the process of petrifaction, in which the original organic object is hardened by minerals that have impregnated its pores and cavities. After such materials as bone or wood have been petrified, they may gradually undergo *replacement*—molecule by molecule, the organic substance is dissolved away and replaced with inorganic materials such as silicates. So slow is this process and so faithful the replacement that even cellular details may be preserved. Thin objects such as leaves cannot be petrified but may merely leave a flat *imprint* in the hardening sediment. Where ground water dissolves away the organic material too rapidly for petrifaction and replacement to take place, the fossil may consist only of a cavity or *mold* in the rock, recording only the object's external shape; this mold may gradually fill with minerals until a *cast* results, keeping outer form without internal detail.

Fossils may also be evidences of life other than traces of the organisms themselves. Burrows of worms, footprints, and even dinosaur gizzard stones remain to give us information on ancient life. "Water biscuits," resembling rounded cobbles but actually composed of concentric layers of calcium carbonate, form a record of the lime-depositing activities of some of the earliest known organisms, cyanophytes.

The history of earth through approximately the past 10^9 years is divisible into major blocks of time (Table 8.2) which were separated from one another by major periods of geological transformation: for example, orogenic (mountain-building) periods, often accompanied by concomitant withdrawals of the temporary seas that repeat-

Table 8.2 □ Geologic time chart

ERA	PERIOD	WHEN PERIOD OR ERA BEGAN, 10^6 YEARS AGO	SIGNIFICANT GEOLOGIC AND BIOTIC EVENTS
Cenozoic	Quaternary	2 (±0.5)	*Cascadian revolution:* now in progress; mountain building, glaciation, man appears
	Tertiary	65 (±2)	First placental mammals; monocots appear; mammals diversify
			Laramide revolution: mountain building; massive extinctions; cooling climate
Mesozoic	Cretaceous	135 (±5)	Extensive submergence of North America; climax of dinosaurs and ammonites, followed by their extinction; flowering plants appear
	Jurassic	160 (±5)	First birds; first mammals; reptiles dominant; ammonites abundant
	Triassic	230 (±10)	Conifers dominant; dinosaurs appear; sharks begin to rediversify
			Appalachian revolution: mountain building; possible time of breakup of ancient supercontinents and drifting apart of the fragments; climate becoming cooler and drier; scattered glaciation; massive extinctions of both terrestrial and marine species
Paleozoic	Permian	280 (±10)	Amphibians beginning to decline; reptiles diversifying; deserts widespread
	Carboniferous	345 (±10)	Climate predominantly warm and moist; great forests of tree ferns, scale trees, and conifers; amphibians abundant; first reptiles
	Devonian	405 (±10)	Diversification of fishes; first amphibians; first ammonites; first seed plants; wingless insects
	Silurian	425 (±10)	First land plants (mosses, ferns) and land invertebrates; first jawed vertebrates (placoderms); aquatic invertebrates abundant
	Ordovician	500 (±10)	Major continental resubmergence; first vertebrates (ostracoderms)
	Cambrian	600 (±50)	Extensive continental submergence; all major invertebrate animal phyla (source of oldest abundant fossils, trilobites being the most common); ending in withdrawal of continental seas, extinction of two-thirds of trilobite families
			Infracambrian glaciation: extensive continental erosion causing changes in seawater composition
Precambrian time		>4,500	Appearance of life; algae and invertebrates (oldest dated algae $\pm 2.6 \times 10^9$ years)

edly have invaded continental lowlands. At such times, widespread changes in environmental conditions bring about numerous extinctions of species. Such periods of diastrophism are followed by much longer periods during which the continents are gradually eroded to featureless lowlands, which are progressively encroached upon by the seas. During these tectonically quiescent periods, life proliferates and many species arise in the available habitats. The most severe geological disturbances are those which have heralded the close of one major *era* and the advent of the next. From its origin somewhat more than 4.5×10^9 years ago up until about $6 (\pm 0.5) \times 10^8$ years ago, the history of earth is roughly divided into the *Azoic* ("no life"), *Archeozoic* ("ancient life"), and *Proterozoic* ("first life") Eras, which together are referred to as Precambrian time (Table 8.2). The boundaries between these earlier eras are indistinct, but it is generally agreed that procaryotic cellular life—bacteria and cyanophytes—appeared during the Archeozoic, following a period of unknown length during which the molecular phase of organic evolution took place. The Proterozoic occupied the last 1.5×10^9 years of Precambrian time. During the Proterozoic all life was aquatic and the major phyla of lower plants came into being, as did most (if not all) animal phyla, but life had not yet surged forward into its phase of extraordinary proliferation and diversification.

Then, approximately 6×10^8 years ago, there took place a massive glaciation, which covered perhaps a third of the earth's surface. Its traces remain today in every continent as well as in deposits of glacier-deposited rubble on the sea floor. The evidences of this glaciation, in particular the orientation of glacial scratches or striae in rock formations already in existence at that time, are such that they suggest the possibility that the continents then constituted a single mass, which later split into two continents: *Gondwanaland,* comprising present-day India, Africa, Australia, Antarctica, and South America, and *Laurasia,* comprising North America, Eurasia, and Greenland. The further breakup of these two great land masses into the elements recognizable today and the drifting apart of the fragments due to convection currents in the earth's mantle may have begun as recently as 2×10^8 years ago, by which time life was well established on land. Even now continental drift is proceeding at an estimated rate of 5 cm/year, which would be able to displace a land mass some 5,000 km over a period of 10^8 years.

A The Paleozoic Era

The glacial period that closed Precambrian time severely eroded the land, releasing large quantities of minerals that were carried into the sea in solution. This "abrupt" change in seawater composition, together with the ensuing period of warm climate that typified the Cambrian Period (about the first 10^8 years of the Paleozoic Era) appear to have been instrumental in triggering an explosive upsurge in the evolution of animal life in particular. That a number of invertebrate phyla existed prior to this time is evident from certain well-preserved Precambrian fossil deposits, and is implicit in the fact that this "biotic explosion" mostly took place during the first 4×10^7 years of the Cambrian Period. Early Cambrian strata are the first to show a varied fauna including echinoderms, brachiopods, molluscs, arthropods, and sponges, together with some puzzling fossils of animal groups now long extinct. Certainly the increase of calcium ion in the sea, resulting from the glacial erosion of the continents, would have stimulated, among other things, the production of calcareous shells and skeletal parts. Minimum concentrations of sodium, potassium, chloride, and calcium ion are also required for effective nerve and muscle activity.

During much of the Cambrian Period shallow seas overlay the still low-lying continents. At the end of this period, the continents once more rose above sea level and the resulting reduction in shallow-water habitats brought about the extinction of two-thirds of the 60 families of trilobites (Figure 8.21*b*), a group of arthropods dominant throughout the Cambrian.

The Paleozoic Era lasted for some 3.5×10^8 years. Its second and third periods, the Ordovician and Silurian, together constituting nearly 10^8 years, saw the appearance of cephalopods and vertebrates (ostracoderms and placoderms) and invasion of the land by plants and arthropods. The earliest known vascular plants are fossilized in Silurian rocks. The fourth period of the Paleozoic, or Devonian Period (some 6×10^7 years) is termed the "Age of Fishes" for it saw the first adaptive radiation of bony and cartilaginous fishes. During the Devonian the lobe-finned fishes also arose, and from one branch of this group came the first amphibians. At the same time, the diversification of land plants proceeded, and primitive wingless insects appeared.

Figure 8.22 □ **Landscapes of the past. (*a*) Carboniferous forest (Mississippian and Pennsylvanian Periods), showing scale trees, sphenopsids (giant horsetails), and a giant dragonfly. (*b*) Dinosaurs of the Cretaceous Period, especially the herbivorous *Triceratops* preparing to defend itself against *Tyrannosaurus rex*, the largest of carnivorous dinosaurs. (*c*) Marine reptiles of the Mesozoic Era, the serpent-necked plesiosaurs and fishlike ichthyosaurs. (*Murals by Charles R. Knight, Field Museum of Natural History.*)**

(*a*)

(*b*)

(*c*)

The fifth and sixth periods of the Paleozoic (the Mississippian and Pennsylvanian Periods, together constituting the "Carboniferous" or coal-producing age) were characterized by a prolonged period of worldwide warm, moist climate lasting for perhaps 6.5×10^7 years. These climatic conditions favored the growth of lush forests, which at this time included all kinds of vascular plants except for the angiosperms. Gymnosperms, tree ferns, lycopsids, and giant horsetails were dominant in this rich flora (Figure 8.22*a*). So abundant were these plants that certain coal deposits are made of only their accumulated spores! Undecayed remains of the great forests of this time were later compressed to form the coal deposits on which much of our present economy depends. Such vegetation often flourished in swampy conditions which were also favorable to amphibians and made possible their adaptive radiation. The Carboniferous is therefore known also as the "Age of Amphibians," a time when small-brained, sprawling tetrapods one or two meters in length waddled through the vegetation, feeding upon it and each other. At this time there also appeared winged insects, some kinds of which attained relatively giant size. Dragonflies with wingspreads spanning a meter must have been an impressive sight, although it is unlikely that such monsters could have been the proficient aerialists that their smaller descendants are today.

Some time during the Pennsylvanian Period, a population of amphibianlike vertebrates (primitive reptiles) laid the first amniote eggs on land (see Figure 4.3c). These eggs may originally have been laid on land for protection from aquatic carnivores or to avoid being trapped in the drying mud of evaporating ponds. Under the moist conditions at first prevailing, the original amniote egg need not have been very efficient in protecting the embryo against desiccation. The cooling climate and increasing aridity of the ensuing Permian Period no doubt served as a selective factor toward the increased efficiency of both the amniote egg and the reptilian skin in resisting dehydration. The climatic changes (including an extensive glaciation) that characterized the Permian Period (about the last 5×10^7 years of the Paleozoic) mitigated against the amphibians, many of which became extinct during this period. As the niches that they had occupied became vacant, the radiative adaptation of reptiles was accelerated.

The Paleozoic Era ended in an extensive period of geological disturbance known as the *Appalachian revolution* from the fact that the present generation of Appalachian Mountains was at that time uplifted in a great chain reaching from Newfoundland to Alabama. This event was of course only one incident in the worldwide tectonic upheaval. That the end of the Permian represented a severe crisis in the history of life is indicated by the fact that during this time nearly *half* of the *families* of animals living at that time became extinct. This represented a loss of some 24 superfamilies or orders. The massive withdrawal of continental seas terminated the fusulinid (giant foraminiferan) and trilobite lines, and nearly finished off the sharks and brachiopods as well. The brachiopods have never recovered their prominence, but a successful new adaptive radiation of modern sharks and rays has taken the place of the Paleozoic sharks.

The history of the changes in the atmosphere and the composition of the ocean that took place during the Appalachian revolution can be reconstructed through the analysis of the mineral content of evaporites, crystalline sedimentary rocks such as gypsum and halite that are formed by the evaporation of standing water. The composition of evaporites, especially microscopic droplets of brine entrapped within the crystals, reflects the composition of the sea at the time when they were formed. Similarly, analysis of sedimentary rocks such as shales formed beneath the surface of the sea provides a means for determining the proportions of various minerals being fixed in the rocks of the earth's crust. Determination of the relative proportions of two forms of sulfur, ^{32}S and ^{34}S, in evaporites and shales, allows us to estimate the contemporary rate of activity of sulfur bacteria, for only these bacteria are known to affect the $^{32}S/^{34}S$ ratio (because of their selective preference for materials containing the lighter form, ^{32}S). The ratio of ^{32}S to ^{34}S in Permian seas and muds has been found to be radically different from that found today (as indicated by measuring the relative amounts of the two forms of sulfur in shales and evaporites of late Permian times). How can we explain this discrepancy? It would appear that the elevation of land masses during the Appalachian revolution accelerated the erosion of sedimentary rock formed in earlier times and liberated large quantities of minerals, including sulfides, that were washed into the sea. Here the increased sulfide promoted the activity of sulfur-oxidizing bacteria, which converted large amounts of sulfide to sulfate. The concentration of sulfate in water trapped in evaporites formed during this time provides a clue to the amount of oxygen needed to produce this much sulfate by the bacterial oxidation of sulfide. So high is the concentration of sulfate that some authorities believe the atmospheric oxygen content must have dropped to only about 15 percent of what it is today (about 3 percent)! If this estimate is correct it is not remarkable that so many kinds of organisms became extinct; it is surprising that such a large number survived.

B The Mesozoic Era

The close of the Appalachian revolution opened a new era in the history of life, a period of some 1.7×10^8 years termed the Mesozoic ("middle life") Era. It took the biotic world some 1.5 to 2×10^7 years to recover from the blow sustained at the close of the Paleozoic. The time of predominance of amphibians had irretrievably passed and many of their niches were taken over by reptiles; the reptilian invasion of land habitats was so successful that the entire Mesozoic is known as the "Age of Reptiles." Most of the earlier vascular plants—the psilopsids, lycopsids, and sphenopsids—never regained their hold; the most promising survivors among land plants were seed ferns, cycads, and conifers.

As well as witnessing the adaptive radiation and ecological dominance of reptiles, cycads, and conifers, the Mesozoic saw the origins of three groups that were to become dominant in the following era, namely the angiosperms, birds, and mammals.

The radiative adaptation of reptiles was the most dramatic event of the Mesozoic Era. From the squat amphibianlike stem-reptiles (cotylosaurs) came groups adapted to living in a great variety of habitats. Turtles ranged on land and in the water. The sea was reinvaded by forms that evolved into long-necked plesiosaurs (which attained lengths of 15 m and had limbs modified into efficient swimming paddles), fishlike ichthyosaurs (which were necessarily live-bearing since they could not come ashore to lay their eggs), and serpentlike mosasaurs 10 m or more in length. Winged pterosaurs glided aloft, probably diving to feed on fish and taking off from the crests of waves after the manner of modern albatross. On land arose two important groups: the *therapsids* (mammallike reptiles, the probable ancestors of mammals) and the *archosaurs,* small agile forms that walked on their hind legs (the ancestors of crocodilians, birds, and dinosaurs, as well as the stock leading to modern lizards and snakes). The first bird to appear in the Paleozoic was *Archaeopteryx,* which may almost be thought of as a sparsely-feathered reptile, for it had sharp-toothed jaws, a scaly skin, a long tail bearing feathers only along each side, and arms that, although feathered, still ended in five claw-bearing fingers. Two separate orders of dinosaurs arose (Figure 8.22*b*): *saurischians* ("lizard hip"), with a typical reptilian pelvic structure, and *ornithischians* ("bird hip"), featuring the wide pubic gap characteristic of birds (although they were not ancestral to birds).

Dinosaurs were the most successful terrestrial vertebrates of the time. Ranging in size from tiny bipeds to the most enormous terrestrial animals ever to heave themselves erect on monstrous limbs, the dinosaurs occupied most of the terrestrial niches then available for vertebrate occupancy. Each order underwent diversification into several types. The saurischian line produced bipedal carnivores and herbivorous quadrupeds with elongated necks and tails. The latter were amphibious, depending in part upon water to buoy up their great mass while they browsed upon aquatic vegetation. Extending up to 30 m in length, they were the largest terrestrial animals ever to have lived. One of the most formidable bipedal carnivores, *Tyrannosaurus rex,* which lived in the latter part of the Mesozoic, stood 6 m tall and sported a bright array of 10-cm-long teeth mounted in jaws that approached 2 m in length (Figure 8.22*b*).

The three major groups of ornithischians were the herbivorous plated dinosaurs, ceratopsians, and duck-billed dinosaurs. The plated dinosaurs and ceratopsians were quadrupedal, although their long hind legs, raising the hips higher than the rest of the back, betrayed their bipedal ancestry. Both groups were heavily armored against predators, plated forms such as *Stegosaurus* having a dorsal double row of upright plates and a formidably spiked tail. The ceratopsians were armored over the entire anterior third of their bodies by a huge dorsal shield that projected anteriorly as one or more horns. The largest known ceratopsian, *Triceratops,* was armed with three forward-directed horns. This heavy-necked, relatively short-tailed dinosaur was a browsing animal which, despite its 10-m length, was so proportioned that it might have been able to charge at predators much in the manner of modern rhinoceros. The duck-billed dinosaurs were amphibious bipeds with webbed feet and flattened tails useful in swimming. Their skulls often bore bony crests and their jaws protruded as a flattened "duck's bill" which no doubt served these reptiles as the bills of ducks do today, for grubbing plant roots and shellfish out of muddy river bottoms.

The land animals of the Mesozoic Era had no grasses, fruits, or nectar to feed upon but browsed upon the foliage of ferns, seed ferns, and gymnosperms. The predominant land plants of the time were cycads and conifers. Cycads were perhaps the most conspicuous flora of early and middle Mesozoic times, but they declined and mostly became extinct by the end of this era. The rise and fall of cycads so closely matches that of the dinosaurs that some believe the two groups to have been interdependent, although no direct evidence of this exists. Herbivorous dinosaurs (on which the carnivores fed) could have depended mainly for food on cycad foliage and during the contact might even have been contaminated with pollen and aided in its transfer. Whether or not the dinosaurs were of any such value to the cycads, the latter's decline may have accelerated the extinction of the former by limiting their food supply.

The conifers, which were mainly wind-pollinated, evolved rapidly in the Mesozoic, gradually coming to resemble present-day forms. Most of the modern families of conifers—including pines, yews, cypress, redwoods, and araucarias—had appeared by the beginning of the Cretaceous Period (the last 5 to 6×10^7 years of the Mesozoic). These plants were able to withstand the climatic changes that accompanied the end of the Mesozoic and most have survived to the present, although becoming of increasingly restricted distribution.

Few flowers brightened Mesozoic landscapes, for angiosperms only began to appear during the Cretaceous and did not diversify greatly until the Cenozoic Era. One group of gymnosperms (cycadeoids) bore showy flowerlike structures and may have been insect-pollinated, but most insects of the day had chewing mouthparts for feeding on foliage rather than mouthparts specialized for sucking nectar; it is thus unlikely that any regular pollinator relationships had come into being. The cycadeoids became extinct at the end of the Mesozoic and true flowering plants took their place. The latter evolved from seed ferns—plants with fernlike foliage that, however, bore pollen and seeds. Unlike their predecessors, the angiosperms had their seeds enclosed within fruits and, as we have already noted, such fruits have proved to be a major means of dispersal of angiosperms over the face of the earth.

During the Cretaceous Period the earth's mean temperature again began to decline while shallow seas spread extensively across the continents. Nearly all of North America was inundated during the Cretaceous submergence and ichthyosaurs, plesiosaurs, and mosasaurs frolicked in the waves that rolled over what is now the Great Plains of North America (Figure 8.22c). Large coil-shelled cephalopods [ammonites (Figure 8.21c)] were also abundant in these seas. But then a new period of tectonic activity, the *Laramide revolution,* commenced, during which the continental masses were folded and elevated to unprecedented altitudes, the continental seas drained away, and the spiny backbone of the Cordillera lifted its mighty ridge from the Aleutian Islands to Tierra del Fuego. In this disturbance about one quarter of all known families of animals, constituting some 16 superfamilies and orders, became extinct. It must not be thought that these catastrophes were abrupt events; they took place against the background of a diastrophic cycle which took some millions of years to accomplish. By the end of the Cretaceous the ecological dominance of reptiles was broken; the saurischians, ornithischians, ichthyosaurs, plesiosaurs, pterosaurs, and mosasaurs all were gone, leaving behind only a small remnant of the great reptilian radiation: the turtles, the crocodilians, and the ancestors of modern snakes and lizards.

C The Cenozoic Era

The climax of the Laramide revolution marks the end of the Mesozoic and the beginning of the Cenozoic Era, dating from some 6.5×10^7 years ago to the present. Now began a new period of biotic diversification, involving the radiative adaptation of the birds, mammals, and angiosperms, groups that first appeared in the Mesozoic but had not gained impetus until after the end of this era.

The most outstanding event characterizing the Cenozoic Era, an event that transformed most terrestrial biomes and shaped the evolution of modern land animals, was the adaptive radiation of the angiosperms. Diversifying into more than 250,000 species the flowering plants spread over the globe at an explosive rate, invading every type of land and freshwater habitat from tundra to tropics. Angiosperms formed the basis for many new biotic communities and provided unprecedented quantities of food for herbivorous animals. Edible seeds, fruits, nectar, and foliage abounded, providing the sustenance required by homoiothermal animals,

Figure 8.23 □ Rate of appearance of new vertebrate genera, as indicated by the fossil record. [*After E. D. Hanson,* Animal Diversity (2nd ed.) (*Englewood Cliffs, N.J.: Prentice-Hall, Inc., 1964*).]

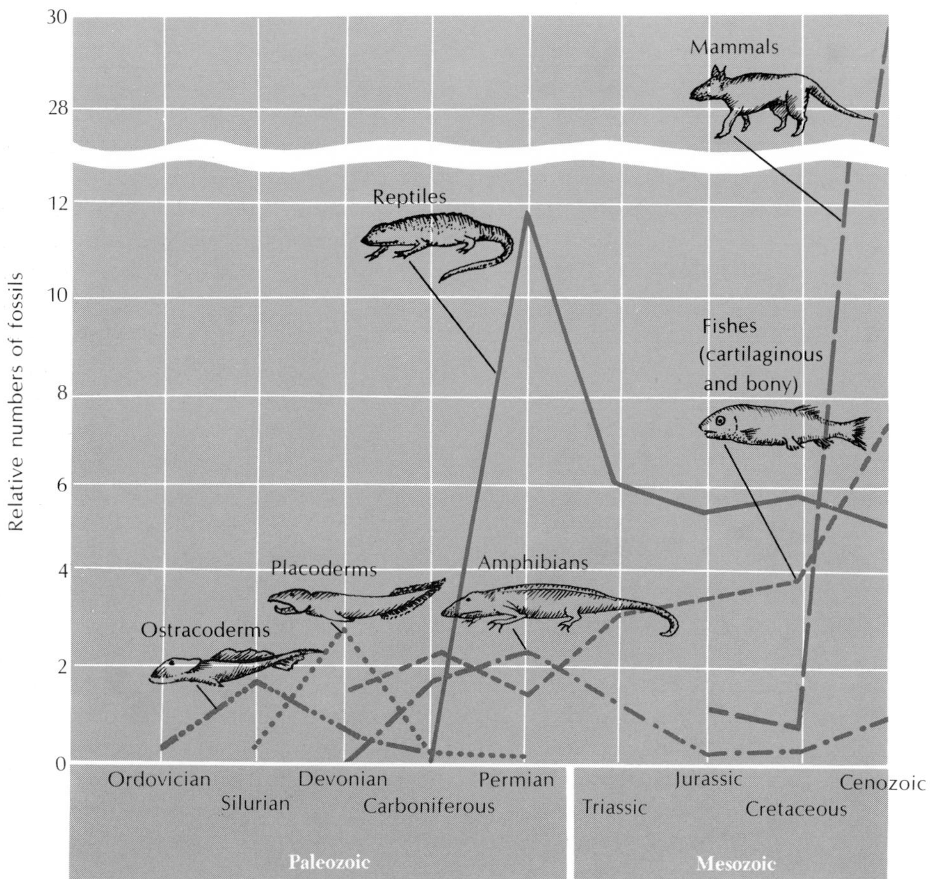

which must expend large amounts of energy merely to maintain their body temperature. Insect life also flourished as never before, diversifying into modern orders containing not only the countless species adapted to feed upon flowering plants but also numerous species predatory on other insects. These insects also provided food for many new types of insectivorous birds, mammals, and lizards.

Almost the entire economy of modern terrestrial communities rests upon the angiosperms. The evolved interrelationships between these plants and terrestrial animals would require many volumes to describe. Various floral types have appeared, which are attractive to specific groups of animals that serve to spread pollen and disperse seeds. Vast numbers of angiosperm species have cospecialized with butterflies, moths, bees, and hummingbirds. There are flowers that attract flies by having the appearance and odor of rotting meat. There are trees that bear flowers or fruits on erect or pendulous stalks accessible to bats that feed upon nectar and transfer pollen during the blooming season and later eat the fruits and void the seeds over their range of flight.

Along with the dramatic rise of angiosperms and modern insects, the mammals and birds increased and diversified; the mammals in particular took over niches previously occupied by reptiles during Mesozoic times. The rate of appearance of new mammalian fossil genera is compared in Figure 8.23 with that of reptiles, amphibians, and fishes. The mammalian radiation that took place during the Cenozoic Era produced many more genera than the comparable reptilian radiation (seen in Figure 2.46) that characterized the Mesozoic. The fact that so many more species of terrestrial animals have arisen in the Cenozoic than ever lived before indicates that present land communities have a more complex web of biotic interrelationships, consisting of more specific niches, than have characterized the biosphere at any earlier age.

During the earlier part of the Cenozoic marsupial mammals became very successful and diversified; they thrived in the tropical and temperate angiosperm woodlands that covered most of the continents. Then, as eutherian mammals gained prominence, the marsupials generally fell before their onslaught wherever the two groups came into direct competition. Several times during the Cenozoic, land bridges connected Eurasia, North America, and South America, and mammals that had evolved in each of these major biogeographical realms migrated into the others with resultant competition and mass extinction. In most cases it took from 10^6 to 10^7 years for the native forms to succumb to the immigrant faunas. Over some of the land bridges there also passed roving bands of primitive men, following their prey: the mammoths, mastodons, camels, antelope, and wild oxen.

The most recent important event in angiosperm evolution, one which had further crucial impact on animal life, was the origin of the monocots—lilies, palms, reeds, and especially grasses—only about 3 to 4×10^7 years ago. Grasslands began to spread, pushing back the forests and creating a new type of habitat, one suitable for swiftly running animals that tended to graze or hunt in bands. Mammals representing new orders, the even-toed and odd-toed hoofed animals, forsook the woodlands and moved out upon the prairies, becoming abundant some 2×10^7 years ago. The advent of grazing mammals is of especial significance, for various predators followed these herbivores out of the forest onto the grasslands; and among these predators were, we now believe, the primate stocks that led to man (see Figure 8.24).

The *hominoid* line leading to man and the apes (gibbons, gorillas, chimpanzees, and orangutans) probably diverged from the prosimian line leading to monkeys some 5×10^7 years ago, before the advent of grasslands and their grazing fauna. Hominoids differ from monkeys in several important respects: they are generally larger, with a greater cranial expansion; their thumbs are often opposable; they are tailless; and, when arboreal, they favor brachiation (swinging hand-over-hand) instead of clambering like monkeys. Brachiation may have favored modification of the skeleton toward a more upright stance even before bipedal walking became possible. Modern apes can walk on their hind legs only for short distances and except for the gorillas are still mainly arboreal. Gorillas live on the ground and do not brachiate, but they walk laboriously and with the aid of the knuckles of one or both hands.

Hominid (manlike) types leading to modern man may have split off from the stock leading to modern apes as early as 2×10^7 years ago. Ancestral hominids may gradually have forsaken the forests to move out across the prairies in search of meat to supplement their formerly vegetarian diet. Probably at first they threw stones and sticks to drive scavengers away from carcasses; later they may have discovered that such objects could be used to subdue prey.

Most modern apes live in social groups: chimpanzee bands are even seen on rare occasions to encircle and kill small game cooperatively, although as a rule they remain creatures of the forest and eat meat only irregularly. Hominid social groups may eventually have evolved into cooperative hunting bands, for in this manner they could stalk and kill prey too large and fleet-footed to be subdued by a solitary hunter. Adoption of social hunting as a regular mode of life introduced new selective factors in hominid evolution, promoting advancement over their apelike predecessors in three major respects: (1) Greater ease of bipedal locomotion became advantageous, for sustained walking and running could be carried on while the hands remained free to grasp sticks and stones useful in disabling prey. (2) A coadaptive evolution of the hand and the motor areas of the forebrain was set in motion: increased use of the hand for grasping and throwing promoted further development of the parts of the brain concerned with the control of the hand; in turn, improvement in these brain areas made possible still more sophisticated use of the hand so that, as a next step, stones could be chipped and shaped to make jagged edges for cutting meat and tough hides. (3) Development of vocal signals having specific meaning increased the success of cooperative hunting bands by more effectively coordinating their efforts; further development of the brain areas concerned with speech and tongue movements therefore became advantageous for survival.

Figure 8.24 □ Proposed pathways of the primate (and anthropoid) radiation (approximate dates parenthetical).

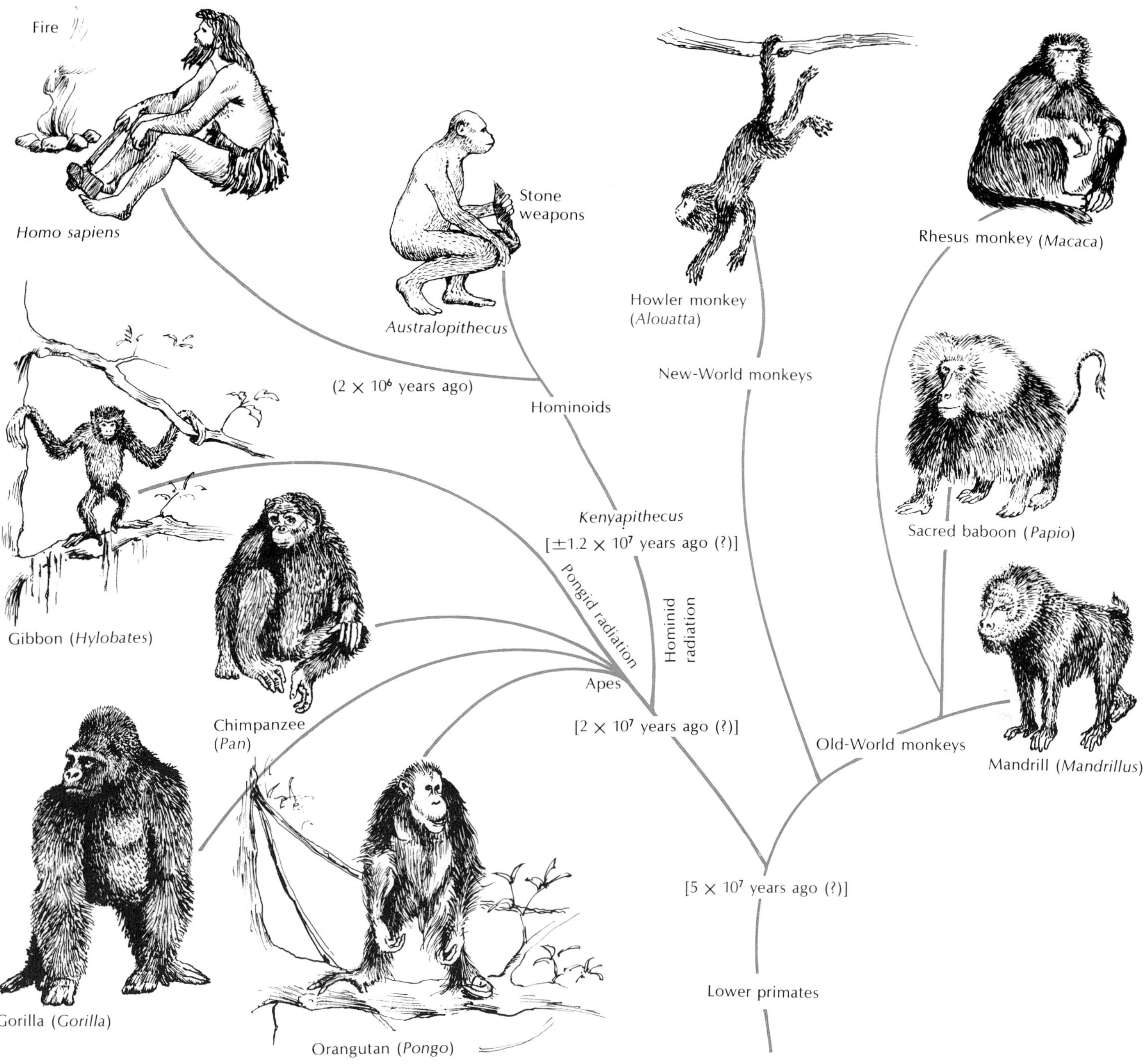
Fire
Homo sapiens
Stone weapons
Australopithecus
Howler monkey (Alouatta)
Rhesus monkey (Macaca)
(2 × 10⁶ years ago)
Hominoids
New-World monkeys
Sacred baboon (Papio)
Kenyapithecus
[±1.2 × 10⁷ years ago (?)]
Pongid radiation
Hominid radiation
Gibbon (Hylobates)
Apes
Chimpanzee (Pan)
[2 × 10⁷ years ago (?)]
Old-World monkeys
Mandrill (Mandrillus)
[5 × 10⁷ years ago (?)]
Lower primates
Gorilla (Gorilla)
Orangutan (Pongo)

The development of these capabilities did not proceed independently of one another: each advancement in one area facilitated further advancement in the others. Nevertheless, millions of years were required to refine these capabilities to their present level. As early as 1.4×10^7 years ago a manlike form, the oldest known hominid, *Ramapithecus* (first named *Kenyapithecus* when its fossil remains were discovered in Kenya, Africa, but later renamed because of its close resemblance to fossil fragments discovered years earlier in India), ranged throughout East Africa and India. *Ramapithecus* is considered a form of early man rather than an ape mainly because its palate and teeth are much more like that of man than of any modern or fossil ape. *Ramapithecus* may already have been a hunter, or at least a scavenger, for in Africa its remains are found associated with smashed skulls and other skeletal fragments of such open-country animals as antelope and giraffe. Furthermore, some of these bones show depressed fractures as if they had been smashed by stones or other implements.

Hominid fossils still must be discovered to fill out the 10^7 years or more between *Ramapithecus* and the next known hominids. Perhaps the most outstanding discoveries of early man have been made by Louis and Mary Leakey, excavating in the Olduvai Gorge of Tanzania, East Africa. In Pliocene strata dated by the potassium-argon method as being approximately 2×10^6 years old, remains have been found of not one but *three* apparently distinct but contemporary hominids, all adapted for fully bipedal locomotion and upright stance. *Paranthropus,* a form with a very low forehead, a long face, and an enormous jaw, had a cranial capacity no larger than that of a gorilla (approximately 600 cm^3); it is thought to have made no tools and to represent an evolutionary dead-end leaving no modern descendants. *Australopithecus,* known first from fossils discovered in South Africa, also lived in Tanzania; the Olduvai fossils are apparently more primitive than those found in South Africa. *Australopithecus* also had a powerful jaw necessitating the development of cranial ridges for attachment of the massive jaw muscles. There is disagreement upon the manner in which the powerful jaws of these two hominids were put to use: some believe they served in crushing vegetable matter; others, that they may have been used for cracking bones. In both lines, the specialization toward an enormous jaw apparatus may have limited further cranial expansion as a result of the pressure of the temporal muscle masses upon the growing skull. Nevertheless, *Australopithecus* seems to have become the ancestor of a more advanced man, *Homo erectus,* who had a cranial capacity averaging 1,000 cm^3 and was a fire-using toolmaker ubiquitous throughout Africa, Europe, and Asia from 10^6 to perhaps 5×10^5 years ago, possibly overlapping the advent of *Homo sapiens.* Many anthropologists claim an australopithecine line as the direct ancestor of modern man: they believe that some population of *H. erectus* actually evolved into *H. sapiens.* However, a third hominid found in Olduvai Gorge, has been named *Homo habilis* by its discoverers (the Leakeys) and proposed as another possible ancestor of *H. sapiens.* Standing little over a meter tall, in comparison with the 1.3-m *Australopithecus* and 1.6-m *Paranthropus,* the delicately formed *H. habilis* had a more modern-type foot and a high-domed cranium lacking the specializations associated with massive jaw development and therefore capable of further expansion free of the counterpressure of heavy temporal muscles. The hand structure evidences capability for using the typically human "precision grip" (in which the distal joint of the thumb opposes the tips of the first and second fingers), rather than only the "power grip" characteristic of apes (in which the thumb folds *over* the clenched fingers, a grip such as we use in wielding a hammer).

Although the status of *H. habilis* remains controversial, some argue that the cranial ridges developed for jaw muscle attachment in the australopithecines and retained by *H. erectus* (such as Java man), may rule out *H. erectus* as a direct ancestor of modern man since such evolutionary specializations, once developed, seldom disappear in favor of a less specialized condition. If this is the case, *H. erectus* may represent only the final and most advanced product of the australopithecine line, being a parallel but less successful type of man than *H. sapiens* proved to be. On the other hand, two skulls thought to represent an extremely early form of *H. sapiens* and dating from about 2 to 3×10^5 years ago (the Swanscombe skull from England and the Steinheim skull from Germany), show evidence that the cranium was ballooning out posteriorly into an enlarged brain case, while the massive facial ridges still persisted but were becoming less pronounced than in *H. erectus.* Although the establishment of modern man's ancestry beyond doubt is of great interest, it is actually more important to realize that over the past 10^7 years a hominid radiation has taken place with several forms starting on the road to fully human status but only one persisting to the present day. Possibly the most advanced type brought about the extinction of less advanced contemporaries (if any), even as early man is held responsible for the extinction of many large Quaternary mammals including the mammoth, mastodon, woolly rhinoceros, and cave bear.

Homo sapiens apparently subdivided at some early date into two subspecies, *H. sapiens neanderthalis* (Neanderthal man), known from Europe, Africa, and the Middle East, and *H. sapiens sapiens,* the line that leads to modern man, of which remains actually do not appear in definitive form until about 37,000 years ago when a population (now known as Cro-Magnon man) entered Europe from the Middle East and coexisted for a time with the Neanderthalers. Neanderthal man stood about 1.6 m tall, nearly 10 cm shorter than Cro-Magnon man; his brow bore a massive bony ridge lacking in Cro-Magnon. It might be thought that the two belonged to different species save for the fact that earlier Neanderthal fossils actually seem to resemble modern man somewhat more than those of a later date. Both the Neanderthal and Cro-Magnon men had cranial capacities within the usual limits for modern man (1,400 to 1,700 cm^3) although the average for Neanderthaler lay near the lower limit of this range. Both made tools and weapons of stone, bone, and ivory, wore hides, and were cave-dwellers or nomadic hunters. Neither practiced agriculture or the domestication of animals. Ultimately Neanderthal man either became extinct or was assimilated by interbreeding with Cro-Magnon man.

In summary, the distinctively human characteristics that developed during the hominid ascent included the following: (1) Adaptations for upright carriage involved shortening of the pelvis, lengthening of the leg and arching of the foot, alignment of the toes, with the great toe's no longer being opposable and useful in grasping (as it is in apes), and movement of the opening for the spinal cord (the foramen magnum) from the rear to the base of the skull, allowing the head to be held erect upon the vertical spinal column. (2) The manipulative capability of the hand was improved, with development of the precision grip and concomitant expansion of the portion of the forebrain devoted to controlling the hand and fingers. (3) A spoken language developed, along with increased complexity of the speech areas of the forebrain, making possible the transmission of abstract ideas and laying the basis for cultural evolution. (4) A prodigious increase in the size of the forebrain took place, starting from prehominid stock with a brain the size of a newborn human infant (300 to 400 cm^3) to the present size of about 1,700 cm^3, and with an even greater increase in the total area of cerebral cortex (the outer portion of the forebrain). (5) Art and other evidences of abstract thought, such as burial of the dead, appeared in Cro-Magnon man.

Physically, modern man had evolved to his present form by about 50,000 B.C., which may also have marked the beginnings of human culture; an acceleration of psychosocial or cultural evolution has since been accompanied by a diminution of the rate of man's organic evolution: although man seems to be on the way to losing his wisdom teeth and fifth toes, there is little evidence that he has undergone any significant structural alterations during the last 50,000 years. Evolutionarily, of course, this is a very short period of time, but through the development of a complex language structure permitting the storage and transmission of human knowledge man has already altered the action of natural selection upon his species. His survival now depends less on further adaptive changes in physique than on his further psychical and ethical development so that he can regulate his behavior and his use of the environment.

REVIEW AND DISCUSSION

1 A mare (19 pairs of chromosomes) bred to a jackass (33 pairs of chromosomes) produces a mule. Explain the sterility of the mule on the basis of chromosome behavior in meiosis.

2 Hemophilia is due to a recessive sex-linked gene in man. Will a hemophiliac man transmit this trait to his sons? Explain, using a diagram to show the transmission of hemophilia through three generations.

3 A strain of sepia-eyed, hairy-bodied *Drosophila* (homozygous, since both of these are due to recessive alleles) are bred with normal (wild-type) flies. The heterozygous F_1 are bred back to the sepia-eyed, hairy-bodied strain. In the resulting progeny only two phenotypic classes predominate: wild type and sepia-hairy. Two other categories, sepia-eyed, normal-bodied, and normal-eyed, hairy-bodied, occur in only a few of the F_2. Explain these results.

4 In cats a sex-linked gene controls coat color. The genotype *BB* produces black hair, while *bb* produces yellow hair. The heterozygous genotype *Bb* results in a mottled coat known as tortoise-shell. Explain why you can tell the sex of a tortoise-shell cat from its coat color alone.

5 A man with blood type O is married to a woman of blood type AB. A baby is born with blood type AB, and the husband sues for divorce. Does he have grounds? Explain, with diagrams showing possible genotypes and phenotypes.

6 Juvenile amaurotic idiocy is due to homozygosity for a recessive allele. The condition appears in about one infant in 10,000. Calculate the relative frequencies of this gene and its normal allele. Since amaurotic idiots die in infancy, two recessive alleles are removed from the population by each such death. If it would also be possible to identify nearly all the persons carrying this allele in the heterozygous state and to convince these persons *not* to bear children, what reduction could be effected in the total frequency of the allele for amaurotic idiocy in one generation of selection? [Refer to the formula in Section 8.2C (page 308)]. Without such artificial selection against this proportion of the heterozygotes, what reduction in the frequency of the allele for amaurotic idiocy would occur in one generation, due to the death of homozygotes alone?

7 If the difference between negroid and caucasoid pigmentation in man is due to equal and additive effects of two gene pairs, *SSTT* producing full melanistic skin color and *sstt* restricting melanin production so that the skin is "white," what skin color would be expected in individuals of the genotype *SsTt*? If, in several matings involving persons of the genotype *SsTt*, around 30 children are produced, how many of these could be expected to show full skin pigmentation? Caucasoid pigmentation? What selective factors may have served in selecting for pale skin in northern European caucasoids and for melanistic skin in negroid peoples?

8 Can two normal persons produce a genetically feebleminded child? Explain. If the feeblemindedness is due to a recessive allele, what is the probability of the first child of heterozygous parents being feebleminded? If the parents produce three children, what is the probability that all three would be feebleminded?

9 Due to the influence of male sex hormone, the allele for baldness will exert its effects on the male phenotype when only one such allele is present. Women, however, must be homozygous for the baldness allele if they are to become bald. Indicate the possible genotypes and phenotypes of the sons and daughters that could be produced by a bald man and a woman whose father was bald. Baldness is an autosomal, not a sex-linked trait.

10 A genetic deformity in chickens, "creeper" (so-called because of the abnormally shortened legs and wings), is the phenotypic expression of a pair of alleles in the heterozygous state. When two creeper fowl (Cc) are mated, their offspring are one-third normal and two-thirds creeper. Can you account for this unusual phenotypic ratio? Can you think of any other data which might support your hypothesis?

11 Explain the adaptive value of diploidy. Distinguish between autopolyploidy, allopolyploidy, and aneuploidy, indicating the evolutionary significance of each.

12 Enumerate and explain various ways in which the genome of a population may be enriched by addition of new genetic material.

13 Explain the "blending theory" and "particulate theory" of inheritance, and show how Mendel's experiments helped to establish one of these theories. What observations had lent support to the theory that Mendel discredited?

14 Summarize the major characteristics of organic evolution, giving illustrative examples of each. Explain the process by which cave fish usually become eyeless.

15 Discuss the significance of the deme as a testing ground for genetic changes.

16 Distinguish among *balanced* genetic polymorphism, *transient* polymorphism, and *indifferent* polymorphism, with examples of each. What heterospecific relationship affects the human genome with respect to the allele for sickle-cell anemia?

17 Compare the processes of speciation (origin of new species) through schistic evolution and through phyletic evolution.

18 What is meant by sex chromosomes? By sex linkage? How does sex determination differ in birds and mammals? How does it differ in man and *Drosophila?*

19 Summarize the two Mendelian laws of heredity, and explain the physical (cellular) basis for these laws.

20 How is it possible to map the linear sequence of genes on chromosomes?

21 Summarize experimental evidence showing that mutations occur at random and not in response to a specific need. Explain the process by which certain insects have become DDT-resistant.

22 Summarize the different ways in which *parts* of chromosomes can be duplicated.

23 Each of the following is a cytological phenomenon occurring during meiosis; specify the *cause* of each: (*a*) The chromosomes are unable to synapse. (*b*) One member of a pair of synapsing homologs is thrown into a loop. (*c*) A chromosome synapses partly with its homolog and partly with a member of another chromosome pair. (*d*) When homologs synapse, one of the two shows a buckled region that is not in contact with the homolog. (*e*) During synapsis the chromosomes as a whole are distorted into loops and peculiar configurations in which only partial synapsis can take place, and several different pairs of chromosomes are all trying to synapse together. (*f*) One pair of homologs are quite unequal in size, so that most of the longer member of the pair synapses with nothing at all.

24 Explain the significance of the Hardy-Weinberg equilibrium principle, and specify the factors responsible for disturbing equilibrium.

25 Explain the implication of the statement, "Evolution is a population phenomenon."

26 Summarize the important biotic events of the Archeozoic, Proterozoic, Paleozoic, Mesozoic, and Cenozoic Eras. How are these eras set off from each other?

REFERENCES

BAKER, W. K. *Genetic Analysis.* Boston: Houghton Mifflin Company, 1965. A short volume that builds upon the basic material presented in this chapter, providing excellent insight into the technical methods and problems of modern genetics.

COLBERT, E. H. "The Ancestry of Mammals," *Sci. Amer.,* **180** (1949).

COLLIAS, N. E. "Evolution of Nest Building," *Nat. Hist.,* **74** (1965).

CROW, J. E. "Ionizing Radiation and Evolution," *Sci. Amer.,* **201** (1959). Considers the possible role of background radiation in bringing about hereditary changes prerequisite to evolutionary advancement.

DELEVORYAS, T. *Morphology and Evolution of Fossil Plants.* New York: Holt, Rinehart and Winston, Inc., 1962. A valuable reference on paleobotany.

DILLON, L. S. "The Life Cycle of the Species: An Extension of Current Concepts," *Systematic Zool.,* **15** (1966). Proposes that most species pass through certain well-defined stages from origin to extinction.

DOBZHANSKY, T. "The Present Evolution of Man," *Sci. Amer.,* **203** (1960). A renowned geneticist discusses how selection may be operating on man today.

ERICSON, D. B., AND G. WOLLIN "Micropaleontology," *Sci. Amer.,* **207** (1962).

FLOWER, J. W. "On the Origin of Flight in Insects," *J. Insect Physiol.,* **10** (1964). Speculates on the nature of selective forces operating in the evolution of insect wings.

GLAESSNER, M. F. "Pre-Cambrian Animals," *Sci. Amer.,* **204** (1961).

HURLEY, P. M. "Radioactivity and Time," *Sci. Amer.,* **181** (1949).

——— "The Confirmation of Continental Drift," *Sci. Amer.,* **218** (1968). Present continents may have been formed by the breakup and drifting apart of supercontinents, beginning in the late Paleozoic and extending through the Mesozoic Era.

JARVIK, E. "The Oldest Tetrapods and Their Forerunners," *Sci. Monthly,* **80** (1955).

KETTLEWELL, H. B. D. "Selection Experiments on Industrial Melanism in the Lepidoptera," *Heredity,* **9** (1955). Evolution is seen in action in the shift toward a dark phase of the peppered moth in industrialized Britain.

KORMONDY, E. J. *Introduction to Genetics.* New York: McGraw-Hill Book Company, 1964. Provides a useful program for self-instruction in the fundamentals of genetics.

KURTÉN, B. "Continental Drift and Evolution," *Sci. Amer.,* **220** (1969). The mammalian radiation may have been particularly diverse because of continental drift during the Cenozoic Era.

LEDERBERG, J., AND E. LEDERBERG "Replica Plating and Indirect Selection of Bacterial Mutants," *J. Bact.,* **63** (1952). Describes the replica plating technique and its application to the problem of detecting preadaptive mutants in bacterial cultures.

LERNER, I. M. *The Genetic Basis of Selection.* New York: John Wiley & Sons, Inc., 1958.

LURIA, S. E., AND M. DELBRÜCK "Mutations of Bacteria from Virus Sensitivity to Virus Resistance," *Genetics,* **28** (1943).

MENDEL, G. "Experiments in Plant-Hybridization," in *Classic Papers in Genetics,* J. A. Peters, ed. Englewood Cliffs, N.J.: Prentice-Hall, Inc., 1959. The classic paper describing experiments that disclosed the quantitative laws of behavior is reprinted in translation.

METCALF, R. L. "Insects vs. Insecticides," *Sci. Amer.,* **187** (1952).

MONTAGU, A. "Chromosomes and Crime," *Psychology Today,* **2** (1968). Chromosome studies indicate a genetic predisposition toward antisocial behavior.

MÜLLER, H. J. "Radiation and Human Mutation," *Sci. Amer.,* **192** (1955).

NEWELL, N. D. "Crises in the History of Life," *Sci. Amer.,* **208** (1963). Possible causes of mass extinctions in the geologic past are considered.

RYAN, F. J. "Evolution Observed," *Sci. Amer.,* **189** (1953).

SHEPPARD, P. M. *Natural Selection and Heredity.* New York: Harper & Row, Publishers, 1960. A succinct discussion of evolutionary processes.

SIMPSON, G. G. *Life of the Past.* New Haven, Conn.: Yale University Press, 1953. An excellent description of ancient life, by a renowned paleontologist.

——— *The Major Features of Evolution.* New York: Columbia University Press, 1953.

SPIETH, H. T. "Sexual Behavior and Isolation in *Drosophila,* II. The Interspecific Mating Behavior of Species of the *Willistoni* Group," *Evolution,* **3** (1949). The breakdown of courtship prior to copulation was studied in 30 combinations of *Drosophila* males and females of different species. Courtship behavior was therefore found to be significant in preventing heterospecific matings.

STEBBINS, G. L. "Cataclysmic Evolution," *Sci. Amer.,* **184** (1951).

——— *Processes of Organic Evolution.* Englewood Cliffs, N.J.: Prentice-Hall, Inc., 1966. A highly recommended discussion of various evolutionary mechanisms, especially those in populations of modern plants.

STERN, C. "Man's Genetic Future," *Sci. Amer.,* **186** (1952).

TERRY, K. D., AND W. H. TUCKER "Biologic Effects of Supernovae," *Science,* **159** (1968). Cosmic radiation from supernovae is proposed as a possible cause of the mass extinctions of the fauna of the land and shallow seas that have taken place several times in the post-Cambrian period.

TYLER, S. A., AND E. S. BARGHOORN "Occurrence of Structurally Preserved Plants in Pre-Cambrian Rocks of the Canadian Shield," *Science,* **119** (1954). Reports the finding of fossil algae, fungi, and flagellates, with well-preserved fine structure, in strata nearly 2×10^9 years old.

VON WAHLERT, G. "The Role of Ecological Factors in the Origin of Higher Levels of Organization," *Systematic Zool.,* **14** (1965). Summarizes major theories concerning evolution and cites case histories in which the animal's behavior serves as the first selective force toward the evolution of new functional patterns.

WALLACE, B. *Chromosomes, Giant Molecules and Evolution.* New York: W. W. Norton & Co., Inc., 1966. Reviews cytogenetic and biochemical evidences of evolution.

WATSON, D. M. S. "The Evolution of the Mammalian Ear," *Evolution,* **7** (1953). Traces the history of the sound-conducting apparatus of the vertebrate ear.

Part 3

THE ORGANIZATION OF LIFE

Beautiful, angular, and bare the machinery of life will lie exposed, as it now is, to my view. There will be the thin, blue skeleton of a hare tumbled in a little heap, and crouching over it I will marvel, as I marvel now, at the wonderful correlation of parts, the perfect adaptation to purpose, the individually vanished and yet persisting pattern which is now hopping on some other hill. I will wonder, as always, in what manner "particles" pursue such devious plans and symmetries. I will ask once more in what way it is managed, that the simple dust takes on a history and begins to weave these unique and never recurring apparitions in the stream of time. I shall wonder what strange forces at the heart of matter regulate the tiny beating of a rabbit's heart or the dim dream that builds a milkweed pod.

L. EISELEY

The evolution of life has been characterized by a stepwise progression from one level of structural and functional organization to another of greater complexity into which the functional units of the preceding levels are integrated. The adaptive potential of each level of organization is improved upon until a module is evolved that can serve as a unit of structure and function from which a still more complex level of organization may emerge. Thus, the earliest self-maintaining, self-reproducing systems were solely molecular, their architecture reflecting the spontaneous arrangements that organic molecules assume today. Such molecular units could not independently carry out such advanced activities as photosynthesis, but could grow and obtain energy by incorporating other organic materials that were present in their environment. In the modern world the only persisting forms of "molecular life" are viruses, which today can grow and reproduce only by using organic materials found within the cells of a living host.

The integration of molecular complexes to form primitive cells was a milestone in the advancement of life. The construction and maintenance of cellular units required the evolution of new processes by which mass and energy could be obtained from the environment with increasing efficiency. It also demanded the development of control mechanisms by which a cell could conserve its steady state (homeostasis), react as a unit, and perpetuate itself. The cell is in fact the simplest biotic unit that under present circumstances independently demonstrates *all* of the characteristics of life—adaptability, irritability, motility, and the means for obtaining materials and energy from the environment for growth, self-maintenance, and reproduction.

Originally adapted only for independent existence, the cell proved also to be a module suitable for the construction of multicellular units of all degrees of complexity, from protozoan colonies to the human body. Although building a multicellular body requires large investments of mass and energy, these investments are repaid by the advantages resulting from cell diversification and by the prolongation of individual life made possible through the development of more effective adaptations for exploiting and controlling the environment.

The evolution of social and colonial units made up of a number of multicellular individuals represented advancement to yet another level of biotic complexity, for here the organism itself, rather than the cell, serves as the basic organizational module. Once more, the increased costs of maintaining these supraorganismal units have been offset by the benefits made possible through cooperation and division of labor among the members of the society or colony.

The development of life's successive levels of complexity has not come about so much through a gradual unfolding of potentialities already present as through a process of trial-and-error by which adaptation was achieved at one level of life, and this success in turn opened the way for advancement to a new level of organization, the characteristics of which proved to be more than the sum of the parts. To develop these characteristics demanded at each step that the individual parts become *coadapted,* that is, integrated into the life of the whole. This need for co-adaptation within the biotic unit is as essential to survival as is successful adaptation to external factors. Not only must the organism be adapted to live within its habitat, society and community, but its various tissues and organs must also be adapted to function together effectively or the organism cannot survive. Not only must each cell become adapted to function within the body of the multicellular organism, but the subcellular molecular machinery must also function harmoniously or the cell cannot survive. Any genetic variation must therefore stand the test of both internal and external selective factors; it will persist and contribute to the advancement of life only if it is compatible with the need both for internal coadaptation and for adaptation to environment.

In this part we shall study the organizational levels of life from molecular to organismal. At the molecular level we shall pay particular attention to the giant molecules of life—proteins and nucleic acids—and the smaller molecular units used in their construction. Here we shall make our first acquaintance with the submicroscopic units that make up cellular structures and shall find that all perpetuation of life depends fundamentally on the capacity of certain giant molecules to reproduce themselves.

Two levels of cellular organization, the procaryotic and eucaryotic, will be studied in Chapter 10. Among the protists (the basically unicellular phyla described in Chapter 2), the adaptive potential of the single cell has met the needs for survival. In these one-celled organisms the individual life span is brief but paradoxically can also be thought of as perpetual, for the line of descent is through an unbroken succession of cell divisions in which the parent, by dividing, becomes its own progeny. Metaphytes and metazoans have, however, gone on to profit by those increases in size and complexity made possible by a multicellular body plan. In Chapter 11 we shall examine the developmental processes through which the body of each new multicellular organism comes into being by means of interactions and coadaptive specializations of its constituent cells. In Chapter 12 we shall review a selection of basic body plans representative of the organismal level of life at varying degrees of complexity. In each case we shall see that the internal structure of the organism reflects the cardinal characteristics featured by the living world as a whole: (1) its constituent parts have undergone diversification; (2) these parts demonstrate adaptation toward harmonious integration, thereby allowing the body to function as an effective living unit.

Chapter 9  THE MOLECULAR BASIS OF LIFE

EARLY EVIDENCE THAT A BASIC UNITY of life exists at its molecular level was obtained by fragmenting cells and separating their components by means of high-speed centrifugation. When these components were isolated they were found capable of carrying on many of their normal metabolic activities outside the living body (for instance, in a test tube). Such a preparation is called an *in vitro system.* It was an exciting moment in the history of biology when chlorophyll-containing units taken from *spinach* leaf cells were found capable of interacting with energy-releasing bodies (mitochondria) obtained from *rat* tissues, so that a rat-spinach in vitro system could effectively carry on the processes of photosynthesis, energy-transfer, and oxidation! Other experiments have followed in which, for example, protein-synthesizing bodies (ribosomes) isolated from the cells of one species proved capable of synthesizing proteins in vitro, according to a code provided by nucleic acid molecules isolated from the tissues of another species. Such findings as these indicate that *underlying the apparent diversity of living things are molecular mechanisms common to many or all.*

Ultimately, explanations of biotic activities must be sought at the molecular level, since the performance of the organism itself—its responsiveness, motor activity, and capacity for converting mass and utilizing energy—is the product of biochemical and biophysical changes in molecules. In fact, in the course of evolution living systems have expanded their capability for synthesizing a wider and wider variety of metabolically useful molecules.

Living bodies are composed of the same basic substances (elements) that comprise the earth itself, as can be proved by qualitative chemical analysis. Such analysis, however, necessarily involves the destruction of the living matter being analyzed. Merely identifying the chemical constituents of living matter gives little information concerning the manner in which these constituents interact functionally. However, we can reach a further understanding of how life is organized at the molecular level by resorting to methods of investigation that do not totally disrupt the living systems. These include the aforementioned in vitro isolation of particular substances that can function outside the intact organism and the application of *radioactive isotopes* to trace the fate of specific atoms both in vitro and *in vivo* (within the intact body).

The initial sections of this chapter will provide background information relevant to understanding the chemistry of life. We shall see that even the manner in which atoms of the element carbon (C) bond together affects the shape and behavior of those *organic* (carbon-based) compounds which make up all living things. The properties of atoms affect those of molecules, and these in turn determine the nature of life. An understanding of atomic structure and how this structure affects the properties of molecules is therefore an essential part of the modern biology curriculum, for without this understanding any study of living processes must remain superficial. As well as providing necessary background, this chapter should prove useful for reference during the reading of such later material as nutrition.

9.1 □ ATOMS AND ELEMENTS

Because living things are composed entirely of materials obtained ultimately from the abiotic environment, it follows that there can be no uniquely biological kinds of *atoms*. Stars, planets, and organisms are all constructed of various proportions of atoms comprising the approximately 90 naturally occurring *elements*. In Table 9.1 we see that 99.99 percent of living matter consists of only 12 elements, of which oxygen (combined as water) is by far the largest constituent by weight. In fact, 99 percent of living matter is made up of only *four* elements—oxygen, carbon, hydrogen, and nitrogen. Many elements not listed in this table are present in minute or trace quantities, including copper, zinc, cobalt, and manganese. Analysis of the elemental composition of living matter is of limited value, for such information is meaningful mainly in terms of the compounds formed from these elements.

Each element is made up of atoms with a specific and constant number of *protons*, or positively charged units of mass, in the atomic nucleus. The number of protons represents the *atomic number* of the element. Elements may be arranged in series from atomic number 1 to 92, from the lightest element, hydrogen (H), with a single proton, to the heaviest naturally occurring element, uranium (U), with 92 protons. Still heavier than U, isotopes of elements numbering from 93 to 103 have been "artificially" produced under laboratory conditions; all are radioactive and many of extremely short half-life.

Atomic nuclei also contain uncharged particles of mass termed *neutrons*, the number of which is approximately equal to the number of protons present. The sum of protons and neutrons represents the *atomic weight* (*atomic mass*), shown as a superscript number to the left of the symbol for the element (for example, ^{238}U).* Outside the nucleus are rapidly moving negatively charged particles of low apparent mass (*electrons*), which equal the protons in number. Thus, oxygen, with eight protons, also has eight electrons.

Isotopes An *element* is conveniently defined as mass composed of a single kind of atom, but this is not strictly the case. All atoms of an element have the same number of nuclear protons, but may differ with respect to the number of *neutrons* present. Such related atoms are known as isotopes. Isotopes have the same atomic number, but

*The mass of a *molecule* (unit formed by the chemical combination of two or more atoms) is calculated as the sum of the atomic masses of its constituent atoms; the mass (*molecular weight*) of H_2O, for instance, is 18 (1 + 1 + 16), and that of CO_2 is 44 (12 + 16 + 16). For ease of calculation, we shall consistently use atomic-mass values rounded to the nearest whole number.

differ in atomic mass. In calculating atomic mass, both protons and neutrons are given a value of one. Three isotopes of hydrogen are: ^1H, or ordinary hydrogen, with one proton but no neutron, therefore having an atomic mass of *one;* ^2H, or *deuterium,* with one proton and one neutron per atom, and an atomic mass of *two;* ^3H, or *tritium,* with one proton and two neutrons. Tritium is radioactive, with a half-life of 12.5 years, and is useful to biologists in tracing hydrogen-containing compounds in metabolism.

Radioactive isotopes Some isotopes are unstable and undergo nuclear changes that eventually bring them to a condition of stability. These changes are known as *radioactive decay,* for they involve the emission from the atomic nucleus of high-speed particles (α and β) and shortwave radiation (γ rays). Alpha (α) particles are relatively massive, consisting of two protons and two neutrons. They can cause severe injury if introduced into the tissues by way of the digestive tract or bloodstream, but are unlikely to penetrate intact skin. Beta (β) particles are *nuclear* electrons. They readily penetrate living tissue because of their high initial velocity and low mass. Both α and β particles, bearing electrical charges of $+2$ and -1, respectively, may cause *ionization effects* within the cells through which they pass. (By ionization effects we mean that electrons are stripped away from certain compounds, causing them to become electrically charged.) Such effects can produce severe cellular damage and even death. Gamma (γ) rays are similar to short X rays, being highly penetrative and therefore capable of inducing ionizations that can kill the cell, change its hereditary material, or alter its behavior so that it may become malignant (cancerous).

Radioactive decay proceeds continuously for each radioisotope, terminating when the reorganization of the atomic nucleus has been concluded and stability has been achieved. If the atomic number is changed by a loss of protons* during radioactive decay, the end product is a different element. Many kinds of stable atoms may be artificially converted into their unstable radioisotopes by exposure to the high-speed neutron emissions of fissionable materials. Iodine-131 (^{131}I), with a half-life of 8.04 days, is particularly useful to physiologists engaged in tracing the fate of thyroid hormones. Relatively large amounts of ^{131}I taken internally may be monitored from the exterior of the body. Emissions from single atoms may also be detected by the tracks which these particles make on film placed in contact with a tissue preparation. Tritium may be used to tag virtually any organic compound, since essentially all such compounds contain hydrogen. Radioactive sulfur (^{35}S), with a half-life of 87.1 days, is valuable in tagging proteins, whereas radioactive phosphorus (^{32}P), with a half-life of 14.3 days, is especially useful in tracing nucleic acid molecules. Radioisotopes have thus become invaluable tools of biological research, particularly in unraveling the skein of molecular reactions that go on within living cells.

9.2 □ INTERACTIONS AMONG ELEMENTS

Few types of atoms exist in an uncombined state. In general they combine with other atoms to form *molecules.* Even as atmospheric gases, nitrogen and oxygen do not exist as free atoms but mainly as the molecules N_2 and O_2. The most abundant elements of the earth's crust, oxygen, silicon, aluminum, and iron, occur mainly in iron oxides and aluminum silicates, in other words, as compounds. A *compound* is formed whenever atoms of more than one kind are chemically bonded together.

Interactions among atoms and molecules primarily depend upon their having sufficient kinetic energy (energy of movement) to produce *effective collisions.* Such collisions may be facilitated by favorable conditions of temperature, by sources of energy such as light or ultraviolet radiation, and by the presence of other substances that may catalyze the reaction. A *catalyst* is any substance that changes the rate of a chemical reaction without being permanently altered by the reaction; small amounts of catalyst may over a period of time catalyze the interaction of great numbers of reacting molecules. Life could not exist without metabolism-accelerating catalysts.

*These protons are lost as part of the α particles.

Table 9.1 □ **Elemental composition of living matter**

ELEMENT	SYMBOL	AVERAGE PERCENTAGE BY WEIGHT
Oxygen	**O**	**76.0**
Carbon	**C**	**10.5**
Hydrogen	**H**	**10.0**
Nitrogen	**N**	**2.5**
Phosphorus	**P**	**0.3**
Potassium	**K**	**0.3**
Chlorine	**Cl**	**0.1**
Sodium	**Na**	**0.04**
Calcium	**Ca**	**0.02**
Magnesium	**Mg**	**0.02**
Sulfur	**S**	**0.02**
Iron	**Fe**	**0.01**

A Common types of reactions

SYNTHESIS Compounds are formed from elements by synthesis. When an electrical spark is passed through a mixture of gaseous hydrogen (H_2) and oxygen (O_2), the elements react to form water:

$$2H_2 + O_2 \longrightarrow 2H_2O$$

Synthesis also takes place when two or more smaller molecules combine to form a single larger one, as when water and carbon dioxide unite to form carbonic acid:

$$H_2O + CO_2 \longrightarrow H_2CO_3$$

DECOMPOSITION The reverse of synthesis is decomposition, in which larger molecules are broken down into smaller molecules or into atoms. An example would be the reverse of either of the above reactions (this is shown by reversing the arrows so that they point to the left instead of to the right).

EXCHANGE REACTIONS Reactions may also take place between molecules of different kinds, with atoms or groups of atoms exchanged between molecules. Such an exchange reaction can take place between copper oxide (CuO) and hydrogen gas, producing the substances water and elemental copper:

$$CuO + H_2 \longrightarrow Cu + H_2O$$

B How do electrons determine the bonding properties of atoms?

The arrangement and energy content of an atom's electrons determine the manner in which it can react with other atoms to form molecules. In this section we can present only a highly compressed discussion of the essential features of atomic bonding; further understanding of this complex subject may be obtained by consulting a modern chemistry textbook.*

The energy associated with electrons does not form a continuous range of energy values but exists as a series of discrete values or quanta. Because of this, each electron is spoken of as occupying a specific energy level known as a *quantum level* or shell. Electrons of lowest energy content occupy the first shell, closest to the atomic nucleus, while those of higher energy content occupy shells successively farther away from the nucleus (Figure 9.1a). For an electron to move from one quantum level to the one next higher requires its energy content to be increased by a value corresponding to the absorption of a quantum ("packet") of energy in the electromagnetic spectrum. An electron that absorbs this additional quantum and moves to a higher shell is said to be "excited." It can occupy this higher shell only for so long as it possesses this extra energy; as this energy is given up the electron returns to "ground state," that is, to the quantum level originally occupied. The excitement of electrons by absorption of light energy and the subsequent biotic utilization of this excess energy will be considered in Chapter 13, for it is the basis of photosynthesis, the major reaction by which energy enters the living world from its surroundings. Most of our present discussion pertains to electrons at ground state, but in later chapters we should recall that electrons used in making energy-rich compounds within living cells still possess excess energy obtained by absorbing sunlight.

*One good reference is H. B. Gray and G. P. Haight, Jr., *Basic Principles of Chemistry* (New York: W. A. Benjamin, Inc., 1967).

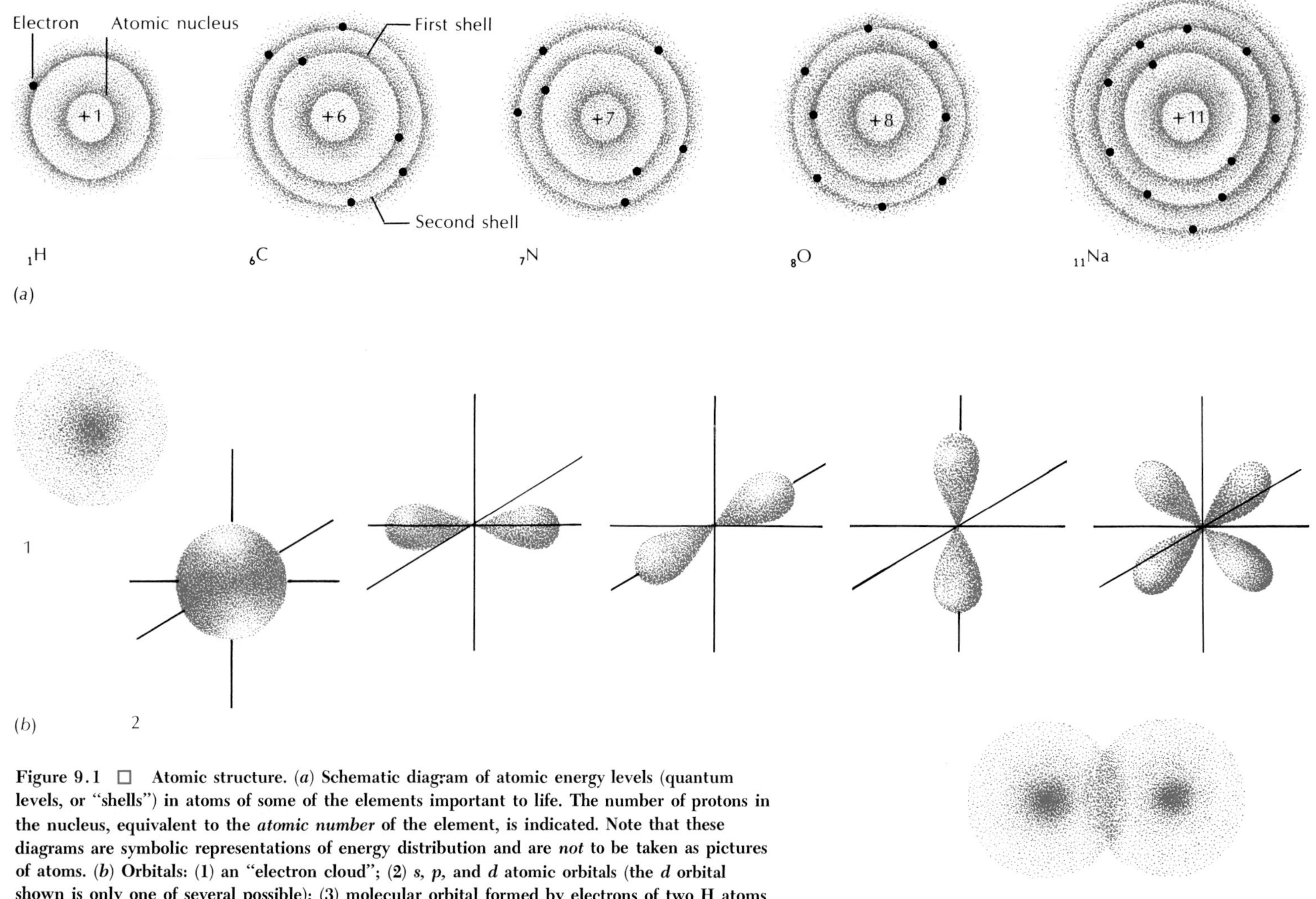

Figure 9.1 □ **Atomic structure. (*a*) Schematic diagram of atomic energy levels (quantum levels, or "shells") in atoms of some of the elements important to life. The number of protons in the nucleus, equivalent to the *atomic number* of the element, is indicated. Note that these diagrams are symbolic representations of energy distribution and are *not* to be taken as pictures of atoms. (*b*) Orbitals: (1) an "electron cloud"; (2) *s*, *p*, and *d* atomic orbitals (the *d* orbital shown is only one of several possible); (3) molecular orbital formed by electrons of two H atoms in molecular hydrogen, H_2.**

Within any given quantum level the probable location and energy content of electrons can be represented in space by figures called *orbitals.* If we could take a series of photographs of a single electron as it moved about the atomic nucleus and could then superimpose all of these frames, we would obtain a composite photograph in which the position of the electron at each moment would appear as a dot; the distribution of dots in all the superimposed frames would form an "electron cloud" of characteristic shape and volume [Figure 9.1*b*(1)]. This cloud would be the visible evidence of the orbital for that electron; within the orbital, the density of dots would reflect the probability that the electron was occupying that part of the orbital at any given moment. Although the outlines of the cloud are fuzzy, it is convenient to picture an orbital as having a distinct boundary; the boundary line is drawn at a distance from the atomic nucleus that encloses 90 to 99 percent of the electron density. Of course it is not actually possible to make such a photograph with available equipment; but the shape and volume of electron orbitals can be described mathematically, and these mathematical descriptions are found to be consistent with the observed properties of atoms and molecules. In fact, most characteristics of chemical compounds can be explained through considerations of orbitals.

Two major properties of orbitals are volume and shape. The overall volume of an orbital is defined by the energy content of the electrons occupying it: the greater the energy content, the larger the volume of the orbital. An orbital at the first quantum level has a smaller radius than an orbital at the second level, and so forth.

The shape of the region within which an electron moves can be designated as an *s*, *p*, *d*, or *f* orbital [Figure 9.1*b*(2)]. An *s* orbital is spherical. The hydrogen atom, with a single electron, has but a single shell comprised of a single orbital; the latter, called a 1*s* orbital (indicating that it is spherical and occupies the first quantum level), is a sphere approximately 10^{-8} cm in diameter. The helium atom also has a single 1*s* orbital, which is occupied by two electrons. In all other elements the orbital electrons occupy more than one shell and orbitals of other than spherical shape occur. The *p* orbitals are bilobed. At any quantum level above the first, three sets of *p* orbitals can exist, each extending from the nucleus at right angles to the other two. The *d* and *f* orbitals are more complex, but they need not concern us here because the three elements other than H most important in organic compounds (C, N, and O) have but two shells, containing only *s* and *p* orbitals.

Within any given shell electrons tend to occupy available orbitals according to three general rules: (1) orbitals of lower energy state tend to be filled before orbitals of higher energy state can be occupied; (2) each orbital can be occupied by no more than two electrons (an electron pair); (3) when filling orbitals of equivalent energy level each orbital tends to be occupied by one electron before any orbital is free to accept a second.

For our present purposes we shall not concern ourselves with the distribution of all of the electrons in a given atom, but only with those few electrons that occupy the orbitals of an atom's highest quantum level, for it is these electrons that are most important in chemical reactions. These *valence electrons* occupy *s* and *p* orbitals in the atom's outermost shell; no more than four electron pairs can occupy this outer shell, which contains one *s* and three *p* orbitals. Any of these four orbitals which contains two electrons (when the atom is in an unbonded state) is known as a *nonbonding orbital,* for it is not usually free to engage in the formation of chemical bonds with another atom. On the other hand, any orbital of the outer shell that contains but one electron is termed a *bonding orbital,* for this orbital can be occupied by one more electron which, if shared by another atom, contributes to the formation of a *chemical bond.* If all of the orbitals of the outer shell are filled, the element does not usually tend to enter into chemical reactions—it possesses no bonding orbitals and is considered to be an *inert* element. Helium, mentioned earlier, has no bonding orbitals and is therefore an inert gas. In most elements, however, one or more orbitals of the outer shell contain but one electron apiece and can therefore accept one more.

The number and arrangement of these bonding orbitals determine how atoms can combine to form molecules and also dictate the length and angle of the bonds formed and the shape of the resultant molecules. Molecular shape in turn dictates how these molecules will behave in living systems. By way of example, let us see how a water molecule is formed and why H_2O is angular molecule,

H
|
O—H

rather than a linear molecule,

H—O—H

The O atom, with only six electrons in its outer shell, has two bonding orbitals, giving it an ordinary combining power (valence) of 2. The electronic configuration of the outer shell can be represented as:

:Ȯ·
¨

In this figure the paired dots represent electrons occupying the same orbital, whereas the unpaired dots represent electrons in the bonding orbitals. An O atom therefore can

Figure 9.2 □ **The sp^3 hybridization and its implications for the shapes of molecules important to life: (*a*) sp^3 orbitals of carbon atom; (*b*) water molecule; (*c*) methane molecule; (*d*) ammonia molecule. Note that, in H_2O, NH_3, and CH_4, the properties of the central atom determine the bonding angles of the peripheral atoms.**

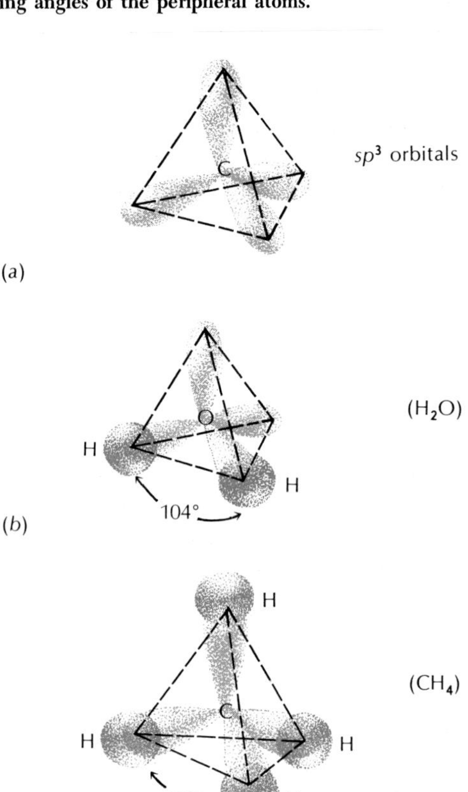

combine chemically with any other atom or atoms having one or more bonding orbitals, for one bonding orbital of each atom can interpenetrate to form a *molecular orbital* containing an electron pair, one electron being contributed by each of the atoms entering into the combination [Figure 9.1*b*(3)]. When a molecular orbital is formed, the two atoms that have contributed electrons to this orbital are chemically bonded to form a molecule. This type of bond, in which a pair of electrons is shared by the two reacting atoms, is known as a *covalent bond.* An O atom, with two bonding orbitals, can form covalent bonds with *two* H atoms, for the 1*s* orbital of H contains only one electron of the two possible. When the electron of H pairs with the electron in one of the bonding orbitals of O, a molecular orbital is formed and the two atoms are held together by means of this shared electron pair. The combination of O with *two* H atoms produces a stable configuration, H_2O, a molecule in which all bonding orbitals are filled. This can be represented as

H
:Ö:H
 ··

in which black dots represent electrons of O and colored dots electrons of H. This combination can be formed whenever effective collisions take place between O and H atoms; providing energy in the form of heat or electrical discharges increases the number of effective collisions taking place in a mixture of the two gases.

The figure shown above indicates that H_2O is a nonlinear molecule, the O atom holding the two H atoms apart at an angle of 104°. To understand why H_2O has this shape, we must examine the arrangement of the orbitals in the outer shell of the O atom. We have said above that the orbitals of the outer shell constitute one *s* and three *p* orbitals; however, in such biotically important elements as O, N, and C, these four orbitals interact or *hybridize* to form four identical *sp^3 hybrid* orbitals that extend outward from the atomic nucleus toward the corners of a tetrahedral volume of space (Figure 9.2*a*). Electrically charged particles of like charge repel one another; this repulsion causes the electrons to be spaced out at some distance from one another. Within any given orbital, an electron pair behaves like one unit, repelling the electron pair in each adjacent orbital. If each of the four sp^3 orbitals contained an electron pair, or if each contained but one electron, the repulsive forces operating among these electrons would be equalized, and the angle between any two orbitals would approximate 109°. However, in the O and N atoms the angles between these four orbitals are not perfectly symmetrical, for the nonbonding orbitals, each containing an electron pair, exert an electrostatic repulsion on the other orbitals that is stronger than the repulsion exerted by the single electrons of the bonding orbitals. In consequence the bonding orbitals are forced closer together and are therefore spaced only 104° apart. This produces the angular configuration

H
| 104°
O—H

when H_2O is formed (Figure 9.2*b*).

Why is an understanding of bond angles important to an understanding of life processes? We shall answer this question in two ways: (1) by considering how bond angles affect the properties of water molecules (which are certainly biotically significant, since living things consist more than 80 percent of water and most biochemical reactions take place with the reactants in solution in water); (2) by considering how the arrangement of the bonding orbitals of the C atom affects the shapes of organic molecules. With respect to H_2O, we find that the bond angle causes the water molecule to be asymmetrical: the O atom is to one side while the two much smaller H atoms are to the other side. The nucleus of the O atom, with eight protons, exerts a stronger attraction upon electrons than can the nuclei of the H atoms, each of which contain only one proton. Consequently, the shared electron pairs tend to be drawn closer to the nucleus of the O atom and farther away from the nuclei of the H atoms. This causes the O part of the water molecule to be somewhat negatively charged and the H part to be somewhat positively charged. The H_2O molecule is accordingly *polarized*—it is an electric dipole and tends to establish electrostatic fields of attraction with neighboring H_2O molecules so that water has a crystalline structure. (The crystalline structure is most apparent when water is in the solid state as ice.) This property causes water to be *cohesive,* which is essential for such biotic processes as the upward transport of water in trees. Furthermore, polar molecules tend to ionize under certain conditions. When undergoing *ionization,* a molecule of H_2O splits into two electrically charged particles, or *ions:* the hydroxyl ion, OH^-,

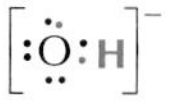

$$[:\ddot{\underset{..}{O}}:H]^-$$

which bears a negative charge because it has one more electron than it has protons, and the hydrogen ion, H^+, which is positively charged because it is simply a proton. Both H^+ and OH^- have important effects on life because they affect the acidity and alkalinity of solutions.

Coming next to the C atom, we must first note that in its unexcited or ground state this atom has only two rather than three *p* orbitals in its outer shell; four electrons are present, two occupying a 2*s* orbital, and one, each of the two *p* orbitals,

$$:\dot{C}.$$

In this state C has a combining power of only 2, and if combined with O will form poisonous carbon monoxide gas, CO. However, if the atom absorbs only a slight amount of energy, one of the two electrons occupying the 2*s* orbital is sufficiently excited that it can move to the previously unoccupied third *p* orbital, creating *four* bonding orbitals, each with one electron:

$$\cdot\dot{\underset{\cdot}{C}}\cdot$$

This raises the combining power of C to 4, a fact of great significance, for with a combining power of only 2, C atoms could not form the branching chains characteristic of the chief compounds in living systems.

One further change takes place: the 2*s* and 2*p* orbitals of the excited C atom now hybridize to form four identical sp^3 hybrid orbitals (Figure 9.2*a*). Since all four of these sp^3 orbitals are alike in containing a single electron apiece, they all repel one another with equal force so that each forms an angle of 109°28′ with any other orbital. Now if each of these orbitals were to share an electron pair with one H atom, a perfectly symmetrical, tetrahedral molecule, CH_4 (methane gas), would be formed (Figure 9.2*c*). Being symmetrical, CH_4 is not a polar molecule like H_2O. Its electronic configuration can be depicted as

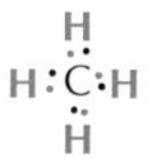

$$\begin{array}{c} H \\ H:\ddot{\underset{..}{C}}:H \\ H \end{array}$$

The bond angles are difficult to portray without a three-dimensional model, but can be approximated thus:

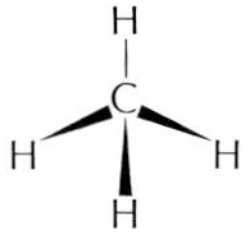

```
      H
      |
      C
H ◄   |   ► H
      H
```

The full significance of the tetrahedral arrangement of its bonding orbitals becomes apparent when carbon forms bonds, not with four identical atoms but with four *unlike* atoms or groups. An example of this is when an amino acid such as alanine is formed. The partial structural formula of alanine is conventionally represented as

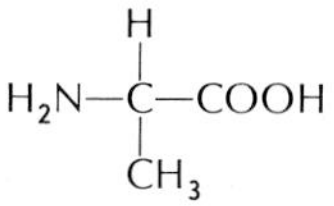

```
        H
        |
H2N—C—COOH
        |
        CH3
```

in which we see that the central C atom is bonded with four different groups: a single H atom, an amino group ($—NH_2$), a carboxyl group (—COOH), and a methyl group ($—CH_3$). The tetrahedral bonding dictates that alanine shall actually be depicted

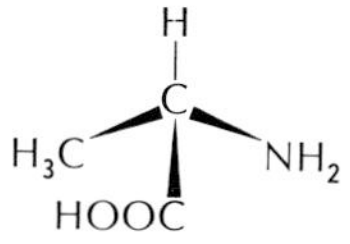

```
          H
          |
          C
H3C            NH2
      HOOC
```

Alanine

However, this tetrahedral configuration permits a mirror image of the alanine molecule to exist, as shown:

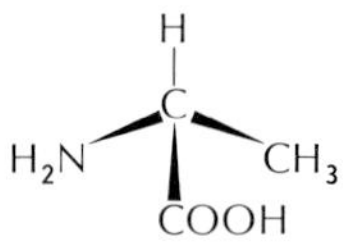

```
     H
     |
     C
H2N/ | \CH3
   COOH
```

Mirror image

These two molecules are *stereoisomers* ("right-handed" and "left-handed" configurations). They may be distinguished by the effect that a solution of each has on a beam of polarized light. When light is polarized, its waves are so aligned that they all vibrate in the same plane. When a beam of polarized light is passed through an alanine solution, the plane of polarization is rotated clockwise, that is, to the right; accordingly, the molecules accomplishing this rotation are termed *dextrorotatory.* A solution containing the mirror image of alanine, on the other hand, rotates the plane of polarization counterclockwise, that is, to the left, so that the molecule is termed *levorotatory.* Thus we recognize two forms of alanine: *dextro-* or *d*-alanine, and *levo-* or *l*-alanine. This difference might seem to be inconsequential, but it actually has marked biotic effects: an animal fed upon "right-handed" amino acids will thrive, while one given only "left-handed" amino acids will starve because the relevant enzyme systems are able to handle only dextrorotatory stereoisomers.

The covalent bonds discussed up to this point have been those formed when a single electron pair is shared by two atoms. In writing formulas (such as that shown above for alanine), each *single* covalent bond is represented by a single line, —, as in the organic compound ethane,

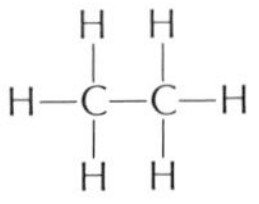

```
  H H
  | |
H—C—C—H
  | |
  H H
```

or the inorganic compound ammonia (Figure 9.2*d*),

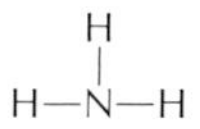

```
  H
  |
H—N—H
```

However, covalent bonds can also be formed in which two atoms share two or three electron pairs. When two molecular orbitals are formed between the two atoms, we say that a *double bond* has been formed, and represent this conventionally as a double line, ═, as in ethylene,

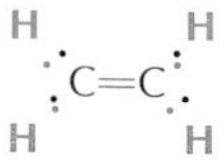

```
H      H
 ˙:C═C:˙
H      H
```

When three electron pairs are shared and three molecular orbitals consequently established between the two atoms, a *triple bond* is formed. This is represented as ≡, such as in the compound molecular nitrogen, N_2,

:N≡N:

or in acetylene,

H:C≡C:H

The more electron pairs that are shared between two atoms, the more closely the two atomic nuclei are drawn together, creating a bond that is shorter and stronger than a single bond. The strength of a chemical bond (*bonding energy*) is measured as the amount of heat that must be applied to break the bond. Nearly twice as much heat is required to break the C═C bond of ethylene as to break the C—C bond of ethane, and nearly three times as much is required to break the C≡C bond of acetylene as is needed for ethane.

C Isomers and structural formulas

The term "CO_2" is an *empirical formula.* An empirical formula consists of the symbols of the elements involved in a compound, together with subscript numerals indicating the number of atoms of each element which the molecule contains. It gives no information other than the kinds and numbers of atoms in the molecule. The configuration O═C═O, on the other hand, is a partial *structural formula,* that is, one which attempts to depict in part the actual spatial arrangements of the atoms and the bonding involved. Structural formulas are of course subject to the limitations that exist whenever three-dimensional objects must be represented two-dimensionally. Despite these limitations, structural formulas convey much more information than do empirical formulas and thus are frequently employed for organic compounds, which are the major concern of biologists. For example, the empirical formula $C_6H_5O_2N$ for the vitamin niacin provides only the information that this compound contains six atoms of carbon, five of hydrogen, two of oxygen, and one of nitrogen. The structural formula

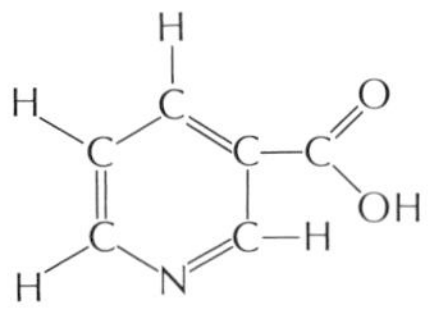

```
         H
         |
H        C
 \     /   \\      O
  C          C—C//
  ||         |     \
  C          C—H    OH
 /     \\   /
H        N
```

reveals the important information that the niacin molecule is not a chain but a ring, contains double bonds, and bears a carboxyl group

$$-C\begin{matrix}\nearrow O \\ \searrow OH\end{matrix}$$

making it an organic acid.

Another limitation of empirical formulas is that they do not allow us to distinguish between isomers. *Isomers* are molecules having the same atoms present but differing in the arrangement of those atoms. We have just considered the mirror-image *stereoisomers* of the amino acid alanine. This type of isomerism is also known as *optical* isomerism, from the effects (explained above) that the isomers have on polarized light.

Geometrical isomerism occurs in molecules in which a double bond prevents the atoms on each side of the bond from rotating freely. This restriction of rotation can be understood by picturing a ball-and-stick model: when two balls are held together by a single rod (representing one molecular orbital), the two balls can be turned in opposite directions; now if a second joining rod is inserted, the two balls no longer can rotate separately. A single bond usually does not keep the conjoined atoms from rotating independently of one another. For instance, in the compound *ethane,* two methyl groups ($-CH_3$) are joined by a single covalent bond, and each group can rotate freely about the C—C bond:

$$H_3C-CH_3$$

In the similar compound ethylene, however, the double bond prevents the conjoined groups from rotating independently:

$$H_2C=CH_2$$

This illustration serves to introduce the phenomenon of geometrical isomerism, for when the two groups joined by a double bond differ in their spatial orientation, *cis*- and *trans*-isomers are formed:

H ╲ ╱ H C=C HOOC ╱ ╲ COOH	H ╲ ╱ COOH C=C HOOC ╱ ╲ H
cis	*trans*

In this figure, the *cis*-isomer is maleic acid, which differs in melting point and other properties from its *trans*-isomer, fumaric acid. The geometric configuration of an isomer, like its left- or right-handedness, may influence its biotic activities profoundly, for (as was the case with left- and right-handed stereoisomers) enzyme systems adapted to handle a *cis*-isomer may be unable to deal with a *trans*-isomer, and vice versa.

Structural isomers are those in which the atoms forming the main skeleton of the molecules are differently arranged:

H — C(H)(H) — O — C(H)(H) — H	H — C(H)(H) — C(H)(H) — OH
Dimethyl ether	*Ethanol*

Such isomers can be very different in their action within living systems. In this example, the ether would act as an anesthetic, causing unconsciousness when inhaled; the alcohol, taken as a beverage, would act as a stimulant in small doses and as a depressant in larger doses.

We can thus see that when biologists wish to know the isomeric state of a compound, they must determine its exact structural formula. Complete structural formulas in which each atom is designated by its symbol are unwieldy when dealing with large organic molecules. Therefore certain simplifications are standard, such as omitting the symbols of all carbon atoms within a ring and showing only the bonds and those atoms other than C. The symbols of H atoms are also often omitted from the ring or main chain, or may be shown as short protruding lines. Thus the niacin molecule shown earlier may be depicted simply as

[Pyridine ring with N, short protruding lines, and C(=O)OH group]

Once the structure of a carboxyl group is understood, it may be represented instead as —COOH. In our discussions of organic compounds we may employ a complete structural formula to introduce a compound, but wherever feasible will use simplified structural formulas thereafter.

D Ionic bonding

Most of the molecules that make up living things are formed by covalent bonding (that is, they are covalent compounds). However, there is another category of compounds, known as *ionic compounds,* which may not properly be thought of as consisting of molecules at all. Instead, they are produced by *electrostatic* attraction among electrically charged atoms termed *ions.* As we have seen, most atoms are electrically neutral, since the sum of the positive units of charge provided by their nuclear protons is balanced by an equivalent number of orbital electrons. However, there are a number of elements, notably alkali metals, which have a relatively low affinity for the electrons of their outer shell and tend to lose these electrons when in the vicinity of other elements that have a high affinity for electrons. Elements which readily lose or give up electrons, are termed *electropositive,* for after having given up their outermost electrons the atoms of these elements have more positive than negative charges and are therefore called positive ions or *cations. Electronegative* elements are nonmetals which have such a strong *affinity* for electrons that they tend to "kidnap" them. As a result, these atoms come to have more electrons than they do protons, and thus gain a net negative electrical charge. Negatively charged atoms are called *anions.*

Ions are attracted to other ions of opposite charge, forming compounds by electrostatic or ionic bonding rather than by covalent bonding. In ionic bonding, the interacting ions are held in regular positions by intersecting lines of force, forming a lattice which as it grows may become visible as a crystal. Table salt (sodium chloride, NaCl) is an ionic compound that forms cubical crystals (Figure 9.3) composed of regularly arranged sodium ions, Na^+, and chloride ions, Cl^-. The element sodium (Na) is a gray metal that readily yields its single outer electron to elements with greater electron affinity. The nonmetallic element chlorine (Cl) is a toxic gas characterized by a strong electron affinity. When a chlorine atom captures one electron, its outer shell is filled (now containing eight instead of seven electrons) and it is rendered stable; however, now having one more electron than its total number of protons (18 electrons to 17 protons), it must be considered an *ion* instead of an atom.

Figure 9.3 □ **Ions in a crystal of sodium chloride. [*After J. Quagliano,* Chemistry (3rd ed.) (*Englewood Cliffs, N.J.: Prentice-Hall, Inc., 1969*).]**

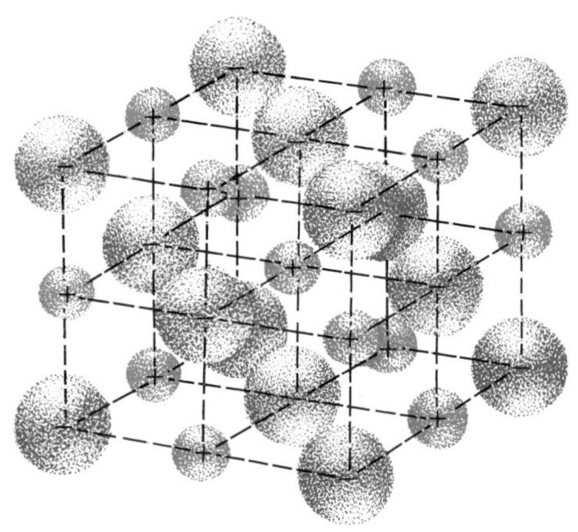

Ions behave quite differently from the elemental atoms from which they are derived. Most living things need a certain amount of *chloride ion* (Cl^-) for correct bodily function—yet they would be killed by exposure to elemental chlorine (Cl). By the same token, when we speak loosely of "needing calcium in the diet" we do not actually mean the element calcium per se, which is a poisonous metal, but rather the calcium ion (Ca^{2+}), which living things do require in their cells and body fluids.

Ionic compounds comprise two major categories: bases and salts. When dissolved in water, both dissociate into their constituent ions. *Bases* such as sodium hydroxide (NaOH) release *hydroxide ion* (OH^-), making the solution basic or alkaline. Since the acidity and alkalinity of solutions are determined by the relative amounts of hydrogen ion (H^+) and hydroxide ion (OH^-) present, the dissociation of *salts* would not seem to affect the acid-base balance, for salts are ionic compounds that do not themselves directly release either H^+ or OH^-. However, some salts may react with water through a reaction known as *hydrolysis* to alter the H^+ concentration. For example, the salt Na_2CO_3 (sodium carbonate) releases carbonate ion (CO_3^{2-}), which combines with H^+ furnished by water as follows,

$$CO_3^{2-} + 2H^+ \longrightarrow H_2CO_3$$

thus reducing the H^+ concentration and causing the solution to become alkaline.

Electrostatic or ionic bonding plays little direct role in living systems, although the ions released by the dissociation of ionic compounds in solution are essential components of cells and body fluids. The ionic composition of body fluids is maintained with a high degree of constancy. Only a few ionic compounds as such form actual parts of organisms, including vertebrate bones and teeth, mollusc shells, and crustacean exoskeletons, all of which are made rigid by crystalline calcium carbonate or phosphate.

Ions. Some ions are *monoatomic,* consisting of only one atom, for example, Na^+, Mg^{2+}, Ca^{2+}, Cl^-. Sodium ion, Na^+, bears a positive electrical charge because the Na atom loses one electron in forming the ion; Mg^{2+} and Ca^{2+} bear two positive charges because two electrons are lost in forming each ion; Cl^- on the other hand bears a negative electrical charge because it gains one electron in forming the ion.

A number of other ions are *polyatomic,* consisting of a group of two or more atoms, usually combined by covalent bonding, which acts as a unit, and which, as a unit, is either electropositive or electronegative. The only common electropositive polyatomic ion is the ammonium ion (NH_4^+).

Common electronegative polyatomic ions include the hydroxide ion (OH^-), the sulfate ion (SO_4^{2-}), the carbonate ion (CO_3^{2-}), the bicarbonate ion (HCO_3^-), the phosphate ion (PO_4^{3-}), and the nitrate ion (NO_3^-). These are of great importance in living systems, as summarized in Table 13.2.

E Ionization

Certain *covalent* compounds also yield ions when in aqueous solution. This event is known as *ionization*. Some yield relatively few ions and are said to be weakly ionizing. Others release a large proportion of ions, and are said to be strongly ionizing. *Acids* are one type of covalent compound which tends to ionize in solution. When dissolved in water, the gas HCl ionizes strongly, releasing hydrogen ion (H^+) and chloride ion (Cl^-). HCl is actually a covalent compound, but the electronegativity or high electron affinity of the chlorine part of the molecule results in the shared electron pair being held more closely to the chlorine atom than to the hydrogen atom:

H :C̈l:

rather than

H:C̈l:

This unequal distribution of the shared electron pair causes the molecule to be polar. Polar molecules, especially in the presence of a polar solvent (such as H_2O), are particularly susceptible to ionization. As we have said, HCl ionizes strongly in water, releasing equal numbers of H^+ and Cl^-. A solution that contains more free H^+ ions than OH^- ions is said to be acidic, and so HCl dissolved in water produces hydrochloric acid. An *acid* is any substance that releases H^+ when in solution.

Organic compounds having a carboxyl group,

$$-C\begin{matrix}\diagup\!\!\!\!=O\\ \diagdown OH\end{matrix}$$

ionize in solution to yield H^+ ions. The rest of the molecule (which may be relatively large) is thus rendered electronegative

$$\left[R-C\begin{matrix}\diagup\!\!\!\!=O\\ \diagdown O\end{matrix}\right]^-$$

where R symbolizes the "remainder" of the molecule. Such compounds are known as organic or *carboxylic acids*. They include a group of highly significant compounds, the *amino acids*, which are constituents of proteins. The capacity of amino acids to ionize means that entire protein molecules can be electrically polarized. This affects their behavior significantly, and also (as we shall find in Section 16.2A) enables them to regulate cell acidity and alkalinity.

pH The symbol pH (potential H) is used to designate the relative degree of acidity or alkalinity of a solution. Acidity or alkalinity is an expression of the relative proportions of H^+ and OH^- ions present in the solution. This can be expressed on a scale of pH values running from 0 to 14. The midpoint of this scale, 7, represents neutrality, and is the negative log of the H^+ concentration of pure water at 25°C, 1×10^{-7} g/liter. If sufficient OH^- is added to the solution to lower the H^+ concentration to 1×10^{-8} g/liter, the pH is said to be 8. On the other hand, should enough acid be added to the solution to increase the H^+ concentration to 1×10^{-6} g/liter, the pH would be 6. Any solution with a pH greater than 7 is alkaline, while any with a pH lower than 7 is acidic. Note that with each change in the integral value of pH, there is a *tenfold* change in H^+ concentration. Thus a solution of pH 1 is ten times as acid as a solution of pH 2, and a solution of pH 10 is one hundred times as alkaline as a solution of pH 8. Both ionic compounds and ionizing covalent compounds affect pH. Living systems must maintain careful homeostatic regulation of their internal pH, which often may not safely fluctuate as much as one tenth of a point (see Section 16.2A).

F Hydrogen bonding

Some molecules which are polarized by the unequal distribution of their bonding electrons nevertheless do not readily ionize in solution. However, the electron imbalance that makes them electric dipoles results in the establishment of attractive electrostatic forces between these molecules and other nearby dipole molecules. This attraction is much weaker than that of a covalent bond, but it is an extremely important factor in stabilizing compounds such as water, nucleic acids, and proteins. This type of bonding is called *hydrogen bonding*. Hydrogen bonds form between the oxygen (electronegative) part of one water molecule and the hydrogen (electropositive) part of another, and are responsible for the cohesive properties and crystalline structure of water, mentioned earlier. Hydrogen bonds are constantly being broken and reformed, but as the temperature is lowered the kinetic energy of the molecules is reduced and the hydrogen bonds do not dissociate so freely. Larger and larger clumps of water molecules coalesce by hydrogen bonding, and eventually grossly visible ice crystals appear.

The characteristic of hydrogen bonds that makes them of cardinal importance in living systems is that they both rupture and form rapidly and easily, without requiring the presence of catalysts. If they are disrupted by a mild increase in temperature, for instance, they reform spontaneously when the temperature is lowered. Slight changes in cell pH can also cause hydrogen bonds to break or form. The value of hydrogen bonds in stabilizing the structure of proteins and nucleic acids will be explained in a later section of this chapter.

9.3 □ ORGANIC COMPOUNDS

The greater proportion by volume of any living thing is the simple *inorganic* compound, water, comprising from 70 to 99 percent of the mass of an organism. The properties of water that render it so essential to life processes have been summarized earlier (see Section 4.1A). However, the structural characteristics and activities of living matter are primarily dependent upon molecules known as *organic compounds,* which constitute the other 1 to 30 percent. These compounds are mainly built up by the covalent bonding of carbon atoms. In nature most organic compounds are produced only within the bodies of living things, although many may now be synthesized in the laboratory.

A Properties of Carbon

The element carbon occurs in an enormous number of compounds, probably greatly exceeding 2×10^6; the total number of all known compounds that do not contain carbon is well under 2×10^5. C—C covalent bonds are particularly stable and permit these atoms to form the long chains and rings characteristic of organic compounds. Outside the chemist's laboratory, C—C bonds are almost exclusively formed within living cells, through the mediation of enzymes occurring in those cells. The vast variety of actual or potential carbon compounds accounts for the fact that no two species, in fact, no two individual organisms, are likely to be biochemically identical. [Another element that has bonding properties similar to those of carbon is silicon (Si), with an atomic number of 14 and an atomic weight of 28. It is thought that under the appropriate conditions Si rather than C could be the basis of the molecules of life; if so, organisms built of silicon compounds would weigh more than twice as much, for their size, as organisms produced by the evolution of carbon compounds.]

In order to serve as the basis for the construction of the complicated branched chain molecules on which life processes depend, an element must meet certain requirements. (1) Its atoms must be capable of forming bonds with other atoms of the same kind. (2) The bond must have a spatial configuration which would favor some versatility in the way adjacent atoms fit together. (3) The bond must contain sufficient energy so that it will not tend to break at normal temperatures. (4) The element must be capable of forming at least *three* such covalent bonds; otherwise *branching* molecules cannot be formed, but only simple chains and rings.

Most elements do not fulfill these four prerequisites. Elements which normally have a combining power of only 1 or 2 cannot build branching molecules. Metallic elements rarely form suitable bonds with other atoms of the same kind. Phosphorus and nitrogen can form three covalent bonds, and branching molecules are known that are built with P—P or N—N bonds. However, the P—P bond breaks rather readily in the presence of water and is therefore unstable in an aqueous medium, and the N—N bond possesses a low bonding energy and is also relatively unstable. Only carbon and silicon are thought to possess the necessary properties for building stable branching chains, and since under terrestrial conditions silicon compounds are rarely gaseous and dissolve with difficulty in water, while carbon compounds exist both as gases [notably CO_2 and CH_4 (methane)] and in solution (for example, as CO_3^{2-} or HCO_3^-), carbon qualifies as the element most "fit" to produce the compounds needed for the evolution of complex self-maintaining and self-perpetuating molecular systems. Furthermore, the C—C bond is relatively high in *bonding energy.* As we have said, the energy of a covalent bond is estimated as the amount of heat that must be applied to the bond to disrupt it. Since it is quite difficult to measure the amount of heat needed to break the covalent bond between any two atoms, it is better expressed as the amount of heat needed to break one *mole* of molecules containing these bonds. (A mole is the molecular weight of a compound expressed in grams; one mole of water equals 18 g, and one mole of CO_2, 44 g.) To break down one mole of a compound built with C—C bonds requires 83 kcal (kilocalories), whereas only 38 kcal are needed to break a mole of N—N bonds. (A kilocalorie is the amount of heat required to raise the temperature of one liter of water by 1°C.)

B Small organic molecules

Organic molecules can undergo a nearly infinite series of permutations, but may still be categorized into a manageable number of types. We shall focus our attention upon those which are of the greatest importance to life. Many of the molecules most essential to life are constructed of smaller constituent molecules. When the constituent molecules are of only one or two types, the resultant giant molecule or macromolecule is called a *polymer.* Each of the reiterated molecular units that form the polymer is known as a *monomer.* A heteropolymer is a molecule built up of two or more somewhat different monomers. Starches, proteins, and nucleic acids all are large polymers built up of simpler, repeated, monomeric units. These units, which may exist independently as well as contributing to larger molecules, may themselves be linear, branching, or ring-shaped. Many have characteristic *functional groups* that affect their properties and reactivity. We shall now consider a few types of relatively simple organic compounds that are important as metabolic intermediates or as constituents of larger molecules.

ALCOHOLS An organic molecule which bears the functional group —OH (the *hydroxyl group*) is known as an alcohol, such as ethanol,

```
   H  H
   |  |
H—C—C—OH
   |  |
   H  H
```

Alcohols appear mainly as transient intermediates in metabolic pathways such as glycolysis (the breakdown of the simple sugar glucose). *Glycerol,*

```
   H    H    H
   |    |    |
H—C——C——C—H
   |    |    |
   OH   OH   OH
```

with three —OH groups, is essential in the formation of triglyceride fats and phospholipids, while other alcohols are concerned in the synthesis of other types of lipids.

CARBOXYLIC ACIDS As we saw above, a molecule possessing one or more *carboxyl groups,*

```
    O
   //
—C
   \
    OH
```

also conveniently represented as —COOH, will ionize in solution to release H^+, and is therefore known as an organic acid or carboxylic acid, such as acetic acid,

```
   H   O
   |  //
H—C—C
   |  \
   H   OH
```

Many carboxylic acids occur as metabolic intermediates, such as in the Krebs citric acid cycle (see Section 14.3C). *Fatty acids* are short- to long-chain carboxylic acids in which a carbon chain containing from 3 to 20 or more carbon atoms terminates in a —COOH. Fatty acids are constituents of fats, oils, waxes, and lipoproteins. A small fatty acid that will serve as an example of this type of compound is capric acid, found in butter:

```
   H  H  H  H  H  H  H  H  H   O
   |  |  |  |  |  |  |  |  |  //
H—C—C—C—C—C—C—C—C—C—C
   |  |  |  |  |  |  |  |  |  \
   H  H  H  H  H  H  H  H  H   OH
```

or $C_9H_{19}COOH$.

Amino acids, which will be considered separately below, are the units that make up protein molecules.

ALDEHYDES An aldehyde is an organic molecule chiefly characterized by the *formyl group*

```
    O
   //
—C
   \
    H
```

also represented by —CHO. Some sugars such as glucose (the common sugar found in the bloodstream of man) are aldehydes. An important metabolic intermediate is acetaldehyde (see page 350).

```
     H
     |    O
     |  //
H—C—C
     |    \
     H     H
```

KETONES When the hydrogen atom of the formyl group of an aldehyde is replaced by some other organic group such as $—CH_3$, the aldehyde becomes a ketone. Ketones are characterized by the configuration

```
    O
   //
—C—R
```

in which R represents the variable group which may replace the H. In the case of acetone, R is a methyl group,

```
   H  O  H
   |  ‖  |
H—C—C—C—H
   |     |
   H     H
```

The sugar fructose is a ketone, and other ketones appear as metabolic intermediates in the breakdown of fat.

ESTERS Replacement of the hydrogen atom of a carboxyl group by some other organic group converts a carboxylic acid into an ester with the configuration

```
    O
   //
—C—O—R
```

as seen in the formula for methyl acetate

```
   H  O     H
   |  ‖     |
H—C—C—O—C—H
   |        |
   H        H
```

Some esters produced by plants have fruity or flowery odors, which attract hungry animals and thus assist the processes of pollination and seed dispersal. Tricarboxylic fats such as ordinary body fat are esters formed when three molecules of fatty acids are bonded through their carboxyl groups to one molecule of glycerol.

The following formulas exemplify the relationship of alcohols, aldehydes, carboxylic acids, ketones and esters:

```
   H  H
   |  |
H—C—C—OH
   |  |
   H  H
Ethanol (an alcohol)
   |
   | −2H
   ↓
   H                              H  O  H
   |   O           −H             |  ‖  |
   |  //       ---------→     H—C—C—C—H
H—C—C    <    +CH3            |     |
   |   \                          H     H
   H    H                     Acetone (a ketone)
Acetaldehyde
                                   H
                                   |   O
                  ---------→       |  //
                     +O        H—C—C
                                   |   \
                                   H    OH
                               Acetic acid
                                   |
                               −H  | +CH3
                                   ↓
                                H  O     H
                                |  ‖     |
                             H—C—C—O—C—H
                                |        |
                                H        H
                          Methyl acetate (an ester)
```

AMINES Amines are organic compounds containing the functional group $—NH_2$, an *amino group.* If ethanol, shown above, were to be *aminated,* the resultant compound would be ethylamine,

```
   H  H
   |  |
H—C—C—NH2
   |  |
   H  H
```

The transferral of an amino group from one molecule to another is termed *transamination:* the *deamination* of the first is coupled with amination of the second. Most amines are intermediary compounds produced during the breakdown of amino acids, and may by deamination be converted into other small molecules which may be further degraded. However there are certain aromatic (ring-shaped) amines that are used as building blocks in a number of important larger molecules. One such aromatic amine is the *pyrrole* ring,

```
H—C———C—H
   ‖       ‖
H—C       C—H
    \     /
      N
      |
      H
```

which is especially important as a constituent of *tetrapyrroles,* rings consisting of four pyrroles centered upon one metallic atom. Three biotically essential molecules which include tetrapyrrole rings are cytochrome, hemoglobin, and chlorophyll (Figure 9.4), the functions of which will be discussed further in Chapters 13 and 14.

AMINO ACIDS A carboxylic acid which also bears an amino group is known as an amino acid. As we have said, amino acids are the molecular units from which protein molecules are constructed. Accordingly they are of cardinal importance to the biotic world. They are produced primarily in plant cells by the amination of carboxylic acids, and are used in the manufacture of plant proteins. When plant proteins are ingested by animals, the individual amino acids are set free during digestion, but are shortly recombined (polymerized) within the tissues to produce the needed animal proteins. Since they can be made up of about 20 different kinds of amino acids occurring in various proportions and ar-

Carbon atoms

Hydrogen atoms

Nitrogen atoms

Oxygen atoms

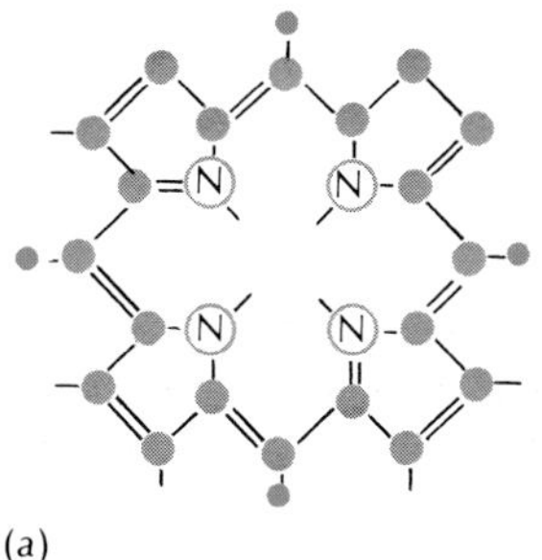

(a)

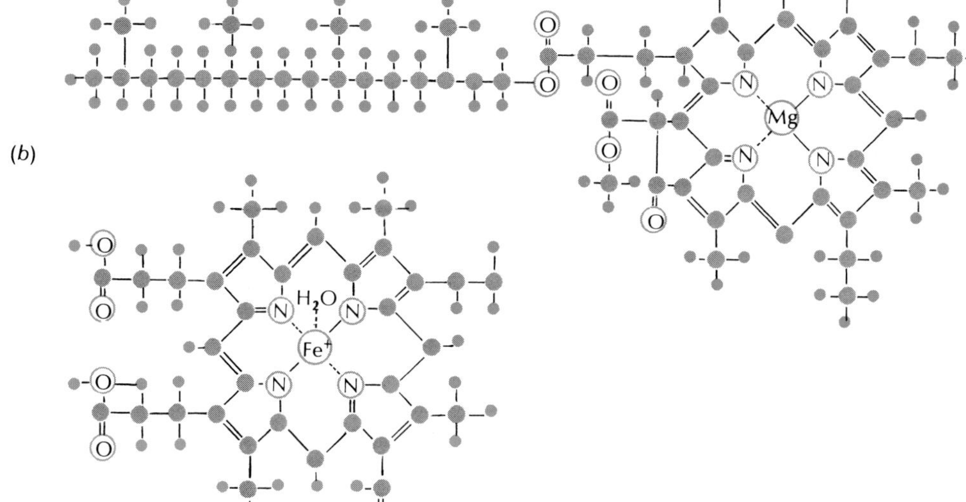

(b)

(c)

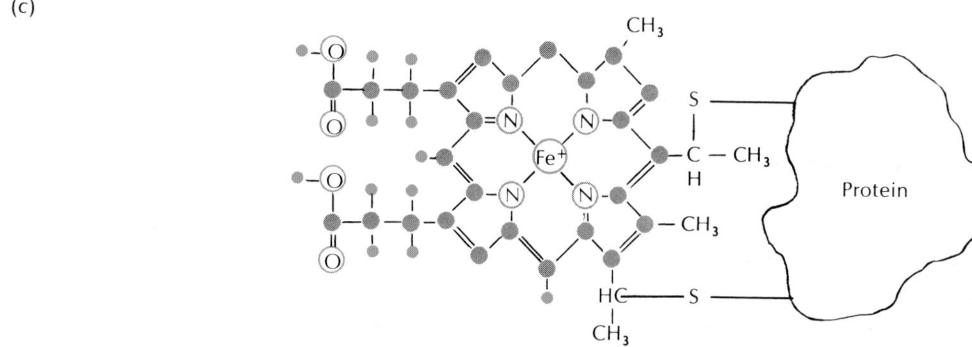

(d)

Figure 9.4 □ Important tetrapyrrole compounds. Tetrapyrroles occur universally in living matter. The basic ring (*a*) is made up of four individual pyrrole units, rings containing four carbon atoms and one nitrogen atom apiece. (*b*) Chlorophyll a, the most widely occurring form of chlorophyll, consists of a hydrocarbon side chain bonded to a tetrapyrrole centered on a magnesium atom; this molecule functions in the trapping of radiant energy for photosynthesis. (*c*) Heme, the oxygen-carrying group of hemoglobin and myoglobin, is a tetrapyrrole centered on an iron atom; the rest of the hemoglobin or myoglobin molecule is protein. (*d*) Cytochrome, an electron-carrier involved in transfer of energy and building of ATP.

rangements, the potential variety of proteins is almost unlimited.

All amino acids share this formula:

$$H_2N-\underset{|}{\overset{\overset{\displaystyle H}{|}}{C}}-COOH$$

The carbon atom which bears both of the functional groups is designated the alpha-carbon (α-C). The unoccupied bond of the α-C in the above formula represents a covalent bond to any one of the alternative sidechains shown in Table 9.2. Two other units that enter into the construction of proteins are the *imino* acids proline and hydroxyproline, also shown in Table 9.2. Imino acids contain the configuration

$$-\overset{|}{N}-H$$

In the prolines the side chain is bonded to the imino group to form a ring. Proline rings are so bulky that the protein molecule may be bent at points where these occur. This effect on the shape of a protein molecule may determine its performance in the living body.

The linking of amino acids into chains involves the covalent bonding of the N of the amino group of one amino acid with the C of the carboxyl group of the next:

$$H_2N-\underset{H}{C}-\overset{O}{\overset{\|}{C}}-OH \quad H-\overset{H}{N}-\overset{H}{C}-COOH \;\longrightarrow\; H_2O$$

Since this reaction involves the elimination of one molecule of water for each bond established, it is called *dehydration synthesis.* In this case dehydration synthesis

Table 9.2 □ Amino and imino acids commonly found in proteins

NAME AND ABBREVIATION (AND BASIC STRUCTURE)	SIDE CHAIN (R—)
Amino acids $\left(R-\overset{NH_2}{C}-H,\ COOH\right)$	
Glycine (gly)	H—
Alanine (ala)	H_3C-
Serine (ser)	$HO-CH_2-$
Phenylalanine (phe)	$C_6H_5-CH_2-$
Tyrosine (tyr)	$HO-C_6H_4-CH_2-$
Tryptophan (try)	$C_8H_6N-CH_2-$
Histidine (his)	$C_3H_3N_2-CH_2-$
Amino acids (continued)	
Valine (val)	$(CH_3)_2CH-$
Arginine (arg)	$H-NH-C(=NH)-NH-CH_2-CH_2-CH_2-$
Lysine (lys)	$H_2N-CH_2-CH_2-CH_2-CH_2-$
Aspartic acid (asp)	$HO(O)C-CH_2-$
Glutamic acid (glu)	$HO(O)C-CH_2-CH_2-$
Glutamine (gluN)	$H_2N(O)C-CH_2-CH_2-$
Leucine (leu)	$(CH_3)_2CH-CH_2-$
Amino acids (continued)	
Isoleucine (ileu)	$CH_3-CH_2-CH(CH_3)-$
Threonine (thr)	$CH_3-CH(OH)-$
Cysteine (cys)	$H-S-CH_2-$
Methionine (met)	$CH_3-S-CH_2-CH_2-$
Imino acids $\left(R\text{–}\overset{NH}{C}-H,\ COOH\right)$	
Proline (pro)	$-CH_2-CH_2-CH_2-$
Hydroxyproline (hpro)	$-CH_2-CH(OH)-CH_2-$

results in a *carboxyamino* linkage. Four such linkages produce a short *peptide* chain:

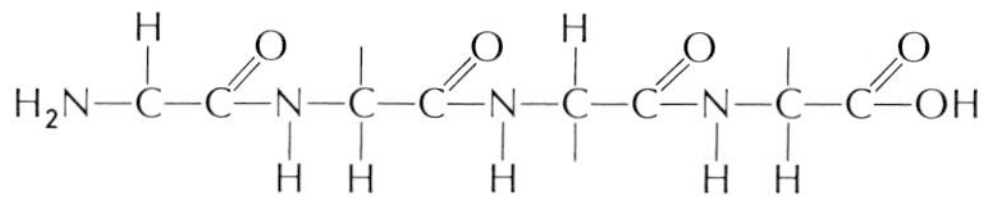

The characteristics of the side chains of the amino acids determine the properties of the peptide chain; therefore it is essential that the sequence of amino acids in the chain be nonrandom. This requires that when a protein molecule is synthesized, the amino acid units be assembled according to some fixed pattern or template on which the chain is built. The nature of this template will be discussed later (Section 9.7D).

NITROGENOUS BASES *Heterocyclic* compounds (that is, ring compounds con-

Figure 9.5 □ Nitrogenous bases and nucleotides: (*a*) important pyrimidines, (*b*) important purines. Note that the side groups on the sixth carbon atom determine how bases can pair during nucleic acid replication: a 6-oxypurine must bond with a 6-aminopyrimidine, and a 6-aminopurine with a 6-oxypyrimidine. (*c*) Important free nucleotides. These compounds are involved in energy transfer and other essential aspects of metabolism. The most versatile of these is ATP (adenosine triphosphate), which upon loss of one phosphate group becomes ADP (adenosine diphosphate) or by the loss of two phosphate groups becomes AMP (adenosine monophosphate).

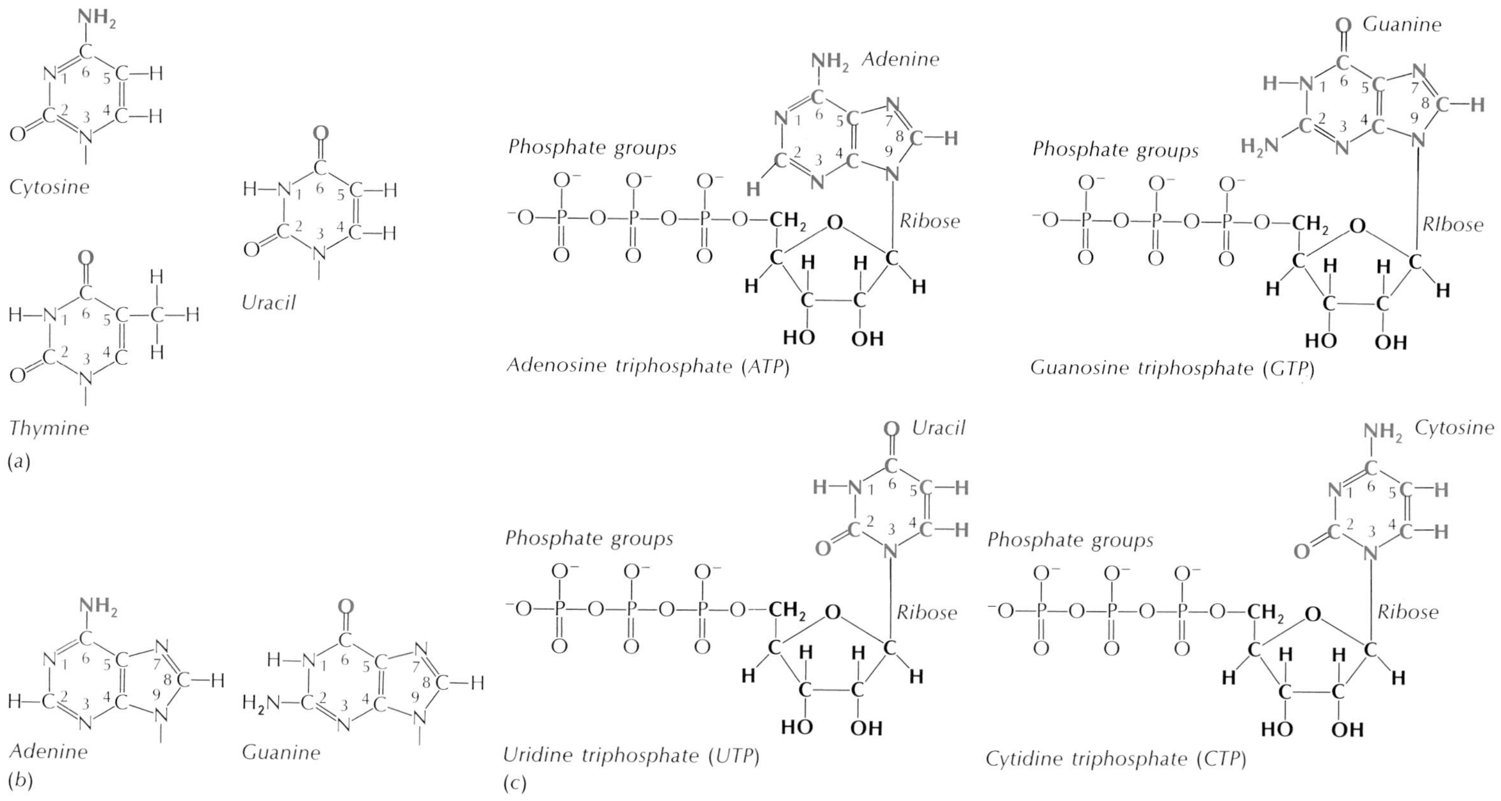

Cytosine

Uracil

Thymine

(*a*)

Adenine

Guanine

(*b*)

Phosphate groups — *Adenine* — *Ribose*

Adenosine triphosphate (ATP)

Phosphate groups — *Guanine* — *Ribose*

Guanosine triphosphate (GTP)

Phosphate groups — *Uracil* — *Ribose*

Uridine triphosphate (UTP)

(*c*)

Phosphate groups — *Cytosine* — *Ribose*

Cytidine triphosphate (CTP)

taining atoms other than C in the ring skeleton) known as purines and pyrimidines (*nitrogenous bases*) are essential to life as components of nucleic acids and certain compounds significant in energy transfer, such as adenosine triphosphate (ATP). A pyrimidine ring contains four carbon and two nitrogen atoms, whereas a purine is a double-ring molecule:*

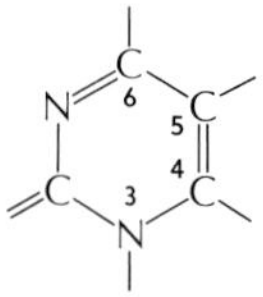

Pyrimidine

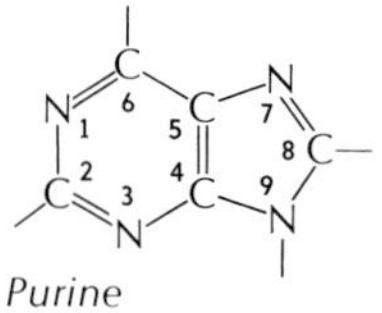

Purine

*For convenient comparison to the purine ring, geneticists and other biologists number the atoms in the pyrimidine ring from 1 to 6 in the same order that the atoms are numbered in the purine ring. This allows side groups occupying equivalent positions on the two kinds of rings to be readily compared, as is necessary when discussing hydrogen bonding between bases in the case of nucleic acids. Chemists adopt a convention for naming compounds that requires the atoms in the pyrimidine ring to be numbered in reverse sequence to the numbering of atoms in the purine ring. Thus, the chemical name of cytosine is 2-oxy-4-aminopyrimidine; uracil is 2,4-dioxypyrimidine; thymine is 5-methyl-2,4-dioxypyrimidine. However, in the interests of conformity to accepted biological usage, we shall use the biological rather than the chemical names for these compounds and shall number the atoms in parallel so that, for instance, the number-6 carbon in the purine ring is also numbered 6 on the pyrimidine ring.

Specific purines and pyrimidines are differentiated by the particular functional groups attached to two or three of the C atoms in the ring. Three pyrimidines important as constituents of nucleic acids and free nucleotides are *cytosine, uracil,* and *thymine* (Figure 9.5*a*). Two purines that are regular constituents of nucleic acids and free nucleotides are *adenine* and *guanine* (Figure 9.5*b*).

NUCLEOTIDES When a purine or a pyrimidine is covalently bonded to a small carbohydrate molecule [either the pentose (5-carbon sugar) *ribose,* or the pentose *deoxyribose*] and this in turn is linked to one or more *phosphate* groups,

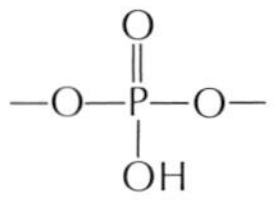

a molecular unit known as *nucleotide* is formed. Nucleotides are important individually as agents of energy transfer in metabolism; furthermore they are the units from which are assembled giant polymeric molecules—the nucleic acids—that govern heredity.

One of the most ubiquitous nucleotides involved in energy transfer during metabolism is adenosine triphosphate [ATP (Figure 9.5c)], a molecule composed of the purine adenine, the sugar ribose, and three phosphate groups. Energy is transferred to reacting molecules when ATP is dephosphorylated by the loss of one or two phosphate groups, becoming adenosine diphosphate (ADP) or adenosine monophosphate (AMP). The energy-bearing phosphate group is passed to another molecule that is thereby made more reactive (this will be considered further in Chapter 13); ATP is then regenerated by means of some other energy-releasing metabolic process such as cell respiration (see Section 14.3C).

Another adenine-containing nucleotide involved in energy transfer is *nicotinamide adenine dinucleotide* (NAD), which upon phosphorylation becomes *nicotinamide adenine dinucleotide phosphate* (NADP).† The metabolic roles of NAD and NADP will be taken up in Chapters 13 and 14, but examining their structural formulas at this time will show that the vitamin nicotinamide (an amine form of niacin, which was pictured above in the text) forms part of these nucleotide molecules (Figure 9.6).

Other nucleotides that play specific roles in cell function include uridine triphosphate (UTP) containing the base uracil, cytidine triphosphate (CTP) containing cytosine, and guanosine triphosphate (GTP) containing guanine. The adaptive value of having such a variety of compounds involved in energy transfer is that they serve like coins of different denomination: each can transfer a somewhat different quantity of energy to a reaction, and for each reaction the compound involved in transferring this energy is the one that most closely gives the "right change," thereby wasting little energy. In addition to their roles in energy transfer, uridine nucleotides serve as carriers of simple sugar molecules during the construction of large carbohydrate molecules such as starch, while CTP serves as a carrier of nitrogenous bases during phospholipid synthesis.

†In the older literature NAD is sometimes seen as diphosphopyridine nucleotide (DPN) and NADP is known as triphosphopyridine nucleotide (TPN).

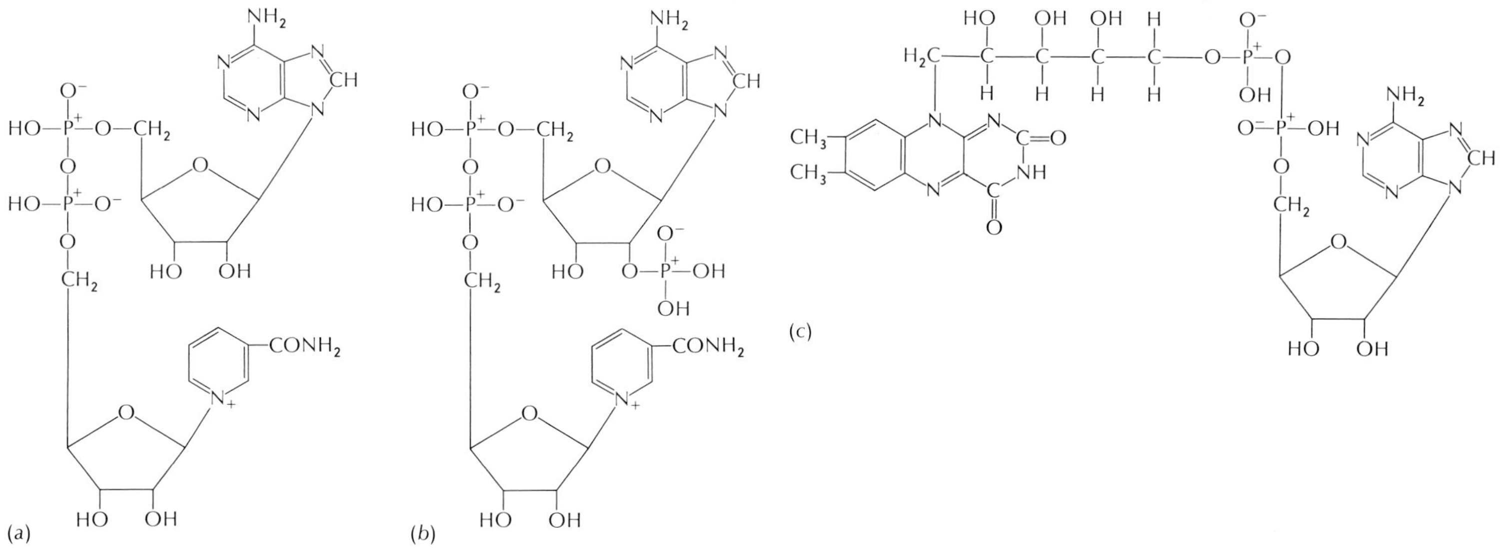

Figure 9.6 □ Nucleotides used as coenzymes in hydrogen-transfer reactions: (*a*) nicotinamide adenine dinucleotide (NAD^+); (*b*) nicotinamide adenine dinucleotide phosphate ($NADP^+$); (*c*) flavin adenine dinucleotide (FAD). Each of these coenzymes contains a B vitamin: (*a*) and (*b*) contain a form of niacin (nicotinamide), and (*c*) contains riboflavin.

Nucleotides behave like acids because (as shown in Figure 9.5c) their phosphate groups can give up H^+, leaving the rest of the molecule negatively charged. This affects the properties both of free nucleotides and of the nucleic acids built up by the linear polymerization of individual nucleotides. The two important nucleic acids are *ribonucleic acid* (RNA) which is composed of the *ribose* nucleotides of the purines adenine and guanine and the pyrimidines cytosine and uracil, and *deoxyribonucleic acid,* made up of the *deoxyribose* nucleotides of the bases adenine, guanine, cytosine and thymine (see Figure 9.18). The properties and functions of nucleic acids will be taken up in Section 9.7.

9.4 □ CARBOHYDRATES

Carbohydrates include sugars, starches, gums, and many other compounds of biotic significance. They range in molecular size from trioses ($C_3H_6O_3$) of low molecular weight to giant polysaccharide macromolecules with a molecular weight of several million. Despite this tremendous range in size, all carbohydrates basically consist of units in which carbon, hydrogen, and oxygen atoms are usually present in the proportions C : 2H : O. Monosaccharides are the simplest carbohydrates, and all larger carbohydrate molecules are merely linked chains constructed of repeated monosaccharide units.

A Monosaccharides

These *simple sugars* are mainly manufactured by plant cells during photosynthesis. Their molecular bonding energy is ultimately that obtained by trapping radiant energy from the abiotic environment. Oxidation of sugar releases this energy, which may then be used in carrying out cell work. Monosaccharides can also be transformed into building blocks for other types of organic molecules: they can be converted into amino acids, nitrogenous bases, carboxylic acids, and so forth.

Monosaccharides are classified according to the number of carbon atoms present in the molecule: *trioses* have three carbon atoms, *pentoses* five, *hexoses* six, and so forth. Of especial importance are the pentoses *ribose* ($C_5H_{10}O_5$) and *deoxyribose* ($C_5H_{10}O_4$), which as we have seen are constituents of nucleotides. Hexoses are the most common monomers out of which large storage and structural polysaccharide molecules are built. They include such sugars as *glucose, fructose,* and *galactose,* structural isomers with the same empirical formula, $C_6H_{12}O_6$ (Figure 9.7a). These hexoses can exist either in straight-chain form or as ring-shaped molecules, usually assuming the ring form when polymerized. In their straight-chain form glucose and galactose are aldehydes, terminating in the group

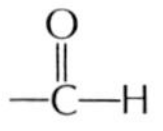

$$-\overset{\displaystyle O}{\overset{\|}{C}}-H$$

while fructose is a ketone, containing subterminally the configuration on page 358:

Figure 9.7 □ Carbohydrates. (*a*) Hexose monosaccharides, shown in straight-chain form: at left, galactose; center, glucose; right, fructose. (*b*) α and β isomers of glucose; a chain made up of the former units is easily digested by animal enzymes, whereas a chain made up of the latter units (such as cellulose) is impossible for most animals to digest. (*c*) Glucose units shown as monomers in a polysaccharide chain; note that the glucose must assume its ring form to be polymerized. (*d*) A portion of the molecule of the polysaccharide glycogen, showing highly branching chains of glucose molecules.

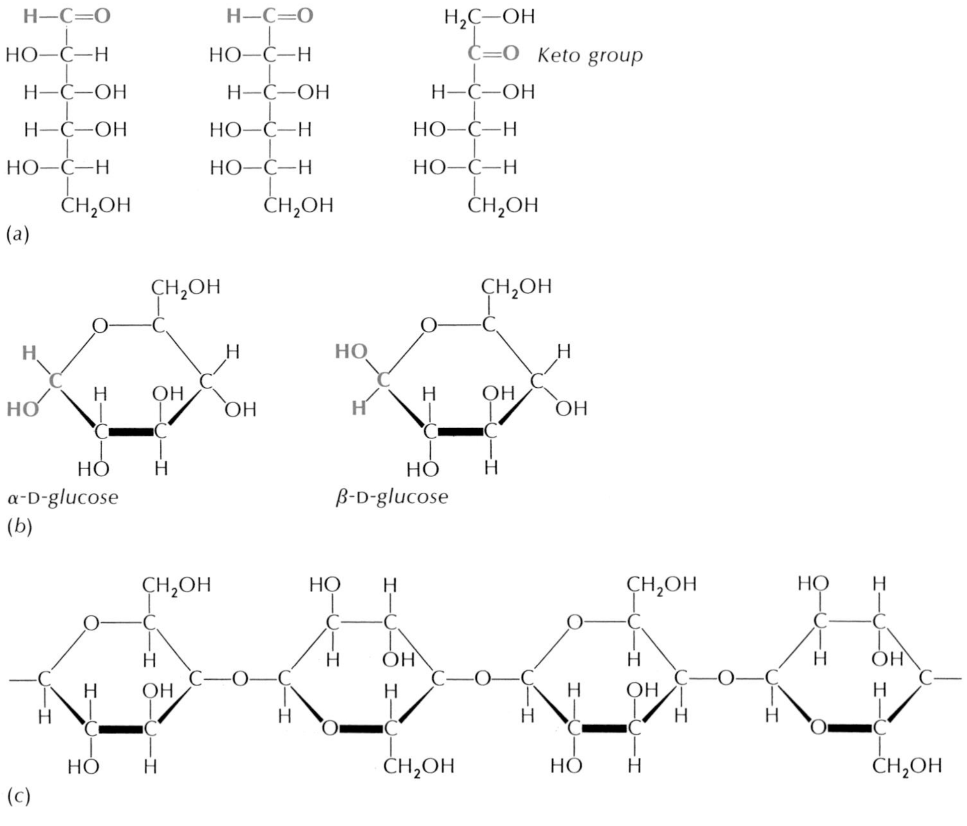

Keto group

(*a*)

α-D-glucose

β-D-glucose

(*b*)

(c)

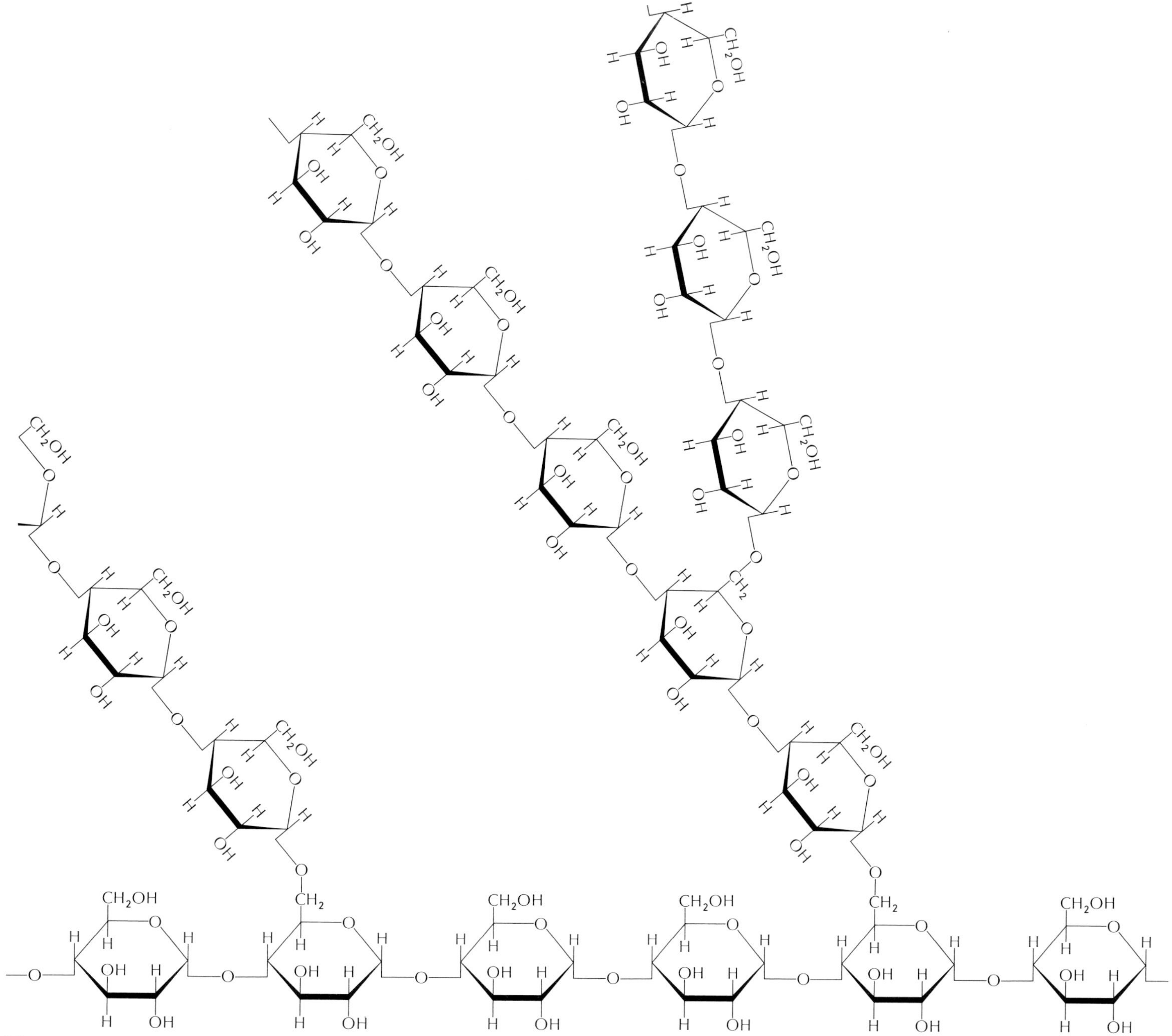

(*d*)

$$\overset{O}{\underset{}{\overset{\|}{—C—}}}$$

Glucose appears to be exceptionally capable of polymerization, and is the major hexose occurring in the animal body. Glucose can exist in a number of isomeric states, two of the most important of which are the geometrical isomers shown in Figure 9.7*b*. The difference between α-D-glucose and β-D-glucose may appear slight, but whereas starch, a polysaccharide constructed of α-D-glucose units, is readily digested by animals, cellulose, a polymer of β-D-glucose, is generally indigestible. In cellulose the spatial relations of the bonds linking individual glucose units are such that animal digestive enzymes cannot attack these bonds.

B Oligosaccharides

Oligosaccharides are built up of two or a few monosaccharide units by dehydration synthesis. Important *disaccharides* ($C_{12}H_{22}O_{11}$) include *sucrose* (cane sugar), *maltose* (malt sugar), and *lactose* (milk sugar). Each disaccharide molecule is built by the covalent bonding of two monosaccharides with the elimination of one molecule of water:

$$C_6H_{12}O_6 + C_6H_{12}O_6 \xrightarrow{\text{Enzyme}} C_{12}H_{22}O_{11} + H_2O$$

Disaccharides serve mainly as a soluble storage form of sugar constituting a reservoir of quickly available energy. They pass through cell membranes less readily than monosaccharides do and consequently can be stored within the large vacuoles occurring in plant cells.

Sucrose, of wide occurrence in fruits and sap, is made up of one glucose and one fructose molecule. Maltose (malt sugar) consists of two glucose molecules, and is obtained from grains and by the partial digestion of starch. Lactose (milk sugar), a disaccharide consisting of glucose and galactose, is widely distributed throughout the animal kingdom, but it takes its common name from its high concentration in mammalian milk.

C Polysaccharides

These high-molecular-weight carbohydrates are polymers made up of many simple sugar units, most commonly hexoses (Figure 9.7*c*). They are built up by dehydration synthesis:

$$n(C_6H_{12}O_6) \xrightarrow{\text{Enzyme}} (C_6H_{10}O_5)_n + n(H_2O)$$

According to their biotic use, polysaccharides may be classified as (1) *storage* molecules and (2) *structural* components.

STORAGE CARBOHYDRATES The polysaccharides *amylose, amylopectin,* and *glycogen* are important as relatively inert storage molecules that do not tend to diffuse out of the cells in which they are found to be stored.

Starch is a mixture of amylose and amylopectin, and is abundant in fruits, seeds, and tubers, where it is stored as intracellular granules. Amylose (*soluble* starch) is a water-soluble polymer of α-D-glucose—a simple, unbranched chain of variable length containing from about 300 to over 1,200 glucose units and therefore ranging from molecular weight 50,000 to 200,000. Starch granules contain up to 90 percent amylopectin, or *insoluble* starch. This too is a polymer of α-D-glucose, but differs from amylose in being a much-branched molecule of 70,000 to 1,000,000 molecular weight and sometimes containing more than 60,000 glucose units. Glycogen (Figure 9.7*d*) is the major storage form of carbohydrate in *animals.* It is a water-soluble polymer of α-D-glucose and resembles amylopectin except that glycogen is still larger, but more finely branched, with shorter, more numerous chains. The adaptive significance of this branching is that enzymes can attack a branched polysaccharide molecule starting from the free end of every branch. Accordingly, the more branched the macromolecule, the more rapidly it can be broken down. The rapid degradability of glycogen makes this compound of especial value to animals, which, being more active than plants, must mobilize their energy reserves more rapidly. In the vertebrate body the highest glycogen concentrations occur in the liver and muscles. Liver glycogen has a molecular weight of 5×10^6, and muscle glycogen a molecular weight of 1×10^6. When muscle glycogen is depleted in the course of exercise, it is quickly replenished by blood glucose, which in turn is replenished by glucose released from the liver by the breakdown of liver glycogen.

STRUCTURAL POLYSACCHARIDES The structural use of polysaccharides is common to both plants and animals. Such polysaccharides are ordinarily highly insoluble long-chain polymers. Perhaps the best known is *cellulose,* of which the rigid supportive walls around the cells of most plants are formed; it rarely occurs in animals. Cellulose molecules are unbranched chains of

Figure 9.8 □ **Animal structural polysaccharides. (*a*) Amino sugars: above, galactosamine, a monomer of chitin and hyaluronic acid; below, glucosamine, a monomer (with glucuronic acid) of chondroitin sulfate. (*b*) Glucuronic acid, a sugar acid, a constituent of hyaluronic acid and chondroitin sulfate in animals and pectin in plants. These substances form intercellular cement. (*c*) Portion of chitin molecule, used in arthropod exoskeletons. (*d*) Cicada and its molted exoskeleton. The chitinous exuvium retains the insect's entire form and still grasps a branch with clawed feet. (*Los Angeles County Museum of Natural History.*)**

(*a*)

(*b*)

(*c*)

(*d*)

β-D-glucose, the molecular weight of which is ±300,000. Herbivorous animals must break down the cell walls of plant tissue by thorough chewing, to gain access to the digestible materials within. A portion of the masticated cellulose can then be digested by microorganisms living within their alimentary tract, notably the rumen protozoa and bacteria of cattle and other cud-chewing (ruminant) mammals. The complete nutritional dependence of termites on their cellulose-digesting protozoan symbionts has already been noted. Cattle too can starve with stomachs full of hay, if their rumen bacteria have been chemically destroyed.

The tough structural material of oat hulls and corn cobs consists of polysaccharides known as *pentosans,* which are chains of pentose sugars. Plant *gums,* and the well-known seaweed extract, *agar,* are polymers of galactose rather than those of glucose.

Three polysaccharides that are structurally important in the animal world are *chitin, hyaluronic acid,* and *chondroitin sulfate,* the monomers of which are shown in Figure 9.8. Hyaluronic acid (together with some chondroitin sulfate) forms the *intercellular* cement which binds together the cells of animal tissues. It is an unbranched heteropolymer composed of two kinds of monomers: (1) *glucuronic acid,* a derivative of glucose, and (2) *glucosamine,* an amino sugar, or hexose in which one —OH group is replaced by an amino (—NH_2) group. Chondroitin sulfate is an important constituent of *connective tissue.* It is made up of alternating units of glucuronic acid and an amino sugar, *galactosamine.*

Chitin is a polymer of the amino sugar

glucosamine. It forms the exoskeleton of arthropods (Figure 9.8*d*), the bristles and jaws of annelids, and occurs sporadically in other phyla. It can be digested by only a few organisms, notably several species of bacteria, without which even the vast reservoir of atmospheric nitrogen would be depleted by massive arthropod incorporation of nitrogen. If these bacteria were destroyed it is likely that life on earth would shortly become extinct, when no more nitrogen remained available for plant growth.

D Conjugated carbohydrates

A monosaccharide may be conjugated with a lipid molecule to form a *glycolipid,* or with a protein to form a *glycoprotein.* Glycolipids will be discussed in the next section. Glycoproteins occur in vertebrate bones and tendons. Conjugation of glucosamine with a protein produces the glycoprotein *mucin,* a component of mucus, the slimy secretion of epidermal, salivary, and intestinal glands. Mucus serves not only to lubricate food for swallowing, but may also be exuded to serve as "mucus traps" for entangling prey or as a glue in binding materials for tubes and nests (such as those of paper wasps). Three hormones secreted by the vertebrate pituitary gland (follicle-stimulating hormone, luteinizing hormone, and thyrotrophin) are also found to be glycoproteins.

9.5 ☐ LIPIDS

Lipids constitute a rather heterogeneous variety of compounds that are relatively insoluble in water but are soluble in "fat solvents" such as ether and carbon tetrachloride. The most important classes of lipids are *triglycerides* (fats and oils), *phospholipids, waxes,* and *steroids.* They may also be conjugated with nonlipid molecules, forming *glycolipids, lipoproteins,* and *proteolipids.* Their biotic uses are as diverse as their molecular structure, and so the physiological and structural significance of each major group will be taken up separately.

A Triglycerides

Fats and oils stored within the cells provide an extensive reservoir of potential energy for both animals and plants. Aside from the fact that oils are liquid at room temperature whereas fats are solid, the two are chemically similar. Fats and oils are triglycerides, esters formed by the bonding of three fatty acid molecules to one molecule of the alcohol glycerol. As we saw earlier, fatty acids consist of two main parts: (1) a carbon chain, from 3 to 25 carbon atoms in length; (2) a terminal carboxyl (—COOH) group. The carbon chain is *hydrophobic* ("water-hating"), whereas the carboxyl group is *hydrophilic* ("water-loving"). This property causes fatty acid molecules to spread out into a thin uniform layer on the surface of water, and is important to the capacity of various lipids to contribute to the formation of cellular membranes.

The three fatty acids that enter into a given triglyceride molecule may be alike or different. A large number of different fatty acids exist, and since these can form many combinations, there are a great many specific kinds of fats and oils. Even a single organism can store different kinds of fat. "Brown fat," for instance, is concentrated under the skin of the back in infant mammals and serves as a particularly important source of energy for generating body heat. Some triglycerides are unique to individual species, so that "lamb fat," for instance, is distinct from the human fat into which it may be metabolized. Triglycerides are synthesized as follows:

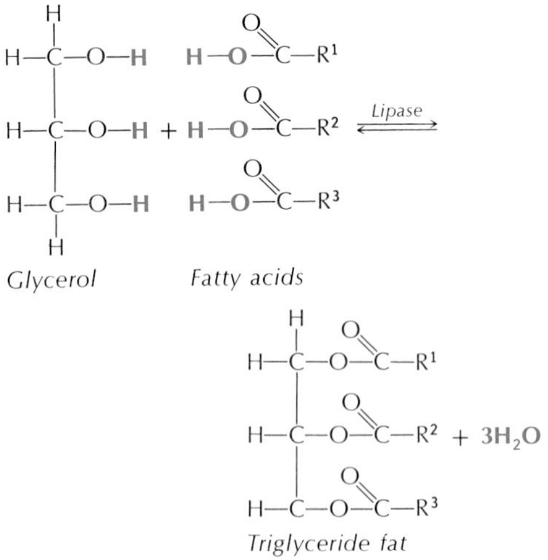

$$
\begin{array}{c}
\mathrm{H} \\
| \\
\mathrm{H{-}C{-}O{-}H} \\
| \\
\mathrm{H{-}C{-}O{-}H} \\
| \\
\mathrm{H{-}C{-}O{-}H} \\
| \\
\mathrm{H} \\
\textit{Glycerol}
\end{array}
\; + \;
\begin{array}{c}
\mathrm{H{-}O{-}\overset{\overset{\displaystyle O}{\|}}{C}{-}R^1} \\
\\
\mathrm{H{-}O{-}\overset{\overset{\displaystyle O}{\|}}{C}{-}R^2} \\
\\
\mathrm{H{-}O{-}\overset{\overset{\displaystyle O}{\|}}{C}{-}R^3} \\
\textit{Fatty acids}
\end{array}
\;\overset{\textit{Lipase}}{\rightleftharpoons}\;
\begin{array}{c}
\mathrm{H} \\
| \\
\mathrm{H{-}C{-}O{-}\overset{\overset{\displaystyle O}{\|}}{C}{-}R^1} \\
| \\
\mathrm{H{-}C{-}O{-}\overset{\overset{\displaystyle O}{\|}}{C}{-}R^2} \\
| \\
\mathrm{H{-}C{-}O{-}\overset{\overset{\displaystyle O}{\|}}{C}{-}R^3} \\
\textit{Triglyceride fat}
\end{array}
\; + \; 3H_2O
$$

The reaction by which the fat molecule is formed is a *dehydration synthesis,* for one molecule of water is liberated for each covalent bond formed. The breakdown of the fat molecule into fatty acids and glycerol is known as *hydrolysis* because a water molecule is used for each bond broken. Besides constituting a reservoir of potential energy, subcutaneous fat deposits help to conserve body heat, while pads of adipose tissue around the viscera (internal organs) help to protect them from injury.

B Phospholipids

Phospholipids are concerned in the formation of membranes around and within cells (see Figure 14.6), and in the structural framework of such cellular components as mitochondria and chloroplasts. Specific phospholipids are found in especially high concentrations in vertebrate brain and nerve tissue, where they occur both within the cells and in the fatty sheaths that cover many nerve fibers (see Figure 11.41*d*).

A phospholipid is usually a *diglyceride* (a lipid composed of *two* fatty acid molecules united by dehydration synthesis with a glycerol molecule), which is also bonded to a phosphoric acid molecule that in turn is linked to any one of several possible small water-soluble organic molecules:

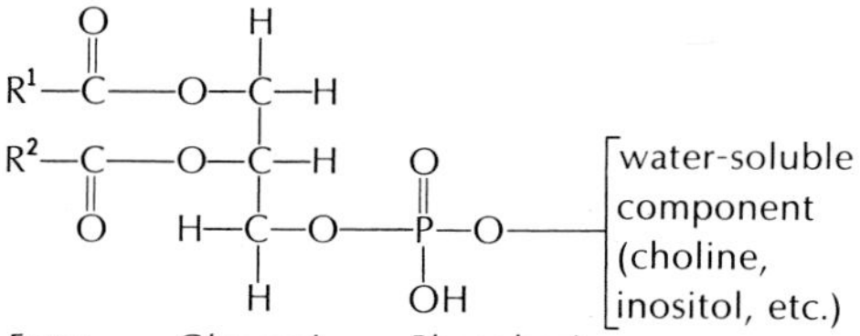

```
       O         H
       ‖         |
R¹—C——O—C—H
                 |
R²—C——O—C—H      O              ⎡water-soluble
       ‖         |          ‖              ⎢component
       O      H—C—O——P—O——⎢(choline,
                 |          |              ⎣inositol, etc.)
                 H          OH
Fatty       Glycerol    Phosphoric
acids                   acid
```

The carbon chains of the two fatty acids often lie parallel so that the phospholipid molecule is two-legged, with hydrophobic "legs" and a hydrophilic "head." In the case of the common phospholipid *lecithin* (found in vertebrate eggs, liver, and blood plasma), the molecule bonded to the phosphoric acid is *choline:*

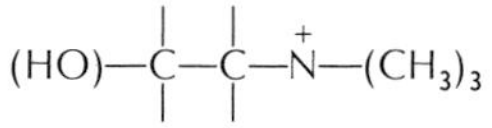

$$(HO)—\overset{|}{\underset{|}{C}}—\overset{|}{\underset{|}{C}}—\overset{+}{N}—(CH_3)_3$$

C Waxes

Waxes are produced by both plants and animals. They are esters formed by the bonding of fatty acids with a high molecular weight alcohol. Plant waxes form the cuticle that protects leaves from excessive water loss. Two waxes formed by sperm whales are *sperm oil* (long used by man as a high-quality lubricant) and *spermaceti* (used in candles). *Wool wax* is a component of lanolin (sheep fat). *Bees' wax,* secreted by the wax glands of honeybees, is the substance from which they construct the honeycomb. In vertebrates, a wax formed by the bonding of the steroid cholesterol with palmitic acid is carried in suspension in the blood plasma. Though apparently a normal product of the body's metabolism, cholesterol palmitate may be involved in the deposition of fatty plaques in the arterial walls, leading to arteriosclerosis (hardening of the arteries).

D Steroids

Steroids are compounds that are characterized by a structure of four connected carbon rings (designated *A, B, C,* and *D*) constituting a "steroid nucleus" (Figure 9.9*a*). Different side groups may be attached, and in a variety of steroids specific bonds within the individual rings may be double bonds.

Cholesterol (Figure 9.9*b*) is a steroid alcohol (sterol) of widespread occurrence in animal cells, although lacking in many echinoderms. It is probably used in the synthesis of a number of other essential steroids including cholic acid, vitamin D, and the steroid hormones. In vertebrates, salts of cholic acid form part of the bile that is secreted by the liver into the small intestine. These salts assist fat digestion by emulsifying the fat (coating the fat droplets so that they cannot coalesce on contact), and they also facilitate the absorption of fatty acids through the lining of the intestine.

The *steroid hormones* of vertebrates include male and female sex hormones (see Figure 17.28), and hormones of the adrenal cortex. The sex hormones control sexual maturation, behavior, and reproductive capacity. Adrenocortical hormones (Figure 15.53) regulate carbohydrate metabolism, and control the retention and excretion of Na^+ and K^+. Certain invertebrate hormones are also steroids, notably the ecdysones (molting hormones of arthropods).

E Conjugated lipids

Glycolipids consist of a hexose (usually galactose) and a long-chain fatty acid, both of which are combined with a nitrogenous base. Their metabolic significance is as yet poorly understood, but they are of wide

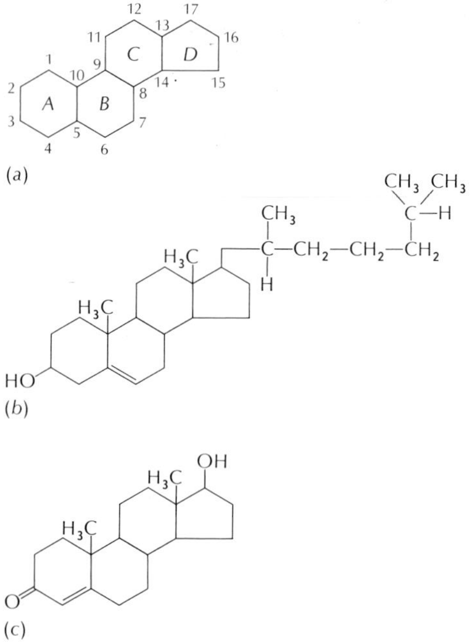

Figure 9.9 □ Steroids. (*a*) **Steroid nucleus;** (*b*) **cholesterol;** (*c*) **testosterone, a steroid hormone (compare with others shown in Figure 17.28).**

distribution, particularly in nervous tissue (hence their alternative name, *cerebrosides*).

Lipoproteins consist of lipids conjugated with proteins. The phospholipids in cell membranes and organelles are typically conjugated with proteins to form lipoproteins.

9.6 □ PROTEINS

Proteins are giant molecules that display an incredible functional versatility, which is a product of their nearly infinite structural variability. Their molecular weights generally range from 10^4 to 10^7. *Simple* proteins are those which consist only of polypeptide chains of amino and imino acids; *conjugated* proteins have one or more polypeptide chains bonded to such other units as carbohydrates, tetrapyrroles, or lipids. A simple protein can contain some 20 possible kinds of amino and imino acids, all combined by carboxyamino linkages, but differing from one another with respect to their side chains (Table 9.2). Not all 20 types of monomers are necessarily found in any single protein. In order to give some idea of the potential variability of proteins, if a particular protein contained 100 amino acids of only *ten* kinds, the number of possible linear arrangements of these 100 units would be 10^{100}! However, only a small proportion of the chemically possible protein molecules are actually significant to life. Each living thing produces several thousand kinds of proteins, a number of which are unique to that particular species. Because of this it is possible for a criminologist to determine if a drop of blood has come from man or from some nonhuman species, and also whether the blood has come from some particular individual.

A Characteristics of enzymes

Many proteins function as catalysts in facilitating biochemical reactions. Without these enzymes reactions could not take place rapidly enough at ordinary body temperatures to sustain life. Most organic reactions are inherently too slow to take place at rates compatible with life unless they are accelerated either by heat or by adding a catalyst. As a general rule raising the temperature 10°C doubles the rate of an uncatalyzed reaction, but living systems usually cannot operate at temperatures exceeding 65°C and therefore must rely on organic catalysts.

Certain generalizations may be made concerning enzymatic activity:

1 Enzymes probably form temporary combinations with the reacting molecules (*substrates*), holding them in particular positions which will facilitate the reaction; by so doing, they *decrease the amount of energy needed to initiate the reaction* (see Figure 13.2).

2 Enzymes *affect only the speed and not the direction* of a reaction; for example, a glycosidase catalyzes both the polymerization of sugar units to form a polysaccharide,

and the breakdown of a polysaccharide into its component sugars as well. The direction in which a reaction proceeds is affected by other factors, in particular the relative proportion of substrate and end-products in the milieu. For instance, if the concentration of simple sugar molecules is high, it is more likely that the surface of the enzyme will be occupied by simple sugar units, which will then be polymerized and released. On the other hand, if most of the available carbohydrate is bound in storage form (as polysaccharides such as starch or glycogen), it is more likely that the reactive surface of the enzyme will be occupied by a portion of the polymer molecule, which will then be broken down.

3 Enzymes display a high degree of *specificity* with respect to the type of reaction that they can catalyze. (In Chapter 13 we shall consider various types of enzymes in relation to the kinds of reaction they catalyze.) Enzymes may also be relatively specific with respect to the range of substrates that they will accept. By way of example, the enzyme invertase catalyzes only the reaction

$$\text{Glucose} + \text{fructose} \rightleftharpoons \text{sucrose}$$

while succinic dehydrogenase functions by removing two hydrogen atoms from succinic acid, which thereby becomes fumaric acid:

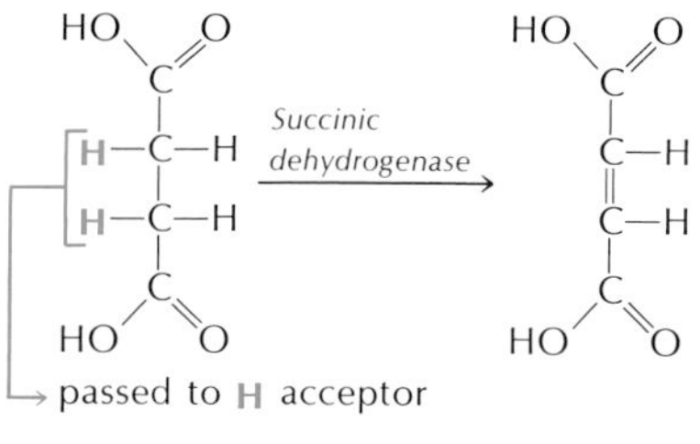

$$\mathrm{HO(O{=})C{-}CH_2{-}CH_2{-}C({=}O)OH} \xrightarrow{\text{Succinic dehydrogenase}} \mathrm{HO(O{=})C{-}CH{=}CH{-}C({=}O)OH}$$

(H—C—H, H—C—H: H passed to H acceptor)

This specificity is explainable in terms of the "lock-and-key theory" of enzyme action. According to this theory, a small part of the surface of the enzyme molecule (the *active site*) is so shaped, three-dimensionally, that into it will fit only certain molecules of complementary shape (Figure 9.10), like a key into a lock. It is small wonder, then, that slight changes in the shape of an enzyme molecule (due perhaps to a genetic mutation) may by changing the shape of the lock interfere with the fit of the key. The lock-and-key theory also makes possible an explanation of the mode of action of certain compounds which act as enzyme *inhibitors* (Figure 9.10*d*). A molecule that is not the normal substrate of an enzyme, but which conforms closely to the shape of that substrate, may compete for the occupancy of the active site. The "fit" of the inhibitor may be such that it "jams in the lock," that is, remains attached to the enzyme and thus permanently inactivates it.

4 Enzyme activity is adversely affected by changes in temperature exceeding the range to which the enzyme is adapted. Poikilothermic animals such as fish and invertebrates may live in polar seas where temperatures rarely far exceed 0°C; these species have evolved enzymes that function at such low temperatures and in fact may be quickly inactivated at higher temperatures. The enzymes of homoiotherms, on the other hand, must function optimally at temperatures close to 40°C. Like other proteins, enzymes are readily denatured at temperatures well below the boiling point of water (that is, usually 65°C or below), but some kinds are more thermosensitive than others. A temperature-sensitive mutant enzyme affecting pigment production produces the Himalayan coloration in rabbits, the fur being white except for dark paws, nose, and ears. This coloration results from the fact that the mutant enzyme is inactivated at normal body temperatures and can function in pigment production only in the cooler extremities of the body.

5 A given enzyme usually requires a specific pH range in which it can operate effectively. The protein-splitting enzyme *pepsin* works best in a highly acid medium (pH 1 to 2), which is provided by dilute hydrochloric acid secreted by the gastric glands. On the other hand, the pancreatic enzyme *trypsin* requires an alkaline medium (about pH 8).

6 Many enzymes are stored within the cell in an inactive state (proenzyme or zymogen), becoming activated only under particular circumstances. Pepsin and trypsin are produced as the inactive forms, *pepsinogen* and *trypsinogen,* which are not activated until they have been secreted into the cavity of the digestive tract. The activation of pepsinogen is accomplished by HCl, whereas that of trypsinogen involves the intervention of an activating protein, *enterokinase,* produced by glands of the small intestine. Certain enzymes such as pepsin and trypsin are capable of attacking the cells in which they are produced; inhibiting such autodigestion is essential to survival. Since the great majority of enzymes must function *intra*cellularly, the production of each is carefully controlled and its action integrated with the cell's other biochemical activities.

7 Because enzymes form only temporary complexes with their substrates, the *enzymes themselves are not permanently altered or used up* in the course of the reaction. A very small quantity of enzyme

Figure 9.10 □ **Characteristics of enzyme action. (*a*) Enzyme-substrate interaction during a chemical reaction. Together, both compounds fit the active site and can combine. (*b*) The shape of the enzyme's active site is such that the compound could fit the active site but cannot approach it; hence it cannot act as a substrate. (*c*) Each of the two compounds can approach and completely fit the active site; they will thus *compete* for its occupancy. (*d*) The compound serves as an enzyme *inhibitor:* it fits the active site but "jams" it and cannot be liberated. (*e*) The compound cannot fit the site and therefore does not serve as a substrate.**

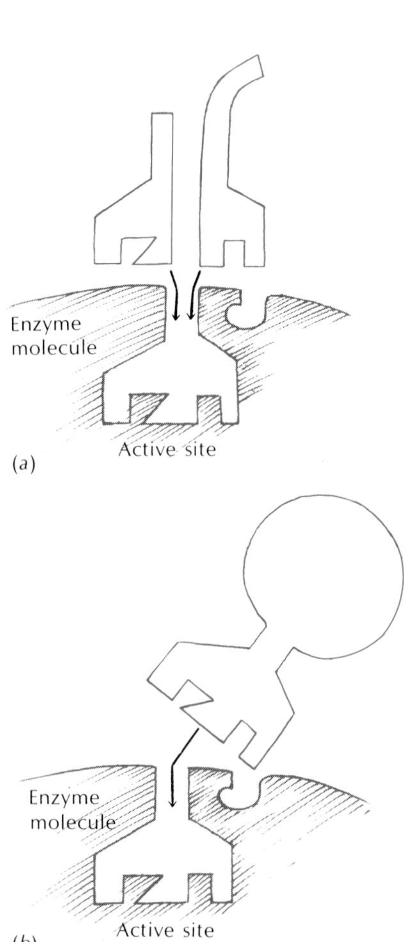

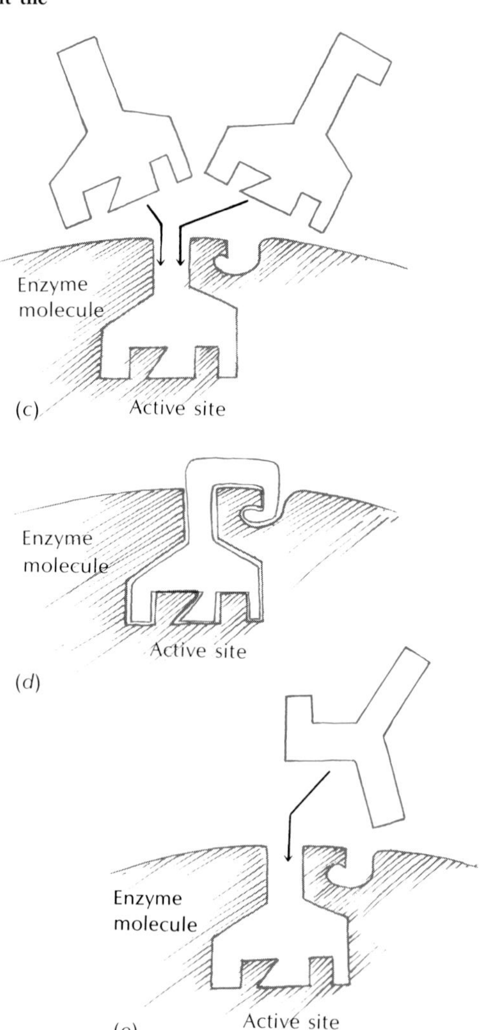

may therefore be capable of transforming relatively huge quantities of substrate.

8 Many enzymes depend for their action upon the presence of another substance, which may serve either as a coenzyme or as a prosthetic group. A *coenzyme* is a molecule which unites only *temporarily* with the enzyme to facilitate one phase of its activity. Several vitamins such as pantothenic acid (B_3) and thiamin (B_1) serve as parts of coenzymes (see Figure 14.40). *Prosthetic groups* are small, nonpeptide molecules, often containing metallic ions such as cobalt ion (Co^{2+}), copper ion (Cu^{2+}), and zinc ion (Zn^{2+}), which unite *permanently* with the enzyme and are essential to its activity. Certain vitamins also function as prosthetic groups. Riboflavin (B_2) is the prosthetic group of a *flavoprotein* enzyme involved in H transfer. Cyanocobalamin (B_{12}), containing Co^{2+}, is thought to serve as prosthetic group to an enzyme involved in the maturation of red blood corpuscles.

B Other functions of proteins

Although the majority of proteins act as enzymes, others are functionally and structurally important in a variety of ways, which we shall enumerate in this section.

1 The *structural framework* of the cell consists largely of proteins. These proteins can undergo changes in *colloidal state* as shown in Figure 10.10, making parts of the cell more or less viscous under different conditions. Alterations in colloidal state involve viscosity changes by which the protein molecules temporarily associate into a crystalline *gel* or dissociate to form a less viscous *sol.* Reversible sol-gel changes may

be induced by slight changes in temperature or pH. Proteins in a *gel* state form a firm outer cortex that helps a protozoan or a body cell to maintain its characteristic shape. Sol-gel changes also accompany cytoplasmic streaming and amoeboid movement.

2 During cell division the chromosomes are drawn to opposite ends of the dividing cell by the shortening of the *spindle fibers,* which are made up of protein (see Figure 10.15).

3 Proteins, although themselves produced by genes, in turn may be instrumental in the *regulation of genes.* In the chromosomes of multicellular organisms, DNA is conjugated with a basic protein (a *histone*). Some investigators claim that chromosomal histones serve to *inactivate* the genes with which they conjugate, but this remains open to debate. Such selective inactivation of certain genes may be essential to the capacity of cells to differentiate into various specialized tissues, for specialization is thought to involve the activation of some genes and the simultaneous repression of others.

4 Certain *hormones* are proteins or peptides. Protein and peptide hormones of vertebrates include the pancreatic hormones *glucagon* and *insulin,* and all of the eight known *pituitary* hormones.

5 The capacity for *motility* depends upon cellular proteins. The contractility of muscle is a product of the interaction of fibrils composed of the proteins *actin* and *myosin,* present in dense concentrations within muscle tissue (see Figure 11.35). Cilia and flagella also contain protein fibrils thought responsible for their movement.

6 Structurally important proteins such

Figure 9.11 □ **Defensive uses of keratin by mammals. (*a*) Porcupine, with keratinous quills. (*Photograph by R. K. Couch, U.S. Bureau of Sport Fisheries & Wildlife.*) (*b*) Armadillo, with keratinized skin serving as armor. (*Photograph by W. P. Taylor, U.S. Bureau of Sport Fisheries & Wildlife.*) (*c*) Pangolin, protected by overlapping keratinized scales. Note the powerful claws, also made of keratin. (*Zoological Society of San Diego photo by Ron Garrison.*)**

(*a*)

(*b*)

(*c*)

as *collagen* are secreted from the cells in which they are produced, to form connective fibers that bind animal tissues together. Collagen also contributes to intercellular cement, and to the matrix of cartilage and bone. Individual molecules (tropocollagen) secreted from the connective tissue cells spontaneously aggregate in such a way that a cablelike fibrillar structure, "native collagen," is built up (Figure 10.7*d*).

7 Proteins that serve as *respiratory pigments* (such as hemoglobin) occur widely throughout the animal kingdom. By combining with oxygen, respiratory pigments greatly increase the amount of oxygen that can be held in the cells or body fluids. Vertebrate muscle cells contain large quantities of the respiratory pigment *myoglobin,* which furnishes a reservoir of oxygen for use during exertion. *Hemocyanins* are Cu^{2+}-containing respiratory pigments found in the blood of many invertebrates. Their molecular weight sometimes exceeds 6×10^6.

8 Soluble proteins are instrumental in maintaining an *osmotic balance* between the cells and the body fluids. Proteins in the blood plasma serve to reduce the tendency for water to pass from the bloodstream into the tissues.

9 Cellular and blood proteins can both liberate and take up H^+; this allows them to serve as *buffers* in the regulation of the pH of cells and body fluids (see Section 16.2A).

10 *Antibodies* are defensive proteins derived from the plasma protein γ-globulin, which serve to combat parasitic invasion (see Section 6.3E).

11 The insoluble protein *keratin* is important to tetrapod vertebrates in several ways. Keratin is synthesized and stored in epidermal cells, which eventually die and serve as a horny covering that protects terrestrial vertebrates against desiccation. Keratinized plates and scales guard the bodies of most reptiles and such mammals as the armadillo. Keratinized cells form claws, nails, spines, and quills (Figure 9.11). They also form bird feathers and mammalian hair.

C Protein structure

Determinations of molecular structure have been completed for only a few proteins such as insulin, myoglobin, ribonuclease, and human hemoglobin. These determinations are complicated by the fact that proteins exhibit not only a primary structure (their amino acid composition), but a secondary and tertiary structure as well (discussed below). All of these must be elucidated if the biotic properties of a protein are to be understood. The first protein to have its primary structure completely analyzed was beef insulin (Figure 9.12a), a task that took ten years to complete!

PRIMARY STRUCTURE The primary structure of a protein is the linear sequence of amino acids in each polypeptide chain that composes it. The number of polypeptide chains in the protein may be determined by identifying the number of amino acids which expose a terminal $—NH_2$ group; one of these marks the free end of each polypeptide chain. Each terminal $—NH_2$ group can be identified because it will form a bright yellow compound with the reagent fluorodinitrobenzene (FDNB). Insulin has been found to consist of two different polypeptide chains, hemoglobin of four, myoglobin of only one.

The total number of different amino acids present in a protein is determined by digesting (hydrolyzing) the protein and separating the individual amino acids. Unfortunately, merely knowing the kinds of amino acids present in the protein gives little clue as to their arrangement. Analysis must proceed, therefore, by fragmenting the polypeptide chains and determining the sequence of amino acids in each fragment. FDNB can be used in this determination also, for the yellow compound formed when FDNB reacts with an amino acid at the $—NH_2$ end of a peptide chain survives hydrolysis, allowing the amino acid so marked to be identified after its removal. When this amino acid is removed from the chain, the next amino acid is exposed, combines with FDNB, and so forth.

SECONDARY STRUCTURE After the primary structure of the protein has been determined, we still must analyze its secondary and tertiary structure to understand its role in the living body. The secondary structure of a protein is the way in which the polypeptide chains are joined together and the geometrical arrangement of the "backbone" of each—by which we mean

```
        |  O        |  O        |  O        |  O
        |  ‖        |  ‖        |  ‖        |  ‖
—N—C—C—N—C—C—N—C—C—N—C—C—
  |  |       |  |       |  |       |  |
```

Stability of the backbone is increased by hydrogen bonds formed between amino acids located some distance from each other along the chain. Perhaps the commonest type of protein secondary structure is the *α helix,* a spiral arrangement stabilized by hydrogen bonds, each of which extends from the amino part of one amino acid to the oxygen of the carboxyl part

Figure 9.12 □ **Small proteins. (*a*) Beef insulin, a hormone. (*b*) Ribonuclease, an enzyme.**

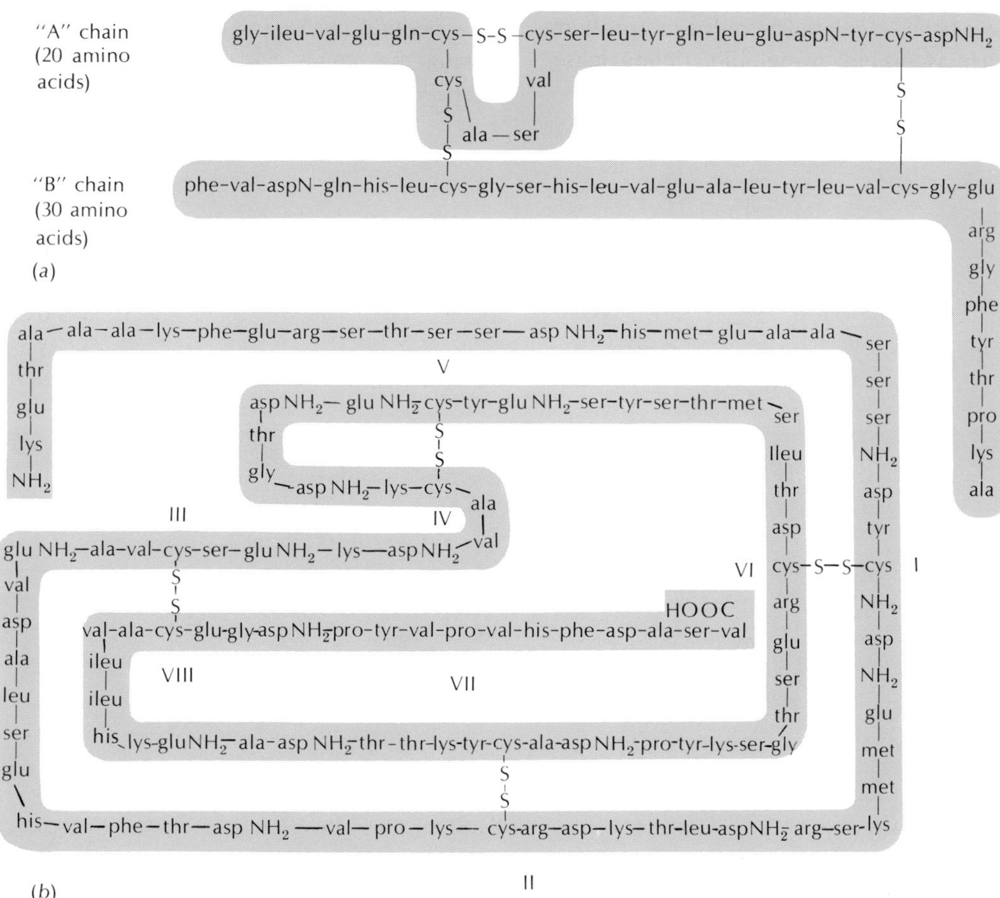

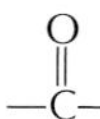

of the amino acid third removed from it (Figure 9.13). The α helix confers rigidity, and makes it impossible for the side chains of the amino acids to rotate around the axis of the backbone.

A helical structure results from the geometrical arrangement of each monomer relative to the one preceding it in the chain. In some long-chain polymers the monomers are simply arranged end-to-end. But in most polymers found in living systems each monomer is both *translated* and *rotated* with respect to the one preceding it. (By translation is meant a shift in the position of the center of each monomer relative to the center of the one preceding it; by rotation is meant a turning of the monomer on its axis.) When both translation and rotation occur with mathematical regularity, a *helix* is produced. Many helical or partly helical macromolecules occur in nature, including DNA (see Figure 9.19). Helical configurations stabilize macromolecules, for they permit the establishment of hydrogen bonds between those monomers that line up directly with each other in the helix.

Some proteins are largely nonhelical, but may be stabilized at particular points by a short helical region. Any protein that is completely helical will necessarily be rod-shaped or fibrous. Tropocollagen, for instance, is a straight molecule forming a helix that makes one complete turn every 640Å.

TERTIARY STRUCTURE The tertiary architecture of a protein is its final, folded configuration. Few proteins in living systems are fibrous; most are *globular*—folded up into a roundish, highly specific configuration, the shape of which is essential to the

Figure 9.13 □ Secondary structure of protein. The amino acid chain is stabilized in the form of a helix by hydrogen bonds. A protein molecule helical thoughout its entire length is long and straight, or fibrous.

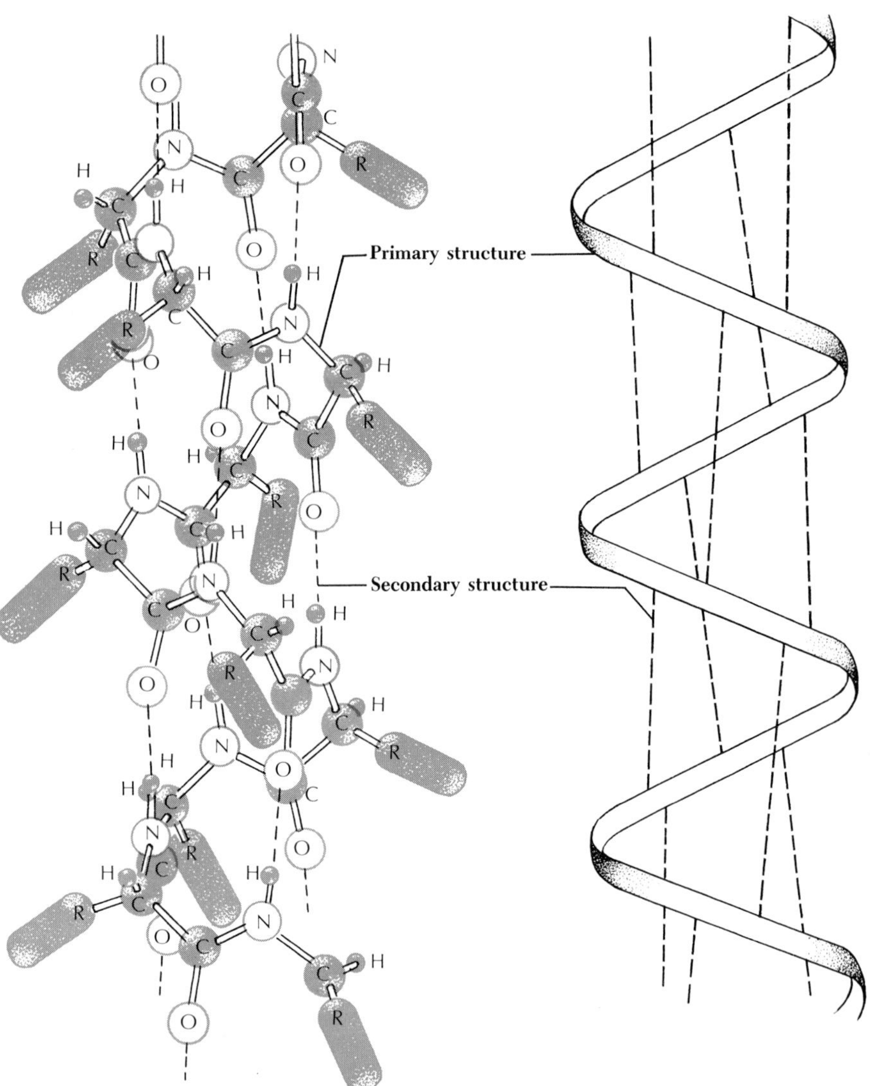

biotic activity of the protein (Figure 9.14). A globular protein may be *denatured* by heat or chemicals. During denaturation the bonds that form the tertiary (and sometimes secondary) structure of the protein are disrupted, and the molecule tends to assume an elongate or fibrous condition. Enzymes which have been denatured by heat never regain their biotic activity.

Stabilization of the tertiary configuration of the protein involves various types of attractive forces operating mainly between the side chains of the amino acids. One such bond is the *cystine bridge* (disulfide bridge), formed between the S atoms of juxtaposed cysteine molecules:

```
     |  H    O
     |  |   //
  —N—C—C—
        |
        C
        |
        S
        |
        S
        |
        C
        |       O
        |     //
  —N—C—C—
     |  |
```

The tertiary structure of the enzyme ribonuclease is stabilized by four such disulfide bridges (Figure 9.12*b*).

Other forces that assist in stabilizing the tertiary structure of proteins include hydrogen bonds, electrostatic (ionic) bonds, and hydrophobic ("water-hating") bonds. Hydrophobic bonds are formed between amino acids having relatively long carbon side chains, which coalesce with one another in preference to being dissolved in water. Polypeptide chains, in fact, demonstrate a remarkable degree of "stickiness," that is, they spontaneously tend to cohere into a compact mass that provides maximal

Figure 9.14 □ A globular protein, β chain of the hemoglobin molecule. The heme group is shown as a colored disc. Human hemoglobin contains four folded chains (two α and two β chains) per molecule. (*After M. F. Perutz.*)

opportunity for internal contact. This cohesiveness is of great help in building structural elements such as cell membranes, organelles, and connective fibers, and probably was prerequisite to the very origin of life, as discussed in Section 10.1C.

9.7 □ NUCLEIC ACIDS

The nucleic acids *deoxyribonucleic acid* (DNA) and *ribonucleic acid* (RNA) are macromolecules, which possess the unique properties of being capable of self-replication and, at the same time, of encoding meaningful information by which proteins may be built. Nucleic acids are the primary hereditary materials by which information is transmitted from one generation of cells or organisms to the next. They are also the basic agents through which metabolic activities are initiated and regulated. Nucleic acids are subject to change by mutation, and it is these changes in nucleic acid molecules which provide the genetic variability that is prerequisite to organic evolution.

Six major questions arise concerning these nucleic acids: (1) What experimental evidence supports the hypothesis that nucleic acids are the primary carriers of the hereditary code? (2) What is the molecular structure of DNA and RNA? (3) How does DNA replicate? (4) How do nucleic acids control metabolism? (5) What is the nature of the genetic code? (6) How is this code altered by mutation? The pursuit of the answers to these questions represents one of the most intriguing quests of modern biology, for in these answers lie the understanding and possibly the control of heredity and metabolism.

A Identification of nucleic acids as primary determinants of heredity

Early investigators of the chemical composition of living matter were struck by the universal occurrence of one type of material, which they therefore named "protein" (meaning *first* or *of first importance*). Nucleic acids, which in most organisms are intimately associated with certain proteins to form complexes known as *nucleoproteins,* were not then recognized as being capable both of replicating themselves and of governing the manufacture of proteins. At the present time we believe that the protein portion of a nucleoprotein complex serves, at least in part, a *repressive* function with respect to the nucleic acid. Nucleic acids seem to be capable of carrying on their normal activities in vitro when separated from the proteins with which they are usually associated. The elevation of nucleic acids to preeminence in the thinking of biologists came as a result of several key experiments, which we shall now review.

BACTERIAL TRANSFORMATION In 1929 a milestone was passed when the English bacteriologist F. Griffith succeeded in permanently altering the heredity of pneumonia bacteria. In his experiments two

Figure 9.15 □ Bacterial transformation. (*a*) Virulent (capsulated) pneumococci injected into mice cause death. (*b*) Avirulent (nonvirulent, noncapsulated) pneumococci do not cause death when injected. (*c*) Heat-killed virulent pneumococci do not cause death. (*d*) A mixture of living avirulent and heat-killed virulent pneumococci proves fatal because of proliferation of living virulent (capsulated) bacteria within the host; this implies that the heredity of the living non-capsulated pneumococci was altered by some factor (obtained from the dead bacteria) that allowed them to construct the protective capsules. (*e*) Virulent pneumococci are killed and fractionated, and the capacity of the purified fractions to transform the heredity of the avirulent bacteria is tested by injecting living avirulent bacteria that have been exposed to one particular fraction; only the DNA fraction proves capable of altering the avirulent bacteria's heredity. (*Based upon experiments of F. Griffith, O. T. Avery, and others.*)

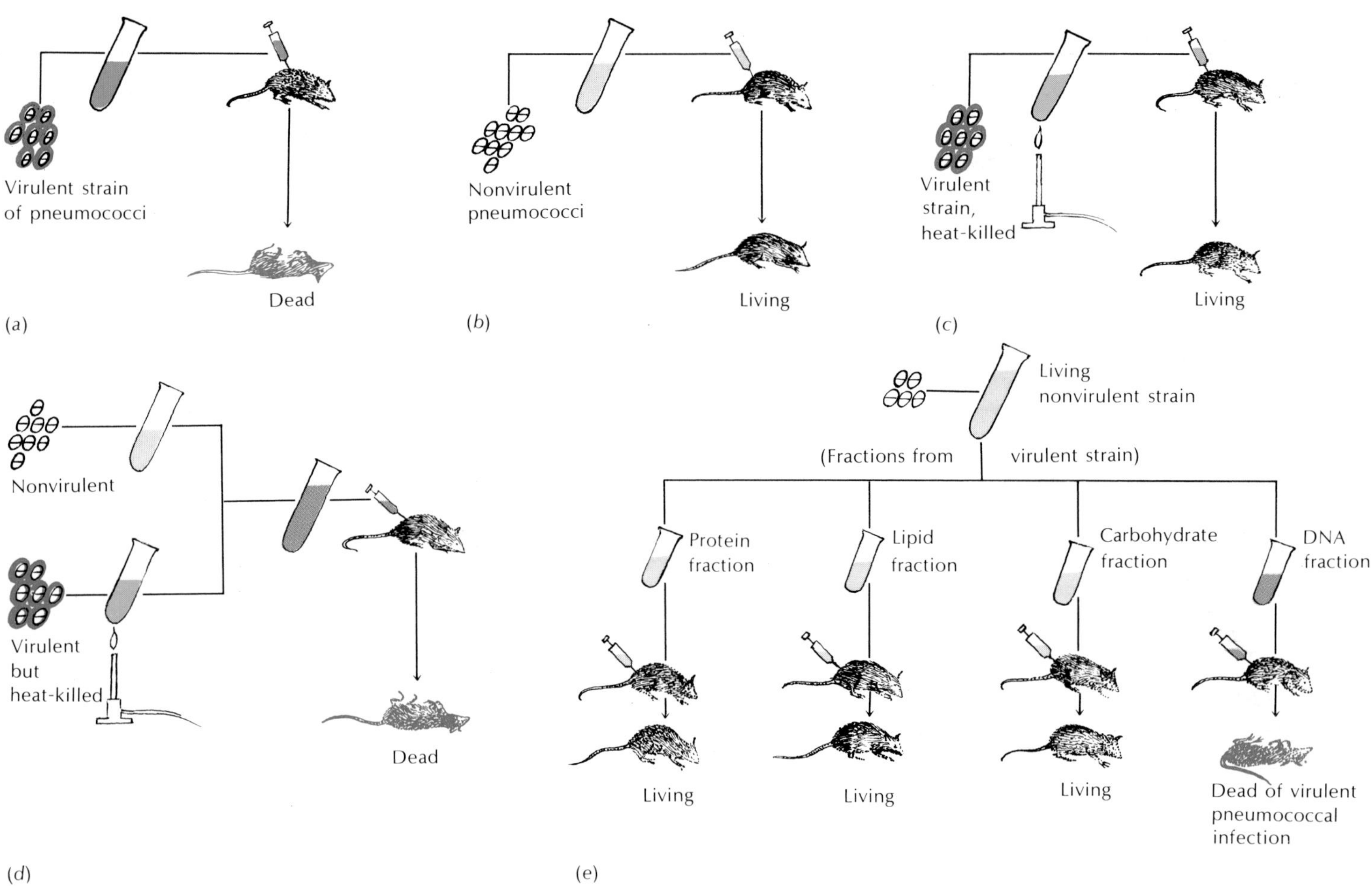

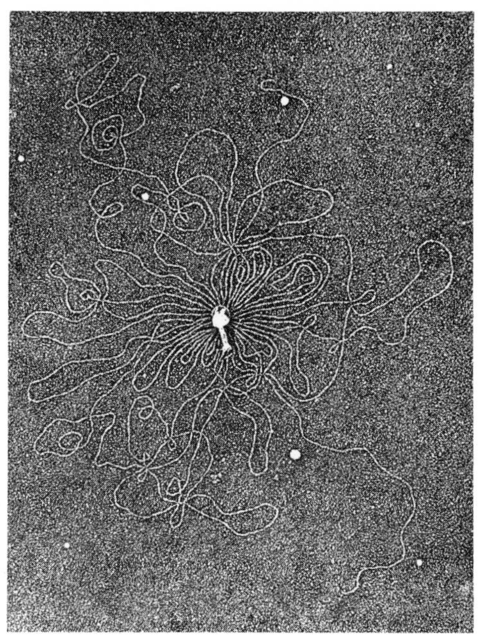

Figure 9.16 □ **Bacteriophage T2 ruptured by osmotic shock, showing protein coat and the single chromosome, a strand of DNA.** [*Courtesy of A. K. Kleinschmidt, D. Lang, D. Jacherts, and R. K. Zahn, "Darstellung und Längenmessungen des Gesamten Desoxyribonucleinsäure-Inhaltes von T_2-Bakteriophagen,"* **Biochim. Biophys. Acta, 61** *(1962). With permission of Elsevier Publishing Co.*]

strains of pneumococci were cultured. One of these, a *virulent* strain, produced pneumonia symptoms and death when inoculated into laboratory animals. The other strain was *avirulent* (that is, produced no symptoms of disease), for it was genetically incapable of manufacturing the antigenic carbohydrate capsule characteristic of the virulent strain. Griffith found that if avirulent pneumococci were cultured in the presence of *heat-killed* virulent pneumococci, a small percentage of the avirulent bacteria became virulent and produced virulent progeny. The "transformed" cells multiplied and produced pneumonia in the animals into which they were injected (Figure 9.15). Apparently some factor that was not destroyed when the virulent bacteria were killed was taken up by some of the living avirulent bacteria and changed their heredity, restoring their capacity for manufacturing the antigenic capsules. The nature of this transforming material was determined by later investigators, who fractionated the chemical constituents of bacterial cells and found that no component except DNA was capable of bringing about transformation of the bacterial genome. An avirulent pneumococcus became capsulated and virulent only by incorporating an appropriate fragment of DNA from the killed virulent cells.

EXPERIMENTS WITH BACTERIOPHAGE The importance of nucleic acids in heredity was also established by using radioactive isotopes to trace the DNA and protein components of bacteriophage viruses. Bacteriophages are relatively complex in form (Figure 2.2). The "head," "tail," and tail filaments of the bacteriophage are proteinaceous. Within the head, which is only 0.1 nm long, is one tightly packed coil of double-stranded DNA around 30 nm in length (Figure 9.16). When a bacteriophage attacks a bacterium, it adheres by means of its tail filaments to the outer membrane of the bacterium, and proceeds to inject into the host cell *only* the DNA thread. The protein portion of the bacteriophage remains outside and eventually deteriorates, or can be removed by the shearing forces generated in a high-speed blendor.

Virus DNA may be tagged with radioisotopes by allowing the viruses to reproduce within bacteria that have previously been cultured on medium containing ^{32}P. The ^{32}P is first incorporated into bacterial cells, and then is taken up by their virus parasites as a constituent of DNA. When ^{32}P-tagged viruses are inoculated into a bacterial culture free from ^{32}P, it is found that the viral ^{32}P is injected into the host (Figure 9.17*a*).

Another experiment is required to determine the fate of the protein portion of bacteriophage. The protein is tagged by letting the viruses reproduce within bacteria that have been grown on a medium containing ^{35}S (a radioisotope of sulfur) (Figure 9.17*b*). This isotope is incorporated into the protein coats of the viruses. When these viruses attack a new host, it is found that the ^{35}S does *not* enter the host cell but remains behind with the discarded coat. It may be concluded from these two experiments together that (1) viral DNA does enter the host cells and (2) viral protein does *not* enter the host cells, at least not in appreciable quantities. Within approximately 30 minutes after the virus has injected its DNA into the host the bacterium ruptures and dies, releasing a number of bacteriophages, where only one may have infected the cell. Reproduction of the viruses has occurred, under the sole control of the viral DNA. This reproduction has two aspects: (1) production of more viral DNA; (2) production of specific viral proteins. Therefore it may be concluded that the viral DNA displays two major capacities—it can replicate itself, and it governs the production of the necessary viral proteins.

FRACTIONATION OF TMV DNA is the primary hereditary material in all plants and animals, and in all but a few kinds of viruses as well. In several viruses such as the *tobacco mosaic virus* (TMV), hereditary information is not encoded in DNA, but in RNA instead. With TMV it has again been demonstrated that the nucleic acid part of the virus and *not* the protein component is responsible for the capacity of the virus to reproduce itself. This can be experimentally shown by using two strains of TMV, one producing whitish lesions on tobacco leaves, and the other producing black lesions.

If both strains of TMV are separately fractionated, and the "white" RNA mixed with protein from the "black" TMV, viruses are produced in which the RNA of the one strain is combined with the protein of the other. However, when a solution of these "hybrid" viruses is applied to tobacco leaves, the resultant lesion is always *white*, indicating that the "black" protein was not transmitted to the new generations of TMV reproducing within the host cells. Corresponding results are obtained with the reciprocal "black" RNA plus "white" protein.

Experiments such as these have established beyond doubt the importance of the nucleic acids (especially DNA) in transmitting hereditary information.

Figure 9.17 □ Experimental evidence that DNA is the hereditary material of bacteriophage viruses. (*a*) Experiment 1: virus DNA has been tagged with ^{32}P by being grown in hosts reared on medium containing ^{32}P, and the marked bacteriophages are allowed to attack unmarked hosts. The protein coats are sheared off and separated from the bacteria after the virus DNA has been injected. It is seen that most of the virus DNA has entered the host and therefore must be responsible for the production of new viruses. (Radioactive particles are shown in color.) (*b*) Experiment 2: bacteriophage viruses are tagged with ^{35}S and are allowed to attack hosts not bearing the radioactive marker. Again, after the virus DNA strand has entered the host, the protein coats are removed. Now it is found that almost none of the ^{35}S-labeled virus protein remains with the host; accordingly, the protein cannot be responsible for production of new viruses within the host.

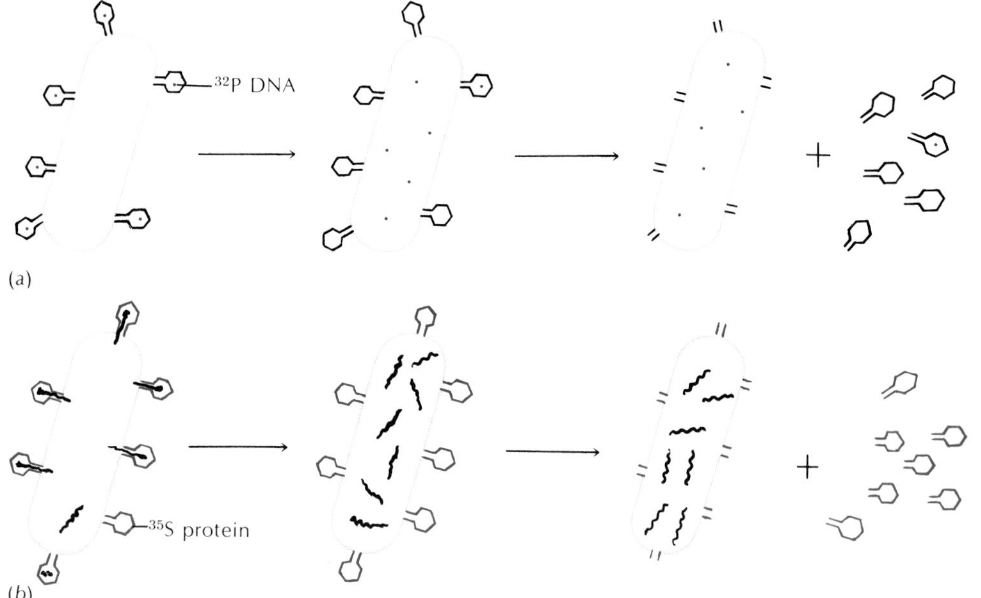

B The molecular structure of DNA and RNA

Nucleic acids are giant linear heteropolymers built up of covalently bonded nucleotide units. We have seen that a nucleotide consists of a *pentose* molecule bonded to a *nitrogenous base* (purine or pyrimidine) and one or more *phosphate* groups (see Figures 9.5 and 9.18*a*). There are eight commonly occurring nucleotides in nucleic acids, four each in DNA and RNA.

Figure 9.18 □ **Components of DNA: (*a*) the subunits of one DNA nucleotide; (*b*) DNA nucleotides; (*c*) portion of a DNA molecule.**

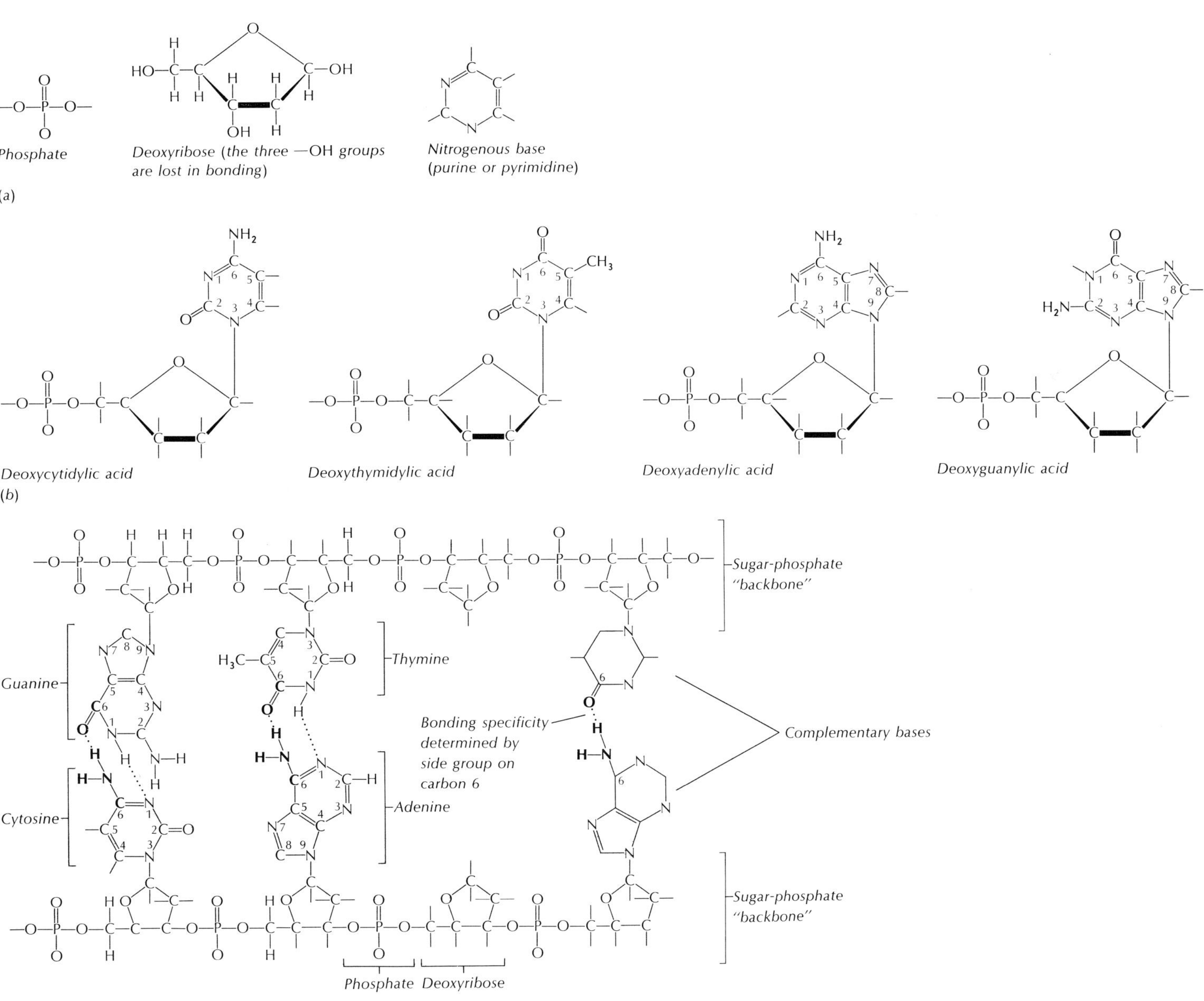

DNA MONOMERS The nucleotides of DNA all contain the pentose *deoxyribose*. They are shown in Figure 9.18*b*. These nucleotides are joined, in any order and in various proportions, by way of covalent bonds between the phosphate group of one nucleotide and the deoxyribose of the next. Although only four types of nucleotides are present, the linear sequence and proportions of these can be varied almost infinitely. (Of course only certain sequences would have biotic significance.) DNA has been found, partly on the basis of X-ray diffraction studies, to exist ordinarily as a double-stranded molecule in which the two strands are held together by hydrogen bonding between complementary bases (Figure 9.18c). Simple geometrical considerations based upon the known diameter of the double-stranded molecule (11 Å or 1.1 nm) indicate that these bonds always occur between a purine and a pyrimidine. Two purine molecules are too bulky to fit into the space known to be present between the sugar-phosphate backbones of the two strands. Two pyrimidines, on the other hand, are so small that in a molecule of this diameter too much space would exist between the strands to permit hydrogen bonds to be formed. A combination of one purine and one pyrimidine conforms admirably to the measured diameter of the DNA molecule.

RNA MONOMERS The nucleotides of RNA contain ribose instead of deoxyribose, and while three of the bases are the same as those in DNA—namely, adenine, guanine, and cytosine—the fourth DNA base, thymine, is changed in RNA to the base *uracil*. The four nucleotides of RNA are shown in Figure 9.5c. When these join together two of the phosphate groups are liberated from each nucleotide, furnishing energy needed to make the bond.

RNA is a *single-stranded* molecule built up of ribose nucleotides. It does not form regularly occurring hydrogen bonds between the bases of complementary strands but is stabilized by occasional hydrogen bonds between bases on the same strand.

Since nucleotides differ primarily with respect to the nitrogenous base which they include we commonly speak merely of *bases* rather than entire nucleotides, and use the first letter of the base (A, G, C, T, and U) to represent the whole nucleotide. Although the sugar and phosphate portions of the nucleotides unite to form the linear backbone of the nucleic acid, it is mainly the bases which confer individuality upon the nucleotide. Protruding at right angles to the pentose-phosphate backbone, the bases are responsible for establishing hydrogen bonds with complementary bases, an event prerequisite both to nucleic acid replication and to protein synthesis.

DNA BASE RATIOS A nucleic acid chain may be broken down by hydrolysis into its constituent nucleotides, which in turn may be isolated by kind, making it possible to determine the relative proportions of the four nucleotides present. These proportions are expressed as *base ratios,* that is, the relative proportions of nucleotides containing the bases A, G, C, and T (or, for RNA, A, G, C, and U). In the case of DNA, the ratios C:G and A:T are found always to be nearly constant, but the two ratios vary independently from one another. In other words, there is always just about as much adenine present as thymine, and just as much cytosine as guanine. A reexamination of the structural formulas of these bases (Figure 9.5) may reveal why this is so. In each case, the functional group attached to the carbon atom designated by the number 6 is *reciprocal* for the two interacting bases of the complementary strands. Adenine, with an amino group ($—NH_2$) on C-6, establishes hydrogen bonds only with thymine, which bears an oxygen atom on C-6. Guanine, with an oxygen on C-6, establishes hydrogen bonds with cytosine, which has an amino group on C-6. Proper hydrogen bonding thus can occur only between a *purine* with an amino group on C-6, and a *pyrimidine* with an oxy group on C-6, or between a *purine* bearing an oxy group on C-6 and a *pyrimidine* with an amino group on C-6. This regularity is of cardinal significance in permitting DNA to replicate itself, as seen in Section 9.6C below.

HELICAL CONFIGURATION OF DNA In its primary structure (Figure 9.18c), DNA resembles a ladder in which the "uprights" are the pentose-phosphate chains and the "rungs" are the bases that protrude at right angles to the "uprights." This primary structure is stabilized by assuming a helical or spiralling secondary structure, much as a very long ladder could be stabilized if twisted into a spiral staircase. The secondary structure of DNA is an α helix (Figure 9.19). The helix makes one complete turn every four consecutive nucleotides, permitting hydrogen bonds to be established between a nucleotide and the fourth one away.

C How does DNA replicate?

The replication of nucleic acid must precede all types of biotic reproduction, cellular or organismal. It is by means of this

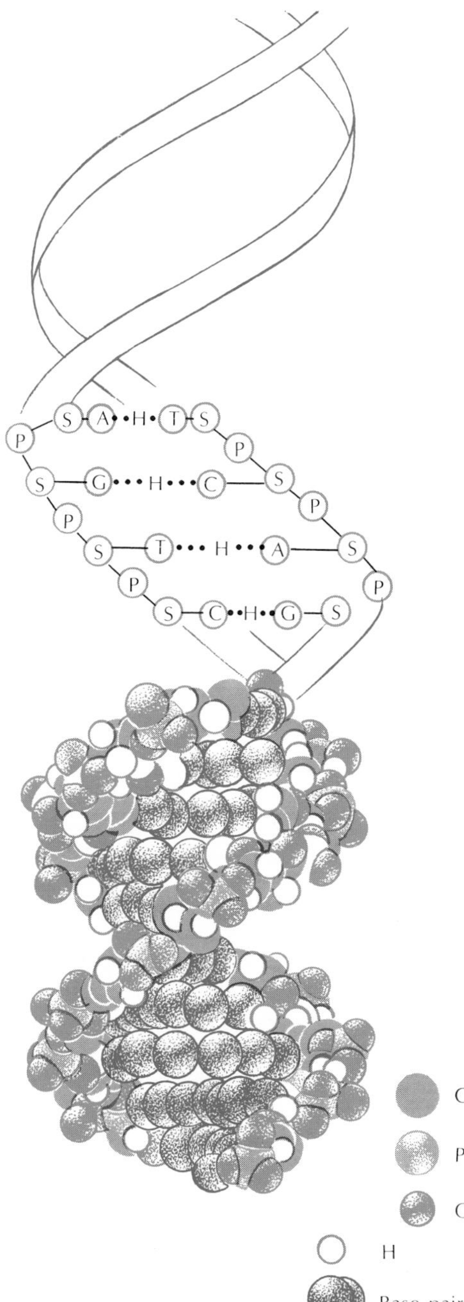

Figure 9.19 □ **Portion of DNA molecule, showing α helix. Above, schematic representation with phosphate-sugar "runners" and base crosspieces. Center, groups designated by encircled letters: phosphate, Ⓟ; sugar (deoxyribose), Ⓢ; adenine, Ⓐ; guanine, Ⓖ; cytosine, Ⓒ; thymine, Ⓣ; hydrogen bonds, dots. Below, ball model, spherical atoms and base units. (*After C. P. Swanson.*)**

precise replication that hereditary information may be transmitted intact from one generation to the next and from one cell to its daughter cells. And it is through occasional *errors* in the replication process that there arise those genetic alterations which permit living things to change and to adapt. The entire DNA strand which constitutes the chromosome of the colon bacillus can replicate in only 16 minutes, requiring the incorporation of some 6×10^5 nucleotides per minute.

The mechanism of DNA replication is thought to involve: (1) separation of the two complementary strands by the breaking of hydrogen bonds between opposing bases; (2) the formation of new hydrogen bonds between the bases of each intact strand and free triply phosphorylated deoxyribose nucleotide units that are available in the milieu as products of cell metabolism; and (3) the polymerization of these units while they are held in proper sequence on the template provided by the old DNA strand. Polymerization involves the formation of covalent bonds, in the presence of a specific enzyme (*DNA-polymerase*). As polymerization proceeds, two phosphate groups are released from each nucleotide added to the new strand, this dephosphorylation furnishing energy to the polymerization reaction (Figure 9.20). This sequence of events is more properly designated "replication" than "duplication," for although the end result is two identical double-stranded DNA molecules, each has been produced by the alignment of a *complementary*, not an *identical* series of nucleotides along each of the preexisting strands. We can easily predict the sequence of bases on the new strand, if we know the base sequence of the old strand. Each exposed adenine will form hydrogen bonds with any triply phosphorylated nucleotide bearing a thymine; each exposed guanine will bond to a cystosine; thus the strand

A-T-A-C-G-G-T-A-C

will replicate the strand

T-A-T-G-C-C-A-T-G

and so forth.

Inferential evidence that the hereditary material generally conserves the same linear arrangement or organization from one generation to the next and from one cell division to the next was available long before more direct evidence was obtained with respect to DNA replication. Most of the DNA component of plant and animal cells exists within the elongate *chromosomes*. Unfortunately, individual chromosomes are not readily distinguishable in most nondividing cells, for when a cell is carrying on its metabolic functions the chromosomes are in a stretched-out condition, and intricately intertwined in the cell nucleus. However, the giant chromosomes of the larvae of two-winged flies such as *Drosophila* are distinguishable in nondividing cells and exhibit distinctive banding patterns that can easily be recognized as being the same from cell to cell and from organism to organism (Figure 8.13). Furthermore, whenever it has been possible to map the linear sequence of genes on such chromosomes, these genes have been found to occupy the same relative positions from generation to generation. These findings support the idea that genes are linearly arranged portions of DNA molecules, but only recently have we obtained direct experimental evidence that DNA actually does conserve its linear organization during replication.

Figure 9.20 □ **DNA replication. Each old strand serves as a template on which a new complementary strand is built by assembling free nucleotides. (*a*) Hydrogen bonds hold new nucleotides in correct position until the "backbone" of the new chain is formed by covalent bonding through enzyme action. Two phosphates and H_2O are set free for each bond made between the sugar and phosphate groups of adjacent nucleotides. (*b*) Requirements for DNA replication: (1) old DNA strand, separated from its complement by the breaking of hydrogen bonds; (2) free triply phosphorylated deoxyribose nucleotides; (3) enzyme, a DNA-polymerase. Products: (1) new DNA strand complementary to the old; (2) pyrophosphate, (P)—(P); (3) H_2O.**

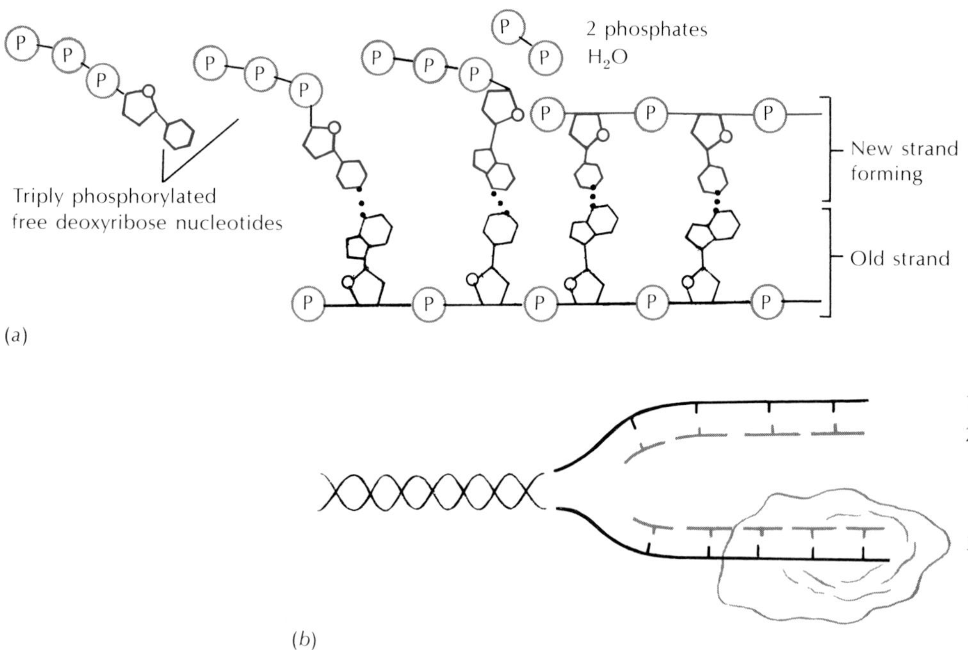

EXPERIMENTAL EVIDENCE CONCERNING DNA REPLICATION Direct evidence that each DNA strand remains structurally intact while replicating was originally obtained by investigations in which a heavy (but not radioactive) isotope of nitrogen (^{15}N) was used to tag the DNA of colon bacilli. The bacteria were first cultivated for several generations on a medium in which all nitrogen available was ^{15}N rather than the usual ^{14}N, so that all nitrogenous compounds present in the bacterial cells eventually contained only ^{15}N. At this point, bacteria were transferred to a medium containing only ^{14}N. They were allowed to complete one generation of reproduction, following which samples were taken for analysis of DNA content. The cells were ruptured and their components separated by ultracentrifugation. The DNA fraction was thereupon found to be intermediate in density between normal DNA containing ^{14}N and a DNA containing only ^{15}N. It was suspected on the basis of these findings that the DNA occurring in progeny of the first generation was actually made up half of ^{14}N-DNA and half of ^{15}N-DNA, but another generation of reproduction was required to prove this hypothesis. After a second generation of progeny were produced, still on medium containing only ^{14}N, samples were again taken, ultracentrifuged, and the DNA layer examined. Now it was found that *two* distinct DNA layers were formed: the denser ^{14}N-^{15}N-DNA and the less dense ^{14}N-DNA. In this generation the two layers were of equal size, but at each subsequent generation the thickness of the ^{14}N-DNA layer increased while that of the ^{14}N-^{15}N-DNA decreased. The ^{15}N-DNA did not disappear even after several more generations had gone by, but due to the production of new ^{14}N-DNA at each replication, the proportion of ^{15}N-DNA in the samples declined in each generation. These findings indicated that DNA did not break up and reassemble itself between cell divisions, but that each old strand remained intact and served as the template for a new one. Therefore, in the first generation produced by culture on the ^{14}N medium, each bacterial chromosome consisted of one old ^{15}N-DNA strand and one new ^{14}N-DNA strand.

D How do nucleic acids control metabolism?

HEREDITARY METABOLIC DEFECTS IN MAN In his pioneering volume, *Inborn Errors in Metabolism* (1909), the British physician A. E. Garrod presented evidence that certain hereditary diseases of man result from alterations in specific biochemical reactions essential to normal metabolism. This was the earliest study that pointed to the role of the hereditary material, the genes (which we now know are composed of DNA), in controlling metabolism. One of the disorders to which Garrod gave consideration was *alcaptonuria*. Persons homozygous for a particular recessive allele are unable to degrade alcapton, an intermediate compound produced in the biochemical pathway leading to the synthesis of the black pigment melanin. It therefore accumulates in the bloodstream, and is excreted in the urine. Urine containing alcapton turns black upon exposure to air. This alone would not prove especially troublesome, but alcaptonurics also suffer from an abnormal hardening and blackening of their cartilaginous tissues. Garrod found that patients fed increased amounts of the amino acids phenylalanine and tyrosine excreted greater quantities of alcapton. He concluded correctly that this substance is normally produced during the metabolic utilization of these amino acids, but because of a hereditary defect can be metabolized no further.

Another inheritable metabolic error in a biochemical pathway involving phenylalanine and tyrosine results in *phenylketonuric idiocy*. The afflicted person, who has received a recessive allele from each parent, is incapable of converting phenylalanine to tyrosine. Instead, the former is deaminated to phenylpyruvic acid, which is excreted in the urine. The high concentration of phenylalanine remaining in the tissues, however, leads to mental retardation. Mental impairment can be avoided only if the defect is detected at birth, and the individual reared on an artificial diet low in phenylalanine.

It is particularly significant that the livers of phenylketonurics lack a specific enzyme (phenylalanine parahydroxylase), which catalyzes the conversion of phenylalanine to tyrosine by the addition of a hydroxyl group to the ring. When it is found that individuals homozygous for a particular mutant gene lack a certain enzyme, it may be suspected that in its normal state that gene has a role in the production of that enzyme. An exhaustive investigation of this possibility was undertaken by the geneticists George W. Beadle and Edward L. Tatum, using the pink bread mold, *Neurospora*, as their test organism.

GENETICS OF NEUROSPORA *Neurospora* proved to be an invaluable subject of genetic investigation, coming to hold a position with respect to *biochemical* genetics comparable to that which *Drosophila* had earned in the analysis of hereditary *transmission*. Its useful attributes include the fact that the cells of the mycelium are monoploid during most of the life cycle, hence any mutant gene present is able to exert an immediate effect upon the phenotype, and need not be present in double dose, as is the case with recessive alleles in diploid organisms (Figure 9.21a). Furthermore, *Neurospora* reproduces sexually as well as asexually, forming diploid zygotes by the fusion of two monoploid cells. These zygotes promptly undergo meiosis (see Figure 8.4) within a fruiting body, the *ascus*, producing monoploid *ascospores*. Each ascospore may be dissected out of the ascus and transferred to a culture dish, where it germinates into a new mycelium. Each cell of the mycelium is normally capable of carrying out all of the biochemical reactions necessary to manufacture amino acids, nitrogenous bases, and various vitamins out of a minimal culture medium containing only sugar, minerals, and the vitamin biotin. The irradiation of *Neurospora* with X rays or ultraviolet light greatly increases the incidence of mutation. By repeated irradiation of *Neurospora* cultures, the investigators

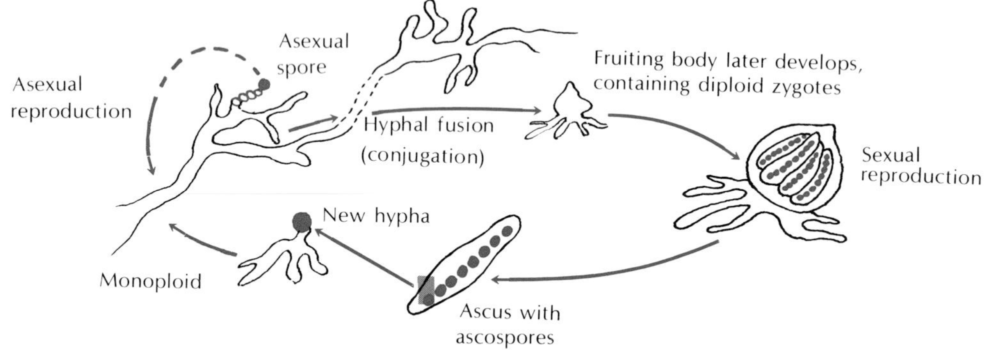

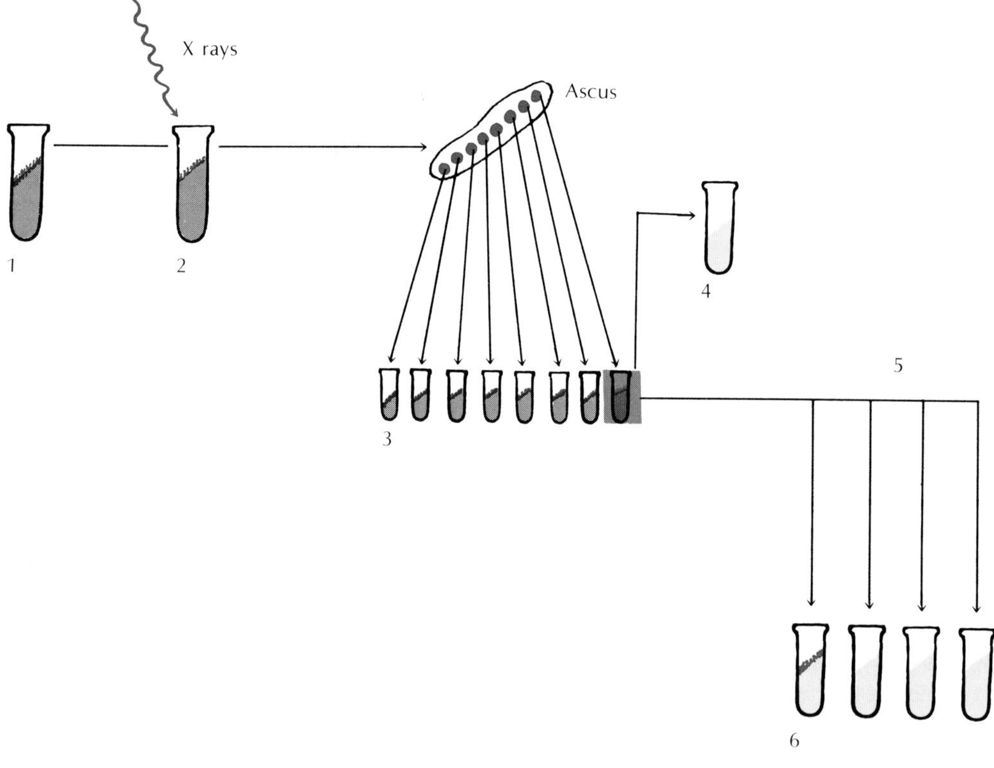

were able to accumulate a large number of mutant strains incapable of manufacturing one or more of the organic compounds that the wild-type mold could synthesize. These strains could survive only if the minimal medium that would sustain wild-type *Neurospora* were supplemented by the missing compound or a precursor.

Such nutritional mutants must be identified by a process of elimination. The irradiated (and possibly mutated) spores must first be germinated on a medium enriched with a wide variety of substances normally synthesized by *Neurospora,* including vitamins, amino acids, purines and pyrimidines. Subcultures are then made by inoculating a series of culture tubes, each of which contains the minimal medium plus *one*

Figure 9.21 □ *Neurospora crassa*, pink bread mold. (*a*) Life cycle: in sexual reproduction zygotes form by mycelial-cell conjugation; each zygote then undergoes meiosis in an ascus. (*b*) Technique for inducing and identifying mutations in *Neurospora:* (1) Wildtype mold grows on agar slant of "minimal medium" of known composition (containing only carbohydrate, the vitamin biotin, and inorganic nutrients, including NH_4^+). (2) Wild-type mold is irradiated with X rays. (3) Spores are dissected out of asci and individually cultured on enriched medium (containing amino acids, purines, pyrimidines, and vitamins). (4) To identify mutants, portions of each culture are now transferred to minimal medium; if any fails to grow, a *mutation* may be responsible. (5) Spores of the suspected mutant strain are then transferred to a series of tubes, each containing minimal medium plus one possible additional requirement (for instance, a vitamin, one amino acid, or one nitrogenous base). (6) This mutant survives on minimal medium plus the amino acid arginine. Accordingly, the mutation caused the loss of the capacity to synthesize arginine, and the new mutant is designated *arg*$^-$, the normal type being *arg*$^+$.

added compound—amino acid, vitamin, or nitrogenous base. If, for example, a mutant is found that flourishes in the culture tube containing minimal medium plus the amino acid arginine, but perishes in all other subcultures, it may be concluded that this particular mutant lacks the capacity for manufacturing arginine (Figure 9.21*b*). It would then be classified as an arginineless mutant (arg^-). On the other hand, the normal strains, which could produce arginine, would be designated arg^+, for they would possess a normally functioning gene involved in arginine synthesis.

As more and more of these mutant stocks were developed, it became apparent that each type of nutritional mutant actually represented a number of separate mutations involving *different* genes concerned with the same sequence of reactions. For instance, a number of arg^- mutants could be recovered, in which different steps of the metabolic sequence leading to the production of arginine were blocked. Sexual recombination between two such different arg^- strains would produce arg^+ progeny, for each mutant stock would contain a normal gene lacking in the other.

THE "ONE GENE–ONE ENZYME–ONE ACTION" THEORY The data accumulated by Beadle and Tatum led these geneticists to conclude that: (1) metabolic sequences consist of series of reactions, each of which produces the substrate needed for the next reaction; (2) each such reaction is enzymatically controlled; and (3) gene mutations block these reactions because of the failure of the mutant alleles to produce the necessary enzymes. On the basis of these conclusions they formulated the *one gene–one enzyme–one action hypothesis* (Figure 9.22). According to this hypothesis, to which few exceptions have been found to date, the majority of genes function by producing an enzyme needed for a particular metabolic reaction. If the gene is mutated, the enzyme it produces is altered and may be incapable of catalyzing the reaction. Failure of the reaction to occur may block an entire metabolic pathway. A few cases have been found in which two or more genes are required for the production of an especially large protein, each being responsible for contributing one polypeptide chain to the macromolecule.

Many gene mutations appear to have multiple effects on the phenotype. How

Figure 9.22 □ One gene–one enzyme–one action hypothesis. (*a*) The number of genes involved in a given metabolic pathway can be calculated according to whether or not a cross between two nutritional mutants lacking the same capacity yields normal progeny ($_1arg$, $_2arg$, and $_3arg$ can be concluded to be different genes involved in the arginine-synthesis pathway; $_3arg$ and $_4arg$ are probably identical). (*b*) Such data have shown that metabolic sequences involve a number of enzyme-mediated steps, each enzyme controlled by a single gene. (*c*) A mutation in one gene blocks the path since the next substrate is not produced.

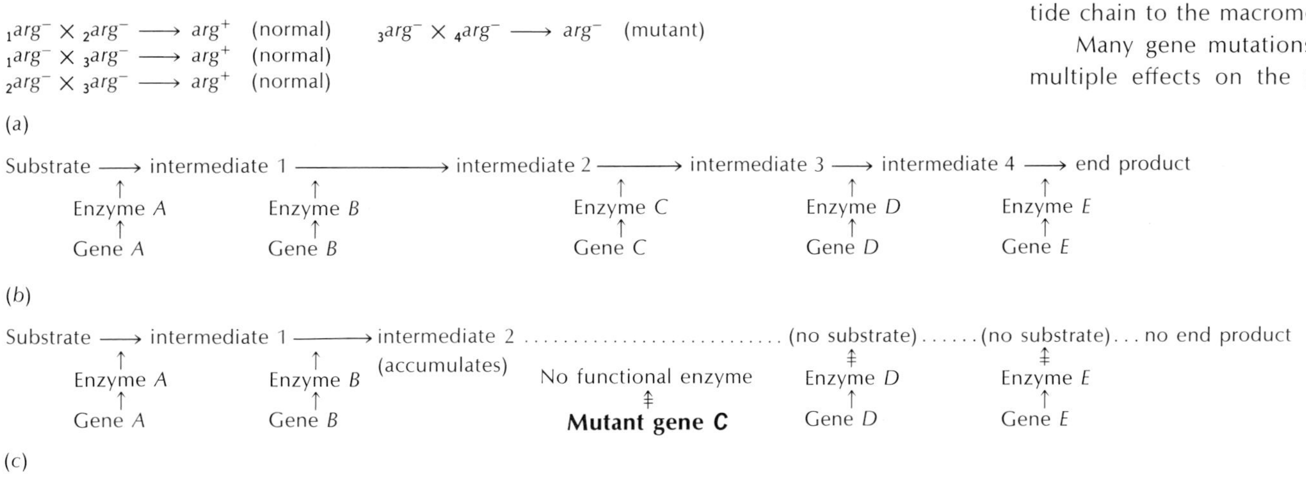

$_1arg^- \times {_2arg^-} \longrightarrow arg^+$ (normal)
$_1arg^- \times {_3arg^-} \longrightarrow arg^+$ (normal)
$_2arg^- \times {_3arg^-} \longrightarrow arg^+$ (normal)

$_3arg^- \times {_4arg^-} \longrightarrow arg^-$ (mutant)

(*a*)

Substrate ⟶ intermediate 1 ⟶ intermediate 2 ⟶ intermediate 3 ⟶ intermediate 4 ⟶ end product

↑ Enzyme *A* ↑ Gene *A* | ↑ Enzyme *B* ↑ Gene *B* | ↑ Enzyme *C* ↑ Gene *C* | ↑ Enzyme *D* ↑ Gene *D* | ↑ Enzyme *E* ↑ Gene *E*

(*b*)

Substrate ⟶ intermediate 1 ⟶ intermediate 2 (accumulates) .... (no substrate) ...... (no substrate) ... no end product

↑ Enzyme *A* ↑ Gene *A* | ↑ Enzyme *B* ↑ Gene *B* | No functional enzyme ⇞ **Mutant gene C** | ⇞ Enzyme *D* ↑ Gene *D* | ⇞ Enzyme *E* ↑ Gene *E*

(*c*)

does this fact jibe with the one gene-one enzyme-one action theory? In many cases we simply do not know, for it is still not possible to ascertain the basic metabolic action of many of the genes of higher organisms, in which such multiple effects are most apt to appear. However, it is thought that when the fundamental action of a gene is understood, it will be possible to demonstrate how these multiple effects relate to that fundamental action. A case in point is a lethal gene in the rat that produces a variety of symptoms, including abnormalities of the ribs and lungs, a humped back, blunt snout, and teeth that fail to meet properly. Death, when it occurs, may be the immediate result of suffocation, starvation, pulmonary hemorrhage, or heart failure. It would seem difficult to lay this variety of defects and causes of death at the door of a single gene mutation, and yet this conclusion is inescapable in the light of the fact that the condition is inherited as a single Mendelian factor: it is a monogenic trait. However, it is possible to trace all of these effects back to a basic defect in cartilage metabolism. Such disturbance in a biochemical pathway involved in cartilage development adequately explains the humped back, deformed ribs and snout, and abnormal position of the teeth. These skeletal defects in turn would cause respiratory difficulties leading to suffocation, or, more gradually, to abnormal enlargement of the lungs, pulmonary hemorrhages, and compensatory enlargement of the heart with eventual cardiac failure. Alternatively, the malformed snout and poorly occluding teeth could cause earlier death from starvation, since the process of feeding would be seriously impaired.

EXPERIMENTAL PROOF OF ENZYME PRODUCTION BY GENES More recently, the hypothesis that genes are responsible for determining the configuration of enzymes has gained additional support through investigations concerned with the enzyme *tryptophan synthetase* ("t'ase"), which catalyzes the production of the amino acid tryptophan from the precursors indole and serine. Over a period of time, a large number of mutant strains of *Neurospora* lacking tryptophan synthetase had been isolated. This query then arose: Did these t^- stocks in fact contain no protein at all similar to t'ase, or was some kind of t'ase-like protein still being produced that lacked the catalytic activity of t'ase itself? This question was answered by applying serological techniques.

First, an antibody against t'ase ("anti-t'ase") was produced by injecting the purified enzyme into rabbits, in which, being a foreign protein, it elicited antibody formation. The anti-t'ase was then isolated from rabbit serum. Crude extracts of t^- cells were then mixed with anti-t'ase in vitro, in a system containing also the substrates (indole and serine) needed for tryptophan production. Since the extracts were taken from a t^- strain, no tryptophan production could take place at this point. Shortly after the addition of the anti-t'ase antibody, a small amount of purified, active t'ase was added to the in vitro system. Finally, the system was analyzed for the presence of tryptophan.

By this method it was found that the various t^- strains could be divided into two categories, on the basis of whether or not tryptophan was finally recovered from the in vitro system. Why should tryptophan be produced in some of these systems, but not in others? This may be clarified if we examine the rationale for employing the anti-t'ase antibody. An antibody combines with a specific antigen to form a complex that inactivates that antigen. In this experiment, if the original extract of t^- cells contained any protein so similar to t'ase that it would react with anti-t'ase, the reaction would tie up both that protein and the antibody that had been introduced into the system. If so, when t'ase itself is then added, no free anti-t'ase remains to inactivate this added enzyme and the enzyme can proceed to catalyze the linking of indole to serine, producing tryptophan. In this way it was discovered that most of the t^- strains did produce a protein so similar to t'ase that it would react with anti-t'ase. In contrast to these, a minority of t^- strains not only failed to produce active t'ase, but also lacked *any* protein which was similar enough to t'ase to combine with its antibody. In these strains, the in vitro system never yielded tryptophan, since when t'ase was added to the system, free antibody still remained to inactivate the enzyme.

These data indicate that many of the mutations which result in the inability to synthesize tryptophan from its immediate precursors do not prevent the genes from producing a protein very similar to t'ase, even though enzymatically inactive. The fact that a protein molecule may be so similar to t'ase as to react with anti-t'ase antibody, and yet be incapable of catalyzing the reactions carried out by t'ase, is not surprising when we consider that the capacity of an enzyme for catalyzing a reaction depends upon its specific folded configuration. The unique shapes of enzyme molecules enable them to combine with substrate molecules, holding them in positions that favor their interaction.

Many gene mutations result in a change of only one or two amino acids in a protein molecule. This change might seem to be insignificant, but the effect upon the final folded configuration of the protein may be profound. For example, of importance among the forces that stabilize protein molecules in folded configurations are S—S bonds between cysteine units (Figure 9.12*b*). If a mutation caused a tyrosine, for instance, to be incorporated at one of these sites instead of a cysteine, no S—S bond could be formed at that location, and the folded configuration of the protein might be drastically altered, ruining its capacity for interacting with the substrates. Therefore, mutation of the gene responsible for producing t'ase might change the amino acid content of this protein so slightly that it would still react with anti-t'ase but at the same time have its tertiary structure altered sufficiently so that it could no longer serve as an enzyme.

DEFINITION OF THE GENE The above investigations, and many more, have lent strong support to the hypothesis that nucleic acids are organized into informational units each of which controls the production of a particular protein molecule, most commonly an enzyme, which in turn catalyzes one or more of the biochemical reactions that in the aggregate constitute the organism's metabolic activities. Each of these functional units is termed a *gene* or *cistron.* Within each cistron, the linear sequence of nucleotides specifies the sequence of amino acids in a specific protein or polypeptide chain.

The term cistron is derived from the *cis-trans test* which can be used to determine the total length of a gene in a chromosome. This test depends on the fact that crossing over between homologous chromosomes (as discussed in Section 8.3A) can take place anywhere *within* the length of a gene as well as between adjacent genes, for a gene is merely a portion of a DNA molecule, and may be several thousand nucleotides in length. For purposes of explanation, let us designate the first half of the gene A as A_1 and the second half as A_2. An individual heterozygous for gene A and its mutant allele a will have a normal phenotype only if no crossing over occurs within the cistron and both A_1 and A_2 remain on the same chromosome, that is, in the *cis* position,

$$\frac{A_1 \quad A_2}{a_1 \quad a_2}$$

However, when crossing over occurs within the cistron, placing A_1 and A_2 in the *trans* position, the genotype of the heterozygote becomes

$$\frac{A_1 \quad a_2}{a_1 \quad A_2}$$

and a *mutant* phenotype is produced. The cistron therefore represents that portion of a chromosome of which the linear order must be preserved intact so that correct function may be carried out. As defined by the *cis-trans* test, the cistron thus actually is taken to represent the functional unit of heredity, the gene.

Crossing over within a cistron can also permit a functional gene to be produced from a recombination of parts of two mutant alleles. If, for example, in one mutant strain a mutation had occurred in the first half of cistron A, the genotype of that strain would really be

$$\frac{a_1 \quad A_2}{a_1 \quad A_2}$$

which would produce a mutant phenotype. In a reciprocal mutant strain in which a mutation had taken place in the second half of cistron A, the genotype would be

$$\frac{A_1 \quad a_2}{A_1 \quad a_2}$$

again resulting in a mutant phenotype. The hybrid progeny resulting from a cross between these two strains would have the *trans* genotype,

$$\frac{a_1 \quad A_2}{A_1 \quad a_2}$$

and consequently would also be phenotypically mutant although two normal half-cistrons are present in the genotype. However, in a certain proportion of F_2, crossing over within cistron A would take place, making possible the reappearance of the normal phenotype, by restoration of an intact cistron $\underline{A_1 \quad A_2}$ on one chromosome.

The experiments reviewed up to this point strongly support the following conclusions: (1) DNA, a double-stranded nucleic acid, is the primary determinant of heredity. (2) It replicates by separation of the two strands, each of which then serves as a template on which free nucleotides with bases complementary to those of the old strand are held in place while being bonded together enzymatically. (3) That portion of a DNA molecule which encodes the amino acid sequence of a protein or a peptide chain constitutes a gene; the total length of a gene may be defined by means of the *cis-trans* test. (4) Mutations taking place in a gene cause metabolic disturbances resulting from the failure of the mutant gene to produce a protein capable of acting as an enzyme; however, serological tests show that the mutant gene may still govern the synthesis of a protein little different from the normal one but changed enough that it cannot serve as an enzyme.

We are now ready to examine the genetic code, the ways in which this code may be changed by mutation, and the manner in which the code serves to direct the process of protein synthesis. We shall see that the contribution of a gene is threefold—it furnishes the molecular basis of *reproduction,* of *evolution,* and of *metabolic control* (Figure 9.23). The code can be *replicated,* in the organization of new DNA, *transcribed* into the somewhat modified language of messenger RNA (a compound with which we shall soon become acquainted), and *translated* into the completely different language of protein structure.

Figure 9.23 □ **Activities of DNA.**

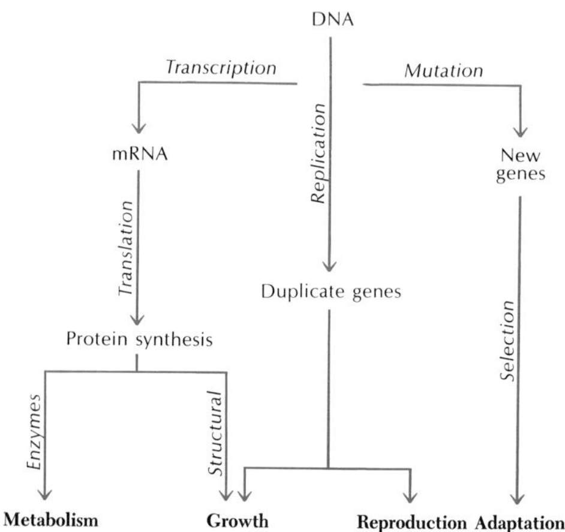

THE GENETIC CODE We know that both DNA and RNA are each constructed mainly out of only four different commonly occurring nucleotide units. The nearly infinite variability of nucleic acids thus can reside only in the *linear sequence and proportions of the four nucleotides present.* The Morse code, with only two symbols, can express every word in the English language. The genetic code has *four* symbols, each represented by one kind of nucleotide. Used *singly,* these would not produce a code of sufficient variety to code for the linear sequence of some 20 amino acids. If we postulate that the "letter" of the genetic code consists of two adjacent nucleotides (AG, CT, etc.), we would only have 16 possible combinations, still too few to carry out the function of determining the sequence of 20 different kinds of amino acids. However, if the "letter" of the genetic code were to consist of *three* consecutive nucleotides, 64 possible combinations would result, more than ample to encode 20 amino acids. Like the Morse code, the genetic code must translate an alphabet of many symbols into a code with few symbols—only two, a dot and a dash for Morse code, but four for the genetic code. But, unlike Morse, it would appear that each "letter" of the genetic code has the same number of unit symbols (three), while "letters" in Morse consist of from one to five unit symbols. Since the nucleotides of DNA differ only with respect to their nitrogenous base, it is convenient to refer to three consecutive nucleotides (on the same strand) as a *base triplet.* Each base triplet or *codon* represents the code by which one amino acid is positioned within a protein molecule. For instance, the triplet AAA is the DNA codon for the amino acid phenylalanine. A given gene must contain at least as many codons as there are amino acids in the protein or polypeptide chain being encoded. Therefore, a gene that encodes a protein having 1,000 amino acid units must itself consist of some 3,003 nucleotides, grouped into 1,001 codons. One thousand of these codons specify amino acid sequence in the protein, while any one of three codons, ATT, ATC, or ACT, serve to mark the end of a gene and terminate the "message" at that point. These chain-terminating codons are the "period" at the end of a genetic "sentence," and each marks one end of a cistron.

The genetic code, as determined for the colon bacillus, *Escherichia coli,* is summarized in Table 9.3. However, the codons shown in this table are RNA rather than DNA codons, for the gene first transcribes its code into the form of an RNA molecule known as messenger RNA, and in the process of transcription the deoxyribose nucleotides attract complementary ribose nucleotides. For instance, the DNA codon AAA is transcribed into the RNA codon UUU, for adenine bonds with uracil.

There is a considerable margin of safety in the genetic code, in that as many as four possible codons may code for a single amino acid. Although data are still inadequate, it is presently assumed that the genetic code determined for *E. coli* is fundamentally like those of all species throughout the biotic world. If this should not prove to be the case, such disparity could be taken as evi-

Table 9.3 □ The genetic code of *Escherichia coli* expressed in RNA codons[a]

FIRST LETTER	SECOND LETTER U		C		A		G		THIRD LETTER
U	UUU	phe	UCU	ser	UAU	tyr	UGU	cys	U
	UUC	phe	UCC	ser	UAC	tyr	UGC	cys	C
	UUA	leu	UCA	ser	UAA[b]		UGA[b]		A
	UUG	leu	UCG	ser	UAG[b]		UGG	try	G
C	CUU	leu	CCU	pro	CAU	his	CGU	arg	U
	CUC	leu	CCC	pro	CAC	his	GCG	arg	C
	CUA	leu	CCA	pro	CAA	gluN	CGA	arg	A
	CUG	leu	CCG	pro	CAG	gluN	CGG	arg	G
A	AUU	ileu	ACU	thr	AAU	aspN	AGU	ser	U
	AUC	ileu	ACC	thr	AAC	aspN	AGC	ser	C
	AUA	ileu	ACA	thr	AAA	lys	AGA	arg	A
	AUG	met or f-met[c]	ACG	thr	AAG	lys	AGG	arg	G
G	GUU	val	GCU	ala	GAU	asp	GGU	gly	U
	GUC	val	GCC	ala	GAC	asp	GGC	gly	C
	GAA	val	GCA	ala	GAA	glu	GGA	gly	A
	GUG	val or f-met[c]	GCG	ala	GAG	glu	GGG	gly	G

[a] Notice that the first and second letters are more crucial than the third in specifying the amino acids.

[b] One of the three chain-terminating codons.

[c] At the start of an mRNA molecule, AUG and GUG encode the position of a formylated methionine unit. It is not yet known whether this code holds for other species.

dence that more than one self-replicating system evolved during the beginnings of life and that contemporary organisms might represent the outcome of several parallel lines of descent.

MESSENGER RNA In most organisms DNA is not directly involved in protein synthesis, but instead produces a single-stranded molecule of *messenger RNA* (mRNA), which directly serves as the template for the protein. DNA replication and transcription are mutually exclusive events; a gene which is in the process of self-replication (as occurs prior to each cell division) is not capable of simultaneously producing messenger RNA. Whether a gene will replicate or transcribe at any given time is determined by conditions within the cell, such as the relative rates at which ribose and deoxyribose nucleotides are accumulating, and the relative proportions of the enzymes DNA-polymerase and RNA-polymerase. Replication is a *chromosomal* event, whereas transcription involves only the *individual* gene. Not all genes may be actively producing messenger RNA at any single moment, but when *replication* occurs, the whole strand must participate.

When producing mRNA, the complementary DNA strands must separate from one another, at least in part, presenting exposed bases for hydrogen bonding with free nucleotides (Figure 9.24). Chain-breaking codons located between each gene and the next assure that the manufacture of an RNA strand will be confined to the length of a single gene. As in the case of DNA replication, free triply-phosphorylated nucleotides (this time *ribose* nucleotides) are taken up by hydrogen bonding with complementary bases on the DNA strand, and are then polymerized in the presence of the enzyme RNA-polymerase. Given a supply of the appropriate ribose nucleotides, an energy source (ATP), and some RNA-polymerase, DNA can produce RNA in vitro. The size of an RNA molecule is determined by the length of the cistron or functional unit of DNA. When it is fully synthesized, the RNA molecule is released from its DNA template, becoming messenger RNA. The mRNA passes away from the chromosomes into the cytoplasm, and becomes associated with organelles known as *ribosomes*. Ribosomes themselves contain RNA, which accounts for their capacity to form specific hydrogen bonds with mRNA.

A number of ribosomes become attached like beads to the mRNA molecule (Figure 9.25). Apparently this arrangement permits multiple use of one mRNA strand by several ribosomes. The first ribosome becomes attached to the "starting end" of the mRNA molecule, and begins to produce a peptide chain by polymerizing amino acids

Figure 9.24 □ **The metabolic activity of DNA: synthesis of mRNA. (*a*) mRNA being produced on DNA template by incorporation of free ribose nucleotides. (*b*) RNA-polymerase, the enzyme responsible for synthesizing mRNA from nucleotides held in place on DNA strand by hydrogen bonding: above, arrows indicate RNA-polymerase molecules attached to DNA strands; below, single molecule of RNA-polymerase, showing that it consists of six subunits arranged in a hexagon (lower electron micrograph at 400,000× magnification). (*Courtesy of Dr. H. Fernández-Morán.*)**

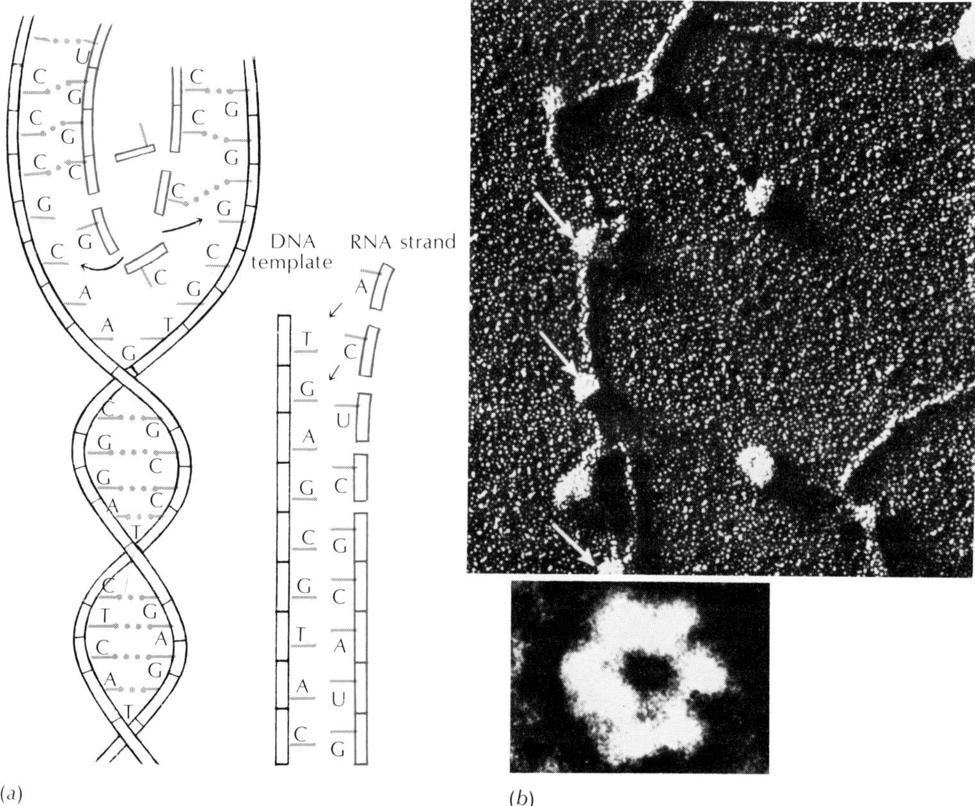

that are held in place on the mRNA template. As it does so, the ribosome moves down the length of the mRNA strand, "reading" one portion of the message at a time. Finally, that ribosome reaches the opposite end of the mRNA molecule and is set free, at the same time releasing the completed chain of amino acids. Meanwhile, another ribosome becomes attached to the starting end of the mRNA and in turn reads the code, moving along the length of the strand and feeding out a second chain of amino acids, identical to that produced by the first ribosome. As soon as one ribosome has moved past the starting end of the mRNA, another can become attached; eventually a long message will bear an entire string of ribosomes spaced out along its length, each synthesizing an amino acid chain as it moves along.

The adaptive value of mRNA is that it *amplifies the metabolic activity of DNA*. If DNA itself had to be directly concerned in protein manufacture (as it probably was in primitive cells), the latter would necessarily proceed at a much slower pace. As it is, DNA can go on reproducing RNA messages while each previously synthesized mRNA is engaged in protein synthesis. The existence of mRNA also permits protein synthesis to take place at a distance from the nucleus, in regions of the cell where the needed nutrients and enzymes are present. The protein-synthesizing activity can thus be spread throughout the cytoplasm.

Some types of mRNA have a short life and must be replenished as needed. Other types are very stable, these being involved in syntheses which must be carried on regularly throughout the life of the cell. One of the shortest-lived mRNA's known is that

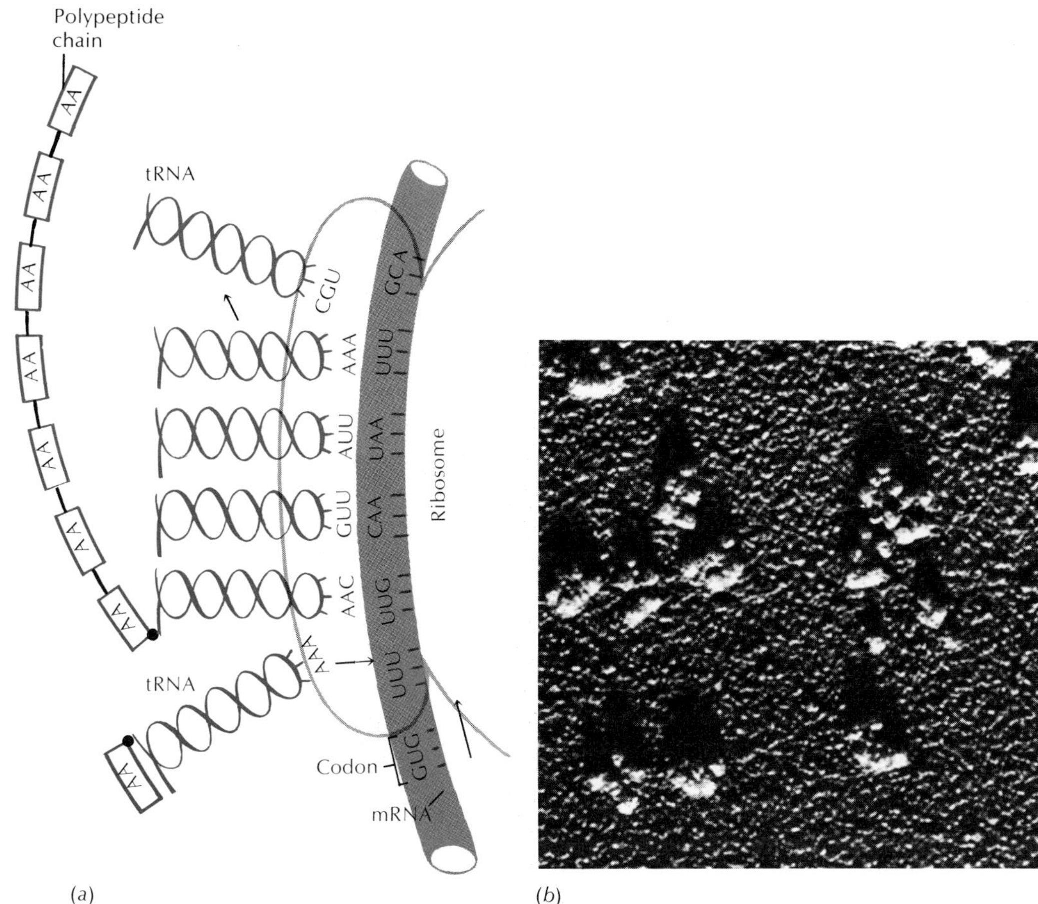

Figure 9.25 □ **Protein synthesis at the ribosome. (*a*) Schematic representation, showing amino acid-tRNA complexes approaching complementary sites on mRNA molecule and polymerization of amino acid units into a peptide chain through action of ribosome. (The actual form of tRNA is less regular than that shown here.) (*b*) Polysomes: clusters of ribosomes associated with long mRNA strand. (*Courtesy of Dr. Alexander Rich.*)**

for a sugar-digesting enzyme, β-galactosidase, which can manufacture only about ten of these enzyme molecules during its life. One of the most persistent is the messenger for hemoglobin, which persists at least 24 hours after the red blood cell has lost its nucleus. Bound mRNA may also be stored in the cytoplasm, for later activation.

TRANSFER RNA How is the message of mRNA translated into the linear order of amino acid units in a protein molecule? This was a baffling question until the significance of still another variety of RNA was clarified. We have previously distinguished the high molecular weight types, mRNA, and ribosomal RNA (rRNA), the latter permanently associated with and forming part of the ribosomes. Another RNA fraction, consisting of smaller molecules of relatively low molecular weight, may also be distinguished. This RNA fraction is known as *soluble RNA,* also designated *transfer RNA* (tRNA) since it serves the function of transferring particular amino acids to appropriate locations on the mRNA molecule.

The source of the soluble RNA fraction is not surely known. Since each gene is made up of *two* complementary strands of DNA, it is speculated that two complementary strands of RNA can be produced simultaneously, one forming on the template provided by *each* DNA strand. While one strand of RNA remains intact to serve as the messenger, its complement may then be fragmented into smaller segments, which would be complementary to short portions of each mRNA molecule and might well serve as a source of tRNA. However, tRNA always contains certain bases such as inosine (I) and pseudouracil (ψ), that are not characteristic of mRNA.

Figure 9.26 □ **Experiment establishing role of tRNA in the positioning of amino acids in protein molecules. The catalyst Raney nickel is used to remove S from cysteine, converting this amino acid to alanine after it has already combined with the cysteine-carrying type of tRNA. Alanine is then incorporated into the protein at each site where cysteine should be. We may conclude that it is the tRNA and not the amino acid that interacts with mRNA and determines the sites at which the amino acid will be incorporated.**

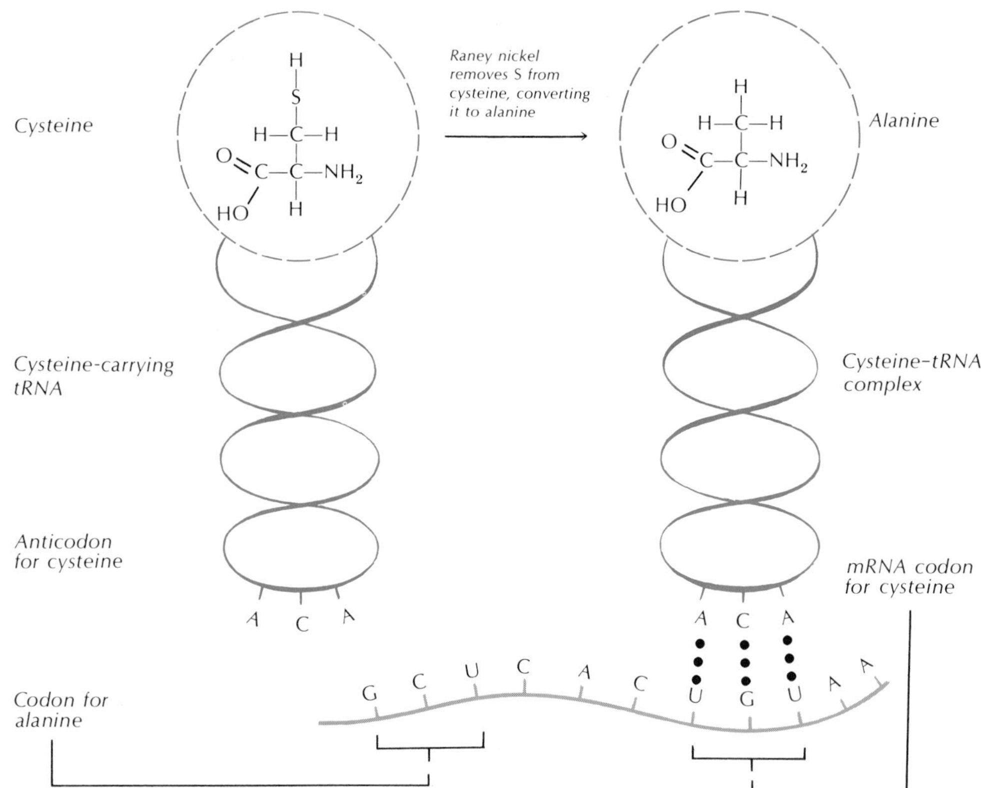

Transfer RNA molecules are short chains of about 75 nucleotides. One end of the chain starts with a guanine, while the other terminates with the base sequence CCA. Internally all types of tRNA contain the sequence GTψCG, which may serve for attachment to the ribosome. In other respects the chains are dissimilar, for more than 20 kinds of tRNA are known. For each amino acid which normally occurs in proteins, there is at least one type of tRNA which serves as an *adaptor* for that amino acid, transporting it to the correct site on the mRNA molecule, and helping to fit it into the reactive site of a ribosome. Transfer RNA molecules stabilize more or less in the form of a cloverleaf or a twisted hairpin: they double back on themselves and the parallel strands, though not complementary, form occasional hydrogen bonds at favorable locations. This bending back of the tRNA molecule upon itself is thought to expose a specific base triplet at the bend, this exposed triplet being thereby positioned favorably for the formation of hydrogen bonds with a complementary base triplet on the mRNA molecule (Figure 9.25). Whereas each base triplet of mRNA is termed a codon, the complementary base triplet of tRNA is termed an *anticodon.*

Transfer RNA forms temporary complexes with amino acid molecules present in the milieu. Such a complex is formed only if the amino acid is previously activated by being united with ATP. The enzyme *amino acyl-sRNA synthetase* then bonds the amino acid by way of its carboxyl group to the terminal adenosine of the tRNA, releasing AMP and pyrophosphate.

Just because tRNA molecules are found associated with amino acids does not necessarily mean that tRNA is involved in the correct placement of the amino acids in a growing peptide chain. The fact that tRNA is so involved was proven by a simple experiment. The question being tested was as follows: if one amino acid were changed into another *after* having formed a complex with tRNA, would that amino acid then be wrongly incorporated into the protein, where the original amino acid should have been? If this question were to be answered affirmatively, there would be grounds for concluding that the RNA part of the complex, and not the amino acid portion, was instrumental in positioning the amino acid within the protein molecule being constructed.

Amino acid–tRNA complexes may be formed in vitro, in a system that includes the soluble RNA fraction, ATP, amino acids, and the enzymes needed for combining the amino acids with ATP and the activated amino acids with tRNA. If the only amino acid provided in the in vitro system is, for example, cysteine, the only complex formed will be that between cysteine and its specific tRNA. After the cysteine–tRNA complexes have formed, a catalyst, Raney nickel, may be added to the system. Raney nickel removes the —SH group of the cysteine, which thereupon becomes the amino acid *alanine* (Figure 9.26). The result is that the tRNA that should be carrying a cysteine is now carrying an alanine instead. At this point isolated ribosomes and a simple synthetic mRNA are added to the system. The synthetic mRNA can be put together so as to be capable only of building a chain composed of a single amino acid, such as cysteine. Would the mRNA that should produce a polycysteine chain now accept the alanine units carried by the cysteine–tRNA? If so, a polyalanine chain instead of a polycysteine chain would be produced. This is in fact the outcome, indicating that the tRNA that normally carries cysteine now delivers the wrong amino acid to the mRNA, which thereupon builds a polyalanine chain. The positioning of amino acid units in a protein is thereby shown to depend strictly upon the complementarity of mRNA codons with tRNA anticodons.

E Gene mutation

Many mutations involve no more than a single nucleotide in a gene. Therefore, a gene potentially has at least as many allelic states as it possesses nucleotides. Mutation often seems to involve a replication error, in which the wrong nucleotide is accidentally incorporated into the new chain (Figure 9.27). In addition, sometimes a base within an existing chain may be altered by *deamination* (the loss of the amino group on C-6), a change that can affect both replication and transcription. The effectiveness of many mutagenic agents is in fact thought to rest upon their ability to render a base unstable or to cause it to lose an important functional group.

BASE SUBSTITUTION As shown in Figure 9.27*a*, adenine in the presence of nitrous acid (HNO_2), a mutagenic chemical, is *deaminated* to the purine hypoxanthine. Guanine may similarly be deaminated to xanthine, as may cytosine, to uracil. Uracil is not itself a normal component of DNA, but at the next replication forms hydrogen bonds with a nucleotide containing adenine. This in turn, at the subsequent replication, incorporates a thymine-containing unit into the complementary strand. Thus, in two successive replications, the base pair C-G has been replaced by the base pair A-T. A DNA codon that formerly read "CAT" would now read "AAT." This would produce a messenger RNA codon with the bases UUA instead of GUA, with the result that the amino acid *leucine* would be incorporated into the protein to be manufactured, in lieu of the correct one, *valine*.

Hypoxanthine and xanthine, both bearing an oxy group on C-6 behave like guanine during replication and transcription. Thus, when a guanine is converted into xanthine, no demonstrable change takes place in the code, but when *adenine* is deaminated to hypoxanthine, at the next replication it can be expected that a cytosine instead of a thymine will be incorporated in the complementary strand:

$$A\text{-}T + HNO_2 \longrightarrow \text{H-T} \rightarrow \{\text{H-C} \rightarrow (\text{H-C},\ \textbf{C-G}),\ \text{T-A} \rightarrow (\text{T-A},\ \text{A-T})\}$$

Mutant (C-G)

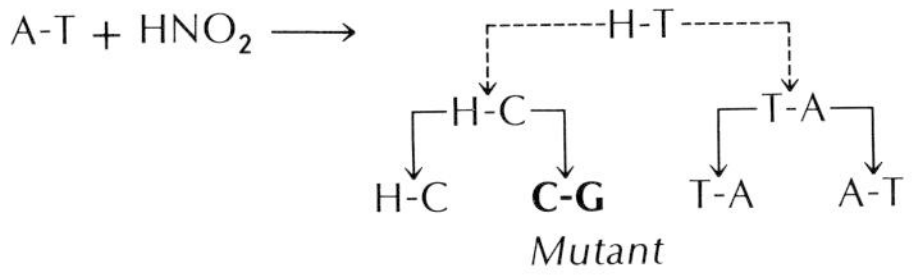

This is an example of mutation by *base substitution*. Only a single codon is altered, but this alteration may considerably change the meaning of the sentence:

THE FAT CAT ATE THE RED RAT

could by base substitution become

THE FAT CAT ATE THE RED HAT

an unusual accomplishment, to say the least. That a change in a single codon may have drastic metabolic effects is well shown in the case of sickle-cell anemia (Figure 8.3), a human malady resulting from the production of a mutant hemoglobin, Hb-S.

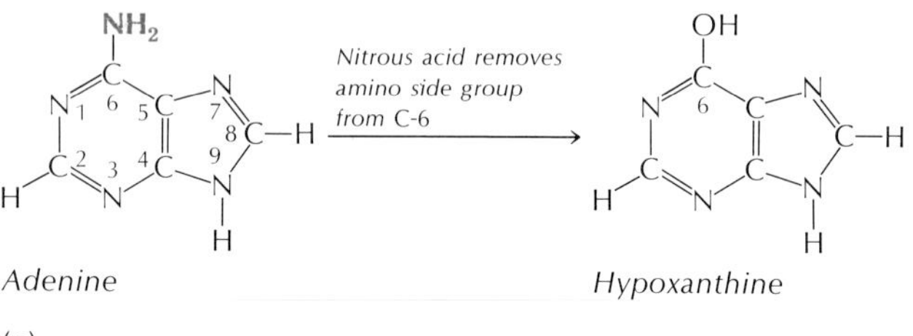

(a)

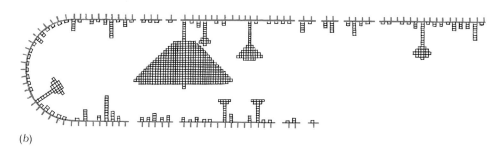

(b)

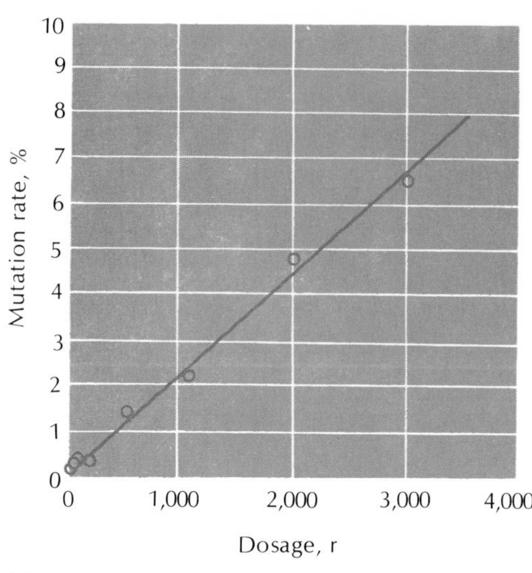

(c)

Figure 9.27 □ Gene mutation. (*a*) Mutation by base substitution, caused by a mutagenic chemical, nitrous acid; by the loss of its amino side group, adenine is converted to hypoxanthine, which at the next replication will incorporate cytosine instead of thymine into the complementary strand. Explain why this error will take place. (*b*) Mutation map of a single gene in the chromosome of bacteriophage T2; number of squares at each locus indicates number of times a mutation has been found to occur at that site (each locus represents one nucleotide so that it can be seen that certain nucleotides appear to be much more unstable than others. [*From S. Benzer,* Proc. Natl. Acad. Sci. 47, *410* (*1961*).] (*c*) Relation between mutation rate and dosage of X rays in *Drosophila;* note that X rays can cause mutation at *any dosage*—there is no "safe" level of exposure. [*From R. P. Wagner and H. K. Mitchell,* Genetics and Metabolism (2nd ed.) (*New York: John Wiley & Sons, Inc., 1964*).]

The hemoglobin molecule is one of the few proteins which to date have been completely analyzed chemically: the position of every single amino acid is known with certainty. This prodigious analytical feat revealed that each hemoglobin molecule consists of four polypeptide chains: two identical α chains, and two β chains. In one portion of each β chain the amino acid sequence normally reads

val-$\overset{+}{\text{his}}$-leu-thr-pro-$\overset{-}{\text{glu}}$-$\overset{-}{\text{glu}}$-$\overset{+}{\text{lys}}$ . . .

while in Hb-S, the sequence is

val-$\overset{+}{\text{his}}$-leu-thr-pro-*val*-$\overset{-}{\text{glu}}$-$\overset{+}{\text{lys}}$. . . .

The designations − and + indicate that the amino acid bears a positive or a negative electrical charge due to the loss of either a proton or an electron. As we can see, in Hb-S a *valine* unit has been substituted for a glutamic acid molecule. Since the missing glutamic acid unit in each β chain bore a *negative* electrical charge, while the substituted valine does not, the entire Hb-S molecule differs from normal hemoglobin by a net loss of two negative units of charge (that is, it possesses two more electrons than it should). This affects the behavior of the entire hemoglobin molecule.

Since the DNA codons for glutamic acid may be CTT or CTC, while those for valine may be CAT or CAC, it is apparent that the amino acid substitution and the altered electrical properties of the Hb-S molecule may be the result of a point mutation involving a *single base substitution.* Strange to think that this minor chemical change spells death to the homozygous individual! Other mutant hemoglobins are known, and where these have been fully analyzed, they also appear to involve a single amino acid substitution resulting from a change in one codon.

Another way in which base substitution can affect the gene is if such a substitution changes an *amino-acid-specifying* codon to a *chain-terminating* codon, for example, ATA (coding for tyrosine) to ATT (chain terminator). In this event the message is broken into two fragments, neither of which may be effective alone.

BASE ADDITION OR DELETION A replication error may result in the *deletion* of a single nucleotide from a gene, or in the accidental repetition of one nucleotide, a *base addition*. Either of these events may have much more drastic effects on the genetic code than a base substitution. Since the code apparently reads off in base triplets from the beginning to the end of one cistron, if a nucleotide is added or deleted, the "sentence" from that point on reads for a completely different amino acid sequence, which in functional terms may be "nonsense." As the result of a single nucleotide deletion, the message

THE FAT CAT ATE THE SAD RED RAT

would become

THE FTC ATA TET HES ADR EDR AT

Wrong information is thus provided for every location beyond the point of deletion. The gene product will be so drastically altered as to be unrecognizable.

Similarly, the above sentence could also be greatly changed by the addition of one base:

THE FAT CAT ATE THE SAD RED RAT

becoming

THH EFA TCA TAT ETH ESA DRE DRA T

Because of the interruptions afforded by chain-terminating codons, any mutation affecting one cistron will not ordinarily affect the code of adjacent ones. Occasionally, however, the "period" may be lost by a deletion which crosses that region of the chromosome. In such a case, a base addition or deletion in the first gene would scramble the code of the second gene as well.

The slightly or drastically modified proteins produced as a result of a base substitution, addition, or deletion are often incapable of mediating essential biochemical activities. If no normal allele is present on a homologous chromosome, the condition may be lethal. On the other hand, where alternative metabolic pathways are available, or where diploidy makes possible the retention of the mutant allele in a harmless recessive state, these altered proteins are available for the eventual assumption of some new role in metabolism or development—they serve as raw materials for evolutionary change. In fact, as the amino acid sequence is determined for more proteins, it should be possible to fathom past evolutionary changes that occurred in the genetic material of allied species, for changes in proteins reflect changes in the corresponding genes. A single amino acid substitution would reflect mutation in a single codon. Knowledge of the genetic code would also permit recognition of cases in which a drastic modification in amino acid composition may have resulted from a simple base deletion or addition. The extent of evolutionary changes in proteins could then be used as a guide to reconstructing phylogeny and to determining the degree of relatedness among various existing taxonomic groups.

REVIEW AND DISCUSSION

1 What types of orbitals occur in the four elements that are of most general occurrence in organic compounds? Explain how sp^3 hybridization affects the biotic world. How do the bonding properties of the oxygen atom affect the behavior of the water molecule?

2 What properties of carbon make it especially suitable as a basis for the development of living systems? What other element has similar properties? How do the bonding properties of carbon affect the shapes of organic molecules?

3 Differentiate, with examples, among stereoisomerism, geometrical isomerism, and structural isomerism. Does the existence of stereoisomers of common organic compounds have any especial biotic significance?

4 Specify the small molecules which make up each of the following: (*a*) protein;

(*b*) nucleic acid; (*c*) phospholipid; (*d*) starch; (*e*) cellulose; (*f*) hyaluronic acid; (*g*) chitin; (*h*) triglyceride fat; (*i*) wax; (*j*) agar; (*k*) mucin.

5 Explain the functional roles of (*a*) phospholipids; (*b*) salts of cholic acid; (*c*) steroid hormones; (*d*) chitin; (*e*) pentosans; (*f*) collagen; (*g*) keratin; (*h*) ribose; (*i*) pyrrole; (*j*) chondroitin sulfate.

6 What are the functional characteristics of enzymes?

7 Summarize the functional roles played by proteins, other than as enzymes.

8 Summarize experimental evidence that: (a) nucleic acids are the primary hereditary determinants; (b) transfer RNA determines how amino acids are bonded with messenger RNA; (c) each strand of DNA retains its linear integrity during replication.

9 Compare the events involved in DNA replication and in transcription from DNA to RNA.

10 Summarize the process by which genes determine the manufacture of proteins. Evaluate the one gene–one enzyme–one action hypothesis, citing experimental evidence in support of the hypothesis. What exceptions may there be to this hypothesis as a general rule?

11 Contrast the effect on the genetic code of a base substitution, addition, or deletion. Under what conditions is a base substitution likely to have the most profound effects? What keeps a mutation in one gene from affecting the next gene in line?

12 Explain what is meant by each of the following: (*a*) codon; (*b*) anticodon; (*c*) valence; (*d*) valence shell; (*e*) isotope; (*f*) ion.

13 Compare ionic, covalent, and hydrogen bonding, and explain how each is important to the biotic world.

14 What is meant by the primary, secondary, and tertiary architecture of a protein? If the genetic code determines only the primary structure, how do the secondary and tertiary arrangements come about? What is the significance of helical arrangements in the case of proteins and of nucleic acids?

REFERENCES

ANFINSEN, C. B. *The Molecular Basis of Evolution.* New York: John Wiley & Sons, Inc., 1959.

AVERY, O. T., C. M. MACLEOD, AND M. MCCARTY "Studies on the Chemical Nature of the Substance Inducing Transformation of Pneumococcal Types. Induction of Transformation by a Desoxyribonucleic Acid Fraction Isolated from Pneumococcus Type III," *J. Exp. Med.,* **79** (1944). A classic paper establishing the role of DNA in heredity.

BEADLE, G. W. "Genes and Chemical Reactions in *Neurospora,*" *Science,* **129** (1959).

BENZER, S., AND E. FREESE "Induction of Specific Mutation with 5-Bromouracil," *Proc. Natl. Acad. Sci. U.S.,* **44** (1958).

BONNER, D. M., Y. SYAMA, AND J. A. DEMOSS "Genetic Fine Structure and Enzyme Formation," *Federation Proc.,* **19** (1960).

CAIRNS, J. "The Bacterial Chromosome," *Sci. Amer.,* **214** (1966).

CLARK, B. F. C., AND K. A. MARCKER "How Proteins Start," *Sci. Amer.,* **218** (1968). A formylated methionine unit is found always to be incorporated at the beginning of a peptide chain in *E. coli,* perhaps furnishing means for "recognizing" the starting end of the molecule.

COMPANION, A. L. *Chemical Bonding.* New York: McGraw-Hill Book Company, 1964. A useful reference, providing information on orbitals and bonding.

CRICK, F. H. C. "The Genetic Code: III," *Sci. Amer.,* **215** (1966). The third in a series of articles reporting progress made in deciphering the genetic code of *E. coli.*

DEERING, R. A. "Ultraviolet Radiation and Nucleic Acid," *Sci. Amer.,* **207** (1962).

FIESER, L. F. "Steroids," *Sci. Amer.,* **192** (1955).

FRAENKEL-CONRAT, H. "The Genetic Code of a Virus," *Sci. Amer.,* **211** (1964).

GORINI, L. "Antibiotics and the Genetic Code," *Sci. Amer.,* **214** (1966).

GROSS, J. "Collagen," *Sci. Amer.,* **192** (1955). The ultrastructure of an important protein is explored.

HANAWALT, P. C., AND R. H. HAYNES "The Repair of DNA," *Sci. Amer.,* **216** (1967). Radiation-resistant bacteria are found to possess an enzyme capable of excising a radiation-damaged segment of the bacterial chromosome and replacing the defective nucleotides with normal ones.

HERSHEY, A., AND M. CHASE "Independent Functions of Viral Protein and Nucleic Acid in Growth of Bacteriophage," *J. Gen. Physiol.,* **36** (1952).

HERSKOWITZ, I. H. *Basic Principles of Molecular Genetics.* Boston: Little, Brown and Company, 1967. A concise, readable reference for the interested student seeking further knowledge in this key area.

HOLLEY, R. W. "The Nucleotide Sequence of a Nucleic Acid," *Sci. Amer.*, **214** (1966).

INGRAM, V. "Abnormal Human Haemoglobins 1. The Comparison of Normal Human and Sickle-cell Haemoglobins by 'Fingerprinting,'" *Biochim. et Biophys. Acta*, **28** (1958). A classic experiment in which the difference between a normal and mutant protein was determined.

KENDREW, J. C. "The Three-dimensional Structure of a Protein Molecule," *Sci. Amer.*, **205** (1961).

KORNBERG, A. "Biologic Synthesis of Deoxyribonucleic Acid," *Science*, **131** (1960).

——— "The Synthesis of DNA," *Sci. Amer.*, **219** (1968). The biochemical pathway of DNA synthesis is elucidated by the production of biologically active virus DNA in a cell-free system.

MERRIFIELD, R. B. "The Automatic Synthesis of Proteins," *Sci. Amer.*, **218** (1968). Once the amino acid sequence of a protein has been identified, the protein can be synthesized in the laboratory by a solid phase technique involving incorporation of amino acids on the surface of microscopic polystyrene beads.

MESELSON, M., AND F. STAHL "The Replication of DNA in *Escherichia coli*," *Proc. Natl. Acad. Sci. U.S.*, **44** (1958). A now classical research paper describing a historical experiment on the replication of bacterial chromosomes.

PERUTZ, M. F. "The Hemoglobin Molecule," *Sci. Amer.*, **211** (1964).

PRESTON, R. D. "Cellulose," *Sci. Amer.*, **197** (1957). Examines the properties of a polysaccharide of nearly universal occurrence throughout the Plant Kingdom.

RICH, A. "Polyribosomes," *Sci. Amer.*, **209** (1963). Considers the functional significance of ribosomal clusters seen by way of the electron microscope.

SCHMITT, F. O. "Giant Molecules in Cells and Tissues," *Sci. Amer.*, **197** (1957).

SPIEGELMAN, S. "Hybrid Nucleic Acids," *Sci. Amer.*, **210** (1964).

STEIN, W. H., AND S. MOORE "The Chemical Structure of Proteins," *Sci. Amer.*, **204** (1961). Describes procedures used in working out the structural formulas of insulin and ribonuclease.

WATSON, J. D. "Involvement of RNA in the Synthesis of Proteins," *Science*, **140** (1963). Reviews in narrative style the research work leading to our present understanding of the mechanism of protein synthesis.

——— *The Molecular Biology of the Gene*. New York: W. A. Benjamin, Inc., 1965.

——— *The Double Helix*. New York: Atheneum Press, 1968. An entertaining account of the discovery of the molecular organization of DNA.

WHITE, E. H. *Chemical Background for the Biological Sciences*. Englewood Cliffs, N.J.: Prentice-Hall, Inc., 1964. Useful reference for students lacking experience in chemistry.

YANOFSKY, C. "Gene Structure and Protein Synthesis," *Sci. Amer.*, **216** (1967). Analysis of the amino acid sequence of mutant forms of tryptophan synthetase, and of the nucleotide sequence of the relevant genes, provides evidence of the colinearity of gene and protein.

Chapter 10 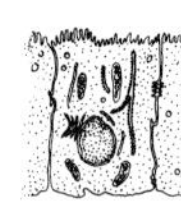 THE ORGANIZATION OF CELLS

TWO FUNDAMENTAL QUESTIONS MUST be considered in any discussion of the development of biotic organization: (1) how did life originate and evolve to its present level of structural complexity; (2) how do living systems conserve their organization from generation to generation? The latter question involves two subproblems: (*a*) how do cells and cellular constituents reproduce themselves; (*b*) how do cells differentiate into specialized types that interact during the course of development to produce a multicellular body? These problems will be the concern of this chapter and the next.

10.1 □ THE ORIGIN OF LIFE

A study of present-day developmental processes sheds less light than might be thought on the question of how life originated, for development now takes place through the mediation of enzymes and according to the specifications of a highly evolved nucleic acid code. New cells arise only from preexisting cells and are from their outset complex units of organization equipped with the genetic materials and energy sources required for growth and maturation. The highly complex functional organization achieved over 3×10^9 years of organic evolution is now replicated and transmitted intact from one generation to the next. Concrete evidence bearing upon the origin of life at the molecular level and its subsequent evolution to the cellular level is still fragmentary and inferential. Any attempt to formulate a coherent account of the sequence of events by which cellular life originated must therefore be considered speculative.

A Hypotheses regarding the origin of life

Proposed explanations of how life arose occur in the mythology and religious literature of most of the world's peoples as well as in scientific writings. These explanations have included the following:

1 *Life on earth was supernaturally created* This belief is not subject to experimental testing and hence lies outside the competence of scientific inquiry. However, its relevance is affected by the credibility of alternative hypotheses.

2 *Life on earth is of extraterrestrial origin* Proposed by the Swedish physical chemist Svante Arrhenius, this theory suggested that bacterial spores might escape from the atmosphere of one planet and drift through interstellar space, propelled by the pressure of light until captured by another planet's gravitational field. Unfortunately, any theory proposing that terrestrial life has originated elsewhere in the universe leaves unanswered the question of how life arose wherever it *did* have its start.

3 *Complex living things can arise de novo from nonliving material at any time* This belief, the so-called *spontaneous generation theory,* was widely held as long as humanity was limited to the evidence of its unaided eyesight. The abrupt appearance of horsehair worms in a horse's watering trough or of maggots on spoiling meat was taken as the clearest proof that these animals had been spontaneously generated from the inanimate horsehair or the dead meat. The theory of spontaneous generation was attacked experimentally in 1688 by the Italian physician Francesco Redi, who demonstrated that no maggots developed on meat if the vessel containing it were covered with cloth to exclude flies. The final blow to this long-lived theory was dealt 200 years later by Louis Pasteur, who found that broth boiled within a flask with a thin S-shaped neck remained sterile indefinitely. The neck of the flask remained open to the exterior, permitting air to enter, but microbes were trapped on the curving sides. When the neck was later snapped off, the broth then developed a growth of microorganisms, proving that it had been capable of supporting such growth all along.

With the collapse of the theory of continuous spontaneous generation, the concept "all life from preceding life" (Pasteur's aphorism, *Omne vivum e vivo*) became widely accepted; although generally accepted at present, the latter concept placed the scientific community in a peculiar position of circularity—if all living things came from other living things, could they *ever,* at any time, have originated spontaneously from the nonliving world? As long as the concept of "fixity of species" prevailed—that species are today as they were first created—any hypothesis of the spontaneous origin of life foundered on the unanswerable argument that it was beyond reason for over a million distinct forms of life to have arisen spontaneously in their present form from nonliving materials. However, only a year before Pasteur's experiments were made public, Charles Darwin and A. R. Wallace published simultaneously and independently their theory that living things do *not* remain the same, but evolve through the agency of natural selection. The gradual acceptance of this evolutionary theory, together with accumulating evidence concerning the fundamental unity of organization in living things, lent support to a new hypothesis concerning the origin of life.

4 *Primordial life could have arisen spontaneously, under favorable conditions, from the abiotic materials of the primeval earth and its atmosphere.* This is the modern theory of *abiogenesis,* the origin of life from the inanimate (Figure 10.1). It assumes prerequisite conditions of the primitive earth different from those of the present.

B The primitive earth

Certain assumptions have been made by scientists concerning the conditions that prevailed on earth at the time when life originated—probably 3 to 4×10^9 years ago. The most ancient definite traces of cellular life found to date exceed 2×10^9 years old, as estimated by radioactive dating of the

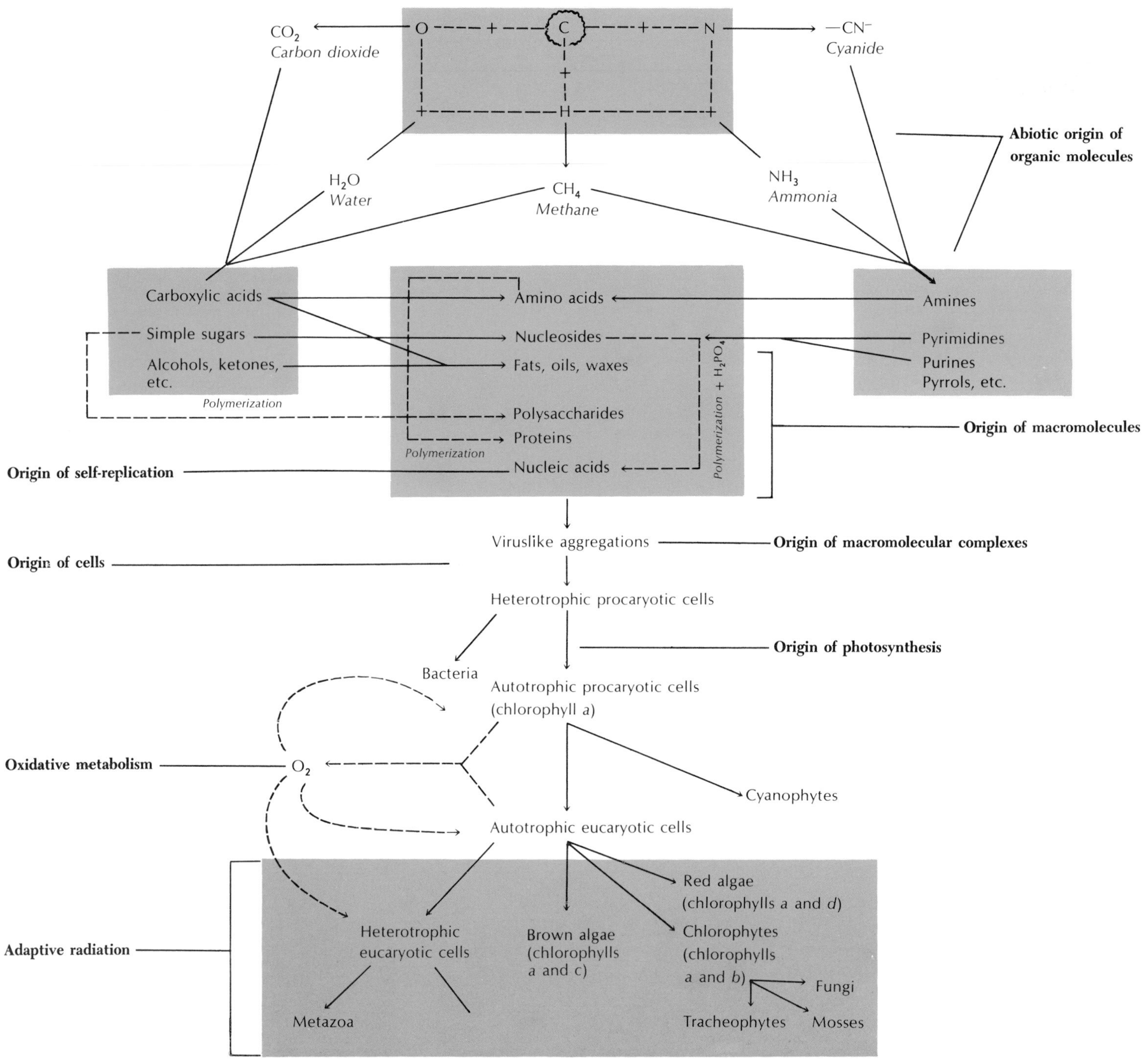
CO_2
Carbon dioxide
O
C
N
H
$-CN^-$
Cyanide
H_2O
Water
CH_4
Methane
NH_3
Ammonia
Abiotic origin of organic molecules
Carboxylic acids
Simple sugars
Alcohols, ketones, etc.
Polymerization
Amino acids
Nucleosides
Fats, oils, waxes
Polysaccharides
Proteins
Nucleic acids
Polymerization
Polymerization + H_2PO_4
Amines
Pyrimidines
Purines
Pyrrols, etc.
Origin of macromolecules
Origin of self-replication
Viruslike aggregations
Origin of macromolecular complexes
Origin of cells
Heterotrophic procaryotic cells
Origin of photosynthesis
Bacteria
Autotrophic procaryotic cells (chlorophyll a)
Oxidative metabolism
O_2
Cyanophytes
Autotrophic eucaryotic cells
Red algae (chlorophylls a and d)
Heterotrophic eucaryotic cells
Brown algae (chlorophylls a and c)
Chlorophytes (chlorophylls a and b)
Fungi
Adaptive radiation
Metazoa
Tracheophytes
Mosses

Figure 10.1 □ Important events in the history of life.

sedimentary rocks in which they occur. Well preserved fossil bacteria have been identified in rocks of this age. Before then, there must have been a period of at least equal length of *molecular evolution* during which organic compounds and macromolecular complexes originated and evolved to the cellular level of organization. A wide variety of organic compounds and possibly even evidence of cellular life have been discovered in rocks as old as 3×10^9 years! The total age of our sun and its planets is now estimated at somewhat more than 5×10^9 years, which would mean that life may have existed on earth for more than half the planet's total age.

The theory is no longer generally held that the planets of our solar system arose as molten pieces torn from our sun by the close passage of another star. Instead, considerable mathematical and physical evidence supports the alternative hypothesis that planets and suns alike arise by the condensation of dust and gases. According to this hypothesis, dust and gases tend to collect into globular clouds of matter, each of which may evolve into a solar system. As such a cloud of prestellar material condenses, it begins to rotate, at first slowly but then more and more rapidly in accordance with the law of conservation of angular momentum. This law is familiar to ice skaters, who know that a slow spin executed with outspread arms is converted into a rapid spin when the arms are drawn in against the trunk. As a primordial cloud of matter condenses and rotates, it tends to collapse into the form of a disk; within this rotating disk subsections begin to rotate separately, creating foci of condensation in the center and at intervals toward the edge of the disk. Most of the mass of the cloud lies in the central focus of condensation, and this becomes a star; the much smaller peripheral masses become its planets. If this hypothesis is correct, a large proportion of the stars must be accompanied by planetary systems.

A planet's gravitational field impedes the escape of lighter elements into space, and these accordingly remain to form an atmospheric envelope about the planet. Was the atmosphere of earth 4×10^9 years ago much as it is today? Probably it was very different, and may have contained many of the materials that even today characterize the atmospheres of the giant planets of our system, such as Jupiter and Neptune. The atmospheres of these planets contain hydrogen (H_2), helium (He), ammonia (NH_3), and methane (CH_4), mostly in the liquid state. The lighter gases, hydrogen and helium, have long since escaped from the attraction of our relatively small planet, but are still held by the greater mass of the giant planets. If hydrogen escapes from the atmosphere, methane and ammonia will not long remain, for they tend to break down under the influence of light, liberating more hydrogen gas, which escapes in turn.

Many geophysicists believe that the earth's primeval atmosphere was similar to that of the giant planets. Others contend that the primordial atmosphere originated mainly by the escape from the earth's interior of hot gases, which interacted with materials of the earth's crust to produce an atmosphere composed mainly of carbon dioxide, carbon monoxide, nitrogen, and hydrogen; such a combination of gases interacts when irradiated by ultraviolet light, to produce the compound hydrogen cyanide ($HC{\equiv}N$).

Despite lack of agreement on particulars, it is generally accepted as a tentative working hypothesis that the primeval earth's atmosphere lacked free oxygen and contained hydrogen or hydrogen compounds, and thus was not an oxidizing but a *reducing* atmosphere. (That is, it could have served as a source of hydrogen for reduction reactions, but it could not furnish oxygen for oxidations.) This concept is of great significance to biologists, since one objection to abiogenetic hypotheses of the origin of life had been the fact that if any organic compounds did arise spontaneously in the presence of an oxidizing atmosphere (such as that of the present day), they would have been oxidized rapidly upon exposure to oxygen and thus could not have persisted long enough to interact effectively. If the primitive atmosphere were indeed a reducing atmosphere, it could have changed into its present form by the gradual escape of hydrogen into space, which would promote further liberation of hydrogen by the breakdown of hydrogen-containing compounds; eventually this hydrogen also would have escaped into space. Meanwhile oxygen could have accumulated gradually in the atmosphere, at first only in such relatively minor quantities as might be liberated through the photolytic effect of sunlight on water, but later, after photosynthesizing organisms had evolved, in much greater quantities. Photolysis of water is a self-limiting process, for as O_2 is released it diffuses into the upper atmosphere and acts as a filter which screens out the ultraviolet radiation that is most effective in causing photolysis. This self-limitation is thought to operate at an O_2 concentration only some 0.01 percent of the present level (the Urey effect). On the other hand, O_2 can be liberated by photosynthesis without any known self-limiting effect. Consequently, photosynthesis is considered responsible for nearly the entire atmospheric O_2 content. Indeed, it has been estimated that the present photosynthetic activity of plants would be sufficient to replenish the oxygen content of the atmosphere in a period of only a few decades.

A second provisional conclusion concerning primitive earth conditions has been that although the planets probably did not cool from a molten state, considerable heat might still have been generated during the condensation of material to form a planet. If so, the climate of the primeval earth could have been substantially hotter than at present. Heat escaping from the interior, coupled perhaps with a higher level of radiation from the young sun, could have produced many environments—shallow parts of the sea, hot freshwater pools, and the like—where temperatures hovered around 90°C., facilitating chemical reactions. Possible sources of additional reaction energy may have been electrical discharges in the atmosphere and ultraviolet radiation in amounts greater than can penetrate the atmosphere as it is now constituted.

On the basis of these tentative conclusions regarding the composition of the primordial atmosphere and the availability of radiant, thermal, or electrical energy, a number of scientists have set up controlled conditions thought to resemble those of the primeval earth to see whether simple inorganic materials interact under these conditions to form organic compounds. The results have been highly gratifying; in summarizing them we must bear in mind that the investigators did *not* in fact *synthesize* the resulting compounds—they only set up the conditions in which certain reactions might occur *spontaneously*.

C Evolution from molecule to cell

In their now classic experiment (1953) Stanley Miller and Harold Urey circulated a mixture of CH_4, NH_3, H_2, and water vapor through a spark-discharge apparatus in which the energy of electrical discharges simulated lightning. In the presence of this energy source these simple compounds interacted to produce a number of different amino and carboxylic acids. (Methane, although classified as an organic compound, is known to occur abiotically, usually as a product of volcanic activity.) Subsequently, other investigators employed ultraviolet light or mild sustained heat as energy sources, and obtained comparable results. Proponents of the hypothesis that cyanide was a principal atmospheric component have found that HCN when irradiated with ultraviolet light will also contribute to the formation of amino acids and other organic molecules. (We should note that cyanide is poisonous only to organisms that require O_2; bacteria that can respire anaerobically are not harmed by cyanide. The first forms of cellular life must have obtained energy strictly by anaerobic processes and could therefore tolerate an atmosphere containing cyanide.)

Amino acids themselves are incapable of self-replication, but under some circumstances, such as drying or being heated to between 70° and 80°C in the presence of phosphate, spontaneously form chains termed *proteinoids*. Proteinoids spontaneously associate in bacteria-sized spherules (*microspheres*), which in turn tend to aggregate in chains. The behavior of proteinoid microspheres is intriguing and may shed light on how membranes might form spontaneously, surrounding water droplets or aggregations of other organic molecules. Microspheres enlarge as they attract additional amino acids and eventually "reproduce" by fission. Such division is merely a surface-tension phenomenon reflecting the physical properties of colloids and is not to be equated with actual cell division, which is much more complex.

Amino acids themselves cannot mediate the production of more amino acids, or proteins the formation of new protein. However, nucleic acids *can* accomplish their own replication. Is there evidence that nucleotides too can arise spontaneously and possibly aggregate to form chains? This question appears to be answerable affirmatively. At least, spontaneously formed adenine, guanine, ribose, and deoxyribose have been isolated from ammonia-methane-water mixtures and have been found to combine into nucleotides such as adenosine triphosphate in the presence of inorganic phosphate and with application of mild heat (±90°C).

Such experiments enable us to reconstruct a possible sequence of events leading to the appearance of mutable, self-replicating macromolecular complexes, perhaps similar to some of the simpler viruses, and the origin from these of the first cellular life. We may divide this sequence into seven possible steps:

1 *Formation of simple organic compounds* Since a variety of small organic molecules have been experimentally shown to arise spontaneously under putative "primitive earth conditions" (in which simple compounds abundant in the abiotic environment are protected from free oxygen while being subjected to energy in the form of mild heat, electrical discharges, or ultraviolet radiation), it is likely that such compounds arose spontaneously during some period when conditions were favorable. As these compounds accumulated, the sea and other bodies of water became rich in substrates needed for building more complex molecular units.

2 *Formation of very large molecules* Small organic molecules have a tendency to coalesce spontaneously to form more stable groupings held together by hydrogen bonds. This increases the probability that they may stay together long enough to form covalent bonds. Today the formation of covalent bonds in living systems depends upon the activity of enzymes; however, catalysts merely facilitate reactions that in time may occur *spontaneously.* In the absence of destructive free oxygen and without preexisting organisms to eat them, even without catalysis abiotically generated amino acids eventually can link to form peptides, and nucleotides combine into nucleic acid chains. Eventually certain macromolecular aggregations may have developed rudimentary properties of life, particularly the capacity to reproduce.

3 *Formation of a self-replicating molecule* The self-replicating capacity of nucleic acids could have been realized whenever a single chain of adequate length was formed by the union of spontaneously formed free nucleotides, probably in the presence of inorganic phosphate. (As we shall see later, compounds gain reaction energy when they form bonds with inorganic phosphate.) Adenosine triphosphate, the most abundant nucleotide generated abiotically, could also have furnished energy for the polymerization. The original polynucleotide could then have served as a template on which free nucleotides from the milieu could have been incorporated in a complementary sequence, much as DNA replicates itself today. Such growth and reproduction by the *selective* incorporation of organic compounds from the environment would have represented the most primitive instance of true nutrition. (The nonselective incorporation of amino acids into a proteinoid microsphere is not exactly a nutritional process, since the incorporation is random and does not take place on an already formed template such as is provided by DNA.)

What is the minimum length at which a DNA molecule becomes capable of self-replication? Investigations have been carried out on bacteriophage viruses in which chain-terminating codons arising through base-substitution mutation cause the virus chromosome to break during its formation, so that only a portion of the total strand is produced. Infecting bacteria with these chromosome fragments demonstrates that the minimum length of a DNA strand capable of self-replication is on the order of 500 nucleotide units. Strands shorter than this fail to replicate. The 500-nucleotide chain, probably considerably shorter than most individual genes, thus appears to represent the simplest "living" system isolated to date.

4 *Protein-building by "protogenes"* In addition to replicating themselves, primordial nucleic acids could also have served as catalysts promoting the formation of proteins from amino acids that had coalesced about the nucleic acid strand. Such catalysis of protein synthesis by nucleic acids would not necessarily have required the presence of tRNA and mRNA, which may have been adaptive refinements developed later that permitted DNA to exert its effects at a distance.

The innate "stickiness" or cohesiveness of the proteins formed in this manner would have increased the likelihood that they would remain in the neighborhood of the protochromosome, possibly assuming the characteristics of a colloidal gel. (Living cytoplasm is a colloidal complex.)

5 *Formation of cell membranes* Many organic molecules exhibit tendencies toward *spontaneous architecture*—the assumption of orderly geometric configurations that might have facilitated the production of cell-like aggregations. For instance, mixtures of lipid molecules (lecithin, cholesterol, and saponin) arrange themselves into membranelike sheets that are actually double-layered sandwiches in which the molecules lie parallel with their fat-soluble ends oriented inward and their water-soluble ends directed outward. If such a lipid film were to coalesce on the surface of a proteinoid microsphere that had previously condensed around a nucleic acid strand, a primitive forerunner of a cell membrane would result, enclosing a very simple cell-like unit. This protocell would tend to grow,

since the surrounding membrane would be porous enough to allow small molecules such as amino acids to enter, but would prevent their escape once they had been combined into larger molecules. Thus, if the DNA strand catalyzed the polymerization of amino acids within the space enclosed by the membrane, the protein molecules formed would be too large to be able to pass out through the membrane. If one of these trapped protein molecules proved capable of catalyzing reactions between various kinds of small molecules present in solution, other large molecules such as fats and polysaccharides could be formed and also remain trapped within the membrane. In this manner the protocell could accumulate food reserves or new structural materials.

Figure 10.2 □ **Possible continuity of internal and external cell membranes, suggesting that cell structure may have evolved partially by complicated infoldings or outgrowths of the original bounding membrane.** (*After J. D. Robertson.*)

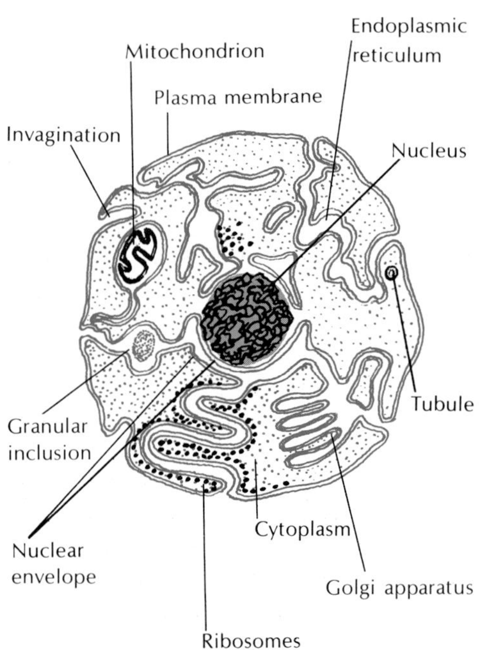

6 *Expansion of cell membranes* Electron micrograph studies of the fine structure of modern cells show that cells are not merely bounded externally by their membranes but that much of their internal structure is membranous as well. In particular, the complex series of internal membranes known as the endoplasmic reticulum (Figure 10.2) seems to be continuous with both the nuclear membrane surrounding the chromosomes and the plasma membrane enclosing the entire cell. Such apparent continuity of cell membranes suggests that protocells may have grown in size and complexity by the expansion of their bounding membranes, which either folded inward or pocketed outward to give rise to the membrane layers that make up the bulk of the cytoplasm of higher cells.

7 *Evolution of eucaryotic cells* We shall examine, later on in this chapter, the possibility that a number of the formed bodies or organelles of regular occurrence within the eucaryotic cells characteristic of all forms of life other than bacteria and blue-green algae actually originated as symbiotic viruslike or bacterialike units that became geared to the life of the host cell, although remaining capable of self-replication. In this manner more primitive living units could have sacrificed independent existence in contributing to the evolution of a cell more complex and versatile than are the procaryotic types that must have appeared earlier.

D Primitive nutrition

The capacity for photosynthesis probably did not evolve at once, for primordial cellular and subcellular organisms could have relied on *heterotrophic* nutrition, utilizing the small, spontaneously formed organic molecules that were then abundant in the milieu. In fact, the success of laboratory experiments in abiogenesis has led to the suggestion that shallow bodies of water on the primeval earth must have been somewhat like dilute soup—warm and filled with nourishing materials. The time would have come at last, however, when the spontaneous production of organic compounds declined to negligible values. This might have resulted from reduced solar output, a decline in the earth's mean temperature, a reduction in the intensity of volcanic activity, or a decrease in the frequency of electrical storms that could have furnished reaction energy. When organic molecules ceased to be generated spontaneously, only those protocells would have survived that could continue to build the materials needed for growth and reproduction from the substrates that remained available. If, as the remaining supply of organic nutrients dwindled, none of these protocells had become capable of trapping radiant energy to use in the synthesis of organic materials from inorganic substrates, life might have become extinct on this planet before it gained more than a toehold. (Such extinction may in fact have taken place innumerable times on other planets throughout the universe.) To be sure, some energy could have been obtained by the further oxidation of inorganic compounds such as oxides of iron and sulfur, but since there was probably less than 0.1 percent oxygen in the atmosphere at that time such oxides were undoubtedly much less abundant than they are at present.

The biotic world's great breakthrough came with the evolution of chlorophyll *a*—a compound that permitted the direct exploitation of solar energy by living things. A nucleotide sequence capable of building chlorophyll-synthesizing enzymes need have arisen only once in the billion or two years of available time. Chlorophyll-containing procaryotic cells (which may have been much like modern blue-green algae) would now have been able to maintain themselves and proliferate without reliance on organic food. They in turn could provide organic matter to sustain their heterotrophic contemporaries, which might have resembled the bacteria or viruses of today. Finally, the incorporation of tiny, chlorophyll-containing cells as symbionts within the larger eucaryotic cells that might have been evolving at the same time, would have led to the appearance of the first autotrophic higher cells. Modified by their symbiotic existence, these primitive procaryotic cells may have been the precursors of modern chloroplasts (see Figure 13.4).

The development of photosynthesis brought about extensive environmental changes. For one thing, molecular oxygen, a by-product of photosynthesis, began to accumulate in the atmosphere, contributing to the oxidation of both inorganic and organic materials. Up to this time, cellular life probably obtained energy solely by anaerobic processes such as the fermentation reactions by which yeasts obtain energy by converting sugar to alcohol. A number of modern bacteria are *facultative anaerobes:* when oxygen is not available they obtain energy anaerobically, but when the oxygen supply reaches a certain threshold concentration they switch over to aerobic respiration, a much more efficient means of obtaining energy. This event, the *Pasteur effect,* takes place at oxygen concentrations that are only about 10 percent of the present concentration of atmospheric oxygen. It seems likely, then, that as the level of atmospheric oxygen reached this critical threshold, the Pasteur effect would have taken place in all primitive organisms having the needed metabolic machinery to make use of oxygen. The significance of this use of oxygen becomes apparent when we compare the amount of energy that can be obtained by the anaerobic fermentation of glucose to lactic acid (52 kcal/mole) with the amount obtained when glucose is degraded aerobically to carbon dioxide and water (283 kcal/mole). The anaerobic reaction is less than 20 percent as efficient as the aerobic process.

From this we see that photosynthesis enabled life to persist despite the depletion of organic nutrients and, coupled with aerobic respiration, put the living world on a profit economy, capable of synthesizing an abundance of organic materials and of degrading these efficiently to liberate stored energy.

Primitive autotrophic cells were probably the ancestors of both plants and animals. Most of the original heterotrophic protocells must have perished with the decline of the organic materials on which they depended, while others gave rise to bacteria or took refuge as viruses or other symbiotic particles within the autotrophic cells. As mentioned earlier, the first true animals were probably flagellated eucaryotic cells that through mutation lost the capacity to produce chlorophyll and subsequently reverted to heterotrophism.

Records of early life are inadequate to resolve the question as to whether all existing forms of life arose *monophyletically* (from a single ancestral protocell) or *polyphyletically* (from a number of parallel lines evolving from independent biogenetic events). If the latter was the case, the structural and biochemical similarity of modern cells would constitute a remarkable instance of parallelism.

A The cell principle

The French microbiologist André Lwoff* has clearly set forth the principle of unity underlying biotic diversity:

A cell contains some 2,000 to 5,000 species of macromolecules. Moreover, nature has produced an immense variety of categories of different organisms. Yet, when the living world is considered at the cellular level, one discovers unity. Unity of plan: *each cell possesses a nucleus imbedded in protoplasm.* Unity of function: *the metabolism is essentially the same in each cell.* Unity of composition: *the main macromolecules of all living beings are composed of the same small molecules. For, in order to build the immense diversity of the living systems, nature has made use of a strictly limited number of building blocks. The problem of diversity of structures and functions, the problem of heredity, and the problem of diversification of species have been solved by the elegant use of a small number of building blocks organized into specific macromolecules.*

A cell may be defined *structurally* as a unit of living matter which includes one or more chromosomes and is bounded by a differentially permeable membrane (DPM). *Functionally* it is definable as the simplest unit of life that is capable of surviving and reproducing in a medium free of other cells. Viruses are not *cellular:* they are not bounded by a lipoprotein DPM and can replicate only in a host cell.

The cellular structure of living matter was first noted by Robert Hooke† in 1665, who actually observed not the living units but the cavities remaining in a piece of cork after the death of the cells. He wrote,

. . . casting the light on it with a deep plano-convex Glass, I could exceedingly plain perceive it to be all perforated and porous, much like a Honey-comb, but that the pores of it were not regular . . . these pores, or cells, were not very deep, but consisted of a great many little Boxes . . . our Microscope informs us that the substance of Cork is altogether filled with Air, and that that Air is perfectly enclosed in little Boxes or Cells distinct from one another . . .

The term *cell* persisted in all later literature, although most cells, especially those of animals, are not boxlike. During the next 170 years, the cellularity of many organisms was confirmed with the extension of the use of the microscope. In 1838 and 1839 the zoologist Theodor Schwann and the botanist M. J. Schleiden independently formulated their conclusion that (1) *the cell is the unit of structure of all living things* and (2) *the cell is the unit of function of all living things.* This statement of fact has come to be known as the *cell principle.* Twenty years later a third precept was added to the cell principle by the embryologist R. Virchow: (3) *every cell comes from a previously existing cell.*

Continued investigation has required little modification of the cell principle. Certain groups of organisms, such as ciliate protozoans, have developed multiple nuclei and complex organelles without becoming multicellular; such organization is sometimes spoken of as *acellular,* but this does not affect the fundamental validity of the cell principle. Lwoff's modern restatement, cited above, needs qualification only in that procaryotic cells lack a true nucleus and that the term *protoplasm* ("first matter") becomes more and more illusory as the fine structure of cells is studied by the modern methods of molecular biology. The concept of protoplasm as an amorphous or granular, colorless "jelly" was the product of technical limitations. With the development of new instruments and techniques for cytological analysis, the matter of cells has been found to be highly organized—layered membranes and organelles constitute nearly all of the mass that was formerly thought of as protoplasm; although the term may be retained for convenience to designate living matter, it is more accurate to specify the particular components of protoplasm that have functional significance.

**Biological Order* (Cambridge, Mass.: The M.I.T. Press, 1962), pp. 10, 11.

†*Micrographia* (London: Royal Society, 1665), p. 113.

Figure 10.3 □ Tissue and organ culture. (*a*) Hanging-drop technique. (*b*) Salivary-gland rudiment from 13-day-old mouse embryo, following 3 days in organ culture. (*Courtesy of Dr. C. Grobstein.*)

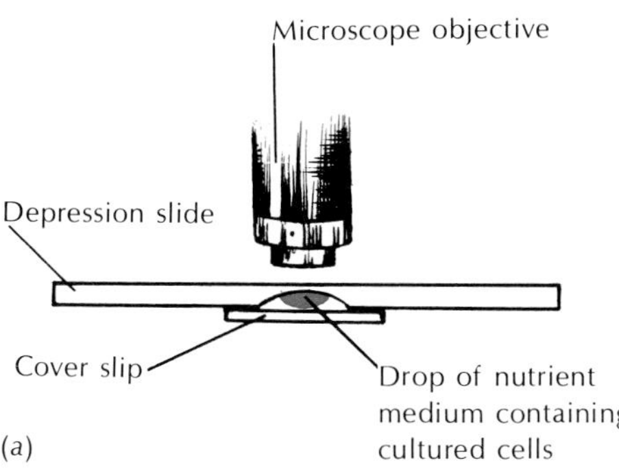

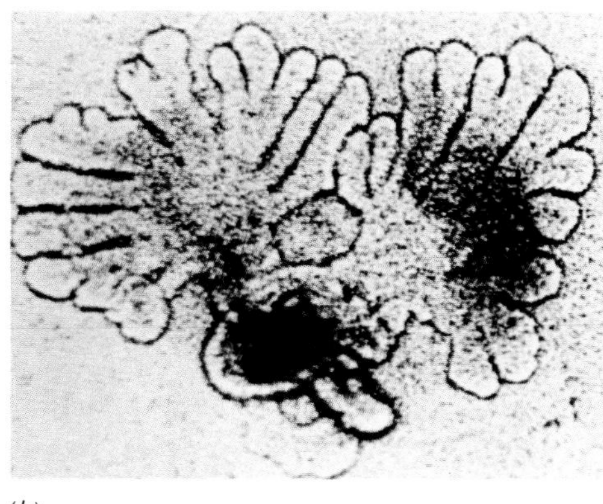

(*b*)

B Cytological instruments and techniques

Knowledge of the existence of cells was first made possible by the development of the light microscope, with lens systems providing magnification up to about 2,000 diameters. The human eye may view objects directly with the light microscope, but this instrument is limited in resolving power by the limits of the wavelengths of visible light. The smallest resolvable objects are about 0.2 μm, or about one half the wavelength of the shortest visible light rays (4,000 Å, or 0.4 μm). The value of light microscopes has been enhanced by the preparation of tissue sections only one or two cells thick; this requires that the tissue be impregnated with paraffin or a plastic, and sectioned with a microtome. Various cellular constituents have been rendered visible by taking advantage of differences in their affinity for particular dyes (differential stains). They can also be differentiated on the basis of the extent to which they bend or break up beams of light. The *phase-contrast* microscope takes advantage of differences in the *refractive index* of different cell components, that is, the angle at which light rays striking the object are refracted or bent. The *interference* microscope allows cell components to break up light as a prism does according to differences in density and other properties, producing multicolored images.

A good *electron microscope* can resolve objects smaller than 0.001 μm (10 Å), by employing a beam of high-speed electrons that is spread by magnetic fields rather than glass lenses. The human eye cannot see electrons and therefore cannot view the image directly, but since photographic emulsions are affected by electrons, the image may be photographed.

The study of intact living cells has been aided by the techniques of tissue and organ culture in vitro (Figure 10.3). Particularly useful is the *hanging-drop* technique, in which a small mass of excised tissue is placed in a sterile drop of nutrient medium on a depression slide, the preparation is sealed with petroleum jelly and a coverslip, and is inverted so that the drop hangs suspended between slide and coverslip. As the cells reproduce, they migrate outward individually or in thin sheets. Their growth and movements may then be recorded by time-lapse cinephotography.

Microdissectors, simple or sophisticated, make possible surgical manipulations upon single cells. For instance, the nucleus of one cell may be removed and transplanted into another cell, providing information on nuclear function.

The functions of specific cell components can also be investigated by the use of nutrients labeled with radioisotopes. The localization of these within the intact cell may be revealed by autoradiographs. It is also possible to disrupt the cells and isolate the particular compounds into which the isotope has been incorporated. By performing this analysis at set intervals, complicated biochemical sequences have been worked out, since the isotope moves from compound to compound during the sequence.

Chemical analysis of individual cell components is facilitated by the *ultracentrifuge.* The cells are ruptured by "osmotic shock" (that is, they are placed in distilled water so that they swell and burst) and the fragments are ultracentrifuged at speeds that produce centrifugal forces up to 500,000*g* (500,000 times the force of gravity). This causes the cell constituents to separate into layers according to density. The fractions may be separated further, and the organelles either left intact for study in an in vitro system, or broken down into their constituent macromolecules. These in turn may be digested enzymatically, and analyzed by chromatographic, electrophoretic, and other techniques of chemical separation.

C The size of cells

The great majority of cells have diameters ranging from 0.5 to 20 μm. The true magnitude of this range becomes apparent when, by applying the formula $4\pi r^3/3$, we find that a spherical cell with a diameter of 20 μm has a volume more than 64 thousand times greater than that of a cell with a diameter of 0.5 μm! A protozoan with a diameter of 100 μm, such as a large amoeba, has a volume 125 times greater than that of a cell of 20-μm diameter. There are instances of cells becoming very much larger. The yolks of the eggs of birds and reptiles are ova which are tremendously distended with stored food material; the amount of living matter present is actually quite small. The unicellular green alga *Acetabularia* (Figure 10.13) attains a length of 9 or 10 cm, but since it is not spherical, its mass is not so great as this length would seem to indicate.

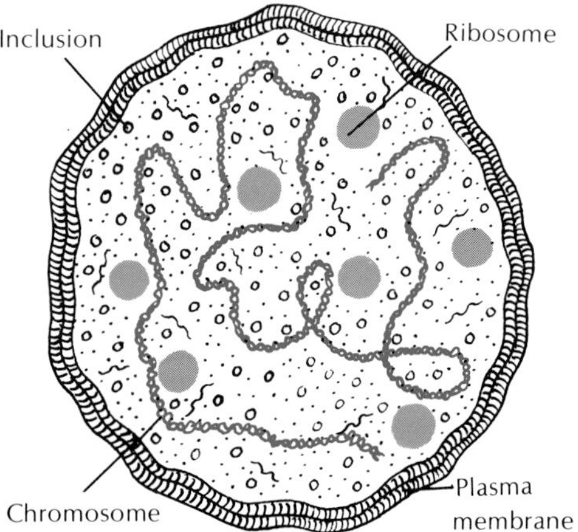

Figure 10.4 □ Pleuropneumonialike organism (PPLO), the smallest known cell. Total diameter is about 0.1 μm. The cell is bounded by the plasma membrane, and the cytoplasm contains ribosomes, a chromosome, and various inclusions, such as stored nutrients.

WHAT FACTORS SET THE LOWER LIMITS OF CELL SIZE? The smallest known cells are those of *pleuropneumonia-like organisms* (PPLO) (Figure 10.4), which somewhat resemble diminutive bacteria but are even smaller than some of the larger viruses. An actively metabolizing PPLO is a spherical cell with a diameter of only 0.25 μm; a still smaller form of PPLO with a diameter of 0.1 μm has also been discovered, but these "elemental bodies" are not metabolically active. Theoretically it should be possible for a cell to have a diameter of only 0.05 μm, but cells so small have yet to be discovered. Several factors set the lower limit of cell size at 0.05 μm: (1) a cell membrane is about 0.01 μm thick, and unless the cell were more than 0.02 μm in diameter, it would be all membrane and no interior; (2) the minimum number of discrete metabolic reactions that a cell must carry out is estimated as 100 to 500. If each reaction requires a special enzyme, the cell must be large enough to contain not only 100 or more kinds of enzyme molecules, but the equivalent number of genes (and perhaps mRNA units as well). A cell of 0.05 μm diameter could contain only a few hundred macromolecules, so few that there might be less than a dozen molecules of a given enzyme. Any metabolic system operating with so few constituents would be extremely delicate and its stability would be jeopardized by even the random thermal movements of its atoms.

WHAT FACTORS SET THE UPPER LIMITS OF CELL SIZE? Two sets of ratios determine the maximum size of cells: (1) the ratio of chromosomal material to the amount of cytoplasm; (2) the ratio of cell surface to cell volume. The total amount of chromosomal material present in a cell must be sufficient to produce the quantity of mRNA needed to manufacture the cell's proteins. Secretory cells that synthesize and release large quantities of proteinaceous material usually possess nuclei very large in proportion to the amount of cytoplasm present. On the other hand, cells such as mature striated muscle fibers, which may no longer be highly active in protein synthesis, need possess relatively little nuclear material compared to their total mass. There are several ways in which larger cells can solve the problem of maintaining an adequate proportion of DNA with respect to their other components. (1) The chromosomes of such cells may become *polynemic* ("many threads") as in the giant cells of larval flies; here the DNA replicates repeatedly until each chromosome becomes a giant cable containing a large number of intertwined DNA strands. (2) The cell may become *multinucleate*. (3) One or more of

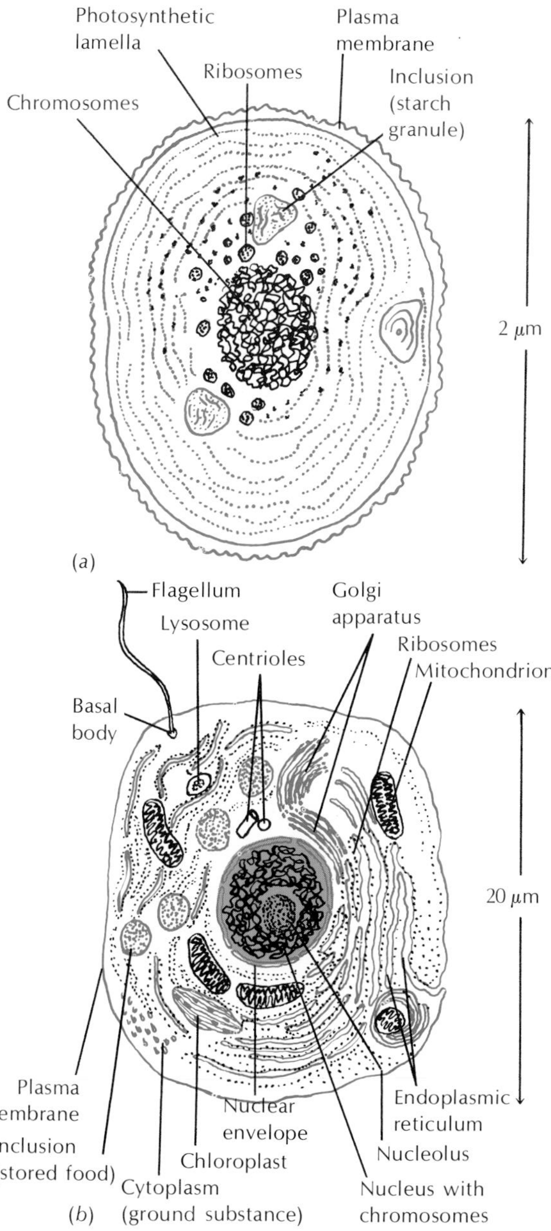

Figure 10.5 □ **Cell structure: (*a*) procaryotic cell of blue-green alga; (*b*) typical eucaryotic cell.**

the nuclei may become *polyploid,* as in vertebrate liver cells. (4) The DNA may be constantly active in producing mRNA. (5) The life of individual mRNA molecules may be prolonged. Whenever increased cell size favors survival, cells in one way or another have solved the problem of maintaining an adequate nuclear-cytoplasmic ratio.

As a spherical cell grows, its surface area increases according to the square of its radius ($4\pi r^2$), while its volume increases according to the *cube* of the radius ($4\pi r^3/3$). If in the process of growth a cell doubles its original radius, its volume increases eightfold. When the surface-to-volume ratio becomes such that molecular traffic through the cell membrane is congested and the nutritional maintenance of the internal part of the cell is impaired, the cell has three alternatives: (1) it may divide; (2) it may cease to grow; (3) it may change shape. A cell which is flattened or elongate or which has numerous processes will have a much greater surface area than a spherical cell of comparable volume. Animal cells are more likely than plant cells to assume such irregular shapes, but in plant cells a similar favorable adjustment of the ratio of surface to volume results from the fact that the interior of many plant cells is occupied by a large storage vacuole so that the cytoplasm is restricted to a thin peripheral sheet surrounding the vacuole.

D Procaryotic cells

Procaryotic cells, those which lack true nuclei, are probably the evolutionary progenitors of eucaryotic cells, those in which the chromosomal material is enclosed by a nuclear membrane. Present-day bacteria possess procaryotic cells. The heterotrophic cell of a PPLO has been seen above. An autotrophic procaryotic cell (of a blue-green alga) is shown in Figure 10.5*a*. It may be seen that the chromosomes of a procaryotic cell may occupy only the central portion, or be spread throughout the cell. Neither a nuclear membrane nor a nucleolus is present. Ribosomes are abundant and a typical cell membrane is present, but mitochondria, plastids, centrioles, and lysosomes, organelles characteristic of many eucaryotic cells, are absent. The cyanophyte cell contains chlorophyll, but this is organized in simple layers (the photosynthetic lamellae) rather than being located within discrete bodies, the plastids.

E Eucaryotic cells

The average eucaryotic cell (Figure 10.5*b*), with a diameter of about 20 μm, is much larger than procaryotic cells, which ordinarily do not exceed 2 μm in length or diameter. They are characterized by a true *nucleus,* bounded by a double nuclear membrane (or envelope), which encloses the chromosomes and one or two ovoid nucleoli. The cytoplasm is organized into complex series of parallel membranes constituting the endoplasmic reticulum, which at points is continuous both with the plasma membrane, bounding the cell's exterior, and with the nuclear envelope, and which communicates with a complicated series of canals and vesicles forming the Golgi apparatus. The cytoplasm is filled not only with inert inclusions of stored food material and secretory products, but with a variety of formed bodies or organelles, some capable of self-replication, that subserve specific functions in the life of the cell. In the following sections the structure and function of various cellular components will be considered in depth. Eucaryotic cell structure is characteristic of organisms of all phyla except Schizophyta and Cyanophyta. Protozoans, diatoms, dinoflagellates, and many green algae are modern forms of life in which cell and organism are one and the same. Metaphytes and metazoans are larger and more complex, but cells remain the basic units of which their bodies are made.

10.3 □ THE CELL SURFACE

A The plasma membrane

Externally, cells are bounded by the *plasma membrane,* a lipoprotein structure averaging 100 Å in thickness, which is apparently continuous with but not necessarily structurally identical to the intracellular membranes of the endoplasmic reticulum. To date, the molecular organization of the plasma membrane has mostly been deduced inferentially from functional properties displayed by the membrane. A conventional interpretation depicts the plasma membrane as a lipid-protein sandwich in which an inner and an outer layer of protein molecules enclose a double layer of phospholipid molecules, polarized with their lipophilic (fat-soluble) ends together and their hydrophilic (water-soluble) ends directed toward the protein layers (Figure 10.6). Scattered pores of about 8 Å diameter may perforate the membrane. An alternative interpretation pictures the plasma membrane as a single protein layer with hammer-shaped lipid molecules protruding through the interstices. Both of these hypotheses are consonant with the membrane's behavior.

The plasma membrane's unique quality of *differential permeability* is essential to the life of the cell. This differential permeability, by which the passage of some substances is facilitated and that of others impeded, is not merely a matter of "mesh gauge" or pore size, for the plasma membrane cannot simply be likened to a gravel sieve that lets through smaller particles and excludes larger ones. Small molecules such as H_2O, CO_2, and O_2 pass through readily and are not subject to regulation by the membrane. But the cell possesses mechanisms for actively controlling the passage of larger molecules and of ions. Associated with the membrane, and probably even forming part of the membrane itself, are enzyme molecules involved in active transport systems that facilitate passage of particular substances, sometimes even against an existing concentration or electrochemical gradient (see Section 14.1B).

Cells are known actively to "drink" liquids [a process termed *pinocytosis* (Figure 14.8)] or engulf solid particles (*phagocytosis*). Pinocytosis and phagocytosis are essentially identical phenomena in which localized inpouchings of the plasma membrane are formed and pinched off internally as cytoplasmic vesicles. Conversely, secretory cells seem to release large molecules by rupturing portions of the plasma membrane, which are then rapidly regenerated.

Whatever the details of its fine structure ultimately may prove to be, the most remarkable characteristic of the plasma membrane is its *dynamism*—the potential for regulating its permeability in ways adaptive to changing circumstances. *Cell surface materials* attached to the exterior of the membrane proper are thought responsible for much of the membrane's reactivity. The cohesiveness of sponge cells, for instance, depends upon cell surface materials that are loosened and dissolved away when the sponge is placed in sea water free of Ca^{2+} and Mg^{2+}. These materials can be built up once more when the needed ions are restored. In at least some cases cell surface materials may exist in the form of proteinaceous organelles having a diameter of 100 to 200 Å; these organelles have only recently been recognized, and their functions remain to be defined.

B Extracellular materials

Both unicellular organisms and the individual cells of multicellular creatures are frequently invested by protective or sup-

Figure 10.6 □ **The cell surface. (*a*) Model of structure of plasma membrane. (*b*) Plasma membrane (unit membrane) of human red blood corpuscle, showing darker protein layers enclosing pale lipid layer. (*Courtesy of Dr. J. D. Robertson.*) (*c*) Plasma membrane and extraneous coat of giant amoeba, *Chaos* (*Pelomyxa*); the plasma membrane is 80 Å in diameter and consists of inner and outer protein layers (each 20 Å thick) enclosing a 40-Å lipid layer; a coating of cell-surface materials 200 Å thick is seen covering the outer surface of the plasma membrane; from this arise filamentous extensions about 2,000 Å long. The significance of this extraneous coat is obscure. (*Courtesy of Dr. P. W. Brandt.*)**

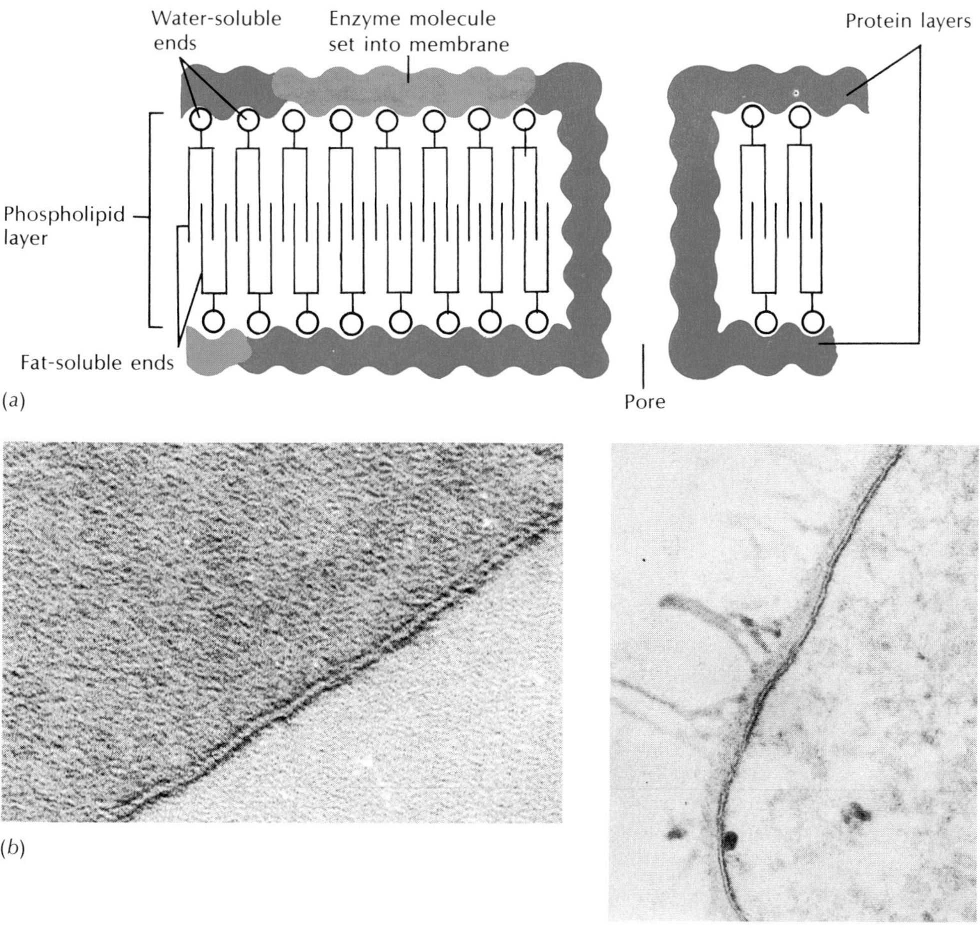

portive materials secreted by the cytoplasm (Figure 10.7). These materials serve, for instance, as intercellular cement, which causes cells to cohere in organized masses or sheets. They may also provide a semirigid support that permits the cell to maintain a characteristic shape. Protozoans such as *Paramecium* (Figure 2.10) maintain a consistent body form by dint of a proteinaceous *pellicle* exterior to the plasma membrane. This pellicle is not rigid: it can be deformed to permit the animal to turn about in a limited space, and it can elastically resume its original shape. The pellicles of ciliates show species-specific markings that are useful for purposes of identification (Figure 12.5).

Plantlike unicellular organisms secrete capsules of polysaccharide and proteinaceous material. The rigid cellulose casing (cuirass) of an armored dinoflagellate (Figure 2.11) provides structural rigidity and, in some genera bears long spines that aid flotation.

Bacteria secrete cell walls primarily consisting of *mucopeptides* made up of amino acid and amino-sugar units. Immediately exterior to the cell wall of bacteria and cyanophytes lies a slime capsule composed of polysaccharides or glycoproteins (Figure 10.7*a*). In some parasitic bacteria, presence of the capsule correlates with pathenogenicity, for the capsule may frustrate the host's defensive mechanisms. Slime capsules also invest many types of algal cells and may be concerned with regulating the water content of the cells in cases where they and their milieu are not in osmotic balance with each other.

The cells of metaphytes secrete a *cell wall* several layers thick (Figure 10.7*c*). The

Figure 10.7 □ **Extracellular materials in various organisms. (*a*) Bacteria and blue-green algae and photograph of *Klebsiella pneumoniae*, capsules appearing white (*courtesy of Carolina Biological Supply Company*). (*b*) Protozoans; *Stentor*. See also Figure 2.10, *Paramecium*. (*c*) Eucaryotic plants; unicellular green alga, metaphyte tissue, with supportive cell wall and adhesive middle lamella holding cells together, and electron micrograph of cellulose cell wall in *Valonia*, showing regular deposition of cellulose fibers in three directions, each oriented 60° from the one immediately below it [*F. C. Steward and K. Mühlethaler, "The Structure and Development of the Cell Wall in the Valoniaceae As Revealed by the Electron Microscope,"* Ann. Botany (London), 17 (*1953*); *by permission of Clarendon Press, Oxford*]. (*d*) Metazoan epithelial membrane, showing protective mucous coating and basement membrane that affixes epithelium to underlying tissues, and electron micrograph of basement membrane of frog epidermis (*Rana clamitans*), with banded collagen fibrils deposited in regularly alternating layers, each oriented 90° from those adjacent (collagen deposition is less regular in most types of basement membranes) (*courtesy of Dr. M. M. Salpeter*). (*e*) Cartilage cells embedded in solid matrix that they have secreted.**

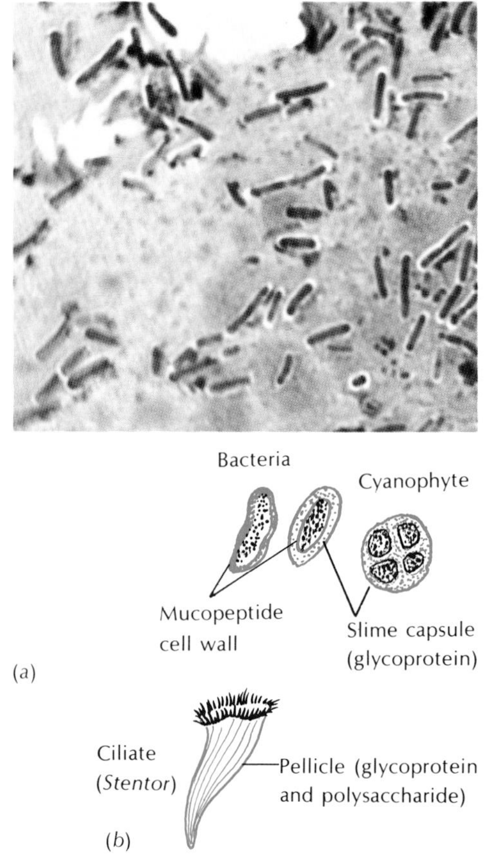

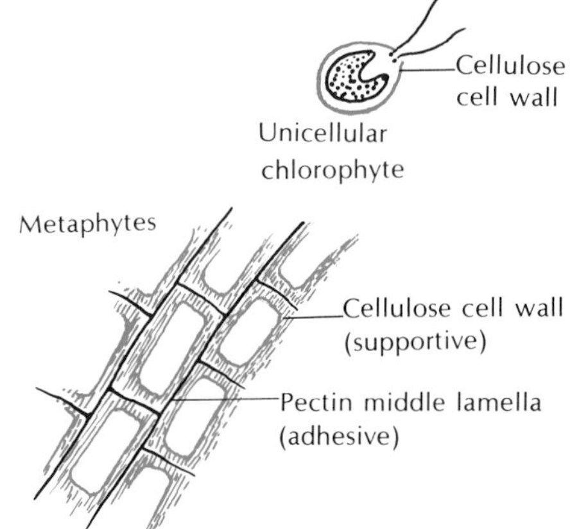

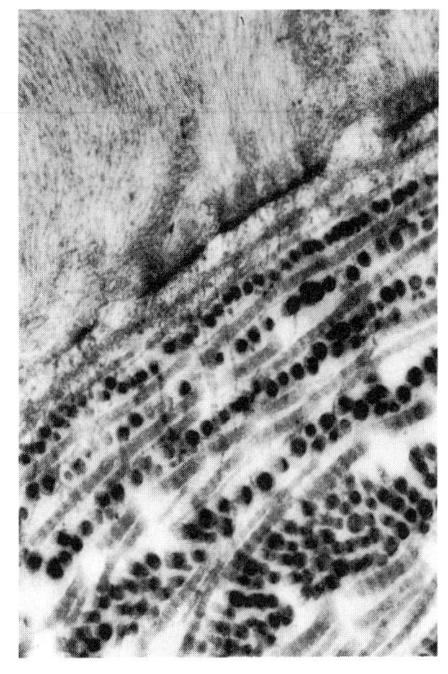

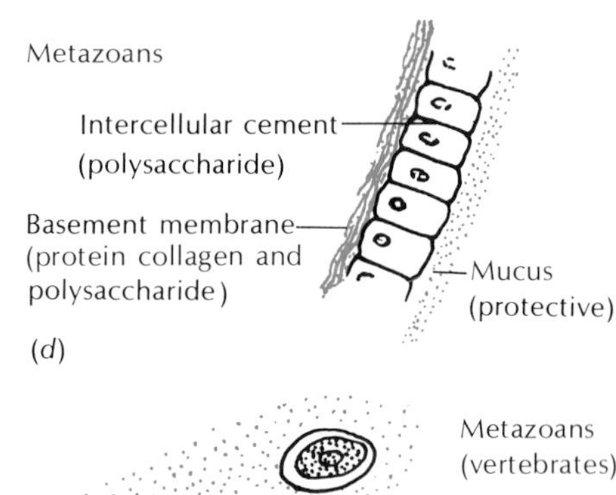

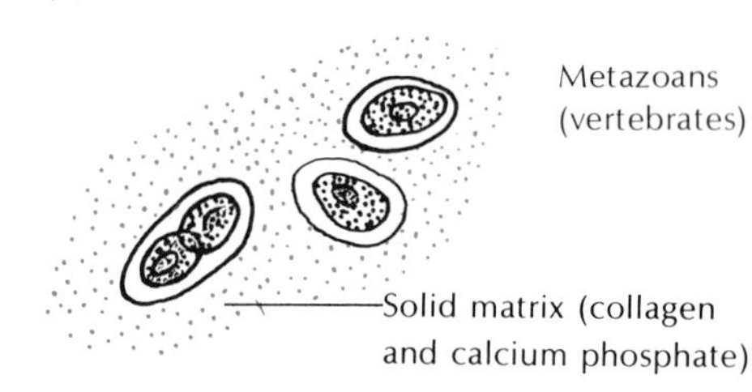

central layer, or middle lamella, serves as the intercellular cement. It first appears as the *cell plate,* which forms crosswise in the cytoplasm between new daughter cells in late mitosis (Figure 10.14*a*) and is composed mainly of the polysaccharide pectin. The role of pectin in promoting the cohesion of cells is reflected by its property of causing fruit jelly to "set." On either side of the middle lamella the cytoplasm secretes a *primary* cell wall composed mainly of cellulose. During the growth of the cell the primary wall remains thin and capable of great distention, but it becomes thick and rigid after cell growth ceases. It is then reinforced by the secretion of a *secondary* wall of varying thickness, lying between the cytoplasm and the primary wall. The composition of the secondary wall varies according to the type of cell secreting it.

The basic framework of the secondary cell wall is a meshwork of cellulose fibrils, which may be impregnated with other substances. Plant epidermal cells secrete secondary walls impregnated with lipids—cutin and waxes—which form an outer *cuticle* that is impervious to water. The cuticle is particularly thick in xerophytic species. The structural strength of woody and fibrous plants depends upon fibers and lignified cells (see Figure 11.36). Fibers represent secondary cell walls usually made of pure cellulose, in which the molecules are grouped like strands in a cable into progressively larger bundles that are flexible but provide tensile strength. Lignified cells confer structural rigidity. During lignification the secondary wall is impregnated with a stony, nonfibrous polysaccharide, *lignin.* The functional performance of plant conductive tissues is also dependent upon the structure of their secondary walls, which must be sturdy yet readily permeable to water and solutes (see Figure 11.40).

Animal cells lack rigid polysaccharide cell walls, and are consequently more deformable than plant cells. A fuzzy coating of filaments containing polysaccharide covers exposed surfaces of certain protozoa and metazoan cells. Such polysaccharide coats, invisible or plainly seen by electron microscopy, may in fact be universally characteristic of animal cells. The shape of individual cells in membranes and tissue masses may be largely influenced by the pressure of adjacent cells, much like a soap bubble that tends to be spherical when solitary and becomes faceted when surrounded by other bubbles. When separated by the enzymatic digestion of the intercellular cement, animal cells often do not simply round up and remain stationary, but may become amoeboid, wandering about and perhaps aggregating with other cells of similar type.

Extracellular materials secreted by specialized cells provide cohesiveness and structural support for the metazoan body (see Figures 4.29 and 11.37). We have already noted the chemical structure of such important substances as collagen, chitin, hyaluronic acid, and chondroitin sulfate, and will consider the organization of supportive and connective tissues at greater length in the next chapter.

10.4 □ CYTOPLASM

The cytoplasm is that part of a cell which lies between the plasma membrane and the nuclear envelope. It is the site of most metabolic activities, including protein synthesis and cellular respiration. Although capable of a liquidlike flow ("cytoplasmic streaming"), it is in fact organized to a high degree of complexity, interpenetrated by a network of fine membranes that can be dissolved and reformed with great rapidity. A variety of organelles are of regular occurrence in the cytoplasm, along with droplets and granules of storage products (Figure 10.8). Specific secretory products and intracellular structures of sporadic occurrence, such as contractile and conductive fibrils, may be found in various kinds of cells that are adapted to perform special functions.

A The endoplasmic reticulum

Much of the cytoplasm is organized into a complex network of double lipoprotein membranes enclosing narrow channels (Figure 10.9). This system of intracellular membranes tremendously increases the

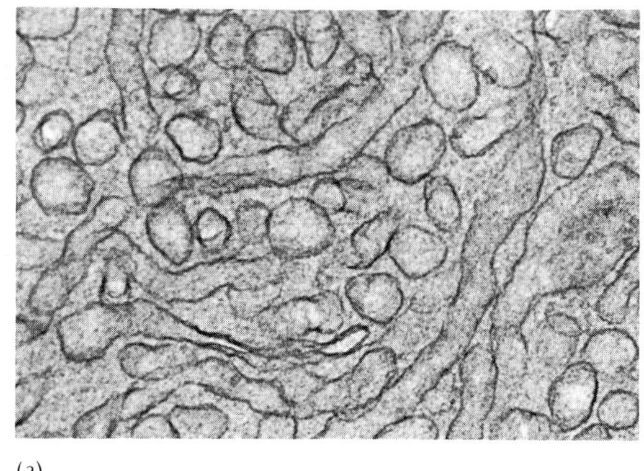

(a)

Figure 10.8 □ Electron micrograph (18,600×) showing portion of eucaryotic cell from frog pancreas. (*Courtesy of Dr. Keith R. Porter.*)

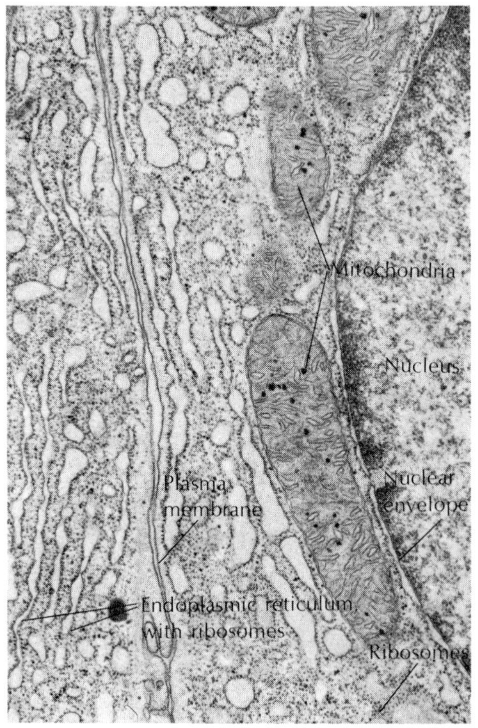

(b)

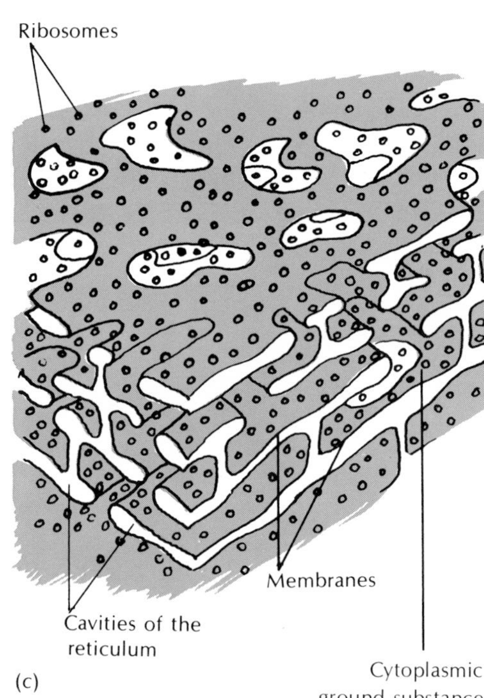

(c)

Figure 10.9 □ (*a*) Agranular (smooth) endoplasmic reticulum from interstitial cell of testis and (*b*) granular (rough) endoplasmic reticulum from pancreas. (*Courtesy of D. W. Fawcett, M.D.*) (*c*) Three-dimensional representation of granular endoplasmic reticulum, showing ribosomes attached to cytoplasmic surfaces of the membranes.

surface area through which materials may pass to and from the nonmembranous parts of the cell. It is thought to furnish passageways for the rapid transport of materials to various parts of the cell, and between the nucleus and the plasma membrane, for the endoplasmic reticulum is apparently continuous both with the nuclear envelope and with the plasma membrane. A large portion of the reticulum is known as the *rough* or *granular* reticulum because the cytoplasmic side of its membranes is heavily studded with ribosomes (Figure 10.9*b*). Proximity of the ribosomes to the reticulum may be adaptive because protein synthesis is facilitated by ready access to amino acids in solution within the channels of the reticulum. Other parts of the reticulum are *smooth* or *agranular,* but may bear adsorbed enzyme molecules and furnish surfaces on which reactions can occur. The extreme lability of the reticulum, parts of which are constantly breaking down or being reconstituted, suggests that membrane precursors are present in the hyaloplasm, which can swiftly associate in response to various stimuli.

B Hyaloplasm

Occupying the interstices between the organized parts of the cytoplasm is a clear matrix, the hyaloplasm, a watery medium containing a variety of ions and molecules in solution and suspension. Besides serving as a reservoir of small nutrient molecules, the hyaloplasm contains proteins which, by undergoing changes in colloidal state, alter the viscosity of the cytoplasm. Perhaps as a result of local pH adjustments, these proteins undergo reversible *sol-gel* changes. They may associate to form a continuous crystalline lattice, the "gel" state of a colloid, which imparts a viscous, jellylike consistency to the cell. When the molecules dissociate, the hyaloplasm passes from a gel to a liquid "sol" state (Figure 10.10). Ordinarily the peripheral hyaloplasm remains in a gel state, forming a cell *cortex* that provides support to the plasma membrane. Changes in colloidal state are thought to accompany cytoplasmic streaming and amoeboid locomotion.

Figure 10.10 ☐ **Changes in colloidal state of cytoplasmic proteins.**

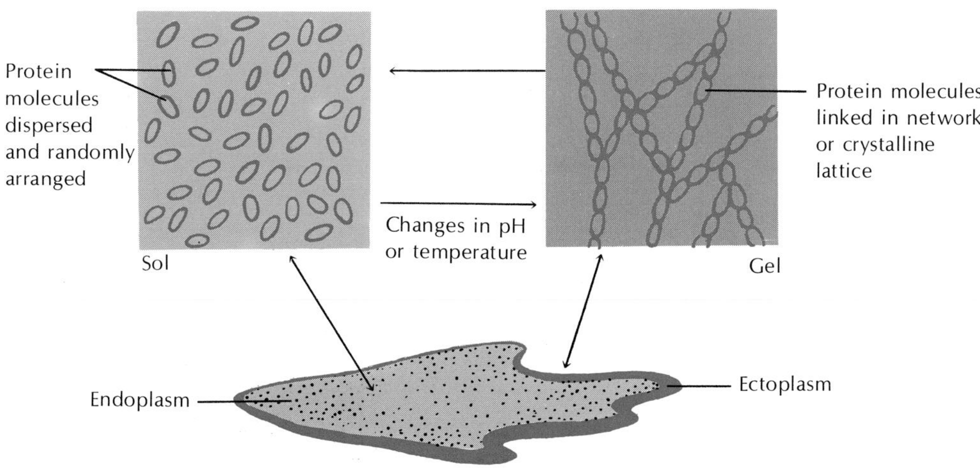

C Mitochondria

An average cell contains several hundred elongate (usually sausage-shaped) mitochondria (see Figure 10.8). The proportion of mitochondria to the total cell volume correlates directly with the cell's rate of oxidative metabolism, for the mitochondria house many enzymes concerned with the oxidative breakdown of nutrients. They are the cell's major source of energy and site of ATP production. A mitochondrion is typically about 0.5 μm in diameter and 1.5 to 2 μm in length—about the size of a bacillus. It consists of outer and inner lipoprotein membranes, the latter deeply infolded, forming parallel internal partitions (cristae) that extend about halfway across the diameter of the mitochondrion. The cristae bear knobbed projections that seem to be enzyme complexes, as seen in Figure 14.54. Between the external and internal membranes and within the internal membrane are fluid-filled spaces. In the core of each mitochondrion is a strand of DNA that contains the code needed for constructing new mitochondria. The enzymes DNA polymerase and RNA polymerase are also present, indicating that these organelles are capable both of DNA replication and of protein synthesis (as would indeed be necessary for mitochondrial reproduction). At each cell division the existing mitochondria are randomly segregated into the daughter cells, and the full cellular complement is then restored by the reproduction of these mitochondria.

Much of the outer mitochondrial membrane consists of a mosaic of enzyme molecules arranged in configurations that permit an "assembly-line" progression of molecules through the series of reactions constituting the Krebs cycle (see Section 14.3C); by means of this cycle small organic molecules are degraded with the release of CO_2, H^+, and electrons. The electrons and H^+ are then apparently transferred from the site of their release on the exterior of the mitochondrion to the knoblike assemblies studding the surfaces of the cristae, where further reactions take place that result in the synthesis of ATP and water. The knob units seem to be specifically concerned with transferring energy from the oxidative reactions to those concerned with the synthesis of ATP. Since the mitochondria contain the cell's most effective mechanisms for energy release and transfer, these organelles are known as the "powerhouses" of the cell.

Mitochondria are bacteria-sized; they contain DNA, can reproduce themselves, and possess the enzymes needed for obtaining energy by oxidative metabolism: they are therefore thought by some investigators to have originated as bacterial symbionts that associated with eucaryotic cells early in the evolutionary history of the latter. If so, mitochondria have become totally adapted for life within the host cells and have lost the capacity for independent life, even as the host cells have come to depend for survival on their mitochondria.

D Ribosomes

All cells (procaryotic and eucaryotic) contain from hundreds to thousands of spheroidal organelles about 0.23 μm in diameter. These bodies, the ribosomes, consist of approximately 64 percent RNA and 36 percent protein by weight. They interact with mRNA in protein synthesis (see Figure 9.25). Many ribosomes are located along the cytoplasmic surface of the membranes of the endoplasmic reticulum, presumably a favorable location for access to nutrients.

Ribosomal RNA (rRNA) is a transcript of a portion of a chromosome representing at least 3,000 DNA nucleotides. In eucaryotic cells rRNA is produced by genes in what is known as the nucleolus organizer region of one particular pair of chromosomes. This region is involved in the production of a nuclear structure called the nucleolus (discussed in Section 10.5B). At each cell division materials accumulated in the nucleolus since its formation after the previous cell division are thought to be liberated into the cytoplasm, furnishing the rRNA needed for formation of new ribosomes in each daughter cell. The proteins associated with the ribosomes include enzymes required for polymerizing amino acids into peptide chains.

Each ribosome bears two active sites: an amino acid site and a peptide site. When the ribosome attaches to an mRNA molecule bearing amino acid–tRNA complexes (held in place by hydrogen bonds between the mRNA codons and the complementary tRNA anticodons), the amino acid bonded to tRNA is adsorbed onto the *amino acid site* of the ribosome. As the ribosome moves along the mRNA strand, the amino acid is then passed to the ribosome's *peptide site*, at which it is covalently bonded to the growing peptide chain. Meanwhile, a new amino acid–tRNA unit can be taken up at the amino acid site as the next mRNA codon moves into position.

A number of ribosomes temporarily bonded along the length of a strand of mRNA constitute a *polysome* (see Figure 9.25*b*). The number of ribosomal units in a polysome serves as an indication of the length of the genetic message and hence of the size and complexity of the protein being formed. Individual ribosomes in a polysome are separated from one another by gaps of 500 to 1,000 nm, and hence do not function cooperatively; each is an independent center of protein synthesis and produces a peptide chain in accordance with the codon sequence of mRNA. New ribosomes are added to the polysome at the starting end of the "message," while those which have completed the reading of the message and have finished the production of a complete peptide chain drop off at the opposite end.

E Lysosomes

Lysosomes are membrane-bounded vacuoles similar in size and shape to mitochondria but distinguishable from the latter by the absence of cristae. The lipoprotein membrane encloses concentrations of *hydrolytic enzymes* (hydrolases), the containment of which is necessary to protect the cell from their destructive action. When the cell dies, autodigestion quickly commences as the lysosomes break down and release these hydrolases.

In phagocytic cells intracellular digestion takes place within temporary *food vacuoles* that originate as invaginations of the plasma membrane and are pinched off to form a complete membrane around the ingested morsel. One or more lysosomes then empty their contents into the food vacuole, converting it into a temporary "stomach" (see Figure 13.21). In nonphagocytic cells large molecules perhaps can be taken from the cytoplasm into the lysosome and there hydrolyzed, or conversely the hydrolases may be released into the cytoplasm in controlled quantities that represent no threat to the cell's integrity.

Figure 10.11 □ **Centrioles: electron micrograph, 49,920×, from embryonic rat liver. Note 90° orientation of the two centrioles. (*Courtesy of Dr. Keith R. Porter.*)**

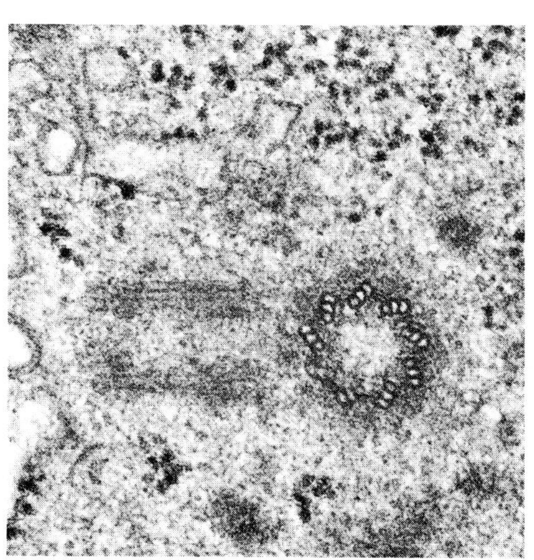

F Centrioles

Centrioles are regular constituents of animal cells and of flagellated plant cells, in which they serve as centers for the synthesis of spindle fibers during cell division. They are constant in size and organization —short cylinders about 0.15 μm in diameter by 0.3 to 0.5 μm in length, each containing a ring of nine longitudinally oriented fibrillar elements. Each of these elements in turn comprises a bundle of three hollow microtubules (Figure 10.11). Cell division is heralded by the separation of the two centriole pairs, that normally lie close to the nucleus. They move directly apart to opposite ends of the cell, forming the poles of the spindle (see Figure 10.15). This migration of the centrioles could be due to their being pushed apart by the tubular spindle fibers elongating between them. After cell division the single centriole pair remaining to each daughter cell separates, and each centriole then seems to replicate, restoring the original complement of two pairs. The new centriole seems to grow out of the old one at right angles to the longitudinal axis of the latter, and eventually separates from it, but retains the same spatial orientation. Accordingly, the two centrioles of a pair are always positioned at right angles to one another. The functional significance of the microtubular internal organization of centrioles, and of their consistent positions relative to one another is not yet known.

The capacity of centrioles to reproduce depends upon a strand of intrinsic centriolar DNA. The region of the chromosome to which the spindle fibers attach during cell division (the centromere) is intriguingly similar to a centriole, as are the basal bodies of cilia and flagella (kinetosomes). Centrioles, centromeres, and kinetosomes all contain intrinsic DNA and can reproduce themselves. Along with the mitochondria, all three of these may be particles of foreign origin (*episomes*)—possibly viral or bacterial symbionts that have become specialized during the course of evolution toward performance of specific functions that enhance survival of the host cell.

G Cilia and flagella

Cilia and flagella are slender contractile structures that protrude from the surfaces of many types of cells. Those of eucaryotic cells are covered externally by extensions of the plasma membrane, and their internal

Figure 10.12 □ (*a*) Cross section of cilia on gill epithelium of freshwater clam (100,000×) and (*b*) longitudinal section of basal portion of cilia, showing rootlets extending into cytoplasm, from gill epithelium of freshwater clam (35,000×). (*Courtesy of Dr. I. R. Gibbons.*) (*c*) Modes of insertion of flagellum, with internal filament (rhizoplast) extending to centriole near nucleus, and cilium, showing basal body (kinetosome) and "roots."

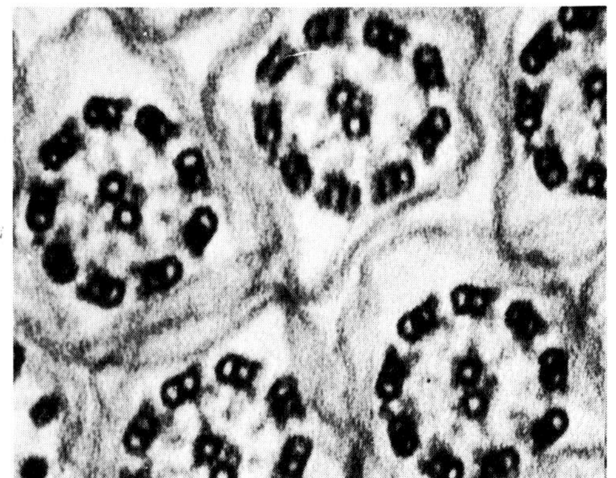

(*a*)

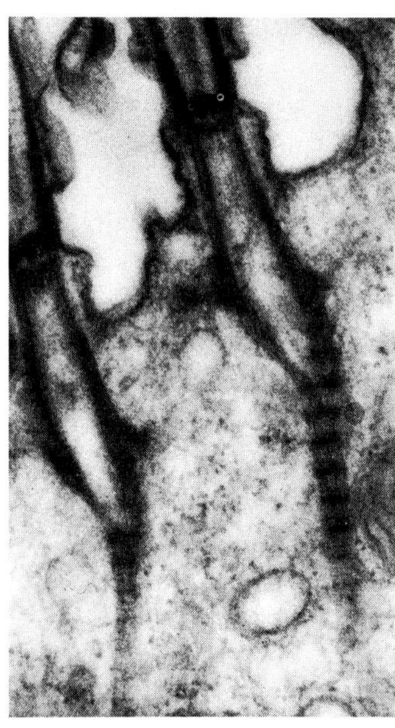

(*b*)

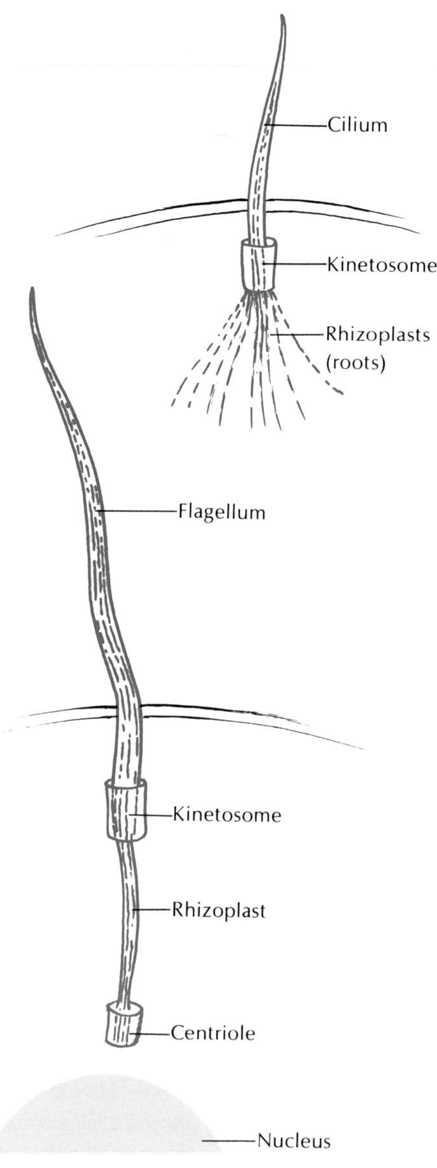

(*c*)

structure is highly reminiscent of that of centrioles, for they contain a ring of nine longitudinally oriented double microtubules surrounding a central pair—the so-called 9 + 2 arrangement (Figure 10.12). The microtubules of the cilium or flagellum extend deeply into the cell, where they are found to arise from basal bodies or *kinetosomes,* which are virtually identical in structure to centrioles. The nine peripheral sets of microtubules extend through the kinetosome and radiate out into the cytoplasm. Kinetosomes contain DNA and are capable of self-replication. When a flagellated unicellular organism divides, the basal body also divides and each daughter kinetosome produces a new flagellum.

Cilia are considerably shorter than flagella. This affects their beat, so that they move in a short, stiff stroke, bending only at the place where they emerge from the cell. The stroke of a flagellum, on the other hand, travels outward from base to tip, describing a spiral or a sine wave (see Figure 16.33). Flagella usually occur on solitary motile cells, the locomotion of which is brought about by the beating of a single to several dozen flagella. In the case of euglenophytes, the flagellated end of the cell moves forward, pulled through the medium by the spiral, rotatory stroke of the flagellum. Flagellated sperm cells on the contrary move with the flagellated end directed posteriorly, the stroke pushing against the medium so that the cell body is driven forward.

Flagella occur widely in both procaryotic and eucaryotic cells. Cilia occur only on animal cells. Few to many cilia may cover all or part of the outer surfaces of protozoans and certain metazoans such as flatworms and many types of larvae, where their coordinated beat brings about locomotion. Unlike flagella, cilia may be interconnected within the cell cortex by "neurofibrils" (see Figure 15.35), which enable them to beat in a coordinated rather than a random fashion. Each cilium becomes rigid during the backward, effective stroke, while the forward recovery stroke seems to be less forceful and consequently does not oppose the action of the backward stroke. The internal cavities and intestinal tracts of many invertebrates are ciliated, as are the respiratory passages and oviducts of vertebrates. Inside the body ciliary action serves to circulate fluids or to move materials such as food, mucus, or ova, from one end of a passage to the other. Ciliary and flagellar action will be considered in further depth in Section 16.3G.

Propagation of a wave of contraction from the base to the tip of a cilium or flagellum must involve conduction of a stimulus, such as occurs along the membrane of a muscle fiber or a nerve cell. This property of conduction may be important to the potential of certain ciliated cells to evolve into sensory receptors. The sensory cilia which such modified cells bear are nonmotile, and lack the central two microtubules, possessing only the peripheral ring of nine sets. Cells that bear such modified nonmotile cilia are often referred to as *hair cells.* The sense of smell (olfaction) in vertebrates depends upon special neuroepithelial hair cells located in the nasal passages (see Figure 15.15). The free end of each of these cells bears sensory cilia; the inner end is elongated to form a conductile process extending to the olfactory lobe of the brain. Similar hair cells are located in the inner ear, where they generate impulses that are carried by the acoustic nerve (see Figure 15.30*d*). Statocysts [gravity receptors (see Figure 4.37)] also are typically provided with sensory hair cells.

Perhaps the most dramatic instance of the evolution of a cilium into a receptor structure is reflected by the maturation of the rod and cone cells of the vertebrate retina. These cells contain visual pigments that undergo photochemical reactions by means of which light energy is converted into the energy of a nerve impulse. During the embryonic development of a rod (see Figure 15.18*d*) a single long cilium, typical in structure save for the absence of the two central microtubules, grows out from one end of the cell. The plasma membrane covering this cilium then expands, folding into a series of transverse platelike layers. These stacked plates are supported by the ciliary microtubules that extend along one side of the mature rod. The visual pigments are closely associated with the lipoprotein membrane forming the plates. The evolution of ciliated cells into numerous types of sensory receptors throughout the Animal Kingdom is a remarkable example of the acquisition of new functions by preexisting structures.

H The Golgi apparatus

The Golgi apparatus is a series of parallel, convoluted, cytoplasmic membranes, continuous with but distinguishable from the endoplasmic reticulum. It is usually located near the nucleus, and its surfaces are not associated with ribosomes. The Golgi apparatus is of wide, perhaps universal, occurrence in eucaryotic cells, but is largest and most conspicuous in active secretory cells, including neurons and gland cells, where its cavities become packed with secretion granules or droplets. The protein constituents of the secretory products are produced at the ribosomes; they then collect within the Golgi apparatus, where polysaccharide components are synthesized and added to the proteins to form glycoproteins and mucosaccharides. In mucus-secreting cells, mucin is synthesized in the Golgi apparatus and "packaged" in a vacuolar membrane pinched off the Golgi membranes. In plant cells the Golgi apparatus is differentiated into a *forming face* and a *maturation face;* as materials are accumulated and synthesized within the cavities of the Golgi apparatus, vesicles bud off of the maturation face and carry the Golgi products to other parts of the cell. In dividing plant cells these vesicles accumulate in the midspindle region, where they contribute to the formation of the plasma membrane and cell plate separating the daughter cells. Pectin, a polysaccharide, is known to be synthesized within the Golgi apparatus and is secreted to contribute to the new cell wall. In addition to its primary role as the cell's major site of polysaccharide synthesis, the Golgi apparatus is also considered a possible site of production of the new membranes required by growing cells, and as a place where the water equilibrium of the cell may be regulated.

I Plastids

Plastids are self-replicating organelles that occur only in eucaryotic plant cells. They contain their own intrinsic DNA and, like mitochondria, may have arisen by the coadaptive evolution of symbionts, perhaps primitive blue-green algae cells. New plastids arise either by the fission of mature plastids (mainly in algae), or by the production and subsequent growth of minute organelles called *proplastids.* As they mature, plastids develop a *lamellar* or "stacked plate" internal organization similar to that seen in vertebrate rod cells (see Figure 13.4). This organization fails to develop in starch-storing plastids (*leucoplasts*). Pigment-containing plastids include chromoplasts, which contain heavy concentrations of yellow or red pigments and are important in the coloration of fruits and flowers, and chloroplasts, which contain mostly chlorophyll and are the sites of photosynthesis in eucaryotic cells.

Structure and function are indeed intimately associated in the chloroplast. The lamellar portions or *grana* are thought to contain chlorophyll and other pigment molecules arranged in monomolecular layers between lipoprotein layers. The grana are so oriented that light must pass through them at right angles to the lamellae, thus necessarily penetrating many layers of chlorophyll molecules. This arrangement facilitates the absorption of light by electrons of the chlorophyll molecules. Furthermore, electron-acceptor molecules are apparently organized along the lamellae, sandwiched between the pigment layers, in such a manner that excited electrons from chlorophyll may readily be captured and their energy transferred to the carbohydrate-building cycle. The enzymes that catalyze the reactions by which sugar is manufactured are also located along the lamellae of the grana, always occurring in intimate association with the chlorophyll and electron-acceptor compounds.

The number of chloroplasts per cell differs from one species to another, and among different tissues within the same species. Each cell of the filamentous green alga *Spirogyra* (see Figure 17.10*b*) contains a single, spirally wound, strap-shaped chloroplast. The unicellular alga *Chlamydomonas* has a single large cup-shaped chloroplast (see Figure 2.13). On the other hand, a single leaf cell of a tracheophyte may contain some 50 ovoid chloroplasts.

J Inclusions

Cytoplasmic inclusions are accumulated products of cell metabolism. Their specific character depends upon the particular species or type of cell under consideration.

Secretions are synthesized and temporarily retained as inclusions in the cytoplasm of secretory cells including gland cells and neurons. Digestive gland cells contain granules of zymogen (inactive proenzyme), cells of endocrine glands contain accumulated hormones, and the swollen endings of nerve fibers contain vesicles filled with transmitter substance; these secretions are released from the cytoplasm upon appropriate stimulation.

In other cases, the materials synthesized remain within the cell. The epidermal cells of terrestrial vertebrates accumulate the horny protein keratin. Various pigments (including the black pigment melanin) are concentrated in the cytoplasm of animal *chromatophores* (see Figure 16.39). Intracellular *fibrils* may be synthesized in the cytoplasm, affecting the cell's contractile or conductive capacities. Muscle cells of various animals contain from few to many contractile myofibrils (see Section 16.3F). Conductive neurofibrils serve to coordinate the ciliary action of protozoans.

Solid *excretory products* may also be retained as cytoplasmic inclusions. A common method of excretion among invertebrates involves the accumulation of metabolic waste materials by amoeboid cells, which convert them into inert solids and later transport them to points at which they can be eliminated from the body (see Section 16.2A).

Various *storage products* constituting a nutrient reservoir may be accumulated as granules or crystals, or as droplets invested by a bounding membrane to form a *vacuole.* Plant cells typically contain a large central sap vacuole that serves for the storage of water and sugar. Lipid droplets are stored in diatom cells, in the adipose tissues of metazoans, and to a lesser degree in many other kinds of cells. Granules of starch, glycogen, paramylum, and other high-molecular-weight carbohydrates are also stored as cytoplasmic inclusions. In storage tissues such as occur in roots and tubers, nutrient inclusions may occupy most of the cell, the cytoplasm and nucleus being displaced to the periphery.

K Episomes

Episomes are intracellular particles of *foreign origin,* which are self-replicating and may exist either as *free episomes* in the cytoplasm or as *integrated episomes* attached to the chromosomes. Earlier we noted that certain organelles of widespread occurrence among eucaryotic cells contain intrinsic DNA and may well have originated as symbiotic viral, algal, or bacterial constituents that evolved toward complete integration into the life of the host cell. These possibly episomal organelles include the plastids, mitochondria, centrioles, kinetosomes, and centromeres. Of these, only the last are regularly associated with the chromosomes. The episomal origin of these organelles is difficult to verify, for they now exist as regular constituents of eucaryotic plant cells, animal cells, or both. It is intriguing to speculate that much of the elaborate structure of eucaryotic cells may have come about by the incorporation of procaryotic cells (primitive bacteria or blue-green algae), first as symbionts, then as episomes, finally as part of the cell's regular machinery.

A number of episomal factors are known that are more restricted in distribution and are in fact *contagious,* being transmitted from the carrier cells to cells formerly free of these factors. Episomal factors found in bacteria are either known or suspected to be viral in nature. The *lambda* factor (λ) is an integrated episome: it originates as all or part of the chromosome of a bacteriophage virus that fails to kill its host, but instead remains attached to the host's chromosome as a symbiotic factor, conferring immunity against further attack by viruses of the same type (that is, λ phage). The integrated λ factor replicates in phase with the host's cycle of reproduction and is thereby transmitted to the daughter cells.

The *F* (fertility) and *R* (antibiotic-resistance) factors are also cytoplasmic particles thought to represent symbiotic viral DNA, but they are passed from one bacterium to another only by an act of *conjugation:* the cell wall disappears between the bacteria and a cytoplasmic exchange ensues (see Figure 17.9). Sexual reproduction in such bacteria as *Escherichia coli* appears to depend upon the episomal *F* factor, for F^- strains never mate; F^+ strains, which carry *F* particles in the cytoplasm, act as "males." In the presence of F^- cells, a filamentous projection forms on the cell wall of the "male." This makes contact with the cell wall of the "female" and a conjugation bridge is formed, penetrating both cell wall and plasma membrane. Through this tubule *F* particles pass from the F^+ to the F^- cell. The *F* factors then reproduce in the cytoplasm of the new host and are transmitted to its progeny, which consequently are also F^+. Occasionally the *F* factor becomes attached to one of the host's chromosomes, causing the chromosome (which ordinarily takes the form of a closed ring) to break open at the point of attachment. When conjugation next occurs, this chromosome will pass across the conjugation bridge, with the *F* factor still attached, to be incorporated into the genome of the "female" cell. Thus a true sexual transfer of chromosomal material takes place, as an outcome of the action of an episome.

The *R* factor in bacteria is a free episome consisting of a ring of DNA that bears several functional regions that confer resistance to a number of known antibiotics. An unusual characteristic of this factor is that it facilitates conjugation even between bacteria of different genera. When R^+ bacteria are exposed to any one of the antibiotics to which *R* is competent to respond, this exposure constitutes a stimulus that activates a conjugation-facilitating site on the episome. Moving to the cell periphery, the *R* factor causes a projection to be put forth that forms a conjugation bridge when the R^+ cell comes in contact with an R^- bacterium (which need not be of the same species). The *R* factor thereupon infects the R^- cell, reproduces, and is passed to the progeny, which are accordingly R^+. Exposure to antibiotics therefore serves to promulgate antibiotic-resistance by activating the transmission of the *R* episome.

The episomes *kappa* and *mu* are considered to be degenerate forms of bacterial symbionts that inhabit the cytoplasm of certain strains of the familiar protozoan *Paramecium.* These factors can be transmitted during conjugation (see Figure 17.11) but can be maintained in the cytoplasm only when the host's genotype contains specific alleles, to wit, the *kappa*-supporting gene *K*, and the *mu*-supporting gene *M*. Individuals of the genotypes *mm* or *kk* may be infected with these episomes, but the latter are unable to reproduce and soon disappear. When infected with *kappa,* individuals of the genotypes *KK* or *Kk* become "killers." In the presence of *kk* individuals, the killer secretes a chemical that soon kills the *kk* protozoans. Similarly, the mate-killer factor *mu* persists only in the cytoplasm of *MM* or *Mm* individuals. If in the course of sexual exchange a *Paramecium* gives up its *M* allele and becomes *mm*, the *mu* particles disappear from the cytoplasm of its descendants within about 18 generations of cell division. They apparently stop reproducing as soon as the gene *M* is lost.

Bacterial symbionts less degenerate than *kappa* and *mu* inhabit the cells of many insects. Like those which are endosymbiotic in the root nodules of legumes (see Figure

4.17), they appear to aid the host's metabolism in specific ways. The existence of such intracellular bacterial symbionts suggests that episomes might have arisen by regressive simplification, with retention only of those parts necessary for the life or well-being of the host.

These known instances of cytoplasmic or intranuclear episomes that alter the phenotype of the host have led to much speculation on the extent to which episomes may also occur in the tissues of man and other mammals. Those which have evolved to the status of regularly occurring cell components cannot be recognized as episomes; those less well adapted to the host cell may occasionally be responsible for disease. Viral episomes transmitted in the egg cytoplasm from mother to offspring may be responsible for the production of cancer in later life. The factor may cause cancer only when the host-episomal integration is disturbed by exposure to chemical irritants, X-rays, or contributory physiological states of the host. Persons susceptible to cold sores actually carry herpes simplex virus at all times within their cells, but the virus is activated only during certain physiological states such as fever; the virus then produces ulcers, usually on the lips but occasionally on the genitalia, on the eyeball, or within the mouth. There is a possibility, however, that chronic carriers of herpes simplex virus may gain immunity to certain types of viral encephalitis. If this should prove to be the case, the "cold sore" virus may be of benefit to the life of the host. Further investigations are in order to ascertain what roles episomes play in the normal functioning of the tissues. Also of great medical interest are the circumstances under which an apparently latent cancer-producing episome may be activated to cause the host cell to become malignant.

10.5 □ THE NUCLEUS

The nucleus of a cell is usually its most conspicuous internal feature. It is often located close to the center of the cell and is typically oval, though occasionally kidney-shaped, lobed, or irregular in form. Its prominence is accentuated by differential staining, since the nucleoprotein material of the chromosomes and nucleolus stains a rich purple in the presence of basic dyes. First described and named by Robert Brown in 1831, the nucleus excited much curiosity. A number of experiments involving nuclear extirpation and transplantation were begun.

A Nuclear function

The importance of the nucleus in cell regeneration was first noted in 1851 by the neurologist A. V. Waller, who found that nerve fibers degenerated when severed from the cell body, whereas the cell body (the central part containing the nucleus) was able to regenerate new fibers. In similar fashion, it was discovered that if an *Amoeba* were cut into two parts the nucleated portion would grow into a normal individual while the enucleate part would survive and move about for some time, but eventually would dwindle and die.

An elegant series of experiments on nuclear function was conducted by J. Hämmerling on the green alga *Acetabularia* (Figure 10.13). Although several centimeters long, *Acetabularia* possesses only a single nucleus, located in the basal part of the stalk (*rhizoid*). At the other end of the stalk is an expanded portion or *cap,* the shape of which is different in two species of the genus. In *A. mediterranea* the cap is discoid with scalloped edges, whereas in *A. crenulata* the cap is crenulated—its margins are so deeply incised that the cap consists of separate rays. These morphological distinctions permit the caps of the two species to be distinguished readily. Hämmerling found first that a decapitated stalk could regenerate a new cap, whereas the isolated cap could not regenerate a stalk or rhizoid. Next he grafted an enucleate section of the stalk of one species onto the cut end of a decapitated stalk of the other species. He found that although the first cap produced was intermediate in character, after several decapitations the cap which regenerated showed the characteristics of the species to which the basal nucleated part belonged: the intervening cytoplasmic graft did not permanently influence cap morphogenesis. Thus, an *A. mediterranea* stalk grafted onto

Figure 10.13 ☐ **Nuclear influence upon regeneration and cap morphogenesis in *Acetabularia.* (*a*) Clump of *Acetabularia mediterranea.* (*Courtesy of General Biological, Inc., Chicago.*) (*b*) Experiments on nuclear function. Above, stalk segments of *A. mediterranea* are grafted onto nucleated base of decapitated *A. crenulata,* and vice versa; the caps ultimately produced are characteristic of the species contributing the nucleus and not of that contributing the stalk. Below, decapitated basal portions of the two species are grafted together, producing a cap of intermediate form but favoring whichever species contributes the larger number of nuclei.**

(*a*)

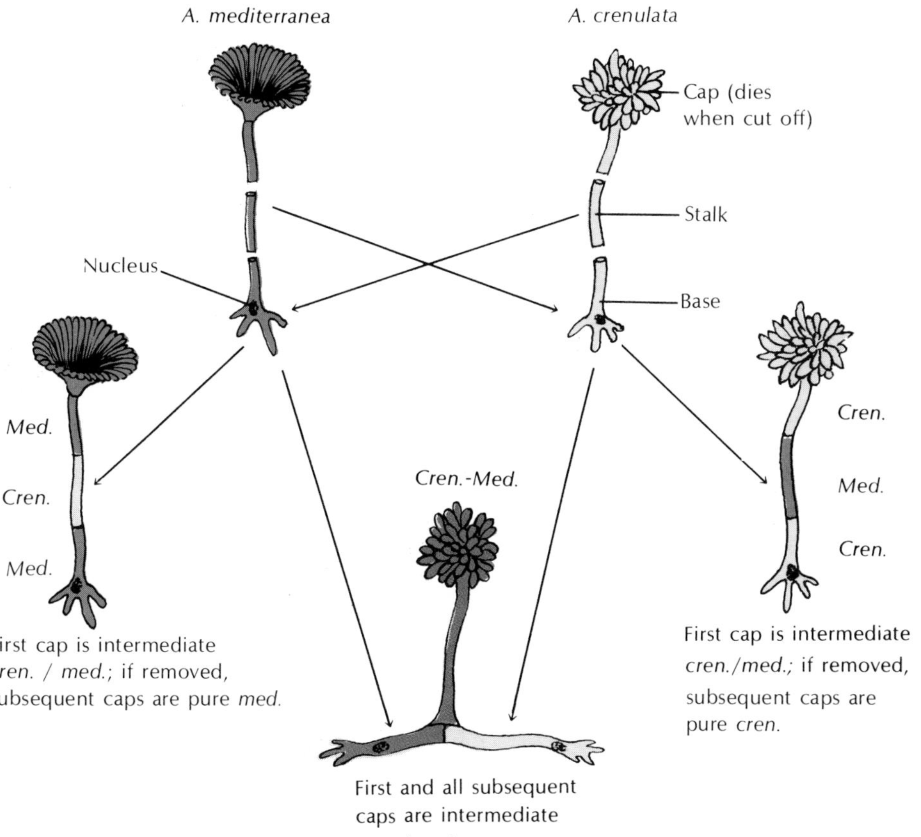

A. mediterranea
A. crenulata
Cap (dies when cut off)
Stalk
Nucleus
Base
Med.
Cren.
Med.
Cren.
Med.
Cren.
Cren.-Med.
First cap is intermediate cren. / med.; if removed, subsequent caps are pure med.
First cap is intermediate cren./med.; if removed, subsequent caps are pure cren.
First and all subsequent caps are intermediate cren./med.

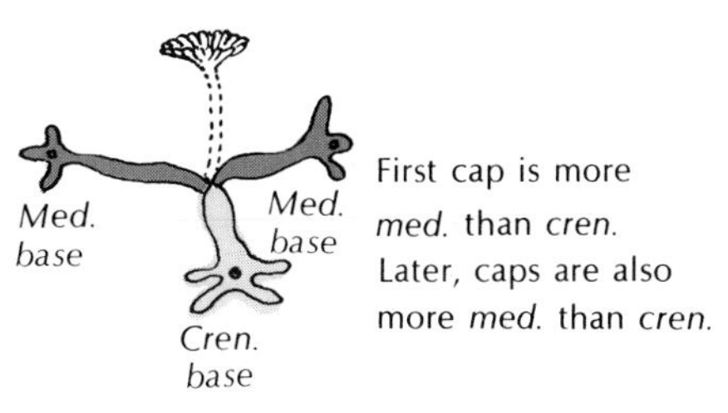

Med. base
Med. base
Cren. base
First cap is more med. than cren. Later, caps are also more med. than cren.

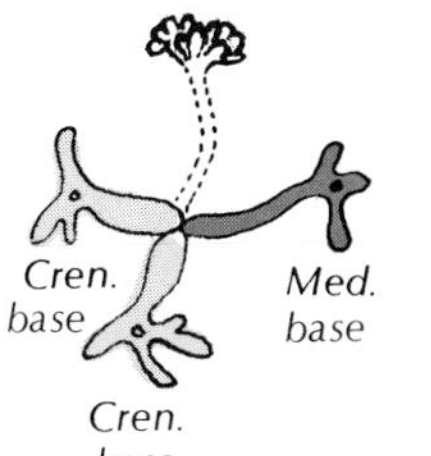

Cren. base
Med. base
Cren. base
First cap is more cren. than med. Later, caps are more cren. than med.

(*b*)

a nucleated rhizoid of *A. crenulata* eventually produced a *crenulata* cap rather than a *mediterranea* cap, and vice versa. Further experiments involved decapitating cells of both species and grafting their stalks together. Such a preparation contained two nuclei, one of each species, and regenerated a single cap which showed characteristics of both species: the hybrid cap was crenulated as in *A. crenulata,* but the ends of the rays were rounded as in *A. mediterranea* rather than pointed as in *A. crenulata.* Thus each nucleus was shown to have influenced the morphogenesis of the cap. Other preparations involved grafting together unequal numbers of decapitated stalks of the two species. In these cases, the new cap more closely resembled that of the species which contributed the greater number of nuclei to the preparation. Hämmerling's experiments with *Acetabularia* demonstrated that the nucleus directs morphogenesis and does so in a quantitative fashion, so that if more than one nucleus is present each contributes to produce a cap of intermediate phenotype. These regenerative and morphogenetic capacities depend of course upon the chromosomes contained within the nucleus.

B Nuclear constituents

THE NUCLEAR ENVELOPE The nuclear membrane or envelope consists of lipoprotein membranes, and is apparently continuous with the membranes of the endoplasmic reticulum. The envelope is double, with a narrow fluid-filled space between the inner and outer membrane (see Figure 10.8). It does not enclose the nuclear materials completely, but appears to have octagonal pores through which large molecules can pass between nucleus and cytoplasm. Not only must high-molecular-weight RNA chains pass from nucleus to cytoplasm, but large molecules involved in gene regulation must pass in the opposite direction. Some cytologists believe that the pores are plugged openings, used only for certain types of transport, while messenger RNA exits from the nucleus by way of *blebs* which may be seen under the electron microscope. A bleb is an outpocketing of the nuclear membrane into which a portion of a chromosome protrudes. The bleb is eventually pinched off and becomes part of the cytoplasmic membranes. It is thought that the chromosome involved in bleb formation may be in the act of releasing messenger RNA into the bleb, which, upon becoming detached, carries the mRNA into the cytoplasm.

CHROMOSOMES The chromosome of most viruses is a simple thread of double- or single-stranded DNA. In all *cells,* however, chromosomes are found to consist of DNA conjugated with protein. The exact arrangement of DNA in the chromosome is not yet clear; certainly it retains a linear organization that persists from one generation to the next and is sufficiently constant to permit the mapping of genes. The polynemic giant chromosomes of dipteran flies consist of a large number of identical DNA strands that display characteristic light and dark banding patterns (see Figure 8.13). Specific genes are found to be associated with identifiable bands: a deletion that eliminates a particular band also eliminates a certain gene. It is thought likely that polynemy may be of widespread occurrence, particularly in mature, nondividing cells. Polynemic chromosomes would be capable of producing many times the mRNA which could be synthesized on a single DNA strand, hence polynemy would multiply the metabolic capabilities of the chromosome.

Chromosomes are composed of about 39 percent DNA, 39 percent histone protein, and 9 percent insoluble residual protein. Histones are water-soluble proteins containing large proportions of the basic (diamino) amino acids lysine, arginine, and histidine (see Table 9.2). The histones associated with chromosomal DNA may serve as gene repressors. Metabolically active portions of the chromosome may be identified by the presence of mRNA at its sites of synthesis. RNA does not seem to be an integral part of the chromosomes, but does seem to assist in the bonding of histones to specific genes.

Each chromosome bears a region known as the *centromere,* which separates the two "arms" of the chromosome. A strand of DNA apparently originating from the centromere extends for a short distance in each direction along the central axis of each arm of the chromosome. The centromere is the only part of the chromosome that can bind with the spindle fibers during cell division. The centromere replicates along with the chromosome but is the last part to divide completely, so that the daughter chromosomes are held together at the centromere during the early stages of mitosis. After it has become attached to the spindle fibers the centromere finishes dividing and anchors each chromosome to the spindle while the spindle fibers shorten, drawing the daughter chromosomes to opposite ends of the dividing cell (see Figure 10.15). The centromere is essential for the migration of the

Cryptic resemblance to foliage. Many insects and other animals escape the notice of predators by faithfully resembling leaves. The resemblance has arisen independently in various groups of insects and illustrates evolutionary convergence among species not closely related. (*a*) A locust, *Microcentrum*, with compressed leaflike form. (*Los Angeles County Museum of Natural History.*) (*b*) A praying mantis, *Chaerododis*, with depressed leaflike form. (*Ward's Natural Science Establishment, Inc.*) (*c*) *Epicnaptera*, a moth. (*Los Angeles County Museum of Natural History*. (*d*) The dead-leaf butterfly, *Kallima*, exhibiting changes in color that match changes in foliage during the dry and rainy seasons. (*Ward's Natural Science Establishment, Inc.*)

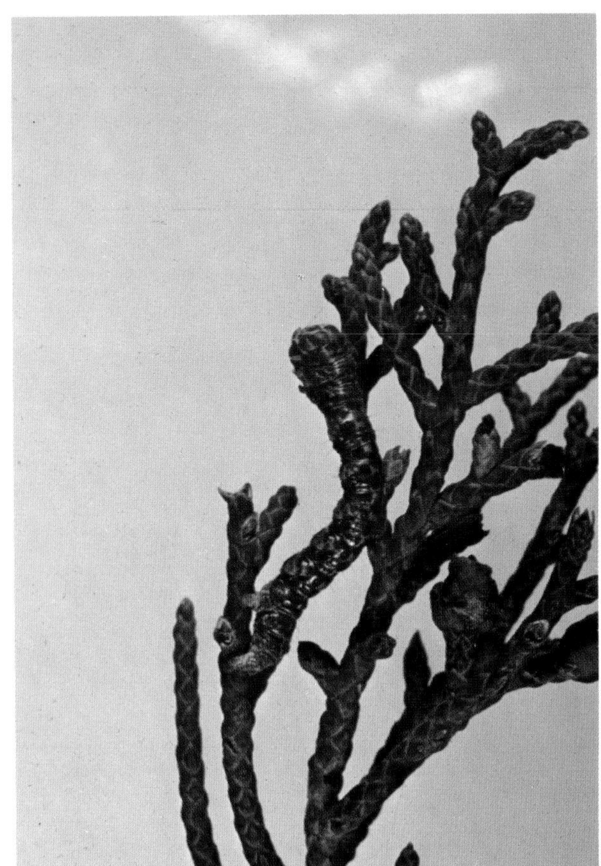

(*a*)

Crypsis and catalepsy. Protective resemblance to leaves, twigs, and bark is effective only if the animal correctly positions itself against the background and preserves throughout the day an attitude of cataleptic immobility, moving about only by night. (*a*) The larva of a geometrid moth holds its body stiffly at the angle at which twigs emerge from the juniper branch on which this species rests. (*b*) A desert plume moth remains immobile, in plain sight yet protected by its physical and positional resemblance to the stem spine clusters of the cactus that is its preferred resting place. (*Los Angeles County Museum of Natural History.*)

(*b*)

Batesian mimicry, the resemblance of an edible mimic to a noxious model, is exemplified by (*a*) the viceroy butterfly and its model, the larger monarch butterfly, and (*b*) a robber fly and its model, the tarantula wasp, *Pepsis*. In each pair, model and mimic occur sympatrically, the model tending to outnumber the mimic. (*Los Angeles County Museum of Natural History.*) *Müllerian* mimicry, the mutual resemblance among a group of sympatric species all of which are unpalatable, is demonstrated in (*c*) several types of butterfly which are not closely related but which have converged in appearance and now constitute a typical Müllerian complex. (*Ward's Natural Science Establishment, Inc.*)

(*a*)

(*c*)

(*b*)

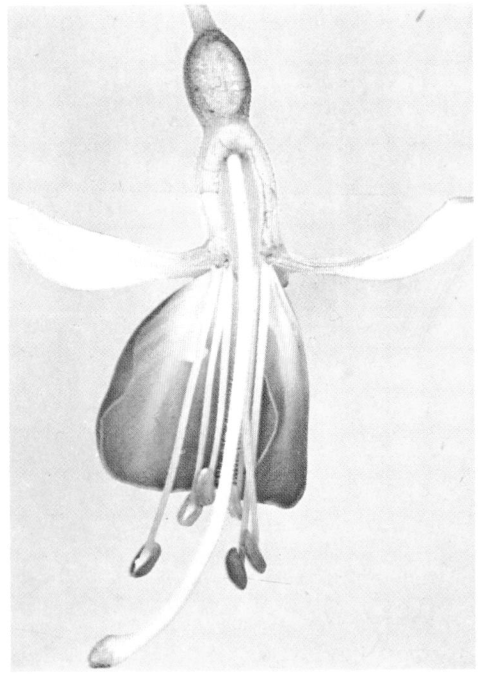

(a)

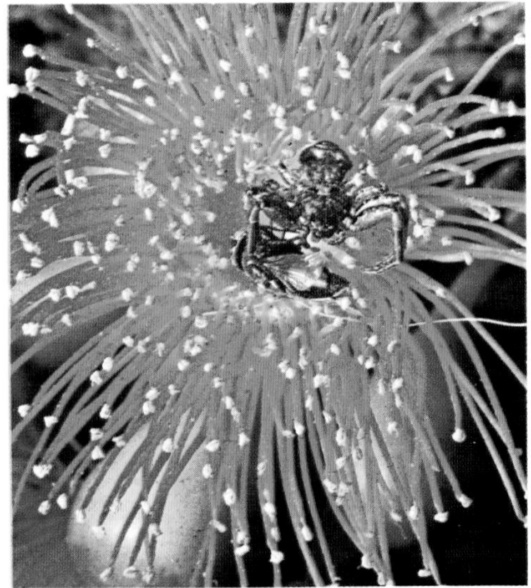

(b)

(c)

Flowers. (*a*) The *perfect* flower of a fuchsia possesses all types of floral structure. The long pistils and stamens protrude from the brightly pigmented calyx and corolla and contact the bodies of hummingbirds that visit the flowers to probe the deep-lying nectaries. (*Ward's Natural Science Establishment, Inc.*) (*b*) The *imperfect* blossom of a eucalyptus lacks petals, but the pistils and stamens are brilliantly colored and attractive to pollinator insects, one of which has here fallen victim to a spider concealed among the stamens. (*Los Angeles County Museum of Natural History.*) (*c*) The *inflorescence* (*head*) of a composite, a member of the most diverse and successful of all dicot orders. The numerous, fertile disc flowers are encircled by conspicuous, but often sterile, ray flowers that help to attract insects. Here a cryptic spider awaits the next visitor. (*Los Angeles County Museum of Natural History.*)

chromosomes during mitosis. Occasionally an abnormal chromosome is produced which lacks a centromere; such an *acentric* chromosome is incapable of attaching to the spindle and fails to move during cell division.

NUCLEOLUS One or more nucleoli, commonly two, are produced anew after each cell division. They are produced by specific chromosomes that have a *nucleolar organizer region*. Genes in this region are thought to produce ribosomal RNA. The nucleoli become densely packed with ribonucleoprotein, which is set free when the nucleolar-bounding membrane disappears during cell division.

NUCLEOPLASM The nucleoplasm is the aqueous medium in which the nucleoli and chromosomes lie. It is probably continuous with the hyaloplasm exterior to the nucleus, and it contains ions and also nutrient molecules in both solution and suspension.

10.6 □ CELL REPRODUCTION

Every time that a cell divides, its internal organization is partly conserved, and partly must be built up again. Some of the cell's organelles, such as chromosomes, plastids, and mitochondria, replicate themselves with fidelity, conserving their organization from one cell generation to the next. Other structures, such as the nuclear envelope and nucleolus, undergo dissolution when the cell divides and are apparently reformed *de novo*. During the growth of each daughter cell, the membranes must grow, and those organelles which are incapable of self-replication must be manufactured until they reach a number characteristic of the mature cell.

Those cellular features most apt to disappear at the time of cell division are the ones that have to do with the differentiation of cells into specialized types. It is generally the case that, the more highly differentiated a cell, the less likely it is to be capable of undergoing mitosis. Cell division is usually the prerogative of undifferentiated cells. Mature, nondividing cells that are explanted and cultured in vitro typically lose many of their structural specializations and, apparently regaining a more or less juvenile state, resume mitotic activity.

The *reproduction* of organisms, both sexually and asexually, depends upon the capacity of cells for reproducing themselves. In addition, the *growth* of organisms depends mainly on the proliferation of their constituent cells. If all daughter cells were to reproduce synchronously through only 30 consecutive divisions, a single fertilized egg would give rise to a body composed of around a billion cells; in actuality, as cells differentiate and mature, cell division becomes restricted to relatively few tissues—those on surfaces exposed to wear, germinal tissues, and some others.

Cell division, as it occurs in eucaryotic plant and animal cells, is a process of remarkable uniformity throughout the biotic world. Common mechanisms are seen to be at work, and a description of mitotic events in the cell of an onion root tip would apply with reasonable fidelity to those occurring in the cell of a man.

Descriptions of cell division formerly rested upon the microscopic examination of cells that had been killed, sectioned, and stained, having been arrested in various stages of division. Plant roottips and animal embryos (Figure 10.14) provided mitotically active material in which many cells could be found in the process of dividing. However, the analysis of mitotic events in *living* cells was later made possible by the application of phase-contrast microscopy to individual cells, such as those of aquatic embryos or cells grown in sterile culture media. By such techniques a consistent description of the mitotic process has been arrived at, but little is yet known concerning the molecular dynamics of the event. We still do not know what triggers the replication of DNA, how entire chromosomes reproduce, how the spindle fibers form (with or without centrioles), lengthen, and shorten, how the centromeres and spindle interact, how the planes of consecutive cell divisions are determined, or how the division of the cytoplasm comes about. Reasonable hypotheses have been formulated to answer these questions, but none is yet firmly established. In these basic respects our ignorance still outweighs our knowledge.

We may conclude with some certainty

Figure 10.14 □ **Mitosis. (*a*) Onion root tip: (1) metabolic (nondividing) stage, (2) prophase, (3) metaphase, (4) anaphase, and (5) telophase. (*Courtesy of Carolina Biological Supply Company.*) (*b*) Whitefish embryo (blastula). (*Courtesy of General Biological, Inc., Chicago.*)**

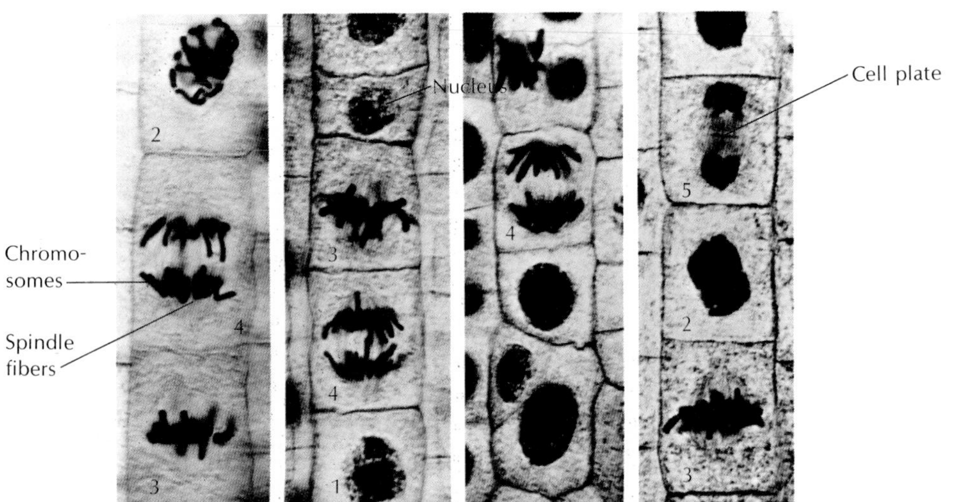

(*a*)

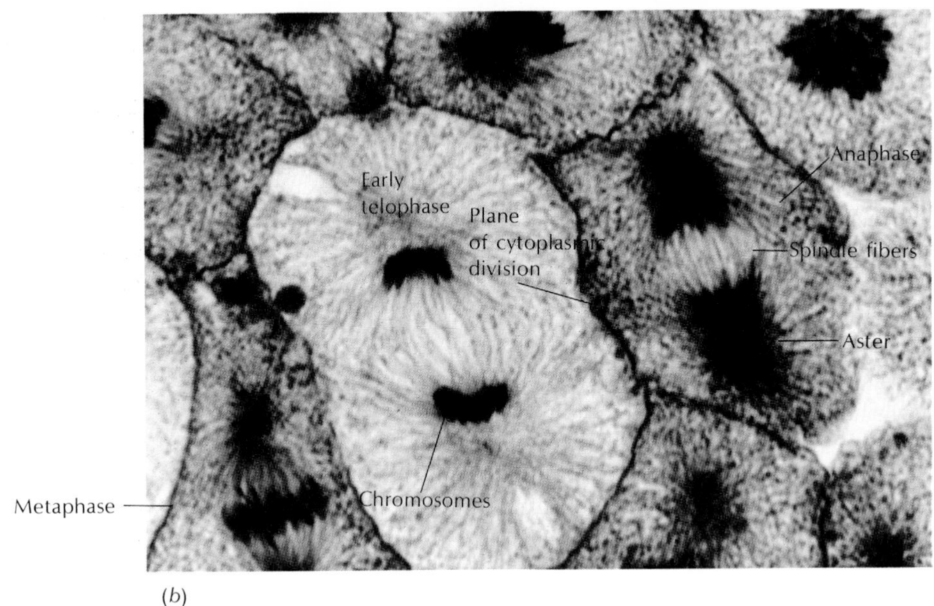

(*b*)

that mitosis consists of a highly ordered sequence of events by which the potentiality for organization is conserved and perpetuated nearly intact to the daughter cells resulting from the division. The precise and orderly movement of chromosomes and centrioles during mitosis reflects the patterned grace of an elaborate dance—but is infinitely more mysterious. Unlike certain biochemical sequences that can be carried out in vitro, separated from the intact cell, mitosis is a uniquely cellular event, involving the entire cell. Such events, unfortunately, leave no fossils, hence the evolution of this beautifully adaptive process cannot be traced. It may be assumed, however, that the process had developed to a sophisticated level before eucaryotic cellular life began to radiate into different phyla—perhaps before plants and animals began to diverge.

The evolution of biotic organization from the molecular to the cellular level probably involved a series of events so fortuitous and rare that perhaps only one protocell ever evolved from subcellular aggregations and survived. Any processes, therefore, which could enhance the conservation of cellular organization during reproduction would have high adaptive value. The orderly events of mitosis as we observe them today have probably passed through an evolutionary history some 2.5 to 3×10^9 years in length, during which the mitotic interactions of cell components underwent selection toward greater precision and predictability of outcome. An intracellular process is subject to selection and evolutionary change, even as is the wing of a bird or the cryptic form of a thorn insect. The ultimate outcome of the events seen in mitosis is the *precise distribution of the genetic material to each of the daughter cells.* Ordinarily (but not invariably) there is also an equal division of cytoplasm, with an accompanying fairly equal apportionment of cytoplasmic organelles, but the *essential* outcome is that each daughter cell is genetically identical, barring mutation.

A Events preceding mitosis

The reproduction of the chromosomes and centrioles does not occur *during* mitosis but at an earlier stage. Centriolar division may follow closely upon the *previous* cell division. Chromosomal duplication takes place within the nuclear envelope at a time when the chromosomes are very elongate and tenuous, hence impossible to make out with accuracy even with a phase-contrast or electron microscope. In at least certain types of cells, the chromosomes become multistranded (polynemic) before they become metabolically active; this multiplication would probably begin immediately after the completion of cell division. In other cases, DNA replication and the subsequent doubling of the chromosomes takes place only after the cell has become fully grown, being perhaps initiated by changes in cellular nutrition resulting from a critical reduction of cell surface compared with cell volume. In this case, chromosome duplication would follow a period of metabolic activity, but would nonetheless take place before the visible onset of mitosis. During early embryonic development, on the other hand, one cell division follows another without an intervening growth period, so that DNA replication must commence almost immediately after the preceding division.

Two more or less distinct events must occur during the reproduction of the chromosomes: (1) the *DNA* must replicate, each strand serving as a template for the polymerization of a complementary strand (Figure 9.20); (2) the *proteinaceous* elements of the new chromosomes must also be organized. Since we presently know almost nothing of the events involved in the reproduction of the parts of the chromosome other than DNA, we may best speak of this process not as "replication," which implies a molecule-by-molecule copying on a template, but only imprecisely, as "duplication." The phrase "division of chromosomes" is commonly employed, but should be restricted to the physical separation of the previously formed daughter chromosomes (*chromatids*) during mitosis; it does not imply that daughter-chromosome production results from lengthwise splitting.

Short applications of tritiated thymidine make possible the determination of the time of DNA synthesis, for this radioactive marker is incorporated only into the DNA molecule. By this means it has been found that DNA is manufactured *not* during mitosis, but during the preceding period of metabolic activity, that it is not formed all at once, but that certain chromosomes or parts thereof typically reproduce earlier or later in the metabolic period. The histone proteins (which are specific to chromosomes) are produced synchronously with the DNA.

B Mitosis

PROPHASE The first visible event presaging mitosis (Figure 10.15) in animal cells is the separation of daughter centrioles, which have remained together since their reproduction at an earlier time. These move directly apart, as though by mutual repulsion. As they move apart tubular spindle fibers lengthen between them. The final position of the centrioles at the end of their migration determines the *polarity* of the dividing cell, while the midline of the spindle that forms symmetrically between the two centrioles marks the *plane of cleavage* of the cytoplasm. This plane may or may not be close to the equator of the cell. (In the unequal divisions of the maturing ovum, as seen in Figure 17.24, cytoplasmic division is highly unequal, but the plane of cleavage still passes through the equator of the *spindle,* even though this is far from the equator of the cell.)

While the spindle fibers are forming and elongating between the retreating centrioles, other fibers of similar appearance grow out radially from the centrioles toward the cortex (peripheral portion) of the cell. The star-shaped configuration thus produced is known as an *aster.* In the cells of higher plants, which lack definitely demonstrable centrioles, the spindle fibers form nonetheless, but no aster is produced. It is thought, therefore, that the centrioles of animal cells may be particularly concerned with the formation of the aster, rather than just the spindle, and that the aster in turn may be involved in cytoplasmic cleavage. The establishment of these temporary fiber systems probably involves the organization of cytoplasmic proteins into chains with the formation of secondary bonds involving sulfhydryl (—SH) groups and the arrangement of these chains into microtubular paracrystalline configurations. These may grow in length by the addition of new

Figure 10.15 □ Division of an animal cell. (*a*) In the *nondividing* cell, DNA replication takes place, producing identical chromatids that are so intimately entwined as to be visibly indistinguishable. (*b*) During *early prophase*, the centrioles migrate toward the poles, aster and spindle fibers appear, the nuclear envelope disappears, and the chromosomes thicken and shorten. (*c*) In *late prophase*, the chromosomes are short and thick and the chromatids easily discernible although still joined at the centromere; the spindle is fully developed. (*d*) At *metaphase*, the chromosomes are aligned at the midline of the spindle, and the centromeres divide and become attached to spindle fibers. (*e*) During *anaphase*, the chromatids move toward opposite poles of the cell, apparently drawn by the shortening of the spindle fibers attached to the centromeres; meanwhile the entire spindle elongates, stretching the cell, and the cytoplasm begins to indent along the equator of the spindle. (*f*) During *telophase*, cytokinesis is completed, the chromosomes begin to revert to their appearance as in the nondividing cell, the centrioles reproduce, the spindle and asters disappear, and the nuclear envelopes form. The two daughter cells are identical in chromosome content.

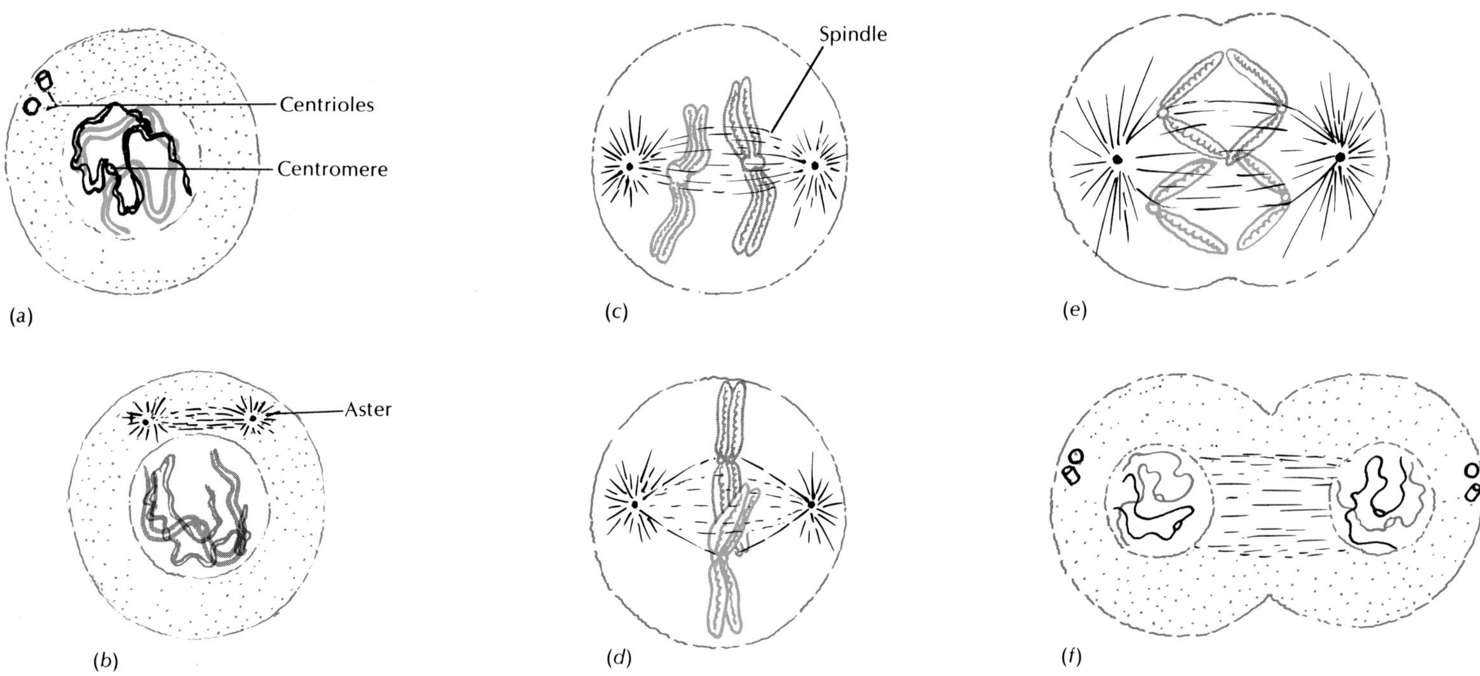

molecules at the centriolar end (the centrioles perhaps being responsible for this "polymerization"), and may subsequently shorten by casting off terminal or subterminal components.

During the period of spindle and aster formation, *nuclear* changes are also in progress. These are first seen as the condensation of the nucleoprotein material, which is present in the metabolically active nucleus as extremely tenuous threads known as *chromonemata* (which probably represent the metabolically active form of the chromosomes). During prophase these threads gradually thicken and shorten, ultimately becoming recognizable as the rodlike chromosomes typical of dividing cells. It should be recalled that except in unusual cases such as the giant cells of fly larvae, chromosomes have not yet been seen as complete entities within the nondividing cell; they are so attenuated and intertwined that only portions are detectable even with benefit of electron microscopy. However, when bacterial cells are burst by osmotic shock, the chromosomes can be clearly seen as filaments some 20 μm long, or about ten times the length of the entire bacterium! Descriptions of chromosomes are usually based upon their appearance in dividing cells. Explanations of the changes that occur in the chromosomes during the onset of mitosis are still hypothetical. Folding or coiling may take place; previously diffuse DNA strands may condense close against the central axis of the chromosome; thickening of the elements by hydration may occur: any or all of these changes may be involved. Eventually the nuclear envelope and nucleolus both disappear, and the chromosomes are seen as relatively short and sturdy bodies lying free in the cytoplasm. As they continue to shorten and thicken, it becomes apparent that each chromosome at this time already consists of two daughter chromosomes or chromatids, which are separate entities except at the undivided centromere.

Each pair of chromatids moves (actively or passively, it is not known which) toward the midplane or equator of the spindle, where the attachment of spindle fibers to the centromeres takes place. This rather involved series of events, conveniently referred to as *prophase,* terminates when the chromosomes are briefly poised at the equator of the spindle.

METAPHASE The midpoint of the mitotic process is the brief period during which the chromosomes are stationary at the equator of the spindle. At this time the centromeres divide, and some type of bond or attraction is set up between each daughter centromere and one or more spindle fibers. Daughter centromeres always must bond with spindle fibers which, by shortening, can draw them *apart,* to opposite poles of the spindle. Thus we can see that as the centromeres divide, the plane of their division must be at right angles to the orientation of the spindle.

ANAPHASE After the division of the centromeres, the two daughter centromeres of each pair of chromatids begin to move directly apart, toward opposite poles of the spindle. The two arms of each chromatid trail backward, so that the ends of the chromosomes are the last part to separate. During this movement to the poles, the chromosomes therefore assume V-shaped configurations, the apex of the V being the centromere. The centromeres appear to be drawn along by the shortening of the attached spindle fibers. As the two retreating groups of daughter chromosomes move apart, the pole-to-pole spindle fibers (which are not attached to the centromeres) continue to lengthen, so that the entire cell is elongated, and the cytoplasm begins to cleave through the midline of the spindle (*cytokinesis*). One hypothesis concerning the role of the aster in animal cells is that, if the astral fibers are in fact anchored to the cell cortex, such a lengthening of the *spindle* without a concomitant lengthening of the *aster* would tend to collapse the cell surface inward along the midline; further shortening of the astral fibers would deepen the cleavage furrow until the constriction was complete. Unfortunately for this attractive hypothesis, it has been found that cytokinesis occurs even after the aster and spindle have been dissected out of cells which have begun anaphase, but in which cytoplasmic cleavage is not yet apparent. On the other hand, application of mitotic arrestants such as colchicine to cells in late prophase, demonstrates that the spindle fibers are normally essential to both chromosomal separation and cytokinesis. In such colchicine-treated cells the spindle disappears and the chromosomes are unable to migrate to opposite poles; cytokinesis fails to occur, and the cells eventually return to a metabolic condition, now possessing a double (tetraploid) chromosome complement.

TELOPHASE The terminal stages of mitosis as they pertain to the nucleus are the reverse of the preliminary stages. The chromosomes, having completed their migration to the poles of the spindle, begin to lengthen and become thinner. They aggregate in a dense mass, and a nuclear membrane forms about them. Meanwhile, the aster and spindle fibers shorten to the point of disappearance and cytokinesis proceeds to completion. In animal cells, cytokinesis involves the progressive constriction of the cytoplasm. In plant cells no such constriction takes place, but a partition of pectin, the *cell plate,* is secreted across the equator of the spindle, becoming the middle lamella of the new cell wall. A new plasma membrane then grows inward along each side of the cell plate. At the close of telophase, two daughter cells, each with a complete nuclear complement, but with only half the cytoplasm of the original cell, exist where before there was but one.

Among protozoa and certain lower plants it is usual for mitosis to take place within the intact nuclear membrane, the spindle forming *intranuclearly.* The nucleus then divides and the daughter nuclei move apart. Nuclear division may precede or accompany cytoplasmic division.

REVIEW AND DISCUSSION

1 Explain why it is not strictly correct to say that investigators such as S. L. Miller actually *synthesized* organic compounds from inorganic materials.

2 Explain what is meant by the Urey effect and the Pasteur effect. What implications have these effects for organic evolution?

3 Why does the study of cell division and maturation *not* shed much light on the origin and evolution of cell structure? How may protocells have evolved?

4 What properties do macromolecules exhibit that might have helped them to stabilize in quasicellular aggregations during the early evolution of biotic organization? At what point in this process could we say that "life" came into being?

5 Compare procaryotic and eucaryotic cells in terms of average size, internal organization, and occurrence.

6 Compare and contrast plant and animal cells in terms of cellular componentry and types of extracellular materials secreted. On the basis of this comparison, would you say that plant and animal cells are more different than they are alike, or more alike than they are different?

7 What factors limit the upper and lower extremes of cell size? In what ways do certain cells circumvent the factors that usually set the upper limits of cell size?

8 Summarize the functional significance of: (*a*) ribosomes; (*b*) lysosomes; (c) mitochondria; (*d*) plastids; (e) centromeres; (*f*) the plasma membrane.

9 What roles are thought to be played by the Golgi apparatus, the centrioles, and the nucleoli?

10 Propose reasons why specialized cells such as muscle fibers rarely divide after reaching maturity.

11 What are some of the things that we do *not* know about the process of cell reproduction?

12 Summarize the events which characterize each stage of mitosis, and compare the outcome of mitosis with that of meiosis.

REFERENCES

ALLISON, A. "Lysosomes and Disease," *Sci. Amer.,* **217** (1967). The escape of lysosomal enzymes may be important in the occurrence of chromosome breakage, in the causation of cancer, and development of the symptoms associated with silicosis, asbestosis, and gout.

BRACHET, J., AND A. E. MIRSKY, EDS. *The Cell,* Vols. I–VI. New York: Academic Press, 1959. One of the most compendious treatments of cell structure and function undertaken to date. Particularly noteworthy are discussions of methods in cell biology (Vol. I) and Mazia's discussion of mitosis (Vol. III). Cell differentiation and the morphology and function of specialized cells are also considered in depth.

BUTLER, J. A. V. *The Life of the Cell.* London: George Allen & Unwin, Ltd., 1964. A brief exposition of the fundamentals of cell biology with consideration of specialized and neoplastic cells, and discussion of the origin of life.

DAVIS, B. D., AND L. WARREN *The Specificity of Cell Surfaces.* Englewood Cliffs, N.J.: Prentice-Hall, Inc., 1967. A compilation of recent findings concerning the nature of the plasma membrane and cell surface materials; technical yet succinct and readable.

DE DUVE, C. "The Lysosome," *Sci. Amer.,* **208** (1963).

DIPPELL, R. V. "Ultrastructure of Cells in Relation to Function," in *This Is Life,* W. H. Johnson and W. C. Steere, eds. New York: Holt, Rinehart and Winston, Inc., 1962. The structural organization of cellular function is revealed at the organelle level, with particular reference to the mitochondrion.

EGLINTON, G., AND M. CALVIN "Chemical Fossils," *Sci. Amer.,* **216** (1967). The occurrence of organic compounds in very ancient strata is described and its significance evaluated.

FOX, S. W. "The Evolution of Protein Molecules and Thermal Synthesis of Biochemical Substances," *Amer. Scientist,* **44** (1956).

——— "How Did Life Begin? Recent Experiments Suggest an Integrated Origin of Anabolism, Protein, and Cell Boundaries," *Science,* **132** (1960).

GIBOR, A. "*Acetabularia:* A Useful Giant Cell," *Sci. Amer.,* **215** (1966).

GREEN, D. E., AND Y. HATEFI "The Mitochondrion and Biochemical Machines," *Science,* **133** (1961). Reviews the functional organization of mitochondria.

HÄMMERLING, J. "Nucleo-cytoplasmic Relationships in the Development of *Acetabularia,*" *Intern. Rev. Cytol.,* **2** (1953). Explores the role of the nucleus in regeneration and morphogenesis of a giant unicellular alga.

HOLWILL, M. E. J. "Physical Aspects of Flagellar Movement," *Physiol. Rev.,* **46** (1966). A comprehensive treatise on flagellar structure and action, with application of hydrodynamic equations to the movement of microorganisms.

JENSEN, W. A. *The Plant Cell.* Belmont, Calif.: Wadsworth Publishing Company, Inc., 1964. A useful reference on the structure of plant cells.

——— AND R. B. PARK *Cell Ultrastructure.* Belmont, Calif.: Wadsworth Publishing Company, Inc., 1967. A fine short electron photomicrographic atlas with explanatory comments.

KEOSIAN, J. *The Origin of Life.* New York: Reinhold Publishing Corporation, 1964. A brief, simple discussion of evidence concerning the abiogenetic origin of life, including an excellent bibliography of periodical articles.

MAZIA, D., AND K. DAN "The Isolation and Biochemical Characterization of the Mitotic Apparatus of Dividing Cells," *Proc. Natl. Acad. Sci. U.S.,* **38** (1952).

MILLER, S. L. "A Production of Amino Acids under Possible Primitive Earth Conditions," *Science,* **117** (1953). Reports upon a classic experiment in abiogenesis.

MOROWITZ, H. J., AND M. E. TOURTELLOTE "The Smallest Cells," *Sci. Amer.,* **206** (1962). Examines the organization of pleuropneumonialike organisms (PPLO), cellular systems smaller than some viruses.

MORRISON, J. H. *Functional Organelles.* New York: Reinhold Publishing Corporation, 1966. A concise consideration of the manner in which the cell's basic machinery is incorporated as an inseparable part of the organization of cell organelles.

NEUTRA, M., AND C. P. LEBLOND "The Golgi Apparatus," *Sci. Amer.,* **220** (1969). Reviews evidence of the role of the Golgi apparatus in polysaccharide synthesis and preparation of materials for secretion.

OVENDEN, M. W. *Life in the Universe.* Garden City, N.Y.: Doubleday & Company, Inc., 1962. A simple, scientifically sound discussion of the possibility of extraterrestrial life, for the nonscientist.

PONNAMPERUMA, C., C. SAGAN, AND R. MARINER "Synthesis of Adenosine Triphosphate under Possible Primitive Earth Conditions," *Nature,* **199** (1963). Abiotically generated adenine and ribose react with phosphate to produce ATP, a compound which could have served to transfer energy into other abiogenetic reactions concerned with the origin of life.

RACKER, E. "The Membrane of the Mitochondrion," *Sci. Amer.,* **218** (1968). The functional organization of the inner mitochondrial membranes is studied by disassembling and reassembling their macromolecular units.

ROBERTSON, J. D. "The Membrane of the Living Cell," *Sci. Amer.,* **206** (1962). The hypothetical structure of the plasma membrane is described.

SATIR, P. "Cilia," *Sci. Amer.,* **204** (1961).

SWANSON, C. P. *The Cell,* 3rd ed. Englewood Cliffs, N.J.: Prentice-Hall, Inc., 1969. A concise source of additional information on the organization of cells.

ZALOKAR, R. B. "Sites of Protein and Ribonucleic Acid Synthesis in the Cell," *Exptl. Cell Research,* **19** (1960).

Chapter 11 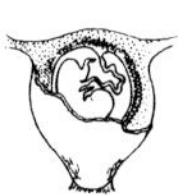 DEVELOPMENT

FEW EVENTS ARE AS INTRIGUING AS those involved in development of the individual organism. Through these events we see unfolding in a brief span of time a pattern that is the net product of the operation of natural selection upon the genomes of ancestral populations throughout the history of life. The genetic code of the species defines the developmental capabilities of each new individual life. These capabilities are regulated and their expression influenced by a complex web of environmental factors, some internal and others external to the organism. Analysis of the control and coordination of developmental processes is one of the most important concerns of modern biological research, and many biologists are actively engaged in this area.

Although developmental biology remains today a challenging field of investigation in which many of the most fundamental questions are still unanswered and new findings often produce more riddles than they solve, the day may not be far removed when the understanding of development now being sought may form the basis of practical applications once beyond the pale of credibility. Individual lifespans may then be extended by replacement of diseased organs with spare ones cultured from cells donated in youth by the future recipient of the implant and kept in reserve pending need. Such autografts would not raise the problems of immune response and resultant graft rejection that complicate current organ transplantation. Even today, in the case of plants, and one known animal species (the African clawed frog), it is possible to produce entire new organisms from single somatic cells or nuclei taken from the adult body and cultured under conditions conducive to their regaining full developmental plasticity. It is conceivable that some day these techniques may be extended to higher animals and even to man.

11.1 □ THE NATURE OF DEVELOPMENT

Development is not simply synonymous with *embryogeny* (embryonic development). It encompasses all processes of maturation, both embryonic and postembryonic, and is therefore better known as *ontogeny,* the development of the individual from conception to maturity (or even beyond maturity to senescence and death). In many species ontogeny is a gradual, more or less continuous process, whereas in others it is marked by a series of more or less abrupt metamorphoses from one developmental stage to the next. In such species the immature or larval stages have evolved specializations relevant to their own mode of life but more or less irrelevant to the life of the adult.

Although ontogeny may be thought to encompass the entire life history of the individual, we shall concern ourselves here primarily with early development, for it is in these initial stages that the most dramatic ontogenetic events take place. Metabolism and growth are carried on more rapidly in embryonic life than at any later time, and form and function unfold swiftly.

A Aspects of development

Development has three main aspects: (1) *growth;* (2) the attainment of form (*morphogenesis*); (3) the specialization of cells (*cytodifferentiation*).

Growth is chiefly accomplished by cellular growth and proliferation, involving assimilation of nutrients, synthesis of new cytoplasmic components, DNA replication, and mitosis.

Morphogenesis mainly results from a combination of directed cell movements (*morphogenetic movements*), differential rates of growth in different parts of the body, and programmed cell death, each of which we shall consider separately. Curiously enough, although the evolution of life appears to have proceeded from molecular to cellular to multicellular, once an organizational pattern has been evolved and need but be produced anew in each generation, development of the pattern proceeds from the general to the particular. Cells of course are present from the start, but their final functional and structural differentiation is one of the *last* events of early development. Instead, the overall body form is first "roughed out" much as a sculptor makes a statue by first crudely blocking out its shape in stone. Later stages of both sculpture and biotic development are chiefly concerned with filling in the details.

One of the first events of animal development is establishment of the body's basic symmetry and polarity. By *symmetry* we refer to the way in which body parts may be mirror images of one another when the body is sectioned along particular planes (see Figure 12.1), whereas by *polarity* we refer to the axes along which some contrast in form or function is manifested. For instance, most animals are polarized along their anteroposterior axis, with marked contrasts existing between the anterior and posterior poles of that axis. Comparable differences also become established along a second axis passing from the dorsal (upper) to the ventral (lower) surface of the body. Symmetry and polarity are two of the most fundamental aspects of body plan, and the first to be established in development.

Cell specialization is one of the major adaptive advantages of the multicellular condition, for grouped cells can afford to maximize certain capabilities at the expense of others. Cytodifferentiation is foreshadowed in such simple colonial forms as the green alga *Volvox* (see Figure 2.13) in which quite different somatic and reproductive cells can be distinguished. *Somatic* cells are those which do not become gametes and mostly are concerned with maintenance of the individual organism rather than with reproduction. In metazoans and advanced metaphytes somatic cells are further specialized for the performance of particular duties. Even as diversification of organisms promotes the success of the biotic community, so diversification and interaction of different cell types permits advancement of the multicellular organism.

By undergoing diversification, individual cells normally sacrifice their capacity for independent existence. In fact, development in unicellular and multicellular organisms differs in one profound respect. A unicellular organism such as a protozoan may develop complex adaptive regional specializations (see Figure 12.4) but these must not impair its self-sufficiency as an independent being. In multicellular organisms, on the contrary, cytodifferentiation must place a restriction on the cell's performance, for cell individualism (as in cancer) can threaten the integrity of the whole body. Unless cell and organism are coextensive, cytodifferentiation must be governed by the needs of the organism rather than by the requirements for separate cell existence. Usually this involves such specialization of the cell's metabolism that independent survival is precluded under normal circumstances.

Functional specialization usually entails structural differentiation, so that we readily distinguish among muscle, glandular, nervous cells, and so forth. Overt specialization tends to disappear when differentiated cells are explanted and grown in culture, but such apparent "dedifferentiation" does not preclude the persistence of some degree of functional differentiation. For instance, a strain of rat pituitary tumor cells is known that continues to secrete chemically normal growth hormone when cultured in vitro.

The functional effectiveness of specialized cells depends on their being aggregated into organized masses or sheets termed *tissues*. Individual muscle fibers, for instance, are so oriented that entire masses contract in the same plane; in fact, groups of fibers share a common nerve supply and thus contract synchronously. Only in such simple metazoans as sponges are there specialized cell types which are not actually organized into tissues (see Section 12.3). Each cell of the sponge body exhibits much independence of action, and although certain amoebocytes may cooperate briefly in the secretion of skeletal elements they go their separate ways when the task is complete. True *histogenesis* (tissue formation) involves the aggregation and functional integration of many similar cells, such as the epithelium lining the intestinal tract. In higher plants and most metazoans functional efficiency is further improved by the integration of different tissues into *organs* that in turn are functionally associated in *organ systems*. However, although we may conveniently think of cells as being grouped into tissues, tissues into organs, and organs into organ systems, we should remember the following: during development it is the general body plan that first appears; next, the main features of the organ systems are manifested before the individual organs are formed; and the cells that form these organs coalesce into masses reflecting the future shape of the organ well before their specialization into distinct functional types takes place.

The principle just summarized is exemplified in early human development. The embryo arrives in the mother's uterus some 4 to 7 days after fertilization in the oviduct, being at this age a spherical "blastocyst" in which the part actually to become the body of the new individual is a mere flattened disc of undifferentiated cells. At approximately two weeks of age the embryo is about 0.15 mm long and still little more than an ovoid plate, but the membranes of the amniote egg have now formed around it. Three weeks after fertilization the embryo proper is around 1.5 mm long and displays bilateral symmetry and certain features specifically characteristic of its phylum: a notochord, a tubular central nervous system forming dorsal to the notochord, and a ventral "heart field" (where the heart is developing). Its anteroposterior polarity is already much in evidence, the growth rate of the anterior portion so far exceeding that of the posterior parts that at this stage some three-fourths of the embryo consists of rudimentary head structures. By the fourth week the central nervous system is formed but the brain is still only a linear series of hollow vesicles, and nerves have yet to grow from the central nervous system to the periphery. The eyes are now partly developed and the heart has begun to beat though it is still a simple U-shaped tube undivided into chambers. By the fifth week limb buds appear as paired mounds of cells lacking resemblance to the arms and legs that they will form (Figure 11.1). By the eighth week the embryo is about 2 cm long, and its human form is becoming barely recognizable, like a clay doll modeled by a child. Once the species can be determined, the young organism is better called a *fetus* than an embryo. By the twelfth week after fertilization the distal ends of the limbs bear fingers, initially unjointed. Gradually the joints of limbs and digits are molded, the facial features appear and sharpen, and internally the organs and tissues undergo further differentiation and refinement. The fetal genitalia are sexually indifferent at first, and only later become recognizably male or female. Throughout the whole process we can see development of general characteristics in advance of the specific, and even after the humanity of the fetus becomes unmistakable, individuality still remains to be impressed upon its features.

B Programmed death

Ontogeny involves not only growth and differentiation, but programmed senescence and dissolution of particular structures or cell masses as well. By "programmed" we mean that such death takes place at a specific time and is correlated with other developmental processes. During insect metamorphosis, for instance, the larval structures retrogress. Last to disappear are segmental muscles which must not degenerate until they have served to expand the wings of the adult, but which thereafter quickly break down, presumably as a delayed response to a hormonal cue received earlier. The human thymus, essential only at the time of origin of the body's future defensive cells, is largest in fetal life and has largely undergone retrogression by the age of ten: the thymus is senile while the organism as a whole is still young.

Localized cell death plays an important role in morphogenesis. During development of a vertebrate limb the shape of the limb is refined through the death of particular groups of cells in the moundlike limb bud. In this manner the connection of limb with trunk becomes narrowed, the tissue between the digits disappears and the elbow joint is sculptured. Metamorphosis of a tadpole into the adult frog involves the carefully synchronized resorption of the tail, much of the intestine, the gills, and the larval kidneys. During this "remodeling" the tissues are found to contain unusually high concentrations of *collagenase* (collagen-digesting enzyme) and *cathepsins* (intracellular protein-digesting enzymes). Collagenase begins to be secreted in response to some regulatory cue, breaking down the extracellular supportive framework in specific parts of the body. At the same time the cathepsins are liberated from the lysosomes in which they have been stored, causing autodigestion of tissues in the affected regions. The cue for both collagenase secretion and cathepsin release is probably furnished by thyroid hormone, in the absence of which the larval amphibian cannot undergo metamorphosis to adulthood. However, the mode of action of this hormone requires further study.

Local cell death also characterizes the process of sexual differentiation in vertebrates. During embryonic life the vertebrate develops primordial organs of both sexes. It remains sexually indifferent until the sex-determining genes begin to take effect, whereupon those structures characteristic of the opposite sex commence to regress and disappear or become vestigial. In the gonad itself the medullary (central) and cortical (outer) tissues are at first approximately equally represented, but gradually either medulla or cortex regresses while the other becomes predominant. The gonadal medulla predominates in the male's testis, the cortex in the female's ovary. This differential fate of the somatic tissues of the gonads in turn determines whether the germinal cells maturing within this stroma will become ova or sperm.

As well as playing such roles as these in animal development, the programmed death of certain tissues may also be an essential aspect of development in plants.

Figure 11.1 □ Five-week-old human embryo seen within its amniotic sac. (*Courtesy of Carolina Biological Supply Company.*)

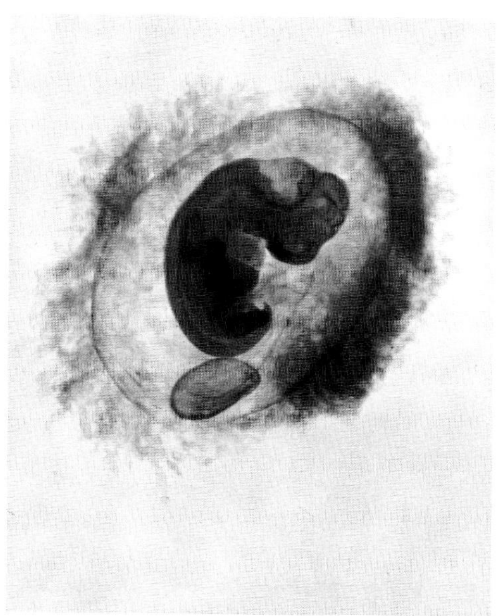

In cereals, for instance, food reserves accumulated during maturation of the seed are stored within the endosperm tissue. When the seed germinates, the embryo secretes a small quantity of hormone (*gibberellin*) that stimulates a layer of cells covering the endosperm to liberate hydrolytic enzymes. These enzymes attack and destroy the endosperm cells, setting free not only the contained food reserves but certain products of protein and nucleic acid breakdown that serve as growth-promoting factors for the embryo. Throughout the life of the plant additional cells die in performance of their function: cork cells secrete the outer bark and die, xylem cells perish after producing the hollow vascular elements that conduct water upward from the roots, and fiber cells die after completing the production of a fiber.

Not only does programmed cell death play a role in development, but the maximum life span of the entire individual organism may also be genetically defined as a result of natural selection, so that the length of individual life is geared to the species' rate of recruitment (rate at which new breeding individuals are added to the population) and the carrying capacity of the habitat. Rate of aging often appears somewhat independent of contributory environmental factors. With advancing senescence the probability increases that death will result when the individual's failing homeostatic mechanisms are unable to cope with environmental stress, but even when guarded from such stress the organism ages and eventually must die. Programmed death comes about abruptly in some species, such as those moths which cannot feed as adults and live only long enough to mate and lay eggs. Fish such as salmon also cease to feed when about to spawn, although apparently still physically capable of feeding. They die after spawning, presumably as a result of exhaustion and malnutrition. Death after reproduction is common among both plants and animals, serving to preserve the resources of the habitat for the coming generation.

It was once thought that tissues of higher organisms could perpetuate themselves indefinitely when cultured in vitro, without undergoing pathological changes. However, this is apparently not the case: cultures that have survived years of growth and transfer prove to be either malignant or abnormal in chromosome content. Human fibroblasts (connective tissue cells) taken from an embryo remain normal in tissue culture through only 50 ($\pm$10) generations of cell division, and then die as if this were the upper limit of their capacity for normal division. Fibroblasts donated by individuals from birth to 20 years of age can reproduce normally only 30 ($\pm$10) times in culture, and those taken from persons over 20 years old divide only 20 ($\pm$10) times before dying. These findings imply that even under optimal conditions human tissues may be incapable of surviving much longer than the average upper limit of human life (about 80 years). Cells taken from the embryos of mammals of shorter life span show a correspondingly shorter period of proliferation in tissue culture: tissues of hamsters, rats, and chickens, for instance, can divide only about 15 times without becoming abnormal. This limitation of normal cell division may reflect the rate at which the cells' genetic mechanisms are irreversibly impaired by accumulated replication errors and other mutations.

Whether senescence is gradual or nearly instantaneous, the processes leading to death of the individual organism may be genetically orchestrated just as are the processes of maturation; they may also be subject to selection toward a maximum life span that is geared to keeping each species in balance with the rest of the natural community.

C Regeneration

In most plants development never completely ceases and lost parts are routinely replaced. This capacity for continued growth and regeneration (replacement of lost parts) rests on the fact that regions of embryonic tissue persist throughout life. In vascular plants the two major regions are the *apical meristem* at the tip of each stem and root (a mound of rapidly dividing cells responsible for growth in length and formation of new buds) and the *vascular cambium* (which produces new conductive cells and is responsible for growth in diameter of the root or shoot); see Figures 12.12 and 12.13.

In most animals growth largely ceases at maturity, although certain tissues such as the epidermis and gut lining renew themselves constantly. However, histogenesis and morphogenesis may sometimes be resumed following injury, in the process of regeneration. Animal capacity for regeneration is widespread but of variable extent and is most limited in higher animals such as insects and vertebrates. However, even such complex creatures as newts and crabs can replace lost legs, and when a starfish is cut in pieces, each fragment containing part of the central disc can regenerate an entire animal (Figure 11.2*a*).

Figure 11.2 □ Regeneration. (*a*) Entire starfish being regenerated from one arm. (*Ward's Natural Science Establishment, Inc.*) (*b*) Regeneration error: two-tailed gecko. (*Zoological Society of San Diego.*) (*c*) Regeneration of hind limb of newt after amputation through thigh.

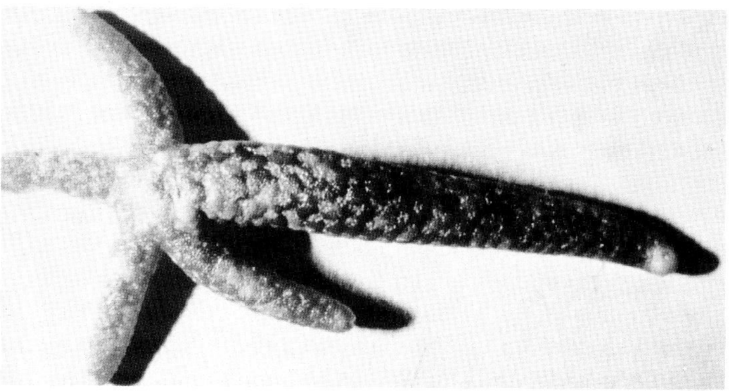

(*a*)

(*b*)

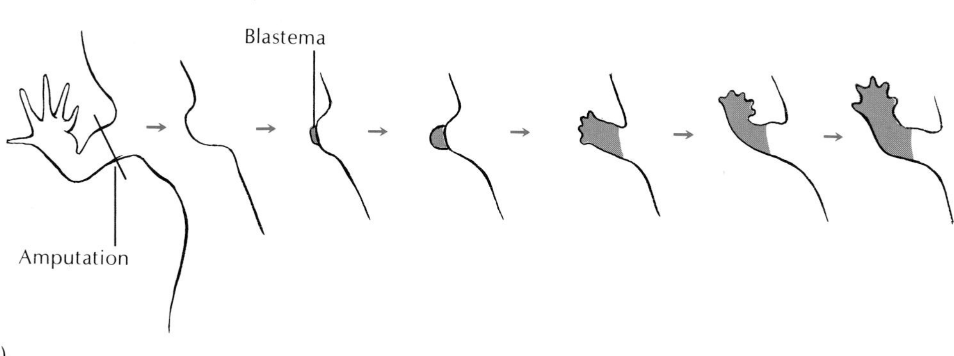

(*c*)

Extensive regenerative capacity is often concomitant to a defensive response known as *autotomy* ("self-cutting"), in which the jeopardized animal may actively discard limbs, tail, or internal organs along preformed fracture lines that allow clean separation without hemorrhage. Disturbed sea cucumbers are perhaps the most notable examples of this form of activity, for they can cast out first their entire respiratory organs and later their whole intestinal tract by way of the anus. These internal organs must all be regenerated, but their loss serves well, for the sticky tissues may ensnare would-be predators. A lizard can autotomize its tail, which writhes about, distracting the predator while the animal makes good its escape. The gecko shown in Figure 11.2*b* had the distinction of regenerating two tails instead of one, a case of developmental error.

Regeneration of limbs has been most extensively studied in salamanders. The tissues in the stump revert to an embryonic appearance and, under the influence of regenerating nerve fibers, form a *blastema,* or mound of cells resembling the original limb bud, from which the new limb gradually emerges (Figure 11.2c). What are the properties inherent in one kind of animal that allow it to grow back lost parts, while another kind cannot? If we could answer this question, we might be able to induce regrowth of human limbs after amputation. We know that the influence of nerve fibers is required for the regeneration of limbs in salamanders. In fact, even a frog, which normally lacks the capacity to replace a lost limb, may be induced to grow a new arm (albeit imperfectly) if the large nerve trunk serving the hindleg is cut and redirected into the stump of the amputated forelimb, providing an enriched nerve supply. This leads us to speculate that nerve tissue may secrete some growth-promoting factor that someday will be isolated, analyzed, and synthesized for medical use.

One of the interesting facets of regeneration is the modification of growth rate in the regenerating part. When a part is being regenerated on the body of a still-growing animal, the growth rate for that part may greatly exceed that for the body as a whole until it reaches the proper proportions, whereupon its growth slows to the rate characteristic of the rest of the body. The mechanism of such synchronization remains to be clarified.

D Differential growth rates

Organisms do not grow at a constant rate. The growth rate for an animal is highest in the earliest stages of development and declines progressively toward maturity. However, because the absolute weight gain is greatest toward the middle of the growth period, a graph of body weight from conception to maturity describes a sigmoid curve like that characteristic of the growth of populations (see Figure 6.1). The growth rate for any point on this curve can be calculated by use of the logistic equation

$$\frac{dW}{dt} = bW\frac{L - W}{L}$$

W being the size of the organism at a given time t, b the potential growth rate, and L the maximum size attained upon maturity. This equation shows that growth is essentially exponential, the rate of mass increase (dW/dt) being proportional to the size already attained. When $W = L$, growth reaches the zero level, that is, ceases. A number of fishes and reptiles never cease to grow entirely, but the growth rate declines progressively and the curve flattens out toward maturity.

Growth rate for any body part correlates inversely with the extent to which cytodifferentiation has set in; many organs such as the brain and kidneys cease to grow when mature, for they lack reservoirs of undifferentiated cells that serve as growth centers. The epidermis and lining of the alimentary tract, on the other hand, maintain a high rate of proliferation but cannot contribute to an overall increase in body size.

During development the growth rates of different parts of the body are seldom identical. Because some parts grow more rapidly than others, body proportions change throughout development. The vertebrate central nervous system actually grows particularly slowly so that, although in the early embryo the head (then mostly brain) at one time amounts to more than half the overall length of the embryo, the relative size of head to body declines consistently during growth until at maturity the head is smaller in comparison with the rest of the body than it is at any earlier time.

Modification of the growth rate of one part of the body, or of the entire body along one of its growth axes while other axes remain unchanged, can greatly alter final form (Figure 11.3). This indicates that marked variation in form can take place with relatively slight genetic modification, for the basic morphogenetic processes may be unaltered despite a change in the direction or rate of growth.

When two body parts grow at the same rate, they are said to grow *isometrically;* when they grow at different rates, growth is *allometric*. An allometric growth formula

$$y = bx^k$$

shows the different sizes of two body parts under comparison at any given time. In this formula y equals the size of one organ, x equals the size of a second organ at the same time, b equals y/x, or the proportion of one organ to the other, and k is an exponent representing the growth ratio (or relation of the growth rates of the parts being compared). If the growth ratio is greater than one, the body part y grows more rapidly than part x; if the ratio is less than one, part y grows more slowly than part x. If the size of x at a given time is known, that of y can be calculated (and vice versa).

The control of growth rate is another riddle of development. Why do the two claws of the male fiddler crab grow isometrically up to a certain age, after which the growth of the left pincer rapidly exceeds that of the right one until the two claws are markedly different in size? This pattern of allometric growth is essential for the perpetuation of the species, for the females are sexually responsive to the male's "fiddling" with his large claw and remain unattracted to small-clawed males. Reversion to isometric pincer growth would mean "genetic death" to a male fiddler crab: he would be doomed to celibacy and have no progeny.

Differential growth of body parts in metaphytes seems to be hormonally controlled (as we shall see in Section 15.4D). *Auxins* regulate stem and root elongation, promoting elongation when present in low concentrations but inhibiting elongation

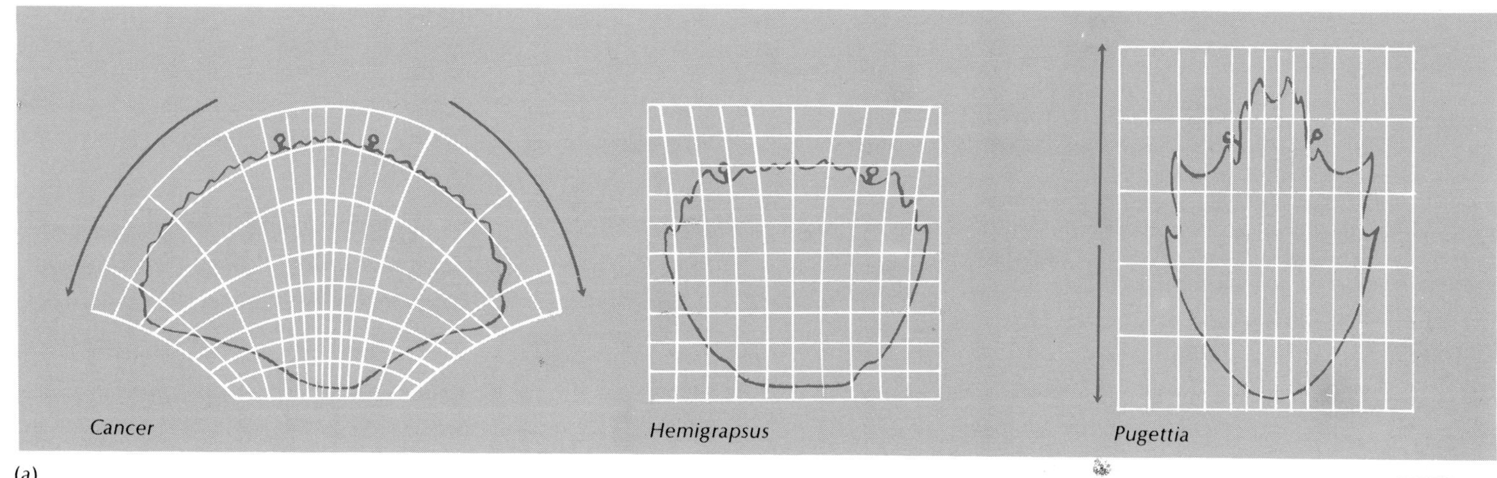

(b)

Figure 11.3 □ Effects on body form of differential growth rates. (*a*) Differences in crab-carapace shape explained on the basis of altered growth coordinates. (*b*) Allometric growth of chelipeds of fiddler crab. In a young male both claws grow at the same rate (colored portion); but upon the onset of sexual maturity the left claw begins to grow more rapidly than does the right until adult proportions are finally achieved.

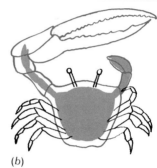

when present in greater concentrations. These hormones affect body form by suppressing the growth of lateral buds. *Gibberellins* are thought responsible for the abrupt elongation of flower-bearing stems, serving to elevate the blossoms above surrounding foliage. A hormone may also promote the maturation of flowers while it represses the growth of other parts. It is not yet clear how the flow of these various hormones is synchronized so that the growth of different plant organs may be selectively regulated.

11.2 □ PLANT GROWTH AND ITS REGULATION

Plant development is less complex than that of higher animals and will therefore be considered first. As just mentioned, it is controlled by certain hormones, the actions of which will be summarized in Chapter 15: their effects are not restricted to early development and they serve as the plant's major agents of integration throughout life.

We usually think of plant growth as commencing with the germination of the seed. In point of fact, the development of a seed plant is divided into two phases separated by a period of dormancy: (1) development from the fertilization of the egg to the maturation of the seed; (2) devel-

Figure 11.4 □ Germination. (*a*) Longitudinal section of plant embryo (*Capsella*) prior to germination: (1) cotyledons and (2) suspensor cells. (*Triarch Incorporated, Geo. H. Conant, Ripon, Wis.*) (*b*) Stages in germination of a bean seed. The radicle first elongates and begins to absorb water; the seed swells, bursting the seed coat; the hypocotyl then elongates, pulling the cotyledons above the surface of the soil; upon exposure to light, the cotyledons turn green and commence photosynthesis; the stem above the cotyledons (*epicotyl*) next elongates as the first foliage leaves enlarge and assume photosynthetic function; the cotyledons wither and are shed.

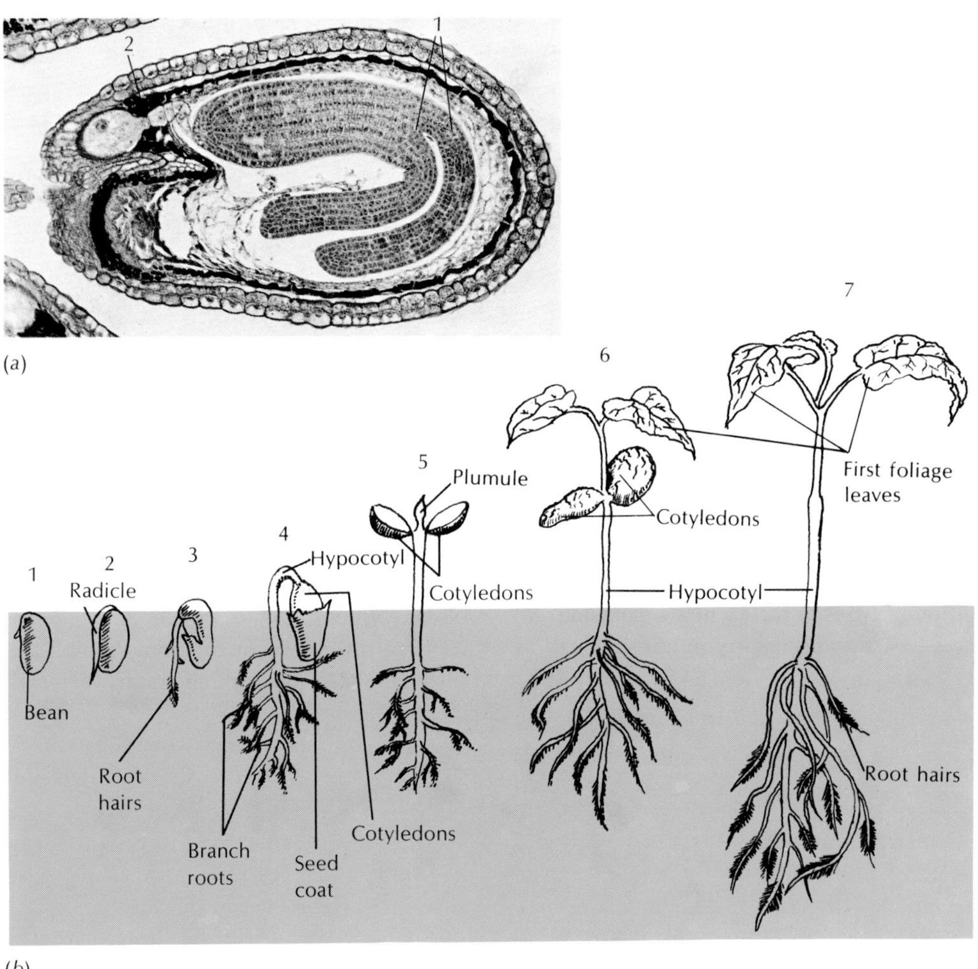

opment from germination of the seed to maturity. The earlier phase will be taken up in Chapter 17, in our study of reproduction. At this time we shall consider only the period of germination and formation of the seedling and shall trace the development of adult structures more fully in the next chapter.

At the time the seed has ripened and the embryo becomes dormant, the latter consists of the "seed leaves" (*cotyledons*), and two inconspicuous nubs of tissue oriented more or less in opposite directions, one of which represents the future primary shoot (*plumule*), the other the primary root (*radicle*). The cotyledons are single in monocots, paired in dicots, and several in conifers. They may be plump with stored food, or lie embedded in a nutrient-rich tissue, the endosperm, on which the seedling draws during germination. Embryo and endosperm are enclosed by a protective *seed coat.*

A Germination

Germination requires favorable conditions of moisture and temperature. In certain species it may also require the preliminary weakening of the seed coat by charring, so that such seeds do not germinate until fire sweeps the area. First the germinating seed swells by imbibing water and bursts the seed coat (Figure 11.4). Cells begin to elongate in two localized regions of the dicot seed: just behind the tip of the radicle, and in an area known as the *hypocotyl* just above the radicle and below the cotyledons. This elongation is directionally oriented: the first growth response of the seedling is expressed as *geotropism,* or growth oriented by gravity. As a result of differential elongation on opposite sides of the growing root or shoot (controlled by auxins), the radicle turns downward while the hypocotyl pushes upward. This comes about even if the seed has been buried upside down in the soil, which proves the geotropic effect.

As the radicle elongates, an absorptive region develops just behind the tip, where the surface cells put forth threadlike extensions, the *root hairs* (see Figure 12.13). Now the primary root can begin to take up water and minerals from the soil.

Meanwhile, the hypocotyl forces the cotyledons upward into the light. In dicots the hypocotyl takes the brunt of abrasive soil particles as it pulls the cotyledons upward, straightening out only after reaching the surface. The seed coat protects dicot seed leaves during this period; in conifers, where the cotyledons themselves form the leading point thrust upward through the soil, and in monocots, where the cotyledons remain below ground and the delicate plumule itself must penetrate the soil, the growing point is protected instead by a tough sheath that is shed after the surface of the soil has been breeched.

The cotyledons of the dicot seedling spread apart and turn green when exposed to light, typically becoming the first leaves to engage in photosynthesis. They are simple in form and rarely resemble the adult foliage. After the stored food they contain has been used up, they manufacture the rest of the materials needed for the initial growth of the plumule and formation of the first postembryonic leaves and then wither away.

Even at an early stage specialized tissues begin to develop within the body of the seedling, differentiating in the growth regions behind the tips of the root and shoot. Conductive tissues must develop rapidly to expedite the flow of materials to the growing tips from the sugar-producing regions of the cotyledons and the absorptive root hair zone of the radicle. These specialized tissues will be described below and their organization further considered in Section 12.5.

It is interesting to note that even after they are mature and fully differentiated, plant cells can be isolated from the plant body and cultured singly in a nutrient medium. An individual cultured cell soon loses visible evidence of specialization and proliferates to form a *callus,* a mass of apparently embryonic tissue. Upon the addition of growth hormones to the culture medium, the callus begins to differentiate and puts forth roots and shoots with the result that an entire new plant is formed. This indicates that plant cells retain the genetic capacity for developing along new lines if their differentiated state is disturbed. To date comparable experiments with animal tissue have not met with success, for although animal tissues can be maintained in vitro they do not redifferentiate into different types to form a new organism (see, however, the discussion on transnucleation experiments in Section 11.4A).

B Plant morphogenesis and differentiation

FACTORS AFFECTING PLANT FORM In algae and fungi, development of form is accompanied by only slight cytodifferentiation, and both are profoundly affected by the planes in which successive cell divisions occur. When successive cell divisions occur in tandem, a filamentous plant body develops, like that of *Spirogyra* (see Figure 17.10); if the planes of cell division are randomized the plant body becomes nodular. Regular patterns of branching may emerge as an outcome of periodic shifts in the plane of division.

The very first division of spore or zygote may polarize all subsequent development (for example, *Fucus;* see Section 11.4C). The plane of cell division in turn may be influenced by conditions external to the cell (but often internal to the organism). For instance, plant cells subjected to compression tend to divide in a plane parallel to the direction of the compressive force, whereas cells put under tension divide along a plane transverse to the direction of the pull. Although the basic symmetry of the plant body is genetically determined and first manifested in the spacing of lateral buds forming in the apical growth regions of the shoot (see Figure 12.14), environmentally generated pressure and tension may force these parts to be redistributed around a new center of gravity, changing the overall form while preserving balance, as in the case of windblown cypress.

The development of strengthening tissues can also be influenced by external factors. A shoot experimentally kept in traction develops more fibrous tissue than would otherwise be the case. For example, sunflower shoots grown under a traction of around 300 g develop tensile strength some 56 percent greater than that of control shoots not reared under traction.

While plant cells are young, the direction in which they can expand is determined by the relative deformability of the cell wall on each side. Cells usually elongate parallel to the long axis of the shoot or root, thereby increasing the plant's length. The extent of elongation can be affected by light and other factors. When a plant is shaded excessively its shoots grow abnormally long and slender, such *etiolation* serving to bring their tips into a better illuminated area. Similarly, the blades of shaded leaves tend to be larger than those of the same species grown in full sun. Such leaf enlargement proceeds only to that point at which the total area of foliage is adequate to absorb the amount of light needed to sustain a normal growth rate for that species. We have mentioned that phototropic and geotropic growth responses result from differential elongation, with one side of the shoot or root elongating more rapidly than the other, causing the tip to turn. In any tropistic response, the direction of growth is successively adjusted by feedback so that it oscillates about a mean longitudinal growth axis; this causes the stem tip to wave to and fro as the stem elongates (this waving is, of course, in "slow motion").

Apical dominance Correlation of growth in different regions of the plant body involves active growth of some parts and the simultaneous suppression of growth in others. Shoots exhibit *apical dominance,* growth of lateral buds being suppressed as long as the terminal buds are actively growing. Similarly morphogenesis of the heart-shaped fern prothallium (see Fig. 2.21) depends on inhibitory effects exerted upon the surface and marginal tissues by a small region of actively proliferating cells in the apical notch region. Excision of this region allows the formerly repressed cells to proliferate, destroying the developing symmetry.

The definitive shape of the plant body is greatly influenced by whether apical dominance resides in a single growing point or in a number. In species in which a single apical region dominates the entire plant, growth is *excurrent* and the shape of the crown conical or columnar. Growth in height can take place only at the apex. In single-trunked palms excision of the terminal bud leads to death since no replacement leaves can be formed. "Topping" a conifer, such as may be done to harvest a "Christmas tree," is not fatal, but may limit further growth in height if a new apical bud does not develop from a previously dormant lateral bud. The growth of most dicots is *deliquescent,* progressively branching to form a spreading crown. In these species removal of a single growing tip does not block further growth in height, for the growth of other branches can be directed vertically (Figure 11.5).

Production of reproductive organs such as flowers is correlated with at least a temporary arrestment of somatic growth. Flowering in fact may presage the death of the plant. The regulatory mechanism that switches growth from vegetative to reproductive lines is not known, but it may be hormonal. An immature shoot grafted onto a plant which is ready to flower will itself be induced to flower, but this is not necessarily a hormonal effect, for the pattern of metabolism typical of the reproductive state may be so pervasive as to operate throughout the whole plant body, even across graft unions.

CELL POSITION AND DIFFERENTIATION The transformation from the vegetative to the reproductive state is of especial interest in slime molds [Phylum Myxomycophyta (see Figure 2.16)], for in these simple organisms the fate of individual cells can be traced through the changes in form that accompany the formation of the fruiting body. In the genus *Dictyostelium* the unicellular myxamoebas aggregate to form a multicellular *pseudoplasmodium* (so called because its constituent cells remain separated by intact cell walls, whereas in a true plasmodium the cells fuse together to form a multinucleate mass). The pseudoplasmodium is simple in outline and is nicknamed "slug" from its superficial resemblance to the mollusc. The slug has a definite anteroposterior polarity, for one end consistently moves forward, and this slenderly pointed anterior end is morphologically distinguishable from the broad, bluntly rounded posterior end. The slug secretes a slime sheath through which it creeps by the coordinated pseudopodial movements of its member cells. Interestingly, although individual myxamoebas show no demonstrable response to light, the entire slug is attracted to faint light (such as that emitted by luminescent bacteria).

When the period of movement and feeding is terminated (mainly by declining humidity), the slug begins its transformation into a stalked fruiting body. This is initiated by the curling of the anterior tip backward over the main part of the body, after which the cells formerly constituting the anterior end push down through the mass of the pseudoplasmodium to the ground below, where they secrete the base of a cylindrical stalk. Other cells formerly located just back of the anterior end then move up the stalk, secreting cellulose that adds to its length. Finally cells formerly constituting the posterior portion of the slug reach the top of the stalk and there form a mass of spores. About 15 percent of the cells of the slug are expended to produce the supportive base and stalk, while the balance form the spores from which a new generation of myxamoebae eventually will arise. These proportions remain relatively constant, for if comparatively few myxamoebae are at hand to form a slug, the fruiting body produced will be perfectly shaped but miniature.

How can we demonstrate experimentally that the future fate of specific cells is determined by their position in the slug? We can do this simply by culturing one group of myxamoebas on a medium containing pigmented bacteria, while a second culture is fed upon colorless bacteria. One colony therefore forms a colored slug, the other a colorless one. Each slug can now be cut in two transversely and the posterior half of each can be allowed to fuse with the anterior half of the other (Figure 11.6). In each case, pigmented and unpigmented cells are found not to mix together but to retain their original positions in the new bicolored slug. When the fruiting bodies are formed, the slug with colored anterior and colorless posterior halves produces a pigmented stalk and unpigmented spores, whereas the slug with the unpigmented anterior and pigmented posterior halves forms a colorless stalk and colored spores. Thus so long as its position remains undisturbed, the contribution of a given cell to the fruiting body is determined long before that body is formed. On the other hand, if a single slug is cut into several pieces and these prevented from fusing together again, each fragment will behave as an independent slug, and when the fruiting body is formed cells that in the original pseudoplasmodium would perhaps have contributed to the base

Figure 11.5 □ **Plant-growth patterns: an expression of the degree of apical dominance. (*a*) Excurrent-growth form in palm and conifer. (*b*) Deliquescent-growth form in a dicot such as oak.**

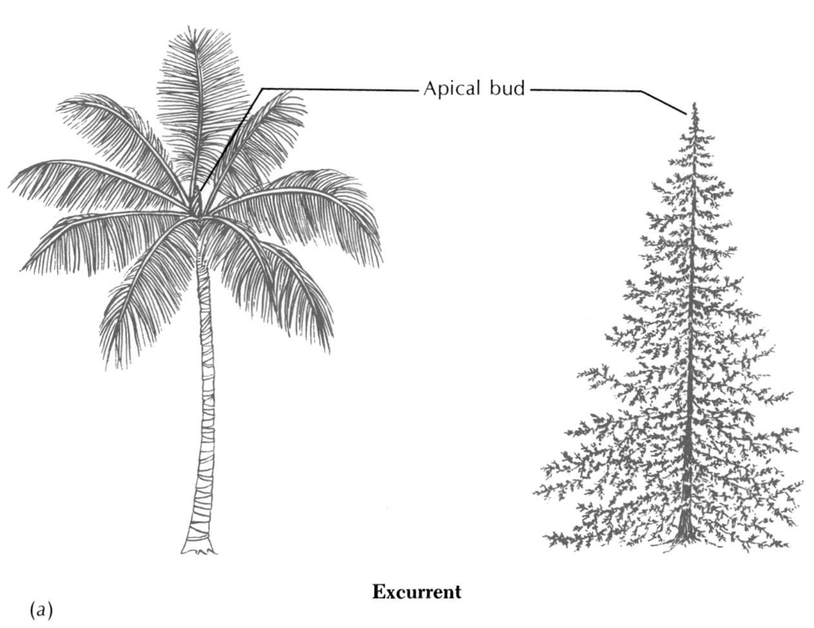

or stalk may now instead become spores, and vice versa. Here the position occupied in the new organism produced by fragmenting the old determines the cells' future differentiation.

This rather simple case, in which cell position determines the manner in which cells can differentiate, is reflected many times over in the process of cytodifferentiation in the body of a vascular plant, which is of course much more difficult to analyze. However, we can say at least as a general principle that within any growing mass of cells physiological gradients are set up so that all cells in the mass do not have the same environment. Access to nutrients is unequal, as is exposure to such growth-regulating factors as light, hormones, and so forth. In the vascular plant a radial physiological gradient is established at each growing tip, where the apical meristem proliferates new cells, dividing at right angles to the long axis of the root or shoot. The effects of this gradient are projected backward from the tip as a result of differential permeability of the maturing tissues, which affects the distribution of nutrients and chemical growth regulators. The vascular cambium, on the other hand, divides radially, whereupon cells proliferated from its inner surface form the water-conducting xylem elements, and those proliferated on its outer surface contribute to the sap-conducting phloem (see Figure 11.40). Differentiation of these cells is therefore influenced by their position relative to the cambium and other tissues. As long as a plant continues to grow, all stages in cytodifferentiation can be found in its younger parts, and the developmental effects of cell position can thus be easily noted.

Figure 11.6 □ Growth and morphogenesis in the slime mold *Dictyostelium*.

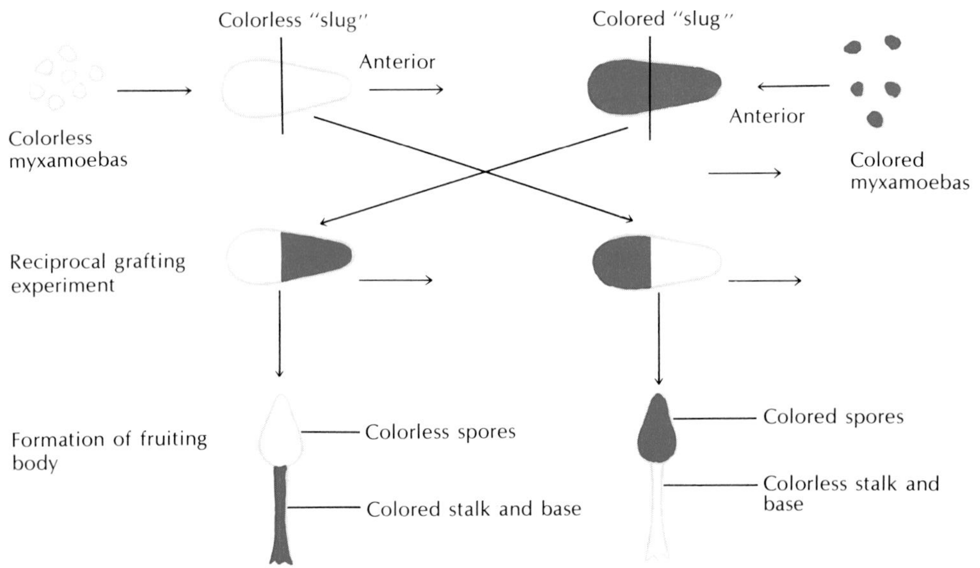

A Initiation of development

THE GAMETES Two highly specialized cells, ovum and sperm, initiate the life of the new individual. These cells are produced by the process of gametogenesis (described in Section 17.2C), one phase of which is the meiotic reduction of chromosome number from diploid to monoploid (see Figure 8.4). The two gametes contribute the entire hereditary blueprint for making a new organism according to the plan of its species.

The specializations of the ovum are important in facilitating the initial stages of development, and chiefly consist of the accumulation and organization of precursors for making new cell constituents during the period when the embryo is unable to obtain food from outside sources. Even an egg that lacks visible yolk (such as that of man) is relatively huge in comparison with most other types of cells of the same species. The diameter of the human egg proper (minus investments) is 89 to 91 μm as compared with an average of 20 μm for a "typical" cell and 8 μm for a blood cell. Frog eggs have a moderate amount of yolk and range in size from 0.7 mm (for the green frog) to 10 mm (for the marsupial frog). This range in size reflects the length of time before the young frog can feed; the green frog becomes an independent tadpole after only a few days' development, whereas the marsupial frog develops to the adult form within a protective pouch on the parent's body and accordingly cannot feed during this entire period.

An egg having stored food evenly dispersed throughout the cytoplasm is termed *isolecithal.* When a greater quantity of yolk is present, it tends to be most concentrated at one end of the egg, and such a *telolecithal* egg is both visibly and metabolically polarized. The metabolic rate is lowest at the yolky *vegetal* pole and highest at the opposite end, the *animal* ("lively") pole, where cells divide most rapidly after fertilization. The telolecithal eggs of the leopard and bull frogs are commonly used for studies in development, for only a moderate amount of yolk is present, and the darkly pigmented animal hemisphere is easily distinguished from the yellowish vegetal hemisphere, so that the basic polarity of the egg is readily kept track of while its early development is observed through the transparent protective coats. *Centrolecithal* insect eggs also have a relatively large amount of yolk, but this is gathered into the center of the egg rather than being concentrated at one end. The pattern of yolk distribution reflects the overall cytoplasmic organization of the ovum and profoundly affects the pattern of cleavage of the fertilized egg.

Even in an isolecithal egg nutrients and other cytoplasmic constituents are not dispersed randomly. During maturation of the egg a nonrandom distribution is established that is partially maintained even throughout cleavage. The egg cytoplasm therefore displays a *morphogenetic gradient* that serves to establish differences among the cells resulting from the cleavage of the egg. Even in nearly yolkless mammalian eggs, the nucleus lies closer to the animal pole, which is marked by a high concentration of RNA, whereas the cytoplasm at the vegetal pole is relatively low in RNA and highly vacuolated. The animal pole of the mammalian egg corresponds to the future dorsal aspect of the embryo, the vegetal pole to its ventral aspect. When the mammalian egg undergoes reduction division, the excess set of chromosomes is extruded at the animal pole, in the form of a small *polar body* (see Figure 17.24).

Two cytoplasmic regions can be distinguished in the ovum: the cortex, and the inner cytoplasm. The *cortex* is an outer layer 2 to 3 μm thick which is in a viscous (gelated) state such that its components cannot readily be displaced even by centrifugation. This viscosity is important in preserving cortical organization during the rotation of the cortex relative to the inner cytoplasm that occurs upon activation of the egg, as we shall see below. The cortex may contain certain materials lacking in the inner cytoplasm, such as pigments, but little can be said concerning the functional significance of these substances.

The egg is covered by two types of membranes: primary membranes and secondary membranes. The innermost primary membrane is the *plasma* membrane, which is elaborated into fingerlike microvilli (see Figure 14.8) that increase surface area for the absorption of nutrients during the egg's maturation. A second primary membrane (commonly called the *vitelline* membrane), consisting of mucopolysaccharides and fibrous proteins, is secreted between the microvilli. In insects, a third primary membrane (the chorion) is secreted over the vitelline membrane. Secondary membranes are those added to the egg by gland cells lining the oviduct. In amphibians these form a gelatinous protective coat; in fish they often constitute a leathery egg case. The complex secondary membranes of birds' eggs include (from innermost to outermost): (1) a fibrous layer fused with the vitelline membrane; (2) the egg white (albumen); (3) two shell membranes composed of matted keratin fibers; (4) the shell, consisting of calcium carbonate ($CaCO_3$) and having pores plugged by collagen. These membranes are secreted one on top of the other as the egg passes along the oviduct.

Like the egg, the sperm undergoes meiotic division to the monoploid state, but unlike the egg it is specialized for motility, not food storage, and its differentiation must be completed before it is capable of fertilization. Many eggs, on the contrary, become quiescent when their cytoplasmic organization is fully established but before reduction division is completed, and do not resume meiosis until fertilized.

Except for their long flagella sperm are among the tiniest of eucaryotic cells. They almost completely lack cytoplasm. A human sperm cell can be considered fairly typical of animal sperm (see Figure 11.8*a*). Its "head" is about 2 μm wide by 4 μm long and consists of the condensed nucleus containing the chromosomes, capped with a conical structure, the *acrosome,* derived from the Golgi apparatus and containing enzymes (lysins) that attack the egg membranes. The sperm's "tail" is a flagellum some 30 to 50 μm in length, extending from the end opposite the acrosome. Joining head and tail is a "middle piece" containing one or more centrioles, the basal body of the flagellum, and a densely packed mass of mitochondria that provide energy during the sperm's active period.

FERTILIZATION The life of the new individual begins with the fusion of ovum and sperm, or fertilization, which brings together the hereditary contributions of the two parents. In this process we can distinguish several important phases: (1) the sperm and egg come in contact; (2) the egg is activated; (3) the sperm penetrates the egg; (4) sperm and egg nuclei come together and may fuse.

The encounter of sperm and egg The random swimming movements of the sperm may eventually bring it in contact with an egg. When egg and sperm are of widely different species it is unlikely that further interaction will take place, but to date no species-specific chemical attractants have been identified that might serve to direct sperm toward eggs of their own kind. Some aquatic invertebrates display a curious antigen-antibody reaction between eggs and sperm of the same species, which causes sperm to agglutinate (stick together) on the surface of the egg. The antibodylike substance coating the sperm (*antifertilizin*) reacts with a material (*fertilizin*) thought to be of complementary molecular shape, which coats the egg. The agglutinated sperm cannot penetrate the egg, but may serve gradually to reduce the protective fertilizin coat until eventually one sperm can break through. This helps insure that only sperm of the same species will be able to penetrate the egg.

Activation and the establishment of basic symmetry and axes of polarity The egg responds positively to sperm contact, being at the moment of contact set irrevocably upon its developmental pathway. Activation of the egg occurs before the sperm head penetrates the egg's plasma membrane. In fact, an egg may be activated by agencies other than sperm (a variety of chemical, mechanical, and even electrical stimuli may serve), resulting in parthenogenetic development (see Section 17.1B). In most animals activation is marked by an abrupt increase in rate of oxidative metabolism and protein synthesis. In some eggs (such as the sea urchin) a "fertilization membrane" lifts away from the cortex. This membrane has been thought to prevent the entry of all sperm except the first to make contact. However, this interpretation remains in doubt, for a number of sperm may make contact simultaneously, and the fertilization membrane requires nearly a minute to develop. As a matter of fact, in a number of animals (including reptiles and birds) several sperm do penetrate the egg, but only one survives to contribute to the embryo. (Scattered cases are on record in man where one person apparently consists of a mosaic of cells of two different heredities, due to the fusion of one sperm with the true egg nucleus and the fusion of a second sperm with the maternal chromosomes that should have been cast off in the second polar body at the second meiotic division! This mosaicism is most evident where it affects eye or skin pigmentation.)

In essence, activation of an egg involves its change from a quiescent, more or less stable condition to one in which a number of changes rapidly take place. If the reduction divisions have not previously been completed, they now are. At this time *rotation* of the cortex over the surface of the internal cytoplasm takes place (Figure 11.7). In the frog egg, this rotation is readily visible because it involves the movement of pigmented cytoplasm. The point of sperm contact establishes the primary meridian of rotation. Following this meridian, the cortex slides over the deeper cytoplasm in such a way that the deeply pigmented cortical cytoplasm of the animal hemisphere rises above the equator on the embryo's future dorsal side, and sinks below the equator on the embryo's future ventral side. Where the deeply pigmented layer rises above the equator, a pale crescentic area (the *gray crescent*) appears, bisecting the meridian of rotation. Why is the gray crescent such an important feature of the frog egg? In the first place, it is decidedly more permeable than other regions of the cortex, and must be the primary site of exchanges of materials between the egg and its surroundings; in the second, it will take the lead in the great morphogenetic movement known as gastrulation (to be discussed below). Furthermore, when the fertilized egg divides for the first time, the plane of cleavage bisects the gray crescent, dividing the embryo into right and left halves.

Figure 11.7 □ **Activation of frog egg and establishment of basic axes of symmetry. Sperm entry initiates rotation of darkly pigmented cortex that moves downward over the point of sperm entry, producing a less-pigmented region (the gray crescent) on the side opposite. The gray crescent marks the embryo's future posterior end, and the plane of the first cleavage of the zygote will bisect the gray crescent, dividing the embryo into right and left halves.**

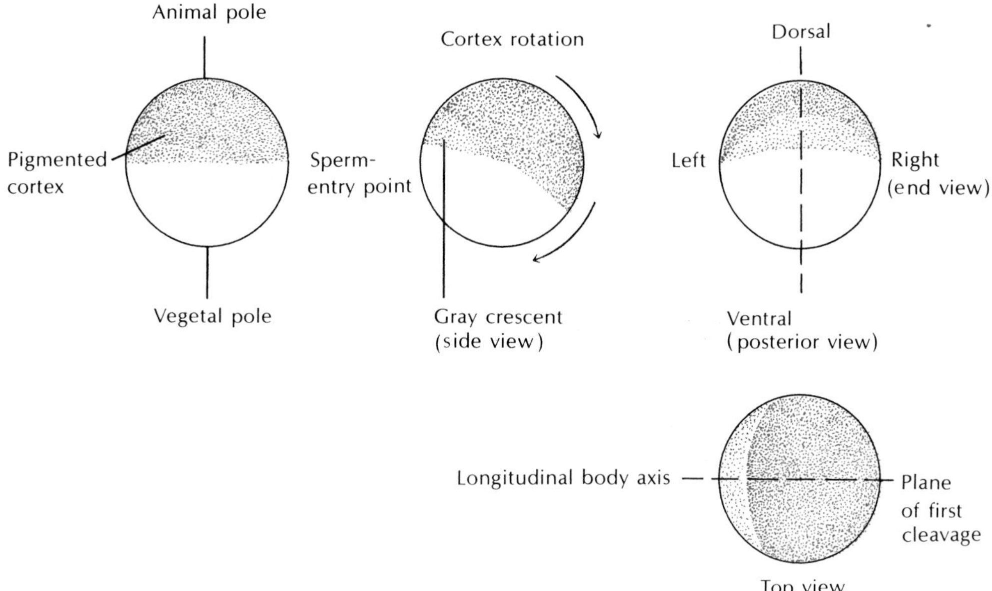

We should note that although the sperm may not yet have fully penetrated the egg, both the dorsoventral axis and the bilateral symmetry of the embryo have already been determined! The factors involved in establishing these cardinal features of body plan include: (1) the original location of the animal and vegetal poles; (2) the point of extrusion of the polar bodies; (3) usually (but not invariably) the point of sperm entry; and (4) the meridian of cortical rotation, which establishes a unique cortical area, the gray crescent (or, presumably, its less visible equivalent in unpigmented eggs). Even the embryo's future anteroposterior axis is already latently established, for in amphibian development the gray crescent is the point from which the major longitudinal supportive rod, the notochord, will later grow forward along the midline of the embryo, marking the future location of the vertebral column. One end of the anteroposterior axis comes to be marked by the blastopore, an opening that appears below

Figure 11.8 □ **Fertilization: (*a*) morphology of mature human sperm; (*b–f*) successive stages in sperm penetration. N, nucleus; VM, vitelline membrane; PM, plasma membrane.**

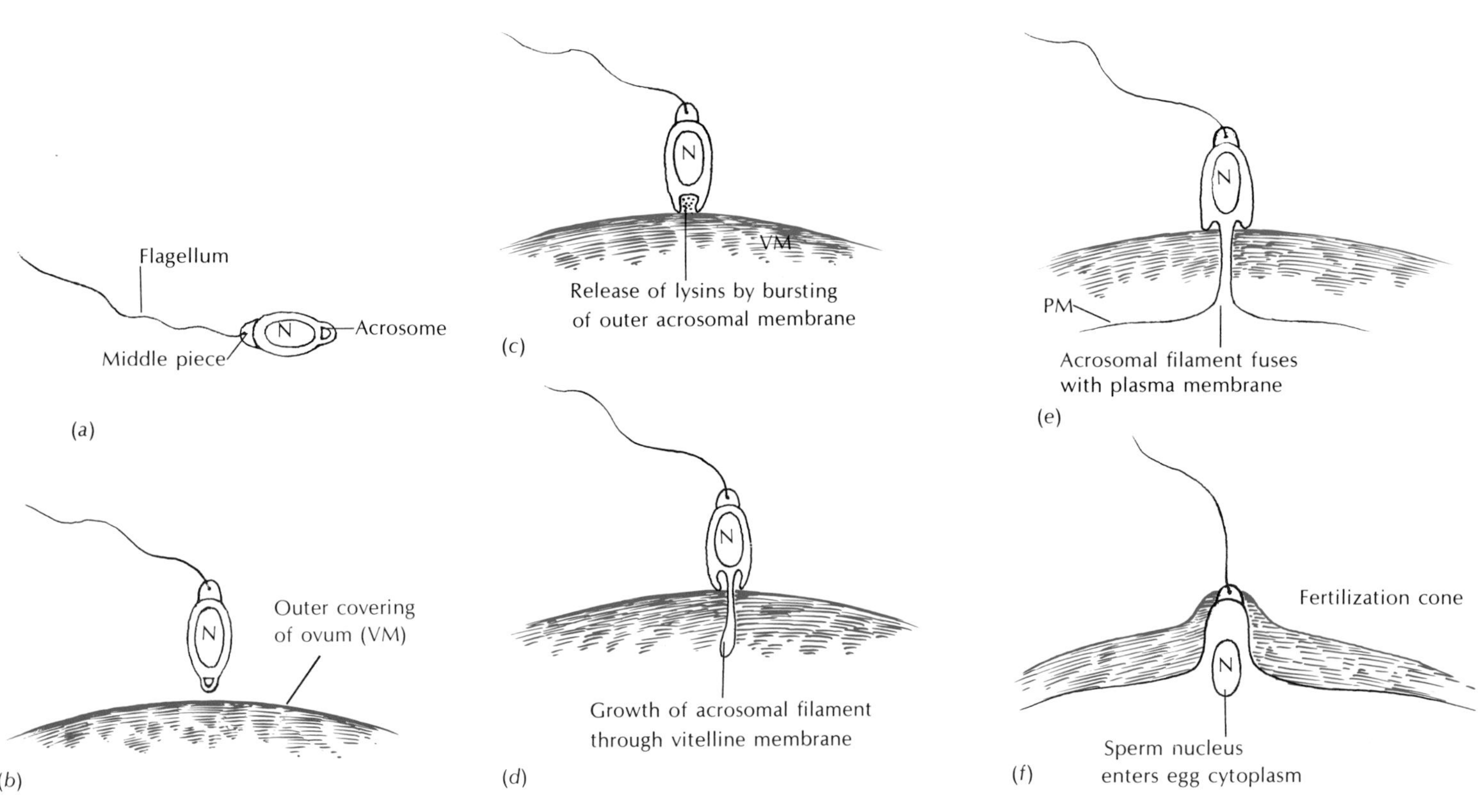

the gray crescent during gastrulation and eventually becomes the anus or posterior opening of the tadpole's digestive tract.

Fusion of sperm and egg In insects, all vertebrate fish except lampreys, and a number of molluscs and echinoderms, sperm can penetrate the egg only by way of a small pore through the outer egg membranes. In other species sperm penetrate at their first point of contact, releasing lysins from the acrosome that dissolve away the membranes at this point. Fertilization of the mammalian egg must be preceded by a more widespread enzyme action, for when shed from the ovary this egg is coated with smaller cells (the cumulus oophorus) that must be removed before the egg is accessible for entry. Mammalian sperm, ascending the oviduct in large numbers, attack the cumulus oophorus with the enzyme hyaluronidase, which digests the hyaluronic acid in the intercellular cement so that the cells are loosened. Although normally only one sperm enters the egg, many are required for dissolution of the cumulus.

After the outer acrosomal membrane ruptures, releasing the lysins that begin to open a path through the egg membranes, the inner acrosomal membrane extrudes a slender filament that elongates until it contacts the egg's plasma membrane (Figure 11.8*b*). Formation of the acrosomal filament seems to be elicited by some chemical in the egg, for its formation can be induced experimentally by placing sperm in water in which ripe eggs have been soaked. When the acrosomal filament contacts the egg's plasma membrane, the egg cortex bulges out at that point in a cylindrical or pseudopodiumlike *fertilization cone* that seems literally to engulf the sperm, carrying the latter inward as it retracts. At the same time the acrosomal membrane may fuse with the egg's plasma membrane, so that a passage is opened for the sperm nucleus to enter the egg cytoplasm. How much of the sperm enters the egg varies in different animals. In mammals the entire sperm usually enters, in many other animals the tail is left behind, and in others only the sperm nucleus and centriole may enter.

Approximation of pronuclei The monoploid sperm and egg nucleus are referred to as *pronuclei* to distinguish them from the diploid *fusion nucleus* that the two will form. The sperm pronucleus swells in size by imbibing water as it moves (by what means we do not know) through the cytoplasm toward the egg pronucleus. The sperm centriole accompanies it, beginning to form an aster typical of mitosis.

As the sperm pronucleus moves through the egg cytoplasm, the latter responds dramatically. We have seen that cortical rotation is triggered by the initial sperm contact. Now, massive streaming pervades the inner cytoplasm as well, as a result of which final rearrangements and definitive morphogenetic cytoplasmic gradients are established, which will be stabilized and preserved throughout cleavage.

When the two pronuclei come together, their nuclear envelopes may break at the point of contact and fuse as one envelope. Fertilization is now complete, and the egg has become a *zygote*. In some species the zygote may enter a period of quiescence before cleavage begins, whereas in others the envelope of the fusion nucleus promptly disintegrates and mitosis begins. In still other cases the pronuclei do not fuse, but their two envelopes disappear and the paternal and maternal chromosomes move to the midline of the first cleavage spindle.

B Early postzygotic development

CLEAVAGE Through a series of mitotic divisions known as cleavage the zygote is transformed into a group of cells that eventually assumes the form of a hollow ball, the *blastula,* surrounding a central cavity (blastocoel). Cleavage differs from ordinary cell division in two major respects: (1) Usually cells grow for a while between consecutive divisions; during cleavage they do not grow, but one division follows the next without pause, and as a result after each division the daughter cells (*blastomeres*) are but half the size of the preceding cell generation. (2) The plane of each successive division is precisely rotated with respect to the preceding one, and is at first coordinated for all blastomeres.

Radial and spiral cleavage The embryos of echinoderms and chordates cleave *radially,* those of most other phyla, *spirally* (Figure 11.9). The difference between the two cleavage patterns is manifested at the third division. The first division follows the future anteroposterior axis, and divides the embryo into right and left halves. The second division is at right angles to this, bisecting the embryo transversely across the anteroposterior axis, producing four cells. The third division takes place through a plane at right angles to each of the preceding two, bisecting the embryo into dorsal and ventral portions and producing two tiers of four blastomeres each. When cleavage is radial, the spindles of the third division are oriented straight up and down, so that the

Figure 11.9 □ **Radial and spiral cleavage. Radial cleavage is characteristic of deuterostomate phyla, including echinoderms and chordates, whereas spiral cleavage occurs in protostomate phyla, such as annelids and molluscs. In both cases the egg cleaves in the same way to the four-cell stage, but at the third cleavage the difference between the two becomes apparent. In radial cleavage succeeding divisions produce tiers of cells directly on top of each other; in spiral cleavage the spindles of successive divisions are so oriented that one tier is displaced clockwise from the next, and the blastomeres are arranged spirally around the axis of polarity. In the spirally cleaving embryo the future contribution of each blastomere and its descendants is determined even at the early developmental stages shown here.**

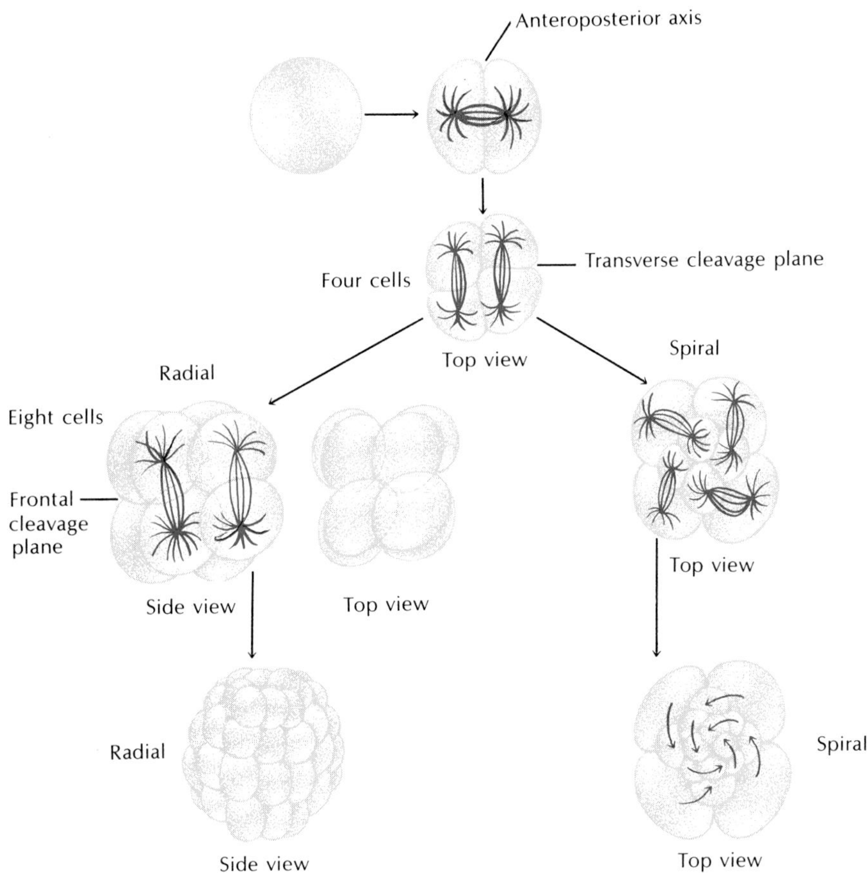

cells of the second tier will lie directly below those of the upper tier. This regularity persists throughout the following several divisions so that subsequent generations of blastomeres form regular rows extending from the dorsal to the ventral pole. In spiral cleavage, on the other hand, the spindles of each division are obliquely oriented so that the cells of each tier do not lie directly under the ones above, but are rotated clockwise (dextrally) or counterclockwise (sinistrally) with reference to the next tier. During successive divisions the orientation of the spindle shifts through 90° so that the blastomeres are shifted dextrally and sinistrally in alternation.

Holoblastic, meroblastic, and superficial cleavage Cleavage is greatly affected by the amount of yolk in the egg. When yolk is abundant it tends to retard or even inhibit cleavage in that part of the embryo. If the amount of yolk is not so great but that the embryo can cleave throughout its entire mass, *holoblastic cleavage* (Figure 11.10*a*,*b*) results. An egg with very little yolk, like that of the starfish or amphioxus, cleaves regularly to produce blastomeres of nearly equal size. A frog egg, with somewhat more yolk, exhibits *unequal* holoblastic cleavage, with small, more numerous blastomeres produced in the upper hemisphere and larger, fewer blastomeres in the lower, yolk-encumbered hemisphere. During the first and second cleavage of the frog egg, the cleavage furrows first appear at the top of the egg and move gradually downward to the ventral pole, cutting inward through the yolk-laden cytoplasm to separate the blastomeres. Once the third division takes place, however, separating upper and lower hemispheres, the former is freed of the encum-

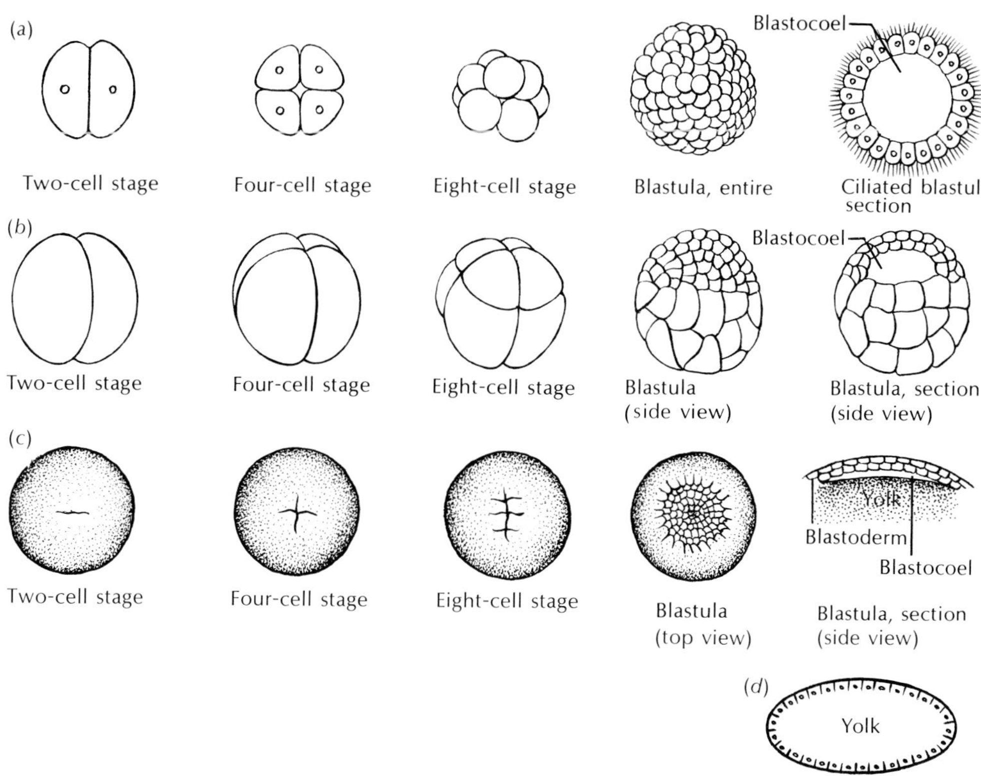

Figure 11.10 □ Cleavage: (*a*) holoblastic equal, characteristic of eggs with very little yolk (starfish); (*b*) holoblastic unequal, characteristic of eggs with slight to moderate quantities of yolk (frog); (*c*) meroblastic, characteristic of eggs with large quantities of yolk and producing a discoidal embryo (bird); (*d*) superficial, showing insect egg.

brance imposed by its previous unity with the lower hemisphere, and from that stage on (in this type of egg) the blastomeres of the upper hemisphere cleave much more rapidly than those of the lower half.

Eggs with even greater concentrations of yolk than are found in the frog are unable to cleave throughout their entire mass, but must cleave either *superfically* or *meroblastically*. The insect egg cleaves superficially, over the entire surface of the yolk. The much larger eggs of reptiles, birds, and monotremes (along with a number of fishes) must cleave meroblastically (Figure 11.10c). (Eutherian eggs, though yolkless, also cleave meroblastically, which is not surprising since they are not likely to deviate much from ancestral cleavage patterns even though their placental attachment makes a large supply of yolk unnecessary.) In meroblastic species, cleavage takes place only at the top of the egg, forming a small disc of cells, the *blastoderm*, that rests upon the yolk. The blastoderm piles up several cells deep, and eventually produces a yolk sac membrane that sheets out over the yolk mass and encloses it, but the cleavage pattern and form of the developing embryo is much altered by the restriction of its development to the top of the yolk.

Blastula formation Cleavage is initially synchronous in an egg with little yolk, so that the embryo consists successively of 2, 4, 8, 16, 32, and 64 cells, and so forth. As cleavage continues, the blastomeres rearrange themselves around a hollow cavity, the *blastocoel*, forming a layer at first usually one cell thick. The blastomeres now adhere to one another more firmly on their contacting surfaces, forming a true epithelium. This represents the first of the embryonic *germ layers*, the *ectoderm*. In the frog embryo the blastocoel is confined to the dorsal hemisphere, and appears first as crevices among the blastomeres, gradually expanding to form a distinct cavity. A frog blastula contains about 8,000 to 16,000 cells, most of which are the small blastomeres of the upper hemisphere. An egg cleaving meroblastically forms only a narrow blastocoel enclosed by a convex disc of blastoderm above, but open to the yolk below. The centrolecithal insect egg develops no blastocoel at all, the space being occupied instead by the central yolk mass.

Blastula formation marks the end of cleavage. In summary, this period has seen

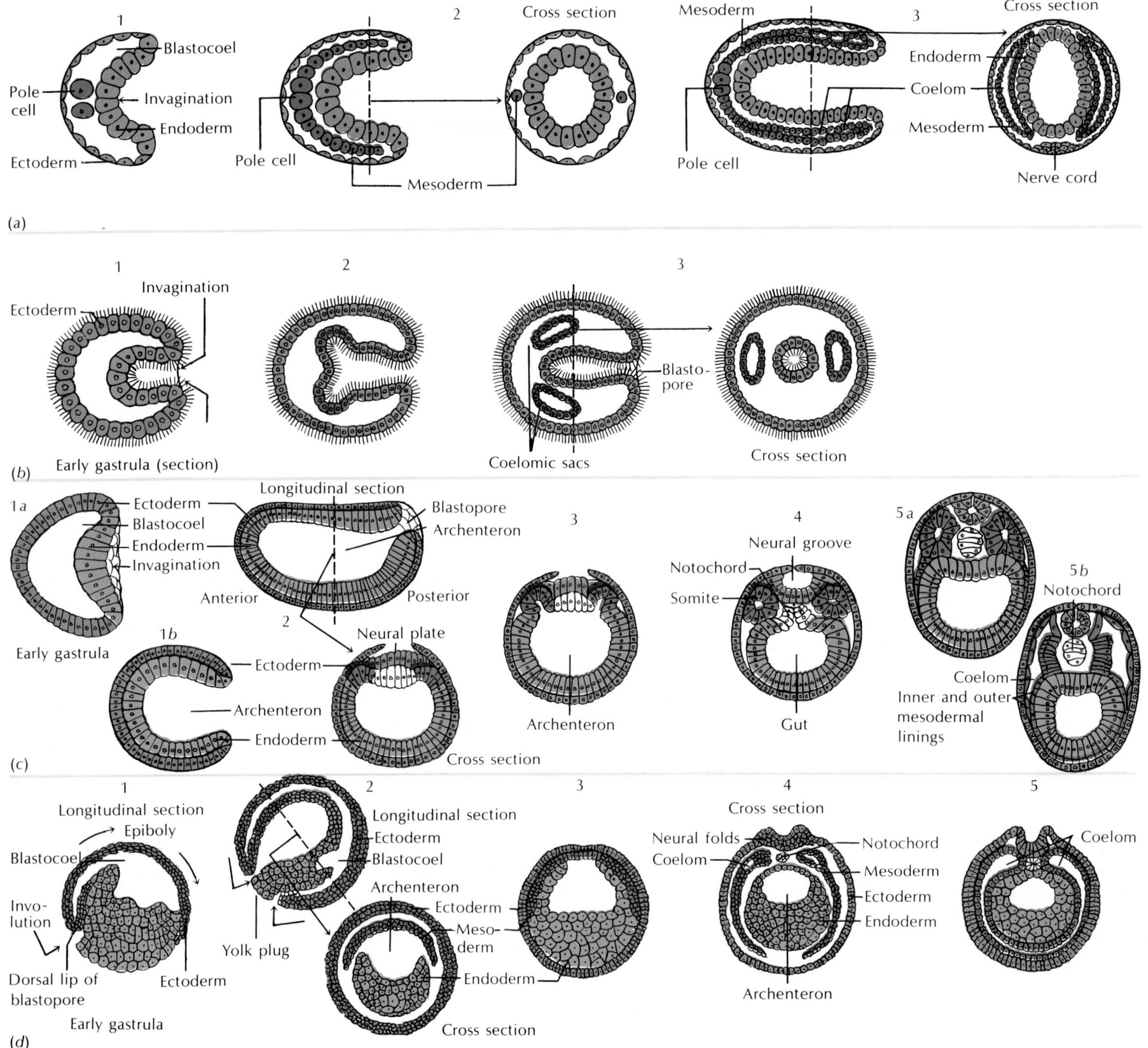

1
Blastocoel
Pole cell
Invagination
Endoderm
Ectoderm
2
Cross section
Pole cell
Mesoderm
Mesoderm
3
Cross section
Endoderm
Coelom
Mesoderm
Pole cell
Nerve cord
(a)
1
2
3
Invagination
Ectoderm
Blasto-
pore
Early gastrula (section)
Coelomic sacs
Cross section
(b)
1a
Ectoderm
Blastocoel
Endoderm
Invagination
Early gastrula
Longitudinal section
Blastopore
Archenteron
Anterior
Posterior
2
1b
Neural plate
Ectoderm
Archenteron
Endoderm
Cross section
3
Archenteron
4
Neural groove
Notochord
Somite
Gut
5a
5b
Notochord
Coelom
Inner and outer
mesodermal
linings
(c)
1
Longitudinal section
Epiboly
Blastocoel
Invo-
lution
Dorsal lip of
blastopore
Ectoderm
Early gastrula
2
Longitudinal section
Ectoderm
Blastocoel
Yolk plug
Archenteron
Ectoderm
Meso-
derm
Endoderm
Cross section
3
4
Cross section
Neural folds
Coelom
Notochord
Mesoderm
Ectoderm
Endoderm
Archenteron
5
Coelom
(d)

the subdivision of the original zygote into hundreds or even thousands of cells, *without growth,* for although food reserves are mobilized and used in the production of new cell materials, few if any nutrients are taken in from the environment. Following the cytoplasmic reorganization at the time when the egg is activated, the cytoplasmic constituents resist any further displacement throughout cleavage; accordingly they are parceled out differentially among the blastomeres. Although the overall mass of the embryo at the blastula stage is no greater than that of the zygote, the nuclear-cytoplasmic ratio has shifted markedly, for the original quantity of cytoplasm is now divided up among many blastomeres, each of which has a nucleus. Synthesis of DNA is accordingly one of the most intensive chemical activities carried on during cleavage, for precursors stored in the egg cytoplasm before fertilization must be mobilized to construct the chromosomes of the hundreds or thousands of cells contributing to the blastula.

GASTRULATION Just after the blastula is formed a major morphogenetic movement, gastrulation, takes place. Morphogenetic movements are *irreversible*: they create new shapes and bring cells into new relationships that affect their future course of development. Each such movement is prerequisite to those following, and so gastrulation must precede all subsequent morphogenetic movements whereby the rudiments of organs and organ systems become established.

In such a nearly yolkless egg as that of amphioxus, gastrulation takes place by *invagination* of the ectoderm at the vegetal pole, until the embryo is transformed into a double-walled cup (Figure 11.11), the *gastrula.* The opening of this cup is the *blastopore,* which gradually becomes constricted. The layer of cells lining the cup constitutes the second embryonic germ layer, or *endoderm,* which lines the primitive gut (*archénteron*). In deuterostomate ("second mouth") phyla (including echinoderms and chordates), the blastopore represents the future anus and the mouth later forms at the end opposite. In protostomate ("first mouth") phyla (annelids, molluscs, arthropods, and others) the blastopore becomes the mouth and the anus forms secondarily at the opposite end. Since in coelenterates and flatworms the mouth forms from the blastopore and remains the only opening of the digestive tract, the protostomate condition is considered the more primitive. The polarity of the anteroposterior axis may by chance have been reversed in the ancestral form leading to the deuterostomate line.

Gastrulation in the frog egg involves two major movements: *epiboly* and *involution.* The dorsal ectoderm begins actively to expand, forcing the leading edges to sheet out over the top of the larger ventral blastomeres. This overgrowth is epiboly. In the gray crescent area, however, these cells do not overgrow the region, but, reaching the dorsal edge of the gray crescent, begin actively to change shape. At this point, the cells become bottle-shaped, their inner ends expanding and their outer ends constricting. This has the effect of squeezing them inward, and as they move inward they actively migrate away from this point of involution (the blastopore) and sheet out along the inner surface of the dorsal ectoderm. Most involution takes place over the dorsal lip of the blastopore, but when the cells overgrowing the ventral part of the embryo by epiboly reach the ventral lip of the blastopore, they too begin to involute to some extent.

The experimental embryologist Hans Spemann, one of the first to investigate the properties of development by excising and transplanting parts of the embryo, discovered that the tissue forming the dorsal lip of the blastopore has unusually far-reaching developmental significance. He found that when this region was excised from one embryo and transplanted into the flank of another, it had the power to induce the development of a complete second embryo upon the body of the first (Figure 11.12)! This discovery led to the conclusion that the dorsal lip tissue is the primary *organizer* of the amphibian embryo; the actual mechanism is still not clarified but is under intensive investigation.

In the bird embryo prior to gastrulation, meroblastic cleavage has produced a discoidal blastoderm two cell layers thick, lying upon the uncleaved yolk. Only the central portion of this *blastodisc* contributes to the further development of the embryo proper, the periphery going to form the various embryonic membranes characteristic of the amniote egg (see Figure 4.3). The lower tier of cells of the blastodisc (the hypoblast)

Figure 11.11 □ Gastrulation and mesoderm and coelom formation in holoblastic eggs. Comparable sequences are shown in (*a*) earthworm, (*b*) starfish, (*c*) amphioxus, and (*d*) frog; but coelom development is traced farther in the two chordates than it is in the echinoderm and annelid. Stages: (1) gastrulation; (2–5*b*) mesoderm formation and appearance of coelom.

Figure 11.12 □ **Spemann's classic experiment demonstrated the inductive role of an organizer region (dorsal lip of blastopore) in the amphibian embryo. A block of tissue excised from this region (full color) and implanted into the blastocoel of another embryo induces development of a secondary larva (tint of color) oriented upside down to the host larva. Embryonic tissue induced by the graft includes notochord, muscle tissue, kidneys, central nervous system, and so forth. [*After J. Holtfreter and V. Hamburger, in* Analysis of Development, *B. Willier, P. Weiss, and V. Hamburger, eds.* (*Philadelphia: W. B. Saunders Co., 1955*).]**

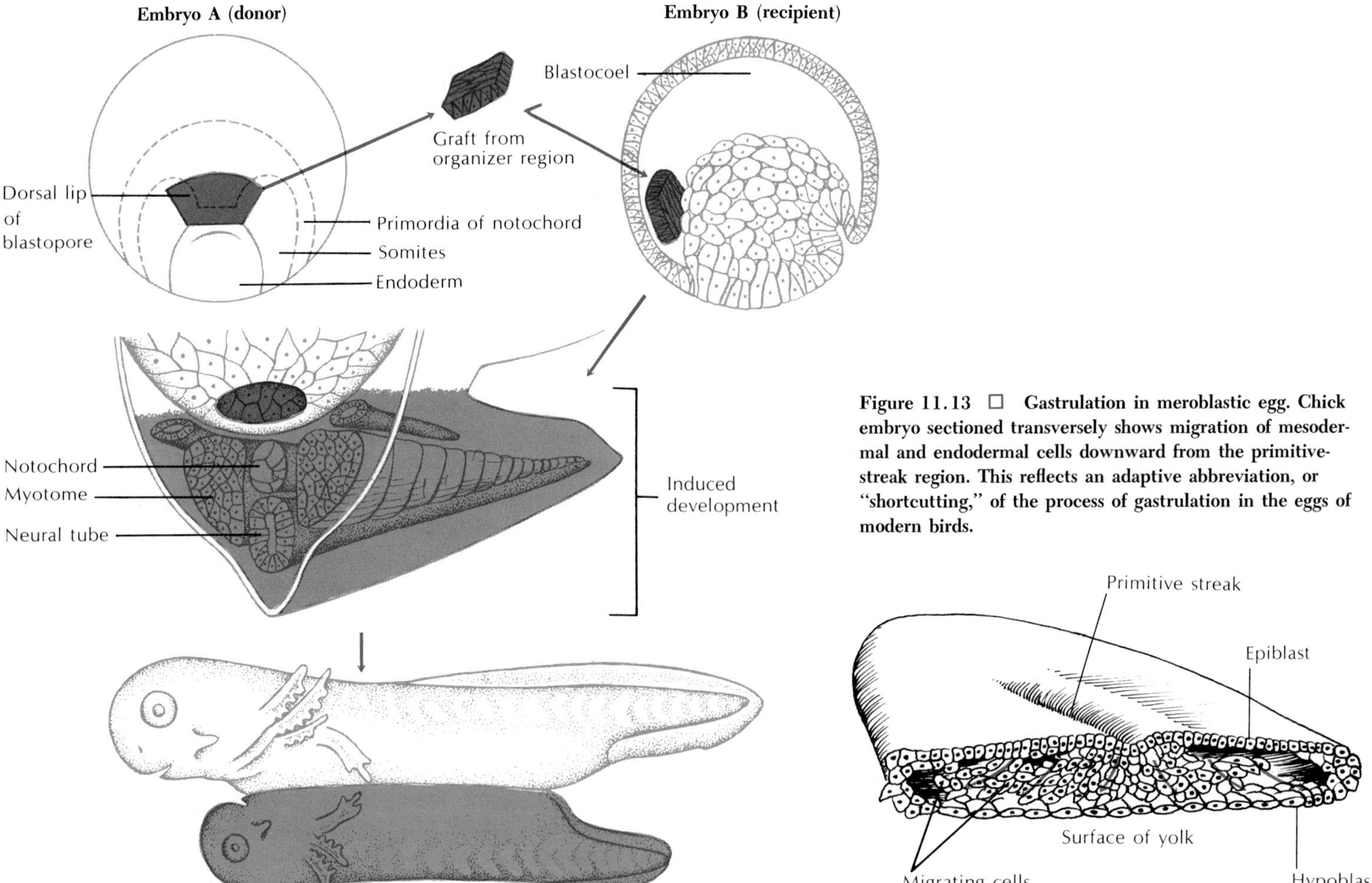

Figure 11.13 □ **Gastrulation in meroblastic egg. Chick embryo sectioned transversely shows migration of mesodermal and endodermal cells downward from the primitive-streak region. This reflects an adaptive abbreviation, or "shortcutting," of the process of gastrulation in the eggs of modern birds.**

mostly contributes to the endoderm. Since gastrulation cannot take place by an infolding of cells under the outer edge of the blastodisc (for this would interfere with growth of the embryonic membranes), it must take place only within the central portion of the blastodisc. Here, cells of the upper tier (epiblast) begin to converge toward the midline in the posterior region of the embryo, producing a thickened area known as the primitive streak. Cells of the epiblast then begin to move downward from the midline of the primitive streak into the space between the epiblast and hypoblast. This is not a movement involving an entire sheet of cells, as seen in invagination and involution, but instead the cells migrate singly, although many move in the same direction. This ingrowth is therefore termed *immigration* (Figure 11.13).

Throughout gastrulation the embryo's mass does not change although its shape is much altered. Cell division continues but no actual growth occurs, and any expansion in one dimension demands contraction in another. The embryo elongates along its anteroposterior axis, so that the endoderm begins to form a tube extending from the blastopore forward. In meroblastic eggs this tube, the lining of the embryonic gut, remains open to the yolk for some time. From this point on the polarity of the anteroposterior axis expresses itself as a metabolic and developmental gradient, for the growth rate of the anterior end soon begins to outstrip that of posterior parts, head structures appearing in advance of those lying farther to the rear.

The onset of gastrulation marks the beginning of extensive morphogenesis involving movements of large portions of the embryo, and migrations of cells both as individuals and in masses. These movements require energy, and it is not surprising that the rate of oxidative metabolism climbs sharply at the start of gastrulation. In amphibian embryos glycogen is an important fuel, and during gastrulation over 30 percent of the glycogen in the dorsal lip region is consumed, whereas in other parts the glycogen content declines by only 1 to 9 percent. However, at this time the highest rate of oxygen consumption is actually at the animal pole, the lowest rate at the vegetal pole. These differences reflect the proportion of cytoplasm to yolk material, for yolky cells respire more slowly. The yolk serves instead as a source of materials for protein synthesis, which increases several fold during gastrulation. New and different proteins now begin to be synthesized at the expense of the yolk proteins. As we might expect, this dramatic increase in protein synthesis is accompanied by an equivalent increase in mRNA synthesis (as shown by rate of incorporation of radioactive precursors). This is the first instance that the genes are known to become metabolically active during amphibian development, providing new supplies of mRNA that augment or replace those stored in the egg cytoplasm.

MESODERM FORMATION AND FURTHER ORGANOGENESIS Following gastrulation the third germ layer, called the *mesoderm,* appears and begins to occupy a position between the ectoderm and endoderm. At this time the cells of the three primary germ layers, although not yet outwardly differentiated, have already begun to follow diverging developmental pathways. Unless abnormal disturbances intervene, ectoderm cells will give rise only to nervous and epidermal tissues (and such derivatives as pigment cells and the cells that secrete tooth enamel), endoderm cells will form the gut lining and the epithelial portions of glands and other organs arising from the gut, while mesoderm cells will eventually become muscle fibers, connective tissue cells, blood corpuscles, wandering defensive cells, portions of the excretory organs, and the somatic tissues of the gonads (see Figure 11.32).

Mesoderm cells are the most mobile embryonic components. In the vertebrate body they provide the structural framework of all organs except the brain, form the heart and blood vessels and the musculature of contractile organs, and produce the skeleton and skeletal muscles, along with the other contributions summarized above. Its most common embryonic form is *mesenchyme,* star-shaped cells capable of amoeboid movement and of fusing together to form multinucleate units. The final positions occupied by various tissues and organs derived from the mesoderm are generally far removed from the original location of the mesodermal portions contributing to each derivative, attesting to widespread cell migrations. Because the origins and fate of the mesoderm in various animal groups are too diverse for tracing here, we shall confine our attention to the amphibian embryo which is reasonably typical of vertebrates as a whole.

During gastrulation of the amphibian egg, most of the cells slated to become mesoderm pass into the interior over the ventral and lateral lips of the blastopore, and move anteriorly as a sheet of cells spreading between the endoderm and ectoderm. The dorsal portion of the mesoderm at first forms the roof of the archenteron, but the archenteron soon closes to become a complete endodermal tube. Just dorsal to the archenteron the *notochord* separates from the mesoderm that remains flanking it to each side. The notochord originated as a longitudinal supportive rod in ancestral chordates, and although its supportive function has been taken over by the vertebral column, it still is of major importance in development because of the influence it exerts on nearby tissues; for instance, the notochord influences the ectoderm lying above it to become the central nervous system.

Figure 11.14 □ **Mesodermal derivatives in the vertebrate embryo. (*a*) Differentiation of mesoderm into epimere, mesomere, and hypomere: (1) early cell movements establishing major mesodermal derivatives; (2) further differentiation of epimere, mesomere, and hypomere, showing sclerotome developing into skeleton, dermatome into dermis of skin, myotome into skeletal muscles; mesomere becomes urogenital ridge, and hypomere differentiates into peritoneum, serosa, and visceral musculature. (*b*) Formation of limb bud by migration of mesenchyme from parietal hypomere.**

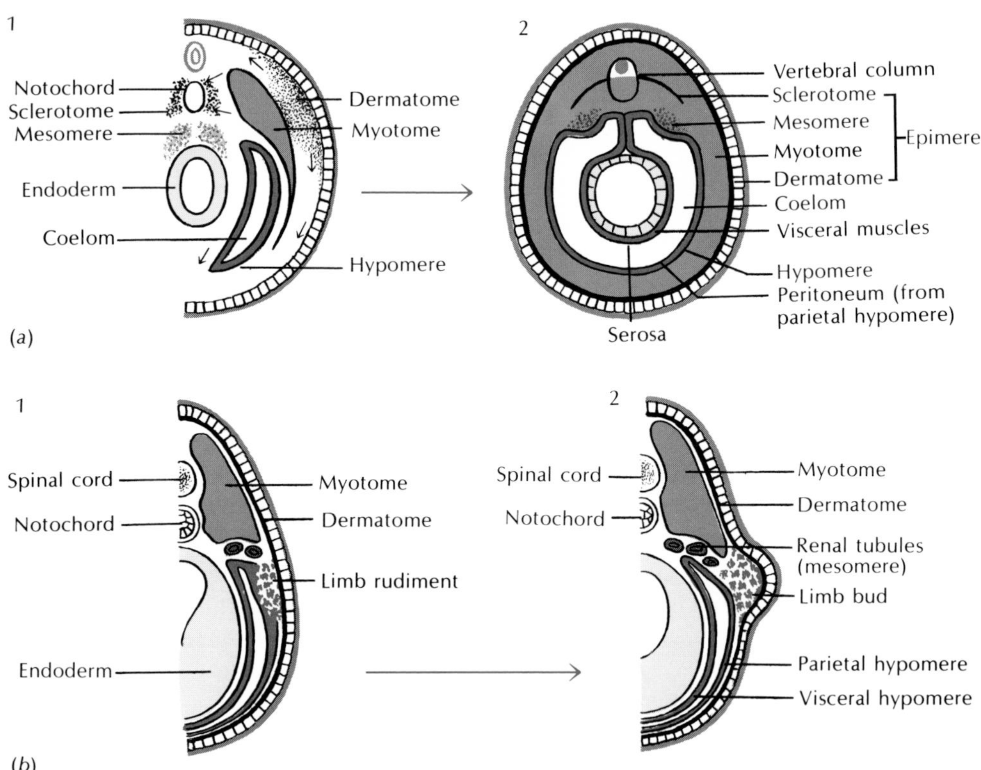

Three major regions of the mesoderm are the epimere, mesomere, and hypomere (Figure 11.14). The *hypomere* consists of mesenchyme cells that spread ventrally and laterally between the ectoderm and endoderm, until they meet at the midline below the gut. These cells tend to adhere more firmly to the ectoderm and endoderm layers with which they come in contact than to one another, and therefore a split soon appears, separating the hypomere into an inner *visceral* layer adhering to the endoderm and an outer *parietal* layer lying against the ectoderm. The cavity formed within the hypomere becomes the *coelom,* or major body cavity. The coelom provides space for the expansion of the viscera and the lengthening and coiling of the gut. The visceral mesoderm gives rise to the involuntary muscles of the internal organs, and to the mesenteries and serosal covering of the viscera. The mesenteries support the coelomic viscera and provide pathways for nerves and blood vessels to reach these viscera from the body wall. The parietal hypomere becomes the peritoneum, or outer lining of the coelom.

Dorsal to the coelom lie paired longitudinal strands constituting the *mesomere.* This forms the *urogenital ridge* from which develop the kidneys, adrenal cortex, and gonads.

The dorsal mesoderm remaining immediately to each side of the notochord constitutes the *epimere.* One group of cells (the *dermatome*) migrates from the epimere

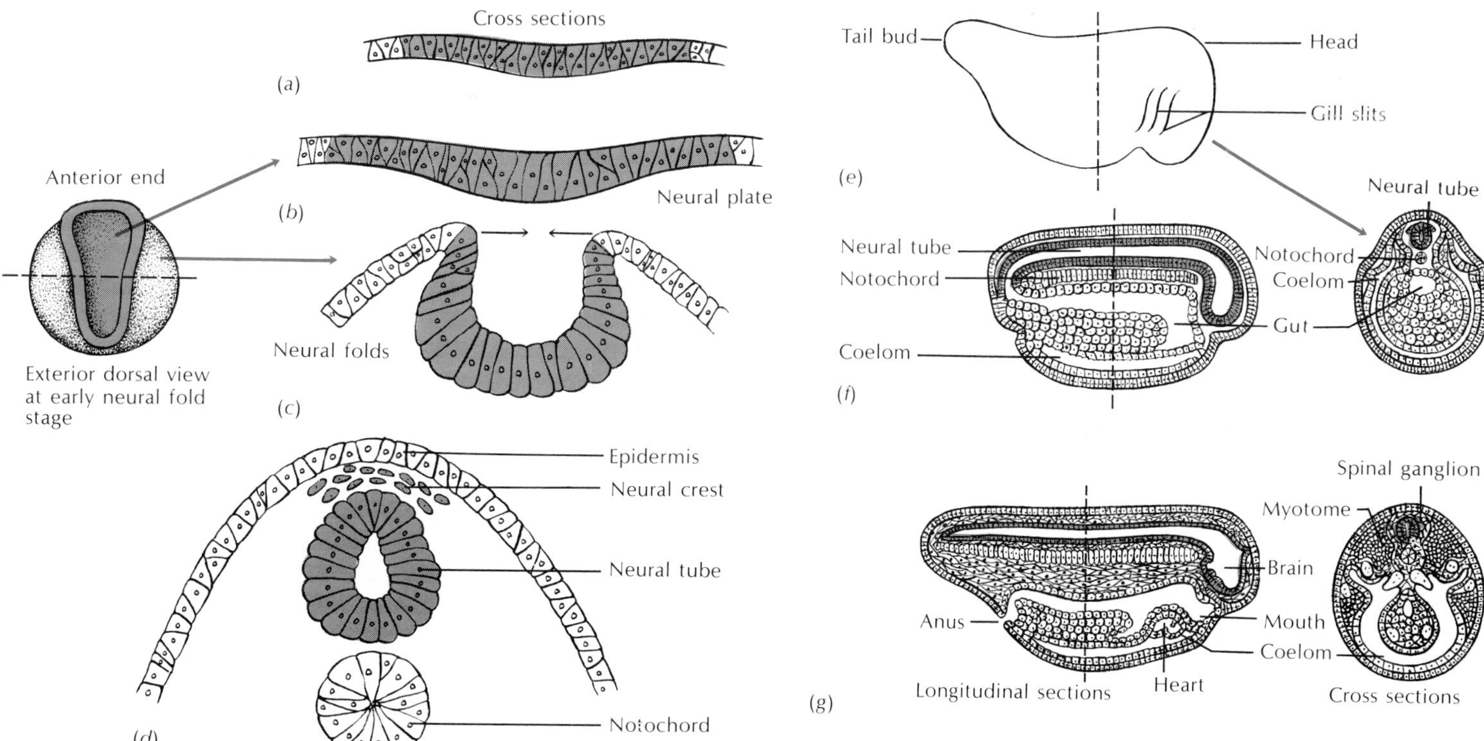

Figure 11.15 □ **Neurulation in the amphibian embryo. The notochord is essential in inducing overlying ectoderm to form the neural tube. Peripheral nerves will grow out from the neural crests and from the neural tube (spinal cord). *(a)* to *(d)* are greatly enlarged over the whole embryos in *(e)* to *(g)*.**

to lie against the ectoderm and sheet out below it, becoming the dermis, or deeper layer of the skin. Another group migrates medially to lie beneath the notochord as segmentally arranged blocks of mesenchyme (the *sclerotome*) that will become the vertebral column and give rise to other skeletal components as well. The rest of the epimere, or *myotome,* also splits into segmental blocks lying along each side of the sclerotome. Each of these segmental blocks then spreads laterally and ventrally to lie between the dermatome and the peritoneum, eventually becoming the skeletal muscles of the body wall.

NEURULATION The central nervous system of vertebrates first appears as a thickening of the dorsal ectoderm lying along the median longitudinal axis above the notochord and anterior portion of the archenteron. The center of this *neural plate* gradually becomes depressed and *neural folds* rise along either side of the depressed area (Figure 11.15). As these folds meet and fuse in the midline, a longitudinally oriented, hollow *neural tube* is formed, constituting the future brain and spinal cord (the central nervous system). This is covered by a sheet of ectoderm that closes over the top to form an unbroken epidermis covering the entire exterior of the body. Flanking the neural tube to each side remain segmentally arranged cell clusters, the *neural crests,* from which will arise the spinal and sympathetic ganglia (masses of nerve cell bodies located outside the central nervous system). Groups of neuroblasts (embryonic nerve cells) also migrate from the neural crests to positions near each kidney, where they become the glandular cells of the adrenal medulla that will secrete adrenaline.

Nerve fibers later grow peripherally from the neural tube and crests to innervate all parts of the body, terminating in the skin, muscles, and internal organs. The growth of motor nerve fibers (innervating the muscles) appears to antedate the establishment of sensory connections between the central nervous system and the periphery. Spontaneous movements of the embryo therefore constitute the earliest form of behavior to be exhibited, for they commence while the embryo is still lacking sensory input by way of specific receptors and is accordingly still incapable of reflex movements in response to particular stimuli.

FURTHER FATE OF THE ENDODERM The major part of the endoderm remains as the epithelial lining of the alimentary tract (except for the linings of mouth and rectum which are instead derived from ectoderm). A large portion of this lining becomes glandular and produces mucus and digestive juices. The alimentary tube becomes differentiated into distinct functional regions (pharynx, esophagus, stomach, and intestines) and may lengthen so much that it must coil and fold within the coelom. Meanwhile, a number of other organs arise as buds or diverticula from the gut, and although the connective tissue framework of these organs is derived mesodermally, their epithelial parts are of endodermal origin. In vertebrates such buds give rise to the salivary glands, anterior pituitary, thyroid, parathyroids, trachea, lungs, liver, and pancreas (Figure 11.16). The endocrine glands mentioned above eventually lose all direct connection with the digestive tube, but the salivary glands, liver, and pancreas remain in communication by way of endodermally lined ducts.

Figure 11.16 □ **Endodermal derivatives in the vertebrate embryo, schematically showing glands and respiratory organs arising as buds from the embryonic alimentary tract.**

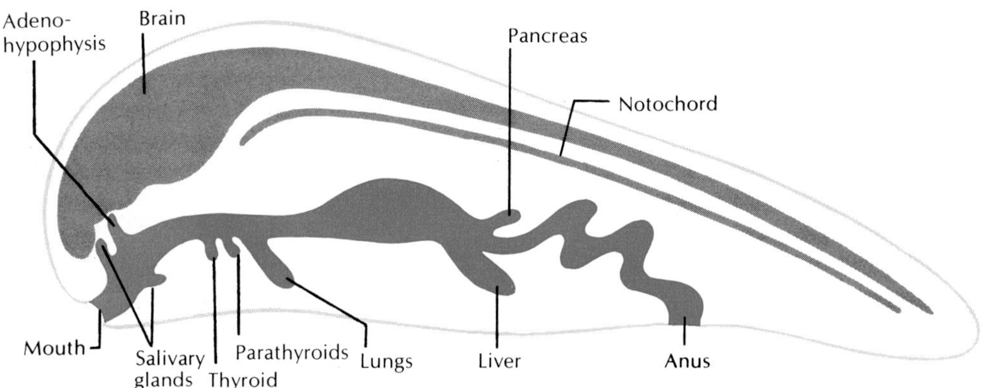

CELL MOVEMENTS AND SELECTIVE AFFINITIES How are morphogenetic movements instigated and directed? We still have much to learn about this, but we think that they can be explained at least in part on the basis of changes in the affinities of embryonic cells for other cells with which they come in contact. The tendency for cells of the same type to adhere together (*homoadhesion*) may at different times be stronger or weaker than their tendency to adhere to cells of some other type (*heteroadhesion*). Such a change in adhesive tendencies is seen during the migration of presumptive mesenchyme cells from the surface into the interior of the early sea urchin gastrula. This event has been recorded by time-lapse cinephotography, which accelerates the cell movements so that they can be studied easily. The cytoplasm on the inner side of the presumptive mesenchyme is seen first to bulge out as broad pseudopodia. This movement involves withdrawal of cytoplasm from the opposite end of the cell, so that the cells lose contact with one another and gradually creep out into the blastocoel. This migration reflects a loss of the tendency to adhere to adjacent future mesenchyme cells present in the epithelium. The mesenchyme cells do not come together in the blastocoel, but remain apart and put forth long pseudopodia. If a pseudopod comes in contact with the inner surface of the ectoderm, the cell is attracted and begins to move by amoeboid streaming along the underside of the ectoderm. In this manner a layer of mesoderm eventually is formed below the ectoderm.

Studies of dissociated cells Selective affinities of cells can be studied by experimentally separating them and allowing them to come back together again by amoeboid movement. Sponge cells were the first to be experimentally dissociated, simply by being forced through the mesh of a finely woven cloth. The embryos of marine invertebrates were next tested and were found to separate into individual blastomeres when placed in Ca^{2+}-free sea water. These blastomeres would then reaggregate when Ca^{2+} was added to the water. More recently, cells of embryos of higher animals such as chicks and mice have been successfully dissociated by enzymatically digesting the intercellular cement.

When reaggregating, dissociated cells exhibit certain remarkable properties: (1) Many cells "recognize" correct *spatial relationships.* A hydra reacts to certain chemicals by turning its saclike body completely inside out by way of the mouth. This places the outer cell layer, or epidermis, to the inside, while the layer of digestive cells, the gastrodermis, lies to the exterior. If the animal fails to turn itself right side out, the individual cells take the initiative and migrate past one another until eventually all gastrodermal cells are once more to the inside and all epidermal cells to the outside. This is reminiscent of the morphogenetic migrations of embryonic cells of higher animals. (2) Many cells "recognize" other cells of the same *species.* If dissociated cells of two differently colored sponges of different species are mixed together, they move about until clumps are formed containing cells of only one color (and hence of only one species). (3) Cells often "recognize" other cells of the same tissue *type,* though not necessarily of the same species. When dissociated cells of various chick embryonic tissues are mixed together, they first clump as a whole, and then further sort out according to type, kidney cells aggregating with other kidney cells, liver with liver cells, and so forth.

The comparative strengths of "species recognition" and "type recognition" vary with different species, and it is impossible to predict in advance of testing whether cells will tend to aggregate primarily according to species or tissue type. Mixtures of dissociated chick and mouse embryonic cells produce chick-mouse tissues in which mouse and chick cells of the same type combine. Coaggregated kidney cells organize themselves into tubules in which both mouse and chick cells (distinguishable on the basis of nuclear differences) participate. On the other hand, attempts to produce chimeric tissues combining cells of two different species of amphibians fail, since amphibian cells seem to sort out by species rather than by type.

To explain these phenomena, cells of still younger embryos have been dissociated so that the behavior of cells of different germ layers could be observed. These cells are found to sort themselves out not only by type but by position relative to the total cell aggregate. When dissociated ectoderm and endoderm cells are mixed together, they creep about until a stable configuration is achieved in which the ectoderm covers the outside of the mass, coating the endoderm. When ectoderm and mesoderm cells are mixed together, the mesoderm clumps to form a nodule at the core and is then covered by a sheet of ectoderm (Figure 11.17). This might be expected on the basis of their relative positions in the intact embryo, but in addition, if a piece of mesoderm tissue is placed near a fragment of *endodermal* tissue, the latter sheets out to enclose the former, so that the endoderm, usually the most interior tissue in an intact embryo, here is the more exterior tissue.

These results can be explained in terms of two types of cell movements, *cell sorting* and *cell spreading,* which reflect the relative strengths of the homoadhesive and heteroadhesive tendencies mentioned above. When cells sort themselves out by kind, they tend to reduce the number of adhesions made with cells of different type and increase the number of those made with cells of like type. When cells spread, they decrease adhesions made with others of the same type and increase the number made with cells of a different type. In other words, sorting maximizes *homo*adhesions and minimizes *hetero*adhesions, whereas spreading maximizes heteroadhesions and minimizes homoadhesions. Through a combination of these two processes the cells involved move toward an equilibrium state that is the same whether it is arrived at primarily by sorting or by spreading. The same end-state is achieved regardless of whether two cell types have been mixed together as suspensions of separated cells, or whether chunks of two tissues have been placed in contact with one another and one allowed to spread over the other. Many of the properties of morphogenetic systems can be explained on the basis of such systems of differential adhesion in cells capable of spontaneous motility, which can adhere with various

Figure 11.17 ☐ **Selective affinities of embryonic cells result in cell movements. (*a*) Mixture of dissociated mesoderm and epidermal cells results in outward movement of epidermal cells and inward movement of mesoderm that eventually becomes mesenchyme and forms coelomic spaces and blood corpuscles. (*b*) Mixture of mesoderm and endoderm cells results in inward migration of mesodermal cells, leaving endoderm to the exterior. In both experiments the mesoderm proves more homoadhesive and less heteroadhesive than do the other cell types.**

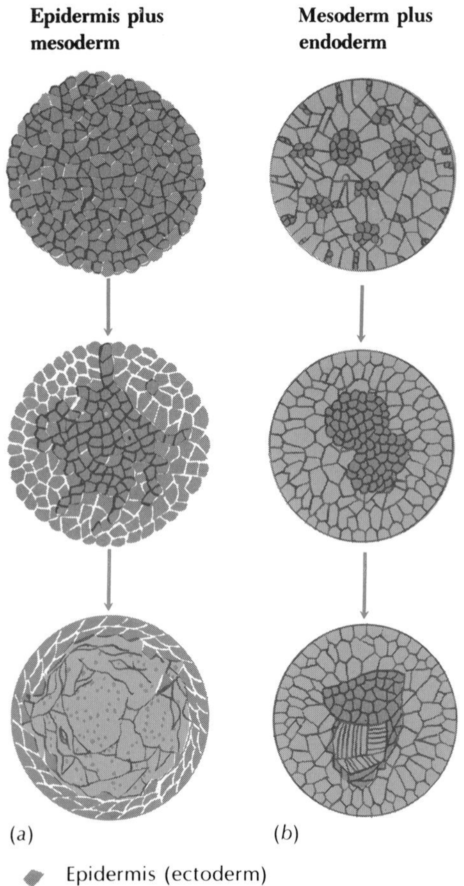

strengths yet retain the power to rearrange themselves still further should these compatabilities change. The final arrangement assumed by such cell mixtures always depends on the relative strengths of homo- and heteroadhesive tendencies, and in any mixture containing different types of embryonic cells, the most homoadhesive tissue goes to the interior of the mass and is overlain by less homoadhesive cells. For example, when dissociated embryonic chick liver, heart, and cartilage cells are mixed together, stability is reached when the cartilage cells have formed a spheroidal mass at the center, covered by a layer of heart cells that in turn is enclosed by a layer of liver cells, which are the least homoadhesive of these three cell types.

Except for slime mold myxamoebas, which aggregate chemotactically due to secretion of the attractant acrasin by the cells initiating the aggregation, cells in general do not seem to associate by chemotaxis. We can readily demonstrate the chemotactic nature of the response of myxamoebas: if a slime mold aggregation is kept in flowing water during its period of formation, myxamoebas on the downstream side are seen to turn and move upstream toward the aggregation, whereas those on the upstream side of the aggregation remain unaffected. Dissociated cells of other kinds of organisms do not behave in this manner, but move about randomly, closely bypassing others of like kind if they do not happen actually to make contact. If in the course of these random movements they touch cells of unlike type, they move past without sign of recognition. If they contact cells of the same type, however, they cease to move. Such immobilization or *contact inhibition* seems to depend on homoadhesive reactions between cell-surface materials. Cells of the same type usually have some degree of homoadhesiveness, although if this were exceeded by their heteroadhesiveness such cells would form not solid masses but open tubules or flat sheets in which the area of contact with cells of the same type is minimized. The above explanation of morphogenetic movements is consonant with the cells' observed behavior, but the real questions remain unanswered: what is the physical basis of homo- and heteroadhesion; and how are changes in these adhesive properties governed so that effective timed movements take place?

Stabilization of cell associations The aggregative capacity of cells of higher animals declines with developmental age. Dispersed cells of 7-, 9-, 11-, 14-, and 17-day-old chick embryos form progressively smaller clumps, while cells from embryos of 19 days or older fail entirely to reaggregate. This loss of embryonic homo- and heteroadhesive tendencies requires that there be various means by which definitive cell arrangements, once achieved, can be made permanent.

What means exist for stabilizing cell aggregations, particularly epithelial sheets which often occupy exposed surfaces and at no time display strong homoadhesive tendencies? Different degrees of intimacy between adjacent cells can be achieved, depending on the extent to which the adhesion must be strengthened or the flow of materials between cells facilitated (Figure 11.18). (1) Deposition of *intercellular cement* consisting of a polysaccharide matrix interpenetrated by collagen fibrils is the most common means of stabilizing cell aggrega-

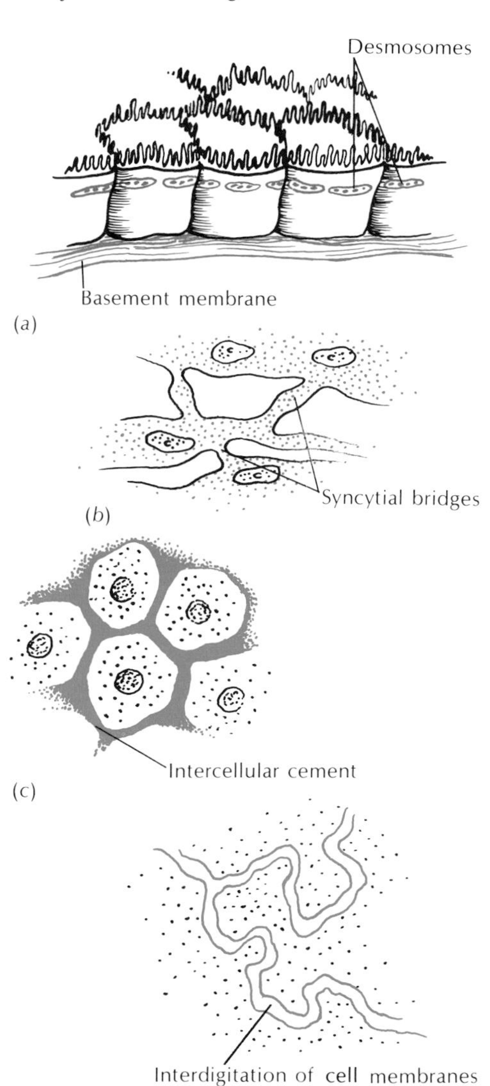

Figure 11.18 □ Stabilization of cell aggregations. **(*a*) Desmosomes hold adjacent epithelial cells together, and basement membrane anchors epithelium to underlying tissues. (*b*) Syncytial bridges unite cytoplasm of adjacent cells. (*c*) Intercellular cement promotes cohesion. (*d*) Membranes of adjacent cells interdigitate.**

tions, and it is this material that must be digested away if cells of embryos old enough to contain stabilized aggregations are to be dissociated for experimental study. (2) The adhesion of epithelial sheets to underlying tissues is reinforced by the secretion of a *basement membrane* (see Figure 10.7*d*) similar to intercellular cement but thicker and built up of layers of collagen fibrils running in regularly alternating directions. (3) Epithelial cells may be attached to one another by special attachment bodies known as *desmosomes,* which form on the contacting surfaces and are particularly well developed in epithelial sheets only one cell thick. (4) The plasma membranes of adjacent cells may *interdigitate* like complementary pieces of a jigsaw puzzle. (5) Where close functional synchrony is essential or a very strong connection demanded, the cells may actually fuse by way of cytoplasmic extensions, forming a *syncytium.* (6) A wide variety of cells communicate by way of *junctional membrane regions* that permit relatively unrestricted exchange of materials across the junction. At these regions of contact, permeability to small ions may be as much as 10^4 times greater than at other points on the cell surface. Such regions are also highly permeable to molecules of up to 1,000 molecular weight. The junctional region is stabilized and insulated from the exterior by a perijunctional insulative material. This acts as a diffusion barrier so that passage of materials is restricted to exchanges between the communicating cells, substances being unable to enter from the milieu because of this protective barrier. Junctional communication persists in such mature tissues as liver epithelium, where it serves to facilitate the distribution of metabolites and enhance functional coordination, but temporary junctional communication may also be causatively involved in cytodifferentiation, facilitating the passage of regulatory substances between adherent cells of unlike type. For example, in embryonic amphibian tissues molecules of the vital dye neutral red pass freely from one cell to another across the contacting membranes for a short period, during which the future development of the cell on the receiving end is presumably being influenced. Following this, the junctional region is "uncoupled" and the flow of the visible dye (and the visually indetectable regulatory substance) ceases.

C The ontogeny of behavior

The behavior of an animal undergoes development, just as its body form does, with the distinction that whereas a bodily structure may change little after attaining a certain stage of maturation, behavior is an ongoing *process* more or less subject to modification throughout life. Throughout embryonic and postembryonic life new patterns of behavior appear, many of which reflect either maturational changes in the nervous system or the effect of priming stimuli that allow a pattern of behavior already latently encoded in the nervous system finally to be expressed. Many new behavior patterns develop as a result of learning, the possible physical basis for which is discussed below and in Section 15.3A. But on the other hand, many other behavior patterns which appear for the first time at different stages in the animal's life history are less the result of learning than the outcome of maturation which permits expression of an action pattern that is genetically determined in the same sense that any other trait is inherited. Obviously, we do not actually inherit blue eyes or a five-fingered hand, but only a genetic blueprint that determines developmental potentials at a molecular level.

MATURATION VERSUS LEARNING How can we tell whether the appearance of some new form of behavior is the result of learning or of maturation allowing expression of an inherited potential? One way of approaching this problem is by analyzing the behavior of embryos and then interfering with this behavior to see the effect that early experience (or the lack of this experience) has on later performance.

The first movements of fish and amphibian embryos are diffuse, generalized trunk movements resembling swimming; out of these generalized movements specific motor patterns later emerge. In the embryos of birds and mammals on the other hand, discrete movements of individual limbs begin at a very early age and are preceded by even earlier rhythmic head nodding. In the chick head nodding begins about the fourth day of incubation, some four days before sensory connections are established. These rhythmic movements therefore probably reflect some endogenous activity cycle in the central nervous system that is expressed as volleys of motor discharges. Reflex movements in response to exogenous stimulation cannot appear until sensory connections are formed.

By its side-to-side trunk movements is the embryonic fish or newt learning to swim? Are the nodding head movements of the unhatched chick a means of learning to peck for food? These questions are not yet fully resolved, but a number of studies have indicated that such embryonic movements are *not* necessary prerequisites for the later normal performance of the postembryonic behavior. If these movements constituted a form of learning, depriving the individual of such practice should impair the postembryonic performance, at least initially. However, salamander embryos kept under constant generalized anesthesia swim just as well as unanesthetized control animals when allowed to recover from the anesthetic at an age comparable to that at which the control group begins to swim. Although having been deprived both of sensory stimulation and of the chance to "practice" swimming by the trunk flexions normally seen, such experimental animals are reported to swim as expertly as the normal controls.

In comparable experiments with birds, nestlings have been reared in tubes that prevent wing movements from taking place from the time of hatching until the birds are old enough to fly. Released at that age, such restrained fledglings have been found to fly as well as their unrestrained nestmates. Flying therefore, like swimming in salamanders, appears to depend solely on neuromuscular maturation and not on learning by practice. Expertise in landing, however, does improve with experience.

The improvement of pecking aim shown by chicks in the first few days after hatching was once held to be due to learning but is now considered more an outcome of neuromuscular maturation, as shown by an experiment in which chicks were outfitted with prismatic goggles that caused kernels of grain to be seen to one side of where they actually lay. No amount of practice allowed these chicks to correct their aim so as not to miss the grain! Nevertheless, their misdirected pecks came to cluster more accurately upon the spot where the grain seemed to lie. This improvement took place despite the failure to secure food, thereby reflecting maturation; if true learning were involved the chicks should have been able to correct their aim to hit the grain, but this they could never do.

Throughout maturation, a young animal may suddenly display new but fully formed unitary motor patterns, and other patterns may gradually be added to these until a complete reaction chain is formed, having an adaptive function that the separate components did not. Such unitary behavioral components may also appear in random order and only later become reorganized into functional sequences. Components of mating behavior appear in sexually immature animals that cannot perform the entire mating act. Furthermore, immature animals such as chicks but a few days old will attempt to behave like full-grown cocks when given injections of male sex hormone. Such hormone administration primes the chick physiologically and permits release of patterns of sexual behavior already encoded in the infant brain. The injected chick crows (ridiculously, with juvenile vocal apparatus) and does its best to mount its perplexed siblings.

Certain behavior patterns function only early in life and then vanish from the repertory in a manner reminiscent of the regression of such larval structures as the tail of a tadpole. At the time of hatching, the young bird releases itself from the shell in a typical, stereotyped manner. It pips the shell in a circle following the edge of the air sac and then pushes out the loosened end. Never again does it need or show this behavior. Nest parasites (see Section 6.3C) such as the cuckoo and honeyguide briefly display specific responses to objects detected within the nest. The young cuckoo takes such objects on its back and pushes them out of the nest. The infant honeyguide stabs them with its fiercely sharp beak. In either case, the parasite removes potential competitors and needs share the nest with none. These responses then wane and do not reappear.

The above examples serve to indicate that although new behavioral patterns may emerge throughout life as the result of learning, many instances of presumed learning are actually due to maturational changes in neuromuscular equipment and the overall physiological state of the organism, much as certain phases of physical development take place at particular times in ontogeny. Behavior that is predominantly genetically programmed during development, rather than being primarily brought about through the agency of exogenous relevant stimuli, is considered to be *innate*. To call a behavior innate need not imply that it is genetically determined to the absolute exclusion of environmental influences, for no trait of any kind can develop if the environment will not allow expression of the genetic potential. A person who has the genetic capacity to grow tall may remain short if deprived of adequate nourishment or if born with a defective pituitary gland, but this does not mean that genes determining stature are not present. Therefore, to call a given behavior "learned" or "innate" is merely to express the relative extent to which it is genetically programmed and subject to natural selection, compared to the extent to which it develops during the life of the individual as a result of experience.

IMPRINTING One of the earliest types of learning seen in young animals, particularly precocial birds, is an oddly ineradicable event known as *imprinting*. Imprinting serves as an excellent example of *critical periods* in development, showing the importance of *timing* in the action of an external stimulus on the developing organism. When a precocial bird (one that hatches with eyes open and is ready to walk about within a few hours) such as a duckling hatches, its tendency to follow a moving object has already been internally programmed—it is an innate tendency. Normally the first moving object seen by the duckling is its mother, and as she moves away from the nest, the following tendency becomes oriented to the mother and therefore serves to keep the infant with its parent (Figure 11.19). The optimum effect for visual imprinting takes place about 12 hours after hatching. (There is also evidence that acoustic imprinting can take place before hatching as the unhatched chick listens to its mother's vocalizations as she broods the nest). If ducklings are hatched in incubators, in isolation from each other, and are kept out of visual contact with any moving object until the critical period is well past, their following response will never develop properly. If during the critical period a duckling is exposed to a moving object other than an adult female duck (for instance a man, a balloon, or a dummy), it will thereafter be programmed to follow this object in preference to an adult female of its species, and will be unable to redirect its tendency to follow a mother duck. If, on the other hand, a duckling has been exposed during incubation to the recorded "follow me" calls of a mother duck, it is reported to follow the sound in preference to a dummy female duck.

The brief visual (or perhaps sometimes acoustic) experience which brings about imprinting is thought not only to program the final link in the following response, but simultaneously to channelize the future sexual preferences of the individual. Birds that have been heterospecifically imprinted to man or some other species show persistent tendencies when mature to court (if male) or accept sexual overtures from (if female) the species on which it was imprinted in preference to individuals of its own kind. The consistent failure of hand-reared Andean condors to mate in captivity has been laid to their being imprinted on man. This conclusion was reached on the basis of observations on a captive male condor (in the Zurich zoo), which would attempt to copulate with any trouser-clad leg in preference to its willing but untried mate.

Difficult as it may be to determine how the potential for a specific kind of behavior can be genetically encoded and subject to development like an anatomical structure, the problem of acquisition of behavior by *any* means presents a great challenge. Is the learning of an entire language by a human child much less puzzling than the genetic acquisition of unlearned knowledge of its migratory route by a bird? Learning must have a physical basis in terms of changes brought about in the nervous system as a result of stimuli experienced and actions practiced. Innate behavior must also have a physical basis, but one that is capable of

Figure 11.19 □ **(*a*) Female wood duck with young following; visual and acoustic imprinting fix the following response upon the mother. (*Zoological Society of San Diego.*) (*b*) Apparatus used for imprinting, with duckling being imprinted upon a balloon. The rotating arm moves at a typical duck pace.**

(*a*)

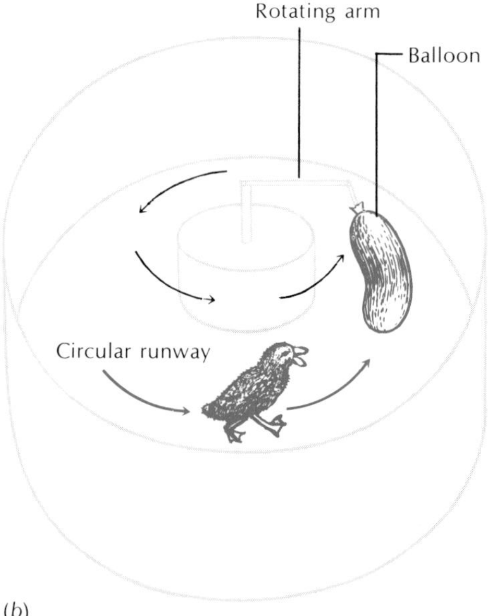

(*b*)

genetic transmission. Although we shall discuss this in later chapters, we shall now consider the formation of a hypothetical entity termed the *engram* because of its relevance to cytodifferentiation and the possible resemblance of engram formation to other developmental events such as determination.

ENGRAM FORMATION Certain experimental evidence indicates that changes involving RNA and protein synthesis must take place in brain cells to consolidate learning and result in a lasting memory of an event. Other data from human subjects undergoing brain surgery while conscious (with local anesthesia applied to the scalp) indicate that, when such biochemical changes are completed, they may be as ineradicable as a definitive morphological developmental event. Let us consider each of these evidences as they relate to the nature of the "memory trace," also called the *engram*.

Various experimental animals including mice and goldfish have been found to forget the results of training if treated before or soon after the training session with some drug that suppresses either protein synthesis or mRNA production. Mice treated with acetyloxycycloheximide just before learning a simple task will forget what they have learned within a few hours. If this drug, which suppresses 90 percent of cerebral protein synthesis, is administered directly after the training session, it also inhibits retention of learning. However, if it is given after a delay of only 30 min, long-term memory of the training is unimpaired. Apparently, within the first half hour of the training session, some event takes place in the brain that involves protein synthesis and brings about a lasting change in the neurons affected. A macromolecular configuration may be formed, constituting the hypothetical engram and being in fact the final step in the differentiation of that neuron. Like the duckling's following response, latently developed but requiring only a single external stimulus for complete programming, the neuron may develop to a state of nearly complete functional differentiation, its differentiation to be finalized at the time of engram formation by the application of an appropriate stimulus. If such a biochemical event constitutes the physical basis of learning (or at least one of several alternative bases), it would be possible for the hereditary programming of behavior to involve the production of such macromolecular configurations by genetic means. In other words, the engram might be formed, completing the physiological differentiation of the neuron, in the course of development without the intervention of relevant experience. Comparable changes in the patterns of mRNA and protein synthesis accompany all cytodifferentiation. If memory is indeed based upon the final programming of neurons by the production of specific macromolecular configurations, such configurations must be constantly renewed by protein and mRNA synthesis. Thus, engram formation may involve definitive regulation of gene action in the affected neurons, after which the activated genes would then serve to perpetuate the modified pattern of neuron activity.

What ground have we for belief that engram formation has as lasting effects as other aspects of cell differentiation? Possibly relevant observations have been made upon human subjects in which localized areas of the brain have been stimulated while the skull is opened for surgery. The brain itself is immune to pain, for it lacks sensory receptors. However, feeble electrical stimulation of discrete portions of the cerebral cortex can cause specific long-gone events apparently to be reexperienced by the subject. Although much is lost to conscious recollection, a far more complete tapestry of remembered experience appears to persist in the human mind than was hitherto believed.

There is no better means of citing these data that imply the permanent effects of engram formation than to quote directly from the records of the investigators* who first published observations on human patients subjected to direct brain stimulation during surgery:

When, by chance, the neurosurgeon's electrode activates past experience, that experience unfolds progressively, moment by moment. This is a little like the performance of a wire recorder or a strip of cinematographic film on which are registered all those things of which the individual was once aware—the things he selected for his attention in that interval of time. Absent from it are the sensations he ignored, the talk he did not heed.

Time's strip of film runs forward, never backward, even when resurrected from the past. It seems to proceed again at time's own unchanged pace. It would seem, once one section of the strip has come alive, that the response is protected by a functional all-or-nothing principle. A regulating inhibitory mechanism must guard against activation of other portions of the film. As long as the electrode is held in place, the experience of a former day goes forward. There is no holding it still, no turning back, no crossing with other periods. When the electrode is withdrawn, it stops as suddenly as it began.

A particular strip can sometimes be repeated by interrupting the stimulation and then shortly reapplying it at the same or a nearby point. In that case it begins at the same moment of time on each occasion. The threshold of evocation of that particular response has apparently been lowered for a time by the first stimulus. . . .

No man can voluntarily reactivate the record. Perhaps if he could, he might become hopelessly confused. Man's voluntary recollection must be achieved through other mechanisms. And yet the recorded patterns are useful to him, even after passage of many years. They can still be appropriately selected by some scanning process and activated with amazing promptness for the purposes of comparative interpretation.

If engram formation *is* comparable to the last step in cytodifferentiation, it is probably little different from other types of metabolic differentiation undergone by maturing tissues. Although we find it easiest to describe development in terms of morphological changes, these changes are accompanied by basic modifications in cell performance that define that cell's role in the adult body. Eventually therefore, all maturational events, whether morphological, physiological, or behavioral, must be understood in terms of biochemical alterations taking place within each individual cell. Changing patterns of protein synthesis, governed by the mRNA-synthesizing activity of genes, characterize the developmental process. Mounting evidence suggests that the coordination of developmental events is primarily a matter of controlling the timing of gene action. Some of these timing factors are environmental; others have been "built in" to the genetic code itself through the action of selective factors during the course of evolution.

11.4 □ REGULATION: THE CONTROL OF DEVELOPMENT

Perhaps no topic in biology other than the deciphering of the genetic code has posed such an enduring and fascinating problem as that of the regulation of development. *Regulation* encompasses all processes by which developmental events are controlled and integrated in space and time. It involves the action of factors both genetic and environmental, the latter including cytoplasmic influences as well as those originating outside the maturing cell or even outside the embryo.

The genome determines only the developmental potential of the organism. Through the process of regulation the genetic potential is realized, but in such a way that only particular capabilities of develop-

*W. Penfield and L. Roberts, *Speech and Brain Mechanisms* (Princeton, N.J.: Princeton University Press, 1959), pp. 53–55.

Figure 11.20 □ Control of development.

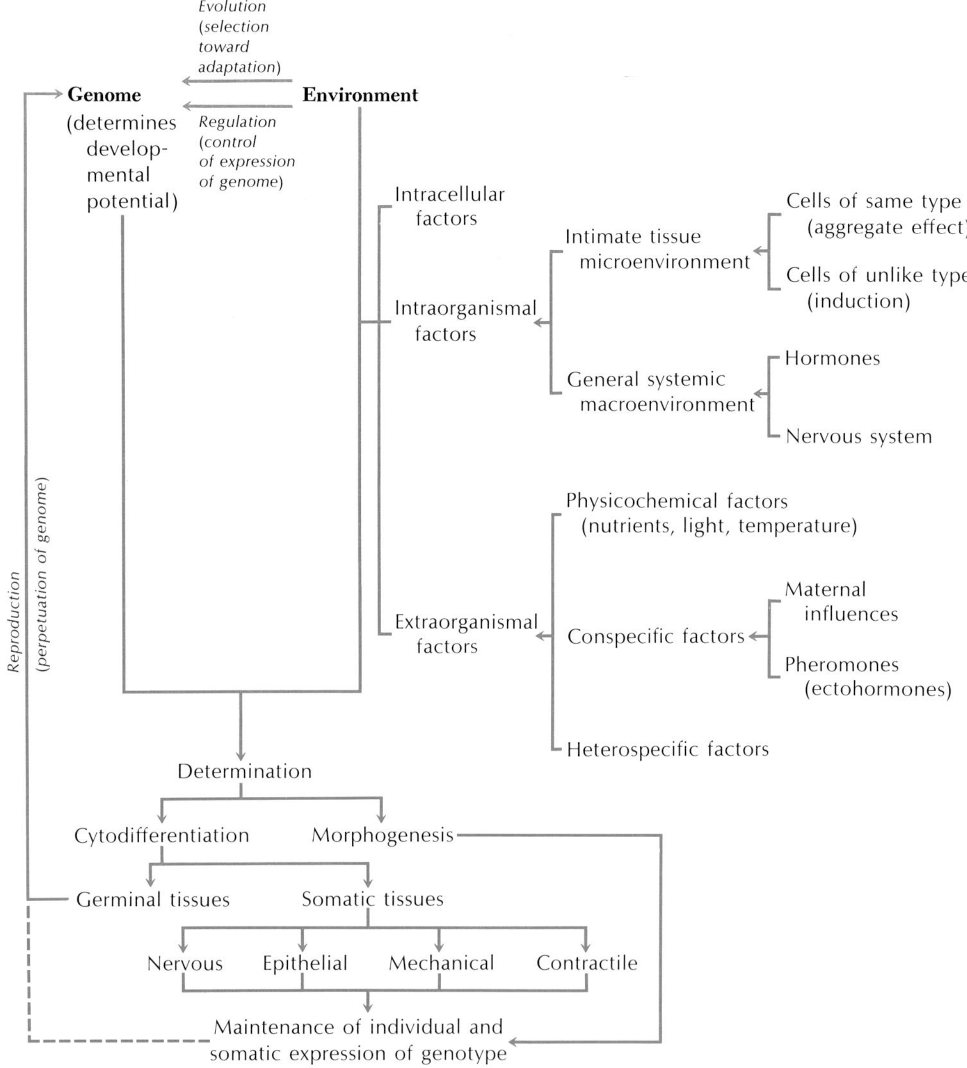

ing cells are brought to expression. In this section we shall consider the roles of genes in development, and how genetic systems may be controlled by various regulatory agents in their environment. This environment consists of: (1) the *intracellular* environment, comprising other genes, the cytoplasm, and the cell periphery; (2) the intimate *tissue microenvironment* within which cells exert regulatory effects upon the development of immediately adjacent tissues; (3) the general *systemic macroenvironment,* including nervous and endocrine agents that coordinate development at the level of the entire organism; and (4) the *external environment,* comprising factors outside the organism, both abiotic and biotic, that can regulate development (Figure 11.20).

A Determination

By determination we mean the progressive restriction of the developmental plasticity of a cell. The zygote is considered *totipotent,* for it is capable of giving rise to all of the specialized cell types (some 100 types in man) which form the body of the multicellular organism. As development proceeds, the cells lose this plasticity, perhaps irrevocably, but the loss is gradual and progressive until a point is reached at which each cell's fate is definitively and specifically determined. It is only at this point that the cell's final morphological and functional differentiation is manifested.

THE MORPHOGENETIC LANDSCAPE An analogy useful in portraying the gradual character of determination is that of the "morphogenetic landscape" (Figure 11.21). The zygote is pictured as a ball poised at the top of a gullied hill, where many channels lead downward in progressively diverging directions. However the zygote must behave as no ball can: it must divide repeatedly as it "rolls downhill." In each cell generation the descendants of the zygote find themselves following increasingly specific pathways, until reaching the bottom of the hill they achieve stability, assuming their final positions and roles in the organism.

In the course of normal development, determination is not usually capable of reversal or redirection into new channels, any more than a ball can roll uphill, but experimentation can give some clue as to how far determination may have gone at any given time, and how capable of reversal or redirection the process still may be. For instance, ectodermal cells that would ordinarily become epidermis may instead become neuroblasts if transplanted to the region from which nervous tissue will arise. This new environment contains factors that alter the course of determination. Similarly the differentiation of cells grown in vitro may be shifted into new channels by exposure to chemical agents. Explanted epidermal cells treated with lithium chloride have been reported to give rise to neurons, pigment cells, and even muscle fibers (which normally arise only from mesoderm).

DETERMINATE AND INDETERMINATE CLEAVAGE The onset and primary stabilization of determination is differently timed in the ontogeny of various species. Protostomate phyla generally show *determinate cleavage:* the developmental plasticity of their cells becomes restricted very early in development and determination is not disturbed thereafter by such experimental procedures as separation of the blastomeres. For instance, one specific cell produced in the sixth cleavage of the annelid egg gives rise to all mesodermal tissue. Should this cell be destroyed, the embryo will lack all mesodermal structures and be unable to survive. Deuterostomate phyla on the contrary display *indeterminate cleavage:* although determination may begin quite early, it is not stabilized until a considerably later time and can be disturbed by experimental separation of the blastomeres.

Figure 11.21 □ Determination. (*a*) The "morphogenetic landscape," showing progressive channelization of cell developmental potential. (*b*) A determinative path (colored arrows).

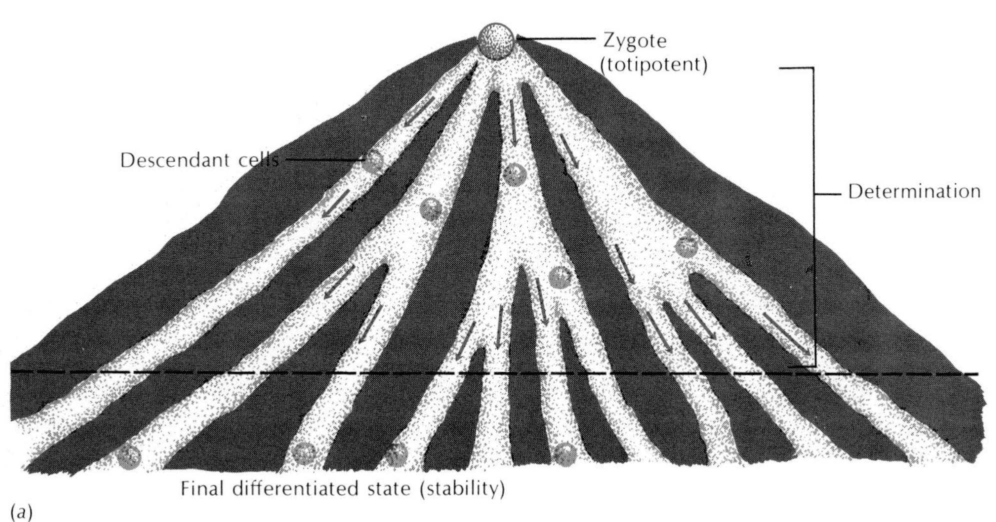

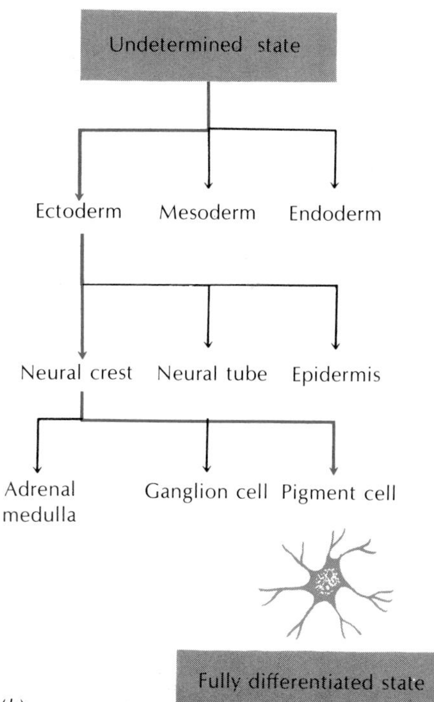

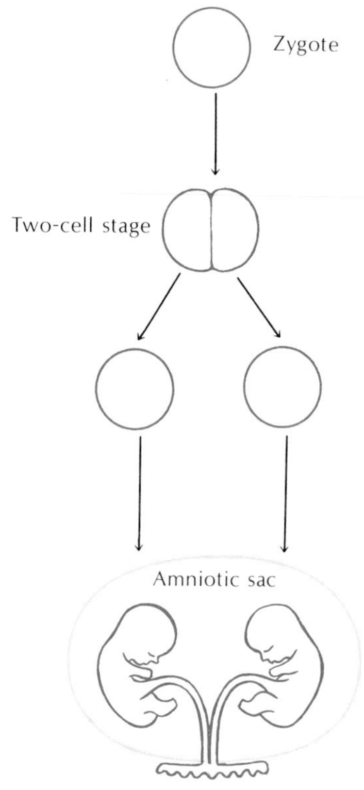

(a)

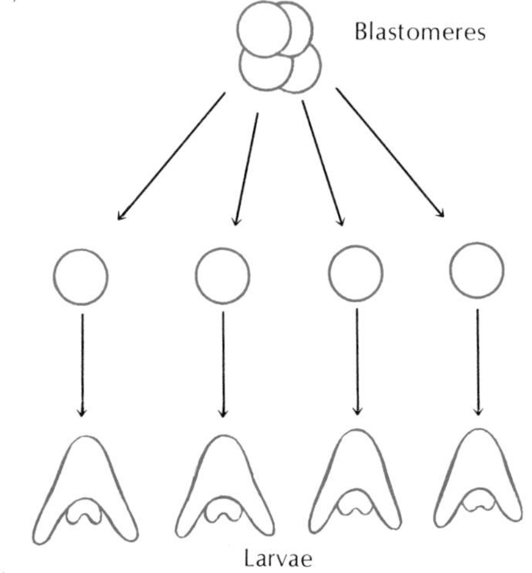

(b)

(c)

Figure 11.22 □ Identical twinning: (*a*) natural; spontaneous separation of blastomeres of human embryo at two-cell stage, producing two babies in one amniotic sac; (*b*) induced: sea urchin embryo placed in Ca^{2+}-free sea water, with resultant separation of blastomeres to produce four identical larvae. (*c*) Siamese twins: incomplete separation of twin embryos produced the two-headed king snake here seen celebrating its sixth-year birthday. (*Zoological Society of San Diego.*)

Twinning When an indeterminately cleaving embryo like that of sea urchin is placed in calcium-free sea water at the two- or four-celled stage, the blastomeres separate. If kept from reaggregating, each proves capable of developing into a normal larva. The natural production of *identical twins* no doubt involves the spontaneous separation of blastomeres. Identical twins share the same heredity, for both come from the same zygote (Figure 11.22). (*Fraternal* twins on the other hand are the products of two different eggs fertilized independently, and thus frequently differ in sex and appearance.) Identical twins tend to be mirror-images: in man, one twin will often be right-handed and the other, left-handed; the hair of one may sprout from the scalp in a clockwise whorl and that of the other, counterclockwise.

Incomplete separation of blastomeres results in *Siamese twins* (structurally conjoined individuals, called "Siamese" after the famous circus pair). If the union is limited to the skin and superficial muscles, the twins may be successfully separated by surgery, but if vital organs are shared in common, as in the two-headed king snake in Figure 11.22c, separation is impossible.*

*Studies on a two-headed human baby helped disprove the "fatigue-poisons" hypothesis of sleep, for one head often slept while the other was wide awake. It was once thought that exercise caused toxic waste products to accumulate in the bloodstream and that these poisons depressed the nervous system to bring about sleep, forcing the body to rest until they could be removed. Were this a valid explanation of sleep, both heads would have slept at the same time (for both would have been equally exposed to such toxins in the bloodstream).

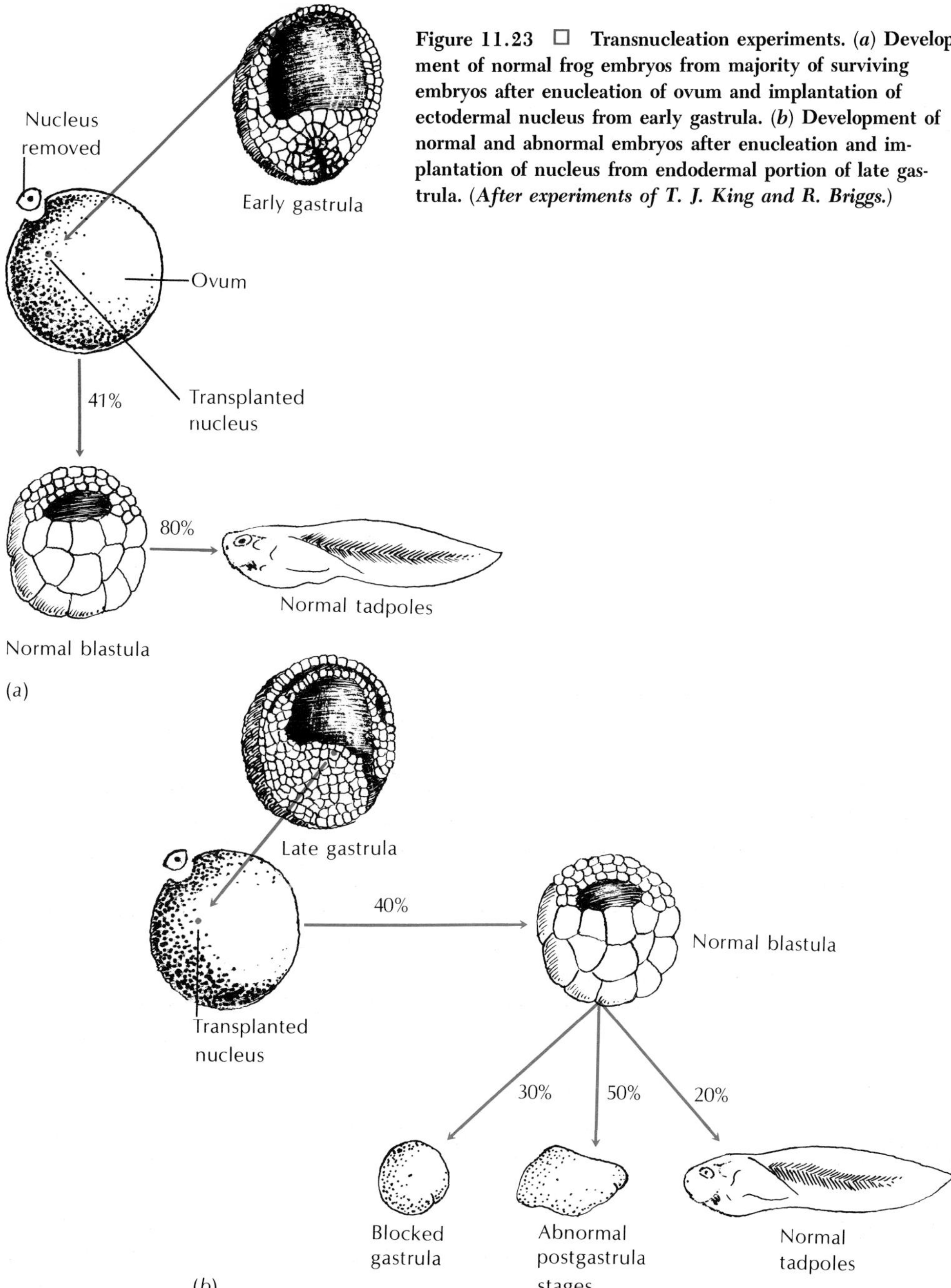

Figure 11.23 □ Transnucleation experiments. (*a*) **Development of normal frog embryos from majority of surviving embryos after enucleation of ovum and implantation of ectodermal nucleus from early gastrula.** (*b*) **Development of normal and abnormal embryos after enucleation and implantation of nucleus from endodermal portion of late gastrula.** (*After experiments of T. J. King and R. Briggs.*)

EXPERIMENTAL TRANSNUCLEATION

The point at which the loss of full developmental plasticity normally becomes irreversible can be identified by nuclear transplantation experiments in which the nucleus of a cell from an older embryo is freed from its own cytoplasm and introduced into the presumably less restrictive environment provided by the cytoplasm of an enucleated egg. Under these conditions a nucleus that has not had its developmental plasticity irreversibly restricted proves capable of initiating the development of a completely normal embryo. On the other hand, nuclei that have undergone some degree of irreversible determination can produce only abnormal embryos under conditions of this kind.

The transnucleation procedure is exacting, requiring first that the egg be enucleated without otherwise being harmed, and next that the transplant nucleus be freed from its own cytoplasm without injury. The technique developed by R. Briggs and T. J. King involves drawing an isolated cell from a donor embryo into a micropipette, the bore of which is slightly less than the cell's diameter. This ruptures the cell membrane without dispersing its contents. The micropipette is then inserted into a previously enucleated egg and its contents forced out just enough to release the intact nucleus. These investigators have reported that when nuclei from the ectoderm of early frog gastrulas are transplanted into egg cytoplasm about 41 percent of these eggs cleave to normal blastulas, and of this number 80 percent continue to develop into normal tadpoles. On the other hand, although endodermal nuclei from late gastrulas can also sustain development to the blastula stage, only 20 percent of these go on to become tadpoles, indicating some irreversible restriction of the plasticity of these transplanted nuclei (Figure 11.23).

Experiments such as these make it possible to determine the time at which a given nucleus becomes incapable of directing the development of a normal embryo. However, conclusions drawn from one species cannot safely be extrapolated to others even closely related. Whereas transplanted endoderm nuclei of the frog *Rana* display total developmental plasticity only up to the late gastrula stage, transplanted nuclei of the African clawed frog (*Xenopus*) have been reported to exhibit full plasticity even when taken from the adult frog. Such reversibility of determination under experimental conditions gives little clue as to factors operating in vivo to bring about or to upset determination.

FATE MAPS The fate of particular blastomeres can be traced through their subsequent divisions and morphogenetic displacements if these cells are marked for future identification. This can be done by permeating cellophane with vital dyes and applying it to the surface of the embryo. The dyes are taken up by the cells with which they come in contact, and tend to remain restricted to these cells and their descendants. Such color coding of single cells or groups of cells makes it possible to define their later contribution to the embryo. This method is to be preferred either to excising certain cells in order to note the defect produced by such excision or to transplanting one part of the embryo to another location, for vital staining does not interfere with normal development.

Through such experiments with vital stains, "fate maps" can be superimposed on

Figure 11.24 □ Fate maps showing early determination of regions of amphibian embryo. (*a*) Vital-staining technique used to work out fate map; each numbered region had been dyed a different color; tissues arising from each region can be traced, despite subsequent cell movements, by persistence of the dyes. (*After Vogt.*) (*b*) Fate map of early gastrula of larval *Amblystoma* (axolotl), dorsal view, worked out by means of vital staining. (*Data after Pasteels.*)

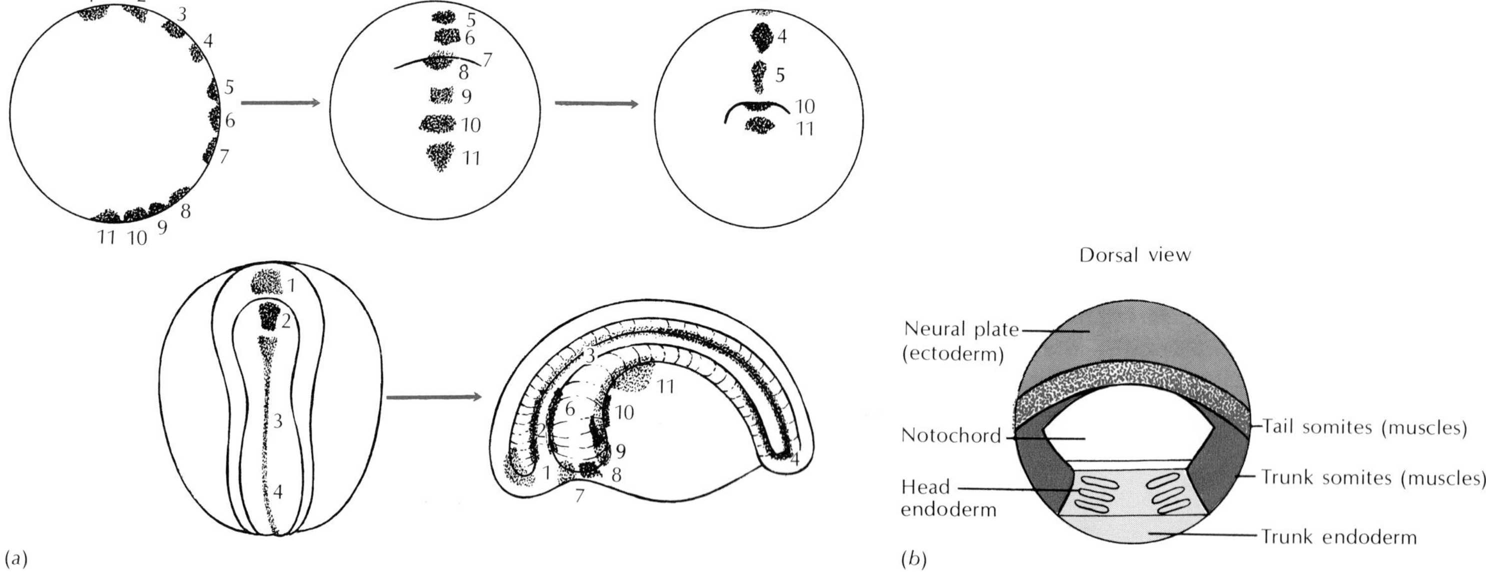

the early embryo, indicating the portion of that embryo which will contribute to particular parts of the adult body (Figure 11.24). These maps show that the final position occupied by descendants of a given blastomere may bear little relationship to the location of the original stained cell. Furthermore, since fate maps are identical for all embryos of the same age of a given species, they show that determination sets in almost at the very onset of development and proceeds in an orderly and predictable manner.

B Gene action in development

Genes are of course the primary determinants of body form and function. An embryo typical of its species must develop according to the genetic "blueprint" contained within the zygote. Actual traits of course are not inherited; that which is inherited is in fact only a DNA code for the synthesis of specific proteins, mainly enzymes catalyzing particular metabolic reactions. Obviously, we have far to go to explain the inheritance of form, but the fact is indisputable that basic structural patterns are determined by heredity. For instance, transplantations carried out between embryos of different species, such as newts and frogs, have shown that although the new tissue environment into which the graft is placed may influence its developmental pathway, the end-product will express the genetic constitution of the donor rather than that of the host. What happens when ectoderm cells are taken from the flank of a frog embryo and transplanted into the mouth region of a salamander embryo? As might be expected, the graft is influenced to develop into teeth instead of skin; however, the teeth produced are those of a frog instead of a salamander! The inescapable evidence of a salamander with a mouthful of frog teeth forces us to conclude that while frog tissues are susceptible to the influence of regulatory factors emanating from salamander tissues, the structures they produce necessarily conform to the genetic code of their own species.

GENETIC CONTROL OF MORPHOGENESIS: TWO EXAMPLES The developmental role of a specific gene can sometimes be defined indirectly in terms of the morphogenetic defects caused by the mutant allele of that gene. In most instances we are still limited to describing the developmental effect of a gene without having any clear idea as to how this effect is produced. Wing shape in *Drosophila* and comb shape in the domestic chicken will be considered as examples of gene interactions in morphogenesis.

Wing morphogenesis in Drosophila The use of X rays to induce mutations in *Drosophila* have allowed a large number of genes involved with normal wing development to be identified; these factors have been named according to the most conspicuous effect of their mutant alleles. A few of the genes involved in wing morphogenesis include *vestigial, dumpy, blistery, xasta, broad, veinlet, net,* and *cubitus interruptus.*

The insect wing first appears as a bud at each side of the thorax. This bud enlarges by cell division, becoming a sac which is finally inflated by the pumping of body fluids from the thoracic cavity into its hollow interior. During the final stages of development the inflated wing contracts, producing the definitive pattern of wing venation. The genes mentioned above act at different times during wing development. Formation of the wing bud requires the action of the normal alleles of *xasta* and *vestigial. Broad* acts during the subsequent period of cell proliferation in the bud, and determines the final breadth of the wing. *Dumpy* operates during the phase of contraction, the mutant allele causing excessive contraction and producing an abnormally short, squared-off wing. *Net* also operates during contraction, its mutant allele causing insufficient contraction. *Veinlet* and *cubitus interruptus* affect the pattern of wing venation, their mutant alleles disturbing this pattern in specific ways.

Additional genes influence development of the posterior pair of wings, which in two-winged flies such as *Drosophila* merely form small balancers (halteres). Various mutant alleles of these genes can cause the halteres to develop into full wings. When this change is brought about through the action of a single gene, it is often inseparable from other developmental effects that cause death. However, full development of the posterior wings can also be brought about through the cumulative action of a number of inoffensive genes, each of which merely produces a tendency toward the transformation of halteres into wings. This type of polygenic inheritance may allow a major developmental change to be brought about without gross harm to the organism.

Comb morphogenesis in chickens Despite the many centuries through which men and chickens have lived in association, the heredity of the chicken is still much more fragmentarily known than that of *Dro-*

Figure 11.25 □ Comb-shape inheritance in domestic chicken. Two pairs of independently assorting genes interact to determine fowl comb shape.

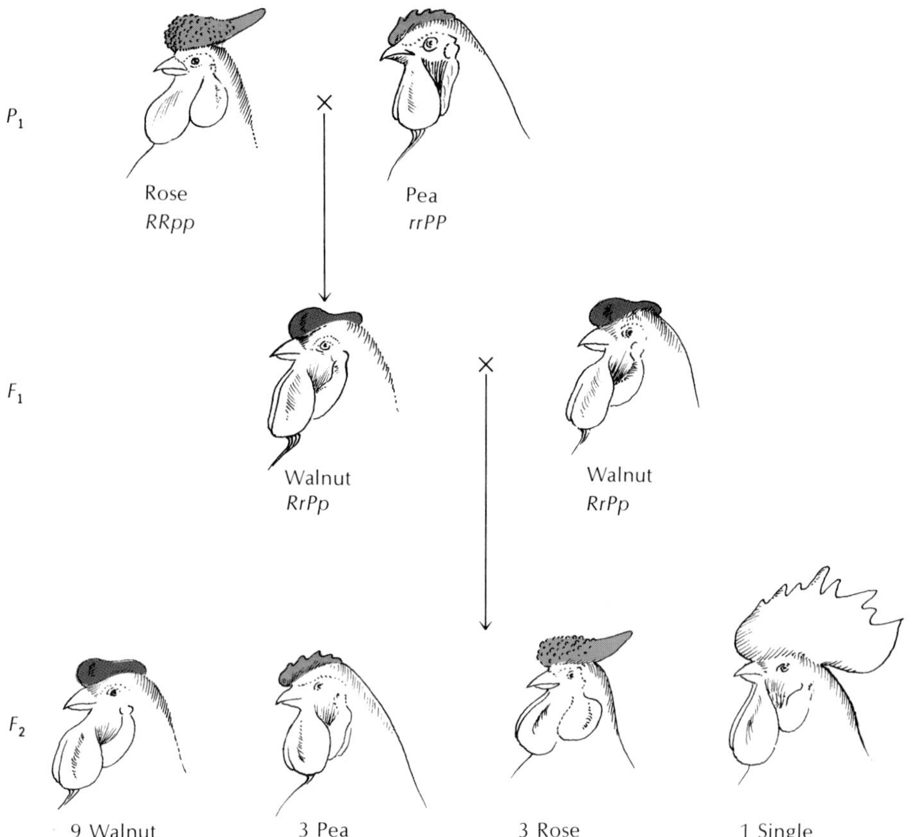

sophila, and only a few genes have been identified of the many that must be involved in the development of the comb. The four major comb shapes found in chickens are known respectively as single, rose, pea, and walnut comb. These four shapes result from the interaction of two independently assorting gene pairs. The allele *R* in the absence of the allele *P*, produces rose comb. The allele *P* in the absence of *R* produces pea comb. Chickens with the genotypes *RRpp* and *Rrpp* are consequently rose-combed, and those with the genotypes *rrPP* and *rrPp* are pea-combed. The mating of a homozygous pea-combed fowl (*rrPP*) with one homozygous for rose comb (*RRpp*) yields progeny all of which have the genotype *RrPp* and are walnut-combed. Walnut comb accordingly results from the interaction of the genes *R* and *P* (Figure 11.25). When two walnut-combed birds are mated their progeny exhibit four different comb types in the 9:3:3:1 ratio of independent assortment with complete dominance: $^9/_{16}$ are walnut-combed (*R_P_*); $^3/_{16}$ rose-combed (*R_pp*); $^3/_{16}$ pea-combed (*rrP_*), and $^1/_{16}$ single-combed (*rrpp*). Since single comb is actually the shape most prevalent among fowl, it is likely that the dominant alleles *R* and *P* are of more recent origin and more restricted distribution than their recessive alleles.

Unfortunately few morphogenetic gene systems can be worked out on the basis of specific abnormalities or phenotypic deviations caused by mutant alleles, for usually such mutations merely cause development to cease at some point, with lethal effects upon the developing organism.

TIMING OF GENE ACTION Experiments in which nuclei of one species are transplanted into enucleated eggs of another species indicate that up to the gastrula stage the pattern of cleavage is cytoplasmically determined and the genes play no role other than serving as templates for the production of new DNA. Only after gastrulation begins do certain genes become metabolically active and begin to produce mRNA. Although the zygote contains the entire genome of the new individual, and although (with few exceptions) all cells receive complete sets of genes and therefore possess the entire genetic potential of the zygote, it is probable that only a proportion of the genes present become metabolically activated in any given tissue.

In our later consideration of how cell metabolism is regulated (see Section 16.1) we shall examine current theories of how genes may be repressed and derepressed. The same models may well apply to the activation and deactivation of genes during development, with two notable differences: (1) genes that will never play a role in the specialized metabolism of a given type of mature tissue may be permanently inactivated at some point during development, rather than being subject to the reversible repression and derepression that seems to characterize metabolic control; (2) genes that have no role to play in maturity may function during development (such genes must be activated at the precise time their action is needed, and when no longer needed may be permanently repressed).

What evidence have we that particular genes are activated during development while others are repressed? Such evidence comes from several different lines of experimentation. As mentioned earlier, experiments with single differentiated plant cells isolated and cultured in vitro have shown that such individual cells still possess the genetic capacity to give rise to all types of specialized plant tissues if their differentiated state is disturbed. Comparable experiments with nuclei taken from the intestinal epithelium of adult clawed frogs and implanted into enucleated eggs show that this mature tissue also has the genetic capacity to produce a complete new organism: apparently no genes are destroyed during the maturation of tissues, but many become inactivated, functioning again only under these unusual circumstances.

A different line of experimentation has focused upon the significance of "puff patterns" observed in the giant chromosomes characteristic of the larvae of two-winged flies. In these larvae the chromosomes of different tissues exhibit characteristic distributions of puffed-up regions known as Balbiani rings. The locations of these puffs on the chromosomes differ from one tissue to another but are the same for all cells in the same tissue (Figure 11.26). The Balbiani rings have been interpreted as regions in which the genes are metabolically active and the DNA is spread out diffusely in such a way as to facilitate mRNA production. It has been found that injection of the molting hormone *ecdysone* causes specific puffs to appear, indicating that this hormone may be responsible for the activation of one or more specific genes in the puffed region. However, the significance of chromosome puff patterns remains in doubt, for when their formation is experimentally inhibited development is still able to proceed normally. This may merely indicate that activated genes can produce mRNA even when the multiple strands of these polynemic chromosomes are not allowed to unravel.

Analysis of the changes that take place in cell metabolism during maturation also support the hypothesis that cells generally retain their full complement of genes, but that certain genes are repressed during development. For example, it has been found that in the young chick embryo all tissues can synthesize vitamin C. Later, this capacity is restricted to a number of internal organs including the stomach and liver. Finally, all organs except the kidney lose the capacity to synthesize vitamin C, and the kidney tissue therefore becomes responsible for the body's entire intrinsic supply of this vitamin throughout postembryonic life. The loss by all other tissues of the capacity to synthesize vitamin C has been found to result from the disappearance of a single enzyme, one catalyzing the final reaction in a sequence leading to vitamin C. Repression of the gene (or genes) responsible for this one enzyme leaves the rest of the reaction pathway intact, for it is also needed for the synthesis of similar compounds.

These and other lines of experimentation make it fairly certain that during development the tissues generally do retain the full gene complement of the zygote, but that through the action of various regulatory factors in each type of tissue only certain genes relevant to adult function remain active while other genes are repressed. By analogy we may think of the organism's genome as equivalent to a map of the entire world carried by a traveler. All information is present for directing the traveler anywhere, and yet he need use only one area of the map to find his way about in any given country. The entire map is there, but only the relevant portions need be consulted. Thus, each cell contains a complete

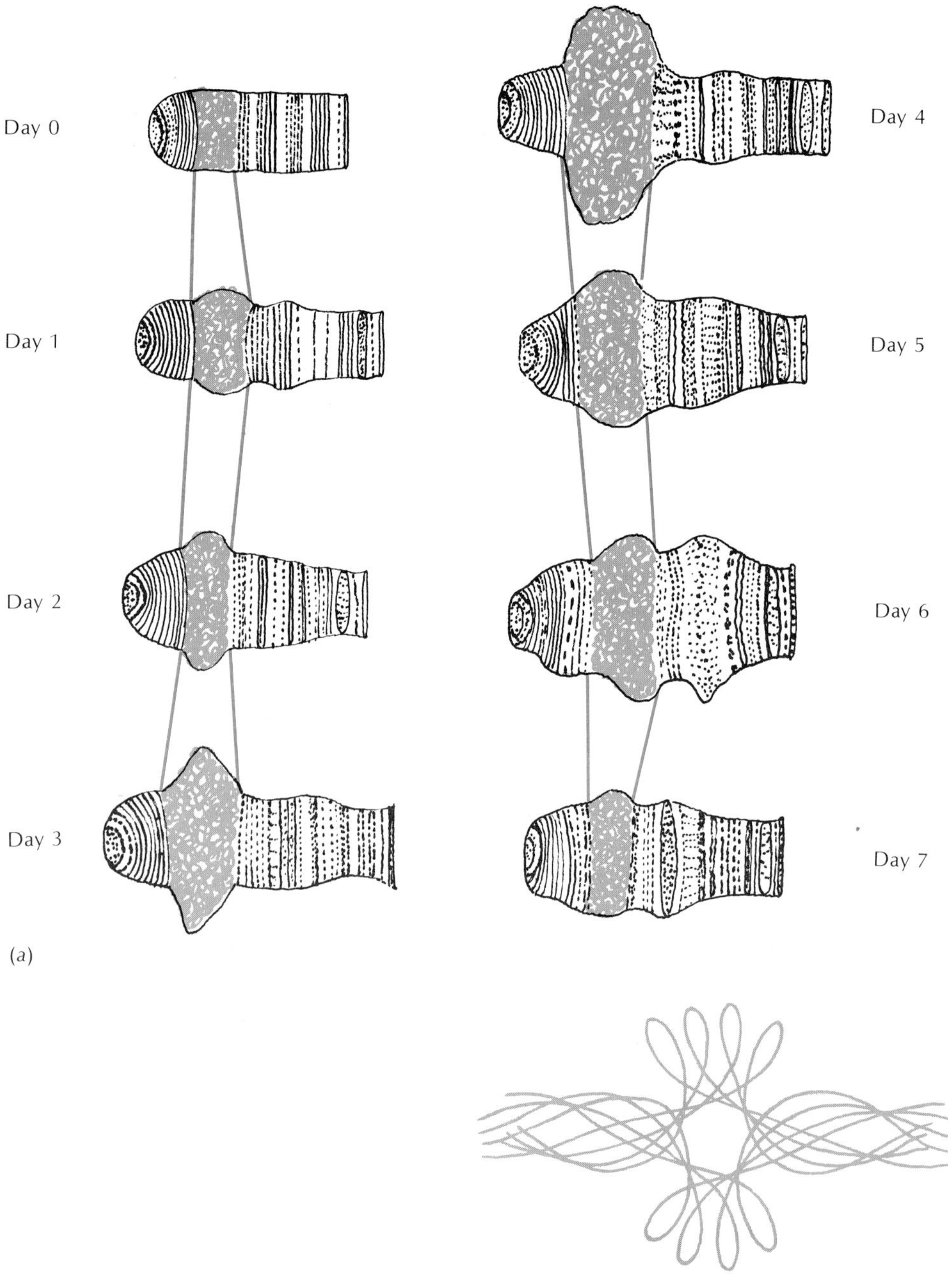

Figure 11.26 □ **Chromosome puffs. (*a*) One week's history of a chromosome puff on giant chromosome of the Brazilian fungus fly (*Rhynchosciara angelae*). Puffs may represent regions in which genes are active in mRNA production. (*Adapted from Breuer and Pavan, courtesy of Springer-Verlag.*) (*b*) Interpretation of arrangement of chromosome fibrils in a puffed region, showing only a few of the several thousand fibrils present in a giant chromosome. (*After Beermann.*)**

"genetic map" for the whole organism, but in any given cell only the pertinent instructions on this map are being "read."

C The role of environment in regulation

COMPETENCE A complex series of gene-environment interactions occurs during the developmental process. These interactions must occur in correct sequence, for those occuring earlier condition the *competence* of tissues with respect to factors operating later. By *competence* we mean the capacity of a tissue to respond to some regulatory factor.

For certain aspects of development there appear to be brief critical periods during which the cell or organism is most responsive to particular regulatory factors present in its environment. If exposure to these factors should be either premature or unduly delayed, competence may be so reduced that an effective interaction cannot take place.

In the following paragraphs, as we examine the effects of certain regulatory factors on the developmental process, one important fact should be borne in mind: the riddle of regulation seems to lie less with the nature of the regulatory agents themselves (for sometimes a bewildering variety of agents can bring about the same effect) than with the responsiveness (competence) of the tissues affected. The reacting cells must be "ready" to respond to the regulatory factor. This critical period is usually quite transitory. For instance, at only one particular time will ectoderm respond to the influence of underlying notochordal tissue by beginning to form a neural tube; the presence of notochord has no demonstrable effect before a certain time, and conversely, should the notochord be removed for the duration of the critical period and then replaced, the competence of the ectoderm is lost and neurulation will not occur.

Furthermore, the same regulatory factor may exert opposite effects on different tissues, and this must be explained in terms of the reactivity of the tissues affected. Amphibian metamorphosis takes place under the influence of thyroid hormone, but when we analyze the responses of specific tissues to this hormone we find that some are totally unaffected, others begin to undergo dissolution, and still others are stimulated to proliferate and form adult structures. Competence, then, is a property of the tissue being regulated; the regulatory agents merely furnish the stimuli that elicit a programmed response.

THE INTRACELLULAR ENVIRONMENT Besides furnishing food required by the embryo until it can assimilate nutrients from the environment, the egg cytoplasm regulates the early stages of development. In the first place, the organization of the egg cytoplasm determines the planes and axes of cleavage, which we have seen establish the fundamental symmetries and polarities of the embryo. In fact, a nucleus need not even be present during cleavage, for enucleated eggs can be activated and will cleave almost normally until the blastula stage. In the second place, cytoplasmic factors established in the ovum may influence gene activity in early stages of determination.

Experimental zygote ligation and section The effects of cytoplasm on the developmental plasticity of nuclei can be shown by experiments in which a zygote is either cut in half, or constricted by means of a loop of human hair (Figure 11.27). When a sea urchin zygote is cut in half bilaterally along a plane passing through the animal and vegetal poles the nucleated half develops into a normal (although small) larva whereas the enucleated half eventually perishes; however, when the zygote is sectioned along a plane at right angles to this one, that is, along the equator between the animal and vegetal poles, the enucleated half dies and the nucleated part develops into an *abnormal* larva. Two kinds of abnormal larvae are recovered: if the nucleus was restricted to the animal hemisphere, the embryo formed consists mainly of ectodermal tissues. If the nucleus was confined to the vegetal hemisphere, the resultant embryo consists mainly of *endo*dermal tissues. In either event, normal development cannot be sustained and the embryo eventually dies. The bilaterally and equatorially sectioned zygotes each have the same amount of cytoplasm, but the qualitative differences from animal to vegetal pole are such that development is regulated differently in the two types of cytoplasm. This difference cannot be ascribed merely to a greater quantity of yolk in the vegetal half, for the sea urchin egg contains very little yolk.

By means of a hair loop, an amphibian egg can be constricted along the midline in such a way that although one half is without a nucleus it is not deprived of all contact with the nucleated portion; as cleavage proceeds a nucleus may cross the cytoplasmic bridge connecting the halves. Two categories of results are obtained with such constricted newt eggs, according to the plane in which the hair loop is applied. (*a*) If the constriction separates future right and left halves of the embryo, twin normal embryos result. The half in which nucleation is delayed will not begin to cleave until a nucleus slips across the intervening bridge, but it then divides at a faster rate that soon allows it to catch up with its twin. (*b*) If the hair loop constricts the zygote midway between the animal and vegetal poles, normal development takes place only in the animal hemisphere. If the zygote nucleus is confined to the vegetal hemisphere, cleavage will be initiated there, but only when a nucleus escapes into the previously uncleaved animal hemisphere does development begin which leads to a normal embryo. The embryo developing from the vegetal hemisphere ceases to develop by the late gastrula stage. The zygote nucleus being in all cases the same, we can conclude that the capacity of this nucleus to produce a normal embryo depends on the quality of the surrounding cytoplasm. The time a nucleus spends in the vegetal hemisphere before escaping into the animal hemisphere is also critical; as late as the 16-cell stage, if a nucleus escapes into the animal hemisphere it can initiate the development of a normal embryo, but only one or two cleavages later this capacity has apparently been lost and irreversible changes have taken place in either the nucleus or the cytoplasm.

Figure 11.27 □ **Experimental zygote section to demonstrate effect of egg cytoplasm on sea-urchin development. Both halves have equal amounts of cytoplasm whether the zygote is (*a*) sectioned vertically (through the animal and vegetal poles) or (*b*, *c*) horizontally (midway between the animal and vegetal poles), but qualitative differences in the cytoplasm results in formation of two types of abnormal larvae in the equatorially sectioned embryos.**

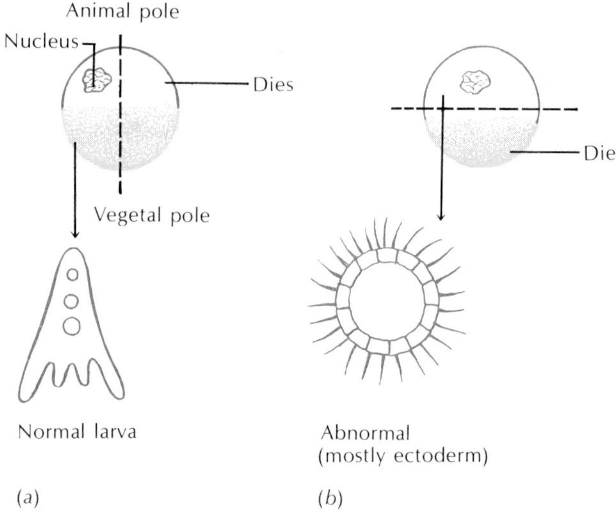

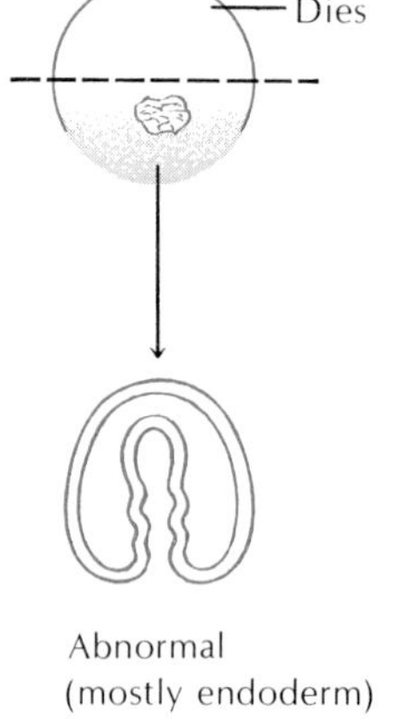

These experiments indicate that egg cytoplasm is organized in a nonrandom manner such that during cleavage the newly formed nuclei become enclosed by cytoplasmic elements having special properties that affect the developmental potential of the nuclear material. Such regionalization of the egg cytoplasm is well shown in amphioxus and tunicate eggs, where there are sharply demarcated cytoplasmic regions that are found to give rise to particular body constituents (Figure 11.28). Destruction of one of these limited regions does not kill the egg but results in an embryo lacking the part for which that area of the egg was responsible. In these species "fate maps" (such as we noted earlier) can be worked out—not only during cleavage but also for the uncleaved egg!

Effects of foreign cytoplasm Intriguing results are obtained when nuclei of one species are required to function in cytoplasm of another species. When enucleated eggs of one species are fertilized by sperm of a related species, the sperm nucleus furnishes the entire chromosomal content of the zygote. Sperm entry activates the egg and cleavage ensues, producing a monoploid "hybrid" embryo in which paternal genes must interact with maternal cytoplasm. When such a hybrid is formed between different genera of sea urchins, the paternal genes are found not to influence the rate of cleavage, this being determined only by the cytoplasm. Characteristics of the paternal species begin to show up at the time of gastrulation, indicating that the genes are becoming influential in development at that time.

Such hybrids produced between different species of amphibians cleave normally

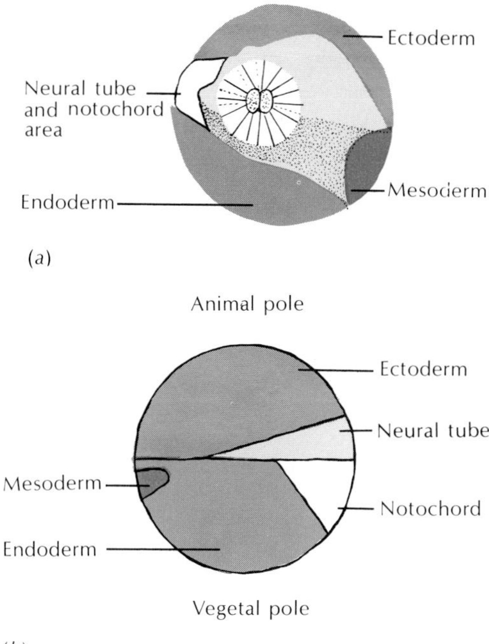

Figure 11.28 □ Cytoplasmic regionalization in (*a*) amphioxus and (*b*) tunicate eggs, showing tissues that will develop from each region.

at first, but about the start of gastrulation nucleocytoplasmic incompatability is expressed by arrestment of development. However, it has been reported that if a nucleus is removed from one of these hybrid embryos before it dies, and is replaced into an enucleated egg of the *paternal* species, surprising results are obtained. This transplantation places the genes of the paternal species back into their appropriate cytoplasmic environment, where it might be assumed that they would initiate normal development. However, this is not the case. When sperm of the frog *Rana pipiens* have fertilized enucleated eggs of *R. sylvatica,* so that *pipiens* nuclei are required to reproduce several times in foreign cytoplasm before being transplanted into enucleated *pipiens* eggs, it is found that the period spent in the *sylvatica* cytoplasm has impaired their capacity to develop normally. The longer the period spent in foreign cytoplasm before transplantation, the more gross is the impairment. This has been tentatively explained in terms of massive chromosomal replication errors brought about by incorporating precoded DNA fragments already built up in the egg cytoplasm. Although this hypothesis needs further testing, it is true that the egg cytoplasm must contain the precursors for building some 2,000 to 25,000 sets of chromosomes. We still do not know how much (if any), of these precursors exist as precoded nucleotide sequences built up during maturation of the egg. Certainly such precoding would be adaptive in conserving the energy resources of the embryo, which would be more heavily drained were it necessary to construct new chromosomes by incorporating nucleotides one at a time. If precoded strands were present in the egg cytoplasm, they might well be incorporated on the partially homologous chromosomes of related species, and this would account for the numerous replication errors that seem to take place. However, the existence of such precoded DNA in egg cytoplasm has yet to be demonstrated.

THE TISSUE MICROENVIRONMENT The immediate environment of a cell during development contains other cells of the same type as well as those which will differentiate along other lines. The interactions among these cells that lie in intimate communication with one another are profoundly significant in regulation of development.

The aggregate effect Cytodifferentiation is a *population* phenomenon: isolated cells will not differentiate and in fact an irreducible minimum of cells of the same type must be present before differentiation will proceed. This aggregate effect can be demonstrated experimentally by swirling dissociated plant cells in a rotating flask containing liquid nutrient medium. Swirling prevents the cells from settling to the bottom but still allows cells with adhesive tendencies to clump together. Only when the clumps reach a certain size will cytodifferentiation set in. In fact, when this is done with carrot cells a number of clumps differentiate into embryolike structures that upon further culture on solid medium actually develop into mature carrot plants!

Cultured animal cells must also occur at a certain minimum density before they can begin to differentiate. The tendency of cells in tissue culture to spread out may account for their loss of apparent differentiation. This may be due to the fact that isolated animal cells are remarkably "leaky," that is, they are unable to retain needed metabolites for further use. When cultured sparsely, cells actually capable of synthesizing particular amino acids or vitamins must instead have these added to the culture medium, for these materials escape from the cells in which they are produced and are dissipated throughout the milieu. However, when the same cells are densely grouped, the composition of the intercellular milieu comes into equilibrium with the cytoplasm so that substances escaping from the cells are easily reabsorbed.

Induction: the effect of cells of unlike type The morphogenetic movements of embryonic cells bring them into contact with cells of different origin. The interaction of these cells, usually reciprocal, is termed *induction* and is one of the most powerful of regulatory forces. In *synergistic* induction, each tissue makes possible the further development of the other.

During induction regulatory agents known as *evocators* (or organizers) are thought to pass from one type of cell to the other, bringing about cytodifferentiation and morphogenetic interactions. During the time these agents are being given off, the tissues of their origin are called *inductors*. In most cases, induction is a reciprocal process, that is to say, two or more inductors exert regulatory effects upon one another.

The development of the mammalian kidney depends on such a synergistic interaction between two tissues of different origin. A portion of the mesomere can develop into the outer (cortical) portion of the kidney when another tissue is present that grows out from the sides of the embryonic cloacal region. When these budlike outgrowths reach the region in which the kidneys are to develop, they begin to branch to form the kidney duct system, while the mesomeric cells differentiate into the cortical tissues. If one of the paired buds is removed surgically, no kidney will develop on that side. Conversely, if the cells that are to become cortical tissue are removed, the bud on that side produces no duct system and again no kidney is formed.

Synergistic induction between epithelial and mesenchyme cells in developing salivary glands has been studied in organ culture. When either tissue is cultured singly, the organized clusters of epithelial cells (acini) characteristic of salivary gland structure do

Figure 11.29 □ **Inductive interaction between salivary epithelium and mesenchyme in organ culture. (*a*) Movement of protein molecules across filter from mesenchyme toward epithelium is traced by use of the amino acid proline tagged with tritium ($^3H^*$), of which black dots record the radioactive emissions. (*b*) Collagen fibers forming between cultured mesenchyme and epithelium, marking development of basement membrane; these fibers, visible by electron microscopy, represent crystalline aggregations of the radiolabeled tropocollagen molecules in (*a*). (The large black dot is merely a size marker.) Mesenchyme cultured alone does not secrete tropocollagen, nor will salivary epithelium cultured alone form acinar clusters. (*Courtesy of F. Kallman and C. Grobstein.*)**

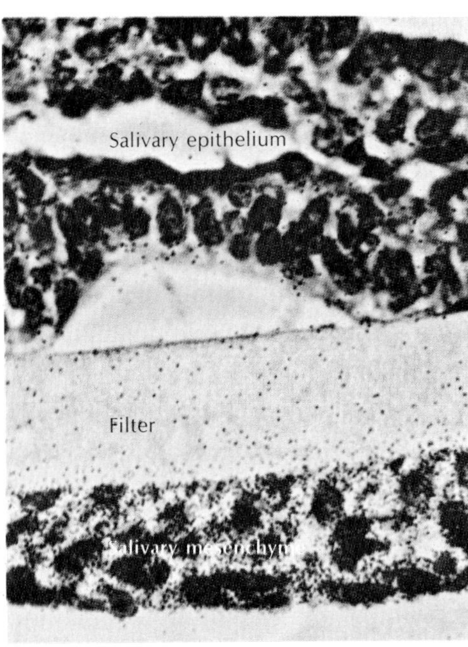

(*a*)

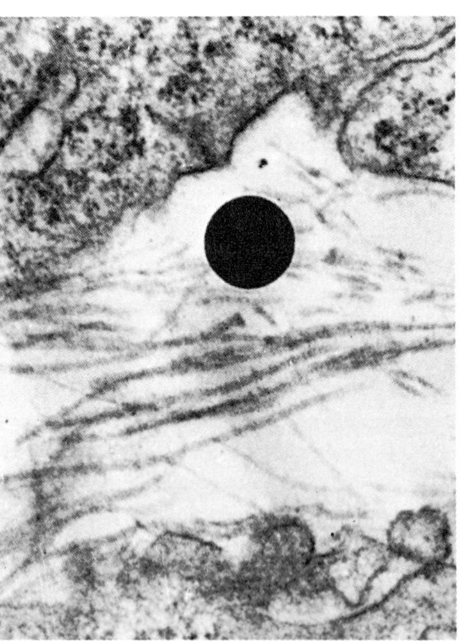
(*b*)

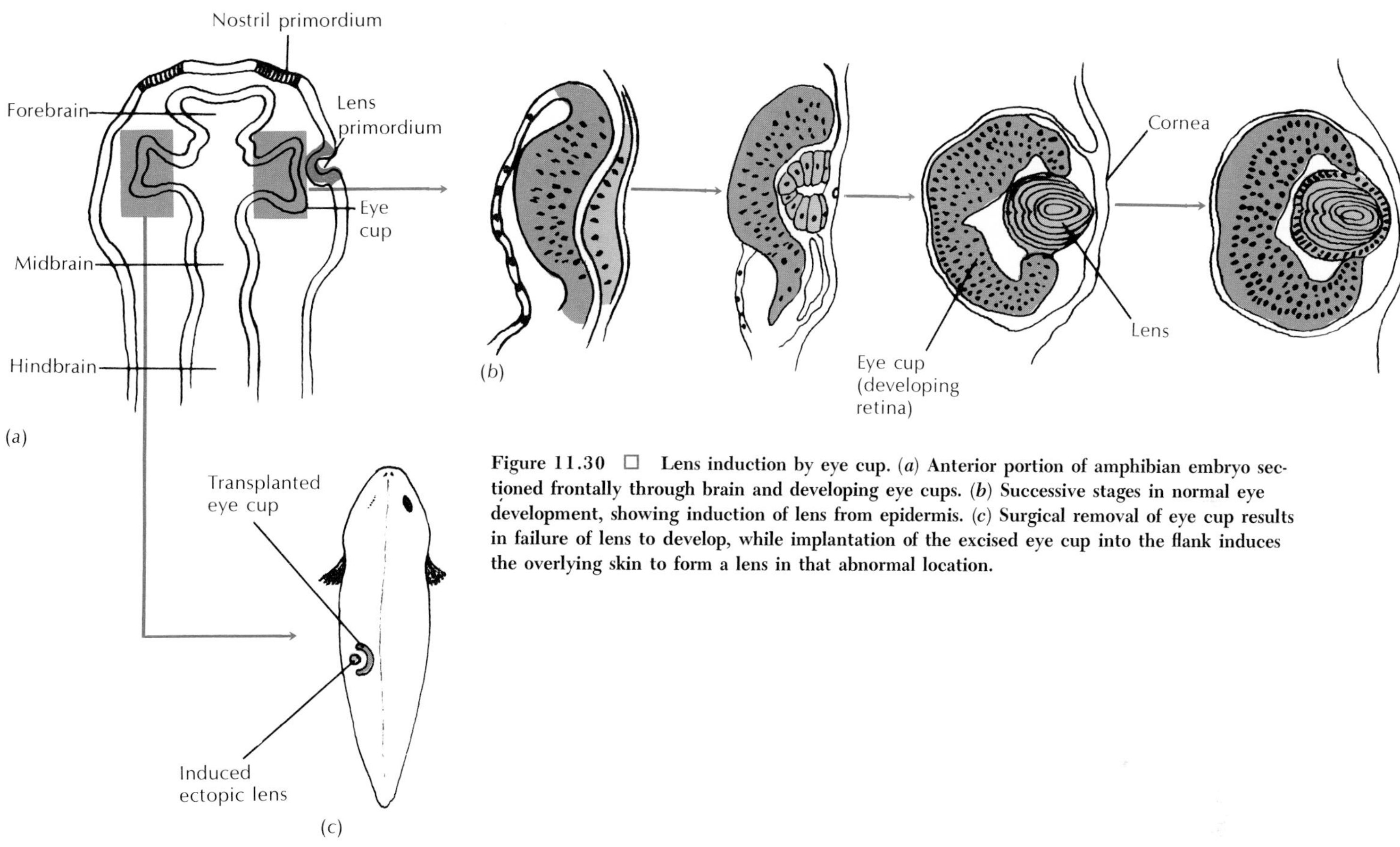

Figure 11.30 □ Lens induction by eye cup. (*a*) **Anterior portion of amphibian embryo sectioned frontally through brain and developing eye cups.** (*b*) **Successive stages in normal eye development, showing induction of lens from epidermis.** (*c*) **Surgical removal of eye cup results in failure of lens to develop, while implantation of the excised eye cup into the flank induces the overlying skin to form a lens in that abnormal location.**

not develop. But when these tissues are cultured together, acini are formed. It is thought that the epithelial cells stimulate the nearby mesenchyme to secrete molecules of a protein, tropocollagen, which organize spontaneously into collagen fibers forming the basement membranes to which the epithelial cells are anchored to form the acini (Figure 11.29). This inductive interaction of salivary epithelium and mesenchyme will operate across a gap of up to 20 μm and even through a filter that excludes the passage of cells.

The inductive interaction of brain tissue and epidermis is seen in the formation of the eye in the amphibian embryo. The vertebrate eye originates as an outgrowth from the side of the brain. As this outgrowth approaches the surface of the body, it expands and then invaginates to form a double-walled eye cup. The ectoderm immediately overlying the eye cup is then induced to form the lens (Figure 11.30). This inductive system can also operate if the eye cup is transplanted to some other part of the body. Even in an abnormal location, the eye cup can induce the overlying ectoderm to form a lens and the surrounding connective tissues to contribute to the formation of the eyeball.

THE SYSTEMIC MACROENVIRONMENT Inductive substances promote local developmental effects, but the overall synchronization of development at the level of the whole organism depends on factors such as hormones that can be disseminated throughout the entire body. A number of hormones exert effects on development, but their mode of action generally remains obscure. We have already cited the requirement of thyroid hormone for amphibian metamorphosis. Vertebrate somatic growth in general is promoted by thyroid hormone, and skeletal growth in particular by the pituitary growth hormone, somatotrophin. Development of secondary sexual characteristics is promoted by male and female sex hormones produced by the gonads.

There may be no fundamental difference between the action of hormones on developing cells and the effect of evocators during induction, except that because of their widespread distribution hormones are capable of affecting simultaneously all tissues competent to be affected. However, while both the nature and mode of action of evocators remains in doubt (some may be hormonelike chemicals but it is probable that many are not), we now have evidence that certain hormones act more or less directly to derepress specific genes. The following evidence has come from studies on mature organisms rather than upon embryos, but the regulatory effects observed here may well also operate during embryonic development.

When a labeled hormone is injected into an animal from which the gland producing that hormone has been removed, the uptake of the hormone can be traced by its radioactivity. In this manner it has been found that certain hormones, including estrogen and the adrenocortical factor aldosterone, concentrate in the nucleus. In addition to this suggestive fact, injection of any of a number of hormones (including estrogen, androgen, aldosterone, somatotrophin, ACTH, thyroxine, and insulin) is shortly followed by dramatic increases in protein and RNA synthesis in some or all tissues. For instance, administration of estrogen to a castrated female mammal elicits as much as a 300 percent increase in protein synthesis within the lining of the uterus. Similarly, estrogen injected into cocks or castrated hens causes their liver tissue to commence synthesis of specific egg yolk proteins normally produced only by egg-laying hens.

How can we tell whether or not the increase in RNA and protein synthesis that follows hormone injection is due to the activation of a gene? To clarify this point, the antibiotic actinomycin-D may be administered in advance of the hormone injection. Actinomycin binds to DNA and blocks subsequent synthesis of mRNA. DNA-dependent protein synthesis will then cease as soon as the available mRNA is exhausted. When estrogen is injected into a mammal previously treated with this antibiotic, the expected increase in uterine protein synthesis does not occur. This lends strong support to the hypothesis that estrogen, at least, activates particular genes in those tissues competent to be affected.

The hormonal synchronization of developmental processes (especially sexual maturation) with changes in external conditions (such as seasonal changes) is under the control of the nervous system. In insects and vertebrates particularly, the nervous and endocrine systems are so integrated that development is not only synchronized throughout the organism, but is also brought into phase with relevant environmental conditions.

THE ABIOTIC ENVIRONMENT Temperature, light, and various nutritional factors in the external environment play important roles in regulating development. They may act directly upon the embryo or in later life by way of the sense organs and neuroendocrine control mechanisms. Ova of the rockweed, *Fucus* (see Figure 5.23a), are initially unpolarized, but become polarized before the first cleavage. At the first cleavage the *Fucus* zygote divides into two cells, one of which will give rise to the holdfast (basal attachment structure) whereas the other is the progenitor of the thallus (blades and stipes). The plane of the first cleavage occurs at right angles to a protuberance arising at one end of the zygote that marks the location of the future holdfast cell. The location of this protuberance can be determined by any of several physicochemical factors, including temperature, pH, CO_2 concentration, and light. The protuberance may arise on the shaded side of the zygote, on its warmer side, on the more acid side, or on the side exposed to higher CO_2 concentration. When *Fucus* zygotes are clustered, the side of each zygote which is nearer the others gives rise to the holdfast cell. Thus, the direction of future growth of the *Fucus* plant can be oriented with respect to any one of several environmental factors.

Temperature affects development both by influencing the rate of metabolism and by modifying the expression of certain temperature-sensitive genes or enzymes. The gene *tetraptera* in *Drosophila* is one of those that cause the balancers to develop into full wings. This gene has a relatively low penetrance (*penetrance* is the extent to which genotype and phenotype coincide), and its penetrance is influenced by the mean temperature at which development takes place. At 25°C its penetrance is 35 percent (meaning that 35 percent of the flies with the *tetraptera* genotype actually develop two full sets of wings), but at 17°C its penetrance drops to 17 percent.

Another example of the effect of temperature on phenotype is the development of Himalayan pigmentation in the rabbit (a white coat except for dark paws, nose, and ear tips). The enzyme produced by the Himalayan allele is needed for the synthesis of the dark pigment melanin. This enzyme is inactivated at the higher body temperatures of the trunk, but at the usually lower temperatures of the extremities it can function normally. If a Himalayan rabbit is wrapped in ice while the fur is growing, it will produce dark fur over the entire body. Conversely, artificial warming of the extremities results in a completely white rabbit.

Light affects development in both plants and animals, with the duration, intensity, and direction of illumination all having their effect. We are familiar with the phototropic growth response of the shoot. Light is also required for the normal formation of chloroplasts and synthesis of chlorophyll. Length of daylight, acting by way of the eyes and brain, affects such processes as dormancy, metamorphosis, and sexual maturation in insects and vertebrates. In man, interestingly enough, light aids normal skeletal development, for ultraviolet irradiation transforms human skin oils into vitamin D, which is needed for the absorption and utilization of calcium phosphate [$Ca_3(PO_4)_2$] in the bones. Vitamin D deficiency results in the deformations characteristic of rickets.

Nutritional factors are of course essential for development after the food stores of the egg have been exhausted. In addition to this general requirement, specific nutritional states may alter development by affecting particular genes. For example, in *Drosophila* an allele that suppresses development of the antenna only exerts its effect if the diet is poor in the vitamin riboflavin.

Toxic chemicals may severely disturb normal development if exposure takes place during a critical period. The importance of the sensitivity of the affected part is well seen in the case of infection with the German measles (rubella) virus. According to the time at which a pregnant woman contracts this disease, her baby may be born blind, deaf, or mentally retarded. The precise effect depends on the relative sensitivity of various organs at the time of exposure to the virus. During 1960 a number of nearly limbless infants were born to women treated with the sedative thalidomide during pregnancy. This drug suppressed development of the long bones of the arms and legs so that hands and feet seemed to sprout directly from the shoulders and hips. In larger doses the drug completely suppressed limb development.

CONSPECIFIC INFLUENCES Organisms of a given species are often capable of regulating the development of other individuals of the same species. We may note especially that the development of normal social behavior in birds and mammals is dependent upon interactions between parents and progeny or within peer groups at critical periods during maturation. There is also evidence that the visual and acoustic cues provided by a courting male may induce sexual maturation in female ring doves and other birds.

Pheromonal regulation of development Sexual maturation in the water mold *Achyla* is pheromonally induced (the term *pheromone* is used here to denote any regulatory chemical secreted by organisms of a species that affects the physiology as well as the behavior of conspecifics). *Achyla* forms a mycelium of branching hyphae from which spore-producing or gamete-producing bodies arise. A single mycelium may produce either male or female sexual structures, but not both. When male and female mycelia are cultured together, as the filaments grow toward one another the male hyphae begin to produce large numbers of branching, gnarled shoots. This apparently is in response to a pheromone secreted by maturing female hyphae. As these distinctive male shoots approach the female hypha, they secrete the first male pheromone. If the female hypha is sufficiently mature, it responds to the male pheromone by elaborating a large sac on the side nearest the male shoots. The tissues of this sac, the presumptive oogonium, now release a second female pheromone, which induces the male shoots to direct their growth toward the oogonium and to spread out over its surface. A second male pheromone is then released, which induces the oogonium to produce female gametes. Finally, perhaps under the influence of a third female pheromone, the male shoots put forth tubules that penetrate the oogonium and permit fertilizing nuclei to pass from the male shoots and enter the female gametes (Figure 11.31).

Figure 11.31 □ **Pheromonal induction of reproductive differentiation in the water mold *Achyla:* (*a*) female filaments (shown in color throughout) secrete ♀ pheromone 1; (*b*) male plant (shown in black throughout) puts forth antheridial filaments and begins to secrete ♂ pheromone 1; (*c*) female plant responds by producing oogonial initiates and ♀ pheromone 2; (*d*) male antheridial hyphae are attracted toward the female and spread out over the oogonia on contact, producing ♂ pheromone 2; (*e*) ♂ pheromone 2 causes female cytoplasm to congeal about egg nuclei, forming mature gametes, and ♀ pheromone 3 may cause antheridial filaments to put forth germ tubes and penetrate ♀ gametes (*f*).**

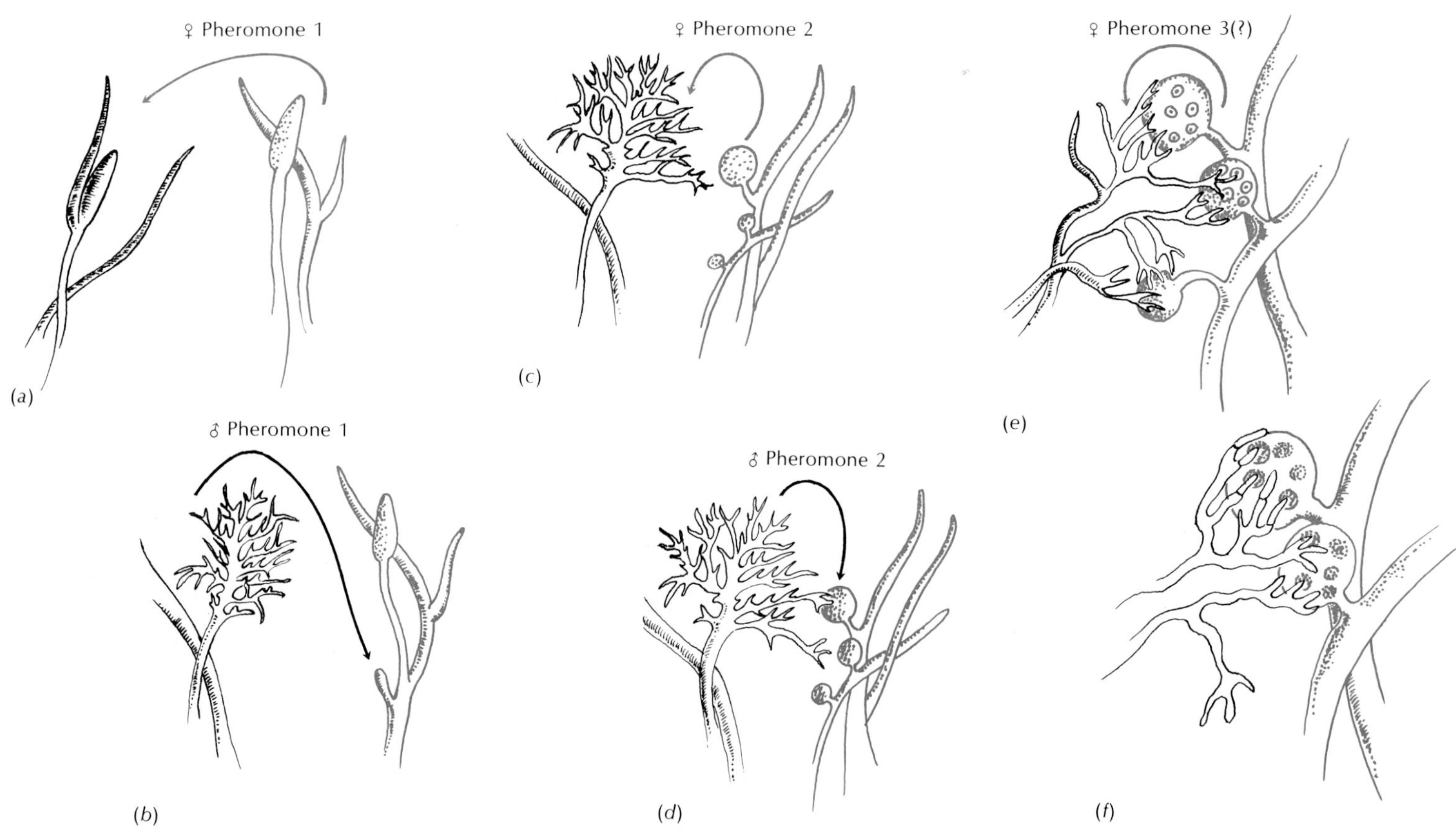

Morphogenesis itself can be profoundly influenced by conspecific factors. We have seen that the sexually indifferent larvae of the marine worm *Bonellia* differentiate into females when maturing in the absence of mature female *Bonellia,* but in the presence of mature females develop instead into minute, degenerate males nutritionally dependent upon the female and inhabiting her body (see Figure 7.20).

Maternal influences Conditions in the ovary or uterus quite often influence the maturation of offspring. A clear-cut example of maternal influence is the determination of direction of coiling of the shell in snails of the genus *Lymnaea.* The tendency to twist to the left or to the right is determined by a single pair of alleles in the genotype of the *mother.* The direction of coiling of the future shell is in fact determined even while the egg is within the ovary. At this time a group of six follicle cells arrange themselves asymmetrically on the surface of the maturing ovum. Two alternative patterns of distribution of these follicle cells may be found, which are mirror images of one another. One configuration predisposes the embryo to coil its shell dextrally, the other to coil the shell sinistrally. Since it is the mother's genotype that determines how the follicle cells will be arranged on the surface of the ovum, the maternal genes accordingly dictate shell coiling in the embryo.

HETEROSPECIFIC INFLUENCES In Chapter 6 we learned that the course of organic evolution is profoundly influenced by interactions among various species that form part of the same community. The development of some specific body form, behavior, or physiological capability, is adaptive only insofar as this attribute contributes positively to the individual's capacity to survive in its biotic milieu.

As well as their selective effect on the evolution of form and function, individuals of one species sometimes exert particular regulatory effects on the development of organisms of other species. An example of such heterospecific induction is seen in the morphogenesis of the rotifer *Brachionus.* This species bears prominent posteriorly directed spines on each side of the carapace. When *Brachionus* develops in the presence of a certain predatory rotifer (*Asplanchna*) its body form is altered, particularly with respect to the size and orientation of the lateral spines. These spines grow larger, and become movable so that they can be directed to the side as well as backwards. This makes it impossible for the larger *Asplanchna* to swallow *Brachionus.* How does the predator exert this effect on the development of *Brachionus?* We can only surmise that it releases some substance into the water, perhaps a by-product of its own metabolism, and that the tissues of *Brachionus* have an evolved sensitivity to this material, so that it has come to serve as an evocator, inducing this interesting protective change. This change is not due to a genetic mutation, for the next generation of *Brachionus* reverts to normal if *Asplanchna* is no longer present.

Drastic morphogenetic effects are exerted on the adult form of the parasitic wasp *Trichogramma* by factors in the host environment within which the larval life is spent. A larva that parasitizes a moth or butterfly develops into an adult which is winged and has plumose antennae. On the other hand, if larval life is spent within the body of an alder fly, the adult wasp is wingless and has club-shaped antennae! These modifications of body form are attributed to differences in the nutritional environments provided by the two types of host.

In summary, we are only now beginning to appreciate the profound significance of environmental factors in regulation of development. That successful expression of the genotype depends on the availability of adequate nutrients is axiomatic. But in addition to nutrients, the developmental environment, from the egg cytoplasm to the entire biotic community, must furnish a series of cues that determine how the genome will be expressed. Even such specific characteristics as the number of cells that develop in the mammalian brain may be markedly influenced by the overall amount of stimulation to which the individual is subjected during maturation. Rats raised in stimulus-poor environments have been reported to possess less than half the number of cells found in the cerebral cortex of rats reared in stimulus-enriched environments. It is interesting to speculate as to how much of human intelligence is due strictly to heredity, and how much may depend upon a developmental hypertrophy stemming from stimulation during ontogeny, particularly social stimulation resulting from association with other human beings and their cultural products. This does not imply that the environment can elicit a type or degree of development which genetic factors disallow, but that the full genetic potential may not be realized in the absence of eliciting environmental factors. Therefore, although development and differentiation must follow the pattern encoded within the genetic material inherited by the zygote, the course of development is determined by a complex series of interactions, including those shown on the right:

Gene ⟷ gene
Gene ⟷ cytoplasm
Cell ⟷ physicochemical milieu
Cell ⟷ cell
Organism ⟷ habitat
Organism ⟷ organism

11.5 □ CYTODIFFERENTIATION: THE DEVELOPMENT OF SPECIALIZED TISSUES

After the major body pattern has been established, cells begin to differentiate into various specialized types adapted for carrying out particular functions in the mature plant or animal body. Cytodifferentiation is the final manifestation of the process of determination. At this point the cell usually becomes incapable of further growth and division, and begins to perform the specific task toward which it has become both morphologically and metabolically specialized.

Certain kinds of mature cells are not rigidly differentiated, but remain capable of undergoing *modulations,* reversible changes in form and function resulting from changes in the cellular environment. Modulation reflects a cell's capacity to respond flexibly to changing circumstances. Whereas differentiations are stabilized changes that long survive the duration of the initiating factors, modulations are transitory changes that last only as long as the eliciting conditions persist.

The presence of excess lipids in the bloodstream brings about the modulation of fibroblasts, cells which at other times secrete connective fibers, into adipose cells that accumulate and store this fat. The presence of antigens (proteins foreign to the body) triggers the modulation of lymphocytes into antibody-secreting plasma cells. The modulation of skeletal muscle fibers in response to exercise consists of the enlargement of individual fibers due to increased synthesis of contractile proteins.

Changes in the quantity of vitamin A cause modulations in both the morphology and physiological performance of mammalian epidermal cells. Usually these form a stratified layer several cells thick, and become horny by accumulating keratin. Vitamin A suppresses keratin synthesis. When this vitamin is deficient, too much keratin is formed and the skin and even cornea of the eye become excessively horny. But when a very great excess of the vitamin is given experimentally, the epidermal cells may grow long and columnar, sprout cilia, and begin to secrete mucus, as though they were epithelial cells lining the windpipe! Since this effect is reversed when the excess vitamin is used up, it is considered a modulation rather than a differentiation.

The mature tissues of plants and animals can be grouped into several major types. Analogous types are often found in higher plants and in animals, for similar functions must be fulfilled in both groups. Human tissues derived from each of the primary germ layers are shown in Figure 11.32. The major tissue types fall into the following two categories:

1 *Somatic tissues* (concerned primarily with the maintenance of the individual): epithelium; muscle tissue (animals only); mechanical (supportive and connective) tissue; parenchyma (mainly plants); vascular tissue; nervous tissue (animals only).

2 *Germinal cells* (potential gametes).

We shall now consider the major characteristics of each of these two important kinds of cells.

A Somatic tissues

Somatic tissues are primarily concerned with the survival of the individual organism. They form the framework of the body and are responsible for its protection, movement, nutrition, and irritability. In accordance with this spectrum of functions, somatic cells constitute a number of diverse structural types.

EPITHELIUM Epithelial cells commonly form sheets which cover body surfaces and line body cavities. When massed, they frequently form hollow acini or tubules. They consistently tend to expose one free surface that may front upon the external environment or upon the cavity of a hollow

Figure 11.32 □ Tissue derivatives of primary germ layers in man.

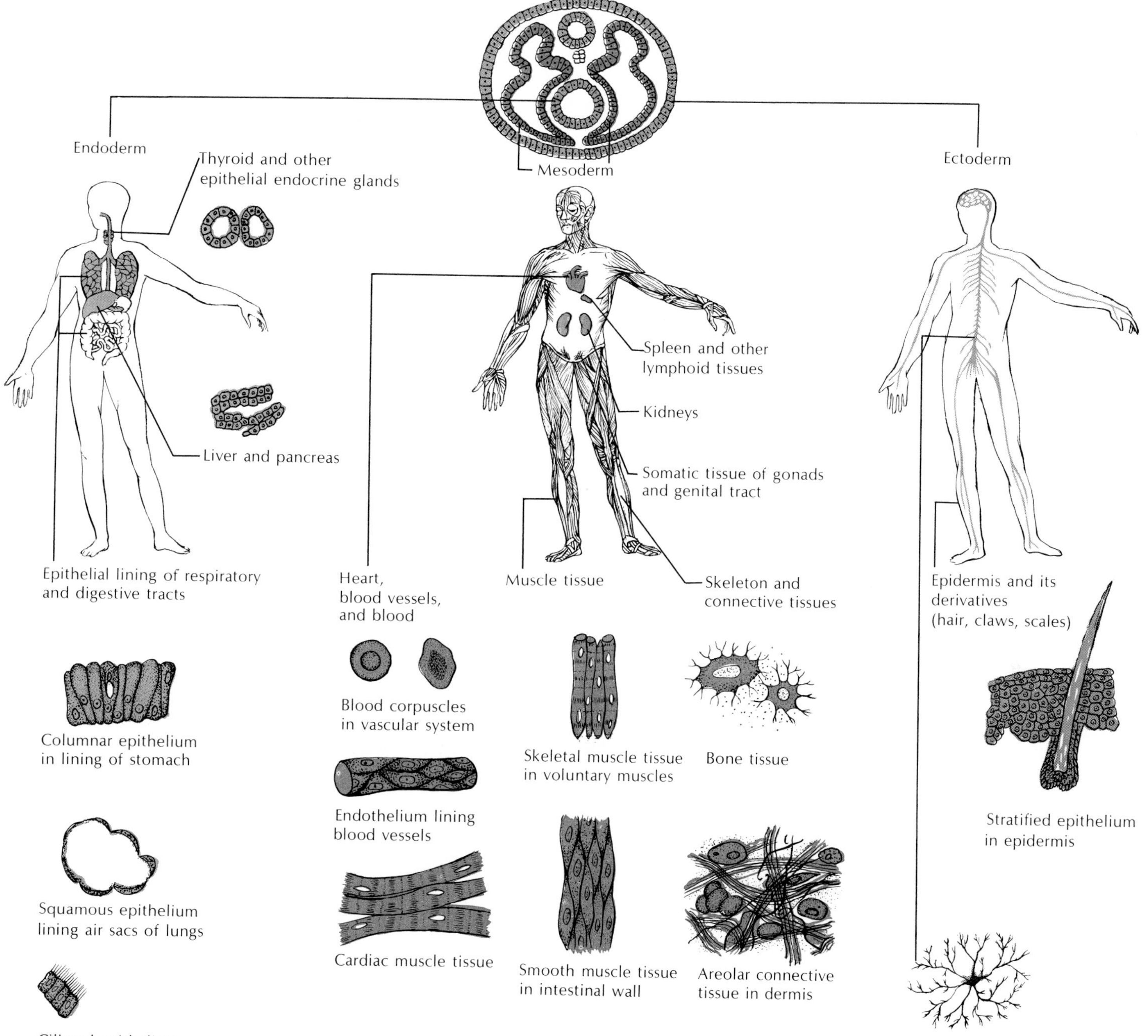
Endoderm
Thyroid and other
epithelial endocrine glands
Mesoderm
Ectoderm
Liver and pancreas
Epithelial lining of respiratory
and digestive tracts
Spleen and other
lymphoid tissues
Kidneys
Somatic tissue of gonads
and genital tract
Heart,
blood vessels,
and blood
Muscle tissue
Skeleton and
connective tissues
Epidermis and its
derivatives
(hair, claws, scales)
Columnar epithelium
in lining of stomach
Squamous epithelium
lining air sacs of lungs
Ciliated epithelium
lining bronchial tract
Blood corpuscles
in vascular system
Endothelium lining
blood vessels
Cardiac muscle tissue
Skeletal muscle tissue
in voluntary muscles
Bone tissue
Smooth muscle tissue
in intestinal wall
Areolar connective
tissue in dermis
Stratified epithelium
in epidermis
Nervous tissue

organ, duct, or tubule (Figure 11.33). This tendency predisposes them to certain functions such as secretion, absorption, and detection of stimuli. Some receptors do appear to be modified epithelial cells.

The end of an epithelial cell opposite its free surface is anchored to a basement membrane, while other surfaces may bear desmosomes that strengthen the attachment between adjacent epithelial cells. The free surface is often specially modified. Epithelial sensory cells and those specialized for absorption of materials from the milieu often have their ends elaborated into numerous fingerlike projections or microvilli, visible to the electron microscope (see Figures 13.24c and 14.8). These greatly increase the surface area of the exposed end. Animal epithelium may be ciliated. When located exteriorly, ciliated epithelium permits the animal to swim or glide by ciliary action. Ciliated epithelium also lines internal tracts such as the nasal passages, trachea, and oviducts, where the cilia serve to move materials along the tracts.

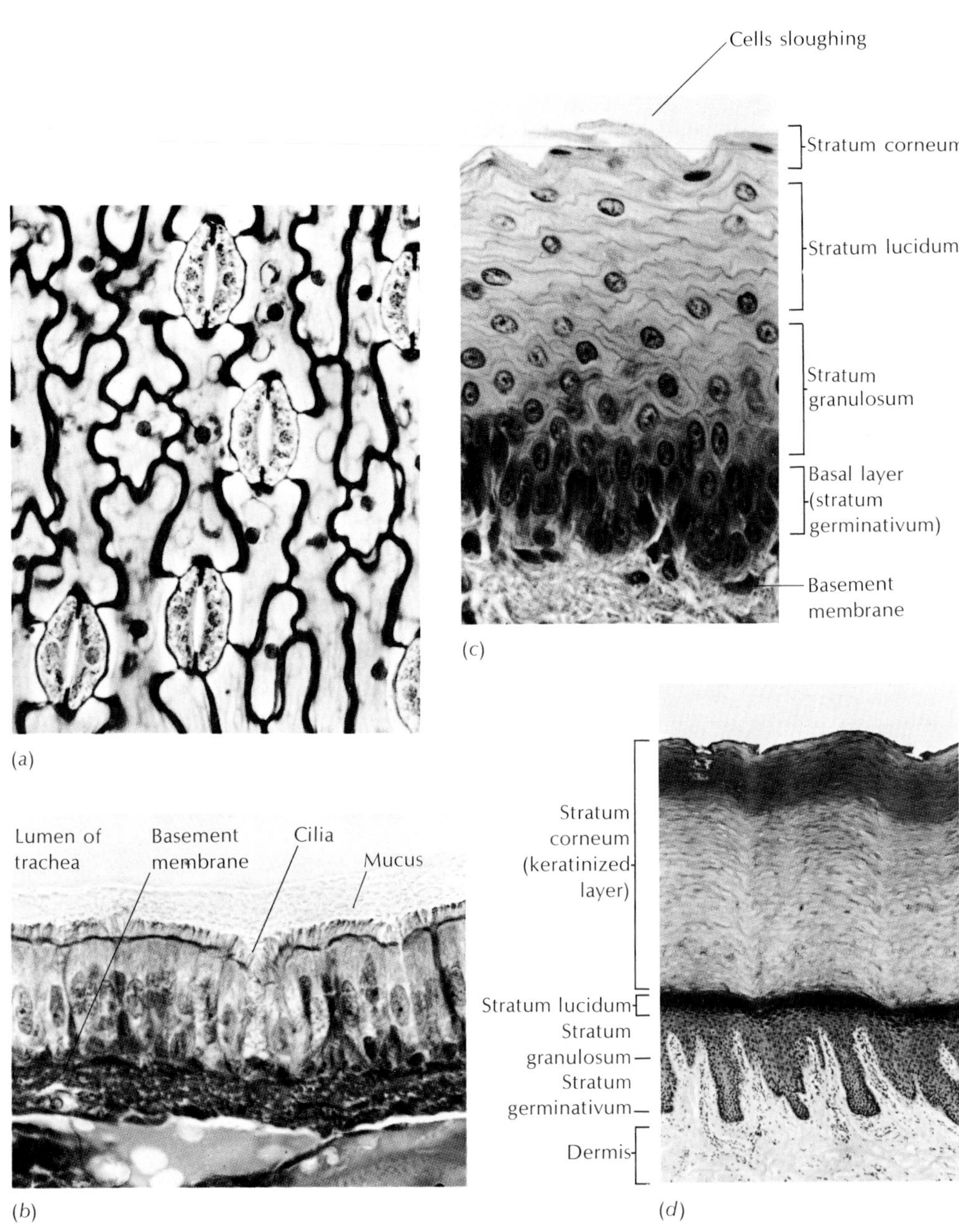

Figure 11.33 □ **Sheet epithelium. (*a*) Plant epidermis (lily leaf); epidermal nuclei are darkly stained; five entire stomates with guard cells are seen. (*Ward's Natural Science Establishment, Inc.*) (*b*) Pseudostratified ciliated columnar epithelium from mammalian trachea. (*Courtesy of Carolina Biological Supply Company.*) (*c*) Stratified squamous epithelium from human esophagus, showing basal layer against basement membrane and progressive flattening of outer layers of epithelium (outermost cells are shed and replaced by new cells produced mitotically in the basal layer); (*d*) stratified squamous epithelium from sole of foot, showing thick layer of horny, keratinized cells protecting deeper layers from injury and wear. (*Courtesy of D. W. Fawcett, M.D.*)**

Figure 11.34 □ **Epithelial glands. (*a*) Types of exocrine glands. (*b*) Relationship of secretory epithelium to bloodstream in an endocrine gland. [In (*a*) and (*b*) the secretory cells are colored.] (*c*) Numerous sweat glands in squirrel footpad (exocrine). (*Triarch Incorporated, Geo. H. Conant, Ripon, Wis.*) (*d*) Follicles of thyroid gland (endocrine); the accumulated colloidal secretion seen within the follicles shrinks during microscopic preparation of the tissue, producing a gap between colloid and follicular cells that is not present in life. (*Ward's Natural Science Establishment, Inc.*)**

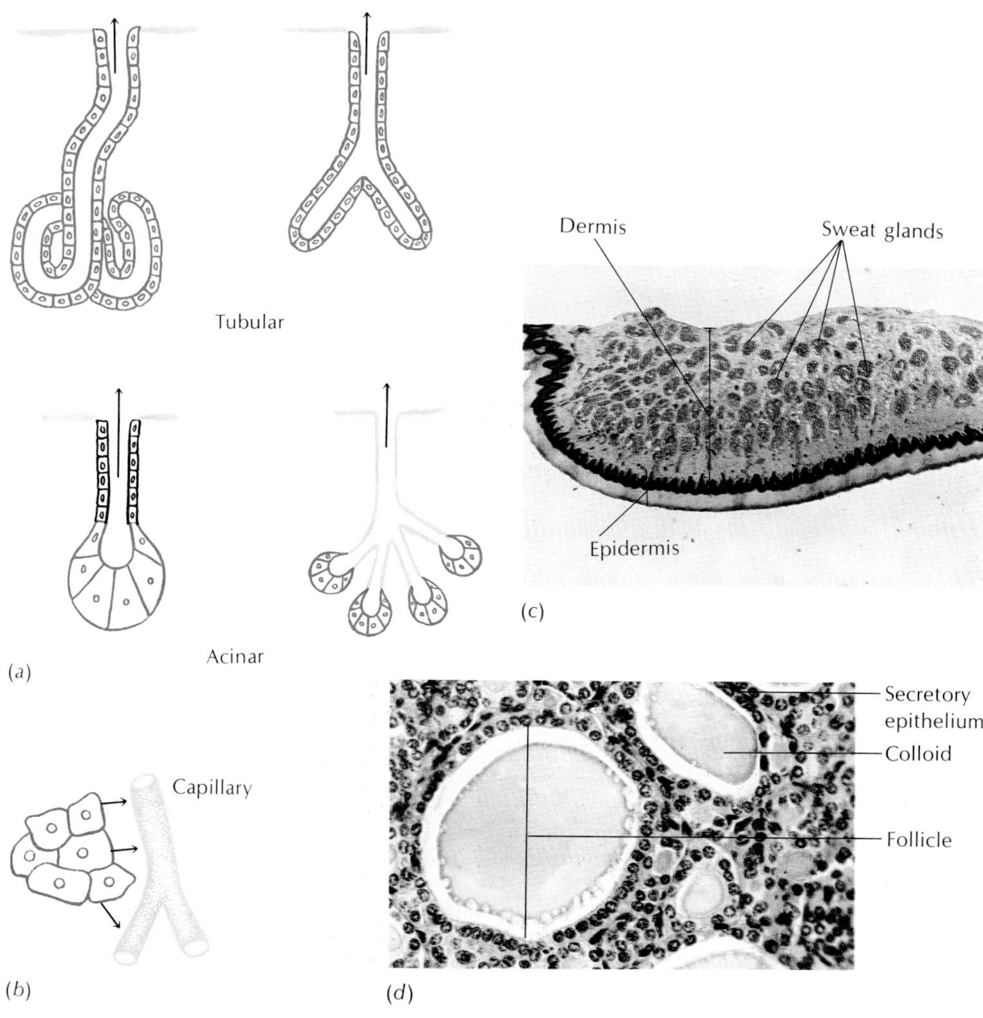

Secretory epithelium constitutes all exocrine and many endocrine glands (Figure 11.34). *Exocrine* glands are those that release their secretions into ducts or onto the free surface of an epithelial sheet. The two main types of exocrine glands are *tubular* and *acinar*. The former consists of branched or unbranched tubules that are of approximately the same diameter throughout their length and may be secretory for much of that length. In acinar glands the tubular portion is nonsecretory, serving only as a duct, whereas the secretory cells form globular clusters (acini) at the inner end of the tubules. Salivary glands are acinar; intestinal and sweat glands are tubular.

Some kinds of exocrine cells are not grouped in glands, but occur as part of an epithelial sheet. This is the case with scattered mucus-secreting cells in the epidermis of fish, amphibians, and most invertebrates. The entire epidermis of many plants is secretory, producing a protective covering such as the waxy cuticle of terrestrial plants. Certain epidermal plant cells also bear specialized glandular "hairs" which release protective exudates when broken off. The shell of a mollusc is secreted by the mantle epithelium, and an arthropod's exoskeleton is secreted by its epidermis. Other products of animal exocrine glands are mucus, saliva, venom, digestive enzymes, skin oils, sweat, milk, bile, and pheromones.

Endocrine glands have no direct connection with an epithelial surface but merely release their products (hormones) into the tissue spaces, whence they diffuse into the bloodstream. Most vertebrate endocrine glands are epithelial, although a few consist of nervous tissue.

MUSCLE TISSUE The distinctive

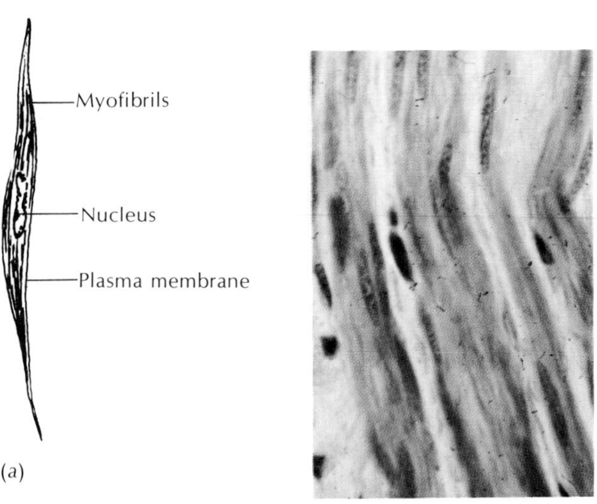

(a)

Figure 11.35 □ (*a*) Smooth muscle: drawing of a single cell (muscle fiber), with nucleus and tapering form; the photomicrograph shows the nuclei darkly stained and boundaries between adjacent cells poorly differentiated. (*Courtesy of General Biological, Inc., Chicago.*) (*b*) Striated (skeletal) muscle: left, portions of several striated fibers, particularly blunt ends and multinucleate condition, with myofibrils filling cell interior restricting nuclei to periphery; middle above, a photomicrograph (*Ward's Natural Science Establishment, Inc.*); middle below, an electron micrograph of tadpole striated muscle (*courtesy Dr. Keith R. Porter*). (*c*) Cardiac muscle: above, a photomicrograph of human heart muscle (*courtesy of Carolina Biological Supply Company*); below, an electron micrograph (*courtesy of D. W. Fawcett, M.D.*).

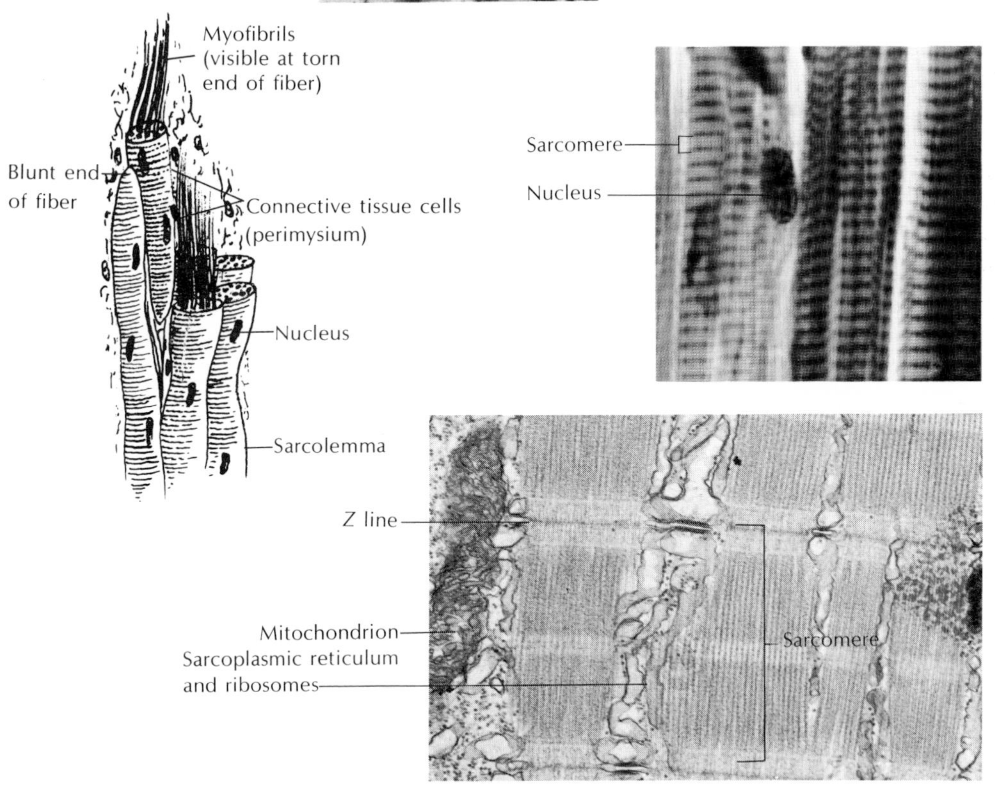

(b)

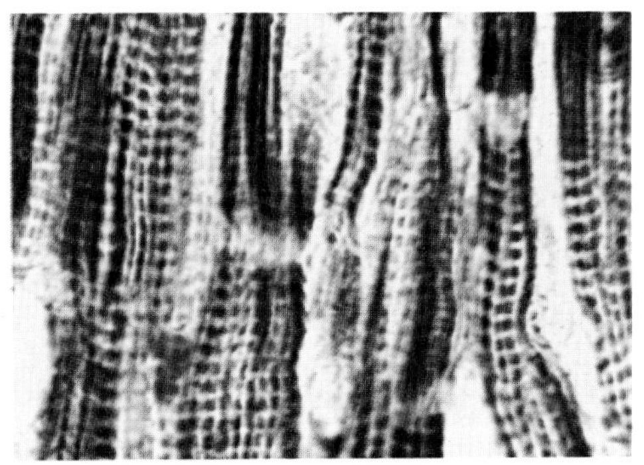

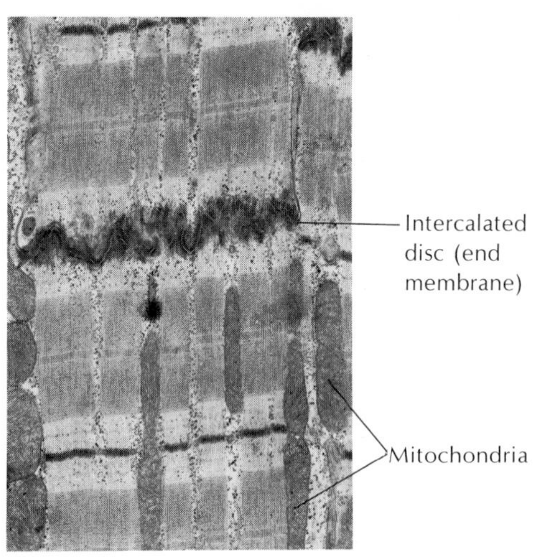

(c)

functional property of muscle tissue (Figure 11.35) is contractility. The cytoplasm of a muscle cell (*muscle fiber*) contains numerous longitudinally oriented contractile units or *myofibrils* made up of regularly arranged filaments of the proteins *actin* and *myosin*, which interact to bring about shortening of the myofibrils and consequent shortening of the entire muscle fiber. Vertebrate muscle fibers have been most intensively studied to date (see Figure 16.31), and we are not yet sure how well the fine details of cell organization as worked out for vertebrate muscle apply to invertebrates, although there appear to be many similarities.

The development of muscle tissue begins with the transformation of mesenchyme into rounded *myoblasts*. These soon put forth a slender process from each end of the cell body, and later become spindle-shaped. Myoblasts that will become smooth muscle remain mononucleate and retain the spindle form, while those that will become striated muscle commence to fuse successively until a tubular, multinucleate muscle fiber, 10 to 100 μm in diameter by several centimeters in length, is formed.

Smooth muscle is characteristically visceral: it is responsible for the motility of the digestive tract, uterine contractility, regulation of the bore of blood vessels, and other involuntary muscular actions. Generally speaking, smooth muscle contracts more slowly and in a more sustained manner than striated muscle. In the vertebrate body smooth muscle is involuntarily controlled by way of the autonomic nervous system, whereas striated muscle is generally under voluntary control and serves to move the skeleton.

Striated muscle fibers appear to be cross-banded because the individual myofibrils are so aligned that their patterns of cross banding coincide. This orderly arrangement may underlie the capacity of striated muscle to contract swiftly and powerfully. The individual myofibril is 1 to 2 μm in diameter and is constructed on a repeating molecular pattern, the *sarcomere*, a unit of function 2 to 3 μm long, in which actin and myosin filaments occur in orderly array. The light and dark banding pattern that characterizes striated muscle is an optical effect resulting from differences in density at parts of the sarcomere in which myosin filaments only, actin filaments only, or actin and myosin filaments together, are present.

Energy is furnished for muscular activity by mitochondria that are densely packed among the myofibrils. (The biochemical mechanism involved in muscle contraction will be discussed in Section 16.3F.)

Vertebrate cardiac muscle fibers are more slender than skeletal muscle fibers, and their nuclei are centrally rather than peripherally located. Each consists of a number of cells arranged in tandem, each cell separated from the next by folded cell membranes (intercalated discs) which may be specialized to facilitate the spread of excitation from cell to cell so that coordinated waves of contraction can sweep through the entire mass of heart tissue. Vertebrate heart muscle (and that of certain invertebrates as well) beats spontaneously, pulsating rhythmically; nervous impulses can alter the rate of beating but are not required to sustain the regular beat. After each contraction the fibers are briefly unresponsive to stimulation (the refractory period); because of this pause, the heart muscle will not fatigue as skeletal muscle does.

MECHANICAL TISSUE In both plants and animals supportive and connective tissues consist mainly of extracellular deposits that have rigidity or tensile strength. These materials are secreted by specialized cells. We have already noted the role of secretory epithelium in producing mollusc shells and arthropod exoskeletons. Among land vertebrates certain supportive or protective structures such as scales, armor, nails, claws, horns, hair, and feathers, are made up of more or less densely packed, keratinized epidermal cells. In this case an insoluble product of cell metabolism, the protein keratin, is retained within the epithelial cell, which dies and contributes to the structure being formed. Most mechanical tissues however are not epithelial in nature.

Plant mechanical tissues Terrestrial plants, lacking the support furnished by an aquatic medium, require supportive tissues analogous to those of higher animals if they are to achieve an upright habit of growth. The cellulose walls common to all kinds of plant tissues contribute to structural rigidity, but in tracheophytes certain cells have specialized toward the production of a thicker and more elaborate cell wall that may be impregnated with rigid, stony substances in addition to cellulose. The major supportive tissues are collenchyma, sclerenchyma, and fibers, each consisting of extracellular materials secreted by specialized cells of the same name (Figure 11.36). *Collenchyma* is the first mechanical tissue to be developed and thus occurs in the younger parts of the shoots. The secondary walls, consisting of alternating layers of pectin and cellulose, are thickened only at the angles. *Sclerenchyma* cells secrete thick secondary walls that become impregnated with *lignin*, a stony ma-

Figure 11.36 □ Plant mechanical tissues (secondary cell wall, consisting of supportive materials, shown in color). (*a*) Collenchyma, longitudinal (left) and cross (right) sections (open spaces occupied by cells). (*b*) Fibers from liquidambar xylem, longitudinal (left) and cross (right) sections. (*c*) Sclerenchyma, stone cells from walnut shell.

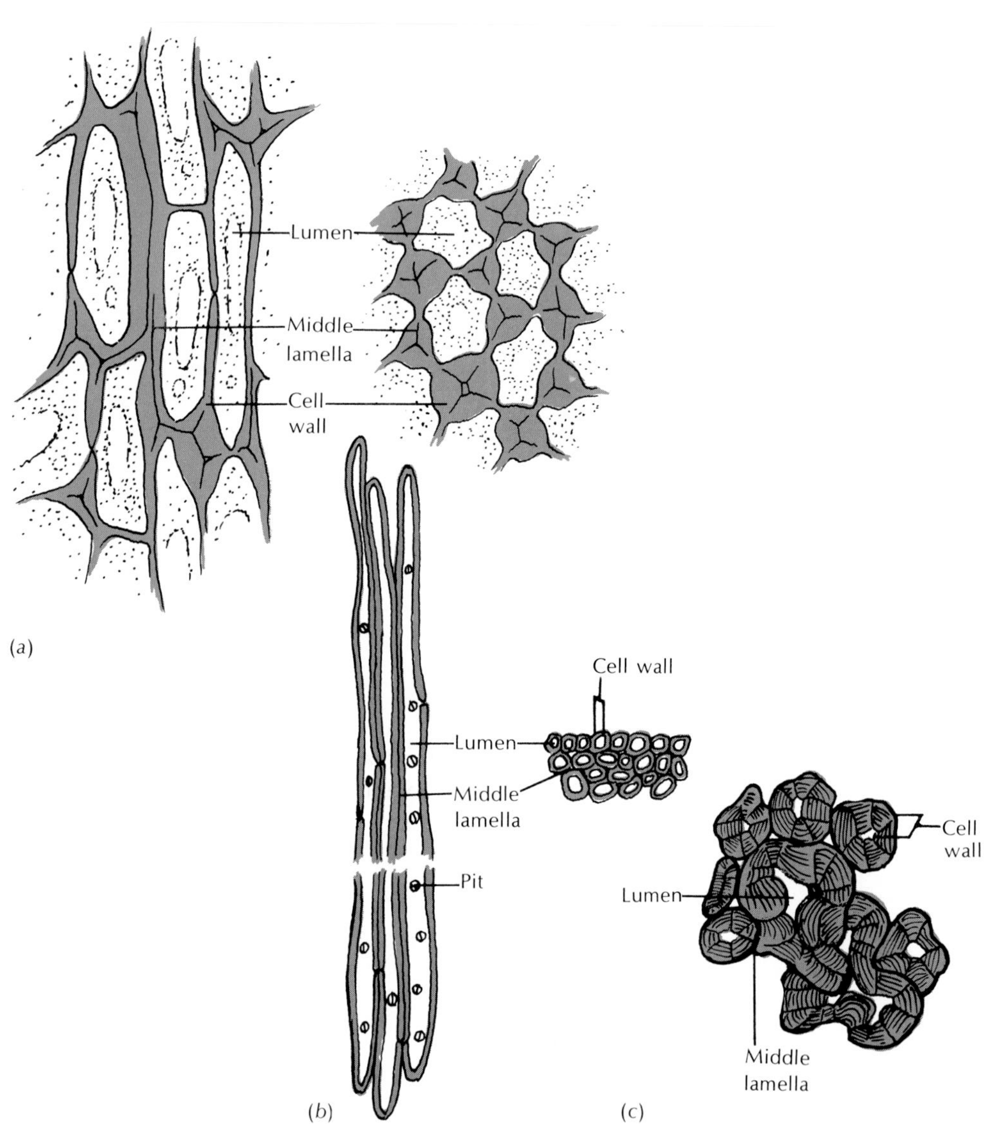

terial. The sclerenchyma cells usually die, leaving hollow cavities within the lignified walls. *Fibers* are secreted by cells which elongate until their length may be some 2,000 times their diameter, and then secrete a thick secondary wall composed of cellulose microfibrils. Upon completion of the secondary wall the fiber cell dies and the wall collapses inward, obliterating the central cavity. For example, a single cotton fiber, the secretory product of one fiber cell, may contain 10^{13} cellulose molecules, deposited in concentric layers in which the molecules in each layer are oriented at an angle to those in adjacent lamellae. This arrangement (similar but not identical to that seen in Figure 10.7c) furnishes great tensile strength without rigidity.

Animal mechanical tissues Other than the aforementioned production of supportive structures by keratinized cells and secretory epithelium, mechanical tissues of animals are extracellular products of amoeboid wandering cells (Figure 11.37). In vertebrates, connective fibers, cartilage, and bone are products of secretory cells derived from mesenchyme that are basically mobile but may become entrapped within the matrix they secrete (see Figure 4.29). *Chondroblasts* secrete cartilage matrix, and *osteoblasts* secrete bone. *Fibroblasts* secrete protein molecules that spontaneously associate to form elastic or collagenous fibers. Chondroblasts and osteoblasts become trapped in small spaces within the solid matrix (and when thus immobilized are known as chondrocytes and osteocytes, respectively), but erosion of this matrix restores them to mobility and secretory activity. Fibroblasts remain mobile and exhibit great capacity for modulation; indeed, we remain uncertain as to

Figure 11.37 □ **Animal connective and supportive tissues. (*a*) Fibroelastic areolar connective tissue (left), showing fibrous (collagenous) and slender elastic fibers and scattered amoeboid wandering cells; elastic cartilage (right), showing cartilage matrix interpenetrated by elastic fibers. (*Courtesy of Carolina Biological Supply Company.*) (*b*) Possible modulations of a basic connective-tissue cell type.**

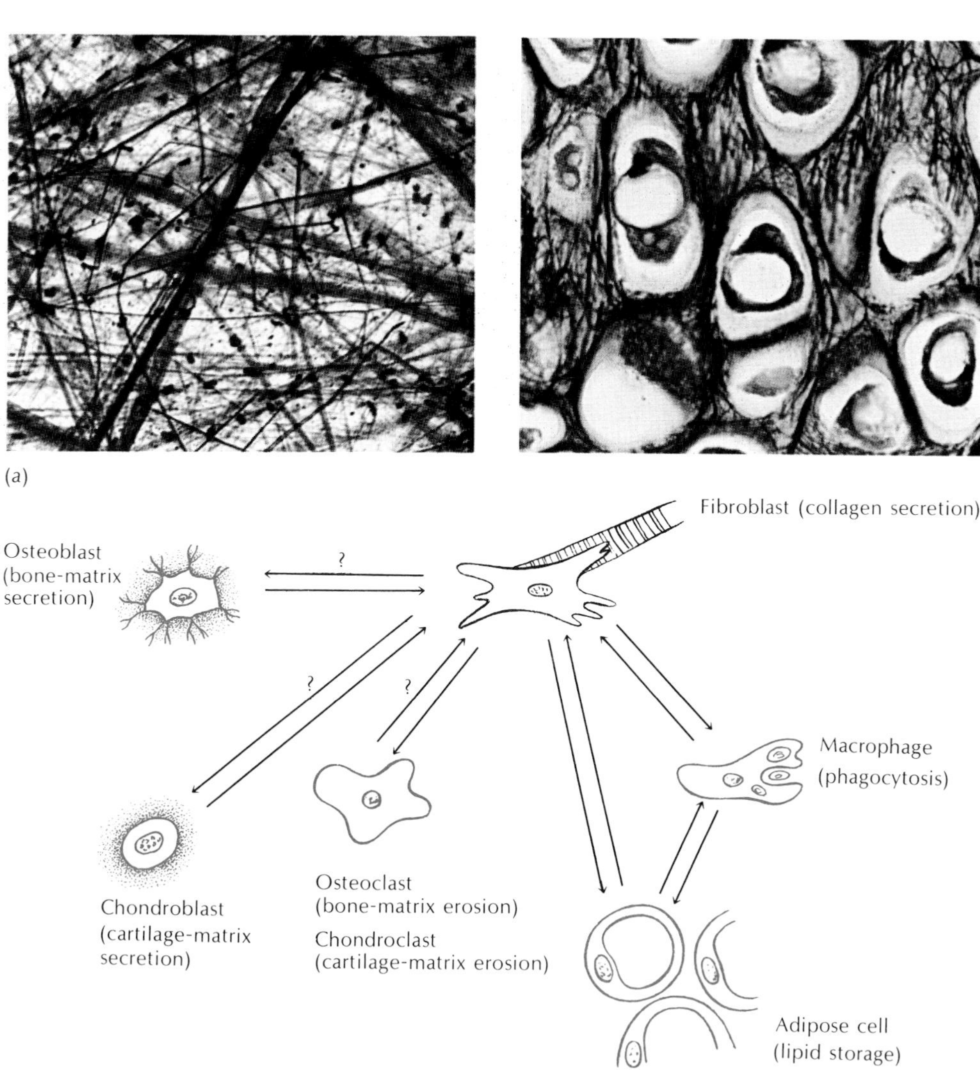

how many of the body's wandering phagocytic cell types may in fact be modulated fibroblasts. Fibroblasts secrete the proteins tropocollagen (the molecular unit of collagen fibrils), elastin, and reticulin. Elastin is a major component of elastic connective tissue (found especially in vertebrate skin and the walls of arteries) and elastic cartilage (such as supports the pinna of the mammalian ear). Reticulin forms extremely fine fibers in loose (areolar) connective tissue and in the intercellular cement. Collagen forms the tough, inelastic, fibrous, or white connective tissue that makes up fasciae, tendons, and ligaments. It contributes to the matrix of bone and fibrocartilage, to intercellular cement and basement membranes; as scar tissue, collagen repairs wounds.

Blood In its origin, although not in its function, blood is allied to animal mechanical tissues, for the cells that give rise to the blood corpuscles stem from the same mesenchymal source as fibroblasts and various tissue wandering cells (Figure 11.38). In fact, during vertebrate postnatal life a principal site of blood-corpuscle formation is the red bone marrow. *Leucocytes* are amoeboid cells capable of phagocytosis and of secreting antibodies. (We have discussed their roles in combating infection in Section 6.3E.) Vertebrate red blood corpuscles, or *erythrocytes,* contain hemoglobin and are mainly concerned with the transport of O_2 and CO_2; their function will be discussed in Chapter 14. The matrix in which these cells are suspended is an aqueous solution, the *plasma,* containing proteins in colloidal dispersion, emulsified lipids, and various other materials including foods, wastes, ions, and hormones (see Section 14.2B).

Figure 11.38 □ (*a*) Blood-forming tissue in bone marrow, showing maturing red corpuscles (small cells) and leucocytes (larger cells); (*b*) mature human blood corpuscles, one granulocyte with irregular nucleus and one lymphocyte with large ovoid nucleus among enucleated erythrocytes. (*Ward's Natural Science Establishment, Inc.*)

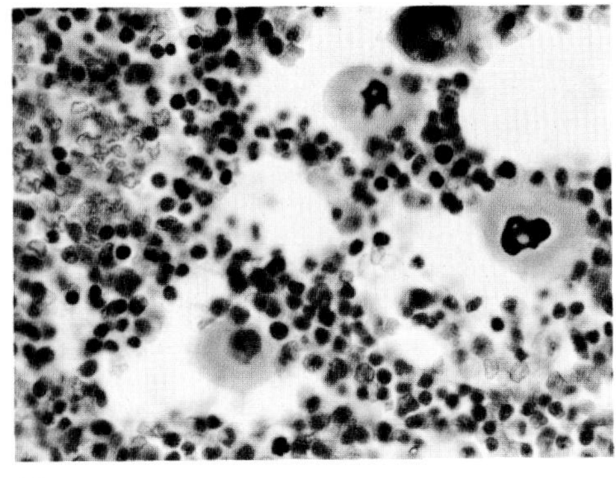

(*a*)

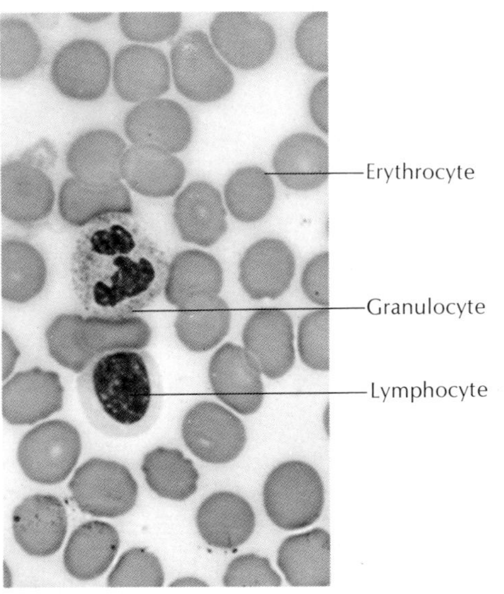

(*b*)

Figure 11.39 □ Storage parenchyma in ranunculus root, showing leucoplasts filled with starch granules. (*Ward's Natural Science Establishment, Inc.*)

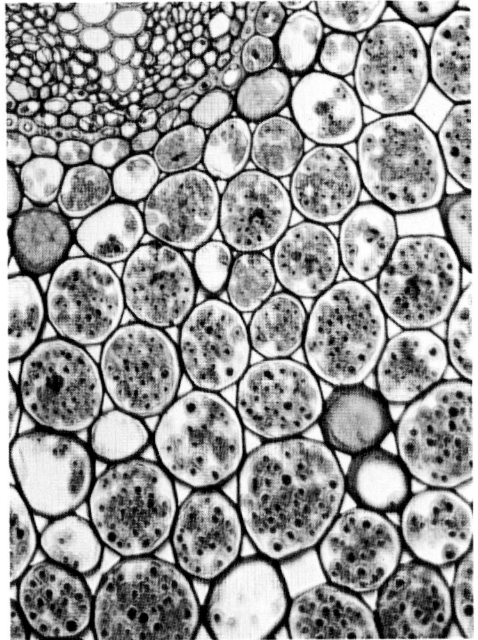

PARENCHYMA Much of the tissue of leaves, flowers, fruits, and young stems and roots consists of loosely packed, rounded, or columnar cells with thin cellulose walls. Such parenchyma cells serve to store water and food reserves, and those which contain chloroplasts (*chlorenchyma*) are sites of photosynthesis (Figure 13.4). Each parenchyma cell often has a large central vacuole containing oils or sugar-rich sap. The cytoplasm of storage parenchyma may be congested with leucoplasts containing starch granules (Figure 11.39).

The term parenchyma is also applied to a somewhat different tissue found in such animals as flatworms and ribbonworms, which are among the simplest animals to develop a true mesoderm. Here the potential for mesodermal differentiation is only partially realized, and much of the mesodermal tissue located between the epidermis and gastrodermis consists of cells that appear to be relatively unspecialized and, being phagocytic, serve to store nutrients. During starvation the animal consumes its own parenchyma and dwindles away like the Cheshire cat.

VASCULAR TISSUES In the sense employed here, vascular tissues consist of cells that are specially modified for the conduction of liquids throughout the body of the organism. Animals have no tissues uniquely specialized for this function other than the flattened epithelium (endothelium) that forms the uninterrupted lining of the entire circulatory system. The tubular phloem and xylem cells of tracheophytes represent true vascular tissues in the sense used here, for they furnish cellular channels through which liquids are transported.

The major types of vascular tissue are

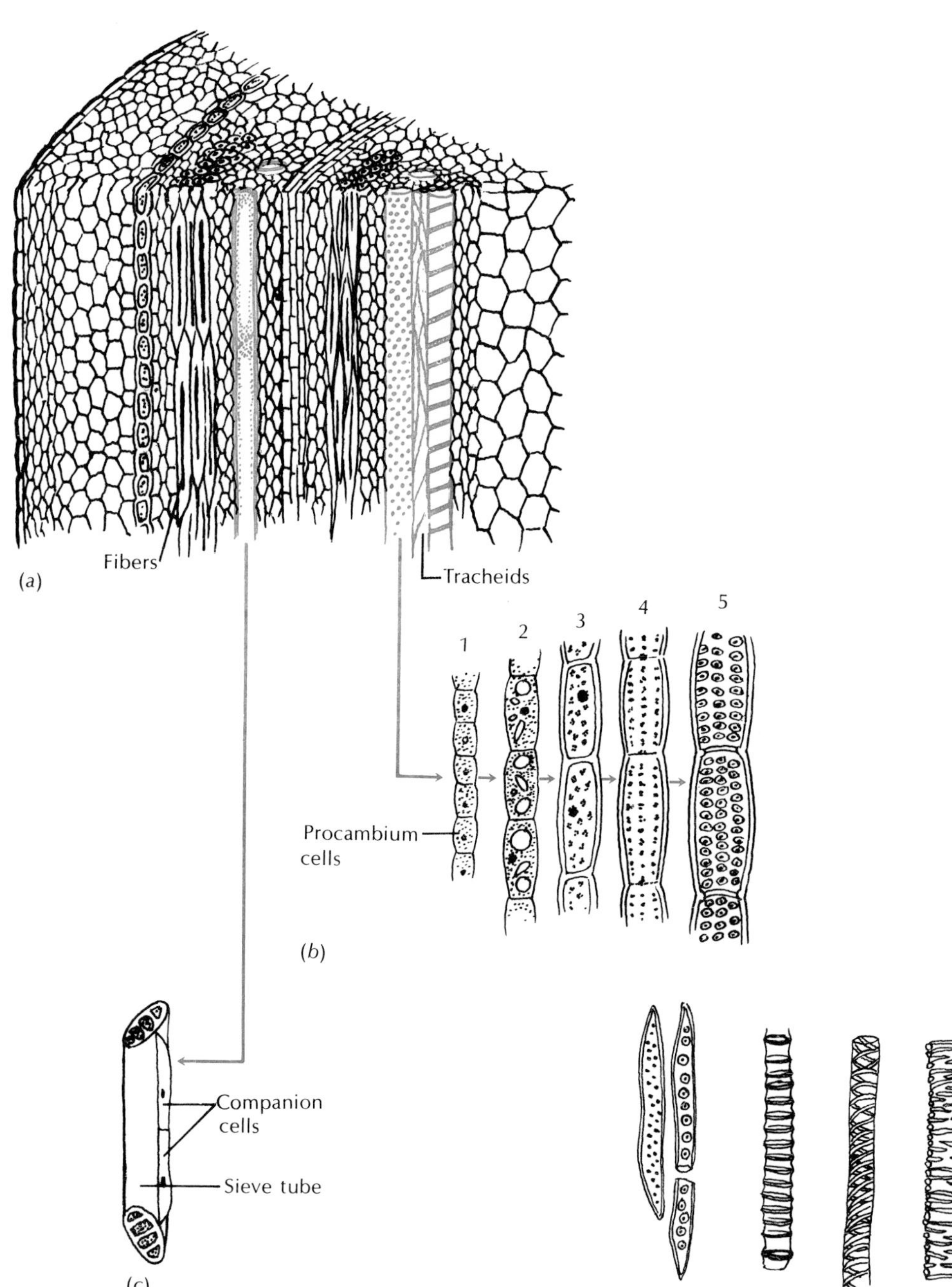

sieve tubes, tracheids, and vessels (Figure 11.40). *Sieve tubes* are the major elements of *phloem,* the tissue within which sap moves from the leaves to the roots and the growing points. They are elongated and stacked in vertical columns. Their end walls are thickened and perforated like a sieve with minute pores through which cytoplasmic strands continue unbroken from one cell to the next, uniting each column syncytially. As the sieve tube matures it loses its nucleus and the cytoplasm is confined to a thin peripheral layer surrounding a huge vacuole through which slender cytoplasmic strands run lengthwise. Solutes are transported through the vacuolar sap and across the cytoplasmic intercellular bridges. Associated with sieve tubes are nucleated *companion cells,* which may support the sieve tubes nutritionally.

Tracheids and vessels are concerned with the upward movement of water and solutes from roots to leaves; in the aggregate they constitute the *xylem* (Figure 14.12). Unlike sieve tubes, which remain alive, tracheid and vessel cells die after completion of the secondary wall. Composed of cellulose and often lignin, these walls are partially thickened according to one of several distinct morphogenetic patterns: spiral, annular, pitted, or scalariform. The alternation of thin and thickened portions

Figure 11.40 □ Plant vascular tissue. (*a*) Radial section of typical dicot stem, showing vascular tissues in situ. (*b*) Stages in development of pitted vessel from procambium (*adapted from Bonnier and Sablon*). (*c*) Sieve tube and companion cells. (*d*) Portions of elongate xylem elements: tracheids (left) and vessels (right). Living cells are absent in the mature xylem tissue.

confers structural strength while allowing freedom of exchange of materials with the surrounding tissues. *Tracheids* are individual, longitudinally oriented elements with tapering ends. Mature *vessels* consist of a vertical column of secondary walls with the end plates completely dissolved away, forming a hollow tubule that may be many centimeters long. In the perennial stems of woody plants the older xylem elements cease to function as vascular tissue, becoming occluded with solid deposits such as resins, gums, and tannin. Old xylem thus becomes supportive in function as it ceases to be conductive. New phloem and xylem continue proliferation from both sides of the vascular cambium (Figure 12.15).

NERVOUS TISSUE Nervous tissue occurs in all metazoans, probably excepting sponges. It is specialized for irritability and the conduction of information in the form of nerve impulses (see Section 15.1A). Nerve cells (*neurons*) are sometimes extremely elongate, facilitating rapid transmission of impulses throughout the body (Figure 11.41). The *sensory* processes of neurons terminate near body surfaces and within the muscles and viscera, where they may be associated with specialized receptor cells. *Motor* fibers activate glands and muscle fibers, bringing about secretory or contractile responses. *Association* neurons lie entirely within the central nervous system and are concerned with integration and storage of information, as well as with selection of appropriate responses.

Neuroblasts are the embryonic progenitors of nerve cells. As they mature they put forth processes that occasionally attain great length. A single motor neuron, with its cell body located in the spinal cord, may send out processes extending the length of a limb. The volume of such a neuron has been estimated at 10^6 μm^3 and in larger vertebrates (and giant squid) its length may well exceed 1 m. Each maturing neuron develops one or more *dendrites,* branching processes that are excitable and that conduct this excitation toward the neuron cell body. The cell body gives off a single *axon* that conducts impulses toward the *synapse,* or point of junction with another neuron, a muscle fiber, or a gland cell. The axon may branch, giving off collaterals, or remain unbranched until the terminal arborescence, where it divides into branchlets that may end in expanded knobs. These endings may lodge in depressions in the plasma membrane of the cell innervated, but the two membranes remain separated by a synaptic gap of at least 200 Å. The cytoplasm at the axon ending is filled with neurofibrils of unknown function and with synaptic vesicles containing the *transmitter substance,* which is released at the moment of excitation (see Section 15.1B).

The neuron cell body contains a large nucleus with a conspicuous nucleolus. Its cytoplasm is rich in a basically staining *Nissl substance,* which consists of rough endoplasmic reticulum densely studded with ribosomes. The prominence of the Nissl substance reflects the extent to which neurons engage in protein synthesis. Although the transmitter substances themselves are not proteinaceous, their synthesis depends on the maintenance in the cytoplasm of the needed enzymes and ribosomes. The cytoplasm also contains other inclusions of obscure significance, including lipid bodies, yellow or black granules of sporadic occurrence, and fibrils.

In the central nervous systems of vertebrates, annelids, arthropods, and molluscs, neurons are associated with numerous smaller branching cells, the *neuroglia.* These are supportive cells and also are thought to be involved in nutritional maintenance of neurons. Some neuroglia pulsate rhythmically, possibly circulating the interstitial fluid that bathes the densely packed processes and cell bodies of neurons and neuroglia alike. Vertebrate brain capillaries are found to be totally encased by glia, which suggests that these cells may mediate the passage of materials between the bloodstream and the interstitial fluid of the brain. These cells are thus thought to constitute a regulatory "blood-brain barrier."

In peripheral nerves and the white tracts of the central nervous system, nerve fibers are often invested with a coating of lipid materials (the *myelin sheath*). Vertebrate nerve fibers lying outside the central nervous system are enveloped by *Schwann cells,* which are of importance in nerve cell nutrition and regeneration. The myelin sheaths of these peripheral nerve fibers are found to consist of a tightly wrapped spiral of Schwann cell membrane. The sheath is interrupted at nodes that are merely the point at which one Schwann cell stops and the next begins. However, not all Schwann cells produce this much membrane material; *amyelinated* fibers are merely covered by a flat Schwann cell that elaborates no extra membrane. Regeneration of severed nerve fibers depends on the survival of the Schwann cells. If the sheath formed by successive Schwann cells (the neurilemma) is excessively mutilated, the nerve fiber cannot regenerate, for the intact neurilemma must be present to guide its growth.

Figure 11.41 □ (*a*) Structure of a motor neuron. (*b*) Photomicrograph of motor neurons in ox spinal cord, showing only cell bodies and proximal portions of fibers. (*Courtesy of Carolina Biological Supply Company.*) (*c*) Electron micrograph of Schwann cell, with nucleus and plasma membrane forming sheath around axon (seen in cross section). [*Courtesy of Dr. H. deF. Webster, from W. Bloom and D. W. Fawcett,* A Textbook of Histology (*Philadelphia: W. B. Saunders Co., 1962*).] (*d*) Electron micrograph of myelin sheath; it is made up of multiple layers of Schwann cell membrane. (*Courtesy of Dr. J. D. Robertson.*) (*e*) Detail of a synaptic terminal, showing axon ending on membrane of cell innervated. (*f*) Other neuron types: (left) neuron from cerebellum; (right) unipolar sensory neuron. [In (*a*) and (*f*) arrows indicate direction of propagation of nerve impulse.]

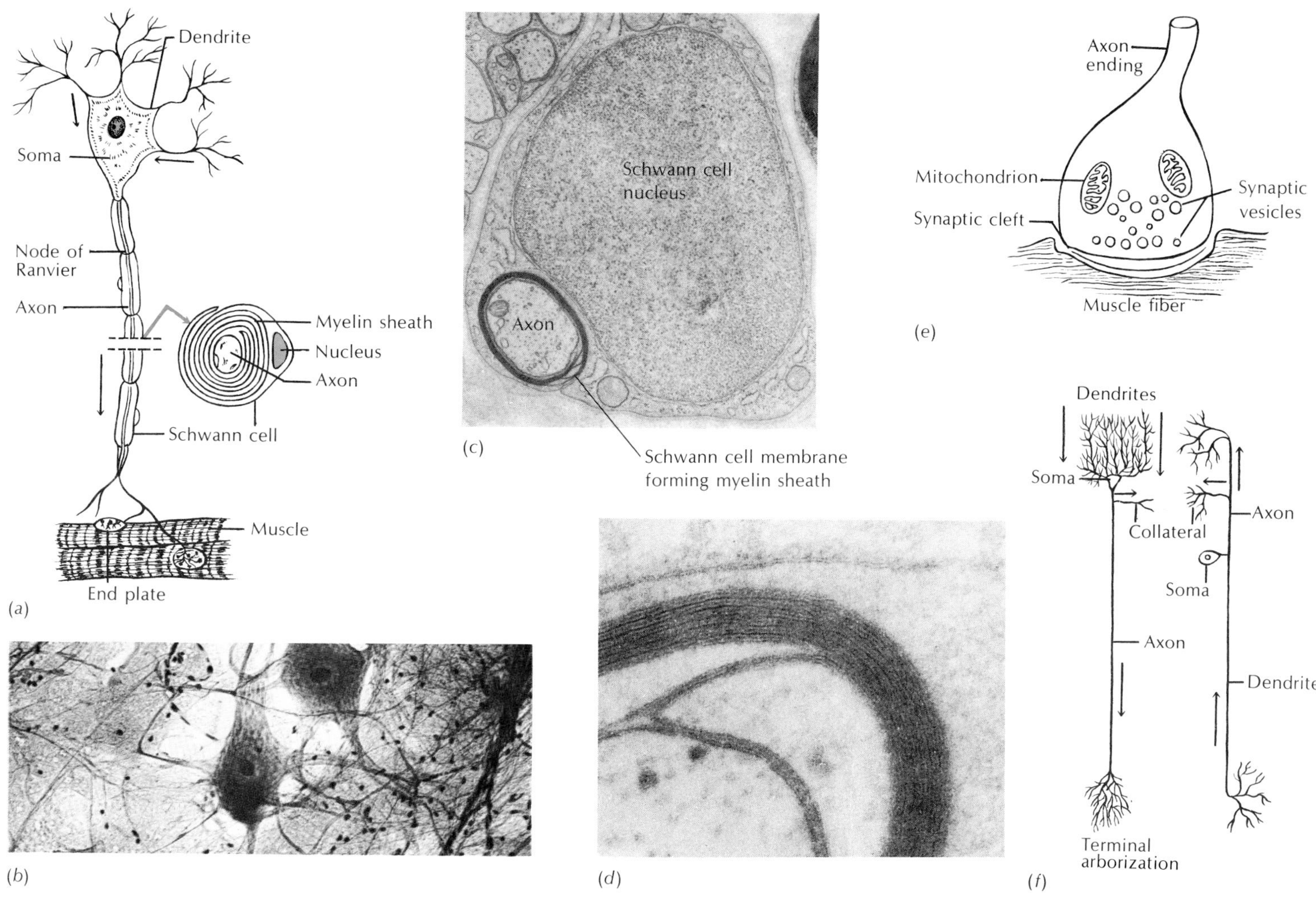

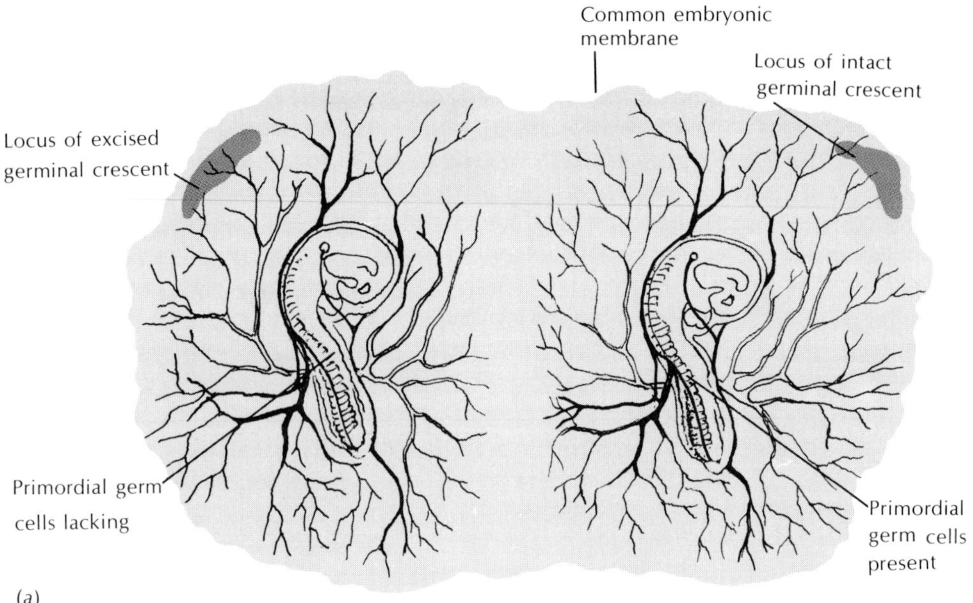

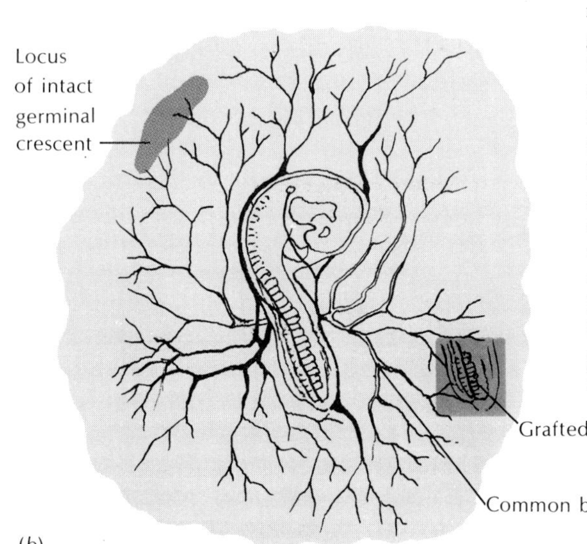

Figure 11.42 □ Origin of germinal cells in the chick. (*a*) Experiment 1: two embryos are joined by way of their extra-embryonic membranes, their bloodstreams remaining separated. Prior to the union, the germinal crescent had been removed from the membranes of the left embryo; later, this embryo was found to lack germinal cells in its gonads. The germinal crescent was left intact in the embryo at right, which was later found to have germinal cells in its gonads. (*b*) Experiment 2: the posterior half of one embryo, containing the future genital region, is grafted to membranes of intact embryo to establish a common blood supply. Both the intact and the half embryo will then have received germinal cells from the germinal crescent, by way of the common bloodstream.

B Germinal tissue

The gamete-producing organs, or *gonads,* of animals are the *ovaries* and *testes. Ova* mature in the former, *sperm* in the latter (see Figure 17.26). Gonadal analogues in plants are *archegonia,* within which maturation of the female gametes takes place, and *antheridia,* which produce sperm cells. Maturation of animal gametes involves the reduction of chromosome number by meiosis (see Figure 8.4). In lower plants, meiosis may be a generation removed from gametogenesis, but in higher plants, with the progressive abridgement of the gametophyte generation, meiosis is less widely separated in time from the formation of the reproductive cells. Sperm and ova as such are not formed in flowering plants. Instead, the monoploid sperm nucleus, which will fertilize the egg nucleus, is part of a multinucleate pollen grain or male gametophyte, and the egg nucleus remains within the cytoplasm of the small female gametophyte in the plant's "ovary." The archegonium of an alga, the ovary of a flowering plant, and the ovary of an animal are *analogous,* for within each organ one or more ova or egg nuclei mature, but they are very different in structure and cannot be considered to be even remotely *homologous.*

Sex organs consist of a framework or stroma of somatic tissues, within which the *germinal cells* mature. The origin of these germinal cells in animals is still subject to question. Are they differentiated from somatic cells, or do they arise very early in embryonic development from otherwise undetermined cells, and later migrate into the stroma of the developing gonad? In 1885 August Weismann published his *theory of continuity of the germ plasm,* which set forth the concept that there are two types of protoplasm: *somatoplasm,* which dies with each generation and does not influence inheritance; and *germ plasm,* which carries the genetic information from one generation to the next. We no longer seriously consider the possibility of two distinct types of protoplasm, but the basic implication of the theory—that germ cells may become isolated from the pathway of somatic development very early in ontogeny, rather than being differentiated later from the somatic cells of the gonads—still stands.

The search for the origin of germ cells has mainly involved amphibian embryos. Histological evidence indicates that the large, rounded primordial germ cells migrate into the developing gonads from elsewhere in the embryo. In frog zygotes (*Rana pipiens* and *R. temporaria*) an area of cytoplasm near the vegetal pole takes up the dye azure A (which stains nucleic acids), permitting the fate of this part of the embryo to be traced through subsequent cell divisions and movements. As cleavage proceeds, this stained cytoplasm is incorporated within only about two dozen cells, which migrate dorsally, around the archenteron, later moving laterally into the area of the developing gonads.

The extragonadal origin of the germ cells is also indicated by experiments on chick embryos. As an amniote egg develops, only a portion of this egg becomes the embryo proper, other tissues contributing to the formation of the extraembryonic membranes, including the yolk sac and amnion. If we extirpate the *germinal crescent,* a small patch of cells in the yolk-sac membrane, germ cells will be completely absent from the chick's gonads (Figure 11.42)! This implies that cells from this area, so far removed from the embryo proper, must at some point migrate into the gonads, there to remain and later mature. If the posterior half of one chick embryo is grafted onto the extraembryonic membranes of an intact embryo, both the gonads of the engrafted half-embryo and those of the intact embryo become populated by germ cells disseminated by way of the common blood flow uniting host and graft.

Such experiments raise more questions than they answer. If primordial germ cells are indeed separated from the line of somatic differentiation very early in ontogeny, what is the significance of this? Why do these cells so long retain their rich content of cytoplasmic nucleic acids? What unique qualities of such cells as those of the germinal crescent predispose them to develop into gametes? What governs their migration from their point of origin into the somatic stroma of the gonads, where they will be regulated to develop into ova or sperm?

Having reached the gonads, the differentiation of the germinal cells is influenced by the relative proportions of medullary and cortical gonadal tissue. As noted earlier, if the gonadal cortex predominates, the germ cells eventually become ova, while if there is a preponderance of medullary tissue, the germ cells will develop into sperm.

11.6 □ EVOLUTIONARY TRENDS IN DEVELOPMENT

A The principle of paleogenesis

As organisms have evolved toward complexity the maturational period has become longer. It is usually extended by the addition of new stages toward the end of embryonic development. Due to this tendency the development of the individual may seem to repeat the evolutionary history of its group. E. H. Haeckel's aphorism, "ontogeny recapitulates phylogeny," which influenced evolutionary thought through three-quarters of a century, is misleading as originally stated, and should be amended as follows: *the ontogeny of descendant species tends to recapitulate the ontogeny of their ancestors.* In no case does the *embryo* of one species closely resemble the *adult* of another. For example, mammalian embryos develop pharyngeal openings ("gill slits"). Such slits also appear in fish embryos, persisting into adult life and functioning in breathing. In mammalian embryos these clefts normally close and disappear as ontogeny proceeds. At early stages, fish embryo

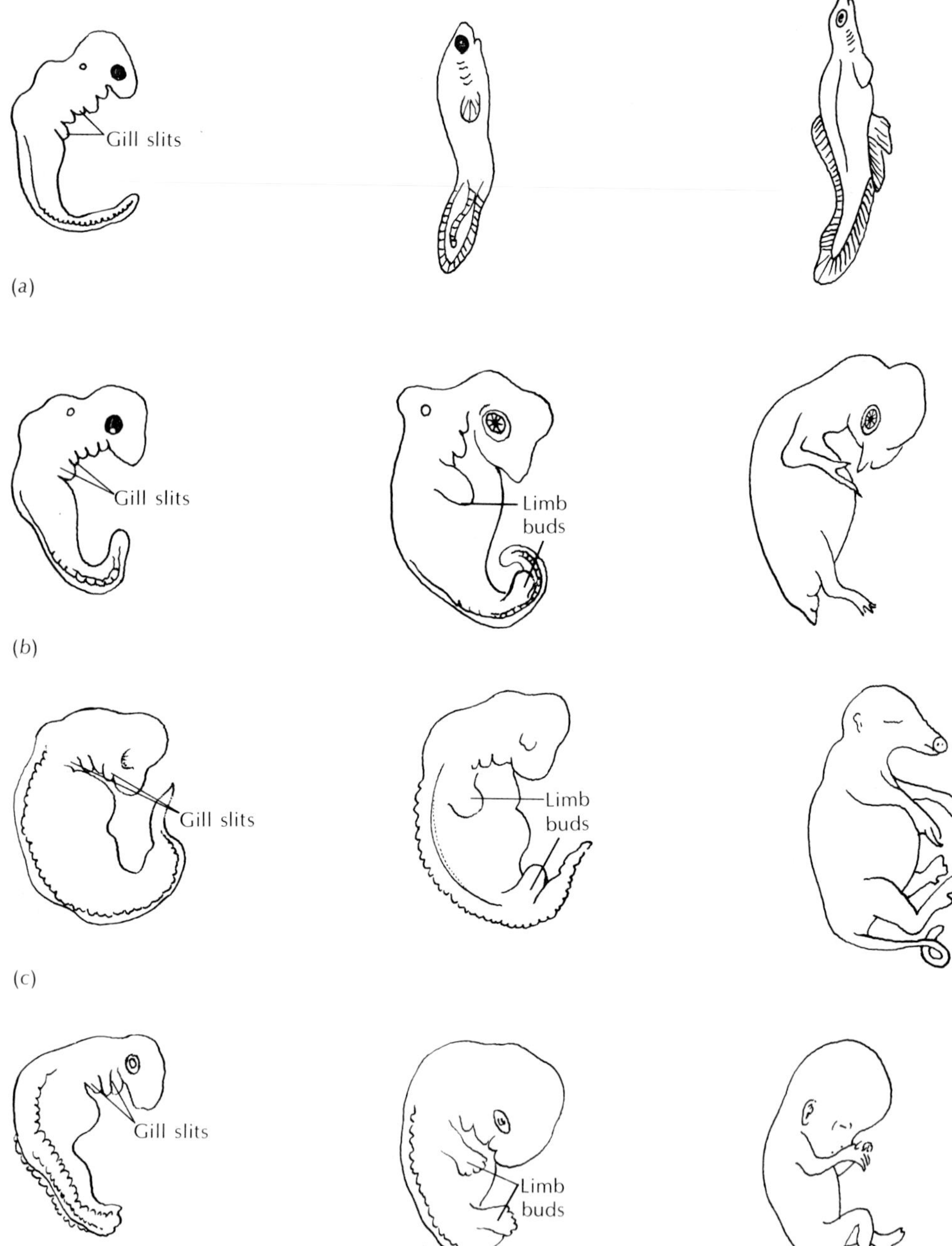

Figure 11.43 □ Comparable stages of embryonic development in (*a*) fish, (*b*) bird, (*c*) pig, and (*d*) man. Note marked similarity of all four vertebrate embryos in earlier stages, distinctive characteristics of class and species becoming apparent later. Embryonic development of higher forms appears to recapitulate ancestral ontogenies.

and mammalian embryo do indeed resemble one another in this and other respects, but at no stage does the mammalian embryo closely resemble an *adult* fish (Figure 11.43).

Since a mammal does not use pharyngeal clefts in feeding or respiration at *any* stage in its development, we may wonder why the embryo expends its energy first to elaborate these functionless structures and then to cause them to disappear. The answer lies of course in an understanding of genes and gene mutation. When a structure is no longer needed, the genes that govern its development do *not* perforce become "silent" or mutate in a useful direction. The ontogeny of advanced species is freighted with a load of redundant maneuvers that remain part of the developmental process of those species merely because the ancestral pattern of ontogeny *necessarily* incorporated those steps. During early development the eutherian embryo elaborates a yolk sac, and then proceeds to develop as a flat disc on top of the nonexistent yolk. Such discoidal cleavage is mandatory for eggs encumbered by huge quantities of yolk, such as those of reptiles, birds, and monotremes; it seems nonsensical in a yolkless egg. However, the mammal has evolved from reptilian ancestors that laid large-yolked eggs and although the placenta has replaced stored yolk in the nutrition of eutherian embryos, the mam-

Figure 11.44 □ Terminal adaptation seen in flatfish development. (*a*) Larval halibut, head structures still symmetrical and body still "typical" fish shape; four days later the left eye had migrated to top of head. (*Photograph by G. Mattson, U.S. Bureau of Commercial Fisheries.*) (*b*) Head of adult halibut, showing left eye located at top of head and mouth skewed toward right side (the animal lies on its left side). (*Scripps Institution of Oceanography.*)

(*a*)

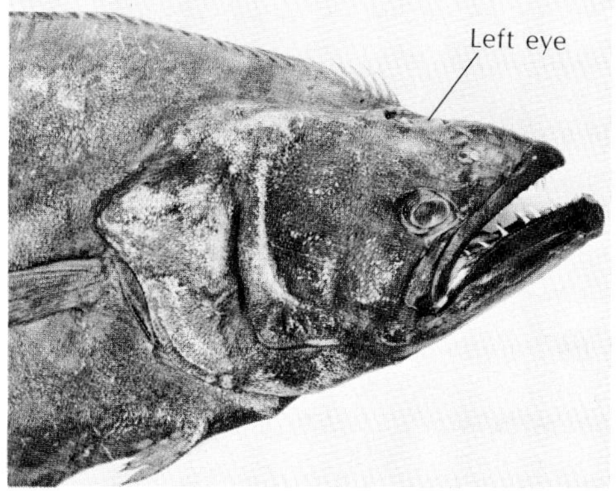

(*b*)

malian egg continues to develop as though it still had a yolk. It is bound to ancestral patterns by still unmutated genes.

In fact, loss mutations are not always advantageous despite the possible energy savings, for an embryonic structure of no persisting value may nevertheless regulate the development of structures that *will* persist. The notochord, for instance, though having no postnatal role in higher vertebrates, is indispensible in development because its presence is required for the induction of neurulation and the differentiation of the vertebral column.

The manner in which development of body form is shaped by natural selection is brought out particularly well in cases where specific modifications occur late in development, representing adaptations for some specialized mode of life. The entire evolution of body form is, of course, a part of the process of adaptation: form, function, and way of life all are integrally related, and those morphogenetic processes that have served to produce body forms most favorable to survival have tended to persist. The body form of a typical fish reflects selection toward proficiency of swimming. However, several groups of fish known commonly as "flatfish" (including halibut, flounder, hake, and sole) have adopted a way of life in which little swimming is done and the fish lies on its side on the bottom, lurking in ambush for its prey. As larvae, flatfish first develop the usual structural adaptations characteristic of fish generally (Figure 11.44). When these larvae undergo metamorphosis to the adult form, however, final morphogenetic changes take place that fit these species to their peculiar mode of life. These changes include the migration of one eye from the future lower side around (or even through) the head, to its final position on the animal's future upper side. This gives the flatfish binocular vision (permitting depth perception) even while lying sideways on the bottom. The mouth also moves around toward the future upper side. As a result of these changes the head becomes much distorted. Although these changes take place in the course of only a few days, the pattern of development actually retraces in accelerated form the evolutionary history of these adaptations. Presumably adoption of a new behavior (the technique of lying on one side, hidden by cryptic coloration from sight of prospective prey) led to selection toward morphogenetic changes that would actually have constituted detrimental abnormalities in fish of more conventional habit.

AN EXAMPLE OF PALEOGENESIS: THE AORTIC ARCHES All vertebrate embryos develop six pairs of arteries arising from the ventral aorta, the large blood vessel that passes forward from the heart to the head and pharynx. These segmentally-arranged vessels, the aortic arches, pass upward between consecutive pharyngeal clefts, and unite to form the roots of the dorsal aorta, the major vessel in which blood flows posteriorly to the trunk, limbs, tail, and internal organs. In modern fishes, all but the most anterior two pairs of aortic arches persist into postembryonic life, developing into the branchial arteries that supply the gills which form in the walls of the pharyngeal clefts. Here the blood of the fish is oxygenated. A gill circulation is also required to oxygenate the blood of larval amphibians, but in adult amphibians and all amniotes gills are lacking and blood is oxy-

Figure 11.45 □ **Recapitulation exemplified by ontogeny and phylogeny of aortic arches. (*a*) Anterior portion of fish embryo, showing aortic arches and heart as seen from right. (*b*) Circulatory system of chick embryo, showing aortic arches and pharyngeal clefts on right side; note marked similarity to condition in fish embryo. (*c*) Fate of aortic arches in classes of vertebrates (top view); arches that disappear are shown by dashed lines.**

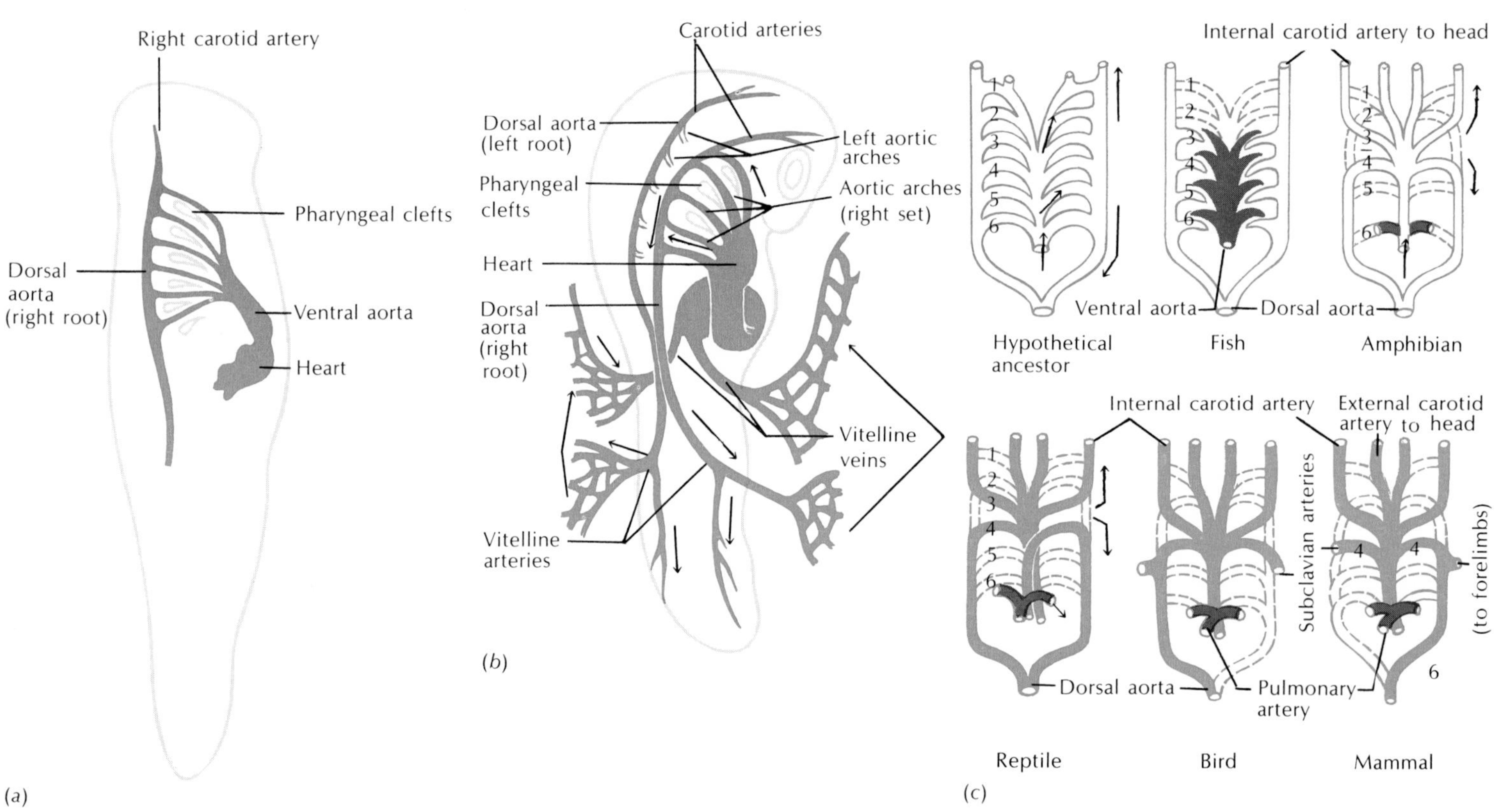

genated in the lungs. Nevertheless, the development of this part of the circulatory system tends to retrace the ancestral pattern of ontogeny, and the six pairs of arches are now formed only to undergo various transformations: some become vestigial and disappear, while others assume new functions that they will perform throughout life.

In Figure 11.45*a* and *b* we see the aortic arches as they appear in fish and chick embryos. For ready reference the arches are numbered I to VI, from anterior to posterior. In the fish, arches I and II will soon disappear while arches III through VI will subdivide to form capillaries within the gills. In the chick embryo shown here the first two pairs of arches have already disappeared, but the posterior four pairs are still present, connecting the ventral and dorsal aortas. The arrangement of the aortic arches in the chick is dictated by the positions of the pharyngeal clefts that make a transient appearance but soon disappear.

The fate of the aortic arches in various classes of living vertebrates is compared in Figure 11.45c. All arches that appear during embryonic development are represented, but only those that persist into adult life are solidly shaded. Several important events can be noted in the tetrapods. (1) The section of each root of the dorsal aorta lying between arches III and IV becomes constricted and eventually disappears; this causes all blood entering arch III from the ventral aorta to be directed forward into the head, providing an increased flow of blood to the brain. (2) Arch IV persists as the *systemic arch,* a shunt between the heart and the dorsal aorta. In reptiles the systemic arch is paired, but in birds and mammals one half of the arch has been eliminated, leaving but a single route for blood to pass from the heart to the dorsal aorta. The left systemic arch persists in mammals, the right in birds. In each of these two classes, the ventral portion of the lost arch remains as a channel for blood flow to the forelimb on that side (the artery serving the opposite forelimb springing instead from the systemic arch). (3) Arch V disappears in all tetrapods, and tends to be produced only imperfectly in the embryonic development of higher tetrapods. (4) The ventral portion of arch VI remains as the pulmonary arteries serving the lungs, but the dorsal portion connecting this arch with the dorsal aorta is lost. In mammals, however, this portion persists long enough to serve throughout fetal life as a circulatory shunt (ductus arteriosus) allowing blood to bypass the lungs (oxygenation of blood occurs in the placenta).

Through this example we have seen that the ontogeny of the aortic arches in modern vertebrates tends to recapitulate ontogenetic patterns developed during the evolutionary history of the group. Although six pairs of arches are formed (presumably the ancestral number), only those persist which have a function to perform in postembryonic life. Gene mutations have not yet made possible the complete deletion of those arches which will not be needed in later life, and so the embryos of higher vertebrates continue to expend materials and energy in retracing the ancestral developmental route.

B The prolongation of development

The foregoing example illustrates the tendency of ontogenetic processes to be conservative, retaining ancestral developmental pathways long past the time when they cease to be useful. Combined with this *ontogenetic conservatism,* the addition of new terminal stages makes the development of more complicated organisms a circuitous, prolonged affair. Human maturation is an extreme example of prolongation of development: a 9-month intrauterine period is succeeded by 12 years of prepubertal maturation during much of which survival depends upon appropriate parental care. About 8 more years ensue from the onset of sexual maturation until somatic growth is largely completed. Further maturational changes, especially in the nervous system, may take place even later.

Two kinds of adaptations have been evolved to cope with the problem of delayed maturation: (1) adaptations for tolerating such prolongation of development; (2) adaptations for shortening the developmental period.

TOLERATIVE ADAPTATIONS Adaptations for enduring the prolongation of development include one or more of the following: (1) the capacity to be self-sustaining from an early stage; (2) storage in the ovum of ample food supplies; (3) elaboration of protective egg membranes; (4) viviparity—development within the parental body; (5) parental behaviors which provide pre- and postnatal care to the young.

Larval independence Many animals become self-sustaining so early in ontogeny that the larval stage little resembles the adult but may with some fidelity recapitulate forms thought perhaps to represent ancestral adult types. This is the case with advanced crustaceans, which pass through larval stages successively resembling other less advanced crustacean types (Figure 11.46).

Figure 11.46 □ **Recapitulation in crustacean development. Larval stages of more advanced species resemble adult stages of lower species. Note that new stages are added terminally, lengthening the developmental period. (Adult stages are shown in full color; a circle indicates a stage taking place within the egg prior to hatching.)**

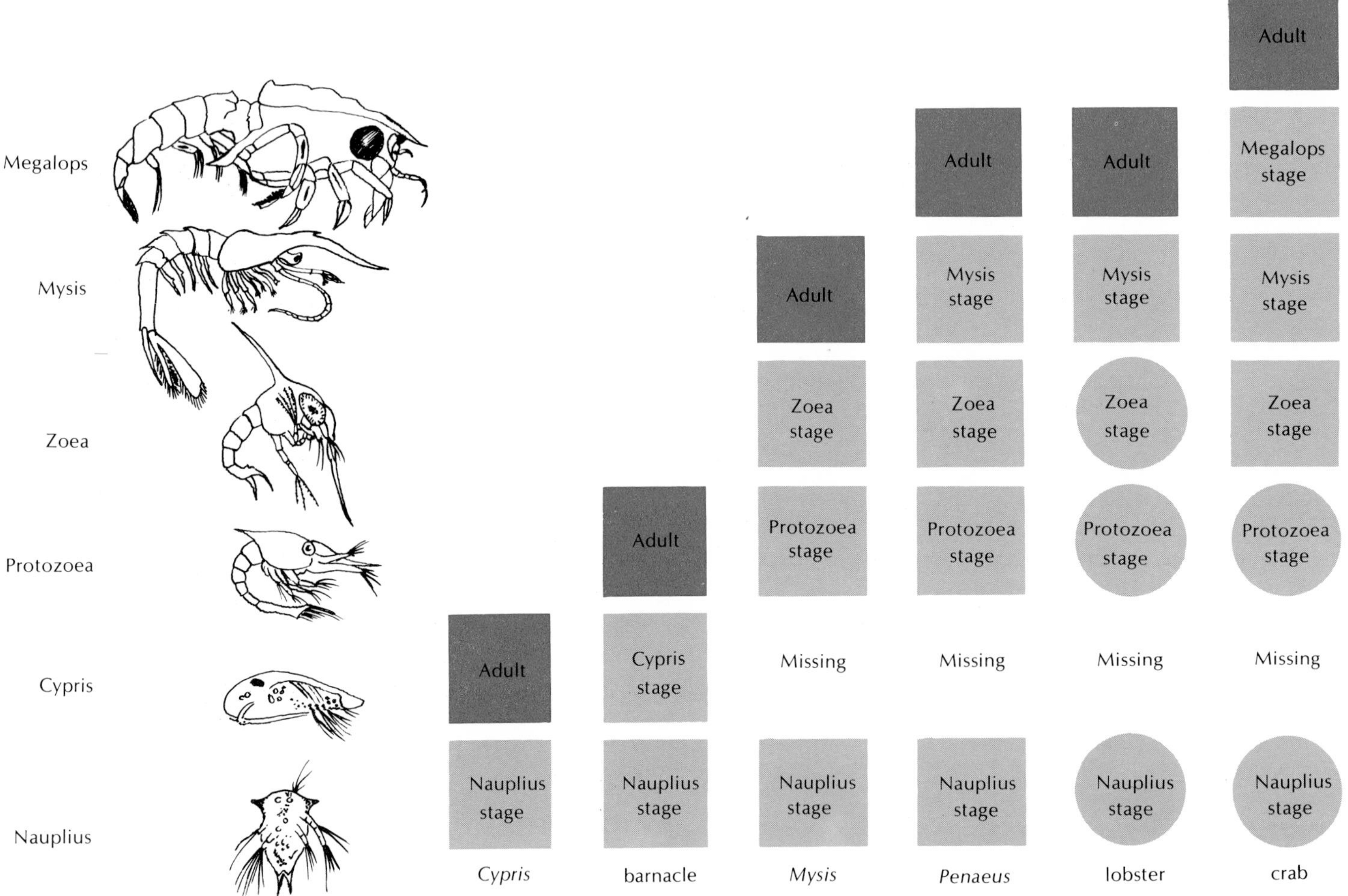

However, larval stages are not merely advanced embryonic stages. Each larval stage has had to adapt to its particular mode of existence, which may differ radically from that at other times of life. Caterpillars possess chewing mouthparts markedly different from the tubular sucking apparatus characteristic of adult moths and butterflies. Their coloration may be cryptic, but matches the background on which the larva (but not the adult) lives. Most benthonic marine crustaceans pass their larval stages in the plankton, which requires that they possess buoyancy adaptations. In the final molt these adaptations are discarded and those suited to adult life appear.

The self-sufficient larval stages are advantageous in that they circumvent the necessity for storage of large amounts of fuel in the egg and, by playing different roles in the biotic community, they do not compete with adults of the same species. However, larvae are exposed to the dangers of predation and starvation: they must develop means of obtaining food and of minimizing the chances of themselves becoming prey; if they are unable to accomplish these tasks as effectively as adults of their species, they may compensate for this by sheer force of numbers. Planktonic invertebrate larvae are prodigiously abundant, but only an extremely small percentage survive to adulthood. Being much more vulnerable to predators than the adults, the larvae form essential components of the nutritional biomass pyramid (see Figure 6.7), and are fed upon by many juvenile and adult forms larger than themselves. Survival to adulthood thus largely depends upon the tremendous fecundity of the adults. A single egg mass produced by the sea hare *Aplysia* (a gastropod) contains some 5×10^9 eggs, yet the number of adults remains in equilibrium with the rest of the littoral community.

Storage of nutrients The storage of food in the ovum may be substantially increased to allow the embryo a longer period of protected development before it must fend for itself. The largest single cells are the yolk-swollen ova of birds, turtles, and certain sharks. We have already noted the way in which large amounts of yolk will alter the pattern of cleavage and later development (see Figure 11.10c).

Egg membranes While of benefit to any species, protective egg membranes are essential to those with long developmental periods. They may provide attachment to the substratum, protection against predators, or against excessive water loss when the egg is laid on land. In Chapter 17 we shall consider the adaptive attributes of amniote egg membranes.

Viviparity Embryos retained within the mother's body during development are well protected against the vicissitudes of a long developmental period. Protection from dehydration, predators, adverse temperatures, parasites, and mechanical injury is afforded merely by remaining within the uterus, as is the case with *ovoviviparous* fishes and reptiles. However, unless nourishment can somehow be obtained from the parent's body, the egg must still be provided with a large amount of yolk. *Euviviparity,* a condition in which the young derives nutrition from the mother during intrauterine development, has been fully realized only by eutherian mammals. In Chapter 17 we shall also consider the viviparous condition and the structure of the placenta.

Parental care Many animals, including invertebrates, protect their eggs from harm. In birds such nurture has the additional function of keeping the eggs warm, as is necessary in homoiothermal species. Postnatal care is also given, regularly by birds and mammals, sporadically among other groups. We shall later (Chapter 17) learn about a number of interesting and unusual means of pre- and postnatal care.

ADAPTATIONS FOR SHORTENING THE DEVELOPMENTAL PERIOD Although the prolongation of development may be tolerated by the means summarized above, there is also considerable survival value in inheritable changes that make possible either the abbreviation or the acceleration of development.

Accelerative adaptations By elevating the temperature within physiologically tolerable limits, metabolism and hence development may be accelerated. Even among homoiotherms, intrinsic temperature regulation is ineffective during prenatal life. Young homoiotherms are unable to maintain a stable body temperature for some time after birth and must spend substantial periods in contact with the body of the parent. The brooding behavior of parent birds serves to warm the eggs and later promotes survival of the nestlings. A comparable effect is obtained in mammals by development within the uterus and marsupium. Eggs of poikilothermal species do not usually perish if chilled but develop more rapidly when warmed; thus, laying of the eggs in sunny places may favor survival.

Abbreviative adaptations Abbreviation of developmental sequences depends upon chance genetic changes by which certain stages are abridged or deleted. It is a general evolutionary rule that that which is unused is lost. There is, of course, survival value in any mutations that prevent the embryo from wasting its reserves on formation of structures that will later have no adaptive value. Such conserving mutations do not take place on demand, or the developmental process would certainly be much less circuitous than we know it to be. However, the organism can also profit from any genetic changes that lead to the *incomplete* development of a structure which is unneeded.

The effect of use and disuse has long been noted. At the start of the nineteenth century, J.-B. P. Lamarck formulated a theory that attempted to explain organic evolution in terms of inheritance of acquired characteristics, implying the acquisition of new traits on the basis of need and their loss through disuse. Despite the consistent lack of experimental verification, Lamarckian theory continues to influence popular thinking with respect to heredity and evolution. How, but for Lamarckianism, may we explain why cave animals are often eyeless? According to Lamarck, if an eye is needed it is acquired, if not needed it is quickly lost. Let us view this from another angle: we know that genetic mutation causes any population to become diversified. Any mutation that even slightly increases the adaptive potential of a characteristic is more likely to be perpetuated than its less effective allele, and this is true whether its adaptive value is defined by exogenous or endogenous selective factors. Mutations that alter the course of development are common enough, but these are ordinarily detrimental or lethal under the conditions of existence which have influenced the evolution of the species to that point. If, however, a population of normal fish were to become established in a totally dark habitat, selection pressure would no longer operate against mutations that interfered with the development of eyes; in fact, since an eye is an elaborate structure requiring considerable expenditure of energy for its production and maintenance, any mutations through which the development of the eye were abridged or deleted would now have positive survival value.

Many similar examples have been noted by students of development. The pharyngeal pouches develop only partially in amniotes. Aortic arch V, doomed to quick involution, makes but a transient appearance in the mammalian embryo. Often such ontogenetic vestiges are traced out in but token fashion—the pattern still is partially represented in the genetic code of the species; since the structure is now useless, however, abridgement of its development is not only tolerable but welcome.

Cenomorphosis Occasionally, part of the load from the past can be shucked off by the complete deletion of some portion of the developmental process. Deletion of subterminal stages in maturation is termed *cenomorphosis* ("new form"), although in fact shortcuts or alternative routes are used in the production of adult structures that may be essentially unchanged. It is as though the "goal" of adult form, having been genetically established, can now be reached by cutting across some of the bends in the circuitous route by which the goal was first attained. Occasionally, quite new paths may be followed in reaching the final destination. Such new pathways are rare, and usually only certain curves are eliminated in shortening the ontogenetic path.

Pedomorphosis Development can also be abbreviated if sexual maturation can be achieved at a stage earlier than the ultimate somatic expression of the genome. Such abbreviation constitutes *pedomorphosis* ("child shape"), a phenomenon in which either sexual maturity is precocious or somatic maturation is retarded. The final result is that certain late developmental stages are omitted at the end of the maturational sequence and formerly juvenile characteristics appear in the adult. A "larval" stage becomes capable of reproduction and constitutes the new adult form. Neotenic salamanders such as *Necturus* retain the gills and other larval characteristics into adulthood. Some students of evolution hold that the ancestor of vertebrates was a neotenic form that failed to change into a sedentary, filter-feeding adult but retained into the adult state a tadpolelike form that is somewhat reminiscent of the larvae of modern tunicates.

We may conclude that as organisms evolve toward increasing complexity, their developmental sequences tend to become circuitous and prolonged. This necessitates the evolution of adaptations for tolerating such lengthening of development, and also promotes retention of mutant genes that act to abbreviate or accelerate the maturational process. Development is rather like a "long, long trail a-winding," for it retains the vestiges of the adaptive requirements of ancestral species and mirrors the long journey of life from its beginnings to the present. Any shortcuts represent *intrinsic adaptations*—genetic changes that are adaptive not so much with respect to external conditions as to the internal integration of the organism itself.

REVIEW AND DISCUSSION

1 Why is development better called *ontogeny* than *embryogeny?*

2 Distinguish between activation and fertilization. Summarize the basic events leading up to cleavage.

3 How and when are the dorsoventral axis and symmetry of an amphibian embryo determined?

4 Summarize experiments indicating that the cytoplasm of the ovum is regionalized even prior to fertilization and that this regionalization affects the determination of cells in the later embryo.

5 Explain, with examples, what is meant by competence, determination, and differentiation.

6 What experimental means may be used to determine whether a certain pattern of behavior develops through learning and practice or through neuromuscular maturation only?

7 How may engram formation resemble other aspects of cytodifferentiation?

8 Summarize experimental evidence indicating how hormones might be involved in the regulation of development.

9 What evidence is there that determination and cytodifferentiation involve the repression of certain sets of genes and the activation of others?

10 Explain, giving examples, what is meant by induction.

11 How may morphogenetic movements be explained in part on the basis of changing affinities among embryonic cells?

12 How are cell aggregations formed and stabilized?

13 Explain how environmental factors affect each of the following: (*a*) penetrance of the antennaless gene in *Drosophila;* (*b*) morphogenesis in *Trichogramma;* (*c*) sexual maturation in *Achyla;* (*d*) polarization of *Fucus* zygotes; (*e*) sex determination in *Bonellia;* (*f*) shell coiling in *Lymnaea;* (*g*) spine morphogenesis in *Brachionus.*

14 What adult structures or tissues in man are derived from each of the three primary germ layers?

15 Summarize the major kinds of tissues occurring in metazoans and tracheophytes, indicating how the form of each reflects function. Why are sponges not considered to have true tissues?

16 Explain and evaluate the principle of paleogenesis. Why must developmental sequences be conservative?

17 Explain why the Lamarckian theory has proved to be so tenacious. Furnish alternative explanations for the acquisition of useful new structures and the loss of useless ones.

18 Summarize the types of adaptations that permit organisms to survive long developmental periods.

19 Contrast *cenomorphosis* and *pedomorphosis,* with examples. Some biologists consider that man is a pedomorphic species; discuss this possibility.

20 What changes in cleavage and gastrulation are brought about when large amounts of yolk are stored in an ovum? Which of these changes may be an outcome of mere mechanical obstruction and which the result of selection toward a new developmental pathway?

21 Discuss the sociological implications of techniques for creating new individuals by implantation of nuclei from cells of the adult body into enucleated human ova.

REFERENCES

ALLEN, R. D. "The Moment of Fertilization," *Sci. Amer.,* **201** (1959).

BARTH, L. J. *Development.* Reading, Mass.: Addison-Wesley Publishing Company, Inc., 1964. Interesting compilation of experimental data concerning the regulation of development.

BEERMANN, W. "Cytological Aspects of Information Transfer in Cellular Differentiation," *Amer. Zool.,* **3** (1963). Specific patterns of chromosome puffs appear during maturation of insect larvae, some of which may be controlled by molting hormone.

BONNER, J. T. *The Evolution of Development.* London and New York: Cambridge University Press, 1958.

——— "How Slime Molds Communicate," *Sci. Amer.,* **209** (1963). Reviews experiments demonstrating the action of a chemical attractant in the formation of multicellular aggregations.

EDWARDS, R. G. "Mammalian Eggs in the Laboratory," *Sci. Amer.,* **215** (1966).

EPHRUSSI, B., AND M. C. WEISS "Hybrid Somatic Cells," *Sci. Amer.,* **230** (1969). Fusion of cells of different species in tissue culture assists the study of cytodifferentiation and facilitates chromosome mapping.

ERICKSON, R. O. "Patterns of Cell Growth and Differentiation in Plants," in *The Cell,* J. Brachet and A. E. Mirsky, eds., Vol. I. New York: Academic Press, Inc., 1959. An advanced reference for the enterprising student.

ETKIN, W. "How a Tadpole Becomes a Frog," *Sci. Amer.,* **214** (1966). The process and regulation of amphibian metamorphosis are considered.

FISCHBERG, M., AND A. W. BLACKLER "How Cells Specialize," *Sci. Amer.,* **205** (1961).

GORDON, J. B. "Transplanted Nuclei and Cell Differentiation," *Sci. Amer.,* **219** (1968). Nuclei of intestinal cells from adult African clawed frogs prove capable of developing into normal tadpoles when transplanted into enucleated eggs.

GROSS, J. "Studies on the Biology of Connective Tissues: Remodelling of Collagen in Metamorphosis," *Medicine,* **43** (1964). The possible action of thyroid hormone is examined in changing patterns of enzyme secretion.

HADORN, E. "Transdetermination in Cells," *Sci. Amer.,* **219** (1968). The development of larval *Drosophila* tissues may be switched into alternative pathways by transplantation into adult flies and subsequent retransplantation into other larvae.

HAYFLICK, L. "Human Cells and Aging," *Sci. Amer.,* **218** (1968). Human fibroblasts are found capable of only about 50 generations of normal cell division before becoming senescent.

KELLENBERGER, E. "The Genetic Control of the Shape of a Virus," *Sci. Amer.,* **215** (1966). Explores the role of genes in the morphogenesis of a simple biotic system.

KING, T. J., AND R. BRIGGS "Changes in the Nuclei of Differentiating Gastrula Cells, as Demonstrated by Nuclear Transplantation," *Proc. Natl. Acad. Sci. U.S.,* **41** (1955). A remarkable technique is described for transplanting cell nuclei, and the results of these transplants are presented and analyzed.

KOLLER, D. "Germination," *Sci. Amer.,* **200** (1959).

KONIGSBERG, I. R. "The Embryological Origin of Muscle," *Sci. Amer.,* **211** (1964).

LOEWENSTEIN, W. R. "Some Reflections on Growth and Differentiation," *Perspectives in Biol. and Med.,* **11** (1968).

MOORE, J. A. *Heredity and Development.* London and New York: Oxford University Press, 1963. A concise, easily understandable reference.

MOSCONA, A. A. "How Cells Associate," *Sci. Amer.,* **205** (1961). Reviews experiments with dissociated cells of sponges and higher animals.

NIU, M. C., AND V. C. TWITTY "The Differentiation of Gastrula Ectoderm in Medium Conditioned by Axial Mesoderm," *Proc. Natl. Acad. Sci. U.S.,* **39** (1953). This classic experiment demonstrates the existence of chemical factors operating in induction.

SINGER, M. "The Regeneration of Body Parts," *Sci. Amer.,* **199** (1958).

SKOOG, F., AND C. O. MILLER "Chemical Regulation of Growth and Organ Formation in Plant Tissues Cultured *in vitro,*" *Symp. Soc. Exp. Biol.,* **11** (1957).

STERN, C. "Two or Three Bristles," *Amer. Scientist,* **42** (1954). Considers a morphogenetic problem in the fruit fly.

STEWARD, F. C., WITH L. M. BLAKELY, A. E. KENT, AND M. O. MAPES "Growth and Organization in Free Cell Cultures," *Brookhaven Symp. in Biol.,* **16** (1963). Describes techniques for in vitro culture of isolated plant cells and the subsequent growth of entire plants from such cells.

SUSSMANN, M. *Animal Growth and Development.* Englewood Cliffs, N.J.: Prentice-Hall, Inc., 1960. A concise, readable reference covering both descriptive and regulative aspects of development.

SZOLLOSI, D. G., AND H. RIS "Observations on Sperm Penetration in the Rat," *Biophys. and Biochem. Cytol.,* **10** (1961). An electron-micrographic analysis of the process of fertilization as observed in a mammalian egg.

VAN OVERBEEK, J. "The Control of Plant Growth," *Sci. Amer.,* **219** (1968). Describes the action of an inhibitor and various hormones in the control of dormancy, germination, and growth.

WADDINGTON, C. H. *How Animals Develop.* New York: Harper & Row, Publishers, 1962.

WESSELLS, N. K., AND W. J. RUTTER "Phases in Cell Differentiation," *Sci. Amer.,* **220** (1969). Biochemical and cytological changes in pancreatic tissue cultured in vitro indicate three phases in cytodifferentiation.

WILSON, H. V. "On Some Phenomena of Coalescence and Regeneration in Sponges," *J. Exp. Zool.,* **5** (1907). A pioneer investigation into the formation of aggregations by dissociated cells.

Chapter 12  BODY PLAN

THE OUTCOME OF DEVELOPMENTAL processes is the production of a functional *organism,* capable of maintaining itself and of contributing to the perpetuation of its kind. The individual organism represents the basic structural and functional level at which life interacts with the environment. An organism is not merely the sum of its parts but manifests a new level of complexity arising out of the coordinated interaction of those parts. It also displays certain regularities of construction that constitute its *body plan.* The body plan is the ultimate expression of morphogenesis: the form of all constituent parts must be integrated so as to produce a harmonious whole, both structurally and physiologically, if the organism is to survive within the competitive-cooperative framework of its community.

The evolution of body plans of greater complexity from ancestral forms of simpler design has not entailed extinction of less complex types, for great diversity can be encompassed within the intricate web of interdependencies that constitutes the planetary ecosystem. Accordingly, we can see today organisms representing a wide spectrum of organizational complexity, from unicellular protists to vertebrates having bodies composed of many billions of specialized cells. Every phylum represents a group of organisms presumably descended from a common ancestor and sharing a common body plan. This plan has often undergone radiative adaptation as various members have adopted different roles in their communities, but the underlying principles that govern bodily design have necessarily remained inviolate.

Alteration in one part of the body necessitates compensatory modifications of other parts. For example, the overall mass of the head determines the relative thickness of neck and shoulder muscles used in the support and mobility of that head. The total mass of the trunk determines the thickness and length of the appendages. A mouse enlarged to elephantine proportions could no longer look or act like a mouse. Its legs, if held to the original relative proportions, could not support the torso. It is thus no coincidence that the elephant has sturdy legs like tree trunks.

In this chapter we shall consider cardinal principles that govern body organization and then shall examine certain organisms that may be considered exemplary of

Figure 12.1 ☐ **Planes and axes of symmetry: (*a*) asymmetrical; (*b*) spherical; (*c*) radial; (*d*) bilateral; (*e*) the various planes of symmetry in a higher animal (rat).**

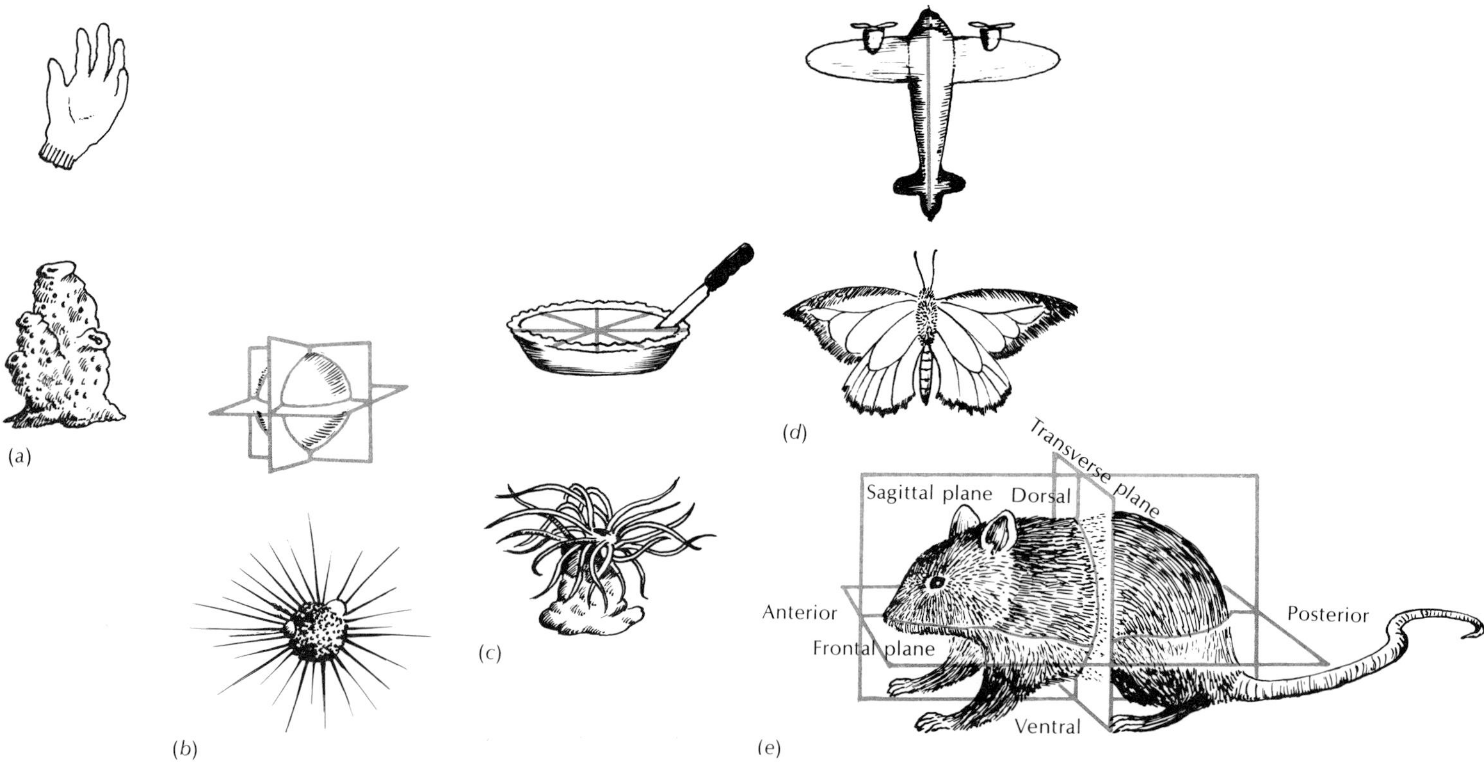

Figure 12.2 □ (*a*) Diatom (*Arachnoidiscus*), showing radially symmetrical arrangement of surface pattern of test. (*Bausch & Lomb.*) (*b*) Sea gooseberry, *Pleurobrachia* (Phylum Ctenophora), fishing with extended tentacles. The bilateral placement of the tentacles and their sheaths makes this animal *biradially* symmetrical. The mouth is located at the lower pole of the ovoid body, and the ciliated comb plates used in swimming are seen extending in rows from the aboral (upper) to the oral (lower) pole. Invertebrates and small fish are captured by adhesive cells (*colloblasts*) on the tentacles. (*Courtesy of Dr. Douglas P. Wilson.*)

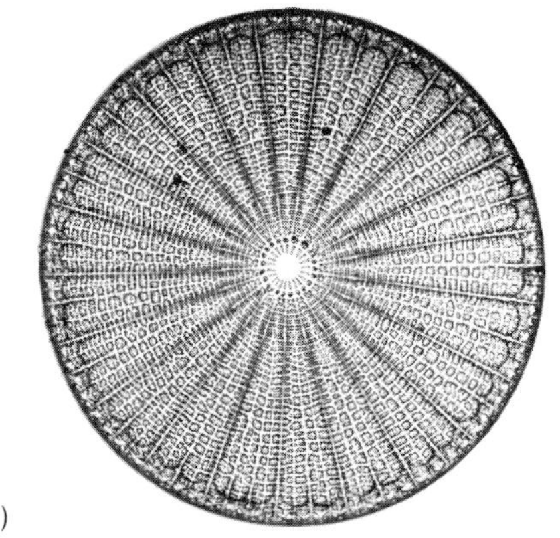

(*a*)

(*b*)

organization at the acellular, cellular, tissue, organ, and organ-system levels of organization. At the organ-system level we shall consider animals representative of several major lines of evolutionary ascent, comparing body plans which are the concrete manifestations of the process of adaptation in the molluscan, arthropodan, and vertebrate lines. These three lines have attained the highest level of organizational complexity realized to date at the organismal level.

A Symmetry

Some organisms are asymmetrical—no plane of section can divide their bodies into equal halves. However even in these forms the necessity for balance requires some regularity of form, so that appendages or branches tend to be placed regularly and the body's mass is oriented about its center of gravity. Most *animals* display definite symmetry, there being at least one plane along which their bodies can be divided into approximately identical halves that are mirror images of one another (Figure 12.1). *Plant* symmetry is less definite but usually tends toward a semblance of radial symmetry because of the need for balanced distribution of foliage and branches.

Although most protozoans are asymmetric, floating types such as heliozoans and some radiolarians (see Figure 4.23) favor *spherical* symmetry—their bodies are globular with stiff axopods projecting in all directions from the center, and can be divided into similar halves along a nearly infinite number of planes.

Coelenterates and comb jellies display *radial* or *biradial* symmetry. In the radially symmetrical organism the body plan is discoidal or columnar, with parts radiating from the central axis like spokes of a wheel (Figure 12.2*a*). The body is usually divisible into equal halves along at least two planes oriented at right angles to one another. In jellyfish these planes bisect the *oral-aboral axis.* (The mouth-bearing surface is *oral;* that opposite it is *aboral.*) Sea anemones and tentaculate comb jellies are *biradially* symmetrical, in that although the body plan is fundamentally radial, the placement of certain structures prevents the body from being divisible into equal halves along any plane but one. The body of the comb jelly *Pleurobrachia* is ovoid, bearing series of ciliated plates along several meridians passing between the aboral and oral poles (Figure 12.2*b*). However, the animal also possesses one pair of tentacles, retractible into sheaths placed 180° apart around the circumference. Accordingly there is only one plane through which the body can be sectioned into identical halves, each bearing one tentacle and sheath.

On the basis of primary body symmetry, metazoan phyla are grouped into two categories: (1) Radiata (phyla with primary radial symmetry); (2) Bilateria (phyla with primary bilateral symmetry). Radiata include coelenterates and comb jellies (ctenophores), mainly sessile or floating species which must meet the environment with equal facility on all sides. Bilateral symmetry favors an actively locomotory mode of life, even though certain Bilateria may become sedentary in adulthood, thereupon often assuming a secondary radial symmetry. The bilaterally symmetrical body can be divided into approximately identical left and right halves, along a *sagittal* plane passing through the midline of the body from the upper (dorsal) to the lower (ventral) surface, in parallel with the longitudinal axis. Sectioning the body along *transverse* planes that intersect the longitudinal axis at right angles does not yield equal halves since any bilaterally symmetrical animal is *polarized,* that is, its anterior end is different from its posterior end. A *frontal* section divides the body into dorsal and ventral halves, but again these halves are dissimilar. Bilaterally symmetrical body plans have proven most conducive to evolutionary advancement, for they promote the development of anteroposterior polarity, with *cephalization* of the anterior end.

Figure 12.3 □ Forty-hour chick embryo, showing axial gradient, as evidenced by more rapid development of anterior end. (*Ward's Natural Science Establishment, Inc.*)

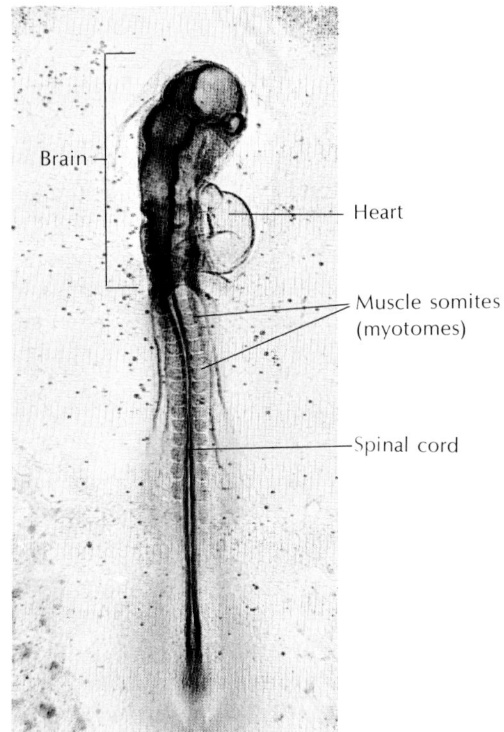

B Cephalization

Neural tissue and receptors of stimuli originating in the external environment tend to concentrate at the anterior end of a bilaterally symmetrical animal. Such concentration is adaptive in that as the animal moves forward its anterior end contacts the environment first. Rudimentary cephalization is shown by planarians, in which the head bears a pair of eyes and a concentration of chemical receptors, communicating with a pair of cephalic ganglia that constitute a simple brain. The mouth of a planarian is not located in the head, but ventrally near the midpoint of the body. In most Bilateria the mouth is placed anteriorly along with an increasing variety of sensory receptors.

C Axial gradient

The anteroposterior polarization of bilaterally symmetrical animals is accompanied by the establishment of a physiological and developmental gradient along that axis of the organism. This *axial gradient* is reflected by the fact that development proceeds more rapidly in the anterior part of the body, and a great proportion of the embryo's energy is spent in the elaboration of head structures. This developmental gradient is well shown in a 40-hr chick embryo (Figure 12.3), in which the head and brain dwarf the more posterior parts of the body. Throughout life, a concomitant *metabolic gradient* exists, with the basal metabolic rate (the rate at which oxygen is consumed by the resting organism) declining from anterior to posterior.

12.2 □ ACELLULAR ORGANIZATION

According to whether structural complexity has been developed through cell differentiation or through the specialization of cell *parts,* organisms may be termed *acellular* or *multicellular.* If multicellular, they may exhibit a *cellular, tissue, organ,* or *organ-system* level of construction. We shall consider each of these levels, as exemplified in the body plans of representative organisms. In so doing, we must bear in mind that relative simplicity of structure at the organismal level does not imply a concomitant simplicity at the molecular level, and that even apparently simple organisms such as *Amoeba* must be able to reproduce and to carry out a number of complex metabolic activities.

The simplest organisms are not multicellular, but consist of a more or less complicated mass of cytoplasm containing one or commonly several nuclei. Such organisms may be thought of as *unicellular;* in fact, however, many attain a level of structural complexity at which they are better considered *acellular,* developing within the confines of a single bounding membrane specialized regions functionally analogous to the organs of multicellular creatures. Ancestral unicellular forms have evolved toward complexity in one of two ways: some have become multicellular (permitting increase in size and division of labor through cell specialization); others have developed multiple nuclei and specialized cell *organelles,* effecting greater competency without usually bringing about any significant increase in size. Largeness has its value, but smallness may also be adaptive. The smaller the organism, the tinier the habitat needed to sustain a population of the species. A puddle in which not a single fish could survive may be the home of innumerable bacteria, desmids, protozoans, and the like. Smallness increases the amount of genetic material in the gene pool: one kilogram of protozoans would possess a gene pool capable of greater heterogeneity (and hence, of flexibility) than that possessed by two 0.5-kg fish. Obviously a population of some 10^{12} protozoa can incorporate many more potentially adaptive alleles than can be found in the genomes of a pair of fish, even though the *individual* genome of the fish is much more elaborate. Accordingly microorganisms can make genetic adjustments much more rapidly than populations of larger organisms can.

We find therefore that although many organisms have evolved toward larger size and complexity at the multicellular level, others have evolved toward an increased complexity that is compatible with smallness. When an organism becomes more highly organized without dividing into a mass of separate cells, it not only saves space that would be occupied by the plasma membranes of those cells, but circumvents the problems of intercellular communication and coordination which all multicellular organisms must solve.

AN EXAMPLE: CILIATE PROTOZOANS Ciliates range in size from <10 μm to >2mm. They use cilia for locomotion and food gathering, and possess two kinds of nuclei: a *macronucleus* and one or more *micronuclei* (Figure 12.4). Micronuclei are typical diploid nuclei, whereas the macronucleus is polyploid, containing multiple chromosome sets and thereby amplifying the organism's mRNA-producing potential. Such chromosomal multiplication is to be expected in view of the relatively large size and high activity rate of many ciliates. The macronucleus thus meets the organism's metabolic demands, whereas the micronucleus functions primarily in the reproductive process.

The cytoplasm contains not only those organelles common to all heterotrophic eucaryotic cells (see Figure 10.8) but additional specialized supportive, coordinative, osmoregulatory, or contractile organelles. The cytoplasm constitutes two distinct regions, the outer *ectoplasm* and the inner *endoplasm.* The former is a clear colloidal gel in which are embedded fibrils, the basal bodies of cilia, and trichocysts. The latter is more fluid and contains stored nutrients, mitochondria, ribosomes, lysosomes, and food vacuoles in various stages of digestion.

Digestive organelles Protozoa ingest solid food (bacteria, algae, and other protozoans) phagocytically. A portion of the plasma membrane invaginates and breaks free internally to form a *food vacuole* enclosing the prey. In sarcodines, food vacuoles may be formed at any point on the cell surface, but in ciliates they form only at the "cell mouth" (*cytostome*), a point at which the plasma membrane is not overlain by the supportive pellicle. The cytostome is often located at the bottom of a pit or groove (the *cytopharynx*) lined with cilia (separate or fused into undulating membranelles) that sweep food into the cytostome. Lysosomes discharge their stored enzymes into the food vacuoles; the digested material passes through the vacuolar membrane into the cytoplasm, while indigestible residues remain within the vacuole and are ultimately discharged to the exterior by way of another opening through the pellicle, the "cell anus" (*cytopyge*). During the digestive process food vacuoles circulate slowly through the endoplasm, finally reaching the cytopyge where they disgorge their remaining contents and vanish. In certain complicated ciliates such as *Epidinium,* the food vacuoles discharge into a rectumlike invagination, from which the accumulated wastes are subsequently discharged to the exterior.

Osmoregulatory and excretory organelles Freshwater organisms must coun-

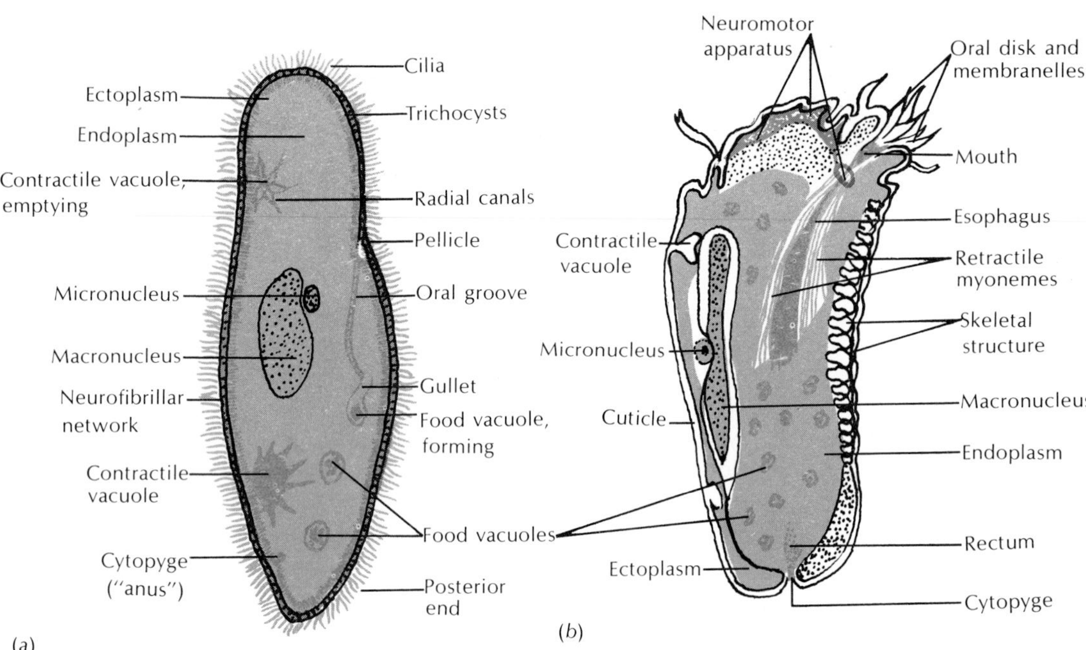

Figure 12.4 □ Acellular level of organization: (*a*) *Paramecium* and (*b*) *Epidinium*. *Epidinium* inhabits the digestive tract of cud-chewing mammals and in internal organization is one of the most complex protozoans.

teract the tendency of water to enter their cells by osmosis. Protozoans collect and expell excess water by means of *contractile vacuoles,* from which radiate a number of collecting canals. The contractile vacuoles of most ciliates are located in the ectoplasm and are fixed in position, communicating either with the cytopyge or with a separate excretory pore opening through the pellicle. A contractile vacuole usually empties from 1 to 15 times per hour in freshwater species, but only once every 3 to 4 hr in marine forms. In the latter it is needed less for the elimination of water than for ionic regulation and some excretion of metabolic wastes.

The mechanisms involved in the filling and emptying of contractile vacuoles are still under investigation. The main vacuole is often formed by the coalescing of the membranes of smaller vesicles that form at the medial ends of the collecting canals. During filling, the viscosity of the surrounding cytoplasm is low; at the time of discharge, the cytoplasmic viscosity abruptly increases. This suggests that a change in colloidal state may take place during "contraction" of the vacuole.

Protective and supportive organelles The exterior of the ciliate is invested with a *pellicle* of extreme thinness and considerable elasticity, capable of resuming its original shape after distortion. The pellicle is often elaborately patterned with strengthening ridges or polygons (Figure 12.5). *Endoskeletal* rods or plates confer rigidity when present (for instance, in *Epidinium*). In some ciliates the cytopharynx is encircled by endoskeletal rods forming a supportive "oral basket."

Trichocysts are cylindrical organelles of disputed function, embedded in the ectoplasm perpendicular to the body surface. Upon appropriate mechanical or chemical stimulation they discharge long filaments into the milieu. In some species these filaments seem to be toxic and may immobilize prospective prey, while in others they may be protective, or may provide anchorage against water currents.

Locomotory organelles Cilia, or membranous or bristlelike organelles formed by the fusion of cilia, are used for locomotion. Each cilium originates in a basal body or *kinetosome* embedded within the cytoplasm (see Figure 10.12). Rows of cilia may be fused into membranelles or triangular cirri, which the ciliates employ as legs, moving them in coordinated sequence so that they can literally walk upon the substratum. For effective locomotion, the action of cilia or cirri must be coordinated by means of neurofibrils. The effective strokes of the cilia must normally all be in the same direction; nevertheless the stroke is reversible, for ciliates can swim not only forward but in reverse as well.

Myonemes are contractile fibrils, possibly structurally homologous with the myofibrils of the muscle cells of higher animals (see Figure 16.31). They may be restricted to the cytoplasm, or may constitute a contractile stalk by which the animal may withdraw from noxious stimuli. *Cytoplasmic* myonemes permit the animal to contract instantaneously into a sphere when subjected to mechanical pressure; in this shape it is best able to withstand such pressure.

Sensomotor apparatus An anastomosing system of coordinative neurofibrils interconnects all cilia and cirri. *Intercilary* fibrils radiate from the *motorium,* which serves as a "brain." When fibers from the motorium are severed, the cilia beat at random. Just within the pellicle runs a network of fibrils associated with presumably sensory bristles extending outward from the cell surface. The neurofibrils of ciliates may function both in the transmission of impulses from sensory areas and in the coordination of motor responses. If so, these complicated acellular organisms have achieved a very creditable analog to the nervous systems of metazoans!

Figure 12.5 □ Pellicle and cortex of *Paramecium.*

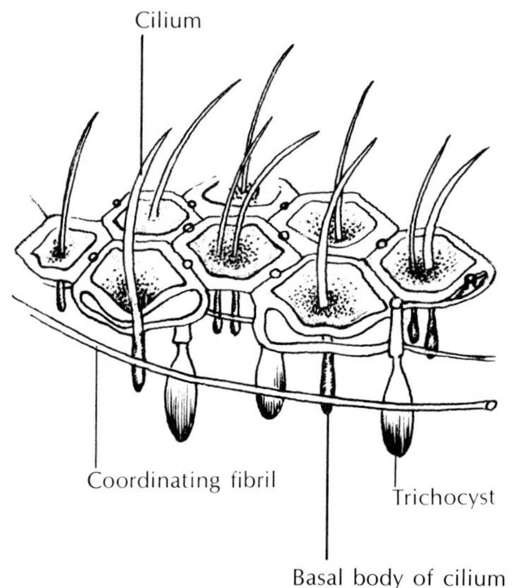

12.3 □ MULTICELLULAR ORGANISMS AT THE CELLULAR LEVEL OF CONSTRUCTION

The least complex forms of multicellular organisms consist of aggregations of cells that are not yet organized into true tissues, although cell specialization may occur.

AN EXAMPLE: SPONGES Sponges are multicellular, but their cells show little tendency to aggregate into true tissues. Nevertheless, cells are differentiated into several types, permitting division of labor (Figure 12.6).

The sponge body plan consists of a body wall perforated by numerous *pores* leading to canals that converge upon a central cavity, the *spongocoel.* Water entering the spongocoel through the pores exits by way of a single excurrent opening, the *osculum.* Three types of construction are recognized—*asconoid, syconoid,* and *rhagonoid* (Figure 2.24). The simplest is the asconoid type, in which the body wall is not

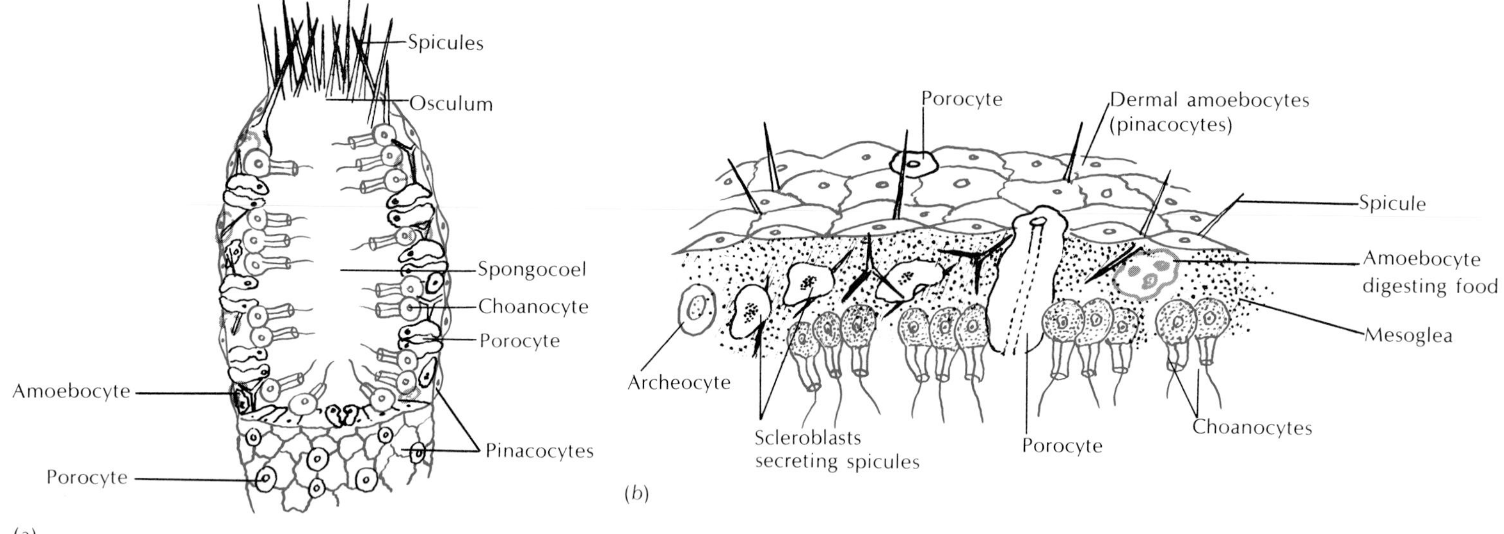

Figure 12.6 **Cellular level of organization. Body plan and cell types of an asconoid sponge: (*a*) longitudinal section through entire sponge (cells shown disproportionately large for clarity); (*b*) cell types seen in section of body wall. True integrated tissues are lacking, each cell responding and performing as an individual.**

convoluted and the pores (ostia) that perforate the body wall open *directly* into the spongocoel, which is lined with flagellated collar cells (*choanocytes*) that maintain a flow of water in through the pores and out by way of the osculum. The body wall of syconoid sponges is elaborated into numerous fingerlike projections containing extensions of the spongocoel, the *radial canals.* Choanocytes line the radial canals and are absent from the spongocoel proper. In rhagonoid sponges, further increase in internal surface area is made possible by complex, branching canals leading from the outside to the much reduced spongocoel. Along these canals are numerous small chambers lined with choanocytes, where food capture takes place.

Since all digestion in sponges takes place within food vacuoles in individual cells, the material that is ingested must be of subcellular dimensions. Larger particles are prevented from entering the spongocoel by the size of the incurrent pores; animals that might actively enter through the osculum are usually discouraged by a ring of needlelike spicules guarding that orifice. The food consists mainly of unicellular phytoplankton swept into the sponge in the current of water circulated by the flagellary action of the choanocytes, and ingested either by these cells or by amoebocytes.

Amoebocytes perform many functions in sponges. They wander freely through the gelatinous matrix that constitutes much of the body wall. Several functional types are recognized, but it is likely that the functional state of a given amoebocyte can be modulated according to the needs of the organism. *Archeocytes* are large amoebocytes having big nuclei and blunt pseudopodia. They are capable of differentiating into eggs or sperm, or presumably into any other cell type in demand. They are also instrumental in digesting and distributing nutrients. Those particularly rich in stored food serve as nurse cells to maturing ova, passing their food reserves into the cytoplasm of the latter.

Scleroblasts are amoebocytes that secrete the supportive and protective *spicules.* We do not know how spicule shape is regulated during their secretion, but many elaborate types are produced, some of which are highly species-specific and therefore of use in taxonomic identification. *Monaxon* spicules are rodlike, curved, or straight, and may be pointed, knobbed, or hooked on one or both ends. Other types of spicules have three, four, six, or many rays, extending in three dimensions. In glass sponges the spicules may be united into a skeletal lattice (see Figure 4.25). Calcareous sponges form spicules of $CaCO_3$, while other sponges produce siliceous spicules. The skeleton of horny sponges consists mainly of anastomosing fibers of *spongin* (a protein similar to silk) secreted by amoeboid *spongioblasts.*

The outer surface of the sponge is covered by a thin layer of polygonal, highly contractile *pinacocytes,* which may be modified amoebocytes. A contracting pinacocyte humps up by retracting its flattened margins; when this reaction is generalized, the diameter of the entire sponge decreases slightly. Other contractile cells are the spindle-shaped *myocytes,* similar to smooth muscle cells of higher animals, which are distributed sparsely except in a ring about the osculum, which they can close defensively. Sponge larvae are flagellated and swim freely, but the adults are not motile. Despite the apparent absence of nerve cells,

Figure 12.7 □ **Sponge reproduction and development.**

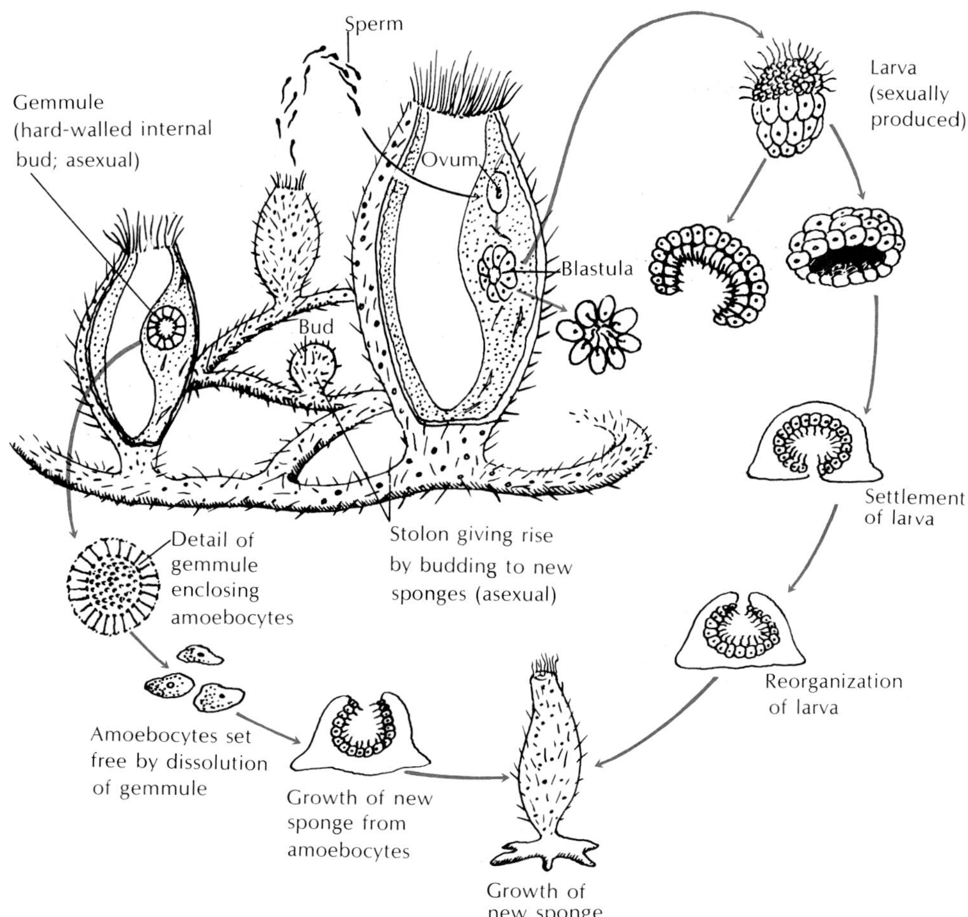

sponges respond to aversive stimuli by limited contractility and closure of their orifices.

Porocytes are cells restricted to asconoid sponges, forming hollow cylinders oriented at right angles to the thickness of the body wall. The openings through the porocytes serve as the incurrent pores. Porocytes can contract, thereby closing these pores; remarkably, they never seem to attempt to capture the prey which passes through them, but rely upon nutrients diffusing from other cells.

A sponge profits by division of labor among its various specialized or functionally versatile cells. Multicellularity confers enhanced efficiency in obtaining food. The composite flagellar activity of the choanocytes produces a brisk current that brings a constant supply of plankton through the sponge. Sperm cells liberated by other sponges are also brought in with this current, enhancing the probability that the ova will be fertilized. A choanocyte which engulfs a sperm cell of its own species behaves oddly. Instead of digesting the sperm, the choanocyte becomes amoeboid and creeps through the matrix until it reaches a mature ovum with which it fuses, thereby bringing about fertilization.

The developing embryos are protected by passing their early developmental period embedded within the body wall of the parent, developing to a flagellated blastula-like stage before breaking free and passing to the exterior by way of the osculum (Figure 12.7). Reproduction also takes place asexually, by budding or by formation of hardwalled overwintering bodies known as gemmules, which contain archaeocytes that can give rise to new sponges.

It could be contended that the layers of choanocytes and pinacocytes constitute actual tissues, but in fact these layers tend to be discontinuous, separated by areas where the nonliving matrix is exposed. In any event, the essence of a tissue is *functional integration.* Although sponge cells exhibit remarkable instances of cooperative effort (such as when scleroblasts congregate to build the spicular wall of a gemmule), each cell actually performs as an individual and most exhibit considerable potential for adopting alternative roles in the organism. No hormonal or nervous mechanism seems to exist for the generalized coordination of all cells.

12.4 □ THE TISSUE LEVEL OF CONSTRUCTION

When cells aggregate with others of the same type, they form functionally integrated masses or layers termed *tissues;* but when there is no concomitant tendency for these tissues to associate in turn to form organs, the organism may be thought of as existing at the tissue level of organization. Coelenterates exemplify this level of construction, for in a strict sense they lack true organs, although their cells are functionally integrated into tissues.

AN EXAMPLE: HYDRA   The hydra is a simple polyp often employed as a type organism in the study of coelenterates, although in fact its morphology is considerably less complex than that of most coelenterates and it is therefore not truly representative of the phylum. The body is a cylindrical column constructed of two layers of cells (Figure 12.8). The intervening layer of nonliving matrix, the *mesoglea,* so characteristic of coelenterates, is absent in hydra. The body wall encloses the large *gastrovascular cavity* (GVC), which functions both in digestion and distribution of nutrients. Hydra glides upon a pedal disc at one end of the column, while the opposite end bears the mouth, ringed with six tentacles. The tentacles are constructed of two cell layers, like the body wall, and contain narrow extensions of the GVC. Hydra is actively raptorial, capturing small animals and employing the tentacles in a coordinated manner to bring the prey into the mouth. The mouth distends enormously under the influence of chemical stimuli (particularly glutathione, released from the wounded prey). The prey is ingested whole and digestion is begun extracellularly, within the GVC. As the prey is dissolved by digestive juices, small fragments are engulfed by individual cells lining the GVC, and digestion is completed intracellularly.

The two cell layers which form the body wall and tentacles are the outer *epidermis* (derived from the embryonic ectoderm) and the inner *gastrodermis* (of endodermal origin). Each layer contains several types of cells,

Figure 12.8 □ Tissue level of organization. Body plan and cell types of *Hydra*, a simple coelenterate: (*a*) cutaway view of body structure; (*b*) photomicrograph of cross section, showing numerous pale glandular cells in the gastrodermis and scattered, pale, spherical nematocysts in the epidermis (*Triarch Incorporated, Geo. H. Conant, Ripon, Wis.*); (*c*) detail view of body wall.

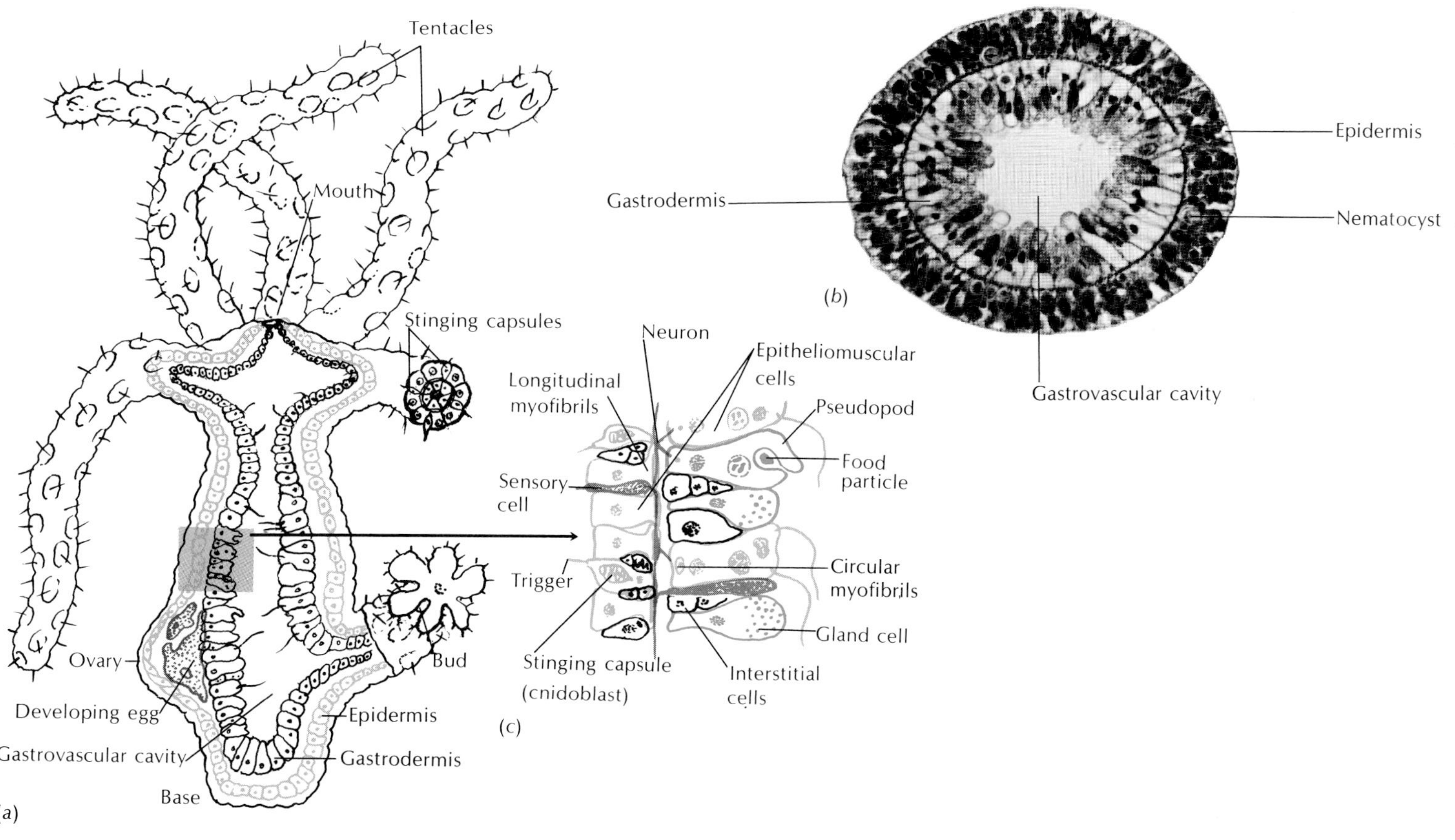

some of which occur in both layers while others are restricted to but one.

Epitheliomuscular cells are the most abundant type in both layers. They are so called because the cell bodies are columnar and constitute a true epithelium, while the base of each cell is contractile, and is drawn out into a flat bar like the crossbar of a "T." Myonemes run the length of this expanded base. The *epidermal* cells are all oriented with myonemes parallel to the long axis of the body column. Coordinated contraction of these cells shortens the body column. The *gastrodermal* epitheliomuscular cells have their bases oriented at right angles to those of the epidermis, and hence at right angles to the long axis of the body. Their contraction decreases the diameter of the body column and consequently lengthens it. The free ends of epitheliomuscular cells form most of the body surface and the lining of the gastrovascular cavity. Many of the gastrodermal cells contain food vacuoles and their free ends bear two flagella employed in stirring the contents of the GVC and capturing particles for intracellular digestion.

Figure 12.9 □ **Nematocysts of *Hydra littoralis*. (*a*) Undischarged penetrant; (*b*) undischarged glutinant (*streptoline*); (*c*) undischarged glutinant (*stereoline*); (*d*) undischarged volvent; (*e*) discharged volvent wrapped around integumentary bristle of copepod (a small crustacean eaten by hydra). (*Courtesy of Carolina Biological Supply Company.*)**

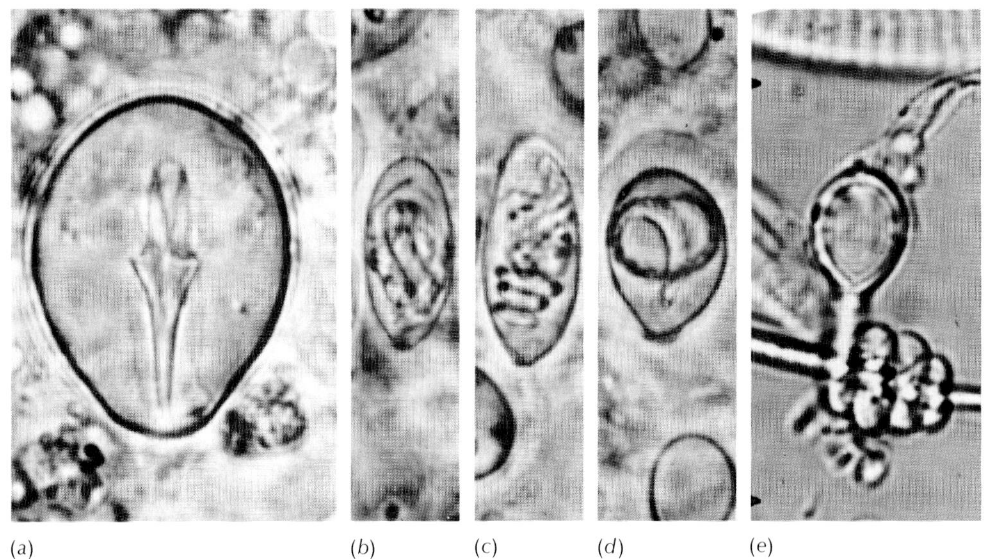

Gland cells occur in the gastrodermis and particularly in the pedal region of the epidermis. The pedal gland cells produce an adhesive secretion used in anchoring hydra to the substratum. Gastrodermal gland cells secrete digestive enzymes. Gland cells near the mouth secrete mucus, facilitating ingestion of prey.

Cnidoblasts are restricted to the epidermis, being most densely aggregated on the tentacles. These ovoid cells produce the stinging elements, or *nematocysts* (Figure 12.9). Each nematocyst consists of an ovoid capsule enclosing a coiled tube that is continuous with the capsular wall. When the nematocyst discharges, the capsular fluid is forced into the tube which, being sealed at its free end, is perforce turned inside out, exposing the barbs and adhesive material that were formerly on the inner surface. The action of a nematocyst is readily illustrated by invaginating the fingers of a rubber glove and then blowing forcibly into the glove's open end. The increased pressure everts the fingers, forcing them outward. Once a nematocyst is discharged it is lost, and the cnidoblast regenerates another. Three major types of nematocysts are penetrants, glutinants and volvents. *Penetrants* are armed with recurved spines and pierce the prey's integument, discharging a paralyzing toxin. *Glutinants* bear a sticky secretion which causes them to adhere to any surface they strike. *Volvents* are short threads which twine securely about bristles on the body of the prey. This diversity in nematocysts suggests a comparable genetic diversity in the cnidoblasts that produce them, although no separate morphological types of the latter have been distinguished.

Interstitial cells are small, undiffer-

Figure 12.10 □ Nerve plexus of hydra. Synaptic gaps are exaggerated for clarity; the nerve cells are separate and do not form an anastomosing network as was once thought. No brain is present in this simplest known type of multicellular nervous system.

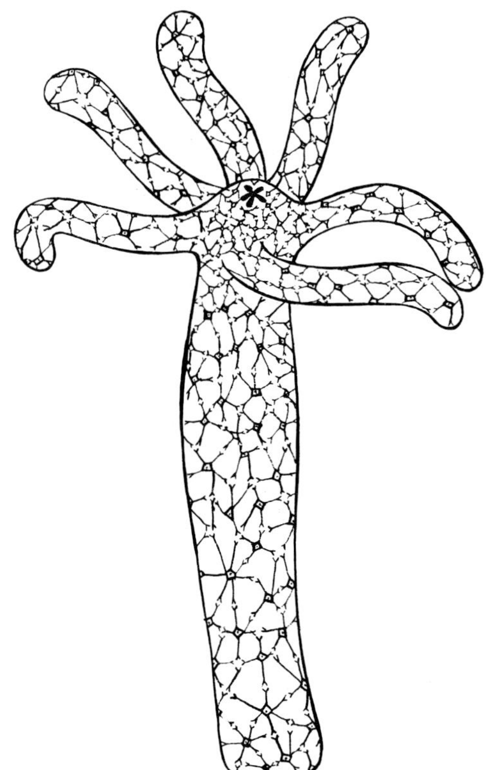

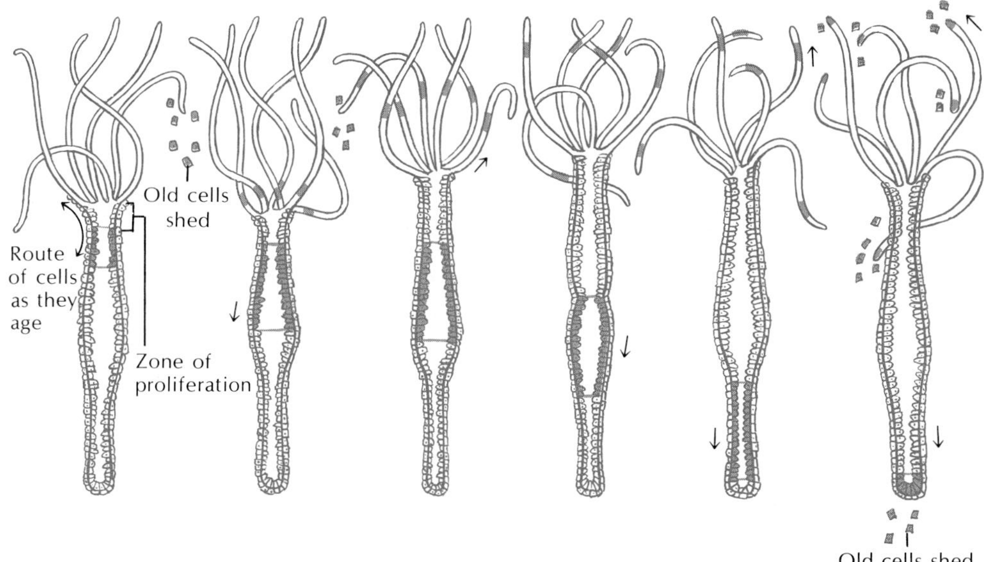

Figure 12.11 □ The potential immortality of hydra. Vital-staining experiments show that new cells are continuously formed in a growth zone at the top of the body column and move toward the base of the column and tips of the tentacles, pushing the older cells ahead until they are shed from the base and the tentacle tips. Such continued self-renewal is unusual among metazoans.

entiated cells scattered among the bases of the epitheliomuscular cells of both layers. They can mature into cnidoblasts or germinal cells, or may initiate a bud from which a new individual is asexually produced. The germinal cells mature in temporary "gonads," which form swellings on the body column. A single ovum matures within an "ovary," whereas a "testis" may produce many sperm (see Figure 17.15). Both ovaries and testes may occur on a single hydra, although most species are dioecious.

Sensory cells permit the organism to respond to stimuli. The outer end of a sensory cell usually terminates in a flagellated point; from the base springs a process branching into fibrils that make contact with the nerve plexus directly underneath the epidermis.

The *nerve plexus* is responsible for coordinated movement (Figure 12.10). It consists of a network of neurons, the processes of which contact those of adjacent cells at junctional regions known as synapses. In coelenterates these synapses are unpolarized; that is, impulses cross them in either direction, so that a diffuse wave of excitation spreads out from any point of stimulation. This excitation is usually damped out as the distance from the origin of the impulses increases, so that only part of the animal, such as a single tentacle, may respond to a stimulus. Intense or generalized stimulation usually invokes a total body response. The coelenterate nerve plexus represents the simplest appearance of true nervous tissue. There is neither a central integrative mass of neurons (brain) nor major nerve cords, although particular regions of the plexus may be specialized for rapid through-conduction. Motor processes of the nerve plexus terminate on the bases of the epitheliomuscular cells, which contract when stimulated.

Hydra is of additional interest in being one of the most advanced animals to renew its body cells so continuously that it does not appear to age and is therefore considered to be potentially immortal (Figure 12.11). Whether the nerve tissue of hydra is also self-renewing remains in doubt, but if cell replacement is truly 100 percent, hydra remains perpetually young. Such cell renewal is impossible in higher animals, in which most types of mature tissue lack mitotic activity.

A number of *colonial* coelenterates have effectively exploited polymorphism as a means of achieving functional as well as structural diversification, for they give rise to zooids that are specialized to assume particular roles on behalf of the entire colony and thus serve as *analogs of the organs of higher animals!* The Portuguese man-of-war (see Figure 7.4), commonly thought of as a single organism, is actually a colony of zooids the activities of which are so effectively integrated that their individual existence is submerged in the life of the whole.

12.5 □ THE ORGAN LEVEL OF CONSTRUCTION

In most *animals* capable of elaborating true organs, these organs become functionally and often structurally associated to form integrated organ systems. Tracheophytes, on the other hand, develop various specialized tissues associated to form *organs,* but these organs are not grouped into organ systems in quite the sense that we find organ systems existing in higher animals. Tracheophytes possess four kinds of organs: *leaves, stems, roots,* and reproductive structures such as *cones* or *flowers.* The designations "leaf," "stem," and "root" are best reserved for those organs in vascular plants. Analogous but much simpler structures occur in nonvascular metaphytes such as mosses and algae; their tissues are poorly differentiated, and they consist mainly of parenchyma cells.

Reproductive organs of plants are more or less intermittent or seasonal in occurrence. They are basically of two types: *spore-producing* bodies (sporangia), produced by the sporophyte generation, and *gamete-producing* bodies, produced by the gametophyte generation (see Figure 17.17). In lower metaphytes, the gamete-producing organs are *antheridia* (sacks within which the sperm mature) and *archegonia,* which produce ova. In seed plants we think of cones and flowers as being reproductive organs, but in fact they do not directly produce gametes. They bear instead minute, dependent gametophytes which develop from monoploid spores borne in the cones or flowers. The gametophytes in turn give rise to sex cells, and upon fertilization diploid zygotes are formed that become the seeds or embryos of the next sporophyte generation. The cones and flowers of seed plants are actually organs derived from the somatic tissues of the sporophyte, which give rise to and protect the gametophyte. The organs which we shall consider in the following section are those of the sporophyte, and are therefore made up of diploid cells.

AN EXAMPLE: THE ANGIOSPERM SPOROPHYTE Angiosperms are structurally the most advanced plants. They have successfully adapted to terrestrial habitats, and their unique evolutionary innovation, the production of *fruits* as devices for seed dispersal, has facilitated their dissemination into many diverse habitats to which they have had to become adapted. The organs of the angiosperm body—*roots, stems, leaves,* and *flowers* (the ovaries of which become *fruits*)—are interconnected by vascular tissue and are influenced by hormonal substances produced in the growing tips, but these organs are not actually organized into organ systems (Figure 12.12).

Roots The primary growth of a root

Figure 12.12 □ **Organ level of organization. (*a*) Body plan of a flowering plant; (*b*) median section through stem tip, showing growing point (apical meristem) and rudimentary leaves (leaf primordia) (*Triarch Incorporated, Geo. H. Conant, Ripon, Wis.*); (*c*) root sectioned at point of origin of branch root, which arises from vascular core (stele) of primary root (*Ward's Natural Science Establishment, Inc.*).**

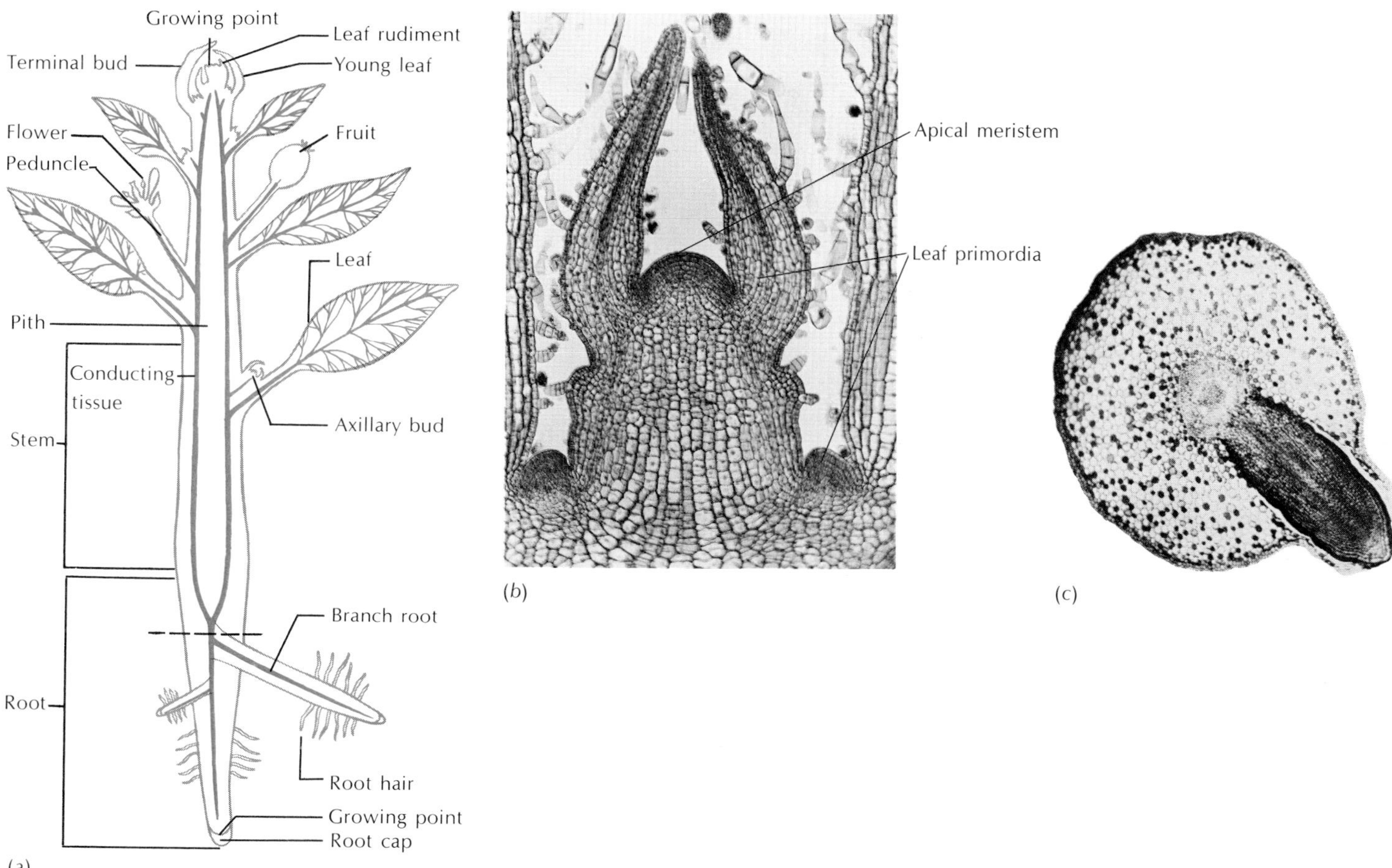

occurs near its tip, in the *meristematic region,* where the cells are unspecialized and mitotically active (Figure 12.13). A protective *root cap* is formed, which is forced through the soil by the elongation of the young cells that lie just above the meristematic region. The root cap takes the brunt of mechanical damage and is constantly abraded and regenerated from the meristem. The meristematic region moves forward as the root grows, and just behind it in a *region of elongation* the newly formed cells imbibe water and rapidly grow in length. In this region most epidermal cells put forth slim lateral outgrowths (*root hairs*), which increase the surface area available for absorption. Root hairs occur at 100 to 200 per square millimeter in this *root hair zone.* Only in this zone can roots absorb water and nutrient minerals. Root hairs grow to a maximum length of 1 cm and persist for only a few days, new ones being produced in the younger part of the root. Thus although a root system may be many meters long, only a few centimeters near the tip of each root represent the absorptive portion.

Following elongation, cytodifferentiation occurs in the *region of maturation.* Here, vascular elements (see Figure 11.40) begin to form a central conductive core, the *stele.* The *xylem,* tissue which conducts the water and solutes imbibed by the root hairs, usually forms a cross in the center of the stele, while pockets of *phloem* (tissue that transports sugar-rich sap from the leaves to other parts of the plant) occupy the angles between the arms of the cross. (The transport function of xylem and phloem will be considered further in Section 14.2A.) Bounding the cylindrical stele is a single layer of modified parenchyma, the *endodermis,* the

Figure 12.13 □ Growth zone of a root. (*a*) Longitudinal section. (*b*) Root tip and root-hair zone of germinating bean seedling. (*Ward's Natural Science Establishment, Inc.*)

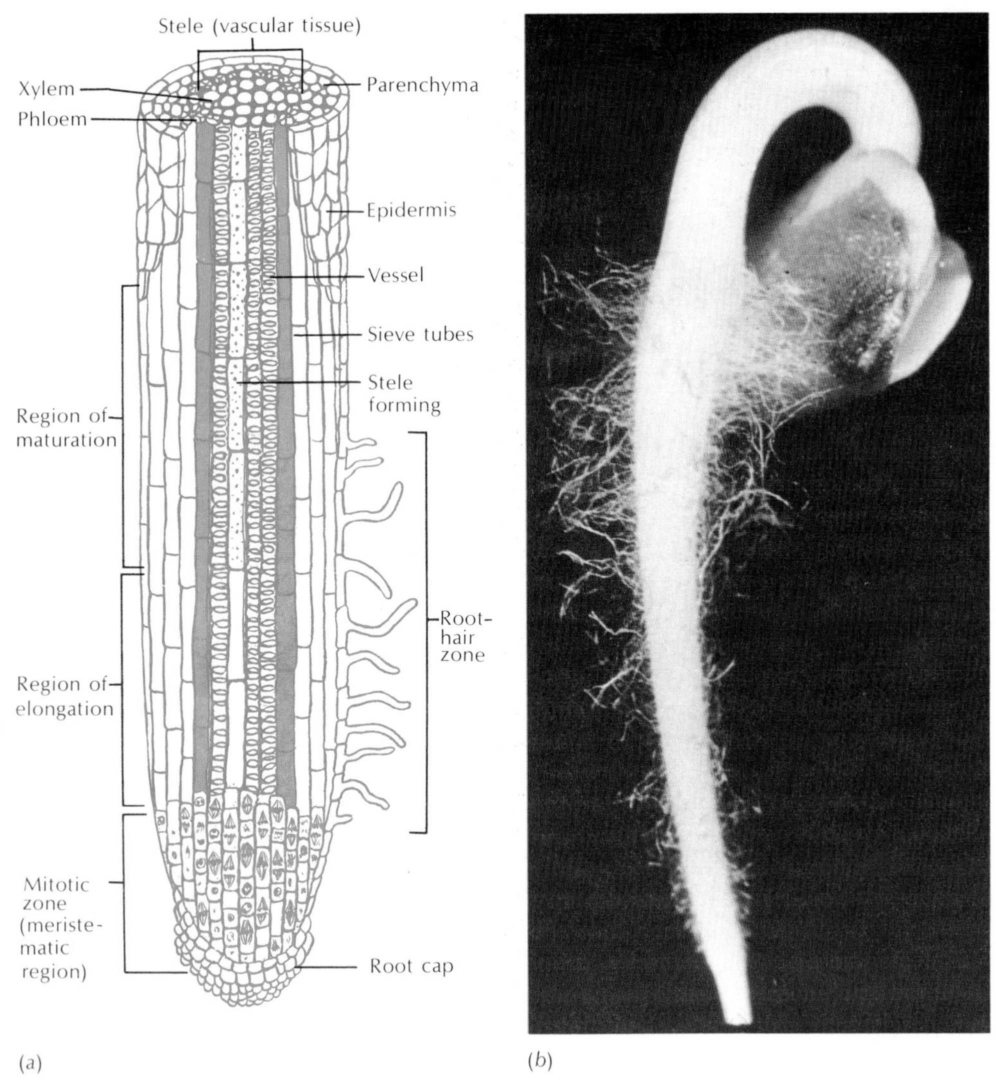

cells of which secrete secondary walls of water-impervious *suberin.* Water being conducted upward is trapped within the stele by this suberized layer; only small amounts pass out through occasional thin-walled cells scattered among the suberized ones. Outside the endodermis lies a *cortex* of large, loosely packed parenchyma often engorged with stored nutrients. The exterior of the young root is covered by a layer of *epidermis.*

Between the vascular cells and the endodermis lies a layer of small, undifferentiated cells, the *pericycle,* from which arise branch roots (see Figure 12.12). These penetrate through the cortex and epidermis to reach the exterior. In perennial roots, the pericycle gives rise to the cork cambium, and contributes to the vascular cambium, a meristematic layer responsible for growth in diameter. During the second year of growth, the mitotically active *cork cambium* develops in the pericycle; the cells formed on its outer surface become highly suberized cork cells. As the cork layer thickens, the overlying endodermis, cortex, and epidermis, deprived of nourishment, disintegrate. Thereafter, cork forms the protective outer covering of the older root. Meanwhile the *vascular cambium* arises between the phloem and xylem. The cells of this layer divide radially so that one of the two daughter cells produced in any division lies on the inside and the other, on the outside. Cells proliferated from the *inner* side of the vascular cambium become xylem, whereas those produced on the *outer* side become phloem. In each subsequent year of growth, an *annual growth ring* is formed, and the diameter of the root increases. As the secondary phloem and xylem expand, they compress the vascular tissue produced earlier. Xylem formed during previous years tends to remain functional, but each succeeding year's growth crushes the phloem formed the preceding year, so that the ring of functional sieve tubes and their companion cells moves constantly outward, ahead of the expanding cambium.

Roots, like other plant organs, grow throughout the life of the plant. The growing tips are constantly exposed to new areas of soil in which fresh nutrients may be available. In the young root the cortical cells are rich in stored food that aids the primary growth. In older regions the cortex is lost and food is stored instead in the phloem. When winter dormancy is broken materials stored in the roots are mobilized to provide nourishment for the first growth of the season. A deciduous plant is totally dependent on these nutrient stores, for until new foliage is produced photosynthesis cannot resume.

Stems Like roots, stems are dependent upon two meristematic regions for growth in length and diameter: the *apical meristem* (at the tip of each shoot) and the *vascular cambium* (lying between the phloem and xylem). Shoots, like roots, grow in length only at their tips, where the apical meristems proliferate new cells that subsequently lengthen in the region of elongation just below the tip (Figure 12.14). After elongating, the cells differentiate in the region of maturation. First to differentiate is the surface layer, which becomes an epidermis, with guard cells and epidermal hairs. Just within the epidermis appear strands of narrow, dense cells, the *procambium,* arranged in a broken ring. These strands produce the cylindrical *stele* composed of

Figure 12.14 □ Longitudinal section of growth zone of a stem.

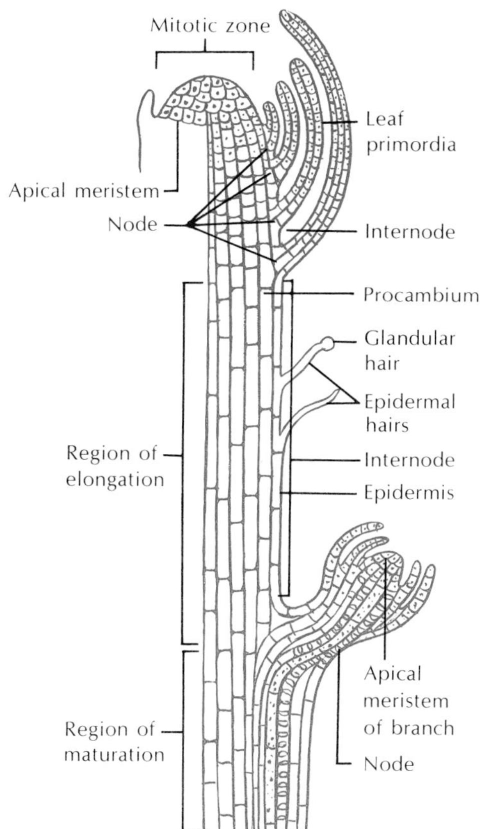

Figure 12.15 ☐ **Tracheophyte cross-sectional stem anatomy. (*a*) Herbaceous dicot (*Aristolochia*): vascular cambium is a slender dark line connecting one vascular bundle to the next; pith (parenchyma) occupies the core of the stem. (*b*) Monocot (portion) (*Zea*): epidermis visible, and vascular bundles are scattered among parenchyma cells. (*Ward's Natural Science Establishment, Inc.*) (*c*) Woody (*Pinus*): three rings, each representing one year's growth; active phloem lies outside the youngest (outermost) ring of xylem. (*Courtesy of Carolina Biological Supply Company.*)**

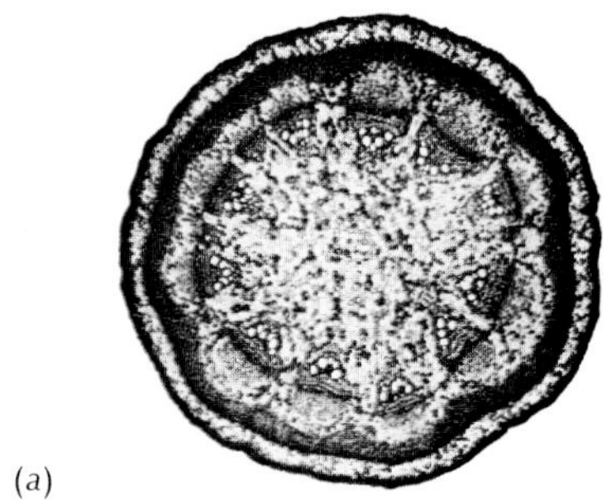

(*a*)

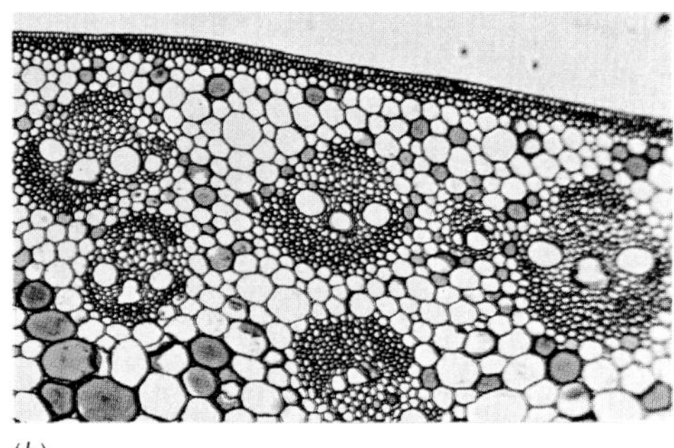

(*b*)

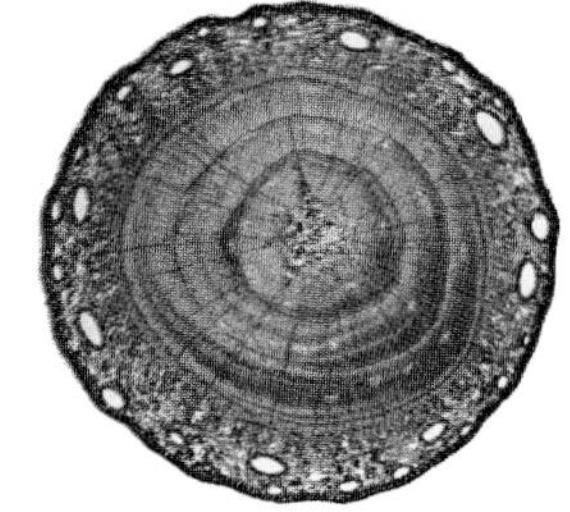

(*c*)

phloem and xylem. The stele does not originate at the core of the stem but as a ring enclosing parenchymal cells that become *pith,* a water- and food-storing tissue.

The *cortex* lies between the stele and the epidermis, and some of its cells mature into mechanical tissues—collenchyma, sclerenchyma, and fibers. In younger stems, cortical parenchyma contains chlorophyll and carries on photosynthesis. The innermost cells of the cortex form the endodermis and the pericycle. Many cells of the latter produce fibers (see Figure 11.36*b*).

Meanwhile, the procambial strands mature into phloem and xylem. In *dicots* (see Section 2.5) the separate strands eventually may fuse to form a complete vascular cylinder, or *continuous* stele; alternatively they may remain separate, forming a *dissected* stele, with pith rays extending outward to the cortex between the separate vascular bundles (Figure 12.15*a*). In *monocots* the vascular bundles are scattered throughout the pith (Figure 12.15*b*).

In perennial stems, the second year finds certain cortical parenchyma cells apparently returning to a meristematic condition to become the cork cambium. The cells produced on the outer surface of this cambium become suberized so that a corky layer makes up the *outer bark.* The cork is penetrated at intervals by *lenticels,* pores permitting gaseous exchange. The epidermis and cortex, deprived of nourishment by the cork layer, slough off, and the stem thereafter lacks photosynthetic capacity. The *inner bark* consists of the inner cortex and the phloem. *Girdling* (removal of both outer and inner bark in a ring around the entire trunk) usually results in death due to interruption of phloem conduction.

Also in the second year a vascular cambium appears between the phloem and xylem, and, as in roots, proliferates phloem to the outside and xylem to the inside, producing a new growth ring each year (Figure 12.15*c*). These growth rings are formed by the xylem, for each year the previous season's phloem is crushed by the expanding stele. The wood is therefore made up of xylem. Older xylem elements, plugged with tannins, resins, and lignin, serve as mechanical tissue.

Annual growth rings furnish clues to climatic conditions in the past, for in years of favorable precipitation and temperature they are wider than in years of drought. During any given year, xylem produced early in the season contains larger elements and is thus less dense than xylem produced later in the season.

As long as it is capable of further elongation, the tip of each stem bears a *terminal bud.* A bud is essentially a conical mound of meristem, along the sides of which arise *leaf primordia* which eventually develop into leaves (see Figure 12.12). Leaf primordia arise at regular intervals along the sides of the apical meristem. These intervals or *nodes* are the only places where leaves or branches will normally arise from the stem. They are separated by *internodes,* which are at first very short but lengthen by the elongation of the young cells. Elongation of the internodes separates adjacent nodes. Each node develops one or more *lateral buds* capable of giving rise to leaves and branch stems. Each lateral bud contains one or more leaf primordia, in the axils of which arise smaller outgrowths, the branch primordia. The bud may remain dormant, encased in protective bud scales, until stimulated to

Figure 12.16 □ Leaves specialized for trapping insects. (*a*) Venus flytrap: above, entire plant with leaf rosette, most leaf blades being partially folded (*courtesy of Carolina Biological Supply Company*); below, leaf capturing fly, six dark trigger hairs seen on the pink inner surface of the closing leaf (*Ward's Natural Science Establishment, Inc.*). (*b*) Australian pitcher plant: opening of pitcher at top of photo, smaller pitcher at right. Note ridges that prevent insects from crawling out over rim of pitcher, of which the inside is an attractive pink serving as a lure. (*Ward's Natural Science Establishment, Inc.*)

(a)

(b)

develop. Rising ambient temperatures may initiate growth in a previously dormant bud. Destruction of the terminal bud permits formerly repressed lateral buds to become active, so that a plant responds to pruning by becoming bushy.

Leaves Leaf primordia arising from the apical meristems may mature at once or remain dormant for some time within a bud. Leaves serve primarily as the major organs of photosynthesis, and the structure of typical leaves reflects many adaptations relevant to the efficient performance of this function (see Figure 3.1). As a leaf grows, its surface-to-volume ratio is affected both by intensity of illumination and by relative humidity, so that plants of the same species may have large, thin leaves when grown in the shade or under conditions of high humidity, and smaller, thicker leaves when exposed to full sun and grown under conditions of low humidity. Leaf morphology appears to be somewhat more subject to adaptive modifications than is that of other plant organs.

Leaves may also undergo modification adapting them to functions other than the basic nutritional role. Modified leaves serve as protective *spines,* as protective *bud scales,* as the *sepals* which enclose flower buds, as clinging *tendrils,* and as thickened food- or water-storage organs. *Bulbs* are thickened, underground leaves, which form the perennial part of the bulb plant and store nutrients for the next season's growth. Certain bog plants have solved the problem of nitrogen deficiency in their habitat by developing modified leaves that enable them to capture insects. These insectivorous plants include the pitcher plant, the sundew, and the Venus' flytrap (Figure 12.16). The inner surface of the trumpet-shaped leaves

Figure 12.17 □ **Leaf morphology: (*a*) venation; (*b*) leaf form.**

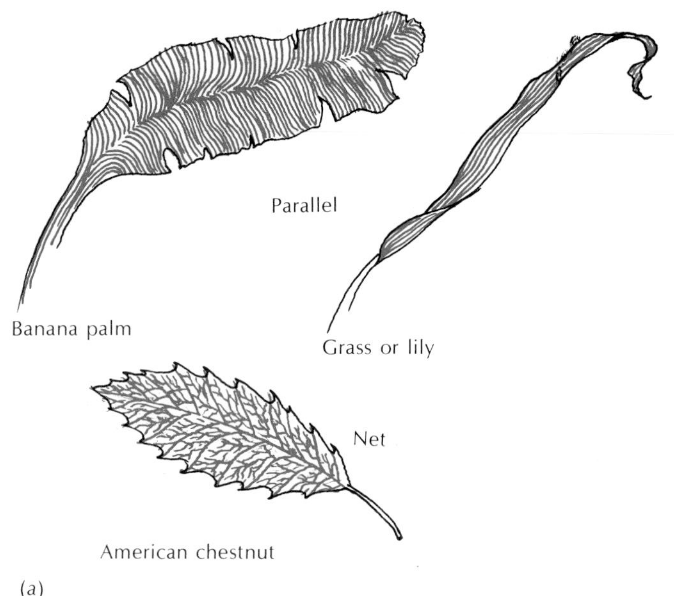

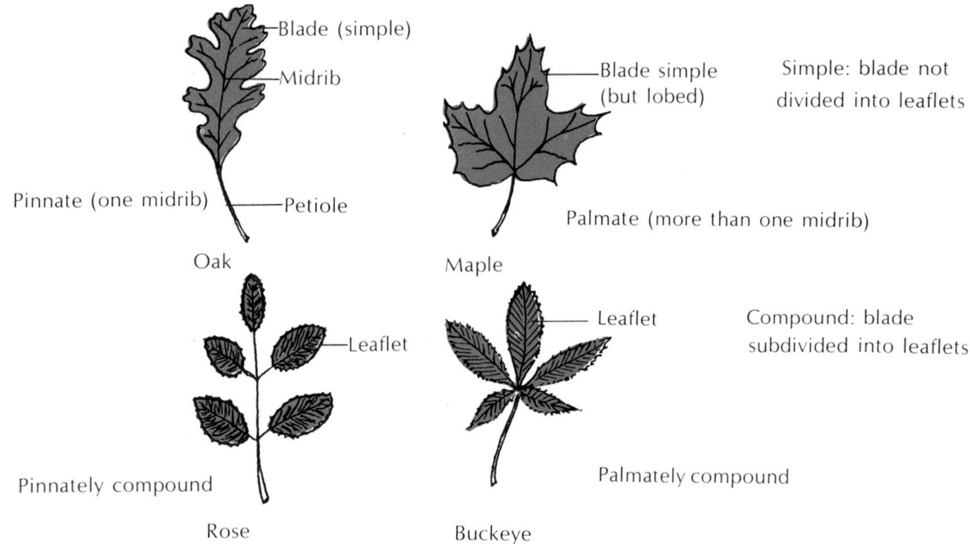

of the pitcher plant bears downward-directed spines which prevent the escape of insects that enter the pitcher, attracted by the odor of the fluid in its base. The leaves of the sundew bear sticky glandular hairs that capture insects, which are then digested by enzymes exuded by other epidermal glands. Each modified leaf of the Venus' flytrap bears a stiff row of marginal bristles, and on the inner surface of the blade are epidermal hairs serving as tactile receptors. When these hairs are touched, a prompt change occurs in the turgor pressure of cells along the midrib, causing the two halves of the leaf to fold together.

In gross structure a typical foliage leaf consists of a *petiole* (the stalk which forms the attachment to the stem) and the flattened *blade* (the expanded, photosynthetic portion). The main vascular bundles of the blade form the *leaf venation,* which is *parallel* in monocot and *netted* in dicot leaves (Figure 12.17*a*). Blade and petiole alike are covered with epidermis, which secretes a waxy cuticle that is especially thick on the upper surface of the blade; the lower surface bears the stomates or pores through which gases are exchanged. Between the upper and lower epidermal layers is the chlorophyll-containing chlorenchyma (see Figure 3.1). The *palisade chlorenchyma* is a single layer of columnar cells, directly underlying the upper epidermis, with their long axes oriented at right angles to the leaf surface. Light passing through the leaf must traverse the entire length of these palisade cells. Below the palisade layer is the loosely packed *spongy* chlorenchyma, among the cells of which are anastomosing air spaces leading to the stomates. The vascular bundles or veins branch among the spongy chlorenchyma, and not only serve for conduction, but also to support the blade.

Leaves display tremendous diversity in blade morphology and veining pattern. Some of this variability may be the incidental product of genetic variation, but much of it is functional with respect to increasing the perimeter of a leaf, relative to its overall area. It is along the margin of a leaf that guttation occurs. Guttation, we should recall, is the exudation of water droplets from the ends of the veins and from special glandular cells located along the margin of the blade (see Figure 4.6). Guttation, like transpiration (the loss of water by evaporation through the stomates), is responsible for xylem conduction, for it serves to draw water upward from the roots (see Figure 14.14).

The blade of a leaf may be *pinnate,* with a single median midrib from which secondary veins arise at about a 45° angle, or *palmate,* with three or more major veins springing radially from the tip of the petiole (Figure 12.17*b*). The leaf margin may be entire, toothed, or scalloped. The blade itself may be entire, or may be divided into lobes by indentations extending from the margin toward the petiole. If these indentations actually reach the major veins, the blade is subdivided into *leaflets* and is said to be *compound.* Pinnately compound leaves, such as those of the rose and the date palm, bear a series of leaflets arising on each side of the midrib. Clover, buckeye, and fan palm have palmately compound leaves, in which the leaflets radiate from the tip of the petiole. Guttation, and consequently the upward movement of water from the roots, should proceed more rapidly in a plant with compound leaves bearing sawtoothed margins (such as the strawberry) than in a plant bearing leaves with undivided blades and smooth margins.

Flowers Flowers are complex structures or compound organs, consisting of four kinds of floral organs known as *sepals, petals, stamens,* and one or more *pistils* (Figure 12.18). These floral organs are modified leaves arising from the apical meristem of a *flower bud.* In contrast to stem growth, the internodes remain short in a flower, so that the floral organs are closely spaced. Floral organs consist of the same somatic tissues as form other parts of the plant: they are covered with epidermis, contain parenchyma among which vascular bundles ramify, and are supported by these veins together with a certain amount of mechanical tissue. The parenchyma often contains pigments that make the flowers conspicuous to pollinator animals.

Sepals are usually obviously leaflike, although in some flowers they are pigmented like the petals; together they constitute the *calyx,* which protects the flower bud. The *petals* lie just distal to the sepals and are most conspicuous in insect- or bird-pollinated species. At their bases lie *nectaries* containing sugar-rich fluid that entices pollinators to probe deeply into the flower, thus becoming contaminated with pollen. In wind-pollinated angiosperms petals are often lacking. The petals in aggregate constitute the *corolla.* The sepals and petals may remain separate or may fuse more or less completely.

Stamens are organs which produce the monoploid *spores* that develop into the pollen grains (the *male gametophytes*). The stalklike *filament* bears at its top the expanded *anther,* within which meiosis and the maturation of the male gametophytes take place. When these are mature, the anther splits open, exposing the pollen to the wind or to pollinators (Figure 12.18*c*).

The *pistil* is the organ within which the *female gametophytes* mature, are fertilized by the sperm nuclei of pollen, and give rise to the *seed* of the next sporophyte generation. The parts of the pistil are the terminal *stigma,* which exposes a sticky surface to which pollen adheres, the more-or-less elongate *style,* which supports the stigma and expands basally into the *ovary.* The ovary is not truly analogous to the female gonads of animals, nor to the archegonia of lower plants, for it is *not* fundamentally an ovum-producing organ. Instead, it contains ovules that are the sites of formation of the *spores* that develop into the monoploid female gametophytes (Figure 12.18*d*; see also Figure 17.22). Each of these microscopic female gametophytes develops an egg nucleus that is ultimately to be fertilized by a sperm nucleus provided by the pollen grain. After fertilization, the cytoplasm of the female gametophyte is absorbed by the growing sporophyte embryo. The ovary then forms a container for these maturing seeds and develops into a fruit. A pistil consists of one or more modified leaves known as *carpels.* [Each carpel and each stamen represents a *sporophyll* (spore-bearing leaf). In a *compound* pistil more than one carpel is present and, although the stigmas and styles sometimes fuse, the compounding is always apparent in the number of chambers located within the base of the pistil, for each of these chambers (locules) represents the internal cavity of a single ovary, and contains from one to many *ovules.* Each ovule can become a seed.

Figure 12.18 □ **Organization of a flower. (*a*) Longitudinal section of a typical flower. (*b*) Longitudinal section of a succulent flower, showing ovules developing within ovary and fleshy receptacle and sepals that serve for water storage. (*Los Angeles County Museum of Natural History.*) (*c*) Cross section of mature anther shedding pollen. (*Ward's Natural Science Establishment, Inc.*) (*d*) Detail of ovule with mature female gametophyte; the egg nucleus and endosperm nuclei will be fertilized by sperm entering the micropyle.**

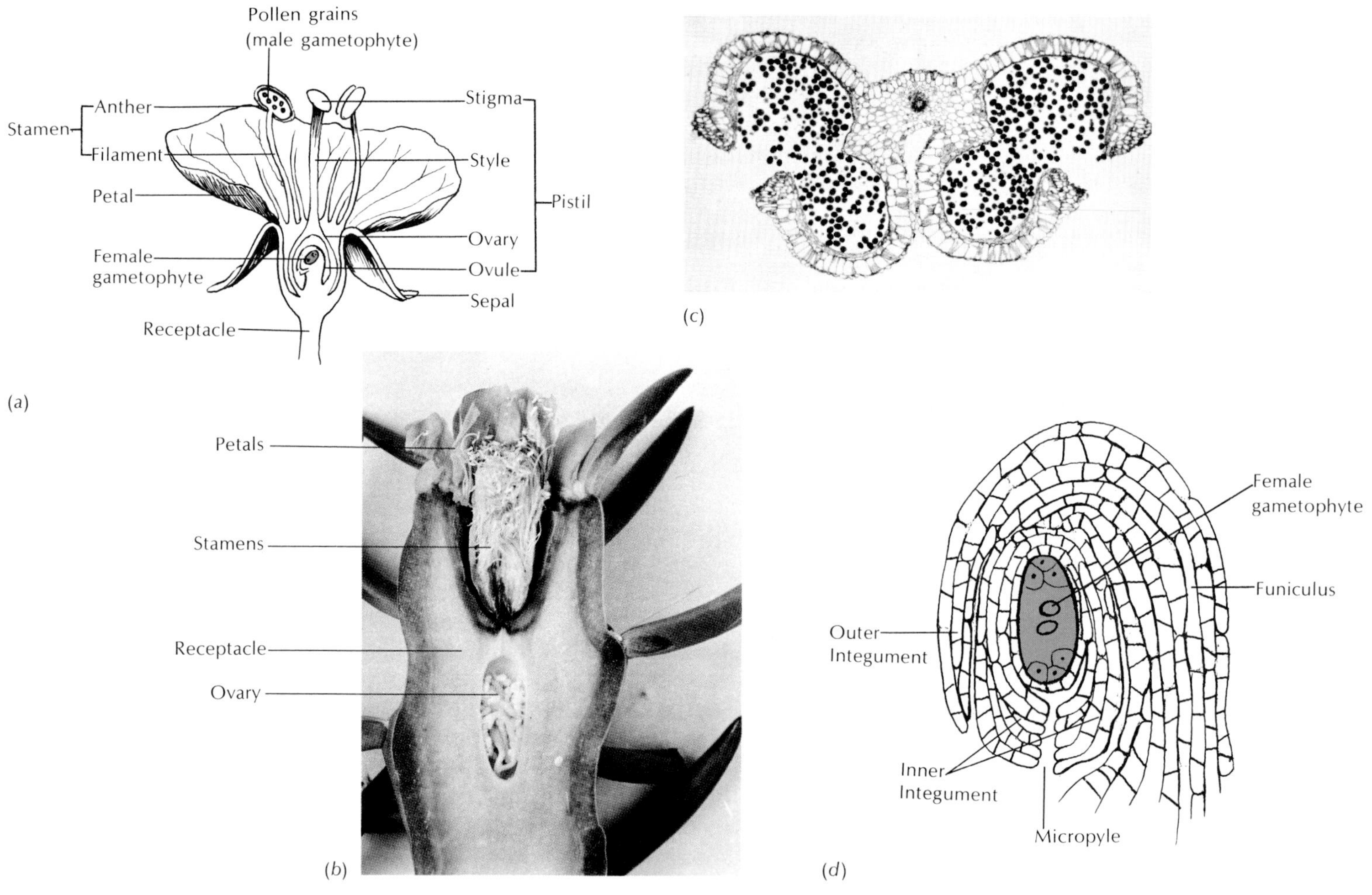

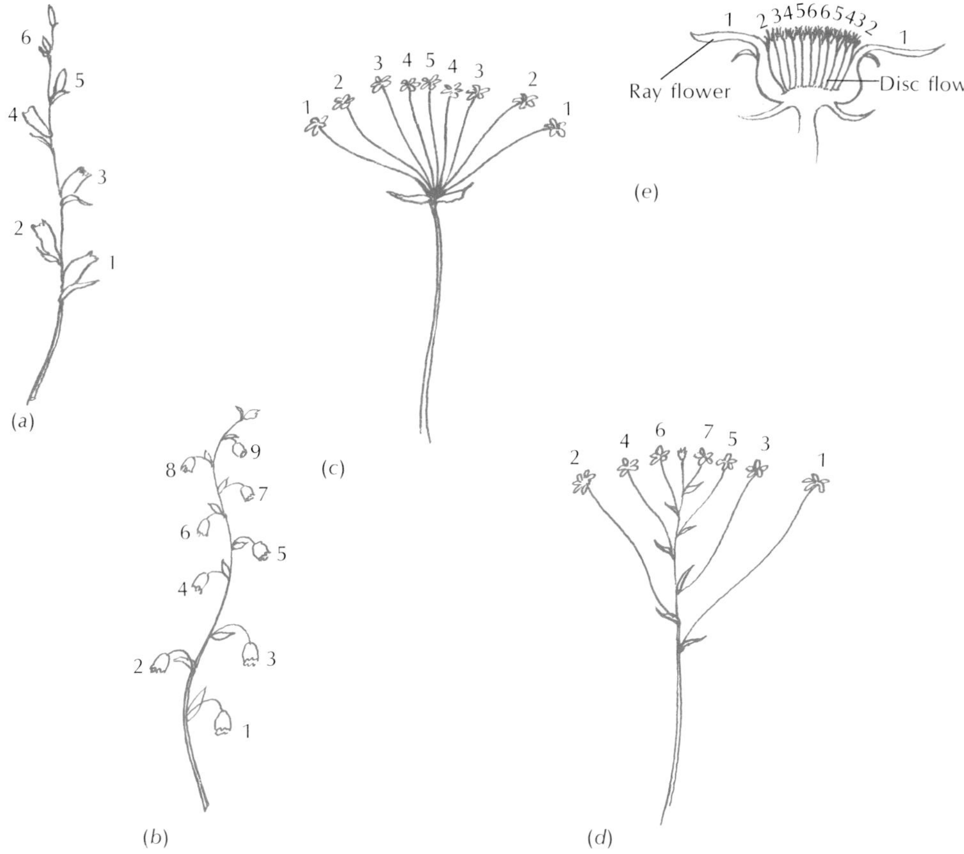

Figure 12.19 □ Types of inflorescence: (*a*) spike; (*b*) raceme; (*c*) umbel; (*d*) corymb; (*e*) head. Numerals indicate the order in which the flowers develop. Can you identify species native to your region that show each type of inflorescence?

Flowers possessing all four kinds of floral organs are termed *complete;* those lacking any of these are *incomplete.* A flower containing both stamens and pistils is termed *perfect,* while one which is staminate only, or pistillate only, is *imperfect* (see Plate 8*a, b*). A *monoecious* plant either bears perfect flowers, or both staminate and pistillate ones. In *dioecious* species staminate flowers are borne on "male" and pistillate flowers on "female" plants.

Flowers may be borne singly, or in clusters termed *inflorescences* (Figure 12.19). The adaptive significance of the inflorescence is that (1) as a whole it is more conspicuous than the single flowers and permits less energy and materials to be expended in elaborating showy petals for each flower, and (2) when the flowers are closely clustered, chances are good that pollen from a number of them will adhere to the bodies of visiting pollinators. A solitary flower containing a single ovary (or only a few, at most) is less adaptive than an inflorescence containing dozens of flowers, each bearing ovaries. *Composites,* species in which the flowers are tightly packed to form an inflorescence known as a *head,* are the most successful of dicot families (see Plate 8*c*).

Fruits The ovarian wall (*pericarp*) ripens into a fruit that encloses the seeds, protecting them and usually providing for their dispersal. The pericarp commonly differentiates into three layers, the thickness and consistency of which differ according to the species (Figure 12.20). These are the outer *exocarp,* consisting of epidermis, the *mesocarp* or middle layer, which may be dry or fleshy, and the inner *endocarp,* which also may be fleshy or dry. The exocarp of edible fruits often becomes brilliantly pigmented

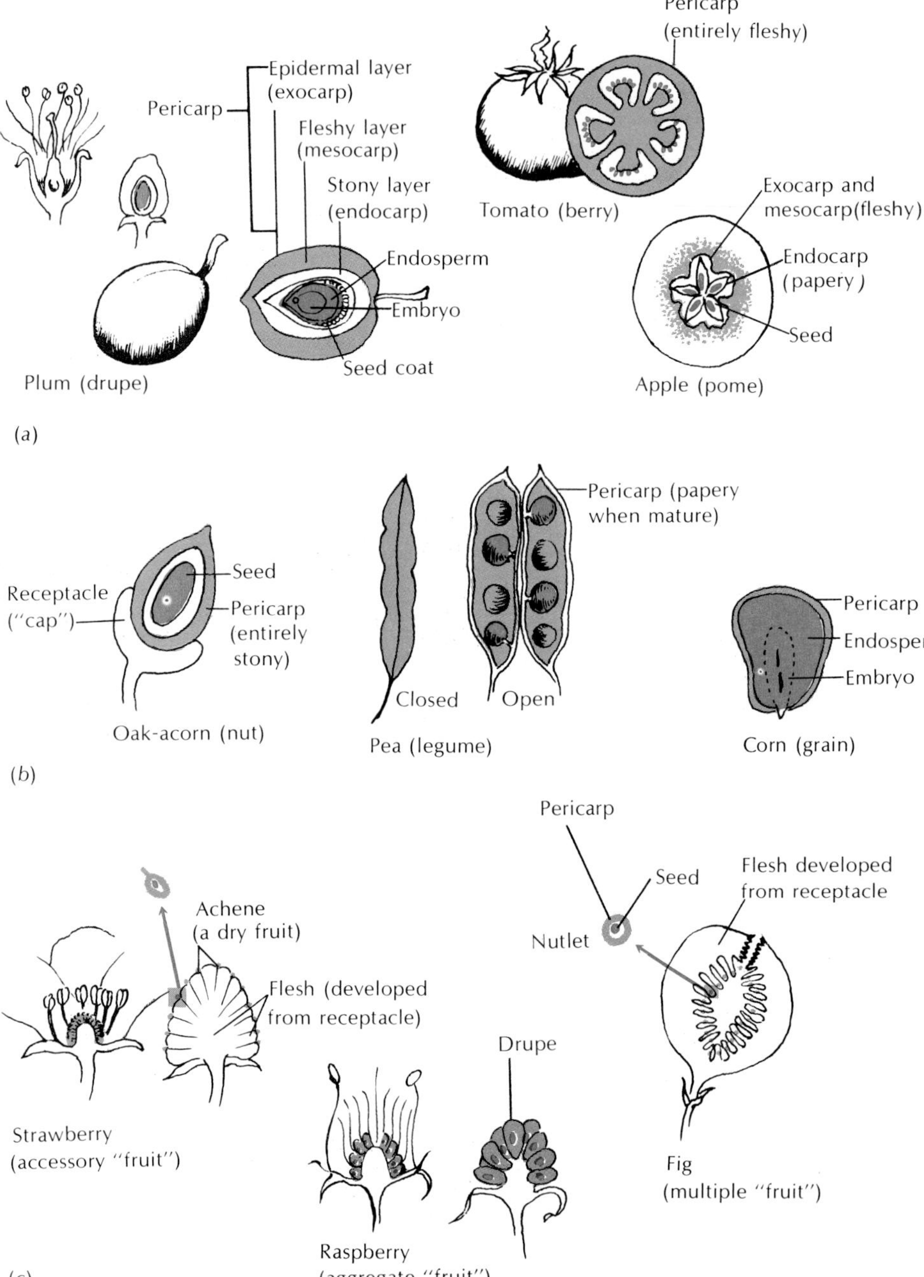

Figure 12.20 □ Types of fruit. (*a*) Fleshy simple fruits. Most of the pome's flesh is derived from the receptacle. (*b*) Dry simple fruits. Most "nuts" are not true nuts: almonds and walnuts are drupes, Brazil nuts are seeds. In a grain, seed and fruit are nearly indistinguishable. (*c*) Compound fruits. In an accessory fruit, the actual fruit containing the seed is the achene; in an aggregate fruit, each fruitlet is a drupe; in the multiple fruit, the actual fruits are seed-bearing nutlets.

when the seeds are ripe, attracting birds that feed upon the fruits and carry away the seeds in their alimentary tracts, to be voided at some distance from the parent plant. *Fleshy* fruits are often (but not always) edible, featuring a nutrient-rich parenchyma. *Berries* (such as oranges, squash, and tomatos) are fleshy fruits in which the entire pericarp is soft. In *drupes* (such as almonds, peaches, and olives) the mesocarp is fleshy, but the endocarp is stony, forming a protective *pit* around the single seed.

Dry fruits are those in which the mature pericarp is often papery or stony. These fruits, with the exception of grains, are seldom edible unless taken while immature (as with string beans). They may aid seed dispersal by splitting open, ejecting the seeds forcibly, or by bearing projections that facilitate wind dispersal or allow the fruit to become entangled in the fur of mammals (see Figure 7.7). In other cases, the stony pericarp may not particularly facilitate dissemination, but may delay germination even for years, by which time the parent plant may have died. In fact, certain plants produce seed coats or pericarps so impervious that germination cannot occur until the outer covering is charred by fire; such species can quickly recover burned-over areas.

Figure 12.21 □ **Multiple exposure of vetch pod opening for the ejection of seeds.** (*Courtesy of Carolina Biological Supply Company.*)

Seed-eating animals also play an important role in the dispersal of dry fruits, for many are carried away and cached, and only relatively few of these are later recovered and eaten.

Dehiscent dry fruits have pericarps that split open along one or more seams when mature, allowing the seeds to be scattered. A *legume* is a dehiscent fruit in which the pericarp splits along *two* seams, at the same time usually twisting so that the seeds are forcibly ejected (peas, acacias) (Figure 12.21). Another type of dehiscent fruits is the *follicle,* which splits open along *one* seam (larkspur). *Indehiscent* dry fruits do not split open; they include nuts, achenes, and grains. A *grain* (corn, wheat) contains a single seed so completely fused with the pericarp that the two are nearly indistinguishable. An *achene* (sunflower, dandelion) also contains a single seed, but this is not fused with the pericarp. A *nut* resembles an achene but has an excessively thickened and stony pericarp. Acorns and chestnuts are true botanical nuts. Other "nuts," in the popular sense, may not be true nuts at all: walnuts, coconuts, and almonds are drupes, while peanuts are legumes.

Accessory fruits are those in which the pericarp itself is enclosed by other tissues, mainly of the *receptacle,* or part of the stem which forms the expanded base for the flower. A strawberry is an accessory fruit in which the fleshy, edible receptacle bears the actual fruits, which are hard-walled achenes. A *pome,* such as a pear or apple, is a core fruit in which the flesh is derived from the receptacle and the pericarp forms only the core.

An *aggregate* fruit such as the raspberry arises from a single flower having multiple pistils; each fruitlet possesses its own pericarp, but all are borne on the same base or receptacle. Flowers that form a compact inflorescence (in which the blossoms are tightly squeezed together) sometimes produce a single *compound* fruit—for instance, a pineapple.

The life span of perennial plants is less limited than that of metazoans, in which maturity soon yields to senescence. As long as the meristems remain active, such plants can continue to grow and regenerate lost organs. Death by fire, disease, drought, or human intervention is the likely fate of the larger perennial plants.

12.6 □ THE ORGAN-SYSTEM LEVEL OF CONSTRUCTION

Most *triploblastic* metazoans—those in which all three of the primary germ layers, ectoderm, endoderm, and mesoderm, are well developed—have achieved an organ-system level of organization. A rudimentary mesoderm consisting of scattered cells in a noncellular matrix does appear in coelenterates, but a dense mesenchyme representing a true third germ layer first develops in flatworms. In platyhelminths the potential of the mesoderm is only partially realized. Ultimately, this germ layer contributes to all organ systems, providing their musculature, connective stroma, and blood vessels.

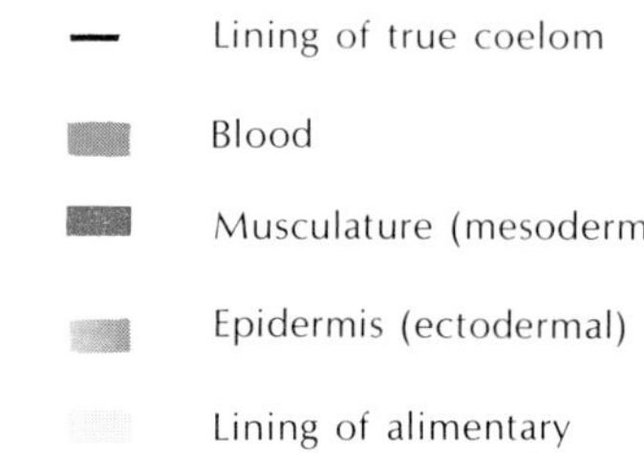

Figure 12.22 ☐ **Comparison of (*a*) acoelomate (ribbon worm), (*b*) pseudocoelomate (nematode), and (*c*) eucoelomate (general schema) body plans. In some eucoelomates (annelids and vertebrates), blood flows in a closed system, and the coelom is not reduced; in others (arthropods and some molluscs), blood flows into expanded spaces (hemocoel), and the true coelom is much reduced.**

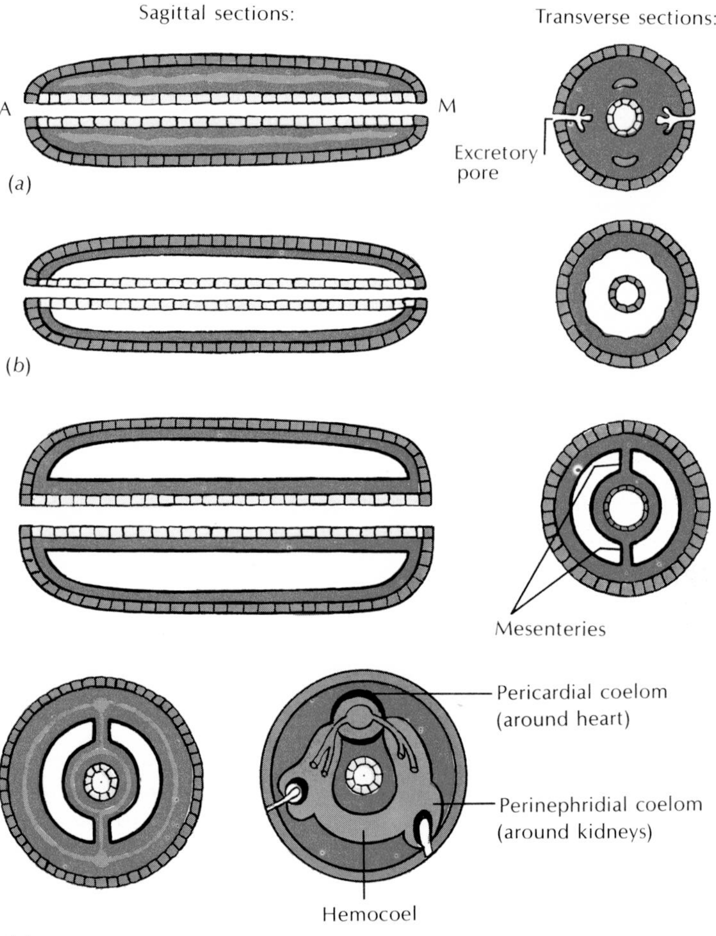

A Tube-within-a-tube body plan

The more primitive triploblastic metazoans, flatworms and ribbonworms, are *acoelomate:* they have not developed a body cavity separating the body wall from the internal organs or viscera (Figure 12.22). The internal organs—reproductive, excretory, and alimentary—are solidly embedded in poorly differentiated mesodermal tissue (mesenchyme or parenchyma) interpenetrated by muscle fibers. An acoelomic body plan limits visceral expansion and precludes independent contractility of the gut. The development of a body cavity represents an evolutionary innovation of great significance. All Bilateria above the level of ribbonworms have a fluid-filled body cavity in which the viscera lie. In these *coelomate* phyla, the body wall forms a hollow tube enclosing a cavity that extends most of the length of the anteroposterior axis; within this cavity lies the alimentary canal, a second hollow tube, extending from mouth to anus. Thus the coelomate body plan is that of a tube (the gut) suspended within another tube (the body wall).

The *body wall* is covered externally by the integument, which encloses two or more layers of muscle fibers. A skeleton, when present, covers or lies within the body wall. When a skeleton is lacking, locomotion is effected by peristaltic waves of contraction sweeping the length of the body wall, in which circular and longitudinal muscle layers contract alternately, shortening and lengthening sections of the body. The incompressability of the fluid within the body cavity (which is compartmentalized in the

Figure 12.23 □ **Comparison of pseudocoelomate and eucoelomate body plans. (*a*) *Ascaris*, a roundworm, in cross section. Note absence of intestinal musculature. (*b*) *Lumbricus* (earthworm) in cross section. Note development of gut musculature in this eucoelomate animal. (*Ward's Natural Science Establishment, Inc.*)**

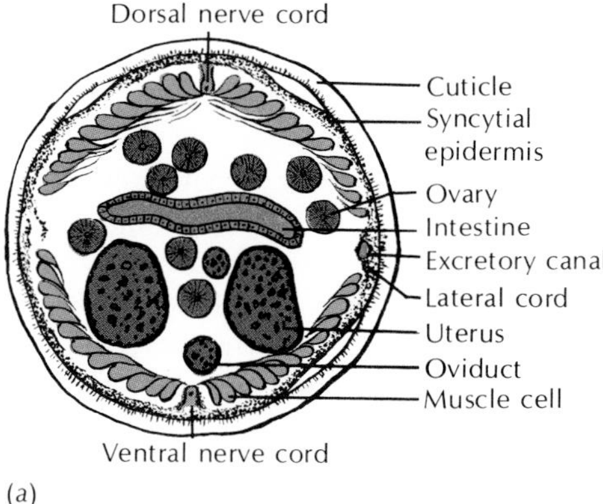

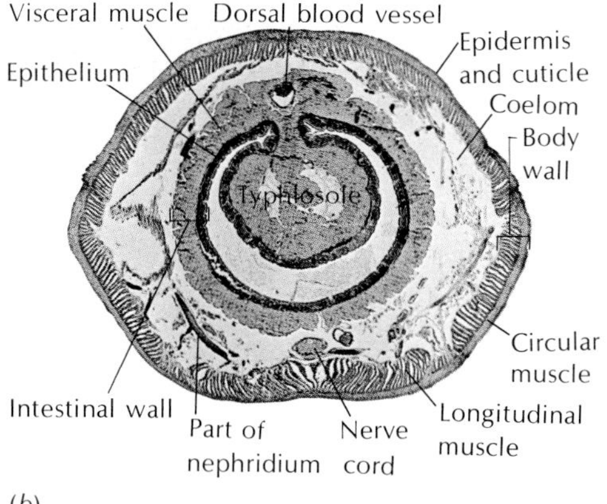

case of annelids such as the earthworm) makes the contracting portions rigid, creating a temporary *hydrostatic skeleton* that facilitates burrowing.

The body cavity provides a fluid-filled space into which metabolic wastes from the cells and digested nutrients from the alimentary tract may diffuse. Excretory tubules of coelomate invertebrates collect and expel the waste-filled coelomic fluid, or alter its composition by the selective removal of materials. A body cavity increases the proportion of free surfaces through which materials can diffuse between the cells and the body fluids. It also provides space for the expansion of the viscera. A more compact trunk (such as is compatible with locomotion upon only a few limbs) is made possible by the folding of the alimentary tube within the body cavity. The reproductive organs also occupy the body cavity, which furnishes room for their distention during egg production or pregnancy.

Two major types of body cavities are recognized: (1) the *pseudocoel,* which arises *between* the endoderm and the mesoderm; (2) the true *coelom,* which develops *within* the mesoderm (Figure 12.23). The difference between the two is significant. In *pseudocoelomate* animals such as roundworms, the gut remains a simple epithelial tube lacking an investing musculature, and movement of materials through the gut is accomplished by ciliary action or pressure exerted by contractions of the muscles of the body wall. Lacking in pseudocoelomates is *peristalsis,* the muscular activity so characteristic of the digestive tract of *eucoelomate* animals; these involuntary contractions of the intestinal wall liquefy and churn the food, facilitating both digestion and absorption.

A true coelom occurs in annelids, arthropods, molluscs, chordates, and echinoderms, as well as other minor eucoelomate phyla. (Its ontogeny may be reviewed by reference to Section 11.3B and Figure 11.11.) The coelom is lined, internally and externally, with an uninterrupted serous membrane that secretes a slick, watery fluid which lubricates the contacting surfaces of body wall and viscera. The coelom partitions the mesoderm into parietal and visceral portions—an evolutionary innovation of great significance. The association of the visceral mesoderm with the gut and other coelomic organs makes possible the development of a supportive visceral connective tissue stroma, an intrinsic visceral musculature, and the vascularization of the viscera. Blood vessels from the body wall ramify within the mesenteries (by means of which the viscera are suspended within the coelom) and penetrate the tissues of the internal organs. The gut lining becomes richly vascularized, providing for efficient transport of absorbed nutrients. The coelom furnishes space within which the digestive tube can be folded, so that much more length can be provided for digestion and absorption. The digestive tract of man, for instance, is some 9 m long and occupies most of the abdominal part of the coelom. The heart and lungs fill the thoracic part of the human coelom. The intrinsic visceral musculature provides for the contraction of various hollow organs, such as the vertebrate gall bladder, the urinary bladder, and the gut. Peristaltic waves of contraction sweep the food along the length of the intestinal tract, while localized segmenting and pendular (back-and-forth) contractions retard the food until it is digested and absorbed.

The significance of the coelom to animal evolution is apparent in the fact that all advanced animal phyla are eucoelomate. Even in the arthropods, where the coelom becomes vestigial and is replaced during ontogeny by the blood-filled *hemocoel,* it makes its contribution during development, by assuring that part of the mesoderm shall be associated with the tissues that are of endodermal derivation.

B Metamerism

Three major phyla, Annelida, Arthropoda, and Chordata, have successfully exploited metamerism as an organizing principle in their body plans (Figure 12.24). Metamerism, the serial repetition of body parts, is a genetically economical device whereby increase in body size and complexity can be achieved without preliminary diversification of the genetic code. Since genes are the primary determinants of structure, if one "package" of structural genes suffices for the construction of one metamere (segment), a dozen or a hundred such metameres may be constructed according to the same code, by a process that may originally have resembled a budding of new individuals from the posterior end of the body. Such budding does in fact occur in certain microscopic annelids, and before their separation, the new individuals resemble cars in a train. A similar process also occurs in tapeworms and scyphozoans.

The most primitive form of segmentation is *homonomous* metamerism, illustrated by the majority of annelids, in which the metameres are nearly identical. If appendages are present, such as the parapodia of the clamworm *Nereis* (see Figure 1.10), they occur one pair per metamere and tend to be identical throughout the length of the body.

Homonomous metamerism provides an economical and efficient body plan, but in addition, it opens the way for further evolutionary advancement in that the genes controlling the development of each metamere can be diversified through mutation, so that the metameres may gradually become different from one another. In arthropods and chordates segmentation has become *heteronomous,* permitting the organizational potential of metamerism to be more effectively exploited in these phyla than in the annelids. The greatest contribution to arthropod success has been the diversification of their segmental appendages, which stem from a simple *biramous* (two-branched) pattern. In the primitively biramous appendage, two tapering sections, one medial (*endopodite*) and one lateral (*exopodite*), arise from a single basal portion (*protopodite*) so that the appendage is Y-shaped (see Figure 1.11). This primitive pattern is retained by a number of crustaceans, but in most arthropods considerable modifications have taken place and the segmental appendages, although serially homologous, are adapted for diverse employment. In the lobster, *antennules* and *antennae* are richly provided with chemical and tactile receptors and are thus primarily sensory. The antennular exopodite and endopodite are both long, slender, and flexible. The antennal exopodite forms a flat, short blade but the endopodite is extremely attenuated and is deployed with whiplike movements as the animal probes its environment for hints of food or danger.

The *mandibles, maxillae,* and *maxillipeds* are concerned with food processing. The mandibular protopodite forms a sturdy chitinous food-crushing jaw, aided by the endopodite, a jointed palp which helps hold the food during chewing. In keeping with their origin as paired legs, arthropod mandibles are placed one to each side of the midline and accordingly move from side to side rather than up and down like vertebrate jaws (see Figure 1.11). The maxillary protopodites are thin and flattened and used in manipulating food. The exopodite of the second maxilla forms an enlarged blade (scaphognathite) which, deployed like an oar, ventilates the gills by drawing water under the carapace. The three pairs of maxillipeds are small, biramous, food-handling legs also well provided with tactile and chemical receptors. The second and third each bears a gill on the protopodite.

Five pairs of legs are used in walking, although the first pair or *chelipeds* are powerful pincers used in defense, attack, and food capture. The walking legs are uniramous, lacking an exopodite. The protopodite of each bears a gill, hence walking helps to ventilate the gills.

The abdominal appendages are small, biramous *pereiopods.* In the male the first two pairs serve as copulatory organs. The posterior three pairs feature flattened endopodites and exopodites and are used by the female to hold the eggs during development. Fanning movements of the pereiopods also set up water currents about the lobster, assisting ventilation and sensory reception. At the end of the abdomen, flanking the flattened telson, are the most posterior appendages, the *uropods,* with large, bladelike endopodites and exopodites.

Figure 12.24 □ Metameric architecture of mammalian body. (*a*) Mammalian embryo, showing metameric arrangement of trunk muscles and developing vertebrae. (*b*) Pig embryo, showing metameric construction of skeleton in situ. (*Courtesy of Carolina Biological Supply Company.*) (*c*) Segmental distribution of human integumentary nerves. Each trunk segment is innervated by one pair of spinal nerves; nerves of several segments are directed into the limbs.

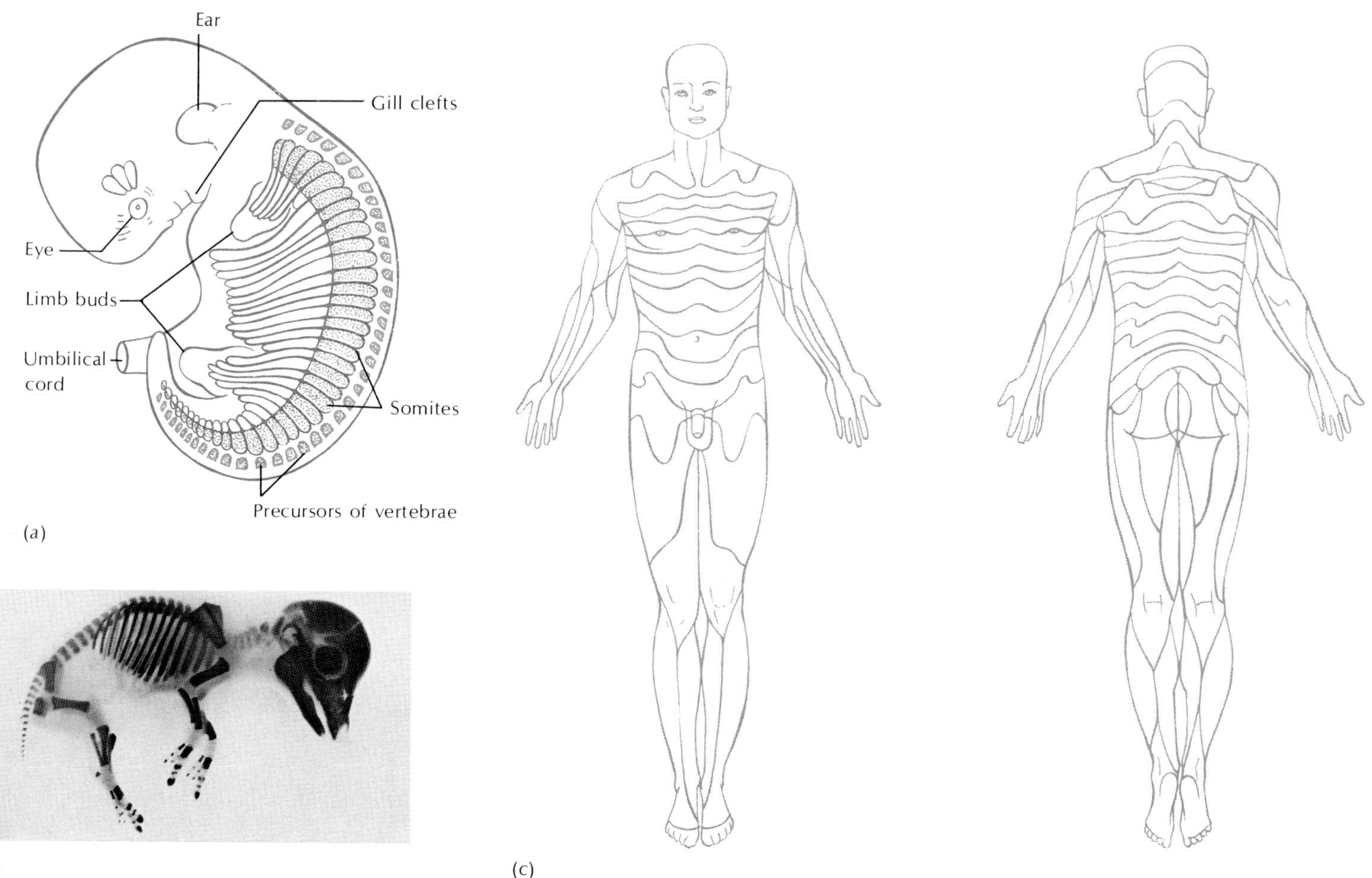

When spread, these, with the telson, form a *tail fan,* used in rapid backward propulsion by strong flexing of the abdomen.

From this example we see that the life of an arthropod depends upon its diversified, serially homologous appendages, an outcome of the effect of genetic variation upon a metameric body plan. Metamerism is a biotic innovation that probably originated more than once during animal evolution. Unless a common metameric ancestor gave rise to both annelids and chordates (which seems unlikely in light of the fact that other deuterostome phyla are unsegmented), it is probable that at two different times the Animal Kingdom has experimented with metameric body plans; both have been conspicuously successful.

C Metazoan organ systems

Ten organ systems are represented in most animal phyla. Nine of these are *somatic* systems, primarily concerned with the maintenance of the individual organism, whereas the tenth, the reproductive system, is concerned with perpetuation of kind. Organ systems concerned primarily with *protection and support* are the *integumentary* and *skeletal* systems. Those concerned mainly with *nutrition* are the *digestive, circulatory* and *respiratory* systems. Those primarily involved in *regulation, integration,* and *response* are the *excretory, nervous, endocrine,* and *muscular systems.*

INTEGUMENTARY SYSTEM Though the functions of the integument and its derivatives are diverse, their primary concern is the protection of internal structures. The integument proper consists of an outer epithelial *epidermis* undergirded in vertebrates especially by a *dermis* containing connective tissue, blood vessels, the bases of integumentary glands, and so forth (Figure 12.25). The unbroken integument furnishes protection against parasitic invasion. Integumentary glands may secrete waterproofing oils, mucus, or secretions noxious to predators. They may also secrete sex attractants and other types of pheromones. In terrestrial animals the integument protects the body from desiccation. Integumentary pigments may protect the animal by furnishing cryptic coloration; conversely, these may be brilliant and serve as warnings to predators, or as social signals between conspecifics (see Plate 4).

In lower metazoans the integument serves as a major organ of *respiration,* and portions of it may be elaborated into extensions (external gills), providing additional surface area for gaseous exchange.

The integument may assist *locomotion.* In animals in which the epidermis secretes an *exoskeleton,* this not only serves a protective function, but in arthropods strengthens and supports the jointed appendages and allows the body to be lifted free of the substratum on which the animal walks. Insect wings are largely integumentary. In other metazoans the integument may be ciliated, facilitating swimming or creeping, and integumentary glands may secrete a mucus path on which the animal can glide.

Occasionally the integument plays a *nutritional* role. Modified integumentary glands produce milk in mammals. Man depends mainly on his skin oils for a supply of vitamin D, for steroid components of these oils are activated upon exposure to ultraviolet radiation, thereupon becoming capable of regulating calcium and phosphate metabolism.

Because it constitutes the interface between organism and environment, the integument must contain a variety of *sensory receptors* that detect stimuli emanating from the external environment. The arthropod exoskeleton is penetrated by hollow sensory bristles containing the endings of tactile and chemical receptors (see Figure 15.14). Many insects taste with their feet as well as with their mouthparts. The vertebrate integument is well provided with tactile, pressure, and thermal receptors.

Integumentary derivatives include the arthropod exoskeleton (see Figure 4.27) and in vertebrates, dermal bone, dermal scales, epidermal scales, and such special keratinized structures as nails, claws, horns, hooves, quills, hair, and feathers (see Figure 9.11). Many of these serve protectively or are useful in locomotion or food getting. Hair and feathers are very important to homoiotherms in conservation of body heat.

SKELETAL SYSTEM Extracellular protective and supportive materials are found in almost all animal phyla, but true skeletal *systems* occur only in those animals in which the individual organs of the skeleton (bones, exoskeletal segments, and the like) are *articulated* (joined) with one another in ways that not only provide support but facilitate locomotion as well. Attachment of the voluntary muscles to the skeleton occurs in arthropods and vertebrates (see Figure 4.28): the skeletal components are worked like levers, thus increasing the muscles' mechanical advantage.

Individual bones of the vertebrate skeleton are bound one to another by *ligaments* of collagenous connective tissue. Muscles attach to the skeleton by way of tough fibrous *tendons*. The bones articulate by way of unions that allow varying degrees of movement (Figure 12.26). *Synarthroses* such as sutures unite bones immovably. *Amphiarthroses* (such as symphyses) are tight fibrous or fibrocartilage junctions that permit only limited movement or expansion (as when the pubic symphysis uniting portions of the pelvic girdle stretches during the birth of young). *Diarthroses* are movable joints in which the articular surfaces of the bones are protectively capped with cartilage and covered by a lubricative *synovial membrane*. Diarthrotic unions include gliding, hinge, and ball-and-socket joints. Gliding joints permit limited slipping of articular surfaces upon one another, as between adjacent vertebrae, or between the vertebrae and ribs. Hinge joints occur at the knee and elbow and permit angular movement through 180° in one plane only. Ball-and-socket joints occur where the limbs articulate with the pectoral and pelvic girdles; at the latter, the globular head of the femur is received into a cuplike depression in the pelvic bone.

MUSCULAR SYSTEM The muscular system consists of the muscles of the body wall, which usually attach to the skeleton if one is present and which bring about the coordinated movement of the body and its parts (see Figure 16.29). In arthropods and vertebrates these *skeletal muscles* are conspicuously striated, having an internal organization thought to favor rapid contractility (see Figure 16.31). Skeletal muscles contract only upon nervous stimulation.

A skeletal muscle is a true organ. Its basic contractile elements are the individual, elongate muscle fibers, organized into bundles by means of connective tissue sheaths.

Figure 12.25 □ Integumentary system: mammalian-skin section. Mammalian skin represents one of the most complex developmental levels of the integumentary system; Figures 11.34*c* and 11.33*d* show some other aspects of this complexity.

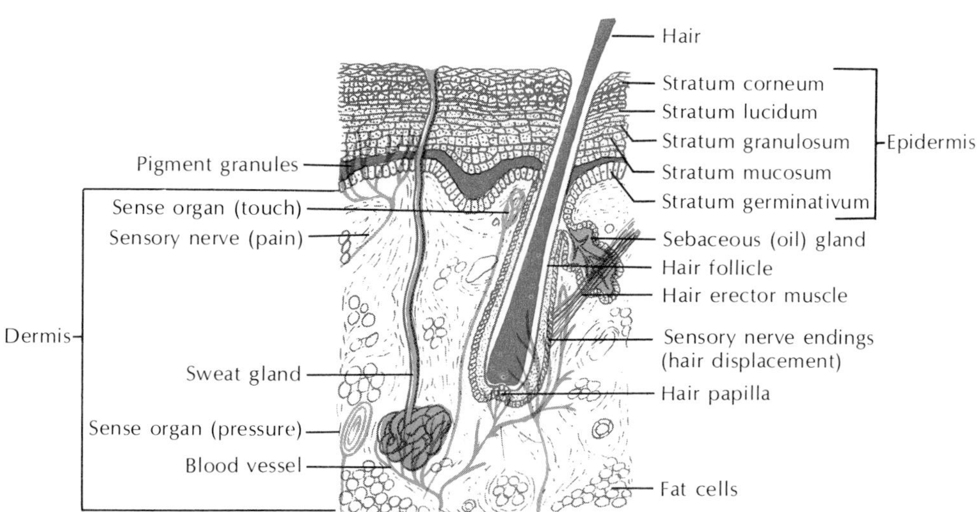

Figure 12.26 □ **Articulation in the skeletal system. Individual bones articulate by way of connections that allow varying degrees and types of movement; fibrous ligaments hold the bones together: the most freely movable joints are protected by synovial structures; less movable joints, such as the pubic and sacroilial symphyses, lack synovial structures, and the bones are closely bound by way of fibrocartilage; skull bones are locked together by sutures.**

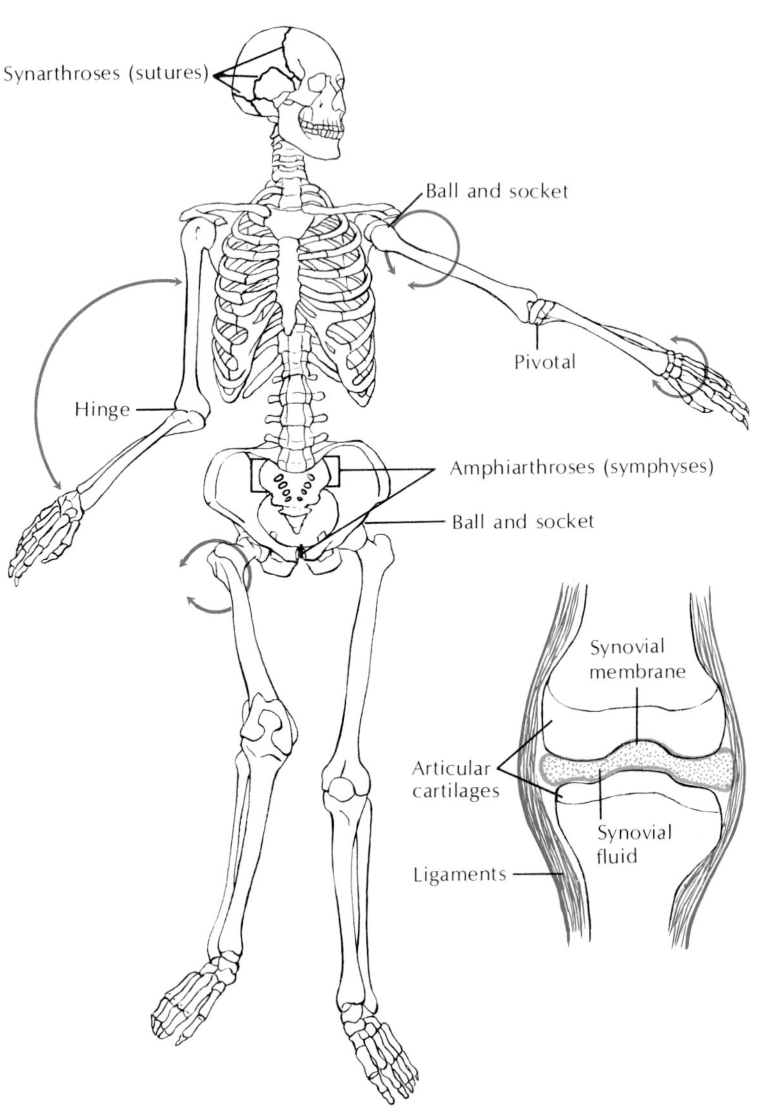

Among these bundles run blood vessels (in the case of vertebrates) and nerves. The entire muscle is bound by a tough connective tissue *fascia,* which is continuous at each end with fibrous tendons that connect the muscle to two or more bones. Pressure and stretch receptors located within the muscles relay sensory information to the central nervous system, eliciting reflexive corrections in posture and muscle tone. Muscles typically operate in *antagonistic* pairs: when one, the *agonist,* shortens in an *isotonic* contraction, the opposing *antagonist* is inhibited from shortening but increases its tone in an *isometric* contraction that does not involve a change in length. As a result of this opposing action, bodily movements are performed smoothly rather than jerkily. Muscles, along with glands, are considered to be the organism's major *effectors,* for they carry out the body's responses to stimuli. The major functional categories of skeletal muscles are given in Figure 16.29.

DIGESTIVE SYSTEM The digestive organs include the *alimentary tube* itself together with associated accessory organs. Animals with true digestive systems have tubular digestive tracts with specific functional regions (Figure 12.27): (1) the *mouth* and buccal cavity, associated with mandibles and teeth for grasping, cutting, and masticating food; (2) a muscular *pharynx,* which initiates swallowing; (3) an *esophagus,* through which food is carried peristaltically to (4) the *stomach,* a dilated chamber within which food is temporarily stored and liquefied; (5) the *intestine,* in which most chemical digestion and absorption are carried out. In many vertebrates the intestine terminates posteriorly in an expanded chamber, the *cloaca,* into which open ducts from the

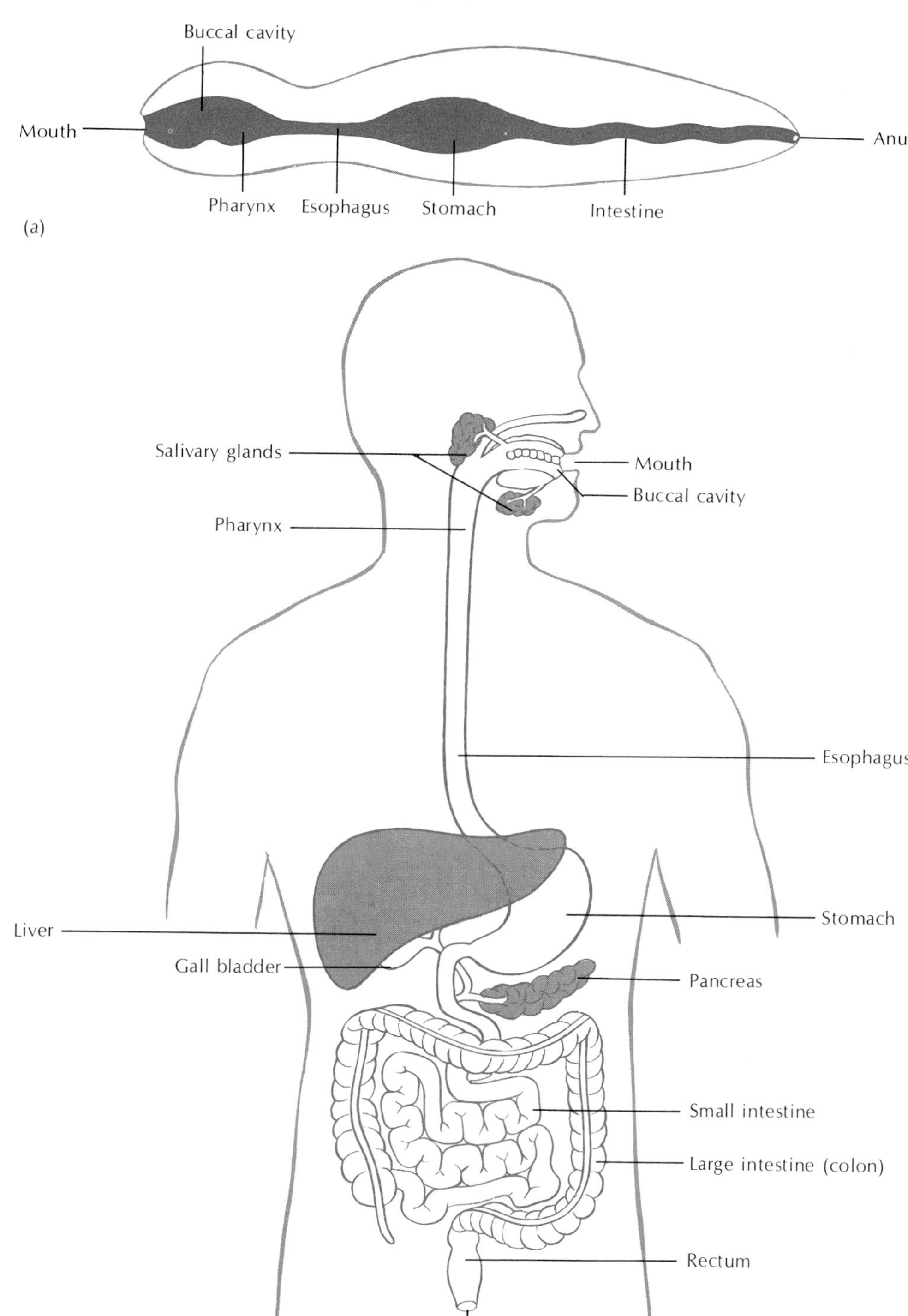

Figure 12.27 □ Digestive system. (*a*) Typical regionalization of digestive tract in a coelomate animal; various glands may be associated with the alimentary tube along its length. (*b*) Human digestive system, showing alimentary tract and associated organs.

urinary bladder and gonads and which communicates to the exterior by way of the *anus.* If the terminal part of the intestine is not associated with reproductive and excretory ducts, it is known instead as a *rectum.* The posterior portion of the esophagus (or the anterior part of the stomach) is sometimes expanded into a nonmuscular storage pouch (*crop*), in which event the muscular part of the stomach is termed the *gizzard.* The vertebrate intestine is usually further divisible into an anterior *small intestine,* the major site of chemical digestion and absorption, and the posterior, shorter *colon* (large intestine), in which indigestible materials are stored prior to defecation (during which time they may be attacked by intestinal bacteria), and much water absorption may take place.

Accessory digestive organs vary with the animal group being considered, but in vertebrates include jaws, teeth, tongue, salivary glands, liver, and pancreas. The lining of the alimentary tube itself is often glandular, and the *gastric* and *intestinal glands* produce many essential enzymes as well as lubricative mucus. Through the integrated performance of these digestive organs the activities of ingestion, mechanical digestion (pulverization and liquefaction), chemical digestion (hydrolysis), absorption of digested nutrients, and egestion or elimination of intestinal wastes (defecation) take place.

RESPIRATORY SYSTEM A respiratory system includes organs such as gills or lungs, in which gaseous exchange takes place between the organism and its environment, together with such structures as are responsible for ventilating the respiratory organs proper (Figure 12.28; see also Figure 14.30). In mammals the respiratory organs are the lungs, and organs that ventilate the lungs include the air passages that communicate with the exterior (nostrils, nasal cavity, pharynx, trachea, and bronchi) and muscles that regulate the expansion and contraction of the thoracic cavity (diaphragm, abdominal, and rib muscles).

Figure 12.28 □ **Human respiratory system. (For more detailed structure of lung, see Figure 14.32.)**

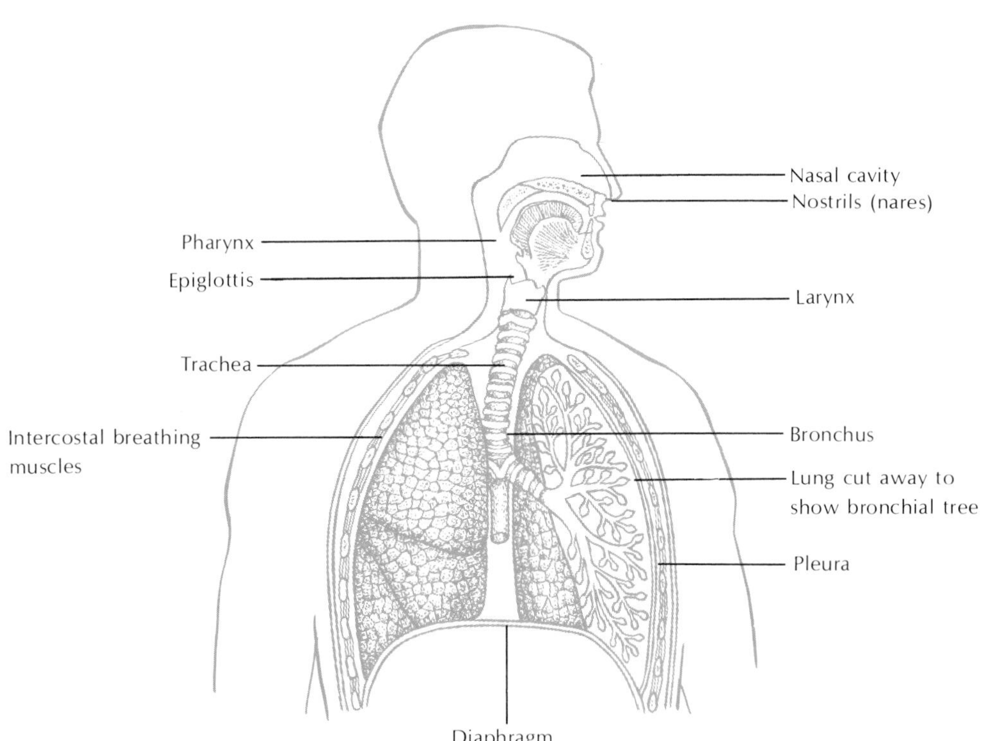

CIRCULATORY SYSTEM A circulatory system assists the internal transport of water and solutes. It may constitute either a *closed* system of blood vessels (arteries, capillaries, and veins) or an *open* system of arteries and blood sinuses (see Figures 14.18 and 14.20). Circulation of the blood is maintained by the rhythmic pulsations of a muscular *heart*. The simplest hearts are merely muscular blood vessels along which pass peristaltic waves of contraction. More advanced hearts are dilated chambers within which the blood is collected prior to being expelled by a forcible pulsation or *heartbeat*. The larger and more active an animal is, the more it must depend on an efficient system of internal transport for: (1) distribution of *nutrients* from the digestive tract to the body cells; (2) transport of *gases* from respiratory organs to the body cells and vice versa; (3) transport of *metabolic wastes* from the tissues to the excretory organs; (4) transport of *hormones* from endocrine glands to the cells they affect. The fluid in which these and other substances such as antibodies are carried is known as *blood*. Although this word commonly brings to mind the richly red, corpuscle-laden fluid of the vertebrate circulatory system, in most phyla blood is colorless or contains red or blue respiratory pigments, and has a sparse corpuscular content.

EXCRETORY SYSTEM The maintenance of correct water, ion, and organic solute concentrations, and the removal from the body of metabolic wastes, are functions of excretory systems. Excretory organs are commonly known as *kidneys,* although in different phyla the analogous organs so designated may vary widely in actual structure (see Figures 16.9 and 16.11). Kidneys concentrate wastes from the blood or other body fluids and void them to the exterior by way of *excretory ducts.* A *urinary bladder* may be present for temporary retention of the urine. Kidneys are important homeostatic organs, for they regulate the chemical composition of body fluids.

NERVOUS SYSTEM An animal's *central* nervous system consists of the major ganglia and fiber tracts that make up the brain and nerve trunks, while its *peripheral* nervous system includes nerves, sense organs, and peripheral ganglia (Figure 12.29). Ganglia are concentrations of neuron cell bodies, from which emanate axons and dendrites contributing to nerves or fiber tracts.* Central ganglia tend to be concentrated along the body's longitudinal axis to form a brain and major nerve trunks. In metameric phyla these major axial trunks constitute a linear series of segmental ganglia, although the segmental character of the arthropod and annelid nerve trunks is more obvious than is that of the vertebrate spinal cord. The latter betrays its metameric origin mainly by giving off paired spinal nerves in each body segment.

Nerves consist only of the peripheral processes of neurons, together with associated nutritive cells, blood vessels, and connective tissue, all bound in a fibrous sheath (see Figure 15.36). Nerves transmit impulses to the central nervous system from the receptors, and from it to the effectors.

Sense organs are responsible for the detection of stimuli arising within the body or externally. They contain receptors which may simply be modified peripheral nerve endings (dendrites) responsive to certain types of stimuli (mechanical, chemical, or electromagnetic), but more rarely consist of specialized receptor cells that communicate with neurons. A sense organ also contains accessory tissues that enhance the efficiency of the receptors.

ENDOCRINE SYSTEM Cells secreting hormones may be aggregated into definite masses or *endocrine glands,* or may be scattered among other types of cells so that no true secretory organ is recognizable. In all eumetazoans *neurohormones* produced by secretory neurons are known to exist, although distinct endocrine tissues other than these may not be discernable. Endocrine glands are concerned with integration and response. They mediate both behavioral and physiological responses and regulate metabolism, growth, and reproduction. They interact closely with the nervous system. The endocrine tissues of arthropods and vertebrates, at least, form true systems, for not only are demonstrable glands present but these interact in sophisticated relationships by which the output of each gland is regulated in terms of the activity of others (see Figure 15.47). Synergism and regulation by negative feedback are characteristic of endocrine systems. (Neuroendocrine coordination, the cornerstone of organismal regulation, will be discussed in Chapter 15.)

REPRODUCTIVE SYSTEM Perpetuation of kind involves the coordinated performance of the whole organism, for reproduction depends on appropriate nutritional state, endocrine regulation, behavior, and so forth. The reproductive system proper includes the *gonads,* which produce gametes, and various accessory organs that function in mating and in the prenatal and postnatal care of the young (see Figures 17.25 and 17.26). Organs of the male reproductive system include the *testes* and *sperm ducts,* and often a copulatory organ or *penis* together with *accessory glands* that may serve to attract mates or to protect and activate the sperm. Reproductive organs of oviparous females include *ovaries, yolk glands, shell glands,* and *oviducts.* The oviduct is dilated to form a *uterus* in some oviparous and all live-bearing species. Euviviparous species lack yolk and shell glands because the nutrition of the embryo is served by the *placenta,* a temporary organ of the eutherian reproductive system. When fertilization is delayed until egg laying, the female reproductive system often includes a *seminal receptacle* within which sperm received during mating are stored. Female reproductive ducts open to the exterior by way of the *cloaca,* by way of a *urogenital sinus* that accommodates urine as well as gametes, or through a separate passage termed the *vagina.*

*In discussing the vertebrate nervous system, the term *ganglion* is often reserved for concentrations located outside the central nervous system and the term *nucleus* for an equivalent concentration *within* the central nervous system; this distinction is not usually observed, however, when considering the nervous systems of invertebrates.

Figure 12.29 □ **Types of nervous systems: (*a*) flatworm; (*b*) scaphopod; (*c*) earthworm; (*d*) shrimp; (*e*) salamander; (*f*) man.**

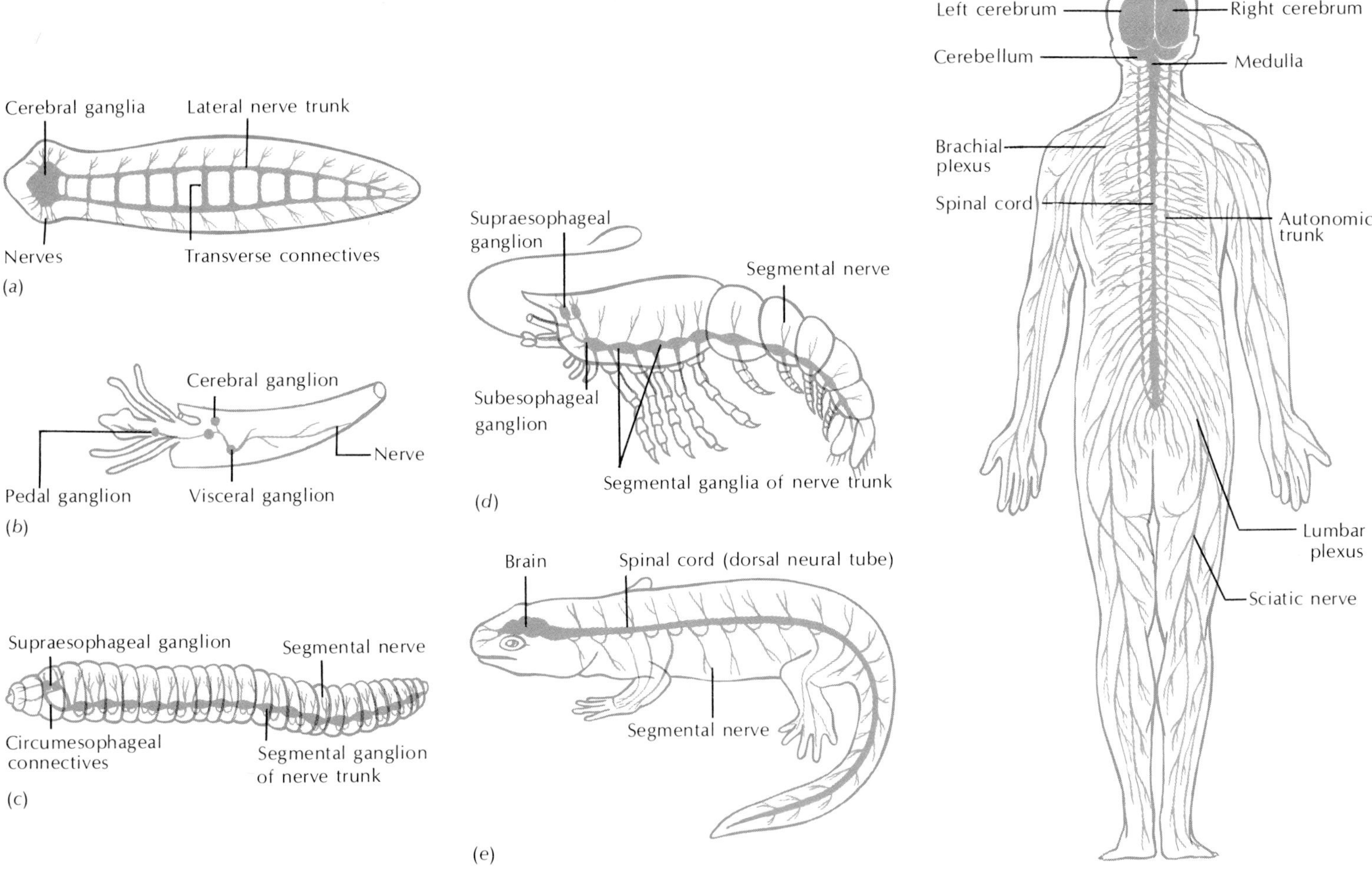

Particulars of metazoan organ systems in three representative organisms will be illustrated next, and their functional aspects will be further considered in the remaining chapters.

A Body plan of an advanced mollusc: *Loligo*, a squid

GENERAL ARCHITECTURE Areas of the body common to the molluscan body plan are the ventral muscular *foot,* the dorsal *visceral hump,* a more or less well developed *head,* and an external *mantle* that typically secretes one or more *shells* (see Figure 2.34). In modern cephalopods, considered to be the most advanced molluscs, the shell is reduced and internalized, and the foot, used for creeping and digging in other molluscs, is subdivided into a *siphon* and a number of prehensile *arms* (Figure 12.30*a*). Cephalopod locomotion is accomplished by crawling upon the arms, or by ejecting water forcibly from the mantle cavity through the funnel-like siphon. Squid are primarily nektonic and pelagic, and their body form reflects their nature as active swimmers, for it is elongated and streamlined along the dorsoventral axis (the functional anteroposterior axis of a swimming squid), and the conical mantle bears finlike stabilizers. The arms, numbering ten, trail backward during swimming. Eight are short, stout arms, bearing a double row of stalked suction cups along their inner surface; two, termed *tentacles,* are twice as long as the rest, and bear suction cups only on their spatulate ends. The two tentacles are employed in seizing prey, which is then held by the arms during ingestion. The mouth is central to the arms, and the head, which protrudes from the mantle, bears two large eyes.

INTEGUMENTARY SYSTEM The integument of *Loligo* consists of the *epidermis,* bearing mucus glands, and the *dermis,* which contains muscles, connective tissue, and numerous pigment sacs (*chromatophores*). Cephalopod chromatophores are distinct from those of other phyla. Each is a spheroidal cell containing a central mass of yellow, reddish, or black pigment; to this cell are connected radial muscles controlled by opposing sets of excitatory and inhibitory nerves (see Figure 16.39*a*). Contraction of these muscles flatten the pigment cell into the form of a disc, the broad surface of which lies parallel to the surface of the skin. The pigment within the expanded chromatophore is thus made more conspicuous. Expansion of different chromatophores in varying proportions brings about a rapid and precisely executed series of color changes.

SKELETON The squid skeleton consists of a horny bladelike *pen,* which supports the long axis of the body, and a cartilagelike endoskeleton developed within the head and mantle wall. The anterior edge of the mantle (collar) is reinforced with cartilaginous ridges that slide into corresponding grooves on the siphon, fitting together snugly during exhalation. Cartilage plates strengthen the mantle, surround the "neck," and encase the brain.

MUSCULATURE The mantle wall and arms contain striated fibers capable of rapid contraction. The mantle muscles contract to peak tension within only 60 msec of stimulation. The circular and longitudinal mantle muscles contract alternately during swimming. During the inhalant phase water is taken into the mantle cavity, which is enlarged by contractions of the longitudinal muscles. When the mantle cavity is filled, the longitudinal muscles relax and the circular muscles contract, reducing the volume of the cavity and forcing the water out through the siphon. Separate muscles control the mobility of the siphon, which can be directed laterally, allowing the animal to turn left or right, or even bent into a U, permitting the animal to move with its head going forward and arms leading instead of trailing.

DIGESTIVE SYSTEM The digestive system is complex (Figure 12.30*b*). The mouth, ringed by the arms, opens into the buccal cavity, and bears a pair of horny jaws forming a beak. The beak can bite off large chunks of flesh. *Loligo* kills its customary prey, young mackerel, by biting a triangular piece out of the neck, severing the spinal cord. Food is pulled into the buccal cavity

Figure 12.30 □ **Squid body plan. (*a*) Living squid. (*b*) Lateral view of internal organs, showing mainly digestive and reproductive organs.**

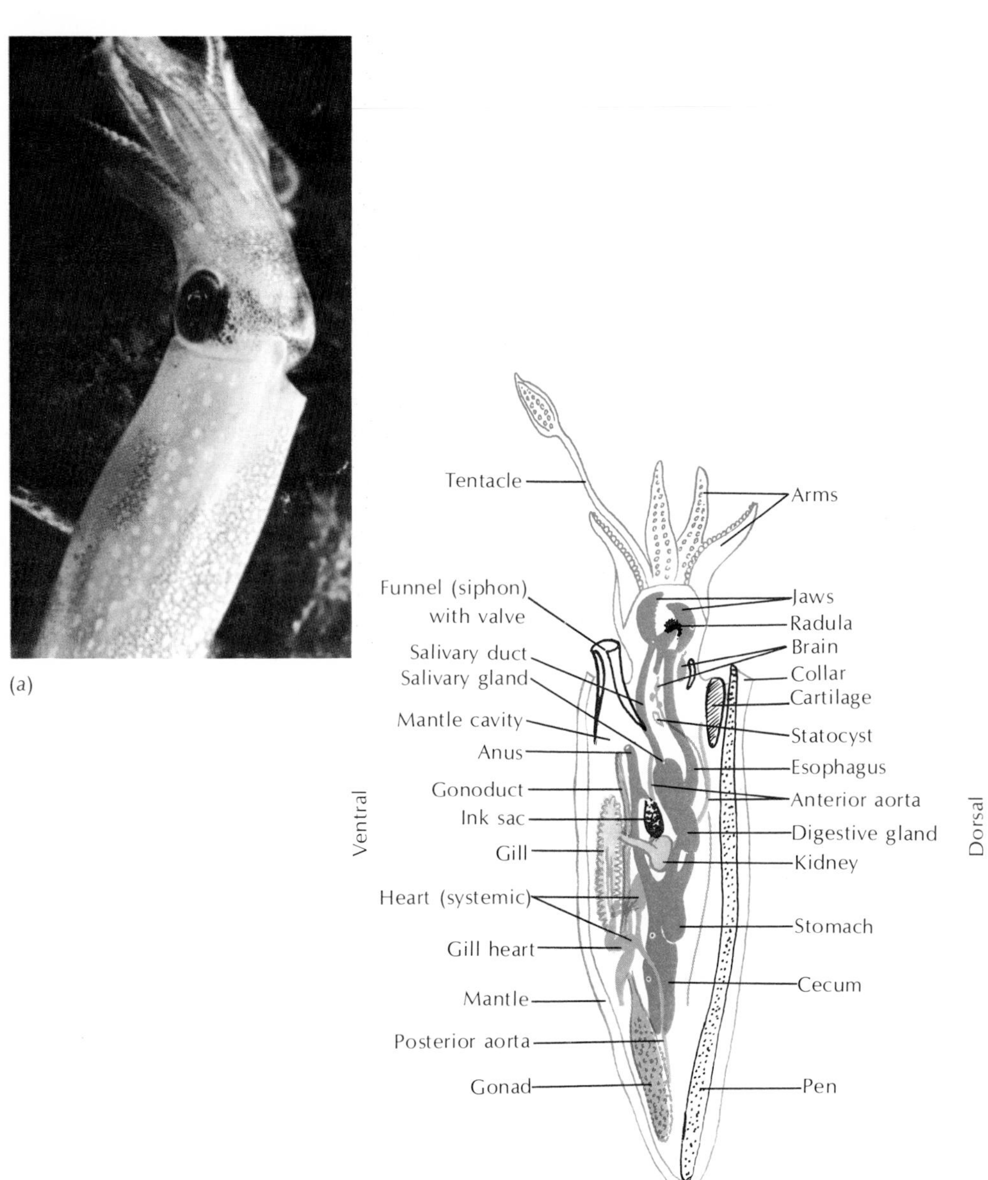

by tonguelike movements of the radula, a membrane bearing recurved chitinous teeth (which is the main feeding organ of such molluscs as chitons and snails). One pair of salivary glands secretes mucus and enzymes into the buccal cavity; a second pair, in reality a poison gland used in subduing large prey, empties into the anterior part of the esophagus. The alimentary tube is U-shaped and muscular, one arm of the U being formed by the esophagus and the other by the intestine, with the stomach occupying the apex of the U. The stomach communicates with a blind pouch (cecum), which receives ducts from a large digestive gland. This gland is divided into two parts, a "pancreas," which continually secretes enzymes that are stored in the cecum, and a "liver," which secretes enzymes only during feeding. Digestion commences in the stomach, where the food is churned and mixed with digestive juices, and is completed in the cecum, where most absorption takes place. The indigestible residue is returned to the stomach and passes into the intestine, being voided through the anus into the mantle cavity, from which it is expelled during exhalation.

An *ink gland* opens into the rectum just anterior to the anus. Discharge of this gland is controlled by the nervous system. The "ink," rich in the black pigment melanin, is employed defensively. Some investigators claim that the ink paralyzes olfaction (the sense of smell) in would-be predators, others that the discharged ink mass hangs in the water as a distracting "ghost-shape" while the cephalopod makes off in another direction. Evidence based upon the behavior of "inked" predators lends support to both of these hypotheses.

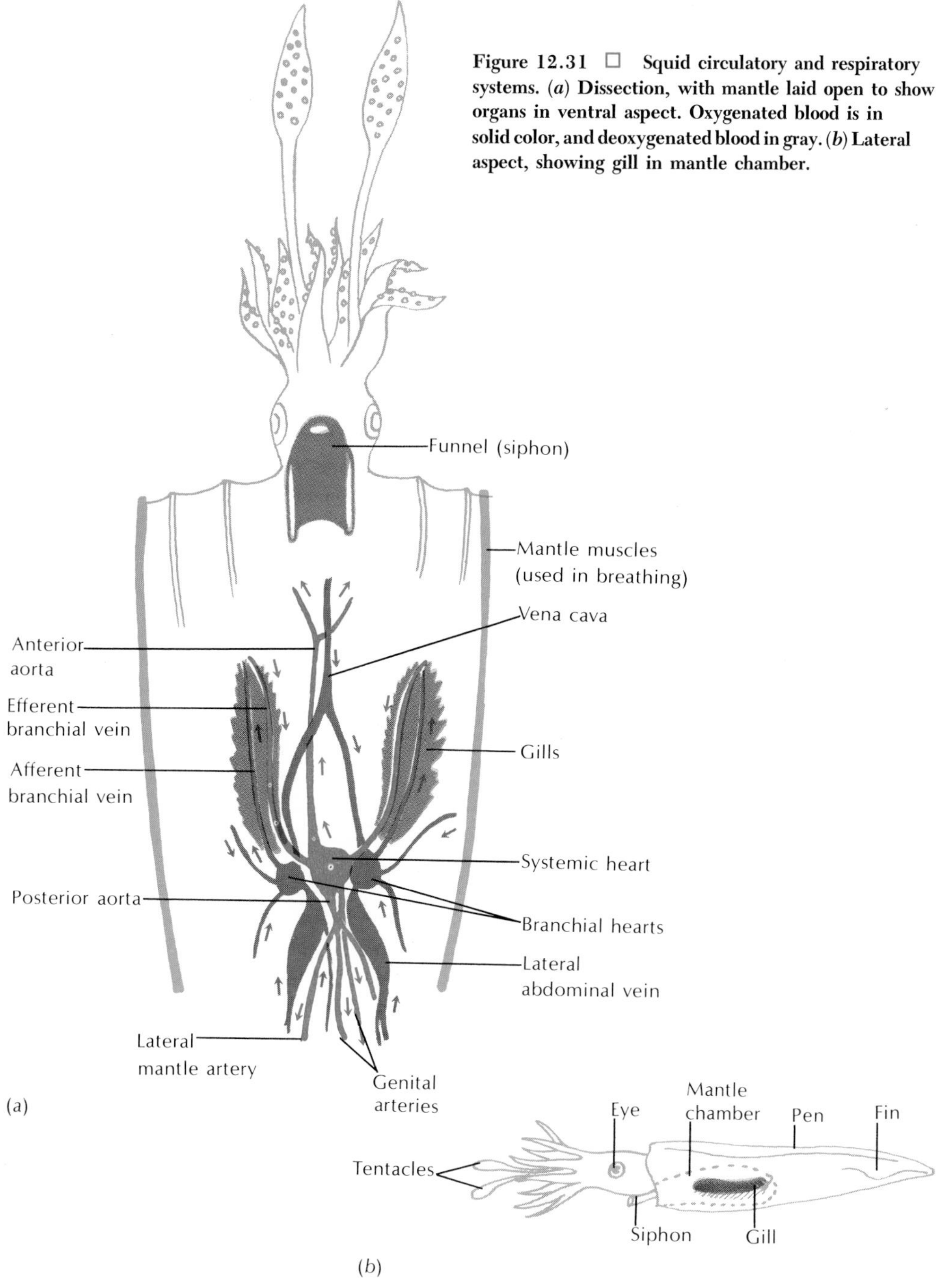

Figure 12.31 □ **Squid circulatory and respiratory systems. (*a*) Dissection, with mantle laid open to show organs in ventral aspect. Oxygenated blood is in solid color, and deoxygenated blood in gray. (*b*) Lateral aspect, showing gill in mantle chamber.**

RESPIRATORY SYSTEM Exchange of gases between the capillaries and the water in the mantle cavity takes place through a pair of finely divided gills (*ctenidia*), which occupy the mantle cavity (Figure 12.31). The mantle itself aids respiration, for its contractions ventilate the ctenidia.

CIRCULATORY SYSTEM The circulatory system of the squid (Figure 12.31a) consists of a closed circuit of arteries, capillaries, and veins, through which the blood, containing the blue respiratory pigment *hemocyanin,* is pumped by the action of three hearts. A *branchial heart* at the base of each ctenidium pumps deoxygenated blood through the gill capillaries. Oxygenated blood from the branchial veins is sucked into the two lateral atria (auricles) of the main *systemic heart.* The atria open into the single muscular *ventricle,* which pumps the blood into an anterior and a posterior aorta. These branch into progressively smaller arteries and eventually into capillaries, where exchanges between the blood and the cells can take place. Deoxygenated blood returning from the head and arms is carried by smaller veins that converge upon a large vein (vena cava). This divides into right and left branches leading toward the branchial hearts, and each branch receives a vein from the mantle and viscera just before entering the branchial hearts that pump the blood to the gills. Thus the blood receives *two propulsive surges* for each complete circuit of the body: one at the gill hearts and one at the systemic heart, a situation analogous to that in tetrapod vertebrates (see Figure 14.20).

EXCRETORY SYSTEM The *pancreas* and the paired *nephridia* are the major organs of excretion. The nephridia are saclike organs opening distally into the mantle cavity by way of nephridiopores and conjoined anteriorly. From the point of junction a large sac arises enclosing the pancreas, which secretes wastes into this sac. Posteriorly, each nephridium encloses one branch of the vena cava, encasing the vein with glandular cells that collect wastes from the blood and secrete them into the cavity of the nephridium. Such association of the bloodstream and the pancreas with the nephridia points to a high level of homeostatic regulation (maintaining the body's chemical stability) during urine production.

Figure 12.32 □ **Squid nervous system. The brain consists of paired dorsal *cerebral ganglia*, anterior *brachial ganglia*, ventral *pedal ganglia*, and posterior *visceral ganglia*.**

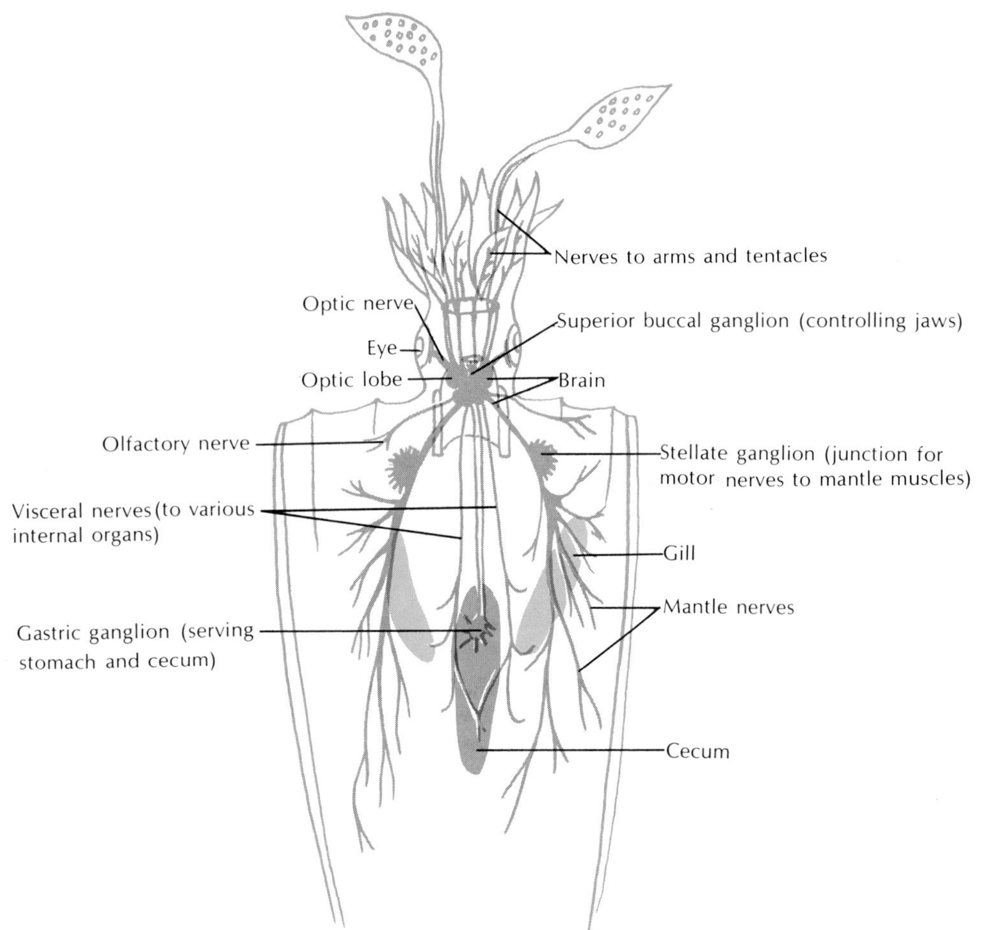

NERVOUS AND ENDOCRINE SYSTEMS The nervous system (Figure 12.32) and sense organs of cephalopods are complex and sophisticated. Motor actions are precise, subtle, and rapidly executed. Experiments performed with octopus (more readily maintained in aquaria than squid) have revealed a high level of learning and discriminative capacity, comparable to that of vertebrates. Several major ganglia are concentrated to form a brain that encircles the esophagus. These ganglia are functionally differentiated and contain centers that control specific activities of different parts of the body. The large *cerebral* or supraesophageal *ganglia,* located above the esophagus, for instance, contain centers that control forward swimming and closure of the suckers; each cerebral ganglion receives a large optic nerve from the eye and gives off buccal nerves to the mouth. The *pedal ganglia* lie below the esophagus and give off nerves to the siphon and arms. Certain evidence suggests that although the brain initiates muscular responses, these are executed without direct feedback to the brain from the periphery: the animal can *see* what its arms are doing, but may not be able to make postural adjustments on the basis of information received. The posterior part of the brain is formed by the *visceral ganglia,* which furnish nerves to the mantle and internal organs.

A balance organ (statocyst) is embedded in the cartilages to each side of the brain. The cephalopod eye is excellently developed and closely resembles the vertebrate camera eye (see Figure 15.20c). The arms are well supplied with receptors sensitive to chemical and mechanical stimuli and probably also to thermal changes.

As well as having neurosecretory tissue, cephalopods possess a pair of nonneuronal endocrine glands, the *optic glands,* situated on the eye stalks that connect the eyes with the brain. The optic glands secrete *gonadotrophins,* which stimulate the maturation of the gonads. In immature animals the optic glands are suppressed by inhibitory nerve fibers from the brain. In young octopus, certain surgical procedures have been found to derepress the optic glands, resulting in sexual precocity. Such procedures include removal of the optic lobe of the brain, interruption of the inhibitory fiber tract, or severance of the optic stalk.

REPRODUCTIVE SYSTEM A single gonad and accessory organs form the reproductive system. *Loligo* is dioecious. In the male, sperm are formed in the wall of the saccular *testis* and pass into the *vas deferens,* which leads to the *seminal vesicle.* Here the sperm are encased in *spermatophores.* Each of these contains a sperm mass, a cement body which serves to attach the spermatophore within the female's body, and a coiled ejaculatory organ that is released when the spermatophore is taken from the storage reservoir (Needham's sac). Cephalopods lack a penis, but one of the two long tentacles is modified (hectocotylized) into a sperm-carrying arm. Mating is preceded by courtship. When the female expresses acquiescence, the male reaches the tip of his hectocotylized tentacle into his Needham's sac, withdraws a mass of spermatophores and inserts these under the female's mantle or into her seminal receptacle. In some species, the male merely snaps off the hectocotylized arm, with its load of spermatophores, and the arm alone goes in search of a female.

The female's saccular *ovary* leads into an *oviduct* at the end of which are glands that furnish each egg with a capsule and invest the entire egg mass with a gelatinous covering which attaches it to the substratum. When the egg mass passes out of the mantle cavity it is held by the female's arms while being fertilized with sperm ejected from her seminal receptacle and is then affixed to the substratum.

B Body plan of an insect: *Dissosteira,* a locust

GENERAL ARCHITECTURE Grasshoppers of various genera are favorite organisms for the study of generalized insect anatomy (Figure 12.33). Locusts undergo gradual metamorphosis, each immature stage closely resembling the adult save for being sexually immature and unable to fly. Growth entails a series of molts and is uninterrupted by pupation. The body is metameric, the original number of segments being seen only in the embryo, for fusion of certain metameres occurs during maturation. The three major body divisions are *head, thorax,* and *abdomen.* The head is formed by a fusion of six embryonic metameres. It bears two large compound eyes, three ocelli (simple eyes), one pair of antennae bearing chemical and tactile receptors, and an assortment of modified legs serving as mouthparts (Figure 12.34). The latter include the single *labrum* (upper lip), the tonguelike *hypopharynx,* paired *mandibles,* paired *maxillae,* and a single *labium* bearing paired palps. The thorax comprises three metameres (prothorax, mesothorax and metathorax), each bearing a pair of uniramous walking legs. The latter two bear wings as well. In the locust the anterior pair of wings is leathery, the posterior membranous, but both are employed in flight. The wings are cuticular outgrowths of the body wall, secreted by a double layer of epidermal cells lying between the dorsal and lateral body plates; they are strengthened by branching "veins" that are actually chitinous thickenings around air tubules. Each walking leg has five segments—a basal coxa, a trochanter, a femur, and tibia (so named because of their analogy to the upper and lower vertebrate leg bones), distal to which is a tarsus or foot comprising three segments plus terminal claws. The claws are retractible by means of a cordlike tendon that originates on the tibia and extends through the hollow tarsus.

The abdomen originally consists of 11 metameres, but only seven are recognizable in the adult. During embryogeny, each abdominal metamere bears a pair of vestigial appendages, but these vanish, leaving the abdomen with only a pair of sensory filaments (cerci), and copulatory organs (in the male) or ovipositor (in the female).

Figure 12.33 □ **Grasshopper body plan. (*a*) External aspect. (*b*) Internal organs in situ, lateral aspect. The reproductive system is shown in grayed color; the circulatory system, in a tint of color; the nervous system, in gray; and the digestive system, in solid color.**

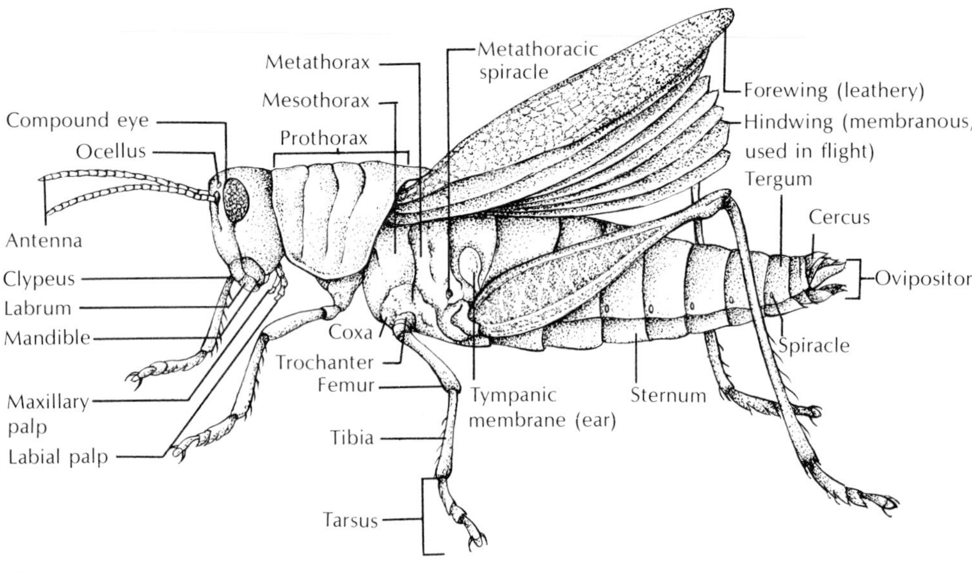

(*a*)

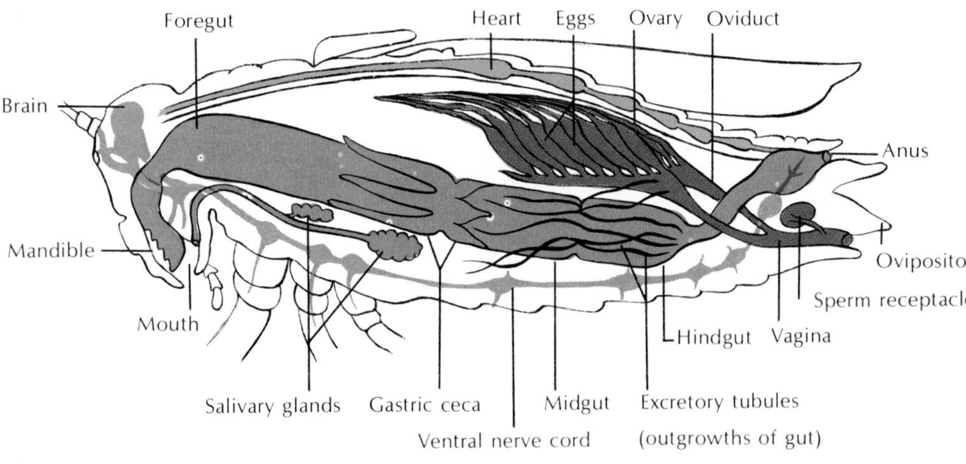

(*b*)

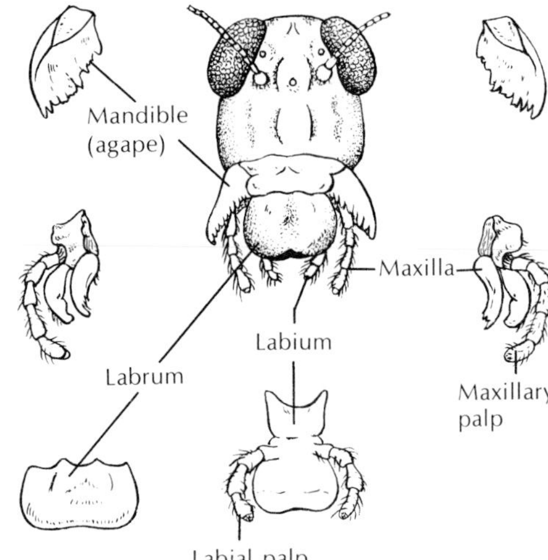

Figure 12.34 □ **Grasshopper mouthparts.**

INTEGUMENT AND SKELETON The integument is a single layer of epithelium which secretes the chitinous exoskeleton. The exoskeleton remains thin and flexible at the joints between segments, but forms four fairly rigid plates—one dorsal, two lateral, and one ventral—encasing each trunk segment. Sensory bristles, pegs, and pits stud the surface of the exoskeleton.

MUSCULATURE The exoskeleton serves not only for support and protection, but for attachment of the several thousand *skeletal muscles.* These muscles are striated and resemble vertebrate muscles in being organized into masses attached to the skeleton by connective fasciae or tendons (see Figure 4.27). Well-developed muscles move the limbs, the mouthparts, the genitalia, and the ovipositor (used by female locusts for excavating holes in the ground, into which the eggs are laid). The muscles of the abdominal wall are responsible for ventilating the tracheae.

The wing muscles proper merely bring the wings from the resting position to a "ready" position at right angles to the thorax, or return them to the resting position. The *flight* muscles, which move the wings through a looping figure-eight circuit, are *not* attached to the wings themselves, but occupy the thoracic cavity (Section 4.3B).

Figure 12.35 □ **Grasshopper respiratory system. Only the main air sacs and tracheal tubes are shown; microscopic tracheoles extend to all tissues.**

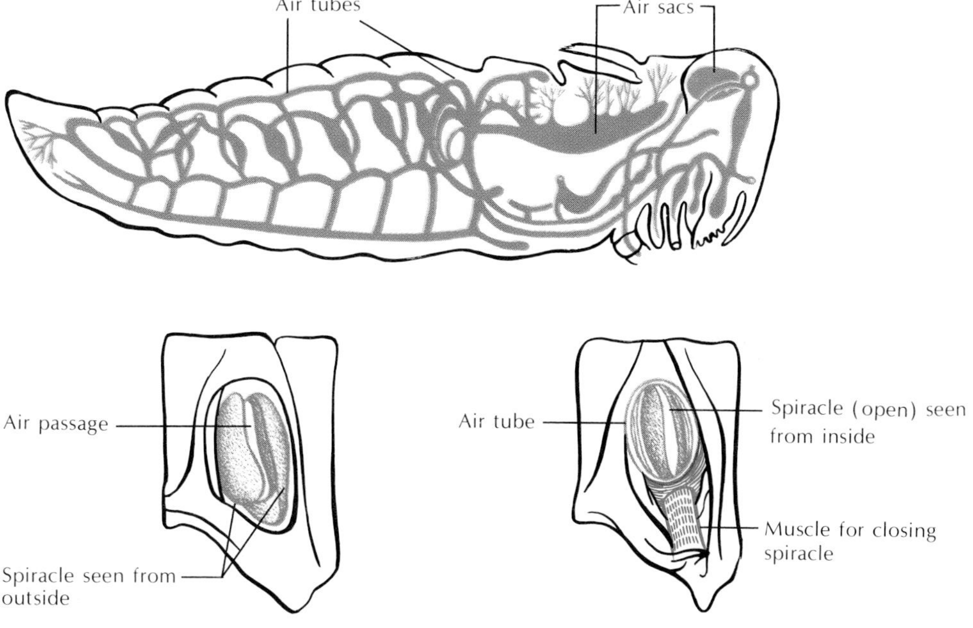

DIGESTIVE SYSTEM The digestive system includes the *mouthparts,* described above, the *salivary glands,* and the alimentary tract itself. The latter is differentiated into three regions: the mouth, pharynx, esophagus, crop, and proventriculus form the *foregut;* the stomach and gastric ceca comprise the *midgut;* and the intestine, rectum, and anus constitute the *hindgut* (Figure 12.33*b*). The foregut and hindgut are lined with chitin; consequently, the absorption of nutrients is largely restricted to the midgut. This chitinous lining is shed during molting, along with the cuticle covering the body externally. The food is held with the other mouthparts while being masticated by the mandibles and mixed with saliva. It is swallowed, passes down the esophagus, and is temporarily held in the thin-walled crop. From there it passes into the proventriculus, where it is ground by contractions of the gut musculature. The food then passes to the stomach, into which eight pairs of cone-shaped pouches, the *gastric ceca,* empty their digestive secretions. Here digestion is completed and absorption takes place. The indigestible residue then passes through the hindgut and is eliminated.

RESPIRATORY SYSTEM The respiratory system of insects represents a successful adaptation to terrestrial life, efficient but at the same time compensating for the open circulation that arthropods adopted long before flight placed additional oxygen demands upon the organism. Gaseous exchange takes place through a branching series of minute chitinous tubules, the *tracheae,* which communicate with the exterior by way of segmentally arranged *spiracles* (Figure 12.35). The tracheae form a diffuse, interconnected network of air passages that penetrate far into the body so that no cell lies far from a direct air supply. The blind terminal branchlets (*tracheoles*) are fluid-filled and often lie in direct contact with the membranes of the cells served. Some tracheae are dilated into thin-walled air sacs that are readily compressible; air is squeezed out of these sacs by contraction of muscles of the body wall; when these muscles relax, air is pulled into the sacs by suction. Internal air sacs also reduce the density of the body, thereby facilitating flight. Breathing is accomplished by rhythmic contractions of the abdominal muscles, which force air out of the tracheal system; new air is sucked in through the spiracles when these muscles relax. The locust has three thoracic and seven abdominal pairs of spiracles, the action of which is synchronized so that the anterior four pairs open during inspiration and close during expiration while the posterior six pairs close during inspiration and open during expiration. This alternation forces air through longitudinal tracheae that connect the segmental ones.

CIRCULATORY SYSTEM Insects possess an open circulation. Blood, a colorless fluid containing only a few amoeboid phagocytes, is expelled from the open ends of large arteries and floods the body spaces within which the organs lie. The true coelom is reduced and the definitive body cavity is a blood-filled *hemocoel.* Capillaries and veins are wanting. The tubular heart consists of a longitudinal series of chambers into each of which a pair of ostia (pores) open. The heart lies along the dorsal surface of the abdomen just beneath the body wall, and is partially enclosed in a *pericardial sac.* Blood from the hemocoel drains into this sac and enters the heart by way of the ostia. When the heart is filled, valves close the ostia and the heart contracts in a wave that sweeps anteriorly, forcing the blood into the single artery, the *aorta,* which opens into the hemocoel in the head region. Blood circulates sluggishly through the hemocoel and is gradually sucked through the ostia by the vacuum created when the heart empties itself. That so active an organism as an insect can tolerate such relative inefficiency of blood circulation is due to the fact that insects do not depend upon the blood for transport of gases, but only for distribution of nutrients. No respiratory pigment is present to augment the oxygen-carrying capacity of the blood, and the tissues must rely upon the tracheal system, almost all cells being in intimate contact with the end of an air tubule.

EXCRETORY SYSTEM Excretion is accomplished by a cluster of slender *Malpighian tubules,* all of which end blindly in the hemocoel and open into the *hindgut* (see Figure 16.9c). Wastes extracted from the blood are secreted into the hindgut, which functions in reabsorption of valuable materials, chiefly water.

NERVOUS SYSTEM The metameric nervous system of an insect includes a dorsal brain (*supraesophageal ganglion*) formed of three pairs of fused ganglia, from which a pair of circumesophageal connectives pass ventrally around the esophagus and join the *subesophageal ganglion.* This ganglion actually represents a fusion of the three pairs of ganglia which innervate the mouthparts. The supraesophageal and subesophageal ganglia together represent the six pairs of ganglia of the six embryonic metameres which form the insect head. A paired *ventral nerve trunk* extends posteriorly from the subesophageal ganglion, running along the floor of the hemocoel just within the body wall. One large paired ganglion occurs in this nerve trunk in each thoracic segment and controls the pair of legs borne on that segment. The segmental ganglia of the abdomen, originally numbering eleven pair, become fused during development so that only five pairs remain in the adult to serve the seven abdominal metameres. The virtual absence of appendages on these abdominal metameres makes this reduction feasible.

A separate ganglionic chain arises from the brain and passes to the muscles of the alimentary tract, the reproductive organs, and the spiracles; this separate innervation of muscles associated with visceral functions is analogous with the autonomic division of the vertebrate nervous system, responsible for involuntary actions.

Integumentary tactile and chemical receptors occur over the body but are especially concentrated on the feet, antennae, and mouthparts. The *compound eyes* cover the sides of the head, together commanding nearly a 360° visual field. The *ocelli* or simple eyes probably lack fine resolution but only monitor photoperiod and light intensity. Acoustic reception of air-borne vibrations is made possible by sensory cells in contact with the eardrum or *tympanic membrane,* a thin oval area occupying most of the lateral plate on each side of the first abdominal segment. Proprioceptors in muscles and joints register position and muscle tension, permitting reflexive postural adjustments and the coordination of limb movements.

ENDOCRINE SYSTEM Hormonal

control in insects is extensive, involving the interaction of neurosecretory tissue and epithelial (nonneurosecretory) endocrine glands. (Details of endocrine regulation in insects and other invertebrates will be considered in Section 15.4B.)

REPRODUCTIVE SYSTEM Sexes are separate and distinguishable externally by the female's conspicuous *ovipositor* and the male's *external genitalia.* The former consists of three pairs of movable plates at the tip of the abdomen, employed in excavating burrows into which the eggs are laid. The female reproductive system (Figure 12.36), includes as well the paired *ovaries* made up of bundles of egg tubules (ovarioles), within which the ova mature, and the *oviducts,* which unite posteriorly into a common *vagina.* During maturation in the ovarioles the eggs are furnished with yolk and a protective, water-impervious shell. A *seminal receptacle* opening near the vaginal orifice stores sperm received during copulation. Sperm are released from the seminal receptacle to fertilize the eggs as they are laid.

The male reproductive system consists of paired *testes,* from each of which sperm pass into a coiled *vas deferens* that dilates posteriorly into a *seminal vesicle* (Figure 12.36). These unite to form a common ejaculatory duct. At the tip of the abdomen are the external genitalia, consisting of movable plates that clasp the female and a *penis* used in copulation. At ejaculation, fluid secreted from an accessory gland is added to the sperm, activating them as they enter the female's genital tract.

Figure 12.36 □ **(*a*) Male and (*b*) female reproductive systems of the grasshopper.**

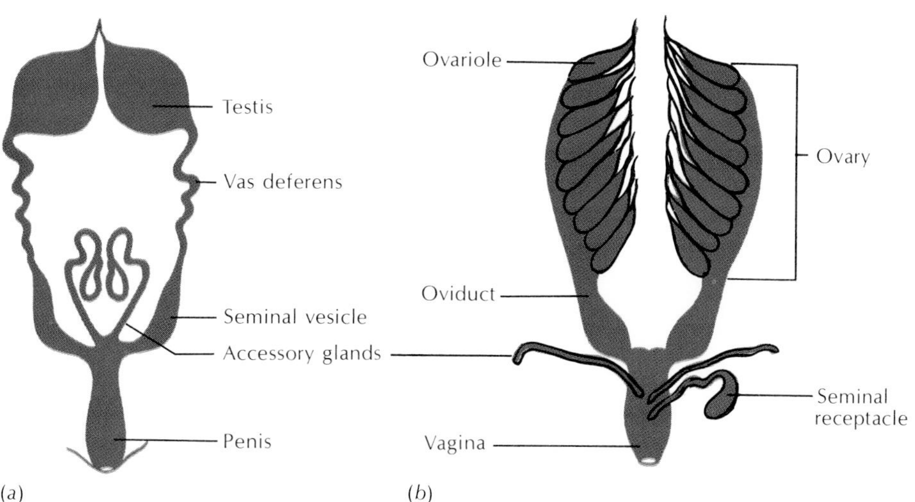

C Body plan of a representative vertebrate: *Squalus*, a shark

GENERAL ARCHITECTURE In their external aspect most vertebrates do not display markedly the metamerism that is an essential feature of their body plan. There are but two pairs of serially homologous appendages, and the body is divisible simply into *head, trunk,* and postanal *tail* (Figure 12.37*a*). In tetrapods these regions are easily distinguishable, but in fish a swimming habit has favored the development of a streamlined body contour in which head, trunk, and tail grade smoothly together. The head bears two lateral eyes, paired nostrils, and an anterior or ventral mouth. The pharyngeal clefts, through which water circulates while passing over the gills, are visible externally in sharks as a series of six metamerically arranged openings on each side of the throat. The trunk contains the viscera, enclosed in the coelom, and bears the two pairs of appendages. The tail lacks appendages but in fish terminates in an expanded *caudal fin.* The tail of fish is strongly muscular and is the main propulsive organ, its caudal fin providing a broad plane which is pushed against the water, driving the body forward.

Squalus, a cartilaginous fish, is considered representative of the primitive vertebrate body plan, although of course it possesses many adaptations relevant to its own mode of life, and the lack of bone stems from the loss of a bone-synthesizing capacity common to ancestral vertebrates. The body is streamlined, the head bluntly pointed and flaring to a broader trunk,

Figure 12.37 □ **Schematic representation of primitive vertebrate architecture. (*a*) External features. (*b*) Endoskeleton (limb bones are differentiated from limb girdles by lighter gray). (*c*) Musculature.**

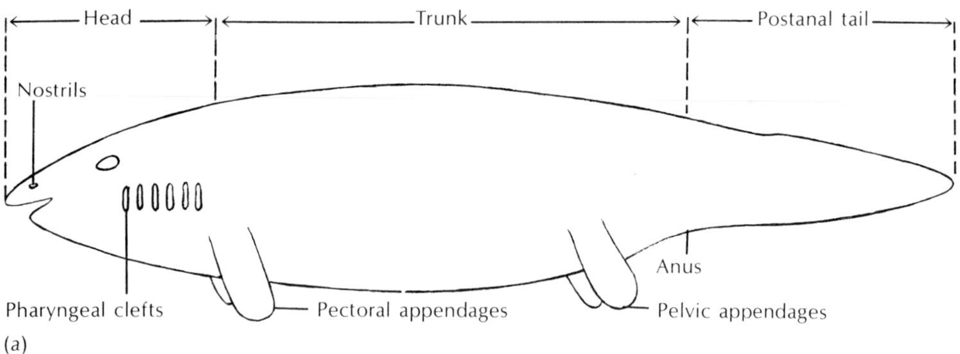

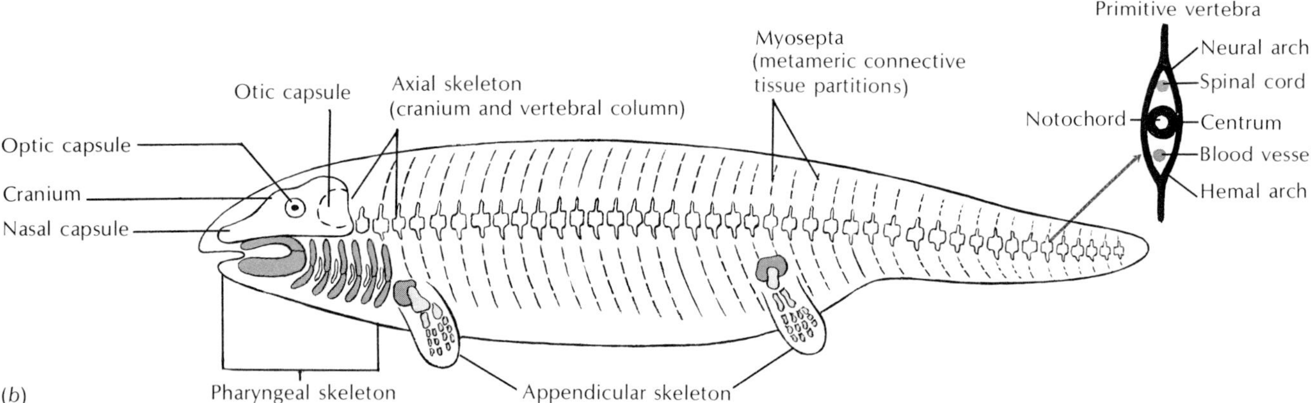

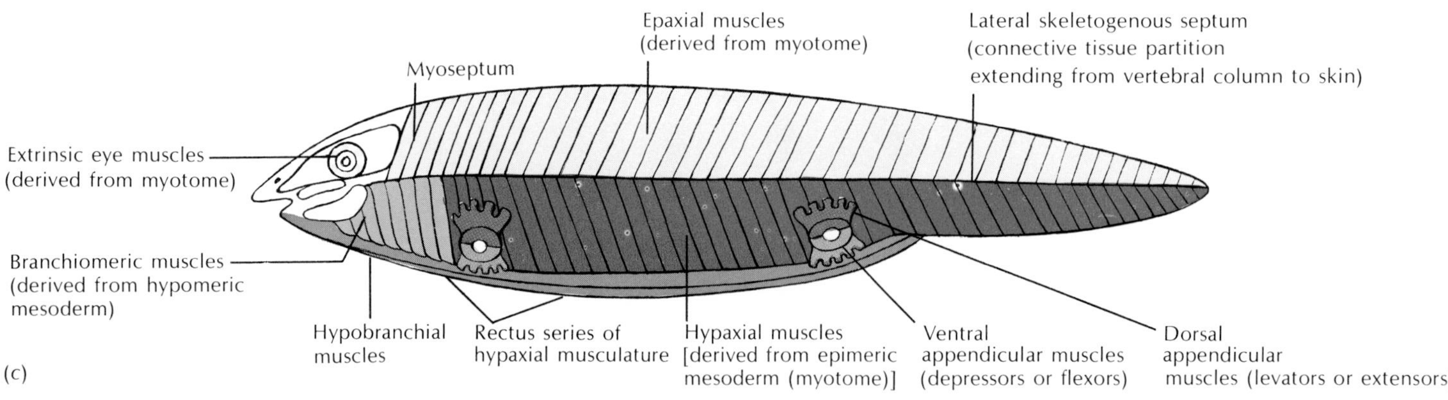

Figure 12.38 □ Mako shark (*Isurus oxyrhynchus*), exhibiting rows of teeth homologous with placoid scales. (*Photograph by G. Mattson, U.S. Bureau of Commercial Fisheries.*)

which then tapers smoothly to the tail. Head and trunk are somewhat flattened dorsoventrally. A snout or rostrum, bearing the nares (nostrils), overhangs the ventral mouth, both jaws of which sport multiple rows of teeth (Figure 12.38). The eyes, set well to the sides of the head, scan separate lateral fields of view, forward vision being restricted. The trunk bears a median dorsal fin and the broad-based, nonmaneuverable *pectoral* and *pelvic fins.* The flaring caudal fin features a large dorsal lobe that serves to impart a downward force that compensates for the tendency to rise caused by the flattened anterior part of the shark's body.

INTEGUMENT The integument consists of an ectodermally derived *epidermis,* composed of stratified squamous epithelium, overlying a mesodermally derived *dermis,* largely made up of connective tissue containing blood vessels, nerves, and sensory endings. The stratification of the epidermis is a unique vertebrate characteristic. The epidermis is rich in mucus-secreting cells, and is penetrated by the sharp posteriorly curved spines of the *placoid scales.* These scales are unlike those of other fish, but are considered homologous with teeth. They make the shark's skin smooth to stroke from front to back, but extremely rough and abrasive when stroked in the opposite direction.

SKELETON The endoskeleton of sharks (Figures 12.37*b* and 12.39*a*) is representative of the basic vertebrate plan, but is atypical in that it lacks bone and consists of cartilage hardened by additional calcium deposits. The axial skeleton includes the *cranium, vertebral column,* and *pharyngeal skeleton.* The cranium protects the brain and laterally has three pairs of sensory capsules: (1) the *nasal capsules,* lined with olfactory receptor cells; (2) the *optic capsules,* that do not ossify but form the tough sclerotic coat of the eyeballs; (3) the *otic capsules,* which encase the *labyrinth,* the balance and acoustic organs of the inner ear (Figure 12.39*b*). The vertebral column of the shark is not regionally specialized. The embryonic notochord is persistent, passing through the hollow centers of the vertebrae.

The pharyngeal skeleton consists of the *jaws* and the *gill arches,* which support the walls of the pharynx and bear the gills. The upper jaw is not fused to the cranium and the homology of the jaws with the gill arches is readily apparent.

The *appendicular skeleton* as seen in Figure 12.39*a*, is rudimentary compared with that of tetrapods (see Figure 4.34), but has certain basic homologies. The *pectoral girdle,* which supports the pectoral fins, forms a simple U composed of a ventral transverse bar (the coracoid) and two lateral, vertically directed elements (the scapulae). (In tetrapods these elements persist, but the coracoid is reduced and fused with the scapula, and a dermal bone, the clavicle, is added to the girdle.) The *pelvic girdle* supports the pelvic fins. It is simply a transverse bar located near the posterior end of the trunk, consisting of paired *puboischiac* cartilages fused midventrally. These elements are considered homologous with the pubis and ischium of the tetrapod pelvis (see Figure 4.36). Laterally each bears a short, dorsally directed *iliac process,* foreshadowing the large, flat ilium of the tetrapod pelvis. In *Squalus* neither limb girdle articulates with the vertebral column. The fins are supported by radially arranged cartilages not closely homologous with tetrapod limb bones.

MUSCULATURE The vertebrate muscular system, consisting mainly of striated skeletal muscles, forms seven major groups seen in *Squalus* in a relatively typical and unspecialized condition: (1) *epaxial* trunk muscles; (2) *hypaxial* trunk muscles; (3) *branchiomeric* muscles; (4) *hypobranchial* muscles; (5) *extrinsic* eye muscles; (6) *intrinsic* eye muscles; (7) *appendicular* muscles (Figure 12.37c).

The epaxial and hypaxial muscles form the body wall musculature of the trunk and tail. A *horizontal septum* of connective tissue divides the body frontally at the level of the vertebral column. Ventral to this septum lies the hypaxial musculature, forming ventral and lateral longitudinal bundles, which in the trunk region become modified

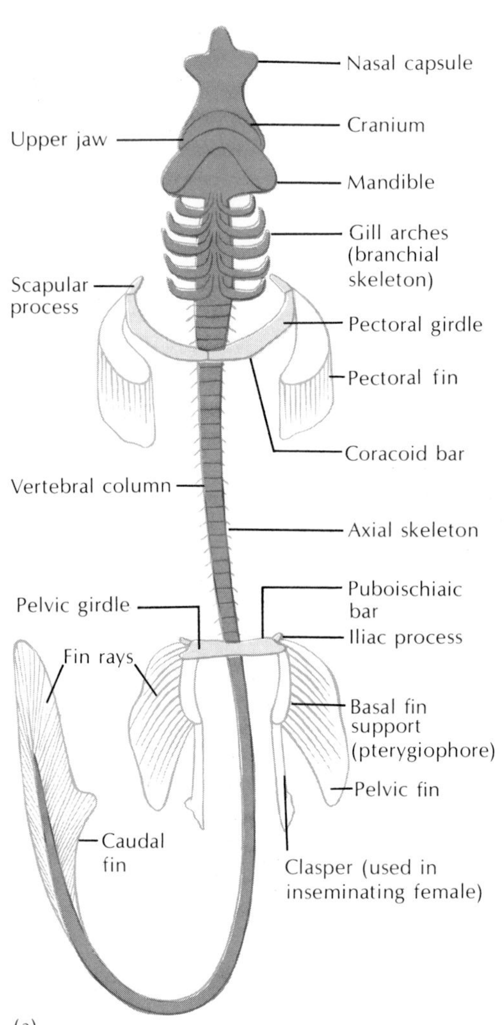

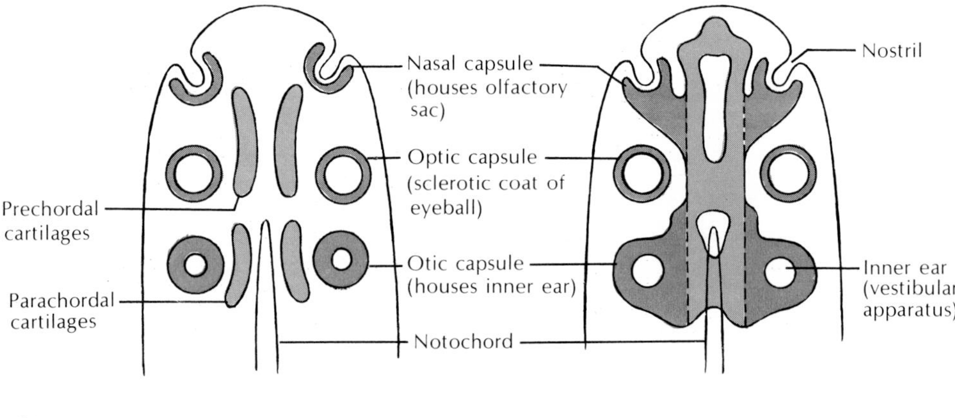

Figure 12.39 □ (*a*) Entire skeleton of male shark (ventral aspect). (*b*) Schematic representation of development of shark cranium (dorsal aspect). At left, paired parachordal and prechordal cartilages form ventral to the brain; these are flanked by three pairs of sensory capsules. At right, prechordal and parachordal cartilages expand and fuse, forming brain case; nasal and otic capsules fuse to cranium; optic capsules remain free, forming sclera of eyeballs.

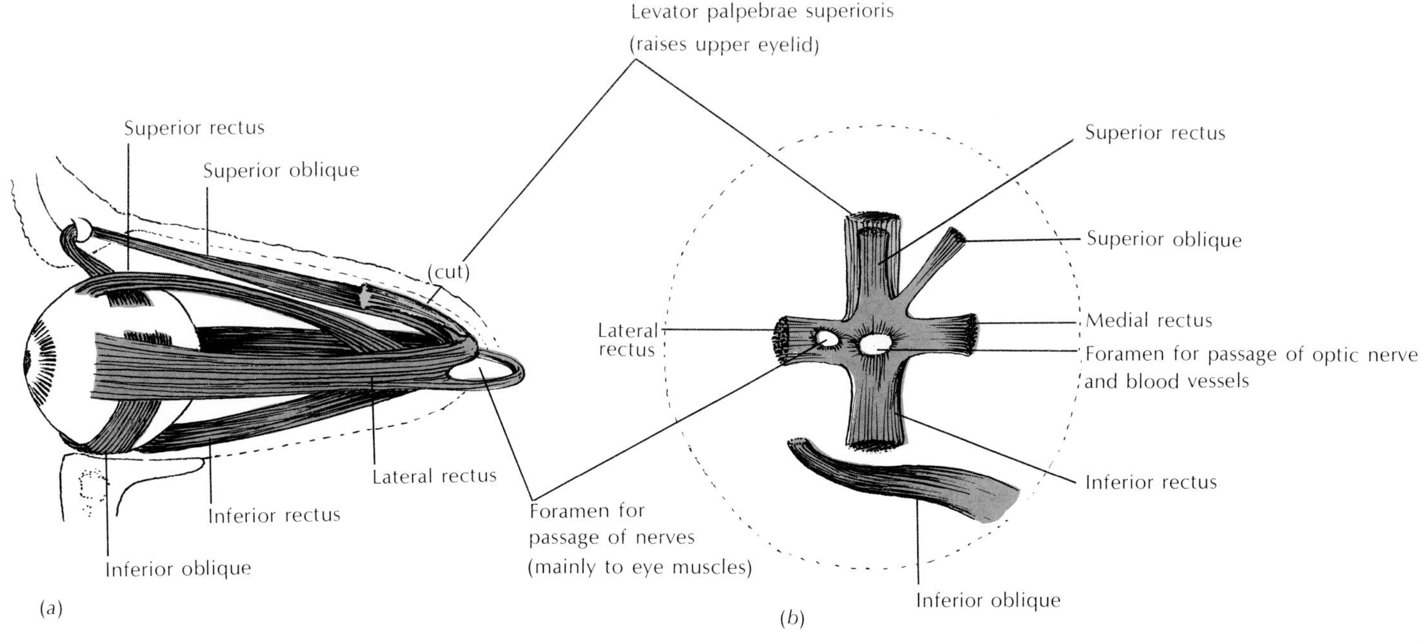

Figure 12.40 □ Extrinsic eye muscles of man. (*a*) Lateral view of eye in situ, with side of orbit (eye socket) removed. (*b*) Rear of orbit, eyeball removed to show muscle attachments.

into sheets that envelop the body cavity. Above the septum lie the epaxial muscles, dorsal longitudinal bundles which parallel the vertebral column, giving off slips that attach to the vertebrae and help flex the column from side to side. The epaxial and hypaxial muscles bear the imprint of their metameric origin, for their fibers form linear series of *myotomes* regularly interrupted by vertical connective tissue partitions (*myosepta*). The epaxial and hypaxial muscles of the trunk and tail are the major muscles of propulsion in fish.

The *branchiomeric* muscles operate the pharyngeal skeleton—the jaws and gill arches in the shark, or their derivatives in tetrapods. The *hypobranchial* muscles represent anterior continuations of the hypaxial ventral longitudinal bundles; their contraction elevates the floor of the mouth cavity (as in swallowing) and opens the mouth by pulling down the lower jaw.

The vertebrate eye features two sets of muscles: *intrinsic* and *extrinsic.* The intrinsic eye muscles are the *iris* (which controls the size of the pupil as seen in Figure 15.23), and the *ciliary muscles* (which modify the shape and position of the lens). Six extrinsic muscles move each eyeball in its socket. Four of these are *rectus* muscles, which attach to the eyeball at right angles to one another: the *superior rectus* turns the eye upward; the *inferior rectus* turns it downward; the *internal* (*medial*) *rectus* rolls the eye toward the nose; and the *lateral* or *external rectus* turns it outward. Two *oblique* muscles, one *superior* and one *inferior,* rotate the eyeball on its axis. The arrangement of these eye muscles in man (Figure 12.40) is very similar to that seen in the shark.

The *appendicular* muscles move the limbs and limb girdles. In fish they are poorly developed, and consist only of a dorsal set, the *levators,* which raise the fins, and a ventral set, the *depressors,* which lower them. In tetrapods the appendicular musculature is extensive; proximally it fans out over the trunk muscles, attaches to the girdles, and distally inserts on the limb bones. The appendicular muscles originate as segmental buds from the embryonic trunk muscles. These buds are few in *Squalus,* but in amniotes (reptiles, birds, and mammals) a large number of myotomes are recruited to the production of buds that contribute to the limb musculature.

DIGESTIVE SYSTEM The alimentary tract, pancreas, and liver are the major organs of the shark's digestive system (Figure 12.41a). The former is divisible into the *mouth, buccal cavity, pharynx, esophagus-stomach, small intestine, colon, cloaca,* and *anus.* Internally the alimentary tube is lined with epithelium including mucus-secreting cells. Particularly in the stomach and small intestine this epithelium grows down into the underlying connective tissue layer to form *gastric* and *intestinal glands* that secrete enzymes. The mouth of *Squalus* is wide and armed with many rows of serrate, triangular teeth that are produced and shed throughout life. The teeth are not differentiated into various functional types as is the case with mammals, but are able to cut great chunks of flesh from the prey. The tongue lies along the floor of the buccal cavity, and in fish is nearly immovable, being therefore unable to assist mastication and

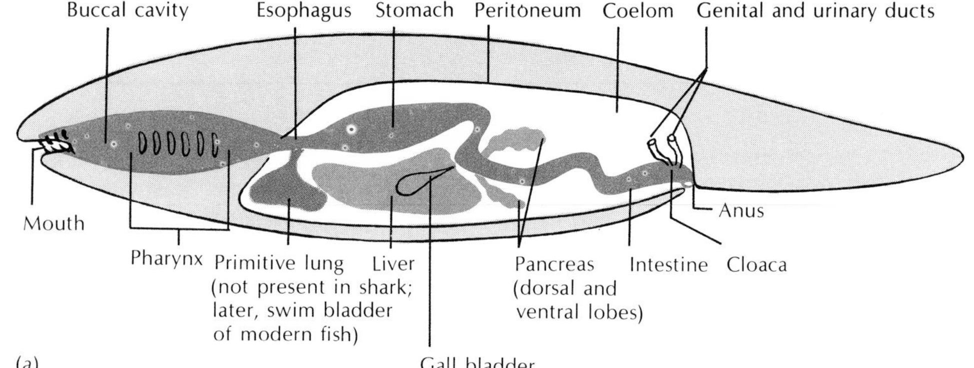

(*a*)

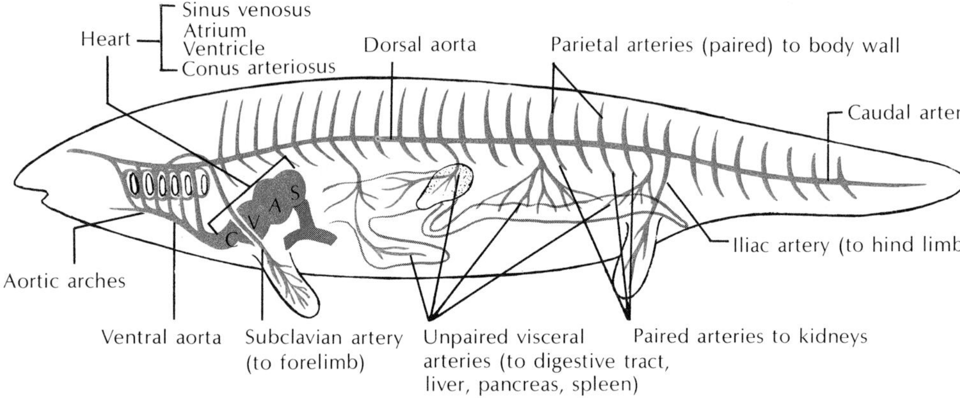

(*b*)

Inferior jugular
Hepatic veins
Hepatic portal capillaries in liver
Hepatic portal (formed of branches from viscera)
Parietal veins (from body wall)
Lateral abdominal vein
Femoral vein (from hind limb)
Caudal vein
Heart (in pericardial cavity)
Anterior cardinal
Common cardinal
Subclavian vein
Gonadal sinus (in gonad)
Posterior cardinal
Kidney
Renal portal
Anus

(*c*)

Figure 12.41 □ Primitive vertebrate architecture. (*a*) Digestive and respiratory systems (lateral aspect). (*b*) Arterial portion of circulatory system (lateral aspect). (*c*) Venous portion of circulatory system (dorsal aspect).

swallowing. The salivary glands too are rudimentary, secreting only mucus. The buccal cavity expands posteriorly into the pharynx, the walls of which are perforated by the gill openings. During feeding, water taken into the mouth with the prey is disgorged through the gill slits before swallowing occurs. Each gill arch bears hooked rakers that prevent the escape of food through the gill slits. Food passes from the pharynx into a wide esophagus which in sharks is not externally differentiated from the stomach. Food is held in the stomach while being churned and liquefied. A muscular ring (the *pyloric sphincter*) prevents food from leaving the stomach prematurely. The first portion of the small intestine, the *duodenum,* contains the greatest concentration of intestinal glands and receives the *bile duct* from the liver and the *pancreatic ducts* from the pancreas. Posteriorly lies the *valvular* intestine, having an unusual *spiral valve,* a partition resembling a spiral ramp that greatly increases the distance the food must traverse without increasing the actual structural length of the alimentary tube. The *colon* is short and terminates in a *cloaca.*

RESPIRATORY SYSTEM The vertebrate respiratory and alimentary tracts are intimately associated in both evolution and ontogeny, and a common epithelial membrane lines both. A fish's mouth serves both for feeding and for ventilating the gills. The lining of the pharyngeal pouches is elaborated into lamellar *gills* with numerous rows of highly vascularized gill filaments. The paired lungs of tetrapods originate as outgrowths from the posterior end of the pharynx, and thus can be considered derivatives of the alimentary tract.

CIRCULATORY SYSTEM The vertebrate circulatory system is unique in comprising two major portions: a *cardiovascular* system consisting of heart, arteries, capillaries, and veins, and containing *blood;* and a *lymphatic* system consisting of lymph capillaries, lymphatics, lymph sinuses, and lymph hearts, and containing *lymph.* The cardiovascular system is a closed circuit through which the blood flows comparatively slowly in fishes but relatively rapidly in tetrapods. The lymphatic system is considered to be a closed system in higher vertebrates where the lymph capillaries terminate distally as blind fingers among the tissues (see Figure 14.20), but is an open system in anamniotes, communicating with the coelomic spaces. Lymph is fundamentally a blood plasma filtrate formed by leakage of fluid from the capillaries. It collects in the lymph sinuses, coelom, and tissue spaces, and is drained away by the lymph capillaries. These converge upon lymphatics which in turn unite like tributaries of a river. Closely set *valves,* paired flaps which open freely in one direction but close together at the midline when forced in the opposite direction, prevent backflow of the lymph, even as similar valves prevent blood backflow in the veins. *Lymph nodes* stud the length of the lymphatics, filtering the lymph and removing invading microorganisms. They produce *lymphocytes* which pass into the lymph and thereby eventually reach the cardiovascular circuit. Other lymphoid organs such as tonsils, thymus, and spleen, are considered part of the lymphatic system, and are important in defense against infection, but the major role of the lymph vessels proper is removal of excess tissue fluids and their return to the cardiovascular portion of the circulatory system. The major lymphatics open into the large veins, the flow of lymph into the bloodstream being facilitated by pulsations of lymph hearts, present in all vertebrates save mammals.

Primitively, as we see in *Squalus,* the vertebrate cardiovascular system is a *single* circuit, in which blood passes only once through the heart for each transit of the body. Since in its course the blood must flow first through the gill capillaries and then through the systemic capillaries, blood pressure is low in all parts of the system except that between the heart and the gill capillaries. (In Chapter 14 we shall consider the evolution of the vertebrate cardiovascular system from a single to a double circuit in which the blood passes from the heart through the pulmonary circuit and then returns to the heart to receive additional impetus before passing to the other body tissues.)

The shark heart reflects the primitive tubular construction of the vertebrate heart (see Figure 14.22*a*), for it consists of four chambers, in linear order from posterior to anterior, the *sinus venosus, atrium, ventricle,* and *conus arteriosus.* Blood enters the posterior end of the heart, whereupon contraction of the thin-walled sinus venosus initiates a forward-sweeping wave of contraction that moves the blood successively through the atrium and into the ventricle, the powerful contraction of which impels the blood through the conus arteriosus into the ventral aorta (Figure 12.41*b*). Valves between the heart chambers and within the conus prevent backflow. As we have seen (see Figure 11.45), the ventral aorta divides into two branches that give off the *afferent branchial* arteries to the gills. These break up into the gill capillaries, which reunite as the *efferent* branchial arteries, carrying the now oxygenated blood upward to the roots of the dorsal aorta, whence some is diverted to the head and the balance passes posteriorly in the dorsal aorta. This great artery gives off segmental *parietal* arteries to the body wall and limbs, and occasional *visceral* arteries to the internal organs. Posteriorly the dorsal aorta continues as the *caudal* artery serving the tail. Ultimately all arteries stemming from the dorsal aorta ramify into capillaries within the integument, skeletal muscles, and walls of the viscera, where the blood gives up much of its oxygen content and nutritional exchanges are effected. The blood must then return to the heart by way of the veins, some of which in *Squalus* form enlarged venous sinuses.

The major portion of the primitive vertebrate venous system describes a letter H with doubled legs (Figure 12.41c). The two anterior pairs of vessels drain the head—the larger being the *anterior cardinal* veins, the smaller the *internal jugular* veins. At the level of the heart these join the two posterior pairs of veins draining the trunk and tail. The latter include the large *posterior cardinals,* the major veins of the trunk, receiving branches from the body wall, kidneys, and gonads, and the smaller *lateral abdominal* veins receiving branches from the body wall and fins. These four pairs of veins unite to form the left and right *common cardinal* veins, which drain medially into the sinus venosus.

The sinus venosus also receives a pair of *hepatic* veins draining the liver. The vertebrate liver has a double blood supply: it receives oxygenated blood from the hepatic artery and also venous blood from the *hepatic portal vein.* Primitively this vein carries blood from both the tail and viscera, but in higher vertebrates loses its caudal connection and carries only blood draining from the organs of the coelom, including the gut, spleen, and pancreas. In the liver the hepatic portal vein branches into many irregular capillaries termed *sinusoids,* which allow the blood intimate contact with the liver cells. Since much of this blood has come from the wall of the alimentary tract and is rich in nutrients and possibly contaminated with toxic materials inadvertently consumed, this arrangement is highly adaptive in permitting the liver cells to act upon the materials in the blood before they can reach the general circulation. The liver detoxifies the blood and removes and converts many nutrients; its activities are so varied that it constitutes the vertebrate body's major "chemical factory." Blood from the hepatic artery mixes at the capillary level with that from the hepatic portal vein, and leaves the liver by way of the aforementioned hepatic veins.

The venous vascularization of the liver just described constitutes the *hepatic portal system.* A portal system is one characterized by the branching out of a *vein* into capillaries before returning to the heart. Three portal systems primitively characterize vertebrates: the hepatic portal, the hypophyseal portal, and the renal portal, the latter becoming vestigial in higher vertebrates. The *hypophyseal portal* system receives blood from capillaries serving a ventral part of the brain, and promptly ramifies into capillaries supplying the pituitary gland (hypophysis).

The *renal portal* system (shown in Figure 12.41c) aids excretion in fishes and amphibians and has left a curious legacy to the kidneys of higher vertebrates. Blood returning from the shark's tail is partially diverted into a renal portal vein that enters each kidney. Here each branches into capillaries, so that the kidney like the liver has *two* capillary beds—one contributed by the renal artery and carrying oxygenated blood, the other contributed by the renal portal vein and carrying deoxygenated blood. The tail is so important in propulsion in fishes that blood returning from this part of the body is laden with wastes produced during muscular exertion; diversion to the kidneys of that quantity of blood which these organs can accomodate is adaptive in that it reduces the level of these wastes in the general circulation. The renal portal capillaries are intimately associated with the renal tubules (excretory tubules), facilitating exchange of wastes between the bloodstream and urine. Both sets of capillaries then converge upon the renal vein, which empties into the posterior cardinal of that side of the body. In its later evolution in tetrapods, which rarely use the tail as their major organ of propulsion, the renal portal vein itself gradually disappears, but its capillaries persist, remaining associated with the renal tubules and joining with the capillaries of the renal artery so that the renal tubules are still associated with two capillary beds. This improves their efficiency, for the one set of capillaries nourishes the kidney tissue and also yields a filtrate that passes into the proximal ends of the renal tubules, while the other carries away essential materials reclaimed from this filtrate (see Figure 16.11).

In higher vertebrates the cardiovascular system has become considerably modified from the ancestral plan, but its descent is reflected in its embryonic development as well as being revealed by comparative studies.

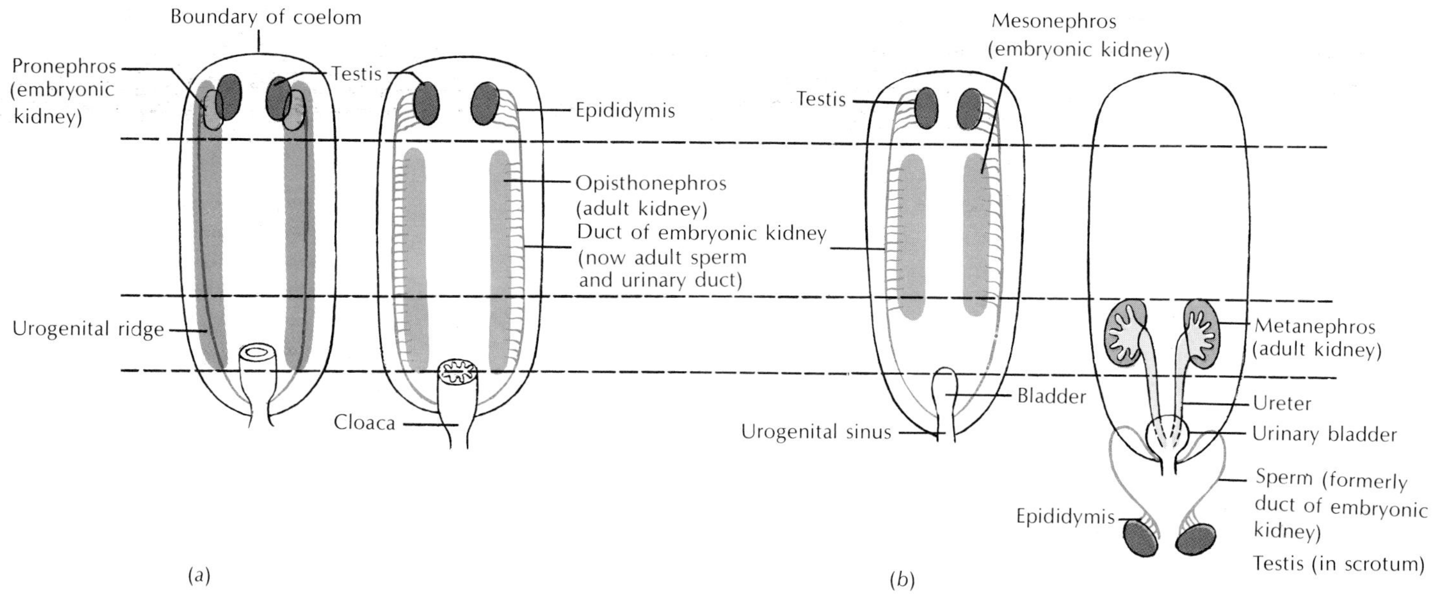

Figure 12.42 □ Comparison of vertebrate kidneys and their duct systems. (*a*) Anamniotes: embryo (left) and adult (right). (*b*) Amniote (mammal): embryo (left) and adult (right). The extent of the urogenital ridge is shown in gray, and the duct of the embryonic kidney, becoming a sperm duct, is shown in solid color. Note posterior displacement of testes out of coelom into scrotum. The size scale of the embryos has been exaggerated the better to show the relation of embryonic and postembryonic kidneys to one another and to the coelom.

UROGENITAL SYSTEM The development and evolution of the vertebrate excretory and reproductive systems are so intimately related that these two systems are often treated as one despite their different functions. Both the gonads and the kidneys arise from the urogenital ridges, paired strands of mesoderm running dorsal to the coelomic cavity. Furthermore, urinary ducts associated with the embryonic kidney often carry sperm in the adult male.

Interestingly, in all vertebrates the embryo's needs for excretion are met by a pair of kidneys that functions only during embryonic life while the definitive postembryonic kidneys are still developing (Figure 12.42). The embryonic kidney of the shark and other anamniotes (*pronephros*) occupies only a few segments in the anteriormost part of the coelom and drains posteriorly to the cloaca by way of a *pronephric duct.* The postembryonic anamniote kidney (*opisthonephros*) develops posterior to the pronephros and extends most of the length of the coelom. Urine passes from the opisthonephros to the cloaca by way of the same duct utilized in embryonic life, now called the opisthonephric (*Wolffian*) duct.

The shark's gonads lie far anterior in the coelom, and gametes pass posteriorly to the cloaca by way of the Wolffian ducts, in the male, or the oviducts, in the female (Figure 12.43). In modern sharks the Wolffian duct continues to carry urine throughout life, but in the male its greater portion has become so thoroughly preempted for the function of carrying sperm that urine drains into this duct only near its posterior end. Just anterior to the point at which urine enters, each

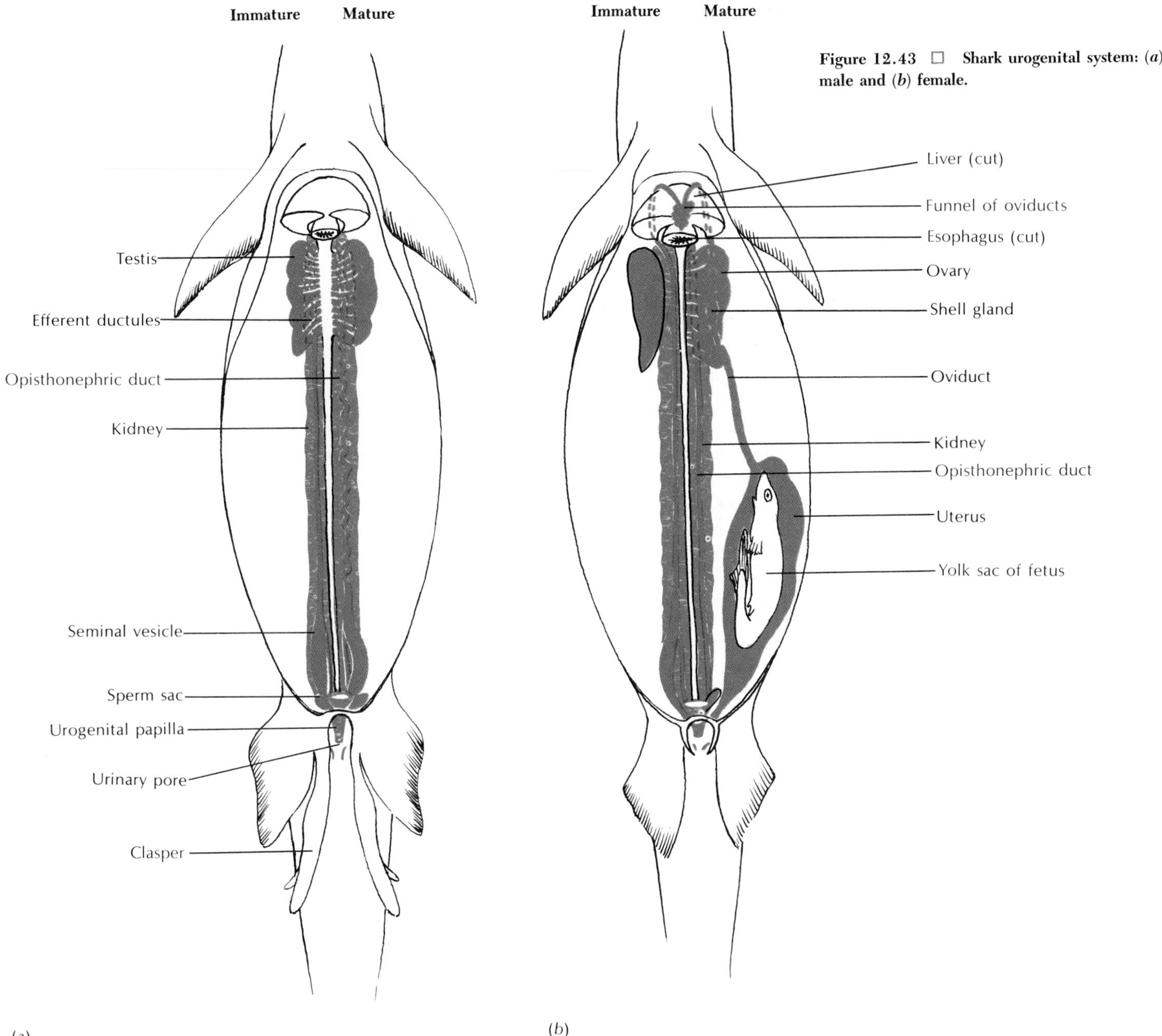

Figure 12.43 □ Shark urogenital system: (*a*) male and (*b*) female.

Wolffian duct is expanded into a chamber, the seminal vesicle, that holds sperm pending mating. Sperm and urine enter the cloaca through a common urogenital opening.

During mating, sperm are introduced directly into the female's cloaca by means of the male's modified pelvic fins (claspers). Each of these fins bears a rigid extension that can be used in the manner of a penis; when the two extensions are pressed together a channel is formed between them through which semen flows during ejaculation. Few groups of fish have developed such successful means of internal fertilization.

The ovaries do not shed their eggs into the Wolffian ducts but right into the coelom close to the ciliated openings of the oviducts. Ciliary action then sweeps the eggs into the oviducts. Each oviduct is dilated posteriorly to form a uterus. In live-bearing sharks such as *Squalus* the eggs remain in the female's genital tract until hatching, about three embryos developing within each uterus.

The development of the amniote urogenital system generally parallels that of the primitive vertebrate plan as seen in the shark. Again, a kidney that will function during embryonic life is first to appear, but in amniotes this temporary kidney (the *mesonephros*) develops from the central portion of the urogenital ridge posterior to the pronephros. The latter is never a functional kidney in amniotes, but its legacy remains to the male reproductive system in the form of the *epididymis,* a cluster of coiled tubules that connect the testis with the anterior part of the Wolffian duct. The postembryonic kidney of amniotes (*metanephros*) develops posterior to the mesonephros. Here, however, a significant departure takes place: the metanephros develops a new duct system, unknown in anamniotes, that is independent of the Wolffian duct. This innovation is made possible by the appearance of paired epithelial buds that arise in the cloacal region and grow laterally until they contact and interact with the embryonic tissue of the urogenital ridge. The development of these new kidney ducts, the *ureters,* is important in that it allows for the separation of the passages carrying urine and sperm. The Wolffian duct, which transports urine during embryonic life, accordingly carries only sperm in the adult male and is functionless in the adult female. This separation of sperm and urinary ducts is adaptively significant, for it minimizes the exposure of sperm to toxic wastes present in the urine.

NERVOUS SYSTEM The vertebrate nervous system has two major parts: (1) the *somatic motor-sensory* division, which includes most of the brain and spinal cord, sensory nerve fibers from receptors in the head and body wall, and motor nerves serving the skeletal muscles; (2) the *autonomic* division, which innervates the glands and the involuntary musculature of the blood vessels and viscera. Curiously, most of the internal organs are *doubly* innervated, receiving two kinds of autonomic fibers, *sympathetic* and *parasympathetic,* largely antagonistic in their action (see Figure 15.37). Most "conscious" activities are controlled by the somatic motor-sensory division, whereas physiological regulation is the domain of the autonomic division. These two divisions are of course integrated at the level of the brain.

The primitive arrangement of the vertebrate brain is well shown in *Squalus* (Figure 12.44). It consists of a linear series of hollow vesicles enclosing a cavity, the *neurocoel,* which contains nutritive cerebrospinal fluid. The most anterior vesicle is the forebrain (*prosencephalon*), which includes the telencephalon (cerebrum) and the diencephalon. In sharks the *telencephalon* retains its primitive olfactory role, but in higher vertebrates it becomes a major integrative center for correlating various sensory data and initiating voluntary motor responses. The *diencephalon* also receives and integrates sensory data but mainly initiates autonomic (involuntary) responses. Its ventral portion, the *hypothalamus,* controls endocrine function by way of the hypophysis. The *mesencephalon* (midbrain) serves primitively as the major center for analysis of *visual* data. The *rhombencephalon* (hindbrain) includes the metencephalon and myelencephalon. The most prominent part of the *metencephalon* is the *cerebellum,* which controls posture and the *coordination of skeletal muscles.* The *myelencephalon* (medulla oblongata) is an important autonomic center, and is also the source of most *cranial nerves* (see Figure 15.40). It is continuous posteriorly with the spinal cord, which gives off a pair of *spinal nerves* in each body segment. Each spinal nerve contains both motor and sensory fibers, and also gives off fibers to the segmental series of *sympathetic ganglia* that flank the spinal column.

Vertebrates possess a variety of sensory receptors, most of which have their analogs among invertebrates. Receptors sensitive to *stretch* and *pressure* are found in the mesenteries, joints, muscles, tendons, and walls of the viscera and major blood vessels. *Chemical* receptors occur in the mouth, olfactory sacs, and the walls of certain arteries. The

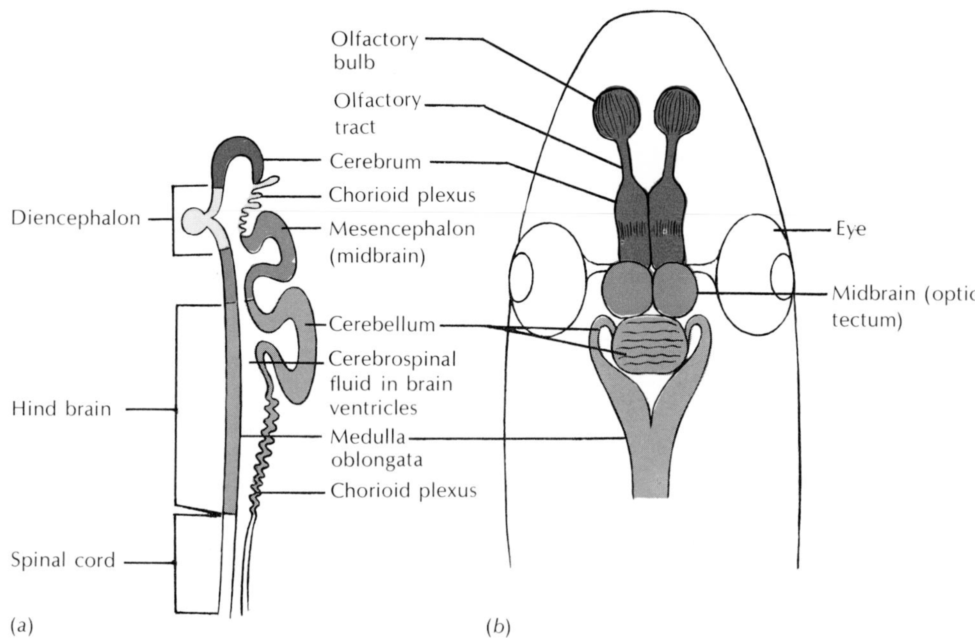

Figure 12.44 □ Brain of *Squalus* in (*a*) medial section and (*b*) dorsal aspect.

integument is richly provided with tactile, pressure, and thermal receptors. Fish have a concentration of cutaneous receptors along a *lateral line system* (see Figure 15.28) that detects water currents and also probably functions in chemical, thermal, and acoustic reception. The *eyes* are of the camera type, capable of accomodation (change in focal length), and in most vertebrates can distinguish colors (see Figure 15.18). The labyrinth (inner ear), a complex structure with an interesting evolutionary history, serves mainly for position and equilibrium detection in fishes, and retains these functions while acquiring an enhanced acoustic function in tetrapods (see Figure 15.29).

ENDOCRINE SYSTEM The vertebrate endocrine system is complex, and includes epithelial glands, diffuse endocrine tissues, and neurosecretory organs. The action of most of these is integrated through the mediation of the nervous system and a "master" gland, the *hypophysis* (see Figure 15.48).

REVIEW AND DISCUSSION

1 Differentiate, with examples, among the various types of body symmetry seen in different animals. Explain why most organisms tend to adopt some kind of symmetry, rather than being completely asymmetrical. With what modes of living would you expect to find the different types of symmetry associated?

2 Contrast the advantages and the problems of multicellularity and acellularity. What structures analogous to those of metazoans have been developed by some acellular organisms?

3 Compare the processes of ingestion and digestion in a ciliate, a sponge, and hydra. How are these processes made more efficient in a grasshopper?

4 Why may it be correct to say that division of labor in sponges is as much an outcome of cell versatility as of cell differentiation?

5 Compare the means by which the male and female gametes are brought together in sponges, squid, and *Squalus*.

6 Explain why it would be inaccurate to think of a flower as a reproductive organ in the sense that a testis or ovary is. In particular, contrast an angiosperm ovary with an animal's ovary.

7 Explain the ecological significance of: (a) the development of floral nectaries; (*b*) the grouping of flowers in inflorescences; (c) the angiosperm pericarp; (*d*)

pericarp dehiscence.

8 Give examples of some of the ways in which pericarps are adaptively modified. Compare berries, drupes, pomes, achenes, legumes, and nuts.

9 Compare and contrast the development and internal organization of a dicot root and stem.

10 What advances does a hydra show over a typical sponge? What advantages may a sponge enjoy, if any?

11 Can a monoecious plant bear imperfect flowers? Explain.

12 Discuss the importance of metamerism as an organizational principle. Specify how this is exemplified in the case of the lobster.

13 Compare the organization of the brain of cephalopods and vertebrates as exemplified by *Loligo* and *Squalus*.

14 Compare the acoelomate, pseudocoelomate, and eucoelomate condition. What advantages does a eucoelomate animal have over one which is pseudocoelomate?

15 Make a chart summarizing the organ systems of metazoa and specifying the functions of these organ systems. Enumerate the major organs of each system, indicating the functional significance of each.

16 Summarize the types of articulation which can occur between bones of the vertebrate endoskeleton, and specify the kind or degree of movement which each type of joint permits.

17 Explain how skeletal muscles are organized functionally to make a true organ system. Summarize the major anatomical groups of vertebrate skeletal muscles and specify the functions of each.

18 Compare the circulatory systems and patterns of blood flow in a locust, a squid, and a shark. Which of these three systems might be considered most efficient? Defend your selection.

19 Compare the manner in which the respiratory organs of locusts, squid, and sharks are ventilated.

20 Compare the excretory organs of the locust, the squid, and the shark. How does it happen that each nephron of a vertebrate kidney has *two* sets of capillaries associated with it?

21 What is the functional significance of the three vertebrate portal systems?

22 Contrast a nerve and a ganglionic nerve trunk (like the spinal cord).

23 Specify the function of each of the following: (*a*) ovipositor; (*b*) seminal vesicle; (*c*) seminal receptacle; (*d*) uterus.

REFERENCES

BROWN, F. A., JR., ED. *Selected Invertebrate Types.* New York: John Wiley & Sons, Inc., 1950.

DOUGHTERY, E. C., ED. *The Lower Metazoa.* Berkeley, Calif.: University of California Press, 1963.

ESAU, K. *Anatomy of Seed Plants.* New York: John Wiley & Sons, Inc., 1960. A classic reference for plant morphology.

GRIFFIN, D. R. *Animal Structure and Function.* New York: Holt, Rinehart & Winston, Inc., 1962. A short, easily read introduction to metazoan organ systems.

JOLIE, M. *Chordate Morphology.* New York: Reinhold Publishing Corporation, 1962. An advanced reference emphasizing vertebrate anatomy.

MOMENT, G. B. "On the Way a Common Earthworm, *Eisenia foetida,* Grows in Length," *J. Morphol.,* **93** (1953).

PITELKA, D. R. *Electron-microscopic Structure of Protozoa.* New York: Crowell Collier and Macmillan, Inc., 1963. Discloses the fine anatomy of acellular animals.

SALISBURY, F. R., AND R. V. PARKE *Vascular Plants: Form and Function.* Belmont, Calif.: Wadsworth Publishing Company, Inc., 1964.

SMITH, H. M. *Evolution of Chordate Structure.* New York: Holt, Rinehart & Winston, Inc., 1960. An advanced but lucid textbook emphasizing the phylogeny of vertebrate organ systems.

Part 4

MAINTENANCE OF THE INDIVIDUAL

...as natural selection works solely by and for the good of each being, all corporeal and mental endowments will tend to progress towards perfection.

CHARLES DARWIN

In the preceding chapters we have seen that in form, function, and behavior the organism is the product of interactions between environmental factors and the intrinsic capabilities of living matter. We have noted that the cell is the simplest organizational unit of life capable of maintaining itself in a medium free of other cells, and that although in some phyla cell and organism are coextensive, in most the cell serves as a module for the construction of multicellular bodies. Survival of the organism, whether its body is made up of a single cell or many billions, rests upon the effective integration of vital processes that basically are organized at a molecular level.

The precise coordination of the cell's machinery for synthesis and energy transfer has come about through evolutionary processes favoring the perpetuation of those versions of the genetic code which have promoted the efficiency of such interactions. In similar fashion selection has operated toward the establishment and perpetuation of integrative mechanisms by means of which the activities of different kinds of cells in the multicellular body have become functionally coadapted. In the multicellular organism, cell independence must be subordinated to the life of the whole, such subordination being brought about by induction during development, followed by neuroendocrine regulation throughout life.

Integrative mechanisms, whether cellular or systemic, cannot be concerned solely with coadaptation of processes *within* the individual body but must also be concerned with the integration of organism and environment. For instance, detection and procurement of nutrients must precede their metabolic use within the tissues. Such detection and procurement demand that animals have means of sensory perception and, usually, means of locomotion. Furthermore, the survival of the individual may not even depend entirely upon the effectiveness of its own integrative mechanisms but may often be dependent upon its being integrated into a social group, with death's being the price of isolation.

In the following four chapters we shall study the life of the individual organism as it is maintained through integrative processes that enable the body to function as a harmonious unit. First we shall study cellular and systemic adaptations by which nutrients are obtained from the environment and processed to meet the organism's needs. Next we shall concentrate upon the coordination of body activities and the means by which organisms adapt to changes in both internal and external environments, either behaviorally or by way of adjustments in cellular and systemic physiology. During these studies we should bear in mind that the finely adjusted adaptive mechanisms through which the life of the individual is maintained are products of selection of favorable genetic variants over countless generations.

Today we see in operation complex cellular mechanisms that may have evolved to their present level of functionality more than

2 billion years ago and need merely be conserved and perpetuated. But in addition to these, there operate within higher organisms mechanisms of synthesis and integration that are probably of much less ancient origin and even now may be undergoing further evolutionary improvement. A case in point is the evolution of mammalian neuroendocrine control mechanisms. Less than 70 million years have passed from the beginning of the Age of Mammals to the advent of art, music, literature, and science. Whereas other maintenance activities may already have reached an adaptive peak at which little further improvement is to be expected, the interaction of organism and environment at a *behavioral* level, moderated by the activity of the brain, may yet undergo significant further evolutionary advancement. It is at the behavioral level that organisms interact with greatest sophistication, both with one another and with their habitat; it is through these interactions that life exerts the most far-reaching effects on its environment.

On this planet, man has a literal "head start" in behavioral complexity and adaptability, but the survival value of intelligence is so great that (if man allows other creatures to survive long enough) we may look for its further development in other evolutionary lines. Cognitive processes are even now not solely man's prerogative, but whether through increased intelligence or by the continued selection of genetic patterns favoring more effective innate behaviors, we can expect that improvements in neural mechanisms will greatly influence the further evolution of organisms and biotic communities.

Chapter 13  NUTRITION: OBTAINING MASS AND ENERGY

LIVING THINGS ARE UNIVERSALLY DEpendent upon the material and energy resources of their environment. Their capacity for growth, repair, and reproduction is in essence a capacity for obtaining molecules from the environment and incorporating them into a living, dynamic fabric. To use these molecules for growth and to perform other kinds of work as well necessitates the transformation of energy, which is also obtained from the environment and ultimately from the sun. The processes involved in acquiring and transforming materials and energy are termed *nutrition*. These include: (1) procuring nutrients; (2) if necessary, digesting them; (3) transporting nutrients throughout the organism; (4) transporting them across cell membranes; (5) utilizing the nutrients intracellularly in *metabolic processes* including *biosynthesis* (construction of new molecules) and *bioenergetics* (carrying out the necessary energy transformations for performing work); (6) gaseous exchange and transport; (7) processing metabolic wastes. The most universal aspects of nutrition are those which take place within cells. The photosynthetic process, for instance, is probably essentially identical in nearly all autotrophs. Furthermore, while autotrophs alone can make organic compounds out of inorganic materials, *all* living things have a common heritage of cellular mechanisms for interconverting and breaking down organic compounds. Onto this heritage have been superimposed specializations by which various species exploit different food sources and carry out their own unique metabolic tasks.

The laws of thermodynamics describe the nature of energy throughout the universe; accordingly, these principles also define the energetics involved in the evolution and functioning of biotic systems. Energy may be considered as the capacity to do work. Biotic systems use energy for carrying out *osmotic* work (such as moving substances against a concentration gradient), *mechanical* work (such as contraction), and *chemical* work (such as biosynthesis); see Figure 13.1. Every cell contains a number of energy-transforming systems, organized at a molecular level. These systems are not only miniaturized to a far greater degree than any energy-transforming systems of human manufacture, but can also undertake operations that no artificial system can yet perform at an economically practical level. Expensive and sophisticated devices are now being employed to deionize sea water or to extract specific minerals from it, but any cell membrane can perform equivalent tasks with greater economy, efficiency, and selectivity. In studying the transformations of mass and energy in biotic systems we should note that these events must be consonant with thermodynamic principles and that these principles in fact can be applied to explain how such systems have evolved.

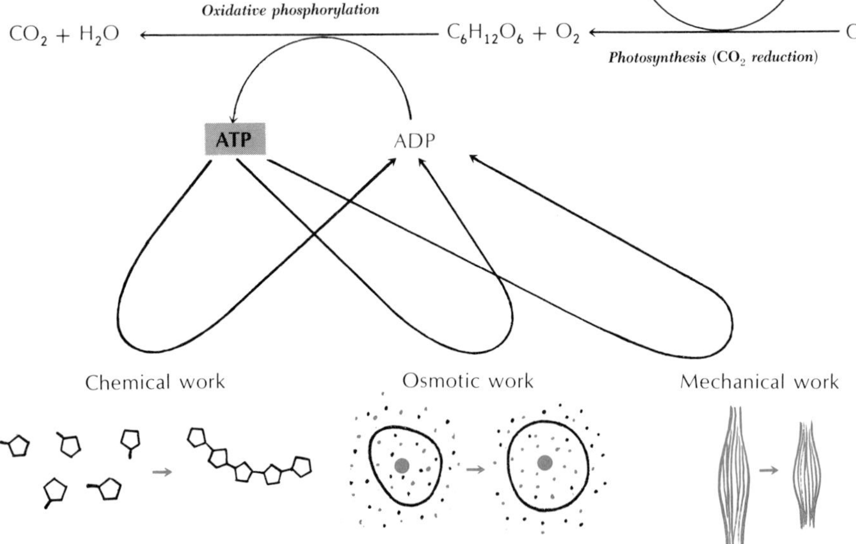

Figure 13.1 □ Biotic mechanisms of energy transfer, showing the key position of the ATP-ADP (adenylic acid) system. The examples of work shown (left to right) are biosynthesis, such as the conversion of glucose to starch, active transport, the maintenance of concentration of substances within a cell different from those in the surrounding environment, and muscle contraction.

A The laws of thermodynamics

In the language of thermodynamics a *system* is any part of the physical universe, the properties of which are under investigation; a system is separated from the rest of the universe, its *surroundings,* by a boundary, real or conceptual. If the boundary allows no interaction between a system and its surroundings, that system is said to be *isolated,* for any change in the system produces no change in the surroundings; if mass and energy can pass across the boundary, however, the system is said to be *open,* and any change in the system will have a corresponding effect on the surroundings. The most commonly studied thermodynamic systems in the biotic world are the cell, the organism, and the ecosystem. All of these systems are open, for their boundaries allow interaction with the surroundings. Although the flow of mass and energy in the ecosystem is largely cyclic, there still must be a constant flow of solar energy across the boundary, and this energy gain by the ecosystem spells an equivalent loss of energy from its surroundings. Cells and organisms of course constantly exchange materials across their boundaries to and from the surroundings: nutrients are taken in, heat and wastes are lost; a net gain on the input side results in growth, while a sustained net loss leads ultimately to death. As long as the input of materials and energy at least balances their loss, a steady state of organic "health" persists.

The *first law of thermodynamics* states that in the universe as a whole energy is conserved: it may change state but is neither gained nor lost. If there is an increase in the internal energy of a system there must be an equivalent decrease in the energy of the surroundings, and vice versa.

There are various kinds of energy: (1) *kinetic energy* (energy possessed by a body by virtue of its movement); (2) *potential energy* (energy possessed by a body as a result of its position in a force field, such as an electrical or gravitational field); (3) *thermal energy* (energy possessed by a body by virtue of its temperature). The forms that kinetic and potential energy can assume include nuclear, chemical, electrical, mechanical, and radiant energy. Nuclear energy is that found within atomic nuclei; it does not change state in biotic systems and therefore will not concern us here. Electrical energy is the result of a flow of electrons in an electrical force field. Mechanical energy is involved in causing mass to be moved (such as when a weight is lifted). Radiant energy makes up the electromagnetic spectrum that includes radio waves, heat, light, ultraviolet, and X rays (see Figure 4.8). Any form of energy is completely and reversibly changeable into any of the other forms.

The first law can be expressed as

$$\Delta E = q - w$$

where ΔE represents the change in the total internal energy content of a system, q represents the exchange of heat between the system and its surroundings, and w represents the work done. For example, water on a mountaintop has energy of position (potential energy); this is translated into kinetic energy as the water flows downhill. If the moving water is made to turn a turbine or waterwheel, work is done: a portion of its kinetic energy is converted to mechanical energy; the turbine may in turn generate electrical energy. At the same time some of the kinetic energy is converted to heat as a result of frictional resistance, and this portion does not perform work. The kinetic energy of flowing water can also be partially converted into heat with no work done at all: when water plunges over a falls without passing through a turbine no work is done, but the water at the bottom of the falls has less energy of position than it did at the top; this loss in potential energy is balanced by a slight but measurable increase in the temperature of the water at the foot of the falls.

Thermodynamics is concerned only with the initial and final states of energy and not with the path between those two states. It allows a precise mathematical prediction of the ultimate outcome of energy changes in a system and its surroundings, regardless of the path followed in passing from the initial to the final state. By way of example, whether a load of materials is carried up a mountain by packhorse or lowered from a helicopter, the potential energy of the material moved has been increased by the same amount: the path does not matter. The respective values of q and w depend upon the path, but the difference between q and w (ΔE) is independent of the path.

The first law of thermodynamics specifies only that the total energy content of the system plus its surroundings does not change although energy may pass through various transformations. This would seem to allow complete reversibility of any natural process; we know, however, that any change in a system has a "preferred" direction and that such a change will not spontaneously tend to reverse itself: when wood is burned, carbon dioxide and water are liberated and chemical energy is converted to heat; if these compounds are placed in a closed container with appropriate heat, they do not again turn into wood (even though the first law of thermodynamics admits this possibility). This tendency for natural processes to have a preferred direction is expressed in the *second law of thermodynamics,* which states that the entropy of a system tends to increase while its free energy tends to decrease. *Free energy* is that portion of the internal energy of a system that is available to do work; in mathematical expressions it is often given the symbol G. *Entropy* is a property of thermodynamic systems that can be interpreted in terms of the randomness of the distribution of atoms and molecules in space, or in terms of the transformation of energy into a form that is unavailable to do work. All spontaneous changes tend to proceed in the direction that results in some increase in the disorderliness or randomness of the system plus its surroundings; this can be stated as an increase in entropy, given the symbol S in mathematical expressions. Entropy provides a means of conferring a numerical value on any increase in randomness or disorderliness.

Any change in the free energy of a system is correlated inversely with a change in the entropy of that system:

$$\Delta G = \Delta H - T\,\Delta S$$

where ΔG is the change in free energy of the system, ΔH is the heat transfer between the system and its surroundings, T is the absolute temperature, and ΔS is the entropy change of the system. The change in the free energy of a system is equal to the amount of heat liberated or taken up by the system minus the product of the absolute temperature and the change in entropy. If no heat exchange takes place between the system and its surroundings, ΔG and $T\,\Delta S$ are equal but of opposite sign:

$$\Delta G = -T\,\Delta S \qquad \text{or} \qquad -\Delta G = T\,\Delta S$$

However, if heat is lost from the system to its surroundings (during the course of a chemical reaction, for instance), the decline in the free energy of the system is greater than its increase in entropy. Conversely, if during the reaction the system absorbs heat from its surroundings, the increase in entropy exceeds the decline in free energy.

Heat and temperature must be taken into account in considering the inverse relationship between entropy and free energy, for heat involves the random movement of atoms and molecules and contributes to disorderliness. We know that if two bottles of volatile materials such as ether and perfume are uncapped in the same room, the random thermal movement of the molecules of the two substances will cause them eventually to become evenly dispersed throughout the available space; this diffusion will take place more rapidly if the room is hot than if it is refrigerated. However, unless the temperature is absolute zero (in which case there would be no thermal movement of molecules), eventually the entropy of the system will be maximized and its free energy minimized—the two substances will be randomly dispersed.

The relation of free energy to work capacity, on the one hand, and to entropy, on the other, may be clarified by another example: water will eventually evaporate from a kettle even at normal room temperatures because the random thermal movements of its molecules cause them one by one to escape into the air. This escape is accelerated if the water is heated to the boiling point. Now the molecules escape at such velocities that their kinetic energy can be made to do work: the steam generated could, for instance, be made to turn a pinwheel (a miniature analog of a steam turbine). Whether or not work is done, the free energy of the system declines as its disorderliness increases; eventually the water molecules will have dispersed throughout the air and can no longer be harnessed to make anything move.

The tendency toward increase in entropy and decrease in free energy is therefore a universal property that serves as a driving force in all reactions. Any reaction that increases entropy and/or decreases free energy is thermodynamically favored. Biotic systems can temporarily decrease their entropy and increase their internal energy, but can do so only at the cost of an equivalent increase in the entropy and decrease in the free energy of their surroundings. Furthermore, each energy transformation or exchange increases the total entropy of the universe. Unless some cosmogenic force operates periodically to reverse or counteract this tendency for entropy to increase and free energy to decrease (as proposed in the oscillating-universe theory) the universe must eventually "run down" to a state of total disorder in which all energy will have been reduced to a nonusable form and all matter will be disorganized. From this general downhill movement the living world is not exempt; it succeeds momentarily in trapping a small portion of the energy being lost daily by the sun and in using this energy to maintain its high degree of organization. Since it is unavoidable that a portion of this trapped energy will be lost as heat, biotic activities inexorably contribute to the total entropy of the universe.

The major means by which energy enters the biotic world is through photosynthesis, wherein radiant (solar) energy is converted to chemical bonding energy. This constitutes a gain in free energy that reverses or staves off randomization. The more elaborate the organizational state attained by a living system, the greater must be the energy required to develop and maintain it. Man, an extreme example, must expend vast quantities of energy not only to maintain the organization of his own complex body but also to run his machines. Only a fraction of this energy of combustion can be used to do work, while the rest is dissipated; thus man is undoubtedly a major contributor to entropy on this planet.

The industrial use of chemical energy usually involves its conversion to *heat* (as when wood or oil is burned to convert water into steam, which in turn powers an engine). Cells, on the other hand, can transform chemical energy into various types of work with a minimum evolution of heat. Reactions occurring outside of living cells are termed exothermic or endothermic, according to whether they release heat to the surroundings (*exothermic*), or must absorb heat to take place (*endothermic*). Energy conversions within living cells are commonly *isothermal,* meaning that they take place without a significant change in temperature. Warm-blooded animals of course must generate considerable heat to maintain a stable body temperature (which substantially increases their need for food), but plants and poikilothermal animals expend little energy as heat. Reactions in living systems are accordingly better described as *exergonic* (liberating energy) or *endergonic* (requiring energy), rather than as exothermic and endothermic. (In point of fact, we shall find in Chapter 14 that little energy is actually *liberated* by any biotic process; instead, energy is conserved in chemical bonds and subsequently *transferred* to another molecule.)

Although metabolic processes are generally isothermal, their energy transfers are conveniently measured in terms of the amount of heat that would be generated if that amount of chemical energy were completely converted to heat. The chemical energy present in a quantity of organic material is estimated in terms of calories of heat released by its combustion. A *calorie* is the amount of heat required to raise the temperature of 1 g of water from 14.5° to 15.5° C. A *kilocalorie* (the "Calorie" of dietetics) is equal to 1,000 calories, and it is the amount of heat required to raise the temperature of 1 *kg* of water from 14.5° to 15.5°C. When 1 g of glucose is burned in a calorimeter to CO_2 and H_2O, 3.74 kcal are evolved, representing a release of 686 kcal/mole. The combustion of the amino acid glycine yields 3.12 kcal/g, or 234 kcal/mole. A typical triglyceride fat such as tripalmitin yields about 9.3 kcal/g or 7,500 kcal/mole. Average caloric values for organic nutrients are

Carbohydrates	4 kcal/g
Fats	9 kcal/g
Proteins	4 kcal/g

A physically active man must consume nutrients with an energy content equivalent to at least 4,000 kcal daily, or around 1.5×10^6 kcal/year!

B The energetic role of phosphate compounds

We have mentioned that most metabolic energy-conversion mechanisms have evolved so that they function isothermally. This is an outcome of natural selection, for exothermic reactions transfer thermal energy to their surroundings as kinetic energy of molecules, and such random thermal molecular movements tend to disrupt living systems. Isothermal reactions are of adaptive significance because they not only conserve free energy by minimizing the proportion converted to heat but also protect the cell's molecular architecture from thermal disruption. Energy is stored by the bonding within one molecule and is transferred in very small "packets" to another. In this manner amounts of energy approximating that needed can be mobilized, there being little excess wasted. By analogy, it is better to light a candle with a match than with a blowtorch, for the latter produces much more heat than is actually needed, probably even melting the candle instead of lighting it. Similarly, mobilization of energy in too large amounts would not only waste the cell's fuel reserves but would probably kill the cell by increasing the random thermal movements of its molecules.

To produce and conserve such small useful energy packets, cells rely on certain *high-energy phosphate compounds.* The distribution of electrons within the molecules of such a compound causes energy to be concentrated in an *organic phosphate group*

```
   O
   ‖
—P—OH
   |
  OH
```

(often simply designated Ⓟ) that can later be transferred to another molecule engaged in some endergonic reaction. The phosphate group is often represented as being attached to the molecule by way of a "high-energy" P∼O bond. Although it is convenient to speak of a high-energy phosphate bond and to designate one by the symbol ∼, the term actually refers to the change in energy content of a molecule upon liberating the phosphate group. The actual energy of a

Table 13.1 □ Energy released by hydrolysis of phosphate compounds

COMPOUND	ENERGY, CAL/MOLE
Phosphoenolpyruvate	12,800
1,3-Diphosphoglyceric acid	11,800
Phosphocreatine	10,500
Acetyl phosphate	10,100
Adenosine triphosphate (ATP)	7,600
Glucose-1-phosphate	5,000
Fructose-6-phosphate	3,800
Glucose-6-phosphate	3,300
3-Phosphoglyceric acid	3,100

covalent bond is estimated as the amount of energy required to break the bond. The P∼O bond is actually more labile than a "low-energy" P—O bond, for less energy need be applied to break the P∼O bond. Nevertheless, rupturing a P∼O bond releases roughly double the amount of energy liberated by breaking an ordinary P—O bond, and sometimes substantially more than that. The amount of energy liberated by some of the cell's important phosphate compounds when a phosphate group is removed by hydrolysis is shown in Table 13.1, which should be used for reference upon later mention of these phosphate compounds. The transfer of Ⓟ and energy characteristically (but not invariably) proceeds "downhill" from a higher- to a lower-energy compound, that is, from compounds shown higher in this table to those shown below them.

When any comparatively low-energy (that is, relatively stable) molecule receives a phosphate group from a high-energy phosphate compound, an amount of energy equal to (or possibly considerably more than) that released by hydrolysis of the phosphate compound in vitro, is transferred to the low-energy compound. The latter is thereupon energized or "activated"—its energy content is raised so that it can perform some type of work (for instance, participate in a chemical reaction).

The so-called high-energy phosphate bond is produced by electrostatic repulsion generated between ionized atoms of like charge. The most important phosphate compound, adenosine triphosphate (ATP) (see Figure 9.5c), bears three phosphate groups, of which the terminal pair forms the configuration

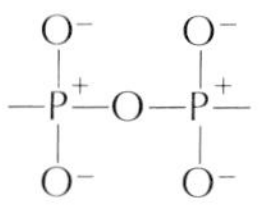

$$-\overset{O^-}{\underset{O^-}{P^+}}-O-\overset{O^-}{\underset{O^-}{P^+}}-$$

in which four negatively charged oxygen atoms are forced into proximity. Because they are held together covalently, the two Ⓟ groups will not separate spontaneously, but strong electrostatic repulsive forces are set up which are relieved when the P∼O bond is broken. When it is broken by hydrolysis, the excess energy escapes as heat; when it is broken during the transfer of Ⓟ from one compound to another, the energy is redistributed in the bonds of the compound phosphorylated.

There are four major kinds of reactions by which high-energy phosphate compounds are produced:

1 *Substrate level oxidative phosphorylation* An example of this is glycolysis, the breakdown of glucose to pyruvic acid with the production of ATP by the phosphorylation of adenosine diphosphate (ADP); (see Figure 14.51).

2 *Phosphoroclastic reactions* A number of bacteria mobilize energy by "phosphoroclastic" reactions in which the energy needed for building a high-energy phosphate compound is obtained by disrupting a covalent C—C, C—S, or C—N bond.

3 *Intramolecular oxidation-reduction* A transfer of electrons from one compound to another involves changes in the energy states of both donor and recipient. A loss in electrons is known as *oxidation* and results in a lowered energy state; a gain of electrons, or *reduction,* characteristically increases the energy content of the molecule or atom. Shifts in the distribution of electrons can also take place *within* a given molecule, altering the internal distribution of its energy so that a high-energy group may be generated. The dehydration of 2-phosphoglyceric acid to phosphoenolpyruvate

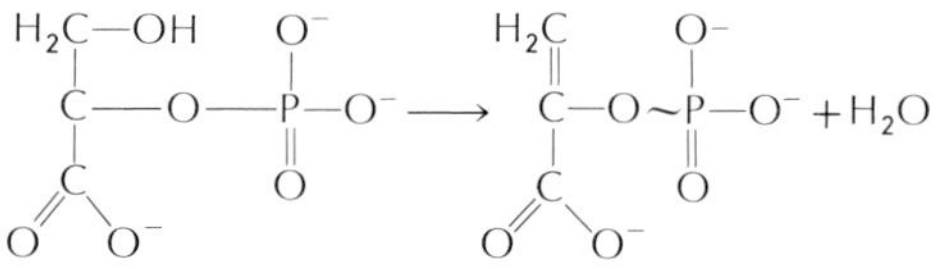

$$H_2C(OH){-}C(COO^-){-}O{-}P(O^-)(=O){-}O^- \longrightarrow H_2C{=}C(COO^-){-}O{\sim}P(O^-)(=O){-}O^- + H_2O$$

increases the concentration of electrons about the central carbon atom, which is consequently partially reduced while the terminal carbon atom is partially oxidized. This in turn causes a change in bond structure, pulling together the negatively charged carboxyl (—COO⁻) and phosphate groups, and generating the electrostatic repulsion mentioned above. Phosphoenolpyruvate (PEP) is therefore capable of transferring more energy to other compounds than any other phosphate compound.

4 *Phosphorylation linked with electron transport* The three types of reactions summarized above mainly take place

with the reactants and enzymes in solution. Those belonging to this fourth category are mainly "solid-state" reactions, occurring with some of the components occupying fixed positions, such as membrane-bound enzyme molecules and electron carriers. *Photophosphorylation* takes place during photosynthesis, the excess energy of a photochemically excited electron being used to phosphorylate ADP to ATP (see Figure 13.7). *Mitochondrial oxidative phosphorylation* involves the oxidation of small organic molecules to CO_2 and H_2O, with electrons being passed to carrier molecules that transfer energy to ATP-building reactions (see Figures 14.53 and 14.55).

The most ubiquitous and versatile high-energy phosphate compound is ATP. Both photophosphorylation and mitochondrial oxidative phosphorylation concentrate useful metabolic energy in the terminal phosphate group of ATP, which therefore constitutes the major carrier of energy available for cellular work. This relationship is shown in Figure 13.1, which shows that in the green plant the energy of sunlight is directly used to power the photophosphorylation reactions by which ADP unites with inorganic phosphate (H_3PO_4, designated P_i) to form ATP. The energy of ATP is then used to build carbohydrates (the term *photosynthesis* being used here in the strict sense of sugar production). When energy stored in the bonds of these sugars (and other organic compounds derived from them) is mobilized during oxidative phosphorylation, more ATP is built from ADP and P_i. The ATP then serves to provide energy to the reactions involved in the performance of cell work.

C Energetic coupling

Transfer of energy from one series of chemical reactions (metabolic pathway) to another requires that both pathways converge upon a *common intermediate*—a compound present in both systems as either a reactant or a product. If the *product* of one chemical reaction becomes one of the *reactants* in a subsequent reaction, it serves as a common intermediate. Any two reactions that share a common intermediate are termed *coupled reactions*. Coupling represents a great principle of biotic energy transfer, for the common intermediate usually carries energy from one reaction to the other. Because of such energetic coupling, energy need not actually be *liberated* by one reaction and taken up by another, but can be conserved by such means as the transfer of a high-energy phosphate group. The *adenylic acid system* (ATP–ADP–AMP: the tri-, di-, and monophosphate adenine ribose nucleotides) is the most frequently occurring common intermediate and serves to transfer energy between a great many different kinds of exergonic and endergonic reactions. For example, energy yielded by glucose during its breakdown to CO_2 and H_2O in mitochondrial oxidative metabolism is mostly used to phosphorylate ADP to ATP. The ATP then serves as a common intermediate, passing this energy to enzyme systems involved in biosynthesis, contractility, membrane transport, and so forth. If metabolic reactions were not coupled through such common intermediates, there would be no means for energy "liberated" by one cellular activity to be used in the performance of other activities.

13.2 □ ROLE OF ENZYMES IN THE BIOTIC USE OF MASS AND ENERGY

A *catalyst* is a substance that alters the rate of a chemical reaction without itself being destroyed or appearing in the end-product of the reaction. Enzymes are proteins that serve as catalysts for metabolic reactions (review Section 9.6A). Enzymes are essential to survival, for they not only *accelerate* chemical reactions to rates compatible with maintaining life but they also permit these reactions to go on *isothermally*. Heat, as we know, accelerates chemical reactions, but the architecture of cells is so delicate that it can be disrupted by even a slight increase in temperature above the optimum to which the cells have become adapted in the course of evolution.

A How do enzymes alter reaction rates?

Enzymes facilitate reactions by *lowering the activation energy* required of the reactants. *Activation energy* (the amount of energy that must be applied to the reactants for a given reaction to take place) constitutes an energy barrier to the spontaneous occurrence of a reaction. It can be measured in terms of the amount of heat needed to maximize the rate of a reaction in an uncatalyzed in vitro system. Because heat harms living systems, any means whereby reaction rates can be maximized at *lower* activation energies will have adaptive value (Figure 13.2).

Enzymes form temporary complexes with their substrates, holding them in spatial relationships that favor the accomplishment of the reaction. Reactions that would take place spontaneously at rates too slow to sustain life, proceed much more expeditiously when the reactants are absorbed onto specific *active sites* on the surface of giant enzyme molecules. Since the structure of enzymes is determined by their amino acid composition as specified by genes, we can see that if various mutant forms of a given gene were to encode enzymes differing somewhat in shape, the one which held the reactants in the position most effective in lowering reaction energy would improve the metabolic efficiency of the organism and would thus tend to be perpetuated. Enzymes are therefore just as much subject to the operation of natural selection and to evolution as are the more conspicuous morphological characteristics of an organism.

Figure 13.2 □ Activation energy and catalysis. The conversion of compound A to B is an exergonic reaction, for the free-energy level of B is lower than that of A. Nevertheless, energy must be added to the system for the reaction to proceed, as indicated by the solid line, showing the changing energy level. The shaded area represents the amount of activation energy for the reaction to occur. Less of this energy is required in the presence of a catalyst, as shown by the dashed line.

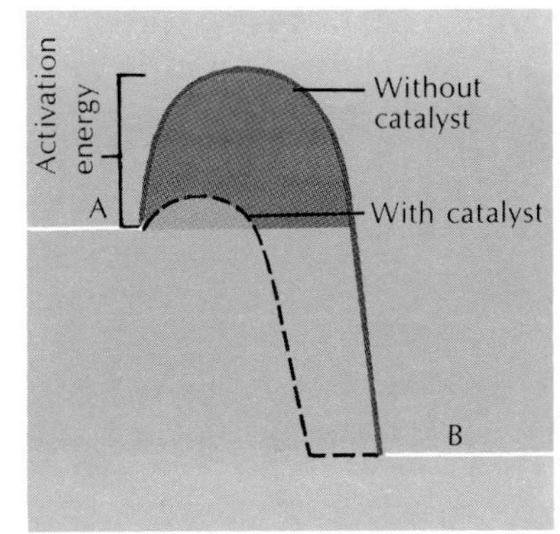

The effectiveness of enzymes in lowering the amount of energy required for the activation of the reactants can be shown by a few examples: (1) hydrolysis of sucrose by the enzyme *yeast invertase* requires less than 50 percent of the activation energy of the same reaction catalyzed by H^+; (2) decomposition of hydrogen peroxide (H_2O_2) by the enzyme *liver catalase* requires less than 31 percent of the activation energy required for the reaction to proceed without catalysis; (3) hydrolysis of the protein casein can be catalyzed by HCl as well as by the enzyme *trypsin,* but the latter reaction requires only about 56 percent of the activation energy of the former.

Enzymes merely alter the *rate* of a reaction, but do not determine its *direction.* The latter is influenced by the relative amounts of reactants and products in the milieu. The enzyme's active site can be occupied equally well by a single reactant molecule slated to be broken into two product molecules, or by two of these product molecules that are to be combined into one. The net direction of a reaction may be first in one direction and then in the other. In life a given enzyme may catalyze a reaction primarily in one direction simply because the products of the reaction do not accumulate in the vicinity, but diffuse away or are tied up at once in some other reaction. For instance, during digestion as large molecules are broken down to smaller ones, these products are absorbed into the bloodstream and carried away. In other cases a reaction proceeds in one direction because that direction is thermodynamically favored. For every chemical reaction there is an equilibrium point at which the concentrations of reactants and products remains constant; at this point the enzyme catalyzes the reaction equally in both directions.

B Relative activity of enzymes

Within the intact cell the rate of enzyme activity is influenced by the availability of substrates. Purified enzymes in solution, provided with a surplus of substrate, show characteristic maximal functional rates that are reflected by the *turnover number,* or number of substrate molecules that can react per minute per molecule of enzyme. The values for three representative enzymes are: β-amylase, 250,000/min; catalase, 5,000,000/min; cholinesterase, 20,000,000/min. The incredible speed with which organic reactions can take place in the presence of enzymes shows how essential these substances are for the maintenance of life. It has been estimated that a single bacterium is able to synthesize some 1,400 molecules of protein and over 12,000 molecules of lipid *per second,* a biochemical feat that would be quite impossible except for the action of enzymes.

C Significance of "enzyme cascades"

Certain reactions, particularly those which must take place rapidly on an extensive scale, are facilitated by an "enzyme-cascade" sequence, a series of reactions in which one enzyme catalyzes the conversion of another enzyme from the inactive (*proenzyme*) condition to the active state, and this enzyme in turn catalyzes the activation of the next enzyme, down to the activation of the last enzyme, which catalyzes the final reaction:

$$\text{Proenzyme A} \xrightarrow{(Initial\ stimulus)} \text{Enzyme A}$$
$$\text{Proenzyme B} \xrightarrow{(Enzyme\ A)} \text{Enzyme B}$$
$$\text{Proenzyme C} \xrightarrow{(Enzyme\ B)} \text{Enzyme C}$$
$$\text{Final substrate} \xrightarrow{(Enzyme\ C)} \text{Final product}$$

Such a cascade provides a means for amplifying the response, so that a much smaller quantity of the initial stimulant is required than if the initial stimulus had to activate every molecule of the final enzyme in the series. If each enzyme in the series had a turnover number of 100,000 substrate molecules per minute, the amplification possible with a four-step cascade would be $100{,}000^3$—one molecule of enzyme A would activate 100,000 molecules of enzyme B, *each* of which would activate 100,000 molecules of enzyme C, each of which would catalyze 100,000 of the final reaction. In only three steps, one molecule of the original enzyme thus produces 10^{15} final reactions!

An extracellular enzymatic response that must take place rapidly is the clotting of blood during hemorrhage. Human blood coagulation depends upon the conversion of immense numbers of molecules of the protein fibrinogen into the fibrous form known as fibrin. This reaction occurs at the end of an enzyme cascade thought to contain as many as a dozen steps. The initial stimulus may be some type of "wound substance," released by injured cells. The first several substances converted from proenzyme to enzyme status are proteins that occur in the plasma in such minute quantities that their presence is deduced only by the incidence of hereditary hemorrhagic diseases in which the factor is lacking. The cascade terminates with the activation of large quantities of the proenzyme *prothrombase* to the active form *thrombase,* which catalyzes the massive conversion of fibrinogen to fibrin at a rate that allows the clot to form more rapidly than it can be swept away by the flowing blood. Other biochemical reactions, such as the photochemical alteration of visual pigments (see Section 15.2D), may also be facilitated by cascades.

Table 13.2 □ Types of enzymes

1 **Enzymes concerned with *addition or removal of water:***
Hydrolases **catalyze hydrolysis and dehydration synthesis. Phosphatases add or remove phosphate groups (for example, ATPase). Glycosidases polymerize monosaccharides and break down polysaccharides (for example, amylase, sucrase). Nucleases construct and break down nucleic acids, and build up or break down nucleotides (for example, ribonuclease and DNAase). Proteases combine amino acids into proteins, and break down proteins into amino acids (for example, pepsin, trypsin).**
Hydrases **catalyze reactions that involve incorporation of the elements of water into or their removal from the substrate molecule. Enolase converts 2-phosphoglycerate to phosphoenolpyruvate. Carbonic anhydrase combines carbon dioxide and water to make carbonic acid. Aconitase converts citric acid to *cis*-aconitic acid and isocitric acid in Krebs cycle (see Section 14.3C)**

2 **Enzymes concerned with *transfer of electrons:***
Oxidases **catalyze the reaction of substrates with molecular oxygen. Catalase converts hydrogen peroxide (H_2O_2) to water and oxygen. Cytochrome oxidase combines hydrogen with molecular oxygen to make water.**
Dehydrogenases **remove hydrogen from the substrate and carry it by means of a coenzyme or a prosthetic group. Riboflavin dehydrogenases have FMN or FAD as coenzymes. Pyridine nucleotide dehydrogenases have NAD or NADP as coenzymes. Some cytochrome *c* reductases have riboflavin prosthetic groups.**

3 **Enzymes involved in *transferring radicals (transferases):***
Transaminases **transfer amino groups ($—NH_2$).**
Transphosphorylases **transfer phosphate groups.**
Transmethylases **transfer methyl groups ($—CH_3$).**
Transglycosidases **transfer monosaccharide units, and the like.**

4 **Enzymes involved in *disrupting* C—C *bonds:***
Desmolases **(for example, amino acid decarboxylase, which catalyzes the removal of the carboxyl group, —COOH, from amino acids).**

D Types of enzymes

Over 1,000 types of enzymes are known, most of which must be present in any given cell to carry out the required metabolic reactions. One scheme of enzyme classification, with examples, is given in Table 13.2. This classification scheme may be used for reference in identifying the general action of specific enzymes mentioned in subsequent sections.

13.3 □ NUTRIENTS

Nutrients are substances obtained from the environment that are utilized in biosynthesis or degraded with the release of energy. Organisms vary in their specific nutritional requirements, the greatest distinction being between autotrophic and heterotrophic species. Autotrophs rely only on simple inorganic substrates, whereas heterotrophs require both organic and inorganic substrates but are not able to synthesize organic compounds from inorganic precursors.

A Inorganic nutrients

Elements required by plants are obtained in the form of ions and small inorganic molecules. According to the quantities needed these elements may be termed macronutrients or micronutrients. *Macronutrients* are required in amounts equal to or greater than 1 mg-atom/liter of nutrient solution. (A *milligram-atom* is equal to the atomic mass of the element taken in milligrams; thus, in the case of nitrogen, with an atomic mass of 14, 14 mg constitute a milligram-atom.) *Micronutrients* are needed in quantities less than 1 mg-atom/liter of nutrient solution.

The macronutrient elements C, H, and O, are obtained by plants in the form of CO_2 and H_2O. Molecular oxygen (O_2) is required only as a hydrogen acceptor in the oxidative metabolism of both autotrophs and heterotrophs. For heterotrophs CO_2 is no nutrient, but a toxic waste; for autotrophs it is the source of the carbon and most of the oxygen atoms that enter into the construction of organic compounds. Water serves as a donor of H in photosynthesis and is incorporated into organic molecules through such reactions as hydrolysis, for example, in the conversion of sucrose to simple sugar:

$$C_{12}H_{22}O_{11} + H_2O \longrightarrow 2C_6H_{12}O_6$$

Water as such constitutes some 80 percent of most living things, serving as a solvent, medium of transport, and favorable milieu for chemical reactions (see Section 4.1A).

Certain micronutrient elements or "minerals" are universally required by both heterotrophs and autotrophs, whereas others may be needed only for special syntheses in restricted groups of organisms. Some occur in the body mainly as ions, including Ca^{2+}, Mg^{2+}, Na^+, K^+, and Cl^-. Phosphorus occurs as the inorganic phosphate ion ($H_2PO_4^-$, HPO_4^{2-}, and PO_4^{3-}), and as organic phosphate, which may dissociate as

$$-\overset{\overset{\displaystyle O}{\|}}{\underset{\underset{\displaystyle OH}{|}}{P}}-OH \quad \text{or} \quad -O-\overset{\overset{\displaystyle O}{\|}}{\underset{\underset{\displaystyle OH}{|}}{P}}-OH$$

Certain metallic elements, including iron, copper, manganese, zinc, and molybdenum, are bound to organic molecules by *chelation,* that is, they are held in the center of a ring-shaped molecule by a type of bonding in which atoms within the ring share their electrons with the metallic atom or ion. The heme group of hemoglobin and cytochrome exemplifies this: it consists of an iron ion held by chelation within a tetrapyrrole ring (see Figure 9.4). The chelated element retains its capacity to form ionic bonds with ionized compounds of opposite charge. Other micronutrient elements such as sulfur and nitrogen are bonded covalently into the basic structure of such compounds as proteins, but in much smaller quantities than are the macronutrient elements (C, H, and O).

The biotic uses of micronutrients are varied and are summarized only in part in Table 13.3. Even such uncommon elements as selenium and vanadium have essential roles in the metabolism of specific groups of organisms. Minimal requirements for normal plant growth can be determined by rearing plants *hydroponically* in liquid culture media of known composition rather than in soil (Figure 13.3). Any lack of substances needed even in trace amounts can seriously impair growth. On the other hand, many micronutrients, particularly the metals, are highly toxic when they are taken in excess.

Table 13.3 ☐ Roles of micronutrient elements in living systems

ELEMENT	FUNCTION
S (sulfur)	As atom, constituent of proteins (as part of cysteine, methionine), vitamins (biotin, thiamin); as SO_4^{2-}, constituent of chondroitin sulfate, etc.
N (nitrogen)	Constituent of amino acids, nucleotides, nitrogenous bases, tetrapyrroles B vitamins
P (phosphorus)	As phosphoric acid group, Ⓟ, forms part of nucleic acids, ATP, NAD, NADP, phospholipids, etc.; increases reactivity of molecules by forming high-energy bond (~P); as part of phosphate ion, contributes to skeletal materials and regulates intracellular pH
Ca (calcium)	Mainly as Ca^{2+}, component of skeletal materials in plants and animals (shell, bone, pectin, intercellular cement); essential for blood clotting and for normal nerve and muscle function: regulates cation balance between cells and milieu along with Na^+, K^+, and Mg^{2+}; cofactor of enzymes (such as succinic dehydrogenase)
Mg (magnesium)	As ion (Mg^{2+}), important in ionic balance with Na^+, K^+, and Ca^{2+}; as atom, constituent of chlorophyll and cofactor for many enzymes (carboxylases, dehydrogenases, and almost all activation enzymes)
K (potassium)	Major intracellular cation; involved in ionic balance and in maintenance of electrochemical potential across cell membrane; promotes protein synthesis
Na (sodium)	Major extracellular cation; helps retain water and maintain osmotic balance; involved in production of action currents in excited cell membranes; promotes nuclear uptake of amino acids and intranuclear protein synthesis
Cl (chlorine)	Major inorganic anion (Cl^-); helps maintain isosmoticity of tissue fluids; serves as catalyst in cytochrome electron transfers in photosynthesis; component of vertebrate gastric HCl; cofactor for salivary amylase
Fe (iron)	Component of cytochromes, catalase, hemoglobin, myoglobin; essential for synthesis of a number of B vitamins (including folic acid, needed for erythrocyte production)
Mn (manganese)	Cofactor of many enzymes (dipeptidases, carboxylases, phosphorylases, etc.); promotes synthesis of vitamins C, B_{12}, biotin, choline, niacin; essential for chlorophyll synthesis; affects Ca^{2+} metabolism
Cu (copper)	Constituent of hemocyanin (major invertebrate blood pigment); required for synthesis of hemoglobin and iron-containing enzymes; component of many enzymes (especially those involved in synthesis of the black pigment melanin)
Zn (zinc)	Cofactor of enzymes including carbonic anhydrase, catalase, phosphatases; mitotic accelerator, concentrating in spindle; required for synthesis of tryptophan and carboxylase
Si (silicon)	Widely used among plants and animals in supportive structures; especially in feathers, grasses, sphenopsids, siliceous sponges, shells of diatoms, radiolarians, etc.
Co (cobalt)	Constituent of vitamin B_{12} (cobalamin); promotes synthesis of iron-containing pyrroles including heme; activates peptidases and other enzymes
Mo (molybdenum)	Cofactor for flavoprotein enzymes, including one needed for conversion of NO_2^- to NO_3^- by bacteria, hence essential in nitrogen cycle
I (iodine)	Constituent of vertebrate thyroid hormones, spongin (silklike protein of bath sponges), coral skeletons, purple dyes of some molluscs
Ni (nickel)	Required for synthesis of pancreatic hormone insulin; antianemic factor; activator of enzymes (mostly those also activated by Co)

B Organic nutrients

Originally products of autotrophic nutrition, organic nutrients are obtained by heterotrophs through consumption of the tissues or residues of plants and animals. A hawk devouring a snake that fed upon mice in the last analysis is subsisting upon organic nutrients manufactured by plants, the seeds of which were consumed by the mice. No matter how intricate the nutritional web of a community, its origins are always traceable to its autotrophic component, the component that alone is capable of tapping the matter and energy resources of the abiotic environment.

CARBOHYDRATES Taken in as soluble sugars or polysaccharides, most carbohydrates are digested to simple sugars and thereafter built into polysaccharides, converted to lipids and other types of organic compounds, or degraded to carbon dioxide and water with the release of energy (see Section 9.4).

LIPIDS Fats may be consumed as such or may be manufactured within heterotrophic cells by the transformation of carbohydrates or amino acids (see Section 9.5). Triglyceride fats serve mainly as energy reserves, being broken down or converted to carbohydrate as needed. Thick deposits under the skin insulate the body against excessive heat loss. Phospholipids are essential structural components of cell membranes. Certain steroids with vitamin activity must be included in the diet, whereas others can be manufactured by heterotrophic cells from organic precursors.

PROTEINS In order to be incorpo-

Figure 13.3 ☐ Tracing plant uptake and use of minerals. Tomato plants grown in culture solution containing radioactive zinc (^{65}Zn) concentrate this element in the seeds. Plants deprived of Zn will not form seeds. Radioautographs made by positron emission from ^{65}Zn show the isotope concentrated in the seeds and visible as points of light within the vascular tissue. Only about 3×10^{-9} g of Zn is present in one seed. (*Courtesy of Dr. P. R. Stout.*)

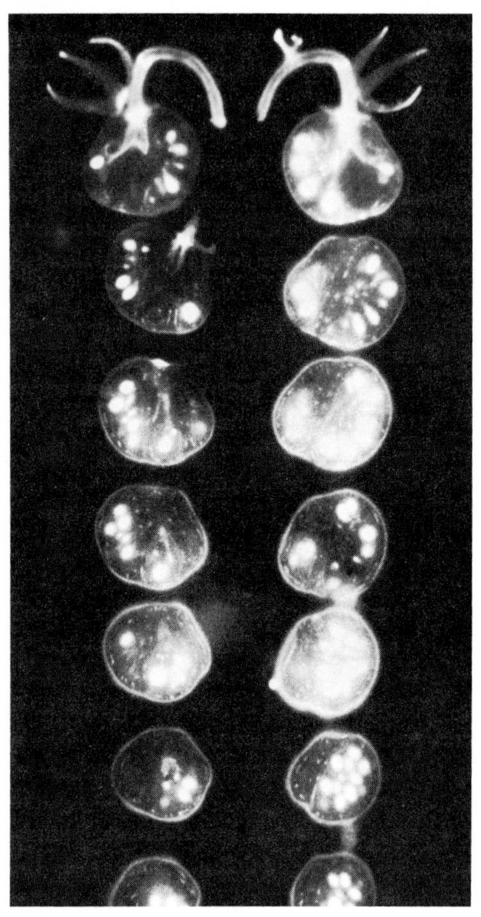

rated by heterotrophs, proteins must first be digested to their constituent amino acids; these are then utilized metabolically in the construction of enzymes and structural proteins (see Section 9.6). Amino acids may also be *deaminated* by the removal of the $—NH_2$ group and converted into carbohydrate or lipid reserves, or further broken down with the release of energy. Heterotrophs are incapable of manufacturing all needed amino acids; by transferring $—NH_2$ groups from one molecule to another (*transamination*), they can convert certain amino acids into others, but they cannot make all amino acids in this way. The amino acids that cannot be made by transferral of an amino group to a suitable carboxylic acid, or by changing the side group of an existing amino acid, must be included in the diet. Such amino acids are termed *essential.* For mammals the essential amino acids are lysine, tryptophan, histidine, phenylalanine, leucine, isoleucine, threonine, valine, arginine, and methionine (see Table 9.2). From these ten, another ten or more *nonessential* amino acids can be made from carbon skeletons (basic chains or rings of carbon atoms from which distinctive groups have been removed), using energy derived from the breakdown of carbohydrates.

VITAMINS Vitamins are relatively small organic molecules of considerable diversity which are essential to life and when eaten are absorbed without having to be digested. In comparison with other organic nutrients, they are needed in only small quantities. Autotrophs and certain heterotrophic microorganisms can manufacture all vitamins needed in their metabolism, whereas other heterotrophic microorganisms may need to take in one or two from the environment. On the other hand most higher animals, including man, require a larger number of vitamins in their diet. Vitamins play specific roles in metabolism, several serving as coenzymes. Their functions will accordingly be discussed in Chapter 14.

13.4 ☐ AUTOTROPHIC NUTRITION

Autotrophs use small inorganic substrates to build organic compounds, obtaining bonding energy from the abiotic environment. A few microbes (such as nitrite, nitrate, and iron bacteria) obtain this energy by catalyzing reactions in which inorganic compounds (for example, ammonia, nitrite, and iron oxides) are converted to a lower energy state (see Section 4.3C); the energy made available by such exergonic reactions is utilized in various energy-requiring synthetic pathways. Most autotrophic nutrition, however, depends upon *photosynthesis,* in which *radiant* energy (of sunlight) is exploited rather than energy from inorganic chemical reactions.

The existence of a photosynthetic process was not suspected until about 200 years ago. For many centuries men had thought that the soil provided all materials needed for plant growth. This was a logical supposition but proved false when finally put to the test by the Flemish physician J. B. van Helmont in 1648. Van Helmont's experimental procedure was beautifully simple: he placed a weighed quantity of dried soil in a tub within which he then planted a willow seedling. The tub was protected from the entry of dust and other foreign solids and over a period of 5 years rainwater or distilled water was added regularly but the soil was not replenished. At the end of this time van Helmont uprooted the willow and weighed both the tree and the remaining soil after drying. He found that, contrary to popular belief, the materials needed for growth of the tree had not come from the soil: the soil weighed only about 60 g less than it had originally but the tree weighed over 360 kg! This did not even include the additional mass of the foliage shed during four autumns. Van Helmont proposed that since only water had been added to the tub during the period of growth, water must have contributed the necessary materials for the tree's observed gain in mass. Far from solving the riddle of plant growth, van Helmont had demonstrated that a riddle existed: the soil, with its apparently rich nutrient content is *not* the primary source of materials for plant growth; could so simple a substance as water actually provide all of these materials?

During the ensuing 100 years several investigations pointed to the fact that some additional material for plant growth came from the atmosphere. Air seemed even more improbable than water as a source of such material until Joseph Priestley, discovering oxygen in 1772, proved that air has a substantial nature. Priestley then proceeded to demonstrate that plants not only liberate oxygen but can purify air rendered poisonous by the exhalations of an animal kept in an airtight container. A mouse sealed into a glass container will quickly suffocate but will survive if a living plant of adequate size is also sealed into the container. By the close of the eighteenth century it was known that carbon dioxide is the gas used for plant growth and that green plants do give off oxygen—but only when they have been illuminated.

Throughout the nineteenth century various attacks were made on the problem of plant nutrition and its main outlines were established: in the presence of light, chlorophyll-bearing plants build sugar and starch and liberate molecular oxygen. In 1898 the term *photosynthesis* was coined to designate this process, for it had been correctly concluded that the process involves the conversion of light energy to chemical bonding energy.

Important questions still were unanswered, however. Do carbon dioxide and water interact directly? What is the source of the oxygen liberated? Reviewing Figure 4.21 we see the experimental means by which it was eventually proven that all oxygen given off by a photosynthesizing plant comes from water and not (as was formerly thought) from carbon dioxide. The chemical reactions by which carbon dioxide and hydrogen atoms from water are used to produce carbohydrates defied analysis until 1950, when an ingenious experimental procedure was adopted by Melvin Calvin and his associates. This procedure will be summarized in Section 13.4D; without looking ahead at this point, what do you think may have been the essential features of his experimental approach?

In green plants water is the hydrogen donor for photosynthesis, and a simplified equation may be given:

$$CO_2 + H_2O \xrightarrow[\text{112* kcal/mole}]{\text{Radiant energy}} CH_2O + O_2$$

However, since hexose is the most common photosynthetic product and since water is reconstituted in the reaction as well as used, the balanced equation should read:

$$6CO_2 + 12H_2O \xrightarrow[\text{673 kcal/mole}]{\text{Radiant energy}} C_6H_{12}O_6 + 6O_2 + 6H_2O$$

We should note that these so-called photosynthetic equations are not meant to be true representations of the process but merely specify the original substrates, the source and amount of energy required, and the basic end-products. Actually, there intervenes a complicated series of reactions, which depend upon the action of a number of enzymes. The pigment chlorophyll *a* is also essential to the reaction for it serves to trap solar energy.

Some sulfur bacteria can also carry on photosynthesis, but these organisms do not require chlorophyll and use hydrogen sulfide (H_2S) as a source of hydrogen atoms instead of water. Elemental sulfur is released as a by-product of this reaction rather than O_2. A simplified representation of this process is

$$CO_2 + H_2S \xrightarrow{\text{Radiant energy}} CH_2O + S$$

but again we should note that the organic product of the reaction is not simply CH_2O but some multiple of this hypothetical unit, such as a hexose.

*Actually slightly more than 112 kcal are required, for when taken six times the reaction requires about 673 (not 672) kcal to build 1 mole of hexose sugar.

Figure 13.4 □ **The photosynthetic apparatus. (*a*) Chloroplasts seen in cross section of chlorenchyma cell of tobacco plant; a large sap vacuole occupies the center of the cell, the cytoplasm being restricted to the periphery. Most of the cytoplasm is occupied by chloroplasts. The darker striated areas within each chloroplast are grana. (*Courtesy of Dr. H. W. Israel.*) (*b*) Single granum seen at higher magnification. (*Courtesy of Dr. H. W. Israel.*) (*c*) Hypothetical model of molecular organization of lamellae within granum.**

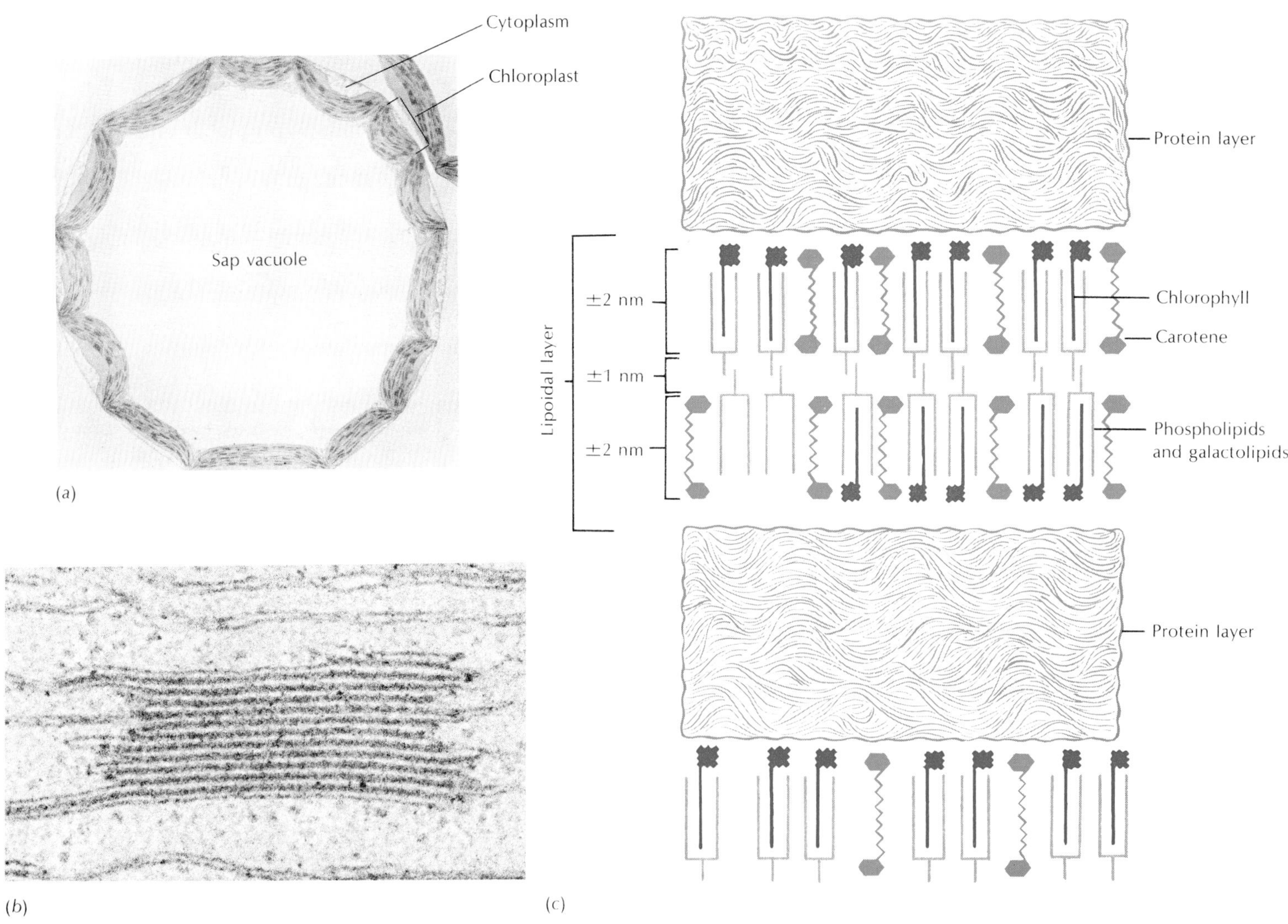

The evolution of plant structure must be viewed in the light of the photosynthetic process: this process evolved before the advent of multicellular forms of life, and the success of autotrophic metaphytes has depended upon the degree to which their gross form and tissue differentiation have contributed toward photosynthetic efficiency.

A Organization of the photosynthetic apparatus

In the procaryotic cells of blue-green algae, chlorophyll occurs throughout the cytoplasm in concentrically arranged photosynthetic lamellae (see Figure 10.5*a*). In the eucaryotic cells of higher plants, such lamellae are confined to the chloroplasts, within which they are periodically grouped into tight stacks, like piles of coins (Figure 13.4). These stacks, the *grana,* are separated from one another by *intergrana*—spaces in which the lamellae are fewer and more loosely arranged in an aqueous matrix. By dry weight, each chloroplast consists of about 10 percent pigments, particularly chlorophylls and carotenoids, 50 percent proteins, and the remaining 40 percent mainly lipids, carbohydrates, and nucleic acids (including a strand of DNA, which enables the chloroplast to reproduce itself).

Each photosynthetic lamella in the chloroplast is single in the intergrana and doubled in the grana, which are the actual sites of photosynthesis. The molecular organization of the grana reflects a high degree of adaptation for trapping and utilizing light energy. In the grana each lamella averages 200 Å in thickness and consists of alternating layers of protein and of galactolipids associated with pigments. The arrangement of these molecules may follow the typical membrane structure shown in Figure 13.4c, or may be considerably different from this. Each protein layer, consisting of enzymes and electron carriers, is thought to be in contact on both surfaces with a pigment-bearing lipoidal layer; for convenience these two layers have been designated pigment systems I and II. Both systems contain chlorophyll *a,* which is nearly universal among photosynthesizers, and various accessory pigments that vary according to the plant group (see Chapter 2). In green algae and land plants a variant, chlorophyll *b,* is present, differing from chlorophyll *a* only in having a formyl group,

$$-\mathrm{C}{\overset{\displaystyle /\!\!/ \mathrm{O}}{\underset{\displaystyle \diagdown \mathrm{H}}{}}}$$

where the former bears a methyl group,

$$-\mathrm{CH_3}$$

(Figure 13.5). This minor difference causes the two pigments to differ in absorption properties. Chlorophyll *c* (restricted to brown algae, diatoms, dinoflagellates and related forms), and chlorophyll *d* (found in the red algae), also have distinctive *absorption spectra.* The chlorophylls mainly absorb light of shorter (violet) and longer (red) wavelengths; reflecting light of intermediate wavelengths, they consequently appear green. Chlorophylls *b, c,* and *d,* and other accessory pigments function in each pigment system as absorbers of light, but cannot themselves engage in photosynthesis, serving only to transfer energy to chlorophyll *a.* These accessory pigments serve to absorb light of wavelengths other than those absorbed by chlorophyll *a,* thereby making more radiant energy available for photosynthesis.

The major absorption peak for chlorophyll *a* within the intact granum is at 685 nm, but this is actually a composite of three separate peaks occurring at 670, 683, and 695 nm. Since upon purification all chlorophyll *a* is found to be identical, these differences in absorptive properties are thought to result from the manner in which the chlorophyll *a* is (or is not) associated with protein. In each pigment system occasional molecules of chlorophyll *a* are thought to occupy exposed positions, protruding from the lipoid layer into the adjacent protein layer, where they are favorably located to pass electrons to acceptors in the protein layer. These exposed molecules in system I are termed *P*700 because of their absorption maximum close to this value (actually probably the 695 nm fraction mentioned above). Comparable exposed positions are occupied in system II by chlorophyll *a* molecules designated *P*680, for their major absorption peak is at 683 nm. The rest of the chlorophyll *a,* along with the accessory pigments, may transfer energy by resonance to the key molecules *P*700 and *P*680, which are thought to be the only ones capable of donating excited electrons to the ATP- and carbohydrate-building pathways. Thus each protein layer in a photosynthetic lamella is geared to receive and utilize the energy of electrons from each of the pigment layers flanking it.

The basic macromolecular complex that represents the functional unit of photosynthesis is thought to consist of (1) a certain minimum number of accessory pigment

Figure 13.5 ☐ **Pigments involved in photosynthesis: (*a*) Chemical formulas. Chlorophyll *b* and bacteriochlorophyll differ from chlorophyll *a* only in the groups shown in color. β-Carotene is an accessory light-absorptive pigment. (*b*) Absorption spectra of chlorophylls *a*, *b*, *c*, and *d*. (*c*) Absorption spectra of chlorophyll *c* and carotenoid pigments.**

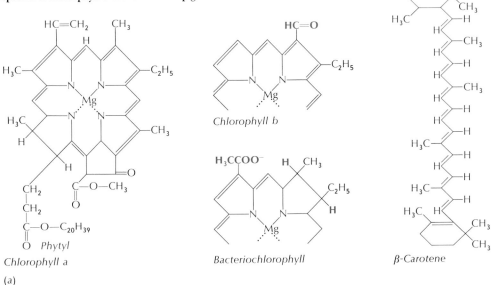

Chlorophyll a

Chlorophyll b

Bacteriochlorophyll

β-Carotene

(*a*)

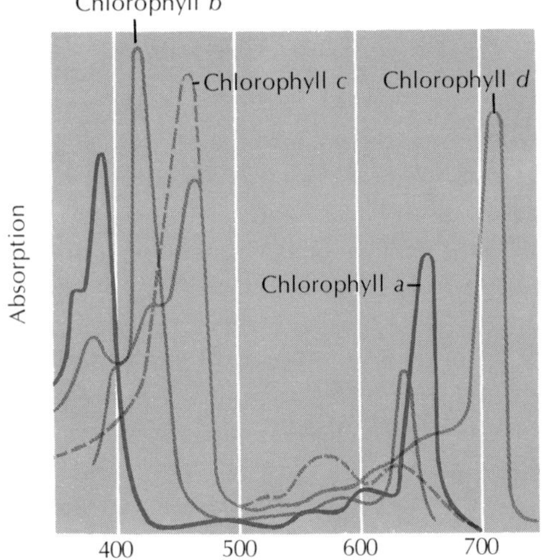

(*b*)

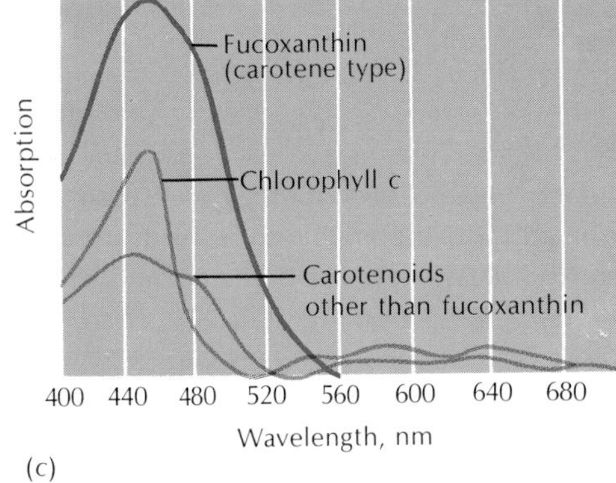

(*c*)

molecules that center upon (2) one of the exposed molecules, *P700* or *P680*, (3) the electron carriers that make possible the production of ATP (photophosphorylation), and (4) the enzymes involved in the carbohydrate-producing reaction cycle. Millions of these functional units must make up each granum.

B The photosynthetic process

The thermodynamic and biochemical events of photosynthesis can be divided into "light reactions" and "dark reactions" (see Figure 13.9). The former are directly dependent on radiant energy, whereas the latter are not.

The light reactions include: (1) absorption of light, resulting in the *excitement of an electron* in each of the exposed chlorophyll *a* molecules; the energy of these excited electrons is passed by coupling to the subsequent reactions; (2) *photophosphorylation* of ADP to ATP; (3) *hydrolysis of water* into hydrogen and oxygen, with the uptake of electrons by electron-transfer enzymes and chlorophyll; (4) movement of protons from H_2O to nicotinamide adenine dinucleotide phosphate (NADP; see Figure 9.6) forming NADPH + H^+.

The dark reactions involve the combination of CO_2 and hydrogen (from NADPH + H^+) to produce sugar. This *reduction* of CO_2 is accomplished in a circular metabolic pathway, the carbohydrate-synthesizing *Calvin cycle*.

The hydrolysis of water, the shifting of hydrogen from H_2O to CO_2, and the phosphorylation of ADP to ATP are all *endergonic* processes dependent upon the light-absorptive capacity of the plastid pigments. The excited electrons of *P*700 and *P*680 are thought to be responsible for transferring energy into these reactions.

The excitation of an electron is an all-or-none event; precisely that amount of energy must be absorbed which equals the energy needed to move one electron from its normal orbital to one farther away from the atomic nucleus. For *P*700, absorption of one quantum of light of approximately 700-nm wavelength provides just the amount of energy needed to excite the particular electron to be taken up by the electron-transport series. (Which atom of the chlorophyll molecule yields this electron is not yet known.) The energy content of light quanta varies according to the wavelength. Briefly, the shorter the wavelength, the higher the energy content of a single light quantum (*photon*). Violet light (395 nm) has nearly twice the energy per quantum as far-red light (750 nm).

C The light reactions

The splitting of water and the subsequent transport of hydrogen is thermodynamically an "uphill" process powered by the excited electrons of chlorophyll. Energy must be invested equivalent to 1.2 eV (electron volts) per electron transported, or 112 kcal of CO_2 reduced (or about six times this amount, 673 kcal per mole of *hexose* produced). To understand the light reactions during which this energy is absorbed into the system from the abiotic environment, we must consider both the thermodynamics of the situation and the pathway that hydrogen must follow to its final union with carbon dioxide. But first, some background information may be helpful.

OXIDATION-REDUCTION Transfer of hydrogen from water to CO_2 is termed an *oxidation-reduction* reaction. As defined earlier, *oxidation* is the loss of electrons from a compound, whereas *reduction* is a gain in electrons by a compound. The molecule that donates electrons (the electron donor) is termed the *reductant,* while the molecule that takes them up (the electron acceptor) is the *oxidant.* The movement of one or more electrons from the reductant to the oxidant oxidizes the former and reduces the latter; thus an oxidation and a reduction always occur simultaneously, being like opposite faces of the same coin. The transfer of an electron from donor (reductant) to acceptor (oxidant) results in a change of the electrical properties of both compounds. Electron donors may be arranged in a graded series from those which have a high *electron pressure* (tendency to get rid of electrons) to those with a low electron pressure. Electron acceptors may be ranked in an equivalent series according to the strength of their *electron affinity* (tendency to take up electrons). Electron pressure and affinity can be indirectly measured as equivalent to the voltage of electrical current that flows between a given compound and its reduced or oxidized form [this is termed a *couple:* for example, O_2 and its reduced form, H_2O, or CO_2 and its reduced form, $(CH_2O)_n$, that is, carbohydrate.] This flow of electrons between members of a couple constitutes the *oxidation-reduction potential* of the couple. In biochemistry, electron donors with high electron pressure are said to have a high negative oxidation-reduction potential, while electron acceptors of high affinity have a high positive oxidation-reduction potential. The more different the potentials of two couples are, the greater the amount of energy which is either required or liberated when electrons are transferred from one couple to the other. In Figure 13.6 we can see that the oxidation-reduction potentials of the couples H_2O/O_2 and $CO_2/(CH_2O)_3$ or PGAL (the first carbohydrate product of photosynthesis), differ by 1.2 eV, and this accordingly is the amount of energy needed to move one electron from the first couple to the second. Conversely, the same amount of energy (per electron) is liberated when electrons are moved from carbohydrate to O_2, thereby oxidizing the carbohydrate to CO_2 and reducing O_2 to H_2O. This takes place when sugar is burned, or when it is oxidized within the cell in the course of cell respiration.

Ordinarily, electron transfer proceeds thermodynamically "downhill," from a negative compound to one which is somewhat less negative. In such a downhill electron-transport series, energy is released as the electron passes from each carrier to the next (see Figure 14.55). Moving an electron in the reverse direction, from a compound with a positive oxidation-reduction potential to one having a negative potential, requires energy. The amount of energy that must be invested to move the electron "uphill" is equivalent to the potential difference between the original donor (the reductant) and the final acceptor (the oxidant).

ELECTRON TRANSPORT FROM WATER TO NADP The major energy investment of photosynthesis is that required to move the electrons of water uphill to a final combination with CO_2. As we have said, to

Figure 13.6 □ **Proposed scheme of noncyclic electron transport in photosynthesis. Two major events occur: noncyclic photophosphorylation of ADP to ATP and transport of protons (H^+; solid color) and electrons (e^-; color tint) to NADP. Protons are accepted by NADP when it is reduced by $2e^-$ from ferredoxin. During transport from water to ferredoxin (or unidentified acceptor "X"), electrons undergo changes in energy state as indicated by the vertical scale of oxidation-reduction potential. Energy enters the system in two distinct light events, one involving chlorophyll *a P*680 in pigment system II, the other involving chlorophyll *a P*700 in pigment system I. Electrons from *P*680 and *P*700 also go into a cyclic electron-transport system that generates ATP. Transfer of H atoms is shown by gray arrows. (See also Figure 13.7).**

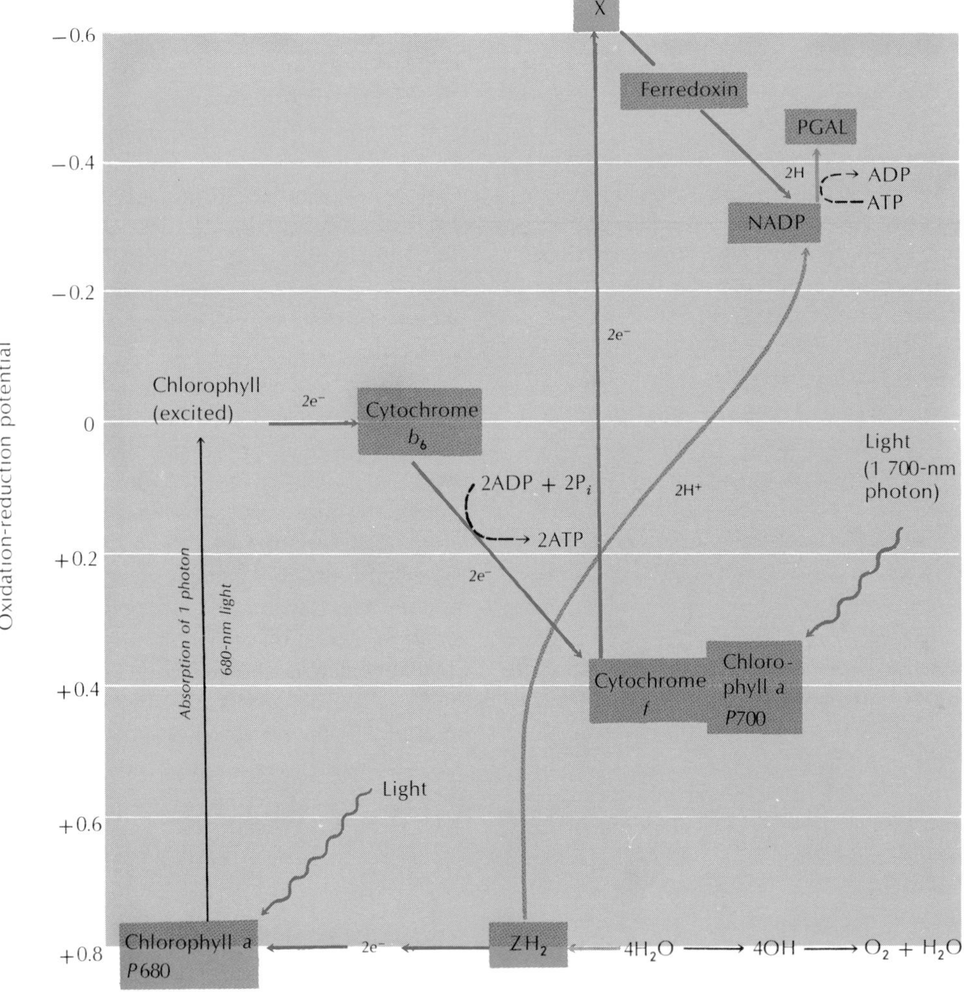

transport one electron from water (with an oxidation-reduction potential of +0.82) to CO_2 (with a potential of −0.43) requires an energy investment equal to +0.82 minus −0.43, or roughly 1.2 eV.

We are speaking in terms of *electron* transfer, and yet in the final analysis it is hydrogen *atoms* that are transported from water to CO_2. This apparent contradiction is easily resolved when one reconsiders the nature of the hydrogen atom, which consists of a single nuclear proton (H^+) and one orbital electron (e^-). The hydrolysis of water is thought to proceed as follows:

$$4H_2O \longrightarrow [4H^+, 4e^-] + 4OH$$

$$[4H^+, 4e^-] \xrightarrow{\text{To enzyme Z}} 2ZH_2 \qquad 4OH \longrightarrow O_2,\ 2H_2O$$

It may be seen that two water molecules are reconstituted for every four hydrolyzed. The hydrogen atoms (H^+ plus e^-) are taken up by an enzyme (known as "Z" since it is as yet unidentified). In subsequent transfers, however, the carrier molecules are specifically involved with e^-, whereas the proton "short-circuits" the pathway, being directly taken up by reduced NADP.

Thermodynamically it is convenient to view photosynthesis as an uphill process of e^- transfer, while *chemically* it consists of the removal of H atoms from water, and their transfer to CO_2. The uphill transport of two e^- from each water molecule is thought to involve two separate boosts by which light energy is fed into the system (Figure 13.6). The unidentified enzyme, Z, catalyzes the hydrolysis of H_2O; Z must have an oxidation-reduction potential equivalent to that of water itself, so that little energy expenditure is involved in its reduction to

ZH_2 and the corresponding oxidation of the donor (H_2O). But to move $2e^-$ from Z to the electron-transfer enzyme *cytochrome* b_6 involves an input of approximately 0.8 V per electron, for the potential of Z is probably about +0.8 while that of cytochrome b_6 is close to zero. This first boost is thought to be provided by light energy absorbed by chlorophyll *P*680 in pigment system II. This molecule, ionized by the escape of a light-excited electron, is free to accept another electron from a donor such as ZH_2. This electron in turn is excited by absorption of a photon and passes into the electron transport system associated with *P*680. At this point, two courses are open: (1) The electron may travel along a cyclic chain of electron carriers that reduce its energy state in a series of steps, using this energy to build ATP from ADP and inorganic phosphate (P_i), and then be returned to chlorophyll. (2) Alternatively, the excited electron may pass from cytochrome b_6 to cytochrome *f*, thereby leaving the cyclic transport system and reentering the noncyclic transport pathway. The movement of electrons (in pairs, as $2e^-$) from cytochrome b_6 to cytochrome *f* is exergonic (thermodynamically downhill); the excess energy is used to build two molecules of ATP from ADP and P_i, for each pair of electrons transported.

To move next uphill from cytochrome *f* to ferredoxin, the electrons must now be energized by means of the light energy absorbed in pigment system I. This boost, equal to the energy of a quantum of 700-nm light, is adequate to permit the electrons to move to ferredoxin. [Some investigators believe that electrons pass from cytochrome *f* to an unidentified compound ("X") with an oxidation-reduction potential of around −0.6, and then proceed downhill from X to ferredoxin.] The electrons then go downhill once more, from ferredoxin to NADP, producing reduced NADP; this $NADP_{red.}$ now has a high affinity for protons (H^+) and can take up those released by the breakdown of water and subsequent ionization of hydrogen atoms; ($NADPH + H^+$) then passes hydrogen atoms to phosphoglyceric acid (PGA), a component of the carbohydrate-producing Calvin cycle, and hydrogen at this point enters the so-called dark reactions.

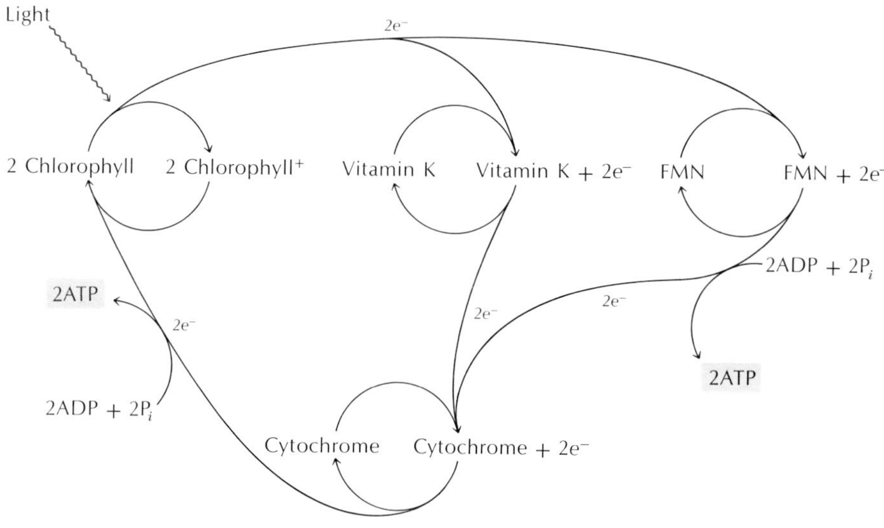

Figure 13.7 □ Proposed scheme of cyclic photophosphorylation. Ionized chlorophyll is designated by $^+$. Electron acceptors include vitamin K, cytochrome, and flavin mononucleotide (FMN).

NONCYCLIC AND CYCLIC PHOTOPHOSPHORYLATION OF ADP The energy absorbed by pigment systems I and II not only must suffice for the uphill transport of electrons and protons from water to their point of union with CO_2 in the dark reactions but must also produce enough ATP to meet the energy needs of the carbohydrate-synthesizing reactions. We have just seen that photophosphorylation of ADP is accomplished by means of energy from electrons excited by light. *Noncyclic* photophosphorylation takes place when energy made available during the exergonic transfer of electrons from cytochrome b_6 to cytochrome *f* is used to bond ADP to inorganic phosphate (P_i) to make ATP. The amount of energy made available is such that one molecule of ATP can be generated for each electron transported through this noncyclic (that is, one-way) system (see Figure 13.6). Noncyclic photophosphorylation, however, is inadequate to meet all the energy needs of the dark reactions. The balance is provided by *cyclic* photophosphorylation, in which excited electrons from chlorophyll pass through a series of electron carriers, including cytochromes, flavin mononucleotide (FMN), and vitamin K, and return in a deenergized state to chlorophyll (Figure 13.7). Since all of the excess energy of the excited electrons can be used to generate ATP, each cycle can yield 4 ATP molecules per $2e^-$ transported. Each pigment system is thought to be associated with one such cyclic ATP-building electron-transport system.

As mentioned above, according to present thinking the electron transport system associated with *P*680 not only yields ATP but shunts high-energy electrons into the noncyclic pathway leading to the dark reactions; the system can then take up other electrons from chlorophyll, which upon being ionized accepts more low-energy electrons from ZH_2. The electron transport system associated with *P*700 is energetically coupled to the noncyclic pathway to provide energy as needed for movement of electrons to X or ferredoxin. Such donations to the noncyclic pathway must of course reduce the net yield of the ATP-building system, but adequate quantities of ATP are still produced to meet the needs of the dark reactions.

At least one of the reactions involved in photophosphorylation is dependent on oxygen (Figure 13.8), for the process is inhibited when nitrogen gas replaces air in a closed in vitro system containing intact chloroplasts. On the other hand, CO_2 fixation does not depend upon the availability of O_2 but seems actually to be facilitated under anaerobic conditions.

Figure 13.8 □ **Effect of anaerobic (O_2-free) conditions (represented by dashed lines and broken bars) on rates of CO_2 fixation (line graphs) and photophosphorylation (histogram) by isolated chloroplasts, N_2 replacing air in the system. Note that lack of O_2 severely depresses photophosphorylation, whereas CO_2 fixation actually proceeds more rapidly in the absence of O_2. Rates under aerobic conditions are shown by solid line and bars. [*Data from D. I. Arnon, M. B. Allen, and F. R. Whatley*, Nature, 174 (*1954*).]**

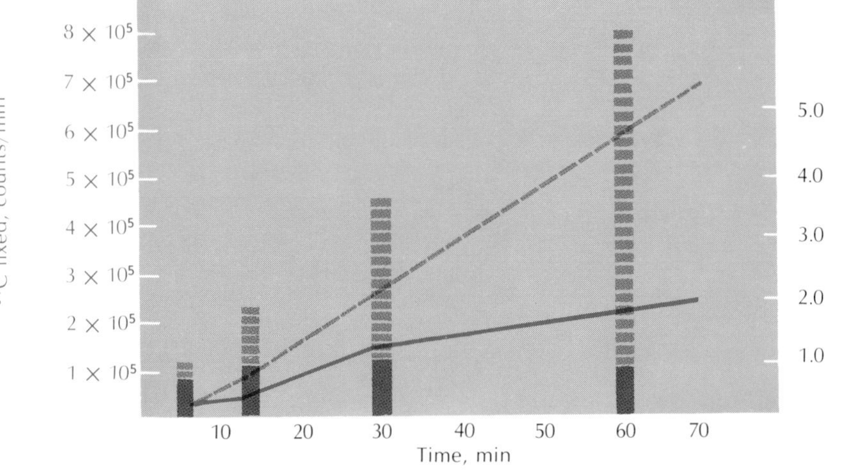

When the cyclic electron-transport systems are in full operation, they may be thought of as "bucket brigades," each carrier simultaneously giving up an electron to the next in line while receiving another electron from the one preceding. By the time a given electron has made a full circuit, it has yielded all of its excess energy to the ADP–ATP system and is ready to return to ground state and occupy its original orbital in the chlorophyll molecule. While adequate light persists, however, the electron does not remain at ground state but, absorbing another photon, jumps to an outer orbital and once again moves along the electron-transfer chain. If needed for the carbohydrate-building process, the excited electron may pass instead into the noncyclic transport chain leading to NADP, and the chlorophyll then makes up its loss by receiving an electron set free during the breakdown of water (Figure 13.9).

In summary, the events of the light reactions appear to be as follows:

1 Water is broken down, with the transfer of 2H per H_2O molecule to enzyme Z, forming the combination ZH_2.

2 The hydrogen atoms dissociate to yield $2e^-$ and $2H^+$; the former pass (directly or indirectly) to chlorophyll *P*680 where they

Figure 13.9 □ **A composite scheme of the events of photosynthesis. Compare with Figures 13.6, 13.7, and 13.10 for details of noncyclic and cyclic electron-transport systems and the Calvin cycle; see text for explanation.**

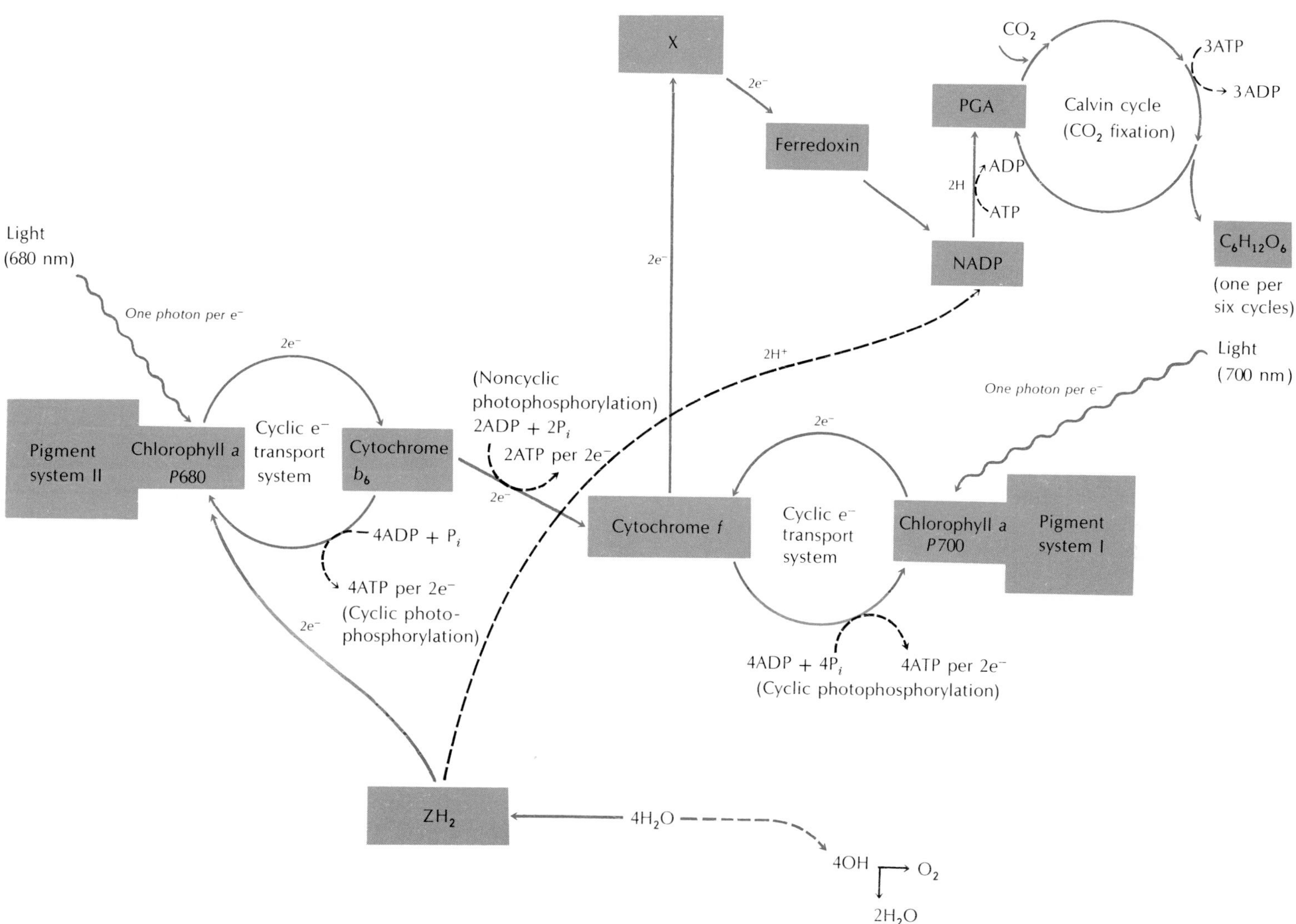

can be energized by the absorption of light; the protons can directly be taken up by $NADP_{red.}$.

3 After $NADP_{red.}$ accepts $2H^+$, it passes two hydrogen atoms (2H) into the dark reactions and is then again reduced by accepting more electrons.

4 NADP receives electrons by way of a noncyclic electron transport pathway leading from water to ferredoxin; since this requires an investment of energy (1.2 eV per electron), the noncyclic system must receive energy from the light-absorbing pigment systems.

5 Two independent light events occur in photosynthesis, one involving chlorophyll *P*680, the other involving *P*700. Absorption of photons of 680-nm light allows *P*680 to donate excited electrons to the noncyclic pathway, as well as building ATP. Absorption of photons of 700-nm light by *P*700 permits this chlorophyll molecule to donate electrons to a cyclic ATP-generating pathway that is energetically coupled to the noncyclic pathway of electron transport and can therefore be called upon to furnish energy to move electrons from cytochrome *f* to X or ferredoxin.

6 Since two such thermodynamic boosts, each equivalent to a photon of red light, are needed to move one from ZH_2 to NADP and since 4H are passed into the dark reactions by $NADPH + H^+$ for each molecule of CO_2 fixed, an investment of 48 photons is required to build one molecule of hexose ($C_6H_{12}O_6$).

7 The dark reactions themselves require energy for the fixation of CO_2; this energy is obtained by the dephosphorylation of ATP built during the light reactions. Cyclic and noncyclic photophosphorylation together furnish enough ATP to power the dark reactions, so that the latter are not dependent upon any energy-mobilizing system located outside the chloroplast. Each cyclic electron transport system can generate 4ATP for every two electrons transported, while the noncyclic pathway can yield 2ATP for every two electrons. In the dark reactions 18ATP must be dephosphorylated to ADP for each molecule of hexose built.

D The dark reactions: the Calvin cycle

The light-dependent phase of photosynthesis terminates with the transfer of hydrogen to NADP. The subsequent reactions, resulting in the fixation of CO_2 and the production of sugar, are not directly light-dependent, although in fact they must cease as soon as the products of the light reactions have been exhausted. The dark reactions involve the addition of CO_2 and hydrogen atoms from $NADPH + H^+$ to a cyclic metabolic pathway in which 3-, 4-, 5-, 6-, and 7-carbon sugars and their phosphate esters are produced (Figure 13.10). The major product to leave this pathway, the Calvin cycle, is the three-carbon sugar *phosphoglyceraldehyde* (PGAL). Some of this triose may be used at once in the cell of its origin, but for storage in the cell's sap vacuole or for transport to other parts of the plant body, most of the PGAL is converted to hexose. This requires a series of reactions in which two PGAL molecules unite to form one molecule of fructose 1,6-diphosphate; the latter molecule gives up a phosphate group to become fructose 6-phosphate, which undergoes rearrangement to become its isomer, glucose 6-phosphate (see Figure 14.43). Glucose ($C_6H_{12}O_6$) is therefore generally considered to be the major product of photosynthesis, although the immediate product is PGAL. Carbohydrate is most commonly stored in plant sap vacuoles or transported through the vascular tissues as the disaccharide sucrose, formed by the dehydration synthesis of one molecule each of glucose and fructose:

$$2C_6H_{12}O_6 \longrightarrow C_{12}H_{22}O_{11} + H_2O$$

A more stable storage product is starch, built up by dehydration synthesis from many glucose units (see Figure 9.7c) and stored as granules within colorless plastids (leucoplasts).

The dark reactions were originally traced by a team of investigators headed by Melvin Calvin. Essentially, the experimental procedure consisted of culturing unicellular algae in a medium to which CO_2 tagged with radioactive ^{14}C was added. Samples of the culture were withdrawn and quickly killed at various intervals following the introduction of the tagged CO_2. The cells were then disrupted and their constituents separated by chromatographic procedures. The compounds containing the tagged CO_2 at any given moment could then be identified by placing a sheet of X-ray film in contact with the chromatogram; spots where the film was exposed represented compounds containing the radioisotope.

By these techniques it was found that in cells killed after only 2-sec exposure to tagged CO_2, the radioactive carbon was concentrated in a single compound, *phosphoglyceric acid* (PGA). If the cells were exposed to tagged CO_2 for as long as 30 sec before fixation, ^{14}C was found already to have been incorporated into many com-

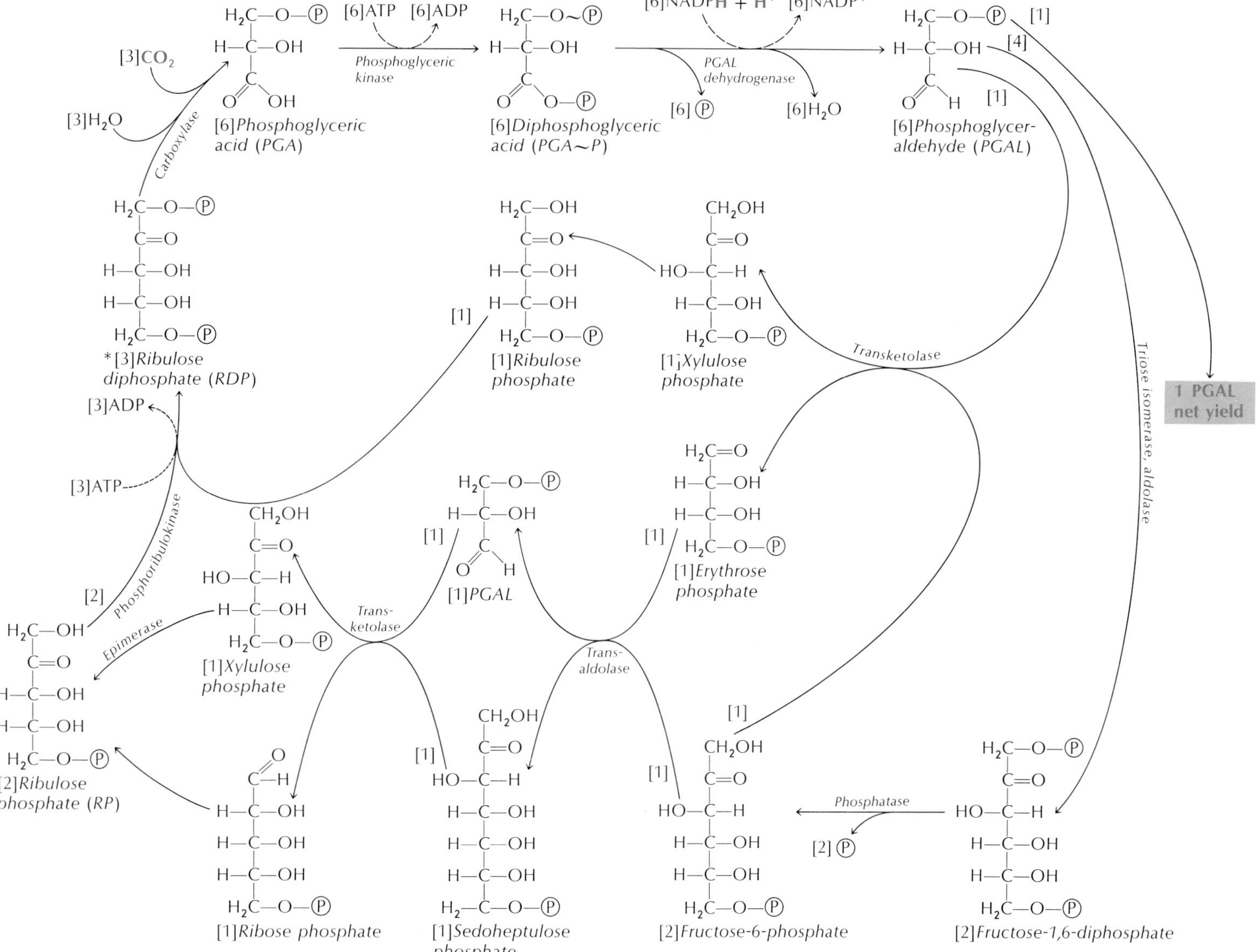

Figure 13.10 □ **Major reactions of the Calvin cycle. Bracketed numerals indicate the number of molecules entering into, or formed by, a reaction; Ⓟ represents organic phosphate group. Note points at which building materials, CO_2 and 2H (in color), enter the cycle. Net product of the cycle is one molecule of the triose PGAL per $3CO_2$ fixed.**

pounds, including amino acids. Most of the study therefore depended upon fixation and analysis of cells that had been permitted to incorporate the tagged CO_2 for less than half a minute!

The reactions involved in the Calvin cycle constitute no less than 10 steps, which can be understood by studying Figure 13.10 along with the following discussion. The 5-carbon sugar *ribulose 1,5-diphosphate* (RDP) can be used as a starting point for studying this cycle, for, in experimental in vitro systems at least, this is the compound with which CO_2 unites to enter the cycle. An unstable intermediate is formed which immediately splits by hydrolysis into two molecules of 3-carbon PGA:

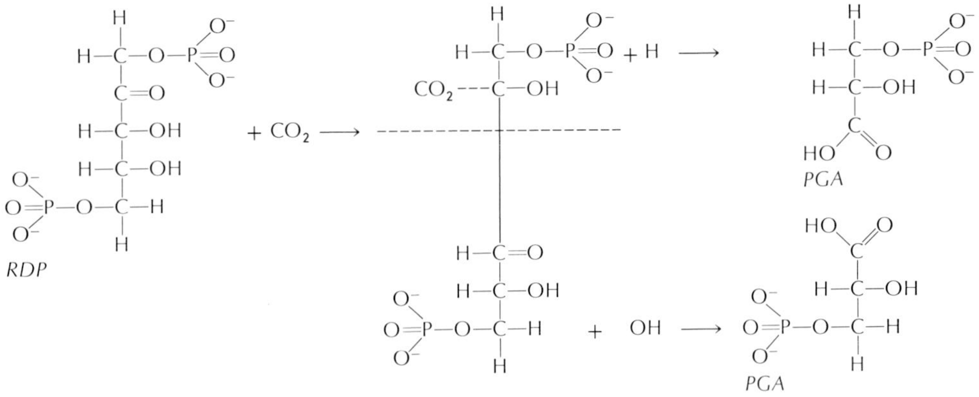

```
         H                               H      O⁻                                H       O⁻
         |      O⁻                       |     /                                  |      /
    H—C—O—P=O                       H—C—O—P=O  + H  ⟶                      H—C—O—P=O
         |      \                        |     \                                  |      \
        C=O     O⁻              CO₂---C—OH     O⁻                            H—C—OH    O⁻
         |                               |                                        |
    H—C—OH          + CO₂ ⟶   ----------+----------                              C
         |                               |                                     HO   \\O
O⁻  H—C—OH                               |                                     PGA
 \       |                               |
O=P—O—C—H                                |                                   HO   O
 /       |                               |                                      \//
O⁻       H                          H—C=O                                        C
RDP                                      |                                        |
                              O⁻    H—C—OH                         O⁻      H—C—OH
                               \         |                          \             |
                              O=P—O—C—H      +   OH   ⟶          O=P—O—C—H
                               /         |                          /             |
                              O⁻         H                         O⁻             H
                                                                   PGA
```

The water used in the hydrolysis of the intermediate to PGA is *not* the source of hydrogen for the Calvin cycle, but is reconstituted and liberated from the cycle at the time of the reduction of PGA to PGAL.

The essential reduction which characterizes the Calvin cycle takes place when PGA, an organic acid, is reduced to the aldehyde PGAL, which as we have said above, is the primary organic product of the cycle. Before this reduction can take place, however, the energy level of PGA must be elevated by phosphorylating it with a second Ⓟ derived from ATP:

PGA + ATP ⟶
PGA~Ⓟ (1,3-diphosphoglyceric acid) + ADP

By reference to Table 13.1 we can see that the phosphorylation of PGA to PGA~Ⓟ raises its energy content from 3,100 to 11,800 cal/mole: a relatively low-energy compound is made reactive by being converted to a high-energy compound. Now, two PGA~Ⓟ molecules each can accept a hydrogen atom from ($NADPH + H^+$) oxidizing this to $NADP^+$ ($NADP_{ox.}$) and using the energy of the phosphate bond to accomplish the reduction. At the same time, water is formed by the combination of hydrogen with the oxygen atom removed from each molecule of PGA~Ⓟ during its reduction to PGAL. Just three reactions constitute the essence of the Calvin cycle:

RDP + CO_2 + H_2O ⟶ 2PGA
PGA + ATP ⟶ PGA~Ⓟ + ADP
PGA~Ⓟ + ($NADPH + H^+$) ⟶
PGAL + Ⓟ + $NADP_{ox.}$ + H_2O

The rest of the cycle is concerned with the regeneration of ribulose 1,5-diphosphate. These regenerative reactions are not unique to photosynthesis, for in reverse they also are found in the pentose phosphate pathway, an important carbohydrate-degrading pathway that we shall study in Chapter 14 (see Figure 14.57). In fact, the essential reduction of PGA to PGAL is exactly reversed in glycolysis, the breakdown of glucose to pyruvate, which we shall also study later. We can see in Figure 13.10 that for every six molecules of PGAL formed by the Calvin cycle, five remain in the cycle and are used to reconstitute ribulose 1,5-diphosphate. If we consider hexose to be the major end-product, the net input and output of six turns of the Calvin cycle can be summarized:

$$6CO_2 + 12(NADPH + H^+) + 18ATP \longrightarrow C_6H_{12}O_6 + 12NADP_{ox.} + 6H_2O + 18ADP + 18P_i$$

The photosynthetic process is one of the cardinal achievements of the living world, an outcome of some 10^9 years of mutation, genetic enrichment, and natural selection. The complex genetic basis of photosynthesis may be perceived if we consider the number of enzymes involved not only directly in the photosynthetic reactions but indirectly in the production of such essential constituents as chlorophyll, ADP, NADP, FMN, vitamin K, ferredoxin, and various accessory but necessary plastid pigments. The Calvin cycle alone involves no less than nine enzymes, each encoded by a separate gene. In the evolution of all of these enzymes, two kinds of selection pressure have operated: one, extrinsic, selecting toward those alleles that brought about the production of compounds most effectively geared for trapping and using energy and matter from the environment; the other, intrinsic, selecting toward enhanced internal coordination of the total process, with persistence of the most economical and expeditious pathways of energy transfer and biosynthesis, and the elimination of those less efficient.

E Factors affecting the rate and efficiency of photosynthesis

Factors that influence the rate and efficiency of photosynthesis include: the intensity and quality (wavelength composition) of light; the availability of water, CO_2, and mineral nutrients; temperature; and certain intrinsic factors. Regardless of the adequacy of other factors, whichever of these is *least* adequate constitutes the *limiting factor* for the entire process. A favorable balance must be maintained between the plant's needs for growth and regeneration and its rate of oxidative metabolism. Unless there is a consistent net gain, growth cannot be sustained. Many species are adapted to conditions under which the rate of photosynthesis is far from maximal; the price of such tolerance is often a slow rate of growth, which may be compensated by longevity.

LIGHT Photosynthesis ceases at night and may be substantially reduced on overcast days. Under experimental conditions, for many plants a maximal rate of photosynthesis is obtained when the intensity of illumination approximates 2,000 ft-c (footcandles), a brightness equivalent to that of full sunlight on a clear day in the temperate zone. Only about 2 percent of the solar energy that reaches the earth's surface is absorbed by plants, the rest being reflected or passing through the foliage without being captured. About 35 percent of light of 685-nm wavelength is trapped and converted to chemical energy, representing in fact a very efficient order of conversion. In addition, a certain amount of light of other wavelengths is absorbed by accessory pigments, these being especially important to seaweeds living at depths where the red light taken up by chlorophyll has been absorbed by the overlying water.

WATER AND MINERALS Land plants obtain and conserve water by various adaptive devices (see Section 4.1). When too little water is present the stomates close, xylem transport nearly comes to a halt, and photosynthesis must soon cease for want of H_2O. (In fact, stomate closure actually limits photosynthesis by depriving the cells of access to CO_2.) Freezing of water prevents its absorption and transport, therefore photosynthesis cannot proceed as long as water is solidly frozen, even though the plant may be evergreen.

Lack of any essential element can derange metabolism and accordingly affect the rate of photosynthesis. In particular, Mg is required for chlorophyll synthesis and severe deficiency may be fatal.

CARBON DIOXIDE For most plants grown under natural conditions, the concentration of atmospheric CO_2 is the effective limiting factor for photosynthesis when light and water are abundant. Photosynthesis is maximized when the concentration of CO_2 is around 0.3 percent, about *eight times* greater than the present average atmospheric concentration (0.044 percent). Even in cities, where the CO_2 concentration averages some 0.1 percent, the level is well below the saturation point for the photosynthetic process. As a matter of conjecture, it is unlikely that photosynthesis could ever be long sustained at its maximal rate even if an adequate amount of CO_2 were initially present. One reason is that such concentrations of CO_2 would create a "greenhouse" effect, which would elevate mean world temperatures. The elevated temperature itself could then become a limiting factor. Also, as the atmospheric concentration of O_2 (a photosynthetic by-product) rises, diffusion of O_2 from the photosynthesizing cells is progressively impeded, thereby slowing down the enzymatic breakdown of water.

TEMPERATURE The optimal temperature range for photosynthesis in a number of plant species tested is about 25 to 30°C, but this range varies according to the native latitudinal distribution of the species. The thermal optimum for the North American potato, for instance, is only 20°C. At temperatures below the optimum, photosynthesis is retarded by the reduction in the kinetic energy of molecules, resulting in a slower rate of exchange between the cells and their environment. Below O°C photosynthesis ceases for want of liquid H_2O. Above the species' thermal optimum, the rate of photosynthesis may for a time be increased but its net yield declines owing to a proportionately greater acceleration of oxidative metabolism (cellular respiration). At still higher temperatures photosynthesis ceases, probably because of the thermolability of vital enzymes.

INTRINSIC FACTORS The molecular machinery of photosynthesis is a product of genetic evolution, and as such is subject to its own inherent limitations. Any genetic defect that prevents the normal synthesis of chlorophyll or of any of the enzymes involved in photosynthesis can result in the death of the organism. "Albinism" in plants is a recessive lethal condition in which no chlorophyll is produced; the seedling dies as soon as its nutritional reserves are depleted.

If all environmental factors are kept at optimal levels, intrinsic limitations to the rate and efficiency of photosynthesis can then be defined. Some of these may reside in the grosser architecture of the plant (for instance, the amount of surface area provided by leaves and roots for the uptake of water and CO_2 and the absorption of light) but the ultimate limitation occurs at the molecular level, and is determined by the length of time required by the *slowest* single reaction in the entire photosynthetic sequence. At lower light intensities the "bottleneck" seems to be one of the light reactions. At higher light intensities, it is one of the dark reactions which limits the rate of photosynthesis. This probably represents the time required for one of the enzymes to unload its substrate. Even this "slowpoke" reaction which retards the whole process takes only 0.01 to 0.02 sec! The entire Calvin cycle can "turn around" once every 0.06 sec. Given this possible maximum rate, it is clear that photosynthesis is more likely to be limited by environmental factors than by intrinsic ones. Intrinsically, photosynthesis is by far the most rapid and efficient photochemical process known.

F Amino acid synthesis in plants

The micronutrient element required by plants in greatest quantity is nitrogen. Its cyclic conversions within the ecosystem should be reviewed (Section 4.3C). Nitrate production is essential for making nitrogen available to most plants. The utilization of nitrate is thought to involve the following conversions, mediated by a series of enzymes (reductases):

$$NO_3^- \xrightarrow[H_2O]{2H} NO_2^- \xrightarrow[H_2O]{2H} \tfrac{1}{2}(N_2O_2^{2-}) \xrightarrow[H^+]{2H} NH_2OH \xrightarrow[H^+ \; H_2O]{2H} NH_4^+$$

The hydrogen needed for these reductions can be obtained from NADPH + H^+. Amino acid synthesis is thought to be closely linked with the basic Calvin cycle of sugar synthesis, and the transfer of H atoms from NADPH + H^+, a common intermediate, to NO_3^- would permit ammonium ion (NH_4^+) to be formed at its site of use. However, conversion of NO_3^- to NH_4^+ and the further conversion of the latter to the amino group ($-NH_2$) of an amino acid also takes place in the roots almost as rapidly as nitrate can be absorbed. The major amino acid first formed in *glutamic acid* (see Table 9.2), which is then transported upward in the xylem to the leaves, where it is used as a source of amino groups for building other amino acids by *transamination*. Incorporation of NH_4^+ into an organic compound is accomplished by the *amination* of an α-keto carboxylic acid [that is, an organic acid bearing an oxygen atom ($=O$) on the α-carbon]:

$$R-\overset{\overset{\displaystyle O}{\|}}{C}-COOH + NH_4^+ \xrightarrow{\text{Dehydrogenase}} R-\underset{\underset{\displaystyle H}{|}}{\overset{\overset{\displaystyle NH_2}{|}}{C}}-COOH + H_2O + H^+$$

Plants can build more than 20 amino acids by transferring $-NH_2$ from glutamic acid to various appropriate α-keto carboxylic acids.

13.5 ☐ HETEROTROPHIC NUTRITION

Heterotrophic organisms include animals and saprophytic or parasitic plants. Heterotrophic plants absorb small organic molecules from the surrounding milieu, often assisting the process by secreting digestive fluids into the medium that bring about the dissolution of solid materials and large molecules. Saprophytes such as most bacteria and fungi are the major agencies of decay and are therefore responsible for the reclamation of much organic material from the bodies of deceased organisms. We shall concern ourselves here mainly with heterotrophic nutrition in animals, for it is in animal life that the need to hunt for food has been translated into form and activity. More than any other selective factor, the loss of the capacity to construct needed organic molecules from universally available inorganic materials has shaped the course of animal evolution, favoring those muta-

Figure 13.11 □ **Disposition of energy content of ingested food. Kilocalorie estimates (derived from data of Brody) indicate that only about 50 percent of the energy taken in is actually available for growth and maintenance. The proportions of net energy used for maintenance, growth, and storage vary with age, amount of exercise, and other factors. (*Specific dynamic action*, mentioned in this analysis, is the stimulation of exergonic metabolism that accompanies the digestive process and is required to furnish energy for muscular contractions of the gut and other digestive processes.)**

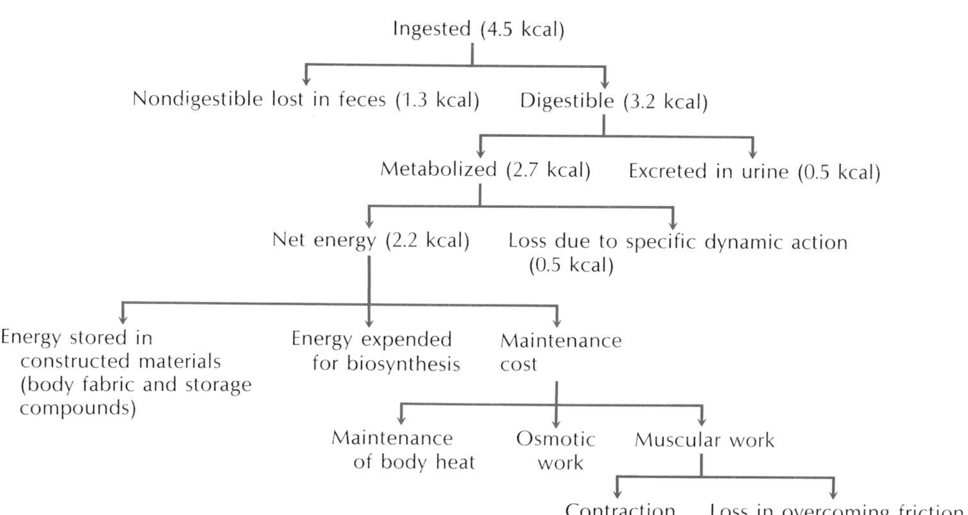

tions which enhance the efficiency of perception and motor response. Location, ingestion, and digestion of nutrients, the major tasks of animal existence, are generally foreign to plant life. Furthermore, utilization of materials for growth is less efficient in animals than in plants, for not only is a proportion lost through the inefficiency of the digestive process, but a high toll must be paid in the energy expended in hunting for food and digesting it. An analysis of the fate of ingested nutrients (with proportions reckoned in kilocalories per gram), shows that only half of the ingested food is available to provide free energy, and of this amount over one third is consumed as maintenance cost (Figure 13.11). At the very most, an estimated *one-sixth* of the nutrients taken in are converted into new organic material, the rest being lost or oxidized to provide energy needed for all cell functions. However, we have seen earlier that generally the net ecological efficiency of animal species is actually only around 10 percent (see Section 6.2D).

A Food selection

Chemical senses (taste and olfaction or their equivalents) are most universally employed in food detection. More recently evolved (and hence less universal) receptors such as ears and image-forming eyes usually assist the food-hunting process only in the terminal stages, after the initial gap has been closed by response to chemical cues.

Most animals display both a *qualitative* and a *quantitative* appetite, which determine food selection and the amount ingested over a particular period of time. Even

Amoeba has been found to favor prey of particular species, turning to less preferred kinds only when these have been depleted.

Qualitative appetite serves to correct nutritional deficiencies. Specific cravings are evoked by need for water, protein, fat, carbohydrate, salt, calcium, and so forth. A need for salt drives herbivorous mammals to travel long distances to salt licks, where their need for these ions can be satisfied. Starvation overrides normal qualitative discrimination so that normally distasteful or toxic materials may be ingested. *Quantitative* appetite determines the average amount of food eaten. In nature few animals become obese, except as a temporary condition related to specific prehibernatory, premigratory, or reproductive physiological states. Unfortunately, obesity is a problem in man, particularly when the normal cues of qualitative and quantitative appetite are subverted by artificial circumstances, such as the addition of flavorful extracts to relatively worthless material. Furthermore, according to A. E. Needham,*

The preservation and processing of human food therefore has introduced a great nutritional danger since it may destroy differentially a few components in the stable foods, leaving them almost as palatable as when fresh, but possibly inferior in nutritive value. Moreover when the resulting deficiency does find expression in an appetite demand, this is quite likely to be for the same food—because in its natural state it would have supplied the components which are now lacking. The unbalance therefore is further exacerbated, since the components which are present increase the requirement for the others and a vicious circle is established. . . . On the other hand, some foods possibly lose more in "palate" than in nutritive value by processing, and this again may adversely affect the wisdom of quality choice.

* *The Growth Process in Animals* (Princeton, N.J.: D. Van Nostrand Company, Inc., 1964), p. 283.

The evolution of *palatability* is a topic of interest. It is not usually to the particular benefit of the eaten that its flesh be palatable to the eater; edible fruits are an exception to this, for it is thus that seeds may be carried far from the parent plant. Generally, we must assume the obverse: it is to the benefit of the *consumer* that its system of taste values correlate with nutritional worth and lack of toxicity. A "good flavor" normally leads to the ingestion of an appropriate food item, while a "bad taste" discourages intake of noxious materials. Occasionally, a species may subsist upon only one particular kind of food organism, which it appears to select instinctually. However, such selectivity may sometimes be based upon prior experience. A female butterfly, for instance, may lay her eggs only upon plants of the particular species on which she herself was reared, even though she belongs to a species having a wider host-plant selectivity. Specialization of food demands is ecologically significant, for by such diversification heterospecific competition in the community is alleviated. Nevertheless, some *omnivorous* animals display considerable versatility of appetite (Figure 13.12).

Figure 13.12 □ **Diet of an omnivore: stomach contents of racoons taken during fall and winter months in New York. The diet varies seasonally according to food items available and their ease of procurement. [*After W. J. Hamilton, Jr.,* American Mammals *(New York: McGraw-Hill Book Company, Inc., 1939).*]**

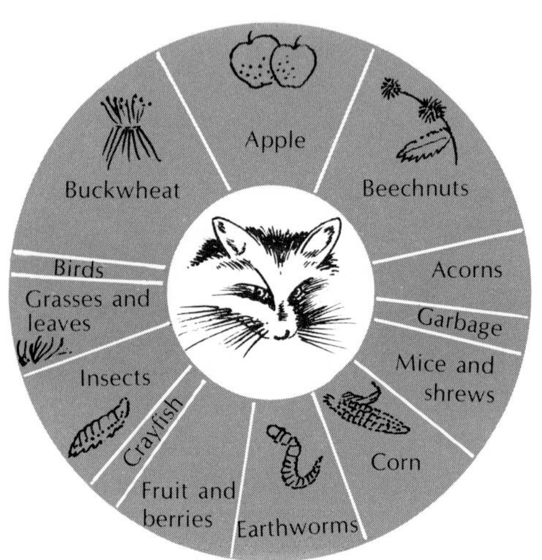

B Feeding mechanisms

These may be categorized according to the *texture* of the materials ingested: they may be composed of liquid or soft material, small particles, or large particles.

Figure 13.13 □ Saprophagous animals. (*a*) Sea cucumber, *Cucumaria frondosa*, a detritus feeder, is nourished by organic debris ingested in mud and sand. (*Courtesy of Carolina Biological Supply Company.*) (*b*) Silphid beetle larva feeding on carrion. The abdominal cavity of the dead rodent has been opened to show the large beetle larva feeding on the decaying tissue. This larva hatched from an egg laid upon the freshly dead mammal. (*Los Angeles County Museum of Natural History.*)

(*a*)

(*b*)

Animals that feed upon *liquids or soft materials* include detritus feeders and saprozoites, which ingest dead and decomposing materials (Figure 13.13), parasites, and certain predators which only suck out the soft tissues and body fluids of their prey (Figure 13.14). Ectoparasites [including fleas, aphids, true bugs (hemipterans), ticks, and leeches] possess mouthparts adapted for piercing the host's integument and withdrawing fluids. Endoparasites either may ingest blood or other soft tissues of their hosts or may directly absorb organic molecules from the intestinal contents or tissue fluids. Predators that only suck out the blood or soft tissues of their prey and discard the rest include most spiders, which lack chewing apparatus and must pierce the prey with venomous fangs and then withdraw the body contents by powerful contractions of a "sucking stomach," leaving only a shrivelled husk. The formidable stylet of the giant water bug is as long as the insect's entire body and may be used to kill prey even larger than the bug itself, following which the stylet serves to withdraw the victim's body fluids (Figure 13.14*b*).

Animals feeding upon solid particles much smaller than their own size (which they usually swallow whole) must feed almost continually, employing some type of *filter-feeding* device that concentrates large numbers of particles. These devices include structural sieves, ciliary traps, and mucus traps. *Structural sieves* are formed by such parts of the body as the pharynx, body wall, or appendages. They form a mesh that traps particles (usually plankton) of optimal size, while allowing smaller ones to escape and simultaneously excluding items too large to be handled. Structural sieves include the

Figure 13.14 □ **Animals that feed on blood and body fluids. (*a*) Section through anterior end of hookworm (*Ancylostoma*), showing worm sucking blood from intestinal villus, the tip of which has been chewed away. As a microscopic larva, this centimeter-long nematode enters the body by burrowing through the thin skin between the toes; like the North American hookworm (*Necator*) it can cause severe anemia in the host. (*Ward's Natural Science Establishment, Inc.*) (*b*) Giant water bug sucking on 20-cm water snake that it has killed with its piercing stylet. (*Courtesy of Dr. Ross E. Hutchins.*) (*c*) Lamprey feeding on whitefish. When satiated, the lamprey will release its host, leaving a circular wound at the point of attachment. The host usually is killed only if the rasping teeth of the lamprey penetrate the entire thickness of the body wall and perforate the coelom. (*U.S. Fish and Wildlife Service.*)**

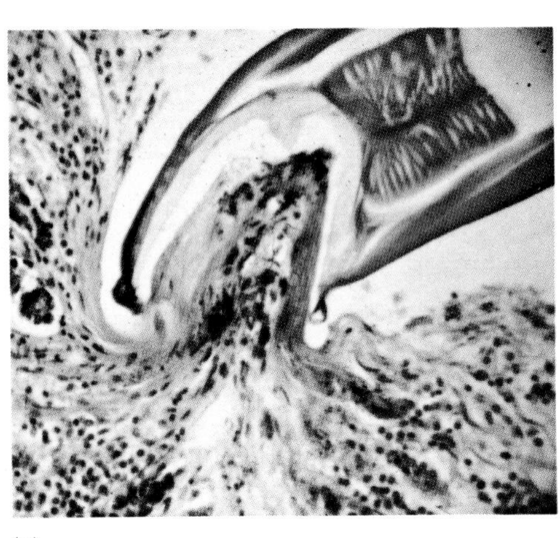

(*a*)

(*b*)

(*c*)

whalebone plates of baleen whales, which are fringed along the edges so that shrimp-like crustaceans taken in with a mouthful of water will be kept in the mouth while the water is pushed out with the tongue. Pharyngeal filters of mosquito larvae (Figure 13.15*a*,*b*), tunicates (see Figure 2.43), and amphioxus (see Figure 2.44), are also used in filter feeding, as are the fringed appendages of barnacles (Figure 13.15c).

Ciliary traps for food collection are often used by sedentary animals to collect microscopic food particles. Currents of water set up by the beating of cilia or flagella provide a constant supply of microorganisms; in the case of sponges these are then ingested by individual cells, whereas in higher animals such as clams the particles are trapped in mucus and swept toward the mouth by ciliary action. Bivalves combine breathing with feeding: the cilia covering the gills maintain a flow of water that enters through the incurrent siphon, passes over the gills, and is expelled by way of the excurrent siphon (Figure 13.16); during this process particles are caught in the mucus covering the gills and are then carried forward to the mouth by the beating of cilia. In similar fashion, ciliated grooves and channels converge toward the mouths of coelenterates, echinoderms, and other animals that may combine filter feeding with the ingestion of much larger food items.

Mucus traps are used by certain tube-dwelling animals such as the worm *Urechis* (see Figure 6.2) and the tube snail, *Serpulorbis,* which do not depend on ciliary action but instead secrete long strands of slime that are later pulled in and eaten together with whatever organic material has become ensnared within them.

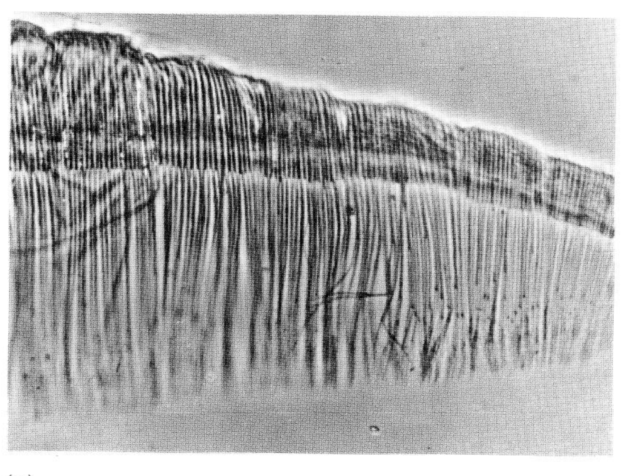

(a)

(b)

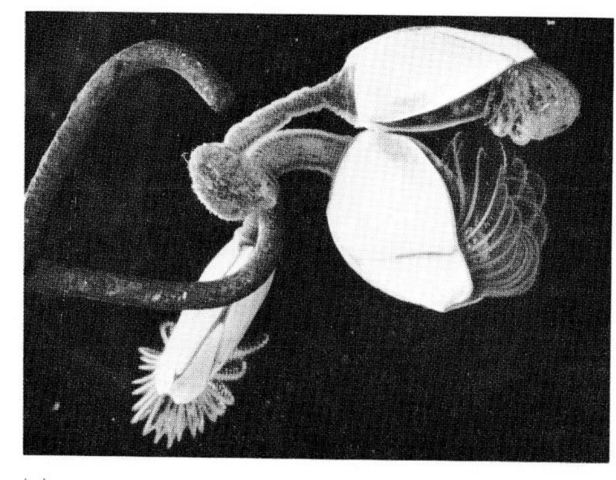

(c)

Figure 13.15 □ Filter-feeding devices. Food comb (*a*) and food brush (*b*) from pharyngeal filter of mosquito larva. (*Courtesy of Thomas Eisner.*) (*c*) Goose barnacle, showing legs extended for feeding. As the legs are rhythmically extended and retracted, planktonic organisms are trapped by the chitinous bristles borne on the legs that form a food-trapping basket. (*Scripps Institution of Oceanography.*)

Figure 13.16 □ Ciliary feeding in a clam: (*a*) constant beating of the cilia clothing the mantle and gills draws water in through the incurrent siphon and drives it out the excurrent siphon; meanwhile, food particles, primarily plankton, are trapped in mucus on the gills and are carried forward to the mouth by the beating of other cilia. The feeding current also serves to aerate the gills. (*b*) Cross section of clam. (*c*) Section through portion of gill.

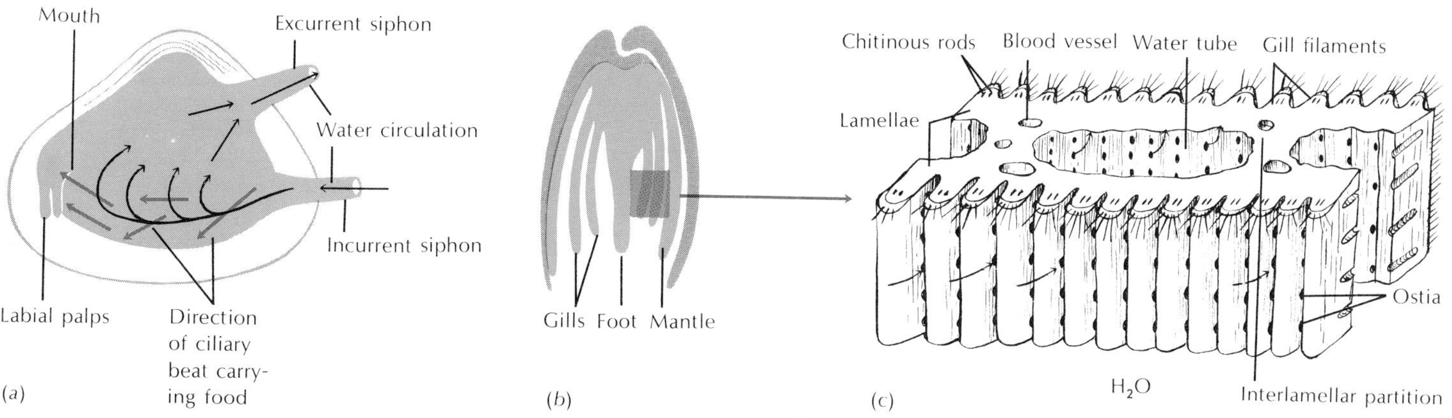

(a)

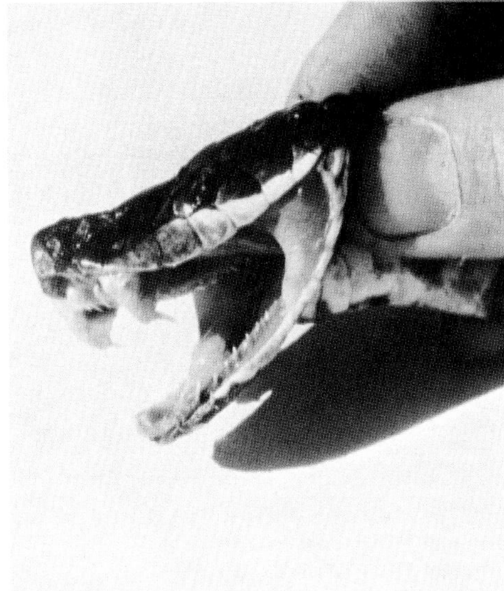

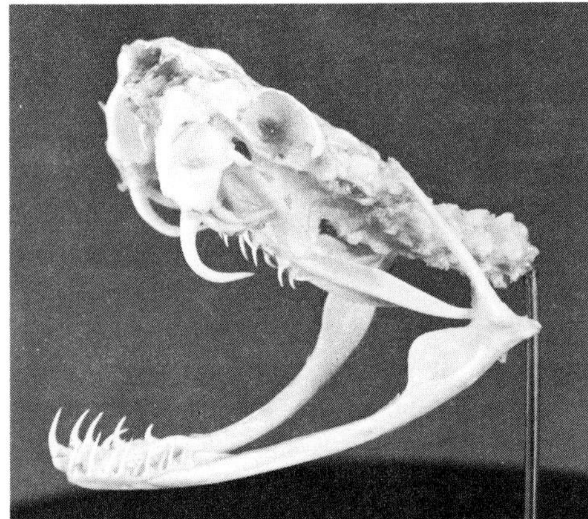

(b)

Most kinds of animals do not rely on filter feeding but ingest relatively large food items, which they may either swallow entire or may first reduce to morsels of suitable size for ingestion. Examples of such feeding are too numerous and diverse to list here. The ability to devour large food items is adaptive in that feeding need only be intermittent: one item may suffice for some time. Remarkably ambitious in this regard is the small egg-eating snake *Dasypeltis* (Figure 13.17*a*), whose impressive performance depends on its unusually distensible jaws and long, pointed vertebral processes that crack the shell when the egg is far enough back so that its contents will run down the throat. The pharyngeal muscles then crush the egg and the shell is spat out. Snakes that eat prey less passive than eggs often kill first by constriction or venom (Figure 13.17*b*).

Raptorial animals (those which capture

Figure 13.17 □ Feeding adaptations of snakes. (*a*) Three stages in the ingestion of a whole egg by the egg-eating snake *Dasypeltis scabra.* Elastic ligaments permit the upper and lower jaws to spread apart and the right and left halves of each jaw to be separated, facilitating ingestion of large food items without chewing. When the egg is well back in the throat, spines at the back of the pharynx break its tip; the throat muscles then contract, crushing the shell, while the contents run down the snake's gullet; the shell fragments are then disgorged. (*Zoological Society of San Diego photos by J. H. Tashjian.*) (*b*) Pit vipers ingest their prey (usually rodents) entire but first kill it by means of venom injected through the hollow fangs that fold back against the roof of the mouth when not in use. Above is a water moccasin (*Agkistrodon piscivorous*), which feeds upon rodents and fish. Below is a rattlesnake skull (*Crotalus*); note jaw modifications for support and fang movement. (*Courtesy of Carolina Biological Supply Company.*)

and devour other animals) require means of subduing their prey—claws, teeth, venom, tentacles, and so forth; these are not needed by herbivores, which feed on plants and mainly require means of rasping or grinding the vegetable materials to free the digestible matter from the indigestible cellulose cell walls.

Anemones and jellyfish capture their prey with nematocyst-armed tentacles and swallow it entire. Nemerteans also swallow their prey whole, but capture it by means of the long eversible proboscis characteristic of members of this phylum (see Figure 2.27). Such advanced predators as octopus combine several means of subduing prey; for instance, the tentacles may seize a crab, its exoskeleton will then be pierced by the rasping buccal organ (the radula) or be crushed by the beaklike jaws, and a paralytic salivary venom will be injected into the wound. After the venom has taken effect, jaws, tentacles, and radula are employed in dextrously dismembering, rending, and crushing the victim.

A starfish approaches the problem of predation differently, using its tubefeet to

Figure 13.18 ☐ **Invertebrate marine carnivores.** (*a*) **An arrow worm (Phylum Chaetognatha),** ***Sagitta hexaptera,*** **a planktonic carnivore only 1 to 2 cm long that feeds upon animals up to its own size.** (***Courtesy of Dr. A. Alvariño de Leira and Scripps Institution of Oceanography.***) (*b*) **Starfish,** ***Asterias forbesi,*** **a benthonic carnivore, here shown opening a bivalve shell by means of its tube feet.** (***Courtesy of General Biological, Inc., Chicago.***)

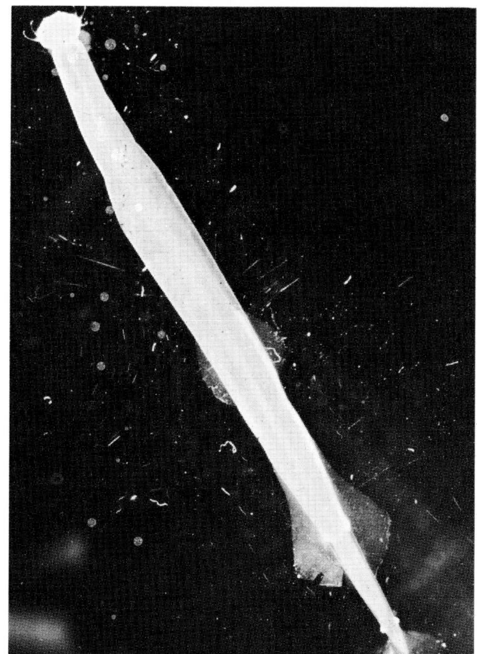

(*a*)

(*b*)

(*a*)

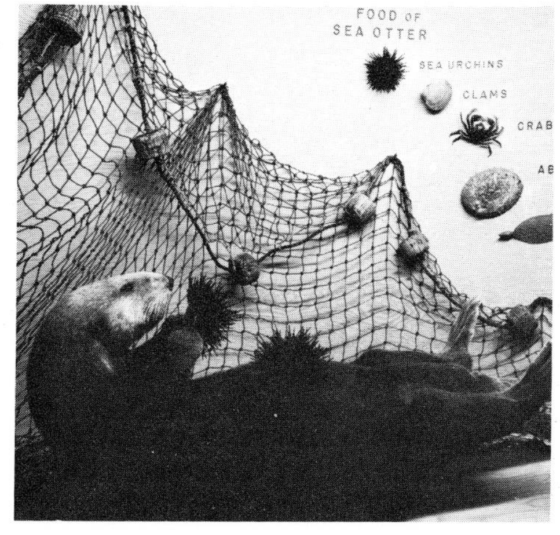

(*b*)

Figure 13.19 ☐ **Vertebrate marine carnivores.** (*a*) **A trained female killer whale, Shamu, 1,600 kg and 5 m long, performs a leap for which she will be rewarded by receiving a fish. Killer whales feed upon fish, seals, and porpoises and in packs may attack even much larger baleen whales.** (***Courtesy of Sea World.***) (*b*) **Museum exhibit of sea otter in preferred feeding position, with a sea urchin, a dietary staple, balanced on abdomen while a second urchin is being held in the paws before consumption. The otter may employ stones brought from the bottom to break the urchin shells. Other dietary items are displayed behind.** (***San Diego Natural History Museum.***)

Figure 13.20 □ Evolutionary trends in digestion: (*a*) intracellular digestion is exemplified by protozoans and poriferans; (*b*) extracellular digestion, within a saccular digestive tract, is shown by coelenterates; (*c*) nemerteans have a tubular digestive tract and separate the digestive and distributive functions; (*d*) a regionalized digestive tract with the development of intrinsic gut musculature is characteristic of the annelids; (*e*) lower vertebrates show an increase in length and surface area of the digestive tract and the development of accessory organs (teeth, digestive glands, and the like); (*f*) in the higher vertebrates, the digestive processes are regulated by the neuroendocrine system, and there is a diversification of dentition.

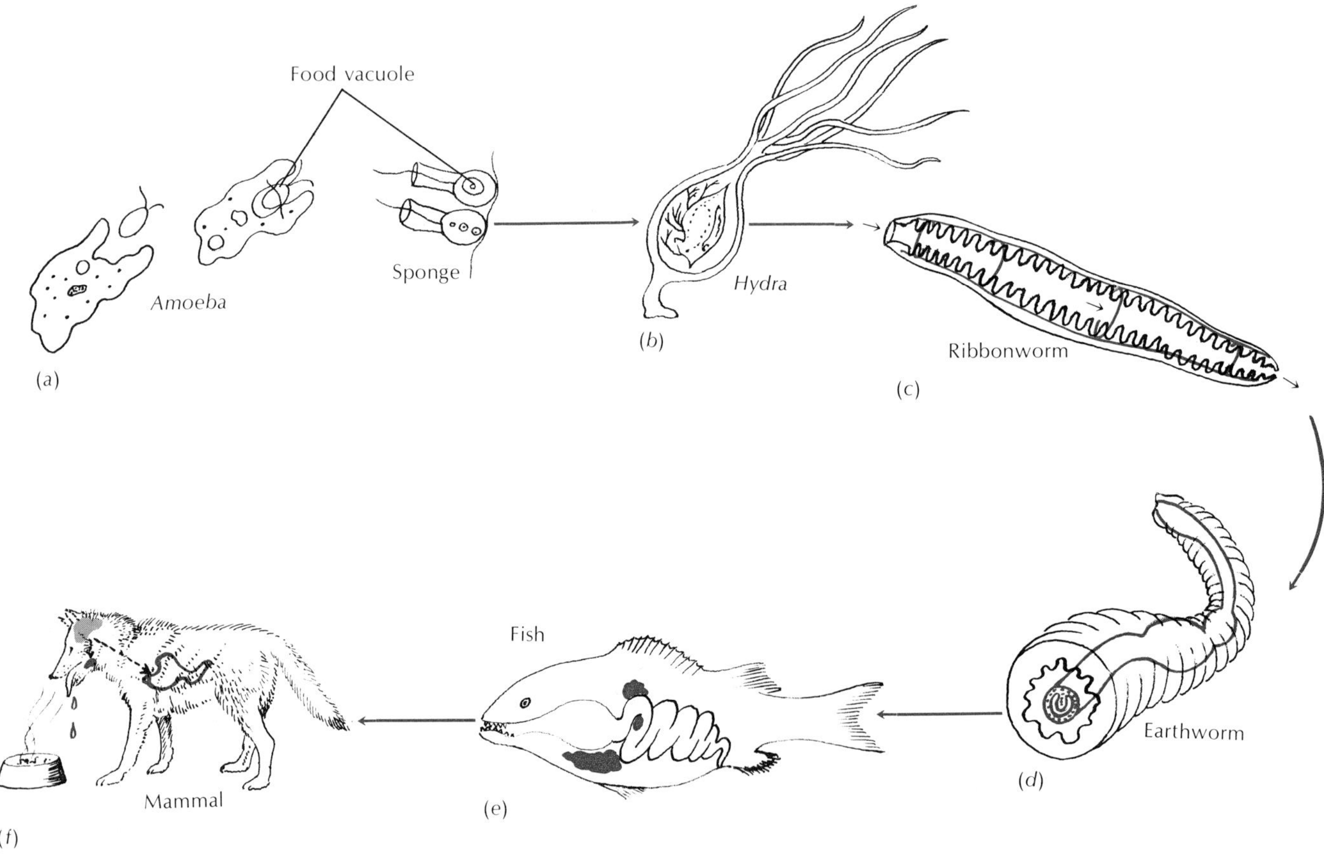

open the valves of a mollusc, and then inserting its stomach through the aperture to digest the unfortunate creature on the half-shell (so to speak).

In Figures 13.18 and 13.19 we see a variety of carnivores of the marine community, invertebrate and vertebrate. One of the largest of raptorial animals, the killer whale—a mammal that is itself virtually exempt from predation by others—is shown executing a leap for which she will be rewarded by receiving a fish from her trainer. Killer whales also eat seals and in packs may even attack the much larger baleen whales. We should recall that in any community, marine, freshwater, or terrestrial, the peak of the biomass pyramid of matter and energy conversion (see Figure 6.7) is occupied by a relatively few species of such ultimate predators—carnivores that rarely succumb to the attacks of other predators but usually must endure the encroachment of parasites; ultimately, of course, they are fated to appear on the menu of scavengers and decay organisms.

C Digestion

The digestive process is basically the same throughout the animal world: ingested material must be pulverized and liquefied and its larger molecules broken down. Similar hydrolytic enzymes that break down carbohydrates, lipids, and proteins occur almost universally, but the *structural* equipment involved in digestion varies. Several evolutionary trends may be detected by comparative study of the digestive apparatus of animals of different phyla (Figure 13.20). These trends include:

1 A change from *intracellular* digestion to *extracellular* digestion.

2 A shift from *saccular* digestive tracts with only one orifice to *tubular* tracts with both mouth and anus.

3 *Separation of digestive and distributory functions,* so that the digestive tract is concerned only with digestion, while distribution of digested nutrients becomes a function of a circulatory system.

4 With the development of the coelom, the acquisition of an *intrinsic gut musculature,* followed by a functional and morphological *regionalization* within the digestive tract.

5 *Increase in surface area* for secretion of enzymes and absorption of the products of digestion.

6 *Development of accessory structures* that improve the efficiency of the digestive tract, including structures for pulverizing the food (teeth, radula, and such) and special digestive glands (liver, pancreas, and the like).

7 Development of *hormonal regulatory mechanisms* that coordinate digestive activities (see Section 15.4C).

INTRACELLULAR AND EXTRACELLULAR DIGESTION Protozoa and sponges lack a digestive cavity and rely exclusively on intracellular digestion. Most coelenterates combine extracellular and intracellular digestion, beginning the process in the gastrovascular cavity and completing it within the gastrodermal cells.

For digestion within the individual cell the morsels are enclosed within a food vacuole or *phagosome,* an invagination of the plasma membrane that pinches off and circulates freely in the cytoplasm (Figure 13.21). Digestive enzymes pass into the phagosomes from lysosomes that fuse with the vacuolar membrane. As hydrolysis proceeds, digested materials pass through the vacuolar membrane into the cytoplasm, whereas the indigestible residue is subsequently extruded through the plasma membrane.

Planarians combine extracellular *mechanical* digestion with intracellular *chemical* digestion. The food—dead animal tissue or living prey—is first mechanically disrupted by strong sucking actions of the proboscis and is then drawn into the multibranched gastrovascular cavity as tiny fragments that are engulfed by phagocytic cells lining the cavity. Other nonparasitic flatworms have a distensible ruffled pharynx that allows prey to be swallowed whole and then to be attacked chemically in the gastrovascular cavity prior to final intracellular digestion.

Extracellular digestion allows the animal to make use of food particles of greater-than-cellular dimensions. This augments nutritional efficiency, for fewer items need be captured and ingested. The most primitive digestive cavities are the saccular gastrovascular cavities of coelenterates and flatworms, which may be either simple or much branched. These cavities serve for both digestion and distribution, blood vessels being absent.

Most metazoans have complete tubular digestive tracts, extending from the anterior mouth to a posterior anus; this is an efficacious arrangement permitting ingestion, digestion, and elimination to proceed simultaneously.

From its primitive condition as a simple linear tube (as seen in ribbonworms and nematodes), the digestive tract has evolved

Figure 13.21 □ **Intracellular digestion. Phagosomes (food vacuoles) within cytoplasm of living *Paramecium.* Solid food within the vacuoles appears dark; pale phagosomes are those in which digestion is advanced, the food having been liquefied by means of enzymes secreted into the phagosomes.**

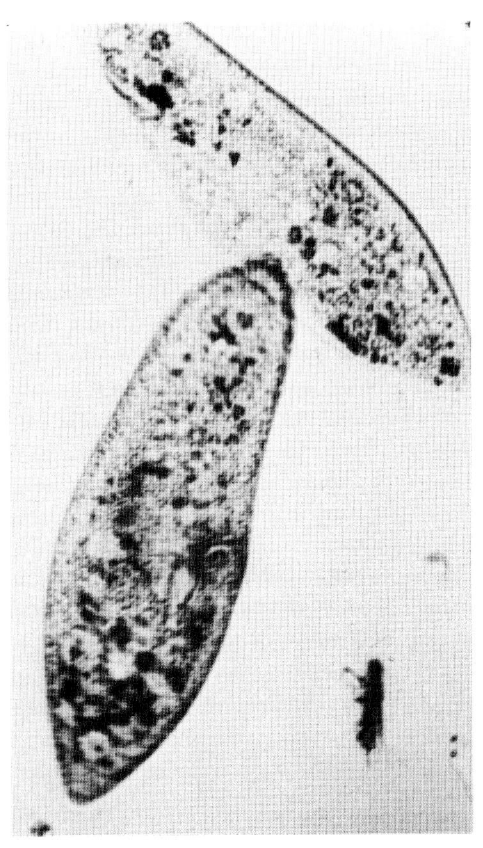

toward *regionalization,* with different functions being assumed by different parts of the tract. This regionalization has been abetted by the development of the involuntary musculature of the gut wall, such as is found in all eucoelomate animals. Gut motility is neurally controlled and several types of contraction are typical. *Peristalsis* is a propagated wave of alternate contraction and relaxation moving posteriorly along the tract; it is opposed by localized contractions that impede the onward movement of the food and mix it with secretions. Circular muscle bands (*sphincters*) retain the food within particular portions of the tract, for storage or prolonged digestion. In vertebrates the *pyloric sphincter* guards the posterior end of the stomach and the *anal sphincter* constricts the anus, retaining material within the colon. The *ileocolic valve* separates the mammalian small and large intestines, preventing backflow of colonic contents.

Analogous or homologous regionalization of the digestive tube is common among the eucoelomate phyla, the regions, from anterior to posterior, being the *mouth, buccal cavity, pharynx, esophagus, stomach, intestine,* and *anus* (see Figure 12.27). The anterior part of the tube (*foregut*) is usually primarily concerned with *mechanical* digestion, the middle portion (*midgut*), with *chemical* digestion, and the posterior part (*hindgut*), with *absorption* of nutrients and also with *concentration of residues* before defecation.

The alimentary tubes of higher metazoans are associated with various accessory organs. Those that assist mechanical digestion are located in or near the mouth, and include such structures as *teeth, tongue, feeding appendages,* and *salivary glands. Skeletal muscles* associated with the jaws and tongue assist mastication. The midgut often receives ducts of accessory *glands* that produce secretions facilitating chemical digestion; in vertebrates these glands include the *liver* and *pancreas.* The vertebrate liver is functionally versatile, but its major contribution to the digestive process is the production of *bile,* a complex mixture of metabolic wastes and steroid salts that assists in fat digestion. The pancreas is a source of several major hydrolases, which are released into the duodenum, the first portion of the small intestine.

The wall of the alimentary tube itself is richly grandular and much of its epithelial lining is elaborated into tubular pits that secrete enzyme-containing digestive juices. Such glands are particularly abundant in the stomach and duodenum. The *gastric glands* of mammals mainly secrete pepsin and dilute HCl, whereas the *duodenal glands* produce an alkaline fluid containing a variety of hydrolases as well as several substances that activate the pancreatic proenzymes.

In cross section, the vertebrate gut displays several distinct layers (Figure 13.22). The outer surface is covered by a thin epithelial *serosa,* continuous with the mesenteries. Just within the serosa is a layer of *longitudinal muscle* fibers, the long axes of which are roughly parallel with the length of the digestive tube. Interior to these is a layer of *circular muscle* fibers, wrapping the tube in a close spiral. Nerve fibers controlling these muscle layers form a network (plexus) between them. Additional muscle layers are present in the stomach. The muscle layers enclose a *submucosa* of scat-

Figure 13.22 □ **Microscopic anatomy of vertebrate small intestine. (*a*) Cross section of amphibian intestine (duodenum), showing several villi. (*Ward's Natural Science Establishment, Inc.*) (*b*) Portion of intestinal mucosa showing goblet cells (mucus-secreting cells) and basement membrane. (*Courtesy of Carolina Biological Supply Company*) (*c*) Detail of section through intestinal gland (jejunum), showing secretory cells containing zymogen (inactive enzyme) granules and large, pale droplets of mucus. (*Courtesy of General Biological, Inc., Chicago.*) (*d*) In submucosa, four Peyer's patches, lymph nodules that destroy bacteria that may penetrate the mucosa. (*Ward's Natural Science Establishment, Inc.*)**

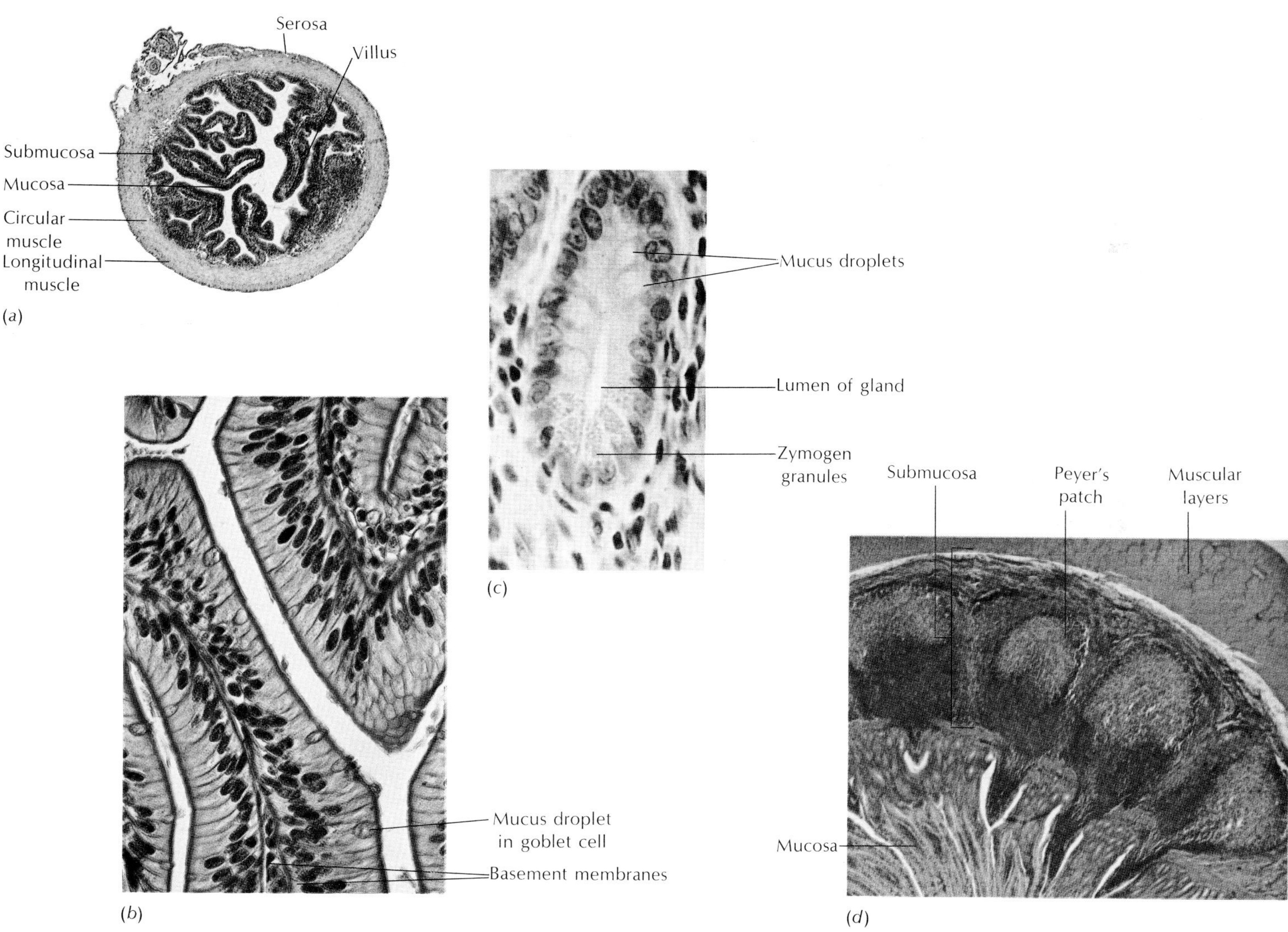

Figure 13.23 □ Comparison of length of gut in (*a*) tadpole (herbivorous) and (*b*) adult frog (carnivorous), demonstrating tendency for the alimentary tract of a herbivore to be distinctly more lengthy than that of a carnivore.

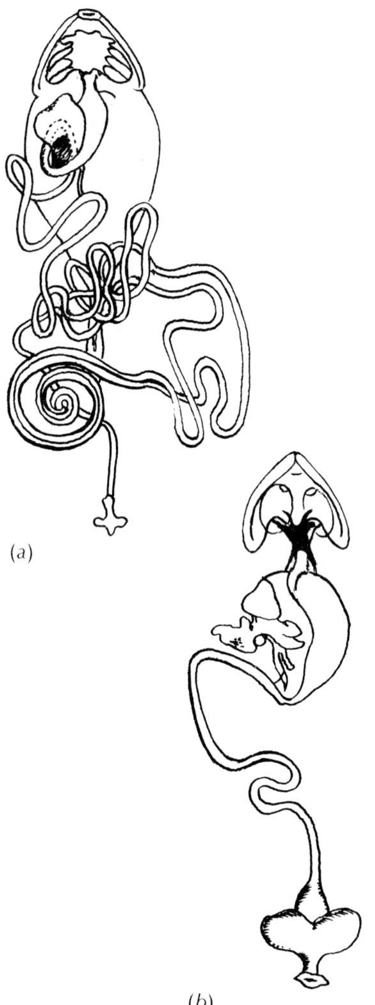

tered connective tissue and muscle fibers, interpenetrated by blood vessels. In the large intestine lymphoid nodules containing concentrations of defensive cells occur in the submucosa where they serve to destroy bacteria that may penetrate the intestinal lining (Figure 13.22*d*). The *mucosa* (innermost layer of the alimentary tube) consists of an epithelium, commonly columnar, underlain by loose (alveolar) connective tissue and a thin muscle layer (muscularis mucosae). The tubular mucosal glands penetrate far into the submucosa. Many cells of the mucosal epithelium secrete lubricative mucus.

The surface area available for secretion and absorption can be increased in coelomate animals by the lengthening of the entire alimentary tube, for this can coil upon itself within the body cavity. The total length of the tube correlates with diet, carnivorous animals usually having a considerably shorter tract than related herbivorous species. A marked shortening of the gut takes place when the vegetarian tadpole changes into the adult frog (Figure 13.23). Surface area can be further augmented by internal folding and protrusion of the mucosa. The mucosa of the vertebrate small intestine bears a large number of fingerlike or leaf-shaped *villi* barely detectable to the unaided eye (Figure 13.24a). In addition, the free surface of the mucosal epithelium is clothed with *microvilli* individually discernible only by electron microscopy (Figure 13.24*b*, c). This large surface area is needed to handle the heavy molecular traffic of digested materials that pass through the plasma membranes of the mucosal cells.

In vertebrates the hindgut consists of the small intestine posterior to the duodenum and a more or less clearly demarcated colon, which terminates in a rectum or cloaca. The mixing of food with duodenal and pancreatic secretions continues as it passes along the length of the small intestine, the products of digestion being absorbed through the mucosal lining. By the time the material enters the colon it consists primarily of indigestible residues, sloughed cells, bacteria, and bile. Water is absorbed from the fecal material while this is held in the colon, where colonic bacteria act upon the residues, producing certain vitamins that are absorbed by the host. Herbivorous mammals feature a large storage chamber, the *cecum,* at the anterior end of the colon, within which cellulose-containing residues are acted upon by bacteria, with further recovery of carbohydrate by absorption of sugars through the cecal mucosa (Figure 13.25). The cecum is vestigial in man and is mainly represented by the apparently nonfunctional *appendix.*

MECHANICAL DIGESTION By a process of *mechanical digestion* food is reduced from a solid to a liquid state without being molecularly altered. Mechanical digestion makes available for immediate absorption those small molecules (such as vitamins, simple sugars, and mineral salts) which need no further reduction in size before being absorbed and distributed to the tissues. This process also exposes to the action of digestive enzymes those larger molecules which require hydrolysis prior to absorption. Thorough mechanical digestion is needed for processing uncooked plant material, owing to the indigestibility of cellulose.

The varied diet of omnivores such as

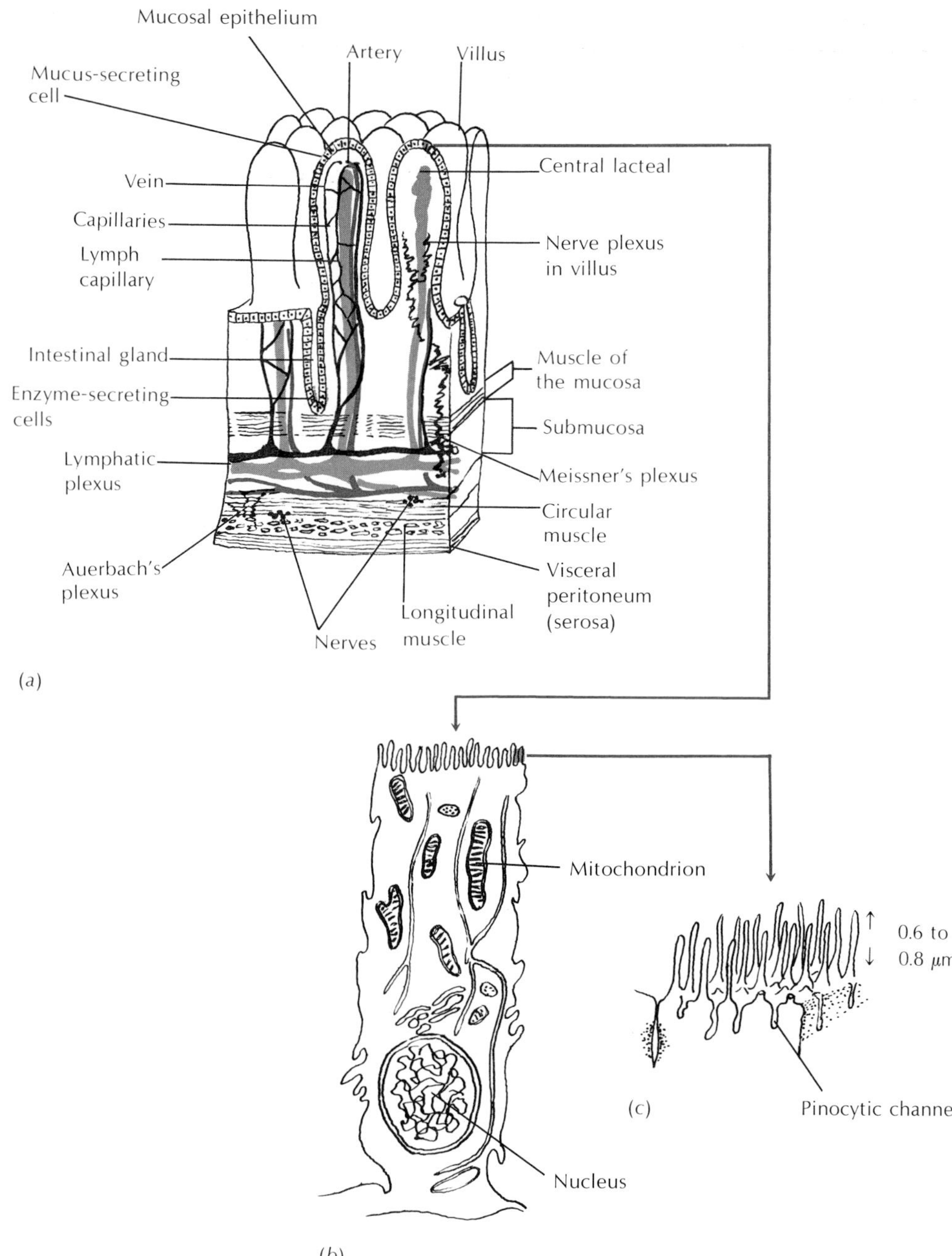

Figure 13.24 □ Adaptations for increased surface area of the lining of the vertebrate small intestine. (*a*) Three-dimensional representation of intestinal wall, showing villi and intestinal glands. (*b*) Single cell of mucosal epithelium, with microvilli that increase free-end surface area. (*c*) Enlargement of microvilli. An individual lining cell may bear 3,000 microvilli; there may be 2×10^8 microvilli per square millimeter of intestinal surface (see also Figure 14.8).

man requires *dental diversification* so that both plant and animal materials may be adequately masticated (Figure 13.26). The mammalian tooth types, all present in man, are cutting *incisors,* tearing *canines,* and grinding *premolars* and *molars.* Many vertebrates constantly replace worn teeth (the shark, for instance; see Figure 12.38), but in mammals there is only partial tooth replacement: they have two basic sets—one deciduous, the other permanent—and the two sets do not usually contain the same number of teeth. The human deciduous set totals 20: 8 incisors, 4 canines, and 8 premolars. These are shed and replaced gradually by the permanent set consisting of 8 incisors, 4 canines, 8 premolars, and 12 molars. This total of 32 is 12 less than the supposed primitive eutherian dentition which includes 12 incisors, 4 canines, 16 premolars and 12 molars, as seen in the mole and (save for 2 molars) in the dog. A few eutherians such as the freshwater dolphin and other cetaceans (Figure 13.26c) have a greater number of teeth, but the general tendency has been for mammals to have fewer teeth and for these to become specialized for diverse diets (Figure 13.26*d,e*). Rodents, for instance, have only 4 incisors (which grow throughout life and must be kept worn down by constant gnawing), and 12 molars; they lack canines and premolars.

The fish tongue is nearly immovable and lies on the floor of the mouth where it may serve mainly as an organ of taste, but the tongue of tetrapod vertebrates is mobile and useful in both food-getting and mastication. In such animals as anteaters and African chameleons the tongue is the main food-capturing organ (Figure 13.27). In mastication the tongue serves to press the food between the teeth, mix it with saliva, and compress it into a compact mass (bolus) for swallowing. It then initiates swallowing by forcing the chewed food backward into the pharynx. The upper surface of the tongue is studded with papillae, the sides of which bear *taste buds* (see Figure 15.16). These buds contain receptor cells that discriminate only among four kinds of substances: salty, sour, sweet, and bitter. During chewing additional nuances of flavor are detected by olfactory receptors in the nasal lining.

Mammalian salivary glands secrete both serous (watery) and mucous (viscid) saliva. Serous saliva helps to liquefy the food and also contains a starch-digesting enzyme. Mucous saliva holds the food together during chewing and causes it to cohere in a sticky bolus for swallowing.

The food does not long remain in the esophagus, except in species where the posterior end of this portion of the digestive tube is dilated for storage (Figure 13.28). In birds the thin-walled distensible *crop* permits the bird to feed intensively when the opportunity presents itself, and to digest the material at leisure. Several chambers of the complex "stomach" of *ruminant* (cud-chewing) mammals are derived from the esophagus. Food is initially swallowed without intensive mastication, and is stored in the most anterior chamber, the *rumen,* until regurgitated for lengthy chewing while the ruminant rests in some patch of shade, the picture of "contentment." The remasticated food is then swallowed once more and passes into the more posterior chambers (*reticulum* and *omasum*), where it is held while the cellulose is hydrolyzed by symbiotic bacteria. Finally the material passes into the true stomach (the *abomasum*), where it is churned and mixed with gastric juices. Herbivores lacking a ruminant stomach must depend for cellulose digestion on the bacterial flora of the cecum.

Mechanical digestion is largely completed in the stomach, where the food is retained until thoroughly liquefied by the churning, rhythmic contractions of the gastric musculature, and is mixed with enzymes secreted by the gastric glands. In vertebrates hydrochloric acid, as well as activating pepsin, plays a role in mechanical digestion, for it can dissolve calcium-containing materials such as bone and cartilage and is thus of considerable importance in the digestive processes of carnivores.

Figure 13.25 □ Digestive system of an herbivorous mammal (rabbit), showing extensive cecum at junction of small intestine and colon. Undigested residues are held in the cecum while being attacked by cellulose-digesting bacteria. Compare this figure with the human digestive system in Figure 12.27; the human cecum is vestigial and is mostly represented by the vermiform appendix.

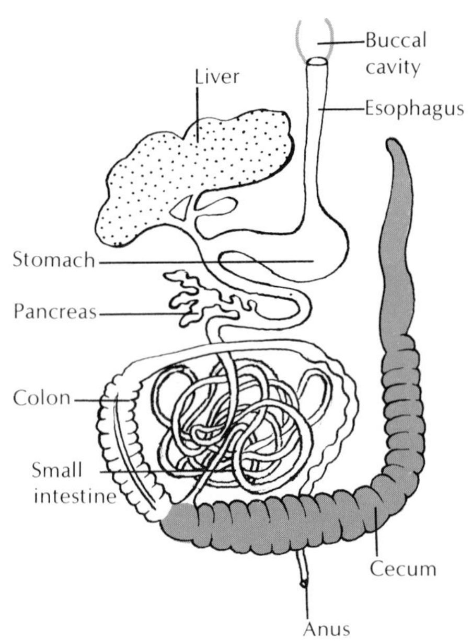

Figure 13.26 □ Mammalian dentition. (*a*) Tooth structure. (*Courtesy of Ward's Natural Science Establishment, Inc.*) (*b*) Tooth diversification in the dog and the human being. (c) Undiversified dentition of a fish-eating mammal, the freshwater dolphin. (*Courtesy of Sea World.*) (*d*) Dental specialization in rodent (beaver); note prominent, canines of this extinct species were used in stabbing. (*San Diego Natural History Museum photo by Dallas Clites.*) (*e*) Tooth reduction and specialization in rodent (beaver); note prominent, chisel-shaped incisors (which continue to grow throughout life) and absence of canines and premolars.

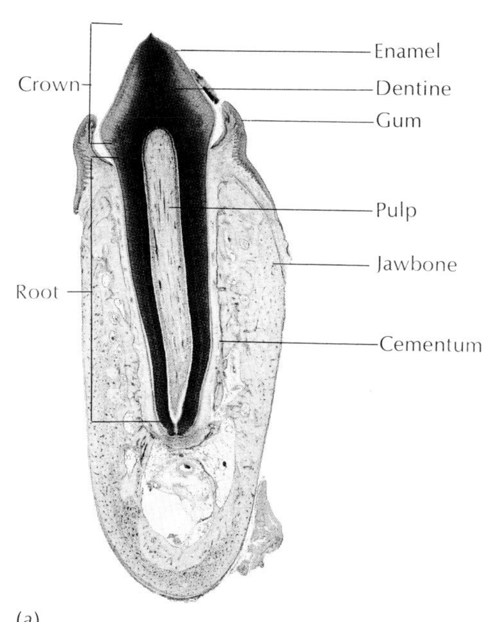
Crown
Enamel
Dentine
Gum
Pulp
Jawbone
Root
Cementum
(a)

(c)

(d)

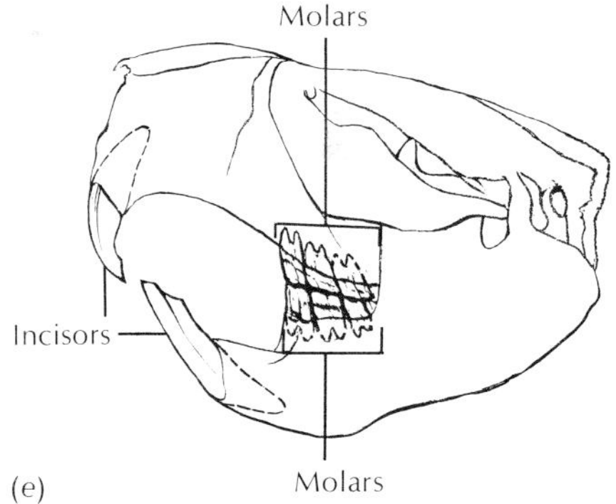
Molars
Incisors
Molars
(e)

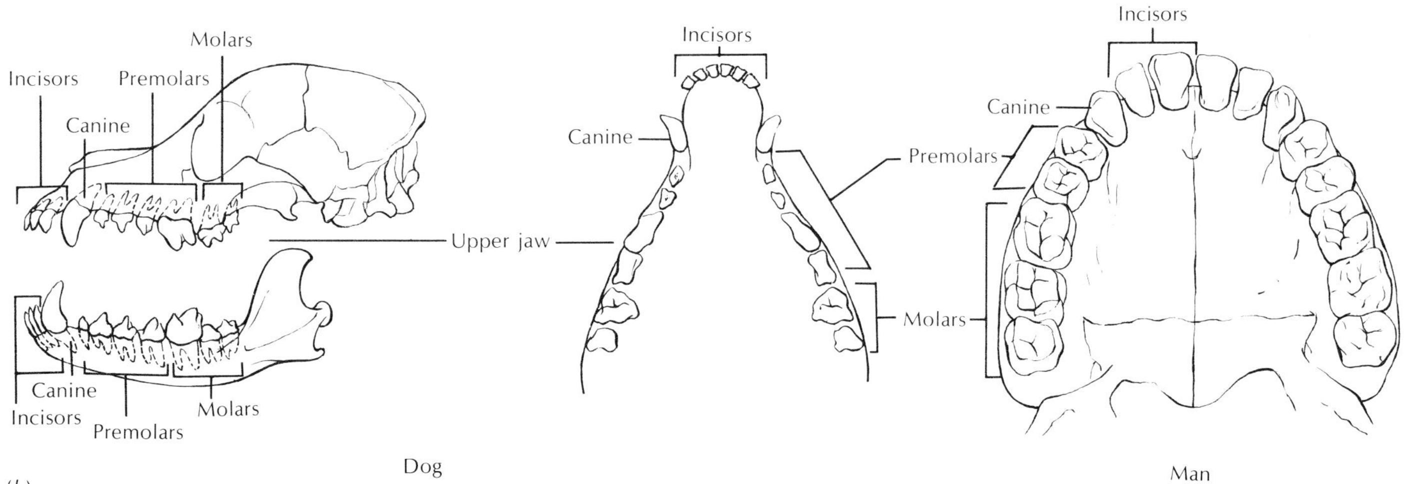
Molars
Incisors
Premolars
Canine
Upper jaw
Canine
Incisors
Premolars
Molars
Incisors
Canine
Premolars
Molars
Incisors
Canine
Premolars
Molars
Dog
Man
(b)

Figure 13.27 □ **These two vertebrates employ the tongue in food capture; in both the tongue has become unusually elongated and mobile. (*a*) African chameleon (*Chameleo*) catching fly. Note prehensile tail bracing the lizard during a capture; the eyes bulge prominently and move independently, allowing the lizard both to see binocularly —thus to estimate when the prey is within striking distance—and to scan separate visual fields with each eye. (*b*) Giant anteater (*Myrmecophaga*). The dietary specialization of this mammal has led to modification of the snout into a slender proboscis housing the extremely long, thin tongue; the powerful forefoot claws, folded under when walking, can rip open anthills. (*Zoological Society of San Diego.*)**

(*a*)

(*b*)

Figure 13.28 □ **Specializations of esophagus and stomach. (*a*) A bird's food is stored in the thin-walled, highly distensible crop. (*b*) Vegetation ingested by a ruminant passes into the rumen, where it can be acted upon by cellulose-digesting bacteria. It then enters the reticulum, from which it is regurgitated as the cud for further chewing. When reswallowed, the cud passes into the omasum and finally enters the abomasum, or true stomach.**

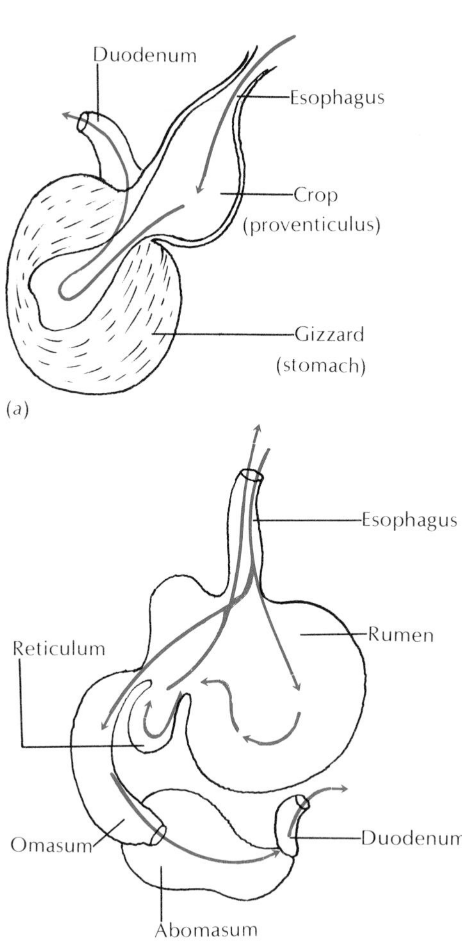

CHEMICAL DIGESTION Most animals can digest lipids, carbohydrates, proteins, and nucleic acids by the use of appropriate *hydrolases,* examples of which are listed in Table 13.4.

Lipases hydrolyze lipids, attacking the bonds which hold the fatty acids to the alcohol part of the molecule. In the case of triglycerides, the three bonds indicated below must be attacked:

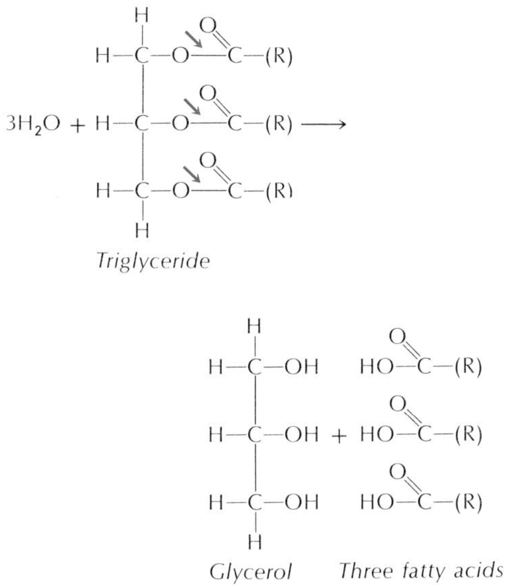

$$3H_2O + \begin{array}{l} H-\overset{H}{C}-O-\overset{O}{\overset{\|}{C}}-(R) \\ H-C-O-\overset{O}{\overset{\|}{C}}-(R) \\ H-\underset{H}{C}-O-\overset{O}{\overset{\|}{C}}-(R) \end{array} \longrightarrow$$

Triglyceride

$$\begin{array}{l} H-\overset{H}{C}-OH \\ H-C-OH \\ H-\underset{H}{C}-OH \end{array} + \begin{array}{l} HO-\overset{O}{\overset{\|}{C}}-(R) \\ HO-\overset{O}{\overset{\|}{C}}-(R) \\ HO-\overset{O}{\overset{\|}{C}}-(R) \end{array}$$

Glycerol *Three fatty acids*

The action of lipase is facilitated by *emulsifying* agents, which coat microscopic fat droplets, preventing their coalescence; such *colloidal fat* can be attacked by lipase on all its exposed surfaces. The role of emulsifier is played in vertebrates by *bile,* a complex mixture of cholesterol salts and pigments derived from the breakdown of hemoglobin. Bile is secreted by the liver and stored in the gall bladder, from which it is expelled into the duodenum when fatty material enters the intestine.

Table 13.4 □ Major constituents of mammalian digestive fluids

SUBSTANCE	SITE OF PRODUCTION	SITE OF ACTION	MAJOR ACTION
Salivary amylase (ptyalin)	Salivary glands	Mouth (stomach)	Hydrolyzes starch to dextrin and disaccharides
Pepsin	Gastric glands	Stomach	Hydrolyzes proteins to polypeptides
Rennin	Gastric glands	Stomach	Clots milk, hydrolyzes only specific milk proteins
Hydrochloric acid	Gastric glands	Neck of gastric glands	Activates pepsinogen to pepsin
Trypsin	Pancreas	Anterior part of small intestine	Hydrolyzes proteins and polypeptides to smaller peptide fragments
Chymotrypsin	Pancreas	Anterior part of small intestine	Hydrolyzes proteins and polypeptides to smaller peptide fragments
Pancreatic carboxypeptidase	Pancreas	Anterior part of small intestine	Hydrolyzes peptides by removing amino acids with exposed —COOH groups
Amylopsin (pancreatic amylase)	Pancreas	Anterior part of small intestine	Hydrolyzes polysaccharides to disaccharides
Steapsin (pancreatic lipase)	Pancreas	Anterior part of small intestine	Hydrolyzes lipids to fatty acids and glycerol
Bile salts	Liver	Anterior part of small intestine	Emulsify fats, aid absorption of fatty acids
Enterokinase	Duodenal glands	Anterior part of small intestine	Activates trypsinogen to trypsin
Sucrase	Duodenal glands	Anterior part of small intestine	Hydrolyzes sucrose to glucose and fructose
Lactase	Duodenal glands	Anterior part of small intestine	Hydrolyzes lactose to glucose and galactose
Maltase	Duodenal glands	Anterior part of small intestine	Hydrolyzes maltose to glucose
Nucleases	Duodenal glands	Anterior part of small intestine	Hydrolyze nucleic acids
Carboxypeptidase	Duodenal glands	Anterior part of small intestine	Hydrolyzes peptides by removing amino acids with exposed —COOH groups
Aminopeptidase	Duodenal glands	Anterior part of small intestine	Hydrolyzes peptides by removing amino acids with exposed $-NH_2$ groups
Dipeptidases	Duodenal glands	Anterior part of small intestine	Separate pairs of amino acids by hydrolysis

Glycosidases (carbohydrases) hydrolyze carbohydrates to their constituent sugar units:

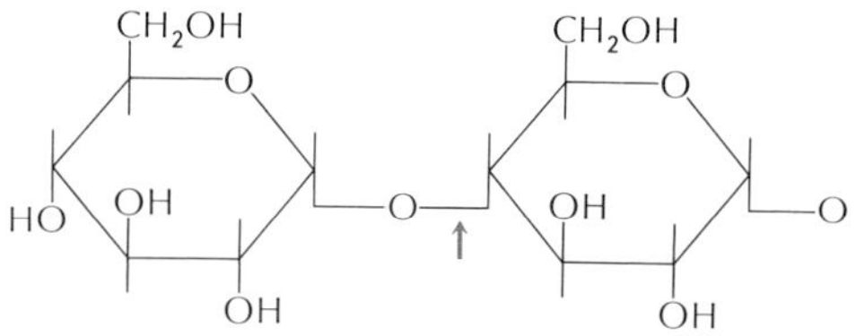

Amylases break down polysaccharides such as amylose (starch) to two-sugar units, by attacking every other bond in the chain. *Disaccharidases* (maltase, sucrase, and lactase) then attack specific disaccharides (maltose, sucrose, and lactose, respectively), reducing these to monosaccharides. In mammals amylases are secreted by the salivary glands and pancreas, and disaccharidases by the duodenal glands. *Chitinases,* which hydrolyze chitin to amino sugars, are mainly restricted to certain bacteria, but these enzymes also occur sporadically among arthropods, molluscs, and insectivorous vertebrates.

Nucleases hydrolyze nucleic acids into their constituent nucleotides, and then break these down further into their base and pentose units; they are products of the duodenal glands in vertebrates.

Proteolytic enzymes attack the carboxy-amino linkages which bind amino acids. Many are species-specific and consequently represent *families* of enzymes rather than specific chemical entities. *Proteases* attack large protein molecules internally, fragmenting them into shorter chains that are then subject to attack by a succession of *peptidases. Pepsin,* a gastric enzyme, initiates protein hydrolysis in vertebrates. The process is continued by the pancreatic proteases *trypsin* and *chymotrypsin.* Next the peptide fragments are attacked by pancreatic and duodenal peptidases. *Carboxypeptidase* and *aminopeptidase* cleave off amino acids from the ends of each fragment, working from opposite ends of the chain. *Dipeptidases* then separate the remaining pairs of amino acids, completing the digestive process.

Proteolytic enzymes are specific in

terms of the bonds they attack. *Endopeptidases* such as pepsin, trypsin, chymotrypsin, and dipeptidase, attack bonds between amino acids internal to the chain. Mammalian pepsin hydrolyzes bonds between the carboxyl group of a dicarboxylic amino acid and the amino group of phenylalanine or tyrosine (both of the latter being amino acids which contain a benzene ring in the molecule; Table 9.2). Chymotrypsin splits bonds on the carboxyl side of phenylalanine, tyrosine, leucine, methionine, and tryptophan. Trypsin acts on the carboxyl side of the basic (diamino) amino acids, lysine and arginine. There appear to be a number of dipeptidases, each restricted to splitting only certain bonds, that is, between serine and glutamic acid, between leucine and aspartic acid, and so forth. *Exopeptidases* such as carboxy- and aminopeptidase split amino acids off each end of a peptide chain. Carboxypeptidase removes amino acids that expose a carboxyl group (—COOH) at one end of the chain. Aminopeptidase removes amino acids that expose amino groups (—NH_2) at the opposite end of the chain (Figure 13.29). Many of these proteolytic enzymes or their analogs occur in invertebrates, but pepsin, which favors an intensely acidic medium (pH 1 to 2), exists only in vertebrates. Because of the bone-dissolving action of HCl, selection may have favored the evolution of an acid-tolerant protease in primitive fish that fed upon their heavily-armored vertebrate contemporaries. Bone must have been virtually indigestible for predatory arthropods of the time, such as eurypterids (see Figure 8.21*a*).

Proteolytic enzymes are capable of damaging the cells that produce them. In consequence they must be stored and secreted in inactive proenzyme status and activated only within the phagosome or in the cavity of the digestive tract. Pepsin is secreted as *pepsinogen,* which is activated by HCl; trypsin, as *trypsinogen,* which can be activated either by *enterokinase* (a duodenal secretion) or by free trypsin itself. The latter also activates *chymotrypsinogen* and carboxypeptidase.

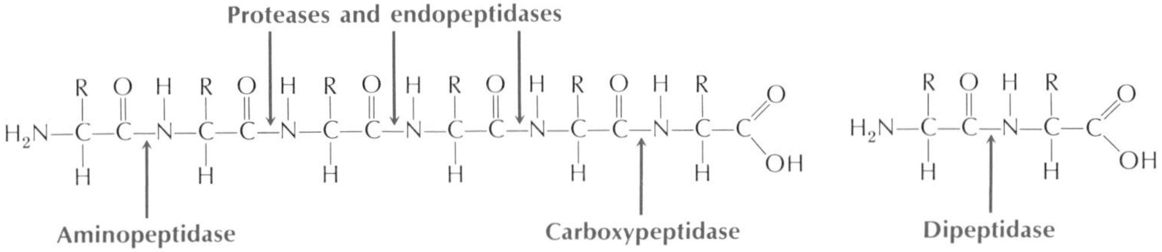

D Absorption

While nutrients are restricted to the interior of a food vacuole, or to the cavity of the digestive tract, they are not, strictly speaking, part of the body proper. They must be transported across a differentially permeable membrane—the bounding membrane of the phagosome, or the plasma membrane of the gut mucosal cells—to become true body constituents. This uptake of nutrients from the site of digestion into the tissues is termed absorption. Materials that fail to be absorbed are ultimately egested and are not incorporated into the body.

Absorption of small nutrient molecules and ions can take place promptly through the *gastric* mucosa, since their hydrolysis is unnecessary. Final water absorption takes place in the hindgut, since considerable water is needed in the digestive process up to that point to aid in liquefaction and hydrolysis. Most organic nutrients require hydrolysis before they can be absorbed, since molecular size per se can represent an absorption barrier. Proteins, polysaccharides, and undigested fats are virtually nonabsorbable, while their hydrolysates—amino acids, monosaccharides, fatty acids, and glycerol—are more easily absorbed. However, absorption is not merely a matter of passive diffusion of molecules from regions of higher concentration to regions of lower concentration, for the mucosal epithelium "stands guard" between the intestinal contents and the body tissues, and by expending energy actively regulates the process of absorption. Membrane transport, considered in Chapter 14, involves not only *passive* processes such as simple diffusion, but *active* processes in which energy is expended to move materials rapidly or to move them against a concentration gradient. Thus, valuable nutrients such as amino acids and sugars do not merely diffuse passively along their con-

Figure 13.29 □ Action of protein-digesting enzymes (R stands for various side chains).

Proteases and endopeptidases

Aminopeptidase **Carboxypeptidase** **Dipeptidase**

centration gradients until an equilibrium is reached, but are instead nearly totally absorbed. On the other hand, molecules of similar size but lacking nutritive value may be rejected. Curiously, simple sugars, though of small size, are in fact not absorbable until they have been *phosphorylated* on the surface of the mucosal cells. Even after phosphorylation, there is a difference in the rate of absorption of the isomers glucose, fructose, and galactose, fructose being absorbed most readily, and galactose most slowly.

The absorption of particular nutrients may be facilitated or inhibited by other substances present in the alimentary tract. Undigested lactose in the intestine promotes the growth of acidophilous ("acid loving") bacteria, which in turn apparently promote the absorption of Ca^{2+} and phosphates. Conversely, intake of food containing oxalate (such as spinach) inhibits Ca^{2+} absorption since this ion reacts with oxalate, forming insoluble calcium oxalate.

Bile salts, which serve first as fat emulsifiers, also facilitate the absorption of fatty acids by increasing their miscibility in water. These salts also aid the absorption of fat-soluble vitamins (A, D, E, and K). After being absorbed, the bile salts dissociate from the lipid or vitamin molecules and, returning to the liver by way of the bloodstream, are secreted once again. Finely emulsified fats (in negatively charged droplets less than 0.5 μm in diameter) can be absorbed without prior digestion. These and the products of lipid hydrolysis pass through the mucosal epithelium and enter the lymphatic drainage (in the case of vertebrates), thereby bypassing the hepatic portal circulation (see Section 12.7C). Amino acids, monosaccharides, and other solutes of low molecular weight pass instead into mucosal capillaries of the blood vascular system and are carried to the liver. Prompt removal of absorbed substances from the mucosal region is necessary for continued absorption.

In this chapter we have compared nutrient procurement and processing in autotrophs and heterotrophs. Next we shall see how these materials are transported through the body of the multicellular organism and to what uses they are put within the body cells.

REVIEW AND DISCUSSION

1 How do the nutritional requirements of autotrophic and heterotrophic organisms differ? Explain why it is inaccurate to say that "plants make their own food," or that "plants do not depend on their environment for food."

2 Explain why the matter-and-energy relationships of living things may constitute a "steady state," but can never attain a true equilibrium. How do living things contribute to the entropy of the universe while reducing their own tendency toward randomization?

3 Summarize the major types of chemical reactions by which high-energy phosphate compounds are built by living systems. What is the nature of the "high-energy" phosphate bond?

4 Why is it better to say that biochemical processes in living cells are exergonic and endergonic, rather than exothermic and endothermic? Define *calorie* and *kilocalorie*. Explain why the caloric value of a food gives only inferential evidence concerning its use in the body. What is the difference between "burning" food in the body, and burning it in a calorimeter?

5 Explain how enzymes alter reaction rates. What is meant by "turnover number"? Summarize the four major kinds of enzymes, with an example of each. To what category do the digestive enzymes pepsin and amylopsin belong? What is the functional significance of an "enzyme-cascade"?

6 How does the structural organization of the granum enhance its functional efficiency? What are the presumed roles of chlorophyll molecules *P700* and *P680*?

7 Explain the probable functional role of each of the following substances in photosynthesis: (*a*) accessory plastid pigments; (*b*) enzyme Z; (*c*) cytochrome b_6; (*d*) cytochrome *f*; (*e*) pigment system II; (*f*) pigment system I; (*g*) ferredoxin; (*h*) NADP; (*i*) water.

8 Trace the path of an electron from a water molecule to its ultimate union with CO_2. Do H_2O and CO_2 combine directly to make sugar? At what point in this pathway is ATP manufactured? What other photosynthetic pathway yields ATP? How will this ATP be used in photosynthesis?

9 Must the photosynthetic "dark reactions" take place in the dark? Why are they called *dark reactions?* How many turns of the Calvin cycle are required to make one molecule of hexose? What is the total energy cost of building a mole of glucose? Explain in terms of oxidation-reduction potentials why energy is required to move H from water to CO_2.

10 Explain how various environmental factors affect photosynthesis. What single factor seems to limit the rate of photosynthesis under natural conditions?

11 Similar ways of food getting are used by many kinds of animals; summarize some of the main means of food gathering, giving examples drawn from different phyla.

12 Can you suggest a means by which physiological need might control qualitative appetite in an animal that cannot consciously analyze its needs?

13 What important evolutionary trends may be perceived through comparative study of the digestive apparatus of various animal phyla?

14 Summarize the major hydrolases found in the mammalian body, which catalyze the hydrolysis of (*a*) lipids; (*b*) proteins; (*c*) carbohydrates. Why are there such a variety of protein-digesting enzymes?

15 Explain the nutritional significance of each of the following: (*a*) molars; (*b*) incisors; (*c*) canines; (*d*) enterokinase; (*e*) bile salts; (*f*) gastric HCl; (*g*) saliva; (*h*) taste buds.

16 What factors determine the absorbability of a given substance? How do we know that absorption is not merely a passive process involving the diffusion of molecules that are too small for the cell membrane to exclude?

REFERENCES

ARNON, D. I. "The Role of Light in Photosynthesis," *Sci. Amer.*, **203** (1960).

———, M. B. ALLEN, AND F. R. WHATLEY "Photosynthesis by Isolated Chloroplasts," *Nature*, **174** (1954). This classic experiment demonstrated that chloroplasts contain all the necessary determinants for synthesizing ATP and fixing CO_2 without the addition of other enzymes.

BASSHAM, J. A. "The Path of Carbon in Photosynthesis," *Sci. Amer.*, **206** (1962). Describes techniques used to trace the biochemical pathway of carbohydrate synthesis.

CALVIN, M. "The Path of Carbon in Photosynthesis," *Science*, **135** (1962). Reviews the Calvin cycle of carbon fixation and sugar production.

——— "New Keys to Life Processes," *Perspectives in Biol. and Med.*, **11** (1968). Reviews the impact of radioisotopes on metabolic research.

FRENCH, C. S. "Photosynthesis," in *This Is Life*, W. H. Johnson and W. C. Steere, eds. New York: Holt, Rinehart and Winston, Inc., 1962.

FRIEDEN, E. "The Enzyme-substrate Complex," *Sci. Amer.*, **201** (1959).

——— "The Biochemistry of Copper," *Sci. Amer.*, **218** (1968). The metabolic roles of an essential micronutrient are summarized.

GIBOR, A. "Chloroplast Heredity and Nucleic Acids," *Amer. Nat.*, **99** (1965). Reviews evidence that chloroplasts are self-replicating organelles possessing the necessary genetic determinants in the form of intrinsic DNA.

HILL, R. "Oxygen Produced by Isolated Chloroplasts," *Proc. Roy. Soc. London, Ser. B*, **127** (1939). Describes the procedure whereby the evolution of molecular oxygen from chloroplasts (the now-famous Hill reaction) was first discovered.

LEHNINGER, A. L. *Bioenergetics.* New York: W. A. Benjamin, Inc., 1965. An interesting, succinct discussion of energy conversions in photosynthesis and metabolism for the able student.

NASH, L. K. *Elements of Chemical Thermodynamics.* Reading, Mass.: Addison-Wesley Publishing Company, Inc., 1962. A sound introduction to principles of thermodynamics.

NEURATH, H. "Protein-Digesting Enzymes," *Sci. Amer.*, **211** (1964). Use of small synthetic substrates facilitates investigation of the nature of the active sites of proteases and the specific characteristics of the types of bonds each can attack.

PHILLIPS, D. C. "The Three-dimensional Structure of an Enzyme Molecule," *Sci. Amer.*, **215** (1966).

RABINOWITCH, E. I., AND GOVINDJEE "The Role of Chlorophyll in Photosynthesis," *Sci. Amer.*, **213** (1965). Excitation of an electron in each of two key chlorophyll molecules per photosynthetic unit provides energy needed to build ATP and boost H into the Calvin cycle.

Chapter 14  NUTRITION: TRANSPORT AND METABOLISM

IN CHAPTER 13 WE EXAMINED THE MEANS by which autotrophic and heterotrophic organisms obtain energy and raw materials for growth and maintenance. We found that autotrophs take in simple inorganic nutrients and utilize energy from their abiotic environment to convert these into organic compounds. The energy used in this construction is trapped as bonding energy in the compounds built, and a portion of it can be reclaimed as free energy when these substances are broken down. Unlike autotrophs, heterotrophs must procure organic as well as inorganic nutrients, and generally must digest these to compounds of more modest molecular dimensions before they can be absorbed into the tissues.

Whether taken in as preformed nutrients or synthesized within the cell, organic compounds serve both as fabric materials and as reservoirs of energy for cell work. We found that in photosynthesis the essential reaction by which the primary organic product, phosphoglyceraldehyde (PGAL), is formed is a *reduction*—the union of phosphoglyceric acid (PGA, formed by the interaction of ribulose diphosphate with CO_2 and water) with hydrogen atoms from NADPH + H^+. Consequently, it follows that cells tap the energy stored in PGAL and the more complex compounds for which PGAL is a precursor by a series of *oxidative* reactions: the compounds that are broken down yield electrons to electron carriers, which in turn transfer some of the energy of these electrons to high-energy phosphate compounds such as ATP. These oxidations constitute the principal energy-mobilizing metabolic system, and they are referred to in the aggregate as *cell respiration.*

Cell respiration may be either aerobic or anaerobic, that is, it may or may not require the presence of molecular oxygen. Reliance on O_2 as a final acceptor of the hydrogen liberated in cell respiration is so widespread that few organisms other than certain bacteria are able to survive under anaerobic conditions. However, in our earlier consideration of the origin of life, we noted that the primitive atmosphere of earth was probably devoid of oxygen and thus the earliest creatures must have relied exclusively on anaerobic processes for mobilization of energy. Not until the onset of photosynthesis did the earth's atmosphere begin to accumulate appreciable concentrations of O_2, a by-product of newly burgeoning plant life. Since even today 90 percent of the world's photosynthesis is carried on by marine algae (mainly diatoms, dinoflagellates, and other phytoplankton), it is clear that the absence of land plants did not hamper the buildup of molecular oxygen in the atmosphere.

In studying cell respiration later in this chapter we shall become reacquainted with a number of compounds introduced in Chapter 13. We shall find in fact that a number of the energy-mobilizing reactions of cell respiration are just the reverse of some of the photosynthetic reactions. This complementarity strongly suggests that much of the metabolic machinery used in photosynthesis had already been evolved for extraction of energy from spontaneously formed organic compounds, and that much later the evolution of chlorophyll made possible the direct trapping of radiant energy to power the construction of such compounds within cells. Once this means of trapping solar energy by the excitation of electrons was available, then the preexisting biochemical machinery might be put to a new use. In a number of cases even the same enzymes could be used, for enzymes merely affect the rate and not the direction of a reaction. In other words, during the evolution of the photosynthetic process cells probably were able to adapt metabolic pathways that had previously evolved for obtaining energy from chemical compounds.

Before we probe further into the means by which cells utilize the products of photosynthesis, we must first consider how these materials are moved to the regions of the body where they are needed. As organisms became larger and more complex, this problem of internal transport of materials became critical and required increasingly elaborate solutions.

In green plants, for example, some metabolites (that is, products of metabolism) of course will be utilized right in the cells in which they are made, but a much greater proportion is needed in the growing tips of the shoots and roots, where photosynthesis is *not* occurring. In addition, storage materials must be accumulated to provide for the plant's growth needs at the start of each growing season, especially in deciduous plants that must put on new foliage before they can resume photosynthesis.

Similarly, in the multicellular animal body, nutrients must be transported from their site of digestion and absorption to all tissues, particularly to regions of growth and to such organs as muscles which have high energy demands.

In the plant body, the major problems of distribution are (1) the exchange of gases (also termed respiration) and their movement between the cells and the stomates and lenticels, (2) the conduction of water and minerals from the roots to the foliage, and (3) the translocation of organic compounds from the leaves to the growing points and storage tissues. In the animal body, gases must be transported between the respiratory organs and the tissues; because of the comparatively high rate at which cell respiration must be carried on in animals, such transport must be much more rapid and efficient than it is in plants. In addition, a constant supply of nutrients must be distributed throughout the body, from the digestive tract and from such storage regions as the body fat and the vertebrate liver. At the same time wastes liberated by the cells must be uninterruptedly and efficiently carried away.

Internal transport therefore is an essential prerequisite to the metabolic use of nutrients in the multicellular body, both in terms of supplying the tissues with nutrients and in preventing them from being poisoned by their own wastes.

Internal transport can be considered to have four phases (Figure 14.1). (1) The materials must be *absorbed* into the body proper—from the external milieu in the case of plants, or from the digestive cavity or interior of a food vacuole in animals. (Note that in animal nutrition no material is actually *within* the body until it has been taken into the cells that line the gut, and even the food of an amoeba is not properly within the amoeba's body as long as it is bounded by the membrane of the phagosome.) (2) Following this initial uptake, nutrients and other materials are transported from the site of absorption to other parts of the body by

Figure 14.1 □ **Extracellular and intracellular transport. Transport across membranes is indicated by arrows in color, transport through body or cellular fluids by gray arrows, and diffusion within interstitial spaces by tinted color arrows.**

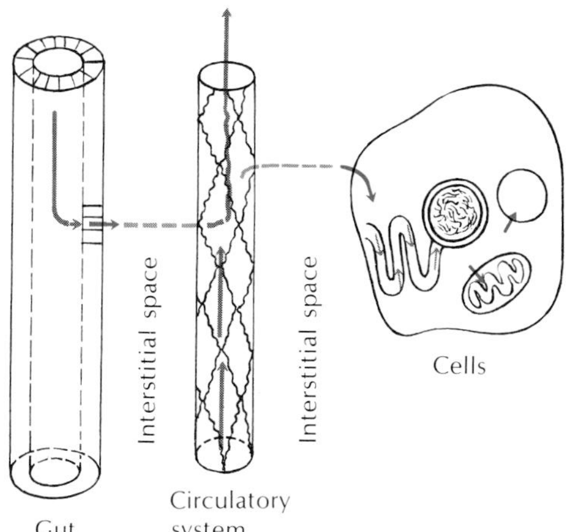

way of the body fluids. This *fluid transport* may proceed by simple diffusion but is typically hastened by some means of propulsion and circulation of body fluids. (3) After distribution, nutrients are taken up from the body fluids into the cells in which they will be metabolized. This, like their initial absorption, demands that they pass across the plasma membrane into the cytoplasm, a process of *membrane transport.* (4) Further transport takes place *intracellularly,* by way of the fluids in the endoplasmic reticulum (see Figure 10.9) and by transport across the membranes of various organelles.

Of these four processes, membrane transport probably involves the most universal mechanisms, for the basic structure and physiology of cell membranes is thought to be very similar throughout the living world, and the movement of materials across these membranes must be governed by mechanisms evolved when cellular life was just beginning. On the other hand, transport through the body fluids, which we shall term fluid transport, depends on a variety of adaptations evolved independently by different lines of multicellular descent. Usually an organism can attain no great size without adequate means of internal distribution of materials: even the smallest vertebrate fish leads such an active life that it cannot survive without most of its cells being in contact with capillaries through which a swift flow of blood is maintained by the rhythmic pulsations of a heart; a relatively sluggish creature like a jellyfish, however, can sometimes attain great size despite having to rely only on the system of canals branching off its gastrovascular cavity. Since the mechanisms of fluid transport are fairly varied whereas those of membrane transport may be virtually universal, the latter will claim our attention first.

14.1 □ MEMBRANE TRANSPORT

The plasma membrane consists 60 percent of protein and 40 percent of lipids, and the generally accepted model for its structure is that of a double layer of phospholipid molecules sandwiched between two layers of protein molecules. The latter are studded with globular proteins, probably membrane-bound enzymes.

The plasma membrane is a differentially permeable membrane (DPM) that governs exchanges of materials between the cell and its environment. Its mesh is calculated at about 3 Å, or around the diameter of a water molecule, but certain measurements indicate that the membrane is also penetrated by larger pores spaced some 200 Å apart. The diameter of these pores is between 7 and 8.5 Å, and their length, if they wind tortuously through the membrane instead of penetrating it directly, may be 200 to 300 Å. Passage of materials through these pores depends primarily on particle size, since the diameter of the particle cannot exceed that of the pore (unless the latter is elastic), and also on whether the particle is electrically charged. Sodium and chloride ions (Na^+ and Cl^-), though of around the same size, behave differently, for Cl^- can pass readily through the pores while Na^+ cannot. This suggests that the walls of the pores are studded with ions or ionized molecules of positive charge, which repel cations such as Na^+. The rate at which water passes through these pores can be determined by immersing red blood corpuscles in an isosmotic solution containing radioactive water (in which the hydrogen atoms are ^3H, tritium). Within only *20 msec* the ratio of H_2O to ^3H_2O has reached equilibrium between the cells and their milieu! The equilibrium attained is actually a constant bidirectional flux, with equal numbers of water molecules passing through the membrane in either direction.

Discussions of the permeability properties of cell membranes are both more interesting and more uncertain today than a generation ago, when it was thought that passage of substances across the plasma membrane simply depended on the size of the particles and the gauge of the mesh of the cell membrane, which was thought to act as a sieve. Now we know that this is not the case, for under certain circumstances even large molecules such as proteins can be taken into the cell, and (conversely) relatively *few* substances even of low molecular weight pass through the membrane as a result of random thermal movements, or simple diffusion. Gases and water can pass by diffusion, along with uncharged solutes of less than 7 Å diameter. The facility with which larger molecules pass through the membrane correlates directly with their degree of miscibility in lipids, suggesting that they dissolve into the membrane and then diffuse out the other side.

Permeability properties are not identical for all cell membranes. They vary even with respect to the facility with which water can pass through the membrane. An interesting situation pertains in most plant cells, in which the large central sap vacuole is bounded by a DPM termed the *endoplast,* which is discontinuous with the external plasma membrane (called the *ectoplast* in this instance to differentiate it from the vacuolar membrane). The endoplast is considerably less permeable to sugar than the ectoplast, and accordingly confines sugar-rich sap to the vacuole until it must be mobilized. Furthermore, when cells are exposed to radioactive KCl, it can be seen that this salt readily passes through the ectoplast but is repelled by the endoplast and therefore remains outside the vacuole. A number of anions that penetrate the ectoplast can be transported across the cell and out the opposite surface without ever entering the vacuole.

A Passive transport: osmosis, dialysis, and solvent drag

The passage of substances across cell membranes proceeds by "passive transport" or "active transport," the two mechanisms differing in that the cell itself must provide energy for the latter. The driving force of passive transport is *diffusion,* the tendency of any substance to randomize itself within whatever volume of space is available to it. Diffusion is brought about by the thermal agitation of molecules, and the rate at which randomization proceeds depends upon the amount of thermal activity. If in the course of these random movements, a particle should pass across a cell membrane, the result would be passive transport, since the cell expends no energy in bringing about such transport. During passive transport each uncharged molecule tends to follow its own concentration gradient into or out of the cell, while each ion moves as well in accordance with the relative distribution of anions and cations.

The passive (diffusion-driven) transport of *water* across a DPM is termed *osmosis.* The cells of the metazoan body are in *osmotic equilibrium* with the surrounding tissue fluids, and so the movement of water into and out of the cells is equalized. Cells can never achieve osmotic equilibrium with pure water, for they always must contain some proportion of solutes and dispersed particles. Therefore, for a fluid to be *isosmotic* to the cells it bathes, it must contain an equivalent concentration of solutes and *colloidal particles* (those with diameters of 0.1 to 1 μm), although these need not be identical in kind with those found within the cell. These particles must be of such character that they cannot pass readily through the membrane, or their concentration would soon be equalized on both sides. Accordingly, ions and colloidal particles such as proteins are of great importance in maintaining the isosmoticity of tissue fluids—the latter because of their large size, the former because the cell membrane bears an electric charge that renders it difficult for some ions to pass through it by diffusion. If the solute concentration of the surrounding fluid were to be diluted by the addition of excess water, the milieu would be rendered *hyposmotic* to the cells, and the net tendency of water would be to enter the cells, causing them to swell and burst (Figure 14.2). (Plant cells do not burst because of their sturdy cell walls, but become distended or *turgid.*) If, on the other hand, the solute concentration of the milieu were elevated by removing water or adding solutes, it would become *hyperosmotic* to the cells, with the result that more water molecules would tend to leave the cells than enter them, and the cells would become dehydrated and eventually die. In each instance, the tendency of water molecules to follow their own concentration gradient (going, so to speak, "downhill" from a region where there is a proportionately higher

Figure 14.2 □ Response of red blood cells (shown in profile) to changes in osmotic pressure. (*a*) Cell in isosmotic medium; concentrations of water and nondialyzable solutes (plasma proteins and cellular proteins that cannot pass the cell membrane) are in equilibrium on both sides of the cell membrane. (*b*) Cell in hyposmotic medium; fewer nondialyzable solutes are present in the medium than within the cell; accordingly there is a higher concentration of water outside the cell than inside, and the net movement of water molecules is *into* the cell. (*c*) Cell in hyperosmotic medium; the concentration of nondialyzable solutes is greater in the medium than within the cell; hence there is a higher initial concentration of water within the cell, and the net movement of water will be *out* of the cell. (Note that the medium does not fit into any of these categories simply by its own properties but by their relation to those of the particular cell under discussion.)

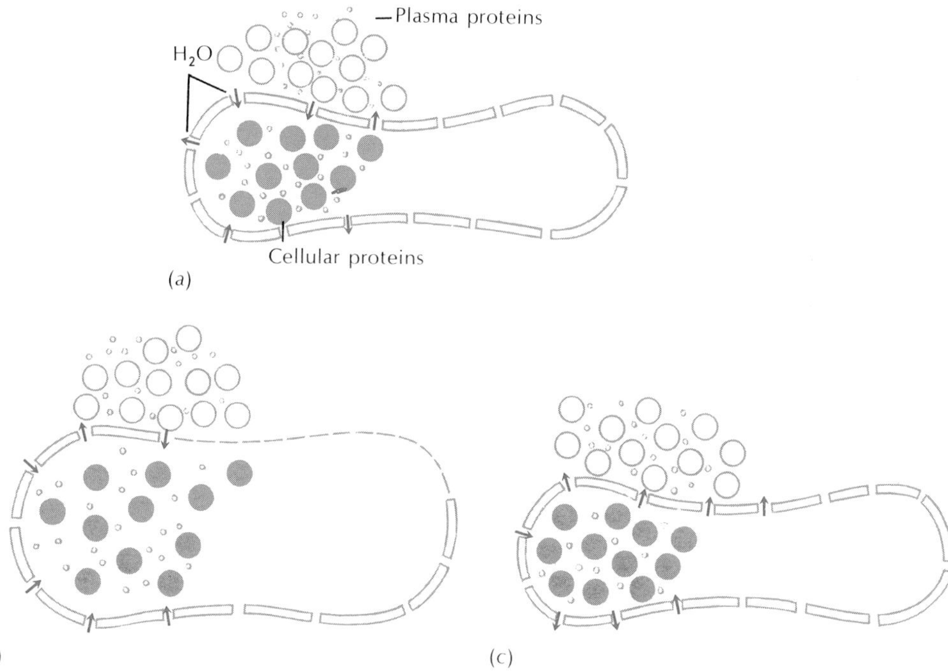

concentration of water molecules to a relatively lower one), produces an *osmotic pressure* reflected by the rate at which water enters or leaves the cells. (Osmotic pressure can be measured as the amount of mechanical pressure required to stop the flow of water across a DPM.) In an artificial system in which a vessel is divided into two compartments by a nonliving DPM, if water containing a solute that cannot pass through the membrane is placed in one compartment and pure water in the other, the net movement of water molecules between the two compartments will bring about a gradual rise in the water level on the side containing solute (Figure 14.3). If one compartment contains only pure water, osmotic equilibrium can never be achieved, and water will continue to pass into the compartment containing solute until at last the weight of the standing column exerts sufficient *hydrostatic* pressure on the DPM that further osmosis is impeded.

Osmotic pressure is directly related to the concentration of solutes and colloidal particles in a solution; it also varies according to temperature, since the higher the temperature the greater is the random thermal movement of molecules and the more rapid the rate of diffusion. Furthermore, each different kind of solution or colloid has unique diffusion characteristics expressible numerically as its diffusion constant. The osmotic pressure (OP) generated when a given solution is separated by a DPM from pure water can therefore be calculated by a simple formula,

$$\mathrm{OP} = CRT$$

which indicates that osmotic pressure is the product of the concentration of the solution

(C), the diffusion constant of the solution (R), and the absolute temperature (T). Solving this formula for a 1.0 M (*molar,* or mole/liter) solution of NaCl separated by a DPM from pure water at 20°C gives a value of 46.5 atm osmotic pressure. A 1.0 M solution of glucose, on the other hand, has an osmotic pressure of about 27.7 atm at this temperature.

Whereas osmosis is the diffusion-driven movement of water molecules across a DPM, the passive transport of small *solute* molecules should be termed *dialysis.* Once it was thought that most compounds of low molecular weight crossed cell membranes by dialysis, but now we know that this is often not the case. Glucose passes through a *nonliving* DPM by dialysis, but when it crosses a *living* DPM, simple dialysis does not occur. Instead, glucose must first be phosphorylated to glucose 6-phosphate (that is, a phosphate group is taken up by carbon atom number 6 at one end of the glucose molecule), this reaction taking place on the cell surface in the presence of the enzyme *hexokinase.* Such a *cell-surface reaction* requires energy in the form of Ⓟ transferred from ATP, and therefore constitutes *active* transport.

Figure 14.3 □ Demonstration of osmosis. One arm of a U tube is filled with 10-percent sucrose solution, the other with 5-percent solution. A differentially permeable membrane separating the two arms of the tube is impermeable to sucrose but allows water to pass freely. (*a*) At the start of the experiment, the net movement of water molecules is to the left until (*b*) an osmotic equilibrium is established, in which the two solutions are at the same concentration and equal numbers of water molecules move across the membrane in either direction.

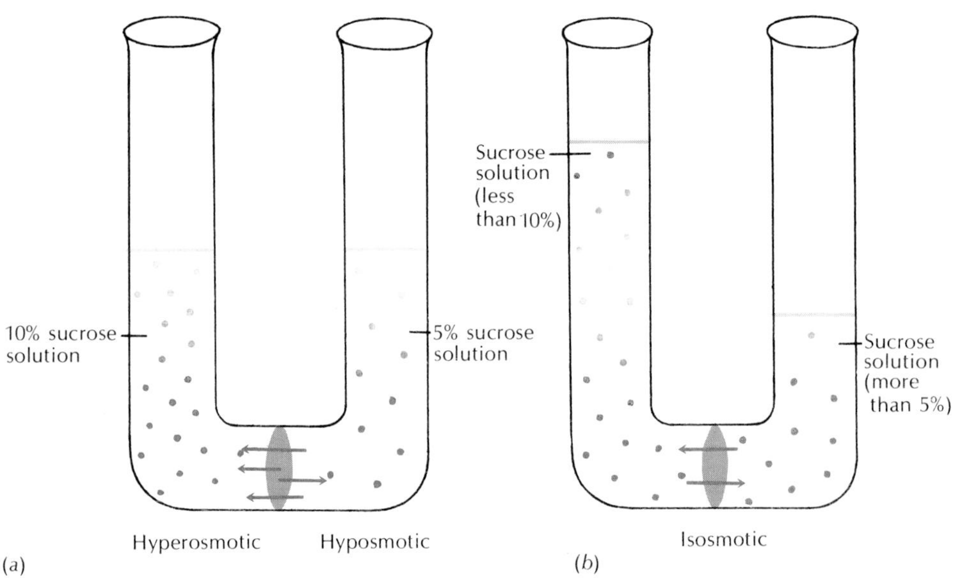

Even the absorption of water by a cell may not always proceed by passive transport. In the insect rectum, water is reclaimed from the urine and feces with such efficiency that the residue is nearly moisture-free. Such movement of water against its concentration gradient is often tied to the active transport of some solute (in our gall bladder, for instance, the transport of water is linked with that of NaCl), but this does not seem to be the case in water absorption by the insect rectal lining. Water absorption by plant root hairs may also involve active transport, for when the roots are deprived of O_2 the rate of water absorption declines, indicating that maintenance of the absorption rate depends upon metabolic activity in the root cells.

Unless a special mechanism exists for the active transport of a given ion, it will cross the plasma membrane by diffusion until a *Donnan equilibrium* is established (wherein the diffusion tendency is counterbalanced by the repulsive force exerted by the electrochemical potential set up across the membrane by the unequal distribution of cations and anions).* Because the trans-

*For more information concerning Donnan equilibria, reference may be made to T. C. Ruch and H. D. Patton, *Physiology and Biophysics,* 19th ed. (Philadelphia: W. B. Saunders Co., 1966), p. 71.

port of many ions is selectively controlled by active transport mechanisms, diffusion of ions *not* so controlled is restricted by differences in net charge on the two sides of the membrane. For example, each Cl^- entering a cell increases the net electronegativity of the cell's interior while decreasing that of the milieu until the difference in charge is such that further passage of Cl^- into the interior is impeded despite a favorable concentration gradient.

Solvent drag is the passive transport of solutes against an electrochemical or concentration gradient by a massive flow of *solvent*. This can occur during extrusion of fluid from a contractile vacuole, or during rapid water imbibition.

B Active transport

Living membranes are characterized by their use of specific active transport mechanisms to move many substances (Figure 14.4). The dependence of these mechanisms upon exergonic metabolic processes is shown in several ways. First, active transport results in a higher consumption of oxygen by the cell. To move Na^+ across frog skin requires the consumption of one molecule of O_2 per 3.4 Na^+ ions transported; in frog muscle four Na^+ ions can be transported at the cost of one O_2. In mammalian kidney tubules, due to improvement in the efficiency of the transport mechanism, 29 Na^+ can be transported per molecule of O_2

Figure 14.4 □ Proposed models of how materials move across cell membranes. (*a*) The coupled-transport system transports two different substances in opposite directions (as Na^+ out and K^+ in). (*b*) Pores through membranes allow molecules of less than 8-Å diameter to pass through by diffusion but impede the movement of anions and cations because the walls of the pores are lined with positively charged compounds serving to bind anions and repel cations. (*c*) Mobile carrier molecules migrate through the membrane carrying substrates in either direction. (*d*) Fixed carriers are polarized molecules that can transport substrates in one direction only. Transport mechanisms (*a*), (*c*), and (*d*) require energy.

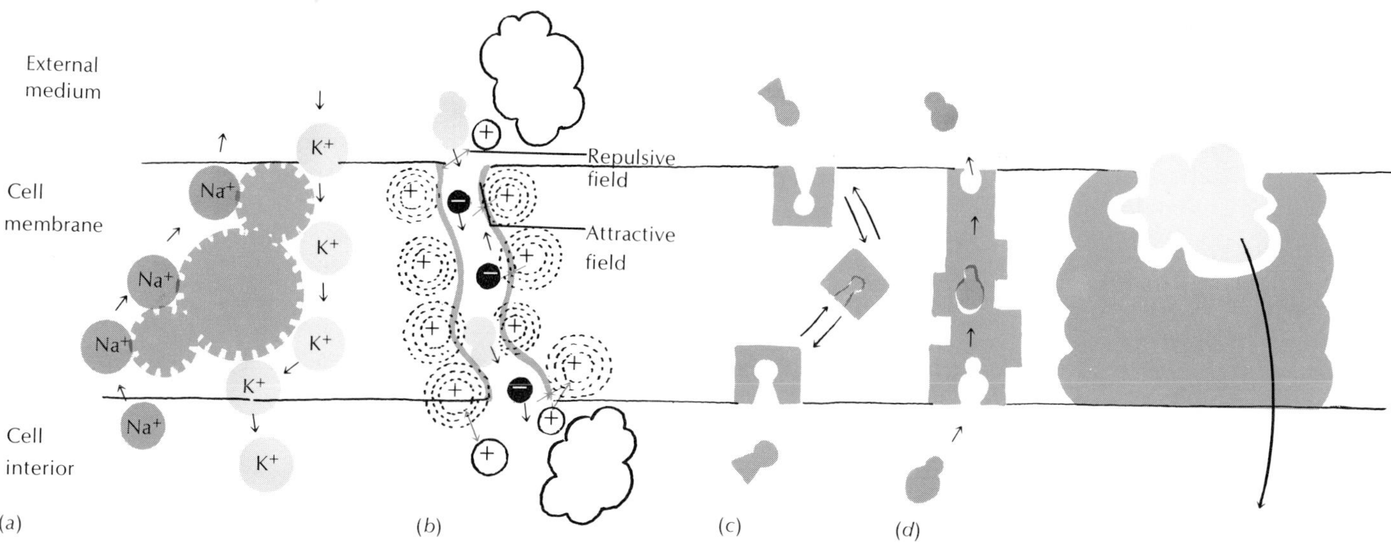

consumed. Second, various metabolic inhibitors—poisons that block particular exergonic pathways and therefore interfere with ATP production—abolish active transport. Cyanide and carbon monoxide, for instance, block active transport in amoeba, including pinocytosis (see Section 14.1C) and the pulsation of the contractile vacuole. Fluoride, which specifically blocks the action of *enolase* (the enzyme required for the conversion of 2-PGA to PEP), inhibits the mechanism by which Na^+ and K^+ are exchanged across the membrane.

Active transport is used by cells in acquiring nutrients, in rapidly ridding themselves of metabolic wastes, and in maintaining homeostasis of their solute and ion content. These important ends are accomplished in two ways: (1) molecules may be moved against concentration gradients and ions against an opposing electrochemical potential; (2) the process of diffusion can be *accelerated* so that the substance, although passing along its concentration or electrochemical gradient in the "right" direction (thermodynamically speaking), does so more rapidly than it could by simply diffusing through a given volume of space. By way of analogy, a ball will reach the bottom of an incline if it is merely allowed to roll from the top, but it will descend more rapidly if impelled by an initial blow from a mallet. This process of *facilitated diffusion* has the same end-result as ordinary diffusion, namely, the attainment of equilibrium in the concentration of the material on each side of the membrane; however, in facilitated diffusion less time is required for equilibrium to be reached.

Sometimes materials are moved against concentration gradients of amazing steepness, the energetic equivalent of rolling a ball *up* an almost vertical incline. Sea urchin ova, for instance, absorb phosphate against a gradient of $1:10^6$, or one part of phosphate in the milieu to one million parts within the cytoplasm. The need for investment of energy in active transport is reflected by the fact that in cells heavily engaged in such transport, gut and kidney epithelia, for instance, the mitochondria (the major sites of ATP production by oxidative metabolism) concentrate close to the plasma membrane on the side of the cell through which active transport is taking place.

Active transport mechanisms share certain characteristics. (1) They move substances against concentration or electrochemical gradients, or facilitate diffusion, altering the velocity of transport in the latter instance without affecting the equilibrium ultimately achieved. (2) They involve the expenditure of energy by the cell, probably made available by the dephosphorylation of ATP. (3) They are highly specific in terms of the substrates carried; specific transport mechanisms are thought to exist for many different ions and compounds. (4) A given mechanism works in one direction only—it either moves a substance across the membrane into the cell or moves it out, but not both. (5) The rate of active transport is independent of the concentration gradient (unlike osmosis and dialysis), but is maximized by an optimal concentration of substrate on the side of the membrane on which transport is initiated. (6) Specific transport mechanisms can be blocked by certain molecules or ions which are chemically related to the proper substrate. This *competitive inhibition* takes place whether the competing substances are actually transported or not. It much resembles enzyme-inhibition by a competing substrate that may permanently block the active site (see Figure 9.10). (7) The application of certain metabolic inhibitors can abolish all active transport.

Certain active transport mechanisms are *coupled,* in that two different substances are transported simultaneously, in the same direction, or in opposite directions. The uptake of glucose seems to be coupled with a sodium-uptake mechanism. Exchange of NH_4^+ appears to be related to Na^+ transport. In general, Na^+ and K^+ transport are coupled, with K^+ being concentrated within the cytoplasm and Na^+ being selectively extruded (see Figure 14.4). The mechanism does not effect a one-to-one exchange of Na^+ and K^+; instead, more Na^+ is extruded than K^+ is brought in. However, the interdependence of the transport of these two ions is shown by the fact that a deficiency of K^+ in the external milieu inhibits the extrusion of Na^+ from the cells. Similarly, Cl^- transport is coupled with that of HCO_3^-. When Cl^- is actively absorbed by goldfish gill tissue, an equivalent extrusion of HCO_3^- takes place. In our consideration of gaseous transport mechanisms we shall find that the movement of HCO_3^- between the erythrocytes and blood plasma is compensated by a characteristic "chloride shift," that is, a transfer of Cl^- in the opposite direction.

Homocellular transport involves movements of materials into and out of a given cell that are governed by the cell's own nutritional state and required homeostatic equilibrium. In addition, the irritability of cells seems to depend on their maintenance of an electrochemical potential across

Figure 14.5 □ **Transcellular transport. Absorptive epithelial cells such as those lining digestive tracts must move materials across the cytoplasm from the mucosal surface to the serosal surface, where they pass out of the cells and into the bloodstream. Transcellular transport of sugar (S) and Na^+ are shown here. (1) A directionally polarized coupled-transport system may carry both Na^+ and sugar into the cell together. Separate unidirectional transport systems may govern the removal of sugar and Na^+. (2) Sugar may leave the cell by simple dialysis or by means of an active-transport mechanism. (3) The mechanism for Na^+ removal requires energy and is independent of the sugar-transport system but related to cytoplasmic concentration of Na^+.**

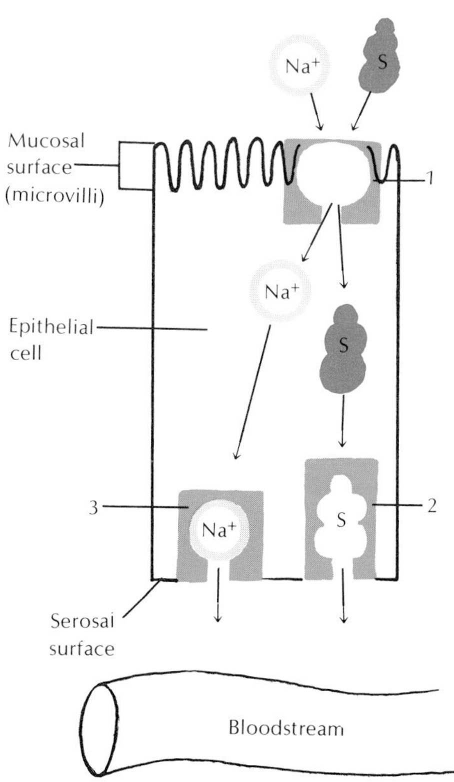

the plasma membrane that may amount to 100 mV; this potential is generated by differences in ionic concentration that are actively maintained across the membrane.

Transcellular transport, on the other hand, involves movement of substances *across* a layer of cells separating two fluid compartments of the body (Figure 14.5). For example, the epithelial cells of the alimentary mucosa expose one surface to the lumen of the digestive tract, whereas the opposite surface is in contact with the interstitial fluids and in proximity to the blood and lymph. Kidney tubule cells bear a comparable relationship to the bloodstream and the lumen of the renal tubules. Such cells absorb materials from one fluid compartment, and actively *secrete* them into the other. The entry and exit mechanisms are distinct. Gastric gland cells are noteworthy in that they concentrate H^+ from the bloodstream (at pH 7.4), and secrete into the stomach a highly acid fluid at pH 1. Cells engaged in transcellular transport are in an unusual predicament, in that they expose opposite surfaces to fluids of quite different solute and ionic composition; they must transport certain substances across their cytoplasm from one compartment to the other and yet maintain their own internal steady state, unlike that of either of the fluid compartments they separate!

The exact mechanisms of active transport remain in doubt. Enzymes termed *permeases* are known to be associated with the plasma membrane of bacterial cells, and it is generally accepted that enzyme molecules either are fixed within the plasma membrane of eucaryotic cells (as they are in the mitochondrial and plastid membranes), or are at least intimately associated with it. The hypothesis that enzyme molecules are fixed within the membrane is favored on the grounds that each specific transport mechanism is *unidirectional,* transporting materials across the membrane in one direction only. This polarized action would result if an enzyme's active site were so shaped that substrate molecules could be adsorbed onto the active site from one direction only, while products could be liberated only in the opposite direction. This explanation remains hypothetical, however, because the three-dimensional structure of the enzymes involved in active transport is not known.

Another proposed type of active transport mechanism involves the action of a mobile *carrier* molecule that unites with a substance on one side of the membrane and then migrates through the membrane and releases its burden on the opposite side. But whether transport depends upon a migratory carrier molecule or upon an enzyme occupying a fixed position, various substances (such as some amino acids) may compete for transport: *l*-alanine inhibits the transport of glycine; leucine inhibits that of valine. Such competition suggests that there is an active selectivity in amino acid transport and that a simple process of diffusion is probably not involved.

The enzymatic role of some of the membrane proteins is fairly well established, but recent investigations have also pointed to the involvement of the membrane *phospholipids* in certain types of active transport. Five different phospholipids occur in the plasma membrane (Figure 14.6). The simplest, *phosphatidic acid,* is a diglyceride bearing only a phosphate group and lacking any additional water-soluble component.

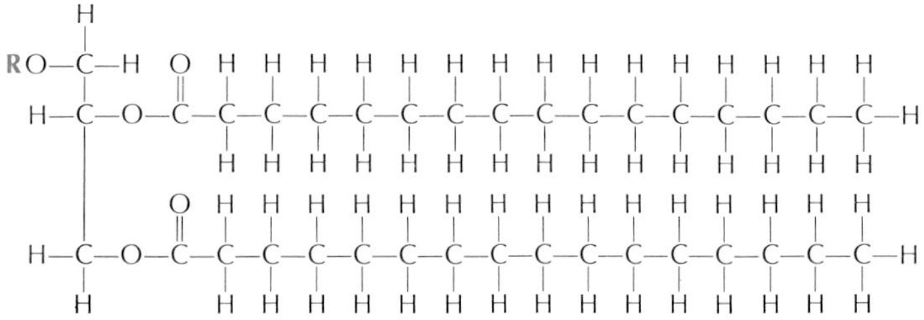

Figure 14.6 □ Lipid components of cell membranes. The type formula is at the right, and below are various groups substituting R in that formula.

$$RO-CH_2-CH(-O-C(=O)-(CH_2)_{14}-CH_3)-CH_2-O-C(=O)-(CH_2)_{14}-CH_3$$

PHOSPHOLIPID	R
(Precursor diglyceride)	H
Phosphatidic acid	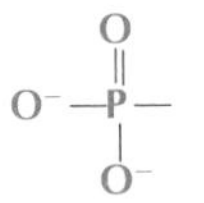 $^{-}O-P(=O)(O^{-})-$
Phosphatidyl inositol	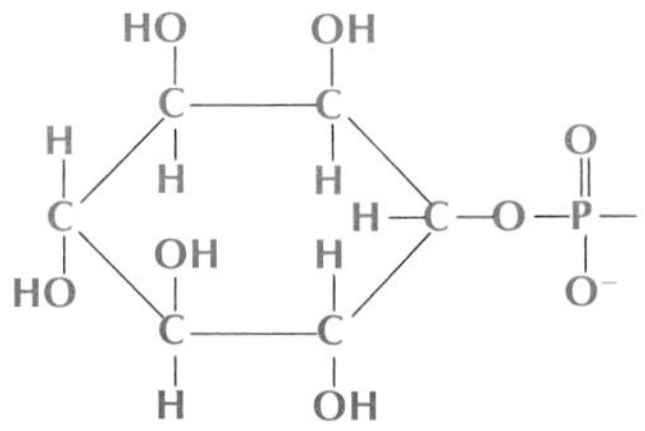 inositol ring $(C_6H_6(OH)_5)-O-P(=O)(O^{-})-$
Phosphatidyl choline (lecithin)	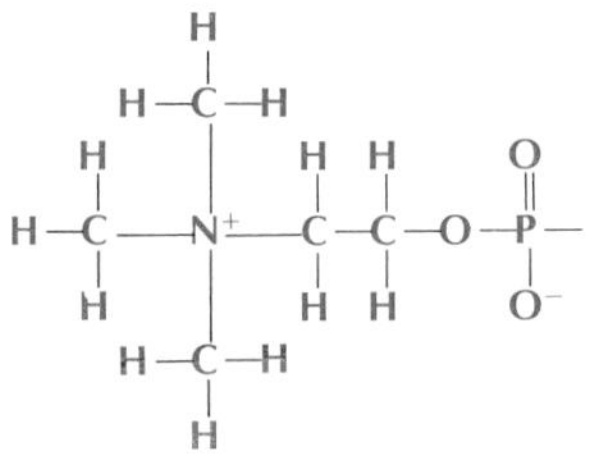 $(CH_3)_3N^{+}-CH_2-CH_2-O-P(=O)(O^{-})-$

Each of the other four bears a different group attached to the phosphate. By far the most abundant of these is lecithin (*phosphatidyl choline*), in which the water-soluble group is the vitamin choline. In the other three, the water-soluble groups are, respectively, *inositol* (another vitamin), *serine* (an amino acid), and ethanolamine (an amine and alcohol). During salt secretion by the nasal salt-glands of seabirds, a portion of the inositol-bearing phospholipid (*phosphatidyl inositol*) gives up both its inositol and phosphate groups, becoming a simple diglyceride; ATP then donates a phosphate to this diglyceride, converting it to phosphatidic acid. When the stimulus eliciting secretion is removed, a recovery period ensues in which phosphatidic acid changes back to phosphatidyl inositol. This fraction of the membrane phospholipid content therefore seems to be involved in ion (especially Na^+) transport, but its exact role remains to be clarified. Figure 14.7 shows the change that takes place in the rate of incorporation of radioactive phosphorus into phosphatidyl inositol in pancreatic cells when these cells are stimulated to secrete protein. The secretion of large protein molecules may require rapid regeneration of portions of the plasma membrane. This regeneration would necessarily be accompanied by an increase in the rate of phospholipid synthesis.

The permeability of cell membranes can be regulated by factors extrinsic to the cell, such as certain hormones (see Section 15.4). Insulin, a product of the vertebrate pancreatic islets, facilitates glucose transport and perhaps also that of amino and fatty acids, as well as other monosaccharides. The adrenocortical hormone aldosterone regulates Na^+ and K^+ transport at the kidneys, salt glands, and other tissues actively engaged in the excretion or absorption of these ions (see Section 16.2A). Reabsorption of water and ions from mammalian urine is promoted by the neurohypophyseal hormone vasopressin (antidiuretic factor). The experimental application of epinephrine (adrenaline) to frog skin causes a dramatic change in the membrane's behavior with respect to Cl^-, for the transport of this ion abruptly changes from a passive flow in one direction to active transport in the opposite direction, thereby elevating the membrane potential (electrochemical difference across the membrane). Although we know that these hormones do affect the permeability properties of the plasma membrane, their precise mode of action has yet to be discovered.

Figure 14.7 □ Rate of synthesis of a membrane phospholipid (phosphatidyl inositol) in pancreatic cells fixed during active secretion of proenzyme (colored bars) and nonsecretory period (gray bars), measured by rate of incorporation of ^{34}P. (*Data from L. E. Hokin* and *M. R. Hokin.*)

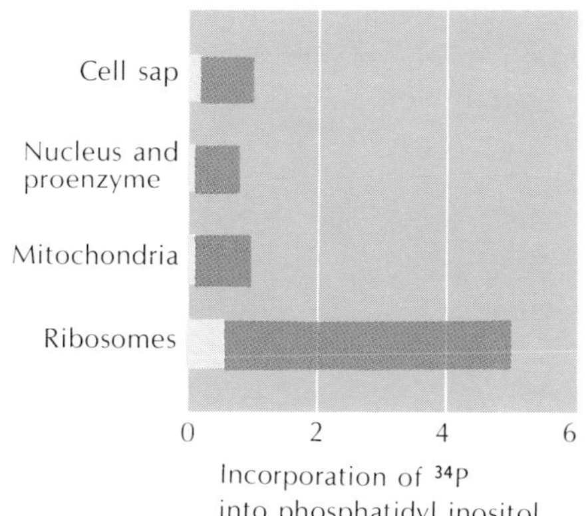

C Pinocytosis, phagocytosis, and exocytosis

These three cell activities abet the processes of active and passive membrane transport. All three probably involve the same fundamental changes in membrane behavior. The major differences are that pinocytosis involves the ingestion by the cell of *liquid* materials, phagocytosis involves the ingestion of *solids,* and *exocytosis* results in the extrusion, rather than the uptake, of such substances as cellular secretions of high molecular weight. In all three instances, the materials involved are enclosed within *vacuolar membranes,* for transport either into or out of the cell.

Pinocytosis and phagocytosis are initiated by the adsorption of certain molecules onto specific binding sites on the exterior of the plasma membrane. This adsorption induces the membrane to invaginate at that point. If the inducing materials (which include amino acids, proteins, and certain salts) are in solution, pinocytosis is initiated. The cell forms large numbers of slender invaginations termed *pinocytic channels,* wherever a binding site is occupied (Figure 14.8). Each channel dilates inwardly as a *pinocytic vesicle* (pinosome), which eventually pinches free and passes into the cytoplasm with its contents. A great number of these tiny vacuoles may be present in the cytoplasm at one time, providing a very effective increase in membrane surface through which active and passive transport can take place. Cells that regularly engage in pinocytosis, including those of the alimentary mucosa, have the plasma membrane of their free surface extended as numerous fingerlike *microvilli,* which much increase the membrane area of this surface (see Figure 13.24).

Phagocytosis is initiated when the material that induces invagination of the plasma membrane is particulate rather than in solution, providing an intense but localized stimulus. The invagination formed is at least as large as the object to be engulfed. When the object is completely surrounded, the plasma membrane closes over the invagination, forming a free vacuole or phagosome in which digestion occurs. Phagocytosis thus not only increases the amount of membrane area available for transport, but makes it possible for amoeboid cells to capture and ingest living prey.

The most universal exocytotic process is probably *secretion.* Secretory cells must release quantities of relatively large molecules that cannot escape either by dialysis or by the usual active transport mechanisms. Such materials include proenzyme molecules, hormones (some of which are polypeptides), mucus (a glycoprotein), lipids, milk, and so forth. These materials are synthesized and retained within the cells until their release is elicited, usually by neural or hormonal stimulation. The flow of saliva is directly instigated by nervous excitation. On the other hand, milk secretion and ejection is hormonally controlled, via the pituitary hormones prolactin and oxytocin. The organic constituents of milk accumulate in the gland cells and when released are diluted by a massive movement of water into the mammary ducts. If the udder of a cow is removed and its milk content expressed, less than a liter of milk can be obtained from an udder that regularly had yielded several

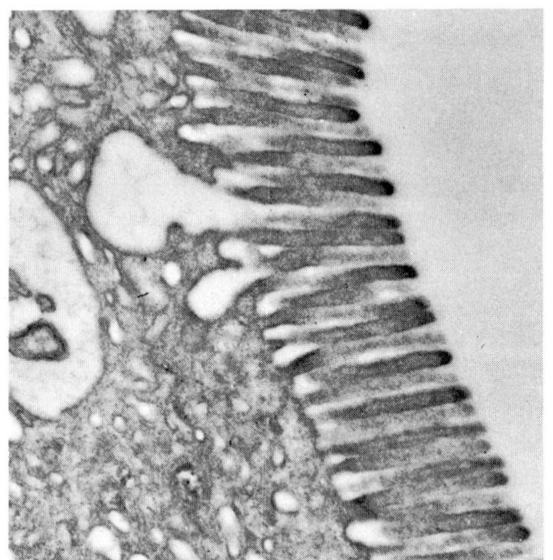

Figure 14.8 □ Portion of mucosal border of epithelial cell (12,500×) from mouse intestine, showing microvilli that serve to increase surface area and pinocytic vesicles that form at microvilli bases and are liberated into cytoplasm; proteins and other colloidal materials are taken into the cytoplasm in this manner. (*Courtesy of Dr. Sam L. Clark, Jr., and* Journal of Biophysical and Biochemical Cytology.)

Figure 14.9 □ Modes of secretion (for clarity, the size of the secretory vesicles is highly exaggerated relative to the size of the cell—processes of merocrine secretion are visible only by electron micrography). (*a*) Merocrine secretion: left, material liberated by fusion of vesicular membrane with plasma membrane; right, material liberated by formation and pinching off of "blebs." (*b*) Apocrine secretion: entire secretory surface of cell ruptures and is regenerated. (*c*) Holocrine secretion: cell disintegrates entirely, liberating accumulated secretory materials.

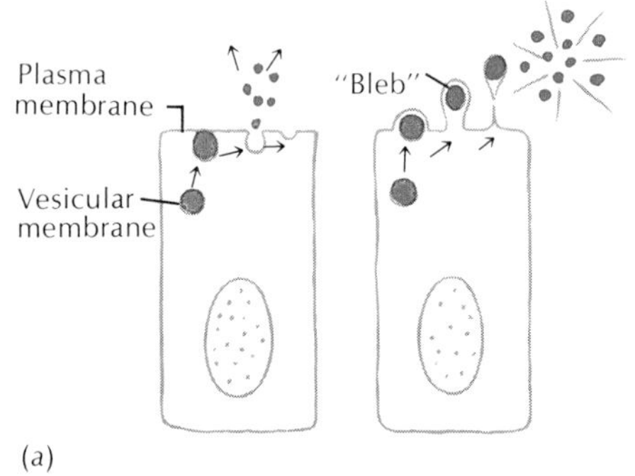

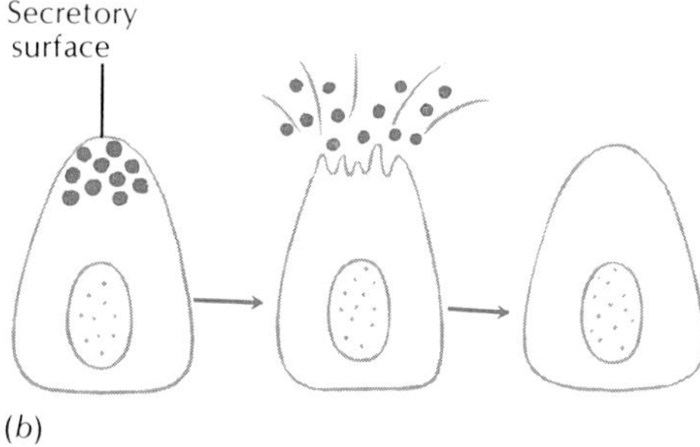

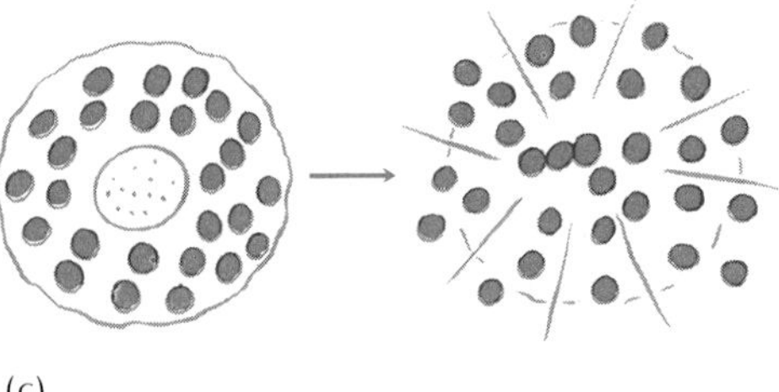

liters per milking. This indicates a rapid refilling of the duct system during the actual process of milking.

Secretion is an active process that is usually not carried on continuously, but is elicited by appropriate stimulation of the secretory cells. In moving such relatively large molecules or droplets out of the cell, and in doing so rapidly, a greater or smaller area of the plasma membrane on the secreting surface of the cell must be ruptured and reconstituted. In pancreatic cells studied in vitro, proenzymes first appear in cytoplasmic vesicles, the membranes of which are heavily studded with ribosomes. These "rough" membranes are continuous with vesicles having "smooth" (ribosome-free) walls, in which the secretion is stored. Being thus enclosed by a membrane through which it cannot pass, the secretion is now in much the same state as undigested material within a phagosome—it is enclosed by the cell but is no longer actually within the cytoplasm. When secretion is induced, these storage vesicles cluster at the exit surface and their membranes fuse at the points of contact with the plasma membrane; the latter then opens at these points and the contents of the secretory vesicles are disgorged (Figure 14.9). A similar secretory phenomenon has been reported, in which the secretion accumulates within numerous small protrusions of the plasma membrane ("blebs"), which are then set free by the pinching together and closure of the plasma membrane across the attached end of each bleb. Freed blebs eventually disintegrate, releasing the enclosed secretion. Bleb formation and release would appear to be precisely the reverse of the process by which a pinocytic vesicle is formed and pinched

Figure 14.10 □ Channels for intracellular transport in striated muscle fibers. The *T*, or *transverse, system* (dark color) consists of invaginations of the muscle-fiber plasma membrane that penetrate into the interior of the fiber at the level of each Z line. The *sarcoplasmic reticulum* (paler color) is homologous with the endoplasmic reticulum of other cells; its channels mainly run lengthwise from one Z line to the next. Membranes separate the channels of the transverse system from those of the sarcoplasmic reticulum. The transverse system is especially involved in conducting electrical excitation from the periphery of the fiber to its interior, but it probably also carries nutrients.

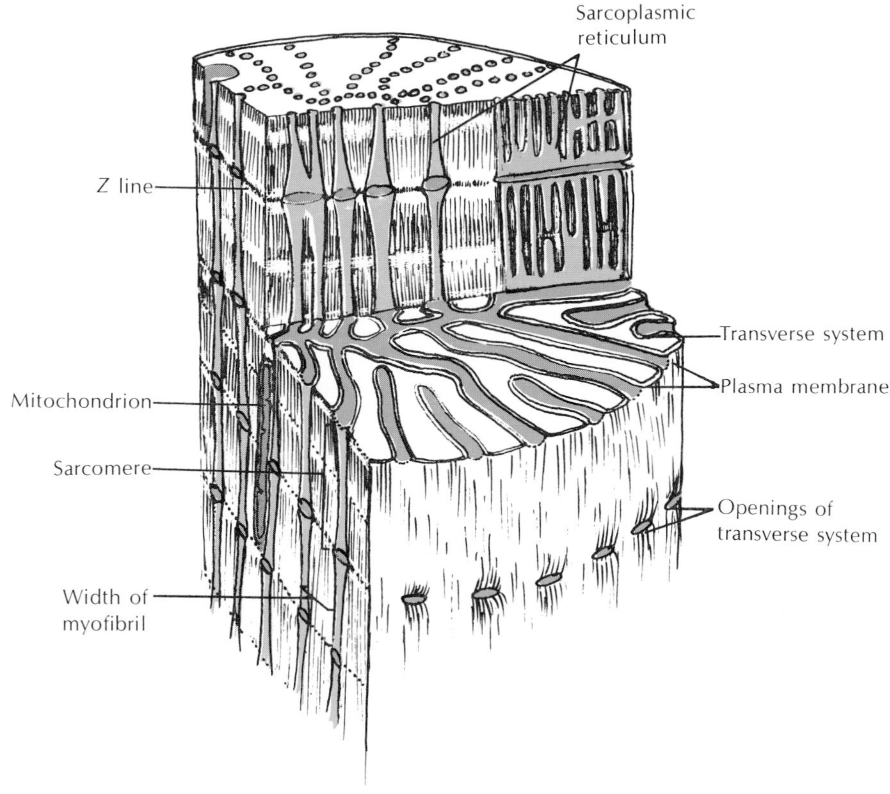

off *internally*. In the case of bleb formation, it is likely that the inducing molecules (the secretion) act on the *inner* side of the plasma membrane in the same manner that nutrient molecules act upon its exterior.

Three kinds of secretory processes—merocrine, apocrine, and holocrine—have been described for mammalian glandular cells. *Merocrine* secretion causes no visible rupture of the plasma membrane. Most glands, both *exocrine* (duct glands) and *endocrine* (ductless glands that secrete into the bloodstream), are merocrine secretors, and although the necessary electron-microscope verification has not yet been forthcoming in all cases, it is probable that the phenomenon of merocrine secretion, formerly so puzzling to histologists, can now be explained in terms of the mechanisms described above. Such glands as the mammary gland must rapidly release large accumulations of high-molecular-weight secretory material. This is accomplished by *apocrine* secretion, in which the plasma membrane of the exit surface appears to be grossly ruptured and regenerated. A third and still more drastic process, *holocrine* secretion, occurs in mammalian sebaceous (skin oil) glands. In this case, as the cell accumulates its lipid secretions, it eventually breaks loose and disintegrates, thus being killed in the process of releasing its products. Its loss is compensated by the production of new gland cells by mitosis.

D Intracellular transport

After substances have entered the cells they must still be distributed throughout the cytoplasm and into various organelles. Both intracellular *fluid* transport and *membrane* transport are involved. The former occurs primarily by way of the endoplasmic reticulum (see Figure 10.9), a canal system that occupies much of the cytoplasm of many cells. Certain channels may even open to the exterior, providing rapid means for transport between the cell core and periphery while also providing much surface for membrane transport. ATP, for instance, can be carried through the reticulum from its major sites of production to particular areas of energy need. In fact the endoplasmic reticulum as well as the plasma membrane bear phosphotransferase enzyme complexes ("ATPase systems") that catalyze removal of Ⓟ from ATP, probably providing energy to the active transport systems of those membranes.

Vertebrate skeletal muscle has been found to have two systems for intracellular transport: (1) the *sarcoplasmic reticulum* resembles the endoplasmic reticulum of other tissues, and serves for the transport of enzymes and nutrients throughout the muscle fiber; (2) the so-called *transverse system* penetrates the fiber at the level of each *Z* line, or boundary between adjacent sarcomeres (Figure 14.10). The transverse system is bounded by internalized portions of the plasma membrane (sarcolemma) of the fiber, and may be formed during the embryonic differentiation of muscle tissue by the partial persistence of the plasma membranes of the individual embryonic cells that fuse to form the striated muscle fiber. It serves especially to conduct excitation from the periphery to the interior, allowing the fiber to contract as a whole.

Such organelles as mitochondria, plastids, and vacuoles possess differentially permeable membrane systems that apparently differ in structure and permeability from the plasma membrane. Mitochondria in vitro, for instance, accumulate Ca^{2+}, Mn^{2+}, and phosphate against their concentration gradients, and we have already noted that the endoplast of plant sap vacuoles differs in behavior from the plasma membrane. Mitochondrial membranes seem to be made up of repeating units consisting of enzyme complexes; there may be some 10,000 such units representing about 70 kinds of enzyme complexes in each mitochondrion.

The organization and properties of subcellular membranes needs much further analysis, as do those of cell membranes in general. It seems likely from chemical and functional analyses performed to date that plasma membranes may become specialized during cytodifferentiation, so that those of various mature tissues become somewhat different, both structurally and functionally. The proportions of the various phospholipids present may differ, as well as the amount of glycosphingolipids (also called *gangliosides:* compounds having molecular weights of 1,000 to 3,000 that contain sialic acid, glucose, galactose, galactosamine, and fatty acid subunits). Gangliosides, though present in relatively small amounts, are important in ion transport, and unite readily with cationic compounds. They are thought to be important in promoting cell cohesion, and also serve as "receptor sites" to which specific compounds that serve as excitors or inhibitors can bind.

Cellular membranes are clearly not mere containers holding the cytoplasm together; they are dynamic, adaptable, and complex, and provide many more riddles for scientists to solve.

14.2 □ FLUID TRANSPORT

The success with which multicellular organisms have solved the problem of effective internal transport has largely dictated their upper limits of size and metabolic efficiency. Only comparatively simple metazoans can do without a circulatory system, relying on random distribution of nutrients, first through the alimentary tract, and then through the tissue spaces; the digestive tract may be much-branched, thus coming in close contact with a large proportion of the body cells (Figure 14.11), but since an effective propulsive mechanism is lacking, no regular circulation is maintained and traffic of materials is relatively sluggish and haphazard. Similarly, nonvascular plants must rely upon passage of substances from cell to cell (sometimes abetted by cytoplasmic streaming) and by diffusion through air- or fluid-filled spaces; lack of a transport system represents no insurmountable barrier to size increase in aquatic plants, however, for the plants' whole surface may serve for exchanges with the environment. Attainment

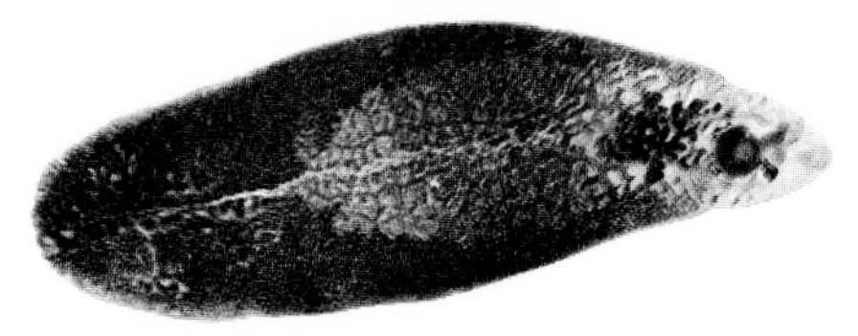

Figure 14.11 □ **Sheep liver fluke (*Fasciola hepatica*) stained to show gastrovascular cavity that branches throughout the tissues, serving for both digestion and internal distribution of nutrients. (*Ward's Natural Science Establishment, Inc.*)**

of appreciable size in terrestrial plants, to the contrary, correlates directly with the efficiency of fluid transport, for solutes and water must be elevated from the roots to the leaves, and organic products of photosynthesis carried from the leaves to the roots and growth regions.

A Fluid transport in vascular plants

Translocation of solutes from one part of the plant body to another takes place by way of the sieve tubes of the phloem and the vessels and tracheids of the xylem (see Figure 11.40). No direct communication exists between xylem and phloem, but at any level materials can pass out of the vascular elements into the tissues and may ultimately reach the other vascular system (Figure 14.12). The phloem is concerned mainly with downward transport of organic metabolites from the leaves to other regions in which they will be stored or utilized, but must also transport materials upward to the growing tips of the shoots. The xylem is the site of upward passage of water and minerals absorbed by the root hairs, and of organic solutes mobilized from storage tissues in the lower parts of the plant and destined for use in the growing tips. The mechanisms of phloem and xylem conduction have long claimed attention, and are still subjects of investigation.

XYLEM TRANSPORT Fluid can rise in the xylem at the impressive rate of 75 cm/min or 1.25 cm/sec. This ascent is caused by the interaction of two forces: root pressure and shoot tension.

Root pressure A positive pressure is generated in roots due to the active and osmotic transport of water from the soil into the root tissues. Osmotic pressure is increased when the root hairs are actively engaged in concentrating ions, or when large quantities of sugar are being mobilized from their site of storage in the root parenchyma. Root pressure builds up at night but is relieved during the daytime by the opening of the stomates, permitting water loss by evaporation (*transpiration*). If the rate of xylem transport is such that the pressure is not adequately relieved by transpiration, water droplets are secreted by glands along the leaf margins (*hydathodes*), which receive the distal ends of the leaf veins; such loss of water by exudation of droplets is called *guttation* (see Figure 4.6).

Root pressure seldom exceeds 2 atm and by itself would be incapable of elevating a column of water to a height exceeding 20 m. For small plants, root pressure can be measured by cutting off the shoot and affixing a vertical length of glass tubing to the severed trunk by means of a rubber collar. If the glass tubing is bent as shown in Figure 14.13, and is filled partially with water and partially with mercury, root pressure forces the mercury column upward in the distal (unattached) arm of the apparatus (called a *manometer*). In an experiment conducted with fuchsia plants, the mercury rose 40 cm in the manometer, indicating a root pressure adequate to raise a column of *water* to a height of about 5 m.

Shoot tension When the stomates are open and the plant is both using water in photosynthesis and losing it by transpiration, water molecules are removed from the top of the xylem columns faster than they can enter at the bottom. This causes the columns of water to move upward, as the pressure within the xylem falls below that of the atmosphere. At the same time, the water columns are put under tension, for their upward movement is opposed by gravity. The columns would snap were it not for the strong *cohesive* tendency of water molecules. Water molecules cling together by means of hydrogen bonds established between the oxygen atom of each molecule and a hydrogen atom of one adjacent. When water molecules at the top of the xylem column are removed, all of the water molecules below are pulled upward as if all were part of one fabric. However, the fact that this fabric is under tension is demonstrated when a xylem column is interrupted: when a tree is felled a hissing sound may be heard, caused by air rushing into the severed xylem elements as the broken columns of fluid retract in both directions from the cut. This retraction can also be observed under the microscope, when a fluid-filled xylem channel is punctured by a fine needle. The puncture allows air to rush in and the fluid column is broken, producing an *air embolism.* During winter freezing such embolisms commonly develop, and if root pressure is inadequate to force the water column to the

Figure 14.12 □ **Vascular system of a tracheophyte. (*a*) Pathways of conduction through the plant body are shown for simplicity as lines; in actuality, phloem and xylem tissue each form a hollow cylinder in the shoot, the phloem enclosing the xylem and the xylem enclosing either pith or wood formed in previous years. Enlarged sections show microscopic structure of xylem and phloem elements and the detail of a sieve plate in phloem. (*b*) Surface view of vascular tissue in cleared *Fothergilla* leaf. (*Ward's Natural Science Establishment, Inc.*) (*c*) Vascular core (stele) of *Ranunculus* root: above, entire root cross section; below, stele only, shown at higher magnification. (*Triarch Incorporated, Geo. H. Conant, Ripon, Wis.*)**

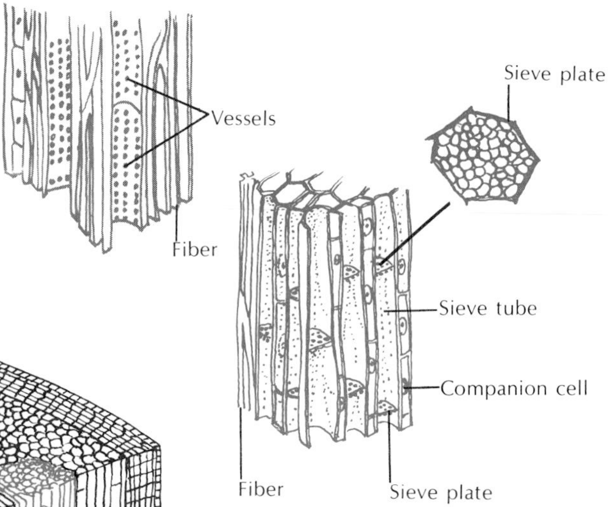

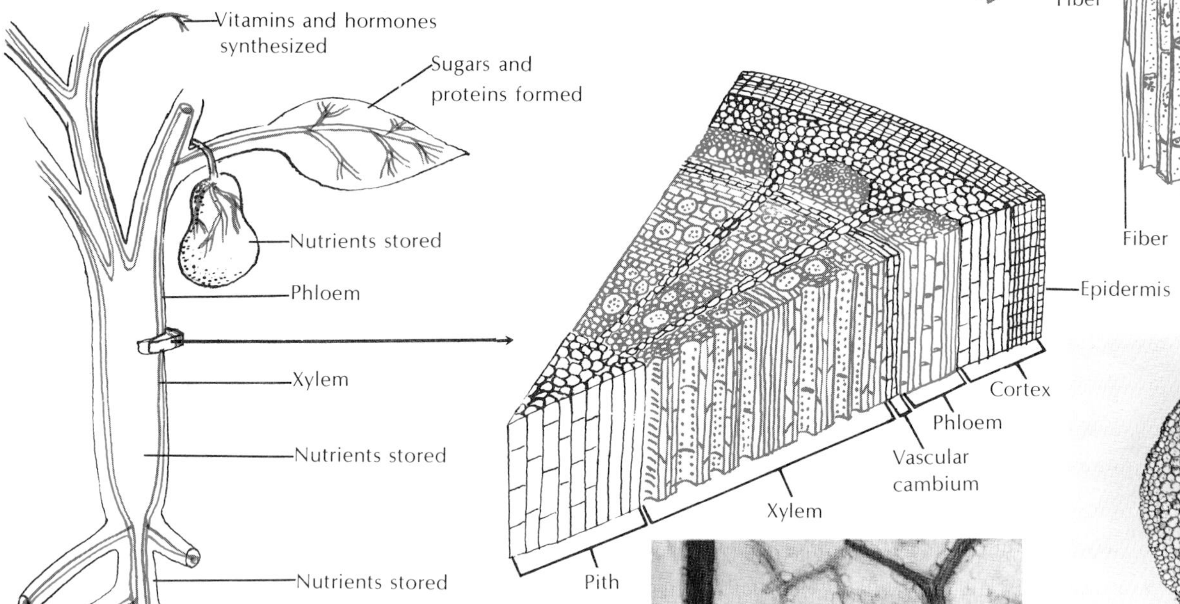

Vitamins and hormones synthesized
Sugars and proteins formed
Nutrients stored
Phloem
Xylem
Nutrients stored
Nutrients stored
H_2O and minerals absorbed· amino acids synthesized

(*a*)

Vessels
Fiber
Sieve plate
Sieve tube
Companion cell
Fiber
Sieve plate
Epidermis
Cortex
Phloem
Vascular cambium
Xylem
Pith

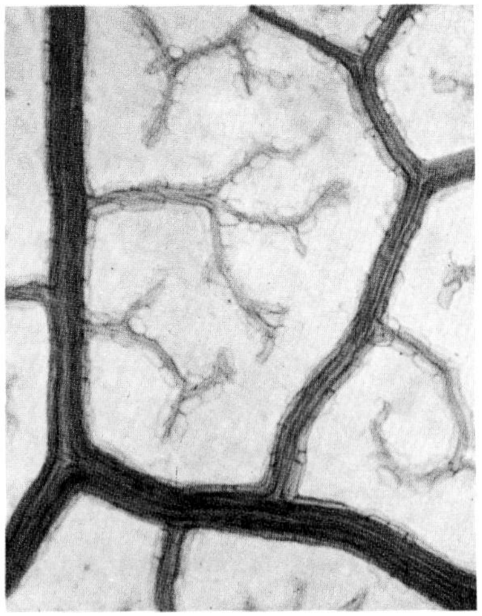

(*b*)

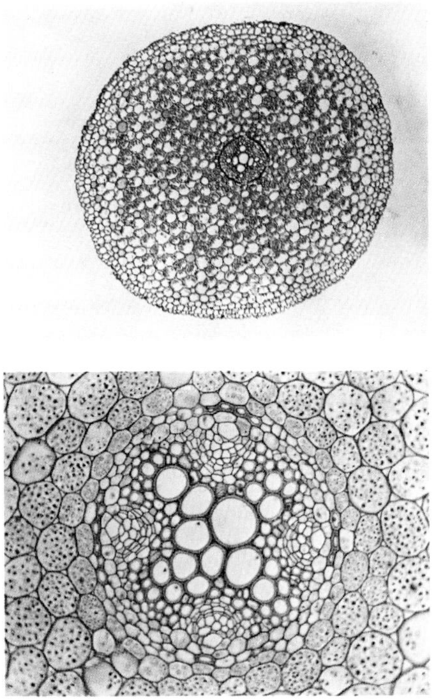

(*c*)

Figure 14.13 □ **Experiment demonstrating root pressure. A glass manometer is attached by rubber tubing to the cut stump of a living plant. The manometer is filled partly with water and partly with mercury. (*a*) At the beginning of the experiment, the level of mercury is the same in both arms of the U tube, but (*b*) as the roots absorb water, pressure develops that forces the mercury upward in the right arm of the tube. A 40-cm rise in the mercury level would indicate a root pressure sufficient to elevate water to a height of over 5 m.**

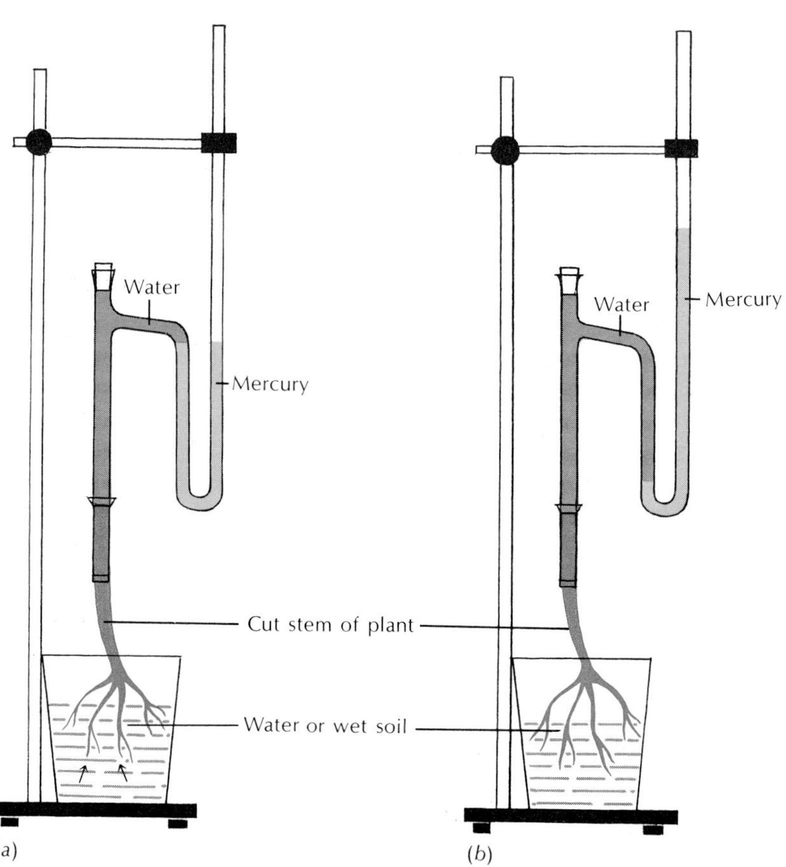

tip of the shoot, thereby clearing the channel of the embolism, the element may be permanently blocked. Such an air pocket may sometimes be bypassed by the transfer of fluid through openings in the side walls of the xylem elements. When an embolism cannot be dislodged, the element soon becomes plugged with solid deposits (lignins and tannins), and thereafter functions as supportive rather than vascular tissue.

The columns of fluid standing in the xylem lengthen as the plant grows. While the plant is small, root pressure alone is adequate to maintain the column intact from root to shoot tip. As the plant gains height, shoot tension becomes increasingly important, not only in maintaining the column, but in causing it to move upward. It is estimated that to maintain a column of water as tall as the tallest trees (about 120 m), a pressure equal to 12 atm must be maintained. We must add to this figure a component of about 18 atm, required for overcoming the frictional resistance between the water and the walls of the xylem elements and allowing the water to move upward. Thus we see that the pressure required to move water to the top of the tallest trees need not exceed 30 atm. Furthermore, this figure may prove excessive, for recent evidence suggests that xylem transport is facilitated by an interaction between water molecules and colloidal proteins associated with the transport system. This interaction is probably at least as important as root pressure in accounting for the massive upward movement of sap in such deciduous trees as sugar maple, just before the new foliage is put on.

Shoot tension can be measured by sev-

Figure 14.14 □ Experiment demonstrating shoot tension, the water-lifting power of transpiring leaves. (*a*) At start of experiment, a cut stem is inserted through a cork sealing the upper end of a water-filled length of glass tubing, the lower end of which is immersed in a vessel of mercury. (*b*) As the shoot loses water by transpiration, mercury is drawn upward into the tube. The 27-cm column of mercury shown here is equivalent to a column of water over 3.5 m tall. (*c*) Mechanical analog of this experiment: as water evaporates from the porous clay vessel capping the tubing, mercury is pulled upward to a height that depends largely on the radius of the column.

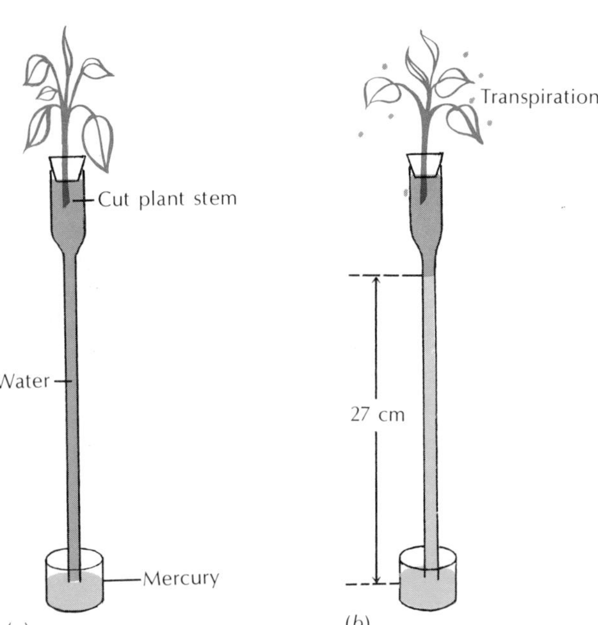

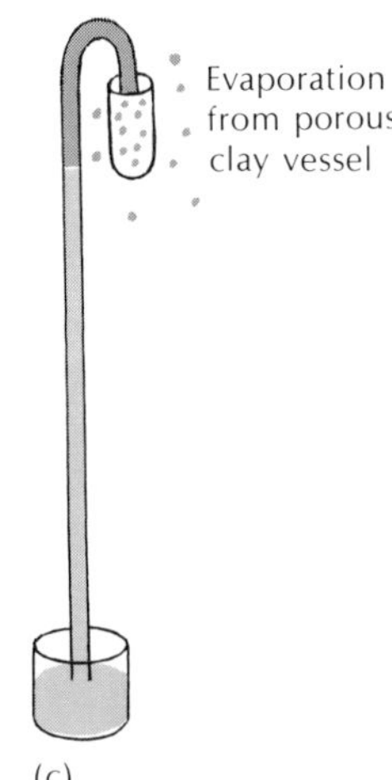

ering a leafy shoot and affixing the cut end to a vertical piece of glass tubing, filled with water (Figure 14.14). The lower end of the tubing is immersed in a vessel of mercury, so that as transpiration proceeds and the intraxylem pressure falls, the pressure of the atmosphere upon the surface of the mercury in the open vessel forces the column of mercury steadily higher in the tubing. The partial vacuum produced by shoot tension is such that a column of mercury originally 76 cm tall can be elevated to heights exceeding 100 cm. Shoot tension is probably the major motive force for xylem transport during most of the life of the plant. It also helps to account for the rapid rate of water uptake from the soil: water is literally pulled through the tissue spaces into the xylem.

PHLOEM TRANSPORT The translocation of organic metabolites from their site of formation in the leaves to other parts of the plant occurs much more slowly than xylem transport but still too rapidly to be explicable on the basis of simple diffusion. According to V. A. Greulach and J. E. Adams,*

> *Calculations show that sugars are transported to a developing pumpkin fruit at rates ranging from 500 to 1000 cm./hr., and rates of 100 cm./hr. or so are quite commonly found in many species of plants. In contrast, sugar diffusing from a 10% solution would take about two and a half years to diffuse a distance of 100 cm. If diffusion were the only means of food transport in plants no plant more than a few centimeters in size could survive, unless its chlorenchyma tissues were distributed throughout the plant.*

* *Plants: An Introduction to Modern Botany* (New York: John Wiley & Sons, Inc., 1967), p. 330.

Figure 14.15 □ Cytoplasmic-streaming hypothesis of phloem transport. Materials may move from one end of a sieve tube to the other by means of cyclic cytoplasmic streaming (cyclosis) and then cross the sieve-plate region by active transport. Reversal of the polarization of the active-transport mechanisms could (*a*) allow materials to pass only in one direction or the other or (*b*) might even allow some substances to move only in one direction while others moved only in the opposite direction. Failure to verify this hypothesis by direct observation of cyclosis may be due to extreme sieve-tube sensitivity to conditions under which such observations must be made.

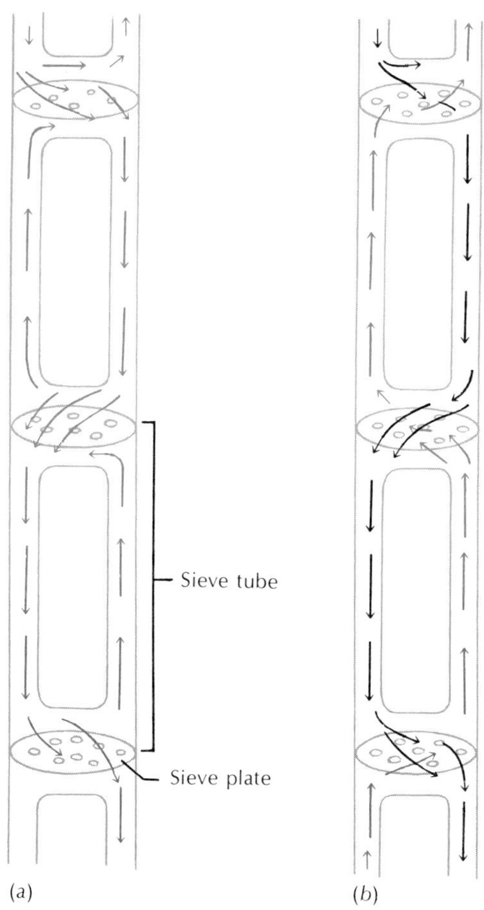

The enucleate but living *sieve tubes* are the transportive elements of the phloem. They are arranged end-to-end in vertical columns, and their end walls are perforated by numerous pores through which cytoplasmic strands communicate from one sieve tube to the next. The phloem sap is under *positive pressure* (that is, a pressure higher than that of the atmosphere), which is made evident when the phloem is punctured. In this event sap is exuded until the bleeding is stopped by the formation of a *callose*—a permanent polysaccharide plug secreted across the sieve plates of the damaged columns. Callose formation occurs on an extensive scale each time a leaf falls and the vascular bundles are severed. This mechanism for controlling bleeding frustrated investigations of phloem transport until a technique was devised for taking advantage of the sap-drinking proclivities of plant lice (aphids). The piercing stylet of an aphid is of prodigious length relative to the insect's body, and can penetrate deeply into the plant tissue to puncture an individual sieve tube. Phloem pressure then forces sap through the aphid's body at such a rate that droplets are exuded from the insect's anus. If the aphid's body is gently severed from the inserted mouthparts, sap will continue to be exuded for hours or even days, at rates up to 5 cm/hr. Such a rate of exudation would require the punctured sieve tube to refill from three to ten times per second!

Although the direction of phloem transport is generally downward, from the photosynthesizing parts to the stems and roots, organic metabolites can also move upward in the phloem from the older leaves to the growing tips and developing fruits or flowers. It is not known whether the direction of phloem transport is subject to reversal in accordance with need, or whether the movement of sap is always upward in some columns, but downward in the majority. The composition of the phloem sap is best analyzed by the aphid technique just described, and is found to have a solute concentration of 10 to 30 percent near the leaves, the solute being mainly sucrose, together with small amounts of amino acids, some other nitrogenous and phosphorylated compounds, and mineral ions. As the distance from the leaves increases, the solute content of the phloem sap declines, due to withdrawal of materials into the parenchyma for storage or growth.

No satisfactory explanation for phloem transport has yet been worked out. As we have noted, the rate of flow is much faster than can be accounted for on the basis of simple diffusion. Cyclic cytoplasmic streaming (*cyclosis*) has been proposed as a means by which solutes entering the upper end of a sieve tube may be moved rapidly to the opposite end, but to date cytoplasmic streaming has only rarely been observed in mature sieve tubes. Cyclosis would, however, make it possible for the same phloem elements simultaneously to transport materials upward and downward (Figure 14.15).

An alternative hypothesis of phloem transport by *mass flow* attributes the movement of solutes to a flow of solvent. The concentration of solutes being highest at the leaves, osmotic pressure would cause water to enter the phloem at that point, carrying with it even those solutes that are present in only low concentrations (Figure 14.16). In support of this hypothesis, it has been found that substances such as hormones, which are present in leaf cells in very low concentra-

Figure 14.16 □ **Mass-flow hypothesis of phloem transport. According to this hypothesis, the production of sugar within the leaf tissues causes these tissues to take up water at such a rate that sugar-rich sap is also forced out of the tissue as turgor pressure counteracts osmotic pressure, the solutes being carried along in a mass flow of solvent (water). This sap cannot enter the xylem because of the opposing xylem pressure (root pressure plus shoot tension) and consequently tends to enter the phloem. Here it is transported in a mass flow maintained by the loss of sugar and water in the lower parts of the phloem system. Sugar tends to leave the phloem in any region where a favorable diffusion gradient is maintained by either the oxidation of sugar within the cells or its conversion to starch.**

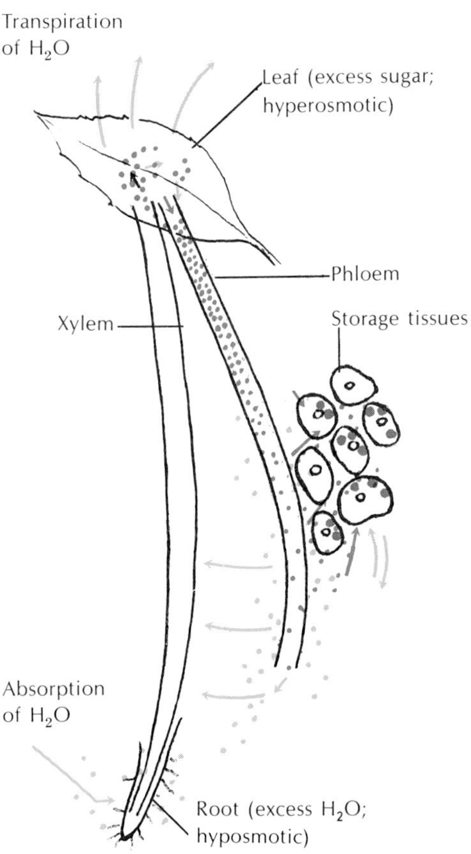

tions, are translocated from the leaves only when sugar is being made and transported. However, the mass flow theory fails to account for the fact that phloem transport slows down when the sieve tubes are deprived of oxygen. Furthermore, the tissues toward which the sap is being carried may have a water or solute concentration equivalent to that in the tissues from which it is being translocated, which would tend to counteract the osmotic pressure acting at the upper end of the system. Even if mass flow should prove to be a factor in phloem transport, it is still too slow to explain the speed at which translocation takes place.

If a tree is *girdled* by cutting away a complete ring of the outer and inner bark from the trunk, the tissues below the cut are deprived of further access to organic materials formed in the leaves. Growth in diameter ceases in the part below the girdle and, after the previously accumulated food reserves are exhausted, the root tissues starve. Since water absorption takes place only in the young tissue near the root tip, cessation of root growth causes eventual death of the girdled shoot due to water deprivation.

B Fluid transport in advanced animals

Efficient means of internal transport become especially critical in those metazoans in which gaseous exchange cannot take place over the entire body surface but is confined to special respiratory organs such as lungs and gills. In such animals special means for gaseous transport become essential, and a true circulatory system may prove indispensible to life. A large fluid-filled body cavity can assist internal distribution but is inadequate if the animal is large, if the body cavity is crowded with organs, or if metabolic demands are high.

FLUID COMPARTMENTS Body fluids are generally confined to several compartments separated by layers of epithelium, so that passage of fluid from one compartment to another usually requires transcellular transport across these epithelia, although some fluid may pass by leaking out between adjacent cells. The major fluid compartments of the animal body (excepting the cavity of the enteron) are: (1) *interstitial spaces* among the tissues, filled with *tissue fluid* that is not confined to epithelium-lined tubes or cavities; (2) in coelomate phyla, a *coelom* or *pseudocoel*, containing *coelomic fluid* which is circulated by ciliary action or by pressure exerted by adjacent muscles; (3) a *circulatory system* including vessels and expanded spaces such as the arthropod *hemocoel,* and in vertebrates constituting both *cardiovascular* and *lymphatic* vessel systems, the former containing *blood* and the latter *lymph;* (4) in chordates only, the *neurocoel* (the cavity of the central nervous system), containing *cerebrospinai fluid.* Exchanges occur among these compartments (Figure 14.17), the motive forces being provided by diffusion, pressure filtration, and active transport. In vertebrates the volume of tissue fluid is increased by pressure filtration of plasma from the capillaries; this in turn promotes movement of materials into the lymphatics, which ultimately drain into the cardiovascular system. Tissue fluid, blood plasma, and lymph are similar in composition, but not identical, differing mainly in protein content and waste concentration. Exchanges between the circula-

Figure 14.17 □ **Movement of water among the extracellular fluid compartments of the vertebrate body: (1) capillary endothelium (lining of cardiovascular system); (2) peritoneum, or serosa, lining coelom; (3) endothelium of lymph capillaries; (4) ependyma (lining of neurocoel); (5) epithelium of renal tubules. Direct communication is shown in color tint, pressure filtration in solid color, and osmosis (grading into pressure filtration as volume in a compartment increases) in gray.**

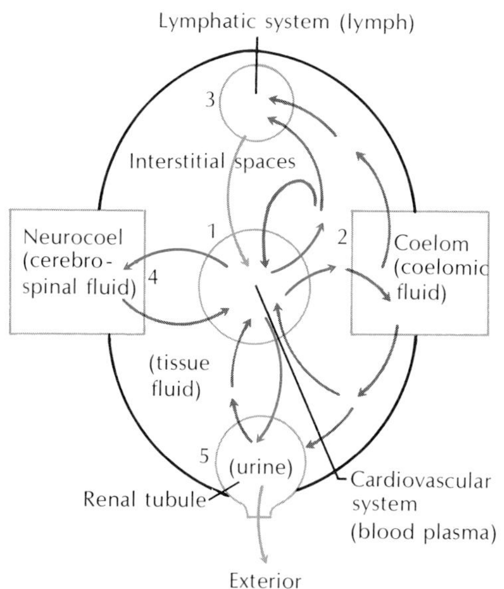

tory system and the cerebrospinal fluid takes place at localized capillary *plexuses* (networks of interlacing blood vessels) within the membranes roofing some of the cavities of the brain.

The circulatory system is the most dynamic of these fluid compartments, for the rapidity with which its contained fluids are circulated promotes exchanges between the blood and the external environment, and between the bloodstream and the adjacent fluid compartments. Rhythmic pulsations of contractile blood vessels or, more effectively, of a hollow pulsatile organ—the heart—maintain circulation of the blood, often creating such pressure that leakage of plasma occurs at the arterial end of the capillaries; this elevates hydrostatic pressure in the adjacent fluid compartments and thus instigates a reverse flow into the venous end of the capillaries, where blood pressure is lowest. In both open and closed circulatory systems (Figure 14.18) a more or less orderly flow of blood is maintained by the heart, which is little more than a contractile blood vessel in nemerteans and annelids, but comes to have chambers, valves, and a thickened muscular wall in higher animals.

THE PATTERN OF HUMAN CIRCULATION We have previously examined representative open and closed circulatory systems, and these should be reviewed by reference to the appropriate descriptions in Sections 12.6C and 12.7A, B, and C. The shark cardiovascular system displays the primitive vertebrate pattern of circulation. Comparing it with the major blood vessels of man (Figure 14.19), the similarity of the human circulatory system to the basic vertebrate plan may not at first be apparent, but on close examination is very much in evidence—especially during embryonic development. The most fundamental changes between the cardiovascular systems of fish and mammals concern the structure of the vertebrate heart, which has undergone significant changes in the adaptation to a land existence. These evolutionary changes will be discussed a little later in this chapter.

The cardiovascular system When first formed the human heart is tubular like the fish heart with blood entering the posterior end and exiting anteriorly, but during development it folds upon itself and ultimately becomes completely subdivided into a "left heart" and a "right heart." After birth, the left heart carries only oxygenated blood and the right heart only deoxygenated blood. The left atrium receives blood from the lungs via the pulmonary veins and pumps it into the left ventricle, from which it is expelled into the aorta. The aorta gives off the arteries of the *systemic circuit* (that serving all regions except the lung alveoli): first, a coronary artery into the heart wall itself; then, carotid arteries to the head and subclavian arteries to the arm (the right subclavian and common carotid spring together from the systemic arch of the aorta as the brachiocephalic artery, whereas the left subclavian and common carotid arteries arise separately, this asymmetry being a reminder of their evolutionary origin from the aortic arches; see Figure 11.45). Passing posteriorly, the aorta now gives off parietal arteries to the body wall and paired and unpaired visceral arteries to internal organs (including renal arteries to the kidneys, coeliac artery to stomach, liver, and spleen, and superior and inferior mesenteric arteries to the intestines). At the end of the trunk, the aorta branches into the common iliac

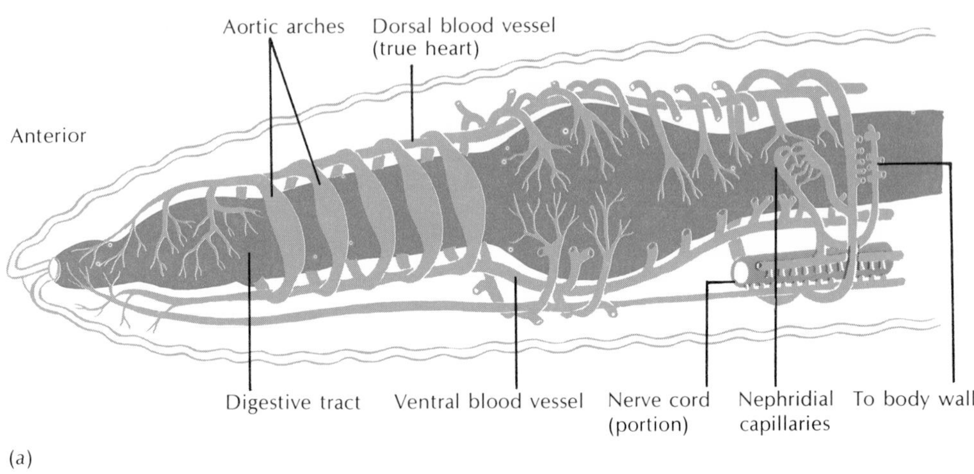

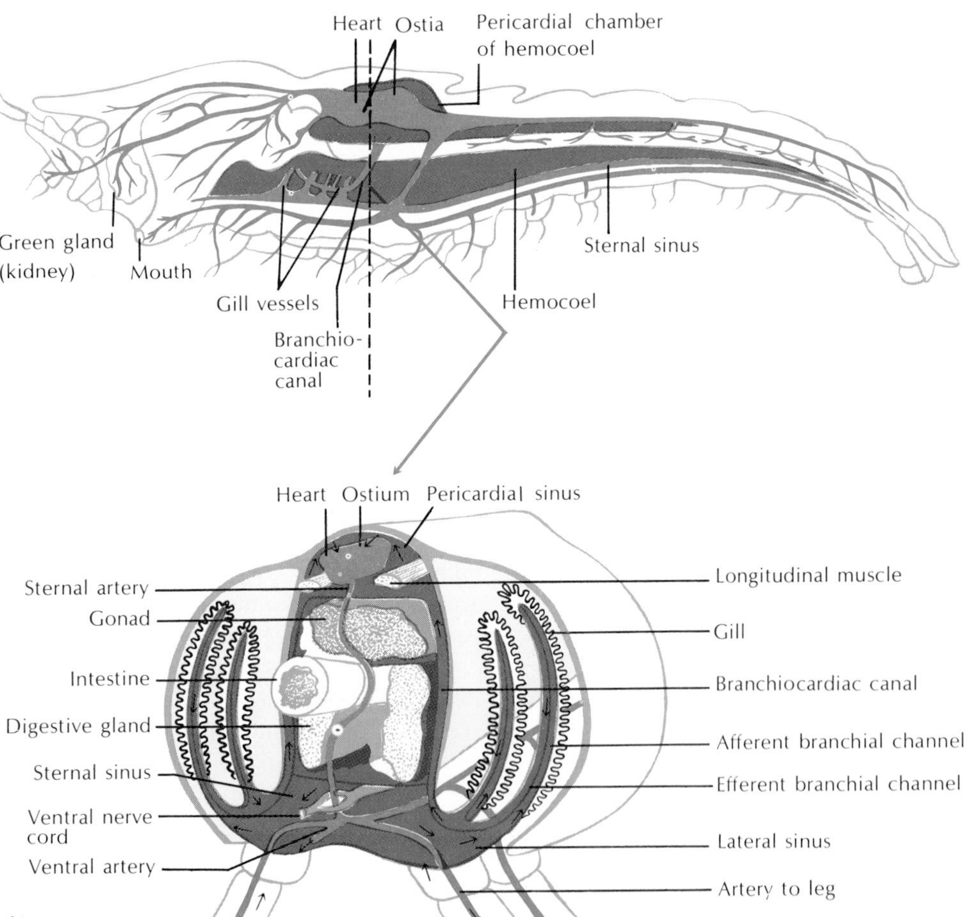

arteries serving the legs. The human arterial system is therefore much like that of the shark except for changes that have taken place in the anterior part of the body: in fish the aortic arches provide the gill circulation; they are present also in amniote embryos, but undergo changes that cause some of them to disappear and others to contribute to the pulmonary artery, carotids, and subclavians.

The systemic arteries branch into progressively finer vessels, the smallest of which are the *arterioles,* leading into the capillaries. The capillaries are the only blood vessels where exchanges can be made between the blood and the body cells. They unite to form the smallest veins (*venules*), which in turn come together to form progressively larger veins. Veins differ from arteries in having thinner walls with much less elastic connective tissue and smooth muscle. Their inner lining, the *endothelium* (the epithelial membrane which continues uninterruptedly throughout the entire

Figure 14.18 □ Invertebrate circulatory systems. (*a*) Earthworm circulatory system, exemplifying pattern of *closed* circulation, in which blood is carried through a closed circuit of blood vessels; the pulsatile dorsal blood vessel serves as a heart to sweep the blood anteriorly, the blood passing ventrally through the paired aortic arches encircling the esophagus and thence posteriorly in the ventral blood vessel that gives off subsidiary vessels in each body segment (see also squid, Figure 12.31). (*b*) Lobster circulatory system, exemplifying pattern of *open* circulation, in which blood escapes from the open ends of the arteries into expanded spaces among the tissues (hemocoel); blood is sucked into the heart from the pericardial portion of the hemocoel, and veins are lacking. The blood-filled spaces and channels of the hemocoel and the heart and arteries are shown in differing shades of color.

Figure 14.19 ☐ **Major human blood vessels. (The hepatic portal vein, draining blood from the alimentary tract, pancreas, and spleen into the liver, is not shown.)**

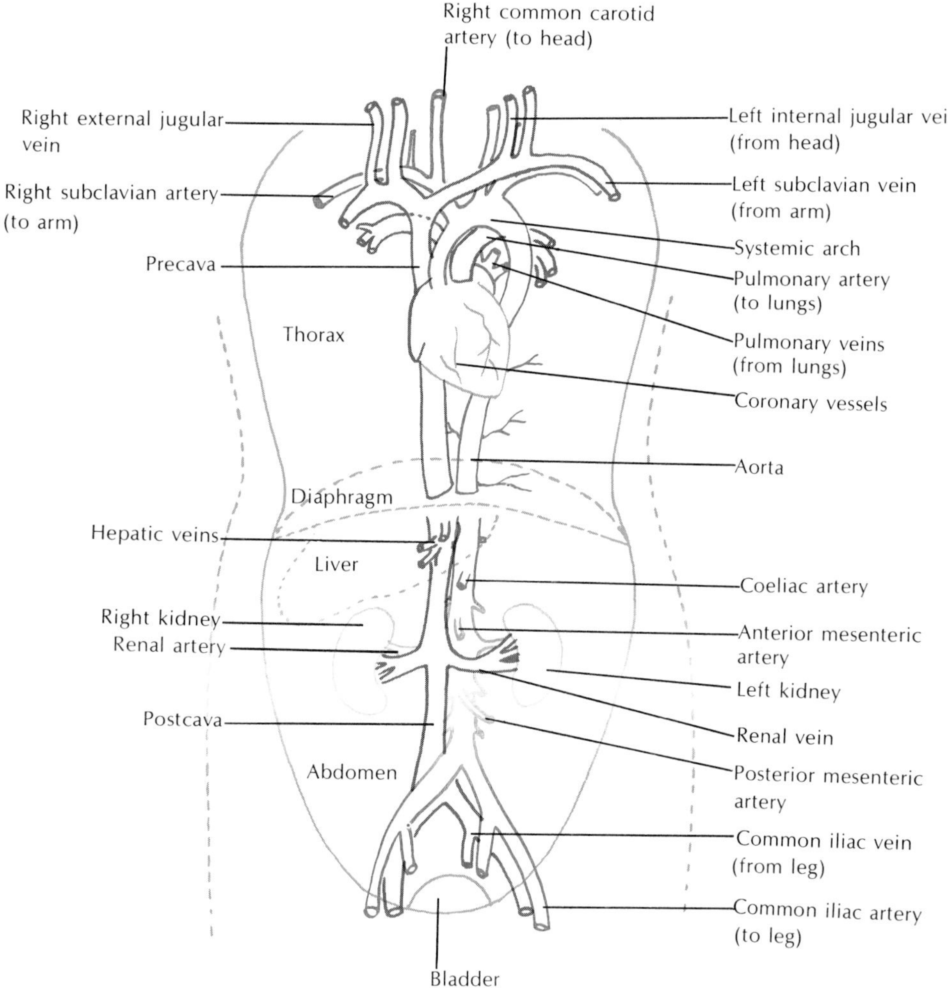

cardiovascular and lymphatic system), is expanded to form pairs of flaps that serve as valves to prevent backflow [and resemble those in lymph vessels (see Figure 14.21*b*)].

Blood is drained from the legs by the common iliac veins that unite at the posterior end of the trunk to form a great vessel, the postcava, which receives parietal veins from the body wall, and veins from the kidneys (renal) and gonads (genital). The postcava is a vessel of complicated evolutionary history, derived in part from the ancient posterior cardinal, which we saw in the shark. All blood draining from the alimentary tract, spleen, and pancreas passes into the hepatic portal system, as in the shark, permitting the liver cells direct access to this nutrient-rich blood. The venous capillaries of the hepatic portal vein come together to form the hepatic veins, which exit from the liver and join the postcava just before the latter enters the right atrium of the heart. The right atrium receives blood from the head and arms by way of the precava, formed mainly by the union of the brachiocephalic veins, each of which in turn is formed by union of the jugular vein from the head and subclavian vein from the arm. Blood from the coronary circulation serving the heart muscle also enters the right atrium from the coronary sinus.

All of the deoxygenated blood collected in the right atrium from the precava, postcava, and coronary sinus is then pumped into the right ventricle, from which it passes on into the pulmonary artery and to the lungs. The passage of blood from the right heart to the lungs, through the pulmonary capillaries, and back to the left heart by way of the pulmonary veins constitutes the *pulmonary circuit;* oxygenation occurs here.

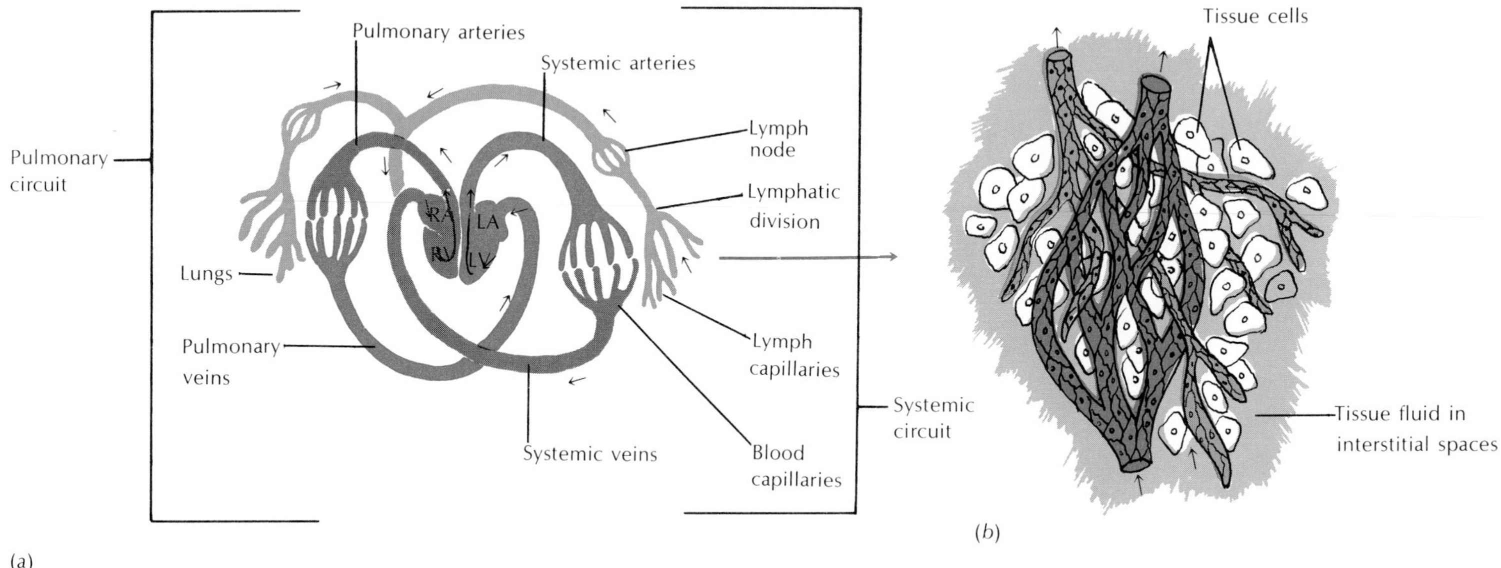

Figure 14.20 □ **Scheme of circulation and relation between cardiovascular and lymphatic divisions of the mammalian circulatory system: (*a*) general scheme of lymph and blood flow; (*b*) lymph and blood capillaries branching among body tissues. (LA and RA mean left and right auricles; LV and RV, left and right ventricles.)**

Figure 14.20 shows the relationships between the pulmonary and systemic circuits of the human cardiovascular system, and between the cardiovascular and lymphatic divisions of the circulatory system.

The lymphatic system Lymph capillaries, like blood capillaries, consist only of the thin layer of endothelium that lines the entire circulatory system; however, they do not communicate at both ends with larger vessels, but end as blind, closed fingers in the tissue spaces, where they are bathed in interstitial fluid (Figure 14.21). A rise in hydrostatic pressure in the interstitial fluid compartment causes tissue fluid (a filtrate of blood plasma to which are added cell secretions and wastes) to enter the lymph capillaries. The lymph capillaries join to form progressively larger *lymphatics,* thin-walled vessels similar to veins but with even thinner walls and with more closely spaced valves along their length, giving them a beaded appearance. As the lymph drains from the periphery it is filtered through lymph nodes populated by defensive lymphocytes (see Section 6.3E). Lymph from the legs and lower trunk is collected in an expanded lymph space (*cisterna chyli*), which continues anteriorly as the thoracic duct that also receives branches from the left arm and the left side of the chest and head. The thoracic duct also receives the *lacteal* drainage from the alimentary tract, this lymph often being milky with lipids absorbed from the intestines during digestion of a fatty meal. Lymphatics from the right side of the head and chest and the right arm drain instead into the right lymphatic duct. The thoracic duct empties into the left brachiocephalic vein, the right lymphatic duct into the right brachiocephalic vein. The importance of the lymphatic drainage becomes dramatically apparent when it is blocked by the bodies of roundworms (*Wuchereria bancrofti*) transmitted by the bite of a mosquito. The affected part of the body becomes grossly swollen, a condition termed *elephantiasis* (Figure 14.21c).

Figure 14.21 □ (*a*) Diagram of human lymphatic system. (*b*) Lymph vessel sectioned to show valve that prevents backflow. (*Courtesy of General Biological, Inc., Chicago.*) (*c*) An advanced case of elephantiasis, a condition resulting from the blockage of lymphatics by the parasitic nematode *Wuchereria;* the subject is a native of French Polynesia. (*Courtesy of Dr. John F. Kessel.*)

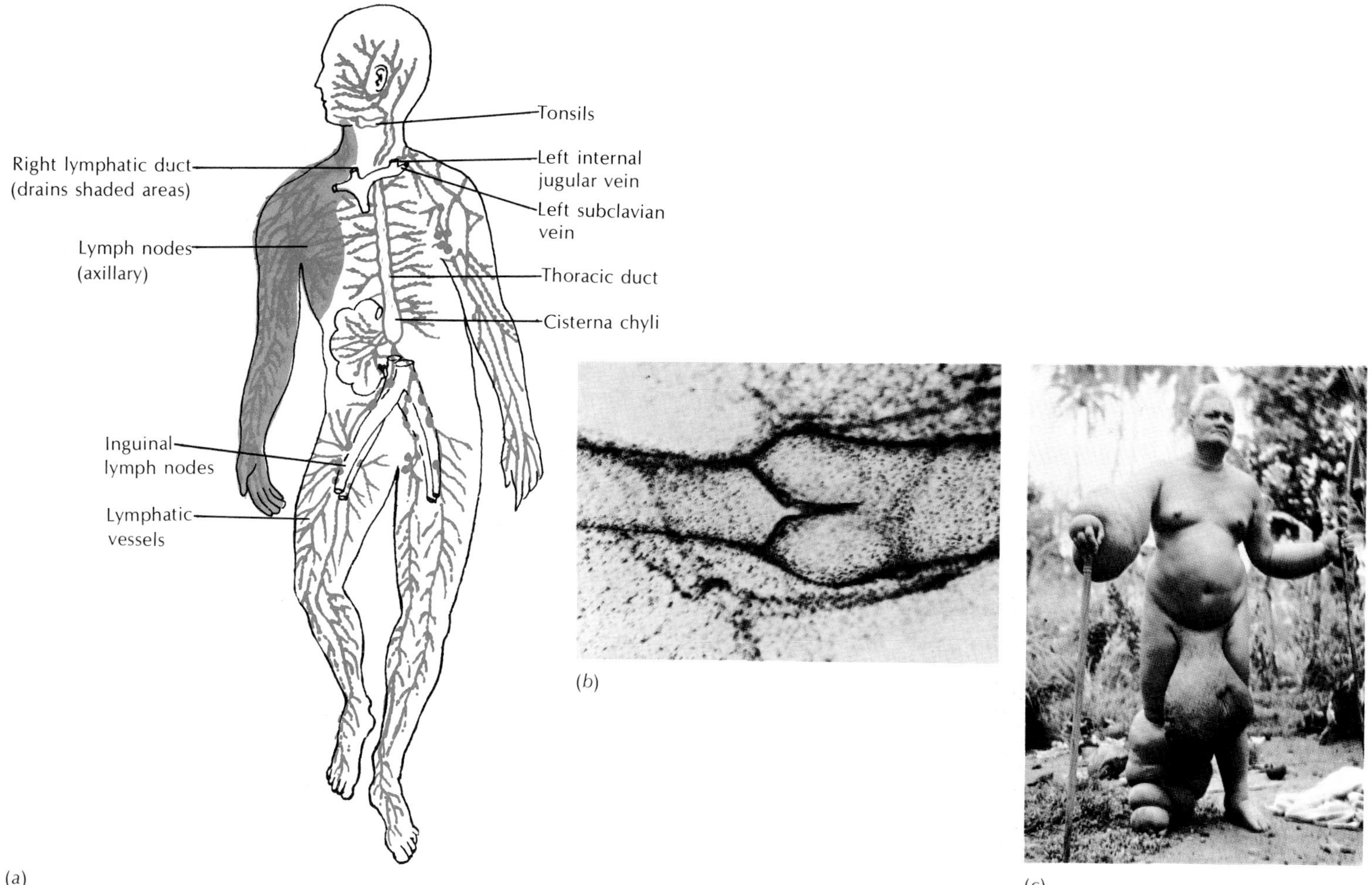

EVOLUTION OF THE VERTEBRATE HEART The fish heart, representing the primitive vertebrate type, consists of a linear series of four chambers, these being the sinus venosus, atrium, ventricle, and conus arteriosus (from posterior to anterior—the direction of blood flow). Valves between atrium and ventricle and in the walls of the conus prevent backflow. The heartbeat is initiated in the sinus venosus and sweeps anteriorly, carrying the deoxygenated blood forward to the gills. In land vertebrates the need for a more efficient circulation has led to the evolution of a *double blood circuit,* in which blood receives *two* propulsive surges for each complete circuit of the body. The first occurs before it passes through the lung capillaries (the *pulmonary* circuit); the second, before it is sent to the capillaries of the other body tissues (the *systemic* circuit). We have already seen how an equivalent double propulsion is furnished separately by the systemic and branchial hearts of cephalopods. In the vertebrates a similar outcome has been achieved by evolutionary changes in the organization of the heart itself (Figure 14.22). Fish, as we learned in Chapter 12, have a *single* blood circuit, in which the blood must traverse from two to four sets of capillaries in each complete circuit, that is, while being pumped through the heart only once (see Figure 12.41*b*); the blood pressure in the systemic arteries is low because of frictional resistance encountered in the branchial capillary bed.

Figure 14.22 □ Evolution of the vertebrate heart as seen in (*a*) fish, (*b*) amphibian, (*c*) reptile, and (*d*) bird or mammal (branches of the aorta and postcava are omitted). Arrows indicate direction of blood flow, and oxygenated blood is designated by colored dots and deoxygenated blood by gray. A progressive trend toward separation of the right and left sides of the heart is apparent, beginning with the partitioning of the atrium and conus arteriosus and extending to the ventricle in amniotes. (V, ventricle; A, atrium; SV, sinus venosus.)

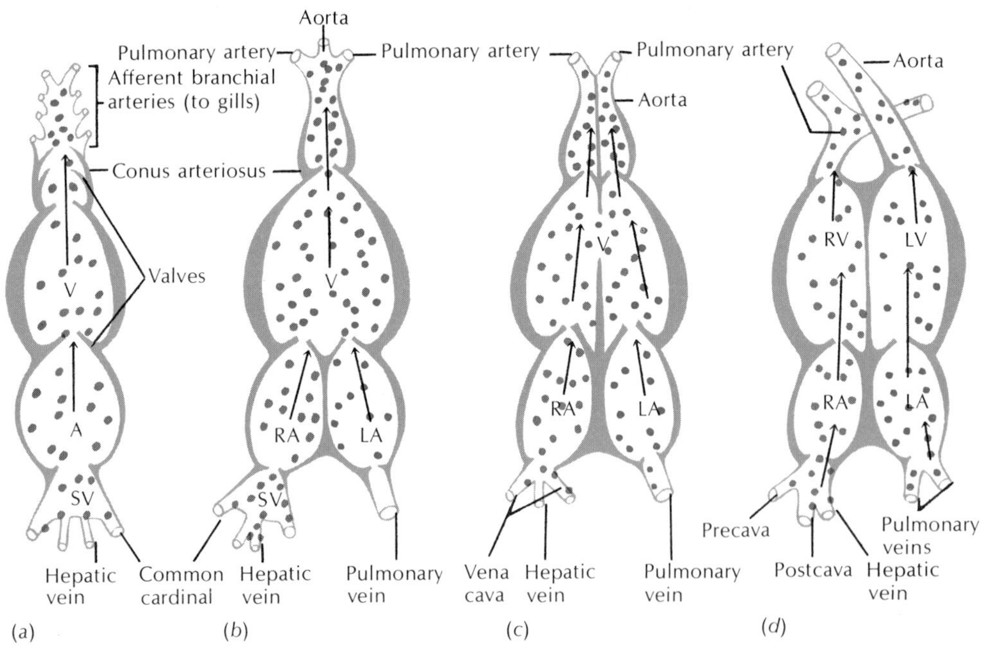

The increased transport requirements of tetrapods has favored a return of blood to the heart from the lungs, and a partitioning of the heart into right and left halves, which do not normally communicate during postnatal life. The fish heart's linear four-chambered organization is still reflected in the heart of the tetrapod embryo, and a comparative study of living vertebrates indicates that there has been a gradual reduction of the sinus venosus, a partitioning of the atrium and ventricle, and a splitting of the conus arteriosus into separate pulmonary and systemic arterial trunks. In the amphibian condition, the atrium is fully subdivided into right and left chambers. The right atrium receives only deoxygenated blood from the systemic veins; the left, only oxygenated blood from the pulmonary veins. This blood mixes to some extent in the single ventricle, though in the highly evolved hearts of modern frogs and toads this mixing is minimized. Two arterial trunks, pulmonary and aortic, spring from the am-

Figure 14.23 □ Mammalian fetal circulation. Note that only the umbilical vein carries fully oxygenated blood, having obtained oxygen from the mother's bloodstream. The mixed blood entering the heart can bypass the pulmonary circuit by way of an opening between the right and left atria (the foramen ovale) or by way of a shunt from the pulmonary artery to the aorta (the ductus arteriosus). Heavy colored and gray arrows mark the locations of these circulatory shunts. At birth, the umbilical circulation is interrupted, and the foramen ovale and ductus arteriosus close, directing blood into the pulmonary circuit and establishing the adult pattern of circulation as shown in Figure 14.20.

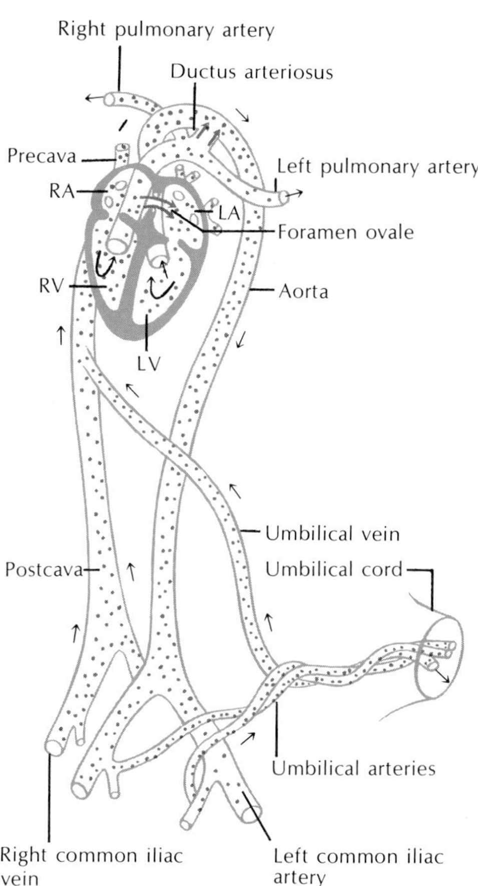

phibian ventricle. Separation of the ventricle into right and left halves began in the reptiles, although in most of these the ventricular septum remains incomplete. Complete separation of right and left ventricles is seen in both birds and mammals. Accordingly, as we saw for man, the "right heart" carries only deoxygenated blood, which it pumps out to the pulmonary artery, and the "left heart" carries only oxygenated blood, received from the pulmonary veins and pumped out to the aorta for systemic distribution.

Thus in homoiotherms, where need for oxygen is greatest, a complete double circuit has evolved: blood passes from the right heart to the pulmonary circuit, returns to the left heart, whence it passes into the systemic circuit, and is finally returned to the right heart. This double impetus elevates the blood pressure in the systemic circuit and consequently accelerates the rate of flow. In fetal mammals the right and left atria communicate by way of an orifice (*foramen ovale*) that allows most of the blood entering the right heart to bypass the pulmonary circuit. This shunt is assisted by the ductus arteriosus, a persistent segment of aortic arch VI that connects the aorta with the pulmonary artery. (This pulmonary bypass is adaptive in that fetal blood is not oxygenated in the lungs but in the placenta.) At birth the foramen ovale normally closes (although occasionally it remains open and requires surgical repair), while the ductus arteriosus constricts to a nonfunctional vestige (Figure 14.23).

THE HEARTBEAT AND ITS REGULATION A heart exhibits *pulsation,* a rhythmic activity in which a nearly synchronous contraction, *systole,* alternates with a period of relaxation and filling, *diastole.* A single pulsation, the *cardiac cycle,* consists of the heartbeat itself and a *refractory period* during which the heart cannot be stimulated to beat and consequently is allowed to rest. In a resting man one cardiac cycle lasts 0.8 sec (Figure 14.24). Atrial systole takes 0.2 sec, following which the atria relax and fill for the remainder of the cycle. Ventricular systole immediately follows atrial contraction, lasting only 0.3 sec, after which the ventricle relaxes and fills for 0.5 sec. During exercise or emotional excitement the entire cardiac cycle is abbreviated as the heart rate accelerates; since each part of the cycle is proportionately shortened, however, the heart still remains at rest for approximately half of each cycle. This refractory period prevents the heart from becoming fatigued.

Initiation of the heartbeat The heartbeat may be myogenic or neurogenic. In *myogenic* hearts such as those of vertebrates and, presumably, molluscs, pulsation is an inherent property of cardiac muscle fibers and is exhibited independent of innervation. *Neurogenic* hearts such as those of decapod crustaceans (crabs, lobsters and true shrimp) and the "horseshoe crab" *Limulus* (actually a chelicerate), can be identified by the fact that their walls are associated with ganglionic nerve cells, removal of which causes the heartbeat to cease. Myogenic hearts may also have associated cardiac ganglia, but in this case removal of the nerves does not abolish the heartbeat. The heartbeat of insects and decapods is myogenic in larval life, but becomes neurogenic in adulthood. Most animals with a myogenic heartbeat develop neural connections to the heart during ontogeny, so that although the heart continues to beat intrinsically, the rate and force of pulsation are subject to the modulatory influence of the nervous system. In some groups (such as hagfish, brine shrimp, and fairy shrimp) the heart permanently lacks innervation, but is subject instead to hormonal control.

The intrinsic rhythmicity of myogenic cardiac muscle manifests itself very early in ontogeny, before nerves have grown out to the heart. The fetal rat heart begins to beat during the tenth day of development. Autonomic nerves (see Section 15.3C) make contact with the heart about the sixteenth day, but the heart remains unaffected until a day or two before birth. At this time, sympathetic nerves begin to exert an excitatory effect, but the restraining influence of the parasympathetic fibers is not demonstrated until about 16 days *after* birth. Similarly, the heart of the chick embryo begins to pulse during the thirtieth hour of incubation, considerably before any neural connections are established. The beat is initially confined to the right ventricle, but somewhat later the right atrium starts to beat at a faster rate that causes the ventricular pulsation to accelerate synchronously. Still later the sinus venosus begins to pulsate, at a still more rapid rate, once more stimulating the slower chambers to accelerate.

Figure 14.24 □ **Each division of the circle graph represents one-eighth of a cardiac cycle of the human heart. The atrial and ventricular systoles (shaded portions) take up only half the cycle; during the remainder, the heart is refractory to stimulation, and it relaxes and fills. In a resting man, one cardiac cycle typically lasts 0.8 sec, giving a value of 0.1 sec for each division, but during exercise, the entire cycle may be greatly accelerated, without, however, altering the proportions required for systole, diastole, and filling.**

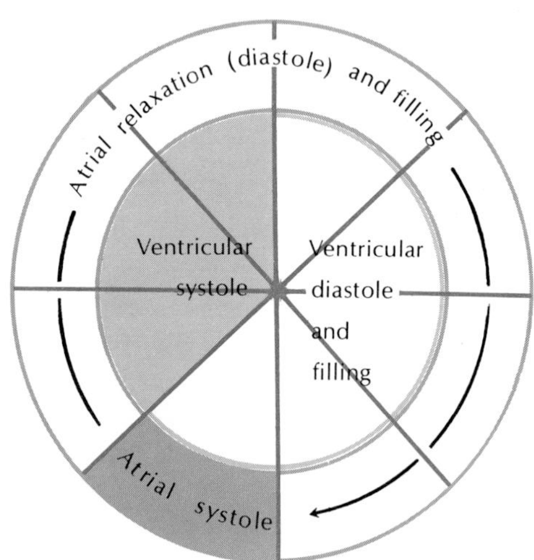

Cells from different parts of the vertebrate heart are characterized by different endogenous rates of pulsation. These are exhibited when heart muscle fibers are separated by trypsin digestion and maintained in vitro. As long as the cultured cells remain apart, each beats at its own characteristic rate, but when the cells reaggregate, the most rapidly pulsating cell in the group acts as pacemaker for the rest. The intrinsic rate of pulsation for the whole heart is set by that region which has the shortest period of oscillation. This basic rate is subject to influence by extrinsic factors, and also changes with age.

In man the neonatal heart beats about 140 times per minute, declining to 90 times in childhood, to 75 during adulthood, and to 70 in old age. There is also a sexual difference which becomes apparent even during fetal life, for the heart of a female human fetus beats at a rate of 140 to 145 times per minute and that of a male 130 to 135 times. Among homoiotherms, heart rate correlates inversely with body size, a mouse heart beating 700 times a minute while an elephant's beats but 25 times.

Heart rate may also differ among related species despite a correspondence in size. When the hearts of salamanders of closely related species are exchanged by transplantation during embryonic life, we find that each heart maintains a rate characteristic of its own species, and neither accelerates nor decelerates to the rate characteristic of the host species. Although appropriate nerve connections may develop, the fundamental heart rate is not altered by factors present in the body into which the heart has been transplanted.

During development certain muscle fibers of the myogenic heart usually become differentiated into *pacemakers*. The cells of a pacemaker region are deficient in contractile properties, but have great spontaneous excitability. Their morphology is usually distinctive, and their pacemaker function can be verified by localizing the point in the heart at which is generated the electrical impulse that is detectable by electrocardiography. The tunicate heart is tubular and has a pacemaker at each end. The excitability of the two pacemakers fluctuates alternatively, so that the heart's wave of contraction sweeps in one direction for a number of beats and then reverses, causing blood to flow in the opposite direction. Interestingly, these two pacemakers cause the heart to beat at different rates.

In the fish heart the *sinus venosus* serves as pacemaker, setting the rate for the entire heartbeat. With the disappearance of this chamber in higher vertebrates, a vestige remains as the *sinatrial node*, an oval swelling in the wall of the right atrium close to

Figure 14.25 □ **Intrinsic excitatory system of the human heart. Nerves terminating at the sinatrial (S-A) node, the heart's pacemaker, merely modify the rate of its discharge and are not responsible for its basic rhythmic firing. Conductive Purkinje fibers (modified muscle tissue) propagate the excitation from the S-A node through the walls of the atria to the atrioventricular (A-V) node, which initiates ventricular contraction by way of Purkinje fibers descending in the interventricular septum and branching out into the ventricular walls. An impulse can propagate from the A-V node to the most distant parts of the ventricular wall in only about 0.065 sec.**

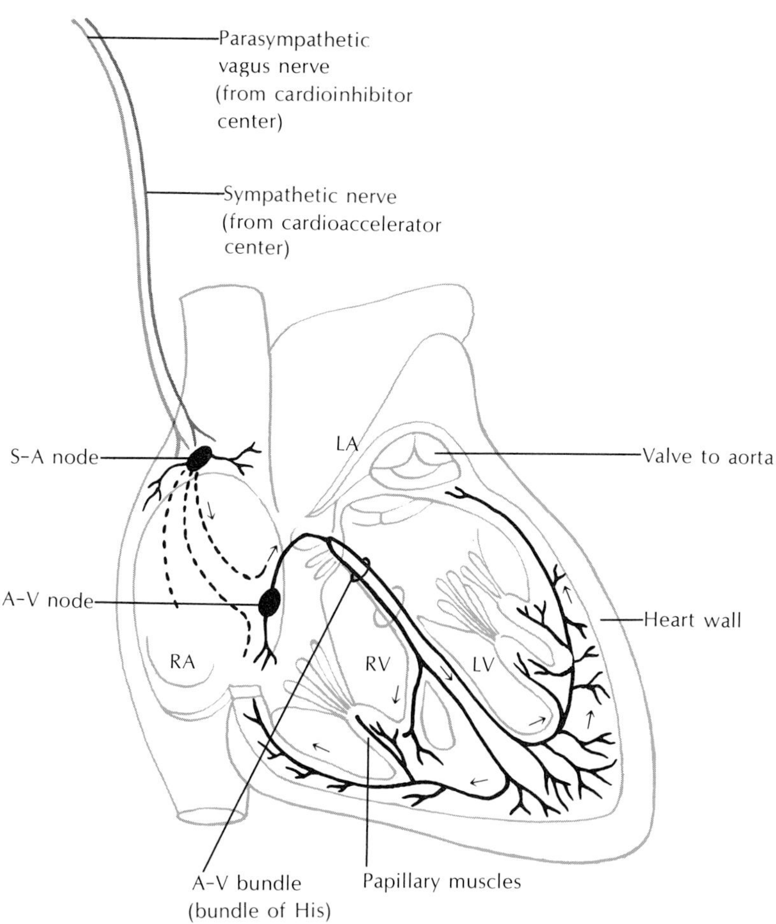

the point of entrance of the precava (the great vein draining the head and forelimbs). The firing of the sinatrial node initiates a wave of excitation (an "action potential") that propagates through the atrial wall at the rate of 1 cm/0.01 sec. Reaching a second group of modified excitable muscle fibers, the *atrioventicular node,* located at the junction of the right atrium and ventricle, the excitation causes this node to fire in turn, propagating the excitation through the ventricular walls and interventricular septum. This propagation is accelerated by means of *Purkinje fibers,* bundles of elongated, noncontractile muscle fibers that serve as intracardiac conductile elements (Figure 14.25). The excitation travels through the Purkinje fibers at the relatively rapid rate of 5.6 cm/0.01 sec, thus making possible a nearly synchronous contraction of all parts of the ventricles.

The most conspicuous physiological feature of myogenic cardiac muscle fibers is that they exhibit a regular, spontaneous fluctuation in membrane polarity. In section 14.1B we noted that the selective permeability of the plasma membrane to various ions results in an ionic distribution that causes the interior of the membrane to be electronegative to the exterior, creating a *transmembrane potential.* When at rest the interior of a cardiac muscle fiber is 70 to 100 mV negative to the exterior, due to a preponderance of anions in the cytoplasm. Upon contraction, this potential reverses, as cations enter the cell until the interior is about 20 mV *positive* to the exterior. This change is similar to that which occurs during the excitation of nerve and skeletal muscle fibers (see Section 15.1A), but a characteristic distinction is that the membrane potential of a cardiac muscle cell declines spontaneously (without the need for nervous stimulation) to a critical point at which a sudden inflow of cations takes place. This serves as a trigger to excite the cell's contractile mechanisms. The rhythmic contraction of heart muscle may therefore be due to an innate periodicity in the behavior of the cell membrane's ion transport mechanisms. It appears as if the membrane of a cardiac muscle fiber periodically allows cations gradually to leak into the cytoplasm until a threshold is reached at which a wave of electrical excitation is triggered, whereupon the fiber contracts. The role of ionic exchanges in the excitation of heart muscle is so important that it is not surprising to find that a proper balance of cations in the surrounding fluid is essential to normal heart action. If an excised heart is perfused with a solution such as NaCl, which contains only a single cation, it will soon cease to beat. An excess of either Na^+ or K^+ arrests the heart in diastole, while Ca^{2+} arrests it in systole. Each of these three cations is highly toxic by itself; all three must be present in the right proportions for the heart to beat normally.

The pacemaker of a neurogenic heart is the group of nerve cells that form its *cardiac ganglion.* In the lobster this ganglion consists of only nine neurons: four small "pacemaker cells" and five larger "follower cells." If any one of the smaller cells fires an action potential, the rest fire almost synchronously, initiating an immediate discharge by the follower cells. This excitation is sufficient to rouse the entire heart to contraction.

The sum total of the changes in membrane potential that accompany the heartbeat is so great that an electrical current is set up which can be monitored by electrodes applied to the exterior of the body. A recording—an electrocardiogram (ECG)—of a beating fish heart displays a characteristic wave for the contraction of each chamber (sinus venosus, atrium, ventricle, and conus arteriosus, in that order). In the mammalian heart the ECG shows only *two* distinct waves, one reflecting the excitation of the atria and the other the excitation of the ventricles.

In lower vertebrates a number of other pulsatile organs, the *lymph hearts,* are located at points where large lymphatics enter the veins. Contractions of these hearts force lymph into the venous flow. The walls of the lymph hearts contain branching striated fibers that more closely resemble skeletal than cardiac muscle. Contractions of these fibers are initiated reflexively by the spinal cord in response to impulses from stretch receptors in the walls of the lymph hearts, but when deprived of a nerve supply they continue to show a spontaneous but sporadic pulsation.

Modulation of the vertebrate heartbeat Both the frequency and amplitude of the heartbeat can be adjusted in response to need. The heart itself responds to stretching by contracting more forcibly, increasing its *stroke volume,* or quantity of blood ejected per systole ("Starling's law"). In trained athletes stroke volume may be so great that the resting heart rate is as low as 50 beats per minute. The output of the heart is a function of both stroke volume and frequency of beat, the *minute volume* being the product of the stroke volume times the number of beats per minute. A characteristic minute volume in man is 9.5 liters, but this may greatly increase during exercise. Exercise accelerates the rate of venous return, due to the pressure of skeletal muscles, massaging the blood inward from the periphery. This increases the amount of blood which enters the heart during diastole, with the result that (up to the heart's physiological limits) the ensuing systole will be more powerful.

In vertebrates the hormones *noradrenaline* and *thyroxine* act directly upon the heart muscle to accelerate the heartbeat. In addition the heart is supplied with two sets of nerves that act in opposition: excitatory *sympathetic* and inhibitory *parasympathetic* nerve fibers. The dual innervation of the vertebrate heart is not exclusive to this group, for the cardiac ganglion of the lobster heart has also been found to receive both excitatory and inhibitory fibers from the central nervous system. The parasympathetic innervation of the vertebrate heart, through the vagus nerve, acts as a brake upon the intrinsic pace. The resting heart rate of a dog is about 90 beats per minute. This increases to 250 per minute when parasympathetic transmission is blocked. Conversely, when sympathetic transmission is interrupted by severing these fibers, the heart rate declines to 65 per minute. When both sets of nerves are severed, the dog heart continues to beat at a rate of 110 per minute, which is probably the intrinsic rhythm set by its pacemaker. Such findings indicate that parasympathetic nerves serve to keep the heartbeat slower than its intrinsic pace, whereas sympathetic nerves accelerate the heartbeat to meet the need for increased blood flow at times of emergency, such as fighting or fleeing from danger.

Separate *cardioinhibitory* and *cardioaccelerator centers* exist in the vertebrate hindbrain (Figure 14.26). These receive impulses from sensory receptors located in the walls of certain blood vessels, and are also influenced by the output of higher brain centers. Inhibitory reflexes are initiated by the stimulation of stretch receptors in the branchial arteries of fish, or by homologous receptors in the aortic and carotid bodies of tetrapods. These bodies are small nodules (2 to 5 mm diameter in man) located in the walls of the aorta and carotid arteries, that contain both mechanical and chemical receptors. When blood pressure is elevated in the aorta and carotid arteries, impulses are sent from the stretch receptors to the brain's

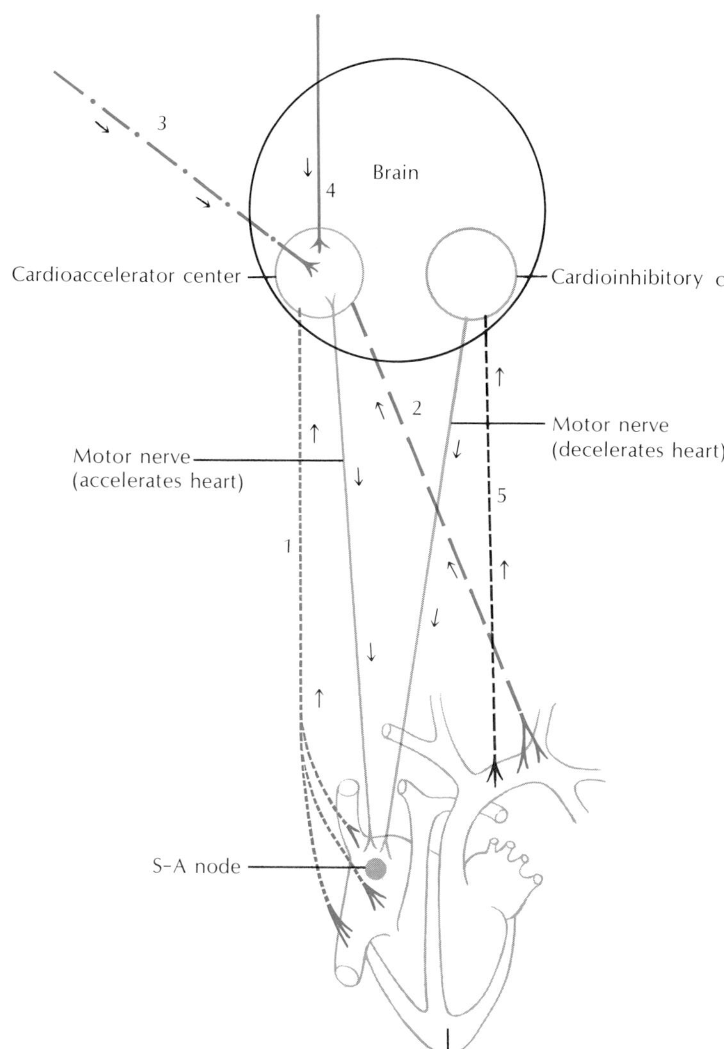

Figure 14.26 □ **Reflex control of heart rate. (1) Acceleration of venous return to the heart causes distention of great veins and right atrium; stretch receptors in the walls of these vessels respond by sending impulses to cardioaccelerator center of brain, from which motor impulses are relayed to the S-A node, causing the heartbeat to be accelerated. (2) Chemoreceptors in the aortic and carotid bodies respond to changes in blood CO_2 and O_2 content and pH, sending impulses to the brain's cardioaccelerator center that cause the heartbeat to accelerate; this increases the rate of blood flow through the pulmonary circuit, thereby lowering blood CO_2 and elevating blood O_2. (3) Sensory nerves from chemoreceptors in throat respond to smoke inhalation (for example) by sending impulses to the cardioaccelerator center, thereby increasing the rate of heartbeat. (4) Impulses from higher brain centers, such as the hypothalamus, concerned with emotional responses excite the cardioaccelerator center and accelerate the heartbeat. (5) Distension of the great arteries (aorta and carotid), when blood is pumped into them faster than it can be transported peripherally, excites stretch receptors that send impulses to the brain's cardioinhibitory center, from which impulses are sent to the S-A node that decelerate its rate of firing and therefore cause the heart to slow down.**

cardioinhibitory center, which sends additional inhibitory impulses by way of the vagus, thereby slowing the heart.

Acceleratory reflexes can be initiated by a number of different factors. Stretch receptors in the walls of the right atrium and the great veins are stimulated when an increased amount of blood enters these veins and the right side of the heart. Chemical receptors in the aortic and carotid bodies respond to changes in pH caused by increased levels of CO_2 in the blood, and may also be sensitive to lowered O_2 tension. These stretch and chemical receptors send impulses to the brain's cardioaccelerator center. This center also responds directly to both lowered oxygen tension and changes in pH, accelerating the heart by way of sympathetic nerves. The cardioaccelerator center is also influenced by input from other receptors, so that stress, pain, smoke inhalation, and so forth cause a reflexive acceleration of heart rate, which probably constitutes a defensive response. A general fall in blood pressure such as may occur during hemorrhage also causes the heart to accelerate, although the force of the beat may actually be weakened.

Figure 14.27 ☐ **Human blood pressure as measured in different parts of the circulatory system. Spacing between lines originating on the horizontal axis reflects the relative length of passage through each type of vessel. Near the heart, venous pressure falls below zero as a result of the suction created each time the heart empties itself.**

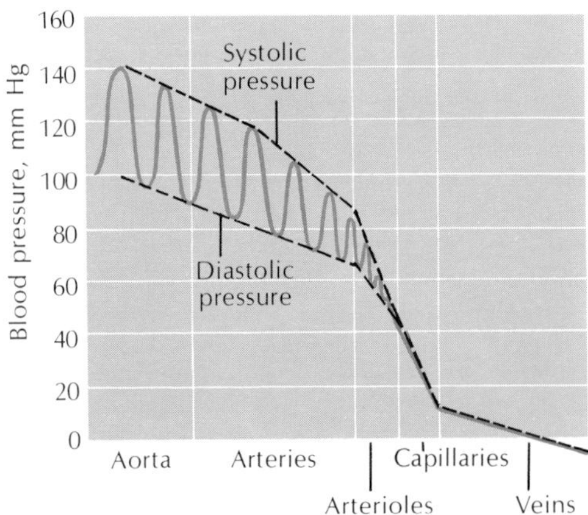

PERIPHERAL CIRCULATION AND ITS CONTROL Blood pressure is highest in the arteries, through which the blood flows in surges that represent the peripheral propagation of the heartbeat. Each surge is detectable as a "pulse" wherever an artery lies close to the body's surface (such as the carotid artery at the base of the neck and the radial artery at the wrist). Human arterial pressure measured at the upper arm is normally equivalent to about 120 mm Hg systolic and 80 mm Hg diastolic [by which we mean the height to which the blood pressure elevates a column of mercury (Hg) in a mercury manometer or sphygmomanometer]. Blood pressure is usually measured indirectly as the pressure exerted *laterally* upon the air in an inflated cuff encircling the upper arm, rather than as the *forward* surge of blood through the vessels (Figure 14.27).

As the arteries become smaller toward the periphery, increasing frictional resistance causes blood pressure to decline rapidly until it equals only 30 to 35 mm Hg at the arteriolar end of the capillaries. The capillary wall is so delicate that it allows not only water and small solute molecules to pass through it by pressure filtration, but some colloidal particles—mainly plasma proteins—to escape as well. The movement of such materials out of the capillaries near their arteriolar end is due to the fact that hydrostatic pressure within the capillaries exceeds the osmotic pressure of the blood colloids that would act toward retaining water within the bloodstream (Figure 14.28). As the blood passes through the capillaries, its hydrostatic pressure continues to decline, falling to 15 mm Hg at the venous end. At this point the combined effect of the osmotic pressure of blood proteins and the hydrostatic pressure of the accumulated tissue fluid in the interstitial spaces causes water and small solute molecules to return to the bloodstream. However, colloidal particles that were forced out of the capillaries at their arteriolar end cannot reenter the bloodstream, but must be removed instead by the lymph capillaries, in which hydrostatic pressure is close to zero. If the lymphatic drainage is blocked (as we saw in elephantiasis) or if abnormally high blood pressure causes excess loss of colloids from the blood, the osmotic pressure of the tissue fluid may rise due to the accumulation of colloidal particles, and impede the flow of water back into the bloodstream. The resulting retention of water in the tissues is known as *edema*.

The bore of a capillary is such that several hours may be required for a single milliliter of blood to traverse its length. Nevertheless, the total cross-sectional area of all the capillaries is so tremendous that the approximately 6 liters of blood in the body of an adult man can make a complete circuit in little over 2 min! The total length of capillaries in an adult human body is estimated at 10^5 km, but blood does not flow through all of these capillaries at the same time. Instead, localized constrictions of small blood vessels (*vasoconstriction*) shunt blood from one capillary bed to another, depending on current physiological need. During digestion the gut capillaries are maximally distended, and blood flow to the skeletal muscles is compensatorily decreased. If the organism must undertake strenuous muscular activity while digesting a heavy meal, the simultaneous opening of both capillary beds may tax the heart's capacity to maintain an adequate blood pressure and rate of flow. *Shock* constitutes a dangerous sequel to emotional crisis or physical injury. During shock the blood pressure may drop fatally, due to failure of vasomotor control and the simultaneous dilation of most of the body's capillaries. Precise control mechanisms must operate to

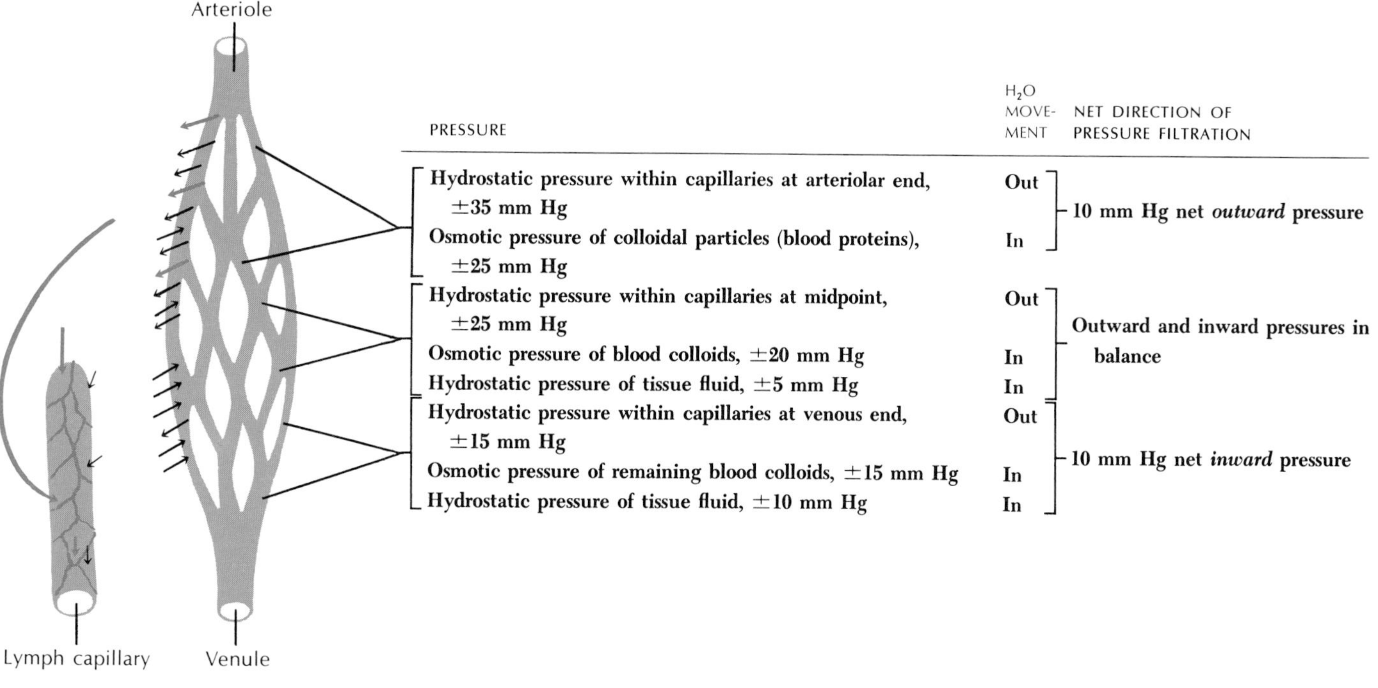

PRESSURE	H_2O MOVEMENT	NET DIRECTION OF PRESSURE FILTRATION
Hydrostatic pressure within capillaries at arteriolar end, ±35 mm Hg	Out	10 mm Hg net *outward* pressure
Osmotic pressure of colloidal particles (blood proteins), ±25 mm Hg	In	
Hydrostatic pressure within capillaries at midpoint, ±25 mm Hg	Out	Outward and inward pressures in balance
Osmotic pressure of blood colloids, ±20 mm Hg	In	
Hydrostatic pressure of tissue fluid, ±5 mm Hg	In	
Hydrostatic pressure within capillaries at venous end, ±15 mm Hg	Out	10 mm Hg net *inward* pressure
Osmotic pressure of remaining blood colloids, ±15 mm Hg	In	
Hydrostatic pressure of tissue fluid, ±10 mm Hg	In	

Figure 14.28 □ Summary of factors causing pressure filtration at the capillaries. At the arteriolar end, the net outward pressure forces water and solutes (shown by black arrows) and colloidal particles, mainly plasma proteins (color arrows), out of the bloodstream into the interstitial spaces. This loss of material reduces hydrostatic pressure within the capillary and lowers its osmotic pressure while elevating the hydrostatic pressure of the tissue fluid. At the venous end of the capillaries, the hydrostatic pressure within the bloodstream has declined to a point at which the net combined effect of the osmotic pressure of blood colloids and of the hydrostatic pressure of the tissue fluids causes water and solutes to reenter the bloodstream. The colloidal particles lost from the blood cannot return at this point but pass instead into the lymph capillaries. If the lymphatic drainage is blocked, the accumulation of colloidal particles in the tissue fluid elevates the osmotic pressure so that water tends to be retained in the tissues (see also Figure 14.21*c*).

equate the proportion of open capillaries with the total blood volume and thus maintain a steady blood pressure.

The decline with increasing distance from the heart of blood pressure and rate of flow is due mainly to the frictional resistance which the blood encounters as it enters progressively smaller vessels. Resistance to flow increases as the fourth power of the radius (r^4), therefore slight changes in the diameter of the smaller blood vessels can have great effects on blood pressure upstream. If by the contraction of its muscular walls the bore of a small artery is reduced to half its previous diameter, only one-sixteenth the amount of blood can flow through that vessel in the same period of time. An increase in blood pressure near the heart must be countered by dilation of the small muscular arteries, reducing peripheral resistance to blood flow. Conversely, should pressure decline in the major arteries, it is bolstered by a compensatory peripheral vasoconstriction.

The great arteries are called *elastic arteries* because their walls contain much elastic and collagenous connective tissue but little smooth muscle. These arteries are accordingly adapted to withstand the powerful surges of blood near the heart where pressure is highest, and in fact their resilience serves to damp these surges so that a smoother pulse is propagated toward the smaller arteries. The latter are termed *muscular arteries* because their walls consist proportionately of less connective and more muscular tissue. The bore of the muscular arteries is controlled by sympathetic *vasomotor nerves.* These nerves are of two types: *vasoconstrictor* nerve fibers which reduce the diameter of the blood vessel, and *vasodilator* fibers which cause its dilation. Both types of fibers emanate from the *vasomotor center* of the hindbrain. This center receives sensory data from stretch receptors in the walls of the large arteries, so that when these vessels are distended by an excess of blood, nerve impulses relayed via the vasodilator fibers cause general peripheral vasodilation. Conversely, a fall in blood pressure in these great arteries results in reflexive general peripheral vasoconstriction, mediated by the vasoconstrictor nerves (Figure 14.29). The vasomotor center is highly sensitive to changes in pH which reflect changes in the concentration of circulating CO_2. An increase of CO_2 in the blood causes generalized peripheral vasoconstriction through its effect on the vasomotor center, but the *local* effect of CO_2 at the capillaries is just the opposite, and promotes dilation of these smallest vessels. The combined outcome of the local and systemic effects of increased CO_2 is that the blood supply is increased to those tissues which are liberating the most CO_2 at that moment, and is decreased to all other peripheral body parts.

If all of the estimated 10^5 km of capillaries in the human body were to be open at any one time, they could hold the body's entire blood volume, which is equivalent to 5 percent of the total body weight. It is apparent that blood flow through the capillaries must be carefully regulated, both to meet specific regional needs and to maintain adequate pressure throughout the system.

The bypassing of capillary beds is made possible by *thoroughfare channels,* which directly connect the arterioles with the venules. The capillaries open off these channels, but at the point of origin of each is a muscular ring, the *precapillary sphincter,* which controls the flow of blood in that capillary. Constriction of a precapillary sphincter closes the capillary, while its relaxation allows blood to enter. In the event that all of the capillaries along a thoroughfare channel are closed off, the blood is shunted directly from the arterial to the venous system without passing through the capillaries or exchanging materials with the cells. The precapillary sphincters relax and constrict periodically, allowing blood to enter different portions of the capillary bed, so that no cells are long deprived of nourishment.

Capillaries themselves, as we have said, consist of but a single thickness of the flattened endothelium that lines the entire vertebrate circulatory system. At the arterioles, the endothelium is spirally wrapped by a single layer of smooth muscle fibers, which become fewer in the thoroughfare channels. The muscle fibers of these smallest contractile vessels are not innervated, but they are in intimate contact with the blood within, and the tissue fluid without. They are thus in a position to respond directly both to the composition of the tissue fluid (which alters as cellular waste products accumulate) and to chemical modulators in the bloodstream. During exercise the oxygen demands of skeletal muscle increase to ten times that of other tissues. Each thoroughfare channel in skeletal muscle tissue gives rise to some 20 to 30 capillaries, most of which remain closed when the muscles are at rest. The opening of nearly all of these capillaries during exertion makes possible a rapid circulation of blood that delivers O_2 to the contracting fibers and carries away excess lactic acid. Such efficient circulation is required for sustained muscular activity, but is unnecessary during rest.

Figure 14.29 □ **Reflex control of the diameter of peripheral arteries. (*a*) A rise in aortic blood pressure increases the frequency at which impulses are relayed by sensory nerve fibers from the aortic stretch receptors to the vasomotor center of the brain (number of arrows is a rough indicator of frequency of nerve impulses); in response, an increased flow of impulses is sent from this center by way of vasodilator nerves to the peripheral arteries, causing these arteries to dilate, with a resultant generalized fall in blood pressure. (*b*) A fall in aortic blood pressure causes fewer impulses to be sent from the aortic receptors to the vasocontrol center; this apparently releases vasoconstrictor nerves from inhibition, and these nerves send an increased flow of impulses to the peripheral arteries, causing their constriction and thereby bringing about an increase in general systemic pressure.**

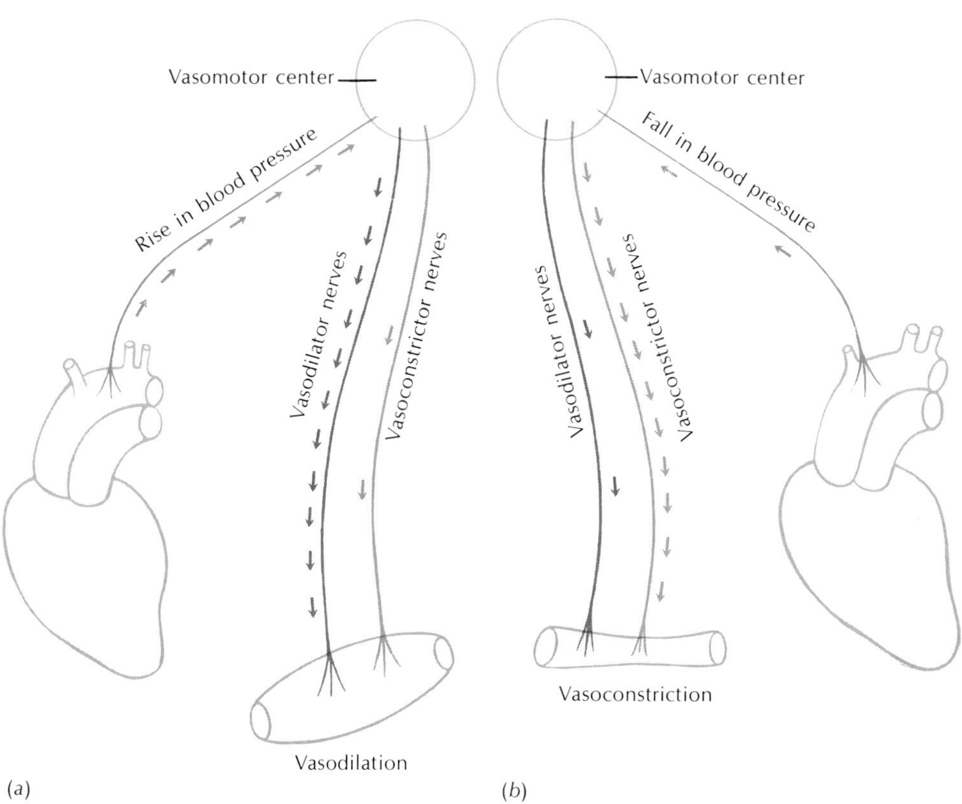

The control of the capillary circulation is dependent upon the chemical sensitivity of the smooth muscle fibers of the arterioles and precapillary sphincters. The injection of only 0.001 μg of adrenaline into a capillary bed suffices to close all of its precapillary sphincters. Larger amounts affect in sequence first the sphincters, then the thoroughfare channels, next the arterioles, and finally the venules. This variable sensitivity permits the capillaries themselves to be closed while the thoroughfare channels remain open. The primary function of arteriolar vasoconstriction is to elevate the blood pressure upstream, which must be done by reducing blood flow to the peripheral tissues. Acetylcholine or other dilatory substances bring about vasodilation in the same order: the smallest doses dilate the precapillary sphincters, while larger doses dilate the thoroughfare channels, and still larger doses dilate the arterioles and venules. A possible source of vasocontrol substances may be amoeboid cells (mast cells) that congregate in the tissue spaces around the smaller blood vessels. These cells secrete heparin, histamine, and serotonin—chemicals known to have profound circulatory effects when given in pharmaceutical doses.

Once blood has passed through the capillaries it must return to the heart by way of the veins. Venous return can only partially be brought about by the pressure of blood entering the veins from the capillaries. A person who stands motionless for a prolonged period may faint due to lowered blood supply to the brain resulting from the stasis of blood in the lower legs. The pressure of adjacent skeletal muscles against the veins is instrumental in massaging the blood toward the heart, valves in the veins preventing backflow. Nearer the chest, changes in intrathoracic pressure caused by breathing help to suck blood into the thoracic veins, from which blood is drawn into the heart by the pressure reduction created each time the heart empties itself. The problem of venous return is aggravated in man by his upright posture. It is not surprising therefore that the veins of human legs are more subject to such maladies as varicosity and phlebitis, than the limb veins of quadrupedal mammals, for in the latter once blood reaches the trunk it need not rise much farther to enter the heart.

BLOOD The fluid tissue transported by an animal circulatory system is known as blood. In most animals it is a colorless fluid containing but few corpuscles, and these are most typically amoeboid phagocytes. Mammalian blood has an unusually high content of corpuscles, which make up about 50 percent of the total blood volume and are mostly red blood corpuscles involved in gaseous transport.

Plasma The liquid portion of blood is known as *plasma.* The main constituent of plasma is water, which serves as an agent of transport for all other substances carried by the blood. Water is also important in maintenance of normal blood volume and pressure, and after hemorrhage the most essential requirement for preserving life is to replace the loss of water (either by the injection of isosmotic saline solution or by having the patient drink large amounts of water).

Other than water, the blood plasma contains a large variety of materials in solution and suspension. These materials are of two main types: (1) those which are present in carefully regulated quantities as constant blood constituents; (2) those which fluctuate according to rate of intake and release, such as various nutrients and wastes. Many plasma constituents are in transit between the alimentary tract and the tissues or between the tissues and the organs of respiration and excretion. Hormones are carried from the glands where they are produced to the various organs they affect. The nutrient content of plasma includes sugar (in man this is mainly glucose), amino acids, lipids, and various vitamins and ions.

The plasma ions are important in regulating osmotic pressure and, although they are constantly being exchanged, an overall steady state is preserved so that the concentration of each ion is stable. About half of the ions are Na^+ and Cl^-; the rest include Ca^{2+}, Mg^{2+}, SO_4^{2-}, HCO_3^-, K^+, and phosphate ($H_2PO_4^-$, HPO_4^{2-}, PO_4^{3-}).

The major nitrogenous waste product found in mammalian blood is urea; in other animals, depending upon the method of nitrogen catabolism, more or less urea, ammonia, uric acid, or creatinine may be present.

Proteins in colloidal dispersion are constant constituents of blood plasma; they are particularly essential in maintaining an osmotic pressure that both largely counteracts the tendency of water to leave the circulatory system as a result of hydrostatic pressure and maintains an osmotic equilibrium between the blood and tissues. Plasma proteins perform many other important functions. Some, especially gamma globulin in vertebrates, serve as antibodies that combat infection. Many assist in stabilizing blood pH, for they can give up either H^+ or OH^- (see Section 16.2A). Other plasma proteins are concerned with blood clotting, as we shall see below. In most phyla a plasma protein is present that serves as a *respiratory pigment* assisting the transport of gases. Only among vertebrates and a few invertebrates such as ribbonworms is the respiratory pigment confined within blood corpuscles rather than freely dispersed in the plasma. Types and properties of respiratory pigments will be dealt with in Section 14.2C.

Corpuscles The blood of most invertebrates contains only a few corpuscles; they are nearly always phagocytic and serve in defense against invading microorganisms or for the concentration and removal of metabolic wastes. Vertebrate blood corpuscles are very numerous and consist of two major types. *Leucocytes* (white blood corpuscles) are amoeboid and either phagocytic or involved in antibody production. We have considered them in conjunction with our earlier discussion of defenses against parasitic invasion (see Figure 6.30). In human blood, leucocytes average 7,500 per cubic millimeter, but the count may double or triple during infection. Lymphocytes are formed in the lymphoid organs and enter the bloodstream from the lymphatics; granulocytes are mainly produced in the bone marrow.

Vertebrate *erythrocytes* (red blood corpuscles) contain hemoglobin and are concerned with the transport of O_2 and CO_2. Except in mammals, they are ovoid and contain nuclei; mammalian erythrocytes lose their nuclei before entering the circulation from their sites of formation (red bone marrow, liver, or spleen). These biconcave discoidal cells are among the smallest and most numerous cells in the body. Each human erythrocyte averages 7 to 8 μm in diameter, and contains about 2.8×10^8 molecules of hemoglobin. The erythrocyte count is normally about 4.5×10^6 per cubic millimeter in women and 5.5×10^6 per cubic millimeter in men. They survive in the bloodstream some 100 to 120 days, but their death rate is such that in man new erythrocytes must be produced at an estimated rate of 2×10^6 per second! We shall discuss the functions of erythrocytes in the next section.

Blood clotting Mammalian blood plasma contains a number of different factors required for normal blood clotting. Most of these are proteins present in very minute amounts that probably exist as proenzymes activating one another in a stepwise enzyme-cascade sequence (see Section 13.2C) until at the end of the sequence large numbers of molecules of the proenzyme *prothrombase* are converted to the active form, *thrombase*. This in turn catalyzes the conversion of the dispersed plasma protein *fibrinogen* into a nondispersed form, *fibrin*, which aggregates and forms cross links to produce a meshwork, the *clot*. Proper clot formation also depends on the presence of adequate Ca^{2+}.

One factor required for completion of the clotting process in mammals is an enzyme contained within tiny bodies known as platelets (*thrombocytes*). Thrombocytes are actually cytoplasmic fragments containing mitochondria and secretion droplets of the enzyme *thrombokinase* (thromboplastin), which activates prothrombase. They are liberated by giant cells (megakaryocytes) that are formed in the red bone marrow and may grow to a diameter of 300 μm before breaking up to yield some 2,000 thrombocytes apiece. Thrombocytes occur in the bloodstream at the rate of 250,000 per cubic millimeter. They can actively plaster themselves over small breaks in the walls of blood vessels, but disintegrate during more massive hemorrhage, releasing the thrombokinase. This substance, or one similar in activity, is also liberated by wounded tissues.

Because the roles of the many other factors known to be involved in the clotting reaction (the antihemophiliac factor, the Stuart factor, the Christmas factor, and so forth) are still problematic, we may for the present summarize the clotting reaction as a mere three-step process, although in fact it probably involves a seven- to ten-step enzyme cascade leading up to these final reactions:

$$\begin{array}{l} \text{Thrombocytes} \xrightarrow{\textit{Release}} \text{thrombokinase} \\ \qquad\qquad\qquad\qquad\qquad\qquad \downarrow \\ \qquad\qquad \text{prothrombase} \xrightarrow[Ca^{2+}]{} \text{thrombase} \\ \qquad\qquad\qquad\qquad\qquad\qquad\qquad \downarrow \\ \qquad\qquad\qquad \text{fibrinogen} \longrightarrow \text{fibrin} \end{array}$$

The fibrin thus produced forms a meshwork that entangles the blood corpuscles and interrupts the hemorrhage. Later, as the clot contracts, it squeezes out a yellowish fluid, *serum*, identical with blood plasma save for the absence of the clotting factors. Since serum may contain antibodies, it can be administered medically as a means of overcoming infection.

Blood clots occasionally form within the circulatory system. Usually this is the result of hard, limy deposits that roughen the arterial lining in arteriosclerosis, or is the outcome of venous inflammation in phlebitis. Such an intravascular clot (thrombus) may break free and be swept along until it becomes lodged in a vessel too small to allow it to pass through; if the occluded vessel serves a critical organ such as the brain or heart muscle, death may result from the condition produced (cerebral or coronary thrombosis).

C Gaseous exchange and transport

Gas molecules are small and pass readily through cell membranes. Whether a particular gas will tend primarily to enter or leave the body of an organism depends on its relative concentration within the body and in the surrounding milieu. Gases diffuse along their own concentration gradients, equalizing their distribution by random thermal movements. The rate of diffusion varies according to temperature and the steepness of the concentration gradient. In the human lungs, for instance, concentration gradients for both O_2 and CO_2 exist between the pulmonary capillaries and the air in the air sacs (alveoli) of the lungs. These gradients differ in direction and steepness, so that each gas diffuses independently of the other. More CO_2 tends to leave the bloodstream than to enter it, whereas more O_2 tends to enter the bloodstream than to leave it. The extent of gaseous exchange can be measured in terms of differences in the O_2 and CO_2 content of air inhaled and exhaled. Air being taken into the lungs contains nearly 21 percent O_2 but only 0.044 percent CO_2; air being exhaled contains only 16 percent O_2 but 4 percent CO_2! This indicates that the concentration gradient for CO_2 is much steeper than that for O_2 since a hundredfold change has taken place in the concentration of CO_2.

Although gases diffuse much more rapidly in air than in water, they must pass into solution before they can be absorbed into

Figure 14.30 □ Types of respiratory organs: (*a*) integument of earthworm; (*b*) external gills of tadpole; (*c*) internal gills in fish; (*d*) alveolar lung of mammals; (*e*) cloacal diverticula in sea cucumber; (*f*) book lung of spiders; (*g*) tracheal tubes in insects.

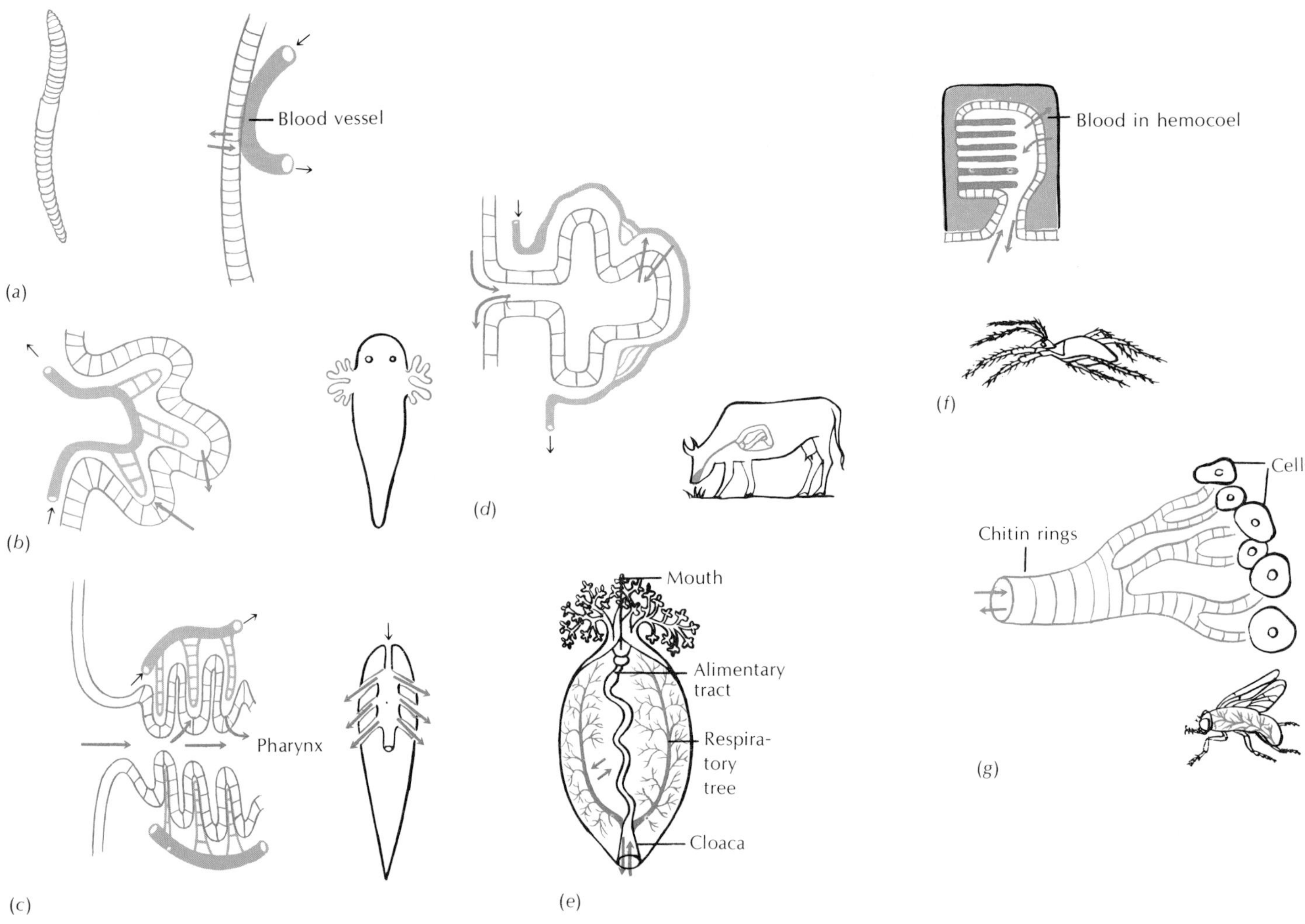

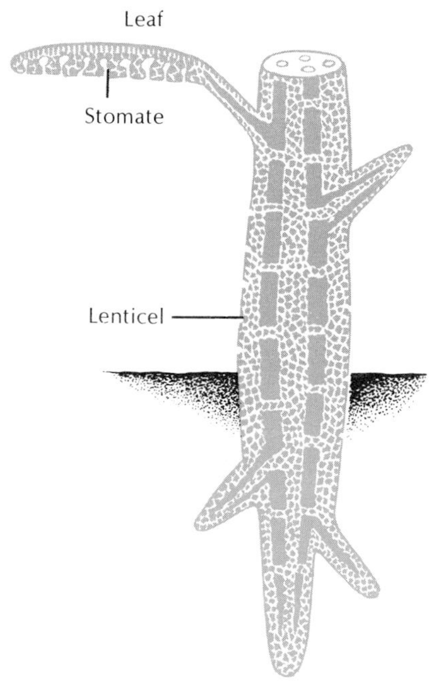

(a)

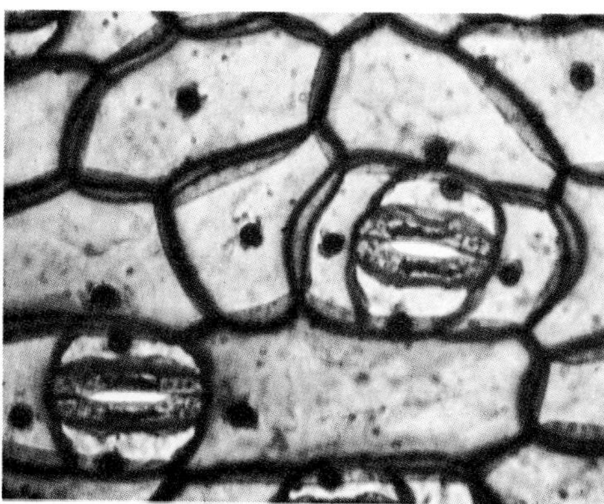

(b)

Figure 14.31 □ Gaseous exchange in plants. (*a*) In the aeration system of a vascular plant, the intercellular air spaces communicate to the exterior by way of stomates and lenticels. (*b*) Leaf surface, showing stomates and guard cells.

the tissues. This requires either that organisms be aquatic or that the surfaces through which gaseous exchange takes place be coated by a film of water.

RESPIRATORY ORGANS Effective gaseous exchange between an organism and its environment requires a respiratory membrane which (*a*) is *moist;* (*b*) presents a *large surface area* to the milieu; (*c*) is usually *well-vascularized;* and (*d*) is *well-ventilated,* or adequately refreshed by a breathing mechanism that brings new air or water into contact with it. Metazoans generally possess at least one of the types of respiratory structures shown here (Figure 14.30):

AQUATIC ANIMALS	TERRESTRIAL ANIMALS
The integument	**Alveolar lungs**
External gills	**Book lungs**
Internal gills	**Tracheae**
Buccal or cloacal lining	

In vascular plants an *aeration system,* consisting of intercellular air spaces that communicate with the exterior via the stomates and lenticels, facilitates gaseous exchange for the internal tissues (Figure 14.31). This system of air passages permits O_2 to diffuse through the plant some 3×10^5 times more rapidly than it diffuses when in aqueous solution. Aquatic plants require particularly extensive aeration systems.

Gaseous exchange through an unmodified epidermis might meet the metabolic requirements of a polyp, flatworm, or earthworm, but is unable to satisfy the needs of larger and more active animals. The simplest specialization for enhanced gaseous exchange is the evagination of the epidermis into filamentous *external gills,* a simple means of augmenting the integumentary surface area available for respiration. Gills can be protected and thus even more delicately branched, when recessed into a cavity, as *internal gills.* In the internal lamellar gills of modern bony fish, the capillaries are arranged in rows in which the direction of blood flow is opposite to the flow of water past the gills. This constitutes a *countercurrent exchange* mechanism which is so efficient that an up to 85 percent exchange of oxygen can take place. (Countercurrent exchange is further discussed in Section 16.2A with respect to urine formation.)

Further internalization of the respiratory membranes is required of terrestrial animals to conserve moisture. Even so, in an arid climate much water is discharged to the atmosphere by evaporation from the lungs, an unavoidable loss that is compensated by increased thirst and production of a more concentrated urine. Internalized respiratory organs must communicate with the exterior by way of a more or less lengthy series of air passages. In vertebrates these include the nasal and buccal cavities, pharynx, trachea, and bronchi. Sound-producing organs such as the larynx and syrinx may be located along the air passages, permitting *vocalization* (see Figure 16.37).

The need for increased surface area has led toward ever finer subdivision of the vertebrate lung, which has evolved from a simple sac developing from the rear of the pharynx, to a spongy mass of microscopic *alveoli* that are ventilated by means of a densely branching system (bronchial tree) of air tubes (Figure 14.32). Amphibian lungs are simple sacs with alveoli developed only in the walls. Bronchial trees are lacking, and

Figure 14.32 □ Evolutionary changes in the vertebrate lung: (*a*) amphibian lungs; (*b*) reptilian lungs; (*c*) bird lungs (note communication with coelomic air sacs, allowing the lungs to be fully ventilated at each breath); (*d*) mammalian lungs, with detail of air sacs with alveoli. Comparison of living vertebrates indicates evolutionary trend toward greater alveolation, most fully expressed in the mammalian lung. Multiplication of alveoli greatly increases the amount of membrane surface available for gaseous exchange.

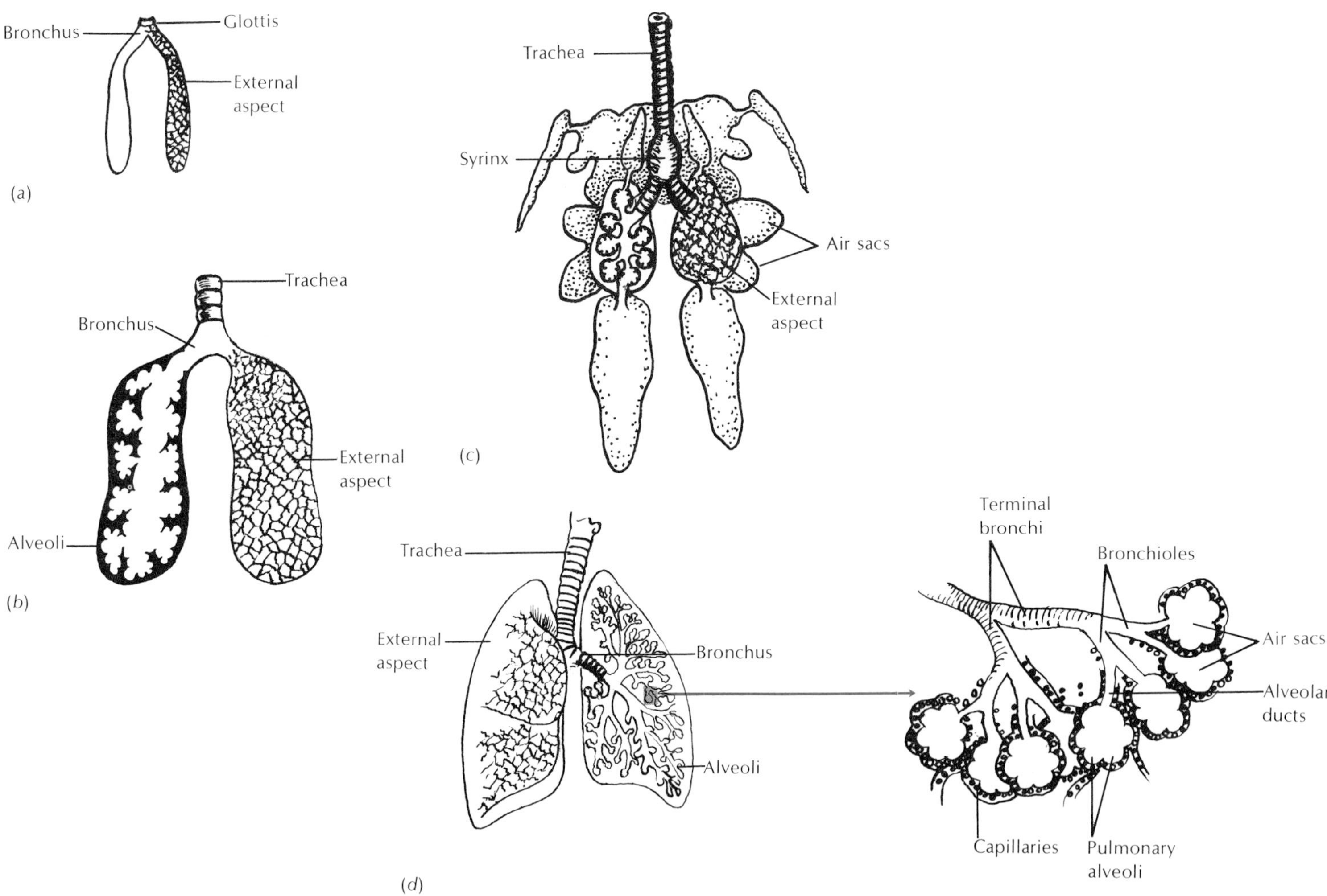

each lung opens directly into the pharynx by way of the *glottis,* a slitlike opening between the paired arytenoid cartilages, forerunners of the larynx. In reptiles, alveolar structure becomes more pronounced and the lungs are divided into several major lobes, each served by a major secondary bronchus. These unite anteriorly to form the primary bronchi that join medially as the trachea, which passes forward to join the pharynx by way of the larynx.

Bird lungs are well-alveolated and are continuous with coelomic air sacs and with an air cavity within each upper arm bone, thus making it possible for the lungs to be completely ventilated (by total air exchange) with each breath. At the point where the two main bronchi converge lies the syrinx, the vocal organ. (In birds the larynx merely guards the glottal opening and is not used in sound production.)

The mammalian larynx is well developed for sound production, and is protected against the accidental entrance of food by the flaplike *epiglottis* that covers the glottis during swallowing. The lungs of mammals are fully alveolated. In man the total surface provided for gaseous exchange is estimated at 125 m^2. Such alveolar proliferation has demanded progressively more extensive subdivision of the bronchi. These air tubes are ringed with cartilage to prevent their collapse, but the rings extend only to the terminal, muscular *bronchioles* that reflexively control the flow of air into each alveolar cluster. (In asthma, an allergic condition, bronchiolar spasms following inhalation lead to difficulty in exhaling.)

Effective gaseous exchange between the air and the bloodstream takes place only in the alveoli. Each alveolus consists of a single layer of squamous epithelium lying in intimate contact with capillaries that branch in the interalveolar spaces. Amoeboid phagocytes inhabit these spaces, ingesting bacteria, soot, and dirt particles that may enter the alveoli. Most such contaminants, however, are trapped on the mucus-lined, ciliated surfaces of the air passages and are carried forward to the pharynx.

The tracheal system of insects represents another effective adaptation of respiratory organs to life on land. It has been described in Section 12.7B (which see).

BREATHING If the respiratory organs are externally located, movements of the animal's body usually suffice to circulate the medium past the membranes. But when these membranes are internalized, special means of ventilation are required. Ventilation can be accomplished by ciliary action (in clams, for instance) or by muscular movements termed *breathing* (Figure 14.33). Crustacean gills are often mounted on the legs; thus, the animal breathes by merely walking or swimming. This is also true of clamworms, in which the legs (parapodia) *are* the respiratory organs. A fish inhales by drawing water into its mouth (by spreading the gill arches and lowering the floor of the mouth, thereby increasing the volume of the pharynx), and exhales by closing the mouth and forcing the water out through the pharyngeal pouches, the walls of which bear the gill lamellae. Nonmammalian tetrapods must use their throat and trunk muscles to force air in and out of the lungs. In vertebrates generally, *inspiration* (breathing in) is the active phase of breathing, and *expiration* is normally passive. For insects the reverse is true. Air is forcibly expelled from the tracheae by contractions of muscles attached to the dorsal and ventral exoskeletal plates (tergum and sternum) of each segment. As these plates are pulled closer together, the internal body spaces are compressed and expiration takes place. When the muscles relax, air is drawn into the tracheae.

Inspiration in mammals is brought about mainly by contractions of the *diaphragm,* a domed muscle that separates the thoracic and abdominal cavities. Contraction of the diaphragm, elicited by impulses from the *phrenic nerve,* causes it to move posteriorly (or downward, in man), thus increasing the depth of the thoracic cavity. Simultaneously, contraction of the intercostal muscles between the ribs raises the ribs and thereby increases the diameter of the thorax. The expansion of the thorax causes the lungs to swell passively. As a result, the air within the lungs becomes rarified (that is, the intrapulmonary atmospheric pressure becomes lower than the external atmospheric pressure) and air rushes into the lungs. Expiration is usually passive, resulting from a reduction in chest volume as the diaphragm relaxes, bowing upward, and the ribs fall back to their original position. During exertion, additional air is expelled from the lungs by *forced* expiration, the volume of the thoracic cavity being further diminished by contractions of muscles that compress the rib cage and that force the abdominal organs forward against the diaphragm.

During rest or moderate activity, only a fraction of the intrapulmonary air is exchanged at each breath. In man this *tidal air* flow approximates only 500 ml. However, the total capacity of the lungs—the *vital capacity*—is reckoned as the amount of air that can be expelled forcibly following the deepest forced inspiration. An average vital capacity for the human lung is 4.5 liters. Even after the most forcible expiration, an additional liter of *residual air* remains in the human lung. The presence or absence of residual air is used in legal medicine to determine whether an infant was stillborn or breathed even once before death.

The rate and depth of breathing are subject to voluntary modulation, but are primarily controlled by nerve impulses from the hindbrain. The frequency of these im-

Figure 14.33 □ Methods of breathing. (*a*) A clamworm's respiratory organs are its legs (parapodia), which are ventilated by ordinary swimming movements. (*b*) The lobster's gills are borne on the basal segments of its legs, and walking causes a current of water to flow through the gill chamber that is located beneath the shieldlike carapace (cut away on this side). When at rest, the lobster breathes by moving its smaller feeding legs, one pair of which bears oarlike blades (scaphognathites) that serve to fan water past the gills. (*c*) A clam breathes by the action of gill cilia, water being drawn in through the incurrent siphon, directed across the gill surfaces, and expelled from the excurrent siphon (see also Figure 13.16). (*d*) In man, inspiration is an active process in which the volume of the thoracic cavity is enlarged, causing air to be drawn into the lungs. This enlargement is due to contractions of various muscles including the diaphragm (which moves downward) and the external intercostals (which pull the ribs upward and outward). Expiration is usually passive, air being forced from the lungs by the decrease in thoracic volume that results when the diaphragm relaxes (bulging upward) and the other muscles of inspiration relax, allowing the ribs to fall inward and downward.

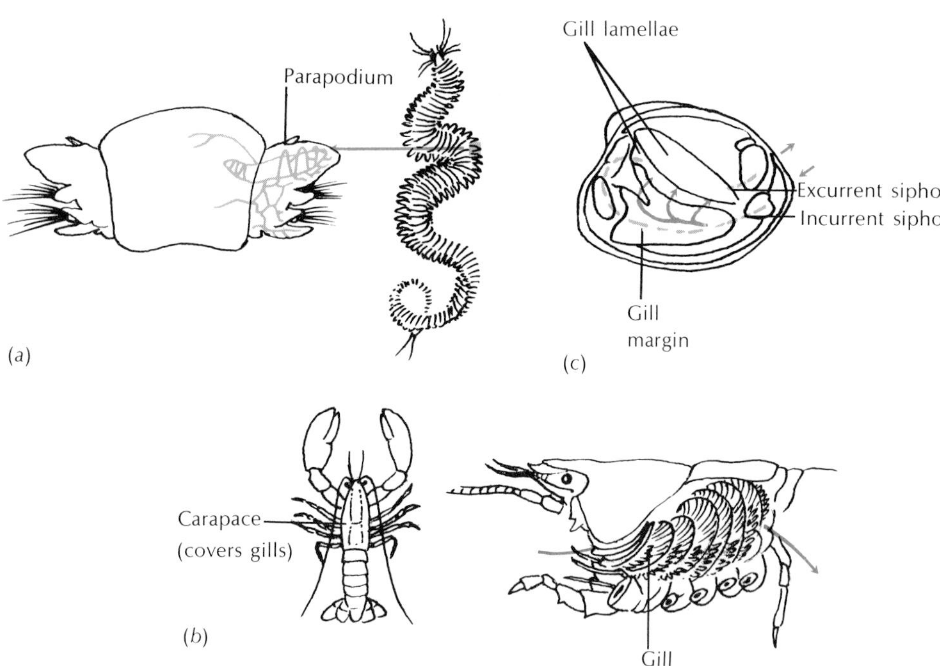

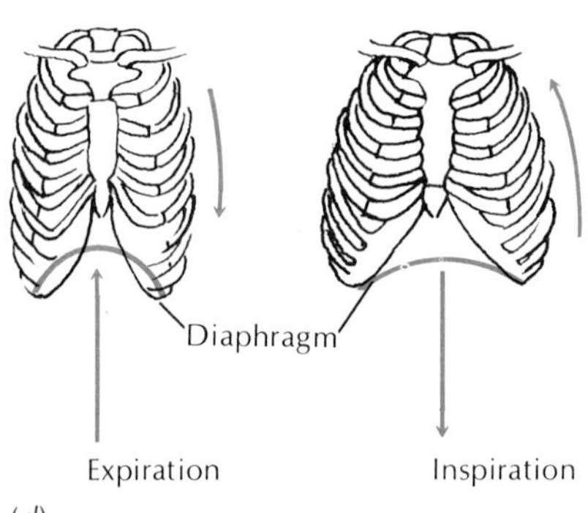

pulses is in turn regulated by information relayed from internal sensory receptors.

Regulation of breathing Providing the cells with O_2 and removing the CO_2 they generate is one of the most critical and precisely regulated activities of the animal body. The influence of four factors must be integrated, these being (1) the rate of oxidative metabolism in the cells; (2) the effectiveness of ventilation; (3) the velocity of internal convection, which is largely determined by the rate and force of the heartbeat; (4) the concentration of gases in the external milieu.

Both short-term and long-term adjustments may be called into play in meeting the organism's gaseous exchange requirements. Short-term adjustments involve modulations in breathing rate and velocity of circulation. Long-term changes include developmental changes in the respiratory organs, modification of the amount of respiratory pigment present, and—in vertebrates—adjustment of the quantity of circulating erythrocytes (which can also be altered on a short-term basis by the storage of excess red cells in the spleen and their liberation by contraction of the spleen). Oxygen concentration exerts specific effects on development. Children reared at high altitudes develop larger lungs and a greater chest expansion than those reared at sea level. Aquatic insect larvae grown under hypoxic (low-oxygen) conditions develop abnormally large numbers of air tubules. On the other hand, tadpoles reared under high-oxygen concentrations develop stunted, thickened gills.

Breathing consists of a rhythmic cycle of inspiration and expiration controlled by impulses from nerve centers that exhibit a characteristic rhythmic activity. The basal breathing rate is seen only in the resting individual, for with exercise the body's demands for gaseous exchange are greatly raised. A resting man requires about 250 ml of O_2/min and liberates 200 ml of CO_2 in the same period, but during strenuous exercise O_2 consumption may increase to 4 or 5 liters/min and the rate of evolution of CO_2 to 6 liters/min. The *minute volume* of the lungs of a resting man is only about 8 liters (of air inhaled and exhaled per minute), but this may exceed 100 liters during exertion. Such adaptive modulation of the rate and depth of breathing requires that the brain centers controlling breathing be responsive to body need.

The spontaneous breathing rhythm of mammals is thought to be set by a pacemaker in the hindbrain, the *medullary respiratory center,* which initiates and terminates inhalation. Two additional breathing-control areas in the brain, a *pneumotaxic center* and an *apneustic center,* have been located slightly anterior to the medullary respiratory center, and it is probably the interaction among these three centers that maintains the breathing rhythm (Figure 14.34).

The medullary respiratory center is thought to be organized into distinct inspiratory and expiratory centers: it sends impulses both to the muscles of inspiration and to those that bring about forced expiration. Elevation of the CO_2 level of the blood or brain tissue increases the rate at which volleys of impulses are sent from this center to the inspiratory muscles. As a breath is taken, stretch receptors in the walls of the alveoli begin to transmit impulses to the brain that inhibit further inspiratory discharges from the medullary respiratory center. The inspiratory muscles then relax and the lungs are deflated.

The apneustic center seems to be somewhat more sensitive to increased CO_2 than the medullary respiratory center and therefore promotes the inspiratory activity of the latter. The pneumotaxic center, on the other hand, sends inhibitory impulses to the medullary respiratory center that shorten the period of inhalation and produce quiet, shallow breathing.

The basic breathing rhythm is modulated by many factors involving sensory input from various parts of the body. Arousal, attentiveness, pain, anxiety, and even the mere thought of physical exertion all can accelerate the rate of breathing. Profound fixation of attention, on the contrary, can make one temporarily "forget to breathe." Emotional excitement may quicken breathing, and we are all familiar with the emotional connotations of the deep inhalation and exhalation called a sigh.

Increases in arterial blood pressure inhibit inspiration by means of impulses sent to the brain from pressure receptors in the walls of the aorta and pulmonary and carotid arteries. Conversely, chemical receptors in the walls of these vessels cause the breathing rate to be accelerated in response to lowered blood pH (resulting from increased CO_2 or from lactic acid liberated from the muscles during exercise). These receptors can also be aroused by lack of oxygen (anoxia), but this sensitivity plays little role in the normal control of breathing for they are excited by blood pH changes long before they respond to anoxia.

Reflexive acceleration of breathing during exercise is not due only to the increased liberation of CO_2 and lactic acid but also to impulses generated by stretch receptors in the skeletal muscles. Thus, as soon as exercise begins, breathing increases in advance of actual physiological need! Following exercise, forced breathing continues until the blood levels of CO_2 and lactic acid have returned to normal.

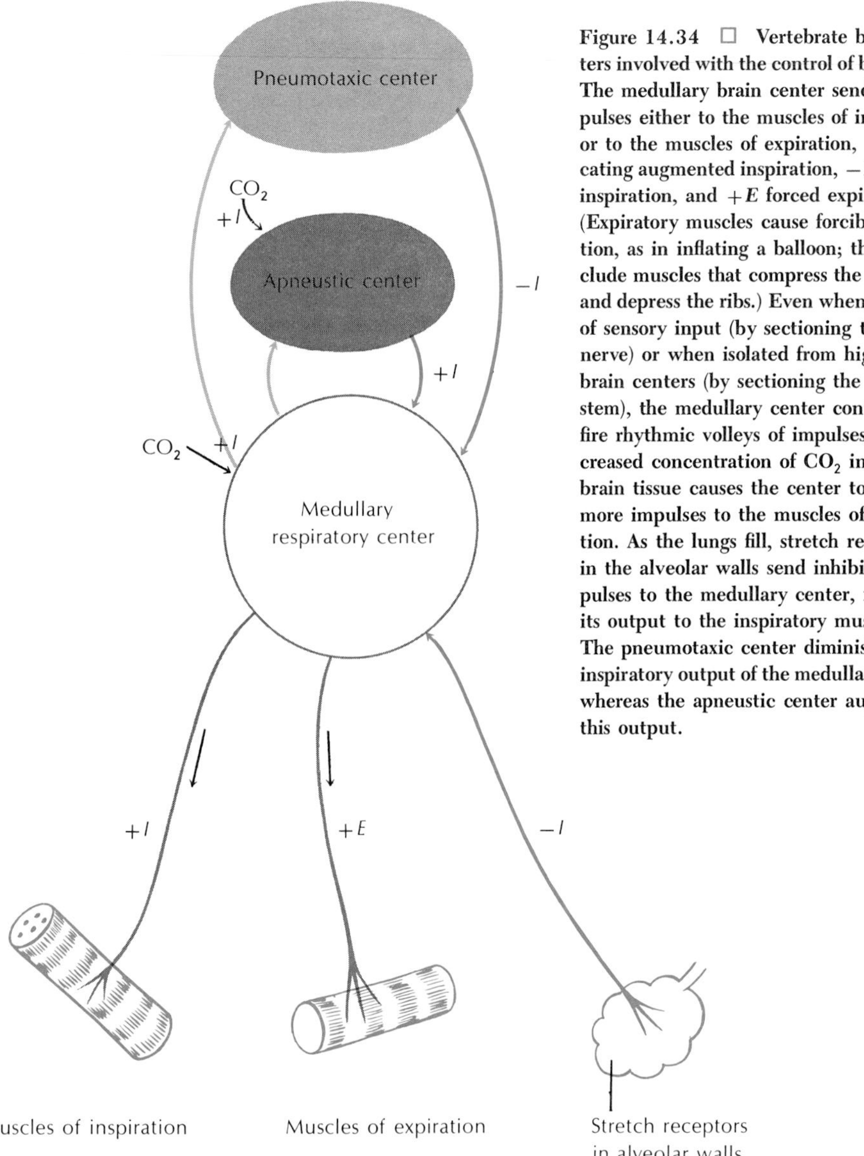

Figure 14.34 □ Vertebrate brain centers involved with the control of breathing. The medullary brain center sends impulses either to the muscles of inspiration or to the muscles of expiration, $+I$ indicating augmented inspiration, $-I$ reduced inspiration, and $+E$ forced expiration. (Expiratory muscles cause forcible exhalation, as in inflating a balloon; these include muscles that compress the abdomen and depress the ribs.) Even when deprived of sensory input (by sectioning the vagus nerve) or when isolated from higher brain centers (by sectioning the brain stem), the medullary center continues to fire rhythmic volleys of impulses. An increased concentration of CO_2 in the brain tissue causes the center to send more impulses to the muscles of inspiration. As the lungs fill, stretch receptors in the alveolar walls send inhibitory impulses to the medullary center, reducing its output to the inspiratory muscles. The pneumotaxic center diminishes the inspiratory output of the medullary center, whereas the apneustic center augments this output.

Cough and *sneeze reflexes* serve to clear the respiratory passages of obstructions. Inhalation of irritants first causes a reflexive closure of the glottis that may prevent these materials from entering the windpipe. This *glottal reflex* is usually followed promptly by coughing, a series of short, forcible expirations. Both types of reflexes are depressed in unconscious individuals, which increases the danger of choking if liquids are given at such times. If irritant particles entering the air passages are less than 1 μm in diameter, they may not cause coughing but by settling upon sensory cells in the lining of the lower respiratory tract cause a *bronchiolar reflex* to be initiated. The bronchiolar muscles contract, constricting the entrance to the alveolar air sacs. Inhalation of cigarette smoke causes a bronchiolar constriction sufficient to increase the airpath resistance by 200 to 300 percent so that breathing must become more forcible. Chronic bronchiolar constriction eventually may lead to emphysema, a disease in which some air sacs are totally blocked and become abscessed; during coughing they may rupture into adjacent air spaces.

The control of breathing and circulation in diving mammals has proven of great interest, for these animals (including whales and seals) can endure prolonged apnea (cessation of breathing) during submersion.

Sperm whales can submerge for up to 1.5 hr, while harbor seals and beavers routinely dive for up to 15 min. Harbor seals have proven cooperative research subjects, for they can be trained voluntarily to submerge their muzzles in a tub of water, leaving the rest of the body convenient for physiological testing, and also divorcing the effects of submersion from those of exercise (Figure 14.35). These diving mammals actually do not have a ratio of lung volume to body weight much greater than that of land mammals, but their tidal air exchange *is* much greater (80 percent in porpoises as compared with less than 20 percent in man). The oxygen-carrying capacity of their blood is not especially increased either, but their muscles contain large quantities of the respiratory pigment *myoglobin,* that serves as an oxygen reservoir. Indeed the myoglobin of whale muscles is reported to hold half the body's total oxygen supply!

Diving mammals exhibit remarkable tolerance for carbon dioxide: even when at rest a seal may breathe only two or three times a minute. This tolerance may be due in part to a special sphincter lacking in other mammals that rings the postcava at the level of the diaphragm and may serve to trap blood in the posterior part of the body during diving. This would restrict the amount of CO_2 and lactic acid reaching the chemoreceptive regions of the great arteries. The postcaval occlusion, lowering as it does the amount of blood entering the right atrium, leads to a dramatic deceleration of heart rate, which drops from 80 to 10 beats per minute in a submerged seal. These studies underline the extent to which an essential physiological process and the neural mechanisms by which it is regulated can be adapted to meet the needs generated by a species' particular mode of life.

Figure 14.35 □ **Harbor seal, a tractable subject for investigations of the physiology of diving mammals. The animal is trained to hold its head under water until a signal is given by the investigator. In this manner the effects of submergence can be analyzed independently of the effects of muscular exertion and water pressure and the emotional results of forcible restraint. (*Courtesy of Dr. Robert Elsner and Scripps Institution of Oceanography.*)**

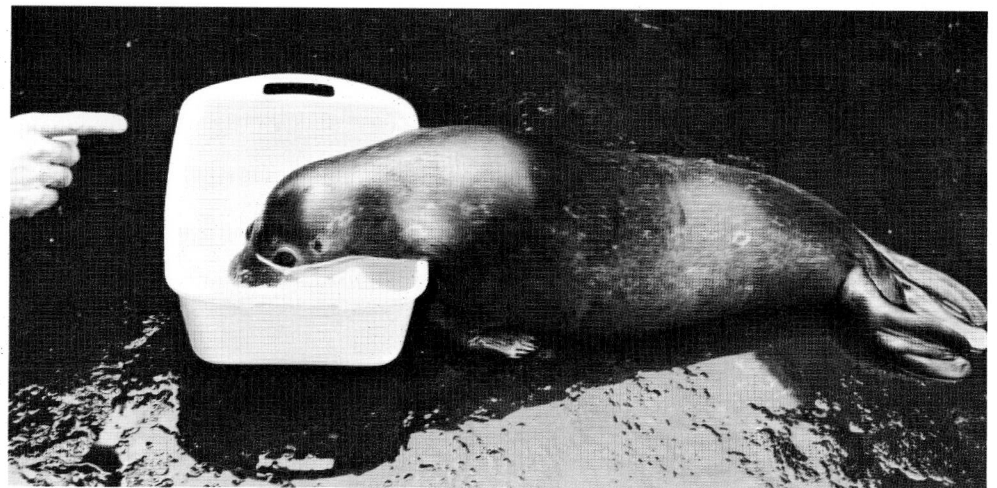

OXYGEN TRANSPORT Oxygen in aqueous solution diffuses at a rate only 0.00003 times that at which it diffuses in air. Its distribution throughout the metazoan body therefore must usually be carried out by convection rather than by simple diffusion. Furthermore, the solubility of O_2 in water declines at higher temperatures, so that whereas the body fluids of animals adapted to living in frigid waters may carry enough O_2 to satisfy their metabolic needs, mammalian blood at 37°C can carry in solution only about 0.3 cm^3 of O_2 per 100 cm^3 of plasma. This amount of O_2 would be totally inadequate to sustain life. However, due to the presence of hemoglobin ("Hb"), mammalian blood can in fact transport nearly 20 cm^3 of O_2 per 100 cm^3 of blood, accordingly being nearly in equilibrium with the concentration (partial pressure) of O_2 in the alveolar air. The *partial pressure* of a gas is that proportion of the total atmospheric pressure which is attributable to that specific gas. The total atmospheric pressure at sea level is about 760 mm Hg. This means that the weight of air upon the exposed surface of a reservoir of mercury (Hg) will force the mercury to a height of 760 mm in a vertical tube from which air has been evacuated. Since O_2 constitutes slightly less than 21 percent of the atmosphere, its partial pressure is about 155 mm Hg. When a gas is in solution, we often speak of its partial pressure as *tension,* that is, its concentration in solution expressed in terms of partial pressure rather than in cubic centimeters per 100 cm^3 of blood. In human lung alveoli, because a certain proportion of stagnant air remains, the partial pressure of O_2 is only about 100 mm Hg, and as the blood passes through the pulmonary capillary bed its O_2 tension (partial pressure of O_2) rises from as little as 20 mm Hg to 100 mm Hg, at which point it is in equilibrium with the alveolar air concentration.

The characteristics of O_2 transport can be understood in terms of the properties of the respiratory pigments involved in this transport. Although a number of aquatic animals can get by without a respiratory pigment (as can insects, because gases are carried through the air-filled tracheal system rather than by way of the blood), blood pigments are of widespread distribution in the animal kingdom. Four different families of respiratory pigments occur in animal blood: hemoglobins, chlorocrurins, hemocyanins, and hemerythrins.

A *hemoglobin* is any blood pigment consisting of a protein conjugated with the iron-bearing tetrapyrrole (porphyrin) *heme* (Figure 9.4c). Heme is very widely distributed in the living world, and occurs in all bilaterally symmetrical animal phyla, where it is associated with a variety of proteins to form either an oxygen transport compound or an oxygen storage compound. The latter occurs only in the cytoplasm, whereas the former may occur either intracellularly or free in the blood plasma. *Oxygenated hemoglobin* ($HHbO_2$) is orange-red, *deoxygenated hemoglobin* (HHb) purplish. The oxygenation and deoxygenation of hemoglobin is *not* an oxidation-reduction reaction, for electrons are neither gained nor lost. Instead, the Fe atom of heme forms a reversible covalent bond with O_2:

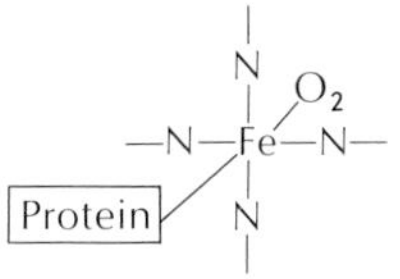

```
              |
              N   O2
              |  /
         —N—Fe—N—
            /  |
[Protein]/     N
               |
```

On the other hand, if Hb is exposed to carbon monoxide gas (CO), a toxic constituent of tobacco smoke and automobile exhaust, it *is* oxidized by the conversion of its ferrous iron (Fe^{2+}) to the ferric state (Fe^{3+}), and becomes the stable form *methemoglobin,* which can no longer associate with O_2. The hemoglobin of all vertebrates except cyclostomes has a molecular weight of about 68,000, and consists of four polypeptide chains, two of a kind, each bearing a heme group. Consequently, each hemoglobin molecule can carry four O_2. Cyclostome Hb consists of but one polypeptide chain bearing a single heme. In this respect it much resembles *myoglobin,* the heme-containing storage pigment of muscle tissue. Invertebrate hemoglobins usually occur freely in the plasma rather than being intracellular. They characteristically consist of one heme combined with a protein of high molecular weight (generally over 10^6). Hemoglobin is the main blood pigment of annelids, and also of certain crustaceans and molluscs.

Chlorocrurins are porphyrin pigments that are green in dilute solution and red in concentrated solution. The basic subunit of the molecule is a polypeptide associated with an iron-bearing tetrapyrrole (chlorocruroheme) only slightly different from heme. These subunits are grouped into macromolecules of up to 3×10^6 molecular weight and containing as many as 190 Fe atoms. This pigment occurs in the blood of certain marine annelids, occasionally along with hemoglobin.

Hemocyanin is the most important respiratory pigment of invertebrates, occurring in solution in the blood plasma of many arthropods, cephalopods, chitons, and gastropods. It is a copper-containing pigment, colorless when deoxygenated and blue when oxygenated, and is built up of a number of subunits having a molecular weight of 50,000 to 74,000, each bearing two atoms of copper which together can bind one O_2. These subunits combine to form macromolecules with molecular weights of several hundred thousand in crustaceans, or several million in molluscs. One of the largest hemocyanins is that of the garden snail, having a molecular weight of 6.6×10^6.

Hemerythrin is a violet-pink, iron-containing respiratory pigment that has no porphyrin component and occurs sporadically in several groups of invertebrates, where it is always enclosed in cells found in the coelomic fluid.

Although physiologically analogous, various blood pigments, even those in fairly closely related species, may differ significantly in their combining characteristics. Each pigment has a characteristic *dissociation curve* derived by calculating the partial pressures at which it will "load" and "unload" O_2. A valuable point of reference is p_{50}, the partial pressure of O_2 at which a pigment is 50 percent saturated with O_2. If the p_{50} value is high, the pigment has a relatively low affinity for O_2 and will give it up at comparatively high O_2 tensions. If the p_{50} value is low, the pigment has a high affinity for O_2 and will release it only at very low O_2 tensions. For example, the hemoglobin of the burrowing marine annelid *Arenicola* is 90 percent saturated with O_2 at tensions of only 5 to 10 mm Hg, and has a p_{50} of about 1.8 mm Hg. The water which enters the burrow of *Arenicola* has an O_2 tension of only about 6.5 mm Hg, which allows the hemoglobin to saturate, and the latter then begins rapidly to unload at the tissues at just under 5 mm Hg. *Arenicola* hemoglobin is consequently admirably adapted for the needs of an animal living in oxygen-poor waters, and tolerant of extremely low O_2 tensions.

Similarly, the exchange of O_2 across the placental barrier in mammals depends on the fact that mammals have two kinds of hemoglobin: fetal hemoglobin, which disappears soon after birth, and adult hemoglobin. The former has the greater affinity for O_2, and is 90 percent saturated at an O_2 tension of only 40 mm Hg, a concentration at which adult hemoglobin, which is 90 percent saturated at 80 mm Hg, has already started to unload. The p_{50} value for adult hemoglobin of cattle is in the neighborhood of 35 mm Hg, while that for fetal hemoglobin is only 12 mm Hg. Therefore as hemoglobin in the mother's bloodstream unloads its O_2 at the placental capillaries, the hemoglobin in the fetal bloodstream takes it up.

Except during exercise, human adult hemoglobin seldom unloads more than 40 percent of its O_2 content, for the O_2 tension of the "resting" tissues is about 32 mm Hg, while p_{50} is around 25 mm Hg.

CARBON DIOXIDE TRANSPORT As CO_2 is liberated in the tissues as a waste product of oxidative metabolism, it follows its diffusion gradient out of the cells into the surrounding milieu. Here its solubility is such that even at the internal temperatures of mammalian blood about 2.5 cm^3 of CO_2 per 100 cm^3 of blood plasma can be transported as free plasma CO_2. However, animals with high metabolic rates liberate much more CO_2 than may be transported in this fashion. Mammalian blood may carry 60 cm^3 of CO_2 per 100 cm^3 of plasma, but not in the form of the unbound gas.

A small proportion of CO_2 is combined with hemoglobin as *carbaminohemoglobin,* but by far the largest proportion is transformed into HCO_3^-. This conversion primarily takes place within the erythrocytes, which contain the enzyme *carbonic anhydrase* that catalyzes the reaction:

$$CO_2 + H_2O \longrightarrow H_2CO_3$$

Carbonic acid ionizes almost completely at normal blood pH values, yielding H^+ and HCO_3^-. The H^+ liberated might acidify the blood were it not for the buffering effect of hemoglobin and the plasma proteins. A major proportion of hemoglobin normally exists as the potassium salt, KHb (potassium hemoglobinate). In the presence of free H^+, K^+ is set free and the H^+ taken up to form HHb. The K^+ then associates with HCO_3^- within the erythrocytes. However, much of the H_2CO_3 formed passes out of the erythrocytes into the plasma, where the H^+ dissociated is in large measure bound with plasma proteins, primarily by exchanging places with Na^+. The displaced Na^+ then becomes associated with HCO_3^- as sodium bicarbonate ($NaHCO_3$).

This sequence of events proceeds in reverse as the blood passes through the capillaries of the respiratory organs, for here the free plasma CO_2 tends to leave the bloodstream. This creates a diffusion gradient along which CO_2 now also leaves the red blood cells, altering the substrate-end-product ratio of the carbonic anhydrase reaction. Accordingly, this enzyme proceeds to catalyze the reverse reaction, breaking down carbonic acid to H_2O and CO_2. As the available H_2CO_3 is broken down, HCO_3^- diffuses into the erythrocytes, its transport being compensated by a movement of Cl^- out of the cells. This rise in intracellular HCO_3^- prompts the release of H^+ by Hb, which again may associate with K^+. The conversion of H_2CO_3 to H_2O and CO_2 goes on until the blood passes beyond the respiratory capillary field, then again reverses.

All of the blood CO_2 is never removed, and in fact it is essential that some persist for the normal functioning of the brain respiratory control centers. Extensive forced hyperventilation so lowers the blood CO_2 content that dizziness and unconsciousness may result. The symptoms of "altitude sickness" are in fact due less to oxygen deficiency than to lowered blood CO_2. The symptoms can often be alleviated by breathing into a bag so that exhaled air is rebreathed and blood CO_2 elevated.

Table 14.1 compares the O_2 and CO_2 content of human oxygenated ("arterial") and deoxygenated ("venous") blood. We should bear in mind that arterial blood is not always high in O_2, for the blood going to the lungs by way of the pulmonary arteries is deoxygenated; conversely, the pulmonary veins returning to the heart from the lungs contain oxygenated blood.

Table 14.1 □ Comparison of human oxygenated (arterial) and deoxygenated (venous) blood in cubic centimeters of gas per 100 cm^3 of blood

GAS	OXYGENATED BLOOD	DEOXYGENATED BLOOD	CHANGE AT LUNGS
O_2	19	12–14	6 ± 1
CO_2	52	58	6

Figure 14.36 □ Oxygen dissociation curves, showing the Bohr effect in human blood (grayed-color lines) at 38°C and cuttlefish blood (solid-color lines) at 14°C. The two curves toward the left of the graph are characteristic of arterial blood with relatively low CO_2 concentration, whereas the curves toward the right are characteristic of venous blood with higher CO_2 concentration. When the cuttlefish lies in wait for prey, it is nearly buried in sand; under these low-O_2 conditions, its blood pigment (hemocyanin) must have a high O_2 affinity. When the cuttlefish is actively swimming, the O_2 affinity of its blood must be much reduced so that plentiful O_2 is made available to the muscles.

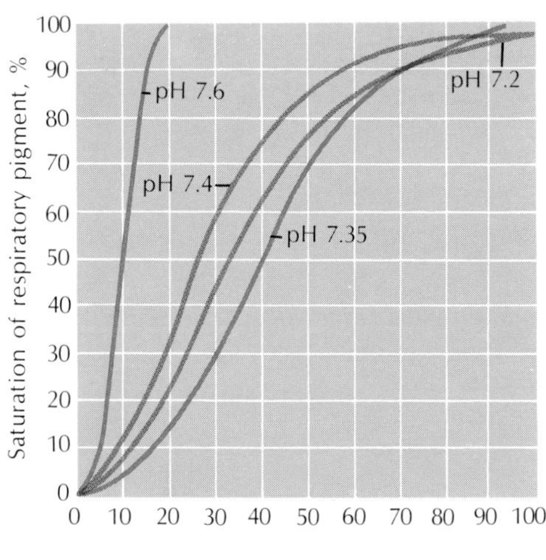

The transient lowering of blood pH that takes place when CO_2 is taken up from the tissues facilitates the dissociation of oxygen from hemoglobin, for the O_2 affinity of hemoglobin declines with increased acidity of the medium [the Bohr effect (Figure 14.36)]. This is physiologically important, for it means that during exercise the increased blood content of CO_2 and lactic acid will have the effect of causing more O_2 to be liberated at the tissues. Animals which lead very active lives tend to show a pronounced Bohr effect, whereas changes in blood pH may have very little influence on O_2 dissociation in more sedentary species.

14.3 □ METABOLISM

When we become involved with the intricacies of digestion, respiration, and internal transport, we may tend to lose sight of the causal factors in the evolution of these adaptive features. Alimentary tract, heart and blood vessels, respiratory organs, vascular tissues, all exist as mere appurtenances to the need of individual cells to obtain nourishment and carry on metabolism. When we speak of the metabolism of a whole organism, we are in fact referring to the sum of the differentiated but coordinated metabolisms of its component cells. When we measure the metabolic rate of an organism as a function of rate of O_2 consumption (Figure 14.37), the value we obtain is actually the mean of various rates of oxidative metabolism in the different tissues. Although the survival of a multicellular organism depends upon the effective coordination of metabolic activities in all of its various tissues, metabolism itself is fundamentally an *intracellular* phenomenon and must accordingly be approached through an analysis of intracellular mechanisms for mobilizing energy and using it for work and biosynthesis. These fundamental intracellular events in the aggregate constitute the dynamic life of both cell and organism. Therefore we must turn again to that triumph of miniaturization: the microscopic chemical factory that is the living cell. Here we shall examine some of the most important pathways of biosynthesis and the fundamental processes involved in cell respiration, whereby energy is mobilized.

By metabolism we mean basically all of the processes by which cells make use of nutrients to perform work and to synthesize fabric materials, storage compounds, and special secretions. *Anabolism* ("constructive metabolism") includes processes that result in a net gain in materials synthesized, whereas *catabolism* ("destructive metabolism") results in a net decrement of material. However, this is no hard and fast distinction, for such catabolic processes as the breakdown of sugar contribute to the formation of ATP and other high-energy phosphate compounds, and also yield carbon skeletons that are needed for building other important compounds. Both anabolism and catabolism involve *both* endergonic and exergonic reactions, for energy must be liberated from some compounds if it is to be transferred to others. Even if catabolism is the ultimate outcome, the materials to be degraded must often first be raised to a higher energy level before they become reactive. This interdependence of anabolic and catabolic processes must be kept in mind in reading the following sections, for although we must dissect out particular aspects of metabolism for separate inspection, in the living cell these mechanisms do not run independently of one another but are intermeshed like sets of gears (Figure 14.38). Little wonder it is then, that a gene mutation resulting in the lack of one essential enzyme usually causes death—the collapse of the whole intricate and fragile construct maintaining life.

Figure 14.37 □ Metabolic rate of various animals, measured as a function of rate of O_2 utilization and plotted on the basis of body weight: (1) barnacle (*Balanus*); (2) crustaceans; (3) gastropod (*Littorina*); (4) gastropod (*Nassarius*); (5) nematodes and polychaetes; (6) mussel (*Mytilus*); (7) planarians and annelids; (8) crustaceans; (9) fish; (10) birds and mammals. Note that in each group larger individuals consume less O_2 per unit of body weight per hour: the metabolic rate of a mouse would be close to the top of curve 10, whereas that of an elephant would be toward the bottom.

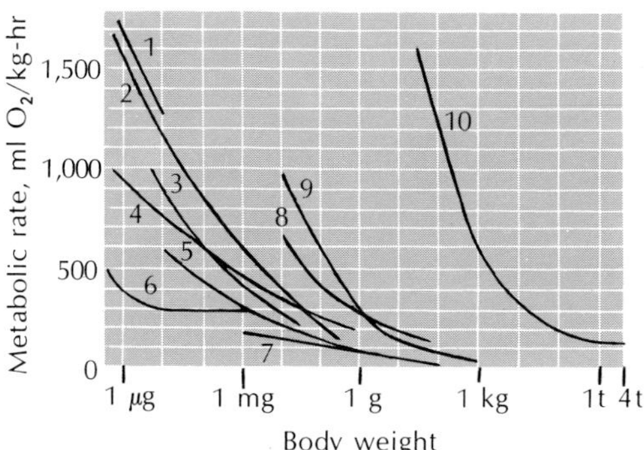

The processes of *intermediary metabolism* yield cell constituents, secretions, and storage compounds at the anabolic end and carbon dioxide, water, and nitrogenous waste compounds at the catabolic end. The intermediates formed are often of such transient existence that they cannot actually be detected by chemical analysis of the tissues. Tracing metabolic pathways has accordingly been one of the great "detective stories" of science, and many techniques including organ culture and use of radioisotopes have been brought to bear on the problem. Beadle and Tatum's use of radiation to cause mutations in *Neurospora* made it possible to work out the steps in a number of synthetic pathways leading to the production of amino acids and vitamins by this mold, for the gene mutations were found to block reaction sequences at whatever points essential enzymes were lacking. The resulting accumulation of specific intermediates in the medium gave clues as to their position in the pathway. One of the most fruitful research techniques has been that of isolating enzymes and substrates in vitro and seeing what conversions take place in such a nonliving cell-free system. By these means many portions of the metabolic web have been traced, but we may not conclude that the whole riddle has been solved, particularly since metabolic pathways in intact cells may not always be those preferred in cell-free in vitro systems. It is wise in this regard (and in fact in many respects where science studies life) to bear in mind the following precautionary statement of Robert Hooke,* discoverer of cells and many other microscopic structures, who warns the reader against too trusting an acceptance of his conclusions:

> *Whereever he finds that I have ventur'd at any small Conjectures, at the causes of the things I have observed, I beseech him to look upon them only as* doubtful Problems, *and* uncertain ghesses, *and not as unquestionable* Conclusions, *or matters of unconfutable Science; I have produced nothing here, with intent to bind his understanding to an* implicit *consent . . .*

Before examining a few of the most important metabolic pathways, we should orient ourselves with respect to where in the cell these reactions actually occur, for generally they are associated with specific regions that can be analyzed morphologically with the aid of the electron microscope. We already know that the synthesis of DNA, messenger RNA, ribosomal RNA, and transfer RNA is apparently restricted to the nu-

**Micrographia* (London: The Royal Society, 1665), Preface.

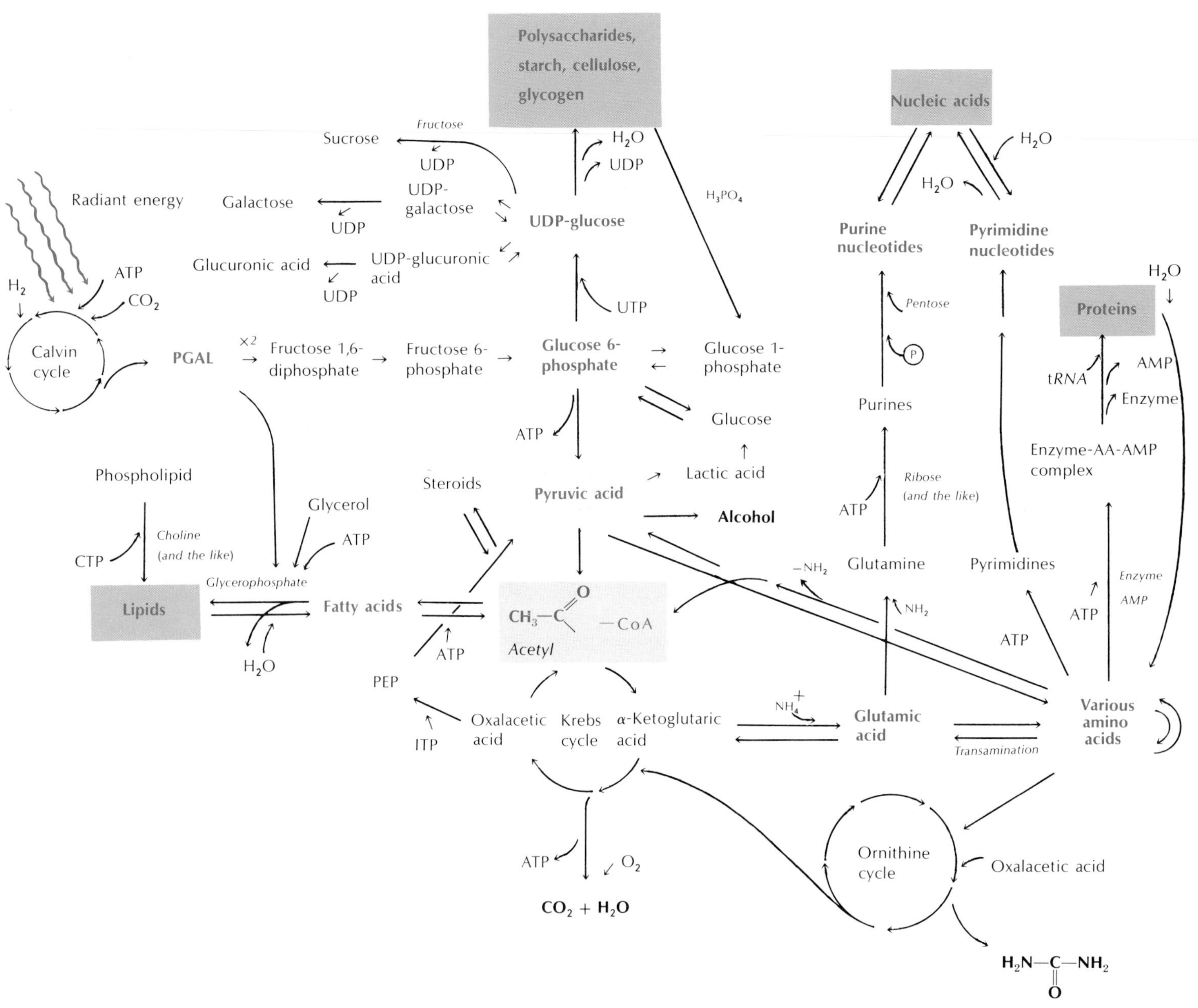
Polysaccharides, starch, cellulose, glycogen
Nucleic acids
Sucrose
Fructose
UDP
H_2O
UDP
Radiant energy
Galactose
UDP-galactose
UDP
UDP-glucose
H_3PO_4
H_2O
Purine nucleotides
Pyrimidine nucleotides
Glucuronic acid
UDP-glucuronic acid
UDP
ATP
H_2
CO_2
UTP
Pentose
H_2O
Proteins
Calvin cycle
PGAL
×2
Fructose 1,6-diphosphate
Fructose 6-phosphate
Glucose 6-phosphate
Glucose 1-phosphate
P
tRNA
AMP
Enzyme
Purines
Glucose
ATP
Enzyme-AA-AMP complex
Lactic acid
Phospholipid
Steroids
Pyruvic acid
Ribose (and the like)
Glycerol
ATP
Alcohol
ATP
CTP
Choline (and the like)
Glycerophosphate
$-NH_2$
Glutamine
Pyrimidines
Enzyme
AMP
Lipids
Fatty acids
$CH_3—C(=O)—CoA$
Acetyl
NH_2
ATP
ATP
ATP
H_2O
PEP
Various amino acids
NH_4^+
Oxalacetic acid
Krebs cycle
α-Ketoglutaric acid
Glutamic acid
ITP
Transamination
Ornithine cycle
Oxalacetic acid
ATP
O_2
$CO_2 + H_2O$
$H_2N—C(=O)—NH_2$

Figure 14.38 □ **Major pathways of the metabolic web. In this simplified representation many interconnections have been omitted. Tinted-color boxes indicate macromolecules that are final products of biosynthetic pathways; colored boldface, especially significant smaller molecules that serve as substrates or intermediates in reaction pathways; black boldface, waste products. (CoA means coenzyme A.) Nucleotides used as energy sources include inosine triphosphate (ITP), adenosine triphosphate (ATP), cytidine triphosphate (CTP), and uridine triphosphate (UTP).**

cleus (except for such DNA replication as may take place during the reproduction of centrioles, plastids, and mitochondria). Protein synthesis takes place at the ribosomes, which are mostly associated with the membranes of the so-called granular or "rough" endoplasmic reticulum. The channels of the "smooth" or agranular endoplasmic reticulum (that is, not associated with ribosomes) contain degradative enzymes for glycolysis, and for lipid and amino acid breakdown, as well as enzymes involved in fatty acid, steroid, and phospholipid synthesis. Certain electron-transport agents such as NAD^+ are also found mainly within the smooth endoplasmic reticulum. Biosynthetic systems for glycogen synthesis are associated with, but not contained within, the ribosomes.

As they are produced in the rough endoplasmic reticulum, enzymes potentially harmful to the cell (such as acid phosphatase, acid ribonuclease, acid deoxyribonuclease, α-glucosidase, and proteases) are collected into enlarged spaces that give rise to the lysosomes. "Programmed cell death" spoken of in Chapter 11, may well be implemented by a "self-destruct" mechanism whereby the lysosomes break down, releasing these enzymes destructive to the integrity of the cell's actual framework. Normally the contained enzymes are passed into pinosomes or phagosomes, or are otherwise liberated as needed.

The synthesis of glycoproteins and mucosaccharides in mucus-secreting glandular cells has been localized (by use of ^{35}S and radiolabeled glucose) to the Golgi complex. These synthetic pathways make use of the nucleotides uridine diphosphate (UDP) and guanosine diphosphate (GDP; see Figure 9.5c) as energy sources, and so it is not surprising that the enzymes most consistently found in the Golgi complex are those that catalyze the dephosphorylation of UDP to UMP and P_i, GDP to GMP and P_i, and so forth.

The mitochondria house the membrane-bound enzymes responsible for the Krebs tricarboxylic acid cycle, the terminal oxidations, and other major pathways of cell respiration, and are therefore the cell's major site of ATP production. Chloroplasts (discussed earlier) are the sites of photophosphorylation and carbohydrate production from inorganic substrates. From our present state of fragmentary knowledge we can look forward hopefully to a time when all metabolic systems have been traced to specific cell components, and when the molecular architecture of these components has been worked out so thoroughly that the interaction of structure and function is apparent, even on the molecular level.

A The metabolic roles of vitamins

As a preliminary to our study of metabolism, we should survey the metabolic roles of a heterogeneous category of small organic molecules termed *vitamins,* since the presence of these in small amounts is indispensible for normal metabolism (Figure 14.39). Vitamins are seldom involved as structural components of cells, and in a number of instances we still do not know their exact mode of action. In most cases where the action is known, the vitamin proves to be an enzyme cofactor or prosthetic group—the nonprotein part of an enzyme molecule (Figure 14.40; see also Figure 9.6). The discovery of vitamins first came about through the study of vitamin-deficiency diseases in man and experimental animals, which were found to be alleviated by adding to the diet certain foods containing the required factor. Such deficiency diseases include beriberi, pellagra, rickets, and scurvy. We now know that these symptoms are merely the overt expression of a metabolic derangement involving, in most cases, *all* of the body cells. These regulatory substances are synthesized by autotrophs, and certain of them are also synthesized by heterotrophs. Those which are universally required as catalytic factors must once have been capable of synthesis in all organisms. We have seen that the loss of the capacity to synthesize chlorophyll was probably responsible for initiating the evolutionary divergence of animals from their autotrophic predecessors. By the same token, the inability to synthesize universally required vitamins can be attributed to mutations by which the synthetic capacity was lost. Such *loss mutations* occur in irradiated *Neurospora,* a mold that normally requires the addition of only one vitamin to its culture medium. Tolerance of such loss is possible if the organism can continue to obtain the needed factor from the environment.

Figure 14.39 □ Representative vitamins (carbon atoms are not shown within rings): (*a*) water-soluble; (*b*) fat-soluble.

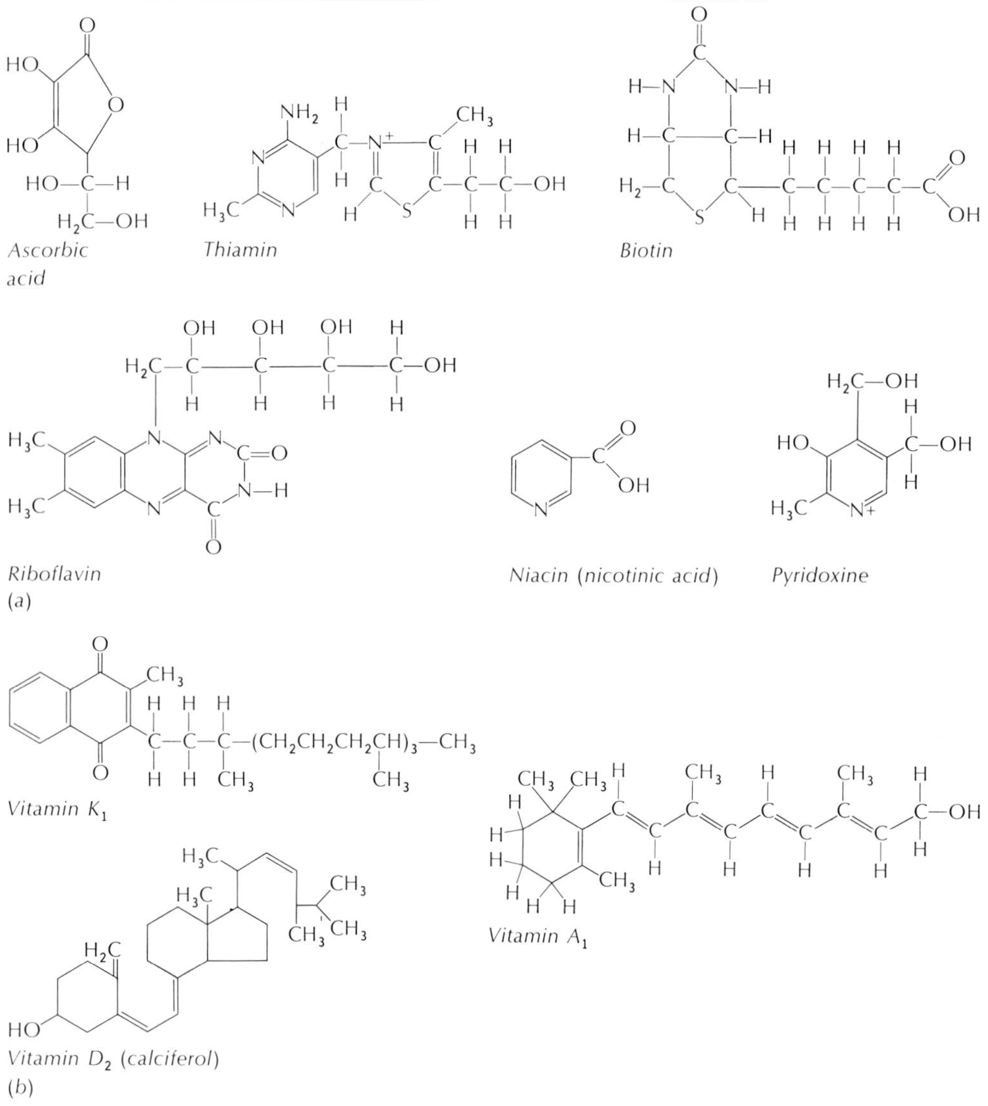

Ascorbic acid *Thiamin* *Biotin*

Riboflavin *Niacin (nicotinic acid)* *Pyridoxine*

(*a*)

Vitamin K_1 *Vitamin A_1*

Vitamin D_2 (calciferol)

(*b*)

Thus we find that although a certain amount of vitamin synthesis takes place in the animal body, by and large animals must satisfy their vitamin requirements by ingesting foods that contain these factors. Often the metabolic function of an ingested vitamin in the animal body is similar to its role in the plant tissues in which it was produced. In certain cases, however, vitamins have assumed new roles in addition to their original functions.

Vitamins are chemically heterogeneous but may be classified on the basis of solubility into fat-soluble and water-soluble groups. In general, the water-soluble vitamins appear to be the most universally required factors, and most of them can be synthesized by bacteria as well as by autotrophs. Where their fundamental action is known, the water-soluble vitamins are found to serve as constituents of coenzymes or enzyme prosthetic groups and thus are required for metabolism in all cells.

The fat-soluble vitamins, on the other hand, are more sporadic in distribution. They have not (as yet) been definitely proven to serve as catalysts, and their functions may vary among different groups of organisms. They can be synthesized by some heterotrophs but are not needed by all, and are thought to be lacking in bacteria. These vitamins contain only C, H, and O, whereas most of the water-soluble vitamins also contain N.

Some thirty compounds are known to have vitamin activity. Each water-soluble vitamin is a unique compound, the action of which cannot be duplicated by a closely related molecule. On the other hand, the fat-soluble vitamins comprise families of related compounds with similar biological

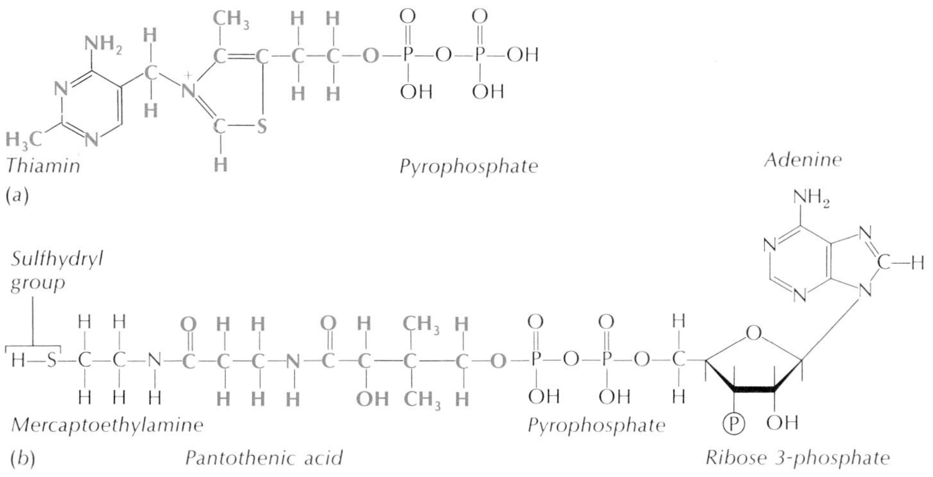

Figure 14.40 □ **Important coenzymes formed with vitamin molecules: (*a*) thiamin pyrophosphate (TPP), "cocarboxylase"; (*b*) coenzyme A (CoA or CoA—SH). (Refer to Figure 9.6 for formulas of the vitamin-containing nucleotide coenzymes FAD, NAD, and NADP.) Coenzyme A bonds through its —SH group to an acetyl group: $H_3C{-}\overset{\overset{\displaystyle O}{\|}}{C}{\sim}S{-}$, and the —C~S— bond is of high energy, making acetyl CoA reactive.**

activity. Accordingly, each water-soluble vitamin has its own distinctive name—ascorbic acid, thiamin, cobalamin, and so forth—while the fat-soluble ones are usually identified by letter, for example, the A, D, E, and K groups. In Table 14.2 the biological activities of the vitamins are summarized, along with the conspicuous systemic effects of their deficiency.

THE WATER-SOLUBLE VITAMINS *Ascorbic acid* (vitamin C) is a hexose derivative required for the normal synthesis of collagen and intercellular cement in the animal body. Its prolonged insufficiency leads to weakened connective tissues, capillary hemorrhages, and probably impaired immunological response, presenting in man the well-known syndrome of *scurvy,* which can be alleviated by consumption of citrus fruits and tomatoes. Long a scourge of seafarers, scurvy was first controlled by the British naval practice of provisioning ships with raw limes (hence the colloquial term "limey" to designate the British sailor). Ascorbic acid is a reversible oxidation-reduction agent and is thought to be a coenzyme for a number of enzymes including certain intracellular proteases (cathepsins).

Inositol is a hexose isomer, the fundamental action of which remains obscure. It is a constituent of the phospholipid *phosphatidylic inositol,* an essential component of cell membranes that is concerned with ion transport. It also promotes cellular growth and mitosis in vitro.

Nicotinic acid (*niacin*) is a constituent of the hydrogen-carriers NAD (nicotinamide adenine dinucleotide) and NADP (nicotinamide adenine dinucleotide phosphate). We have previously noted the role of NADP in feeding H into the Calvin cycle of photosynthesis and will shortly consider the role of NAD as an H acceptor in glycolysis and the Krebs cycle.

Thiamin is a component of cocarboxylase, a coenzyme to carboxylase; this enzyme serves to remove —COOH from pyruvic acid (a product of glycolysis), converting it to acetaldehyde (see Figure 14.52). Acetaldehyde is then taken up by coenzyme A, which is formed by the vitamin *pantothenic acid.* Coenzyme A transfers acetaldehyde into the Krebs cycle and also catalyzes many other important reactions. Thiamin has an additional role in autotrophs, where it appears to be involved in CO_2 fixation.

Riboflavin is a precursor of FMN (flavin mononucleotide), which serves as a coenzyme to a number of dehydrogenases. When bonded to adenylic acid, FMN becomes flavin adenine dinucleotide (FAD), a prosthetic group to flavoproteins in the terminal oxidations and other sequences involving electron transfer (see Figure 14.55). Flavoproteins also require the presence of certain metallic ions (Cu, Fe, Mo, or Mn) for proper function.

Biotin serves as a coenzyme to transferases engaged in the transfer of amino and carboxyl groups. A deficiency of this vitamin is rarely known, since it (along with a number of other B vitamins) is synthesized in the gut by symbiotic bacteria. Biotin, thiamin, and pyridoxine all serve to promote the synthesis of lipids.

Table 14.2 □ Important vitamins

VITAMIN	ACTION	DEFICIENCY
Water-soluble:		
Ascorbic acid (C)	Oxidation-reduction agent; coenzyme to intracellular protease; essential to synthesis of collagen and intercellular cement	*Scurvy;* hemorrhage, weakened connective tissue
Inositol	Constituent of cell membrane lipid (phosphatidylic inositol); involved in active transport; essential action in growth undetermined	Connective tissue abnormalities
Nicotinic acid (B_5 or niacin)	Constituent of NAD and NADP, thus involved in H transfer	*Pellagra;* dermatitis, gastric and nervous disorders
Thiamin (B_1)	Thiamin pyrophosphate is coenzyme to carboxylase, concerned with decarboxylations	*Beriberi;* nervous and circulatory disorders
Pantothenic acid (B_3)	Precursor of coenzyme A; moves acetaldehyde into Krebs cycle or into pathways of lipid or amino acid synthesis	Rare; dermatitis, graying, neural and circulatory disorders
Riboflavin (B_2)	Precursor of FMN and FAD, involved in e^- transport	Dermatitis, corneal vascularization, lesions at mouth angles
Biotin	Precursor of coenzyme to transferases involved in transaminations and transcarboxylations	Rare; dermatitis, graying; growth impairment
Pyridoxine (B_6)	Coenzyme to transferases involved in transaminations; promotes NH_3 fixation and deamination and decarboxylation of amino acids	Rare; dermatitis
Choline	Constituent of lecithin; coenzyme to transferases engaged in transmethylations	Fatty liver
Cobalamin (B_{12})	Extrinsic antipernicious anemia factor; coenzyme to transferases involved in transferring one-carbon units	Anemia
Folic acid	Coenzyme to transferases of formyl groups	Anemia; dermatitis, hemorrhage; nervous disorders
'at-soluble:		
Vitamin A group	Form retinal, a constituent (enzyme inhibitor) of visual pigments; restrict epithelial keratinization	Night blindness; excessive epidermal keratinization; corneal keratinization
Vitamin D group	Control Ca and P absorption and metabolism	*Rickets;* excessive Ca and P excretion; bone erosion
Vitamin E group	Essential action unknown; antisterility factor in rats; may affect lipid and nucleic acid metabolism	Sterility in rats; perhaps embryonic eye defects in man
Vitamin K group	Electron transfer agent in photosynthesis; involved in prothrombase synthesis in mammals	Clotting abnormalities in mammals

Figure 14.41 □ (*a*) **Xerophthalmia in rat due to vitamin A deficiency.** (*b*) **Eyes restored to normal by feeding 3 U.S.P. units (about 0.001 mg) of vitamin A daily.** (*E. R. Squibb & Sons, Inc.*)

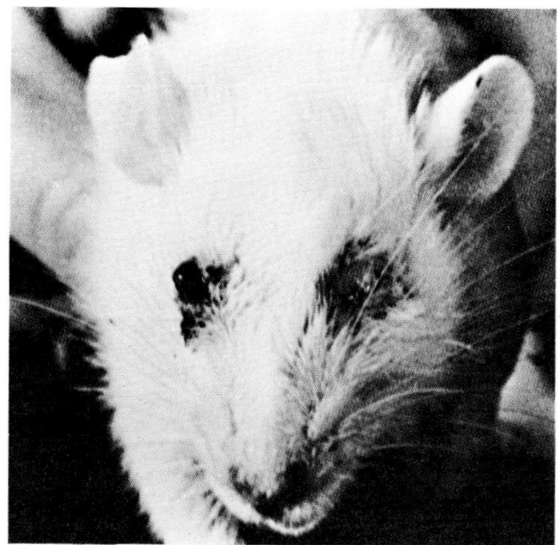

(*a*)

(*b*)

Pyridoxine is chemically similar to niacin but functions as coenzyme to transferases involved in transaminations. Pyridoxine enzymes also catalyze the initial fixation of NH_3 by plants. In addition, they bring about deamination and decarboxylation of amino acids.

Choline is a constituent of the diglyceride lecithin (see Figure 14.6), an essential constituent of cell membranes. It also serves as coenzyme to transferases engaged in the transfer of methyl groups ($—CH_3$), for it can reversibly take up and donate these groups.

Cobalamine (B_{12}) is a relatively complex molecule including a tetrapyrrole ring like that of hemoglobin but centered upon a cobalt instead of an iron atom. Its most familiar role is as the *erythrocyte-maturing* or *extrinsic antipernicious anemia factor* in mammals, for its lack causes pernicious anemia. It forms a coenzyme involved with various isomerizations, and another that is essential to the synthesis of methyl groups from serine or formaldehyde. It also plays a part in mobilizing fats by assisting the synthesis of choline, which in turn promotes the oxidation of triglycerides.

Folic acid is also an antianemic factor and a general growth factor in all animals tested. A reduced form, *tetrahydrofolic acid* ("FH_4"), serves as carrier for activated one-carbon formyl units:

$$—C\overset{\displaystyle O}{\underset{\displaystyle H}{\lessgtr}}$$

In this capacity it is essential to the synthesis of purine nucleotides (see Figure 14.50).

Lipoic acid serves as a coenzyme in oxidizing α-keto acids to acetyl moieties:

$$CH_3—\overset{\displaystyle O}{\overset{\|}{C}}—$$

It reacts with thiamine pyrophosphate and coenzyme A to move acetyl groups into the Krebs cycle (see Figure 14.52), and at the same time serves as a hydrogen acceptor and transfer agent.

THE FAT-SOLUBLE VITAMINS The *vitamin A family* consists of vitamins formed in the animal body by hydrolysis of one molecule of the yellow pigment *carotene*, obtained by consuming plant tissue, into two molecules of vitamin A. The most universal role of the A vitamins is as *retinal* (vitamin A–aldehyde), a constituent of visual pigments such as rhodopsin and iodopsin. Instead of being a coenzyme, retinal appears to be an *enzyme inhibitor*, which is broken off the enzyme (opsin) when exposed to light (see Figure 15.22). In mammals and birds, vitamin A seems to have adopted additional roles in promoting growth and maintaining the integrity of epithelial membranes. Its deficiency leads to excessive keratinization of the epidermis and cornea of the eye (Figure 14.41). It is required for normal embryonic development, for its lack during pregnancy may cause the young to be eyeless and limbless. It also seems to promote growth of the brain and cranial nerves by causing bone resorption on the inside of the cranium and around the openings through which nerves must exit from the skull.

The *vitamin D* group consists of steroids or related compounds that control calcium and phosphate absorption, retention, metabolism, and deposition in teeth and bone. Its mode of action is unknown, but a prolonged deficiency in mammals leads to *rickets*, a

Figure 14.42 □ **Mechanisms of biosynthesis: (*a*) template control (free nucleotides assembling on preexisting DNA template); (*b*) self-assembly (four peptide subunits assembling by noncovalent bonding); (*c*) enzyme control (substrates forming covalent bonds on active site of enzyme molecule).**

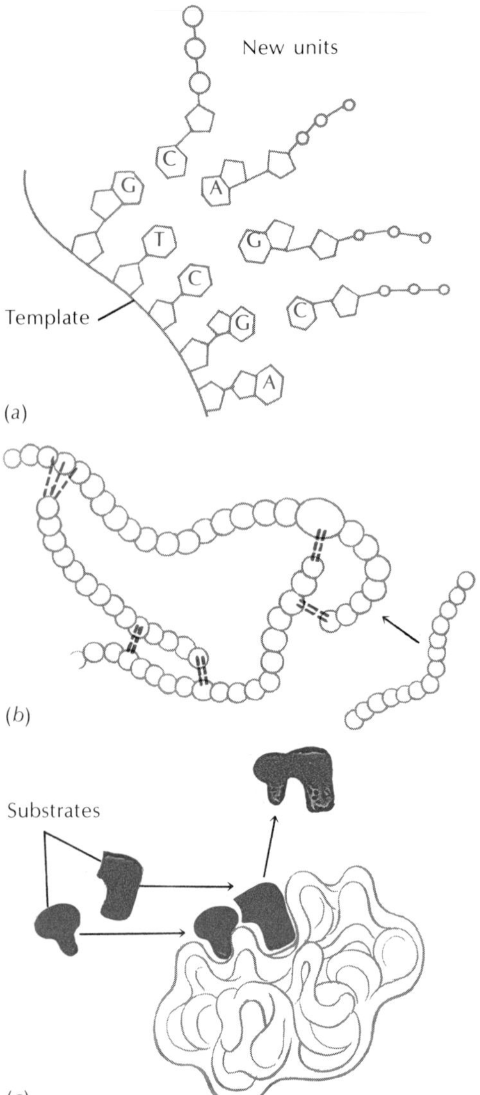

disease in which the teeth and bones are eroded and deformed.

The most important vitamin of the *E* group is *α-tocopherol,* best known as an antisterility factor in rats. The effects of its deficiency are undetermined in man, although its lack during pregnancy is thought to contribute to eye defects in the offspring. Its essential action is unknown, but it appears to be involved in oxidative reactions, especially affecting the metabolism of nucleic acids and unsaturated fats. It is thought to protect sensitive mitochondrial systems from being irreversibly inhibited by lipid peroxides, for in vitro it acts as an antioxidant and prevents mitochondrial deterioration.

The *vitamins K* are growth-promoting factors that have various functions in the different groups of organisms in which they occur. In mammals, K_1 is well known as an antihemorrhagic agent essential to the synthesis of *prothrombase* by the liver. In autotrophs, vitamin K serves as a transfer agent of electrons from chlorophyll.

B Biosynthesis

The synthesis of biotic structures at all levels of complexity is governed by two general principles: (1) the thermodynamic principle of minimum energy, which dictates that favored reactions are those leading toward a state at which the free energy of the system is at the lowest realizable level; (2) the biological principle of evolution by natural selection, which determines that from the multitude of energetically possible reactions only those that are most adaptive will be conserved. Free energy is here defined as the net driving force that makes chemical reactions occur; it is expressed as the sum of two separate driving forces—the tendency of a system to lose heat (enthalpy), and the tendency toward randomness or disorderliness (entropy). A molecular configuration will persist only if energy barriers of sufficient magnitude prevent it from assuming some other potentially more stable configuration. Most molecular configurations found in biotic systems do not represent the lowest state of free energy possible for their components, therefore they have a low margin of stability. The addition of a relatively slight amount of activation energy allows these configurations to undergo transitions to a more stable state. If this state is also the most functional state, the transition need not be reversed by use of energy. But if a less stable state is more adaptive, it must constantly be renewed. New configurations must continuously be built up in an orderly manner relevant to the needs of the cell or organism.

Biotic structures are built up through some combination of three major mechanisms: (1) *template control;* (2) *self-assembly;* (3) *enzymatic control* processes (Figure 14.42). The linear order of amino acids in a polypeptide chain is template-controlled, through the transcription of the base sequence of a DNA cistron (gene) to mRNA, and the subsequent coupling of mRNA with tRNA. The maximum molecular weight of a polypeptide is in the neighborhood of 40,000, or some 1,000 amino acid units, which appears to be about the maximum practical size for a unit produced by a template-control mechanism. Many proteins are much larger than this, but are found to consist of several polypeptide chains that have become associated by spontaneous self-assembly, with the formation of noncovalent bonds. Many of the proteins thus formed by a combination of template control and self-assembly then serve as enzymes, constituting enzymatic control mechanisms for the synthesis of nonprotein compounds.

The self-assembly of subunits is a most significant aspect of biosynthesis, and results not only in the formation of macromolecules but in the orderly grouping of subunits into crystalline lattices and other forms. The existence in different tissues, or in the same tissue at different stages of maturation, of *isozymes* (variants of a given enzyme molecule) is in part explicable on the basis of randomness in this self-assembly process. For example, the isozymes of lactic dehydrogenase are made up of four polypeptide chains representing two types. They differ only in the number of chains of each type present, and this in turn is a function of the relative synthetic activity of the two genes involved. For instance, if at one time in ontogeny chain "A" were synthesized at a significantly greater rate than chain "B," an isozyme consisting of three A and one B chains would tend to predominate. Later, changing conditions might promote the activity of the gene controlling chain B, whereupon isozymes with two A and two B or even one A and three B chains would become relatively more abundant. The occurrence of many such isozymes reflects a degree of randomness in the self-assembly process that would make many assembly errors unavoidable. However, the noncovalent bonds characteristic of self-assembled units are readily reversible, and in conformity with the law of minimum free energy such self-assembled units will tend spontaneously to pass through various alternative configurations until ultimately the most stable state, that with the lowest realizable free energy, is reached. This configuration will tend to persist, since any further change would be a thermodynamically "uphill" process, requiring an input of energy for its completion. However, if this thermodynamically most stable state is *not* at the same time the most functionally efficient (in the biotic sense), natural selection will operate in favor of perpetuating some more adaptive though less stable configuration, even at considerable energy cost. Biotic systems do in fact contain many adaptively valuable but not very stable configurations that can be maintained only by constant energy investment.

We have already studied template-controlled biosyntheses in our consideration of DNA replication and mRNA production (see Figure 9.20), and will review these only briefly in the present chapter. We shall also say no more about self-assembly processes, important as they are, for to do so would involve us in consideration of the three-dimensional organization of macromolecules and the forces underlying the spontaneous assumption of these characteristic shapes, which are beyond the scope of this book. Most of the reactions we shall examine during the balance of this chapter are enzymatically controlled. We need only to remind ourselves that to form the enzymes on which these reactions depend requires both template control and self-assembly processes.

Table 14.3, which summarizes the rate of synthesis of essential macromolecules in the colon bacillus, serves to give us an idea of how rapidly enzyme-controlled reactions may proceed. It is estimated that each *E. coli* cell has to convert 2.5×10^6 molecules of ATP to ADP *per second* (with a release of between 7,000 and 12,000 cal/mole) merely to synthesize new materials rapidly enough to keep up with the observed rate at which this bacillus can multiply!

In discussing both synthetic and degradative intermediary metabolism we shall make ample use of figures showing structural formulas for the substrates, intermediates, and products. These formulas are intended to serve as a highway map does a motorist, not to overwhelm with detail. They need not be memorized, nor learned any more than the motorist learns his map, but studying them should make quite clear what is taking place in any given reaction sequence. Where necessary, reference may be made to the pertinent sections of Chapter 9 for review of the basic chemistry required and the conventions used in writing simplified structural formulas.

CARBOHYDRATE BIOSYNTHESIS The simplest usable carbohydrate formed by autotrophic cells from inorganic precursors is phosphoglyceraldehyde (PGAL; see Figure 13.10). This is presumably too reactive a material to accumulate in quantity, but is the basic substrate from which monosaccharides of higher molecular weight—such as hexoses and pentoses—are built. Pentoses may be obtained for use in nucleotide synthesis either directly from the Calvin cycle or by the partial degradation of hexose in the pentose phosphate pathway (see Figure 14.57). When PGAL leaves the Calvin cycle, the first conversion that it undergoes is the joining of two PGAL molecules to form one molecule of fructose 1,6-diphosphate. This

Table 14.3 □ Biosynthetic capacities of a bacterial cell[a,b]

CHEMICAL COMPONENT	PERCENT OF DRY WEIGHT	APPROXIMATE MOLECULAR WEIGHT	NUMBER OF MOLECULES PER CELL	NUMBER OF MOLECULES SYNTHESIZED PER SECOND	NUMBER OF MOLECULES OF ATP REQUIRED (FOR SYNTHESIS) PER SECOND	PERCENT OF TOTAL BIOSYNTHETIC ENERGY REQUIRED
DNA	5	2,000,000,000	4[c]	0.0033	60,000	2.5
RNA	10	1,000,000	15,000	12.5	75,000	3.1
Protein	70	60,000	1,700,000	1,400	2,120,000	88.0
Lipids	10	1,000	15,000,000	12,500	87,500	3.7
Polysaccharides	5	200,000	39,000	32.5	65,000	2.7

[a] From A. L. Lehninger, *Bioenergetics* (New York: W. A. Benjamin, Inc., 1965), p. 174.

[b] A cell of *Escherichia coli* is about 1 by 1 by 3 μm in size, has a volume of 2.25 μm^3, a total weight of 10×10^{-13} g, and a dry weight of 2.5×10^{-13} g. The rates of biosynthesis given were averaged over a 20-min cell-division cycle.

[c] The exact molecular weight and number of DNA molecules in *E. coli* cells are not known, but it is probable that there are only a few molecules, each of which is of great size.

gives up a phosphate group as inorganic phosphate (P_i), to become fructose 6-phosphate, which in turn isomerizes to form glucose 6-phosphate (Figure 14.43). Glucose 6-phosphate is one of the most important of metabolic intermediates, for it stands at the "crossroads" of the pathways of carbohydrate degradation or further synthesis and isomerization. It is the major form in which carbohydrate enters the glycolytic (Figure 14.51) and pentose phosphate pathways. In animals particularly it can be dephosphorylated to glucose, the major sugar found in the blood and therefore the main form in which carbohydrate is transported through the animal body. A meticulous balance must be maintained between the amount of free glucose and polysaccharide present. If the blood glucose concentration falls below tolerable levels, glycogen is mobilized to repair the deficit; if blood glucose exceeds normal levels, it is either transformed to glycogen or excreted through the kidneys.

The primary means by which glucose 6-phosphate is converted to other hexoses such as glucuronic acid and galactose, or is built up into oligosaccharides and polysaccharides, is by its isomerization to glucose 1-phosphate and the combination of this form with the free nucleotide, UTP, (uridine triphosphate; see Figure 9.5c) to form uridine diphosphoglucose (UDP-glucose) with the release of pyrophosphate (Figure 14.44). Regeneration of UTP from UDP requires the transfer of ~Ⓟ from ATP.

LIPID BIOSYNTHESIS The synthesis of fatty acids and other essential cell constituents proceeds by the repetitive addition of an activated two-carbon condensation unit to the lengthening chain. This condensation unit is often an activated acetyl group,

$$CH_3{-}\overset{\overset{\large O}{\|}}{C}{\sim}$$

bonded through a high-energy linkage to coenzyme A (see Figure 14.40*b*). Coenzyme A is a modified adenine nucleotide linked with pantothenic acid (a vitamin) and an amine bearing a terminal —SH (sulfhydryl group). The reactive compound formed by the combination of acetyl with coenzyme A (CoA) is briefly designated

$$CH_3{-}\overset{\overset{\large O}{\|}}{C}{\sim}S{-}CoA$$

or merely acetyl CoA. Other organic fragments can also be activated by bonding with CoA as acyl CoA complexes,

$$R{-}\overset{\overset{\large O}{\|}}{C}{-}{\sim}S{-}CoA$$

such as malonyl CoA, succinyl CoA, and so forth:

$$\underset{\textit{Malonyl CoA}}{\overset{\overset{COOH}{|}}{CH_2}{-}\overset{\overset{\large O}{\|}}{C}{\sim}S{-}CoA} \qquad \underset{\textit{Succinyl CoA}}{\overset{\overset{COOH}{|}}{CH_2}{-}CH_2{-}\overset{\overset{\large O}{\|}}{C}{\sim}S{-}CoA}$$

Malonyl CoA is the actual condensing unit

in the synthesis of fatty acids. It itself can be produced by the union of acetyl CoA with CO_2. The CO_2 must first be activated by being joined to a biotin enzyme, using energy from ATP:

1 Co_2 + biotin enzyme + ATP $\longrightarrow$
CO_2-biotin enzyme + ADP + P_i
2 CO_2-biotin enzyme + acetyl CoA $\rightleftharpoons$
malonyl CoA + biotin enzyme

The actual synthesis of a fatty acid chain takes place on the surface of a carrier protein containing pantothenic acid and bearing a terminal sulfhydryl group to which the acyl moieties can link. This protein, known as *acyl carrier protein* (ACP-SH), receives the activated acyl groups from CoA. (This is shown in reactions 1 and 2 of Figure 14.45, which should be referred to during the following discussion.)

The first condensation (reaction 3) takes place between an acetyl and a malonyl group, forming a four-carbon acetoacetyl unit linked with ACP. It might appear simpler for two acetyl-ACP units to unite, but this is too readily reversible to favor the production of a long hydrocarbon chain. The incorporation of malonyl, on the other hand, is highly favorable for the growth of such a chain, for it simultaneously is *decarboxylated*. This loss of CO_2 prevents the reaction from spontaneously proceeding in reverse. Reactions 4, 5, and 6 are needed now only as a preliminary to the next condensation (reaction 7). The acetoacetyl unit is first reduced, obtaining hydrogen from NADH • H^+, then dehydrated with the loss of H_2O, and then reduced once more with 2H from NADH • H^+. The product of reaction 6 is butyryl-ACP, which if released by hydrolysis would be the low molecular weight fatty

H₂C—O—Ⓟ
H—C—OH
H—C=O
+
H—C=O
H—C—OH
H₂C—O—Ⓟ
2PGAL

Aldolase

H₂C—O—Ⓟ
C=O
HO—C—H
H—C—OH
H—C—OH
H₂C—O—Ⓟ
Fructose 1,6-diphosphate

Phosphatase
P_i

H₂COH
C=O
HO—C—H
HC—OH
HC—OH
H₂C—O—Ⓟ
Fructose 6-phosphate

Phosphohexose isomerase

H—C=O
H—C—OH
HO—C—H
H—C—OH
H—C—OH
H₂—C—O—Ⓟ
Glucose 6-phosphate

Figure 14.43 □ Formation of glucose 6-phosphate from PGAL. Note that fructose is a *keto* sugar (ketose), characterized by a keto group, $-\underset{|}{R}-\overset{O}{\overset{\|}{C}}-R$, whereas glucose is an *aldehyde* sugar (aldose), characterized by an aldehyde group, $R-\overset{O}{\overset{\|}{C}}-H$. Names of enzymes catalyzing each reaction appear over the arrows. Organic phosphate is represented as Ⓟ; inorganic phosphate, as P_i.

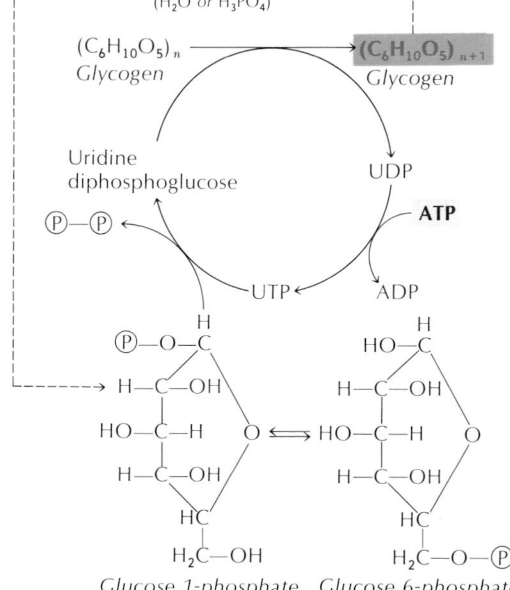

Figure 14.44 □ Means by which one glucose unit is added to a glycogen molecule. Dashed arrow indicates that a glucose unit can be removed from glycogen either by hydrolysis (as in digestion) or by phosphorolysis. Here Ⓟ—Ⓟ stands for pyrophosphate; UTP, for uridine triphosphate; UDP, for uridine diphosphate.

Figure 14.45 □ **Synthesis of a fatty acid: (1) activation of acetyl group by bonding to ACP (acyl carrier protein); (2) activation of malonyl group by bonding to ACP; (3) condensation reaction, producing acetoacetyl-ACP, with liberation of CO_2 (decarboxylation); (4) reduction of acetoacetyl-ACP with H_2 from $NADH_2$ (representing an energy gain); (5) dehydration of hydroxylbutyryl-ACP; (6) reduction of crotonyl-ACP with H_2 from $NADH_2$, producing butyryl-ACP; (7) condensation of another malonyl with product of steps 1 to 6.**

1 $$H_3C-\overset{O}{\overset{\|}{C}}\sim S-CoA + ACP\text{-}SH \xrightarrow{\textit{Acetyl transacylase}} H_3C-\overset{O}{\overset{\|}{C}}-S-ACP + CoA$$

Acetyl CoA → *Acetyl-ACP*

2 $$H_2\overset{COOH}{\overset{|}{C}}-\overset{O}{\overset{\|}{C}}\sim S-CoA + ACP\text{-}SH \xrightarrow{\textit{Malonyl transacylase}} H_2\overset{COOH}{\overset{|}{C}}-\overset{O}{\overset{\|}{C}}-S-ACP + CoA$$

Malonyl CoA → *Malonyl-ACP*

3 $$H_3C-\overset{O}{\overset{\|}{C}}-S-ACP + H_2\overset{COOH}{\overset{|}{C}}-\overset{O}{\overset{\|}{C}}-S-ACP \xrightarrow{\textit{β-Ketoacyl ACP synthetase}} H_3C-\overset{O}{\overset{\|}{C}}-CH_2-\overset{O}{\overset{\|}{C}}-S-ACP + \mathbf{CO_2} + ACP-S\mathbf{H}$$

Acetoacetyl-ACP

4 $$H_3C-\overset{O}{\overset{\|}{C}}-CH_2-\overset{O}{\overset{\|}{C}}-S-ACP + NAD\mathbf{H} + \mathbf{H}^+ \xrightarrow{\textit{β-Ketoacyl ACP reductase}} H_3C-\underset{\mathbf{H}}{\underset{|}{\overset{\mathbf{OH}}{\overset{|}{C}}}}-CH_2-\overset{O}{\overset{\|}{C}}-S-ACP + NAD^+$$

Hydroxylbutyryl-ACP

5 $$H_3C-\underset{H}{\underset{|}{\overset{\mathbf{OH}}{\overset{|}{C}}}}-\underset{H}{\underset{|}{\overset{\mathbf{H}}{\overset{|}{C}}}}-\overset{O}{\overset{\|}{C}}-S-ACP \xrightarrow{\textit{Enoyl ACP hydrase}} H_3C-CH{=}CH-\overset{O}{\overset{\|}{C}}-S-ACP + \mathbf{H_2O}$$

Crotonyl-ACP

6 $$H_3C-CH{=}CH-\overset{O}{\overset{\|}{C}}-S-ACP + NAD\mathbf{H} + \mathbf{H}^+ \xrightarrow{\textit{Enoyl ACP reductase}} H_3C-\underset{H}{\underset{|}{\overset{\mathbf{H}}{\overset{|}{C}}}}-\underset{H}{\underset{|}{\overset{\mathbf{H}}{\overset{|}{C}}}}-\overset{O}{\overset{\|}{C}}-S-ACP$$

Butyryl-ACP

7 $$H_3C-CH_2-CH_2-\overset{O}{\overset{\|}{C}}-S-ACP + \mathbf{H_2}\overset{COOH}{\overset{|}{C}}-\overset{O}{\overset{\|}{C}}-S-ACP \xrightarrow{\textit{β-Ketoacyl ACP synthetase}} H_3C-CH_2-CH_2-\overset{O}{\overset{\|}{C}}-CH_2-\overset{O}{\overset{\|}{C}}-S-ACP + \mathbf{CO_2} + ACP-S\mathbf{H}$$

β-Ketohexanoyl-S-ACP

acid, butyric acid. However, butyryl–ACP can now take up another malonyl unit, lengthening the chain by two more carbon atoms. We can see (in Figure 14.45) that reaction 7 is actually a repetition of reaction 3, and is catalyzed by the same enzyme, β-ketoacyl–ACP synthetase. It is not difficult to see that if we were to schematize the synthesis further, reaction 8 would be a reduction (repeating 4), 9 a dehydration (repeating 5), and 10 another reduction (repeating 6), following which the chain would be ready to add another malonyl condensing unit. This stepwise, repeating pattern is typical of most biosynthetic pathways.

To interject a word about enzyme nomenclature, we can see by inspecting the names of the enzymes needed to catalyze these reactions that the first part of the name indicates the enzyme's substrate (say, acetyl), and the latter part the general category to which the enzyme belongs (say, a reductase or a transacylase*). Finally, the ending -*ase* indicates that the compound is an enzyme. No fewer than six enzymes are required to build a fatty acid chain, and all of these appear to form a complex on the surface of ACP, which—being itself unaltered by the reactions—also serves a catalytic function.

This reaction sequence beautifully demonstrates some of the cardinal aspects of biosynthesis. (1) The reactants must be energized, in this case by forming high-energy links with CoA. (2) A series of specific enzymes are required, each catalyzing a particular type of reaction, such as a condensation, a reduction, or a dehydration. (3)

*A *transacylase* is a transferase that transfers acyl groups.

1 $2R{-}C(=O)OH$ + CoA—SH ⟶ **$2R{-}\overset{O}{\overset{\|}{C}}{\sim}S{-}CoA$**

Fatty acid

2 Glycerol (H—C—OH / H—C—OH / H—C—OH) + **ATP** ⟶ **H—C—OH / H—C—OH / H—C—O—Ⓟ** + ADP

Glycerol *Glycerophosphate*

3 Glycerophosphate + $2R{-}\overset{O}{\overset{\|}{C}}{\sim}S{-}CoA$ ⟶ **H—C—O—C(=O)—R / H—C—O—C(=O)—R / H—C—O—Ⓟ** + 2CoA—SH

Phosphatidic acid

4 Phosphatidic acid ⟶ (P_i) **H—C—O—C(=O)—R / H—C—O—C(=O)—R / H—C—OH**

Diglyceride

5 **Choline** + ATP ⟶ **Phosphorylcholine** + ADP

6 Phosphorylcholine + CTP ⟶ **CDP—choline** + Ⓟ—Ⓟ

7 CDP—choline + diglyceride ⟶ **Phosphatidyl choline (lecithin)** + CMP

Figure 14.46 □ Phospholipid synthesis: lecithin formation. (See Figure 14.6 for additional structural formulas.) Substrates are printed in color boldface; on first appearance, intermediates are printed in black boldface.

Vitamins are involved as coenzymes: biotin in the CO_2-activating enzyme, pantothenic acid in CoA and ACP, and so forth. (4) Nicotinamide adenine dinucleotide (NAD or DPN) serves as a hydrogen-transfer agent. (5) Energy is required for the reaction. In this case it is provided by ATP (in the activation of CO_2), by CoA (via the generation of a high-energy C∼S linkage), and by the two reductions (in which the energy of electrons is transferred with 2H from NADH + H^+, thereby simultaneously oxidizing the carrier while reducing and raising the energy level of the substrate). (6) A given metabolic pathway can often be found to consist of a repeating functional module (in this instance a series of four consecutive reactions—condensation, reduction, dehydration, reduction) that is reiterated as often as necessary to build up a long-chain molecule, adding the same group (here, the two-carbon unit,

$$-CH_2-\overset{O}{\overset{\|}{C}}-$$

from malonyl) each time.

After fatty acids have been built up they can be linked together by way of an alcohol such as glycerol to form di- and triglycerides and phospholipids (see Section 9.5). Phospholipid biosynthesis is of particular interest because several different types of substrates—fatty acids, glycerol, and a water-soluble component such as the vitamin choline—are linked together, with energy derived from several different sources.

In Figure 14.46 we can trace the biosynthesis of the phospholipid *lecithin* (phosphatidyl choline). We see first that each of the substrates must be made reactive before all can be linked together. The fatty acids are activated by combination with coenzyme A, which as we saw above generates a high-energy C~S link. Glycerol and choline are each phosphorylated by receiving a high-energy phosphate group from ATP. The glycerophosphate formed condenses with two fatty acid–CoA complexes, yielding diglyceride, P_i, and CoA. Before bonding with this diglyceride, the phosphorylcholine must be further activated by linking to another energy carrier, cytidine triphosphate (CTP; see Figure 9.5c), forming cytidine diphosphocholine (CDP-choline) and also releasing pyrophosphate; CDP-choline and diglyceride can then undergo condensation with the formation of lecithin and the release of CMP (cytidine monophosphate).

This reaction sequence has largely been powered by energy mobilized by the dephosphorylation of high-energy phosphate compounds, namely ATP and CTP. The CTP is now regenerated by the expenditure of more ATP, two ATP being converted to ADP for each molecule of CMP phosphorylated to CTP. The ATP must then be reconstituted by energetic coupling from some exergonic pathway such as glycolysis.

AMINO ACID AND PROTEIN BIOSYNTHESIS The initial biosynthesis of amino acids in green plants is the *reductive amination* of α-ketoglutaric acid to glutamic acid, as shown at the top of the next column.

α-Ketoglutaric acid is an intermediate formed in the Krebs cycle during cell respiration, and is consequently always available. Pyruvic acid, formed as a product of glycolysis, can also enter a pathway leading to amino acid synthesis by reductive amination. First pyruvic acid must be carboxylated

$$\underset{\alpha\text{-Ketoglutaric acid}}{HOOC-CH_2-CH_2-C(=\mathbf{O})-COOH} + NAD\mathbf{H} + \mathbf{H}^+ + NH_3 \xrightleftharpoons{\text{Glutamic dehydrogenase}} \underset{\text{Glutamic acid}}{HOOC-CH_2-CH_2-CH(NH_2)-COOH} + NAD^+ + \mathbf{H_2O}$$

by the addition of CO_2 to form oxalacetic acid:

$$\underset{\text{Pyruvic acid}}{CH_3-C(=O)-COOH} + \mathbf{CO_2} \longrightarrow \underset{\text{Oxalacetic acid}}{(\mathbf{COOH})CH_2-C(=O)-COOH}$$

This is *oxidative* CO_2 fixation, not to be confused with the *reductive* CO_2 fixation of photosynthesis. Any cell can fix CO_2 oxidatively, but only autotrophic cells can fix it reductively. Oxalacetic acid is then reductively aminated to form the amino acid, aspartic acid:

$$(COOH)CH_2-C(=\mathbf{O})-COOH + NAD\mathbf{H}\cdot\mathbf{H}^+ + NH_3 \longrightarrow (COOH)CH_2-CH(NH_2)-COOH + NAD^+ + \mathbf{H_2O}$$

Note the role played by NAD as a hydrogen carrier in amino acid synthesis as well as fatty acid synthesis.

Glutamic acid is especially important in the production of other amino acids because of the ease with which it participates in *transamination* reactions whereby the amino group ($-NH_2$) is transferred to various α-keto acids (Figure 14.47). By such transaminations all other needed amino acids may be made.

Amino acids formed either by reductive amination or transamination can then be linked together to form proteins. This cannot be done directly, but by means of an *amino acid activation system.* Through the action of an *activating enzyme* specific to that amino acid, a complex is formed between ATP and the amino acid, with the release of pyrophosphate:

$$\underset{ATP}{\textbf{Adenine-ribose}-O-P(=O)(OH)-O-P(=O)(OH)-O-P(=O)(OH)-OH} + \underset{\text{Amino acid}}{{}^{-}O-C(=O)-CH(NH_2\cdot H^+)-R} \xrightarrow{\text{Activating enzyme}}$$

$$\underset{\text{Amino acyl adenylate}}{\textbf{adenine-ribose}-O-\overset{(+)}{P}(O^{(-)})-O-\overset{(+)}{C}(O^{(-)})-CH(NH_2\cdot H^+)-R} + \underset{\text{Pyrophosphate}}{HO-P(=O)(OH)-O-P(=O)(OH)-OH}$$

The manner in which the amino acid is represented above indicates that it tends to give up a proton from the carboxyl end and gain one at the amino group, which consequently becomes strongly electropositive. The distribution of electrons between the phosphorus atom and the oxygen atom with which it is linked by an atypical covalent

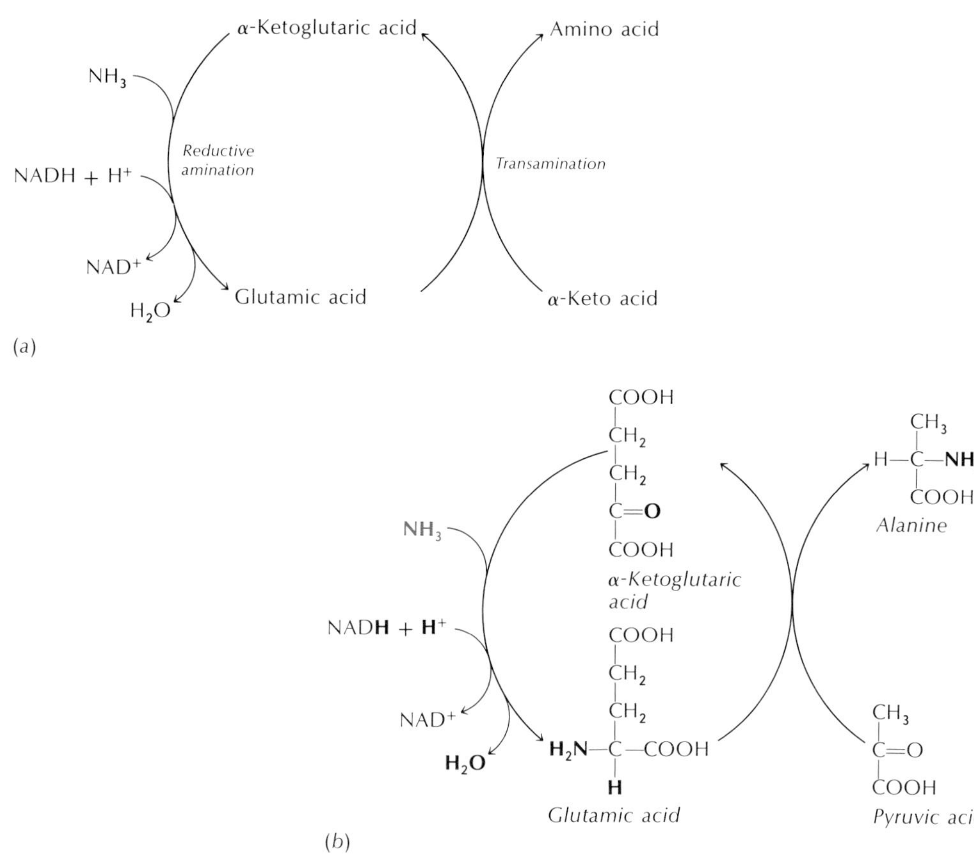

Figure 14.47 □ Amino acid biosynthesis. (*a*) General scheme, showing formation of glutamic acid by amination of α-ketoglutaric acid and subsequent formation of other amino acids by transfer of $-NH_2$ from glutamic acid, thereby regenerating α-ketoglutaric acid. (*b*) An example: formation of alanine by amination of pyruvic acid. Note that carboxylic acids participating in amino acid formation must bear a keto group (=O) on the α carbon (the carbon atom that will bear both carboxyl and amino groups in the amino acid).

bond often represented as a double line, also makes the P atom somewhat electropositive, so that it is represented here as $P^{(+)}$. An electrostatic repulsion is accordingly generated between the P atom and the amino group, making the P—O—C linkage highly labile. The lability of this linkage renders the amino acyl adenylate complex exceedingly reactive, and it is stabilized only by remaining associated with the activating enzyme that catalyzed its formation.

As well as recognizing only one specific amino acid, each kind of activating enzyme will pass its amino acyl adenylate complex to only one particular type of transfer RNA. (We already have seen that tRNA is a low-molecular-weight nucleic acid serving as a specific adapter which holds an amino acid in place on an mRNA template during bonding onto a peptide chain.) For an amino acid-tRNA complex to be formed, the appropriate tRNA must become associated with the activating enzyme, whereupon the amino acyl adenylate complex splits at its labile bond, releasing AMP and furnishing energy for the bonding of the amino acyl group with its tRNA:

$$\textbf{Adenine-ribose}\text{—O—}\overset{O^{(-)}}{\overset{\|}{P^{(+)}}}\text{—O—}\overset{O^{(-)}}{\overset{\|}{C^{(+)}}}\text{—}\underset{H}{\overset{NH_2 \cdot H^+}{C}}\text{—R} \;+$$

Amino acyl adenylate

$$\text{tRNA} \longrightarrow \text{tRNA—}\overset{O}{\overset{\|}{C}}\text{—}\underset{H}{\overset{NH_2 \cdot H^+}{C}}\text{—R} \quad + \text{AMP}$$

Amino acyl-tRNA complex *Adenosine monophosphate*

By carefully reviewing the relevant portions of Section 9.7D at this time, we will recall that the primary structure (amino acid sequence) of a protein is dictated by the linear sequence of codons in mRNA and that this in turn is specified by the DNA codon sequence in a gene. When an amino acid-tRNA unit comes into the vicinity of an mRNA strand associated with ribosomes, hydrogen bonds are established between

Figure 14.48 □ Molecules that contribute to formation of (*a*) pyrimidine ring and (*b*) purine ring.

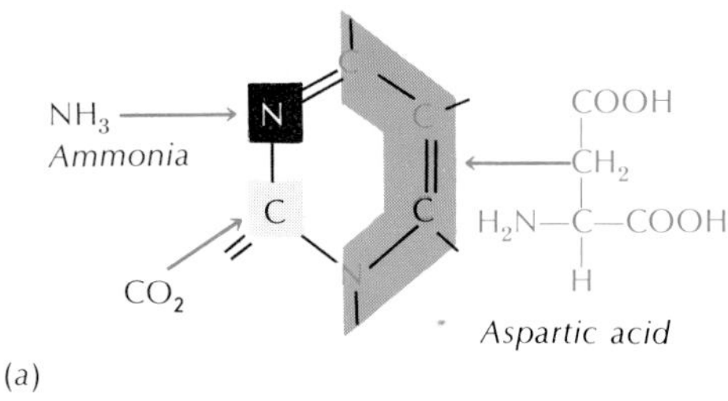

(*a*)

(*b*)

each mRNA codon and the reciprocal tRNA anticodon. This holds the amino acids in correct order while they are joined together by carboxyamino linkages formed through the mediation of ribosomal enzymes.

A polypeptide chain grows by the addition of a new amino acid to the carboxyl end of the preceding amino acid. The first amino acid in the chain exposes its amino group at the starting end of the chain, and is therefore designated the "N-terminal." As a ribosome moves along an mRNA strand linking amino acids into a polypeptide chain, it eventually reaches a chain-terminating codon that permits no amino acid to be incorporated. At this point the completed chain is released from the ribosome, presumably with the aid of GTP (guanosine triphosphate) and a releasing enzyme. The last amino acid exposes its carboxyl group at the end of the chain, and therefore constitutes the "C-terminal." As we saw in Chapter 13, during digestion some peptidases can attack a chain only from its amino end, others only from the carboxyl end.

The rest of the story of protein synthesis must be told in terms of spontaneous self-assembly. Individual polypeptide chains stabilize themselves by the formation of hydrogen bonds within the chain, forming helices in the straight parts of the molecule and loops or buckles in the folded parts. Disulfide (S—S) bridges are formed between juxtaposed cysteine units, and hydrophobic bonds between amino acids that bear side groups having fatty characteristics. In addition, we have seen that polypeptide chains of different kinds spontaneously associate to form even larger protein molecules. The manner in which the secondary and tertiary structure of the protein develops is of course dependent upon its amino acid sequence as determined by mRNA.

NUCLEOTIDE BIOSYNTHESIS In Chapter 9 we studied the composition of nucleic acids and found that they consist of a linear sequence of units known as nucleotides, each made up of a phosphate, a pentose, and a nitrogenous base. We found that nucleic acids, DNA or RNA, are built up on a template of preexisting DNA, first by the establishment of hydrogen bonds between nitrogenous bases of reciprocal character (that is, a 6-oxypurine with a 6-aminopyrimidine, and a 6-aminopurine with a 6-oxypyrimidine). In the presence of an appropriate enzyme, free triply phosphorylated nucleotides held in place on the primer strand are joined together with the release of pyrophosphate, energy being provided by phosphorolysis (see Figure 9.20). Thus the nucleotide sequence of the old strand dictates the nucleotide sequence of the new, and the replication of DNA or its transcription to mRNA is template-controlled.

Nucleotides not only are the building blocks of nucleic acids, but are involved in energy transfer as the triply phosphorylated molecules ATP, CTP, UTP, and GTP, all of which we have mentioned earlier as sources of energy for various metabolic pathways. They also are constituents of the hydrogen acceptors NAD, NADP, FMN (flavin mononucleotide) and FAD (flavin adenine dinucleotide).

Purine nucleotides and pyrimidine nucleotides are formed by two different synthetic pathways. Both pathways are fairly complicated, but deserve examination because they show admirably how a complex ring molecule may be built up by the condensation of components donated by a

$NH_3 + CO_2 \xrightarrow{\text{Carbamyl kinase}} H_2N-\overset{O}{\overset{\|}{C}}-O-\overset{O}{\overset{\|}{P}}-OH$

ATP ADP

OH

Carbamyl phosphate

+

N-Carbamyl aspartic acid

P_i

Aspartic acid

Ring closure by dehydration ($-H_2O$)

Dihydroorotic acid

FAD $FADH_2$

Orotic acid

+

AMP ATP

Ribose 5-phosphate

5-Ribosyl-1-pyrophosphate

($-CO_2$)

Orotidine monophosphate (OMP)

Uridine monophosphate (UMP)

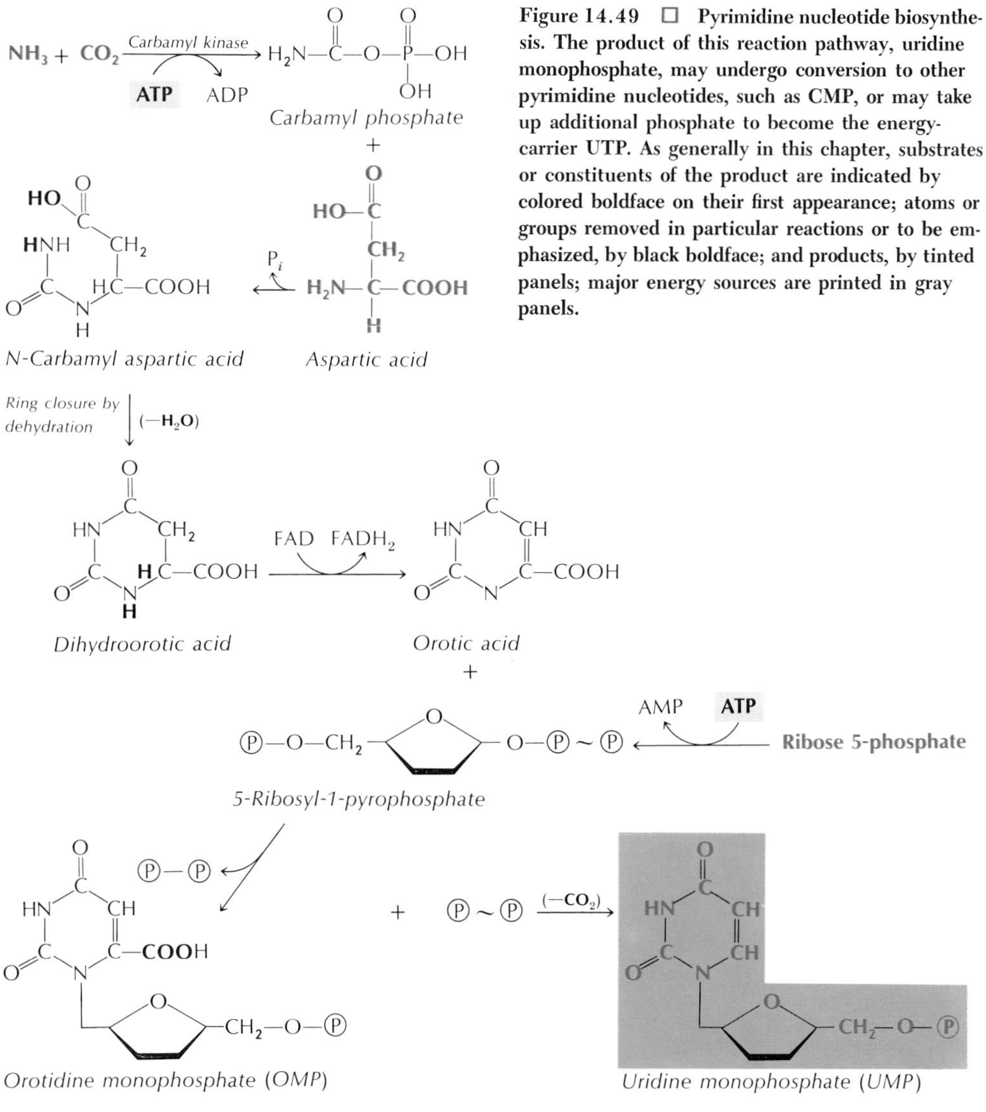

Figure 14.49 □ **Pyrimidine nucleotide biosynthesis. The product of this reaction pathway, uridine monophosphate, may undergo conversion to other pyrimidine nucleotides, such as CMP, or may take up additional phosphate to become the energy-carrier UTP. As generally in this chapter, substrates or constituents of the product are indicated by colored boldface on their first appearance; atoms or groups removed in particular reactions or to be emphasized, by black boldface; and products, by tinted panels; major energy sources are printed in gray panels.**

variety of other compounds (Figure 14.48). The basic pyrimidine ring is built first, and is then joined with ribose phosphate to form a nucleotide, whereas a purine ring is built up with its precursor already linked with ribose phosphate, so that the unit is not a purine alone, but a purine nucleotide.

The pathway of pyrimidine nucleotide biosynthesis is summarized in Figure 14.49. Energy is furnished to the pathway by ATP, and FAD serves as a hydrogen acceptor. Ammonia and CO_2 are condensed and simultaneously phosphorylated to the reactive form, carbamyl phosphate. This is then dephosphorylated while being joined with the amino acid aspartic acid, forming a ring molecule that closes by dehydration. This molecule is then oxidized by giving up 2H to FAD, forming orotic acid. The latter then condenses with ribosyl pyrophosphate, formed from the reaction of ribose phosphate with ATP. Pyrophosphate is released and the nucleotide orotidine monophosphate (OMP) is formed. This is not itself a constituent of nucleic acids, but undergoes decarboxylation to uridine monophosphate (UMP), which is a constituent of RNA and of the uridylic acid system (UMP-UDP-UTP); UMP can also undergo further changes to yield the pyrimidine nucleotides of cytosine and thymine.

Purine nucleotide synthesis (Figure 14.50) involves a formidable sequence of reactions powered by phosphorylations and dephosphorylations, starting with the further phosphorylation of ribose 5-phosphate, a pentose intermediate available from either the Calvin cycle or the pentose phosphate pathway. The product, 5-ribosyl-1-pyrophosphate, then receives an amino group by transamination from glutamine, at the same

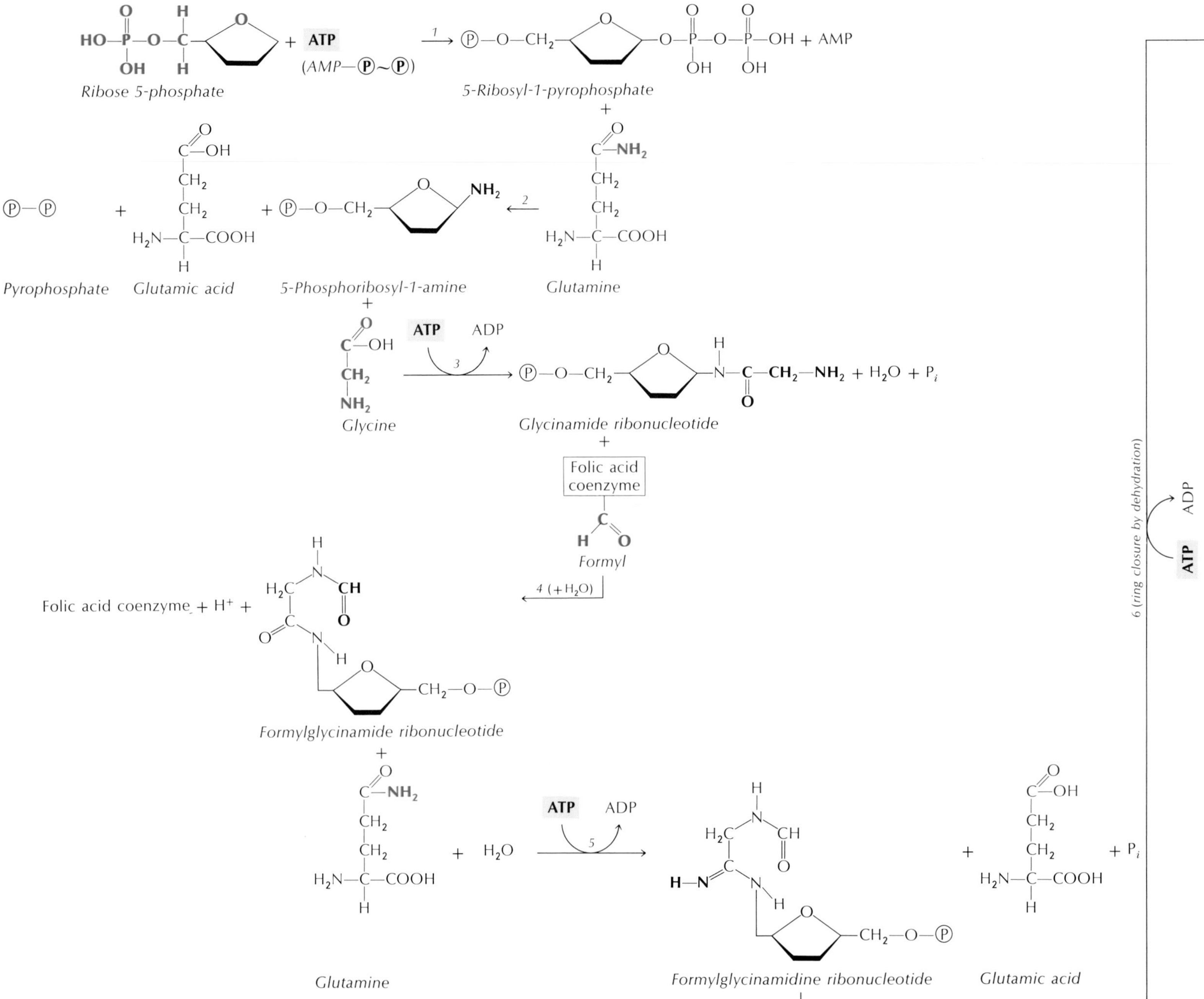

Ribose 5-phosphate + ATP ($AMP—Ⓟ\sim Ⓟ$) —1→ 5-Ribosyl-1-pyrophosphate + AMP

5-Ribosyl-1-pyrophosphate + Glutamine —2→ Pyrophosphate + Glutamic acid + 5-Phosphoribosyl-1-amine

5-Phosphoribosyl-1-amine + Glycine + ATP —3→ Glycinamide ribonucleotide + ADP + H_2O + P_i

Glycinamide ribonucleotide + Folic acid coenzyme (Formyl) —4 ($+H_2O$)→ Formylglycinamide ribonucleotide + Folic acid coenzyme + H^+

Formylglycinamide ribonucleotide + Glutamine + H_2O + ATP —5→ Formylglycinamidine ribonucleotide + ADP + Glutamic acid + P_i

6 (ring closure by dehydration) ATP → ADP

Figure 14.50 □ **Purine nucleotide biosynthesis.**

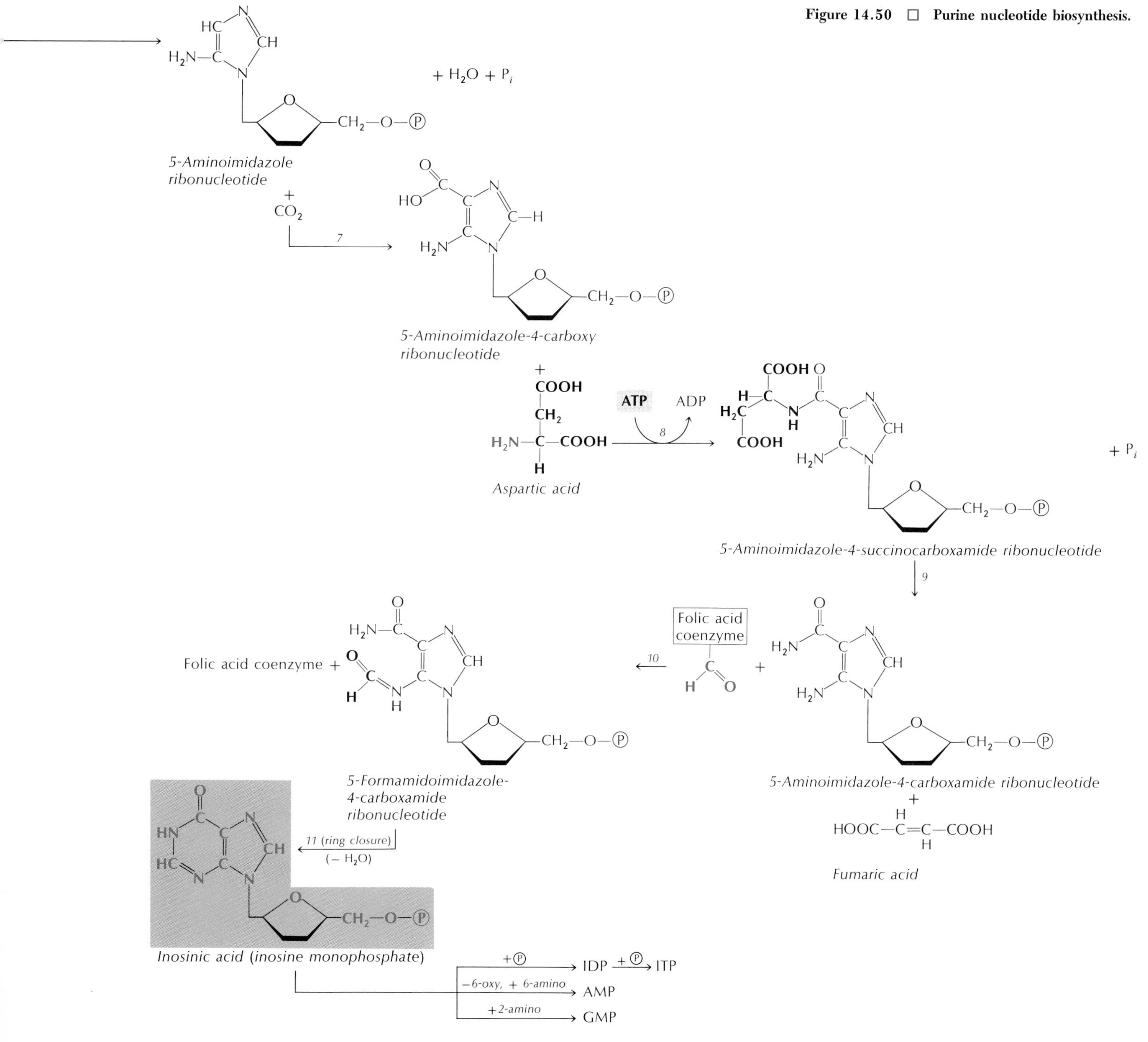

5-Aminoimidazole ribonucleotide + H_2O + P_i

5-Aminoimidazole ribonucleotide + CO_2 →(7) *5-Aminoimidazole-4-carboxy ribonucleotide*

5-Aminoimidazole-4-carboxy ribonucleotide + *Aspartic acid* →(8; ATP → ADP) *5-Aminoimidazole-4-succinocarboxamide ribonucleotide* + P_i

5-Aminoimidazole-4-succinocarboxamide ribonucleotide →(9) *5-Aminoimidazole-4-carboxamide ribonucleotide* + *Fumaric acid*

5-Aminoimidazole-4-carboxamide ribonucleotide + Folic acid coenzyme (formyl) →(10) *5-Formamidoimidazole-4-carboxamide ribonucleotide* + Folic acid coenzyme

5-Formamidoimidazole-4-carboxamide ribonucleotide →(11 (ring closure) (− H_2O)) *Inosinic acid (inosine monophosphate)*

Inosinic acid (inosine monophosphate):
- + Ⓟ → IDP + Ⓟ → ITP
- −6-oxy, + 6-amino → AMP
- +2-amino → GMP

time giving off pyrophosphate. This aminated ribose phosphate now condenses with glycine by dehydration synthesis, using energy from ATP. The glycinamide ribonucleotide thus formed now takes up H_2O and a formyl group from a folic acid coenzyme, and next receives another amino group from glutamine, again using energy from ATP. Now the first ring of the purine nucleus can be closed by dehydration, with energy from ATP. Then the components of the second ring are assembled by the addition of CO_2, aspartic acid, and another formyl group from a folic acid coenzyme. This ring is now closed by dehydration, completing the basic purine ring and forming the purine nucleotide, *inosinic acid* (inosine monophosphate, IMP). This product functions as a free nucleotide in the IMP–IDP–ITP energy-transfer system, but also can be converted to guanosine monophosphate and adenosine monophosphate. It also occurs in tRNA.

By these means, ribose nucleotides are formed, which can be reduced to the corresponding *deoxy*ribonucleotides, for instance:

$$\underset{\textit{Cytidine monophosphate}}{\text{CMP}} \xrightarrow{\text{ATP} \;\; \text{ADP}} \text{CDP} \xrightarrow{\textit{CDP reductase}} \underset{\textit{Deoxycytidine diphosphate}}{\text{dCDP}}$$

This schematic example also shows that di- and triphosphate nucleotides are built up from the monophosphates by the donation of high-energy phosphate groups from ATP:

$$\text{CMP} + \text{ATP} \longrightarrow \text{CDP} + \text{ADP}$$
$$\text{CDP} + \text{ATP} \longrightarrow \text{CTP} + \text{ADP}$$

C Cell respiration

Cell respiration includes all processes by which cells obtain energy from fuel molecules. These fuels are not derived solely from storage compounds, for few cell constituents, even fabric materials, are stable enough to endure for long. Even a relatively long-lived mRNA, for instance, probably persists no more than 2 or 3 days. Proteins, lipids, carbohydrates, and nucleic acids all continuously are degraded to more stable end-products via series of enzyme-regulated reactions that permit a substantial proportion of the bonding energy contained in these materials to be used in making high-energy phosphate compounds. These in turn serve as common intermediates to transfer energy by coupling to various energy-requiring pathways. ATP is the major high-energy compound produced by cell respiration, and this can serve in turn to produce GTP, UTP, CTP, and creatine phosphate, energy carriers which may transfer energy packets of a value more suited to the requirements of the reactions they serve than are those transferred by ATP itself. (For instance, ATP may yield around 12,000 cal/mole by phosphate transfer within the living cell; if the reaction to which this is passed requires only 5,000 cal/mole, the rest will be dissipated as heat. If another phosphate compound is used that transfers energy in packets of 6,000 cal/mole, only 1,000 cal/mole is lost as heat at the time of that reaction.)

As we consider several of the most important pathways of cell respiration, we should note that biotic systems employ only a few kinds of reactions to produce high-energy compounds from low-energy precursors. These are (1) the formation of a high-energy phosphate group in the dehydration of phosphoglyceric acid to phosphoenolpyruvic acid; (2) the formation of a high-energy phosphate group in converting the triose phosphoglyceraldehyde to 1,3-diphosphoglyceric acid; (3) the formation of thioester (such as acetyl CoA), with production of a high-energy acyl group; (4) the "downhill" transport of electrons from a compound with a negative oxidation-reduction potential to one with a less negative potential. (This is complementary to the "uphill" transport of electrons in photosynthesis, and serves to transfer some of the energy gained by those electrons during photosynthesis.) A fifth type of energy-mobilizing reaction that occurs in cell respiration is hydrolysis, which mainly liberates heat. However, even heat may be useful when released in minute, carefully regulated increments, for in such amounts it serves to accelerate chemical reactions without jeopardizing the intricate internal organization of the cell.

Hydrolysis, in which water is used to break covalent bonds, is the first phase of cell respiration, for it breaks down proteins to amino acids, lipids to fatty acids and glycerol, nucleic acids to nucleotides, nucleotides to nitrogenous bases and pentose phosphates, and polysaccharides to monosaccharides (pages 604 to 606). Since a cell's major fuel compound is likely to be a polysaccharide such as glycogen or starch, it is not surprising that phosphorolysis rather than hydrolysis is the major means of polysaccharide breakdown within the living cell. Phosphorolysis, as we have seen, generates little heat and liberates not glucose but glucose 1-phosphate.

Following hydrolysis or phosphorolysis, sugars are broken down further via either the glycolytic or the pentose phosphate pathway (see Figure 14.58). Glycolysis yields pyruvic acid, which under aerobic conditions is free to be converted to activated acetyl and enters the Krebs cycle in the form of the high-energy acyl group of acetyl CoA. Other hydrolysates such as amino and fatty acids may also be converted to acetyl CoA, or may enter the Krebs tricarboxylic acid cycle as one of the organic acid intermediates of the cycle. The nitrogen portion of amino acids and nitrogenous bases must be processed for excretion as urea, uric acid, or other nitrogenous wastes, mainly by way of the urea cycle.

In the Krebs cycle the residues are broken down to CO_2 and 2H, the latter being passed to a series of hydrogen or electron carriers constituting the respiratory chain, at the end of which 2H is combined with O as water (see Figure 14.55). The passage through this chain is thermodynamically downhill due to the decreasing negativity (or increasing positivity) of the oxidation-reduction potentials of the carriers, and the energy liberated during this passage is used to build ATP.

GLYCOLYSIS Glycolysis is the major pathway in all cells by which glucose is prepared for complete oxidation. It consists of the breakdown of glucose 6-phosphate to yield two molecules of pyruvic acid, with a net gain of two molecules of ATP per molecule of glucose utilized. This represents a recovery of at least 14,000 cal/mole of glucose, or 27 percent of the 52,000 cal/mole liberated by glycolysis, with the balance of the energy being lost as heat.*

There are eight major reactions in the glycolytic sequence, if we consider glucose 6-phosphate to be the starting substrate. Glucose 6-phosphate can be obtained by either of two alternative pathways:

(1) In any cells where polysaccharides are available to be broken down with the release of sugars, glucose 1-phosphate is liberated by the *phosphorolysis* of the storage compound:

$$(C_6H_{10}O_5)_n + n(H_3PO_4) \xrightarrow{\textit{Phosphorylase}} n(\text{glucose 1-phosphate})$$

This reaction involves little change in free energy and is readily reversible. In phosphorolysis, phosphoric acid (H_3PO_4) acts as water does in hydrolysis: it attacks the bond between the first carbon (C-1) of one hexose unit and the fourth (C-4) of the next, contributing hydrogen to C-4 of one glucose and the phosphate residue to C-1 of the other. (We should note that during the digestion of carbohydrates, water contributes H to C-4 of one hexose and —OH to C-1 of the other.) In a second reaction, glucose 1-phosphate is converted to glucose 6-phosphate in the presence of the enzyme phosphoglucomutase. This reaction is reversible, but in fact strongly favors the conversion to glucose 6-phosphate so that in an equilibrium mixture containing the enzyme and the two of these phosphate sugars 95 percent of the mixture eventually will be glucose 6-phosphate.

(2) A second kind of reaction leading up to glycolysis uses glucose itself as a substrate, when polysaccharide reserves are not available for use. Glucose is phosphorylated to glucose 6-phosphate in the presence of the enzyme hexokinase, and with the expenditure of one ATP:

$$\text{Glucose} + \text{ADP}\sim\text{Ⓟ} \xrightarrow{\textit{Hexokinase}} \text{glucose 6-phosphate} + \text{ADP}$$

In this reaction (and others shown later) we shall write ATP as ADP~Ⓟ so as to keep in mind that dephosphorylating ATP involves the transfer of a high-energy phosphate group, ~Ⓟ. When this high-energy group is transferred to glucose, its energy is redistributed internally within the glucose molecule and the P—O link becomes an ordinary covalent bond, O—Ⓟ, possessing only half the energy of hydrolysis of the high-energy bond (~). Since the hydrolysis of glucose 6-phosphate to glucose liberates only 3,000 cal/mole, whereas hydrolysis of ATP to ADP yields 7,000, we can see that the direct conversion of glucose to glucose 6-phosphate involves a loss in free energy amounting to around 4,000 cal/mole. This means of obtaining glucose 6-phosphate is not nearly as economical as the preceding reactions in which it was derived indirectly from phosphorolysis of starch or glycogen.

Glycolysis may best be understood if we consider it step by step, referring to Figure 14.51 for an overall summary of the process:

*Different figures can be arrived at, for some investigators consider the high-energy phosphate group of ATP to be capable of transferring some 12,000 cal/mole within the living cell, as opposed to a release of only about 7,000 cal/mole when ATP is hydrolyzed to ADP in vitro. If the higher figure is used instead of the lower, the energy conservation achieved in glycolysis may be estimated at 46 percent rather than 27 percent. In either event, it is never possible to save all of the energy that was originally invested to build glucose, but the amount that is recovered to do cellular work represents an efficiency equivalent to that of a very good man-made machine.

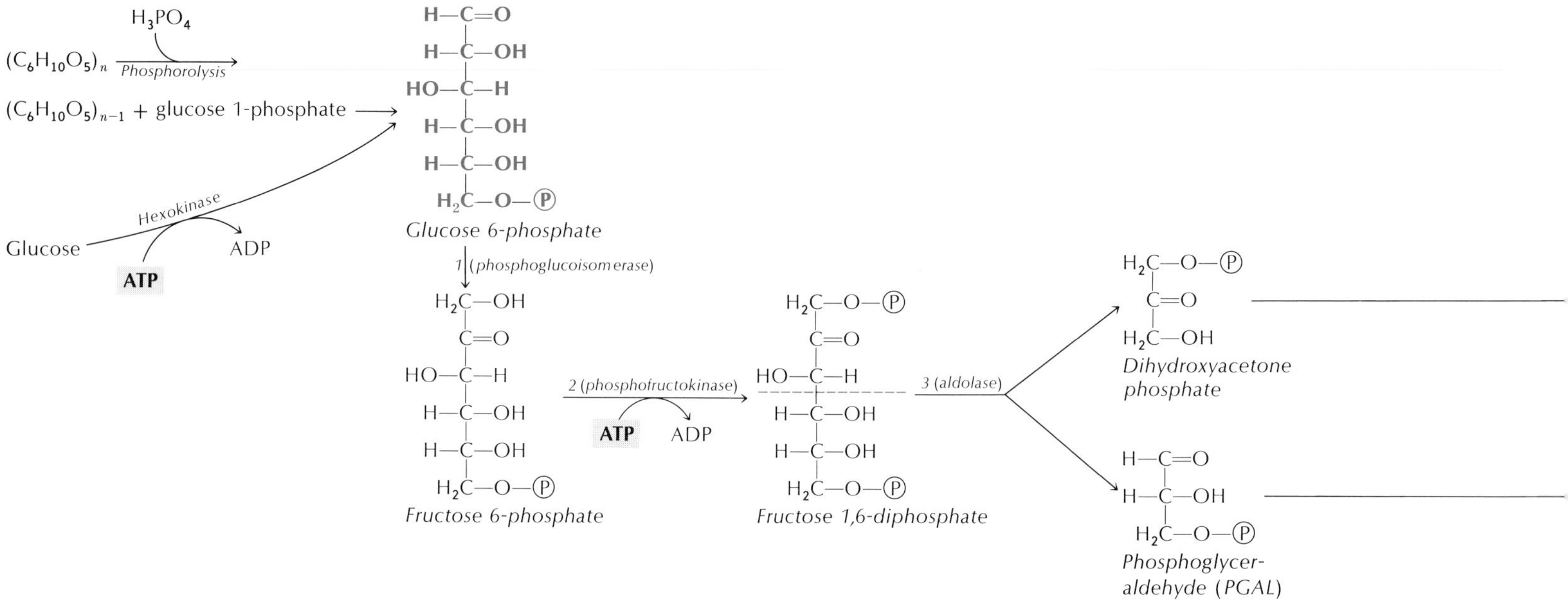

H_3PO_4

$(C_6H_{10}O_5)_n \xrightarrow{\text{Phosphorolysis}}$

$(C_6H_{10}O_5)_{n-1}$ + glucose 1-phosphate →

Glucose —Hexokinase (ATP → ADP)→

H—C=O
H—C—OH
HO—C—H
H—C—OH
H—C—OH
H_2C—O—Ⓟ
Glucose 6-phosphate

↓ 1 (*phosphoglucoisomerase*)

H_2C—OH
C=O
HO—C—H
H—C—OH
H—C—OH
H_2C—O—Ⓟ
Fructose 6-phosphate

→ 2 (*phosphofructokinase*) (**ATP** → ADP)

H_2C—O—Ⓟ
C=O
HO—C—H
H—C—OH
H—C—OH
H_2C—O—Ⓟ
Fructose 1,6-diphosphate

→ 3 (*aldolase*)

H_2C—O—Ⓟ
C=O
H_2C—OH
Dihydroxyacetone phosphate

H—C=O
H—C—OH
H_2C—O—Ⓟ
Phosphoglyceraldehyde (PGAL)

Reaction 1 Glucose 6-phosphate is isomerized to fructose 6-phosphate,

Glucose 6-phosphate $\xrightarrow{\text{Phosphoglucoisomerase}}$ fructose 6-phosphate

Reaction 2 Fructose 6-phosphate is phosphorylated to fructose 1,6-diphosphate,

Fructose 6-phosphate + ADP~Ⓟ $\xrightarrow{\text{Phosphofructokinase}}$ Ⓟ—fructose—Ⓟ + ADP

Once more we have shown ATP as ADP~Ⓟ to indicate that a high-energy phosphate bond is transformed into a low-energy bond—a link that yields some 7,000 to 12,000 cal/mole has been expended to form a link requiring only about 3,000 cal/mole. The balance has been liberated as heat: this is a substantial loss in free energy, and therefore the reaction is not directly reversible.

Reaction 3 Fructose 1,6-diphosphate is broken down to yield two molecules of three-carbon sugar: one, phosphoglyceraldehyde (PGAL), shown here as glyceraldehyde—Ⓟ; the other dihydroxyacetone phosphate, which readily isomerizes to PGAL in the presence of the enzyme triose phosphate isomerase:

Ⓟ—fructose—Ⓟ $\xrightarrow{\text{Aldolase}}$ glyceraldehyde—Ⓟ + dihydroxyacetone—Ⓟ

dihydroxyacetone—Ⓟ ⇅ (*Triose phosphate isomerase*) PGAL

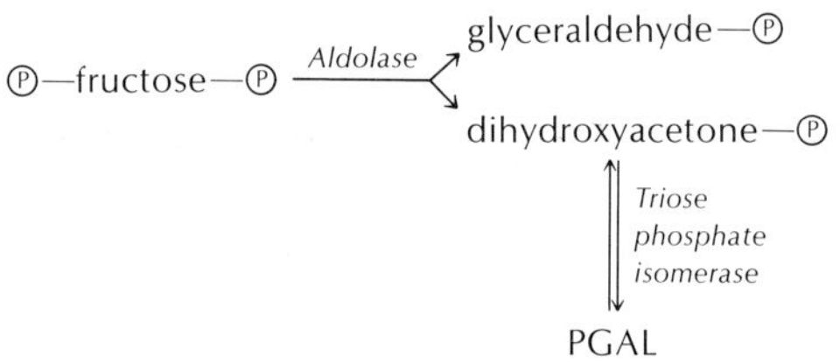

All reactions to this point have been merely preparatory. No ATP-producing oxidations have yet taken place, but instead ATP has actually been "spent" to provide activation energy. The reactions described to this point are just the reverse of those by which PGAL produced in the Calvin cycle of photosynthesis is built into glucose.

Figure 14.51 □ Glycolysis, with two modes of entry into the glycolytic pathway shown. Note expenditure and net gain of ATP in conversion of one glucose molecule to two of pyruvic acid. One ATP is spent to move glucose into the cycle, and a second to activate fructose phosphate so that it splits to triose phosphate. A high-energy phosphate group (~Ⓟ) is created when PGAL is phosphorylated and dehydrogenated to 1,3-diphosphoglyceric acid; ~Ⓟ is then transferred to ADP to make ATP. Since this reaction is taken twice (once for each molecule of PGAL), two ATP molecules are gained. Another high-energy phosphate group is generated by the dehydration of 2-PGA to PEP, and this too is transferred to ADP, making ATP. Since this reaction also is taken twice, we see that glycolysis yields a net gain of two ATP molecules per molecule of glucose broken down. The $NADH+H^+$ that is produced during glycolysis is also a source of energy, for it transfers 2H to FAD, thereby creating a high-energy group that is used in generating ATP. (See also Figure 14.55.) If glycolysis is carried out anaerobically, pyruvic acid must serve as a hydrogen acceptor, becoming lactic acid.

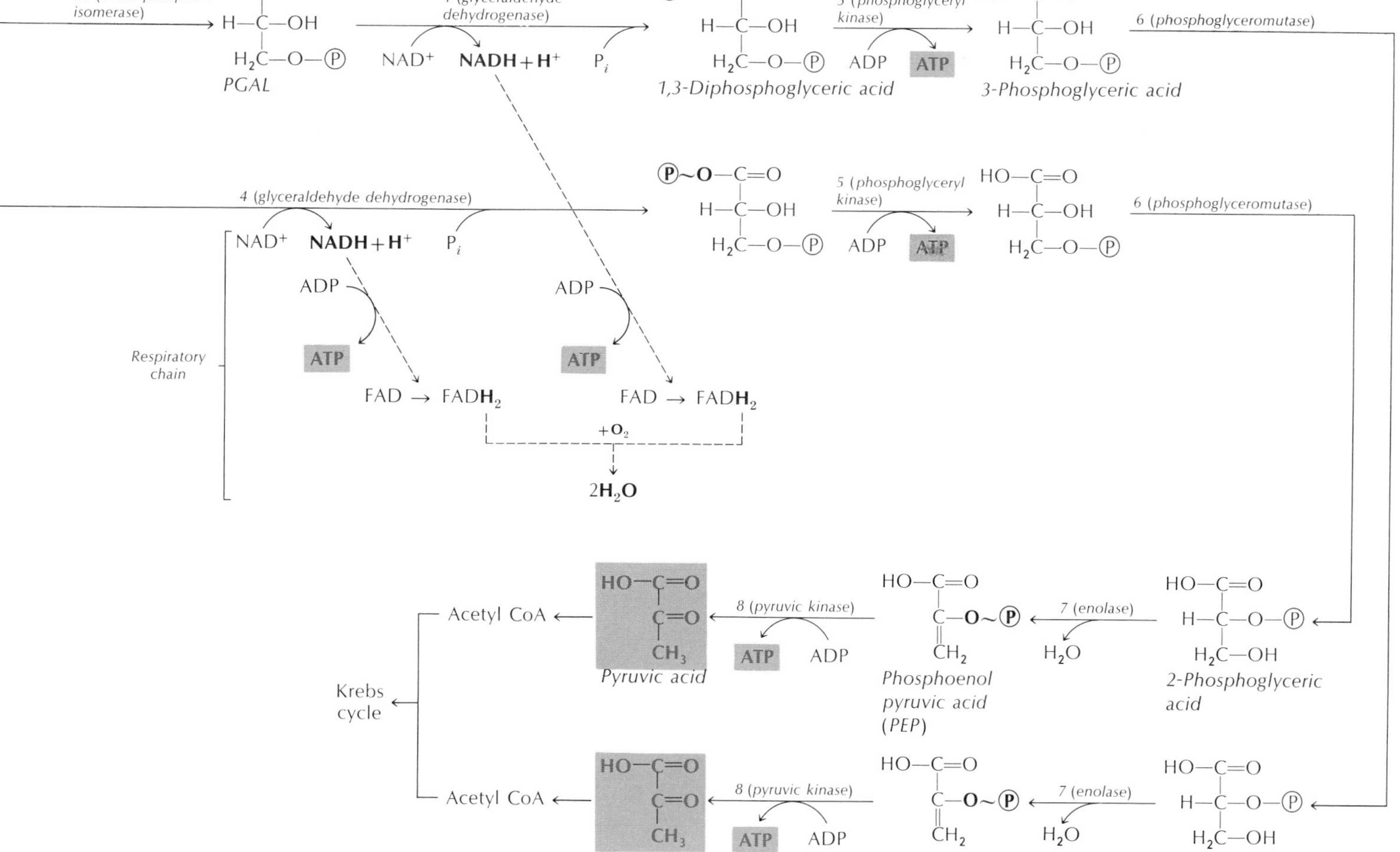

All following reactions must be taken twice, since two molecules of PGAL are produced from each hexose molecule.

Reaction 4 Now the first oxidation-reduction reaction takes place, in which a high-energy phosphate group is generated that will be transferred to ADP to make ATP in reaction 5; PGAL is simultaneously phosphorylated and dehydrogenated (oxidized) to 1,3-diphosphoglyceric acid. This oxidation causes an electron redistribution that concentrates energy in the phosphate group linked with C-1; NAD^+ serves as hydrogen acceptor:

$$\text{PGAL} + \text{NAD}^+ + \text{H}_3\text{PO}_4 \xrightarrow[\text{dehydrogenase}]{\text{PGAL}} \text{PGA}{\sim}Ⓟ + \text{NADH} + \text{H}^+$$

Oxidized NAD (NAD^+) takes up an electron, becoming electrically neutral (NAD), and then accepts one entire H atom to become NADH, leaving a free proton (H^+). Although it is not part of the glycolytic sequence proper, we should note that under aerobic conditions NADH + H^+ will pass 2H to another acceptor, a flavoprotein with the prosthetic group FAD, which transfers electrons to a chain of carriers (cytochromes) and liberates protons that combine with oxygen. As shown in Figure 14.51 (see also Figure 14.55), the transfer of hydrogen from NADH to FAD is a thermodynamically downhill electron shift liberating enough energy to phosphorylate one ADP to ATP per electron moved.

Reaction 5 The high-energy phosphate group is now transferred from 1,3-diphosphoglyceric acid to ADP:

$$\text{PGA}{\sim}Ⓟ + \text{ADP} \xrightarrow[\text{kinase}]{\text{Phosphoglyceryl}} \text{PGA} + \text{ADP}{\sim}Ⓟ^*$$

*That is, ATP.

Now we can make a net statement, summing reactions 4 and 5:

$$\text{PGAL} + \text{NAD}^+ + \text{ADP} + \text{H}_3\text{PO}_4 \longrightarrow \text{PGA} + \text{NADH} + \text{H}^+ + \text{ATP}$$

which shows that the oxidation of an aldehyde to a carboxylic acid has concentrated energy in a high-energy phosphate group which is ultimately transferred to ADP, yielding ATP. This is the first place where energy is actually transferred in glycolysis to make a high energy phosphate compound, which in turn can pass this energy by coupling to other reaction pathways.

Reaction 6 The organic acid produced by the preceding reaction is 3-phosphoglyceric acid [a phosphate group is attached to the number 3 carbon (C-3) by way of a low-energy phosphate bond]. Now, in preparation for the ensuing reaction, 3-PGA is converted to 2-PGA by transferring the Ⓟ from C-3 to C-2. This shift is accomplished enzymatically with little expenditure of energy, and is therefore readily reversible:

$$\text{3-PGA} \xrightleftharpoons{\text{Phosphoglyceromutase}} \text{2-PGA}$$

Reaction 7 Now there can take place an oxidative dehydration which produces another high-energy phosphate group: 2-PGA is converted to phosphoenolpyruvate (PEP) with a liberation of H from C-2 and —OH from C-3 to make H_2O:

$$\text{2-PGA} \xrightarrow{\text{Enolase}} \text{PEP} + \text{H}_2\text{O}$$

This reaction has already been used as an example of an intramolecular oxidation-reduction that concentrates electrons around C-2 and causes electrostatic repulsive forces to be generated in the phosphate group (see Section 13.1B). This dehydration reaction is freely reversible, for it involved little expenditure of energy, but because of the electrostatic repulsion generated, the total energy of the molecule is changed dramatically: hydrolysis of 2-PGA yields only 3,100 cal/mole; hydrolysis of PEP yields 12,800 cal/mole! However, in the living cell PEP is not fated for hydrolysis, but will serve as a source of high-energy phosphate for building ATP.

Reaction 8 Phosphoenolpyruvate is now converted to pyruvic acid, with the transfer to ADP of the high-energy phosphate group created in reaction 7

$$Ⓟ{\sim}\text{EP} + \text{ADP} \xrightarrow[\text{kinase}]{\text{Pyruvic}} \text{pyruvic acid} + \text{ADP}{\sim}Ⓟ$$

This reaction is not readily reversible, for the free energy of hydrolysis of ATP is significantly less than that of PEP. *Two* ATP molecules were gained in reaction 5 and *two* more in reaction 8 for each molecule of glucose 6-phosphate entering the glycolytic pathway. When calculating the net ATP yield of glycolysis, *glucose* is taken as the initial substrate and the molecule of ATP "spent" to convert glucose to glucose 6-phosphate is deducted as an energy cost of glycolysis. Since one more ATP is required to change fructose 6-phosphate to fructose 1,6-diphosphate, the net yield is considered to be *two* molecules of ATP per molecule of glucose converted to pyruvic acid. The essential equation for glycolysis can therefore be given as:

$$\text{C}_6\text{H}_{12}\text{O}_6 + 2\text{ATP} + 2\text{H}_3\text{PO}_4 + 2\text{NAD}^+ \longrightarrow \underbrace{2\text{CH}_3\text{—}\overset{\text{O}}{\overset{\|}{\text{C}}}\text{—COOH}}_{\textit{Pyruvic acid}} + 4\text{ATP} + 2\text{ADP} + 2\text{H}_2\text{O} + 2\text{NADH} + \text{H}^+$$

(The water generated by the reaction comes

from the dehydration of 2-PGA to PEP.)

The glycolytic sequence itself terminates with the production of pyruvic acid, but for glycolysis to continue, a supply of oxidized NAD (NAD^+) must be available to serve as a hydrogen acceptor. Accordingly, reduced NAD ($NADH + H^+$) must unload two hydrogen atoms before it is available to accept more. There are three different pathways by which $NADH + H^+$ can be reoxidized. Two of these are anaerobic, whereas the third (and most frequently used) involves O_2 as a hydrogen acceptor.

The first way in which glycolysis can terminate anaerobically is the pathway of *alcoholic fermentation,* found today mainly in such microorganisms as yeasts, but probably one of the most ancient biotic means of obtaining energy, antedating the evolution of the aerobic pathways that are dependent on an ample supply of atmospheric O_2. In yeast metabolism, pyruvic acid is decarboxylated to acetaldehyde and CO_2, by action of the enzyme α-carboxylase. This enzyme is active only in the presence of a coenzyme, thiamine pyrophosphate ("cocarboxylase"):

$$CH_3\overset{\overset{\displaystyle O}{\|}}{C}—COOH \xrightarrow[\textit{Cocarboxylase}]{\alpha\textit{-Carboxylase}} \underset{\textit{Acetaldehyde}}{CH_3C\overset{\displaystyle O}{\diagup\!\!\diagup}\!\!—H} + CO_2$$

The acetaldehyde produced by the above reaction is now used as a hydrogen acceptor, yielding ethyl alcohol and oxidized NAD:

$$CH_3C\overset{\displaystyle O}{\diagup\!\!\diagup}\!\!—H + NADH + H^+ \xrightarrow[\textit{dehydrogenase}]{\textit{Alcohol}} CH_3—\overset{\overset{\displaystyle H}{|}}{\underset{\underset{\displaystyle H}{|}}{C}}—OH + NAD^+$$

A second way in which $NADH + H^+$ can give up 2H anaerobically is found in muscle tissue, where a portion of the pyruvic acid produced by glycolysis is itself recruited as a hydrogen carrier, becoming the substance lactic acid:

$$\underset{\textit{Pyruvic acid}}{CH_3—\overset{\overset{\displaystyle O}{\|}}{C}—COOH} + NADH + H^+ \xrightleftharpoons[]{\textit{Lactic dehydrogenase}} \underset{\textit{Lactic acid}}{CH_3—\overset{\overset{\displaystyle OH}{|}}{\underset{\underset{\displaystyle H}{|}}{C}}—COOH} + NAD^+$$

Lactic acid must be removed from the muscle tissue to be further metabolized, and causes muscle fatigue if it accumulates to excess. In the liver it can be oxidized to pyruvic acid and either used to rebuild carbohydrate or further oxidized to CO_2 and H_2O in the presence of oxygen. Since muscle tissue can obtain O_2 from myoglobin as well as from the bloodstream, during moderate exercise little lactic acid is generated.

When O_2 is available, glycolysis terminates aerobically with O_2 used as a final hydrogen acceptor:

$$NADH + H^+ + \tfrac{1}{2}O_2 \longrightarrow NAD^+ + H_2O$$

This equation should not be taken to mean that NADH and O_2 react directly. Instead, as mentioned above and shortly to be discussed at further length, $NADH + H^+$ transfers hydrogen to a "respiratory chain" of flavoprotein and cytochromes ending with the transfer of hydrogen to oxygen. During this series of transfers some of the potential energy of the hydrogens' electrons is used to build ATP. When this aerobic pathway can be used, none of the pyruvic acid produced by glycolysis need be converted to lactic acid or acetaldehyde for use as a hydrogen acceptor, and all can be decarboxylated and combined with coenzyme A to enter the Krebs cycle.

Glycolysis itself is responsible for the mobilization of energy amounting to only around 7 percent of the total energy released when glucose is oxidized to CO_2 and H_2O (686 kcal/mole). Further energy recovery requires the breakdown of pyruvic (or lactic) acid to CO_2 and H_2O via the Krebs cycle and the respiratory chain.

To enter the Krebs cycle, pyruvic acid must be decarboxylated to acetyl [activated by combination with coenzyme A (Figure 14.52)]. Pyruvic acid is first taken up by thiamine pyrophosphate (cocarboxylase) and transferred to the vitamin lipoic acid, thus liberating CO_2 and the thiamine coenzyme. S-Acetyl lipoic acid then reacts with coenzyme A, producing acetyl CoA, a thioester with energy concentrated in the acetyl group (as indicated by the high-energy C∼S linkage). In this activated state the acetyl group can be passed into the Krebs cycle with the liberation of CoA. Meanwhile, the dihydrolipoic acid produced transfers 2H to NAD^+, and this in turn can pass it to FAD in the respiratory chain, thus providing energy sufficient to build one molecule of ATP.

THE KREBS TRICARBOXYLIC ACID CYCLE

All organisms capable of aerobic oxidative metabolism do so by way of a self-regenerating cyclic series of conversions of carboxylic acids known as the *tricarboxylic* acid cycle* (or as the *Krebs cycle* after the English biochemist who worked out most of its details). In essence, this cycle takes

*That is, having three —COOH groups.

Figure 14.52 □ **Conversion of pyruvic acid to activated acetyl. This pathway is required for moving pyruvic acid, the product of glycolysis, into the Krebs tricarboxylic acid cycle. Three vitamins are involved in this pathway: lipoic acid, thiamine (as part of the coenzyme TPP), and panthothenic acid (in coenzyme A). Lipoic acid serves as a hydrogen acceptor, passing 2H to NAD⁺, which then transfers it to FAD with the formation of one molecule of ATP.**

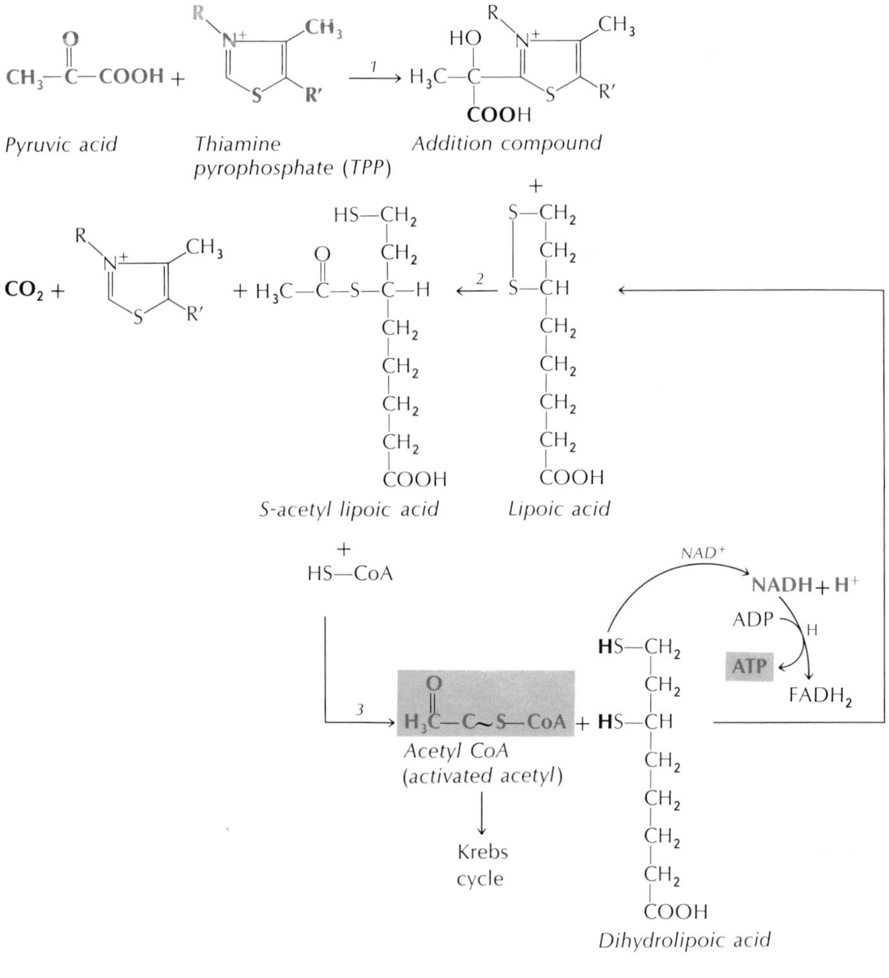

$CH_3-\overset{O}{\overset{\|}{C}}-COOH$ + Thiamine pyrophosphate (*TPP*) $\xrightarrow{1}$ Addition compound ($H_3C-C(OH)(COOH)-$TPP)

Pyruvic acid *Thiamine pyrophosphate (TPP)* *Addition compound*

Addition compound + Lipoic acid $\xrightarrow{2}$ CO_2 + TPP + $H_3C-\overset{O}{\overset{\|}{C}}-S-$(S-acetyl lipoic acid)

S-acetyl lipoic acid *Lipoic acid*

S-acetyl lipoic acid + HS—CoA $\xrightarrow{3}$ $H_3C-\overset{O}{\overset{\|}{C}}\sim S-CoA$ + Dihydrolipoic acid

Acetyl CoA (activated acetyl) → Krebs cycle

Dihydrolipoic acid + NAD^+ → $NADH + H^+$; ADP → **ATP**; H → $FADH_2$

in one activated acetyl per turn of the cycle, liberates two CO_2, produces one molecule of ATP at the substrate level (that is, by generation of a high-energy phosphate group on one of the intermediates of the cycle), and gives off four pairs of hydrogen atoms, one pair of which goes directly to FAD, the other three to NAD⁺. Summing up:

$$CH_3-\overset{O}{\overset{\|}{C}}\sim S-CoA + 4H_2O + 1GDP + 3NAD^+ + 1FAD \longrightarrow HS-CoA + 2CO_2 + 1H_2O + 1GTP + 3(NADH + H^+) + 1FADH_2$$

Note that the only high-energy phosphate compound produced in the cycle proper is guanosine triphosphate, which reversibly interchanges Ⓟ with ATP.

The cycle is best studied by reference to Figure 14.53, in which uptake of activated acetyl is considered the starting point. Materials can also enter the cycle as any one of the four-, five-, or six-carbon organic acids that are intermediates of the cycle, this being the common mode of entry for the α-keto acids resulting from the deamination of amino acids. The increased energy content of the acetyl group (generated by its C∼S linkage with CoA) provides activation energy for the cycle. Furthermore, transfer of 2H to NAD⁺ and FAD is a thermodynamically "downhill" process that liberates more energy than it requires.

The uptake of acetyl liberates CoA and converts 4-carbon oxalacetic acid to six-carbon citric acid (hence another name for the pathway, the *citric acid cycle*). This may isomerize directly to isocitric acid, or go to isocitric by way of *cis*-aconitic acid. Isocitric acid now undergoes oxidative decarboxyla-

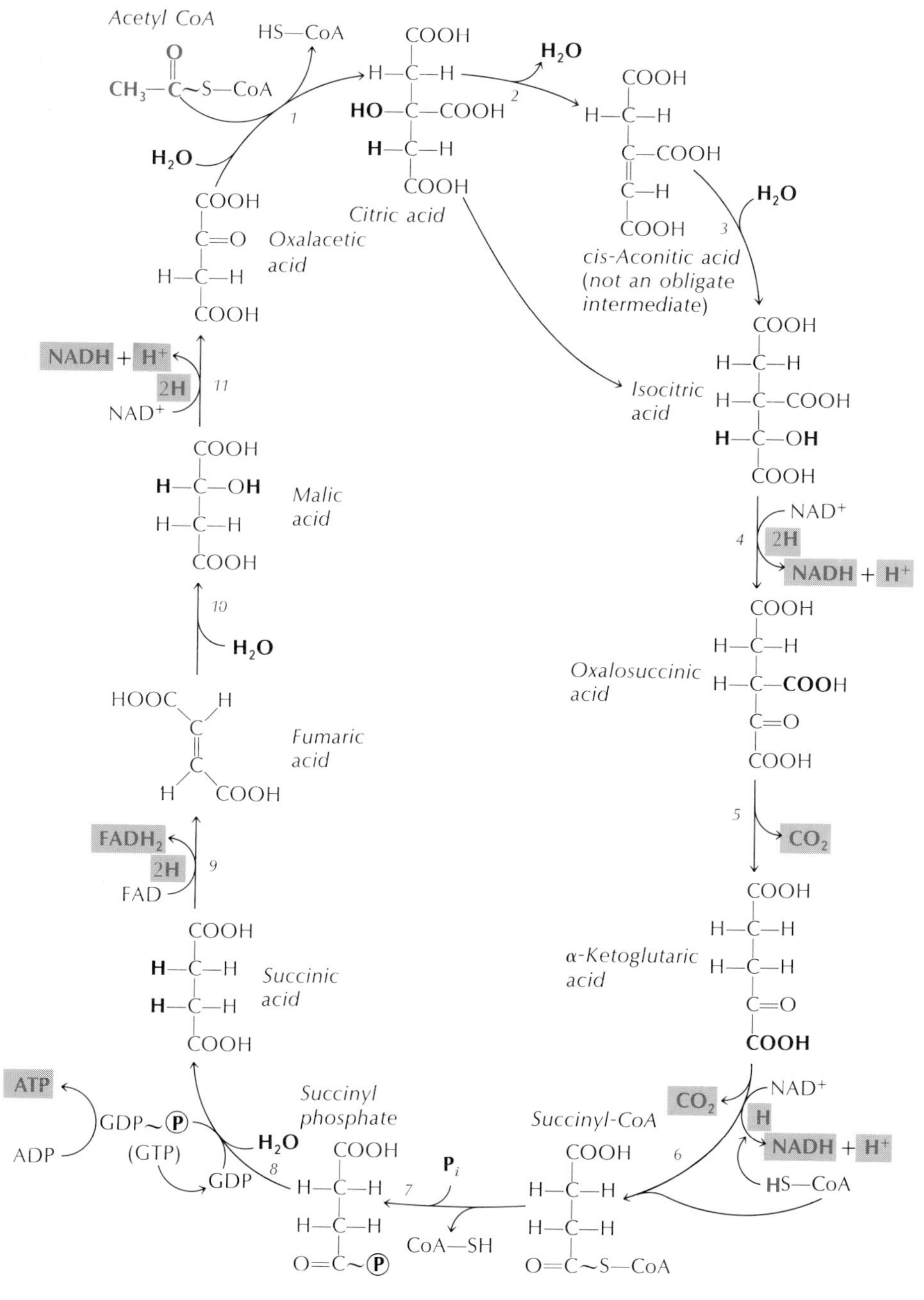

Figure 14.53 □ The Krebs tricarboxylic acid cycle. Note that, for each acetyl group entering the cycle, two CO_2 are given off, four NADH + H^+ are made from NAD^+, and one ATP is formed by transfer of ~Ⓟ from GTP to ADP. Enzymes are (1) condensing enzyme, (2) and (3) aconitase, (4) and (5) isocitric enzyme, (6) α-ketoglutaric acid oxidase, (7) and (8) succinyl thiokinase, (9) succinic dehydrogenase, (10) fumarase, and (11) malic dehydrogenase.

tion, with NAD^+ serving as the oxidant and CO_2 being liberated. In Figure 14.53, this conversion is shown in reactions 4 and 5, which may be considered as one since the oxalosuccinic acid formed is not a free intermediate but remains enzymebound during its conversion to α-ketoglutaric acid.

In the next step (reaction 6) α-ketoglutaric acid undergoes oxidative decarboxylation with release of CO_2 and formation of NADH + H^+, and at the same time combines with coenzyme A as activated succinyl (succinyl CoA). In the following reactions (7 and 8, which may also be considered as one) succinyl CoA reacts with inorganic phosphate (H_3PO_4), releasing CoA and redistributing the energy of the acyl group to form a high-energy phosphate group, which is transferred to GDP to form GDP~Ⓟ, that is, GTP. The GTP can then transfer the high-energy phosphate to ADP to produce ATP

The succinic acid (product of reaction 8) now is dehydrogenated through the action of the enzyme succinic dehydrogenase, two hydrogens being transferred to FAD, a prosthetic group bound to that enzyme through a peptide linkage. The resulting fumaric acid incorporates H_2O to form malic acid, which is then dehydrogenated to oxalacetic acid with the production of NADH + H^+.

Figure 14.54 □ **The mitochondrion: (*a*) cutaway representation, showing stalked-knob subunits lining inner membranes; these may contain respiratory assemblies. (*b*) Electron micrographs of stalked-knob units, shown at two levels of magnification. (*Courtesy of Dr. H. Fernández-Morán.*)**

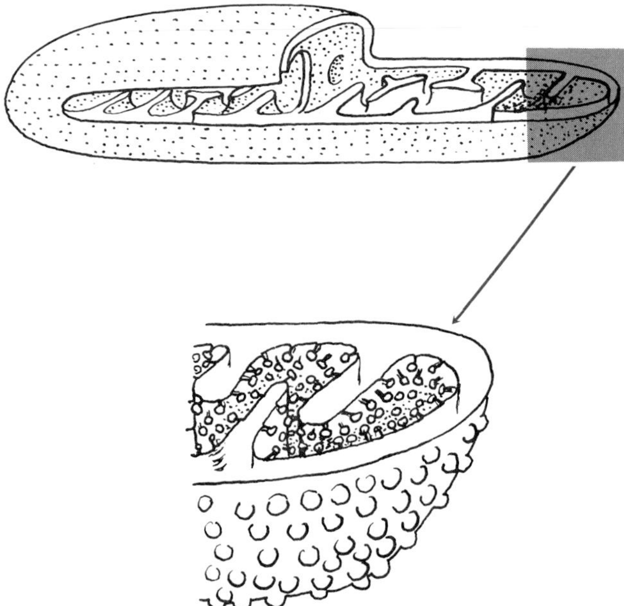

(*a*)

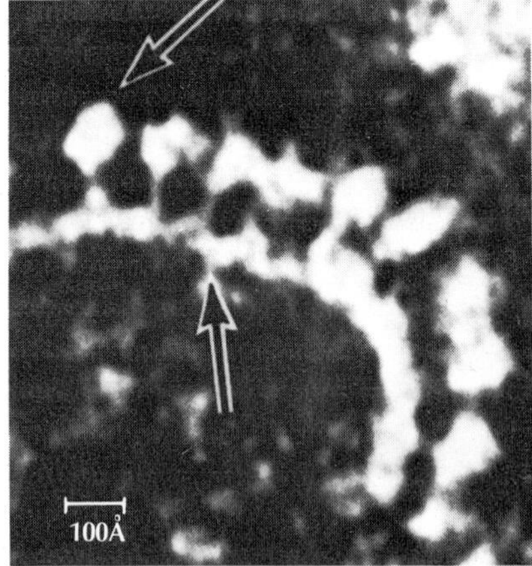

(*b*)

The enzymes catalyzing this finely geared cyclic mechanism are located in the mitochondria (of eucaryotic cells) in proximity to the enzymes of the respiratory chain, for it is the latter which accepts the eight hydrogen atoms liberated at each turn of the Krebs cycle and, in the process of transferring these atoms to oxygen to make water, produces the greatest yield of ATP.

OXIDATIVE PHOSPHORYLATION: THE RESPIRATORY CHAIN The glycolytic sequence, the conversion of pyruvic acid to activated acetyl, and the Krebs cycle, all transfer H into the respiratory chain, a sequence of hydrogen and/or electron carriers including NAD, flavoprotein, and cytochromes. These carriers are thought to occupy "assembly-line" configurations in the inner mitochondrial membranes (Figure 14.54). In considering the respiratory chain we shall (as with photosynthesis) speak in terms of electron transfer, while recognizing that some steps actually involve transfer of the entire H atom. In the final step, when hydrogen is bonded with oxygen via the enzyme cytochrome oxidase, the proton (H^+) and electron (e^-) must be reunited, for the cytochromes that constitute the bulk of this chain carry electrons only. Furthermore, whereas NAD^+ and FAD each can handle two electrons or hydrogen atoms at a time, the cytochromes can handle but one. Therefore in Figure 14.55 the number of cytochrome molecules is shown doubled. The chain as given depicts those particular cytochromes functioning in animal tissue; others are known to occur in bacteria and plants. In all cases cytochromes contain heme, and the electron is taken up by the ferric ion (Fe^{3+}) converting it to the ferrous ion (Fe^{2+}); see Figure 9.4*c*,*d*.

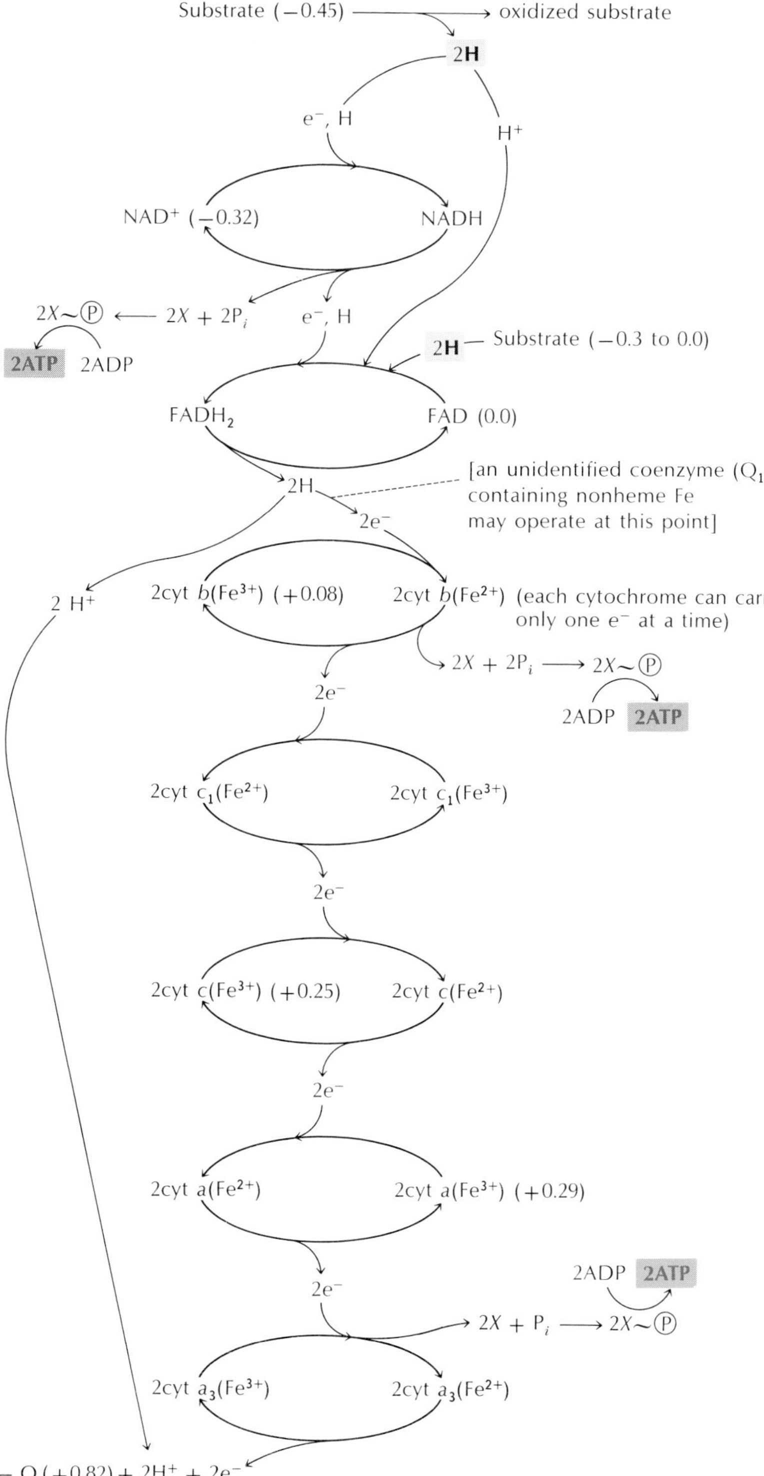

Figure 14.55 □ **The respiratory chain, with redox potentials of representative compounds given. This thermodynamically "downhill" electron transport liberates energy to convert 3ADP to ATP per e^- transported. A final hydrogen acceptor is O_2. This pathway transfers into the bonds of ATP much of the energy invested during the "uphill" transport of e^- from H_2O to NADP in photosynthesis (see Figure 13.6).**

The probable evolution of the respiratory chain is a matter of some interest. Since NAD^+ is used in all oxidative e^- transfers, both aerobic and anaerobic, it is thought to be the most ancient carrier involved in oxidative phosphorylation. It can function in an atmosphere lacking O_2, for it cannot react with O_2, but instead transfers 2H either to substrates or to flavoproteins. Flavoproteins can pass 2H directly to oxygen, but if they do so, toxic hydrogen peroxide (H_2O_2) rather than H_2O is produced. A number of bacteria termed *facultative anaerobes* can use either aerobic or anaerobic pathways with equal facility, and if in the course of anaerobic respiration H_2O_2 is produced, it is enzymatically broken down; however, to bacteria that are *obligate anaerobes* O_2 is actually a poison, for the H_2O_2 formed cannot be degraded and accumulates to kill the organism.

Although a number of cytochromes may have evolved before the atmosphere came to contain appreciable O_2, they have proven most adaptive where O_2 is available to serve as a hydrogen acceptor, for they make possible the production of H_2O instead of H_2O_2. A few anaerobes such as the sulfur bacterium *Desulfovibrio* use cytochrome transport in the absence of O_2, sulfate being the final e^- acceptor, as shown in the fol-

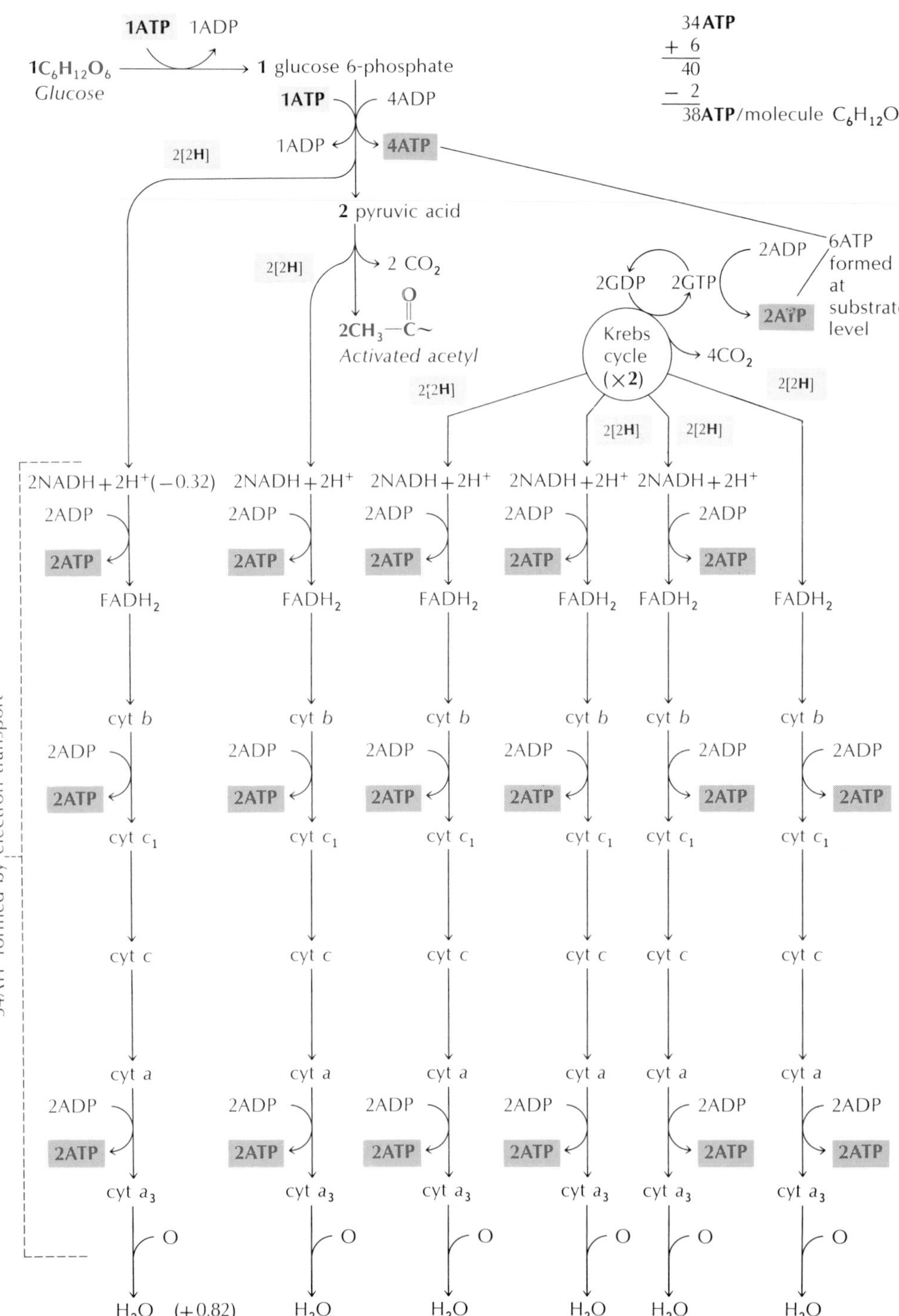

lowing reaction:

$$\text{Cytochrome } c_3(Fe^{2+}) + SO_4^{2-} + 2H^+ \longrightarrow \text{cytochrome } c_3(Fe^{3+}) + SO_3^{2-} + H_2O$$

The *Desulfovibrio* respiratory chain consists of NAD^+, FAD, and cytochromes b, b_3, and c_3. (Various cytochromes differ in the subgroups on the tetrapyrrole ring, as well as in the protein with which they are associated.)

For each transit of the respiratory chain by 2H from NAD to oxygen, three molecules of ADP are phosphorylated to ATP. This phosphorylation uses the energy made available when electrons are passed from a reductant with a negative oxidation-reduction ("redox") potential to an oxidant with a less negative (or a positive) redox potential. To understand this, we should refer to Section 13.4C where it was pointed out that a major part of the energy investment of photosynthesis consists of moving hydrogen (or e^-) thermodynamically "uphill" from water to its final reduction of CO_2. It is estimated that 1.2 eV must be invested for each e^- moved from H_2O with a redox potential of +0.82 to CO_2 with a redox potential of −0.6. This is the energy required to remove an electron from a substance with a high electron affinity and donate it to one with a comparatively low electron affinity. The same amount of energy is liberated when an electron is moved in the reverse

Figure 14.56 □ Formation of ATP during oxidation of glucose to CO_2 and H_2O. (Summary of Figures 14.51 to 14.53 and 14.55.) It may be seen that there is a net gain of 38ATP per molecule of glucose oxidized to CO_2 and H_2O, 34 of which are formed by electron transport in the respiratory chain.

direction. Each e^- moved through the respiratory chain passes through a series of transfers that are thermodynamically favored, for they involve e^- transfer from substances with lower e^- affinity to substances with higher e^- affinity.

Hydrocarbon compounds are relatively unstable, for they are holding electrons for which they have low affinity, and with the input of a little activation energy will readily relinquish these to oxidants with high electron affinity. When hydrocarbon compounds are burned, the transfer of electrons from carbon to oxygen proceeds in one step with the evolution of heat and light. The adaptive function of the respiratory chain is to release this energy in small increments that can be trapped in the high-energy groups of ATP. If NAD (−0.32) were to transfer 2H directly to O_2 (+0.82), 54 kcal would be released per mole of NADH + H^+ oxidized. Released in small consecutive steps this amount of energy is more than enough to account for the 3 moles of ATP made per mole of NADH + H^+ oxidized.

The respiratory chain forms a great final common pathway for transporting hydrogen from carbon compounds to O_2. Figure 14.56 summarizes ATP formation in the breakdown of a single molecule of glucose to CO_2 and H_2O: 40 molecules of ATP are produced, 6 at the substrate level (4 in glycolysis, 2 for every two turns of the Krebs cycle) and 34 by electron transport through the respiratory chain. Since two ATP were "spent" to phosphorylate glucose and to produce fructose 1,6-diphosphate, the net yield is 38 ATP formed per glucose molecule fully oxidized. This is equivalent to between 276 and 456 kcal recaptured as bonding energy per mole of glucose oxidized (the considerable range between these two values is due to uncertainty as to how much energy ATP can actually transfer in the intact cell). The total energy investment made during photosynthesis is 673 kcal/mole (when expressed as heat, or 686 kcal/mole when expressed as free energy, a distinction with which we need not concern ourselves unduly at this time). Therefore, of the energy yielded by the oxidative metabolism of glucose, from 40 to 66 percent is recovered as energy available to do work, and the balance is dissipated as heat. Even using the more conservative estimate of 7 kcal as the energy of hydrolysis of ATP, the fixation of 40 percent of the energy released, as bonding energy of ATP, attests to the remarkable efficiency of the cell's machinery for oxidative metabolism.

The rate at which an organism carries out aerobic cell respiration can be estimated in terms of the rate at which O_2 is consumed. This in turn varies in man with age, sex, thyroid activity, ratio of body surface to body weight, state of exercise, and so forth. When a person is fasting and at rest the *basal metabolic rate* (BMR) can be determined. Under such basal conditions a human adult uses around 14 liters of O_2/hr, which is equivalent to oxidation of glucose at the rate of 18 g/hr.

THE PENTOSE PHOSPHATE PATHWAY ("HEXOSE SHUNT") Carbohydrate degradation can also take place in solution in the cytoplasm rather than within the mitochondria. This is by means of the pentose phosphate pathway, so called because for each turn of the cycle *six* hexose phosphate molecules *each* give up (CH_2O) to become pentose phosphate. Then through a series of regenerative reactions involving three-, four-, five-, and seven-carbon sugar-phosphate intermediates, *five* hexose phosphate molecules are formed and a new one must enter the cycle to restore the original number of six (Figure 14.57).

For each equivalent of a hexose molecule ($C_6H_{12}O_6$) broken down in this cycle, $6H_2O$ enter the cycle and $6CO_2$ and 12 pairs of hydrogen atoms are given off. The hydrogen passes to $NADP^+$, which like NAD^+ takes up an electron and a H atom, leaving H^+ free. This gain of twelve NADPH + H^+ is an important consequence of the pentose phosphate pathway, for NADPH is a hydrogen donor in many reductions including the synthesis of long-chain fatty acids, certain steroids, and the amino acid tyrosine. We have already noted the role of $NADP^+$ in photosynthesis, where it takes up two hydrogen atoms and passes them into the Calvin cycle.

The pentose phosphate pathway occurs very widely, and although its contribution is insignificant in the metabolism of skeletal muscle, in such tissues as brain, liver, and the mature leaves of plants, it may provide up to 90 percent of the cells' energy needs. This is possible because when NADPH + H^+ need not serve as hydrogen donor to some reduction, it can transfer 2H to NAD^+ across the mitochondrial boundary, thereby passing electrons into the respiratory chain. For each glucose molecule entering the cycle, if the full amount of hydrogen liberated is passed through the respiratory chain to O_2, 36 molecules of ATP are evolved. Deducting the cost of one ATP to phosphorylate glucose to glucose 6-phosphate, we are left with a net yield of 35 ATP per glucose oxidized to $6CO_2$ and $6H_2O$, which compares quite favorably with the net yield of

Figure 14.57 □ The pentose phosphate pathway. In this alternative to the glycolytic and Krebs cycles, for each six turns of the cycle, one molecule of glucose is broken down to $6CO_2$ and $6H_2O$, with the reduction of $12NADP^+$ to $NADPH + H^+$. The latter can then transfer 2H to NAD^+, which transports 2H into the respiratory chain.

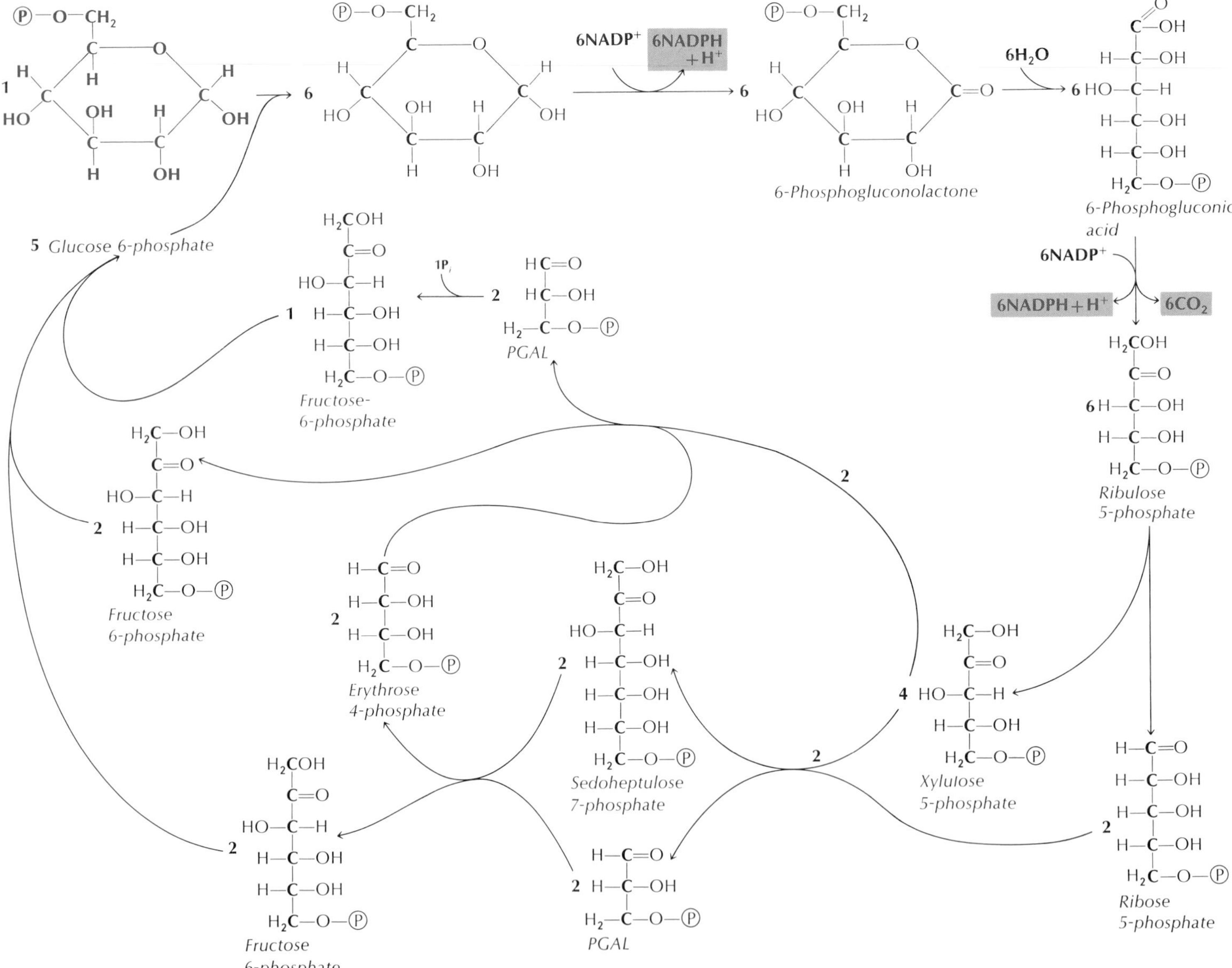

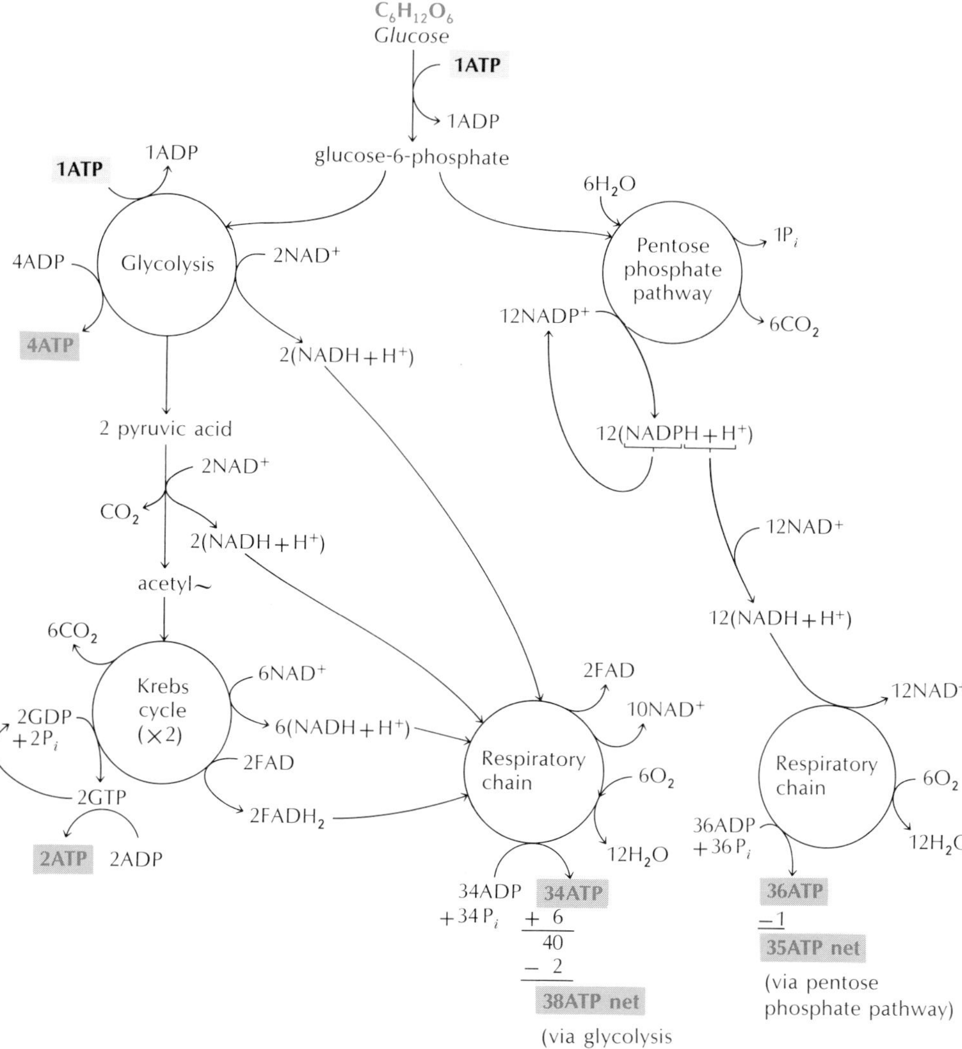

Figure 14.58 □ Pathways of glucose respiration: simplified scheme, showing relationships of major pathways diagrammed in preceding figures. Note that the pentose phosphate pathway yields a net gain of 35ATP per molecule of glucose broken down, as compared with the 38ATP representing the net gain of glycolysis and the Krebs cycle.

38 for glycolysis and the Krebs cycle (Figure 14.58).

As well as serving as a source of ATP and NADPH + H^+, the pentose phosphate pathway is adaptively valuable as a means of interrelating the metabolism of three- to seven-carbon sugars, and provides a ready source of pentoses for nucleotide synthesis.

LIPID CATABOLISM Lipids are first degraded hydrolytically into their constituent fatty acid and alcohol components. Glycerol, the most characteristic alcohol occurring in lipids, may then be phosphorylated and oxidized to 3-phosphoglyceraldehyde (PGAL), which enters the glycolytic sequence at its midpoint:

```
   H
   |
H—C—OH
   |
H—C—OH  +  NAD⁺  +  ATP  ⟶
   |
H—C—OH
   |
   H
```
Glycerol

```
 H—C=O
    |
 H—C—OH      +  NADH  +  H⁺  +  ADP
    |
H₂—C—O—Ⓟ
```
PGAL

Fatty acids are broken down by a process known as *β-oxidation,* from the fact that the second (*β*-)carbon in the chain is oxidized with the result that the chain breaks between the *α*- and *β*-carbons. The two-carbon fragment that is split off enters the Krebs cycle as acetyl CoA. The entire sequence is now repeated and the new two-carbon terminal portion is broken off next (Figure 14.59). This continues until the entire chain has been reduced to two-carbon fragments coupled with CoA.

Figure 14.59 □ **Fatty acid β oxidation. Only six carbon atoms of the fatty acid chain are shown, the rest of the chain being represented by R. Successive two-carbon units are differentially shaded to aid identification through successive steps. Only one ATP need be spent to initiate the sequence. For each acetyl CoA liberated, one FAD is reduced to $FADH_2$ and one NAH^+ to $NADH + H^+$.**

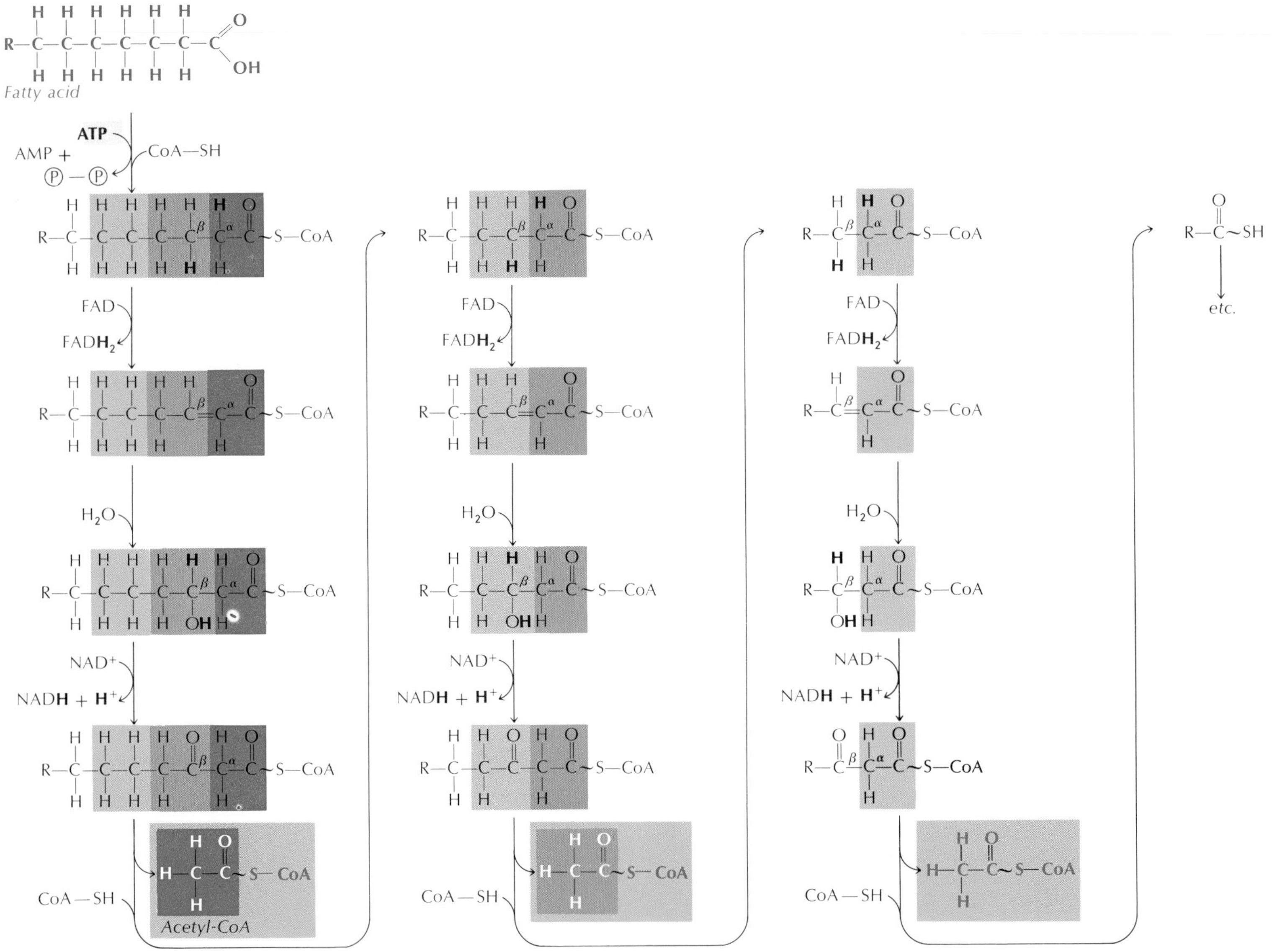

The "cost" of the first β-oxidation is one ATP degraded to AMP and pyrophosphate, as is needed to form the initial acyl CoA:

$$R-\overset{\overset{\displaystyle O}{\|}}{C}\sim S-CoA$$

From this point on, no more ATP need be expended no matter how long the fatty acid chain may be, for energy is made available in the transfer of hydrogen to FAD and NAD^+, and the high-energy C$\sim$S linkage makes the thioesters highly reactive.

NITROGEN CATABOLISM Nitrogenous compounds present a somewhat special metabolic problem, in that they can only enter the Krebs cycle as acetyl residues, or by conversion to one of the carboxylic acids which are part of the cycle. This requires that they be *deaminated,* and that the nitrogen-containing portion be prepared for excretion by some pathway other than that by which carbohydrates and lipids are degraded. Nitrogen excretion poses no problem for plants, for their continued growth requirements demand the construction of new proteins and nucleic acids. The greater energy needs of animals result in a more rapid turnover of materials, including the nitrogenous compounds. There are storage forms of both carbohydrate and lipid, which may be drawn upon when needed, but protein ingested in excess of immediate need tends to be degraded. The initial phase of nitrogen catabolism is the hydrolysis of the polymers—proteins and nucleic acids—to their constituent amino acid or nucleotide units. The further degradation of nucleotides requires the separation of the nitrogenous bases from the pentose phosphate.

Purine catabolism proceeds through a series of conversions to *uric acid* (2,6,8-oxypurine). This may be excreted as such, or first one ring and then the other may be broken, converting uric acid to *allantoin* and then to *allantoic acid,* and finally to *urea,* which may in turn be further degraded to CO_2 and NH_3 (Figure 14.60). We should note that *any one* of these compounds may be the major excretory product of purine breakdown in a given animal group. Fish and amphibia may carry the reactions to urea, while aquatic invertebrates carry them all the way to CO_2 and ammonia. Purine catabolism in birds and most reptiles goes only as far as uric acid, but most mammals (excepting man and other primates) convert uric acid to allantoin. How far the series can be carried depends on the enzymes that are present; stopping short of the complete degradation is probably attributable to loss mutation.

Amino acid and *pyrimidine catabolism* both lead to the formation of urea, but in birds, snakes, and lizards the need to conserve water during excretion has favored the conversion of urea to uric acid, since the latter is nontoxic and can be stored and excreted as a solid waste, while urea is somewhat more toxic and must be excreted in aqueous solution. Ammonia is the most toxic nitrogenous waste, and must either be removed promptly from the body (as can be done with aquatic species), or must be detoxified by conversion to urea or uric acid. *Ammonotelic* animals are those in which the major nitrogenous waste is ammonia; these include most invertebrates, bony fish, and larval amphibians. Ammonia excretion is practical where excretion can take place through any part of the body surface (as in protozoa, sponges, and coelenterates), or where water is amply available for production of a copious, dilute urine. *Ureotelic* animals, which excrete mainly urea, include adult amphibians, aquatic turtles, mammals, and cartilaginous fishes. Urea synthesis has been put to the unusual adaptive use of regulating the water balance of sharks and rays, for rather than actively secreting salts from their tissues to the hyperosmotic seawater, these fish remain in osmotic equilibrium with their environment by tolerating large quantities of urea, which increase the osmotic pressure of their blood and tissue fluids. *Uricotelic* animals have achieved the most effective means of reducing water loss during excretion, for their principle nitrogenous waste is solid uric acid. Uricotelic groups include insects, birds, snakes, lizards, and tortoises. In moths and butterflies, the nitrogenous waste materials are converted into pigments that accumulate in the wing scales. We also find solid nitrogenous products being concentrated in parts of the vertebrate body which are eventually shed, including the hair, nails, and outer epidermis. Possibly accumulation of keratin in the tetrapod epidermis was originally an excretory adaptation for removing excess nitrogen without water loss. The waterproofing effect of keratinized epidermis would then provide an adaptive bonus that would favor even more extensive keratin synthesis and deposition.

The major terminal pathway of protein catabolism in animals is the *urea cycle* (also known as the ornithine cycle; see Figure 14.61). Nitrogen enters this cycle from two sources: as NH_3 released by deamination reactions from amino acids and nitrogenous bases; and as nitrogen from the amino acid *aspartic acid.* The $-NH_2$ from other amino

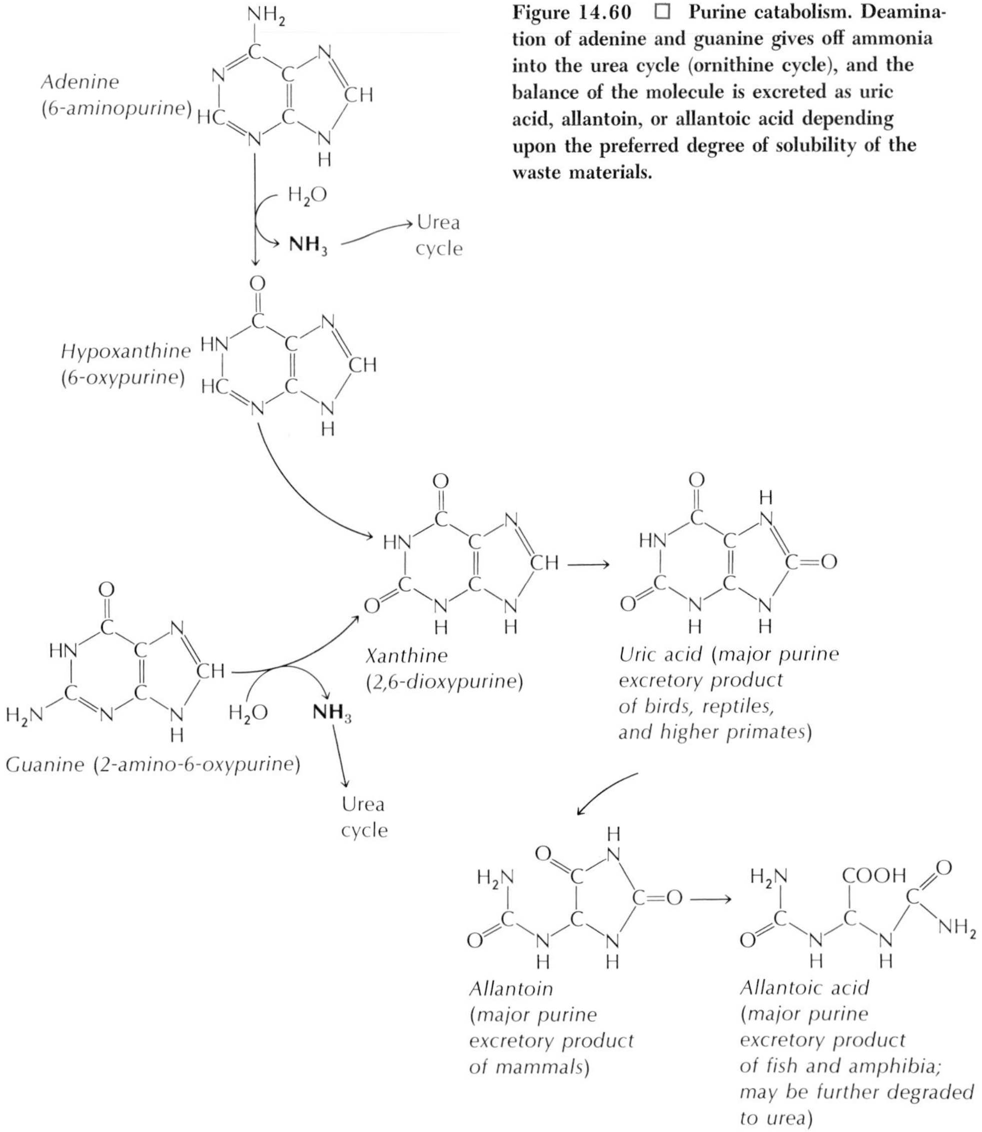

Figure 14.60 □ Purine catabolism. Deamination of adenine and guanine gives off ammonia into the urea cycle (ornithine cycle), and the balance of the molecule is excreted as uric acid, allantoin, or allantoic acid depending upon the preferred degree of solubility of the waste materials.

acids reaches the urea cycle through transamination reactions in which the amino group is passed to oxalacetic acid to form aspartic acid. The cycle is regenerative, as shown, and its major product is urea. Three ATP must be expended for each molecule produced of

$$H_2N{-}\overset{\displaystyle O}{\overset{\|}{C}}{-}NH_2$$

In an ammonotelic animal the urea is then broken down to CO_2 and ammonia. In uricotelic species urea must enter a synthetic pathway leading to the synthesis of uric acid, the excretion of this relatively insoluble and nontoxic waste being, as we have said, a water-conserving adaptation.

The urea cycle is also important as the body's major source of the important amino acid arginine. It is dependent upon the Krebs cycle for a supply of oxalacetic acid, and in turn gives off fumaric acid into the Krebs cycle. The keto acid residues remaining from amino acid deamination can also enter the Krebs cycle either directly (if they represent intermediates of that cycle) or by conversion to acetyl CoA.

D Whole-organism metabolism

In this chapter and Chapter 13 we have traced the fate of materials in the body of the individual organism—their procurement, distribution, and ultimate metabolic use—giving special attention to those biosynthetic and energy-mobilizing pathways that appear to be of most universal occurrence in the biotic world. We have attempted to approach metabolism at the cellular level, for in the last analysis whole-organism metabolism must be considered the product of individual cell metabolisms. However, in dealing with metabolic processes in higher animals particularly, we must keep two things in mind: (1) that cell metabolism can undergo differentiation and specialization even as can cell morphology; and (2) that control mechanisms are necessary which allow the metabolic activities of various tissues to be effectively coordinated.

Probably through selective gene repression, many mature tissues sacrifice their capacity to carry on certain reactions of which they are genetically capable. This allows them to specialize toward the performance of particular metabolic activities relevant to their role in the life of the organism. For instance, vertebrate erythrocytes specialize in hemoglobin synthesis, and skeletal muscle tissue in the synthesis of the contractile proteins myosin and actin. Such metabolic specialists become dependent on other tissues to process for them nutrients and wastes that are transported by way of the bloodstream.

The vertebrate liver, for example, is essential to the life of other organs, for it not only detoxifies blood draining into it from the gut by way of the hepatic portal vein, but serves as the body's major site for biochemical conversion of nutrients (Figure 14.62). Its versatility in both synthesizing and degrading materials relieves the metabolic burden upon other organs such as glands, muscles, and the brain, which must concentrate upon their particular commitments to the exclusion of certain basic maintenance functions. The liver converts fructose and galactose to glucose, and glucose to glycogen, which is accumulated and released to the bloodstream on demand as blood sugar.

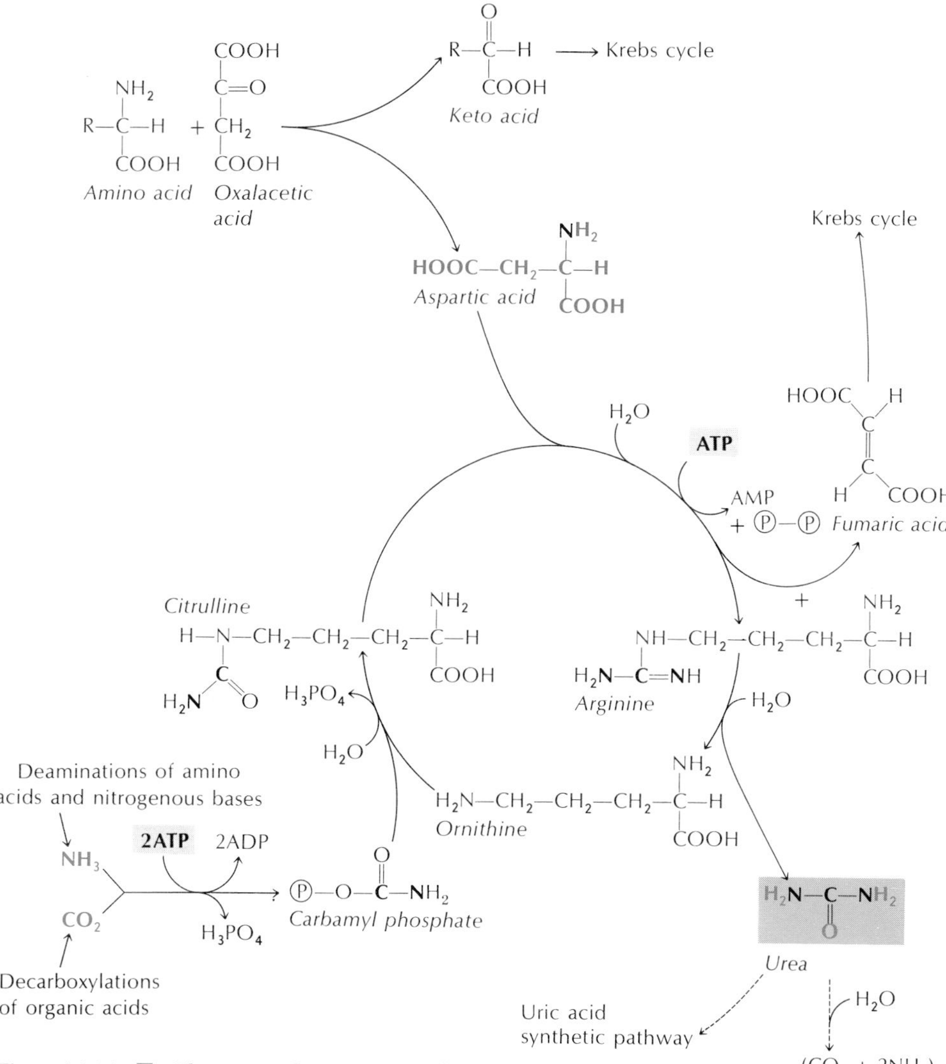

Figure 14.61 □ The urea cycle. Ammonia and CO_2 enter the cycle as carbamyl phosphate; amino nitrogen ($-NH_2$) enters as part of the aspartic acid molecule. Aspartic acid + citrulline + $H_2O \rightarrow$ arginine + fumaric acid. Arginine, an intermediate of the cycle, gives off urea by hydrolysis and forms ornithine, the next intermediate of the cycle. This reacts with H_2O and carbamyl phosphate to form citrulline, the third intermediate, giving off H_3PO_4. The energy cost per molecule of urea built is 3ATP.

After storing glycogen to capacity, the liver converts excess sugar to lipids that pass by way of the circulation to regions in which adipose tissue accumulates. It synthesizes plasma proteins of many types, and regulates the blood level of each specific amino acid by converting those in excess to glucose and urea and replenishing others by performing transaminations and other conversions. Serving in early life as a source of red blood cells and a site of hemoglobin synthesis, the liver later becomes the major organ through which substances released by the disintegration of aged erythrocytes are processed and excreted as bile constituents. The metabolic versatility of the liver, by relieving other tissues of responsibility for many tasks requisite to their own survival, makes it possible for them to assume metabolic functions not required of less advanced organisms.

Figure 14.62 □ **Electron photomicrograph of liver epithelium, showing bile capillary between cells.** (*Courtesy of D. W. Fawcett, M.D.*)

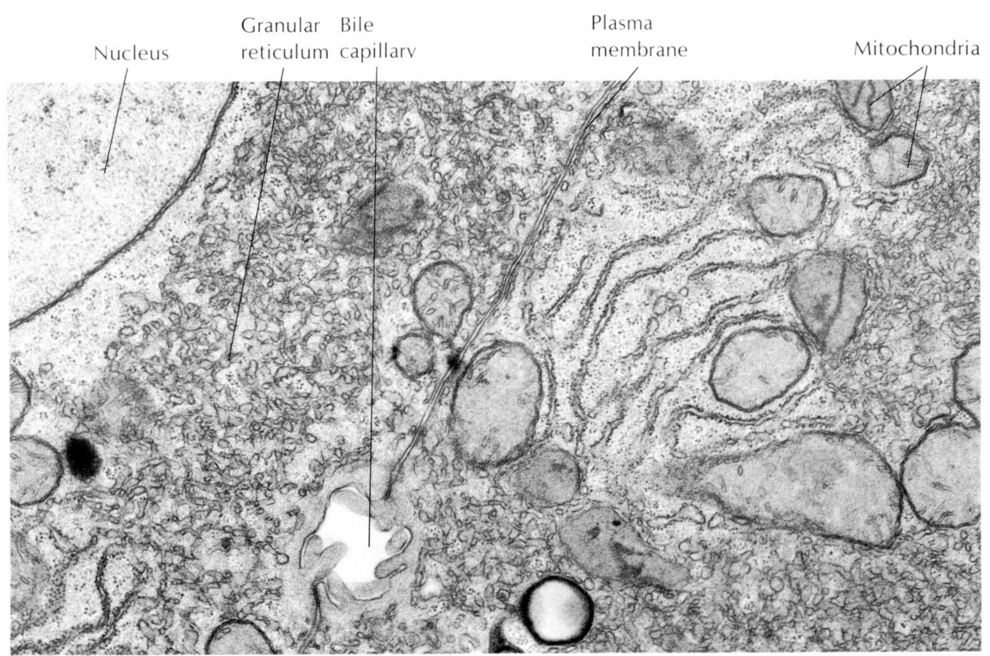

Organic evolution has not only led toward increased structural complexity but toward a concomitant increase in the complexity of metabolic processes. As we saw in Chapter 8, during the course of evolution advance in complexity has been made possible by the accumulation of new increments of genetic coding material. Since higher organisms such as arthropods and vertebrates possess so much more genetic material than do bacteria, it is not surprising that they can synthesize more kinds of enzymes and carry on a wider variety of metabolic functions than can bacteria or other simpler forms of life. The genomes of advanced species must contain an irreducible minimum of genes requisite for the performance of those fundamental and universal processes that are basic to cell survival, but they must also contain genes encoding enzymes controlling those more recently evolved reactions that make possible a higher order of existence. However, we should bear in mind that animal cells are unable to carry on many synthetic reactions of which most bacteria and plants are capable, such as the construction of many vitamins and amino acids, and must therefore obtain these in the diet. In such cases this is not due to gene repression during cytodifferentiation but to gene mutations that have taken place during animal evolution. As a result of such mutations, no cell of the animal body is now able to carry on these reactions.

Coordination of specialized cell metabolisms to maintain an effective level of metabolism throughout the organism depends in part upon the existence of so-called *primitive control mechanisms* by which cell metabolism responds adaptively to changes in the intracellular concentrations of various substances, including wastes and substrates, and in part upon more modern *neuroendocrine control mechanisms* superimposed on these. Such adaptive modulations in cell behavior are essential for effective responses of the whole organism; both the "primitive" and the neuroendocrine mechanisms for regulating cell and organismal metabolism are discussed in Chapters 15 and 16.

REVIEW AND DISCUSSION

1 How do pinocytosis and phagocytosis facilitate the process of membrane transport? How do these processes resemble and differ from each other? What processes are involved in merocrine, apocrine, and holocrine secretion?

2 What are the characteristics of active transport systems? What evidence is there that not even amino acid or glucose membrane transport are mainly the result of passive diffusion? Explain why active transport requires an energy expenditure by the cell. How do hormones affect membrane transport?

3 How do solutes move *within* living cells? Cite evidence that indicates that intracellular membranes may have different permeability properties than the outer plasma membrane.

4 Differentiate between root pressure and shoot tension, and assess the importance of each in xylem transport in small shrubs and tall trees. Compare the manner in which fluid moves in the phloem and in the xylem.

5 What is the functional significance of a plant's aeration system? Can you explain why aquatic tracheophytes have aeration systems that are so much more extensive than those occurring in terrestrial tracheophytes?

6 Compare the anatomy and functions of the vertebrate lymphatic and cardiovascular systems. Under what pathological conditions might the transportive function of the lymphatics be most dramatically demonstrated?

7 Explain the adaptive significance of the changes that the vertebrate heart has undergone in its evolution from the fish to the mammalian condition. What is the function of the foramen ovale?

8 Summarize the cardiac cycle, and explain how its organization prevents the heart from fatiguing. How is this cycle modified during exercise?

9 Compare lung structure and methods of ventilation of amphibians, reptiles, birds, and mammals. In which group is ventilation most effective? How are the respiratory organs ventilated in crustaceans (such as lobsters) and insects?

10 What are respiratory pigments? What is the distribution of the major respiratory pigments throughout the Animal Kingdom? Explain how vertebrate erythrocytes function in *both* O_2 and CO_2 transport. Why is it incorrect to say that animals "breathe in oxygen and breathe out carbon dioxide"?

11 Summarize the essential action of each of the major water-soluble vitamins and of each group of fat-soluble vitamins. Compare the distribution and adaptive roles of water-soluble and fat-soluble vitamins in general. Vitamin A has apparently taken on a new function in mammals. Can you think of analogous situations in which some other structure or substance has changed functions, or gained a new function, in the course of evolution?

12 The polymerization of monosaccharide, nucleotide, and amino acid units cannot take place directly. Summarize the major steps involved in forming a polysaccharide, nucleic acid, and peptide chain.

13 Compare the method of synthesis of a long-chain fatty acid, with the method by which it is broken down. Why is β-oxidation an economical process?

14 Compare the energy output, in terms of ATP produced, of the glycolytic sequence, the pentose phosphate pathway, the Krebs cycle, and the respiratory chain. How does their energy *conserved* compare with their total energy *released?*

15 Compare ammonotelic, ureotelic, and uricotelic modes of nitrogenous excretion; correlate them with ecological factors.

16 Lungfish undergo a metabolic shift during estivation from ureotelism to uricotelism. Explain the adaptive significance of this shift. Can you think of any reason why selection has operated against these fishes' remaining uricotelic throughout the year?

17 What are the major differences between plants and animals with regard to the synthesis, utilization, and catabolism of nitrogenous compounds?

REFERENCES

ASIMOV, I. *The Bloodstream: River of Life.* New York: Collier Books, 1961. A lively popular account dealing mainly with the composition and functions of blood.

BIDDULPH, S., AND O. BIDDULPH "The Circulatory System of Plants," *Sci. Amer.,* **200** (1959). Radioactive isotopes trace paths of translocation within the vascular plant.

BOSMANN, H. B., AND S. S. MARTIN "Mitochondrial Autonomy: Incorporation of Monosaccharides into Glycoprotein by Isolated Mitochondria," *Science,* **164** (1969). In vitro studies demonstrate that mitochondria are genetically equipped to carry on synthesis of proteins and glycoproteins needed for their own structure.

CHRISTENSEN, H. N. "Some Transport Lessons Taught by the Organic Solute," *Perspectives in Biol. and Med.,* **10** (1967). Reviews the history and present status of active transport theory.

CLEMENTS, J. A. "Surface Tension in the Lungs," *Sci. Amer.,* **207** (1962). Mitochondria in the alveolar lining of the mammalian lung secrete a lipoprotein coating that reduces surface tension and prevents capillary fluid from leaking into the alveoli.

COMROE, J. H., JR. "The Lung," *Sci. Amer.,* **214** (1966). Good overview of pulmonary structure and function, including mechanics and neural control of breathing and effects of respiratory irritants.

DOWLING, J. E. "Night Blindness," *Sci. Amer.,* **215** (1966). Discusses the role of vitamin A in vision and changes in retinal ultrastructure resulting from prolonged vitamin A deficiency.

FENN, W. O. "The Mechanism of Breathing," *Sci. Amer.,* **203** (1960). Describes the pulmonary pressure changes that cause inhalation to take place.

FOX, H. M. "Blood Pigments," *Sci. Amer.,* **182** (1950).

GIESE, A. C. "Energy Release and Utilization," in *This Is Life,* W. H. Johnson and W. C. Steere, eds. New York: Holt, Rinehart and Winston, Inc., 1962.

GREEN, D. E. "The Synthesis of Fat," *Sci. Amer.,* **202** (1960).

——— "The Mitochondrion," *Sci. Amer.,* **210** (1964).

GREULACH, V. A. "The Rise of Water in Plants," *Sci. Amer.,* **187** (1952). Describes the mechanisms thought responsible for xylem transport.

HOKIN, L. E., AND M. R. HOKIN "The Chemistry of Cell Membranes," *Sci. Amer.,* **213** (1965). Considers the structure of membrane phospholipids and their possible role in secretion of enzymes from pancreatic cells.

HOLTER, H. "How Things Get Into Cells," *Sci. Amer.,* **205** (1961). Discusses passive and active transport.

MAYERSON, H. S. "The Lymphatic System," *Sci. Amer.,* **208** (1963). Reviews the anatomy of the lymphatic system, the ultrastructure of lymph capillaries, and the causes of lymph formation.

PONDER, E. "The Red Blood Cell," *Sci. Amer.,* **196** (1957).

PORTER, K. R., AND C. FRANZINI-ARMSTRONG "The Sarcoplasmic Reticulum," *Sci. Amer.,* **212** (1965). Electron microscopy shows that striated muscle fibers are penetrated by two separate tubule systems that provide for internal transport and the rapid spread of excitation.

REDMOND, J. R. "Transport of Oxygen by the Blood of the Land Crab, *Geocarcinus lateralis,*" *Amer. Zool.,* **8** (1968). Describes procedures for determining O_2-equilibrium curves of land crab blood; concludes that this blood has a higher O_2 capacity than that of aquatic crustaceans and transports more O_2 per unit volume.

ROBERTSON, J. D. "The Membrane of the Living Cell," *Sci. Amer.,* **206** (1962). A model for the structure of the plasma membrane is based upon functional properties displayed by the membrane.

RUSTAD, R. C. "Pinocytosis," *Sci.

Amer., **204** (1961). A mechanism is described whereby large solute molecules may enter the cytoplasm in minute vesicles that are pinched off the inner surface of the plasma membrane.

SCHAYER, R. W. "A Unified Theory of Glucocorticoid Action. II. On a Circulatory Basis for the Metabolic Effects of Glucocorticoids," *Perspectives in Biol. and Med.*, **10** (1967). Proposes that the diverse metabolic effects of some important adrenal hormones can be explained in terms of their primary action as promoters of microvascular constriction.

SELVERSTON, A. "Structure and Function of the Transverse Tubular System in Crustacean Muscle Fibers," *Amer. Zool.*, **7** (1967). Considers the selective ion permeability of the transverse system and notes similarities to and differences between those which are seen in vertebrate striated muscle.

SOLOMON, A. K. "Pores in the Cell Membrane," *Sci. Amer.*, **203** (1960). Describes an ingenious technique that demonstrates the existence of pores through the cell membrane and provides information on the size of these openings.

——— "Pumps in the Living Cell," *Sci. Amer.*, **207** (1962). Considers active transport of ions.

VROMAN, L. *Blood.* Garden City, N.Y.: The Natural History Press, 1967. An entertaining yet instructive account of the composition and functions of blood.

WEIS-FOGH, T. "Functional Design of the Tracheal System of Flying Insects as Compared with the Avian Lung," *J. Exp. Biol.*, **41** (1964).

WILLIAMS, C. B. "Insect Breathing," *Sci. Amer.*, **188** (1953).

WOOD, J. E. "The Venous System," *Sci. Amer.*, **218** (1968). Distended veins serve as a reservoir for as much as 70 percent of the body's total blood supply; their active constriction allows the volume of circulating blood to be precisely regulated.

WOODWARD, J. D. "Biotin," *Sci. Amer.*, **204** (1961). Discusses the nature of a member of the vitamin B family.

ZIMMERMANN, M. H. "Movement of Organic Substances in Trees," *Science*, **133** (1961). Using the severed mouthparts of living aphids, the sap from individual phloem columns may be collected and information obtained on the composition and rate of flow of this fluid.

——— "How Sap Moves in Trees," *Sci. Amer.*, **208** (1963). Reviews mechanisms of xylem transport.

ZWEIFACH, B. W. "The Microcirculation of the Blood," *Sci. Amer.*, **200** (1959). Describes the organization of the microcirculation and considers the mechanisms by which blood flow through capillary beds is regulated.

Chapter 15 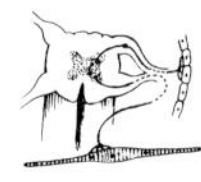 INTEGRATIVE MECHANISMS

A MAJOR TREND IN ORGANIC EVOLUtion has been toward increasing awareness by living things of their environment and a concomitant development of ever more effective responses on the basis of the information received. The adaptive value of this trend is twofold: (1) higher organisms can exploit and manipulate their environment to greater advantage than can less advanced creatures; (2) higher organisms are more capable of maintaining their own internal stability despite changes in the environment, and are therefore protected to some degree from the effects of those changes.

The first of these adaptive advantages is realized at the *behavioral* level: to make better use of its surroundings, an animal may perform some act or a plant orient its growth in one direction. The second is an outcome of the evolution of *physiological* regulatory mechanisms that preserve the organism's internal economy in a steady state of dynamic equilibrium (*homeostasis*).

The level at which adaptive responses, both behavioral and physiological, are carried out depends upon the complexity of the organism's mechanisms for (1) obtaining information on external and internal conditions, (2) transmitting and analyzing this information, and (3) executing the necessary responses. These three functions must, of course, be efficiently integrated: the value of having excellent sensory equipment, for instance, may be limited by the extent to which the data received can be analyzed. A bird with visual acuity far exceeding that of man cannot use all the sensory data it receives because of the limitations of its

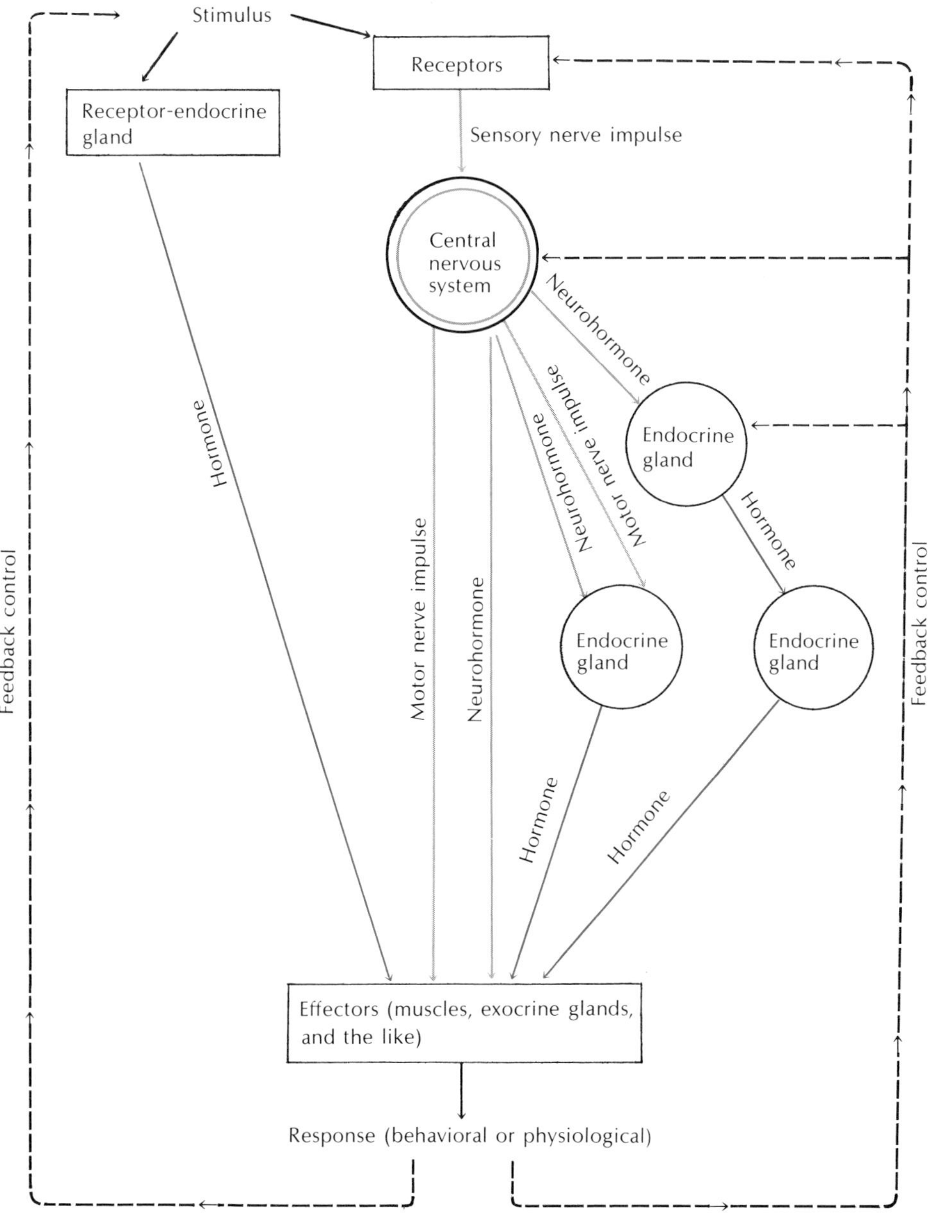

Figure 15.1 □ Integratory mechanisms of the animal body. Neurohormones are shown in color tint, other hormones in solid color, and nerve impulses in gray.

brain. On the other hand, a mole, which is nearly blind, cannot analyze visual data even though it may have a complex brain. Again, the nature and effectiveness of the response depends not only on the sensory and integrative mechanisms available, but on the potentialities of the organism's motor equipment. Despite the complexity of its brain, a porpoise or whale cannot perform manipulative tasks—lacking, as it does, a grasping hand.

Sensory acuity, neural and neuroendocrine organization, and motor capacity have all generally coevolved in close relation to one another, however, for selection pressure would rarely have tended to drive any one of them very far ahead of the others. In other words, any failure of one to advance would limit the opportunity for evolutionary advancement of all three.

Integration operates on two major levels: (1) it must maintain internal functional harmony within the body of the organism; (2) it must maintain an effective relationship between the organism and its environment. In this chapter we shall review the sensory, neural, and hormonal equipment that living things have evolved for obtaining information and generating appropriate responses (Figure 15.1). In Chapter 16 we shall consider the two basic categories of response: (1) *physiological regulation* at both cellular and systemic levels, whereby internal harmony is maintained and the organism's steady-state preserved in the face of environmental inconstancy; (2) *behavior,* that is, the overt response involving movement, production of light and sound, and other devices by which organisms interact with both living and nonliving factors in their environment.

All cells are to some extent *irritable* (capable of responding to certain environmental changes that act as *stimuli*). Unicellular motile organisms respond by changing their direction and/or rate of locomotion when exposed to changes in illumination, temperature, or the chemical composition of their surroundings. However, in multicellular organisms certain tissues tend to be more sensitive than others to such changes, partially on the basis of their degree of exposure to these factors. In plants the youthful, mitotically active tissues located close to the body surface are most susceptible to stimulation. These can propagate their excitation to adjacent cells, possibly electrochemically, but also bring about generalized systemic effects by secreting hormones that are distributed throughout the plant by way of the vascular channels.

All metazoans except sponges have well-developed nervous tissue (see Figure 11.41) specialized for the particular functions of receiving stimuli and propagating the excitation to other parts of the body. Neurons occasionally are associated with epithelial cells that amplify the stimulus energy and transduce it into a form capable of eliciting a nerve impulse. In such cases it is the *receptor* cell and not the neuron that is specialized for sensitivity to some particular type of stimulation. However, epithelial receptor cells are uncommon and are generally restricted to vertebrates. Accordingly, the neuron itself must usually be receiver, amplifier, transducer, conductor, and transmitter, all in one. This is a formidable requirement, and one which has been met not only by the diversification of neurons into a number of more or less distinct morphological and functional varieties, but also by the development in any given neuron of three functionally distinct regions: the *generator, conductor,* and *transmitter* regions (Figure 15.2).

The generator region of a neuron is the part most susceptible to stimulation. It may be directly excitable by some particular type of stimulus from the environment, or receive excitation from another neuron or an epithelial receptor cell. The generator region may consist of no more than the very tips of the dendrites or may include the entire, highly branched "dendritic tree" and the cell body as well. In the vertebrate brain, each cell body directly receives stimulation from the transmitter endings of other neurons and accordingly serves as the major generator region of these central neurons. Sensory neurons serving the periphery are by contrast normally excited only at the tips of their dendrites.

The conductor region of a neuron consists of its *nerve fibers*—the dendrites and axon. Excitation is conducted from the dendritic endings toward the cell body, and thence along the axon to the latter's terminal arborization ("end-brush"). In *bipolar* neurons the cell body is involved in conductance for it lies between the dendrites and axon, whereas in *unipolar* neurons the cell body lies to one side of the conductance pathway, allowing the excitation to pass without interruption along the entire combined length of the nerve fibers (Figure 15.2c). Because conduction speed is increased when one or a few, rather than many, neurons serve as the pathway, natural selection has operated toward the lengthening of the conductor region. Many neurons located entirely within the central nervous system (brain and major nerve trunks) have a very short, highly-branching conductive region. Such *association* neurons do not need to conduct the excitation far, but must be capable of receiving stimulation from a number of other neurons and of exciting a number more, in turn. *Sensory* and *motor* neurons, on the other hand, must usually be relatively long, for the former must conduct excitation from the periphery into the central nervous system whereas the latter must conduct excitation from the central nervous system to the *effectors* (muscles and glands). The short dendrites and the cell bodies of vertebrate olfactory cells are located peripherally, in the nasal mucosa, and conduction to the brain is by way of the long axons of these cells. On the other hand, in the vertebrate body pain and pressure are detected by the dendritic endings of sensory neurons, the cell bodies of which lie close to the spinal cord, so that in this case the conductor region consists of a very long dendrite and a much shorter axon. The

Figure 15.2 □ Functional regions of neurons: (*a, b*) bipolar neurons; (*c*) unipolar neuron. The generator regions are shown in color, conductor regions in gray, and transmitter regions in color tint.

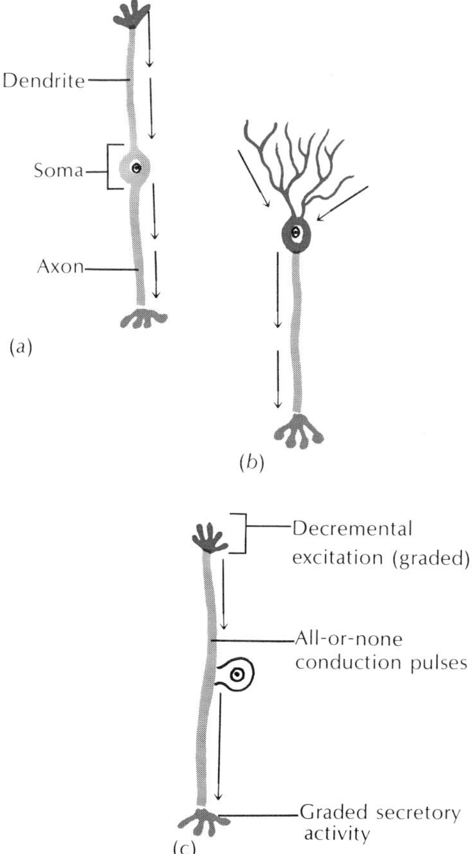

longest of all vertebrate neurons are *proprioceptive* ("self-sensing") sensory neurons, the dendritic endings of which terminate in tension-sensing organs located in muscles and joints. The conductive pathway of these neurons passes into the spinal cord and forward to the brain without interruption, a distance of many meters in such huge vertebrates as whales. Cells of such extreme length (despite a diameter of only a few micrometers) allow the animal to make rapid adjustments in posture and muscle tone. In contrast to sensory neurons, the conductive portion of a *motor* neuron consists mainly of the long axon, extending from the central nervous system to the effector being innervated.

The transmitter portion of a neuron consists of its axon endings. As a rule these secrete chemical transmitter substances (to be discussed below) capable of arousing the cells with which they come in contact; these substances are secreted across a junction known as a *synapse*. The neuron's transmitter region has undergone selection toward secretory performance and toward the increased surface area that is needed to excite the cell on the far side of this synaptic junction.

To summarize, in the course of evolution neurons have tended to become regionally specialized, their generator regions increasingly sensitive (but usually only with respect to specific types of stimuli), their conductor regions more elongate (when necessary), and their transmitter regions better adapted for the excitation of other cells. These adaptations have facilitated the acquisition and transmission of data and the speedy instigation of appropriate responses to such data.

A Excitability and the behavior of cell membranes

In Chapter 14 we found that cell membranes are capable of selectively regulating the materials that pass through them. As we shall see, the irritability of cells generally seems to depend on this capability for active transport and selective permeability with respect to ions. The excitation of a cell is accompanied by a flow of these electrically-charged particles across the cell membrane, which generates an electrical current that can be monitored by such instruments as a galvanometer or oscilloscope.

When a cell is stimulated at one point, a wave of excitation can be set up that will spread without decrement over the entire cell surface. This wave of excitation, the *action potential,* is an all-or-none event: it either occurs at maximum intensity or does not occur at all. The stimulus must reach a certain *threshold* strength before an action potential is set off; at subthreshold levels a localized change in membrane behavior is elicited, which initiates a graded wave of excitation that spreads *decrementally* from the point of stimulation. This decremental current, the *generator potential,* if strong enough constitutes the primer that sets off the action potential.

To clarify the above, let us consider the following analogy. Only a gun which is loaded can be fired. The cocked hammer has potential energy that is converted to kinetic energy when the trigger is squeezed. When the hammer falls upon the cartridge, the chemical energy of the stored gunpowder is transformed into the kinetic energy of the speeding bullet. The pressure of the finger on the trigger can be graded, like the generator potential, but when the bullet is fired, this is an all-or-none event, like the action potential. Before excitation a cell is like a loaded pistol ready to be fired. The potential energy to be transformed into the generator and action currents is present in the form of an *unequal distribution of ions* across the plasma membrane (Figure 15.3): both anions and cations are unequally distributed.

1 More *anions* occur within the cytoplasm than in the extracellular fluid. Whereas the most abundant extracellular anion is Cl^-, cytoplasmic anions are predominantly proteins that ionize negatively at the pH typical of living cells. Due to an excess of negatively charged ions within the cell, an electrochemical gradient amounting to 75 to 100 mV exists across the plasma membrane of the unexcited cell. The membrane is consequently polarized, for its inner surface is electronegative to its outer surface.

2 Although the total concentration of *cations* is about the same outside and within the cell, the major cations in each compartment are not the same. The cell selectively excludes one cation (usually Na^+) while retaining equivalent amounts of another (K^+). Each cation must be restrained from following its concentration gradient across the membrane, a task that requires uninterrupted energy expenditure by the cell. Upon excitation, however, the membrane at the point of stimulation seems briefly to be unable to prevent these cations from crossing it in accordance with their diffusion tendency. The essential effect of a stimulus may therefore be a momentary arrestment of the active transport mechanisms by

Figure 15.3 □ **Ion distribution within animal cell and milieu. Note that the extracellular milieu is electrically neutral because of balance between anions and cations, whereas the cell interior is electronegative to the exterior because of a preponderance of anions, which are mainly cytoplasmic proteins (Pr^-). The major cytoplasmic cation is K^+, whereas the major extracellular cation is Na^+. These cations are prevented from attaining equilibrium by the cell's active-transport mechanisms that exclude Na^+ and concentrate K^+ within the cell. Cations are shown in gray, and anions in solid color.**

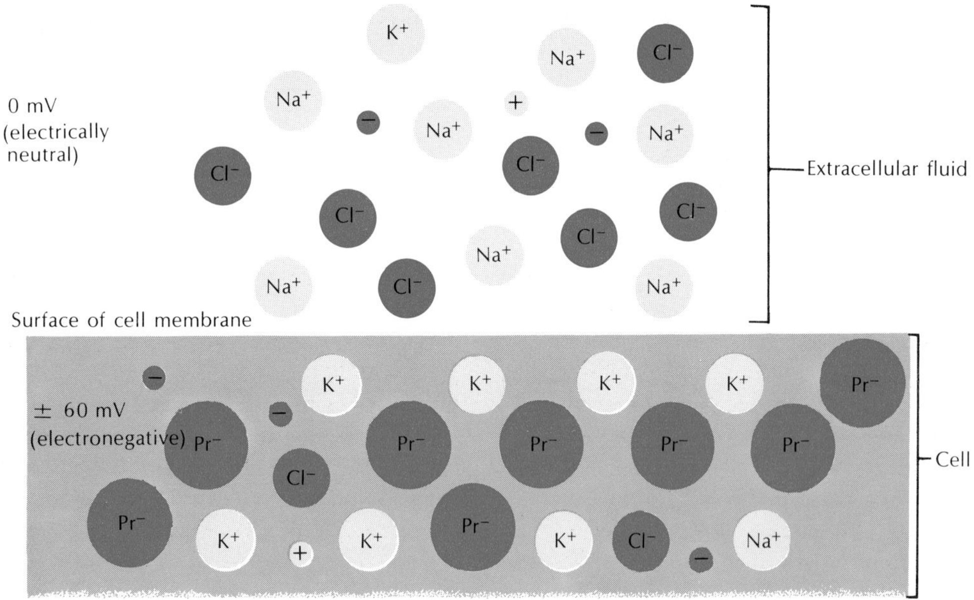

which one ion is excluded from the cell and the other kept in. The resulting cation flow alters the electrochemical potential across the membrane, for both cations do not move at the same moment. First, the ion usually excluded leaks into the cell at the point of stimulation, rendering it less electronegative (or even electropositive) with respect to the environment. This depolarization or reversal of polarity sets up a flow of electrical excitation between the affected region and adjacent points on the membrane, exciting these in turn, so that the excitation propagates as a wave sweeping across the entire membrane. Immediately after one part of the membrane has been excited, its original potential is restored by an equivalent outflow of the major cytoplasmic cation. This reestablishes the former interior electronegativity and in effect "reloads the gun for the next shot."

INVESTIGATIONS WITH GIANT ALGAL CELLS Both plant and animal cells respond similarly to stimulation. The major difference is in the greater *speed* with which animal cells respond. Giant cells of the fresh water alga *Chara* may be 15 cm long and 1.5 mm in diameter and make excellent subjects for experimentation, for a stimulus can be applied at one point on the cell membrane and its effect registered at a point some distance away. Furthermore such cells are large enough for electrodes to be inserted easily into their interior without demonstrable harm.

When a point stimulus is applied to the membrane of a *Chara* cell a decremental wave of excitation (the generator potential) is set up. This damps out with distance but should the stimulus be of great enough intensity or sufficient duration, the membrane polarity in the excited region gradually declines to some 75 to 90 percent of its "resting" value. Somewhere within this range a threshold is crossed that triggers an all-or-none event, the aforementioned *action potential.* At this moment the membrane (in the excited region) becomes fully permeable to the major cation usually excluded from the cell (in *Chara* this ion is Ca^{2+}), and the sudden influx of this cation causes a fluctuation of about 100 mV from the resting potential. Because this change is sufficient to affect the permeability of adjacent parts of the membrane to the extent that these parts too reach the threshold of full excitation, the action current spreads out nondecrementally at the rate of a few centimeters per second in all directions from its point of origin until the whole cell has been affected.

The wave of excitation which is the action potential appears on an oscilloscope as a *spike* having a wave form and propagation speed characteristic of the particular kind of cell. In a *Chara* cell such a spike takes about 20 sec to develop and return to normal, as compared with a spike duration of about 1 msec for a mammalian neuron or 2 msec for a squid giant axon. The ascending slope of the spike reflects the inflow of Ca^{2+}; the descending slope, the efflux of K^+ which restores the resting potential. During these seconds of recovery the alga cell is *refractory* (unresponsive) to further stimulation. By contrast, a mammalian neuron recovers from the passage of an action potential in only 0.5 to 2 msec, so that one spike after another can travel along the nerve fiber, spaced little more than this brief interval apart.

The functional significance of the action potential in plant cells remains open to speculation. In some plants it may spread from cell to cell, but it does not do so in *Chara.* It may have some effect on the plant's tropistic growth movements. Certainly it is interesting to find the mechanism of excitation to be so similar in cells as far apart phylogenetically as an alga cell and an animal neuron.

THE NERVE IMPULSE A nerve impulse is an action potential set up across the membrane of a neuron. Much of our present understanding of the nerve impulse rests on investigations of the behavior of giant squid axons, which may exceed 1 mm in diameter and remain excitable for some time after removal from the animal's body.

Due to the unequal distribution of ions, an electrical potential of about 60 mV exists across the membrane of the resting axon, the interior of the membrane being electronegative to the exterior. When a stimulus is applied to one point on the axon membrane, the membrane at that point undergoes a reversal of polarity due to an increase in its permeability to Na^+, which is usually excluded from the cell. As Na^+ enters the cell at this point, the inside of the membrane becomes about 40 mV *positive* to the exterior, an overall change of about 100 mV. This change is registered by oscilloscope as the ascending arm of the spike (Figure 15.4). At the instant of maximal deviation from the resting potential, the axon membrane once more becomes impermeable to Na^+, but now becomes permeable to K^+. This cation now follows *its* concentration gradient, moving out of the cell and thereby restoring the original polarity of the membrane. This phase is recorded as the descending arm of the spike, and represents the *absolute* refrac-

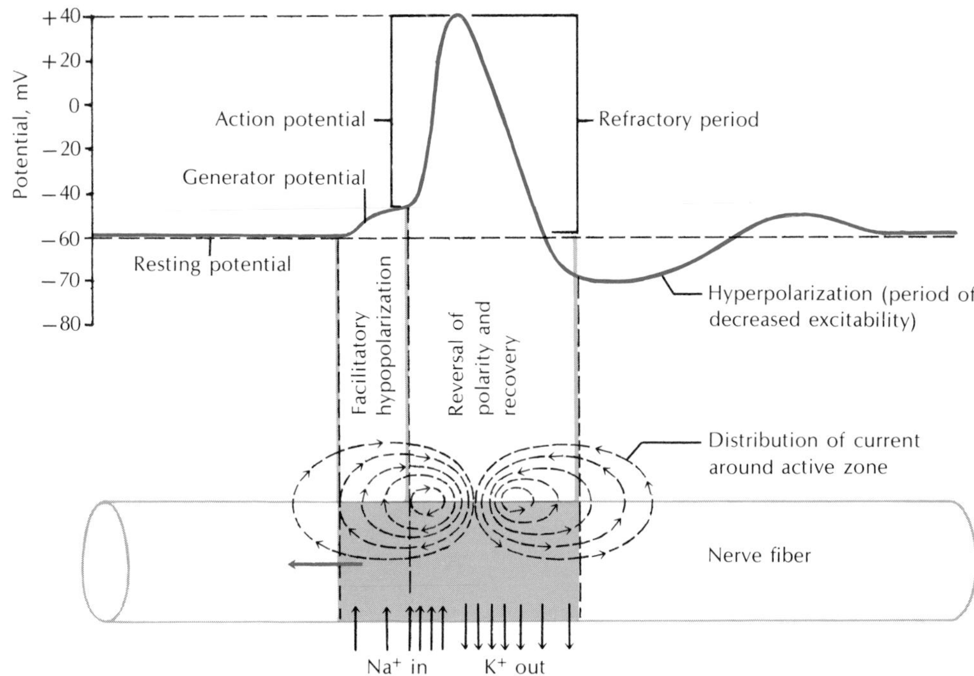

Figure 15.4 □ The nerve impulse: a single impulse, or "spike," as recorded by oscillograph, is correlated with changes in ionic distribution across the membrane of the nerve fiber. The color arrow indicates the direction of propagation of the nerve impulse.

tory period, during which the membrane at that point is unexcitable. Usually a little more K^+ is lost than is needed to just restore the resting potential. This loss constitutes an "overshoot," for the brief duration of which the membrane is *hyperpolarized* by the excessive interior electronegativity, and is therefore partially refractory to stimulation.

How is it possible to measure the ionic exchange involved in generating a nerve impulse? This has been done by use of the radioisotopes ^{24}Na and ^{42}K. Axons soaked in seawater containing ^{24}Na were found to take up very little Na^+ except when excited. On the other hand, axons soaked in seawater containing ^{42}K without being stimulated soon became saturated with this isotope, after which they were removed to plain seawater for testing. Here they were found to give up a certain amount of ^{42}K at the passage of each impulse. Measurement of the amount of radioisotope taken up or lost at the passage of each impulse indicated that the squid axon takes up 3.5 pmole* of Na^+ per square centimeter of membrane, and loses approximately the same quantity of K^+. This is actually a very limited exchange of ions per impulse, but with repeated excitation eventually both cations would be randomly distributed if the cell had no means of reversing this flow. Should Na^+ and K^+ continue to change places even in such small increments, they would eventually reach equilibrium on both sides of the membrane and the cell would no longer be excitable. However, this does not take place, for the ionic flow accompanying excitation is opposed by an energy-requiring recovery process whereby the cell's cation-pump mechanisms expell Na^+ and accumulate K^+ against their respective concentration gradients. These "pumps" function at all times other than the precise moment at which a generator or action potential is traversing a given region of the cell membrane. Their action requires O_2 and ATP.

Although much attention has been given the nerve impulse, which is of particular adaptive significance in propagating excitation from one part of the body to another (say, from a sense organ to the central nervous system or from the latter to the muscles), within the central nervous system itself many neurons have fibers so short that the decremental generator current can spread to all parts of the membrane and bring about the release of transmitter substances at the synapses. Such association neurons may never have occasion to fire a nerve impulse. *Decremental conduction* is especially significant in the functioning of the brain, for its graded (rather than all-or-

*Picamole; 1 pmole equals 10^{-12} mole.

none) character makes possible a more precisely graduated effect at the synapse.

SPEED OF CONDUCTION Coordination of the rapid and complex movements executed by higher animals depends upon the rapidity with which nerve impulses can travel throughout the body. The conduction rate characteristic of a given neuron increases with temperature (which explains in part why a lizard warmed by the sun will react to danger so much more swiftly than one which is chilled), but its upper limit is determined by the fiber's diameter and the nature of its myelin sheath (see Figure 11.41*c, d*).

Because internal resistance to the spread of the action potential varies inversely with fiber diameter, large fibers conduct impulses more rapidly than do those of smaller diameter. Speed of conductance typically increases as the square of the fiber's diameter. Accordingly, one evolutionary pathway toward increased conduction speed has led to development of giant nerve fibers. This was the route followed by advanced invertebrates, which developed nerve fibers so large that they are often easily visible to the unaided eye. Unfortunately, achieving increased speed of conduction in this way levies a penalty on the future evolution of such nervous systems, for any increase in the size of individual neurons means that fewer neurons can be present. The nervous systems of advanced invertebrates must therefore be parsimonious in construction, with relatively few cells present to control even the complicated forms of instinctive behavior such invertebrates often show.

Vertebrates pursued another and ultimately more successful evolutionary pathway toward increased conduction speed: that of *saltatory conduction,* as made possible by *nodal* myelin sheaths. (By *saltatory* we mean "leaping": that is, excitation leaps from one point on the fiber to the next without exciting intervening portions.) Reviewing Figure 11.41*d,* we see that the myelin sheaths covering the fibers of many vertebrate peripheral neurons are made up of spirally wrapped layers of the membranes of Schwann cells that surround these fibers. The bare nerve fiber is exposed only at the *nodes,* or gaps in the sheath where one Schwann cell ends and the next begins. Between nodes the myelin sheath serves to insulate the fiber membrane from excitation. An action potential reaching the first node sets up a circuit that flows through the extracellular fluid to the next node in line, depolarizing the membrane at this point until the threshold is reached, at which another action potential is generated, and so on. In effect the excitation leaps from node to node, leaving all intervening parts of the membrane at rest (Figure 15.5). Because the resistance to conductance encountered in the milieu is so much less than that within the cell, the impulse can travel by such leaps much more rapidly than if it had to move along the entire membrane.

Although invertebrate nerve fibers often have thin myelin sheaths that protect them from stimulation along their length, only vertebrate neurons have nodally interrupted myelin sheaths that permit saltatory conduction (as just described). These myelin sheaths are also much thicker than those of invertebrates and may account for some 50 percent of the fiber's total diameter. As a result of saltatory conduction, cat myelinated fibers only 15 to 17 μm in diameter can conduct at a rate of 78 to 102 m/sec, whereas a giant squid axon 200 μm in diameter, but invested with a thin, non-nodal myelin sheath, can conduct at a rate of only 20 m/sec despite its much greater size.

Saltatory conduction has been of tremendous significance for the evolution of vertebrate nervous systems, for it has en-

Figure 15.5 □ Saltatory conduction.

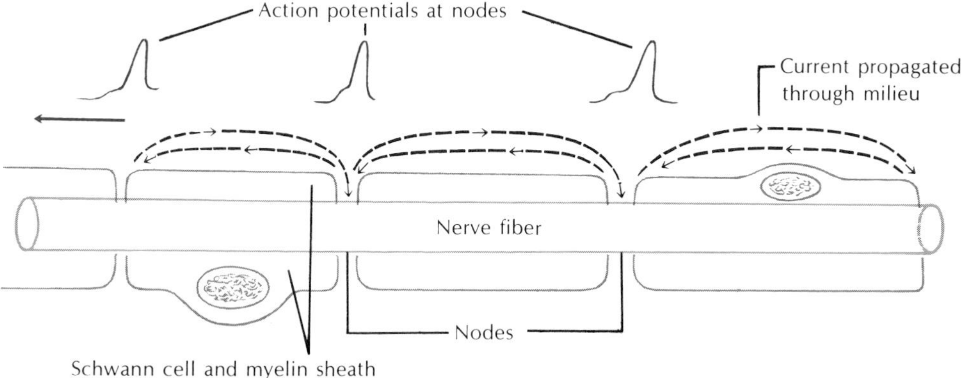

Figure 15.6 □ **Demonstration showing that stimulation of the vagus nerve of one excised heart (1) results in liberation of a chemical responsible for deceleration of heart 2. This experiment supports the hypothesis that chemical transmitter substances are released at nerve endings. In the graphs, each spike records one heartbeat; *S* represents electrical stimulus.**

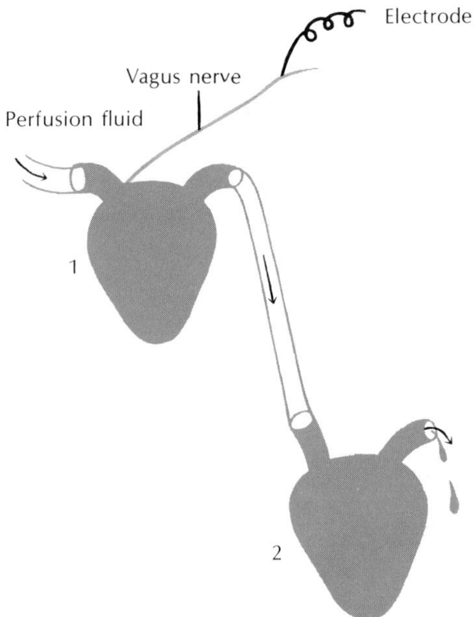

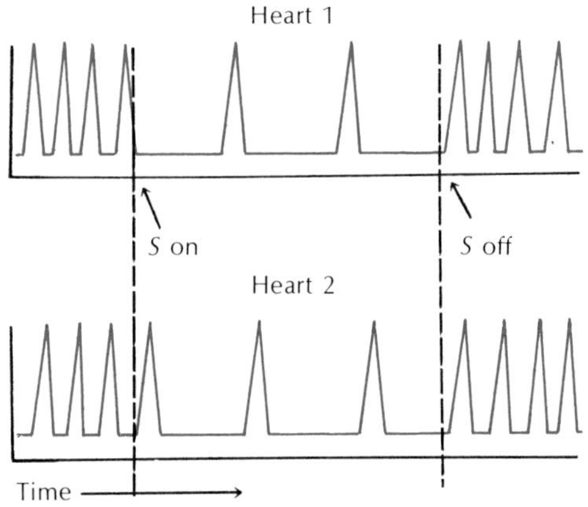

couraged *miniaturization* of the systems' components. If the speed of conduction necessary for advanced motor performance can be achieved with fibers of small diameter, much space can be saved as compared to that needed to accomodate giant fibers. This helps to explain why the lobster's nervous system contains less than 10^6 neurons, whereas that of the much smaller mouse contains at least 10^{11}.

B Synaptic transmission

A synapse is the junction between one neuron and the next, the term usually being extended as well to the junctions of neurons with the effector cells (gland cells and muscle fibers) they serve. A synapse consists of the axon endings (the presynaptic membrane), the membrane of the cell being affected (the postsynaptic membrane), and an intervening gap (the synaptic cleft), some 200 to 500 Å wide. An action potential cannot ordinarily jump across a synapse, and any effect exerted on the next cell is almost always chemically mediated. The *transmitter substances* are synthesized in the cell body of the neuron and flow through the cytoplasm of the axon to the terminals; here they are stored in vesicles of 200 to 400 Å diameter. When an action potential traveling down the axon reaches the terminals, it triggers a brief discharge of transmitter material, but many such discharges are required to exhaust the accumulated secretion and block further transmission ("synaptic fatigue").

Although electrochemical synaptic transmission is known to occur in a few cases, the chemical hypothesis of synaptic transmission has gained support from a number of experimental studies. One of the most striking in its simplicity was that of Otto Loewi, who perfused two excised turtle hearts with an isosmotic saline solution (Ringer's solution) so that it passed first through one heart and then through the chambers of the other (Figure 15.6). Like other myogenic hearts (see Section 14.2B), the turtle heart continues to beat when deprived of a nerve supply. However, if a mild electrical shock is applied to the stump of the severed vagus nerve, the heartbeat will slow down. With his perfusion arrangement, Loewi found that repeated stimulation of the vagus nerve of the first heart caused the second heart to slow down as well. This could be explained only on the basis of some chemical that was released by the tissues of the first heart and carried in the perfusion fluid to the second. This material was identified as acetylcholine, the first known transmitter substance.

The fact that synaptic transmission is usually brought about by chemical means has several significant corollaries. (1) Synaptic transmission is much slower than is the rate of conduction of a nerve impulse. Accordingly, the longer the nerve fiber, and the fewer the synaptic interruptions, the more rapidly may propagation of excitation occur. Even in such simple creatures as coelenterates there are usually a few "through-conduction" nerve fibers interconnecting synapses in distant parts of the body. (2) Except in coelenterates, synapses are directionalized, since only axon terminals are capable of liberating transmitter substance. If a nerve fiber is stimulated at some point along its length, excitation can spread in both directions from this point, but only that which reaches the axon terminals elicits secretion of transmitter material. (3) Synaptic transmission ceases when the accumulated transmitter substance is depleted, such synaptic fatigue continuing until a new supply of this material has been synthesized. (4) Both temporal and spatial *summation* can take place upon the postsynaptic membrane, since repeated or widespread exposure to small concentrations of transmitter substance can exert the same effect as a single larger dose. By *temporal* summation we mean that if subthreshold excitation is applied to one point at a high enough frequency, the postsynaptic membrane may gradually be depolarized to the level at which an action potential will finally be generated. By *spatial* summation we mean that the axons of several different neurons may terminate at different points on the same postsynaptic membrane, so that simultaneous low-intensity excitation from a number of these endings may reach threshold value by extending the generator potential over a larger area of the membrane. (5) Since neurons can produce different kinds of transmitter substances, the effect on the postsynaptic membrane may be either excitatory or inhibitory, according to whether the substance causes the membrane to become depolarized or hyperpolarized. In fact, there is evidence that one and the same neuron can release an excitatory transmitter substance from some of its axon endings and an inhibitory material from others.

IPSP AND EPSP *Inhibitory* transmitter substances make the cell *less* excitable by *increasing* its electronegativity to a level even higher than when it is "at rest." They do this by increasing the membrane's permeability only to smaller ions such as Cl^- and K^+ (Na^+ is larger than either of these because when hydrated it is covered by a thick sheath of water molecules). The interior of the cell becomes more electronegative either by taking up Cl^- or losing K^+. The resultant hyperpolarized condition of the cell membrane is termed an *inhibitory postsynaptic potential* (IPSP).

Excitatory transmitter substances *decrease* the cell's interior electronegativity by slightly increasing the membrane's permeability to Na^+. The resultant local partial depolarization of the membrane is known as an *excitatory postsynaptic potential* (EPSP), which is simply a generator current set up by the action of a transmitter substance on the postsynaptic membrane.

Both excitatory and inhibitory terminals may terminate on the generator region of the same neuron, especially within the central nervous system, so that the average membrane potential of such a neuron is a blend representing the sum of all EPSPs and IPSPs generated (Figure 15.7). As many as 1,000 axon endings may encrust the generator region (including the cell body) of each neuron in the mammalian brain, and the depolarizing and hyperpolarizing stimuli provided by these endings may be in such delicate balance that only the most minute change in their proportions will suffice to make the neuron fire. Some neurons in fact seem to undergo a spontaneous oscillation in cation permeability which, superimposed on a basal state of near-threshold arousal, may cause them to fire periodic bursts of impulses without any new external stimulation. Axons ending on these neurons may serve mainly to inhibit such spontaneous bursts when they are not needed.

TYPES OF TRANSMITTER SUBSTANCES

Figure 15.7 □ EPSPs and IPSPs being generated on dendrites and soma of an association neuron. Whether or not this neuron will fire depends on the net hypo- or hyperpolarization of its membrane, as determined by the sum of excitatory and inhibitory discharges upon the membrane. IPSPs are shown by concentric circles around the inhibitory terminals (in gray), and EPSPs, around the excitatory terminals (in color tint).

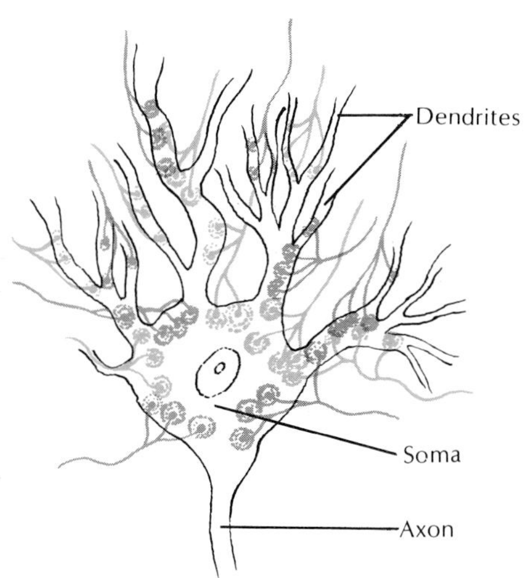

The most widely occurring synaptic transmitter substance is acetylcholine:

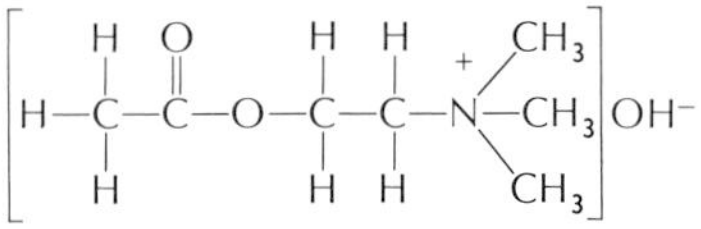

$$\left[\begin{array}{c} \text{H O H H CH}_3 \\ \text{H—C—C—O—C—C—N}^+\text{—CH}_3 \\ \text{H H H CH}_3 \end{array}\right] OH^-$$

Acetylcholine

Synapses at which acetylcholine are released are termed *cholinergic,* and include myoneural junctions (between nerves and muscle fibers) and all other known excitatory peripheral junctions in the vertebrate body, except the endings of sympathetic fibers on the organs they serve. The enzyme *cholinesterase* is also released at cholinergic junctions, serving to inactivate acetylcholine within 2 msec of its release. This allows each spurt of acetylcholine to act as a fresh stimulus upon the postsynaptic membrane, allowing the membrane's polarity to regenerate between stimuli.

Adrenergic synapses, those at which *adrenaline* (or sometimes *noradrenaline*)

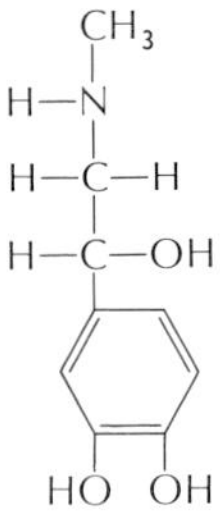

Adrenaline (epinephrine)

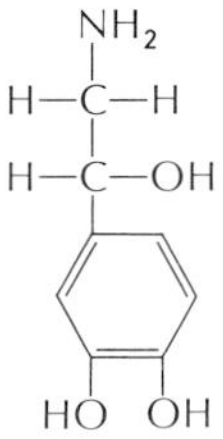

Noradrenaline (norepinephrine)

is liberated, occur at least in arthropods, molluscs, annelids, and vertebrates. In vertebrates, adrenergic synapses are restricted to glands and visceral muscles, including the heart.

Transmitter substances released within the central nervous system await further identification. *Serotonin* (5-hydroxytryptamine, or 5-HT), known as a peripheral transmitter substance in invertebrates, may also activate parasympathetic centers in the vertebrate brain. γ-*Aminobutyric acid* (GABA), an amino acid isolated from the mammalian brain in significant quantities, has been cited as a possible inhibitory transmitter, but this requires further evidence.

15.2 □ RECEPTION

We have noted that in most kinds of animals a receptor is simply the generator ending of a sensory neuron, specialized for particular sensitivity to some specific type of stimulus. Certain vertebrate receptors are specialized epithelial cells that can transduce the stimulus energy into some form capable of exciting the dendritic endings of the sensory neurons that terminate upon these receptor cells.

A *sense organ* is formed when one or more receptors are grouped with nonreceptor cells that somehow enhance their performance. One of the simplest of vertebrate sense organs is the Pacinian corpuscle (Figure 15.8), a pressure-sensing organ barely visible to the naked eye and consisting of concentric layers of modified connective tissue investing the sensory dendritic ending. This ending is still excitable if the covering is removed, but the capsule normally serves to equalize pressure over the entire receptor ending, thereby widening the area of membrane over which a generator potential is elicited. A much more complex sense organ is an eye, the receptors of which are photosensitive cells that are often associated with a lens, connective tissue, muscles that allow the eye to be moved and its focal length to be altered, and so forth. Before considering specific types of sense organs let us review the fundamental properties of stimuli and receptors in a more general way.

A The nature of stimuli

A *stimulus* is a change in the external or internal environment that causes a response in a receptor cell. Its *intensity* must exceed a certain minimum threshold value for the receptor to be excited, although (as we have said) subthreshold stimuli administered in rapid enough sequence may summate to cause excitation. The effectiveness of a stimulus also depends on the *rate of change.* Constant conditions do not act as stimuli, since receptors adapt to such conditions and are not excited by them. If a change takes place so slowly that it is kept

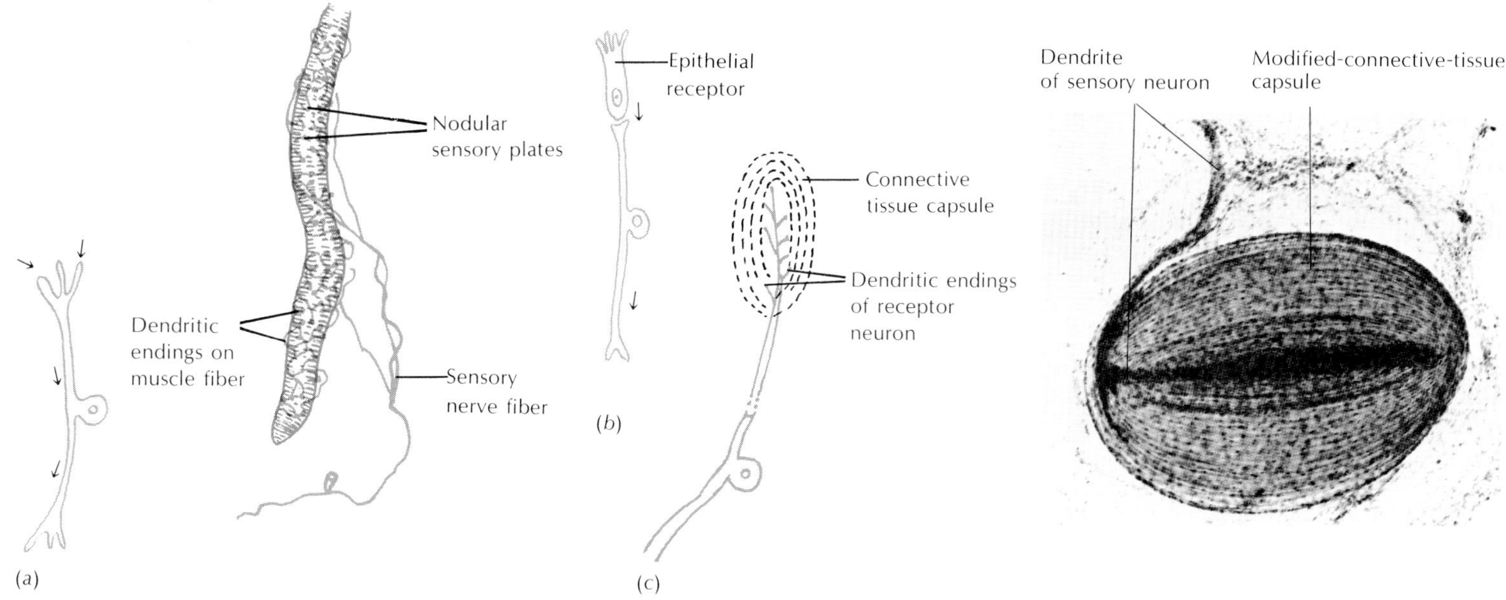

Figure 15.8 □ **Receptor and sense organ: (*a*) left, diagram of receptor neuron and, right, arborization of receptor-neuron dendrites on muscle fiber; (*b*) a sensory neuron; (*c*) left, a simple sense organ and, right, photograph of a sense organ, a Pacinian corpuscle (*courtesy of Carolina Biological Supply Company*).**

pace with by adaptation, the change will be undetected. If we were to watch a flower opening through the length of a day, we would not actually see the petals unfolding, for the rate of change is so slow that our eyes cannot detect the change while it is occurring. Furthermore, a change in the environment will not act as a stimulus if it is outside the *range of acuity* of the organism's receptors. We perceive as light only those electromagnetic vibrations lying between 400 and 700 nm, whereas some other species detect much shorter wavelengths but are blind to the red end of the spectrum. Vibrations of the air ranging from about 20 to 20,000 Hz (hertz)* are detected as sound by the human ear, whereas the acoustic sensitivity of bats may extend as high as 150,000 Hz. Sensitivity to such high frequencies is related to the bat's ability to emit short bursts of ultrasound (beyond the human acoustic range) that are reflected off solid objects and enable the bat to avoid obstacles and detect flying insects by *echo location* (Figure 15.9).

How can one set about determining experimentally the limits of an animal's sensory acuity? This is a difficult feat, but if the animal being tested is amenable to training, it can be taught to perform some action upon presentation of a signal, for instance a musical tone. The pitch can then be varied, and the points at which the animal fails to respond for apparent want of signal detection can be taken as the limits of its sensory acuity. Within this range, its ability to discriminate between adjacent tones can also be tested by rewarding its response to one tone and not giving a reward if the subject wrongly responds to a tone that differs by a few hertz. With practice, human subjects can learn to discriminate among some 15,000 different pitches,

*One hertz equals one vibration per second.

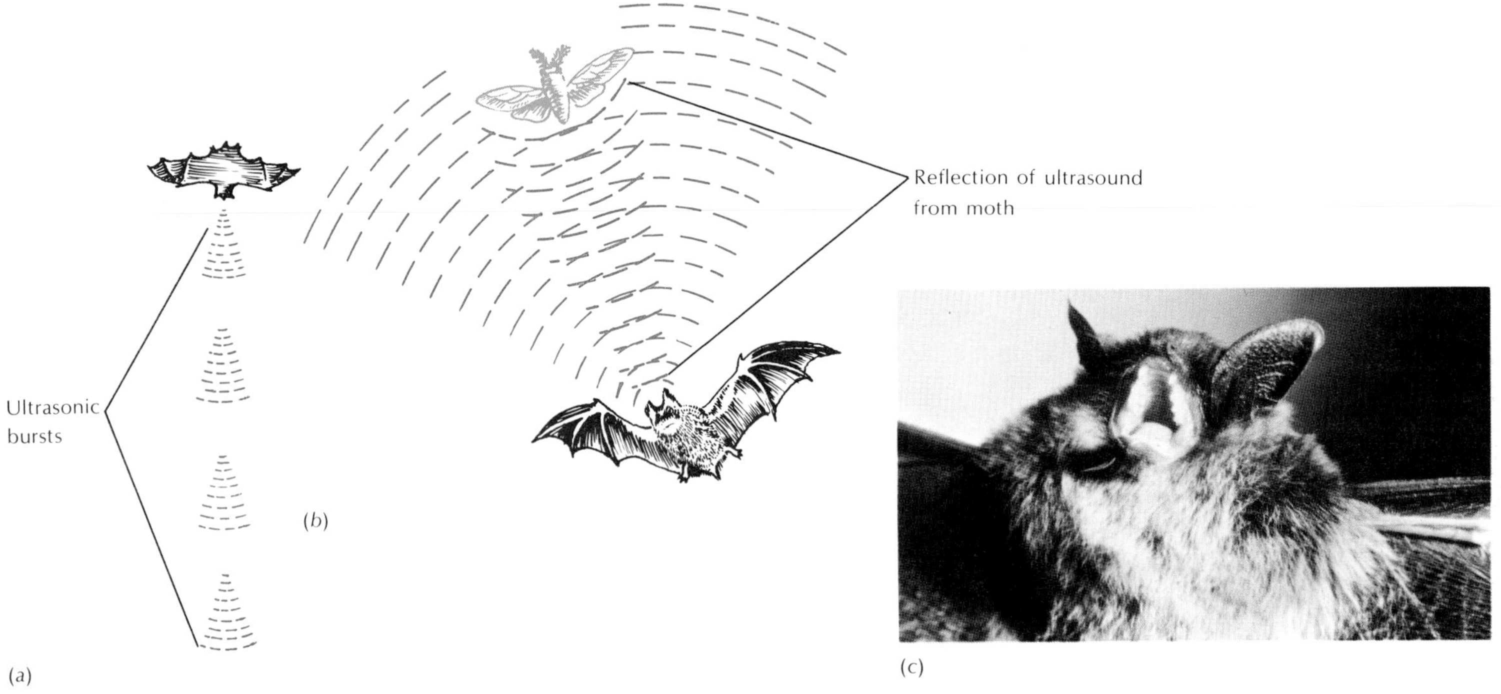

Figure 15.9 □ **Echolocation: (*a*) bats emit short bursts of ultrasound that are reflected (*b*) off solid objects. (*c*) The photograph shows large external ears (pinnas) that collect these rebounding sound waves. (*Los Angeles County Museum of Natural History.*)**

successive tones differing by little more than 1 Hz!

A stimulus may furnish either a positive or negative signal. Usually a stimulus involves energy *input,* but receptors sensitive to cold, for example, are excited by a *reduction* in energy level, caused by a loss of thermal kinetic energy. Either a positive or a negative signal can excite a receptor or inhibit it, according to whether the change hyperpolarizes or depolarizes the cell membrane. If a certain environmental change acts as a stimulus, then a change back to the original condition serves as a stimulus of opposite sign—that is, if the initial change is excitatory, cessation of the signal will be inhibitory for a brief moment. We are all familiar with the fact than when an engine starts up, we are aroused by the sound but soon become unaware of it if it remains a constant drone. When at last it stops we are momentarily aroused by what seems a profound silence. Thus the cessation of sound can serve as a stimulus just as much as the onset of sound.

Although a stimulus may be sufficient to promote a response (such as an action potential) in the single receptor cell, no response is usually forthcoming by the organism unless a *number* of receptors fire together for some period of time: when a continuous inflow of impulses excites association neurons in the central nervous system, the process of integration begins. We shall consider integration a bit later, but should now note that even though a stimulus may both excite the receptors and arouse the central nervous system, a response by the organism may still not be forthcoming if the stimulus does not constitute a meaningful part of the animal's *Umwelt* (the succinct German term for its "perceptual world"). Reception is the role of the receptors, but *perception* is largely the result of integration of data in the central nervous system. Despite the acuity of the animal's receptors, if the signal is not meaningful at the *perceptual* level, the organism will not respond to it. On the other hand, certain stimulus configurations are so significant that they trigger specific responses even when presented out of meaningful context. In Section 4.2D we noted that such *sign stimuli* (releasers) can often be identified by the use of simplified models that elicit the response while a realistic model lacking the sign stimulus evokes no response (see Figure 4.13).

According to the type of energy involved, stimuli may be classified as *radiant, thermal, chemical, electrical,* and *mechanical.* The latter include changes in pressure and tension caused by stretching, vibration, compression, and so forth. Receptors are specialized to respond only to stimuli of one modality. The so-called *adequate stimulus* is that specific stimulus energy capable of eliciting the greatest change in the cell's excitability. An acoustic receptor will not normally respond to light, or an eye to sound. Nevertheless, if the receptor should be stimulated by an inappropriate stimulus, the resultant sensation will be interpreted in terms of the usual function of that receptor. For instance, pressure applied at the inner corner of the eye affects the retina and produces the sensation of a ring of light. This is because nerve fibers from the retina run to the *visual* centers of the brain and not to the pressure-sensing areas.

B Properties of receptors

A receptor's location in the body influences the type and source of the information it can gather. Those located near the body surface are best fitted for monitoring external conditions. Animal skin is richly provided with a variety of such *exteroceptors.* The skin of a man, for instance, is estimated to contain some 4×10^6 pain endings, 5×10^5 touch and pressure receptors, and 1.5×10^5 cold and 1.6×10^4 heat receptors. These are not evenly distributed over the body surface. Touch receptors, for instance, are much more closely spaced on the fingertips and face than on the back.

Vertebrate exteroceptors tend to be most concentrated in the head. The portrait of a rattlesnake (Figure 15.10) shows some of the ways in which the snake is provided with detailed information on its surroundings. The nostrils lead into the nasal cavity where receptors sensitive to odors are located. The snake's tongue collects air-borne molecules on its moist forked tip, which is then thrust into a special organ of taste or smell located in the roof of the mouth (the vomeronasal organ). The eyes of course are responsible for vision. There are no external ear openings shown in this picture, because these are lacking in snakes, but sense organs of balance and hearing are both located in the inner ears, buried within the skull bones in back of the eyes. Anterior to each eye is a deep facial pit, the sensory function of which was established experimentally. It was once thought that rattlesnakes depended mainly on the sense of smell to locate prey in the dark. It there-

Figure 15.10 □ **Concentration of external receptors in the head of a rattlesnake. The tongue is used to introduce air-borne molecules into the olfactory Jacobsen's organ in the roof of the mouth. Thermoceptive pits that detect warmth are visible between the eyes and nostrils. The vertical pupil, allowing the eye to function efficiently under a wide range of illumination, is characteristic of a number of species that hunt both by night and by day. (*Zoological Society of San Diego.*)**

fore came as a surprise to find that a hungry snake would strike a balloon as readily as it would a rat, provided that the balloon was filled with warm air! Neither a cold balloon nor a cold, dead rat would prompt the snake to strike. What other tests might also be used to determine the relative importance of different senses in the food-getting success of various animals?

Internal conditions are monitored by receptors located deep within the body (*interoceptors*), in the muscles, joints, the walls of hollow organs, and the mesenteries. *Proprioceptors* are internal receptors concerned with postural maintenance and monitoring the body's position in space.

TYPES OF RECEPTORS According to the type of stimulus detected, receptors are classified into radioreceptors, thermoreceptors, chemoreceptors, mechanoreceptors, and electroreceptors. The senses of man are summarized in Table 15.1. It is easy to see that, despite tradition, many more than five senses can be enumerated. It is doubtful that man possesses specific electroreceptors, but the other types of receptors are present in abundance.

Radioreceptors are sensitive to radiations of the electromagnetic spectrum. Experiments are still in progress to discover the full variety of radioreceptors possessed by various animals. Most animals apparently see as light the band of frequencies visible to our own eyes, but the range of acuity may be shifted toward one end of the spectrum or the other: some animals can see in the ultraviolet but are blind to red, whereas others may detect infrared but not blue light. We detect infrared waves as heat rather than light.

Whereas we ourselves can be bathed in

Table 15.1 □ The senses of man

SENSE	LOCATION OF RECEPTORS		GENERAL TYPE OF RECEPTOR
Taste (4 acuities)	Taste buds of tongue	Restricted to head	Chemoreceptor
Olfaction ($\pm$ 7 acuities)	Nasal epithelium	Restricted to head	Chemoreceptor
Sight (in dim light; scotopic)	Retina of eye (rods)	Restricted to head	Radioreceptor
Color vision (photopic)	Retina of eye (cones)	Restricted to head	Radioreceptor
Hearing	Cochlea of inner ear	Restricted to head	Mechanoreceptor
Head position (static balance)	Saccule and utricle of inner ear	Restricted to head	Mechanoreceptor
Head movements in space (dynamic balance)	Semicircular canals of inner ear	Restricted to head	Mechanoreceptor
Touch (hairless skin)	Dermis of skin (Meissner's corpuscles)		Mechanoreceptor
Touch (on hairs)	Dermis of skin (plexus around hair follicles)		Mechanoreceptor
Heat	Dermis of skin (Ruffini ending), wall of alimentary tract, hypothalamus of brain		Unknown (radio- and/or mechano-receptor
Cold (reduction in molecular kinetic energy)	Probably similar distribution (Krause's end bulb in skin)		Probably mechano-receptor
Pain	General somatic and visceral (except brain)		Probably chemo-receptor
Thirst[a]	Back of pharynx		Probably osmo-receptor[b]
Muscle position and state of tension	Muscles, tendons, joints (muscle spindles)		Mechanoreceptor
Distension of hollow organs	Walls of blood vessels, alimentary tract (aortic and carotid bodies, and the like)		Mechanoreceptor
Blood pH and CO_2 concentration	Walls of large arteries, portions of brain concerned with regulation of breathing and heart rate		Chemoreceptor
Blood osmotic pressure	Hypothalamus of brain		Osmoreceptor
Pressure, surface and internal	Pacinian corpuscles in dermis, mesenteries, and the like		Mechanoreceptor

[a] Thirst is considered a specific sense, but hunger is a complex *sensation* arising not only from the increased motility of an empty stomach but from psychogenic factors as well.

[b] Osmoreceptors may be a kind of chemoreceptor.

a lethal flood of X rays and injured beyond hope of recovery while our senses give no warning, such insects as moths seem to be able actually to see X rays. Two types of experimental findings support this conclusion: (1) the insect retina begins to fire impulses when exposed to mild doses of X rays; (2) moths kept in the dark until their eyes are dark-adapted begin to fly when exposed to X rays in doses as low as 0.01 roentgens/sec. Since this response is not given by moths whose eyes have had no time to become dark-adapted before being stimulated, we know that they do not merely feel the rays instead of seeing them. There is also some evidence that a number of animals may be sensitive to the "lines of force" of the earth's magnetic field and use these in their orientation. However, attempts to prove that migratory birds use magnetic cues are open to question.

Thermoreceptors seem to be of two distinct types: those that respond to being warmed and those that respond to chilling. We do not yet know exactly what the nature of the stimulus is to which thermoreceptors are attuned. It seems likely that they respond to changes in the thermal kinetic energy of molecules, or that some thermosensitive metabolic reaction within the receptor undergoes a significant rate change that is responsible for the cell's excitation.

Although attempts have been made to associate thermoreception with definite formed organs (such as the Ruffini and Krause endings in human skin), in the most carefully investigated cases thermoreceptors seem to be merely free dendritic endings. Such free branches innervate the aforementioned facial pits of rattlesnakes. These are the most acute thermoreceptive organs known. A rattlesnake requires but 0.5 sec to detect a rat-sized object placed in its cage at a distance of 40 cm if the object is but 10°C warmer than its surroundings!

Cold receptors are thought to be excited by a reduction in thermal kinetic energy or perhaps by the cessation of some specific heat-dependent chemical reaction. Their distinctness from heat receptors is indicated by the fact that in human subjects the distribution of "cold spots" on the skin (that is, spots where the subject reports a cold sensation when touched with a chilled needle) is different from the distribution mapped for "hot spots."

Chemoreceptors are excited by contact with certain molecules or ions. Olfactory receptors detect volatile molecules borne in air or water from external and often distant sources. Taste receptors also detect materials from the external milieu but respond to relatively few types of substances and require these in considerably greater concentrations. Internal chemoreceptors respond to changes in blood pH and osmotic pressure.

Mechanoreceptors are excited by the mechanical distortion of their membranes, as by pressure, tension, or vibrations of the medium. There is a wide variety of mechanoreceptors, some monitoring external environmental conditions, others informing the organism on the state of its own body. Sensations of touch, of fullness in the hollow organs, of muscle tension and body position in space, all are due to impulses sent to the brain by various mechanoreceptors. Acoustic receptors detect vibrations of the external milieu within a certain range of frequencies, and the brain interprets these vibrations as sound.

Electroreceptors that detect weak electrical currents are undoubtedly possessed at least by those electric fishes that generate weak electrical fields for aid in "radar" location of prey (see Section 16.31). Any receptor can of course be stimulated by direct electric shock, but such a stimulus is interpreted in terms of that receptor's own acuities, based on the part of the brain to which those fibers run. A mild shock applied to the tongue, for instance, is experienced as taste, for the fibers stimulated run to the gustatory centers of the brain.

RANGE FRACTIONATION An important evolutionary trend has been for receptors and the neurons with which they communicate to divide up the range of sensory acuity so that much more information can be obtained. For instance, color vision depends on there being present several types of photoreceptor, each most sensitive to a specific part of the spectrum. Furthermore, analysis of vertebrate retinal organization shows that the receptors and the neurons on which they converge form functional units that respond maximally only to certain aspects of the stimulus. For instance, the retina of a frog's eye is a mosaic of no less than four types of unit differing in excitability. Some units are excited only when the photoreceptors in one part of the unit are illuminated and the balance shaded; these serve as "edge detectors," for they sharpen the outlines of objects seen. Other units that respond to light-dark interfaces (but only when these are moving) allow the frog to detect large moving objects, such as predators. The frog's escape reaction—a mighty leap—is best triggered by the excitation of retinal units that respond only when suddenly thrown into total shadow. Most essential to survival are the units that act as "bug detectors," excited only by small opaque objects that move against the background. (Frogs cannot recognize motionless insects as prey and, if offered only dead flies, will starve in the midst of plenty.) This type of functional diversification characterizes not only the retina but many parts of the vertebrate brain as well.

There is a proprioceptive sense organ in the crab leg that provides another and simpler example of range fractionation. The fact that arthropod nervous systems contain so few cells is helpful in these studies, for only a few nerve fibers have to be tested. Besides receptors that continue to monitor position when the leg is held still, this organ has been found to contain two kinds of motion detectors: one of these fires most strongly when the leg is moved slowly through about 1° of arc per second, whereas the other responds to more rapid movements amounting to at least 100°/sec. These three kinds of receptors keep the crab's brain informed as to the position of its legs when at rest and also provide information on the rate and extent of leg movement when in motion.

There are many other examples of ways in which a certain range of acuity is divided up among a number of receptors in such a way that more specific information can be sent to the brain. Sometimes range fractionation is due directly to a narrowing of the receptor's own range of sensitivity, while in other cases it may be due to some other property of the sense organ. Man's ability to distinguish between sounds of different pitch is thought to be due to the fact that the basilar membrane of the inner ear (see Section 15.2F) vibrates in sections to particular frequencies, so that only a fraction of the acoustic receptors are stimulated by any given tone. Here range fractionation is an outcome of the behavior of a portion of the sense organ larger than the individual receptor.

STIMULUS AMPLIFICATION Receptors can amplify stimulus energy at the same time that they transduce it into the energy of a nerve impulse. The cell's response may be dramatically out of proportion to the quantity of stimulus energy applied to its membrane. The hair cells of the mammalian inner ear are known to respond to displacements of less than the diameter of a hydrogen atom (1Å), and a single photon may suffice to excite some photoreceptors. The chemoreceptors on the antennae of a male moth are so sensitive that they respond to only one or two molecules of the sex-attractant secreted by the female.

Such extreme sensitivity has yet to be satisfactorily explained at the molecular-biological level. In the case of photoreception, at least, it has been proposed that absorption of one photon may initiate an enzyme cascade (see Section 13.2C) that allows the cell's final response to be catalyzed on a grand scale.

As well as the amplification effected by the receptors themselves, complex sense organs have often evolved additional means of intensifying the signal reaching the receptors. The mammalian middle ear bones serve to increase manyfold the pressure of sound entering the inner ear. The lens and cornea of an eye gather light from a wide visual field and focus it upon the much tinier retinal field. In addition, the retinas of many nocturnal animals are backed by a reflective pigment layer, the *tapetum,* that reflects light back through the retina for a 100 percent gain that allows these animals to see well in dim light. When struck by a beam of light the tapetum glows red in crocodiles, orange in bears and skunks, yellow in racoons, and so forth; thus a "guidebook to eyeshine" might be a worthwhile survival aid for those who like to walk abroad in the wilds at night (Figure 15.11).

PERIPHERAL AND CENTRAL MODULATION OF RECEPTION While responsible for feeding information into the central nervous system, receptors themselves are under the control of other neurons, both central and peripheral. Many receptors, or the neurons associated with them, receive axon collaterals (side branches) from nearby sensory cells. In all known cases impulses from these collaterals are *inhibitory.* This means that when a given sensory neuron is excited, it may be capable both of sending excitatory impulses toward the central nervous system and at the same time sending inhibitory impulses to neighboring sensory neurons. (This is understandable if we assume that in a single neuron some axon terminals are specialized to liberate an excitatory substance while others secrete an inhibitor.)

This type of *peripheral modulation* of reception can result in more meaningful information being sent to the brain, because of the screening effect possible at the level of the sense organ itself. In the insect compound eye, for example, each of the individual visual units (*ommatidia*) that make up this eye can, when excited, inhibit adjacent ommatidia from firing. This has the effect of sharpening contrasts between light and shadow and strengthening the outline of the object seen.

Figure 15.11 □ **Eyeshine of kit foxes. The reflective layer backing the retina enhances visual acuity under conditions of dim illumination.** (*Courtesy of C. E. Short.*)

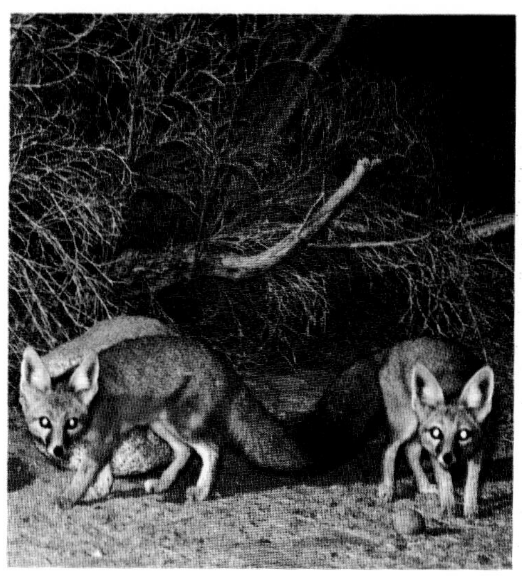

Central modulation can affect reception in a number of different ways. One clear-cut example of this is seen in the way that contraction of mammalian skeletal muscles is brought about through the action of nerve fibers from the central nervous system upon small tension-sensing organs (*muscle spindles*) located in the skeletal muscles themselves (Figure 15.12). Muscle spindles consist of small bundles of modified muscle fibers innervated by both sensory and motor neurons. The central portion of these fibers is noncontractile, whereas the two ends are contractile. Sensory nerve fibers terminating on the noncontractile section are stimulated either when the contractile portions of the spindle shorten, or when the whole region is put under load (that is, when the muscle is weighted). Motor fibers known as *γ-efferents* serve the contractile portions of the spindle. These fibers are axons of neurons located in the spinal cord, which are controlled in turn by impulses from three sources: (1) sensory impulses relayed from the sensory neurons serving the muscle spindle; (2) excitatory and inhibitory impulses from a region of the brain known as the reticular activating system (RAS) that form a constant tonic background onto which are superimposed (3) excitatory impulses from fibers originating in the motor areas of the cerebral cortex, the part of the mammalian brain where voluntary movements are initiated. The muscle spindles are accordingly under both peripheral and central control.

When a muscle is stretched its spindles relay impulses to the spinal cord. A *stretch reflex* is elicited whereby motor neurons in the cord send impulses to the skeletal muscles, causing them to contract against the load. Whenever we initiate a voluntary movement a remarkable series of events is set in motion involving the central control of the muscle spindles. First, our brain sends impulses to the γ-efferent neurons in the cord. These send impulses to the muscle spindles, causing them to contract. As the spindles contract, the tension placed upon their central noncontractile portions stimulates the sensory neurons to relay information back to the spinal cord that causes other motor neurons to send excitatory impulses to the skeletal muscles proper, and the desired movement is brought about. This circuitous procedure may well be the most economical way of bringing about a coordinated movement, for cerebral control is merely superimposed upon stretch-reflex machinery evolved probably earlier. Since afferent fibers from the spindle receptors may branch to make contact with many association neurons in the cord and these in turn excite many more motor neurons, axons from the motor areas of the forebrain need excite only a few γ-efferent cells; the stretch reflex machinery can take care of the rest of the response. This is another excellent example of the way in which the evolutionary process takes advantage of preexisting mechanisms, putting them to new uses.

In a more general sense, the brain controls sensory reception by instigating movements that change the animal's position in the stimulus field. For instance, if a sound is difficult to localize, the animal may respond by turning its head, thereby changing the time required for the stimulus to reach each ear. Detection of a faint stimulus often induces an animal to approach the source until further data permit determination of

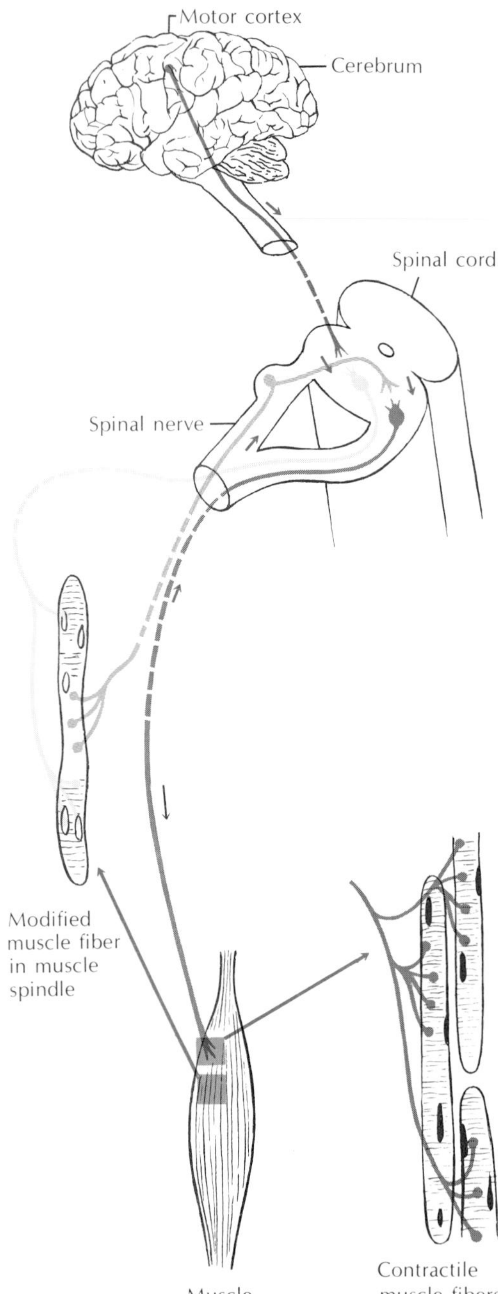

Figure 15.12 □ **Voluntary muscle contraction brought about via muscle-spindle γ-efferent system and stretch-reflex arc. The neuron from the motor areas of the cerebral cortex is shown in dark color; the γ-efferent motor neuron to the muscle spindle, light gray; the sensory neuron, light color; the motor neuron serving the skeletal muscle fibers, dark gray.**

whether closer approach or avoidance would be more advantageous. Such behavior seems to us an exhibition of "curiosity," yet we should not interpret animal behavior in human terms. Conversely, much human curiosity may have its evolutionary roots in an innate tendency to approach and examine unfamiliar stimuli. Rodents characteristically explore new quarters thoroughly, memorizing various cues that are not necessarily immediately meaningful. Such investigatory behavior permits *latent learning* to take place, for if a food reward is later placed in a maze that a rat has already explored, the rat familiar with the maze will learn to recognize the feeding place much more rapidly than one strange to the maze. Investigatory behavior serves to acquaint the animal with the stimuli characteristic of its environment and consequently facilitates recognition of new stimuli when these are introduced.

C Olfaction and taste

OLFACTION AND TASTE IN INVERTEBRATES In aquatic invertebrates no demonstrable difference exists between the senses of olfaction and taste, for all substances detected by external chemoreceptors are present in solution in the milieu. The capacity to distinguish between substances may range from a simple acceptable-unacceptable discrimination in the case of food procurement to apparently specific recognition of particular compounds that elicit distinctive responses. In the latter category we have the approach response of a symbiont to its host or of an individual of one sex to an attractant exuded by the opposite sex. We find too that prey species may have become selectively responsive to chemicals secreted by their major predators; this is the case with sand dollars, which burrow into the sand when approached by starfish of one species predatory upon them but permit themselves to be literally walked upon by other starfish without attempting any sort of evasive response.

Terrestrial animals generally have different receptors for air-borne molecules and those in solution. Insects have two distinct kinds of integumentary chemoreceptors which, although morphologically similar, differ functionally in that the olfactory receptors detect volatile materials in the air whereas the taste receptors must be immersed in solutions of the materials to which they are sensitive. The olfactory receptors are often concentrated on the antennae; the taste receptors are concentrated on the feet and mouthparts (Figure 15.13).

A single arthropod integumentary sense organ (*sensillum*) may contain several kinds of receptors together with glandular cells that secrete the cuticular housing of the sensillum. Sensilla take the form of pits, pegs, or bristles (Figure 15.14). Sensory bristles housing chemoreceptors have perforated tips through which materials can enter, contacting the endings of ciliary pro-

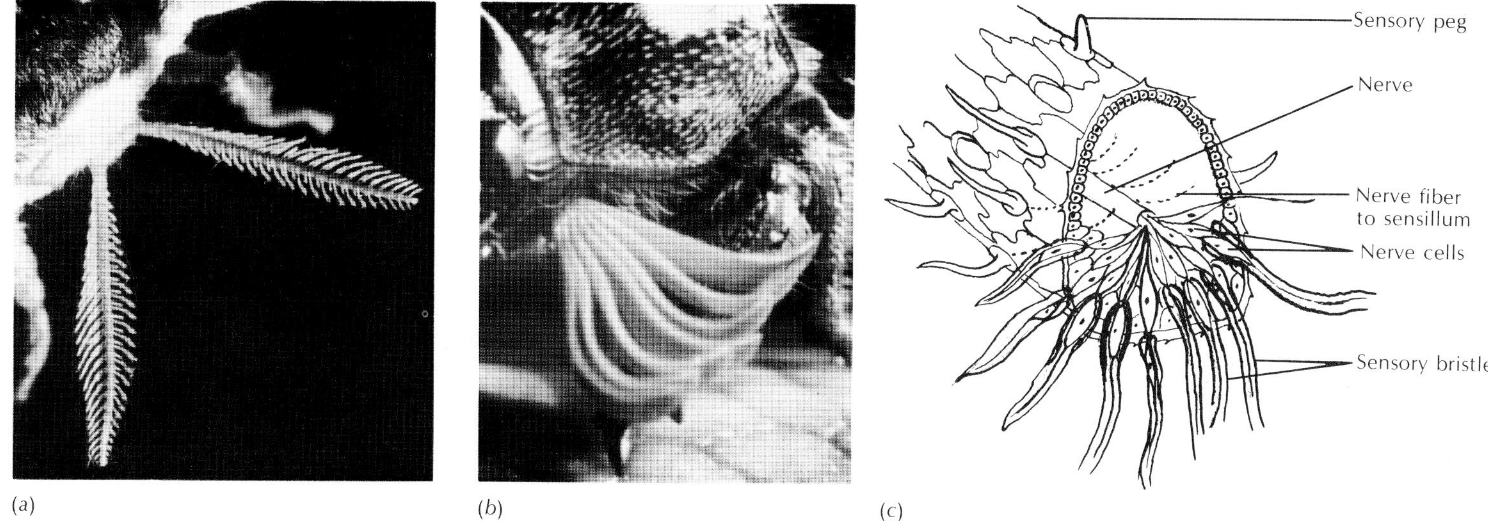

Figure 15.13 □ Insect antennae: (*a*) the immense plumose antennae of the male moth enable him to locate the female over a distance of more than 1 km; (*b*) the distal portion of the antennae of this scarabid beetle is elaborated into a parallel series of leaflets, thereby increasing the surface area for olfactory sense organs. (*Los Angeles County Museum of Natural History.*) (*c*) Structure of a typical antenna.

cesses extending from sensory neurons the cell bodies of which are located in the socket of the sensillum. A typical sensillum houses two secretory cells (one producing the bristle, the other its socket), a mechanoreceptor that registers touch, and two or more different chemoreceptive cells. Thus the whole sense organ may have only five or six cells, each with its own distinct function!

Taste reception in the blowfly *Phormia* and related genera has been investigated by taking advantage of the fly's automatic proboscis-extension reflex. When a hungry fly's feet are dipped into a nutrient solution (such as sugar water) its proboscis is lowered and it begins to feed. This is a purely involuntary response that can be elicited repeatedly until the fly is satiated. When the feet of a feeding fly are transferred to a solution of some unacceptable material (say, salt water), the proboscis is quickly withdrawn. (One enterprising entomologist discovered an excellent means of preserving butterfly internal organs for later microscopic examination. When a butterfly's feet are placed in a sugar solution, it uncoils its long proboscis to feed; if the tip of the proboscis is then redirected into a vial of fixative, the sensations arising from the tarsal receptors override the contradictory signals from the mouthparts, and the insect will then continue with its feeding until it falls dead, perfectly and efficiently embalmed from within!)

By use of the proboscis-extension reflex, *Phormia* has been found to discriminate among only four categories of materials: sugars (or other compounds with similar ring-shaped molecules), proteins (in reproductive females at least), water, and unacceptable materials (salts, acids, and such). Its sensitivity is remarkably keen: immersing a single sensillum containing but one sweet-receptor in a 0.00001 mole sucrose solution evokes the complete proboscis extension reflex in a hungry fly! Rejection (as indicated by proboscis withdrawal or inhibition of its

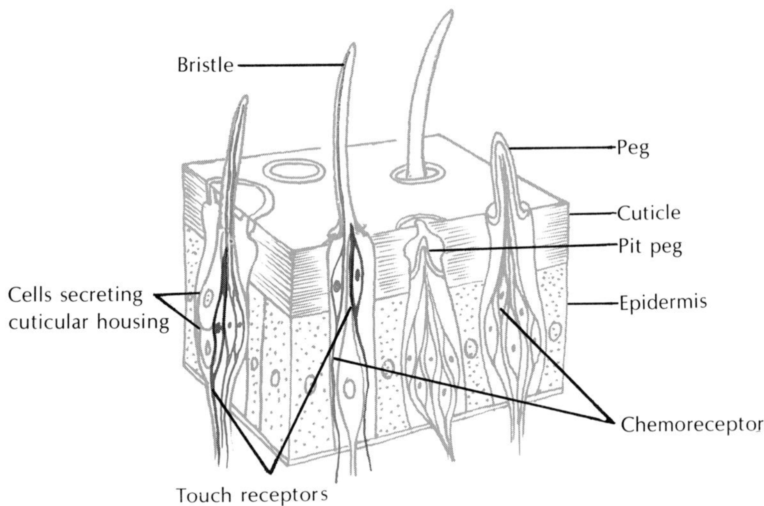

Figure 15.14 □ Types of insect sensilla. Tactile and chemical receptors are associated with these pegs, pits, and bristles.

extension) can be brought about in two ways: (1) by stimulation of a rejection receptor thought specifically sensitive to monovalent ions; (2) by inhibition of the acceptance receptors by means of substances that specifically block the excitation of these receptors without at the same time exciting the rejection receptor. When many sensilla are stimulated simultaneously by a mixed solution containing both acceptable and unacceptable materials, whether or not the proboscis will be extended depends strictly upon the relative numbers of rejection receptors stimulated and acceptance receptors excited or inhibited.

OLFACTION AND TASTE IN VERTEBRATES Vertebrates, whether aquatic or terrestrial, have two quite different sets of sensory equipment for olfaction and taste. The olfactory receptors are sensory neurons, the short dendrites and cell bodies of which are located in the lining of the nasal cavity, and the axons of which pass into the forebrain by way of the olfactory nerve (Figure 15.15). In mammals the olfactory receptors are restricted to a small area (about 2 cm^2 in man) in the upper part of the nasal cavity, and olfaction is intensified by *sniffing,* which draws air currents through this part of the nasal cavity. Sniffing is a nearly reflexive response, as witnessed by how often we draw a full noseful of some offensive odor before remembering that we had better *not* sniff!

Vertebrate olfactory cells are often called "neuroepithelium," for they display characteristics of both neurons and epithelial cells. Electron microscope studies of frog olfactory receptors show that each dendrite terminates distally in several (±6) ciliumlike processes about 200 μm long. The ciliary derivation of these nonmotile sensory "hairs" is evidenced by the characteristic ring of nine tubule doublets (see Figure 10.12) in the proximal portion of each process (the number and arrangement of these doublets being less orderly in the distal part). As with cilia, these tubule doublets spring from basal bodies in the dendritic cytoplasm. Such modified sensory cilia are found on a wide variety of receptors in many phyla, including vertebrate receptors of sound, light, and gravity and the sensillar chemoreceptors of insects that were described earlier.

Vertebrate taste receptors are specialized epithelial cells clustered in *taste buds* occupying depressions in the lining of the mouth and throat and the surface of the tongue (Figure 15.16). The free ends of these gustatory cells bear microvilli two or more micrometers long, whereas the opposite ends contain vacuoles enclosing secretions thought to excite the dendritic endings of the sensory neurons that synapse with these receptors. Afferent nerve fibers pass from the taste buds to the brain by way of cranial nerves V, VII, and IX (see Figure 15.40). Subjective responses from human subjects, together with electrode monitoring of impulses generated in the gustatory nerve fibers, suggest that only four taste modalities are discriminated: sweet, bitter, salt, and acid. It is still uncertain as to whether there are four distinct kinds of receptor cells, fractionating the range of acuity, or whether there is some difference in the excitability of the associated sensory neurons that accomplishes the same thing. Excitation is not strictly of the all-or-none type, for some

Figure 15.15 □ **Vertebrate olfactory receptors. (*a*) Sagittal section of human head, showing location and detail of olfactory epithelium and its relation to the nasal cavity and pharynx. (*b*) Parasagittal section of frog head through plane of left external nostril, olfactory nerve, and olfactory lobe of brain. Receptor cells shown at higher magnification are modified neurons (neuroepithelium), bearing nonmotile ciliary processes at their dendritic endings while their axons form the fibers of the olfactory nerve.**

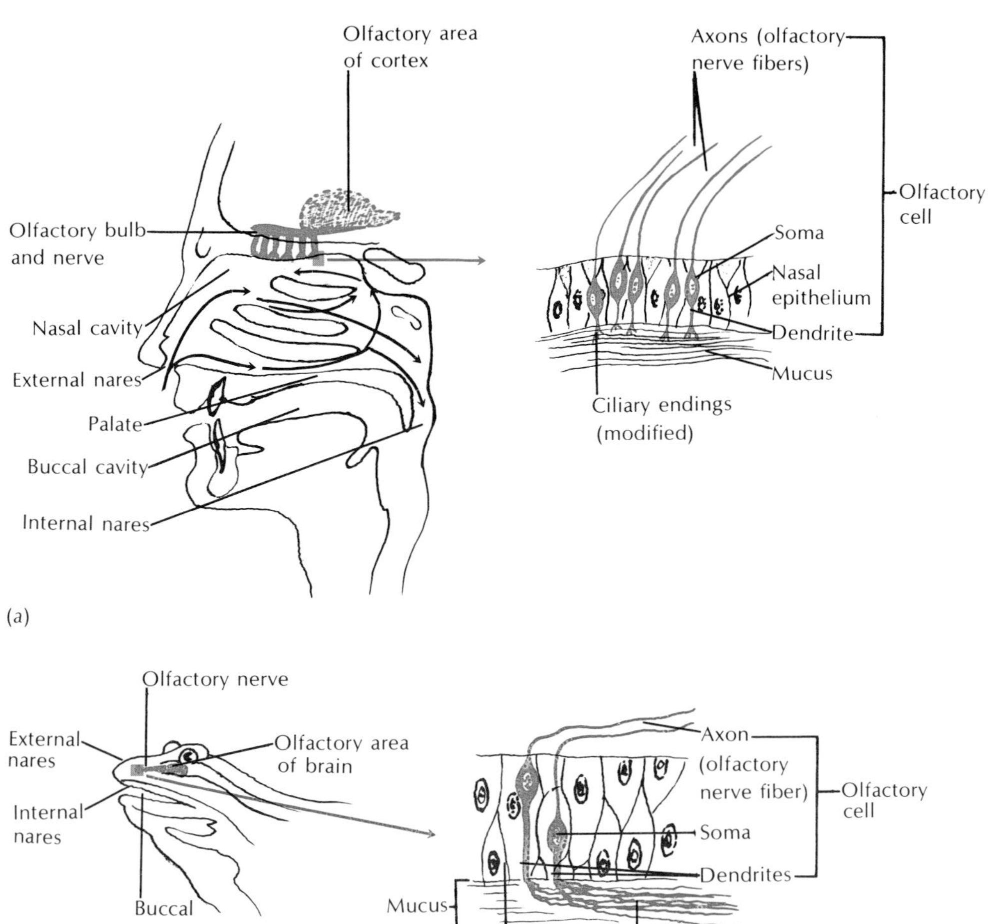

degree of arousal is elicited even by substances that do not exactly fall into any of these categories. However, most flavor sensations result from the excitation of olfactory as well as gustatory receptors. During chewing volatile molecules pass from the mouth into the nasal passages by way of the pharynx. When the nasal passages are clogged with mucus (as during a head cold) food becomes nearly tasteless. A homing salmon probably both tastes and smells its way back to the stream where it was hatched: when one gives a salmon an artificial "cold" by plugging its nostrils with vaseline, it is very likely to get lost. Covering the salmon's eyes has less effect, but the unfortunate fish will most likely reach home with a badly scraped nose from running into obstacles while sniffing out its course.

According to the *stereochemical hypothesis* of taste and olfaction, each kind of chemoreceptor bears on its exposed surface a number of receptor sites of specific three-dimensional configuration, and the cell is excited only by those molecules of complementary shape which can fit correctly into the receptor sites (Figure 15.17). This would be similar to the proposed "lock-and-key" conformity of enzyme and substrate or antigen and antibody. It is really very difficult to describe an odor, and a number of different schemes of classifying odors have been proposed. One of the most recent of these recognizes seven distinct types: floral, musky, camphoraceous, ethereal, pepperminty, putrid, and pungent. A chemically purified compound would have a relatively "pure" odor if its molecules fit into only one of the proposed seven different kinds of receptor sites. It would be odorless if its molecules fit none of these

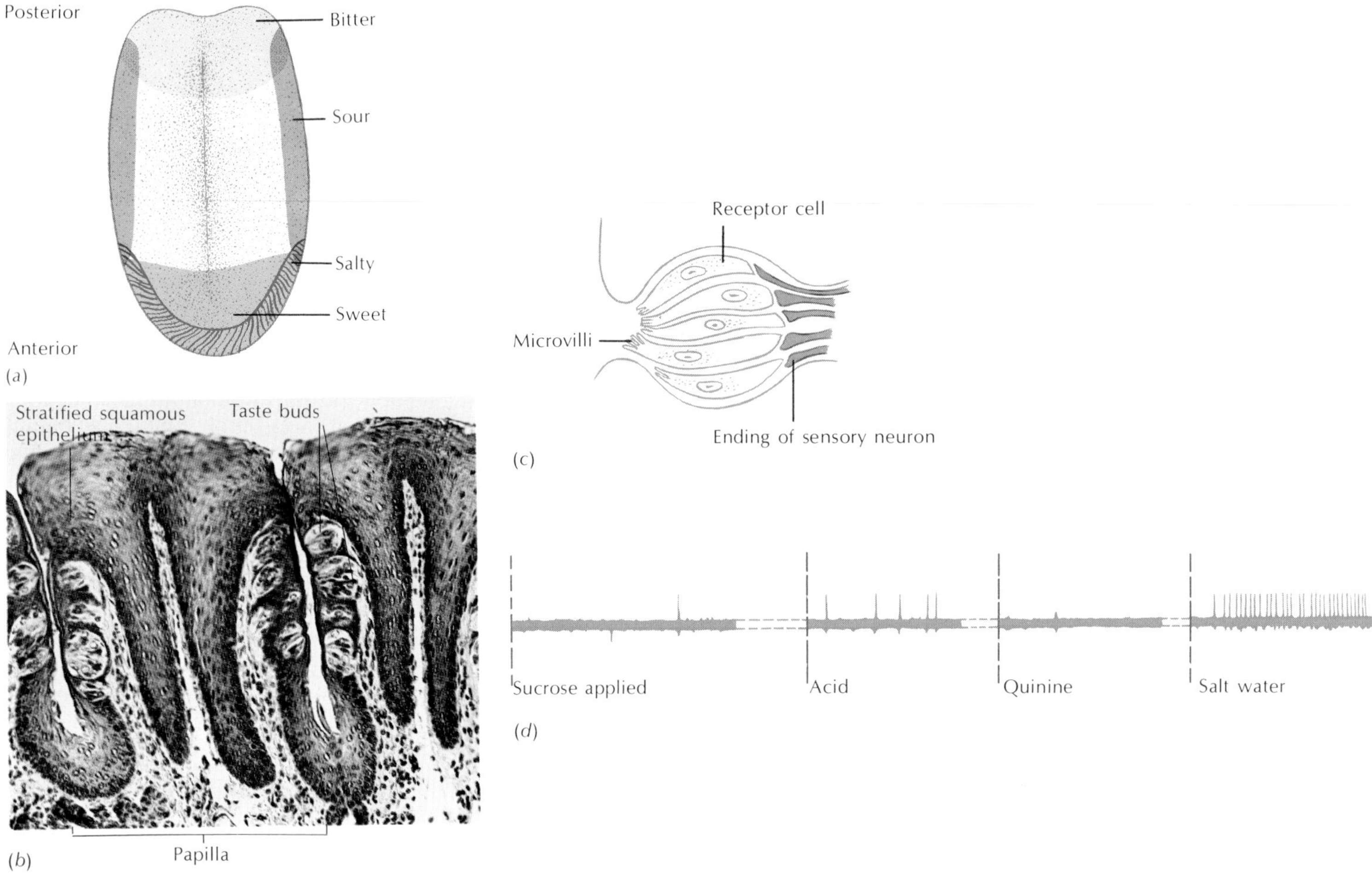

Figure 15.16 □ Taste. (*a*) Distribution of sensory acuities on surface of human tongue. (*b*) Section through papilla of rabbit tongue, showing taste buds. (*Courtesy of Carolina Biological Supply Company.*) (*c*) Structure of a taste bud. (*d*) Record of nerve impulses from a single gustatory nerve fiber when various substances are applied to the tongue; salty substances activate this fiber, whereas sweet, acid, and bitter substances do not.

sites. A mixed solution would have a complex odor, the qualities of which would reflect the various proportions of the different receptors stimulated. The stereochemical hypothesis has gained preliminary support from results with human subjects said to respond predictably when presented with volatile material of molecular geometry supposedly complementary to the shape of one of the hypothesized receptor sites. Altering the geometry of a molecule produces an isomer with a very different odor.

Although this hypothesis cannot yet be considered as proven, it represents an important starting point for research into sensory physiology.

Figure 15.17 □ J. E. Amoore's stereochemical hypothesis of olfaction. Three-dimensional receptor sites on the exposed membrane of an olfactory receptor are thought to take up molecules of complementary shape. Each receptor cell is considered to bear only one kind of active site, odor qualities being determined by the proportions of various receptors excited.

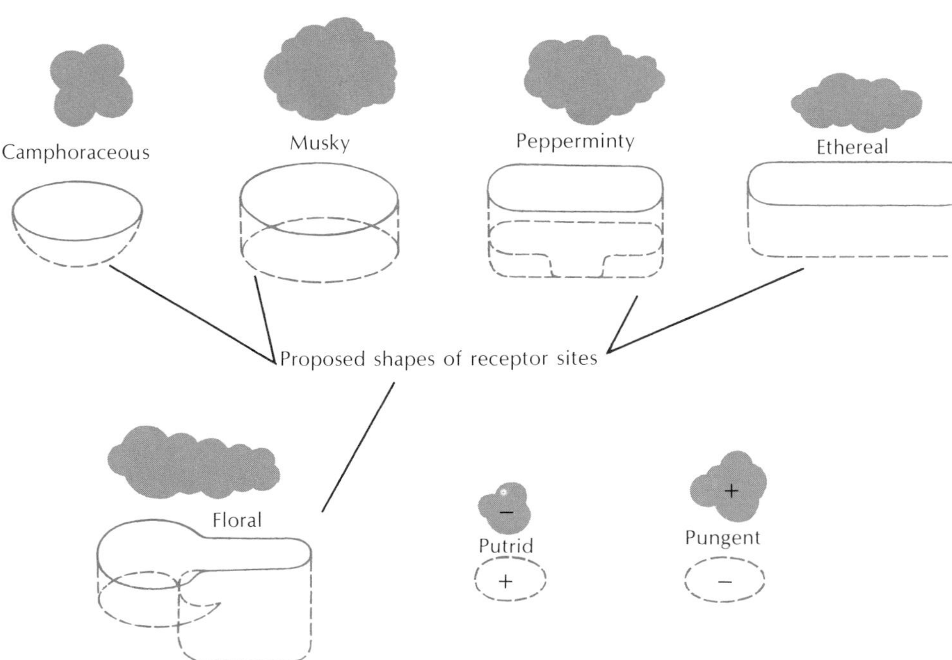

D Photoreception

Many organisms that are eyeless can respond to changes in the direction and intensity of illumination. Plants grow toward light by phototropic bending. A number of unicellular autotrophs exhibit *phototaxis* (a directionalized locomotory response to light) by virtue of a localized concentration of photosensitive pigment forming an "eyespot" in the cytoplasm. Unicellular creatures lacking such eyespots cannot execute phototactic movements but do exhibit *photokinesis,* a random locomotory response to light that allows a photophobic ("light hating") organism to escape gradually into more dimly lit regions. Animals of most phyla have a *dermal light sense* due to the photosensitivity of unidentified cutaneous receptors. This sense is presumably responsible for the "shadow reflexes" shown by a number of animals that lack demonstrable photoreceptors but behave defensively when a shadow suddenly falls upon them. Sudden shading causes tubeworms to retract instantly and certain sea urchins to direct their spines toward the object casting the shadow.

Such diffuse light sensitivity has its value, but much more information can be obtained if eyes are present. So great is the survival value of vision that many different animal groups have evolved eyes. Because an effective eye must have certain components and can have only a few functionally pos-

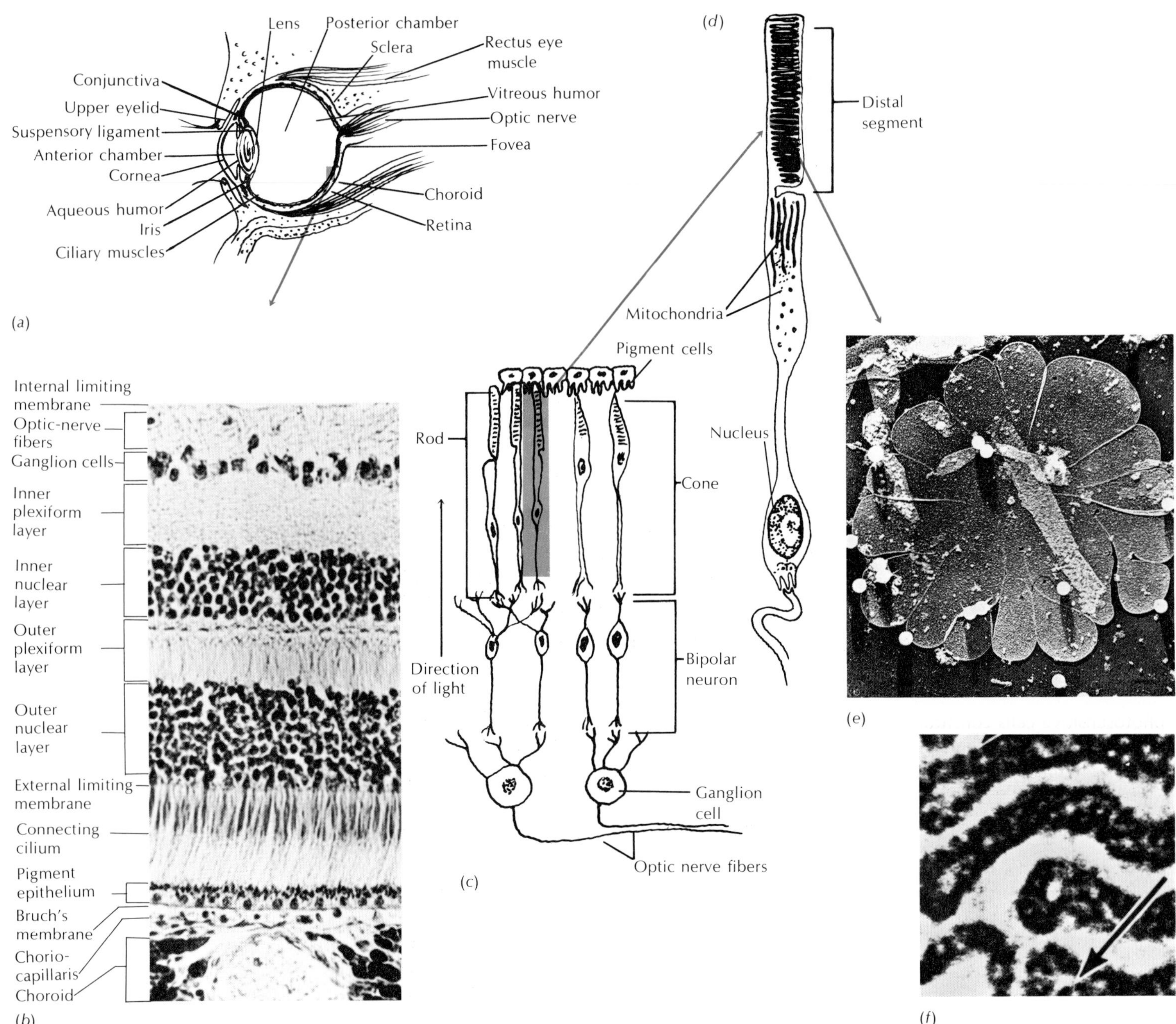
Lens
Posterior chamber
Sclera
Rectus eye muscle
Conjunctiva
Upper eyelid
Vitreous humor
Optic nerve
Suspensory ligament
Anterior chamber
Fovea
Cornea
Choroid
Aqueous humor
Iris
Retina
Ciliary muscles
(a)
(d)
Distal segment
Mitochondria
Pigment cells
Nucleus
Internal limiting membrane
Optic-nerve fibers
Ganglion cells
Inner plexiform layer
Inner nuclear layer
Outer plexiform layer
Outer nuclear layer
External limiting membrane
Connecting cilium
Pigment epithelium
Bruch's membrane
Choriocapillaris
Choroid
(b)
Rod
Cone
Direction of light
Bipolar neuron
Ganglion cell
Optic nerve fibers
(c)
(e)
(f)

Figure 15.18 □ **Vertebrate eye structure. (*a*) Section of mammalian eye through plane of optic nerve. (*b*) Retinal structure of rhesus monkey (*courtesy of Dr. Kenneth T. Brown*). Note that light must penetrate through the layers of nerve fibers and ganglionic cells to reach the layer of photoreceptors. (*c*) Retinal structure at higher magnification. (*d*) Structure of a rod; the outer segment of the rod consists of a perpendicular stack of discs supported along one edge by a single modified cilium. (*e*) Electron micrograph, showing surface structure of a single disc isolated from the outer segment of a frog-retina rod (*courtesy of Dr. H. Fernández-Morán*). The modified cilium (marginal cord) is in cross section at one side of the disc. Latex particles (diameter, 2,800 Å) have been added to the preparation to allow disc to be measured. (*f*) Portion of compound membrane of discs magnified 700,000 times, showing dense 40-Å subunits (*courtesy of Dr. H. Fernández-Morán*).**

sible forms, eyes that have evolved independently in different phyla often resemble one another closely in both form and physiology. For instance, some type of vitamin A compound serves as a photosensitive pigment in all types of animal visual systems that have been identified and studied up to the present.

EYE STRUCTURE A cluster or layer of photosensitive cells constitutes a *retina,* the one indispensible element of an eye. Invertebrate retinas consist of sensory neurons differentiated from the maturing skin. Vertebrate retinas, while also of ectodermal origin, arise as direct outgrowths of the embryonic brain. Consequently, the vertebrate retina is functionally upsidedown, for its photoreceptors (the rods and cones) occupy the deepest layers of the retina and are overlain by blood vessels, neurons, and nerve fibers through which light must penetrate to reach the photoreceptive cells (Figure 15.18*a, b, c*). This unavoidable circumstance has been partially compensated for during the evolution of the vertebrate eye: at the point on the retina where light rays would come into focus from an object being looked at directly, the layer of overlying blood vessels and nerve fibers virtually disappears and the photoreceptors are most densely spaced. This area, the *fovea,* is the part of the retina where visual acuity is most keen. In man it is a mere 300 μm in diameter but, because each photoreceptor within the fovea is responsible for stimulating one fiber of the optic nerve, the region of the brain involved with foveal vision is much larger than that devoted to all of the rest of the retina.

Outside the fovea several photoreceptors converge upon a single intermediate neuron, and several of these converge in turn upon one ganglionic neuron which sends a fiber (its axon) to the brain. The farther to the sides of the retina the cells are located, the greater this convergence. This means that while foveal vision is most acute in terms of resolving detail, peripheral vision is best adapted to seeing in dim light. A quantity of light too slight to make a foveal neuron fire can excite a neuron in the periphery of the retina because impulses from a number of photoreceptors summate upon that one neuron.

The fine structure of photoreceptors Most vertebrates have two morphologically distinct kinds of photoreceptors: *rods,* that function best in dim light; and *cones,* that are responsible for color vision. Most mammals, being nocturnal (or coming from nocturnal ancestors), lack color vision, but man and other primates can discriminate among various hues.

At the level of magnification possible with the electron microscope, we find that photoreceptors of both vertebrates and invertebrates display a stacked membrane-pigment lamellar organization remarkably reminiscent of the photosynthetic grana of plant chloroplasts (Figure 15.18*d;* see also Figure 13.4). In the columnar distal segments of the photoreceptive cells, layers of visual pigment alternate with folds of the plasma membrane, forming a stack of either discs or tubules through which light must penetrate vertically, allowing the greatest opportunity for absorption of photons. In deuterostome phyla (chordates and echinoderms), such a stack consists of a column of discs that arise as outgrowths of the plasma membrane on one side of an acentrically positioned sensory cilum (Figure 15.18*e, f*). In protostome phyla, an analogous photosensitive column, the *rhabdomere,* arises along the distal segment, which in this case is the dendritic portion of a sensory neuron, the *retinula* (Figure 15.19*a, b*). The rhabdomere consists of densely packed tubules oriented at right angles to the long axis of the dendrite. These tubules appear to be *microvilli,* bounded by the plasma membrane and containing concentrations of visual pigment. Thus we find membrane-pigment sandwiches evolving by two different routes: (1) by modification of a cilium; (2) by modification of vertical arrays of microvilli. Despite their different origins, these types of photoreceptors are alike in that (1) their photosensitive apparatus presents an extensive membrane surface in which proteins (presumably enzymes) are associated with the visual pigment; (2) the lamellae are oriented at right angles to the direction of light penetration; (3) large

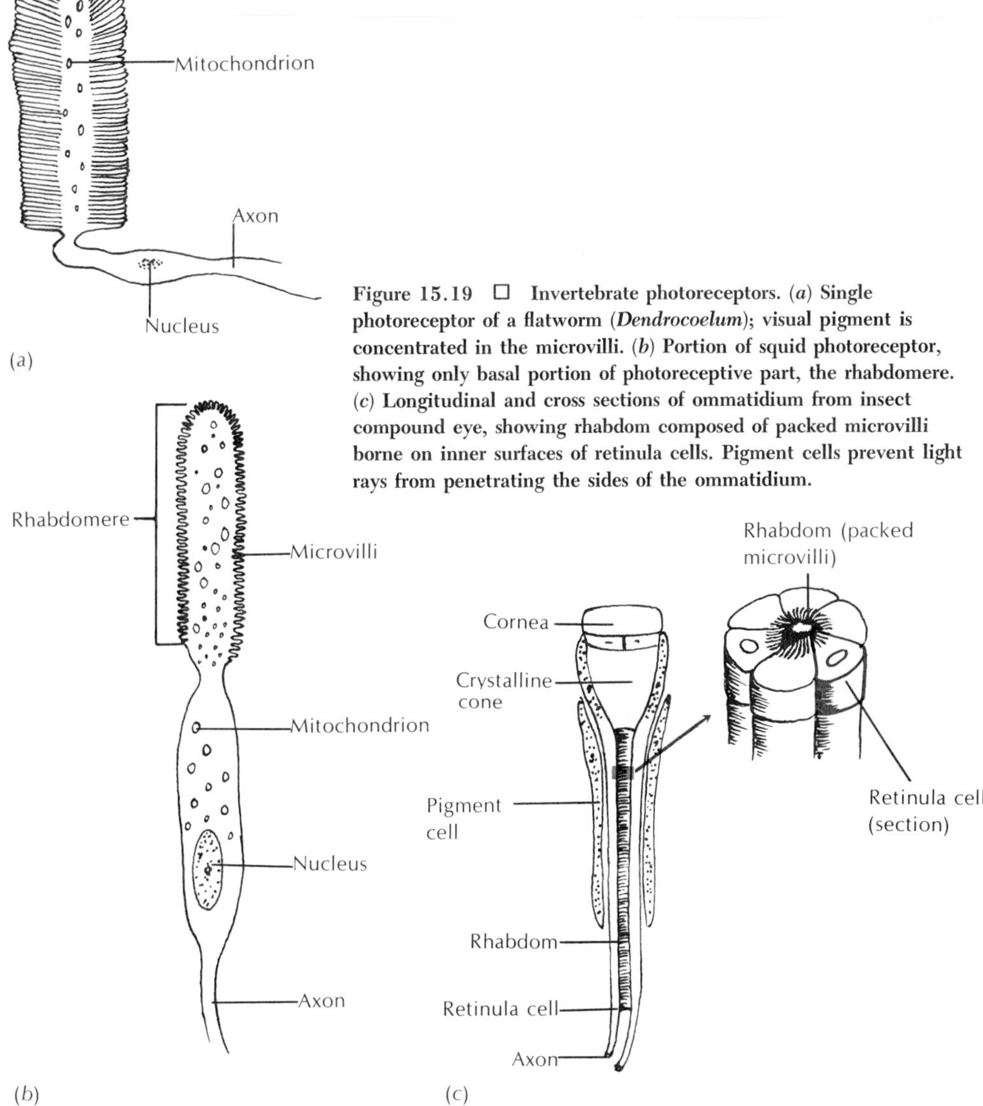

Figure 15.19 □ Invertebrate photoreceptors. (*a*) Single photoreceptor of a flatworm (*Dendrocoelum*); visual pigment is concentrated in the microvilli. (*b*) Portion of squid photoreceptor, showing only basal portion of photoreceptive part, the rhabdomere. (*c*) Longitudinal and cross sections of ommatidium from insect compound eye, showing rhabdom composed of packed microvilli borne on inner surfaces of retinula cells. Pigment cells prevent light rays from penetrating the sides of the ommatidium.

numbers of mitochondria are associated with the lamellar apparatus, suggesting involvement of oxidative metabolism with the processes of amplification and/or transduction.

Insect retinula cells usually are grouped in small functional units known as *ommatidia,* in which only six to eight receptor cells are arranged about a central axis, with their closely juxtaposed rhabdomeres forming a composite photoreceptive structure, the *rhabdom* (Figure 15.19c).

Types of eyes Photoreceptors and their accessory tissues may be categorized into four different morphological types of eyes (Figure 15.20 and 15.21): *flat* eyes, *cup* eyes, *vesicular* eyes, and *compound* eyes. The first three types may occur together within a single phylum, even one so simple as Coelenterata, having perhaps arisen by independent evolution in different groups within the phylum. Compound eyes have been found only in insects, a number of crustaceans and annelids, and a few molluscs.

1 *Flat eyes* like those of the jellyfish *Aurelia* are patches of photosensitive cells lying flat to the epidermis and usually lacking a lens. Even in these simplest eyes, a concentration of dark pigment underlies the retina, serving to absorb light that has passed through the retina and preventing light from striking the retina from below (as would, of course, be possible in cases where the animal is small and its tissues are translucent).

2 *Cup eyes* are concave depressions in the epidermis, lined with photoreceptors and often enclosing an immovable crystalline lens. Some cup eyes like those of *Nautilus* (a cephalopod) approach the vesicular

Figure 15.20 □ **Types of simple eyes: (*a*) flat, (*b*) cup, and (*c*) vesicular. All three types may occur in a single phylum.**

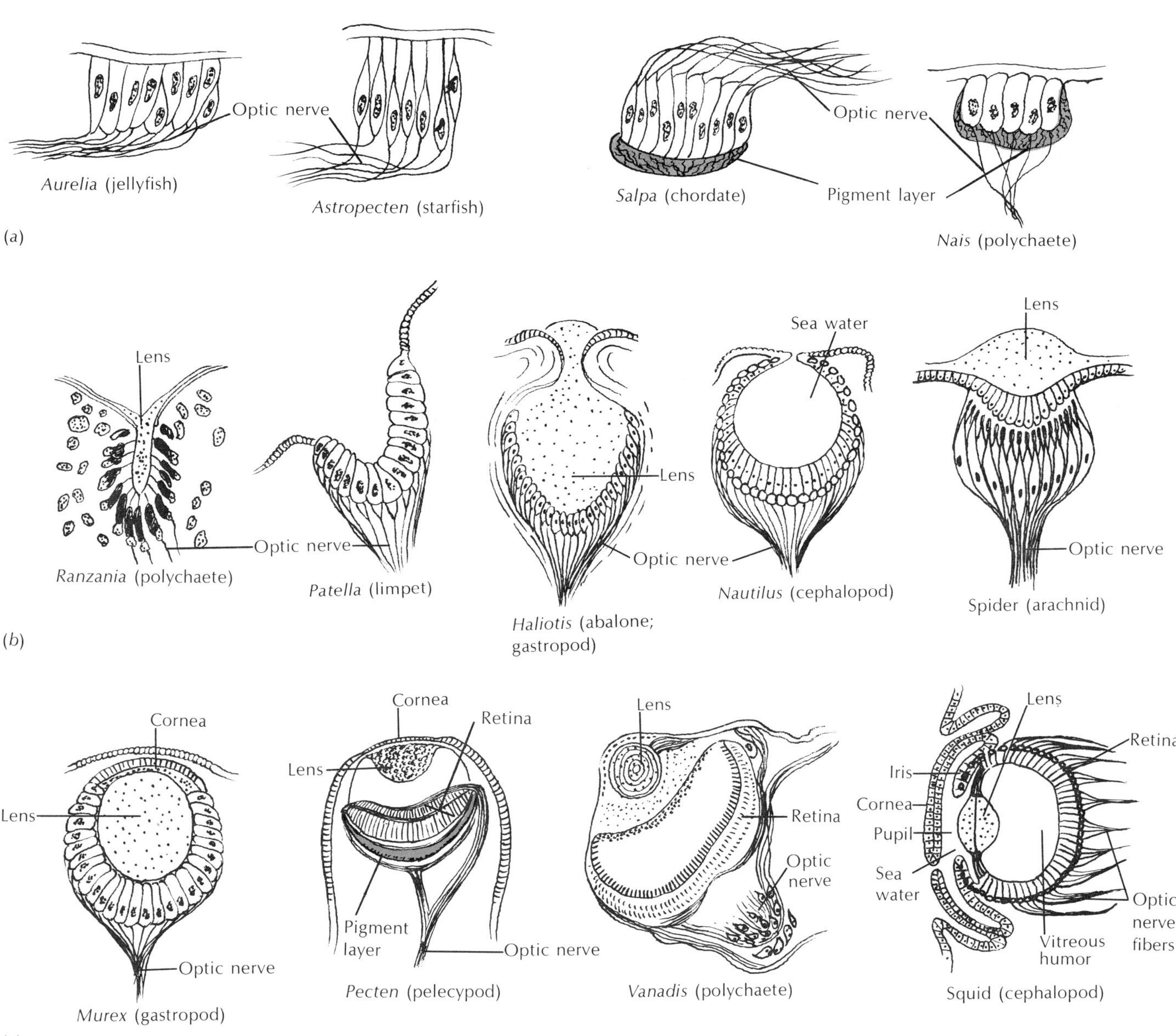

Figure 15.21 □ **Compound-eye structure. (*a*) The huge eyes of the dragonfly, composed of many ommatidia, nearly cover the head, enabling the insect to see in all directions simultaneously. (*Los Angeles County Museum of Natural History.*) Dragonflies locate their prey (other insects) visually and capture them in midflight. (*b*) The reduced army-ant eye, with few ommatidia, suggests that this insect does not hunt visually but locates its prey by olfaction. (*Los Angeles County Museum of Natural History.*) Compare relative sizes of eyes and antennae in dragonfly and army ant. (*c*) Diagram of the structure of the insect compound eye. Each facet represents the lens of a single ommatidium. (*d*) Insect visual acuity depends on the number of ommatidia per unit area of the eye surface. Moving objects (or stationary objects seen in flying) register on successive groups of ommatidia.**

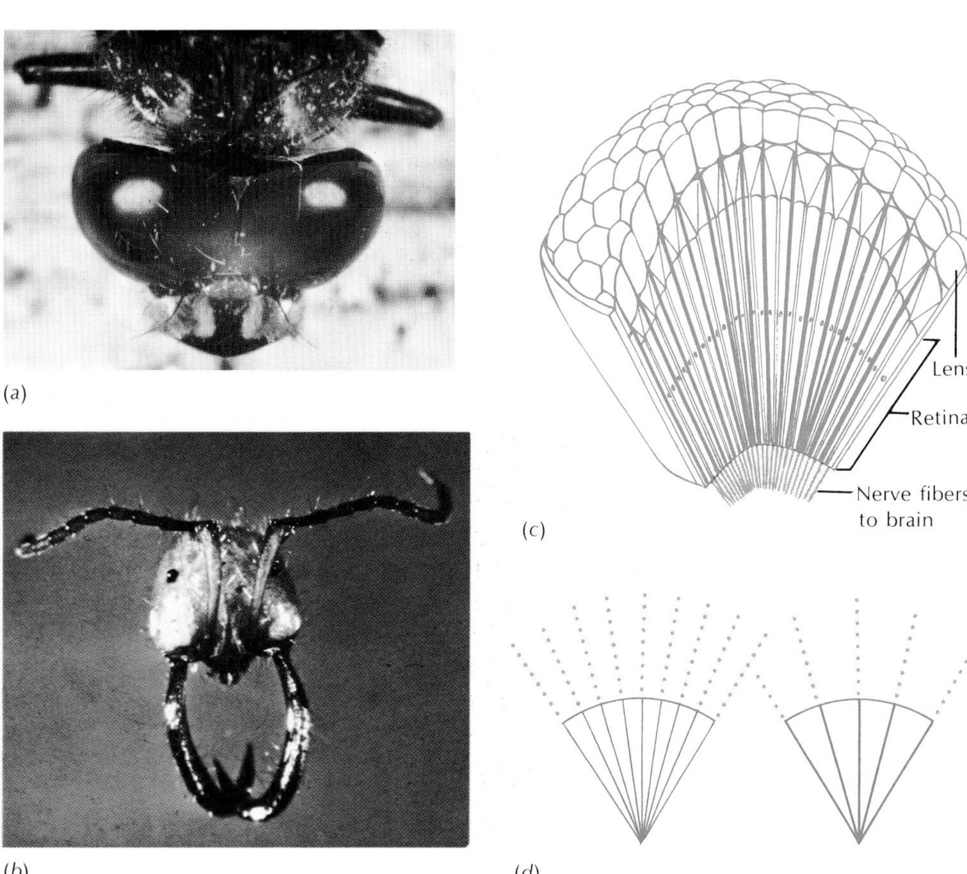

condition, being fluid-filled spheres communicating with the exterior only by way of a pinhole opening located in the front of the eye.

3 *Vesicular eyes* are hollow spheres (vesicles) lined with photoreceptors except at the front, which is covered by a transparent *cornea.* The vesicle is filled with clear fluid or gelatinous material (vitreous humor) that helps the eyeball hold its shape. Usually a lens is present, which may be movable and/or deformable, allowing the eye to change the angle at which light rays are bent to focus upon the retina.

The advanced vesicular eyes of cephalopods and vertebrates are closely convergent in both structure and function. Both are housed in skeletal sockets to which are anchored muscles that move the eyeball in its socket (see Figure 12.40). The muscles of the octopus eye rotate the eyeball in its socket so that the rectangular pupil, which admits light in a horizontal band, is always oriented with its long axis at right angles to the pull of gravity. This reflex, important in keeping the octopus' visual world rightside up, is abolished by destruction of the animal's gravity receptors. In both groups, a thin epidermal *conjunctiva* covers the cornea, which forms the front of the eye's anterior chamber (see Figure 15.18*a*). The anterior chamber, filled with *aqueous humor* or sea water, is bounded posteriorly by the pigmented *iris,* a muscle that controls the passage of light through the *pupil,* the opening into the eye's posterior chamber. Behind the pupil lies the lens, suspended by ligaments controlled by *ciliary muscles* that regulate the position and curvature of the lens, permitting modification of the eye's focal length. The posterior chamber is lined by the retina, which is underlain by the *choroid,* a layer containing blood vessels and light-absorptive black pigment. The choroid is continuous anteriorly with the iris. The outer coat of the eyeball is the tough, collagenous *sclera,* which is continuous with the cornea at the front of the eye.

4 *Compound* eyes are most highly developed in insects and higher crustaceans. They are convex organs made up of a number of columnar ommatidia, each of which monitors a small portion of the visual field. The focusing apparatus of each ommatidium consists of a *corneal lens* (a transparent section of the cuticle) and, below this, the *crystalline cone.* These structures gather light rays and focus them upon the rhabdom formed by the underlying cluster of retinula cells. The axons of these cells form the optic nerve that passes to the optic lobe of the brain. Insect compound eyes may nearly cover the head, together comprising thousands of ommatidia and commanding a visual field of almost 360° (Figure 15.21). What kind of image is seen with these eyes remains a matter for speculation. A photograph taken through the stripped-off retina of the insect eye gives us the impression that the insect sees numerous repetitions of the same small image. But in life the ommatidia are screened by pigment from all light rays except those entering directly parallel to the long axis of the ommatidium; since (as we have mentioned) stimulated ommatidia also have the capacity to inhibit adjacent ones with which their visual field may overlap, the image produced may really be quite clear, although somewhat grainy like a newsprint photograph. Studies with bees indicate that these insects have color vision and that the ommatidia have an image-retention time so brief that a bee would see a motion picture (projected at the normal speed of 32 frames per second) as a series of still frames. This brief image-retention time may permit the insect to resolve details of structures past which it is flying rapidly; this would permit the bee to avoid the blurred effect that we experience when viewing nearby objects from a rapidly moving train.

THE PHYSIOLOGY OF VISION The initial event involved in photoreception is a photochemical reaction in which molecules of *visual pigment* undergo isomerization and partly break down. Visual pigments consist of a vitamin A aldehyde known as *retinal,* conjugated with any one of a number of related proteins (probably enzymes) known as *opsins.* Differences in the absorptive properties of various visual pigments are due to the fact that as well as there being a number of different kinds of opsins there are two kinds of retinal: retinal$_1$, an aldehyde of vitamin A_1, and retinal$_2$, an aldehyde of vitamin A_2 (Figure 15.22). Two general functional categories of opsins are distinguished: scotopsins, that function well in dim light, and photopsins, that require more intense illumination.

The visual pigments of vertebrate rods are *rhodopsin* (retinal$_1$ plus scotopsin) and *porphyropsin* (retinal$_2$ plus scotopsin). The latter, which is restricted to freshwater fish and some reptiles and amphibians, absorbs light most strongly at 522 nm, whereas the absorptive maximum for rhodopsin is 491 nm. Several vertebrate cone pigments or *iodopsins* (retinal$_1$ plus photopsin) are known. Chicken iodopsin absorbs maximally at 562 nm. Turtles have a cone pigment (cyanopsin, containing retinal$_2$) that has an absorptive maximum at 620 nm.

When a visual pigment such as rhodopsin is extracted from the retina in the dark and is then illuminated, the first apparent event is that the retinal molecule changes from a bent (*cis*) to a straight (all-*trans*) configuration. This isomerization is accompanied by a sudden change in the light-absorptive properties of the solution, which turns from pinkish to yellow. Upon continued illumination retinal then dissociates entirely from scotopsin and the solution turns white. A current interpretation of the physiological significance of these events is that a bent retinal molecule can inhibit the catalytic activity of an opsin molecule by covering up its active site, while isomerization of retinal to its straight form liberates the enzyme's active site so that a reaction can be initiated that will terminate in the excitation of a neuron. This reaction may be the first step in an enzyme cascade (see Section 13.2C) by which the stimulus energy is amplified into a whole-cell reaction that provides sufficient energy to trigger a nerve impulse.

A visual pigment can absorb light only when the retinal and protein components are associated. Neither component alone is light-absorptive. Consequently, to be capable of repeated stimulation the molecular system must be allowed to regenerate. Rhodopsin regenerates only under conditions of very low illumination; this explains why we are nearly blind when coming into a dark room after being in full daylight (which requires a switch from cone vision to rod vision), but after about 15 min can discern many details in this comparative darkness. This is about the time required for a solu-

Figure 15.22 □ **Biochemistry of vision. (*a*) Generalized model of the visual-pigment cycle. (*b*) Structural formulas, showing changes that take place in retinal portion of retinal-opsin complex. (*c*) Hypothetical role of retinal in regulating enzymatic activity of opsin. Step 3 represents the substrate approaching the action site as the first step in the reaction sequence leading to the generation of the nerve impulse.**

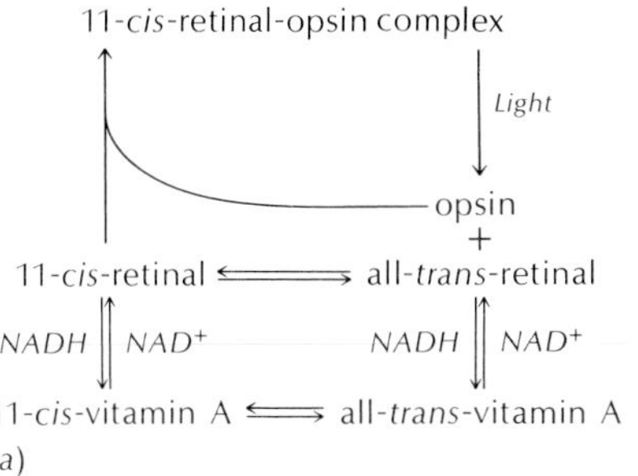

11-cis-retinal$_1$

(*b*)

All-trans-retinal$_1$

NADH NAD^+

Vitamin A_1

(*c*)

11-*cis*-retinal

Active site

Opsin molecule

1

All-*trans*-retinal

Photon absorbed

2

Vitamin A

Substrate

3

tion of dissociated rhodopsin to regenerate when placed in the dark.

DAY AND NIGHT VISION An animal that is exclusively nocturnal may have only scotopic receptors present in its retina. A few strictly diurnal animals (squirrels and certain waterfowl) may have only photopic receptors, for the visual pigments of these receptors do not require darkness to regenerate. These animals are literally blind at night. The day vision of some waterfowl is undoubtedly more acute than that of man (at the receptor level), for the fovea is larger than that of the human eye and contains cones at a density of 10^6 per square millimeter as compared with 1.4×10^5 per square millimeter in the human fovea. Most vertebrates have both rods and cones, the proportions differing according to how much the animal tends to be active by day or by night.

Visual acuity is sacrificed in the predominantly scotopic eye in favor of light sensitivity. As we have noted, impulses from a number of rods must summate upon a single neuron to make it fire. A dark-adapted human rod is excited by one photon, but for a point of light to be seen no fewer than five to ten rods must be excited simultaneously. The human fovea contains only cones, therefore limiting foveal vision to the daytime, the proportion of cones decreasing and of rods increasing toward the edges of the visual field. The increasing light sensitivity toward the periphery of the retina probably explains why it is that many legends of ghosts and goblins arise: when at night we catch sight of an object at the edge of our field of vision, our automatic response is to turn our eyes to look full at that object; this places it upon the fovea,

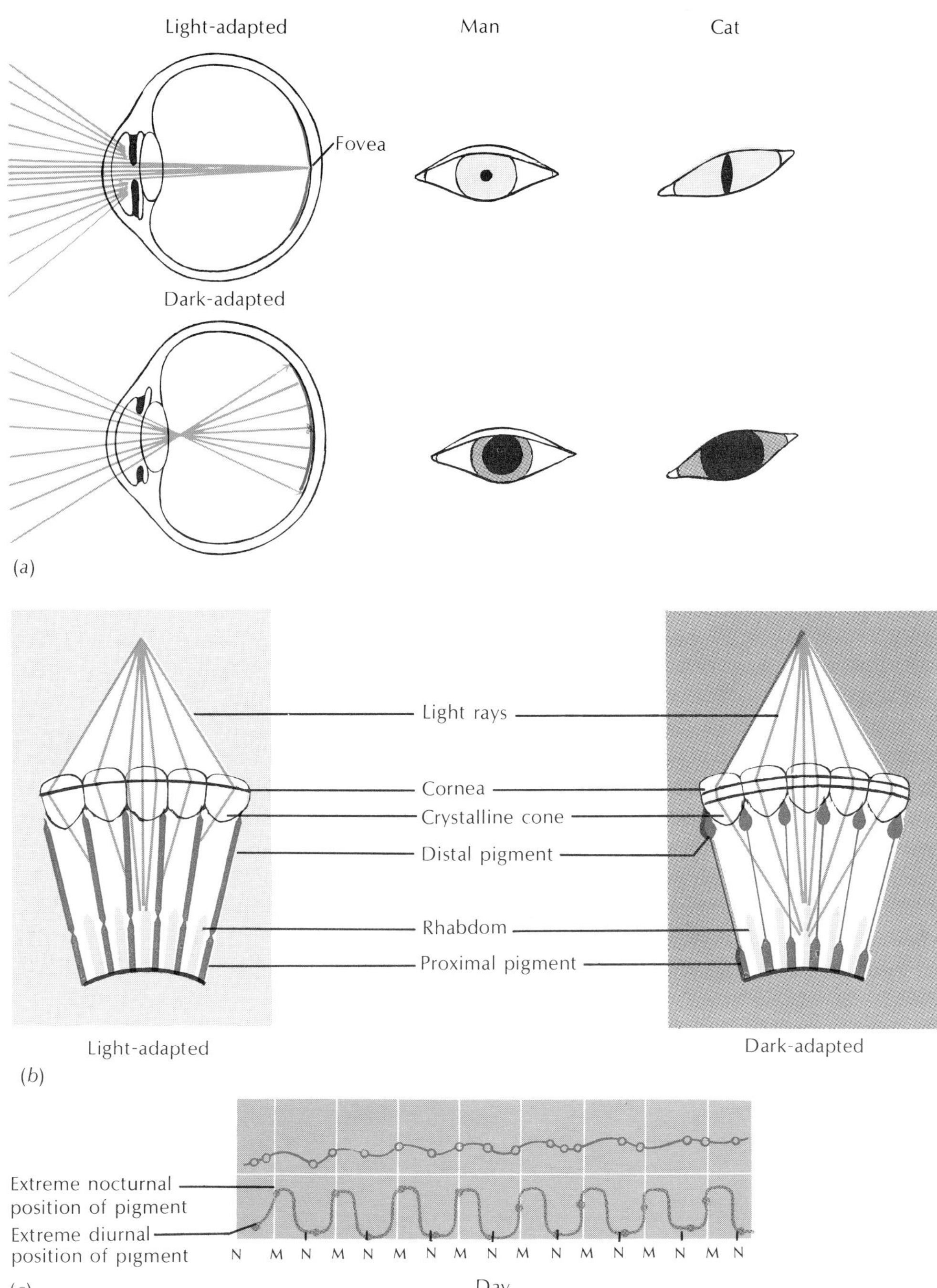

whereupon it instantly vanishes—and a new ghost story is born! This effect can be tested by watching the twilight sky for the first glimpse of a star, which can be seen by rod vision and out of the "corners" of the eye. Until the sky has darkened sufficiently, a star looked at directly will tend to disappear from view.

Responses to changes in light intensity When an animal is active both night and day, its eyes must adapt to a wide range of light intensity. Certain changes accompany the shift from photopic to scotopic vision and vice versa. In such vertebrates the iris responds to changes in light intensity by adjusting the pupillary diameter so that more or less light strikes the retina. This *pupillary reflex* is mediated by the brain and autonomic nerve fibers to the iris musculature. The muscle fibers of the human iris are arranged in radial and concentric sets that act in opposition, so that the iris dilates and constricts like a diaphragm (Figure 15.23*a*).

Figure 15.23 □ Optic responses to changes in light intensity. (*a*) In the light-adapted vertebrate eye, constriction of the pupil causes a narrow beam of light to fall upon the fovea. In the dark-adapted eye, peripheral vision is enhanced by dilation of the pupil, allowing light to fall upon a large area of the retina. (*b*) In the light-adapted arthropod eye, pigment shields each ommatidium, preventing oblique light rays from penetrating into adjacent ommatidia. In the dark-adapted eye, the pigment collar is withdrawn and rays can be transmitted through the transparent walls of the ommatidia, producing a blurred image but allowing the arthropod to see in dim light. (*c*) Movements of distal pigments in eyes of a nocturnal shrimp (N, noon, M, midnight). Shrimp kept in perpetual darkness (lower graph) exhibit a circadian rhythm of pigment movement nearly abolished when kept under constant illumination (upper graph). (*Modified from Welsh.*)

Figure 15.24 □ **Absorption properties of human rods and cones. Difference spectra for individual rods and cones indicate that three distinct functional types of cone exist in the human retina. (A difference spectrum is obtained by subtracting the absorption value obtained in the light from the value obtained in the dark.) (*Data from G. Wald.*)**

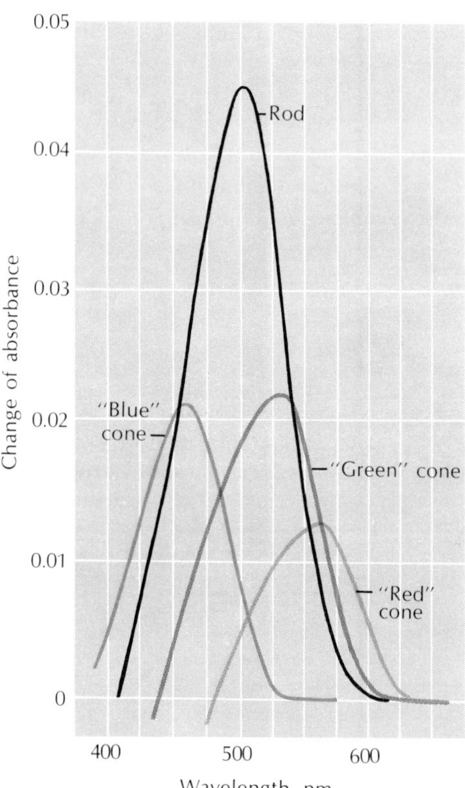

The pupil is enlarged when the radial muscles contract, and made smaller when the concentric fibers contract. Although the human pupil may be constricted in bright light to less than the diameter of a pinhead, the iris diaphragm is less versatile than the curtain-type iris seen in the cat, where the muscles form two "curtains" that can pull widely apart so that the pupil can occupy almost the whole diameter of the iris or can close together so that the pupil becomes a mere slit. The iris pigment prevents light from entering the posterior chamber of the eye except through the pupil. When this pigment is abnormally restricted, as in albino and blue-eyed individuals, vision is often impaired in bright light. (The vertebrate eye never contains *blue* pigment—a blue effect is obtained by refraction when only scanty amounts of black and yellow pigment are present.)

We have noted previously that a number of nocturnal animals have a mirrorlike pigment layer, the tapetum, underlying the retina, that reflects light back through the retina and enhances light sensitivity. The reflective property of the tapetum is due to concentrations of such materials as crystalline guanine and riboflavin. If the animal is partly diurnal, black pigment may disperse by day to cover the reflective materials.

A pupillary reflex is obviously impossible in a compound eye, but adjustments to changes in illumination are accomplished by movements of the pigment that by day shields each ommatidium from the oblique penetration of light rays. At night the pigment granules, formerly dispersed throughout the cytoplasm of the branching pigment cell (chromatophore), draw in around its nucleus, allowing oblique rays to penetrate through the sides of the now unshielded ommatidium (Figure 15.23*b*). This permits more light to reach the retina but must produce a blurred series of multiple and partially overlapping images. The loss of visual clarity is however compensated by the increased ability to discern moving (hence, probably menacing) objects at night. The chromatophore response seems to be neurally regulated in insects but hormonally controlled in crustaceans.

Color vision Objects viewed by scotopic vision are seen in various shades of gray. Photopic vision includes color discrimination only when more than one kind of photopic receptor is present. Vertebrate cones are morphologically alike, but recent evidence suggests that three functional types are present: (1) blue-sensitive cones (containing a form of iodopsin called *cyanolabe* (a pigment labile in blue light) with an absorption maximum at 4,470 Å; (2) red-sensitive cones (containing *erythrolabe,* a red-labile iodopsin) with an absorption maximum at 5,770 Å; and (3) green-sensitive cones (containing *chlorolabe* a green-labile iodopsin) with an absorption maximum at 5,400 Å. The absorption curves for these three kinds of cones, as determined for man, are shown in Figure 15.24. Note that the curves for erythrolabe and chlorolabe overlap substantially, whereas cyanolabe absorbs across a somewhat narrower range of wavelengths in the blue-violet region of the spectrum, and its absorption curve overlaps the other two much less.

There is considerable support for the hypothesis that all color sensation is due to the stimulation of various proportions of the three varieties of cones. Several kinds of hereditary colorblindness are known to occur in man, all thought to be due to sex-linked recessive alleles, which explains why men are colorblind so much more frequently than women (see Figure 8.7). The two major types of red-green colorblindness are *protanopia* (in which erythrolabe is lacking but the other pigments are produced normally) and *deuteranopia* (in which chlorolabe is wanting). A less common type of colorblindness known as "blue weakness," involving poor discrimination only at the short end of the spectrum, is due to the absence of cyanolabe. Rare individuals that are completely colorblind are found to lack any two of these three pigments.

Despite the evident existence of three distinct functional types of cones, electromonitoring of optic nerve fibers indicate that this three-color information must be conducted to the brain in the form of a binary "on-off" code. The neurons serving the cones fire under two conditions: (1) when the cones are stimulated by light of frequencies to which they are most sensitive; (2) when exposure of the eye to certain *other* wavelengths ceases. This can be explained if we hypothesize that each ganglionic neuron sending a fiber from the retina to the brain forms synapses with intermediate neurons that are stimulated by at least two different kinds of cones. For instance, one class of ganglionic cell may receive excitatory impulses from intermediate neurons activated by red cones and inhibitory impulses from intermediate neurons activated by green cones. Whether this ganglionic cell fires when the retina of the eye is illuminated by light of mixed wavelengths depends on the relative quantity of red and green rays present, determining the ratio of excitatory and inhibitory impulses it receives (in other words, what blend of EPSPs and IPSPs exists across its membrane). When the eye is exposed to a beam of light containing both red and green wavelengths, any ganglionic cell excited by neurons serving red cones and inhibited by those serving green cones will fire if the red wavelengths predominate or cease to fire if the green wavelengths predominate. A ganglionic cell repressed by green light will also fire when the green light goes off and the green cones cease to be excited. Thus each optic nerve fiber transmits data on two of the three basic colors. At least six basic "on-off" code combinations are possible by means of which the brain may receive information concerning the relative proportions of different wavelengths present in light falling upon the eye.

IMAGE-FORMATION AND ACCOMMODATION An eye can form an image, rather than merely detecting changes in illumination, if light reflected from each point of the object viewed can be focused upon a comparable point of the retina. A *camera* eye like that of vertebrates forms a complete image of the object seen upon the retinal field. Since most objects seen are obviously much larger than the area provided by a retina, light rays reflected from that object must be made to converge so that they illuminate an area of the retina of the same shape but much reduced in size (Figure 15.25*a*). Light rays from a tree 40 m tall and seen at a distance of 2 km are bent (*refracted*) so that they converge as they pass first through the cornea and then through the lens, with the result that an inverted image of the tree only 0.3 mm tall falls upon the retina. This is small enough to fit entirely within the diameter of the fovea. The cornea is responsible for most refraction. It is bowed so that light striking its edges are bent more strongly than those striking nearer its center. This means that rays striking the upper portion of the cornea will be bent to fall upon the lowest part of the retina occupied by the image, while rays passing through the lower part of the cornea are bent to fall upon the upper part of the retina; this is what causes the image to be inverted.

Small as the fovea is, the fact that we can clearly see all parts of an object projecting a much larger image on the retina is due to the fact that our eye muscles constantly cause small flicking movements that bring first one part of the object and then another upon the fovea. These flicking movements are important in keeping the eye from adapting to an object kept in constant view. In fact, if a contact lens is used to hold an object immovably in the field of view (fixed so that it moves with each movement of the eyeball), the image perceived soon begins to disintegrate and is seen only as fragments that fade out and reappear.

Accommodation The functional efficiency of an image-forming eye is improved if it is capable of *accommodation,* or adjusting the degree to which light rays are refracted to come into focus upon the retina. Light rays are reflected in all directions off a solid object, but when it is more than a few meters away the only rays reaching the eye will be traveling roughly parallel and will not require strong refraction to be brought into focus upon the retina. Some of the light rays striking a human eye from objects viewed closer at hand are still diverging when they reach the cornea, and these rays will not be

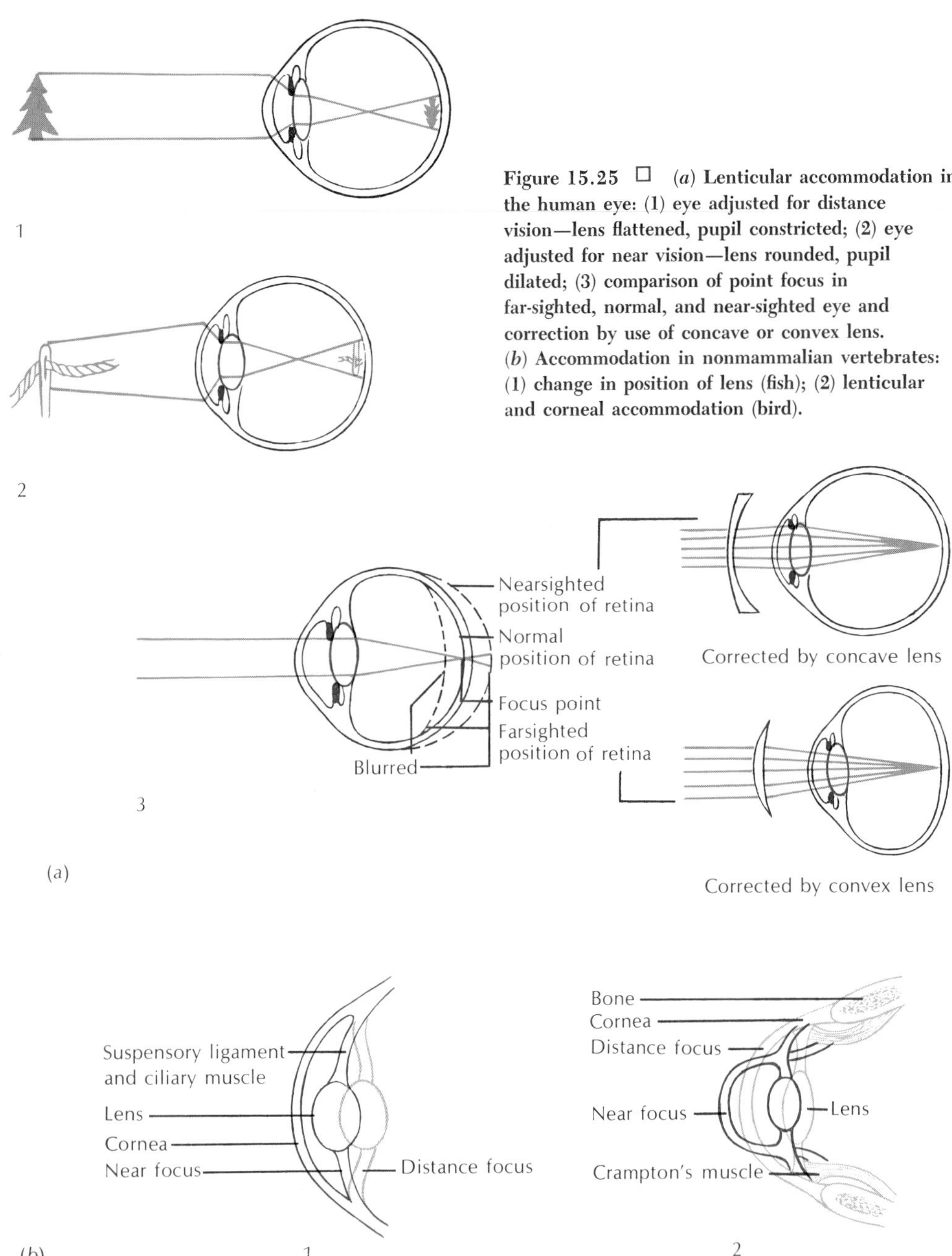

Figure 15.25 □ **(*a*) Lenticular accommodation in the human eye: (1) eye adjusted for distance vision—lens flattened, pupil constricted; (2) eye adjusted for near vision—lens rounded, pupil dilated; (3) comparison of point focus in far-sighted, normal, and near-sighted eye and correction by use of concave or convex lens. (*b*) Accommodation in nonmammalian vertebrates: (1) change in position of lens (fish); (2) lenticular and corneal accommodation (bird).**

in focus unless they can be bent more strongly. In the human eye the lens is the major structure involved in accommodation. When the eye is at rest it is accommodated for distance vision, and the elastic lens is kept relatively flattened by tension exerted upon it by the suspensory ligaments that hold it in place. To adapt for close work, the ciliary muscles within the eyeball must contract. This relieves the tension on the suspensory ligament and allows the lens to recoil into a more rounded shape. Light passing through this rounded lens is more strongly bent and accordingly comes into focus in a shorter focal length. Nearsightedness (myopia) in man is usually due to a dominant hereditary trait that causes the eyeball to grow too long from back to front. Parallel light rays passing through cornea and lens reach a focal point in front of the retina and are out of focus once more by the time the rays actually reach the retina. This condition can be corrected by wearing concave lenses that spread the light rays so that they are diverging when they strike the cornea. A longer focal length will be required to bring these rays into focus.

Close work is tiring for the normal human eye, for the required accommodation demands that the ciliary muscles be kept in a state of contraction. For the congenitally farsighted (hypermetropic) eye the situation is even worse, for the eyeball is too short from front to back and a beam of diverging light rays coming from a close object cannot be brought into focus in the available focal length. While distant objects can be viewed with clarity, the farsighted individual must don convex lenses to read, these lenses serving to initiate the convergence of light rays before they strike the cornea. The aging human eye loses its capacity to accommodate as the lens becomes less elastic, and fails to round up when released from tension. As a result, reading glasses may be needed in later life by individuals who were not farsighted in youth.

Changing the shape of the lens is only one of several ways by which the eyes of vertebrates and a few invertebrates (some worms, cephalopods, and certain other molluscs) can adjust their focal length. These other means include (1) changing the degree to which the cornea is bowed and (2) changing the distance of the lens from the retina (Figure 15.25*b*). Amniotes use a combination of corneal and lenticular accommodation, but bony and cartilaginous fishes and amphibians accommodate by moving the lens. The resting eye of a bony fish is adapted for near vision, the lens being moved posteriorly for distance vision. The lens of the eye of a shark or a frog is normally positioned toward the rear, and is moved forward for focusing upon nearby objects. Lenticular accommodation in amniotes involves changes in lens shape. The lenses of birds and reptiles are flattened and accommodated for distance vision when at rest. For close vision, the lens is made round by pressure exerted by the surrounding ciliary muscles. We have already noted that in the mammalian eye the lens rounds up spontaneously when released from tension.

Figure 15.26 □ (*a*) **The eyes of this young orangutan are favorably placed for binocular vision, allowing depth perception. Like man, the eyes track synchronously (conjugate fixation), each viewing the same object but from a slightly different angle. (*Zoological Society of San Diego.*) (*b*) Visual pathway from retina to brain, showing physical basis for conjugate fixation and depth perception.**

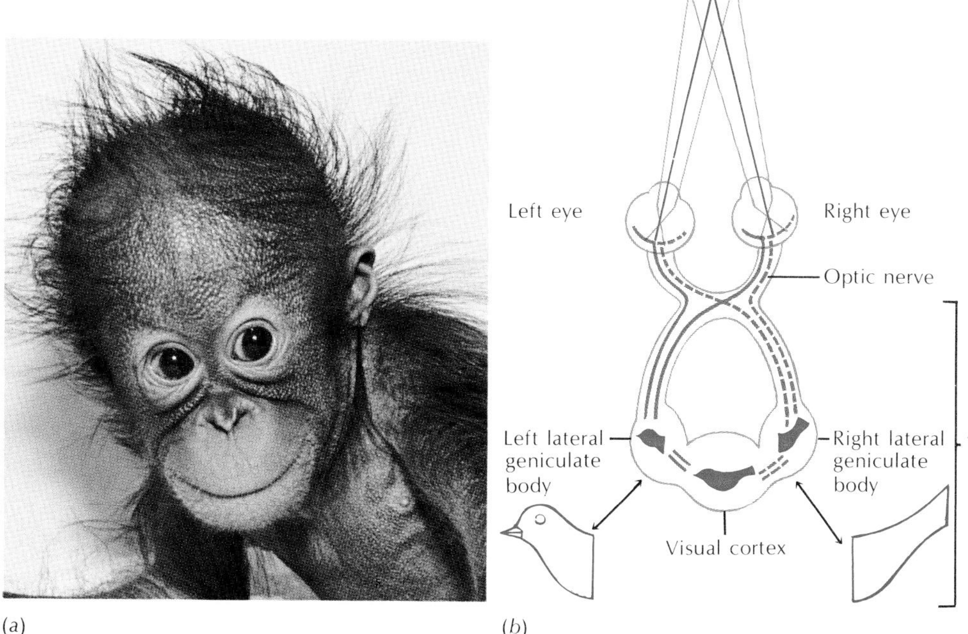

Depth perception Many animals view separate visual fields with each eye. However, if both eyes can be brought to bear upon the same point simultaneously, the slightly different perspective obtained by each eye allows a near object to be perceived as three-dimensional and its distance from the observer to be estimated. Depth perception demands (1) that the eyes be forward-directed, producing a *binocular* field of vision, and (2) that the eye muscles be capable of *conjugate fixation,* that is, of moving the eyes so that a single point is brought onto the foveae of both eyes at once (Figure 15.26). Failure to fixate conjugately results in double vision (seeing two overlapping images).

F Mechanoreception, especially hearing

Mechanoreceptors are excited when deformed by pressure, tension, or vibrations. Those located near the body surface monitor external pressure, water currents, and vibrations of the milieu, including those interpreted as sound. Those located more deeply register body position, movements, tension

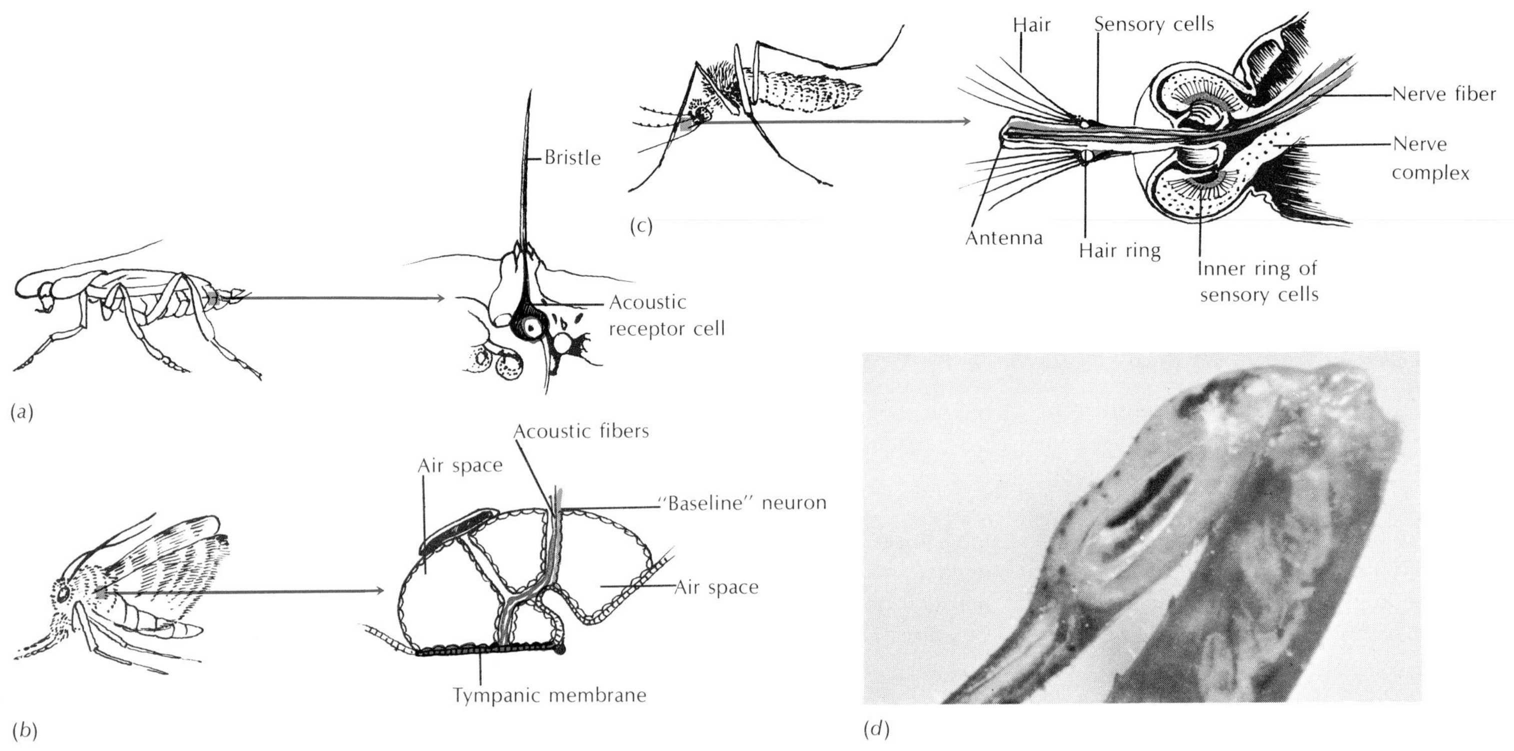

Figure 15.27 □ Hearing organs of invertebrates: (*a*) cockroach hearing hairs, each containing one nerve fiber; (*b*) tympanic membrane of a moth, each ear having three nerve fibers (*after K. D. Roeder and A. G. Treat*); (*c*) hearing apparatus of a mosquito, each ear containing about 30,000 nerve fibers (*modified from Risler*); (*d*) photo of tympanic membrane on foreleg of long-horned grasshopper (*courtesy of Dr. Ross E. Hutchins*).

in muscles and joints, and distension of hollow organs. Many basically reflexive activities such as tonal and postural muscular adjustments, breathing, urination, defecation, and regulation of heart rate and blood pressure, are initiated or regulated by means of impulses from internally located mechanoreceptors. Intake of food is quantitatively controlled by stretch receptors in the stomach wall. Insects with these sensory pathways surgically interrupted may continue to feed until their stomachs actually burst!

The capacity to detect sound, that is, oscillatory vibrations of the milieu within a given frequency range, has proven of great significance in the integration of organism and environment. Acoustic organs help the animal to detect prey, avoid enemies, and recognize other individuals of the same species. Probably almost all animals have some degree of acoustic sensitivity, for even general pressure receptors can detect sound vibrations transmitted through water, but special organs of hearing seem to be limited to insects and vertebrates.

HEARING IN INSECTS The acoustic organs of insects are modified sensilla that lie upon elastic strands suspended within the body cavity. These sensilla are excited by being stretched, especially by vibratory displacements of the exoskeleton at points where the supporting strands are anchored. Insects with sensitive hearing often possess large, thin tympanic membranes (eardrums) located on each side of the thorax. Behind each eardrum lies an air-filled cavity within which is suspended the sensillum with its sensory cells.

Actually, such a variety of acoustic organs occurs in insects (Figure 15.27) that few generalizations can be made about them except that they are extremely sensitive to changes in intensity and rhythm but seem insensitive to changes in pitch or timbre (tonal quality). The ear of a mosquito occupies the base of its antenna and contains some 30,000 neurons. The ear of a katydid is housed in its leg. That of a noctuid moth lies in the thorax and contains but three neurons; such parsimonious construction has simplified analysis of its function.

The ears of moths are specifically adapted for detecting the ultrasonic pulses emitted by hunting bats, the moths' worst enemy. Each of the three neurons in the ear has a distinct function. One emits a spontaneous rhythmic pulse at 10 to 20 sec intervals that seems to provide a base level of stimulation meaning "no bat." The other two cells are acoustic receptors, differing in sensitivity and responsible for triggering two distinct behavior patterns on the part of the moth when it is approached by a bat: (1) when the bat is detected at a distance, only one of the two acoustic receptors is excited in each ear and the slight difference in time needed for the sound to strike each ear makes it possible for the moth to perceive the direction from which the sound has come and to alter its flight path so as to move away from the source; (2) when the bat is close by, the second receptor, responsive only to sounds of high intensity, also begins to fire—causing the moth to engage in erratic maneuvers that are the best means of eluding a bat during its final closing swoop. Whereas many insects produce and detect sounds of characteristic rhythm that serve to attract mates, only a few species of moths are known to emit sounds that specifically serve to confuse a predator. Upon detection of a bat near at hand, these talented insects give vent to a burst of ultrasound in the bat's own frequency range (but at much lower intensity). This has the effect of causing the bat to swerve or fall silent, listening. During this instant the moth folds its wings and dives to the ground, undetected by the bat's sonar detection system.

HEARING IN VERTEBRATES The evolution of vertebrate sound reception must be interpreted in relation to the movement of tetrapods from water to the land. Many changes have come about, especially in the sound-conduction system but also in the actual receptive portion of the ear; these changes have increased the range of vibrations to which the tetrapod ear is sensitive and have made the ear more susceptible to stimulation by air-borne vibrations.

Hearing and equilibrium sense in fish Fish have two different organs of hearing. Probably the better developed of these is the *lateral line system,* which detects water currents, pressure changes, and water-borne vibrations—including those in the frequency range we know as sound (Figure 15.28). The lateral line system consists of a longitudinal canal running beneath the skin

Figure 15.28 □ **Section through portion of lateral line system of a fish.**

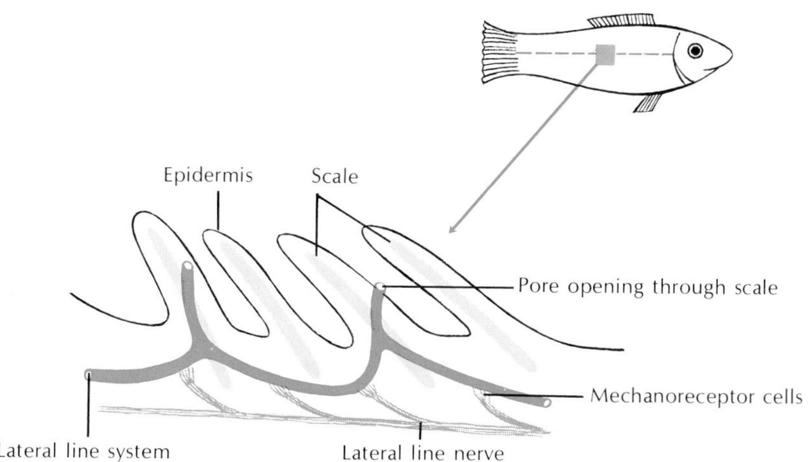

Figure 15.29 □ The membranous labyrinth, of which portions concerned with position and balance are colored: (*a*) man, showing prominent cochlea concerned with hearing and chair analogy of relative positions of semicircular canals (*after B. Hardy*); (*b*) receptors in ampulla of semicircular canal, concerned with detection of head movements, (*c*) fish, showing otoliths in gravity-sensing chambers (lagena, utriculus, sacculus); (*d*) reptile, showing increased length of lagena with heightened acoustic function.

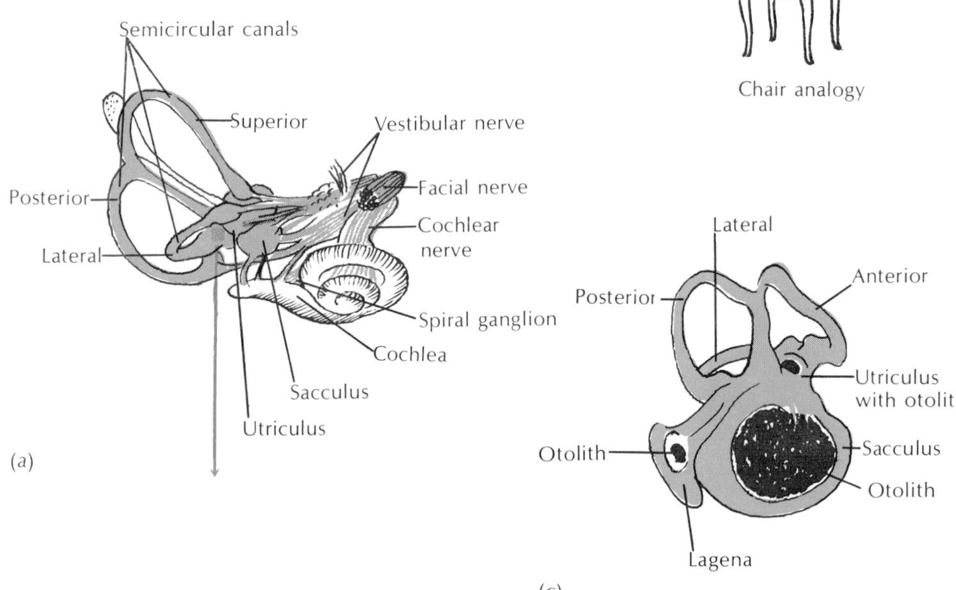

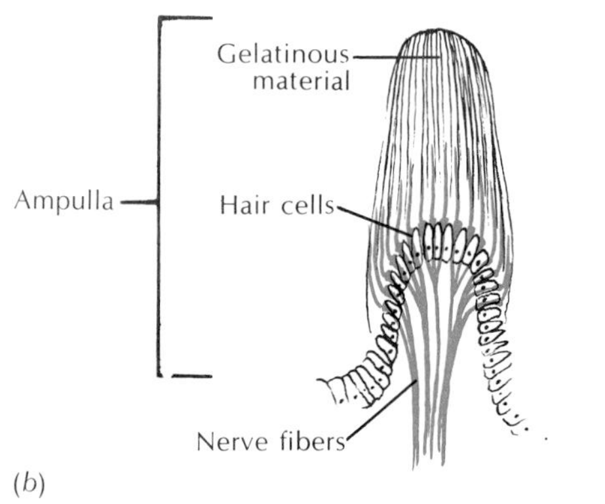

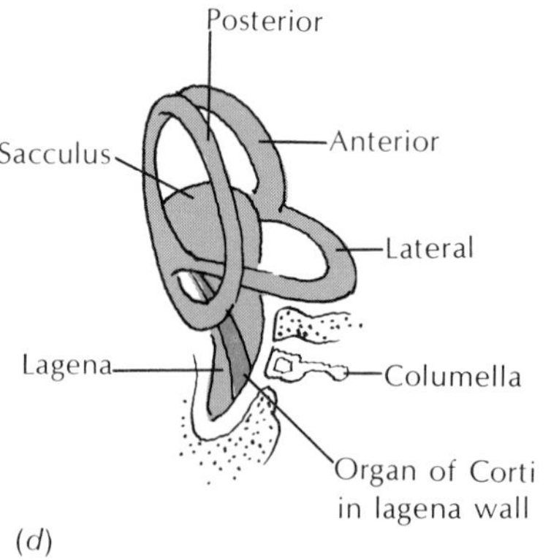

along each side of the body and partially lined with mechanoreceptive cells that are excited when their ciliary processes are bent or stretched. The second organ, concerned with equilibrium as well as hearing, is the *labyrinth,* a hollow, fluid-filled membranous organ of complex shape embedded in the skull bones on each side of the head. The labyrinth retains its equilibratory function in all vertebrates; its acoustic function, still rudimentary in fishes, becomes increasingly important during the transition from water to land.

The mechanoreceptors that line a portion of the labyrinth are quite similar to those of the lateral line system, suggesting that the labyrinth evolved by modification of the anterior portion of that system.

The labyrinth consists of three saccular chambers, the *lagena, sacculus,* and *utriculus,* and three *semicircular canals,* each arranged at right angles to the other two, like the back, arm, and seat of a chair (Figure 15.29). All of these spaces interconnect and are filled with a common fluid, the *endolymph.* Awareness of position in the earth's gravitational field depends upon receptors housed in the sacculus and utriculus, and primitively also in the lagena. In each of these chambers the ciliary processes of the sensory cells are embedded in a gelatinous material that covers a calcareous nodule, the *otolith.* As the otolith moves within the cavity in response to changes in head position, its weight pulls upon these ciliary processes, generating nerve impulses that inform the brain as to the head's position relative to the gravitational field of the earth.

The semicircular canals detect head movements. Within these canals are clusters of receptors, the processes of which are embedded in gelatinous cones (cupulae) that are displaced when the endolymph rotates within the canals as the head moves about. We do not know if a fish escaping from a whirlpool feels dizzy, but in our own experience rapid rotation of the head causes dizziness due to the fact that when the head comes to rest inertia causes the fluid in the semicircular canals to continue to rotate, giving a sensation of spinning when no movement is actually in progress. Information relayed to the brain by way of the acoustic nerve is essential for maintaining equilibrium; disease of the inner ear, as well as causing deafness, can have the disastrous effect of destroying the sense of balance and also of causing chronic sensations of dizziness.

The lagena, still a gravity-sensing organ in fishes, bears in its wall the *organ of Corti,* which contains the acoustic receptors. During its evolution in tetrapods, the lagena lengthens and coils, giving rise to the *cochlea* of the mammalian ear (Figure 15.30). The organ of Corti lengthens too, with a concomitant increase from less than 5,000 to as many as 40,000 nerve fibers serving the organ.

The mammalian ear The membranous labyrinth occupies a cavity in the mammalian temporal bone, which is of complementary shape and is known as the *osseous labyrinth;* together, they constitute the inner ear (*vestibule*). Only the cochlear portion of the mammalian vestibule is very different from that of lower vertebrates. The cochlear membranous labyrinth is long but coiled. It forms the endolymph-filled cochlear duct, within the wall of which lies the ribbonlike organ of Corti. The cochlear membranous labyrinth is suspended within the bony labyrinth in such a way that the latter is subdivided into two parallel canals, the vestibular and tympanic canals, which are continuous with one another at the smallest turn of the cochlea. These canals are occupied by a fluid (*perilymph*) distinct from the endolymph filling the cochlear duct. The detection of sound depends on the setting up of vibrations within the canals of the *osseous* labyrinth; these vibrations are then propagated to the hair cells of the organ of Corti.

While still in the water or even crawling upon the ground, vertebrates could rely on the transmission of vibrations to the inner ear by bone conduction. The effective detection of air-borne vibrations, however, required the evolution of a sophisticated sound-conduction pathway by which these vibrations could, in effect, be "focused" upon the inner ear. The amniote ear communicates with the exterior by way of an external ear canal. In mammals this canal is framed by the expanded *pinna*—the usually movable organ (which we inaccurately call the "ear") that collects sound vibrations and aids in their localization. The sound waves travel down the external ear canal to its inner terminal, the thin eardrum, which starts to vibrate. Interior to the eardrum lies the air-filled middle ear cavity, communicating with the pharynx by way of the Eustachian canal. This passage allows air pressure to be equalized on both sides of the eardrum: when the Eustachian canal is blocked during infection, any extensive change in altitude may cause extreme ear pain. The middle ear cavity also serves as a place into which vibrations that have traveled through the cochlear fluid can be dissipated: the air in the cavity is compressible while the fluid is not.

Vibrations of the eardrum are transmitted across the middle ear cavity by tiny bones (ossicles), of which there is only one (the columella) in nonmammalian tetrapods, but three (the hammer, anvil, and stirrup) in mammals, derived from bones earlier involved in jaw suspension (see Figure 8.19). The "footplate" of the stirrup is cemented to a membrane stretched across an *oval window* into the vestibular canal of the cochlea. In the passage of vibrations from eardrum to stirrup, their amplitude is reduced but the sound pressure is multiplied some twentyfold, for the vibration of a comparatively large membranous surface is being transformed into the pistonlike movements of a much tinier bone.

Pulsing rhythmically against the oval window, the stirrup sets up vibrations in the fluid (perilymph) that are propagated up the vestibular canal and back down the tympanic canal, being dissipated through the membrane-covered *round window,* which opens into the middle ear and bulges out each time the oval window bulges inward. As these vibrations pass down the tympanic canal from the apex of the cochlea, they set in sympathetic motion sections of the *basilar membrane,* which bears on its inner surface the organ of Corti. The organ of Corti is sandwiched between the basilar membrane below and the *tectorial membrane* above. The latter protrudes like a shelf into the cochlear canal and is covered with a gelatinous material in which are embedded the hairlike processes of the receptor cells of the organ of Corti. When the basilar membrane vibrates, the ciliary processes of the receptor cells, adhering to the tectorial membrane,

Figure 15.30 □ (*a*) Section through human ear, showing middle ear bones in situ and membranous labyrinth suspended within bony labyrinth in temporal bone of skull. (*After Weichert.*) (*b*) Section through cochlea, showing fibers of acoustic nerve arising from organ of Corti in wall of cochlear canal. (*c*) Diagram of cochlea unrolled, showing relationships of cochlear canal with vestibular and tympanic canals of the osseous labyrinth. Arrows indicate pathway of sound vibrations. (*d*) Section through organ of Corti, showing action of basilar and tectorial membranes in exciting the receptor cells: (1) fluid pressure against basilar membrane creates shearing force on tectorial membrane; (2) shearing force set up between tectorial membrane and organ of Corti excites receptor cells. The membranous labyrinth is shown in pale color throughout.

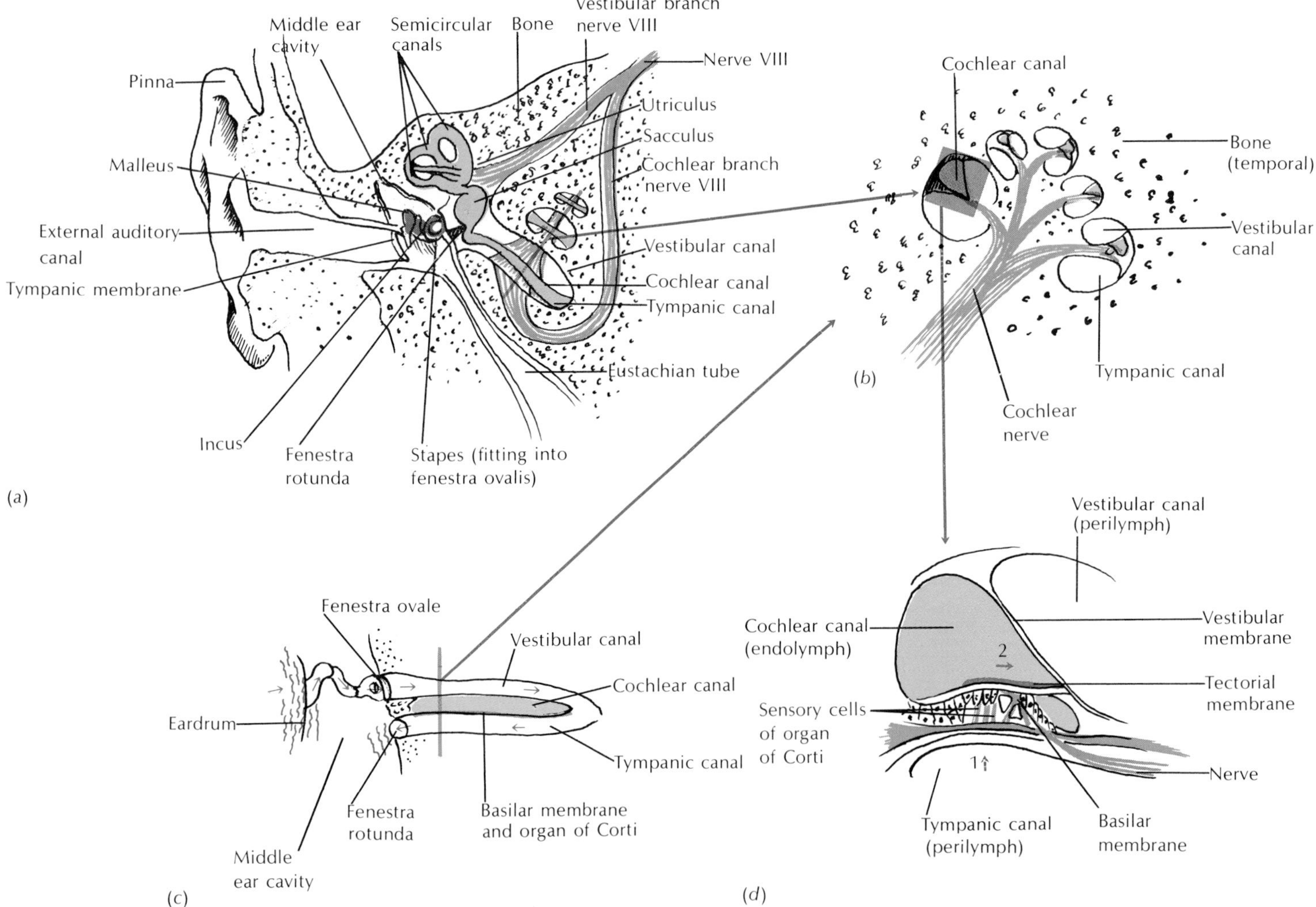

are yanked and stretched. This mechanical stimulation excites the receptors, which in turn trigger nerve impulses that travel to the brain, where they may be "translated" at the perceptual level into a meaningful signal.

But how can we explain the fact that we also discriminate between sounds of different pitch (frequency), loudness (amplitude), and tonal quality (timbre)? Detection of sound amplitude is the simplest to explain. The louder the sound, the stronger the vibrations set up along the sound-conduction pathway and within the cochlea. More receptors are excited, and more nerve impulses fired. Discrimination of pitch and timbre depend upon the capacity of the basilar membrane to vibrate *in sections* rather than always as a whole. Timbre, the quality that makes the tone of an individual voice or musical instrument distinctive, results from the fact that most vibrating bodies not only give off vibrations at one main frequency (the primary tone) but also by vibrating in parts give off *overtones* of other frequencies. Sounds of less than 50 Hz set the entire basilar membrane in motion and are heard as a roar or rumble. Sounds of frequencies above 50 Hz set into motion only those parts of the basilar membrane that resonate in response to the primary tone and overtones. The section of the basilar membrane nearest the apex of the cochlea vibrates most strongly at low frequencies, whereas the highest frequencies are detected close to the round window. With advancing age our ears lose their sensitivity to sounds of high pitch. This partial deafness is more pronounced in men; thus the husband who becomes deaf to his wife's voice may not (as she is likely to conclude) be guilty of inattentiveness.

15.3 ◻ THE FUNCTIONAL ORGANIZATION OF NERVOUS SYSTEMS

Through its sensory windows the organism looks out upon the world, sampling stimuli and initiating responses on the basis of meaningful cues. By way of its interoceptors, the organism also monitors its own body conditions, setting in motion those largely unconscious physiological responses essential to proper body function. Information from receptors flows in constantly to the central nervous system, where perception, integration, and response selection take place. Here sensory data of various modalities can be simultaneously compared and may also be assessed in terms of past experience. Then, according to the way in which the physical basis of response has been organized in the brain, a response may be selected partially at random (that is, by trial and error), or on the basis of previous experience; or, alternatively, the sensory data may trigger an innate response, shaped by natural selection and not dependent on previous experience or on some "free-will" decision-making process.

Many interesting discoveries are being made at this time on the organization and functioning of animal nervous systems—from coelenterate to man. Of all areas in biology, the study of the nervous system and animal behavior may represent the most exciting field for current investigation. We are beginning to understand more about how nervous systems *may* function and how information *may* be stored in the brain, but few definitive statements can yet be made as to how these vital functions actually are carried out. Without doubt we are finding that even the realm of human thought, so unique in the biotic world, is subject to natural laws and may eventually be explicable in physicochemical and molecular biological terms.

A The integratory functions of nervous systems

Integration is one of the most significant activities of nervous systems. Its essential feature is that an informational input is used to generate relevant output: for instance, a hawk sights a rabbit (input) and dives upon it (output). Integration involves the performance by the nervous system of three basic functions: (1) a *relay* function; (2) a *modulatory* function; and (3) a *storage* function. The relay function merely involves the transmission of excitation from receptor to effector by way of a more or less complicated *reflex arc*. The modulatory function involves information coding, reinforcement or inhibition of signals, and the selection of one response out of several possible alternatives. The storage function involves the formation of *engrams* ("memory traces"), whereby certain responses are reinforced and made habitual, and data are conserved for purposes of later comparison. The latter function also bears upon the interesting problem of how behavioral patterns may be *genetically* acquired.

REFLEX ARCS A reflex arc (that is, a neural pathway from receptor to effector) is the basic organizational unit of the nervous system. Although broadly speaking almost any response is initiated and carried out by way of such an arc, the term applies mainly to those simpler pathways by which reflex actions are brought about. A *reflex* is a simple, essentially automatic physiological or behavioral response, such as acceleration of the heartbeat during exercise, or the jerking away of a hand idly placed on a hot stove.

Reflex arcs of three levels of complexity may be distinguished: (1) the one-neuron reflex arc; (2) the two-neuron sensomotor reflex arc; (3) the polysynaptic reflex arc involving one or more association neurons as well as the sensory and motor neurons (Figure 15.31). But to consider these three levels as equal in importance would be to make the mistake of the savage who knows only three numerals: *one, two,* and *more-than-two.* For the third category opens up broad vistas of complexity: inclusion of association neurons in the neural pathway allows a strictly automatic stimulus-response relationship to be replaced by a wide variety of behavioral alternatives; a vast network has thus been formed for neural conduction, modulation, and storage.

The one-neuron reflex arc In this simplest type of relay, found only in the tentacles of coelenterates, a single neuron

Figure 15.31 □ Types of reflex arc. (*a*) Independent effector: a coelenterate epitheliomuscular cell serves as both receptor and effector. (*b*) One-neuron reflex pathway in coelenterate tentacle. (*c*) Two-neuron reflex arc, shown controlling knee-jerk response in man; a blow of the hammer below the knee elicits a stretch stimulus on the tendon above the kneecap. (*d*) Simple polysynaptic reflex involving only three neurons, shown eliciting withdrawal from painful cutaneous sensation. Arrows indicate the direction of the nerve impulses elicited by the stimulus *S*.

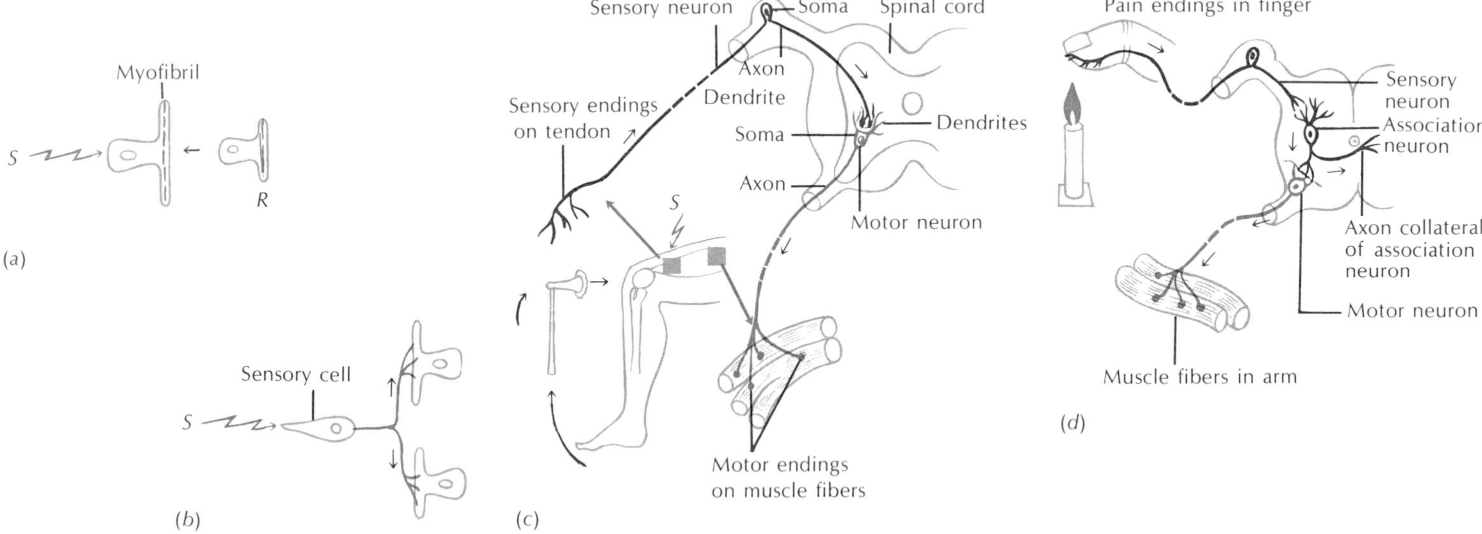

receives the stimulus at its generator region and transmits the excitation directly to the effector (a contractile or glandular cell) by way of its axon, which therefore constitutes the only possible signal pathway. No flexibility exists in this relay, for there is no opportunity for excitation to follow alternative pathways. Nevertheless, a variation in number of impulses conducted in a given amount of time can cause a weak or strong response at the neuroeffector junction.

The two-neuron sensomotor reflex arc This type of arc basically involves only two neurons: one sensory and one motor. An *afferent* sensory fiber transmits excitation from the receptor to the central nervous system, and an *efferent* motor fiber conducts it out from the central nervous system to the effector. The knee-jerk reflex in man is an example of a simple response mediated by a sensomotor arc: a smart tap administered on the tendon below the kneecap causes sudden contraction of the muscles that straighten the leg. The pathway is inflexible, but there is opportunity for the signal to spread if the sensory neuron gives off axon collaterals to more than one motor neuron. Also, the response may be blocked by synaptic fatigue or, on the other hand, the synapse may be *facilitated* (made easier to cross) by repeated use of the pathway. *Summation* may also play a role here, for if a given motor neuron is served by axon terminals from several sensory neurons, impulses from more than one sensory neuron may be required to make this motor neuron fire.

The polysynaptic reflex arc The role of central modulation in determining what stimuli will actually evoke a response and what the character of that response will be increases in importance when association neurons are involved in the pathway between sensory and motor neurons. These polysynaptic arcs mainly occur in the *central* nervous system (brain and major neural trunks such as the spinal cord), where many neuron-to-neuron synapses are available. Branching, converging, and even circular pathways of varying degrees of complexity can now intervene between the sensory input and the efferent impulse to the effector. In a complex association field such as that provided by the vertebrate brain, a great abundance of alternative pathways exist: the strictly reflexive character of the stimulus-response relationship dissolves into a flexible modulating system in which one or more appropriate efferent pathways are selected on the basis of high-speed comparisons between present input and arrays of previously stored data.

CENTRAL MODULATION All factors that intervene between stimulus and response may be considered modulatory whether these occur peripherally, at receptor or effector, or within the central nervous system. We shall confine ourselves to considering mainly what may go on in the central nervous system, for here lies the greatest capacity for modulation. The questions with which we shall deal are the following. (1) How is information encoded in the nerve impulse (or in the decremental conduction current characteristic of many central neurons)? (2) How are signals reinforced or diminished? (3) What is the significance of pathway facilitation?

Informational codes used in conduction A nerve cell need not give off a strict "go–no-go" signal to other cells with which it is in synaptic contact. At least three different informational codes are known that can affect the character of synaptic transmission and the response of the cell being affected at the synapse. These are (*a*) frequency code, (*b*) duration code, and (*c*) pulse code (Figure 15.32).

A *frequency code* is the number of impulses transmitted in a given unit of time as compared with the maximum number a neuron is able to transmit. Up to this physiological limit, the frequency code gives information on the *intensity* of the stimulus, for the stronger the stimulus, the higher the frequency will be.

A *duration code* is possible for neurons that fire like machine guns instead of like pistols, emitting volleys rather than single shots for each pull on the trigger. The length of these impulse bursts may alter the quality or intensity of response by the postsynaptic cell.

Pulse coding appears to be characteristic of many central neurons that display a high degree of "spontaneous" activity. These neurons emit impulses in patterned sequences, not unlike Morse code but fixed and repetitive. Even when action potentials are not generated, the decremental conduction current and/or the synaptic discharge can be pulse coded. An example of pulse coding is the "dash-dot-dash-dash, dash-dot-dash-dash" signal endlessly emitted by the lobster cardiac ganglion. The frequency may change, accelerating or decelerating the heartbeat, but the pulse remains the same. Recent evidence suggests that some two-axon neurons are capable of transmitting two different pulse codes simultaneously, one via each axon!

One of the intriguing aspects of pulse coding is that in some cases the pattern characteristic of a given neuron may prove to be genetically determined, while in other cases the pulse code may be set up or modified as a result of changes that take place in a neuron during learning.

Modification of signal strength An organism could never react effectively if it had to react to *all* stimuli reaching its brain from the receptors. One of the most essential aspects of central modulation is the screening of afferent signals so that some will be strengthened and reacted to, whereas others will be ignored or blocked out before they even reach the level of conscious perception. Particularly significant in this regard is the reticular activating system (to be discussed in Section 15.3C), which protects the animal from the distracting effect of excessive stimulation while at the same time directing its attention to significant signals, even though these be faint.

Such modulatory action occurs in our daily lives whenever we must pick one thread of conversation out of the mixed voices of a crowded room. Although significant differences in volume may be lacking, we usually experience little difficulty in following the conversation on which our attention is centered. But let another voice give out one "cue word" of special significance to us (for instance, our own name), and without conscious effort our attention stream may be diverted to this new channel, now "tuning out" the signals previously noted.

How such screening and selection of signals is accomplished we have yet to learn. Reduction in the amount of signal "noise"* propagated throughout the nervous system may be partially due to the fact that excitatory synaptic contacts from a number of other neurons may be necessary to make a given central neuron fire. We have noted the necessity for such spatial summation in the activation of ganglionic neurons in the retina. In turn, excitation from several of these sensory neurons may be required to arouse one neuron in the brain, and so forth. The firing of central neurons may also be actively inhibited by impulses from nerve cells that release inhibitory transmitter substances upon their membranes. Still a third way in which a signal may be damped out is during the process of decremental conduction through the elaborate dendritic "tree" characteristic of many association neurons. Unless the signal is sufficiently strong, it will fade out before reaching the axon of that neuron.

Augmentation, the reinforcement of excitation, may be due partly to *pathway facilitation.* As mentioned earlier, repeated use causes a synapse to become easier for

Figure 15.32 □ **Methods of information coding in nervous conduction: (*a*) frequency code (low frequency represents low stimulus intensity; high frequency, high stimulus intensity); (*b*) duration code; (*c*) pulse code.**

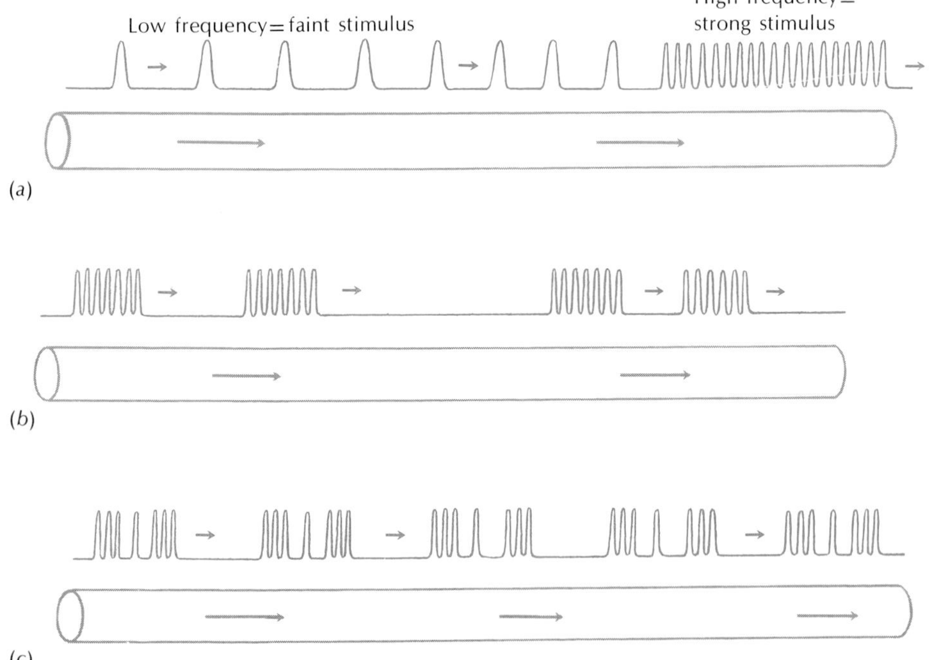

*The term *noise* is used here in the sense of irrelevant input that interferes with perception of meaningful data.

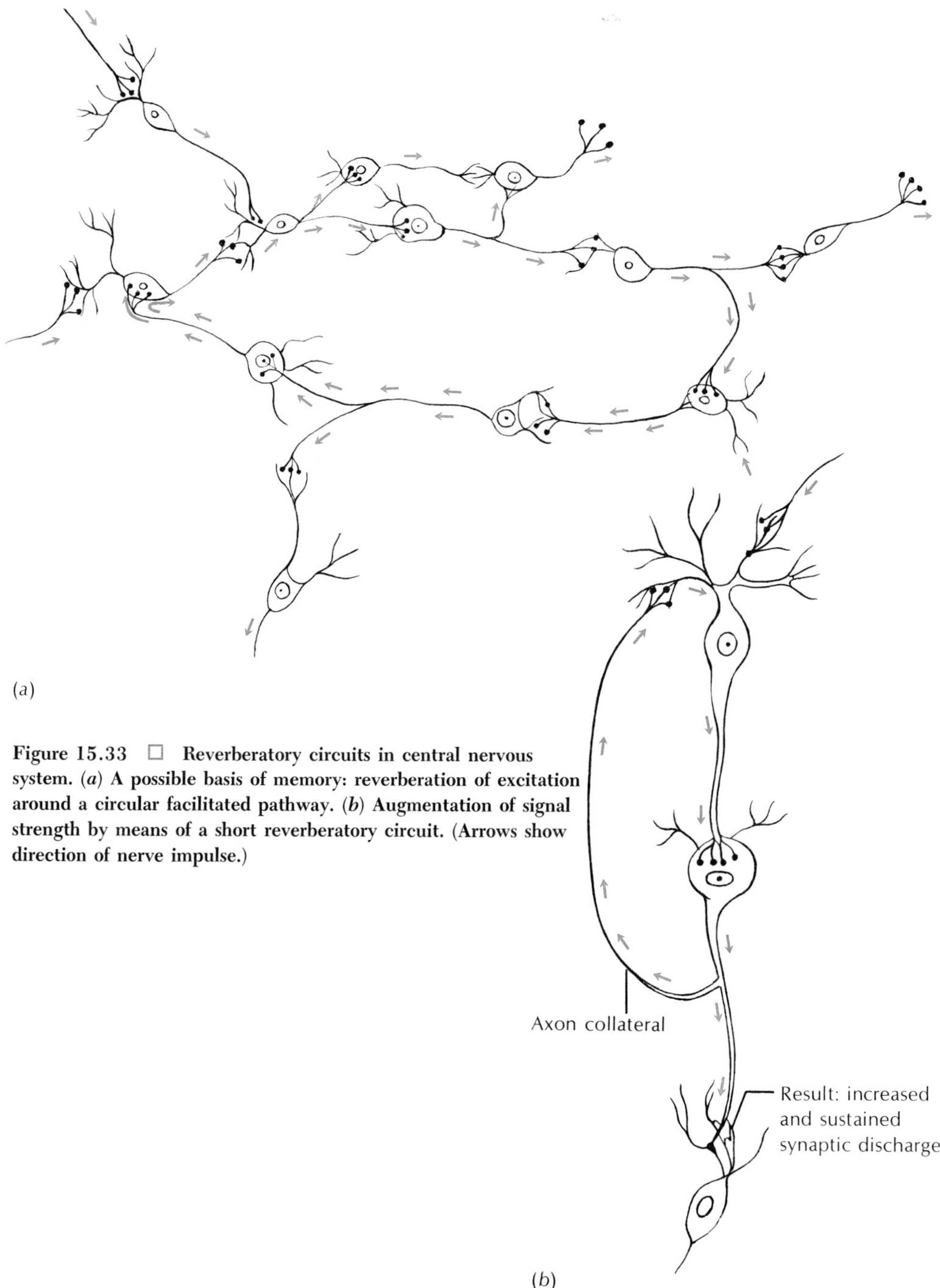

Figure 15.33 □ **Reverberatory circuits in central nervous system. (*a*) A possible basis of memory: reverberation of excitation around a circular facilitated pathway. (*b*) Augmentation of signal strength by means of a short reverberatory circuit. (Arrows show direction of nerve impulse.)**

an impulse to cross. Within the association fields of the central nervous system, where many alternate pathways exist for synaptic transmission, such synaptic facilitation may have important long-term consequences. If neuron *A* gives off terminals upon both neurons *B* and *C* but at the first excitation chances to stimulate *B* instead of *C*, upon each consecutive stimulation it is even more likely to continue to excite *B* instead of *C*. Where a number of neurons are involved, gradually an entire pathway through the association field is facilitated; each time the pathway is used thereafter the facilitation is strengthened, so that it becomes more and more probable that this pathway rather than others will continue to be followed. Such pathway facilitation seems to be the basis for formation of habits and the improvement of motor skills by repetition (practice).

The reinforcement of excitation may also be due to the establishment of one or more *reverberatory circuits* along the neural pathway. These are circular pathways around which the excitation may propagate itself endlessly (Figure 15.33a). With only occasional sensory input, a reverberatory circuit may persist indefinitely, maintaining the facilitation of the pathway and also serving to keep the neurons in a basal state of arousal that allows them to reach peak excitation when only a slight increase in signal input takes place. This type of cyclic self-excitation may also constitute one of the major means by which information is stored in the brain.

Positive feedback in short reverberatory circuits may be an important means of increasing the strength of specific signals. In this case, axon collaterals of a given neuron circle back to the neuron that excited it. The excitation of the first neuron is thus augmented and it then excites the second neuron more strongly than before (Figure 15.33*b*). Unless it is interrupted by an inhibitory input, this reverberatory circuit will continue to function until it is turned off by synaptic fatigue.

Even when sleeping, the brain may unceasingly trace over circular facilitated pathways, its activity being phased in such a way that rhythmic, spontaneous discharges of electricity are given off, which are so great that they can be monitored by electrodes applied to the outside of the cranium and recorded (by an electroencephalograph). These *brain waves* indicate that large numbers of neurons are discharging *synchronously* rather than at random. Such smooth waves of spontaneous activity are rare in the brains of invertebrates, where individual neurons fire more independently and spasmodically. How this synchrony is maintained we do not know, but its existence suggests an intrinsic rhythmicity of brain function onto which the changing pattern of sensory input and response is merely superimposed.

Sensation One of the least well understood aspects of nervous activity is the production of *sensations*. We recognize sensations as pervasive subjective states that are to some extent either pleasurable or painful, or both. Pleasurable sensations promote responses that prolong or intensify exposure to the stimulus; however, prolonged or intensified exposure can modify the sensation produced by the stimulus, and a more or less painful or obnoxious sensation may then develop, leading to responses that lessen the intensity of the stimulation or remove the organism from that stimulus. Interestingly, many stimuli that produce pleasurable sensations at lower intensities may become aversive at higher intensities (for instance, music played at moderate volume may evoke pleasurable sensations but may instead produce confusion and even dizziness and nausea, if played at very high intensities).

Painful and pleasurable sensations both have adaptive value, for the former result in the organism's removing itself from a potentially injurious situation, whereas the latter encourage performance of activities that enhance the well-being of the individual or help to perpetuate the species. Pleasurable sensations are often associated with the performance of such basic functions as eating, mating, and suckling of young. It is therefore not surprising to find that, when slender needle electrodes are inserted into brain centers associated with these activities, an animal such as a rat or monkey can learn to turn on such pleasurable stimulants electrically and will then do so for hours, sometimes even in preference to performing the genuine acts!

Pain as a sensation is more difficult to analyze, for its intensity appears to be greatly influenced by such factors as past experience. Animals reared in isolation, protected from all hurts, are found deficient in the perception of pain. Puppies reared in this manner were found later even to sniff at flames, not giving evidence of pain although actually burned. Pain receptors seem to be naked, unmodified dendrites, but what the stimulus may be that excites them still requires clarification. An actual wound may cause the release of chemicals from the damaged tissues that could arouse the pain receptors, but pain can also be induced by strong pressure, heat, intense cold, muscle spasm, and so forth. Internal pain is unusual in being *referred* to the body wall, often in parts distant from the affected organ. Thus one symptom of heart trouble is pain referred to the inside of the left arm and the left chest muscles (*angina pectoris*). The explanation of referred pain is that it is referred to the skin areas innervated by the same spinal segment from which the visceral sensory fibers arose. The brain itself has no pain receptors, but "headaches" may originate in the membranes (*meninges*) covering the brain.

Any sensory input of sufficient magnitude is interpreted by the brain as a sensation. Light and color are sensations, and so are warmth, cold, hunger, and sound. Why does the squeaking of chalk on a blackboard often produce an aversive "chill" of almost unbearable intensity? Why do a succession of tones recognized as "music" evoke lively feelings of enjoyment? Why do other sounds produce neither pleasure nor pain? These are riddles of perception that await solution.

INFORMATION STORAGE: MEMORY Without some means of recording the passing moment, an organism must exist like a clockwork mechanism, responding only to present stimuli and incapable of changing its response to such stimuli. Short-term modifications of response, implying at least brief retention, are seen even in the simplest animals. Place a paramecium in a sealed tube little larger than its own diameter and you will find that upon reaching the end of the tube it will butt fruitlessly against the closed end for only a limited number of times before laboriously executing a jackknife turn that enables it to swim in the opposite direction. Long-term modifications of response require equally long-term retention. We have already seen (Section 11.3C) that consolidation of memory can be interfered with if a drug capable of suppressing either RNA synthesis or protein synthesis is administered shortly after a training period, but that such administration is without effect if it takes place after the time required for "fixing" the memory has elapsed. These and other lines of investigation indicate that long-term retention is accompanied by ineradicable changes in brain cells that involve RNA and/or protein synthesis. It is postulated that during this period a macromolecular configuration representing the intracellular *engram* (memory trace) is formed and thereafter is maintained or renewed as necessary.

This lasting change may be brought about by the repeated stimulation involved when a facilitated, reverberatory pathway is set up; it may in turn stabilize and perpetuate this circuit by altering the neuron's sensitivity to stimulation or the manner in which it transmits the impulse.

Although we have previously likened a neuron to a gun, inactive except when fired, a neuron is a *living* unit and a gun is not. It is not inert when unstimulated, nor is it always fully "fired" when stimulated. It may conduct excitation as bursts or coded pulses. Furthermore, it is not necessarily restricted to transmitting only one type of message. Especially in association fields, where neurons seldom exceed 1 mm in total length, the decremental conduction current described earlier is likely to be the sole language of communication. A neuron that has undergone the final differentiation of intracellular engram formation may "speak a different language" than it did before: once the macromolecular engram has been formed, the behavior of that cell may be irreversibly changed.

Also noted in Section 11.3C was the fact that localized stimulation of the cerebral cortex of unanesthetized human subjects strongly supports the idea that the record of experiences, in man at least, is preserved nearly intact: even trivial events are ineradicably recorded; only those things that were not consciously noted at the time may be omitted. Such detailed retention implies that the human brain has a storage capacity of staggering magnitude. The storage of so many bits of information (using "bit" in the computer sense of an item evoking a single *yes-no,* or *on-off* response) suggests that not only the estimated 10^{10} cerebral neurons but also the estimated 10^{11} neuroglial cells may be involved in the process of retention. This does not even take into account the storage capacity of the vast subcortical association fields of the thalamus and other important brain areas.

One estimate of the storage capacity of the human brain, based upon "bit" analysis of the record of retention revealed by direct brain stimulation, is that the brain must be capable of storing no less than 2.8×10^{20} bits of information during an average lifetime. However, psychological tests indicate that no one can consciously deal with more than about 25 bits per second; accordingly, one essential aspect of brain function must be the suppression of stored data so that they reach the conscious level only at appropriate times and in manageable quantities. Should this suppressive function fail, the past might come flooding in upon the mind with the vividness of the present, perhaps causing the complete derangement sometimes seen clinically in cases of severe psychosis.

B The evolution and functional organization of nervous systems

TECHNIQUES OF INVESTIGATION Anatomical studies of nervous systems are revealing, but much less so than such studies of other organ systems. Even the best histological techniques usually cannot trace a single neuron along its entire length and locate every one of its synaptic connections. Furthermore, even if such anatomical connections could be determined, we would still not know which synapses were excitatory and which inhibitory. It is evident that real understanding of the organization of nervous systems must come through techniques other than those of strict morphology. Various approaches to analyzing the functional organization of nervous systems include the following. (1) The basic circuitry or "wiring pattern" of the nervous system can be mapped by severing individual fiber tracts close to the cell bodies of the neurons from which they arise. Such tract interruption may produce well-defined deficiencies in perception or motor performance that shed light on the functional significance of that tract. In addition, the detached portion of the fibers degenerate, with changes that are visible to microscopic inspection and can be traced to the synapses. (2) Larger portions of the nervous system can be destroyed in situ, and the resultant behavioral deficits observed. The extent to which various mammals are dependent on the cerebral cortex has been defined by surgically stripping away certain amounts of cortex. By this means it has been found that a fully decorticated rat has no demonstrable motor impairment although it no longer can make complex visual discriminations. A decorticated cat moves like a sleepwalker and seems actually to be unconscious, although responding appropriately to painful stimuli. Decorticated monkeys become nearly blind and are partially paralyzed; decorticated human beings are not only totally blind and severely paralyzed but soon die—even though their essential vegetative functions are not fundamentally impaired. Decortication involves the removal of many billions of neurons; at the other extreme, it is possible to destroy single nerve cells by using laser beams of microscopic diameter. Such destruction is most useful in analyzing the organization of arthropod brains in which few cells are present and every cell may have a distinct job to perform. (3) Recording electrodes can be used to detect electrical changes in the brain and nerves when certain fibers or receptors are stimulated. The production of glass microelectrodes with tips less than 0.5 μm in diameter has even made it possible to record the activity of single neurons in vivo, although it cannot be certain that inserting even so small an instrument into a fiber or cell body only some 10 to 40 μm in diameter may not somehow modify its behavior. (4) Direct stimulation of localized areas of the brain have been very useful in "mapping" the functional regions of the brain. In addition to mild electrical stimulation of the exposed surface of the brain, as can be done in the course of brain surgery, needle electrodes can be inserted deeply into the brains of experimental animals and allowed to remain in place indefinitely without detectable harm. Mild stimulation via these electrodes sometimes evokes specific reactions. For instance electrode stimulation of the *amygdala* of the cat (a part of the brain concerned with emotional responses) causes it to growl, switch its tail, and attack models. If a nearby but functionally distinct spot is stimulated, the cat instead hisses defensively and attempts vigorously to escape. When both centers are stimulated simultaneously, the animal displays a complex, ambivalent behavior in which both escape and attack tendencies are exhibited. All that is then needed to identify the part of the brain concerned with a given response is to sacrifice the animal and then locate (by microscopic inspection of the fixed tissues) the precise region where the tip of the electrode was lodged. (5) Histochemistry, the chemical analysis of small tissue samples, has proven especially useful for studying the occurrence of various synaptic transmitter substances in different parts of the brain. Allied to this type of analysis is the application of such drugs as chlorpromazine (a tranquilizer) to determine specific effects on learning and motor performance.

All of these techniques must be brought to bear and others must be devised if the intricacies of nervous systems are to be unraveled and the physical basis of behavior is to be understood.

MAJOR TRENDS IN THE EVOLUTION OF NERVOUS SYSTEMS Evolutionary trends in neural organization and function can to a point be deduced by a comparative study of living species that have attained varying degrees of nervous complexity. However, even when there are strong morphological similarities, it is unsafe to assume functional parallelism, especially across phylum lines. An earthworm, for instance, has a brain in its head, but removal of the head does *not* abolish the memory of previous training. Quite to the contrary, once the new brain regenerates the worm then tends to "forget," since the new, untrained brain interferes with the performance of the posterior parts of the nervous system, which still retain the previous training!

Another fallacious assumption is that learning and the performance of complex patterns of behavior require a large number of cells in the brain. Despite having so few brain cells, insects display entire repertories of elaborate albeit inflexible patterns of activity associated with food getting, mating, care of the young, defense, and so forth. Furthermore, a hunting wasp with a brain the size of a pinhead has been found capable of memorizing at one glance all the landmarks needed to locate the burrows in which each of her eggs are laid. This infallible memory is necessary for her successful return to the burrows with fresh provisions, but she is thrown off if the landmarks are removed (see Figure 16.17).

Six major trends can be discerned in the evolution of nervous systems: (1) increased speed of conduction; (2) centralization; (3) increase in number of association neurons; (4) cephalization; (5) development of cephalic dominance; and (6) organization of complex association fields.

Increased speed of conduction has been achieved (*a*) by the evolution of the action potential (probably of more recent origin than decremental conduction); (*b*) by the lengthening of nerve fibers and minimization of synaptic interruptions; (*c*) by increase in fiber diameter (invertebrates); or (*d*) by nodal myelination and saltatory conduction (vertebrates).

Centralization involves the condensation of nervous tissue into one or more major neural trunks or masses from which the nerves arise. These concentrations have tended to form along the body's longitudinal axis, and have further tended to become fused into one major axial trunk, running either ventral or dorsal to the gut. These neural trunks are more like the brain than they are like nerves, for nerves consist only of nerve fibers given off by cell bodies located elsewhere, whereas neural trunks ("nerve cords") contain neuron cell bodies as well as fibers, and therefore synapses can take place within these trunks. Due to the axial concentration of nervous tissue the nervous system has become subdivided into *central* and *peripheral* portions, the latter consisting of the nerves and receptors, the former of the neural trunks and (later) the brain.

Association neurons have increased to far outnumber sensory and motor neurons in the brains of higher animals. The central nervous systems of higher animals accordingly have ceased to be mere relay stations on the pathway from receptor to effector. The multiplication of interneuron synapses has perhaps reached its ultimate expression in the mammalian brain, where individual association neurons may receive up to 1,000 axon terminals from other neurons.

Cephalization is the tendency of neural tissue and exteroceptors to become concentrated in the head, the anterior end of the longitudinal body axis. This phenomenon (although apparent even in flatworms) is most pronounced in vertebrates in which organs of sight, olfaction, taste, balance, static position, and hearing all have come to be located in the head, and the skin of the face is especially rich in receptors of heat, cold, pain, touch, and pressure. The presence of ganglia (masses of nerve tissue) in the head may lead us to conclude that these ganglia constitute a brain capable of exerting control over the rest of the nervous system (cephalic dominance), but such dominance is actually characteristic only of the brains of higher animals. In lower animals such cephalic ganglia may be concerned mainly with analysis of sensory data from the receptors concentrated in the head.

Cephalic dominance, the tendency of the anterior neural centers to assume control over the more posterior centers, is particularly characteristic of vertebrate nervous systems, in which a distinct hierarchy of control centers has evolved, with conscious control moving to ever more anterior centers. Among invertebrates cephalic dominance either is lacking, or may take the form of the *repression* of more posterior centers by those in the head. The longitudinal neural trunks of the insect nervous system have considerable autonomy, and the brain is mainly concerned with vision and sensations from receptors on the antennae and mouthparts. They are much smaller than, and exert little control over, the massive thoracic ganglia that receive acoustic and proprioceptive fibers and send motor impulses to the wings and legs. Cephalic inhibition represses such activities as copulation. In fact, copulatory activities in the praying mantis are found to increase in intensity if the head is removed; such decapitation is not infrequent in nature, for so voracious is the female mantis that she often seizes her mate as he approaches and begins to eat him head first. However, once the rest of the body is freed from the inhibitory effects of the brain, the headless male begins to walk in a circle, pulling himself free of her grasp, and while constantly performing strong S-shaped copulatory movements mounts upon her back and successfully copulates. Not being able to see what he is mounting, a decapitated male will attempt to inseminate any object of appropriate size presented to his touch. (Similar release from cephalic inhibition may be seen in the violent muscular spasms of the beheaded chicken, but these movements have no adaptive significance.)

Complex *association fields* that receive little direct sensory input have become most important in vertebrates and advanced invertebrates. The *neuropile* is the major type of association field seen in invertebrates. It consists of a dense meshwork of nerve fibers, highly branching and presenting innumerable synaptic connections. The cell bodies are not part of the neuropile, but are located around the edges (Figure 15.34). The association fields of vertebrates include not only intermeshing fibers but the cell bodies as well; thus synaptic connections may be made directly upon the cell bodies in addition to the dendrites. In vertebrate evolution, association areas have progressively increased in importance, coming to have many times the number of neurons in regions concerned strictly with sorting of sensory data. Large areas of the human cerebral cortex, particularly in the frontal lobe, have not been demonstrated either to receive sensory fibers or directly to give off motor ones but instead receive fibers from other parts of the brain; they are therefore

Figure 15.34 □ **In the optic ganglion of a fly the central association field is a neuropile consisting of a mesh of synapsing fibers, the neuron cell bodies being restricted to the periphery. (*After S. Ramón y Cajal and D. Sánchez.*)**

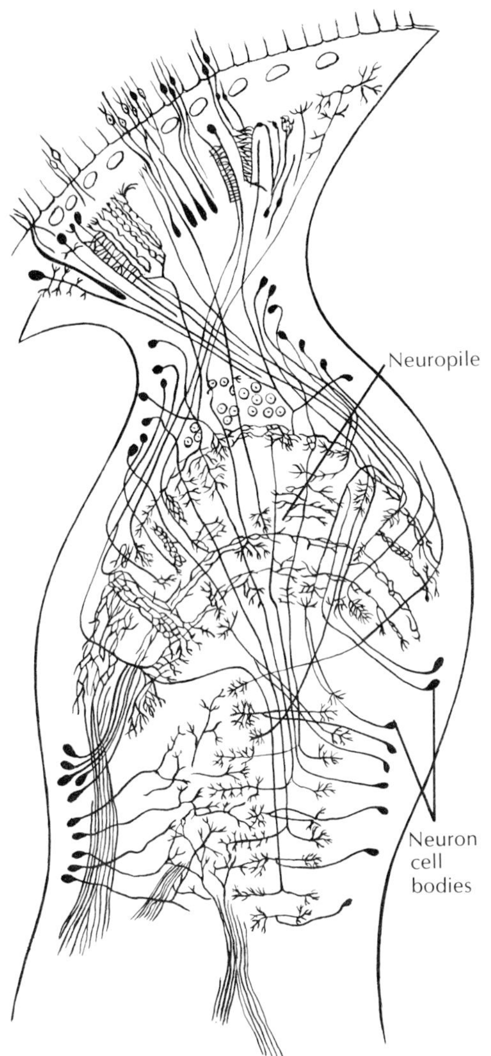

able to correlate data from all areas of the sensory system. Thus, the area of the brain concerned with specific sensory and motor systems has been proportionally diminishing relative to those areas concerned with correlation and storage of data. Similar areas are rare among invertebrates, where such correlation as is possible is largely restricted to the neuropile. However, the octopus has a large correlation area (the *verticalis complex*) in the optic lobe of its brain; removal of this region prevents the animal from remembering what it has learned for more than about 15 min.

PHYLETIC COMPARISONS Subcellular analogs of nerve fibers and "brain" occur in some complex protozoans. The neurofibrils coordinate the beating of the cilia, and may be controlled in turn by a central integrative body, the motorium (Figure 15.35). Well-developed nervous tissue may not exist in sponges, but the individual cells are *independent effectors,* that is, are capable of detecting stimuli and responding accordingly.

Coelenterates have an uncentralized nerve plexus in which the processes of bipolar and multipolar neurons crisscross and occasionally synapse. Most of the synapses are symmetrical, synaptic transmission occurring in either direction with equal facility (see Figure 12.10). Conventional polarized synapses also are found. Excitation is propagated decrementally throughout the plexus in all directions from the point of stimulation, its spread involving both facilitation and summation. Both excitatory and inhibitory synapses occur in the coelenterate nerve plexus, and in jellyfish there are also long through-conduction tracts of large fibers that interconnect different parts of the plexus and conduct more rapidly than the plexus itself. These through-conduction tracts make possible the generalized contractions used in swimming. Despite their long evolutionary history, coelenterates have advanced no farther toward centralization than the grouping of fibers into these through-conduction tracts; this may be due to some intrinsic limitation in the evolutionary potential of the radially symmetrical body plan.

Modern flatworms display a variety of nervous systems ranging from a diffuse nerve plexus (like that of hydra) to a highly centralized system consisting of paired ventral nerve trunks and a "brain" in the head. The so-called brain serves mainly as a relay station between the sensory receptors in the head and the longitudinal nerve trunks, which are the actual motor control centers and thus the worm's true brain. Between these extremes fall intermediate types having both a nerve plexus and up to eight longitudinal trunks, but lacking important ganglia in the head.

Centralization is far advanced in annelids and arthropods. The ventral series of paired segmental ganglia contain a well-developed neuropile and are interconnected by giant fiber tracts. The cell bodies of their sensory neurons are not located in the central nervous system as a rule, but peripherally, in the sensilla. Some degree of cephalic dominance is seen, at least in that the head ganglia may inhibit the more posterior centers. The most highly organized invertebrate nervous systems are those of insects and cephalopod molluscs, which we have previously considered (see Section 12.7A, B, and Figure 12.32). The arthropod brain shows a degree of organization higher than that

Figure 15.35 □ Neuromotor system of cytopharyngeal region in *Paramecium.* This network of fibrils controls the long cilia that sweep food particles into the cytopharynx. (*After E. E. Lund.*)

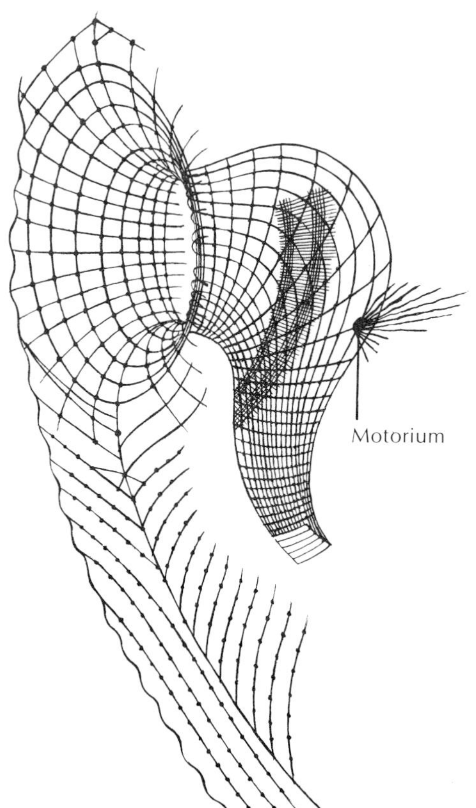

of the neuropile, for its fibers are arranged in orderly layers rather than being randomly intertwined.

The vertebrate nervous system is both centralized and highly cephalized. The cell bodies of sensory neurons are either located peripherally or in ganglia close to the central nervous system. The latter is unique in the animal kingdom in that it is basically a *hollow tube* rather than a solid cord or mass. Development of the central cavity (neurocoel), filled with nutritive cerebrospinal fluid, seems to have been at least partially responsible for allowing the vertebrate central nervous system to evolve to a size and complexity unknown among invertebrates. The food and oxygen requirements of the brain cells can be met on both surfaces of this hollow tube. Most of the increase in brain size, as in the expansion of the cerebral hemispheres, has resulted from development of fiber tracts; the neuron cell bodies still tend to be located either on the outer surface or around the neurocoel. The vertebrate nervous system is also unusual in having a high degree of cephalic dominance and in having its autonomic portion divided into sympathetic and parasympathetic divisions so that most organs are supplied with two sets of nerves that generally act in opposition. Each organ thus has both an "accelerator" and "brakes," permitting precise regulation of visceral processes.

C The vertebrate nervous system

THE PERIPHERAL SYSTEM The peripheral nervous system consists of the cranial and spinal nerves, springing from the brain and spinal cord, respectively, the sensory and autonomic ganglia, the receptors and associated peripheral neurons located in sense organs such as the eye and ear, and a few nerve plexuses such as those that run in the walls of the alimentary tract and control its contractility.

The somatic sensory-motor system The cranial and spinal nerves are given off segmentally, in pairs. With one major exception (the vagus nerve), most of the fibers making up these nerves are *somatic* sensory and motor fibers serving the body wall instead of the internal organs. Somatic sensory and motor fibers are involved with detection of external and proprioceptive stimuli and initiation of voluntary movements. *Autonomic* nerve fibers, on the contrary, are concerned with visceral sensation and response (glandular secretion and the contraction of involuntary muscles).

The cranial nerves will be considered below in conjunction with the brain, for brain function is intimately related to the flow of information through these nerves. Some cranial nerves are entirely sensory, containing only *afferent* (sensory) fibers conducting impulses to the brain from the nose, eyes, and ears. Others are exclusively motor, containing only *efferent* (motor) fibers transmitting impulses to the muscles of the tongue, neck, and eyeballs. Still other cranial nerves are *mixed* nerves containing both afferent and efferent fibers serving the tongue and throat, and the skin and muscles of the face. As we have said, nerves are bundles of fibers, bounded by a sheath of connective tissue (Figure 15.36). Larger nerves contain small blood vessels serving the Schwann cells and fibers. Like a telephone cable, a nerve carries messages to and fro, uninterrupted by synaptic connections.

Figure 15.36 □ Cross section of a peripheral nerve, showing nerve sheath (at bottom); myelin sheaths of individual fibers are stained black with osmic acid. No neuron cell bodies or synaptic junctions occur within a nerve. (*Ward's Natural Science Establishment, Inc.*)

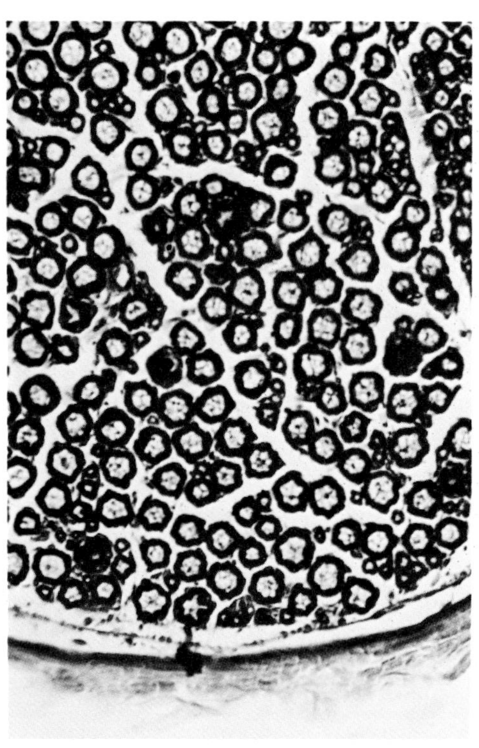

The spinal nerves arise as separate dorsal and ventral roots that quickly unite to form a common fiber trunk. Upon the dorsal root is situated the dorsal root ganglion, containing the cell bodies of sensory neurons. The dorsal root is exclusively sensory, the ventral root exclusively motor. This can be proven simply by severing one root while leaving the other intact. Dorsal root section causes loss of sensation in the affected body segment, while the motor capabilities are unimpaired. Conversely, ventral root section paralyzes the muscles of that segment but does not affect sensation. The spinal somatic motor fibers serve the skeletal muscles of the trunk and limbs, the sensory fibers, receptors in the skin, muscles, and joints.

The autonomic system Besides somatic sensory and motor fibers, the spinal and some of the cranial nerves also carry autonomic fibers. Some of these arise from the brain, others from motor neurons in the spinal cord (Figure 15.37). The autonomic fibers arising from the central nervous system are called *preganglionic fibers,* for they terminate in *autonomic ganglia* that either lie close to the spinal cord, or close to or actually within the organs served. These ganglia contain the cell bodies of neurons that send *postganglionic fibers* to the organ's smooth muscle and glandular tissues.

Autonomic fibers are of two types: parasympathetic and sympathetic. *Parasympathetic* fibers arise either from the brain or from the most posterior portion of the spinal cord; their long preganglionic fibers end in parasympathetic ganglia close to or within the organs served. Those fibers arising from the spinal cord leave the spinal nerves to enter the body cavity as the *pelvic plexus,* which serves the genitalia, urinary bladder, and distal colon. The major parasympathetic outflow, however, is not from the spinal cord but from the brain, mainly as the *vagus* nerve that serves the heart, respiratory tract, and digestive organs. Both preganglionic and postganglionic parasympathetic fibers are unmyelinated, and the synapses are *cholinergic* (acetylcholine being the transmitter substance).

Throughout the middle portion of the spinal cord, *sympathetic* fibers are given off with each pair of spinal nerves; however, these fibers leave the spinal nerves almost at once to enter the sympathetic ganglia that flank the spinal cord on each side. Longitudinal fibers link each ganglion to the next in line to form a *sympathetic chain.* The preganglionic fibers that run from the cord to the ganglia are myelinated and as a rule are much shorter than the amyelinated postganglionic fibers running from the ganglia to the viscera. Some postganglionic fibers emerge from the ganglia and rejoin the spinal nerves, flowing peripherally to innervate the arterioles of the skeletal muscles, and such integumentary structures as the sweat glands and hair-erector muscles. Fibers from the more anterior sympathetic ganglia pass forward to serve head structures such as the lacrimal (tear) glands and the pupillary and ciliary muscles of the eye. Some fibers from these anterior ganglia also flow peripherally to form the *cardiac plexus* serving the heart and lungs. A few sympathetic ganglia are located near the organs served, rather than close to the spinal cord, and must therefore be served by long preganglionic fibers. These are the *celic ganglion,* serving the liver, pancreas, and adrenals, and the alimentary tract from esophagus to colon (the latter via a secondary

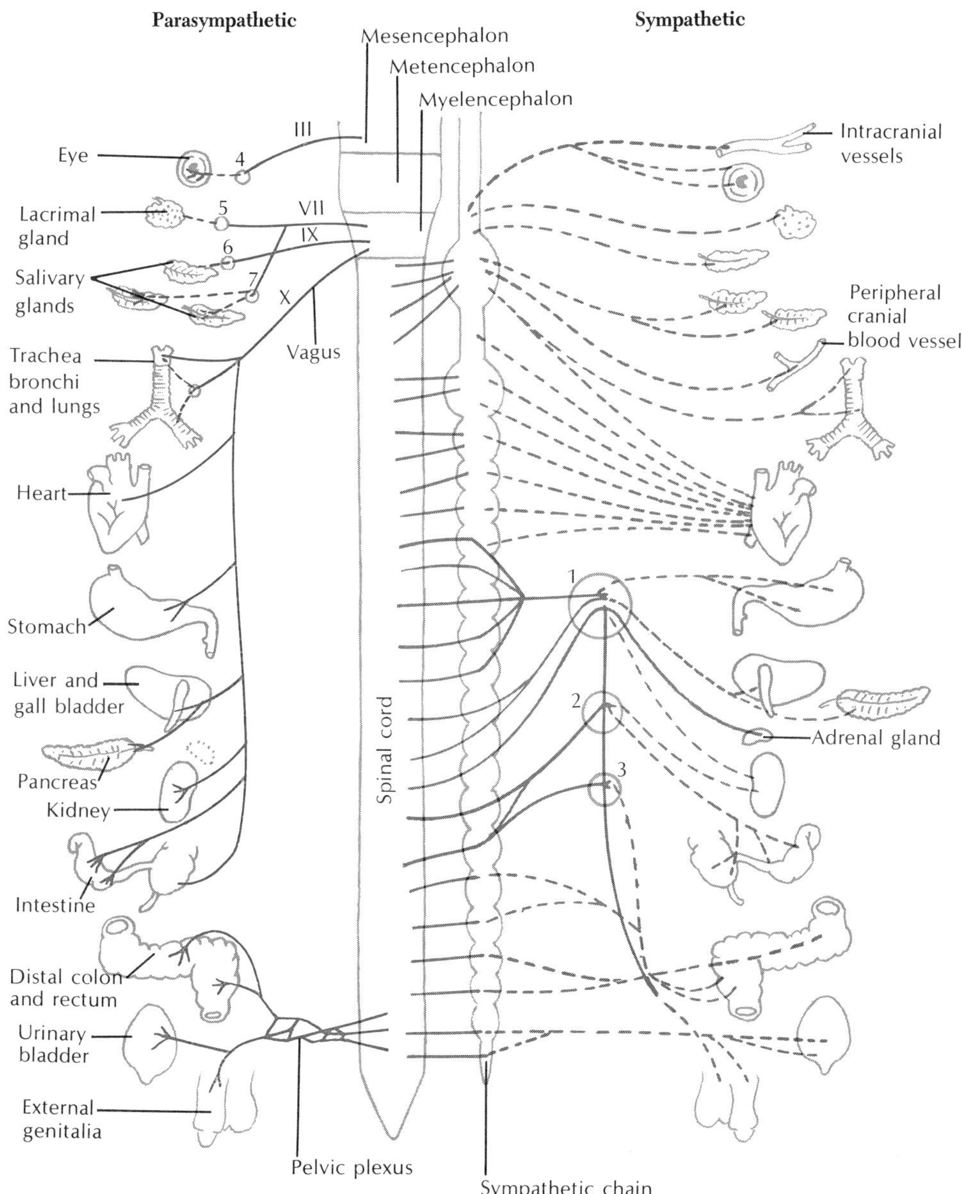

Figure 15.37 □ **Autonomic division of mammalian nervous system, with parasympathetic outflow on left and sympathetic outflow on right. Circles represent peripheral ganglia: (1) celiac, (2) anterior mesenteric, (3) posterior mesenteric, (4) ciliary, (5) sphenopalatine, (6) otic, and (7) submaxillary. Note that only sympathetic fibers innervate the adrenal gland (medullary portion) and cranial blood vessels. (Sympathetic vasomotor nerves to other blood vessels are not shown.) The preganglionic fibers are shown as solid lines, and the postganglionic as dashed. Both types of parasympathetic fibers are cholinergic, as are the sympathetic preganglionic fibers. The sympathetic postganglionic fibers are adrenergic.**

ganglion, the *anterior mesenteric*), and the *posterior mesenteric ganglion* serving the posterior colon, kidney, urinary bladder, gonads, and genitalia. Most sympathetic postganglionic synapses are *adrenergic,* adrenaline or noradrenaline being the transmitter substance. However, synapses within the sympathetic ganglia, together with the postganglionic synapses serving the uterus, sweat glands, and arterioles of the skeletal muscles are cholinergic.

Usually, sympathetic and parasympathetic nerves act in opposition at their visceral synapses: this is understandable in the light of the fact that different transmitter substances are secreted at the two types of synapses. Parasympathetic nerves usually promote normal physiological activities, whereas sympathetic nerves are mainly concerned with preparing the organism to cope with emergency conditions, such as an encounter with a rival or a predator. In man, the sympathetic "fight-or-flight" syndrome is associated with subjective sensations of fear or rage. Sympathetic impulses cause

(a)

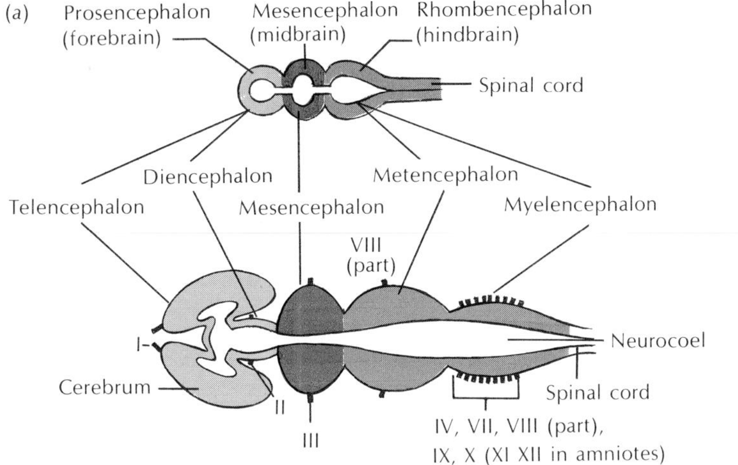

Prosencephalon
(forebrain)
Mesencephalon
(midbrain)
Rhombencephalon
(hindbrain)
Spinal cord
Diencephalon
Metencephalon
Telencephalon
Mesencephalon
Myelencephalon
VIII
(part)
I
Neurocoel
Cerebrum
II
III
Spinal cord
IV, VII, VIII (part),
IX, X (XI XII in amniotes)

(b)

1

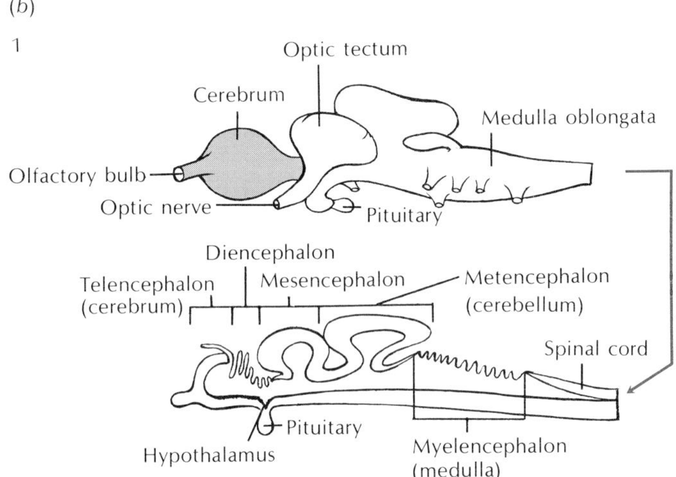

Optic tectum
Cerebrum
Medulla oblongata
Olfactory bulb
Optic nerve
Pituitary
Diencephalon
Telencephalon
(cerebrum)
Mesencephalon
Metencephalon
(cerebellum)
Spinal cord
Pituitary
Hypothalamus
Myelencephalon
(medulla)

2

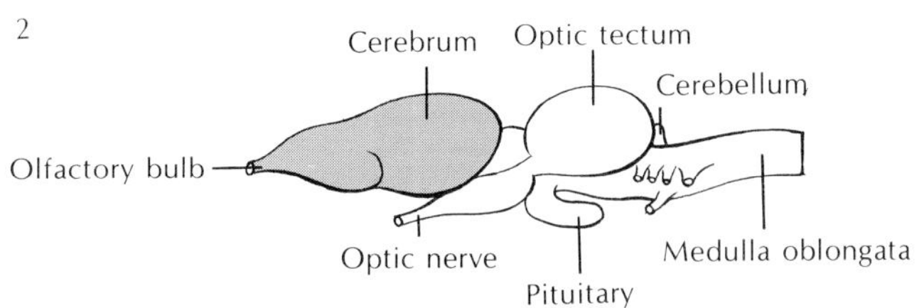

Cerebrum
Optic tectum
Cerebellum
Olfactory bulb
Optic nerve
Medulla oblongata
Pituitary

3

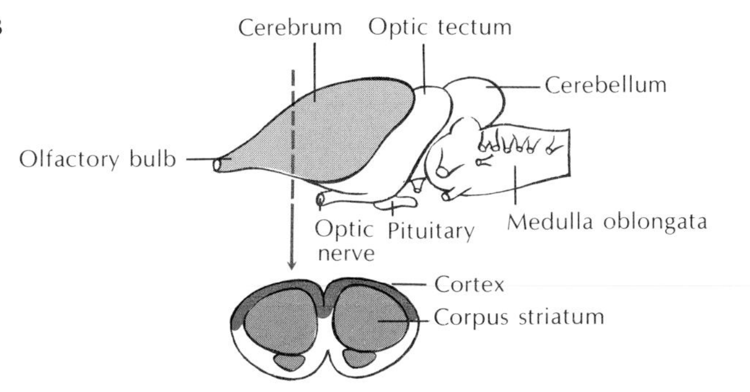

Cerebrum
Optic tectum
Cerebellum
Olfactory bulb
Optic
nerve
Pituitary
Medulla oblongata
Cortex
Corpus striatum

4

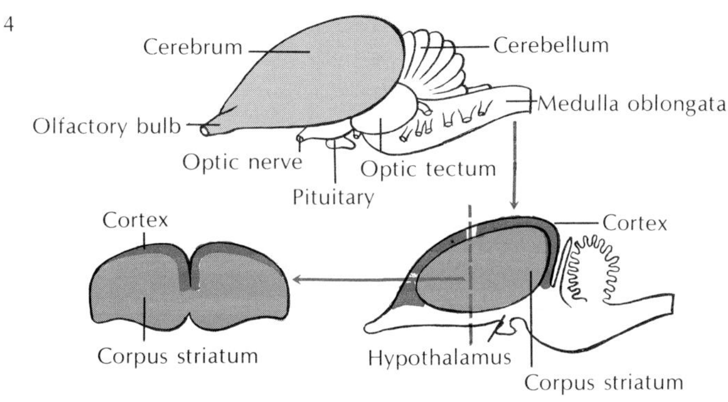

Cerebrum
Cerebellum
Medulla oblongata
Olfactory bulb
Optic nerve
Optic tectum
Pituitary
Cortex
Cortex
Corpus striatum
Hypothalamus
Corpus striatum

5

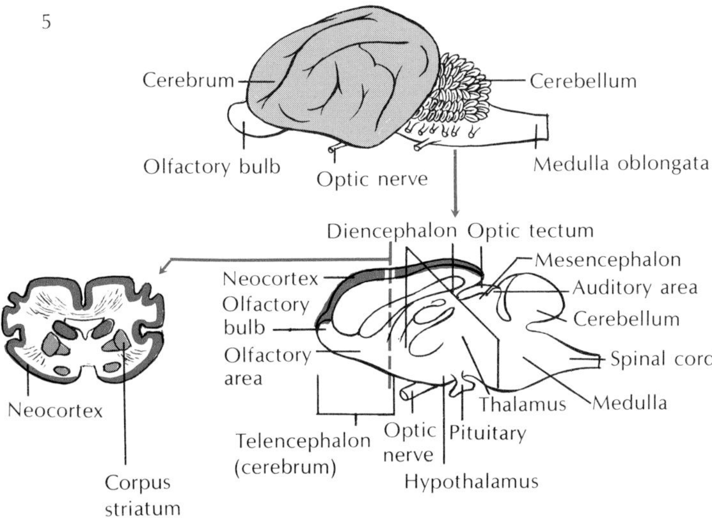

Cerebrum
Cerebellum
Olfactory bulb
Optic nerve
Medulla oblongata
Diencephalon
Optic tectum
Mesencephalon
Neocortex
Auditory area
Olfactory
bulb
Cerebellum
Olfactory
area
Spinal cord
Neocortex
Thalamus
Medulla
Optic
nerve
Pituitary
Telencephalon
(cerebrum)
Hypothalamus
Corpus
striatum

secretion of adrenaline and/or noradrenaline by the adrenal glands; these hormones augment and prolong the sympathetic action. The heartbeat is accelerated, pupils are dilated, sweat glands are activated, and digestion, salivation, urination, and defecation are inhibited. On the other hand, parasympathetic impulses decelerate the heartbeat, constrict the pupils, and promote the normal motility of the gut, secretion of saliva, contraction of the urinary bladder, and so forth. The two subdivisions of the autonomic system are not always opposed in action, for only parasympathetic fibers control the ciliary muscles that focus the eye, and only sympathetic nerves supply the integumentary glands, hair-erector muscles, and the smooth muscles of blood vessels generally. Some of these sympathetic *vasomotor* nerves are dilatory, whereas others cause vasoconstriction (see Figure 14.29).

THE CENTRAL NERVOUS SYSTEM With the exception of the cerebral and cerebellar cortex (structures best developed in mammals), the *gray matter* of the vertebrate central nervous system is located internally, around the neurocoel, and is surrounded on all sides by *white matter.* The gray matter consists of neuron cell bodies, amyelinated fibers, and neuroglia, and it is only here that synaptic connections take place. The white matter consists of myelinated fiber tracts that interconnect various levels of the central nervous system. One and the same fiber may be myelinated when running within a fiber tract and amyelinated when it leaves the tract and enters a region of gray matter.

Figure 15.38 □ The vertebrate brain.
(*a*) Embryonic development (frontal section).
(*b*) Phyletic comparisons: (1) fish, with parasagittal section; (2) amphibian; (3) reptile (alligator), with cross section; (4) bird, with parasagittal and cross sections; (5) mammal (monkey), with parasagittal and cross sections. Note relative size of cerebral cortex and cerebral basal nuclei (corpus striatum) in cross sections of alligator, bird, and monkey brains. Note also expansion of cerebrum relative to size of other brain lobes during the course of vertebrate evolution. The cerebral cortex is shown in solid color and the corpus striatum in color tint.

In the spinal cord, the primitive arrangement persists in which the spinal gray matter is located around the neurocoel and is surrounded by longitudinal white fiber tracts. In the brains of anamniotes the same arrangement is found: masses of gray matter (sometimes called "nuclei") occur around the neurocoel; the outer portion of the brain consists of white fiber tracts, the dorsal tracts being sensory and the ventral tracts motor. Additional areas of gray matter have been formed mainly in the forebrain by the spreading of gray matter onto the outer surface of the cerebrum to form the *cerebral cortex* (also called the *pallium:* "cloak"). In a portion of the hindbrain of mammals a comparable eruption to the surface has taken place to form the *cerebellar cortex,* essential in controlling the newly evolved motor areas of the cerebral cortex.

The primitive function of each part of the vertebrate brain may be determined by examining the distribution of cranial nerves, which arise from the same parts of the brain in all vertebrates although their origins are most clearly seen during embryonic development (Figure 15.38). We shall review the parts of the vertebrate brain starting from the posterior end, for the more posterior centers have tended to retain their ancient functions, whereas the most significant changes in function have taken place in the forward portions. Comparative study of living vertebrates indicates that the posterior centers have gradually come under the control of the more anterior centers, although remaining essential to vegetative functions. This evolutionary tendency toward development of a hierarchy of control centers, with the highest level of conscious control residing in those most anterior, is shown in Figure 15.39 with reference to the auditory pathway.

The hindbrain The hindbrain consists of two parts: the myelencephalon (*medulla oblongata*) and the *metencephalon,* which includes the *cerebellum.* The medulla oblongata is continuous with the spinal cord. It contains a number of essential sensory and motor nuclei, both autonomic and somatic. From the medulla arise the trochlear (IV), trigeminal (V), abducens (VI), facial (VII), glossopharyngeal (IX), and vagus (X) nerves, the cochlear branch of the acoustic nerve (VIII), and in amniotes, the spinal accessory (XI) and hypoglossal (XII) nerves as well (Figure 15.40). The *trochlear* and *abducens* nerves each control one of the muscles that turn the eyeball in its socket. The *trigeminal* and *facial* are mixed nerves serving the head, tongue, and throat (the trigeminal being mainly sensory; the facial, predominately motor). The *glossopharyngeal* is a mixed nerve serving the tongue and pharynx, receiving sensory impulses associated with taste and thirst, and controlling some of the muscles involved in swallowing. The *hypoglossal* and *spinal accessory* are motor nerves serving the tongue, hypobranchial muscles, and branchiomeric muscles of the throat (see Figure 12.37c). Responsible for gill breathing in fishes, these nerves—formerly spinal—have become associated

Figure 15.39 □ **Integrative centers along the auditory pathway. During vertebrate evolution, the centers of acoustic analysis in the midbrain and forebrain have gained prominence. The midbrain may be considered the highest sensory integrating center in fish and amphibians, the thalamus in reptiles, birds, and lower mammals, and the cerebral cortex in higher mammals. By this means a hierarchy of control centers has evolved, with the most anterior centers dominating the older, more posterior centers.**

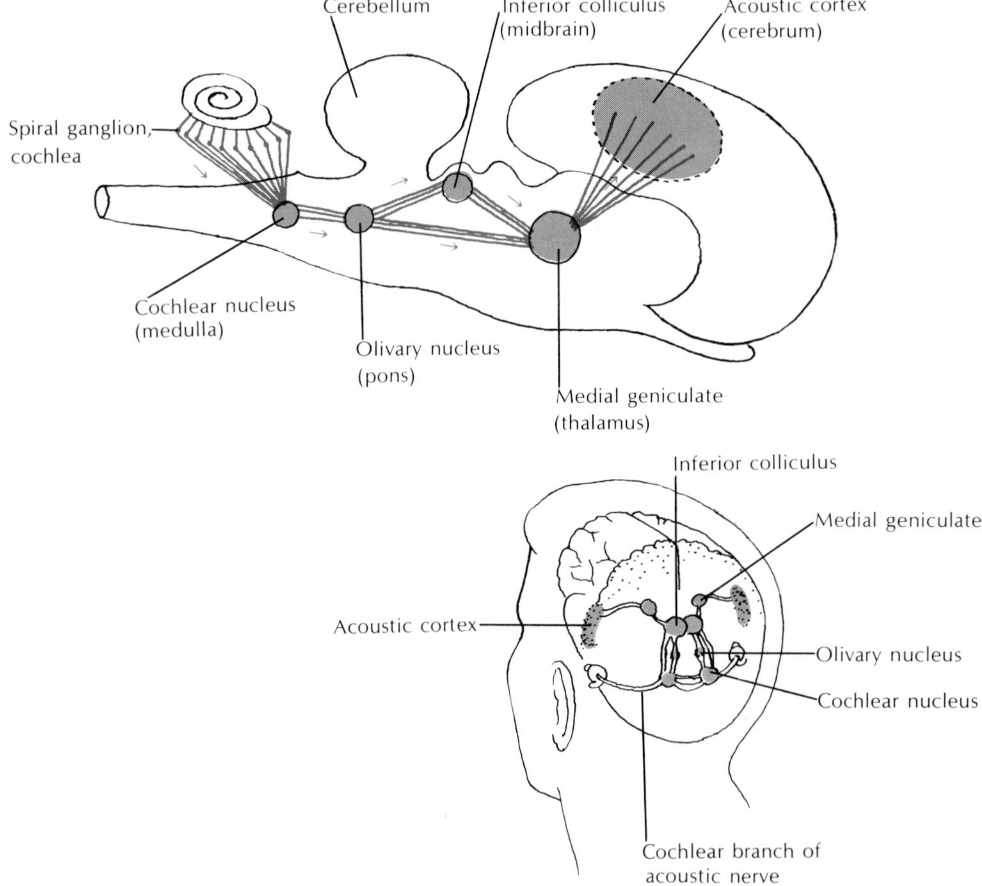

with the hindbrain in amniotes and are important in the mobility of head and tongue. In man the hypoglossal is the major nerve controlling tongue movements in speech. The *vagus* is the major parasympathetic nerve serving the viscera, and also carries sensory fibers for cardiovascular and respiratory reflexes.

The nuclei of the medulla oblongata are of three types: (1) *motor nuclei,* from which arise the efferent fibers of the somatic mixed and motor cranial nerves; (2) *sensory nuclei,* which are the first relay stations in the brain for afferent impulses, the sites of synapses controlling somatic reflexes (such as blinking the eye), and the source of association fibers running to higher brain centers; (3) *autonomic nuclei,* including the breathing-control, vasoconstrictor, and cardiac-inhibitory centers. Clearly the medulla was once the most important part of the brain for all sensory analysis other than visual, olfactory, and acoustic sensations, and also controlled head movements and autonomic responses; in higher vertebrates the medulla is controlled in turn by more anterior parts of the brain.

The metencephalon (anterior part of the hindbrain) is roofed by the *cerebellum,* which originally was mainly concerned with equilibrium and maintenance of posture. In mammals, however, the cerebellum gives off massive fiber tracts to the motor areas of the cerebral cortex, which in all known cases act *inhibitorily* upon the motor cortex and are essential to the smooth performance of voluntary movements. This new function has required the development of a large new association area, the *cerebellar cortex,* lacking in nonmammalian vertebrates, while the ancient functions of equilibrium and pos-

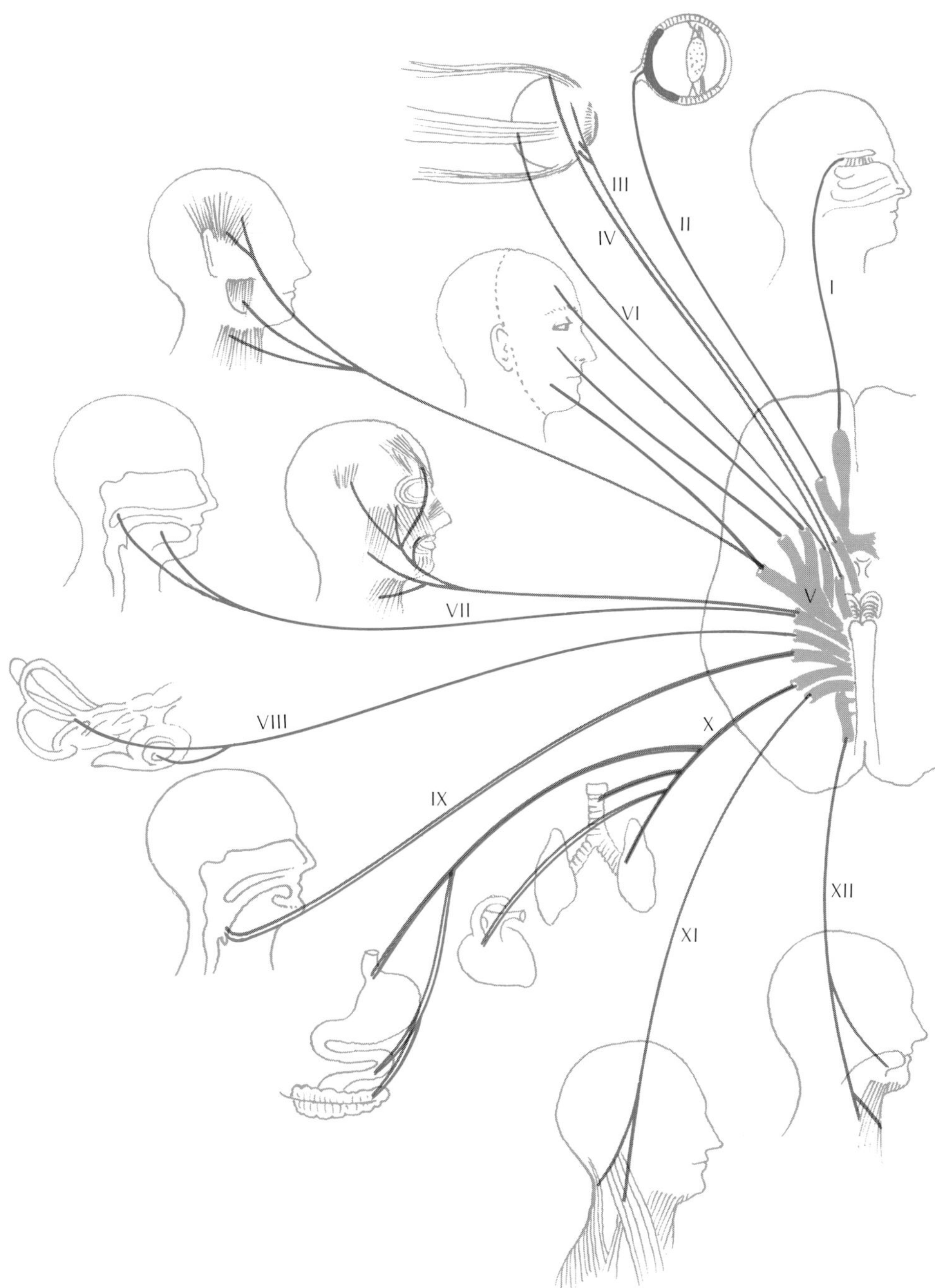

Figure 15.40 □ **Distribution and functions of human cranial nerves: I, the olfactory nerve, leads to the nasal lining and functions in the sense of smell; II, the optic nerve, leads to the retina and functions in vision; III, the oculomotor nerve, leads to four eye muscles and controls eye movement; IV, the trochlear nerve, leads to the superior oblique eye muscles and also contributes to eye movement; V, the trigeminal nerve, leads to the facial skin and jaw muscles and functions in cutaneous sensation and chewing; VI, the abducens nerve, leads to the lateral rectus eye muscle and contributes to eye movement; VII, the facial nerve, leads to the facial muscles, tongue, and uvula and functions in expression and taste; VIII, the acoustic nerve, leads to the labyrinth and functions in both hearing and balance; IX, the glossopharyngeal nerve, leads to the tongue and pharynx and functions in thirst, swallowing, and taste; X, the vagus nerve, leads to the viscera, functioning in visceral sensation and control of visceral action; XI, the spinal accessory nerve, leads to neck muscles and functions in head mobility; XII, the hypoglossal nerve, leads to the tongue and throat muscles, controlling speech. Sensory fibers are colored; motor fibers, dark gray.**

tural maintenance continue to be the concern of internally located cerebellar nuclei. The cerebellum receives sensory input from the vestibular branch of the acoustic nerve (serving the semicircular canals, utriculus, and sacculus), and receives proprioceptive information from the trunk and limbs, relayed via certain nuclei of the medulla. In mammals the cerebellum also receives collateral tracts from visual, tactile, and auditory pathways.

The assumption of cerebellar control over the motor areas of the cerebral cortex required the development in the ventral portion of the mammalian metencephalon of a huge mass of fiber tracts, the *pons*. So large is the pons that it has come to surround certain nuclei formerly associated with the medulla oblongata, so that in mammals the nuclei of the trigeminal and facial nerves and the olivary nucleus (a way-station for auditory impulses) are considered to be pontine nuclei.

The midbrain The midbrain (mesencephalon) is the most important part of the brain for visual analysis in anamniotes. Impulses entering the diencephalon (posterior part of the forebrain) from the optic nerve are relayed posteriorly to an association area, the *optic tectum,* forming the roof of the midbrain. The tectum is considered to be the highest center of consciousness in anamniotes, for the anamniote cerebrum is mostly concerned with olfaction. In keeping with this functional prominence, the optic tectum of fishes forms two large rounded humps on the dorsal surface of the brain (the anterior colliculi). In amphibians, a new set of acoustic integration centers (the posterior colliculi) appear in the midbrain, but these form visible bulges only in mammals, in which their enlargement parallels the evolution of the cochlea. During the evolution of amniotes, visual pathways have tended to be directed forward into the cerebrum, rather than posteriorly to the tectum, and a large area for acoustic analysis has also arisen in the cerebrum, taking over much of the function of the posterior colliculi. Accordingly, the midbrain of mammals is concerned only with eye movements (via the *oculomotor nerve,* III, controlling four of the extrinsic eye muscles), and with performance of certain acoustically oriented reflexes. In the cat, much visual and acoustic discrimination occurs in the midbrain: its destruction abolishes these capacities; decortication merely impairs them.

The ventral portion of the midbrain (tegmentum) consists of fiber tracts descending from the forebrain to the spinal cord. In mammals there appears in this region an important new motor integration center, the *red nucleus,* that receivers fibers from the cerebellum and is involved in a feedback circuit controlling the cerebral motor cortex.

The forebrain The telencephalon (cerebrum) and the more posterior diencephalon make up the forebrain. The latter is that section of the brain from which the optic cups arise during embryonic development, and it remains the site of entry of the *optic nerve* (II) and the first relay station for visual impulses. Its concern with vision is further reflected by the fact that two bodies, the parietal and pineal organs, which arise medially from its roof, are believed to have once served as accessory eyes. In fact, the visual function of the pineal organ has persisted in amphibians (where it responds to changes in light although covered by the thin skull bones) and even in a number of reptiles [including the New Zealand tuatara (*Sphenodon*), last survivor of the ancient order *Rhynchocephalia*]. The endocrine function of the mammalian pineal organ has been discussed in Section 8.2D.

The diencephalon contains two association centers of great importance: the thalamus and the hypothalamus. The *thalamus* is the most important center in nonmammalian amniotes for the integration of sensory data and even in mammals remains important in this respect although some of the more complex aspects of sensory integration have been assumed by the cerebral cortex. The thalamus receives fibers from the sensory nuclei of the hindbrain and projects fibers to the various sensory areas of the cerebrum (other than those concerned with olfaction). The *lateral geniculate bodies* of the thalamus are the first synaptic relay stations on the visual pathway; these give off fibers to the midbrain and especially to the visual area of the cerebral cortex. The *medial geniculate bodies* of the thalamus are centers for acoustic integration, receiving fibers from the posterior colliculi and giving off tracts to the acoustic areas of the cerebral cortex.

Within the thalamus lies the anterior portion of an extremely important association field, the *reticular formation* (or RAS, reticular-activating system), the significance of which was not realized until recently. The reticular system, about the size of a finger in man, extends through the core of the hindbrain, midbrain, and thalamus. It consists of a dense meshwork of small neurons with short fibers, and receives collaterals from every ascending and descending pathway. By receiving this extensive information flow, the reticular system can serve as a selective filter, screening out distracting sensory impulses, augmenting others, modifying the intensity of motor responses, and generally allowing the conscious brain to focus its attention upon particular relevant stimuli. Even during sleep as well as during inattentive wakefulness, the reticular system continues to monitor the sensory field, serving as an arousal system that activates higher brain centers such as the cerebral cortex. Its importance is shown by the fact that if the reticular system is damaged, the individual slips into a deep coma from which no awakening is possible.

Ventral to the thalamus lies the *hypo-*

thalamus, the most important control center for visceral functions. The hypothalamus coordinates autonomic responses with sensory data (especially olfaction), and is concerned with emotional states, sexual impulses, sleep, appetite, thirst, and temperature control. Electrode stimulation of specific parts of the hypothalamus cause an animal to behave as if in extreme rage, fright, pain, or pleasure. The "pleasure centers" mentioned earlier are located in the hypothalamus, close by the centers concerned with pain or fright.

Parasympathetic functions are controlled by the anterior hypothalamic nuclei; sympathetic functions, by the posterior nuclei. By way of its control over the medulla oblongata, the hypothalamus constantly "resets the baseline" for various visceral functions; for instance, it causes elevation of the blood pressure during exercise to a level considerably higher than that maintained during rest.

The hypothalamus is also the center of *neuroendocrine* control over many of the body's endocrine glands. It contains clusters of neurosecretory cells that secrete *hypophyseal release factors* that are taken up by the bloodstream and distributed to the nearby pituitary gland (hypophysis), where they control the secretion of pituitary hormones (see Section 15.4C). Furthermore, the posterior portion of the pituitary gland (neurohypophysis) actually consists of the axons of hypothalamic neurosecretory cells that liberate certain hormones (vasopressin and oxytocin) directly into the bloodstream. It is evident that some of the hypothalamic nuclei are actually endocrine glands of immense significance in the control of both behavioral and physiological responses.

The *telencephalon* consists of the *cerebral cortex* and the *cerebral basal nuclei.* Originally the cerebrum was mainly concerned with olfactory analysis and initiation of motor responses guided by olfactory cues, for it is to this part of the brain that olfactory signals are brought by way of the *olfactory nerve* (I). The cerebral basal nuclei are the highest motor control centers in nonmammalian vertebrates. The largest of these, the *corpus striatum,* forms a huge, solid mass within the cerebrum of birds and modern bony fishes and is thought to be a major center in which are organized the stereotyped instinctive behaviors characteristic of most vertebrates other than mammals.

Of particular interest is the evolutionary history of the cerebral cortex. The anamniote cerebrum is roofed by a thin layer of gray matter representing the most primitive version of the cerebral cortex, the *archipallium* ("first cloak"), an association area concerned with olfactory perception. In reptiles the archipallium persists, but a new cortical area, the *paleopallium* ("old cloak"), appears; this receives fibers from the sensory analyzing centers posterior to the cerebrum and correlates these with olfactory data. The increased significance for land animals of visual and auditory perception promoted the extension of the paleopallium, which spread over the surface of the cerebral white matter as a true outer cloak or cortex. However, in the reptilian line leading to mammals there appeared still a third version of the cerebral cortex, showing a more complex tissue organization than either of the older cortical areas. This most modern version, the *neopallium* ("new cloak"; also called the neocortex), underwent extensive development during mammalian evolution, while remaining rudimentary in contemporary reptiles. As the neopallium spread, it ballooned out over the more ancient but persistent archipallium and paleopallium, hiding them from surface view. The increase in fiber tracts extending from the neocortex and interconnecting various cortical regions contributed to the swelling of the cerebral hemispheres, which have become so large in advanced mammals as to have overgrown both the midbrain and most of the hindbrain—now best seen by sectioning the mammalian brain along its midsagittal plane (Figure 15.41a). During its growth the neocortex has thickened little but has folded into grooves and ridges (sulci and gyri) that allow a greater amount of cortical material to be compacted into a comparatively small space (Figure 15.41*b*). The principal interconnections between the neocortex and lower brain centers are shown diagrammatically in Figure 15.42.

The evolution of the neopallium has not led to the disappearance of the older cerebral association areas. These persist as centers responsible for olfactory analysis. Pathways from the paleopallium to the hypothalamus allow autonomic functions and emotional states to be correlated with olfactory sensations. Even in man, whose olfactory sense is much less keen than that of other mammals, odors frequently trigger a number of interesting emotional states—as the users (and advertisers) of perfume well know!

Although of course cross connections between the two cerebral hemispheres existed before the appearance of the neocortex, the latter's growth necessitated the development of a great transverse fiber tract new to mammals, the *corpus callosum.* Sectioning the corpus callosum has been found

Figure 15.41 □ **Brains of higher mammals. (a) Median section of human brain, showing inner surface of left cerebral hemisphere and lower brain centers. (*b*) Brains of two marine mammals, killer whale (left) and dolphin (right), viewed from the posterior end and showing the convolutions of the cerebral cortex and cerebellar cortex. (*Los Angeles County Museum of Natural History.*) The cortical surface area compares favorably with that of the human brain, but brain size in man is greater relative to total body size. Note enormous cerebellum of killer whale, a portion of the brain that controls the motor area of the cerebral cortex.**

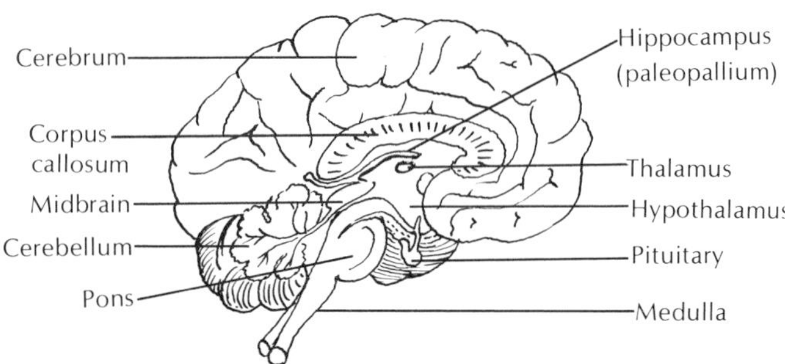

(*a*)

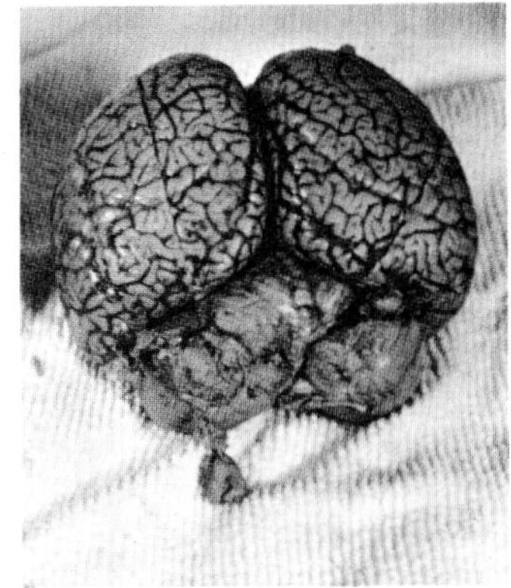

(*b*)

to relieve certain kinds of epileptic seizures, and this medical procedure has led to the intriguing discovery that such "split-brained" individuals behave as though they have two separate brains! Fiber tracts entering and leaving the brain mostly cross over during their ascent so that, for example, sensations from the right side of the body are projected to the left cerebral hemisphere, and vice versa. The visual field seen with the right half of each retina is registered on the left side of the brain, because half of the fibers in each optic nerve cross over before reaching the brain. Apparently, whatever we experience with one half of our cerebral cortex is usually transferred at once to an equivalent point in the opposite hemisphere, so that what the left hemisphere experiences the right half does second-hand, and vice versa. After the corpus callosum is severed, such transferral can no longer take place. Thereafter, a task learned by one hand has to be learned separately by the other, so that a split-brained monkey can even be trained to perform contradictory actions with right and left hands.

These curious results indicate that with one important exception, the two halves of the cerebral cortex mirror each other in their recording of the experiential record. The exception is that in man the left hemisphere (the dominant one in most right-handed persons) contains a speech area that stops developing in the right hemisphere at about the age of four. Although the right cerebral hemisphere of a right-handed split-brained person understands the spoken word, it cannot initiate either speaking or writing! Why this one area should not faithfully mirror the equivalent portion of the dominant hemisphere remains a mystery.

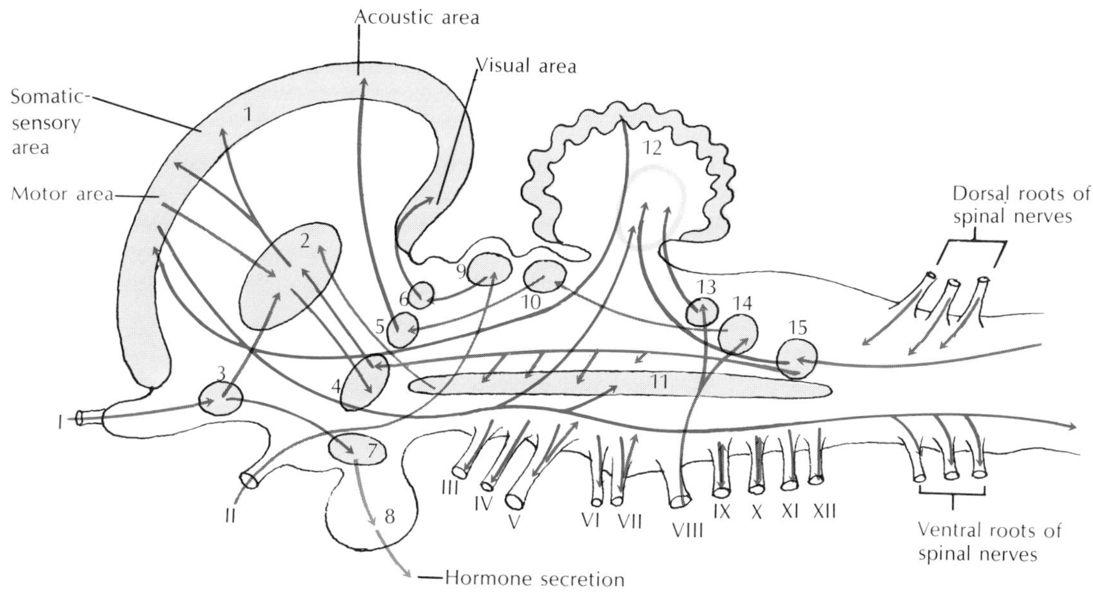

Figure 15.42 □ Major pathways of the mammalian brain (tracts interconnecting various regions of the cerebral cortex are not shown). (1) Neocortex, (2) corpus striatum and other cerebral basal nuclei, (3) old cortex (olfactory), (4) thalamic nuclei, (5) medial geniculate body (thalamus), (6) lateral geniculate body (thalamus), (7) hypothalamus, (8) pituitary gland, (9) anterior colliculus (optic, midbrain), (10) posterior colliculus (acoustic, midbrain), (11) reticular formation, (12) cerebellum, (13) vestibular nucleus (medulla), (14) cochlear nucleus (medulla), and (15) hindbrain somatic-sensory relay centers. The cranial nerves are numbered I to XII (Figure 15.40). Pale-gray areas represent concentrations of gray matter of the brain. Afferent impulses are shown in color, efferent impulses in dark gray, and hormone secretion into the bloodstream in color tint.

By electrode probing it has been possible to map the functional regions of the cerebral cortex in a number of different mammals, although this can be done most satisfactorily with human subjects who can describe sensations felt at the time of stimulation. Distinct cortical sensory, motor, and association areas have been mapped (Figure 15.43). The proportion of the cortex given over to specific sensory and motor functions diminishes in higher mammals relative to the amount of association area and becomes least in man. However, the remaining sensory and motor areas are found to be precisely organized so that specific regions receive sensations from particular body parts, and other specific areas project motor impulses to those parts. Interestingly, areas concerned with adjacent parts of the body lie adjacent on the cortex. The motor area concerned with movements of the thumb lies next to that controlling the index finger, which is next to the area controlling the middle finger; next comes the area controlling the ring finger, and finally that controlling the little finger. Stimulation of each area in turn causes the subject involuntarily to move first one finger and then the next. If all body parts were represented in the organization of the cortex according to their actual relative size, the cortex might be thought of as bearing a functional "image" of the entire body. To a point this is true, but all body parts are not of equal importance in sensation and response. The motor region controlling the human hand is larger than the entire region controlling the arm and leg, and that concerned with vocalization is also relatively huge. Sensations from the face and especially the lips occupy more area in the sensory cortex than do cutaneous sensations from all the rest of the body. Localization of specific functions in the association cortex is more difficult, but so far three distinct areas concerned with verbalization (that is, speech and written language) have been mapped. Damage to very small portions of these speech areas (such as caused by a mild "stroke," that is, a cerebral hemorrhage) can result in curious impairments that may be limited to the loss of only a few words from the written and spoken vocabulary. One case history relates the loss from a patient's memory of the word "squirrel"; this individual could still describe the animal but remained quite unable to bring the proper term to mind. Somehow the physiological equivalent of the term "squirrel" had been expunged by a small cerebral accident.

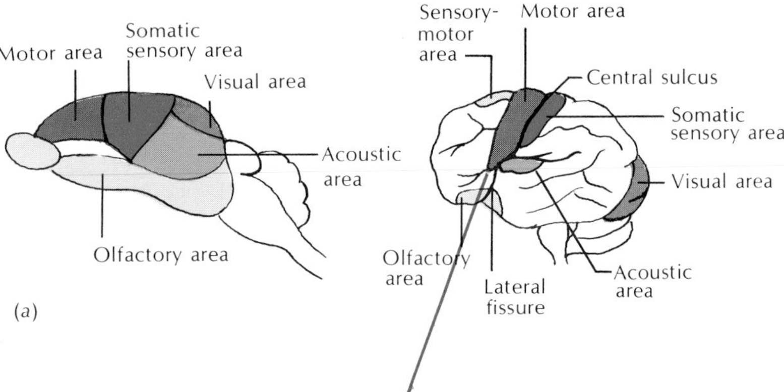

Figure 15.43 □ **Functional regions of the cerebral cortex. (*a*) Comparison of brains of (left) shrew and (right) man. Unshaded regions represent association areas not committed to any single sensory or motor function; these areas predominate in the human cerebral cortex. (*Shrew brain after G. E. Smith.*) (*b*) Transverse section of human cerebral hemisphere through motor and somatic-sensory areas. Although the motor area lies slightly anterior to the somatic-sensory area, the functional mapping of the two regions has been superimposed here for ease of comparison, motor functions shown to the inside and sensory to the outside. Note relatively large proportions of the sensory and motor areas devoted to the hand and mouth.**

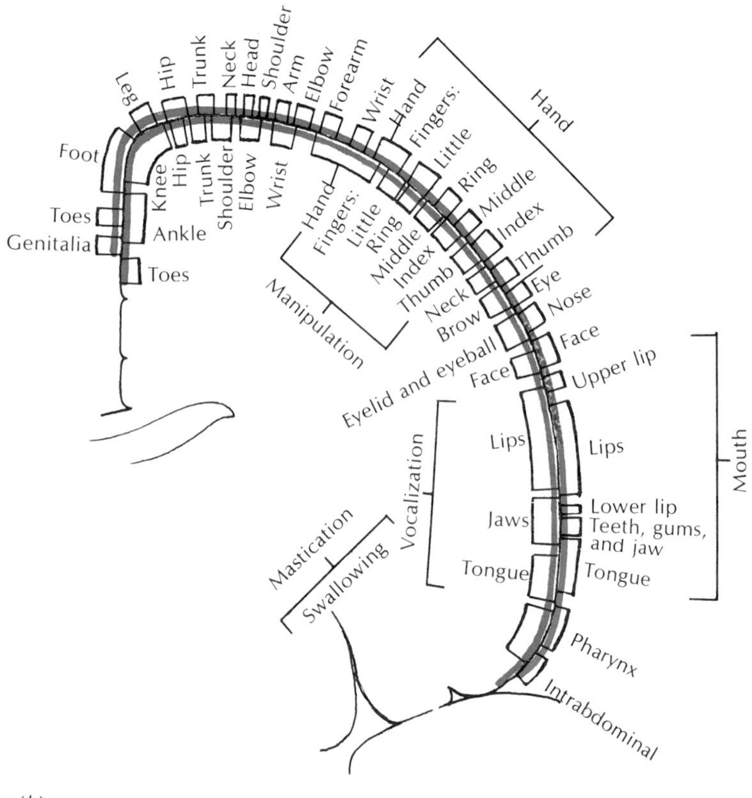

There seems little doubt that even "civilized" man makes only partial use of the vast correlative area provided by the enormous expansion of the neocortex. On a number of occasions in the history of life we find that some innovation has taken place that outstripped the immediate use to which it was put and laid the foundation for some future adaptive breakthrough. Necessity is generally the driving force of evolution, but genetic change must precede selection. A change that is sufficiently beneficial under one set of circumstances will tend to be perpetuated, and this change may continue even further in the same direction if the genetic trend does not become actually harmful. In this way genetic change can move ahead of the immediate need.

Such "preadaptation" in a simple manner is shown by the occurrence in bacterial cultures of antibiotic-resistant mutants that have never known exposure to the antibiotic. Another possible example is that keratin began to be deposited in vertebrate skin long before it came to accumulate in quantities sufficient to form an actual protective shield; perhaps the initial tendency was merely an additional means of ridding the body of nitrogenous wastes, until the keratin buildup became so great as to constitute an adaptive advantage in quite a new direction, namely, migration to land. Still another example is that a number of animals seem to have sense organs capable of providing much more information than their brains can analyze. The evolution of an efficient eye, for instance, unavoidably brings the ability to see printed words on a page. But the visual resolution of such printing does not mean that a fish or bird can really learn to read: the sensory equipment is there; the brain capacity is not.

The concept just expressed is consistent with a statement made much earlier in this book: namely, that genetic change does *not* take place in response to need. It is a random process, and if it takes place at all, can do so at any time in *advance* of need. If a preadaptive change does not take place in a population, that population may simply perish when finally faced with a need it cannot meet.

Returning to the evolution of the neocortex in man, even the most "uncivilized" human tribe seems to have the cerebral capability for mastering any aspect of culture developed by other human groups, if properly educated from infancy. The genetic capacity in such cases far exceeds the cultural uses to which the capacity is put. Furthermore, we have good reason to believe that, even under the best systems of modern education the full genetic potentialities of the human brain have not yet been exploited.

Man's unusual brain has already created many unique problems for our species that no living being before has had to face. We live in a "dream world" of our own creation—a conceptual world as real to us as the actual physical world. Our fears and hates are often based mainly upon *imagined* possibilities and consequences, rather than upon those actually realized. Natural selection may operate little further on the overall structure of the human body, for we have compensated by machines and other cultural devices for its physical inadequacies. However, there is no reason to suppose that selection will not operate further on the human brain, for it is the manner in which we develop and grow conceptually that will, more than any other factor, determine whether or not our species is to survive and, if it does, what its future will be. Because of his unprecedented brain development, man has cast off the instinctive safeguards that protect other creatures from destroying themselves and laying waste the biotic communities in which they live. The ultimate test of survival will be whether or not man can direct his remarkable cognitive faculty toward evaluating the outcomes of his actions and restoring rather than further despoiling the world in which he lives.

15.4 □ HORMONES: AGENTS OF CHEMICAL CONTROL

A nervous system is required for performance of the rapid responses that characterize animal life in general. However, both behavioral and physiological responses are also subject to control through the agency of those chemical regulators called hormones. Hormones are known to occur in vascular plants and most invertebrates as well as all vertebrates. Primitively, animal hormones may mainly have been products of neurosecretory neurons, which served merely to augment the action of the nervous system and to extend its effects to tissues not directly innervated (Figure 15.44). In the most highly evolved animals, such neurosecretory neurons also dominate epithelial endocrine glands in such a way that a precisely correlated system of neuroendocrine control is established. Through this system the physiological activities of various tissues are coordinated at the level of the whole organism. Accordingly, except when dealing with plants, we cannot consider the subject of hormonal regulation without reference to nervous control, for in bringing about appropriate responses both systems in effect operate as one. This will be made especially clear in our ensuing discussions of how the constancy of the internal environment is maintained, and especially the chemical constancy of body fluids (Section 16.2A), and how reproductive cycles and pregnancy are controlled (Section 17.2D).

In every cell, metabolic processes are carried out in accordance with the needs and genetic potentialities of that cell. These

Figure 15.44 □ Neurosecretion.

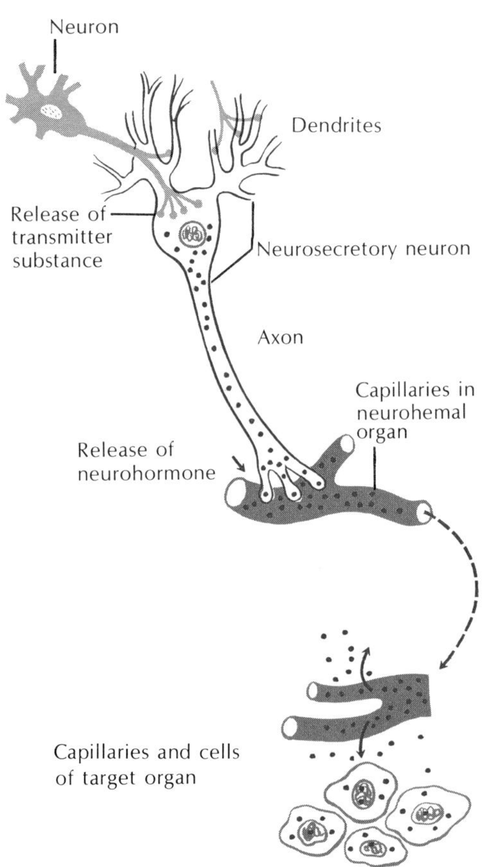

processes of mass and energy conversion (reviewed in Chapter 14) are controlled by intracellular regulatory mechanisms to be further considered in Chapter 16. Such intracellular mechanisms no doubt functioned long before the evolution of multicellular life, but with multicellularity came the problem of coordinating the performance of individual cells so that the multicellular organism could act as a unit. When the growth needs of one particular organ demand an enriched supply of nutrients, storage tissues elsewhere in the body must be made to give up these nutrients. When the time is appropriate for the organism to switch from a vegetative to a reproductive state, widespread changes in behavior and physiology must take place and the nutritional demands of somatic tissues must be subordinated to the needs of tissues concerned with the production and care of young. Hormones are chemical regulators, disseminated throughout the body from their tissues of origin, which serve as exogenous agents that bring the metabolism of individual cells under control of the whole organism. They exert specific effects upon various tissues according to the capacity of these tissues to respond to hormonal influence. They are effective in very low concentrations, which suggests that they may act as coenzymes, somewhat as vitamins do. However, radioisotope studies indicate that (whether as coenzymes or not) certain hormones may exert their effects by activating or repressing particular genes, thereby promoting or suppressing the synthesis of specific enzymes.

In most cases we still can say little concerning the specific role played by hormones in controlling the activities of individual cells. We are generally confined to reporting the systemic effects of hormone excess or insufficiency and deducing from these malfunctions the role normally played in physiological and behavioral regulation. Furthermore, no hormone acts in isolation from other hormones. Some hormones are synergistic, enhancing one another's effectiveness. Others seem to act in opposition. One hormone may alter the physiological state of a tissue so that the response of that tissue to a second hormone is altered. A complete analysis of the neuroendocrine regulation of any one aspect of whole-organism metabolism is still beyond our means, even were we to defer the more basic questions as to exactly what hormones do within the cells they affect.

It is even often a challenge to determine whether or not a given response is hormonally mediated at all, and it may be difficult to prove whether a tissue suspected of having an endocrine function does indeed produce hormones. Years of controversy only recently have been brought to a close by an experiment demonstrating that the vertebrate thymus (see Section 6.3E) actually is a source of hormone, but this factor still has not been isolated or identified.

Several routine procedures can be used in determining whether or not a tissue is hormone-secreting. Basically they commence with the surgical removal of the tissue in question, followed by a period of observation and testing during which resultant derangements can be analyzed. After deficiency symptoms have developed, their alleviation is attempted in one of three ways: (1) by replacing the organ that was removed with one taken from another individual; (2) by injecting cell-free extracts of the tissue; (3) by creating a parabiotic union (that is, a joining of bloodstreams) between the experimental subject and a normal individual. If any of these procedures results in correction of the defects, the presence of a hormone is indicated. Another technique involves grafting into a younger individual supposed endocrine tissue from an adult member of the species to see whether precocious maturation can be induced. By such techniques the existence of a hormone may be established long before the factor itself is isolated and its chemical nature determined.

As hormones have been isolated one by one, they have been found to be chemically diverse. Most known plant hormones are organic acids. Some animal hormones are small proteins and polypeptides, whereas others are steroids, alcohols, or amino acids. This chemical diversity suggests that all hormones do not act in the same manner, and this is borne out by radioisotope studies that determine where in the cell a hormone may concentrate. Some hormones are found to concentrate within the nuclei of affected cells, where they stimulate RNA and protein synthesis. Some remain within the cytoplasm, apparently exerting their effects extranuclearly. Still others seem to participate in cell-surface reactions without necessarily entering the affected cell at all.

A The evolution of endocrine function

Although the demonstrated function of hormones is to serve as chemical agents of integration throughout the entire body, this could not very well have been their original function. Their original adaptive value must have resided in their action within the cells producing them. At first every individual cell must have needed to manufacture enough of these regulatory materials to control its own metabolism. Should one tissue particularly well adapted for secretion start to produce larger quantities of the material than needed for its own immediate use, this potential endocrine gland would begin to exert regulatory effects on the surrounding tissues. Should the secretory activity of the potential gland continue to increase, the time would come when the factor would be liberated in concentrations great enough to be systemically distributed. Until this point was reached, all body tissues would have to produce enough of the factor to meet their own needs for metabolic regulation. However, when a supply of the material began reaching them by way of the circulation, these tissues could afford to give up making the regulator and rely entirely on the exogenous source. Once this step had been taken, selection would operate strongly toward enhanced (and reliable) secretory capability of the developing gland, for its failure to meet the needs of all tissues would probably result in death of the organism.

The availability of the regulator from an outside source would probably have had the immediate effect of repressing those metabolic pathways involved in the synthesis of the factor, for the presence of adequate end-product often serves as a means of "turning off" the synthetic mechanism involved in producing that substance. However, this reversible suppression must at some point become permanent: upon removal of a gland, other tissues cannot simply begin to produce the needed factor. In our study of development we noted that although all cells of a multicellular organism usually retain the full genetic makeup of the zygote, during maturation many genes apparently cease to function; only those remain active which are relevant to the final role of the specialized cell. If this is true, then all body tissues must have the genetic capacity to produce any hormone needed by the body, but following the process of cytodifferentiation this capacity is no longer evident in all cells other than those specializing toward the endocrine function.

The *first* animal hormones were probably neurohormones secreted by specialized nerve cells. Epithelial endocrine glands are known to exist in only a few groups of animals, but neurohormones have now been found to occur in all metazoan phyla save sponges and coelenterates. The evolution of endocrine glands in animals can therefore be viewed as having first been a means whereby the nervous system could exert its effects more widely and steadily than before by making use of the bloodstream as well as existing synaptic connections.

Neurosecretory neurons synthesize and liberate polypeptide neurohormones in lieu of the transmitter substances released by other neurons. They are aided in this by the fact that their axons frequently terminate in *neurohemal organs,* bodies in which these axon endings can make intimate contact with the bloodstream. The pars nervosa of the vertebrate posterior pituitary gland and the sinus gland of crustaceans are examples of neurohemal organs. The axons ending within these organs do not actually originate there, but in some nearby portion of the brain.

A variety of actions are attributed to various neurohormones. These include: (1) regulation of pigment movement in chromatophores; (2) stimulation of visceral muscles (including the musculature of the heart, gut, uterus, mammary ducts, oviduct, and so forth); (3) maintenance of water balance (osmoregulation); (4) control of the deposition and resorption of such skeletal materials as bone and chitin; (5) regulation of somatic growth and development (including control of diapause and metamorphosis in insects); (6) enzyme activation; (7) maintenance of daily (circadian) activity rhythms; (8) activation or repression of other endocrine glands; (9) regulation of sexual maturation and reproductive activities. Such versatility suggests that, even when epithelial endocrine glands have failed to evolve, quite a sophisticated level of neuroendocrine control can still exist by action of the nervous system alone.

We should note that although new hormones have certainly evolved from time to time (and variations of a basic molecule have arisen by mutation in related animal groups), the *uses* to which hormones are put appear to evolve more rapidly than do the hormones themselves. The chemical architecture of certain hormones remains much the same throughout widely disparate groups of organisms, but the manner in which they are put to use must change according to how various tissues respond to their presence. For instance, estrogens (female sex hormones in animals) are actually found even in plant tissues, but we do not yet know whether they have a regulatory function there or are present merely as metabolic intermediates. If the latter, we have another example of how some previously evolved capability in living matter may come eventually to have some great new adaptive value.

The pituitary hormone prolactin is of especial interest in this regard. Though very similar in all vertebrates studied, this polypeptide appears to control such diverse activities as: (1) osmoregulation in fish that migrate from salt to fresh water and vice versa; (2) newt "water drive," a prespawning migration from land to water; (3) development of mating colors by various fish; (4) secretion by pigeons of "crop milk," a rich exudate on which the young are fed by regurgitation; (5) lactation in mammals; (6) stimulation of various kinds of care-giving parental behaviors. This versatile hormone may still have other roles to play in the evolution of life.

In the following sections dealing with invertebrate and vertebrate hormones we shall restrict ourselves to considering the functions of hormones in somatic integration and maintenance of the individual organism. We shall reserve for Chapter 17 consideration of their important roles in reproduction and mating. Essential as hormones are to the internal coordination of body processes, they are also essential in integrating the individual organism into its social group, in regulating its physiology and behavior with respect to relevant environmental factors (such as season), and in making it possible for living things to perpetuate their kind.

B Invertebrate hormones

HORMONAL ACTION IN ANNELID WORMS Growth and regeneration in such annelids as the clamworm appear to be regulated by neurohormones released from the dorsal pair of cephalic ganglia (the so-called cerebral ganglia or brain). If the cerebral ganglia are removed at the same time that the posterior region of the body is amputated, regeneration of the lost segments fails to occur. However, regeneration will take place if the decerebrate (brainless) worm receives an implant of cerebral tissue from another worm that has had its own hind end amputated about three days before the transplantation. If the brain of the donor worm is not transplanted until the fifth day after the hind end of that worm was removed, subsequent removal of the brain will neither impede regeneration in this worm nor will its implantation stimulate regeneration in the recipient. These findings indicate (1) that the act of amputation initiates the synthesis and accumulation in the cerebral ganglia of a neurohormone responsible for eliciting regeneration; (2) that it takes about 3 days for this product to accumulate; (3) that it is totally discharged to the circulation by the fifth day after amputation. Furthermore, its secretion need not be sustained: once the injured parts have received the hormonal cue, they regenerate without further exposure to the factor.

CRUSTACEAN HORMONES Neurohormones control color changes and molting in crustaceans. These neurohormones are secreted by clusters of neurosecretory cells lying within a ganglion located in each eyestalk. Axons from these cells lead from the *eyestalk ganglion* to a neurohemal organ, the *sinus gland,* where their secretions can be released into an adjacent blood sinus (Figure 15.45). This release is governed by impulses from the brain, allowing color changes to be coordinated with relevant visual data, for some of the hormones secreted by the cells of the eyestalk ganglion are *chromatophorotrophins,** which regulate the distribution of pigment granules within the chromatophores (pigment cells). These hormones can even regulate the distribution of more than one pigment within a single cell, causing one to concentrate about the nucleus while another is made to disperse throughout the cytoplasm. Chromatophorotrophic action is not identical in all crustaceans. In some species removal of the sinus gland causes permanent darkening due to the dispersion of black pigment. In other species, the same operation results in blanching due to the concentration of red and black pigments about the nuclei and the simultaneous dispersion of white pigment throughout the cytoplasm. In a third group removal of the sinus gland causes the tail to darken temporarily while the rest of the body blanches.

No consistent picture has yet been obtained concerning the hormonal regulation of the migration of the eye pigments that serve as a tapetum by night and screen the ommatidia from one another by day (see

Figure 15.45 □ Neuroendocrine system of a crab. Dotted lines indicate circulatory distribution of hormones. Only one cell or a few cells of a type are shown for simplicity.

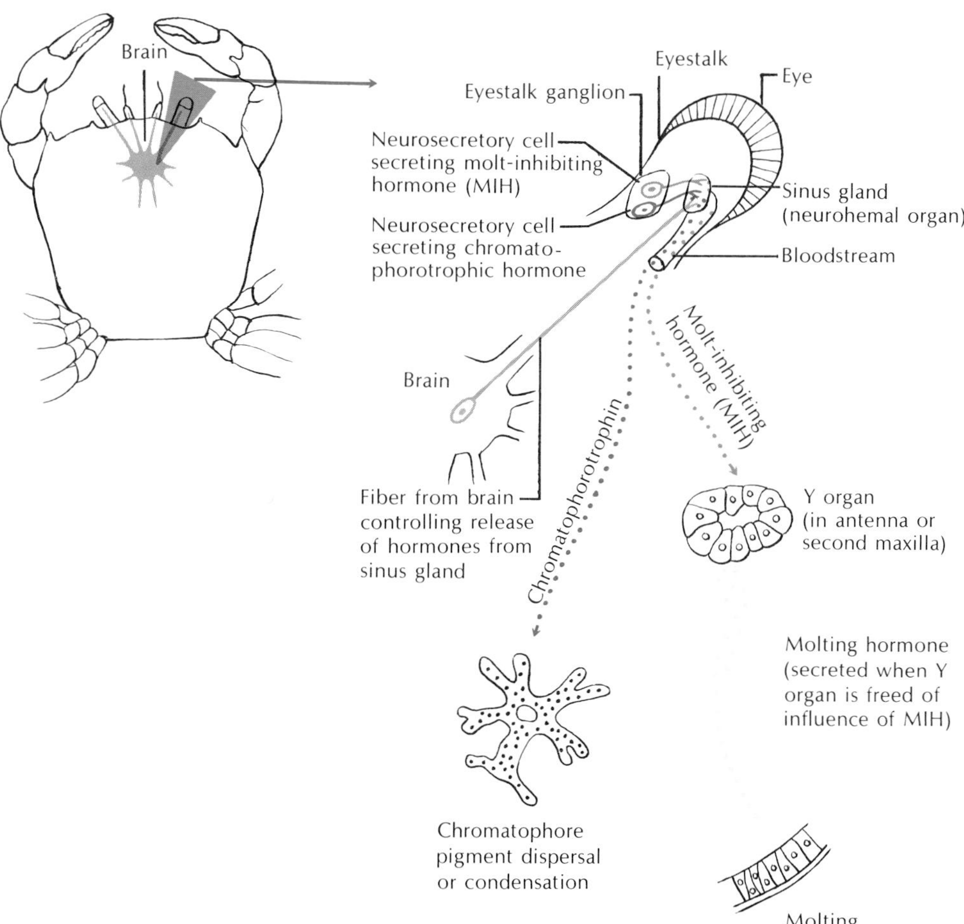

*The literature of endocrinology is complicated by inconsistencies in spelling arising from disagreement concerning the derivation of the term "trophin." Some writers use the suffix "-trophin," from *trophe,* meaning to nourish or stimulate, to describe hormones that sustain or stimulate the activity of some other tissue, usually another endocrine gland. Others use the suffix "-tropin," derived from *trope,* meaning to turn toward. Since the derivation from *trophe* appears more consistent with the actual meaning of the term -trophin, this suffix will be used herein. The student should recognize however that -tropin is favored by many.

Figure 15.46 □ Neuroendocrine control of insect molting and metamorphosis.

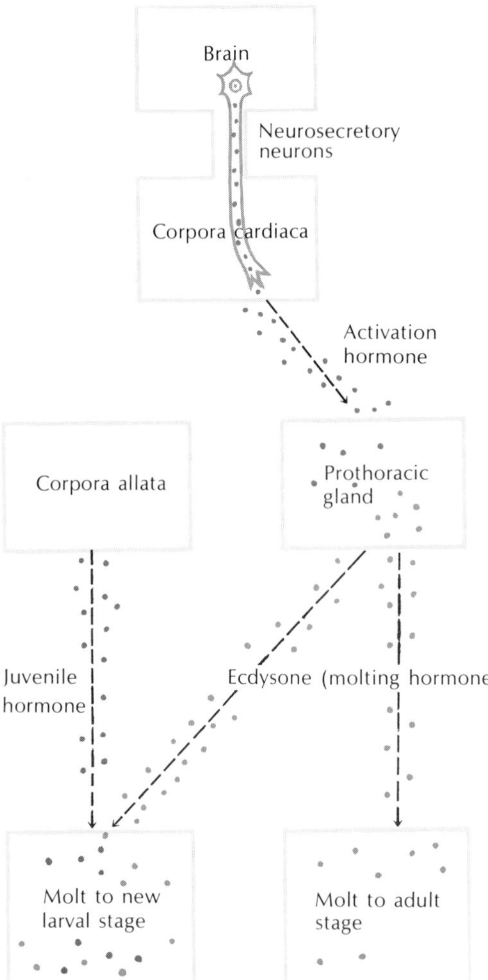

Figure 15.23). Injecting eyestalk extracts into a dark-adapted shrimp causes concentration of the black pigment while leaving the white reflective pigment unaffected. There is some evidence to suggest the existence of distinct dark- and light-adapting neurohormones.

A molt-inhibiting hormone is also secreted by the eyestalk ganglion and released from the sinus gland. This hormone inhibits the secretory activity of the *Y organs* (epithelial endocrine glands lying within either the antennae or the second maxillae): if the Y organs of a crab are removed during the intermolt period, the molting cycle is permanently abolished, being restored only by the implantation of new Y organs; on the other hand, if the sinus glands are removed, the initiation of a premature molt will result.

HORMONES IN INSECTS The bug *Rhodnius* was one of the first subjects selected for the study of endocrine function in insects (Figure 15.46). *Rhodnius* passes through several *instars* (growth intervals separated by periodic molts) and finally attains the adult form without an intervening pupal stage. An area of *Rhodnius'* brain (the *pars intercerebralis*) contains neurosecretory cells that produce an *activation hormone* (AH). This hormone passes along the axons to the *corpora cardiaca,* paired neurohemal organs from which it is liberated. The corpora cardiaca are located behind the brain in intimate contact with the aorta, favoring the prompt dissemination of AH throughout the hemocoel.

The flow of AH is controlled by nervous impulses generated by sensory input to the brain during feeding. As the bug consumes a blood meal, its abdomen becomes distended, exciting stretch receptors in the abdominal wall. Stimuli from these receptors to the brain set in motion metabolic changes that bring about a flow of AH about 8 days after the blood meal was consumed. A bug decapitated after feeding but before 8 days have elapsed will not molt, but one decapitated after the passage of 8 days will molt normally several weeks later, despite the absence of a head. Parabiotic linking of the bloodstreams of two bugs—one beheaded immediately after its blood meal, the other decapitated more than 8 days later—allows both insects to molt successfully due to the spread of AH from the second individual into the first through their conjoined circulatory systems.

Activation hormone acts by stimulating the *prothoracic gland* (an epithelial endocrine gland lying within the thorax) to secrete the molting hormone *ecdysone.* Ecdysone, a steroid hormone cited earlier for its effect in promoting the development of chromosome puffs, excites mitotic activity in the epidermis and stimulates the epidermal cells first to deposit new cuticle beneath the old and then to secrete a molting fluid of which the function is to loosen the outer cuticle.

Until the final molt to adulthood, larval structures are maintained by the secretion of *juvenile hormone* (JH) from the *corpora allata,* a pair of epithelial endocrine glands located in the head. By the end of the fifth larval instar the production of JH has diminished while the flow of ecdysone has increased, so that metamorphosis to the sexually mature, fully winged adult takes place at the last molt.

Studies of diapause in the silkworm (see Section 5.1) indicate that the immediate cause of diapause is the arrestment of neurosecretory activity of the pars intercerebralis, with consequent cessation in the flow of AH. The larva must be chilled and rewarmed before neurosecretory activity can be resumed and diapause broken. If the brain of a chilled larva is transplanted into a larva that has not been chilled, the recipient will immediately be aroused from diapause.

Figure 15.47 □ Human endocrine system. Hormones are in parentheses following the names of glands.

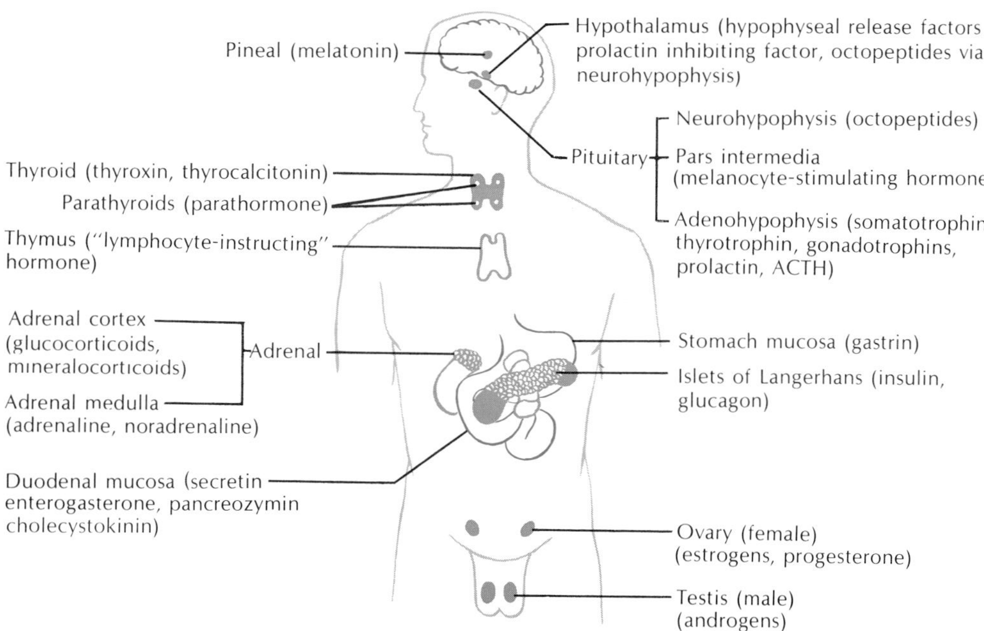

C Vertebrate hormones

The vertebrate endocrine control system includes neurohormones, hormones secreted by epithelial endocrine glands, and tissue hormones secreted by cells not grouped into demonstrable endocrine glands (Figure 15.47). Some of these hormones are under the direct or indirect control of the nervous system, whereas others are released in response to such cues as changes in blood pressure or chemistry. The most sophisticated aspect of neuroendocrine regulation involves the hormones controlled by the *hypothalamo-hypophyseal axis,* a regulatory circuit involving the hypothalamus of the brain, the hypophysis (pituitary gland), and the various endocrine glands controlled by the hypophysis (gonads, adrenal cortex, thyroid); see Figure 15.48. All components of this axis are linked in a negative feedback circuit in which any rise in the level of circulating hormones secreted by the tertiary glands acts suppressively on the hypothalamus, diminishing its stimulatory effects upon the hypophysis, which in turn ceases to liberate the trophic hormones that promote the activity of those tertiary glands. Conversely, as the blood level of the tertiary hormones declines, the

Figure 15.48 □ The hypothalamo-hypophyseal control axis. **(*a*) Hormones and other factors: adenohypophyseal hormones are shown in gray; melanocyte-stimulating hormones, pale color tint; release factors from hypothalamus, black; a possible neurohormone controlling the pars intermedia, dark color tint; and the octopeptides secreted by neurosecretory neurons terminating in the neurohypophysis, solid color. (*b*) The control cycle: *H*, the hypothalamus; *A*, the adenohypophysis.**

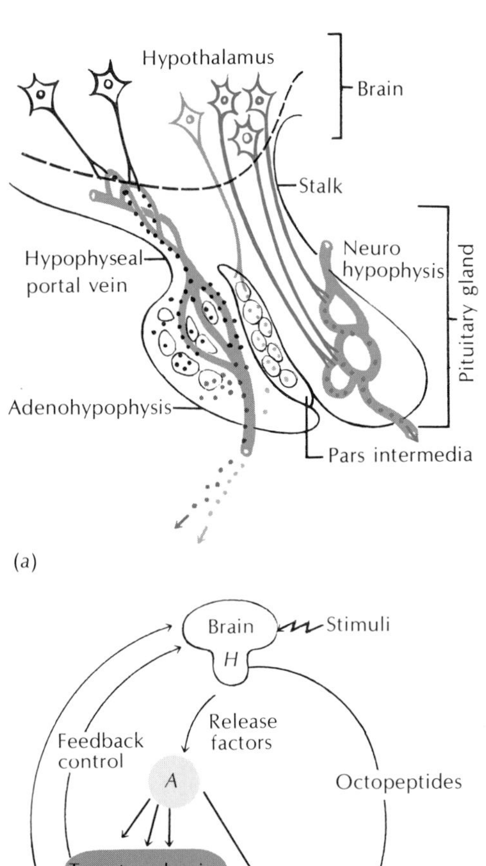

hypothalamus is reactivated and in turn excites the pituitary (Table 15.2).

VERTEBRATE NEUROHORMONES Apart from mammals, in which the pineal organ is now considered to have an endocrine function and to secrete the gonad-regulating hormone *melatonin* (see Section 8.2D), the hypothalamus is the only known source of neurohormones in the vertebrate brain. The hypothalamus is particularly influenced by input from the ancient olfactory association areas of the old cortex (the "limbic system"), and from the thalamus, that great subcortical correlative center which receives all types of sensory data and projects fibers to (as well as receiving them from) the cerebral cortex. In addition to this neural control, the hypothalamus is also affected by the hormones secreted by glands under its direct or indirect control.

The octopeptides Axons from two hypothalamic nuclei descend through the pituitary stalk to terminate upon capillaries in the neurohypophysis (posterior pituitary), which accordingly constitutes a neurohemal organ like the crustacean sinus gland. In mammals two hormones are released by these axons: *vasopressin* (also known as antidiuretic hormone, ADH) and *oxytocin* (Figure 15.49). These hormones and equivalent factors in lower vertebrates are octopeptides made up of eight amino acids. The various octopeptides differ from one another in only a couple of amino acid substitutions, and their basic function seems to relate to the control of the excretion of ions (mainly Na^+) in aquatic vertebrates and water excretion or retention in terrestrial species. It has also been suggested that the octopeptides may first have served as a communications link from the brain to the adenohypophysis.

Figure 15.49 □ Octopeptides secreted from the mammalian neurohypophysis.

ileu——tyr——cys

gluNH$_2$—aspNH$_2$—cys—pro—**leu**—glyNH$_2$

Oxytocin

phe——tyr——cys

gluNH$_2$—aspNH$_2$—cys—pro—**arg**—glyNH$_2$

Vasopressin

The fact that mammals have two octopeptides differing in only two amino acids suggests that these factors are products of duplicated genes that have undergone base substitution mutations (see Section 9.7E). Vasopressin serves to promote water retention by the kidneys. Its lack in man produces diabetes insipidus,* a condition in which up to 30 liters of dilute urine are voided daily, a loss of water that must be balanced by equally copious drinking to avoid death. Vasopressin also elevates blood pressure when injected, but this may not be a normal physiological effect. Oxytocin, on the other hand, exerts its main effect on smooth muscle. It promotes milk release during suckling by stimulating contractions of the myoepithelial cells forming the mammary ducts, and when injected causes uterine contractions and brings on labor.

Hypophyseal release factors Capillaries around certain clusters of neurosecretory cells in the hypothalamus take up other neurohormones known as the hypo-

*Not to be confused with diabetes mellitus, an insulin-deficiency syndrome.

Table 15.2 □ Mammalian hormones

HORMONE	SITE OF FORMATION	ACTION
Somatotrophin release factor (STRF)	Hypothalamus	Stimulates adenohypophysis to secrete somatotrophin
Corticotrophin release factor (CTRF)	Hypothalamus	Stimulates adenohypophysis to secrete adrenocorticotrophic hormone
Thyrotrophin release factor (TTRF)	Hypothalamus	Stimulates adenohypophysis to secrete thyrotrophin
Gonadotrophin release factors (FSH-RF and LH-RF)	Hypothalamus	Stimulate adenohypophysis to secrete gonadotrophins (FSH and LH)
Prolactin inhibiting factor (PIF)	Hypothalamus	Inhibits adenohypophysis from secreting prolactin
Melatonin	Pineal	Regulates gonadal annual cycle (?)
Vasopressin	Hypothalamus (via neurohypophysis)	Promotes water retention in kidneys
Oxytocin	Hypothalamus (via neurohypophysis)	Promotes milk release, uterine contractions (?)
Melanocyte-stimulating hormone (MSH)	Pars intermedia of pituitary	Stimulates melanin synthesis
Somatotrophin (growth hormone)	Adenohypophysis (anterior pituitary)	Promotes somatic (especially skeletal) growth
Adrenocorticotrophin (ACTH)	Adenohypophysis	Stimulates adrenal cortex to secrete glucocorticoids
Thyrotrophin (TTH)	Adenohypophysis	Stimulates release of thyroid hormones
Follicle-stimulating hormone (FSH)	Adenohypophysis	Promotes maturation of ovarian follicles, secretion of sex hormones
Luteinizing hormone (LH) (same as ICSH)	Adenohypophysis	Promotes growth of corpus luteum, secretion of sex hormones
Prolactin	Adenohypophysis	Promotes milk production, parental behavior
Thyroxine	Thyroid	Stimulates oxidative metabolism, promotes somatic growth
Thyrocalcitonin	Thyroid	Lowers blood Ca^{2+} level
Parathormone	Parathyroid	Elevates blood Ca^{2+} level
Glucocorticoids (corticosterone and the like)	Adrenal cortex	Regulate carbohydrate metabolism
Mineralocorticoids (aldosterone and the like)	Adrenal cortex	Regulate excretion and retention of Na^+ and K^+
Adrenaline and noradrenaline	Adrenal medulla	Reinforce action of sympathetic nervous system
Insulin	Pancreatic islets (Islets of Langerhans)	Promotes passage of glucose into cells, lowers blood sugar level
Glucagon	Pancreatic islets	Promotes breakdown of glycogen, elevates blood sugar level
Estrogens (estradiol, estrone, and the like)	Ovaries	Promote female secondary sexual characteristics, development of genital tract
Progesterone	Ovaries, corpus luteum	Promotes and maintains pregnancy
Androgens (testosterone, androsterone, and the like)	Testes	Promote male secondary sexual characteristics, sexual drive
Gastrin	Gastric mucosa	Promotes flow of gastric juice
Enterogasterone	Duodenal mucosa	Inhibits flow of gastric juice
Secretin	Duodenal mucosa	Excites flow of watery component of pancreatic juice
Pancreozymin	Duodenal mucosa	Stimulates secretion of pancreatic enzymes
Cholecystokinin	Duodenal mucosa	Stimulates contraction of gall bladder and release of bile
Angiotensin	Blood factor activated by renin from kidney	Elevates peripheral blood pressure, stimulates adrenal cortex to secrete aldosterone
Thymic hormone	Thymus	Promotes immunological competence of lymphoid tissues
Chorionic gonadotrophin	Placenta	Maintains pregnancy by promoting growth of corpus luteum of pregnancy
Relaxin	Placenta	Relaxes pubic symphysis before partuition

physeal release factors. These factors appear to be polypeptides, and there is probably a specific one controlling each hormone liberated by the adenohypophysis. These release factors are transported to the pituitary by way of the *hypophyseal portal system,* blood vessels that drain the capillaries serving the hypothalamic neurosecretory cells and deliver blood to the capillary bed within the hypophysis. The dependence of the adenohypophysis on these release factors can be demonstrated experimentally. If the pituitary stalk is sectioned, the endocrine glands controlled by the adenohypophysis atrophy for want of the pituitary trophic hormones that stimulate their activity. The hypothalamic domination of the adenohypophysis can also be shown by implanting small pellets of a hormone secreted by a gland under hypophyseal control into the tissues of either the hypothalamus or the hypophysis itself. Such pellets are without demonstrable effect if implanted into the pituitary, but pellets implanted into the hypothalamus cause suppression of the gland secreting that hormone by inhibiting the liberation of the appropriate pituitary trophic hormone. For example, implantation of estrogen into the basal part of the hypothalamus causes atrophy of both the ovaries and the uterus; on the other hand, estrogen implanted into the hypophysis has no such effect.

In modern bony fish a new source of neurohormones has appeared. Neurons in the posterior portion of the spinal cord give off axons that liberate neurohormones within a neurohemal organ, the *urophysis*. These factors have been found to affect osmoregulation, a matter of critical concern to bony fish, which inhabit waters either hyposmotic or hyperosmotic to their tissues.

HORMONES OF THE ADENOHYPOPHYSIS AND PARS INTERMEDIA The intermediate lobe of the pituitary secretes one hormone, *melanocyte-stimulating hormone* (MSH), a peptide containing from 13 to 21 amino acids that elicits pigment-dispersion in the melanocytes of lower vertebrates and stimulates melanin synthesis in mammalian skin. Release of MSH is controlled by axons from the hypothalamus, which terminate upon the MSH-secreting cells.

Most adenohypophyseal hormones are trophic hormones, the major action of which is to promote the development and secretory activity of other endocrine glands. Exceptions are prolactin, the multiple effects of which were summarized earlier and will be considered further in Chapter 17, and the growth hormone, *somatotrophin,* a protein with a molecular weight of 25,000 to 50,000 that contains 188 amino acid units in man (Figure 15.50). Somatotrophin promotes general somatic growth, particularly stimulating bone deposition and protein synthesis while depressing amino acid catabolism. Lack of this factor in early life leads to pituitary dwarfism; its excess, to pituitary giantism. When moderate this effect produces a good basketball player, but when extreme can lead to a stature of more than 2.5 m. Such pituitary giants are well-proportioned but usually suffer from circulatory troubles resulting from the difficulty of returning the blood from the legs to the heart. Excess production of somatotrophin in maturity, when most of the skeleton has ceased to grow, leads to acromegaly (a disfiguring condition in which there is continued bony deposition in the facial areas and extremities).

Thyrotrophin (TTH, also known as thyroid-stimulating hormone or TSH) is a glycoprotein that specifically stimulates the thyroid gland to release its accumulated products. The flow of thyrotrophin itself is controlled by negative feedback regulation of the hypothalamus by the circulating thyroid hormones, as was explained earlier in this section.

Adrenocorticotrophin (ACTH) stimulates the growth and secretory performance of the adrenal cortex, particularly with regard to the glucocorticoids, or cortical hormones controlling sugar metabolism. It is a polypeptide containing up to 39 amino acids, of which a sequence of nine are in common with the smaller MSH molecule, suggesting a common evolutionary origin (Figure 15.51). The secretion of ACTH is controlled by negative feedback like that for TSH. Circulating glucocorticoids suppress the secretion by the hypothalamus of the ACTH release factor, and the lack of this factor in turn causes the adenohypophysis to cease secreting ACTH. However, some investigators contend that prolonged physical or emotional stress, such as may result from overcrowding, harrassment of a subordinate individual by a dominant member of the group, and so forth, can cause the central nervous system to override this feedback control, causing more ACTH to flow despite a high level of circulating cortical hormones. This would lead to the hyperstimulation of the adrenal cortex, its enlargement, and eventual exhaustion atrophy, which very often terminates in death of the individual.

The adenohypophysis also secretes two *gonadotrophins, follicle-stimulating hormone* (FSH), and *luteinizing hormone* (LH), and a hormone, prolactin (luteotrophin or lactogenic hormone), which promotes lactation and has many other reproductively oriented functions in mammals and nonmammalian vertebrates; FSH and LH are glycoproteins (molecular weight 50,000 to 100,000), whereas prolactin is a small protein (molecular weight 25,000). The control of reproduction by these hormones, their corresponding hypothalamic release factors, and the sex hormones which they control will be taken up in Chapter 17.

ENDOCRINE GLANDS CONTROLLED BY THE HYPOTHALAMO-HYPOPHYSEAL AXIS The thyroid, adrenal cortex, and secretory tissues of the ovaries and testes are primarily under control of the hypothalamus via the anterior pituitary; they in turn influence the functioning of the hypothalamus by negative feedback.

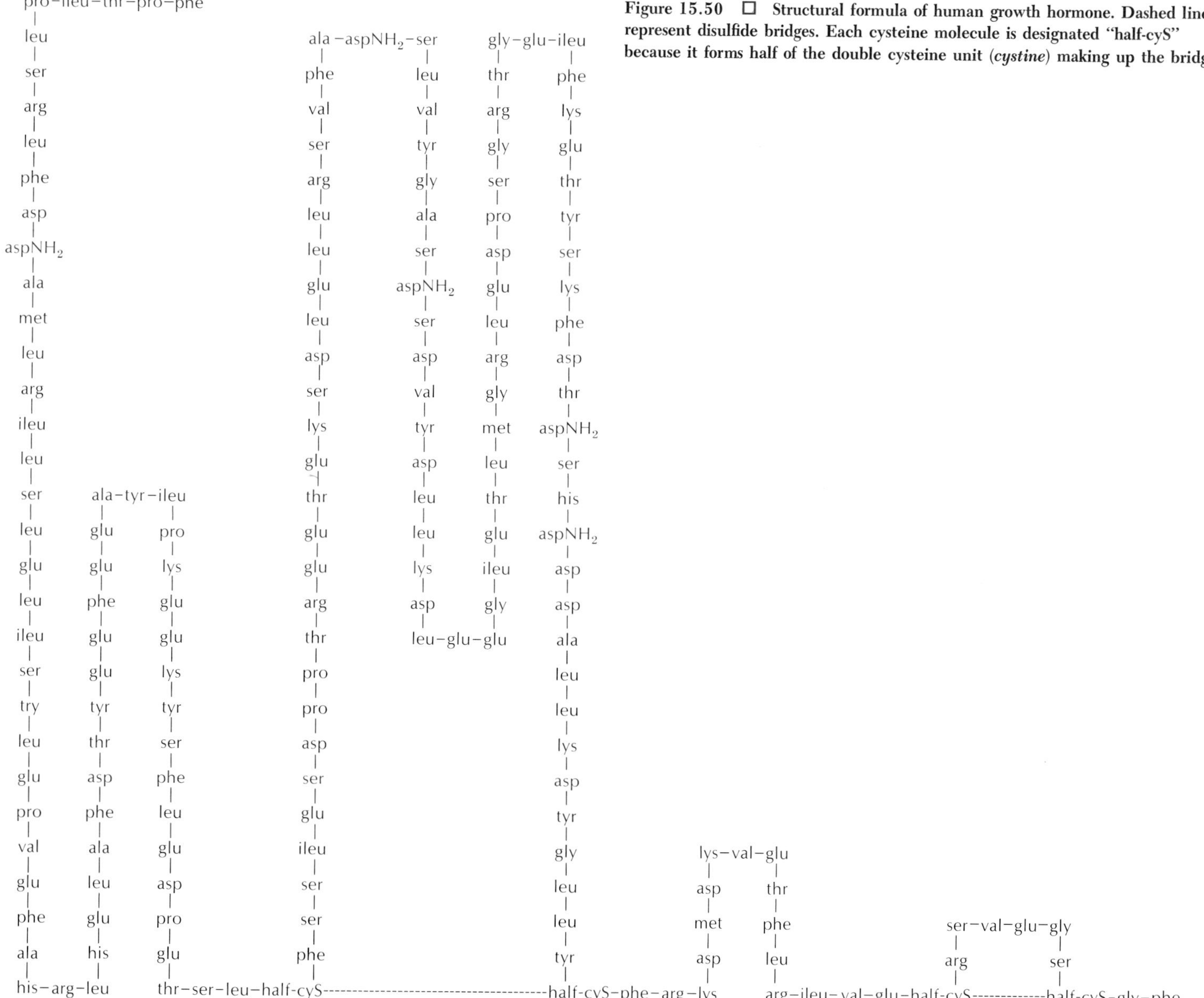

Figure 15.50 □ **Structural formula of human growth hormone. Dashed lines represent disulfide bridges. Each cysteine molecule is designated "half-cyS" because it forms half of the double cysteine unit (*cystine*) making up the bridge.**

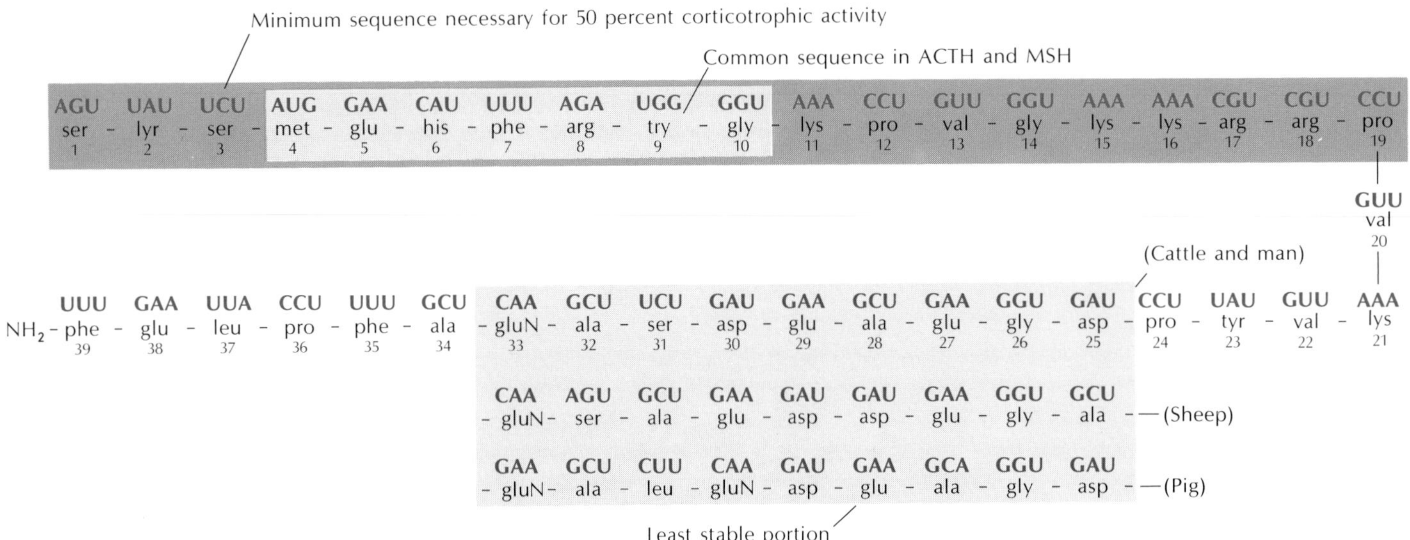

Figure 15.51 □ ACTH: adrenocorticotrophic hormone. Chemical analysis of ACTH of man, cattle, sheep, and pig shows the hormone to be identical with respect to the critical 19-amino acid sequence responsible for 50 percent corticotrophic activity. In the less stable 9-amino acid sequence designated above, mutations have taken place that result in several amino acid substitutions. RNA codons are shown for each amino acid, indicating base sequence of mRNA encoding the ACTH molecule. Note that in most cases a one-base substitution mutation would be sufficient to change the amino acid present at that point in one species to the amino acid occurring in that position in one of the other two species.

The thyroid gland *Thyroxine* and *triiodothyronine* are thyroid hormones concerned with regulating biosynthesis and cell respiration. Both are amino acids bearing four and three iodine atoms, respectively (Figure 15.52). Thyroxine is more abundant, but triiodothyronine has the greater physiological activity.

Production of these hormones depends on the dietary acquisition of iodides. When these are insufficient (such as in foods raised on soils leached by glacial action, as in central Europe and the Great Lakes area), the thyroid remains chronically overstimulated by TSH and enlarges to form a *simple goiter.* (Simple goiter was once so common in central Europe as to be considered a mark of feminine beauty.) Physiologically, the goiterous individual may be otherwise normal or may display signs of *hypo*thyroidism, such as depressed metabolism, mental dullness, and thickened skin. Simple goiter is corrected by adding iodides to the diet, usually in the form of iodized table salt. A more dangerous condition, *exophthalmic goiter,* characterized by bulging eyes and symptoms of *hyper*thyroidism (high metabolic rate, loss of weight, nervousness, and even hallucinations) is actually due to malfunction of either the hypothalamus or the hypophysis, for TSH continues to be released even in the presence of adequate thyroid hormone.

Thyroxine has been found to suppress amino acid catabolism while simultaneously stimulating the breakdown of glycogen and the oxidative catabolism of carbohydrates and lipids. It is synergistic with somatotrophin, that is, the two together promote

Figure 15.52 □ **Major thyroid hormones, bearing four or three iodine atoms attached to the rings.**

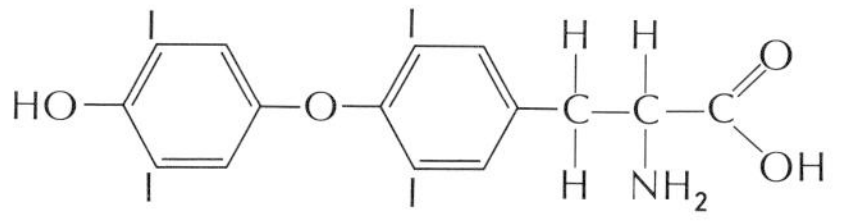

Thyroxine

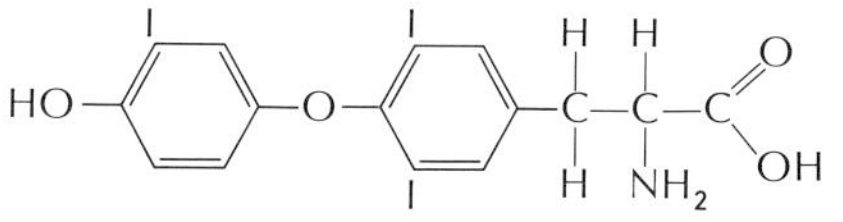

Triiodothyronine

growth more effectively than either alone. Thyroid insufficiency in early life causes cretinism, a condition of dwarfism accompanied by severe mental retardation. In later life pronounced hypothyroidism leads to myxedema, a condition characterized by low metabolic rate, thickened skin, mental dullness, lassitude, and obesity. The essential mode of action of thyroxine remains obscure. Its control of metamorphosis in amphibians may involve repression and derepression of entire sets of genes, but this effect may be indirect.

The thyroid gland of mammals secretes another hormone, *thyrocalcitonin,* which is not controlled by the hypothalamo-hypophyseal axis and is instead secreted in response to a rise in blood calcium level. Thyrocalcitonin acts in opposition to parathormone and will be discussed at further length in conjunction with the latter.

The gonads Both ovaries and testes produce three kinds of steroid hormones: *estrogens, androgens,* and *gestagens,* the primary roles of which have to do with reproduction and will therefore be considered in Chapter 17. However, we should note here that the sex hormones also play important roles in somatic development, particularly in sexually dimorphic species where overall body size, coloration, and proportions are influenced by these hormones, as well as such specific traits as hair and fat distribution and voice quality. Many behaviors controlled by sex hormones (such as singing by male birds) are only indirectly associated with mating. The concentration of circulating testosterone, for instance, correlates directly with an animal's position in the social hierarchy and its capacity to hold a territory.

The adrenal cortex At least part of the activity of the adrenal cortex is under hypophyseal control via ACTH. The adrenal cortex forms the outer rind of the adrenal gland, an organ which in mammals consists of two tissues of different origin: the cortex is epithelial and derived from the mesoderm; the medulla is derived from neuroblasts of the embryonic neural crests. The adrenal cortex secretes a number of steroid hormones. Some of these are sex hormones resembling those of the gonads (but considered mainly to be metabolic intermediates). Because of the preponderance of cortical androgens, adrenal tumors cause sexual precocity in boys and have a masculinizing effect in women, promoting beard growth and other male traits.

The major adrenocortical hormones are of two types that actually blend in their effects: *mineralocorticoids,* which primarily control the excretion or retention of ions (particularly Na^+ and K^+), and *glucocorticoids,* which mainly control carbohydrate metabolism and other biochemical conversions.

Only the glucocorticoids seem to be controlled by ACTH. A number have been isolated, of which by far the most abundant are *cortisone* and *hydrocortisone* (Figure 15.53). These hormones promote the synthesis of glycogen and depress glycolytic processes, while stimulating protein catabolism. They also influence water and ion metabolism, and are essential to life; destruction of the adrenal cortex in man leads to a fatally terminating syndrome (Addison's disease) that is arrested only by glucocorticoid-replacement therapy.

By far the most active mineralocorticoid is *aldosterone,* which also influences carbo-

Figure 15.53 □ **Major hormones of the adrenal cortex: (*a*) glucocorticoids; (*b*) mineralocorticoids.**

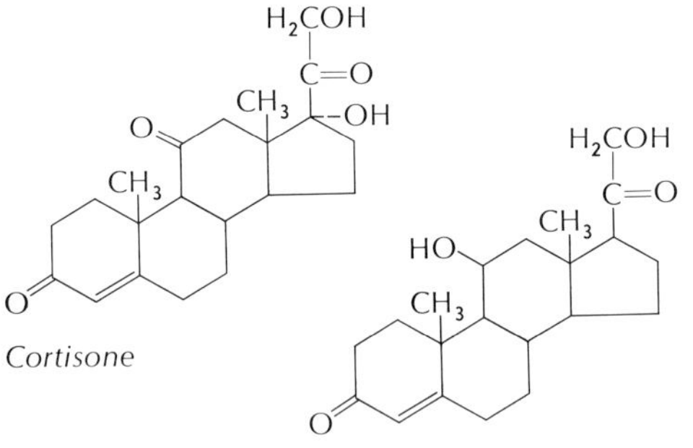

(*a*) *Cortisone*; *Cortisol*

(*b*) *Aldosterone*; *11-Desoxycorticosterone*

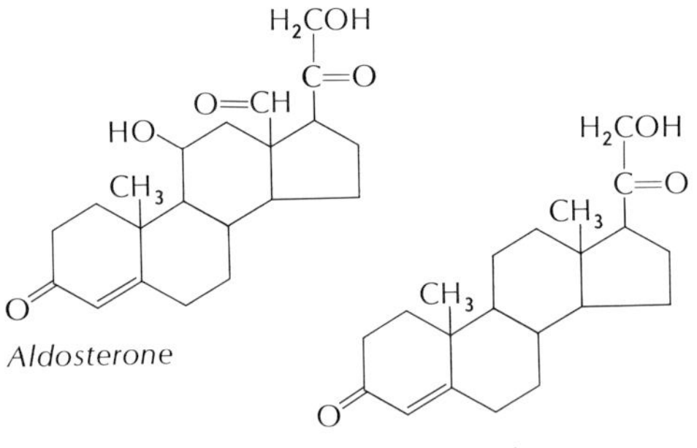

hydrate metabolism but mainly serves to regulate the Na^+/K^+ balance, promoting the retention of the Na^+ in the mammalian kidney and concomittant loss of K^+ and H^+. In animals that drink sea water, on the other hand, the mineralocorticoids promote *excretion* of Na^+ and other ions taken in excess. In marine fish, mineralocorticoid injections increase Na^+ secretion by the gill tissues. Equivalent salt excretion takes place in sea birds by way of the nasal salt glands, and these too are controlled by the adrenal cortex as shown by their failure to secrete following adrenalectomy. The release of mineralocorticoids seems to be largely independent of ACTH and to be controlled instead by angiotensin, a blood constituent, as well as by a recently discovered release factor from the diencephalon.

Some forty compounds with hormonal activity have been isolated from adrenocortical extracts, although only ten are present in appreciable amounts. Most of the others may be present only as metabolic intermediates on the pathways of synthesis or degradation of the physiological hormones.

ENDOCRINE GLANDS THAT ARE CHEMICALLY REGULATED The adrenal medulla, parathyroids, pancreatic islets, and the tissues secreting gastrointestinal hormones release their products when stimulated by certain specific chemicals that are not hormonal in nature. All but the first of these are free of direct control by the nervous system.

The adrenal medulla The adrenal medulla liberates *adrenaline* and *noradrenaline* in response to the secretion of the transmitter substance, acetylcholine, by preganglionic sympathetic fibers terminating within the medulla. In effect, the adrenal medulla serves as a modified sympathetic ganglion, for the hormones it produces are the same as the transmitter substances released at the endings of postganglionic sympathetic fibers. However, instead of liberating these materials only at adrenergic synapses, the adrenal medulla releases them into the general circulation, promoting a systemic effect that augments and sustains the action of sympathetic nerves and intensifies the emergency "fight-or-flight" syndrome described earlier.

The physiological effects of adrenaline and noradrenaline are similar but not identical. Adrenaline increases the flow of blood through the muscles, heart tissue, liver, and brain, whereas noradrenaline constricts blood vessels in general, excepting those of the muscles and liver. Adrenaline promotes glycogenolysis in the liver (Figure 15.54), thereby promptly raising the blood sugar level; noradrenaline has a similar effect but is only 25 percent as effective. Both promote glucose oxidation. The distinction between adrenaline and noradrenaline may be more significant than we now realize: studies with human subjects indicate that sensations of fear and anxiety are associated with increased adrenaline flow, whereas sensations of rage appear linked to increased noradrenaline output. In one such investigation male college students were tested under conditions in which their answers were invariably declared wrong. Under such frustration two groups emerged: (1) those who resorted to self-blame and anxiety, and who were found mainly to secrete adrenaline; (2) those who turned their frustration outward in anger at the examiners, and who secreted mainly noradrenaline. These differences matched certain sharp differences in social

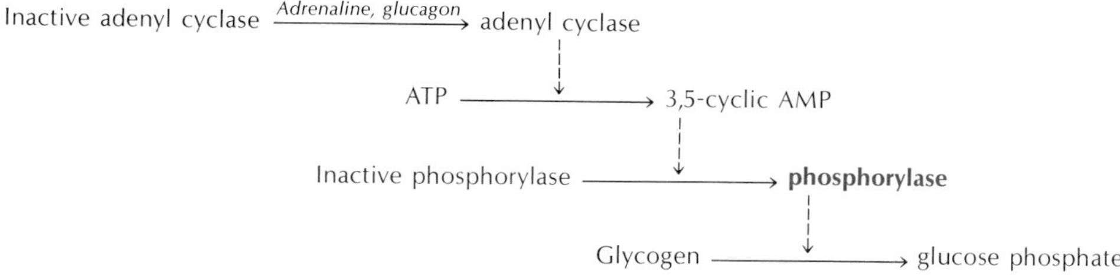

Figure 15.54 □ Proposed mode of action of adrenaline and glucagon in the mobilization of liver glycogen.

background: the anxious self-denigrators had come from protected home environments; the enraged students from slum situations in which aggressive "toughness" was prerequisite to social and economic success. Thus early experience seems to have lasting effects on the manner in which our bodies are physiologically geared to meet stress. Through habit either the "fight" or the "flight" aspect of the sympathetic syndrome can predominate.

The pancreatic islets Embedded within the enzyme-secreting tissue of the pancreas are clusters of endocrine cells known as the pancreatic islets (*islets of Langerhans*). Within each islet are two major types of secretory cells that can be discriminated by differential staining: β cells, which secrete the hormone *insulin* in response to a rise in blood sugar level; and α cells, which secrete the hormone *glucagon* in response to a drop in the level of circulating glucose. These two polypeptide hormones thus largely act in opposition.

Insulin is of historic interest as the first protein to be subjected to complete chemical analysis (see Figure 9.12). It is composed of 51 amino acids organized in two chains that are connected by disulfide (cysteine) bridges. Separation of these chains by breaking the disulfide bridges destroys the compound's hormonal activity. Insulin acts in two distinct ways. First, it appears to activate the gene that controls the production of *hexokinase,* the enzyme responsible for catalyzing the reaction,

$$\text{Glucose} + \text{ATP} \longrightarrow \text{glucose 6-phosphate} + \text{ADP}$$

which we should recall is a cell-surface reaction prerequisite to the absorption of glucose. Second, insulin activates the glucose-transport mechanism, thus promoting the movement of glucose 6-phosphate across the plasma membrane into the cells. This active transport of glucose into the cells causes a lowering of the blood sugar level, which in turn serves as the stimulus for glucagon release.

Glucagon mobilizes liver glycogen by promoting the production of *phosphorylase* (presumably by gene activation), which catalyzes the phosphorolytic breakdown of glycogen to glucose 1-phosphate. As the simple sugar diffuses from the cells into the bloodstream, the rising blood sugar level signals the cessation of glucagon release and triggers that of insulin. In this manner these two hormones maintain a sensitive homeostatic control over the equilibrium of glucose in the cells and in the body fluids.

Destruction of the pancreas leads in many mammals to an insulin-deficiency disease known as *diabetes mellitus,* in which glucose accumulates in the bloodstream and is excreted in the urine, and the cells instead attack their proteins and lipid reserves. By-products of this excessive lipid catabolism (ketone bodies) may enter the bloodstream in such quantities that blood pH is deranged and diabetic coma or death may ensue. However, sensitivity to lack of insulin is variable, and some vertebrates remain unaffected by removal of the pancreas.

The parathyroids The parathyroids are small glands essential to life, embedded within the tissues of the thyroid gland. They secrete a calcium-controlling factor (*parathormone*) that acts in opposition to the previously mentioned thyroid factor, thyrocalcitonin. Together these factors regulate the blood level of Ca^{2+}, and since both are liberated in response to changes in blood calcium level it is significant that they are placed close together and can therefore sample the blood at the same location in the body. These hormones constitute the body's "calcistat," for, like the thermostat of a furnace, their combined role is to maintain a steady state (here, an unchanged blood calcium level).

Parathormone is secreted in response to a decline in blood Ca^{2+}. It promotes the bone-eroding activity of osteoclasts, amoeboid cells that digest the bony matrix and make possible the dynamic adjustment of bone to changing stress (see Section 4.4D). Parathormone also promotes the excretion of phosphate by the kidneys, for when calcium is mobilized from the bones, phosphates are released as well—and would mount to excess in the bloodstream if not removed by the kidneys.

During parathormone insufficiency in mammals the number of osteoclasts declines, the level of blood Ca^{2+} drops dramatically, and the individual succumbs to convulsions and asphyxiation brought on by spasms of the respiratory muscles. Mild parathyroid hyperactivity is normal in pregnancy, making supplies of calcium and phosphate available to the fetal skeleton, but gross hyperactivity as in parathyroid tumor leads to the withdrawal of so much of the bones' mineral content that the skeleton can no longer support the body's weight and becomes limber as rubber!

Thyrocalcitonin is secreted in response to rising blood Ca^{2+} and acts to lower it. Its mode of action is obscure but may consist of direct inhibition of osteoclast activity, thereby suppressing bone resorption.

The gastrointestinal tissue hormones The *gastrointestinal endocrine complex* consists of a number of hormonal factors secreted by the epithelial lining of the stomach and duodenum in response to the presence of particular food materials within the digestive tract. Some of these factors remain hypothetical, and all have yet to be isolated and chemically identified. Even the cells that secrete these hormones defy final identification for they are scattered among the other secretory cells of the mucosal glands.

One of the first gastrointestinal hormones to be recognized was *gastrin,* secreted by the stomach lining. The existence of gastrin was established through the researches of the renowned Russian physiologist I. P. Pavlov. He approached the study of gastric secretion by severing the animal's esophagus and directing the cut ends to the surface of the body so that food properly swallowed could not reach the stomach and would pass out by way of this esophageal fistula resulting in "sham feeding." The fistula also allowed food to be introduced directly into the stomach without being either tasted or swallowed. Sham-fed dogs were found to secrete only about 25 percent of the normal amount of gastric juice, and even this flow could be abolished by cutting the nerves serving the stomach wall. Direct insertion of fresh meat into the stomach failed to elicit gastric secretion, but if the meat were partially digested before insertion it not only triggered a normal flow of gastric juice but did so even when the nerve supply was interrupted! That this effect was not due to direct stimulation of the gastric glands by some chemical in the partially digested meat was shown by tying off part of the stomach to form an isolated pouch into which food could be introduced separately. When partially digested food was placed in the pouch, gastric juice began to flow in the main part of the stomach, which lacked direct contact with the food. From Pavlov's experiments it could be concluded that during normal feeding the initial flow of gastric juice is neurally instigated but that when digestion reaches a certain stage, substances released from the partly digested meat trigger the secretion of a hormone (gastrin). This hormone enters the general circulation and eventually returns to the stomach, where it stimulates the gastric glands to secrete their products (mainly HCl and pepsin).

Fats entering the duodenum from the stomach trigger the secretion of the hormone *enterogasterone,* which opposes gastrin, inhibiting the release of gastric juice (especially HCl) and thereby retarding the release of food from the stomach. Another duodenal hormone, *cholecystokinin,* is also secreted in response to fats within the duodenum, but this hormone causes contraction of the gall bladder, thereby expelling the accumulated bile into the intestinal cavity. *Secretin* is released into the bloodstream when acidic material enters the duodenum from the stomach. It causes the pancreas to secrete the watery, alkaline component of pancreatic juice, and stimulates the liver cells to secrete bile. *Pancreozymin,* also from the duodenum, elicits the secretion of the pancreatic hydrolases, its own secretion being triggered by the presence of proteins within the duodenal cavity.

Other organs concerned with hormone production are the kidneys and the thymus. The *thymus,* a lymphoid organ, has only recently been found to produce a hormone involved in the induction of immunological competence in the other lymphoid tissues of the body. The elegant experiments by which the existence of thymic hormone was established have been detailed in Section 6.3E. To date we do not know how thymic secretion is controlled.

The hormone *angiotensin* is actually not secreted by any gland but is produced in the bloodstream by the action of a protease, *renin,* upon a precursor, *angiotensinogen,* which like most plasma proteins is probably produced in the liver. Renin is secreted by kidney cells in response to lowered renal blood pressure. Angiotensin acts to elevate peripheral blood pressure generally and also promotes the secretion of aldosterone by the adrenal cortex. This too would affect blood pressure, for the aldosterone-induced retention of sodium by the kidneys also causes additional water retention with a resultant increase in blood volume and hence in blood pressure. In mammals maintenance of an adequate renal blood pressure is essential to urine production, which depends on pressure filtration of plasma.

AN EXAMPLE OF NEUROENDOCRINE REGULATION: CONTROL OF CARBOHYDRATE METABOLISM Sugar utilization may be taken as an example of the way in which an important bodily process is controlled by neuroendocrine regulation. We shall mention only those relationships which are most direct and best understood, keeping in mind that other hormones also affect the use of sugars in a less direct way.

The initial digestion of carbohydrates is brought about through the action of salivary and pancreatic amylases, secretion of the former being under the control of nerves via a *salivary reflex* triggered by visual, olfactory, and gustatory cues. Secretion of pancreatic amylase is regulated by the duodenal hormone *pancreozymin.* After digestion, the absorption of glucose into the bloodstream and thence into the tissues is promoted by *insulin.* Especially within liver and muscle tissue, glucose is then built up into glycogen, a synthesis promoted by *glucocorticoids* from the adrenal cortex. Secretion of these glucocorticoids is in turn controlled by *ACTH* from the pituitary, the flow of this hormone being regulated by the *ACTH-release factor* from the *hypothalamus.*

During muscular exertion, which in nature is often associated with an emergency situation such as fighting a rival or escaping from a predator, the muscle glycogen reserves are depleted and blood glucose must be used to repair the deficit. The sympathetic responses that assist the animal in fighting or running away are controlled by the *hypothalamus* by way of sympathetic nerves to the viscera and adrenal medulla. The hypothalamus must of course have received the necessary cues from other parts of the brain, which set the sympathetic response in motion. During the duration of the emergency, *adrenaline* promotes the breakdown of liver glycogen, keeping the blood sugar level high enough so that ample supplies remain available to the muscles. After the emergency, adrenaline flow falls off and further mobilization of liver glycogen is brought about by *glucagon,* which only comes into action when the blood sugar concentration declines below permissible levels. Glucagon continues to maintain the blood sugar level while the muscles draw upon the blood sugar for materials with which to rebuild their glycogen stores. Again, insulin and the glucocorticoids are involved in this uptake of blood sugar and its synthesis to glycogen.

During periods of rest as well as during exercise, glycolysis and carbohydrate respiration must continue, promoted by the *thyroid* hormones. Flow of these hormones is dependent upon *thyrotrophin* from the pituitary, and this in turn is controlled by the *TTH-release factor* from the hypothalamus.

Sex hormones and gonadotrophins also enter the picture, mainly influencing the conversion of sugars to lipids and the accumulation of fat in particular body regions: development of the breasts and rounded hips of women is due to the *estrogenic* control of fat deposition. Estrogen secretion is controlled by the pituitary *gonadotrophins,* which in turn are regulated by the *gonadotrophin-release factors* from the hypothalamus. Fat synthesis and storage before migration or breeding probably are influenced by both the brain and sex hormones.

These delicately regulated processes reveal the complex interaction of nervous system and endocrine glands. Although the hypothalamus has been mentioned repeatedly as being the control center for visceral responses and pituitary function, we should remember that the hypothalamus itself is subject to control by other parts of the brain, particularly the olfactory limbic system, the thalamus, and the neocortex by way of the thalamus. The storage and mobilization of carbohydrates is thus regulated with regard to various external stimuli as well as to internal physiological states.

D Plant hormones

As in the case of animals, somatic growth and reproduction in plants appear to be orchestrated by precisely timed interactions of a number of regulatory substances: some of these promote somatic growth or flowering; others repress growth and induce dormancy and the shedding of fruit or foliage. Our understanding of the fundamental action of these chemical regulators is fragmentary (as is our understanding of how animal hormones act), but available evidence suggests that they control rates of enzyme synthesis, and activate or repress enzyme systems already present.

How the secretion of plant hormones is regulated is yet to be determined, but photoperiod may play an important role in such regulation.

Figure 15.55 □ **Experiments establishing existence of auxin. (*a*) Removal of growing tip retards growth of shoot; capping the cut shoot with an agar block into which material has diffused from the severed tip causes growth to be accelerated. (*b*) Capping a cut shoot asymmetrically with an agar block into which material has diffused from the severed tip causes the shoot to bend during growth owing to greater elongation of cells on side of shoot directly below agar block.**

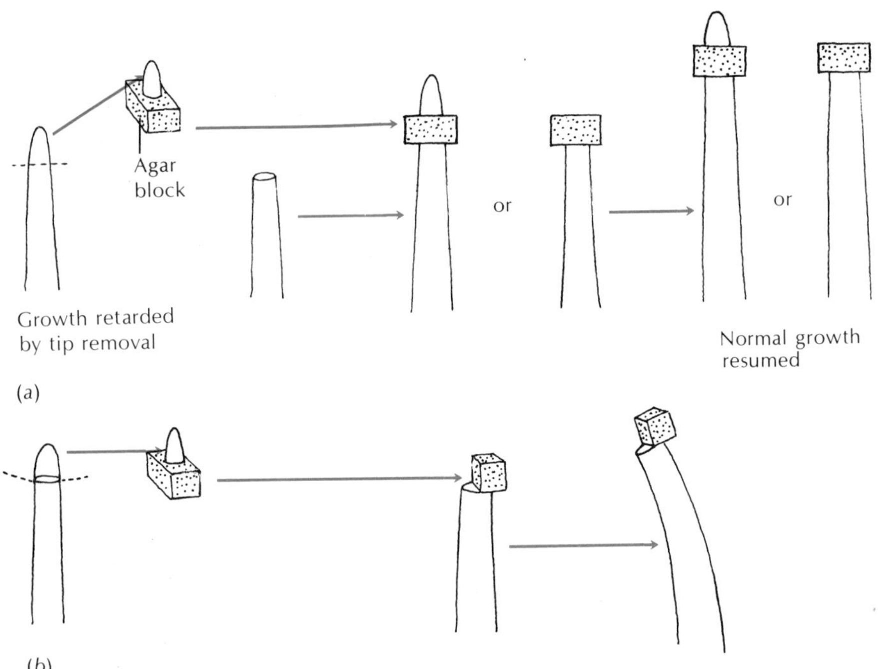

AUXINS The first conclusive evidence that hormones play important roles in regulating plant growth came from the discovery that an oat seedling with its growing tip removed would resume growth if the cut end were covered with a block of agar into which substances had been allowed to diffuse from severed stem tips (Figure 15.55). Furthermore, when such an agar block was placed asymmetrically on the cut stem, it promoted growth most effectively in the part directly beneath it, causing the stem to curve. These growth-promoting substances produced in the growing tips of flowering plants were named *auxins*. They have since been found to bring about stem lengthening by altering the plasticity of the cell walls in the young stem's region of elongation (see Figure 12.14).

Auxin application is found to be followed by an increased rate of RNA and protein synthesis. The heightened cell-wall plasticity that precedes cell lengthening may be brought about by enzyme activity, with auxin possibly involved in promoting the synthesis of the relevant enzymes. However, cell lengthening in oat and pea tissue is initiated within only 10 to 15 min after auxin application, which suggests that the hormone's immediate effect may be upon the cell wall proper or upon some preformed enzyme that only required activation. A period of 40 to 60 min (about four times as long) is required before increased protein is detectable within the cells.

The first auxin to be identified was a complex material, *auxin a*. Auxin *a* is responsible for *phototropic* responses, that is, curvature of the stem so that the tip grows toward a directional source of illumination. Light does not abolish auxin production on

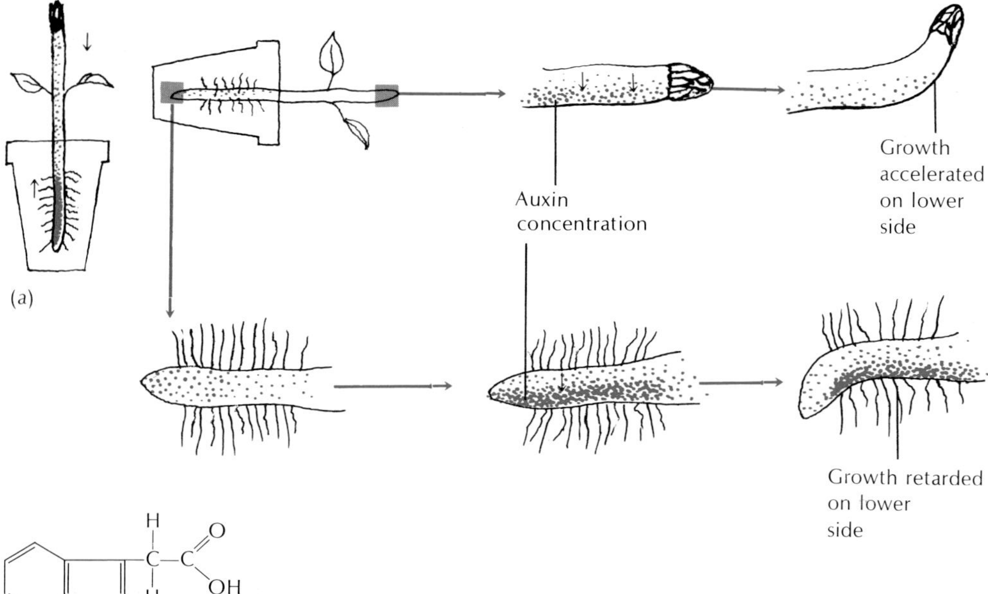

Figure 15.56 □ **Geotropism and auxin. (*a*) Geotropic response of shoot and root in terms of auxin action: in a growing plant, under normal conditions, the diffusion (black arrows) of auxin downward from the stem tip and upward from the root tip creates an auxin concentration gradient (represented by density of stippling), with greatest density in the root tissue above the tip (sketch at upper left). When the plant is turned on its side, auxin diffuses to the lower side of stem and root. In the stem, it stimulates growth, and the stem tip turns upward, as it elongates more on the lower side. In the root, it inhibits growth, and the root turns downward as elongation on the lower side is retarded. (*b*) Indole acetic acid, an auxin of known geotropic effect.**

the illuminated side of the stem but does seem to cause molecules of auxin a to migrate toward the shaded side, where they diffuse downward in the phloem, stimulating the cells on the shaded side to elongate more than the cells on the lighted side.

The negative *geotropic* response of stems (turning upward away from the pull of gravity) is attributable to the diffusion of auxin to the lower side of a horizontally placed shoot (Figure 15.56). This effect can be mediated by auxins such as *indole acetic acid* (IAA), which are structurally much simpler than auxin *a*. However, since IAA does not migrate along a light gradient it can play no part in a plant's response to light. The positive geotropism of roots has been explained only provisionally, on the basis of the observation that high concentrations of auxin in shoots can actually inhibit rather than stimulate elongation. Root tissue may contain fairly high concentrations of auxin, which both flows downward from the stem tissues and upward from the root tips. Any further increase, such as might occur on the lower side of a root laid horizontally, might serve to inhibit elongation on that side, whereupon the greater elongation of cells on the upper side would cause the root tip to turn downward into the soil.

Some 20 substances with auxinlike activity are found widely among higher plants. The minimum structural requirements for these compounds are that they must be organic acids with a ring in the molecule, that this ring must contain a double bond, and that the latter must bear a certain spatial relationship to the acid's carboxyl group. This suggests that auxins may have a two-point mode of attachment to a substrate, by way of the double bond, and that this attachment may place the —COOH group in a favorable position to enter into a reaction. Synthetic herbicides such as 2,4-dichlorophenoxyacetic acid (2,4-D) have certain auxinlike properties, but it is not yet known whether their lethal effect is due to enzyme blockage such as results when two similar molecules compete for association with an enzyme, or whether it may be due to the generally observed fact that hormonelike materials which are beneficial in small quantities often are severely detrimental in excess.

Auxins promote similar effects in all higher plants tested. Although their most typical effect is on stem elongation, they produce a variety of other responses, probably due less to the physiological virtuosity of auxins than to the competence of the reactive tissues. Auxins produced in the terminal bud repress development of the lateral buds (which explains the fact that these buds may begin to develop only when the terminal bud is excised). Auxin sprayed onto fruit trees delays the development of an abscission layer across the stalks of leaves and fruits, thus preventing preharvest fruit drop in commercial orchards. In greater concentrations, auxin sprays have the opposite effect upon less mature fruit, causing abscission layers to form and the fruit to drop, with the result that the crop is thinned and the remaining fruit attain greater size. Auxins also make possible the development of seedless fruit in species that normally require pollination for fruit production. *Parthenocarpy* (the development of fruit without seeds) is uncommon in nature, but its artificial induction by auxin sprays has been useful especially in the production of seedless tomatos.

Auxins stimulate root development from stem cuttings, an effect of great value to commercial plant propagators. A complex response is induced in which cells of the pericycle become dedifferentiated and then mature into root tissues. A similar effect is noted when calluses (undifferentiated cell masses) grown in tissue culture from isolated plant cells are treated with auxin, differentiating to produce a complete plant.

CYTOKININS Cytokinins occur widely in bacteria and higher plants. They may contribute to the formation of tRNA molecules: the cytokinin IPA (isopentenyladenosine) is found in various tRNAs. However, it is not known whether this is the major hormonal role of cytokinin or whether IPA liberated upon the breakdown of tRNA is then translocated to target tissues where a hormonal effect is exerted. For instance, the cytokinins responsible for bud formation in mosses appear to be only loosely bound to the cells they affect, for they are easily extracted.

GIBBERELLINS Gibberellins (so called because the first known was isolated from the parasitic fungus *Gibberella*) are of wide distribution. These plant hormones are best known for the exaggerated stem elongation produced in plants that are treated with them. A gibberellin-treated plant that is genotypically a dwarf strain becomes phenotypically indistinguishable from nondwarf strains, whereas plants of normal stature become spindly giants. This increase in stem length is not, however, accompanied by a commensurate gain in the plant's dry weight and is therefore of limited value to the horticulturist. One important function of the gibberellins could be in promoting a rapid last-minute elongation in a flower-bearing stem ("bolting"). In species which bolt, the stems which will bear the flower heads grow at a much faster rate than the normal vegetative growth rate, thereby raising the inflorescence well above the other foliage and making the flowers more conspicuous to pollinators. Long-day (short-night) plants treated with gibberellin will sometimes flower (Figure 15.57), but flowering cannot be induced in short-day (long-night) species.

The primary action of gibberellin during germination appears to be the promotion of enzyme synthesis, specifically of α-amylase, protease, and ribonuclease. Its action in cell elongation remains obscure but seems to relate to a modification of mRNA synthesis. Gibberellin-treated pea nuclei, for instance, show enhanced incorporation of cytidine triphosphate.

MISCELLANEOUS SOMATIC REGULATORS Other plant growth regulators are known. A wound hormone, *traumatin,* secreted by damaged bean tissues, promotes the formation of scar tissue. In *Mimosa* (the "sensitive plant") a hormone is released by cells excited by a pinch or tap; this is carried through the phloem to cells at the leaf joints, which respond by causing the halves of the leaf to fold together. This *leaf-folding hormone* may alter the membrane permeability of the effector cells. If the aversive stimulus continues, the entire leaf folds down against the stem.

Ethylene is a naturally occurring growth regulator which, being gaseous, spreads readily from the sites of its production to the tissues it affects. Its secretion is promoted by auxin and, since ethylene acts mainly as a growth inhibitor, brings an end to auxin-induced growth. Ethylene also may promote transverse cell expansion, in contrast to auxins and gibberellins, which promote cell elongation. Ethylene also plays a role in the ripening of fruit and the abscission of fruit and foliage; in the latter case, it promotes RNA synthesis and enzyme activity in the abscission zone (where the stalk of the leaf or fruit breaks off). Increased cellulase activity brings about the dissolution of cell walls in the abscission zone.

Abscisic acid is thought to be of ubiquitous occurrence in plants, but to date its role in promoting dormancy is deduced only from the observed effects of externally applied synthetic abscisic acid. Such application causes inhibition of germination, cessation of stem elongation, and formation of resting buds. The primary action of abscisic acid is still in doubt, but in barley seeds it inhibits the synthesis of α-amylase (which, we have seen, is promoted by gibberellin). In various species abscisic acid is found to repress DNA or RNA synthesis, with corresponding repression of protein synthesis.

THE CONTROL OF FLOWERING Changes in temperature and photoperiod stimulate very young buds to shift from a vegetative condition (in which new leaves are formed and growth in stem length takes place) to a generative state in which stem growth is repressed and flowers develop. Grafting experiments indicate that this change is hormonally activated, and the hormone—although it remains elusive—has received the provisional name of *florigen.* If a plant is kept under conditions of artificial photoperiod that induce it to flower out of normal season, grafting a cutting from this plant to another which has not been exposed to the inducing photoperiod will cause this plant also to bloom. This effect can be propagated by grafting the second plant to a third, and so on. An even more dramatic experiment demonstrated that cocklebur plants (a long-night species) could be induced to flower by exposing only 1 cm^2 of a single leaf to the inducing photoperiod (9 hr or more of uninterrupted darkness)! Furthermore, the various physiological changes that were set in motion in this leaf not only spread to the entire plant bearing the leaf but also could be passed on across graft unions to a series of several other plants.

Flowering is regulated by photoperiod: long-night species bloom only when exposed to unbroken periods of darkness of at least 9-hr duration; short-night species bloom only when the darkness is broken into shorter intervals. The photosensitivity of flowering plants has been found to be due to a pigment, a protein that can exist in two forms, known respectively as *R-phytochrome* and *F-phytochrome:* R-phytochrome changes abruptly to the F form when exposed to red light (with or without light of other wavelengths); F-phytochrome then slowly reverts to the R form in the dark, but this conversion can be greatly hastened by exposing the plant to a burst of far-red light (730 nm wavelength) in the absence of the shorter red wavelengths. On the other hand, exposing the plant during the night to even a flash of light including the shorter red wavelengths will interrupt the regeneration of R-phytochrome and cause it to change back to the F form. Thus the plant's internal clock is set back to zero as if an entire day had passed. This effect of red light can however be reversed once more if the plant is next subjected to a flash of far-red light, and the night continues as though it had never been interrupted. These effects must be taken into account by floriculturists if they are successfully to bring plants into bloom out of their natural season.

Figure 15.57 □ Response of rhododendron to gibberellin application. Left to right, untreated control, one drop of 1 percent gibberellin applied once, one drop of 1 percent gibberellin applied eight times at 3-day intervals. The untreated plant is not flowering although a tight bud has formed, whereas the two treated plants are in full bloom. (*U. S. Department of Agriculture.*)

The phytochrome conversions may be summarized:

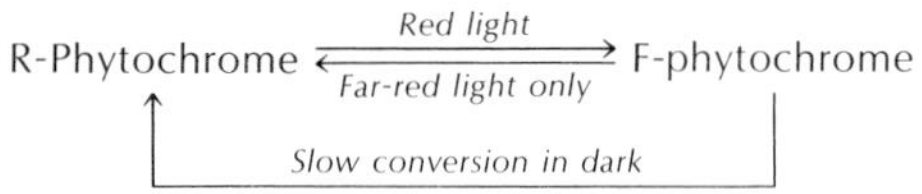

R-Phytochrome ⇄ F-phytochrome (Red light →; ← Far-red light only; F-phytochrome → R-Phytochrome: Slow conversion in dark)

The identity of the flowering hormone is only one of many riddles remaining to baffle the biologist. Despite all that we now know concerning the mechanisms of integration and regulation, many basic questions remain virtually unresolved. We still do not know the fundamental action of stimuli upon receptors, the basic effects of hormones, the physical basis of memory, or the means by which some patterns of behavior are shaped by heredity and selection and then passed on to new generations without benefit of the relevant learning experience. Each year a few more pieces are added to the growing mosaic of scientific fact that promotes our understanding of life, and each new piece of data better reveals the nature of the pattern remaining to be disclosed.

REVIEW AND DISCUSSION

1 Explain why it is adaptive for the regulation of body processes to be under the control of hormones as well as the nervous system. What is a neurohemal organ? What is *neuroendocrine regulation?*

2 Why does the maintenance of an electrochemical potential across the plasma membrane depend upon the membrane's capacity for differential permeability? How does a stimulus disturb this condition?

3 Explain the difference in effect upon the cell membrane of inhibitory and excitatory stimuli. Distinguish between a generator potential and an action potential. Which one behaves as an all-or-none event?

4 What are the implications of the fact that synaptic transmission is most commonly effected by the secretion of a chemical transmitter at the axon ending? Distinguish between adrenergic and cholinergic synapses. Where do each occur?

5 What is meant by an adequate stimulus? Explain why a visual sensation is elicited when pressure is applied to the outer cornea of the eye. Why is it advisable to define a stimulus as an environmental energy that causes a *receptor* to respond, rather than as an energy that causes an *organism* to respond? Give an example of a case in which an animal may respond strongly to a signal at one time, but fail to respond at others.

6 What are the roles of temporal and spatial summation and of synaptic facilitation in the functioning of the nervous system?

7 Compare the response to stimulation of a neuron with that of nonneural cells such as those of the freshwater alga, *Chara*. What animal tissues other than neurons might you expect to produce particularly strong and detectable action currents when stimulated? Summarize the events that take place during the propagation of a nerve impulse along a nerve fiber.

8 What are the functional regions of a neuron? How is each region specialized for more efficient performance of its function? Define and discriminate between: (*a*) dendrite and axon; (*b*) afferent neuron and efferent neuron; (*c*) motor neuron and sensory neuron; (*d*) nerve fiber and nerve; (*e*) ganglion and nucleus; (*f*) white matter and gray matter.

9 Enumerate, with examples, the various functional types of receptors. Distinguish between a receptor and a sense organ. Explain, with examples, the adaptive significance of range fractionation.

10 What different morphological kinds of eyes are found in the animal kingdom? What evidence is there also for a "dermal light sense"? What are the essential components of any eye? Explain how each of the following augments the functional efficiency of the eye: (*a*) iris; (*b*) lens; (*c*) tapetum; (*d*) ciliary muscles; (*e*) extrinsic eye muscles; (*f*) cornea.

11 Summarize the biochemical events concerned with rod and cone vision. How is color perception thought to occur?

12 Compare the process of accommodation in various kinds of vertebrate eyes. What is the adaptive value of accommodation?

13 By what means do invertebrate and vertebrate eyes adapt to changes in intensity of illumination? Explain, in terms of the organization of the vertebrate retina, why vision under conditions of dim illumination is much less acute than day vision even though some photoreceptors respond to as little as one quantum of light. Compare scotopic and photopic receptors.

14 How would you define "sound" in terms that would apply to any hearing animal? What must be the essential qualities of a phonoreceptor? Trace the anatomical and functional changes that have taken place in the evolution of the vertebrate labyrinth. Explain the function of each of the following: (*a*) pinna; (*b*) Eustachian tube; (*c*) ossicles; (*d*) columella; (*e*) basilar membrane; (*f*) perilymph; (*g*) round window; (*h*) organ of Corti.

15 Explain ways in which the central nervous system affects sensory input to specific receptors.

16 Where do chemical receptors occur in the vertebrate body? What conditions specifically do these receptors monitor? Explain the stereochemical theory of chemoreception, especially as it applies to olfaction.

17 Compare the primitive functions of the vertebrate telencephalon, diencephalon, mesencephalon, metencephalon, and myelencephalon, with their functions in mammals. What phylogenetically ancient areas remain in the mammalian cerebrum, and how may these areas affect behavior?

18 Discuss the role of invertebrate hormones in molting and metamorphosis.

19 What vertebrate hormones are directly secreted by neurosecretory cells? Which are directly under control of the hypothalamus? Which are under the control of the hypothalamic-hypophyseal axis by means of pituitary trophic hormones? Which are controlled by sympathetic nerves? What endocrine tissues respond directly to chemical stimuli in the milieu?

20 Specify what hormones are directly concerned with each of the following, and the results of their action: (*a*) regulation of carbohydrate metabolism; (*b*) regulation of ion metabolism, retention and excretion; (*c*) responses to stress; (*d*) regulation of digestion; (*e*) regulation of adenohypophyseal activity; (*f*) regulation of brain centers, with concomitant activation or suppression of specific behaviors.

REFERENCES

AGRANOFF, B. W. "Memory and Protein Synthesis," *Sci. Amer.*, **216** (1967). Retention of a conditioned response in goldfish is blocked if chemical inhibitors of protein synthesis are injected shortly after the training period.

AIKEN, D. E. "Photoperiod, Endocrinology and the Crustacean Molt Cycle," *Science*, **164** (1969). Discusses effects of photoperiod on the secretion of molt-controlling hormones.

AMOORE, J. E., J. W. JOHNSTON, JR., AND M. RUBIN "The Stereochemical Theory of Odor," *Sci. Amer.*, **210** (1964). Proposes a mechanism of olfaction based on the complementarity of air-borne molecules with sites in the membrane of the receptor cell.

BARRINGTON, E. J. W. *Hormones and Evolution.* London: The English Universities Press, Ltd., 1964. A brief volume in which evolutionary changes in the structure and function of hormones are discussed.

BERN, H. A., AND N. TAKASUGI "The Caudal Neurosecretory System of Fishes," *Gen. Comp. Endocrin.*, **2** (1962). Neurosecretory fibers arising from the caudal region of the spinal cord and ending in a neurohemal organ, the urophysis, are thought to secrete a factor involved in osmoregulation.

BULLOCK, T. H. "In Search of Principles of Integrative Biology," *Amer. Zool.*, **5** (1965). Summarizes recent advances and fundamental issues concerning the ways in which nervous systems function.

DAVIDSON, E. H. "Hormones and Genes," *Sci. Amer.*, **212** (1965). Reviews lines of evidence that certain hormones may function by activating genes.

DIAMOND, I. T., AND W. C. HALL "Evolution of Neocortex," *Science*, **164** (1969). Investigation of the visual cortex of two "primitive" mammals indicates divergent and convergent lines of cortical evolution in different mammalian orders.

ECCLES, J. "The Synapse," *Sci. Amer.*, **212** (1965).

ETKIN, W. "How a Tadpole Becomes a Frog," *Sci. Amer.*, **214** (1966). Describes the multiple events triggered by thyroid hormone.

FRENCH, J. D. "The Reticular Formation," *Sci. Amer.*, **196** (1957). The importance of a previously little-known area of the brain is discussed.

GALSTON, A. W., AND P. J. DAVIES "Hormonal Regulation in Higher Plants," *Science*, **163** (1969). Presents evidence that all known plant hormones exert their effects by controlling nucleic acid metabolism.

GELLHORN, E. "The Tuning of the Nervous System: Physiological Foundations and Implications for Behavior," *Perspectives in Biol. and Med.*, **10** (1967). Adjustments of hypothalamic function not only affect autonomic responses but also affect behaviors controlled by the cerebral cortex.

HARTLINER, H. K. "Visual Receptors and Retinal Interaction," *Science*, **164** (1969). Analysis of a comparatively simple retina (*Limulus*) permits study of patterns of discharge from individual receptors.

HELD, R. "Plasticity in Sensory-Motor Systems," *Sci. Amer.*, **213** (1965).

HODGSON, E. S. "Taste Receptors," *Sci. Amer.*, **204** (1961). Experiments on receptors in sensory bristles of the blowfly reveal that feeding is controlled by only two major types of receptor cells.

HUBBARD, R., AND A. KROPF "Molecular Isomers in Vision," *Sci. Amer.*, **216** (1967). Light-induced isomerization of retinal is basic to vision processes in all animals.

JOST, E. "Full or Partial Maturation of Fetal Endocrine Systems under Pituitary Control," *Perspectives in Biol. and Med.*, **11** (1968). Experiments with normal and decapitated rat fetuses indicated that prenatal pituitary activity is required for normal differentiation and development of other endocrine glands, especially the adrenals and thyroid.

KATZ, B. *Nerve, Muscle, and Synapse*. New York: McGraw-Hill Book Company, 1966. A brief but comparatively advanced treatment of neuromuscular physiology.

KEYNES, R. D. "The Nerve Impulse and the Squid," *Sci. Amer.*, **199** (1958). Experiments with isolated giant axons show ionic exchanges to be causally involved in the propagation of nerve impulses.

LEVINE, S. "Sex Differences in the Brain," *Sci. Amer.*, **214** (1966).

LI, C. H. "Current Concepts on the Chemical Biology of Pituitary Hormones," *Perspectives in Biol. and Med.*, **11** (1968). This important review article points up ten key concepts concerning hormone chemistry and functional behavior.

LOEWENSTEIN, W. R. "Biological Transducers," Experiments with isolated pressure receptors probe the question as to how receptors transform stimulus energy into the energy of a nerve impulse.

MACKIE, G. O. "Conduction in the Nerve-free Epithelia of Siphonophores," *Amer. Zool.*, **5** (1965). Describes the conductive properties of epithelial cells in colonial coelenterates lacking demonstrable nerve tissue.

MACNICHOL, E. F., JR. "Three-pigment Color Vision," *Sci. Amer.*, **211** (1964). Microspectrophotometric methods capable of measuring light absorption by single cone cells reveal that the primate retina contains three distinct types of cone cells.

MCCASHLAND, B. *Animal Coordinating Mechanisms*. Dubuque, Iowa: William Brown Company Publishers, 1968. A concise, up-to-date introduction to the study of animal nervous systems.

MCKUSICK, V. A., AND D. L. RIMOIN "General Tom Thumb and Other Midgets," *Sci. Amer.*, **217** (1967). Considers the inheritance of pituitary dwarfism in man.

NACHMANSOHN, D. "Chemical Factors Controlling Nerve Activity," *Science*, **134** (1961).

NATAPOFF, A. "The Consideration of Evolutionary Conservatism Toward a Theory of the Human Brain," *Perspectives in Biol. and Med.*, **10** (1967). Proposes a simple evolutionary mechanism by which selection toward development of a critical faculty was initiated by a genetic dysfunction in short-term memory.

MICHAEL, C. R. "Retinal Processing of Visual Images," *Sci. Amer.*, **220** (1969). Compares two principle types of visual systems in vertebrates, in one of which visual signals are extensively processed within the retina before transmission to the brain.

NEISSER, U. "The Processes of Vision," *Sci. Amer.*, **219** (1968). Reviews recent findings concerning the nature of visual perception and recall in man.

ROCK, I., AND C. S. HARRIS "Vision and Touch," *Sci. Amer.*, **216** (1967). Experiments on human subjects indicate that when visual and tactual cues are contradictory, vision predominates.

ROEDER, K. D. "Moths and Ultrasound," *Sci. Amer.*, **212** (1965). Bats' hunting cries excite one or both of the two acoustic fibers serving the moth ear and evoke specific types of evasive behavior.

ROSENZWEIG, M. R. "Auditory Localization," *Sci. Amer.*, **205** (1961). Reviews classic and modern investigations into how mammals localize sounds, presenting evidence that slight differences in time of stimulation results in larger response from the cerebral hemisphere opposite the ear first stimulated.

SCHARRER, B. "The Neurosecretory Neuron in Neuroendocrine Regulating Mechanisms," *Amer. Zool.*, **7** (1967). In animals of many phyla, neurosecretory neurons form a means whereby the central nervous system exerts control over endocrine glands and their target organs.

SCHNITZLEIN, H. N. "Correlation of Habit and Structure in the Fish Brain," *Amer. Zool.*, **4** (1964). Reviews neural connections and homologies with the brains of other vertebrates.

SIMPSON, L., H. A. BERN, AND R. S. NISHIOKA "Survey of Evidence for Neurosecretion in Gastropod Molluscs," *Amer. Zool.*, **6** (1966). Histological evidence suggests that reproduction, hibernation, and water balance may be under neuroendocrine control.

STAGER, K. A. "Avian Olfaction," *Amer. Zool.,* **7** (1967). Presents evidence for behaviorally significant olfactory acuity in several orders of birds and points out the hazards of generalizing from particular "type organisms" such as the pigeon.

STEBBINS, R., AND R. M. EAKIN "The Role of the 'Third Eye' in Reptilian Behavior," *Amer. Mus. Novitates,* **1870** (1958).

STEPHAN, H., AND O. J. ANDY "Quantitative Comparisons of Brain Structures from Insectivores to Primates," *Amer. Zool.,* **4** (1964). Points out certain significant trends in the phylogeny of the mammalian brain, as indicated by comparative anatomical and functional studies.

STETTNER, L. J., AND K. A. MATYNIAK "The Brain of Birds," *Sci. Amer.,* **218** (1968). Reviews the performance of birds in various learning tests and concludes that rudimentary cortical development does not preclude significant behavioral flexibility via subcortical centers.

VILLEE, C. A. "Hormonal Expression through Genetic Mechanisms," *Amer. Zool.,* **7** (1967). Reviews current concepts of the mechanisms of hormone action, presenting evidence that some hormones control the synthesis of mRNA by genes.

WEBSTER, D. B. "Ear Structure and Function in Modern Mammals," *Amer. Zool.,* **6** (1966). Compares ear structures and function with especial attention to adaptations of certain mammals for detection of extremely high or low frequencies.

WILLIAMS, C. M. "Third Generation Pesticides," *Sci. Amer.,* **217** (1967). Insect juvenile hormone has potential as a selective insecticide against which resistance cannot be developed.

Chapter 16  ADAPTIVE RESPONSE

IN THE COURSE OF ORGANIC EVOLUTION many groups of organisms have succeeded in making themselves less vulnerable to the effects of change in their environment. Animals in particular have developed a rich repertory of responses over and above those primitive control mechanisms governing cell metabolism in all forms of life (mechanisms which also will be considered in this chapter).

Response at the organismal level has two major aspects: (1) behavioral responses by which an organism responds adaptively to its external environment; (2) physiological responses by which it maintains the constancy of its internal environment (Figure 16.1). The nervous and hormonal regulatory mechanisms just reviewed in Chapter 15 operate primarily to modulate the activity of individual body cells, coordinating these cell-level responses in such a way that the organism can react effectively as a whole. Every response, therefore, fundamentally involves some quantitative or qualitative change in cell metabolism, but it is by no means certain just how the *cellular* response may be translated into the response of the whole organism. Here remain some of the most challenging areas for biological research.

In this chapter we shall first review the salient points of present knowledge bearing on the adaptive regulation of cell metabolism, and then shall turn our attention to whole-organism physiological and behavioral responses. In the area of physiological regulation we shall examine two aspects of homeostasis: (1) maintenance of the *chemical constancy* of the internal milieu, particu-

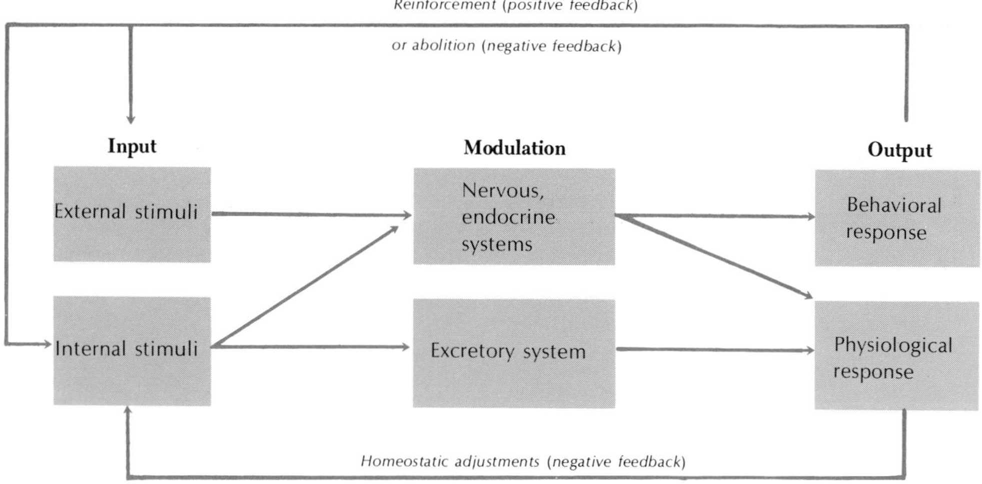

Figure 16.1 □ Flow diagram, showing relationships of mechanisms of stimulation, modulation, and response.

larly by means of selective excretion; (2) maintenance of a *stable body temperature* in homoiothermal animals.

In the area of behavior we shall emphasize the mechanisms and patterns of *motor response,* for movements of the body and its parts constitute the means by which most behavioral patterns are manifested. To understand the cellular basis of motor responses we must consider current hypotheses of muscular contraction, of amoeboid movement, and of ciliary and flagellar action. Lower organisms (primarily unicellular forms) commonly rely on ciliary, flagellar, or amoeboid movement, whereas metazoans generally carry out their major motor responses by means of contraction of muscle fibers. The physical analysis of most forms of animal behavior will therefore ultimately involve identification of (1) the specific muscles used to bring about each movement contributing to a behavioral sequence and (2) the neural pathways governing this muscular activity.

In addition to motor responses we shall review several other categories of response considered behavioral at least when triggered by such external stimuli as the approach of predators or prey, or of members of the animal's own species to which it must relate in a social manner. These responses include the production of sound, light, and electrical discharges, and the execution of color changes (especially when such changes constitute communication signals). The cellular mechanisms underlying each of these types of response will be discussed, at least insofar as they are currently understood.

16.1 □ THE CONTROL OF CELL METABOLISM

In the tale *The Sorcerer's Apprentice,* we may recall that the lazy apprentice conjured a broom into carrying buckets of water for him—but then the broom would not stop carrying water, and the apprentice nearly drowned. From this fable we draw the moral that too much of a good thing can bring disaster. The metabolic machinery of the cell poses the same problem for survival as the apprentice's broom: evolved for extreme efficiency and speed of response in carrying on the activities essential to life, how can this machinery be governed so that any given reaction system may be slowed down or halted when not needed, and reactivated when needed once again?

The first problem in metabolic control arises during embryonic development, when the differentiating cells must give up many of the activities of which they are genetically capable and begin to specialize toward activities relevant to the role each cell will finally play in the life of the whole organism. This phenomenon, probably involving permanent repression of genes no longer needed for cell function, is characteristic only of multicellular organisms. So too is the system of neuroendocrine controls superimposed on the basic intracellular control mechanisms evolved earlier. The cellular effects of these nervous and hormonal control systems common to multicellular life require much further study; although we have noted earlier that certain hormones appear to be involved in the reversible activation and repression of specific gene or enzyme systems, there is little evidence to date as to how they may do this.

Because of their comparative simplicity, bacteria and other microorganisms have been used as subjects of investigations into the regulation of cell metabolism, and it remains to be seen to what extent the control mechanisms discovered in these organisms apply as well to the eucaryotic cells of higher organisms.

A "Primitive" metabolic control mechanisms

A living cell is in part a multiple *servo-control system,* that is, a system in which each basic reaction pathway is controlled by "negative feedback": as an activity proceeds, it progressively alters intracellular conditions until they become unfavorable for continuance of that activity, which thereupon is discontinued. The discontinuation of the activity then causes intracellular conditions to change in the opposite direction until that activity is elicited once more. Metabolic pathways also tend to interact so that activation of any one may demand repression of another.

Four types of control mechanisms are known to operate within individual cells (these "primitive" control mechanisms are probably found throughout the living world and furnish the basic substratum onto which nervous and hormonal controls are imposed in higher organisms): (1) inhibition of a reaction by its end-product; (2) obligatory coupling; (3) dependence on shared cofactors; (4) repression or induction of specific enzymes.

END-PRODUCT INHIBITION The accumulation of the end-product of a reaction pathway may inhibit this pathway in one of two ways.

First, in reversible reactions there is a *mass action* effect whereby an equilibrium tends to become established between the relative amounts of substrate and end-product present. At the equilibrium point, the relative proportions of substrate and product are such that enzyme action swings back and forth, driving the reaction first in one direction and then in the other. An example of this is seen in the glutamic dehydrogenase system, where at equilibrium the conversion

$$\text{Glutamic acid} \rightleftharpoons \alpha\text{-oxoglutarate} + NH_3$$

is held in balance. The equilibrium point for any reversible reaction can be calculated according to the formula

$$k_1 A \cdot B = k_2 C \cdot D$$

where the velocity of formation v_1 of the products C and D from the substrates A and B is expressed as $k_1 A \cdot B$, and the velocity of the reverse reaction v_2 is expressed as $k_2 A \cdot B$ (k_1 and k_2 are known reaction constants based on the thermodynamics of each reaction.) At equilibrium the velocity of the forward reaction is equal to the velocity of the reverse reaction (that is, $v_1 = v_2$), so that just as much A and B are changed to C and D, as C and D are changed to A and B. At the equilibrium point for most reversible reactions the concentrations of A and B are quite different from the concentrations of C and D, since one or the other of the reactions tends to be thermodynamically favored. If the energy barrier is lower for the conversion of A and B to C and D than it is for the conversion of C and D to A and B, at equilibrium more C and D will be present than A and B.

Although generally applicable to chemical reactions, however, the above law of mass action does not seem to play as important a role in regulating metabolic activities as was once thought. Instead a second, more common form of end-product inhibition occurs in living systems, in which the end-product acts to inhibit the pathway *not* at the final reaction, but at some point much closer to its beginning.

According to the law of mass action, control of a pathway by end-product inhibition would be as shown in the following series of reactions:

$$\text{Reaction } A \xrightarrow{Enz.\ 1} \text{reaction } B \xrightarrow{Enz.\ 2} \text{reaction } C \xrightarrow{Enz.\ 3} \text{reaction } D \underset{\uparrow\_\_\_\_\_\_\_\_\_\_\_\_\_\_\_\_\_\_\_\_\_\_\_\_\_\_\_\_\_\_\_\_\_\_\_\_\_\_\_\_\_\_\_\_\_\_\_\_\_\_\_\_\_\_\_\_\_\_\_\_\_|}{\overset{Enz.\ 4}{\rightleftharpoons}} \text{end-product}$$

However, in most cases of end-product inhibition in living systems, the block operates much earlier in the sequence:

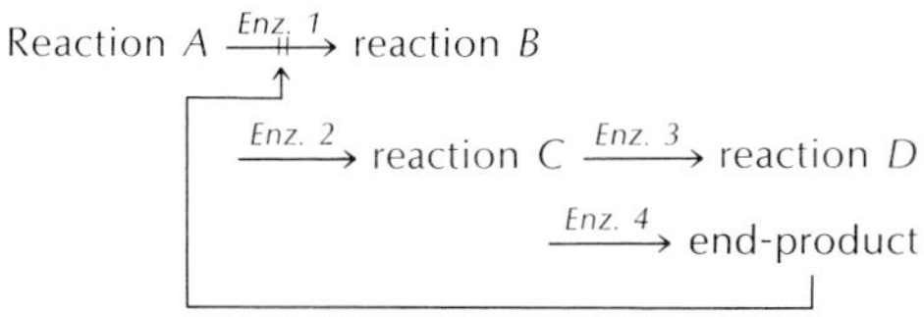

$$\text{Reaction } A \xrightarrow{\text{Enz. 1}} \text{reaction } B \xrightarrow{\text{Enz. 2}} \text{reaction } C \xrightarrow{\text{Enz. 3}} \text{reaction } D \xrightarrow{\text{Enz. 4}} \text{end-product}$$

(end-product feeds back to inhibit Enz. 1)

Such control exerted at an early point in the pathway is more economical in conserving the cell's energy resources than is control exerted upon the final step, for the series of reactions leading up to that step not only may consume energy but also produces intermediates that are of no immediate use. This second type of end-product inhibition is called *enzyme suppression* to distinguish it from the mass action effect.

OBLIGATORY COUPLING A reaction is subject to control when it is coupled to some other pathway—one that furnishes substrates or energy to the reaction, or accepts energy or materials from it. For example, the rate of cell respiration is governed less by the availability of sugars and other materials to be broken down than by the availability of ADP and inorganic phosphate (P_i) from which ATP is built. As was shown in Figure 14.55, an obigatory coupling exists between the electron carriers of the respiratory chain and (ADP + P_i). When most of the available ADP has become converted to ATP, the rate of cell respiration decreases. Similarly, endergonic pathways rely on energy furnished by specific high-energy compounds such as CTP, UTP, GTP, and ATP, and the reactions may continue only as long as a supply of the needed energy carrier is available.

DEPENDENCE ON SHARED COFACTORS Many pathways of cell metabolism share certain cofactors required for some reaction of pivotal importance. For instance, we have seen that most substrates enter the Krebs cycle in combination with coenzyme A (see Figure 14.53). This compound theretore represents a "bottleneck" in oxidative metabolism: acetyl groups can enter the Krebs cycle only as rapidly as coenzyme A can react with them. Competition exists among substrates for the use of these common cofactors. What determines the outcome of this competition is not yet clear, but it has been noted that as a rule metabolic *intermediates* compete successfully against the materials that are the substrates for the beginning of a metabolic sequence. This is important because it means, for instance, that once the breakdown of a large molecule (such as starch, fat, or glycogen) has begun, another large molecule will not be attacked until the breakdown of the first has been entirely completed.

ENZYME REPRESSION AND INDUCTION We now recognize that cells synthesize two classes of enzymes: *constitutive* enzymes, which are constantly required by the cell and must therefore always be present, and *inducible* enzymes, the synthesis of which can be repressed at either the gene or the ribosome. In the latter category are enzymes that need not constantly be present but tend to be produced "on order" in response to particular substrates or certain modulators such as hormones. Inducible enzymes are not absolutely essential to the life of the individual cell but enable it to take advantage of a wider range of nutrient substrates; such enzymes are indispensible to the special activities that cells in a multicellular body must carry out on behalf of the whole organism. The production of egg yolk proteins by bird liver cells, for instance, is not essential to the survival of the liver cells but *is* essential to the perpetuation of the species. The production of enzymes only as needed saves the cell from needlessly wasting its resources and simultaneously protects it against the accumulation of unneeded quantities of reaction products.

Suppression of enzyme action by accumulation of the end-product (mentioned earlier in this section) has the advantage that it swiftly inhibits further production of that material while not interfering with the synthesis of the enzymes themselves. Enzyme *repression,* on the other hand, involves some little delay: it cannot become effective until the enzyme molecules already present have been exhausted and must be replenished. In this case, further enzyme *synthesis* is inhibited, either at the gene (blocking its production of mRNA) or at the ribosome (preventing the actual synthesis of the protein on the mRNA template.) Suppression is therefore a highly sensitive, rapidly acting means for bringing about short-term adjustments in cell metabolism, whereas repression is even more economical in energy expenditure (enzyme synthesis being a costly process) but is less responsive and tends to act over a longer period of time (Figure 16.2). Together these processes allow cell metabolism to be constantly and subtly adjusted in response to changing conditions within the body of the organism.

Analysis of the β-galactosidase control system The existence of inducible enzymes in bacteria has long been known. A bacterial culture using sucrose as an energy source does not contain appreciable quantities of the enzyme needed to hydrolyze milk sugar (lactose). But should lactose be added

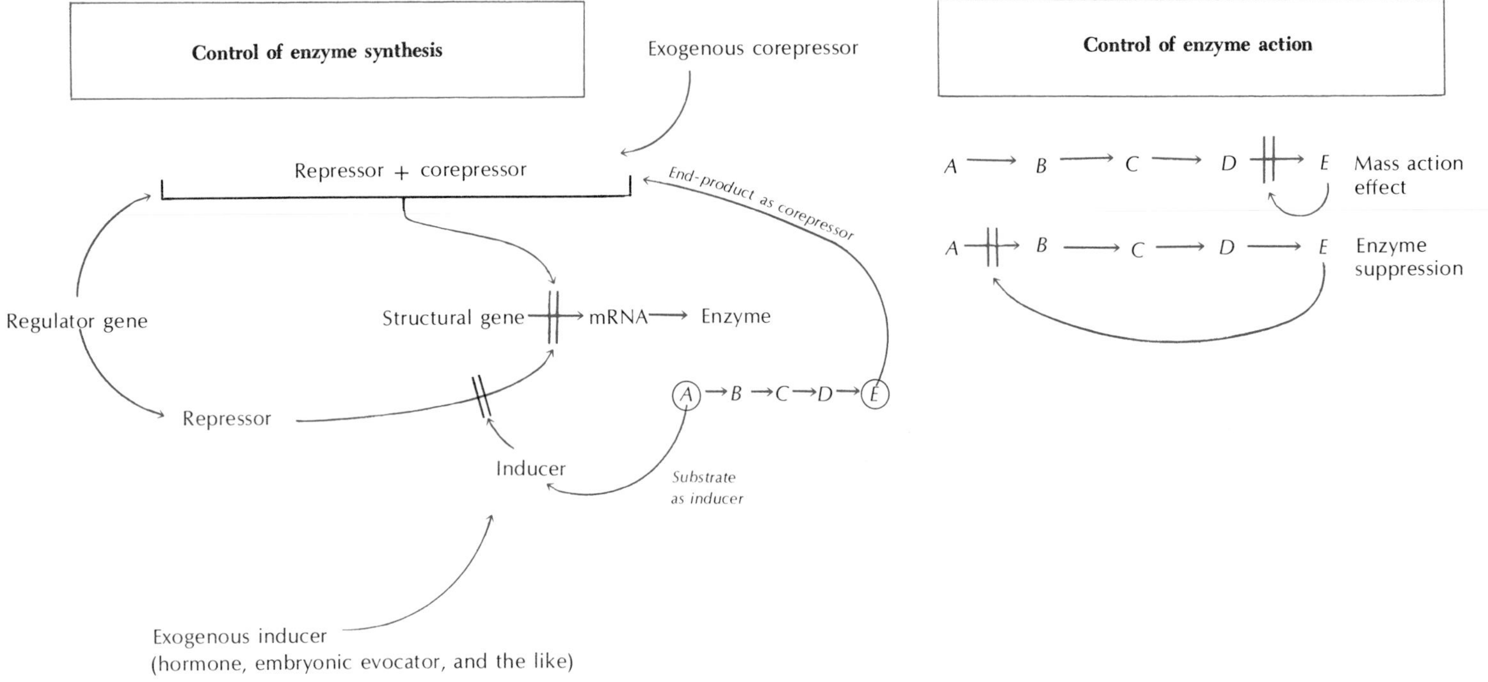

Figure 16.2 □ Model of proposed scheme of control of cell metabolism. Double vertical lines indicate points at which inhibition can take place: colored lines designate blocks in enzyme synthesis or action; black lines indicate inhibition of a *repressor* with resultant activation of the enzyme-synthesis system.

to the medium, within as little as 3 min detectable quantities of two new enzymes appear: (1) a permease responsible for the active transport of lactose into the bacterial cell; (2) a hydrolase, β-galactosidase, responsible for splitting lactose into simple sugars (glucose and galactose). In time the concentration of β-galactosidase rises until this one enzyme constitutes some 3 percent of the cell's total protein content! But, should the bacteria then be transferred back to a medium free of lactose, the concentration of the two enzymes again declines to negligible levels (Figure 16.3). The fact that the decline in β-galactosidase begins 2.5 to 3 min after transfer indicates that the mRNA responsible for its synthesis is very short-lived, and as it ceases to be replenished in the lactose-free medium the enzyme synthesis stops. Obviously, the more short-lived the mRNA, the more rapidly enzyme repression can take effect.

It can be concluded from these observations that β-galactosidase is an inducible and not a constitutive enzyme—it is made only when needed. Its synthesis appears to be activated by the presence of the appropriate substrate. However, once the synthetic process has been set in motion, how is it turned off again once the enzyme is no longer needed? A clue to the answer to this riddle was obtained through studies on mutant colonies of the colon bacillus (*Escherichia coli*). Certain colonies were found to be unable to utilize lactose at any time, due to a mutation in the gene encoding the amino acid sequence of the enzyme β-galactosidase. Under no circumstances could these colonies produce the functional enzyme and so utilize lactose. However, a second type of mutant was also found, in which synthesis of β-galactosidase not only took place, but was carried on at all times—that is, its synthesis was constitutive rather than inducible, even in the absence of lactose! (Like the sorceror's apprentice, the mutant bacteria could not turn off their brooms.) The recessive mutation causing synthesis of the enzyme to become nonrepressible was found to occur in a different gene from that actually encoding the enzyme (the so-called *structural* gene). In fact, the gene governing repressibility was located far enough away from the structural gene along the chromosome that one could be separated from the other by interrupting the process of bacterial conjugation.*

Figure 16.3 □ Enzyme induction by addition of lactose to bacterial growth medium. The lactose-concentration curve is shown in color tint, while that for β-galactosidase is in solid color.

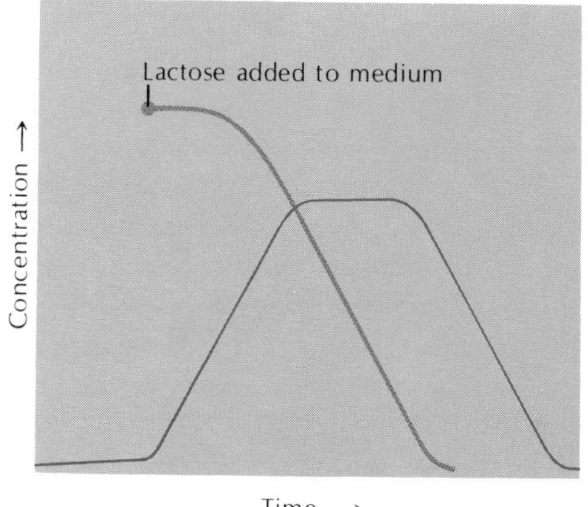

The structural gene for β-galactosidase has been designated z^+ and its mutant allele z^-; the alleles of the gene seemingly in control of the structural gene are called i^+ and i^-. When wild-type male bacteria of the genotype z^+i^+ (both capable of synthesizing β-galactosidase and of having this synthesis repressed) are allowed to mate with female bacteria of the genotype z^-i^-, conjugation can be interrupted at a point at which the female cell receives only gene z^+ but not i^+. Its progeny accordingly are capable of synthesizing β-galactosidase (which could not be done prior to conjugation), but must do so *constitutively*. If on the other hand, conjugation is allowed to be completed so that the female cell receives both genes z^+ and i^+, the progeny not only become capable of synthesizing the functional enzyme, but will do so only in the presence of lactose—that is, both the normal capacity for enzyme synthesis and the capacity for inducibility have been transferred.

Clearly, then, at least two different genes are involved in controlling the synthesis of the enzyme β-galactosidase: as indicated, genes such as z^+, which actually produce the mRNA template that manufactures the enzyme, are called *structural* genes; it has been proposed that genes such as i^+ (capable of repressing structural genes) be termed *regulator* genes.

Regulator genes are thought to govern the production of specific *repressor* substances (possibly proteins) that inhibit the activity of structural genes. However, there appear to be two ways in which these repressor substances can act (Figure 16.4). One class of repressors seems capable of binding directly to the structural gene (or its mRNA product); they are prevented from forming this combination only by the presence of an *inducer*. In the case of the β-galactosidase system, the inducer is lactose, which combines with the repressor molecules as they are formed and prevents them from blocking the gene or mRNA. But, as soon as the lactose is used up, free repressor molecules again begin to accumulate and once more repress enzyme synthesis.

The other class of repressors can inhibit the structural gene only when they form complexes with some substance of low-molecular weight (the *corepressor*). In some cases the corepressor may be the end-product of the reaction pathway; in other cases it may be some substance (such as a hormone) originating outside the cell.

The importance of this difference between the two classes of repressors is that the first type can act at all times except when *inactivated* by some substance (typically the *substrate* of the reaction to be catalyzed), whereas repressors of the second type can act only when a corepressor (such as the reaction's *end-product*) is available. In the latter case, the system of enzyme synthesis will probably be "on" most of the time, but may be repressed on occasion; in the former instance the system of enzyme synthesis will probably be "off" most of the

*During *conjugation* (sexual mating) an entire bacterial chromosome several times the length of the whole bacterium must pass slowly across a narrow conjugation bridge joining the male and female cells. If during this process the bacteria are sheared apart by being agitated in a high-speed liquefier, the chromosome is broken at the point occupying the bridge at that moment, and only the genes that have already passed across can affect the heredity of the female cell.

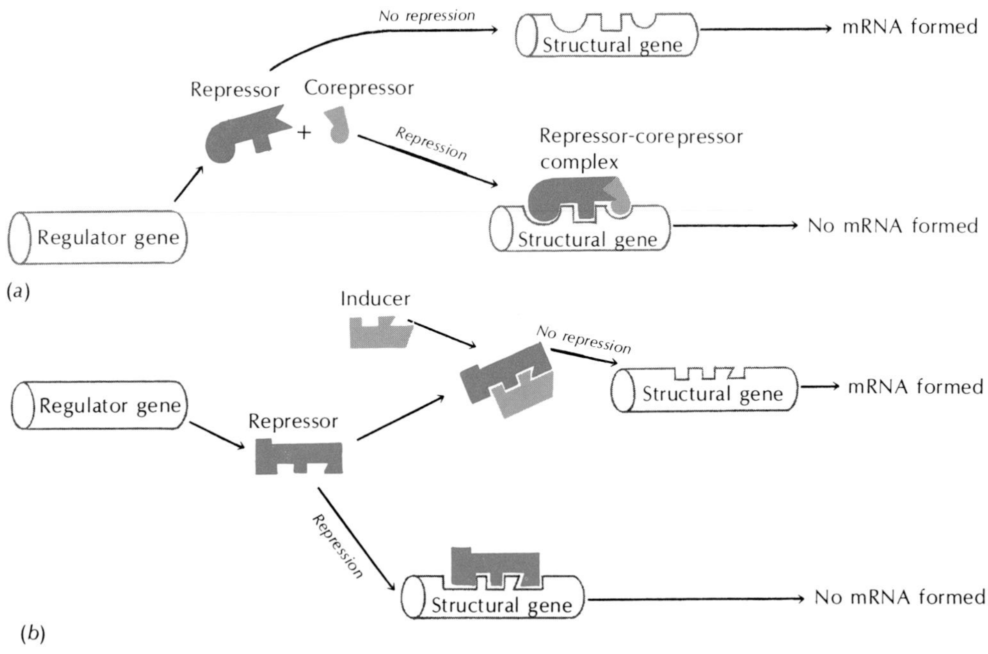

Figure 16.4 □ **Proposed modes of gene repression and activation. (*a*) Repressor activated by corepressor. (*b*) Repressor inactivated by inducer.**

time, but be capable of being activated at specific times.

The operon concept Is the control of structural genes by regulator genes the full story of how enzyme synthesis is regulated? Apparently not. Still another class of mutants of *E. coli* has been identified, in which mutation of a gene immediately adjacent to the structural gene (z) on the bacterial chromosome causes synthesis of β-galactosidase to become constitutive even in the presence of the repressor gene i^+! The discovery of this second type of gene (now called an *operator* gene), involved in governing the activity of structural genes, led to the development of the *operon* hypothesis by F. Jacob and J. Monod. According to this hypothesis, in bacteria (at least) the structural genes concerned with producing the enzymes needed for some particular reaction pathway tend to lie in linear sequence along the chromosome, and their template activity in producing mRNA is controlled by a single operator gene lying at the end of the sequence from which mRNA transcription must proceed. The entire unit of operator gene together with the structural genes it controls is known as an operon (Figure 16.5). Analysis of the *lac* operon (that is, the genes concerned with lactose utilization) of *E. coli* indicates that it consists of one operator and three structural genes. One of the latter is the above-mentioned gene z encoding the primary structure of β-galatosidase; the second is the gene y that encodes the permease needed for the uptake of lactose into the cell; the third, a, does not seem directly concerned with lactose metabolism but produces a transacetylase (an enzyme catalyzing the transfer of acetyl groups,

$$H_3C{-}\overset{\displaystyle O}{\overset{\|}{C}}{-}$$

such as might be produced during further breakdown of the sugars yielded by lactose hydrolysis).

What could be the adaptive value of having genes grouped into operons? Probably the value would rest in the fact that only one repressor need be produced to control the whole operon as one unit. As long as several structural genes involved in the same reaction pathway were to remain in linear sequence along the chromosome, they could all be turned on and off together, by the action of a single regulator gene producing a repressor capable of binding to the operator gene controlling the operon. The energetic advantage to the cell is similar to our own saving of effort when, by flipping a single switch, we can turn on or off all the lights in a room, rather than having to walk from lamp to lamp. We do not yet know if the operon concept, with its economical one regulator–one operator relationship, can be extended to higher organisms.*

*See P. E. Hartman and S. R. Suskind, *Gene Action,* 2nd ed. (Englewood Cliffs, N.J.: Prentice-Hall, Inc., 1969), pp. 195–203.

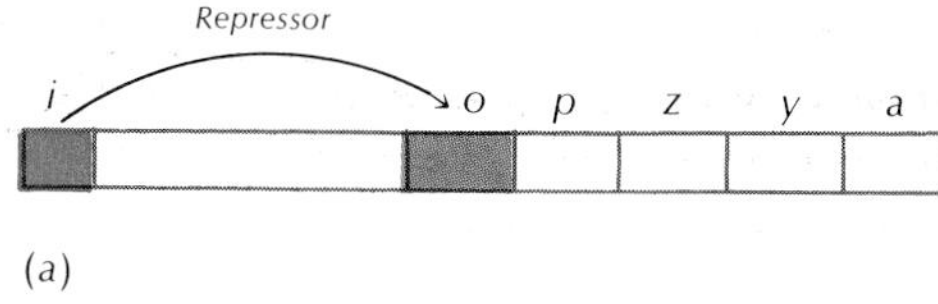

(a)

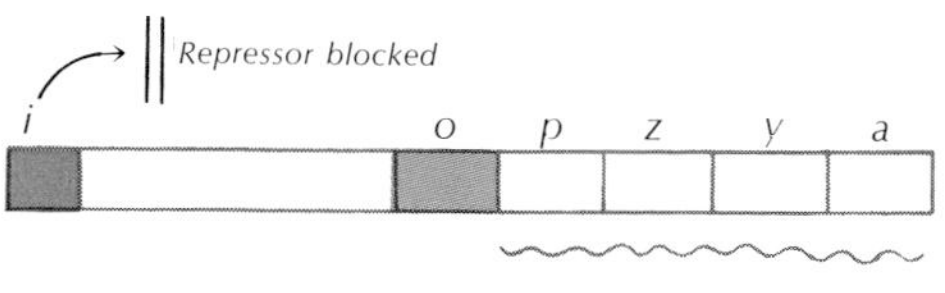

(b)

Figure 16.5 □ The *lac* operon in *Escherichia coli:* (*a*) inactive; (*b*) mRNA produced. *i* indicates a regulator gene, shown in color, and *o* an operator gene, shown in color tint; *p*, *z*, *y*, and *a* are structural genes "turned on" when *o* is derepressed.

Figure 16.6 □ Effect of hydrocortisone on enzyme activity and RNA synthesis. (*Data from Kennedy and Kull.*)

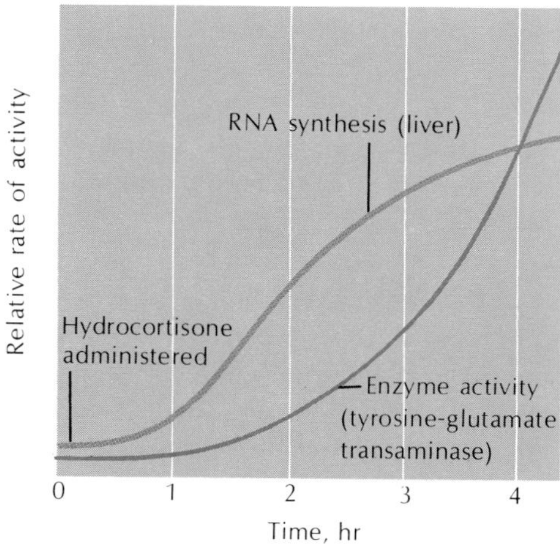

No doubt we have so far traced only a portion of the control network that regulates cell metabolism, but at least it seems probable that the major *types* of "primitive" control mechanisms have been correctly defined, although specifically worked out for only a few systems (and these mainly in bacteria). The increased importance of hormonal inducers and corepressors in multicellular organisms further complicates the control mechanism in these creatures.

B Neuroendocrine regulation of cell metabolism

We will say relatively little on this significant topic; few things can be said at present that are not inconclusive or highly fragmentary. The quest continues, aided by such techniques as use of radioactive isotopes, but it is obviously much more difficult to work out the factors regulating the metabolism of a cell within a multicellular body than it is to discover those controlling bacterial metabolism. Synaptic discharges from a nerve fiber ending on a gland or muscle cell do change that cell's behavior, but in what specific ways? Hormones do alter the pattern of cell metabolism. but exactly *how* do they exert their effects?

In Chapter 15 we noted that carbohydrate metabolism, to take one example, is regulated by a number of hormones, each with a specific role to play in the control process. For some, these roles still remain obscure, but a specific hormone-enzyme relationship has been detected in the following cases. (1) Insulin promotes synthesis of the enzyme hexokinase (responsible for the phosphorylation of glucose in preparation for its transport into the cell). (2) Glucagon promotes synthesis of the enzyme phosphorylase (which catalyzes the phosphorylation and hydrolysis of glycogen). (3) Adrenaline brings about the activation of adenyl cyclase (an enzyme involved in the pathway leading to glycogen breakdown). (4) Cortisone and hydrocortisone promote the synthesis of several enzymes, including phosphatases and transaminases (Figure 16.6).

It is too early to say, however, whether these hormones actually serve as inducers, directly preventing a repressor from acting upon a gene and consequently freeing that gene for action, or whether their point of operation is further removed from the mechanisms of gene control and enzyme synthesis. The puzzle must be put together a piece at a time until the composite data yield a meaningful picture.

C Circadian rhythms in metabolism

The mechanisms controlling cell metabolism at both the so-called primitive and systemic levels have evolved toward a more precise "fit" of the organism's metabolic cycles to the daily cycles of light and darkness under which most creatures live. Of course a metabolic rhythm is imposed on autotrophic plants by the presence or absence of light needed for photosynthesis. But even organisms much less directly dependent on light often exhibit circadian physiological rhythms that approximate the length of the 24-hr cycle. Circadian rhythms have been mentioned earlier (Section 5.5E) during our discussion of tidal, daily, and lunar rhythms in marine organisms. We noted then that one way of determining the existence of endogenous rhythms is to isolate the organisms from external cues and to note whether any activity—physiological or behavioral—continues to oscillate rhythmically. Circadian rhythms do in fact tend to persist under constant environmental conditions, and when liberated from the influence of external stimuli that normally "reset the clock" are found to have innate periods of oscillation slightly longer or shorter than 24 hr, but rarely exactly the length of the terrestrial day. A great variety of organisms have been found to show circadian rhythms, not only in motor activity (with concomitant changes in rate of cell respiration) but in such particulars as osmotic pressure, membrane permeability, and sensitivity to light, temperature, and various chemical substances. In fact, an understanding of circadian rhythms is important even to the physician, for daily fluctuations in drug sensitivity may explain why a medicine administered at one time of day may be beneficial but actually prove fatal if given at the time of maximum sensitivity! It has long been noted that a significant increase in human births and deaths takes place from 2:00 to 3:00 A.M. This period may represent the nadir of vital functions in the cycle of human circadian rhythms.

The attempt to establish beyond doubt the existence of inborn circadian physiological rhythms has led investigators to remarkable lengths. In one of the most carefully controlled investigations a variety of organisms including molds, higher plants, insects, and rodents were transported to the South Pole and there were kept under constant lighting conditions upon a turntable set to rotate one cycle per day in a direction opposite the earth's spin. In this way it was hoped that all possible clues to the earth's daily cycle would be abolished and that the rhythms exhibited by these organisms would tend to persist (as indeed they did); it was therefore felt that these rhythms could truly be considered innate.

The adaptive significance of circadian rhythms is easily seen: at the organism's most active time of day (which may be night for nocturnal species) its metabolism must be most fully recruited for locomotion and feeding. Later it must be geared for those activities (like digestion and absorption) that take place more efficiently when the organism is muscularly at rest. The full story of circadian rhythms has yet to be worked out, but only a few years ago they were not even suspected to exist.

16.2 □ PHYSIOLOGICAL RESPONSE: TWO EXAMPLES OF HOMEOSTASIS

The maintenance of an internal steady state (homeostasis) is one of the most crucial responsibilities of physiological regulatory mechanisms at the level of the whole organism. The control mechanisms must themselves be adjusted through series of negative feedback loops, and these "servo" controls must be sufficiently sensitive so that the system will not tend to swing too far to either side of the optimum. By analogy, a relatively insensitive thermostat set for 20°C may actually allow room temperature to drop to 18°C before turning on the furnace or allow it to rise to 22°C before turning the furnace off. If our own body thermostat behaved like this, we could not survive. In many respects the body shows very little tolerance of fluctuations in its internal conditions, and its servo mechanisms must be more like a thermostat set for 20°C that is sensitive enough to turn the furnace on at 19.9°C and turn it off again at 20.1°C. The sensitivity of physiological control mechanisms is enhanced by the fact that more than one control system may affect the same process; these systems may function in opposition so that they tend to counteract one another's tendencies to deviate and together serve to prevent fluctuations in internal state more effectively than either could alone. In Chapters 13 and 14 we noted the importance of maintaining a balance between food intake, on the one hand, and growth and energy requirements, on the other, and we also examined some of the factors involved in keeping blood pressure and blood CO_2 and O_2 content within tolerable limits. Now we shall focus upon two other major aspects of homeostatic regulation: (1) maintenance of the chemical constancy of the internal milieu; (2) thermoregulation and the maintenance of a stable internal body temperature in homoiotherms. We cannot attempt to present a complete picture, but only the essential features.

Figure 16.7 □ Types of cells involved in selective secretion. (*a*) Excretophores absorb wastes from body fluids, storing them as inclusions and returning useful materials to the body fluids. (*b*) Renal epithelium absorbs wastes from fluids bathing the renal tubules and selectively removes useful materials from the urine and returns them to the body fluids.

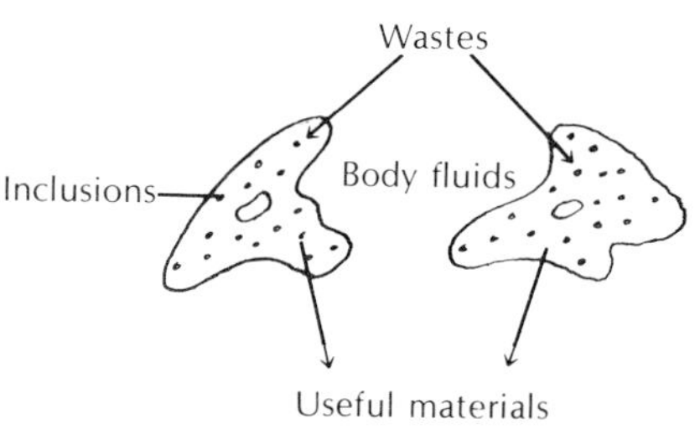

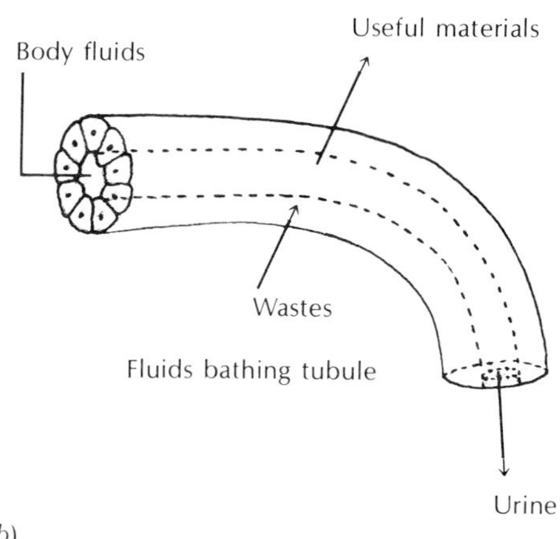

A Regulation of the chemical composition of body fluids

Both the composition and the volume of body fluids must be kept steady. Only slight deviations in pH are tolerable and uncontrolled variations in solute concentration can lead to serious osmotic disturbances. Depletion of the nutrient pool carried by the body fluids (solutes and colloidal particles including lipids, glucose, and amino acids) can quickly lead to cell starvation, whereas unrelieved accumulation of any of these materials, however useful, can also prove fatal, as can the excessive accumulation of metabolic wastes. Changes in the total volume of body fluids can on the one hand lead to water accumulation in the tissues (edema), and on the other to a possibly fatal decline in blood pressure. To remove metabolic wastes (or indeed any material present in excess), to adjust the volume, pH, and ion content of the body fluids, and at the same time to conserve nutrients and other useful materials, highly versatile homeostatic mechanisms are required.

SELECTIVE EXCRETION Chemical regulation of the body fluids is achieved mainly through the capacity of certain cells to exercise selectivity in the kinds of materials they withdraw from or return to those fluids. In addition, neuroendocrine mechanisms play a regulatory role in higher organisms.

There are two major types of cells in the animal world that are charged with the duty of selective excretion: (1) *excretophores,* which are often independent, amoeboid phagocytes; (2) *renal epithelium,* which forms the lining of excretory tubules or *nephridia* (Figure 16.7). Excretophores have been identified definitely only in invertebrates, where they often constitute the major excretory tissue. These wandering cells accumulate waste materials from the coelomic fluid and convert them into inert storage compounds. For the invertebrate, excretophores perform many of the biochemical conversions carried on in the vertebrate body by the liver. Absorbing materials from the body fluids, excretophores process these substances, liberating useful products while retaining nonusable compounds as solid inclusions. Eventually these inclusions become so numerous as to cause the death of the excretophore, but before this takes place aging excretophores tend to concentrate in the neighborhood of the excretory tubules, where the residue released by their disintegration can readily be expelled to the exterior. Alternatively (in the absence of excretory tubules), excretophores glutted with wastes may simply migrate through the body wall to the exterior, committing suicide while ridding the organism of their load of wastes.

The membrane forming or lining the ducts through which liquids must pass on their way to the exterior consists of renal epithelium. In the sense in which we are employing this term, it applies only to those portions of the duct system that are actively involved in determining the composition of the urine, not merely in conducting it to the outside. Epithelium with such regulatory potential probably forms part of the excretory apparatus of any animal having protonephridia, metanephridia, Malpighian tubules, or nephrons (as described below).

Originally, the epithelium forming any

Figure 16.8 □ **Active salt reabsorption in the kidney of the crayfish, a freshwater crustacean. (*a*) Crayfish excretory system, with designation of points from which urine samples were removed for analysis. (*b*) Results of urine-sample analysis; measurement of Cl^- indicates active removal of this ion as the urine passes along the nephridial canal, thereby conserving the Cl^- concentration of blood and tissue fluid. (*Data from Parry.*)**

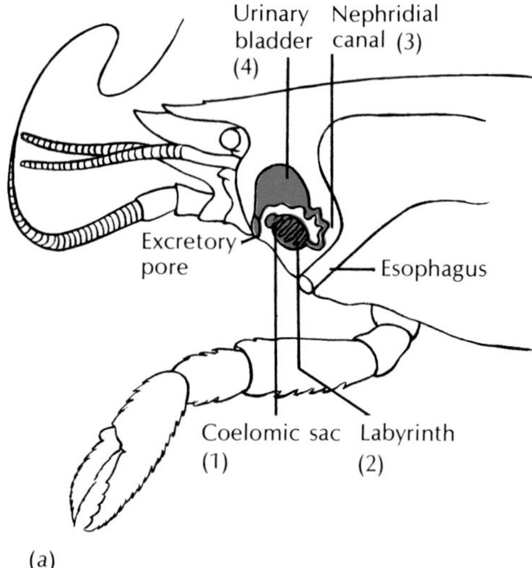

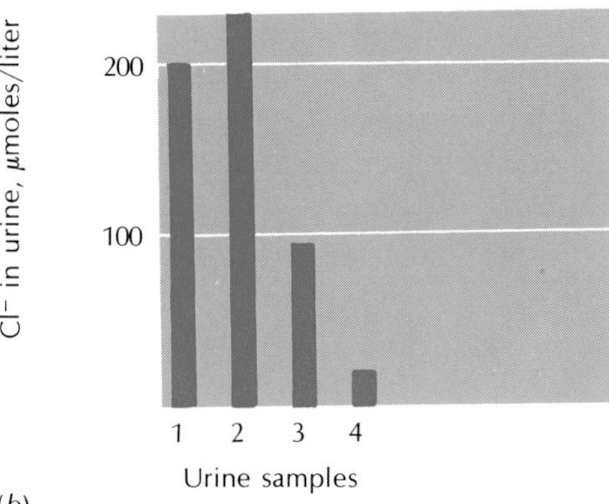

such tubular system may have had no special capacity to alter the composition of the fluids inside and outside the tubules in any selective manner. Bathing the tubule on its outer surface was tissue fluid, coelomic fluid, or blood. When the primitive renal epithelium lacked any regulatory capability, the unmodified fluid that passed through it into the tubule had to be voided, accomplishing the removal of excess water and solutes but also involving the loss of many valuable constituents. But when in the course of evolution the epithelium began to develop the capacity to shunt materials *selectively* (see Figure 14.5) from one fluid compartment to the other, the advantages of the savings thus effected were so great that all genetic changes which tended to make this process of selective transport more efficient henceforth were favored.

In freshwater animals one of the major tasks of the kidney is to rid the body of excess water while salvaging needed ions (Figure 16.8). On the other hand, in marine vertebrate fishes and all terrestrial animals the major problem becomes one of *retaining* water while removing wastes and excess ions. We shall mention below some of the adaptations undergone by the vertebrate kidney in its adjustments to life on land, in the sea, and in fresh water. Without knowing the nature of the animal whose kidney he is examining, the biologist can usually determine the animal's habitat merely through an analysis of renal structure.

The regulatory behavior of the renal epithelium is modulated (in higher animals at least) by hormonal factors. In the last analysis, however, it is the renal epithelium itself that is responsible for monitoring conditions in the two fluid compartments which it separates and for transporting materials between these two compartments. The major effect exerted by systemic modulators such as hormones may be merely to alter the *renal threshold* for a given substance, that is, the concentration the substance must reach in the body fluids before it begins to appear in the urine.

INVERTEBRATE EXCRETORY ORGANS Protonephridia, metanephridia, and Malpighian tubules are the major functional units making up the kidneys of invertebrates (Figure 16.9). A *protonephridium* (as found in flatworms, ribbonworms, rotifers, certain annelids, amphioxus, and others) is an excretory tubule that terminates blindly at its inner end in a cluster of ciliated or flagellated cells (known respectively as flame cells or solenocytes). Substances cannot flow directly into the protonephridium from the body cavity or tissue spaces, but must cross the epithelial membrane forming the protonephridium. During this process selectivity can be exercised, for the epithelium may transport some materials in preference to others and therefore determine the composition of the urine. Fluids accumulating within the protonephridium are propelled to the exterior by the beating of the terminal cilia or flagella.

The kidneys of molluscs, crustaceans, and many annelids are *metanephridia*. A metanephridium is an excretory tubule that communicates directly with the coelom by way of an open, usually ciliated funnel which collects coelomic fluid and carries it toward the exterior. Such removal of coelomic fluid lowers the hydrostatic pressure in the body cavity so that more fluid tends to enter the coelom from the bloodstream or tissue spaces, permitting the excretory

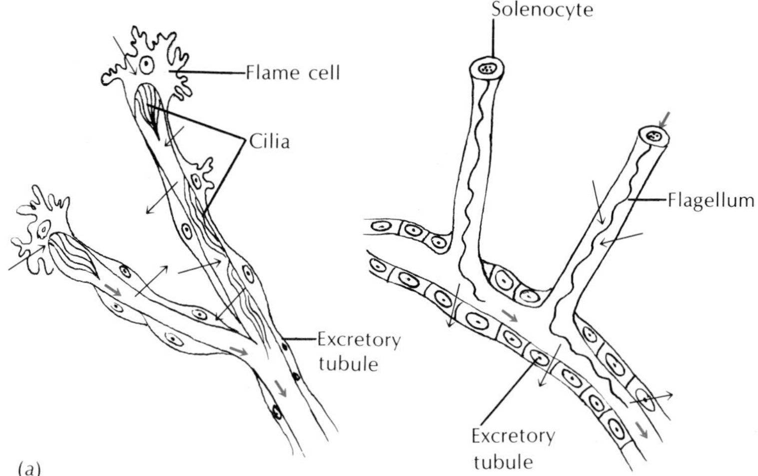

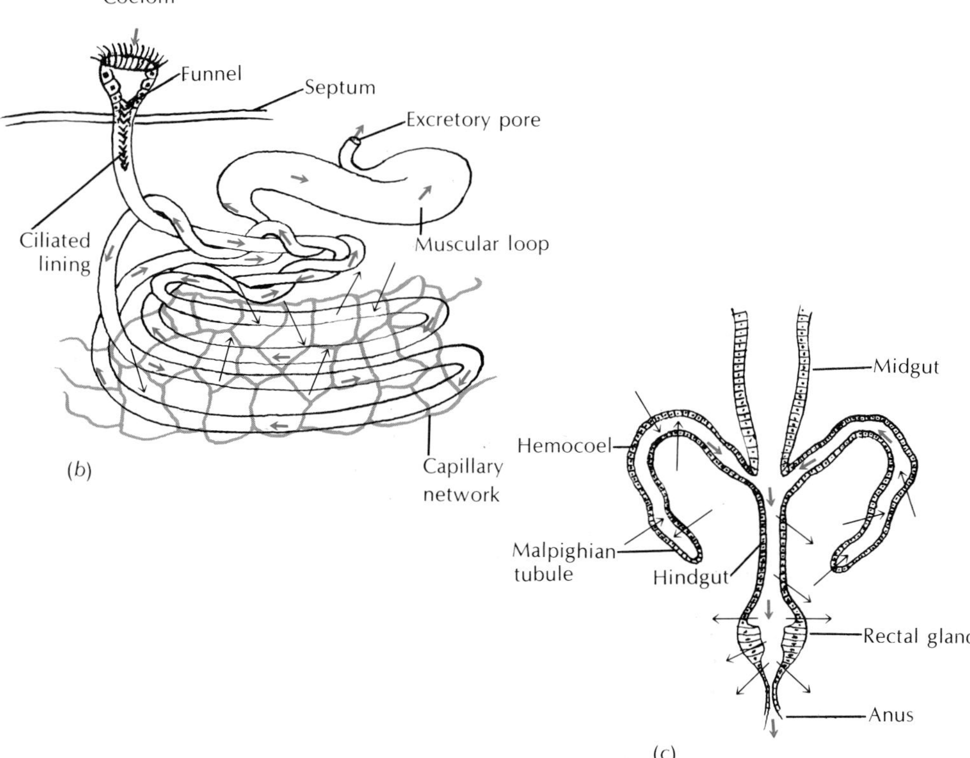

Figure 16.9 □ **Types of invertebrate excretory organs. (*a*) Protonephridia: Left, excretory tubules of a flatworm, terminating internally in ciliated flame cells; right, excretory tubules of a polychaete, terminating internally in flagellated solenocytes. (*b*) Metanephridium of earthworm (cell structure shown only near coelomic funnel). Note capillary bed associated with renal tubule, allowing addition of materials to, or their removal from, the urine. The urine initially consists of unmodified coelomic fluid. (*c*) Malpighian tubules and hindgut of an insect. Materials are absorbed from the blood into the Malpighian tubules, and selective reabsorption takes place in the hindgut. The thin black arrows indicate excretion pathways and selective reabsorption. Heavy color arrows show intratubular flow.**

process to continue. As it transports the coelomic fluid toward the exterior, the metanephridium may be associated along its length with blood capillaries, or (in arthropods and some molluscs) may pass through blood-filled spaces (the hemocoel), allowing materials to be reclaimed from the urine and transferred to the bloodstream, or additional wastes to be transferred from the blood to the urine.

Insects and a number of other terrestrial arthropods have developed special excretory organs that are in fact tubular *glands* arising from the alimentary tract at the union of midgut and hindgut. These *Malpighian tubules* lie coiled within the hemocoel, but their ends are closed so that urine must be formed entirely by the transport of water, ions, and solutes, across the epithelium forming the tubules. These materials are emptied into the hindgut, which functions in the recovery of water and useful solutes. The hindgut must therefore be considered to have a renal function in these arthropods. The mechanism for active reclamation of water in the insect hindgut is so efficient that nearly dry excreta can be produced; this mechanism has yet to be satisfactorily explained.

THE VERTEBRATE KIDNEY AND ITS EVOLUTION The functional unit of the vertebrate kidney is the *nephron,* a tubular unit in which a renal epithelium is associated with a capillary tuft (*glomerulus*). In the course of evolution the renal tubule appears to have changed from a simple metanephridium carrying coelomic fluid to a closed-ended tubule (not homologous with a protonephridium) deriving its fluids entirely from the bloodstream instead of the coelom (Figure 16.10).

The vertebrate kidney is the most elaborate and efficient of animal excretory organs. Indeed, during embryonic development of the complex kidney that is to function throughout postembryonic life, another, simpler kidney must first be utilized to meet the temporary needs of the embryo. The evolution of the vertebrate kidney may be provisionally outlined by study of its embryonic development in modern vertebrates. The ancestral kidney is thought to have been a segmental organ extending the full length of the coelom and bearing in each segment a pair of metanephridia opening by way of a ciliated funnel into the coelom and leading at the opposite end into a longitudinal urinary duct that emptied into the cloaca.

Figure 16.10 □ **Evolution of the vertebrate nephron. (*a*) Hypothetical ancestral condition: glomeruli lacking and coelomic fluid drained by means of segmental metanephridia (only a representative number of nephridial units are shown). (*b*) External glomerular stage: glomerular capillary tufts protruding into coelom near each coelomic funnel. (*c*) Formation of Bowman's capsules around glomeruli, enhancing opportunity for materials to be filtered from blood directly into renal tubules. (*d*) Disappearance of coelomic openings (in adult anamniotes), leaving glomeruli as only source of fluid for renal tubules. (*e*) Development of ureter with new drainage system for kidney (adult amniotes).**

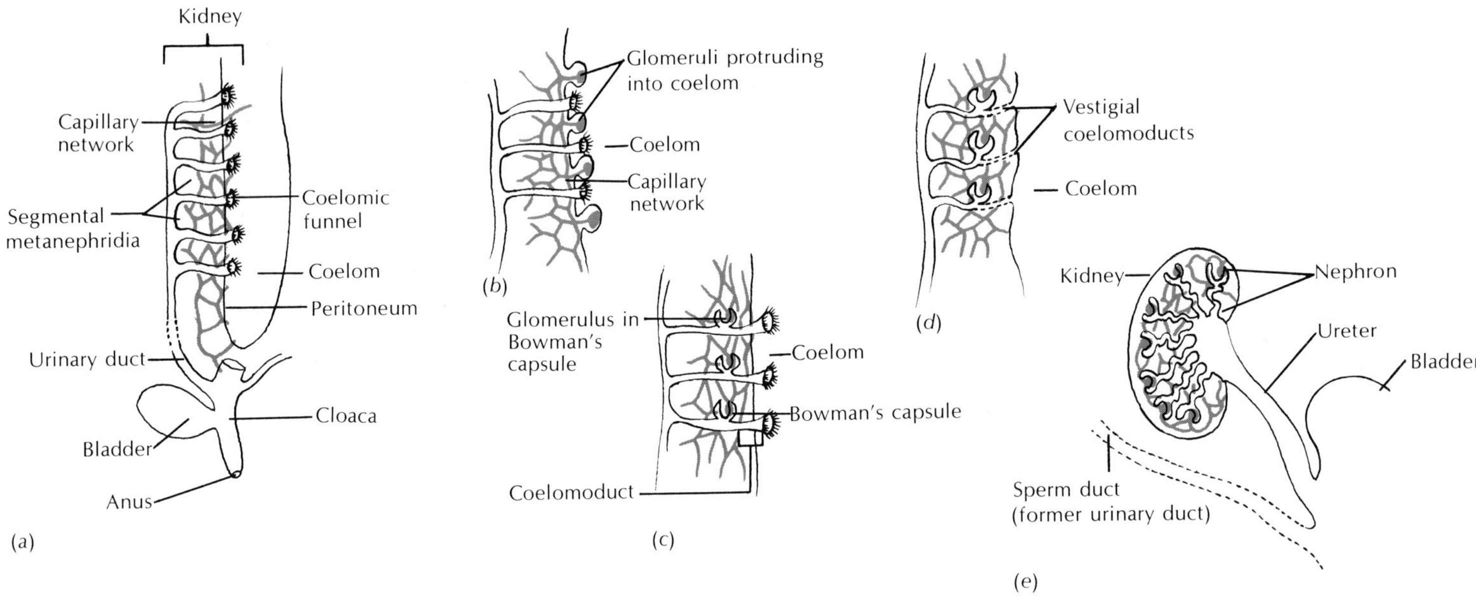

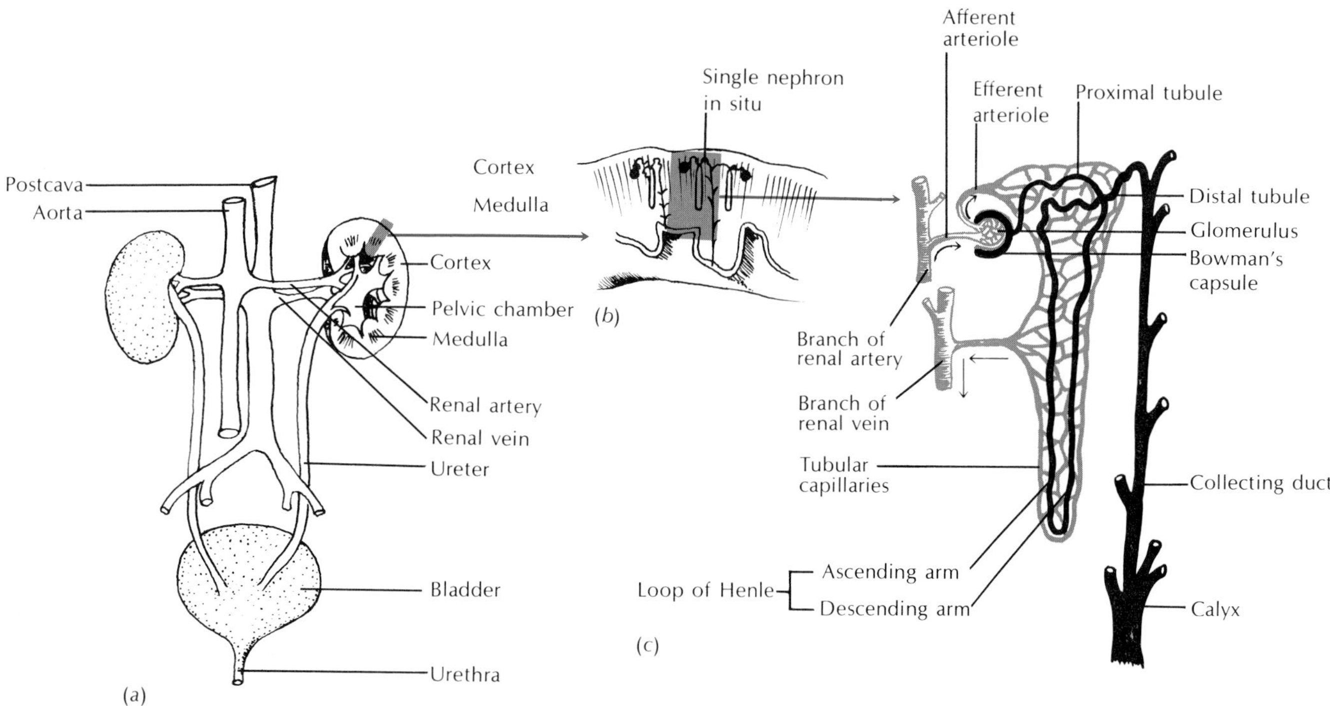

Figure 16.11 □ Human excretory system. (*a*) Entire excretory system, dorsal aspect. (*b*) Enlarged portion of kidney, showing a few nephrons in situ. (*c*) Enlargement of a single nephron, with blood vessels and collecting tubule. Arrows indicate direction of blood flow.

Since the first vertebrates probably lived in fresh water, they had to rid their tissues of excess water. This led to the development of capillary knots (glomeruli) that protruded into the coelom from the body wall, close to the open ends of the metanephridia. The blood pressure in the glomeruli being higher than the fluid pressure within the coelom, a plasma filtrate was formed that passed into the coelom and was carried away by the metanephridia. This functional association between the glomeruli and excretory tubules promoted their structural intimacy. We can only speculate about the transitional stages. Probably the glomeruli first came to rest directly against the coelomic funnels of the metanephridia, then sank into the tissue of the kidney, each becoming encased in a cuplike expansion (Bowman's capsule) arising along the length of the excretory tubule. Thereafter, the opening of the renal tubules into the coelom became redundant and accordingly tended to close, leaving the glomerulus as the only source of fluid for each nephron. Functional openings into the coelom persist today only in the embryonic kidneys of anamniotes but vestiges are also seen in the adult kidneys of amphibians.

As an outcome of this possible evolutionary progression, each nephron in the kidneys of amniotes (as well as the postembryonic kidneys of anamniotes) arises proximally as a double-walled epithelial cup, Bowman's capsule, enclosing a glomerulus (Figure 16.11). A second set of capillaries, evolutionarily derived from the renal portal system (see Figure 12.41c), branches about each nephron along its length, facilitating further exchanges with the bloodstream. The individual nephrons drain into collecting tubules, which then empty into the expanded pelvic chamber leading into the ureter.

Development of a kidney unit adapted for the removal of excess water by production of large amounts of dilute urine met the needs of freshwater vertebrates, but when fish moved down to the sea and amphibians emerged upon the land, new renal adaptations were required that resulted in modifications of kidney structure and functional changes in the processes of selective excretion. The capability of the renal tubule cells to regulate urine composition by selective membrane transport has been accentuated in both marine and terrestrial vertebrates. Among marine fish, water conservation is accomplished by reduction or loss of the glomeruli, most if not all of the urine being formed by active secretory processes in the renal tubules. In addition to this, excess ions are removed by salt-secreting tissues in the gills. Among amniotes, two courses of water-conservation have been followed. Most birds and reptiles solved the problem by the metabolic conversion of more toxic soluble nitrogenous wastes (such as urea) that must be voided in water into harmless solid urates that can be voided as solid excreta. However, blood is still filtered through the glomeruli for removal of other materials, and in consequence renal epithelium still plays an important role in the selective reclamation of useful solutes from the urine. In the mammalian kidney a special adaptation for water retention has evolved: there has been a lengthening of the nephron, with differentiation of a new portion, the hairpin-shaped *Henle's loop,* which enables mammals to void a liquid urine *hyperosmotic* to their tissues, a feat unique in the animal world.

In addition to the changes taking place in the structure of the nephron during the evolution of the vertebrate kidney, it should also be noted that the number of nephrons per kidney has greatly multiplied. From the presumed ancestral condition of one pair of tubules per body segment, the number of nephrons has so increased that about a million of these units occur in each human kidney. This is at least twice the number required for survival, for removal of one kidney seems in no way to impair health.

URINE FORMATION IN THE MAMMALIAN KIDNEY Formation of urine in the nephron is a three-step process involving filtration, reabsorption, and augmentation. First, a glomerular filtrate is formed by the pressure filtration of plasma from the glomerulus into the cavity of Bowman's capsule. Blood pressure is unusually high in the mammalian glomerulus, in part due to the fact that the blood vessel leaving the glomerulus has a considerably smaller bore than the vessel entering it. This elevated intravascular pressure results in *ultrafiltration,* with nearly 20 percent of the blood plasma that enters the glomerulus being forced out into the Bowman's capsule. Some 170 liters of plasma filtrate are formed daily by the human kidney; normally, about 1.5 liters of urine are voided daily (less if perspiration is copious or water intake restricted).

Glomerular filtrate resembles the blood plasma except that it is protein-free—since the plasma proteins are too large normally to escape from the capillaries. Obviously the filtrate contains so much water and so many valuable solutes that the second step in the urine-forming process, *tubular reabsorption,* must be extremely efficient. The passage of such great volumes of glomerular filtrate through the nephron allows the renal epithelium to exercise close regulation of the composition of the body fluids, for the original makeup of the filtrate of course reflects the composition of the blood. However, this rate of filtration and reabsorption, while making the mammalian kidney the most effective known organ for chemical homeostasis, also makes it extremely sensitive to changes in blood pressure. The nephrons are especially vulnerable to damage from high blood pressure, such damage being heralded by the appearance of plasma proteins in the urine. Conversely, a fall in blood pressure so reduces the rate of glomerular filtration that urinary excretion may not keep pace with the body's needs. Toxic nitrogenous wastes, particularly urea, then begin to accumulate to excess in the blood, leading to convulsions and death.

In the light of this sensitivity to changes in blood pressure it is not surprising that the kidney itself has become capable of regulating blood pressure. In the walls of the renal blood vessels are stretch receptors that double as glandular cells: when blood pressure declines they release the substance *renin,* which interacts with the plasma factor *angiotensinogen* to form the hormone *angiotensin.* This hormone promotes peripheral vasoconstriction throughout the body, resulting in a general elevation of blood pressure. The ability of these receptors both to monitor blood pressure and to secrete the pressure-regulating factor makes rapid response possible, thus warding off injurious changes in renal blood pressure.

During its passage through the renal tubules, the composition of the glomerular filtrate is greatly altered. About 80 percent

Figure 16.12 □ **Production of hyperosmotic urine in mammalian kidney by means of countercurrent exchange of Na^+ in Henle's loop. The active removal of Na^+ from the urine in the ascending arm of Henle's loop (shown by solid color arrows) and its reabsorption into the descending arm (dashed color arrows) constitute a cyclic movement of Na^+ that sets up a salinity gradient in the surrounding tissue fluid, as indicated by the background shading: increasing intensity of shading means increasing salinity. As the collecting tubule passes through the salty tissue fluid of the kidney medulla, a massive osmotic withdrawal of water from the urine takes place (thin black arrows), producing a urine hyperosmotic to the blood. Water does not accumulate in the tissue fluid, for it enters the capillaries and is carried away. (Urine flow is represented by grayed arrows, and reabsorption of solutes by pale-color arrows.)**

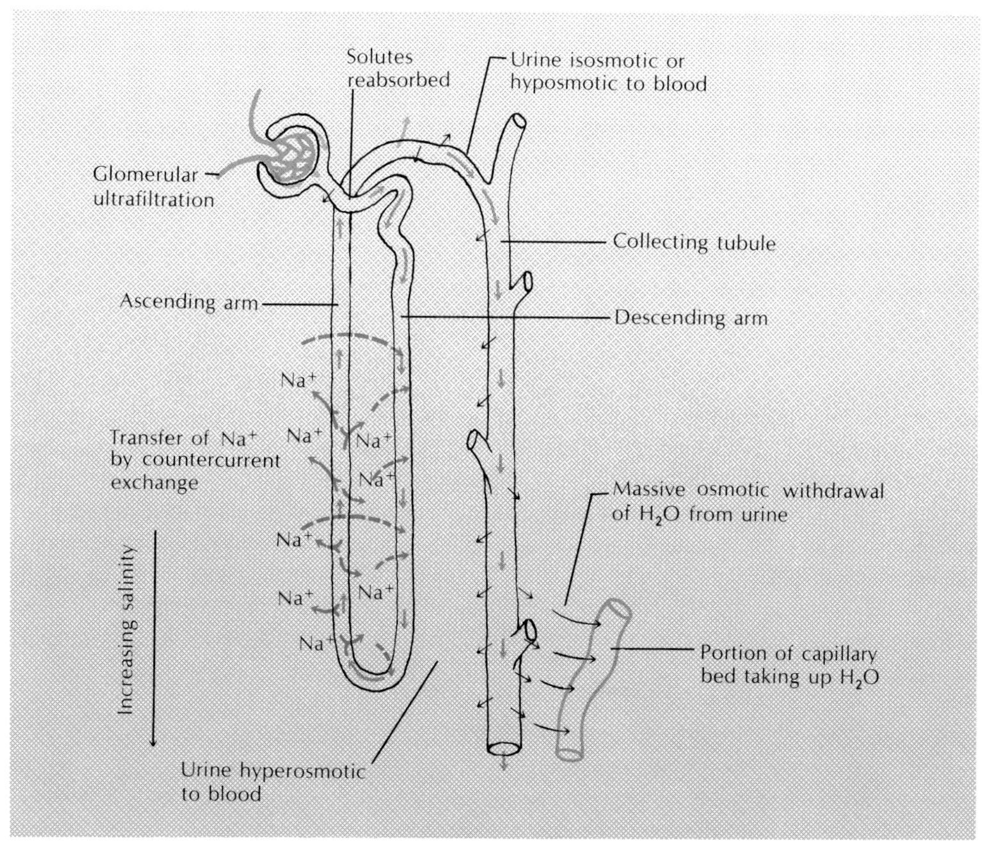

of the water content is reabsorbed osmotically in the proximal convoluted tubule and up to 99 percent of the remainder can be reclaimed osmotically in the collecting tubules as a result of a countercurrent exchange system formed by Henle's loop (as described below). In addition, various solutes are recovered by active transport in both the proximal and distal convoluted tubules (see Figure 16.11c). Such *low-threshold* solutes as glucose are usually recovered totally. *Intermediate-threshold* compounds such as urea are partially reabsorbed, whereas certain *nonthreshold* substances such as creatinine and sulfates are not reabsorbed at all. In addition to carrying on the selective reabsorption of materials from the urine, the renal epithelium is also responsible for the third process in urine formation, *tubular augmentation*—the active secretion of additional materials by transcellular transport from the interstitial fluid into the urine. We have mentioned the cardinal importance of this process for urine production in the kidneys of many marine fish, where glomeruli are lacking. Tubular augmentation is probably considerably less important in mammals, due to their dependence on glomerular filtration.

The remarkably efficient reabsorption of water that results in production of a hyperosmotic urine in mammals is a topic of much interest. Henle's loop and the collecting tubule into which individual nephrons drain are the parts of the kidney particularly involved in this process. The unique function of Henle's loop is the maintenance of a salinity gradient in the interstitial fluid through which the loop passes in its long hairpin descent into the renal medulla and return to the renal cortex (Figure 16.12). A *countercurrent exchange* system* is set up between the descending and ascending limbs of the loop, which is responsible for maintaining this salinity gradient.

The mammalian nephron is some 40 to 50 mm long, and at least half of this length lies within Henle's loop. Fluid passing from Bowman's capsule into the proximal convoluted tubule next enters the descending limb of Henle's loop and flows toward the medulla of the kidney, only to reverse its direction and flow outward once more in the ascending limb of the loop. The two limbs lie parallel to one another and constitute a countercurrent exchange system for sodium ion. The *ascending* limb (leading to the distal convoluted tubule) is *impervious to water,* but its epithelium removes some of the Na^+ from the urine and secretes it into the interstitial fluid. From here Na^+ is actively reabsorbed into the *descending* limb of the loop. Since Na^+ is taken up all along the length of the descending limb, the urine in this limb becomes more and more salty, but then as it turns and flows outward in the ascending limb the progressive removal of Na^+ makes the urine less and less salty. However, since additional Na^+ continues to enter Henle's loop in the glomerular filtrate even while Na^+ is being excreted from the ascending limb into the tissue fluid, to be taken back up into the descending limb through which it has already passed, the concentration of Na^+ tends to build up in the tissue fluid until that of the renal medulla becomes some *four times saltier* than the blood plasma! The tissue fluid in the renal medulla is also at least 400 percent saltier than the urine at the time the latter flows from the distal convoluted tubule into the collecting tubule. On its way to the pelvis of the kidney, where it will join the ureter, the collecting tubule must therefore pass through interstitial fluid of progressively higher salinity. Sodium ion does not escape into the bloodstream or diffuse into the collecting tubule because of the tendency of cell membranes to exclude Na^+. Water, on the other hand, is free to move along its concentration gradient, and does so. A massive, diffusion-driven movement of water out of the collecting tubule into the interstitial compartment takes place. Osmotic equilibrium is not reached because water can then pass into the bloodstream and be carried away, whereas the ions making the tissue fluid hyperosmotic to the urine cannot move out of the compartment. As a result of this osmotic withdrawal of water, the urine in the collecting tubule becomes more and more concentrated, so that the final product is nearly as briny as the medullary tissue fluid. Mammalian kidney structure therefore is particularly adaptive in that it allows for a highly efficient means of water recovery with minimal energy expenditure. Otherwise, the energetic cost of processing such quantities of glomerular filtrate might be prohibitive.

**Countercurrent exchange* originally referred to heat exchange between parallel channels in which liquid is circulating in opposite directions (as in some engineering applications); it now applies to other phenomena besides heat exchange, including those found in several important biological systems. When two streams of fluid flow in opposite directions in parallel channels separated by a differentially permeable membrane, a highly efficient exchange of solvent or solutes can take place between the two streams. Such countercurrent exchange systems occur in salt glands, mammalian kidneys, the placenta, the walls of fish bladder, and various parts of the circulatory system (to be discussed later).

NERVOUS AND HORMONAL CONTROL OF BODY FLUIDS The kidneys are seldom the only organs involved in regulating the chemical constancy of the internal milieu. Besides the elimination of CO_2 through the gills or lungs, with a concomitant reduction in circulating HCO_3^-, kidney function must be integrated with the activities of such organs as nasal salt glands (in seabirds and marine reptiles), sweat glands (in mammals), salt-secreting gill tissues (in marine fishes), and the integument (in amphibians). Such integration requires central control, however this control is furnished not primarily by nerves but by hormones.

In mammals we can distinguish three major control systems involved in regulating the concentration and volume of body fluids: (1) the *hypothalamic drinking center;* (2) the hypothalamic neurohormone *vasopressin;* (3) the *angiotensin-aldosterone control axis.*

Water-seeking and -drinking behaviors are activated by the hypothalamic drinking center, which in turn receives input from receptors in the lining of the mouth and pharynx that are sensitive to drying. The control of drinking is sufficiently precise that after enough liquid has been imbibed to dilute the blood to normal concentrations, drinking will cease even before the ingested water has been absorbed from the gut into the bloodstream. However, the sensation of thirst itself can be alleviated by moistening the pharyngeal mucosa, even though the body is in need of water.

If the body's water needs cannot be satisfied by drinking, other central control mechanisms go into action, which promote

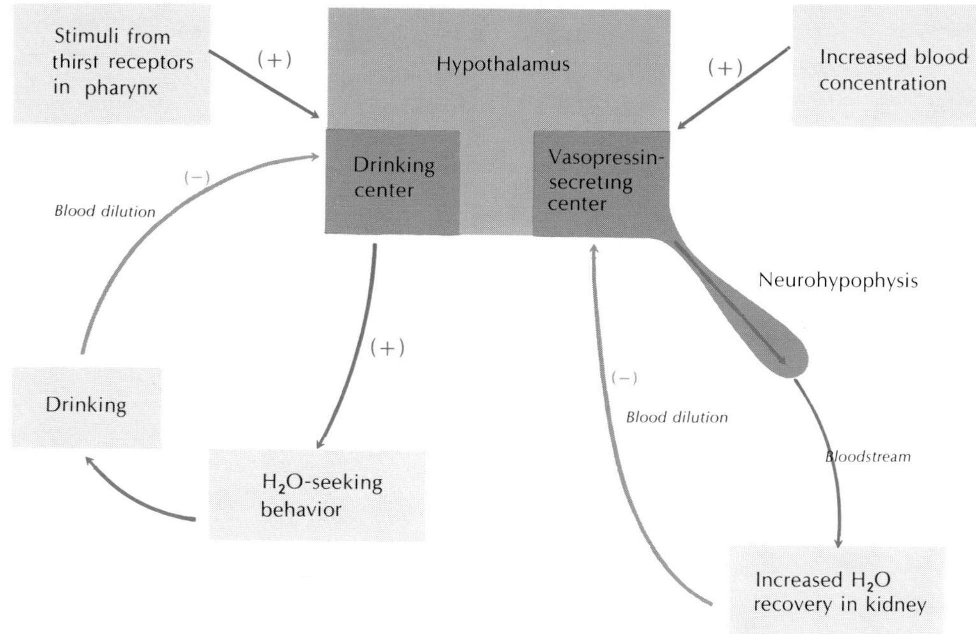

Figure 16.13 □ Hypothalamic control of blood volume.

additional water retention by the kidneys. *Osmoreceptors* thought to be located within the hypothalamus proper respond to increases in the solute concentration of the blood and tissue fluids by triggering *vasopressin* release. This neurohormone acts upon the renal tubules to increase water recovery, thus diluting the blood and increasing the volume of body fluids. As blood volume increases, stretch receptors in the walls of the atria and larger blood vessels send impulses to the brain that result in the inhibition of further vasopressin release (Figure 16.13).

Angiotensin, the vasoconstrictor effect of which was noted above, is thought to be the major factor promoting the secretion of aldosterone by the adrenal cortex. *Aldosterone,* we may recall, increases Na^+ retention, which in turn results in more extensive water recovery. As the blood volume rises, the renin-secreting cells in the kidney cease to liberate renin and as a result no more angiotensin is formed and the flow of aldosterone slacks off (Figure 16.14).

The efficiency of these control mechanisms is well demonstrated when the system is challenged by hemorrhage. Hemorrhage results in an abrupt reduction in blood volume and attendant lowering of blood pressure. This is first compensated for by constriction of the arterioles, thereby reducing capillary blood pressure to a point at which water tends to be drawn into the circulation from the tissue fluid compartment. In this way blood volume is restored to normal (provided that bleeding is controlled), but its solute concentration is reduced. This dilution is soon corrected by means of the Na^+-conserving action of aldosterone, while the overall body fluid volume is gradually restored by a vasopressin-controlled reduction in urine volume.

In addition to the control systems discussed so far that are responsible for maintaining the chemical constancy of the body fluids, we should again make mention of other hormones responsible for maintaining precise control over the concentration of specific materials in the body fluids. In particular there are two sets of hormones acting in opposition to one another that deserve review. The body's "glucostat," which regulates the glucose content of the body fluids by mobilizing glycogen or increasing the cellular absorption and utilization of glucose, consists of the pancreatic hormones *insulin* and *glucagon.* These act in opposition, not upon the same processes but in different ways that result in keeping a balance between sugar release and sugar utilization. As noted in Chapter 15, insulin promotes glucose absorption and the building of glycogen, whereas glucagon promotes the breakdown of glycogen, thereby raising the blood sugar level. The pancreatic islet cells seem to be directly responsive to changes in blood glucose level.

The body's "calcistat," which regulates the levels of blood Ca^{2+} and phosphate, consists of the opposing hormones parathormone and thyrocalcitonin. The glandular cells secreting these factors are directly sensitive to changes in blood Ca^{2+} level. As described in Section 15.4B, these two hormones interact to regulate the rate at which calcium phosphate is deposited in or mobilized from the supportive tissues and the extent to which Ca^{2+} and phosphate ions are reabsorbed from the urine.

REGULATION OF pH The concentration of H^+ in the body fluids is only one millionth that of the concentration of Na^+, yet the mechanisms controlling hydrogen ion concentration must be especially precise, for cell metabolism is greatly disturbed by even slight changes in the amount of H^+ present. This is because H^+ is highly reactive with cell proteins. Association of H^+ with an enzyme molecule causes redistribution of electrical charges throughout the molecule and may profoundly affect the enzyme's capacity to combine with its substrates. Intracellular pH is maintained almost exactly at neutrality, or pH 7 as measured by means of microelectrodes made of pH-sensitive glass that can be directly inserted into the cytoplasm. Human blood is normally slightly alkaline, pH 7.4, but deviations between pH 6.8 to 7.7 are not fatal. The normal mild alkalinity is adaptive, for the body must deal mainly with excess acidity rather than with excess alkalinity. Cells produce and excrete a number of organic acids such as lactic acid, and phosphoric and sulfuric acids are also generated to excess during muscular exercise. By far the most common acid produced in the body is carbonic acid, H_2CO_3, which is formed during CO_2 transport (see Section 14.2C): CO_2 passing from the tissues into the mammalian bloodstream reacts with H_2O to form H_2CO_3. Within the red blood cells this reaction is catalyzed by carbonic anhydrase. Carbonic acid is considered a weak (that is, weakly ionizing) acid, but at normal blood pH it actually tends to ionize completely, to H^+ and HCO_3^-. The quantity of H^+ liberated would represent a serious problem were it not for the presence of hemoglobin (Hb). This protein, best known for its role in oxygen transport, tends to take up H^+ at normal blood pH, to become *acid hemoglobin* (HHb). This exchange of one acid for another might not seem to be much of an improvement, but in fact HHb does not ionize appreciably unless the blood becomes more alkaline than usual. Then HHb dissociates to yield H^+, thereby helping to counteract the alkaline deviation.

The tendency of hemoglobin to take up H^+ at one pH and to relinquish it at another is characteristic of a *buffer* substance. Buffers titrate body fluids, liberating H^+ when the fluids become more alkaline and taking up H^+ when they begin to become more acidic. In other words, buffers act as acids (H^+ donors) at higher pH values, and as bases (H^+ acceptors) at lower pH values. Because of the presence of buffers, the

Figure 16.14 □ Control of blood volume and pressure by angiotensin and aldosterone.

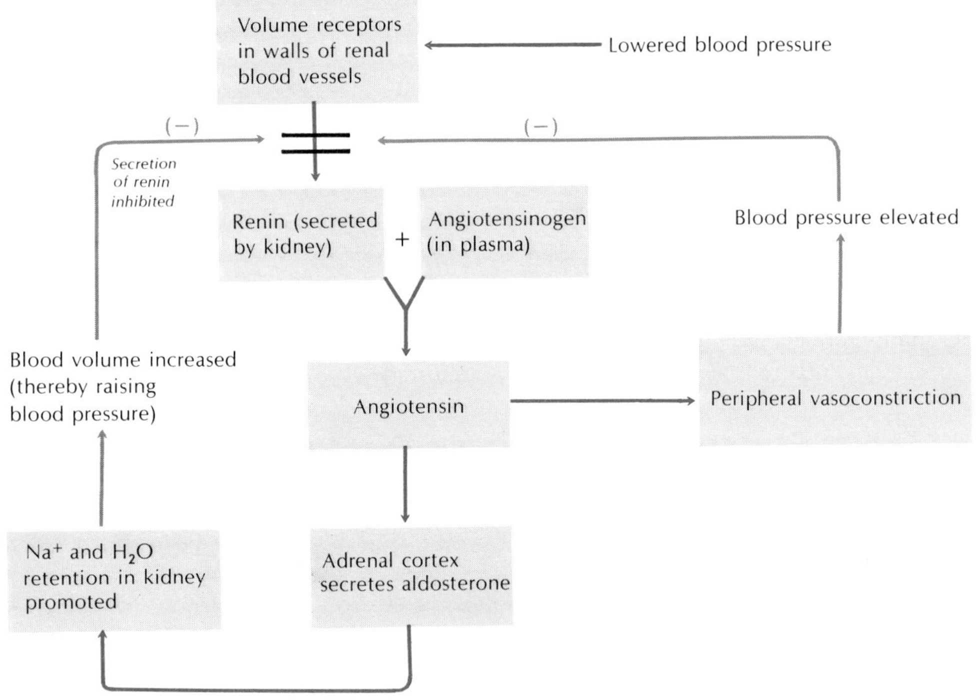

addition of a strong acid to blood causes little change in pH until the point is reached at which the capacity of the buffers has been exceeded, after which pH alters rapidly. The most important buffers in living systems are *buffer anions*. Within the cells these anions are mainly protein and various phosphate anions. (Proteins can act either as acids or bases, but tend to dissociate as anions at the H^+ concentration characteristic of living systems.) In the human bloodstream the major buffer anions are ionized hemoglobin (Hb^-), plasma proteins, and phosphate and bicarbonate ions.

The carbonic acid–bicarbonate system is particularly important in regulating the pH of the bloodstream. The formation of H_2CO_3 (concomitant with CO_2 transport) and its subsequent ionization to H^+ and HCO_3^-, with the H^+ being taken up by hemoglobin, leaves relatively large amounts of HCO_3^- available in the plasma to serve as an H^+ acceptor. If a strong acid such as HCl is added, the total ionic reaction is

$$Na^+ + HCO_3^- + H^+ + Cl^- \longrightarrow H_2CO_3 + Na^+ + Cl^-$$

The fate of the H_2CO_3 formed is then influenced by the equilibrium existing between the plasma concentrations of CO_2 and HCO_3^-. At equilibrium human blood plasma contains 1.2 mmoles free CO_2/liter and 24 mmoles HCO_3^-/liter. Every time the blood cycles through the lungs, CO_2 is removed, lowering the plasma CO_2 level, and the equilibrium must be reestablished by means of the reaction

$$H_2CO_3 \xrightarrow{\text{Carbonic anhydrase}} H_2O + CO_2$$

This raises the plasma CO_2 level back to the equilibrium state and at the same time results in the binding of the former excess H^+ as part of a water molecule.

The blood HCO_3^-/CO_2 equilibrium can be related to the pH value through the Henderson-Hasselbalch equation,

$$\log K' = \log\,[H^+] + \frac{[HCO_3^-]}{\log 0.03P_{CO_2}}$$

where K' is the equilibrium constant characteristic of the reaction, $[H^+]$ represents the blood pH, and $0.03P_{CO_2}$ is the partial pressure of CO_2 in the plasma. Studying the relations in this equation it can be seen that the values for HCO_3^- concentration and P_{CO_2} control the pH value.

Maintaining neutrality within the cell involves two different regulative systems. The first of these includes the intracellular buffers—cytoplasmic proteins and, especially, various phosphate anions. Phosphoric acid, a regular cell constituent, can dissociate stepwise, as follows:

$$H_3PO_4 \rightleftharpoons H^+ + H_2PO_4^-$$
Dihydrogenphosphate

$$H_2PO_4^- \rightleftharpoons H^+ + HPO_4^{2-}$$
Monohydrogenphosphate

$$HPO_4^{2-} \rightleftharpoons H^+ + PO_4^{3-}$$
Phosphate

The anions formed serve as H^+ acceptors. For instance, PO_4^{3-} can take up H^+ to form HPO_4^{2-}, which does not contribute toward cell acidification.

The second system involved in maintaining cellular neutrality appears to be some factor that opposes the tendency of H^+ to enter the cell. Due to the fact that the interior of the cell is electronegative to the exterior there is actually a strong tendency for H^+ to enter the cell, and in fact its concentration in human muscle tissue does amount to around 2.5 times that in the interstitial fluid. However, the transmembrane potential (−90 mV) is so great that enough H^+ should enter to bring the cytoplasmic pH from 7 to 5.9 despite the action of its buffers. How is it then that this much H^+ is not found within the cell? Since hydrated H^+ is so much smaller than either hydrated Na^+ or K^+, it seems less likely that the cell membrane is actually impervious to H^+ than that H^+ is continuously being pumped out of the cell by means of some specific active transport mechanism.

Ultimately the body's buffers, both intracellular and extracellular, would become saturated with H^+ were it not that H^+ is continuously removed from the body, especially by way of the kidneys. Excess water (including that formed by the breakdown of carbonic acid), dihydrogenphosphate and monohydrogenphosphate anions, and H^+ itself are excreted in the urine. In man the urinary excretion of H^+ may be great enough to produce urine as acid as pH 4.4; H^+ appears to be excreted into the urine by active transport in the renal tubules, the transport mechanism probably being linked with the Na^+/K^+ pump mechanism mentioned earlier. In addition, ammonia (NH_3) produced in the kidney cells takes up H^+ to form NH_4^+, which is also excreted in the urine.

B Thermoregulation

Physiological regulation of body temperature is possible only for homoiotherms ("warm-blooded" animals), although as we have seen earlier poikilotherms ("cold-blooded" animals) often maintain reason-

Figure 16.15 □ **Thermoregulation.**

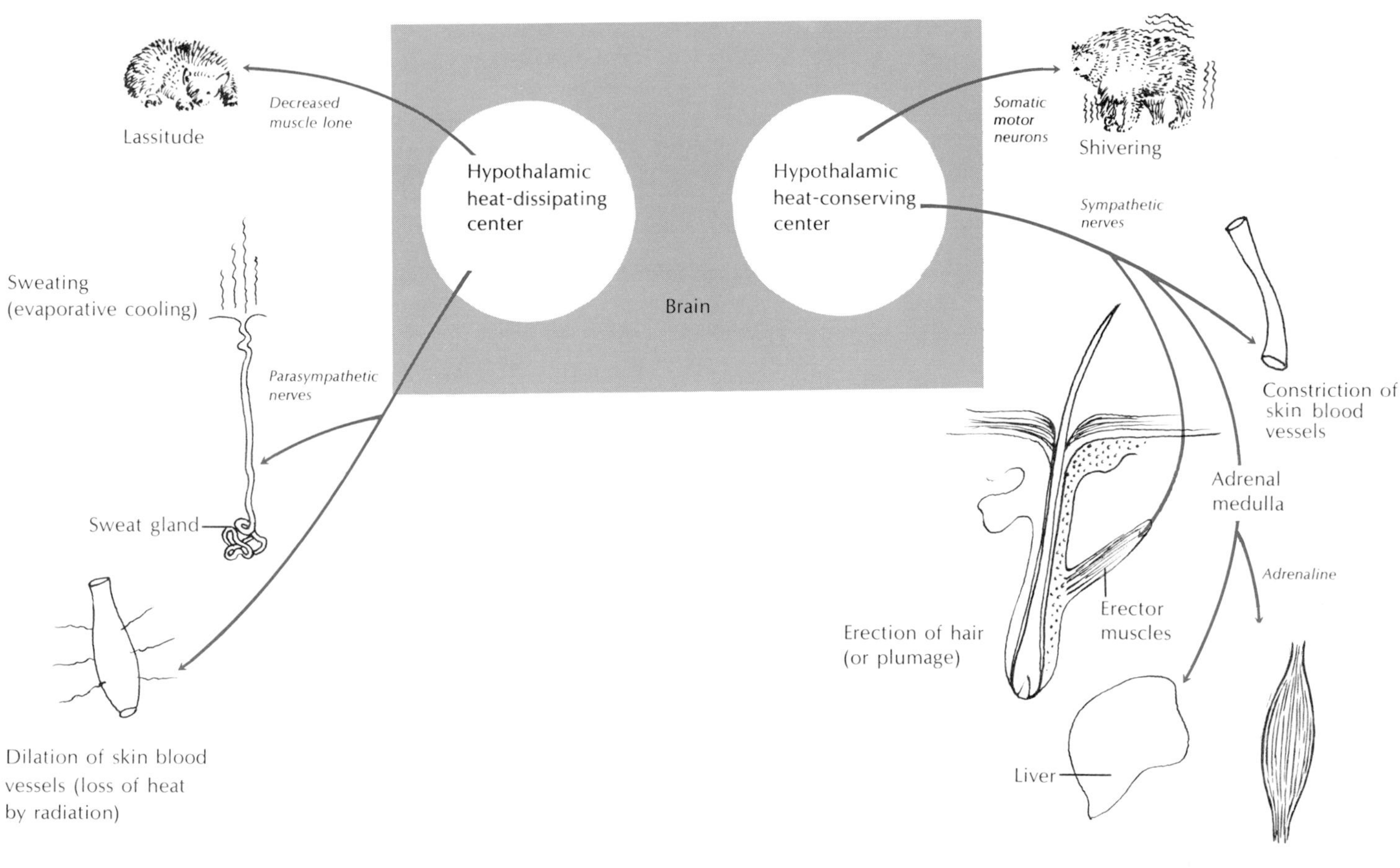

Decreased muscle lone
Lassitude
Hypothalamic heat-dissipating center
Hypothalamic heat-conserving center
Somatic motor neurons
Shivering
Sympathetic nerves
Brain
Sweating (evaporative cooling)
Parasympathetic nerves
Sweat gland
Dilation of skin blood vessels (loss of heat by radiation)
Constriction of skin blood vessels
Adrenal medulla
Adrenaline
Erector muscles
Erection of hair (or plumage)
Liver
Breakdown of liver and muscle glycogen

able thermal stability by behavioral means such as thermotactic movement into a preferred temperature range (see Figure 4.9). The effectiveness of the homeostatic mechanisms of many homoiotherms is evidenced by their capacity to endure fluctuations in ambient (external) temperature of as much as 100°C, while undergoing internal temperature changes of only 1 to 2°C.

Homoiotherms show both physiological and behavioral thermoregulation. Physiological regulation of body temperature is governed by the *hypothalamus* by way of autonomic nerves (Figure 16.15). Two distinct regulatory mechanisms can be distinguished: (1) *heating mechanisms* and (2) *cooling mechanisms. The thermally neutral zone* for a given species may be fairly narrow, if this is defined as the temperature range over which the animal can maintain its *basal* metabolic rate without either gradually losing body heat or accumulating a heat load. The lower limit of this range is more readily determined than the upper limit, and for man and other basically tropical mammals has been cited as 25 to 27°C. Animals adapted to colder climates can maintain the basal metabolic rate without a change in body temperature at environmental temperatures well below freezing. How hard the body's thermoregulatory mechanisms must work depends upon the species' range of thermal tolerance, the breadth of its thermally neutral zone, and how widely the ambient temperature deviates from this range both daily and seasonally. The human hypothalamus has been found to respond to blood temperature changes of only a few thousandths of a degree. The thermosensitive cells are located in the hypothalamus proper, and monitor the temperature of blood within the nearby internal carotid artery. Peripheral thermoreceptors seem to play no important role in physiological thermoregulation, but undoubtedly influence the individual's selection of surroundings having a comfortable temperature.

A *heat conserving center* in the posterior hypothalamus responds to cooling by initiating adjustments mediated by way of sympathetic nerves. Heat conservation is promoted by the constriction of blood vessels of the skin, by the inhibition of sweating, and by constriction of the muscles which erect the hair or feathers. Heat production is also increased by both physical and chemical means. *Physical thermogenesis* involves the generation of heat by contractions of the skeletal muscles, either during exercise or by rapid involuntary tremors (shivering). *Chemical thermogenesis* involves the increased oxidation of carbohydrates and lipids, especially liver and muscle glycogen.

A *heat-dissipating center* is located in the anterior hypothalamus. This center responds to increases in blood temperature in the internal carotid artery by evoking *para*sympathetically mediated adjustments. Loss of heat by evaporation is promoted by sweating (which in man can amount to a flow of 4 liters/hr). In birds, ventilation is stimulated, increasing heat loss by evaporation from the internal air sacs. Panting also increases heat loss by evaporation from the lungs and lining of the mouth and throat. In addition, heat causes the blood vessels of the skin to dilate, thus increasing heat loss by radiation. At the same time, decreased muscle tone accompanied by lassitude reduces internal heat production.

Behavioral adaptations are as important in the toleration of excess heat as they are in avoiding cold. We have spoken in Section 5.3A of adaptations of desert animals, including estivation, burrowing, nocturnality, and tolerance of heat load. In addition, mammals often respond to overheating by seeking shade, panting, and becoming lethargic. Kangaroos cool themselves by licking their paws and chests, and then standing with outspread arms so that evaporation is facilitated. Elephants spray themselves with their nasal exudates, and wood storks urinate upon their legs every minute or so, an unusual cooling device resorted to by a species that cannot sweat.

Physiological adaptation to seasonal temperature changes is known as *acclimatization.* This is mainly regulated by photoperiod and is hormonally controlled. As winter approaches, the animal's insulation is increased by the thickening of its fur or feathers and by the subcutaneous deposition of fat. At the same time changes take place in the skin, including reduction in its blood supply. A higher proportion of unsaturated fats (which remain liquid at low temperatures) are found in the skin and extremities of animals living in frigid climates.

According to how extensively they thermoregulate, homoiotherms may be termed obligate, stubborn, or facultative. *Obligate* homoiotherms cannot survive more than a few degrees' fluctuation in internal temperature. Polar species that are obligate homoiotherms conserve heat by tolerating the cooling of their extremities to nearly the freezing point. Countercurrent exchange systems,* in which arteries con-

*See the footnote on page 802.

taining hot blood from the central regions are surrounded by veins containing cold blood returning from the extremities, have been identified in the legs of polar birds and mammals, and in the tail and flukes of whales. The arteries and veins serving these extremities form a complicated network of parallel channels in which chilled venous blood and hot arterial blood run in opposite directions. So effective is the heat exchange that blood leaving the trunk at 30°C is chilled to nearly 0°C by the time it reaches the extremities, *without* the organism suffering appreciable heat loss. Instead, the heat has been transferred to the venous flow, warming the blood to around 28°C before it reenters the trunk. Such differences in body temperature from the interior to the body surface and from trunk to extremities require local cellular adaptations. For instance, nerve fibers in the extremities continue to conduct impulses at temperatures well below those that inactivate nerve fibers in warmer parts of the body. Enzymes located in peripheral tissues must operate at temperatures more than 35°C lower than those at which enzymes must operate in deeper tissues of the trunk. Fat deposits in the trunk may have a melting point of about 40°C, while those in the footpads remain liquid at 0°C.

Stubborn homoiotherms such as poorwills and deer mice maintain an even body temperature despite wide environmental fluctuations, but do hibernate in winter if deprived of food. If food is provided in abundance, these species do not become torpid, although their body temperature may decline a few degrees from its summer level. *Facultative* homoiotherms, on the other hand, relax their thermal control when asleep, their nightly temperatures falling to ambient levels. For homoiotherms as small as hummingbirds, this capacity means survival, for the high ratio of body surface to volume means that much heat is lost by radiation. It has been calculated that if a hummingbird had to maintain its body temperature at daytime levels while sleeping it would need to consume 10 kcal of food each day; but, due to the nightly fall in body temperature, it actually requires only 7.6 kcal/day—a saving of nearly 25 percent (Figure 16.16).

Figure 16.16 □ Obligate and facultative homoiothermy. Rates of metabolism of shrew and male Anna's hummingbird over a 24-hr period. The shrew, a mammal, is an obligate homoiotherm that must maintain a nearly constant body temperature or die. The hummingbird is a facultative homoiotherm that becomes torpid at night, thereby avoiding depletion of the body's energy reserves at night, when the hummingbird cannot feed. (*From Yapp, after Pearson.*)

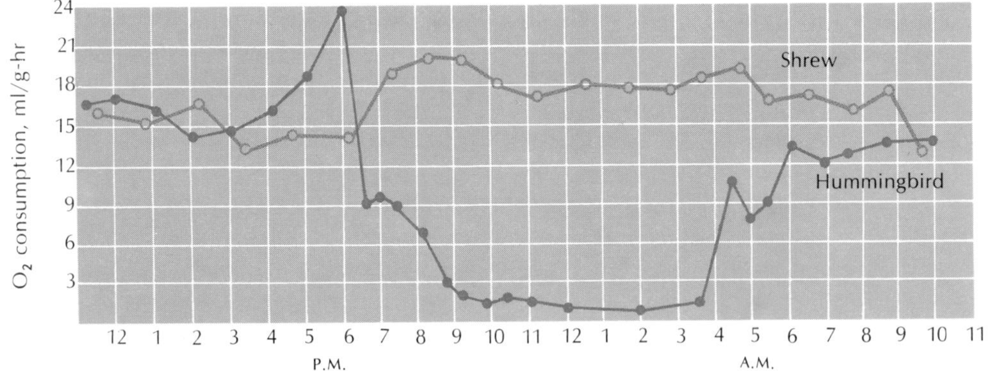

There are a number of interesting differences between *hibernators* and facultative homoiotherms. The latter (like poikilotherms) are subject to *cold narcosis,* an obligate torpor that overcomes them as ambient temperatures sharply decline. Arousal is dependent upon an external source of heat and is not spontaneous as in hibernators. Hibernation, on the contrary, is an event for which the animal becomes physiologically prepared by a prehibernatory period of overeating and rapid fat deposition. Special depots of brown fat, a tissue containing unusually high concentrations of unsaturated triglycerides and phospholipids, are accumulated. Large quantities of Mg^{2+} are also stored by hibernating species (increases of from 25 to 92 percent have been recorded). This ion does not seem to be involved in the onset of hibernation, but its sedative effect on the nervous system promotes quiescence.

Hibernation may begin in food-deprived ground squirrels even when ambient temperatures exceed 30°C. Metabolic activities decline dramatically during hibernation, thyroid activity being depressed and the basal metabolic rate declining to values ranging from 1 to 30 percent of the waking level. In the ground squirrel, breathing declines from 100 to 200 per minute to 4 per minute. Breathing continues even at a body temperature of 5°C in a hibernator (but ceases at a body temperature of 19°C in a cold-narcotized homoiotherm*), and exhibits positive feedback control, for it follows a periodic pattern known as Cheyne-Stokes respiration that is also typical of infant and dying mammals. This periodic breathing is interrupted by a long interval of apnea (lack of breathing); at last a short, shallow breath is taken, followed by a series of progressively deepening breaths until a peak is reached at which breathing is abolished and another apneic period ensues. During hibernation brain activity (as monitored by electroencephalograph) declines to only 10 percent of its waking level, but this residual activity seems to be nonrandom and to be centered in regions concerned with physiological regulation.

Excess cold may actually arouse a hibernator, for if its tissues should come dangerously close to freezing, internal heat production is stepped up. An interesting oddity of hibernatory species is that their adrenal cortex not only fails to respond to cold with the cold-stress response usual in nonhibernators, but in fact adrenalectomized animals entirely fail to hibernate. When adrenalectomized hamsters and ground squirrels are injected with glucocorticoids, they regain the capacity to hibernate.

A hibernator can be aroused by the application of external heat, but the breaking of hibernation does not require this. Instead, internal heat production increases very suddenly, resulting in a rise in body temperature of around 20°C/hr. The oxidation of brown fat may be an especially good heat source. During arousal, heat production in the marmot may equal 3,000 kcal/m^2 a day.

The thermoregulatory mechanisms of both birds and mammals come into play gradually during maturation. Some species such as caribou are effective thermoregulators at birth, while others are virtually poikilothermic for some days, and must depend on the parents' body heat or be able to bear chilling. For instance, a young rat is capable of complete thermoregulation only after it is about 2.5 months old.

16.3 □ BEHAVIOR

An organism's behavior consists of observable changes in motor activities in response to external or internal stimulation. Five major types of behavioral responses can be distinguished: (1) a change in the rate and direction of *locomotion* or *movement of body parts* (which may involve interruption of a previous activity as well as the initiation of movement); (2) production of *sound,* often by some type of vocal or stridulatory apparatus and usually as a means of communication; (3) production of *electrical discharges,* when such discharges can be modulated in frequency or amplitude and when they are emitted in self-defense, to stun prey, or to facilitate orientation; (4) generation of *light,* especially in patterned bursts such as firefly flashing "codes" that serve as recognition signals between conspecifics; (5) *color changes* in the presence of conspecifics or as a response to danger.

Whatever the specific character of the response, behavior serves to modify the organism's stimulus situation in such a way that either the behavior is reinforced and continues to be performed (positive feedback) or else it is abolished (negative feedback) and a new behavior substituted. For example, as an animal approaches a food source the stimuli emanating from the food are intensified, promoting further movement in the same direction. On the other hand, detection of a noxious stimulus causes the animal to move away from it, until eventually the animal is so far from the stimulus that it no longer is operative and the avoidance reaction ceases. Similarly, internal stimuli that produce the sensation of hunger promote feeding behavior; then, as feeding continues other internal stimuli are substituted, such as feelings of fullness in the stomach, and food intake is discontinued.

*Such cessation of breathing is tolerable because cell metabolism is nearly arrested and the need for oxygen is negligible.

A Approaches to the study of behavior

The analysis of the characteristics, causes, and underlying mechanisms of behavior represents an important field of investigation in which many vital questions await answer. Because it is difficult to observe an animal's performance without equating it with our own behavior and motivation, and because we often find the latter very difficult to analyze in scientific terms, the study of behavior was long hampered by anthropomorphism (a tendency to explain the actions of animals in human terms) and vitalism (a doctrine that asserts the behavior of organisms to be inexplicable in terms of physiological mechanisms and hence views it as ultimately outside the range of scientific analysis). In 1893 C. Lloyd Morgan set forth an empirical statement of philosophy that significantly changed the climate for behavioral research by rejecting both anthropomorphic and vitalistic frames of reference: "In no case may we interpret an action as the outcome of the exercise of a higher psychical faculty, if it can be interpreted as the outcome of one which stands lower in the psychological scale." Morgan's canon, rigidly interpreted, has not been found to suffice in all instances, especially when one is dealing with the behavior of higher vertebrates, but it served to liberate the study of behavior from its previous philosophical impasse and launched the first scientific attack upon an area which had heretofore been thought impregnable.

This attack has become interdisciplinary in nature, for scientists of various backgrounds and persuasions are converging upon the problem of behavioral analysis: *ethologists,* who as biologists with basic interests in heredity and ecology seek mainly to disclose the adaptive relevance, evolutionary history, and genetic basis for the organism's behavior in its natural milieu; *psychologists,* who as social scientists are often primarily concerned with analysis of human behavior and learning processes, but who have also contributed significantly to the study of animal behavior; and *neurophysiologists,* who are investigating the neuroendocrine mechanisms underlying reception and response.

The major techniques of ethology include the following. (1) The organism is preferably first observed in its natural environment, without experimental intervention. In this way the outward physical characteristics of the behavioral pattern may be analyzed in the circumstances under which it normally occurs. Excellent field studies conducted recently upon wild chimpanzees revealed hitherto unsuspected facets of their normal behavior (such as the ability to modify twigs into tools suitable for probing into termite hills) that had gone undetected through the many years in which these primates were used as laboratory animals. Similarly, the study of the communication systems of honeybees has mainly involved observation of free-ranging bees, although the investigator must use a hive in which the interior can be viewed and may modify the situation to a point by setting out feeding stations at known locations. (2) The *field experiment* has proven a powerful tool, especially as employed by such perceptive investigators as N. Tinbergen. Here the animal remains in its natural habitat (or some reasonable facsimile) while the experimenter intervenes to a restricted extent. In this way the use of memorized landmarks by the hunting wasp *Philanthus* was discovered, simply by setting up such landmarks and then moving them (Figure 16.17). The effectiveness of stimuli can also be tested in the field, by such means as presenting gull chicks with simplified models of the adult's head, offering a bird a giant egg, or displacing birds' eggs or nestlings to discover whether they will be recognized and retrieved. The responses of animals to predators and to others of their own kind have been tested in the field in such ways as playing a recording of the song of a male bird within the established territory of another male of the same species, playing recordings of the songs of male locusts (which are found to attract females from a distance), and setting out simplified models, such as crude owl shapes with painted eyes. (3) After having conducted whatever studies are possible in the field, the ethologist may then resort to laboratory procedures to investigate those aspects of behavior which are not particularly amenable to analysis with free-ranging animals. Experiments conducted on confined subjects are usually oriented toward further definition of the inducing stimuli, toward clarification of the extent to which a given behavior is genetically programmed or must be acquired on the basis of individual experience and the like. Many significant data have been obtained by such means as (*a*) rearing animals in isolation and then exposing them to normal and abnormal sensory cues, (*b*) cross fostering of birds' eggs or newborn mammals to adults of another species, and (*c*) obtaining interracial and interspecific hy-

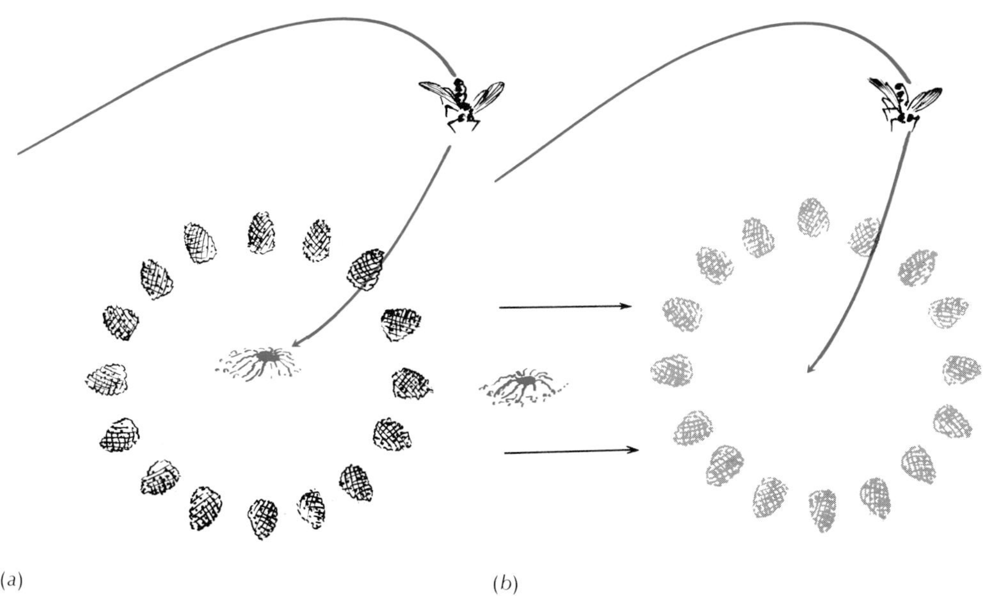

Figure 16.17 □ **Field experiment on homing in the wasp *Philanthus*. (*a*) *Philanthus* nest ringed with 16 pine cones. (*b*) Ring of cones shifted away from nest; misdirection of wasp indicates that she had used the ring of cones as a landmark in locating the nest. Such landmarks are memorized by the insect in only a few seconds before she first leaves the vicinity of the nest. (*After N. Tinbergen.*)**

brids (by artificial insemination if necessary), which may exhibit hybrid behavior patterns.

The strengths and weaknesses of psychological approaches to the analysis of behavior more or less complement those of ethology, which make the two sciences good teammates. Ethologists often deal with multiple variables, recognizing that the more carefully a stimulus situation is controlled, the less apt is the behavior to follow its natural course. In fact animals confined in artificial environments often develop pathological behavior, which at best is a distorted reflection of the normal patterns. However, multivariant situations are often nearly impossible to analyze and present difficulties that may also lead to mistakes in interpretation. Psychologists, on the other hand, have tended to emphasize the one-variable experimental situation, carefully controlled and subject to statistical analysis. Where possible they may simplify their measurement of response to a clean-cut "yes-no" alternative, which purposely ignores nuances meaningful to the ethologist (such as subtle intention movements and expressions of ambivalence) for the sake of obtaining a readily quantifiable set of data. Despite the artificialities of the test situation, these techniques have yielded much valuable insight, particularly upon the nature of learning. However, when human-oriented psychologists attempt to extend to nonmammals techniques that have proven successful with mammals (in order, for instance, to compare "intelligence"), they must recognize the fact that experimental situations suitable for mammals may be completely irrelevant for other animals. Rats and mice are naturally investigative in strange quarters, so maze-running conforms with their normal approach to things; a bird, on the other hand, may thoroughly catalog its environment visually without moving from its perch, and it would never "cross its mind" to run through a maze. Furthermore, even if the test performance appears similar, it cannot be concluded that the learning processes correspond. Both rats and ants learn to run mazes with facility, and yet there is evidence that the learning processes involved are drastically different. Some investigators have concluded that ants learn a maze from start to finish, and gradually cut out alternative routes that do not lead to the feeding place, whereas rats learn a maze from the goal backwards. Originally locating the feeding place by chance (as ants also must do), rats seem first to memorize the final turns leading to the goal, then the turning points farther away from the goal, and so forth, until they know the route from the starting place.

Neurophysiologists employ the techniques summarized in Chapter 15. Whereas ethologists and psychologists tend more or less to deal with the intact animal and study whole-organism responses to changes in external conditions, neurophysiologists pry the lid off the "box" and try to work out its "wiring diagram" (Figure 16.18). This can be done by removing glands or parts of the nervous system, by glandular transplants, by surgically displacing limbs or receptors or creating artificial nerve connections, and by electrode stimulation. The results obtained are often difficult to correlate with observed behavior, but in this respect quite promising techniques have involved the use of implanted electrodes to locate specific brain centers that control particular behaviors. Such work done with invertebrates has revealed the existence of *command neurons,* individual cells which, when stimulated by microelectrodes, trigger an entire behavioral sequence. Several such command neurons have been identified in the brain of a sea slug (*Tritonia*), any of which can evoke the animal's entire "escape response."

Figure 16.18 □ Comparison of approaches to behavioral analysis. (*a*) Ethological: left, observor *O* and subject *S* free-ranging and interacting; right, observer hidden in blind, subject ranging free and undisturbed. (*b*) Psychological: observer free, subject confined in controlled test situation. (*c*) Neurophysiological: observer opens the "black box" (the intact organism) to examine internal mechanisms.

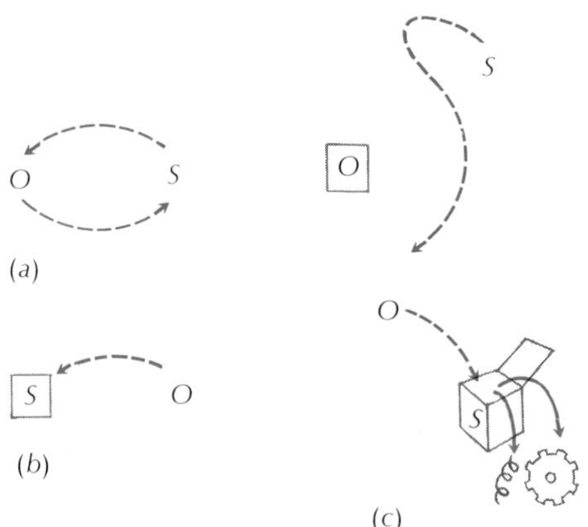

B The concept of intervening variables

During their early attempts to apply Morgan's canon, students of behavior attempted to reduce to series of reflexes and forced movements (*tropisms*) even the most complex action patterns. To a point it is true that a number of animals seem to move automatically along a stimulus gradient (although we now call this type of oriented movement a *taxis* instead of a tropism) and, if we choose to include in the term "reflex" even neural pathways which include many interneurons, almost any form of behavior may be considered reflexive. Yet both of these concepts imply an automatic response to each stimulus (in which case the animal should always respond in the same way), and this of course is simply not the case, even with so-called lower animals. Between stimulus and response stand many intervening variables, so that the response is not fully predictable; instead, the *probability* of a given response's being performed can be estimated with more or less confidence by identifying and weighting these variables. Some of the most important variables include: (1) the factor of selective input; (2) central inhibition when conflicting stimuli are presented; (3) motivation or "drives"; (4) the effect of enduring physiological states; (5) the effects of previous experience.

SELECTIVE INPUT Sensory and perceptual filters operate at all levels, from the receptor to the highest brain centers, determining that certain stimuli may provoke no response at the organismal level, whereas others may bring about a response so intense as to appear quite disproportionate. As we shall note below, perception is greatly influenced by previous experience, for the animal may learn to ignore stimuli that lack relevance while at the same time becoming sensitized to other stimuli, however slight, that furnish meaningful cues. We are all familiar with the sight of a household pet napping while the television blares forth the din and clash of a "blood-and-thunder" epic, yet awakening instantly to the faint click of the refrigerator door. Selective sensitization to specific stimuli can also be genetically programmed in the course of evolution, for (as we have seen) certain sign stimuli, the significance of which need not be learned, can trigger the animal's total response even when presented in irrelevant contexts (see Figures 4.13 and 7.18).

It has been proposed that such stimuli be termed *releasers,* for they serve to release patterns of innate behavior (that is, behavior which is not primarily based on learning) by activating the brain centers that govern such behavior. In some cases, very discrete stimuli are found to have releaser value. For example, a red spot near the tip of a sea gull's beak directs its chick's pecking response (which in turn provokes food regurgitation

Figure 16.19 □ **Supernormal stimuli.** **(*a*) Oystercatcher attempts to brood artificial giant egg in preference to her own egg or to a herring gull's egg. [*After N. Tinbergen,* The Study of Instinct *(Oxford: The Clarendon Press)*]. (*b*) Stimuli provided by cuckoo nestling divert food-bearing parent birds bound for their own nests and cause them to feed the young cuckoo instead. (*Courtesy of Karoly Koffán.*)**

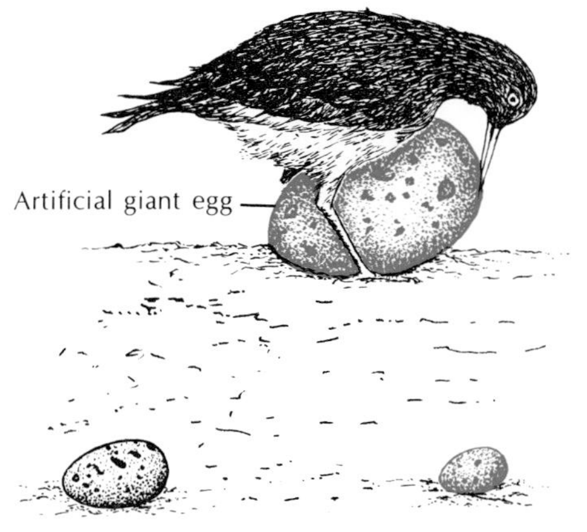

(*a*)

(*b*)

by the parent) more effectively than does the total head shape. If the spot is displaced on a model, the pecking response is still directed toward the spot and not toward the tip of the beak. Sometimes a stimulus can be found which has even greater releaser value than the normal one. When a gull or oystercatcher is presented with an artificial egg much larger than a real one, the bird ignores its own egg and struggles to pull the giant egg into the nest (Figure 16.19). The neural centers that control innate behaviors can also be affected by internally generated stimuli, for such behaviors are known sometimes to take place in the absence of the appropriate releasers.

CENTRAL INHIBITION When conflicting stimuli are presented together, the animal may respond to only one. This need not involve conscious choice. For example, if the spinal cord of a dog is severed just below the point at which the phrenic nerve is given off to the diaphragm, the animal remains alive but is unable to initiate voluntary movements. However, it can still respond by spinal reflex arcs to stimuli applied to the trunk or limbs. Electrical stimulation of an area of skin covering much of the back and sides triggers a scratch reflex, in which the leg on the same side is lifted and moved rhythmically at the rate of about four strokes per second. If a painful shock is given to one paw, a withdrawal reflex is evoked. Now, if one simultaneously presents stimuli that should elicit both reflexes, there is no behavioral conflict: the scratching reflex is instantaneously abolished and the withdrawal reflex immediately activated. Here central inhibition is operating at the level of the spinal cord: only one of the two stimuli determines the response, and the activation of one pathway inhibits the other.

MOTIVATION No area of study is more plagued with imprecise language than that relating to the more or less transient internal states determining whether at a given moment an animal will feed, attempt to copulate, or pick up a piece of nesting material. The very term *motivation* seems to imply conscious foreknowledge of the results of a behavior pattern. Watching a bird building a nest, we are tempted to believe that the bird "knows" it is preparing a shelter for its future young. In higher vertebrates we cannot rule out the possibility that hunger, for instance, conjures up a "mental picture" of the accustomed feeding place, whereupon the animal moves in that direction. But generally speaking it is doubtful that such an image of the goal is held; it is more probable that the animal merely responds in accordance with its internal state, without predicting the outcome.

The internally motivated urge to behave in a certain way is known as a *drive.* The drive concept has little value when we equate it with categories that are too broad, such as a drive toward "maternal behavior." Maternal behavior has many aspects and correspondingly involves many different drives, not all of which operate at any given moment. A drive can be generated by some disturbance of physiological homeostasis. We have seen earlier in this chapter that animals may thermoregulate behaviorally, moving into the sun when chilled and retreating to the shade when warmed. We have also noted that water-seeking and drinking responses are evoked from hypothalamic control centers that gauge increases in blood solute concentration.

However, all drives cannot be equated with clear-cut physiological needs: a well-fed cat may exhibit a drive to hunt and may then toy with the prey instead of eating it; a rat placed in new quarters has an investigative drive that leads it to explore every nook and cranny.

The strength of a drive may be either intensified or reduced by deprivation. Starvation merely intensifies the urge to eat, up to the point at which physiological derangements become so acute that behavior is no longer normal. Isolation may generate a drive to seek and come into contact with other members of one's species. On the other hand, absence of appropriate stimulation may in time cause a drive toward mating to wane. In general, however, performing a *consummatory act* (one that satisfies the drive, such as eating, drinking, or mating) reduces the intensity of the drive.

Figure 16.20 □ Peacock courtship display misdirected toward Burmese jungle fowl. Performance of a social behavior pattern in the absence of an appropriate stimulus object indicates that internal factors (such as sex hormones) disposing the individual toward this behavior have reached a high level of intensity. These birds range freely in the San Diego Zoo. (*Courtesy of H. Warren.*)

The strength of a drive can be experimentally estimated in terms of the amount of punishment an animal will withstand in attempting consummation. When its need becomes sufficiently acute, an animal will cross an electrified grid to reach food, drink, its mate, or its young. If an animal is placed in an isolation chamber in which it can learn to press separate buttons for food, drink, or the sight of another animal, the relative strengths of the three drives can be estimated from the number of times each button is pressed in a given period. As we saw in Chapter 15, electrodes inserted into hypothalamic centers associated with various essential functions (such as eating, drinking, and mating) and connected to a circuit that permits the animal to stimulate its own brain may result in repeated self-stimulation, sometimes even replacing the actual consummatory act. Thus, fulfillment of a drive may evoke a pleasurable sensation (by stimulation of the relevant brain centers), reinforcing the performance of that behavior.

ENDURING PHYSIOLOGICAL STATES
Fluctuations in drive intensity are superimposed onto the animal's basal physiological state, which also influences its behavior. The individual's overall state of development is important, for the appearance of certain behavior patterns depends upon attainment of the appropriate level of neuromotor maturation. For instance, the feeding behavior of a butterfly will differ drastically from that of the caterpillar it once was. In alleviating a hunger drive a butterfly may respond to a floral odor, alight, and then probe the nectaries with its long proboscis. As a larva it would instead have sought out certain kinds of foliage and attacked them with its biting jaws.

Reproductive rhythms are associated with relatively long-term fluctuations in hormonal state, which in turn determine how an animal is likely, say, to respond to a potential mate or rival, or to the sight of a nest box. If the animal is physiologically prepared to mate, the lack of a partner may cause its sexual behavior to be directed toward some inappropriate stimulus object. Free-ranging peacocks in the San Diego Zoo have been seen courting anything from a jungle fowl (Figure 16.20) to an emu. What is more, a rooster reared in isolation may direct otherwise normal courting behavior toward such objects as a feather plucked from his own body and tossed repeatedly into the air. Since he cannot copulate with a feather, the drive cannot be satisfied by completing the consummatory act, and this abberant behavior may tend to persist for as long as the rooster's hormonal state so predisposes him.

EFFECTS OF PREVIOUS EXPERIENCE
An animal's behavior may change from day to day, on the basis of what has gone before. One cause of changing behavior is that the animal learns which responses are most effective, and tends to repeat those. An animal placed in a test situation where the performance of a learned task has some desirable consequence may even "learn to learn," that is, develops *learning set;* by this we mean that once the initial association is made between the test situation and the possibility of reward, an animal of sufficient acumen will become responsive to its test

surroundings, as though actively seeking stimuli toward which reward-producing responses may be directed. The importance of learning as an intervening variable is so great that we shall consider it in detail later.

Antecedent events may also change the animal's behavior in ways that do not involve learning. A virgin screw fly responds positively to the presence of a courting male, but having once mated she will copulate no more, rejects all suitors, and begins instead to search for an appropriate host on which to lay her eggs. Similar but more involved sequences are seen in birds, where the completion of each step in a progression of events abolishes the previous behavior pattern and activates the next. Thus, completion of the nest abolishes nest-building activity (destruction of the nest may initiate it once more) and stimulates copulatory and egg-laying activities. The sight and/or feel of an appropriate clutch of eggs in the nest in turn abolishes copulatory behavior and egg laying, and stimulates incubating behavior. This in turn gives way to feeding and hovering patterns when the eggs hatch and new stimuli emanate from the nestlings. Finally, the attainment of a certain state of maturity by the young causes their effectiveness as stimuli to wane, the feeding and care-giving responses diminish, and the parents now may abandon the young, which should be capable of fending for themselves.

C The organization of behavior

An animal tends to respond to any intensification of internal motivation by beginning to move about more or less randomly, until it eventually finds itself in the presence of a stimulus that releases the terminal response, or *consummatory act,* whereby the drive is satisfied. For instance, a female mammal in heat (estrus) displays her sexual receptivity by restlessly running about, apparently seeking a mate. If caged alone, she may translate this restlessness into vigorous use of her exercise wheel.

The preliminary activity leading up to the release of the consummatory act is known as *appetitive behavior;* it is at this stage that behavior is most subject to modification by learning. In general, consummatory acts are those such as eating, drinking, courting, mating, nest building, and various aspects of the care of young, which are so essential to the survival of the individual or the species that their completion cannot be left to chance. Instead, they tend to consist of stereotyped *fixed action patterns* that have evolved along with other characteristics of the species.* On the other hand, appetitive behavior tends to be more flexible and is governed by the situation at hand. Plasticity in appetitive behavior not only increases the likelihood that the animal will be able to place itself in a situation stimulating release of the consummatory act, but that with experience it can minimize the expenditure of time and energy required to find the same situation again.

In these two types of activity, appetitive and consummatory, we find the two major adaptive components of animal behavior: (1) the fixed action pattern, simple or elaborate, primarily determined by the inherited properties of the muscular and nervous systems and, although subject to some degree of individual variation, tending by and large to be typical of the species; (2) the modifiable action pattern, primarily organized through learning and representing the variable aspect of adaptive behavior.

*Although subject to individual variation (like any presumably polygenically inherited trait), the fixed action pattern is sufficiently predictable when studied at a population level to be useful even to taxonomists as a trustworthy criterion of the animal group under consideration.

FIXED ACTION PATTERNS Two types of fixed action patterns are the *reflex* and the *instinct.* The former is a relatively simple and highly automatic stimulus-bound response that represents a fundamental unit of behavior. A reflex is a unit of motor response, such as jerking away from a painful stimulus or blinking when some object rapidly approaches the head. Balance, muscle tone, and physiological response also depend on reflexes. As we saw in Chapter 15, a reflex depends upon an organizational unit in the nervous system, termed the reflex arc, which usually consists of a sensory neuron, interneuron, and motor neuron. Although highly automatic, reflexes can be modified or suppressed by higher brain centers. A reflex can also be *conditioned* by presenting a conditioning stimulus along with the normal stimulus, such as ringing a bell before mealtime; eventually salivation will come to be elicited by the dinner bell alone, without food being presented.

An *instinct* is characterized by the fact that a single stimulus (or more often a series of related stimuli) triggers a complex set of actions that appear to be programmed within the central nervous system. Criteria of an instinct include the following: (1) it is constant in form and characteristic of the species; (2) it is more complex than a simple reflex and often involves the coordination of several organ systems; (3) its release is dependent upon specific environmental stimuli that the animal seeks out by appetitive behavior impelled by internal drives; (4) it appears in animals reared in isolation from their own kind and in animals prevented from learning it during development; (5) it can, at least within the limits of neuromuscular development, be prematurely evoked by hormone injections (if the instinctive behavior is one which depends on the animal's hormonal state, such as mating).

ACTS AND ACT SYSTEMS Complex action patterns, whether fixed or modifiable, can often be analyzed in terms of unitary components termed *acts*. An act is a relatively simple and distinct behavioral unit: the term reflex implies the existence of a sensory-association-motor neural circuit, whereas when we speak of an act we imply nothing concerning the causative neural organization but refer only to the behavior itself. Some acts may indeed depend upon reflex arcs; others may arise from impulses generated internally without immediate reference to sensory input. During development, acts are gradually correlated into more elaborate sequences called *act systems*. If the organization of acts into an act system is mainly determined by heredity, the act system corresponds to a fixed action pattern or instinct. The acts that make up a given act system may appear in correct sequence during maturation ($A + B + C + D. . .$) but the adaptive significance of the response may not be apparent until the entire system has developed. On the other hand, individual acts may first be performed at random and later be automatically assembled into the right sequence at the proper stage of maturation; alternatively, they may become sometimes correlated as a result of learning.

An excellent study of cocoon-spinning behavior in the American silkworm (*Cecropia*) showed that this apparently complex act system can be resolved into only three or four unitary motor patterns or acts. The first of these ("stretch-bend"), performed with the caterpillar head-upright on a vertical support, consists of extreme bending of the anterior part of the body to one side, a movement that brings the caterpillar's head into contact with a horizontal surface below and allows a radial thread of silk to be attached. The larva turns around at fixed intervals; during the spinning of the outer part of the cocoon turning about takes place approximately every 40 min. The next act ("swing-swing") is performed with the caterpillar head-down, swinging its anterior end from side to side and spinning out a flat web of silk. When the animal's weaving brings it into contact with threads already laid down, a figure-eight movement of the head is added to the basic body movement. When about 60 percent of the silk has been spun out of the silk glands, the animal starts to spin the cocoon's dense lining, using the same acts but within a progressively diminishing space, turning about only every 170 min. The essence of this system is that a few acts are rhythmically repeated and alternated to produce a functionally effective sequence.

Hybridization of species or races is particularly revealing in the analysis of act systems, for the hybrid progeny may exhibit portions of the two parental act systems and if these are incompatible certain adaptive responses may be blocked. Several species of lovebirds (*Agapornis*) collect nesting materials by clipping strips of paper (when provided) or other vegetable material. According to the species of lovebird, these strips are then carried to the nesting cavity, either held singly in the beak or tucked into the tail feathers (Figure 16.21). The clip-and-tuck behavior involves at least three identifiable acts: clipping, tucking, and letting go of the material once it has been secured in the plumage. Hybrids produced by mating a clip-and-tuck species with a clip-and-carry species are found to be capable of both clipping and tucking, but at this point the act system breaks down, for the hybrids are unable to open their bills to release the material which has been tucked into the tail feathers and it is brought away from the plumage in the beak. Prolonged and frustrating sessions of tucking and attempting to let go ensue, which end in the hybrid's flying off to the nest bearing a single strip in its beak. Eventually the tucking attempt wanes but even after several years persists as abortive intention movements.

Resistance to the infectious disease of honeybees known as American foulbrood has been found essentially to depend upon a two-act system. The two acts appear to be controlled by genes that assort independently. After a period of feeding the larvae, worker bees cap the larval cells in preparation for pupation. If larvae die within the sealed cells, the foulbrood-resistant strain responds by uncapping the cells and removing the dead larvae from the hive. Susceptible strains neither uncap the cells nor remove dead larvae, which therefore remain as foci from which disease-producing bacteria can spread. Note that although this behavior is manifested only by workers, its genetic basis is transmissible only through the reproductive castes, which do

Figure 16.21 □ **Acts in the nest-building sequence of the peach-faced lovebird, *Agapornis roseicollis:* (*a*) clipping paper strips for use as nest material; (*b*) tucking strips into the rump feathers for transport to the nest hole. Fischer's lovebird (*A. fischeri*) also clips strips of material but carries each strip singly in the beak instead of tucked into the plumage. Hybrids produced by crossing *A. roseicollis* and *A. fischeri* attempt to tuck the clippings into their rump feathers but are unable to complete this act successfully and eventually must carry the materials in the beak. (*Courtesy of Dr. William C. Dilger.*)**

(*a*)

(*b*)

not engage in such activities. When queens of the resistant strain are mated with drones of the susceptible strain (or vice versa), the F_1 progeny fail to perform these defensive activities. If an F_1 hybrid queen is now test-crossed by being mated with a drone of the resistant strain, four classes of progeny are produced in equal proportions: (1) workers which can both uncap cells and remove dead larvae; (2) workers which uncap cells containing dead larvae, but then fail to remove the larvae; (3) workers which cannot uncap the cells, but will remove the dead larvae if the human investigator intervenes and uncaps the cells; (4) workers which are unable to uncap the cells and fail to remove the larvae even after the cells have been uncapped by the investigator. These results can be explained on the basis of inheritance of two independently assorting genes, which we shall call *A* and *B*—one concerned with the uncapping act, the other with removal of dead larvae. The recessive allele of gene *A* allows uncapping to be carried out successfully, whereas this motor pattern is not expressed in workers carrying the dominant allele; similarly, the recessive allele of gene *B* is concerned with the act of removal, which cannot be performed by workers carrying the dominant allele. The possible inheritance of the two-act system can thus be summarized as shown in the following schema:

This does not imply that genes *A* and *B* are the only ones involved in the genetic organization of each act. Each may instead control but one step in a sequence of reactions by which the act is encoded in the bee's nervous system.

DISPLACEMENT BEHAVIOR AND RITUALIZATION Displacement behavior involves the insertion of apparently irrelevant acts into the particular act system being performed. It appears when the performance of the appropriate act system is somehow being inhibited. This may occur when a stimulus situation evokes conflicting tendencies, such as a tendency to attack and a tendency to flee. A male stickleback restrained from attacking a rival male by a glass partition dividing the aquarium may resort to vigorous displacement digging, an activity that is a normal constituent of the nest-building sequence but in this case is pursued to such lengths that the animal may literally dig itself into the substratum, disappearing into a yawning pit. A pair of avocets engaged in fighting may suddenly turn away, tucking their heads under their wings and apparently falling immediately asleep. So-called displacement grooming is seen in many kinds of animals when they are caught in a dilemma as to which of two courses of action must be chosen or when they find themselves in a situation where an appropriate course of behavior is blocked.

Susceptible queen; no uncapping or removing	*AABB*♀ × *aabb*♂ ↓	Resistant drone; uncapping and removing
F_1	*AaBb*	Heterozygous; workers neither uncap nor remove
Hybrid queen	*AaBb*♀ × *aabb*♂ ↓	Testcross to resistant drone
	¼ *A_B_*	Can neither uncap nor remove
	¼ *aaB_*	Uncap but fail to remove
	¼ *A_bb*	Cannot uncap but can remove
	¼ *aabb*	Both uncap and remove

The evocation of displacement behaviors has yet to be satisfactorily explained in neurophysiological terms but may be an outcome of the organization of the central nervous system, which allows excitation to be transferred into alternative pathways if the appropriate one is somehow blocked. An interesting phenomenon discovered in locusts may shed light both on the neural basis of some types of displacement behavior, as well as how new acts may be recruited into a given act system in the course of behavioral evolution. Electrode monitoring has revealed that when impulses are sent from the central nervous system to sets of muscles engaged in carrying out a particular activity (such as walking), identical patterns of discharge—but at lower frequencies—are simultaneously sent through other, irrelevant motor channels. For example, during walking the pattern of impulses sent to the legs is mirrored by a pattern sent to the wing muscles but at a frequency too low to trigger any actual wing movements. This would appear to indicate that the control sequence for a new act may already be present at subthreshold levels. Should the threshold for expression be lowered, the new act may appear and undergo selection in a different context, perhaps becoming useful in communication rather than in locomotion. For instance, wing vibrating in the fly *Drosophila* is not a locomotory act but instead is one of several acts constituting the courtship ritual.

Figure 16.22 □ **"Facing away" display of the black-headed gull. This appeasement posture reduces the intensity of aggressive tendencies and serves during courtship to accustom potential mates to one another's physical proximity. The facial mask (worn only in breeding) acts as a distance-increasing adaptation, for it intimidates and repels other gulls. (*Courtesy of N. Tinbergen.*)**

It is essential to bear in mind that when we term a behavior "displacement" and assume it to be irrelevant to the situation at hand, we are actually defining relevancy in terms of our expectations. There may in fact be no such thing as true displacement behavior. Displacement grooming, for instance, may not be irrelevant but may serve adaptively to quiet the nervous system by reducing tension built up in the conflict situation.

Under some conditions what may possibly be displacement behavior may be recruited into a new context and come to appear as a regular element of that behavior. Again, this may well reflect ambivalence or generation of conflicting behavioral tendencies. Courtship rituals often reflect such ambivalence, since the close approach necessary for mating may also give rise to aggressive-defensive (agonistic) tendencies. In this event, placatory ("appeasement") gestures may serve to relieve the tensions apparently generated by such unavoidable proximity. The "facing away" display of black-headed gulls (and related species) serves to break eye contact and reduce the probability of an actual attack taking place during an agonistic encounter (Figure 16.22). As a tension-alleviating device this display is also useful in the courtship ritual, although not immediately relevant to the act of mating. Ethological analysis of courtship behavior often shows it to be an amalgam of approach tendencies intermixed with threat and appeasement gestures, also showing elements of parental behavior.

Recruitment of patterns of behavior into new contexts often infuses them with a communicative significance that leads toward their ritualization. In our earlier discussion of animal communication (see Section 7.3C) we noted that communicative displays tend to evolve toward stereotyped patterns. This applies as well to any displacement behavior recruited into a new act system—its performance may become ritualized, often exaggerated (in a motor sense), as seen in the displacement preening of courting drakes (see Figure 7.17). The exaggeration and "artificiality" of a ritualized behavior usually makes unlikely its being confused with the original act from which it was derived.

The recruitment of any preexisting behavior into a context other than that in which it evolved implies that the behavior becomes *emancipated* from those stimuli that formerly evoked its performance and falls instead under the control of cues relevant to the new association. Since this is not a learned or conditioned change, but one that is genetically based, we must eventually seek to understand behavioral emancipation and recruitment in terms of the "wiring" of the nervous system as determined by heredity.

D Learning

Behavioral flexibility depends upon the organism's ability to modify its responses on the basis of experience. All forms of learning involve *retentivity*—the capacity to remember the outcome of a previous response to a given stimulus. More complex forms of learning also involve *ideational* capabilities (which permit the animal to compare alternatives and in some cases to invent new solutions on the basis of associations derived from previous experiences).

In order to be learned, a given behavior must ordinarily be *reinforced.* Reinforcement is commonly used to denote a reward or desirable outcome following performance of the behavior (such as the finding of food at the end of a maze), but it may equally refer to a painful outcome which the animal learns to avoid. If, for instance, an animal is placed in a training box furnished with a lever that it can move, should pressing this lever bring a reward the animal quickly associates this act with the reward and repeats it. If, on the other hand, pressing the lever produces an electric shock, the animal learns to avoid the lever. If no reinforcement, either positive or negative, results from moving the lever, the animal will henceforth ignore it. The process of acquiring a behavior by associating its performance with a reinforcement is termed *operant conditioning.* After a behavior has been acquired by operant conditioning, it may undergo *extinction* upon removal of the reinforcement: if the animal has learned to associate food with lever pressing and then no more food is given in this manner, lever pressing will soon be given up as an unprofitable pastime. Extinction does not necessarily involve *forgetting,* for the same response will be relearned more rapidly a second time.

TYPES OF LEARNING At least four important types of learning can be recognized: habituation, trial-and-error, latent learning, and insight learning. These categories intergrade and all contain examples of widely varying complexity. *Habituation* involves the relatively permanent waning of a response, when that response fails to change the stimulus situation or when the stimulus proves to be meaningless in terms of reinforcement. For example, if a snail is given a mild electrical shock on the tip of one tentacle, it initially responds by withdrawing the tentacle, but should the shocks continue despite such withdrawal the animal eventually will extend the tentacle again and will "ignore" the shock. Habituation is also seen when a male Siamese fighting fish is presented with a model of another male; at first it attacks the model promptly and with enthusiasm, but since the latter does not counterattack or retreat the response wanes and eventually the model is ignored.

Trial-and-error is a common form of learning even in man. It results from the association of a stimulus with a response that, when tried by chance, has proven adaptive in meeting that situation. When faced with a novel stimulus situation, the organism responds by trying out various courses of action. Eventually the most effective response (the one most consistently reinforced and demanding least effort) tends to be adopted, with elimination of less effectual modes of behavior.

Insight learning occurs in higher mammals at least, and involves a grasp of relationships that permits learned responses acquired in different but relevant situations experienced earlier to be used in new ways. In this manner the animal may solve a problem by abridging or skipping the process of trial-and-error. It is as though alternatives are mentally reviewed and on the basis of the visualized outcomes the one apparently most appropriate is selected for overt expression.

Latent learning takes place in the absence of identifiable reinforcement, and the fact that learning has taken place at all may not be recognized until much later. Latent learning may consist of familiarization with a stimulus situation, allowing a more effective choice to be made among alternative responses at a subsequent time when some reinforcement is introduced. As mentioned earlier, a rat allowed to familiarize itself with a maze before food is placed in the goal box will learn the pathway leading to the goal box when food is placed there much more rapidly than a rat unfamiliar with the maze. In other words, latent learning has taken place in the course of random exploration of the maze and may be put to use when food is introduced.

Imprinting (discussed in Section 11.3C) may constitute a form of latent learning, for it may have delayed effects not detectable until the imprinted animal reaches maturity. In precocial birds imprinting involves the fixation of an innate tendency to follow any moving object, upon the first moving object seen during a critical period soon after hatching; however, the longer-term value of imprinting is that it may also serve normally to acquaint a young animal with the adult of its species, allowing it later to recognize a suitable mate. Under experimental conditions imprinting may result in redirection of the mating drive toward some inappropriate object. This redirection may be so compulsive as to make normal mating impossible when the animal reaches maturity.

Another example of latent learning is seen in the case of certain species of birds such as chaffinch that learn their species' song upon hearing it only once as a juvenile. Chaffinches reared in isolation and not permitted to hear the song of their own species during youth prove incapable of singing a complete song later on. However if a chaffinch being reared in isolation is even once allowed to hear a recorded chaffinch song, it will begin to sing this song months later when mature!

INNATE LEARNING TENDENCIES Lately we have come to recognize that although learning involves acquired associations and selection of responses on the basis of their reinforcement, an animal may have an innate tendency to learn certain types of things more readily than others. *Preferential learning* is seen in birds that readily learn songs of their own species but fail to learn songs of other species. It has been found that bluebirds reared in isolation from before hatching until 6 months of age do not develop an innate song but sing normally only when allowed to hear a recorded bluebird song. When exposed to the songs of other species, such isolated bluebirds proved unresponsive and failed to learn thrush or oriole songs. But when allowed to hear a bluebird song played *backward,* these birds promptly evidenced interest and upon hearing the same song played forward began to mimic it (at first crudely) within less than a minute. Apparently, only the song to which they are genetically primed to respond can be learned. Chaffinches, on the other hand, develop a rudimentary song even when reared in acoustic isolation, but will also learn and incorporate into their final song elements of the songs of other species played to them during the critical period of learning. However, in the wild, where young chaffinches are routinely exposed to the songs of other sympatric species as well as to those of their own kind, they do not tend to develop such "hybrid" songs but learn only that of their own species. In the absence of experimentation it is impossible to ascertain how much of a bird's song develops as an expression of its genetic constitution and how much is determined by songs heard by the individual during maturation.

MEMORY The essential prerequisite for learning is that a change takes place in the nervous system as a result of experience and that this change brings about a more or less lasting modification of the individual's behavior. The possible nature of this change has been discussed in Sections 11.3C and 15.3A, in which the possible significance of facilitated neural pathways (especially reverberatory circuits) and macromolecular changes within neurons (DNA, RNA, or protein engrams) were taken up. Despite many areas of uncertainty we have reason to believe that the processes involved in short-term and long-term remembering are unalike. If learning is to be retained, the learning experience must be followed by a period of *consolidation.* Short-term learning, not fixed in this manner, is abolished soon after the needs of the moment have been met. Long-term learning, on the other hand, appears to be virtually ineradicable, for once the consolidation process has been completed permanent changes appear to have taken place in the nervous system. The information may not always be rapidly retrieved when needed, but in man the completeness of recall under hypnosis (as well as the apparent reliving of an experience evoked by direct brain stimulation) testifies to the permanence of the change. The process of consolidation can be interrupted by electrical shock as well as by administration of any of several chemicals that inhibit mRNA synthesis or protein synthesis. Consolidation of learning in goldfish is blocked by injecting the antibiotic puromycin, during (or within the first half hour after) training sessions in which the fish has learned simple reinforced responses. Puromycin, which blocks protein synthesis at the ribosomes without inhibiting mRNA synthesis, apparently obliterates all memory of training when injected immediately after the conditioning session, whereas an injection given 1 hr after the session does not impair retention at all. These studies correspond well with those reported in Section 11.3C, in which long-term learning in mice was inhibited by injection of another chemical inhibitor of protein synthesis. Presumably any change in the pattern of protein synthesis in a brain cell would require a corresponding change in the gene encoding the mRNA template for the protein. A number of different studies point to the possible "transfer of learning" in planarians and even mammals when RNA extracted from the brains of trained individuals is injected into untrained individuals before the latter are trained to perform the same task (RNA from untrained individuals is said not to have such an effect). The possibility of such chemical transfer of learning certainly deserves further investigation.

Figure 16.23 □ **Comparison of releasing stimulus and directing stimulus in gaping response of young birds. (*a*) Nest is jarred, and birds with unopened eyes gape vertically; finger serves as mechanical stimulus releasing the gaping response, but the response is oriented to gravity (days 1 to 10). (*b*) Finger serves as visual stimulus that releases gaping, but the response is still oriented to gravity (days 10 to 12). (*c*) Finger serves as visual releaser and also orients the gaping response (after day 11 or 12). (*Data from N. Tinbergen.*)**

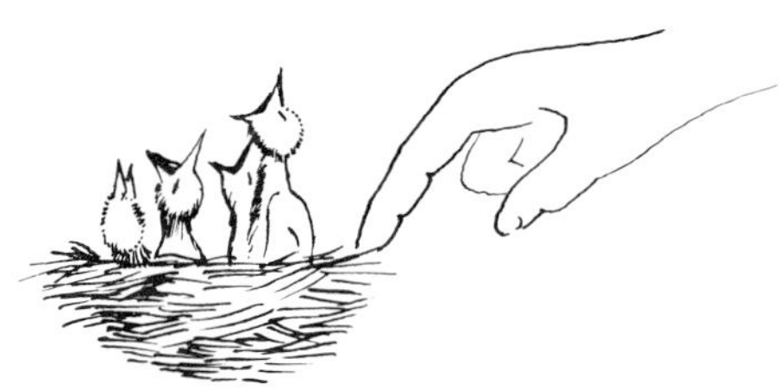

Day 1

(*a*)

Day 10

(*b*)

Day 12

(*c*)

E Orientation: the directional component of behavior

A motor response is usually oriented with respect to particular external stimuli. Movement may be directed toward a stimulus (such as prey) or away from it, or some stimulus (such as light) may be used as a means for steering a course that maintains a constant angle to the stimulus source. The stimulus guiding the direction of a response may or may not be the same as that instigating the response. For example, when a young nestling with unopened eyes is stimulated by touching its beak or jarring the nest a gaping response is released that is directed *not* toward the releasing stimulus but *vertically.* Here the tactile stimulus initates gaping but gravity determines the directional component of the response. Only after the nestling's eyes have been open for a few days does gaping come to be directed instead toward objects seen at the side of the nest and above the nestling's eye level (Figure 16.23). In the same vein, migratory behavior in birds is actually initiated by physiological changes that in turn are geared to changes in photoperiod, but the direction of travel and choice of migratory route seem to be determined by innate and/or acquired recognition of landmarks and celestial cues, particularly constellations.

The least complicated type of oriented movement and the one accordingly most amenable to analysis is the *taxis.* A taxis is a locomotory response guided by a directional stimulus that serves as a sensory "beacon." The animal's path of travel may be toward or away from, or at an angle to the stimulus source. For many animals a taxis partakes of the compulsory quality of a reflex, but for others the response may be less automatic. No organism can orient itself by means of a directional stimulus unless it is capable of detecting the direction from which the stimulus is coming. An animal lacking this capacity may nevertheless respond to the stimulus by means of an unoriented response known as a *kinesis,* in which the stimulus affects the rate of locomotion and the frequency of turning, but does not determine the *direction* of movement. The difference between a kinesis and a taxis may be seen by placing in a beam of light two photophobic (light-avoiding) species, one of which can determine the direction from which the beam is emanating whereas the other cannot. The first will turn and move directly away from the light source. The second will begin to move more rapidly, turning this way and that, at random. Eventually this procedure will bring it out of the range of the aversive stimulus: the more closely it approaches the light, the higher its frequency of turning becomes; the farther it moves away from the light, the more its turning tendency declines and the resultant tendency to move in a straight line then brings it into progressively darker regions (Figure 16.24*a*).

Klinotaxis, tropotaxis, and telotaxis are three kinds of movements along a stimulus gradient, directly toward or away from the stimulus source. The first involves *consecutive* comparisons of the intensity of stimulation affecting each side of the body. *Klinotaxis* is shown by maggots which, having a single median photoreceptor, swing their anterior ends from side to side as they move away from light, monitoring the intensity of illumination first to one side and then to the other. *Tropotaxis,* on the other hand, involves *simultaneous* comparison of stimulus intensity on both sides of the body. This requires the presence of bilaterally positioned receptors, such as paired eyes. A photopositive animal that orients tropotactically will, when illuminated from the left, turn left until light falls equally upon both eyes, whereupon it will pursue a straight line toward the light without engaging in the oscillatory correcting movements characteristic of animals orienting by klinotaxis (Figure 16.24*b*). It is possible to tell whether or not an animal orients to light tropotactically simply by blinding it in one eye. As a result, as it attempts to move along the light gradient, it instead will continue to turn in circles, toward the blinded side if negatively phototactic or toward the sighted side if positively phototactic (Figure 16.24*c*).

If an animal that orients either klinotactically or tropotactically is presented simultaneously with two attractive stimulus sources, such as two pieces of food, it tends to pursue a straight course that brings it not to one object or the other but to a point midway between the two. The line of travel represents the distance from each source at which the tendencies to turn left or right are equal (Figure 16.24*d*). There are many species, however, that exhibit tactic behavior but do not pursue such a course when presented with two stimulus sources, instead moving directly toward (or away from) one while apparently ignoring the other. These animals, including hermit crabs, which can orient to only one source out of

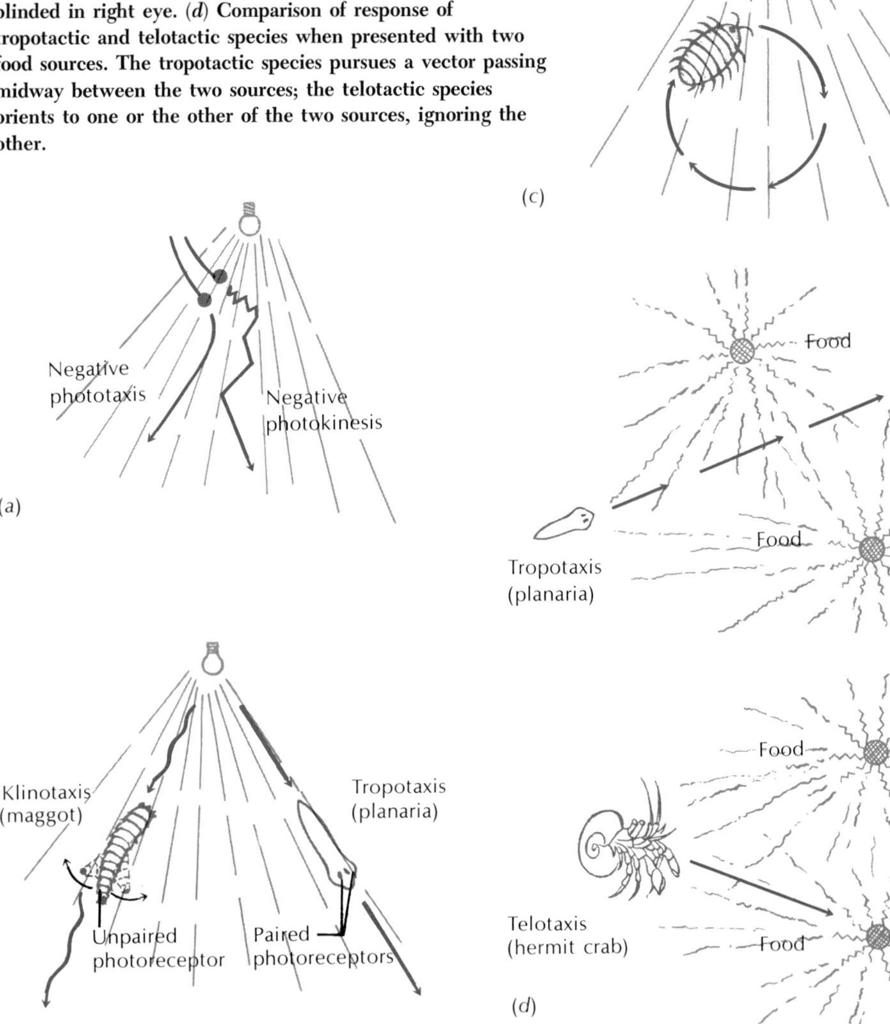

Figure 16.24 □ **Oriented movements. (*a*) Comparison of phototaxis and photokinesis (the dots indicate the positions of the animals when the light is turned on). (*b*) Comparison of klinotaxis and tropotaxis. (*c*) Response to light of a tropotactic, photophobic species, such as a sow bug, when blinded in right eye. (*d*) Comparison of response of tropotactic and telotactic species when presented with two food sources. The tropotactic species pursues a vector passing midway between the two sources; the telotactic species orients to one or the other of the two sources, ignoring the other.**

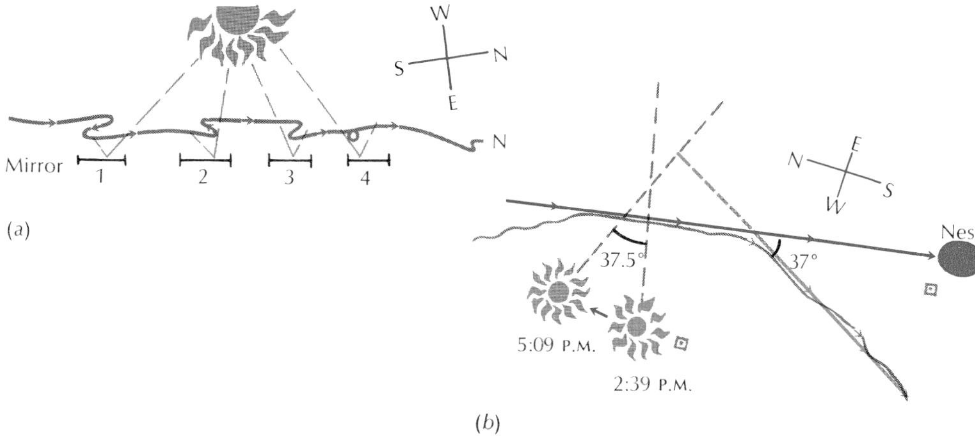

Figure 16.25 □ Light-compass reaction (menotaxis) in ants. (*a*) Field experiment demonstrating menotaxis: an ant returning to the nest with the sun at its left can be made to reverse course whenever the sun's direct rays are shielded and its image is projected by means of a mirror placed on the right side of the animal's original line of travel (points 1 to 4). The correct direction is taken again as soon as the ant is allowed to see the sun directly. (*After F. Santschi.*) (*b*) An ant is trapped while en route to its nest with the sun shining from the right at an angle of 90° to its line of travel. Released after 2.5 hr, the ant adopts a new path of travel that deviates from the correct one by an angle equivalent to that through which the sun has moved during the 2.5-hr period. Solid-color line indicates former (and correct) direction of travel toward nest; tinted line indicates new (and incorrect) direction of travel oriented to the later position of sun. (*After R. Brun.*)

several of identical value, are said to exhibit *telotaxis*. Such selectivity probably demands that an initial tendency to respond to one stimulus out of the several presented be strengthened by simultaneous inhibition of tendencies to respond to the others. This is not unlike the manner in which an animal may respond to a sign stimulus, apparently oblivious to other, possibly contradictory cues. Unlike tropotactic species, an animal orienting by telotaxis will not tend to move in circles when unilaterally blinded, but follows the information provided by the one remaining eye, correcting its tendency to turn to one side.

Menotaxis differs from other tactic responses in that the animal orients, not directly toward or away from a stimulus source, but at an angle to the source. Since the stimulus most often used in such orientation is the sun, menotaxis is also known as the *light-compass* response. Ants may return home menotactically as their odor trail fades away. If a mirror is used to change the sun's apparent position, the ants become confused and reorient their course relative to the reflected sun (Figure 16.25*a*).

A menotactic species can make better use of the capacity to maintain a constant compass direction if it also possesses innate means for measuring the passage of time. Many organisms have such a time sense, or "biological clock," which functions with amazing accuracy (Figure 16.25*b*). A number of insects and crustaceans, as well as migratory birds, apparently orient menotactically, compensating accurately for the earth's rotation. Interestingly, although bees are known to rely on the position of the sun when foraging or returning to the hive, they do not need to see the sun itself but can detect and orient to the plane along which the sun's rays are polarized as they pass through the atmosphere.

Most oriented movements are not the result of simple tactic responses, but depend on the animal's ability to make use of a number of different kinds of sensory cues. Some animals no doubt memorize salient landmarks, whereas others may genetically "recognize" stellar patterns useful in maintaining migratory bearings. Homing sea turtles and fish use odors for guidance when returning to their breeding grounds. Green turtles migrate from South America across the open Atlantic to Ascension Island (a mere speck in the vastness of the sea, 2,300 km east of Brazil), on the beaches of which the females lay their eggs. Perhaps this great migration is initially oriented by negative *rheotaxis,* the tendency to swim directly into an opposing current, for the turtles swim against the flow of the South Equatorial Current. At what point they begin to detect faint olfactory cues that guide the rest of the journey has not yet been determined.

F The physical basis of motor response

Most behavior consists of movements brought about by the contraction of skeletal or voluntary muscles under the control of motor nerve fibers. The functional organization of voluntary muscles is especially fascinating in that we can trace this organization from the organismal to the molecular level with relatively few serious gaps remaining in our knowledge. At each level, muscle structure beautifully reflects adaptation to function, so that through cytochemical and electron-microscopic study of muscle ultrastructure we can actually obtain a clear picture of the manner in which a movement is brought about at the level of the organism as a whole.

In our consideration of the physical basis of motor response we shall accordingly begin at the level of the whole organism in its community and descend by stages to the molecular level. An organism's behavior allows it to relate to the world in which it lives by responding in a nonrandom manner to stimuli emanating from the environment. The ultimate test of the effectiveness of a given motor response is how well it contributes toward the survival of the individual. Whether or not a particular act is innate, acquired through practice, or both, the neural and muscular mechanisms involved are subject to evolutionary change and advancement. If survival demands that an animal be fleet-footed in capturing prey or escaping from predators, in both predator and prey populations selective factors promote the conservation of any genetically based improvements in nervous and muscular organization that make possible more rapid locomotion. If a population adopts an arboreal mode of life, facility in climbing and grasping branches becomes essential and any inheritable changes taking place in the functional organization of the muscular system and in the motor nerve centers controlling these muscles will tend to persist. The development of opposable digits capable of grasping branches has taken place independently in a number of arboreal vertebrates including most birds and some primates and lizards. The African chameleon, which must brace itself steadily while shooting out its tongue to capture prey, not only has grasping feet with two digits opposing the other three but employs a prehensile tail as well, wound tendril-fashion around the branch (Figure 13.27). The feet of perching birds (passerines) not only have three toes directed forward and one back (as is characteristic of most birds), but in addition tendons passing over the "heel" of the foot cause the toes to flex when the leg is folded as the bird settles down to rest (Figure 16.26). This pulley mechanism allows the bird to perch without tiring or loosening its hold during sleep. The opposable thumb developed by the arboreal ancestors of apes and men as an aid to climbing also provided the functional and structural basis upon which manipulative skills could be built through further refinement of the neural control of the hand.

LOCOMOTION Locomotory behavior is relatively simple when compared to movements functioning in social contexts, for the latter often consist of ritualized acts derived from various other systems. To detail the variety of movements used in social communication would require a treatise, as would a catalog of muscular activities contributing to self-maintenance, including grooming, bathing, feeding, and drinking. We shall limit our analysis, therefore, to a few major types of locomotion used by terrestrial mammals and use them as examples of the way in which muscular activity is coordinated to bring about effective movement of the whole organism.

Quadrupedal walking and running in

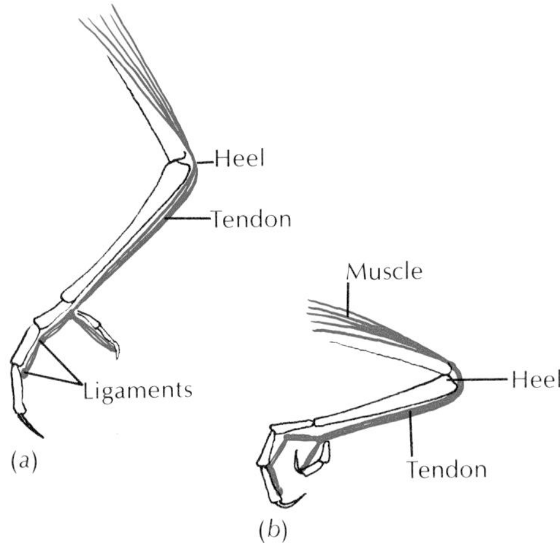

Figure 16.26 □ Songbird perching mechanism: (*a*) waking position. (*b*) When the passerine settles down to sleep, its ankle joint is flexed. The tendon extending over the heel to the ends of the toes is thereby put under tension, causing the toes to lock about the branch.

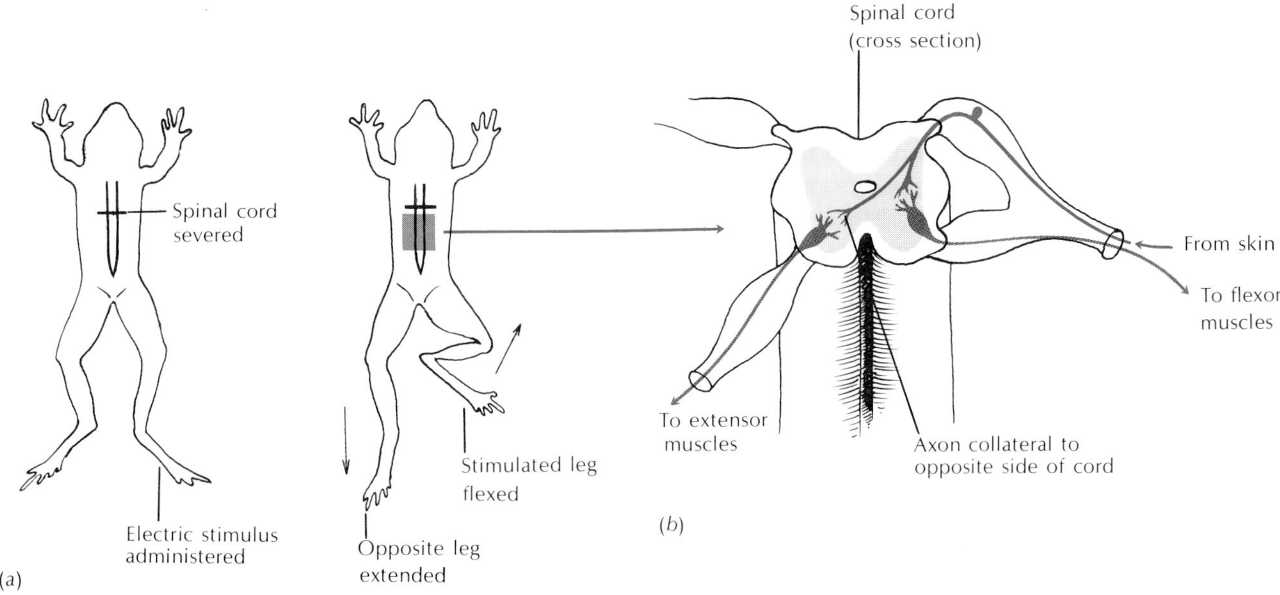

Figure 16.27 □ The reflex basis of vertebrate locomotion. ***(a)*** **A frog with severed spinal cord responds to shock applied to its right foot by flexing the right leg (nociceptive flexion reflex) and simultaneously straightening the left leg (crossed extension reflex). This coupling of flexion and extension reflexes at the level of the spinal cord constitutes an organizational basis for alternate leg movements seen in walking.** ***(b)*** **Cross section through spinal cord showing in simplified fashion the transmission of excitation to motor neurons on the opposite side of the cord, thereby eliciting the crossed extension reflex.**

vertebrates always follows the same basic pattern (see Figure 4.33). One leg at a time is flexed (bent) to elevate it from the ground, is swung forward through an arc by contraction of the shoulder or hip muscles, and then is straightened to bear the body's weight. This extension is an expression of a reflex, as shown by the involuntary straightening of a load-bearing limb when the one opposite it is flexed. In fact, both quadrupedal and bipedal walking or running may involve the rhythmic operation of flexion and crossed-extension reflexes, first in one pair of legs and then in the other. In a *crossed-extension* reflex, sensory fibers responsible for initiating a flexion response in one limb send axon collaterals to the opposite side of the spinal cord that synapse with motor fibers controlling the extensor muscles of that limb; as a result the bending of one limb is accompanied by the straightening of the one opposite (Figure 16.27).

In Chapter 15 we noted that cerebral motor control is superimposed upon spinal reflex machinery evolved earlier; accordingly it is not surprising that a voluntary behavior such as walking makes use of spinal reflex arcs, and although we can consciously modify the direction, rate, length, and pattern of gait, the control of walking is basically subconscious, mediated through subcortical brain centers. Even such an obviously learned maneuver as a dance step tends to become automatic with practice so that cerebral monitoring of the activity is minimized.

Quadrupedal walking and running thus involves a leg progression in which *diagonally* opposite legs are moved at nearly the same moment while the limbs *directly* opposite the ones flexed are straightened to bear the body's weight. In walking, three legs tend to bear the weight of the trunk while the fourth is advanced. In running, diagonally opposite legs tend to move at the same time so that body weight rests upon the other two: left front and right rear move forward while right front and left rear are fully extended, right front and left rear are then advanced while left front and right rear support the trunk and provide forward thrust. Another locomotory rhythm is seen in a few mammals including camels and bears, that *amble* rather than run. In ambling, both front and rear legs on one side are flexed and moved forward at the same time, while both legs on the side opposite are extended, thrusting backward. Camels are justifiably nicknamed "ships of the desert," for the rider is tilted from side to side to such an extent that the inexperienced may become "seasick"!

In all types of locomotion on land, the vertebrate's rear legs are responsible for generating most forward thrust and accordingly tend to be more muscular than the front legs. Indeed, a number of basically quadrupedal lizards resort to bipedal running when in haste. Bipedal walking and running was first characteristic of the ancient reptiles (archosaurs) ancestral to both dinosaurs and birds. Once the hind limbs only were used for locomotion, the front limbs could be used for manipulation. Such dinosaurs as *Tyrannosaurus* (see Figure 8.22*b*) were fully bipedal, with nearly vestigial front limbs. Others, including *Triceratops* (also seen in Figure 8.22*b*), were quadrupedal but their bipedal ancestry remained evident in the large size of the hind legs and pelvis, the back sloping downward anteriorly to the comparatively small forequarters. A swelling larger than the brain, located in the posterior region of the dinosaur vertebral column, indicates either that these animals required a large mass of nervous tissue (almost a second brain!) in the cord to operate their massive hindquarters or else that energy was provided to the nervous tissue in this region by a glycogen body such as that characteristic of modern birds.

The mammalian gait permitting most rapid locomotion is the *gallop*, or its bipedal version, the *hop*. A horseback rider cannot fail to notice the change that takes place when his mount switches from a fast trot to a gallop. The horse's diagonal pattern of leg movement is suddenly replaced by one in which both rear legs are extended simultaneously, while both front legs are flexed and swung forward. Then as the two front legs touch the ground together, they bear the body's weight while the two rear feet are lifted and, as the back is arched, swung forward to a position actually ahead of the front feet. The rear legs are then extended once more and the vertebral column is simultaneously straightened while the front legs are flexed, swung forward, and extended, to come down once more side by side. A "hopping" rabbit is actually galloping like a horse, for the forelegs bear the body's weight between thrusts of the hind legs. Kangaroos, however, actually do hop when in haste, but gallop when moving slowly. This is not a play on words, but makes sense in terms of the actual gaits described by the terms "hop" and "gallop." When moving

Figure 16.28 □ Kangaroos bounding. (*Courtesy of Australian News and Information Bureau.*)

slowly, the kangaroo places both forepaws on the ground and then with the aid of its muscular tail lifts both hind feet free of the ground and swings them forward to touch ground once more to either side of the front feet, which can then be lifted and advanced in turn. On the other hand, when fleeing from danger the kangaroo carries tail and forelegs off the ground, and leaps by extending both hind legs together, flexing the legs in midair while executing a bound as much as 10 m in length (Figure 16.28).

At full gallop large antelopes can clock better than 70 km/hr and cheetahs more than 120 km/hr for a short distance. The development of such speeds has involved changes in the skeleton involving a shortening of the leg and lengthening of the foot, so that weight rests only upon the toes (in a *digitigrade* animal such as a cat) or upon hooves derived from one or more toenails (in an *unguligrade* animal such as an antelope or horse). The leg muscles are bunched close to the trunk and operate to move the limb as a unit, by way of long tendons that control the foot in such a way that a relatively slight movement of the thigh can swing the foot rapidly through a wide arc.

A major problem in behavioral analysis is that of determining how the nervous system orchestrates muscular activity so that contraction and inhibition of different sets of muscles are effectively timed. In locomotion such timing is basically rhythmic and a few activity patterns are repeated over and over; in various nonlocomotory activities timing may be either rhythmic or arhythmic, and the actions performed sequentially may be either alike or different. Analyzing the control of order and timing of heterogeneous behavior sequences may be much more difficult than analyzing the neural control of locomotion.

FUNCTIONAL ORGANIZATION OF THE MUSCULAR SYSTEM Body movements such as those described above reflect the manner in which the voluntary muscles are organized and attached to the skeleton. Muscles function in only one way: they *shorten* by contracting. The only way that effective body movements can be executed is for muscles to be arranged in opposing sets. Even the earthworm, lacking a true skeleton, can crawl by virtue of alternating contractions of the circular and longitudinal muscle sheets that form its body wall. The front end is first thrust forward by contraction of the circular muscles and then is anchored in place while the posterior end is brought forward by contractions of the longitudinal muscles.

Arthropods and vertebrates are the only animals to evolve an articulated skeleton that furnishes sites for attachment of the voluntary (*skeletal*) muscles (see Figures 4.28 and 12.26). The structure of the joint and the position of muscle attachments to the skeleton dictate the type of movement possible. In order to move the skeleton, a muscle must attach by way of tendons to more than one bone. The *origin* of a muscle is its proximal, usually more fixed point of attachment; its *insertion* is the more distal, movable attachment.

The major opposing sets of skeletal muscles are the following. (1) *Flexors* bend limbs or arch the trunk so that head and tail are brought together ventrally; *extensors* straighten limbs or arch the trunk in a "backbend." (2) *Levators* elevate a body part (such as the head or the lower jaw) and *depressors* lower those parts. (3) *Adductors* pull a limb toward the body's median longitudinal axis, and *abductors* pull them away from the midline. (4) *Supinators* rotate a limb so that (for instance) the hand turns palm up and *pronators* rotate the limb in the opposite direction (Figure 16.29). In each set the muscles contracting are termed the *agonists*. Those opposing them (the *antagonists*) are inhibited from shortening at the same time but rather than remaining fully relaxed tend to assume a state of mild *isometric* contraction (in which muscle tonus increases without a corresponding change in length). As a result of this opposing action bodily movements tend to be smoothly coordinated rather than jerky and abrupt. Careful study of the skeletal attachments of the muscles shown in Figure 16.29 should make it clear how opposing sets of muscles serve to move the skeleton.

Each vertebrate skeletal muscle is a distinct organ, composed of muscular and connective tissues, served by blood vessels and nerves, and containing receptors sensitive to changes in pressure and tension. The muscle may be sheetlike, rhomboidal, triangular, or spindle-shaped, and is subdivided by internal connective tissue partitions into bundles of striated muscle fibers (see Figure 11.35). Muscle contraction can be studied at the organ level by removing a single muscle from the body and stimulating it either directly by mild electrical shock or by a stimulus applied to the stump of its nerve. In this manner it has been found that the stimulus must attain a certain minimum threshold value for a single contraction (twitch) to take place. A latent period of 0.0025 to 0.004 sec intervenes between application of the stimulus and the onset of the twitch. The twitch itself consists of a

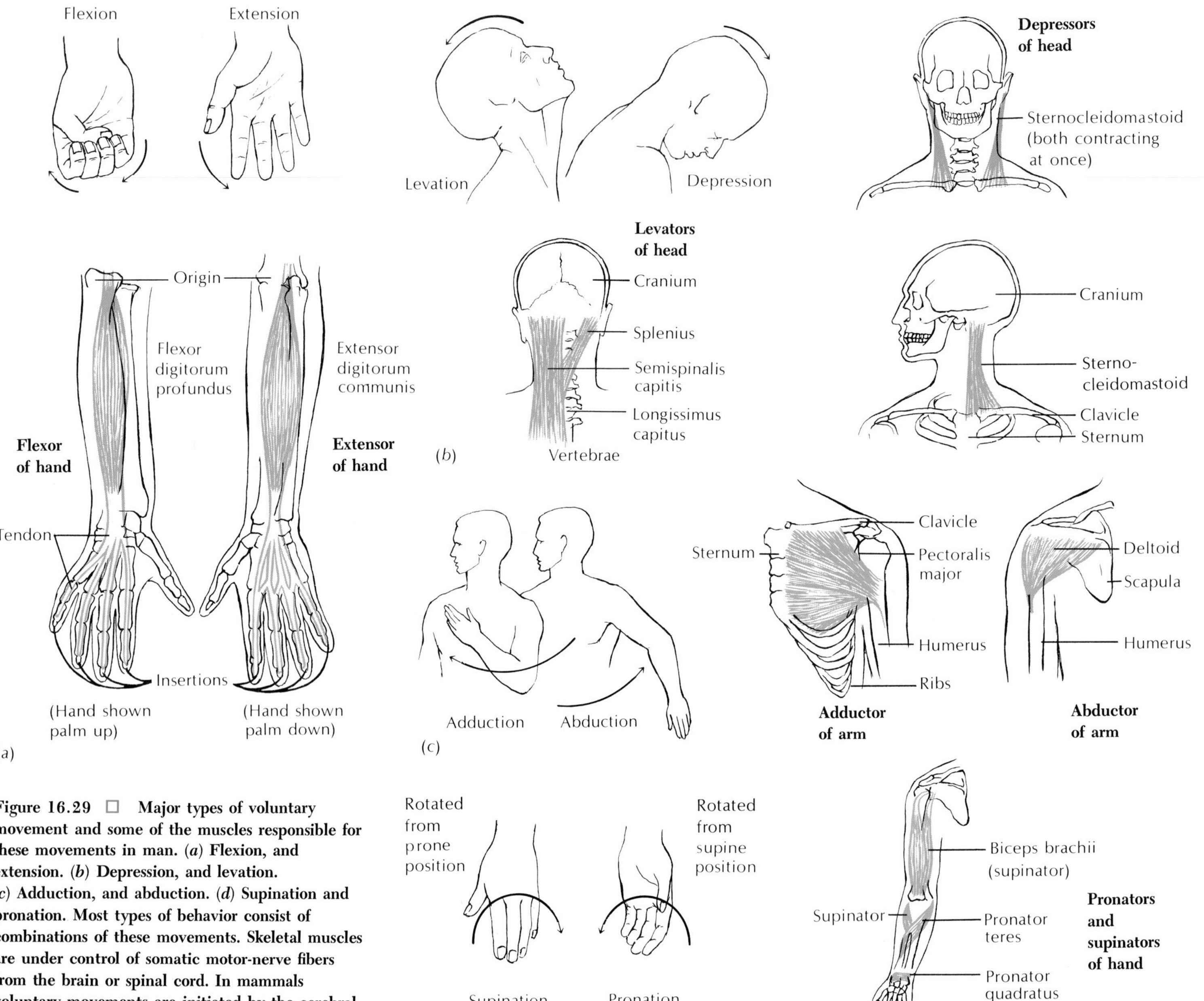

Figure 16.29 □ Major types of voluntary movement and some of the muscles responsible for these movements in man. (*a*) Flexion, and extension. (*b*) Depression, and levation. (*c*) Adduction, and abduction. (*d*) Supination and pronation. Most types of behavior consist of combinations of these movements. Skeletal muscles are under control of somatic motor-nerve fibers from the brain or spinal cord. In mammals voluntary movements are initiated by the cerebral motor cortex, which sends fibers to various levels of the spinal cord.

contraction phase of about 0.04 sec followed by a *relaxation phase* about 0.05 sec long. If the stimulus is sustained, successive twitches fuse into a more extensive contraction known as *tetanus* that continues until stimulation is interrupted or fatigue sets in (Figure 16.30). A muscle in tetanus contracts as strongly as possible, but its capacity to sustain the contraction depends on the fact that even during such a strong contraction not all of the muscle fibers comprising the muscle contract simultaneously. We find instead that a muscle is functionally subdivided into a number of *motor units*. Each motor unit consists of a group of muscle fibers served by a single motor neuron. When this neuron fires, all the fibers in that motor unit contract at one time. While some motor units are contracting, others are in a state of recovery. An "all-or-none" law is said to apply to vertebrate muscle, but applies only to the individual muscle fiber and not to the muscle as a whole. The individual fiber contracts to its fullest extent, if it contracts at all; the reaction of the whole muscle, however, is graded, depending on the number of motor units excited at any given time. This in turn depends on the number of motor neurons firing and the frequency of the impulses conducted.

Despite the staggering of the contraction of different motor units, a tetanic contraction eventually causes the muscle as a whole to fatigue. This is due in part to exhaustion of the muscle glycogen reserves and in part to the fact that pressure of contracting muscle fibers on adjacent vascular channels reduces oxygen supply to the tissues and causes the accumulation of lactic acid, a product of glycolysis conducted under anaerobic conditions (see Figure 14.51). Eventually the muscle must relax, restoring blood flow and allowing lactic acid to be carried away to the liver for further metabolism and glucose to be taken into the muscle cells for immediate use or to be built into glycogen.

FUNCTIONAL ORGANIZATION AT THE CELLULAR LEVEL As seen in Figure 11.35, each skeletal muscle fiber is an elongate, multinuclear cell with rounded ends, cylindrical in cross section and measuring from 10 to 100 μm in diameter by as much as several centimeters long. The nuclei are pushed to the periphery, for the cytoplasm is occupied by from 1,000 to 2,000 longi-

Figure 16.30 □ **Muscular activity. (*a*) Apparatus for making kymograph record of muscle activity. (*b*) Kymograph record of twitches and tetanus in isolated skeletal muscle. A twitch follows each stimulus, but as the frequency of stimuli is increased, successive twitches fuse into a plateau of contraction (tetanus) that persists until stimulation is discontinued or muscle fatigue sets in.**

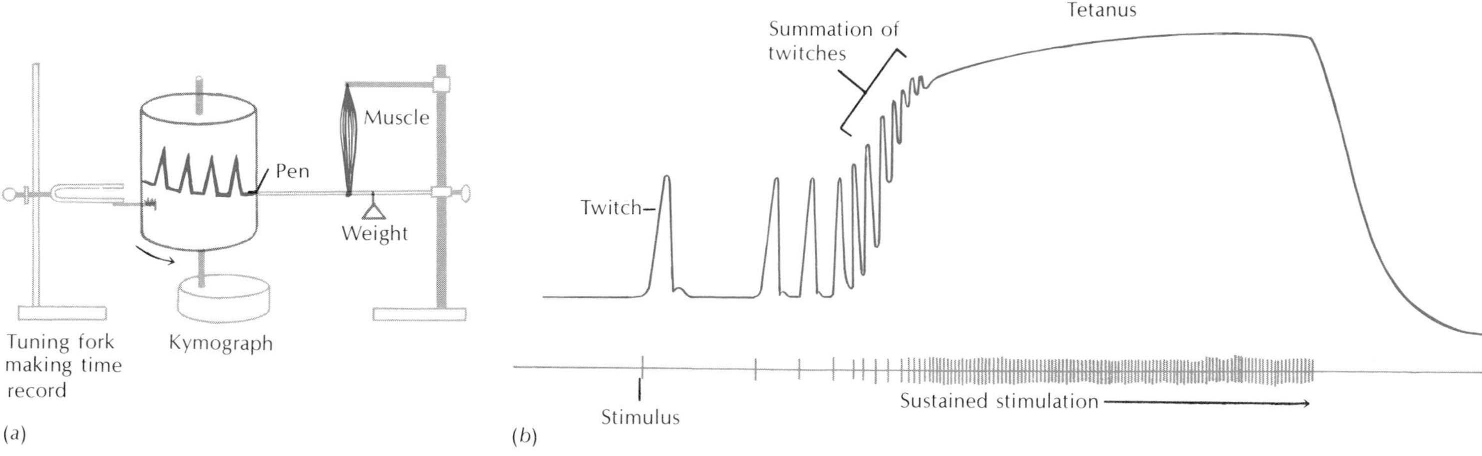

tudinally oriented contractile units (*myofibrils*), the organization of which is basic to muscle contractility, as discussed below. Between the myofibrils are clusters of mitochondria, among which run the channels of the endoplasmic (or sarcoplasmic) reticulum. At regular intervals tubular extensions of the plasma membrane (sarcolemma) penetrate into the interior of the fiber as the *transverse system* (Figure 14.10). The "T-system" provides channels by which nutrients can more readily reach the cell interior, but serves mainly as a means whereby excitation initiated at the myoneural junction can be transmitted throughout the fiber so rapidly that all of its myofibrils contract simultaneously.

A muscle fiber can contract to about 65 percent of its resting length. The contraction is initiated by the discharge of acetylcholine at the myoneural junction where the motor nerve axon terminates upon the sarcolemma. Like other plasma membranes, the sarcolemma at rest is electronegative on the inside with a potential difference of about 90 mV across the membrane. Acetylcholine makes the membrane locally permeable to Na^+, depolarizing the membrane until a threshold is reached at which membrane polarity abruptly reverses and an all-or-none wave of excitation, the action potential (similar to the nerve impulse studied in Chapter 15) sweeps across the entire sarcolemma, spreading evenly in all directions from its point of origin. This wave of excitation prompts the onset of contraction, but the exact connection between the membrane phenomenon and the contractile response has yet to be clarified. As in nervous tissue the resting membrane potential is restored immediately by the outflow of K^+ but the original distribution of Na^+ and K^+ must be restored later by action of the membrane's Na^+/K^+ "pump." Vertebrate muscle fibers are innervated only by excitatory synapses, but invertebrate muscle cells are known in some cases to be doubly innervated with excitatory fibers that release transmitter substances depolarizing the membrane and with inhibitory fibers that release substances hyperpolarizing the membrane and rendering it resistant to excitation. Invertebrate muscle fibers are less committed to an all-or-none response than vertebrate muscle fibers seem to be, but can give a graded contractile response due to decremental conduction of excitation along the cell membrane. This makes possible a wider range of response from the comparatively few fibers that may be present.

Energy for the contractile response is directly derived from ATP generated in the mitochondria. During contraction ATP is dephosphorylated to ADP, but this can in turn take up Ⓟ from other high-energy phosphate compounds present in the cytoplasm, namely creatine phosphate (in deuterostomes) or arginine phosphate (in protostomes). These *phosphagens* can only replenish ATP for several seconds of activity, but during this time muscle glycogen reserves can be mobilized and glycolysis begun, furnishing energy for the formation of new high-energy phosphate compounds. During mild exercise glycolysis can terminate aerobically, with transfer of activated acetyl to the Krebs cycle and subsequent generation of ATP in the respiratory chain (see Figures 14.51, 14.52, and 14.53). This aerobic respiration is facilitated by stores of molecular oxygen in the cytoplasm, loosely held by the respiratory pigment *myoglobin.* When the myoglobin has been fully deoxygenated, glycolysis must terminate anaerobically by the use of pyruvic acid as a hydrogen acceptor, thereby forming lactic acid. During muscle recovery some of this lactic acid is removed via the bloodstream to be rebuilt as glycogen in the liver. The rest must be metabolized in the muscle tissue by being converted to pyruvic acid, a reaction which requires O_2 to be available as an H acceptor. The muscle tissue must accordingly take up large amounts of O_2 from the bloodstream to pay off the "oxygen debt" incurred by anaerobic glycolysis. Oxygen must also be taken up and stored in combination with myoglobin. Some of the pyruvic acid formed is oxidized to provide energy for rebuilding the cell's phosphagen and ATP reserves and to allow the rest of the pyruvic acid present to be reconverted to glucose, which is rebuilt to glycogen. As a result of these regenerative processes, the only material actually expended during muscle contraction is a portion of the muscle glycogen stores, and since up to 80 percent of the lactic acid formed can be reconverted to glycogen, relatively little glucose must be taken up from the bloodstream to restore the glycogen reserves. So efficient are the processes of energy conversion within muscle cells that some kinds of fibers are capable of contracting up to 100 times/sec and of producing mechanical work equivalent to nearly 1,000 times their own weight.

FUNCTIONAL ORGANIZATION AT THE MOLECULAR LEVEL: THE MYOFIBRIL The macromolecular functional unit of a muscle fiber is the myofibril, a cylinder from 1 to 2 μm in diameter composed mainly of the contractile protein *actomyosin*—actually a complex of two different proteins, *actin* and *myosin,* neither of which is contractile in vitro unless in the presence of the other. The designations "actin" and "myosin" should really be considered generic terms, for the specific contractile proteins may differ somewhat from one phylum to another. Vertebrate actin can undergo a reversible globular-fibrillar transformation. In a solution lacking salts it dissociates into globular units (G-actin) having a molecular weight of 70,000. These units polymerize spontaneously to form long fibrils (F-actin) in the presence of ATP, K^+, and Cl^-. The fibrils are arranged as a double helix with 13 units of G-actin per turn of the helix. Vertebrate myosin has a molecular weight of about 450,000 and when extracted from muscle tissue appears as spindle-shaped fibrils some 100 Å in diameter by 1,500 Å long. These units bind ATP and cations, especially Mg^{2+}. Two kinds of myosin make up these units: (1) a lighter component about 20 Å in diameter makes up the "backbone" of the filament; (2) a heavier component forms a helix about the backbone, bearing projections that extend from the sides of the helix and operate as cross bridges during contraction.

If actin and myosin are extracted from muscle tissue and combined in solution, they associate spontaneously to form a loose complex of actomyosin, from which artificial fibrils may be prepared. These can then contract in vitro in the presence of ATP. Myosin is found to perform a catalytic function in the dephosphorylation of ATP and in fact nearly all of the ATP that can be extracted from muscle tissue is found to be associated with the heavy myosin fraction. In vitro contraction, although serving to identify the contractile elements of muscle tissue, did not show the manner in which contraction actually takes place. Did the actomyosin molecule fold up or was some other reaction possible?

Studies of the ultrastructure of myofibrils of vertebrate skeletal muscle have lent support to the *sliding filament hypothesis* of muscle contraction (proposed independently by H. E. Huxley and A. F. Huxley, both of Great Britain). This hypothesis is centered on the molecular architecture of the myofibril, as revealed by the electron microscope (Figure 16.31*a*). The striped appearance of skeletal or striated muscle is due to the fact that the individual myofibrils are themselves cross banded, and that the myofibrils lie side by side in such a way that their individual patterns of cross striation reinforce rather than cancel the banding pattern for the whole cell. Myofibrils from smooth muscle fibers appear homogeneous along their length, whereas those from striated muscle are constructed of a repeating molecular unit, the *sarcomere,* a module about 3 μm long when not in a state of contraction (see Figure 11.35). Each sarcomere is separated from the next in line by a dense cross partition, the *Z line,* from either side of which spring longitudinal filaments about 50 Å in diameter that are found to consist of F-actin. These filaments are arranged in a hexagonal pattern in which each hexagon is centered upon one of the thicker myosin filaments. The myosin filaments are not anchored to the *Z* lines but occupy the center portion of the sarcomere, forming the dark, birefringent* *A zone* (the anisotropic zone). The regions at each end of the sarcomere, where only the thinner actin filaments are present, do not refract light in two planes and therefore constitute the pale *I zones* (isotropic zones). The darker portions of the *A* zone lie to each side of the center of the sarcomere, for here the actin and myosin filaments overlap and create an effect of greater optical density. The actin filaments do not extend all the way to the center of the sarcomere, so that a less dense region, the *H disc* (Hensen's disc), is seen transecting the *A* zone.

During contraction the *I* zone and the *H* disc narrow markedly, whereas the *A* zone does not change in length. This suggests that the actin filaments slide along the myosin filaments toward the center of the sarcomere, pulling the *Z* lines toward each other and shortening the sarcomere to about two-thirds its resting length. The mechanism of this sliding action remained obscure until photographs taken at even higher resolution demonstrated the existence of cross bridges projecting from the myosin filaments and apparently attaching to active sites on the adjacent actin filaments (Figure 16.31*b, c, d*). These cross bridges arise at intervals of 60 to 70 Å, and each bridge is angularly displaced by 60° from the preceding one so that one complete turn about the fiber takes place every 400 Å. This means that each actin filament is linked once every 400 Å by a bridge from the same myosin filament. The hexagonal arrangement permits every myosin filament to form cross bridges with six actin filaments, and every actin filament to contact bridges from three myosin filaments.

The current hypothesis concerning the action of the cross bridges is that in the

**Birefringence* is the property of refracting light in two planes—one plane of refraction is parallel to the long axis of the fibrils and the other plane crosses the long axis.

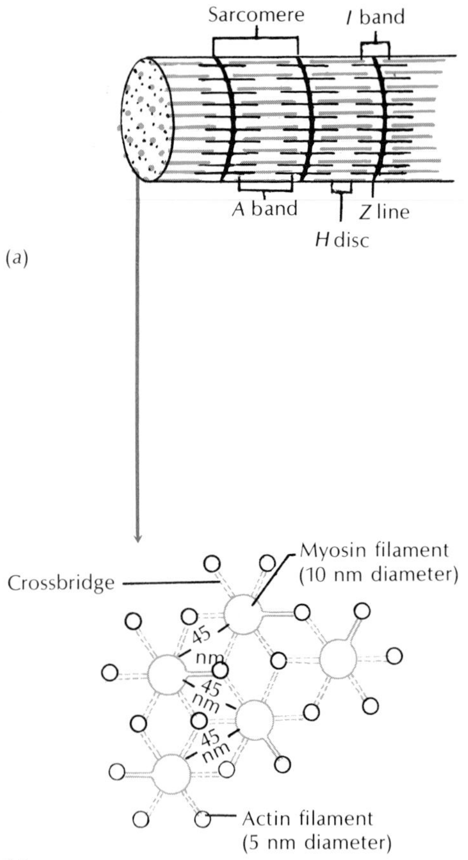

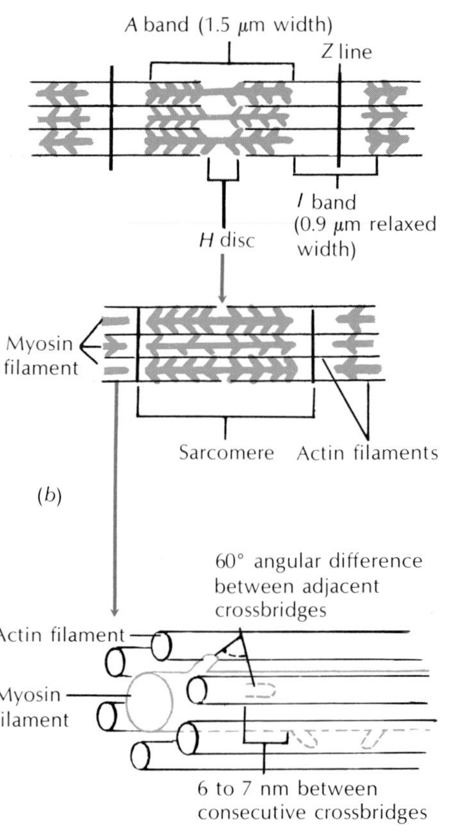

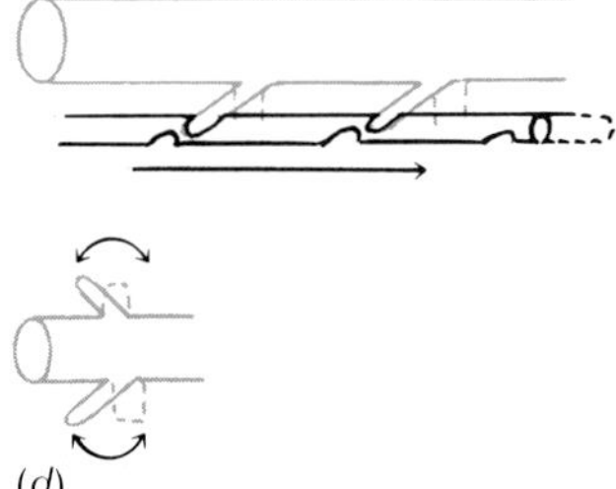

Figure 16.31 □ Model of striated muscle ultrastructure and function. (*a*) Portion of myofibril; each functional unit or sarcomere is 2 to 3 μm long. (*b*) Portion of sarcomere in relaxed (above) and contracted (below) states; note that actin filaments move together until they touch but that neither the length of the actin filaments nor that of the myosin filaments is changed though there is a change in the angles of the cross bridges. (*c*) Myosin and actin filaments in cross section, showing regular spacing and location of cross bridges ("ghosted" cross bridges are below the plane of section). (*d*) Longitudinal representation of portion of single myosin filament (above) and surrounding actin filaments, showing placement of cross bridges, and (below) proposed action of cross bridges. Each lengthened bridge is bound to an active site on the actin filament; shortening of the bridge (involving expenditure of one molecule of ATP) pulls the actin filament forward. The bridge then lengthens once more and attaches to the next active site in line. (The ghosts indicate the new positions of bridges and actin fibers, after the bridges have shortened).

resting sarcomere each bridge is conjugated with a terminally located ATP unit. The initial event caused by excitation is thought to be the release of Ca^{2+} from the sarcoplasmic reticulum into the cytoplasm, where the ions diffuse to a site between the cross bridge and an ADP-containing site on the actin filament. Here they establish a chelate or electrostatic link between the myosin and actin. This link diminishes the electronegativity characteristic of the fully extended cross bridge, and allows the bridge to contract by coiling into a helix. As the bridge shortens, the ATP is brought into contact with a site having ATPase activity, its terminal phosphate group is split off, and the link between the actin and myosin is broken. The myosin-bound ADP is then rephosphorylated by taking up Ⓟ from phosphagen, thereby recharging the bridge negatively and causing it to extend once more. Each time the bridge shortens, the actin filament bound to the bridge is drawn forward along the length of the myosin filament (Figure 16.31e). When the link is broken and the bridge extends once more it comes in contact with another active site further along the actin filament and the cycle of shortening, pulling, and releasing is repeated. On the basis of the number of cross bridges that actually can be counted in rabbit muscle, together with the observed rate of contraction of this tissue, it has been estimated that each cross bridge must undergo a complete activity cycle from 50 to 100 times/sec, using up one molecule of ATP per cycle. Each myosin filament seems to consist of two halves polarized in opposite directions so that the cross bridges in each half work oppositely. This would allow the actin filaments to be drawn together from both ends of the sarcomere until they meet at the midline, at which point no further contraction can take place. Now sarcomere, myofibril, and muscle fiber all have shortened to their maximal extent, for the contraction of all three of them is in fact to be considered a single event.

What causes the myofibril to return to its relaxed state? The answer to this question seems to involve a *relaxing factor* associated with membrane-lined vesicles of the sarcoplasmic reticulum. This factor binds Ca^{2+}, resulting in inhibition of ATPase activity. Apparently the excitation of muscle tissue causes the release of Ca^{2+} from the sarcoplasmic reticulum into the cytoplasm, whereas muscle relaxation involves the active pumping of Ca^{2+} from the cytoplasm back into the reticulum. Another protein, tropomyosin, found associated with the *Z* lines is thought to react with Ca^{2+} to control the actin–myosin interaction.

The precise molecular architecture characteristic of striated myofibrils is not seen in myofibrils from unstriated muscle, but this does not mean that a different mechanism of contraction need exist. In fact, traces of actomyosin have been detected in nearly all cells tested, suggesting that cytoplasmic streaming (cyclosis and amoeboid movement) and ciliary action may also be ultimately explained in terms of a sliding interaction between actin and myosin filaments, even when these are not organized into identifiable myofibrils.

G Nonmuscular movement

Unicellular and small multicellular organisms often move and collect food by ciliary action or amoeboid streaming. Ciliary movement depends on the rhythmic oscillations of cilia and flagella. Amoeboid movement involves protrusion of temporary projections of the cytoplasm known as pseudopodia, into which the less viscous internal cytoplasm flows. Strange to say, although the flagellar action of sperm cells and the sedate creeping of the common amoeba were some of the earliest phenomena known to microscopists, the mechanism of these nonmuscular types of movement is still less well understood today than is the mechanism of muscle contractility. The student first making the acquaintance of *Amoeba proteus* (see Figure 2.6) might well note that contemporary biologists are as perplexed by this living riddle almost as much as were the first explorers into the microbial world.

AMOEBOID MOVEMENT Spontaneous protoplasmic movements are of general occurrence in the living world. Some of these movements involve single organelles such as the nucleus, and their value to the organism is not yet clarified. For instance, the nuclei of epithelial cells lining the human nasal cavity rotate continuously at a rate of one turn each 4.3 min, and such nuclear rotation has been noted in a number of other tissues as well. Possibly the rotation aids in circulation of nutrients or in facilitating the passage of nuclear products into the cytoplasm. Similar speculation may be directed toward the rotary streaming (cyclosis) of cytoplasm in plant cells, which may reach velocities of 80 μm/sec.

Protoplasmic movements may result in amoeboid locomotion when part of the cell is in contact with some solid substratum that offers purchase. Portions of the cell surface may be deformed into temporary extensions (pseudopodia). These extensions may be broad and lobose, and in fact the entire anterior end of a creeping leucocyte may form a single pseudopod. The pseudopods of *A. proteus,* one of the organisms in which this type of locomotion has been most intensively studied, end bluntly and tend to contact the substratum only at their tips. Other protozoans such as foraminiferans have extremely long, delicate, pseudopods fused into a network of cytoplasm. Amoeboid movement in the slime mold *Physarum polycephalum* (Figure 2.16) is unusual in that the cytoplasm flows in one direction in any given portion of the plasmodium for about a minute, then stops and reverses for the same interval. A little forward progress is made, however, because the forward flow is slightly more rapid than the backflow. This streaming is accompanied by rhythmic pulsations of the entire plasmodium, somewhat like the beating of a heart.

So diverse are the types of cells capable of amoeboid movement and the specific characteristics of the movement itself that it is possible that there are different types of amoeboid movement, brought about by dissimilar mechanisms. In addition to cells and organisms that consistently employ amoeboid movement, we find that most types of embryonic cells can move about in this way when taken from the body and cultured in vitro. This implies that, at least up to a certain point in the process of differentiation, the capacity for amoeboid movement is present in almost all cells.

Amoeboid movement as seen in *A. proteus* has been painstakingly described and, although a description per se does not constitute an explanation of the phenomenon, it may serve to generate hypotheses concerning the causative mechanisms of this type of locomotion. The cytoplasm of *Amoeba* is differentiated into several distinct layers: a narrow zone of clear, relatively stiff ectoplasm covers the entire cell; within this lies a layer of granular ectoplasm which apparently exists in the state of a colloidal gel (Figure 16.32), for the inclusions found within this layer occupy fixed positions relative to one another; interior to this lies the apparently more fluid endoplasm that flows in the direction of travel. However, not all of the endoplasm exists in the state of a colloidal sol: the central core seems to exist as a gel in the form of a hollow tube. As the amoeba crawls, the endoplasm flows forward into the advancing pseudopodia, each of which ends in a transparent region (hyaline cap) that may consist of a bubble of water squeezed out by contraction of the gel just back of the tip. In this region, designated the "fountain zone," the endoplasm turns aside and, undergoing a change of colloidal state, becomes part of the granular ectoplasm. Occasionally some of the streaming endoplasm appears to burst foward from the fountain zone into the hyaline cap, and at such times the tip of the pseudopodium advances as much as 4 μm/sec. Meanwhile, at the posterior end of the cell the granular ectoplasm enters a "recruitment zone" where its viscosity is much reduced and here it flows medially to join the central core of endoplasm.

Figure 16.32 □ Proposed organization of a flowing amoeba (lateral aspect). In the recruitment zone, ectoplasm becomes endoplasm by solation; in the fountain zone, endoplasm becomes ectoplasm by gelation. The shear zone is symbolized by a dashed line. Compare with Figure 2.6.

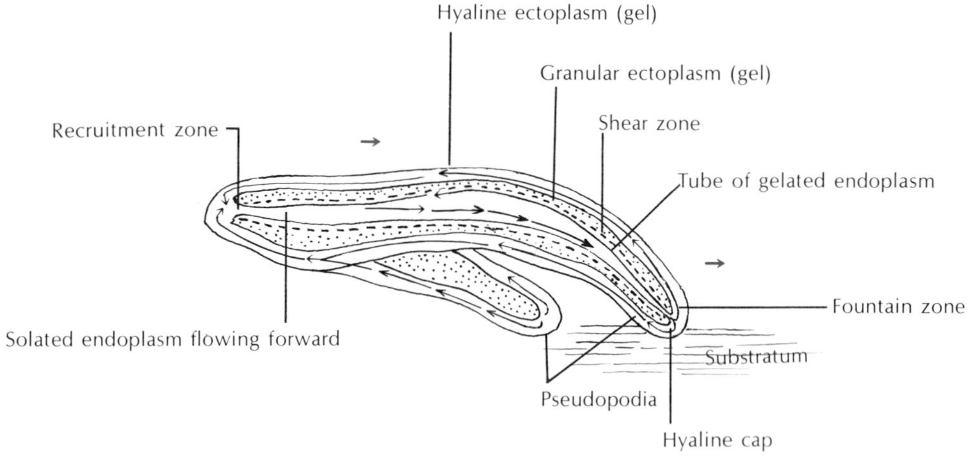

A number of ingenious interpretations of the events just described have been advanced. One is that the contraction of the gel in the fountain zone serves to pull the rest of the cytoplasm forward, much like a man lifting himself by his own shoelaces. Conversely, it has been proposed that contraction of the gel in the posterior part of the cell could push the rest of the cytoplasm forward like toothpaste being squeezed out of a tube (the outer tube of viscous ectoplasm serves to direct the force of hydraulic pressure toward the anterior end). Discovery of an inner tube of endoplasmic gel suggests the possibility that this tube may grow in length at the posterior end and simultaneously give up material to the ectoplasm at the anterior end so that new materials are always moving forward.

According to yet another hypothesis a shear zone exists between the ectoplasm and endoplasm, where some type of oriented ratchet mechanism may operate at the interface so that the endoplasm slides forward and the ectoplasm backward: ". . . one gel filament shears on the other like two millipeds traveling in opposite directions, the legs of one pushing back and of the other forward."* This is perhaps very similar to the proposed action of the cross bridges between the myosin and actin filaments of skeletal muscle. In the latter case the sliding filament hypothesis gains support from electron microscope studies of myofibrillar structure, whereas equivalent evidence has not been forthcoming with other cells. However, some supportive evidence has come from studies of cytoplasmic streaming in the giant cells of the freshwater alga *Nitella*. Placing a single cell under partial vacuum to prevent collapse of the cell wall, the lower end of the cell may be immersed in a saline solution and amputated so that although the ectoplasm remains in place droplets of the flowing endoplasm are extruded. Droplets of pure endoplasm collected in this way lack all locomotory properties even though the endoplasm before separation has been busily engaged in cyclosis. Droplets containing both endoplasm and ectoplasm, however, exhibit pulsatile or streaming movements! In such mixed droplets, rotating fibers have been seen that are thought to be the elements responsible for generating the shear force between ectoplasm and endoplasm.

The final explanation of amoeboid movement may prove to be a combination of several of the hypotheses summarized above, for they are not mutually exclusive. They are all worthy of serious study, for in cytoplasmic streaming and the internal forces that generate it we come to close grips with one of the fundamental properties of all living matter.

CILIARY MOVEMENT Specialized filamentous extensions, cilia and flagella, are widely used for locomotion of protozoans, small metazoans, free-swimming larvae, unicellular and colonial algae, and motile gametes. Cilia are also used to maintain flows of material along internal passages of the metazoan body. In man the windpipe, nasal cavity, and oviducts are lined by ciliated epithelium. Despite their widespread occurrence within the metazoan body, cilia originally must have served only as motive organelles of small aquatic organisms.

Cilia and flagella are remarkably similar in ultrastructure (excepting bacterial flagella, described below), but their mode of beating shows considerable variation (Figure 16.33). Flagella often occur singly whereas cilia tend to be numerous. An estimated 17,000 cilia clothe the body of a paramecium. Cilia are usually much shorter than flagella and their beating tends to resemble the rowing of a boat, in that the entire cilium bends at the base in a stiff, forceful power stroke that is followed by a flaccid, more gentle recovery stroke. However, whereas some types of cilia beat in only one direction and move back and forth in a single plane, other cilia (such as those of protozoans) can reverse the direction of the power stroke so that the animal may swim backward as well as forward. The recovery stroke of protozoan cilia does not follow the path of the power stroke, but describes an arc to one side of that path. Protozoan cilia can even rotate clockwise or counterclockwise so that the tip of the cilium moves through a circle. Flagella may also rotate so that the tip describes an arc, or they may undulate with waves of contraction passing from base to tip.

Two questions arise in the study of ciliary movement: (1) what mechanism is responsible for the beating of the individual cilium or flagellum; (2) how is ciliary action coordinated so that all cilia beat in the same direction and at the same rate? When we closely examine a swimming ciliate we see that during forward locomotion each wave of ciliary action begins at the anterior end and sweeps backward in a spiral course. In a plane at right angles to the direction of motion all the cilia in one transverse row beat together; but if we observe a row of cilia running from anterior to posterior, we note that a wave of excitation appears to be propagated rearwards so that each cilium begins to beat slightly after the one in front of it has begun its stroke (Figure 16.33*b*). Cutting through the system of neurofibrils that interconnects the cilia (see Figure 12.5) destroys the synchrony of their action. No equivalent system of fibrils seems to be present to coordinate the beating of a ciliated epithelium, but the action is nevertheless synchronous. If a small piece of epithelium (as from the frog pharynx) is removed and replaced in a reversed position, the cilia of the graft continue to beat synchronously, and in a direction opposite to that of the surrounding intact membrane: either they cannot be influenced to reverse the direction of their beating or they may be structurally incapable of doing so. The cilia of an isolated epithelial cell will also

*C. L. Prosser and F. A. Brown, Jr., *Comparative Animal Physiology,* 2nd ed. (Philadelphia: W. B. Saunders Company, 1961), p. 471.

Figure 16.33 □ (*a*) Patterns of flagellar action (heavy color arrows indicate direction of locomotion). (*b*) Ciliary action: power stroke (left) and recovery stroke (middle). At the right is a representation of the metachronous beating of the cilia of paramecium.

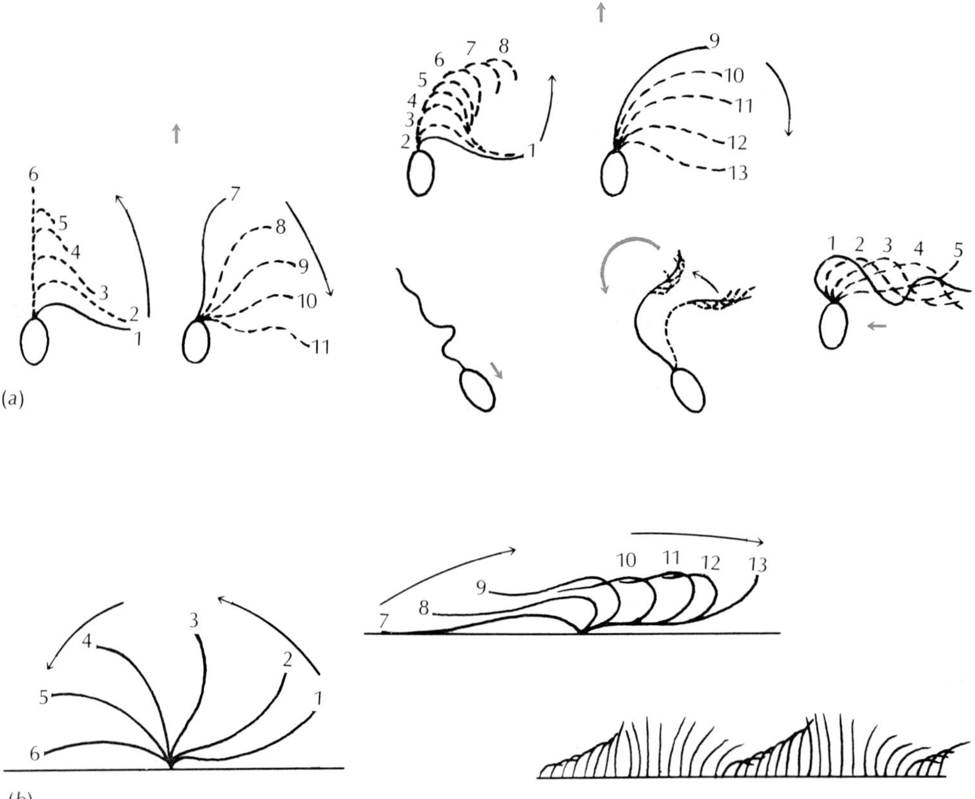

continue to beat normally, showing independence of nervous or hormonal stimulation.

We have no definite explanation as yet for the inner mechanism of ciliary or flagellar action. Unlike myofibrils, these motile filaments do not visibly shorten. Nevertheless, some localized contraction almost certainly takes place. Even an isolated flagellum will undulate in the presence of ATP if the length of the fragment exceeds a certain critical minimum. This implies that rhythmic beating is an inherent property of cilia and flagella, and that a study of their ultrastructure may reveal the physical organization underlying this property.

The whiplike flagella of bacteria differ in fine structure from the cilia and flagella of eucaryotic cells. They are as long as a typical cilium (3 to 12 μm) but are no more than 190 Å in diameter, as compared with a typical diameter of 2,000 Å for a cilium. Any bacterial flagellar structure visible to the light microscope is actually a compound structure consisting of many individual flagella fused together (see Figure 2.3*b*). Bacterial flagella consist 99 percent of one characteristic protein. In *Proteus vulgaris* three spiral filaments of this protein form each flagellum; the filaments are twisted about one another like strands of a cable and the cable itself describes a helix around a hollow core. If a flagellum is cut off, the bacterium rapidly grows a new one at a rate of as much as 0.5 μm/min, halting the synthesis when the regenerated filament attains a length characteristic of the species. Compound flagella located at one end of a bacterial cell may characteristically beat in a circle at as much as 40 cycles/sec, causing the bacterial cell to rotate in the opposite direction at about one-fourth this rate. Since most bacteria are slightly curved or spiral in form, they may thus literally drill their way through the medium.

We have examined the structure of the cilia and flagella of eucaryotic cells in Figure 10.12, noting that the most constant feature of their anatomy is a nine-plus-two arrangement of longitudinal tubular filaments that characteristically spring from a basal body (kinetosome) or may actually show continuity with the centrioles. The central pair of tubules are slightly larger than the surrounding ring of tubule doublets. The existence of nonmotile sensory cilia lacking the central pair of tubules but still having the peripheral circle of nine suggests that the central two may somehow be necessary for the excitation of the other nine. A current hypothesis holds that the central pair are responsible for the rapid conduction of excitation from the kinetosome through the core of the cilium, thus causing the peripheral filaments to respond almost simultaneously along their full length. Sudden contraction of five of the peripheral units is thought to bring about the power stroke, while the flaccid recovery stroke is due to a slow wave of contraction sweeping from base to tip of the other four doublets.

The molecular organization of the longitudinal tubules will probably furnish the most definite clue to the mode of ciliary action, but so far we can describe these filaments much less satisfactorily than we can the organization of a sarcomere. Each peripheral doublet presents a cross-sectional area about 200 Å across by 350 Å long, and the part that lies slightly closer to the center of the cilium is often seen to possess a pair of "arms" about 150 Å long. The tubules themselves consist of protein. A protein having ATPase activity reminiscent of that of myosin is localized in the arms of the peripheral doublets. The two central tubules are each about 240 Å in diameter and are spaced about 60 to 100 Å apart. The positioning of the pair is significant, for a cilium appears to be bilaterally symmetrical! (By this we mean that a plane passing between the two central tubules divides the cilium into "right" and "left" halves; this plane is characteristically also the plane of the ciliary stroke.)

So far our position with regard to ciliary action is somewhat like that of an aborigine who finds a rocket grounded in the jungle: he may work out an excellent description of the vehicle without having more than a vague notion as to what made it fly. We have come full circle back to the same problem: how do cilia beat? Probably the tubule doublets do contract, for a mere 6 percent contraction would suffice to bring about a full ciliary stroke, but whether or not this contraction can be explained in terms of the sliding filament hypothesis has yet to be determined. Certainly the motile elements are the tubules, for isolated fragments of flagella beat rhythmically on exposure to ATP, even when stripped of their outer membrane (an extension of the plasma membrane) and reduced to little more than the nine-plus-two structural unit.

H Sound production

In our study of animal communication (see Section 7.3C), we found that animals communicate in various ways—by means of colors, movements, postures, and odors, as well as by acoustic signals. The latter, commonly in use among vertebrates and certain insects, are capable of almost limitless diversification. They can be rigidly patterned to serve as species-specific mating calls operating across a distance much greater than that across which visual signals are effective. They can also be modulated to permit recognition of one individual by another or to reflect with accuracy such nuances as the relative intensity of the individual's aggressive and courting tendencies. A male bird may sing vigorously as a means of territorial defense when another individual first enters his territory, but upon perceiving that the intruder is a female of his species may continue the same song, but in a less strident manner that now serves to entice the female rather than repel a potential rival. Vocalizations also serve to reduce actual conflict between individuals or social units. Howler monkeys (Figure 16.34) have unusually well-developed voice boxes from which issue howls detectable across several kilometers that allow neighboring troops to ascertain and avoid each other's locale, and thus actual territorial defense is never required.

Sound production results from some muscular activity that sets into vibration the molecules of the surrounding medium (air or water). This muscular activity may involve the rhythmic movement of limbs against trunk or wings, sudden pressure of trunk muscles against a swim bladder, vibrations of laryngeal muscles, and other devices. Three kinds of biotically generated sounds may be distinguished, any of which may serve for communication: (1) incidental sounds; (2) stridulations and other nonvocal sounds; (3) vocalizations.

Figure 16.34 □ **Male red howler monkey vocalizing. Howls of remarkable volume, produced by means of the unusually large voice box, are primarily used to advertise the location of one troop to neighboring troops, thereby avoiding territorial encroachments and aggressive encounters. (*Zoological Society of San Diego.*)**

Figure 16.35 □ **Stridulatory organs of katydid (*Microcentrum*). Scraper at base of right wing rubs against file at base of left wing, producing stridulations that attract mates. (*Courtesy of Dr. Ross E. Hutchins.*)**

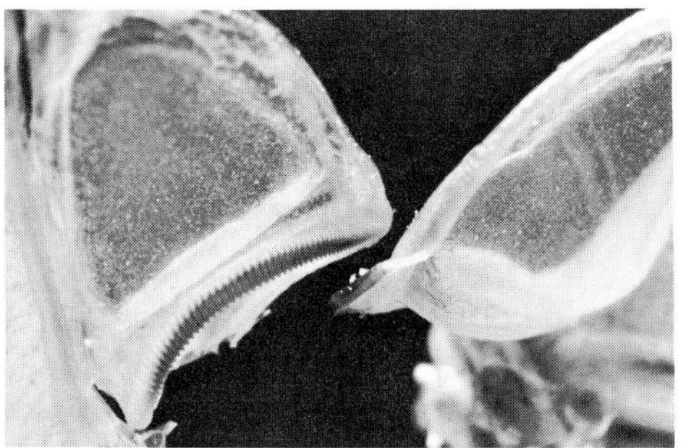

Incidental sounds are merely by-products of other activities. They include noises generated during swimming (hydrodynamic sounds), the rending and chewing sounds that accompany feeding, and the tramp of hooves or click of marching claws. Such sounds have not evolved as special communicatory signals but still may modify the behavior of those overhearing them. Hydrodynamic sounds may help schooling fish to remain together during the night. Feeding noises may prompt others nearby to feed—an example of social facilitation.

Stridulations are sounds produced by scraping, rubbing, or striking one body part against another. These are the sounds characteristically produced by arthropods (Figure 16.35). Insect stridulatory organs are modified portions of the chitinous exoskeleton; for instance, the margin of one wing may become specialized as a file and the edge of the wing opposite as a scraper that is rubbed against the file. Both the structure of the sound-producing apparatus and the action of the skeletal muscles moving the parts affect the quality of sound produced. The actual characteristics of the sound itself—frequency (pitch), amplitude (volume), and timbre (tonal quality or overtone characteristics)—may have been modified in the course of evolution to produce a species-specific signal; in addition, patterned neural discharges to the muscles produce a series of sound pulses of specific duration and rhythm. Used as mating calls, stridulations are extremely important as *reproductive isolating factors* that reduce the likelihood of hybrid matings occurring between individuals of related species. How can we actually demonstrate this function? Quantitative data can be collected here as in any other area of biological investigation. For instance, it has been suspected that the emission of certain sounds might serve as an isolating mechanism between the sympatric insect species *Chorthippus biguttulus* and *C. brunneus*. In captivity heterospecific matings do take place but very infrequently. However, when the two prospective sexual partners are caged together so that they can hear the songs of individuals of opposite sex belonging to their own species (both male and female *Chorthippus* sing), they tend to become so stimulated that the incidence of heterospecific mating greatly increases, though never reaching the frequency of normal conspecific matings (Figure 16.36). What these results show is that (1) matings *can* take place between individuals of the species *C. brunneus* and *C. biguttulus*—that is, morphological features do not prevent mating; (2) hearing the song of the other species releases mating behavior so imperfectly that the incidence of copulation remains insignificant even in captivity; (3) merely hearing the song of an individual of opposite sex and of the same species is sufficient to release mating behavior so that a significant increase in heterospecific copulations does take place under these circumstances.

Reproductive isolation continues to operate in the next generation, for a hybrid male produces a song that almost completely fails to attract females of either parental species! (A hybrid female fares slightly better than does the male, for her song occasionally attracts a male of one parental species or the other.) Thus we see that in this case "survival of the fittest" consists of being capable of producing a song that will release mating behavior in

Figure 16.36 □ **Effect of hearing song on frequency of heterospecific mating of *Chorthippus brunneus* and *C. biguttulus*. Individuals of one species are designated by black symbols for male (♂) and female (♀); those of the other species, by colored symbols. Encircled symbols indicate individuals present but enclosed in tubes so that they could be heard but not seen or contacted. Note that the frequency of heterospecific matings is greatest when each of the mating individuals can hear the song of a member of its own species of opposite sex. (*Data from Perdeck.*)**

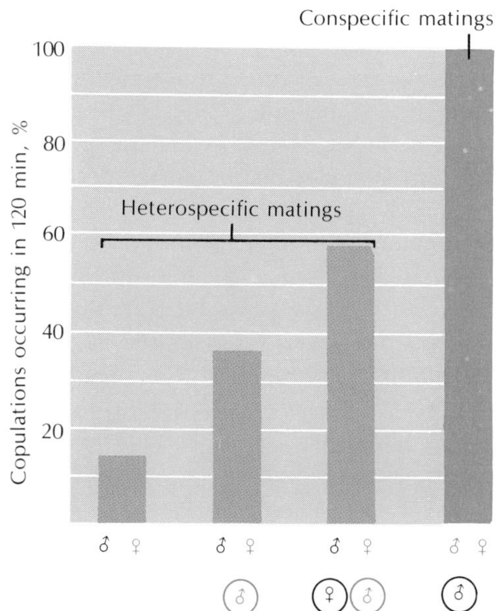

individuals of the opposite sex and of the correct species. Failure to produce such a song actually operates as a *genetic lethal* (defined earlier as any inheritable trait that prevents the individual from leaving progeny), for although the hybrid locusts do not seem to be physically impaired they rarely have progeny for want of a mate.

Nonvocal sounds are also produced by fish: drumming, honking, and groaning noises are generated mainly by the contraction of trunk muscles that rub against the wall of the swim bladder, which serves as a resonance chamber. Some species also use the internal portions of the bony fin supports (fin rays), beating these like drumsticks against the membrane of the swim bladder. The communicative significance of these sounds is not always clear, but some are produced in significant contexts, such as during courtship, when a male of the same species enters another's territory, and when the fish is seized by a predator. Other nonvocal sounds having communicative significance are produced even by species capable of vocalizing: a beaver warns others of danger by slapping its tail against water or the ground, and courting peacocks reinforce the visual display of their spread tail fans by producing a rattling whir with feathers specialized for this use.

Vocalizations are sounds generated in the air passages and are therefore characteristic of animals having lungs. During exhalation air passes through a vocal apparatus that can be set into vibration by the contractions of skeletal muscles; this in turn sets the air into vibration. Tetrapods (except birds) use the *larynx* (voice box) in sound production (Figure 16.37). Paired folds, the vocal folds or "cords," arise from each side of the larynx. The tension of these folds and the width of the air passage between them may be regulated by movements of the arytenoid cartilages, allowing sounds of different frequencies to be produced. The avian larynx lacks vocal cords; sound is produced instead by vibrations of the *syrinx,* an organ located at the point where the trachea branches to form the bronchi. The air sac located between the clavicles ("wishbone") can be made to vibrate by contractions of adjacent skeletal muscles and this vibration is transmitted in turn to the membranous walls of the syrinx, setting up vibrations in the air being exhaled through the syrinx. These basic sounds are modulated by movements of the beak, throat, and tongue, and their tonal quality is influenced by the shape of the larynx and buccal cavity.

The types of sounds an animal can produce—its "vocabulary"—may be genetically determined. Their character is then defined strictly by the anatomy of the sound-producing apparatus and the inherited organization of the nervous system that directs the performance of this apparatus. However, many homoiotherms not only have an innate vocabulary but may through experience develop in addition a rich variety of other acoustic signals. Songbirds, for instance, often have a language of about twenty distinct *call* notes and from one to five *songs* that have a more complex acoustic structure than simple calls. The calls may tend to be genetically fixed, but a subtle interplay of heredity and learning is often seen in the development of a bird's song. The first version expressed by the immature bird, the *subsong,* consists of an apparently unpatterned mixture of calls and subdued warbling. This is eventually replaced by the

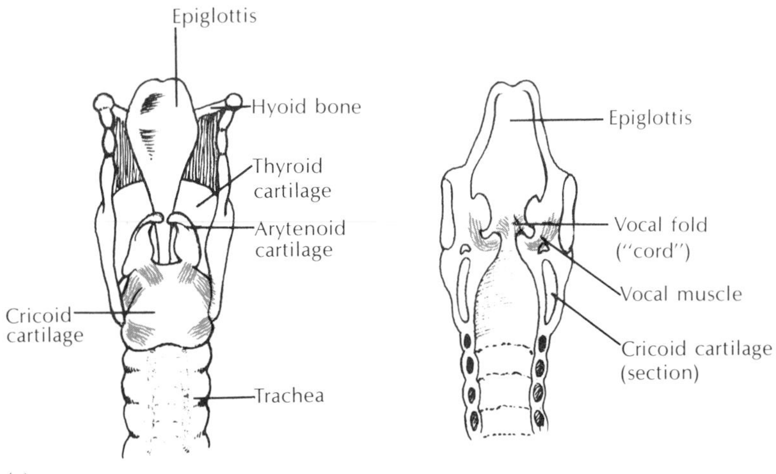

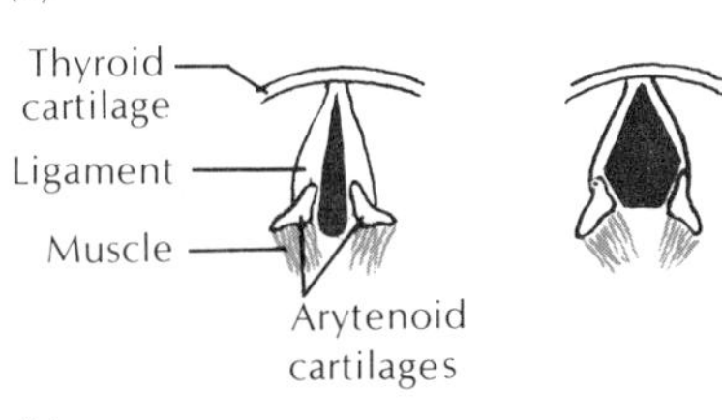

Figure 16.37 □ The human larynx. (*a*) Left, viewed from behind and, right, viewed from behind and sectioned through air passage. Note position of vocal folds (vocal cords) and the muscles that control them. (*b*) Position of arytenoid cartilages and width of glottal aperture: left, during quiet breathing and, right, during deep inhalation. (*c*) Vocal folds viewed from above, showing change in position and size of glottis from quiet breathing to voicing (*Bell Telephone Laboratories.*)

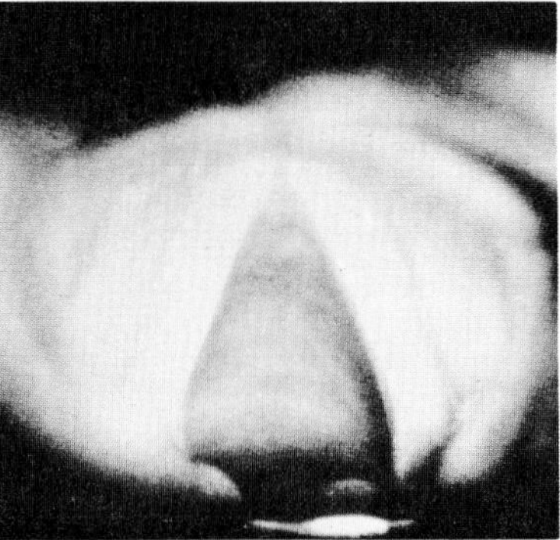

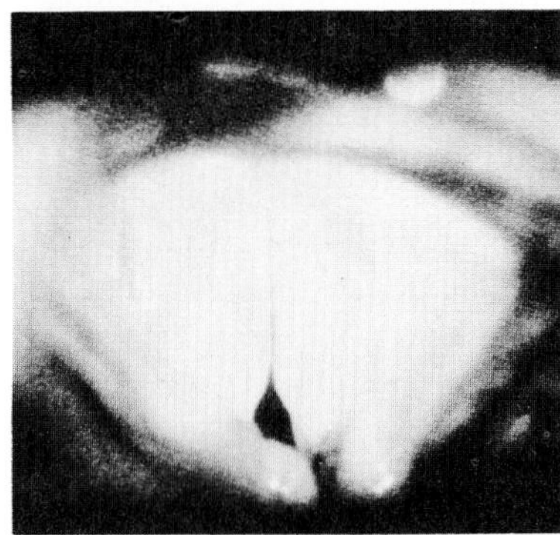

(c)

rehearsed song. This patterned singing develops into the song (the *primary song*) characteristic of the mature male bird in his reproductive state. The tendency to sing the subsong appears to be innate and forms the substratum onto which additional patterns will be added during maturation. Ordinarily the patterns added will be only those characteristic of the bird's own species, but such vocal mimetics as the mockingbird and lyre bird may also acquire the songs of other species and sing these with such remarkable fidelity as to drive from their territories not only rival males of their own kind but those of the other species as well. The effects of learning can be seen in development of the chaffinch's primary song, which tends to resemble more closely that of the breeding aggregation within which a bird is raised than it does the songs of other chaffinch populations. The finer details of a bird's primary song apparently are individual, no matter how closely the overall pattern conforms to that of the species: male birds learn to recognize and get used to songs sung by neighboring males in established territories but respond aggressively when the recorded song of a strange male is played nearby.

To be fully effective as a means of communication, animal sounds must usually be amplified. Sound amplification may or may not be subject to voluntary modulation. Insect stridulations are sometimes amplified by having the sound-producing organs centered within a flared extension of the thoracic shield that acts as a sound reflector. Male cicadas amplify their calls by stridulating in chorus, producing synchronized waves of sound that surge through the forest like swells breaking on some distant beach. This chorus summons females across a range

Figure 16.38 □ Electric organs. (*a*) *Torpedo*, the electric ray, showing electric organ on left side, served by nerves from brain. (*b*) Microscopic structure of electroplaques, lateral aspect, with innervated and noninnervated faces of several electroplaques in one column.

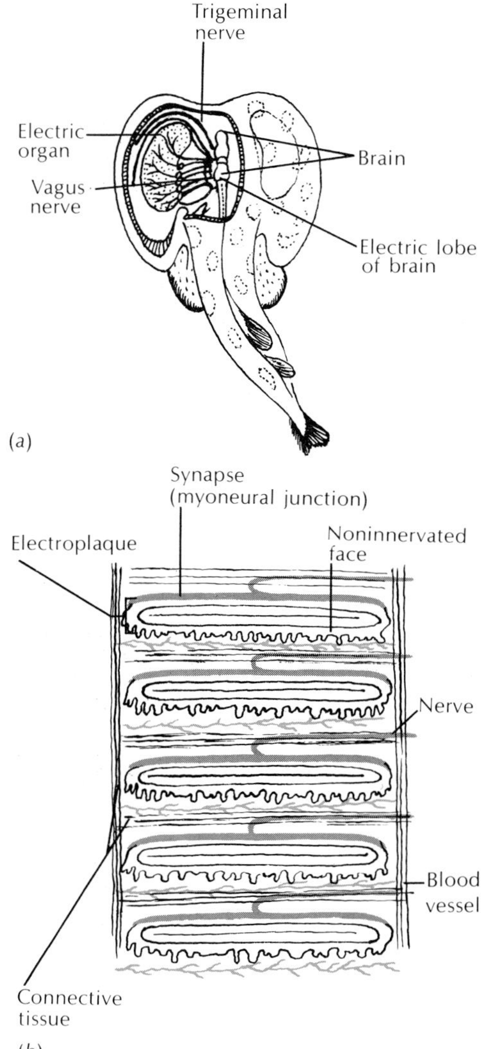

much greater than possible for the individual male.

In vertebrates the air passages lying anterior to the larynx or syrinx serve for sound amplification, especially the nasal cavities of mammals and the throat pouches (gular sacs) of frogs and toads, which act as resonance chambers. The enormous throat sac of the male tree frog ("spring peeper") allows the diminutive creature to attract his mate with nearly the volume and vocal authority of a bullfrog.

I Production of electrical discharges

All cells generate electricity in the form of a potential set up across the cell membrane due to the unequal distribution of ions in the cytoplasm and the external milieu. Muscle contraction is accompanied by an electrical discharge. The discharge that takes place when all fibers of a heart ventricle contract almost simultaneously is great enough to be registered externally by means of electrocardiograph.

Some of the skeletal muscles of certain fish have become specialized as *electric organs* capable of generating bioelectricity in amounts much greater than that generated and discharged during ordinary muscular contractions. The discharge of electricity is controlled by nerve fibers that branch profusely and make numerous synaptic contacts with one face of the platelike, noncontractile muscle fibers (*electroplaques*) which make up the electric organ (Figure 16.38). Many electroplaques are grouped (like coins stacked with all "heads" up) to form columns in which the innervated faces of the electroplaques all face in the same direction. As a rule the electroplaques in each column are oriented in the same direction as those in all other columns. In the South American electric eel there are several thousand electroplaques in each column. Nervous impulses reach all electroplaques in all columns at the same moment, causing simultaneous excitation of all of the innervated faces. As in excited nerve or muscle tissue, a reversal of the membrane charge takes place with the inside of the cell membrane briefly becoming electropositive. While this reversal of membrane polarity is taking place on the innervated faces, the noninnervated faces either retain their resting potential (as in the electric eel and the electric ray, *Torpedo*) or else also undergo depolarization, but only after the excitation of the innervated faces has been completed (as in most other freshwater electric fishes).

At the moment of excitation the inside of the membrane of the innervated face of each electroplaque becomes about 100 mV electropositive relative to the noninnervated face, so that each column momentarily consists of alternating positive and negative "plates" like those of a voltaic pile. The voltage generated correlates directly with the length of the column and the number of electroplaques lined up in series, whereas the strength of the current (amperage) correlates directly with the surface area of each electroplaque and the number of columns lined up parallel to one another.

In the electric eel the columns of the electric organs are few but long, running most of the length of the fish; thus, although the amperage is low, several hundred volts can be discharged from each column, generating a shock that can stun or even kill fairly large animals. If a caiman (South

American alligator) were to blunder into a pond infested with electric eels, it might be attacked by a number of eels, shocked into unconsciousness, and drowned. Another fish that can generate strong shocks is the electric ray, *Torpedo*. The ray's body is very much flattened from top to bottom, as a result of which the columns of the electric organs are short, but so many lie in parallel that the current generated measures several amperes although only about 60 V are discharged at one time. Most fish that produce powerful electric discharges do so to immobilize prey or when threatened by predators. Other species that generate weak electrical fields typically produce regular pulses employed in echo location, as we use radar and bats use ultrasound (see Figure 15.9). Such pulses may be given off uninterruptedly night and day at species-specific rates ranging from 4 to 2,000 discharges *per second* throughout life! If a moving object is detected in the "radar field," the fish often respond by varying the rate at which the pulses are emitted, this presumably helping them to locate the object more accurately.

J Photogenic responses

Production of light may serve to attract prey or bring potential mates together, as mentioned in our earlier discussions of deep-sea animals and fireflies. Unless an animal luminesces constantly, light production usually is a definite photogenic response set off by appropriate stimuli. A male firefly in search of a mate and a wingless female lurking in the grass both emit light signals at low frequencies; when one of them perceives the other's signal, it begins to flash at a higher rate and as a result the signals are reinforced until the two insects come together.

Certain deep-sea shrimp escape predators by discharging a glowing cloud of luminescent material as effective in their dark environment as the ink of cuttlefish in the lighted world above. In this case potentially photogenic materials react only when discharged and exposed to O_2. More usually, production of light is an intracellular response involving reactions different from those of regular metabolism. Emission of energy as visible light requires that it be liberated in packets equaling 40 to 60 kcal, a "burst" up to four times greater than the usual amount released by dephosphorylation reactions. The light-producing reaction depends on the enzymatically controlled oxidation of any of a number of different potentially luminescent compounds known as *luciferins;* the enzymes catalyzing the reaction are termed *luciferases*. The reaction requires O_2 and in the firefly also demands a supply of ATP and Mg^{2+}. Evidence suggests that before the cell can luminesce a luciferin–Mg^{2+}–luciferase–ATP complex is formed, which breaks down when the cell is excited and releases energy in the form of a light quantum.

In many bioluminescent species the photogenic response is so precisely controlled by the nervous system that species-specific flashing patterns are emitted to which only individuals of the same species will respond (see Figure 7.22). In luminescent fish the light-producing cells (photophores) are directly stimulated by sympathetic nerve fibers, whereas in the firefly the nerves seem not to control the photophores themselves but to govern the flow of air to the cells by regulating the bore of the tracheoles. (As mentioned above, the photogenic response of the firefly requires O_2.) We need not assume that there is any one universal mechanism for light production in the animal world, for the capability has arisen independently in unrelated species or even in a few families of an otherwise nonluminescent group.

K Color change as a behavioral response

Seasonal changes in the color of skin, hair, or feathers may serve to protect an animal (as when an arctic hare turns white in winter) or may advertise breeding state (as when the belly of the male three-spined stickleback reddens). Such changes take place gradually under hormonal regulation and cannot themselves be considered behavioral responses, although certainly important in eliciting certain types of behavior. However, relatively rapid short-term color changes do take place in cephalopods and a number of crustaceans, fishes, and reptiles that may enable the animal to match its background or to communicate with other individuals of its species. We all know the communicative value of blushing, even though we cannot voluntarily control the color change and would usually prefer that it not take place at all. Blushing results from the dilation of skin capillaries, but most forms of color change depend on the reactions of pigment cells (*chromatophores*).

The cephalopod chromatophore is a spherical cell with a highly elastic plasma membrane to which are attached from 6 to

20 radially arranged smooth muscle fibers (Figure 16.39*a*). Contraction of these fibers stretches the pigment cell into the form of a thin disc, the flat surface of which lies parallel to the surface of the skin. When the muscle fibers relax the chromatophore elastically rounds up once more. The muscle fibers governing the chromatophore are themselves controlled by nerve fibers. Each chromatophore contains but one kind of pigment, but the expansion or contraction of various proportions of the several types present make possible a number of distinctive color responses. White, red, yellow, and black chromatophores may be present, and the neural control over them is so elaborate that complex patterns may be produced such as the zebra striping of male cuttlefish, used as a threat display (Figure 16.39*b*). So important to the cephalopod is color change that three entire brain centers are concerned with this response: one center inhibits chromatophore expansion; a second receives and correlates visual, acoustic, and equilibratory sensations; it in turn relays impulses to the third or chromatophore motor center, from which motor nerve fibers pass to the muscles serving the chromatophores.

Chromatophores found in other animals are much-branched cells within which the distribution of pigment granules is altered by cytoplasmic streaming (Figure 16.39c). A pigment becomes more conspicuous by being evenly dispersed throughout the cytoplasm and becomes inconspicuous when concentrated about the nucleus. The cytoplasmic streaming that affects pigment distribution is so controlled that in the very same cell one pigment may disperse while another concentrates about the nucleus. Crustaceans that match their backgrounds by appropriate color changes depend for the response on the action of the neurohormones (chromatophorotrophins) released from the sinus gland, as mentioned in Chapter 15. Hagfish, elasmobranchs, and amphibians may gradually change color under hormonal influence, but the pigment cells of modern bony fishes are also typically controlled by autonomic nerve fibers—sometimes sympathetic only and sometimes both sympathetic and parasympathetic fibers, with the former promoting darkening and the latter blanching. In this manner some reef fishes can pass from one color pattern to another in only a few minutes.

Perhaps the most sophisticated type of chromatophore control among vertebrates is seen in the African chameleon. In this lizard the chromatophores each contain several pigments, the distribution of which is under the control of pigment-dispersing and pigment-concentrating nerve fibers.

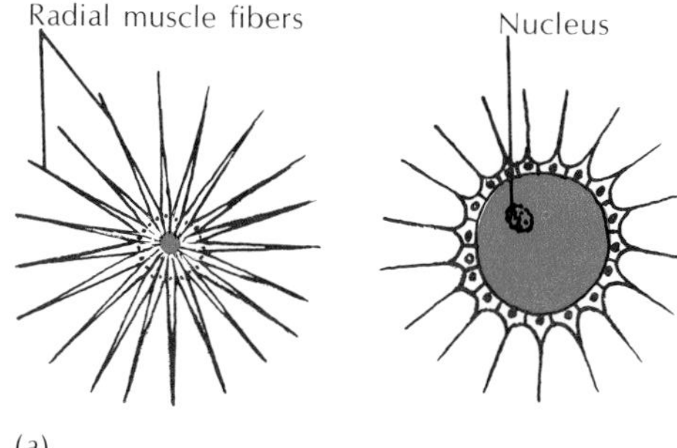

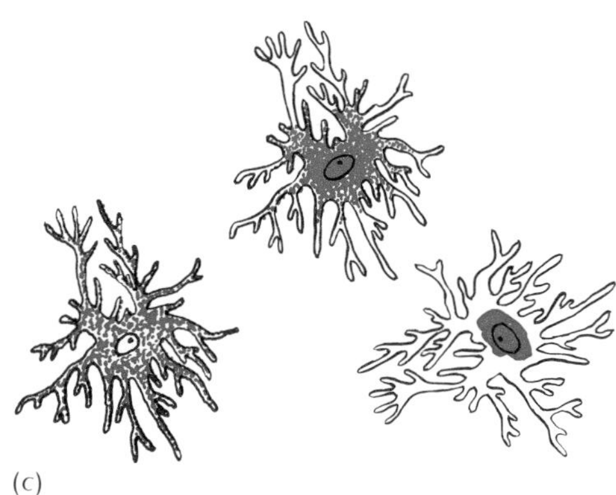

Figure 16.39 □ Chromatophore responses. (*a*) Cephalopod chromatophore: left, muscle fibers relaxed and pigment cell contracted and, right, muscle fibers contracted, expanding the pigment cell. (*b*) Aggressive zebra-stripe threat display of male cuttlefish (*Sepia*). This vivid pattern is often displayed while the males hover side by side, facing in opposite directions. (*Courtesy of Dr. Douglas P. Wilson.*) (*c*) Response of crustacean chromatophore to change in background color. Left, shrimp on black background and black pigment granules fully dispersed throughout cytoplasm of pigment cell, affording the animal protective coloration. Center, same chromatophore after shrimp has been on white background for 0.5 hr. Right, same cell after shrimp has been on white background for 2 hr; pigment granules are now fully concentrated about the nucleus, leaving the cell nearly colorless.

In a number of species physiological color changes associated with breeding state are "advertised" by specific patterns of behavior that serve to make the colored area more conspicuous, as when the male frigate bird inflates his scarlet throat pouch. By such means, as well as by the chromatophore responses that have just been described, an animal may use color changes as a form of communication with others of its own kind.

L Behavior as a factor in animal evolution

Behavior plays a leading role in the evolution of higher animals. It serves as a selective factor influencing the further development of body parts that enable the behavior to be performed more profitably. By way of example, if a bird were to feed by slicing the surface of the water with its open bill while flying just above water level, such feeding behavior would make adaptive any changes in bill structure that increased the effectiveness of prey capture. The black skimmer (*Rhynchops*), a seabird that feeds in this manner, has an unusually long and heavy mandible (much out of proportion to the smaller upper bill) that serves to cut the water more deeply as the bird skims across the waves hunting. Of course it may be argued that this odd bill evolved first and the bird then adopted a mode of food-getting that would put the bill to use, but it seems unlikely that a morphological change would proceed to such extremes without there being already some adaptive value in the specialization. It is equally unlikely that penguins lost the power of flight and then took up swimming; conversely, birds that swam in pursuit of fish might readily undergo selection toward greater speed and maneuverability in the water, even at the cost of losing the ability to fly, which in this case would be less relevant to survival than would an increased proficiency in swimming.

Behavior also acts as a selective factor in the evolution of structures having releasing value, that is, serving as stimuli to promote or trigger certain behavioral responses. We have already noted that the gaping response of young birds releases feeding behavior on the part of the parents. The effectiveness of the signal has been enhanced in many species, not only by the outsized beak of the nestlings, but also by the fact that the sides of the mouth may be brightly outlined with yellow and the lining of the mouth may contrast with the external coloration, even to the extent of being brightly spotted. In Chapter 17 we shall see that the tendency of the females of some species to mate with males capable of the most striking display of plumage seems to have promoted the development in the male of breeding plumage so cumbersome as to menace his very survival. Field experiments with artificial eggs have shown that an egg larger than that normal to the species can evoke incubation attempts more strongly than an actual egg does (see Figure 16.19). The effectiveness of such *supernormal* stimuli clearly demonstrates the manner in which behavior and morphology can interact to promote evolutionary change. If an oystercatcher will abandon its own egg to attempt to straddle an impossibly large dummy egg, it is apparent that a selective force is in operation that should cause birds of this species to produce ever larger eggs. Despite behavioral preferences, the actual limits to egg size must eventually be dictated by the anatomical limitations of the female's reproductive tract as well as by the fact that an egg too large to hover efficiently cannot be kept warm enough to hatch. However, the tendency of a bird to show preference for larger eggs may save it from fruitlessly brooding an abnormally small, possibly yolkless egg, and this may explain in part the adaptive value of such a behavioral preference.

Adoption of some new behavior may also be the first step leading to speciation—the splitting of one original species to form new species. Any factor that restricts gene flow within a population can lead to speciation. Restriction in gene flow is likely first to occur by the selection of a new habitat, particularly for breeding. In Figure 6.14 we saw that some species of cormorants nest on cliffs beside the sea, whereas others migrate inland and nest in trees. Such diversification of nesting preference effectively isolates the species, for although both feed at sea and may occur sympatrically except during the reproductive season, isolation during breeding prevents heterospecific matings from taking place. Of course, these cormorants already represent two different species, but we can see that differences in nest-site preference could cause speciation to occur. If one population within a species were by chance to adopt a new breeding place, that population would from that point on fail to interbreed with other members of the species.

We have already noted that behavior also serves as a reproductive isolating mechanism operating between species. Species-specific courtship displays and mating calls greatly reduce the probability of heterospecific matings between sympatric populations of related species. Any isolating factor that operates so early in the mating process contributes more effectively to survival of the population than does one that operates later, such as hybrid sterility or death of the embryo during development.

REVIEW AND DISCUSSION

1 Discuss the regulation of enzyme synthesis and action. Explain the operon hypothesis.

2 Specify the role of each of the following in the regulation of body fluids: (*a*) angiotensin; (*b*) aldosterone; (*c*) vasopressin; (*d*) kidney tubule cells; (*e*) hypothalamus; (*f*) parathormone; (*g*) glucagon.

3 What adaptive modifications have taken place during the evolution of the vertebrate kidney? How has it become modified in marine fishes? How does the structural organization of the mammalian nephron, together with its permeability properties, assist the recovery of water?

4 Compare the structure and occurrence of protonephridia, metanephridia, and Malpighian tubules. Compare kidney structure and the process of urine formation in vertebrates and insects.

5 Discuss the adaptive value of countercurrent exchange systems in the animal body.

6 Compare cold narcosis with hibernation, and summarize the special adaptations characteristic of hibernator species.

7 What are the benefits and penalties of facultative homoiothermy as compared with obligate homoiothermy and with poikilothermy? Under what conditions might facultative homoiothermy be necessary for survival?

8 Explain the concept of the "act" as a unit of behavior and cite cases in which the neural organization responsible for the performance of specific acts appears to be inherited through the mediation of Mendelian factors.

9 Contrast the appetitive and consummatory aspects of behavior. Which types of behavior are most likely to consist of unlearned fixed action patterns?

10 Distinguish between: (*a*) habituation and extinction; (*b*) reward and reinforcement; (*c*) latent, insight, and trial-and-error learning.

11 How could you determine on the basis of observed behavior whether a given species responds to light menotactically, klinotactically, or tropotactically? How would the behavior of a photokinetic species differ from one that is phototactic? What additional capacity must be present for the most effective exploitation of menotaxis?

12 Speculate concerning the genetic and neurophysiological basis of each of the following: (*a*) displacement behavior; (*b*) behavior directed toward an inappropriate stimulus object; (*c*) the releasing capacity of a sign stimulus; (*d*) the breakdown of the nest-material-carrying act system in hybrid *Agapornis*.

13 Summarize the intracellular events that take place during muscular contraction and recovery. What are the specific roles of acetylcholine, glycogen, ATP, phosphagen, actin, myosin, and oxygen in muscular activity?

14 How are electrical discharges generated by electric fishes? How is survival enhanced by the capacity to produce such discharges?

REFERENCES

ALLEN, R. D. "Amoeboid Movement," *Sci. Amer.,* **206** (1962). Describes possible mechanisms of pseudopodial locomotion.

BENZINGER, T. H. "The Human Thermostat," *Sci. Amer.,* **204** (1961). A brain mechanism sets the baseline for maintenance of body temperature.

BOGERT, C. M. "How Reptiles Regulate Their Body Temperature," *Sci. Amer.,* **200** (1959). Behavioral thermoregulation may compensate for physiological incapacity to maintain a stable body temperature.

BOYCOTT, B. B. "Learning in the Octopus," *Sci. Amer.*, **212** (1965). Operant conditioning indicates the nature of perception and learning capacity in this sophisticated mollusc.

CHANGEAUX, J. "The Control of Biochemical Reactions," *Sci. Amer.*, **212** (1965). Summarizes current theory regarding metabolic control systems at the molecular level.

DAVIS, W. J., JR. "Cricket Wing Movements during Stridulation," *Anim. Behav.*, **16** (1968). High-speed cinephotography is applied to the analysis of the motor patterns whereby crickets produce acoustic signals.

DILGER, W. C. "The Behavior of Lovebirds," *Sci. Amer.*, **206** (1962). Describes the behavior of several species of the African lovebird, *Agapornis*, with particular reference to the collecting and transport of nesting materials in birds of each species and interspecific hybrids.

DU BRUL, E. L. "Pattern of Genetic Control of Structure in the Evolution of Behavior," *Perspectives in Biol. and Med.*, **10** (1967). Embryological evidence suggests that genetically based changes in skeletal muscles affect the development of relevant parts of the nervous system.

EDNEY, E. B. "Water Balance in Desert Arthropods," *Science*, **156** (1967).

FRAENKEL, G. S., AND D. L. GUNN *The Orientation of Animals.* New York: Dover Publications, Inc., 1961. This classic work defines major types of oriented movements and reviews relevant experimental work.

GOTTSCHALK, C. "Osmotic Concentration and Dilution in the Mammalian Nephron," *Circulation*, **21** (1960).

HARDY, J. D. "Physiology of Temperature Regulation," *Physiol. Rev.*, **41** (1961).

HUXLEY, H. E. "The Mechanism of Muscular Contraction," *Sci. Amer.*, **213** (1965). Proposes a sliding-filament theory of contraction based on studies of striated muscle ultrastructure.

IRVING, L. "Adaptations to Cold," *Sci. Amer.*, **214** (1966).

JOHNSGARD, P. A. *Animal Behavior.* Dubuque, Iowa: William C. Brown Company, Publishers, 1967. An excellent short introduction to the biological study of animal behavior, including consideration of the ecology, evolution, and ontogeny of behavior.

KAMAMOTO, F. I., K. N. KATO, AND L. E. TUCKER "Neurosecretion and Salt and Water Balance in the Annelida and Crustacea," *Amer. Zool.*, **6** (1966). Evidence is presented for the neuroendocrine control of water and ion balance in the species studied.

KENNEDY, D. "Small Systems of Nerve Cells," *Sci. Amer.*, **216** (1967). Analysis of invertebrate behavior is facilitated by the fact that complete behavioral systems may be controlled by a very few neurons, the activity of which can be monitored by microelectrodes.

LANGLEY, L. L. *Homeostasis.* New York: Reinhold Publishing Corporation, 1965. A brief, elementary introduction to problems of steady-state mechanisms concerned with body weight, respiration, heartbeat, movement, and body fluids.

LISSMANN, H. W. "Electric Location by Fishes," *Sci. Amer.*, **208** (1963).

MCCULLOUGH, C. B. "Pacemaker Interaction in *Hydra*," *Amer. Zool.*, **5** (1965). The behavior of a simple coelenterate is explained in terms of the interaction of two distinct through-conduction networks, each controlled by its own pacemaker.

MROSOVSKY, N. "The Adjustable Brain of Hibernators," *Sci. Amer.*, **218** (1968). Rhythmic fluctuations characterize the hypothalamic brain centers that regulate feeding behavior and body temperature.

PRIBRAM, K. H. "The Neurophysiology of Remembering," *Sci. Amer.*, **220** (1969). Experiments suggest that recall may be associated with holographic brain activation in which discrete mnemic events are simultaneously activated to form a coherent whole.

ROTHENBUHLER, W. "Behavior Genetics of Nest Cleaning in Honey Bees. IV. Responses of F_1 and Backcross Generations to Disease-killed Brood," *Amer. Zool.*, **4** (1964). Uncapping of brood cells and removal of dead larvae appear to be controlled by independently assorting genes.

SCHMIDT-NIELSEN, K. "Salt Glands," *Sci. Amer.*, **200** (1959). Special salt-excreting glands enable marine birds and reptiles to drink sea water.

SEILACHER, A. "Fossil Behavior," *Sci. Amer.*, **217** (1967). Tracks and burrows of Paleozoic invertebrates shed light on the evolution of patterns of food-seeking behavior.

SHARPE, R. S., AND P. A. JOHNSGARD "Inheritance of Behavioral Characters in F_2 Mallard × Pintail (*Anas platyrhynchos L.* × *Anas acuta L.*) Hybrids," *Behaviour*, **27** (1966). The motor patterns of courting hybrid drakes are compared with those of the two parental species.

SMITH, D. S. "The Flight Muscles of Insects," *Sci. Amer.*, **212** (1965).

SMITH, W. J. "Vocal Communication of Information in Birds," *Amer. Nat.*, **97** (1963). In the tyrant flycatchers variation on but a few basic vocal patterns provides means of modifying information content.

TAYLOR, C. R. "The Eland and the Oryx," *Sci. Amer.*, **220** (1969). Living in arid habitats, these antelopes control body and brain temperature and conserve water through several unique physiological and behavioral adaptations.

UNGAR, G. "Molecular Mechanisms in Learning," *Perspectives in Biol. and Med.,* **11** (1968). Reviews evidence of intraneuronal molecular changes associated with the learning process and presents a hypothesis whereby these changes bring about activation of a previously nonfunctional neural channel.

VAN DER KLOOT, W. G. "Membrane Depolarization and the Metabolism of Muscle," *Amer. Zool.,* **7** (1967). Considers the question of how the respiration of frog muscle fibers is increased at the time of excitation.

WELLS, M. J. "Invertebrate Learning," *Nat. Hist.,* **75** (1966). Experiments with octopus indicate lack of peripheral feedback for proprioceptive control of motor activities.

WILSON, D. M. "The Flight Control System of the Locust," *Sci. Amer.,* **218** (1968). Neurophysiological experiments indicate that wing movements in flight are controlled both by a genetically programmed central mechanism and by reflexes elicited by relevant proprioceptive, visual, and tactile stimuli.

WILSON, V. J. "Inhibition in the Central Nervous System," *Sci. Amer.,* **214** (1966). Muscular activity involves the stimulation of certain motor neurons and the simultaneous inhibition of others.

Part 5

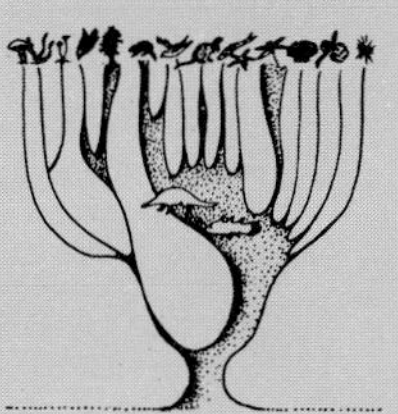

THE CONTINUANCE OF LIFE

A thing . . . never returns to nothing, but all things after disruption go back into the first bodies of matter . . . then goodly crops spring up and boughs are green with leaves upon the trees, trees themselves grow and are laden with fruit; by them in turn our race and the race of wild beasts are fed, by them we see glad towns teem with children and the leafy forests ring on all sides with the song of new birds; through them cattle wearied with their load of fat lay their bodies down about the glad pastures and the white milky stream pours from the distended udders; through them a new brood with weakly limbs frisks and gambols over the soft grass, rapt in their young hearts with the pure new milk. None of the things therefore which seem to be lost is utterly lost, since nature replenishes one thing out of another and does not suffer any thing to be begotten, before she has been recruited by the death of some other.

LUCRETIUS

The lifespan of the individual organism is finite. Even such potential immortals as hydra must eventually succumb to unfavorable environmental conditions or injuries. No matter whether the life of the individual be reckoned in hours or millenia, the persistence of any species depends on its ability to compensate for the mortality of the individual by the production of new ones. Conversely, the persistence of any biotic *community* depends also on the effective *limitation* of increase by each species within the community; each thus normally remains in homeostatic equilibrium with other members of the community. Only those communities endure in which mortality is balanced by reproduction and fecundity by limitations on rate of increase. Although predators and parasites play important roles in maintaining populations at an asymptote (the point at which a population growth curve levels off so that mortality and reproduction remain in balance; see Figure 6.1), in many species restriction in rate of increase appears to rest ultimately upon regulatory factors operating within the individual species. Some of these factors have been considered in Chapter 7. Both effective population control and successful perpetuation of kind depend to some extent on group interactions within the species. A field of plants must come into flower at the same time if cross pollination is to succeed. An aggregation of sea urchins must shed eggs and sperm synchronously if adequate numbers of zygotes are to be formed. So important are these interactions that, in effect, the study of reproduction in higher animals becomes the study of social behavior, both with respect to mating and subsequent care of the young. The social aspects of reproduction will therefore be one of the major topics that are to be considered in detail in the following chapter.

Reproduction depends ultimately on the template replication of nucleic acids, by which certain nutrient materials are reorganized to produce copies of the genetic code of the species; this code is then transmitted to each new cell or organism. It is through such template replication that adaptive advances made by previous generations have been passed on to the new, making possible a gradual increase in the complexity of life.

We have previously considered the mechanisms of nucleic acid and cellular reproduction (see Sections 9.7 and 10.6) and will now devote our attention primarily to perpetuation of kind at the level of the organism and the community. Perpetuation of life involves more than the replication of a genetic code and the growth and division of cells—the lives of each generation must be shaped toward the successful creation of the next generation and, as far as possible, toward safeguarding these offspring through their precarious beginnings.

Chapter 17  PERPETUATION OF KIND

PERPETUATION OF KIND INVOLVES MORE than the mere act of reproduction, for it also includes whatever means a species may use for minimizing the mortality of gametes and young. Although many organisms are capable of some type of asexual or vegetative proliferation requiring no exchange of genetic material between individuals, the vast majority also rely on sexual processes that necessarily require the interaction of two or more individuals of the same species. This interaction may be so brief as to accomplish only the union of gametes or it may be so prolonged that the products of the union can be nurtured within a family unit from conception to young adulthood. Whatever the extent of interaction, integrative mechanisms must be brought into play that assure the effectiveness of the reproductive process and make it possible for each new generation approximately to equal the numbers of the one preceding. Although numbers of individuals do not remain exactly the same from one generation to the next, any decline must eventually be offset by a rise in prolificacy (or extinction will result), while any increase beyond tolerable levels must be met either by increased predation, disease, and starvation, or by intraspecific population-limiting devices. These latter include pregnancy block, abortion, forced emigration, and the intensified aggression and slaughter of conspecifics that may come as a result of tensions generated by overcrowding.

Most successful species offset mortality both by prolificacy and by energy-saving adaptations that reduce the mortality of sex cells and progeny. We shall consider both of these facets of successful perpetuation.

Proliferation is accomplished by both asexual and sexual means in most kinds of living things. Asexual reproduction provides a safety factor, especially in species that must maintain a high rate of increase, for no mating is necessary and should but a single organism survive to maturity it can give rise to a clone of identical progeny. Sexual reproduction is less certain to occur, for two mature individuals of appropriate sex or mating type must usually come together to effect the exchange of hereditary material; nevertheless its adaptive value is tremendous, as is attested to by the fact that nearly all existing organisms, including most bacteria and protozoans, at least occasionally resort to processes of sexual exchange. Such genetic recombination augments a population's chance of survival by increasing its variability.

17.1 □ ASEXUAL REPRODUCTION

A Fission

Many unicellular organisms rely primarily upon asexual reproduction by binary or multiple fission, although sexual union often intervenes after a number of generations of asexual increase (Figure 17.1a). *Binary fission* is the splitting of one organism into two, and is in essence identical with cell division (Figure 17.2). However, it involves not only the precise apportionment of chromosomes between the two daughter cells (as shown in Figures 10.14 and 10.15), but also the reproduction of flagella and various other specialized organelles characteristic of the more complex acellular organisms. The formation of the spindle and

Figure 17.1 □ **Types of asexual reproduction. (*a*) Fission of unicellular organisms: left to right, longitudinal binary fission, transverse binary fission, multiple fission, and unequal fission ("budding"). (*b*) Vegetative proliferation in multicellular organisms: left to right, budding from common stalk of colonial hydroid, budding from body column of solitary polyp, strobilation, fragmentation by posterior decay, and two examples of growth of new individuals along stolons (runners).**

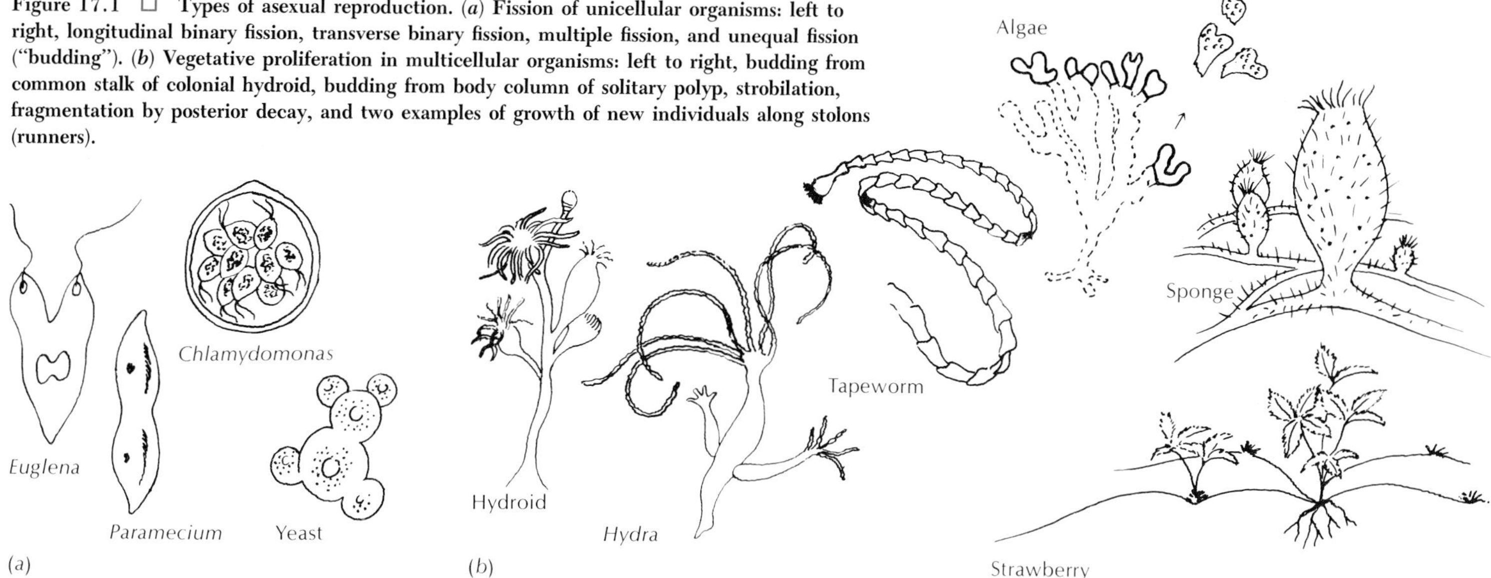

separation of chromatids during fission often takes place within the intact nuclear envelope. During *multiple fission,* several (rather than only two) identical cells are formed by the repeated division of the original protoplast, following which the outer wall is ruptured and the progeny escape. *Unequal fission* (budding), with the daughter cells receiving the necessary nuclear material but little cytoplasm, is characteristic of yeasts.

Figure 17.2 □ (*a*) Electron micrograph of *Bacillus subtilis* in process of fission. (*Courtesy of Dr. George B. Chapman.*) (*b*) Three successive stages in transverse fission of *Paramecium;* the macronucleus stains darkly. (*Ward's Natural Science Establishment, Inc.*)

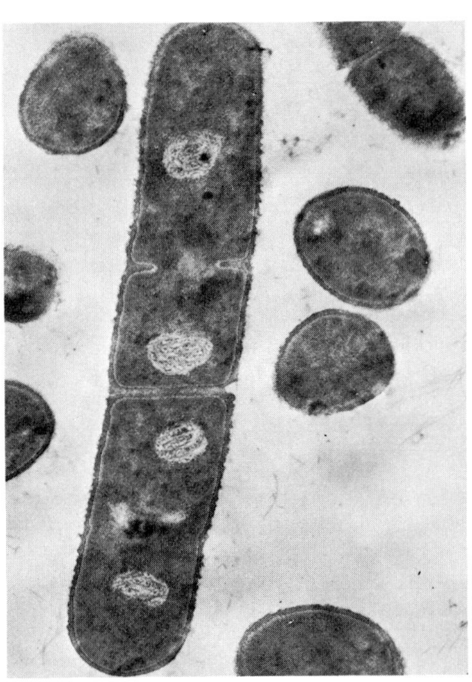

(*a*)

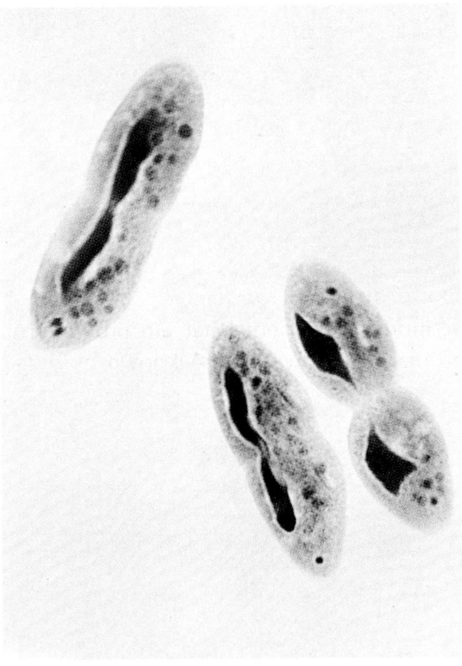

(*b*)

B Asexual reproduction in multicellular organisms

VEGETATIVE PROLIFERATION Several avenues of vegetative proliferation are open to multicellular organisms. *Budding* (Figure 17.3*a*) is a process in which a somatic cell of a preexisting individual begins to cleave like a zygote, forming a new individual that remains attached to the parent's body for some time, receiving nourishment. The *bud* either eventually pinches free to assume an independent existence or else remains attached to the parent, forming part of a colony. Sponges, coelenterates, and flatworms bud frequently, and *strobilation* (Figure 17.3*b*) is a normal aspect of the life cycles of jellyfish and tapeworms.

Spontaneous *fragmentation* is less common than budding, but does serve as a regular means of proliferation in some species. Algae and liverworts can propagate by a type of fragmentation in which the older parts of the thallus die (*posterior decay*), leaving the separated tips to develop into new individuals. Fragmentation of the vegetative mycelium of fungi also produces new individuals, for each hyphal fragment can

Figure 17.3 □ **Asexual reproduction in coelenterates: (*a*) hydra with bud (*Ward's Natural Science Establishment, Inc.*); (*b*) strobilating *Aurelia* polyps develop up to four segments, each of which becomes a young medusa (*courtesy of Dr. Dorothy Spangenberg and* The American Biology Teacher).**

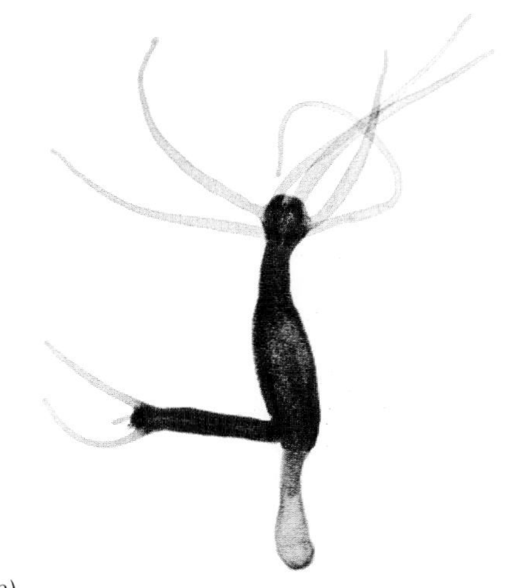

(*a*)

(*b*)

form a new mycelium. The capacity of starfish to regenerate after being torn apart is well known, but this is not a normal mode of reproduction. However, at least one kind of starfish is known to fragment spontaneously when subjected to noxious stimulation such as an electrical shock. When a shock is applied to the central disk, the animal divides into five equal parts, each ray creeping away from the others and eventually developing into a new starfish.

Lateral stems and horizontal roots serve for asexual increase in a number of plants and in such animals as sponges and colonial hydroids, corals, and bryozoans. Many tracheophytes including the strawberry, the strawberry-begonia, and a number of grasses and ferns put forth lateral stems (*stolons*) at the nodes of which new roots and vertical shoots arise. After the new plants are established, disintegration of the intervening stolon may take place, liberating the progeny from the parent plant.

SPOROGENY *Spores* are asexually produced reproductive cells, which may be flagellated and motile or hard-walled and nonmotile (but then may be disseminated by wind or water). Most plants produce spores of some type (Figure 17.4). Diploid or monoploid spores that are products of ordinary cell division are known as *mitospores.* Spores which arise from a *meiotic* division (see Figure 8.4) are always monoploid and are termed *meiospores.* Meiospores are formed in the sporangia of ferns and mosses, capsules within which diploid *spore mother cells* undergo meiosis to become the monoploid spores. Meiospores are also produced by flowering plants, within the ovaries and anthers, but these spores are not set free, instead remaining within these organs to develop into the monoploid gametophyte generation (see Figure 17.22).

In Phycomycetes such as the black mold, *Rhizopus,* true zygotes are formed by conjugation (see below) in which nuclear materials of two hyphal cells are combined. The zygote is often termed a "zygospore" because of its hard protective wall, but in fact is a product of sexual union and hence not a spore in the usual sense of the term. However, as soon as the zygote germinates, it gives rise to a sporangium, within which meiosis takes place and a number of meiospores are produced, each of which can generate a new hypha (Figure 17.5).

The sac fungi (Ascomycetes) and club fungi (Basidiomycetes) each produce two kinds of spores. Mitospores (*conidia*) are borne on vertical offshoots of the hyphae. In addition, sexual union (by conjugation) takes place between young hyphae, so that each cell of the mature mycelium has two nuclei containing homologous but not necessarily identical sets of genes. Both of these nuclei affect the cell's metabolic activities, but they do not fuse except in cells that will give rise to meiospores. In sac fungi, the meiospore-forming body, or *ascus,* is a slender sac enclosing one cell which divides meiotically to form four monoploid spores each of which divides once more to make eight. Asci are commonly clustered into cup-shaped fruiting bodies (Figure 17.6). Large clublike cells (*basidia*) develop within the fruiting bodies of club fungi, such as along the margins of mushroom "gills." Within each basidium the two monoploid nuclei fuse to form a diploid nucleus. This fusion nucleus, equivalent to a zygote, undergoes meiosis to produce four monoploid nuclei, each of which is pinched off with

Figure 17.4 □ **Types of sporogeny: (*a*) production of diploid mitospores; (*b*) production of monoploid mitospores; (*c*) production of monoploid meiospores.**

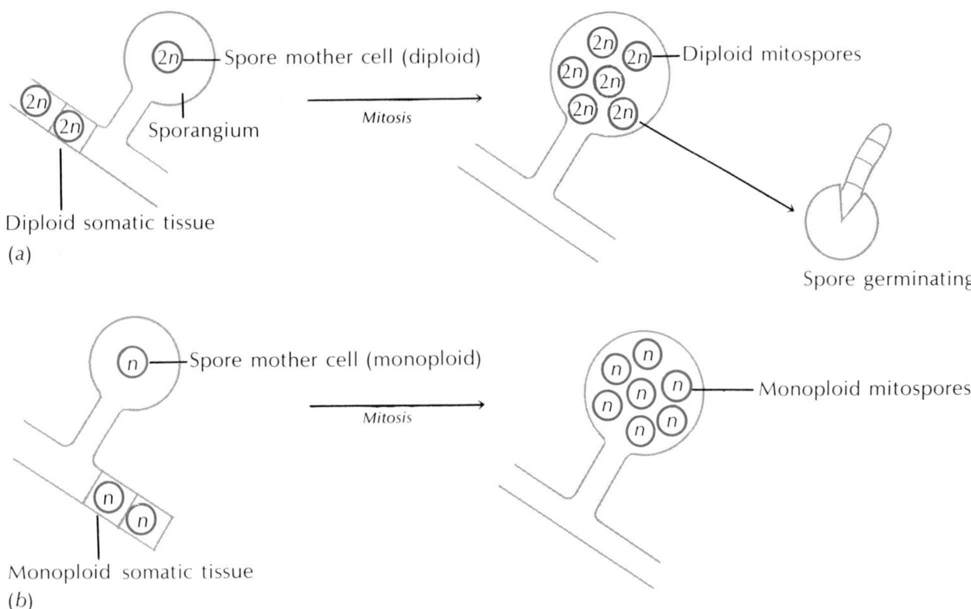

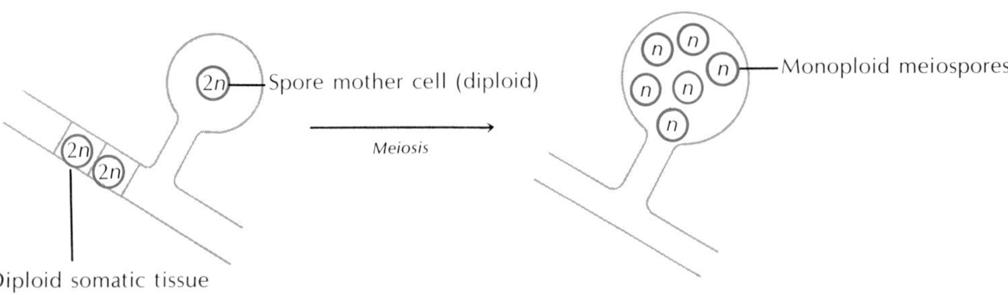

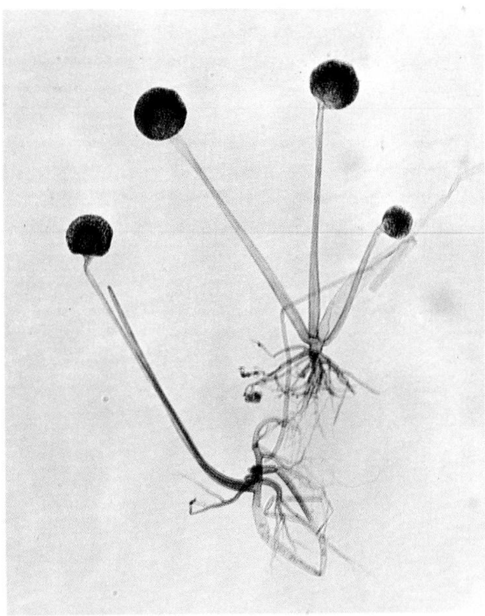

Figure 17.5 □ **Black bread mold, *Rhizopus*, showing sporangia arising from mycelium. (*Courtesy of Carolina Biological Supply Company.*)**

Figure 17.6 □ **Conjugation and sexual-ascospore formation in an ascomycete. (*a*) Section through fruiting body of *Peziza* and (*b*) higher magnification of portion of fruiting body, showing several asci with ascospores. (*Triarch Incorporated, Geo. H. Conant, Ripon, Wis.*) (*c*) Life cycle of a typical ascomycete.**

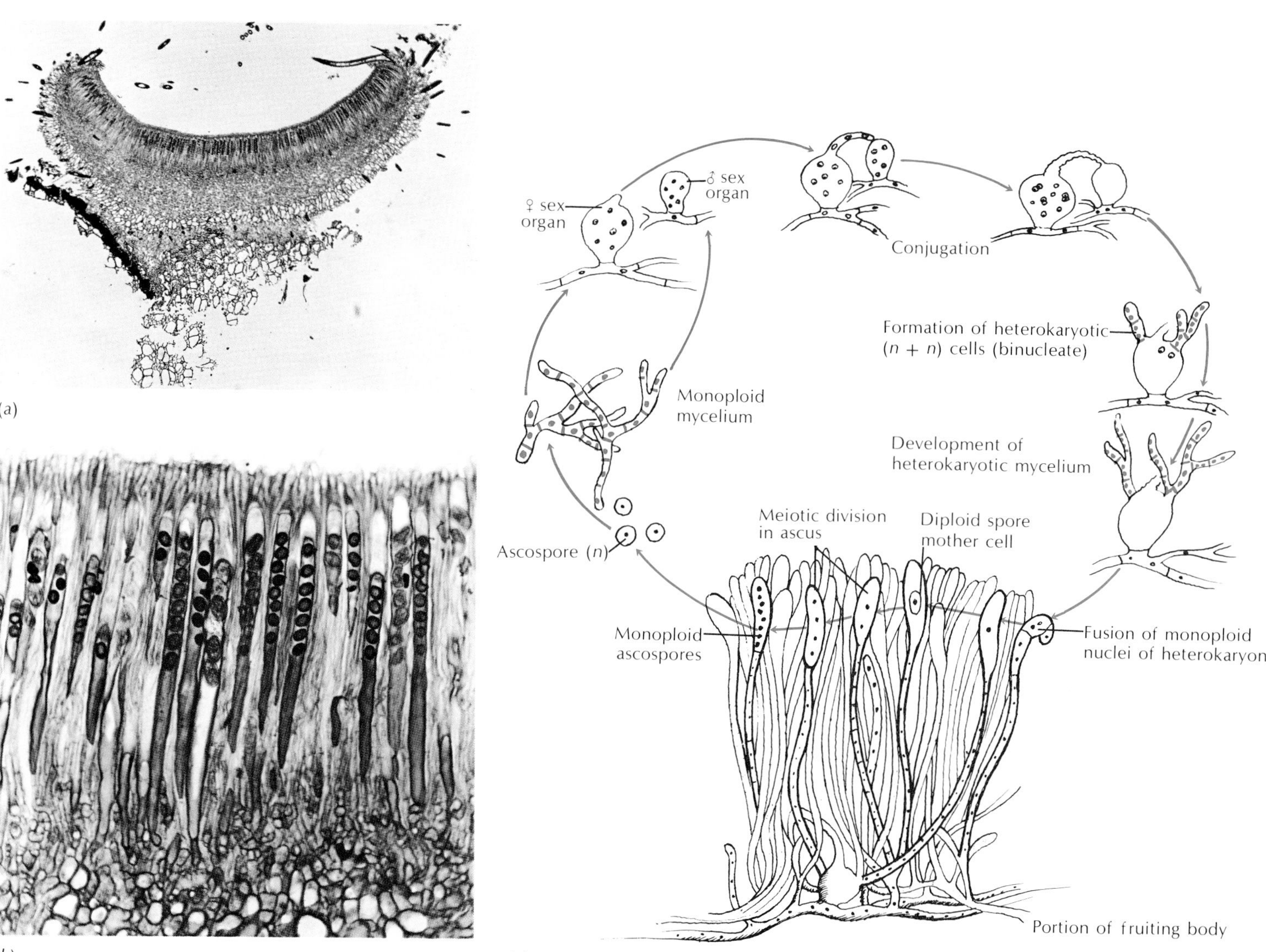

a small amount of cytoplasm to form a spore (Figure 17.7). Both meiospores and mitospores are capable of directly giving rise to new hyphae.

PARTHENOGENESIS A regular form of asexual proliferation in certain metazoans and an emergency survival device in others is parthenogenesis, in which unfertilized eggs develop into new individuals (Figure 17.8). Any gamete-producing species is probably capable of some degree of spontaneous parthenogenesis (and parthenogenetic development can also be experimentally induced by applying a variety of chemical or mechanical stimuli to activate the unfertilized ovum), but in only a few groups has this device been adopted nearly to the exclusion of normal sexual reproduction.

Three types of parthenogenesis may be distinguished, one of which produces monoploid individuals whereas the other two yield diploid individuals. All three types are widespread among insects. *Monoploid parthenogenesis* (cleavage of the monoploid ovum), gives rise to male individuals that have only one set of chromosomes in their cells. In the honeybee, such unfertilized eggs develop into drones whereas fertilized eggs produce females: queens or workers. *Automictic* parthenogenesis takes place when an ovum that has undergone reduction division has its diploid chromosome complement restored by a fusion of two nuclei. These are usually the nucleus of the egg and that of the second polar body (see Figure 17.24), but sometimes the diploid condition is restored by the failure of the cytoplasm to divide after the nucleus of an activated but unfertilized egg has divided once. Instead, the two cleavage nuclei fuse and the now diploid cell again begins to divide. In *apomictic* parthenogenesis such as is typical of aphids, no reduction division takes place during the maturation of the egg; instead, the diploid eggs develop into females and males may be virtually unknown. Since the daughters receive a full diploid set of chromosomes from their mother they can be heterozygous for a number of alleles, and in fact heterozygosity is bound to increase through the generations by the accumulation of new mutations. Automictic and monoploid parthenogenesis, on the other hand, tend to promote homozygosity and may lead to the establishment of a number of genetically distinct populations representing incipient species.

Figure 17.7 □ Basidiospore formation and life cycle of a basidiomycete.

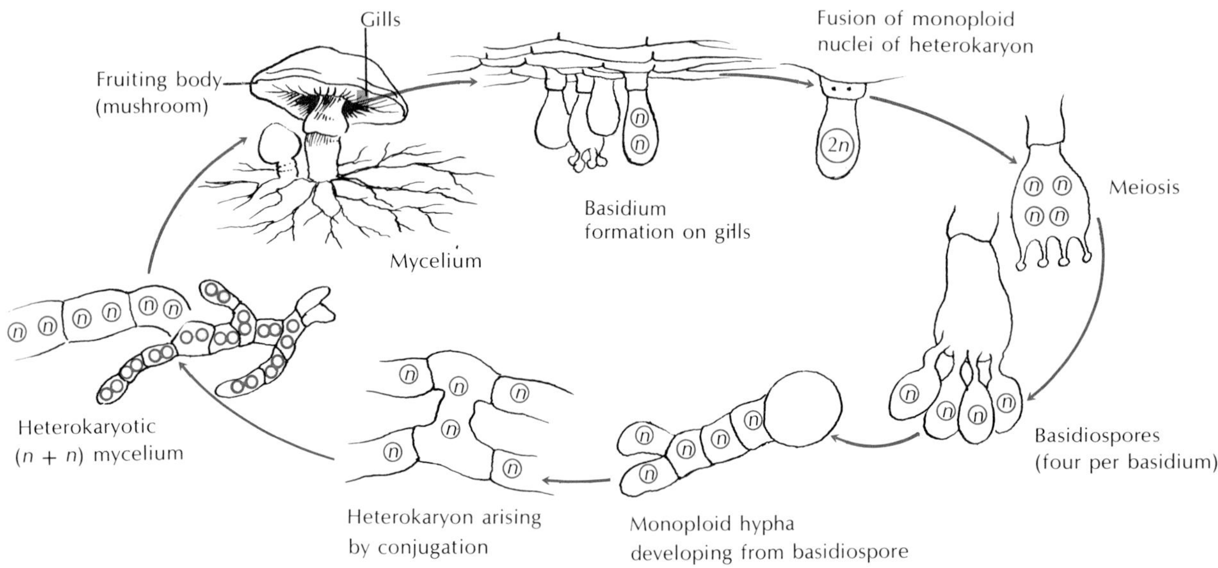

Figure 17.8 ☐ (*a*) **Monoploid parthenogenesis: cleavage of unfertilized ovum produces individual not genetically identical with parent.** (*b*) **Automictic parthenogenesis: egg fertilized by polar-body nucleus develops into diploid individual not necessarily genetically identical with parent.** (*c*) **Apomictic parthenogenesis: ovum cleaves without undergoing reduction division, producing diploid individual genetically identical with parent.**

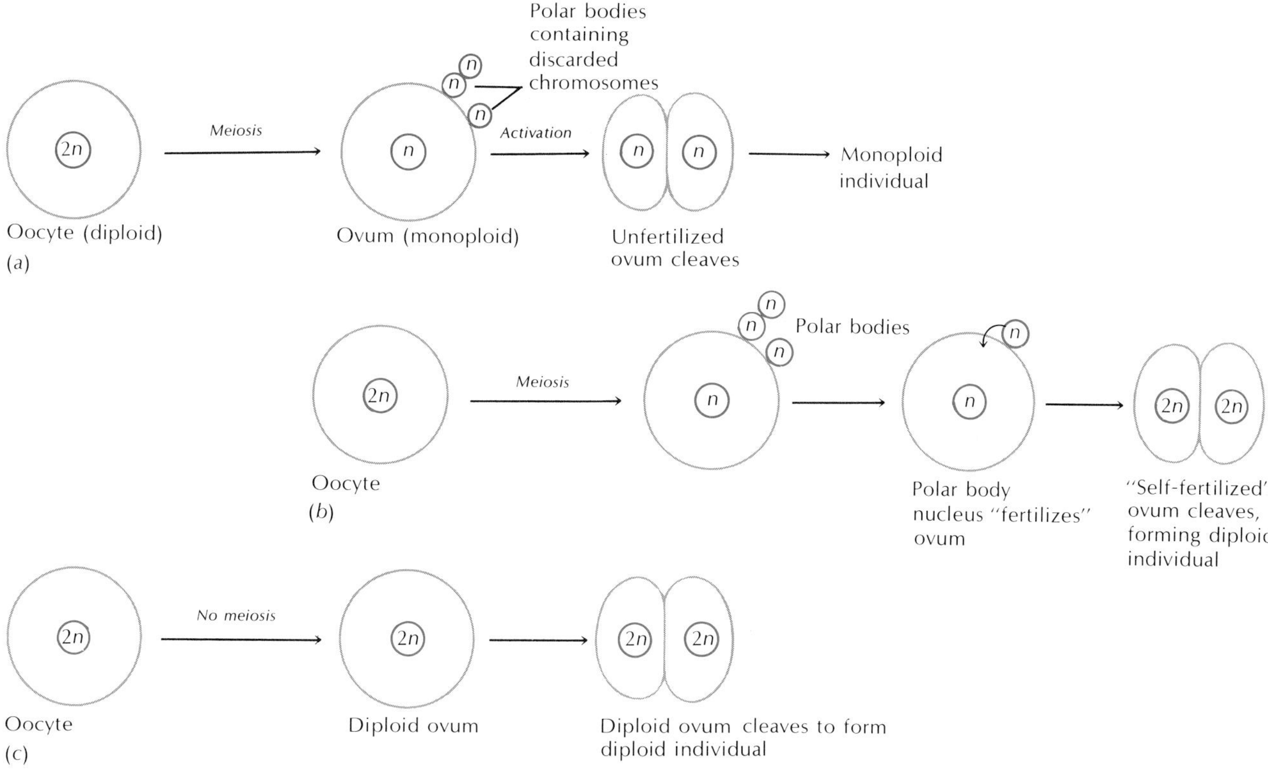

17.2 ☐ SEXUAL REPRODUCTION

Organisms need not have a *sex* in order to engage in sexual reproduction. The latter requires merely that genetic materials from two individuals be conjoined in the production of a new organism. We usually think of a plant or animal as having a sex only if it is at least potentially capable of generating sperm and/or eggs. An organism may be genetically male or female even though it is a juvenile or a neuter. Worker bees, for instance, are female, but due to pheromonal repression of their sexual development remain *neuter.* A *hermaphrodite* is not a neuter, but is *both* male and female, that is, capable of producing both eggs and sperm simultaneously or sequentially. *Protandrous* hermaphrodites such as slipper shells (*Crepidula*) produce sperm when young and eggs when older; *protogynous* species that produce first eggs and later sperm also occur but are less common.

A Types of sexual reproduction

Sexual reproduction can take place with or without gametes, and if gametes are involved they may be alike or dissimilar.

Figure 17.9 □ Bacterial conjugation. The smaller cell acts as a male, initiating the formation of a conjugation bridge that unites it with the female while one of the male's chromosomes migrates across the bridge. (*Courtesy of Thomas F. Anderson, Elie L. Wollman, and François Jacob, L'Institut Pasteur, Paris.*)

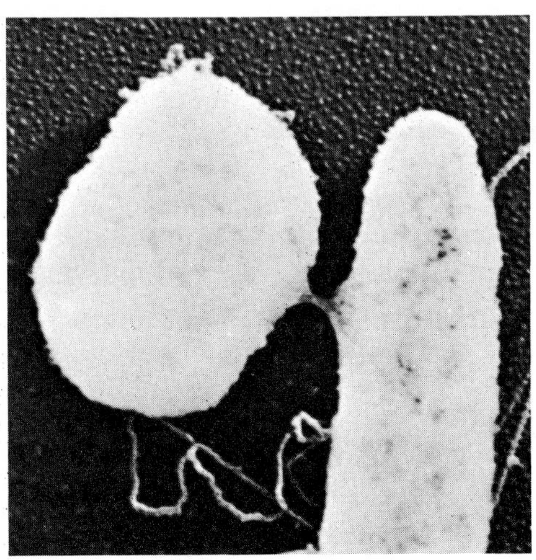

Conjugation and *syngamy* are forms of sexual reproduction that do not require the union of actual gametes. *Isogamy* involves the production and union of gametes of like form, whereas *heterogamy* involves the production and union of dissimilar gametes, notably eggs and sperm.

CONJUGATION A one-way or reciprocal exchange of hereditary materials can take place between two cells or organisms which come together and partially fuse as *conjugants.* Bacterial conjugation takes place when a protuberance arising on the membrane of a "male" bacterium fuses with the membrane of a "female" cell, forming a narrow conjugation bridge across which one of the chromosomes of the male can slowly pass (Figure 17.9). Certain strains of bacteria display an unusually high frequency of sexual recombination, due to the presence of an episomal virus particle, the *F* (fertility) *factor.* The *F* factor stimulates the formation of the conjugation bridge, across which it can pass to infect new bacterial hosts. When the *F* factor attaches to one of the host's chromosomes, this chromosome also passes across the bridge, bringing about changes in the genotype of the new host. Infection with the *F* factor transforms the former female into a male, for at the next mating this cell can now initiate the conjugation act; F^+ (male) bacteria can only mate with F^- individuals.

Conjugation in the mold *Rhizopus* takes place between cells of adjacent hyphae (Figure 17.10*a*). Conjugation tubes arise from the near sides of both conjugants and meet midway between the hyphae. The nuclei of the two cells then migrate into the tube and unite at the midline to form a zygote. Many green algae such as *Spirogyra* also mate by conjugation (Figure 17.10*b*). The more usual type, *scalariform* (ladderlike) conjugation, involves the union of cells of different filaments, whereas *lateral* conjugation takes place between adjacent cells of the same filament. In each case, the entire cell body of one conjugant creeps through the conjoined region and unites with the protoplast of the opposite conjugant, leaving behind an empty cell wall. The zygote thus produced secretes a protective casing within which it can survive freezing or desiccation. At the time of germination, the zygote undergoes meiosis, following which three of the monoploid nuclei disintegrate. The remaining monoploid cell (meiospore) then germinates to become a new filament.

Conjugation in ciliates such as *Paramecium* is preceded, rather than followed, by meiosis (Figure 17.11). The micronucleus of each conjugant divides meiotically into four monoploid nuclei: three of these, together with the polyploid macronucleus, disintegrate; the remaining monoploid micronucleus divides once more, and then one micronucleus of each conjugant passes across the conjugation bridge that joins the two animals. At this point, the genotypes of both conjugants are altered—they are genetically different individuals than they were prior to conjugation. The conjugants then separate and the two monoploid micronuclei in each (one its own, the other donated by its partner) unite to become a single diploid fusion nucleus. Soon this divides repeatedly to yield eight identical diploid nuclei, of which three disintegrate, four begin to enlarge to form new macronuclei, and one remains as the definitive micronucleus. This nuclear reorganization is shortly followed by two consecutive events

Figure 17.10 □ Conjugation in molds and algae. (*a*) ***Rhizopus:*** outgrowths from adjacent filaments fuse at their tips, and a diploid zygote is formed by the fusion of the nuclei of the two conjugating cells; a hard wall secreted about the zygote protects it until conditions favor germination. (*b*) ***Spirogyra,*** a green alga: (1) filament prior to conjugation; note spiral, straplike chloroplast characteristic of this genus; (2) conjugation tubes forming between cells of adjacent filaments; (3) one entire cell (protoplast) migrates through each conjugation tube and fuses with its conjugant; (4) the zygotes thus produced secrete protective casings; note compartments left vacant by migration of protoplasts (*courtesy of Carolina Biological Supply Company*).

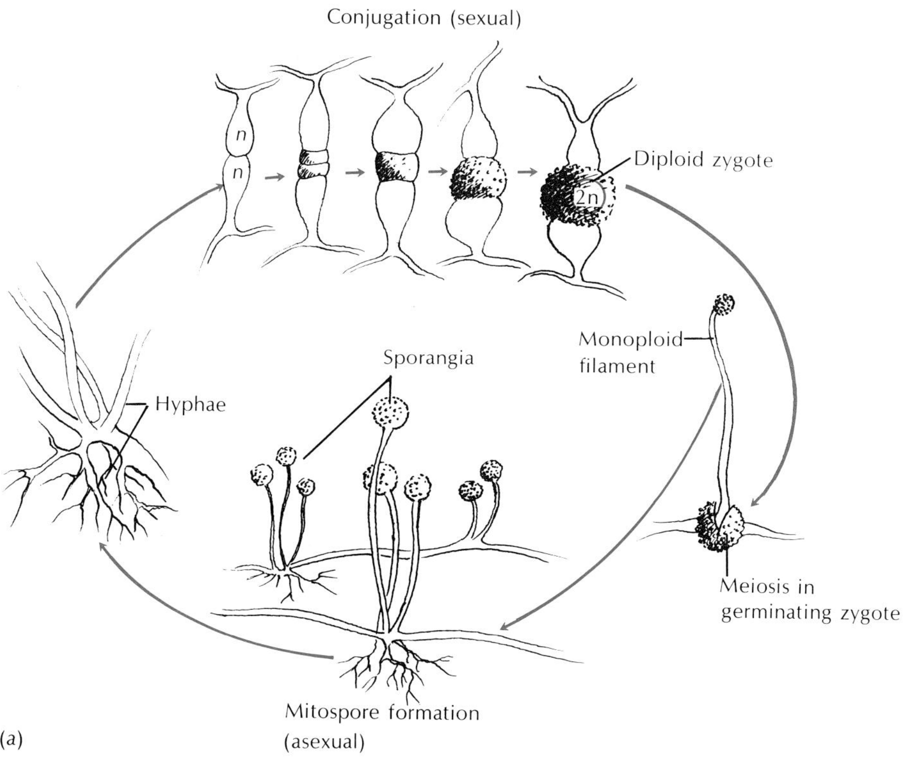

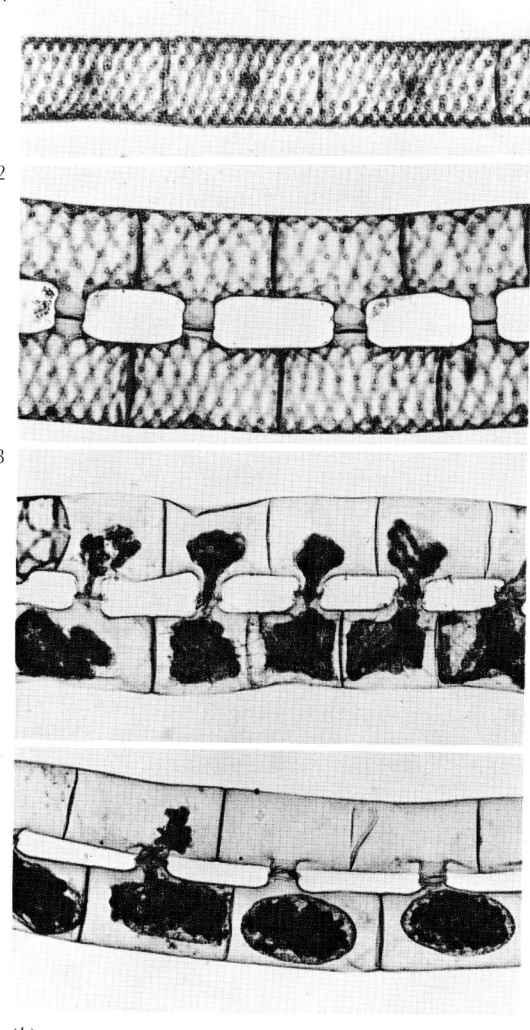

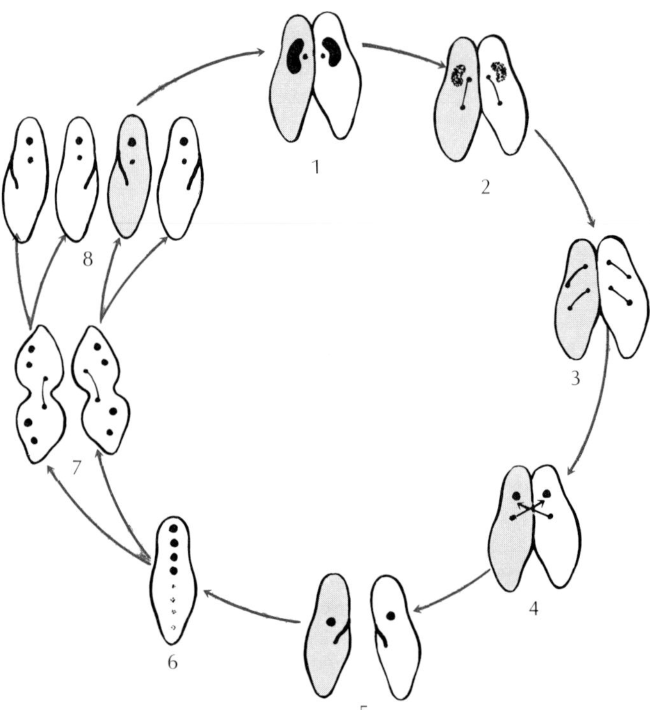

Figure 17.11 ◻ Conjugation in *Paramecium*. Clockwise from top: (1) conjugants of reciprocal mating type come together and fuse through their oral grooves. (2) Each macronucleus degenerates while the micronuclei divide, probably meiotically. (3) After the second meiotic division, three of the now-monoploid micronuclei degenerate. (4) The remaining micronucleus in each conjugant divides unequally, and the smaller micronucleus of each animal then migrates across the conjugation bridge. (5) The two micronuclei in each conjugant fuse, reconstituting a diploid fusion micronucleus; the conjugants then separate. (6) The fusion micronucleus divides three times, producing eight micronuclei, four of which become macronuclei, while one remains a micronucleus and the other three degenerate. (7) Two successive events of binary fission then take place, resulting in the production of four progeny (8) from each of the original conjugants. During fission the four developing macronuclei are parceled out—one to each daughter cell—and the micronucleus divides so that each daughter cell also receives one micronucleus.

of binary fission, producing four identical progeny. In conjugating species, sexual union may be separated from the reproductive act by a substantial period of time. In the sac and club fungi the hyphal conjugation that produces the doubly nucleated cells of the mature mycelium takes place at the beginning of mycelial growth, considerably before the production of meiospores in the asci or basidia.

SYNGAMY The act of syngamy, which occurs in phytoflagellates such as *Chlamydomonas,* requires no production of special gametes. Instead, two monoploid unicellular organisms, identical in appearance but of complementary mating types, come together and fuse as though they were gametes (Figure 17.12). Their individual identities are merged in the production of a diploid zygote. Subsequently this zygote undergoes meiosis, giving rise to four flagellated monoploid progeny that escape when the zygote wall ruptures.

ISOGAMY Isogamous species typically are simple multicellular algae like *Ulothrix* (Figure 17.13), in which single cells of the thallus change into unicellular *gametangia* that undergo multiple fission to produce a number of flagellated, identical gametes (*isogametes*). Meiosis need not occur at this time, because the entire algal filament is monoploid. The isogametes are released by the bursting of the gametangium. They swim about and eventually fuse with gametes of identical form that must, however, come from a different filament. *Ulothrix* also reproduces asexually, by means of monoploid mitospores formed by the multiple fission of cells constituting unicellular *sporangia.* These spores are distinguishable from the isogametes only in that they bear four flagella instead of two and do not participate in gametic fusion, instead settling directly to the substratum where each generates a new filament. Union of isoga-

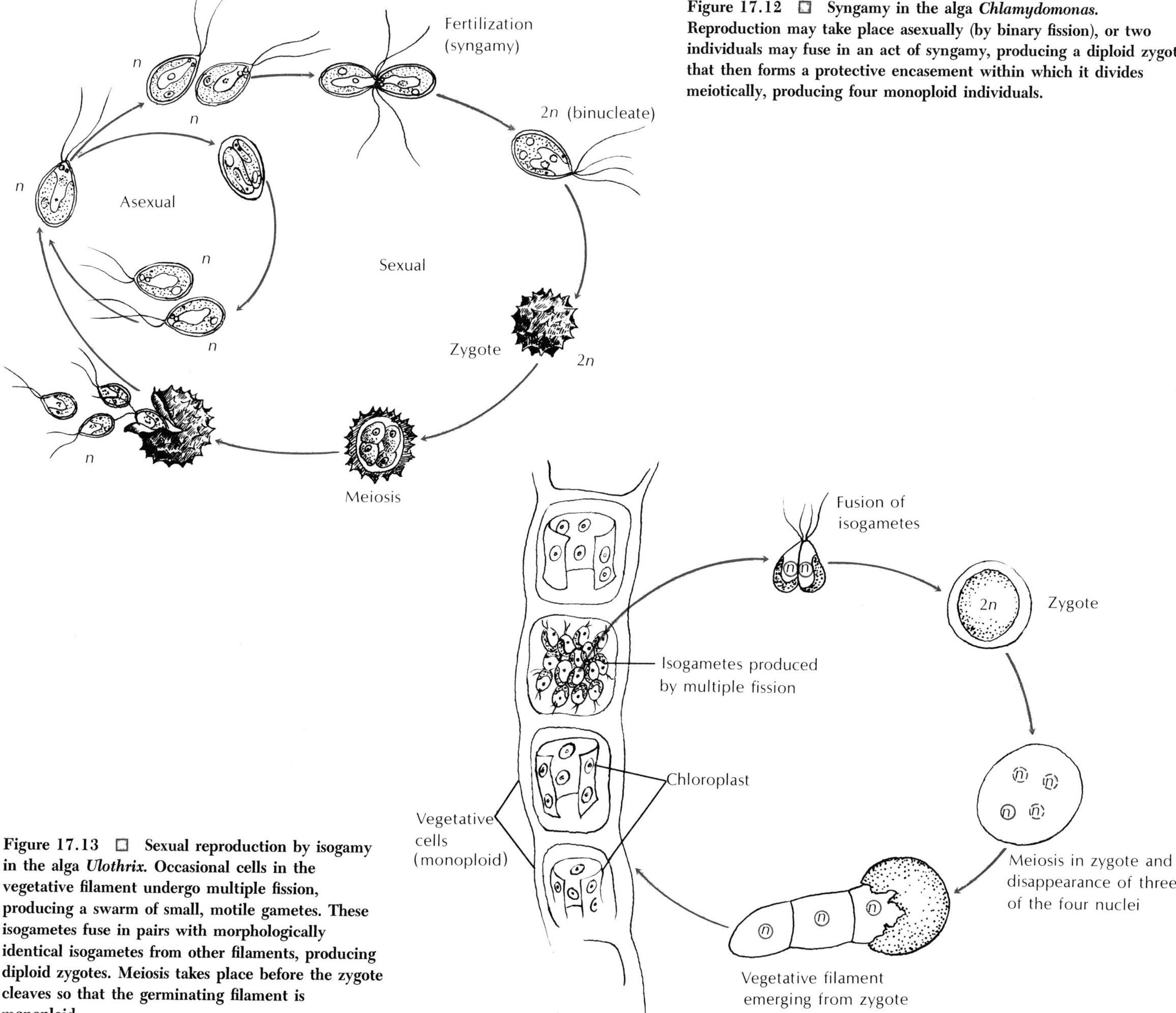

Figure 17.12 ◻ **Syngamy in the alga *Chlamydomonas*. Reproduction may take place asexually (by binary fission), or two individuals may fuse in an act of syngamy, producing a diploid zygote that then forms a protective encasement within which it divides meiotically, producing four monoploid individuals.**

Figure 17.13 ◻ **Sexual reproduction by isogamy in the alga *Ulothrix*. Occasional cells in the vegetative filament undergo multiple fission, producing a swarm of small, motile gametes. These isogametes fuse in pairs with morphologically identical isogametes from other filaments, producing diploid zygotes. Meiosis takes place before the zygote cleaves so that the germinating filament is monoploid.**

metes, on the contrary, produces a diploid zygote, which as in *Spirogyra* undergoes meiotic division with only one of the four monoploid nuclei persisting to give rise to a new filament.

HETEROGAMY The specialization of gametes into two types—one small and motile, the other less motile and swollen with nutrients—is of great adaptive significance. It makes possible storage of nutrients sufficient to meet early developmental needs and also permits the "expensive" nutrient-storing gamete to remain in a relatively protected position until fertilization. Heterogamy is typical of metazoans and all higher plants, and is also common among algae such as "sea lettuce" (*Ulva*), as shown in Figure 17.14, and certain groups of protozoans including sporozoans and foraminiferans. In metazoans the differentiation of male and female gametes reaches its extreme expression in *oogamy,* with the formation of nonmotile, relatively enormous ova, which are fertilized by the tiny, usually flagellated sperm (Figure 17.15).

Figure 17.14 □ **Sexual reproduction by heterogamy in the alga *Ulva*. Motile gametes of two morphological types (heterogametes) are produced and fuse in pairs; the zygote undergoes meiosis before germinating to form a new thallus.**

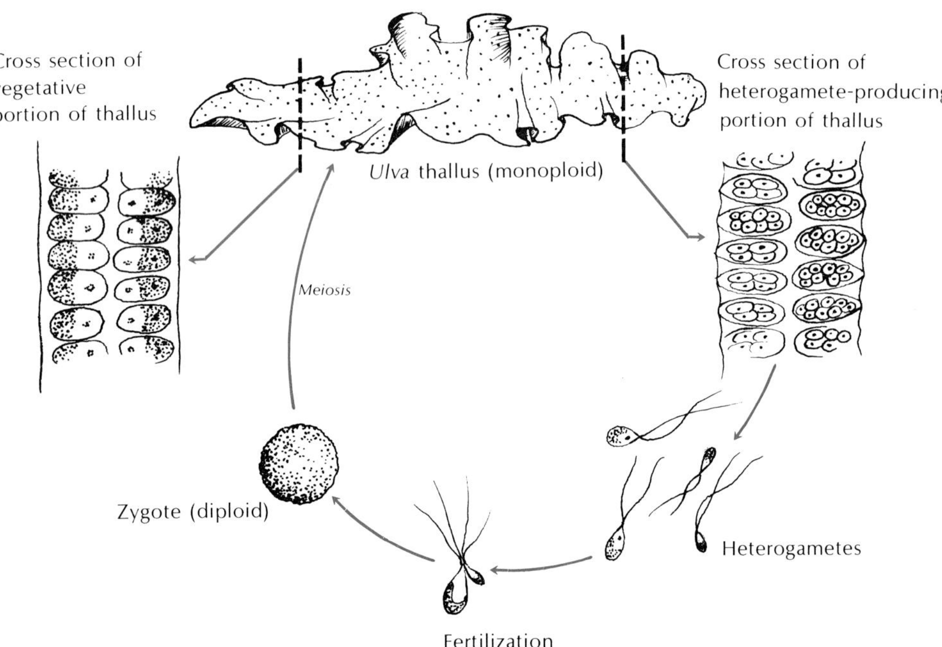

Relatively few eggs mature compared with the number of sperm produced. For each diploid cell which undergoes meiosis in the ovary, only *one* can become an ovum; for each diploid cell that undergoes meiosis in the testis, *four* monoploid sperm are formed. Furthermore, in mammals at least, few of the potential egg cells ripen, for such maturation is a prolonged, energy-consuming process. Ordinarily only one egg is liberated during each human menstrual cycle, and 28 days later another egg is shed, usually from the opposite ovary. Accordingly, no more than about 450 mature ova are shed by a woman during her entire reproductive life. In fact, the number is usually much less,

Figure 17.15 □ **Production of sperm and eggs by *Hydra*. (*a*) Hydra bearing spermaries, temporary gonads within which large numbers of sperm mature. (*b*) Hydra bearing amoeboid ovum. When fertilized, the egg remains within the parent's body wall during early development of the embryo. (*Ward's Natural Science Establishment, Inc.*)**

Figure 17.16 □ **Sexual reproduction in *Fucus*, a phaeophyte.**

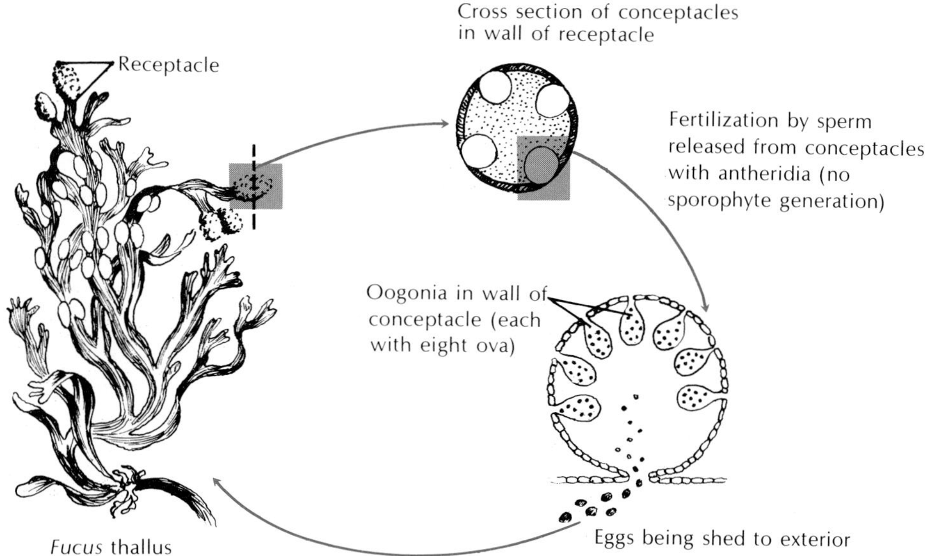

for the maturation of ova is inhibited throughout pregnancy and usually during the subsequent period of lactation as well.

Production of such large eggs as those of birds and reptiles requires intensive physiological preparation that enables the female to release eggs frequently during the mating season. This time is brief, and a long recuperative period intervenes before the next breeding season. Sperm production does not demand the energy investment required for the production of a yolky egg. Accordingly, billions of sperm can be produced for each ovum that matures. (Females of such species as the cod and the blood fluke, however, perform the prodigious feat of laying millions of eggs; female codfish are known to lay 6×10^6 eggs in a single breeding season.)

The heterogametes of green, red, and brown algae are produced by single, specialized sperm- or egg-producing cells known respectively as *antheridia* and *oogonia*. The antheridia and oogonia of phaeophytes are clustered within hollow bodies (conceptacles) which may contain one or the other, or both, kinds of gamete-producing cells. The eggs and sperm are voided to the exterior through an opening in the wall of the conceptacle (Figure 17.16). The sex organs of bryophytes and tracheophytes are multicellular. The sperm-producing type is still termed an antheridium, whereas the female organ is known as an *archegonium*. The archegonium also shelters the embryo during development and accordingly these two phyla are often grouped as Subkingdom Embryophyta.

Metazoans typically produce gametes in multicellular organs termed *gonads*, that provide a framework of supportive tissues in which the developing sex cells are embedded. Gonadal tissues also produce sex hormones in vertebrates. A sperm-producing gonad is a *testis;* an egg-producing gonad is an *ovary.* (In some hermaphroditic species a single gonad, the *ovotestis,* produces both types of heterogametes.) Gametogenesis (gamete formation) must be preceded by meiosis, but in plants meiosis usually takes place at a different time in the life cycle from gamete production, while in animals it is part of the gametogenetic process.

Figure 17.17 □ Alternation of generations in plant life cycles: (*a*) equal and independent generations (for example, certain red algae); (*b*) sporophyte generation dependent nutritionally upon gametophyte generation (for example, mosses); (*c*) unequal but independent generations (for example, fern, with sporophyte dominant); (*d*) unequal generations, with gametophyte nutritionally dependent on sporophyte (for example, angiosperms).

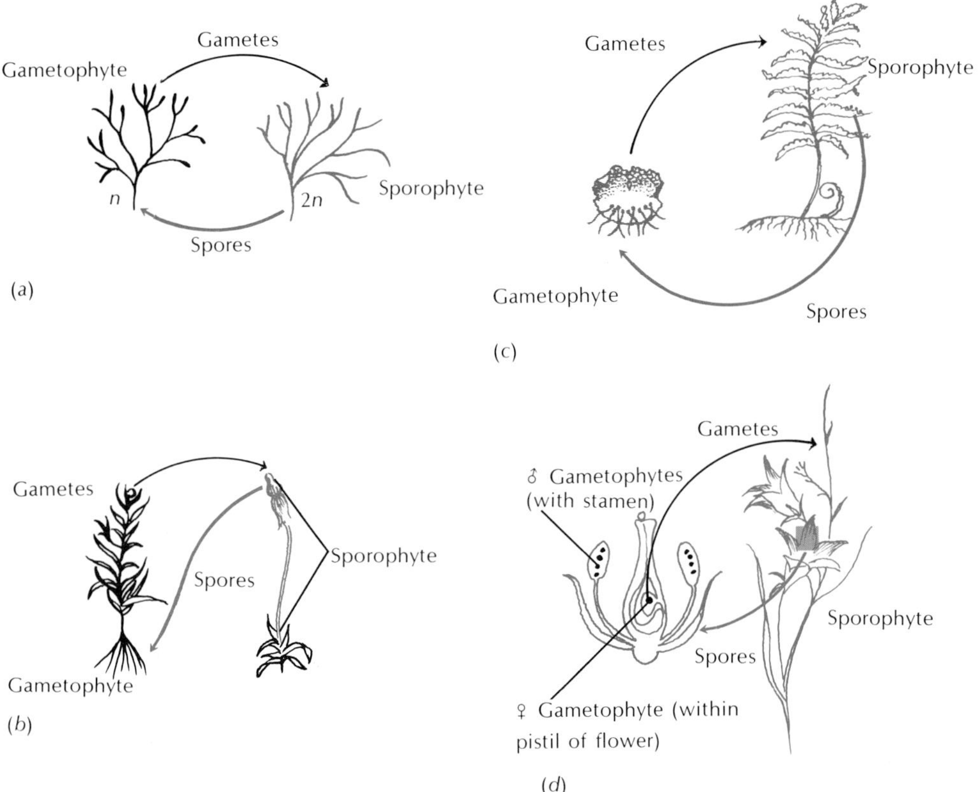

B Reproductive cycles of metaphytes

Metagenesis, the alternation of sexual and asexual generations in the life history, is characteristic of multicellular plants, with a diploid meiospore-producing generation, the *sporophyte,* alternating with a monoploid gamete-producing generation, the *gametophyte.* According to the plant group, the two generations may be equally conspicuous and both capable of independent existence; or the gametophyte may be relatively more persistent and conspicuous and the sporophyte dependent upon it; or the two generations may be unequal in size, but independent; or the sporophyte dominant and the gametophyte reduced and dependent (Figure 17.17). The adaptive advantages of diploidy have favored the increased predominance of the sporophyte so that this has become the conspicuous generation in ferns and seed plants. Nevertheless, the gametophyte generation cannot be utterly deleted without sacrificing the adaptive benefits of sexual recombination. The compromise reflected in the life cycle of seed plants is that the vegetative form is the diploid sporophyte, which nurtures and protects the minute, dependent gametophyte on which sexual reproduction still depends.

RED ALGAE Metagenesis with equal and independent generations is exemplified by the rhodophyte *Polysiphonia* (Figure 17.18). The lacy thallus of the gametophyte is grossly indistinguishable from that of the sporophyte, but has monoploid rather than diploid tissues. *Polysiphonia* is dioecious, with sperm formed in antheridia on the male plant and ova in carpogonia on the female plant. The sperm are not flagellated, but are released into the water at a time when the female organs are mature, where they drift until captured by adhesive hairs protruding from the carpogonia. After fertilization the zygote proliferates mitotically, putting forth filaments that terminate in urn-shaped bodies, the diploid carposporophytes within which diploid mitospores are produced. These are shed into the water, each settling and growing into a diploid sporophyte thallus (the tetrasporophyte). When mature the tetrasporophytes elaborate sporangia, within which meiosis takes place and tetrads of monoploid meiospores are formed. These are released to the milieu and grow into the monoploid gametophytes.

BRYOPHYTES Mosses and liverworts are metagenetic, with the sporophyte transient and dependent on the gametophyte (see Figure 17.17*b*). The leafy shoots and underground rhizoids of a moss represent the gametophyte generation, which germinates from a monoploid meiospore. The gametophyte can reproduce asexually by means either of lateral runners or of groups of cells termed *gemmae,* which bud from the leaflets or shoot tips. In liverworts the gemmae are borne in shallow cups on the upper surface of the broad and prostrate thallus.

Many bryophytes are dioecious, with sperm and eggs borne on separate plants (Figure 17.19). The multicellular antheridia and archegonia serve to protect the germinal cells from the rigors of a terrestrial habitat. However, bryophyte adaptation to the land is imperfect, for fertilization is still dependent upon moisture being sufficient for the sperm to swim from the antheridia of one plant to the archegonium of another. The single egg that matures in each archegonium is retained therein while it grows into the sporophyte generation.

The sex organs of liverworts such as *Marchantia* (see Figure 2.19*b*) are borne in clusters at the top of vertical stalks. The

Figure 17.18 □ Life cycle of the rhodophyte *Polysiphonia*.

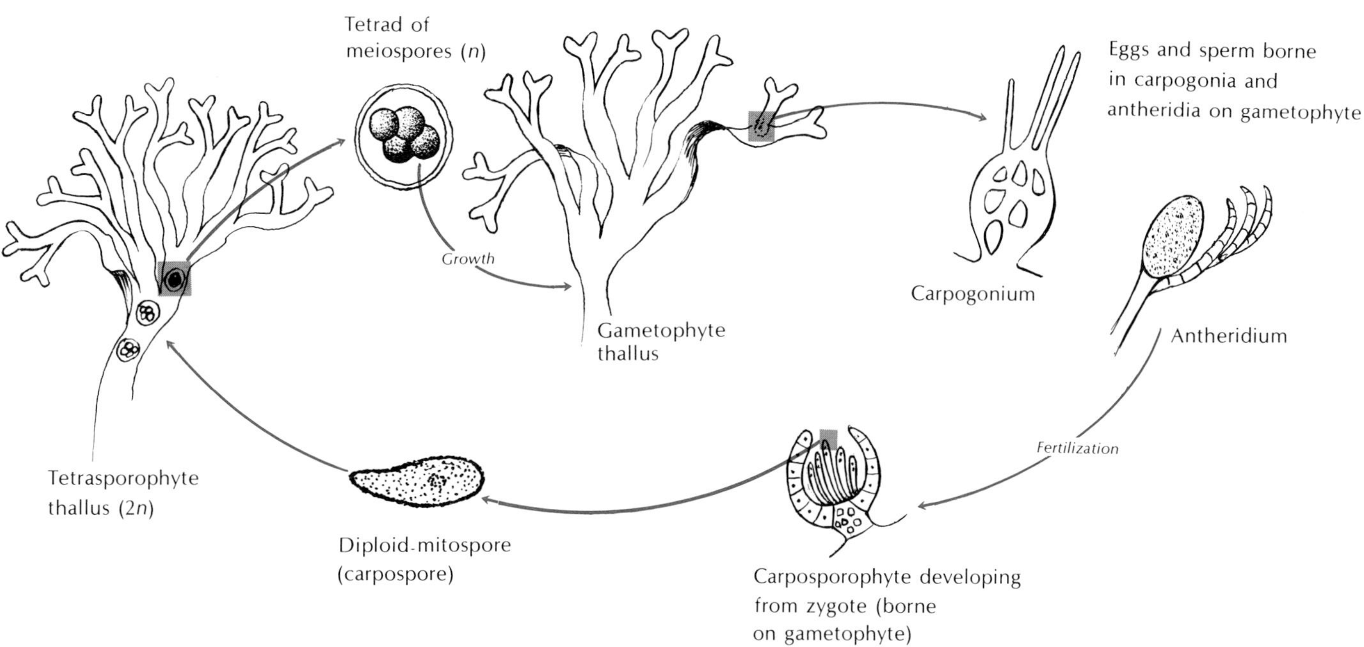

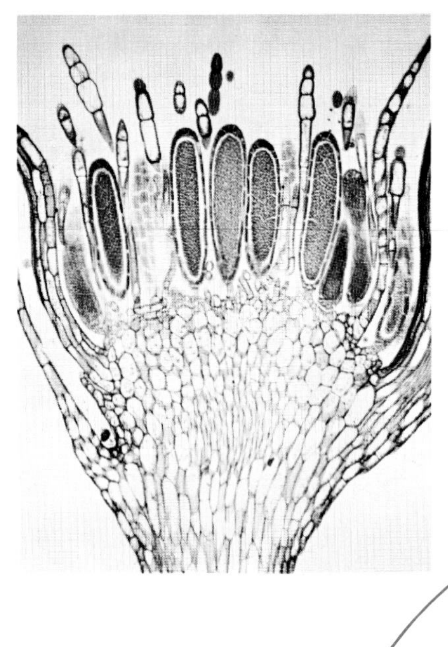

Figure 17.19 □ **Life cycle of a moss. The photograph shows five antheridia in median longitudinal section borne at the apex of the gametophyte shoot and containing developing sperm. (*Ward's Natural Science Establishment, Inc.*)**

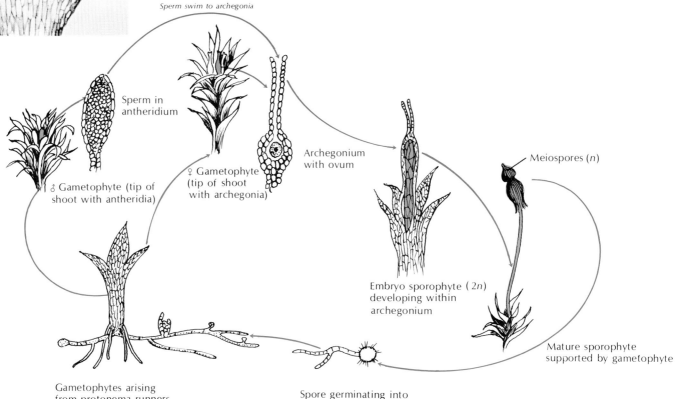

Sperm swim to archegonia

Sperm in antheridium

♂ Gametophyte (tip of shoot with antheridia)

♀ Gametophyte (tip of shoot with archegonia)

Archegonium with ovum

Embryo sporophyte ($2n$) developing within archegonium

Meiospores (n)

Mature sporophyte supported by gametophyte

Spore germinating into protonema stage of gametophyte

Gametophytes arising from protonema runners

Figure 17.20 □ **Fern life cycle. Various stages are not drawn to the same scale; the gametophyte is only about 2 to 3 mm in diameter.**

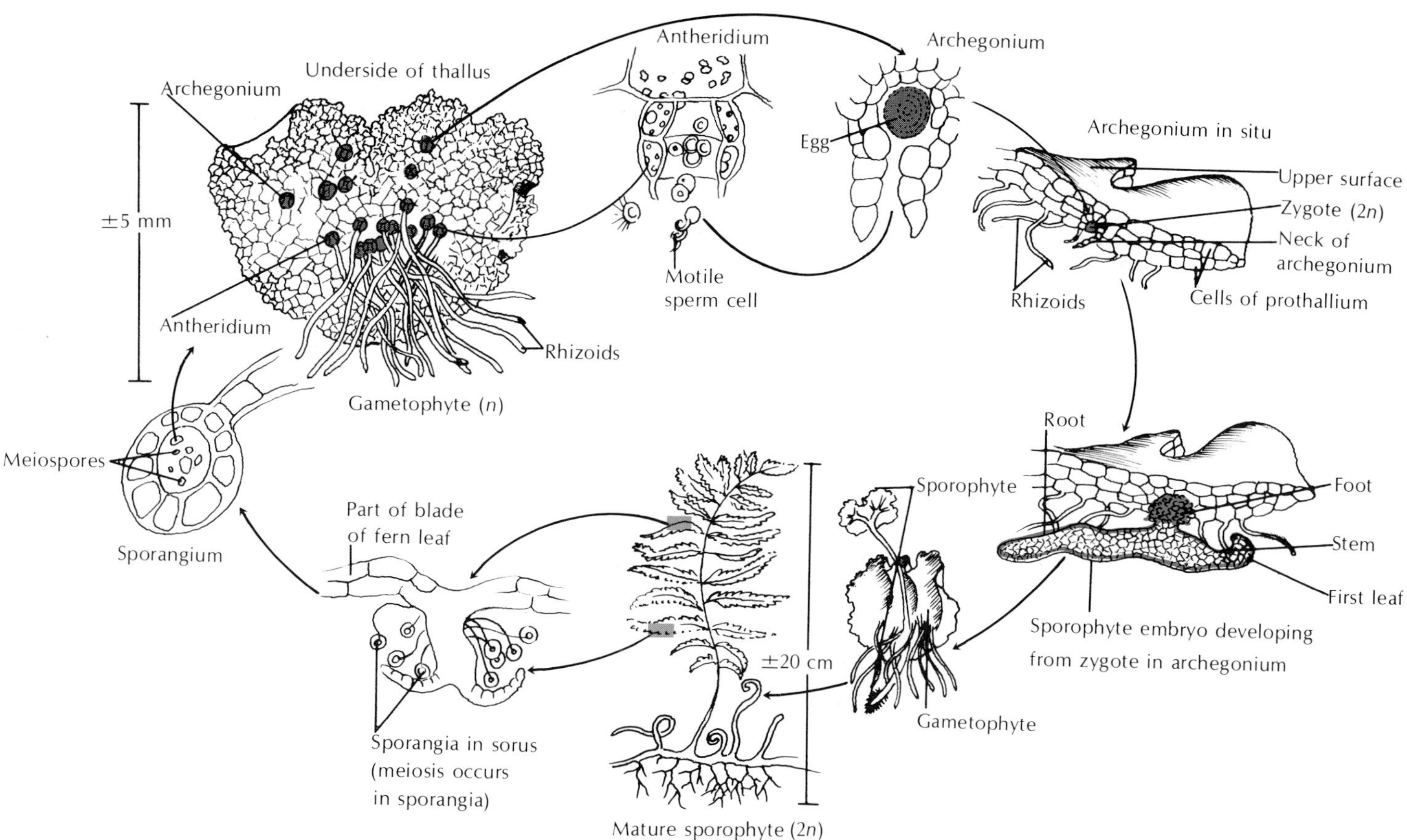

sporophytes that develop from the fertilized eggs are small and hang down from the underside of the archegonia. The moss sporophyte, on the other hand, rises as a slender erect filament from the apex of the gametophyte shoot. Each sporophyte produces a terminal sporangium containing diploid spore mother cells that undergo meiosis to form the meiospores.

FERNS The fern life cycle is characterized by a small but independent gametophyte generation and a dominant sporophyte that may attain heights of 25 m in the tree ferns (see Figure 2.21). The sporophyte consists of true roots, stems, and leaves, contains vascular tissues, and is well adapted for terrestrial existence. It can proliferate indefinitely by vegetative processes and also produces meiospores in sporangia clustered on the underside of the leaves (Figure 17.20). These meiospores require humid conditions

Figure 17.21 □ **Reproduction in conifers. (*a*) Male and female pine cones in various stages of maturation. (*Courtesy of Carolina Biological Supply Company.*) (1) Ovulate (female) cones at time of pollination; before fertilization these immature strobili must mature for an additional year, during which the pollen tube grows slowly inward to the ovule. (2) Female cone (part) in median longitudinal section through sporophylls, showing ovules within which sporophyte embryos are developing. (3) Mature female cone with scales spread for shedding the ripe seeds. (4) Cluster of staminate (male) cones. (5) Mature male strobilus in median longitudinal section, showing ripe pollen. (*b*) Pine life cycle.**

for successful growth into the flat, simple thallus of the gametophyte generation, the *prothallium* (Figure 2.21*b*). The prothallium is autotrophic and from its underside arise rootlike rhizoids and multicellular sex organs—a cluster of antheridia toward the apex of the heart-shaped thallus, and a group of archegonia near the notched end. As in the bryophytes, water is required for fertilization, for the sperm must swim to the eggs in the archegonia, usually of another thallus. The sporophyte embryo is nourished by the gametophyte while its primary root and first leaf are being formed. It then becomes self-nourishing while the gametophyte withers away.

CONIFERS The reproductive organs of conifers are unisexual *cones,* on the scale-like spore-bearing leaves (*sporophylls*) of which the small, dependent, short-lived gametophytes are borne (Figure 17.21). The

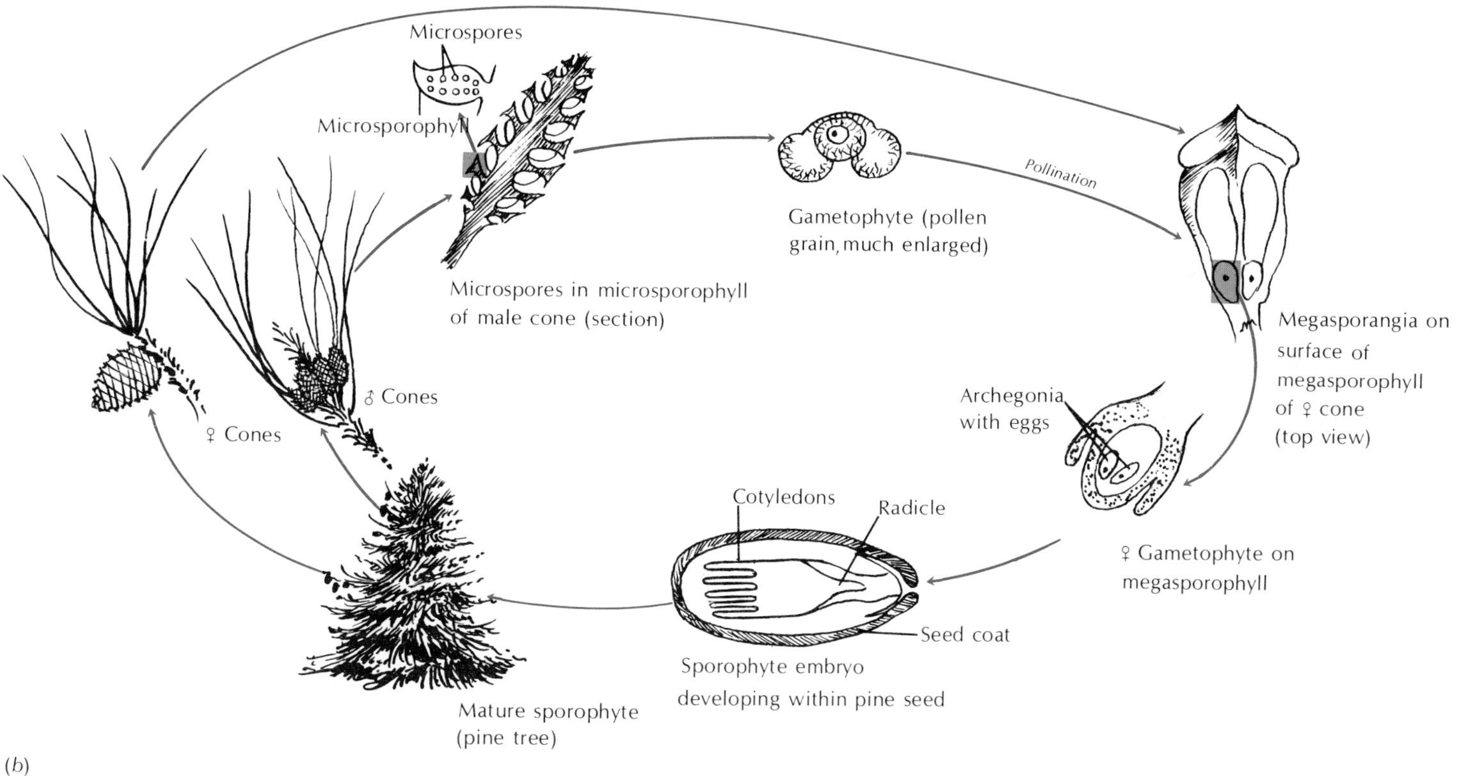

(*b*)

male cones are small and occur in clusters. They consist of numerous microsporophylls (that is, "small spore leaves"), which spring spirally from the central axis of the cone. Each microsporophyll bears a pair of sporangia within which diploid *microspore mother cells* undergo meiosis to produce small meiospores known as microspores. Each microspore then divides mitotically to produce a male gametophyte consisting of four cells of unequal size: two vegetative cells, one generative cell, and one tube cell. At this stage, the male gametophyte (pollen grain) is shed, covered by a winged protective coat (see Figure 4.2). Further development of the pollen takes place only when it makes contact with a female cone and begins to grow inward toward the female gametophyte.

Female cones bear large, thickened megasporophylls, each of which bears two large sporangia on its upper surface. Within each sporangium, a *megaspore mother cell* undergoes meiosis, producing four megaspores (large meiospores), three of which disintegrate. The survivor develops into an ovoid, multicellular female *gametophyte*. This small sexual organism is encased in a covering of protective tissues, the *ovule*, which consists of somatic tissues of the sporophyte. At one end the ovule bears a pore (the micropyle) through which pollen may enter. At the end nearest the micropyle, the female gametophyte develops two or three archegonia, each enclosing a single ovum.

Fertilization in the pine may not occur until a year after pollination and an additional year may be required for seeds and cone to become mature. Pollination takes place when a pollen grain falls upon the sticky fluid exuded from the micropyle and is drawn in through the micropyle as this fluid contracts upon drying. This event activates the male gametophyte. Bursting its protective coat, the male gametophyte forms an elongate *pollen tube,* into which the tube cell and generative cell enter. The nucleus of the tube cell remains near the tip of the pollen tube, perhaps controlling its growth. The generative cell now divides into a stalk cell and a body cell. As the pollen tube grows chemotropically toward the archegonia of the female gametophyte, the body cell divides to form two cells each of which matures into a sperm bearing whorls of cilia. When the tip of the pollen tube reaches the archegonia, the tube disintegrates, releasing the two sperm, which swim the small remaining distance to the egg. (Months have been required for the growth of the pollen tube to this point.) Now, one of the sperm fertilizes an egg, forming the zygote of the new sporophyte generation. In fact, all of the eggs in the archegonia of the female gametophyte may be fertilized, but usually only one embryo survives to complete development. The zygote nucleus divides to form about 1,000 nuclei, after which cell walls form and the pine embryo takes shape.

Elongation of suspensor cells at its base forces the pine embryo deep into the remaining gametophyte tissues, which now constitute the nutritive *endosperm.* The outer integument of the ovule meanwhile hardens into a protective *seed coat,* and at this time the *seed,* consisting of embryo, endosperm, and seed coat, may be shed from the cone. The cones of the jack pine remain closed, protecting the seeds, until forest fire sweeps the area. The cones then release the seeds, providing for rapid reestablishment of the pine community.

ANGIOSPERMS The life cycle of the flowering plant is fundamentally very similar to that of the conifer, although there is even further reduction of the gametophyte generation. Both meiospores and gametes are formed within special, complex reproductive organs—the flowers (see Figure 12.18). Flowers are homologous with cones although their sporophylls are not scalelike, but form the *stamens* and *pistils,* respectively (Figure 17.22). Within the *anther* of each stamen are the microspore mother cells that undergo meiosis to produce tetrads of monoploid microspores. The nucleus of each microspore then divides, so that a male gametophyte is formed which is actually unicellular but has two nuclei. One of these is a *tube nucleus* that probably aids in the development of the pollen tube after pollination; the other is a *generative nucleus* that later divides to form two sperm nuclei. When the pollen grains are mature the anther splits open and turns inside out, so that the pollen is exposed to wind or the bodies of visiting insects.

The pistil consists of one or more modified leaves (*carpels*), which bear ovules

Figure 17.22 ☐ **Angiosperm gametophyte production. (*a*) Maturation of female gametophyte. Photographs: left, median section through ovule in *Lilium* ovary, showing developing gametophyte at two-nucleus stage (*Triarch Incorporated, Geo. H. Conant, Ripon, Wis.*); right, *Lilium* gametophyte at four-nucleus stage (*Ward's Natural Science Establishment, Inc.*). (*b*) Maturation of male gametophytes. Photograph: pollen tetrads from lily anther (*Ward's Natural Science Establishment, Inc.*).**

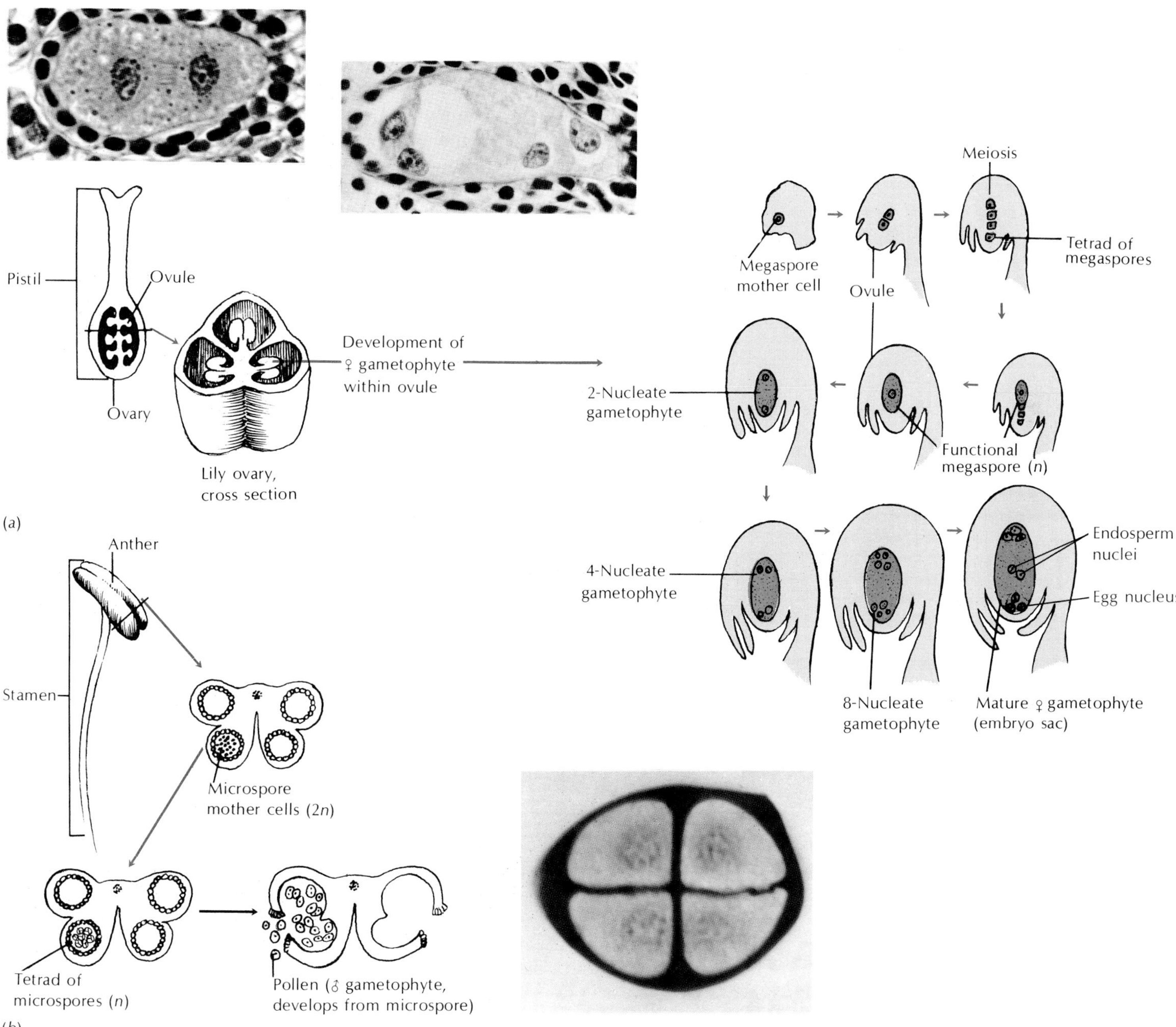
Pistil
Ovule
Ovary
Lily ovary, cross section
Development of ♀ gametophyte within ovule
(a)
Meiosis
Megaspore mother cell
Ovule
Tetrad of megaspores
2-Nucleate gametophyte
Functional megaspore (n)
4-Nucleate gametophyte
8-Nucleate gametophyte
Endosperm nuclei
Egg nucleus
Mature ♀ gametophyte (embryo sac)
Anther
Stamen
Microspore mother cells (2n)
Tetrad of microspores (n)
Pollen (♂ gametophyte, develops from microspore)
(b)

along their edges. The margins of a carpel are turned inward and fused along the line of meeting to form a hollow, cylindrical chamber enclosing the ovules. A pea pod develops from a pistil having a single carpel and the peas develop from the ovules borne within the cavity of that carpel. Each ovule consists of diploid somatic cells that enclose and nourish a megaspore mother cell. This cell divides meiotically into four megaspores, three of which die while the fourth grows into an ovoid female gametophyte having eight monoploid nuclei (Figure 17.22a). Five of these nuclei eventually disappear, but the two central ones persist as *endosperm nuclei,* while the one nearest the micropyle becomes the egg *nucleus.*

Pollination occurs when a pollen grain adheres to the stigma, the sticky terminal portion of the pistil. In many flowers that contain both stamens and pistils, the stamens develop ahead of the pistils (or vice versa) thereby ensuring cross pollination. In some species if pollination fails to occur while the pistil is young, the style then splits, allowing the lobes of the stigma to curl downward until they come in contact

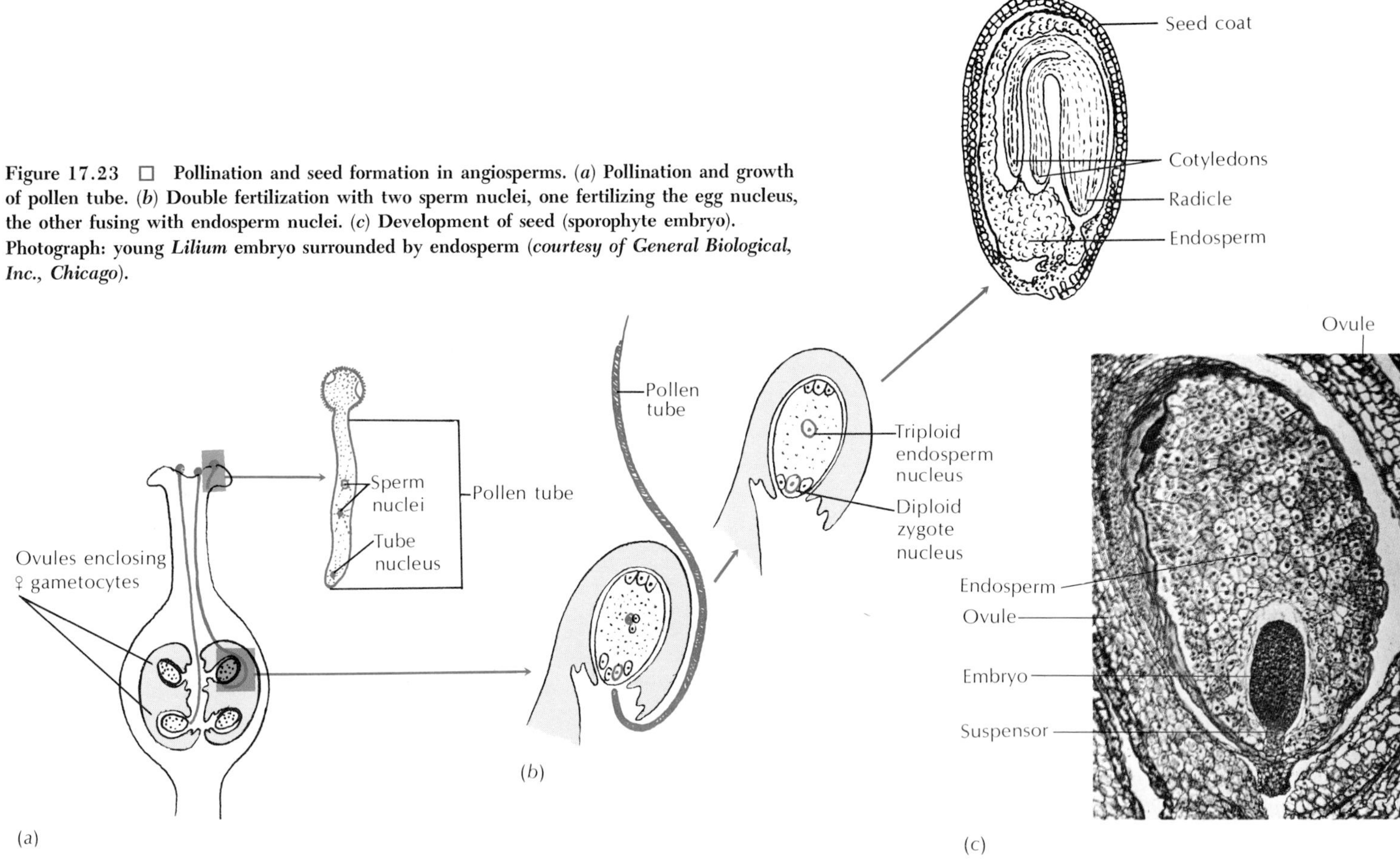

Figure 17.23 □ Pollination and seed formation in angiosperms. (*a*) Pollination and growth of pollen tube. (*b*) Double fertilization with two sperm nuclei, one fertilizing the egg nucleus, the other fusing with endosperm nuclei. (*c*) Development of seed (sporophyte embryo). Photograph: young *Lilium* embryo surrounded by endosperm (*courtesy of General Biological, Inc., Chicago*).

with the anthers of the same flower, resulting in self-fertilization. Contact with the stigma activates the male gametophyte, which bursts the wall of the pollen grain and forms a pollen tube that grows the length of the style to the ovary (Figure 17.23). The angiosperm pollen tube may lengthen several centimeters in only a few hours, in marked contrast to that of conifers, which requires a year to grow a few millimeters. As the pollen tube elongates, the generative nucleus of the male gametophyte divides into two sperm nuclei, each of which is invested with a small amount of cytoplasm that assumes a spiral, tapering form. When the tip of the pollen tube penetrates through the micropyle and reaches the female gametophyte within the ovule, these two sperm cells are released, to participate in a unique *double fertilization* event. One sperm joins the egg nucleus to form the zygote, while the other penetrates into the center of the female gametophyte and there joins with *both* of the endosperm nuclei to form a *triploid* endosperm fusion nucleus. This polyploid condition probably serves to fortify the metabolic activities of the endosperm cells, which must synthesize large amounts of protein and accumulate heavy food reserves to provide for the growth of the seedling.

Shortly after the endosperm fusion nucleus begins to divide to form the endosperm tissue, the zygote also starts to divide, producing the diploid tissues of the embryo proper. The embryo may remain enclosed by the endosperm, on which it gradually draws for nourishment. Alternatively, the nutrients stored within the endosperm may be digested and taken up by the *cotyledons* (seed leaves) of the embryo, which become plump and serve as a source of nourishment during germination. At this time the seed is mature and further development of the embryo ceases. The seed remains dormant until conditions are favorable for resuming growth. Meanwhile, the sporophyte tissues that made up the flower's ovary change to become the *fruit,* which is specialized for seed protection and/or dispersal (see Figure 12.20).

Plant evolution reflects a trend toward ever more effective protection of the gametes and progeny. First, the development of multicellular antheridia and archegonia enhances the protection afforded the gametes and later the sporophyte embryo. Next, in seed plants generally we find the gametophyte generation protected by tissues of the parent sporophyte. Finally, in angiosperms the entire ovarian wall of the preceding sporophyte generation is specialized for the protection and dissemination of the next sporophyte generation.

C Animal reproductive systems

GAMETOGENESIS The essential commitment of the gonads is gametogenesis, the production of gametes: oogenesis takes place in the ovary; spermatogenesis, in the testis. The nuclear events of oogenesis are identical with those of spermatogenesis in that the chromosome complement is reduced to the monoploid state (see Figure 8.4). The first significant *difference* between the two processes is that at each meiotic division the cytoplasm is *equally* apportioned in spermatogenesis but is very *unequally* divided in oogenesis (Figure 17.24). In each case, a primordial, diploid cell—the *oogonium* or the *spermatogonium*—undergoes a period of enlargement, becoming the *primary oocyte* or *primary spermatocyte.* This cell then undergoes a reduction division, in which homologous chromosomes first synapse and then are separated during the ensuing anaphase.

In the oocyte, the spindle develops just within the cell membrane; since the plane of cytokinesis is determined by the equator of the spindle rather than that of the cell, the two daughter cells produced are a large *secondary oocyte* and a small *polar body* containing the discarded set of chromosomes. Division of the primary spermatocyte on the other hand, produces two *secondary spermatocytes* of equal size.

A second meiotic division follows the first without any intervening DNA or chromosomal replication; this division separates the chromatids. Since the chromatids are the daughter chromosomes formed prior to the onset of the first meiotic division, they are fundamentally identical except for possible crossing over. The first meiotic division is therefore mainly *reductional* and the second division *equational.* (Less commonly the chromatids separate at the *first* division and homologous chromosomes at the second.) Cleavage of the cytoplasm again occurs equally in the male, producing two *spermatids* from each secondary spermatocyte, and unequally in the female, yielding a large *ootid* and another small polar body. The first polar body divides in synchrony with the secondary oocyte, but all three polar bodies eventually disintegrate.

The ootid then grows into the mature *ovum,* whereas the four spermatids formed by the two divisions of each primary spermatocyte now undergo differentiation into

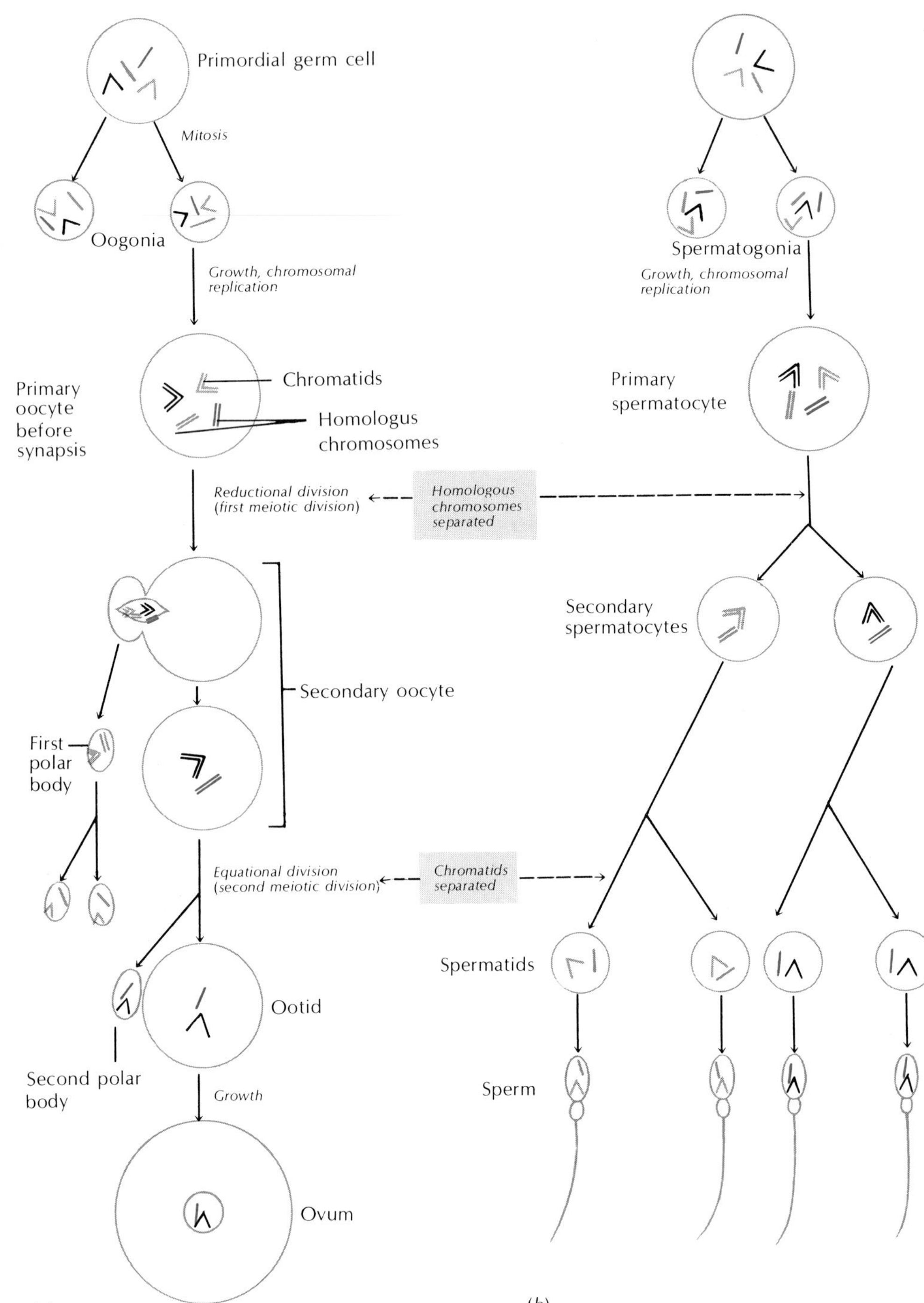

Figure 17.24 □ **Gametogenesis: (*a*) oogenesis; (*b*) spermatogenesis.**

mature sperm. Each sprouts one or more flagella and its "head" is capped with an *acrosome* filled with enzymes that will later serve to penetrate the egg membranes (see Figure 11.8). The mitochondria are retained during this metamorphosis. In vertebrates they are closely packed within the "middle piece" lying between the chromosome-bearing "head" and the motile "tail." Sperm when activated will have great need for the energy generated in the mitochondria. During its final differentiation most of the cytoplasm of the spermatid is used up, so that in volume (though not in length) sperm are among the smallest of cells.

GENITAL ORGANS Gonads, genital tract, and external genitalia (when present) constitute the animal reproductive system (Figure 17.25). The somatic tissues of the gonads support the germinal cells both structurally and nutritionally, and in vertebrates have also assumed an endocrine function and control the maturation and functional state of the genital tract, external genitalia, and other target organs.

After meiosis, the ova remain within the ovary while accumulating their stores of yolk (Figure 17.26*a*). The eggs of vertebrates (and a number of invertebrates) ripen singly, within *ovarian follicles*. These are composed of epithelial cells which synthesize food storage materials that are passed to the ovum. The plasma membrane of the ovum is often covered with microvilli (as is typical of cells intensively engaged in absorption) and pinocytic vesicles (see Figure 14.8) have

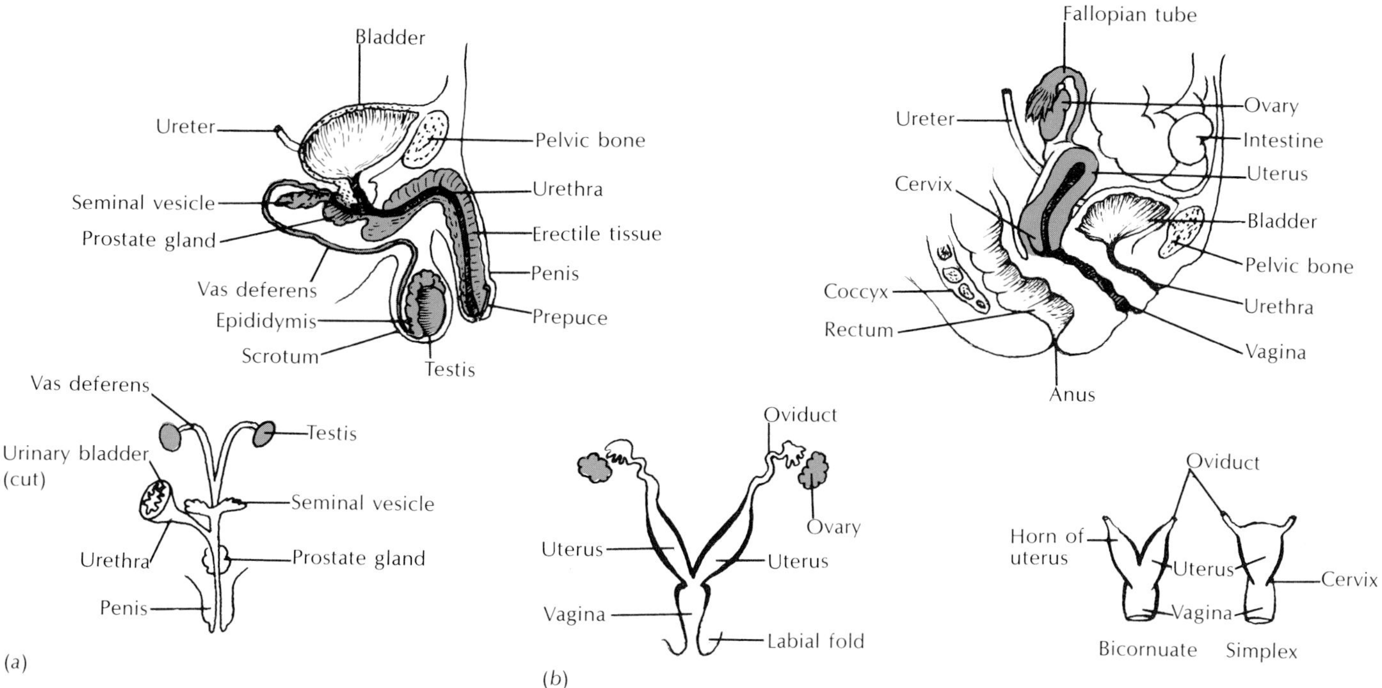

Figure 17.25 □ **Mammalian genital tracts. (*a*) Male: below, male genital tract prior to testicular descent into scrotum (ventral aspect); above, human male genital tract (lateral aspect). (*b*) Female: left below, typical mammal (ventral aspect); right below, lower tracts showing degrees of uterine fusion; above, human female genital tract (lateral aspect).**

been noted. The requirement for yolk-formation often far exceeds the synthetic capabilities of a single cell. Even the ova of organisms as simple as sponges and coelenterates obtain food stores by engulfing smaller neighboring cells or by taking up materials liberated by nurse cells. The cells forming the ovarian follicle can also act as phagocytes, devouring the yolk left when some of the ova degenerate instead of attaining maturity. On maturation, the ripe eggs are liberated by the rupturing of the follicles (*ovulation*).

In a number of invertebrates such as insects the ovaries are tubular and continue uninterruptedly into the upper part of female genital tract (*oviduct*). In this case the oogonia are located at the proximal ends of the ovarian tubules (ovarioles), and the eggs pass along as they ripen, being shed at last to the exterior by way of a genital pore. As they pass through the oviduct the eggs are usually invested by protective secretions forming a shell or a gelatinous capsule. In vertebrates and a number of coelomate invertebrates the ovaries are saccular and the eggs are shed directly into the coelomic cavity, whence they pass into the flared ciliated inner ends of the oviducts. The bird oviduct is functionally regionalized; as the egg passes along, it is first coated with albumen and then receives a shell membrane and outer limy shell. Finally, a slick

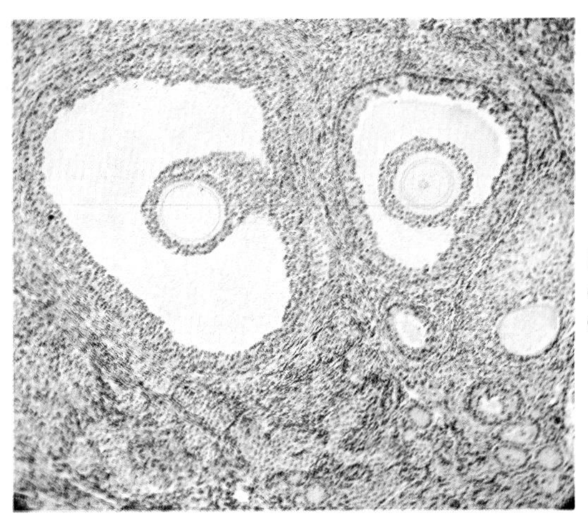

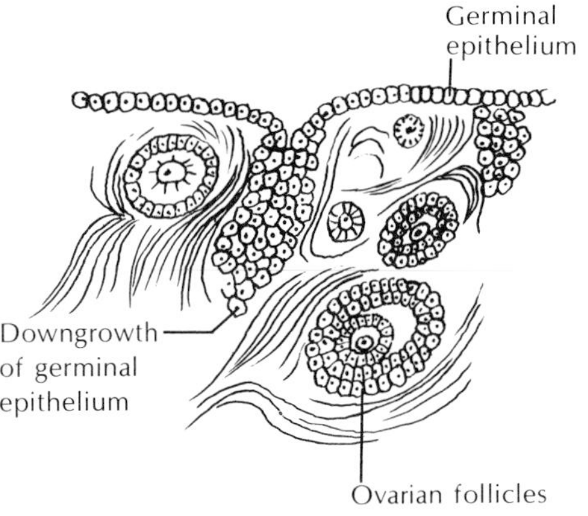

(*a*)

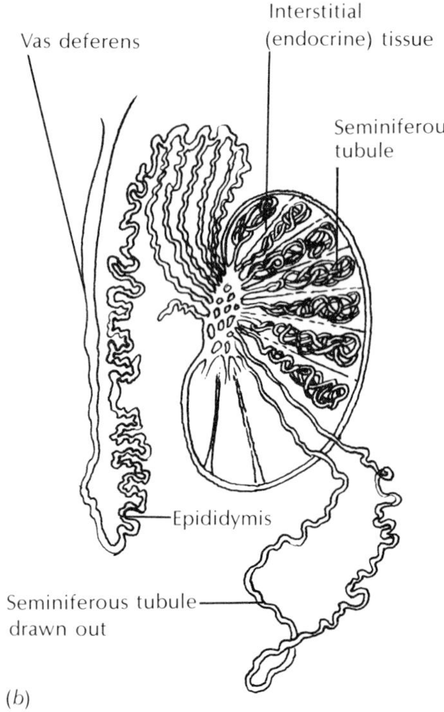

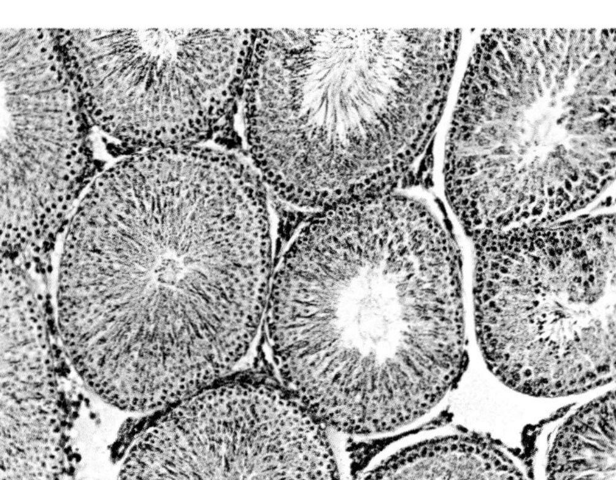

(*b*)

Figure 17.26 □ Mammalian gonads. (*a*) Ovary: left, portion of cat ovary, showing two nearly mature follicles with ova and a number of immature follicles and ripening ova (*Ward's Natural Science Establishment, Inc.*); right, cell detail, showing downgrowth of germinal epithelium to form new follicles. (*b*) Testis: left, section through entire human testis, showing seminiferous tubules and epididymis; right, section of rat testis, showing seminiferous tubules with spermatozoa maturing in their walls (*Triarch Incorporated, Geo. H. Conant, Ripon, Wis.*). Hormone-secreting interstitial cells occupy the spaces among the tubules.

mucus coating seals the pores of the shell and prevents infection (see page 440).

The distal portion of the female genital tract is often dilated to form a *uterus* or more often paired uteri that open to the exterior separately or by way of a common *vagina.* Uteri are of course analogous rather than homologous when they occur in different phyla, but they all serve to store the eggs internally until a time propitious for their release. The paired uteri of monotremes and all nonmammalian vertebrates open separately into the vagina or directly into the cloaca, and are easily recognizable as the somewhat inflated distal portions of the oviducts. The vagina originally opened into the cloaca, but during mammalian evolution has become progressively separated from the intestinal and urinary tracts. Only in female primates, however, do the urethra, vagina, and anus each open individually to the exterior. Uterine evolution in mammals has favored the gradual fusion of the two uteri into one chamber providing space for fewer but larger young. A *simplex* uterus is characteristic of primates and normally accomodates but one fetus at a time. Partially fused, Y-shaped uteri occur in other eutherians, with embryos developing in each uterine horn.

In a number of invertebrates the female reproductive system includes an organ (*seminal receptacle,* or, in insects, *spermatheca*) that receives the sperm during mating and holds them pending later fertilization of the eggs.

Female *external genitalia* are well developed in insects, and serve to clasp and guide the male's copulatory apparatus during mating. The *ovipositor* aids in placing the eggs during laying, and may be used to dig a burrow in the soil or to pierce the tissues of a host. Human female genitalia include the paired labia major and smaller labia minor (which fold protectively over the vaginal and urethral openings) and the clitoris, a homolog of the penis that generates erotic sensations upon tactual stimulation, thus reinforcing the sexual receptivity of the female.

Testes are usually made up of microscopic tubules (*seminiferous tubules*), within the walls of which spermatogenesis proceeds. These tubules are continuous with the male genital tract, the sperm ducts (Figure 17.26*b*). In the vertebrate testis the spaces among the seminiferous tubules are occupied by hormone-secreting *interstitial cells.*

Vertebrate testes primitively lie far anterior in the coelom (see Figure 12.43), but have tended to move posteriorly, until in mammals they usually reside outside the body cavity within a *scrotum.* Testicular descent into the scrotum is permanent in ungulates and primates, but occurs only at the breeding season in rodents, bats, and shrews. This displacement of the testes into the scrotal sac is dictated by the inability of most types of sperm to withstand the high internal body temperatures of the homoiothermal animal. When the testes fail to descend in man, sterility and diminished production of male hormones result. Bird testes are cooled by their proximity to the large internal air sacs, and the sperm are stored close beneath the skin; testicular displacement is accordingly not required in these homoiotherms.

The vertebrate male genital tract is differentiated into a proximal, much convoluted cluster of small tubules, the *epididymis,* and the larger, more distal *vas deferens.* Opening into the vas deferens are accessory glands that secrete *seminal fluid,* which with the sperm comprises the *semen.* In mammals various components of the seminal fluid are contributed by the seminal vesicles, prostate, and bulbourethral glands. The seminal fluid is buffered, protecting the sperm from unfavorable pH changes in the female tract. It serves as a medium for sperm transport and also contains nutrients (chiefly fructose in mammals) that provide for the energy needs of the sperm (which have no food reserves).

Invertebrate male genital tracts consist of a duct, the *vas deferens,* that expands distally to form a *seminal vesicle* (not analogous with the vertebrate gland of the same name), within which the sperm are stored until ejaculation. Various accessory glands are associated with invertebrate genital tracts. If, as in squid and many insects, the sperm are transferred to the female encased in a spermatophore, this body must be formed in a special spermatophore-producing organ.

Male external genitalia include such aids to mating as claspers that hold the female during copulation, and/or *intromittent* (copulatory) organs that introduce sperm directly into the female tract. The external genitalia of insects are complex and so diverse in form that they often frustrate mating attempts between misguided insects of different species. (This marked species specificity is frequently a great help to taxonomists who are attempting to differentiate between two species.)

The vertebrate *penis* probably originated as a specialized portion of the cloaca, for in some vertebrates which lack a penis (such as birds) copulation is achieved by the partial protrusion of the cloaca from the anus and its insertion into the anus of the sexual partner. In birds the cloacal end of the oviduct is everted and thrust into the anus of the male. Male lizards and snakes have *hemipenes,* paired sacs that protrude from each side of the cloaca and are inserted into the female's body during coitus. Turtles and mammals have a true penis, which is erectile when engorged with blood. Along the midventral wall of the turtle cloaca runs a spermatic groove flanked on each side by spongy erectile tissue, the corpora cavernosa. When these are filled with blood they enclose the spermatic groove to form a temporary duct leading from the vas deferens to the exterior. In mammals this duct is permanent, forming an extension of the urethra. It is flanked by three masses of erectile tissue (corpus spongiosum and corpora cavernosa). In a number of mammals such as cattle a penial bone (*baculum*) develops in the connective tissue between the corpora cavernosa, imparting permanent rigidity to the penis.

D The physiology of vertebrate reproduction

THE NEUROENDOCRINE CONTROL OF REPRODUCTION All aspects of vertebrate reproduction from sexual maturation to parental behavior are under the joint control of the nervous system, the pituitary gland, and sex hormones secreted by the gonads (Figure 17.27). The hypothalamus is the part of the brain most directly concerned with the control of reproduction. It regulates the adenohypophysis by secreting neurohormones that govern the release of the hypophyseal hormones (see Figure 15.48). The hypothalamus in turn is controlled by hypophyseal and gonadal hormones and also by other parts of the brain that receive and interpret sensory data. Thus not only may the internal events leading up to reproduction be coordinated, but they may also be synchronized with relevant environmental factors.

The hypothalamus and reproduction Implantation of electrodes or of small hormone pellets directly into the hypothalamus has demonstrated that this part of the vertebrate brain contains a number of specific, localized control centers that govern various aspects of reproductive behavior and physiology.

The hypothalamus exerts control over the adenohypophysis by way of neurohormones that reach the pituitary via the hypophyseal portal blood vessels. Two hypothalamic neurohormones are the *gonadotrophin release factors* (FSH-RF and LH-RF), which respectively cause the hypophysis to secrete the *gonadotrophins* FSH (follicle-stimulating hormone) and LH (luteinizing hormone), which in turn affect the gonads and control their secretion of male sex hormones (*androgens*) and female sex hormones (*estrogens*). A third neurohormone secreted by the hypothalamus, the *prolactin-inhibiting factor* (PIF) prevents the pituitary from secreting prolactin. The existence of these neurohormonal control factors may be experimentally demonstrated by liberating the pituitary from hypothalamic influence. This can be accomplished in vivo simply by interrupting the hypophyseal portal circulation. Alternatively, the hypophysis may be removed and maintained in organ culture. In either event, the pituitary stops secreting gonadotrophins but secretes greater amounts of prolactin.

In addition to these neurosecretory centers that affect reproduction by way of the pituitary, the hypothalamus houses other centers, some of which govern specific reproductive behaviors, whereas others act to stimulate or inhibit the centers that produce FSH-RF, LH-RF, and PIF. For example, there appears to be a specific area that inhibits the center which produces FSH-RF and LH-RF. When this area is experimentally destroyed in the rat, the animal enters puberty precociously. On the other hand, destruction of another area considered to excite the RF-producing center causes the animals to remain permanently prepubertal (sexually immature). Still another area constitutes an ovulation center. Impulses from this center evoke a sudden brief upsurge in the secretion of LH by the pituitary, which brings about ovulation. If this center is destroyed, a female mammal is arrested indefinitely in a state of behavioral *estrus* (intense sexual hunger and receptivity).

The hypothalamus, by withholding its release factors, prevents an animal from maturing sexually until its somatic growth is largely completed. Both the pituitary and the gonads are actually competent to function reproductively at a much earlier time. This can be shown by transplanting a juvenile pituitary into an adult animal from which the pituitary has been removed. Under the influence of the mature hypothalamus, the young pituitary begins at once to secrete gonadotrophins. Similarly, an immature gonad implanted into a mature, castrated animal responds to the presence of gonadotrophins by promptly beginning to secrete sex hormones.

In a number of recent investigations minute amounts of solidified sex hormone have been introduced directly into the brain in quantities too minute to leak into the systemic circulation and cause effects on other tissues. The results obtained reveal that sex hormones act upon the brain directly, both to suppress the secretion of the gonadotrophin release factors and to control reproductive behavior patterns that are activated in hypothalamic or other nearby brain areas. The existence of separate brain centers for courting and copulatory behavior in birds has been demonstrated by implanting male sex hormone into one specific site in the brain of a castrated male. When placed in this location (the preoptic region) the implanted hormone induces copulatory behavior but does not trigger courtship behavior.

Ovariectomized female cats promptly become sexually unreceptive. Receptivity can be restored either by introducing female sex hormones directly into the hypothalamus or by injecting them in larger amounts

Figure 17.27 □ **Neuroendocrine regulation of reproduction in vertebrates. Hormones secreted by hypothalamus are in solid color; by adenohypophysis, color tint; by gonads, black.**

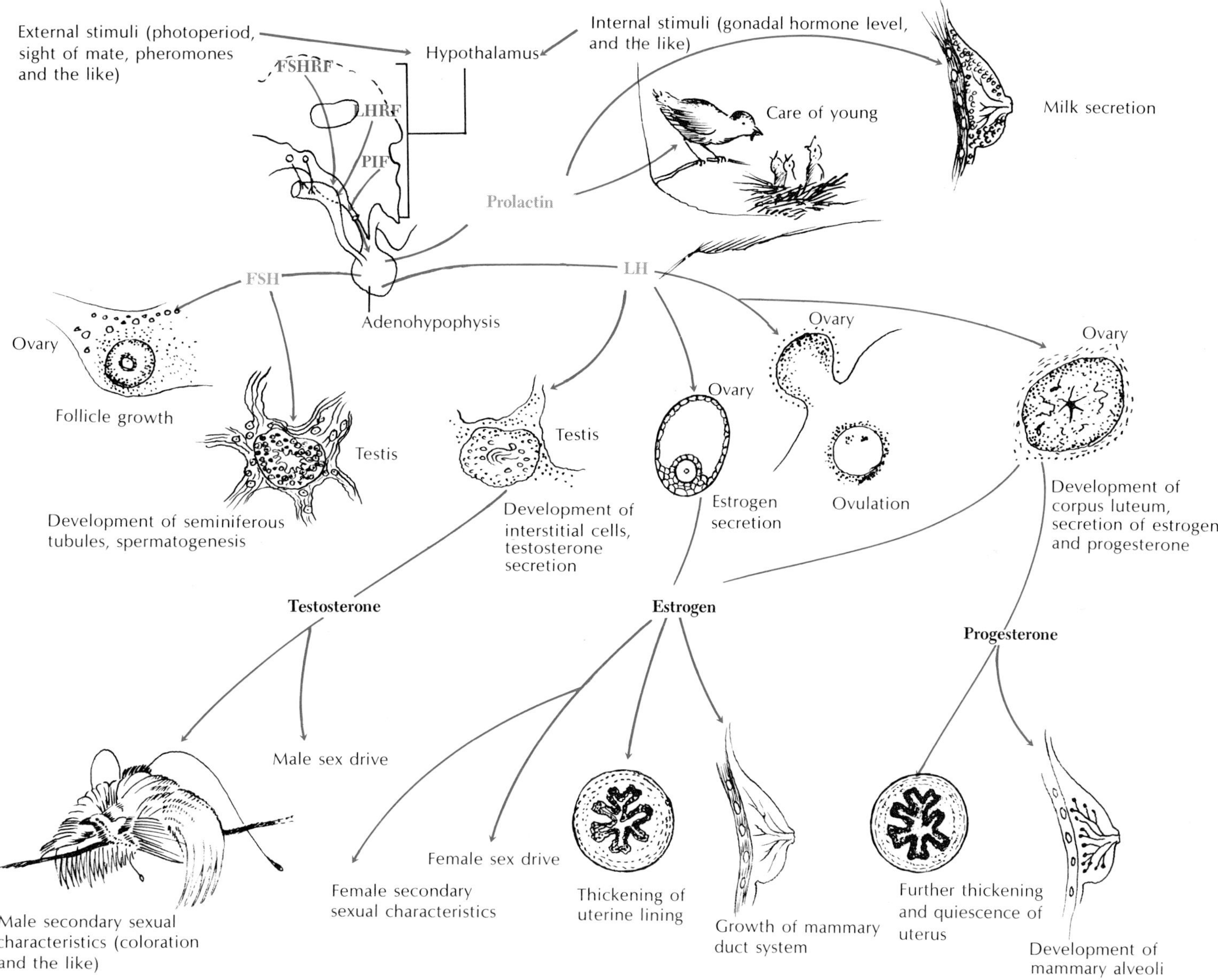

into the general circulation. If an intravenous injection of radioactive estrogen is given, the only parts of the brain found to take up the tagged hormone molecules are the hypothalamus and nearby preoptic region. The radioactivity reaches its peak in the brain within a few hours after the injection and then gradually wanes. However, during the brain's brief exposure to estrogen, behavioral changes have been induced which do not become manifest for several days, long after the brain radioactivity has completely vanished. This indicates that the estrogen serves as a trigger only, setting in motion neurophysiological processes that finally produce overt expression of the behavior.

Injecting young mammals with sex hormones at certain critical times during development may have lasting effects on reproductive behavior, inducing irreversible changes in the brain. Both masculine and feminine behavior patterns appear to be latently organized in the brains of both sexes. If a certain minimum amount of androgen (male sex hormone) is present in the bloodstream during this critical period, it will cause the feminine behavior patterns to be permanently suppressed and will promote differentiation of the male patterns (although these will not actually be expressed until much later when circulating androgen reaches concentrations typical of the mature state). However, if a basal level of androgen is lacking in males during this critical period, *feminine* patterns will later emerge! The critical period for rats appears to be within 4 days after birth, for the majority of males castrated during this time and left hormonally untreated later demonstrate feminine types of behavior. On the other hand, estrogen (female sex hormone) injected into newborn male rats does *not* induce feminine behavior in either castrated or intact animals. Furthermore, estrogen injected into newborn *female* rats actually interferes with the differentiation of female patterns so that feminization never takes place and the animal is sexually unreceptive when mature! This demonstrates that the feminization of reproductive behavior is dependent *not* upon the presence of estrogen, but upon the *absence* of androgen during the critical developmental period.

After the initial sexual differentiation of the brain, reproductive behavior patterns are triggered mainly by the action of gonadal or hypophyseal hormones upon the appropriate brain centers. Removal of the gonads before puberty causes mammals of both sexes to remain sexually immature, both physiologically and behaviorally. Ovariectomizing mature female mammals usually causes loss of sexual drive and receptivity. In the cat the full spectrum of reproductive behavior may be quickly restored by implanting estrogen directly into the posterior hypothalamus. The implant also causes a decline in pituitary gonadotrophin release, due to feedback repression of the centers secreting FSH-RF and LH-RF. Castration of a sexually experienced cat or man leads to a gradual waning of sexual drive and potency, which however may persist for some months before disappearing. Again, normal behavior is instantly restored by androgen injections or implants.

In the human female neither ovariectomy nor the natural failure of estrogen secretion that follows menopause abolishes erotic sensations or sexual drive. However, occasionally a woman must have her adrenal glands surgically removed along with her ovaries. In this event she does suffer diminution or loss of sexual drive and responsiveness. This leads us to believe that such loss of libido is due not the absence of estrogen, but to the lack of adrenal *androgens,* for the adrenal cortex typically secretes small amounts of sex hormones and is a source of male hormones in the female.

Adenohypophyseal reproductive hormones Under hypothalamic control the anterior pituitary secretes three hormones concerned with reproduction: the two gonadotrophins (FSH and LH) and prolactin (lactogenic hormone); FSH and LH are glycoproteins having a molecular weight of 40,000 to 100,000 (sheep LH represents the lower figure, swine LH the upper). Follicle-stimulating hormone promotes the growth of the ovarian follicles in females and stimulates spermatogenesis in males. Luteinizing hormone induces ovulation in the female and promotes the secretion of the gonadal hormones in both sexes. In the male, LH induces differentiation of the endocrine interstitial tissue of the testis; in the female it promotes the secretion of estrogen by the ovarian follicle cells and later promotes the transformation of these cells into a yellow mass of glandular tissue, the *corpus luteum.* LH then promotes the secretion of estrogen and a second hormone, progesterone, by the luteal cells.

All vertebrates studied to date have been found to produce both FSH and LH, but in various proportions. Even with mammals markedly different FSH/LH ratios are found. In general, the higher the proportion of LH to FSH, the longer is the duration of sexual receptivity in the female. The ratio of LH to FSH increases successively in the following: cattle, with a sexually receptive period of only 12 to 18 hr; sheep, with a receptive period of 30 to 36 hr; pigs, which are receptive for 48 to 72 hr; horses, with a receptive period of 5 to 10 days; and finally women, who are sexually receptive at almost all times.

Secretion of FSH and LH is regulated by a feedback mechanism, in which a rise in circulating sex hormones causes suppression of FSH-RF and LH-RF secretion by the hypothalamus, with a consequent suspension of FSH and LH release from the pituitary. This in turn results in a decline in circulating sex hormones until a certain lower threshold is reached, whereupon the hypothalamus once more begins to secrete its release factors.

Prolactin, a protein with molecular weight ranging from 22,000 to 35,000 (according to the species), is a hormone of many talents. Its name derives from the fact that it is responsible in mammals for the secretion of milk by the mammary glands. However, it occurs in all vertebrates studied to date and has varied physiological and behavioral effects. In a few mammals (such as the rat) prolactin rather than LH is responsible for the secretory activity of the corpus luteum. Prolactin injections cause hens to become broody, pigeons to secrete "crop milk" (used to feed the young), and roosters to show some (but not all) types of parental behavior. We have noted earlier that prolactin induces "newt water drive," the prespawning migration that brings salamanders back to the water for mating and egg laying. Prolactin also cooperates with MSH (melanocyte-stimulating hormone) in bringing about pigmentary changes in fish that advertise the breeding state. In euryhaline fishes prolactin is important to osmoregulation, assisting the physiological adjustments involved in migrations from the sea to fresh water and vice versa.

Sex hormones Sex hormones are steroid compounds (see Figure 9.9) that are primarily secreted by endocrine cells in the gonads. They are responsible for the differentiation, development, and maintenance of the genital tract and various secondary sexual characteristics. Sex hormones also suppress or activate sexual behavior patterns and exert subtle influences on other behaviors not strictly concerned with reproduction. Androgen level, for instance, correlates directly with an animal's position in a social hierarchy, for individuals with higher androgen concentrations tend to be more aggressive. Accordingly, androgen injections may elevate a low-ranking male or even a female to social prominence. The sex hormones profoundly influence somatic development, especially in sexually dimorphic species where male and female may differ in overall size, color, and body proportions. Despite the role of the chromosomes in the determination of sex (see pages 290–291), sexual differentiation during embryonic development may be interfered with if the androgen-estrogen ratio is abnormal. Estrogens promote the development of female sexual characteristics (including feminine distribution of body fat, growth of the mammary glands, and the like) *in either sex* and cause feminization of the previously indifferent genital tract and gonad. Androgens (especially testosterone in man) are specific for male secondary sexual characteristics (including beard growth in man, antlers in deer, male plumage in roosters, and so forth) and for the masculinization of the gonad and genital tract. If during the critical period of development the sex hormone balance does not match up with the genetic sex, differentiation of the reproductive system may be reversed and the individual come to be of the opposite sex. Such sex-reversed individuals are often normal in all respects save for the lack of agreement of genotype and phenotype. A man who is actually a sex-reversed female can only have daughters, however, for he lacks the male-determining Y chromosome. Disturbance of sex hormone balance at a somewhat later time can lead to improper masculinization or feminization of an already partially committed reproductive system, and hermaphroditism (usually with sterility) may result. Castrating a young male kangaroo, for instance, causes the developing scrotum to change into a typical female pouch! In cattle twins of mixed sex, the female twin is a sterile, masculinized *freemartin.* This is an outcome of the flow of androgens through the partially conjoined placental circulations typical of cattle twins.

Both ovaries and testes secrete estrogens and androgens, as well as pregnancy-supporting hormones (*gestagens*). All three types of sex hormones are also secreted in small amounts by the adrenal cortex in both sexes. In consequence, the sex hormone balance differs *quantitatively* rather than qualitatively in males and females, for both male and female hormones occur in both sexes, although one or the other predominates. In fact, synthesis of sex hormones seems to be linked into a common metabolic pathway, which broadly speaking leads from cholesterol to gestagens, to androgens, and finally to estrogens.

The mammalian ovary contains two

major endocrine tissues: follicles and corpora lutea. During the maturation of an ovarian follicle the follicular cells secrete estrogens together with a lesser quantity of the gestagen progesterone. After ovulation, the follicular cells are transformed into *luteal* cells, which proliferate within the cavity of the ruptured follicle. In anamniotes the corpus luteum is probably not an endocrine gland at all; as far as we know, monotremes (such as the duckbilled platypus) are the most primitive vertebrates in which pituitary LH serves to trigger endocrine activity on the part of the corpus luteum. In other vertebrates the luteal cells are phagocytic and seem to be involved principally with cleaning up debris left in the ruptured follicle. In mammals they produce large quantities of progesterone and smaller amounts of estrogen.

The principal vertebrate estrogens are estradiol, estrone, and estriol (Figure 17.28), all three of which may be present in various proportions. Estradiol is the main estrogen occurring in women. Estrogens are responsible for the growth and maintenance of the oviduct and uterus, the preovulatory thickening of the uterine lining, and the secretion of vaginal lubricants during coitus. Estrogens also occur in plants, where they act as mitotic stimulators. Perhaps in their early evolution estrogens originally acted upon some basic metabolic system common to both plants and animals, and only later assumed a distinct reproductive function. In fact, estrogens in invertebrates are thought not to affect sexual characteristics, but to promote yolk synthesis and mitotic activity in the ovarian follicles.

In mammals a major evolutionary innovation is that the corpus luteum comes under the control of LH from the pituitary and becomes the body's major source of *progesterone,* the hormone promoting gestation. Increased supplies of progesterone paved the way for the actual placental attachment of an embryo to the mother's uterine wall. We shall discuss intrauterine development further in a later section, but should note here that in noneutherian vertebrates the embryo, although it may be retained within the uterus, seldom becomes actually embedded in the uterine lining. The spongy thickening of this lining, which prepares the uterus for implantation of the embryo, occurs under the influence of progesterone. Progesterone stimulates the growth and secretory activity of the uterine glands and suppresses uterine contractions. If pregnancy occurs the corpus luteum persists and enlarges further, so that the secretion of progesterone continues to rise. During early pregnancy progesterone keeps the uterus muscularly quiescent, preventing possible loss of the embryo. It also acts in combination with estrogen to bring the mammary glands to a state of full develop-

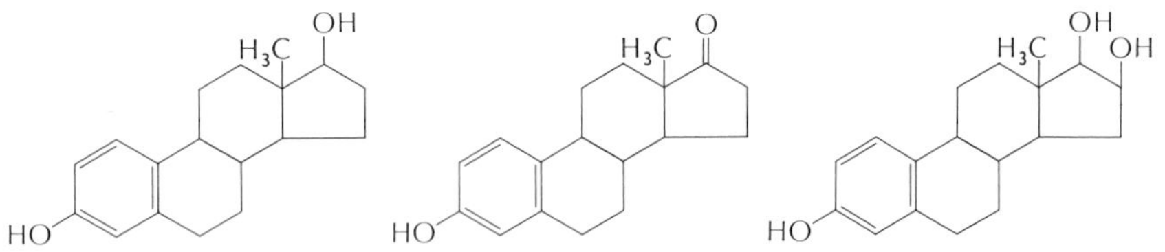

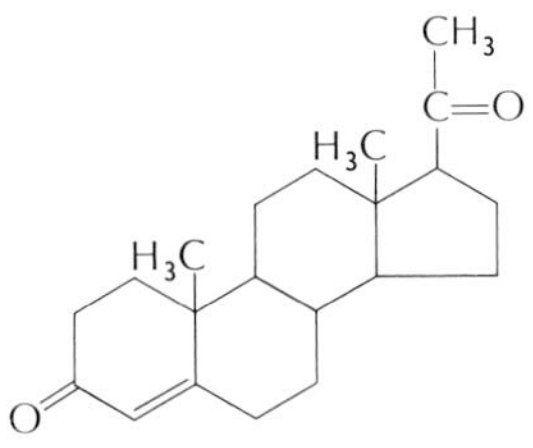

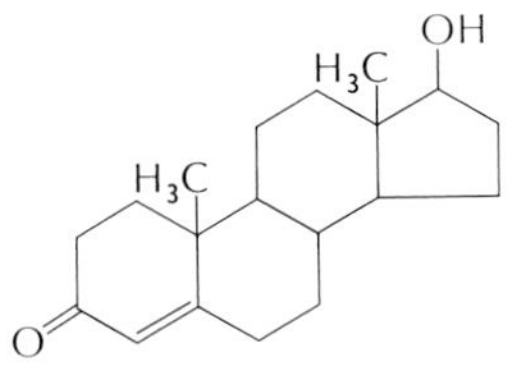

Figure 17.28 □ **Gonadal hormones: (*a*) major estrogens; (*b*) progesterone, a pregnancy-supporting factor; (*c*) testosterone.**

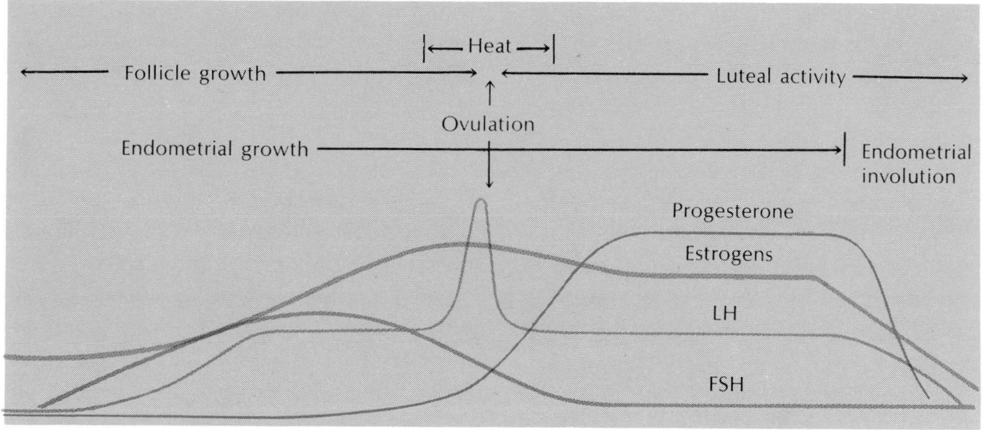

Figure 17.29 □ **Estrus cycle. Relative levels of four important hormones are graphed through one complete estrus cycle and are correlated with relevant ovarian, uterine, and behavioral events. Total duration of an estrus cycle and the number of cycles per year vary according to species.**

ment, promoting extreme branching of the ducts and growth of clusters of secretory cells at the ends of the ducts. Progesterone is also known to trigger certain reproductive behavior patterns. For example, injected into nonpregnant mice, progesterone induces them to build large, fluffy brood nests (such as pregnant females build) rather than the usual small sleeping nests.

REPRODUCTIVE CYCLES Rhythmic fluctuations occur in gonadal activity, in gametogenesis, in the condition of the genital tract, and in sexual drive. These reproductive cycles are fundamentally endogenous, but may be influenced by certain environmental rhythms, particularly photoperiod. The basic cycle is often an annual one, but several shorter cycles may occur during a single breeding season. Only a few species of vertebrates breed freely throughout the year: female rats and mice have 4- to 5-day reproductive cycles, and nonpregnant human females have 28-day cycles approximately from the age of 12 to 45.

Because the mammalian reproductive cycle is usually characterized by a brief period of intense female sexual receptivity ("heat"), it is known as an *estrus* ("frenzy") *cycle* (Figure 17.29). The female in heat moves about restlessly and often actively seeks a mate. This period of receptivity lasts only a few hours or days, its peak coinciding with ovulation and the presence of ova in the genital tract, together with the thickening of the uterine lining. These gonadal, uterine, and behavioral events require precise synchronization or reproduction may fail. Furthermore, the reproductive physiology of male and female must also be synchronized. If breeding is seasonal, the male must come into the reproductive state at the same time as the female. However he exhibits no marked cyclical fluctuation of sexual activity within the breeding season, being capable of inseminating the female whenever she becomes receptive. Species in which females continue to have estrus cycles throughout the entire year are characterized by a nearly perpetual state of sexual readiness in the male.

The human *menstrual cycle* is a modified estrus cycle, differing in two main respects. First, the woman does not enter an intense estrus state in which mating becomes obligatory, nor is she sexually unreceptive throughout the rest of the cycle. Second, toward the end of each cycle (if pregnancy has not occurred) the outer layers of the thickened uterine lining slough off with some bleeding (menstruation). Menstruation is typical only of higher primates; in other eutherians the thickened part of the lining is absorbed without sloughing or blood loss. The emancipation of women from the strict cyclicity of estrus and anestrus (nonreceptivity) has facilitated the strengthening of the bond between male and female that must endure during the long period of dependency of human offspring. Although her receptivity undergoes no measurable cyclic fluctuation, a woman's fertile period is actually restricted to about 24 hr of each cycle, and in consequence relatively few copulations can result in conception.

Unless it is fertilized, the human ovum begins to degenerate within 12 to 24 hours after ovulation; sperm can survive for only a day or two in the human female genital tract: therefore, unless coitus takes place on the day of ovulation or during the preceding two days, conception is unlikely. However, the time of ovulation varies among individuals and may even change from one cycle to another depending upon psychogenic and physiological factors, and it is therefore impossible to predict exactly the so-called *safe* period by any method presently known. Since ovulation is usually suppressed during lactation (which in primitive peoples especially may be allowed to continue for many months), during this time the mating act may be repeated frequently without resulting in pregnancy. Contraceptive pills now in use consist of synthetic estrogenlike and progesteronelike substances that alter the flow of gonadotrophins just enough to suppress ovulation. Besides preventing conception, they may also be used to combat sterility; by taking them over a period of time a woman can correct certain hormonal imbalances so that when she ceases to take them she may not only ovulate normally, but may even have multiple ovulations and produce triplets or quadruplets—a true *embarras des richesses!*

The mammalian estrus cycle is divisible into a follicular phase and a luteal phase, separated by the period of ovulation. During the *follicular phase* the ovarian follicles are growing and estrogen is the predominant ovarian hormone (although some progesterone is also secreted). Estrogen promotes the initial phase of uterine thickening and stimulates contraction of the uterine muscles. As its concentration rises, estrogen begins to inhibit FSH (acting by way of the hypothalamus, and not directly upon the pituitary) and simultaneously promotes the secretion of LH. The follicular phase terminates in most mammals with estrus and with the abrupt surge of LH production that induces ovulation. During the *luteal phase* the follicular cells are transformed into the corpus luteum, which under the influence of LH secretes a little estrogen and a great deal of progesterone (the hormone that dominates this phase of the cycle). As the production of progesterone increases, it in turn affects the hypothalamus, suppressing the release of both LH and FSH. The corpus luteum then shrinks and becomes nonfunctional while the thickened portion of the uterine lining is either absorbed or sloughed off.

EFFECTS OF EXTERNAL STIMULI ON REPRODUCTION Throughout the time of breeding and rearing of young, the animal responds to a series of stimuli emanating from the abiotic environment as well as from its mate, its young, and other members of the breeding aggregation. These responses help to correlate intrinsic breeding cycles with environmental factors in such a way that the young are borne at a time of year best suited for survival. The reproductive physiology of potential mates may also be synchronized, and even the reproductive activities of entire breeding groups. Later, certain cues may direct parents in the care of their young.

By way of example, let us trace some of the integrative processes by which the reproductive activities of birds are regulated. The basic annual reproductive cycle is endogenous, but especially in temperature zone species it is susceptible to the influence of seasonal changes in the length of daylight. Initially, a lengthening photoperiod (as in spring) acts upon the brain, causing the flow of hypothalamic release factors to the pituitary with consequent secretion of gonadotrophins and stimulation of the gonads. This photoperiodic effect is probably mainly mediated through the eyes, but the pineal may also be involved, for severing the optic tract does not totally abolish the response.

The gonads, under control of the pituitary gonadotrophins, begin to secrete sex hormones. These in turn regulate other organs, including the liver, which in the female starts to synthesize egg yolk proteins. Under the influence of testosterone, a male bird now assumes his nuptial plumage and shows interest in females. Acting upon the brain, these hormones prime the centers having to do with reproductive behavior so that the animal's behavior toward other members of its species is altered. Prior to this time, sight of another male may produce no particular response; now the male bird establishes a territory (if of a territorial species), advertises it by lusty singing, and defends it by fighting.

The presence of other individuals of the same species provides stimuli that are essential in bringing about ovulation and egg laying. A number of birds (including ring doves and pigeons) will not ovulate unless a nest site and nesting materials are available. However, even in this case a pigeon will not lay eggs if she is isolated from others of her own kind, but will do so in the sight of other pigeons (even females) or even when a mirror is placed in her cage. In other species such as parakeets and canaries, a visually isolated female will build a nest and lay eggs if she is acoustically stimulated by the vocalizations of a male or a breeding pair. The sight of a courting male is most efficacious in causing ring doves to build nests and lay eggs. When the male is castrated (thereupon ceasing to court) this effect wanes.

Interactions among territorial individuals at the boundaries of their territories may be of prime importance in bringing the animals into breeding condition. The recurrent arousal provided by threatening and quarreling at the territorial boundary seems to promote full development of breeding readiness. This may explain why, instead of dispersing as much as possible throughout the available space, territorial animals tend to cluster as closely as their contrary tendency to drive off others of their species permits them. Even though other potential sites may be available, a gull which cannot command a territory in the colony's breeding area will not move away and establish a solitary nest, but simply will not court, mate, or lay eggs.

Actual mating is usually preceded by a series of interactions between male and female, such as we shall discuss in Section 17.2E. Successful courtship terminates in nest building, mating, and egg laying. When a full clutch of eggs has been laid (a number characteristic of the species and usually linked to the ability of the parents to feed the young), the visual and tactile cues furnished by the eggs in the nest inhibit further egg laying and initiate incubation behavior. Prior to this time, a patch of skin on the breast of the female (or of both sexes, if both participate in brooding) has, apparently under the influence of prolactin, become highly vascularized and inflamed and the plumage has molted in that spot. This hot "brood patch" serves to transfer heat from the parent's body to the eggs, and the probably refreshing sensation of resting this inflamed skin against the cooler eggs may be instrumental in encouraging birds to incubate.

After the eggs hatch, the nestlings themselves provide new stimuli that trigger feeding and hovering behavior. Many young birds instinctively stretch their necks and gape widely, at first when the nest is jogged and later when stimulated by the sight of the returning parent. Their wide mouths are often rimmed with a band of bright color that reinforces the releaser effect of gaping and makes it impossible for the parents to withhold food from the young. Other sensory cues are forthcoming as development proceeds. Konrad Lorenz has reported that in the first few days after hatching, naked young jackdaws may be held in the hand without evoking parental retribution. However, as soon as the black pinfeathers erupt, the nestlings become "real" jackdaws and further attempts to handle them are met with fierce attack by the adults.

Through this example we have seen that in any series of reproductive and care-giving activities, the stimuli must proceed in succession, with each response dependent upon prior physiological arousal of appropriate brain centers by specific hormones. The flow of these hormones has previously been triggered by external stimuli. Each successive response, physiological or behavioral, places the animal in a new stimulus situation, permitting the next set of responses to come into play.

Olfactory stimuli have a major influence upon reproductive behavior in most animals (except in birds, where they seem to play no part). Volatile chemicals released by one sex or the other may have pheromonal effects, either directly releasing a sexual behavior or promoting certain physiological changes that in turn lead to the reproductive state. For instance, a male pig gives off an odor that affects the hypothalamus of the sow's brain by way of her olfactory nerves so that FSH-RF and LH-RF are secreted. If the olfactory region of the sow's brain is destroyed experimentally, her pituitary gland will no longer secrete gonadotrophins. Male mammals rely on odors emitted by the female to gauge the approach of estrus. Male insects are often attracted over considerable distances by means of sex attractants released by mature females (although sometimes it is the male which secretes the attractant and lures the female).

The role of olfactory stimuli in the control of reproduction has probably been most extensively investigated in the laboratory mouse. Female mice are *negatively* olfactorily imprinted to their fathers: if they are exposed to the father's odor during a critical period after birth, they will upon maturity refuse to mate with him or in fact with any male of the same inbred strain if males of other strains are available. This olfactory preference is not exhibited when female mice are deprived of contact with their father's odor. The duration and regularity of the mouse estrus cycle is profoundly regulated by the olfactory environment. In all-female groups the mice may remain anestrus for long periods. This mutual suppression is known to be mediated by odor, for it does not occur if the female's olfactory nerves are surgically interrupted. The odor of a male mouse causes the female's estrus period to become shorter and more regular; this effect is fully produced simply by anointing the female's nostrils with male urine and will not be brought about if the female is rendered unable to detect odors.

Since urine from castrated males does not have this effect, the active compound is thought to be a urinary androgen or some by-product of androgen metabolism.

Olfactory pregnancy block has been previously cited (see Section 7.2C) as an intraspecific population-control device that comes into play (in mice at least) as a result of overcrowding. If a female mouse is subjected to the concentrated odor of male mice during the first 5 days after mating, she seldom becomes pregnant. The immediate cause of pregnancy failure is that prolactin is not released and since it is the hormone primarily responsible for the development of the corpus luteum in mice, progesterone also will be wanting and the uterine lining will not be prepared for the implantation of the embryo.

E Mating

In a broad sense we may consider mating to include all aspects of the physiological and behavioral synchronization of two individuals that lead to a one- or two-way transfer of gametes. Such synchronization is vital even when individuals do not come together for physical union and gametes are shed freely into the milieu. Many marine invertebrates synchronize release of gametes either by means of chemical cues (emanating from the animals themselves) or by keeping time to some environmental rhythm (tidal or lunar). Although many organisms mate by this simple means, gamete mortality is bound to be high under such circumstances. Loss of gametes can be reduced if sperm are shed directly over the eggs as they are laid (as in most vertebrate fish) or are transferred directly into the body of the mate. In order to come close enough to each other so that either of these events can take place, many kinds of animals require that some sort of courtship ritual precede the mating act.

We have noted previously that when mature many animals avoid bodily contact with others of their kind and may actually be somewhat aggressive toward them, thus effecting a spacing out of the population within the habitat. For such noncontact species the aversion to bodily contact and aggressive tendencies toward conspecifics must be temporarily suspended. And in the case of predatory species, including spiders and many insects, it is also necessary to suspend prey-capturing behavior for the duration of the mating act—or prospective mates may dine upon one another before the reproductive function can be consummated. Many forms of animal communication (see Section 7.3C) have evolved as aids to the courting and mating process. Since they are so intimately concerned with perpetuation of kind, most animal communication systems are essential for survival of the species (Figure 17.30).

COURTSHIP Premating interactions between prospective mates have several functions: (1) they aid in species recognition; (2) they assist in recognition of individuals that are ready to mate; (3) they help to synchronize the reproductive physiology and behavior of male and female, including the abovementioned overriding of aggressive or predatory inclinations. Although courtship may culminate with the mating act and cease thereafter, in species where both parents are subsequently involved in the nurture of the young, courtship activities may be long extended, serving to maintain the pair bond. Ritual feeding, an important aspect of courtship in many birds, may continue for so long that the female, gaping and fluttering her wings in a revival of juvenile food-begging behavior, may be fed on the nest by the male along with their own fledglings.

Ethological isolation Courtship rituals (or in fact any chemical, visual, or acoustic cues that facilitate mutual recognition) can prevent the loss of time and energy caused by accidental matings with individuals of other species. Even when such heterospecific matings are physically possible, no offspring may result; even when hybrid progeny are produced, they may be sterile or less well adapted than either of the parental species, which occupy specific niches in the community. The earlier in the mating process that a reproductive barrier can operate between species, the greater the economy effected. The most economical reproductive barrier is *ethological isolation,* which acts at the time of courtship. By *ethological isolation* we mean that even when in the same locality, closely related species will not normally interbreed because their courtship or other mate-recognition cues are sufficiently unlike. A female frog can identify males of her own kind by their distinctive call, although the pond may be crowded with vociferous songsters of several species. Similarly, only the stridulations of a male of her own species exerts a hypnotic attraction upon a female katydid so that she moves resistlessly toward the source of the sound, even when blinded.

Ethological isolation is seen dramatically in action on any mud flat occupied by several species of fiddler crabs. The little males

Figure 17.30 □ **Sexual dimorphism and courtship behavior in American eiders. Note that both breeding plumage and behavior help to identify males in reproductive state: male at right is performing the "reaching" display. (*Courtesy of Dr. P. A. Johnsgard.*)**

stand before the entrance to their burrows, busily 'fiddling" with their single large claw. Morphologically the various species may closely resemble one another, as do the gross aspects of the courtship movements. But closer inspection reveals differences in the rate of fiddling, the angle at which the fiddling arm is moved relative to the trunk, and the correlation of general body movements with the fiddling. The efficacy of these slight but vital differences is demonstrated by the behavior of the female: if while scuttling across the flat she comes face to face with a courting male of her own kind, she may be arrested in midrun, spend some time in rapt contemplation of this magnificent creature, and then docilely descend with him into the privacy of his burrow.

Sexual selection We note that the female often acts as the discriminator, both in accepting only males of her own kind (many males, as their internal reproductive drive mounts in intensity, may court and attempt to copulate with quite inappropriate love objects) and in actually choosing a mate from among a number of males of the proper species. This discrimination by the female we call *sexual selection,* and Darwin considered it to be one of the major forces operating to bring about evolution. He probably overestimated its role in this respect, for in many cases it cannot be demonstrated at all and in other cases a female seems drawn more to a given territory than to a particular male. However, it does seem to hold true that where social hierarchies exist, females are especially susceptible to the blandishments of high-ranking males. Wolves and baboons in heat, for example, first "present" (make a gesture inviting coitus) to the group's dominant male. An African antelope, the kob, displays *arena behavior* during the mating season. Most of the males of the herd stake out small territories within which each struts and threatens his neighbors. As the males display within their arenas the estrus females approach, calmly threading their way past the low-ranking males holding peripheral territories to reach dominant males that defend territories in the middle of the arena area. The arena displays of grouse also result in the "master cock" attracting and subsequently mating with a majority of the hens (Figure 17.31).

In other cases, a female may show a distinct preference for a male with the most conspicuous secondary sexual characteristics. Female *Anolis* (American "chameleons") favor males with the reddest dewlaps, and female jewelfish spend the greater portion of their time consorting with the most brightly colored males. Because of sexual selection a "conflict of interests" may be set up in which the overexposed male is placed in jeopardy from predators during the mating season. The enormous tail feathers of peacock, argus pheasant, and lyrebird seriously encumber the breeding males, but because the females of these species disdain males with less massive adornments, natural selection will no doubt continue to move toward ever more splendid and cumbersome

Figure 17.31 ☐ **Sexual selection. The relation of breeding territory to "popularity" of the male is visible in this photograph of a sage grouse lek, or strutting ground. The "master cock," just to the right of center, has attracted six females, shown waiting nearby. A seventh female has just been mounted and is now leaving the lek (left background). Social dominance and territorial possession are influential in a male grouse's breeding success and accordingly affect the genetic composition of the population. (*Courtesy of Dr. P. A. Johnsgard.*)**

male plumage (Figure 17.32). Since only the female of these species cares for the young, the chosen male need live only long enough to perpetuate his genes; little profit it the drabber male if his underdeveloped plumage enables him to evade predators but dooms him to a life of celibacy. If the male's sexual adornments become too unwieldly, such feminine unreasonableness may eventually lead to extinction of the species.

Reproductive synchronization When prolonged, courtship often induces physiological changes that bring both male and female to a peak of breeding readiness. However, even a short courtship involves the behavioral synchronization of potential mates and is one of the surest means of determining that only individuals in breeding state and of the same species will actually perform the mating act. In the integration of male and female reproductive behavior patterns a zigzag stimulus-response sequence may be followed: a signal presented by an individual of one sex releases a specific response in a member of the opposite sex, and this response in turn serves as a stimulus for the release of the next behavior in the first individual. If the stimulus-response chain is broken at any point, it often must be started again from the very

Figure 17.32 □ Courtship displays in (*a*) Argus pheasant (*Zoological Society of San Diego*) and (*b*) lyre bird: left, female and male scratching for food; right, male in courtship display, tail fan completely hiding body (*courtesy of Australian News and Information Bureau*). In these two species the tendency of females to mate with males having the most conspicuous display has resulted in selection toward ever more cumbersome breeding plumage that hampers the males' escape from predators. This adaptive conflict may eventually lead to extinction.

(*a*)

(*b*)

beginning. The mating of the Queen butterfly demonstrates just such a reaction chain (Figure 17.33). The sequence is initiated when a male catches sight of a female. He then engages in aerial pursuit, overtakes the female, and hovers in front of her, brushing her antennae with his "hairpencils," a cluster of bristles that can be extended from the tip of his abdomen. The hairpencils appear to be periodically anointed with a pheromone produced in a glandular pouch on each hindwing. If the female is sexually receptive, she responds to the hairpencilling by alighting. The male then performs a bobbing dance, fluttering in front of the female and continuing to brush her antennae with his hairpencils. Now the female may fold her wings and only if she does so does the male alight, retract his hairpencils, and attempt to copulate. Once coitus is achieved the male flies off, still coupled with the female, who hangs passively upside down from the tip of his abdomen. This short postnuptial flight serves to remove the mating pair from an area in which their courting activities may have made them dangerously conspicuous to predators. Coitus ends with insemination (transfer of the sperm), and the two butterflies separate. In this stimulus-response chain the female may terminate the sequence at any point by failing to provide the male with the next sign stimulus. If interrupted, the sequence may be initiated again; and should this new start occur, the sequence once more follows the same stereotyped course.

Such stereotyped reaction sequences also characterize the courtships of many vertebrates, as observed by the ethologist Niko Tinbergen in the courting of the three-spined stickleback. Prior to mating

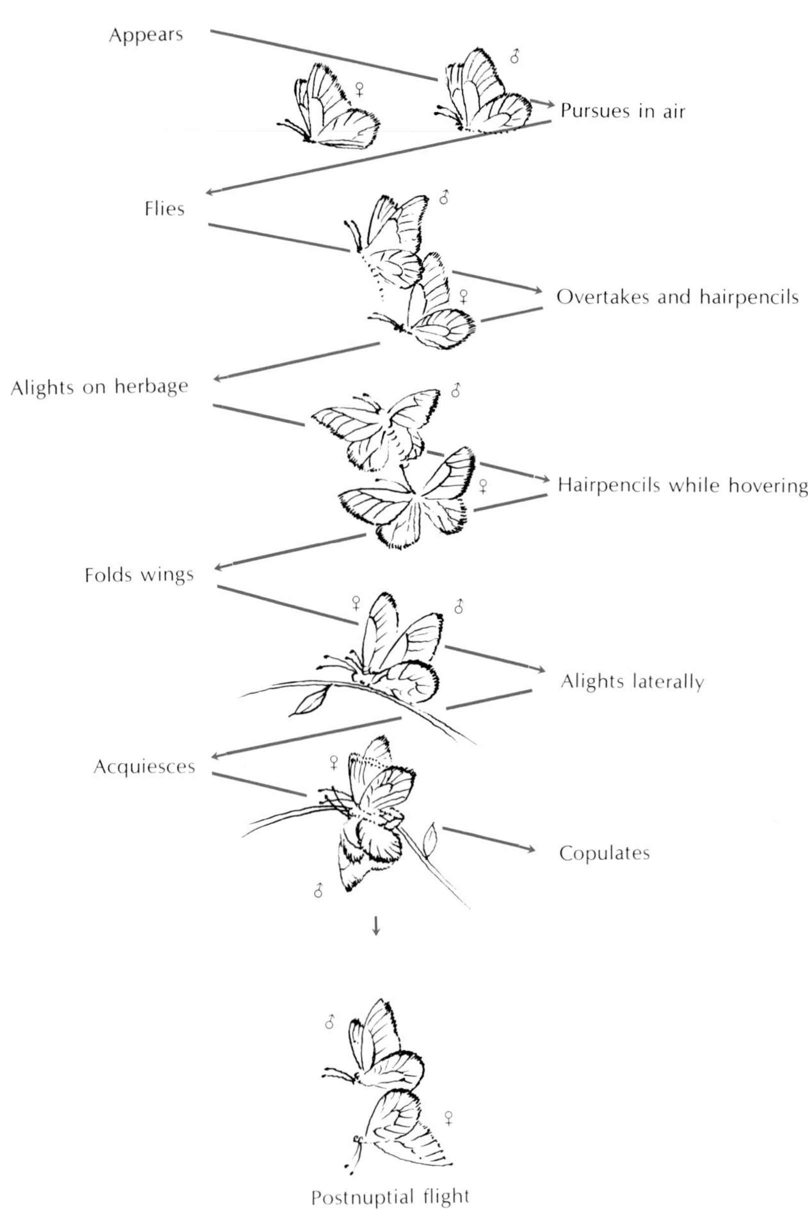

Figure 17.33 □ Stimulus-response reaction chain in the courtship of the queen butterfly (*Danaus gilippus berenice*). [*Adapted from L. P. Brower, J. van Z. Brower, and F. P. Cranston, Zoologica, 50 (1965).*]

these small spike-backed fish migrate from the ocean into fresh water. We do not know what specific physiological changes initiate the prespawning migration, but when the fish reach an estuary the changing salinity triggers a movement into fresh water and upstream. This salinity preference is reversed at the end of the breeding season, when the fish move downstream and back to sea. It is an expression of an intrinsic rhythm and although correlated with the gonadal cycle is not under immediate control of the sex hormones, for it persists despite gonadectomy. Reaching an area suitable for nesting, the stickleback school disperses, the males assuming their red-bellied breeding coloration and becoming belligerent toward other males showing the same distinctive coloration. Eventually territories are established and aggressive behavior diminishes to occasional border skirmishes. This premating aggressive behavior and establishment of territories is dependent upon gonadotrophins and not upon androgens. However, subsequent behaviors such as nest building, nest defense, and incubation are androgenically controlled.

The male gathers vegetation and constructs a cylindrical nest, binding it with secretions from his own body. Then he stands guard against all trespassing fish, especially rival males. An approaching female also first provokes an aggressive rush,

Figure 17.34 □ Stimulus-response chain in courtship of the three-spined stickleback. The male first establishes a territory and builds a nest. Recognition of a gravid female inhibits male's attack, and he turns toward nest, inducing female to follow by means of a "zigzag dance." The male "points the way" into the nest by poking his own head into the opening and withdrawing it. When the female enters the nest, the male taps her tail rapidly with his snout, thereby eliciting egg laying. After this, the female leaves the nest, and the male enters and sheds semen over the eggs. Several females may be courted in turn, each adding her eggs to the nest. (*After N. Tinbergen.*)

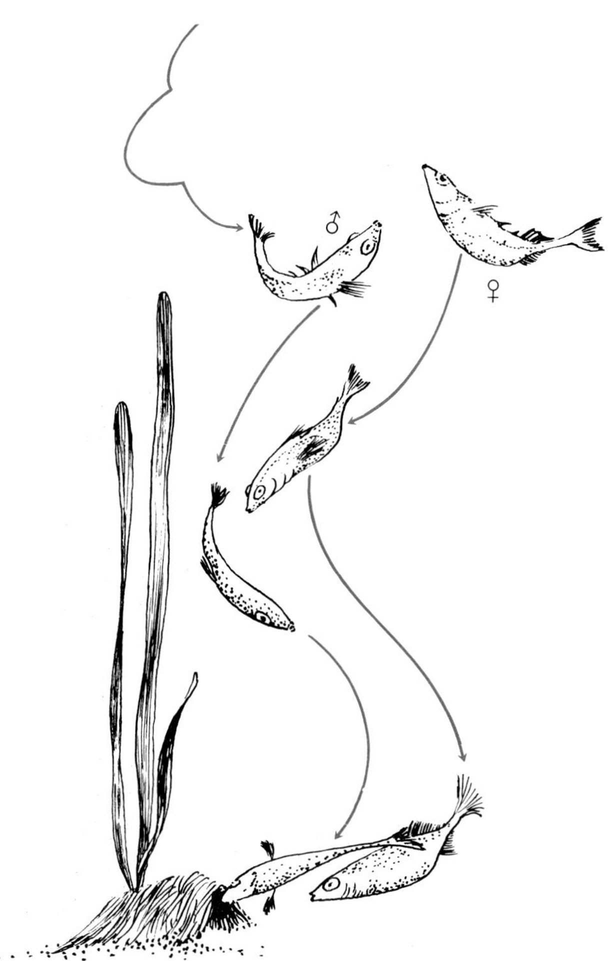

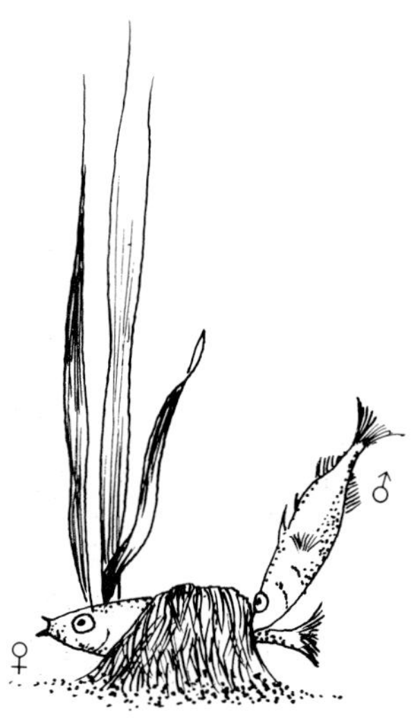

which is arrested as soon as she tilts upward, revealing her egg-swollen belly. This serves as a visual cue that initiates the male's first courtship act, the "zigzag dance" (Figure 17.34). As the male dances he moves gradually toward the nest, and the female follows. He then turns and leads her to the nest, before which he hovers and "points" the entrance like a birddog pointing a covey of quail. As the female enters the nest in response, the male begins to tap his snout against her tail with a quick, vibratory movement. This tactual stimulus (which the investigator can mimic with a glass rod) causes the female to lay her eggs in the nest. When finished the female moves out of the nest and the male enters and sheds semen over the eggs. He repeats this procedure until several females have added their eggs to his nest. Then the male's behavior toward all sticklebacks becomes wholly aggressive, and he now drives off all comers regardless of sex. It is well that he does so because the females are not reluctant to eat their own eggs. Between sorties he ventilates the nest with fanning movements of his fins, and if eggs spill out of the nest he retrieves them in his mouth and replaces them. When the young hatch he continues to guard them for some time, returning them to the nest when danger threatens.

In some species courtship and mating activities cause ovulation to take place. In most mammals ovulation occurs spontaneously when estrogen concentration reaches the threshold for arousing the hypothalamic ovulation center that causes the release of the preovulatory spurt of LH. However, in cats, rabbits, and ferrets, the ova mature but are not shed from the ovary until mating takes place. In such *induced ovu-*

Figure 17.35 □ **Internal fertilization is especially important for terrestrial animals, such as insects and amniote vertebrates. (*a*) Hover flies in copula. (*Los Angeles County Museum of Natural History photo by C. L. Hogue.*) (*b*) Galápagos tortoise mounting. (*Zoological Society of San Diego.*)**

(*a*)

(*b*)

lators courtship activities are aggressive and rowdy, extreme emotional arousal apparently being required to stimulate the ovulation center. Such mating is more reminiscent of an act of intended annihilation than of classical "love making." However, in many other species courtship serves to tone down and control aggressive tendencies that may be prominent in noncontact species or in fact in any species in which individuals become territorial during the breeding season. Because of the tendency of noncontact species always to preserve a certain distance from one another, it is not surprising that courtship acts are found to consist of ritualized elements of the *agonistic* (aggressive-defensive-submissive) repertory, in which both attack and escape tendencies are evident. Such rituals, performed by male and female alike, seem gradually to alleviate both tendencies until a pair bond is formed (see Figure 16.22). Thereafter, male and female stand together, defending their joint territory against intrusive neighbors. For the duration of the breeding season they are a unit, and the requirement for individual distance is suspended.

INSEMINATION Transfer of sperm from male to female (insemination) is not necessarily synonymous with internal fertilization (that is, fertilization of ova within the female genital tract), for in a number of species sperm received during mating are merely stored within the female's body, to be voided to the exterior as the eggs are laid some time later. Whether the eggs are fertilized externally or internally, fertilization need not immediately follow insemination. Delayed fertilization is typical of a number of insects in which the female mates but once, storing within her spermatheca enough sperm to fertilize all the eggs that she shall ever lay. In the honeybee this may require that the sperm survive for one or two years, during which time they are constantly in motion within the spermatheca, their flagella beating several hundred times per minute. This perpetual motion requires that the sperm be provided with nutrients secreted by the spermathecal lining.

Transfer of sperm directly into the body of the female is so much more effective than shedding them into the water (and in fact is the only feasible way for terrestrial animals) that means of insemination have evolved in animals of many different phyla (Figure 17.35). Insemination can be effected without copulatory organs but is of course more efficient when such organs are present. Salamanders, for instance, lack copulatory apparatus, but their courtship ritual makes insemination possible. The female gives off a species-specific pheromone that attracts only males of her own kind. The male often first rubs his snout over the female's body, perhaps verifying recognition, and then moves in front of her, walking slowly forward while the female follows, straddling his tail. He then deposits a gelatinous spermatophore on the substratum and the female, moving forward, picks it up with the lips of her cloaca as she passes over it. Birds also lack a penis, but in response to the male's courtship the female crouches, moves her tail to one side, and raises and everts her cloaca, which may be inserted into the male's as he mounts her and ejaculates.

Earthworms, which are hermaphroditic, achieve efficient mutual insemination without relying on intromittent organs. Extending their anterior ends, each from its own

Figure 17.36 □ **The gamete-containing posterior portion of the palolo worm, a marine annelid, is snapped off and makes its way to the surface. Synchronized by the monthly lunar rhythm, the worms liberate their hind quarters within a few moments of one another so that a massive, frenzied "swarming" takes place, with a high probability that most eggs will be fertilized.**

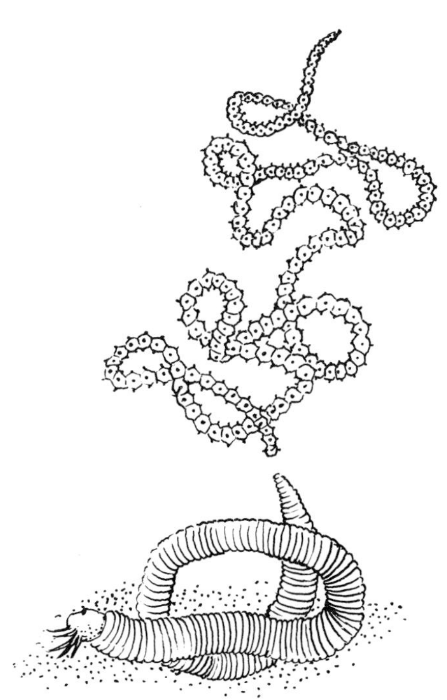

burrow, the two worms press their ventral surfaces together with heads pointing in opposite directions. This places the openings of the seminal receptacles of each worm opposite the clitellum (a girdle of glandular tissue) of the other. The worms cling together by driving bristles into each other's body at the points of contact and by secreting a broad slime tube that binds them together in the contact zone. Each worm then expels semen from the openings of the sperm ducts. The sperm swim along grooves on the worm's ventral surface to the opening of its partner's seminal receptacles. Copulation lasts for about two hours, following which the worms separate. Retracting into their respective burrows, each secretes a cylindrical cocoon from the clitellum and then, crawling slowly backward out of the cocoon, first lays eggs and then voids sperm from the seminal receptacles upon the eggs. By this means cross fertilization is achieved, with both worms serving first as males, then as females.

Although less mandatory for aquatic than for terrestrial species, direct sperm transfer so enhances the probability of fertilization that means of insemination have been independently developed in many aquatic animals. Penial spicules which are inserted into the female's vagina are found in tapeworms, flukes, and nematodes. Modified legs form a penis in crustaceans. A bizarre means of insemination occurs in some leeches, in which one leech deposits a spermatophore on any part of the body of another leech after which the sperm perforate through the body wall into its coelomic cavity, where they fertilize the eggs. A similar but even more unusual means of internal fertilization is seen in certain marine annelids that swarm at the time of mating. Annelids of this type develop gonads only in a series of posterior segments that are lost and regenerated each breeding season. When the worms swarm, the female bites off the male's sperm-filled hindparts and proceeds to eat them. During digestion the sperm are set free within her digestive tract and penetrate the gut wall into the coelom, where the eggs are fertilized.

In a related family of worms [including the palolo (Figure 17.36)], fertilization is external, but is made more effective by a very remarkable type of mating behavior. These worms remain cozily within their burrows but extend and snap off their gamete-filled hind ends. These swim to the surface in large numbers where they writhe about so vigorously that they literally tear themselves asunder, releasing the gametes into the water. Millions of these headless halfworms may be performing their frenzied dance at the same time under a full moon. This response to the lunar cycle greatly increases the incidence of fertilization.

MATING SYSTEMS Social vertebrates exhibit several types of mating: promiscuous, polygynous, polyandrous, seasonally monogamous, or perennially monogamous.

In *promiscuous* species any male and female in the social group may mate, the two consorting only during the mating act or for but a few days. The female may accept several males during a given period of receptivity, while at the same time the mature males attempt to copulate with as many females as are receptive. Social rank may play an important role in determining a given male's access to the receptive females. Promiscuity usually implies that the female alone must assume care of the young, if any; in certain social primates such as baboons, however, the males are responsible for the protection of the entire troop, especially guarding the pregnant females and juveniles.

Polygyny is a common mating system, involving the control of a number of females by a single male for the duration of the breeding season. The social rank of male sea lions and wapiti (North American elks) determines the size of the harems they control. Male sea lions migrate to the breeding grounds in advance of the females and by the time the latter arrive have established territories into which they herd the females. The male firmly dissuades the females from wandering into the territories of rivals, while threatening other males that show intentions of territorial encroachment.

Polyandry, a mating system in which several males mate with but a single female during a breeding season, is relatively uncommon in both human and animal societies. A conspicuous exception is the jacana, a tropical rail-like aquatic bird characterized by long, slender toes that enable it to walk about upon waterlily pads. A female American jacana, aggressive and territorial when in mating condition, is courted in her territory by a number of males, and eventually accepts no more than four, with all of which she may mate even on the same day. She then subdivides her territory into as many subterritories as she has mates, and lays a clutch of eggs in each subterritory. The males then incubate the eggs while the female patrols her territory, ousts intruders, and settles disputes by the simple expedient of threatening or attacking her squabbling husbands.

Figure 17.37 □ Perennial monogamy: Canada geese mate for life. Here the male guards while the female broods the nest. (*Courtesy of General Biological, Inc., Chicago.*)

Seasonal monogamy requires that the pair bond between male and female be maintained only for the length of one breeding season. *Perennial* monogamy demands that the pair bond be reinforced annually or continuously, for the same individuals are mates for as long as they both live (Figure 17.37). A monogamous relationship usually implies that both parents are to be involved for some time in the care of the young. Unusual among reptiles is the monogamous association of the male and female king cobra, which build a nest and share the guardianship of the eggs. Most birds that produce helpless (altricial) young are monogamous, and both parents share their care. [*Altricial* offspring are completely dependent at birth; their eyes may be sealed closed, their skin virtually naked, and they are incapable of locomotion for some time. *Precocial* young are much less dependent, for their eyes are open at birth, their skin covered with fur or down in the case of homoiotherms, and they are capable of coordinated locomotion within a few hours of birth (Figure 17.38).] Monogamous birds reinforce the pair bond by prolonging certain courtship rituals through the entire reproductive season. Both male and female may participate in nest building, in incubation, and in feeding and hovering the young. A "nest-relief ceremony" may be used to stimulate one parent to leave the nest, allowing the other to take over.

Relatively few mammals are monogamous, exceptions being marmosets (tiny monkeys in which the paternal role includes carrying the infant, which is passed to the mother only for nursing), jaguars, and foxes, in which the male's role is primarily that of providing food for the vixen and kits. We do not know if man is naturally monogamous, for both polygamy and promiscuity are established practices in various societies; regardless of the mating system in use, the male generally serves as protector of and provider for the young.

17.3 □ CARE OF THE YOUNG

Figure 17.38 □ Altricial and precocial young just after hatching: (*a*) altricial young lingers in its nest; (*b*) precocial young leaves its nest early.

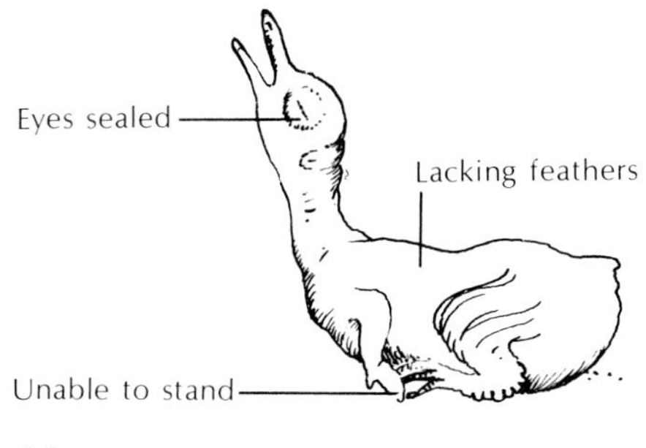

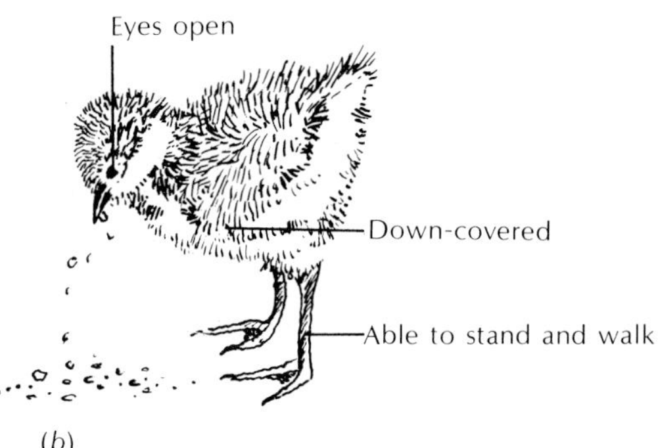

Successful perpetuation of a species requires that the young be protected and nurtured until they are able to fend for themselves. The less the protection afforded and the earlier the stage at which the progeny must meet their own needs, the more prolific must be the species. Protection and nurture can be provided by evolved structures such as egg membranes, uterus, and placenta, as well as by evolved or learned patterns of parental care. When the period of protection and nurture is long the young are afforded more time for growth, which permits development of complex forms of neural organization. Continued association with the parent after birth may extend the period of nurture and guardianship and even make possible the transmission of learned habits from adults to offspring. When the period of dependency is very prolonged, frequently not only the mother but also the father and even other adults of the social group will cooperate in its rearing.

A Egg membranes

Protective egg membranes are particularly required by oviparous (egg-laying) species, especially those which are terrestrial and/or undergo a prolonged developmental period. The egg membranes of certain rock snails are impregnated with noxious chemicals that make the eggs unattractive to predators. The egg cases of skates bear four tendrils that coil about kelp and thus prevent the eggs from being washed ashore or buried in silt during their long period of development (Figure 17.39). Oviparous terrestrial species must lay eggs resistant to desiccation; such *cleidoic* eggs are laid by insects, arachnids, and other terrestrial arthropods, and by reptiles, birds, and monotremes (see Figure 4.3). The *amniote* egg which originated with reptiles has proven the most successful of cleidoic eggs, for its embryonic membranes not only have afforded protection from dehydration, but also have paved the way for the evolution of the placenta and viviparity (Figure 17.40). The amniote egg cleaves meroblastically (see Figure 11.10C) and as the discoid embryo develops additional tissues sheet out to form the embryonic membranes. The outermost of these membranes, the *chorion,* comes to lie just within the shell of avian and reptilian eggs but its role is rudimentary in these groups compared to its later contribution to the mammalian placenta. The *amnion* directly encloses the embryo (see

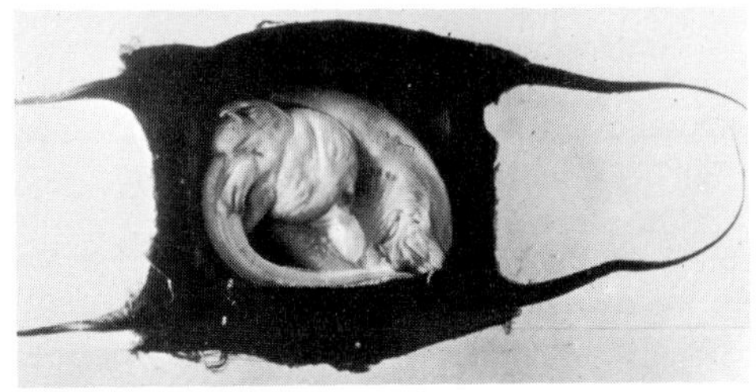

Figure 17.39 □ **Young skate developing within egg case. The tendrils on the case twine about vegetation, preventing the egg from being swept away. (*Courtesy of General Biological, Inc., Chicago.*)**

Figure 17.40 □ **Oviparity: horned lizards hatching. The genus *Phrynosoma* includes both egg-laying (oviparous) and live-bearing (ovoviviparous) species. (*Zoological Society of San Diego.*)**

Figure 11.1), its cavity being filled with amniotic fluid that not only prevents dehydration of the embryo but cushions it against mechanical injury and lubricates it so that adhesions do not develop. The outer layer of amniotic cells, derived from the mesoderm, differentiates into muscle fibers that contract rhythmically, "rocking" the embryo and providing stimulation possibly needed for normal neural and motor development. From the ventral surface of the embryo spring two other embryonic membranes: the *yolk sac,* which encloses stored nutrients in all vertebrates, (Figure 17.41) and the *allantois.* The latter serves in birds, reptiles, and monotremes both as a moist respiratory membrane and as a repository for nitrogenous wastes that accumulate during development. The eutherian allantois contributes to the umbilical cord and placenta.

B Internal development

VIVIPARITY A number of animals do not lay eggs at all but retain the embryos within the body of the adult during the early developmental stages. Such "live-bearing" species are said to be *viviparous.* Viviparity is a very effective means of reducing mortality of the young. It has arisen independently in many animal groups, both invertebrate and vertebrate. Viviparous species are found in all classes of vertebrates except cyclostomes and birds. Most viviparous species are actually *ovoviviparous,* by which we mean that although the eggs are retained internally for development they do not receive appreciable nourishment from the parent's body (Figure 17.42). Eutherian mammals (such as the dolphin shown giving birth in Figure 17.43) are said to be *euviviparous:* there is a placental attachment that permits nutritional exchanges to take place between mother and young. Euviviparity is so advantageous an adaptation that a number of ovoviviparous species seem to be independently evolving toward it, although none so successfully to date as the eutherians. The eggs of euviviparous species have relatively little yolk, for the yolk need not meet all needs of the embryo.

By way of example, let us compare two related sharks: *Squalus acanthias* and *Mustelus canis,* both so-called dogfish. The former is ovoviviparous, with a gestation period of about 22 months. The "pups" are eventually set free by disintegration of the eggs' membranous envelopes. The dry weight of a fertilized egg is 23 to 31 g, whereas that of a pup is only 15 to 25 g. Since the egg weighs more than the pup, it is apparent that no food need be derived from the uterus in which the eggs are held. However, the uterine lining is highly vascularized, suggesting that it plays a role in gaseous exchange and removal of metabolic wastes from the embryo. *Mustelus,* on the other hand, is euviviparous. The gestation

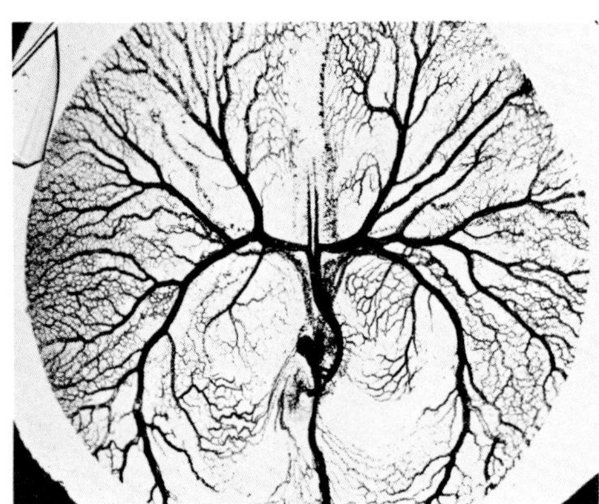

Figure 17.41 □ **Yolk-sac circulation: 56-hr chick embryo with circulatory system injected shows network of blood vessels branching over surface of yolk, providing for absorption of nutrients and their distribution to the embryo. (*Courtesy of Carolina Biological Supply Company.*)**

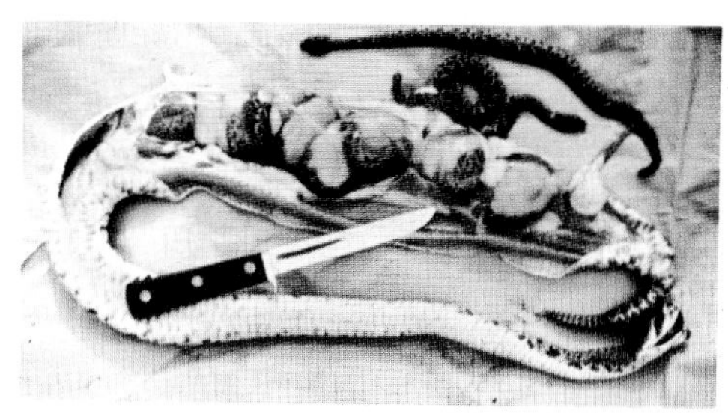

Figure 17.42 □ Ovoviviparous development: Rattlesnake (*Crotalus adamanteus*) dissected to show young developing within uterus. Two young have been removed from the protective embryonic membranes. (*Courtesy of General Biological, Inc., Chicago.*)

Figure 17.43 □ Viviparity: birth of a dolphin. Note that the head emerges last, preventing the infant from drowning. (*Courtesy of Marineland of Florida.*)

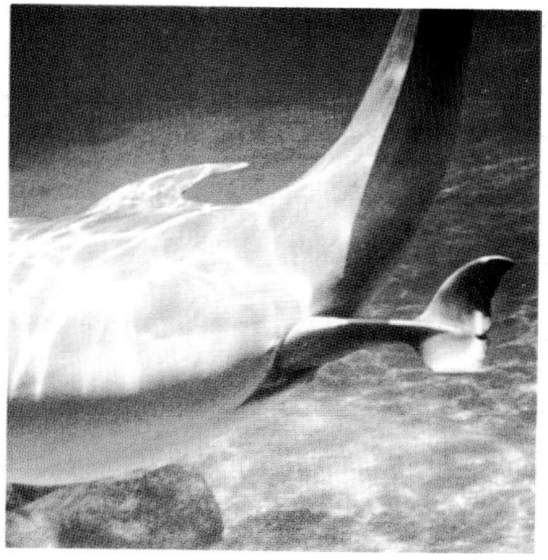

period is only 11 months, during which time the eggs are held in place in the uterus by paired folds of the uterine lining so that each egg is lodged in its own compartment. The embryo's yolk sac then comes into intimate contact with tissues of the uterine lining, forming a true but primitive placenta. The amount of nourishment gained through this connection is reflected by the fact that the dry weight of the ovum is only about 1.6 g while that of the pup at birth averages 20.5 g.

The euviviparous African toad *Nectophyrnoides* retains some ten small-yolked eggs in a richly vascularized section of the oviduct through a gestation period of 9 months. During this time a corpus luteum persists in the ovary, presumably maintaining this condition of the oviduct.

The chorioallantoic placenta developed by early mammals is being achieved at this later date by certain enterprising lizards in which an elliptical well-vascularized portion of the chorion and allantois is held in contact with a correspondingly vascularized, folded part of the uterine lining. This placental association permits a great reduction in the amount of yolk present in the eggs.

In a number of insects the young are held within the mother's body during larval growth and may be even retained until after they pupate. In most cases such internal development is strictly ovoviviparous, but several different means of deriving nourishment from the mother have also been achieved. In the bloodsucking tsetse fly, carrier of African sleeping sickness, a single egg develops within the uterus until hatching. The larva then begins to obtain nourishment by "suckling" at the nipplelike duct of an accessory "milk gland" which opens into the uterus. The larva is born only when ready to pupate and thus never need find itself a host until it has become a winged adult. In certain other viviparous insects the eggs and later the larvae develop within the mother's hemocoel: the egg first absorbs nourishment from the blood through its thin membrane; later the larva feeds upon the mother's tissues and finally escapes to the exterior by penetrating her integument!

THE EUTHERIAN PLACENTA The efficient development of the chorioallantoic placenta from the chorion and allantois of the amniote egg has been an outstanding achievement of eutherians, putting them well to the forefront of vertebrate reproductive evolution. The adaptive value of this achievement can perhaps best be seen by comparing eutherians with their nearest relatives, the marsupials, which with few exceptions have lost ground whenever forced to compete with their eutherian equivalents. The marsupial embryo develops for only a short time in the mother's uterus, without benefit of placental attachment, then rips its way out of the uterus into the birth canal and begins a perilous migration along the mother's body to the opening of her pouch or *marsupium*. If during its journey the embryo should become disoriented or lose hold of the mother's hair, the mother does not rescue it. Only those young survive which reach the pouch and seize a nipple (Figure 17.44). Because suckling is continuous at this stage, if the number of nipples is fewer than the number of young the embryos that fail to take immediate possession of a nipple are doomed to starvation. Marsupial young first release their hold on the nipple and begin to move actively within the pouch, suckling intermittently, only

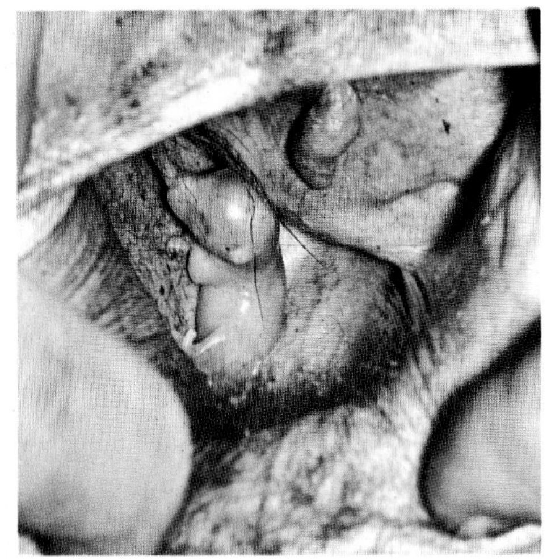

Figure 17.44 □ Compare the size of this newborn marsupial, a wallaby, with the human fingers holding open the lips of its pouch. Still in a fetal condition as compared with newborn eutherians, the wallaby's eyes and ears are covered, and it suckles constantly, the nipple swelling within its mouth so that it cannot lose hold. (*Zoological Society of San Diego photo by Ron Garrison.*)

when they have matured to a stage approximately equivalent to that at which a eutherian infant is born. However, the combined period of marsupial development within the uterus followed by continuous suckling within the pouch is about *50 percent longer* than the time required for a eutherian embryo to develop to the same state of maturation within the mother's uterus! Thus a marsupial female can rear fewer litters during her reproductive life than can an equivalent eutherian. Furthermore, the marsupial brain is poorly developed in comparison with the eutherian brain. The brain of a marsupial "cat," for example, is only half the size of the brain of a eutherian cat of the same body size. In consequence, the behavior of the domestic placental cat reflects a substantially higher level of intelligence than is displayed by its marsupial analog.

Placental nutrition is so efficient that some eutherian species such as the mouse and rat can bear highly developed (but also highly dependent) young only 21 to 22 days after fertilization. The gestation periods of representative eutherians are given in Table 17.1. Primates have the longest gestation period for homoiothermal species with very dependent (altricial) young, in keeping with the high level of neural maturation that must be attained. Other mammals with equivalent or even longer gestation periods bear precocial young. Pregnancy lasts nine months in both man and cow, but the young calf is able to stand, walk about, and seek its mother's udder within a few hours of birth, whereas the human infant may not sit or crawl for several months more. The offspring of whales, elephants, and rhinoceros, which spend from 18 to 24 months in utero are also precocial and able to travel with their roving parents soon after birth.

The chorioallantoic placenta is derived from both maternal and fetal tissues, for the uterine lining as well as two of the embryonic membranes participate in its formation (Figure 17.45). Most mammals (including sheep and cattle) have an *indeciduate* placenta: at the time of birth the chorion separates smoothly from the uterine lining without hemorrhage. The placenta of pri-

Table 17.1 □ Gestation in representative eutherians[a]

SPECIES	AGE WHEN SEXUALLY MATURE	GESTATION PERIOD	TYPICAL LITTER SIZE	NUMBER OF LITTERS PER YEAR
Bear, grizzly (*Ursus horribilis*)	2–3 years	180–225 days	2	<1 (every 2 years)
Cat (*Felis catus*)	6–15 months	52–69 days	4	2–3
Cattle (*Bos taurus*)	6–14 months	210–335 days	1	1
Dog (*Canis familiaris*)	6–8 months	53–71 days	7	1
Elephant (*Elephas maximus*)	8–16 years	510–720 days	1	<1
Horse (*Equus caballus*)	1 year	264–420 days	1	<1
Man (*Homo sapiens*)	12–15.4 years	267 days	1	<1
Mouse (*Mus musculus*)	35 days	19–31 days	6	4–6
Pig (*Sus scrofa*)	5–8 months	101–130 days	9	
Rabbit (*Oryctolagus cuniculus*)	5.5–8.5 months	30–35 days	8	
Rat, Norway (*Rattus norvegicus*)	37–67 days	21–30 days	12	2
Seal (*Arctocephalus pusillus*)	2 years	330–360 days	2	<1
Sheep (*Ovis aries*)	7–8 months	144–152 days	1–4	1
Whale (*Balaenoptera borealis*)	2 years	360 days	1	<1
Woodchuck (*Marmota monax*)	1 year	28 days	4	1

[a] Data mostly from W. S. Spector, *Handbook of Biological Data* (Philadelphia: W. B. Saunders Company, 1956).

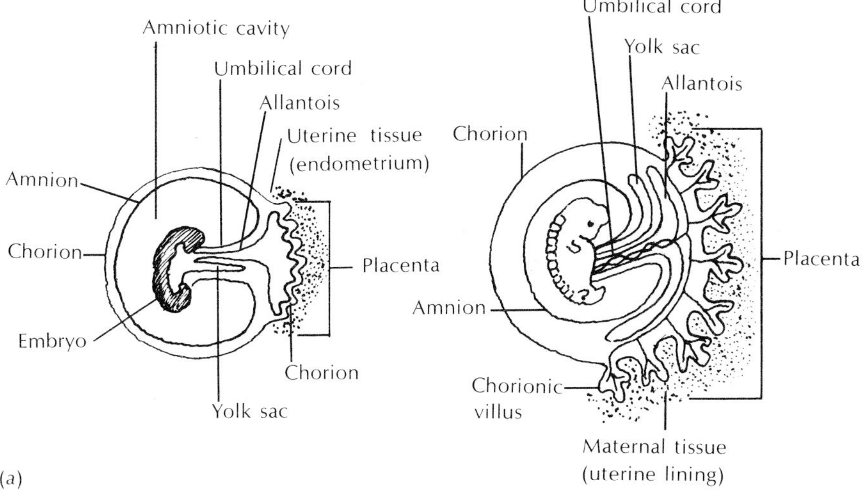

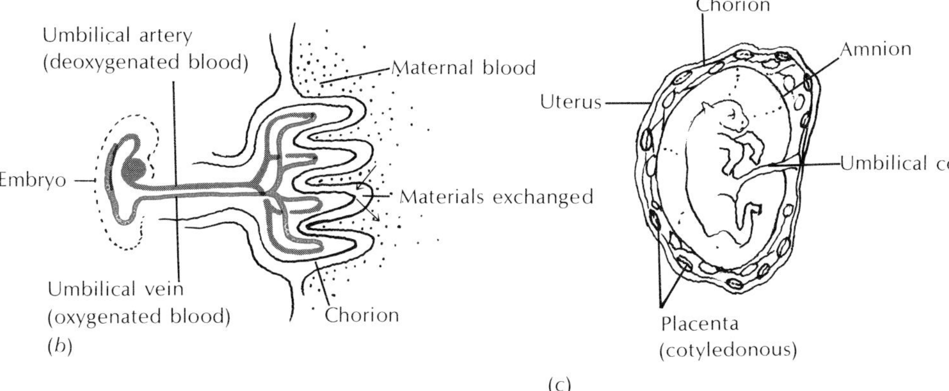

Figure 17.45 □ The eutherian placenta: (*a*) development of discoidal placenta, such as that of man; (*b*) pattern of placental circulation; (*c*) cotyledonous placenta of a hoofed mammal.

mates, carnivores, bats, and insectivores, on the other hand, is *deciduate,* which means that all of the uterine tissues that participated in placental formation are sloughed and pass out of the vagina with the embryonic membranes and the umbilical cord as the "afterbirth." A certain amount of blood loss is unavoidable in this process.

The placenta begins to develop shortly after implantation of the embryo in the uterine lining. Under hormonal control this lining has become thick and spongy before ovulation occurs; if the ovum is fertilized as it passes down the oviduct, the embryo typically enters the uterus as a hollow sphere, the *blastocyst,* consisting of a flattened plate of cells (the embryo proper) sandwiched between two fluid-filled cavities—the amniotic cavity above and the yolk sac cavity below. The outermost cells of the blastocyst represent the developing chorion, and when these contact the uterine lining they cause it to erode away at that spot. In this manner the blastocyst sinks completely into the wall of the uterus, rather than remaining within the uterine cavity as is the case with ovoviviparous vertebrates.

As the embryo grows its surrounding membranes also expand, bulging out into the uterine cavity until the latter is obliterated. At certain points of contact the chorion puts forth fingerlike projections that penetrate the uterine lining and even erode into some of the maternal blood vessels. Capillaries in these chorionic projections therefore permit exchanges to take place between fetal and maternal bloodstreams. The distribution of these points of interaction vary with the species: in horses and swine they are scattered over the entire surface of the chorion, forming a diffuse placenta; in dogs and cats the placenta forms several rings completely encircling the embryo; in human beings the placenta is discoidal, being about the size and shape of a saucer.

Blood poor in oxygen and containing CO_2 and other wastes passes to the placenta from the embryo by way of an artery in the umbilical cord; here exchanges are made with the maternal circulation, and then oxygenated, nutrient-rich blood returns to the fetus by way of the umbilical vein.

Erythroblastosis fetalis, an anemic condition afflicting human infants, is an outcome of the intimate placental union between mother and fetus, when the two are incompatible with respect to a hereditary blood constituent, the *Rh* (rhesus) *factor.* This protein, so named from its initial discovery in the rhesus monkey, occurs on the surface of the erythrocytes of Rh^+ individuals, who constitute a substantial majority of the human population. Rh^+ individuals may be either homozygous or heterozygous for a dominant gene controlling the production of the Rh factor, whereas Rh^- individuals are homozygous for the recessive allele. An Rh^- wife of a heterozygous Rh^+ man has a 50:50 chance of bearing an Rh^+ fetus at each pregnancy. At the time an Rh^+ infant is born, sloughing of the placenta exposes the torn blood vessels of the mother's uterine lining to fetal corpuscles lost from the ruptured blood vessels of the chorion. If enough Rh^+ corpuscles enter her bloodstream, an Rh^- woman will respond by producing an anti-Rh antibody, which may remain in her bloodstream for several years. If she should again bear an Rh^+ fetus, the antibody passing across the placental barrier into the fetal circulation will cause destruction of the fetal red blood cells. If the fetus is not actually killed it is born with the anemic condition named above, appearing "blue" from oxygen lack, and may be rescued only by complete blood transfusion. Recently it has been found that the Rh^- mother's immune response can be avoided if she is given massive injections of gamma globulin during the critical period immediately following the birth of an Rh^+ child.

THE PHYSIOLOGY OF MAMMALIAN PREGNANCY Fertilization of an ovum as it passes through the oviduct and subsequent implantation of the blastocyst in the uterine lining sets in motion a series of endocrine adjustments concerned with the maintenance of pregnancy. In most mammals the embryo implants within 4 to 5 days after the onset of cleavage. Delayed implantation is characteristic of such species as badger, weasels, and bears, in which the blastocyst may remain unattached within the uterus for many months before implantation.

When pregnancy occurs the luteal activity of the ovary increases rather than declines. In women the most recently formed corpus luteum enlarges to form the *corpus luteum of pregnancy.* This produces an increased flow of progesterone which keeps the uterine muscles from contracting and maintains the thickened, secretory condition of the uterine lining. We may recall that in the nonpregnant mammal a rise in circulating progesterone exerts feedback control upon the pituitary by way of the hypothalamus, inhibiting further release of LH, and thereby causing the decline of the corpus luteum. How is this feedback control overridden during pregnancy? The answer seems to lie in the fact that during pregnancy the placenta serves as a new source of gonadotrophin, and is not subject to control by the hypothalamus. In women the chorion is the source of this hormone (*chorionic gonadotrophin*), which is a glycoprotein of approximately 100,000 molecular weight. Chorionic gonadotrophin is secreted in such quantities that some of it is excreted in the urine. It constitutes the basis for most pregnancy tests; its injection triggers ovulation in virgin mice and rabbits, egg laying by toads, and release of sperm by male frogs. The frog test is most rapid, for positive results can be obtained within 8 hours of the injection of pregnancy urine.

As gestation continues, the placenta also becomes a major source of both progesterone and estrogen, so that after the first two months of pregnancy a woman can usually have her ovaries removed without causing loss of the fetus. The endocrine activity of the placenta is of great adaptive significance, for it liberates the hormonal control of pregnancy from hypothalamo-hypophyseal dominance. This is important because the hypothalamus is subject to the effect of external stimuli which might threaten the endocrine stability essential during gestation. Response to external stimuli through neuroendocrine control of the early stages of reproduction is of course vital, but once pregnancy has been achieved such sensitivity to the environment becomes less relevant (and even hazardous); the maintenance of internal stability is now paramount.

Just before birth, placental secretion of estrogen rises abruptly. This may restore uterine motility in preparation for expulsion of the fetus and also synergizes the hormone *relaxin,* which is secreted by the placenta and ovaries. Relaxin acts upon the connections between the pubic bones to relax the pubic symphysis so that the pelvis may expand to accommodate the passage of the fetus. It may also promote dilation of the neck of the uterus (cervix). *Oxytocin,* a neurohormone secreted by the posterior pituitary (see Figure 15.49), causes contraction of the uterine muscles and most likely acts together with estrogen to induce labor.

During pregnancy the mammary glands must be prepared for lactation or the newborn mammal will not long survive. Control of mammary development is incompletely understood. Growth of the duct system and terminal clusters of secretory cells seems primarily to depend upon a complex interaction between estrogen and progesterone, the former priming the mammary glands for the action of the latter. Somatotrophin, prolactin, and some of the adrenocortical hormones may also play roles in this maturation. After birth, the secretion of milk is primarily evoked by prolactin. The milk ejection reflex is due to the effect of oxytocin on the contractile tissue of the mammary ducts. Secretion of oxytocin in turn is brought about by neural factors, mainly the stimulation resulting from suckling.

C **Parental behavior**

Some degree of parental care is given the young by the adults of most species. The more painstaking and prolonged this care, the less will be the mortality of the progeny and the fewer that need be reared. "Parental care" is not exclusively given by the parents, but sometimes also by older siblings or other adults of a social group; in consequence, it is proposed that this type of care-giving behavior be termed *epimeletic* (without reference to the familial relationship between the provider of care and the beneficiary).

Epimeletic behavior may operate only prenatally or be continued postnatally for as long as the young can profit by this care. Such behavior is not usually dependent upon learning, even in such relatively advanced animals as rabbits and rodents, although Harlow's experiments with young rhesus monkeys deprived of contact with mothers and peers indicate that in primates at least, early experience is essential to the development of normal social (including parental) relationships. On the other hand, rats having their first litters build nests and care for their young just as well as experienced animals. Nest building occurs even when rats have been reared under circumstances in which they could not have gained any practice in manipulation. Rabbit nest building does improve with experience, but even virgins build nests of paper strips or other available materials and pregnant females pull fur from their own chests to line the nests before they first give birth, just as they will do with subsequent litters.

PRENATAL CARE Care of the young before birth or hatching takes several forms (Figure 17.46): (1) a nest, burrow, or other suitable place may be prepared by the parents; (2) the parents may remain watchfully near their eggs, protecting them from predators and parasites; (3) alternatively, the eggs or unborn young may be carried about, within or upon the parent's body; (4) especially in species requiring warmth for development, thermoregulation (as by incubation) may be important.

Selection and preparation of site Among mammals one parent or the other often prepares a den well in advance of the birth of young. Here the young are born and are subsequently protected from predators and chilling. Although the duty of den preparation commonly falls upon the mother, the male black ferret is the den builder in this species. He occupies the den only until he finds and subdues an estrus female, which he drags into the den by the scruff of the neck as though she were prey. After mating he abandons both mate and den while the female retains the housing for herself and young.

Birds as a class, together with certain fishes and reptiles, construct more or less elaborate nests, often woven of available plant materials. The nests of weaver birds (see Figure 17.46*d*) are globular and solidly closed except for a small opening at the bottom, making the nest difficult for most predators to enter. Additional protection from snakes is often gained by selecting as a group nesting site some thorny tree overhanging a watercourse. Fish that build nests for their eggs usually remain at hand to protect them from harm, as mentioned in the case of sticklebacks.

Many animals that do not guard their eggs at least conceal them from view within a burrow. Female hunting wasps fill such burrows with food for their young. Unusual among invertebrates is the cooperation seen between male and female dung beetles in preparing and stocking a nursery for the offspring they may never see. While the female excavates a deep shaft, the male carries away the loosened soil upon his flat back. After the shaft has been prepared, the male collects pellets of dung and drops

Figure 17.46 □ Aspects of prenatal care. (*a*) Egg guarding: black widow spider with egg case. (*Los Angeles County Museum of Natural History.*) (*b*) Egg tending and cleaning: *Aequidens portalegrensis* male and female build nest, guard and clean the eggs, and pick out and eat the white unfertilized eggs that might spread fungus infection. (*Los Angeles County Museum of Natural History.*) (*c*) Egg carrying: male giant water bug with eggs cemented to his back by the female, here still nearby. (*Courtesy of Dr. Ross E. Hutchins.*) (*d*) Nest building: captive male rufous-necked weaver bird weaving globular nest from palm-leaf strips. After nest completion, the male begins to court a female; before accepting him, she will enter the nest to inspect it. (*Zoological Society of San Diego.*) (*e*) Incubation: male king penguin incubating egg on his foot. (*Zoological Society of San Diego.*)

them down the shaft to the female. Shaping the dung into sausagelike rolls, she inserts one into each nursery chamber and lays an egg upon it. After this the male departs but the female remains on guard for some time.

Even if a site is not specially prepared for habitation by the young, the selection of an appropriate place for the eggs to be laid may be important to survival. For instance, herbivorous insects must select appropriate food plants on which to lay their eggs, whereas the free-living adults of species with parasitic larvae must lay their eggs in or on the body of living prey (such as caterpillars; see Figure 6.22).

Egg guarding and carrying One of the most effective means of protection of unborn young is achieved by parents that carry them about on or within their own body. Animals of many phyla have developed brood pouches or other structural means of egg carrying; others merely carry the eggs with their legs or in their mouths. Among viviparous species the young are retained within the expanded uterine portion of the mother's genital tract. A number of basically oviparous species have also evolved toward the ovoviviparous state by storing the eggs on or in portions of the body other than the genital tract proper. Such egg placement demands appropriate behavior on the part of one or both parents, cooperation between sexes being not uncommon. The male seahorse takes the eggs as they are laid by the female and places them in his abdominal pouch, the lining of which then develops a dense network of blood vessels that provide for gaseous exchanges during development. After the eggs hatch, the male forcibly and permanently ejects the young from his pouch.

Mouthbreeding fish, on the other hand, hold the eggs within the mouth until hatching, and even after birth the parent's mouth may serve as a refuge for the young. It is usually the male mouthbreeder that incubates the eggs, rolling them about in his mouth and thereby keeping them free of a fungus infection to which they usually succumb if not cleansed in this manner. Generally the father must fast throughout this entire period, but he rarely swallows one of his children. After hatching, the young remain near the parents. When danger threatens, either the young rush into their parents' mouths or the older fish, suspiciously eyeing the intruder, suck them up like vacuum cleaners.

In the prenatal care of the young of Surinam toads, a structural oddity of the female has coevolved with the necessary egg-placing behavior on the part of the male of the species. During the breeding season highly vascularized pits develop in the thickened skin of the female's back. While mating the male clasps the female around the belly and rests upon her back. During egg laying the female's oviduct protrudes from her anus and the male manipulates it over her back in such a manner that each egg slips into one of the pits. Finally a covering forms over the pits, sealing the eggs in place. There being no tadpole stage in the Surinam toad, young toads eventually emerge from the pits. This adaptation not only guards the young from predators but makes it unnecessary for the toads to return to the water to lay their eggs. Comparable independence of the water is seen in a species of South American tree frog in which the male's enlarged vocal sac is used as a brood pouch.

Such crustaceans as isopods and opossum shrimp brood their eggs in an abdominal pouch formed by overlapping plates extending from the basal segments of a number of legs. This protection is especially important for terrestrial crustaceans such as sow bugs, for no crustacean egg is effectively sealed to loss of moisture and humidity must be conserved within the brood chamber.

Egg-guarding behavior is seen in a number of oviparous species that do not carry their eggs about. Web-building spiders such as the black widow hang the globular egg case in the web in constant sight of the mother. The female octopus suspends her eggs from the ceiling of some protected crevice and remains at hand for over 4 months to guard and ventilate them; during this vigil she may actually die of starvation.

Prenatal thermoregulation Young homoiotherms cannot maintain their body temperature effectively and must be protected from chilling both before and after birth. For most mammals thermoregulation is no problem, for the young develop within the mother's uterus and later are kept warm by being held against her body. Monotremes and birds must incubate their eggs throughout development and hover their young until the latter are well provided with hair or feathers. A few poikilotherms also brood their eggs. Skinks incubate their eggs by first sunning themselves and then coiling about the clutch. Pythons also coil about their eggs, but warm them with heat generated by muscular tremors. Other poikilotherms may select sunny places in which to lay their eggs, for warmth accelerates development even when not obligatory for survival. A female alligator will excavate a hole in a sunny river bank and bury her eggs in the mud. Since the latter bakes to a bricklike consistency she must rip open the nest to free the young when she hears them begin to move about.

Truly unusual thermoregulatory behavior is shown by tropical incubator birds, which maintain a stable incubation temperature for their eggs without actually hovering them. The female merely lays her eggs upon the ground, whereupon they are promptly buried by the male. Digging with his disproportionately enormous feet, the male erects a compost pile of soil and decaying vegetation over the eggs. Under humid conditions the internal heat of decomposition within the mound serves to incubate the eggs, which require no further care since the young are fully independent upon hatching. However, changing climate has wreaked a cruel fate upon the Australian incubator bird, for this species must now build its mound under arid, desert conditions where severe daily temperature fluctuations are the rule. The male must compensate for this unfavorable climate by laboring interminably to regulate the internal temperature of the mound. In the heat of the day the patient father periodically plunges his beak into the mound as a means of sensing its internal temperature. If this has risen too high, his huge feet labor to uncover the eggs. When these have cooled somewhat, he covers them again. This indefatigable care continues until the chicks hatch and dash away at once, leaving the worn parent to recuperate.

POSTNATAL CARE Parental responsibility may end with the laying of eggs, or with their hatching, or may continue through the days, months, or years of the young's dependency (Figure 17.47). During this period epimeletic behavior on the part of adults is sustained by care-soliciting behaviors on the part of the young. Care-giving and care-soliciting behaviors are two sides of the same coin, reinforcing one another synergistically. Care-soliciting displays or acoustic signals reinforce the tendency of the care-giving individuals to continue to provide service. Normally care-soliciting behavior wanes as the young mature (although often reappearing between courting adults), but sometimes the changing physiological state of the parents, as they pass out of reproductive condition, leads them to become unresponsive to the young and to reject them. Such rejection must coincide with the progeny's being able to fend for itself. Any inherited tendency toward premature abandonment of young actually operates as a type of genetic lethal, for although the individual carrying the trait does not die, its offspring will, unless their care is taken over by other members of the social group (an event unlikely in most kinds of animals other than man). Natural selection thus operates toward establishment of patterns of parental care that endure throughout the offspring's period of dependency.

Postnatal care may consist mainly of guarding the young from danger. The male stickleback, for instance, not only guards the nest until the young hatch but for some time restricts their activities to the vicinity of the nest and when threatened takes them in his mouth and exhales them into the nest.

When postnatal care involves not only protection but also the provision of food, the situation becomes more complex. The parents must not only attend to their own needs but must provide as well for those of their offspring, often until the latter are fully grown. This often demands that both parents, or the mother together with her social group, be constantly engaged in food gathering for the offspring. Parent birds are helpless to resist the stimuli afforded by crying, gaping young, and an act of abandonment may be required to terminate this dependency. Shearwaters are perennially monogamous seabirds that nest in burrows in the ground, to which they return annually. Both parents feed their single offspring on regurgitated fish until it is so plump as to be unable to pass through the entrance of the burrow. They then abandon it, and it remains trapped within the burrow until the enforced fast slenderizes it to a point at which it can make its escape and trudge to the sea, where its maiden flight is initiated simply by its falling off the cliff edge.

The feeding of young by regurgitation is a common practice in birds and predatory mammals. Observations of semidomesticated wolves have revealed that not only do adult wolves regurgitate undigested caribou meat when solicited by begging pups, but that even adult wolves other than the parents can be induced to part with their meals.

Early postnatal care of young mammals devolves mainly upon the mother: her mammary glands provide the young with milk (Figure 17.47*d*). The suckling response is innate and in turn affects the mother through her nervous and endocrine systems so that lactation and maternal behavior are further stimulated. If lactating rats are furnished with newborn young every one to two weeks, they will continue to yield milk and display care-giving behavior for many months. The stimuli provided by suckling are thought to act through the hypothal-

Figure 17.47 □ Aspects of postnatal care. (*a*) Carrying of young: the hunting spider builds no web but carries her young until they are able to fend for themselves. (*Courtesy of Dr. Ross E. Hutchins.*) (*b*) Carrying of young: the two-toed sloth makes no den but carries her infant as she moves slowly through the tree tops; the young sloth must retain a firm grip on her fur or it may fall and be lost. (*Zoological Society of San Diego.*) (*c*) Feeding of young: nestling cormorants await fish dinner, which their parents will offer by regurgitation. (*Photograph by C. J. Henry, U.S. Bureau of Sport, Fisheries & Wildlife.*) (*d*) Suckling of young: dromedary nursing. (*Zoological Society of San Diego photo by Ron Garrison.*) (*e*) Grooming of young: mother okapi grooms young with her long tongue, also used in pulling foliage from trees; besides maintaining coat health, grooming is important among mammals for social integration and bond strengthening between mother and offspring. (*Zoological Society of San Diego.*) (*f*) Protection of young: as well as guarding her infant against predators, the female hippopotamus prevents it from drowning in deep water by supporting its head upon her broad snout. (*Zoological Society of San Diego photo by Ron Garrison.*)

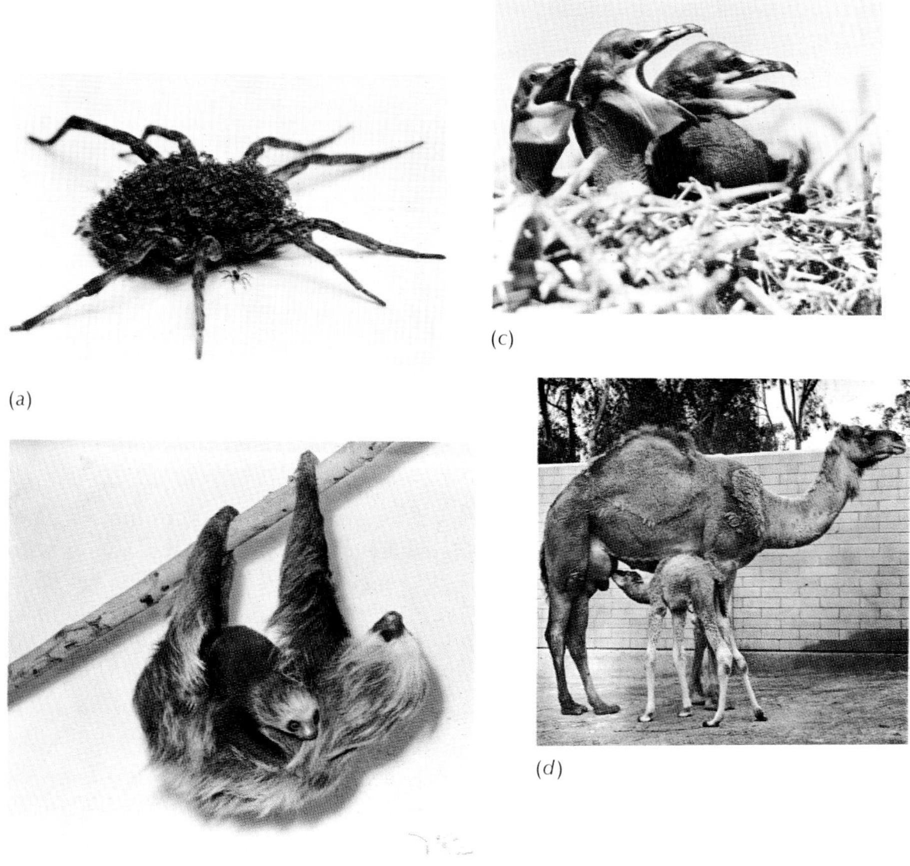

(*a*) (*b*) (*c*) (*d*)

(*e*)

(*f*)

amus upon the pituitary, causing a continued release of prolactin and a corresponding inhibition of gonadotrophins.

That the acquisition of parental behavior in primates is at least partially dependent on experience has been demonstrated by Harlow's experiments (see Figure 7.25) with isolated rhesus monkeys that were reared with cloth or wire surrogate mothers. Despite the comfort and security derived from contact with the cloth mother, female subjects were found incapable of normal mating and maternal behavior when grown. These females refused males even when in heat, and when made pregnant by artificial insemination, ignored or abused their newborn young. These behavioral deficits could not be entirely repaired but were found to be prevented when young monkeys were reared with others of their own age, even when no adult monkeys were present. Early experience with other individuals of the same species is therefore concluded to be essential to the development of normal social behavior, at least in primates.

Figure 17.48 □ **A primate family: male and female proboscis monkeys with their year-old son, born in the San Diego Zoo. The male proved solicitous toward the infant and belligerent toward human trespassers. (*Zoological Society of San Diego photo by Ron Garrison.*)**

The male mammal generally plays much less of a role in postnatal care than do male birds; in consequence the family group consisting of mother, father, and offspring is fairly rare (compared to the situation in birds) but does occur in some species such as the proboscis monkey (Figure 17.48). The social bonds established between mother and young (and among siblings) are the first bonds that integrate the juvenile into the social life of its species. The adult male may even represent a hazard to the young, as in the grizzly bear, where the close association of the cubs with the female extends over two years and takes on the nature of a mutual-defense pact as the cubs grow large. These bonds, although strong, are abruptly terminated when the female approaches estrus and prepares to mate once more; her change in physiological state is heralded by her forcible rejection of the cubs.

Mammals that form herds or troops provide social groups larger than the family in which postnatal care of young is effectively provided. The males of social primates fend off would-be predators and are often demonstrably solicitous of the young. Since most primates are promiscuous, such generalization of paternal responsibility is not surprising. Having no means of identifying his own progeny, the male accepts responsibility for all of the juveniles in his troop. Solicitous attention is also given younger primates by the adolescents and older juveniles, although in larger troops it is typical for youngsters of the same age to play together.

Group care of the young is rare in birds—but has been claimed for the Emperor penguin, at least in that the adults assemble to encircle the massed chicks when antarctic storm winds threaten to snatch them away. Feeding remains strictly the duty of each chick's own parents, however, and remarkably enough chick and parents recognize each other with absolute accuracy and the adults only regurgitate fish for their own offspring.

Care of the young has evolved along different lines in the social insects such as termites, bees, and ants. Here the young are dependent upon the adults for protection, shelter, and food; however, the care-giving adults are not their parents but neuter workers. During group movements, worker ants delicately carry the eggs, larvae, and pupae in powerful jaws (mandibles) that could readily crush them to death (Figure 17.49). The behavior of the worker caste may influence the development of the young. When the concentration of queen pheromone declines as a queen bee ages, the workers begin to construct a few large queen cells. When an egg is placed in a queen cell the size difference between this cell and adjacent ones in which workers are developing furnishes a cue to attendant workers to feed this particular larva a protein-rich diet that allows it to develop into a sexually mature queen. In this way the workers preserve the life of the hive, which otherwise would perish with the senility and

Figure 17.49 □ **African driver ant (*Dorylus*) carrying larva. (*Courtesy of Dr. Ross E. Hutchins.*)**

death of the original queen. In her prime the queen bee controls the social structure of her hive through pheromone secretion; during her decline, but while she is still capable of laying eggs, her workers prepare the way for the "royal succession" and the hive, as a distinct social entity, lives on.

Man and the biosphere Perpetuation of a *cultural* as well as a biological heritage is a privilege reserved to few forms of life, notably man and a few other primates. Cultural transmission has enabled man to reach his present level of achievement in literature, science, technology, and other areas. Without his cultural heritage man would still have a superior hand and brain but would be restricted to profiting by only whatever he could achieve with these tools during one lifetime. When individual lifetimes are long enough to allow several generations to coexist and interact, cultural transmission is facilitated: each new being is integrated into a preexisting social group and assimilates much of its culture as he matures. However, such cultural perpetuation binds as well as liberates and may fetter the growing mind in shackles of past beliefs and attitudes. Not only the discoveries but the mistakes made by one generation are passed on to the next.

Man has employed his intelligence to escape hazards to which other species are subject, and to delay the operation of certain natural laws of which he now erroneously imagines himself free. However, man need remind himself that there are *two* essential prerequisites for long-term success in the perpetuation of one's kind: (1) the actual production and rearing of young; (2) restriction of birth rates to match declining premature death rates. If either factor is neglected, serious harm will eventually befall the species and the ecosystem of which it is a part.

Mindless of the rise and fall of individual species, natural selection has refined and shaped life's genetic heritage, preserving and expanding the biosphere through nearly three billion years of organic evolution. Now this fabric is threatened at every level by the expansion of one species—beings intelligent enough to remake much of the earth's surface yet perhaps lacking perception as to the outcome of present trends or the will to reshape these trends. Most nonhuman organisms maintain their numbers at a level well below the capacity of the habitat. For human populations, should birth rate exceed death rate by only 2 percent a year (as it now does in many parts of the world) the population will double every 50 years. Should reproduction exceed mortality by a mere 0.2 percent a year, the world population will double every 500 years. Eventually, for man as for any other creature birth and death must come into balance. Our concern therefore should be not how to maintain the greatest possible number of human beings, but to define what is the *optimum* population density at which men interact harmoniously and lead a satisfying existence. Valid as it is to improve agricultural techniques, the basic invalidity of attempting to solve man's population problem by increased food production is starkly revealed by statistical comparisons of projected maximum food yields and present observed rates of population growth.

Three problems are inseparable from the problem of uncontrolled fertility.

1 We are destroying the diversity of life. Thousands of species of plants and animals are now endangered, mainly because of the destruction of their habitats, taken over for cultivation and human residence. The one act of filling in south San Francisco Bay for housing development is estimated to have destroyed some 45 percent of the total waterfowl wintering range in the state of California. Reduction in biotic diversity is a threat to the very continuance of life on earth as well as an impoverishment of human experience. To say that future generations will not miss what they have never known is (if true) an absurd excuse for our failure to act now to control human population growth before many more species have disappeared.

2 We are contaminating our planet with the waste products of our cultural "metabolism." It would be a sad indictment of our much-prized intelligence were the rate of population growth curbed, not by planning but through increased premature deaths brought about by the contamination of soil, air, and water. Pesticides are accumulating in the tissues of organisms through-

out the world (including Eskimos in Alaska and penguins in Antarctica); DDT, for instance, is now thought responsible for the increasing failure of birds' eggs to hatch and for a severe decline in photosynthesis by certain key species of marine phytoplankton. Since phytoplankton produces some 80 percent of the world's oxygen supply, this is no trivial matter. Lead, a gasoline additive, is also accumulating exponentially in the ecosystem, and few species of plants and animals are immune to injury from such heavy-metal accumulation. Safe disposal of radioactive materials produced by the use of nuclear power is another growing problem; fission products such as strontium 90 and cesium 137 persist for many years to cycle through food chains and especially to accumulate in the tissues of carnivorous species close to the apex of nutritional pyramids. It should be noted that industrialized nations are now consuming some 80 percent of the world's minerals and fossil fuel resources and are generating an even greater proportion of contaminants. Should other nations achieve a similar level of industrialization, the rate of generation of contaminants may soon far exceed that seen throughout the world at this time.

3 By refusing to face the problem of population planning at the present time, we may sacrifice human freedom for future generations. If population stability is not achieved through voluntary means at a level below the ultimate capacity of the habitat, it will nevertheless be reached at a time not too far away when the limits of food supply and living space are reached. At that point birth and death rates *will* be brought into equilibrium, but at what cost? The world of the future will be largely of man's making. Whether life in that world will be worth living depends much on forces set in motion today. Should we not bend every effort toward preserving not only mankind but the biosphere as a whole, toward restoring the hygiene of our planet, and toward stabilizing the human population at an optimal rather than a maximal density?

For our species the problem of perpetuation of kind is no longer one of keeping our own offspring alive but of looking ahead to ensure the survival of future generations. Moreover, since mankind possesses the ability to eradicate most other forms of life, we also bear the responsibility for the fate of those hosts of fellow creatures which have been our companions on the long evolutionary road.

REVIEW AND DISCUSSION

1 Compare asexual and sexual reproduction, in terms of the adaptive value of each. Cite organisms that regularly enjoy the benefits of both. Differentiate between sporogeny and gametogeny, and between meiospores and mitospores, with examples.

2 Define *sex* and *sexual reproduction*. Are these terms synonymous? Is sexual reproduction possible where sex does not exist? Differentiate between *neuter* and *hermaphrodite*. Describe and compare the process of conjugation as it occurs in *Paramecium* and in an alga or fungus. In each case, how closely are conjugation and meiosis associated?

3 Compare and contrast the processes of oogenesis and spermatogenesis in animals. In what significant aspects are these events different from those involved in sperm and egg formation in algae, mosses, and ferns?

4 Explain why, in the course of plant evolution, selection has favored the increasing dominance of the sporophyte generation. Why is the gametophyte generation not simply deleted from the life cycle of seed plants? What do we mean literally when we speak of a "male" California pepper tree?

5 Compare the events that take place during gametophyte formation in conifers and angiosperms. Specify several reasons why angiosperms have proven more successful than gymnosperms.

6 Why are bryophytes and tracheophytes often classified together as "embryophytes"?

7 What are the functions of animal courtship? Explain why polygynous mating systems have proven more adaptive than polyandrous ones, as indicated by their frequency of occurrence. What conditions promote monogamous rather than polygamous or promiscuous associations?

8 Compare the mammalian male and female reproductive tracts. What is the adaptive significance of the male penis? Cite analogous means of internal fertilization employed among invertebrates and non-mammalian vertebrates.

9 Discuss the roles of the amnion, allantois, and chorion in abetting embryonic development in mammals and other amniotes.

10 Distinguish between ovoviviparity and euviviparity. Cite instances in which an ovoviviparous condition is approached or facsimilated by oviparous species. How else may oviparous types protect their young?

11 Contrast, with examples, the types of postnatal care that must be given by parents of altricial young with that furnished by parents of precocial young.

12 If the basis for successful maternal behavior must be laid during the infancy of monkeys, explain why such a basis can be furnished by experience with a peer group as well as by contact with the mother.

13 How does the prolonged dependency of the young alter the social role of the male primate as compared with that of many other male mammals?

REFERENCES

ÅKERMAN, B. "Behavioural Effects of Electrical Stimulation in the Forebrain of the Pigeon. I. Reproductive Behaviour." *Behaviour,* **26** (1965). Specific components of courtship behavior are elicited by electrode stimulation of discrete forebrain loci.

ASDELL, S. A. *Patterns of Mammalian Reproduction,* 2nd ed. Ithaca, N.Y.: Cornell University Press, 1964. A useful source book.

BASTOCK, M. *Courtship: An Ethological Study.* Chicago: Aldine Publishing Company, 1967. An excellent short discourse on courtship behavior in invertebrates, fish, and birds, including discussion of the evolution and genetic bases of such behavior and the neural and hormonal mechanisms controlling courtship behavior.

BEST, J. B., A. B. GOODMAN, AND A. PIGON "Fissioning in Planarians: Control by the Brain," *Science,* **164** (1969). The planarian brain is found to produce a neurohormonal factor that suppresses fissioning in the presence of other planarians and may constitute an intrinsic means of regulating population density.

BLAKE, J. "Population Policy for Americans: Is the Government Being Misled?" *Science,* **164** (1969). Survey data indicate that despite increased access to contraceptives population growth will continue until traditional views of the female life role are modified.

DEL SOLAR, E., AND H. PALOMINO "Choice of Oviposition in *Drosophila melanogaster,*" *Amer. Nat.,* **100** (1966). *Drosophila* females demonstrate a tendency to lay their eggs in vials already occupied by larvae of their own species; this behavior may provide an important opportunity for intraspecific competition and selection.

EHRMAN, L. "Courtship and Mating Behavior as a Reproductive Isolating Mechanism in *Drosophila,*" *Amer. Zool.,* **4** (1964). The tendency of *D. paulistorum* females to select males of their own species appears to be determined by genes located in all of the three pairs of chromosomes; the importance of this tendency in reducing heterospecific matings is discussed.

——— "Mating Success and Genotype Frequency in *Drosophila,*" *Anim. Behav.,* **14** (1966). Analyzes the "minority effect" in Texan and Californian races of *D. pseudoobscura.*

FRIEDMAN, M., AND D. S. LEHRMAN "Physiological Conditions for the Stimulation of Prolactin by External Stimuli in the Male Ring Dove," *Anim. Behav.,* **16** (1968). Sight of the incubating female serves to induce prolactin secretion and broodiness in the male, provided that certain prerequisites have been met.

GERALL, H. D., I. L. WARD, AND A. A. GERALL "Disruption of the Male Rat's Sexual Behaviour Induced by Social Isolation," *Anim. Behav.,* **15** (1967). Long-term detrimental effects result from lack of early contact with other members of the species.

GREEP, R. O. "The Saga and the Science of the Gonadotrophins," *Perspectives in Biol. and Med.,* **12** (1968). A lively personal account of one scientist's dedication to the investigation of reproductive physiology.

HARDIN, G. "The Tragedy of the Commons," *Science,* **162** (1968). A thoughtful and provocative consideration of the problems of human population control and the overexploitation of the habitat.

——— "Finding Lemonade in Santa Barbara's Oil," *Saturday Rev.,* May 10, 1969. A California oil disaster prompts reexamination of the premises that population expansion and the attendant economic growth are still valid goals of modern society.

HARLOW, H. F. "Love in Infant Monkeys," *Sci. Amer.,* **200** (1959). The use of surrogate mothers reveals the need for development of affectional ties by young rhesus monkeys.

——— AND M. K. HARLOW "Social Deprivation in Monkeys," *Sci. Amer.,* **207** (1962). Lasting behavioral deficits result from lack of contact with mother or peers during infancy.

JANZEN, D. H. "Reproductive Behavior in the Passifloraceae and Some of Its Pollinators in Central America," *Behaviour,* **32** (1968). Movements of the stipes of passion flowers is timed to coincide with the schedules of visitation of pollinator animals.

JONES, J. C. "The Sexual Life of a Mosquito," *Sci. Amer.,* **218** (1968). Describes the processes of mating, fertilization, and egg-laying in *Aedes aegypti.*

KETCHEL, M. M. "Fertility Control Agents as a Possible Solution to the World Population Problem," *Perspectives in Biol. and Med.,* **11** (1968). Discusses the nature and mode of action of chemical fertility control agents and the moral and political implications of their use.

KNIPLING, E. F. "Control of Screw-worm Fly by Atomic Radiation," *Sci. Monthly,* **85** (1957). The monogamous habit of female screw-worm flies makes it possible to control this pest by liberating large numbers of sterilized laboratory-reared males into the wild population.

LEHRMAN, D. S. "The Reproductive Behavior of Ring Doves," *Sci. Amer.,* **211** (1964). Visual cues provided by courting males stimulate the female's reproductive physiology and behavior.

LEVINE, L., AND B. LASCHER "Studies on Sexual Selection in Mice. II. Reproductive Competition Between Black and Brown Males," *Amer. Nat.,* **99** (1965). When males of two inbred strains were placed in competition for a single female, males of one of these strains sired more than 70 percent of the offspring, perhaps due to social dominance rank.

LILL, A., AND D. G. M. WOOD-GUSH "Potential Ethological Isolating Mechanisms and Assortative Mating in the Domestic Fowl," *Behaviour,* **25** (1965). Sexual selection favoring own-breed matings was observed in several strains of domestic fowl; specific courtship displays heighten the sexual arousal of the female.

MANNING, A. "The Control of Sexual Receptivity in Female *Drosophila,*" *Anim. Behav.,* **15** (1967). Analyzes sexual receptivity in female *Drosophila* and discusses possible hormonal control mechanisms.

MICHELMORE, S. *Sexual Reproduction.* Garden City, N.Y.: The Natural History Press, 1964. An interesting short survey of various aspects of sexual reproduction.

NEILL, W. T. "Viviparity in Snakes: Some Ecological and Zoogeographical Considerations," *Amer. Nat.,* **98** (1964). Considers the evolution and adaptive significance of viviparity in several families of snakes.

ROBEL, R. J. "Booming Territory Size and Mating Success of the Greater Prairie Chicken (*Tympanuchus cupido pinnatus*)," *Anim. Behav.,* **14** (1966). Field studies show that the male controlling the largest territory on the display ground inseminates by far the largest percentage of females.

ROTH, L. M., AND R. H. BARTH, JR. "The Sense Organs Employed by Cockroaches in Mating Behavior," *Behaviour,* **28** (1967). Describes normal mating behavior and explores the effects of partial antennal amputation on mating success.

LORD ROTHSCHILD "Unorthodox Methods of Sperm Transfer," *Sci. Amer.,* **195** (1956).

SALMON, M., AND S. P. ATSAIDES "Visual and Acoustical Signalling during Courtship by Fiddler Crabs (Genus Uca)," *Amer. Zool.,* **8** (1968). Compares the communicative behavior of several species of *Uca* and discusses factors operating in the evolution of this behavior.

SELANDER, R. K. "On Mating Systems and Sexual Selection," *Amer. Nat.,* **99** (1965). Examines the influence of monogamous, polygynous, and promiscuous mating systems on the evolution of male secondary sexual characteristics in birds.

SMITH, N. G. "Visual Isolation in Gulls," *Sci. Amer.,* **217** (1967). A field experiment establishes the importance of the eye ring in recognition of appropriate mates.

SMITH, R. J. F., AND W. S. HOAR "The Effects of Prolactin and Testosterone on the Parental Behaviour of the Male Stickleback *Gasterosteus aculeatus,*" *Anim. Behav.,* **15** (1967). Fanning the nest is a behavior controlled by testosterone; prolactin does not influence parental behavior but may control prespawning migratory activities.

TINBERGEN, N. "The Courtship of Animals," *Sci. Amer.,* **191** (1954). Discusses the adaptive significance of courtship.

WASHBURN, S. L., AND I. DEVORE "The Social Life of Baboons," *Sci. Amer.,* **204** (1961). A classic field study discloses the social organization of baboon troops and the roles of adults in care of the young.

WOLLMAN, E. L., AND F. JACOB "Sexuality in Bacteria," *Sci. Amer.,* **195** (1956).

ZAHL, P. A. "The Evolution of Sex," *Sci. Amer.,* **180** (1949).

Glossary

THE FOLLOWING BRIEF DEFINITIONS OF some biological terms in common use are meant to supplement definitions provided in the text and are not intended to be comprehensive but merely to serve for convenient reference. Terms used only occasionally in the text and there defined are not included in this glossary, which is a compilation of terms used repeatedly without redefinition at each use. Names of taxonomic groups are mostly excluded.

A- Prefix meaning "not" or "without," such as *asexual* (not sexual)

ABIOGENESIS Origin of life from the inanimate

ABIOTIC Nonliving, in the sense of never having been alive

ABSORPTION Passage of materials in solution into a cell or organism

ACID A compound that liberates hydrogen ion (H^+) in solution; *acidic,* having a pH less than 7 (opposed to *basic* or *alkaline*)

ACOELOMATE Refers to multicellular animals lacking a body cavity, such as flatworms and ribbonworms

ADAPTABILITY Used herein to refer to the capacity of the individual organism to adapt to changing circumstances without prerequisite changes in heredity

ADAPTATION (1) Process by means of which organisms become better fitted for their particular mode of life; (2) the state of being fitted for one's mode of life; (3) any structure, behavioral pattern, or physiological process that serves to promote fitness

ADAPTIVE RADIATION Divergence from a common ancestral form into various descendent types specialized for different modes of life

ADENOHYPOPHYSIS The anterior part of the pituitary gland of vertebrates (see *pituitary*), which secretes several hormones controlling somatic growth and sexual maturation and is controlled in turn by hormonal release factors from the brain

AEROBIC Dependent upon a supply of free oxygen (O_2); *aerobe,* organism dependent for survival upon oxygen

ALDEHYDE Organic compound containing the group $-C{\overset{O}{\underset{H}{\lessgtr}}}$

ALGA A nonvascular autotrophic plant, uni- or multicellular, restricted to water or moist places; the term *alga* lacks taxonomic significance; there are a number of algal phyla, for instance, Rhodophyta (red algae)

ALKALINE Basic; having a pH of more than 7; opposite of *acidic*

ALLELE One gene of a homologous pair; one of the alternative states of the same gene

ALLOPATRIC Not living in the same habitat

ALTRICIAL Helpless at birth, such as young robins or human infants; opposite of *precocial*

AMINATION Addition of an amino group to a compound

AMINO The $—NH_2$ group; *amino acid,* a carboxylic acid bearing an amino group

AMNION Protective membrane within egg of land vertebrates; encloses the embryo and guards it from dehydration

AMNIOTE A vertebrate that produces a land-adapted egg with protective membranes including the amnion; amniotes include reptiles, birds, and mammals

AMOEBOID Moving and ingesting food by means of pseudopodia

AMPHIBIAN Vertebrate that typically passes through an aquatic, gill-breathing larval stage to a terrestrial, lung-breathing, tetrapod adult stage

AMPHIBIOUS Living both in water and on land, such as an alligator

AMYLASE Starch-digesting enzyme such as ptyalin; hydrolyzes starch to the disaccharide maltose

ANABOLISM Constructive metabolism, including all biosynthetic reactions

ANAEROBIC Not dependent on the availability of free oxygen

ANALOGOUS Of similar function but not necessarily of common origin

ANAMNIOTE Vertebrate that does not produce a land-adapted amniote egg; includes fishes and amphibians

ANATOMY Gross body architecture, or the study thereof

ANDROGEN Male sex hormone, such as testosterone

ANEUPLOIDY Condition in which one or more chromosomes, but not the entire set, are duplicated

ANGIOSPERM Vascular plant having seeds enclosed within a fruit; flowering plant

ANIMAL Any eucaryotic organism that is not a plant

ANION Negatively charged ion such as NO_3^- or Cl^-

ANISOGAMY Production of unlike gametes such as sperm and ova

ANTERIOR Toward the head or front part of the body; opposite of *posterior*

ANTIBODY Defensive substance (protein) synthesized in response to the presence of a foreign protein (*antigen*), which the antibody neutralizes

ANTICODON A sequence of three nucleotides in a transfer RNA molecule that forms H bonds with a complementary triplet (*codon*) of mRNA

ANTIGEN A foreign substance (usually protein) capable of eliciting the formation of an antibody

APPENDAGE Limb, such as a leg or antenna

ASYMPTOTE Portion of a population growth curve at which birth and death are balanced and numerical stability maintained

ATP Adenosine triphosphate, a nucleotide involved in energy transfer in metabolism; mainly formed during cell respiration; serves to transfer energy into endergonic metabolic pathways

AUTO- Prefix meaning *self*

AUTONOMIC Vertebrate nervous functions regulating involuntary physiological processes; the *autonomic division* of the nervous system includes *sympathetic* and *parasympathetic* subdivisions

AUTOSOME Any chromosome other than a sex chromosome; man has one pair of sex chromosomes and 22 pairs of autosomes per body cell

AUTOTOMY Defensive casting off of body parts, such as when a lizard sheds its tail

AUTOTROPHIC Capable of synthesizing organic compounds from inorganic substrates, as in photosynthesis; *autotroph,* organism capable of autotrophic nutrition

AUXIN Plant growth hormone

AXIS A straight line that passes through a body (or body part) and serves as a fixed line of reference: (1) *anteroposterior,* through midline from anterior to posterior; (2) *transverse,* through midline from one side to other at right angles to (1); (3) *oral-aboral,* in radially symmetrical animals, through center from mouth to opposite surface

AXON Process or fiber of a nerve cell that transmits excitation away from the neuron cell body toward the synapse; compare with *dendrite*

BACTERIOPHAGE A complex virus that parasitizes bacteria

BASE (1) The nitrogenous portion of a nucleotide; used by inference to denote an entire nucleotide; for example, "A" denotes the nitrogenous base adenine, in turn referring to an adenine-containing nucleotide; (2) a chemical compound that liberates hydroxyl ion (OH^-) in solution

BENTHONIC Refers to the floor of a body of water; *benthos,* biota living on the bottom of a body of water

BIOME Major habitat type in which the dominant vegetation comprises certain characteristic types reflecting climatic tolerances, such as desert, taiga, and tundra

BIOSPHERE The sum total of all living things inhabiting the earth and its atmosphere

BIOSYNTHESIS Formation of complicated substances from less complex precursors by living organisms, such as the assembling of simple sugars into polysaccharides, or the synthesis of sugars from CO_2 and H_2O

BIOTA The fauna and flora of a region

BIOTIC Living; pertaining to life

BLAST-, -BLAST Prefix or suffix denoting a formative or embryonic unit of living matter, such as *myoblast* (embryonic precursor of a muscle fiber) and *blastodisc* (disc of embryonic cells forming on the surface of a large-yolked egg)

CALORIE The quantity of heat needed to raise the temperature of 1 g of water 1°C; *Calorie,* the calorie of dietetics, a kilocalorie equal to 1,000 calories

CARBOHYDRATE Organic compound consisting of C, H, and O, typically in the ratio C:2H:O; the type formula for a carbohydrate is therefore $(CH_2O)_n$; include sugars, starch, cellulose

CARBONIFEROUS Warm, moist period during the late Paleozoic Era when amphibians flourished and forests grew that later formed coal deposits; in the United States this period is known as the Mississippian and Pennsylvanian Periods

CARBOXYL The —COOH $(\text{—}\overset{\overset{\displaystyle O}{\|}}{C}\text{—OH})$ group characterizing organic acids

CATABOLISM Degradative metabolism, such as cell respiration

CATALEPSY Rigid immobility associated with crypsis (which see below), protecting nocturnal species by day

CATALYST Substance that alters the rate of a chemical reaction without becoming a permanent part of the product; in living systems most catalysts are proteins known as *enzymes*

CATION Positively charged ion such as Na^+ or NH_4^+

CELL Unit of structure and function of plants and animals, typically consisting of a mass of cytoplasm enclosing a nucleus and bounded by a differentially permeable membrane; *cellular,* made up of or pertaining to cells

CELLULOSE Rigid structural polysaccharide forming cell walls of plants

CENOZOIC ERA Interval of geological time extending from about 70 million years ago to the present, characterized by the adaptive radiation of mammals, birds, and flowering plants

CENTRIOLE A self-replicating organelle found in animal and some kinds of plant cells that determines the poles of the dividing cell and apparently forms the spindle fibers

CEPHALIZATION Tendency for sense organs and neural tissue to concentrate at the anterior end of the body, forming a head

CHLOROPHYLL Green pigment responsible for trapping radiant energy for photosynthesis; molecule contains tetrapyrrole ring centered upon a magnesium atom

CHROMATOPHORE Animal pigment cell; *melanocyte,* cell containing the black pigment melanin

CHROMOSOME Elongate intracellular body consisting of DNA (usually associated with protein) and made up of a linear series of functional units known as genes

CILIUM Motile fibril extending from a cell; *ciliate,* a protozoan having cilia; *ciliated,* bearing cilia, such as the epithelium lining the vertebrate nasal passages and windpipe

CIRCADIAN RHYTHM Endogenous physiological or behavioral rhythm that approximates the length of one day

CLEAVAGE Successive divisions of a fertilized egg up to the blastula stage of the embryo

CODON A sequence of three consecutive nucleotides in a gene or an mRNA molecule that specifies the position of one amino acid in a polypeptide

COELOM A true body cavity, developing as a space within the mesoderm

COENZYME A nonprotein group that associates temporarily with an enzyme molecule and is responsible for the latter's catalytic activity, such as coenzyme A

COLLAGEN Fibrous protein forming connective tissue fibers and contributing to intercellular cement

COLLOID A substance divided into small particles in suspension, such as protein molecules in water; the particles of a colloidal suspension are larger than those of a true solution

COLONY (1) A group of individual organisms produced by asexual reproduction and remaining physically attached together, as coral; (2) a social aggregation such as a prairie dog "town"

COMMENSALISM Symbiotic association essential to the survival of one member of the association (the *commensal*) but neither beneficial nor injurious to the other member (the *host*); for example, the relation between shark and remora

COMMUNITY All organisms living in a common habitat; *climax community,* an evolved, stabilized community in which all species tend to exist in a state of natural balance or numerical stability

COMPETENCE The capacity to respond physiologically to relevant environmental factors; for example, during development there are critical periods during which a given tissue is most competent to respond to inductive factors

COMPOUND Substance composed of two or more elements which are chemically bonded; *inorganic compound,* compound not based on carbon and occurring in the abiotic world; *organic compound,* carbon-based compound produced by living things

CONSPECIFIC (1) As adjective, pertains to organisms of the same species or to relationships within a species; (2) as noun, an organism of the same species as the one under consideration

CONVERGENCE Evolutionary process by which organisms or body parts of unlike origin come to resemble one another as an outcome of similar functions or mode of life; for instance, the eyes of vertebrates and cephalopods show convergence

COOPERATION A mutually beneficial ecological relationship between organisms of two species, which however is not obligate to those two particular species; as, the relationship between flowering plants as a whole and various kinds of pollinator insects

COORDINATION Maintenance of harmonious interactions among the subunits of any biotic system

COTYLEDON Seed leaf of an embryonic seed plant: monocots have one cotyledon; dicots, two

COVALENT BONDING Chemical bonding in which one or more pairs of electrons are shared by two atoms

CRYPSIS Protective resemblance to background, as by form- or color-matching; camouflage

CYTO- or -CYTE Prefix or suffix pertaining to a cell, such as *cytoplasm* and *phagocyte*

CYTOLOGICAL Pertaining to cells or to the study of cells

CYTOPLASM Portion of a cell lying outside the nucleus and bounded externally by the plasma membrane; the site of most metabolic processes; contains such organelles as ribosomes, mitochondria, and plastids; much of the cytoplasm consists of a system of membranes, the endoplasmic reticulum

DEHYDRATION SYNTHESIS Building up a larger molecule from smaller ones with the removal of one H_2O for each covalent bond formed; as, linking amino acids to form protein; opposite of *hydrolysis*

DEME A breeding population; an isolated subpopulation of a species

DENDRITE Process of a nerve cell that transmits excitation from its free endings toward the neuron cell body; compare with *axon*

DETERMINATION Progressive restriction or channelization of the developmental potential of an embryonic tissue

DIALYSIS Diffusion-driven passage of solutes across a differentially permeable membrane; form of "passive" transport not requiring cell energy

DIAPAUSE Developmental arrestment during the egg or pupal stage in insects, thought to be hormonally induced; chilling and rewarming are required for breaking diapause

DICOT Member of Order Dicotyledonae, a flowering plant having two seed leaves or cotyledons, usually also characterized by net-veined leaves and floral parts borne in fours or fives

DIFFERENTIATION Process by which embryonic tissues mature into specialized types

DIFFUSION Tendency of molecules to move away from a region of greater concentration to a region of lesser concentration, due to random thermal movements

DIGESTION Process by which ingested foods are prepared for absorption into the cells; *mechanical* digestion includes fragmentation and liquefaction; *chemical* digestion involves hydrolytic breakdown of molecules

DIOECIOUS (1) Being of separate sexes; having only ovaries or testes; producing only eggs or sperm; (2) in flowering plants, bearing only staminate or pistillate flowers on a single plant

DIPLOIDY Condition in which each cell contains two sets of chromosomes constituting homologous pairs; represented as $2n$

DISACCHARIDE A sugar made up of two simple sugar units united by dehydration synthesis, such as sucrose ($C_{12}H_{22}O_{11}$)

DISTAL Situated away from the reference point; as, away from the main part of the body; opposite of *proximal*

DIURNAL (1) Active by day; (2) recurrent each day; (3) having a daily cycle

DNA Deoxyribonucleic acid; a polymer made up of nucleotides containing deoxyribose, phosphate, and the nitrogenous bases adenine, guanine, cytosine, and thymine; generally exists as a double-stranded molecule; DNA is capable of self-replication and is the carrier of heredity in all organisms except a few viruses

DOMINANT Pertaining to a gene which is capable of masking the presence of its allele; most dominant alleles represent the fully functional evolved state of the gene; opposed to *recessive*

DORMANCY State in which life processes are arrested or greatly decelerated; includes *hibernation* (winter dormancy), *aestivation* (drought-induced dormancy), and *diapause* (hormone-induced dormancy in immature insects)

DORSAL Referring to the upper side, as of a bilaterally symmetrical animal; opposite of *ventral*

ECDYSIS Molting, as in insects; *ecdysone,* molt-regulating hormone

ECOLOGY Study of the relationships among organisms and between organisms and their physicochemical environment

ECOSYSTEM Ecological unit within which mass and energy are utilized cyclically with little dependence on external factors other than sunlight; consists of a biotic community together with its physicochemical environment or habitat; when in a state of natural balance, the ecosystem is self-perpetuating

ECTODERM Outermost primary germ layer in the metazoan embryo; develops into the epidermis and nervous system

EFFECTOR Body part responsible for carrying out a response; mainly used with reference to muscle and gland cells

ELECTRON Negatively charged particle of mass outside the atomic nucleus; electrons are involved in the formation of chemical bonds between atoms

ELEMENT Substance composed of only one kind of atom, such as carbon, sulfur, and nitrogen

EMBRYO Early developmental stage of a plant or animal, before it is capable of independent nutrient procurement

EMBRYOPHYTE A multicellular plant in which the embryo of the sporophyte generation remains protectively enclosed within a multicellular organ (the archegonium) of the parent gametophyte; as, mosses, ferns, and seed plants

EMULSIFYING AGENT Substance that stabilizes an emulsion, as of oil in water, such as bile which coats fat droplets and prevents their coalescence

EMULSION Colloidal system in which both the dispersed and continuous phases are liquid

ENDERGONIC Reaction requiring a net investment of energy, such as dehydration synthesis of amino acids to peptides

ENDO- Prefix meaning "within" or "inner"; or "taking in" as opposed to "giving off," such as *endoderm* (the innermost embryonic germ layer) and *endergonic* (taking in or requiring energy)

ENDOCRINE Liberating secretions directly into the tissue fluids or bloodstream and not into a duct or onto a free epithelial surface; as, thyroid and pituitary glands

ENDODERM Innermost primary germ layer in the metazoan embryo; develops into the lining of the gut and the epithelial portion of such organs as liver, pancreas, and lungs

ENDOGENOUS Originating within the system under consideration (such as a cell or organism), as an outcome of the properties of that system. (Opposed to *exogenous.*) May be used to denote hereditary traits as opposed to those mainly of environmental origin

ENDOPLASMIC RETICULUM Extensive system of double membranes enclosing fluid-filled channels and occupying most of the cytoplasm

ENERGY The capacity to do work

ENTROPY A measure of the disorderliness or randomness of a system

ENVIRONMENT Surroundings; the complex of biotic and abiotic factors that affect the growth, survival, and evolution of living units such as cells, organisms, and communities

ENZYME An organic catalyst; a protein responsible for governing the rate of a given metabolic reaction; some enzymes such as pepsin work outside cells but most operate intracellularly

EPIDERMIS (1) Epithelium covering the external surface of a multicellular plant or animal; (2) in vertebrates, the outer layers of the skin (the deeper layers forming the *dermis*)

EPISOME Hereditary particle of possibly foreign origin that exists free in the cytoplasm or may become attached to a chromosome; an example is the F (fertility) factor in bacteria

EPITHELIUM A membranous, often secretory, tissue that covers body surfaces, lines body cavities, and forms exocrine glands and a number of endocrine glands

ERYTHROCYTE Red blood corpuscle, mainly occurring in vertebrates and containing hemoglobin; concerned with oxygen transport

ESTROGEN Female sex hormone, such as estradiol

ESTRUS Period of intense sexual receptivity during the reproductive cycle of female mammals; *anestrus,* not being in estrus

ETHOLOGY The study of animal behavior, usually with respect to its adaptive significance under natural conditions

EU- Prefix meaning "true" or "good," as in *eumetazoan*

EUCARYOTIC Having an advanced cell structure with a nuclear envelope, mitochondria, and often centrioles and plastids; characteristic of all cellular life except bacteria and blue-green algae

EURY- Prefix indicating a broad or wide range of tolerance, as in *euryhaline* (tolerant of a wide range of salinity values) or *eurybathic* (tolerant of great changes in pressure and therefore capable of extensive vertical movements in the sea); opposite of *steno-*

EUTHERIAN Placental mammal

EUVIVIPAROUS Nourishing young within the mother's body prior to birth

EVOCATOR Chemical substance released by an embryonic tissue that induces a particular developmental process in nearby tissues

EVOLUTION Process of change in the genetic constitution of a population through successive generations, eventually giving rise to new forms of life

EX-, EXO- Prefix meaning out of or outside, such as *exothermic* (giving off heat) and *exoskeleton* (external skeleton covering the outside of the body); opposite of *endo-*

EXCRETION Removal of metabolic wastes from a cell or organism

EXERGONIC Liberating energy; opposite of *endergonic*

EXOCRINE Liberating secretions into a duct or onto a free epithelial surface, as mucus and salivary glands

EXOGENOUS Originating outside the system under consideration, such as outside the cell or organism; opposite of *endogenous*

EXOTHERMIC Liberating heat to the surroundings (said of chemical reactions)

EXTEROCEPTOR Sensory receptor receiving stimuli from the exterior of the body

FAUNA The animal species inhabiting a given region or forming part of a particular community

FERTILIZATION The fusion of gametes, such as sperm and ovum, to form a zygote

FETUS Late stage in development before birth or hatching, when the species is identifiable

FISSION Asexual reproduction by division of the body into two or more equal or unequal parts; common among protists

FITNESS A measure of an organism's state of adaptation, expressed as its relative capacity to produce offspring

FLAGELLUM Relatively long motile fibril borne by a cell such as a spermatozoan; *flagellate,* a protozoan bearing one or more flagella

FLORA The plant species inhabiting a given region or forming part of a particular biotic community

FOOD (1) Nutrient materials obtained from the environment (see *nutrient*); (2) fuel substances stored within living tissues, such as starch or glycogen

FORMULA Statement of the elemental composition of a compound or a molecule; an *empirical* formula only designates the elements present and the number of atoms of each; a *structural* formula depicts the arrangement of the constituent atoms

FRUIT The mature ovary of a flower; serves to protect the seeds

GAMETE A monoploid sex cell, such as a sperm or ovum

GAMETOPHYTE The monoploid, gamete-producing generation of a plant life cycle; in mosses and some algae the gametophyte is the most conspicuous and persistent generation, whereas in vascular plants, the gametophyte is inconspicuous and may be nutritionally dependent on the sporophyte

GANGLION Aggregation of nerve cell bodies, considered in the case of vertebrates to be located outside the central nervous system; among invertebrates ganglia also form the central nervous system, the *cerebral ganglia* constituting the brain

GENE Portion of a chromosome bearing the code for amino acid sequence in a specific protein or polypeptide; portion of a chromosome or DNA molecule that carries the hereditary code for development of a specific trait or unit character

GENE POOL All of the genes in a breeding population or species

GENETIC Pertaining to heredity; inherited; *genetics,* the science of inheritance; *genetic code,* the sequence of nucleotides in a nucleic acid that specifies the amino acid sequence in a polypeptide

GENITALIA Organs of the reproductive system, including gonads and accessory organs such as uterus or penis; *genital,* pertaining to the reproductive tract or sex organs

GENOME Total genetic constitution of an organism

GENOTYPE Genetic makeup of an individual with respect to a given hereditary trait; a tall sweet pea plant may have the *homozygous* genotype *TT* or the *heterozygous* genotype *Tt*, the latter carrying a recessive factor for dwarfness

GENUS Taxonomic unit consisting of a group of allied species

GEOTROPISM Gravity-oriented plant growth response

GERM CELL A gamete or an antecedent cell that produces a gamete

GERMINATION Resumption of growth by a seed or spore

GLUCOSE The commonest simple sugar or monosaccharide ($C_6H_{12}O_6$), used by most organisms as their major fuel substance

GLUCOSIDASE Enzyme that digests carbohydrates; hydrolyzes polysaccharides to disaccharides, or disaccharides to monosaccharides

GLYCOGEN Highly-branching polysaccharide which is the major carbohydrate storage compound in animal tissues

GONADS Sex organs, that is, organs in which eggs and/or sperm are produced; male gonads are *testes*, female gonads, *ovaries*

GUTTATION Exudation of water droplets from the leaves, such as from glands on the leaf margins or from the open ends of veins

GYMNOSPERM Vascular plant bearing seeds that are not enclosed within a fruit, such as a cycad or conifer

HABITAT The environment or place in which a plant or animal naturally lives

HALF-LIFE Time required for a radioactive element to lose 50 percent of its remaining radioactivity, that is, for half the atoms in a sample to undergo radioactive decay

HEMO- Prefix meaning "blood," as in *hemoglobin* (an oxygen-carrying blood pigment)

HEMOCOEL A blood-filled body cavity that largely replaces the coelom in animals (such as arthropods) having an open circulatory system

HERBIVORE Animal feeding upon plant materials

HEREDITY The transmission of characteristics from parents to progeny, mainly by way of the chromosomes of the germ cells

HETERO- Prefix meaning "different" or "other"

HETEROPOLYMER A polymer made up of two or more different types of repeating molecular units, for example, chitin, hyaluronic acid, and proteins

HETEROSPECIFIC Having to do with different species, such as relationships between organisms of two species

HETEROTROPHIC Incapable of synthesizing organic compounds from inorganic precursors, hence requiring organic nutrients

HETEROZYGOUS Having alleles of unlike type for a given genetic trait, as when carrying genes for the mutually exclusive traits of tallness (*T*) and dwarfness (*t*)

HEXOSE Six-carbon sugar such as glucose: $C_6H_{12}O_6$

HOLOBLASTIC Type of cleavage in animal embryos in which the entire mass of the egg can divide, as in starfish and amphibians

HOMEOSTASIS Maintenance of a steady state; often refers to maintaining the chemical constancy of body fluids

HOMOIOTHERMAL "Warm-blooded," that is, capable of maintaining a stable body temperature by physiological means

HOMOLOGOUS (1) Being of similar origin in evolution or embryonic development; (2) *homologous chromosomes*, chromosome pairs in diploid organisms, each consisting of a basically identical set of genes; one homologous chromosome of each pair is donated to the individual by its father and one by its mother

HOMOZYGOUS Having identical alleles for a given hereditary trait

HORMONE Secretion that serves to regulate the performance of tissues over a distance from its site of liberation; usually the product of an endocrine gland; *neurohormone*, hormone liberated at the axon endings of a neurosecretory neuron; hypophyseal release factors in vertebrates are neurohormones

HOST An organism on or within which lives a symbiont such as a parasite or commensal

HYBRID Heterozygous individual, especially one produced by crossing two different strains or varieties

HYDROLASE A hydrolytic enzyme such as an amylase or lipase

HYDROLYSIS Process of breaking a larger molecule into smaller components by addition of water into the bond broken; as, digestion of proteins to amino acids; opposite of *dehydration synthesis;* also, splitting of H_2O molecule

HYPER- Prefix meaning "over" or "above," as in *hyperexcitable* (over-excitable)

HYPEROSMOTIC *Hypertonic*; in a comparison of two solutions, refers to the one having the higher concentration of solutes; water tends to diffuse across a differentially permeable membrane from a *hyposmotic* solution to a *hyperosmotic* solution

HYPHA One of the filaments or threads that makes up the mycelium of a fungus

HYPO- Prefix meaning "less" or "below," such as *hypodermic* (below the skin)

HYPOSMOTIC *Hypotonic;* in a comparison of two solutions, refers to the one having the lower concentration of solutes; water tends to pass osmotically from a *hyposmotic* solution to one that is *hyperosmotic;* freshwater organisms live in a medium *hyposmotic* to their tissues

HYPOTHALAMUS Ventral posterior portion of the vertebrate forebrain, responsible for control of autonomic functions and for secreting hormones that regulate the pituitary gland

HYPOTHESIS A tentative explanation or assumption that must be tested by experimentation or direct observation before it is accepted

INDIGENOUS Native to an area, not introduced

INDUCTION Influence exerted by embryonic tissues on the development of adjacent tissues; *inductor*, embryonic tissue that exerts an inductive influence on the differentiation of nearby tissues

INFLORESCENCE A cluster of flowers borne on the same stalk, such as a sunflower head

INGESTION Eating; the process by which an animal takes food into its body

INNATE Inborn; primarily genetically based rather than experientially based; as, *innate behavior* (see *instinct*)

INSTINCT Complex pattern of innate (genetically based) behavior

INTEGUMENT Outer covering, skin

INTER- Occurring between (or among)

two (or more) of the units under consideration, such as *interstitial* (occupying spaces among cells), *interspecific* (concerning relationships between different species), *interphase* (the period of time between consecutive cell divisions)

INTEROCEPTOR Sensory receptor that monitors internal body conditions

INTRA- Prefix meaning within; such as *intracellular* (within the cell), *intraspecific* (within the species); compare with *inter-*

INVERTEBRATE Animal lacking a backbone

IN VITRO Taking place in isolation from the intact organism, for instance in a test tube

IN VIVO Within the living organism; opposed to *in vitro*

INVOLUTION Decrease in size of an organ during process of maturation

ION Electrically charged particle consisting of one or more atoms

IONIZE To dissociate into ions when in solution, such as the *ionization* of sodium chloride (NaCl) into Na^+ and Cl^- or of carbonic acid (H_2CO_3) to hydrogen ion (H^+) and bicarbonate ion (HCO_3^-)

IRRITABILITY Capacity to detect and respond adaptively to stimuli

ISO- Prefix meaning "equal" or "like"; similar to *homo-* and opposed to *aniso-*

ISOMER A molecule having the same empirical formula as some other molecule but differing in the arrangement of the atoms; such as glucose and fructose

ISOSMOTIC *Isotonic;* refers to a solution that contains the same proportions of water and solutes as another solution with which it is being compared; isosmotic solutions are in osmotic equilibrium and the flow of water is equalized between the two solutions (blood and tissue fluids are *isosmotic* to the cytoplasm; although the extracellular and intracellular solutes are not identical their total concentration is in balance)

ISOTHERMAL Taking place without a significant change in temperature: characteristic of chemical reactions within cells

ISOTOPE One of two or more forms of an element, having the same atomic number but differing in atomic mass due to differences in the number of neutrons present in the atomic nucleus; see *radioisotope*

KERATIN Horny, water-impervious protein found in vertebrate epidermis, feathers, scales, hair, claws, and quills; *keratinization,* process by which the skin becomes horny and waterproof through keratin deposition

KETONE Organic compound containing the configuration $-\overset{\overset{\displaystyle O}{\|}}{C}-$

KILOCALORIE Unit of heat required to raise the temperature of one kilogram of water 1°C; equal to 1000 calories; equivalent to the *Calorie* of dietetics

KINESIS Locomotory response in which the stimulus alters the rate of movement or the frequency of turning but does not control the direction of movement

LARVA Sexually immature postembryonic stage in the life cycle of an animal, capable of nutrient procurement but requiring metamorphosis to adulthood

LEUCOCYTE White blood corpuscle; usually amoeboid and of defensive function

LIPASE Enzyme catalyzing the hydrolysis of fats to fatty acids and glycerol

LIPID A fat or fatlike compound such as a true fat, oil, wax, phospholipid, or steroid, all of which are soluble in fat solvents

LYSO-, LYSIS-, -LYTIC, -LYZE Prefix or suffix forms pertaining to a dissolving or disruptive action, such as *proteolytic* (protein-digesting) enzymes

LYSOSOME Membrane-bounded organelle serving to store hydrolytic enzymes within the cytoplasm

MACRO- Prefix meaning "large," as opposed to *micro-*, meaning "small" (*macroscopic,* visible to the unaided eye; *microscopic,* visible only with the aid of a microscope)

MACROMOLECULE Giant molecule such as a protein or nucleic acid; macromolecules may have a molecular weight of several million

MAMMAL A homoiothermal vertebrate having mammary glands and body hair; other distinguishing characteristics include enucleated red blood corpuscles, three middle ear bones, a diaphragm separating thorax from abdomen, sebaceous and sweat glands in the skin, and usually an external ear or pinna protruding from the side of the head; includes *monotremes* (egg-laying mammals), *marsupials* (pouched mammals), and *eutherians* (placental mammals)

MARSUPIAL A nonplacental viviparous mammal (such as the kangaroo), in which the young are protected after birth within a pouch formed by folds of skin enclosing the nipples

MASS That form of energy which occupies space, exhibits inertial properties, and has weight in a gravitational field

MEIOSIS Process by which a diploid cell is reduced to the monoploid condition; occurs during gametogenesis in animals, but at other times in the plant life cycle (such as at the time of gametophyte production)

MEMBRANE Thin sheet or layer: (1) *epithelial* membrane, a thin sheet of cells such as the peritoneum that lines the body cavity; (2) *basement* membrane, an adhesive layer of protein and carbohydrate materials to which an epithelium is anchored; (3) *plasma* membrane, the lipoprotein layer bounding a cell and regulating the passage of materials into and out of the cell

MERISTEM Undifferentiated or embryonic tissue found in growing regions of plants

MEROBLASTIC Type of embryonic cleavage in which the presence of a large quantity of yolk restricts cleavage to a disc resting upon the yolk, as in birds, reptiles, and mammals

MESENCHYME Most common type of mesodermal embryonic tissue, consisting of star-shaped cells capable of amoeboid locomotion; differentiates into bone and connective tissue cells, blood-forming cells, and so forth

MESODERM Primary germ layer in all metazoans except sponges and coelenterates, which develops between the ectoderm and the endoderm and gives rise to muscles, connective tissues, gonads, and excretory organs

MESOZOIC ERA Interval of geological time from about 230 to 70 million years ago, known as the Age of Reptiles

MESSENGER RNA See *RNA*

METABOLISM Sum total of all chemical

reactions taking place within the cells, by which nutrients are utilized for growth, maintenance, and energy (see *anabolism* and *catabolism*)

METAGENESIS Alternation of generations; that is, alternation during the life cycle of a species of a sexual generation and one or more asexual generations, which usually differ conspicuously in body form and often in mode of life; occurs in most metaphytes and in many coelenterates and parasitic flatworms

METAMERE Body segment; somite

METAMERISM Body plan in which the body of an organism is built up of a series of repeated segmental units or metameres

METAMORPHOSIS Gradual or abrupt change in body form during maturation, with or without a pupal stage

METAPHYTE A many-celled plant

METAZOAN A multicellular animal

METRIC SYSTEM A decimal system for measuring length, volume, mass, force, capacity, and area (see Appendix 1)

MIMICRY Protective resemblance, usually between two animal species, at least one of which is inedible or noxious: *Batesian mimicry,* resemblance to a noxious organism (the model) by one which is edible (the mimic); *Mullerian mimicry,* resemblance among a group of inedible or noxious species

MITOCHONDRION Cell organelle serving as the major center of ATP production; site of Krebs cycle and terminal oxidations

MITOSIS Cell division that does not change the total chromosome number from one cell generation to the next; by mitosis diploid cells produce diploid daughter cells and monoploid cells produce monoploid daughter cells

MOLE Molecular weight of a compound taken in grams

MOLECULE Unit made up of two or more atoms that are chemically bonded

MOLECULAR WEIGHT The sum total of the weight or mass of all atoms within a molecule

MONOCOT Member of Order Monocotyledonae, a flowering plant having a single seed leaf or cotyledon; usually also characterized by parallel-veined leaves and by floral parts borne in threes; includes lilies, grasses, grains, palms, orchids

MONOECIOUS (1) Having both male and female sex organs in the same individual; hermaphroditic; (2) in flowering plants, bearing both pistillate and staminate flowers

MONOMER Molecular unit forming a polymer, such as a sugar unit in a starch molecule

MONOPLOIDY Condition in which only one set of chromosomes is present per cell; also termed *haploidy;* represented as *n*

MONOSACCHARIDE A simple sugar such as a triose, hexose, or pentose; the monomer unit from which oligosaccharides and polysaccharides are built

MORPH-, -MORPH Prefix or suffix meaning "form" or "shape"

MORPHOGENESIS Development of form, especially during embryonic development

MORPHOLOGICAL Pertaining to the form or structure of a cell or organism

MUTAGENIC Capable of causing mutations, such as X rays

MUTATION A genetic change, primarily a change in a gene

MUTUALISM A symbiotic association essential to the survival of both members of the association (such as termites and their intestinal protozoans, or yucca and yucca moth)

MYCELIUM Network of filaments (hyphae) making up the body of a fungus

NAD Nicotinamide adenine dinucleotide; a compound that contains adenine, ribose, phosphate, and the vitamin niacin (nicotinamide) and serves as an agent of electron transport in cell metabolism; formerly called DPN (diphosphopyridine nucleotide)

NADP Nicotinamide adenine dinucleotide phosphate; an electron-transfer agent particularly significant in transporting H into the Calvin cycle of photosynthesis; formerly called TPN (triphosphopyridine nucleotide)

NEKTON Actively swimming aquatic organisms such as fish

NERITIC Oceanic habitat zone overlying the continental shelf

NERVE A bundle of nerve fibers, that is, axons and/or dendrites

NEURAL Pertaining to nerves and nervous functions

NEUROHORMONE Hormone produced by a specialized neurosecretory neuron

NEUROHYPOPHYSIS Preferred term designating the posterior part of the vertebrate pituitary gland, from which neurohormones originating in the hypothalamus are liberated into the bloodstream

NEURON A nerve cell

NICHE Specific role in a community played by one particular species

NITRATE NO_3^-, the only form in which most plants can obtain nitrogen for metabolic use

NOCTURNAL Active by night

NUCLEIC ACID Polymer made up of nucleotide units: deoxyribonucleic acid (DNA) is a polymer of deoxyribose nucleotides; ribonucleic acid (RNA), of ribose nucleotides; carrier of code for protein synthesis

NUCLEOTIDE The molecular unit that is the monomer of a nucleic acid chain; consists of a pentose, a phosphate group, and a nitrogenous base; important free nucleotides include ATP and NAD

NUCLEUS Center: (1) *cell nucleus,* central body containing the chromosomes; (2) *atomic nucleus,* central mass consisting of protons, neutrons, and possibly other particles of mass; (3) nucleus in central nervous system consists of a mass of neuron cell bodies; such nuclei are interconnected by nerve fiber tracts

NUTRIENT Substance obtained from the external environment and utilized for growth and maintenance; autotrophs require inorganic nutrients, heterotrophs require both organic and inorganic materials as nutrients

NUTRITION All processes involved in processing and utilizing nutrients, including ingestion, digestion, internal distribution of nutrients, and metabolic processes by which nutrients are used for energy or biosynthesis

OLFACTION The sense of smell, or capacity to detect volatile air- or water-borne molecules

OLIGOSACCHARIDE A low-molecular-weight carbohydrate consisting of two or a few monosaccharide units, such as sucrose

OMNIVORE Animal that eats both meat and plant materials

ONTOGENY (1) Development of the individual from fertilization to maturity; (2) life history of the organism from conception to death

ORAL (1) Pertaining to the mouth; (2) mouth-bearing surface or pole, as of a radially symmetrical animal; opposite of *aboral*

ORGAN A structure of more or less definite form and function that consists of several types of tissues; the stomach is an organ and has a digestive function

ORGANELLE A functional body within the cell, such as a mitochondrion, chromosome, or ribosome

ORGANIC Pertaining to living things or organisms: *organic compound,* carbon-based compound as found in living things; *organic evolution,* process of hereditary change in living things

ORGANISM An individual living thing, such as a bacterium, lion, or tree

OSMOSIS Passage of water across a differentially permeable membrane: *osmotic pressure,* measure of the tendency of water to pass across a membrane due to unequal concentration of solutes on each side of the membrane; water molecules tend to diffuse from the region of their greater concentration (that is, where there are fewer solutes) to a region where they are less concentrated (that is, where there are more solutes and relatively less water); *osmotic equilibrium,* steady-state in which the concentration of water molecules is the same on both sides of a differentially permeable membrane so that water flows equally in both directions; *osmoregulation,* capacity to regulate the retention of water and its loss from the body, as is necessary when the organism lives in a medium with which it is not in osmotic equilibrium

OVARY (1) Egg-producing organ of an animal; (2) ovule-containing organ in a flower, within which the seeds mature

OVIPAROUS Egg-laying, as, birds

OVOVIVIPAROUS Retaining eggs within the parent's body until hatching but without providing nourishment other than by the stored egg yolk

OVULE The part of the ovary of a seed plant within which the megasporangium, female gametophyte, and seed mature successively

OVUM Egg; female gamete, usually nonmotile and enlarged with stored food materials

OXIDATION Loss of hydrogen or electrons; opposite of *reduction*

PALEOZOIC ERA Interval of geological time from about 600 to 230 million years ago, distinguished by the rise of invertebrates and the appearance of fishes, amphibians, reptiles, and land plants

PARASITISM A symbiotic association essential to the survival of one member (the *parasite*) but more or less injurious to the other member (the *host*), such as the relationship between tick and mammal, or Chinese liver fluke and man: *ectoparasitism,* being parasitic on the exterior of the host's body; *endoparasitism,* being parasitic within the host's body

PARENCHYMA (1) Thin walled tissue in plants used for storage and photosynthesis; (2) poorly differentiated mesodermal tissue in flatworms

PARTHENOGENESIS Development of an egg without fertilization by a sperm

PENTOSE Five-carbon sugar such as ribose ($C_5H_{10}O_5$) and deoxyribose ($C_5H_{10}O_4$), especially important as a constituent of nucleotides

PEPTIDE A chain composed of two or more amino acids linked by covalent bonds; a *polypeptide* contains many amino acids; one or more polypeptide chains make up a protein molecule

PERMEABILITY The characteristics of a cell membrane with respect to what types of substances can pass through it; a *differentially permeable* membrane (DPM) can actively regulate the passage of materials

pH Potential H^+; a measure of acidity and alkalinity expressed as the negative log of H^+ concentration: a pH of 7 represents neutrality; a pH of below 7, acidity; above 7, alkalinity

-PHAGE, PHAGO- Suffix or prefix meaning "one that eats," as in *macrophage* (a large amoeboid defensive cell that eats bacteria)

PHAGOCYTOSIS Process by which a cell engulfs solid particles; *phagocyte,* a defensive cell capable of phagocytosis, such as a leucocyte

PHENOTYPE Physical appearance with respect to a given hereditary trait; for instance, eye color is a phenotype

PHEROMONE Chemical secreted by certain members of a species, which alters the physiology or behavior of other members of that species; pheromones causing physiological changes are said to have *primer* effects whereas those eliciting a specific behavior are said to have *releaser* effects

PHLOEM Tissue in vascular plants consisting of living sieve tubes, which conduct solutes from the leaves to other parts of the plant

PHOSPHOLIPID Compound consisting of fatty acids, glycerol, phosphate, and a water-soluble component such as choline or inositol; phospholipids contribute to the formation of cell membranes

PHOSPHORYLATION Addition of a phosphate group to a compound, usually representing a gain in free energy; opposite of *dephosphorylation*

PHOTOPERIOD Length of daylight; *photoperiodism,* physiological or behavioral response to changes in length of day

PHOTOTROPISM Growth movement of a plant toward light

PHYLOGENY Evolutionary history of a group

PHYLUM Major subdivision of a biotic kingdom; composed of a group of related classes

PHYSIOLOGICAL Pertaining to the normal functioning of a cell or organism

PHYTO-, -PHYTE Prefix and suffix referring to a plant, as in *phytoplankton* and *gametophyte*

PHYTOPLANKTON Unattached floating aquatic plants, mostly microscopic, including dinoflagellates, desmids, and diatoms

PINOCYTOSIS "Cell drinking"; process by which cells imbibe droplets of solution often containing large colloidal particles that cannot enter the cell by other means

PISTIL "Female" reproductive organ of a flowering plant; contains the ovary within which the female gametophytes are formed and the seeds later mature

PITUITARY "Master" endocrine gland in vertebrates which controls the activities of other endocrine glands such as the thyroid, gonads, and adrenal cortex

PLACENTA Nutritional structure developing within uterus of pregnant eutherian mammal, providing for exchanges of materials between maternal and fetal bloodstreams

PLANKTON Drifting or weakly swimming aquatic organisms, often minute: *phytoplankton,* planktonic plants; *zooplankton,* planktonic animals

PLASMA MEMBRANE The external membrane bounding a cell, consisting of proteins and phospholipids and characterized by a dynamic capacity to regulate the passage of materials into and out of the cell; the plasma membrane is described as a differentially permeable membrane (DPM)

PLASTID Organelle in plant cells often containing pigments; *chloroplast,* plastid containing chlorophyll; site of photosynthesis

POIKILOTHERMAL "Cold-blooded," that is, unable to maintain stable body temperature by physiological means

POLARIZED Being directionalized along one axis, that is, having two poles with opposite properties; cell membranes are electrically polarized, being electronegative on their inner surface and electropositive on their outer surface; synapses are polarized if the excitation can pass in only one direction, such as from axon to dendrite and not from dendrite to axon; *polarity,* condition of being polarized; for instance, bilaterally symmetrical animals are *polarized* along their longitudinal body axis from anterior to posterior

POLYMER Molecule built up by serial repetition of identical or similar molecular subunits (monomers): polypeptides are *polymers* of amino acids; starch, a *polymer* of glucose

POLYMORPHISM Condition in which individuals of different form and function coexist in the same generation of a colony or society; as, feeding and reproductive hydroid polyps, and worker, soldier, and reproductive termite castes

POLYMORPHISM, GENETIC Condition in which alternative expressions of a genetic trait coexist in a population, as, A, B, AB, and O blood groups in man; a *balanced genetic polymorphism* is one in which natural selection favors the heterozygote over either type of homozygote, as, sickle-cell anemia in malarial areas

POLYPLOIDY Condition in which three or more complete sets of chromosomes are present per cell; triploid individuals are designated $3n$, tetraploid individuals $4n$, and so forth; common among plants and in the somatic tissues of animals

POLYSACCHARIDE Polymer made up of many simple sugar units; for example, starch, cellulose, glycogen

POSTERIOR Toward the tail or rear part of the body; opposite of *anterior*

PRECOCIAL Capable of much independent activity from birth, as domestic chicks and lambs; opposite of *altricial*

PREDATORY Living by predation, the killing of prey

PROCARYOTIC Having a relatively simple cell structure in which a nuclear envelope, mitochondria, centrioles, and plastids are lacking; characteristic only of bacteria and blue-green algae; opposite of *eucaryotic*

PROPRIOCEPTOR "Self-sensing" receptor in muscles, tendons, and joints that monitors posture, movement, and position in space; responsible for equilibrium and muscular coordination

PROSTHETIC GROUP A nonprotein group that unites permanently with an enzyme molecule and is responsible for its catalytic function; a *riboflavin prosthetic group* is responsible for the activity of flavoprotein enzymes in cell respiration

PROTEASE Enzyme such as pepsin which catalyzes the hydrolysis of proteins

PROTEIN A high-molecular-weight polymer made up of amino acids linked to form polypeptide chains

PROTIST Unicellular eucaryotic organism such as a protozoan

PROTON Positively charged unit of mass in the atomic nucleus; the hydrogen ion, H^+, is a proton

PROTOPLASM General designation for the living substance of a cell or of a plant or animal body

PROXIMAL Situated close to the reference point, as, close to the main part of the body; opposite of *distal*

PSEUDOCOEL A "false" body cavity, that is, one developing between the endoderm and mesoderm, as in roundworms

PSEUDOPODIUM Cytoplasmic protusion of an amoeboid cell, used in locomotion and feeding

RADIOACTIVE Spontaneously emitting subatomic particles (α and β particles) and γ rays, as products of the disintegration of atomic nuclei

RADIOISOTOPE Radioactive form of an element; may occur naturally or be artificially produced, as by neutron bombardment of the stable (nonradioactive) element

RECEPTOR A sensory cell that receives stimuli; the *photoreceptors* of the vertebrate eye are rods and cones

RECESSIVE Pertaining to a gene the effect of which is masked by the presence of its dominant allele; most mutations are recessive

REDUCTION Gain in hydrogen or electrons; opposite of *oxidation*

REDUCTION DIVISION Meiotic division in which homologous chromosomes are separated, reducing the daughter cells from a diploid ($2n$) to a monoploid ($1n$) state

REFLEX Simple behavioral unit involving receptor, sensory nerve fiber, motor nerve fiber, and effector

REGENERATION Capacity of an organism to grow back lost parts or to repair injuries

RENAL Pertaining to the kidney

REPTILE Poikilothermal amniote, usually with scaly skin, including lizards, snakes, turtles, crocodilians, and many extinct groups

RESPIRATION (1) Exchange of gases (*a*) between a cell and its milieu, or (*b*) between an organism and its environment; (2) breathing; (3) *cell respiration* involves all metabolic processes, aerobic and anaerobic, whereby energy is mobilized by the breakdown of organic compounds

RESPIRATORY PIGMENT Substance that serves in the transport or storage of oxygen, such as *hemoglobin* in the bloodstream and *myoglobin* in muscle tissue

RETICULUM Network of fibers or minute canals, for example, the *endoplasmic reticulum* within the cytoplasm

RETINA Light-sensitive layer of cells in an

eye; in vertebrates contains *rods* (dim-light receptors), *cones* (color receptors), and ganglion cells

RIBOSOME Cell organelle composed of protein and ribonucleic acid; serves as site of protein synthesis in the cytoplasm; interacts with mRNA to polymerize amino acids on the template provided by mRNA (see *RNA*)

RNA Ribonucleic acid; a polymer of nucleotides made up of ribose, phosphate, and nitrogenous bases, primarily adenine, guanine, cytosine, and uracil: *mRNA* (messenger RNA), a high-molecular-weight strand produced by DNA, which carries a template for protein synthesis to the ribosomes; *tRNA* (transfer RNA), a low-molecular-weight form that establishes complexes with specific amino acids and forms hydrogen bonds with reciprocal groups on the mRNA strand, thereby correctly positioning the amino acid for incorporation into the protein

RUDIMENTARY Being less well developed than at some later stage or time

SAPROPHYTIC Obtaining nourishment from decaying tissues, as a fungus

SCHIZOPHYTA Phylum of the bacteria

SCLERENCHYMA Thick-walled supportive tissue in plants

SEDENTARY Not freely moving about; usually applies to animals that are permanently attached to the substratum, such as barnacles

SEED An embryonic plant in a state of arrested development pending germination

SELECTION, NATURAL Process whereby genetic variations are perpetuated or eliminated on the basis of their effects upon survival of an organism in its natural milieu

SENESCENCE Process of aging; state of being aged

SENSE ORGAN A group of receptors and accessory tissues, such as an eye

SOCIETY An organized group of animals of the same species

SOLUTE Substance dissolved in a solvent, such as sugar in water

SOLUTION A liquid containing a dissolved material; a homogeneous mixture of solvent and solute

SOLVENT Substance capable of dissolving other substances; water is the major solvent in living systems

SOMATIC (1) Pertaining to or concerned with the life of an individual organism, as opposed to the perpetuation of kind; (2) all body tissues except the germ cells; (3) the body wall (skin and musculature) as opposed to internal organs (visceral components)

SPECIES A specific type of plant or animal; a taxonomic group below the rank of genus; a freely interbreeding taxonomic unit that does not usually interbreed outside the group

SPERM Male gamete, usually motile by means of flagella, spermatozoan

SPINDLE Fibrous apparatus responsible for separation of chromosomes during cell division

SPORANGIUM A unicellular structure in which spores are produced

SPORE (1) A single cell encased in a protective coat and capable of germinating to form a multicellular organism such as a fungus, alga, moss, or fern; (2) the encysted form of a bacterium or sporozoan

SPOROPHYTE Diploid generation of a plant life cycle, producing monoploid spores by meiosis; in vascular plants the sporophyte is the dominant generation

STAMEN Part of a flower in which the male gametophytes (pollen) are produced

STARCH A high-molecular-weight polysaccharide made up of glucose units, which is the main food-storage compound of plants

STATOCYST Gravity sensor; sense organ used in detecting a body's position in a gravitational field

STELE Portion of a stem or root containing the vascular tissue

STENO- Prefix denoting a narrow range of tolerance, as in *stenothermal* (capable of surviving only within a restricted temperature range); opposite of *eury-*

STEROID Organic compound with a skeleton of four interconnected carbon rings; includes sex and adrenocortical hormones, cholesterol, vitamin D

STIMULUS Change in the environment that elicits a response

STOMATE Opening in a leaf flanked by guard cells and permitting gaseous exchanges between the atmosphere and the internal air spaces of the leaf

SUBSTRATE Substance worked upon by an enzyme

SUBSTRATUM The solid surface on which an organism lives, such as the bottom of a lake or ocean; may apply to any surface used as a foundation for attachment or support

SUCCESSION A developmental process through which a community reaches a stabilized, climax state

SYMBIOSIS An obligate relationship between organisms of two species that is essential to the survival of one or both members of the partnership (see also *mutualism, commensalism,* and *parasitism*)

SYMMETRY Condition in which a body can be divided into two equal mirror-image halves along one or more planes: *bilateral symmetry,* condition in which the body can be divided into equal right and left halves through one plane only (a sagittal plane passing from dorsal to ventral through the median longitudinal axis); *radial symmetry,* condition in which the body can be subdivided into equal halves through any of a number of planes passing through the oral-aboral axis

SYMPATRIC Refers to species or populations that live in the same habitat and are therefore parts of the same community

SYNAPSE (1) Junction between axon of one neuron and dendrite or cell body of another neuron; (2) junction between axon ending and an effector such as a muscle fiber or gland cell; acetylcholine is liberated at *cholinergic synapses,* adrenaline at *adrenergic synapses*

SYNAPSIS The alignment of homologous chromosomes during meiosis, a necessary preliminary to the reduction division and consequent segregation of alleles

SYNCYTIUM (1) A network of conjoined cells; (2) a multinucleate mass of protoplasm formed by the fusion of many cells

SYSTEMIC Generalized throughout the body of an organism, as opposed to localized or intracellular; as, a *systemic* infection

TAXIS Locomotion oriented with respect to a directional stimulus, such as *phototaxis* or locomotion toward or away from a light source

TAXON A taxonomic group, such as a genus or species

TEMPLATE A pattern on which a duplicate, reciprocal, or other orderly unit can be built; for example, DNA serves as a *template* for building RNA

TERRITORIALITY Tendency of an individual to exclude other members of the same species from the area or space occupied by that individual (or his group)

TETRAPOD A four-footed animal; used to designate amphibians, reptiles, birds, and mammals, as distinguished from fishes

THALLUS A multicellular plant body which is not differentiated into distinct roots, stems, and leaves, and is not composed of complexly organized tissues; *thallophyte,* a multicellular plant the body of which is a thallus, such as an alga, a fungus, or a moss

THEORY Scientific generalization reached by inductive reasoning from experimental or observational data

THERMODYNAMICS Study of energy conversions and exchanges; a *thermodynamic system* is any system the energy properties of which are being considered; the *first law of thermodynamics* states that the total energy content of a system plus its surroundings (the universe) remains constant; the *second law* states that the entropy (degree of randomness) in the system and surroundings tends to increase

TISSUE A functionally integrated mass or sheet of cells of similar type, such as *nervous tissue* and *muscle tissue*

TRACHEA An air-conducting tube, specifically, the vertebrate windpipe; *tracheole,* microscopic air-conducting tubule in an insect

TRACHEOPHYTE Vascular plant, including ferns and seed plants

TRANSDUCTION Transfer of genetic material from one organism to another through the agency of a virus

TRANSLOCATION (1) Transfer of a portion of a chromosome to a different part of another chromosome, usually one that is nonhomologous; (2) transport of soluble organic materials through the body of a vascular plant, from the leaves to the storage tissues and growing regions and from the storage tissues to the growing regions

TRANSPIRATION Loss of water by evaporation, especially from the stomates of leaves

TRIOSE A three-carbon sugar ($C_3H_6O_3$), such as PGAL (phosphoglyceraldehyde)

-TROPH, -TROPHIC Suffixes meaning "to nourish," as in *autotrophic,* ("self-nourishing") and *gonadotrophin* (gonad-nourishing or -stimulating hormone)

TROPISM Growth movement of a plant in response to a directional stimulus: *geotropism,* response directed by gravity; *phototropism,* response directed by light

TURGOR Distention of a plant cell due to uptake of water

UNGULATE Hoofed animal; the term includes members of two different mammalian orders: *Artiodactyla,* the even-toed hoofed mammals such as antelope, camel, cattle, sheep, and swine; *Perissodactyla,* the odd-toed hoofed mammals such as horse, tapir, and rhinoceros

UTERUS Portion of a female reproductive tract within which the young develop until birth, or within which the eggs are retained pending laying or hatching

VACUOLE Fluid-filled cavity or vesicle within a cell; *contractile vacuole,* organelle in freshwater protozoans that collects and expells excess water; *sap vacuole,* large cavity containing stored sap in plant tissues

VASCULAR Pertaining to vessels used for internal transport of materials throughout the body of a multicellular plant or animal; *vascular plant,* plant having vascular tissue for transport of water and other nutrients; fern or seed plant; *cardiovascular system,* blood-containing system including heart and blood vessels

VEIN (1) A blood vessel carrying blood toward the heart; (2) a vascular bundle in the leaf of a tracheophyte

VENTRAL Referring to the lower side or underparts, as of a bilaterally symmetrical animal; opposite of *dorsal*

VERTEBRATE Animal possessing a backbone composed of a series of vertebrae

VESTIGIAL Being less functional or less well developed than at some earlier stage or time; compare with *rudimentary*

VISCERAL Pertaining to internal organs, primarily hollow organs such as the stomach but generalized to refer to other internal organs as well

VISUAL PIGMENT Light-sensitive organic compound found in the retina and responsible for vision; includes *rhodopsin* (rod pigment) and *iodopsin* (cone pigment)

VITAMIN Organic compound required in relatively minute quantities, either ingested as a nutrient or synthesized internally; vitamins of known function generally serve as parts of coenzymes, such as *niacin* in NAD and *pantothenic acid* in coenzyme A

VIVIPAROUS Live-bearing, that is, giving birth to young instead of laying eggs

X CHROMOSOME Sex-determining chromosome occurring paired in one sex and unpaired in the other: in mammals the female has two X chromosomes, the male one; in birds the reverse is true

XEROPHYTE Plant adapted to grow under arid conditions; a desert plant

XYLEM Conductive tissue in vascular plants consisting of nonliving vessels and tracheids that transport water and solutes from the roots to the leaves and growing tips of the plant

Y CHROMOSOME Chromosome occurring in only one sex and having few or no functional genes; in mammals, the Y chromosome carries a maleness determiner

YOLK Stored food material in an egg

ZOO- Prefix denoting an animal, as in *zoology,* the study of animal life; *-zoic* and *-zoite* are suffixes of similar meaning, denoting an animal-like origin or nature

ZOOID Single organism in an animal colony, such as a coral polyp

ZOOPLANKTON Floating or weakly swimming animals, often microscopic, that are carried along in currents of water, for example, copepods, jellyfishes, comb jellies, and krill

ZYGOTE Fertilized egg; diploid cell formed by the fusion of gametes

Appendix 1 THE METRIC SYSTEM

THE METRIC SYSTEM IS A DECIMAL SYSTEM of measurement that has been based on the *meter* (for length), the *gram* (for mass), and the *liter* (for volume or capacity), as shown for the principal units in Table A1.1, which is continued on page 926.

Table A1.1 □ Units commonly used in biology

PREFIX	LENGTH	EQUIVALENCE	MASS	EQUIVALENCE	VOLUME	EQUIVALENCE
kilo-	**kilometer (km)**	**1,000 m, or 10^3 m**	**kilogram (kg)**[a]	**1,000 g, or 10^3 g**		
	***meter* (m)**[b]		***gram* (g)**[c]		***liter* (l)**[d]	
centi-	**centimeter (cm)**	**0.01 m**				
milli-	**millimeter (mm)**	**0.001 m, or 10^{-3} m**	**milligram (mg)**	**0.001 g, or 10^{-3} g**	**milliliter (ml)**	**0.001 liter, or 10^{-3} liter**

[a] Equivalent to 2.2 lb. [b] One meter is equal to 10^{-7} the distance from the equator to the North Pole; it is now measured as 1,650,763.73 times the wavelength of the orange-red line in the spectrum of the element krypton 86 and is roughly equivalent to 39.3 in. [c] One gram is equal to the mass of 1 cm^3 of distilled water at 4°C. [d] One liter is equal to the volume of 1 kg of distilled water at 4°C and is equivalent to 0.908 quart.

Table A1.1 (*cont.*)

PREFIX	LENGTH	EQUIVALENCE	MASS	EQUIVALENCE	VOLUME	EQUIVALENCE
micro-	**micrometer (μm)**[e]	**0.001 mm, or 10^{-6} m**	**microgram (μg)**	**0.001 mg, or 10^{-6} g**	**microliter (μl)**	**0.001 ml, or 10^{-6} liter**
nano-	**nanometer (nm)**[f]	**0.001 μm, or 10^{-9} m**	**nanogram (ng)**	**0.001 μg, or 10^{-9} g**	**nanoliter (nl)**	**0.001 μl, or 10^{-9} liter**
	angstrom (Å)	**0.1 nm, or 10^{-10} m**				
pico-	**picometer (pm)**	**0.001 nm, or 10^{-12} m**	**picogram (pg)**	**0.001 ng, or 10^{-12} g**	**picoliter (pl)**	**0.001 nl, or 10^{-12} liter**

[e] Formerly micron (μ). [f] Formerly millimicron (mμ).

Appendix 2 □ INTRODUCTION TO QUANTITATIVE BIOLOGY

A2.1 □ PROBABILITY AND THE CHI-SQUARE TEST

Probability can be defined in terms of the frequency with which a given event occurs in a given number of trials. For example, the probability that a tossed coin will land heads up is 50 percent, whether this is once out of two trials (1/2) or 50 times out of 100 trials. In actual practice, observed events may deviate from those theoretically expected (the coin, for instance, may fall heads up only 46 times in 100 trials), and it therefore is important to be able to determine whether this deviation of the observed from the expected can be attributed to chance alone. In scientific experimentation, if there is a statistically significant deviation from the expected values, the hypothesis that predicted them must be rejected.

The chi-square (χ^2) test is one means for determining the significance of any deviation in the results obtained from those expected:

$$\chi^2 = \sum \frac{(o - e)^2}{e}$$

that is, χ^2 equals the sum (Σ) of all quotients obtained by dividing the expected numbers in each class (e), into the square of the deviation between the observed numbers (o) and those expected, as shown in Table A2.1. Each value for χ^2 is calculated statisti-

Table A 2.1

CLASS	OBSERVED (o)	EXPECTED (e)	DEVIATION ($o - e$)	$(o - e)^2$	$\frac{(o-e)^2}{e}$
Heads	46	50	−4	16	0.32
Tails	54	50	+4	16	0.32

$$\chi^2 = \Sigma \frac{(o - e)^2}{e} = 0.64$$

Table A 2.2

DEGREES OF FREEDOM	PROBABILITY 0.95	0.90	0.70	0.50	0.30	0.20	0.10	0.05	0.01	0.001
1	0.004	0.016	0.15	0.46	1.07	1.64	2.71	3.84	6.64	10.83
2	0.10	0.21	0.71	1.39	2.41	3.22	4.61	5.99	9.21	13.82
3	0.35	0.58	1.42	2.37	3.67	4.64	6.25	7.82	11.35	16.27
4	0.71	1.06	2.20	3.36	4.88	5.99	7.78	9.49	13.28	18.47
5	1.15	1.61	3.00	4.35	6.06	7.29	9.24	11.07	15.09	20.52

cally to have a certain probability of occurrence. Accordingly, the χ^2 value obtained must be checked against a table of probabilities, of which an abridged sample, calculated only to five degrees of freedom, is given in Table A2.2. The "degrees of freedom" are always one less than the number of classes being dealt with; in other words, with coin tossing one expects only two classes of results, heads or tails, and so there is one degree of freedom. (If dice were used instead of coins, since a die has six faces, the degrees of freedom would be 5.)

A χ^2 value of 0.64 with one degree of freedom as calculated in the table of probabilities (Table A2.2) can be obtained by chance with a probability of between 0.50 and 0.30; $P < 0.05$ is the accepted upper limit for considering a deviation to be *significant*, that is, great enough that it should not be thought merely the result of chance. In other words, the fact that a coin turned up heads 46 instead of 50 times out of 100 does not indicate that any factor other than chance was responsible for this deviation. If, on the other hand, a tossed coin came up heads only 35 times out of 100 trials, the χ^2 value would be 9 and $P = <0.01$. This would indicate with a probability of over 99 percent that some factor other than chance was at work in causing so great a deviation from the expected results. The hypothesis that a tossed coin will land heads up 50 percent of the time would have to be revised; we could amend it to state that "a correctly balanced coin (one with a symmetrical weight distribution) will land heads up 50 percent of the time."

A2.2 □ DETERMINATION OF CENTRAL TENDENCIES

Measuring a population sample for any particular characteristic (such as height) usually yields a range of measurements that cluster about some midpoint, that is, the data exhibit a *central tendency.* There are three major expressions of central tendency: the mean, the mode, and the median. The *mean* is the arithmetical average of the sample, derived by adding together all of the values obtained for the sample and dividing this sum by the number of individuals in the sample. The *mode* is the value that occurs most frequently in the sample; any group of measurements may have more than one mode. The *median* is the value that is in the middle of a range of values, with just as many values below it as above it. In a large sample that yields a symmetrical, bell-shaped ("normal") distribution curve for the trait being measured, the mode and median tend to coincide with the mean. If the distribution curve is asymmetrical, the median may reflect the central tendency more accurately than the mean.

Where the population sample can be graphed as a normal distribution curve with respect to variation in the trait being measured, the mean is the most useful expression of central tendency and the strength of the central tendency can be expressed in terms of the standard deviation and standard error of the mean.

The procedure often used for determining the mean and the extent of deviation from the mean involves first the determination of the *range of variation* for the trait: the height of a number of corn plants of the same age might be found to range from less than 20 cm to more than 95 cm. Within this range it is convenient to group the measurements into a number of equal *class intervals,* and to tally the number of individual plants falling within each interval: a range of values from 0 to 109.9 cm can be subdivided into ten class intervals of 10 cm each, and a midvalue established for each interval (x). The number of individuals falling into each class interval is symbolized f. The mean is then calculated according to the formula,

$$\bar{x} = \frac{\Sigma fx}{\Sigma f}$$

where $\bar{x}$ denotes the mean and Σ indicates the sum of the separate class values (fx) as shown in the example given in Table A2.3. In this example, the height of 100 corn plants is measured and the mean determined. The last column to the right (fx^2) is not needed for computing the mean but for determining the standard deviation.

The actual significance of the mean of the sample shown in Table A2.3 must be defined in terms of the variability of the sample or "spread" about the mean. This can be expressed as the sample's *standard deviation* (s), calculated according to the formula

$$s = \sqrt{\frac{\Sigma fx^2 - \bar{x}^2\Sigma f}{(\Sigma f) - 1}}$$

where $\bar{x}^2$ represents the square of the mean and $(\Sigma f) - 1$ represents the degrees of freedom, which are one less than the number of individuals measured:

$$s = \sqrt{\frac{312{,}300 - (53.2)^2 \times 100}{100 - 1}}$$

$$= \sqrt{\frac{312{,}300 - 283{,}024}{99}} = \sqrt{\frac{29{,}276}{99}}$$

$$= \sqrt{296} = 17.2$$

For the example given above, the mean and standard deviation are written as 53.2 ± 17.2.

Where the data can be graphed as a normal distribution curve, $\bar{x} \pm 1s$ includes 68 percent of the area under the curve, $\bar{x} \pm 2s$ includes 96 percent, and $\bar{x} \pm 3s$ includes more than 99.5 percent of this area. The greater the range of variation, the larger will be the value of s.

The practice of measuring samples taken from a much larger population is necessitated by the impracticality of measuring the entire population. In our preceding example, 100 plants may have been taken as a sample from a field containing many thousands. The *standard error* is a means for expressing the extent to which the means of other similar samples taken from the same larger population can be expected to vary from the mean of the sample measured. This can also be taken as an estimate of the deviation of the sample means from the true mean of the entire population. The standard error (S.E.) is determined by the formula

Table A2.3

CLASS INTERVAL, HEIGHT, CM	CLASS MIDPOINT, x	FREQUENCY, f	fx	fx^2
100.0–109.9	105	0	0	0
90.0– 99.9	95	1	95	9025
80.0– 89.9	85	5	425	36125
70.0– 79.9	75	12	900	67500
60.0– 69.9	65	16	1040	67600
50.0– 59.9	55	24	1320	72600
40.0– 49.9	45	18	810	36450
30.0– 39.9	35	14	490	17150
20.0– 29.9	25	9	225	5625
10.0– 19.9	15	1	15	225
0.0– 9.9	5	0	0	0
		100	5320	312300

$$\bar{x} = \frac{\Sigma fx}{\Sigma f} = \frac{5320}{100} = 53.2$$

$$\text{S.E.} = \frac{s}{\sqrt{\Sigma f}}$$

In our example,

$$\text{S.E.} = \frac{17.2}{\sqrt{100}} = \frac{17.2}{10} = 1.72$$

and the mean and standard error are written as 53.2 ± 1.72. We should therefore expect that the mean of the sample measured deviated by only +1.72 cm or −1.72 cm from the true mean of the larger population. This expectation can be verified by actually measuring all of the plants in the population, subdividing the population into 100-plant samples, determining the number of individuals per sample in each of the 10-cm class intervals, and calculating the mean of each sample. Plotting the sample means in graph form gives us a distribution curve for the entire population. The standard deviation of the distribution of all the sample means is the standard error. Since 68 percent of the area under this curve falls within one standard deviation of the mean, we may conclude that 68 percent of the time the mean of a given sample will fall within 1 S.E. of the true mean of the whole population.

Index

THE PAGE NUMBERS IN ITALICS ARE THOSE ON WHICH FIGURES APPEAR.

M

N

U

V

W

X

Y

Z